ENGLISH-RUSSIAN
RUSSIAN-ENGLISH
DICTIONARY

OTHER BOOKS BY KENNETH KATZNER

A Russian Review Text (1962)
The Languages of the World (1975)

ENGLISH-RUSSIAN
RUSSIAN-ENGLISH
DICTIONARY

KENNETH KATZNER

A Wiley-Interscience Publication

JOHN WILEY & SONS

New York • Chichester • Brisbane • Toronto • Singapore

Composition: Euramerica Translations, Inc.

Library of Congress Cataloging in Publication Data:

Katzner, Kenneth.
  English-Russian, Russian-English dictionary.

  "A Wiley-Interscience publication."
  1. English language—Dictionaries—Russian.

2. Russian language—Dictionaries—English. I. Title.
PG2640. K34 1983   491.73'21   82-24747
ISBN 0-471-86763-2
       0-471-84442-X paperback

Printed in the United States of America

10 9 8 7 6 5 4 3 2 1

Preface

An American contribution to the field of Russian-English lexicography is long overdue.

This dictionary constitutes a first in many respects. It is the first full-size English-Russian or Russian-English dictionary to be compiled and published in the United States. It is the first to be based on American, rather than British, English. And it is the first full-size dictionary published anywhere, including the Soviet Union, to contain English-Russian and Russian-English sections in the same volume.

Soviet bilingual dictionaries are generally one-way only, based on British English, and designed primarily for those whose mother tongue is Russian. Many of the English words and phrases they contain (especially in the case of the English-Russian dictionaries) have a quaint nineteenth-century flavor about them, and some of them make one wonder where they could possibly have been found. Furthermore, grammatical information, such as irregular verb endings, is given for English words only, whereas obviously the English speaker needs such information for Russian words.

This dictionary, by contrast, is aimed primarily at the native speaker of English, though Russian speakers will also find much in it that is useful. All explanatory notes are in English, rather than in Russian. All irregularities in Russian verb conjugations and noun declensions appear at the beginning of the entry for the given Russian word. And in the English-Russian section all English words with more than one meaning have each meaning numbered and defined, thus making it clear which meaning is about to be rendered into Russian.

The two halves of the dictionary mirror each other exactly. Any Russian word given as the equivalent of an English word in the first half appears as an entry in the second half, and vice versa.

While the dictionary is based on American English, British usage and spellings have not been ignored. Where the British spelling of a word differs from the American, the British spelling is both cross-referenced to the American spelling and listed as an alternate spelling under the American spelling.

The initial planning of this dictionary was done by the late Albert H. Morehead, with valuable assistance from Waldemar von Zedtwitz and Salvatore Ramondino. I am particularly indebted to Sima Ficks, of George Washington University, who read over the entire manuscript for accuracy of translation and usage. And many thanks are due to my wife, Betty Katzner, for helping with the numerous chores involved in getting the manuscript ready for publication.

The typesetting has been done by Euramerica Translations Inc., Yuri Radzievsky, President.

KENNETH KATZNER

Washington, D.C.
September 1983

On Using the Dictionary

ALPHABETIZATION

All main entries are listed in strict alphabetical order. Derivative words may be run in under a main entry only if they immediately follow or precede the main entry word — that is, no other entry occurs alphabetically in between.

The numerous two-word lexical items that occur in English, such as *blank verse, light year, maiden name,* and *stumbling block,* are most often listed as separate entries in their regular alphabetical position, not run in under either of the two words which comprise them. For example, *light year* is not run in under either "light" or "year," but occurs as a separate entry after the word "lightweight." In the Russian-English section, however, such Russian items are run in under one of their two components.

LABELING OF MEANINGS

If an English word has more than one meaning, each meaning is identified by a label (usually a synonym) inserted in parentheses just before the Russian equivalent that follows. This label (the "contextual gist" label) should make clear which meaning is about to be rendered into Russian. A simple example might be the word "trunk," which is treated as follows: 1, (of a tree) ствол. 2, (of an elephant) хобот. 3, (torso) туловище. 4, (large box or case) сундук. 5, (of an automobile) багажник. 6, *pl.* (for swimming) плавки. In some cases the label may be a special field label, such as *physics* or *finance.*

GENDER OF NOUNS

The gender of most Russian nouns is self-evident from their ending. For those ending in а ь, the designation *n.m.* indicates masculine and *n.f.* indicates feminine. The *n.m.* designation is also used with nouns such as дядя and слуга, which are masculine despite their -а or -я ending, as well as with many masculine nouns denoting people where the feminine form immediately follows.

The designation *n.m. & f.* is used with a large group of nouns denoting people, which are masculine or feminine depending on the person. The designation *n.m. or f.* is used with a small group of nouns (e.g., колибри) that are both masculine and feminine.

Indeclinable nouns ending in -o may be assumed to be neuter unless otherwise indicated. For those with other endings the gender is always given (e.g., кофе, *n.m. indecl.*).

VERBS

If a Russian verb has both a perfective and imperfective aspect, it is always listed under the imperfective, with the perfective form following immediately in brackets. The perfective verb is also listed separately and cross-referenced to the imperfective verb unless it is alphabetically adjacent to the imperfective verb — that is, no other words occur between. (Even if adjacent it is sometimes included, in order to show an irregularity in its conjugation.)

Reflexive verbs are usually run in under the nonreflexive verb, with only the imperfective aspect given. Unless otherwise indicated, it may be assumed that the perfective of the reflexive verb is formed with the same prefix or ending as the perfective of the nonreflexive verb.

If a prefixed perfective verb is cross-referenced to its nonprefixed imperfective counterpart, it may be assumed that the perfective verb is conjugated like the imperfective verb.

In the treatment of English verbs, intransitive meanings have been set completely apart from transitive meanings, a practice followed by all large dictionaries of English but not, for some reason, by Soviet English-Russian dictionaries.

Abbreviations Used in the Dictionary

abbr.	abbreviation	indecl.	indeclinable
acc.	accusative	indef.	indefinite
adj.	adjective	indeterm.	indeterminate
aero.	aeronautics	indir.	indirect
agric.	agriculture	inf.	infinitive
anat.	anatomy	infl.	inflected
approx.	approximately	instr.	instrumental
archit.	architecture	interj.	interjection
art.	article	interr.	interrogative
astron.	astronomy	intrans.	intransitive
attrib.	attributive	l.c.	lower case
Bib.	Bible, Biblical	ling.	linguistics
biol.	biology	lit.	literature; literal
bot.	botany	loc.	locative
Brit.	British	masc.	masculine
cap.	capital, capitalized	math.	mathematics
chem.	chemistry	mech.	mechanics
colloq.	colloquial	med.	medicine
comm.	commerce	metall.	metallurgy
comp.	comparative	meteorol.	meteorology
conj.	conjunction	mil.	military
contr.	contraction	myth.	mythology
dat.	dative	n.	noun
def.	definite	naut.	nautical
dem.	demonstrative	neg.	negative
dent.	dentistry	neut.	neuter
dim.	diminutive	n.f.	feminine noun
dipl.	diplomacy	n.m.	masculine noun
dir.	direct	nom.	nominative
eccles.	ecclesiastic	obj.	object
econ.	economics	obs.	obsolete
esp.	especially	opp.	opposite
fem.	feminine	Orth. Ch.	Orthodox Church
fig.	figurative	part.	participle
fol.	followed	pers.	personal
gen.	genitive	pert.	pertaining
geog.	geography	pfv.	perfective
geol.	geology	philos.	philosophy
geom.	geometry	phonet.	phonetics
gram.	grammar	photog.	photography
hist.	history	physiol.	physiology
impers.	impersonal	pl.	plural
impfv.	imperfective	polit.	politics, political

poss.	possessive	topog.	topography
prep.	preposition	trans.	transitive
prepl.	prepositional	trig.	trigonometry
pre-rev.	prerevolutionary	U.S.	United States
pres.	present	usu.	usually
pron.	pronoun	v.	verb
pros.	prosody	var.	variant
psychol.	psychology	v. aux.	auxiliary verb
refl.	reflexive	v.i.	intransitive verb
rel.	relative	v. impfv.	imperfective verb
relig.	religion	v. pfv.	perfective verb
R.R.	railroads	v.r.	reflexive verb
sing.	singular	v.t.	transitive verb
superl.	superlative	vulg.	vulgar
theat.	theater	zool.	zoology

REGULAR RUSSIAN DECLENSION PATTERNS

NOUNS

Masculine

Nouns ending in a hard consonant

	Sing.	Pl.
Nom.	билет	билет-ы
Gen.	билет-а	билет-ов
Dat.	билет-у	билет-ам
Acc.	N. or G.	N. or G.
Instr.	билет-ом	билет-ами
Prepl.	билет-е	билет-ах

Nouns ending in ь

	Sing.	Pl.
Nom.	роял-ь	роял-и
Gen.	роял-я	роял-ей
Dat.	роял-ю	роял-ям
Acc.	N. or G.	N. or G.
Instr.	роял-ем	роял-ями
Prepl.	роял-е	роял-ях

Nouns ending in й

	Sing.	Pl.
Nom.	музе-й	музе-и
Gen.	музе-я	музе-ев
Dat.	музе-ю	музе-ям
Acc.	N. or G.	N. or G.
Instr.	музе-ем	музе-ями
Prepl.	музе-е	музе-ях

Feminine

Nouns ending in a

	Sing.	Pl.
Nom.	картин-а	картин-ы
Gen.	картин-ы	картин
Dat.	картин-е	картин-ам
Acc.	картин-у	N. or G.
Instr.	картин-ой	картин-ами
Prepl.	картин-е	картин-ах

Nouns ending in я

	Sing.	Pl.
Nom.	недел-я	недел-и
Gen.	недел-и	недел-ь
Dat.	недел-е	недел-ям
Acc.	недел-ю	N. or G.
Instr.	недел-ей	недел-ями
Prepl.	недел-е	недел-ях

Nouns ending in ь

	Sing.	Pl.
Nom.	цел-ь	цел-и
Gen.	цел-и	цел-ей
Dat.	цел-и	цел-ям
Acc.	цел-ь	N. or G.
Instr.	цел-ью	цел-ями
Prepl.	цел-и	цел-ях

Neuter

Nouns ending in o

	Sing.	Pl.
Nom.	блюд-о	блюд-а
Gen.	блюд-а	блюд
Dat.	блюд-у	блюд-ам
Acc.	блюд-о	блюд-а
Instr.	блюд-ом	блюд-ами
Prepl.	блюд-е	блюд-ах

Nouns ending in ле, ре

	Sing.	Pl.
Nom.	пол-е	пол-я
Gen.	пол-я	пол-ей
Dat.	пол-ю	пол-ям
Acc.	пол-е	пол-я
Instr.	пол-ем	пол-ями
Prepl.	пол-е	пол-ях

Nouns ending in це, ще, же

	Sing.	Pl.
Nom.	чудовищ-е	чудовищ-а
Gen.	чудовищ-а	чудовищ
Dat.	чудовищ-у	чудовищ-ам
Acc.	чудовищ-е	N. or G.
Instr.	чудовищ-ем	чудовищ-ами
Prepl.	чудовищ-е	чудовищ-ах

Nouns ending in ие

	Sing.	Pl.
Nom.	здан-ие	здан-ия
Gen.	здан-ия	здан-ий
Dat.	здан-ию	здан-иям
Acc.	здан-ие	здан-ия
Instr.	здан-ием	здан-иями
Prepl.	здан-ии	здан-иях

Nouns ending in ье, ьё

	Sing.	Pl.
Nom.	ущел-ье	ущел-ья
Gen.	ущел-ья	ущел-ий
Dat.	ущел-ью	ущел-ьям
Acc.	ущел-ье	ущел-ья
Instr.	ущел-ьем	ущел-ьями
Prepl.	ущел-ье	ущел-ьях

The accusative singular of all masculine nouns and the accusative plural of all nouns is the same as the nominative when the noun is inanimate, and the same as the genitive when the noun is animate. Animate nouns include people, animals, birds, fish, insects, and so on.

Special Rules

1   After the consonants г, к, х, ж, ч, ш, щ, the vowel ы is replaced by и (e.g., кни́ги, уро́ки, ножи́, све́чи), and я is replaced by а (e.g., ноча́м, веща́ми).

2   After the consonants ж, ч, ш, щ, ц, the instrumental case endings -ом and -ой become -ем and -ей when unstressed (e.g. му́жем, ты́сячей, ме́сяцем, пти́цей).

3   When stressed, the instrumental case endings -ем and -ей become -ём and -ёй (e.g., рулём, бельём, землёй, статьёй).

4   The prepositional singular ending for nouns ending in -ия is -ии (e.g. а́рмия-а́рмии).

5   The genitive plural of nouns ending in -ая, -ея, -ия, -уя is formed by replacing the я with й (e.g., ста́я-стай, ли́ния-ли́ний).

6   The genitive plural ending for nouns ending in ж, ч, ш, щ is -ей (e.g. ножей, ключей).

7   The genitive plural ending for nouns ending in ц is -ев when unstressed (e.g. ме́сяцев).

Note.   All individual exceptions to the above tables and rules are indicated in the body of the dictionary under the entry for the given word. If only the genitive singular is indicated (e.g., рот – *gen.* рта; лёд – *gen.* льда; за́яц – *gen.* за́йца; ручей́ – *gen.* ручья́) the irregularity occurs throughout the singular and plural declension of the noun. This also applies to shifts of stress — e.g., щит – *gen.* щита́; язы́к – *gen.* языка́; руль – *gen.* руля́ mean that the stress shifts to the ending throughout the singular and plural declension. If only the nominative plural is indicated (e.g., дуб – *pl.* дубы́; дом – *pl.* дома́; страна́ – *pl.* стра́ны; лицо́ – *pl.* ли́ца; колесо́ – *pl.* колёса) the irregularity or shift of stress occurs throughout the plural (but not the singular) declension of the noun.

ADJECTIVES

Adjectives ending in -о́й

	Masc.	Fem.	Neut.	Pl.
Nom.	прям-о́й	-а́я	-о́е	-ы́е
Gen.	прям-о́го	-о́й	-о́го	-ы́х
Dat.	прям-о́му	-о́й	-о́му	-ы́м
Acc.	N. or G.	-у́ю	-о́е	N. or G.
Instr.	прям-ы́м	-о́й	-ы́м	-ы́ми
Prepl.	прям-о́м	-о́й	-о́м	-ы́х

Adjectives ending in -ый

	Masc.	Fem.	Neut.	Pl.
Nom.	но́в-ый	-ая	-ое	-ые
Gen.	но́в-ого	-ой	-ого	-ых
Dat.	но́в-ому	-ой	-ому	-ым
Acc.	N. or G.	-ую	-ое	N. or G.
Instr.	но́вым	-ой	-ым	-ыми
Prepl.	но́в-ом	-ой	-ом	-ых

Adjectives ending in -го́й, -ко́й, -хо́й

	Masc.	Fem.	Neut.	Pl.
Nom.	плох-о́й	-а́я	-о́е	-и́е
Gen.	плох-о́го	-о́й	-о́го	-и́х
Dat.	плох-о́му	-о́й	-о́му	-и́м
Acc.	N. or G.	-у́ю	-о́е	N. or G.
Instr.	плох-и́м	-о́й	-и́м	-и́ми
Prepl.	плох-о́м	-о́й	-о́м	-и́х

Adjectives ending in -гий, -кий, -хий

	Masc.	Fem.	Neut.	Pl.
Nom.	ти́х-ий	-ая	-ое	-ие
Gen.	ти́х-ого	-ой	-ого	-их
Dat.	ти́х-ому	-ой	-ому	-им
Acc.	N. or G.	-ую	-ое	N. or G.
Instr.	ти́х-им	-ой	-им	-ими
Prepl.	ти́х-ом	-ой	-ом	-их

Adjectives ending in -жо́й, -шо́й

	Masc.	Fem.	Neut.	Pl.
Nom.	больш-о́й	-а́я	-о́е	-и́е
Gen.	больш-о́го	-о́й	-о́го	-и́х
Dat.	больш-о́му	-о́й	-о́му	-и́м
Acc.	N. or G.	-у́ю	-о́е	N. or G.
Instr.	больш-и́м	-о́й	-и́м	-и́ми
Prepl.	больш-о́м	-о́й	-о́м	-и́х

Adjectives ending in -жий, -чий, -ший, -щий

	Masc.	Fem.	Neut.	Pl.
Nom.	свѣ́ж-ий	-ая	-ее	-ие
Gen.	свѣ́ж-его	-ей	-его	-их
Dat.	свѣ́ж-ему	-ей	-ему	-им
Acc.	N. or G.	-ую	-ее	N. or G.
Instr.	свѣ́ж-им	-ей	-им	-ими
Prepl.	свѣ́ж-ем	-ей	-ем	-их

Adjectives ending in -ний

	Masc.	Fem.	Neut.	Pl.
Nom.	си́н-ий	-яя	-ее	-ие
Gen.	си́н-его	-ей	-его	-их
Dat.	си́н-ему	-ей	-ему	-им
Acc.	N. or G.	-юю	-ее	N. or G.
Instr.	си́н-им	-ей	-им	-ими
Prepl.	си́н-ем	-ей	-ем	-их

Adjectives ending in -бий, -вий, -зий, -лий, -сий*

	Masc.	Fem.	Neut.	Pl.
Nom.	ры́б-ий	-ья	-ье	-ьи
Gen.	ры́б-ьего	-ьей	-ьего	-ьих
Dat.	ры́б-ьему	-ьей	-ьему	-ьим
Acc.	N. or G.	-ью	-ье	N. or G.
Instr.	ры́б-ьим	-ьей	-ьим	-ьими
Prepl.	ры́б-ьем	-ьей	-ьем	-ьих

*Adjectives with these endings are derived mainly from the words for animals and other living creatures (e.g., коро́вий from коро́ва, ко́зий from коза́, собо́лий from со́боль, ли́сий from лиса́), and include some ending in -ний (оле́ний), -жий (медвѣ́жий), -чий (пти́чий), and -ший (петуши́й).

Regular Verb Conjugation Patterns

I. Verbs ending in -ать

желáть: желáю, желáешь, желáет, желáем, желáете, желáют
дéлать: дéлаю, дéлаешь, дéлает, дéлаем, дéлаете, дéлают

II. Verbs ending in -ять

менять: меняю, меняешь, меняет, меняем, меняете, меняют

III. Verbs ending in -еть

имéть: имéю, имéешь, имéет, имéем, имéете, имéют

IV. Verbs ending in -ить

говори́ть: говорю́, говори́шь, говори́т, говори́м, говори́те, говоря́т
вéрить: вéрю, вéришь, вéрит, вéрим, вéрите, вéрят

V. Verbs ending in -уть

вернýть: вернý, вернёшь, вернёт, вернём, вернёте, вернýт
трóнуть: трóну, трóнешь, трóнет, трóнем, трóнете, трóнут

After the letters ж, ч, ш, щ, the endings -ю and -ят are replaced by -у and -ат.

реши́ть: решý, реши́шь, реши́т, реши́м, реши́те, решáт

The conjugation of verbs with the infinitive endings -оть, -ыть, -сть, -сти, -зти, -зть, -чь, as well as of all irregular verbs and those with shifts of stress, is given in the body of the dictionary under the entry for the given word.

Past Tense

Verbs ending in -ть

	Masculine	Feminine	Neuter	Plural
петь:	пел	пéла	пéло	пéли
мыть:	мыл	мы́ла	мы́ло	мы́ли

In the case of reflexive verbs -ся is added to those forms ending in consonant or ь, and -сь to those forms ending in a vowel.

одевáться: одевáюсь, одевáешься, одевáется, одевáемся, одевáетесь, одевáются

вернýться: вернýсь, вернёшься, вернётся, вернёмся, вернётесь, вернýтся

Past tense: одевáлся, одевáлась, одевáлось, одевáлись

English-Russian Section

A

A,a пе́рвая бу́ква англи́йского алфави́та. —*n.* **1,** (musical note) ля. **2,** (school grade) пятёрка. Get an A, получи́ть пятёрку; получи́ть "отли́чно". Get straight A's, учи́ться на кру́глые пятёрки. —**from A to Z**, от А до Я.

a *indef. art. Generally not rendered in Russian: a young man,* молодо́й челове́к; *a box of matches,* коро́бка спи́чек; *a story about a little girl,* расска́з о ма́ленькой де́вочке. ♦ *Special uses:* **1,** (one) оди́н: *in a word,* одни́м сло́вом; *just a minute,* одну́ мину́тку. *He didn't say a word,* он ни сло́ва не сказа́л. *I didn't hear a thing,* я ничего́ не слы́шал(а). **2,** (a certain) оди́н: *an old friend of mine,* оди́н мой ста́рый друг. **3,** (of someone unknown) не́кий: *a Mr. Smith called,* вас спра́шивал не́кий ми́стер Смит. **4,** (such a) тако́й: *we live at a time when...,* мы живём в тако́е вре́мя, когда́... **5,** (per) в: *twice a week,* два ра́за в неде́лю. **6,** (for the amount specified) за (+ *acc.*): *two dollars a dozen,* два до́ллара за дю́жину.

aardvark *n.* трубкозу́б.

aback *adv., in* **take aback,** озада́чить; огоро́шить. *I was taken aback,* я был озада́чен.

abacus *n.* счёты.

abandon *v.t.* **1,** (leave; desert) покида́ть; оставля́ть; броса́ть. *Abandon a child,* подбра́сывать ребёнка. **2,** (give up, as an attempt) отка́зываться от. *Abandon hope,* оставля́ть наде́жду. —*n.* беззабо́тность. *With abandon,* беззабо́тно. —**abandoned,** *adj.* поки́нутый.

abase *v.t.* унижа́ть. —**abasement,** *n.* униже́ние.

abash *v.t.* смуща́ть; конфу́зить.

abate *v.t.* ослабля́ть. —*v.i.* затиха́ть; утиха́ть; стиха́ть; спада́ть. —**abatement,** *n.* ослабле́ние. *Without abatement,* неосла́бно.

abbess *n.* аббати́са; игу́менья.

abbey *n.* абба́тство: *Westminster Abbey,* Вестми́нстерское абба́тство.

abbot *n.* абба́т; игу́мен; настоя́тель.

abbreviate *v.t.* сокраща́ть. —**abbreviation,** *n.* сокраще́ние.

ABC *n.* а́збука: *learn the ABC's,* вы́учиться а́збуке. *The ABC's of chemistry,* а́збука хи́мии. —**as simple as ABC,** как два́жды два четы́ре.

abdicate *v.t.* отрека́ться от. —*v.i.* отрека́ться от престо́ла. —**abdication,** *n.* отрече́ние от престо́ла.

abdomen *n.* живо́т. —**abdominal,** *adj.* брюшно́й.

abduct *v.t.* похища́ть. —**abduction,** *n.* похище́ние. —**abductor,** *n.* похити́тель.

aberrant *adj.* ненорма́льный.

aberration *n.* аберра́ция.

abet *v.t.* подстрека́ть. *Abet a crime,* соде́йствовать соверше́нию преступле́ния. —**abetment,** *n.* подстрека́тельство. —**abetter; abettor,** *n.* подстрека́тель.

abeyance *n.* (вре́менное) прекраще́ние. *Hold in abeyance,* откла́дывать.

abhor *v.t.* ненави́деть. —**abhorrence,** *n.* отвраще́ние. —**abhorrent,** *adj.* ненави́стный; отврати́тельный.

abide *v.t.* **1,** (await) ждать. **2,** (tolerate) терпе́ть. —*v.i.* **1,** (remain) остава́ться. **2,** (dwell) жить; пребыва́ть. —**abide by, 1,** (live up to, as an agreement) соблюда́ть; приде́рживаться. **2,** (acquiesce in, as a decision) подчиня́ться (+ *dat.*).

abiding *adj.* постоя́нный; неизме́нный.

ability *n.* спосо́бность; уме́ние.

abject *adj.* **1,** (wretched) уни́женный. *Abject poverty,* кра́йняя нищета́. **2,** (despicable) презре́нный.

abjure *v.t.* **1,** (renounce) отрека́ться от. **2,** (retract) отка́зываться от.

ablaze *adj.* в огне́. *Set ablaze,* воспламеня́ть.

able *adj.* уме́лый; спосо́бный. *Be able,* мочь; уме́ть.

able-bodied *adj.* трудоспосо́бный; работоспосо́бный.

abloom *adj.* в цвету́.

ablution *n.* омове́ние.

ably *adv.* уме́ло.

abnegate *v.t.* отка́зываться от; отрека́ться от. —**abnegation,** *n.* отка́з; отрече́ние.

abnormal *adj.* ненорма́льный; анорма́льный. —**abnormality,** *n.* ненорма́льность. —**abnormally,** *adv.* ненорма́льно.

aboard *adv.* **1,** (position) на борту́; на корабле́. **2,** (motion) на́ борт; на кора́бль. Go aboard, сесть на кора́бль. *Take aboard,* брать на́ борт. —**all aboard!,** по ваго́нам!

abode *n.* жили́ще.

abolish *v.t.* отменя́ть; упраздня́ть. —**abolition,** *n.* отме́на; упраздне́ние.

abominable *adj.* отврати́тельный; проти́вный; гну́сный.

abominate *v.t.* ненави́деть; пита́ть отвраще́ние к.

abomination *n.* **1,** (loathing) омерзе́ние. **2,** (loathsome thing) ме́рзость.

aboriginal *adj.* коренно́й; тузе́мный. —**aborigine,** *n.* абориге́н; тузе́мец.

abort *v.t.* **1,** (terminate the pregnancy of) сде́лать або́рт (+ *dat.*). **2,** *fig.* (terminate prematurely) прекраща́ть.

abortion *n.* аборт. *Have an abortion,* сделать аборт. *Perform an abortion upon,* сделать аборт (+ *dat.*).

abortive *adj.* **1,** *med.* абортивный. **2,** *fig.* (unsuccessful) безрезультатный; бесплодный.

abound *v.i.* **1,** (exist in great numbers) иметься в изобилии. **2,** *fol.* **by in** *or* **with** (have in great abundance) изобиловать (+ *instr.*).

about *adv.* **1,** (approximately) около: *about an hour,* около часа. **2,** (nearly) почти: *about ready,* почти готов. **3,** (at hand) кругом; вокруг: *there was no one about,* кругом/вокруг никого не было. —*prep.* **1,** (here and there in) по: *walk about town,* ходить по городу. *Her things lay all about the room,* её вещи валялись по всей комнате. **2,** (concerning) о: *what are you talking about?,* о чём вы говорите? —**be about to,** собираться (+ *inf.*): *I was just about to call you,* я как раз собирался вам звонить. *The train is about to leave,* поезд вот-вот отойдёт. *I was about to ask, but...,* я спросил было, но... —**up and about,** на ногах. —**what about; how about...?,** как насчёт (+ *gen.*)?

about-face *n.* **1,** *mil.* поворот кругом. *About face!,* кругом! **2,** *fig.* (reversal) поворот на сто восемьдесят градусов.

above *prep.* **1,** (over) над: *above sea level,* над уровнем моря. **2,** (in excess of) выше: *above average,* выше среднего. *Five degrees above zero,* пять градусов выше нуля. **3,** (superior to) выше: *head and shoulders above the others,* на голову выше других. **4,** (beyond the reach of) вне: *above suspicion,* вне подозрений. **5,** (too honorable to engage in) выше: *be above prejudice,* быть выше предрассудков. —*adv.* наверху; выше. *From above,* сверху; свыше. —*n.,* preceded by the вышеупомянутое. —**above all, 1,** (most of all) больше всего. **2,** (most importantly) прежде всего.

aboveboard *adj.* открытый; откровенный. —*adv.* открыто; откровенно.

abracadabra *n.* абракадабра.

abrade *v.t.* сдирать (кожу).

abrasion *n.* **1,** (wearing away) истирание. **2,** (abraded area, as on the skin) ссадина.

abrasive *n.* абразив. —*adj.* **1,** (causing abrasion) абразивный. **2,** *fig.* (causing friction or resentment) раздражающий.

abreast *adv.* в ряду; в ряд. *Sit three abreast,* сидеть по трое в ряду. *March three abreast,* маршировать по трое в ряд/ряду. —**keep abreast of, 1,** (keep up with) идти в ногу с. *Keep abreast of the times,* идти в ногу с жизнью *or* со временем. **2,** (keep well-posted on) следить за.

abridge *v.t.* **1,** (shorten) сокращать. **2,** (curtail, as rights) урезывать.

abridgment *also,* **abridgement** *n.* **1,** (act of abridging) сокращение. **2,** (abridged edition) сокращённое издание.

abroad *adv.* **1,** (location) за границей; за рубежом. **2,** (direction) за границу. *From abroad,* из-за границы.

abrogate *v.t.* отменять; аннулировать. —**abrogation,** *n.* отмена; аннулирование.

abrupt *adj.* **1,** (sudden) внезапный; резкий; крутой. *Abrupt departure,* внезапный отъезд. **2,** (steep) крутой; обрывистый. **3,** (brusque) резкий. —**abruptly,** *adv.* резко. —**abruptness,** *n.* резкость.

abscess *n.* абсцесс; нарыв; гнойник.

abscissa *n.* абсцисса.

abscond *v.i.* скрываться; бежать.

absence *n.* отсутствие. *Absence from class,* пропуск занятий *or* уроков. *In the absence of,* в отсутствие *or* за отсутствием (+ *gen.*). *In my absence,* в моё отсутствие. —**absence without leave,** самовольная отлучка.

absent *adj.* отсутствующий. *Be absent,* отсутствовать. —*v.t.* [*usu.* **absent oneself**] отлучаться.

absentee *n.* отсутствующий. —**absenteeism,** *n.* (систематические) прогулы.

absentia *see* **in absentia.**

absently *adv.* отсутствующим взглядом; рассеянно.

absent-minded *adj.* рассеянный. —**absent-mindedly,** *adv.* рассеянно. —**absent-mindedness,** *n.* рассеянность.

absinthe *n.* абсент; полынная водка.

absolute *adj.* **1,** (complete; total) абсолютный; совершенный; полный. **2,** (unlimited; unqualified) абсолютный; безусловный. **3,** (sheer; utter) сплошной; сущий. —*n.* абсолют. —**absolute majority,** абсолютное большинство голосов. —**absolute monarchy,** абсолютная монархия. —**absolute pitch,** абсолютный слух. —**absolute zero,** абсолютный нуль.

absolutely *adv.* **1,** (perfectly; entirely; utterly) совершенно: *absolutely correct/certain,* совершенно правильно/уверен(а). *Absolutely impossible,* совершенно *or* абсолютно невозможно. **2,** (positively) абсолютно; решительно. *Absolutely everything,* решительно всё. *Absolutely nothing,* совершенно/абсолютно/решительно/положительно ничего. **3,** as an exclamation безусловно!

absolution *n.* **1,** (forgiveness) прощение. **2,** (remission of sin) отпущение грехов.

absolutism *n.* абсолютизм. —**absolutist,** *n.* абсолютист. —*adj.* абсолютистский.

absolve *v.t.* **1,** (acquit) оправдывать. **2,** (release) освобождать. *Absolve of responsibility,* снимать ответственность с (+ *gen.*). **3,** (remit, as a sin) прощать; отпускать.

absorb *v.t.* **1,** (take in; suck up) всасывать; впитывать; поглощать. **2,** (engross) поглощать: *absorbed in one's work,* поглощён своей работой; погружён в свою работу. *Become absorbed in,* погружаться *or* углубляться в (+ *acc.*). **3,** (take up completely) поглощать. **4,** (mentally assimilate) воспринимать; усваивать.

absorbent *adj.* всасывающий; поглощающий. —**absorbent cotton,** вата.

absorbing *adj.* увлекательный; захватывающий.

absorption *n.* всасывание; поглощение; абсорбция.

abstain *v.i.* воздерживаться: *abstain from the voting,* воздерживаться от голосования.

abstemious *adj.* воздержанный.

abstention *n.* **1,** (act of abstaining) воздержание. **2,** (failure to vote) воздержавшийся: *ten in favor, six against, five abstentions,* десять за, шесть против, пять воздержавшихся.

abstinence *n.* воздержание.

abstract *adj.* отвлечённый; абстрактный. *Abstract art,* абстракционизм. —*n.* **1,** (synopsis) реферат; конспект. **2,** (something abstract) абстракция. —*v.t.* **1,** (consider separately) абстрагировать. **2,** (make an abstract of) реферировать; конспектировать. —**in the abstract,** абстрактно; отвлечённо.

abstraction *n.* **1,** (abstract idea or concept) абстра́кция; отвлече́ние. **2,** (absent-mindedness) рассе́янность.

abstruse *adj.* мудрёный; замыслова́тый; зау́мный.

absurd *adj.* неле́пый; абсу́рдный. **—absurdity,** *n.* неле́пость; абсу́рд; абсу́рдность.

abundance *n.* оби́лие; изоби́лие. *In abundance,* в изоби́лии; в избы́тке.

abundant *adj.* оби́льный: *abundant harvest,* оби́льный урожа́й.

abundantly *adv.* **1,** (in abundance) оби́льно. **2,** (extremely) преде́льно: *abundantly clear,* преде́льно я́сно.

abuse *v.t.* **1,** (misuse) злоупотребля́ть: *abuse power,* злоупотребля́ть вла́стью. **2,** (revile) руга́ть; обруга́ть. *—n.* **1,** (misuse; corrupt practice) злоупотребле́ние. **2,** (abusive language) ру́гань; брань.

abusive *adj.* руга́тельный; оскорби́тельный.

abut *v.t. & i.* примыка́ть (к).

abutment *n.* **1,** (point of contact) стык. **2,** (support for an arch) пята́. **3,** (support for a bridge) усто́й.

abysmal *adj.* жа́лкий. *Abysmal ignorance,* кра́йнее неве́жество. *Abysmal failure,* по́лный прова́л. *Fail abysmally,* по́лностью провали́ться.

abyss *n.* про́пасть; бе́здна.

acacia *n.* ака́ция.

academic *adj.* академи́ческий.

academician *n.* акаде́мик.

academy *n.* **1,** (learned institution) акаде́мия: *academy of sciences,* акаде́мия нау́к. **2,** (specialized school) шко́ла; учи́лище: *academy of music,* музыка́льная шко́ла; *military academy,* вое́нное учи́лище; *riding academy,* шко́ла верхово́й езды́.

acanthus *n.* ака́нт.

accede *v.i.* [*usu.* **accede to**] **1,** (consent to) согла-ша́ться (на). **2,** (assume, as an office) вступа́ть (в). *Accede to the throne,* вступи́ть на престо́л.

accelerate *v.t.* ускоря́ть. *Accelerated course,* уско́ренный курс. *—v.i.* ускоря́ться. **—acceleration,** *n.* ускоре́ние. **—accelerator,** *n.* ускори́тель; акселера́тор.

accent *n.* **1,** (stress) ударе́ние. **2,** (regional or national manner of speech) акце́нт. **3,** (accent mark) ударе́ние. *—v.t.* **=accentuate.**

accentuate *v.t.* **1,** (pronounce with heavy stress) акценти́ровать; де́лать ударе́ние на. **2,** (emphasize) акценти́ровать; де́лать акце́нт на.

accept *v.t.* **1,** (say yes to) принима́ть: *accept an offer/invitation,* принима́ть предложе́ние/пригла-ше́ние. **2,** (reconcile oneself to) мири́ться: *accept one's fate,* мири́ться со свое́й судьбо́й. **3,** (admit formally) принима́ть: *he was accepted at X college,* он был при́нят в университе́т икс.

acceptable *adj.* прие́млемый.

acceptance *n.* **1,** (act of accepting) приня́тие. **2,** (condition of being accepted) призна́ние: *gain accept-ance,* получи́ть призна́ние.

access *n.* до́ступ: *gain access* to, получи́ть до́ступ к. **—access road,** подъездна́я доро́га.

accessible *adj.* досту́пный. **—accessibility,** *n.* досту́пность.

accession *n.* **1,** (to the throne) вступле́ние; вос-ше́ствие (на престо́л); (to office) вступле́ние (в до́лжность). **2,** (something newly acquired) приобре-те́ние. **3,** (agreement; assent) согла́сие.

accessory *n.* **1,** (extra piece of equipment) приста́в-

ка. **2,** *pl.* (items of equipment) принадле́жности. **3,** *pl.* (extra items of dress) принадле́жности костю́ма. **4,** *law* соуча́стник. *—adj.* **1,** (extra) подсо́бный. **2,** *law* соуча́ствующий.

accident *n.* **1,** (mishap) несча́стный слу́чай; ката-стро́фа; ава́рия. **2,** (chance occurrence) случа́йность. *It is no accident that...,* не случа́йно, что... **3,** (chance) слу́чай. *By accident,* случа́йно.

accidental *adj.* случа́йный; неча́янный. **—acciden-tally,** *adv.* случа́йно; неча́янно.

acclaim *v.t.* **1,** (welcome with applause) приве́тство-вать. **2,** (praise; extol) расхва́ливать. **3,** (proclaim approvingly) провозглаша́ть. *—n.* **1,** (welcoming) шу́мное приве́тствие. **2,** (praise) восхвале́ние.

acclamation *n.* шу́мное одобре́ние. **—by accla-mation,** единоду́шно; без голосова́ния.

acclimate *also,* **acclimatize** *v.t.* акклиматизи́ровать. *Become acclimated,* прижива́ться; акклиматизи́ро-ваться. **—acclimation; acclimatization,** *n.* аккли-матиза́ция.

accommodate *v.t.* **1,** (oblige; help) услу́живать. **2,** (lodge) помеща́ть. **3,** (have space for) вмеща́ть. **4,** (adapt) приспособля́ть. **—accommodating,** *adj.* ус-лу́жливый; сгово́рчивый.

accommodation *n.* **1,** (a favor) услу́га. **2,** (conve-nience) удо́бство: *for the accommodation of,* для удо́бства (*+ gen.*). **3,** (adaptation; adjustment) приспо-собле́ние. **4,** (reconciliation) соглаше́ние: *reach an accommodation,* достига́ть соглаше́ния. **5,** *pl.* (lodg-ings) помеще́ние; жильё. **6,** *pl.* (traveling space) ме́сто.

accompaniment *n.* **1,** (something added) добавле́-ние. **2,** *music* аккомпанеме́нт; сопровожде́ние. **—accompanist,** *n.* аккомпаниа́тор.

accompany *v.t.* **1,** (go along with) сопровожда́ть. *Accompanied by,* в сопровожде́нии (*+ gen.*). **2,** (escort up to a point) провожа́ть. **3,** *music* аккомпа-ни́ровать.

accomplice *n.* сообщник; соуча́стник.

accomplish *v.t.* соверша́ть; осуществля́ть; выпол-ня́ть. *Accomplish a feat/miracle,* соверша́ть по́двиг/ чу́до. *Accomplish a task,* выполня́ть зада́чу. *Accom-plish a great deal,* доби́ться мно́гого.

accomplished *adj.* **1,** (done) совершённый. *Ac-complished fact,* соверши́вшийся факт. **2,** (pro-ficient) зако́нченный.

accomplishment *n.* **1,** (completion) выполне́ние; осуществле́ние. **2,** (an achievement) достиже́ние.

accord *v.t.* **1,** (give; extend) ока́зывать. **2,** (grant; bestow) предоставля́ть. *—v.i.* [*usu.* **accord with**] совпада́ть (с); сходи́ться (с); вяза́ться (с). *—n.* **1,** (an agreement) соглаше́ние. **2,** (harmony) согла́сие. **—of one's own accord,** по до́брой во́ле.

accordance *n.* соотве́тствие. *In accordance with,* в соотве́тствии с; согла́сно.

accordingly *adv.* **1,** (correspondingly) соотве́т-ственно; соотве́тствующим о́бразом. **2,** (conse-quently) таки́м о́бразом.

according to 1, (as stated by) по слова́м (*+ gen.*). **2,** (in accordance with) по; согла́сно; в соотве́тствии с. **3,** (in proportion to) по: *each according to his abil-ity,* ка́ждый по его́ спосо́бностям.

accordion *n.* гармо́ника; аккордео́н. **—accordion pleats,** плиссе́.

accordionist *n.* гармони́ст; аккордеони́ст.

accost *v.t.* подходить к; привязываться к.

account *n.* **1,** (business record) счёт: *open an account,* открывать счёт. **2,** (report; description) отчёт; рассказ: *an account of events,* отчёт/рассказ о событиях. **3,** (importance; worth) значение; важность. *Of no account,* не имеющий значения. **4,** (reason; basis) основание; причина: *on that account,* на этом основании; по этой причине. —*v.i.* [*usu.* **account for**] **1,** (explain) объяснять: *how do you account for the fact that...?,* чем вы объясняете то, что...? *This accounts for his strange behavior,* этим объясняется его странное поведение. **2,** (represent numerically) *inverted in Russian: copper accounts for a third of all exports,* треть всего экспорта приходится на медь. **3,** (give a statement of) отчитываться в: *account for one's expenses,* отчитываться в расходах. **4,** in *all present and accounted for,* все налицо. —**bring to account,** привлекать к ответственности. —**by all accounts,** по общему мнению; по словам всех. —**call to account,** призывать к ответу. —**give a good account of oneself,** хорошо себя зарекомендовать. —**on account of,** из-за; вследствие (+ *gen.*). —**on no account,** ни в коем случае. —**on (someone's) account,** ради: *on my account,* ради меня. —**take into account; take account of,** принимать во внимание/к сведению/в расчёт; учитывать.

accountable *adj.* ответственный; подотчётный. —**accountability,** *n.* подотчётность.

accountant *n.* бухгалтер; счетовод.

accounting *n.* бухгалтерия; счетоводство. *Accounting department,* бухгалтерия.

accouterment *also,* **accoutrement** *n., usu. pl.* снаряжение.

accredit *v.t., dipl.* аккредитовать.

accretion *n.* **1,** (growth in size) прирост. **2,** (accumulated matter) нарост.

accrue *v.i.* **1,** *fol. by* **to** (fall to) доставаться (+ *dat.*). **2,** (accumulate, as of interest) нарастать.

accumulate *v.t.* копить; накоплять. —*v.i.* копиться; накопляться; скапливаться.

accumulation *n.* **1,** (act of accumulating) накопление. **2,** (that which has accumulated) скопление.

accuracy *n.* **1,** (freedom from error) точность. **2,** (precision, as with a weapon) меткость.

accurate *adj.* **1,** (free from error; correct) точный. **2,** (always hitting one's target) меткий. —**accurately,** *adv.* точно.

accursed *adj.* проклятый.

accusation *n.* обвинение.

accusative *adj.* винительный: *accusative case,* винительный падеж.

accusatory *adj.* обвинительный.

accuse *v.t.* обвинять: *accuse someone of lying,* обвинять кого-нибудь во лжи. —**accused,** *n., law* обвиняемый. —**accuser,** *n.* обвинитель.

accustom *v.t.* приучать.

accustomed *adj.* **1,** (habitual) привычный. **2,** *fol. by* **to** (used to) привыкший (к).

ace *n.* **1,** *cards* туз. **2,** (pilot) ас. —*adj., colloq.* первоклассный.

acerbic *adj.* **1,** (astringent) терпкий. **2,** *fig.* (caustic) едкий. —**acerbity,** *n.* терпкость; едкость.

acetate *n.* соль уксусной кислоты; уксуснокислая соль.

acetic *adj.* уксусный. —**acetic acid,** уксусная

кислота.

acetone *n.* ацетон.

acetylene *n.* ацетилен. —*adj.* ацетиленовый.

ache *n.* боль. —*v.i.* болеть.

achieve *v.t.* достигать; добиться. —**achievement,** *n.* достижение.

Achilles' heel ахиллесова пята.

acid *n.* кислота: *sulfuric acid,* серная кислота. —*adj.* **1,** (containing acid) кислотный. **2,** (sour) кислый. **3,** (caustic, as of a remark) едкий.

acidity *n.* кислота; кислотность.

acknowledge *v.t.* **1,** (admit) признавать: *acknowledge one's mistakes,* признавать свои ошибки. **2,** (recognize and reply to) отвечать на: *acknowledge a letter,* отвечать на письмо. *Acknowledge receipt of,* подтверждать получение (+ *gen.*).

acknowledgment *also,* **acknowledgement** *n.* **1,** (act of admitting) признание. **2,** (document confirming receipt) расписка.

acme *n.* высшая точка; верх; вершина. *The acme of perfection,* верх совершенства.

acne *n.* угри.

aconite *n.* аконит.

acorn *n.* жёлудь.

acoustic *also,* **acoustical** *adj.* акустический. —**acoustics,** *n.* акустика.

acquaint *v.t.* знакомить; ознакомлять. *Acquaint oneself with,* ознакомляться с.

acquaintance *n.* **1,** (state of being acquainted) знакомство. *Make someone's acquaintance,* знакомиться с. **2,** (person known to one) знакомый.

acquainted *adj.* знакомый. *Get acquainted,* знакомиться.

acquiesce *v.i.* соглашаться. —**acquiescence,** *n.* согласие. —**acquiescent,** *adj.* уступчивый.

acquire *v.t.* приобретать. —**acquisition,** *n.* приобретение. —**acquisitive,** *adj.* собственнический.

acquit *v.t.* оправдывать: *he was acquitted,* он был оправдан. —**acquit oneself,** вести себя; держаться. *Acquit oneself well,* хорошо себя зарекомендовать.

acquittal *n.* оправдание.

acre *n.* акр.

acrid *adj.* едкий; терпкий.

acrimonious *adj.* едкий; злобный. —**acrimony,** *n.* едкость; злоба.

acrobat *n.* акробат. —**acrobatic,** *adj.* акробатический. —**acrobatics,** *n.* акробатика.

acropolis *n.* акрополь.

across *prep.* **1,** (to the other side of) через: *walk across the street,* перейти через улицу. **2,** (on the other side of) по ту сторону (+ *gen.*). *They live across the street,* они живут напротив. **3,** (athwart) поперёк: *lie across the road,* лежать поперёк дороги. —*adv.* **1,** (to the other side) *usu. rendered by the prefix* пере-: *walk across,* переходить; *swim across,* переплывать. **2,** (in width) в ширину: *the river is two miles across,* река имеет две мили в ширину. —**across from,** напротив.

acrostic *n.* акростих.

act *v.i.* **1,** (take action) действовать; поступать: *act decisively,* действовать/поступать решительно. *We must act at once,* мы должны действовать немедленно. **2,** (behave) вести себя: *act foolishly,* вести себя глупо; *act like a child,* вести себя как ребёнок. **3,** (pretend) притворяться. **4,** (be an actor) играть (на сцене). **5,** *fol.* by **as** (serve as) служить (+*instr.*). —*v.t.* играть. *The play was well acted,* актёры играли хорошо. —*n.* **1,** (deed) поступок; акт. *Catch in the act,* поймать с поличным. **2,** (law) акт. **3,** (part of a play or opera) действие; акт. **4,** (item on a variety program) номер. **5,** (false show) комедия: *put on an act,* разыграть комедию. —**act on, 1,** (act according to) следовать (*e.g.* совету). **2,** (have an effect on) действовать на. —**act out,** разыгрывать. —**act up,** *colloq.* шалить.

acting *n.* **1,** (performance) игра. **2,** (profession) актёрство. —*adj.* исполняющий обязанности (+*gen.*): *acting manager,* исполняющий обязанности заведующего.

actinium *n.* актиний.

action *n.* **1,** (doing something) действие. *Plan of action,* план действий. *Freedom of action,* свобода действий. *Take action,* действовать. *Put out of action,* выводить из строя. **2,** *pl.* (acts; deeds) действия; дела. *Judge someone by his actions,* судить о ком-нибудь по его делам. *Be responsible for one's actions,* отвечать за свои поступки. **3,** (of a play or narrative) действие. **4,** *mil.* (combat) бой: *be killed in action,* пасть в бою. *See action,* воевать. **5,** *law* иск; процесс. *Bring legal action,* начинать судебный процесс; подавать в суд.

activate *v.t.* **1,** (set in motion) приводить в действие. **2,** *mil.* (place on active status) призывать на действительную службу.

active *adj.* **1,** (energetic; busy) активный; деятельный. **2,** (lively; agile) живой. **3,** (functioning; in operation) действующий. *Active volcano,* действующий вулкан. **4,** *gram.* действительный: *active voice,* действительный залог. **5,** *mil.* действительный: *active duty,* действительная служба. —**actively,** *adv.* активно.

activist *n.* активист.

activity *n.* **1,** (action) деятельность. **2,** (vigorous action) активность. **3,** *pl.* (organized pursuits) мероприятия: *extracurricular activities,* внеклассные мероприятия.

actor *n.* актёр. —**actress,** *n.* актриса.

actual *adj.* действительный; фактический. —**actuality,** *n.* действительность. —**actually,** *adv.* действительно; фактически; на самом деле.

actuate *v.t.* **1,** (put into action) приводить в действие. **2,** (impel) побуждать.

acuity *n.* острота.

acumen *n.* проницательность; зоркость.

acupuncture *n.* акупунктура; иглотерапия; иглоукалывание.

acute *adj.* острый. —**acute accent,** острое ударение. —**acute angle,** острый угол.

ad *n.* объявление; реклама.

A.D. нашей эры: *in 200 A.D.,* в двухсотом году нашей эры.

adage *n.* изречение.

adagio *adv. & n.* адажио.

adamant *adj.* непреклонный.

Adam's apple адамово яблоко; кадык.

adapt *v.t.* **1,** (adjust) приспособлять. **2,** (convert to a new medium) переделывать. *Adapt for the stage,* инсценировать. —*v.i.* приспособляться.

adaptability *n.* приспособляемость. —**adaptable,** *adj.* легко приспособляющийся.

adaptation *n.* **1,** (act of adapting) приспособление. **2,** (of a story, play, etc.) переделка. **3,** *biol.* адаптация.

adapter *n.* адаптер.

add *v.t.* **1,** (put additionally) прибавлять; добавлять: *add two cups of sugar,* прибавлять/добавлять две чашки сахара. *Add a line to a letter,* прибавлять строчку к письму. *Add wood to the fire,* подкладывать дров в огонь. **2,** (state additionally) добавлять: *he added that...,* он добавил, что... **3,** *math.* складывать: *add two and two,* складывать два и два. **4,** (join) присоединять: *add one's voice to,* присоединять свой голос к. —*v.i.* **1,** (do addition) складывать числа. **2,** *fol.* by **to** (augment) увеличивать; усиливать. —**add on, 1,** (add additionally) прибавлять: *add on the interest,* прибавлять проценты. **2,** (build on) пристраивать. —**add up, 1,** (figure the total of) суммировать; подытоживать. **2,** *usu. neg.* (seem consistent) (не) сходиться; (не) выдерживать критики. —**add up to, 1,** (amount to) составлять; равняться (+*dat.*). **2,** (signify; come down to) сводиться (к).

added *adj.* дополнительный; добавочный.

addendum *n.* приложение; дополнение.

adder *n.* (snake) гадюка.

addict *n.* **1,** (drug addict) наркоман; морфинист. **2,** (enthusiast) любитель. *Chess addict,* страстный шахматист. —**addicted,** *adj.* пристрастившийся.

addiction *n.* влечение. *Drug addiction,* наркомания.

adding machine счётная машина.

addition *n.* **1,** (act of adding; something added) прибавление; добавление; дополнение. **2,** *math.* сложение. —**in addition,** вдобавок; кроме того; к тому же. —**in addition to,** кроме; в дополнение к; в добавление к.

additional *adj.* дополнительный; добавочный. —**additionally,** *adv.* к тому же.

additive *n.* добавка; присадка.

addle *v.t.* **1,** (spoil) портить. **2,** (confuse) путать.

addled *adj.* **1,** (rotten, as of an egg) тухлый. **2,** (confused; mixed up) путаный.

address *n.* **1,** (dwelling or mailing place) адрес. **2,** (formal speech) выступление. —*v.t.* **1,** (speak to) обращаться к; адресоваться к. **2,** (deliver a speech to) выступать на *or* перед. **3,** (write the address on) адресовать. *A letter addressed to the president,* письмо на имя президента. **4,** (direct, as a remark or question) адресовать. **5,** *in* **address oneself to** (turn to; take up) браться за; приниматься за.

addressee *n.* адресат.

adduce *v.t.* приводить.

adenoid *n.* аденоид.

adept *adj.* искусный.

adequacy *n.* достаточность.

adequate *adj.* достаточный. —**adequately,** *adv.* достаточно.

adhere *v.i.* **1,** (stick fast) прилипать; приставать. **2,** *fol.* by **to** (follow consistently) придерживаться (+*gen.*); держаться (+*gen.*).

adherence *n.* приверженность.

adherent *n.* приверженец.

adhesion *n.* прилипание.

adhesive *adj.* липкий. —*n.* липкое вещество. —**adhesive tape,** липкая лента.

ad hoc специа́льный: *ad hoc committee*, специа́льный комите́т.

adieu *interj.* проща́й! —*n.* проща́ние.

ad infinitum до бесконе́чности.

adipose *adj.* жи́рный.

adjacent *adj.* сме́жный; сосе́дний. —**adjacent angles,** сме́жные углы́.

adjective *n.* и́мя прилага́тельное. —**adjectival,** *adj. Adjectival endings,* оконча́ния имён прилага́тельных.

adjoin *v.t.* прилега́ть к; примыка́ть к. —**adjoining,** *adj.* сме́жный; прилега́ющий.

adjourn *v.t.* закрыва́ть: *declare the meeting adjourned,* объяви́ть заседа́ние закры́тым. *Adjourn a game,* отложи́ть па́ртию. —*v.i.* **1,** (suspend or end proceedings) закрыва́ться; закрыва́ть заседа́ние; объявля́ть переры́в. **2,** *colloq.* (move) переходи́ть. —**adjournment,** *n.* переры́в.

adjudge *v.t.* признава́ть: *he was adjudged insane,* его́ призна́ли душевнобольны́м.

adjudicate *v.t.* суди́ть; выноси́ть реше́ние по.

adjunct *n.* прида́ток.

adjure *v.t.* **1,** (command solemnly) повелева́ть. **2,** (entreat) заклина́ть.

adjust *v.t.* **1,** (make accurate; set right) регули́ровать. *Adjust a clock,* подводи́ть часы́. **2,** (move into the proper position) поправля́ть. **3,** (alter so as to make fit) подгоня́ть. **4,** (compose, as differences) ула́живать. —*v.i.* приспособля́ться. —**adjustable,** *adj.* передвижно́й. —**adjuster,** *n.* нала́дчик.

adjustment *n.* **1,** (adaptation) приспособле́ние. **2,** (regulating; setting) устано́вка; регулиро́вка. **3,** (fixing; setting right) попра́вка: *a slight adjustment,* небольша́я попра́вка. **4,** (composing, as differences) ула́живание.

adjutant *n.* адъюта́нт.

ad-lib *v.t. & i., colloq.* импровизи́ровать.

administer *v.t.* **1,** (manage) управля́ть. **2,** (inflict, as a beating, defeat, etc.) наноси́ть. **3,** (give remedially) дава́ть. *Administer first aid,* ока́зывать пе́рвую по́мощь. *Administer an injection,* сде́лать уко́л. **4,** (give; conduct, as a test) проводи́ть (экза́мен). **5,** (tender, as an oath): *administer the oath to someone,* приводи́ть кого́-нибудь к прися́ге. **6,** (dispense, as justice) отправля́ть (правосу́дие). —*v.i.* [*usu.* **administer to**] ока́зывать по́мощь (кому́-нибудь); удовлетворя́ть (чьи-нибудь) ну́жды.

administration *n.* **1,** (managing) управле́ние. **2,** (managing officials) администра́ция. **3,** (government) администра́ция. **4,** (government bureau) управле́ние.

administrative *adj.* администрати́вный.

administrator *n.* администра́тор.

admirable *adj.* похва́льный; отли́чный.

admiral *n.* адмира́л. —**Admiral of the Fleet,** адмира́л фло́та.

admiralty *n.* адмиралте́йство.

admiration *n.* преклоне́ние; восхище́ние.

admire *v.t.* **1,** (esteem highly) преклоня́ться пе́ред. **2,** (watch with pleasure) любова́ться.

admirer *n.* покло́нник; почита́тель.

admissible *adj.* допусти́мый; прие́млемый.

admission *n.* **1,** (act of admitting or letting in) впуск; до́пуск; приём; приня́тие. **2,** (entry) до́ступ: *gain admission to,* получи́ть до́ступ в *or* на. **3,** (entrance fee) входна́я пла́та. **4,** (acknowledgment) призна́ние: *admission of guilt,* призна́ние вины́. —**admission charge,** входна́я пла́та.

admit *v.t.* **1,** (allow to enter) впуска́ть; допуска́ть; принима́ть. **2,** (acknowledge; confess) признава́ть. **3,** (concede; grant) допуска́ть.

admittance *n.* **1,** (act of admitting) впуск; до́пуск; приём. **2,** (entry) вход: *no admittance!,* вход воспрещён!

admittedly *adv.* пра́вда; призна́ться.

admix *v.t.* приме́шивать.

admixture *n.* при́месь.

admonish *v.t.* **1,** (chide) жури́ть. **2,** (advise; urge) увещева́ть.

admonition *n.* **1,** (mild rebuke) замеча́ние. **2,** (advice; warning) наставле́ние; нравоуче́ние; увеща́ние.

ad nauseam до тошноты́.

ado *n.* суета́. *Without further ado,* без дальне́йших церемо́ний; без да́льних слов. —**much ado about nothing,** мно́го шу́ма из ничего́.

adobe *n.* кирпи́ч-сыре́ц; сама́н. —*adj.* сама́нный; глиноби́тный.

adolescence *n.* о́трочество.

adolescent *n.* подро́сток. —*adj.* о́троческий.

adopt *v.t.* **1,** (take into one's family) усыновля́ть; удочеря́ть. **2,** (vote to accept) принима́ть. **3,** (take up and follow) принима́ть; усва́ивать; перенима́ть; заи́мствовать. —**adopted,** *adj.* приёмный.

adoption *n.* **1,** (taking into one's family) усыновле́ние. **2,** (acceptance and use; vote to accept) приня́тие.

adoptive *adj.* приёмный.

adorable *adj.* преле́стный; восхити́тельный.

adore *v.t.* обожа́ть. —**adoration,** *n.* обожа́ние.

adorn *v.t.* украша́ть. —**adornment,** *n.* украше́ние.

adrenal *adj.* надпо́чечный. —**adrenal gland,** надпо́чечная железа́; надпо́чечник.

adrenalin *also,* **adrenaline** *n.* адренали́н.

adrift *adv.* по тече́нию: *set adrift,* пуска́ть по тече́нию.

adroit *adj.* ло́вкий; прово́рный. —**adroitly,** *adv.* ло́вко. —**adroitness,** *n.* ло́вкость; прово́рство.

adsorb *v.t.* адсорби́ровать. —**adsorption,** *n.* адсо́рбция.

adulation *n.* **1,** (excessive praise) восхвале́ние. **2,** (intense admiration) преклоне́ние.

adult *n. & adj.* взро́слый. *Adult education,* обуче́ние взро́слых.

adulterate *v.t.* фальсифици́ровать; разбавля́ть. —**adulteration,** *n.* фальсифика́ция.

adulterer *n.* прелюбоде́й. —**adulteress,** *n.* прелюбоде́йка. —**adulterous,** *adj.* прелюбоде́йский.

adultery *n.* прелюбодея́ние. *Commit adultery,* соверша́ть прелюбодея́ние; прелюбоде́йствовать.

adulthood *n.* зре́лость; возмужа́лость.

advance *v.t.* **1,** (move forward; further; promote) продвига́ть. **2,** (put forward, as a theory) выдвига́ть. **3,** (lend) ссужа́ть. —*v.i.* **1,** продвига́ться; выдвига́ться. *Troops are advancing on the capital,* войска́ продвига́ются к столи́це. —*n.* **1,** (move forward) продвиже́ние. **2,** *fig.* (important step forward) достиже́ние. **3,** (loan) ссу́да; ава́нс. **4,** *pl.* (overtures) заи́грывания; уха́живания. —*adj.* **1,** (prior) предвари́тельный: *advance sale,* предвари́тельная прода́жа (биле́тов). **2,** (going ahead) передово́й: *advance* *guard,* передово́й отря́д. **—in advance,** зара́нее; предвари́тельно; вперёд; ава́нсом.

advanced *adj.* **1,** (far along) продви́нутый: *advanced student,* продви́нутый учени́к *or* студе́нт. *Advanced course,* курс повы́шенного ти́па. **2,** (modern; progressive) передово́й: *advanced methods,* передовы́е ме́тоды. **3,** (old) прекло́нный: *advanced age,* прекло́нный во́зраст. *Advanced in years,* прекло́нного во́зраста.

advancement *n.* продвиже́ние.

advantage *n.* **1,** (edge; superiority) преиму́щество: *enjoy a clear advantage over,* по́льзоваться я́вным преиму́ществом пе́ред. **2,** (factor giving an edge) преиму́щество; досто́инство. *Advantages and disadvantages,* досто́инства и недоста́тки. *Have a number of advantages over,* име́ть ряд преиму́ществ пе́ред. **3,** (benefit; profit) вы́года; по́льза. *Turn to one's advantage,* обраща́ть в свою́ по́льзу. **—take advantage of, 1,** (avail oneself of) по́льзоваться (*+ instr.*). **2,** (abuse; exploit) злоупотребля́ть; эксплуати́ровать. **—to advantage,** вы́годно; в вы́годном све́те. **—to the best advantage, 1,** (in the best way) наилу́чшим о́бразом. **2,** (in the best light) в са́мом вы́годном све́те.

advantageous *adj.* вы́годный.

advent *n.* наступле́ние; прише́ствие.

adventure *n.* приключе́ние; авантю́ра. *Thirst for adventure,* жа́жда приключе́ний. *—adj.* приключе́нческий; авантю́рный: *adventure story,* приключе́нческий/авантю́рный рома́н.

adventurer *n.* иска́тель приключе́ний.

adventuresome *adj.* сме́лый; предприи́мчивый.

adventurism *n.* авантюри́зм. **—adventurist,** *n.* авантюри́ст. **—adventuristic,** *adj.* авантюристи́ческий.

adventurous *adj.* сме́лый; предприи́мчивый.

adverb *n.* наре́чие. **—adverbial,** *adj.* наре́чный.

adversary *n.* проти́вник.

adverse *adj.* неблагоприя́тный. *Adverse wind,* встре́чный ве́тер. **—adversely,** *adv.* отрица́тельно.

adversity *n.* несча́стье; невзго́да.

advertise *v.t. & i.* реклами́ровать. **—advertisement,** *n.* объявле́ние; рекла́ма.

advertising *n.* рекла́ма. *—adj.* рекла́мный.

advice *n.* сове́т.

advisable *adj.* целесообра́зный. **—advisability,** *n.* целесообра́зность.

advise *v.t.* **1,** (give advice to) сове́товать: *What do you advise me to do?,* что вы мне сове́туете де́лать? *He advised against it,* он сове́товал не де́лать э́того. **2,** (notify) сообща́ть; извеща́ть; уведомля́ть; дать знать.

advised *adj.* осведомлённый. *Keep someone advised,* держа́ть кого́-нибудь в ку́рсе дел. **—advisedly,** *adv.* наме́ренно; обду́манно. *I say this advisedly,* я наме́ренно э́то говорю́.

advisement *n.* рассмотре́ние. **—take under advisement,** рассма́тривать.

adviser *n.* сове́тник.

advisory *adj.* консультати́вный.

advocacy *n.* защи́та; подде́ржка.

advocate *v.t.* стоя́ть за; выступа́ть за. *—n.* **1,** (one who favors a cause) сторо́нник: *an advocate of reform,* сторо́нник рефо́рмы. **2,** *law* защи́тник; засту́пник.

adz *also,* **adze** *n.* тесло́.

aegis *n.* эги́да: *under the aegis of,* под эги́дой (*+ gen.*).

aerate *v.t.* прове́тривать. **—aeration,** *n.* аэра́ция.

aerial *adj.* возду́шный. *Aerial photograph,* аэросни́мок. *—n.* анте́нна.

aerodrome *n.* = **airdrome.**

aerodynamics *n.* аэродина́мика. **—aerodynamic,** *adj.* аэродинами́ческий.

aeronaut *n.* воздухопла́ватель; аэрона́вт. **—aeronautical,** *adj.* авиацио́нный; воздухопла́вательный. *Aeronautical engineer,* авиацио́нный инжене́р. **—aeronautics,** *n.* воздухопла́вание; аэрона́втика.

aerosol *n.* аэрозо́ль.

aerospace *n.* возду́шно-косми́ческое простра́нство. *—adj.* возду́шно-косми́ческий; авиакосми́ческий.

aerostat *n.* аэроста́т. **—aerostatics,** *n.* аэроста́тика.

aesthete *n.* = **esthete. —aesthetic,** *adj.* = **esthetic. —aesthetics,** *n.* = **esthetics.**

afar *adv., in* **from afar,** издалека́.

affable *adj.* приве́тливый. **—affability,** *n.* приве́тливость.

affair *n.* **1,** (event; matter; business) де́ло. *Foreign affairs,* иностра́нные дела́. *State of affairs,* положе́ние дел *or* веще́й. *It's none of your affair,* э́то не ва́ше де́ло. **2,** (amorous relationship) связь; рома́н.

affect *v.t.* **1,** (have an effect upon) влия́ть на. **2,** (touch; concern) затра́гивать. **3,** (touch emotionally) тро́гать. **4,** (feign) притворя́ться; прики́дываться.

affectation *n.* де́ланность; жема́нство; аффекта́ция.

affected *adj.* **1,** (feigned) наи́гранный; напускно́й; аффекти́рованный. **2,** (artificial in manner) жема́нный; мане́рный. **3,** (moved by emotion) тро́нут; растро́ганный. **4,** (afflicted) затро́нутый; заде́тый.

affection *n.* привя́занность. **—affectionate,** *adj.* ла́сковый.

affiance *v.t.* обруча́ть.

affidavit *n.* пи́сьменное показа́ние под прися́гой.

affiliate *v.i.* присоединя́ться. *Be affiliated with,* име́ть связь с. *—n.* филиа́л. **—affiliation,** *n.* принадле́жность.

affinity *n.* **1,** (natural attraction; liking) влече́ние. **2,** (similarity implying common origin) родство́; сродство́.

affirm *v.t.* **1,** (assert positively) заявля́ть о: *affirm one's loyalty,* заяви́ть о свое́й лоя́льности. **2,** (confirm) подтвержда́ть; утвержда́ть.

affirmation *n.* **1,** (firm statement) заявле́ние. **2,** (confirmation) подтвержде́ние.

affirmative *adj.* утверди́тельный. *Answer in the affirmative,* отвеча́ть утверди́тельно. **—affirmatively,** *adv.* утверди́тельно.

affix *v.t.* **1,** (attach) прикрепля́ть. **2,** (stick on) накле́ивать; прикле́ивать. **3,** (write; stamp; imprint) накла́дывать; ста́вить: *affix a seal,* накла́дывать/ста́вить печа́ть. *Affix one's signature to,* ста́вить свою́ по́дпись под (*+ instr.*).

afflict *v.t.* поража́ть. *Be afflicted with,* страда́ть (*+ instr.*).

affliction *n.* **1,** (distress) несча́стье. **2,** (ailment) боле́знь.

affluence *n.* оби́лие; бога́тство. **—affluent,** *adj.* бога́тый; состоя́тельный.

afford *v.t.* **1,** (have the means for) позволить себе: *I can't afford it,* не могу этого себе позволить; это мне не по средствам (*or* не по карману). *I can't afford the time,* мне некогда. **2,** (give; provide) доставлять; предоставлять: *afford pleasure,* доставлять удовольствие; *afford an opportunity,* предоставлять возможность. *The balcony affords an excellent view of the lake,* с балкона открывается прекрасный вид на озеро.

affront *v.t.* оскорблять. —*n.* оскорбление.

Afghan *adj.* [*also,* **Afghanistani**] афганский. —*n.* **1,** (native of Afghanistan) афганец; афганка. **2,** *l.c.* (woolen blanket) шерстяное одеяло.

afield *adv.* от темы: *go rather far afield,* отклоняться от темы. *That would take us far afield,* это завело бы нас далеко.

afire *adj.* в огне. *Set afire,* поджигать.

aflame *adj.* в огне. *Be aflame,* быть в огне; пылать. *Set aflame,* воспламенять.

afloat *adj. & adv.* на воде; на плаву. *Remain afloat,* держаться на воде. *Rumors are afloat,* ходят слухи.

afoot *adv. & adj., obs.* пешком. —**be afoot,** готовиться; затеваться.

aforementioned *adj.* вышеупомянутый.

aforesaid *adj.* вышесказанный.

afraid *adj., used predicatively: I am afraid,* мне страшно. *Be afraid of,* бояться (+ *gen.*). *Be afraid that...,* бояться, что...

afresh *adv.* снова: *start afresh,* начинать снова.

African *adj.* африканский. —*n.* африканец.

aft *adv.* на корме; на корму.

after *prep.* **1,** (subsequent to) после: *after dinner,* после обеда. ♦*With expressions of time* через: *after a year,* через год; *after a while,* через некоторое время. *Ten years after the war,* через десять лет после войны. **2,** (following; behind; in pursuit of) за (+*instr.*): *summer comes after spring,* лето идёт за весной. *Time after time,* раз за разом. *One after the other,* один за другим. *Run/look/clean up/after someone,* бежать/присматривать/убирать за кем-нибудь. **3,** (in telling time) *ten after two,* десять минут третьего. *It is already after six,* уже седьмой час. **4,** (for; in honor of) в честь: *he was named after his grandfather,* его назвали в честь деда. **5,** (in view of) после: *after what went on yesterday,* после того, что произошло вчера. *After all she has been through,* после всего, что она пережила. **6,** (in spite of) несмотря на: *after all he has done for you,* несмотря на всё, что он сделал для вас. —*adv.* **1,** (behind) сзади; позади. **2,** (subsequently) позднее; потом. —*conj.* после того, как: *after he left,* после того как он ушёл. *After you have read the book,* после того, как вы прочтёте книгу. *After learning about what happened,* узнав о случившемся. —**after all, 1,** (despite all; in the end) всё-таки: *I was right after all,* всё-таки я был прав. **2,** (when all is said and done) же; ведь: *after all, she is your sister!,* она же твоя сестра; ведь она твоя сестра. —**after that,** вслед за тем. —**after you!,** прошу вас!

afterbirth *n.* послед.

after-dinner *adj.* послеобеденный.

aftereffect *n.* последствие; отголосок.

afterglow *n.* вечерняя заря.

afterlife *n.* загробная жизнь.

aftermath *n.* отголоски.

afternoon *n.* время после полудня; вторая половина дня. —**in the afternoon,** днём; после обеда; во второй половине дня. *At three o'clock in the afternoon,* в три часа пополудни.

aftertaste *n.* привкус; осадок.

afterward *also,* **afterwards** *adv.* после; потом; впоследствии. *Soon afterward,* вскоре.

again *adv.* опять; снова; ещё раз. *What, again?,* что, опять? *Try again,* попробовать ещё раз. *Meet again,* снова встретиться. *Happen again,* повторяться. —**again and again,** снова и снова. —**but then again,** впрочем. —**now and again,** время от времени. —**time and again,** то и дело; неоднократно.

against *prep.* **1,** (in opposition to; contrary to; compared to) против: *against the wind,* против ветра; *against one's will,* против воли. *Compete/struggle against,* состязаться/бороться с. *Six in favor, three against,* шесть за, три против. **2,** (so as to strike) о (+*acc.*): *beat against the shore,* биться о берег. **3,** (so as to touch) к: *lean against a wall,* прислоняться к стене. *Place the table up against the wall,* поставить стол вплотную к стене. **4,** (as a protection from) от: *insurance against breakage,* страхование от поломки. *Protection against the cold,* защита от холода. **5,** (in anticipation of) на: *against a rainy day,* на чёрный день. **6,** (in contrast to the background of) на фоне (+*gen.*): *stand out against the sky,* выделяться на фоне неба. **7,** (as a debit on) под: *borrow money against an insurance policy,* занимать деньги под страховой полис.

agape *adj. & adv.* разинув рот.

agate *n.* агат. —*adj.* агатовый.

agave *n.* агава.

age *n.* **1,** (years since birth) возраст. *At my age,* в мои годы. *Be the same age,* быть одних лет. *Not to look one's age,* выглядеть моложе своих лет. **2,** (old age) старость: *live to a ripe old age,* дожить до старости. **3,** (adulthood) совершеннолетие: *come of age,* достигать совершеннолетия. *Be of age,* быть совершеннолетним. **4,** (period in history) век; эпоха. *The Stone Age,* каменный век. *The space age,* космический век. **5,** *often pl., colloq.* (a long time) целую вечность: *I haven't seen you for ages,* не видел вас целую вечность. —*adj.* возрастной: *age group,* возрастная группа. —*v.t.* **1,** (make old) старить. **2,** (mature, as wine) выдерживать. —*v.i.* **1,** (grow old) стареть. **2,** (mature, as of wine) созревать. —**at the age of,** в возрасте (+ *gen.*): *at the age of twenty-five,* в возрасте двадцати пяти лет; в двадцатипятилетнем возрасте; в двадцать пять лет.

aged *adj.* **1,** (old) старый; престарелый. **2,** (of a certain age): *a girl aged five,* девочка пяти лет. **3,** (mature, as of wine) выдержанный. —**the aged,** старики.

ageing *adj. & n.* = **aging.**

ageless *adj.* **1,** (seeming not to grow old) вечно молодой. **2,** (eternal) вечный.

agency *n.* **1,** (bureau; department) агентство; бюро; управление; учреждение: *telegraph agency,* телеграфное агентство; *travel agency,* бюро путешествий; *specialized agency,* специализированное учреждение. *Central Intelligence Agency,* Центральное разведывательное управление. **2,** (means; instrumentality) средство. *Through the agency of,* посредством (+ *gen.*); через посредство (+ *gen.*).

agenda *n.* повéстка дня.

agent *n.* **1,** (person) агéнт: *insurance agent,* страховóй агéнт; *intelligence agent,* агéнт развéдки. **2,** (substance) вещество́; сре́дство; аге́нт. —**agent provocateur,** провока́тор.

age-old *adj.* веково́й.

agglutination *n.* агглютина́ция. —**agglutinative,** *adj.* агглютинати́вный.

aggrandize *v.t.* увели́чивать; расширя́ть. —**aggrandizement,** *n.* увеличéние; расширéние.

aggravate *v.t.* **1,** (make worse) ухудша́ть; обостря́ть. **2,** *colloq.* (vex) раздража́ть; досажда́ть.

aggravating *adj.* доса́дный. —**aggravating circumstances,** отягча́ющие вину́ обстоя́тельства.

aggravation *n.* **1,** (making worse) ухудшéние; обострéние. **2,** (vexation) раздражéние; доса́да.

aggregate *adj.* совоку́пный. —*n.* совоку́пность.

aggression *n.* агрéссия. *Act of aggression,* акт агрéссии.

aggressive *adj.* **1,** (militant; hostile) агресси́вный. **2,** (assertive; pushy) напо́ристый.

aggressor *n.* агрéссор.

aggrieve *v.t.* **1,** (distress) огорча́ть. **2,** (wrong) обижа́ть. *The aggrieved party,* потерпéвшая сторона́.

aghast *adj.* в у́жасе.

agile *adj.* прово́рный. —**agility,** *n.* прово́рство.

aging *also,* **ageing** *adj.* старéющий. —*n.* старéние.

agitate *v.t.* **1,** (disturb, as the sea) волнова́ть. **2,** (shake briskly) взба́лтывать. **3,** (perturb) волнова́ть. —*v.i.* агити́ровать. —**agitated,** *adj.* взволно́ванный.

agitation *n.* **1,** (agitated state) волнéние. **2,** *polit.* агита́ция.

agitator *n.* агита́тор.

aglet *n.* **1,** (tip at the end of a lace) наконéчник. **2,** (braid on a uniform) аксельба́нт.

aglow *adj., used predicatively:* be aglow, сия́ть.

agnostic *n.* агно́стик. —*adj.* агности́ческий. —**agnosticism,** *n.* агностици́зм.

ago *adj.* тому́ наза́д: *two years ago,* два го́да тому́ наза́д. —*adv., in* **long ago,** давно́; **not long ago,** неда́вно.

agonize *v.i.* му́читься. —**agonizing,** *adj.* мучи́тельный.

agony *n.* **1,** (intense suffering) му́ка; мучéние. **2,** (throes of death) (предсмéртная) аго́ния.

agrarian *adj.* агра́рный.

agree *v.i.* **1,** (be of the same opinion) быть согла́сным; соглаша́ться: *I agree with you,* я с ва́ми согла́сен (согла́сна). **2,** *fol. by* **to** (consent to) соглаша́ться (*+ inf.*) *or with* на (*+ acc.*): *agree to a draw,* согласи́ться на ничью́. **3,** (reach agreement; make arrangements) договори́ться. **4,** (be in harmony; coincide) сходи́ться. **5,** *fol. by* **with** (be suitable or good for): *married life agrees with him,* бра́чная жизнь ему́ по душé. *Turnips don't agree with me,* мой желу́док не выно́сит рéпы. **6,** *gram.* согласова́ться.

agreeable *adj.* **1,** (pleasing) прия́тный. **2,** (ready to consent) согла́сный. **3,** (amenable) сгово́рчивый.

agreed *adj.* устано́вленный; поло́женный; усло́вный; усло́вленный. *Also,* **agreed-upon.**

agreement *n.* **1,** (harmony of opinion) согла́сие: *complete agreement,* по́лное согла́сие. **2,** (arrange-ment; understanding) соглашéние: *come to an agreement,* приходи́ть к соглашéнию. **3,** *gram.* согласова́ние.

agriculture *n.* сéльское хозя́йство. —**agricultural,** *adj.* сельскохозя́йственный.

agronomy *n.* агроно́мия. —**agronomic,** *adj.* агрономи́ческий. —**agronomist,** *n.* агроно́м.

aground *adj.* на мели́. —*adv.* на мель: *run aground,* сесть на мель.

ah *interj.* а!; ах!

aha *interj.* ага́!

ahead *adv.* **1,** (forward) вперёд: *full speed ahead!,* по́лный ход вперёд! *Set a clock ahead,* поста́вить часы́ вперёд. **2,** (in front of one) впереди́: *ahead lay a river,* впереди́ была́ река́. *There is danger ahead,* впереди́ опа́сность. **3,** (into or for the future) вперёд: *look ahead,* загляну́ть вперёд. *Plan ahead,* плани́ровать зара́нее. *What lies ahead for him?,* что его́ ждёт впереди́? —*adj.* впереди́: *who is ahead?,* кто впереди́? —**ahead of, 1,** (in front of) впереди́ (*+ gen.*): *walk ahead of the others,* идти́ впереди́ остальны́х. *You have your whole life ahead of you,* у вас цéлая жизнь впереди́. **2,** (in advance of) прéжде (*+ gen.*); ра́ньше (*+ gen.*). *Ahead of time,* ра́ньше врéмени; ра́ньше сро́ка. —**get ahead,** продвига́ться (вперёд). —**get ahead of,** опережа́ть. —**go ahead!,** дава́йте! —**straight ahead,** пря́мо.

ahem *interj.* гм!

aid *v.t.* помога́ть. —*n.* **1,** (assistance) по́мощь: *first aid,* ско́рая по́мощь. *Come to the aid of,* прийти́ на по́мощь (*+ dat.*). **2,** (helpful device) аппара́т: *hearing aid,* слухово́й аппара́т. **3,** *pl.* (teaching devices) посо́бия: *visual aids,* нагля́дные посо́бия.

aide *n.* **1,** *mil.* адъюта́нт. **2,** (assistant) помо́щник.

aide-de-camp *n.* адъюта́нт.

aide-mémoire *n.* па́мятная запи́ска.

aiguillette *n.* аксельба́нт.

ail *v.i.* недомога́ть; хвора́ть. —*v.t. What ails you?,* что вас беспоко́ит?

aileron *n.* элеро́н.

ailment *n.* болéзнь; недомога́ние; неду́г.

aim *n.* **1,** (objective) цель: *the aim of the experiment,* цель экспериме́нта. **2,** (act of aiming) прице́ливание. *Take aim at,* прице́ливаться в; взять прице́л на. —*v.t.* направля́ть; наводи́ть; наце́ливать. —*v.i.* **1,** (take aim) прице́ливаться; мéтить. **2,** (aspire) стреми́ться (к); мéтить. *Aim higher,* мéтить вы́ше. **3,** *fol. by* **to** (have as one's goal) имéть цéлью (*+ inf.*).

aimless *adj.* бесцéльный. —**aimlessly,** *adv.* бесцéльно.

air *n.* **1,** (atmosphere) во́здух. *Out in the open air,* на откры́том во́здухе. **2,** (appearance) вид. *Assume an air of importance,* напуска́ть на себя́ ва́жность. **3,** *pl.* (affected manners) *usu. in* **put on airs; give oneself airs,** ва́жничать; кривля́ться; лома́ться; задава́ться; зазнава́ться. **4,** *radio* эфи́р: *on the air,* в эфи́ре. **5,** (tune; melody) пéсня; напéв. —*adj.* возду́шный: *air filter,* возду́шный фильтр. *Air travel,* пое́здки на самолёте. *Air pollution,* загрязнéние во́здуха. —*v.t.* **1,** [*usu.* **air out**] (ventilate) провéтривать. **2,** (express publicly; bring out into the open) разглаша́ть. —**be in the air,** вéять: *spring is in the air,* вéет весно́й. —**be up in the air,** висéть *or* пови́снуть в во́здухе. —**be walking on air,** ног под собо́й не чу́ять. —**by air,** на самолёте; самолётом. —**clear the air,**

разрядить атмосферу. —**take the air**, подышать свежим воздухом. —**vanish into thin air**, как сквозь землю провалиться; как в воду кануть.

air base авиабаза.

airborne *adj.* **1,** (aloft) в воздухе. **2,** *mil.* (transported by air) воздушнодесантный.

air-condition *v.t.* кондиционировать. —**air-conditioned,** *adj.* кондиционированный; с кондиционером. —**air conditioner**, кондиционер. —**air conditioning**, кондиционирование воздуха.

air-cooled *adj.* с воздушным охлаждением.

aircraft *n.* **1,** (airplane) самолёт. **2,** (airplanes collectively) авиация. —**aircraft carrier**, авианосец.

air defense противовоздушная оборона.

airdrome *also,* **aerodrome** *n.* аэродром.

airfield *n.* лётное поле; аэродром.

air force военно-воздушные силы.

air gun духовое ружьё.

air hole отдушина.

airily *adv.* весело; беззаботно.

airing *n.* проветривание.

airless *adj.* душный: *airless room*, душная комната.

airlift *n.* воздушная перевозка; "воздушный мост".

airline *n.* авиакомпания.

airliner *n.* воздушный лайнер.

air mail авиапочта. "(*By*) *air mail*", авиа; авиапочтой.

airman *n.* лётчик.

airplane *n.* самолёт.

air pocket воздушная яма.

airport *n.* аэропорт.

air pressure давление воздуха.

air raid воздушный налёт. —**air-raid shelter**, бомбоубежище. —**air-raid siren**, сирена воздушной тревоги.

air route авиатрасса.

airship *n.* дирижабль.

airsick *adj.* страдающий воздушной болезнью. *I became airsick*, меня укачало на самолёте. —**airsickness,** *n.* воздушная болезнь.

air space воздушное пространство.

airspeed *n.* воздушная скорость.

airstrip *n.* взлётно-посадочная полоса.

airtight *adj.* герметический.

airwaves *n.pl.* эфир.

airway *n.* авиатрасса.

airworthy *adj.* годный к полёту.

airy *adj.* **1,** (with plenty of air) полный воздуха. **2,** (light; thin) воздушный.

aisle *n.* проход.

ajar *adj. & adv.* приоткрытый; полуоткрытый; полуотворенный; неприкрытый. *Leave the door ajar*, оставлять дверь неприкрытой.

akimbo *adj. & adv.* подбоченившись. *Stand with arms akimbo*, подбочениться.

akin *adj.* родственный. *Be akin to*, быть сродни (+*dat.*).

alabaster *n.* алебастр. —*adj.* алебастровый.

à la carte 1, *used adjectivally* порционный. **2,** *used adverbially* по порциям.

alacrity *n.* быстрота. *With alacrity*, быстро; живо.

alarm *n.* **1,** (sudden fear) тревога. **2,** (signal of danger) тревога; набат. *Fire alarm*, пожарная тревога. *Sound the alarm*, бить/забить/ударять тревогу; бить /забить/ударять (в) набат. —*adj.* тревожный; набатный. *alarm signal*, тревожный сигнал; *alarm bell*, набатный

колокол. *Alarm system*, сигнализация. —*v.t.* тревожить. —**alarm clock**, будильник.

alarmed *adj.* встревоженный.

alarming *adj.* тревожный.

alarmist *n.* паникёр.

alas *interj.* увы!

Albanian *adj.* албанский. —*n.* **1,** (person) албанец; албанка. **2,** (language) албанский язык.

albatross *n.* альбатрос.

albeit *conj.* хотя.

albino *n.* альбинос. —**albinism,** *n.* альбинизм.

album *n.* альбом.

albumen *n.* белок.

albumin *n.* альбумин.

alburnum *n.* заболонь.

alchemy *n.* алхимия. —**alchemist,** *n.* алхимик.

alcohol *n.* **1,** (liquid) спирт; алкоголь. **2,** (intoxicating beverages) алкоголь; спиртные напитки.

alcoholic *adj.* спиртной; алкогольный. —*n.* алкоголик. —**alcoholism,** *n.* алкоголизм.

alcove *n.* альков; ниша.

alder *n.* ольха.

alderman *n.* член городского совета.

ale *n.* эль.

alert *n.* тревога. *Place on alert*, поднимать по тревоге. —*adj.* **1,** (watchful) настороженный; бдительный. **2,** (mentally quick) бойкий. —*v.t.* настораживать. —**on the alert**, настороже.

alexandrite *n.* александрит.

alfalfa *n.* люцерна.

algae *n.pl.* водоросль.

algebra *n.* алгебра. —**algebraic,** *adj.* алгебраический.

Algerian *adj.* алжирский. —*n.* алжирец; алжирка.

algorithm *n.* алгоритм.

alias *n.* вымышленное имя. —*adv.* иначе называемый; он же.

alibi *n.* **1,** *law* алиби. **2,** *colloq.* (excuse) отговорка.

alien *n.* иностранец. —*adj.* **1,** (foreign; strange) чужой: *alien customs*, чужие обычаи. **2,** (adverse; hostile) чуждый: *alien ideology*, чуждая идеология. *It is alien to his nature*, это ему чуждо по духу.

alienate *v.t.* отчуждать; отдалять; отталкивать. —**alienation,** *n.* отчуждение; отдаление.

alight *v.i.* **1,** (dismount) сходить. **2,** (settle) садиться.

align *v.t.* **1,** (arrange in a straight line) выравнивать. **2,** *fol. by* **oneself** (ally oneself) присоединяться.

alignment *n.* **1,** (act of aligning) выравнивание. **2,** *mil.* равнение.

alike *adj.* **1,** (similar) похожий. *They look alike*, (внешне) они похожи (друг на друга). **2,** (identical) одинаковый. —*adv.* одинаково.

alimentary canal пищеварительный канал; желудочно-кишечный тракт.

alimony *n.* алименты.

alive *adj.* **1,** (living) живой: *he is still alive*, он ещё жив. *Remain alive*, оставаться в живых. *Take alive*, брать живьём. *Buried alive*, заживо погребённый. *Keep alive*, поддерживать жизнь (+*gen.*). **2,** (lively; animated) живой. *Come alive*, оживать; оживляться. **3,** *fol. by* **to** (aware of; responsive to) чувствительный (к). *Be alive to*, ясно понимать. **4,** *fol. by* **with** (swarming) кишащий: *be alive with bees*, кишеть пчёлами.

alkali *n.* щёлочь. —**alkaline,** *adj.* щелочной. —**alka-**

linity, *n.* щёлочность.

alkaloid *n.* алкалóид.

all *adj.* весь (вся, всё, все): *all day,* весь день; *all the time,* всё врéмя; *all nations,* все стрáны. —*pron.* **1,** (everything) всё: *that's all,* э́то всё. *All is well,* всё хорошó. **2,** (everyone) все: *all agree,* все соглáсны. —*n.* [*usu.* one's all] *Give one's all,* отдавáть все си́лы. *Stake one's all,* постáвить всё на кáрту. —*adv.* **1,** (completely) весь; совершéнно; совсéм. *I got all wet,* я весь промóк; я вся промóкла. *All alone,* совершéнно *or* совсéм оди́н/однá. **2,** *sports: the score was two-all,* счёт был двá-двá. —**all along,** *see* **along.** —**all at once,** *see* **once.** —**all but,** *see* **but.**—**all for,** целикóм за то, чтóбы (+*inf.*). —**all in,** *colloq.* без ног. —**all in all, 1,** (in general) в о́бщем и цéлом. **2,** (altogether) всегó.—**all over,** *see* **over.** —**all the same,** *see* **same.** —**all told,** в о́бщей слóжности. —**at all, 1,** (whatsoever) никакóй: *no difference at all,* никакóй рáзницы. *For no reason at all,* без вся́кой причи́ны. **2,** (in no way) никáк: *That won't help at all,* э́то никáк не помóжет. **3,** (in any event) вообщé: *I doubt whether he'll come at all,* я сомневáюсь, придёт ли он вообщé. *See also* **not at all.** —**in all,** всегó; в о́бщей слóжности. —**not all there,** *colloq.* не в своём умé; не все дóма. —**not at all,** *see* **not.** —**of all,** всегó: *most of all,* бóльше всегó.

Allah *n.* аллáх.

all-around *adj.* всесторóнний.

allay *v.t.* **1,** (lessen; relieve) смягчáть; облегчáть. **2,** (set to rest) успокáивать: *allay suspicion,* успокáивать подозрéние.

all clear отбóй (воздýшной тревóги). *Also,* **all-clear signal.**

allegation *n.* (голослóвное) утверждéние.

allege *v.t.* **1,** (assert) утверждáть. **2,** (offer as an excuse) ссылáться на. —**alleged,** *adj.* предполагáемый: *the alleged murderer,* предполагáемый уби́йца. *For alleged improprieties,* я́кобы за нарушéние прили́чий. —**allegedly,** *adv.* я́кобы.

allegiance *n.* вéрность. *Pledge allegiance,* кля́сться в вéрности.

allegory *n.* аллегóрия; иносказáние. —**allegorical,** *adj.* аллегори́ческий; иносказáтельный.

allegretto *adv. & n.* аллегрéтто.

allegro *adv. & n.* аллéгро.

all-embracing *adj.* всеобъéмлющий.

allergic *adj.* аллерги́ческий. *Be allergic to,* имéть аллерги́ю к; не выноси́ть.

allergy *n.* аллергия.

alleviate *v.t.* облегчáть; смягчáть. —**alleviation,** *n.* облегчéние; смягчéние.

alley *n.* ýзкий переýлок; ýзкий прохóд. —**alley cat,** бродя́чий кот.

alliance *n.* сою́з.

allied *adj.* **1,** (united) сою́зный. *Be allied with,* быть сою́зником (+*gen.*). **2,** (similar; related) смéжный; рóдственный.

alligator *n.* аллигáтор.

alliteration *n.* аллитерáция.

allocate *v.t.* **1,** (allot; appropriate) выделя́ть; ассигновáть; отводи́ть. **2,** (apportion; distribute) распределя́ть. —**allocation,** *n.* ассигновáние; распределéние.

allopath *n.* аллопáт. —**allopathic,** *adj.* аллопати́ческий. —**allopathy,** *n.* аллопáтия.

allot *v.t.* **1,** (parcel out) распределя́ть; наделя́ть. **2,** (allocate) выделя́ть; отводи́ть.

allotment *n.* **1,** (parceling out) распределéние; наделéние. **2,** (allocating) выделéние. **3,** (portion allotted) дóля.

all-out *adj.* развёрнутый; тотáльный. —**go all out,** *colloq.* напрягáть все си́лы; лезть из кóжи вон.

allow *v.t.* **1,** (give permission to) позволя́ть; разрешáть. *He is not allowed to...,* емý не разрешáется (+*inf.*). **2,** (permit to happen) допускáть. *Allow a goal,* пропусти́ть гол. **3,** *fol. by* in (permit to enter) допускáть; впускáть; пропускáть. **4,** (concede) допускáть. **5,** (acknowledge as valid) признавáть справедли́вым. **6,** (provide; allot, as time) отводи́ть. **7,** *fol. by* for (make allowance for) учи́тывать. **8,** *comm.* дéлать скидку (+*dat.*): *allow someone 10%,* дéлать комý-нибудь скидку на дéсять процéнтов.

allowance *n.* **1,** (deduction) скидка. **2,** (money paid or given out) посóбие. **3,** *mil.* (дéнежное) довóльствие. *Housing allowance,* кварти́рные дéньги. *Travel allowance,* командирóвочные дéньги. **4,** (consideration) скидка: *make allowance for,* дéлать скидку на.

alloy *n.* сплав. —*v.t.* сплавля́ть.

all-powerful *adj.* всемогýщий; всеси́льный.

all-purpose *adj.* универсáльный.

all right 1, (expression of assent) лáдно; хорошó. **2,** (O.K.) хорошó. *It's all right with me,* я соглáсен; я не возражáю. **3,** (so-so) так себé. **4,** (unhurt) невреди́м. *Are you all right?,* вы не уши́блись? **5,** (recovered) здорóв. **6,** *preceded by* it's *or* that's (it doesn't matter) ничегó. **7,** (without a doubt) бýдьте увéрены: *that's him all right!,* бýдьте увéрены, э́то он!

all-round *adj.* всесторóнний; универсáльный. *All-round education,* разносторóннее образовáние.

allspice *n.* души́стый пéрец; гвозди́чный пéрец.

all-star *adj.* сборный: *all-star team,* сборная комáнда.

all-time *adj.* непревзойдённый: *all-time record,* непревзойдённый рекóрд. *Prices reached an all-time high,* цéны дости́гли небывáло высóкого ýровня.

allude *v.i.* [*usu.* allude to] ссылáться на; упоминáть; намекáть на.

allure *v.t.* замáнивать; завлекáть. —*n.* [*also,* allurement] примáнка; обольщéние. —**alluring,** *adj.* замáнчивый; маня́щий.

allusion *n.* ссы́лка; упоминáние; намёк.

alluvium *n.* нанóс; аллю́вий. —**alluvial,** *adj.* нанóсный; аллювиáльный.

ally *n.* сою́зник. —*v.t. Ally oneself with,* вступáть в сою́з с. *Be allied with,* быть сою́зником (+*gen.*).

almanac *n.* альманáх.

almighty *adj.* всемогýщий. —**the Almighty,** бог.

almond *n.* **1,** (tree) миндáль. **2,** (nut) миндáльный орéх; (collectively) миндáль. —*adj.* миндáльный: *almond oil,* миндáльное мáсло.

almost *adv.* почти́: *almost never,* почти́ никогдá. ♦*Of something that nearly happened, but did not* едвá не; чуть не: *I almost fell,* я едвá не/чуть не/ упáл.

alms *n.* ми́лостыня. —**almshouse,** *n.* богадéльня.

aloe *n.* алóэ. —**aloes,** *n.* алóэ.

aloft *adj. & adv.* **1,** (on high) наверхý; в высотé. **2,** (airborne) в воздýхе.

alone *adj. & adv.* **1,** (without company) оди́н: *are you alone?,* вы оди́н (однá)? *Be alone with,* быть наединé

с. **2,** (only) оди́н: *God alone knows,* одному́ бо́гу
изве́стно. *Man does not live by bread alone,* не хле́-
бом еди́ным жив челове́к. **3,** (with nothing else
added) (оди́н) то́лько: *this year alone,* то́лько в э́том
году́. *Moscow alone has a population of...,* в одно́й
то́лько Москве́ живёт... —**go it alone,** *colloq.* де́й-
ствовать в одино́чку. —**leave alone, 1,** *literally*
оставля́ть одного́ (одну́, одни́х). **2,** (not bother)
оставля́ть в поко́е. —**let alone, 1,** (leave alone)
оставля́ть в поко́е. **2,** (not to mention) не говоря́
уже́ о.
along *prep.* **1,** (over the length of) по: *walk along the
street,* идти́ по у́лице. *Stop along the way,* останo-
ви́ться по пути́. **2,** (along the side of) вдоль: *houses
along the road,* дома́ вдоль доро́ги. —*adv.* **1,**
(onward) да́льше; вперёд. *Move along!,* проходи́те
вперёд! **2,** (with one) с собо́й: *take along,* взять с
собо́й. —**all along, 1,** (all the time) всё вре́мя; с
са́мого нача́ла. **2,** (along the entire) на всём протя-
же́нии (+gen.). *All along the way,* всю доро́гу; на
протяже́нии всего́ пути́. —**along with,** вме́сте с.
—**get along,** *see* **get.**
alongside *adv.* ря́дом. —*prep.* ря́дом с; во́зле.
Draw (up) alongside, поравня́ться с.
aloof *adv.* в стороне́; особняко́м: *remain aloof,* дер-
жа́ться в стороне́/особняко́м. —*adj.* отчуждён-
ный. —**aloofness,** *n.* отчуждённость.
aloud *adv.* вслух.
alpaca *n.* альпака́.
alpha *n.* а́льфа. —**alpha particle,** а́льфа-части́ца.
—**alpha rays,** а́льфа-лучи́.
alphabet *n.* а́збука; алфави́т. —**alphabetic; alphabetical,** *adj.* алфави́тный. —**alphabetize,** *v.t.* распо-
лага́ть в алфави́тном поря́дке.
Alpine *adj.* альпи́йский.
already *adv.* уже́: *it is late already,* уже́ по́здно. *I
have already eaten,* я уже́ пое́л(а). *This complicates
an already tense situation,* это усложня́ет и без того́
напряжённое положе́ние.
also *adv.* то́же; та́кже.
Altaic *adj.* алта́йский.
altar *n.* алта́рь.
alter *v.t.* **1,** (modify) изменя́ть. **2,** (adjust, as a garment) переде́лывать. —*v.i.* изменя́ться.
alteration *n.* **1,** (change) измене́ние. **2,** (adjustment,
as of a garment) переде́лка.
altercation *n.* перебра́нка.
alternate *v.t.* чередова́ть; перемежа́ть. —*v.i.* черe-
дова́ться; перемежа́ться. —*n.* замести́тель. —*adj.*
1, (alternating) череду́ющийся. **2,** (every other) ка́ж-
дый второ́й. *On alternate days,* че́рез день. **3,** (alternative; substitute) запасно́й; альтернати́вный. **4,**
math. (of an angle) противолежа́щий.
alternately *adv.* попереме́нно; вперемёжку.
alternating current переме́нный ток.
alternation *n.* чередова́ние.
alternative *n.* вы́бор; альтернати́ва. *We have no
alternative,* у нас нет вы́бора. —*adj.* альтерна-
ти́вный.
alternator *n.* альтерна́тор.
although *conj.* хотя́.
altimeter *n.* альтиме́тр; высотоме́р.
altitude *n.* высота́. *At an altitude of,* на высоте́
(+gen.).
alto *n.* альт. —*adj.* альто́вый.

altogether *adv.* **1,** (completely) совсе́м; вполне́. **2,**
(in all; all told) всего́; в о́бщей сло́жности.
altruism *n.* альтруи́зм. —**altruist,** *n.* альтруи́ст.
—**altruistic,** *adj.* альтруисти́ческий.
alum *n.* квасцы́.
aluminum *also, Brit.,* **aluminium** *n.* алюми́ний.
—*adj.* алюми́ниевый.
alumnus *n.* пито́мец; воспи́танник.
alveolus *n.* лу́нка; альвео́ла. —**alveolar,** *adj.* аль-
веоля́рный.
always *adv.* всегда́.
amalgam *n.* амальга́ма.
amalgamate *v.t.* **1,** *chem.* амальгами́ровать. **2,**
(merge) объединя́ть; слива́ть. —*v.i.* объединя́ться;
слива́ться.
amalgamation *n.* **1,** *chem.* амальгама́ция. **2,** (mixture; blend) амальга́ма. **3,** (merger) слия́ние; объ-
едине́ние.
amaranth *n.* амара́нт.
amaryllis *n.* амари́ллис.
amass *v.t.* накопля́ть.
amateur *n.* люби́тель; дилета́нт. —*adj.* люби́тель-
ский; самоде́ятельный. *Amateur photographer,* фо-
то́граф-люби́тель. *Amateur status,* ста́тус люби́те-
ля. —**amateurish,** *adj.* дилета́нтский.
amaze *v.t.* изумля́ть. —**amazement,** *n.* изумле́ние.
—**amazing,** *adj.* изуми́тельный. —**amazingly,** *adv.*
изуми́тельно.
Amazon *n., myth.* амазо́нка.
ambassador *n.* посо́л. —**ambassadorial,** *adj.* по-
со́льский. *At the ambassadorial level,* на у́ровне
посло́в.
amber *n.* янта́рь. —*adj.* янта́рный.
ambergris *n.* а́мбра.
ambiance *also,* **ambience** *n.* среда́.
ambidextrous *adj.* владе́ющий одина́ково сво-
бо́дно обе́ими рука́ми.
ambience *n.* = **ambiance.**
ambiguous *adj.* двусмы́сленный. —**ambiguity,** *n.*
двусмы́сленность.
ambition *n.* **1,** (strong desire to succeed) честолю́-
бие. **2,** (object of one's aspirations) стремле́ние;
мечта́. —**ambitious,** *adj.* честолюби́вый.
ambivalent *adj.* дво́йственный: *ambivalent feelings,*
дво́йственное чу́вство. —**ambivalence,** *n.* дво́йст-
венность.
amble *n.* и́ноходь. —*v.i.* **1,** (of a horse) идти́ и́но-
ходью. **2,** (of a person) идти́ ногá зá ногу.
ambrosia *n.* амбро́зия.
ambulance *n.* маши́на ско́рой по́мощи.
ambulatory *adj.* ходя́чий: *ambulatory patient,*
ходя́чий больно́й. *He is ambulatory,* он мо́жет
ходи́ть.
ambush *n.* заса́да. *Lie in ambush,* быть в заса́де.
—*v.t.* напада́ть на (кого́-нибудь) из заса́ды.
ameba *also,* **amoeba** *n.* амёба.
ameliorate *v.t.* улучша́ть. —*v.i.* улучша́ться.
—**amelioration,** *n.* улучше́ние.
amen *interj.* ами́нь.
amenable *adj.* сгово́рчивый; покла́дистый; усту́п-
чивый; подáтливый.
amend *v.t.* **1,** (revise) исправля́ть. **2,** (add amend-
ments to) вноси́ть попра́вки в.
amendment *n.* попра́вка: *amendment to a bill,*
попра́вка к законопрое́кту.

amends *n.pl.* компенсация; возмещение. —**make amends for,** искупать; заглаживать.

amenity *n.* **1,** (pleasantness) приятность. **2,** *pl.* (conveniences) удобства. **3,** *pl.* (social courtesies) приличия.

American *adj.* американский. —*n.* американец; американка.

americium *n.* америций.

amethyst *n.* аметист. —*adj.* аметистовый.

amiable *adj.* приветливый. —**amiability,** *n.* приветливость.

amicability *n.* дружелюбие.

amicable *adj.* **1,** (of personal relations) дружный; дружеский; дружелюбный. **2,** (of an agreement, settlement, etc.) полюбовный. —**amicably,** *adv.* дружно; полюбовно.

amid *prep.* среди; посреди. *Also,* **amidst.**

amidships *adv.* в середине корабля.

amidst *prep.* = **amid.**

amino acid аминокислота.

amiss *adj.* неладный: *something is amiss,* что-то неладно. —**take amiss,** обижаться на; толковать в дурную сторону.

amity *n.* дружба; согласие; дружеские отношения.

ammeter *n.* амперметр.

ammonia *n.* аммиак. *Liquid ammonia,* нашатырный спирт.

ammonium *n.* аммоний. —**ammonium chloride,** нашатырь; хлористый аммоний. —**ammonium nitrate,** аммиачная *or* аммониевая селитра. —**ammonium sulfate,** сернокислый аммоний.

ammunition *n.* боеприпасы. —**ammunition belt,** патронная лента; патронташ. —**ammunition dump,** склад боеприпасов.

amnesia *n.* потеря памяти.

amnesty *n.* амнистия. *Grant amnesty to,* амнистировать.

amoeba *n.* = **ameba.**

amok *adv.* = **amuck.**

among *prep.* **1,** (in between; surrounded by) среди: *be among friends,* быть среди друзей. *First among equals,* первый среди равных. **2,** (with one another) между (собой): *They quarreled among themselves,* они поссорились между собой. **3,** (in the opinion of many) у: *very popular among young people,* очень популярен у молодёжи. *Also,* **amongst.**

amoral *adj.* аморальный. —**amorality,** *n.* аморальность.

amorous *adj.* любовный; влюбчивый. —**amorousness,** *n.* влюбчивость.

amorphous *adj.* бесформенный; аморфный.

amortize *v.t.* амортизировать. —**amortization,** *n.* амортизация.

amount *n.* **1,** (sum) сумма: *the total amount,* общая сумма. **2,** (quantity) количество: *a huge amount,* огромное количество. —*v.i.* [*usu.* **amount to**] **1,** (equal in total) составлять; выражаться в сумме (+*gen.*). **2,** (be equivalent to) равняться (+ *dat.*); быть равносильным (+ *dat.*). *It amounts to the same thing,* всё равно; это то же самое. **3,** *fol. by* **something, anything,** *etc.* (achieve success): *he'll never amount to anything,* из него никогда ничего не выйдет; из него ничего путного не выйдет.

ampere *n.* ампер.

ampersand *n.* знак &.

amphibian *n.* земноводное животное; амфибия.

amphibious *adj.* **1,** (of an animal) земноводный. **2,** (of a vehicle) плавающий. **3,** *mil.* морской десантный. *Amphibious landing,* высадка морского десанта.

amphitheater *also,* **amphitheatre** *n.* амфитеатр.

ample *adj.* **1,** (abundant) обильный. **2,** (sufficient) достаточный. **3,** (spacious) просторный.

amplification *n.* **1,** (enlargement) расширение. **2,** (fuller statement) уточнение. **3,** *electronics* усиление; звукоусиление. *Amplification system,* система звукоусиления.

amplifier *n.* усилитель.

amplify *v.t.* **1,** (enlarge) расширять. **2,** (enlarge upon, as a statement) уточнять. **3,** *electronics* усиливать.

amplitude *n.* **1,** (extent) широта. **2,** *physics* амплитуда.

amply *adv.* щедро: *amply rewarded,* щедро награждён.

ampule *also,* **ampoule** *n.* ампула.

amputate *v.t.* ампутировать; отнимать. —**amputation,** *n.* ампутация.

amuck *adv., in* **run amuck,** буйствовать; буянить.

amulet *n.* амулет; ладанка.

amuse *v.t.* развлекать; забавлять. *He is not amused,* ему не смешно. —**amuse oneself,** развлекаться; забавляться.

amusement *n.* **1,** (entertainment) развлечение; забава. **2,** (state of being amused) веселье. —**amusement park,** парк с аттракционами; увеселительный сад; луна-парк.

amusing *adj.* смешной; забавный; занимательный.

an *indef. art., var. of* **a.**

Anabaptism *n.* анабаптизм. —**Anabaptist,** *n.* анабаптист.

anachronism *n.* анахронизм. —**anachronistic,** *adj.* анахронический.

anaconda *n.* анаконда.

anaemia *n.* = **anemia.** —**anaemic,** *adj.* = **anemic.**

anaerobe *n.* анаэроб. —**anaerobic,** *adj.* анаэробный.

anaesthesia *n.* = **anesthesia.** —**anaesthetic,** *adj.* & *n.* = **anesthetic.** —**anaesthetize,** *v.* = **anesthetize.**

anagram *n.* анаграмма.

anal *adj.* заднепроходный; анальный.

analgesic *adj.* болеутоляющий. —*n.* болеутоляющее средство.

analogous *adj.* аналогичный.

analogy *n.* аналогия. *By analogy with,* по аналогии с.

analyse *v.* = **analyze.**

analysis *n.* анализ; разбор. —**in the final analysis,** в конечном итоге; в конечном счёте.

analyst *n.* аналитик.

analytic *also,* **analytical** *adj.* аналитический. —**analytic geometry,** аналитическая геометрия.

analyze *also,* **analyse** *v.t.* разбирать; анализировать.

anapest *n.* анапест.

anarchic *adj.* анархичный.

anarchism *n.* анархизм. —**anarchist,** *n.* анархист. —**anarchistic,** *adj.* анархический.

anarchy *n.* анáрхия.
anathema *n.* анáфема. —**anathematize,** *v.t.* предавáть анáфеме.
anatomy *n.* анатóмия. —**anatomical,** *adj.* анатомúческий. —**anatomist,** *n.* анáтом. —**anatomize,** *v.t.* анатомúровать.
ancestor *n.* прéдок. —**ancestral,** *adj.* родовóй. —**ancestry,** *n.* происхождéние.
anchor *n.* я́корь. *At anchor,* на я́коре. —*v.t.* стáвить на я́корь. —*v.i.* станови́ться на я́корь.
anchorage *n.* я́корная стоя́нка.
anchorite *n.* отшéльник; затвóрник.
anchovy *n.* анчóус.
ancient *adj.* дрéвний; старúнный; антúчный. —**the ancients,** дрéвние.
ancillary *adj.* вспомогáтельный; подсóбный.
and *conj.* и: *cause and effect,* причúна и слéдствие.
♦ *Sometimes rendered by* с: *you and I,* мы с вáми; *bread and butter,* хлеб с мáслом. ♦ *When in contrast* а: *he is Russian and she is French,* он рýсский, а онá францýженка.
andante *adv. & n.* андáнте.
andiron *n.* подстáвка для дров.
anecdote *n.* анекдóт. —**anecdotal,** *adj.* анекдотúческий.
anemia *also,* **anaemia** *n.* малокрóвие; анемúя. —**anemic; anaemic,** *adj.* малокрóвный; анемúчный.
anemometer *n.* анемóметр; ветромéр.
anemone *n.* анемóн; вéтреница. —**sea anemone,** актúния.
anent *prep., archaic* относúтельно.
aneroid barometer анерóид.
anesthesia *also,* **anaesthesia** *n.* анестезúя; наркóз. —**anesthesiologist,** *n.* анестезиóлог.
anesthetic *also,* **anaesthetic** *adj.* анестезúрующий; обезбóливающий. —*n.* анестезúрующее/обезбóливающее срéдство; наркóз.
anesthetize *also,* **anaesthetize** *v.t.* анестезúровать; обезбóливать. —**anesthetization,** *n.* обезбóливание.
anew *adv.* снóва; зáново.
angel *n.* áнгел. —**angelic,** *adj.* áнгельский.
angelica *n.* дя́гиль; дýдник.
anger *n.* гнев. *In anger,* в гнéве. —*v.t.* сердúть.
angina *n.* ангúна. —**angina pectoris,** груднáя жáба; стенокардúя.
angle *n.* **1,** *geom.* ýгол: *right angle,* прямóй ýгол. **2,** (aspect; point of view) тóчка зрéния; ýгол зрéния. *Consider a question from all angles,* рассмáтривать вопрóс со всех сторóн (*or* на все лады́).—*v.i.* **1,** (fish) удúть рыбу. **2,** *fol. by for* (slyly try to obtain) напрáшиваться на.
angler *n.* удúльщик.
Anglican *adj.* англикáнский.
Anglicism *n.* англицúзм.
Anglicize *v.t.* англизúровать.
angling *n.* ужéние.
Anglophile *n.* англофúл.
Anglo-Saxon *adj.* англосаксóнский.
angrily *adv.* сердúто.
angry *adj.* сердúтый. *Be angry,* сердúться. *Don't be angry with him,* не сердúтесь на негó. *Become/get angry,* рассердúться. *Make someone angry,* рассердúть когó-нибудь.
anguish *n.* мýка; страдáние. —**anguished,** *adj.*

мучúтельный: *anguished cry,* мучúтельный крик.
angular *adj.* **1,** (having many angles) угловáтый: *angular features,* угловáтые чертú. **2,** (measured by an angle) угловóй: *angular velocity,* угловáя скóрость. **3,** (gaunt) костля́вый. **4,** (lacking grace; stiff) угловáтый.
aniline *n.* анилúн. —**aniline dye,** анилúновая крáска.
animal *n.* живóтное. —*adj.* живóтный: *animal fat,* живóтный жир. —**animal husbandry,** животновóдство.
animate *v.t.* оживля́ть. —*adj.* одушевлённый: *animate creature,* одушевлённое существó.
animated *adj.* оживлённый. —**animated cartoon,** мультипликацóнный фильм.
animation *n.* оживлéние. *With (great) animation,* оживлённо; жúво.
animism *n.* анимúзм. —**animist,** *n.* анимúст. —**animistic,** *adj.* анимистúческий.
animosity *n.* враждéбность; враждá.
anise *n.* анúс. —*adj.* анúсовый.
anisette *n.* анúсовка.
ankle *n.* лодúжка; щúколотка. *Sprain one's ankle,* подвернýть себé нóгу.
annals *n.pl.* аннáлы.
anneal *v.t.* **1,** (heat) отжигáть. **2,** *fig.* (temper) закаля́ть.
annex *v.t.* присоединя́ть; аннексúровать. —*n.* **1,** (subsidiary building) пристрóйка. **2,** (supplement) приложéние (к договóру). —**annexation,** *n.* присоединéние; аннéксия.
annihilate *v.t.* уничтожáть; истребля́ть. —**annihilation,** *n.* уничтожéние; истреблéние.
anniversary *n.* годовщúна; юбилéй. ♦ *Specific anniversaries are rendered with the suffix* -лéтие: *tenth anniversary,* десятилéтие. *The fiftieth anniversary of his death,* пятидесятилéтие со дня егó смéрти. —*adj.* юбилéйный: *anniversary year,* юбилéйный год.
annotate *v.t.* комментúровать. —**annotation,** *n.* комментáрий.
announce *v.t.* **1,** (declare publicly) заявля́ть; объявля́ть; сообщáть. **2,** (state the arrival or presence of) доклáдывать о: *announce a visitor,* доклáдывать о посетúтеле.
announcement *n.* **1,** (statement) заявлéние: *make an announcement,* сдéлать заявлéние. **2,** (public notice) объявлéние.
announcer *n.* дúктор.
annoy *v.t.* досаждáть; раздражáть. —**annoyance,** *n.* досáда. —**annoyed,** *adj.* раздражён. —**annoying,** *adj.* досáдный. *How annoying!,* какáя досáда!
annual *adj.* **1,** (occurring once a year) ежегóдный. **2,** (pertaining to a given year) годовóй. **3,** *bot.* однолéтний. —*n.* **1,** (publication) ежегóдник. **2,** (plant) однолéтнее растéние. —**annually,** *adv.* ежегóдно.
annuity *n.* ежегóдная рéнта.
annul *v.t.* аннулúровать; отменя́ть. —**annulment,** *n.* аннулúрование; отмéна.
Annunciation *n., relig.* благовéщение.
anode *n.* анóд.
anoint *v.t.* помáзывать. —**anointment,** *n.* помáзание.
anomaly *n.* аномáлия. —**anomalous,** *adj.* аномáльный.

anonymity *n.* анони́мность.

anonymous *adj.* анони́мный. —**anonymously**, *adv.* анони́мно.

anopheles *n.* ано́фелес.

another *adj. & pron.* **1**, (one more) ещё (оди́н): *another glass of milk*, ещё стака́н молока́. **2**, (a different) друго́й: *that's quite another matter*, э́то совсе́м друго́е де́ло. —**one another**, друг дру́га. —**one way or another**, так и́ли ина́че.

answer *v.t. & i.* отвеча́ть. *Answer someone*, отвеча́ть кому́-нибудь. *Answer a question*, отвеча́ть на вопро́с. *Answer the telephone*, подходи́ть к телефо́ну. *Answer the door*, открыва́ть дверь. *Answer the purpose*, отвеча́ть це́ли. *Answer for one's actions*, отвеча́ть за свои́ посту́пки. —*n.* **1**, (reply) отве́т. *In answer to*, в отве́т на (+*acc.*). **2**, (solution) реше́ние: *answer to a problem*, реше́ние зада́чи. —**answer back**, груби́ть; дерзи́ть.

answerable *adj.* отве́тственный. *Be answerable for*, отвеча́ть за.

ant *n.* мураве́й.

antagonism *n.* антагони́зм; вражда́. —**antagonist**, *n.* антагони́ст. —**antagonistic**, *adj.* антагонисти́ческий; вражд́бный.

antagonize *v.t.* восстана́вливать про́тив себя́; отта́лкивать.

antarctic *adj.* антаркти́ческий. —**Antarctic Circle**, Ю́жный поля́рный круг.

ante *n.* ста́вка. *Raise the ante*, повы́сить ста́вку.

anteater *n.* муравье́д. —**spiny anteater**, ехи́дна.

antecedent *n.* **1**, (something that goes before) предше́ствующее собы́тие. **2**, *pl.* (ancestors) пре́дки.

antechamber *n.* пере́дняя; прихо́жая; аванза́л.

antedate *v.t.* **1**, (come before) предше́ствовать. **2**, (put an earlier date on) поме́тить за́дним число́м.

antediluvian *adj.* допото́пный.

antelope *n.* антило́па.

antenna *n.* анте́нна.

anterior *adj.* **1**, (forward; front) пере́дний. **2**, (coming earlier) предше́ствующий.

anteroom *n.* пере́дняя; приёмная; аванза́л.

anthem *n.* гимн: *national anthem*, госуда́рственный гимн.

anther *n.* пы́льник.

anthill *n.* мураве́йник.

anthology *n.* антоло́гия; сбо́рник.

anthracite *n.* антраци́т. —*adj.* антраци́тный; антраци́товый.

anthrax *n.* сиби́рская я́зва.

anthropoid *n.* антропо́ид. —*adj.* человекообра́зный.

anthropology *n.* антрополо́гия. —**anthropological**, *adj.* антропологи́ческий. —**anthropologist**, *n.* антропо́лог.

anthropomorphism *n.* антропоморфи́зм. —**anthropomorphic**, *adj.* антропоморфи́ческий. —**anthropomorphous**, *adj.* человекообра́зный.

antiaircraft *adj.* зени́тный.

anti-American *adj.* антиамерика́нский. —**anti-Americanism**, *n.* антиамериканизм.

anti-ballistic missile антираке́та.

antibiotic *n.* антибио́тик.

antibody *n.* антите́ло.

antic *n., usu. pl.* ша́лости; вы́ходки.

Antichrist *n.* анти́христ.

anticipate *v.t.* **1**, (foresee) предви́деть. **2**, (expect) ожида́ть. **3**, (foresee and deal with in advance) предупрежда́ть; предвосхища́ть.

anticipation *n.* **1**, (expectation) ожида́ние; предви́дение: *in anticipation of*, в ожида́нии/предвиде́нии (+ *gen.*). **2**, (dealing with in advance) предвосхище́ние. **3**, (eagerness) нетерпе́ние.

anticommunism *n.* антикоммуни́зм.

anticommunist *n.* антикоммуни́ст. —*adj.* антикоммунисти́ческий.

antidote *n.* противо́йдие.

antifreeze *n.* антифри́з.

antigen *n.* антиге́н.

antimatter *n.* антивещество́.

antimony *n.* сурьма́.

anti-party *adj.* антипарти́йный.

antipathetic *adj.* **1**, *fol. by* **to** (averse) настро́ен про́тив. **2**, (causing antipathy) антипати́чный.

antipathy *n.* антипа́тия.

anti-personnel *adj., mil.* оско́лочный; противопехо́тный.

antiquary *n.* антиква́р. *Also*, **antiquarian**.

antiquated *adj.* устаре́лый; устаре́вший.

antique *adj.* стари́нный; антиква́рный. —*n.* антиква́рная вещь. *Antique dealer*, антиква́р. *Antique shop*, антиква́рный магази́н.

antiquity *n.* **1**, (ancient times; great age) дре́вность; анти́чность. **2**, *pl.* (ancient relics) дре́вности.

antireligious *adj.* антирелигио́зный.

anti-Semite *n.* антисеми́т. —**anti-Semitic**, *adj.* антисеми́тский. —**anti-Semitism**, *n.* антисемити́зм.

antisepsis *n.* антисе́птика.

antiseptic *adj.* антисепти́ческий. —*n.* антисепти́ческое сре́дство.

antisocial *adj.* **1**, (harmful to society) антиобще́ственный. **2**, (unsociable) необщи́тельный.

anti-Soviet *adj.* антисове́тский.

antitank *adj.* противота́нковый.

antithesis *n.* **1**, (opposite) анти́теза. **2**, *logic* анти́тезис. —**antithetical**, *adj.* антитети́ческий.

antitoxin *n.* антитокси́н. —**antitoxic**, *adj.* антитокси́ческий.

antiwar *adj.* антивое́нный.

antler *n.* (оле́ний) рог.

antonym *n.* анто́ним.

anus *n.* за́дний прохо́д.

anvil *n.* накова́льня.

anxiety *n.* беспоко́йство; озабо́ченность.

anxious *adj.* **1**, (worried) озабо́ченный; неспоко́йный; трево́жный. *Anxious moment*, трево́жный моме́нт. **2**, (eager): *be anxious to*, о́чень хоте́ться (+ *dat.*). *We are very anxious to see you*, мы вас о́чень ждём.

anxiously *adv.* с нетерпе́нием: *anxiously await*, ждать с нетерпе́нием.

any *adj. & pron.* **1**, (no matter which; every) любо́й; вся́кий: *any time*, в любо́е вре́мя; *in any case*, во вся́ком слу́чае; *at any price*, любо́й цено́й; *any of you*, любо́й из вас. **2**, (some) како́й-нибудь: *have you any questions?*, у вас есть каки́е-нибудь вопро́сы? *Have you any money?*, у вас есть де́ньги? ♦*In neg. sentences* никако́й: *I didn't buy any books*, я не покупа́л(а) никаки́х книг. *We haven't any flour today*, у нас сего́дня нет муки́. *I don't see any*, не ви́жу ни одного́. **3**, *Any minute*, с мину́ты на минуту; *any day* (*now*), со дня на день. —*adv. Not rendered in Russian: is he any better today?*, ему лучше сегодня? ♦ *In neg. sentences* нисколько: *he is not any better today*, ему сегодня нисколько не лучше. —**any more, 1,** (some more) ещё: *have you any more questions?*, у вас есть ещё вопросы? **2,** (no more) больше: *I haven't any more money*, у меня нет больше денег. *See also* **anymore.**

anybody *pron.* = **anyone.**

anyhow *adv.* **1,** (in any case) во всяком случае. **2,** (just the same) всё-таки; всё же.

anymore *adv.* больше: *I don't go there anymore*, я больше не хожу туда.

anyone *pron.* **1,** *in affirmative sentences* любой; всякий; каждый; кто угодно: *anyone can do it*, любой/всякий/каждый может это сделать. *Ask anyone*, спросите кого угодно. **2,** *in interr. and hypothetical sentences* кто-нибудь: *did you see anyone?*, вы видели кого-нибудь? **3,** *in neg. sentences* никого: *I didn't see anyone*, я никого не видел(а). *Neither he nor anyone else*, ни он и никто другой.

anyplace *adv., colloq.* = **anywhere.**

anything *pron.* **1,** *in affirmative sentences* всё; всякое; всё, что угодно. *Anything is possible*, всё возможно; всякое бывает. *I would give anything to...*, всё отдам, чтобы... **2,** *in interr. and hypothetical sentences* что-нибудь: *do you want anything to drink?*, вы хотите что-нибудь выпить? **3,** *in neg. sentences* ничего: *I don't know anything*, я ничего не знаю. —**anything but,** совсем не: *anything but cheap*, совсем не дешёвый.

anytime *adv.* **1,** (at any time) в любое время; когда угодно. **2,** (whenever) когда бы ни; всякий раз, когда.

anyway *adv.* = **anyhow.**

anywhere *adv.* **1,** *in affirmative sentences* где *or* куда угодно; где *or* куда бы то ни было. **2,** *in interr. and hypothetical sentences* где-нибудь; куда-нибудь. **3,** *in neg. sentences* нигде; никуда.

aorta *n.* аорта.

apace *adv.* полным ходом: *proceed apace*, идти полным ходом.

apart *adv.* **1,** (separately) врозь; порознь; отдельно. **2,** (into pieces) на части. *Take apart*, разбирать. —**apart from,** помимо. —**tell apart,** различать.

apartheid *n.* апартеид.

apartment *n.* квартира. —**apartment house,** жилой дом.

apathetic *adj.* апатичный.

apathy *n.* апатия.

ape *n.* обезьяна. —*v.t.* обезьянничать. —**ape-like,** *adj.* обезьяний; обезьяноподобный. —**ape-man,** *n.* обезьяночеловек.

aperture *n.* отверстие; апертура.

apex *n.* вершина.

aphasia *n.* афазия.

aphelion *n.* афелий.

aphorism *n.* афоризм. —**aphoristic,** *adj.* афористический; афористичный.

apiary *n.* пасека; пчельник.

apiece *adv.* **1,** (per item) за штуку. **2,** (per person) за *or* на каждого.

aplomb *n.* апломб.

apocalypse *n.* апокалипсис. —**apocalyptic,** *adj.* апокалипсический.

Apocrypha *n.pl.* апокрифы.

Apocryphal *adj.* **1,** (pert. to the Apocrypha) апокрифический. **2,** *l.c.* (of doubtful authenticity) недостоверный.

apogee *n.* апогей.

apolitical *adj.* аполитичный.

Apollo *n.* Аполлон.

apologetic *adj.* извиняющийся. *He was very apologetic*, он очень извинялся. —**apologetically,** *adv.* извиняющимся тоном.

apologetics *n.* апологетика.

apologia *n.* апология.

apologist *n.* апологет.

apologize *v.i.* извиняться.

apology *n.* извинение.

apoplexy *n.* апоплексия. —**apoplectic,** *adj.* апоплексический.

apostasy *n.* отступничество. —**apostate,** *n.* отступник. —*adj.* отступнический.

a posteriori **1,** *used adverbially* апостериори. **2,** *used adjectivally* апостериорный.

apostle *n.* апостол. —**apostolic,** *adj.* апостольский.

apostrophe *n.* апостроф.

apothecary *n.* аптекарь.

apotheosis *n.* апофеоз.

appall *also*, **appal** *v.t.* ужасать; приводить в ужас. *Be appalled*, ужасаться; быть в ужасе; приходить в ужас. —**appalling,** *adj.* ужасный; вопиющий.

apparatus *n.* **1,** (device) аппарат; прибор. **2,** (group of instruments) аппаратура. **3,** *sports* гимнастические снаряды. **4,** (system of organization) аппарат: *spy apparatus*, шпионский аппарат.

apparel *n.* одежда; наряд. *Apparel shop*, магазин готового платья.

apparent *adj.* видимый: *for no apparent reason*, без видимой причины. *It is apparent that...*, видно, что...

apparently *adv.* видимо; по-видимому.

apparition *n.* видение; призрак; привидение.

appeal *v.i.* **1,** (earnestly request) обращаться; призывать. *Appeal to someone for help*, обращаться к кому-нибудь за помощью. *Appeal for unity*, призывать к единству. **2,** *fol. by* **to** (strike favorably) нравиться. *It doesn't appeal to me*, это мне не улыбается. **3,** *law* апеллировать; подавать кассационную жалобу. —*v.t.* обжаловать: *appeal a verdict*, обжаловать приговор. —*n.* **1,** (call for aid or support) обращение; призыв; воззвание. **2,** (attraction) привлекательность. **3,** *law* (general procedure) обжалование: *right of appeal*, право обжалования; (request so made) апелляция; кассационная жалоба. —**appealing,** *adj.* привлекательный.

appear *v.i.* **1,** (come into view) появляться. **2,** (present oneself; show up) являться; представать: *appear in/before the/court*, явиться в суд; предстать перед судом. **3,** (perform) выступать (на сцене). **4,** (be published) выходить (в свет). **5,** (seem) казаться; представляться. *The rain appears to have stopped*, дождь как будто кончился.

appearance *n.* **1,** (coming into sight) появление. *Put in an appearance*, появляться. **2,** (coming into public view) выступление: *television appearance*, выступление по телевидению. **3,** (outward aspect) вид; облик. *External appearance*, внешность; наружность. *For appearance's sake*, для вида. —**from**

all appearances, по всей ви́димости.

appease *v.t.* **1,** (placate) умиротворя́ть. **2,** (assuage, as hunger) утоля́ть. **—appeasement,** *n.* умиротворе́ние.

appellate *adj.* апелляцио́нный: *appellate court,* апелляцио́нный суд.

appellation *n.* назва́ние; наименова́ние.

append *v.t.* прилага́ть.

appendage *n.* прида́ток.

appendectomy *n.* удале́ние аппе́ндикса.

appendicitis *n.* аппендици́т.

appendix *n.* **1,** (of a document or book) приложе́ние. **2,** *anat.* аппе́ндикс.

apperception *n.* апперце́пция.

appertain *v.i.* относи́ться; принадлежа́ть.

appetite *n.* **1,** (desire for food) аппети́т. **2,** (craving) жа́жда; влече́ние. *Sexual appetite,* полово́е влече́ние.

appetizer *n.* заку́ска.

appetizing *adj.* аппети́тный; вку́сный.

applaud *v.i.* аплоди́ровать; рукоплеска́ть. *—v.t.* **1,** (clap to show approval of) аплоди́ровать (+ *dat.*). **2,** (approve of; commend) приве́тствовать.

applause *n.* аплодисме́нты; рукоплеска́ния.

apple *n.* я́блоко. *—adj.* **1,** (made of apples) я́блочный: *apple pie,* я́блочный пиро́г. **2,** (of an apple tree) я́блоневый: *apple blossom/orchard,* я́блоневый цвет/сад. **—apple of discord,** я́блоко раздо́ра. **—apple of one's eye,** зени́ца о́ка.

applecart *n.* теле́жка с я́блоками. **—upset the applecart,** спу́тать все ка́рты; испо́ртить всю му́зыку.

applesauce *n.* я́блочное пюре́.

apple tree я́блоня.

appliance *n.* прибо́р; приспособле́ние.

applicable *adj.* примени́мый. **—applicability,** *n.* примени́мость.

applicant *n.* претенде́нт; кандида́т.

application *n.* **1,** (applying; putting on) наложе́ние. **2,** (putting to use) примене́ние; приложе́ние. **3,** (formal request) заявле́ние: *submit an application,* подава́ть заявле́ние. **4,** (diligence) прилежа́ние; стара́тельность.

applied *adj.* прикладно́й: *applied sciences,* прикла́дные нау́ки.

appliqué *n.* аппликация.

apply *v.t.* **1,** (lay on) накла́дывать; ста́вить. *Apply makeup/a bandage/to,* наложи́ть грим/повя́зку на (+ *acc.*). **2,** (put to use) применя́ть: *apply one's knowledge to,* применя́ть свои́ зна́ния к. *Apply the brakes,* тормози́ть. *Apply pressure to,* ока́зывать давле́ние на. **3,** (credit, as to an account) зачи́тывать. *—v.i.* **1,** (submit an application) обраща́ться; подава́ть заявле́ние. *Apply for a job as a typist,* подава́ть заявле́ние на до́лжность маши́нистки. **2,** *fol. by* **to** (be applicable to) относи́ться (к): *this applies to all,* э́то отно́сится ко всем. *The rule does not apply to/in this case,* пра́вило неприменимо в да́нном слу́чае. **—apply oneself to,** налега́ть на; принале́чь на.

appoint *v.t.* **1,** (designate) назнача́ть: *appoint someone to a position,* назнача́ть кого́-нибудь на до́лжность. *He was appointed plant manager,* он был назна́чен дире́ктором заво́да. **2,** *usu. passive* (furnish) обставля́ть: *well-appointed rooms,* хорошо́ обста́вленные ко́мнаты.

appointment *n.* **1,** (act of appointing or being appointed) назначе́ние. **2,** (scheduled meeting) свида́ние; (делова́я) встре́ча. *I have an appointment,* мне назна́чена делова́я встре́ча. *Make an appointment with the doctor,* записа́ться к врачу́. *I have a doctor's appointment,* мне назна́чено прийти́ к врачу́. **3,** *pl.* (furnishings) обстано́вка.

apportion *v.t.* распределя́ть; выделя́ть. **—apportionment,** *n.* распределе́ние; выделе́ние.

apposition *n., gram.* приложе́ние.

appraisal *n.* оце́нка.

appraise *v.t.* оце́нивать. **—appraiser,** *n.* оце́нщик.

appreciable *adj.* заме́тный; ощути́мый.

appreciate *v.t.* **1,** (see the value of; recognize gratefully) цени́ть. **2,** (realize; be aware of) понима́ть; отдава́ть себе́ отчёт в. *—v.i.* повыша́ться в цене́.

appreciation *n.* **1,** (gratitude) призна́тельность. **2,** (sensitive awareness) понима́ние. **3,** (rise in value) повыше́ние сто́имости.

appreciative *adj.* призна́тельный.

apprehend *v.t.* **1,** (take into custody) аресто́вать; брать под стра́жу. **2,** (comprehend; grasp) постига́ть.

apprehension *n.* **1,** (arrest) задержа́ние; аре́ст. **2,** (intuitive understanding) восприя́тие. **3,** (fear; dread) опасе́ние.

apprehensive *adj.* озабо́ченный; беспоко́йный. **—apprehensiveness,** *n.* озабо́ченность; беспоко́йство.

apprentice *n.* учени́к; подмасте́рье. *—v.t.* отдава́ть в уче́ние. **—apprenticeship,** *n.* уче́ние; учени́чество.

apprise *v.t.* извеща́ть; осведомля́ть; уведомля́ть; информи́ровать.

approach *v.i.* подходи́ть; приближа́ться. *—v.t.* **1,** (walk up to; draw near to) подходи́ть к; приближа́ться к. **2,** (make an appeal or proposal to) обраща́ться к. **3,** (begin to deal with) подходи́ть к. *—n.* **1,** (drawing near) приближе́ние. **2,** (way by which a place is reached) подхо́д. *The approaches to a city,* подсту́пы к го́роду. **3,** (method of approach, as to a problem) подхо́д.

approachable *adj.* досту́пный.

approbation *n.* одобре́ние; апроба́ция.

appropriate *v.t.* **1,** (allot; allocate) ассигнова́ть. **2,** (take possession of) присва́ивать. *—adj.* **1,** (what is suitable or needed) соотве́тствующий; подходя́щий; надлежа́щий. **2,** (apt) уме́стный. **—appropriately,** *adv.* уме́стно.

appropriation *n.* **1,** (allotment of funds; funds so allotted) ассигнова́ние. **2,** (taking over; seizure) присвое́ние.

approval *n.* одобре́ние.

approve *v.i.* [*usu.* **approve of**] одобря́ть. *—v.t.* утвержда́ть; одобря́ть: *approve a plan,* утвержда́ть/одобря́ть план.

approving *adj.* одобри́тельный. **—approvingly,** *adv.* одобри́тельно.

approximate *adj.* приблизи́тельный. *—v.t.* приближа́ться к. **—approximately,** *adv.* приблизи́тельно; приме́рно. **—approximation,** *n.* приблизи́тельный подсчёт.

appurtenance *n.* **1,** (adjunct) прида́ток. **2,** *pl.* (accessories) принадле́жности.

apricot *n.* абрико́с. *Dried apricots,* курага́; урю́к. *—adj.* абрико́совый.

April *n.* апрель. —*adj.* апрельский.
a priori 1, *used adverbially* априори. **2,** *used adjectivally* априорный.
apron *n.* передник; фартук. —**be tied to someone's apron springs,** быть под башмаком у кого-нибудь.
apropos *adv.* кстати. —*adj.* уместный. —**apropos of,** относительно; в связи с.
apse *n.* апсида. *Also,* **apsis.**
apt *adj.* **1,** (pertinent) удачный; меткий. **2,** (quick to learn) способный. **3,** *fol. by* **to** (inclined; likely) склонный (к). *In such weather one is apt to catch cold,* в такую погоду можно легко простудиться.
aptitude *n.* способности: *an aptitude for languages,* способности к языкам.
aptly *adv.* уместно; удачно.
aqualung *n.* акваланг.
aquamarine *n.* аквамарин. —*adj.* аквамариновый.
aquarium *n.* аквариум.
Aquarius *n.* Водолей.
aquatic *adj.* водяной. *Aquatic sports,* водный спорт.
aquatint *n.* акватинта.
aqueduct *n.* акведук.
aquiline *adj.* орлиный: *aquiline nose,* орлиный нос.
Arab *n.* араб. —*adj.* арабский: *Arab countries,* арабские страны.
arabesque *n.* арабеска.
Arabian *adj.* аравийский.
Arabic *adj.* арабский. —*n.* арабский язык. *Speak Arabic,* говорить по-арабски. —**Arabic numerals,** арабские цифры.
arable *adj.* пахотный.
Aramaic *adj.* арамейский. —*n.* арамейский язык.
arbiter *n.* **1,** *law* арбитр; третейский судья. **2,** (one who decides) законодатель: *arbiter of fashions,* законодатель мод.
arbitrary *adj.* произвольный; самоуправный; самочинный. —**arbitrarily,** *adv.* произвольно. —**arbitrariness,** *n.* произвол; самоуправство.
arbitrate *v.t.* решать в арбитражном порядке. —**arbitration,** *n.* арбитраж. *Court of arbitration,* третейский суд. —**arbitrator,** *n.* арбитр; третейский судья.
arbor *also,* **arbour** *n.* беседка.
arboretum *n.* дендрарий.
arc *n.* дуга.
arcade *n.* **1,** *archit.* аркада. **2,** (covered passageway with shops) пассаж.
arcane *adj.* заумный.
arch *n.* **1,** (curved structure) арка; свод. **2,** (curve of the foot) свод стопы. *Fallen arches,* плоскостопие. —*adj.* **1,** (sly) лукавый. **2,** [*usu.* arch-] (notorious) архи-: *arch-liar,* архилгун. —*v.t.* выгибать: *arch one's back,* выгибать спину.
archaeology *n.* = archeology. —**archaeological,** *adj.* = archeological. —**archaeologist,** *n.* = archeologist.
archaic *adj.* архаический; устаревший. —**archaism,** *n.* архаизм.
archangel *n.* архангел.
archbishop *n.* архиепископ.
archdeacon *n.* архидьякон; *Orth. Ch.* протодьякон.
archdiocese *n.* епархия архиепископа.
archduke *n.* эрцгерцог. —**archduchess,** *n.* эрцгерцогиня. —**archduchy,** *n.* эрцгерцогство.
arched *adj.* арочный; сводчатый; дугообразный.

archenemy *n.* заклятый враг.
archeology *also,* **archaeology** *n.* археология. —**archeological,** *adj.* археологический. —**archeologist,** *n.* археолог.
archer *n.* стрелок из лука. —**archery,** *n.* стрельба из лука.
archetype *n.* прототип; образец.
archimandrite *n.* архимандрит.
archipelago *n.* архипелаг.
architect *n.* архитектор.
architecture *n.* архитектура; зодчество. —**architectural,** *adj.* архитектурный; зодческий.
archives *n.pl.* архив. —**archivist,** *n.* архивист.
arch support супинатор.
archway *n.* сводчатый проход.
arctic *adj.* арктический; полярный. —**Arctic Circle,** Северный полярный круг. —**Arctic Ocean,** Северный Ледовитый океан.
ardent *adj.* страстный; ревностный; пылкий; горячий. —**ardently,** *adv.* страстно; горячо.
ardor *also,* **ardour** *n.* пыл; жар; рвение; задор.
arduous *adj.* трудный; тяжёлый.
area *n.* **1,** (two-dimensional extent) площадь: *the area of a circle,* площадь круга. **2,** (district) район: *residential area,* жилой район. **3,** (place; ground; site) площадка: *loading area,* погрузочная площадка. **4,** (field, as of study or interest) область. *Area studies,* страноведение.
arena *n.* арена.
Argentinean *adj.* [*also,* **Argentine**] аргентинский. —*n.* аргентинец; аргентинка.
argon *n.* аргон.
argot *n.* арго; жаргон.
argue *v.i.* (engage in an argument) спорить. —*v.t.* **1,** (plead, as a case) вести (дело). **2,** (contend) утверждать; доказывать.
argument *n.* **1,** (quarrel) спор. *Have an argument,* спорить. **2,** (objection) возражение. *And no argument!,* без возражений!; без разговоров! **3,** (reason for or against) довод; аргумент: *strong argument,* сильный довод/аргумент. —**argumentation,** *n.* аргументация. —**argumentative,** *adj.* любящий спорить.
aria *n.* ария.
arid *adj.* сухой; засушливый; безводный. —**aridity,** *n.* сухость.
Aries *n.* Овен.
arise *v.i.* **1,** (get up) вставать. **2,** (come about) возникать; создаваться.
aristocracy *n.* аристократия. —**aristocrat,** *n.* аристократ. —**aristocratic,** *adj.* аристократический; аристократичный.
arithmetic *n.* арифметика. —*adj.* [*also,* **arithmetical**] арифметический.
ark *n.* **1,** (boat) ковчег: *Noah's ark,* ноев ковчег. **2,** (receptacle in the synagogue) ковчег. *Ark of the covenant,* ковчег завета.
arm *n.* **1,** (part of the body) рука: *carry in one's arms,* нести на руках. *Under one's arm,* под мышкой. **2,** (of a chair, sofa, etc.) ручка. **3,** (of a dress, river, etc.) рукав. **4,** *pl.* (weapons) *see* **arms.** —*v.t.* вооружать. —*v.i.* вооружаться. —**arm in arm,** под руку. —**at arm's length,** на почтительном расстоянии. —**with open arms,** с распростёртыми объятиями.
armada *n.* армада.

armadillo *n.* броненóсец.

armament *n.* **1,** (act of arming) вооружéние. **2,** *pl.* (arms) вооружéния. *The armaments industry,* воéнная промы́шленность.

armature *n.* я́корь; арматýра.

armband *n.* (нарукáвная) повя́зка.

armchair *n.* крéсло. —*adj.* кабинéтный: *armchair strategist,* кабинéтный стратéг.

armed *adj.* вооружённый. —**armed forces,** вооружённые си́лы.

Armenian *adj.* армя́нский. —*n.* **1,** (person) армяни́н; армя́нка. **2,** (language) армя́нский язы́к.

armful *n.* охáпка.

armhole *n.* прóйма.

armistice *n.* переми́рие.

armor *also,* **armour** *n.* **1,** (worn by medieval knights) броня́; пáнцирь; доспéхи; лáты. *Suit of armor,* лáтные доспéхи. **2,** (for warships, tanks, etc.) броня́. **3,** *mil.* (armored vehicles) бронирóванные маши́ны. —*v.t.* бронировáть.

armored *adj.* **1,** (protected by armor) броневóй; бронирóванный. *Armored car,* бронеавтомоби́ль; броневи́к. *Armored personnel carrier,* бронетранспортёр. **2,** (equipped with armored vehicles) бронетáнковый: *armored division,* бронетáнковая диви́зия.

armor plate броневáя плитá; броневóй лист. *Also,* **armor plating.**

armory *also,* **armoury** *n.* арсенáл; склад орýжия.

armour *n.* = **armor.** —**armoury,** *n.* = **armory.**

armpit *n.* подмы́шка.

armrest *n.* подлокóтник.

arms *n.pl.* орýжие. *Arms race,* гóнка вооружéний. *Arms control,* контрóль над вооружéниями. —**be up in arms over,** встрéтить в штыки́. —**under arms,** под ружьём.

army *n.* áрмия. —*adj.* армéйский: *army corps,* армéйский кóрпус.

aroma *n.* аромáт. —**aromatic,** *adj.* аромáтный; души́стый.

around *prep.* **1,** (encircling) вокрýг: *travel around the world,* путешéствовать вокрýг свéта. **2,** (so as to avoid or get past) *rendered by the prefix* об-: *walk around the puddle,* обходи́ть лýжу. **3,** (by turning) за: *around the corner,* за углóм. **4,** (here and there in) по: *walk around town,* ходи́ть по гóроду. **5,** *colloq.* (approximately) óколо: *around six dollars,* óколо шести́ дóлларов. —*adv.* кругóм; вокрýг. *Turn around,* повáрачиваться (кругóм); оборáчиваться. *There is no one around,* никогó нет кругóм. *For miles around,* за мнóго миль.

arouse *v.t.* **1,** (awaken) буди́ть. **2,** (stir to action) возбуждáть. **3,** (evoke, as a feeling) возбуждáть; вызывáть.

arpeggio *n.* арпéджио.

arquebus *n.* пищáль.

arraign *v.t.* привлекáть к судý. —**arraignment,** *n.* привлечéние к судý.

arrange *v.t.* **1,** (put in correct order) располагáть; расставля́ть. **2,** (organize) устрáивать. **3,** *music* аранжи́ровать. —*v.i.* **1,** *fol. by inf.* (agree) договáриваться; услáвливаться; сговáриваться. **2,** *fol. by for* (see to it that) распоряжáться, чтóбы.

arrangement *n.* **1,** (act of arranging; order) расположéние; устрóйство. *A flower arrangement,* ком-

поз́иция цветóв; букéт. *Table arrangement,* сервирóвка столá. **2,** (agreement) соглашéние; (terms of same) поря́док: *I suggest this arrangement,* я предлагáю такóй поря́док. **3,** (way something is to be done) план; вариáнт: *I suggest a different arrangement,* я предлагáю другóй план/вариáнт. **4,** *pl.* (plans; preparations) мéры; приготовлéния. **5,** *music* аранжирóвка; переложéние.

arrant *adj.* **1,** (notorious) отъя́вленный. **2,** (downright) сýщий.

array *n.* **1,** (arrangement) расположéние. **2,** *mil.* боевóй поря́док. **3,** (imposing collection or display) коллéкция; вы́ставка. —*v.t.* **1,** (arrange) располагáть. **2,** *mil.* выстрáивать.

arrears *n.pl.* задóлженность; недо́ймка. *Be in arrears,* имéть задóлженность.

arrest *v.t.* **1,** (take into custody) арестóвывать; задéрживать. **2,** (check, as growth, a disease, etc.) задéрживать; останáвливать. **3,** (capture, as one's attention) прикóвывать. —*n.* **1,** (detention) арéст. *Under house arrest,* под домáшним арéстом. *Place under arrest,* посади́ть под арéст; взять *or* заключи́ть под стрáжу. **2,** *med.* останов́ка: *cardiac arrest,* останóвка сéрдца.

arresting *adj.* поражáющий; захвáтывающий.

arrival *n.* **1,** (act of arriving) прибы́тие; прихóд; приéзд. **2,** (one who has just arrived) новоприбы́вший.

arrive *v.i.* **1,** (come to a place) приходи́ть; приезжáть; прибывáть. **2,** (come, as of a time or season) наступáть. **3,** *fol. by* at (reach, as a conclusion) приходи́ть (к).

arrogant *adj.* высокомéрный; надмéнный; занóсчивый. —**arrogance,** *n.* высокомéрие; надмéнность; занóсчивость.

arrogate *v.t.* присвáивать себé.

arrow *n.* **1,** (projectile fired from a bow) стрелá. **2,** (pointer; indicator) стрéлка.

arrowhead *n.* наконéчник стрелы́.

arsenal *n.* арсенáл.

arsenic *n.* мышья́к. —*adj.* мышьякóвый.

arson *n.* поджóг. —**arsonist,** *n.* поджигáтель.

art *n.* **1,** (creative work or skill) искýсство. *Work of art,* произведéние искýсства. **2,** *pl.* (liberal arts) гуманитáрные наýки. —*adj.* худóжественный. *Art exhibit,* вы́ставка карти́н. *Art gallery,* карти́нная галерéя.

artel *n.* артéль.

arterial *adj.* **1,** *anat.* артериáльный. **2,** (of a highway) магистрáльный.

arteriosclerosis *n.* артериосклерóз.

artery *n.* артéрия.

artesian well артезиáнский колóдец.

artful *adj.* **1,** (wily) хи́трый. **2,** (skillful) лóвкий.

arthritis *n.* артри́т. —**arthritic,** *adj.* артрити́ческий.

artichoke *n.* артишóк. *Jerusalem artichoke,* земляня́я грýша.

article *n.* **1,** (item) предмéт. *Toilet articles,* туалéтные принадлéжности. **2,** (composition written for publication) статья́. **3,** (paragraph of a treaty, constitution, etc.) статья́. **4,** *gram.* арти́кль; член.

articulate *v.t.* **1,** (enunciate) выговáривать. **2,** (express in words) выражáть. —*v.i.* артикули́ровать. —*adj.* членораздéльный. —**articulation,** *n.* артикуля́ция.

artifact *n.* предмёт человёческого трудá.

artifice *n.* улóвка.

artificial *adj.* искýсственный. —**artificial limb**, протёз. —**artificial respiration**, искýсственное дыхáние. *Give artificial respiration to*, откáчивать.

artificiality *n.* искýсственность.

artificially *adv.* искýсственно.

artillery *n.* артиллёрия. —*adj.* артиллерийский: *artillery fire*, артиллерийский огóнь. —**artilleryman**, *n.* артиллерист.

artisan *n.* ремёсленник.

artist *n.* **1,** (one who draws or paints) худóжник. **2,** (performer) артист.

artistic *adj.* **1,** (of or pert. to art) худóжественный. **2,** (showing good taste or a talent for art) артистический. —**artistry**, *n.* артистичность; худóжественность.

artless *adj.* **1,** (ingenuous) простодýшный; бесхитростный. **2,** (done without skill; crude) бездáрный.

Aryan *adj.* арийский. —*n.* áриец; *pl.* арийцы.

as *conj.* **1,** (to the same degree that) как: *thin as a rail*, худóй как щёпка. **2,** (according to what) как: *as is known*, как извёстно; *as you can see*, как вúдно. *Do as you are told*, дёлайте как вам вёлено. **3,** (while) когдá; в то врёмя как: *he arrived as I was leaving*, он пришёл, когдá я уходúл. **4,** (because; since) так как: *we must be leaving as it is already late*, нáдо уйтú, так как ужё пóздно. **5,** (to the degree that) по мёре тогó, как: *as it became warmer*, по мёре тогó, как становúлось теплёе. **6,** (though; however) как ни: *as smart as he is, he could not solve the problem*, как он ни умён, он не мог решúть задáчу. —*adv.* **1,** (equally) так же; такóй же: *our house is just as large*, наш дом такóй же большóй. **2,** (for example) как; как напримёр. *Such important people as...*, такúе вáжные лúца, как... *African languages, as Swahili*, африкáнские языкú, как напримёр суахúли. —*prep.* (by way of; in the capacity of) как; в кáчестве (+ *gen.*). *As an example*, в кáчестве примёра. *I give you this advice as a friend*, совётую это вам, как друг. ♦*Also rendered by the instrumental case: work as a salesman*, рабóтать продавцóм; *serve as a pretext*, служúть предлóгом. —**as...as**, так (*or* такóй) же...как (и). *He is as tall as you*, он такóй же высóкий как вы. —**as for...**, что касáется (+ *gen.*). —**as if**, (как) бýдто; как бы; слóвно. *As if you didn't know!*, как бýдто вы не знáете! —**as it were**, так сказáть. —**as of**, на: *as of June 1*, на пёрвое июня. —**as though**, *see* **though**. —**as well**, *see* **well**. —**as you were!**, *mil.* отстáвить!

asbestos *n.* асбёст. —*adj.* асбёстовый.

ascend *v.i.* поднимáться; всходúть. —*v.t.* поднимáться по; всходúть на. *Ascend the throne*, взойтú *or* вступúть на престóл.

ascendancy *n.* власть; госпóдство.

ascendant *adj.* **1,** (rising) восходáщий. **2,** (dominant) госпóдствующий.

ascension *n.* **1,** (ascent) восхождёние. **2,** *cap., relig.* вознесёние.

ascent *n.* **1,** (upward movement) восхождёние; подъём. **2,** (slope) крутизнá; подъём.

ascertain *v.t.* выяснять; устанáвливать.

ascetic *n.* аскёт; подвúжник. —*adj.* аскетúческий. —**asceticism**, *n.* аскетúзм.

ascorbic acid аскорбúновая кислотá.

ascribe *v.t.* приписывать: *the play is sometimes ascribed to Shakespeare*, пьёсу иногдá приписывают Шекспúру.

asepsis *n.* асёптика. —**aseptic**, *adj.* асептúческий.

asexual *adj.* беспóлый.

ash *n.* **1,** (tree) ясень. *Mountain ash*, рябúна. **2,** *usu. pl.* (residue after burning) пёпел; золá. **3,** (fine lava) пёпел: *volcanic ash*, вулканúческий пёпел. **4,** *pl.* (ruins) пёпел: *rise from the ashes*, поднимáться из пёпла. **5,** *pl.* (human remains) прах.

ashamed *adj., used predicatively:* *be ashamed*, стыдúться. *I am ashamed*, мне стыдно. *Aren't you ashamed!*, как вам не стыдно! *You ought to be ashamed of yourself!*, вам должнó быть стыдно!

ash can мýсорный ящик.

ashen *adj.* **1,** (of the color of ashes) пёпельного цвёта. **2,** (extremely pale) помертвёлый.

ashore *adv.* на бёрег; к бёрегу. *Go/put/wash ashore*, сходúть/высáживать/выносúть на бёрег. *Swim ashore*, плыть к бёрегу. *The body was washed ashore*, труп прибúло к бёрегу.

ashtray *n.* пёпельница.

Asian *also*, **Asiatic** *adj.* азиáтский. —*n.* азиáт.

aside *adv.* в стóрону. *Joking aside*, шýтки в стóрону; крóме шýток. *Put/set aside*, отклáдывать (в стóрону); сберегáть. —**all else aside**, помúмо всегó прóчего. —**aside from**, помúмо.

asinine *adj.* дурáцкий; идиóтский.

ask *v.t.* **1,** (put a question to; inquire about) спрáшивать: *I'll ask her*, я её спрошý. *Ask a passer-by*, спросúть у прохóжего. *Ask the way*, спросúть дорóгу. *Ask a question*, задавáть вопрóс. **2,** (request) просúть: *ask someone to do the dishes*, просúть когó-нибудь помыть посýду. *Ask him to come in*, попросúте егó войтú. *I have a favor to ask of you*, у меня к вам прóсьба. **3,** (invite) приглашáть; звать. **4,** (charge, as an amount of money) просúть; спрáшивать. **5,** (demand; expect) трёбовать. —*v.i.* спрáшивать: *if you don't know, ask*, ёсли не знáешь, спросú. *She asked about you*, онá о вас спросúла. —**ask for**, **1,** (request) просúть; спрáшивать: *ask for a book*, просúть/спрáшивать кнúгу: *ask for permission*, просúть/спрáшивать разрешёния. *Ask for help*, просúть (о) пóмощи. **2,** (ask to see) спрáшивать: *someone was asking for you*, вас спрáшивал какóй-то человёк. **3,** (invite, as trouble) напрáшиваться на (неприятности). *See also* **asking.**

askance *adv.* кóсо: *look askance*, смотрёть кóсо.

askew *adv.* кóсо; крúво.

asking *n. It's yours for the asking*, стóит тóлько попросúть. —**asking price**, запрáшиваемая ценá.

aslant *adv.* кóсо; нáискось.

asleep *adj., used predicatively* **1,** (sleeping): *be asleep*, спать. *Fall asleep*, засыпáть. **2,** (numb): *my foot is asleep*, я отлежáл нóгу.

asp *n.* áспид.

asparagus *n.* спáржа. —*adj.* спáржевый: *asparagus soup*, спáржевый суп.

aspect *n.* **1,** (appearance) вид. **2,** (part; feature) сторонá; момёнт; аспёкт. *Consider a question in all its aspects*, рассмáтривать вопрóс со всех сторóн. *Negative aspects*, отрицáтельные момёнты. **3,** *gram.* вид: *imperfective aspect*, несовершённый вид.

aspectual *adj., gram.* видовóй.

aspen *n.* осúна. —*adj.* осúновый.

asperity *n.* рéзкость; грýбость.

asperse *v.t.* клеветáть; чернúть; порóчить.

aspersion *n.* клеветá. *Cast aspersions on,* бросáть тень на.

asphalt *n.* асфáльт. —*adj.* асфáльтовый. —*v.t.* асфальтúровать.

asphyxia *n.* асфúксия.

asphyxiate *v.t.* удушáть. —**asphyxiation,** *n.* удушéние; асфúксия.

aspic *n.* заливнóе.

aspirant *n.* претендéнт.

aspirate *n. & adj.* придыхáтельный. —*v.t.* произносúть с придыхáнием.

aspiration *n.* 1, (ambition) стремлéние. 2, *phonet.* придыхáние.

aspire *v.i.* [*usu.* **aspire to**] стремúться (к); претендовáть (на). *Aspire to the role of,* претендовáть на роль (+ *gen.*).

aspirin *n.* аспирúн. *Aspirin tablet,* таблéтка аспирúна.

ass *n.* 1, (donkey) осёл. 2, *slang* (dope; jerk) болвáн. *Make an ass of oneself,* опростоволóситься. 3, *slang* (buttocks) зад.

assail *v.t.* 1, (assault) нападáть на. 2, (denounce) обрýшиваться на. 3, *fig.* (beset) мýчить: *be assailed by doubts,* мýчиться сомнéниями.

assailant *n.* налётчик.

assassin *n.* убúйца.

assassinate *v.t.* убивáть. *Attempt to assassinate,* покушáться на. —**assassination,** *n.* убúйство. *Assassination attempt,* покушéние (на).

assault *n.* нападéние; штурм; атáка. —*v.t.* нападáть на; атаковáть. —**assault and battery,** избиéние; оскорблéние дéйствием.

assay *v.t.* 1, (attempt) пытáться. 2, (estimate) оцéнивать.

assemblage *n.* 1, (gathering of persons) собрáние. 2, *mech.* сбóрка; монтáж.

assemble *v.t.* собирáть. —*v.i.* собирáться; сходúться; съезжáться. —**assembler,** *n.* сбóрщик.

assembly *n.* 1, (act of meeting or assembling) собрáние: *freedom of assembly,* свобóда собрáний. 2, (deliberative body) собрáние; ассамблéя. 3, *mech.* сбóрка; монтáж. —**assembly hall,** áктовый зал. —**assembly line,** сбóрочный конвéйер.

assent *v.i.* соглашáться. —*n.* соглáсие.

assert *v.t.* 1, (aver) утверждáть. 2, (claim and forcefully defend) отстáивать; предъявлять: *assert one's rights,* отстáивать/предъявлять свои правá.

assertion *n.* утверждéние.

assertive *adj.* напóристый.

assess *v.t.* 1, (evaluate) оцéнивать. 2, (levy, as a fine) налагáть. 3, (levy a payment upon) облагáть.

assessment *n.* 1, (evaluation) оцéнка. 2, (amount assessed) обложéние.

asset *n.* 1, (something advantageous) преимýщество; цéнное кáчество. 2, *usu. pl., comm.* актúв.

assiduous *adj.* прилéжный; старáтельный; усúдчивый. —**assiduousness; assiduity,** *n.* прилежáние; старáтельность; усúдчивость.

assign *v.t.* 1, (appoint; designate) назначáть. 2, *mil.* прикомандировáть. 3, (allocate) отводúть. 4, (give out, as a task, lesson, etc.) задавáть.

assignment *n.* 1, (appointment) назначéние. 2, (task) поручéние; задáние. *Homework assignment,* домáшнее задáние.

assimilate *v.t.* 1, *physiol.* ассимилúровать; усвáивать. 2, (absorb mentally) усвáивать; воспринимáть. —*v.i.* ассимилúроваться. —**assimilation,** *n.* ассимиляция; усвоéние.

assist *v.t. & i.* помогáть; содéйствовать. —**assistance,** *n.* пóмощь; содéйствие.

assistant *n. & adj.* помóщник. *Assistant director,* помóщник дирéктора. —**assistant professor,** ассистéнт.

associate *n.* сотрýдник; коллéга. —*v.t.* соединять; связывать; ассоциúровать. *The problems associated with it,* связанные с этим проблéмы. —*v.i.* общáться. —**associate member,** член-корреспондéнт. —**associate professor,** доцéнт.

association *n.* 1, (act of associating) общéние. 2, (an organization) óбщество; объединéние; ассоциáция. 3, (connection in the mind) ассоциáция.

assonance *n.* созвýчие; ассонáнс. —**assonant,** *adj.* созвýчный.

assort *v.t.* сортировáть. —**assorted,** *adj.* рáзные; рáзного рóда.

assortment *n.* выбор; подбóр; ассортимéнт.

assuage *v.t.* 1, (allay) смягчáть; облегчáть. 2, (calm) успокáивать. 3, (appease, as hunger) утолять.

assume *v.t.* 1, (suppose) предполагáть; допускáть: *let us assume that...,* предположим/допýстим, что... 2, (take on; take over) принимáть: *assume a pose,* принимáть пóзу; *assume command,* принимáть комáндование. *Assume responsibility,* принимáть (*or* брать) на себя отвéтственность. *Assume the offensive,* переходúть в наступлéние. *Assume office,* вступúть в дóлжность. *Assume an injured look,* принимáть обúженный вид. *Assume a threatening character,* принимáть *or* приобретáть угрожáющий харáктер.

assumed *adj.* 1, (supposed; presumed) предполагáемый. 2, (fictitious) вымышленный. *Under an assumed name,* под чужúм úменем.

assumption *n.* 1, (supposition) предположéние. *Proceed on the assumption that...,* исходúть из предположéния (*or* из тогó), что... 2, (taking on; taking over) принятие (на себя). 3, (accession, as to a position) вступлéние. 4, *cap., relig.* успéние. *Cathedral of the Assumption,* Успéнский собóр.

assurance *n.* 1, (positive statement) увéрение; заверéние. *Give assurances,* давáть заверéния. 2, (certainty) увéренность. 3, (confidence) самоувéренность.

assure *v.t.* 1, (promise confidently) уверять; заверять. 2, (make certain) обеспéчивать. —**you may rest assured,** мóжете быть увéрены.

assuredly *adv.* несомнéнно.

Assyrian *adj.* ассирúйский. —*n.* ассирúец.

astatine *n.* астатúн.

aster *n.* áстра.

asterisk *n.* звёздочка.

astern *adv.* 1, (behind a ship) за кормóй. 2, (at the rear of a ship) на кормé.

asteroid *n.* астерóид.

asthma *n.* áстма. —**asthmatic,** *adj.* астматúческий. —*n.* астмáтик.

astigmatism *n.* астигматúзм. —**astigmatic,** *adj.* астигматúческий.

astir *adj.* **1**, (in motion) в движе́нии. **2**, (out of bed) на нога́х. **3**, (excited) взволно́ванный.

astonish *v.t.* изумля́ть. —**astonishing**, *adj.* изуми́тельный. —**astonishment**, *n.* изумле́ние.

astound *v.t.* изумля́ть; поража́ть. —**astounding**, *adj.* изуми́тельный; порази́тельный.

astraddle *prep.* верхо́м на (+ *prepl.*).

astrakhan *n.* кара́куль. —*adj.* кара́кулевый.

astray *adv.* с пути́. *Go astray*, сбива́ться с пути́; заблуди́ться. *Lead astray*, сбива́ть с пути́; вводи́ть в заблужде́ние.

astride *prep.* верхо́м на (+ *prepl.*).

astringent *adj.* **1**, (tending to constrict) вя́жущий. **2**, (harsh) те́рпкий. —*n.* вя́жущее сре́дство. —**astringency**, *n.* те́рпкость.

astrolabe *n.* астроля́бия.

astrology *n.* астроло́гия. —**astrologer**, *n.* астро́лог; звездочёт. —**astrological**, *adj.* астрологи́ческий.

astronaut *n.* космона́вт.

astronomy *n.* астроно́мия. —**astronomer**, *n.* астроно́м. —**astronomic(al)**, *adj.* астрономи́ческий.

astrophysics *n.* астрофи́зика. —**astrophysical**, *adj.* астрофизи́ческий. —**astrophysicist**, *n.* астрофи́зик.

astute *adj.* проница́тельный; то́нкий. —**astuteness**, *n.* проница́тельность.

asunder *adv.* на ча́сти; на куски́.

asylum *n.* **1**, (refuge) убе́жище; прию́т. **2**, (institution) сумасше́дший дом.

asymmetric *also*, **asymmetrical** *adj.* асимметри́чный; несимметри́чный. —**asymmetry**, *n.* асимметри́я; несимметри́чность.

at *prep.* **1**, (in; attending) в; на (+ *prepl.*): *at the theater*, в теа́тре; *at work*, на рабо́те. *At home*, до́ма. **2**, (near; by) у: *at the window*, у окна́. **3**, (indicating arrival) в; на (+ *acc.*): *arrive at school*, прийти́ в шко́лу. **4**, (at the home of) у: *at my uncle's*, у моего́ дя́ди. **5**, (seated at) за: *be seated at the table*, сиде́ть за столо́м. **6**, (indicating the target or object of something) в; на (+ *acc.*): *look at one's watch*, посмотре́ть на часы́; *fire at a target*, стреля́ть в мише́нь. **7**, (indicating pace or speed) *rendered by the instrumental case: at a trot*, ры́сью; *at a snail's pace*, черепа́шьим ша́гом. **8**, (indicating a certain time) в (+ *acc.*): *at noon*, в по́лдень; *at three o' clock*, в три часа́; *at that time*, в то вре́мя. ♦ *But notice: at night*, но́чью; *at dawn*, на рассве́те; *at what time?*, в кото́ром часу́? **9**, (indicating a state or condition) на (+ *prepl.*): *at liberty*, на свобо́де; *at anchor*, на я́коре; *at one's leisure*, на досу́ге. **10**, (in accordance with) по: *at the request of*, по про́сьбе (+ *gen.*); *at one's discretion*, по своему́ усмотре́нию. **11**, (in reaction to) при: *at the sight of*, при ви́де (+ *gen.*); *shudder at the thought of*, содрога́ться при мы́сли о. **12**, *in various miscellaneous expressions: at fault*, винова́т; *at large*, на свобо́де; *at rest*, в поко́е. —**at all**, *see* **all**. —**at last**, наконе́ц. —**at once**, *see* **once**. —**at that**, **1**, (after all) в конце́ концо́в: *not so bad at that*, в конце́ концо́в не так уж пло́хо. **2**, (besides) причём: *he solved all the problems, and rather quickly at that*, он реши́л все зада́чи, причём дово́льно бы́стро. *Only one tie, and a frayed one at that*, то́лько оди́н га́лстук, да и то поно́шенный.

ataman *n.* атама́н.

atavism *n.* атави́зм. —**atavistic**, *adj.* атависти́ческий.

ataxia *n.* атакси́я.

atheism *n.* атеи́зм; безбо́жие. —**atheist**, *n.* атеи́ст; безбо́жник. —**atheistic**, *adj.* атеисти́ческий.

Athenian *adj.* афи́нский.

athlete *n.* спортсме́н; атле́т.

athletic *adj.* атлети́ческий. —**athletics**, *n. pl.* атле́тика.

athwart *prep.* поперёк.

Atlantic *adj.* атланти́ческий. —**Atlantic Ocean**, Атланти́ческий океа́н.

atlas *n.* а́тлас.

atmosphere *n.* **1**, (air) атмосфе́ра. **2**, *fig.* (setting; surroundings) обстано́вка; атмосфе́ра. —**atmospheric**, *adj.* атмосфе́рный.

atoll *n.* ато́лл.

atom *n.* а́том. *Atom-free zone*, беза́томная зо́на.

atomic *adj.* а́томный. —**atomic bomb**, а́томная бо́мба.

atomize *v.t.* распыля́ть. —**atomizer**, *n.* распыли́тель; пульвериза́тор.

atonal *adj.* атона́льный. —**atonality**, *n.* атона́льность.

atone *v.i.* [*usu.* **atone for**] искупа́ть. —**atonement**, *n.* искупле́ние.

atop *prep.* на верху́ (+ *gen.*).

atrocious *adj.* **1**, (cruel; brutal) зве́рский. **2**, *colloq.* (abominable) отврати́тельный.

atrocity *n.* зве́рство.

atrophy *n.* атрофи́я. —*v.i.* атрофи́роваться.

atropine *n.* атропи́н.

attach *v.t.* **1**, (fasten) прикрепля́ть: *attach an antenna to the roof*, прикрепля́ть анте́нну к кры́ше. **2**, (append) прилага́ть: *attached hereto*, при сём прилага́ется. **3**, (ascribe) придава́ть: *attach great importance to*, придава́ть большо́е значе́ние (+ *dat.*). **4**, *mil.* (assign) придава́ть. **5**, *law* налага́ть аре́ст на. *See also* **attached.**

attaché *n.* атташе́.

attached *adj.* **1**, (fastened) прикреплённый. **2**, (affiliated): *he is attached to the university*, он рабо́тает при университе́те. **3**, *fol. by* **to** (devoted) привя́занный (к).

attachment *n.* **1**, (attaching) прикрепле́ние. **2**, (affection) привя́занность. **3**, (accessory) приста́вка. **4**, *law* наложе́ние аре́ста.

attack *v.t.* **1**, (assault) напада́ть на. **2**, (criticize sharply) обру́шиваться на. **3**, (begin working on) бра́ться за. **4**, *med.* (strike) поража́ть. —*v.i.* наступа́ть; атакова́ть. —*n.* **1**, (assault; offensive) нападе́ние; ата́ка. **2**, (denunciation) вы́пад; *pl.* напа́дки. **3**, *med.* (seizure) припа́док; при́ступ. *Heart attack*, серде́чный припа́док; инфа́ркт.

attain *v.t.* достига́ть; доби́ться. —**attainable**, *adj.* достижи́мый. —**attainment**, *n.* достиже́ние.

attempt *v.t.* пыта́ться. *Attempt suicide*, покуша́ться на самоуби́йство. —*n.* **1**, (endeavor) попы́тка. **2**, (attack) покуше́ние: *attempt on someone's life*, покуше́ние на чью́-нибудь жизнь. *Make an attempt on someone's life*, покуша́ться на чью́-нибудь жизнь.

attend *v.t.* **1**, (be present at) прису́тствовать на. **2**, (go to regularly, as school) посеща́ть. **3**, (take care of; minister to) уха́живать за. —*v.i.* [*usu.* **attend to**] делать; заниматься; заботиться о. *Attend to a customer*, заниматься покупателем. *I have some things to attend to*, у меня есть кое-какие дела.

attendance *n.* **1,** (act of attending) посещение: *compulsory attendance*, обязательное посещение. **2,** (regularity of or number attending) посещаемость: *poor attendance*, плохая посещаемость.

attendant *n.* обслуживающее лицо; служитель. —*adj.* сопутствующий: *attendant circumstances*, сопутствующие обстоятельства.

attention *n.* **1,** (heed; care) внимание: *pay attention to*, обращать внимание на. *Bring/come to someone's attention*, доводить/доходить до чьего-нибудь сведения. **2,** *mil.* стойка "смирно"; строевая стойка. *Attention!*, смирно! *Stand at attention*, стоять по стойке "смирно"; стоять *or* стать смирно; стоять навытяжку; стать во фронт; принимать строевую стойку; вытянуться в струнку.

attentive *adj.* внимательный. —**attentively,** *adv.* внимательно. —**attentiveness,** *n.* внимательность.

attest *v.t.* удостоверять. —*v.i.* [*usu.* **attest to**] свидетельствовать о. —**attestation,** *n.* удостоверение.

attic *n.* чердак.

attire *n.* наряд; платье. —*v.t., usu. passive,* одевать: *smartly attired*, шикарно одетый.

attitude *n.* **1,** (feeling; disposition) отношение: *his attitude toward me*, его отношение ко мне. **2,** (position; posture) поза: *strike an attitude*, принимать позу.

attorney *n.* адвокат; поверенный. —**power of attorney,** доверенность.

attorney general министр юстиции.

attract *v.t.* привлекать. *Attract attention*, привлекать к себе внимание; обращать на себя внимание.

attraction *n.* **1,** (power to attract; pull) притяжение; тяготение. *Hold no attraction for*, не привлекать кого-нибудь. **2,** (something that attracts) приманка. **3,** (public entertainment) аттракцион.

attractive *adj.* привлекательный. —**attractiveness,** *n.* привлекательность.

attribute *v.t.* приписывать: *to what do you attribute...?*, чему вы приписываете...? —*n.* **1,** (characteristic) свойство; атрибут. **2,** *gram.* определение; атрибут.

attribution *n.* ссылка: *not for attribution*, без ссылки на источник.

attributive *n.* атрибут. —*adj.* атрибутивный.

attrition *n.* убыль персонала. —**war of attrition,** война на истощение.

attune *v.t.* **1,** (tune) настраивать. **2,** (bring into accord) согласовывать.

atypical *adj.* атипический.

auburn *adj.* русый; каштановый.

auction *n.* аукцион; торги. —*v.t.* продавать с аукциона/с торгов/с молотка. —**auctioneer,** *n.* аукционист.

audacious *adj.* **1,** (bold) смелый. **2,** (brazen) дерзкий; наглый. —**audacity,** *n.* смелость; дерзость; наглость.

audibility *n.* слышимость.

audible *adj.* слышный. —**audibly,** *adv.* слышно. *Speak audibly*, говорить вслух; говорить громко.

audience *n.* **1,** (spectators; listeners) аудитория; зрители; слушатели; публика. **2,** (formal interview) аудиенция.

audio *adj.* звуковой. —*n.* звук.

audit *n.* проверка отчётности; ревизия. —*v.t.* **1,** (conduct an audit of) ревизовать. **2,** (attend, as a course) слушать.

audition *n.* **1,** (hearing) слушание. **2,** (test performance) проба (на роль).

auditor *n.* ревизор; контролёр.

auditorium *n.* аудитория; зрительный зал.

auditory *adj.* слуховой.

Augean stables авгиевы конюшни.

auger *n.* бурав.

augment *v.t.* увеличивать; прибавлять. —**augmentation,** *n.* увеличение.

augur *n.* авгур. —*v.t.* предвещать. —*v.i.* [*usu.* **augur well**] предвещать хорошее.

augury *n.* предзнаменование.

august *adj.* величественный; внушительный.

August *n.* август. —*adj.* августовский.

auk *n.* гагарка.

aunt *n.* тётя; тётка.

aura *n.* ореол: *aura of mystery*, ореол таинственности.

aureole *n.* ореол.

auricle *n.* **1,** (chamber of the heart) предсердие. **2,** (external part of the ear) ушная раковина.

aurochs *n.* **1,** (extinct wild ox) тур. **2,** (European bison) зубр.

aurora *n.* **1,** (atmospheric phenomenon) сияние: *aurora borealis*, северное сияние. **2,** *poetic* (dawn) аврора.

auscultate *v.t.* выслушивать. —**auscultation,** *n.* выслушивание.

auspice *n., usu. pl.* покровительство: *under the auspices of*, под покровительством (+ *gen.*).

auspicious *adj.* благоприятный.

austere *adj.* строгий; суровый.

austerity *n.* строгая экономия. *Austerity program*, режим экономии.

Australian *adj.* австралийский. —*n.* австралиец; австралийка.

Austrian *adj.* австрийский. —*n.* австриец; австрийка.

authentic *adj.* подлинный. —**authenticate,** *v.t.* устанавливать подлинность (+ *gen.*). —**authenticity,** *n.* подлинность.

author *n.* автор.

authoritarian *adj.* авторитарный.

authoritative *adj.* авторитетный.

authority *n.* **1,** (power; jurisdiction) полномочие. **2,** *pl.* (those in charge) власти. **3,** (expert) авторитет. **4,** (source of information) источник: *on good authority*, из достоверных источников.

authorization *n.* разрешение. *By authorization of*, по уполномочию (+ *gen.*).

authorize *v.t.* **1,** (empower) уполномочивать. **2,** (give permission to publish) авторизовать.

authorized *adj.* уполномоченный; авторизованный. *Authorized translation*, авторизованный перевод.

authorship *n.* авторство.

auto *n., colloq.* машина.

autobiography *n.* автобиография. —**autobiographical,** *adj.* автобиографический.

autocracy *n.* самодержавие; автократия; единовластие. —**autocrat,** *n.* самодержец; автократ.

—**autocratic,** *adj.* самодержа́вный; автократи́ческий; единовла́стный.

autogiro *n.* автожи́р.

autograph *n.* авто́граф. —*v.t.* надпи́сывать. *Autographed copy,* именно́й экземпля́р.

automat *n.* рестора́н-автома́т.

automate *v.t.* автоматизи́ровать.

automatic *adj.* автомати́ческий. —**automatically,** *adv.* автомати́чески.

automation *n.* **1,** (science) автома́тика: *the age of automation,* век автома́тики. **2,** (act) автоматиза́ция: *automation of production,* автоматиза́ция произво́дства.

automaton *n.* автома́т.

automobile *n.* автомоби́ль. —*adj.* автомоби́льный.

automotive *adj.* автомоби́льный.

autonomous *adj.* автоно́мный. —**autonomy,** *n.* автоно́мия.

autopsy *n.* вскры́тие.

autosuggestion *n.* самовнуше́ние.

autumn *n.* о́сень. *In autumn,* о́сенью. —*adj.* [*also,* **autumnal**] осе́нний: *autumn sky,* осе́ннее не́бо.

auxiliary *adj.* вспомога́тельный. —**auxiliary verb,** вспомога́тельный глаго́л.

avail *v.t.* приноси́ть по́льзу (+ *dat.*). *His efforts availed him nothing,* его́ уси́лия не принесли́ ему́ по́льзы; его́ уси́лия пропа́ли да́ром. —*n.* по́льза; вы́года. *To no avail,* напра́сно. —**avail oneself of,** воспо́льзоваться (+ *instr.*).

availability *n.* нали́чие; досту́пность.

available *adj.* име́ющийся; нали́чный; досту́пный. *Be available,* име́ться; быть в нали́чии.

avalanche *n.* лави́на.

avant-garde *n.* авангарди́сты. —*adj.* авангарди́стский

avarice *n.* жа́дность. —**avaricious,** *adj.* жа́дный.

avenge *v.t.* мстить (за); вымеща́ть. —**avenger,** *n.* мсти́тель.

avenue *n.* **1,** (wide street) проспе́кт; авеню́. *Fifth Avenue,* Пя́тая авеню́. **2,** *fig.* (means of achieving something) путь: *avenue to success,* путь к успе́ху.

aver *v.t.* утвержда́ть.

average *adj.* сре́дний. —*n.* сре́днее число́. *Above /below average,* вы́ше/ни́же сре́днего. —*v.t.* **1,** (find the average of): *average figures together,* выводи́ть о́бщее число́. **2,** (amount to as an average) составля́ть в сре́днем: *average five percent,* составля́ть в сре́днем пять проце́нтов. —**on the average,** в сре́днем.

averse *adj., used predicatively* не распо́ложен. *Not be averse to,* быть не прочь (+ *inf.*).

aversion *n.* отвраще́ние; антипа́тия. *Have an aversion to,* пита́ть отвраще́ние к; испы́тывать антипа́тию к; бре́згать (+ *inf.*).

avert *v.t.* **1,** (turn away) отводи́ть. **2,** (prevent) предотвраща́ть.

aviary *n.* вольёр.

aviation *n.* авиа́ция. —*adj.* авиацио́нный.

aviator *n.* лётчик; авиа́тор.

avid *adj.* **1,** (greatly desirous) жа́дный. *Avid for power,* жа́ждущий вла́сти. **2,** (ardent; enthusiastic) стра́стный. —**avidity,** *n.* жа́дность. —**avidly,** *adv.* жа́дно; с жа́дностью.

avocado *n.* авока́до.

avocation *n.* побо́чное заня́тие.

avocet *n.* шилоклю́вка.

avoid *v.t.* **1,** (keep away from; refrain from) избега́ть. *In order to avoid,* во избежа́ние (+ *gen.*). **2,** (evade, as a blow) уклоня́ться от.

avoidance *n.* уклоне́ние. *Avoidance of military service,* уклоне́ние от вое́нной слу́жбы.

avow *v.t.* откры́то признава́ть. —**avowal,** *n.* призна́ние. —**avowed,** *adj.* при́знанный.

await *v.t.* ждать; ожида́ть.

awake *v.t.* **1,** (wake up) буди́ть. **2,** (stir; arouse, as a feeling) пробужда́ть. —*v.i.* **1,** (wake up) просыпа́ться. **2,** *fol. by* **to** (become aware of) осознава́ть. —*adj. Be awake,* не спать; бо́дрствовать.

awaken *v.t. & i.* = **awake.** —**awakening,** *n.* пробужде́ние.

award *n.* награ́да. —*v.t.* награжда́ть; присужда́ть; присва́ивать; удоста́ивать.

aware *adj. Be aware* (of), знать; сознава́ть; отдава́ть себе́ отчёт в (+ *prepl.*). —**awareness,** *n.* понима́ние; созна́ние; осозна́ние.

away *adv.* прочь; вон. *Away with you!,* вон отсю́да! ♦ *Usually rendered by a prefixed verb: carry away,* уноси́ть; *go away,* уходи́ть; уезжа́ть; *pass away,* сконча́ться; *run away,* убега́ть; *throw away,* выбра́сывать; *waste away,* ча́хнуть. —*adj.* **1,** (absent; gone) в отъе́зде; в отлу́чке. *Be away,* уе́хать; отсу́тствовать; быть в отъе́зде/отлу́чке. **2,** (distant) на расстоя́нии (+ *gen.*): *ten miles away,* на расстоя́нии десяти́ миль. *Christmas is three months away,* до Рождества́ оста́лось три ме́сяца.

awe *n.* страх; благогове́ние. *Be in awe of,* преклоня́ться пе́ред. —*v.t.* внуша́ть страх (+ *dat.*).

awesome *adj.* стра́шный; гро́зный.

awful *adj.* **1,** (very bad) ужа́сный; отврати́тельный. **2,** (inspiring awe) гро́зный. *An awful stillness,* гробова́я тишина́. —**an awful lot of,** ма́сса (+ *gen.*).

awfully *adv.* **1,** (very badly) ужа́сно; отврати́тельно. **2,** (very; extremely) ужа́сно; о́чень: *awfully tired,* ужа́сно уста́л; *awfully kind of you,* о́чень любе́зно с ва́шей стороны́.

awhile *adv.* немно́го; не́которое вре́мя. *Wait awhile!,* подожди́те немно́го!

awkward *adj.* **1,** (clumsy) неуклю́жий; нело́вкий. **2,** (embarrassing; embarrassed) нело́вкий: *awkward situation,* нело́вкое положе́ние; *feel awkward,* чу́вствовать себя́ нело́вко. —**awkwardly,** *adv.* неуклю́же; нело́вко. —**awkwardness,** *n.* неуклю́жесть; нело́вкость.

awl *n.* ши́ло.

awning *n.* наве́с; тент; зонт.

awry *adv.* **1,** (askew) ко́со; на́бок. **2,** (amiss) насма́рку: *go awry,* идти́/пойти́ насма́рку.

ax *also,* **axe** *n.* топо́р.

axial *adj.* осево́й.

axil *n.* па́зуха.

axiom *n.* аксио́ма. —**axiomatic,** *adj.* аксиомати́ческий.

axis *n.* ось.

axle *n.* ось.

ayatollah *n.* аятолла́.

aye *adv.* да. —*n.* за: *three ayes, two nays,* три за, два про́тив. *The ayes have it,* большинство́ за. —**aye aye, sir!,** есть!

azalea *n.* аза́лия.

azimuth *n.* а́зимут.

azure *n.* лазу́рь. —*adj.* голубо́й; лазу́рный.

B

B, b втора́я бу́ква англи́йского алфави́та. —*n.* **1,** (musical note) си. **2,** (school grade) четвёрка.

baba au rhum ро́мовая ба́ба.

babble *v.i.* **1,** (prattle) лепета́ть. **2,** (of a brook) журча́ть. —*n.* **1,** (prattle) ле́пет. **2,** (of a brook) журча́ние.

babe *n.* **1,** (baby) младе́нец. **2,** *slang* (girl) де́вка.

babel *n.* смеше́ние языко́в; вавило́нское столпотворе́ние. —**Tower of Babel,** вавило́нская ба́шня.

baboon *n.* павиа́н.

babushka *n.* плато́к.

baby *n.* **1,** (infant) ребёнок. **2,** (young or newborn animal, bird, etc.) детёныш. *Baby elephant,* детёныш слона́; слонёнок. *Baby bird,* птене́ц. —*adj.* де́тский: *baby talk,* де́тский ле́пет. *Baby brother,* брати́шка. *Baby sister,* сестрёнка. —*v.t.* ня́нчиться с. —**baby carriage,** де́тская коля́ска. —**baby grand piano,** кабине́тный роя́ль. —**baby tooth,** моло́чный зуб.

babyish *adj.* ребя́ческий.

Babylonian *adj.* вавило́нский.

baby sitter приходя́щая ня́ня.

baccalaureate *n.* сте́пень бакала́вра.

baccarat *n.* баккара́.

bachelor *n.* **1,** (unmarried man) холостя́к. **2,** (holder of a bachelor's degree) бакала́вр. *Bachelor's degree,* сте́пень бакала́вра. —*adj.* холосто́й; холостя́цкий. *Bachelor apartment,* холостя́цкая кварти́ра. —**bachelorhood,** *n.* холоста́я жизнь.

bacillus *n.* баци́лла; па́лочка.

back *n.* **1,** (part of the body) спина́. **2,** (part of a chair, garment, etc.) спи́нка. **3,** (rear) зад; за́дняя часть; за́дняя сторона́. *In the back of the book,* в конце́ кни́ги. **4,** (reverse side) оборо́т; оборо́тная сторона́. *Back of a card,* руба́шка. *Back of the hand,* ты́льная сторона́ руки́. **5,** *sports* (defenseman) защи́тник. —*adj.* **1,** (dorsal) спинно́й. **2,** (rear) за́дний: *back seat,* за́днее сиде́нье. *Back door,* чёрный ход. **3,** (remote) глухо́й. *Back street,* закоу́лок. *Back country,* глушь. **4,** (of a past date) ста́рый: *back issue,* ста́рый но́мер. —*adv.* **1,** (backward) наза́д: *step back,* шага́ть наза́д. **2,** (to or toward where one began) обра́тно. *On the way back,* на обра́тном пути́. *When will he be back?,* когда́ он вернётся? **3,** (to the original possessor) наза́д; обра́тно: *give back,* отда́ть наза́д; *get back,* получи́ть обра́тно. **4,** (ago) тому́ наза́д: *a while back,* не́которое вре́мя тому́ наза́д. ♦ *Often rendered by a prefixed verb: come back,* возвраща́ться; *hold back,* уде́рживать; *pay back,* отпла́чивать. —*v.t.* **1,** fol. by **up** (move backward) отодви-

га́ть. **2,** (support) подде́рживать. **3,** *fol.* by **up** (substantiate) подкрепля́ть. **4,** (put money into) финанси́ровать; субсиди́ровать. **5,** (bet on) ста́вить на. *Back the wrong horse,* ста́вить не на ту ло́шадь. —*v.i.* [*usu.* **back up**] **1,** (move backward) подвига́ться *or* отодвига́ться наза́д; пя́титься. **2,** (go into reverse) дава́ть за́дний ход. —**back and forth,** взад и вперёд. —**back down,** отступа́ть; бить отбо́й. —**back off,** отступа́ть. —**back out (of),** отступа́ть (от). —**back to back,** спина́ (*or* спино́й) к спине́. —**behind someone's back,** за чьей-нибудь спино́й. —**go back on,** наруша́ть; не сдержа́ть. *Go back on one's word,* наруша́ть своё сло́во; идти́ на попя́тный. —**in back of, 1,** (position) за (+ *instr.*). **2,** (motion) за (+ *acc.*). —**there and back,** туда́ и обра́тно. —**turn one's back on,** отвора́чиваться от.

backache *n.* боль в спине́.

backboard *n.* **1,** (board supporting the back) доска́. **2,** *basketball* щит.

backbone *n.* **1,** (spine) позвоно́чник; спинно́й хребе́т. **2,** (fortitude) твёрдость хара́ктера. **3,** (mainstay) станово́й хребе́т; станова́я жи́ла; костя́к.

backbreaking *adj.* непоси́льный; ка́торжный.

backdate *v.t.* поме́тить за́дним число́м.

backdrop *n.* **1,** *theat.* за́дник. **2,** *fig.* (background) фон.

backer *n.* **1,** (supporter) сторо́нник. **2,** (patron) покрови́тель.

backfire *v.i.* дать осе́чку; возыме́ть обра́тное де́йствие; оберну́ться про́тив самого́ себя́.

backgammon *n.* триктра́к.

background *n.* **1,** (setting) фон; за́дний план; по́ле. **2,** (secondary place or position) за́дний план: *remain in the background,* остава́ться на за́днем пла́не. **3,** (underlying events) канва́. **4,** (training; experience) подгото́вка. **5,** (origin; ancestry) происхожде́ние; род.

backhand *n.,* *tennis* уда́р сле́ва. —*adj. & adv.* сле́ва.

backhanded *adj.* **1,** = **backhand. 2,** (equivocal) сомни́тельный: *backhanded compliment,* сомни́тельный комплиме́нт.

backing *n.* **1,** (supporting material) подкла́дка. **2,** (endorsement) подде́ржка.

backlog *n.* **1,** (accumulation) скопле́ние. **2,** (reserve supply) запа́с.

backrest *n.* опо́ра для спины́.

backside *n.,* *colloq.* зад; я́годицы.

backstage *adv.* **1,** (location) за кули́сами. **2,**

(motion) за кулисы. —*adj.* закулисный.

backstroke *n.* плавание на спине.

back talk возражения. *No back talk*!, без возражений!; без разговоров!; никаких разговоров!; не разговаривать!

backtrack *v.i.* **1**, (return over the same route) возвращаться по своим следам (*or* стопам). **2**, *fig.* (reverse oneself) давать задний ход.

backward *adv.* [*also*, **backwards**] **1**, (toward the back) назад. **2**, (in reverse order) наоборот; в обратном порядке. **3**, (in the reverse direction) задом. *Move backward*, пятиться. **4**, (with the back foremost) задом наперёд: *put one's hat on backwards*, надеть шапку задом наперёд. —*adj.* **1**, (rearward) обратный. **2**, (retarded) отсталый. —**bend/lean over backwards**, всячески стараться; лезть из кожи вон. —**know backwards and forwards**, знать (что-нибудь) вдоль и поперёк.

backwardness *n.* отсталость.

backwards *adv.* = **backward.**

backwater *n.* заводь; затон.

backwoods *n.pl.* глушь. —*adj.* глухой.

bacon *n.* бекон; копчёная грудинка.

bacteria *n.*, *pl. of* **bacterium.** —**bacterial**, *adj.* бактериальный.

bacteriology *n.* бактериология. —**bacteriological**, *adj.* бактериологический. —**bacteriologist**, *n.* бактериолог.

bacterium *n.* бактерия.

bad *adj.* **1**, (not good) плохой; дурной. *Bad weather*, плохая погода. *Bad habits*, дурные привычки. *That's bad*, это плохо. *Smell bad*, плохо пахнуть. **2**, (wicked) злой: *the bad fairy*, злая фея. **3**, (naughty) озорной; непослушный. **4**, (harmful) вредный: *bad for one's health*, вредно для здоровья. **5**, (sore; defective) больной: *a bad heart*, больное сердце. **6**, (severe) сильный: *a bad cold*, сильный насморк. —**get in bad**, *colloq.* впадать в немилость. —**go bad**, **1**, (degenerate) вырождаться. **2**, (become tainted) портиться. —**go from bad to worse**, становиться всё хуже и хуже. —**not a bad** (+ *noun*), неплохой. —**not bad**, неплохо; ничего. —**too bad**, очень жаль. *It's too bad that...*, жаль, что...

badge *n.* значок; бляха.

badger *n.* (animal) барсук. —*v.t.* (pester) приставать к; травить.

badly *adv.* **1**, (poorly) плохо; дурно; скверно. **2**, (very much; greatly) очень; сильно. **3**, (severely) сильно; тяжело; больно: *badly damaged*, сильно повреждён; *badly wounded*, тяжело ранен; *cut oneself badly*, сильно порезаться.

badminton *n.* бадминтон.

baffle *v.t.* озадачивать. —**baffled**, *adj.* озадаченный. —**bafflement**, *n.* озадаченность. —**baffling**, *adj.* недоуменный.

bag *n.* **1**, (for carrying something) сумка. **2**, (sack) мешок. **3**, (paper bag) пакет; пакетик. **4**, (suitcase) чемодан. **5**, (handbag) сумка; сумочка. **6**, (game killed in hunting) добыча. **7**, *pl.* (pouchlike folds of skin) мешки (под глазами). —*v.t.* **1**, (put in a bag) класть в мешок. **2**, (capture) схватывать. **3**, (kill, as game) убивать; настрелять. —**bag and baggage**, *colloq.* со всеми пожитками. —**be left holding the bag**, *colloq.* остаться с носом; остаться при пиковом интересе. —**it's in the bag**, *colloq.* дело в шляпе.

bagel *n.* баранка; бублик.

baggage *n.* багаж. —*adj.* багажный: *baggage car*, багажный вагон. —**baggage compartment**, багажник. —**baggage room**, камера хранения (багажа).

baggy *adj.* мешковатый.

bagpipe *n.* волынка. *Also*, **bagpipes.**

bah *interj.* тьфу!

bail *n.* поручительство; порука. *Release on bail*, отпускать на поруки. —*v.t.* [*usu.* **bail out**] **1**, (remove, as water; remove the water from) вычёрпывать. **2**, (put up bail for) брать на поруки. **3**, (help out of difficulty) выручать. —*v.i.* [*usu.* **bail out**] выбрасываться с парашютом.

bailiff *n.* судебный исполнитель; *pre-rev.* судебный пристав.

bailiwick *n.* часть: *not in my bailiwick*, не по моей части.

bait *n.* наживка; приманка. *Take the bait*, попасться на удочку. —*v.t.* **1**, (apply bait to) наживлять. **2**, (entice) заманивать; приманивать. **3**, (torment; harass) травить.

baize *n.* байка. —*adj.* байковый.

bake *v.t.* **1**, (cook in an oven) печь. **2**, (treat with heat, as bricks) обжигать. —*v.i.* **1**, (do baking) печь. **2**, (become baked) печься. *Bake in the sun*, печься (*or* жариться) на солнце.

baked *adj.* печёный.

bakelite *n.* бакелит.

baker *n.* пекарь; булочник. —**baker's dozen**, чёртова дюжина.

bakery *n.* **1**, (store) булочная; хлебный магазин. **2**, (baking establishment) пекарня.

baking *n.* печение; выпечка. —*adj.* пекарный: *baking powder*, пекарный порошок. —**baking sheet**, противень. —**baking soda**, питьевая сода.

balalaika *n.* балалайка.

balance *n.* **1**, (scale) весы. **2**, (equilibrium) равновесие: *lose one's balance*, потерять равновесие. **3**, *bookkeeping* баланс; сальдо. **4**, (remainder) остаток. —*v.t.* **1**, (keep in a state of equilibrium) уравновешивать. *Balance oneself*, балансировать. *Balance a basket on one's head*, балансировать корзиной на голове. **2**, *bookkeeping* балансировать. *Balance the books*, подводить баланс. —*v.i.* **1**, (be in equilibrium) балансировать. **2**, (tally) сходиться. —**balance of payments**, платёжный баланс. —**balance of power**, равновесие сил. —**balance of trade**, торговый баланс. —**hang in the balance**, зависеть от исхода дела. —**on balance**, в общем и целом.

balanced *adj.* сбалансированный. *Balanced budget*, сбалансированный бюджет. *Balanced diet*, рациональная диета.

balancer *n.* **1**, (acrobat) эквилибрист; балансёр. **2**, *mech.* стабилизатор.

balance sheet балансовый отчёт.

balance wheel маятник; балансир.

balcony *n.* балкон.

bald *adj.* лысый; плешивый. *Become bald*, лысеть; плешиветь.

bald eagle орлан.

balderdash *n.* белиберда; галиматья.

baldheaded *adj.* лысый; плешивый.

baldness *n.* плешивость.

bald spot лысина; плешь.

bale *n.* **1,** (bundle) тюк. **2,** (amount) кипа: *bale of cotton,* кипа хлопка. —*v.t.* укладывать в тюки.

baleful *adj.* **1,** (maleficent) пагубный. **2,** (sinister; ominous) зловещий.

balk *v.i.* (refuse) артачиться; упрямиться. —*v.t.* (thwart) расстраивать; срывать.

Balkan *adj.* балканский.

balky *adj.* упрямый; с норовом.

ball *n.* **1,** (sphere) шар. **2,** (used in games) мяч. *Play ball,* играть в мяч. *Billiard ball,* бильярдный шар. **3,** (of thread, yarn, etc.) клубок. *Curl up into a ball,* свернуться клубком. **4,** (projectile) ядро: *cannon ball,* пушечное ядро. **5,** (formal dance) бал. —*v.t.* [*usu.* **ball up**] *colloq.* перепутывать. —**have a ball,** *colloq.* веселиться. —**on the ball,** *colloq.* расторопный. —**start the ball rolling,** пустить дело в ход.

ballad *n.* баллада.

ballade *n.* баллада.

ball-and-socket joint шаровой шарнир.

ballast *n.* балласт.

ball bearing шарикоподшипник; шариковый подшипник.

ballerina *n.* балерина.

ballet *n.* балет. —*adj.* балетный: *ballet company,* балетная труппа. *Ballet dancer,* артист(ка) балета. —**ballet master,** балетмейстер.

ballistic *adj.* баллистический: *ballistic missile,* баллистическая ракета. —**ballistics,** *n.* баллистика.

balloon *n.* воздушный шар. *Weather balloon,* зонд. —*v.i.* раздуваться. —**balloonist,** *n.* аэронавт; воздухоплаватель.

ballot *n.* **1,** (voting ticket) (избирательный) бюллетень. **2,** (vote; voting) голосование; баллотировка. *Secret ballot,* тайное голосование, —**ballot box,** избирательная урна.

ball park стадион.

ball-point pen шариковая ручка.

ballroom *n.* танцевальный зал.

ballyhoo *n., colloq.* шумиха. —*v.t., colloq.* поднимать шумиху вокруг; трубить о.

balm *n.* **1,** (balsam) бальзам. **2,** *fig.* (something that comforts) бальзам; елей.

balmy *adj.* **1,** (mild) мягкий. **2,** *slang* (daft) сумасбродный.

baloney *n.* **1,** = **bologna. 2,** *slang* (nonsense) вздор.

balsam *n.* бальзам.

Baltic *adj.* балтийский; прибалтийский.

baluster *n.* балясина.

balustrade *n.* балюстрада.

bamboo *n.* бамбук. —*adj.* бамбуковый.

ban *v.t.* запрещать; налагать запрет на. —*n.* **1,** (prohibition) запрет; запрещение. **2,** *eccles.* анафема; отлучение от церкви.

banal *adj.* банальный; избитый. —**banality,** *n.* банальность.

banana *n.* банан. —*adj.* банановый: *banana peel,* банановая корка *or* кожура.

band *n.* **1,** (strip for binding) лента. *Armband,* повязка. *Hatband,* околыш. *Rubber band,* резинка. **2,** (stripe) полоса. **3,** (group) группа. **4,** (gang) банда. **5,** (orchestra) оркестр. **6,** *radio* диапазон. —*v.t.* связывать. —*v.i.* [*usu.* **band together**] объединяться.

bandage *n.* повязка; бинт. —*v.t.* перевязывать; бинтовать.

bandanna *also,* **bandana** *n.* цветной платок.

bandbox *n.* картонка для шляпы.

bandit *n.* разбойник; бандит. —**banditry,** *n.* разбой; бандитизм.

bandmaster *n.* капельмейстер.

band saw ленточная пила.

bandstand *n.* эстрада для оркестра; (оркестровая) раковина.

bandy *v.t.* **1,** (toss back and forth) перебрасываться (+ *instr.*). **2,** (circulate; spread) распространять. *Rumors are being bandied about,* ходят слухи.

bandy-legged *adj.* кривоногий.

bane *n.* отрава. *The bane of one's existence,* отрава *or* проклятие чьей-нибудь жизни.

baneful *adj.* пагубный; губительный; гибельный.

bang *n.* **1,** (blow) удар. **2,** (sound) хлопок. **3,** *pl.* (of hair) чёлка. —*v.t.* **1,** (strike; pound) ударять; стучать; хлопать: *bang one's fist on the table,* ударять/стучать/хлопать кулаком по столу. **2,** (bump accidentally) ударяться; стукаться: *bang one's head on the door,* удариться/стукнуться головой о дверь. —*v.i.* **1,** (make a loud noise) хлопать. **2,** *fol. by* **on** (pound) бить (по); ударять (по); стучать (в). **3,** *fol. by* **into** *or* **against** (bump) ударяться о. —*interj.* бах!; бац! *Bang bang!,* бах-бах! —*adv., colloq.* прямо: *bang on the mark,* прямо в цель.

bangle *n.* браслет.

banish *v.t.* **1,** (exile) изгонять; высылать; ссылать. **2,** (expel) выгонять; прогонять. **3,** *fig.* (dismiss, as a thought) отгонять. —**banishment,** *n.* изгнание; высылка; ссылка.

banister *also,* **bannister** *n.* перила.

banjo *n.* банджо.

bank *n.* **1,** (financial institution) банк. **2,** (river edge) берег. **3,** (long mound) вал. *Sandbank,* песчаная мель. **4,** (of snow) занос. **5,** (of clouds) гряда. **6,** (row; set) ряд. **7,** *aero.* крен. **8,** *games* банк: *break the bank,* сорвать банк. —*adj.* банковый; банковский. —*v.t.* **1,** (deposit in a bank) класть в банк. **2,** (heap up into a bank) сваливать в кучу; наваливать. **3,** (tilt, as an aircraft) накренять. —*v.i.* **1,** (maintain a bank account) держать деньги (в банке). **2,** *fol. by* **on** (count on) рассчитывать (на); делать ставку (на).

bank account счёт в банке.

bankbook *n.* банковская книжка; сберегательная книжка.

banker *n.* **1,** (bank executive) банкир. **2,** (in a game) банкомёт.

banking *n.* банковое дело.

bank note банкнот; кредитный билет.

bankroll *n.* денежные средства; финансовые ресурсы.

bankrupt *adj.* обанкротившийся. *Go bankrupt,* обанкротиться. —*v.t.* привести к банкротству. —**bankruptcy,** *n.* банкротство.

bank shot *billiards* дуплет.

banner *n.* знамя. —*adj.* рекордный: *banner year,* рекордный год. *Banner headlines,* аршинные заголовки.

bannister *n.* = **banister.**

banquet *n.* банкет; пир. —*adj.* банкетный: *banquet table,* банкетный стол.

banter *n.* болтовня.

baobab *n.* баобаб.

baptism *n.* креще́ние. —**baptism of fire,** боево́е креще́ние.

baptismal *adj.* крести́льный.

Baptist *n.* бапти́ст. —*adj.* бапти́стский. —**John the Baptist,** Иоа́нн Предте́ча.

baptistery *also,* **baptistry** *n.* **1,** (place for baptism) баптисте́рий. **2,** (baptismal font) купе́ль.

baptize *v.t.* крести́ть. *Be baptized,* крести́ться.

bar *n.* **1,** (of wood, metal, etc.) брусо́к. **2,** (of gold) сли́ток (зо́лота); (of soap) кусо́к; брусо́к (мы́ла); (of chocolate) пли́тка (шокола́да). **3,** (bolt) засо́в. **4,** (obstacle; barrier) прегра́да; барье́р. **5,** *sports* перекла́дина; *pl.* бру́сья; (in high jumping) пла́нка. **6,** (tavern) бар. **7,** (counter) сто́йка. **8,** (legal profession) адвокату́ра. **9,** *fig.* (place of judgment) суд. **10,** *music* такт. **11,** (unit of pressure) бар. —*v.t.* **1,** (bolt) запира́ть на засо́в. **2,** (block; obstruct) закрыва́ть; прегражда́ть; загражда́ть; загора́живать. **3,** (exclude) исключа́ть. **4,** (forbid) запреща́ть. —*prep.,* *in* **bar none,** без исключе́ния. —**behind bars,** за решёткой.

barb *n.* **1,** (of an arrow, fishhook, etc.) зубе́ц. **2,** (caustic remark) ко́лкость.

barbarian *n.* ва́рвар. —*adj.* ва́рварский.

barbaric *adj.* ва́рварский.

barbarism *n.* **1,** (barbarity) ва́рварство. **2,** *ling.* варвари́зм.

barbarity *n.* ва́рварство.

barbarous *adj.* ва́рварский.

barbecue *n.* **1,** (grill) ра́шпер. **2,** (roasted meat) зажа́ренная ту́ша. —*v.t.* жа́рить.

barbed *adj.* **1,** (containing barbs) колю́чий. **2,** *fig.* (cutting) ко́лкий. —**barbed wire,** колю́чая про́волока.

barbell *n.* шта́нга.

barber *n.* парикма́хер.

barberry *n.* барбари́с.

barbershop *n.* парикма́херская.

barbiturate *n.* барбитура́т.

barcarole *n.* баркаро́ла.

bard *n.* бард.

bare *adj.* **1,** (naked; uncovered) го́лый; наго́й. *With one's bare hands,* го́лыми рука́ми. *Bare feet,* бо́сые но́ги. *In one's bare feet,* босико́м. *Sleep on the bare floor,* спать на го́лом полу́. **2,** (just sufficient): *the bare/barest necessities,* са́мое необходи́мое. *Bare majority,* незначи́тельное большинство́. —*v.t.* **1,** (uncover) обнажа́ть; оголя́ть; раскрыва́ть. **2,** (reveal) обнажа́ть; раскрыва́ть. *Bare one's soul to,* откры́ть *or* раскры́ть ду́шу пе́ред. —**lay bare,** обнажа́ть; выкла́дывать.

bareback *adv.* без седла́.

barefaced *adj.* бессты́дный; неприкры́тый. *Barefaced lie,* на́глая ложь.

barefoot *adj.* босо́й; босоно́гий; разу́тый. —*adv.* босико́м.

barehanded *adj. & adv.* го́лыми рука́ми.

bareheaded *adj. & adv.* с непокры́той голово́й; простоволо́сый.

barely *adv.* едва́; е́ле; чуть.

bargain *n.* **1,** (deal) сде́лка. **2,** (advantageous purchase) вы́годная поку́пка. —*v.i.* торгова́ться. —**bargain for,** ожида́ть. —**into the bargain,** в прида́чу.

barge *n.* ба́ржа. —*v.i.* [*usu.* **barge into**] ворва́ть-

ся в. —**bargeman,** *n.* бурла́к.

barite *n.* бари́т.

baritone *n.* барито́н. —*adj.* барито́нный.

barium *n.* ба́рий. —**barium sulfate,** сернокислый ба́рий.

bark *n.* **1,** (cry of a dog) лай. **2,** (covering of a tree) кора́. **3,** (sailing vessel) барк. —*v.i.* **1,** (of a dog) ля́ять. **2,** (of a person) га́ркать. —*v.t.* выкри́кивать: *bark (out) a command,* вы́крикнуть кома́нду. —**bark up the wrong tree,** *colloq.* быть на ло́жном пути́.

barley *n.* ячме́нь. —*adj.* ячме́нный.

barmaid *n.* буфе́тчица.

barman *n.* буфе́тчик.

barn *n.* **1,** (for storing crops) амба́р. **2,** (for stabling livestock) хлев; коро́вник.

barnacle *n.* усоно́гий рак. *Acorn barnacle,* морско́й жёлудь. *Goose barnacle,* морска́я у́точка. —**barnacle goose,** белощёкая каза́рка.

barn owl сипу́ха.

barnstorm *v.i.* гастроли́ровать (в прови́нции).

barn swallow дереве́нская ла́сточка; каса́тка.

barnyard *n.* пти́чий двор.

barometer *n.* баро́метр. —**barometric,** *adj.* барометри́ческий.

baron *n.* **1,** (nobleman) баро́н. **2,** (magnate) магна́т. —**baroness,** *n.* бароне́сса.

baronet *n.* бароне́т.

baronial *adj.* баро́нский. —**barony,** *n.* баро́нство.

baroque *n.* баро́кко. —*adj.* в сти́ле баро́кко; баро́чный.

barracks *n.pl.* каза́рмы.

barrage *n.* **1,** *mil.* загради́тельный ого́нь; огнево́й вал. **2,** (torrent) пото́к; град.

barrel *n.* **1,** (cask) бо́чка. **2,** (unit of measure, esp. of oil) ба́ррель. **3,** (of a firearm) ствол. —**cash on the barrel,** де́ньги на бо́чку.

barrel organ шарма́нка.

barren *adj.* **1,** (of land) беспло́дный; неплодоро́дный. **2,** (of a woman) беспло́дная. —**barrenness,** *n.* беспло́дие; неплодоро́дность.

barricade *n.* баррика́да. —*v.t.* баррикади́ровать.

barrier *n.* **1,** (obstruction) барье́р. *Police barriers,* полице́йские рога́тки. **2,** (gate at a railroad crossing) шлагба́ум. **3,** *fig.* (obstacle) барье́р: *racial/trade barriers,* ра́совые/торго́вые барье́ры. —**language barrier,** языково́й барье́р. —**sound barrier,** звуково́й барье́р.

barring *prep.* исключа́я.

barrister *n., Brit.* адвока́т.

barroom *n.* бар.

barrow *n.* **1,** (wheelbarrow) та́чка. **2,** (burial mound) курга́н.

bartender *n.* буфе́тчик.

barter *n.* товарообме́н; менова́я торго́вля. —*v.t.* обме́нивать; проме́нивать.

basal metabolism основно́й обме́н.

basalt *n.* база́льт. —*adj.* база́льтовый.

base *n.* **1,** (foundation) осно́ва; основа́ние; ба́за. **2,** (installation) ба́за: *naval base,* морска́я ба́за. **3,** *chem.; math.* основа́ние. —*adj.* **1,** (low; mean) ни́зкий; ни́зменный; по́длый. *Base motives,* ни́зменные побужде́ния. **2,** (of a base) ба́зовый: *base hospital,* ба́зовый го́спиталь. **3,** (used as a starting point) ба́зисный: *base period,* ба́зисный перио́д. *Base pay,* основно́й за́работок. **4,** *in* **base metal,** небла́городный металл. —*v.t.* осно́вывать; стро́ить; бази́-ровать. *Based on facts,* осно́ванный на фа́ктах. —**be off base,** *colloq.* заблужда́ться. —**not** (*or* **never**) **get to first base,** *colloq.* ничего́ не дости́г-нуть; не сдви́нуться с ме́ста.

baseball *n.* бейсбо́л.

baseless *adj.* необосно́ванный; неоснова́тельный; безоснова́тельный.

basement *n.* подва́л. —*adj.* подва́льный: *basement window,* подва́льное окно́.

baseness *n.* ни́зость; по́длость.

bash *v.t., colloq.* хло́пать; шлёпать.

bashful *adj.* засте́нчивый; ро́бкий. —**bashfulness,** *n.* засте́нчивость; ро́бость.

basic *adj.* основно́й. —*n., usu. pl.* осно́вы. —**basic training,** основна́я *or* первонача́льная подгото́вка.

basically *adv.* в основно́м; по существу́.

basil *n.* бази́лик.

basilica *n.* базили́ка.

basin *n.* **1,** (container) таз. **2,** (lowland) бассе́йн.

basis *n.* осно́ва; основа́ние; ба́зис; ба́за. *On the basis of,* на основа́нии (+ *gen.*); на осно́ве (+ *gen.*).

bask *v.i.* гре́ться; не́житься (на со́лнце).

basket *n.* корзи́на; корзи́нка.

basketball *n.* баскетбо́л. *Basketball player,* баскет-боли́ст. —*adj.* баскетбо́льный.

Basque *adj.* ба́скский. —*n.* **1,** (person) баск; бас-ко́нка. **2,** (language) ба́скский язы́к.

bas-relief *n.* барелье́ф. —*adj.* барелье́фный.

bass[1] (beis) *n., music* бас. —*adj.* басо́вый: *bass clef,* басо́вый ключ.

bass[2] (bas) *n.* (fish) о́кунь.

bass baritone баритона́льный бас.

bass drum туре́цкий бараба́н.

basso *n.* бас.

bassoon *n.* фаго́т. —**bassoonist,** *n.* фаготи́ст.

bass viol контраба́с.

bast *n.* лы́ко; луб; моча́ло. —*adj.* лы́ковый; лубяно́й.

bastard *n.* **1,** (illegitimate child) внебра́чный ребё-нок. **2,** *slang* (scoundrel) сво́лочь. —*adj.* внебра́ч-ный; незаконнорождённый.

baste *v.t.* **1,** (sew) мета́ть; смётывать; намётывать; замётывать. **2,** (moisten) полива́ть.

bastion *n.* **1,** (fortification) бастио́н. **2,** *fig.* (bulwark) опло́т.

bat *n.* **1,** (cudgel) дуби́на; дуби́нка. **2,** *sports* бита́; лапта́. **3,** (flying mammal) лету́чая мышь. —*v.t.* **1,** (hit) бить. **2,** (wink) морга́ть: *without batting an eye,* гла́зом не моргну́в. *He didn't bat an eye,* он и бро́вью не повёл. —**go to bat for,** *colloq.* заступа́ться за; хлопота́ть за. —**right off the bat,** *colloq.* с ме́ста в карье́р.

batch *n.* **1,** (of bread) вы́печка. **2,** (of letters, papers, etc.) па́чка. **3,** (lot, as of merchandise) па́ртия.

bated *adj., in* **with bated breath,** не дыша́; затаи́в дыха́ние; с затаённым дыха́нием.

bath *n.* **1,** (bathing) ва́нна. **2,** (bathtub) ва́нна. **3,** (bathroom) ва́нная ко́мната. **4,** (public bath) ба́ня.

bathe *v.t.* **1,** (place in liquid; give a bath to) купа́ть. **2,** (apply liquid to for healing) обмыва́ть; промыва́ть. **3,** *fig.* (cover; flood) залива́ть: *bathed in sunlight,* за́литый со́лнцем. —*v.i.* купа́ться. —**bather,** *n.* купа́льщик.

bathhouse *n.* купа́льня.

bathing *n.* купа́ние. —**bathing cap,** купа́льная

шапочка. —**bathing suit,** купа́льный костю́м.

bathrobe *n.* хала́т.

bathroom *n.* **1,** (for bathing) ва́нная; ва́нная ко́мна-ната. **2,** (lavatory) убо́рная.

bath towel ба́нное полоте́нце.

bathtub *n.* ва́нна.

batiste *n.* бати́ст.

baton *n.* **1,** (symbolic staff) жезл. **2,** (rod used by a conductor) (дирижёрская) па́лочка. **3,** *sports* эстафе́та; эстафе́тная па́лочка.

battalion *n.* батальо́н; дивизио́н. —*adj.* баталь-о́нный.

batten *v.t.* [*usu.* **batten down**] задра́ивать.

batter *v.t.* **1,** (pound) би́ться о; колоти́ть. **2,** (damage by repeated blows) измя́ть. **3,** *fol. by in* (bash in) вда́вливать. —*n.* взби́тое те́сто.

battering-ram *n.* тара́н.

battery *n.* **1,** (storage battery) батаре́я; аккумуля́-тор. **2,** (small, as for a flashlight) батаре́йка. **3,** *mil.* батаре́я. —**assault and battery,** *see* **assault.** —**battery-operated,** *adj.* батаре́йный.

batting *n.* ва́тин.

battle *n.* бой; би́тва; сраже́ние. *The battle of Stalingrad,* би́тва под Сталингра́дом. *The battle of Borodino,* би́тва при Бородине́. *He died in battle,* он поги́б в бою́. —*adj.* боево́й: *battle cry,* боево́й клич. —*v.t. & i.* сража́ться (с); боро́ться (с).

battlefield *n.* по́ле бо́я; по́ле би́твы; по́ле сраже́-ния. *Also,* **battleground.**

battle-hardened *adj.* закалённый в боя́х; обстре́-лянный.

battlement *n.* зу́бчатая крепостна́я стена́.

battleship *n.* лине́йный кора́бль; линко́р.

battleworthy *adj.* боеспосо́бный.

batty *adj., slang* сумасше́дший. *Drive batty,* своди́ть с ума́.

bauble *n.* безделу́шка.

bauxite *n.* бокси́т. —*adj.* бокси́товый.

Bavarian *adj.* бава́рский.

bawdy *adj.* са́льный; поха́бный.

bawl *v.i.* вопи́ть; ора́ть; реве́ть. —**bawl out,** *colloq.* брани́ть; разноси́ть.

bay *n.* **1,** (body of water) зали́в; бу́хта. **2,** *archit.* пролёт. **3,** (bark) лай. **4,** (tree) лавр. —*adj.* (color of a horse) гнедо́й. —*v.i.* (bark) ла́ять. —**at bay,** за́гнанный; затра́вленный. —**bring to bay,** загоня́ть; (за)трави́ть.

bay leaf ла́вровый лист.

bayonet *n.* штык. —*v.t.* коло́ть штыко́м.

bay window фона́рь.

bazaar *n.* база́р.

bazooka *n.* противота́нковый гранатомёт.

B.C. до на́шей э́ры: *in 200 B.C.,* в двухсо́том году́ до на́шей э́ры.

be *v.i.* **1,** (expressing condition, location, etc.) быть: *I was home,* я был (была́) до́ма. *I will be home,* я бу́ду до́ма. ♦*Generally omitted in the present tense: he is ill,* он бо́лен; *she is not here,* её нет. *Sometimes rendered by* есть *or* бу́дет: *an order is an order,* прика́з есть прика́з. *If nothing is done,* е́сли ниче́го не бу́дет сде́лано. **2,** (constitute; represent) явля́ться; составля́ть; представля́ть собо́й. —**be that as it may,** как бы то ни́ было. — **it was not to be,** не тут-то бы́ло. —**so be it,** так и быть; пусть бу́дет так. —**there is; there are,** *see* **there.** *See also* **were.**

beach *n.* пляж. —*adj.* пляжный: *beach umbrella,* пляжный зонт.

beachhead *n.* (приморский) плацдарм.

beacon *n.* **1,** (signal light) сигнальный огонь. **2,** (radio beacon) радиомаяк.

bead *n.* **1,** (single bead) бусина; бисерина. **2,** *pl.* (string of beads) бусы; бисер. **3,** *pl.* (rosary) чётки. **4,** (drop, as of perspiration) капля. —**draw a bead on,** взять на прицел; взять на мушку.

beaded *adj.* бисерный.

beagle *n.* гончая.

beak *n.* клюв.

beaker *n.* **1,** (laboratory container) мензурка. **2,** (goblet) кубок.

beam *n.* **1,** (of wood, metal, etc.) балка; брус. **2,** (of light) луч. *Turn up/turn down/the high beams,* включить/притушить дальный свет. —*v.t.* **1,** (radiate) излучать. **2,** (transmit) передавать; направлять. —*v.i.* сиять; *fig.* сиять от радости.

bean *n.* боб. *Kidney bean,* фасоль. *String beans,* стручковая фасоль. *Coffee beans,* зёрна кофе. —*adj.* бобовый; фасолевый. *Bean soup,* фасолевый суп. —**spill the beans,** *colloq.* проговориться; проболтаться.

beanpole *n., colloq.* каланча.

bear *n.* медведь. —*adj.* [*also,* **bear's**] медвежий: *bear hunt,* медвежья охота. —*v.t.* **1,** (carry) нести; носить. *Bear arms,* носить оружие. **2,** (bring and tell) приносить: *bear glad tidings,* приносить радостное известие. **3,** (bring forth; produce) приносить: *bear fruit,* приносить плоды. **4,** (give birth to) рожать; рождать. **5,** (have; show) носить: *bear traces,* носить следы; *bear one's name,* носить чьё-нибудь имя. *Bear a resemblance,* иметь сходство. *Bear no relation to,* не иметь никакого отношения к. **6,** (hold; harbor) (за)таить: *bear a grudge,* (за)таить обиду *or* злобу. **7,** (support, as weight) выдерживать. **8,** (shoulder, as expense or responsibility) нести. **9,** (endure; withstand) выдерживать; выносить; терпеть; переносить. **10,** *fol. by* **oneself** (conduct) вести себя: *bear oneself with dignity,* вести себя с достоинством. —*v.i.* забирать: *bear right,* забирать вправо. —**bear down,** натуживаться. —**bear down on,** нажимать на. —**bear in mind,** иметь в виду. —**bear on** *or* **upon,** иметь отношение к. —**bear out,** подтверждать. —**bear up,** крепиться. —**bring to bear,** оказывать (давление); напрягать (все силы).

bearable *adj.* сносный; терпимый.

beard *n.* борода.

bearded *adj.* бородатый. —**bearded vulture,** бородач; ягнятник.

beardless *adj.* **1,** (having no beard) безбородый. **2,** *fig.* (callow) безусый.

bearer *n.* **1,** (of news) вестник. **2,** (of a check, document, etc.) податель; предъявитель.

bearing *n.* **1,** (carrying) ношение. **2,** (carriage) выправка; осанка. **3,** *mech.* подшипник: *ball bearing,* шариковый подшипник. **4,** (relevance) отношение: *have no bearing on,* не иметь отношения к. **5,** *pl.* (sense of direction) ориентация: *lose one's bearings,* потерять ориентацию. *Get one's bearings,* ориентироваться. **6,** *navigation* пеленг. *Take a bearing on,* пеленговать.

bearskin *n.* медвежья шкура. —*adj.* медвежий: *bearskin coat,* медвежья шуба.

beast *n.* зверь; животное. —**beast of burden,** вьючное животное. —**beast of prey,** хищный зверь.

beastly *adj.* **1,** (bestial) зверский. **2,** *colloq.* (nasty; awful) скверный; зверский.

beat *v.t.* **1,** (strike repeatedly) бить. *Beat a carpet,* выбивать ковёр. **2,** (thrash; whip) бить; избивать. *Beat to death,* забить до смерти. **3,** (whip; churn) взбивать. **4,** (clear, as a path) пробивать (тропу). **5,** (mark, as time) отбивать (такт). **6,** (defeat) (по)бить; побеждать; выигрывать *у;* обыгрывать. **7,** (get ahead of; reach a goal ahead of) опережать. **8,** *in* **beat a retreat,** бить отбой. —*v.i.* **1,** (pulsate, as of the heart) биться. **2,** (sound when struck, as of drums) бить. **3,** *fol. by* **against** (dash; strike) биться (о); стучать (в); хлестать (в). —*n.* **1,** (beating) биение; бой. *The beat of hoofs,* стук *or* цокот копыт. **2,** (rounds; patrol) обход; дозор. **3,** *music* ритм; такт. —*adj., slang* (exhausted) без ног. —**beat back,** отбивать. —**beat down, 1,** (flatten) прибивать. **2,** (of the sun) палить; припекать. —**beat it!,** *slang* вон отсюда!; пошёл вон! —**beat off,** отбивать. —**beat up,** избивать.

beaten *adj.* **1,** (whipped up, as of eggs) взбитый. **2,** (defeated) разбитый; побеждённый. **3,** (crushed in spirit) убитый. **4,** (well-worn; familiar) избитый; проторённый: *the beaten track,* избитая/проторённая дорога.

beatific *adj.* блаженный.

beatify *v.t.* причислять к лику блаженных. —**beatification,** *n.* причисление к лику блаженных.

beating *n.* **1,** (pulsation, as of the heart) биение. **2,** (act of whipping or thrashing) избиение. **3,** (a whipping or thrashing) побои; порка. **4,** (defeat) разгром.

beatitude *n.* блаженство. —**the Beatitudes,** заповеди блаженства.

beat-up *adj., colloq.* **1,** (threadbare) поношенный. **2,** (dilapidated) полуразрушенный.

beau *n.* поклонник; кавалер.

beautician *n.* косметичка.

beautification *n.* украшение.

beautiful *adj.* красивый; прекрасный. —**beautifully,** *adv.* красиво.

beautify *v.t.* украшать.

beauty *n.* **1,** (beautifulness) красота. **2,** (beautiful woman) красавица. **3,** (beautiful thing) красавец; красавица.

beauty parlor косметический кабинет.

beauty spot 1, (cosmetic patch) мушка. **2,** (birthmark) родинка.

beaver *n.* **1,** (animal) бобр. **2,** (fur) бобёр; бобровый мех.

becalm *v.t.* успокаивать.

because *conj.* потому что. —**because of,** из-за. *It's all because of...,* это всё из-за...; всему виной (+ *nom.*).

beck *n.* кивок. —**be at someone's beck and call,** быть у кого-нибудь на побегушках.

beckon *v.t. & i.* манить; подзывать.

becloud *v.t.* заволакивать; затуманивать.

become *v.i.* становиться; делаться. *Become ill,* заболеть. *Become angry,* рассердиться. —*v.t.* **1,** (show to advantage) идти (+ *dat.*); быть к лицу (+ *dat.*). **2,** (befit) подобать (+ *dat.*); быть к лицу

(+ *dat.*). —**become of,** стать с; ста́ться с: *What's become of him?,* что с ним ста́ло/ста́лось?

becoming *adj.* **1,** (suitable; fitting) подоба́ющий. **2,** (attractive) к лицу́.

bed *n.* **1,** (for sleeping) посте́ль; крова́ть. *Hospital bed,* (больни́чная) ко́йка. *Go to bed,* ложи́ться спать. *Put to bed,* укла́дывать. **2,** (quarters): *bed and board,* кварти́ра и стол; (accommodations): *bed and breakfast,* ночле́г и за́втрак. **3,** (flower bed) клу́мба; гряда́; гря́дка. **4,** (riverbed) ру́сло. **5,** (roadbed) полотно́. **6,** *geol.* пласт: *lava bed,* пласт ла́вы. **7,** in *oyster bed,* у́стричная ба́нка. —*adj.* посте́льный: *bed linen,* посте́льное бельё. —**get up on the wrong side of the bed,** встать с ле́вой ноги́. —**take to one's bed,** слечь в посте́ль.

bedazzle *v.t.* ослепля́ть.

bedbug *n.* клоп.

bedclothes *n.pl.* посте́льное бельё.

bedding *n.* **1,** (items for a bed) посте́льные принадле́жности. **2,** (material for an animal to sleep on) подсти́лка. **3,** *geol.* напластова́ние.

bedeck *v.t.* украша́ть.

bedevil *v.t.* му́чить; терза́ть.

bedlam *n.* бедла́м; ха́ос.

Bedouin *n.* бедуи́н.

bedpan *n.* подкладно́е су́дно.

bedpost *n.* сто́лбик крова́ти.

bedraggled *adj.* растрёпанный; взъеро́шенный.

bedridden *adj.* прико́ванный к посте́ли.

bedrock *n.* **1,** *geol.* материко́вая поро́да. **2,** *fig.* (fundamental principles) суть: *get down to bedrock,* добра́ться до су́ти де́ла.

bedroom *n.* спа́льня. —**bedroom slippers,** дома́шние ту́фли; шлёпанцы.

bedside *n. At one's bedside,* у посте́ли.

bedsore *n.* про́лежень.

bedspread *n.* покрыва́ло.

bedstead *n.* крова́ть.

bedtime *n.* вре́мя ложи́ться спать. *It is bedtime,* пора́ спать.

bee *n.* пчела́. —*adj.* пчели́ный. *Bee sting,* уку́с пчелы́.

beech *n.* бук. —*adj.* бу́ковый.

beechnut *n.* бу́ковый оре́шек.

beechwood *n.* бук. —*adj.* бу́ковый.

beef *n.* **1,** (meat) говя́дина. *Roast beef,* ро́стбиф. **2,** *slang* (complaint) жа́лоба. —*adj.* говя́жий; мясно́й. *Beef cattle,* мясно́й скот. —*v.t.* [*usu.* **beef up**] попо́лнять. —*v.i., slang* (complain) ныть.

beefsteak *n.* бифште́кс.

beef stroganoff беф-стро́ганов.

beefy *adj.* мяси́стый; му́скулистый.

beehive *n.* у́лей.

beekeeper *n.* пчелово́д; па́сечник. —**beekeeping,** *n.* пчелово́дство.

beep *n.* **1,** (sound of a horn) гудо́к. **2,** (short high-pitched note) высо́кий звук. —**beeper,** *n.* зу́ммер.

beer *n.* пи́во. —*adj.* пивно́й: *beer mug,* пивна́я кру́жка.

beeswax *n.* пчели́ный воск.

beet *n.* свёкла. —*adj.* свеко́льный: *beet soup,* свеко́льный суп.

beetle *n.* жук.

beetle-browed *adj.* с нави́сшими бровя́ми.

beet sugar свеклови́чный са́хар.

befall *v.t.* постига́ть; выпада́ть (+ *dat.*); обру́шиваться на.

befit *v.t.* подоба́ть. —**befitting,** *adj.* подоба́ющий.

before *prep.* **1,** (prior to) до; пе́ред: *before the war,* до войны́; *before dinner,* пе́ред обе́дом. *Two years before his death,* за два го́да до его́ сме́рти. *That was before my time,* э́то бы́ло ещё до меня́. **2,** (ahead of; sooner than) пре́жде (+ *gen.*); ра́ньше (+ *gen.*). **3,** (in front of) пе́ред: *appear before the court,* предста́ть пе́ред судо́м. —*conj.* пре́жде чем; пе́ред тем, как; до того́, как. *Before leaving the house,* пре́жде чем (и́ перед тем, как) вы́йти из дому. *Before I came to America,* до того́, как я прие́хал в Аме́рику. *Before it is too late,* пока́ не по́здно. —*adv.* ра́ньше; пре́жде. *I have never been here before,* я никогда́ ра́ньше здесь не быва́л. *You should have thought of that before!,* на́до бы́ло ду́мать об э́том ра́ньше! —**as before,** по-пре́жнему. —**before last,** позапро́шлый: *the year before last,* позапро́шлый год. —**before long,** в ско́ром вре́мени. —**long before,** задо́лго до. —**never before,** никогда́ ещё. —**shortly before,** незадо́лго до.

beforehand *adv.* зара́нее; предвари́тельно.

befriend *v.t.* подружи́ться с.

befuddle *v.t.* **1,** (cloud, as the mind) дурма́нить. **2,** (confuse; baffle) озада́чивать.

beg *v.t.* **1,** (ask earnestly; plead with) умоля́ть; упра́шивать. **2,** (ask for earnestly) проси́ть: *beg permission,* проси́ть разреше́ния. **3,** (evade; sidestep) обходи́ть (вопро́с) —*v.i.* **1,** (solicit alms) ни́щенствовать; проси́ть ми́лостыню. *Go begging to,* идти́ на покло́н к. **2,** *fol. by* **of** (ask earnestly) о́чень проси́ть; умоля́ть: *I beg of you,* я вас о́чень прошу́; умоля́ю вас. **3,** *fol. by* **for** (plead for) проси́ть: *beg for mercy/forgiveness,* проси́ть поща́ды/проще́ния. **4,** *fol. by inf.* (used in certain forms of politeness): *I beg to differ,* позво́лю себе́ не согласи́ться. **5,** (of a dog) служи́ть. —**beg off,** отгова́риваться. —**go begging,** не име́ть спро́са. —**I beg your pardon, 1,** (please excuse me) извини́те! прости́те! прошу́ проще́ния! **2,** (what did you say?) прости́те, что вы сказа́ли? **3,** (I disagree) извини́те!

beget *v.t.* **1,** (father; sire) роди́ть. **2,** *fig.* (generate) порожда́ть.

beggar *n.* ни́щий. —*v.t.* не поддава́ться: *beggar description,* не поддава́ться описа́нию. —**beggarly,** *adj.* ни́щенский. —**beggary,** *n.* ни́щенство.

begin *v.t.* **1,** *fol. by a noun* начина́ть: *begin work,* начина́ть рабо́ту. **2,** *fol. by inf.* начина́ть; стать: *he began to write,* он на́чал/стал писа́ть. —*v.i.* **1,** (start) начина́ть: *let us begin,* начнём. **2,** (commence) начина́ться: *The meeting is beginning,* собра́ние начина́ется. **3,** *preceded by* **can't** (do in the slightest degree): *I can't begin to tell you,* не могу́ да́же сказа́ть; *I can't begin to compare with...,* э́то не идёт ни в како́е сравне́ние с... —**to begin with,** во-пе́рвых.

beginner *n.* начина́ющий.

beginning *n.* нача́ло. *In the beginning,* снача́ла; внача́ле. *From beginning to end,* с нача́ла до конца́. —*adj.* начина́ющий. —*prep.* начина́я с: *beginning July 1,* начина́я с пе́рвого ию́ля.

begone *interj.* убира́йся!; прочь!

begonia *n.* бего́ния.

begrudge *v.t.* **1,** (envy) зави́довать. **2,** (give reluctantly) жале́ть; зави́довать.

beguile *v.t.* **1,** (trick) обольща́ть. **2,** (charm) очаро́вывать.

behalf *n., in* **on/in behalf of, 1,** (speaking for; representing) от и́мени (+ *gen.*). **2,** (in the interest of; for the benefit of) в по́льзу (+ *gen.*).

behave *v.i.* **1,** (conduct oneself) вести́ себя́; держа́ть себя́. **2,** (comport oneself properly) вести́ себя́ хорошо́.

behavior *also,* **behaviour** *n.* поведе́ние. —**behaviorism,** *n.* бихевиори́зм.

behead *v.t.* обезгла́вливать. —**beheading,** *n.* обезгла́вливание.

behemoth *n.* бегемо́т.

behest *n. At the behest of,* под дикто́вку (+ *gen.*).

behind *prep.* **1,** (on the far side of) за (+ *instr.*): *behind the scenes,* за кули́сами. **2,** (to the far side of) за (+ *acc.*): *fall behind the couch,* упа́сть за дива́н. **3,** (lagging behind) *be behind schedule,* отстава́ть. *Be behind the times,* не идти́ в но́гу с ве́ком. **4,** (underlying) за (+ *instr.*): *What's behind all this?,* что за э́тим кро́ется? —*adv.* позади́; сза́ди. *Lag behind,* отстава́ть. —*n., colloq.* (buttocks) зад. —**from behind,** из-за (+ *gen.*). *Sneak up on someone from behind,* подкра́дываться к кому́-нибудь сза́ди. —**leave behind, 1,** (get way ahead of) оставля́ть позади́. **2,** (leave after departure or death) оставля́ть по́сле себя́.

behind-the-scenes *adj.* закули́сный.

behold *v.t.* смотре́ть; созерца́ть; зреть. —*interj.* смотри́(те)!

beholden *adj.* обя́занный.

behoove *v.t.* сле́довать (+ *dat.*); надлежа́ть (+ *dat.*): *it behooves you to...,* вам сле́дует (+ *inf.*).

beige *n.* цвет беж. —*adj.* бе́жевый.

being *n.* **1,** (existence) бытие́. **2,** (creature) существо́. *Human being,* челове́к. —**being as/that,** *colloq.* так как. —**come into being,** возника́ть. —**for the time being,** пока́; до поры́ до вре́мени.

belabor *also,* **belabour** *v.t.* **1,** (pummel) колоти́ть. **2,** (assail verbally) обру́шиваться на. **3,** (harp upon) пережёвывать.

belated *adj.* запозда́лый.

belch *v.i.* рыга́ть. —*v.t.* **1,** *fol. by* **up** (cough up) отры́гивать. **2,** *fol. by* **forth** (eject violently) изрыга́ть. —*n.* отры́жка.

beleaguer *v.t.* осажда́ть.

belfry *n.* колоко́льня.

Belgian *adj.* бельги́йский. —*n.* бельги́ец; бельги́йка.

belie *v.t.* опроверга́ть; противоре́чить.

belief *n.* **1,** (faith; trust) ве́ра: *belief in God,* ве́ра в бо́га. **2,** (opinion; conviction) убежде́ние: *suffer for one's beliefs,* страда́ть за свои́ убежде́ния. *It is my belief that...,* я счита́ю, что... —**beyond belief,** невероя́тно.

believable *adj.* правдоподо́бный.

believe *v.t.* **1,** (trust the word of; accept as true) ве́рить: *I believe you,* я вам ве́рю. *I can't believe it,* я не могу́ э́тому пове́рить. *I don't believe a word he says,* я не ве́рю ни одному́ его́ сло́ву. *I couldn't believe my eyes,* я не ве́рил(а) свои́м глаза́м. *Believe it or not,* хоти́те ве́рьте, хоти́те нет. **2,** (be of a certain opinion) счита́ть: *I believe him to be mistaken,* я счита́ю, что он ошиба́ется. **3,** (think; be more or less sure) ду́мать: *I believe he left,* ду́маю,

что он ушёл. —*v.i.* **1,** (have religious faith) ве́рить. **2,** *fol. by* **in** (have faith in) ве́рить в: *believe in God,* ве́рить в бо́га. —**make believe,** притворя́ться.

believer *n.* ве́рующий.

belittle *v.t.* умаля́ть; принижа́ть.

bell *n.* **1,** (device to be rung) ко́локол; колоко́льчик. **2,** (electrical device, as a doorbell) звоно́к. **3,** (small sphere, as in sleigh bells) бубене́ц; бубе́нчик. **4,** *pl.* (musical instrument) колокола́. **5,** (flare of a wind instrument) растру́б. **6,** *naut.* (ship's bell) ры́нда; (30-minute period) скля́нка: *four bells,* четы́ре скля́нки. —**ring a bell,** *colloq.* быть знако́мым: *the name rings a bell,* и́мя мне знако́мо. *The name doesn't ring a bell,* э́то и́мя мне ничего́ не говори́т.

belladonna *n.* белладо́нна.

bell-bottom *adj., in* **bell-bottom trousers,** брю́ки клёш.

bellboy *n.* коридо́рный. *Also,* **bellhop.**

belle *n.* краса́вица. —**the belle of the ball,** цари́ца ба́ла.

bellflower *n.* колоко́льчик.

bellicose *adj.* вои́нственный. —**bellicosity,** *n.* вои́нственность.

belligerence *n.* вои́нственность.

belligerency *n.* состоя́ние войны́.

belligerent *adj.* **1,** (waging war) вою́ющий. **2,** (bellicose) вои́нственный. —*n.* вою́ющая сторона́.

bellow *v.i.* мыча́ть; реве́ть. —*n.* мыча́ние.

bellows *n.* мехи́.

bell ringer звона́рь.

bell tower колоко́льня.

belly *n.* **1,** (abdomen) живо́т; брю́хо. **2,** *colloq.* (paunch) брю́шко; пу́зо.

bellyache *n.* боль в животе́. —*v.i., slang* (gripe) ныть.

bellyband *n.* подпру́га.

bellybutton *n., colloq.* пуп; пупо́к.

belong *v.i. Usu. rendered with* ме́сто: *I belong here,* моё ме́сто здесь. *This chair belongs in the basement,* э́тому сту́лу ме́сто в подва́ле. *Where do these things belong?,* где ме́сто э́тим веща́м? —**belong to, 1,** (be the property of) принадлежа́ть (+ *dat.*). **2,** (be a member of) принадлежа́ть к; состоя́ть в. **3,** (be one of; be a part of) принадлежа́ть к; относи́ться к.

belongings *n. pl.* пожи́тки.

beloved *adj. & n.* возлю́бленный.

below *adv.* **1,** (at a lower place or level) ни́же; внизу́. *From below,* сни́зу. *They live a floor below,* они́ живу́т этажо́м ни́же. **2,** (to a lower place or level) вниз. —*prep.* ни́же; под. *Below zero,* ни́же нуля́. *Below average,* ни́же сре́днего. *Sink below the horizon,* скры́ться за горизо́нтом.

belt *n.* **1,** (waistband) по́яс; реме́нь. **2,** (zone) по́яс; полоса́. **3,** *mech.* реме́нь: *fan belt,* реме́нь вентиля́тора.

beluga *n.* **1,** (white whale) белу́ха. **2,** (white sturgeon) белу́га.

bemoan *v.t.* се́товать на.

bemused *adj.* **1,** (dazed; bewildered) ошеломлённый; растёрянный. **2,** (lost in thought) заду́мчивый; мечта́тельный.

bench *n.* **1,** (seat) скамья́; скаме́йка; ла́вка. **2,** (work table) верста́к.

bench mark репе́р; пике́т.

bend *v.t.* **1,** (curve) гнуть; сгибáть; изгибáть. *Bend out of shape,* искривлять. **2,** (exert, as efforts) прилагáть; направлять; напрягáть. **3,** (force to submit) подчинять: *bend to one's will,* подчинять своéй вóле. —*v.i.* **1,** (become bent) гнýться; сгибáться. **2,** (curve, as of a road) повора́чивать. **3,** *fol. by* **over** (stoop) наклоня́ться; склоня́ться; нагибáться; сгибáться. **4,** (yield) гнýться. —*n.* изгиб; сгиб; извилина; излучина. *See also* **bent.**

bends *n.* кессóнная болéзнь. —*prep.* **1,** (below) под. **2,** (unworthy of) нúже: *beneath someone's dignity,* нúже чьегó-нибудь достóинства. *It is beneath him to lie,* лгать недостóйно егó.

benediction *n.* заключительная молитва.

benefactor *n.* благодéтель.

beneficence *n.* **1,** (generosity; kindness) великодýшие. **2,** (beneficent act) благодея́ние.

beneficent *adj.* **1,** (kind; generous) великодýшный. **2,** (beneficial) благотвóрный; благодéтельный.

beneficial *adj.* благотвóрный.

beneficiary *n.* наслéдник.

benefit *n.* **1,** (advantage; good) вы́года; пóльза. *For the benefit of,* рáди. **2,** *pl.* (pecuniary aid) пособие. **3,** *theat.* бенефис. —*v.t.* приносить пóльзу (+ *dat.*). —*v.i.* извлекáть пóльзу. *Both sides benefit,* óбе стороны́ выи́грывают.

benevolent *adj.* доброжелáтельный; благожелáтельный. —**benevolence,** *n.* доброжелáтельство; благожелáтельность.

Bengali *adj.* бенгáльский. —*n.* **1,** (person) бенгáлец; бенгáлка. **2,** (language) бенгáльский язык.

benign *adj.* **1,** (kind; gracious) милостивый. **2,** (mild; favorable) благотвóрный. **3,** *med.* доброкáчественный.

bent *adj.* **1,** (curved) изóгнутый. **2,** *fol. by* **on** (determined) реши́вшийся (на); имéющий твёрдое намéрение. —*n.* склóнность; наклóнность; влечéние; тяга.

benzene *n.* бензóл.

benzine *n.* бензин.

benzoin *n.* рóсный лáдан; бензойн.

benzol *n.* бензóл.

bequeath *v.t.* завещáть.

bequest *n.* посмéртный дар.

berate *v.t.* ругáть; бранить.

bereave *v.t.* лишáть. —**bereavement,** *n.* тяжёлая утрáта. —**bereft,** *adj.* лишённый.

beret *n.* берéт.

beriberi *n.* бéри-бéри.

berkelium *n.* беркéлий.

berry *n.* я́года.

berserk *adj.* бéшеный; обезýмевший; исступлённый. *Go berserk,* взбеси́ться; обезýметь; приходить в исступлéние.

berth *n.* **1,** (on a train) (спáльное) мéсто; пóлка. *Upper berth,* вéрхнее мéсто; вéрхняя пóлка. *Lower berth,* ни́жнее мéсто; ни́жняя пóлка. **2,** (on a ship) мéсто; кóйка. **3,** (place of moorage) я́корная стоя́нка; причáл.

beryl *n.* берилл.

beryllium *n.* берилий.

beseech *v.t.* умоля́ть; упрáшивать.

beset *v.t.* **1,** (attack) обрýшиваться на. **2,** (hem in) сти́скивать. **3,** (plague) мýчить: *be beset with doubts,*

мýчиться сомнéниями. **4,** (stud) усыпáть.

beside *prep.* **1,** (alongside) ря́дом с; вóзле; пóдле. **2,** (other than) крóме; помимо. —**beside oneself,** вне себя́: *beside oneself with joy,* вне себя́ от рáдости. —**beside the point,** не к дéлу; некстáти; не по существý.

besides *prep.* крóме; помимо. —*adv.* крóме тогó; к томý же.

besiege *v.t.* **1,** (lay siege to) осаждáть. **2,** (overwhelm, as with offers) засыпáть; осаждáть.

besmirch *v.t.* **1,** (soil) пáчкать. **2,** (tarnish; dishonor) чернить; пятнáть; порóчить.

besom *n.* вéник.

bespatter *v.t.* забры́згивать.

bespeak *v.t.* **1,** (be indicative of) говорить о. **2,** (presage) предвещáть.

bespectacled *adj.* в очкáх.

besprinkle *v.t.* обры́згивать; окропля́ть; опры́скивать.

best *adj.* лýчший; сáмый лýчший; наилýчший. *Best wishes,* наилýчшие пожелáния. —*adv.* лýчше всегó; бóльше всегó. *I like this one best,* э́тот мне нрáвится бóльше всегó. —*n.* [*usu.* **the best**] лýчший; лýчшее: *one of the best,* один из лýчших. *It's all for the best,* всё к лýчшему. *Hope for the best,* надéяться на лýчшее. *Turn out for the best,* обернýться к лýчшему. —*v.t.* побеждáть: *best one's rival,* победить сопéрника. —**all the best!,** всегó хорóшего!; всегó дóброго!; всегó лýчшего! —**at best,** в лýчшем слýчае. —**be at one's best,** быть в удáре; быть на высотé. —**do one's best,** сдéлать всё возмóжное. —**get the best of,** брать верх над. —**had best,** бы лýчше (+ *dat.*): *you had best go right away,* вам бы лýчше пойти сейчáс же. —**make the best of,** мириться с. —**to the best of my ability,** по мéре сил; по мéре спосóбностей. —**to the best of my knowledge/belief,** наскóлько мне извéстно.

bestial *adj.* звéрский; живóтный. —**bestiality,** *n.* звéрство.

best man шáфер.

bestow *v.t.* **1,** (give as a gift) дарить; даровáть; жáловать. **2,** (confer; award) присуждáть; присвáивать; награждáть. —**bestowal,** *n.* присуждéние; присвоéние; награждéние.

bestrew *v.t.* **1,** (scatter about) разбрáсывать. **2,** (cover with things scattered) усыпáть.

best seller бестсéллер.

bet *n.* пари́. —*v.i.* держáть пари́: *do you want to bet?,* хотите держáть пари́? *Bet on a horse,* дéлать стáвку (*or* стáвить) на лóшадь. —*v.t.* стáвить; спóрить на: *bet ten dollars,* стáвить (*or* спóрить на) дéсять дóлларов. *I'll bet you that...,* держý пари́, что... *I bet him ten dollars that...,* я поспóрил с ним на дéсять дóлларов, что... —**you bet!,** конéчно!; бýдьте увéрены!

beta *n.* бéта. —**beta particle,** бéта-частица. —**beta rays,** бéта-лучи́.

betake *v.t.* [*usu.* **betake oneself**] отправля́ться.

betel *n.* бéтель.

betide *v.t.* случáться с; постигáть. *Woe betide...!,* гóре (+ *dat.*)!

betray *v.t.* **1,** (be a traitor to; be disloyal to) изменять; предавáть. **2,** (disappoint, as someone's trust) обмáнывать. **3,** (reveal; give away) выдавáть. —**betrayal,** *n.* предáтельство; измéна.

betroth v.t. обручáть; помóлвить. —**betrothal,** n. обручéние; помóлвка. —**betrothed,** adj. обручённый; помóлвленный.

better adj. **1,** modifier лýчший. **2,** predicate лýчше: he is (feeling) better today, емý лýчше сегóдня. Get better, стать лýчше; улучшáться. —adv. лýчше: play better when it's warm, игрáть лýчше, когдá теплó. I like this one better, этот (эта, это) мне бóльше нрáвится. —n. **1,** (something better) лýчшее: change for the better, перемéна к лýчшему. To change for the better, изменúться в лýчшую стóрону. **2,** pl. (one's superiors) стáршие. —v.t. **1,** (improve) улучшáть. Better oneself, выдвигáться. **2,** (surpass) улучшáть: better the world record, улýчшить мировóй рекóрд. —**get the better of,** брать верх над. —**never better,** как нельзя лýчше; как никогдá. —**so much the better,** тем лýчше. —**think better of it,** одýматься. —**you had better...,** вам бы лýчше (+ inf.).

betterment n. улучшéние.

bettor n. держáщий парú.

between prep. мéжду. In between, посредú. —**between you and me,** мéжду нáми.

betwixt prep., archaic мéжду. —**betwixt and between,** ни то ни сё.

bevel n. **1,** (tool) наугóльник. **2,** (sloping part) скос. —v.t. скáшивать.

beverage n. напúток.

bevy n. **1,** (group) грýппа. **2,** (flock) стáя.

bewail v.t. сéтовать на.

beware v.i. [usu. beware of] берéчься; остерегáться.

bewilder v.t. озадáчивать; сбивáть с тóлку. —**bewildered,** adj. озадáченный; недоумéнный; недоумевáющий. —**bewildering,** adj. недоумевáющий. —**bewilderment,** n. недоумéние; растéрянность.

bewitch v.t. **1,** (cast a spell over) заколдóвывать; околдóвывать; завораживать. **2,** (captivate) очаровывать; зачарóвывать; обворáживать; завораживать. —**bewitched,** adj. заколдóванный; зачарóванный. —**bewitching,** adj. очаровáтельный; обаятельный; обворожúтельный.

beyond prep. **1,** (past) за; дáльше. Beyond the bounds of, за предéлами (+ gen.). The matter never got beyond the talking stage, дáльше разговóров дéло не шло. **2,** (after) пóзже (+ gen.). **3,** (in addition to; over and above) крóме. **4,** (surpassing; exceeding) вне; выше; свыше; сверх. Beyond compare, вне сравнéния. Beyond any doubt, вне всякого сомнéния. Beyond belief, невероятно. Beyond all expectations, сверх всякого ожидáния. Beyond my comprehension, выше моегó понимáния. Live beyond one's means, жить не по свойм срéдствам.

bias n. **1,** (oblique line) косáя лúния. **2,** (partiality) пристрáстие. **3,** (prejudice) предубеждéние; предвзятость.

biased adj. **1,** (partial) пристрáстный. **2,** (prejudiced) предубеждённый.

bib n. нагрýдник.

Bible n. бúблия. —**Biblical,** adj. библéйский.

bibliography n. библиогрáфия. —**bibliographer,** n. библиóграф. —**bibliographic,** adj. библиографúческий.

bibliophile n. библиофúл; книголюб; кнúжник.

bicameral adj. двухпалáтный.

bicarbonate of soda двууглекúслая сóда; питьевáя сóда.

bicentennial adj. двухсотлéтний. —n. двухсотлéтие. Also, **bicentenary.**

biceps n. двуглáвая мышца; бúцепс.

bicker v.i. спóрить; вздóрить; пререкáться.

bicuspid n. мáлый кореннóй зуб.

bicycle n. велосипéд. —adj. велосипéдный: bicycle racing, велосипéдные гóнки. —v.i. éздить на велосипéде. —**bicyclist,** n. велосипедúст.

bid v.t. **1,** (order) велéть. **2,** (ask) просúть. **3,** (say): bid farewell, прощáться; bid welcome, привéтствовать. **4,** (offer, as a price) предлагáть. **5,** cards объявлять. —v.i. **1,** (make a bid) предлагáть цéну. **2,** fol. by inf. (strive) добивáться тогó, чтóбы (+ inf.). —n. **1,** (offer) предложéние. **2,** (attempt) попытка. **3,** cards объявлéние. —**bid fair,** обещáть.

bidding n. **1,** (making of bids) предложéние цен. **2,** (ordering; directing) диктóвка: at someone's bidding, под чью-нибудь диктóвку. Do someone's bidding, выполнять чью-нибудь вóлю.

bide v.t., in **bide one's time,** выжидáть удóбный слýчай.

biennial adj. двухлéтний. —n. двухлéтнее растéние.

bier n. катафáлк.

bifocal adj. двухфóкусный. —**bifocals,** n.pl. очкú с двухфóкусными стёклами.

bifurcate v.i. разветвляться. —**bifurcation,** n. разветвлéние.

big adj. **1,** (large) большóй: big house, большóй дом. **2,** (elder) стáрший: my big sister, моя стáршая сестрá. **3,** (important; prominent) крýпный. **4,** (outstanding in its way) большóй: big secret/risk/liar, большóй секрéт/риск/лгун.

bigamist n. двоежéнец.

bigamy n. двоебрáчие; двоежéнство.

Big Dipper Большáя Медвéдица.

big game крýпный зверь. Big-game hunting, охóта на крýпного звéря.

big-hearted adj. великодýшный.

bighorn n. снéжный барáн.

bigmouth n. пустозвóн.

bigot n. фанáтик; изувéр. —**bigoted,** adj. фанатúческий; нетерпúмый. —**bigotry,** n. фанатúзм.

big shot slang шúшка.

bigwig n., colloq. туз; ворóтила.

bike n. & v., colloq. = **bicycle.**

bilateral adj. двусторóнний.

bile n. жёлчь. —**bile duct,** жéлчный протóк.

bilge n. **1,** (bottom of a ship) днúще. **2,** colloq. (twaddle) пустослóвие.

bilingual adj. двуязычный. —**bilingualism,** n. двуязычие.

bilious adj. жёлчный.

bilk v.t. надувáть; обжýливать.

bill n. **1,** (statement of charges) счёт: water bill, счёт за вóду. **2,** (bank note) бумáжка; купюра: ten-dollar bill, десятидóлларовая бумáжка/купюра. **3,** (draft of a proposed law) законопроéкт; билль. **4,** (schedule of theatrical entertainment) прогрáмма. **5,** (poster) афúша. **6,** (beak) клюв. —v.t. **1,** (present with a bill) подавáть счёт (+ dat.). **2,** (advertise) анонсúровать. —**bill and coo,** воркóвать. —**fill the**

bill, годи́ться; отвеча́ть тре́бованиям.

billboard *n.* рекла́мный щит.

billet *n.* помеще́ние; кварти́ра. —*v.t.* расквартиро́вать; ста́вить на посто́й. —**billeting,** *n.* расквартирова́ние; посто́й.

billfold *n.* бума́жник.

billiard *adj.* билья́рдный: *billiard table,* билья́рдный стол.

billiards *n.* билья́рд.

billion *n.* миллиа́рд. —**billionth,** *adj.* миллиа́рдный.

bill of exchange ве́ксель.

bill of fare меню́.

bill of lading накладна́я; коносаме́нт.

Bill of Rights билль о права́х.

billow *n.* вал. —*v.i.* вздыма́ться; волнова́ться. —**billlowy,** *adj.* вздыма́ющийся.

billy *n.* дуби́нка. *Also,* **billy club.**

billy goat козёл; ко́злик.

bimetallic *adj.* биметалли́ческий. —**bimetallism,** *n.* биметалли́зм.

bimonthly *adj.* двухме́сячный. —*adv.* раз в два ме́сяца. —*n.* двухме́сячник.

bin *n.* **1,** (for grain) ларь; за́кром. **2,** (for coal) бу́нкер (для угля́).

binary *adj.* **1,** (having two components) двойно́й. **2,** *chem.; math.; astron.* бина́рный.

bind *v.t.* **1,** (tie up) вяза́ть; свя́зывать: *bind sheaves,* вяза́ть снопы́; *bind hand and foot,* связа́ть по рука́м и нога́м. **2,** (link closely) свя́зывать. **3,** *usu. fol. by* **up** (bandage) перевя́зывать. **4,** (obligate) обя́зывать: *this does not bind you to anything,* э́то вас ни к чему́ не обя́зывает. **5,** (fasten together, as a book) переплета́ть. *See also* **bound.**

binder *n.* **1,** (bookbinder) переплётчик. **2,** (holder of loose-leaf sheets) скоросшива́тель.

bindery *n.* переплётная.

binding *n.* **1,** (tying) вяза́ние. **2,** (covering of a book) переплёт. —*adj.* **1,** (obligatory) обя́зывающий; обяза́тельный. **2,** *med.* крепи́тельный.

bindweed *n.* вьюно́к.

binge *n., colloq.* кутёж; вы́пивка. *Go on a binge,* проку́тить.

bingo *n.* лото́.

binoculars *n.pl.* бино́кль.

binomial *n.* бино́м; двучле́н. —*adj.* двучле́нный. —**binomial theorum,** бино́м Нью́тона.

biochemistry *n.* биохи́мия. —**biochemical,** *adj.* биохими́ческий. —**biochemist,** *n.* биохи́мик.

biography *n.* биогра́фия. —**biographer,** *n.* био́граф. —**biographical,** *adj.* биографи́ческий.

biology *n.* биоло́гия. —**biological,** *adj.* биологи́ческий. —**biologist,** *n.* био́лог.

bionics *n.* био́ника.

biophysics *n.* биофи́зика.

biopsy *n.* биопси́я.

bipartisan *adj.* двухпарти́йный.

bipartite *adj.* двусторо́нний.

biped *adj.* двуно́гий. —*n.* двуно́гое живо́тное.

biplane *n.* бипла́н.

birch *n.* берёза. —*adj.* берёзовый. *Birch bark,* берёста. *Birch forest,* березня́к.

bird *n.* пти́ца. —*adj.* [*also,* **bird's**] пти́чий: *bird's nest,* пти́чье гнездо́. —**a bird in the hand is worth two in the bush,** не сули́ журавля́ в не́бе, а дай сини́цу в ру́ки. —**birds of a feather,** *see* **feather.**

—kill two birds with one stone, уби́ть двух за́йцев одни́м уда́ром.

birdcage *n.* пти́чья кле́тка.

birdie *n.* пти́чка.

birdlime *n.* пти́чий клей.

bird of paradise ра́йская пти́ца.

birdseed *n.* пти́чий корм.

bird's-eye view вид с пти́чьего полёта.

birth *n.* **1,** (being born) рожде́ние. *Blind from birth,* слепо́й от рожде́ния *or* от приро́ды. **2,** (giving birth) ро́ды. **3,** (lineage; descent) происхожде́ние. *He is Italian by birth,* он ро́дом из Ита́лии. —**give birth (to),** рожа́ть. *She gave birth to a son,* у неё роди́лся сын.

birth certificate свиде́тельство о рожде́нии; ме́трика.

birth control контро́ль над рожда́емостью. *Practice birth control,* применя́ть противозача́точные сре́дства.

birthday *n.* день рожде́ния. *Birthday present,* пода́рок ко дню рожде́ния.

birthmark *n.* роди́мое пятно́; ро́динка.

birthplace *n.* ме́сто рожде́ния.

birth rate рожда́емость.

birthright *n.* пра́во перворо́дства.

biscuit *n.* пече́нье; суха́рь; гале́та.

bisect *v.t.* разреза́ть.

bisexual *adj.* двупо́лый.

bishop *n.* **1,** (prelate) епи́скоп. **2,** *chess* слон. —**bishopric,** *n.* сан епи́скопа.

bismuth *n.* ви́смут.

bison *n.* **1,** (American) бизо́н. **2,** (European) зубр.

bit *n.* **1,** (small piece) кусо́чек. *Smash to bits,* разбива́ть вдре́безги. **2,** (small amount) чу́точка. **3,** (mouthpiece of a bridle) удила́. **4,** (boring device) пёрка. —**a bit,** немно́го; немно́жко. *He is a bit of a coward,* он трусова́т. —**bit by bit,** ка́пля за ка́плей; ка́пля по ка́пле. —**bit part,** выходна́я роль. —**do one's bit,** внести́ свою́ ле́пту. —**every bit,** всё без оста́тка. —**not a bit,** ниско́лько; ничу́ть; ни ка́пли; ни на йо́ту. *You haven't changed a bit!,* вы совсе́м не измени́лись! —**take the bit in one's teeth,** закуси́ть удила́.

bitch *n.* су́ка. —**son of a bitch,** *vulg.* су́кин сын.

bite *v.t.* **1,** (grip or cut with the teeth) куса́ть. *Bite one's nails,* грызть *or* куса́ть но́гти. **2,** (sting) жа́лить. —*v.i.* **1,** (grip something with the teeth) куса́ть. **2,** (tend to bite, as of a dog) куса́ться. **3,** (take the bait, as of a fish) клева́ть. **4,** *fig.* (take the bait; be tricked) попа́сться на у́дочку. —*n.* **1,** (act of biting; wound inflicted by biting) уку́с: *mosquito bite,* комари́ный уку́с. **2,** (snack; morsel) заку́ска. *Have a bite to eat,* закуси́ть. **3,** *dent.* прику́с. —**bite off,** отку́сывать. —**bite one's tongue,** прикуси́ть язы́к.

biting *adj.* **1,** (sharp, as of a wind) ре́зкий; хлёсткий. **2,** (caustic; mordant) е́дкий; ко́лкий; хлёсткий.

bitter *adj.* **1,** (acrid) го́рький: *bitter lemon/taste,* го́рький лимо́н/вкус. **2,** (intense) жесто́кий; лю́тый; ожесточённый. *Bitter cold,* лю́тый хо́лод. *Bitter enemy,* злейший враг. *Bitter hatred,* лю́тая не́нависть. *Bitter struggle,* ожесточённая борьба́. *Bitter disappointment,* го́рькое *or* жесто́кое разочарова́ние. **3,** (hard to accept) го́рький: *the bitter truth,* го́рькая пра́вда. *A bitter lesson,* жесто́кий уро́к. **4,** (embittered) озло́бленный. —*adv.* о́чень; ужа́сно.

Bitter cold, ужа́сно хо́лодно. —**to the bitter end,** до са́мого конца́; до после́днего.

bitterly *adv.* го́рько: *cry/complain bitterly,* го́рько пла́кать/жа́ловаться. *Be bitterly disappointed,* жесто́ко разочарова́ться.

bittern *n.* выпь.

bitterness *n.* **1,** (bitter taste) го́речь. **2,** (bitter feeling) го́речь; озлобле́ние; ожесточе́ние.

bitters *n.pl.* го́рькая.

bitumen *n.* биту́м. —**bituminous,** *adj.* битумино́зный; биту́мный.

bivalent *adj.* двухвале́нтный.

bivalve *adj.* двуство́рчатый. —*n.* двуство́рчатый моллю́ск.

bivouac *n.* бива́к. —*v.i.* стоя́ть *or* располага́ться бива́ком.

biweekly *adj.* двухнеде́льный. —*adv.* раз в две неде́ли. —*n.* двухнеде́льник.

bizarre *adj.* стра́нный; дико́винный; экстравага́нтный.

blab *v.i.* (chatter) болта́ть. —*v.t.* (give away, as a secret) разба́лтывать; выба́лтывать.

blabbermouth *n., colloq.* болту́н.

black *adj.* чёрный. *Turn black,* черне́ть. *Paint the door black,* кра́сить дверь в чёрный цвет. —*n.* **1,** (color) чёрный цвет. *Dressed in black,* оде́т(а) в чёрное. **2,** (negro) негр; чёрный. **3,** *chess* чёрные: *black wins,* чёрные выи́грывают. —**black out, 1,** (extinguish all the lights in) затемня́ть. **2,** (lose consciousness) потеря́ть созна́ние.

black-and-blue *adj.* в синяка́х. *Beat black-and-blue,* избива́ть до синяко́в.

black-and-white *adj.* чёрно-бе́лый. *In black-and-white,* чёрным по бе́лому.

blackball *v.t.* забаллоти́ровать.

blackberry *n.* ежеви́ка. —*adj.* ежеви́чный.

blackbird *n.* чёрный дрозд.

blackboard *n.* доска́.

blacken *v.t.* черни́ть. —*v.i.* черне́ть.

black eye подби́тый глаз. *Give someone a black eye,* подби́ть глаз кому́-нибудь.

black grouse те́терев.

blackguard *n.* подле́ц; негодя́й; мерза́вец.

blackhead *n.* у́горь.

blacking *n.* ва́кса.

blackjack *n.* **1,** (weapon) дуби́на; дуби́нка. **2,** (card game) два́дцать одно́.

blacklist *n.* чёрный спи́сок. —*v.t.* вноси́ть в чёрный спи́сок.

black magic чёрная ма́гия.

blackmail *n.* шанта́ж. —*v.t.* шантажи́ровать. —**blackmailer,** *n.* шантажи́ст.

black market чёрный ры́нок.

blackness *n.* чернота́.

blackout *n.* **1,** (extinguishing of lights) затемне́ние; светомаскиро́вка. **2,** (fainting spell) поте́ря созна́ния; о́бморок.

black sheep парши́вая овца́ (в семье́).

blacksmith *n.* кузне́ц.

blackthorn *n.* тёрн; терно́вник.

bladder *n.* пузы́рь.

blade *n.* **1,** (of a tool) ле́звие. **2,** (of a weapon, esp. a sword) клино́к. **3,** (of an oar, propeller, etc.) ло́пасть. **4,** (of a saw) полотно́. **5,** (of a fan, windmill, etc.) крыло́. **6,** (of an ice skate) по́лоз. **7,** (of a leaf)

пласти́нка. **8,** (of grass) трави́нка; были́нка. **9,** *colloq.* (dashing young man) у́харь; хват. —**razor blade,** ле́звие бри́твы. —**shoulder blade,** лопа́тка.

blame *v.t.* вини́ть: *don't blame me!,* не вини́те меня́! *You have only yourself to blame,* вы должны́ вини́ть то́лько самого́ себя́. —*n.* **1,** (responsibility) вина́: *place the blame on,* возлага́ть вину́ на. **2,** (censure) порица́ние: *deserve blame,* заслу́живать порица́ния. —**be to blame,** быть винова́тым: *I am to blame,* я винова́т(а).

blameless *adj.* невино́вный; неви́нный.

blameworthy *adj.* заслу́живающий порица́ния.

blanch *v.t.* (bleach) бели́ть. —*v.i.* (turn pale) бледне́ть.

bland *adj.* **1,** (mild; not irritating) мя́гкий. *Bland diet,* лёгкая дие́та. **2,** (flavorless; dull) пре́сный; бесцве́тный.

blandishment *n.* угово́р.

blank *adj.* **1,** (not written on) чи́стый. *Blank space,* пусто́е ме́сто. **2,** (of a cartridge, shot, etc.) холосто́й. **3,** (solid, as of a wall) глухо́й. **4,** (vacant, as of a look) отсу́тствующий; неви́дящий. —*n.* **1,** (space) пусто́е ме́сто. **2,** (form) бланк; анке́та. **3,** (blank cartridge) холосто́й патро́н. **4,** (loss of memory) прова́л па́мяти: *my mind is a complete blank,* у меня́ по́лный прова́л па́мяти. —**draw a blank,** ничего́ не доби́ться. —**go blank, 1,** *My mind went blank,* у меня́ отши́бло па́мять. **2,** *The screen went blank,* карти́на исче́зла с экра́на.

blanket *n.* **1,** (bed covering) одея́ло. **2,** *fig.* (mantle) покро́в: *blanket of snow,* сне́жный покро́в. —*adj.* о́бщий; огу́льный. —*v.t.* оку́тывать.

blankly *adv.* отсу́тствующим взгля́дом.

blank verse бе́лые стихи́.

blare *v.t. & i.* труби́ть. —*n.* тру́бный звук.

blarney *n.* лесть.

blasé *adj.* пресы́щенный.

blaspheme *v.i.* богоху́льствовать; кощу́нствовать. —*v.t.* поноси́ть; хули́ть.

blasphemous *adj.* богоху́льный; кощу́нственный. —**blasphemy,** *n.* богоху́льство; кощу́нство.

blast *n.* **1,** (gust of air) поры́в (ве́тра); струя́ (во́здуха). **2,** (loud sound, as of a trumpet) (тру́бный) звук. **3,** (explosion) взрыв. **4,** *colloq.* (verbal attack) вы́пад. —*v.t.* **1,** (blow up) взрыва́ть: *blast rock,* взрыва́ть скалу́. **2,** *colloq.* (assail) обру́шиваться на. —*v.i.* [*usu.* blast off] старто́вать; отрыва́ться от земли́. —**(at) full blast,** по́лным хо́дом.

blasted *adj., colloq.* прокля́тый.

blast furnace до́мна; до́менная печь.

blasting *n.* взрывны́е рабо́ты. —**blasting powder,** ми́нный по́рох.

blast-off *n.* старт.

blatant *adj.* **1,** (noisy) крикли́вый. **2,** (obvious) я́вный.

blather *n.* пустосло́вие.

blaze *n.* пла́мя. —*v.i.* **1,** (burn) горе́ть; пыла́ть. **2,** (give off great heat) пали́ть: *the blazing sun,* паля́щее со́лнце. **3,** *fol. by away* (fire rapidly) открыва́ть ого́нь. —*v.t., in* blaze a trail, прокла́дывать путь. —**like blazes,** *colloq.* со всех ног; сломя́ го́лову.

blazer *n.* спорти́вная ку́ртка.

blazon *n.* герб.

bleach *v.t.* бели́ть; отбе́ливать. —*n.* бели́льное сре́дство. —**bleached,** *adj.* белёный.

bleaching *n.* беле́ние. —*adj.* бели́льный. —**bleaching powder,** хло́рная и́звесть.

bleak *adj.* **1,** (desolate) пусты́нный. **2,** (dismal; unpromising) мра́чный.

bleary-eyed *adj.* осолове́лый; посолове́лый.

bleat *v.i.* бле́ять. —*n.* бле́яние.

bleed *v.i.* кровоточи́ть. *His nose is bleeding,* у него́ кровь течёт и́з носу. *He is bleeding profusely,* он истека́ет кро́вью. *My heart bleeds for you,* моё се́рдце за вас кро́вью облива́ется. —*v.t.* **1,** (take blood from) пуска́ть кровь (+ *dat.*). **2,** *colloq.* (extort money from) обира́ть; обдира́ть. —**bleed white,** обобра́ть до ни́тки.

bleeding *n.* кровотече́ние. —*adj.* истека́ющий кро́вью.

blemish *n.* пятно́. —*v.t.* пятна́ть.

blend *v.t.* сме́шивать. —*v.i.* **1,** (merge; unite) сме́шиваться; слива́ться. **2,** (go well together) гармони́ровать; сочета́ться. —*n.* смесь; смеше́ние.

blender *n.* смеси́тель.

bless *v.t.* **1,** (ask divine favor for) благословля́ть: *God bless you!,* да благослови́т тебя́ Бог. ♦*After a sneeze* будь здоро́в(а)!; бу́дьте здоро́вы! **2,** (endow) наделя́ть: *blessed with outstanding ability,* наделён исключи́тельными спосо́бностями. *Be blessed with good health,* по́льзоваться хоро́шим здоро́вьем.

blessed *adj.* **1,** (holy) свяще́нный. **2,** (blissful) блаже́нный. *Of blessed memory,* блаже́нной па́мяти.

blessing *n.* **1,** (benediction) благослове́ние. **2,** (that which gives happiness) бла́го. **3,** (approval) благослове́ние: *with the blessing of,* с благослове́ния (+ *gen.*).

blight *n.* **1,** (plant disease) ожо́ги расте́ний. **2,** *fig.* (plague) бич. —*v.t.* вреди́ть; губи́ть.

blind *adj.* слепо́й. *Go blind,* слепну́ть. *Blind in one eye,* слепо́й на оди́н глаз. —*adv.* вслепу́ю. —*v.t.* ослепля́ть. —*n.* што́ра. *Venetian blinds,* подъёмные жалюзи́. —**turn a blind eye to,** закрыва́ть глаза́ на; смотре́ть сквозь па́льцы на.

blind alley тупи́к.

blinders *n.pl.* шо́ры; нагла́зники.

blindfold *n.* повя́зка (на глаза́х). —*v.t.* завя́зывать глаза́ (+ *dat.*).

blindfolded *adj.* с завя́занными глаза́ми. —*adv.* вслепу́ю.

blinding *adj.* ослепи́тельный.

blindly *adv.* сле́по; вслепу́ю.

blindman's bluff жму́рки.

blindness *n.* слепота́.

blink *v.i.* **1,** (wink; flash) мига́ть; морга́ть. **2,** *fol. by* **at** (pretend not to see) смотре́ть сквозь па́льцы (на). —*v.t.* мига́ть; моргну́ть (глаза́ми). *Without blinking an eye,* гла́зом не моргну́в. —**on the blink,** *colloq.* не рабо́тает.

blinker *n.* **1,** (flashing light) мига́лка. **2,** *pl.* (shades for a horse's eyes) нагла́зники; шо́ры.

bliss *n.* блаже́нство. —**blissful,** *adj.* блаже́нный.

blister *n.* волды́рь; пузы́рь.

blistering *adj.* **1,** (of heat) паля́щий. **2,** (scathing, as of criticism) разно́сный.

blithe *adj.* весёлый; беспе́чный; жизнера́достный.

blitzkrieg *n.* молниено́сная война́.

blizzard *n.* мете́ль; вью́га; пурга́; бура́н.

bloat *v.t.* вздува́ть; раздува́ть. —**bloated,** *adj.* взду́тый; разду́тый.

blob *n.* ка́пля; ша́рик.

bloc *n.* блок.

block *n.* **1,** (solid piece) глы́ба: *block of ice,* глы́ба льда. **2,** (block of wood) чурба́н. **3,** (chopping block) коло́да; (execution block) пла́ха. **4,** *usu. pl.* (children's building blocks) ку́бики. **5,** (city block) кварта́л. **6,** (mold for shaping hats) болва́н. **7,** (large building brick) блок. **8,** (pulley) блок. **9,** (in an engine) блок: *cylinder block,* блок цили́ндров. **10,** (obstruction) прегра́да; зато́р. **11,** *philately* блок. **12,** *slang* (head) башка́. *Knock one's block off,* всы́пать по пе́рвое число́. —*v.t.* **1,** (obstruct) прегражда́ть; загражда́ть; заго́раживать; перекрыва́ть. **2,** *fol. by up* (clog) забива́ть. **3,** (prevent; thwart) меша́ть; срыва́ть. **4,** *sports* блоки́ровать. **5,** *fol. by* **out** (outline) намеча́ть; набра́сывать.

blockade *n.* блока́да. —*v.t.* блоки́ровать.

blockage *n.* **1,** (act of blocking) прегражде́ние. **2,** (obstruction; jam) прегра́да; зато́р. **3,** *med.* непроходи́мость; заку́порка.

blockhead *n.* болва́н; тупи́ца.

blockhouse *n.* блокга́уз.

block letters печа́тные бу́квы.

blond *n.* [*fem.* **blonde**] блонди́н; блонди́нка. —*adj.* белоку́рый.

blood *n.* кровь. *It's in his blood,* э́то у него́ в крови́. —*adj.* **1,** (pert. to blood) кровяно́й. **2,** (related by blood) кро́вный. —**in cold blood,** хладнокро́вно.

blood bath крова́вая ба́ня.

blood clot сгу́сток кро́ви.

bloodcurdling *adj.* душераздира́ющий.

bloodhound *n.* ище́йка.

bloodless *adj.* бескро́вный.

bloodletting *n.* **1,** (drawing of blood) кровопуска́ние. **2,** (bloodshed) кровопроли́тие.

blood orange королёк.

blood poisoning зараже́ние кро́ви.

blood pressure кровяно́е давле́ние.

bloodshed *n.* кровопроли́тие.

bloodshot *adj.* нали́тый кро́вью. *Become bloodshot,* нали́ться кро́вью.

bloodstain *n.* кровяно́е *or* крова́вое пятно́. —**bloodstained,** *adj.* окрова́вленный.

bloodstream *n.* ток кро́ви.

bloodsucker *n.* **1,** (leech) пия́вка. **2,** (extortionist) кровопи́йца.

blood test ана́лиз (*or* иссле́дование) кро́ви.

bloodthirsty *adj.* кровожа́дный.

blood transfusion перелива́ние кро́ви.

blood type гру́ппа кро́ви.

blood vessel кровено́сный сосу́д.

bloody *adj.* крова́вый. —*v.t.* окрова́вить. *Bloody someone's nose,* расква́сить кому́-нибудь нос.

bloom *v.i.* цвести́. —*n.* цвет: *in full bloom,* в по́лном цвету́. *Burst into bloom,* расцвета́ть; зацвести́. *Lose its bloom,* отцвета́ть.

blossom *n.* цвет: *apple blossom,* я́блоневый цвет. —*v.i.* цвести́; расцвета́ть.

blot *n.* пятно́. *Inkblot,* кля́кса. —*v.t.* **1,** (stain) пятна́ть. **2,** (dry; soak up) промока́ть. —**blot out, 1,** (hide; cover; obscure) затмева́ть. **2,** (efface; erase) изгла́живать. **3,** (destroy) уничтожа́ть.

blotch *n.* **1,** (spot) пятно́. **2,** (blemish on the skin) прыщ.

blotter *n.* промока́шка.

blotting paper промокáтельная (*or* пропускнáя) бумáга.

blouse *n.* блýзка; кóфточка.

blow *n.* **1,** (hard stroke; shock) удáр: *with one blow,* одни́м удáром. *They came to blows,* у них дошлó до дрáки. *A blow to the family,* удáр для семьи́. **2,** (blast of air) дуновéние. *Blow out the candles with one blow,* задýть свéчи одни́м дуновéнием (*or* вы́дохом). —*v.i.* **1,** (of the wind) дуть. **2,** (of a horn, whistle, etc.) гудéть. **3,** (puff) дуть: *blow on one's fingers,* дуть на пáльцы. **4,** (be carried by the wind) летéть. *The paper blew away,* бумáжка улетéла. **5,** (of a fuse) перегорéть. —*v.t.* **1,** (drive by blowing) гнать (ли́стья); развевáть (флáги). *Blow dust from the shelf,* сдувáть пыль с пóлки. *Blow smoke in someone's face,* пускáть дым в лицó (+ *dat.*). **2,** (make, as glass, bubbles, etc.) выдувáть (стеклó); пускáть (мы́льные пузыри́). **3,** (cause to sound, as a trumpet) труби́ть (в трубý); (a whistle) дать (свистóк); (a car horn) гудéть. **4,** (clear, as one's nose) сморкáть (нос); сморкáться. **5,** *slang* (squander) транжи́рить; спускáть. **6,** in *blow a kiss,* послáть воздýшный поцелýй. **7,** *in* blow a fuse; blow one's top; blow one's stack, *colloq.* взорвáться. —**blow down,** свáливать. —**blow off, 1,** (blow away) сдувáть. *My hat blew off,* шля́пу у меня́ сдýло. **2,** (give off, as steam) выпускáть. **3,** in *blow off steam, fig., colloq.* дать вы́ход своим чýвствам. —**blow out, 1,** (extinguish by blowing) задувáть; туши́ть. **2,** (remove by blowing) выдувáть. **3,** (clean out by blowing) продувáть. **4,** (burst, as of a tire) лóпнуть. **5,** (fail, as of a bulb) перегорéть. **6,** in *blow one's brains out,* пусти́ть себé пýлю в лоб. —**blow over, 1,** (topple) свáливать. **2,** (be forgotten) проходи́ть; миновáть. **3,** (subside) затихáть; утихáть. —**blow up, 1,** (inflate) надувáть. **2,** (destroy) взрывáть; подрывáть. **3,** *photog.* (enlarge) увели́чивать. **4,** (exaggerate) раздувáть. **5,** (of a storm) налетáть. **6,** *colloq.* (lose one's temper) взорвáться.

blower *n.* вентиля́тор.

blowgun *n.* духовóе ружьё.

blowout *n.* разры́в (ши́ны).

blowpipe *n.* пая́льная трýбка.

blowtorch *n.* пая́льная лáмпа.

blubber *n.* вóрвань.

bludgeon *n.* дуби́на; дуби́нка. —*v.t.* бить дуби́ной; дубáсить.

blue *adj.* **1,** (color) си́ний (*dark*); голубóй (*light*). **2,** (depressed) уны́лый; подáвленный. —*n.* си́ний цвет; синевá. —*v.t.* подси́нивать. —**appear out of the blue,** с нéба свали́ться. —**from out of the blue,** откýда ни возьми́сь. —**once in a blue moon,** в кóи вéки.

bluebell *n.* колокóльчик.

blueberry *n.* черни́ка. —*adj.* черни́чный.

blue-eyed *adj.* синеглáзый.

bluefish *n.* луфáрь.

blue-gray *adj.* си́зый.

blueprint *n.* си́нька.

blues *n.pl.* **1,** (melancholy) хандрá. **2,** *music* блюз.

bluff *v.t.* обмáнывать; вводи́ть в заблуждéние. —*v.i.* блефовáть. —*n.* **1,** (deception) блеф. **2,** (cliff) обры́в; утёс. —**call someone's bluff,** застáвить (когó-нибудь) раскры́ть кáрты.

bluing *n.* си́нька.

bluish *adj.* синевáтый; голубовáтый.

blunder *n.* прóмах; оплóшность. —*v.i.* грýбо ошибáться; оплошáть.

blunt *adj.* **1,** (not sharp) тупóй. **2,** (frank; straightforward) прямóй. —*v.t.* притупля́ть. —**bluntly,** *adv.* пря́мо; начистотý.

bluntness *n.* **1,** (dullness) тýпость. **2,** (frankness) прямотá.

blur *v.t.* **1,** (obscure) затумáнивать. **2,** (make fuzzy, as a photograph) смáзывать. —**blurry,** *adj.* расплы́вчатый.

blurt *v.t.* [*usu.* blurt out] сболтнýть; вы́палить.

blush *v.i.* краснéть. —*n.* крáска стыдá. —**at first blush,** на пéрвый взгляд.

bluster *v.i.* **1,** (blow stormily) бушевáть. **2,** (speak noisily or threateningly) курáжиться. —*n.* пусты́е словá; пусты́е угрóзы.

boa *n.* **1,** (snake) удáв. **2,** (scarf) боá. —**boa constrictor,** боá.

boar *n.* **1,** (male hog) хряк. **2,** (wild boar) кабáн.

board *n.* **1,** (wooden strip; flat surface) доскá. *Bulletin board,* доскá объявлéний. *Ironing board,* гладильная доскá. **2,** (side of a ship) борт: *on board,* на борту́. **3,** (meals) стол: *room and board,* квартира и стол; пансиóн. **4,** (group of officials) правлéние; управлéние; совéт; коми́ссия. *Board of directors,* совéт директорóв. *Board of inquiry,* слéдственная коми́ссия. *Editorial board,* редакциóнная коллéгия. —*v.t.* **1,** *fol. by up* (cover with boards) забивáть; заколоти́ть. **2,** (get on) сади́ться в *or* на. **3,** (come alongside, as an enemy ship) брать на абордáж. —*v.i.* сесть на самолёт.

boarder *n.* пансионéр.

boarding *n.* посáдка. —**boarding pass,** посáдочный талóн.

boarding house пансиóн.

boarding school шкóла-интернáт.

boardwalk *n.* дощáтый настил (на пля́же).

boast *v.i.* (brag) хвáстаться; хвали́ться. —*v.t.* (proudly possess) быть счастли́вым обладáтелем (+ *gen.*). —*n.* хвастовствó. —**boastful,** *adj.* хвастли́вый.

boat *n.* **1,** (small vessel) лóдка: *motor boat,* мотóрная лóдка. **2,** (ship) парохóд. —*adj.* лóдочный: *boat races,* лóдочные гóнки. —**in the same boat,** в такóм же положéнии. —**miss the boat,** *colloq.* прозевáть удóбный слýчай.

boathouse *n.* лóдочный сарáй.

boating *n.* лóдочный спорт; катáние на лóдке. *Go boating,* катáться на лóдке.

boatman *n.* лóдочник.

boatswain *n.* бóцман.

bob *n.* **1,** (quick jerking motion) рывóк. **2,** (knoblike weight) груз отвéса. **3,** (fishing float) поплавóк. **4,** (short curl or knob of hair) завитóк. —*v.i. Bob up and down,* подпры́гивать. *Bob on the waves,* покáчиваться на волнáх. —*v.t.* (cut short) кóротко стричь.

bobbin *n.* катýшка.

bobby *n., Brit., colloq.* полисмéн.

bobby pin закóлка.

bobcat *n.* америкáнская рысь.

bobsled *n.* бóбслей.

bode *v.t. & i.* предвещáть: *bode well,* предвещáть хорóшее.

bodice *n.* лиф; корсáж.

bodily *adj.* телéсный: *bodily injuries*, телéсные поврежде́ния. —*adv.* со́бственной персо́ной. *Throw someone bodily out of the room*, вы́швырнуть кого́-нибудь из ко́мнаты.

body *n.* **1**, (human form) те́ло: *the human body*, челове́ческое те́ло. **2**, (corpse) труп. **3**, (substance) те́ло: *foreign body*, посторо́ннее те́ло. **4**, (object in space) те́ло: *celestial body*, небе́сное те́ло. **5**, in *body of water*, во́дное простра́нство. **6**, (of various devices) ко́рпус; (of a car) ку́зов; (of an airplane) фюзеля́ж. **7**, (central part, as of a book) основна́я часть. **8**, (group of persons) о́рган; коллекти́в: *legislative body*, законода́тельный о́рган; *student body*, студе́нческий коллекти́в. **9**, (density) пло́тность; про́чность. **10**, (consistency; strength, as of wine) кре́пость. —*adj.*: *body temperature*, температу́ра те́ла. —**body and soul**, душо́й и те́лом. —**keep body and soul together**, подде́рживать существова́ние; перебива́ться.

bodyguard *n.* телохрани́тель.

Boer *n.* бур. —*adj.* бу́рский.

bog *n.* боло́то; тряси́на; топь. —*v.t. Become bogged down* (in), увяза́ть (в); погряза́ть (в). —*v.i.* [*usu.* **bog down**] (peter out) захлебываться.

bogeyman *n.* бука.

boggle *v.t.* потряса́ть: *boggle the mind*, потряса́ть ум.

boggy *adj.* боло́тистый.

bogus *adj.* подде́льный; фальши́вый.

Bohemian *adj.* **1**, (of or from Bohemia) боге́мский. **2**, (unconventional) боге́мный.

boil *v.t.* **1**, (bring to a boiling point, as water) кипяти́ть. **2**, (cook, as eggs) вари́ть. —*v.i.* кипе́ть. —*n.* **1**, (boiling state) кипе́ние: *bring to a boil*, доводи́ть до кипе́ния. **2**, (skin sore) нары́в; фуру́нкул. —**boil down**, **1**, (lessen by boiling) ува́ривать. **2**, (reduce) своди́ть. **3**, *fol. by* **to** (come down to) своди́ться: *the whole thing boils down to this*, все де́ло сво́дится к э́тому. —**boil over**, перекипа́ть.

boiled *adj.* варёный; кипячёный.

boiler *n.* (парово́й) коте́л; куб. —**boiler plate**, коте́льное желе́зо. —**boiler room**, коте́льная; коте́льное отделе́ние.

boilerman *n.* истопни́к.

boiling *adj.* кипя́щий. *Boiling water*, кипято́к. —**boiling hot**, горя́чий как кипято́к. —**boiling point**, то́чка кипе́ния.

boisterous *adj.* шумли́вый; бу́йный.

bold *adj.* **1**, (daring) сме́лый. **2**, (brazen) де́рзкий. **3**, (distinct to the eye) че́ткий. **4**, *printing* жи́рный. —**make bold**, осме́ливаться.

boldface *n.* жи́рный шрифт. —*adj.* жи́рный.

bold-faced *adj.* **1**, (brazen) на́глый. **2**, *printing* жи́рный.

boldly *adv.* сме́ло.

boldness *n.* сме́лость.

boll *n.*, *bot.* коро́бочка. —**boll weevil**, хло́пковый долгоно́сик.

bologna *n.* боло́нская колбаса́.

Bolshevik *n.* большеви́к. —*adj.* большеви́стский.

bolster *n.* ва́лик. —*v.t.* подде́рживать; подкрепля́ть. *Bolster someone's spirits*, поднима́ть чье-нибудь настрое́ние.

bolt *n.* **1**, (metal pin) болт. **2**, (sliding bar that locks) засо́в; задви́жка. **3**, (sliding mechanism for a rifle) затво́р. **4**, (roll of material) руло́н. **5**, (of thunder or lightning) уда́р (гро́ма/мо́лнии). —*v.t.* **1**, (fasten with bolts) скрепля́ть болта́ми. **2**, (lock) закрыва́ть на засо́в *or* на задви́жку; задвига́ть. **3**, (break away from, as a political party) порва́ть с. —*v.i.* **1**, (dash; dart) бро́ситься: *bolt from the room*, бро́ситься вон из ко́мнаты. **2**, (of a horse) понести́. —**bolt from the blue**, гром среди́ я́сного не́ба.

bomb *n.* бо́мба. —*adj.* бо́мбовый: *bomb load*, бо́мбовая нагру́зка. —*v.t.* бомбардирова́ть; бомби́ть. —**bomb out**, разбомби́ть.

bombard *v.t.* **1**, (bomb) бомбардирова́ть. **2**, (shower, as with questions) забра́сывать (+ *instr.*); засыпа́ть (+ *instr.*). —**bombardier**, *n.* бомбарди́р. —**bombardment**, *n.* бомбардиро́вка.

bombast *n.* напы́щенность; высокопа́рность. —**bombastic**, *adj.* напы́щенный; высокопа́рный.

bomb bay бо́мбовый отсе́к.

bomber *n.* бомбардиро́вщик.

bombing *n.* бомбардиро́вка; бомбомета́ние.

bomb load бо́мбовая нагру́зка.

bomb shelter бомбоубе́жище.

bombsight *n.* бомбардиро́вочный прице́л.

bona fide **1**, (made in good faith) добросо́вестный. **2**, (genuine) по́длинный.

bond *n.* **1**, (tie) связь. *Bonds of friendship*, у́зы дру́жбы. **2**, *pl.* (shackles) пу́ты; око́вы. **3**, *finance* облига́ция. **4**, (bail) пору́ка: *post bond for*, брать на пору́ки.

bondage *n.* ра́бство.

bondsman *n.* **1**, (guarantor) поручи́тель. **2**, (slave) раб. —**bondwoman**, *n.* раба́; рабы́ня.

bone *n.* кость. —*adj.* ко́стный: *bone tissue/disease*, ко́стная ткань/боле́знь. —*v.t.* вынима́ть ко́сти из. —*v.i.* [*usu.* **bone up**] *slang* (cram) зубри́ть. —**bag of bones**, ко́жа да ко́сти. —**bone of contention**, я́блоко раздо́ра. —**chilled to the bone**, продро́гший до мо́зга косте́й. —**feel in one's bones**, чу́вствовать всем свои́м существо́м (что...). —**have a bone to pick with**, име́ть счёты с. —**make no bones about**, не де́лать секре́та из.

bonehead *n.*, *slang* болва́н; остоло́п.

bone meal костяна́я мука́.

boner *n.*, *colloq.* про́мах; опло́шность.

bonfire *n.* костер.

bonnet *n.* **1**, (lady's hat) ка́пор. **2**, *Brit.* (hood of a car) капо́т.

bonus *n.* пре́мия.

bon vivant жуи́р.

bony *adj.* **1**, (having many bones) кости́стый. **2**, (skinny) костля́вый.

boo *v.t. & i.* осви́стывать.

booby *n.* болва́н; балбе́с.

booby trap ми́на-лову́шка.

book *n.* кни́га. —*adj.* кни́жный: *book learning*, кни́жные зна́ния. —*v.t.* (reserve) зака́зывать; брать; брони́ровать. *We're all booked up*, все места́ за́няты; свобо́дных мест нет. —**be on the books**, быть на уче́те. —**in my book**, *colloq.* на мой взгляд. —**keep the books**, вести́ кни́ги. —**know like a book**, знать как свои́ пять па́льцев.

bookbinder *n.* переплётчик. —**bookbinding**, *n.* переплётное де́ло.

bookcase *n.* кни́жный шкаф; этаже́рка.

bookend *n.* подста́вка для книг.

bookish *adj.* книжный.

bookkeeper *n.* бухгалтер; счетовод. —**bookkeeping,** *n.* бухгалтерия; счетоводство.

booklet *n.* книжечка; брошюра; буклет.

bookmaker *n.* букмекер.

bookmark *n.* закладка.

bookmobile *n.* библиотека-передвижка.

bookplate *n.* экслибрис; книжный знак.

book review рецензия на книгу.

bookseller *n.* продавец книг. *Secondhand bookseller,* букинист.

bookshelf *n.* книжная полка.

bookstore *n.* книжный магазин.

bookworm *n.* книжный червь.

boom *n.* **1,** (deep rumbling sound) гул; грохот. **2,** (rapid rise) бум. **3,** (arm of a derrick) стрела. —*v.i.* **1,** (make a deep rumbling sound) греметь; грохотать. **2,** (flourish) процветать. —*interj.* бум!

boomerang *n.* бумеранг.

boon *n.* благо; благодеяние. *A boon to the city,* благо для города. *A boon to progress,* толчок к прогрессу.

boondocks *n.pl., slang* глушь; захолустье.

boor *n.* хам; невежа; грубиян. —**boorish,** *adj.* хамский. —**boorishness,** *n.* хамство.

boost *v.t.* **1,** (lift) поднимать. **2,** (raise, as prices) повышать. **3,** (increase) увеличивать. —*n.* **1,** (lift) подъём. **2,** (help) содействие. **3,** (raise) повышение.

booster *n.* **1,** *electricity* усилитель. **2,** *rocketry* ускоритель. **3,** (enthusiastic supporter) патриот. —**booster rocket,** ракетный ускоритель; стартовый ракетный двигатель.

boot *n.* **1,** (shoe) ботинок; сапог. **2,** (kick) пинок. **3,** *Brit.* (trunk of a car) багажник. —*v.t.* **1,** (kick) пинать. **2,** *usu. fol. by* **out,** *slang* (expel) выгнать; вышвырнуть. —**give the boot to,** выгонять с работы. —**lick someone's boots,** лизать пятки (+ *dat.*). —**to boot,** вдобавок; в придачу.

bootblack *n.* чистильщик сапог.

booth *n.* **1,** (small compartment) будка; кабина. *Telephone booth,* телефонная будка. *Voting/polling booth,* кабина для голосования. **2,** (stall; stand) киоск; ларёк; палатка. *Change booth,* разменная касса.

bootlicker *n.* лизоблюд; подлиза.

booty *n.* добыча; трофеи.

booze *n., colloq.* хмельное.

borax *n.* бура.

border *n.* **1,** (boundary) граница. **2,** (trim) кайма; бордюр. —*adj.* пограничный: *border post,* пограничный пост; пограничная застава. —*v.t.* **1,** [*also,* **border on**] (bound; verge on) граничить с. **2,** (put a border or edging on) окаймлять; обшивать. —**border guard,** пограничник.

bore *n.* **1,** (of a firearm) канал. **2,** (tiresome person) скучный *or* нудный человек. —*v.t.* **1,** (drill) сверлить; бурить. **2,** (tire) надоедать.

bored *adj.* скучный. *I am bored,* мне скучно; мне надоело.

boredom *n.* скука.

boric *adj.* борный. —**boric acid,** борная кислота.

boring *adj.* **1,** (used for drilling) буровой; бурильный; сверлильный. **2,** (tiresome) скучный; надоедливый.

born *adj.* **1,** (brought forth by birth) рождённый: *born out of wedlock,* рождённый вне брака. *I was*

born in France, я родился (родилась) во Франции. *He was born to fly,* он рождён летать. **2,** (having the natural talent of) прирождённый: *a born poet,* прирождённый поэт. —**in all one's born days,** за всю свою жизнь.

boron *n.* бор.

borough *n.* городок.

borrow *v.t.* **1,** (take temporarily) брать: *borrow a book from the library,* брать книгу из библиотеки. *May I borrow your pen for a moment?,* можно попросить на минуту вашу ручку? **2,** (receive as a loan) занимать; брать взаймы. *Borrow money from someone,* занимать деньги у кого-нибудь. **3,** (adopt; take over) займствовать. —**borrower,** *n.* заёмщик.

borsch *also,* **borsht, borscht** *n.* борщ.

borzoi *n.* борзая.

bosom *n.* **1,** (breast) грудь. **2,** (space formed by the breast) пазуха: *remove from one's bosom,* вынимать из-за пазухи. **3,** *fig.* (source of feelings) душа. —**bosom friend,** закадычный друг.

boss *n.* **1,** (employer; superior) начальник. **2,** (political chief) босс. —*v.t.* **1,** (manage) управлять. **2,** *fol. by* **around** (order about) командовать над. —**bossy,** *adj.* властный.

botany *n.* ботаника. —**botanical,** *adj.* ботанический. —**botanist,** *n.* ботаник.

botch *v.t.* напутать.

both *adj.* оба; обе: *both boys,* оба мальчика; *with both hands,* обеими руками. *People of both sexes,* лица обоего пола. —*pron.* оба; обе; и тот и другой. —*conj.* и... и; как..., так и: *he speaks both English and Russian,* он говорит и по-английски и по-русски. *Both in London and Paris,* как в Лондоне, так и в Париже.

bother *v.t.* **1,** (disturb; pester) мешать. **2,** (worry; trouble; cause discomfort to) беспокоить. —*v.i.* (take the trouble) дать себе труд. —*n.* **1,** (trouble) беспокойство. **2,** (nuisance; annoyance) досада.

bothersome *adj.* надоедливый.

bottle *n.* бутылка: *bottle of milk,* бутылка молока. *Infant's bottle,* рожок. *Ink bottle,* пузырёк для чернил. *Medicine bottle,* склянка для лекарств. *Perfume bottle,* флакон. —*v.t.* **1,** (put in bottles) разливать по бутылкам. **2,** *fol. by* **up** (stifle) сдерживать. —**hit the bottle,** *slang* выпивать.

bottled *adj.* бутылочный: *bottled beer,* бутылочное пиво.

bottleneck *n.* узкое место.

bottom *n.* дно: *go to the bottom,* идти ко дну. *At the bottom of the page,* внизу страницы. —*adj.* нижний: *the bottom step,* нижняя ступенька. —**at bottom,** в сущности; по существу. —**bottoms up!,** до дна! —**from the bottom of one's heart,** от всего сердца; от всей души. —**from top to bottom,** сверху донизу. —**get to the bottom of,** добраться до сути (+ *gen.*).

bottomless *adj.* бездонный.

boudoir *n.* будуар.

bough *n.* сук.

bouillon *n.* бульон.

boulder *n.* валун.

boulevard *n.* проспект.

bounce *v.i.* **1,** (rebound) прыгать. *Bounce off,* отскакивать от. **2,** (leap; spring) вскакивать: *bounce out of bed,* вскакивать с постели. —*v.t.* **1,** (a ball) бить (мячóм) о зéмлю. **2,** *slang* (dismiss) выгонять. —*n.* **1,** (rebound) рикошéт. **2,** (resiliency) упрýгость. —**bounce back,** оправляться.

bouncer *n., colloq.* вышибáла.

bound *n.* **1,** (leap) прыжóк; скачóк. **2,** *pl.* (limits) грани́цы; предéлы. *Exceed the bounds of...,* вы́йти за предéлы (+ *gen.*). *Know no bounds,* не знать грани́ц. —*adj.* **1,** (tied) свя́занный. **2,** (having a binding) в переплёте. **3,** (obligated) обя́занный. **4,** (headed for): *the train is bound for Moscow,* пóезд направля́ется в Москвý; пóезд слéдует до Москвы́. **5,** (certain; sure): *it was bound to happen,* э́то и должнó бы́ло случи́ться. *He is bound to find out about it,* он непремéнно узнáет об э́том. —*v.i.* **1,** (leap) пры́гать. *Bound over the fence,* перескочи́ть чéрез забóр. **2,** *fol. by* **back** *or* **off** (rebound) отскáкивать (от). **3,** *fol. by* **on** (border on) грани́чить с. *Sweden is bounded on the west by Norway,* на зáпаде Швéция грани́чит с Норвéгией. —**out of bounds,** *sports* вне игры́. **bounds,** *sports* вне игры́.

boundary *n.* грани́ца. —*adj.* пограни́чный: *boundary marker,* пограни́чный знак.

boundless *adj.* безграни́чный; безбрéжный; необозри́мый.

bounteous *adj.* = **bountiful.**

bountiful *adj.* **1,** (generous) щéдрый. **2,** (abundant) оби́льный.

bounty *n.* **1,** (generosity) щéдрость. **2,** (gift) дар. **3,** (reward) награ́да.

bouquet *n.* букéт.

bourgeois *n.* буржуá. —*adj.* буржуáзный. —**bourgeoisie,** *n.* буржуази́я.

bout *n.* **1,** (contest) схвáтка. **2,** (siege, as of illness) при́ступ. —**drinking bout,** запóй; попóйка.

boutonniere *n.* бутоньéрка.

bovine *adj.* бычáчий; бы́чий.

bow[1] (bau) *v.i.* **1,** (bend one's head or body) кла́няться. **2,** *fol. by* **down** (kneel) преклоня́ться. **3,** (yield) подчиня́ться; покоря́ться. —*v.t.* склоня́ть; наклоня́ть: *bow one's head,* склоня́ть/наклоня́ть гóлову. —*n.* **1,** (bending of the head or body) поклóн. *Take a bow,* раскла́ниваться. **2,** (of a ship) нос. —**bow and scrape,** низкопоклóнничать. —**bow out,** выходи́ть; выбывáть.

bow[2] (bo) *n.* **1,** (for shooting arrows) лук. **2,** (for playing the violin) смычóк. **3,** (bowknot) бант.

bowel *n.* **1,** (intestine) кишкá; *pl.* кишки́; кишéчник. *Bowel movement,* стул. *Move one's bowels,* испражня́ться. **2,** *pl.* (innermost part) нéдра: *bowels of the earth,* нéдра земли́.

bower *n.* бесéдка.

bowl *n.* **1,** (deep dish) ми́ска; глубóкая тарéлка. **2,** (vase) вáза. **3,** (of a toilet) унитáз. —*v.i.* (go bowling) игрáть в кéгли. —**bowl over, 1,** (knock down) свали́ть с ног. **2,** (stun) ошеломля́ть.

bowlegged *adj.* кривонóгий.

bowler *n.* **1,** (one who bowls) игрóк в кéгли. **2,** (hat) котелóк.

bowling *n.* (игрá в) кéгли. —**bowling alley,** кегельбáн.

bowls *n.* игрá в шáры.

bowman *n.* стрелóк из лýка.

bowsprit *n.* бушпри́т.

bowstring *n.* тетивá.

bow tie бáбочка.

box *n.* **1,** (container) корóбка; я́щик. **2,** *theat.* лóжа. **3,** (booth) бýдка: *sentry box,* караýльная бýдка. **4,** (blow) пощёчина. **5,** (species of tree) самши́т. —*v.t.* **1,** (put in a box) укла́дывать в я́щик. **2,** (strike) дать пощёчину (+ *dat.*). **3,** *fol. by* **in** (crowd; squeeze) вти́скивать. —*v.i.* боксúровать.

boxer *n.* боксёр.

boxing *n.* бокс. —**boxing glove,** боксёрская перчáтка.

box office (театрáльная *or* билéтная) кáсса. —**box-office receipts,** сбóры.

box seat мéсто в лóже.

boy *n.* мáльчик.

boyar *n.* боя́рин.

boycott *n.* бойкóт. —*v.t.* бойкоти́ровать.

boyfriend *n.* прия́тель.

boyhood *n.* дéтство.

boyish *adj.* мальчи́шеский.

boy scout скáут.

bra *n.* бюстгáльтер.

brace *n.* **1,** (clamp) скобá; скрéпа. **2,** (tool holding a bit) коловорóт. **3,** (pair; couple) пáра. **4,** *pl., Brit.* (suspenders) подтя́жки. —*v.t.* **1,** (fasten) скрепля́ть. **2,** (invigorate) бодри́ть. —**brace oneself,** напряга́ться; собира́ться с си́лами.

bracelet *n.* браслéт.

bracing *adj.* бодря́щий. *The air is bracing,* вóздух бодри́т.

bracket *n.* **1,** (shelf support) кронштéйн. **2,** (staple) скобá. **3,** *pl.* ([ ]) (квадрáтные) скóбки. —*v.t.* **1,** (enclose in brackets) заключáть в скóбки. **2,** (group together) стáвить на однý дóску.

brackish *adj.* солоновáтый.

brad *n.* гвóздик; шпи́лька.

brag *v.i.* хвáстаться.

braggart *n.* хвастýн; бахвáл; фанфарóн.

Brahman *also,* **Brahmin** *n.* брахмáн. —**Brahmanism,** *n.* брахмани́зм.

braid *v.t.* **1,** (plait) заплетáть. **2,** (weave) плести́. —*n.* **1,** (ornamental band) тесьмá. **2,** (of hair) косá.

brain *n., anat.* мозг. **2,** *pl.* (food) мозги́. —*adj.* мозговóй. —**brain drain,** утéчка мозгóв.

brainchild *n., colloq.* дéтище.

brainless *adj., colloq.* безмóзглый; безголóвый.

brainstorm *n.* блестя́щая мысль.

brain trust мозговóй трест.

brain-twister *n.* головолóмка.

brainwash *v.t.* промывáть мозги́ (+ *dat.*).

brainwork *n.* мозговáя рабóта; ýмственный труд.

brainy *adj., colloq.* мозгови́тый; башкови́тый.

braise *v.t.* туши́ть.

brake *n.* тóрмоз. —*adj.* тормознóй: *brake fluid,* тормознáя жи́дкость. —*v.t. & i.* тормози́ть.

brakeman *n.* тормознóй кондýктор.

bramble *n.* кумани́ка.

brambling *n.* вьюрóк; юрóк.

bran *n.* óтруби.

branch *n.* **1,** (limb) ветвь; вéтка. **2,** (commercial subdivision) филиáл; отдéление. **3,** (field) óтрасль: *branch of science,* óтрасль науки. **4,** (arm of a river) рукáв. **5,** *mil.* род войск; слýжба. —*adj.* филиáльный: *branch office,* филиáльное отдéление. —*v.i.* **1,** (divide into branches) разветвля́ться. **2,** *fol. by* **off** (go off in a different direction) ответвля́ться.

brand *n.* **1,** (make; kind) мáрка. **2,** (burning piece of wood) головня. **3,** (mark made on cattle) клеймо; тавро. **4,** (stigma) клеймо. —*v.t.* клеймить. —**branding iron,** клеймо.

brandish *v.t.* размахивать; потрясать.

brand-new *adj.* совсем новый; новенький. *Brand-new suit,* костюм с иголочки.

brandy *n.* коньяк.

brant *n.* (goose) казарка.

brash *adj.* наглый; дерзкий.

brass *n.* **1,** (alloy) латунь. **2,** *slang* (top officials) верхушка; головка. —*adj.* латунный. —**brass band,** духовой оркестр. —**brass knuckles,** кастет.

brassiere *n.* бюстгальтер.

brat *n.* озорник; пострел.

bravado *n.* бравада.

brave *adj.* храбрый. —*v.t.* бравировать. —**bravely,** *adv.* храбро. —**bravery,** *n.* храбрость.

bravissimo *interj.* брависсимо!

bravo *interj.* браво!

bravura *n.* бравурная музыка.

brawl *n.* свалка; дебош. —*v.i.* скандалить; дебоширить. —**brawler,** *n.* драчун; задира; забияка.

brawn *n.* мускулы; мускульная сила. —**brawny,** *adj.* мускулистый.

bray *v.i.* кричать; реветь.

brazen *adj.* **1,** (resembling brass) медный. **2,** (shameless) бесстыдный; беззастенчивый.

brazier *n.* **1,** (worker in brass) медник. **2,** (roasting pan) жаровня.

Brazilian *adj.* бразильский. —*n.* бразилец; бразильянка.

breach *n.* **1,** (break) брешь; пролом. **2,** (violation; infringement) нарушение: *breach of promise,* нарушение обещания. —*v.t.* пробивать; проламывать.

bread *n.* хлеб. —*adj.* хлебный: *bread crumbs,* хлебные крошки. —**take the bread out of someone's mouth,** отбивать хлеб у кого-нибудь.

breadbasket *n.* **1,** (basket for carrying bread) хлебница. **2,** (region that supplies much grain) житница.

breadth *n.* **1,** (width) ширина. **2,** (wide extent; scope) широта.

breadwinner *n.* кормилец.

break *v.t.* **1,** (split; fracture; put out of working order) ломать. *Break one's watch/one's leg,* сломать часы/себе ногу. *Break one's neck,* свернуть себе шею. *Break the ice,* сломать ог разбить лёд. **2,** (smash; shatter) разбивать. *Break a window,* разбить окно. **3,** (fail to keep; violate) нарушать: *break a promise/one's word/the law,* нарушать обещание/слово/закон. **4,** (interrupt; disturb) нарушать; прерывать: *break the silence,* нарушать/прерывать молчание. **5,** (sever, as relations) порывать; разрывать. **6,** (wear down, as resistance) сломить. *Break a strike,* сорвать забастовку. **7,** (divide into smaller units) разрознивать: *break a set of something,* разрознивать комплект чего-нибудь. *Break a dollar,* разменивать доллар. **8,** (surpass, as a record) побить. **9,** (get rid of, as a habit) отучиться от. *Break someone of a habit,* отучать кого-нибудь от привычки. **10,** (convey, as bad news) разорять. *Break the bank,* сорвать банк. **12,** *electricity* размыкать: *break a circuit,* размыкать цепь. **13,** *in various miscellaneous expressions: break a code,* разгадывать код; *break camp,* сниматься с лагеря; *break ranks,* расходиться; *break someone's heart,*

разбить чьё-нибудь сердце. —*v.i.* **1,** (become smashed, cracked, or useless) ломаться; разбиваться. **2,** (snap, as of a rope) рваться. **3,** (stop suddenly, as of one's voice) ломаться; срываться; прерываться. **4,** (make a sudden dash) броситься: *break for the door,* броситься к двери. **5,** (dawn): *day is breaking,* (рас)светает. **6,** *fol. by with* (sever ties with) пор(ы)вать с. *Break with tradition,* порвать с традицией. —*n.* **1,** (burst; rupture) разрыв; прорыв; пролом. *Water-main break,* разрыв водопроводной магистрали. **2,** *fig.* (severing) разрыв: *break in diplomatic relations,* разрыв дипломатических отношений. **3,** (interruption; recess) перерыв: *without a break,* без перерыва; беспрерывно. **4,** *in the break of day,* рассвет. **5,** (sudden dash) бросок. **6,** (escape, as from prison) бегство; побег (из тюрьмы). **7,** *colloq.* (stroke of luck) счастливый случай. *He gets all the breaks,* ему всегда везёт. *The breaks were against us,* нам не везло. —**break apart,** разламываться. —**break away,** вырываться. —**break down, 1,** (smash down, as a door) выламывать. **2,** (overcome, as resistance) сломить. **3,** (divide) разбивать (на группы, категории, *etc.*). **4,** (go out of working order) испортиться; выйти из строя. *Communications broke down,* связь прервалась. **5,** (fail) проваливаться: *all efforts have broken down,* все попытки провалились. *Negotiations broke down,* переговоры зашли в тупик. **6,** (lose one's composure) не выдержать: *she broke down and cried,* она не выдержала и заплакала. —**break even,** оставаться при своих. —**break in, 1,** (enter by force) вламываться. **2,** (interrupt) вмешиваться. **3,** (a car, motor, etc.) обкатывать; (a horse) выезжать; объезжать; (shoes) разнашивать. —**break into, 1,** (enter by force) вламываться в. **2,** (interrupt, as a conversation) вмешиваться в. **3,** (give way to, as laughter) разразиться (+ *instr.*). *He broke into a sweat,* его бросило в пот. *Break into song,* запеть (песню). —**break off, 1,** (sever by breaking) отламывать; откалывать. **2,** (come off) отламываться; откалываться. **3,** (halt abruptly) прекращать; прерывать. **4,** (sever, as relations) порывать; разрывать. **5,** *fol. by from* (split off from, as a group) откалываться (от). —**break open,** взламывать. —**break out, 1,** (start unexpectedly) вспыхнуть; разразиться. **2,** (appear, as of a rash) появляться. **3,** (escape) вырываться. *Break out of prison,* бежать из тюрьмы. —**break through,** прорываться; прорываться сквозь; пробиваться сквозь. —**break up, 1,** (force to disperse) разгонять. **2,** (disperse; split up) расходиться. **3,** (divide into smaller parts) разбивать. **4,** (be divided up) разбиваться. **5,** (cease to exist or function) распадаться.

breakable *adj.* ломкий; хрупкий.

breakage *n.* ломка; поломка; бой.

breakdown *n.* **1,** (failure to function) авария; поломка. **2,** (total failure) развал. **3,** (mental collapse) надрыв; надлом. *Nervous breakdown,* неврастения. **4,** (analysis; classification) разбор.

breaker *n.* (wave) бурун.

breakfast *n.* завтрак. *Have breakfast,* завтракать.

breaking point момент разрыва. *Reach the breaking point* (*fig.*), дойти до точки; дойти до предела.

breakneck *adj., in at breakneck speed,* сломя голову.

breakthrough *n.* прорыв.

breakup *n.* **1,** (splitting into pieces) распа́д; разва́л; ло́мка. **2,** (split between people) разры́в.

breakwater *n.* мол; волноло́м; волноре́з.

bream *n.* (fish) лещ.

breast *n.* **1,** (human) грудь. **2,** (of a coat) борт: *double-breasted,* двубо́ртный. —*adj.* грудно́й; нагру́дный. *Breast pocket,* нагру́дный карма́н. *Breast feeding,* кормле́ние гру́дью. *Breast cancer,* рак моло́чной железы́. —**make a clean breast of it,** всё вы́ложить.

breastbone *n.* груди́на.

breastplate *n.* нагру́дник.

breast stroke брасс.

breastwork *n.* бру́ствер.

breath *n.* **1,** (act of breathing) дыха́ние. *Hold one's breath,* затаи́ть дыха́ние. **2,** (a single breath) вдох. *Take a deep breath,* глубоко́ вдохну́ть. —**be out of breath,** запыха́ться. —**it took my breath away,** у меня́ захвати́ло дух. —**under one's breath,** вполго́лоса; шёпотом.

breathe *v.i.* дыша́ть. *Breathe in,* вдыха́ть. *Breathe out,* выдыха́ть. —*v.t.* **1,** (inhale and exhale) дыша́ть (+ *instr.*). *Breathe new life into,* вдохну́ть жизнь в. **2,** (utter; whisper) проро́нить; обмо́лвиться. *Not breathe a word,* не проро́нить ни сло́ва; не обмо́лвиться ни сло́вом. —**breathe down someone's neck,** стоя́ть над чье́й-нибудь душо́й. —**breathe one's last,** испусти́ть дух.

breather *n.* (respite) передышка.

breathing *n.* дыха́ние. —**breathing space/spell,** переды́шка.

breathless *adj.* запыха́вшийся.

breathtaking *adj.* захва́тывающий.

breech *n.* **1,** (of a gun) казённая часть. **2,** (buttocks) зад.

breeches *n.pl.* бри́джи. *Riding breeches,* рейту́зы; галифе́. *Also,* **britches.**

breed *v.t.* **1,** (mate; raise) разводи́ть. **2,** (produce; generate; give rise to) порожда́ть. —*v.i.* плоди́ться; размножа́ться. —*n.* поро́да.

breeder *n.* (of cattle) скотово́д; (of horses) конево́д. —**breeder reactor,** размножа́ющий реа́ктор.

breeding *n.* **1,** (producing of offspring) размноже́ние. **2,** (raising of animals) разведе́ние. ♦*Usu. rendered by the suffix* -во́дство: *cattle breeding,* ското-во́дство. **3,** (improving of strains) селе́кция. **4,** (good manners) воспи́танность. —**breeding ground, 1,** (of animals) ме́сто размноже́ния; (*of sea mammals*) ле́жбище; (*of fish*) нерести́лище. **2,** *fig.* (conducive place) оча́г; расса́дник.

breeze *n.* (пёгкий) ветеро́к. *Sea breeze,* бриз.

breezy *adj.* **1,** (brisk; windy) све́жий; ве́треный. **2,** (lively; sprightly) живо́й; лихо́й.

brethren *n.pl.* бра́тья; собра́тья.

brevity *n.* кра́ткость.

brew *v.t.* **1,** (make, as beer) вари́ть. **2,** (prepare, as tea) зава́ривать. —*v.i.* собира́ться; надвига́ться: *a storm is brewing,* собира́ется/надвига́ется гроза́.

brewer *n.* пивова́р. —**brewery,** *n.* пивова́ренный заво́д. —**brewing,** *n.* пивоваре́ние.

briar *n.* = **brier.**

bribe *n.* взя́тка. —*v.t.* подкупа́ть. —**bribery,** *n.* взя́точничество; по́дкуп.

bric-a-brac *n.* вещи́цы; безделу́шки.

brick *n.* кирпи́ч. —*adj.* кирпи́чный.

bricklayer *n.* ка́менщик.

brick-red *adj.* кирпи́чный; кирпи́чного цве́та.

brickwork *n.* кирпи́чная кла́дка.

bridal *adj.* сва́дебный; подвене́чный.

bride *n.* неве́ста.

bridegroom *n.* жени́х.

bridesmaid *n.* подру́жка неве́сты.

bridge *n.* **1,** (structure) мост. **2,** (on a ship) мо́стик. **3,** (of the nose) перено́сица. **4,** (of a stringed instrument) кобы́лка. **5,** (mounting for false teeth) мост. **6,** (card game) бридж. —*v.t.* **1,** (build a bridge across) наводи́ть мост че́рез. **2,** (overcome) преодолева́ть. *Bridge the gap,* восполня́ть пробе́л. —**burn one's bridges,** сжига́ть свои́ мосты́ *or* корабли́.

bridgehead *n.* плацда́рм; предмо́стное укрепле́ние.

bridle *n.* узда́; узде́чка. —*v.t.* взну́здывать; обу́здывать. —*v.i.* разозли́ться; вскипе́ть. —**bridle path,** вью́чная тропа́.

brief *adj.* **1,** (short in time) коро́ткий. **2,** (concise) кра́ткий. —*n.* сво́дка; резюме́. —*v.t.* инструкти́ровать. —**in brief,** вкра́тце; кра́тко; коро́че говоря́.

briefcase *n.* портфе́ль.

briefing *n.* инструкта́ж.

briefly *adv.* коро́тко; кра́тко; вкра́тце.

brier *also,* **briar** *n.* **1,** (thorny bush) шипо́вник. **2,** (heath) э́рика.

brig *n.* **1,** (ship) бриг. **2,** (place of confinement) гауптва́хта.

brigade *n.* **1,** *mil.* брига́да. **2,** (organized group) кома́нда; брига́да; дружи́на. *Fire brigade,* пожа́рная кома́нда; пожа́рная дружи́на.

brigadier general генера́л-майо́р.

brigand *n.* разбо́йник. —**brigandage,** *n.* разбо́й.

bright *adj.* **1,** (shining; luminous) я́ркий; све́тлый. *Bright light,* я́ркий свет. *Bright colors,* я́ркие цвета́. *Bright sun,* я́ркое со́лнце. *Bright red,* я́рко-кра́сный; я́рко-кра́сного цве́та. *Bright day,* све́тлый день. *Bright future,* све́тлое бу́дущее. **2,** (clever) смышлё-ный; сообрази́тельный.

brighten *v.t.* **1,** (make bright) озаря́ть. **2,** (bring color or life to) оживля́ть. —*v.i.* **1,** (become bright) светле́ть; проясня́ться. **2,** (become more cheerful) оживля́ться. **3,** (improve) улучша́ться.

brightly *adv.* я́рко.

brightness *n.* я́ркость; све́тлость.

brilliance *n.* блеск.

brilliant *adj.* **1,** (sparkling) я́ркий. **2,** (outstanding) блестя́щий. —**brilliantly,** *adv.* я́рко; блестя́ще.

brim *n.* **1,** (edge) край. *Filled to the brim,* по́лный до краёв. **2,** (of a hat) поля́. —*v.i.* [*usu.* **brim with**] наполня́ться (+ *instr.*).

brine *n.* рассо́л.

bring *v.t.* **1,** (by carrying) приноси́ть: *bring me my shoes,* принеси́ мне боти́нки. **2,** (on foot) приводи́ть: *bring someone to dinner,* приводи́ть кого́-нибудь к обе́ду. **3,** (by conveyance) привози́ть: *bring something from abroad,* привози́ть что́-нибудь из-за грани́цы. **4,** (cause to happen) приноси́ть: *war brings suffering,* война́ прино́сит страда́ния. *It brought tears to my eyes,* э́то вы́звало у меня́ слёзы. **5,** *in various miscellaneous expressions: bring home to,* внуша́ть; втолкова́ть; *bring charges,* предъявля́ть обвине́ние; *bring suit against,* подава́ть в суд на (+ *acc.*); предъявля́ть иск к; *bring to an end,* положить конец (+ *dat.*); *bring to mind,* напоминать; *bring to one's senses,* наводить на ум. —**bring about,** осуществлять; добиться. —**bring around, 1,** (persuade) уговорить. **2,** (revive) приводить в себя. —**bring back,** вернуть. —**bring down, 1,** (carry down) сносить. **2,** (cause to fall) обрушивать. **3,** (succeed in lowering) снижать. **4,** (overthrow) свергать. —**bring forth,** производить на свет. —**bring in, 1,** (carry in) вносить. **2,** (import) ввозить. **3,** (produce, as revenue) приносить. **4,** (render, as a verdict) выносить. —**bring oneself,** решаться: *I can't bring myself to do it,* не могу решиться на это; не могу заставить себя это сделать; у меня рука не поднимается сделать это. —**bring out, 1,** *literally* выносить. **2,** (produce) выпускать. **3,** in *bring out into the open,* выводить на чистую воду. —**bring up, 1,** (raise; rear) воспитывать. **2,** (raise, as a subject) поднимать. **3,** *mil.* подводить: *bring up the reserves,* подводить резервы. **4,** in *bring up the rear,* замыкать шествие.

brink *n.* край; грань.

briny *adj.* солёный.

briquette *n.* брикет.

brisk *adj.* **1,** (quick) быстрый: *at a brisk pace,* быстрым шагом. **2,** (lively) бойкий; оживлённый: *brisk business,* бойкая/оживлённая торговля. **3,** (fresh and invigorating) свежий; бодрящий.

brisket *n.* грудинка.

bristle *n.* щетина. —*v.i.* **1,** (become stiff and erect) щетиниться. **2,** (show sudden anger) (вс)кипеть гневом; щетиниться. —**bristly,** *adj.* щетинистый.

britches *n.pl.* = **breeches.**

British *adj.* английский; британский. —*n., preceded by* **the** англичане. —**British thermal unit,** британская тепловая единица.

brittle *adj.* хрупкий; ломкий.

broach *n.* **1,** (spit) вертел. **2,** = **brooch.** —*v.t.* затрагивать: *broach a subject,* затрагивать вопрос.

broad *adj.* широкий. —**it's as broad as it is long,** что в лоб, что по лбу.

broadcast *n.* передача; радиопередача; трансляция. —*v.t.* передавать по радио *or* в эфир; транслировать. —*v.i.* вести радиопередачу; вещать.

broadcasting *n.* радиовещание. —*adj.* радиовещательный.

broadcloth *n.* сукно.

broaden *v.t.* расширять. —*v.i.* расширяться.

broad-gauge *adj.* ширококолейный.

broad jump прыжок в длину. —**running broad jump,** прыжок с разбега. —**standing broad jump,** прыжок с места.

broadly *adv.* широко: *interpret broadly,* широко толковать. —**broadly speaking,** вообще говоря.

broad-minded *adj.* терпимый; свободомыслящий; с широкими взглядами.

broad-shouldered *adj.* широкоплечий; плечистый.

broadside *n.* **1,** (firing of a ship's guns) залп. **2,** (verbal attack) град упрёков.

broadsword *n.* палаш.

broadtail *n.* каракульча.

brocade *n.* парча. —**brocaded,** *adj.* парчовый.

broccoli *n.* спаржевая капуста; брокколи.

brochure *n.* брошюра.

broil *v.t.* жарить. —*v.i.* жариться.

broiled *adj.* жареный.

broiler *n.* жаровня.

broiling *adj.* палящий.

broke *adj., colloq.* без гроша. —**go broke,** прогорать. —**go for broke,** идти ва-банк.

broken *adj.* **1,** (fractured) сломанный. **2,** (shattered) разбитый. **3,** (not functioning) испорченный. **4,** (crushed; weakened) надломленный. **5,** (imperfectly spoken) ломаный: *in broken English,* на ломаном английском языке. **6,** (violated, as of promises) несдержанный. **7,** (rugged, as of terrain) пересечённый. **8,** *in* **broken heart,** разбитое сердце; **a broken man,** сломленный человек.

broken-down *adj.* ветхий; обветшалый; полуразрушенный.

broken-hearted *adj.* с разбитым сердцем; убитый горем.

broker *n.* **1,** (agent) комиссионер. **2,** (stockbroker) маклер.

brokerage *n.* **1,** (business of a broker) маклерство. **2,** (broker's fee) комиссионные. —**brokerage house,** маклерская фирма.

bromide *n.* **1,** *chem.* бромид. ♦ *In compounds* бромистый: *sodium bromide,* бромистый натрий. **2,** *med.* бром. **3,** *colloq.* (cliché) банальность.

bromine *n.* бром.

bronchi *n.pl.* бронхи.

bronchial *adj.* бронхиальный. —**bronchial tubes,** бронхи.

bronchitis *n.* бронхит.

brontosaurus *n.* бронтозавр.

bronze *n.* бронза. —*adj.* бронзовый. —*v.t.* бронзировать. —**Bronze Age,** бронзовый век.

brooch *n.* брошь; брошка.

brood *n.* выводок. —*v.i.* **1,** (sit on eggs) сидеть на яйцах; высиживать. **2,** (think long and moodily) задумываться (о).

brood hen наседка.

brook *n.* ручей. —*v.t.* терпеть: *brook no delay,* не терпеть отлагательства. —**brook trout,** ручьевая форель.

broom *n.* метла.

broomstick *n.* палка (для) метлы.

broth *n.* бульон.

brothel *n.* публичный дом; дом терпимости.

brother *n.* брат. —**brotherhood,** *n.* братство.

brother-in-law *n.* **1,** (husband's brother) деверь. **2,** (wife's brother) шурин. **3,** (sister's husband; husband's sister's husband) зять. **4,** (wife's sister's husband) свояк.

brotherly *adj.* братский.

brow *n.* **1,** (eyebrow) бровь. **2,** (forehead) лоб.

browbeat *v.t.* запугивать.

brown *adj.* коричневый. *Brown eyes,* карие глаза. *Brown hair,* каштановые волосы. —*n.* коричневый цвет. —*v.t.* подрумянивать. —*v.i.* **1,** (become sunburned) загорать. **2,** *cooking* подрумяниваться.

brown bear бурый медведь.

brownie *n.* (goblin) домовой.

browse *v.i.* смотреть; осматриваться; оглядываться.

bruise *n.* синяк; ушиб; кровоподтёк. —*v.t.* ушибать.

brunet *n.* брюнет. —**brunette,** *n.* брюнетка.

brunt *n.* основная тяжесть: *bear the brunt of,* вынести основную тяжесть (+ *gen.*).

brush *n.* **1,** (implement) щётка: *hairbrush,* щётка для волос. **2,** (paintbrush) кисть. **3,** (encounter; runin) стычка. **4,** (underbrush) заросль. **5,** *electricity* щётка. —*v.t.* **1,** (clean with a brush) чистить щёткой. *Brush one's teeth,* чистить зубы. **2,** (groom with a brush) приглаживать щёткой. **3,** *fol. by off* (sweep off) счищать; смахивать. —*v.i.* [*usu.* **brush against**] задевать. —**brush aside,** отмахиваться от. —**brush away,** отмахиваться от (*e.g.* от мух). —**brush up,** освежать: *brush up one's Russian,* освежать свой русский язык.

brushwood *n.* **1,** (tree branches) хворост. **2,** (underbrush) заросль.

brushwork *n.* кисть.

brusque *adj.* грубый; резкий; бесцеремонный. —**brusquely,** *adv.* грубо; резко; бесцеремонно. —**brusqueness,** *n.* грубость; резкость.

Brussels sprouts брюссельская капуста.

brutal *adj.* зверский. —**brutality,** *n.* зверство. —**brutally,** *adv.* зверски.

brute *n.* животное; зверь. —*adj.* грубый: *brute force,* грубая сила.

bubble *n.* пузырь. —*v.i.* **1,** (give off bubbles) пузыриться. **2,** (make a bubbling sound) клокотать.

bubo *n.* бубон.

bubonic *adj.* бубонный. —**bubonic plague,** бубонная чума.

buccaneer *n.* пират.

buck *n.* **1,** (male of various animals) самец. **2,** *slang* (dollar) доллар. —*v.t., colloq.* (go against) противиться. —**buck up,** *colloq.* не падать духом. —**pass the buck,** сваливать ответственность на другого.

bucket *n.* ведро. —**drop in the bucket,** капля в море. —**kick the bucket,** *slang* сыграть в ящик.

buckle *n.* пряжка. —*v.t.* застёгивать (пряжкой). —*v.i.* **1,** (warp; curl) коробиться. **2,** (give way, as of one's legs) подламываться. —**buckle down,** запрягаться.

buckram *n.* коленкор.

buckshot *n.* крупная дробь; картечь.

buckskin *n.* оленья шкура.

buckthorn *n.* крушина.

bucktooth *n.* торчащий зуб.

buckwheat *n.* гречиха; гречневая крупа. —*adj.* гречневый.

bucolic *adj.* деревенский.

bud *n.* почка; бутон. —*v.i.* давать почки. —**nip in the bud,** *see* nip.

Buddhism *n.* буддизм. —**Buddhist,** *n.* буддист. —*adj.* буддистский.

buddy *n., colloq.* товарищ.

budge *v.t.* сдвинуть с места. —*v.i.* шевелиться.

budget *n.* бюджет. —*adj.* бюджетный: *budget deficit,* бюджетный дефицит. —*v.t.* предусматривать в бюджете. *Budget one's time,* распределять своё время. —**budgetary,** *adj.* бюджетный.

buff *n.* **1,** (leather) буйволовая кожа. **2,** (tan color) беж. **3,** *colloq.* (enthusiast) любитель. —*v.t.* лощить; полировать. —**in the buff,** нагишом.

buffalo *n.* **1,** (Old World animal) буйвол. **2,** (bison) бизон.

buffer *n.* буфер. —**buffer state,** буферное государство. —**buffer zone,** буферная зона.

buffet[1] (buf-it) *v.t.* **1,** (hit; club) ударять; колотить. **2,** (knock about) бросать (*impers.*): *the waves buffeted*

the ship, пароход бросало по волнам.

buffet[2] (bu-fay) *n.* буфет.

buffoon *n.* шут; скоморох; буффон. —**buffoonery,** *n.* шутовство; скоморошество; буффонада.

bug *n.* **1,** (insect) козявка; букашка. **2,** *colloq.* (defect) неполадка. —*v.t., slang* **1,** (install a hidden microphone in) прослушивать: *this apartment is bugged,* эта квартира прослушивается. **2,** (nag) пилить: *don't bug me!,* не пилите меня!

bugaboo *n.* пугало; жупел. *Also,* **bugbear.**

buggy *n.* кабриолет.

bugle *n.* **1,** (horn) горн. *Bugle call,* сигнал на горне. **2,** *pl.* (beads) стеклярус. —**bugler,** *n.* горнист.

build *v.t. & i.* строить: *build a house,* строить дом. *Build a road,* строить *or* прокладывать дорогу. *Build a fire,* разводить *or* раскладывать костёр. *Build a nest,* вить гнездо. —*n.* сложение: *of sturdy build,* крепкого сложения. —**build on,** пристраивать. —**build up, 1,** (create and add to) создавать. **2,** (increase; make larger) увеличивать; наращивать. **3,** (develop, as an urban area) застраивать. **4,** (develop, as endurance or immunity) вырабатывать. **5,** (increase, as strength or confidence) укреплять. *Build up someone's hopes,* подавать надежду (+ *dat.*). **6,** (make better known) рекламировать. *Build oneself up,* набивать себе цену. **7,** (gradually become greater) накопляться.

builder *n.* строитель.

building *n.* **1,** (structure) здание; дом. **2,** (construction) строительство; построение. —*adj.* строительный: *building materials,* строительные материалы.

build-up *n.* **1,** (publicity; praise) реклама. **2,** *mil.* наращивание (сил).

built-in *adj.* вделанный. *Built-in closet,* стенной шкаф.

bulb *n.* **1,** (light bulb) лампочка. **2,** (of a plant) луковица.

bulbous *adj.* луковичный.

Bulgarian *adj.* болгарский. —*n.* **1,** (person) болгарин; болгарка. **2,** (language) болгарский язык.

bulge *v.i.* раздуваться; распухать; оттопыриваться. —*n.* выпуклость; утолщение.

bulk *n.* **1,** (mass) объём. **2,** (the major part) основная масса; большая часть. —**in bulk,** гуртом.

bulkhead *n.* **1,** (on a ship) переборка. **2,** (wall to hold back water) перемычка.

bulky *adj.* громоздкий; объёмистый.

bull *n.* **1,** (animal) бык. **2,** (papal edict) булла. —**bull in a china shop,** слон в посудной лавке. —**take the bull by the horns,** взять быка за рога.

bulldog *n.* бульдог.

bulldozer *n.* бульдозер.

bullet *n.* пуля. —*adj.* пулевой: *bullet wound,* пулевая рана; *bullet hole,* пулевая пробоина.

bulletin *n.* бюллетень. —**bulletin board,** доска объявлений.

bulletproof *adj.* пулестойкий; пуленепробиваемый; пуленепроницаемый.

bullfight *n.* бой быков.

bullfinch *n.* снегирь.

bullion *n.* слитки: *gold bullion,* золото в слитках.

bullock *n.* вол.

bull's-eye *n.* яблоко мишени. *Hit the bull's-eye,* попасть в цель.

bully *n.* задира; забияка. —*v.t.* запугивать.

bulrush *n.* камыш.

bulwark *n.* **1,** (rampart) вал. **2,** *fig.* (bastion) оплот.

bum *n.*, *slang* лодырь; бродяга.

bumblebee *n.* шмель.

bumbling *adj.* неумелый.

bump *n.* **1,** (swelling) шишка. **2,** (in a road) ухаб. **3,** (jolt) толчок. —*v.t.* удариться (+ *instr.*); стукнуться (+ *instr.*). *Bump heads,* стукнуться головами. *Bump one's head on the door,* удариться/стукнуться головой о дверь. —**bump into, 1,** (collide with) наталкиваться на; сталкиваться с. **2,** (meet by chance) наталкиваться на; натыкаться на; набрести на. —**bump off,** *slang* уложить.

bumper *n.* буфер; бампер. —*adj.*, *in* **bumper crop; bumper harvest,** невиданный урожай.

bumpiness *n.* тряска; *aero.* болтанка.

bumpkin *n.* деревенщина.

bumpy *adj.* тряский; ухабистый.

bun *n.* **1,** (pastry) сдобная булка/булочка; пышка. **2,** (hair worn in a roll) пучок.

bunch *n.* **1,** (collection of similar things fastened together) связка; пучок. **2,** (cluster, as of grapes) кисть; гроздь. **3,** *colloq.* (group of people) группа.

bundle *n.* **1,** (number of things bound together) связка; узел; сверток; пачка; вязанка. **2,** (package) пакет. —*v.t.* **1,** (wrap or tie together) связывать в узел. **2,** (wrap snugly) закутывать. **3,** *fol. by* **off** (send away) спроваживать. —*v.i.* [*usu.* **bundle up**] одеваться тепло. —**bundle of energy,** сгусток энергии. —**bundle of nerves,** комок нервов.

bungalow *n.* домик.

bungle *v.t.* напутать.

bunion *n.* мозоль.

bunk *n.* **1,** (bed) койка. **2,** *slang* (nonsense) вздор; чушь.

bunker *n.* **1,** (storage bin) бункер. **2,** *mil.* блиндаж.

bunny *n.* зайчик.

Bunsen burner горелка Бунзена.

bunting *n.* **1,** (fabric) материя (для флагов). **2,** (bird) овсянка. *Snow bunting,* пуночка.

buoy *n.* буй; бакен. —*v.t.* поднимать: *buoy someone's spirits,* поднимать дух (+ *dat.*).

buoyancy *n.* **1,** (ability to keep afloat) плавучесть. **2,** *fig.* (exuberance) бодрость.

buoyant *adj.* **1,** (floating) плавучий. **2,** *fig.* (lighthearted) бодрый; жизнерадостный.

bur *n.* репейник.

burbot *n.* налим.

burden *n.* **1,** (load) ноша. **2,** *fig.* (encumbrance) бремя. *Be a burden to,* быть в тягость (+ *dat.*). —*v.t.* обременять. —**burden of proof,** обязанность доказывать.

burdensome *adj.* обременительный.

burdock *n.* лопух; репейник.

bureau *n.* **1,** (dresser) комод. **2,** (agency) бюро.

bureaucracy *n.* бюрократия. —**bureaucrat,** *n.* бюрократ. —**bureaucratic,** *adj.* бюрократический.

burgeon *v.i.* **1,** (bud) давать почки. **2,** (expand rapidly) разрастаться.

burgher *n.* бюргер.

burglar *n.* взломщик. —**burglarize,** *v.t.* взламывать. —**burglary,** *n.* кража со взломом.

burgomaster *n.* бургомистр.

burial *n.* погребение. —**burial ground,** кладбище.

—burial mound, курган; могильный холм. —**burial place,** место погребения. —**burial vault,** склеп; усыпальница.

burlap *n.* холст; дерюга. —*adj.* холщовый; дерюжный.

burlesque *n.* бурлеск.

burly *adj.* дородный; рослый.

bur marigold череда.

Burmese *adj.* бирманский. *He is Burmese,* он бирманец. —*n.* **1,** (language) бирманский язык. **2,** *preceded by* **the** (people) бирманцы.

burn *v.t.* **1,** (deliberately) жечь. **2,** (accidentally) обжигать: *burn one's finger,* обжигать себе палец. *Burn oneself,* обжигаться. *Burn a hole in,* прожигать дыру в (+ *prepl.*). **3,** (overcook) сжигать; поджигать. **4,** (cause a burning sensation in) жечь; щипать. **5,** (consume, as gas) потреблять. —*v.i.* **1,** (be on fire) гореть. *Burn to the ground,* сгореть дотла. **2,** (of food) гореть; подгорать; перегорать. **3,** (of light, a lamp, etc.) гореть. **4,** (cause a burning sensation; sting) жечь. **5,** (feel hot; smart) гореть. **6,** *fig.* (be consumed with, as an emotion) гореть: *burn with desire,* гореть желанием. —*n.* **1,** (injury) ожог: *suffer burns,* получить ожоги. **2,** (sunburn) загар. *I got quite a burn,* я сильно загорел(а). —**burn down, 1,** (raze) жечь. **2,** (be burned to the ground) сгореть. —**burn one's fingers** (*fig.*), обжигаться. —**burn out, 1,** (destroy by heat) выжигать. **2,** (go out, as of a bulb) перегореть. **3,** (cause to go out) пережигать. —**burn up, 1,** (burn completely) сгорать. **2,** *colloq.* (infuriate) приводить в ярость. —**he has money to burn,** денег у него — хоть пруд пруди; у него денег куры не клюют. —**smell something burning,** чувствовать, как пахнет гарью.

burner *n.* горелка; конфорка. *Gas burner,* газовый рожок.

burning *n.* сжигание: *burning of trash,* сжигание мусора. —*adj.* **1,** (on fire) горящий; пылающий. **2,** (extremely hot) жгучий; палящий. *Burning sensation,* жжение. *Burning question,* жгучий вопрос.

burnish *v.t.* полировать; воронить.

burnt *adj.* жжёный; горелый. —**burnt offering,** жертвоприношение.

burp *n.*, *colloq.* отрыжка. —*v.i.*, *colloq.* рыгать.

burr *n.* **1,** (rough edge on metal) заусеница. **2,** (guttural pronunciation of the letter R) картавость.

burro *n.* ослик.

burrow *n.* нора. —*v.i.* рыть нору. *Burrowing rodent,* роющий грызун.

bursa *n.* сумка.

bursitis *n.* воспаление сумки.

burst *v.i.* **1,** (break open) лопаться; прорываться. *The bubble burst,* пузырь лопнул. *The dam burst,* плотину прорвало. *The boiler burst,* котёл разорвало. **2,** (go off; explode) взрываться; разрываться; лопаться. **3,** *fol. by* **with** (be filled to overflowing) ломиться (от): *the shelves are bursting with books,* полки ломятся от книг. *He is bursting with energy,* энергия в нём бьёт ключом. *She is bursting with envy,* она лопается от зависти. **4,** *fol. by* **into** (come rushing into) врываться (в); вломиться (в). **5,** *fol. by* **into** *or* **out** (give sudden expression to) разразиться (+ *instr.*): *burst into tears; burst out crying,* разразиться слезами; расплакаться. *Burst out laughing,* разразиться смехом; рассмеяться; расхохотáться. *Burst into applause*, разразúться апло-дисмéнтами. **6,** in *burst into flames*, вспы́хнуть плáменем. —*v.t.* прорывáть: *burst the pipes*, про-рывáть трýбы. —*n.* **1,** (explosion) взрыв. *Burst of flame*, вспы́шка огня́. *Burst of thunder*, удáр грóма. *Burst of machine-gun fire*, пулемётная óчередь. **2,** *fig.* (outburst, as of laughter or applause) взрыв. *Burst of anger*, вспы́шка *or* поры́в гнéва. *Burst of energy*, вспы́шка *or* прилúв энéргии. **3,** (spurt) бросóк.

bury *v.t.* **1,** (place in a grave) хоронúть. **2,** (conceal in the ground) закáпывать; зарывáть. **3,** (cover; hide) закрывáть: *bury one's face in one's hands*, закрывáть лицó рукáми. *Bury one's head in a pillow*, зары-вáться головóй в подýшку. —**bury oneself in**, зарывáться в. *Bury oneself in a book*, уткнýть нос в кнúгу.

bus *n.* автóбус. —*adj.* автóбусный: *bus line*, автó-бусная лúния. *Bus driver*, водúтель автóбуса. *Bus stop*, остановка автóбуса. —*v.t.* перевозúть на автóбусе.

bush *n.* куст. —**beat around the bush**, ходúть вокрýг да óколо; говорúть обиняками.

bushed *adj., colloq.* без ног.

bushel *n.* бýшель.

bushing *n.* втýлка.

bushy *adj.* густóй: *bushy eyebrows*, густы́е брóви. *Bushy tail*, пушúстый хвост.

business *n.* **1,** (commercial dealings) дéло: *on busi-ness*, по дéлу; по делáм. *Business is business*, дéло есть дéло. *Get down to business*, приступúть к дéлу. *Talk business*, говорúть по дéлу. **2,** (establishment) предприя́тие; бúзнес. **3,** (one's own affairs) дéло: *it's none of your business*, э́то не вáше дéло. *Mind your own business!*, не сýйся не в своё дéло! *What business is it of yours?*, а вам какóе дéло? —*adj.* деловóй: *business letter*, деловóе письмó. *Business card*, визúтная кáрточка. *Business address*, служéб-ный áдрес. *Business trip*, командирóвка. —**go about one's business**, занимáться своúми делáми. —**have no business** (+ *verb*), не имéть прáва (+ *inf.*). —**make it one's business to...**, стáвить себé цéлью (+ *inf.*). *I'll make it my business to be there*, я бýду там обязáтельно. —**mean business**, не шутúть. —**mix business with pleasure**, сочетáть полéзное с прия́тным.

businesslike *adj.* деловóй; деловúтый.

businessman *n.* предпринимáтель; бизнесмéн.

bust *n.* **1,** (bosom; sculpture) бюст. **2,** *slang* (flop) провáл; неудáча. —*v.t., slang* **1,** (break) разбивáть. **2,** (bankrupt) разоря́ть.

bustard *n.* дрофá. —**little bustard**, стрéпет.

bustle *n.* суетá; суматóха. —*v.i.* суетúться. —**bus-tling**, *adj.* суетлúвый.

busy *adj.* **1,** (occupied) зáнятый: *I am very busy*, я óчень зáнят. *The line is busy*, лúния занятá. **2,** (full of activity, as of a street) оживлённый. —*v.t.* [*usu.* **busy oneself with**] занимáться (+ *instr.*).

busybody *n.* хлопотýн.

but *conj.* но: *slowly but surely*, мéдленно, но вéрно. *But on the other hand...*, но с другóй сторóны... ♦*Also rendered by* а *and* да: *not he, but his brother*, не он, а егó брат. *She would like to go, but she can't*, онá и пошлá бы, да не мóжет. —*prep.* крóме: *everyone but me*, все, крóме меня́. *What could I do but agree?*, что мне оставáлось, как не согла-

сúться? —*adv.* тóлько; лишь; прóсто. *He is but a child*, он лишь ребёнок. *Had I but known!*, éсли бы я тóлько знал! —*n.* "но": *a slight "but"*, мáлень-кое "но". —**all but**, почтú: *all but certain*, почтú увéрен. —**but for**, éсли бы не. —**but then**, затó; впрóчем.

butane *n.* бутáн.

butcher *n.* **1,** (seller of meat) мяснúк. **2,** *fig.* (mur-derer) палáч. —*v.t.* **1,** (slaughter) рéзать; закáлы-вать. **2,** *fig.* (murder, as a language) ковéркать (язы́к). —**butcher shop**, мяснáя лáвка; мяснóй магазúн.

butchery *n.* бóйня; резня́.

butler *n.* дворéцкий.

butt *n.* **1,** (thick end) торéц; (*of an axe*) óбух; обýх. **2,** (rifle butt) приклáд. **3,** (of a cigarette) окýрок. **4,** *fig.* (target) мишéнь: *butt of jokes*, мишéнь для острóт. —*v.t.* бодáть. —*v.i.* бодáться. —**butt in**, *colloq.* совáться.

butter *n.* мáсло. *Butter knife*, нож для мáсла. *Butter dish*, маслёнка. —*v.t.* **1,** (put butter on) намá-зывать мáслом. **2,** *fol. by* up, *colloq.* (flatter) умáс-ливать; замáсливать; подмáзываться к.

buttercup *n.* лю́тик; курослéп.

butterfly *n.* бáбочка.

buttermilk *n.* пáхта.

buttocks *n.pl.* я́годицы.

button *n.* **1,** (for a garment) пýговица. **2,** (push button) кнóпка. —*v.t.* застёгивать. —*v.i.* застёги-ваться. —**on the button**, *colloq.* рóвно; тóчно.

buttonhole *n.* **1,** (for a button) пéтля. **2,** (for a flower, ribbon, etc.) петлúца.

buttress *n.* **1,** *archit.* контрфóрс. **2,** *fig.* (prop) подпóра. —*v.t.* поддéрживать; подпирáть; под-креплять.

butyl *n.* бутúл.

butylene *n.* бутилéн.

buxom *adj.* полногрýдый.

buy *v.t.* покупáть (*pfv.* купúть). *Buy one's wife a present*, купúть подáрок женé. —*n.* **1,** (purchase) покýпка. *You got a good buy*, вы удáчно купúли. **2,** *colloq.* (bargain) вы́годная покýпка. —**buy up**, скупáть; раскупáть; закупáть.

buyer *n.* **1,** (purchaser) покупáтель. **2,** *comm.* (pur-chasing agent) закýпщик.

buzz *v.i.* жужжáть. —*n.* **1,** (buzzing) жужжáние. **2,** (hum; rumble) гул. —**give someone a buzz**, *colloq.* позвонúть комý-нибудь.

buzzard *n.* каню́к; сары́ч.

buzzer *n.* зýммер.

by *prep.* **1,** (near) у; óколо. *Stand by the window*, стоя́ть у окнá. **2,** (beside) пóдле; вóзле; ря́дом с. **3,** (past; beyond) мúмо: *pass by someone's house*, проходúть мúмо чьегó-нибудь дóма. **4,** (through the action or agency of) *rendered by the instr. case*: *done by me*, сдéлан мнóю; *by force of arms*, сúлой орýжия. *What do you mean by that?*, что вы хотúте э́тим сказáть? **5,** (mode of travel) на (+ *prepl.*). ♦*Also rendered by the instr. case*: *go by train*, éхать на пóезде *or* пóездом. **6,** (with verbs of holding, seizing, etc.) за (+ *acc.*): *hold by the hand*, держáть за рýку; *seize by the collar*, схватúть за шúворот. **7,** (means of communication) по: *by telephone*, по теле-фóну. **8,** *expressing various relationships* по: *by mistake*, по ошúбке; *by nature*, по прирóде; *by pro-fession*, по профéссии; *call by name*, называ́ть по и́мени; *judging by this,* су́дя по э́тому. **9,** (according to) по: *by my watch,* по мои́м часа́м. **10,** (before; no later than) к: *by two o'clock,* к двум часа́м. **11,** (born of) от: *a child by her first husband,* ребёнок от пе́рвого му́жа. **12,** (in units of) на: *sell by the pound,* продава́ть на фунт. **13,** (in groups of) по: *one by one,* по одному́; оди́н за други́м; *two by two,* по́ дво́е. **14,** (in succession) за: *step by step,* шаг за ша́гом. *Day by day,* изо дня в день. *Little by little,* ма́ло-пома́лу. **15,** (in or to the amount or degree of) на: *older than you by two years,* ста́рше вас на два го́да. **16,** *in multiplication and division* на: *multiply/divide ten by five,* помно́жить/раздели́ть де́сять на пять. **17,** *with dimensions* на: *six meters by five,* шесть ме́тров на пять. **18,** *in various miscellaneous expressions:* by day, днём; *by night,* но́чью; *by heart,* наизу́сть; *by chance,* случа́йно;

by sight, в лицо́; *by degrees,* постепе́нно; *by candle-light,* при свеча́х. —*adv.* **1,** (near) бли́зко; ря́дом. *Be standing by,* стоя́ть ря́дом. **2,** (past) ми́мо: *pass by,* пройти́ ми́мо. —**by and by,** со вре́менем. —**by and large,** в це́лом; в основно́м. —**by the way,** ме́жду про́чим; кста́ти.

bye-bye *interj.* до свида́нья!

bygone *adj.* мину́вший; было́й. —**let bygones be bygones,** что прошло́, то прошло́.

bylaw *n.* пра́вило; постановле́ние.

bypass *n.* обхо́д. —*v.t.* обходи́ть.

by-product *n.* побо́чный проду́кт.

byroad *n.* просёлок; просёлочная доро́га.

bystander *n.* свиде́тель; очеви́дец.

byword *n.* посло́вица; погово́рка. *Become a by-word,* войти́ в посло́вицу.

Byzantine *adj.* византи́йский.

C

C, c тре́тья бу́ква англи́йского алфави́та. —*n.* **1,** (musical note) до. **2,** (school grade) тро́йка.

cab *n.* **1,** (taxi) такси́. *Cab driver,* шофёр такси́. **2,** (driver's compartment) каби́на.

cabal *n.* **1,** (group of plotters) кли́ка. **2,** (plot) за́говор.

cabana *n.* купа́льная каби́на.

cabaret *n.* кабаре́.

cabbage *n.* капу́ста. *Stuffed cabbage,* голубцы́. —**cabbage butterfly,** капу́стница. —**cabbage soup,** щи.

cabin *n.* **1,** (hut; cottage) хи́жина; до́мик. *Log cabin,* бреве́нчатый до́мик. **2,** (stateroom on a ship) каю́та. **3,** (of an airplane) каби́на. —**cabin boy,** ю́нга.

cabinet *n.* **1,** (cupboard; case) шкаф. *Medicine cabinet,* апте́чка. **2,** (of a radio, television set, etc.) ко́рпус. **3,** (advisory body of a chief executive) кабине́т.

cabinetmaker *n.* столя́р.

cable *n.* **1,** (rope or wire) кана́т; трос. **2,** (underwater telegraph line) ка́бель. **3,** (cablegram) телегра́мма; каблогра́мма. —*v.t. & i.* телеграфи́ровать.

cable car подвесна́я вагоне́тка; фуникулёр.

cablegram *n.* каблогра́мма; телегра́мма.

cable television ка́бельное телеви́дение.

cabriolet *n.* кабриоле́т.

cacao *n.* кака́о.

cache *n.* тайни́к. *Cache of weapons,* та́йный склад ору́жия.

cackle *v.i.* (of a hen) куда́хтать; (of a goose) гогота́ть. —*n.* куда́хтанье; го́гот.

cacophonous *adj.* неблагозву́чный; какофони́ческий. —**cacophony,** *n.* неблагозву́чие; какофо́ния.

cactus *n.* ка́ктус.

cad *n.* хам.

cadaver *n.* труп. —**cadaverous,** *adj.* мёртвенный; помертве́лый.

caddish *adj.* ха́мский.

caddy *n.* ча́йница.

cadence *n.* **1,** (rhythm; beat) ритм; такт. **2,** *music* каде́нция.

cadenza *n.* каде́нция.

cadet *n.* **1,** *mil.* (student) курса́нт. **2,** *cap.* (member of the Russian Constitutional Democrat party) каде́т.

cadmium *n.* ка́дмий.

cadre *n.* ка́дровый соста́в. —**cadres,** *n.pl.* ка́дры.

caecum *n.* = **cecum.**

Caesarean section ке́сарево сече́ние.

café *n.* кафе́.

cafeteria *n.* кафете́рий.

caffeine *n.* кофеи́н.

caftan *n.* кафта́н.

cage *n.* кле́тка. —*v.t.* сажа́ть в кле́тку. *Feel caged in,* чу́вствовать себя́ как в кле́тке.

cagey *also,* **cagy** *adj.* осторо́жный; себе́ на уме́.

cahoots *n.pl., slang, in* **in cahoots with,** в сго́воре с.

caisson *n.* **1,** (watertight chamber) кессо́н. **2,** (ammunition wagon) заря́дный я́щик.

cajole *v.t.* угова́ривать; задо́бривать. —**cajolery,** *n.* угово́ры.

cake *n.* **1,** (pastry) торт; кекс. *Sponge cake,* бискви́т. **2,** (patty of meat or fish) котле́та: *fish cakes,* ры́бные котле́ты. **3,** (bar, as of soap) кусо́к; брусо́к. —*v.i.* спека́ться; ссыха́ться.

calabash *n.* горля́нка.

calamity *n.* бе́дствие. —**calamitous,** *adj.* бе́дственный.

calcify *v.t. & i.* превраща́ть(ся) в и́звесть.

calcium *n.* кáльций. —*adj.* кáльциевый. —**calcium carbide,** углерóдистый кáльций. —**calcium carbonate,** углекúслый кáльций. —**calcium chloride,** хлóристый кáльций. —**calcium oxide,** óкись кáльция.

calculate *v.t.* **1,** (compute) рассчúтывать; подсчúтывать; вычислять; исчислять. **2,** (intend; design) рассчúтывать: *calculated for effect,* рассчúтанный на эффéкт.

calculated *adj.* рассчúтанный: *calculated rudeness,* рассчúтанная грýбость. —**calculated risk,** риск с тóчным расчéтом; обдýманный риск.

calculating *adj.* **1,** (designed to calculate) счéтный: *calculating machine,* счётная машúна. **2,** (shrewd; cautious) расчётливый; себé на умé.

calculation *n.* расчёт; подсчёт; вычислéние; исчислéние.

calculator *n.* калькулятор; арифмóметр.

calculus *n.* исчислéние.

caldron *also,* **cauldron** *n.* котёл.

calendar *n.* календáрь. —*adj.* календáрный: *calendar year,* календáрный год.

calender *n.* калáндр.

calf *n.* **1,** (young of the cow) телёнок. **2,** (young of other animals) детёныш. **3,** (rear part of the leg below the knee) икрá. —*adj.* [*also,* **calf's**] телячий: *calf's liver,* телячья печёнка.

calfskin *n.* телячья кóжа; опóек.

caliber *also,* **calibre** *n.* **1,** (diameter) калúбр. **2,** *fig.* (ability) кáчества: *person of high caliber,* человéк высóких кáчеств.

calibrate *v.t.* калибровáть. —**calibration,** *n.* калибровáние.

calibre *n.* = **caliber.**

calico *n.* **1,** *U.S.* (printed cloth) сúтец. **2,** *Brit.* (unprinted) миткáль. —*adj.* сúтцевый; миткáлевый.

californium *n.* калифóрний.

caliper *also,* **calliper** *n., usu. pl.* кронцúркуль.

caliph *n.* халúф; калúф. —**caliphate,** *n.* халифáт.

calisthenics *also,* **callisthenics** *n.* гимнáстика; зарядка.

calk *v.t.* = **caulk.**

call *v.t.* **1,** (shout to) звать. **2,** (utter in a loud voice) называть: *who called my name?,* кто назвáл моé úмя? **3,** (summon) звать; вызывáть. **4,** (telephone) звонúть; вызывáть. **5,** (name) называть: *what is this called?,* как это называется? *Call it what you will,* называйте, как хотúте. **6,** (describe as specified) называть: *call someone a liar,* назвáть когó-нибудь лжецóм. *You could hardly call her beautiful,* её нельзя назвáть красúвой. **7,** (declare) признавáть: *call the game a draw,* признáть пáртию ничьéй. **8,** (convene) созывáть. **9,** *with various nouns: call a strike,* объявúть забастóвку; *call (someone) names,* обругáть; *call the roll,* дéлать переклúчку; *call attention to,* обращáть (чьё-нибудь) внимáние на. **10,** *in various expressions: call to mind,* напоминáть; *call to order,* призывáть к порядку; *call to arms,* призывáть к орýжию; *call in question,* стáвить под вопрóс. —*v.i.* **1,** (shout) звать: *call for help,* звать на пóмощь. **2,** (phone) звонúть. **3,** (of a ship) захóдить: *call at a port,* заходúть в порт. —*n.* **1,** (cry; shout) крик: *call for help,* крик о пóмощи. **2,** (phone communication; summons) вызов. *Were there any calls for me?,* меня никтó не вызывáл? **3,** (appeal)

призыв: *a call to action,* призыв к дéйствию. **4,** (cry of a bird or animal) крик. *Mating call,* токовáние. **5,** (sound of a horn) сигнáл: *bugle call,* сигнáл на гóрне. **6,** (visit) визúт: *courtesy call,* визúт вéжливости. *Pay a call on,* заходúть к; приходúть с визúтом к. —**call aside,** отводúть в стóрону. —**call back, 1,** (summon back; recall) отзывáть. **2,** (telephone again) звонúть ещё раз. —**call down,** *colloq.* отчúтать. —**call for, 1,** (come and pick up) заходúть за; заезжáть за. **2,** (appeal for; advocate) призывáть к *or* на. **3,** (require) трéбовать. —**call forth,** вызывáть. —**call in, 1,** (summon) вызывáть. **2,** (phone in) сообщáть по телефóну. **3,** (retire from circulation) изымáть из обращéния. —**call off, 1,** (summon away) отзывáть. **2,** (read aloud) называть. **3,** (cancel) отменять. —**call on, 1,** (ask to recite, as in class) спрáшивать; вызывáть. **2,** (allow to speak) предоставлять слóво (+ *dat.*). **3,** (visit briefly) посещáть; заходúть к. **4,** (urge) призывáть. **5,** (appeal to, as for help) обращáться к. —**call out, 1,** (shout) кричáть; выкрúкивать. *Call out one's name,* выкрикнуть своé úмя. **2,** (summon) вызывáть. —**call up, 1,** (call on the telephone) вызывáть; звонúть. **2,** (summon for military service) призывáть.

caller *n.* гость; посетúтель.

calligraphy *n.* каллигрáфия. —**calligraphic,** *adj.* каллиграфúческий.

calling *n.* призвáние: *follow one's calling,* слéдовать своемý призвáнию. —**calling card,** визúтная кáрточка.

calliper *n.* = **caliper.**

callisthenics *n.* = **calisthenics.**

call number шифр.

callous *adj.* **1,** [*also,* **calloused**] (hardened) огрубéлый; загрубéлый; мозóлистый. **2,** *fig.* (unfeeling) чéрствый. —**callousness,** *n.* чéрствость.

callow *adj.* зелёный; безýсый.

call sign позывнóй сигнáл; позывнúе.

call-up *n.* призыв.

callus *n.* мозóль.

calm *adj.* спокóйный: *calm sea,* спокóйное мóре; *calm voice,* спокóйный гóлос. —*n.* **1,** (tranquillity) спокóйствие. **2,** (absence of wind) затúшье. *The calm before the storm,* затúшье пéред грозóй. —*v.t.* успокáивать. —*v.i.* [*usu.* **calm down**] успокáиваться. —**calmly,** *adv.* спокóйно.

caloric *adj.* теплoвóй. *Caloric content,* калорúйность.

calorie *n.* калóрия.

calorimeter *n.* калорúметр; тепломéр.

calumniate *v.t.* клеветáть на. —**calumnious,** *adj.* клеветнúческий. —**calumny,** *n.* клеветá.

Calvary *n.* Голгóфа.

calve *v.i.* телúться.

calyx *n.* чáшечка.

cam *n.* кулáк; кулачóк; эксцéнтрик.

camaraderie *n.* товáрищество.

cambium *n.* кáмбий.

cambric *n.* батúст.

camel *n.* верблюд.

camellia *n.* камéлия.

camel's hair 1, (hair) верблюжья шерсть. **2,** (cloth) верблюжье сукнó. —**camel's-hair,** *adj.* верблюжий.

cameo *n.* камéя.

camera *n.* фотографúческий аппарáт; фотоаппарáт. —**movie camera**, киноаппарáт. —**television camera**, телевизиóнная кáмера.

cameraman *n.* кинооперáтор.

camomile *also*, **chamomile** *n.* ромáшка; пупáвка.

camouflage *n.* маскирóвка. —*v.t.* маскировáть.

camp *n.* лáгерь: *prisoner-of-war camp*, лáгерь для военноплéнных. *Split into two camps*, расколóться на два лáгеря. —*v.i.* **1,** (set up camp) располагáться лáгерем. **2,** *fol. by* **out** (sleep outdoors) жить (как) на бивуáках.

campaign *n.* кампáния; похóд. —*v.i.* проводúть кампáнию.

campanula *n.* колокóльчик.

campfire *n.* костёр.

camphor *n.* камфарá.

campsite *n.* кéмпинг.

campus *n.* университéтский городóк.

camshaft *n.* распределúтельный вал; кулачкóвый вал.

can[1] *v.aux.* **1,** (be able) мочь: *I cannot come today*, я не могý прийтú сегóдня. *What can I do for you?*, чем могý быть полéзен? *Can you see the blackboard?*, вам виднá доскá? *Run as fast as you can*, бегúте как мóжно быстрéе. **2,** (know how) умéть: *can you drive a car?*, вы умéете водúть машúну?

can[2] *n.* **1,** (small container) бáнка. *Tin can*, жестáнка; консéрвная бáнка. *Beer can*, жестáнка из-под пúва. **2,** (large container) бидóн: *milk can*, бидóн для молокá. *Garbage can*, мýсорный áщик. *Watering can*, лéйка. —*v.t.* (preserve) консервúровать. —**can opener**, консéрвный нож.

Canadian *adj.* канáдский. —*n.* канáдец; канáдка.

canal *n.* канáл.

canard *n.* ýтка.

canary *n.* канарéйка. —**canary-yellow**, *adj.* канарéечный; канарéечного цвéта.

cancan *n.* канкáн.

cancel *v.t.* **1,** (call off) отменáть. **2,** (void) отменáть; аннулúровать. **3,** (mark, as a postage stamp) погашáть. **4,** *fol. by* **out** (offset) сводúть на нет. **5,** *math.* сокращáть.

cancellation *n.* **1,** (calling off) отмéна. **2,** (voiding) отмéна; аннулúрование. **3,** (marking of postage stamps) погашéние; (mark so made) гашéние. **4,** *math.* сокращéние.

cancer *n.* **1,** (disease) рак. **2,** *cap.*, *astron.* Рак. —*adj.* рáковый: *cancer cell*, рáковая клéтка. —**Tropic of Cancer**, трóпик Рáка.

cancerous *adj.* рáковый.

candelabrum *n.* канделáбр.

candid *adj.* откровéнный; чистосердéчный.

candidacy *n.* кандидатýра. —**candidate**, *n.* кандидáт.

candied *adj.* засáхаренный.

candle *n.* свечá. —**burn the candle at both ends**, жечь свечý с двух концóв. —**not hold a candle to**, в подмётки не годúться (+ *dat.*). —**the game is not worth the candle**, игрá не стóит свеч.

candlelight *n.* свет свечú: *by candlelight*, при свéте свечú; при свечáх. —**candle-lit**, *adj.* освещённый свечáми.

candlepower *n.* свечá: *bulb of forty candlepower*, лáмпочка в сóрок свечéй.

candlestick *n.* подсвéчник.

candor *also*, **candour** *n.* откровéнность; чистосердéчность. —**in all candor**, со всей откровéнностью.

candy *n.* конфéты. *Piece of candy*, конфéта. —*adj.* конфéтный: *candy wrapper*, конфéтная обёртка.

cane *n.* **1,** (walking stick) пáлка, трость. **2,** (plant) тростнúк; камýш. *Sugar cane*, сáхарный тростнúк. —*v.t.* бить пáлкой. —**cane sugar**, тростникóвый сáхар.

canine *adj.* собáчий. —**canine tooth**, клык.

canister *n.* **1,** (container for tea or spices) корóбка; бáнка. **2,** (part of a gas mask; device for dispensing tear gas) корóбка. —**canister shot**, картéчь.

canker *n.* áзва.

canned *adj.* консервúрованный. *Canned food*, консéрвы. *Canned meat*, мяснúе консéрвы. *Canned vegetables*, овощнúе консéрвы. *Canned fruit*, консервúрованные фрýкты.

cannery *n.* консéрвная фáбрика.

cannibal *n.* людоéд. —**cannibalism**, *n.* людоéдство. —**cannibalistic**, *adj.* людоéдский.

cannon *n.* **1,** (weapon) пýшка. **2,** *Brit.* (carom) карамбóль. —**cannon ball**, пýшечное ядрó. —**cannon fodder**, пýшечное мáсо.

cannonade *n.* пýшечная пальбá; канонáда.

cannot *v.* = **can not**.

canny *adj.* **1,** (cautious) осмотрúтельный. **2,** (shrewd) себé на умé.

canoe *n.* канóэ; чёлн; челнóк; байдáрка. —**canoeist**, *n.* каноúст.

canon *n.* **1,** (religious law; principle; rule) канóн. **2,** (clergyman) канóник. **3,** *music* канóн. —**canon law**, канонúческое прáво.

canonical *adj.* канонúческий.

canonize *v.t.* канонизúровать; причислáть к лúку святúх.

canopy *n.* балдахúн; пóлог.

cant *n.* жаргóн; аргó. *Thieves' cant*, воровскóй жаргóн; блат.

cantaloupe *n.* канталýпа.

cantankerous *adj.* сварлúвый; вздóрный.

cantata *n.* кантáта.

canteen *n.* **1,** (flask) флáга; флáжка. **2,** *mil.* воéнный магазúн; клуб-столóвая.

canter *n.* лёгкий галóп. —*v.i.* идтú лёгким галóпом.

cantilever *n.* консóль. —**cantilever bridge**, консóльный мост.

canto *n.* песнь.

canton *n.* кантóн. —**cantonal**, *adj.* кантонáльный.

cantor *n.* кáнтор.

canvas *n.* **1,** (cloth) парусúна. **2,** (a piece of such material on which to paint) холст. **3,** (painting on canvas) полотнó. **4,** (loosely woven cloth for needlework) канвá. —*adj.* парусúновый.

canvass *v.t.* **1,** (travel through) объéздить. **2,** (poll; survey) опрáшивать.

canyon *n.* каньóн; ущéлье.

cap *n.* **1,** (fur) шáпка; (small) кéпка; (part of a uniform) фурáжка; (fool's, chef's, etc.) колпáк. **2,** (of a mushroom) шляпка. **3,** (covering, as for a bottle) колпачóк. *Lens cap*, крúшка объектúва. **4,** (percussion cap) кáпсюль. —*v.t.* **1,** (cover) покрывáть. **2,** (complete) довершáть. **3,** (exceed; top) превосходúть. —**to cap all**, в довершéние всегó.

capability *n.* **1,** (ability) спосóбность. **2,** *usu. pl.*

(potential ability) возмо́жности.
capable adj. спосо́бный. *Capable of anything*, спосо́бен на всё. **—capably,** adv. уме́ло.
capacious adj. ёмкий; вмести́тельный.
capacitator n. конденса́тор.
capacity n. 1, (ability to hold; volume) вмести́мость; ёмкость. *Filled to capacity*, по́лный до отка́за; битко́м наби́тый. 2, (ability) спосо́бность: *capacity for learning*, спосо́бность к учёбе; *carrying capacity*, пропускна́я спосо́бность. 3, (maximum level of production) мо́щность: *operate at full capacity*, рабо́тать на по́лную мо́щность. 4, (position; function) ка́чество: *in the capacity of*, в ка́честве (+ *gen.*). **—adj.** по́лный: *play to capacity crowds*, де́лать по́лные сбо́ры; идти́ с аншла́гом.
cape n. 1, (point of land) мыс. 2, (garment) накидка; пелери́на.
caper n. 1, (playful leap) прыжо́к. 2, (prank) вы́ходка; прока́за. 3, pl. (condiment) ка́персы.
capillary n. капилля́р. **—adj.** капилля́рный.
capital n. 1, (capital city) столи́ца. 2, econ. капита́л. **—adj.** 1, (containing the seat of government) столи́чный: *capital city*, столи́чный го́род. 2, econ. капита́льный. *Capital investment*, капиталовложе́ния. 3, (punishable by death) наказу́емый сме́ртью. *Capital punishment*, сме́ртная казнь; вы́сшая ме́ра наказа́ния. 4, (of a letter) прописно́й; загла́вный; большо́й. *This word is spelled with a capital letter*, э́то сло́во пи́шется с большо́й бу́квы. 5, colloq. (excellent; first-rate) превосхо́дный; первокла́ссный. **—make capital of,** спекули́ровать на; выезжа́ть на.
capitalism n. капитали́зм.
capitalist n. капитали́ст. **—adj.** [also, **capitalistic**] капиталисти́ческий.
capitalization n. 1, gram. употребле́ние прописны́х букв: *the rules for capitalization*, пра́вила употребле́ния прописны́х букв. 2, econ. капитализа́ция.
capitalize v.t. 1, (write with a capital letter) писа́ть с большо́й бу́квы. 2, (convert into capital) капитализи́ровать. **—v.i.** [usu. **capitalize on**] (use to advantage) испо́льзовать; по́льзоваться.
capitol n. капито́лий.
capitulate v.i. капитули́ровать. **—capitulation,** n. капитуля́ция.
capon n. каплу́н.
caprice n. капри́з; причу́да; при́хоть. **—capricious,** adj. капри́зный; причу́дливый; прихотли́вый.
Capricorn n. Козеро́г. **—Tropic of Capricorn,** тро́пик Козеро́га.
capsize v.t. опроки́дывать. **—v.i.** опроки́дываться.
capstan n. кабеста́н; шпиль.
capsule n. 1, (for enclosing a dose of medicine) ка́псула. 2, (detachable part of a rocket) ка́псула; каби́на. **—adj.** кра́ткий: *capsule summary*, кра́ткое изложе́ние.
captain n. 1, (military rank) капита́н; (naval rank) капита́н пе́рвого ра́нга. 2, (ship's commander) капита́н; командуи́р. 3, sports капита́н.
caption n. 1, (heading) заголо́вок. 2, (of an illustration or cartoon) по́дпись. 3, motion pictures субти́тр.
captious adj. придирчивый.
captivate v.t. пленя́ть; очаро́вывать; восхища́ть. **—captivating,** adj. плени́тельный; очарова́тельный; восхити́тельный.

captive n. пле́нник; пле́нный. **—adj.** взя́тый в плен; пле́нный. **—be taken captive,** попа́сть в плен. **—take captive,** взять в плен. **—hold captive,** держа́ть в плену́.
captivity n. 1, (of people) плен; нево́ля. 2, (of animals) нево́ля: *breed in captivity*, размножа́ться в нево́ле.
capture v.t. 1, (take or seize by force) захва́тывать. 2, (take prisoner) взять в плен. 3, (win in a contest) завоёвывать. 4, chess брать. 5, (record for posterity) запечатлева́ть: *capture on film*, запечатлева́ть на плёнке. **—n.** захва́т; поймка; взя́тие в плен.
capuchin n. 1, cap. (monk) капуци́н. 2, (cloak) плащ с капюшо́ном. 3, (monkey) капуци́н.
capybara n. водосви́нка.
car n. 1, (automobile) маши́на; автомоби́ль. 2, (of a train) ваго́н.
caracul also, **karakul** n. 1, (sheep) кара́ку́льская овца́. 2, (fur) кара́куль.
carafe n. графи́н.
caramel n. караме́ль. **—adj.** караме́льный.
carat n. 1, (unit of weight for gems) кара́т. 2, = **karat.**
caravan n. карава́н.
caravel n. караве́лла.
caraway n. тмин. **—adj.** тми́нный.
carbide n. карби́д.
carbine n. караби́н.
carbohydrate n. углево́д.
carbolic adj. карбо́ловый. **—carbolic acid,** карбо́ловая кислота́; карбо́лка.
carbon n. углеро́д.
carbonate n. карбона́т; углеки́слая соль. **—v.t.** газировать: *carbonated beverages*, газиро́ванные напитки.
carbon copy 1, (copy made with carbon paper) ко́пия. *Make carbon copies*, писа́ть под копи́рку. 2, colloq. (perfect likeness) то́чная ко́пия.
carbon dioxide углеки́слый газ.
carbonic acid углекислота́; у́гольная кислота́.
carbon monoxide уга́рный газ.
carbon paper копирова́льная бума́га; копи́рка.
carborundum n. карбору́нд.
carbuncle n. карбу́нкул.
carburetor also, **carburettor** n. карбюра́тор.
carcass n. ту́ша.
carcinogen n. канцероге́н; карциноге́н. **—carcinogenic,** adj. канцероге́нный.
card n. 1, (piece of stiff paper used for various purposes) ка́рточка: *calling card*, визитная ка́рточка. 2, (playing card) ка́рта: *play cards*, игра́ть в ка́рты. 3, (certificate of membership) биле́т: *membership card*, чле́нский биле́т. **—adj.** ка́рточный: *card trick/catalogue*, ка́рточный фо́кус/катало́г. **—v.t.** чеса́ть: *card wool*, чеса́ть шерсть. **—house of cards,** ка́рточный до́мик. **—it was not in the cards,** ви́дно, не судьба́! **—lay one's cards on the table,** вы́ложить ка́рты на стол.
cardboard n. карто́н. **—adj.** карто́нный.
card file картоте́ка.
cardiac adj. серде́чный.
cardigan n. шерстяна́я ко́фточка.
cardinal adj. основно́й; кардина́льный. *Cardinal principle*, основно́й при́нцип. **—n.** 1, (prelate) кардина́л. 2, (bird) кардина́л. **—cardinal number,**

коли́чественное числи́тельное. —**cardinal point**, страна́ све́та.

cardiogram *n.* кардиогра́мма.

cardiograph *n.* кардио́граф.

cardiology *n.* кардиоло́гия. —**cardiologist**, *n.* кардио́лог.

cardiovascular *adj.* серде́чно-сосу́дистый.

cardsharp *n.* шу́лер.

card table ка́рточный стол; ло́мберный стол.

care *n.* **1,** (concern; source of concern) забо́та: *my chief care*, гла́вная моя́ забо́та. *She hasn't a care in the world*, она́ не име́ет никаки́х забо́т. **2,** (close attention) ухо́д: *care of the sick*, ухо́д за больны́ми; *care of one's car*, ухо́д за маши́ной. *Require constant care*, тре́бовать постоя́нного ухо́да. *He received excellent care*, за ним был прекра́сный ухо́д. **3,** (charge; supervision) попече́ние: *he was left in the care of his grandmother*, он оста́лся на попече́нии ба́бушки. *Under the care of a physician*, под наблюде́нием врача́. **4,** (painstaking application) тща́тельность. *With the greatest of care*, са́мым тща́тельным о́бразом. **5,** (caution) осторо́жность: *handle with care*, обраща́ться с осторо́жностью. —*v.i.* забо́титься: *care about someone*, забо́титься о ком-нибудь. *I don't care*, мне всё равно́. *What do I care?*, како́е мне де́ло? *I don't care what happens*, мне безразли́чно, что бу́дет. —*v.t.* хоте́ть: *I don't care to go*, мне не хо́чется идти́. —**care for, 1,** (tend) забо́титься о; уха́живать за. **2,** (be fond of) люби́ть. **3,** (like; wish) хоте́ть: *would you care for another cup of tea?*, хоти́те ещё ча́шку ча́ю? —**care of**, по а́дресу (+ *gen.*); че́рез; для переда́чи (+ *dat.*). —**take care**, быть осторо́жным. —**take care of, 1,** (care for) забо́титься о; уха́живать за. **2,** (guard; protect) бере́чь; побере́чь. **3,** (attend to) занима́ться (+ *instr.*); выполня́ть. **4,** in *take care of oneself*, побере́чься. —**take care not to**, смотри́те, не (+ *imperative*).

careen *v.i.* крени́ться. *The car careened from side to side*, маши́ну броса́ло из стороны́ в сто́рону.

career *n.* карье́ра. —**careerist**, *n.* карьери́ст.

carefree *adj.* беззабо́тный; беспе́чный.

careful *adj.* **1,** (cautious) осторо́жный. *Be careful!*, осторо́жно!; бу́дьте осторо́жны! **2,** (painstaking) тща́тельный.

carefully *adv.* **1,** (with caution) осторо́жно. **2,** (with great care) тща́тельно. **3,** (with close attention) внима́тельно.

careless *adj.* **1,** (slipshod) небре́жный. *Make a careless mistake*, допусти́ть оши́бку по небре́жности. **2,** (incautious) неосторо́жный. —**carelessly**, *adv.* небре́жно; неосторо́жно. —**carelessness**, *n.* небре́жность; неосторо́жность.

caress *n.* ла́ска. —*v.t.* ласка́ть.

caretaker *n.* дво́рник.

carfare *n.* проездна́я пла́та.

cargo *n.* груз. —*adj.* грузово́й: *cargo ship*, грузово́е су́дно.

caricature *n.* карикату́ра.

caries *n.* костое́да; ка́риес.

carillon *n.* карильо́н.

carious *adj.* карио́зный.

carmine *n.* карми́н. —*adj.* карми́нный; карми́новый.

carnage *n.* резня́; бо́йня.

carnal *adj.* **1,** (of the flesh) пло́тский. **2,** (sexual) полово́й.

carnation *n.* гвозди́ка.

carnival *n.* карнава́л.

carnivore *n.* плотоя́дное живо́тное. —**carnivorous**, *adj.* плотоя́дный.

carol *n.* рожде́ственская пе́сня; коля́дка.

carom *n.* карамбо́ль. —*v.i.* отска́кивать.

carouse *v.i.* кути́ть; гуля́ть. —**carousal**, *n.* кутёж; попо́йка.

carousel also, **carrousel** *n.* карусе́ль.

carouser *n.* кути́ла; гуля́ка.

carp *n.* карп; саза́н; кара́сь. —*v.i.* придира́ться.

carpenter *n.* пло́тник. —**carpentry**, *n.* пло́тничье *or* пло́тничное де́ло; пло́тничество.

carpet *n.* ковёр. —*v.t.* устила́ть ковро́м. —**call on the carpet**, *colloq.* вы́звать на ковёр.

carping *adj.* приди́рчивый.

carriage *n.* **1,** (vehicle) коля́ска; экипа́ж; каре́та. *Baby carriage*, де́тская коля́ска. *Gun carriage*, лафе́т. **2,** *Brit.* (railroad passenger car) ваго́н. **3,** (moving part, as of a typewriter) каре́тка. **4,** (manner of carrying oneself; bearing) оса́нка; вы́правка.

carrier *n.* **1,** (one who carries something) перено́счик. **2,** (person transmitting a disease) носи́тель; (insect doing same) перено́счик. **3,** (aircraft carrier) авиано́сец. —**carrier pigeon**, почто́вый го́лубь.

carrion *n.* па́даль; мертвечи́на.

carrot *n.* морко́вь. —*adj.* морко́вный: *carrot juice*, морко́вный сок. —**carrot and stick**, поли́тика кнута́ и пря́ника.

carrousel *n.* = **carousel.**

carry *v.t.* **1,** (bear) нести́: *carry a child in one's arms*, нести́ ребёнка на рука́х; *carry a pack on one's back*, нести́ ра́нец на спине́. **2,** (have or keep on one's person) носи́ть; держа́ть при себе́. *Carry money in one's pocket*, носи́ть де́ньги в карма́не. **3,** (transport) переноси́ть; (by vehicle) везти́; перевози́ть: *carry passengers and freight*, перевози́ть пассажи́ров и това́ры. **4,** (have in stock) держа́ть; торгова́ть. **5,** (be pregnant with) вына́шивать. **6,** (print, as an article) помеща́ть. **7,** (extend) доводи́ть: *carry to an extreme*, доводи́ть до кра́йности. **8,** *in various miscellaneous expressions*: *carry weight*, име́ть вес; *carry insurance*, быть застрахо́ванным. —*v.i.* **1,** (travel, as of sound) доноси́ться. *His voice doesn't carry*, его́ го́лос пло́хо слы́шен. **2,** (be approved): *the resolution carried*, резолю́ция была́ при́нята. —**be/get carried away**, увлека́ться. —**carry forward**, *bookkeeping* транспорти́ровать. —**carry on, 1,** (engage in; conduct) вести́. **2,** (continue; keep up) продолжа́ть. **3,** *colloq.* (behave wildly) беси́ться; рвать и мета́ть. —**carry oneself**, держа́ться. —**carry out, 1,** *literally* выноси́ть. **2,** (fulfill, as an order, promise, etc.) выполня́ть; исполня́ть. **3,** (conduct, as an investigation, experiment, etc.) проводи́ть; производи́ть. **4,** (execute, as a mission or raid) соверша́ть. **5,** (put into practice, as a plan or program) осуществля́ть. **6,** (implement, as a threat or sentence) приводи́ть в исполне́ние.

cart *n.* **1,** (vehicle pulled by an animal) теле́га; подво́да; двуко́лка. **2,** (handcart) (ручна́я) теле́жка. —*v.t.* **1,** (transport) везти́; перевози́ть. **2,** (carry with great effort) тащи́ть. —**put the cart before the horse**, начина́ть не с того́ конца́.

cartel *n.* картéль.

carter *n.* вóзчик; ломовóй; ломовóй извóзчик.

cartilage *n.* хрящ. —**cartilaginous,** *adj.* хрящевáтый.

cartography *n.* картогрáфия. —**cartographer,** *n.* картóграф. —**cartographic,** *adj.* картографúческий.

carton *n.* картóнка.

cartoon *n.* **1,** (drawing) карикатýра. **2,** (film) мультипликациóнный фильм; мультипликáция. —**cartoonist,** *n.* карикатурúст.

cartridge *n.* патрóн. —**cartridge case,** гúльза. —**cartridge clip,** обóйма. —**cartridge pouch,** подсýмок.

carve *v.t. & i.* **1,** (make by cutting) рéзать; (*specifically in wood*) вырезáть; (*specifically in stone*) высекáть. **2,** (slice, as meat) нарезáть. **3,** *fol. by* **up** (divide up) разделя́ть; разбивáть. **4,** *fol. by* **out** (achieve) ковáть: *carve out a victory,* ковáть побéду. —**carved,** *adj.* резнóй; вырезнóй. —**carver,** *n.* рéзчик. —**carving,** *n.* резьбá; резнáя рабóта.

caryatid *n.* кариатúда.

cascade *n.* каскáд. —*v.i.* низвергáться.

case *n.* **1,** (instance) слýчай: *in most cases,* в большинствé слýчаев. *In any case,* во вся́ком слýчае. *In case...,* в том слýчае, éсли...; на слýчай, éсли... *In case of,* в слýчае (+ *gen.*). *Just in case,* на вся́кий слýчай. *Make an exception in someone's case,* сдéлать исключéние для когó-нибудь. **2,** (the actual state of affairs): *that is not the case,* э́то не так; э́то не вéрно. *If that's the case; that being the case,* в такóм слýчае; éсли дéло обстоúт так. *As the case may be,* в завúсимости от обстоя́тельств. *As is often the case,* как э́то чáсто бывáет. **3,** *law* дéло: *hear a case,* слýшать дéло. **4,** (argument in support of) дóводы: *the case for capital punishment,* дóводы в пóльзу смéртной кáзни. **5,** (person being treated) больнóй: *a mental case,* психúчески больнóй. *It's a hopeless case,* больнóй безнадёжен. **6,** *gram.* падéж: *accusative case,* винúтельный падéж. **7,** (large box) я́щик: *packing case,* упакóвочный я́щик. **8,** (small box) футля́р: *eyeglass case,* футля́р для очкóв. *Cigarette case,* портсигáр. **9,** (cover) чехóл: *case for a camera,* чехóл для фотоаппарáта. **10,** (showcase) витрúна. **11,** (tray for storing type) кáсса.

caseharden *v.t.* цементúровать.

case history истóрия болéзни.

casein *n.* казеúн.

casemate *n.* каземáт.

casement *n.* ствóрка. —**casement window,** ствóрчатое окнó.

cash *n.* налúчные (дéньги): *pay cash,* платúть налúчными. *Short of cash,* не при деньгáх. —*adj.* налúчный: *cash payment,* налúчный расчёт. —*v.t. Cash a check,* **1,** (of a person) получúть дéньги по чéку. **2,** (of a bank) вы́дать дéньги по чéку.

cashbook *n.* кáссовая кнúга.

cash box кáсса.

cashier *n.* кассúр. —*v.t.* увольня́ть со слýжбы.

cashmere *n.* кашемúр. —*adj.* кашемúровый.

cash register кáсса.

casing *n.* кожýх; кóрпус.

casino *n.* казинó.

cask *n.* бóчка; бочóнок.

casket *n.* **1,** (small box) шкатýлка. **2,** (coffin) гроб.

cassava *n.* маниóка.

cassette *n.* кассéта.

cassock *n.* ря́са.

cast *v.t.* **1,** (throw) бросáть; кидáть; метáть. **2,** (cause to fall, drop, or occur) бросáть: *cast anchor,* брóсить я́корь; *cast a glance,* брóсить взгляд. *Cast a shadow,* отбрáсывать тень. *Cast doubt upon,* подвергáть сомнéнию. *Cast a spell over,* заколдóвывать; околдóвывать. *Cast one's lot with,* связáть свою́ судьбý с. **3,** (give, as a vote) подавáть; отдавáть (гóлос). **4,** (draw, as lots) бросáть (жрéбий). *The die is cast,* жрéбий брóшен. **5,** (shape; mold) лить; отливáть. —*n.* **1,** (mold) слéпок. **2,** *med.* гипс. **3,** (actors in a play) состáв исполнúтелей. **4,** (tinge; shade) оттéнок. **5,** *in cast of mind,* склад умá. —**cast about for,** изы́скивать. —**cast aside,** отбрáсывать. —**cast off, 1,** (throw off) сбрáсывать. **2,** (sail off, as of a boat) отвáливать; отчáливать.

castanets *n.pl.* кастанéты.

caste *n.* кáста. —*adj.* кáстовый: *caste system,* кáстовая систéма.

caster *n.* **1,** (founder) литéйщик. **2,** [*also,* **castor**] (small wheel) колéсико; рóлик.

castigate *v.t.* подвергáть сурóвой крúтике; бичевáть.

casting *n.* **1,** (founding) литьё; отлúвка. **2,** (object cast in a mold) отлúвка; *pl.* литьё. **3,** *theat.* распределéние ролéй.

cast iron чугýн. —**cast-iron,** *adj.* чугýнный. *Cast-iron stomach,* лужёный желýдок.

castle *n.* **1,** (fortress) зáмок. **2,** (chess piece) ладья́; турá. —*v.i. chess* рокировáть(ся); дéлать рокирóвку. —**castles in the air,** воздýшные зáмки.

castor *n.* **1,** (cloth) кастóр; бóбрик. **2,** = **caster.** —**castor oil,** кастóровое мáсло.

castrate *v.t.* кастрúровать; холостúть; оскопля́ть. —**castration,** *n.* кастрáция.

casual *adj.* **1,** (chance) случáйный. **2,** (informal; relaxed) непринуждённый; небрéжный. *Casual clothes,* повседнéвное плáтье. **3,** (cursory) бéглый. —**casually,** *adv.* случáйно; мимохóдом; попýтно.

casualty *n.* **1,** (person killed or injured) жéртва: *there were no casualties,* жертв не́ бы́ло. **2,** *pl., mil.* рáненые; потéри. *Heavy casualties,* тяжёлые потéри.

casuist *n.* казуúст. —**casuistic,** *adj.* казуистúческий; —**casuistry,** *n.* казуúстика.

cat *n.* кóшка. *Male cat,* кот. —**let the cat out of the bag,** проговáриваться; пробáлтываться; вы́болтать секрéт.

cataclysm *n.* катаклúзм. —**cataclysmic,** *adj.* катастрофúческий.

catacombs *n.pl.* катакóмбы.

catafalque *n.* катафáлк.

Catalan *adj.* каталóнский; каталáнский.

catalepsy *n.* каталéпсия. —**cataleptic,** *adj.* каталептúческий; калепсúческий.

catalogue *also,* **catalog** *n.* **1,** (source of information) катáлог: *card catalogue,* кáрточный катáлог. **2,** (list of items for sale) прейскурáнт. —*v.t.* каталогизúровать. —**cataloguer,** *n.* каталогизáтор.

catalysis *n.* катáлиз. —**catalyst,** *n.* катализáтор. —**catalytic,** *adj.* каталитúческий.

cat-and-mouse game игрá в кóшки-мы́шки.

catapult *n.* катапýльта. —*v.t.* подбрáсывать в вóздух. —*v.i.* взлетáть; вскáкивать; подскáкивать.

cataract *n.* 1, (waterfall) водопа́д; катара́кт. 2, (opacity of the eye) катара́кта.

catarrh *n.* катáр.

catastrophe *n.* катастро́фа. —**catastrophic**, *adj.* катастрофи́ческий.

catch *v.t.* 1, (grab; trap; capture) лови́ть (*pfv.* пойма́ть): *catch a ball/fish/thief,* пойма́ть мяч/ры́бу/во́ра. 2, (take by surprise) застава́ть: *catch unawares,* заста́ть враспло́х. *Get caught in the rain,* попа́сть под дождь. *Be caught stealing,* попа́сться на кра́же. 3, (catch up to; overtake) догоня́ть. 4, (snag) зацепля́ть: *catch one's sleeve on a nail,* зацепи́ть рукаво́м за гвоздь. 5, (jam, as one's fingers in a door) защемля́ть; прищемля́ть (па́льцы две́рью). 6, (be in time for, as a train) успе́ть на; попа́сть на. 7, (contract, as an illness) получа́ть; нажива́ть; схва́тывать. *Catch cold,* простужа́ться. 8, (understand; grasp) ула́вливать. 9, *colloq.* (hear) расслы́шать. 10, *in various miscellaneous expressions: catch fire,* загоре́ться; *catch sight of,* уви́деть; зави́деть; *catch one's breath,* перевести́ дух; отдыша́ться. —*v.i.* 1, (become snagged) зацепля́ться; задева́ть. 2, (ignite) разжига́ться. —*n.* 1, (act of catching) пои́мка. 2, (quantity caught) уло́в. 3, (fastener) защёлка; язычо́к. 4, (bolt; latch) задви́жка. 5, (game) игра́ в мяч: *play catch,* игра́ть в мяч. 6, *colloq.* (hitch; rub) зацёпка; загво́здка. —**catch it,** *colloq.* доста́ться (+ *dat.*); попа́сть (+ *dat.*): *I'll catch it,* мне доста́нется; мне попадёт. —**catch on, 1,** (become popular) привива́ться. 2, (get the knack) приноравливаться. 3, *colloq.* (grasp the meaning) понима́ть; смека́ть. —**catch oneself,** лови́ть себя́ (*with* на + *prepl.*). —**catch someone's eye, 1,** (get the attention of) лови́ть чей-нибудь взгляд. 2, (happen to be seen by) привлека́ть чьё-нибудь внима́ние; попада́ться на глаза́ (+ *dat.*). —**catch up (with** *or* **to),** догоня́ть. *Catch up on one's sleep,* отсыпа́ться.

catching *adj.* зара́зный; зарази́тельный.

catchy *adj.* легко́ запомина́ющийся.

catechism *n.* катехи́зис.

categorical *adj.* категори́ческий; реши́тельный. —**categorically,** *adv.* категори́чески; реши́тельно.

categorize *v.t.* 1, (classify) относи́ть к (како́й-нибудь) катего́рии. 2, (characterize) характеризова́ть.

category *n.* катего́рия; разря́д.

cater *v.i.* [*usu.* **cater to**] 1, (serve) обслу́живать. 2, (satisfy) удовлетворя́ть. 3, (indulge) потво́рствовать. —*v.t.* обслу́живать.

caterpillar *n.* гу́сеница. —**caterpillar tractor,** гу́сеничный тра́ктор. —**caterpillar tread,** гу́сеничная ле́нта.

catgut *n.* кетгу́т.

catharsis *n.* очище́ние желу́дка. —**cathartic,** *adj.* слаби́тельный. —*n.* слаби́тельное.

cathedral *n.* собо́р.

catheter *n.* кате́тер.

cathode *n.* като́д. —**cathode rays,** като́дные лучи́. —**cathode-ray tube,** като́дная тру́бка.

Catholic *adj.* католи́ческий. —*n.* като́лик. —**Catholicism,** *n.* католици́зм; католи́чество.

catkin *n.* серёжка.

cat-o'-nine-tails *n.* ко́шки.

cattail *n.* рого́з.

cattle *n.* скот. *Herd of cattle,* ста́до коро́в. —**cattleman,** *n.* скотово́д.

catty-corner *adv.* наи́скось.

Caucasian *adj.* 1, (of the Caucasus) кавка́зский. 2, (Caucasoid) европео́идный. —*n.* европео́ид.

caucus *n.* парти́йное собра́ние.

cauldron *n.* = **caldron.**

cauliflower *n.* цветна́я капу́ста.

caulk *also,* **calk** *v.t.* конопа́тить.

causal *adj.* причи́нный. —**causality,** *n.* причи́нность. —**causative,** *adj.* причи́нный.

cause *n.* 1, (that which produces an effect) причи́на: *cause and effect,* причи́на и сле́дствие. *The cause of the fire,* причи́на пожа́ра. *What is the cause of it?,* чем э́то вы́звано? 2, (ground; occasion) по́вод; причи́на. *There is no cause for alarm,* нет причи́н беспоко́иться. 3, (principle; movement) де́ло: *the cause of peace,* де́ло ми́ра. —*v.t.* 1, (be the cause of; bring about) вызыва́ть; причиня́ть. *Cause an argument/accident,* вы́звать спор/катастро́фу. *Cause damage/grief,* причиня́ть вред/го́ре. 2, (prompt; induce) побужда́ть; заставля́ть: *what caused him to...?,* что побуди́ло/заста́вило его́ (+ *inf.*). —**make common cause with,** солидаризи́роваться с.

caustic *adj.* 1, (corrosive) е́дкий; каусти́ческий. 2, (biting; sarcastic) е́дкий; ко́лкий; язви́тельный. —**causticity,** *n.* е́дкость.

caustic soda е́дкий натр.

cauterize *v.t.* прижига́ть; выжига́ть. —**cauterization,** *n.* прижига́ние; выжига́ние.

caution *n.* 1, (wariness) осторо́жность. 2, (warning) предостереже́ние. —*v.t.* предостерега́ть.

cautious *adj.* осторо́жный. —**cautiously,** *adv.* осторо́жно.

cavalcade *n.* кавалька́да.

cavalier *n.* ры́царь. —*adj.* 1, (haughty) надме́нный. 2, (offhand) бесцеремо́нный.

cavalry *n.* кавале́рия; ко́нница. —*adj.* кавалери́йский. —**cavalryman,** *n.* кавалери́ст; ко́нник.

cave *n.* пеще́ра. —*v.i.* [*usu.* **cave in**] обва́ливаться; обру́шиваться; ру́хнуть.

cave-in *n.* обва́л.

cave man пеще́рный челове́к.

cavern *n.* пеще́ра. —**cavernous,** *adj.* похо́жий на пеще́ру.

caviar *also,* **caviare** *n.* икра́.

cavil *v.i.* придира́ться. —*n.* приди́рка.

cavity *n.* 1, (hole; depression) впа́дина. 2, (natural hollow in the body) по́лость: *abdominal cavity,* брюшна́я по́лость. 3, (in a tooth) дупло́; (in the lungs) каве́рна.

cavort *v.i.* 1, (leap about) де́лать прыжки́. 2, (romp; frolic) резви́ться.

caw *v.i.* ка́ркать. —*n.* ка́рканье.

cease *v.t.* 1, (stop doing an action) перестава́ть. 2, (terminate) прекраща́ть. —*v.i.* прекраща́ться.

cease-fire *n.* прекраще́ние огня́.

ceaseless *adj.* непреста́нный; беспреста́нный.

cecum *also,* **caecum** *n.* слепа́я кишка́.

cedar *n.* кедр. —*adj.* кедро́вый.

cede *v.t.* сдава́ть; уступа́ть.

cedilla *n.* седи́ль.

ceiling *n.* потоло́к. —**hit the ceiling,** прийти́ в я́рость; лезть (поле́зть) на сте́ну.

celebrate *v.t.* 1, (observe; commemorate) праздно-

вать; справля́ть. *Celebrate New Year's Eve,* встре-
ча́ть Но́вый год. **2,** (perform, as a mass) служи́ть
(обе́дню). **3,** (extol) прославля́ть. —*v.i.* **1,** (observe
a holiday) пра́здновать. **2,** (engage in merrymaking)
весели́ться. —**celebrated,** *adj.* знамени́тый; про-
сла́вленный. —**celebration,** *n.* пра́здник; пра́здно-
вание; пра́зднество; торжество́.

celebrity *n.* знамени́тость.

celerity *n.* быстрота́.

celery *n.* сельдере́й. —*adj.* сельдере́йный.

celesta *n.* челе́ста.

celestial *adj.* небе́сный. —**celestial navigation,**
астронавига́ция.

celibacy *n.* безбра́чие.

celibate *adj.* безбра́чный; холосто́й. —*n.* холостя́к.

cell *n.* **1,** (in a prison) ка́мера; (in a monastery) ке́лья.
2, *biol.* кле́тка. **3,** (small group) ячейка. **4,** *electricity*
элеме́нт.

cellar *n.* по́греб. *Wine cellar,* ви́нный по́греб.

cellist *n.* виолончели́ст.

cellmate *n.* сока́мерник.

cello *n.* виолонче́ль.

cellophane *n.* целлофа́н. —*adj.* целлофа́новый.

cellular *adj.* кле́точный.

celluloid *n.* целлуло́ид.

cellulose *n.* клетча́тка; целлюло́за.

Celsius *adj.* Це́льсий: *ten degrees Celsius,* де́сять
гра́дусов по Це́льсию.

Celt *n.* кельт. —**Celtic,** *adj.* ке́льтский.

cement *n.* цеме́нт. —*adj.* цеме́нтный. —*v.t.* **1,**
(cover with cement) цементи́ровать. **2,** *fig.* (solidify)
скрепля́ть.

cemetery *n.* кла́дбище.

censer *n.* кади́ло; кури́льница.

censor *n.* це́нзор. —*v.t.* подверга́ть цензу́ре.
—**censorship,** *n.* цензу́ра.

censure *v.t.* порица́ть; осужда́ть. —*n.* порица́ние;
осужде́ние.

census *n.* пе́репись.

cent *n.* цент. *Not have a cent to one's name,* не
име́ть ни гроша́ за душо́й.

centaur *n.* кента́вр.

centenary *adj.* столе́тний. —*n.* столе́тие.

centennial *adj. & n.* = **centenary.**

center *also,* **centre** *n.* **1,** (middle) центр; середи́на.
2, (focal point) центр: *shopping center,* торго́вый
центр. *Be the center of attention,* быть в це́нтре
внима́ния. **3,** *basketball* центрово́й. —*adj.* сре́дний:
center aisle, сре́дний прохо́д. —*v.t.* **1,** (place in the
center) помеща́ть в це́нтре. **2,** (direct toward one
place; concentrate) сосредото́чивать. —*v.i.* сосре-
дото́чиваться. *The conversation centered around one
subject,* разгово́р верте́лся о́коло одного́ предме́-
та. —**center of gravity,** центр тя́жести.

centerfold *n.* разворо́т.

Centigrade *adj.* Це́льсий: *ten degrees Centigrade,*
де́сять гра́дусов по Це́льсию.

centigram *n.* сантигра́мм.

centime *n.* санти́м.

centimeter *also,* **centimetre** *n.* сантиме́тр.

centipede *n.* многоно́жка; сороконо́жка.

centner *n.* це́нтнер.

central *adj.* центра́льный. —**Central Asia,** Сре́дняя
А́зия. —**Central Committee,** центра́льный ко-
мите́т.

centralism *n.* централи́зм. —**democratic centralism,** демократи́ческий централи́зм.

centralization *n.* централиза́ция.

centralize *v.t.* централизова́ть. —**centralized,** *adj.*
централизо́ванный.

centre *see* **center.**

centrifugal *adj.* центробе́жный: *centrifugal force,*
центробе́жная си́ла.

centripetal *adj.* центростреми́тельный.

century *n.* век; столе́тие. *In the 19th century,* в
девятна́дцатом ве́ке.

century plant столе́тник.

ceramic *adj.* керами́ческий. —**ceramics,** *n.* ке-
ра́мика.

cereal *n.* **1,** (grain) (хле́бные) зла́ки. **2,** (breakfast
food) блю́до из хле́бных зла́ков. —*adj.* хле́бный;
зла́ковый.

cerebellum *n.* мозжечо́к.

cerebral *adj.* мозгово́й. —**cerebral hemorrhage,**
кровоизлия́ние в мозг. —**cerebral palsy,** цере-
бра́льный парали́ч.

cerebrum *n.* головно́й мозг.

ceremonial *adj.* церемониа́льный. —*n.* **1,** (ritual)
церемониа́л. **2,** (rite) обря́д.

ceremonious *adj.* церемо́нный.

ceremony *n.* **1,** (formal ritual) церемо́ния. **2,** (formality) церемо́нии. —**stand on ceremony,** церемо́-
ниться.

cerise *adj.* вишнёвый.

cerium *n.* це́рий.

certain *adj.* **1,** (sure; positive) уве́ренный: *I am certain,* я уве́рен(а). **2,** (sure to happen) ве́рный: *certain
death,* ве́рная ги́бель. **3,** (sure; indisputable) несом-
не́нный: *one thing is certain,* одно́ несомне́нно. *He
is certain to be late,* он несомне́нно опозда́ет. *It
is by no means certain that...,* совсе́м не я́сно, что...
4, (known but not specified) определённый: *in certain
cases,* в определённых слу́чаях. **5,** (some but not
others) не́который: *certain people,* не́которые лю́ди.
6, (some but not all) не́который; изве́стный: *to a
certain extent,* до не́которой/изве́стной сте́пени.
7, *preceded by* **a** (unidentified) не́кий; не́кто: *a certain
Mr. Smith,* не́кий/не́кто ми́стер Смит. —**for cer-
tain,** достове́рно; наверняка́: *know for certain,*
знать достове́рно/наверняка́. —**make certain,**
= **make sure** (*see* **sure**).

certainly *adv.* **1,** (of course) коне́чно. **2,** (without
a doubt) несомне́нно. —**certainly not,** ни в ко́ем
слу́чае.

certainty *n.* **1,** (assuredness) уве́ренность. **2,** (anything certain) несомне́нный факт. —**know for a
certainty,** знать наверняка́.

certificate *n.* удостовере́ние; свиде́тельство;
аттеста́т; сертифика́т.

certification *n.* удостовере́ние.

certify *v.t.* удостоверя́ть; заверя́ть.

certitude *n.* уве́ренность.

ceruse *n.* **1,** (white lead) свинцо́вые бели́ла. **2,**
(cosmetic) бели́ла.

cervical *adj.* ше́йный; заты́лочный.

cervix *n.* **1,** (neck) ше́я. **2,** (necklike part of the uterus)
ше́йка ма́тки.

cesium *n.* це́зий.

cessation *n.* прекраще́ние.

cession *n.* усту́пка; сда́ча.

cesspool *n.* выгребная яма; помойная яма.

chafe *v.t.* тереть; натирать; стирать. —*v.i.* **1,** (rub) тереть. **2,** (be irritated or impatient) гореть от нетерпения; горячиться.

chaff *n.* **1,** (husks) мякина. **2,** (fine-cut straw) сечка.

chaffinch *n.* зяблик.

chagrin *n.* огорчение. —**chagrined,** *adj.* огорчённый.

chain *n.* **1,** (connected links) цепь; цепочка. *Put the chain on the door,* запереть дверь на цепочку. **2,** (for a watch, pendant, etc.) цепочка: *watch chain,* цепочка для часов. **3,** *pl.* (shackles) цепи; оковы. *Put (someone) in chains,* заковать (кого-нибудь) в цепи. **4,** (range of mountains) (горная) цепь. **5,** (series) цепь: *chain of events,* цепь событий. **6,** (network, as of stores) сеть. —*adj.* цепной: *chain link,* цепное звено. —*v.t.* [*often* **chain up**] сажать на цепь. *Chain a dog to a post,* приковывать собаку цепью к столбу. —**chain of command,** командные инстанции. —**chain mail,** кольчуга. —**chain reaction,** цепная реакция. —**chain saw,** цепная пила. —**chain stitch,** тамбур; тамбурный шов; тамбурная строчка; цепной стежок.

chain-smoke *v.i.* курить запоем.

chair *n.* **1,** (piece of furniture) стул. **2,** (presiding officer) председатель. **3,** (professorship) кафедра. —*v.t.* председательствовать на (собрании).

chairman *n.* председатель. —**chairmanship,** *n.* председательство.

chaise longue шезлонг.

chalcedony *n.* халцедон.

chalet *n.* шале.

chalice *n.* чаша.

chalk *n.* мел. —*v.t.* натирать мелом. —**chalk up, 1,** (earn; score) одержать (победу); набирать (очки). **2,** *fol. by* **to** (attribute to) относить на счёт (+ *gen.*).

chalky *adj.* меловой.

challenge *v.t.* **1,** (summon to a contest) вызывать. **2,** (call into question; dispute) оспаривать. **3,** (demand identification from) окликать. —*n.* **1,** (summons to a contest) вызов. **2,** (demand for identification) оклик. **3,** *law* отвод. —**challenge cup,** *sports* переходящий кубок.

challenger *n.* претендент.

chamber *n.* **1,** (large room for a certain purpose) камера: *compression chamber,* камера сжатия. *Torture chamber,* застенок. **2,** (bedroom) спальня. **3,** (unit of a legislature) палата. **4,** (of a firearm) патронник.

chamberlain *n.* камергер.

chambermaid *n.* горничная.

chamber music камерная музыка.

chamber of commerce торговая палата.

chamber pot ночной горшок.

chameleon *n.* хамелеон.

chamois *n.* **1,** (antelope) серна. **2,** (soft leather) замша.

chamomile *n.* = **camomile.**

champ *n., colloq.* = **champion.** —*v.i.* чавкать. —**champ at the bit,** грызть удила.

champagne *n.* шампанское.

champion *n.* **1,** (one who is ranked first) чемпион. **2,** (defender, as of a cause) поборник. —*v.t.* бороться за. —*adj. Champion swimmer,* чемпион по плаванию.

championship *n.* **1,** (title) первенство; чемпионство. **2,** (competition) чемпионат; первенство. **3,** (advocacy) борьба; защита.

chance *n.* **1,** (fortune; luck) случай; случайность. *Game of chance,* азартная игра. *Leave to chance,* оставлять на волю случая. **2,** (opportunity) случай; возможность. **3,** (probability) шанс: *one chance in ten,* один шанс из десяти. *Stand a chance,* иметь шансы. **4,** (risk) риск: *take a chance,* идти на риск; рисковать. —*adj.* случайный: *a chance meeting,* случайная встреча. —*v.t.* рисковать: *let's chance it,* рискнём. —*v.i. I chanced to be there,* я случайно был (была) там. —**by any chance,** случайно. —**by chance,** случайно. —**chances are,** скорее всего.

chancellery *n.* канцелярия.

chancellor *n.* канцлер.

chancre *n.* шанкр. —**chancroid,** *n.* мягкий шанкр.

chancy *adj.* рискованный.

chandelier *n.* люстра.

change *v.t.* **1,** (switch) менять: *change jobs,* менять работу. *Change clothes,* переодеваться; *change shoes,* переодевать туфли. *Change planes, trains, etc.,* пересаживаться; делать пересадку. *Change sides,* перейти на другую сторону. *Change hands,* перейти в другие руки. **2,** (alter) изменять: *change tactics,* изменять тактику. *Change color,* менять свою окраску. **3,** (replace) сменять: *change a tire,* сменить шину. **4,** (exchange; switch) меняться (+ *instr.*): *change places,* меняться местами. **5,** (convert, as money) разменивать: *change ten dollars,* разменять десять долларов. **6,** (diaper) пеленать (ребёнка). —*v.i.* **1,** (vary; become different) меняться; изменяться; перемениться. **2,** (of a young man's voice) ломаться. **3,** *fol. by* **off** (alternate) чередоваться. **4,** = **change clothes, change planes,** etc. —*n.* **1,** (alteration; transformation) изменение; перемена: *change in the weather,* изменение/перемена погоды. *Change for the better,* перемена к лучшему. **2,** (replacement) смена: *oil change,* смена масла. **3,** (of planes, trains, etc.) пересадка. **4,** (variety) разнообразие: *for a change,* для разнообразия. *It's a nice day, for a change,* наконец-то хорошая погода! **5,** (small money; coins) мелочь. **6,** (money given back) сдача: *change of a dollar,* сдача с доллара. —**change of life,** климактерий.

changeable *adj.* изменчивый; непостоянный. —**changeability,** *n.* изменчивость.

changeover *n.* переход; переключение.

change purse кошелёк.

channel *n.* **1,** (waterway) пролив. *The English Channel,* Ла-Манш. **2,** (river bed) русло. **3,** *pl.* (means of communication) каналы. **4,** *television* канал. —*v.t.* направлять.

chant *v.t. & i.* **1,** (sing) петь. **2,** (call out rhythmically) скандировать. —*n.* песнопение: *Gregorian chant,* григорианское песнопение.

chaos *n.* хаос. —**chaotic,** *adj.* хаотический; хаотичный.

chap *v.t.* обветрить: *chapped lips,* обветренные губы. —*v.i.* трескаться. —*n., colloq.* (fellow) парень; малый.

chapel *n.* часовня; капелла. *The Sistine Chapel,* Сикстинская капелла.

chaperon *also,* **chaperone** *n.* дуэнья.

chaplain *n.* капеллан.

chapter *n.* **1,** (division of a book) глава́. **2,** (branch of a society) отделе́ние.

char *v.t.* обу́гливать.

character *n.* **1,** (individual nature) хара́ктер. *In character,* хара́ктерно; сво́йственно. *Out of character,* не хара́ктерно; не сво́йственно; не в чьём-нибудь хара́ктере. **2,** (moral excellence) хара́ктер: *man of character,* челове́к с хара́ктером. **3,** (person; personage) ли́чность. **4,** (person in a play or novel) де́йствующее лицо́. **5,** *colloq.* (an eccentric) оригина́л; чуда́к. **6,** *pl.* (symbols used in writing) письмена́; иеро́глифы. **—character actor,** хара́ктерный актёр. **—character reference,** характери́стика.

characteristic *n.* сво́йство; осо́бенность; черта́. **—***adj.* хара́ктерный; сво́йственный.

characterization *n.* характери́стика.

characterize *v.t.* характеризова́ть.

charade *n.* шара́да.

charcoal *n.* древе́сный у́голь.

charge *v.t.* **1,** (replenish, as a battery) заряжа́ть. **2,** (entrust, as with an assignment) поруча́ть. **3,** (accuse) обвиня́ть. **4,** (ask as a price) брать; проси́ть: *how much does he charge for this?,* ско́лько он берёт/про́сит за э́то? *Charge a lot for,* брать до́рого за. *They charged us ten dollars,* с нас взя́ли де́сять до́лларов. **5,** (record as a debt to be paid) запи́сывать: *charge it to my account,* запиши́те э́то на мой счёт. *Do you wish to charge it?,* вам присла́ть счёт? **6,** (attack) атакова́ть. **—***v.i.* **1,** (ask payment) брать де́ньги; взима́ть пла́ту. **2,** (rush violently forward) бро́ситься. **3,** (attack vigorously) бро́ситься в ата́ку. **—***n.* **1,** (quantity of explosives or electricity) заря́д. **2,** (custody) попече́ние: *I leave them in your charge,* оставля́ю их на ва́ше попече́ние. **3,** (ward) подопе́чный. **4,** (assignment; responsibility) поруче́ние. **5,** (accusation) обвине́ние: *press charges against,* предъяви́ть обвине́ние (+ *dat.*). **6,** (money to be paid) пла́та: *admission charge,* входна́я пла́та. *Free of charge,* беспла́тно. *There is an extra charge for that,* за э́то на́до заплати́ть отде́льно. **7,** (attack) ата́ка. **—be in charge,** распоряжа́ться. **—be in charge of,** ве́дать; заве́довать. **—put in charge of,** поста́вить во главе́ (+ *gen.*). **—take charge of,** взять в свои́ ру́ки.

charged *adj.* **1,** *physics* заряжённый: *charged particles,* заряжённые части́цы. **2,** *fig.* (tense) накалённый: *charged atmosphere,* накалённая атмосфе́ра.

chargé d'affaires пове́ренный в дела́х.

charger *n.* **1,** (for batteries) заря́дный агрега́т. **2,** (warhorse) строева́я ло́шадь; боево́й конь.

chariot *n.* колесни́ца. **—charioteer,** *n.* возни́ца.

charitable *adj.* **1,** (kind; generous) милосе́рдный. **2,** (philanthropic) благотвори́тельный. **3,** (lenient in judging) снисходи́тельный.

charity *n.* **1,** (benevolence) милосе́рдие; ми́лость. **2,** (philanthropy) благотвори́тельность. *Raise money for charity,* собира́ть де́ньги на благотвори́тельные це́ли. **3,** (charitable institution) благотвори́тельное учрежде́ние.

charlatan *n.* шарлата́н. **—charlatanism,** *n.* шарлата́нство.

charm *n.* **1,** (delightful quality) пре́лесть: *lose its charm,* теря́ть свою́ пре́лесть. *The charm of country life,* пре́лести жи́зни в дере́вне. **2,** (ability to captivate) очарова́ние; обая́ние; ча́ры. *I succumbed to*

her charm, я подда́лся её очарова́нию. **3,** (ornament) брело́к. **—***v.t.* **1,** (captivate) очаро́вывать. **2,** (cast a spell over) заколдо́вывать.

charmed *adj.* очаро́ванный; заколдо́ванный. *Charmed!,* о́чень прия́тно! **—he leads a charmed life,** он как бы заколдо́ван.

charmer *n.* (man) чароде́й; (woman) чароде́йка; чаро́вница. **—snake charmer,** заклина́тель змей.

charming *adj.* очарова́тельный; обая́тельный; преле́стный.

charred *adj.* обгоре́лый; обу́гленный.

chart *n.* гра́фик; схе́ма; диагра́мма. **—***v.t.* наноси́ть на гра́фик, схе́му, *etc.*

charter *n.* **1,** (grant of rights) ха́ртия. **2,** (constitution) уста́в. **—***v.t.* нанима́ть; взять напрока́т; фрахтова́ть.

chartreuse *adj.* жёлто-зелёный.

charwoman *n.* убо́рщица.

chary *adj.* **1,** (cautious) осторо́жный; осмотри́тельный. **2,** (sparing) скупо́й.

chase *v.t.* **1,** (pursue) гна́ться за: *chase a thief,* гна́ться за во́ром. *Chase up a tree,* загоня́ть на де́рево. **2,** *fol. by* **away** (drive away) отгоня́ть: *chase away a fly,* отогна́ть му́ху. **3,** *fol. by* **out** (drive out) выгоня́ть; прогоня́ть: *chase the children out of the room,* выгна́ть/прогна́ть дете́й из ко́мнаты. **—***v.i.* **1,** *fol. by* **after** (run after) гна́ться за; бе́гать за. *Chase after women,* бе́гать за же́нщинами. **2,** *colloq.* (rush) бе́гать. *Chase all over town,* обега́ть весь го́род. **—***n.* **1,** (pursuit) пого́ня. *Give chase,* погна́ться; пусти́ться вдого́нку. **2,** *preceded by* **the** (hunting) охо́та.

chasm *n.* про́пасть.

chassis *n.* шасси́.

chaste *adj.* целому́дренный.

chasten *v.t.* **1,** (punish) нака́зывать. **2,** (inhibit) стесня́ть.

chastise *v.t.* нака́зывать; кара́ть; бичева́ть.

chastity *n.* целому́дрие.

chasuble *n.* ри́за.

chat *v.i.* бесе́довать. **—***n.* бесе́да.

chattel *n.* дви́жимое иму́щество.

chatter *v.i.* **1,** (click, as of the teeth) стуча́ть. **2,** (jabber; prate) болта́ть; треща́ть. **3,** (utter rapid sounds, as of birds) щебета́ть. **—***n.* **1,** (utterance of birds) щебет. **2,** (idle talk) болтовня́.

chatterbox *n.* болту́н; говору́н; балабо́лка; трещётка.

chatty *adj.* болтли́вый.

chauffeur *n.* шофёр; води́тель.

chauvinism *n.* шовини́зм. **—chauvinist,** *n.* шовини́ст. **—chauvinistic,** *adj.* шовинисти́ческий.

cheap *adj.* **1,** (inexpensive) дешёвый. **2,** (niggardly) скупо́й. **—***adv.* дёшево: *buy/sell something cheap,* дёшево купи́ть/прода́ть что́-нибудь. *Get off cheap,* дёшево отде́латься.

cheapen *v.t.* **1,** (lessen the value of) обесце́нивать. **2,** (debase) опошля́ть.

cheaply *adv.* дёшево.

cheapskate *n.,* *colloq.* скря́га; скопидо́м; сква́лыга.

cheat *v.t.* обма́нывать; надува́ть. *Cheat someone out of two dollars,* обману́ть/наду́ть кого́-нибудь на два до́ллара. **—***v.i.* **1,** (in a game) плутова́ть; жу́льничать. **2,** (on a test) спи́сывать (на экза́мене). **—***n.* [*also,* **cheater**] обма́нщик; плут; жу́лик.

check *n.* **1,** (restraint): *hold/keep in check,* сдéрживать; держáть в уздé. **2,** (test for accuracy) провéрка. **3,** (check mark [✔]) гáлочка; птúчка. **4,** [*also,* **cheque**] (written order to pay money) чек. **5,** (ticket; slip) номерóк. **6,** (bill, as in a restaurant) счёт. **7,** (square in a checkered pattern) клéтка. **8,** *chess* шах. —*v.t.* **1,** (halt) останáвливать; задéрживать. **2,** (hold back) сдéрживать; обýздывать. **3,** (examine for accuracy) проверя́ть. **4,** [*often* **check off**] (mark with a check) отмечáть гáлочкой. **5,** (deposit for safekeeping) сдавáть. —*v.i.* **1,** (make an inquiry) спрáшивать. **2,** (tally) сходúться; совпадáть. —**check in,** регистрúроваться; прописывáться. —**check out, 1,** (settle up and leave) выпúсываться (из гостúницы). *Are you checking out today?,* вы сегóдня уезжáете? **2,** (investigate further) разузнавáть. **3,** (agree; tally) сходúться. —**check (up) on,** проверя́ть.

checkbook *n.* чéковая кнúжка.

checked *adj.* клéтчатый; в клéтку.

checker *n.* **1,** (one who checks) контролёр. **2,** (piece used in the game of checkers) шáшка.

checkerboard *n.* шáхматная (*or* шáшечная) доскá.

checkered *adj.* клéтчатый.

checkers *n.* шáшки.

checkmate *n.* мат. —*v.t.* сдéлать мат (+ *dat.*).

checkpoint *n.* контрóльный пункт.

checkroom *n.* **1,** (for apparel) гардерóб; раздевáлка. **2,** (for baggage) кáмера хранéния.

checkup *n.* осмóтр; обслéдование. *Go into the hospital for a checkup,* лечь в больнúцу на обслéдование.

cheek *n.* **1,** (side of the face) щекá. **2,** *colloq.* (effrontery) нáглость. —**turn the other cheek,** подставля́ть другýю щéку. —**with tongue in cheek,** в шýтку.

cheekbone *n.* скулá.

cheep *v.i.* пищáть. —*n.* писк.

cheer *n.* **1,** (shout of approval) вóзглас; урá. **2,** (encouragement; comfort) ободрéние. *Words of cheer,* ободря́ющие словá. **3,** *in* **be of good cheer,** быть весёлым; не унывáть. —*v.t.* **1,** (acclaim with cheers) привéтствовать (грóмкими вóзгласами); кричáть урá в честь (+ *gen.*). **2,** *fol. by* **up** (gladden) ободря́ть; подбодря́ть; (раз)веселúть. —*v.i.* **1,** (shout cheers) кричáть урá. **2,** *fol. by* **up** (feel encouraged) ободря́ться; подбодря́ться; развеселúться; воспря́нуть дýхом.

cheerful *adj.* бóдрый; весёлый. —**cheerfulness,** *n.* бóдрость; весёлость.

cheerio *interj., colloq.* до встрéчи!; покá!

cheerless *adj.* мрáчный; безрáдостный; безотрáдный.

cheery *adj.* бóдрый. *A cheery smile,* рáдостная улы́бка.

cheese *n.* сыр. —*adj.* сы́рный: *cheese omelet,* сы́рный омлéт.

cheesecloth *n.* мáрля.

cheetah *n.* гепáрд.

chef *n.* шеф-пóвар.

chemical *adj.* химúческий. —*n.* химúческий препарáт; химúческий продýкт. —**chemical engineer,** инженéр-хúмик. —**chemical warfare,** химúческая войнá.

chemise *n.* (жéнская) сорóчка.

chemist *n.* **1,** (specialist in chemistry) хúмик. **2,** *Brit.* (druggist) аптéкарь.

chemistry *n.* хúмия.

chemotherapy *n.* химиотерапúя.

chenille *n.* синéль.

cheque *n., Brit.* = **check,** *n.* (*in sense #4*).

cherish *v.t.* **1,** (hold dear) дорожúть. **2,** (nurture, as hopes) лелéять.

cherry *n.* вúшня. —*adj.* вишнёвый: *cherry jam,* вишнёвое варéнье. —**cherry tree,** вúшня.

cherub *n.* херувúм. —**cherubic,** *adj.* херувúмский.

chess *n.* шáхматы: *play chess,* игрáть в шáхматы. —*adj.* шáхматный: *chess tournament,* шáхматный турнúр. —**chessboard,** *n.* шáхматная доскá. —**chessman,** *n.* шáхматная фигýра. —**chess player,** шахматúст.

chest *n.* **1,** (part of the body) грудь. **2,** (box) я́щик; сундýк. *Medicine chest,* аптéчка. *Chest of drawers,* комóд. —*adj.* груднóй: *chest cavity,* груднáя пóлость. *Chest pain,* боль в грудú.

chestnut *n.* каштáн. —*adj.* каштáновый. *Chestnut horse,* ры́жая лóшадь.

cheviot *n.* шевиóт. —*adj.* шевиóтовый.

chevron *n.* шеврóн; нашúвка.

chew *v.t. & i.* жевáть. —**chew out,** *slang* вы́бранить; разругáть. —**chew the fat** *or* **rag,** *slang* бесéдовать.

chewing *n.* жевáние. —*adj.* жевáтельный: *chewing gum,* жевáтельная резúнка; *chewing tobacco,* жевáтельный табáк.

chic *adj.* шикáрный; стúльный.

chicanery *n.* интрúга; кóзни; кáверза.

chick *n.* **1,** (small chicken) цыплёнок. **2,** *slang* (girl) девчóнка.

chickadee *n.* гáичка.

chicken *n.* **1,** (hen or rooster or its flesh) кýрица. **2,** (young hen or rooster) цыплёнок. —*adj.* курúный: *chicken soup,* курúный бульóн; *chicken livers,* курúная печёнка. —**chicken coop,** куря́тник. —**chicken pox,** ветря́ная óспа; ветря́нка.

chickpea *n.* нут; турéцкий горóх.

chicory *n.* цикóрий.

chide *v.t.* побранúть; журúть.

chief *n.* главá; начáльник. *Chief of staff,* начáльник штáба. *Chief of state,* главá правúтельства. —*adj.* глáвный: *chief question/engineer,* глáвный вопрóс/инженéр. —**chiefly,** *adv.* глáвным óбразом.

chieftain *n.* вождь.

chiffon *n.* шифóн. —*adj.* шифóновый.

chiffonier *n.* шифоньéрка.

chignon *n.* шиньóн.

child *n.* ребёнок. —*adj.* [*also,* **child's**] дéтский: *child labor,* дéтский труд. —**child's play,** пустякóвое дéло; пáра пустякóв. *See also* **children.**

childbearing *n.* деторождéние.

childbirth *n.* рóды. *Die in childbirth,* умерéть от рóдов.

childhood *n.* дéтство. *Since childhood,* с дéтства; с мáлых лет.

childish *adj.* дéтский; ребя́ческий. —**childishly,** *adv.* как ребёнок. —**childishness,** *n.* ребя́чество.

childless *adj.* бездéтный. —**childlessness,** *n.* бездéтность.

childlike *adj.* дéтский; невúнный.

children *n.pl.* дéти. —**children's,** *adj.* дéтский.

Chilean *adj.* чилийский. —*n.* чилиец; чилийка.

chill *n.* **1,** (sensation of cold) простуда; озноб. *Catch a chill,* схватить простуду. *He has a chill,* его знобит. **2,** (coldness in the air) холодок. *There is a chill in the air,* свежо. **3,** (feeling of sudden fear) холод: *a chill ran down my spine,* холод пробежал по моей спине. **4,** (coolness, as in relations) холодок (в отношениях). —*v.t.* охлаждать. *Chilled to the bone,* продрогший до костей.

chilling *adj.* **1,** (freezing) леденящий: *chilling wind,* леденящий ветер. **2,** (frightening; shocking) жуткий.

chilly *adj.* прохладный; свежий: *it is chilly in here,* здесь прохладно/свежо. *It is getting chilly,* свежеет. *I am chilly,* мне прохладно.

chime *n., usu. pl.* куранты. —*v.i.* бить; звучать; звонить. —**chime in,** ввернуть словечко; вступить в разговор.

chimera *n.* химера. —**chimerical,** *adj.* химерический.

chimney *n.* (дымовая) труба. —**chimney sweep,** трубочист.

chimpanzee *n.* шимпанзе.

chin *n.* подбородок. —**keep one's chin up,** не падать духом.

china *n.* **1,** (porcelain) фарфор. **2,** (dishes) посуда. —*adj.* **1,** (made of china) фарфоровый. **2,** (for china) посудный: *china closet,* посудный шкаф.

chinchilla *n.* шиншилла.

Chinese *adj.* китайский. *He (she) is Chinese,* он китаец; она китаянка. —*n.* **1,** (language) китайский язык. *Speak Chinese,* говорить по-китайски. **2,** *preceded by* the (people) китайцы.

chink *n.* **1,** (slit) щель; расщелина; скважина. **2,** (sound) звон; звяканье.

chintz *n.* ситец. —*adj.* ситцевый.

chip *n.* **1,** (fragment) щепка. **2,** (imperfection caused by chipping) щербина. **3,** (counter used in gambling games) фишка. *Bargaining chip,* предмет торга. —*v.t.* **1,** (damage slightly) надбивать. **2,** *fol. by* **away** (cut away, as ice) скалывать. —*v.i.* **1,** (lose a chip) биться. **2,** *fol. by* **off** (break off) отбиваться: *a piece of the cup chipped off,* у чашки отбился край. —**chip in,** внести свою лепту. —**chip off the old block,** сын своего отца. —**in the chips,** при деньгах. —**when the chips are down,** в решающий момент.

chipmunk *n.* бурундук.

chipper *adj., colloq.* бодрый; живой.

chiropody *n.* педикюр. —**chiropodist,** *n.* педикюрша.

chirp *v.i.* чирикать; щебетать; стрекотать. —*n.* щебет.

chisel *n.* долото. —*v.t.* **1,** (cut) вырезать; высекать. **2,** *slang* (swindle) надувать; обжуливать. —**chiseled,** *adj.* (of features) точёный. —**chiseler,** *n., slang* рвач.

chit *n.* талон.

chivalry *n.* рыцарство. —**chivalrous,** *adj.* рыцарский; галантный.

chive *n.* шнитт-лук.

chloric *adj.* хлорный.

chloride *n.* хлорид. ♦ *In compounds* хлористый: *hydrogen chloride,* хлористый водород. —**chloride of lime,** хлорная известь.

chlorinate *v.t.* хлорировать. —**chlorination,** *n.* хлорирование.

chlorine *n.* хлор.

chloroform *n.* хлороформ. —*v.t.* хлороформировать.

chlorophyll *n.* хлорофилл.

chlorous *adj.* хлористый.

chock-full *adj.* битком набитый; набитый до отказа.

chocolate *n.* шоколад. *Hot chocolate,* горячий шоколад. *Box of chocolates,* шоколадный набор. —*adj.* шоколадный: *chocolate cake,* шоколадный торт.

choice *n.* выбор. *He was offered a book of his choice,* ему предложили книгу на выбор. *We have no choice but to...,* нам не остаётся другого выбора (*or* ничего другого), как... —*adj.* отборный; как на подбор.

choir *n.* **1,** (group of singers) хор. **2,** (part of a church) клирос. —**choirboy,** *n.* певчий. —**choirmaster,** *n.* хормейстер.

choke *v.t.* **1,** (prevent from breathing) душить. **2,** (clog) забивать. **3,** (of weeds) заглушать. **4,** *fol. by* **off** *or* **down** (suppress) душить; подавлять. —*v.i.* **1,** (on something caught in one's throat) давиться; поперхнуться. **2,** (with tears, anger, etc.) задыхаться (от). —*n., mech.* дроссель.

cholera *n.* холера. —*adj.* холерный: *cholera epidemic,* холерная эпидемия. —**choleric,** *adj.* холерический.

cholesterol *n.* холестерин.

choose *v.t.* **1,** (select) выбирать. **2,** *fol. by inf.* (elect) решать; решаться; предпочитать. —*v.i.* выбирать; делать выбор.

choosy *adj., colloq.* привередливый.

chop *v.t.* **1,** (hew) рубить; колоть: *chop wood,* рубить/колоть дрова. **2,** (mince) рубить: *chop meat/onions,* рубить мясо/лук. —*n.* (отбивная) котлета. *Lamb chop,* баранья котлета. *Pork chop,* свиная котлета; свиная отбивная. —**chop down,** рубить; срубать; вырубать. —**chop off,** отрубить. —**chop up,** рубить; крошить.

chopped *adj.* рубленый: *chopped meat,* рубленое мясо.

chopper *n.* **1,** (tool) косарь; секач. **2,** *colloq.* (helicopter) вертолёт.

choppy *adj.* **1,** (rough, as of the sea) взволнованный. **2,** (jerky) резкий; порывистый.

chopsticks *n.pl.* палочки для еды.

choral *adj.* хоровой.

chorale *n.* хорал.

chord *n.* **1,** *math.* хорда. **2,** *music* аккорд. **3,** *anat.* *See* **cord. 4,** *fig.* (emotional response) струна: *strike a sensitive chord,* задеть чувствительную струну.

chore *n., usu. pl.* хлопоты: *household chores,* хлопоты по хозяйству.

chorea *n.* хорея.

choreography *n.* хореография. —**choreographer,** *n.* хореограф. —**choreographic,** *adj.* хореографический.

chorister *n.* певчий; хорист.

chorus *n.* **1,** (singing group) хор. **2,** (refrain) припев. **3,** (simultaneous utterance): *chorus of cheers,* дружные возгласы. —**in a chorus,** хором.

chosen *adj.* избранный.

Christ *n.* Христос.

christen *v.t.* **1,** (baptize) крестить. **2,** (name) нарекать.

christening n. **1,** (act) крещёние. **2,** (ceremony) крестйны.

Christian adj. христиáнский. —n. христианйн; христиáнка. —**Christian name,** ймя.

Christianity n. христиáнство.

Christmas n. рождествó. Merry Christmas!, с рождествóм! —adj. рождéственский: Christmas tree, рождéственская ёлка. —**Christmas Eve,** сочéльник.

chromatic adj. хроматйческий.

chrome n. хром. —**chrome alum,** хрóмовые квасцы́. —**chrome plating,** хромйрование; хрóмовое покрытие. —**chrome steel,** хрóмистая сталь.

chromic acid хрóмовая кислотá.

chromite n. хрóмистый железнáк; хромйт.

chromium n. хром.

chromosome n. хромосóма.

chronic adj. **1,** (of an illness or patient) хронйческий. **2,** (inveterate) застарéлый; закоренéлый. **3,** (constant) вéчный: chronic complaints, вéчные жáлобы.

chronicle n. лéтопись; хрóника. —v.t. заносйть в дневнйк, лéтопись, etc. —**chronicler,** n. летопйсец.

chronology n. хронолóгия. —**chronological,** adj. хронологйческий.

chronometer n. хронóметр.

chrysalis n. кýколка.

chrysanthemum n. хризантéма.

chubby adj. пýхлый.

chuck n. **1,** (cut of beef) лопáтка. **2,** (clamp; wedge) патрóн. —v.t. **1,** (toss) швырáть. **2,** colloq. (toss out) вышвыривать.

chuckle n. смешóк. —v.i. посмéиваться.

chum n. товáрищ; прийтель.

chunk n. ломóть.

chunky adj. плóтный; коренáстый.

church n. цéрковь. —adj. церкóвный: church bells, церкóвные колоколá. —**churchwarden,** n. церкóвный стáроста.

churl n. грубийн. —**churlish,** adj. грýбый; злой.

churn n. маслобóйка. —v.t. **1,** (stir) сбивáть; пáхтать. **2,** fol. by **up** (dig up; tear up) изрывáть. **3,** fol. by **up** (cause to swirl, as water) взбивáть.

chute n. жёлоб; лотóк.

cicada n. цикáда.

cider n. сидр.

cigar n. сигáра. —adj. сигáрный: cigar smoke, сигáрный дым.

cigarette n. папирóса; сигарéта. —adj. папирóсный; сигарéтный: cigarette smoke, папирóсный/сигарéтный дым. Cigarette butt, окýрок папирóсы. —**cigarette case,** портсигáр. —**cigarette holder,** мундштýк. —**cigarette lighter,** зажигáлка.

cinch n. **1,** (saddle girth) подпрýга. **2,** colloq. (easy thing to do) пустякй.

cinchona n. хйнное дéрево.

cinder n. пéпел; pl. золá; гарь. —adj. гаревóй: cinder path, гаревáя дорóжка.

Cinderella n. Зóлушка.

cinema n. **1,** preceded by **the** (motion pictures collectively) кинó. **2,** (motion-picture theater) кинó; кинотеáтр.

cinematography n. кинематогрáфия.

cinnabar n. кйноварь.

cinnamon n. корйца.

cipher n. **1,** (zero) нуль. **2,** (code) шифр.

Circassian adj. черкéсский. —n. черкéс.

circle n. **1,** (round figure; circular movement) круг. **2,** geog. круг: Arctic Circle, Сéверный полáрный круг. **3,** (small group) круг: circle of acquaintances, круг знакóмых. Ruling circles, прáвящие кругй. **4,** (social group) кружóк: dramatic circle, драматйческий кружóк. —v.t. **1,** (draw a circle around) обводйть. **2,** (go around) обходйть; объезжáть; облетáть; вращáться; (all with вокрýг). —v.i. кружйть(ся); опйсывать кругй.

circuit n. **1,** aerospace оборóт: three circuits of the earth, три оборóта вокрýг Землй. **2,** (regular journey) обхóд; объéзд. **3,** electricity цепь; кóнтур. Short circuit, корóткое замыкáние. **4,** electronics схéма: integrated circuit, интегрáльная схéма. —**circuit breaker,** прерывáтель. —**circuit court,** окружнóй суд.

circuitous adj. окóльный; обхóдный; крýжный.

circular adj. **1,** (round) крýглый. **2,** (moving in a circle) круговóй; кругообрáзный. —n. циркулáр.

circulate v.i. **1,** (move, as of blood) обращáться; циркулйровать. **2,** econ. (of money) обращáться. **3,** (spread, as of rumors) циркулйровать; распространáться. —v.t. рассылáть; распространáть.

circulation n. **1,** (movement, as of air) циркулáция. **2,** (of blood) обращéние (крóви); кровообращéние: poor circulation, плохóе кровообращéние. **3,** (use) оборóт; обращéние: put into circulation, пустйть в оборóт/в обращéние. **4,** econ. обращéние: withdraw from circulation, изъáть из обращéния. **5,** (number of copies sold) тирáж.

circulatory adj. кровенóсный: circulatory system, кровенóсная систéма.

circumcise v.t. обрезáть. —**circumcision,** n. обрéзание.

circumference n. окрýжность.

circumlocution n. окóличности.

circumnavigate v.t. Circumnavigate the globe, совершáть кругосвéтное плáвание.

circumscribe v.t. **1,** (limit) огранйчивать. **2,** math. опйсывать. —**circumscription,** n. ограничéние.

circumspect adj. осмотрйтельный. —**circumspection,** n. осмотрйтельность.

circumstance n. **1,** (fact; event) обстоáтельство. **2,** pl. (financial condition) обстоáтельства: in straitened circumstances, в стеснённых обстоáтельствах. —**under no circumstances,** ни в кóем слýчае; ни под какйм вйдом; ни при какйх обстоáтельствах; ни при какйх услóвиях.

circumstantial evidence кóсвенные улйки.

circumvent v.t. **1,** (surround; encircle) окружáть. **2,** (go around; bypass) обходйть.

circus n. цирк. —adj. цирковóй: circus performer, цирковóй артйст.

cirrhosis n. циррóз: cirrhosis of the liver, циррóз пéчени.

cistern n. цистéрна.

citadel n. цитадéль.

citation n. **1,** (act of quoting) цитйрование. **2,** (quote) цитáта; ссылка. **3,** (commendation) благодáрность. **4,** (summons) вызов.

cite v.t. **1,** (quote) ссылáться на; цитйровать. **2,** (refer to, as an example) приводйть. **3,** (commend, as for bravery) отличáть. **4,** law привлекáть к отвéтственности.

citizen *n.* граждани́н. —**citizenship**, *n.* гражда́нство.

citrate *n.* цитра́т.

citric acid лимо́нная кислота́.

citrus *n.* ци́трус. —*adj.* цитрусовый.

city *n.* го́род. —*adj.* городско́й: *city council,* городско́й сове́т. —**city hall**, ра́туша.

civet *n.* виве́рра.

civic *adj.* гражда́нский: *civic duty,* гражда́нский долг.

civil *adj.* **1,** (pert. to citizens) гражда́нский. **2,** (polite) ве́жливый. —**civil defense,** гражда́нская оборо́на. —**civil engineer,** инжене́р-строи́тель. —**civil marriage,** гражда́нский брак. —**civil rights,** гражда́нские права́. —**civil servant,** госуда́рственный слу́жащий. —**civil service,** госуда́рственная слу́жба. —**civil war,** гражда́нская война́.

civilian *n.* шта́тский (челове́к). —*adj.* шта́тский; гражда́нский.

civility *n.* ве́жливость.

civilization *n.* цивилиза́ция.

civilize *v.t.* цивилизова́ть. —**civilized,** *adj.* цивилизо́ванный.

clabber *n.* простоква́ша.

clack *v.i.* цо́кать. —*n.* цо́кот.

clad *adj.* оде́тый. *Snow-clad,* заснеженный.

claim *v.t.* **1,** (assert one's right to) тре́бовать: *claim damages,* тре́бовать возмеще́ния убы́тков. **2,** (call for; pick up) востре́бовать. **3,** (maintain; assert) утвержда́ть. —*n.* **1,** (request; demand) прете́нзия; притяза́ние; тре́бование. **2,** (assertion; contention) утвержде́ние. —**lay claim to,** претендова́ть на; предъявля́ть тре́бование *or* пра́во на.

claimant *n.* претенде́нт.

claim check квита́нция.

clairvoyance *n.* яснови́дение.

clairvoyant *adj.* яснови́дящий. —*n.* яснови́дец.

clam *n.* моллю́ск. —*v.i.* [*usu.* **clam up**] *colloq.* замолча́ть.

clamber *v.i.* кара́бкаться.

clamor *also,* **clamour** *n.* **1,** (din) шум; гам. **2,** (public outcry) шум. —*v.i.* крича́ть; шуме́ть.

clamp *n.* зажи́м; скре́па. —*v.t.* скрепля́ть. —**clamp down on,** подтя́гивать; прируни́вать.

clan *n.* клан.

clandestine *adj.* та́йный; скры́тый.

clang *n.* лязг. —*v.t. & i.* ля́згать.

clank *n.* лязг; цо́кот. —*v.t. & i.* ля́згать; бряца́ть; цо́кать.

clannish *adj.* за́мкнутый; обосо́бленный.

clap *v.t.* **1,** (strike together, as one's hands) бить; ударя́ть; хло́пать (в ладо́ши). **2,** (toss, as into jail) упря́тывать; упека́ть. —*v.i.* хло́пать. —*n.* **1,** (act of clapping) хло́панье. **2,** (sound, as of thunder) уда́р; раска́т. *There was a clap of thunder,* уда́рил гром.

clapper *n.* язы́к (ко́локола).

claque *n.* кла́ка. —**claqueur,** *n.* клакёр.

claret *n.* (wine) бордо́. —*adj.* (color) бордо́; цве́та бордо́; бордо́вый.

clarification *n.* разъясне́ние.

clarify *v.t.* разъясня́ть; проясня́ть; выясня́ть.

clarinet *n.* кларне́т. —**clarinetist,** *n.* кларнети́ст.

clarion *n.* фанфа́ра. —*adj.* гро́мкий; зву́чный.

clarity *n.* я́сность.

clash *v.i.* **1,** (come into conflict) ста́лкиваться. **2,**

(not go well together) дисгармони́ровать. —*n.* столкнове́ние.

clasp *n.* **1,** (hook) застёжка. **2,** (grip) объя́тие; пожа́тие. —*v.t.* **1,** (fasten) застёгивать. **2,** (grasp) обнима́ть; обхва́тывать. **3,** in *clasp one's hands,* всплесну́ть рука́ми.

class *n.* **1,** (in most meanings) класс: *the working class,* рабо́чий класс. *Go to class,* идти́ в класс. *Travel first class,* е́хать пе́рвым кла́ссом. **2,** (alumni graduated in one year) вы́пуск: *the class of 1970,* вы́пуск 1970-го го́да. —*adj.* **1,** (pert. to social classes) кла́ссовый: *class consciousness,* кла́ссовое созна́ние. **2,** (pert. to a class in school) кла́ссный. —*v.t.* классифици́ровать.

classic *n.* **1,** (writer) кла́ссик. **2,** (work) класси́ческое произведе́ние; *pl.* кла́ссика. —*adj.* класси́ческий.

classical *adj.* класси́ческий.

classicism *n.* классици́зм. —**classicist,** *n.* кла́ссик.

classification *n.* **1,** (act of classifying) классифика́ция. **2,** *mil.* гриф секре́тности.

classified *adj.* **1,** (grouped) классифици́рованный. **2,** *mil.* секре́тный; засекре́ченный. —**classified ad,** объявле́ние (в газе́те).

classify *v.t.* **1,** (arrange by class) классифици́ровать. **2,** (declare to be secret) засекре́чивать.

classless *adj.* бескла́ссовый.

classmate *n.* однокла́ссник.

classroom *n.* класс; кла́ссная ко́мната.

classy *adj., colloq.* шика́рный; первокла́ссный.

clatter *n.* стук; то́пот; цо́кот. —*v.i.* греме́ть; громыха́ть; цо́кать; тараба́нить.

clause *n.* **1,** (part of a sentence) предложе́ние. **2,** (article; provision) статья́; пункт.

claustrophobia *n.* боя́знь остава́ться в закры́том помеще́нии; клаустрофо́бия.

clavichord *n.* клавико́рды.

clavicle *n.* ключи́ца.

claw *n.* **1,** (of a bird or animal) ко́готь. **2,** (of a lobster or crab) клешня́. **3,** (of a hammer) ла́па. —*v.t.* терза́ть когтя́ми.

clay *n.* гли́на. —*adj.* гли́няный: *clay tablets,* гли́няные табли́чки. —**clayey,** *adj.* гли́нистый.

clean *adj.* чи́стый: *clean shirt/plate,* чи́стая руба́шка/таре́лка. —*adv.* **1,** (so as to be clean) на́чисто: *sweep the floor clean,* на́чисто вы́мести пол. *Lick the plate clean,* обли́зывать таре́лку. **2,** (completely) соверше́нно: *I clean forgot,* я соверше́нно забы́л(а). —*v.t.* чи́стить: *clean a carpet,* чи́стить ко́вер. —**clean out, 1,** (clear of rubbish) очища́ть. **2,** *colloq.* (of a robber) очища́ть; обокра́сть *or* огра́бить до́чиста; (in gambling) обчища́ть; обыгра́ть до́чиста. —**clean up, 1,** (tidy up) убира́ть; прибира́ть. **2,** *colloq.* (finish) зако́нчить. **3,** *slang* (make a lot of money) сорва́ть куш.

clean-cut *adj.* опря́тный; вы́холенный.

cleaner *n.* **1,** (person) чи́стильщик; убо́рщик. **2,** (establishment) химчи́стка: *take to the cleaners,* отдава́ть в химчи́стку.

cleaning *n.* чи́стка. —**cleaning woman,** убо́рщица.

cleanliness *n.* чистота́.

cleanly *adj.* чистопло́тный. —*adv.* чи́сто.

cleanse *v.t.* чи́стить; очища́ть. —**cleanser,** *n.* мо́ющее сре́дство.

clean-shaven *adj.* бри́тый; гла́дко вы́бритый.

clear *adj.* **1,** (bright; easily understood) ясный: *clear day/answer,* ясный день/ответ. *As clear as day,* ясный как божий день. *Make it clear that...,* дать ясно понять, что... **2,** (pure; unblemished) чистый: *clear water/skin/conscience,* чистая вода/кожа/ совесть. **3,** (unobstructed) свободный: *the way is clear,* путь свободен. —*adv.* **1,** (distinctly) ясно: *loud and clear,* громко и ясно. **2,** (all the way): *clear to the top,* до самой вершины. —*v.t.* **1,** (rid of dirt, unwanted objects, etc.) очищать: *clear the windshield,* очищать переднее стекло. *Clear the air,* очищать воздух; *fig.* разрядить атмосферу. *Clear one's throat,* откашливаться. *Clear a forest,* очищать лес. *Clear a path,* расчищать дорожку. *Clear the table,* убирать со стола. *Clear the way,* открывать путь. **2,** (empty; vacate) освобождать; очищать: *clear the premises,* освобождать/очищать помещение. **3,** (remove) убирать; считать. *Clear the dishes from the table,* убирать посуду со стола. *Clear the snow off the sidewalk,* считать снег с тротуара. **4,** (jump over) брать: *clear a hurdle,* брать барьер. **5,** (acquit) оправдывать. **6,** (authorize to see classified information) засекречивать. **7,** (earn; net) выручать. **8,** in *clear one's name,* восстановить своё доброе имя. —*v.i.* проясняться: *the sky is clearing,* небо проясняется. —**clear away,** убирать; считать. —**clear out, 1,** (empty; clean up) очищать. **2,** *colloq.* (depart) убираться. —**clear up, 1,** (clean up) очищать. **2,** (clarify; solve) разъяснять. *The matter was cleared up,* дело разъяснилось. **3,** (grow fair, as of the weather) проясняться. **4,** (disappear, as of a cold, rash, etc.) проходить.

clearance *n.* **1,** (space) зазор. **2,** (sale) распродажа. **3,** = security clearance.

clear-cut *adj.* чёткий.

clearing *n.* **1,** (act of making clear) очистка; очищение; расчистка. **2,** (place cleared of trees) вырубка; поляна. **3,** *comm.* клиринг; безналичный расчёт. —**clearing house,** расчётная палата.

clearly *adv.* **1,** (in a clear manner) ясно. **2,** (without a doubt) несомненно. **3,** (obviously) очевидно.

cleat *n.* шип: *shoes with cleats,* башмаки на шипах.

cleavage *n.* раскол.

cleave *v.t.* раскалывать; рассекать.

cleaver *n.* тяпка; сечка.

clef *n.* ключ.

cleft *n.* расселина; расщелина; трещина. —*adj.* раздвоенный. —**cleft palate,** волчья пасть.

clematis *n.* ломонос.

clemency *n.* милосердие; пощада; помилование.

clench *v.t.* сжимать. *Clenched fists,* сжатые кулаки.

clergy *n.* духовенство. —**clergyman,** *n.* священник; духовное лицо.

cleric *n.* духовное лицо.

clerical *adj.* **1,** (pert. to the clergy) духовный. **2,** (pert. to office work) канцелярский.

clerk *n.* **1,** (office worker) конторский служащий; клерк. **2,** (salesperson) продавец; приказчик. **3,** (record-keeper) регистратор.

clever *adj.* **1,** (bright; intelligent) умный; сообразительный; смышлёный. **2,** (showing skill or wit) ловкий; остроумный. —**cleverly,** *adv.* ловко; остроумно. —**cleverness,** *n.* ловкость; сообразительность.

cliché *n.* клише; штамп.

click *n.* щелчок: *the click of a camera,* щелчок фотоаппарата. —*v.t.* щёлкать (+ *instr.*). *Click one's heels,* щёлкать *or* пристукивать каблуками. —*v.i.* щёлкать: *the camera clicked,* фотоаппарат щёлкнул.

client *n.* **1,** (customer) клиент. **2,** (of a lawyer) подзащитный. —**clientele,** *n.* клиентура.

cliff *n.* утёс; (отвесная) скала. *Fall over a cliff,* упасть со скалы.

climactic *adj.* кульминационный.

climate *n.* **1,** (type of weather) климат. **2,** *fig.* (prevailing conditions) атмосфера. —**climatic,** *adj.* климатический.

climax *n.* **1,** (culmination) кульминационный пункт. **2,** (dénouement) развязка.

climb *v.i.* **1,** (clamber) лезть: *climb up on the roof,* лезть на крышу. **2,** (increase; rise) расти. **3,** (gain altitude) набирать высоту. —*v.t.* лезть на; влезать на; взбираться на. *Climb a tree,* лезть *or* влезать на дерево. *Climb (the) stairs,* подниматься по лестнице. —*n.* **1,** (act of climbing) подъём; восхождение. **2,** *aero.* набор высоты. —**climb down,** слезать. —**climb in,** влезать. —**climb out,** вылезать. —**climb over,** перелезать.

climber *n.* **1,** (mountain climber) альпинист. **2,** (plant) вьющееся растение.

climbing *n.* лазанье. *Mountain climbing,* альпинизм. —*adj.* (of a plant) вьющийся. —**climbing irons,** кошки.

clinch *v.t.* **1,** (secure; fasten) заклёпывать. **2,** *fig.* (settle for good) решать. *Clinch a deal,* заключить сделку.

cling *v.i.* [*usu.* cling to] цепляться (за). *Cling to life,* цепляться за жизнь. *Cling to a hope,* цепляться за надежду.

clinic *n.* клиника. —**clinical,** *adj.* клинический.

clink *n.* **1,** (sound) звон. **2,** *slang* (jail) кутузка. —*v.t.* звенеть (+ *instr.*). *Clink glasses,* чокаться.

clip *n.* **1,** (metal fastener) скрепка. **2,** (piece of jewelry) брошь. **3,** (cartridge clip) (патронная) обойма. **4,** *colloq.* (pace) ход: *at a fast clip,* быстрым ходом. —*v.t.* **1,** (fasten with a clip) скреплять. **2,** (trim) стричь; обрезать; подрезать. **3,** *fol. by* out (cut out) вырезать. **4,** *colloq.* (strike) дать: *clip someone on the ear,* дать кому-нибудь по уху. —**clip someone's wings,** подрезать крылья (+ *dat.*).

clipper *n.* **1,** *usu. pl.* (shears) ножницы. **2,** *usu. pl.* (device for cutting hair) машинка для стрижки. **3,** (ship) клипер.

clipping *n.* вырезка.

clique *n.* клика.

clitoris *n.* клитор; похотник.

cloak *n.* **1,** (garment) плащ; мантия. **2,** *fig.* (guise; cover) покров; ширма; маска. —*v.t.* прикрывать; маскировать.

cloakroom *n.* гардероб; раздевалка. *Cloakroom attendant,* гардеробщик.

clock *n.* часы. *Alarm clock,* будильник. —*v.t.* хронометрировать. —**round the clock,** круглые сутки.

clockwise *adv.* по часовой стрелке.

clockwork *n.,* in **work like clockwork,** работать как часы.

clod *n.* **1,** (lump) ком; глыба. **2,** (dolt) олух; недотёпа.

clog *v.t.* засорять; забивать. *Become clogged,* засоряться.

cloister *n.* **1,** (monastery) монасты́рь. **2,** (covered walk) (кры́тая) арка́да. —*v.t.* **1,** (confine to a monastery) заточа́ть в монасты́рь. **2,** (seclude) уединя́ть.

close[1] (klos) *adj.* **1,** (near) бли́зкий. *Close relative,* бли́зкий ро́дственник. *Close resemblance,* большо́е схо́дство. *Close combat,* бли́жний бой. **2,** (intimate) бли́зкий; те́сный. *Close friend,* бли́зкий друг. *Close connection,* те́сная связь. **3,** (tight; compact; crowded) те́сный. *Close weave,* ча́стое переплете́ние. *Close print,* убо́ристый шрифт. *Close order, mil.* со́мкнутый строй. *In close quarters,* в те́сном сосе́дстве. **4,** (keenly contested) напряжённый. *Close match,* напряжённый матч; упо́рная борьба́. *Close vote,* почти́ ра́вное деле́ние голосо́в. **5,** (rigorous; searching) внима́тельный. *Keep a close watch on,* внима́тельно следи́ть за. **6,** (stuffy) ду́шный: *it is close in here,* здесь ду́шно. —*adv.* бли́зко. *Follow close behind,* идти́ сле́дом за. *Press close to one's bosom,* прижима́ть к груди́. —**close by,** бли́зко; ря́дом. —**close to,** о́коло; бли́зко от; недалеко́ от. *He is close to sixty,* ему́ под шестьдеся́т. —**up close,** вблизи́: *the house looks different up close,* вблизи́ дом вы́глядит ина́че.

close[2] (kloz) *v.t.* **1,** (shut) закрыва́ть: *close the door,* закрыва́ть дверь; *close one's eyes,* закрыва́ть глаза́. **2,** (fill up; stop up) заде́лывать: *close a hole with putty,* заде́лывать ды́ру зама́зкой. **3,** (bring together; join) смыка́ть; спла́чивать: *close ranks,* смыка́ть/спла́чивать ряды́. **4,** (conclude) заключа́ть: *close a deal,* заключи́ть сде́лку. —*v.i.* закрыва́ться: *the window won't close,* окно́ не закрыва́ется. —*n.* закры́тие; коне́ц. *Draw to a close,* приближа́ться к концу́. —**close down,** закрыва́ть; прикрыва́ть. —**close in,** смыка́ть кольцо́ окруже́ния. —**close out,** распрода́ть. —**in closing,** в заключе́ние.

closed *adj.* закры́тый. *The city is closed to foreigners,* го́род закры́т для иностра́нцев.

close-fisted *adj.* прижи́мистый.

close-fitting *adj.* те́сный. *Close-fitting dress,* пла́тье, пло́тно облега́ющее фигу́ру.

close-knit *adj.* спа́янный.

closely *adv.* **1,** (intimately) те́сно: *closely connected,* те́сно свя́занный. **2,** (attentively) внима́тельно; чу́тко.

close-mouthed *adj.* за́мкнутый.

closeness *n.* **1,** (nearness) бли́зость. **2,** (tightness) теснота́. **3,** (stuffiness) духота́.

close-out *n.* распрода́жа.

closet *n.* шкаф. —*v.t.* [*usu.* **closet oneself**] уединя́ться.

close-up *n.* кру́пный план. *Take a close-up of,* снима́ть (кого́-нибудь) кру́пным пла́ном.

closing *n.* **1,** (act of shutting) закры́тие. *Closing time,* вре́мя закры́тия. **2,** (end; conclusion) заключе́ние. —*adj.* заключи́тельный.

closure *n.* закры́тие.

clot *n.* сгу́сток: *blood clot,* сгу́сток кро́ви. —*v.t.* сгуща́ть. —*v.i.* сгуща́ться; запека́ться.

cloth *n.* **1,** (fabric) ткань; сукно́; мате́рия. **2,** (small piece for wiping or dusting) суко́нка; тря́пка. —*adj.* суко́нный: *cloth coat,* суко́нное пальто́.

clothe *v.t.* одева́ть.

clothes *n.pl.* оде́жда; пла́тье. —*adj.* платяно́й: *clothes brush,* платяна́я щётка. —**clothesline,** *n.* верёвка для белья́. —**clothespin,** *n.* прище́пка.

clothier *n.* торго́вец гото́вой оде́ждой.

clothing *n.* оде́жда; пла́тье. —*adj.* вещево́й: *clothing allowance,* вещево́е дово́льствие. *Clothing store,* магази́н гото́вого пла́тья.

cloture *n.* прекраще́ние пре́ний.

cloud *n.* о́блако. *Storm cloud,* ту́ча. *Cloud of dust,* клуб пы́ли. —*adj.* о́блачный: *cloud cover,* о́блачный покро́в. —*v.t.* затемня́ть; омрача́ть; затума́нивать. —*v.i.* [*usu.* **cloud up**] затума́ниваться. —**be up in the clouds,** вита́ть в облака́х.

cloudberry *n.* моро́шка.

cloudburst *n.* ли́вень.

cloudiness *n.* о́блачность.

cloudless *adj.* безо́блачный.

cloudy *adj.* **1,** (full of or covered with clouds) о́блачный. **2,** (murky, as of a liquid) му́тный.

clout *n., colloq.* тума́к.

clove *n.* гвозди́ка.

cloven *adj.* раздво́енный. —**cloven hoof,** раздво́енное копы́то.

clover *n.* кле́вер. —**be in clover,** ката́ться как сыр в ма́сле; жить припева́ючи.

clown *n.* кло́ун. —*v.i.* пая́сничать; дура́читься. —**clownish,** *adj.* кло́унский; шутовско́й.

cloy *v.t.* пресыща́ть. —**cloying,** *adj.* прито́рный; слаща́вый.

club *n.* **1,** (cudgel) дуби́на; дуби́нка. **2,** (golf club) клю́шка. **3,** (association or its headquarters) клуб. **4,** *pl., cards* тре́фы. —*v.t.* избива́ть; дуба́сить.

clubfoot *n.* изуро́дованная ступня́.

club soda со́довая вода́.

cluck *v.i.* клохта́ть. —*n.* клохта́нье.

clue *n.* путево́дная нить. *Leave no clues,* не оставля́ть никаки́х следо́в. *Give someone a clue,* наводи́ть кого́-нибудь на след. *I haven't a clue,* поня́тия не име́ю.

clump *n.* **1,** (cluster) гру́ппа: *clump of trees,* гру́ппа дере́вьев. **2,** (lump) комо́к. **3,** (sound of heavy footsteps) то́пот.

clumsy *adj.* неуклю́жий. —**clumsily,** *adv.* неуклю́же. —**clumsiness,** *n.* неуклю́жесть.

cluster *n.* **1,** (bunch, as of grapes) кисть; гроздь. **2,** (small group) гру́ппа; ку́чка. *Star cluster,* звёздное скопле́ние. —*v.i.* [*usu.* **cluster around**] окружа́ть; обступа́ть.

clutch *v.t.* хвата́ть; схва́тывать. —*v.i.* [*usu.* **clutch at**] хвата́ться за. —*n.* **1,** (grip) хва́тка. **2,** *mech.* му́фта; сцепле́ние. —**fall into the clutches of,** попа́сть в ко́гти к; попа́сть в ла́пы (+ *dat.*).

clutter *v.t.* [*usu.* **clutter up**] загроможда́ть.

coach *n.* **1,** (carriage) каре́та. **2,** (tutor) репети́тор. **3,** *sports* тре́нер. —*v.t.* **1,** (tutor) репети́ровать; ната́скивать. **2,** *sports* трениро́вать. **3,** (prompt) подска́зывать: *no coaching!,* не подска́зывать!

coach house каре́тный сара́й.

coachman *n.* ку́чер; во́зница; изво́зчик.

coagulant *n.* сгуща́ющее сре́дство; коагуля́нт.

coagulate *v.t.* сгуща́ть; свёртывать. —*v.i.* сгуща́ться; свёртываться; запека́ться. —**coagulation,** *n.* свёртывание; коагуля́ция.

coal *n.* **1,** (mineral) у́голь. **2,** *pl.* (embers) у́гли. —*adj.* у́гольный; каменноу́гольный. *Coal mine,* у́гольная ша́хта. —**rake over the coals,** зада́ть жа́ру (+ *dat.*); взять под обстре́л.

coalesce *v.i.* **1,** (grow together) сраста́ться. **2,**

(unite; merge) объединя́ться; слива́ться. —**coalescence**, *n.* сраще́ние; соедине́ние.

coalition *n.* коали́ция. —*adj.* коалицио́нный.

coal tar каменноуго́льный дёготь.

coarse *adj.* **1,** (rough; crude; unrefined) гру́бый. **2,** (not fine, as of sand) кру́пный.

coarsen *v.t.* де́лать гру́бым. —*v.i.* грубе́ть.

coarseness *n.* гру́бость.

coast *n.* **1,** (edge of the land facing the sea) бе́рег: *along the coast,* вдоль бе́рега; *rocky coast,* скали́стый бе́рег. **2,** (region next to the sea) побере́жье: *the West Coast,* за́падное побере́жье. —*v.i.* кати́ться (свобо́дным колесо́м). —**the coast is clear,** путь свобо́ден.

coastal *adj.* бергово́й; прибре́жный.

coast guard 1, (unit guarding a coast) берегова́я охра́на. **2,** *cap.* (U.S. branch of service) морска́я пограни́чная слу́жба.

coastline *n.* берегова́я ли́ния.

coat *n.* **1,** (overcoat) пальто́. *Fur coat,* шу́ба. **2,** (suit jacket) пиджа́к. **3,** (skin; fur) мех; шку́ра. **4,** (layer, as of paint) слой. —*v.t.* покрыва́ть; залива́ть. *My tongue is coated,* у меня́ обложи́ло язы́к. —**coat of arms,** герб. —**coat of mail,** па́нцирь; кольчу́га.

coati *n.* носу́ха.

coating *n.* покры́тие; налёт.

coatroom *n.* гардеро́б; раздева́лка.

coattail *n.* фа́лда.

coauthor *n.* соа́втор. —**coauthorship**, *n.* соа́вторство.

coax *v.t.* **1,** (try to persuade) угова́ривать; убежда́ть. **2,** (obtain by persuasion) выпра́шивать.

coaxial cable коаксиа́льный ка́бель.

cob *n.* поча́ток кукуру́зы.

cobalt *n.* ко́бальт. —*adj.* ко́бальтовый.

cobbled *adj.* булы́жный.

cobbler *n.* сапо́жник.

cobblestone *n.* булы́жник. —*adj.* булы́жный.

cobra *n.* очко́вая змея́; ко́бра.

cobweb *n.* паути́на.

coca *n.* ко́ка.

cocaine *n.* кока́ин.

coccus *n.* кокк.

coccyx *n.* ко́пчик.

co-chairman *n.* сопредседа́тель.

cochineal *n.* коше́ниль.

cock *n.* **1,** (rooster) пету́х. **2,** (faucet) кран. **3,** (hammer of a firearm) куро́к. —*v.t.* **1,** (tilt) зала́мывать (ша́пку). *Cock one's head to one side,* склони́ть го́лову на́бок. **2,** (set, as a firearm) взводи́ть куро́к (пистоле́та). *The gun is cocked,* куро́к на боево́м взво́де.

cockade *n.* кока́рда.

cock-and-bull story небыли́ца; ро́ссказни.

cockatoo *n.* какаду́.

cockchafer *n.* ма́йский жук; хрущ.

cocked hat треуго́лка.

cockerel *n.* петушо́к.

cockeyed *adj.* **1,** (cross-eyed) косогла́зый. **2,** *colloq.* (askew) косо́й. **3,** *colloq.* (absurd) глу́пый; дура́цкий.

cockfight *n.* петуши́ный бой.

cockle *n.* **1,** (weed) ку́коль; пле́вел. **2,** (mollusk) сердцеви́дка. —**cockles of one's heart,** тайники́ се́рдца.

cockpit *n.* каби́на (самолёта).

cockroach *n.* тарака́н.

cockscomb *n.* **1,** (comb of a cock) петуши́ный гре́бень. **2,** (plant) петуши́й гребешо́к.

cocksure *adj.* **1,** (absolutely sure) вполне́ уве́ренный. **2,** (too sure of oneself) самоуве́ренный.

cocktail *n.* кокте́йль.

cocky *adj., colloq.* самоуве́ренный; чванли́вый.

coco *n.* коко́совая па́льма; коко́с. *Also,* **coco palm; coconut palm.**

cocoa *n.* кака́о.

coconut *n.* коко́совый оре́х; коко́с. —*adj.* коко́совый.

cocoon *n.* ко́кон.

cod *n.* треска́.

C.O.D. нало́женным платежо́м.

coddle *v.t.* не́жить; изне́живать.

code *n.* **1,** (body of laws) ко́декс; свод зако́нов. **2,** (system of secret communication) код.

codeine *n.* кодеи́н.

codfish *n.* треска́.

codicil *n.* припи́ска.

codify *v.t.* кодифици́ровать. —**codification**, *n.* кодифика́ция.

cod-liver oil ры́бий жир.

coeducation *n.* совме́стное обуче́ние. —**coeducational**, *adj.* совме́стного обуче́ния.

coefficient *n.* коэффицие́нт.

coerce *v.t.* принужда́ть; заставля́ть. —**coercion**, *n.* принужде́ние. —**coercive**, *adj.* принуди́тельный.

coexist *v.i.* сосуществова́ть. —**coexistence**, *n.* сосуществова́ние.

coffee *n.* ко́фе. —*adj.* кофе́йный: *coffee beans,* кофе́йные бобы́. —**coffee-colored**, *adj.* кофе́йный; кофе́йного цве́та. —**coffee house,** кафе́. —**coffee mill,** кофе́йная ме́льница; кофе́йница. —**coffeepot**, *n.* кофе́йник.

coffer *n.* **1,** (strongbox) (де́нежный) я́щик. **2,** *pl.* (treasury) казна́.

coffin *n.* гроб.

cog *n.* зубе́ц.

cogent *adj.* убеди́тельный. —**cogency**, *n.* убеди́тельность.

cogitate *v.i.* размышля́ть; разду́мывать. —**cogitation**, *n.* размышле́ние.

cognac *n.* конья́к.

cognate *adj.* ро́дственный. —*n.* ро́дственное сло́во.

cognition *n.* позна́ние. —**cognitive**, *adj.* познава́тельный.

cognizance *n.* зна́ние. —**take cognizance of,** обраща́ть внима́ние на.

cognizant *adj.* *Be cognizant of,* осознава́ть; отдава́ть себе́ отчёт в.

cogwheel *n.* зубча́тое колесо́; шестерня́.

cohabit *v.i.* сожи́тельствовать. —**cohabitation**, *n.* сожи́тельство.

cohere *v.i.* слипа́ться; сепля́ться.

coherent *adj.* свя́зный; стро́йный. —**coherence**, *n.* свя́зность.

cohesion *n.* сплочённость. —**cohesive**, *adj.* сплочённый.

cohort *n.* **1,** (band) отря́д. **2,** (associate) посо́бник.

coil *n.* **1,** (roll) вито́к. **2,** *electricity* кату́шка. —*v.t.* нама́тывать; обма́тывать. —*v.i.* ви́ться; обвива́ться.

coin *n.* моне́та. —*v.t.* **1,** (mint) чека́нить. **2,** (invent, as a word or expression) создава́ть. —**the other side of the coin,** оборо́тная сторона́ меда́ли.

coinage n. **1,** (making of coins) чека́нка (моне́ты). **2,** (newly coined word) новообразова́ние.

coincide v.i. совпада́ть.

coincidence n. совпаде́ние: *by a curious coincidence,* по забавному совпаде́нию.

coincidental adj. случа́йный. *It's purely coincidental,* э́то чи́стая случа́йность.

coition n. совокупле́ние. *Also,* **coitus.**

coke n. кокс. —adj. ко́ксовый; коксова́льный: *coke oven,* ко́ксовая/коксова́льная печь. —**coking coal,** коксу́ющийся у́голь.

colander n. дуршла́г.

cold adj. холо́дный. *It is cold,* хо́лодно. *It is getting cold,* холода́ет. *I am cold,* мне хо́лодно. *Get cold (of food),* стыть; сты́нуть; остыва́ть. *Grow cold toward someone,* охладе́ть к кому́-нибудь. —adv., colloq. соверше́нно: *cold sober,* соверше́нно трезв. *Know something cold,* знать что́-нибудь до то́чки. *Turn down cold,* отказа́ть наотре́з. —n. **1,** (low temperature) хо́лод. **2,** (ailment) простуда; на́сморк. *Catch cold,* простуди́ться. —**be left out in the cold,** оста́ться за бо́ртом. —**leave someone cold,** не производи́ть никако́го впечатле́ния на. —**throw cold water on,** обли́ть холо́дной водо́й.

cold-blooded adj. **1,** zool. холоднокро́вный. **2,** (sensitive to cold) зя́бкий. **3,** (callous; heartless) хладнокро́вный.

cold cream кольдкре́м.

coldly adv. хо́лодно.

coldness n. хо́лодность.

cold war холо́дная война́.

coleslaw n. сала́т из шинко́ванной капу́сты.

colic n. ко́лики.

coliseum n. колизе́й.

colitis n. воспале́ние то́лстых кишо́к; коли́т.

collaborate v.i. сотру́дничать. *Collaborate on a book,* совме́стно писа́ть кни́гу. *Collaborate with the enemy,* сотру́дничать с враго́м. —**collaboration,** n. сотру́дничество.

collaborator n. **1,** (associate) сотру́дник. **2,** (one who collaborates with the enemy) коллаборацио́нист.

collapse v.i. **1,** (cave in) ру́шиться; ру́хнуть; обру́шиваться; обва́ливаться; прова́ливаться; разва́ливаться. **2,** (break down completely) ру́хнуть; разва́ливаться; потерпе́ть крах. **3,** (break down physically) свали́ться. —n. **1,** (caving in) обва́л; разва́л. **2,** (failure) распа́д; разва́л; круше́ние; крах. **3,** (extreme prostration) изнеможе́ние.

collapsible adj. складно́й; раскладно́й; разбо́рный; откидно́й.

collar n. **1,** (of a coat) воротни́к; (of a shirt, blouse, etc.) воротничо́к. **2,** (for a dog) оше́йник; (for a horse) хому́т. —v.t., colloq. схва́тывать. —**get hot under the collar,** (раз)горячи́ться. —**seize by the collar,** взять за ши́ворот.

collarbone n. ключи́ца.

collate v.t. слича́ть; сверя́ть.

collateral n. гара́нтия; обеспе́чение. —adj. **1,** (secondary; additional) побо́чный; второстепе́нный; дополни́тельный. **2,** (guaranteed by something pledged) обеспе́ченный.

colleague n. колле́га; сослужи́вец.

collect v.t. **1,** (gather) собира́ть: *collect evidence,* собира́ть доказа́тельства. *Collect one's thoughts,* собира́ться с мы́слями. **2,** (save as a hobby) собира́ть; коллекциони́ровать. **3,** (pick up; call for) заезжа́ть за. **4,** (pick up and take with one) брать: *collect one's mail,* брать по́чту. *Collect the garbage,* брать or увози́ть му́сор. **5,** (receive in payment) получа́ть: *collect a pension,* получа́ть пе́нсию. *Collect taxes,* собира́ть нало́ги. **6,** (gather, as dust) покрыва́ться (пы́лью). —v.i. собира́ться; набира́ться; ска́пливаться; накопля́ться. *Dust collected on the shelf,* пыль собрала́сь на по́лке. —**collect oneself,** овладе́ть собо́й.

collected adj. **1,** (gathered together) со́бранный. *Collected works,* собра́ние сочине́ний. **2,** (cool; calm; composed) хладнокро́вный.

collection n. **1,** (act of collecting) сбор; собира́ние. **2,** (assemblage, as of books, stamps, etc.) колле́кция; собра́ние. **3,** (anthology) сбо́рник. **4,** (soliciting of money) де́нежный сбор. **5,** (pickup of mail) вы́емка.

collective adj. **1,** (joint; common) коллекти́вный. **2,** gram. собира́тельный. —n. коллекти́в. —**collective farm,** колхо́з.

collectively adv. **1,** (through joint efforts) совме́стно; сообща́. **2,** (taken as a whole) в о́бщем; в совоку́пности.

collectivism n. коллективи́зм.

collectivize v.t. коллективизи́ровать. —**collectivization,** n. коллективиза́ция.

collector n. **1,** (one who collects for a hobby) коллекционе́р; собира́тель. **2,** (one who collects money due) сбо́рщик: *tax collector,* сбо́рщик нало́гов. **3,** in *ticket collector,* контроле́р; *garbage collector,* му́сорщик.

college n. **1,** (school of higher learning) университе́т; колле́дж; вуз. **2,** (body) колле́гия: *college of cardinals,* колле́гия кардина́лов. —adj. университе́тский: *a college education,* университе́тское образова́ние.

collide v.i. ста́лкиваться.

collie n. ко́лли; шотла́ндская овча́рка.

collision n. столкнове́ние.

collodion n. колло́дий.

colloid n. колло́ид. —**colloidal,** adj. колло́идный.

colloquial adj. разгово́рный. —**colloquialism,** n. разгово́рное сло́во or выраже́ние.

collusion n. сго́вор: *be in collusion with,* быть в сго́воре с.

Colombian adj. колумби́йский.

colon n. **1,** (punctuation mark) двоето́чие. **2,** anat. ободо́чная кишка́.

colonel n. полко́вник.

colonial adj. колониа́льный. —**colonialism,** n. колониали́зм. —**colonialist,** n. колониза́тор.

colonist n. колони́ст.

colonize v.t. колонизи́ровать. —**colonization,** n. колониза́ция. —**colonizer,** n. колониза́тор.

colonnade n. колонна́да.

colony n. коло́ния.

color *also,* **colour** n. **1,** (hue) цвет; кра́ска. *Local color,* ме́стный колори́т. *Color in one's cheeks,* румя́нец. *Dress in bright colors,* одева́ться в я́ркие цвета́. *Paint in bright colors,* писа́ть я́ркими кра́сками. **2,** pl. (flag; banner) знамя. *Trooping of the colors,* развод карау́ла. *Call to the colors,* призыва́ть на военную службу. —*adj.* цветной: *color television,* цветное телевидение. —*v.t.* **1,** (give color to) раскрашивать. **2,** (influence to some degree) влиять на; сказываться на. —**show one's true colors,** показать своё настоящее лицо. —**with flying colors,** с блеском.

coloration *n.* окраска; раскраска.

coloratura *n.* колоратура. —*adj.* колоратурный.

color blindness дальтонизм.

colored *adj.* цветной.

colorful *adj.* красочный.

coloring *n.* окраска; раскраска.

colorless *adj.* бесцветный.

colossal *adj.* колоссальный.

colossus *n.* колосс.

colour *see* color.

colt *n.* жеребёнок.

column *n.* **1,** (pillar) колонна. **2,** (of smoke) столб (дыма); (of mercury) столбик (ртути). **3,** (in a book, newspaper, etc.) столбец; колонка. **4,** (of figures) колонна; колонка; столбец. **5,** *mil.* колонна.

columnar *adj.* напечатанный столбцами.

columned *adj.* колонный.

columnist *n.* обозреватель; публицист.

colza *n.* сурепица.

coma *n.* кома. —**comatose,** *adj.* коматозный.

comb *n.* **1,** (for the hair) гребень; гребёнка; расчёска. **2,** (crest of certain fowl) гребень; гребешок. —*v.t.* **1,** (someone's hair) причёсывать; расчёсывать. *Comb one's hair,* причёсываться. **2,** (card, as flax) чесать. **3,** (search thoroughly) прочёсывать.

combat *n.* бой. *See combat,* участвовать в бою. —*adj.* боевой: *combat vehicle,* боевая машина. —*v.t.* бороться *с* *or* против. *Combat crime,* бороться с преступностью. —**combatant,** *n.* дерущийся. —**combative,** *adj.* воинственный; драчливый.

combination *n.* сочетание; комбинация. —**combination lock,** замок с секретом.

combine *v.t.* **1,** (join; amalgamate) объединять: *combine two positions,* объединять две должности. *Combine efforts,* объединять *or* соединять усилия. **2,** (mix) сочетать; совмещать; соединять; комбинировать. *Combine colors,* сочетать/комбинировать краски. *Combine business with pleasure,* сочетать/совмещать полезное с приятным. —*v.i.* объединяться. —*n.* **1,** (harvesting machine) комбайн. **2,** (association) комбинат.

combined *adj.* совместный.

combings *n.pl.* очёски.

combustible *adj.* горючий. —*n.* горючий материал. —**combustibility,** *n.* горючесть.

combustion *n.* сгорание; воспламенение.

come *v.i.* **1,** (approach) идти: *Come here!,* иди сюда! *I'm coming!,* иду! *Here he comes,* вот он идёт. **2,** (arrive) приходить; приезжать. *He did not come,* он не пришёл (*or* не приехал). **3,** (of a time or season) наступать; настать; приходить. **4,** (reach) доходить: *the dress comes to her knees,* платье доходит ей до колен. **5,** (progress) идти: *how is your work coming?,* как идёт ваша работа? **6,** (occur; fall) выпадать; приходиться: *New Year's Day comes on a Thursday,* Новый год выпадает/приходится на четверг. *B comes after A,* буква Б следует за буквой А. **7,** (be available): *this dress comes in five colors/sizes,* это платье (можете найти) в пяти

цветах/размерах. **8,** (be due) причитаться: *you have two dollars coming to you,* вам причитается два доллара. *He got what was coming to him,* он получил по заслугам. —**come about,** происходить; случаться. —**come across,** натыкаться на; наталкиваться на. —**come along,** идти; приходить. *He came along with us,* он пришёл вместе с нами. *How are things coming along?,* как идут дела? —**come apart,** распадаться. —**come around, 1,** (revive) приходить в себя. **2,** (recover) оправляться. **3,** (agree in the end) соглашаться. **4,** *colloq.* (come and visit) заходить. —**come away with,** выносить. —**come back, 1,** (return) возвращаться. **2,** *fol. by* **to** (return to one's memory) вспоминаться (+ *dat.*). —**come between,** разъединять: *nothing can come between us,* ничто нас не разъединит. —**come by, 1,** (drop by) заходить. **2,** (obtain) доставать. —**come down, 1,** (descend) сходить. **2,** (fall; decline) падать. *Come down in price,* падать в цене. **3,** *fol. by* **to** (boil down to) сводиться к. **4,** *fol. by* **with** (develop, as an illness) получать. *I think I'm coming down with the flu,* думаю, что у меня начинается грипп. —**come from, 1,** *literally* приходить из. **2,** (originate from): *wine comes from grapes,* вино делают из винограда. *He comes from California,* он родом из Калифорнии. *She comes from a good family,* она из хорошей семьи. *Where did this thing come from?,* откуда взялась эта штука? —**come in, 1,** (enter) входить. **2,** (be received, as of letters, complaints, etc.) поступать. **3,** (finish) приходить: *come in second,* приходить вторым. **4,** *fol. by* **for** (be subjected to) подвергаться (+ *dat.*). —**come into, 1,** *literally* входить в. **2,** (inherit) получить (что) в наследство; доставаться (+ *dat.*). **3,** *with various nouns* входить в: *come into use,* входить в употребление; *come into fashion,* входить в моду. *Come into being,* возникать. *Come into view,* показаться. —**come of,** выходить из: *nothing will come of it,* из этого ничего не выйдет. —**come off,** отделяться; отрываться; срываться; соскакивать; отставать. —**come on!, 1,** (hurry up) живей! **2,** (don't be silly) ну что вы! —**come out, 1,** (emerge; be issued or released) выходить. *The sun came out,* солнце вышло *or* выглянуло. **2,** (make one's debut) дебютировать. **3,** (turn out; end up) сойти; выйти. *Come out well in a picture,* хорошо выйти на снимке. *The picture came out well,* снимок получился хороший. **4,** (of a stain) выводиться. **5,** (take a position) выступать: *come out in favor of/against,* выступать за/против. **6,** *fol. by* **with** (utter) выпаливать. —**come over, 1,** (visit) заходить. **2,** (seize, as of an emotion) овладевать; завладевать. *What's come over you?,* что это на вас нашло?; что это вы? —**come through, 1,** (seep through) просачиваться через. **2,** (endure successfully) переносить: *she came through the operation well,* она хорошо перенесла операцию. —**come to, 1,** (reach, as an end, agreement, etc.) приходить к. **2,** (amount to) составлять. **3,** (result in) сводиться: *come to naught,* сводиться к нулю. **4,** (regain consciousness) приходить в себя. **5,** (be learned by) даваться: *languages come to her easily,* языки даются ей легко. —**come true,** осуществляться; сбываться. —**come under, 1,** (fit into, as a category) относиться к. **2,** (be subjected to) попадать под: *come under suspicion,* попасть под подозрение.

—come up, 1, (rise) поднима́ться; всходи́ть. **2,** (sprout) всходи́ть. **3,** (arise, as in discussion) возника́ть. **—come up to, 1,** (approach) подходи́ть к. **2,** (stand as tall as) достава́ть до: *he comes up to my shoulder,* он мне достаёт до плеча́. **3,** *colloq.* (equal; be as good as) сравни́ться с. **—come up with,** находи́ть. **—come upon,** набрести́ на; напада́ть на; находи́ть на. **—come what may,** будь, что бу́дет. **—how come?,** *see* **how.**

comedian *n.* ко́мик.

comedy *n.* коме́дия.

comely *adj.* хоро́шенький; милови́дный.

comet *n.* коме́та: *Halley's Comet,* коме́та Галле́я.

comfort *v.t.* утеша́ть. **—n. 1,** (solace) утеше́ние. **2,** (ease) комфо́рт; ую́т. **3,** *pl.* (conveniences) удо́бства.

comfortable *adj.* **1,** (providing comfort) удо́бный; комфорта́бельный. **2,** (in a state of comfort; at ease) *rendered by* удо́бно: *are you comfortable?,* вам удо́бно? **3,** (fairly well-to-do) безбе́дный. **—comfortably,** *adv.* удо́бно. *Live comfortably,* жить безбе́дно *or* в доста́тке.

comforter *n.* **1,** (one who comforts) утеши́тель. **2,** (quilted bedcover) стёганое одея́ло.

comforting *adj.* утеши́тельный.

comic *adj.* коми́ческий; шу́точный. **—n. 1,** (entertainer) ко́мик. **2,** *pl.* (cartoon strips) ко́миксы. **—comic opera,** коми́ческая о́пера.

comical *adj.* коми́чный; коми́ческий; смешно́й.

coming *n.* **1,** (arrival) прихо́д; прие́зд. *The Second Coming,* второ́е прише́ствие. **2,** (advent, as of a season) наступле́ние. **—adj.** сле́дующий; бу́дущий; наступа́ющий.

Comintern *n.* Коминте́рн.

comma *n.* запята́я.

command *v.t.* **1,** (order) прика́зывать. **2,** *mil.* (be in command of) кома́ндовать. **3,** (inspire, as respect) внуша́ть. **4,** (bring, as a high price) идти́; продава́ться (по высо́кой цене́). **5,** (afford, as a view): *the room commands a beautiful view of the ocean,* из ко́мнаты открыва́ется прекра́сный вид на океа́н. **—n. 1,** (an order) прика́з; кома́нда. **2,** (authority to command) кома́ндование: *under the command of,* под кома́ндованием (+ *gen.*). *Be in command of,* кома́ндовать (+ *instr.*). **3,** (mastery): *have an excellent command of English,* отли́чно владе́ть англи́йским языко́м. **—adj.** кома́ндный: *command post,* кома́ндный пункт.

commandant *n.* коменда́нт.

commandeer *v.t.* реквизи́ровать.

commander *n.* **1,** *mil.* команди́р; кома́ндующий. **2,** *naval* капита́н второ́го ра́нга. **—commander in chief,** главнокома́ндующий.

commanding *adj.* **1,** (in command): *commanding officer,* кома́ндующий; команди́р. **2,** (authoritative) вла́стный. **3,** (high up; overlooking) госпо́дствующий; домини́рующий. *Commanding heights,* кома́ндная высота́.

commandment *n.* за́поведь.

commando *n.* деса́нтник.

commemorate *v.t.* пра́здновать; ознамено́вать. **—commemoration,** *n.* пра́зднование; ознаменова́ние.

commemorative *adj.* па́мятный; мемориа́льный. *Commemorative stamp,* юбиле́йная *or* па́мятная ма́рка.

commence *v.t.* начина́ть. **—v.i.** начина́ться.

commencement *n.* **1,** (beginning) нача́ло. **2,** (graduation exercises) (выпускно́й) акт.

commend *v.t.* **1,** (praise) хвали́ть. **2,** (recommend) рекомендова́ть.

commendable *adj.* похва́льный.

commendation *n.* **1,** (praise) похвала́. **2,** (award; citation) объявле́ние благода́рности.

commensurable *adj.* соизмери́мый.

commensurate *adj.* соразме́рный.

comment *n.* **1,** (note of explanation) примеча́ние. **2,** (remark) замеча́ние. **—v.i.** де́лать замеча́ние. *Comment on something,* комменти́ровать что́-нибудь. **—no comment,** никаки́х коммента́риев.

commentary *n.* коммента́рий.

commentator *n.* обозрева́тель; коммента́тор.

commerce *n.* торго́вля; комме́рция.

commercial *adj.* торго́вый; комме́рческий. **—n.** рекла́ма.

commingle *v.t.* сме́шивать. **—v.i.** сме́шиваться.

commiserate *v.i.* [*usu.* commiserate with] соболе́зновать (+ *dat.*). **—commiseration,** *n.* соболе́знование.

commissar *n.* комисса́р.

commissariat *n.* **1,** *U.S.S.R.* (ministry) комиссариа́т. **2,** *mil.* интенда́нтство.

commissary *n.* вое́нный магази́н.

commission *n.* **1,** (specially appointed body) коми́ссия. **2,** (fee) комиссио́нные. **3,** (authorization to buy or sell) коми́ссия. **4,** (perpetration, as of a crime) соверше́ние. **5,** *mil.* офице́рское зва́ние. **—v.t.** поруча́ть; назнача́ть; уполномо́чивать. **—out of commission,** в неиспра́вности. *Put out of commission,* выводи́ть из стро́я; приводи́ть в него́дность.

commissioned officer офице́р.

commissioner *n.* комисса́р.

commit *v.t.* **1,** (perpetrate) соверша́ть: *commit a crime,* соверша́ть преступле́ние. *Commit an error,* допусти́ть оши́бку. *Commit perjury,* лжесвиде́тельствовать. *Commit adultery,* соверша́ть прелюбодея́ние. **2,** (obligate) обя́зывать. **3,** (consign, as to a mental institution) помеща́ть. **4,** (give over) предава́ть: *commit to the flames,* предава́ть огню́. **—commit oneself, 1,** (pledge oneself) обя́зываться. **2,** (take a firm position) свя́зывать себя́ сло́вом. **—commit suicide,** поко́нчить жизнь самоуби́йством; поко́нчить с собо́й. **—commit to battle,** вводи́ть в бой. **—commit to memory,** зау́чивать.

commitment *n.* **1,** (confinement, as to an institution) помеще́ние. **2,** (pledge; obligation) обяза́тельство.

committee *n.* комите́т; коми́ссия.

commode *n.* **1,** (chest of drawers) комо́д. **2,** (movable washstand) умыва́льник. **3,** (seat over a chamber pot) стульча́к.

commodious *adj.* вмести́тельный; просто́рный.

commodity *n.* това́р; проду́кт; предме́т потребле́ния. **—commodity exchange,** това́рная би́ржа.

common *adj.* **1,** (general; joint; public) о́бщий. *In common use,* употреби́тельный. *It is common knowledge that...,* общеизве́стно, что... **2,** (widespread) распространённый. **3,** (of the masses; ordinary) просто́й; обыкнове́нный; рядово́й. **4,** (vulgar; coarse) по́шлый. **—have much in common,** име́ть мно́го о́бщего. **—have nothing in common,** не име́ть ничего́ о́бщего.

commonality *n.* общность.

common denominator общий знаменатель.

commoner *n.* человек из народа; простой человек.

common law обычное право. —**common-law marriage**, фактический брак. —**common-law wife**, гражданская жена.

commonly *adv.* обычно.

Common Market Общий рынок.

common noun имя нарицательное.

commonplace *adj.* банальный; избитый. —*n.* банальность; общее место.

common sense здравый смысл.

common stock обыкновенные акции.

commonwealth *n.* содружество: *the British Commonwealth*, Британское содружество.

commotion *n.* суматоха; переполох.

communal *adj.* общинный. *Communal apartment*, коммунальная квартира.

commune *n.* община; коммуна.

communicable *adj.* заразный: *communicable disease*, заразная болезнь.

communicate *v.i.* 1, (express oneself) объясняться. 2, *fol. by* **with** (get in touch with) сообщаться (с); связываться (с); сноситься (с). —*v.t.* сообщать; передавать.

communication *n.* 1, *often pl.* (act or means of communicating) связь; сообщение: *telephone communications*, телефонная связь; телефонное сообщение. *Ministry of Communications*, Министерство связи. *Communications officer*, *mil.* офицер связи. 2, *often pl.* (transportation routes) сообщение; пути сообщения; *mil.* коммуникации. *Railway communications*, железнодорожное сообщение. 3, (message) сообщение: *an urgent communication*, срочное сообщение. —**communications satellite**, спутник связи.

communicative *adj.* откровенный; разговорчивый.

communion *n.* 1, (communication; association) общение. 2, *cap.* (Eucharist) причастие.

communiqué *n.* коммюнике.

communism *n.* коммунизм.

communist *n.* коммунист. —*adj.* коммунистический: *communist party*, коммунистическая партия.

community *n.* 1, (neighborhood) район. 2, (group of people with common ties) община; колония. 3, (identity; likeness) общность. —**community property**, общее имущество супругов.

commutation *n.* смягчение (наказания *or* приговора). —**commutation ticket**, сезонный билет.

commute *v.t.* смягчать (наказание *or* приговор). —*v.i.* ездить (ежедневно). —**commuter**, *n.* ежедневный пассажир.

compact *adj.* плотный; компактный; сжатый. —*n.* 1, (cosmetics container) пудреница. 2, (covenant) соглашение; договор; конвенция.

companion *n.* 1, (comrade) товарищ. 2, (paid attendant) компаньонка. 3, (other of a pair) пара.

companionable *adj.* компанейский.

companionship *n.* компания.

company *n.* 1, (business firm) компания. 2, (companionship; association) компания; общество: *in the company of*, в обществе (+ *gen.*). *Male company*, мужское общество. *Keep company with*, водить компанию с; водиться с. *Keep someone company*, составлять компанию (+ *dat.*). *Part company*, расходиться. 3, (visitors; guests) гости. 4, (troupe) труппа: *touring company*, гастрольная труппа. 5, *mil.* рота.

comparable *adj.* сравнимый.

comparative *adj.* сравнительный. —**comparatively**, *adv.* сравнительно.

compare *v.t.* сравнивать. *Compared to*, по сравнению с. —*v.i.* [*usu.* **compare to** or **with**] сравниться (с). —*n.*, in **beyond compare**, вне сравнения. —**compare notes**, обмениваться впечатлениями.

comparison *n.* сравнение. *There is no comparison between them*, их нельзя сравнивать.

compartment *n.* 1, (space; section) отделение. 2, (on a train) купе.

compass *n.* 1, (instrument for determining direction) компас. *Surveyor's compass*, буссоль. 2, *often pl.* (instrument for describing circles) циркуль. —**compass point**, страна света.

compassion *n.* сострадание. —**compassionate**, *adj.* сострадательный.

compatible *adj.* совместимый. —**compatibility**, *n.* совместимость.

compatriot *n.* соотечественник; земляк.

compel *v.t.* заставлять; принуждать; вынуждать.

compelling *adj.* 1, (convincing) убедительный: *compelling evidence*, убедительное доказательство. 2, (holding one's attention) захватывающий.

compendium *n.* конспект; компендиум.

compensate *v.t.* 1, (recompense; remunerate) вознаграждать. 2, (indemnify) возмещать: *compensate someone for damages*, возмещать кому-нибудь убытки. —*v.i.* [*usu.* **compensate for**] (make up for; offset) компенсировать.

compensation *n.* 1, (restitution) компенсация; возмещение: *compensation for damages*, компенсация/возмещение убытков. 2, (payment for services) вознаграждение.

compensatory *adj.* компенсационный. —**compensatory leave**, отгул.

compete *v.i.* состязаться; соревноваться.

competence *n.* 1, (ability) способность; компетентность. 2, (jurisdiction) компетенция.

competent *adj.* 1, (qualified; capable) компетентный. 2, (legally qualified) правомочный. 3, (responsible for one's actions) дееспособный.

competition *n.* 1, (contest) состязание; соревнование; конкурс. 2, (business rivalry) конкуренция.

competitive *adj.* 1, (involving competition, as of an examination) конкурсный. 2, (able to compete) конкурентоспособный. *Competitive prices*, конкурентоспособные цены.

competitor *n.* конкурент.

compilation *n.* 1, (act of compiling) собирание; составление; компиляция. 2, (something compiled) компиляция.

compile *v.t.* 1, (gather) собирать. 2, (make up; write, as a list or dictionary) составлять.

compiler *n.* составитель; компилятор.

complacent *adj.* самодовольный. —**complacency**, *n.* самодовольство.

complain *v.i.* жаловаться. *Complain about the weather*, жаловаться на погоду. *Complain of a headache*, жаловаться на головную боль. *I can't complain*, я не могу пожаловаться.

complaint *n.* **1,** (grievance) жа́лоба. **2,** (ailment) недомога́ние.

complaisant *adj.* услу́жливый; любе́зный.

complement *n.* **1,** (that which completes) дополне́ние. **2,** (full quota) компле́кт. **3,** *gram.* дополне́ние. —*v.t.* дополня́ть.

complementary *adj.* дополня́ющий друг дру́га. *Complementary colors,* дополни́тельные цвета́.

complete *adj.* **1,** (entire) по́лный: *complete set,* по́лный набо́р. **2,** (finished) зако́нченный: *the job is complete,* рабо́та зако́нчена. **3,** (absolute) по́лный: *complete freedom,* по́лная свобо́да. —*v.t.* **1,** (finish) зака́нчивать; заверша́ть; доверша́ть. **2,** (make whole) укомплектова́ть. *To complete the picture,* для полноты́ карти́ны. —**completely,** *adv.* соверше́нно; вполне́; по́лностью; целико́м. —**completeness,** *n.* полнота́; зако́нченность.

completion *n.* оконча́ние; заверше́ние.

complex *adj.* сло́жный: *a complex matter,* сло́жное де́ло. —*n.* **1,** (large system or unit) ко́мплекс. **2,** *psychoanalysis* ко́мплекс; ма́ния: *inferiority complex,* ко́мплекс неполноце́нности; *persecution complex,* ма́ния пресле́дования. —**complex sentence,** сложноподчинённое предложе́ние.

complexion *n.* **1,** (skin color) цвет лица́: *dark complexion,* сму́глый цвет лица́. **2,** *fig.* (aspect) свет; окра́ска. *Put a different complexion on something,* придава́ть чему́-нибудь другу́ю окра́ску.

complexity *n.* сло́жность.

compliance *n.* **1,** (act of complying) подчине́ние: *compliance with the law,* подчине́ние зако́ну. **2,** (acquiescence) согла́сие. **3,** (disposition to comply) усту́пчивость. —**in compliance with,** в соотве́тствии с.

compliant *adj.* усту́пчивый.

complicate *v.t.* усложня́ть; осложня́ть. —**complicated,** *adj.* сло́жный.

complication *n.* **1,** (something that complicates) осложне́ние; усложне́ние. **2,** *med.* осложне́ние.

complicity *n.* соуча́стие; посо́бничество.

compliment *n.* **1,** (expression of praise) комплиме́нт. **2,** *pl.* (greetings) приве́т; покло́н. —*v.t.* похвали́ть; сде́лать комплиме́нт (+ *dat.*).

complimentary *adj.* **1,** (containing a compliment) ле́стный. **2,** (given free) беспла́тный; даровой. *Complimentary ticket,* контрама́рка.

comply *v.i.* подчиня́ться. *Comply with the rules,* подчиня́ться пра́вилам. *Comply with a request,* удовлетвори́ть *or* испо́лнить про́сьбу.

component *n.* составна́я часть; дета́ль; компоне́нт. —*adj.* составно́й: *component part,* составна́я часть.

comport *v.t.* [*usu.* **comport oneself**] вести́ себя́; держа́ть себя́.

comportment *n.* поведе́ние; мане́ра держа́ть себя́.

compose *v.t.* **1,** (write; draft) составля́ть. **2,** (create, as a poem or work of music) сочиня́ть. **3,** (reconcile, as differences) ула́живать. **4,** *printing* (set in type) набира́ть. —**be composed of,** состоя́ть из. —**compose oneself,** овладе́ть собо́й.

composed *adj.* споко́йный; хладнокро́вный.

composer *n.* компози́тор.

composite *adj.* составно́й; сво́дный; ко́мплексный. —*n.* смесь; соста́в; соедине́ние.

composition *n.* **1,** (musical or literary work; essay for school) сочине́ние. **2,** (make-up; structure) соста́в. **3,** (artistic arrangement, as of a photograph) компози́ция. **4,** *printing* набо́р.

compositor *n.* набо́рщик.

compost *n.* компо́ст.

composure *n.* споко́йствие; самооблада́ние; хладнокро́вие. *Regain one's composure,* овладе́ть собо́й.

compote *n.* компо́т.

compound *n.* **1,** *chem.* соедине́ние. **2,** (enclosed area) огоро́женное ме́сто. —*adj.* составно́й; сло́жный. —*v.t.* **1,** (mix; combine) сме́шивать; соединя́ть. **2,** (add to; intensify) усугубля́ть; осложня́ть. —**compound fracture,** сло́жный перело́м. —**compound interest,** сло́жные проце́нты. —**compound sentence,** сложносочинённое предложе́ние.

comprehend *v.t.* **1,** (understand) понима́ть; постига́ть. **2,** (include) охва́тывать.

comprehensible *adj.* поня́тный; постижи́мый; вразуми́тельный.

comprehension *n.* понима́ние.

comprehensive *adj.* всесторо́нний; развёрнутый; всеобъе́млющий.

compress *v.t.* сжима́ть. —*n.* компре́сс: *hot compress,* согрева́ющий компре́сс. —**compressed air,** сжа́тый во́здух.

compression *n.* сжа́тие. —**compression chamber,** ка́мера сжа́тия. —**compression ratio,** сте́пень сжа́тия.

compressor *n.* компре́ссор.

comprise *v.t.* **1,** (consist of) состоя́ть из; заключа́ть в себе́. **2,** (constitute) составля́ть.

compromise *n.* компроми́сс. —*adj.* компроми́ссный: *compromise decision,* компроми́ссное реше́ние. —*v.i.* идти́ на компроми́сс. —*v.t.* **1,** (adjust by concessions) ула́живать. **2,** (place in a compromising position) компромети́ровать. —**compromiser,** *n.* соглаша́тель.

comptroller *n.* контролёр.

compulsion *n.* принужде́ние.

compulsive *adj.* застаре́лый; неисправи́мый. *Compulsive desire,* неудержи́мое жела́ние.

compulsory *adj.* обяза́тельный.

compunction *n.* угрызе́ния со́вести. *Without compunction,* без зазре́ния со́вести.

computation *n.* вычисле́ние; подсчёт.

compute *v.t.* вычисля́ть; подсчи́тывать.

computer *n.* вычисли́тельная маши́на; вычисли́тель; компью́тер.

comrade *n.* това́рищ. —**comrade in arms,** това́рищ по ору́жию; сора́тник.

comradeship *n.* това́рищество.

con *n.,* **in the pros and cons,** до́воды за и про́тив.

concave *adj.* во́гнутый.

concavity *n.* **1,** (state of being concave) во́гнутость. **2,** (concave area on a surface) впа́дина.

conceal *v.t.* скрыва́ть; ута́ивать. —**concealment,** *n.* сокры́тие; скры́тие.

concede *v.t.* допуска́ть: *I'll concede that...,* допуска́ю, что... —*v.i.* призна́ть своё пораже́ние (на вы́борах).

conceit *n.* самомне́ние. —**conceited,** *adj.* большо́го мне́ния о себе́; самовлюблённый.

conceivable adj. мы́слимый; возмо́жный; допусти́мый. It is quite conceivable that..., вполне́ возмо́жно/допусти́мо, что... Every conceivable precaution, всевозмо́жные ме́ры предосторо́жности.

conceivably adv. возмо́жно; допусти́мо: there might conceivably be others, вполне́ возмо́жно/допусти́мо, что существу́ют и други́е.

conceive v.t. **1,** (form in the mind) заду́мывать. **2,** (become pregnant with) зача́ть. —v.i. **1,** fol. by of (form a mental image of) представля́ть себе́. **2,** (become pregnant) забере́менеть.

concentrate v.t. сосредото́чивать; концентри́ровать. —v.i. сосредото́чиваться; концентри́роваться. —n. концентра́т.

concentration n. **1,** (act of concentrating) сосредото́чение; концентра́ция. **2,** (complete attention) сосредото́ченность. —**concentration camp,** концентрацио́нный ла́герь; концла́герь.

concentric adj. концентри́ческий.

concept n. поня́тие.

conception n. **1,** (mental picture; idea) поня́тие; представле́ние; конце́пция. **2,** (conceiving in the womb) зача́тие.

concern n. **1,** (matter of interest) де́ло. That is not my concern; that is no concern of mine, э́то не моё де́ло; э́то меня́ не каса́ется. **2,** (solicitude) забо́та; уча́стие: show concern, проявля́ть забо́ту/уча́стие. **3,** (anxiety) беспоко́йство; озабо́ченность. A matter of great concern, де́ло большо́й ва́жности. **4,** (business enterprise) предприя́тие; конце́рн. —v.t. **1,** (relate to; affect) каса́ться. As far as I am concerned, что каса́ется меня́. **2,** (trouble; worry) беспоко́ить; трево́жить. —**concern oneself, 1,** (worry) беспоко́иться. **2,** fol. by with (busy oneself) занима́ться (+ instr.).

concerned adj. **1,** (interested; involved) заинтересо́ванный: the parties concerned, заинтересо́ванные сто́роны. **2,** (uneasy; troubled) озабо́ченный; обеспоко́енный.

concerning prep. относи́тельно; каса́ющийся; по по́воду.

concert n. конце́рт. —adj. конце́ртный: concert hall, конце́ртный зал. —**in concert,** совме́стно; сообща́; дру́жно; заодно́.

concerted adj. согласо́ванный; дру́жный.

concertina n. концерти́но.

concertmaster n. концертме́йстер.

concerto n. конце́рт.

concession n. **1,** (something conceded) усту́пка: make concessions, идти́ на усту́пки. **2,** (commercial privilege) конце́ссия.

concessionaire n. концессионе́р.

concessive adj., gram. усту́пительный.

conciliate v.t. мири́ть; примиря́ть. —**conciliation,** n. примире́ние. —**conciliator,** n. примири́тель. —**conciliatory,** adj. примири́тельный.

concise adj. сжа́тый; кра́ткий. —**conciseness,** n. сжа́тость; кра́ткость.

conclave n. **1,** (meeting) совеща́ние. **2,** relig. конкла́в.

conclude v.t. заключа́ть: conclude a deal, заключи́ть сде́лку. Conclude one's speech with a toast, заключи́ть речь то́стом. This leads me to conclude that..., из э́того я заключа́ю, что... —v.i. заключа́ться. —**concluding,** adj. заключи́тельный.

conclusion n. **1,** (close; closing part) заключе́ние.

2, (final judgment or decision) заключе́ние; вы́вод: come to a conclusion, приходи́ть к заключе́нию/вы́воду. —**in conclusion,** в заключе́ние.

conclusive adj. реша́ющий. Conclusive evidence, неопроверж́имые доказа́тельства. —**conclusively,** adv. неопроверж́имо: prove conclusively, неопроверж́имо доказа́ть.

concoct v.t. **1,** (cook) стря́пать. **2,** (devise) приду́мывать. **3,** (make up) выду́мывать. —**concoction,** n. стряпня́.

concomitant adj. сопу́тствующий.

concord n. согла́сие.

concordat n. конкорда́т.

concourse n. **1,** (large open space, as in a station) зал. **2,** (thoroughfare) проспе́кт.

concrete n. бето́н. —adj. **1,** (made of concrete) бето́нный. **2,** (real; specific) конкре́тный. —**concrete number,** именова́нное число́.

concubine n. нало́жница.

concur v.i. **1,** (agree) быть согла́сным. **2,** (occur simultaneously) совпада́ть.

concurrence n. **1,** (agreement) согла́сие. **2,** (coincidence) совпаде́ние.

concurrent adj. совпада́ющий; одновре́менный. —**concurrently,** adv. одновре́менно.

concussion n. сотрясе́ние.

condemn v.t. **1,** (denounce) осужда́ть. **2,** (sentence) осужда́ть; пригова́ривать: condemn to death, осужда́ть на смерть; пригова́ривать к сме́ртной ка́зни. **3,** (doom to an unhappy fate) осужда́ть; обрека́ть. **4,** (declare unfit for use) признава́ть него́дным (для жилья́). —**condemnation,** n. осужде́ние.

condensation n. **1,** (abridgment) сокраще́ние. **2,** (that which is abridged) сокращённое изда́ние. **3,** (reduction of a gas to liquid) конденса́ция.

condense v.t. **1,** (change from gas to liquid) конденси́ровать. **2,** (make thicker or more concentrated) сгуща́ть: condensed milk, сгущённое молоко́. **3,** (abridge) сокраща́ть; сжима́ть.

condenser n. конденса́тор.

condescend v.i. снисходи́ть. —**condescending,** adj. снисходи́тельный. —**condescension,** n. снисхожде́ние; снисходи́тельность.

condiment n. припра́ва.

condition n. **1,** (state) состоя́ние: in good condition, в хоро́шем состоя́нии. **2,** (provision; stipulation) усло́вие. **3,** pl. (circumstances) усло́вия: working conditions, усло́вия труда́. Under such conditions, при таки́х усло́виях. **4,** (state of fitness) фо́рма: out of condition, не в фо́рме. **5,** (ailment) боле́знь: a heart condition, боле́знь се́рдца. —v.t. **1,** (limit by a condition) обусло́вливать. **2,** (train) приуча́ть. —**on condition that...,** при усло́вии, что...

conditional adj. усло́вный. —**conditional mood,** усло́вное наклоне́ние.

conditionally adv. усло́вно.

conditioned reflex усло́вный рефле́кс.

condole v.i. [usu. **condole with**] соболе́зновать (+ dat.). —**condolence,** n. соболе́знование.

condominium n. кондоми́ниум.

condone v.t. проща́ть.

condor n. ко́ндор.

conducive adj. Be conducive to, располага́ть к: the atmosphere is conducive to work, атмосфе́ра располага́ет к рабо́те.

conduct v.t. **1,** (guide; lead) водить; проводить; сопровождать. **2,** (carry out; perform; hold) вести; проводить; производить. *Conduct (i.e. hold) a meeting*, проводить собрание. *Conduct negotiations*, вести переговоры. *Conduct an experiment*, проводить *or* производить опыт. **3,** (direct; run) вести: *conduct (i.e. run) a meeting*, вести собрание; *conduct a lesson*, вести урок. **4,** (direct, as an orchestra) дирижировать. **5,** (convey, as electricity) проводить. —n. **1,** (behavior) поведение. **2,** (management) ведение. —**conduct oneself**, вести себя; держать себя.

conductivity n. проводимость.

conductor n. **1,** (leader; guide) проводник. *Tour conductor*, экскурсовод. **2,** (on a train) проводник; кондуктор; (on a bus or streetcar) кондуктор. **3,** (of an orchestra) дирижёр. **4,** *physics* проводник.

conduit n. трубопровод.

cone n. **1,** (geometric figure) конус. **2,** (fruit, as of the pine) шишка.

confection n. конфета. —**confectioner,** n. кондитер. —**confectionery,** n. кондитерская.

confederacy n. конфедерация.

confederate n. сообщник; соучастник. —adj. конфедеративный. —v.i. объединяться в союз. —**confederation,** n. конфедерация; федерация.

confer v.t. (award) присваивать; присуждать; удостаивать. —v.i. [*usu.* **confer with**] совещаться (с).

conferee n. участник конференции.

conference n. совещание; конференция. *Conference hall*, конференц-зал. *Conference table*, стол переговоров.

confess v.t. **1,** (admit) признавать: *confess one's error*, признавать свою ошибку. **2,** (acknowledge; concede) признаваться: *I must confess I never heard of him*, признаюсь, о нём не слышал. —v.i. **1,** (admit one's guilt) сознаваться. **2,** *fol. by* **to** (admit) признаваться в; сознаваться в. **3,** *relig.* исповедоваться.

confession n. **1,** (admission of guilt) признание. **2,** *relig.* исповедь. —**confessional,** n. исповедальня.

confessor n. **1,** (priest who hears confessions) духовник; исповедник. **2,** (person who confesses) исповедник.

confetti n. конфетти.

confidant n. поверенный.

confide v.t. доверять; вверять; поверять. —v.i. [*usu.* **confide in**] делиться с: *she has no one she can confide in*, ей не с кем поделиться.

confidence n. **1,** (trust) доверие. *Vote of confidence*, вотум доверия. **2,** (assurance; certainty) уверенность. **3,** (self-assurance) самоуверенность. —**in confidence,** по секрету. —**take into one's confidence,** доверять свои тайны (+ *dat.*).

confident adj. **1,** (sure) уверенный: *confident of victory*, уверен в победе. **2,** (self-assured) самоуверенный.

confidential adj. секретный; конфиденциальный.

confidentially adv. **1,** (in confidence) конфиденциально; по секрету. **2,** *as an introductory word* между нами.

configuration n. конфигурация; очертание.

confine v.t. **1,** (limit; restrict) ограничивать. *Confine oneself to*, ограничиваться (+ *instr.*). **2,** (shut in) заключать. *Confined to bed*, прикованный к постели.

confinement n. **1,** (imprisonment) заключение:

solitary confinement, одиночное заключение. **2,** (lying-in) роды.

confines n.pl. пределы: *within the confines of*, в пределах (+ *gen.*).

confirm v.t. **1,** (corroborate) подтверждать. **2,** (approve; ratify) утверждать. **3,** *relig.* конфирмовать.

confirmation n. **1,** (corroboration) подтверждение. **2,** (approval) утверждение. **3,** *relig.* конфирмация.

confirmed adj. **1,** (deeply committed) убеждённый. **2,** (inveterate) закоренелый: *confirmed bachelor*, закоренелый холостяк.

confiscate v.t. конфисковать. —**confiscation,** n. конфискация.

conflagration n. пожар.

conflict n. **1,** (battle; war) конфликт. **2,** *fig.* (clash) столкновение. —v.i. противоречить друг другу. *Conflict with*, противоречить (+ *dat.*). —**conflicting,** adj. противоречивый.

confluence n. слияние; впадение.

conform v.i. [*usu.* **conform to**] сообразоваться с; согласоваться с; соответствовать (+ *dat.*). *Make something conform to something*, сообразовать что-нибудь с чем-нибудь.

conformism n. конформизм.

conformity n. соответствие; сообразность. *In conformity with*, сообразно с. *Also,* **conformance.**

confound v.t. **1,** (bewilder) озадачивать. **2,** (mistake for another) путать.

confounded adj. **1,** (taken aback) озадаченный. **2,** *colloq.* (damned) проклятый.

confront v.t. **1,** (face) стоять лицом к; стоять перед. *The task confronting us*, задача, стоящая перед нами. **2,** (meet boldly) смотреть (чему-нибудь) в лицо.

confrontation n. конфронтация.

confuse v.t. **1,** (mix up; throw off) сбивать с толку; путать. **2,** (mistake) спутывать; смешивать.

confused adj. **1,** (perplexed) недоумённый: *confused look*, недоумённый взгляд. *Become confused*, сбиться с толку; спутаться; запутаться. **2,** (muddled) спутанный: *confused thoughts*, спутанные мысли.

confusing adj. сбивчивый.

confusion n. смятение; замешательство; растерянность.

congeal v.t. замораживать. —v.i. **1,** (harden) застывать. **2,** (coagulate) свёртываться.

congenial adj. **1,** (suited to each other) дружный: *congenial couple*, дружная пара. *Congenial tastes*, сходные вкусы. **2,** (friendly; pleasant) дружеский; тёплый: *congenial atmosphere*, дружеская/тёплая атмосфера. *Congenial host*, приветливый хозяин.

congeniality n. **1,** (likeness) сродство. **2,** (affability) дружелюбие.

congenital adj. врождённый.

congest v.t. переполнять. —**congested,** adj. тесный; переполненный; скученный.

congestion n. **1,** (overcrowding) скученность; переполнение. **2,** (heavy traffic) затор; пробка. **3,** *med.* застой крови.

conglomerate n. конгломерат. —**conglomeration,** n. нагромождение; конгломерат.

congratulate v.t. поздравлять: *congratulate someone on his victory*, поздравлять кого-нибудь с победой.

congratulation n. поздравление. *Congratula-*

tions!, поздравля́ю вас! *Hearty congratulations,* серде́чные поздравле́ния.

congratulatory *adj.* поздрави́тельный.

congregate *v.i.* собира́ться; сходи́ться.

congregation *n.* **1,** (assemblage) собра́ние. **2,** *relig.* прихо́д.

congress *n.* **1,** (assembly) съезд; конгре́сс. **2,** *cap.* (U.S. legislative body) конгре́сс. —**Congress of Vienna,** Ве́нский конгре́сс.

congressional *adj.* относя́щийся к конгре́ссу. *Congressional committee,* коми́ссия конгре́сса.

congressman *n.* конгрессме́н.

congruent *adj., math.* конгруэ́нтный. —**congruence,** *n., math.* конгруэ́нция.

conic *adj.* кони́ческий. *Also,* **conical.**

conifer *n.* хво́йное де́рево. —**coniferous,** *adj.* хво́йный.

conjectural *adj.* предположи́тельный; гада́тельный.

conjecture *n.* дога́дка; предположе́ние; до́мысел. *That is a matter of pure conjecture,* об э́том мо́жно то́лько гада́ть. —*v.t. & i.* гада́ть; стро́ить дога́дки; предполага́ть.

conjugal *adj.* супру́жеский; бра́чный. *Conjugal bed,* бра́чное ло́же.

conjugate *v.t.* спряга́ть. —**conjugation,** *n.* спряже́ние.

conjunction *n.* **1,** (combination) сочета́ние. **2,** (simultaneous occurrence) совпаде́ние. **3,** (part of speech) сою́з. —**in conjunction with,** в связи́ с; в сочета́нии с.

conjunctivitis *n.* конъюнкти́вит.

conjure *v.t.* **1,** (summon by oath or magic spell) заклина́ть. **2,** *fol. by* **up** (evoke) воскреша́ть в па́мяти. —*v.i.* (practice magic) колдова́ть.

conjurer *n.* **1,** (sorcerer) колду́н; чароде́й. **2,** (magician) волше́бник; фо́кусник.

conk *v.t., slang* (bash) тра́хнуть. —*v.i.* [*usu.* **conk out**] *slang* отка́зываться рабо́тать; загло́хнуть.

connect *v.t.* **1,** (link; join) соединя́ть; свя́зывать. **2,** (hook up) подключа́ть. —*v.i.* соединя́ться; сообща́ться.

connecting *adj.* соедини́тельный. *Connecting rooms,* проходны́е ко́мнаты. —**connecting rod,** шату́н; соедини́тельная тя́га.

connection *also,* **connexion** *n.* **1,** (act of connecting) соедине́ние. **2,** (link) связь. **3,** (context) отноше́ние; связь: *in this connection,* в э́том отноше́нии; в э́той связи́. *In connection with,* в связи́ с. **4,** (change of planes, trains, etc.) переса́дка. **5,** (on the telephone) слы́шимость: *we have a bad connection,* слы́шимость плоха́я. **6,** *pl.* (influential associates) свя́зи.

connective *adj.* соедини́тельный. —**connective tissue,** соедини́тельная ткань.

connexion *n.* = **connection.**

conning tower боева́я ру́бка.

connivance *n.* попусти́тельство.

connive *v.i.* **1,** *fol. by* **at** (tolerate) попусти́тельствовать (+ *dat.*). **2,** *fol. by* **with** (conspire with) интригова́ть (с).

connoisseur *n.* знато́к; цени́тель.

connotation *n.* дополни́тельное значе́ние; отте́нок.

connote *v.t.* означа́ть; говори́ть о; подразумева́ть.

connubial *adj.* супру́жеский; бра́чный.

conquer *v.t.* **1,** (defeat; vanquish) завоёвывать; побежда́ть; покоря́ть. **2,** *fig.* (overcome) преодолева́ть; побежда́ть. —**conqueror,** *n.* завоева́тель.

conquest *n.* **1,** (act of conquering) завоева́ние; покоре́ние. **2,** *pl.* (territory conquered) завоева́ния.

consanguineous *adj.* единокро́вный; родстве́нный. —**consanguinity,** *n.* родство́.

conscience *n.* со́весть. *Have on one's conscience,* име́ть на свое́й со́вести. —**in all conscience,** по со́вести говоря́.

conscientious *adj.* **1,** (scrupulous; honest) со́вестливый. **2,** (careful; painstaking) добросо́вестный. —**conscientiousness,** *n.* добросо́вестность.

conscious *adj.* **1,** (capable of thought) созна́тельный: *man is a conscious being,* челове́к — созна́тельное существо́. **2,** (mentally awake) в созна́нии: *be conscious,* быть в созна́нии. **3,** *fol. by* **of** (aware of) созна́ющий: *be conscious of,* сознава́ть (что́-нибудь). **4,** (deliberate) созна́тельный. —**consciously,** *adv.* созна́тельно.

consciousness *n.* **1,** (state of being conscious) созна́ние: *lose consciousness,* потеря́ть созна́ние. *Regain consciousness,* приходи́ть в созна́ние; приходи́ть в себя́; очну́ться. **2,** (awareness) (само)сознание; созна́тельность: *class consciousness,* кла́ссовое (само)созна́ние; кла́ссовая созна́тельность.

conscript *n.* призывни́к. —*v.t.* призыва́ть. —**conscription,** *n.* во́инская пови́нность.

consecrate *v.t.* освяща́ть. —**consecration,** *n.* освяще́ние.

consecutive *adj.* после́довательный. *Four consecutive days,* четы́ре дня подря́д. —**consecutively,** *adv.* после́довательно.

consensus *n.* **1,** (agreement) согла́сие. **2,** (opinion of most) о́бщее мне́ние.

consent *v.i.* соглаша́ться. —*n.* согла́сие.

consequence *n.* **1,** (effect) после́дствие; сле́дствие. **2,** (importance) значе́ние: *of no consequence,* не име́ющий значе́ния.

consequent *adj.* вытека́ющий.

consequently *adv.* сле́довательно.

conservation *n.* **1,** (act of conserving) сохране́ние: *energy conservation,* сохране́ние эне́ргии. **2,** (protection of natural resources) охра́на приро́ды. —**conservationist,** *n.* сторо́нник охра́ны приро́ды.

conservatism *n.* консервати́зм.

conservative *adj.* **1,** (tending to oppose change) консервати́вный. **2,** (moderate; cautious) скро́мный: *conservative estimate,* скро́мный подсчёт. —*n.* консерва́тор.

conservatory *n.* **1,** (greenhouse) оранжере́я. **2,** (school of music) консервато́рия.

conserve *v.t.* сохраня́ть; бере́чь; сберега́ть.

consider *v.t.* **1,** (examine; take up) рассма́тривать. **2,** (think over) обду́мывать; сообража́ть. **3,** (look upon; regard) счита́ть; рассма́тривать. *I consider him my friend,* я его́ счита́ю свои́м дру́гом. *I consider it an honor,* счита́ю за честь. *I consider it madness,* я рассма́триваю э́то как безу́мие. **4,** (take into account) учи́тывать; счита́ться с; принима́ть во внима́ние. *All things considered,* принима́я всё во внима́ние. **5,** (show consideration for) счита́ться с. **6,** (believe; feel) счита́ть.

considerable adj. значи́тельный. —**considerably,** adv. значи́тельно.

considerate adj. внима́тельный; предупреди́тельный.

consideration n. **1,** (careful thought) рассмотре́ние. The matter is under consideration, де́ло сейча́с рассма́тривается. **2,** (factor to be considered) соображе́ние. **3,** (thoughtfulness of others) внима́ние. Have no consideration for others, не счита́ться с други́ми. **4,** (recompense) вознагражде́ние: for a small consideration, за небольшо́е вознагражде́ние. —**in consideration of, 1,** (in view of) принима́я во внима́ние; с учётом (+ gen.). **2,** (in return for) в благода́рность за. —**take into consideration,** принима́ть во внима́ние/в соображе́ние/к све́дению/в расчёт; учи́тывать.

considered adj. обду́манный; проду́манный.

considering prep. принима́я во внима́ние; учи́тывая; ввиду́.

consign v.t. **1,** (entrust to someone's care) поруча́ть. **2,** (relegate) предава́ть: consign to oblivion, предава́ть забве́нию. **3,** comm. (deliver for sale) отправля́ть.

consignment n. **1,** (delivery for sale) отпра́вка. **2,** (something consigned) па́ртия (това́ров); тра́нспорт.

consist v.i. [usu. **consist of**] **1,** (be made up of) состоя́ть из: the book consists of ten chapters, кни́га состои́т из десяти́ глав. **2,** (be; involve) состоя́ть в: what will my work consist of?, в чём бу́дет состоя́ть моя́ рабо́та?

consistency n. **1,** (adherence to pattern) после́довательность. **2,** (firmness) пло́тность; твёрдость; консисте́нция.

consistent adj. **1,** (adhering to a pattern) после́довательный. **2,** fol. by **with** (not contradicting) соотве́тствующий: be consistent with, соотве́тствовать (+ dat.). Not be consistent with, противоре́чить.

consistently adv. **1,** (without contradicting oneself) после́довательно. **2,** (without exception) всегда́.

consolation n. утеше́ние. —**consolation prize,** утеши́тельный приз.

console[1] (kun-sol) v.t. утеша́ть.

console[2] (kan-sol) n. **1,** (bracket) консо́ль. **2,** (cabinet) ко́рпус. **3,** (control panel) пульт.

consolidate v.t. **1,** (make secure) укрепля́ть; закрепля́ть; упро́чивать. **2,** (combine; merge) слива́ть; объединя́ть.

consolidation n. **1,** (making secure) укрепле́ние; закрепле́ние; упро́чение; консолида́ция. **2,** (combining; merging) слия́ние; объедине́ние.

consommé n. бульо́н.

consonance n. созву́чие; консона́нс.

consonant n. **1,** (sound) согла́сный звук. **2,** (letter) согла́сная бу́ква. —adj. **1,** (consonantal) согла́сный. **2,** (harmonious in sound) созву́чный. **3,** fol. by **with** (in keeping with) согла́сный (с). —**consonantal,** adj. согла́сный.

consort n. супру́г; супру́га. —v.i. [usu. **consort with**] обща́ться (с); води́ться (с).

consortium n. консо́рциум.

conspicuous adj. ви́дный; заме́тный; броса́ющийся в глаза́. Be conspicuous by one's absence, блиста́ть свои́м отсу́тствием.

conspiracy n. за́говор. —**conspirator,** n. загово́р-

щик; конспира́тор. —**conspiratorial,** adj. загово́рщический.

conspire v.i. (та́йно) сгова́риваться.

constable n. консте́бль.

constancy n. постоя́нство.

constant adj. постоя́нный. —n. постоя́нная величина́; конста́нта. —**constantly,** adv. постоя́нно.

constellation n. созве́здие.

consternation n. у́жас; замеша́тельство; расте́рянность.

constipate v.t. крепи́ть. He is constipated, его́ крепи́т. —**constipation,** n. запо́р.

constituency n. избира́тельный о́круг.

constituent adj. **1,** (component) составно́й. **2,** (authorized to draw up a constitution) учреди́тельный. —n. **1,** (constituent part) составна́я часть. **2,** (voter) избира́тель.

constitute v.t. **1,** (make up; form) составля́ть: constitute a quorum, составля́ть кво́рум. **2,** (be; represent) представля́ть собо́й: constitute a violation of the law, представля́ть собо́й наруше́ние зако́на.

constitution n. **1,** (charter) конститу́ция. **2,** (physical make-up) (те́ло)сложе́ние. Iron constitution, желе́зное здоро́вье.

constitutional adj. **1,** (of a constitution) конституцио́нный. Constitutional law, госуда́рственное пра́во. **2,** (inherent in one's make-up) органи́ческий. —n. (walk; exercise) моцио́н; прогу́лка для моцио́на.

constrain v.t. **1,** (force) принужда́ть; вынужда́ть. **2,** (inhibit) ско́вывать; стесня́ть.

constraint n. **1,** (something that holds back) стесне́ние. **2,** (lack of ease) ско́ванность; стесне́ние; принуждённость. **3,** (compulsion) принужде́ние.

constrict v.t. **1,** (make smaller or narrower) су́живать. **2,** (produce a tight feeling in) стесня́ть; сжима́ть; сда́вливать; сти́скивать.

constriction n. **1,** (act of constricting) суже́ние. **2,** (feeling of pressure or tightness) стесне́ние; сжа́тие. I feel a constriction in my chest, мне тесни́т грудь.

construct v.t. стро́ить; конструи́ровать. Construct a triangle, стро́ить треуго́льник. Construct a sentence, стро́ить предложе́ние.

construction n. **1,** (act of building) строи́тельство. Be under construction, стро́иться. **2,** (design) констру́кция. **3,** (interpretation) истолкова́ние. **4,** gram. констру́кция. —adj. строи́тельный: construction site, строи́тельная площа́дка.

constructive adj. конструкти́вный.

construe v.t. толкова́ть; истолко́вывать.

consul n. ко́нсул —**consular,** adj. ко́нсульский. —**consulate,** n. ко́нсульство.

consult v.t. **1,** (ask the advice of) сове́товаться с. **2,** (refer to, as a dictionary) справля́ться в; обраща́ться к.

consultant n. консульта́нт.

consultation n. **1,** (act of consulting) консульта́ция. **2,** (meeting between doctors) конси́лиум.

consultative adj. совеща́тельный; консультати́вный.

consulting adj. Rendered by -консульта́нт: consulting engineer, инжене́р-консульта́нт.

consume v.t. **1,** (use, as food, fuel, etc.) потребля́ть. **2,** (eat or drink up) съесть; вы́пить. **3,** (destroy, as by burning) пожира́ть. **4,** (use up, as time, money, etc.) поглощáть. **5,** *fol. by* **with** (fill with, as an emotion) пожирáть; глодáть. *He is consumed with envy,* его глóжет зáвисть.

consumer *n.* потребúтель. —**consumer goods,** товáры широкого потреблéния; ширпотрéб.

consummate *v.t.* завершáть; доводúть до концá. —*adj.* закóнченный: *a consummate artist,* закóнченный артúст. —**consummation,** *n.* завершéние.

consumption *n.* **1,** (using up) потреблéние. **2,** (disease) чахóтка. —**consumptive,** *adj.* чахóточный.

contact *n.* **1,** (touching) контáкт; соприкосновéние. **2,** (being in touch) контáкт; связь. *Be in contact with,* быть в контáкте с. *Come into contact with,* стáлкиваться с. **3,** *usu. pl.* (helpful acquaintances) свЯзи. —*v.t.* **1,** (touch) соприкасáться с. **2,** (get in touch with) связываться с.

contact lens контáктная лúнза.

contagion *n.* зарáза.

contagious *adj.* **1,** *med.* зарáзный. **2,** *fig.* (of a smile, laughter, etc.) зарazúтельный.

contain *v.t.* **1,** (hold; include) содержáть: *meat contains protein,* мЯсо содéржит белóк. *The proposal contains nothing new,* предложéние не содéржит ничегó нóвого. **2,** (restrain) сдéрживать. —**contain oneself,** сдéрживаться; владéть собóй.

container *n.* **1,** (receptacle) сосýд; вместúлище. **2,** (for shipping goods) контéйнер. —*adj.* контéйнерный: *container ship,* контéйнерное сýдно.

contaminate *v.t.* загрязнЯть; заражáть. —**contamination,** *n.* загрязнéние; заражéние.

contemplate *v.t.* **1,** (gaze at) созерцáть. **2,** (consider) соображáть. **3,** (intend) замышлЯть. **4,** (expect) ожидáть. —*v.i.* размышлЯть.

contemplation *n.* созерцáние. *Be lost in contemplation of,* засмáтриваться на; заглЯдываться на.

contemplative *adj.* созерцáтельный.

contemporary *adj.* совремéнный. —*n.* **1,** (person one's own age) свéрстник; ровéсник. **2,** (person living at the same time) совремéнник.

contempt *n.* презрéние. *Contempt of court,* оскорблéние судá. —**contemptible,** *adj.* презрéнный. —**contemptuous,** *adj.* презрúтельный.

contend *v.i.* **1,** (compete) состязáться. *Contend for,* оспáривать. **2,** *fol. by* **with** (cope with) справлЯться с. —*v.t.* (assert) утверждáть.

contender *n.* претендéнт.

content[1] (kan-tent) *n.* **1,** *pl.* (what is in a receptacle) содержúмое. **2,** (subject matter) содержáние. **3,** (substance) содержáние: *form and content,* фóрма и содержáние. **4,** (amount of a substance contained) содержáние: *the fat content of milk,* содержáние жúра в молокé.

content[2] (kun-tent) *adj.* довóльный. —*v.t.* [*usu.* **content oneself with**] удовлетворЯться (+ *instr.*); довóльствоваться (+ *instr.*). —**to one's heart's content,** вдóволь; ввóлю; скóлько душé угóдно.

contented *adj.* довóльный. —**contentedly,** *adv.* довóльно.

contention *n.* **1,** (competition) соревновáние. *Be in contention,* имéть шáнсы. **2,** (strife) раздóр. **3,** (assertion) утверждéние. —**bone of contention,** Яблоко раздóра.

contentious *adj.* задúристый; занóзистый.

contentment *n.* довóльство.

contest *n.* **1,** (struggle; battle) борьбá. **2,** (competition) состязáние; соревновáние; кóнкурс. —*v.t.* оспáривать.

contestant *n.* учáстник состязáния.

context *n.* контéкст. *Take out of context,* вырывáть из контéкста.

contiguity *n.* смéжность; соприкосновéние. —**contiguous,** *adj.* смéжный; соприкасáющийся; прилегáющий; сопредéльный.

continence *n.* воздержáние.

continent *n.* материк; континéнт. —**continental,** *adj.* материкóвый; континентáльный.

contingency *n.* (возмóжный) слýчай.

contingent *adj.* **1,** (possible) возмóжный. **2,** (chance) случáйный. **3,** (dependent): be *contingent on,* завúсеть от. —*n.* контингéнт.

continual *adj.* непрестáнный; беспрестáнный. —**continually,** *adv.* непрестáнно; беспрестáнно.

continuation *n.* продолжéние.

continue *v.t.* продолжáть. —*v.i.* продолжáть(ся): *continue!,* продолжáйте! *The struggle continues,* борьбá продолжáется. —**to be continued,** продолжéние слéдует.

continuer *n.* продолжáтель.

continuity *n.* непрерывность; преéмственность.

continuous *adj.* **1,** (uninterrupted) непрерывный; беспрерывный. **2,** (unbroken) сплошнóй. —**continuously,** *adv.* непрерывно; беспрерывно.

contort *v.t.* искривлЯть. —**contortion,** *n.* искривлéние. —**contortionist,** *n.* человéк-змеЯ.

contour *n.* кóнтур; очертáние. —**contour map,** кóнтурная кáрта.

contraband *n.* контрабáнда. —*adj.* контрабáндный.

contrabass *n.* контрабáс.

contrabassoon *n.* контрафагóт.

contraception *n.* предотвращéние зачáтия.

contraceptive *adj.* противозачáточный. *Contraceptive device,* презерватúв. —*n.* противозачáточное срéдство.

contract *n.* договóр; контрáкт; подрЯд. —*v.t.* **1,** (draw together; reduce in size) сокращáть. **2,** (catch, as a disease) получáть; подхвáтывать; наживáть. **3,** (incur, as debts) дéлать (долги). —*v.i.* **1,** (draw together) сокращáться; сжимáться. **2,** *fol. by* **for** *or inf.* (enter into a contract) заключúть договóр (на).

contraction *n.* **1,** (act of contracting) сокращéние; сужéние. **2,** (condensed form of two words) сокращённое слóво.

contractor *n.* **1,** (one who contracts for anything) подрЯдчик; контрагéнт. **2,** (builder) подрЯдчик-стрóитель.

contractual *adj.* договóрный.

contradict *v.t.* противорéчить. *Contradict oneself,* впадáть в противорéчие. —**contradiction,** *n.* противорéчие. —**contradictory,** *adj.* противорéчивый.

contradistinction *n., in* in contradistinction to, в отлúчие от; в противополóжность (+ *dat.*).

contralto *n.* контрáльто. —*adj.* контрáльтовый.

contraption *n., colloq.* приспособлéние.

contrapuntal *adj.* контрапунктúческий.

contrary *adj.* **1,** (opposite) противополóжный. **2,** *fol. by* **to** (in contradiction with) протúвный (+ *dat.*). *Be contrary to,* противорéчить (+ *dat.*). **3,** (obstinate) упрЯмый; сварлúвый. —*n. Quite the contrary,* как раз наоборóт. *Unless I hear to the contrary,* éсли я не услышу чего-нибудь иного. —**contrary to**, вопреки; наперекор. —**on the contrary**, наоборот.

contrast n. контраст. *In contrast to*, в отличие от. —v.t. сопоставлять; противопоставлять. —v.i. контрастировать.

contravene v.t. 1, (violate) нарушать. 2, (go against; conflict with) идти вразрез с; противоречить. —**contravention**, n. нарушение.

contribute v.t. 1, (donate) жертвовать. *Contribute one's share*, вносить свою долю. 2, (offer, as an idea, suggestion, etc.) вносить; выдвигать. 3, (furnish for publication) писать. —v.i. 1, (give money) жертвовать. 2, (write articles) сотрудничать (в газете, журнале, *etc.*). 3, *fol.* by **to** (help bring about) содействовать; способствовать.

contribution n. 1, (monetary donation) пожертвование. *Make a contribution*, пожертвовать что-нибудь. 2, (that which advances something) вклад: *make a contribution to science*, делать *or* вносить вклад в науку.

contributor n. 1, (donor) жертвователь. 2, (writer of articles) сотрудник (газеты, журнала, *etc.*).

contrite adj. кающийся. —**contrition**, n. раскаяние; покаяние.

contrivance n. 1, (device) приспособление. 2, (scheme) ухищрение.

contrive v.t. 1, (plan; devise) измышлять. 2, *fol.* by *inf.*(manage) ухитряться; умудряться; изловчиться; (succeed through trickery) ухищряться.

control v.t. 1, (regulate the operation of) управлять; регулировать. *This button controls the heat*, это — кнопка отопления. *Control prices*, регулировать цены. 2, (hold sway over; dominate) контролировать; держать под своим контролем. *Control the straits*, контролировать проливы. 3, (keep in check) сдерживать; обуздывать. *Control oneself*, владеть собой. —n. 1, (operation) управление. *Remote contol*, дистанционное управление. 2, (domination) контроль: *gain control of*, брать под свой контроль. 3, (check) контроль: *price controls*, контроль над ценами; *birth control*, контроль над рождаемостью. 4, *pl.* (instruments) рычаги управления. *Be at the controls*, стоять за штурвалом. —adj. контрольный. *Control experiment*, контрольный опыт. *Control post*, контрольный пост. *Control panel*, щит управления; пульт. —**be in control of**, владеть. —**due to circumstances beyond our control**, по не зависящим от нас обстоятельствам. —**get control of oneself**, овладеть собой. —**get out of control**, выйти из-под контроля. —**go out of control**, потерять управление. —**lose control of**, потерять управление (+ *instr.*). —**take control of**, взять под свой контроль. —**under control**, в порядке; нормально: *everything is under control*, всё в порядке; всё нормально. *The fire has been brought under control*, пожар остановлен.

controller n. 1, *finance* контролёр. 2, *aero.* диспетчер: *air traffic controller*, диспетчер воздушного транспорта.

control tower диспетчерская вышка; диспетчерская.

controversial adj. спорный; дискуссионный; полемический.

controversy n. спор; дискуссия; полемика.

contuse v.t. контузить. —**contusion**, n. контузия; ушиб.

convalesce v.i. выздоравливать. —**convalescence**, n. выздоровление. —**convalescent**, n. & adj. выздоравливающий.

convene v.t. созывать. —v.i. собираться.

convenience n. удобство. *For the convenience of*, для удобства (+ *gen.*). *At your convenience*, когда вам будет удобно. *At your earliest convenience*, возможно скорее. *With all the conveniences*, со всеми удобствами. —**marriage of convenience**, брак по расчёту.

convenient adj. удобный.

convent n. (женский) монастырь.

convention n. 1, (assembly) съезд; *hist.* конвент. 2, (agreement between nations) конвенция. 3, (custom) условность.

conventional adj. 1, (established by general agreement) условный; общепринятый. 2, *mil.* (non-nuclear) обычный: *conventional weapons*, обычное оружие.

conventionality n. условность.

converge v.i. сходиться; стекаться; сливаться. —**convergence**, n. стечение; слияние.

conversant adj. осведомлённый; сведущий.

conversation n. разговор; беседа. —**conversational**, adj. разговорный.

converse v.i. разговаривать. —n. (opposite) обратное. —adj. обратный; противоположный. —**conversely**, adv. наоборот.

conversion n. 1, (changing to something else) превращение; обращение. 2, *relig.* обращение; переход: *conversion to Christianity*, обращение/переход в христианство. 3, (changing, as of money) перевод.

convert v.t. 1, (transform) превращать. 2, (cause to change to another religion) обращать (в другую веру). 3, (change to a different unit of measurement) переводить. 4, *finance* конвертировать. —v.i. переходить; обращаться (в другую веру). *Convert to Christianity*, переходить/обращаться в христианство. —n. новообращённый.

converter n. конвертер.

convertibility n. обратимость.

convertible adj. 1, (capable of being converted) обратимый. 2, (of an automobile) открытый. —n. открытый автомобиль.

convex adj. выпуклый. —**convexity**, n. выпуклость.

convey v.t. 1, (carry; transport) везти; перевозить. 2, (impart; communicate) передавать.

conveyance n. 1, (act of conveying) перевозка. 2, (vehicle) перевозочное средство.

conveyer also, **conveyor** n. конвейер; транспортёр. —**conveyer belt**, конвейерная лента; ленточный транспортёр.

convict v.t. осуждать. —n. осуждённый; заключённый; каторжник.

conviction n. 1, (finding guilty) осуждение. 2, (one of a numer of times convicted) судимость. 3, (strong belief) убеждение. 4, (air of certainty) убеждённость. *With conviction*, убеждённо. *Carry conviction*, быть (очень) убедительным.

convince v.t. убеждать: *I am convinced of it*, я убеждён (убеждена) в этом. *He convinced me to stay*, он убедил меня остаться. —**convincing**, adj. убедительный. —**convincingly**, adv. убедительно.

convivial *adj.* **1,** (jovial) весёлый. **2,** (festive) праздничный. **3,** (friendly) дружелюбный. **—conviviality,** *n.* весёлость.

convocation *n.* **1,** (summoning) созы́в. **2,** (ecclesiastic assembly) собо́р.

convoke *v.t.* созыва́ть.

convoluted *adj.* **1,** (twisted) изо́гнутый; изви́листый. **2,** (complicated; intricate) замыслова́тый.

convoy *n.* карава́н; коло́нна.

convulse *v.t.* вызыва́ть су́дорогу *or* конву́льсии у. *Be convulsed with laughter,* надрыва́ть животы́ со́ смеху.

convulsion *n.* су́дорога; конву́льсия. **—convulsive,** *adj.* су́дорожный; конвульси́вный.

coo *v.i.* воркова́ть.

cook *v.t. & i.* гото́вить; стря́пать. **—***v.i.* (of food) вари́ться. **—***n.* (man) по́вар; (woman) куха́рка. **—cook up,** *colloq.* стря́пать. **—what's cooking?,** *colloq.* что происхо́дит?

cookbook *n.* пова́ренная кни́га.

cookery *n.* кулина́рия.

cookie *n.* пече́нье.

cooking *n.* ку́хня; стол: *French cooking,* францу́зская ку́хня; *home cooking,* дома́шний стол. **—***adj.* ку́хонный: *cooking utensils,* ку́хонные принадле́жности.

cool *adj.* **1,** (moderately cold) прохла́дный. **2,** (calm; collected) споко́йный; хладнокро́вный. **3,** (not cordial) холо́дный. **—***v.t.* охлажда́ть. **—***v.i.* **1,** (of soup, tea, etc.) остыва́ть. **2,** *fol. by* **off** (of a person) освежа́ться; (of the weather) стать прохла́днее. **3,** (moderate; wane, as of feelings) остыва́ть. *Passions have cooled,* стра́сти улегли́сь. **4,** *fol. by* **to** (become less enthusiastic about) охладе́ть (к); остыва́ть (к). **—***n.* прохла́да: *the cool of the evening,* вече́рняя прохла́да.

cooler *n.* холоди́льник.

cool-headed *adj.* невозмути́мый. **—cool-headedness,** *n.* невозмути́мость.

coolie *n.* ку́ли.

cooling *n.* охлажде́ние. **—***adj.* прохлади́тельный.

coolly *adv.* прохла́дно: *react coolly,* отнести́сь (к чему́-нибудь) прохла́дно.

coolness *n.* **1,** (relatively low temperature) прохла́да. **2,** (calmness) хладнокро́вие. **3,** (distance, as between people) холодо́к; охлажде́ние.

coop *n.* куря́тник. **—***v.t.* [*usu.* **coop up**] заключа́ть. *Be cooped up,* юти́ться; жить в тесноте́. **—fly the coop,** *colloq.* удра́ть; смы́ться.

cooper *n.* бо́ндарь; боча́р.

cooperate *v.i.* сотру́дничать. **—cooperation,** *n.* сотру́дничество.

cooperative *adj.* **1,** (joint) совме́стный. **2,** (collectively owned and operated) кооперати́вный. **3,** (helpful) услу́жливый. **—***n.* коопера́ция; кооперати́в.

coordinate *v.t.* согласо́вывать; координи́ровать. **—***n., math.* координа́та. **—***adj., gram.: coordinate clause,* сочинённое предложе́ние; *coordinate conjunction,* сочини́тельный сою́з.

coordination *n.* **1,** (act of coordinating) согласова́ние; координа́ция. **2,** (harmony of action) согласо́ванность; координа́ция. *Lack of coordination,* несогласо́ванность; разла́д. **3,** *physiol.* координа́ция.

coot *n.* лысу́ха.

co-owner *n.* совладе́лец.

cop *n., colloq.* полице́йский; полисме́н.

copal *n.* копа́л.

cope *v.i.* [*usu.* **cope with**] справля́ться с.

copier *n.* **1,** (person) перепи́счик; копиро́вщик. **2,** (machine) копирова́льная маши́на.

copilot *n.* второ́й пило́т.

copious *adj.* оби́льный; бога́тый.

copper *n.* **1,** (metal) медь. **2,** (coin) медя́к. **—***adj.* ме́дный.

copperhead *n.* щитомо́рдник.

coppersmith *n.* ме́дник.

copper sulfate ме́дный купоро́с.

coppice *n.* = **copse.**

copra *n.* ко́пра.

copse *n.* переле́сок. *Also,* **coppice.**

Coptic *adj.* ко́птский.

copulate *v.i.* совокупля́ться. **—copulation,** *n.* совокупле́ние.

copulative *adj., gram.* соедини́тельный.

copy *n.* **1,** (duplicate; facsimile) ко́пия. *Rough copy,* чернови́к. **2,** (any of a number of something printed or written) экземпля́р. **3,** (written matter to be printed) материа́л. **—***v.t.* **1,** (transcribe) перепи́сывать; спи́сывать. **2,** (reproduce) копи́ровать; снима́ть ко́пию с. **3,** (imitate) копи́ровать; подража́ть.

copyholder *n.* корре́ктор-подчи́тчик.

copying *n.* копи́рование; копиро́вка. **—copying machine,** копирова́льная маши́на.

copyist *n.* перепи́счик; копиро́вщик.

copyright *n.* а́вторское пра́во.

coquetry *n.* коке́тство.

coquette *n.* коке́тка. **—coquettish,** *adj.* коке́тливый.

coral *n.* кора́лл. **—***adj.* кора́лловый. **coral reef,** кора́лловый риф.

cord *n.* **1,** (string) верёвка. **2,** (electrical wire) шнур. **3,** *anat.: vocal cords,* голосовы́е свя́зки; *spinal cord,* спинно́й мозг; *umbilical cord,* пупови́на. **4,** (rib in fabric) ру́бчик.

cordial *adj.* серде́чный; раду́шный. **—***n.* ликёр. **—cordiality,** *n.* серде́чность; раду́шие. **—cordially,** *adv.* серде́чно; раду́шно.

cordon *n.* кордо́н. **—***v.t.* [*usu.* **cordon off**] оцепля́ть.

corduroy *n.* ру́бчатый вельве́т.

core *n.* **1,** (central part of a fruit) сердцеви́на. **2,** *fig.* (essence) ядро́. **—to the core,** до конца́ ногте́й; до мо́зга косте́й. *Rotten to the core,* наскво́зь прогни́вший.

coreligionist *n.* единове́рец.

coriander *n.* кориа́ндр. **—***adj.* кориа́ндровый.

Corinthian *adj.* кори́нфский.

cork *n.* про́бка. **—***adj.* про́бковый. **—***v.t.* заку́поривать. **—cork oak,** про́бковый дуб.

corkscrew *n.* што́пор.

cormorant *n.* бакла́н.

corn *n.* **1,** (cereal plant or its kernels) кукуру́за. **2,** *Brit.* (grain) зерно́. **3,** (callus) мозо́ль. **—***adj.* кукуру́зный.

corn crake коросте́ль; дерга́ч.

cornea *n.* рогова́я оболо́чка; рогови́ца.

corned beef солони́на.

corner *n.* **1,** (of a room) у́гол: *in the corner,* в углу́. **2,** (street corner) у́гол: *on the corner,* на углу́. *Around the corner,* за угло́м. *Turn the corner,* заверну́ть за́ угол. **3,** (remote region) уголо́к. **—***adj.* углово́й:

corner room, угловая комната. —*v.t.* **1,** (force into a corner) загонять в угол. **2,** *comm.* монополизировать. —**cut corners,** урезывать расходы; экономить. —**just around the corner,** на носу: *spring is just around the corner,* весна на носу.

cornerstone *n.* краеугольный камень.

cornet *n.* корнет.

cornfield *n.* кукурузное поле.

corn flakes кукурузные хлопья.

cornflower *n.* василёк.

cornice *n.* карниз.

cornmeal *n.* кукурузная мука.

corn oil кукурузное масло.

cornstalk *n.* кукурузный стебель.

cornucopia *n.* рог изобилия.

corny *adj., colloq.* банальный; избитый.

corolla *n.* венчик.

corollary *n.* вывод.

corona *n.* корона; венец.

coronary *adj.* венечный: *coronary artery,* венечная артерия. —*n.* [*also,* **coronary thrombosis**] закупорка артерий.

coronation *n.* венчание (на царство); коронация.

coroner *n.* медик судебной экспертизы.

coronet *n.* **1,** (small crown) корона. **2,** (jeweled headband) диадема.

corporal *n.* капрал. —*adj.* телесный: *corporal punishment,* телесное наказание.

corporate *adj.* **1,** (pert. to a corporation) корпоративный. **2,** (joint; common) совместный.

corporation *n.* **1,** (company) корпорация. **2,** *colloq.* (paunch) брюшко; пузо.

corporative *adj.* корпоративный.

corporeal *adj.* телесный.

corps *n.* **1,** (large army unit) корпус. **2,** (specialized branch of the armed forces) служба: *signal corps,* служба связи. *Marine Corps,* морская пехота. **3,** (body of people) корпус: *diplomatic corps,* дипломатический корпус. —**corps de ballet,** кордебалет.

corpse *n.* труп.

corpsman *n.* санитар.

corpulent *adj.* дородный; тучный; грузный. —**corpulence,** *n.* полнота; дородность; тучность.

corpuscle *n., usu. pl.* кровяные тельца; кровяные шарики.

corpus delicti состав преступления.

corral *n.* загон. —*v.t.* загонять; вгонять; сгонять.

correct *v.t.* исправлять; поправлять. —*adj.* **1,** (right; accurate) правильный; верный. **2,** (proper, as of behavior) корректный.

correction *n.* поправка; исправление. —**house of correction,** исправительный дом.

corrective *adj.* исправительный.

correctly *adv.* правильно; верно. —**correctness,** *n.* правильность.

correlate *v.t.* соотносить. —**correlation,** *n.* соотношение.

correlative *adj.* соотносительный.

correspond *v.i.* **1,** *fol. by* **to** (match; conform) соответствовать (+ *dat.*). **2,** (write letters) переписываться.

correspondence *n.* **1,** (agreement; similarity) соответствие. **2,** (communication by letters) переписка; корреспонденция. —**correspondence course,** заочный курс.

correspondent *n.* корреспондент.

corresponding *adj.* соответствующий.

corridor *n.* коридор. *In the corridors,* в кулуарах.

corroborate *v.t.* подтверждать. —**corroboration,** *n.* подтверждение.

corrode *v.t.* разъедать; выедать. —*v.i.* ржаветь.

corrosion *n.* коррозия.

corrosive *adj.* едкий. —*n.* едкое вещество. —**corrosive sublimate,** сулема.

corrosiveness *n.* едкость.

corrugate *v.t.* гофрировать. —**corrugated,** *adj.* гофрированный; рифлёный.

corrupt *adj.* продажный. —*v.t.* развращать.

corruption *n.* **1,** (act of perverting) развращение. **2,** (graft) коррупция.

corsage *n.* букет.

corsair *n.* корсар.

corset *n.* корсет.

cortege *n.* **1,** (procession) кортеж. **2,** (retinue) свита.

cortex *n.* **1,** (bark) кора. **2,** (of the brain) кора головного мозга.

cortisone *n.* кортизон.

corundum *n.* корунд; алмазный шпат.

coruscate *v.i.* сверкать; блистать.

corvette *n.* корвет.

cosecant *n.* косеканс.

cosine *n.* косинус.

cosmetic *n., usu. pl.* косметика. —*adj.* косметический.

cosmetology *n.* косметика.

cosmic *adj.* космический. —**cosmic dust,** космическая пыль. —**cosmic rays,** космические лучи.

cosmogony *n.* космогония.

cosmology *n.* космология.

cosmonaut *n.* космонавт.

cosmopolitan *adj.* космополитический. —*n.* [*also,* **cosmopolite**] космополит. —**cosmopolitanism,** *n.* космополитизм.

cosmos *n.* космос.

Cossack *n.* казак. —*adj.* казацкий.

cost *n.* стоимость: *cost of living,* стоимость жизни. *Sell something at cost,* продать что-нибудь по себестоимости. *At the cost of,* ценой (+ *gen.*). *To one's cost,* на свою беду; на своё горе; на свою голову. —*v.t. & i.* стоить; обходиться. *How much does it cost?,* сколько это стоит? *Cost someone dearly,* дорого обходиться (+ *dat.*). *It cost him his life,* это стоило ему жизни. —**at all costs,** во что бы то ни стало.

costly *adj.* дорогой; дорогостоящий.

costume *n.* костюм. —**costume designer,** костюмер. —**costume party,** костюмированный бал.

cosy *adj.* = cozy.

cot *n.* раскладушка.

contangent *n.* котангенс.

coterie *n.* кружок.

cotillion *n.* котильон.

cottage *n.* коттедж; домик; дача.

cottage cheese творог.

cottage industry кустарный промысел; кустарное производство.

cotton *n.* **1,** (cloth) бумажная ткань; хлопчатобумажная ткань. **2,** (plant from which it comes) хлопчатник; хлопок. **3,** (fibers of this plant) хлопок. *Pick cotton,* собирать хлопок. **4,** (absorbent cotton) вата.

—*adj.* **1,** (pert. to the plant) хло́пковый: *cotton fiber,* хло́пковое волокно́. **2,** (made of cotton) бума́жный; хлопчатобума́жный; си́тцевый. —**cotton gin,** хлопкоочисти́тельная маши́на. —**cotton picker,** сбо́рщик хло́пка.

cottonseed *n.* хло́пковое се́мя. —**cottonseed oil,** хло́пковое ма́сло.

cotyledon *n.* семядо́ля.

couch *n.* куше́тка; дива́н. —*v.t.* (word) облека́ть: *couch in diplomatic language,* облека́ть в дипломати́ческие выраже́ния.

cougar *n.* кугуа́р.

cough *n.* ка́шель. *Cough medicine,* лека́рство от ка́шля. —*v.i.* ка́шлять. —**cough up,** отха́ркивать.

could *v.,* past tense of **can.** *I couldn't have done it without you,* без тебя́ я не мог бы э́того сде́лать. *Could you lend me a dollar?,* не мо́жете ли вы одолжи́ть мне до́ллар?

coulomb *n.* куло́н.

council *n.* **1,** (assembly) сове́т. **2,** *relig.* собо́р. —**councilman,** *n.* член сове́та.

counsel *n.* **1,** (advice) сове́т. **2,** (lawyer) адвока́т. —*v.t.* сове́товать. —**keep one's own counsel,** храни́ть молча́ние. —**take counsel with,** совеща́ться с.

counselor *also,* **counsellor** *n.* **1,** (adviser) сове́тник. **2,** (lawyer) адвока́т.

count *v.t.* **1,** (add up; total) счита́ть [*pfv.* сосчита́ть]. **2,** (regard as; consider) счита́ть [*pfv.* счесть]. —*v.i.* **1,** (name numbers in sequence) счита́ть: *count to ten,* счита́ть до десяти́. **2,** (be of significance) име́ть значе́ние; име́ть ма́лое значе́ние; не име́ть никако́го значе́ния. *That does not count,* э́то не счита́ется; э́то не в счёт. *Every minute counts,* ка́ждая мину́та на счету́. **3,** (be considered) засчи́тываться: *count as time worked,* засчи́тываться в стаж. **4,** *fol. by* **on** (rely on) рассчи́тывать (на); де́лать ста́вку (на). —*n.* **1,** (act of counting) счёт: *lose count of,* потеря́ть счёт (+ *dat.*). **2,** *law* пункт обвине́ния: *guilty on all counts,* вино́вный по всем пу́нктам обвине́ния. **3,** (nobleman) граф. —**count in,** включа́ть. —**count off,** отсчи́тывать. —**count out, 1,** (count while handing over) отсчи́тывать. **2,** (disregard; exclude) сбра́сывать со счето́в. —**not counting,** не счита́я; е́сли не счита́ть.

countdown *n.* обра́тный отсчёт вре́мени.

countenance *n.* **1,** (facial expression) выраже́ние лица́; ми́на. **2,** (composure) самооблада́ние. **3,** (approval) одобре́ние. —*v.t.* **1,** (approve) одобря́ть. **2,** (tolerate) терпе́ть.

counter *n.* **1,** (one who counts; device that records) счётчик. **2,** (flat surface for selling goods) прила́вок; (for serving food) сто́йка. **3,** (token) фи́шка; жето́н. —*adv.* *Run counter to,* идти́ вразре́з с. —*v.t.* пари́ровать. —**under the counter,** из-под полы́.

counteract *v.t.* противоде́йствовать (+ *dat.*). —**counteraction,** *n.* противоде́йствие.

counterattack *n.* контрата́ка. —*v.t. & i.* контратакова́ть.

counterbalance *n.* противове́с. —*v.t.* уравнове́шивать.

counterblow *n.* встре́чный уда́р; контруда́р.

countercharge *n.* встре́чное обвине́ние.

counterclockwise *adv.* про́тив часово́й стре́лки.

counterespionage *n.* контрразве́дка.

counterfeit *adj.* подде́льный; подло́жный; фаль-

ши́вый. —*v.t.* подде́лывать. —*n.* подде́лка. —**counterfeiter,** *n.* подде́лыватель; фальшивомоне́тчик.

counterfoil *n.* корешо́к.

counterintelligence *n.* контрразве́дка.

counterman *n.* буфе́тчик.

countermand *v.t.* отменя́ть (прика́з).

countermeasure *n.* контрме́ра.

counteroffensive *n.* контрнаступле́ние.

counteroffer *n.* контрпредложе́ние.

counterpane *n.* покрыва́ло.

counterpart *n.* собра́т: *the African elephant is larger than its Asian counterpart,* африка́нский слон крупне́е своего́ азиа́тского собра́та. *The Trade Minister conferred with his Japanese counterpart,* мини́стр торго́вли совеща́лся со свои́м япо́нским колле́гой.

counterpoint *n.* контрапу́нкт.

counterpoise *n.* противове́с.

counterproposal *n.* контрпредложе́ние.

counterrevolution *n.* контрреволю́ция.

counterrevolutionary *adj.* контрреволюцио́нный. —*n.* контрреволюционе́р.

countersign *v.t.* скрепля́ть —*n.* паро́ль; про́пуск.

countersignature *n.* скре́па.

counterweight *n.* противове́с.

countess *n.* графи́ня.

countless *adj.* бесчи́сленный; несчётный; неисчисли́мый.

country *n.* **1,** (nation) страна́. **2,** (land of one's birth or allegiance) ро́дина: *love one's country,* люби́ть свою́ ро́дину. **3,** (rural area) дере́вня: *live in the country,* жить в дере́вне. **4,** (region of a specified character) ме́стность: *hilly country,* холми́стая ме́стность. —*adj.* дереве́нский: *country life,* дереве́нская жизнь.

countryman *n.* сооте́чественник; земля́к.

countryside *n.* дере́вня; се́льская ме́стность.

county *n.* (in the U.S.) о́круг; (in Great Britain) гра́фство.

coup *n.* **1,** (brilliant stroke) ло́вкий *or* блестя́щий ход. **2,** (seizure of power) переворо́т: *palace coup,* дворцо́вый переворо́т. —**coup d'état,** госуда́рственный переворо́т.

couple *n.* **1,** (pair) па́ра. **2,** (married couple) супру́жеская па́ра; чета́. **3,** *colloq.* (a few; several) *rendered by* не́сколько: *in a couple of days,* че́рез не́сколько дней. —*v.t.* **1,** (hitch together) сцепля́ть. **2,** *fig.* (link) свя́зывать.

coupling *n.* му́фта; сцепле́ние; связь.

coupon *n.* тало́н; купо́н.

courage *n.* хра́брость; му́жество; отва́га. —**courageous,** *adj.* хра́брый; му́жественный; отва́жный. —**courageously,** *adv.* хра́бро; му́жественно; отва́жно.

courier *n.* курье́р.

course *n.* **1,** (direction) курс: *stray off course,* отклоня́ться от ку́рса. **2,** (curriculum) курс: *history course,* курс исто́рии. **3,** (way of proceeding) курс: *course of treatment,* курс лече́ния. *Course of action,* о́браз де́йствий. **4,** (progress) тече́ние; ход: *in the course of,* в тече́ние (+ *gen.*); в хо́де (+ *gen.*). *Course of events,* ход *or* разви́тие собы́тий. *In the course of time,* с тече́нием вре́мени. *Take its course,* идти́ свои́м чередо́м. **5,** (part of a meal) блю́до: *three-course dinner,* обе́д из трёх блюд. **6,** *sports* площа́дка: *golf course,* площа́дка для го́льфа. *Racecourse,* скаковáя дорóжка. —**as a matter of course,** как нéчто самó собóй разумéющееся. *Take as a matter of course,* принимáть как дóлжное. —**in due course,** своеврéменно; в своё врéмя. —**of course,** конéчно.

court *n.* **1,** (tribunal) суд: *appear before the court,* предстáть пéред судóм. **2,** (courtyard) двор. **3,** (sovereign and his council) двор. **4,** *sports* площáдка. *Tennis court,* тéннисный корт. —*adj.* **1,** (pert. to a court of law) судéбный. **2,** (pert. to the court of a sovereign) придвóрный: *court jester,* придвóрный шут.—*v.t.* **1,** (seek the favor of) зáискивать пéред. **2,** (woo) ухáживать за. **3,** (invite, as trouble) накликáть (бедý). —**pay court to,** ухáживать за.

courteous *adj.* вéжливый; учтúвый; обходúтельный. —**courteously,** *adv.* вéжливо.

courtesan *n.* куртизáнка.

courtesy *n.* вéжливость; учтúвость. *By courtesy of,* благодаря любéзности (+ *gen.*). —**courtesy call,** визúт вéжливости.

courthouse *n.* здáние судá.

courtier *n.* придвóрный.

courtly *adj.* вéжливый; изы́сканный; галáнтный.

court-martial *n.* воéнный суд. —*v.t.* судúть воéнным судóм.

courtroom *n.* зал судá.

courtship *n.* ухáживание.

courtyard *n.* двор.

cousin *n.* двоюрóдный брат; двоюрóдная сестрá. —**second cousin,** троюрóдный брат; троюрóдная сестрá.

cove *n.* бýхточка.

covenant *n.* **1,** (agreement) соглашéние. **2,** *relig.* завéт.

cover *v.t.* **1,** (place something over) покрывáть; закрывáть. **2,** (upholster) обивáть; обтя́гивать. **3,** (lie over, as of snow, dust, etc.) покрывáть. **4,** *fol. by up* (conceal) покрывáть; скрывáть. *Cover up one's tracks,* заметáть следы́. **5,** (include; take in) охвáтывать. **6,** (provide for, as of a law, contract, etc.) предусмáтривать. **7,** (defray, as expenses) покрывáть; окупáть (расхóды). **8,** (traverse, as a distance) проходúть; покрывáть. **9,** *cards* покрывáть. **10,** *in* **cover oneself with glory,** покрывáть себя́ слáвой. —*n.* **1,** (lid) кры́шка. **2,** (anything that covers) чехóл; покрóв. *Under cover of night,* под покрóвом нóчи. **3,** (blanket) одея́ло. **4,** (hard cover of a book) переплёт. *Read from cover to cover,* прочéсть от кóрки до кóрки *or* от доски́ до доски́. **5,** (soft cover of a book or magazine) облóжка. **6,** (paper cover to protect a book) обёртка. **7,** (envelope) конвéрт: *under separate cover,* в отдéльном конвéрте. **8,** (shelter) укры́тие; прикры́тие. *Take cover,* укры́ваться. **9,** (guise; front) прикры́тие. **10,** *mil.* прикры́тие.

coverage *n.* **1,** (treatment in the media) освещéние: *extensive coverage in the press,* ширóкое освещéние в печáти. **2,** (insurance) (страховóе) покры́тие.

covered *adj.* кры́тый; закры́тый. —**covered wagon,** кры́тая повóзка.

covering *n.* покры́тие; покрóв. —**covering letter,** сопроводúтельное письмó.

coverlet *n.* покрывáло.

covert *adj.* скры́тый.

covet *v.t.* желáть; жáждать. —**covetous,** *adj.* жáдный.

covey *n.* **1,** (flock) стáя. **2,** (bevy) грýппа.

cow *n.* **1,** (farm animal) корóва. **2,** (female of certain other animals) сáмка. —*adj.* [*also,* **cow's**] корóвий: *cow's milk,* корóвье молокó. —*v.t.* (intimidate) запýгивать.

coward *n.* трус. —**cowardice,** *n.* трýсость. —**cowardly,** *adj.* труслúвый.

cowberry *n.* бруснúка.

cowboy *n.* ковбóй. —*adj.* ковбóйский: *cowboy hat,* ковбóйская шля́па.

cower *v.i.* приседáть (от стрáха).

cowhide *n.* **1,** (hide of a cow) корóвья шкýра. **2,** (leather) волóвья кóжа.

cowl *n.* **1,** (monk's hood) капюшóн. **2,** *mech.* (cover; hood) колпáк; капóт.

cowpox *n.* корóвья óспа.

cowshed *n.* корóвник.

coy *adj.* **1,** (shy) застéнчивый. **2,** (feigning shyness) жемáнный.

coyote *n.* луговóй волк; койóт.

coypu *n.* нýтрия.

cozy *also,* **cosy** *adj.* ую́тный.

crab *n.* **1,** (shellfish) краб. **2,** *colloq.* (grouch) брюзгá. —*v.i.,* *colloq.* (complain) ворчáть; ныть.

crab apple дúкое я́блоко.

crabby *adj.* злой; брюзглúвый.

crack *v.i.* **1,** (split) дать трéщину; трéснуть; трéскаться. **2,** (make a sharp, snapping sound) трещáть. **3,** (break, as of one's voice) ломáться. **4,** (break down) не вы́держать: *crack under the strain,* не вы́держать напряжéния. —*v.t.* **1,** (break open) колóть; щёлкать (орéхи). **2,** (make a crack in) дéлать трéщину в; надлáмывать. **3,** (snap, as a whip) щёлкать (кнутóм). **4,** *colloq.* (utter, as a joke) отпускáть. **5,** (break open, as a safe) взлáмывать. **6,** (break, as a code) разгáдывать. —*n.* **1,** (fissure) трéщина. **2,** (slight opening) щель; щёлка. **3,** (sound) щелчóк; треск. *Crack of a whip,* щелчóк кнутá. **4,** *colloq.* (attempt) попы́тка. *Take a crack at,* попытáться (+ *inf.*); попрóбовать свои́ сúлы на *or* в. **5,** *colloq.* (remark) острóта. **6,** *in* **at the crack of dawn,** чуть свет. —*adj., colloq.* отбóрный: *crack regiment,* отбóрный полк. —**crack down on,** принимáть круты́е мéры прóтив; приструнивать. —**crack up,** **1,** (have a breakdown) надлáмываться. **2,** *colloq.* (become convulsed with laughter) лóпаться от смéха; надрывáть животы́ (сó смеху).

cracked *adj.* **1,** (split) надтрéснутый. **2,** *colloq.* (nutty) трóнутый.

cracker *n.* **1,** (biscuit) галéта; сухáрь. **2,** (party favor) хлопýшка.

crackerjack *adj., colloq.* отлúчный; блестя́щий.

crackle *v.i.* трещáть; потрéскивать. —*n.* треск; трескотня́; трещáние.

crackling *n.* **1,** (sound) треск; трескотня́; трещáние. **2,** *pl.* (crisp remains of fat after rendering) шквáрки.

crackpot *n., slang* сумасбрóд.

cradle *n.* колыбéль.

craft *n.* **1,** (trade) ремеслó. **2,** (boat) сýдно. —**craft union,** цеховóй профсою́з.

craftsman *n.* **1,** (one engaged in a craft) ремéсленник. **2,** (skilled artisan) мáстер. —**craftsmanship,** *n.* мастерствó.

crafty *adj.* хúтрый; лукáвый.

crag *n.* скала; утёс. —**craggy**, *adj.* скалистый; утёсистый.

crake *n.* курочка.

cram *v.t.* **1,** (stuff into insufficient space) втискивать; впихивать. **2,** (fill beyond normal capacity) набивать. —*v.i., colloq.* (study) зубрить. —**crammer**, *n.* зубрила.

cramp *n.* **1,** (muscle spasm) судорога. *I have a cramp in my leg*, у меня свело ногу. **2,** *pl.* (sharp abdominal pains) схватки. —*v.t.* **1,** (cause a cramp in) сводить. **2,** (confine; restrict) стеснять.

cramped *adj.* тесный.

cranberry *n.* клюква. —*adj.* клюквенный.

crane *n.* **1,** (bird) журавль. **2,** (derrick) подъёмный кран. —*v.t., in* **crane one's neck,** вытягивать шею.

crane fly долгоножка.

cranium *n.* череп; черепная коробка. —**cranial**, *adj.* черепной.

crank *n.* **1,** (device) кривошип; *(for starting a car)* заводная рукоятка. **2,** *colloq.* (eccentric) чудак. **3,** *colloq.* (grouch) брюзга. —*v.t.* **1,** *usu. fol. by* **up** (start with a crank) заводить. **2,** *fol. by* **out** (mass-produce) фабриковать.

crankcase *n.* картер.

crankshaft *n.* коленчатый вал.

cranky *adj.* брюзгливый.

cranny *n.* закоулок: *every nook and cranny*, все закоулки.

craps *n.* игра в кости.

crash *v.i.* **1,** *fol. by* **into** (smash into) врезаться (в). **2,** (fall with great noise) рушиться. **3,** (of an airplane) разбиться; потерпеть аварию. **4,** (of the stock market) потерпеть крах. —*v.t.* **1,** (smash) разбивать. **2,** *colloq.* (come uninvited to) явиться без приглашения на. —*n.* **1,** (sound) грохот; треск. **2,** (collision; wreck) авария; крушение; катастрофа. *Plane crash*, авиационная катастрофа. **3,** (financial collapse) крах. —*adj.* ударный: *crash program*, ударная программа. *Crash course*, ускоренный курс. —**crash helmet**, защитный шлем. —**crash landing,** аварийная посадка.

crass *adj.* грубый.

crate *n.* ящик. —*v.t.* упаковывать в ящик.

crater *n.* **1,** (of a volcano or on the moon) кратер. **2,** (resulting from a bomb) воронка.

crave *v.t.* жаждать.

craven *adj.* трусливый; малодушный.

craving *n.* жажда; страстное желание.

craw *n.* зоб.

crawfish *n.* рак. *Also,* **crayfish.**

crawl *v.i.* **1,** (creep) ползти. *Crawl in*, вползать. *Crawl out*, выползать. **2,** *fol. by* **with** (swarm; teem) кишеть (+. *instr.*). —*n., swimming* кроль. —**at a crawl,** черепашьим шагом.

crawler *n.* **1,** (one who crawls, esp. a baby) ползун; ползунок. **2,** *pl.* (baby's garment) ползунки.

crayfish *n.* = **crawfish.**

crayon *n.* цветной карандаш.

craze *n.* мания. —*v.t.* доводить до бешенства. —**crazed**, *adj.* бешеный; озверелый.

crazily *adv.* как сумасшедший.

craziness *n.* глупость; безумие.

crazy *adj.* сумасшедший; безумный. *Crazy about*, без ума от. *Drive crazy*, сводить с ума; выводить из себя; доводить до безумия. —**like crazy**, *colloq.*

ужасно; безумно. *Run like crazy*, бежать во все лопатки.

creak *v.i.* скрипеть. —*n.* скрип. —**creaky**, *adj.* скрипучий.

cream *n.* **1,** (part of milk) сливки. *Sour cream*, сметана. *Whipped cream*, взбитые сливки. **2,** (substance, as for a cake, for the face, etc.) крем. *Shaving cream*, крем для бритья. *Cold cream*, кольдкрем. **3,** *fig.* (best part) сливки: *the cream of society*, сливки общества. —*adj.* **1,** (of or for cream) сливочный. **2,** (cream-colored) кремовый.

cream cheese сливочный сыр.

creamer *n.* сливочник.

creamery *n.* маслобойня; маслозавод.

cream of tartar винный камень.

creamy *adj.* сливочный.

crease *n.* складка. —*v.t.* **1,** (wrinkle) мять. **2,** (graze) задевать. —*v.i.* мяться.

create *v.t.* **1,** (make; produce) создавать; творить. *Create a work of art*, создавать произведение искусства. *Create difficulties*, создавать трудности. *God created the world*, Бог сотворил мир. **2,** (cause; give rise to) вызывать: *create doubts*, вызывать сомнения.

creation *n.* создание: *creation of capital*, создание капитала. *Creation of the world*, сотворение мира. *A marvelous creation*, замечательное создание.

creative *adj.* творческий; созидательный. —**creativity**, *n.* творческая сила.

creator *n.* творец; создатель.

creature *n.* существо; создание.

credence *n.* вера. *Give credence to; put/place credence in*, верить; давать веру (+ *dat.*).

credentials *n.pl.* верительные грамоты. —**credentials committee**, мандатная комиссия.

credibility *n.* **1,** (of a story or account) вероятность; правдоподобие. **2,** (of a person) надёжность; доверие к себе.

credible *adj.* **1,** (plausible) вероятный; правдоподобный. **2,** (who can be believed) заслуживающий доверия.

credit *n.* **1,** (credence) вера. *Place credit in*, верить. **2,** (praise; approval) похвала. *He deserves a lot of credit*, он очень достоин похвалы. *Give credit to*, отдавать должное *or* справедливость (+ *dat.*). *Give credit to someone for something*, ставить что-нибудь в заслугу (+ *dat.*). *Take credit for*, ставить себе (что-нибудь) в заслугу. **3,** (favor; honor; reputation) честь: *to his credit it must be said that...*, к его чести надо сказать, что... *He is a credit to his profession*, он делает честь своей профессии. *Have to one's credit*, иметь на своём счету. **4,** *comm.* кредит: *buy on credit*, купить в кредит. **5,** *bookkeeping* кредит. —*adj.* кредитный. —*v.t.* **1,** (believe) верить; доверять. **2,** (give credit to for something) ставить (что-нибудь) в заслугу (+ *dat.*). **3,** (apply, as to an account) записывать в кредит (на чей-нибудь счет). **4,** *bookkeeping* (enter on the credit side) приходовать.

creditable *adj.* похвальный.

credit card кредитная карточка.

creditor *n.* кредитор.

credo *n.* кредо.

credulity *n.* легковерие. —**credulous**, *adj.* легковерный.

creed *n.* **1,** (credo) символ веры; кредо. *The*

Apostles' Creed, апо́стольский си́мвол ве́ры. **2,** (one's religion) вероиспове́дание.

creek *n.* **1,** (brook) ручей. **2,** (inlet) за́водь; зато́н.

creel *n.* ве́рша.

creep *v.i.* **1,** (crawl) ползти́. **2,** (sneak) кра́сться. **3,** (of plants) ползти́; стла́ться. —**creep in, 1,** (sneak in) вкра́дываться; залеза́ть. **2,** *fig.* (of doubts, errors, etc.) вкра́дываться; закра́дываться. —**creep up,** подкра́дываться. —**make one's flesh creep,** приводи́ть в содрога́ние.

creeper *n.* **1,** (plant) ползу́чее расте́ние. **2,** (bird) пищу́ха.

creeps *n.pl., colloq.* содрога́ние. *It gives me the creeps,* у меня́ мура́шки бе́гают по спине́; у меня́ моро́з по ко́же подира́ет.

cremate *v.t.* сжига́ть; креми́ровать. —**cremation,** *n.* крема́ция. —**crematorium,** *n.* кремато́рий.

crenelated *adj.* зубча́тый.

Creole *n.* крео́л. —*adj.* крео́льский.

creosote *n.* креозо́т.

crepe *n.* креп; флёр.

crescendo *n.* креще́ндо.

crescent *n.* полуме́сяц; серп луны́.

cress *n.* кресс.

crest *n.* **1,** (comb of a bird) гре́бень; (feathered tuft) хохо́л. **2,** (top, as of a wave or hill) гре́бень. —**crested,** *adj.* хохла́тый.

crestfallen *adj.* уби́тый; пришибленный; как в во́ду опу́щенный.

cretaceous *adj.* мелово́й.

cretin *n.* крети́н. —**cretinism,** *n.* кретини́зм.

cretonne *n.* крето́н. —*adj.* крето́новый; крето́нный.

crevice *n.* расще́лина.

crew *n.* **1,** (of a ship, plane, etc.) экипа́ж; кома́нда. *Train crew,* поездна́я брига́да. **2,** (group of workers) брига́да. **3,** *mil.* расчёт: *gun crew,* оруди́йный расчёт.

crew cut е́жик: *in a crew cut,* е́жиком.

crib *n.* **1,** (child's bed) де́тская крова́ть. **2,** (feeding trough) я́сли. **3,** (bin for storing grain) ларь; за́кром. **4,** *colloq.* (concealed student's notes) шпарга́лка.

crick *n.* су́дорога.

cricket *n.* **1,** (insect) сверчо́к. **2,** (game) кри́кет.

crier *n.* глаша́тай.

crime *n.* **1,** (criminal act) преступле́ние. **2,** (criminality) престу́пность: *the increase in crime,* рост престу́пности.

Crimean *adj.* кры́мский. —**Crimean War,** Кры́мская война́.

criminal *n.* престу́пник. —*adj.* **1,** (constituting a crime) престу́пный: *criminal negligence,* престу́пная небре́жность. **2,** (pert. to the administration of penal law) уголо́вный: *criminal law,* уголо́вное пра́во.

criminology *n.* криминоло́гия. —**criminologist,** *n.* кримино́лог.

crimp *v.t.* **1,** (press into small folds) гофри́ровать. **2,** (curl, as hair) завива́ть. —*n.,* *in* **put a crimp in,** *colloq.* расстра́ивать (*e.g.* пла́ны).

crimson *adj.* мали́новый; багро́вый. —*n.* мали́новый цвет; багря́нец.

cringe *v.i.* **1,** (cower) съёживаться. **2,** (fawn) лебези́ть; раболе́пствовать.

crinkle *v.t.* мо́рщить.

cripple *n.* кале́ка. —*v.t.* **1,** (make a cripple of)

кале́чить. **2,** (deal a crippling blow to) разруша́ть. *Crippling blow,* сокруши́тельный уда́р.

crisis *n.* кри́зис.

crisp *adj.* **1,** (brittle) хрустя́щий. **2,** (invigorating) бодря́щий; живи́тельный. **3,** (terse; pithy) живо́й; пика́нтный. —**burn to a crisp,** сгоре́ть дотла́.

crisscross *v.t.* перекре́щивать. —*v.i.* перекре́щиваться. —*adv.* крест–на́крест.

criterion *n.* крите́рий; мери́ло.

critic *n.* кри́тик. *Film critic,* кинокри́тик.

critical *adj.* **1,** (containing criticism) крити́ческий. **2,** (crucial) крити́ческий; отве́тственный; перело́мный. **3,** (extremely serious) крити́ческий.

critically *adv.* **1,** (gravely) тяжело́: *critically ill/wounded,* тяжело́ бо́лен/ра́нен. **2,** (vitally) жи́зненно: *critically important,* жи́зненно ва́жный.

criticism *n.* кри́тика.

criticize *v.t. & i.* критикова́ть.

critique *n.* реце́нзия; крити́ческий разбо́р.

croak *v.i.* ква́кать. —*n.* ква́канье.

Croat *n.* хорва́т. —**Croatian,** *adj.* хорва́тский.

crochet *v.t. & i.* вяза́ть (крючко́м).

crock *n.* гли́няный сосу́д.

crockery *n.* гли́няная посу́да.

crocodile *n.* крокоди́л. —*adj.* крокоди́ловый. —**crocodile tears,** крокоди́ловы слёзы.

crocus *n.* кро́кус.

crook *n.* **1,** (bend) сгиб: *the crook of one's arm,* сгиб ло́ктя. **2,** (staff) по́сох: *shepherd's crook,* пасту́ший по́сох. **3,** *colloq.* (swindler) плут.

crooked *adj.* **1,** (not straight) криво́й. **2,** *colloq.* (dishonest) нечи́стый. —**crookedness,** *n.* кривизна́.

croon *v.t. & i.* напева́ть.

crop *n.* **1,** (farm product) культу́ра; посе́в. *Winter crops,* ози́мые культу́ры. *The crops are coming up,* посе́вы всхо́дят. *Crop rotation,* севооборо́т. **2,** (yield) урожа́й: *the corn crop,* урожа́й кукуру́зы. *Crop failure,* неурожа́й. **3,** (whip handle) кнутови́ще. **4,** (craw of a bird) зоб. —*v.t.* стричь: *crop someone's hair,* стричь кого́-нибудь под гребёнку. —**crop up,** возника́ть.

croquet *n.* кроке́т.

crosier *also,* **crozier** *n.* по́сох.

cross *n.* **1,** (structure or representation of same) крест. *Sign of the cross,* кре́стное зна́мение; крест. **2,** (hybrid) по́месь: *a mule is a cross between a donkey and a female horse,* мул — по́месь осла́ с кобы́лой. —*adj.* **1,** (transverse) попере́чный: *crossbeam,* попере́чная ба́лка. **2,** (intersecting) пересека́ющийся. **3,** (involving interchange) перекре́стный: *cross-pollination,* перекре́стное опыле́ние. **4,** (ill-tempered) злой. *He is cross with me,* он зол на меня́. —*v.t.* **1,** (traverse) переходи́ть; переезжа́ть; пересека́ть. **2,** (intersect) пересека́ть. **3,** (place crosswise) скре́щивать: *cross swords,* скре́щивать шпа́ги *or* мечи́. *Cross one's legs,* класть но́гу на́ ногу. **4,** (crossbreed) скре́щивать. **5,** (double-cross) обма́нывать: *he doesn't like to be crossed,* он не лю́бит, что́бы его́ обма́нывали. **6,** *in* **cross one's mind,** приходи́ть в го́лову (+ *dat.*). —*v.i.* **1,** (go to the other side) переходи́ть. **2,** (intersect) пересека́ться. **3,** *in* **cross in the mail,** размину́ться. —**cross off,** вычёркивать. —**cross oneself,** крести́ться. —**cross out,** зачёркивать. —**cross up,** подводи́ть.

crossbar *n.* **1,** (crossbeam) попере́чина; перекла́-

дина. **2,** *sports* (for high jumping) пла́нка; (between goal posts) шта́нга.

crossbeam *n.* попере́чная ба́лка; попере́чина; переклади́на.

crossbill *n.* клёст.

crossbow *n.* самостре́л.

crossbreed *v.t.* скре́щивать. —*n.* по́месь. —**cross-breeding,** *n.* скре́щивание; метиза́ция.

cross-country *adj.* **1,** (across a country) че́рез страну́: *a cross-country flight,* перелёт че́рез страну́. **2,** (across open country): *cross-country race,* кросс. **3,** (able to operate on any terrain) вездехо́дный. *Cross-country vehicle,* вездехо́д.

cross-cut saw попере́чная пила́.

cross-examination *n.* перекрёстный допро́с. —**cross-examine,** *v.t.* подверга́ть перекрёстному допро́су; допра́шивать.

cross-eye *n.* косогла́зие. —**cross-eyed,** *adj.* косогла́зый; косо́й.

crossfire *n.* перекрёстный ого́нь.

crossing *n.* **1,** (act of crossing) перехо́д; перее́зд; перепра́ва. **2,** (place to cross) перехо́д; перее́зд. **3,** (intersection) перекрёсток; скреще́ние. **4,** (railroad crossing) перее́зд.

crosspiece *n.* попере́чина; кресто́вина; перемы́чка.

cross-purposes *n.pl., in* **at cross-purposes,** наперекор друг дру́гу.

cross-reference *n.* перекрёстная ссы́лка.

crossroad *n.* **1,** (road that crosses) попере́чная доро́га. **2,** *pl.* (place of intersection) распу́тье; перепу́тье. —**at the crossroads,** на распу́тье; на перепу́тье.

cross section попере́чное сече́ние; попере́чный разре́з.

crosswalk *n.* перехо́д.

crosswise *adv.* крестообра́зно; крест-на́крест.

crossword puzzle кроссво́рд.

crotch *n.* проме́жность. *The trousers are tight in the crotch,* брю́ки у́зки в шагу́.

crotchety *adj.* причу́дливый; сварли́вый.

Croton bug пруса́к.

crouch *v.i.* приседа́ть.

croup *n.* круп.

croupier *n.* крупье́.

crouton *n.* грено́к.

crow *n.* воро́на. —*adj.* [*usu.* **crow's**] воро́ний: *crow's nest,* воро́нье гнездо́. —*v.i.* **1,** (cry, as of a rooster) кукаре́кать. **2,** *colloq.* (boast) труби́ть; прокрича́ть. —**as the crow flies,** по прямо́й.

crowbar *n.* лом.

crowd *n.* толпа́. *Avoid crowds,* избега́ть толпы́. —*v.t.* **1,** (make uncomfortable) тесни́ть; стесня́ть. *Crowd one's neighbor,* тесни́ть сосе́да. **2,** (fill to excess) заполня́ть: *people crowded the stores,* пу́блика запо́лнила магази́ны. *Crowd a room with furniture,* загроможда́ть *or* заставля́ть ко́мнату ме́белью. **3,** (squeeze; cram) вти́скивать. *Crowd six people into a car,* помеща́ть шесть челове́к в маши́не. **4,** *fol. by* **out** (displace) вытесня́ть. —*v.i.* **1,** *fol. by* **into** (squeeze into) набива́ться в; вти́скиваться в. **2,** *fol. by* **around** (cluster around) обступа́ть. **3,** *fol. by* **together** (gather closely together) толпи́ться; столпи́ться; тесни́ться; стесня́ться.

crowded *adj.* те́сный; лю́дный; переполненный.

It is crowded here, здесь те́сно.

crown *n.* **1,** (of a sovereign) коро́на; вене́ц. **2,** (garland; wreath) вено́к. **3,** (of the head) те́мя; маку́шка; (of a tooth) коро́нка; (of a hat) тулья́; (of a tree) кро́на. **4,** (monetary unit) кро́на. —*v.t.* **1,** (enthrone) коронова́ть; венча́ть на ца́рство. **2,** (endow with honor; surmount; make complete) венча́ть. *Be crowned with success,* увенча́ться успе́хом. **3,** *dentistry* ста́вить коро́нку на (зуб). **4,** *checkers* проводи́ть (ша́шку) в да́мки. **5,** *colloq.* (hit on the head) дать по голове́.

crown prince насле́дный принц.

crow's-feet *n.pl.* гуси́ные ла́пки.

crozier *n.* = **crosier.**

crucial *adj.* реша́ющий; крити́ческий; отве́тственный.

crucible *n.* **1,** (vessel) ти́гель. **2,** *fig.* (ordeal) горни́ло.

crucifix *n.* распя́тие.

crucifixion *n.* распя́тие (на кресте́).

cruciform *adj.* крестообра́зный.

crucify *v.t.* распина́ть.

crude *adj.* **1,** (raw; unrefined) сыро́й; необрабо́танный. *Crude oil,* нефть-сыре́ц. **2,** (coarse; unpolished) гру́бый: *crude remark,* гру́бое замеча́ние.

crudely *adv.* гру́бо. *To put it rather crudely,* гру́бо говоря́.

crudeness *n.* гру́бость. *Also,* **crudity.**

cruel *adj.* жесто́кий: *cruel person,* жесто́кий челове́к; *cruel treatment,* жесто́кое обраще́ние. —**cruelly,** *adv.* жесто́ко. —**cruelty,** *n.* жесто́кость.

cruet *n.* у́ксусница. *Cruet stand,* судо́к.

cruise *n.* морско́е путеше́ствие; круйз. —*v.i.* крейси́ровать. *Cruising speed,* кре́йсерская ско́рость. —**cruise missile,** крыла́тая раке́та.

cruiser *n.* кре́йсер.

crumb *n.* кро́шка.

crumble *v.t.* кроши́ть. —*v.i.* **1,** (fall into small pieces) кроши́ться; рассыпа́ться. **2,** (decay; disintegrate) распада́ться; разруша́ться.

crumbly *adj.* ры́хлый; рассы́пчатый.

crummy *adj., slang* дрянно́й; парши́вый.

crumpet *n.* сдо́бная пы́шка; лепёшка.

crumple *v.t.* мять; ко́мкать. —*v.i.* мя́ться.

crunch *v.t. & i.* хрусте́ть. —*n.* хруст.

crusade *n.* **1,** *hist.* кресто́вый похо́д. **2,** (campaign) похо́д; кампа́ния.

crusader *n.* **1,** *hist.* крестоно́сец. **2,** (strong advocate) боре́ц: *crusader for freedom,* боре́ц за свобо́ду.

crush *v.t.* **1,** (mash) дави́ть. *Crush to death,* задави́ть на́смерть. **2,** (grind into small particles) дроби́ть; размельча́ть. **3,** (crease; rumple) мять. **4,** (put down; suppress) подавля́ть; разда́вить. **5,** (defeat; overwhelm) разбива́ть. —*n.* **1,** (pressure from a crowd) да́вка; толче́я; толкотня́. **2,** *colloq.* (infatuation) увлече́ние.

crushed *adj.* **1,** (in small bits) дроблёный. **2,** (creased; wrinkled) мя́тый. **3,** (crestfallen) уби́тый.

crusher *n.* дроби́лка. *Rock crusher,* камнедроби́лка.

crushing *adj.* **1,** (designed to crush) дроби́льный. **2,** *fig.* (devastating) сокруши́тельный: *crushing blow,* сокруши́тельный уда́р. *Crushing defeat,* жесто́кое пораже́ние.

crust *n.* **1,** (of bread) ко́рка. **2,** (hard surface) кора́: *the earth's crust,* земна́я кора́.

crustacean *n.* ракообразное.

crutch *n.* костыль.

crux *n.* суть: *the crux of the matter,* суть дела.

cry *v.i.* **1,** (weep) плакать. *Burst out crying,* расплакаться. **2,** (shout) (за)кричать. **3,** *fol. by out* (shriek) вскрикивать. —*v.t.* **1,** *in* **cry one's eyes out,** выплакать глаза. **2,** *in* **cry oneself to sleep,** плакать пока (он) не заснул. —*n.* **1,** (shout) крик. **2,** (spell of weeping) плач. *Have a good cry,* выплакаться. **3,** (call of an animal or bird) крик. **4,** (rallying call) клич: *battle cry,* боевой клич.

crybaby *n.* плакса.

crying *n.* плач. —*adj.* вопиющий: *crying injustice,* вопиющая несправедливость. *A crying need,* острая необходимость. *It's a crying shame!,* стыд и срам!

crypt *n.* склеп.

cryptic *adj.* загадочный; немногословный; двусмысленный.

cryptogram *n.* криптограмма.

cryptographer *n.* шифровальщик.

cryptography *n.* криптография. —**cryptographic,** *adj.* криптографический.

crystal *n.* **1,** (clear glass) хрусталь. **2,** (solid body) кристалл. **3,** (of a watch) (часовое) стекло. —*adj.* хрустальный.

crystal-clear *adj.* **1,** (of water) кристальный. **2,** *fig.* (obvious) предельно ясный.

crystalline *adj.* кристаллический.

crystallize *v.t.* кристаллизовать. —*v.i.* кристаллизоваться. —**crystallization,** *n.* кристаллизация.

cub *n.* детёныш. ♦*Compounds are rendered by the suffix* -ёнок *or* -онок: *lion cub,* львёнок; *bear cub,* медвежонок.

Cuban *adj.* кубинский. —*n.* кубинец; кубинка.

cube *n.* **1,** (six-sided figure) куб. **2,** (small piece so shaped) кубик: *ice cube,* кубик льда. **3,** *math.* (third power) куб: *the cube of two is eight,* два в кубе — восемь; куб двух равен восьми. —*v.t.* возводить в куб. —**cube root,** кубический корень.

cubic *adj.* кубический.

cubicle *n.* клетушка.

cubism *n.* кубизм.

cubit *n.* локоть.

cuckold *n.* рогоносец. —*v.t.* наставлять рога (+ *dat.*).

cuckoo *n.* кукушка. —*v.i.* куковать. —**cuckoo clock,** часы с кукушкой.

cucumber *n.* огурец. —*adj.* огуречный.

cud *n.* жвачка: *chew the cud,* жевать жвачку.

cuddle *v.t.* обнимать; прижимать к себе. —*v.i.* [*usu.* **cuddle up**] прижиматься.

cudgel *n.* дубина. —*v.t.* дубасить.

cue *n.* **1,** (signal on stage) реплика. **2,** *billiards* кий.

cuff *n.* **1,** (of a sleeve) манжета; обшлаг. **2,** (of trousers) отворот. **3,** (slap) пощёчина. —**off the cuff,** *colloq.* экспромтом.

cuff link запонка.

cuirass *n.* кираса.

cuisine *n.* кухня.

culinary *adj.* кулинарный.

cull *v.t.* **1,** (select) черпать. **2,** (pick; gather, as flowers) собирать.

culminate *v.i.* [*usu.* **culminate in**] кончаться (+ *instr.*); выливаться в. —**culmination,** *n.* кульминация; кульминационный пункт.

culpable *adj.* виновный. —**culpability,** *n.* виновность.

culprit *n.* виновник.

cult *n.* культ.

cultivate *v.t.* **1,** (till) обрабатывать; возделывать. **2,** (grow, as plants) выращивать; разводить. **3,** *fig.* (develop) развивать; воспитывать; культивировать; утончать. **4,** (seek the good will of) заискивать перед; льнуть к.

cultivated *adj.* **1,** (tilled) обработанный. **2,** (cultured) культурный; образованный. **3,** (refined) утончённый.

cultivation *n.* **1,** (tillage) обработка. **2,** (development) развитие; воспитание.

cultural *adj.* культурный.

culture *n.* культура. —**cultured,** *adj.* культурный.

cumbersome *adj.* громоздкий.

cummerbund *n.* кушак.

cumulative *adj.* кумулятивный.

cumulous *adj.* кучевой. —**cumulus,** *n.* кучевые облака.

cuneiform *n.* клинопись.

cunning *adj.* хитрый. —*n.* хитрость.

cup *n.* **1,** (vessel) чашка. *Paper cup,* бумажный стаканчик. **2,** *sports* (trophy) кубок. —*v.t., in* **cup one's hand,** держать руку горстью.

cupboard *n.* шкаф.

Cupid *n.* Купидон.

cupidity *n.* жадность; алчность.

cupola *n.* купол.

cupping glass банка.

cur *n.* ублюдок.

curable *adj.* излечимый.

curative *adj.* лечебный; целебный; целительный.

curator *n.* хранитель.

curb *n.* **1,** (check; restraint) узда. **2,** (edge of a sidewalk) обочина. —*v.t.* обуздывать; укрощать.

curd *n., often pl.* творог.

curdle *v.t.* створаживать. —*v.i.* свёртываться; створаживаться.

cure *v.t.* **1,** (heal; remedy) вылечивать; излечивать: *cure an illness,* вылечивать/излечивать болезнь. *Cure someone of an illness,* вылечивать/излечивать кого-нибудь от болезни. **2,** (preserve, as meat) вялить; солить; коптить. —*n.* **1,** (treatment) курс лечения; излечение. **2,** (recovery of one's health) излечение. **3,** (remedy) средство: *a cure for cancer,* средство от рака.

cure-all *n.* панацея.

curfew *n.* комендантский час.

curia *n.* курия.

curiosity *n.* **1,** (inquisitiveness) любопытство. **2,** (thirst for knowledge) любознательность. **3,** (something that arouses interest) редкость; диковина.

curious *adj.* **1,** (eager to find out; inquisitive) любопытный. *I am curious to know,* мне любопытно знать... *A curious look,* любопытный взгляд. **2,** (eager to learn; inquiring) любознательный. **3,** (odd; strange) курьёзный.

curiously *adv.* любопытно. *Curiously enough...,* как ни странно...

curium *n.* кюрий.

curl *n.* локон; завиток; *pl.* кудри. —*v.t.* **1,** (form into ringlets, as hair) завивать. **2,** (cause to curve, as paper) коробить. **3,** *in* **curl one's lip,** кривить губы. —*v.i.* **1,** (of hair) завиваться; виться. **2,** (of paper) коробиться. **3,** (of smoke) клубиться. **4,** *fol. by* **up** (sit or lie cozily) свёртываться.

curler *n.* бигуди; папильотка.

curlew *n.* кроншнеп.

curlicue *n.* завитушка; крючок.

curling irons щипцы для завивки.

curly *adj.* кудрявый; курчавый; вьющийся.

currant *n.* **1,** (fruit or berry) смородина. **2,** (seedless raisin) коринка.

currency *n.* **1,** (money) валюта; деньги. *Foreign currency,* иностранная валюта. **2,** (prevalence; vogue) хождение: *enjoy wide currency,* иметь широкое хождение. —*adj.* валютный: *currency reform,* валютная реформа.

current *n.* **1,** (flow) течение: *against the current,* против течения. *Air current,* воздушное течение. *A current of air,* струя воздуха. **2,** *electricity* ток. —*adj.* текущий; нынешний; теперешний. *Current events,* текущие события. —**currently,** *adv.* ныне; в настоящее время.

curriculum *n.* курс обучения; учебный план.

currier *n.* кожевник.

curry *v.t.* выделывать (кожу). —**curry favor,** заискивать.

currycomb *n.* скребница.

curse *n.* **1,** (imprecation) проклятие. **2,** (bane) бич. —*v.t.* **1,** (damn) проклинать. **2,** *fol. by* **out** (berate) ругать; обругать. —*v.i.* (swear) ругаться. —**curse word,** бранное слово; ругательство.

cursed *adj.* проклятый.

cursive *adj.* рукописный. *Cursive writing,* скоропись.

cursory *adj.* беглый. —**cursorily,** *adv.* бегло.

curt *adj.* резкий; отрывистый.

curtail *v.t.* сокращать; урезывать. —**curtailment,** *n.* сокращение.

curtain *n.* **1,** (for a window) занавеска. **2,** (on stage) занавес. —*v.t.* завешивать; занавешивать. —**curtain call,** вызов (на сцену). —**curtain rod,** палка для гардин.

curtsy *also,* **curtsey** *n.* реверанс; приседание; книксен. —*v.i.* делать реверанс; приседать.

curvature *n.* кривизна; искривление.

curve *n.* **1,** (arc) кривая. **2,** (bend) изгиб; извилина. **3,** (draftsman's instrument) лекало. —*v.t.* изгибать. —*v.i.* изгибаться.

curved *adj.* изогнутый.

curvilinear *adj.* криволинейный.

cushion *n.* **1,** (pillow) подушка. **2,** (rim of a billiard table) борт. —*v.t.* смягчать (удар).

cuspid *n.* клык.

cuspidor *n.* плевательница.

cuss *v.i.,* *colloq.* ругаться. —*v.t.* [*usu.* **cuss out**] *colloq.* разругать. —*n.,* *colloq.* малый: *a queer old cuss,* странный малый.

custard *n.* заварной крем.

custodian *n.* **1,** (caretaker) хранитель. **2,** (janitor) дворник.

custody *n.* **1,** (guardianship) опёка; попечение. **2,** (detention) арест. *In custody,* под арестом; под стражей. *Take into custody,* брать под арест; брать под стражу.

custom *n.* обычай. *See also* **customs.**

customary *adj.* обычный; привычный. —**customarily,** *adv.* обычно.

customer *n.* заказчик; покупатель; клиент.

custom-made *adj.* сделанный на заказ.

customs *n.pl.* **1,** (agency) таможня. *Pass through customs,* проходить таможенный осмотр. **2,** (duty) пошлина. —*adj.* таможенный: *customs inspector,* таможенный надсмотрщик.

cut *v.t.* **1,** (divide into parts; slice; carve) резать. **2,** (hurt; gash) порезать: *cut one's finger,* порезать себе палец. *Cut oneself,* порезаться. **3,** (trim) подрезать (ногти); стричь (волосы); срезать (цветы). **4,** (mow) косить. **5,** (cut out, as cloth) кроить. **6,** (shape, as gems) гранить. **7,** (divide in two, as of a road or river) рассекать. **8,** (have grown in, as a tooth) прорезаться: *he is cutting a tooth,* у него прорезается зуб. **9,** (reduce, as prices, taxes, etc.) снижать. **10,** (shorten, as a book, article, etc.) сокращать; урезывать. **11,** *cards* снимать (колоду). **12,** *colloq.* (fail to attend, as a class) прогуливать. —*v.i.* **1,** (act as a sharp edge) резать: *the knife does not cut,* нож не режет. **2,** (admit to being cut) резаться: *the meat cuts easily,* мясо легко режется. **3,** *cards* снимать колоду. —*n.* **1,** (gash) порез. **2,** (of meat) кусок. **3,** (style of a garment) покрой. **4,** (deletion) купюра. **5,** (reduction) снижение; сокращение. —*adj.* **1,** (gashed) порезанный. **2,** (trimmed, as of flowers) срезанный. **3,** (of gems, glass, etc.) гранёный. **4,** (reduced) льготный. —**cut across,** пересекать. —**cut back,** урезывать. —**cut down, 1,** (fell) рубить; срубать; вырубать. **2,** (kill) срезать; сражать. **3,** (reduce) урезывать. —**cut off, 1,** (sever) отрезать. **2,** (isolate) разобщать. **3,** (halt) прекращать. **4,** (rudely interrupt) обрывать. **5,** (on the telephone) прерывать; разъединять: *we've been cut off,* нас прервали/разъединили. —**cut out, 1,** (remove by cutting) вырезать. **2,** (shape by cutting, as material) выкраивать. **3,** (remove; delete) вычёркивать. **4,** *colloq.* (discontinue; give up) бросить (курить); отказаться от (мяса). **5,** *slang* (cease) перестать; бросить; прекратить. *Cut it out!,* прекрати! —**cut out for; cut out to be,** созданный для: *he is not cut out for it,* он не создан для этого. *He is not cut out to be a soldier,* он не годится в солдаты. —**cut short,** оборвать. —**cut through, 1,** (cut across) пересекать. **2,** (penetrate) рассекать. —**cut up,** разрезать; резать.

cutaway *n.* визитка. *Also,* **cutaway coat.**

cutback *n.* сокращение.

cute *adj.,* *colloq.* **1,** (pretty) хорошенький; миленький. **2,** (clever) умный; остроумный.

cutlass *n.* тесак.

cutlery *n.* ножевой товар.

cutlet *n.* (отбивная) котлета. *Veal cutlet,* телячья отбивная.

cut-rate *adj.* льготный.

cutter *n.* **1,** (one who cuts) резальщик. *Diamond cutter,* гранильщик. *Wood cutter,* лесоруб. **2,** (of cloth) закройщик. **3,** (tool) резец; резак. **4,** (boat) катер; тендер.

cutthroat *n.* головорез. —*adj.* жестокий; ожесточённый.

cutting *n.* **1,** (act of cutting) резание. **2,** (work of cutting material) кройка. **3,** (plant shoot used for grafting) черенок. —*adj.* **1,** (that cuts) режущий. **2,** (chilling or piercing) резкий. **3,** (sarcastic) колкий.

cuttlefish *n.* каракатица; сепия.

cyanic *adj.* цианновый; цианистый.

cyanide *n.* цианид. —**potassium cyanide,** цианистый калий.

cyanogen *n.* циан.

cyanosis *n.* цианоз; синюха.

cybernetics *n.* кибернетика.

cyclamen *n.* цикламен.

cycle *n.* цикл. —*v.i.* ездить на велосипеде. —**cyclical,** *adj.* циклический.

cyclist *n.* **1,** (rider) велосипедист. **2,** (racer) велогонщик.

cyclone *n.* циклон. —**cyclonic,** *adj.* циклонический.

cyclotron *n.* циклотрон.

cylinder *n.* **1,** (geometric figure; object so shaped) цилиндр. **2,** (rotating part of a revolver) барабан. —**cylindrical,** *adj.* цилиндрический.

cymbals *n.pl.* тарелки.

cynic *n.* циник. —**cynical,** *adj.* циничный. —**cynicism,** *n.* цинизм; циничность.

cypress *n.* кипарис.

Cyrillic alphabet кириллица.

cyst *n.* киста.

cytology *n.* цитология. —**cytological,** *adj.* цитологический.

czar *n.* = **tsar.**

Czech *adj.* чешский. —*n.* **1,** (person) чех; чешка. **2,** (language) чешский язык.

Czechoslovak *adj.* чехословацкий.

D

D, d четвёртая буква английского алфавита. —*n.* **1,** (musical note) pe. **2,** (school grade) двойка.

dab *v.t.* **1,** (pat gently): *dab one's eyes with a handkerchief,* прикладывать платок к глазам. **2,** (apply liquid to) мазать. —*n.* (of paint) мазок; (of rouge) капелька.

dabble *v.i.* [*usu.* **dabble in**] заниматься (поверхностно). —**dabbler,** *n.* любитель; дилетант.

dacha *n.* дача.

dachshund *n.* такса.

dactyl *n.* дактиль. —**dactylic,** *adj.* дактилический.

dad *n., colloq.* папа. *Also,* **daddy.**

daffodil *n.* нарцисс.

daffy *adj., slang* сумасбродный.

daft *adj.* сумасшедший.

dagger *n.* **1,** (knife) кинжал. **2,** *printing* (†) крестик.

dahlia *n.* георгин.

daily *adj.* ежедневный. —*adv.* ежедневно. —*n.* ежедневная газета.

dainty *adj.* **1,** (delicately pretty or graceful) изящный; утончённый. **2,** (delicious and choice) лакомый.

dairy *n.* молочная. —*adj.* молочный: *dairy products,* молочные продукты. —**dairy farm,** молочная ферма; молочное хозяйство. —**dairymaid,** *n.* молочница. —**dairyman,** *n.* молочник.

dais *n.* помост; возвышение.

daisy *n.* **1,** (English daisy) маргаритка. **2,** (oxeye daisy) нивяник; поповник.

dale *n.* долина; ложбина; лощина.

dally *v.i.* **1,** (dawdle) мешкать. **2,** *fol. by* **with** (trifle with; toy with) играть (+ *instr.*).

dam *n.* **1,** (barrier) плотина. **2,** (female parent of an animal) матка. —*v.t.* запруживать; перекрывать.

damage *n.* **1,** (harm; injury) вред; повреждение; ущерб; порча. **2,** *pl.* (compensation for losses) убытки: *suit for damages,* иск за убытки. *Pay damages,* возмещать убытки. —*v.t.* повреждать. *Be damaged,* пострадать. —**damaging,** *adj.* вредный.

damask *n.* штоф. —*adj.* штофный.

dame *n.* **1,** (lady) дама. **2,** *slang* (woman) баба.

damn *v.t.* проклинать. —*adj., colloq.* проклятый. *Damn fool,* набитый дурак. —*adv., colloq.* чертовски. *You're damn right!,* вы совершенно правы. —*interj.* чёрт (возьми)!; проклятие! —**not give a damn,** (на)плевать: *he doesn't give a damn,* ему (на)плевать на это. —**not worth a damn,** гроша медного (*or* выеденного яйца) не стоит.

damnable *adj.* **1,** (meriting damnation) предосудительный. **2,** *colloq.* (accursed) проклятый.

damnation *n.* **1,** (act of damning) проклятие. **2,** (eternal punishment) вечные муки.

damned *adj.* проклятый. *I'll be damned if...,* будь я проклят, если...

damning *adj.* изобличительный.

damp *adj.* сырой; влажный. —*v.t.* [*usu.* **damp down**] тушить.

dampen *v.t.* **1,** (moisten) смачивать. **2,** (cool, as enthusiasm, etc.) омрачать; охлаждать.

damper *n.* заслонка; вьюшка. —**put a damper on,** расхолаживать; омрачать.

dampness *n.* сырость; влажность.

damsel *n.* девица.

dance *v.t. & i.* танцевать. *Ask someone to dance,* пригласить кого-нибудь на танец. —*n.* **1,** (dancing; kind of dance) танец: *folk dance,* народный танец; *modern dance,* новый танец. **2,** (gathering of people for dancing) танцы; танцевальный вечер; бал. *Invite someone to a dance,* пригласить кого-нибудь на танцы. —*adj.* танцевальный: *dance hall,* танцевальный зал. —**dance attendance on,** ходить на задних лапках перед. —**dance to someone's tune,** плясать под чью-нибудь дудку.

dancer *n.* **1,** (one who dances) танцо́р. **2,** (professional dancer) танцо́вщик; танцо́вщица.

dancing *n.* та́нцы: *folk dancing,* наро́дные та́нцы. —*adj.* танцева́льный. *Dancing lessons,* уро́ки та́нцев.

dandelion *n.* одува́нчик.

dander *n., usu. in* get one's dander up, разозли́ться.

dandle *v.t.* кача́ть.

dandruff *n.* пе́рхоть.

dandy *n.* **1,** (fop) щёголь; франт. **2,** *colloq.* (excellent thing) пре́лесть.—*adj., colloq.* преле́стный.

Dane *n.* датча́нин; датча́нка. —**Great Dane,** да́тский дог.

danger *n.* опа́сность. *Danger signal,* сигна́л опа́сности.

dangerous *adj.* опа́сный. —**dangerously,** *adv.* опа́сно. *Dangerously ill,* опа́сно *or* тяжело́ бо́лен.

dangle *v.t.* болта́ть. —*v.i.* болта́ться.

Danish *adj.* да́тский. —*n.* да́тский язы́к.

dank *adj.* сыро́й; промо́зглый.

dapper *adj.* вы́холенный; щеголева́тый.

dapple *v.t.* испещря́ть. —*adj.* = **dappled.** —*n.* подпа́лина.

dappled *adj.* **1,** (spotted) пятни́стый. **2,** (of a horse) в я́блоках; чуба́рый.

dapple-gray *adj.* се́рый в я́блоках.

dare *v.t. & i.* сметь; осме́ливаться. *How dare you...!,* как ты сме́ешь (+ *inf.)! He wouldn't dare to do it,* он не посме́ет э́то сде́лать. —*v.t.* вызыва́ть. *I dare you to...,* а ну (+ *imperative*). —**dare say,** сметь *or* осме́ливаться сказа́ть.

daredevil *n.* смельча́к; лиха́ч; удале́ц; головоре́з; сорвиголова́. —*adj.* опроме́тчивый; безрассу́дный.

daring *adj.* сме́лый. —*n.* сме́лость.

dark *adj.* тёмный. *Dark blue,* тёмно-си́ний. *Dark complexion,* сму́глое лицо́. *Get dark,* темне́ть. —*n.* темнота́; тьма; мрак. *Before dark,* за́светло. *After dark,* по́сле наступле́ния темноты́. —**be/keep in the dark,** быть/держа́ть в неве́дении.

darken *v.t.* затемня́ть —*v.i.* темне́ть.

dark-haired *adj.* темноволо́сый.

darkness *n.* темнота́; тьма; мрак.

darkroom *n.* тёмная ко́мната.

dark-skinned *adj.* темноко́жий.

darling *n.* **1,** (beloved person) ми́лый (ми́лая); дорого́й (дорога́я); ду́шенька; голу́бка. **2,** (someone in great favor) люби́мец; ба́ловень. —*adj.* **1,** (beloved) дорого́й; ми́лый. **2,** *colloq.* (cute; lovely) чуде́сный.

darn *v.t.* што́пать. —*adj., colloq.* [*also,* **darned**] прокля́тый.

darnel *n.* плёвел.

darning needle 1, (needle used in darning) што́пальная игла́. **2,** (dragonfly) стрекоза́.

dart *n.* **1,** (missile) стрела́. **2,** (dash; rush) бросо́к. —*v.i.* бро́ситься; ри́нуться; помча́ться. *Dart out from behind a bush,* вы́лететь из-за куста́.

dash *v.i.* **1,** (dart; rush) бро́ситься; ри́нуться; помча́ться. *Dash out of the room,* вы́бежать из ко́мнаты. **2,** (land with great force) би́ться; ударя́ться: *the waves dashed against the shore,* во́лны би́лись/ударя́лись о бе́рег. —*v.t.* **1,** (throw violently) бро́сить (изо всех сил): *dash to the ground,* бро́сить о зе́млю. **2,** (shatter, as hopes) разбива́ть (наде́жды). **3,** *fol. by* off (write hastily) набра́сывать. —*n.* **1,** (rush) бросо́к. *Make a dash for the door,* бро́ситься к две́ри. **2,** *sports*

бег: *100-meter dash,* бег на сто ме́тров. **3,** (—) тире́. **4,** (bit; touch) при́месь.

dashboard *n.* прибо́рная доска́.

dashing *adj.* лихо́й; бра́вый; молодцева́тый.

dastard *n.* трус; подле́ц. —**dastardly,** *adj.* трусли́вый; по́длый.

data *n.pl.* да́нные. —**data bank/base,** спра́вочно-информацио́нный фонд. —**data processing,** обрабо́тка да́нных.

date *n.* **1,** (day of the month) число́: *what is today's date?,* како́е сего́дня число́? **2,** (statement of calendar time) да́та: *date of birth,* да́та рожде́ния. *Put the date on the letter,* проставля́ть да́ту на письме́. **3,** (day when something is to happen) срок: *by a certain date,* к определённому сро́ку. *Set the date,* назнача́ть срок. *Date of departure,* срок *or* день отъе́зда. **4,** (social engagement) свида́ние: *go out on dates,* ходи́ть на свида́ния. **5,** (fruit) фи́ник. —*v.t.* **1,** (put the date on) дати́ровать; помеча́ть: *the letter was dated May 6th,* письмо́ бы́ло дати́ровано/поме́чено шесты́м ма́я. **2,** (see socially) встреча́ться с. —*v.i.* относи́ться: *this building dates from the 15th century,* э́то зда́ние отно́сится к пятна́дцатому ве́ку. *Date back to ancient times,* восходи́ть к дре́вности. —**to date,** до сих пор. —**up to date,** в ку́рсе де́ла. *Bring up to date,* вводи́ть в курс де́ла. *See also* **out-of-date** *and* **up-to-date.**

dated *adj.* **1,** (marked with a date) дати́рованный. **2,** (outdated) устаре́вший.

date line Ли́ния переме́ны да́ты. *Also,* **International Date Line.**

date palm фи́никовая па́льма.

dative *adj.* да́тельный: *dative case,* да́тельный паде́ж.

daub *v.t. & i.* ма́зать; малева́ть; мара́ть. —*n.* мазня́; пачкотня́.

daughter *n.* дочь. —**daughter-in-law,** *n.* неве́стка; сноха́.

daunt *v.t.* **1,** (make afraid) запу́гивать; устраша́ть. **2,** (dishearten) обескура́живать. —**dauntless,** *adj.* неустраши́мый; бесстра́шный.

dauphin *n.* дофи́н.

davenport *n.* дива́н-крова́ть.

dawdle *v.i.* ме́шкать; ло́дырничать; каните́литься.

dawn *n.* **1,** (daybreak) рассве́т; у́тренняя заря́. **2,** *fig.* (beginning) заря́. —*v.i.* **1,** (begin to grow light) света́ть; рассвета́ть: *day is dawning,* света́ет; рассвета́ет. **2,** *fol. by* on *or* upon (begin to be understood) озаря́ть: *it dawned on me,* меня́ озари́ла мысль.

day *n.* день. —*adj.* дневно́й: *the day shift,* дневна́я сме́на. —**any day (now),** со дня на́ день. —**day after day,** изо дня в день. —**day by day,** день ото дня. —**day off,** выходно́й день. —**in those days,** в те времена́. —**one of these days,** на днях. —**some day,** когда́-нибудь. —**the day before,** накану́не. —**the other day,** на днях. —**to this day,** по сей день.

daybed *n.* дива́н-крова́ть.

daybreak *n.* рассве́т.

daydream *n.* мечта́; грёза. —*v.i.* мечта́ть; грёзить. —**daydreaming,** *n.* мечта́ние.

daylight *n.* **1,** (light of day) дневно́й свет. *In broad daylight,* средь бе́ла дня. **2,** (dawn) рассве́т: *before daylight,* до рассве́та; затемно́. **3,** (daytime) дневно́е вре́мя: *two hours of daylight,* два часа́ дневно́го вре́мени. —**scare the daylights out of,** *colloq.* напуга́ть дó смéрти. —**see daylight,** вúдеть вúход из положéния.

daytime *n.* дневнóе врéмя. *In the daytime,* днем. —*adj.* дневнóй: *daytime activities,* дневнúе занáтия.

day-to-day *adj.* повседнéвный.

daywork *n.* подённая рабóта; подéнщина. —**day-worker,** *n.* подéнщик; подённый.

daze *n.* отупéние. *Be in a daze,* быть (как) в чадý. —*v.t.* ошеломлáть. —**dazed,** *adj.* обалдéлый.

dazzle *v.t.* ослеплáть. —**dazzling,** *adj.* ослепúтельный.

deacon *n.* дьáкон.

deactivate *v.t.* **1,** (disband) распускáть. **2,** (render inoperative) обезврéживать.

dead *adj.* **1,** (of a person) мёртвый. *He is dead,* он ýмер. *Dead body,* труп. *Play dead,* притворáться мёртвым. **2,** (of an animal) дóхлый. **3,** (of trees, leaves, etc.) сухóй. **4,** (failing to operate) заглóхший: *the motor went dead,* мотóр заглóх. **5,** *with certain nouns* мёртвый: *dead languages,* мёртвые языкú; *dead season,* мёртвый сезóн; *dead silence,* мёртвая тишинá; *dead weight,* мёртвый груз. —*adv.* совершéнно: *dead right,* совершéнно прав. *Dead against,* решúтельно прóтив. *Dead tired,* дó смéрти устáлый. *Dead drunk,* мертвéцки пьян. *Stop dead in one's tracks,* остановúться как вкóпанный. —*n.* **1,** *preceded by* **the** (those who have died) мёртвые; умéршие. *Rise from the dead,* воскресáть. **2,** (coldest or darkest point) *rendered by* глубóкий: *in the dead of night/winter,* глубóкой нóчью/зимóй.

dead center мёртвая тóчка: *move off dead center,* сдвúнуть(ся) с мёртвой тóчки.

deaden *v.t.* **1,** (make less intense) заглушáть: *deaden the sound/pain,* заглушáть звук/боль. **2,** (make numb) умерщвлáть: *deaden a tooth,* умерщвлáть нерв зýба.

dead end тупúк.

dead letter 1, (undelivered letter) недостáвленное письмó. **2,** (something no longer valid or enforced) мёртвая бýква.

deadline *n.* срок; послéдний срок; крáйний срок; предéльный срок. *The deadline for payment,* срок платежá.

deadlock *n.* мёртвая тóчка; тупúк. —*v.t.* заводúть в тупúк. *Be deadlocked,* заходúть в тупúк.

deadly *adj.* смертéльный; смертонóсный. —*adv., colloq.* смертéльно: *deadly dull,* смертéльно скýчно.

dead reckoning счислéние путú.

deaf *adj.* глухóй. *Become deaf,* (о)глóхнуть. *Be deaf to,* быть глухúм к. —**fall on deaf ears,** остáться без внимáния. —**turn a deaf ear to,** пропустúть мúмо ушéй.

deaf-and-dumb *adj.* глухонемóй.

deafen *v.t.* оглушáть. —**deafening,** *adj.* оглушúтельный.

deaf-mute *n.* глухонемóй.

deafness *n.* глухотá.

deal *n.* **1,** (transaction) сдéлка. **2,** *cards* сдáча. **3,** *in a* **great** (*or* **good**) **deal,** мнóго: *a great deal of money,* мнóго дéнег. *I learned a great deal,* я мнóгому научúлся. *She is a good deal better today,* ей сегóдня значúтельно лýчше. —*v.t.* **1,** *usu. fol. by* **out** (apportion; distribute) раздавáть; распределáть. **2,** *cards* сдавáть (кáрты). **3,** (administer, as a blow) наносúть (удáр). —*v.i.* **1,** *cards* сдавáть кáрты. *Who deals?,* кто сдаёт? **2,** *fol. by* **in** (sell; trade) торговáть

(+ *instr.*). —**deal with, 1,** (have dealings with) имéть дéло с. **2,** (behave toward) поступáть с. **3,** (handle; take care of) справлáться с. **4,** (take up; treat) рассмáтривать.

dealer *n.* **1,** (merchant; seller) торгóвец. **2,** *cards* тот, кто сдаёт кáрты: *who is the dealer?,* кто сдаёт?

dealing *n.* **1,** (conduct toward others) поведéние: *honest dealing,* чéстное поведéние. **2,** *usu. pl.* (transactions) (торгóвые) делá.

dean *n.* **1,** (university official) декáн. **2,** (of a cathedral) настоáтель. **3,** (senior member) старшинá.

dear *adj.* дорогóй. —*n.,* *used in direct address* дорогóй (дорогáя); мúлый (мúлая). —**oh dear!; dear me!,** бóже мой!; о бóже!; гóсподи!

dearly *adv.* дóрого: *pay dearly for,* дóрого заплатúть за. *It cost him dearly,* это емý дóрого обошлóсь. *Love someone dearly,* горячó любúть когó-нибудь.

dearth *n.* недостáток; нехвáтка.

death *n.* смерть. *Be near death,* быть прú смéрти. *Sentence to death,* приговáривать к смéртной кáзни. *Put to death,* предавáть смéрти. —*adj.* смéртный: *death penalty,* смéртная казнь; *death sentence,* смéртный приговóр. *Death rate,* смéртность. *Death certificate,* свидéтельство о смéрти. —**at death's door,** прú смéрти. —**be the death of,** сводúть в могúлу; сживáть со свéта. —**to death,** дó смéрти: *frighten to death,* напугáть дó смéрти. *Be bored to death,* смертéльно скучáть. —**to the death,** нáсмерть: *fight to the death,* сражáться нáсмерть; борóться (*or* борьбá) не на жизнь, а на смерть.

deathbed *n.* смéртное лóже. *On one's deathbed,* на смéртном одрé.

deathblow *n.* смертéльный удáр.

deathly *adj.* мéртвенный: *deathly pallor,* мéртвенная блéдность. *Deathly silence,* гробовóе молчáние. —*adv.* смертéльно: *be deathly afraid of,* смертéльно боáться (+ *gen.*).

death mask посмéртная мáска.

debacle *n.* катастрóфа.

debar *v.t.* **1,** (shut out) не допускáть. **2,** (prevent) лишáть прáва: *debar from voting,* лишáть прáва гóлоса.

debark *v.t.* высáживать. —*v.i.* высáживаться. —**debarkation,** *n.* высáдка.

debase *v.t.* **1,** (cheapen) обесцéнивать: *debase the currency,* обесцéнивать валюту. **2,** (lower in dignity) унижáть. *Debase oneself,* унижáться.

debatable *adj.* спóрный; оспорúмый; дискуссиóнный. *That's debatable,* это спóрный вопрóс.

debate *v.i.* дебатúровать. —*v.t.* **1,** (discuss) обсуждáть; дебатúровать; дискутúровать. **2,** (consider; weigh) соображáть; взвéшивать. —*n.* **1,** (discussion) дебáты; прéния; дискýссия. **2,** (formal contest) дúспут.

debauch *v.t.* развращáть; совращáть. —**debauchery,** *n.* разврáт; разгýл.

debenture *n.* облигáция.

debilitate *v.t.* ослаблáть; расслаблáть. —**debilitation,** *n.* ослаблéние; расслаблéние.

debility *n.* слáбость; бессúлие.

debit *n.* дéбет. —*v.t.* дебетовáть.

debonair *adj.* **1,** (affable; gracious) любéзный. **2,** (carefree; gay) весёлый; жизнерáдостный.

debris *n.* облóмки.

debt *n.* долг. *I am in your debt,* я у вас в долгý.

debtor *n.* должни́к. *Debtor's prison,* долгова́я тюрьма́; долгова́я я́ма.

debut *n.* дебю́т. *Make one's debut,* дебюти́ровать. —**debutante,** *n.* дебюта́нтка.

decade *n.* десятиле́тие.

decadence *n.* упа́дочничество; декаде́нтство.

decadent *adj.* упа́дочный; упа́днический; декаде́нтский. —*n.* декаде́нт.

decagon *n.* десятиуго́льник.

decahedron *n.* десятигра́нник. —**decahedral,** *adj.* десятигра́нный.

decal *n.* переводна́я карти́нка.

decamp *v.i.* **1,** (break camp) снима́ться с ла́геря. **2,** (depart) удира́ть; смыва́ться.

decanter *n.* графи́н.

decapitate *v.t.* обезгла́вливать. —**decapitation,** *n.* обезгла́вливание.

decathlon *n.* десятибо́рье.

decay *v.i.* **1,** (rot; decompose) гнить; разлага́ться; *(of teeth)* по́ртится. **2,** (deteriorate physically) ветша́ть. *Decaying building,* обветша́лое зда́ние. **3,** *fig.* (go into a decline) приходи́ть в упа́док. —*n.* **1,** (decomposition) гние́ние; разложе́ние. *Tooth decay,* ка́риес зубо́в. **2,** (decline) упа́док. **3,** *chem.; physics* распа́д.

deceased *adj.* поко́йный. —*n., preceded by* the поко́йник; поко́йный; уме́рший.

deceit *n.* обма́н. —**deceitful,** *adj.* обма́нный; лжи́вый.

deceive *v.t. & i.* обма́нывать.

decelerate *v.t.* замедля́ть. —*v.i.* замедля́ть ход. —**deceleration,** *n.* замедле́ние.

December *n.* дека́брь. —*adj.* дека́брьский. —**Decembrist,** *n.* декабри́ст.

decency *n.* прили́чие. *A man without decency,* бессо́вестный челове́к. *He didn't have the decency to apologize,* у него́ хвати́ло со́вести не извини́ться.

decent *adj.* **1,** (proper) прили́чный. **2,** (respectable) поря́дочный. **3,** (adequate; passable) прили́чный. **4,** (kind; thoughtful) любе́зный. —**decently,** *adv.* прили́чно.

decentralize *v.t.* децентрализова́ть. —**decentralization,** *n.* децентрализа́ция.

deception *n.* обма́н. —**deceptive,** *adj.* обма́нчивый.

decibel *n.* издеци́бел.

decide *v.t. & i.* реша́ть; *I decided to leave,* я реши́л(а) уе́хать. *Decide the outcome of,* реша́ть исхо́д (+ *gen.*). *Decide on a course of action,* реши́ться на (како́й-нибудь) посту́пок.

decided *adj.* я́вный; бесспо́рный; реши́тельный. —**decidedly,** *adv.* реши́тельно.

deciduous *adj.* листопа́дный.

decigram *also,* **decigramme** *n.* децигра́мм.

deciliter *also,* **decilitre** *n.* децили́тр.

decimal *adj.* деся́тичный. —*n.* деся́тичная дробь.

decimate *v.t.* разоря́ть; коси́ть.

decimeter *also,* **decimetre** *n.* дециме́тр.

decipher *v.t.* **1,** (decode) расшифро́вывать; дешифри́ровать. **2,** (read; make out) разбира́ть. —**decipherment,** *n.* расшифро́вка; дешифро́вка.

decision *n.* реше́ние.

decisive *adj.* **1,** (forceful; conclusive) реши́тельный: *decisive person,* реши́тельный челове́к; *decisive victory,* реши́тельная побе́да. **2,** (determining the final outcome) реша́ющий: *decisive factor,* реша́ющий фа́ктор. —**decisively,** *adv.* реши́тельно. —**decisiveness,** *n.* реши́тельность.

deck *n.* **1,** (of a ship) па́луба. **2,** (pack of cards) коло́да. —*v.t.* [*usu.* **deck out**] принаряжа́ть: *decked out in a new suit,* принаряжённый в но́вый костю́м.

deckhouse *n.* ру́бка.

declaim *v.t. & i.* деклами́ровать.

declamation *n.* деклама́ция. —**declamatory,** *adj.* декламацио́нный.

declaration *n.* объявле́ние; деклара́ция. *Declaration of love,* объясне́ние в любви́. *Customs declaration,* тамо́женная деклара́ция.

declarative *adj.* **1,** (making a statement or assertion) декларати́вный. **2,** *gram.* повествова́тельный.

declare *v.t.* **1,** (announce formally; proclaim) объявля́ть: *declare war on,* объяви́ть войну́ (+ *dat.*). **2,** (assert; avow) заявля́ть. **3,** (pronounce) признава́ть: *declare someone insane,* призна́ть кого́-нибудь душевнобольны́м. **4,** (make a statement of, as taxable goods) называ́ть. *Have you anything to declare?,* у вас есть что́-нибудь, подлежа́щее обложе́нию по́шлиной? —**declare oneself,** выска́зываться.

declassify *v.t.* рассекре́чивать.

declension *n., gram.* склоне́ние.

declinable *adj.* склоня́емый.

declination *n.* **1,** *astron.* склоне́ние. **2,** (magnetic declination) магни́тное отклоне́ние.

decline *v.t.* **1,** (turn down) отклоня́ть; отка́зываться от. **2,** *fol. by inf.* (refuse) отка́зываться. **3,** *gram.* склоня́ть. —*v.i.* **1,** (refuse to accept something) отка́зываться. **2,** (decrease; go down) уменьша́ться; па́дать. **3,** (deteriorate) приходи́ть в упа́док. —*n.* **1,** (downward slope) склон. **2,** (drop; reduction) паде́ние; сниже́ние. **3,** (deterioration) упа́док.

declivity *n.* склон; спуск; отко́с.

decoction *n.* отва́р.

decode *v.t.* расшифро́вывать. —**decoding,** *n.* расшифро́вка.

décolleté *adj.* декольте́; декольти́рованный. —**décolletage,** *n.* декольте́.

decompose *v.t.* разлага́ть. —*v.i.* разлага́ться. —**decomposition,** *n.* разложе́ние.

decontaminate *v.t.* **1,** (rid of germs) обеззара́живать. **2,** (rid of poisonous or radioactive substances) дегази́ровать. —**decontamination,** *n.* обеззара́живание; дегаза́ция.

decontrol *v.t.* освобожда́ть от контро́ля.

décor *n.* обстано́вка.

decorate *v.t.* **1,** (adorn) украша́ть; декори́ровать. **2,** (furnish) обставля́ть; отде́лывать. **3,** (award a medal to) награжда́ть.

decoration *n.* **1,** (act of decorating) украше́ние. **2,** (ornament) украше́ние. **3,** (award) о́рден; знак отли́чия.

decorative *adj.* декорати́вный.

decorator *n.* декора́тор.

decorous *adj.* прили́чный; присто́йный; чи́нный.

decorum *n.* прили́чие; деко́рум.

decoy *n.* прима́нка. —*v.t.* зама́нивать; прима́нивать.

decrease *v.t.* уменьша́ть. —*v.i.* уменьша́ться. —*n.* уменьше́ние.

decree *n.* указ; декре́т; постановле́ние. —*v.t. & i.* постановля́ть.

decrepit *adj.* дря́хлый. —**decrepitude,** *n.* дря́хлость.

decry *v.t.* осуждать; порицать.

dedicate *v.t.* **1,** (devote; inscribe) посвящать. *Dedicate a book to,* посвятить книгу (+ *dat.*). **2,** (open formally) открывать. —**dedicated,** *adj.* преданный.

dedication *n.* **1,** (act of dedicating) посвящение. **2,** (formal opening) открытие. **3,** (devotion) преданность.

deduce *v.t.* выводить: *from this I deduced that...,* из этого я вывел, что...

deduct *v.t.* **1,** (subtract) вычитать. **2,** (withhold) удерживать; отчислять.

deduction *n.* **1,** (subtraction; withholding) вычет; удержание. **2,** (reasoning) дедукция. **3,** (conclusion) вывод. —**deductive,** *adj.* дедуктивный.

deed *n.* **1,** (act) поступок; дело. *Good deed,* доброе дело. **2,** (exploit) подвиг. **3,** *pl.* (action, as opposed to words) дела. **4,** (legal document) акт; грамота.

deem *v.t.* считать: *deem something necessary,* считать что-нибудь необходимым.

de-emphasize *v.t.* преуменьшать.

deep *adj.* **1,** (extending far down, back or into) глубокий: *deep hole/river,* глубокая яма/река. *Deep cut,* глубокий порез. **2,** (having a specified depth): глубиной в: *ten meters deep,* глубиной в десять метров. **3,** (profound; intense) глубокий. **4,** (of sleep) глубокий; беспробудный. **5,** (absorbed, as in thought) погружённый (в мысли). **6,** (low-pitched) низкий; густой. **7,** (dark, as of a color) тёмный: *deep blue,* тёмно-синий. —*adv.* глубоко: *dig deep,* рыть глубоко. —**deep into,** вглубь (+ *gen.*).

deepen *v.t.* углублять. —*v.i.* углубляться.

deeply *adv.* глубоко.

deep-rooted *adj.* укоренившийся; закоренелый.

deep-sea *adj.* глубоководный. *Deep-sea fishing,* ловля рыбы в глубоких водах. *Deep-sea diving,* водолазное дело.

deep-seated *adj.* укоренившийся.

deer *n.* олень. —*adj.* [*also,* **deer's**] олений: *deer hide,* оленья шкура.

deerskin *n.* оленья шкура. —*adj.* олений: *deerskin coat,* оленья шуба.

deface *v.t.* **1,** (mar; disfigure) уродовать; обезображивать. **2,** (efface; obliterate) стирать; изглаживать.

de facto **1,** *used adverbially* де-факто. **2,** *used adjectivally* фактический: *de facto recognition,* фактическое признание.

defamation *n.* диффамация; поношение; клевета. —**defamatory,** *adj.* клеветнический.

defame *v.t.* поносить; клеветать.

default *n.* **1,** (failure to pay money due) неплатёж. **2,** (failure to appear) неявка. —*v.i.* не выполнять обязательств. —**defaulter,** *n.* неплательщик.

defeat *n.* поражение: *suffer a defeat,* потерпеть поражение. *Admit defeat,* признать себя побеждённым. —*v.t.* **1,** (vanquish) побеждать. **2,** (beat in a game) побеждать; (по)бить; выигрывать у; обыгрывать. **3,** (thwart; frustrate) расстраивать; срывать.

defeatism *n.* пораженчество.

defeatist *n.* пораженец. —*adj.* пораженческий.

defecate *v.i.* испражняться. —**defecation,** *n.* испражнение.

defect *n.* порок; недостаток; дефект; брак; изъян. *Speech defect,* дефект речи. —*v.i.* перебегать; переметнуться.

defection *n.* перебежка.

defective *adj.* **1,** (imperfect; faulty) неисправный;

дефектный; бракованный. **2,** (subnormal in intelligence) дефективный.

defector *n.* невозвращенец; перебежчик.

defence *n.* = **defense.**

defend *v.t.* **1,** (protect) защищать; оборонять. **2,** (uphold) защищать; отстаивать. **3,** (represent in court) защищать.

defendant *n., law* подсудимый; обвиняемый; ответчик.

defender *n.* защитник.

defense *also,* **defence** *n.* **1,** (protection) защита: *self-defense,* самозащита. **2,** *mil.* оборона: *minister of defense,* министр обороны. *Break through the enemy's defenses,* прорвать оборону противника. **3,** *law; sports* защита: *witness for the defense,* свидетель защиты. —**defense attorney,** защитник.

defenseless *adj.* беззащитный.

defenseman *n.* защитник.

defensive *adj.* оборонительный. —*n.* оборона: *on the defensive,* в обороне.

defer *v.t.* (put off) откладывать; отсрочивать. —*v.i.* [*usu.* **defer to**] **1,** (show deference toward) относиться с почтением к. **2,** (yield to; rely on) полагаться на.

deference *n.* уважение; почтение; почтительность. *In deference to,* из уважения к.

deferential *adj.* почтительный.

deferment *n.* отсрочка.

defiance *n.* неповиновение. *In defiance of,* вопреки; наперекор.

defiant *adj.* вызывающий.

deficiency *n.* недостаток.

deficient *adj.* имеющий недостатки; недостаточный.

deficit *n.* дефицит.

defile *v.t.* осквернять; развращать. —*n.* (narrow passage) теснина. —**defilement,** *n.* осквернение; развращение.

define *v.t.* **1,** (give the definition of) определять. **2,** (specify) определять; устанавливать; характеризовать.

definite *adj.* определённый; точный. *Make it definite,* договориться определённо. *Nothing is definite yet,* пока ещё нет ничего определённого. —**definite article,** *gram.* определённый артикль *or* член.

definitely *adv.* **1,** (for sure) определённо: *I can't say definitely,* не могу сказать определённо. **2,** (absolutely) безусловно: *this is definitely the last time,* это безусловно последний раз. **3,** (without fail) обязательно.

definition *n.* **1,** (of a word) определение. **2,** (clarity; sharpness) резкость.

definitive *adj.* окончательный. —**definitively,** *adv.* окончательно.

deflate *v.t.* **1,** (release the air from) спускать. **2,** (puncture the pride of) сбивать спесь с.

deflation *n., econ.* дефляция.

deflect *v.t.* отводить; отклонять; отбивать. —*v.i.* отклоняться. —**deflection,** *n.* отклонение.

deforest *v.t.* обезлесить. —**deforestation,** *n.* обезлесение.

deform *v.t.* уродовать. —**deformation,** *n.* деформация. —**deformed,** *adj.* уродливый. —**deformity,** *n.* уродство.

defraud *v.t.* обманывать.

defray *v.t.* покрывать (расходы). —**defrayal,** *n.* покрытие (расходов).

defrock *v.t.* расстригáть; лишáть духóвного сáна.

defrost *v.t.* разморáживать. —*v.i.* разморáживаться. —**defroster,** *n.* обогревáтель.

deft *adj.* лóвкий; провóрный.

defunct *adj.* бóльше не существýющий.

defuse *v.t.* обезврéживать: *defuse a bomb,* обезврéдить бóмбу. *Defuse tension,* смягчáть напряжéние. *Defuse the situation,* разрядúть атмосфéру.

defy *v.t.* 1, (openly challenge) брóсить вы́зов (+ *dat.*): *defy world opinion,* брóсить вы́зов мировóй обществéнности. 2, (ignore): *defy an order,* пренебрегáть прикáзом; ослýшаться прикáза. *Defy death/danger,* презирáть смерть/опáсность. 3, (dare) *I defy you to do it,* ручáюсь, что вам э́того не сдéлать. 4, (be beyond) не поддавáться (+ *dat.*): *defy description,* не поддавáться описáнию. *His actions defy logic,* егó постýпки противорéчат лóгике (*or* лишены́ лóгики).

degeneracy *n.* вырождéние.

degenerate *v.i.* вырождáться. —*n.* дегенерáт. —*adj.* выродúвшийся. —**degeneration,** *n.* вырождéние; дегенерáция. —**degenerative,** *adj.* вырождéнческий.

degradation *n.* унижéние.

degrade *v.t.* унижáть. —**degrading,** *adj.* унизúтельный.

degree *n.* 1, (extent) стéпень: *to a certain degree,* до извéстной стéпени. *First-degree burns,* ожóги пéрвой стéпени. 2, (unit of measure for angles; unit of temperature) грáдус: *ten degrees below zero,* дéсять грáдусов нúже нуля́. 3, *gram.* стéпень: *comparative degree,* сравнúтельная стéпень. 4, (academic title) (учёная) стéпень: *master's degree,* стéпень магúстра. —**by degrees,** постепéнно.

dehydrate *v.t.* обезвóживать. —**dehydration,** *n.* обезвóживание.

deify *v.t.* обожествля́ть; обоготворя́ть. —**deification,** *n.* обожествлéние; обоготворéние.

deign *v.i.* удостáивать; снисходúть; соизволя́ть; соблаговолúть.

deism *n.* деúзм. —**deist,** *n.* деúст. —**deistic,** *adj.* деистúческий.

deity *n.* божествó.

dejected *adj.* уны́лый; подáвленный; удручённый; угнетённый. —**dejection,** *n.* уны́ние.

de jure де-ю́ре.

delay *v.t.* 1, (cause to be late) задéрживать; замедля́ть. 2, (postpone) откла́дывать; отсрóчивать. —*v.i.* задéрживаться; мéдлить. —*n.* 1, (holdup) задéржка; замедлéние; промедлéние; проволóчка. *Without delay,* немéдленно; без промедлéния; без проволóчек. 2, (short postponement) отсрóчка.

delayed-action *adj.* замéдленного дéйствия.

delectable *adj.* прелéстный.

delegate *n.* делегáт. —*v.t.* 1, (assign) поручáть. 2, (turn over to a subordinate) передавáть.

delegation *n.* 1, (group of persons) делегáция. 2, (turning over) передáча.

delete *v.t.* вычёркивать; исключáть.

deleterious *adj.* врéдный; пáгубный; тлетвóрный.

deletion *n.* 1, (act of deleting) вычёркивание. 2, (that which is deleted) вы́черкнутое слóво, выражéние, *etc.*

delftware *n.* фая́нс.

deliberate *adj.* 1, (intentional) нарочúтый; намé-ренный; умы́шленный. 2, (careful) осторóжный; осмотрúтельный. 3, (unhurried) неторопли́вый. —*v.i.* 1, (think carefully) соображáть. 2, (consult; confer) совещáться.

deliberately *adv.* нарóчно; умы́шленно.

deliberation *n.* 1, (careful thought) размышлéние. 2, (slowness and care) осторóжность; осмотрúтельность. 3, *pl.* (discussion and debate) совещáние.

deliberative *adj.* совещáтельный: *deliberative body,* совещáтельный óрган.

delicacy *n.* 1, (need of tactful treatment) деликáтность; щекотлúвость. 2, (frailty) хрýпкость. 3, (fineness of quality) утончённость. 4, (choice item of food) деликатéс; лáкомство.

delicate *adj.* 1, (gentle; tender; frail) нéжный; хрýпкий; деликáтный. 2, (tactful; subtle) деликáтный. 3, (needing tactful handling) щекотлúвый; деликáтный. 4, (fine; exquisite) тóнкий; утончённый.

delicatessen *n.* 1, (store) гастрономúческий магазúн; магазúн кулинáрии; гастронóм. 2, (food) кулинáрия.

delicious *adj.* óчень вкýсный.

delight *n.* 1, (great pleasure) (большóе) удовóльствие; наслаждéние; отрáда. 2, (something that gives great pleasure) прéлесть. —*v.t.* восхищáть. —*v.i.* [*usu.* **delight in**] наслаждáться (+ *instr.*).

delighted *adj.* óчень рад.

delightful *adj.* прелéстный; восхитúтельный.

delimit *v.t.* разгранúчивать; размежёвывать; отмежёвывать. —**delimitation,** *n.* разграничéние.

delineate *v.t.* 1, (outline) очéрчивать. 2, (describe in detail) обрисóвывать.

delinquency *n.* правонарушéние. *Juvenile delinquency,* дéтская престýпность.

delinquent *adj.* 1, (having done wrong) винóвный. 2, (overdue) неоплáченный. —*n.* (ю́ный) правонарушúтель.

delirious *adj.* бредовóй. *Be delirious,* быть в бредý; брéдить.

delirium *n.* бред.

deliver *v.t.* 1, (take to a place) доставля́ть. 2, (distribute, as mail) разносúть. 3, (save; set free) избавля́ть. 4, (surrender; hand over) сдавáть. 5, (deal, as a blow) наносúть (удáр). 6, (give, as a speech, lecture, etc.) произносúть (речь); читáть (лéкцию). 7, (assist at the birth of) принимáть.

deliverance *n.* избавлéние. —**deliverer,** *n.* избавúтель.

delivery *n.* 1, (transporting; distributing) достáвка. 2, (birth) рóды. 3, (rescue) избавлéние. 4, (manner of speaking) дúкция. 5, *sports* подáча. —**delivery boy/man,** рассы́льный. —**delivery room,** *med.* родúльное отделéние. —**delivery system,** *mil.* срéдство достáвки.

dell *n.* ложбúна; лощúна.

delphinium *n.* живокóсть; шпóрник.

delta *n.* дéльта. —**deltoid,** *adj.* дельтовúдный.

delude *v.t.* вводúть в заблуждéние. *Delude oneself,* обмáнывать себя́.

deluge *n.* 1, (downpour) лúвень. 2, (flood) потóп. 3, (overwhelming influx) потóк; град. —*v.t.* 1, (flood) затопля́ть. 2, (overwhelm) засыпáть.

delusion *n.* заблуждéние: *be under a delusion,* быть в заблуждéнии. —**delusions of grandeur,** мáния величúя.

de luxe роскóшный; -люкс: *de luxe hotel,* гостúница-люкс.

delve *v.i.* [*usu.* **delve into**] углублáться (в); вникáть (в).

demagnetize *v.t.* размагнúчивать.

demagogue *n.* демагóг. —**demagoguery; demagogy,** *n.* демагóгия. —**demagogic,** *adj.* демагогúческий.

demand *v.t.* трéбовать: *demand an apology,* трéбовать извинéния. —*n.* **1,** (insistent request) трéбование. **2,** *econ.* спрос: *supply and demand,* спрос и предложéние. *In great demand,* в большóм ходý. —**on demand,** по предъявлéнии.

demanding *adj.* трéбовательный; взыскáтельный.

demarcate *v.t.* разгранúчивать.

demarcation *n.* демаркáция. *Line of demarcation,* демаркациóнная лúния.

démarche *n.* демáрш.

demean *v.t.* унижáть; ронáть. *Demean oneself,* унижáться; ронáть своё достóинство.

demeanor *also,* **demeanour** *n.* поведéние; манéра держáть себя.

demented *adj.* сумасшéдший; помéшанный. —**dementia,** *n.* сумасшéствие; помешáтельство.

demerit *n.* **1,** (fault; defect) недостáток. **2,** (mark for bad conduct) взыскáние.

demigod *n.* полубóг.

demilitarization *n.* демилитаризáция.

demilitarize *v.t.* демилитаризовáть. *Demilitarized zone,* демилитаризóванная зóна.

demise *n.* кончúна.

demitasse *n.* мáленькая чáшка.

demobilize *v.t.* демобилизовáть. —**demobilization,** *n.* демобилизáция.

democracy *n.* демокрáтия.

democrat *n.* демокрáт. —**democratic,** *adj.* демократúческий.

democratize *v.t.* демократизúровать. —**democratization,** *n.* демократизáция.

demography *n.* демогрáфия. —**demographer,** *n.* демóграф. —**demographic,** *adj.* демографúческий.

demolish *v.t.* **1,** (tear down) сносúть. **2,** (destroy) разрушáть. **3,** *fig.* (refute, as a theory) разбивáть.

demolition *n.* разрушéние. —*adj.* подрывнóй: *demolition work,* подрывнýе рабóты. —**demolition bomb,** фугáсная бóмба.

demon *n.* дéмон. —**demoniac; demonic,** *adj.* демонúческий.

demonstrable *adj.* доказýемый.

demonstrate *v.t.* **1,** (show) демонстрúровать. **2,** (prove) доказáть. **3,** (reveal, as a quality) проявлáть: *demonstrate courage,* проявлáть мýжество. —*v.i.* демонстрúровать: *demonstrate against something,* демонстрúровать прóтив чегó-нибудь.

demonstration *n.* **1,** (show; display) демонстрáция: *demonstration of merchandise,* демонстрáция товáров. **2,** (manifestation) проявлéние: *demonstration of affection,* проявлéние нéжности. **3,** (parade; march) демонстрáция; манифестáция.

demonstrative *adj.* **1,** (given to showing one's feelings) экспансúвный. **2,** (showing clearly; convincing) наглáдный; доказáтельный. **3,** *gram.* указáтельный: *demonstrative pronoun,* указáтельное местоимéние.

demonstrator *n.* **1,** (one who demonstrates some-

thing) демонстрáтор. **2,** (one who participates in a demonstration) демонстрáнт.

demoralize *v.t.* деморализовáть. —**demoralization,** *n.* деморализáция.

demote *v.t.* понижáть (в чúне, по слýжбе, *etc.*). —**demotion,** *n.* понижéние.

demur *v.i.* возражáть.

demure *adj.* **1,** (sedate) степéнный. **2,** (retiring; shy) застéнчивый.

demurral *n.* возражéние.

den *n.* **1,** (lair) лóговище; лóгово; берлóга. *Lion's den,* лóгово льва. **2,** (hideout for illegal activity) притóн: *thieves'/gambling den,* воровскóй/игóрный притóн. *Den of iniquity,* притóн разврáта. **3,** (study) кабинéт.

denature *v.t.* денатурúровать. —**denatured alcohol,** денатурúрованный спирт; денатурáт.

dendrite *n.* дендрúт.

denial *n.* **1,** (act of denying) отрицáние. **2,** (statement of denial) опровержéние. **3,** (refusal to grant something) откáз; отклонéние: *denial of a request,* откáз в прóсьбе; отклонéние прóсьбы. **4,** (repudiation) отречéние.

denigrate *v.t.* порóчить; чернúть; поносúть. —**denigration,** *n.* поношéние.

denizen *n.* жúтель; обитáтель.

denomination *n.* **1,** (name) наименовáние. **2,** (religious group) вероисповéдание. **3,** (value of a coin or bill) достóинство: *coins of small denomination,* монéты мáлого достóинства.

denominator *n.* знаменáтель. *Least common denominator,* наимéньший óбщий знаменáтель.

denotation *n.* **1,** (act of denoting) обозначéние. **2,** (explicit meaning) значéние.

denote *v.t.* **1,** (mean) знáчить; означáть; обозначáть. **2,** (indicate) обозначáть: *on a map blue denotes water,* сúний цвет на кáрте обозначáет мóре.

dénouement *n.* развáзка.

denounce *v.t.* **1,** (condemn) осуждáть. **2,** (inform against) доносúть на.

dense *adj.* **1,** (thick) густóй; плóтный: *dense forest,* густóй лес; *dense fog,* густóй *or* плóтный тумáн. **2,** (thickheaded) тупóй; тупоýмный.

densely *adv.* гýсто; плóтно. *Densely populated,* густонаселённый; плóтно населённый.

density *n.* **1,** (denseness) густотá; плóтность. *Population density,* плóтность населéния. **2,** *physics* плóтность. **3,** (stupidity) тупоýмие.

dent *n.* вмáтина; вýбоина. —*v.t.* вдáвливать; вминáть.

dental *adj.* зубоврачéбный; зубнóй. *Dental school/practice,* зубоврачéбная шкóла/прáктика. *Dental technician,* зубнóй тéхник.

dentifrice *n.* зубнóй порошóк; зубнáя пáста.

dentine *also,* **dentin** *n.* дентúн.

dentist *n.* зубнóй врач; стоматóлог. —**dentistry,** *n.* стоматолóгия.

denture *n.* зубнóй протéз.

denude *v.t.* обнажáть; оголáть.

denunciation *n.* **1,** (condemnation) осуждéние. **2,** (informing against) донóс.

denunciatory *adj.* осуждáющий.

deny *v.t.* **1,** (refuse to acknowledge) отрицáть: *deny one's guilt,* отрицáть свою винý. *He denied that...,* он отрицáл, что... *Deny responsibility for,* не брать на себя ответственности за. *There is no denying that...*, нельзя не признать, что...; слов нет,... **2**, (declare to be untrue) опровергать: *deny a charge*, опровергнуть обвинение. **3**, (refuse to grant) отказывать в: *deny someone's request*, отказывать кому-нибудь в просьбе. *He was denied permission*, ему не дали разрешения. **4**, (deprive) лишать: *denied the right to vote*, лишены права голоса. —**deny oneself (something)**, отказывать себе в (+ *prepl.*).

deodorant *n.* дезодоратор.

depart *v.i.* **1**, (leave) уходить; уезжать; отправляться; отбывать. **2**, *fol. by* from (deviate from) отклоняться (от); отходить (от); отступать (от). —*v.t.* покидать. *Depart this world*, покинуть свет.

departed *adj.* умерший. —*n.* покойник.

department *n.* **1**, (section) отдел; отделение. **2**, (government bureau) ведомство; департамент. **3**, (subdivision of a college) факультет; кафедра.

departmental *adj.* ведомственный.

department store универсальный магазин; универмаг.

departure *n.* **1**, (leaving) отъезд; уход; отход; отправление; отбытие. **2**, (deviation) отклонение; отступление; отход. —**point of departure**, точка отправления.

depend *v.i.* [*usu.* **depend on**] **1**, (be contingent on) зависеть (от). *It (all) depends*, смотря как. **2**, (rely on; count on) полагаться (на); рассчитывать (на). —**depending on**, в зависимости от; смотря по.

dependable *adj.* надёжный. —**dependability**, *n.* надёжность.

dependant *n.* = **dependent**.

dependence *n.* зависимость.

dependency *n.* **1**, = **dependence**. **2**, (dependent territory) зависимая страна.

dependent *adj.* зависимый: *dependent countries*, зависимые страны. *Be dependent on someone for support*, быть на иждивении кого-нибудь. —*n.* [*also*, **dependant**] иждивенец. *How many dependents have you?*, сколько у вас на иждивении? —**dependent clause**, придаточное предложение.

depersonalize *v.t.* обезличивать.

depict *v.t.* изображать.

deplete *v.t.* истощать. —**depletion**, *n.* истощение.

deplore *v.t.* оплакивать; сожалеть о. —**deplorable**, *adj.* прискорбный; плачевный.

deploy *v.t.* развёртывать. —*v.i.* развёртываться. —**deployment**, *n.* развёртывание.

depopulate *v.t.* обезлюдить. *Become depopulated*, обезлюдеть.

deport *v.t.* высылать; ссылать. —**deport oneself**, вести себя; держать себя.

deportation *n.* высылка; ссылка.

deportment *n.* поведение; манеры.

depose *v.t.* свергать; низлагать.

deposit *n.* **1**, (money placed in a bank) вклад. **2**, (anything given as security) залог; задаток. **3**, (accumulation of minerals in the ground) залежь; месторождение. **4**, (natural accumulation) отложение: *calcium/lime deposits*, кальциевые/известковые отложения. —*v.t.* класть; опускать. *Deposit money in a bank*, класть деньги в банк. *Deposit a coin in a machine*, опускать монету в автомат.

deposition *n.* **1**, (act of deposing) низложение. **2**, (written statement used as evidence) показание.

depositor *n.* вкладчик.

depository *n.* хранилище.

depot *n.* **1**, (warehouse) склад. **2**, (train or bus station) вокзал; станция.

deprave *v.t.* развращать. —**depraved**, *adj.* развращённый; порочный. —**depravity**, *n.* развращённость; порочность.

deprecate *v.t.* **1**, (express disapproval of) осуждать. **2**, (belittle) умалять.

depreciate *v.i.* обесцениваться. —*v.t.* **1**, (lessen the value of) обесценивать. **2**, (belittle) умалять.

depreciation *n.* **1**, (decline in value) обесценение. **2**, (allowance made for this in accounting) амортизация.

depredation *n.* грабёж; ограбление.

depress *v.t.* **1**, (dispirit) подавлять; угнетать; удручать. **2**, (press down on) нажимать на. —**depressed**, *adj.* подавленный; удручённый; угнетённый. —**depressing**, *adj.* гнетущий; тягостный; подавляющий.

depression *n.* **1**, (sunken place; hollow) впадина; углубление. **2**, (melancholy) подавленность; упадок духа; депрессия. **3**, (economic crisis) депрессия; кризис.

deprive *v.t.* лишать: *deprive someone of his rights*, лишать кого-нибудь прав. —**deprivation**, *n.* лишение.

depth *n.* **1**, (distance downward) глубина. **2**, *pl.* (deepest part) глубь: *the ocean depths*, морская глубь. **3**, (intellectual capacity or profundity) глубина; глубокомыслие. —**in depth**, глубоко.

depth charge глубинная бомба.

deputation *n.* депутация.

deputize *v.t.* назначать заместителем.

deputy *n.* **1**, (one appointed to act for another) заместитель. **2**, (member of a legislature in certain countries) депутат. —*adj. Deputy director*, заместитель директора.

derail *v.t.* пускать (поезд) под откос. —**derailment**, *n.* сход с рельсов.

derange *v.t.* сводить с ума. —**deranged**, *adj.* сумасшедший; помешанный. *Become deranged*, сойти с ума. —**derangement**, *n.* сумасшествие; умопомешательство.

derby *n.* **1**, (hat) котелок. **2**, *cap.* (race) дерби.

derelict *n.* бродяга; босяк. —*adj. Be derelict in one's duty*, изменить своему долгу.

dereliction *n.* нарушение: *dereliction of duty*, нарушение долга.

deride *v.t.* насмехаться над; осмеивать; высмеивать.

derision *n.* насмешка; осмеяние; издевательство.

derisive *adj.* насмешливый; издевательский.

derivation *n.* **1**, (obtaining) получение. *Derivation of a formula*, вывод формулы. **2**, (origin, as of a word) происхождение.

derivative *adj.* производный. —*n.* **1**, *chem.* производное; дериват. **2**, *ling.* производное слово. **3**, *math.* производная.

derive *v.t.* **1**, (receive, as pleasure, benefit, etc.) получать; извлекать. **2**, (deduce, as a formula) выводить. —*v.i.* (originate) происходить.

dermatology *n.* дерматология. —**dermatologist**, *n.* дерматолог.

derogate *v.i.* [*usu.* **derogate from**] умалять. —**derogation**, *n.* умаление.

derogatory adj. оскорбительный; обидный: derogatory remarks, оскорбительные/обидные замечания.

derrick n. **1,** (crane) дéррик; дéррик-кран. **2,** (oil derrick) буровáя вышка.

dervish n. дéрвиш.

desalinize also, **desalinate** v.t. опреснять. —**desalinization; desalination,** n. опреснéние.

descend v.i. **1,** (go down) сходить; спускáться. **2,** fol. by **on** (visit without warning) нагрянуть к. **3,** fol. by **to** (stoop to) унижáться (до). **4,** fol. by **from** [also, **be descended from**] (spring from a stock or source) происходить (из). **5,** (pass by inheritance) переходить. —v.t. сходить с; спускáться с.

descendant n. потóмок.

descent n. **1,** (downward motion) спуск: descent from a mountain, спуск с горы. Descent of an airplane, снижéние самолёта. **2,** (downward slope) спуск; склон; скат. **3,** (ancestry) происхождéние: of Russian descent, рýсский по происхождéнию.

describe v.t. **1,** (give a description of) описывать. **2,** (depict in a certain way) характеризовáть.

description n. описáние. Of every description, всякого рóда.

descriptive adj. описáтельный. —**descriptive geometry,** начертáтельная геомéтрия.

descry v.t. рассмотрéть; разглядéть.

desecrate v.t. осквернять. —**desecration,** n. осквернéние.

desegregate v.t. десегрегировать. —**desegregation,** n. десегрегáция.

desert[1] (**dez**-ert) n. пустыня. —adj. пустынный. Desert island, необитáемый óстров.

desert[2] (di-**zurt**) v.t. бросáть; покидáть; оставлять. —v.i., mil. дезертировать. —n., often pl. заслýга: get one's just deserts, получить по заслýгам.

deserted adj. безлюдный; пустынный; опустéлый. The streets were deserted, на ýлицах было пýсто.

deserter n. дезертир.

desertion n. **1,** (abandonment) оставлéние. **2,** mil. дезертирство.

deserve v.t. заслýживать. He got what he deserved, он получил по заслýгам. —**deserved,** adj. заслýженный; достóйный. —**deservedly,** adv. по заслýгам; по прáву. —**deserving,** adj. достóйный.

design v.t. **1,** (plan the construction of, as a building) проектировать. A building designed by..., здáние, пострóенное по проéкту (+ gen.). **2,** (plan the external appearance of, as a book, stage set, etc.) оформлять. **3,** (style, as a dress) моделировать. **4,** (intend; mean) предназначáть: the dictionary is designed for children, словáрь предназнáчен для детéй. —n. **1,** (pattern) узóр. **2,** (of a building, aircraft, etc.) констрýкция; (of a book) оформлéние. **3,** (sketch) проéкт; чертёж. **4,** (purpose; intention) зáмысел; ýмысел. By design, с ýмыслом. Have designs on, имéть виды на.

designate v.t. **1,** (indicate; mark) обозначáть. **2,** (appoint) назначáть. —adj. назнáченный.

designation n. **1,** (name; title) назвáние. **2,** (appointment) назначéние. **3,** (mark; sign) обозначéние.

designedly adv. умышленно; с ýмыслом.

designer n. чертёжник; проектирóвщик; констрýктор; оформитель. Aircraft designer, авиаконстрýктор. Dress designer, модельéр. Stage designer, декорáтор; оформитель.

designing adj. интригýющий.

desirable adj. желáтельный. —**desirability,** n. желáтельность.

desire v.t. желáть. Leave much to be desired, оставлять желáть мнóго лýчшего. —n. желáние: a great desire, большóе желáние.

desired adj. желáнный; желáемый. Produce the desired effect, дать желáемый результáт; имéть дóлжный эффéкт.

desirous adj. желáющий.

desist v.i. перестáвать.

desk n. письменный стол. School desk, пáрта. Information desk, спрáвочный стол. —adj. настóльный: desk lamp, настóльная лáмпа. Desk drawer, ящик столá.

desman n. выхухоль.

desolate adj. **1,** (barren) забрóшенный. **2,** (deserted) пустынный; безлюдный. —v.t. **1,** (depopulate) обезлюдить. **2,** (devastate) опустошáть.

desolation n. **1,** (laying waste) опустошéние. **2,** (emptiness; waste) запустéние.

despair n. отчáяние. —v.i. отчáиваться.

desperado n. головорéз.

desperate adj. отчáянный: desperate attempt, отчáянная попытка. I am desperate, я в отчáянном положéнии.

desperately adv. **1,** (with desperation) отчáянно: fight desperately, борóться отчáянно. Try desperately, всéми силами старáться. **2,** (extremely; frightfully) крáйне; ужáсно. Desperately ill, тяжелó бóлен. **3,** (urgently) до зарéзу: he needs money desperately, емý нужны дéньги до зарéзу.

desperation n. отчáяние.

despicable adj. презрéнный; низкий; пóдлый. —**despicably,** adv. низко; пóдло.

despise v.t. презирáть.

despite prep. несмотря на. Despite all, несмотря ни на что.

despoil v.t. грáбить; разорять.

despondent adj. унылый; подáвленный. —**despondency,** n. уныние; подáвленность.

despot n. дéспот. —**despotic,** adj. деспотический. —**despotism,** n. деспотизм.

dessert n. десéрт. For dessert, на слáдкое; на десéрт. —adj. десéртный: dessert spoon, десéртная лóжка.

destination n. мéсто назначéния.

destine v.t. предназначáть. We were not destined to..., нам не суждено́ (or не судьбá) было (+ inf.).

destiny n. судьбá.

destitute adj. обездóленный; обнищáлый. Be left destitute, остáться ни с чем or без средств. —**destitution,** n. нищетá; обнищáние.

destroy v.t. разрушáть; уничтожáть.

destroyer n. **1,** (one who or that which destroys) разрушитель. **2,** (ship) эскáдренный миноносец; эсминец.

destruction n. **1,** (act of destroying) разрушéние. **2,** (heavy damage) разрушéния. —**destructive,** adj. разрушительный.

desultory adj. несвязный; бессвязный; отрывочный.

detach v.t. отделять. —**detachable,** adj. съёмный; отрезнóй.

detached *adj.* **1,** (separate) отде́льный. **2,** (impartial) беспристра́стный.

detachment *n.* **1,** (removal) отделе́ние. **2,** (impartiality) беспристра́стие. **3,** *mil.* отря́д.

detail *n.* **1,** (minute element) подро́бность; дета́ль. *In detail,* подро́бно. *Go into detail,* вдава́ться в подро́бности. **2,** *mil.* (small detachment) наря́д. —*v.t.* **1,** (describe minutely) подро́бно расска́зывать. **2,** *mil.* (assign) наряжа́ть; отряжа́ть.

detailed *adj.* подро́бный; дета́льный.

detain *v.t.* заде́рживать: *don't let me detain you!,* не хочу́ вас заде́рживать. *He was detained by the police,* его́ задержа́ла поли́ция.

detect *v.t.* обнару́живать. —**detection,** *n.* обнаруже́ние.

detective *n.* сы́щик; детекти́в. —**detective story,** детекти́в.

detector *n.* детéктор.

détente *n.* разря́дка.

detention *n.* задержа́ние; содержа́ние под аре́стом. *Be in detention,* быть под стра́жей.

deter *v.t.* уде́рживать.

detergent *n.* мо́ющее сре́дство; стира́льный порошо́к.

deteriorate *v.i.* ухудша́ться; по́ртиться. —**deterioration,** *n.* ухудше́ние.

determinant *n.* определи́тель.

determinate *adj.* определённый; устано́вленный.

determination *n.* **1,** (act of determining) определе́ние. **2,** (firm resolve) реши́мость; реши́тельность.

determine *v.t.* определя́ть: *determine the distance between...,* определя́ть расстоя́ние ме́жду... *Determine the outcome of,* определя́ть *or* реша́ть исхо́д (+ *gen.*).

determined *adj.* реши́тельный; по́лный реши́мости.

determinism *n.* детермини́зм.

deterrent *adj.* сде́рживающий; уде́рживающий. —*n.* сде́рживающий фа́ктор.

detest *v.t.* ненави́деть. —**detestable,** *adj.* отврати́тельный; ме́рзкий. —**detestation,** *n.* не́нависть.

dethrone *v.t.* сверга́ть с престо́ла; низлага́ть. —**dethronement,** *n.* сверже́ние с престо́ла; низложе́ние.

detonate *v.t.* взрыва́ть. —*v.i.* взрыва́ться; детони́ровать. —**detonation,** *n.* детона́ция. —**detonator,** *n.* детона́тор.

detour *n.* объе́зд; крюк. —*v.i.* сде́лать крюк.

detract *v.i.* [*usu.* detract from] умаля́ть. —**detraction,** *n.* умале́ние. —**detractor,** *n.* хули́тель.

detriment *n.* вред; уще́рб: *to the detriment of,* во вред *or* в уще́рб (+ *dat.*). —**detrimental,** *adj.* вре́дный.

deuce *n.* **1,** (two) дво́йка. **2,** *tennis* ра́вный счёт. **3,** *colloq.* (devil; dickens) чёрт: *what the deuce is he doing there!,* како́го чёрта он там де́лает!

deuterium *n.* дейте́рий.

Deuteronomy *n.* Второзако́ние.

devalue *v.t.* девальви́ровать. —**devaluation,** *n.* девальва́ция.

devastate *v.t.* **1,** (lay waste) опустоша́ть. **2,** *fig.* (shatter; demoralize) потряса́ть.

devastating *adj.* **1,** (extremely destructive) опустоши́тельный. *Devastating blow,* сокруши́тельный уда́р. **2,** *fig.* (withering; scathing) уничтожа́ющий.

devastation *n.* опустоше́ние.

develop *v.t.* **1,** (expand; improve) развива́ть: *develop one's muscles,* развива́ть мускулату́ру. *Develop new sources of energy,* развива́ть но́вые исто́чники эне́ргии. **2,** (work out; perfect) разраба́тывать: *develop a method,* разраба́тывать ме́тод; *develop a new aircraft,* разраба́тывать но́вый самолёт. **3,** (acquire gradually) развива́ть; приобрета́ть. *Develop an interest in,* развива́ть интере́с к. *Develop a taste for,* приобрета́ть вкус к. *Develop pneumonia,* получи́ть воспале́ние лёгких. *He has developed the habit of...,* у него́ вы́работалась привы́чка (+ *inf.*). **4,** (build up) застра́ивать. **5,** *photog.* проявля́ть. —*v.i.* **1,** (increase in maturity, scope, etc.) развива́ться. *Developing countries,* развива́ющиеся стра́ны. **2,** (gradually come into being) создава́ться; скла́дываться. **3,** *fol. by* into (gradually become) выраста́ть в; вылива́ться в. **4,** (turn out) вы́ясниться: *it developed that...,* вы́яснилось, что...

developer *n.* **1,** (builder) застро́йщик. **2,** *photog.* проявитель.

development *n.* **1,** (act or process of developing) разви́тие. **2,** (working out; designing) разрабо́тка. **3,** (building up) застро́йка. **4,** (event; occurrence) собы́тие.

deviant *adj.* ненорма́льный; противоесте́ственный.

deviate *v.i.* [*usu.* deviate from] отклоня́ться (от); уклоня́ться (от); отступа́ть (от). —**deviation,** *n.* отклоне́ние; уклоне́ние; отступле́ние.

device *n.* **1,** (apparatus) прибо́р; устро́йство; приспособле́ние. **2,** (something used to achieve an effect) приём. **3,** (scheme) ухищре́ние. —**leave to one's own devices,** предоставля́ть самому́ себе́.

devil *n.* чёрт; дья́вол. *What the devil are you doing?,* како́го чёрта ты де́лаешь? —*adj.* [*usu.* devil's] чёртов. —**between the devil and the deep blue sea,** ме́жду двух огне́й; ме́жду мо́лотом и накова́льней. —**give someone the devil,** дать нагоня́й (+ *dat.*). —**lucky devil,** счастли́вец. —**poor devil,** бедня́га. —**talk of the devil!,** лёгок на помине!

devilish *adj.* чёртовский; дья́вольский. —**devilishly,** *adv.* чёртовски.

devil-may-care *adj.* бесшаба́шный; залихва́тский.

devious *adj.* **1,** (circuitous) око́льный. **2,** (shifty) увёртливый.

devise *v.t.* приду́мывать.

devoid *adj.* [*usu.* devoid of] лишённый (+ *gen.*).

devolve *v.i.* [*usu.* devolve upon] переходи́ть (к).

devote *v.t.* **1,** (dedicate) посвяща́ть. *Devote oneself to,* посвяща́ть себя́ (+ *dat.*); отдава́ться (+ *dat.*). **2,** (give, as time, attention, etc.) уделя́ть. —**devoted,** *adj.* пре́данный. —**devotee,** *n.* покло́нник.

devotion *n.* пре́данность.

devour *v.t.* **1,** (consume) пожира́ть. **2,** *fig.* (read or listen to avidly) поглоща́ть. *Devour every word (when listening),* лови́ть ка́ждое сло́во.

devout *adj.* **1,** (pious) на́божный; благочести́вый. **2,** (earnest) и́скренний: *devout wish,* и́скреннее жела́ние.

dew *n.* роса́. —**dewdrop,** *n.* роси́нка; ка́пля росы́.

dewlap *n.* подгру́док.

dewy *adj.* роси́стый.

dexterity *n.* ло́вкость; прово́рство. —**dexterous,** *adj.* ло́вкий; прово́рный.

dextrose n. декстроза.

diabetes n. диабет; сахарная болезнь. —**diabetic,** adj. диабетический. —n. диабетик.

diabolic adj. дьявольский. Also, **diabolical.**

diacritical adj. диакритический. —**diacritical mark,** диакритический знак.

diadem n. диадема.

diagnose v.t. распознавать; определять (болезнь).

diagnosis n. диагноз.

diagnostic adj. диагностический. —**diagnostician,** n. диагност.

diagonal adj. диагональный. —n. диагональ. —**diagonally,** adv. по диагонали; наискось.

diagram n. схема; диаграмма. —**diagrammatic,** adj. схематический.

dial n. **1,** (of a radio, gauge, etc.) шкала; циферблат. **2,** (tuning knob) ручка (настройки). **3,** (telephone device) диск. —v.t. **1,** (a telephone number) набирать (номер). **2,** radio (tune in) настраивать.

dialect n. диалект; наречие; говор. —**dialectal,** adj. диалектный.

dialectical adj. диалектический. —**dialectics,** n. диалектика.

dialogue n. диалог.

diameter n. диаметр.

diametrical adj. диаметральный. —**diametrically,** adv. диаметрально: diametrically opposite, диаметрально противоположный.

diamond n. **1,** (stone) алмаз. **2,** (gem) бриллиант. **3,** (figure) ромб. **4,** pl., cards бубны. —adj. бриллиантовый; алмазный.

diaper n. пелёнка. —v.t. пеленать.

diaphragm n. **1,** anat. грудобрюшная преграда; диафрагма. **2,** physics; mech. мембрана. **3,** optics; photog. диафрагма.

diarchy n. двоевластие.

diarrhea also, **diarrhoea** n. понос. He has diarrhea, его слабит.

diary n. дневник.

diathermy n. диатермия.

diatonic adj. диатонический.

diatribe n. бранная речь.

dice n.pl. игральные кости. Play dice, играть в кости.

dichotomy n. деление.

dickens n., slang чёрт: what the dickens do you want?, какого чёрта вам нужно? —**give someone the dickens,** дать кому-нибудь нагоняй.

dicker v.i. торговаться.

dickey also, **dicky** n. **1,** (shirt front) манишка. **2,** (bib) нагрудник.

dicotyledon n. двудольное растение. —**dicotyledonous,** adj. двудольный.

dictaphone n. диктофон.

dictate v.t. & i. диктовать. —n. веление: the dictates of one's conscience, веление совести.

dictation n. **1,** (act of dictating, as a letter) диктовка: take dictation, писать под диктовку. **2,** (classroom exercise) диктант.

dictator n. диктатор. —**dictatorial,** adj. диктаторский. —**dictatorship,** n. диктатура.

diction n. дикция.

dictionary n. словарь.

dictum n. **1,** (authoritative pronouncement) постановление. **2,** (saying) изречение.

didactic adj. наставительный; назидательный; дидактический. —**didactics,** n. дидактика.

die v.i. умирать; (of animals) дохнуть; (of plants) гибнуть. —n. **1,** (engraving stamp) штамп. **2,** sing. of **dice.** The die is cast, жребий брошен. —**be dying to,** жаждать; рваться: I am dying to see you, я жажду/ рвусь увидеть вас. I am dying to tell her, меня так и подмывает сказать ей. —**die away,** замолкать; умолкать. —**die down,** замирать; затихать; утихать; стихать; глохнуть. —**die laughing,** умирать со смеху. —**die out, 1,** (of fire) угасать. **2,** (go out of use) отмирать. **3,** (become extinct) вымирать.

dieresis n. две точки.

diesel adj. дизельный. Diesel engine, дизель. Diesel locomotive, тепловоз.

diet n. диета. Go on a diet, сесть на диету. Put on a diet, посадить на диету. —v.i. быть на диете. —**dietary,** adj. диетический.

dietetic adj. диететический. —**dietetics,** n. диететика.

dietitian also, **dietician** n. диетврач.

differ v.i. **1,** (be dissimilar) отличаться; различаться. Differ from the rest, отличаться от остальных. **2,** (disagree) расходиться. We differ on this issue, наши мнения по этому вопросу расходятся.

difference n. **1,** (dissimilarity; variation) разница: the enormous difference between them, огромная разница между ними. Age difference, разница лет or возрастов. Difference in time, разница во времени. A difference of ten dollars, разница в десяти долларах. **2,** (disagreement) разногласие; расхождение. Difference of opinion, разногласие/различие/расхождение во мнениях. **3,** math. разность. —**make a difference:** it makes a great difference, большая разница. It makes no difference (to me), (мне) всё равно. —**what's the difference?,** какая разница?

different adj. **1,** (dissimilar; various) разный; различный. Be different from, отличаться от. In different ways, по-разному. **2,** (another) другой. That's different, это другое дело.

differential n. **1,** (difference) различие; разница: price differential, различие/разница в цене. **2,** math.; mech. дифференциал. —adj. дифференциальный: differential calculus/equation, дифференциальное исчисление/уравнение.

differentiate v.t. & i. различать; разграничивать.

differentiation n. разграничение; дифференциация.

differently adv. **1,** (in a different way) иначе; по-другому. **2,** (in various ways) по-разному.

difficult adj. **1,** (hard to do, solve, or handle) трудный: difficult work, трудная работа; a difficult problem, трудная задача; a difficult child, трудный ребёнок. **2,** (hard to deal or cope with; complex) сложный: difficult matter, сложное дело. **3,** (unpleasant; trying; awkward) трудный; затруднительный; тяжёлый. Difficult times, тяжёлые времена. Under difficult conditions, в трудных условиях. In a difficult situation, в затруднительном положении.

difficulty n. **1,** (quality of being difficult) трудность. With difficulty, с трудом. Without difficulty, без труда. **2,** (difficult situation) затруднение: be in difficulty, быть в затруднении. **3,** (complication; obstacle) затруднение; трудность.

diffidence *n.* застéнчивость; стесни́тельность. —**diffident,** *adj.* застéнчивый; стесни́тельный.

diffuse *v.t.* **1,** (scatter) рассéивать. **2,** (disseminate, as knowledge) распространя́ть. —*adj.* **1,** (scattered) рассéянный. **2,** (verbose) многослóвный.

diffusion *n.* **1,** (dissemination) рассéивание; распространéние. **2,** *physics* диффу́зия. *Diffusion of light,* рассéяние свéта.

dig *v.t.* копáть; рыть: *dig a hole,* копáть/рыть я́му. —*v.i.* копáться; ры́ться: *dig in the sand,* копáться/ры́ться в пескé. —*n., colloq.* **1,** (poke) тычóк. **2,** (gibe) шпи́лька. —**dig in,** окáпываться. —**dig up, 1,** (tear up; churn up) искáпывать; изрывáть. **2,** (unearth) выкáпывать; вырывáть; откáпывать; отрывáть. **3,** *colloq.* (find; discover) выкáпывать; откáпывать; раскáпывать.

digest *v.t.* усвáивать; перевáривать. —*n.* **1,** (synopsis) резюмé. **2,** (collection) сбóрник.

digestible *adj.* удобовари́мый. —**digestibility,** *n.* удобовари́мость.

digestion *n.* пищеварéние. —**digestive,** *adj.* пищевари́тельный.

digger *n.* копáтель; землекóп.

digging *n.* копáние; рытьё.

digit *n.* **1,** (finger; toe) пáлец. **2,** (number) знак: *two-digit number,* двузнáчное числó.

digital computer цифровáя вычисли́тельная маши́на.

digitalis *n.* наперстя́нка.

dignified *adj.* величáвый; степéнный.

dignify *v.t.* придавáть достóинство (+ *dat.*).

dignitary *n.* санóвник; высокопостáвленное лицó.

dignity *n.* достóинство. *Beneath one's dignity,* ни́же чьегó-нибудь достóинства.

digress *v.i.* отклоня́ться; уклоня́ться; отступáть; отходи́ть; отвлекáться. —**digression,** *n.* отклонéние; уклонéние; отступлéние; э́кскурс.

dihedral *adj.* двугрáнный.

dike *n.* дáмба.

dilapidated *adj.* вéтхий; обветшáлый; полуразру́шенный.

dilate *v.t.* расширя́ть. —**dilation,** *n.* расширéние.

dilatory *adj.* мéдленный; медли́тельный.

dilemma *n.* дилéмма. *Be in a dilemma,* стоя́ть пéред дилéммой.

dilettante *n.* дилетáнт; люби́тель. —**dilettantism,** *n.* дилетанти́зм; дилетáнтство.

diligence *n.* прилежáние; стáрательность.

diligent *adj.* прилéжный; старáтельный. —**diligently,** *adv.* прилéжно; старáтельно.

dill *n.* укрóп.

dillydally *v.i.* мéшкáть; лóдырничать.

dilute *v.t.* разбавля́ть; разжижáть; разводи́ть. —**dilution,** *n.* разжижéние.

dim *adj.* **1,** (not bright) ту́склый. **2,** (not clear; hazy; vague) смýтный. —*v.t.* притуши́ть: *dim the headlights,* притуши́ть фáры. —*v.i.* тускнéть. —**take a dim view of,** относи́ться скепти́чески к.

dime *n.* монéта в дéсять цéнтов.

dimension *n.* **1,** (measurable extent) измерéние. *Three-dimensional,* трёхмéрный. **2,** *pl.* (extent) размéры.

diminish *v.t.* уменьшáть. —*v.i.* уменьшáться.

diminuendo *n.* диминуэ́ндо.

diminution *n.* уменьшéние.

diminutive *adj.* **1,** (small) мáленький; миниатю́рный. **2,** *gram.* уменьши́тельный. —*n.* уменьши́тельное существи́тельное.

dimly *adv.* **1,** (not brightly) ту́скло. **2,** (vaguely) смýтно.

dimness *n.* ту́склость.

dimple *n.* я́мочка.

dimwit *n., colloq.* тупоýмный человéк; тупи́ца; тугодýм. —**dimwitted,** *adj., colloq.* тупоýмный; тупоголóвый.

din *n.* грóхот; гвалт. —*v.t.* [*usu.* **din into**] вдáлбливать (чтó-нибудь + *dat.*).

dine *v.i.* обéдать.

diner *n.* **1,** (person dining) обéдающий. **2,** (dining car) вагóн-ресторáн. **3,** (small restaurant) закýсочная.

dinghy *n.* я́лик.

dingy *adj.* ту́склый; мрáчный.

dining car вагóн-ресторáн.

dining room столóвая.

dinner *n.* обéд. *Have dinner,* обéдать. —*adj.* обéденный: *dinner table,* обéденный стол. —**dinner jacket,** смóкинг. —**dinner party,** звáный обéд.

dinnertime *n.* обéденное врéмя.

dinosaur *n.* динозáвр.

dint *n., in* **by dint of,** посрéдством (+ *gen.*); путём (+ *gen.*).

diocese *n.* епáрхия.

diode *n.* диóд.

dioxide *n.* двуóкись.

dip *v.t.* (immerse) погружáть; окунáть; макáть; обмáкивать. —*v.i.* **1,** (immerse oneself) окунáться. **2,** (descend; drop) спускáться; опускáться. **3,** (decline; go down) пáдать; снижáться; пойти́ вниз. —*n.* **1,** (brief swim) *go for a dip,* поплáвать. **2,** (depression, as in a road) впáдина; углублéние. **3,** (drop; decline) падéние; снижéние.

diphtheria *n.* дифтери́я; дифтери́т. —**diphtherial,** *adj.* дифтери́йный.

diphthong *n.* дифтóнг; двуглáсный звук.

diploma *n.* диплóм.

diplomacy *n.* **1,** (dealings between nations) дипломáтия. **2,** (tact) дипломати́чность.

diplomat *n.* дипломáт.

diplomatic *adj.* **1,** (pert. to diplomacy) дипломати́ческий. **2,** (tactful) дипломати́ческий; дипломати́чный.

dipper *n.* **1,** (ladle) ковш; черпáк. **2,** *cap., astron.* Медвéдица. **3,** (bird) оля́пка.

dipstick *n.* щуп.

dire *adj.* **1,** (grave; extreme) крáйний: *dire need,* крáйняя нуждá. **2,** (disastrous) бéдственный: *be in dire straits,* быть в бéдственном положéнии. **3,** (ominous) зловéщий: *dire predictions,* зловéщие предскáзания.

direct *adj.* **1,** (by the shortest way) прямóй: *direct route,* прямóй путь. **2,** (with nothing in between) прямóй; непосрéдственный: *direct connection,* прямáя связь; *direct cause,* непосрéдственная причи́на. **3,** (straightforward) прямóй: *direct answer,* прямóй отвéт. —*adv.* прямо: *direct from the factory,* прямо с завóда. —*v.t.* **1,** (aim) направля́ть; обращáть. **2,** (show the way to) указáть дорóгу (+ *dat.*). **3,** (manage; run) руководи́ть. *Direct traffic,* регули́ровать движéние. **4,** (order) предпи́сывать. **5,** *music* дирижировать. **6**, *theat.* режиссировать. —**direct current,** постоянный ток. —**direct object,** *gram.* прямое дополнение.

direction *n.* **1**, (course) направление; сторона. *In the direction of,* по направлению к; в сторону (+ *gen.*). *In all directions,* во всех направлениях; врассыпную. *Sense of direction,* чувство ориентировки. **2**, (supervision) руководство. **3**, *usu. pl.* (instructions) указания. **4**, *theat.* режиссура.

directional *adj.* направленный: *directional antenna,* направленная антенна. —**directional signal,** указатель поворота.

direction finder (радио) пеленгатор.

directive *n.* директива; установка.

directly *adv.* **1**, (without deviating) прямо. **2**, (immediately) сразу; немедленно.

directness *n.* прямота; прямодушие.

director *n.* **1**, (manager) директор. **2**, *theat.* режиссёр; постановщик.

directorate *n.* **1**, (board of directors) директорат. **2**, (Soviet governmental department) управление.

directorial *adj.* директорский.

directory *n.* справочник; указатель; адресная книга. *Telephone directory,* телефонная книга; телефонный справочник.

dirge *n.* погребальное пение.

dirigible *n.* дирижабль.

dirt *n.* грязь. —*adj.* грунтовой: *dirt road,* грунтовая дорога.

dirt-cheap *adj.* дешевле пареной репы. —*adv.* по дешёвке.

dirty *adj.* **1**, (unclean) грязный. **2**, (obscene) сальный; скабрёзный. **3**, (mean; despicable) подлый. —*v.t.* пачкать; загрязнять. —**dirty look,** укоризненный взгляд. *Give someone a dirty look,* посмотреть на кого-нибудь укоризненно. —**dirty trick,** злая шутка; подлость; гадость. *Play a dirty trick on,* сыграть с (+ *instr.*) злую шутку; подложить свинью (+ *dat.*).

disability *n.* нетрудоспособность; инвалидность.

disable *v.t.* делать нетрудоспособным; выводить из строя.

disabled *adj.* **1**, (incapacitated) нетрудоспособный; неработоспособный; *mil.* небоеспособный. **2**, (of a vehicle) испортившийся.

disabuse *v.t.* [*usu.* **disabuse of**] разубеждать (в); разуверять (в).

disadvantage *n.* **1**, (unfavorable position) невыгода. *Be at a disadvantage,* быть в невыгодном положении. **2**, (drawback) недостаток: *advantages and disadvantages,* достоинства и недостатки. **3**, (detriment) вред: *work to the disadvantage of,* действовать во вред (+ *dat.*). —**disadvantageous,** *adj.* невыгодный.

disaffect *v.t.* отчуждать. —**disaffection,** *n.* отчуждение.

disagree *v.i.* **1**, (have different opinions) не соглашаться; расходиться во мнениях. *I disagree with you,* я с вами не согласен (согласна). **2**, (fail to coincide, as of versions of a story) расходиться; не совпадать; не сходиться. **3**, *fol. by* **with** (upset, as of food) плохо действовать (на).

disagreeable *adj.* неприятный.

disagreement *n.* **1**, (difference of opinion) разногласие; расхождение. **2**, (dispute; quarrel) ссора.

disallow *v.t.* отказывать в (+ *prepl.*); отклонять.

disappear *v.i.* **1**, (pass out of sight) исчезать. *Disappear from view,* скрыться из виду. **2**, (be missing; be lost) пропадать. —**disappearance,** *n.* исчезновение.

disappoint *v.t.* разочаровывать. —**disappointed,** *adj.* разочарованный. —**disappointing,** *adj.* разочаровывающий. —**disappointment,** *n.* разочарование.

disapproval *n.* **1**, (unfavorable attitude) неодобрение. *In disapproval,* неодобрительно. **2**, (rejection) отклонение.

disapprove *v.i.* [*usu.* **disapprove of**] не одобрять. —*v.t.* (reject) отвергать; отклонять. —**disapproving,** *adj.* неодобрительный.

disarm *v.t.* **1**, (seize a weapon from) обезоруживать; разоружать. **2**, (reduce the armed forces or weapons of) разоружать. **3**, (win over) обезоруживать. —*v.i.* разоружаться.

disarmament *n.* разоружение.

disarming *adj.* обезоруживающий.

disarrange *v.t.* расстраивать; (пере)путать; приводить в беспорядок.

disarray *n.* беспорядок; расстройство.

disassemble *v.t.* разбирать (на части).

disassociate *v.t.* = **dissociate.**

disaster *n.* бедствие; катастрофа. *On the brink of disaster,* на краю пропасти. —**disastrous,** *adj.* бедственный; катастрофический; гибельный.

disavow *v.t.* **1**, (deny; disown) отрицать. **2**, (repudiate; renounce) отрекаться от; отказываться от.

disavowal *n.* **1**, (denial) отрицание. **2**, (repudiation) отречение; отказ.

disband *v.t.* распускать. —*v.i.* расходиться; рассеиваться.

disbar *v.t.* лишать права адвокатской практики.

disbelief *n.* неверие. *In disbelief,* не веря своим глазам *or* ушам.

disbelieve *v.t.* не верить.

disburse *v.t.* выплачивать. —**disbursement,** *n.* выплата.

disc *n.* = **disk.**

discard *v.t.* **1**, (throw away) выбрасывать. **2**, *cards* сбрасывать; скидывать; сносить.

discern *v.t.* различать; рассмотреть; разглядеть; распознавать. —**discernible,** *adj.* различимый. —**discerning,** *adj.* проницательный. —**discernment,** *n.* проницательность.

discharge *v.t.* **1**, (unload) выгружать (груз); высаживать (пассажиров). **2**, (release) освобождать; (*from military service*) увольнять; (*from a hospital*) выписывать. **3**, (dismiss from a job) увольнять; рассчитывать. **4**, (perform, as duties) исполнять; выполнять. **5**, (pay, as a debt) выплачивать. **6**, (emit) выпускать; испускать; выделять. **7**, (fire; shoot) выпускать; пускать. **8**, *electricity* разряжать. —*v.i.* **1**, (go off, as of a cannon) выстрелить. **2**, *electricity* разряжаться. —*n.* **1**, (from military service) увольнение; (from a hospital) выписка; (from a job) увольнение; расчёт. **2**, (fulfillment; performance) исполнение; выполнение. **3**, (payment, as of a debt) уплата; покрытие. **4**, (firing; shooting off) выстрел. **5**, (secretion) выделение. **6**, *electricity* разряд.

disciple *n.* **1**, *relig.* апостол. **2**, (pupil; follower) ученик; последователь.

discipline *n.* дисциплина. —*v.t.* дисциплинировать. —**disciplinary,** *adj.* дисциплинарный.

disclaim *v.t.* отрицать: *he disclaimed any knowledge of the incident,* он отрицал, что знал о происшедшем. *Disclaim responsibility for,* не брать на себя ответственности за. —**disclaimer,** *n.* опровержение.

disclose *v.t.* раскрывать. —**disclosure,** *n.* раскрытие.

discolor *also,* **discolour** *v.t.* обесцвечивать. —**discoloration,** *n.* обесцвечивание.

discomfit *v.t.* **1,** (frustrate; thwart) расстраивать. **2,** (disconcert) смущать. —**discomfiture,** *n.* смущение; замешательство.

discomfort *n.* **1,** (lack of comfort) неудобство. **2,** (distress; embarrassment) неудобство; смущение. **3,** (pain): *she is in great discomfort,* ей тяжело; ей очень больно.

discommode *v.t.* затруднять; причинять неудобство (+ *dat.*).

disconcert *v.t.* смущать; сбивать; приводить в замешательство.

disconnect *v.t.* разъединять: *we've been disconnected,* нас разъединили. *Disconnect a telephone,* отключить телефон.

disconnected *adj.* несвязный; бессвязный.

disconsolate *adj.* неутешный.

discontent *n.* [*also,* **discontentment**] недовольство. —*adj.* [*also,* **discontented**] недовольный.

discontinue *v.t.* прекращать. —**discontinuation,** *n.* прекращение.

discord *n.* **1,** (dissension) разногласие; раздор; разлад. **2,** *music* диссонанс.

discordant *adj.* **1,** (not in accord) противоречивый. **2,** (not harmonious in sound) нестройный; несогласный; неблагозвучный.

discount *n.* скидка: *at a discount,* со скидкой. —*v.t.* **1,** *comm.* учитывать (вексель). **2,** (take no account of) не считаться с; не принимать в расчёт. —**discount rate,** учётная ставка; учётный процент.

discourage *v.t.* **1,** (dishearten) обескураживать. **2,** *fol. by* **from** (dissuade) отговаривать (от). —**discouragement,** *n.* обескураженность. —**discouraging,** *adj.* обескураживающий.

discourse *n.* **1,** (conversation) разговор. **2,** (lengthy discussion) рассуждение. **3,** (treatise) трактат. —*v.i.* рассуждать.

discourteous *adj.* невежливый. —**discourtesy,** *n.* невежливость.

discover *v.t.* **1,** (be the first to see) открывать. **2,** (find; detect; realize) обнаруживать. —**discoverer,** *n.* открыватель. —**discovery,** *n.* открытие.

discredit *v.t.* **1,** (damage in reputation) порочить; дискредитировать. **2,** (not believe; discount) не верить; не доверять. **3,** (show to be untrue) развенчивать. —*n. Bring discredit upon,* дискредитировать.

discreet *adj.* благоразумный; тактичный; осторожный. *Discreet distance,* почтительное расстояние.

discrepancy *n.* несоответствие; разногласие.

discretion *n.* **1,** (prudence) благоразумие. **2,** (power to decide) усмотрение: *at (someone's) discretion,* по (чьему-нибудь) усмотрению. *Leave to someone's discretion,* представлять на чьё-нибудь усмотрение. *Use one's discretion,* действовать по своему усмотрению.

discretionary *adj.* дискреционный.

discriminate *v.i.* **1,** (act with prejudice) дискриминировать. *Discriminate against women,* дискриминировать женщин. **2,** *fol. by* **between** (distinguish between) различать (между).

discriminating *adj.* разборчивый. *Discriminating taste,* тонкий вкус.

discrimination *n.* **1,** (injustice) дискриминация. **2,** (discernment) разборчивость. —**discriminatory,** *adj.* дискриминационный.

discus *n.* диск. *Discus throw,* метание диска.

discuss *v.t.* обсуждать.

discussion *n.* обсуждение; дискуссия. *Be under discussion,* обсуждаться.

disdain *v.t.* **1,** (scorn) презирать; гнушаться. **2,** *fol. by inf.* (refuse scornfully) брезгать; гнушаться. —*n.* презрение. —**disdainful,** *adj.* презрительный.

disease *n.* болезнь. —**diseased,** *adj.* больной; заболевший.

disembark *v.t.* высаживать. —*v.i.* высаживаться. —**disembarkation,** *n.* высадка.

disembowel *v.t.* потрошить.

disenchant *v.t.* разочаровывать. —**disenchantment,** *n.* разочарование.

disenfranchise *v.* = **disfranchise.**

disengage *v.t.* разъединять. —*v.i.* разъединяться. —**disengagement,** *n.* разъединение.

disentangle *v.t.* распутывать; выпутывать.

disestablish *v.t.* отделять (церковь) от государства.

disfavor *also,* **disfavour** *n.* немилость; опала. *Fall into disfavor,* впасть в немилость.

disfigure *v.t.* обезображивать; уродовать. —**disfigured,** *adj.* изуродованный. —**disfigurement,** *n.* обезображивание.

disfranchise *v.t.* лишать гражданских *or* избирательных прав.

disgorge *v.t.* извергать; изрыгать.

disgrace *n.* **1,** (shame; dishonor) позор; бесчестье. **2,** (disfavor) немилость; опала. —*v.t.* позорить; бесчестить. —**disgrace oneself,** позориться; покрыть себя позором. *He did not disgrace himself,* он не ударил лицом в грязь.

disgraceful *adj.* позорный. *It's simply disgraceful!,* это просто безобразие!

disgruntle *v.t.* вызывать (чьё-нибудь) недовольство. —**disgruntled,** *adj.* недовольный; в дурном настроении.

disguise *v.t.* маскировать; переодевать. *Disguise one's voice,* менять *or* изменять голос. *Disguise oneself as,* переодеваться (+ *instr.*). —*n.* маскировка. *In disguise,* замаскированный; переодетый.

disgust *n.* отвращение. —*v.t.* внушать отвращение (+ *dat.*).

disgusted *adj. I am/got disgusted,* мне надоело; мне опротивело; мне осточертело.

disgusting *adj.* отвратительный; противный. *It is disgusting to watch,* противно смотреть.

dish *n.* **1,** (small plate) тарелка. **2,** *pl.* (table utensils) посуда: *do the dishes,* мыть посуду. **3,** (particular kind of food) блюдо: *my favorite dish,* моё любимое блюдо. —*v.t.* [*usu.* **dish out** *or* **dish up**] подавать; сервировать.

disharmony *n.* **1,** (dissonance) дисгармония; неблагозвучие. **2,** (discord) дисгармония; разногласие.

dishcloth *n.* посу́дная тря́пка.
dishearten *v.t.* обескура́живать. *Become disheartened,* уныва́ть; па́дать ду́хом.
disheveled *also,* **dishevelled** *adj.* растрёпанный; взъеро́шенный; взлохма́ченный.
dishonest *adj.* нече́стный. —**dishonestly,** *adv.* нече́стно. —**dishonesty,** *n.* нече́стность.
dishonor *also,* **dishonour** *n.* бесче́стье. —*v.t.* бесче́стить. —**dishonorable,** *adj.* бесче́стный.
dishpan *n.* таз (для мытья́ посу́ды).
dishrag *n.* посу́дная тря́пка.
dishtowel *n.* посу́дное полоте́нце.
dishwasher *n.* **1,** (person) судомо́йка. **2,** (machine) посудомо́ечная маши́на; посудомо́йка.
dishwater *n.* помо́и.
disillusion *v.t.* разочаро́вывать. —**disillusioned,** *adj.* разочаро́ванный. *Become disillusioned,* разочаро́вываться. —**disillusionment,** *n.* разочарова́ние.
disinclination *n.* нерасположе́ние; нежела́ние; неохо́та. —**disinclined,** *adj.* не скло́нен (к); не расположен (к).
disinfect *v.t.* дезинфици́ровать; обеззара́живать.
disinfectant *adj.* дезинфици́рующий. —*n.* дезинфици́рующее сре́дство. —**disinfection,** *n.* дезинфе́кция; обеззара́живание.
disinformation *n.* дезинформа́ция.
disingenuous *adj.* нейскренний; непрямо́й.
disinherit *v.t.* лиша́ть насле́дства. —**disinheritance,** *n.* лише́ние насле́дства.
disintegrate *v.i.* распада́ться. —*v.t.* раздробля́ть; измельча́ть. —**disintegration,** *n.* распа́д.
disinter *v.t.* выка́пывать; отка́пывать.
disinterest *n.* **1,** (impartiality) беспристра́стие. **2,** (indifference) равноду́шие. —**disinterested,** *adj.* незаинтересо́ванный; бескоры́стный.
disjoint *v.t.* **1,** (dislocate) вы́вихнуть. **2,** (take apart at the joints) разде́лывать.
disjointed *adj.* **1,** (dislocated) вы́вихнутый. **2,** (disconnected; incoherent) несвя́зный; бессвя́зный; отры́вистый; отры́вочный; обры́вочный.
disjunctive *adj.* раздели́тельный.
disk *also,* **disc** *n.* диск. —**disk brake,** ди́сковый то́рмоз. —**disk harrow,** ди́сковая борона́.
dislikable *adj.* неприя́тный.
dislike *v.t.* не люби́ть. —*n.* [*also,* **disliking**] нелюбо́вь; нерасположе́ние; антипа́тия. *Take a disliking to,* невзлюби́ть; настро́иться про́тив.
dislocate *v.t., med.* вы́вихнуть.
dislocation *n.* **1,** (displacement) перемеще́ние. **2,** *med.* вы́вих.
dislodge *v.t.* выбива́ть; вышиба́ть.
disloyal *adj.* нелоя́льный. —**disloyalty,** *n.* нелоя́льность.
dismal *adj.* мра́чный; тоскли́вый; па́смурный.
dismantle *v.t.* разбира́ть; демонти́ровать.
dismay *v.t.* **1,** (distress) смуща́ть. **2,** (dishearten) обескура́живать. —*n.* **1,** (consternation) смуще́ние. **2,** (alarm) трево́га.
dismember *v.t.* расчленя́ть. —**dismemberment,** *n.* расчлене́ние.
dismiss *v.t.* **1,** (tell to go or disperse) отпуска́ть; распуска́ть. **2,** (remove from office or employment) увольня́ть; рассчи́тывать. **3,** (put out of one's mind) отбра́сывать. **4,** *law* прекраща́ть (де́ло); отклоня́ть (иск).

dismissal *n.* **1,** (ordering or allowing to disperse) ро́спуск. **2,** (discharge; removal) увольне́ние; расчет. —**dismissal notice,** уведомле́ние об увольне́нии.
dismount *v.i.* сходи́ть *or* слеза́ть с ло́шади; спе́шиваться.
disobedience *n.* непослуша́ние; неповинове́ние. —**disobedient,** *adj.* непослу́шный.
disobey *v.t. & i.* не слу́шаться; ослуша́ться.
disorder *n.* **1,** (disarray) беспоря́док. **2,** *often pl.* (public disturbances) беспоря́дки. **3,** (ailment) расстро́йство. —*v.t.* (пере)пу́тать; приводи́ть в беспоря́док.
disorderly *adj.* **1,** (unsystematic) беспоря́дочный. **2,** (unruly) бу́йный. —**disorderly conduct,** хулига́нство.
disorganize *v.t.* дезорганизова́ть. —**disorganization,** *n.* дезорганиза́ция; неорганизо́ванность. —**disorganized,** *adj.* дезорганизо́ванный; неорганизо́ванный; беспоря́дочный.
disorient *v.t.* дезориенти́ровать. —**disorientation,** *n.* дезориента́ция.
disown *v.t.* отрека́ться от; отка́зываться от.
disparage *v.t.* умаля́ть; принижа́ть; поро́чить; хули́ть. —**disparagement,** *n.* умале́ние; приниже́ние. —**disparaging,** *adj.* оскорби́тельный; оби́дный.
disparate *adj.* разли́чный; *disparate elements,* разли́чные элеме́нты. —**disparity,** *n.* ра́зница; несоотве́тствие.
dispassionate *adj.* беспристра́стный.
dispatch *v.t.* **1,** (send off) отправля́ть. **2,** (kill) добива́ть; прика́нчивать. —*n.* **1,** (sending) отправле́ние; отпра́вка. **2,** (message) донесе́ние; депе́ша. **3,** (alacrity) быстрота́.
dispatcher *n.* диспе́тчер.
dispel *v.t.* рассе́ивать; разгоня́ть.
dispensable *adj.* необяза́тельный; без чего́ мо́жно обойти́сь.
dispensary *n.* амбулато́рия.
dispensation *n.* **1,** (distribution) разда́ча. **2,** (release from an obligation) освобожде́ние (от обяза́тельства).
dispense *v.t.* **1,** (distribute) раздава́ть. **2,** (administer, as justice) отправля́ть (правосу́дие). —*v.i.* [*usu.* **dispense with**] обходи́ться без.
dispenser *n.* автома́т.
dispersal *n.* рассе́ивание; разго́н.
disperse *v.t.* рассе́ивать; разгоня́ть. —*v.i.* рассе́иваться; расходи́ться; разбега́ться. —**dispersion,** *n.* рассе́ивание; рассе́яние; *physics* диспе́рсия.
dispirit *v.t.* удруча́ть; угнета́ть. —**dispirited,** *adj.* удручённый; угнетённый.
displace *v.t.* **1,** (force out; supersede) вытесня́ть. **2,** (remove) смеща́ть. —**displaced person,** переме́щённое лицо́.
displacement *n.* **1,** (superseding) вытесне́ние. **2,** (removal) смеще́ние. **3,** (tonnage) водоизмеще́ние.
display *v.t.* **1,** (exhibit) выставля́ть. **2,** (reveal; manifest) проявля́ть; обнару́живать. —*n.* **1,** (showing) пока́з. *Put on display,* выставля́ть напока́з. **2,** (exhibit) вы́ставка. **3,** (manifestation) проявле́ние.
displease *v.t.* не нра́виться. —**displeased,** *adj.* недово́льный. —**displeasure,** *n.* неудово́льствие; недово́льство.
disposable *adj.* одноразо́вого употребле́ния; бро́совый.

disposal *n.* **1,** (arrangement) расположе́ние. **2,** (getting rid of) удале́ние: *waste disposal,* удале́ние отхо́дов. —**at one's disposal,** в чьём-нибудь распоряже́нии. *Have at one's disposal,* располага́ть (+ *instr.*); име́ть в своём распоряже́нии. *Place at someone's disposal,* предоста́вить в чьё-нибудь распоряже́ние. *My room is at your disposal,* моя́ ко́мната к ва́шим услу́гам.

dispose *v.t.* **1,** (place; arrange) располага́ть. **2,** (incline in a certain way) располага́ть; настра́ивать; склоня́ть. —**dispose of, 1,** (get rid of; remove) удаля́ть; убира́ть. **2,** (take care of; finish off) поко́нчить с; разде́латься с; распра́виться с.

disposed *adj.* располо́женный.

disposition *n.* **1,** (arrangement) расположе́ние. **2,** (temperament) нрав; хара́ктер. **3,** (tendency) расположе́ние; скло́нность. **4,** (handling; distribution) распоряже́ние. **5,** *mil.* дислока́ция.

dispossess *v.t.* лиша́ть со́бственности.

disproportion *n.* несоразме́рность; непропорциона́льность; диспропо́рция. —**disproportionate,** *adj.* несоразме́рный; непропорциона́льный. —**disproportionately,** *adv.* несоразме́рно; непропорциона́льно.

disprove *v.t.* опроверга́ть.

disputation *n.* деба́ты; ди́спут. —**disputatious,** *adj.* лю́бящий спо́рить.

dispute *n.* спор: *border dispute,* пограни́чный спор. *Be in dispute,* быть предме́том спо́ра. —*v.t.* оспа́ривать. *Disputed territory,* спо́рная террито́рия.

disqualify *v.t.* дисквалифици́ровать. —**disqualification,** *n.* дисквалифика́ция.

disquiet *v.t.* беспоко́ить; трево́жить. —*n.* [*also,* **disquietude**] беспоко́йство; трево́га. —**disquieting,** *adj.* беспоко́йный; трево́жный.

disquisition *n.* тракта́т.

disregard *v.t.* пренебрега́ть; игнори́ровать. —*n.* пренебреже́ние.

disrepair *n.* неиспра́вность. *Fall into disrepair,* приходи́ть в ве́тхость *or* в него́дность.

disreputable *adj.* по́льзующийся дурно́й сла́вой.

disrepute *n.* дурна́я сла́ва. *Fall into disrepute,* приобрести́ дурну́ю сла́ву.

disrespect *n.* неуваже́ние; непочте́ние; непочти́тельность. —**disrespectful,** *adj.* непочти́тельный.

disrobe *v.t.* раздева́ть; обнажа́ть. —*v.i.* раздева́ться; обнажа́ться.

disrupt *v.t.* наруша́ть; срыва́ть; дезорганизова́ть. —**disruption,** *n.* наруше́ние; дезорганиза́ция.

disruptive *adj.* **1,** (tending to disrupt) подрывно́й. **2,** (unruly) непоко́рный.

dissatisfaction *n.* недово́льство; неудовлетворённость. —**dissatisfied,** *adj.* недово́льный; неудовлетворённый.

dissect *v.t.* **1,** (cut apart) вскрыва́ть; анатоми́ровать. **2,** (analyze closely) разбира́ть.

dissection *n.* **1,** (cutting apart) вскры́тие. **2,** (analysis) разбо́р.

dissemble *v.t.* **1,** (conceal the real nature of) скрыва́ть; маскирова́ть. **2,** (feign) притворя́ться (+ *instr.*). —*v.i.* лицеме́рить; криви́ть душо́й.

disseminate *v.t.* распространя́ть. —**dissemination,** *n.* распростране́ние.

dissension *n.* разла́д; раздо́р.

dissent *v.i.* не соглаша́ться; возража́ть. *Dissenting vote,* го́лос про́тив. —*n.* инакомы́слие. —**dissenter,** *n.* инакомы́слящий.

dissertation *n.* диссерта́ция.

disservice *n.* плоха́я услу́га.

dissidence *n.* инакомы́слие. —**dissident,** *n. & adj.* инакомы́слящий.

dissimilar *adj.* несхо́дный. —**dissimilarity,** *n.* несхо́дство.

dissipate *v.t.* **1,** (dispel) рассе́ивать; разгоня́ть. **2,** (squander) растра́чивать; расточа́ть. —*v.i.* рассе́иваться.

dissipation *n.* **1,** (dispelling) рассе́ивание. **2,** (squandering) расточе́ние. **3,** (dissoluteness) распу́тство.

dissociate *v.t.* разобща́ть. *Dissociate oneself from,* отмежёвываться от.

dissolute *adj.* распу́тный; распу́щенный; развра́тный; беспу́тный. —**dissoluteness,** *n.* распу́тство; распу́щенность; беспу́тство.

dissolution *n.* **1,** (melting) растворе́ние. **2,** (termination) расторже́ние; ликвида́ция. **3,** (dismissal) ро́спуск. **4,** (breaking up) распа́д.

dissolve *v.t.* **1,** (melt) растворя́ть. **2,** (terminate) расторга́ть (брак); ликвиди́ровать (компа́нию). **3,** (dismiss, as an assembly) распуска́ть. —*v.i.* раствора́ться.

dissonance *n.* диссона́нс; неблагозву́чие. —**dissonant,** *adj.* неблагозву́чный; нестро́йный.

dissuade *v.t.* отгова́ривать; отсове́товать.

distaff *n.* пря́лка. —**distaff side,** же́нская ли́ния.

distance *n.* расстоя́ние. *At a distance,* на не́котором расстоя́нии. *In the distance,* в отдале́нии; вдали́; вдалеке́. *Into the distance,* вдаль. *From a distance,* и́здали; издалека́. *Quite a distance from here,* дово́льно далеко́ отсю́да. *Because of the great distance,* за да́льностью расстоя́ния. —**keep one's distance,** держа́ться вдалеке́; держа́ться на почти́тельном расстоя́нии.

distant *adj.* **1,** (remote) далёкий; да́льний; отдалённый. *Distant relative,* да́льний ро́дственник. *Distant resemblance,* отдалённое схо́дство. **2,** (cold; indifferent) холо́дный; сухо́й.

distaste *n.* отвраще́ние; антипа́тия. —**distasteful,** *adj.* неприя́тный.

distemper *n.* **1,** (ill humor) плохо́е настрое́ние. **2,** (disease of dogs) соба́чья чума́. **3,** *painting* те́мпера.

distend *v.t.* надува́ть. —*v.i.* надува́ться. —**distended,** *adj.* наду́тый; напряжённый.

distill *also,* **distil** *v.t.* **1,** (purify) дистилли́ровать: *distilled water,* дистилли́рованная вода́. **2,** (make, as whiskey) перегоня́ть; гнать. —**distillation,** *n.* дистилля́ция; перего́нка; винокуре́ние. —**distiller,** *n.* виноку́р. —**distillery,** *n.* перего́нный *or* виноку́ренный заво́д.

distinct *adj.* **1,** (clear; plain) отчётливый; чёткий. **2,** (evident; marked) я́вный; заме́тный. *Distinct improvement,* заме́тное улучше́ние. *Distinct advantage,* я́вное преиму́щество. **3,** (different) разли́чный: *distinct dialects,* разли́чные диале́кты. —**as distinct from,** в отли́чие от.

distinction *n.* **1,** (differentiation) разли́чие: *make a distinction between,* де́лать разли́чие ме́жду. **2,** (eminence) изве́стность. *Man of distinction,* выдаю́щийся челове́к. **3,** (honor) честь: *dubious distinction,* сомни́тельная честь. *Serve/graduate with distinction,* служи́ть/око́нчить шко́лу/с отли́чием. *He has* *the distinction of being...*, на его до́лю вы́пала честь быть...

distinctive *adj.* **1,** (distinguishing) отличи́тельный. **2,** (characteristic; peculiar) своеобра́зный.

distinctly *adv.* отчётливо; чётко.

distinguish *v.t.* **1,** (tell apart) различа́ть; отлича́ть. *Distinguish colors,* различа́ть цвета́. *Distinguish good from evil,* отлича́ть добро́ от зла. **2,** (make different; set apart) отлича́ть. *Distinguishing characteristic,* отличи́тельная черта́. **3,** (discern) различа́ть. —*v.i.* [*usu.* **distinguish between**] различа́ть (ме́жду). —**distinguish oneself,** отлича́ться.

distinguishable *adj.* различи́мый.

distinguished *adj.* **1,** (eminent) выдаю́щийся. **2,** *in direct address* уважа́емый: *distinguished guests,* уважа́емые го́сти. **3,** (dignified in appearance) импоза́нтный.

distort *v.t.* **1,** (contort) искажа́ть; искривля́ть. **2,** (misrepresent) искажа́ть; извраща́ть. —**distortion,** *n.* искаже́ние; извраще́ние.

distract *v.t.* отвлека́ть: *distract someone from his/ her work,* отвлека́ть кого́-нибудь от рабо́ты.

distraction *n.* **1,** (act of distracting) отвлече́ние. **2,** (something that distracts) поме́ха. **3,** (mental derangement) безу́мие: *love someone to distraction,* люби́ть кого́-нибудь до безу́мия.

distraught *adj.* обезу́мевший (от го́ря).

distress *n.* **1,** (pain; suffering) огорче́ние. **2,** (trouble; danger) бе́дствие. *Distress signal,* сигна́л бе́дствия. *A ship in distress,* су́дно, те́рпящее бе́дствие. —*v.t.* огорча́ть. —**distressed,** *adj.* огорчённый. —**distressing,** *adj.* огорчи́тельный; гнету́щий; тя́гостный.

distribute *v.t.* **1,** (allot; parcel out) распределя́ть. **2,** (hand out) раздава́ть.

distribution *n.* **1,** (parceling out) распределе́ние. **2,** (range of occurrence) распростране́ние. —**distributive,** *adj.* распредели́тельный.

distributor *n.* **1,** (one who distributes) распредели́тель. **2,** *comm.* опто́вая фи́рма; опто́вый торго́вец. **3,** *mech.* распредели́тель.

district *n.* райо́н; о́круг. —*adj.* райо́нный; окружно́й. —**district attorney,** окружно́й прокуро́р.

distrust *n.* недове́рие. —*v.t.* не доверя́ть. —**distrustful,** *adj.* недове́рчивый.

disturb *v.t.* **1,** (bother; interrupt) меша́ть: *I hope I'm not disturbing you,* наде́юсь, что я вам не меша́ю. **2,** (disrupt) наруша́ть: *disturb the balance,* наруша́ть равнове́сие. **3,** (trouble; disquiet) беспоко́ить.

disturbance *n.* **1,** (disruption) наруше́ние. **2,** (interruption; intrusion) беспоко́йство. **3,** (public disorder) волне́ния; беспоря́дки. **4,** *med.* расстро́йство.

disturbed *adj.* **1,** (troubled) обеспоко́енный. **2,** (emotionally unstable) душевнобольно́й.

disturbing *adj.* беспоко́йный; трево́жный.

disunity *n.* отсу́тствие еди́нства; разла́д; разногла́сие.

disuse *n. Fall into disuse,* вы́йти из употребле́ния.

disyllabic *adj.* двусло́жный.

ditch *n.* кана́ва; ров. —*v.t. Ditch a plane over water,* де́лать вы́нужденную поса́дку на́ воду.

ditto *n.* то же. —**ditto marks,** кавы́чки (вме́сто повторе́ния).

ditty *n.* часту́шка.

diuretic *adj.* мочего́нный. —*n.* мочего́нное сре́дство.

diurnal *adj.* дневно́й.

divan *n.* тахта́.

dive *v.i.* **1,** (plunge head first into water) ныря́ть. **2,** (leap; plunge) бро́ситься. **3,** *aero.* пики́ровать. —*n.* **1,** (plunge into water) прыжо́к в во́ду; ныро́к. **2,** *aero.* пики́рование; пике́. **3,** *colloq.* (cheap place) кабачо́к.

dive bomber пики́рующий бомбардиро́вщик.

diver *n.* **1,** *sports* ныря́льщик. **2,** (deep-sea diver) водола́з. *Pearl diver,* иска́тель жемчуга.

diverge *v.i.* расходи́ться. —**divergence,** *n.* расхожде́ние.

divergent *adj.* **1,** (diverging) расходя́щийся. **2,** (different) разли́чный.

diverse *adj.* ра́зный; разнообра́зный.

diversify *v.t.* разнообра́зить. —**diversification,** *n.* диверсифика́ция.

diversion *n.* **1,** (turning aside) отво́д. **2,** (amusement) развлече́ние. **3,** *mil.* диве́рсия; демонстра́ция. —**diversionary,** *adj.* диверсио́нный; демонстрати́вный.

diversity *n.* разнообра́зие.

divert *v.t.* **1,** (draw off in another direction) отвлека́ть: *divert attention from,* отвлека́ть внима́ние от. *Divert a river,* изменя́ть ру́сло реки́. **2,** (entertain) развлека́ть.

divest *v.t.* лиша́ть. —**divest oneself of,** отка́зываться от.

divide *v.t.* **1,** (separate into parts; give out in shares) разделя́ть; дели́ть: *divide something in half,* разделя́ть/дели́ть что́-нибудь попола́м. *Divide up the loot,* дели́ть/разделя́ть добы́чу. **2,** (separate; be a boundary between) отделя́ть. **3,** *math.* дели́ть; разделя́ть. **4,** *fig.* (set apart) разъединя́ть: *the things that divide us,* то, что нас разъединя́ет. *Opinions are divided,* мне́ния расхо́дятся. —*v.i.* разделя́ться; дели́ться: *the road divides,* доро́га разделя́ется/де́лится. *Divide up into two groups,* разделя́ться на две гру́ппы.

dividend *n.* **1,** *finance* дивиде́нд. **2,** *math.* дели́мое.

divider *n.* **1,** (partition) перегоро́дка. **2,** *pl.* (pair of compasses) ци́ркуль.

dividing *adj.* раздели́тельный: *dividing line,* раздели́тельная черта́.

divination *n.* гада́ние; ворожба́.

divine *adj.* боже́ственный. —*n.* богосло́в. —*v.t.* предуга́дывать; разга́дывать.

diving *n.* **1,** *sports* прыжки́ в во́ду. **2,** (deep-sea diving) водола́зное де́ло. —**diving board,** трампли́н. —**diving helmet,** водола́зный шлем. —**diving suit,** водола́зный костю́м; скафа́ндр.

divinity *n.* **1,** (divine nature) боже́ственность. **2,** (deity) божество́. **3,** (study of religion) богосло́вие.

divisible *adj.* **1,** (general term) дели́мый. **2,** *math.* кра́тный: *divisible by two,* кра́тный двум. *Six is divisible by three,* шесть де́лится на три; шесть — кра́тное трём. —**divisibility,** *n.* дели́мость.

division *n.* **1,** (act of dividing) деле́ние; разделе́ние; разде́л. *Division of labor,* разделе́ние труда́. **2,** (section) отде́л. **3,** (military unit) диви́зия. **4,** *math.* деле́ние.

divisional *adj.* дивизио́нный.

divisive *adj.* раско́льнический.

divisor *n., math.* дели́тель.

divorce *n.* развод. —*adj.* бракоразводный: *divorce case,* бракоразводное дело. —*v.t.* **1,** (get a divorce from) разводиться с. **2,** (separate) отделять; отрывать. —**divorced,** *adj.* разведённый. *They are divorced,* они в разводе. —**divorcée,** *n.* разведённая.

divulge *v.t.* разглашать. —**divulgence,** *n.* разглашение.

dizzy *adj.* **1,** (giddy): *I am dizzy,* у меня кружится голова. **2,** (causing dizziness) головокружительный. —**dizziness,** *n.* головокружение.

do[1] (doo) *v.t.* **1,** (perform; attend to) делать: *what are you doing?,* что вы делаете? *Do one's lessons,* делать уроки. *Do the dishes,* мыть посуду. *Do a lot of reading,* много читать. **2,** (work at) работать; заниматься: *what do you do for a living?,* кем вы работаете?; чем вы занимаетесь? **3,** (cause) причинять: *do harm to,* причинять вред *or* зло (+ *dat.*). делать зло (+ *dat.*). *Do someone good,* приносить пользу (+ *dat.*). **4,** (render; perform) делать: *do someone a favor/service,* сделать кому-нибудь одолжение. *What can I do for you?,* чем могу быть полезен (полезна)? **5,** *fol. by to* (hurt) делать: *what did you do to him?,* что вы ему сделали? *What did he ever do to you?,* что он такое вам сделал? *What did you do to your leg?,* что случилось с вашей ногой? —*v.i.* **1,** (act; behave) делать: *do as you are told,* делайте, как вам велено. **2,** (fare): *how are you doing?,* как (ваши) дела? *How did he do?,* как у него получилось? **3,** (be suitable) годиться; подходить. *That won't do,* это не подойдёт. **4,** (be sufficient) хватать: *that will do,* хватит!; этого хватит. —*v.aux.* **1,** *in forming questions: do you speak Russian?,* вы говорите по-русски? **2,** *in forming neg. sentences: I do not speak Russian,* я не говорю по-русски. **3,** *to add emphasis: Do pay us a visit,* пожалуйста, зайдите к нам! *Do be quiet!,* да замолчите же! **4,** *to replace a verb previously expressed or understood: Do you know how to cook? Yes, I do.,* умеете ли вы готовить? Да, умею. *You don't know how to cook. Yes, I do.,* вы не умеете готовить. Неправда, умею. —**do away with,** уничтожать; покончить с. —**do not,** *see* **don't.** —**do over,** переделывать. —**do with,** девать: *what did I do with my glasses?,* куда я дел мой очки? —**do without,** обходиться без. *See also* **doing, done, don't.**

do[2] (do) *n., music* до.

docile *adj.* послушный; покорный. —**docility,** *n.* покорность.

dock *n.* **1,** (place where a ship stands) док: *dry dock,* сухой док. **2,** (pier) пристань. **3,** (prisoner's stand) скамья подсудимых: *in the dock,* на скамье подсудимых. —*v.i.* **1,** (of a ship) причаливать. **2,** (of space vehicles) стыковаться. —*v.t.* (deduct from) урезывать.

docket *n., law* список дел.

docking *n., aerospace* стыковка.

dockyard *n.* верфь.

doctor *n.* **1,** (physician) врач. **2,** (holder of a doctorate) доктор. —*v.t.* **1,** (treat) лечить. **2,** (tamper with) подделывать; фальсифицировать. —**doctoral,** *adj.* докторский. —**doctorate,** *n.* докторская степень.

doctrine *n.* доктрина. —**doctrinaire,** *adj.* доктринёрский.

document *n.* документ. —*v.t.* документировать.

documentary *adj.* документальный. —*n.* документальный фильм.

documentation *n.* документация.

dodder *v.i.* **1,** (tremble) трястись. **2,** (wobble along) ковылять; шататься. *A doddering old man,* ковыляющий старик; старик, еле передвигающий ноги.

dodge *v.t.* уклоняться от; увёртываться от; увиливать от. —*n.* увёртка.

doe *n.* **1,** (female deer) оленуха. **2,** (female of other animals) самка.

doeskin *n.* замша.

doff *v.t.* снимать.

dog *n.* собака. —*adj.* собачий: *dog collar,* собачий ошейник. —*v.t.* **1,** (track; pursue) гнаться по пятам за; увязываться за. *Dog someone's footsteps,* следовать по пятам за. **2,** *fig.* (haunt; hound) преследовать: *dogged by misfortune,* преследуемый несчастьями. —**a dog's age,** целая вечность. —**a dog's life,** собачья жизнь. —**dog tired,** усталый как собака. —**go to the dogs,** пойти прахом. —**it is raining cats and dogs,** дождь льёт как из ведра. —**let sleeping dogs lie,** не тронь лиха, пока спит тихо.

doge *n.* дож.

dogeared *adj.* захватанный.

dogfight *n., aero.* воздушный бой.

dogfish *n.* морская собака.

dogged *adj.* упорный; настойчивый.

doggerel *n.* вирши.

doggone *adj., colloq.* проклятый.

doggy *n.* собачка.

doghouse *n.* конура.

dogma *n.* догма. —**dogmatic,** *adj.* догматический. —**dogmatism,** *n.* догматизм. —**dogmatist,** *n.* догматик.

dog sled нарты.

dogwood *n.* кизил.

doily *n.* салфеточка.

doing *n. Big doings,* большие события. *It is mainly their doing,* это в основном дело их рук. *That will take some doing,* это потребует немало усилий.

doldrums *n.pl.* **1,** *naut.* штилевые полосы. **2,** *fig.* (low spirits) подавленное настроение; уныние.

dole *n.* **1,** (handout) подачка. **2,** *Brit.* (unemployment insurance) пособие (по безработице). —*v.t.* [*usu.* **dole out**] выдавать.

doleful *adj.* скорбный; жалобный.

doll *n.* кукла. *Play with dolls,* играть в куклы. —*v.t. & i.* [*usu.* **doll up**] разодеть(ся). *All dolled up,* весь разодетый; вся разодетая.

dollar *n.* доллар. *Dollar bill,* долларовая бумажка *or* купюра. —**in dollars and cents,** в денежном выражении.

dollhouse *n.* кукольный домик.

dolly *n.* **1,** (doll) куколка. **2,** (cart) тележка.

dolomite *n.* доломит.

dolphin *n.* дельфин.

dolt *n.* глупец; болван; тупица.

domain *n.* **1,** (territory; realm) владение; территория. **2,** (sphere; field) область; сфера; круг.

dome *n.* купол.

domestic *adj.* **1,** (of the home) домашний. *Domestic animals,* домашние животные. **2,** (internal) внутренний. **3,** (produced at home; not imported) местный; отечественный. —*n.* (servant) слуга; прислуга. —**domestic science,** домоводство.

domesticate *v.t.* приручать; одомашнивать. —**domesticated,** *adj.* ручной; приручённый. —**domestication,** *n.* приручение; одомашнивание.

domicile *n.* местожительство.

dominance *n.* господство. —**dominant,** *adj.* господствующий; доминирующий.

dominate *v.t. & i.* **1,** (control) госпо́дствовать: *dominate the sea/air,* госпо́дствовать на мо́ре/в во́здухе. *Dominate other nations,* госпо́дствовать над други́ми стра́нами. **2,** (tower over) домини́ровать над; госпо́дствовать над. —**domination,** *n.* госпо́дство.

domineer *v.t. & i.* вла́ствовать (над); кома́ндовать (над). —**domineering,** *adj.* вла́стный.

dominion *n.* **1,** (sovereignty; rule) владычество. **2,** *pl.* (territory under control) владе́ния. **3,** (self-governing member of the British Commonwealth) доминио́н.

domino *n.* **1,** (masquerade costume) домино́. **2,** *pl.* (game) домино́. **3,** (tile used in this game) кость.

don *v.t.* надева́ть.

donate *v.t.* же́ртвовать. —**donation,** *n.* поже́ртвование.

done *adj.* **1,** (carried out) сде́лан: *the deed is done,* де́ло сде́лано. **2,** (finished) (о)ко́нчен. *Are you done?,* вы ко́нчили? **3,** (adequately cooked) гото́в: *is the meat done yet?,* мя́со уже́ гото́во? **4,** (socially acceptable) при́нят: *that is not done,* э́то не при́нято. —**done for,** пропа́вший; поги́бший: *we are done for,* мы пропа́ли; мы поги́бли.

donkey *n.* осёл.

donor *n.* же́ртвователь. *Blood donor,* до́нор.

don't *contr. of do not, rendered by* не *plus the imperative: don't cry!,* не плачь!; не пла́чьте! *Don't forget!,* не забу́дь!; не забу́дьте!

doom *n.* ги́бель. *Sense of doom,* чу́вство обречённости. —*v.t.* обрека́ть: *doomed to failure,* обречённый на прова́л.

doomsday *n.* день Стра́шного суда́. —**till doomsday,** до второ́го прише́ствия.

door *n.* дверь. —*adj.* дверно́й: *door lock,* дверно́й замо́к. —**behind closed doors,** при закры́тых дверя́х. —**next door,** ря́дом. —**out of doors,** на дворе́. —**show someone the door,** показа́ть кому́-нибудь на дверь.

doorbell *n.* (дверно́й) звоно́к.

doorkeeper *n.* привра́тник.

doorknob *n.* дверна́я ру́чка.

doorman *n.* швейца́р.

doormat *n.* полови́к.

doorpost *n.* (дверно́й) коса́к.

doorstep *n.* поро́г. —**camp on someone's doorstep,** обива́ть поро́ги у кого́-нибудь. —**lay the blame on someone's doorstep,** возлага́ть вину́ на кого́-нибудь.

doorway *n.* дверно́й проём. *In the doorway,* в дверя́х.

dope *n., slang* **1,** (drug) нарко́тик; дурма́н. **2,** (dumbbell) глупе́ц. **3,** (information) све́дения; информа́ция. —*v.t., colloq.* **1,** (drug) дурма́нить. **2,** *fol. by* out (figure out) разга́дывать. —**dope addict; dope fiend,** наркома́н.

dopey *adj., colloq.* **1,** (in a stupor) одурма́ненный. **2,** (dumb) глу́пый.

dormant *adj.* **1,** (sleeping) спя́щий. **2,** (inactive) усну́вший: *dormant volcano,* усну́вший вулка́н. —**lie dormant,** быть забы́тым; быть отло́женным (в сто́рону).

dormer window слухово́е окно́.

dormitory *n.* общежи́тие.

dormouse *n.* со́ня.

dorsal *adj.* спинно́й.

dosage *n.* дозиро́вка.

dose *n.* до́за.

dossier *n.* досье́.

dot *n.* то́чка. *Dots and dashes,* то́чки и тире́. *Polka dots,* горо́шек. —*v.t.* **1,** (mark with a dot) ста́вить то́чку на. **2,** (stud) усе́ивать: *the fields are dotted with flowers,* поля́ усе́яны цвета́ми. —**on the dot, 1,** *with the time of day,* ро́вно. **2,** (exactly on time) мину́та в мину́ту.

dotage *n.* ста́рческое слабоу́мие. *Be in one's dotage,* впада́ть в де́тство.

dote *v.i.* [*usu.* **dote on** *or* **upon**] души́ не ча́ять в; носи́ть на рука́х.

dotted *adj.* в кра́пинку; в горо́шек. —**dotted line,** пункти́рная ли́ния; пункти́р.

dotterel *n.* си́вка глу́пая; хруста́н.

double *adj.* **1,** (dual; twofold) двойно́й; двоя́кий. *Double portion,* двойна́я по́рция. *Double bed,* двуспа́льная крова́ть. *Double room,* ко́мната *or* но́мер на двои́х. *Double chin,* двойно́й подборо́док. *Double exposure,* двойна́я *or* двукра́тная экспози́ция. *Double pneumonia,* двусторо́ннее воспале́ние легких. *Double standard,* двойна́я ме́рка. **2,** *bot.* махро́вый: *double rose,* махро́вая ро́за. —*adv.* вдво́е бо́льше; вдвойне́. *Double the price,* вдво́е доро́же. —*n.* **1,** (perfect likeness) двойни́к. **2,** *pl.,* *tennis* па́рная игра́. —*v.t.* удва́ивать. —*v.i.* удва́иваться. —**double back,** возвраща́ться по свои́м следа́м. —**double up,** скрю́чивать(ся): *he was doubled up in pain,* он скрю́чился (*or* его́ скрю́чило) от бо́ли. —**on the double,** бего́м; на бегу́. —**see double,** дво́иться в глаза́х: *I am seeing double,* у меня́ дво́ится в глаза́х.

double-barreled *adj.* двуство́льный.

double bass контраба́с.

double bassoon контрафаго́т.

double-breasted *adj.* двубо́ртный.

double-cross *v.t., colloq.* обма́нывать; надува́ть.

double-dealer *n.* двуру́шник. —**double-dealing,** *adj.* двуру́шнический. —*n.* двуру́шничество.

double-edged *adj.* обоюдоо́стрый. —**double-edged sword,** па́лка о двух конца́х.

double entendre двусмы́сленность.

double-space *v.t.* печа́тать че́рез два интерва́ла.

doubly *adv.* вдвойне́.

doubt *n.* сомне́ние: *without a doubt,* без вся́кого сомне́ния. *Have doubts about someone,* сомнева́ться в ко́м-нибудь. —*v.t.* сомнева́ться в: *I doubt that,* я в э́том сомнева́юсь. *Doubt someone's honesty,* сомнева́ться в чьей-нибудь че́стности. *I doubt if he'll agree,* я сомнева́юсь (в том), что он согласи́тся. —**be in doubt:** *when in doubt — ask,* е́сли не зна́ешь, спроси́. *The outcome is still in doubt,* исхо́д де́ла еще не я́сен. —**no doubt, 1,** (undoubtedly) без сомне́ния; несомне́нно. **2,** (probably) наве́рно.

doubtful *adj.* **1,** (uncertain): *be doubtful,* сомнева́ться. *It is doubtful,* вряд ли. **2,** (questionable; dubious) сомни́тельный.

doubtless *adv.* **1,** (undoubtedly) несомне́нно. **2,** (probably) наве́рно. *Also,* **doubtlessly.**

douche *n.* душ; облива́ние.

dough *n.* **1,** (flour paste) те́сто. **2,** *slang* (money) моне́та.

doughnut *n.* по́нчик.

doughty *adj.* сто́йкий; отва́жный.

dour *adj.* мра́чный; угрю́мый.

douse *v.t.* **1,** (immerse) погружа́ть; окуна́ть. **2,** (drench) обдава́ть; облива́ть; ока́чивать. **3,** (extinguish) туши́ть; гаси́ть. *Douse a fire,* залива́ть костёр.

dove *n.* го́лубь. —**dovecote**, *n.* голубя́тня.

dovetail *n.* ла́сточкин хвост.

dowager *n.* **1,** (widow) вдова́. *Dowager queen*, вдо́вствующая короле́ва. **2,** *colloq.* (elderly woman) матро́на.

dowdy *adj.* немо́дный; неэлега́нтный.

dowel *n.* шпо́нка; штифт; штырь.

down *adv.* **1,** (to a lower position; toward the ground) вниз: *look down*, смотре́ть вниз. ♦ *Usu. rendered by a single verb: sit down*, сесть; *lie down*, лечь; *go* (or *come*) *down*, сойти́; *climb down*, слезть; *fall down*, упа́сть; *knock down*, повали́ть; сбить с ног; *tear down*, снести́; *burn down*, сгоре́ть; *write down*, записа́ть; *calm down*, успоко́и(ся). **2,** (as a down payment) нали́чными: *forty dollars down and the rest in monthly installments*, со́рок до́лларов нали́чными, а остально́е ежеме́сячными взно́сами. —*adj. The sun is down*, со́лнце зашло́. *Her temperature is down*, её температу́ра пони́зилась. *Strike a man when he is down*, бить лежа́чего. *He is down with the grippe*, он лежи́т с гри́ппом. —*prep.* c: *fall down the stairs*, упа́сть с ле́стницы. *Sail down the river*, плыть вниз по реке́. —*n.* пух: *eider down*, гага́чий пух. —*v.t.* **1,** (shoot down) сбива́ть. **2,** (drink) вы́пить за́лпом. —**down and out**, разорённый; в нищете́. —**down to**, вплоть до. —**down with...!**, доло́й (+ *acc.*)

downcast *adj.* уны́лый; пону́рый.

downfall *n.* паде́ние; круше́ние.

downgrade *n.* склон; укло́н. —*v.t.* **1,** (demote) понижа́ть. **2,** (minimize) умаля́ть. —**on the downgrade**, в состоя́нии упа́дка.

downhearted *adj.* па́вший ду́хом; уны́лый. *Don't be downhearted!*, не унывай!

downhill *adv.* под го́ру.

down payment зада́ток.

downpour *n.* ли́вень.

downright *adj.* я́вный; сплошно́й; су́щий. —*adv.* про́сто; прямо: *it's downright amazing!*, это про́сто/ пря́мо удиви́тельно!

downstairs *adv.* **1,** (location) внизу́. **2,** (motion) вниз. —*n.* ни́жний эта́ж.

downstream *adv.* вниз по тече́нию.

downtime *n.* просто́й.

downtown *n.* центр го́рода; делова́я часть го́рода. —*adj.* центра́льный. —*adv.* в це́нтр(е) го́рода.

downtrodden *adj.* заби́тый; за́гнанный.

downward *adv.* [*also,* **downwards**] вниз; кни́зу; под укло́н. —*adj.* под укло́н: *downward movement*, движе́ние под укло́н.

downy *adj.* пуши́стый; пухо́вый.

dowry *n.* прида́ное.

doze *v.i.* дрема́ть. *Doze off*, задрема́ть; вздремну́ть; забыва́ться.

dozen *n.* дю́жина.

drab *adj.* бесцве́тный; се́рый; однообра́зный. —**drabness**, *n.* бесцве́тность; однообра́зие.

drachma *n.* дра́хма.

draconian *adj.* драко́новский.

draft *n.* **1,** (preliminary version) набро́сок; эски́з. *First draft*, чернови́к. *Final draft*, оконча́тельная реда́кция. *Draft resolution*, прое́кт резолю́ции. **2,** (current of air) сквозня́к. **3,** (device to regulate air intake) тя́га. **4,** (conscription) во́инская пови́нность. **5,** *finance* чек. **6,** *naut.* (depth of a vessel below the water) оса́дка. —*adj.* **1,** (for hauling) тя́гловый. *Draft animals*, (живое) тя́гло; рабо́чий скот. **2,** (drawn from a

cask) разливно́й: *draft beer*, разливно́е пи́во. —*v.t.* **1,** (conscript) призыва́ть (на вое́нную слу́жбу). **2,** (compose in preliminary form) составля́ть; разраба́тывать. *Also, chiefly Brit.*, **draught.**

draft board призывно́й пункт.

draftee *n.* призывни́к.

draftsman *also,* **draughtsman** *n.* чертёжник.

drafty *adj.* *It is drafty in here*, здесь сквози́т.

drag *v.t.* **1,** (pull along the ground) тащи́ть; волочи́ть. *Drag one's feet*, волочи́ть но́ги. **2,** (dredge, as a river) очища́ть (дно реки́). **3,** (force to go against one's will) тащи́ть. **4,** *fol. by* **out** (prolong) тяну́ть; затя́гивать; растя́гивать. —*v.i.* **1,** (trail along) тащи́ться; волочи́ться. **2,** *fol. by* **on** *or* **out** (progress slowly; last a long time) тяну́ться; затя́гиваться. —*n.* **1,** (hindrance) тормоз; обу́за. **2,** *colloq.* (draw, as on a cigarette) затя́жка.

dragnet *n.* **1,** (net) бре́день. **2,** (network for catching a criminal) обла́ва.

dragon *n.* драко́н.

dragonfly *n.* стрекоза́.

dragoon *n.* драгу́н.

drain *v.t.* **1,** (draw off, as water) отводи́ть. **2,** (draw water from) отводи́ть во́ду из; осуша́ть; дрени́ровать. **3,** (drink all the contents of) осуша́ть. **4,** *surgery* дрени́ровать. **5,** *fig.* (exhaust; consume totally) истоща́ть. —*v.i.* впада́ть: *the river drains into the ocean*, река́ впада́ет в океа́н. —*n.* **1,** (channel; pipe) водосто́к; (водо)сто́чная труба́. **2,** *fig.* (continuous outflow) уте́чка. —**go down the drain**, пойти́ насма́рку.

drainage *n.* дрена́ж; осуше́ние. —*adj.* дрена́жный; осуши́тельный; отво́дный; водоотво́дный.

drainpipe *n.* водосто́чная труба́.

drake *n.* се́лезень.

drama *n.* дра́ма. *Drama critic*, театра́льный кри́тик.

dramatic *adj.* **1,** (of drama; stirring) драмати́ческий. **2,** (striking; drastic) ре́зкий: *dramatic change*, ре́зкая переме́на. —**dramatically**, *adv.* ре́зко; кру́то: *change dramatically*, ре́зко/кру́то измени́ться.

dramatics *n.* драмати́ческое иску́сство. —**dramatist**, *n.* драмату́рг. —**dramatize**, *v.t.* драматизи́ровать. —**dramaturgy**, *n.* драматурги́я.

drape *v.t.* драпирова́ть. *The coffin was draped in black*, гроб был обтя́нут чёрным. —*n.* = **drapery.**

drapery *n., usu. pl.* драпиро́вка.

drastic *adj.* круто́й; ре́зкий.

draught *n.* = **draft.**

draughts *n.pl., Brit.* = **checkers.**

draughtsman *n.* = **draftsman.**

draw *v.t.* **1,** (pull) тащи́ть: *the horse draws the carriage*, ло́шадь та́щит каре́ту. *Draw the curtain/blind*, заде́ргивать занаве́ску/што́ру. **2,** (pull tight) натя́гивать: *draw the bow*, натя́гивать лук. **3,** (move in a given direction) отводи́ть: *draw someone aside*, отводи́ть кого́-нибудь в сто́рону. **4,** (take out; withdraw) вынима́ть; выхва́тывать. *Draw one's sword*, вынима́ть шпа́гу из но́жен. *Draw a knife/gun*, выхва́тывать нож/пистоле́т. *Draw a card from the deck*, тяну́ть ка́рту из коло́ды. **5,** (cause to flow) че́рпать: *draw water from a well*, че́рпать во́ду из коло́дца. *Draw blood*, пуска́ть кровь. *Draw a bath*, наполни́ть ва́нну. **6,** (attract) привлека́ть; обраща́ть на себя́. *Draw someone's attention to*, обраща́ть чьё-нибудь внима́ние на. **7,** (elicit) вызыва́ть: *draw enemy fire*, вызыва́ть ого́нь проти́вника. *Draw criticism*, подверга́ться кри́тике. **8,** (sketch) рисова́ть: *draw a picture*, рисова́ть карти́ну. *Draw a line*, проводи́ть ли́-

нию *or* черту́. *Draw a map,* черти́ть ка́рту. **9,** (get or receive by chance) *rendered by* выпада́ть (+ *dat.*): *he drew a tough assignment,* ему́ вы́пало тру́дное зада́ние. **10,** (get or pick at random) тяну́ть: *draw lots,* тяну́ть жре́бий. **11,** (derive as a conclusion) де́лать (вы́вод). **12,** (make, as a comparison) проводи́ть (сравне́ние). **13,** (earn, as a salary, interest, etc.) зараба́тывать. *Draw a good salary,* хорошо́ зараба́тывать. **14,** (issue, as a check) выпи́сывать. **15,** (inhale) вдыха́ть: *draw fresh air into one's lungs,* вдыха́ть све́жий во́здух. *Draw a breath,* передохну́ть. **16,** *naut.* име́ть оса́дку в: *the ship draws 15 feet,* парохо́д име́ет оса́дку в пятна́дцать фу́тов. —*v.i.* **1,** (sketch) рисова́ть. **2,** (move in a certain direction): *draw near,* приближа́ться; *draw to a close,* подходи́ть к концу́. **3,** (draw lots) тяну́ть жре́бий. *Draw for partners,* выбира́ть партнёров по жре́бию. **4,** (play to a tie) сыгра́ть вничью́; сде́лать ничью́. **5,** (take in air) тяну́ть: *the chimney isn't drawing,* труба́ не тя́нет. —*n.* **1,** (act of pulling, attracting, etc.) тя́га. **2,** (tie) ничья́. —**draw aside,** отводи́ть в сто́рону. *Draw aside the curtain,* отдёрнуть занаве́ску. —**draw back, 1,** (pull back) отдёргивать. **2,** (step back) отпря́нуть. —**draw in,** втя́гивать. —**draw off, 1,** (siphon off) отводи́ть. **2,** *mil.* отводи́ть; оття́гивать (войска́). —**draw out,** выта́гивать. —**draw up, 1,** (compose; draft) составля́ть; разраба́тывать. **2,** *fol. by* **to** (pull up to) подъезжа́ть (к).

drawback *n.* недоста́ток.

drawbridge *n.* подъёмный мост; разводно́й мост.

draw curtain раздвижно́й за́навес.

drawer *n.* **1,** (sliding box) я́щик. *Chest of drawers,* комо́д. **2,** *comm.* трасса́нт. **3,** *pl.* (undergarment) кальсо́ны.

drawing *n.* **1,** (art) рисова́ние; черче́ние. *Mechanical drawing,* механи́ческое черче́ние. **2,** (picture) рису́нок. **3,** (sketch; design) чертёж. **4,** (selection of tickets in a lottery) ро́зыгрыш.

drawing board чертёжная доска́.

drawing pin *Brit.* (thumbtack) кно́пка.

drawing room 1, (living room) гости́ная. **2,** (private compartment on a train) купе́.

drawl *n.* протя́жное произноше́ние. —*v.i.* говори́ть врастя́жку; растя́гивать слова́.

drawn *adj.* **1,** (haggard) изможде́нный. **2,** (tied, as of a game) ничейный.

dray *n.* ломова́я теле́га. —**dray horse,** ломова́я ло́шадь. —**drayman,** *n.* ломово́й изво́зчик.

dread *v.t.* боя́ться; страши́ться. —*n.* страх; боя́знь. —*adj.* стра́шный; гро́зный.

dreadful *adj.* стра́шный; ужа́сный.

dreadnought *n.* дредно́ут.

dream *n.* **1,** (thoughts while asleep) сон; сновиде́ние. *Bad dream,* дурно́й сон. *I had a dream,* я ви́дел(а) сон. *Walk around in a dream,* ходи́ть, как во сне. **2,** (cherished hope) мечта́; грёза. —*v.i.* **1,** (have a dream; have dreams) ви́деть *or* сни́ться сон/сны. *Am I dreaming?,* это мне сни́тся? *I dreamt about you,* вы мне сни́лись; я вас ви́дел(а) во сне. **2,** *fol. by* **of** (envision, as in a dream) мечта́ть: *dream of a trip abroad,* мечта́ть о пое́здке за грани́цу. *Dream of becoming an actress,* мечта́ть стать актри́сой. **3,** *fol. by* **of** (consider doing) сни́ться: *I never even dreamt of it,* это мне да́же и не сни́лось. *I wouldn't dream of it!,* и не поду́маю!; об э́том не мо́жет быть и ре́чи. —*v.t.* сни́ться: *I dreamt that...,* мне сни́лось, что... *I never dreamt that...,* мне не приходи́ло в го́лову, что...

—**dream up, 1,** (devise) приду́мывать. **2,** (concoct) выду́мывать.

dreamer *n.* мечта́тель.

dreamland *n.* **1,** (sleep) сон. **2,** = **dreamworld.**

dreamworld *n.* мир грёз; ца́рство грёз.

dreamy *adj.* мечта́тельный.

dreary *adj.* мра́чный; па́смурный; хму́рый. —**dreariness,** *n.* мра́чность.

dredge *n.* дра́га. —*v.t.* очища́ть (дно реки́).

dregs *n.pl.* **1,** (residue) подо́нки; гу́ща. **2,** *fig.* (worst portion) подо́нки: *the dregs of society,* подо́нки о́бщества.

drench *v.t.* прома́чивать; выма́чивать. *Get drenched,* промока́ть; вымока́ть.

dress *n.* **1,** (woman's garment) пла́тье. **2,** (apparel) оде́жда; пла́тье. —*adj.* **1,** (for a dress): *dress fabric,* мате́рия на пла́тье. **2,** *mil.* пара́дный: *dress uniform,* пара́дная фо́рма. —*v.t.* **1,** (clothe) одева́ть. *Get dressed,* одева́ться. **2,** (adorn) украша́ть; убира́ть. **3,** (bandage) перевя́зывать. **4,** (prepare for cooking) чи́стить; разде́лывать; свежева́ть. **5,** *mil.* выра́внивать. —*v.i.* **1,** (put on one's clothes) одева́ться. **2,** (come into alignment) равня́ться: *dress right!,* напра́во - равня́йся! —**dress down,** *colloq.* дать наго́няй *or* взбу́чку (+ *dat.*). —**dress up,** наряжа́ться; приоде́ться. *Dress up as,* переодева́ться (+ *instr.*).

dress circle бельэта́ж.

dresser *n.* **1,** (one who dresses in a certain way): *she is a good dresser,* она́ хорошо́ одева́ется. **2,** (chest of drawers) комо́д.

dressing *n.* **1,** (act of clothing) одева́ние. **2,** (bandage) перевя́зка. **3,** (sauce) припра́ва. **4,** (stuffing) начи́нка; фарш. —**dressing gown,** хала́т. —**dressing room,** *n.* **1,** (of an actor or performer) убо́рная. **2,** (in a gymnasium, public bath, etc.) раздева́льня. **3,** (for trying on clothes) приме́рочная. —**dressing table,** туале́тный сто́лик; туале́т.

dressing-down *n.* наго́няй; взбу́чка.

dressmaker *n.* портни́ха.

dress rehearsal генера́льная репети́ция.

drib *n., in* **in dribs and drabs,** че́рез час по ча́йной ло́жке.

dribble *v.i.* **1,** (drip) ка́пать. **2,** (drool) пуска́ть слю́ни. —*v.t. & i., basketball* вести́ (мяч).

dried *adj.* суше́ный; сухо́й.

drier *n.* = **dryer.**

drift *n.* **1,** *naut.; aero.* дрейф; снос. **2,** (snowdrift) зано́с; сугро́б. **3,** (meaning) смысл: *get the drift of the conversation,* улови́ть смысл разгово́ра. —*v.i.* **1,** (move with the current) плыть; дрейфова́ть. *Drift downstream,* плыть вниз по тече́нию. **2,** (move aimlessly) идти́ самотёком. *Let things drift,* пусти́ть де́ло на самотёк. *Drift from place to place,* переходи́ть с ме́ста на ме́сто. *We drifted apart,* на́ши пути́ разошли́сь. **3,** (stray) отклоня́ться: *drift off course,* отклоня́ться от ку́рса. **4,** (pile up, as of snow) намета́ть; нава́ливать (*both impers.*).

drifter *n.* бродя́га.

driftwood *n.* плавни́к.

drill *n.* **1,** (tool for making holes) сверло́; дрель. **2,** (dentist's drill) бормаши́на. **3,** (training exercise) трениро́вка. **4,** *mil.* строева́я подгото́вка; муштра́; муштро́вка. —*v.t.* **1,** (make, as a hole) пробива́ть; просве́рливать (отве́рстие). **2,** (make a hole in) сверли́ть; просве́рливать. **3,** (bore, as rock) бури́ть. **4,** (teach; train) обуча́ть; тренирова́ть. **5,** *mil.* муштрова́ть. —*v.i.* **1,** (practice) упражня́ться; трениро-

ваться. **2**, *mil.* проводить строевую подготовку.
drillmaster *n.* инструктор строевой подготовки.
drink *v.t. & i.* пить. *Drink to someone's health*, пить за чьё-нибудь здоровье. *Would you like something to drink?*, хотите что-нибудь выпить? —*n.* напиток: *food and drinks*, еда и напитки. *Would you like a drink of water?*, хотите воды? —**drink in**, впитывать. —**take to drink**, спиваться.
drinkable *adj.* годный для питья.
drinker *n.* пьющий.
drinking *n.* питьё. —*adj.* питьевой: *drinking water*, питьевая вода. —**drinking bout**, запой; попойка. —**drinking companion**, собутыльник. —**drinking fountain**, фонтанчик. —**drinking song**, застольная песня.
drip *v.i.* **1**, (of a liquid) капать: *water was dripping from the faucet*, вода капала из крана. *His hands were dripping with blood*, кровь стекала с его рук. **2**, (of a candle) оплывать; отекать. —*v.t.* капать (+ *instr.*). —*n.* капанье.
dripping *adj.* капающий: *dripping faucet*, капающий кран. —*adv.*, *in* **dripping wet**, мокрый, хоть выжми. —*n.*, *usu. pl.* вытекший сок.
drive *v.t.* **1**, (propel) двигать: *steam drives the mechanism*, пар движет механизм. **2**, (operate, as a car) вести; водить (машину); управлять; править (машиной). **3**, (transport in a vehicle) отвозить: *drive someone to the airport*, отвозить кого-нибудь в аэропорт. **4**, (lead; herd, as cattle) гнать. **5**, (force; chase; press) загонять: *drive into a corner*, загонять в угол. *Drive the invaders from the country*, прогонять захватчиков из страны. **6**, (hammer) вбивать; забивать: *drive a nail into a wall*, вбивать/забивать гвоздь в стену. *Drive a wedge between*, вбивать клин между. **7**, (bring to a certain state) доводить (до): *drive to despair*, доводить до отчаяния. *Drive mad*, сводить с ума. —*v.i.* **1**, (go in a vehicle) ехать (на машине). **2**, (operate a vehicle) вести/водить машину; править/ управлять машиной. **3**, *fol. by* **at** (mean; intend) гнуть; клонить: *what are you driving at?*, куда ты гнёшь?; к чему ты клонишь? —*n.* **1**, (ride in a car) езда; прогулка. *A two-hour drive*, два часа езды. *Go for a drive*, ездить на прогулку; кататься на машине; прокатиться; проехаться. *Take for a drive*, катать; прокатить. **2**, (street; avenue) улица; проспект. **3**, (campaign) поход: *economy drive*, поход за экономию. **4**, (energy; ambition) энергия. *Sexual drive*, половое влечение. **5**, *mech.* передача; привод. —**drive away**, **1**, (repel) прогонять; отгонять. **2**, (depart in a vehicle) укатить; (of a vehicle) укатиться. —**drive back**, оттеснять. —**drive home**, **1**, *literally* отвозить домой. **2**, (make someone understand) внушать. —**drive off**, = **drive away**. —**drive out**, **1**, (chase out; expel) выгонять. **2**, (exit in a vehicle) выезжать. —**drive up to**, подъезжать к.
drivel *v.i.* **1**, (drool) пускать слюни. **2**, (talk foolishly) пороть чушь; нести вздор. —*n.* **1**, (saliva) слюни. **2**, (foolish talk) чушь; вздор. —**driveling**, *adj.* слюнявый.
driver *n.* **1**, (of a car or truck) водитель; шофёр. **2**, (of a carriage) кучер; извозчик. **3**, (of cattle) погонщик; гуртовщик. —**driver's license**, водительские права.
drive shaft приводной вал.
driveway *n.* подъезд (к дому).

driving *n.* вождение. —*adj.* **1**, *mech.* приводной: *driving wheel*, приводное колесо. **2**, (violent, as of rain) проливной.
drizzle *n.* изморось. —*v.i.* моросить: *it is drizzling*, моросит.
droll *adj.* забавный. —**drollery**, *n.* шутки; юмор.
dromedary *n.* дромадёр.
drone *n.* **1**, (hum) гул. **2**, (bee; *also fig.* idler) трутень. —*v.i.* **1**, (hum) гудеть; жужжать. **2**, *fol. by* **on** (speak in a monotonous tone) бубнить; дудеть.
drool *v.i.* пускать слюни.
droop *v.i.* свисать; отвисать; обвисать; поникать; никнуть.
drop *n.* **1**, (liquid globule) капля: *drop of water*, капля воды. *Not touch a drop*, капли в рот не брать. **2**, *pl.* (liquid medicine) капли: *eye drops*, глазные капли. *Cough drops*, таблетки от кашля. **3**, *pl.* (small pieces of candy) драже. **4**, (fall; decrease) падение; понижение. —*v.t.* **1**, (accidentally let drop) ронять: *you dropped your comb*, вы уронили гребень. **2**, (deposit) опускать: *drop a letter in the mailbox*, опускать письмо в почтовый ящик. *Drop one's ballot in the box*, опускать бюллетень в избирательную урну. **3**, (let fall from an airplane) сбрасывать: *drop bombs*, сбрасывать бомбы. *Drop by parachute*, сбрасывать на парашюте. **4**, (let off, as from a conveyance) высаживать. **5**, (omit; delete) исключать; опускать. **6**, (give up; abandon) бросить. *Drop the subject*, оставить тему. **7**, (send, as a note) присылать; черкнуть: *drop me a line*, пришлите мне весточку; черкните мне несколько строк. **8**, *colloq.* (utter casually) обронить. *Drop a hint*, сделать намёк. **9**, *in* **drop anchor**, бросить якорь. **10**, *in* **drop a stitch**, спустить петлю. —*v.i.* **1**, (fall) падать. *Drop out of one's hands*, выпасть из рук. *Be ready to drop*, валиться с ног от усталости. *You could have heard a pin drop*, слышно было, как муха пролетит. **2**, (decline) падать; снижаться; пойти вниз. —**at the drop of a hat**, по малейшему поводу. —**drop back**, отступать. —**drop by/in/over**, заходить. —**drop in the bucket**, капля в море. —**drop off**, **1**, (let off, as from a vehicle) высаживать. **2**, (fall asleep) засыпать. **3**, (decrease) падать; снижаться. —**drop out**, **1**, (fall from) выпадать (из). **2**, (withdraw) выходить; выбывать; отсеиваться. **3**, *Drop out of sight*, выпасть из поля зрения.
droplet *n.* капелька.
dropout *n.* тот, кто отсеялся из школы. *Dropout rate*, процент отсева.
dropper *n.* капельница; пипетка.
droppings *n.pl.* помёт.
dropsy *n.* водянка.
droshky *n.* дрожки.
dross *n.* окалина.
drought *n.* засуха.
drove *n.* стадо; гурт. —**in droves**, толпами.
drover *n.* гуртовщик; погонщик.
drown *v.i.* тонуть. *Drowning man*, утопающий. —*v.t.* **1**, (cause to drown) топить. *Drown oneself*, (у)топиться. *Drown one's sorrows in drink*, топить горе в вине. **2**, *fol. by* **out** (muffle, as sound) заглушать; глушить; подавлять; покрывать. —**drowning**, *n.* утопление.
drowse *v.i.* дремать.
drowsy *adj.* сонный; сонливый; дремотный. *I feel*

drowsy, меня клонит ко сну. —**drowsiness,** *n.* сонливость; дремота; забытьё.

drub *v.t.* **1,** (beat) дубасить. **2,** (defeat) разбивать.

drubbing *n.* **1,** (beating) побои. **2,** (defeat) разгром.

drudgery *n.* кропотливая работа.

drug *n.* **1,** (medication) лекарство; медикамент. **2,** (narcotic) наркотик. —*v.t.* накачать наркотиками. —**drug addict,** наркоман.

druggist *n.* аптекарь.

drugstore *n.* аптека.

drum *n.* барабан. —*v.i.* **1,** (beat a drum) бить в барабан. **2,** (tap) барабанить пальцами (*e.g.* по столу). —*v.t.* **1,** *fol. by* **into** (instill) вдалбливать. **2,** *fol. by* **out** (expel) изгонять.

drumbeat *n.* барабанный бой.

drummer *n.* барабанщик.

drumstick *n.* **1,** (stick for beating a drum) барабанная палочка. **2,** (leg of a fowl) ножка.

drunk *adj. & n.* пьяный. *Get drunk,* напиться; опьянеть.

drunkard *n.* пьяница.

drunken *adj.* пьяный; *in a drunken state,* в пьяном виде. *Drunken revelry,* пьяный кутёж. —**drunkenness,** *n.* пьянство.

dry *adj.* сухой. *Dry land,* суша. —*v.t.* **1,** (make dry) сушить; осушать. **2,** (wipe) вытирать: *dry the dishes,* вытирать посуду. *Dry one's eyes,* осушать глаза. —*v.i.* сохнуть; сушиться. —**dry up; run dry,** высыхать; иссыхать; пересыхать; иссякать.

dry cleaning химическая чистка; химчистка.

dry dock сухой док.

dryer *also,* **drier** *n.* сушилка. *Hair dryer,* фен.

dry goods галантерея.

dry ice сухой лёд.

dryly *adv.* сухо.

dry measure мера сыпучих тел.

dryness *n.* сухость.

dry run испытательный пробег.

dual *adj.* **1,** (double) двойной; двоякий; двойственный. *Dual purpose,* двоякая цель. **2,** (joint) совместный. —**dualism,** *n.* дуализм. —**dualistic,** *adj.* дуалистический. —**duality,** *n.* двойственность.

dub *v.t.* **1,** (knight) посвящать (в рыцари). **2,** (nickname) прозывать; окрестить. **3,** *motion pictures* дублировать.

dubious *adj.* **1,** (doubtful): *be dubious,* сомневаться. **2,** (of doubtful worth) сомнительный: *a dubious honor,* сомнительная честь.

ducal *adj.* герцогский.

ducat *n.* **1,** (old coin) дукат. **2,** *slang* (ticket) билет.

duchess *n.* герцогиня.

duchy *n.* герцогство. *Grand duchy,* великое княжество.

duck *n.* утка. —*adj.* [*also,* **duck's**] утиный: *duck feathers,* утиные перья. —*v.t.* **1,** (immerse) окунать. **2,** (dodge) увернуться от. —*v.i.* **1,** (so as to avoid a blow) нырнуть. **2,** (in order to pass under something) нагнуть голову. **3,** *fol. by* **out** (leave suddenly) улизнуть. —**like water off a duck's back,** как с гуся вода.

duckbill *n.* утконос.

duckling *n.* утёнок. —**ugly duckling,** гадкий утёнок.

duckweed *n.* ряска.

duct *n.* проток; канал. *Bile duct,* жёлчный проток.

ductile *adj.* ковкий; тягучий.

ductless gland железа внутренней секреции.

due *adj.* **1,** (owed; payable) следуемый: *the amount due me,* следуемая мне сумма. *Five rubles are due you,* вам причитается пять рублей. *The bill is/falls due on May 1,* счёт подлежит уплате первого мая. **2,** (proper) должный: *with due regard for,* с должным вниманием к. *With all due respect to,* при всём (моём) уважении к. *Give credit where it is due,* отдавать должное. **3,** (expected) должен: *he is due here at noon,* он должен прийти в полдень. —*adv.* прямо на: *due north,* прямо на север. —*n.* **1,** (that which one deserves) должное: *give someone his due,* отдать должное (+ *dat.*). **2,** *pl.* (fee) взносы: *membership dues,* членские взносы. —**due to,** по: *due to illness,* по болезни. *Due to circumstances beyond our control,* по не зависящим от нас обстоятельствам. *Death was due to asphyxiation,* смерть была вызвана удушением. —**in due course; in due time,** своевременно; в своё время.

duel *n.* дуэль; поединок. —*v.i.* драться на дуэли. —**duelist,** *n.* дуэлист.

duet *n.* дуэт.

dugout *n.* **1,** (boat) челнок. **2,** (shelter) землянка; *mil.* блиндаж.

duke *n.* герцог. *Grand duke,* великий князь. —**dukedom,** *n.* герцогство.

dulcet *adj.* сладкий; благозвучный; мелодичный.

dulcimer *n.* цимбалы.

dull *adj.* **1,** (blunt) тупой. **2,** (not bright; not shiny) тусклый. **3,** (gloomy; cloudy) мрачный; пасмурный. **4,** (boring) скучный. **5,** (mentally slow; obtuse) тупой. **6,** (not distinct, as of a sound) глухой; тупой. **7,** (not acute, as of pain) тупой. —*v.t.* **1,** (make less sharp) тупить; притуплять. **2,** (cloud, as the senses) мутить; притуплять. —*v.i.* тупиться.

dullard *n.* тупица.

dullness *n.* тупость.

duly *adv.* **1,** (properly) должным образом; надлежащим образом. **2,** (at the proper time) своевременно.

dumb *adj.* **1,** (mute) немой. **2,** (of animals) бессловесный. **3,** *colloq.* (stupid) глупый.

dumbbell *n.* **1,** (weight for exercise) гиря; гантель. **2,** *slang* (dolt) болван; глупец.

dumfound *also,* **dumbfound** *v.t.* ошарашивать.

dummy *n.* **1,** (mannequin) манекен. **2,** *printing* макет. **3,** *cards* болван. **4,** *slang* (dolt) болван; тупица. —*adj.* ложный; фальшивый.

dump *v.t.* **1,** (drop heavily) валить; сваливать. **2,** (throw out) выбрасывать; вываливать. **3,** *comm.* выбрасывать: *dump goods on the market,* выбрасывать товар на рынок. *Dump shares of stock,* сбрасывать акции. —*n.* **1,** (field for rubbish) свалка. **2,** *mil.* (storage place) склад: *ammunition dump,* склад боеприпасов. —**in the dumps,** в унынии.

dumpling *n.* клёцка; галушка.

dump truck самосвал.

dunce *n.* глупец; тупица. —**dunce cap,** дурацкий колпак.

dunderhead *n.* олух; остолоп; растяпа.

dune *n.* дюна; песчаный холм.

dung *n.* помёт; навоз.

dungarees *n.pl.* рабочие брюки.

dung beetle навозный жук; навозник.

dungeon *n.* темни́ца.

dunghill *n.* наво́зная ку́ча.

dunk *v.t.* **1,** (immerse) погружа́ть; окуна́ть. **2,** (dip, as a doughnut) мака́ть.

duo *n.* па́ра; дуэ́т.

duodenal *adj.* двенадцатипе́рстный. —**duodenum,** *n.* двенадцатипе́рстная кишка́.

dupe *n.* проста́к. —*v.t.* надува́ть; наставля́ть нос (+ *dat.*).

duplex *adj.* двойно́й. —*n.* **1,** (house) двухкварти́рный дом. **2,** (apartment) двухэта́жная кварти́ра.

duplicate *n.* дублика́т; дубле́т; ко́пия. *In duplicate,* в двух экземпля́рах. —*adj.* дуплика́тный. —*v.t.* дубли́ровать. —**duplication,** *n.* дубли́рование. —**duplicator,** *n.* копирова́льная маши́на.

duplicity *n.* двули́чие; двули́чность.

durable *adj.* про́чный. —**durability,** *n.* про́чность.

duralumin *n.* дюралюми́ний.

duration *n.* продолжи́тельность; дли́тельность. *For the duration of,* на вре́мя (+ *gen.*). *Of short duration,* непродолжи́тельный; недолгове́чный.

duress *n.* принужде́ние. *Under duress,* по принужде́нию.

during *prep.* во вре́мя (+ *gen.*); за (+ *acc.*); в тече́ние (+ *gen.*). *During the war/lesson,* во вре́мя войны́/уро́ка. *During that time,* за э́то вре́мя. *During the last year,* за после́дний год. *During the winter,* в тече́ние зимы́. *I'm home during the day,* днём я до́ма. *It rained during the night,* но́чью шел дождь. *During the last two weeks,* в тече́ние после́дних двух неде́ль.

durum *n.* твёрдая пшени́ца. *Also,* **durum wheat.**

dusk *n.* су́мерки. *From dawn till dusk,* от зари́ до зари́.

dust *n.* **1,** (tiny bits, as of earth) пыль. **2,** (mortal remains) прах. —*v.t.* **1,** (wipe the dust from) стира́ть пыль с. **2,** (sprinkle with a powdery substance) опы́ливать: *dust crops,* опы́ливать посе́вы. —*v.i.* стира́ть пыль. —**bite the dust,** упа́сть. —**shake the dust from one's feet,** отрясти́ прах от свои́х ног. —**throw dust in someone's eyes,** втира́ть очки́ (+ *dat.*); пуска́ть пыль в глаза́ (+ *dat.*).

dustbin *n., Brit.* му́сорный я́щик.

duster *n.* **1,** (cloth for dusting) пы́льная тря́пка. **2,** (protective smock) пы́льник.

dust jacket суперобло́жка.

dustman *n., Brit.* му́сорщик.

dustpan *n.* сово́к (для му́сора).

dust storm пы́льная бу́ря.

dusty *adj.* пы́льный.

Dutch *adj.* голла́ндский. —*n.* **1,** (language) голла́ндский язы́к. **2,** *preceded by* **the** (people) голла́ндцы. —**Dutchman,** *n.* голла́ндец.

duteous *adj.* послу́шный. *Also,* **dutiful.**

duty *n.* **1,** (obligation) долг; обя́занность. **2,** *pl.* (work required) обя́занности. **3,** (service; watch) дежу́рство; слу́жба. *Be on duty,* дежу́рить. *Guard duty,* карау́льная слу́жба. **4,** (tariff) по́шлина: *pay duty,* (у)плати́ть по́шлину. —*adj.* дежу́рный: *duty officer,* дежу́рный офице́р. *Duty roster,* расписа́ние дежу́рств. —**in line of duty,** при исполне́нии служе́бных обя́занностей.

duty-free *adj.* беспо́шлинный.

dwarf *n.* ка́рлик. —**dwarfish,** *adj.* ка́рликовый.

dwell *v.i.* **1,** (reside) жить. **2,** *fol. by* **on** (linger) остана́вливаться: *dwell on a subject,* остана́вливаться на вопро́се. —**dweller,** *n.* жи́тель; обита́тель. —**dwelling,** *n.* жили́ще.

dwindle *v.i.* уменьша́ться; истоща́ться.

dye *n.* кра́ска; краси́тель. —*v.t.* кра́сить.

dyed *adj.* кра́шеный. —**dyed-in-the-wool,** *adj.* твердоло́бый.

dyeing *n.* кра́шение. —**dyer,** *n.* краси́льщик.

dyestuff *n.* кра́сящее вещество́.

dye works краси́льня.

dying *n.* умира́ние. —*adj.* **1,** (about to die) умира́ющий. **2,** (uttered just before death) предсме́ртный. —**till one's dying day,** до са́мой сме́рти.

dynamic *adj.* динами́ческий. —**dynamics,** *n.* дина́мика. —**dynamism,** *n.* динами́зм.

dynamite *n.* динами́т. —*adj.* динами́тный. —*v.t.* взрыва́ть динами́том.

dynamo *n.* дина́мо.

dynamometer *n.* динамо́метр; сило́мер.

dynasty *n.* дина́стия. —**dynastic,** *adj.* династи́ческий.

dyne *n., physics* ди́на.

dysentery *n.* дизентери́я.

dyspepsia *n.* диспепси́я.

dysprosium *n.* диспро́зий.

dystrophy *n.* дистрофи́я.

E

E, e пя́тая бу́ква англи́йского алфави́та. —*n.* (musical note) ми.

each *adj. & pron.* ка́ждый: *each participant*, ка́ждый уча́стник. *Each of them*, ка́ждый из них. *To each his own*, ка́ждому своё. —*adv.* (apiece) за шту́ку: *ten cents each*, де́сять це́нтов за шту́ку. *They received five rubles each*, ка́ждый получи́л по пять рубле́й. —**each other**, друг дру́га: *love each other*, люби́ть друг дру́га. *Write to each other*, писа́ть друг дру́гу. *They resemble each other*, они́ похо́жи друг на дру́га. ♦ *Also with the refl. verb: see each other*, ви́деться; *scratch each other*, цара́паться.

eager *adj.* **1,** (ardent) усе́рдный: *eager pupil*, усе́рдный учени́к. *Eager fans*, стра́стные боле́льщики. **2,** *fol. by* **for** (earnestly seeking; impatiently awaiting) жа́ждущий (+ *gen.*): *eager for fame*, жа́ждущий сла́вы. **3,** (anxious): *I am eager to see him*, мне о́чень хо́чется уви́деть его́. *I am eager to begin*, мне не те́рпится нача́ть.

eagerly *adv.* жа́дно; с жа́дностью; с нетерпе́нием.

eagerness *n.* пыл; рве́ние; задо́р.

eagle *n.* орёл. *Bald eagle*, орла́н. *Golden eagle*, бе́ркут. —*adj.* орли́ный: *eagle eye*, орли́ный взгляд. —**eagle owl**, фи́лин.

eaglet *n.* орлёнок.

ear *n.* **1,** (organ of hearing) у́хо. *Whisper in someone's ear*, говори́ть на́ ухо (+ *dat.*). **2,** (sense of hearing) слух: *ear for music*, музыка́льный слух. *Play by ear*, игра́ть по слу́ху. **3,** (of corn) поча́ток. **4,** (of wheat, oats, etc.) ко́лос. —*adj.* ушно́й: *ear drops*, ушны́е ка́пли. —**be all ears**, во все у́ши слу́шать; превраща́ться в слух; быть весь (вся) внима́ние. —**in one ear and out the other**, в одно́ у́хо вошло́, в друго́е вы́шло. —**up to one's ears**, по́ уши (в рабо́те, в долга́х, *etc.*).

earache *n.* боль в у́хе; ушна́я боль.

eardrum *n.* бараба́нная перепо́нка.

earflap *n.* нау́шник.

earl *n.* граф.

early *adj.* ра́нний: *in early autumn*, ра́нней о́сенью. *Since early childhood*, с ра́ннего де́тства. *It is still early*, ещё ра́но. *He is an early riser*, он ра́но встаёт. *In the early 1960s*, в нача́ле шестидеся́тых годо́в. *He is in his early forties*, ему́ лет со́рок с небольши́м. *Early release from prison*, досро́чное освобожде́ние из тюрьмы́. —*adv.* ра́но: *go to bed early*, ложи́ться ра́но. —**early bird**, ра́нняя пта́шка.

earmark *v.t.* предназнача́ть; выделя́ть.

earmuff *n.* нау́шник.

earn *v.t.* **1,** (receive in payment for labor) зараба́тывать. *Earn a living*, зараба́тывать на жизнь. *Earned income*, трудовы́е дохо́ды. **2,** (gain; deserve) заслужи́ть: *earn the right*, заслужи́ть пра́во.

earnest *adj.* **1,** (intent in purpose) серьёзный; добросо́вестный; испра́вный. **2,** (marked by deep feeling) и́скренний. —**in earnest, 1,** (not joking) всерьёз. *Are you in earnest?*, вы э́то всерьёз? **2,** (with determination) вплотну́ю.

earnings *n.pl.* **1,** (wages) за́работок. **2,** (profit) вы́ручка.

earphone *n.* нау́шник.

earring *n.* серьга́.

earshot *n.* преде́л слы́шимости: *within earshot*, в преде́лах слы́шимости.

earth *n.* **1,** *often cap.* (the planet) Земля́: *revolve around the earth*, враща́ться вокру́г Земли́. *The earth's axis/crust*, земна́я ось/кора́. **2,** (land; ground; this world) земля́: *fall to earth*, упа́сть на зе́млю. *Peace on earth*, мир на земле́. —**on earth**, *rendered variously in Russian: why on earth did he say that?*, почему́ же он э́то сказа́л? *Why on earth should I do that?*, с како́й ста́ти мне сде́лать э́то? *How on earth did you find out?*, как вы смогли́ узна́ть э́то?

earthen *adj.* **1,** (made of earth) земляно́й. **2,** (made of baked clay) гли́няный.

earthenware *n.* гли́няная посу́да; гонча́рные изде́лия. —*adj.* гли́няный.

earthly *adj.* **1,** (worldly) земно́й. **2,** (possible; conceivable) *of no earthly use*, соверше́нно бесполе́зный. *For no earthly reason*, безо вся́кой причи́ны.

earthquake *n.* землетрясе́ние.

earthwork *n.* **1,** *usu. pl.* (embankment; fortification) земляно́е укрепле́ние. **2,** (excavation) земляны́е рабо́ты.

earthworm *n.* земляно́й червь.

earthy *adj.* **1,** (of or like earth) земли́стый. **2,** (hearty; spicy) солёный.

ear trumpet слухова́я тру́бка; слухово́й рожо́к.

earwax *n.* ушна́я се́ра.

ease *n.* **1,** (freedom from pain, worry, or trouble) поко́й. *A life of ease*, споко́йная жизнь; приво́льная жизнь. **2,** (facility) лёгкость: *with ease*, с лёгкостью. —*v.t.* **1,** (facilitate; alleviate) облегча́ть. **2,** (move slowly and carefully) (осторо́жно) подвига́ть. **3,** *fol. by* **out** (oust gently) вытесня́ть. —*v.i.* смягча́ться; успока́иваться. —**at ease, 1,** (relaxed) споко́йный. *Set someone's mind at ease*, успока́ивать кого́-нибудь. *My mind is at ease*, у меня́ на душе́ споко́йно.

Feel ill at ease, чувствовать себя неловко. **2,** *mil.* вольно. *At ease!,* вольно!

easel *n.* мольберт.

easily *adv.* **1,** (with ease) легко; без труда. **2,** (beyond question) несомненно; бесспорно. **3,** (very possibly) вполне вероятно: *you may easily be right,* вполне вероятно, что вы правы.

east *n.* восток. *The East,* Восток. —*adj.* восточный: *east wind,* восточный ветер. —*adv.* на восток; к востоку. *East of,* к востоку от; восточнее (+ *gen.*).

Easter *n.* пасха. —*adj.* пасхальный.

easterly *adj.* восточный.

eastern *adj.* восточный. —**easternmost,** *adj.* самый восточный.

eastward *adv.* к востоку. —*adj.* восточный.

easy *adj.* лёгкий: *easy lesson/test/way,* лёгкий урок/экзамен/способ. —**be on easy street,** жить в достатке *or* в довольстве. —**come easy to,** даваться легко (+ *dat.*). —**easier said than done,** легче сказать, чем сделать. —**easy come, easy go,** как нажито, так и прожито. —**take it easy, 1,** (remain calm) не волноваться. **2,** (not hurry) не торопиться. **3,** (relax; rest) отдыхать.

easy chair кресло.

easygoing *adj.* **1,** (good-natured) уживчивый. **2,** (leisurely) неторопливый.

eat *v.t. & i.* есть; кушать. *Have you already eaten?,* вы уже поели? *I do not eat meat,* я не ем мяса. —**eat away,** разъедать; изъедать. —**eat into,** въедаться в; изъедать. —**eat one's heart out,** изводиться. —**eat one's words,** брать назад свои слова. —**eat out,** обедать вне дома. —**eat up,** съесть; пожирать. —**what's eating you?,** какая муха вас укусила?

eatable *adj.* съедобный.

eater *n.* едок.

eau de Cologne одеколон.

eaves *n.* стреха.

eavesdrop *v.i.* подслушивать.

ebb *n.* отлив. *Ebb and flow,* прилив и отлив. —*v.i.* убывать; угасать. —**ebb tide,** отлив.

ebonite *n.* эбонит.

ebony *n.* чёрное дерево; эбеновое дерево. —*adj.* эбеновый.

ebullient *adj.* кипучий.

eccentric *adj.* **1,** (odd) эксцентричный. **2,** *math.* эксцентрический. —*n.* чудак; оригинал.

eccentricity *n.* **1,** (eccentric nature) эксцентричность. **2,** (peculiarity; quirk) странность.

ecclesiastic *adj.* церковный; духовный. *Also,* **ecclesiastical.**

echelon *n.* **1,** (step-like formation) эшелон; ступенчатое расположение. **2,** (section of a military force) эшелон: *rear echelon,* второй *or* тыловой эшелон. **3,** (level of authority) инстанция; звено.

echidna *n.* ехидна.

echo *n.* эхо; отзвук; отголосок. —*v.i.* откликаться *or* отдаваться эхом. —*v.t.* вторить.

éclair *n.* эклер.

eclectic *adj.* эклектический; эклектичный. —*n.* эклектик. —**eclecticism,** *n.* эклектизм.

eclipse *n.* затмение. —*v.t.* затмевать.

ecliptic *n.* эклиптика.

ecology *n.* экология. —**ecological,** *adj.* экологический.

economic *adj.* экономический.

economical *adj.* **1,** (thrifty) экономный. **2,** (efficient; avoiding waste) экономичный.

economics *n.* экономика. —**economist,** *n.* экономист.

economize *v.i.* экономить; соблюдать экономию.

economy *n.* **1,** (thrift) экономия; экономность; бережливость. **2,** (economic system or condition) экономика; хозяйство.

ecstasy *n.* восторг; экстаз. —**ecstatic,** *adj.* восторженный; экстатический. *She was ecstatic,* она была в восторге.

ectoplasm *n.* эктоплазма.

ecumenical *adj.* вселенский. —**ecumenical council,** вселенский собор.

eczema *n.* экзема.

eddy *n.* водоворот.

edelweiss *n.* эдельвейс.

edema *n., med.* отёк.

Eden *n.* Эдем.

edge *n.* **1,** (border; brink) край: *edge of a table/cliff/city,* край стола/обрыва/города. *Edge of a forest,* опушка. *At the water's edge,* на самом берегу; у самой воды. **2,** (cutting part of a blade) остриё. **3,** *colloq.* (advantage) преимущество; перевес. —*v.t.* **1,** (trim) окаймлять. **2,** *Edge one's way,* пробираться; протискиваться. —*v.i.* подвигаться: *edge forward,* подвигаться вперёд. —**on edge,** в нервном состоянии. —**take the edge off,** притуплять.

edgewise *adv.* боком; бочком. —**get a word in edgewise,** ввернуть словечко.

edging *n.* кайма; кант; бордюр; обшивка; оторочка; выпушка.

edgy *adj.* нервный; раздражительный.

edible *adj.* съедобный. —**edibles,** *n.pl.* съестное.

edict *n.* указ.

edification *n.* назидание: *for the edification of,* в назидание (+ *dat.*).

edifice *n.* здание; сооружение.

edify *v.t.* поучать; просвещать. —**edifying,** *adj.* поучительный; назидательный.

edit *v.t.* редактировать. *Edit a film,* монтировать фильм.

edition *n.* **1,** (of a book) издание. **2,** (of a newspaper) выпуск: *the morning edition,* утренний выпуск.

editor *n.* редактор. *Editor's note,* "от редакции." *Letter to the editor,* письмо в редакцию. —**editor in chief,** главный редактор.

editorial *adj.* редакционный; редакторский. *Editorial board,* редакционная коллегия. —*n.* редакционная статья.

educate *v.t.* воспитывать. —**educated,** *adj.* образованный.

education *n.* образование; просвещение.

educational *adj.* **1,** (pert. to education) образовательный; воспитательный. **2,** (providing instruction) учебный: *educational film,* учебный фильм; *educational institution,* учебное заведение. **3,** (instructive) поучительный.

educator *n.* воспитатель; педагог.

eel *n.* угорь.

eerie *adj.* таинственный; призрачный; жуткий.

efface *v.t.* **1,** (erase) стирать. **2,** (blot out; obliterate) изглаживать.

effect *n.* **1,** (result) следствие: *cause and effect,* причина и следствие. **2,** (influence) влияние; действие; воздействие. *Have an effect (on),* оказывать влияние/(воз)действие (на); (по)действовать (на); возыметь действие. *Have a harmful effect on,* вредно действовать на. *The medicine has taken effect,* лекарство подействовало. **3,** (force) сила; действие: *go into effect,* вступать в силу/действие. *Put a law into effect,* вводить закон в действие. **4,** (impression purposely produced) эффект: *done for effect,* рассчитанный на эффект. *Sound effects,* шумовые эффекты. **5,** (meaning) смысл. *To the effect that,* о том, что. *Something to that effect,* что-то в этом духе. **6,** (specific scientific phenomenon) эффект: *Doppler effect,* эффект Доплера. **7,** *pl.* (belongings) имущество; пожитки. *Personal effects,* личные вещи. —*v.t.* производить; совершать; осуществлять. —**in effect, 1,** (in force) в силе. **2,** (in essence) фактически; по существу.

effective *adj.* **1,** (producing the desired result) действенный; эффективный. **2,** (in force) действующий; в силе. *Become effective,* вступать в силу.

effectively *adv.* **1,** (in an effective manner) эффективно. **2,** (in effect) фактически.

effectiveness *n.* действенность; эффективность.

effectual *adj.* эффективный; действенный.

effectuate *v.t.* совершать; осуществлять.

effeminate *adj.* женоподобный.

effervesce *v.i.* **1,** (give off bubbles of gas) шипеть. **2,** *fig.* (show exhilaration) кипеть.

effervescence *n.* **1,** (bubbling state) шипучесть. **2,** (vivacity) кипучесть.

effervescent *adj.* **1,** (sparkling) игристый; шипучий. **2,** (exuberant) кипучий.

effete *adj.* **1,** (exhausted) истощённый. **2,** (barren) бесплодный.

efficacious *adj.* действенный; эффективный. —**efficacy,** *n.* действенность; эффективность.

efficiency *n.* эффективность.

efficient *adj.* **1,** (systematic; not wasteful) эффективный. **2,** (competent; thorough) дельный; аккуратный; расторопный; исполнительный. —**efficiently,** *adv.* эффективно; аккуратно.

effigy *n.* чучело. —**burn/hang in effigy,** сжечь/повесить чучело (кого-нибудь).

effort *n.* усилие: *without effort,* без усилия; без усилий. *Make an effort to,* делать усилия для. *Make every effort,* прилагать все усилия.

effortless *adj.* сделанный без усилий; гладкий. —**effortlessly,** *adv.* без усилий; играючи.

effrontery *n.* наглость; нахальство.

effulgent *adj.* лучезарный.

effusion *n.* излияние.

effusive *adj.* экспансивный.

egalitarian *adj.* уравнительный; эгалитарный.

egg *n.* яйцо. —*adj.* яичный: *egg yoke,* яичный желток. —*v.t.* [*usu.* **egg on**] подстрекать; подбивать; науськивать. —**put all one's eggs in one basket,** поставить всё на одну карту.

egghead *n., slang* интеллигент.

eggplant *n.* баклажан.

eggshell *n.* яичная скорлупа.

egg white белок.

ego *n.* **1,** (the self) личность. **2,** (conceit) самомнение. **3,** (self-esteem) самолюбие.

egoism *n.* эгоизм; себялюбие. —**egoist,** *n.* эгоист. —**egoistic,** *adj.* эгоистический.

egotism *n.* эготизм. —**egotist,** *n.* эгоист. —**egotistical,** *adj.* эгоистический; эгоистичный.

egregious *adj.* вопиющий.

egress *n.* выход.

egret *n.* белая цапля.

Egyptian *adj.* египетский. —*n.* египтянин. —**Egyptian vulture,** стервятник.

Egyptology *n.* египтология. —**Egyptologist,** *n.* египтолог.

eider *n.* гага. —*adj.* гагачий. —**eiderdown,** *n.* гагачий пух.

eight *adj.* восемь. —*n.* **1,** (cardinal number) восемь. **2,** *cards* восьмёрка. —**figure (of) eight,** восьмёрка.

eighteen *n. & adj.* восемнадцать. —**eighteenth,** *adj.* восемнадцатый.

eighth *adj.* восьмой. —*n.* **1,** (eighth part) восьмая часть. **2,** (fraction) восьмая: *one-eighth,* одна восьмая.

eight hundred восемьсот. —**eight-hundredth,** *adj.* восьмисотый.

eighty *n. & adj.* восемьдесят. —**eightieth,** *adj.* восьмидесятый.

einsteinium *n.* эйнштейний.

either *adj.* **1,** (one or the other of two) любой: *in either case,* в любом случае. **2,** (each of two; one and the other) оба: *on either side of the street,* по обеим сторонам улицы. —*pron.* **1,** (either one) любой; и тот и другой. **2,** (neither one) ни тот ни другой: *I don't like either one,* мне не нравится ни тот ни другой. —*adv.* тоже: *I don't know either,* я тоже не знаю. —**either...or,** или...или.

ejaculate *v.t.* извергать. —**ejaculation,** *n.* семяизлияние.

eject *v.t.* **1,** (emit; discharge) выбрасывать; извергать. **2,** (expel; evict) исключать; выгонять.

ejection *n.* **1,** (discharging) выбрасывание. **2,** (expulsion) исключение. —**ejection seat,** катапульта.

eke *v.t.* [*usu.* **eke out**] *Eke out a living,* перебиваться кое-как. *Eke out a narrow victory,* с трудом вырвать победу.

elaborate *adj.* **1,** (worked out carefully and thoroughly) тщательно разработанный. **2,** (intricate; ornate) замысловатый; затейливый. **3,** (lavish; plush) пышный; роскошный. —*v.t.* разрабатывать. —*v.i.* вдаваться в подробности. *Elaborate on a subject,* развивать тему.

elaboration *n.* уточнение: *require no further elaboration,* не требовать уточнения.

eland *n.* оленебык.

elapse *v.i.* **1,** (pass) проходить; протекать. **2,** (expire) истекать.

elastic *adj.* **1,** (resilient) упругий; эластичный. **2,** (flexible; adaptable) гибкий. —*n.* резинка; ластик.

elasticity *n.* **1,** (resiliency) упругость; эластичность. **2,** (flexibility) гибкость.

elate *v.t.* очень обрадовать. —**elated,** *adj.* обрадованный. —**elation,** *n.* восторг; ликование.

elbow *n.* локоть. —*v.t.* толкать локтем. *Elbow one's way,* проталкиваться. —**at one's elbow,** под рукой. —**rub elbows with,** якшаться с.

elbowroom *n.* простор.

elder *adj.* старший. —*n.* **1,** (elder person; senior member) старший. **2,** (shrub) бузина.

elderberry *n.* я́года бузины́.

elderly *adj.* пожило́й.

eldest *adj.* ста́рший.

elicit *v.t.* **1,** (draw out; obtain) выявля́ть: *elicit the facts,* выявля́ть фа́кты. *Elicit information,* выве́дывать информа́цию. **2,** (evoke) вызыва́ть: *elicit applause,* вызыва́ть аплодисме́нты. *Elicit no reply,* не принести́ отве́та.
бо́рная кампа́ния.

elective *adj.* **1,** (chosen by election) вы́борный: *elective office,* вы́борная до́лжность. **2,** (optional) факультати́вный.

elector *n.* вы́борщик. —**electoral,** *adj.* избира́тельный. —**electorate,** *n.* избира́тели.

electric *adj.* электри́ческий. *Electric power,* электроэне́ргия. *Electric shock,* уда́р электри́ческим то́ком. *Electric train,* электропо́езд.

electrical *adj.* электри́ческий. —**electrical engineer,** инжене́р-эле́ктрик; электроте́хник. —**electrical engineering,** электроте́хника.

electric chair электри́ческий стул.

electric eye фотоэлеме́нт.

electrician *n.* (электро)монтёр; эле́ктрик.

electricity *n.* электри́чество.

electrification *n.* электрифика́ция.

electrify *v.t.* **1,** (charge with electricity) электризова́ть. **2,** (provide with electric power) электрифици́ровать. **3,** *fig.* (charge with excitement) электризова́ть.

electrocardiogram *n.* электрокардиогра́мма. —**electrocardiograph,** *n.* электрокардио́граф.

electrocute *v.t.* **1,** (execute) казни́ть на электри́ческом сту́ле. **2,** (kill accidentally by electricity) убива́ть электри́ческим то́ком.

electrocution *n.* казнь на электри́ческом сту́ле.

electrode *n.* электро́д.

electrolysis *n.* электро́лиз.

electrolyte *n.* электроли́т.

electromagnet *n.* электромагни́т. —**electromagnetic,** *adj.* электромагни́тный. —**electromagnetism,** *n.* электромагнети́зм.

electron *n.* электро́н. —*adj.* электро́нный: *electron microscope,* электро́нный микроско́п.

electronic *adj.* электро́нный. —**electronically,** *adv.* с по́мощью электро́нной аппарату́ры.

electronics *n.* электро́ника.

electrostatics *n.* электроста́тика. —**electrostatic,** *adj.* электростати́ческий.

elegance *n.* элега́нтность; изя́щество.

elegant *adj.* элега́нтный; изя́щный. —**elegantly,** *adv.* элега́нтно; изя́щно.

elegiac *adj.* элеги́ческий. —**elegiacs,** *n.pl.* элеги́ческие стихи́.

elegy *n.* эле́гия.

element *n.* **1,** (in most meanings) элеме́нт: *chemical element,* хими́ческий элеме́нт. *Consist of a number of elements,* состоя́ть из ря́да элеме́нтов. *The criminal element,* престу́пный элеме́нт. *The element of surprise,* внеза́пность. **2,** (customary environment) стихи́я: *be in one's element,* быть в свое́й стихи́и. **3,** (trace) до́ля: *element of truth,* до́ля и́стины. *Element of doubt,* тень сомне́ния. **4,** *pl.* (fundamentals) осно́вы; элеме́нты. **5,** *pl.* (weather conditions) стихи́и: *withstand the elements,* противостоя́ть стихи́ям.

elemental *adj.* стихи́йный: *elemental force,* стихи́йная си́ла.

elementary *adj.* **1,** (fundamental) элемента́рный. **2,** (pert. to the first years of schooling) нача́льный: *elementary school,* нача́льная шко́ла.

elephant *n.* слон.

elephantiasis *n.* слоно́вая боле́знь; слоно́вость.

elephant seal морско́й слон.

elevate *v.t.* поднима́ть; повыша́ть; возвыша́ть.

elevated *adj.* **1,** (raised, as of a railroad) надзе́мный. **2,** *fig.* (lofty) возвы́шенный; припо́днятый.

elevation *n.* **1,** (act of elevating) подня́тие. **2,** (height; altitude) высота́. **3,** (raised area) возвы́шенность.

elevator *n.* лифт. *Grain elevator,* элева́тор. —**elevator operator,** лифтёр; лифтёрша.

eleven *n. & adj.* оди́ннадцать. —**eleventh,** *adj.* оди́ннадцатый.

elf *n.* эльф.

elicit *v.t.* **1,** (draw out; obtain) выявля́ть: *elicit the facts,* выявля́ть фа́кты. *Elicit information,* выве́дывать информа́цию. **2,** (evoke) вызыва́ть: *elicit applause,* вызыва́ть аплодисме́нты. *Elicit no reply,* не принести́ отве́та.

eligibility *n.* пра́во: *eligibility for a position,* пра́во на заня́тие до́лжности.

eligible *adj.* **1,** (qualified) име́ющий пра́во. **2,** (desirable for marriage) вы́годный: *eligible bachelor,* вы́годный жени́х.

eliminate *v.t.* **1,** (get rid of) устраня́ть. **2,** (rule out, as a possibility) исключа́ть. **3,** *sports* выводи́ть. *Be eliminated,* выбыва́ть. **4,** *physiol.* (excrete) выделя́ть.

elimination *n.* **1,** (getting rid of) устране́ние. **2,** *physiol.* (secretion) выделе́ние. —**process of elimination,** ме́тод исключе́ния.

elite *n.* эли́та. *Social elite,* сли́вки *or* цвет о́бщества.

elixir *n.* эликси́р.

elk *n.* лось.

ellipse *n.* э́ллипс.

ellipsis *n.* э́ллипсис; э́ллипс.

ellipsoid *n.* эллипсо́ид.

elliptical *adj.* эллипти́ческий.

elm *n.* вяз; ильм.

elocution *n.* ора́торское иску́сство.

elongate *v.t.* удлиня́ть. —**elongated,** *adj.* удлинённый; продолгова́тый.

elope *v.i.* бежа́ть (с возлю́бленным).

eloquence *n.* красноре́чие. —**eloquent,** *adj.* красноречи́вый.

else *adj.* **1,** (different) друго́й: *something else,* что́-то друго́е; *someone else,* кто́-то друго́й; *no one else,* никто́ друго́й. *Everything else,* всё остально́е. *Everyone else,* все други́е; все остальны́е. **2,** (additional) ещё: *what else do you need?,* что ещё вам ну́жно? ♦ *With negatives* бо́льше: *nothing else,* бо́льше ничего́. *Nothing else happened,* ничего́ бо́льше не случи́лось. *No one else knows about it,* никто́ бо́льше об э́том не зна́ет. *There was no one else there,* никого́ бо́льше не́ было там. —*adv.* ещё: *where else did you go?,* куда́ ещё вы е́здили? *Somewhere else,* где́-то в друго́м ме́сте. *Nowhere else in the world,* бо́льше нигде́ в ми́ре. —**or else,** а то; а не то; ина́че. —**someone else's,** чужо́й.

elsewhere *adv.* (где́-нибудь) в друго́м ме́сте; (куда́-нибудь) в друго́е ме́сто.

elucidate *v.t.* разъясня́ть; освеща́ть. —**elucidation,** *n.* разъясне́ние; освеще́ние.

elude *v.t.* избега́ть; уве́ртываться от; ускольза́ть от.

elusive *adj.* неуловимый. —**elusiveness,** *n.* неуловимость.

emaciate *v.t.* истощать. —**emaciated,** *adj.* истощённый; изможденный; исхудалый; тощий.

emanate *v.i.* **1,** (of heat, light, etc.) излучаться. **2,** (originate) исходить; истекать.

emanation *n.* эманация.

emancipate *v.t.* освобождать; эмансипировать; раскрепощать. —**emancipation,** *n.* освобождение; эмансипация; раскрепощение. —**emancipator,** *n.* освободитель; эмансипатор.

emasculate *v.t.* выхолащивать (*lit. & fig.*).

embalm *v.t.* бальзамировать. —**embalmer,** *n.* бальзамировщик.

embankment *n.* **1,** (to hold back water) набережная. **2,** (to support a roadway) насыпь.

embargo *n.* эмбарго.

embark *v.i.* **1,** (go aboard a vessel) садиться на корабль. **2,** *fol. by* **on** *or* **upon** (start out on) начинать; пускаться в. —**embarkation,** *n.* посадка (на корабль).

embarrass *v.t.* смущать. *Be embarrassed,* смущаться. —**embarrassment,** *n.* смущение.

embassy *n.* посольство.

embed *v.t.* **1,** (implant firmly) вделывать. **2,** (fix, as in one's memory) врезать; запечатлевать (в памяти).

embellish *v.t.* **1,** (beautify) украшать. **2,** (embroider; exaggerate) приукрашивать; прикрашивать.

embellishment *n.* **1,** (decoration) украшение. **2,** (fictitious details) прикрасы.

ember *n.* тлеющий уголь. *Live embers,* горячие угли.

embezzle *v.t.* растрачивать. —**embezzlement,** *n.* растрата. —**embezzler,** *n.* растратчик.

embitter *v.t.* озлоблять; ожесточать.

emblem *n.* эмблема. —**emblematic,** *adj.* эмблематический.

embody *v.t.* воплощать; олицетворять. —**embodiment,** *n.* воплощение; олицетворение.

embolism *n.* эмболия; закупорка.

emboss *v.t.* **1,** (cover with raised figures, as a surface) украшать *or* лепить (что-нибудь) рельефом. **2,** (raise upon a surface, as a design) чеканить; гофрировать.

embossed *adj.* **1,** (of a surface) рельефный. **2,** (of a design) тиснёный. —**embossing,** *n.* тиснение.

embrace *v.t.* **1,** (hug) обнимать. **2,** (include; encompass) охватывать. **3,** (take up; adopt) принимать. —*v.i.* обниматься. —*n.* объятие.

embrasure *n.* **1,** (opening for a door or window) проём. **2,** (opening through which a gun may be fired) амбразура; бойница.

embroider *v.t.* **1,** (decorate with needlework) вышивать. **2,** *fig.* (embellish, as a story) приукрашивать; прикрашивать. —*v.i.* вышивать.

embroidery *n.* **1,** (needlework) вышивание; вышивка. **2,** (embroidered design) вышивка.

embroil *v.t.* впутывать; втягивать.

embryo *n.* зародыш; зачаток; эмбрион.

embryology *n.* эмбриология. —**embryologist,** *n.* эмбриолог.

embryonic *adj.* зародышевый; эмбриональный. *In an embryonic state,* в зачаточном состоянии.

emerald *n.* изумруд. —*adj.* изумрудный.

emerge *v.i.* **1,** (come out) выходить. **2,** (come into being) возникать. **3,** (come to light) всплывать; выплывать. —**emergence,** *n.* выход; возникновение.

emergency *n.* крайняя необходимость. *In case of emergency,* в случае крайней необходимости. *State of emergency,* чрезвычайное положение. —*adj.* **1,** (used in an emergency) аварийный: *emergency brake/signal,* аварийный тормоз/сигнал. *Emergency exit,* запасный выход. **2,** (occurring or invoked in an emergency) чрезвычайный: *emergency meeting,* чрезвычайное собрание. *Emergency powers,* чрезвычайные полномочия. *Emergency landing,* вынужденная *or* аварийная посадка.

emeritus *adj.* в отставке. *Professor emeritus,* заслуженный профессор в отставке.

emery *n.* наждак. —*adj.* наждачный.

emetic *adj.* рвотный. —*n.* рвотное; рвотное средство.

emigrant *n.* эмигрант.

emigrate *v.i.* эмигрировать. —**emigration,** *n.* эмиграция.

émigré *n.* эмигрант.

eminence *n.* **1,** (exalted position) знаменитость. **2,** (elevation; hill) возвышенность.

eminent *adj.* выдающийся; знаменитый. —**eminently,** *adv.* весьма; вполне.

emir *n.* эмир. —**emirate,** *n.* эмират.

emissary *n.* эмиссар.

emission *n.* испускание.

emit *v.t.* испускать; издавать.

emotion *n.* чувство; эмоция.

emotional *adj.* **1,** (pert. to the emotions) душевный: *emotional state,* душевное состояние. **2,** (easily aroused to emotion; appealing to emotions) эмоциональный.

empathize *v.i.* [*usu.* **empathize with**] входить в (чьё-нибудь) положение.

empathy *n.* сочувствие; отзывчивость.

emperor *n.* император.

emphasis *n.* ударение; акцент. *Lay/place (the) emphasis on,* делать упор/ударение/акцент на. *Pronounce with emphasis,* произносить подчёркнуто.

emphasize *v.t.* подчёркивать.

emphatic *adj.* решительный; категорический. —**emphatically,** *adv.* решительно; категорически.

emphysema *n.* эмфизема.

empire *n.* империя.

empirical *adj.* эмпирический. —**empiricism,** *n.* эмпиризм. —**empiricist,** *n.* эмпирик.

emplacement *n., mil.* площадка: *machine-gun emplacement,* пулемётная площадка.

employ *v.t.* **1,** (use) использовать; применять. **2,** (hire) нанимать. —*n.* служба: *be in the employ of the government,* быть на государственной службе.

employee *n.* служащий. —**employer,** *n.* наниматель; работодатель.

employment *n.* **1,** (use) использование; применение. **2,** (hiring) наём: *opportunities for employment,* возможности найма. **3,** (work; occupation) работа. **4,** *econ.* занятость: *full employment,* полная занятость.

empower *v.t.* уполномочивать.

empress *n.* императрица.

emptiness *n.* пустота.

empty *adj.* пустой: *empty glass/bus/hall,* пустой стакан/автобус/зал. *Empty seat,* свободное место.

Empty words/promises, пустые слова/обещания. —*v.t.* **1,** (remove the contents of) опоражнивать. **2,** (toss out) выбрасывать: *empty the trash from the wastebasket,* выбрасывать сор из корзины. **3,** *fol. by* **into** (pour into) выливать (в); высыпать (в). —*v.i.* **1,** (become empty) (о)пустеть; опоражниваться. **2,** *fol. by* **into** (flow into, as of a river) впадать (в); нести свои воды (в).

empty-handed *adj.* ни с чем; с пустыми руками.

empty-headed *adj.* пустоголовый.

emu *n.* эму.

emulate *v.t.* равняться по: *emulate one's predecessors,* равняться по своим предшественникам. *Emulate one's father's success,* добиться того же успеха, что и отец.

emulsion *n.* эмульсия.

enable *v.t.* позволять; давать возможность (+ *dat.*).

enact *v.t.* **1,** (make into law) принимать. **2,** (act out) разыгрывать. —**enactment,** *n.* принятие.

enamel *n.* эмаль. —*adj.* эмалевый; эмалированный. —*v.t.* покрывать эмалью; эмалировать. —**enamelware,** *n.* эмалированная посуда.

enamored *also,* **enamoured** *adj.* влюблён. *Be enamored of,* увлекаться (+ *instr.*).

encamp *v.i.* располагаться лагерем.

encampment *n.* **1,** (setting up a camp) расположение лагерем. **2,** (camp; campsite) стоянка.

encase *v.t.* вделывать.

encephalitis *n.* энцефалит.

enchant *v.t.* очаровывать; восхищать; пленять; обвораживать.

enchanted *adj.* **1,** (captivated) зачарованный; очарованный. **2,** (having a seemingly magical quality) заколдованный; зачарованный.

enchanting *adj.* очаровательный; обаятельный; обворожительный; восхитительный. —**enchantment,** *n.* очарование; восхищение; обаяние. —**enchantress,** *n.* чаровница; чародейка.

encipher *v.t.* шифровать.

encircle *v.t.* окружать. —**encirclement,** *n.* окружение.

enclave *n.* анклав.

enclose *v.t.* **1,** (fence in) огораживать; загораживать. **2,** (insert) вкладывать (в конверт); прилагать (к письму). **3,** (place between, as in parentheses) заключать (в скобки).

enclosure *n.* **1,** (act of enclosing) огораживание. **2,** (enclosed area) огороженное место. **3,** (fence) ограда. **4,** (something enclosed with a letter) вложение; приложение.

encode *v.t.* шифровать; кодировать.

encomium *n.* панегирик.

encompass *v.t.* **1,** (encircle) окружать. **2,** (take in; include) охватывать.

encore *interj.* бис. —*n. Give an encore,* исполнить что-нибудь на бис; бисировать.

encounter *n.* **1,** (meeting) встреча. **2,** (contact; clash) столкновение. —*v.t.* встречать; сталкиваться с. *Encounter difficulties,* сталкиваться с трудностями. *Encounter resistance,* встречать сопротивление.

encourage *v.t.* **1,** (hearten) ободрять; подбодрять; обнадёживать. **2,** (stimulate) поощрять. **3,** (help bring about) способствовать. —**encouragement,** *n.* ободрение; поощрение. —**encouraging,** *adj.* ободрительный; поощрительный; обнадёживающий. *Ini-*

tial results are encouraging, первые результаты обнадёживают.

encroach *v.i.* [*usu.* **encroach on** *or* **upon**] посягать (на); покушаться (на). —**encroachment,** *n.* посягательство.

encrust *v.t.* инкрустировать.

encumber *v.t.* **1,** (hinder; hamper) стеснять. **2,** (clutter; obstruct) загромождать.

encumbrance *n.* **1,** (hindrance) препятствие; помеха. **2,** (burden) бремя; обуза.

encyclical *n.* энциклика.

encyclopedia *n.* энциклопедия. —**encyclopedic,** *adj.* энциклопедический. —**encyclopedist,** *n.* энциклопедист.

end *n.* **1,** (extremity; conclusion) конец: *the end of the street,* конец улицы. *Come to an end,* приходить к концу. *Put an end to,* положить конец (+ *dat.*). *To the bitter end,* до самого конца; до последней капли крови. **2,** (goal; purpose) цель: *toward this end,* с этой целью. *The end justifies the means,* цель оправдывает средства. **3,** (death) смерть; кончина: *meet one's end,* найти свою смерть. —*adj.* конечный: *end product,* конечный продукт. *End result,* исход дела. —*v.t.* **1,** (conclude) кончать; заканчивать; заключать. **2,** (halt; put a stop to) прекращать. —*v.i.* кончаться: *all's well that ends well,* всё хорошо, что хорошо кончается. *End in disaster,* кончиться катастрофой. —**at loose ends,** без дела; не у дел. —**be the end of,** сводить в могилу. —**end up,** очутиться. —**in the end,** в конце концов. —**make ends meet,** сводить концы с концами. —**no end of,** отбою нет от; хоть отбавляй. —**on end,** по целым: *for weeks on end,* по целым неделям. —**stand on end, 1,** (set upright) ставить стоймя; ставить на ребро. **2,** (bristle, as of one's hair) вставать *or* становиться дыбом. —**to the ends of the earth,** на край света (*or* земли).

endanger *v.t.* подвергать опасности; ставить под угрозу.

endear *v.t.* сделать дорогим сердцу. *Endear oneself to,* покорять сердце (+ *gen.*). —**endearing,** *adj.* подкупающий; обезоруживающий.

endearment *n.* ласка. —**term of endearment,** ласкательное имя.

endeavor *also,* **endeavour** *v.t.* пытаться; стараться. —*n.* **1,** (attempt) попытка. **2,** (undertaking) предприятие; затея.

endemic *adj.* эндемический.

end game *chess* эндшпиль.

ending *n.* окончание: *verb/chess/nerve endings,* глагольные/шахматные/нервные окончания. *The story has a happy ending,* рассказ имеет счастливый конец.

endless *adj.* бесконечный; нескончаемый. —**endlessly,** *adv.* без конца; бесконечно.

endocrine *adj.* эндокринный. —**endocrine glands,** эндокринные железы; железы внутренней секреции.

endocrinology *n.* эндокринология.

endorse *v.t.* **1,** *finance* индоссировать. **2,** (support, as a candidate) поддерживать кандидатуру (+ *gen.*). **3,** (express one's agreement with) присоединяться к.

endorsement *n.* **1,** (support) поддержка. **2,** (signature on the back of a check) передаточная надпись; индоссамент; жиро.

endow *v.t.* **1,** (provide with funds) обеспе́чивать. **2,** (invest with, as certain qualities) наделя́ть; одаря́ть.

endowment *n.* **1,** (bequest) дар; поже́ртвование. **2,** (natural gift) дарова́ние; одарённость.

endurance *n.* выно́сливость; вы́держка.

endure *v.t.* терпе́ть; выноси́ть; переноси́ть; выдё́рживать. —*v.i.* дли́ться; продолжа́ться. —**enduring,** *adj.* про́чный: *enduring peace,* про́чный мир.

endwise *adv.* **1,** (on end) стоймя́. **2,** (lengthwise) в длину́. **3,** (with the end foremost) концо́м вперёд.

enema *n.* кли́зма.

enemy *n.* враг; неприя́тель; проти́вник. —*adj.* вра́жеский; неприя́тельский.

energetic *adj.* энерги́чный. —**energetically,** *adv.* энерги́чно.

energy *n.* **1,** (general term) эне́ргия. **2,** *pl.* (efforts) си́лы: *direct one's energies to,* направля́ть свои́ си́лы на (+ *acc.*)

enervate *v.t.* обесси́ливать; расслабля́ть.

enfeeble *v.t.* ослабля́ть; обесси́ливать. —**enfeebled,** *adj.* одряхле́вший.

enfold *v.t.* **1,** (surround with a covering) заку́тывать. **2,** (embrace) обнима́ть.

enforce *v.t.* осуществля́ть; проводи́ть в жизнь. —**enforceable,** *adj.* осуществи́мый. —**enforcement,** *n.* осуществле́ние.

enfranchise *v.t.* предоставля́ть избира́тельные права́ (+ *dat.*).

engage *v.t.* **1,** (hire) нанима́ть. **2,** (occupy; absorb) занима́ть; поглоща́ть. *Engage someone in conversation,* занима́ть кого́-нибудь разгово́ром. *Engage someone's attention,* поглоща́ть чьё-нибудь внима́ние. *The work engages much of my time,* рабо́та поглоща́ет у меня́ мно́го вре́мени. **3,** (meet in battle) вступа́ть в бой с. —*v.i.* **1,** *fol. by* in (involve oneself; take part) занима́ться (+ *instr.*). **2,** (mesh) сцепля́ться.

engaged *adj.* **1,** (occupied) за́нятый. *Be engaged in,* быть за́нятым (+ *instr.*); занима́ться (+ *instr.*). **2,** (betrothed) помо́лвленный; обручённый. *Become engaged to,* обруча́ться с.

engagement *n.* **1,** (betrothal) помо́лвка; обруче́ние. **2,** (appointment) свида́ние. **3,** (battle) бой. —*adj.* обруча́льный: *engagement ring,* обруча́льное кольцо́.

engaging *adj.* привлека́тельный; подкупа́ющий.

engender *v.t.* порожда́ть; зарожда́ть.

engine *n.* **1,** (motor) дви́гатель; мото́р; маши́на. **2,** (locomotive) парово́з; локомоти́в. —**engine room,** маши́нное отделе́ние.

engineer *n.* **1,** (one trained in a branch of engineering) инжене́р. **2,** (locomotive operator) машини́ст. —*v.t.* соверша́ть: *engineer an escape,* соверши́ть побе́г. *Engineer a victory,* кова́ть побе́ду.

engineering *n.* инжене́рное де́ло; те́хника.

English *adj.* англи́йский. —*n.* **1,** (language) англи́йский язы́к. *Speak English,* говори́ть по-англи́йски. **2,** *preceded by* the (people) англича́не.

English horn англи́йский рожо́к.

Englishman *n.* англича́нин. —**Englishwoman,** *n.* англича́нка.

engrain *v.* = ingrain.

engrave *v.t.* гравирова́ть. —**engraver,** *n.* гравёр.

engraving *n.* **1,** (art) гравирова́ние; гравиро́вка. **2,** (engraved plate) гравю́ра.

engross *v.t.* поглоща́ть. *Be engrossed in,* быть поглощённым в; углубля́ться в; погружа́ться в. —**engrossing,** *adj.* увлека́тельный; захва́тывающий.

engulf *v.t.* **1,** (of flames, darkness, etc.) охва́тывать. **2,** (of waves, the sea, etc.) поглоща́ть.

enhance *v.t.* увели́чивать; повыша́ть.

enigma *n.* зага́дка. —**enigmatic,** *adj.* зага́дочный.

enjoin *v.t.* **1,** (order; direct) предпи́сывать. **2,** (forbid; prohibit) запреща́ть.

enjoy *v.t.* **1,** (have a good time at): *did you enjoy the play?,* пье́са вам понра́вилась? **2,** (relish; admire) наслажда́ться. **3,** (have, as an advantage, good health, etc.) по́льзоваться; облада́ть. —**enjoy oneself,** хорошо́ проводи́ть вре́мя; получи́ть (большо́е) удово́льствие.

enjoyable *adj.* прия́тный.

enjoyment *n.* **1,** (pleasure) удово́льствие; наслажде́ние. **2,** (possession) облада́ние.

enlarge *v.t.* **1,** (make larger) расширя́ть. **2,** *photog.* увели́чивать. —*v.i.* **1,** (become larger) расширя́ться; увели́чиваться. **2,** *fol. by* upon (treat in greater detail) распространя́ться о.

enlargement *n.* **1,** (act of enlarging) увеличе́ние; расшире́ние. **2,** (enlarged copy) увеличе́ние.

enlarger *n., photog.* увеличи́тель; увеличи́тельный аппара́т.

enlighten *v.t.* **1,** (bring knowledge to) просвеща́ть. **2,** (inform) осведомля́ть. —**enlightened,** *adj.* просвещённый. —**enlightening,** *adj.* поучи́тельный. —**enlightenment,** *n.* просвеще́ние.

enlist *v.i.* (добровольно) поступа́ть (*e.g.* на вое́нную слу́жбу). —*v.t.* **1,** (recruit) вербова́ть. **2,** (secure, as services) заруча́ться. —**enlisted man,** военнослу́жащий рядово́го соста́ва.

enlistment *n.* **1,** (act of enlisting) поступле́ние (на вое́нную слу́жбу). **2,** (term) срок слу́жбы.

enliven *v.t.* оживля́ть.

en masse в ма́ссе.

enmity *n.* вражда́; неприя́знь.

ennoble *v.t.* облагора́живать.

ennui *n.* ску́ка; тоска́.

enormity *n.* **1,** (heinousness) чудо́вищность. **2,** (heinous crime) злодея́ние.

enormous *adj.* огро́мный; грома́дный. —**enormously,** *adv.* в огро́мной сте́пени; чрезвыча́йно.

enough *adj.* доста́точно (+ *gen.*): *enough money,* доста́точно де́нег. *Be enough,* хвата́ть: *that will be enough for today,* э́того хва́тит на сего́дня. *There is enough room for everyone,* на всех хвата́ет ме́ста. —*adv.* **1,** (sufficiently) доста́точно: *old enough to understand,* доста́точно взро́слый, что́бы поня́ть. **2,** (adequately) дово́льно: *he plays well enough,* он игра́ет дово́льно хорошо́. **3,** *in oddly enough,* как ни стра́нно; **sure enough,** *see* sure. —*n.* доста́точно: *I've had enough,* мне уже́ доста́точно. —*interj.* доста́точно!; хва́тит!

en passant 1, (in passing) мимохо́дом. **2,** *chess* на прохо́де.

enrage *v.t.* беси́ть; разъяря́ть; приводи́ть в я́рость. —**enraged,** *adj.* разъярённый. *Become enraged,* приходи́ть в я́рость.

enrapture *v.t.* восхища́ть; восторга́ть.

enrich *v.t.* обогаща́ть. *Enriched uranium,* обогащённый ура́н. —**enrichment,** *n.* обогаще́ние.

enroll *also,* **enrol** *v.t.* запи́сывать; зачисля́ть. —*v.i.* запи́сываться; зачисля́ться.

enrollment *also,* **enrolment** *n.* 1, (act of enrolling) зачисле́ние. 2, (number of students enrolled) число́ уча́щихся.

en route по (*or* в) пути́; по (*or* в) доро́ге.

ensconce *v.t.* устра́ивать. *Ensconce oneself,* устра́иваться; засе́сть.

ensemble *n.* 1, (group) анса́мбль. 2, (attire) наря́д.

enshrine *v.t.* храни́ть; сохраня́ть. *Enshrined in our hearts forever,* наве́чно сохранён в на́ших сердца́х.

enshroud *v.t.* оку́тывать.

ensign *n.* 1, (flag) зна́мя; флаг. 2, (emblem) значо́к; эмбле́ма. 3, (rank) мла́дший лейтена́нт.

enslave *v.t.* порабоща́ть. —**enslavement,** *n.* порабоще́ние. —**enslaver,** *n.* порабо́титель.

ensnare *v.t.* пойма́ть в лову́шку.

ensue *v.i.* 1, (follow) сле́довать. 2, (result) вытека́ть. —**ensuing,** *adj.* после́дующий; вытека́ющий.

ensure *v.t.* обеспе́чивать.

entail *v.t.* влечь за собо́й; быть свя́занным с.

entangle *v.t.* запу́тывать. *Become entangled,* запу́тываться.

enter *v.t.* 1, (go into; come into) входи́ть в: *enter the hall,* входи́ть в зал. *Enter the hospital,* лечь в больни́цу. *Enter one's head,* приходи́ть в го́лову (+ *dat.*). 2, (join; enroll in) вступа́ть в; поступа́ть в. 3, (pierce; penetrate) вонза́ться в; проника́ть в. 4, (begin, as a new era) вступа́ть в. 5, (place, as on a list) вноси́ть; заноси́ть; впи́сывать; зачисля́ть. 6, (place; register, as in school) запи́сывать. 7, (submit formally) заявля́ть: *enter a protest,* заявля́ть проте́ст. —*v.i.* входи́ть. —**enter into,** вступа́ть в; входи́ть в. *Enter into an agreement,* заключа́ть соглаше́ние.

enteritis *n.* энтери́т.

enterprise *n.* 1, (undertaking; business operation) предприя́тие. 2, (economic activity) предпринима́тельство: *private enterprise,* ча́стное предпринима́тельство. 3, (initiative) предприи́мчивость.

enterprising *adj.* предприи́мчивый.

entertain *v.t.* 1, (amuse) развлека́ть; забавля́ть; занима́ть. 2, (extend hospitality to) принима́ть; угоща́ть. 3, (consider) обду́мывать. *Entertain a motion,* принима́ть предложе́ние к рассмотре́нию. 4, (harbor) пита́ть. —*v.i.* принима́ть госте́й.

entertaining *adj.* занима́тельный.

entertainment *n.* 1, (entertaining of guests) приём (госте́й); угоще́ние. 2, (diversion) развлече́ние. 3, (show; performance) варьете́.

enthrall *v.t.* 1, (captivate) увлека́ть; захва́тывать; завлека́ть. 2, *obs.* (enslave) порабоща́ть. —**enthralling,** *adj.* увлека́тельный; захва́тывающий; завлека́тельный.

enthrone *v.t.* возводи́ть на престо́л.

enthusiasm *n.* энтузиа́зм; увлече́ние; воодушевле́ние; подъём. —**enthusiast,** *n.* энтузиа́ст; охо́тник. —**enthusiastic,** *adj.* восто́рженный; по́лный энтузиа́зма.

entice *v.t.* зама́нивать; завлека́ть; прельща́ть.

enticement *n.* 1, (act of enticing) зама́нивание. 2, (that which entices) прима́нка.

enticing *adj.* зама́нчивый; завлека́тельный.

entire *adj.* 1, (whole) це́лый; весь: *an entire day,* це́лый день; *the entire day,* весь день. 2, (complete) по́лный.

entirely *adv.* соверше́нно; совсе́м; вполне́; целико́м; всеце́ло.

entirety *n.* полнота́. *In its entirety,* во всей полноте́; со всей полното́й.

entitle *v.t.* 1, (qualify; authorize) дава́ть пра́во (+ *dat.*). *Be entitled to,* име́ть пра́во на. 2, (name) озагла́вливать. *The book is entitled...,* кни́га называ́ется...

entity *n.* вещь: *separate entities,* ра́зные ве́щи.

entomb *v.t.* погреба́ть.

entomology *n.* энтомоло́гия. —**entomological,** *adj.* энтомологи́ческий. —**entomologist,** *n.* энтомо́лог.

entourage *n.* окруже́ние.

entrails *n.pl.* вну́тренности; требуха́.

entrance[1] (en-trens) *n.* 1, (act of entering) вход. 2, (place to enter) ход. *Back entrance,* чёрный ход. 3, *theat.* вы́ход (на сце́ну). —*adj.* входно́й; вступи́тельный. *Entrance examination,* вступи́тельный экза́мен.

entrance[2] (en-trans) *v.t.* очаро́вывать; завора́живать.

entrant *n.* уча́стник (состяза́ния).

entrap *v.t.* пойма́ть в лову́шку.

entreat *v.t.* умоля́ть; упра́шивать. —**entreaty,** *n.* мольба́.

entrée *n.* 1, (right of entry) пра́во вхо́да. *Have entrée,* быть вхо́жим. 2, (main course) второ́е (блю́до).

entrench *v.t.* 1, (fortify with a trench) ока́пывать. 2, (establish firmly) укореня́ть. *Become entrenched,* укореня́ться.

entrepreneur *n.* предпринима́тель.

entrust *v.t.* доверя́ть; вверя́ть; поруча́ть.

entry *n.* 1, (act of entering) вход. 2, (opening; passage) вход; прохо́д. 3, (notation) за́пись; отме́тка. 4, (item in a reference book) статья́.

entwine *v.t.* 1, (intertwine) вплета́ть; сплета́ть. *Become entwined,* переплета́ться. 2, (twine around) обвива́ть. —*v.i.* [*usu.* **entwine around**] обвива́ться вокру́г.

enumerate *v.t.* перечисля́ть.

enumeration *n.* 1, (act of enumerating) перечисле́ние. 2, (list; catalogue) пе́речень.

enunciate *v.t.* 1, (articulate) выгова́ривать. 2, (state systematically) излага́ть. 3, (announce; proclaim) провозглаша́ть. —*v.i.* произноси́ть.

enunciation *n.* 1, (pronunciation) вы́говор. 2, (formal statement) изложе́ние; провозглаше́ние.

envelop *v.t.* охва́тывать; оку́тывать; обвола́кивать.

envelope *n.* конве́рт.

envelopment *n.* охва́т.

envenom *v.t.* отравля́ть.

enviable *adj.* зави́дный.

envious *adj.* зави́стливый. *Be envious of,* зави́довать (+ *dat.*).

environment *n.* окруже́ние; среда́. *The environment,* окружа́ющая среда́. —**environmental,** *adj.* свя́занный с окружа́ющей средо́й. —**environmentalist,** *n.* сторо́нник охра́ны окружа́ющей среды́.

environs *n.pl.* окре́стности.

envisage *v.t.* предусма́тривать.

envision *v.t.* 1, (picture in the mind) представля́ть. 2, (provide for in the future) предусма́тривать.

envoy *n.* 1, (messenger) посла́нец; по́сланный. 2, (diplomat) посла́нник.

envy *n.* зависть. —*v.t.* завидовать: *I don't envy him,* я не завидую ему.

enzyme *n.* фермент.

eon *n.* вечность.

epaulet *also,* **epaulette** *n.* эполёт; эполёта.

ephemeral *adj.* недолговечный; преходящий; эфемерный.

epic *n.* эпическая поэма; эпопея. —*adj.* эпический.

epicenter *also,* **epicentre** *n.* эпицентр.

epicure *n.* эпикуреец. —**epicurean,** *adj.* эпикурейский.

epidemic *n.* эпидемия. —*adj.* эпидемический.

epidermis *n.* эпидермис.

epiglottis *n.* надгортанник.

epigram *n.* эпиграмма. —**epigrammatic,** *adj.* эпиграмматический.

epigraph *n.* **1,** (inscription) надпись; эпиграф. **2,** (opening quotation) эпиграф.

epilepsy *n.* эпилепсия. —**epileptic,** *adj.* эпилептический. —*n.* эпилептик.

epilogue *n.* эпилог; послесловие.

Epiphany *n.* крещение; богоявление.

episcopal *adj.* епископский.

Episcopalian *adj.* епископальный. —*n.* член епископальной церкви.

episode *n.* эпизод. —**episodic,** *adj.* эпизодический.

epistemology *n.* теория познания.

epistle *n.* эпистола. —**epistolary,** *adj.* эпистолярный.

epitaph *n.* надгробная надпись; эпитафия.

epithelium *n.* эпителий. —**epithelial,** *adj.* эпителиальный.

epithet *n.* **1,** (descriptive word or phrase) эпитет. **2,** (disparaging word or phrase) ругательство. *Hurl epithets at,* осыпать (кого-нибудь) бранью.

epitome *n.* **1,** (perfect example; embodiment) воплощение. **2,** (summary) конспект.

epitomize *v.t.* **1,** (typify) воплощать. **2,** (summarize) конспектировать.

epoch *n.* эпоха. —**epochal,** *adj.* эпохальный.

Epsom salt *also,* **Epsom salts** английская соль.

equable *adj.* **1,** (not fluctuating) ровный; равномерный. **2,** (tranquil; serene) ровный; уравновешенный.

equal *adj.* равный: *equal parts,* равные части. *Equal rights,* равноправие. *In equal measure,* в равной мере. *Other things being equal,* при прочих равных условиях. —*v.t.* **1,** (be equal to) равняться (+ *dat.*): *six plus three equals nine,* шесть плюс три равняется (*or* равно) девяти. *Let x equal y,* пусть икс равен игреку. **2,** (duplicate; tie) повторять: *equal a record,* повторять рекорд. —*n.* равный: *he has no equal,* ему нет равного; он не имеет себе равного. *Treat someone as an equal,* относиться к кому-нибудь как к равному. —**equal to,** на высоте (+ *gen.*): *equal to the occasion,* на высоте положения. *He is not equal to the task,* эта задача ему не под силу.

equality *n.* равенство.

equalize *v.t.* уравнивать. —**equalization,** *n.* уравнение.

equally *adv.* **1,** (in equal parts) поровну. **2,** (uniformly) одинаково; в равной мере; в одинаковой мере. **3,** (by the same token) равным образом.

equal sign знак равенства.

equanimity *n.* спокойствие; самообладание; хладнокровие.

equate *v.t.* равнять; приравнивать.

equation *n.* уравнение.

equator *n.* экватор. —**equatorial,** *adj.* экваториальный.

equestrian *adj.* конный.

equiangular *adj.* равноугольный.

equidistant *adj.* на равном расстоянии.

equilateral *adj.* равносторонний.

equilibrium *n.* равновесие.

equine *adj.* лошадиный.

equinox *n.* равноденствие.

equip *v.t.* оборудовать; снаряжать; оснащать. —**equipment,** *n.* оборудование; снаряжение.

equitable *adj.* справедливый; беспристрастный.

equity *n.* **1,** (fairness) справедливость. **2,** *finance* активы.

equivalent *adj.* равносильный; равнозначный; эквивалентный. —*n.* эквивалент. —**equivalence,** *n.* эквивалентность.

equivocal *adj.* двусмысленный.

equivocate *v.i.* увиливать; вилять. —**equivocation,** *n.* двусмысленность; уклончивость. *Without equivocation,* недвусмысленно.

era *n.* эра; эпоха.

eradicate *v.t.* **1,** (destroy; wipe out) уничтожать: *eradicate pests,* уничтожать вредителей. **2,** *fig.* (eliminate; put an end to) искоренять; уничтожать; ликвидировать. —**eradication,** *n.* искоренение; уничтожение; ликвидация.

erase *v.t.* **1,** (rub out) стирать. *Erase the blackboard,* стирать с доски. **2,** (obliterate, as from one's mind) изглаживать (из памяти).

eraser *n.* **1,** (for something written in pencil) резинка; ластик. **2,** (for blackboards) тряпка.

erasure *n.* подчистка.

erbium *n.* эрбий.

ere *prep., poetic* до; перед. —*conj., poetic* прежде чем.

erect *adj.* стоячий: *erect position,* стоячее положение. *Stand erect,* держаться прямо. *With one's head erect,* с поднятой головой. —*v.t.* (build) сооружать; возводить; воздвигать.

erection *n.* **1,** (construction) сооружение; возведение. **2,** *physiol.* эрекция.

erg *n.* эрг.

ergo *adv.* следовательно.

ergot *n.* спорынья.

ermine *n.* горностай. —*adj.* горностаевый.

erode *v.t.* **1,** (wear away, as of the wind) выветривать. **2,** (wash away, as of water) размывать. **3,** (eat into, as of acid) разъедать. —*v.i.* выветриваться.

erosion *n.* эрозия; выветривание; размыв.

erotic *adj.* эротический. —**eroticism,** *n.* эротизм.

err *v.i.* ошибаться; заблуждаться.

errand *n.* поручение. *Run errands for,* быть у кого-нибудь на посылках *or* на побегушках. —**errand boy,** рассыльный.

errant *adj.* **1,** (wandering) странствующий; блуждающий. **2,** (having gone astray) заблудший; сбившийся с пути.

erratic *adj.* неустойчивый; неровный.

erratum *n.* опечатка.

erroneous *adj.* ошибочный; неверный; ложный. —**erroneously,** *adv.* ошибочно; по ошибке.

error *n.* ошибка. *Be in error*, ошибаться; заблуждаться.

ersatz *adj.* суррогатный.

erstwhile *adj.* прежний.

erudite *adj.* учёный; знающий; эрудированный. —**erudition**, *n.* эрудиция; учёность; начитанность.

erupt *v.i.* **1,** (of a volcano) извергаться. **2,** (of a rash) высыпать; выступать. **3,** *fig.* (of an argument, fight, etc.) вспыхивать.

eruption *n.* **1,** (of a volcano) извержение. **2,** (rash) сыпь.

erysipelas *n.* рожа.

escalate *v.i.* перерастать. —**escalation**, *n.* перерастание; эскалация.

escalator *n.* эскалатор.

escapade *n.* выходка; проделка.

escape *v.i.* **1,** (get free) бежать; убегать. *Escape from prison*, бежать из тюрьмы. **2,** (avoid injury, danger, etc.) спасаться. *He barely escaped*, он едва спасся; он едва ноги унёс. *Escape with minor injuries*, отделаться лёгкими ранениями. **3,** (leak out; seep out) утекать; вытекать. *Gas escaped from the pipe*, газ утекал из трубы. —*v.t.* **1,** (manage to avoid) спасаться от: *escape death*, спасаться от смерти. *There is no escaping the fact that...*, никуда не уйти от того, что... **2,** (be unnoticed or forgotten by) ускользать от: *escape someone's notice*, ускользать от чьего-нибудь внимания. *Nothing escapes him*, от него ничто не укроется. *His name escapes me*, не могу припомнить его имени. **3,** (slip out inadvertently, as from one's lips) срываться (с языка). —*n.* **1,** (breaking out) побег; бегство. **2,** (avoidance of near disaster) спасение: *miraculous escape*, чудесное спасение. *Have a narrow escape*, едва спастись.

escarpment *n.* откос; *mil.* эскарп.

eschew *v.t.* сторониться; чуждаться.

escort *n.* **1,** (one who accompanies) провожатый. **2,** (for a lady) кавалер. **3,** (armed guard) конвоир. *Under police escort*, под конвоем полицейских. **4,** *mil.* (single ship or plane) конвоир; конвойный; (a number of ships or planes) конвой; эскорт. —*v.t.* **1,** (accompany) сопровождать; провожать. **2,** *mil.* конвоировать; эскортировать.

escutcheon *n.* щит герба.

Eskimo *n.* эскимос. —*adj.* эскимосский.

esophagus *also*, **oesophagus** *n.* пищевод.

esoteric *adj.* малодоступный; заумный.

espalier *n.* шпалера.

especial *adj.* особенный; особый.

especially *adv.* **1,** (to a particularly large degree) особенно: *especially pleased*, особенно рад. *What especially struck me*, что меня особенно поразило. **2,** (specifically) специально: *especially for you*, специально для вас. *I came especially to...*, я пришёл специально для того, чтобы... **3,** (the more so) особенно: *especially now/if/when*, особенно теперь/если/когда. *Especially since...*, тем более, что...

Esperanto *n.* эсперанто.

espionage *n.* шпионаж. —*adj.* шпионский: *espionage activity*, шпионская деятельность.

esplanade *n.* эспланада.

espouse *v.t.* выступать за; поддерживать; отстаивать. —**espousal**, *n.* поддержка.

espy *v.t.* рассмотреть; разглядеть.

esquire *n.* эсквайр.

essay *n.* очерк. —*v.t.* **1,** (try out) пробовать. **2,** (attempt) пытаться. —**essayist**, *n.* очеркист.

essence *n.* **1,** (fundamental nature; heart; crux) сущность; существо; суть. **2,** (extract) эссенция. —**in essence**, в сущности; по существу; по сути дела.

essential *adj.* **1,** (absolutely necessary) необходимый. **2,** (fundamental) существенный: *an essential difference*, существенная разница. —*n., usu. pl.* **1,** (necessities) необходимое: *the barest essentials*, самое необходимое. **2,** (heart; crux) суть: *get down to the essentials*, добраться до сути дела. **3,** (fundamentals) основы; элементы.

essentially *adv.* в сущности; по существу.

essential oil эфирное масло.

establish *v.t.* **1,** (found) основывать: *establish a museum/newspaper*, основать музей/газету. **2,** (bring about; set up) устанавливать: *establish order/relations/a dictatorship/*, установить порядок/отношения/диктатуру. **3,** (ascertain; prove) устанавливать: *establish a fact/the cause of something/one's innocence/*, установить факт/причину чего-нибудь/свою невиновность/. —**establish oneself**, устраиваться.

establishment *n.* **1,** (act of establishing) установление; основание. **2,** (institution) учреждение; заведение.

estate *n.* **1,** (piece of landed property) имение; поместье; усадьба. **2,** (possessions of a deceased person) имущество; состояние. **3,** (social class in feudal times) сословие.

esteem *v.t.* **1,** (respect) уважать; ценить. **2,** (regard) deem) считать. —*n.* уважение; почёт. *Hold in high esteem*, высоко ценить. *Be held in high esteem*, пользоваться почётом.

esthete *also*, **aesthete** *n.* эстет. —**esthetic**, *adj.* эстетический. —**esthetics**, *n.* эстетика.

estimable *adj.* достойный уважения; уважаемый; многоуважаемый.

estimate *v.t.* оценивать; исчислять. *Estimate the distance*, определять расстояние глазомером. *Estimated cost*, сметная стоимость. —*n.* оценка; смета.

estimation *n.* мнение; суждение. *Go up in someone's estimation*, выиграть в чьём-нибудь мнении; вырасти в чьих-нибудь глазах. *Go down in someone's estimation*, терять *or* проиграть в чьём-нибудь мнении.

Estonian *adj.* эстонский. —*n.* **1,** (person) эстонец; эстонка. **2,** (language) эстонский язык.

estrange *v.t.* отдалять; отчуждать; разобщать. —**estrangement**, *n.* отдаление; отчуждение.

estuary *n.* лиман.

et cetera и так далее; и тому подобное.

etch *v.t.* гравировать; травить.

etcher *n.* гравёр.

etching *n.* **1,** (process) гравирование; травление. **2,** (figure so made) гравюра; офорт.

eternal *adj.* вечный. —**eternally**, *adv.* вечно.

eternity *n.* вечность. *Seem like an eternity*, казаться вечностью.

ether *n.* эфир. —**ethereal**, *adj.* эфирный.

ethical *adj.* этический; этичный.

ethics *n.pl.* этика.

Ethiopian *adj.* эфиопский. —*n.* эфиоп; эфиопка.

ethnic *adj.* этнический.

ethnography *n.* этнография. —**ethnographer**, *n.*

этнóграф. —**ethnographic,** *adj.* этнографйческий.

ethnology *n.* этнолóгия. —**ethnological,** *adj.* этнологйческий. —**ethnologist,** *n.* этнóлог.

ethyl *n.* этйл. —*adj.* этйловый. —**ethyl alcohol,** этйловый *or* вйнный спирт.

ethylene *n.* этилéн.

etiquette *n.* этикéт.

Etruscan *adj.* этрýсский.

étude *n.* этюд.

etymology *n.* этимолóгия. —**etymological,** *adj.* этимологйческий. —**etymologist,** *n.* этимóлог.

eucalyptus *n.* эвкалйпт. —*adj.* эвкалйптовый.

Eucharist *n.* причáстие; евхарйстия.

eugenics *n.* евгéника. —**eugenic,** *adj.* евгенйческий.

eulogize *v.t.* восхвалять. —**eulogy,** *n.* надгрóбная речь; надгрóбное слóво; панегйрик.

eunuch *n.* éвнух.

euphemism *n.* эвфемйзм. —**euphemistic,** *adj.* эвфемистйческий. —**euphemistically,** *adv.* для прилйчия: *euphemistically called...,* для прилйчия назывáемый...

euphonic *adj.* благозвýчный.

euphonious *adj.* благозвýчный. —**euphoniousness,** *n.* благозвýчность.

euphony *n.* благозвýчие.

euphoria *n.* эйфорйя.

Eurasian *adj.* евразййский.

eureka *interj.* эврика!

European *adj.* европéйский. —*n.* европéец. *The Europeans,* европéйцы.

europium *n.* еврóпий.

Eustachian tube евстáхиева трубá.

evacuate *v.t.* **1,** (remove) эвакуйровать. **2,** (vacate) освобождáть. **3,** (excrete) выделять. —**evacuation,** *n.* эвакуáция. —**evacuee,** *n.* эвакуйрованный.

evade *v.t.* избегáть; уклоняться от; ускользáть от.

evaluate *v.t.* оцéнивать. —**evaluation,** *n.* оцéнка.

evanescent *adj.* мимолётный; минýтный.

evangelical *adj.* евангелйческий.

evangelist *n.* **1,** *cap., Bib.* евангелйст. **2,** (preacher) проповéдник.

evaporate *v.t.* испарять. —*v.i.* испаряться; улетýчиваться. —**evaporated milk,** сгущённое молокó.

evaporation *n.* испарéние.

evasion *n.* **1,** (avoidance) уклонéние: *evasion of military service,* уклонéние от воéнной слýжбы. *Tax evasion,* уклонéние от уплáты налóгов. **2,** (subterfuge) улóвка; увéртка.

evasive *adj.* уклóнчивый. —**evasiveness,** *n.* уклóнчивость.

eve *n.* канýн. *On the eve of,* в канýн (+ *gen.*); наканýне (+ *gen.*). —**Christmas Eve,** сочéльник. —**New Year's Eve,** канýн Нóвого гóда.

even *adj.* **1,** (level) рóвный: *even ground,* рóвная земля. **2,** (uniform) рóвный; равномéрный. **3,** (calm; tranquil) рóвный; уравновéшенный. **4,** *fol. by* **with** (flush with) врóвень с. **5,** (divisible by 2) чётный: *even number,* чётное числó. **6,** (exact) *rendered by* тóчно: *an even dozen,* тóчно дюжина. **7,** (having settled debts, scores, etc.) квйты; в расчёте: *now we are even,* тепéрь мы с вáми квйты/в расчёте/. —*adv.* дáже: *even in winter,* дáже зимóй. *What is even worse...,* что ещё хýже... —*v.t.* **1,** (smooth; level) вырáвнивать; ровнять. **2,** (equalize) равнять.

Even the score, сравнять счёт. —*v.i.* [*usu.* **even out**] вырáвниваться. —**break even,** остáться при свойх. —**even if,** дáже éсли; хотя бы. —**even so,** всё равнó; хоть бы и так. —**even though,** хотя и. —**get even with,** расплáчиваться с; рассчйтываться с; расквитáться с.

even-handed *adj.* беспристрáстный.

evening *n.* вéчер. *In the evening,* вéчером. *This evening,* сегóдня вéчером. *Good evening!,* дóбрый вéчер! —*adj.* вечéрний: *evening dress,* вечéрнее плáтье.

evenly *adv.* рóвно. *Divide evenly,* делйть пóровну. *Evenly matched teams,* равносйльные комáнды.

evenness *n.* рóвность.

event *n.* **1,** (occurrence) событие. **2,** (item on a sports program) нóмер. —**in any event,** во всяком слýчае. —**in the event of,** в слýчае (+ *gen.*). —**in the event that,** в том слýчае, éсли...

even-tempered *adj.* уравновéшенный.

eventful *adj.* пóлный событий.

eventual *adj.* конéчный: *the eventual outcome,* конéчный исхóд.

eventuality *n.* (возмóжный) слýчай; случáйность.

eventually *adv.* в концé концóв.

eventuate *v.i.* **1,** *fol. by* **in** (result in) кóнчиться (+ *instr.*). **2,** (develop; happen) получйться; случйться.

ever *adv.* **1,** (at any time) когдá-нибудь; когдá-либо; *have you ever been there?,* вы когдá-нибудь бывáли там? *The best film I ever saw,* сáмый лýчший фильм, котóрый я когдá-либо вйдел. *More than ever before,* бóльше чем когдá-либо рáньше. ♦ *In neg. constructions* никогдá: *no one has ever been there,* никтó никогдá нé был там. **2,** (at all times) всегдá: *as ever,* как всегдá. —*particle: thank you ever so much!,* большóе вам спасйбо! *What ever do you mean by that?,* что же, сóбственно, вы хотйте этим сказáть? —**ever since,** с тех пор (как). —**hardly ever,** почтй никогдá.

evergreen *adj.* вечнозелёный. —*n.* вечнозелёное растéние.

everlasting *adj.* вéчный.

ever-present *adj.* безотлýчный.

every *adj.* **1,** (each) кáждый: *every day,* кáждый день. **2,** (all possible) все: *have every reason to suppose,* имéть все основáния предполагáть. **3,** (each sequentially) кáждый: *every three hours,* кáждые три часá; *every few minutes,* кáждые нéсколько минýт. —**every now and then; every once in a while; every so often,** врéмя от врéмени. —**every one,** все без исключéния. —**every other,** чéрез; кáждый вторóй; кáждые два: *every other day,* чéрез день. —**every time,** всякий раз. *Every time he speaks,* всякий раз, когдá он говорйт. —**every which way,** *colloq.* врассыпнýю; врозь. —**in every way, 1,** (in every respect) во всех отношéниях. **2,** (using every method) всячески.

everybody *pron.* все.

everyday *adj.* повседнéвный; житéйский; бýдничный. *Everyday occurrence,* обычное явлéние.

everyone *pron.* все.

everything *pron.* всё: *everything is all right,* всё в порядке. *There is a time for everything,* всемý своё врéмя.

everywhere *adv.* вездé; всюду; повсюду. *Every-*

where we went, всюду, куда мы приезжали. *From everywhere,* отовсюду.

evict *v.t.* выселять. —**eviction,** *n.* выселение.

evidence *n.* **1,** (something that tends to prove) свидетельство; доказательство. **2,** (testimony) показание; свидетельство: *give evidence,* давать показания; свидетельствовать. **3,** (incriminating information) улики: *there is no evidence against him,* против него нет никаких улик. —*v.t.* **1,** (indicate) свидетельствовать о. **2,** (evince) проявлять. —**in evidence,** заметный; на виду.

evident *adj.* очевидный. —**evidently,** *adv.* очевидно; по-видимому.

evil *n.* зло: *good and evil,* добро и зло. *Choose the lesser of two evils,* из двух зол выбрать меньшее. —*adj.* злой; дурной: *evil spirit,* злой дух; *evil thoughts,* дурные мысли.

evildoer *n.* злодей.

evil eye дурной глаз.

evince *v.t.* проявлять; выказывать.

eviscerate *v.t.* потрошить.

evoke *v.t.* вызывать.

evolution *n.* эволюция. —**evolutionary,** *adj.* эволюционный.

evolve *v.t.* развивать; разрабатывать. —*v.i.* развиваться; эволюционировать.

ewe *n.* овца.

ex- *prefix* бывший: *ex-president,* бывший президент.

exacerbate *v.t.* обострять. —**exacerbation,** *n.* обострение.

exact *adj.* точный: *exact copy,* точная копия; *exact meaning,* точный смысл. —*v.t.* взыскивать. *Exact payment,* взимать плату. *Exact tribute,* налагать дань.

exacting *adj.* требовательный; взыскательный.

exactitude *n.* точность.

exactly *adv.* **1,** (in an exact manner) точно. **2,** (just) как раз: *exactly what I need,* как раз то, что мне нужно. **3,** (specifically) именно: *where exactly does he live?,* где именно он живёт? **4,** (quite so) вот именно; совершенно верно. —**not exactly,** не совсем; (это) не совсем так.

exactness *n.* точность.

exaggerate *v.t. & i.* преувеличивать. —**exaggeration,** *n.* преувеличение.

exalt *v.t.* **1,** (raise in status) возвышать. **2,** (glorify) возвеличивать. **3,** (extol) восхвалять.

exaltation *n.* восторг; упоение; экзальтация.

exalted *adj.* высокий; возвышенный.

examination *n.* **1,** (scrutiny) осмотр; рассмотрение. *Physical examination,* медицинский осмотр. **2,** (test of knowledge) экзамен. —**examination paper,** экзаменационная работа.

examine *v.t.* **1,** (scrutinize) осматривать; рассматривать. *Examine a patient,* осматривать больного. **2,** (give a test to) экзаменовать.

examiner *n.* **1,** (inspector) контролёр. **2,** (one who gives an examination) экзаменатор.

example *n.* пример. —**for example,** например.

exasperate *v.t.* выводить из себя; изводить; донимать. —**exasperating,** *adj.* досадный. —**exasperation,** *n.* досада; раздражение.

excavate *v.t.* раскапывать. —**excavation,** *n.* раскопка; *pl.* раскопки.

exceed *v.t.* **1,** (be more than; go beyond) превышать:

exceed ten dollars, превышать десять долларов; *exceed the speed limit,* превышать дозволенную скорость. **2,** (surpass) превосходить: *exceed all expectations,* превосходить все ожидания. —**exceedingly,** *adv.* чрезвычайно.

excel *v.t.* превосходить. —*v.i.* выдаваться; выделяться; отличаться.

exellence *n.* высокое качество. *For excellence in studies,* за отличную учёбу.

Excellency *n.* превосходительство: *Your Excellency,* ваше превосходительство.

excellent *adj.* отличный; прекрасный; превосходный. —**excellently,** *adv.* отлично.

excelsior *n.* стружка.

except *prep.* кроме; за исключением (+ *gen.*). *Every day except Sunday,* каждый день, кроме воскресенья. —*conj.* кроме как; разве только: *except in the summertime,* кроме как (*or* разве только) в летнее время. —*v.t.* исключать. *Present company excepted,* исключая присутствующих. —**except for,** за исключением (+ *gen.*); если не считать.

excepting *prep.* исключая; за исключением (+ *gen.*).

exception *n.* исключение. *With the exception of,* за исключением (+ *gen.*). *Make an exception in your case,* делать исключение для вас. —**take exception to, 1,** (take issue with) возражать против. **2,** (take offense at) обижаться на.

exceptional *adj.* исключительный. —**exceptionally,** *adv.* исключительно.

excerpt *n.* выдержка; отрывок; выписка. —*v.t.* выписывать; выбирать (отрывки).

excess *n.* **1,** (surplus) излишек; избыток. **2,** *usu. pl.* (instances of immoderation) излишества; перегибы; эксцессы. —*adj.* лишний: *excess weight,* лишний вес. *Excess profits,* сверхприбыль. *Pay for excess baggage,* доплатить за лишний вес. —**in excess of,** сверх (+ *gen*); свыше (+ *gen.*). —**to excess,** до излишества. *Drink to excess,* перепивать.

excessive *adj.* чрезмерный; непомерный; излишний. —**excessively,** *adv.* чрезмерно.

exchange *v.t.* **1,** (trade for another) менять; обменивать: *exchange one book for another,* менять/обменивать одну книгу на другую. **2,** (interchange) меняться; обмениваться (+ *instr.*): *exchange gifts,* меняться/обмениваться подарками. **3,** (change, as money) разменивать. —*n.* **1,** (swap) обмен: *exchange of views,* обмен мнениями *or* взглядами. *In exchange for,* в обмен на. **2,** (central place for brokers, merchants, etc.) биржа: *stock exchange,* фондовая биржа. **3,** *finance* валюта: *foreign exchange,* иностранная валюта. *Bill of exchange,* вексель. *Rate of exchange,* валютный курс.

exchequer *n.* казначейство; казна.

excise *n.* [*also,* **excise tax**] акциз. —*v.t.* **1,** *med.* вырезать; иссекать. **2,** (delete) исключать; вычёркивать. —**excision,** *n., med.* иссечение.

excitable *adj.* возбудимый. —**excitability,** *n.* возбудимость.

excitation *n.* возбуждение.

excite *v.t.* **1,** (rouse; stir up) возбуждать; волновать. **2,** (evoke) возбуждать; вызывать.

excited *adj.* возбуждённый; взволнованный. *Get excited,* волноваться.

excitement *n.* возбуждёние; волнёние.

exciting *adj.* волнующий; захватывающий.

exclaim *v.t. & i.* восклицать.

exclamation *n.* восклицание. **—exclamation point,** восклицательный знак.

exclamatory *adj.* восклицательный.

exclude *v.t.* исключать. **—excluding,** *prep.* исключая. **—exclusion,** *n.* исключёние.

exclusive *adj.* **1,** (sole) исключительный: *exclusive right,* исключительное право. **2,** (admitting only a select group) для избранных. **—exclusive of,** не считая; исключая.

exclusively *adv.* исключительно.

excommunicate *v.t.* отлучать от цёркви. **—excommunication,** *n.* отлучёние (от цёркви).

excoriate *v.t.* осуждать; разносить.

excrement *n.* испражнёния; кал.

excrescence *n.* нарост; (*on trees*) наплыв.

excrete *v.t.* выделять. **—excretion,** *n.* выделёние. **—excretory,** *adj.* выделительный; выводной.

excruciating *adj.* мучительный.

exculpate *v.t.* оправдывать.

excursion *n.* экскурсия. **—***adj.* экскурсионный.

excusable *adj.* простительный; извинительный.

excuse *v.t.* **1,** (forgive; pardon) прощать. *Excuse me!,* извините!; простите! *Excuse the interruption!,* извините/простите за беспокойство! **2,** (justify; make all right) оправдывать. **3,** (release; let off) освобождать: *excuse from classes,* освобождать от занятий. **—***n.* **1,** (pretext) отговорка; предлог. **2,** (valid reason) извинёние; оправдание. **—excuse oneself,** извиняться; просить прощёния.

execrable *adj.* отвратительный; гнусный.

execrate *v.t.* **1,** (denounce) проклинать. **2,** (detest) ненавидеть.

execute *v.t.* **1,** (carry out; perform) выполнять; исполнять. **2,** (put to death) казнить.

execution *n.* **1,** (carrying out; performance) выполнёние; исполнёние. **2,** (putting to death) казнь.

executioner *n.* палач.

executive *adj.* **1,** (exercising authority) исполнительный: *executive committee,* исполнительный комитёт. **2,** (of an executive) административный: *executive duties,* административные обязанности. **—***n.* руководящий работник.

executor *n.* душеприказчик.

exemplary *adj.* примёрный; образцовый.

exemplify *v.t.* служить примёром (+ *gen.*).

exempt *v.t.* освобождать. **—***adj.* [*usu.* **exempt from**] освобождённый (от); не подлежащий (+ *dat.*).

exemption *n.* **1,** (act of exempting) освобождёние. **2,** (tax deduction) льгота (по налогу).

exercise *n.* **1,** (physical activity) физические упражнёния; зарядка; моцион. *Do one's exercises,* дёлать зарядку. *You should get more exercise,* вам нужно больше физических упражнёний. **2,** (that which develops proficiency) упражнёние: *exercises for the piano,* упражнёния для фортепьяно. **3,** (performance, as of duties) исполнёние; отправлёние. **4,** (act of using or exerting) осуществлёние; применёние. **5,** *pl.* (ceremonies) торжества. *Graduation exercises,* выпускной акт. **6,** *mil.* учёние. **—***v.t.* **1,** (drill; train) упражнять. **2,** (execute; discharge, as duties) исполнять; выполнять. **3,** (use; put into play) осуществлять; применять: *exercise a right,* осущест-

влять право; *exercise authority,* применять власть. **4,** (display, as caution, patience, etc.) проявлять. **5,** (exert, as influence) оказывать. **6,** (worry; upset) расстраивать. **—***v.i.* дёлать моцион; дёлать зарядку.

exert *v.t.* **1,** (strain) напрягать. *Exert oneself,* напрягаться. *Exert every effort,* прилагать все усилия; напрягать все силы. **2,** (exercise; bring to bear) оказывать: *exert pressure,* оказывать давлёние.

exertion *n.* напряжёние.

exhale *v.t. & i.* выдыхать. **—exhalation,** *n.* выдох; выдыхание.

exhaust *v.t.* **1,** (tire out) изнурять; истощать. **2,** (use up; deplete) исчёрпывать; истощать: *exhaust supplies,* исчёрпывать/истощать запасы. *My patience is exhausted,* моё терпёние кончилось *or* лопнуло. **3,** (deal with completely) исчёрпывать: *exhaust a subject,* исчёрпывать тёму. **—***n., mech.* выхлоп. **—***adj.* выхлопной; вытяжной: *exhaust pipe,* выхлопная труба; *exhaust fan,* вытяжной вентилятор.

exhausted *adj.* **1,** (tired out) изнурённый; измученный. *Be exhausted,* замучиться; выбиться из сил; быть без ног. **2,** (depleted) исчёрпанный; истощённый.

exhausting *adj.* утомительный; изнурительный.

exhaustion *n.* **1,** (extreme fatigue) изнурёние; истощёние; изнеможёние. **2,** (depletion) истощёние.

exhaustive *adj.* исчёрпывающий.

exhibit *v.t.* **1,** (put on show) выставлять; экспонировать. **2,** (manifest; give evidence of) проявлять. **—***n.* экспонат.

exhibition *n.* **1,** (display; manifestation) проявлёние. **2,** (public display) выставка: *exhibition of paintings,* выставка картин.

exhibitor *n.* экспонёнт.

exhilarate *v.t.* развеселить; оживлять. **—exhilaration,** *n.* весёлость; приподнятое настроёние.

exhort *v.t.* призывать; увещевать. **—exhortation,** *n.* увещание.

exhume *v.t.* выкапывать; вырывать.

exigency *n.* **1,** (urgency) неотложность. **2,** (urgent situation) (крайний) случай. **3,** *pl.* (requirements) потрёбности.

exile *n.* **1,** (banishment) изгнание; ссылка. **2,** (one who is exiled) изгнанник; ссыльный. **—***v.t.* изгонять; ссылать.

exist *v.i.* существовать.

existence *n.* существование. *Come into existence,* возникать; появляться. *Go out of existence,* перестать существовать. *The best plane in existence,* самый лучший самолёт из всех существующих. *Lead a miserable existence,* влачить жалкое существование.

existent *adj.* существующий.

existential *adj.* экзистенциальный. **—existentialism,** *n.* экзистенциализм. **—existentialist,** *adj.* экзистенциальный. **—***n.* экзистенциалист.

exit *n.* выход. *Exit visa,* выездная виза. **—***v.i.* **1,** (go out) выходить. **2,** (stage direction) "он/она уходит"

exodus *n.* **1,** (outpouring of people) (массовый) отъёзд. **2,** *cap., Bib.* исход; (*book*) Исход.

exonerate *v.t.* оправдывать. **—exoneration,** *n.* оправдание.

exorbitant *adj.* непомёрный.

exorcise also, **exorcize** v.t. изгонять (злых духов). —**exorcism**, n. изгнание злых духов.

exotic adj. экзотический.

expand v.t. 1, (enlarge; extend) расширять. 2, math. разлагать. —v.i. 1, (become larger) расширяться. 2, fol. by on (discuss more fully) распространяться на (тему).

expanse n. пространство; простор; ширь.

expansion n. 1, (enlargement) расширение. 2, (extension of one's territory) экспансия.

expansionism n. экспансионизм. —**expansionist**, adj. экспансионистский; захватнический.

expansive adj. экспансивный.

expatiate v.i. распространяться (о).

expatriate n. экспатриант. —v.t. экспатриировать. —**expatriation**, n. экспатриация.

expect v.t. 1, (anticipate) ожидать; ждать: be expecting company, ожидать or ждать гостей. It was to be expected, этого следовало ожидать. 2, fol. by inf. (plan; intend) думать; предполагать; рассчитывать. 3, (consider due or obligated) требовать: expect too much of, требовать слишком много от. —be expecting, ждать or ожидать ребёнка; быть в положении.

expectancy n. ожидание; предвкушение. —life expectancy, продолжительность жизни.

expectant adj. ожидающий. Expectant mother, беременная женщина.

expectation n. ожидание: contrary to all expectations, вопреки всем ожиданиям.

expectorate v.i. 1, (cough up phlegm) отхаркиваться. 2, (spit) харкать. —v.t. отхаркивать.

expedient adj. целесообразный; выгодный. —**expediency**, n. целесообразность.

expedite v.t. 1, (speed up) ускорять. Expedite a matter, продвинуть дело. 2, (do quickly) (быстро) выполнять.

expedition n. экспедиция. —**expeditionary**, adj. экспедиционный.

expeditious adj. быстрый; скорый.

expel v.t. 1, (discharge; eject) выбрасывать; извергать. Expel air from the lungs, выпускать воздух из лёгких. 2, (dismiss) исключать; выгонять.

expend v.t. тратить; затрачивать; расходовать.

expenditure n. 1, (act of expending) затрата; расходование. 2, (that which is expended) трата; затрата; расход.

expense n. 1, (financial outlay) расход. Go to expense, тратить деньги; тратиться. Put to expense, вводить в расход. At one's own expense, на свой средства. 2, pl. (costs) расходы; издержки; затраты. —at the expense of, за or на счёт (+ gen.): at government expense, за казённый счёт. Jokes at my expense, шутки на мой счёт or по моему адресу.

expensive adj. дорогой.

experience n. 1, (accumulated knowledge) опыт. 2, (something lived through) переживание. —v.t. испытывать; переживать. —**experienced**, adj. опытный.

experiment n. опыт; эксперимент. —v.i. производить опыты; экспериментировать.

experimental adj. экспериментальный; опытный. —**experimentation**, n. экспериментирование.

expert n. эксперт; специалист; знаток. —adj. искусный; опытный. Expert advice, экспертный совет.

expertise n. специальные знания.

expiate v.t. искупать. —**expiation**, n. искупление. —**expiatory**, adj. искупительный.

expiration n. 1, (termination) истечение. 2, (exhalation) выдыхание.

expire v.i. 1, (elapse, as of a time period) истекать. 2, (become invalid) терять силу. 3, (exhale) выдыхать. 4, (breathe one's last) испустить дух.

explain v.t. & i. объяснять. —**explain oneself**, объяснять своё поведение.

explainable adj. объяснимый.

explanation n. объяснение.

explanatory adj. объяснительный; разъяснительный; пояснительный. —**explanatory note**, примечание.

expletive n. 1, (imprecation) бранное слово; ругательство. 2, (word used to fill out a sentence) вставное слово.

explicable adj. объяснимый.

explicit adj. ясный; точный; определённый. —**explicitly**, adv. ясно; недвусмысленно.

explode v.i. взрываться. —v.t. 1, (set off) взрывать. 2, fig. (refute, as a theory) разбивать; уничтожать; опровергать. Explode a myth, развеять миф.

exploit v.t. 1, (capitalize on; take advantage of) использовать; пользоваться. 2, (use selfishly for one's own ends) эксплуатировать. —n. подвиг. —**exploitation**, n. эксплуатация. —**exploiter**, n. эксплуататор.

exploration n. 1, (traveling and studying) исследование. 2, (prospecting) разведка: exploration for oil, разведка нефти; нефтеразведка.

exploratory adj. 1, (involving research or exploration) исследовательский. 2, geol. разведочный. 3, med. пробный: exploratory operation, пробная операция. 4, fig. (sounding out the possibilities) вондирующий.

explore v.t. 1, (travel into and study) исследовать. 2, (look into; investigate) изучать; рассматривать. —v.i. [usu. explore for] разведывать на. —**explorer**, n. исследователь.

explosion n. взрыв. —**population explosion**, демографический взрыв.

explosive adj. 1, (liable to explode) взрывчатый. Explosive bullet, разрывная пуля. 2, fig. (highly volatile) опасный; угрожающий. —n. взрывчатое вещество.

exponent n. 1, (advocate) сторонник; проповедник. 2, math. показатель; экспонент.

export v.t. вывозить; экспортировать. —n., often pl. вывоз; экспорт. —adj. вывозной; экспортный.

exportation n. вывоз.

exporter n. экспортёр.

expose v.t. 1, (bare) раскрывать. 2, (deprive of protection) подставлять. 3, (bring to light; unmask) разоблачать. 4, fol. by to (subject to) подвергать (+ dat.). Be exposed to danger, подвергаться опасности. 5, photog. экспонировать.

exposer n. обличитель; изобличитель.

exposition n. 1, (presentation of subject matter) изложение. 2, (large exhibition) выставка.

expository adj. объяснительный; разъяснительный.

expostulate v.i. [usu. expostulate with] увещевать. —**expostulation**, n. увещание.

exposure n. 1, (act of exposing) раскрытие; разоблаче́ние. **2,** (condition of being exposed): *die from exposure,* поги́бнуть от хо́лода. *Avoid excessive exposure to the sun,* воздержа́ться от чрезме́рного пребыва́ния на со́лнце. **3,** (direction faced): *the room has a southern exposure,* ко́мната выхо́дит на юг. **4,** *photog.* вы́держка; экспози́ция. —**exposure meter,** экспозиме́тр; экспоно́метр.

expound *v.t.* **1,** (set forth) излага́ть. **2,** (interpret) разъясня́ть. —*v.i.* [*usu.* **expound on**] распространя́ться (о).

express *v.t.* выража́ть; выска́зывать. *Express one's opinion,* вы́разить/вы́сказать своё мне́ние. —*adj.* **1,** (explicit) я́сный; то́чный. **2,** (specific) специа́льный: *for the express purpose of,* специа́льно для того́, что́бы. **3,** (rapid) сро́чный: *express telegram,* сро́чная телегра́мма. *Express train,* курье́рский по́езд; экспре́сс. —*adv.* экспре́ссом. —*n.* (train) экспре́сс. —**express oneself, 1,** (make oneself understood) объясня́ться. **2,** (state one's opinion) выража́ться; выска́зываться.

expression *n.* выраже́ние. *Idiomatic expression,* идиомати́ческое выраже́ние. *Expression on one's face,* выраже́ние лица́. *Read with expression,* чита́ть с выраже́нием.

expressive *adj.* вырази́тельный. —**expressiveness,** *n.* вырази́тельность.

expressly *adv.* **1,** (explicitly) я́сно. **2,** (specifically) специа́льно.

expressway *n.* автостра́да; автомагистра́ль.

expropriate *v.t.* экспроприи́ровать. —**expropriation,** *n.* экспроприа́ция.

expulsion *n.* изгна́ние; исключе́ние.

expunge *v.t.* вычёркивать.

expurgate *v.t.* вычёркивать нежела́тельные места́ в (кни́ге).

exquisite *adj.* **1,** (extremely beautiful) прекра́сный. **2,** (delicate; refined) изы́сканный; утончённый.

extant *adj.* сохрани́вшийся; существу́ющий.

extemporaneous *adj.* импровизи́рованный. —**extemporaneously,** *adv.* без подгото́вки; экспро́мтом.

extemporize *v.t. & i.* импровизи́ровать.

extend *v.t.* **1,** (stretch out; hold out) протя́гивать. *Extend one's hand,* протя́гивать *or* подава́ть ру́ку. **2,** (enlarge) расширя́ть; удлиня́ть. **3,** (expand, as influence) распространя́ть. **4,** (prolong in time) продлева́ть. **5,** (give; grant; accord) ока́зывать: *extend aid to,* ока́зывать по́мощь (+ *dat.*). *Extend credit to,* открыва́ть креди́т (+ *dat.*). **6,** (give; convey) передава́ть; выража́ть. *Extend regards/an invitation,* передава́ть приве́т/приглаше́ние. *Extend thanks/sympathy,* выража́ть благода́рность/сочу́вствие. —*v.i.* (stretch) тяну́ться; простира́ться. —**extend oneself,** утружда́ть себя́.

extended *adj.* **1,** (stretched out) протя́нутый; распростёртый. **2,** (lengthy; prolonged) дли́тельный; продолжи́тельный. **3,** (enlarged in scope) расши́ренный.

extensible *adj.* раздвижно́й.

extension *n.* **1,** (extending; expanding) удлине́ние; расшире́ние. **2,** (addition, as to a house) пристро́йка. **3,** (extra time allowed a debtor) отсро́чка; продле́ние сро́ка. **4,** (internal telephone number) доба́вочный: *extension five,* доба́вочный пять. —**extension cord,** удлини́тельный шнур; удлини́тель. —**extension ladder,** раздвижна́я ле́стница.

extensive *adj.* **1,** (vast) обши́рный. **2,** (broad in scope) широ́кий; обши́рный. *Extensive knowledge,* обши́рные зна́ния. *Extensive damage,* больши́е повреждения. *Extensive repairs,* кру́пный ремо́нт.

extensively *adv.* мно́го: *read/travel extensively,* мно́го чита́ть/путеше́ствовать.

extent *n.* **1,** (length) протяже́ние; протяжённость. **2,** (degree) сте́пень; ме́ра: *to a certain extent,* до не́которой *or* до изве́стной сте́пени; в изве́стной ме́ре. **3,** (scope) сте́пень; разме́р: *extent of the damage,* сте́пень поврежде́ния; разме́р уще́рба. *To the full extent of the law,* по всей стро́гости зако́на.

extenuate *v.t.* смягча́ть. —**extenuating circumstances,** смягча́ющие вину́ обстоя́тельства.

exterior *adj.* нару́жный; вне́шний. —*n.* нару́жность; вне́шность.

exterminate *v.t.* уничтожа́ть; истребля́ть; выводи́ть; мори́ть; трави́ть. —**extermination,** *n.* уничтоже́ние; истребле́ние.

external *adj.* вне́шний; нару́жный.

extinct *adj.* **1,** (of an animal, bird, etc.) вы́мерший. *Become extinct,* вымира́ть. **2,** (of a volcano) поту́хший.

extinction *n.* **1,** (extinguishing) гаше́ние; туше́ние. **2,** (dying out) вымира́ние.

extinguish *v.t.* гаси́ть; туши́ть.

extirpate *v.t.* искореня́ть; выкорчёвывать; вырыва́ть с ко́рнем. —**extirpation,** *n.* искорене́ние.

extol *v.t.* превозноси́ть; расхва́ливать; восхваля́ть.

extort *v.t.* вымога́ть (де́ньги); вы́рвать (призна́ние); исто́ргнуть (обеща́ние). —**extortion,** *n.* вымога́тельство. —**extortionate,** *adj.* граби́тельский. —**extortionist,** *n.* вымога́тель.

extra *adj.* **1,** (additional) дополни́тельный: *extra expenses,* дополни́тельные расхо́ды. *Postage is extra,* за пересы́лку берётся осо́бая пла́та. *Pay two dollars extra,* приплачивать два до́ллара. **2,** (spare) ли́шний: *have you an extra pencil?,* есть ли у вас ли́шний каранда́ш? —*adv.* осо́бенно; осо́бо. *Of extra fine quality,* осо́бенно высо́кого ка́чества. —*n.* **1,** *theat.* (supernumerary) стати́ст. **2,** (special edition) э́кстренный вы́пуск.

extract *v.t.* **1,** (draw out; remove) извлека́ть; удаля́ть; выта́скивать; вырыва́ть. **2,** (remove from the ground) добыва́ть. **3,** (obtain by pressing or squeezing) выжима́ть. **4,** (copy out; choose for quotation) выпи́сывать; выбира́ть. **5,** (obtain, as a promise, confession, etc.) вырыва́ть; вынужда́ть; исторга́ть. **6,** *math.* извлека́ть. —*n.* **1,** (excerpt) извлече́ние; вы́держка; вы́писка; вы́борка. **2,** (concentrate) вы́тяжка; экстра́кт; насто́й.

extraction *n.* **1,** (act of extracting) извлече́ние; удале́ние; добы́ча. **2,** (origin; descent) происхожде́ние.

extracurricular *adj.* внекла́ссный.

extradite *v.t.* выдава́ть. —**extradition,** *n.* вы́дача.

extramarital *adj.* внебра́чный.

extraneous *adj.* **1,** (coming from outside; foreign) посторо́нний. **2,** (irrelevant) не име́ющий отноше́ния (к чему́-нибудь).

extraordinarily *adv.* чрезвыча́йно; в вы́сшей сте́пени.

extraordinary *adj.* **1,** (remarkable; exceptional) чрезвыча́йный; необыча́йный. **2,** (special, as of a meeting) чрезвычайный; внеочередной. **3,** (of an envoy) чрезвычайный.

extrapolate *v.t. & i.* экстраполировать. —**extrapolation,** *n.* экстраполяция.

extraterritorial *adj.* экстерриториальный.

extravagance *n.* расточительность.

extravagant *adj.* **1,** (wasteful) расточительный. **2,** (excessive) непомерный.

extreme *adj.* крайний: *extreme caution/poverty,* крайняя осторожность/нищета. *Extreme measures/ views,* крайние меры/взгляды. *Extreme old age,* глубокая старость. —*n.* крайность: *to an extreme,* до крайности. *Go to extremes,* вдаваться в крайности. *Go from one extreme to the other,* ударяться из одной крайности в другую.

extremely *adv.* крайне; чрезвычайно.

extremism *n.* экстремизм.

extremist *n.* экстремист. —*adj.* экстремистский.

extremity *n.* **1,** (end; edge) конец; край. **2,** *pl.* (appendages of the body) конечности.

extricate *v.t.* выпутывать; вытаскивать. *Extricate oneself,* выпутываться; выкарабкиваться.

exuberance *n.* жизнерадостность.

exuberant *adj.* кипучий; жизнерадостный.

exude *v.t.* **1,** (discharge) выделять. **2,** *fig.* (radiate) пыхать (+ *instr.*); сиять (+ *instr.*). —*v.i.* выделяться; проступать.

exult *v.i.* ликовать; торжествовать.—**exultant,** *adj.* ликующий; торжествующий. —**exultation,** *n.* ликование; торжество.

eye *n.* **1,** (organ of sight) глаз. **2,** (of a needle) ушко. —*adj.* глазной: *eye doctor,* глазной врач. —*v.t.* разглядывать; заглядываться на; засматриваться на. —**an eye for an eye,** око за око. —**be all eyes,** смотреть во все глаза. —**before one's very eyes,** на чьих-нибудь глазах; на глазах у кого-нибудь. —**close one's eyes to,** закрывать глаза на. —**give someone the eye; make eyes at,** делать *or* строить глазки (+ *dat.*). —**have an (or one's) eye on,** иметь на примете. —**in the eyes of,** в глазах (+ *gen.*). —**keep an eye on,** присматривать за. —**see eye to eye,** сходиться во взглядах; быть одного мнения.

eyeball *n.* глазное яблоко.

eyebrow *n.* бровь.

eyecup *n.* глазная ванночка.

eyeglasses *n. pl.* очки.

eyelash *n.* ресница.

eyelet *n.* петелька.

eyelid *n.* веко.

eyepiece *n.* окуляр.

eyeshade *n.* наглазник.

eyesight *n.* зрение.

eye socket глазная впадина; глазница.

eyesore *n.* безобразие.

eyestrain *n.* напряжение глаз.

eyetooth *n.* глазной зуб.

eyewash *n.* примочка для глаз.

eyewitness *n.* очевидец.

F

F, f шестая буква английского алфавита. —*n.* **1,** (musical note) фа. **2,** (failing grade) единица.

fa *n., music* фа.

fable *n.* басня. —**fabled,** *adj.* баснословный; сказочный.

fabric *n.* **1,** (cloth) ткань; материя; материал. **2,** *fig.* (basic structure) строй; строение. *The social fabric,* общественный строй.

fabricate *v.t.* **1,** (manufacture) производить; фабриковать. **2,** (make up; invent) фабриковать; выдумывать.

fabrication *n.* **1,** (manufacture) производство; фабрикация. **2,** (falsehood) выдумка; вымысел.

fabulist *n.* баснописец.

fabulous *adj.* баснословный; сказочный.

façade *n.* фасад.

face *n.* **1,** (of a human being) лицо. **2,** (of a clock) циферблат. **3,** (surface) лицо; лик. *Face of the moon,* лик луны. *Vanish from the face of the earth,* исчезнуть с лица земли. **4,** (expression; countenance) лицо; мина; физиономия. *Long face,* вытянутое лицо; мина. **5,** (exaggerated expression) гримаса. *Make faces,* гримасничать; делать *or* строить гримасы. **6,** (front; main side) лицевая сторона; лицо. **7,** (dignity) лицо: *loss of face,* потеря лица. —*v.t.* **1,** (front; look out on) смотреть; выходить (*with* в *or* на). **2,** (stand facing) стоять лицом к. **3,** (confront) стоять перед: *the problems facing us,* проблемы, стоящие перед нами. *We are faced with a difficult task,* нам предстоит трудная задача. *He faces life imprisonment,* ему грозит пожизненное тюремное заключение. **4,** (confront squarely) смотреть в лицо (+ *dat.*): *face death/the truth/,* смотреть смерти/ правде в лицо. **5,** (cover with a layer of something else) облицовывать; обкладывать. —**face down,** лицом вниз; ничком. —**face to face,** лицом к лицу; один на один. —**face up,** лицом кверху. —**face up to,** смотреть в лицо (+ *dat.*). —**in the face of,** перед лицом (+ *gen.*). —**on the face of it,** на первый взгляд. —**to one's face,** в лицо (+ *dat.*).

face card фигура.

face cream крем для лица.

faceless *adj.* безликий; безличный.

face powder пудра для лица.

facet *n.* **1,** (of a gem) грань; фасе́т(ка). **2,** *fig.* (aspect) сторона́.

facetious *adj.* шутли́вый; шу́точный.

face towel полоте́нце для лица́.

face value номина́льная сто́имость. —**take at face value,** принима́ть за чи́стую моне́ту.

facial *adj.* лицево́й. *Facial features,* черты́ лица́. *Facial expression,* выраже́ние лица́. —*n.* масса́ж лица́.

facile *adj.* бе́глый; бо́йкий.

facilitate *v.t.* **1,** (make easier) облегча́ть. **2,** (promote; stimulate) спосо́бствовать.

facility *n.* **1,** (ease) лёгкость. *With facility,* легко́; бе́гло; с лёгкостью. **2,** (aptitude) спосо́бность. **3,** *pl.* (conveniences; services) сре́дства; удо́бства; услу́ги.

facing *n.* **1,** (outer covering) облицо́вка. **2,** (trim) кант; отде́лка.

facsimile *n.* факси́миле.

fact *n.* факт. *It is a fact that...,* факт, что... *The fact that...,* то, что... *The fact is...,* де́ло в том, что... —**after the fact,** за́дним число́м. —**as a matter of fact,** *see* matter. —**in fact,** факти́чески; на са́мом де́ле. —**know for a fact,** знать то́чно; знать наверняка́.

faction *n.* фра́кция. —**factional,** *adj.* фракцио́нный.

factious *adj.* фракцио́нный.

factor *n.* **1,** (contributing element) фа́ктор; обстоя́тельство. *You forgot one important factor,* вы забы́ли об одно́м ва́жном обстоя́тельстве. **2,** (agent) комиссионе́р. **3,** *math.* мно́житель; сомно́житель; коэффицие́нт. —*v.t.* разлага́ть на мно́жители.

factory *n.* фа́брика; заво́д. —*adj.* фабри́чный: *factory worker,* фабри́чный рабо́чий.

factual *adj.* факти́ческий.

faculty *n.* **1,** *usu. pl.* (power of the mind) спосо́бности: *mental faculties,* у́мственные спосо́бности. *The faculty of speech,* дар ре́чи. *In full possession of one's faculties,* в по́лном рассу́дке. *Lose possession of one's faculties,* вы́жить из ума́. **2,** (knack) спосо́бности: *a faculty for languages,* спосо́бности к языка́м. **3,** (department of a university) факульте́т. **4,** (teaching staff) преподава́тельский соста́в.

fad *n.* пове́трие.

fade *v.i.* **1,** (lose color) линя́ть; выцвета́ть. **2,** (wither) вя́нуть; блёкнуть. **3,** (grow dim) бле́кнуть. **4,** (grow inaudible) замира́ть. **5,** (lessen; wane) га́снуть; угаса́ть: *hopes are fading,* наде́жды га́снут/угаса́ют. **6,** (disappear gradually) исчеза́ть: *fade into the distance,* исчеза́ть вдали́. *Fade from view,* скрыва́ться и́з виду. *Fade from memory,* стере́ться в па́мяти. —*v.t.* обесцве́чивать: *sunlight fades the fabric,* со́лнце обесцве́чивает ткань.

faded *adj.* вы́цветший.

faeces *n.* = feces.

fag *v.t.* утомля́ть. *Be fagged out,* замучиться.

fagot *also,* **faggot** *n.* вяза́нка хво́роста.

Fahrenheit *adj.* Фаренге́йт: *forty degrees Fahrenheit,* со́рок гра́дусов по Фаренге́йту.

fail *v.i.* **1,** (be unsuccessful) не удава́ться; терпе́ть неуда́чу; прова́ливаться. **2,** (stop working; cease to function) отказа́ть; отказа́ться рабо́тать. **3,** (decline; deteriorate) слабе́ть; сдава́ть. *His eyesight is failing,* его́ зре́ние слабе́ет; зре́ние ему́ изменя́ет. **4,** (become insolvent) прогора́ть. **5,** (receive a failing grade) прова́ливаться. —*v.t.* **1,** (be of no help to)

изменя́ть: *his strength failed him,* си́лы ему́ измени́ли. *Words fail me,* не нахожу́ слов. **2,** (disappoint; let down) подводи́ть: *don't fail me,* не подведи́те меня́. **3,** *fol. by inf.* (not do): *he failed to answer,* он не отве́тил. *I fail to see the difference,* не ви́жу ра́зницы. **4,** (not pass) прова́ливаться на (*e.g.* экза́мене) *or* по (*e.g.* хи́мии). **5,** (not give a passing grade to) прова́ливать. —**without fail,** обяза́тельно; в обяза́тельном поря́дке.

failing *n.* недоста́ток; сла́бость. —*adj.* **1,** (not passing, as of a mark) неудовлетвори́тельный. **2,** (deteriorating, as of eyesight) слабе́ющий. *She is in failing health,* у неё сла́бое здоро́вье. —*prep.* за неиме́нием (+ *gen.*). *Failing which,* ина́че; в проти́вном слу́чае.

failure *n.* **1,** (lack of success) неуда́ча; прова́л. *Doomed to failure,* обречён на прова́л. *Crop failure,* неурожа́й. **2,** (one who is unsuccessful) неуда́чник. **3,** (non-perfomance) неисполне́ние: *failure to carry out an order,* неисполне́ние распоряже́ния. **4,** (malfunctioning) ава́рия; отка́з; неиспра́вность. *Mechanical failure,* механи́ческая неиспра́вность. *Power failure,* отка́з электропита́ния. **5,** (a becoming bankrupt) крах; банкро́тство.

faint *adj.* **1,** (weak; dim; slight) сла́бый: *faint mark,* сла́бый след; *faint hope,* сла́бая наде́жда. *Faint resemblance,* отдалённое схо́дство. **2,** (ready to faint): *feel faint,* чу́вствовать дурноту́. *I feel faint,* мне ду́рно. —*n.* о́бморок: *in a dead faint,* в глубо́ком о́бмороке. —*v.i.* упа́сть в о́бморок.

fainthearted *adj.* малоду́шный. —**faintheartedness,** *n.* малоду́шие.

faintly *adv.* **1,** (dimly) сла́бо; нея́сно. **2,** (slightly) слегка́.

faintness *n.* **1,** (dimness) сла́бость. **2,** (weak feeling) дурнота́.

fair *adj.* **1,** (beautiful; lovely) прекра́сный. **2,** (light, as of skin) све́тлый. **3,** (blond) белоку́рый. **4,** (clear; sunny) я́сный. **5,** (just and honest) справедли́вый; че́стный. **6,** (fairly large) изря́дный: *a fair amount,* изря́дное коли́чество. **7,** (average; so-so) неплохо́й; посре́дственный; сно́сный. —*adv.* че́стно; поря́дочно; по пра́вилам. —*n.* **1,** (market) я́рмарка. **2,** (exposition) вы́ставка: *world's fair,* всеми́рная вы́ставка. —**bid fair,** обеща́ть. —**fair copy,** чистово́й экземпля́р; чистови́к. —**fair enough!,** согла́сен!; согла́сна! —**fair sex,** прекра́сный пол. —**fair to middling,** так себе́; сно́сно; ни ша́тко ни ва́лко.

fair-haired *adj.* **1,** (light-haired) белоку́рый; ру́сый; светлово́лосый. **2,** (favorite) излю́бленный.

fairly *adv.* **1,** (justly) справедли́во; че́стно. **2,** (rather) дово́льно: *fairly well,* дово́льно хорошо́.

fairness *n.* справедли́вость. —**in all fairness,** справедли́вости ра́ди.

fairy *n.* фе́я. —**fairyland,** *n.* ска́зочная страна́; волше́бное ца́рство. —**fairy tale,** (волше́бная) ска́зка.

fait accompli соверши́вшийся факт. *Present someone with a fait accompli,* поста́вить кого́-нибудь пе́ред фа́ктом.

faith *n.* **1,** (trust; confidence) ве́ра; дове́рие. *Put one's faith in,* полага́ться на. **2,** (belief in God) *faith in God,* ве́ра в бо́га. *Man of faith,* ве́рующий. **3,** (religious denomination) ве́ра; вероиспове́дание. —**bad faith,** недобросо́вестность. *In bad faith,* недобросо́вестно. —**good faith,** и́скренность. *In good faith,* и́скренне; по чи́стой со́вести. —**keep faith with,** остава́ться ве́рным (+ *dat.*). —**take on faith,** принима́ть на ве́ру.

faithful *adj.* ве́рный. —**faithfully,** *adv.* ве́рно. —**faithfulness,** *n.* ве́рность.

faithless *adj.* неве́рный.

fake *v.t.* **1,** (feign) притворя́ться (+ *instr.*). **2,** (forge) подде́лывать. —*v.i.* притворя́ться. —*adj.* подде́льный; подло́жный; фальши́вый. —*n.* подде́лка; фальши́вка.

faker *n.* обма́нщик; притво́рщик. —**fakery,** *n.* обма́н.

falcon *n.* со́кол. —**falconry,** *n.* соколи́ная охо́та.

fall *v.i.* **1,** (lose one's footing; drop) па́дать. *Fall down the stairs,* упа́сть с ле́стницы. *Fall in battle,* пасть в бою́. *Prices fell,* це́ны упали́. *Rain fell during the night,* но́чью шёл дождь. *Dusk is falling,* спуска́ются су́мерки. *Shadows are falling,* те́ни ложа́тся. *His face fell,* его́ лицо́ вы́тянулось. **2,** (be caught or captured) попада́ть; *fall into a trap,* попа́сть в лову́шку. *Fall into the hands of,* попа́сть в ру́ки (+ *gen.*). *Fall victim to,* пасть же́ртвой (+ *gen.*). **3,** (be conquered or overthrown) пасть: *the fortress fell,* кре́пость па́ла. *Fall from power,* лиши́ться вла́сти. **4,** (occur) наступа́ть: *night fell,* наступи́ла ночь. *New Year's Day falls on a Wednesday,* Но́вый год выпада́ет *or* прихо́дится на сре́ду. *The stress falls on the first syllable,* ударе́ние па́дает на пе́рвый слог. **5,** (come by lot or chance) па́дать; выпада́ть: *the lot fell upon him,* ему́ вы́пал жре́бий; жре́бий пал на него́. **6,** (pass into a particular state): *fall asleep,* засыпа́ть; *fall ill,* заболева́ть; *fall silent,* замолка́ть; умолка́ть; *fall in love,* влюбля́ться. **7,** (be classified; belong) относи́ться: *fall into a certain category,* относи́ться к тако́й-то катего́рии. *Fall into three categories,* дели́ться на три катего́рии. *Fall within one's jurisdiction,* входи́ть в чью-нибудь компете́нцию. **8,** *fol. by inf.* (begin; set about) *rendered variously in Russian: they fell to work immediately,* они́ сра́зу взя́лись за рабо́ту. *They fell to quarreling among themselves,* они́ поссо́рились ме́жду собо́й. —*n.* **1,** (loss of footing; drop; collapse) паде́ние. *Take a bad fall,* си́льно разби́ться. *Fall in prices,* паде́ние цен. *The fall of the Roman Empire,* паде́ние Ри́мской Импе́рии. **2,** *pl.* (waterfall) водопа́д. **3,** (autumn) о́сень. *In the fall,* о́сенью. —*adj.* осе́нний: *fall weather,* осе́нняя пого́да. —**fall apart,** распада́ться; развали́ваться. —**fall back,** отступа́ть. —**fall back on,** прибега́ть к. —**fall behind, 1,** *literally* зава́ливаться за (+ *acc.*). **2,** (lag) отстава́ть. —**fall down,** па́дать. —**fall flat,** прова́ливаться. —**fall for, 1,** (be tricked by, as bait) попада́ться на (у́дочку). **2,** (be captivated by) влюбля́ться в; увлека́ться (+ *instr.*). —**fall in, 1,** (cave in) обва́ливаться; прова́ливаться. **2,** *mil.* стро́иться. *Fall in!,* станови́сь! —**fall in with,** попа́сть в: *fall in with a bad crowd,* попа́сть в плоху́ю компа́нию. —**fall off, 1,** (tumble from) упа́сть с; свали́ться с. **2,** (decline) уме́ньшиться; упа́сть. —**fall out, 1,** *literally* выпада́ть; выва́ливаться. **2,** *mil.* выходи́ть из стро́я. —**fall over,** опроки́дываться. —**fall short of,** не достига́ть. *Fall short of expectations,* обма́нывать ожида́ния. —**fall through,** прова́ливаться; срыва́ться.

fallacious *adj.* оши́бочный; ло́жный. —**fallaciousness,** *n.* оши́бочность.

fallacy *n.* **1,** (false notion; error) оши́бка. **2,** (fallaciousness) оши́бочность.

fallen *adj.* па́вший; па́дший. —**fallen arches,** плоскосто́пие. —**fallen woman,** па́дшая же́нщина.

fallible *adj.* подве́рженный оши́бкам.

falling *adj.* па́дающий.

falling-out *n.* ссо́ра. *They have had a falling-out,* они́ в ссо́ре; они́ рассо́рились; ме́жду ни́ми пробежа́ла чёрная ко́шка.

Fallopian tubes фалло́пиевы тру́бы.

fallout *n.* **1,** (particles) радиоакти́вные оса́дки. **2,** (descent of same) выпаде́ние радиоакти́вных оса́дков.

fallow *adj.* парово́й. *Fallow land,* земля́ под па́ром. *Lie fallow,* лежа́ть под па́ром. —**fallow deer,** лань.

false *adj.* **1,** (incorrect; insincere) ло́жный: *false rumor,* ло́жный слух; *false modesty,* ло́жная скро́мность. *False advertising,* лжи́вая рекла́ма. **2,** (forged) фальши́вый: *false passport,* фальши́вый па́спорт. —**false alarm,** ло́жная трево́га. —**false note,** фальши́вая *or* неве́рная но́та. —**false start,** неве́рный старт. —**false step,** ло́жный шаг. —**false teeth,** вставны́е зу́бы. —**under a false name,** под чужи́м и́менем.

falsehood *n.* ложь; непра́вда; вы́мысел.

falsely *adv.* ло́жно.

falsetto *n.* фальце́т; фи́стула. —*adj.* фальце́тный.

falsification *n.* фальсифика́ция.

falsifier *n.* фальсифика́тор.

falsify *v.t.* фальсифици́ровать.

falsity *n.* **1,** (falseness) ло́жность. **2,** (falsehood) ложь.

falter *v.i.* **1,** (hesitate; waver) дро́гнуть. **2,** (lose strength or momentum) слабе́ть.

fame *n.* сла́ва; изве́стность. —**famed,** *adj.* просла́вленный.

familiar *adj.* **1,** (well-known) знако́мый: *a familiar voice,* знако́мый го́лос. *His face is familiar to me,* его́ лицо́ мне знако́мо. **2,** *fol. by with* (having knowledge of) знако́мый с; в ку́рсе (+ *gen.*). *Become familiar with,* знако́миться с; ознакомля́ться с. **3,** (unduly intimate) фамилья́рный; развя́зный; бесцеремо́нный.

familiarity *n.* **1,** (knowledge) знако́мство. **2,** (undue intimacy) фамилья́рность; бесцеремо́нность.

familiarization *n.* ознакомле́ние.

familiarize *v.t.* знако́мить; ознакомля́ть. *Familiarize oneself with,* знако́миться с; ознакомля́ться с.

family *n.* **1,** (parents and children) семья́. **2,** *biol.* семе́йство. **3,** (of languages) семья́. —*adj.* семе́йный; фами́льный. *Family ties,* ро́дственные свя́зи. —**family man,** семе́йный челове́к. —**family name,** фами́лия. —**family planning,** плани́рование семьи́. —**family tree,** родосло́вное де́рево. —**in the family way,** в интере́сном положе́нии.

famine *n.* го́лод. —**feast or famine,** то гу́сто, то пу́сто.

famished *adj.* голо́дный как соба́ка; умира́ющий от го́лода.

famous *adj.* знамени́тый. *Be famous for,* сла́виться (+ *instr.*).

fan *n.* **1,** (manual device) ве́ер. **2,** (machine) вентиля́тор. **3,** *colloq.* (devotee) боле́льщик; люби́тель; покло́нник. —*v.t.* **1,** (cool with a fan) обма́хивать. *Fan* *oneself,* обмáхиваться. **2,** (direct air on, as a fire) раздувáть. **3,** *fig.* (stir up; foment) раздувáть. —*v.i.* [*usu.* **fan out**] развёртываться вéером.

fanatic *n.* фанáтик. —*adj.* [*also,* **fanatical**] фанати́ческий; фанати́чный. —**fanaticism,** *n.* фанати́зм.

fan belt ремéнь вентилятора.

fanciful *adj.* **1,** (imaginary; unreal) фантасти́ческий. **2,** (whimsical) капри́зный.

fancy *n.* **1,** (imagination) фантáзия: *flight of fancy,* полёт фантáзии. **2,** (whim) при́хоть; причýда; фантáзия. **3,** (liking) увлечéние. *Take a fancy to,* увлекáться (+ *instr.*). *Catch the fancy of,* приглянýться (+ *dat.*). —*adj.* **1,** (not plain) замыслова́тый; затéйливый. **2,** *colloq.* (high, as of prices) дýтый. —*v.t.* **1,** (imagine) воображáть. *Fancy oneself as a writer,* воображáть себя писáтелем. **2,** (suppose; surmise) предполагáть; воображáть. **3,** (like): *what do you fancy?,* что вам нрáвится? **4,** (feel like): *I don't fancy...,* у меня нет охóты (+ *inf. or* на+ *acc.*).

fanfare *n.* **1,** (flourish of trumpets) фанфáра. **2,** (ballyhoo) шуми́ха. *Without fanfare,* без затéй.

fang *n.* клык.

fantastic *adj.* фантасти́ческий.

fantasy *n.* **1,** (creative imagination) фантáзия. **2,** (something existing only in the imagination) фантáстика; фантáзия.

far *adj.* **1,** (distant) A, *used predicatively* далекó: *Moscow is far away,* Москвá далекó. *Not far from here,* недалекó отсюда. B, *used as a modifier* далёкий: *the far north,* далёкий сéвер. **2,** (more distant) дáльний: *in the far corner,* в дáльнем углý. —*adv.* **1,** (a long way) далекó: *go too far,* зайти́ сли́шком далекó. **2,** *in comparisons* (by a great deal) горáздо; намнóго: *far better,* горáздо/намнóго лýчше. —**as far as, 1,** (up to) до: *we drove as far as Boston,* мы доéхали до Бóстона. **2,** (to the extent that) наскóлько: *as far as I know,* наскóлько я знáю. *As far as I am concerned,* что касáется меня. —**by far; far and away,** несомнéнно; бесспóрно. —**far and wide,** повсюду; вдоль и поперёк. —**far be it from me to...,** я далёк от тогó, чтобы... —**far from, 1,** *literally* далекó от. **2,** (by no means) далекó не: *far from dumb,* далекó не глуп. —**far from it,** далекó не так; ничегó подóбного. —**go far,** далекó пойти́: *he will go far,* он далекó пойдёт. —**far into,** вглубь (+ *gen.*): *far into the woods,* вглубь лéса. *Far into the night,* до глубóкой нóчи. *Look far into the future,* заглядывать в далёкое будущее. —**how far?,** скóлько нáдо éхать?; скóлько киломéтров? —**so far,** покá что; покá ещё; до сих пор. —**so far, so good,** покá всё хорошó.

faraway *adj.* **1,** (distant) далёкий; отдалённый. **2,** (dreamy, as of a look) отсýтствующий.

farce *n.* фарс. —**farcical,** *adj.* смешнóй.

fare *v.i.* поживáть: *how are you faring?,* как вы поживáете? —*n.* **1,** (price of a trip) плáта за проéзд; стóимость проéзда. *What is the fare to Washington?,* скóлько стóит проéзд *or* билéт в Вашингтóн? **2,** (paying passenger) пассажи́р. **3,** (food) пи́ща; питáние; стол.

Far East дáльний востóк. —**Far Eastern,** дальневостóчный.

farewell *n.* прощáние. *Bid farewell to,* прощáться с. —*adj.* прощáльный; напýтственный. —*interj.* прощáй(те)!

farfetched *adj.* надýманный; притянутый зá волосы.

far-flung *adj.* обши́рный; раздóльный.

farina *n.* мáнная крупá. —**farinaceous,** *adj.* мучни́стый.

farm *n.* фéрма. *Collective farm,* колхóз. —*adj.* сельскохозяйственный: *farm products/machinery,* сельскохозяйственные продýкты/маши́ны. —*v.t.* **1,** (cultivate) обрабáтывать. **2,** *fol. by* **out** (let out) отдавáть на óткуп. —*v.i.* занимáться сéльским хозяйством.

farmer *n.* фéрмер.

farm hand сельскохозяйственный рабóчий; батрáк.

farmhouse *n.* дом на фéрме.

farming *n.* земледéлие.

farmland *n.* пáхотная земля.

farmstead *n.* усáдьба.

farmyard *n.* скóтный двор.

faro *n.* фараóн; банк.

far-off *adj.* далёкий; дáльний.

far-reaching *adj.* далекó идýщий.

farrow *n.* опорóс.

farsighted *adj.* **1,** *med.* дальнозóркий. **2,** (having or showing foresight) дальнови́дный. —**farsightedness,** *n.* дальнозóркость.

farther *adv.* дáльше. *Not a step farther!,* ни шáгу дáльше!

farthing *n.* фáртинг.

fascinate *v.t.* увлекáть. —**fascinating,** *adj.* увлекáтельный.

fascination *n.* **1,** (state of being fascinated) увлечéние. **2,** (charm; attraction) очаровáние.

fascism *n.* фаши́зм.

fascist *n.* фаши́ст. —*adj.* фаши́стский.

fashion *n.* **1,** (current style; vogue) мóда: *be in fashion,* быть в мóде. *The latest fashion,* послéдняя мóда. *Fashion magazine,* журнáл мод. *Fashion show,* покáз модéлей одéжды. **2,** (way; manner) óбраз; спóсоб; манéра. —*v.t.* выдéлывать. *Fashion out of clay,* вылепить из гли́ны. —**after a fashion,** нéкоторым óбразом; в своём рóде.

fashionable *adj.* **1,** (in style) мóдный. **2,** (high-class) фешенéбельный. —**become fashionable, 1,** (of clothes) входи́ть в мóду. **2,** (of a practice) стать мóдно.

fashionably *adv.* мóдно.

fashion plate мóдник; мóдная карти́нка.

fast *adj.* **1,** (swift) бы́стрый; скóрый. *Fast horse,* бы́страя лóшадь. *Fast train,* скóрый пóезд. **2,** (of a timepiece): *my watch is (ten minutes) fast,* мой часы́ спешáт (на дéсять минýт). **3,** (loyal; close, as of friends) вéрный. **4,** (not fading) прóчный: *fast colors,* прóчные крáски. **5,** (dissolute) беспýтный; разгýльный. —*adv.* **1,** (rapidly) бы́стро: *run fast,* бежáть бы́стро. **2,** (firmly) крéпко. *Stand fast,* стóйко держáться. **3,** *He is fast asleep,* он крéпко спит. —*n.* пост: *observe a fast,* соблюдáть пост. —*v.i.* пости́ться.

fasten *v.t.* **1,** (attach) прикреплять: *fasten a mirror to the wall,* прикреплять зéркало к стенé. **2,** (secure) закрепля́ть; скрепля́ть. **3,** (draw and pull tight) застёгивать: *fasten one's seat belt,* застегнýть привязнóй ремéнь. —*v.i.* **1,** *fol. by* **to** *or* **onto** (attach to) прикрепля́ться (к). **2,** (button; hook; clasp) застёгиваться. —**fastener,** *n.* застёжка.

fastidious *adj.* **1,** (neat) чистопло́тный. **2,** (discriminating) разбо́рчивый.

fast-moving *adj.* быстрохо́дный.

fastness *n.* **1,** (remote and secure place) тверды́ня. **2,** (firmness) про́чность.

fat *adj.* **1,** (obese) по́лный; то́лстый; ту́чный. *Get fat,* полне́ть; толсте́ть. **2,** (fatty) жи́рный. —*n.* жир; са́ло.

fatal *adj.* **1,** (mortal; lethal) смерте́льный. **2,** (causing ruin; disastrous) роково́й: *fatal mistake,* роко́вая оши́бка. *Fatal consequences,* ги́бельные после́дствия.

fatalism *n.* фатали́зм. —**fatalist,** *n.* фатали́ст. —**fatalistic,** *adj.* фаталисти́ческий.

fatality *n.* смерте́льный слу́чай: *no fatalities,* ника́ких сме́ртных слу́чаев.

fatally *adv.* смерте́льно.

fate *n.* **1,** (invisible force) судьба́; рок. **2,** (what happens to someone) судьба́; у́часть.

fated *adj.* суждено́: *we were not fated to...,* нам не суждено́ было (+ *inf.*).

fateful *adj.* **1,** (momentous) роково́й. **2,** (telltale) проро́ческий.

father *n.* **1,** (male parent) оте́ц. **2,** *pl.* (ancestors) пре́дки. —*v.t.* роди́ть; производи́ть. —**fatherhood,** *n.* отцо́вство.

father-in-law *n.* **1,** (husband's father) свёкор. **2,** (wife's father) тесть.

fatherland *n.* оте́чество.

fatherly *adj.* оте́ческий.

fathom *n.* морска́я са́жень. —*v.t.* проника́ть в; разга́дывать; разбира́ть.

fatigue *n.* утомле́ние; уста́лость. —*v.t.* утомля́ть. —*v.i.* устава́ть. —**fatiguing,** *adj.* утоми́тельный.

fatten *v.t.* корми́ть на убо́й; отка́рмливать; раска́рмливать.

fattening *adj.* жи́рный. *Avoid fattening foods,* избега́ть жиро́в.

fatty *adj.* жи́рный; жирово́й. —**fatty acid,** жи́рная кислота́.

fatuous *adj.* глу́пый; дура́цкий.

faucet *n.* (водопрово́дный) кран.

fault *n.* **1,** (responsibility; blame) вина́. *It's my fault,* я винова́т(а). *It's all your fault,* э́то всё вы винова́ты. **2,** (flaw; defect) недоста́ток. **3,** *geol.* сдвиг. —*v.t.* придира́ться к; критикова́ть. —**at fault,** винова́т. —**find fault with,** придира́ться к. —**to a fault,** чрезме́рно.

faultfinder *n.* приди́ра; критика́н.

faultless *adj.* безупре́чный; безукори́зненный.

faulty *adj.* неиспра́вный; дефе́ктный.

faun *n.* фавн.

fauna *n.* фа́уна.

faux pas ло́жный шаг.

favor *also,* **favour** *n.* **1,** (good turn) одолже́ние; любе́зность; ми́лость; услу́га. *Do someone a favor,* сде́лать одолже́ние (+ *dat.*). *I have a favor to ask of you,* у меня́ к вам про́сьба. **2,** (friendly regard; approval) ми́лость; благоскло́нность; расположе́ние. *Out of favor,* в неми́лости. *Find favor in someone's eyes,* сниска́ть чье́-нибудь расположе́ние. *Look upon with favor,* относи́ться благоскло́нно к. *Gain favor among,* находи́ть подде́ржку у. —*v.t.* **1,** (oblige) благоволи́ть. **2,** (show partiality toward; prefer) ока́зывать предпочте́ние (+ *dat.*). **3,** (be in favor of; advocate) быть за; стоя́ть за; выступа́ть за. **4,** (facilitate; aid) благоприя́тствовать. **5,** (resemble) уроди́ться в. —**in favor of, 1,** (for; supporting) за: *be in favor of,* быть/стоя́ть/выступа́ть за. **2,** (to the advantage of) в по́льзу (+ *gen.*): 3-2 *in favor of...,* три-два в по́льзу (+ *gen.*). *The matter was settled in our favor,* де́ло реши́лось в на́шу по́льзу.

favorable *also,* **favourable** *adj.* благоприя́тный. *Favorable balance of trade,* акти́вный торго́вый бала́нс.

favorably *also,* **favourably** *adv.* благоскло́нно: *be favorably disposed toward,* относи́ться благоскло́нно к. *Compare favorably with,* выи́грывать в сравне́нии с.

favorite *adj.* люби́мый; излю́бленный. —*n.* **1,** (that best liked) люби́мец; фавори́т. **2,** *sports* фавори́т. —**favoritism** *n.* фаворити́зм.

favour *n.&v.* = **favor.** —**favourable,** *adj.* = **favorable.**

fawn *n.* молодо́й оле́нь. —*v.i.* [*usu.* **fawn on** *or* **upon**] раболе́пствовать (пе́ред); пресмыка́ться (пе́ред); лебези́ть (пе́ред).

faze *v.t., colloq.* смуща́ть; расстра́ивать.

fealty *n.* ве́рность.

fear *n.* **1,** (fright) страх. **2,** (concern) опасе́ние: *arouse fears,* вызыва́ть опасе́ния. —*v.t. & i.* боя́ться: *fear trouble,* боя́ться неприя́тностей; *fear for one's life,* боя́ться за свою́ жизнь. —**for fear of/that,** из стра́ха, что; бойсь, что; из боя́зни, что.

fearful *adj.* **1,** (dreadful) стра́шный. **2,** (apprehensive): *be fearful that...,* боя́ться, что...

fearless *adj.* бесстра́шный; неустраши́мый. —**fearlessness,** *n.* бесстра́шие; неустраши́мость.

fearsome *adj.* стра́шный; гро́зный.

feasible *adj.* выполни́мый; исполни́мый; осуществи́мый. —**feasibility,** *n.* осуществи́мость.

feast *n.* **1,** (sumptuous meal) пир. **2,** (religious festival) пра́здник. —*v.i.* **1,** (have a feast) пирова́ть. **2,** *fol. by* **on** (eat) ла́комиться (+ *instr.*). —*v.t.* че́ствовать. —**feast one's eyes on,** любова́ться (+ *instr.*); упива́ться (+ *instr.*).

feat *n.* по́двиг.

feather *n.* перо́. *Light as a feather,* лёгкий, как пёрышко. —**birds of a feather,** одного́ по́ля я́года. *Birds of a feather flock together,* моря́к моряка́ (*or* рыба́к рыбака́) ви́дит издалека́. —**feather in one's cap,** большо́е достиже́ние; предме́т го́рдости. —**feather one's nest,** нагре́ть ру́ки; наби́ть себе́ карма́н; свить себе́ тёплое гнёздышко.

feather bed пери́на; пухови́к.

feathered *adj.* опере́нный; перна́тый.

feather grass ковы́ль.

feathery *adj.* **1,** (covered with feathers) перна́тый. **2,** (light; soft) пуши́стый.

feature *n.* **1,** (characteristic) черта́; осо́бенность. *Distinguishing feature,* отличи́тельная черта́. **2,** *pl.* (facial appearance) черты́ лица́. **3,** (highlight) гвоздь. —*v.t.* отводи́ть важне́йшее ме́сто (+ *dat.*); помеща́ть на ви́дном ме́сте; выводи́ть в гла́вной ро́ли.

febrile *adj.* лихора́дочный.

February *n.* февра́ль. —*adj.* февра́льский.

feces *also,* **faeces** *n.pl.* кал; испражне́ния.

feckless *adj.* **1,** (careless; irresponsible) неради́вый. **2,** (ineffectual) сла́бый: *feckless attempt,* сла́бая попы́тка.

fecund *adj.* плодови́тый. —**fecundity**, *n.* плодови́-тость.

federal *adj.* федера́льный; федерати́вный; сою́зный. —**federalism**, *n.* федерали́зм. —**federalist**, *n.* федерали́ст.

federate *v.t. & i.* объединя́ть(ся) в сою́з. —**federated**, *adj.* федерати́вный. —**federation**, *n.* федера́ция; сою́з.

fee *n.* **1,** (for professional services) гонора́р. **2,** (for admission, membership, etc.) пла́та; взнос.

feeble *adj.* **1,** (infirm) не́мощный; хи́лый. **2,** *fig.* (ineffective) сла́бый: *feeble attempt,* сла́бая попы́тка.

feeble-minded *adj.* слабоу́мный. —**feeble-mindedness**, *n.* слабоу́мие.

feed *v.t.* **1,** (give food to; help to eat) корми́ть: *feed the baby,* корми́ть ребёнка; *feed oats to the horses,* корми́ть лошаде́й овсо́м. **2,** (keep nourished; sustain) корми́ть; пита́ть. **3,** *in* **feed oneself,** есть самостоя́тельно. *Be able to feed oneself,* мочь сам (сама́) есть. —*v.i.* **1,** (of animals) корми́ться. **2,** *fol. by* **on** (use as food) пита́ться (+ *instr.*). —*n.* корм. —**be fed up,** надое́сть; осточерте́ть: *I am fed up with it,* э́то мне надое́ло/осточерте́ло.

feedbag *n.* то́рба.

feeder *n.* **1,** (branch line) ве́тка. **2,** *electricity* фи́дер.

feeding *n.* кормле́ние. —**feeding bottle,** де́тский рожо́к. —**feeding trough,** корму́шка.

feel *v.t.* **1,** (sense; experience) чу́вствовать; ощуща́ть: *feel pain,* чу́вствовать/ощуща́ть боль. **2,** (touch) щу́пать; ощу́пывать; потро́гать. *Feel someone's pulse,* (по)щу́пать пульс у кого́-нибудь. **3,** *in* **feel one's way,** пробира́ться о́щупью. **4,** (think; consider) счита́ть. —*v.i.* **1,** (be in a certain physical condition) чу́вствовать себя: *how do you feel?,* как вы себя́ чу́вствуете? *Feel ill,* пло́хо себя́ чу́вствовать. **2,** (experience some emotion): *feel sorry for,* жале́ть. *Feel bad about,* сожале́ть о. **3,** (seem, as to the touch) каза́ться: *the water feels warm,* вода́ ка́жется тёплой. —*n.* ощуще́ние; осяза́ние. *Get the feel of,* осво́иться с. —**feel for, 1,** (grope for) иска́ть о́щупью; нащу́пывать. **2,** (sympathize with) сочу́вствовать (+ *dat.*); страда́ть за; боле́ть за. —**feel like,** хоте́ться (+ *dat.*); име́ть охо́ту; быть не прочь. —**make itself felt,** дава́ть себя́ знать; дава́ть себя́ чу́вствовать.

feeler *n.* **1,** *zool.* у́сик. **2,** *fig.* (hint) про́бный шар. *Put out a feeler,* заки́нуть у́дочку.

feeling *n.* **1,** (emotion; sense) чу́вство: *feeling of pride,* чу́вство го́рдости. *Play with feeling,* игра́ть с чу́вством; игра́ть с душо́й., **2,** (sensation) ощуще́ние. *I have no feeling in my arm,* у меня́ рука́ онеме́ла. **3,** *pl.* (sensibilities) самолю́бие: *hurt someone's feelings,* задева́ть чье-нибудь самолю́бие. **4,** (impression; opinion) впечатле́ние; мне́ние. **5,** (presentiment) предчу́вствие.

feign *v.t. & i.* притворя́ться. —**feigned**, *adj.* притво́рный.

feint *n.* финт. —*v.i.* сде́лать финт.

feldspar *n.* полево́й шпат.

felicitate *v.t.* поздравля́ть. —**felicitation**, *n.* поздравле́ние.

felicitous *adj.* уда́чный; ме́ткий.

felicity *n.* **1,** (great happiness) сча́стье; блаже́нство. **2,** (aptness) ме́ткость.

feline *adj.* коша́чий.

fell *v.t.* **1,** (cut down) руби́ть; сруба́ть; выруба́ть. **2,** (knock down) вали́ть; сбива́ть с ног.

fellow *n.* челове́к; па́рень; ма́лый. —*adj.* това́рищ по; со-: *fellow worker,* това́рищ по рабо́те; *fellow citizen,* согражда́нин. *Fellow countryman,* соотéчественник.

fellowship *n.* **1,** (comradeship) това́рищество. **2,** (grant) стипе́ндия.

fellow traveler попу́тчик.

felon *n.* престу́пник. —**felonious**, *adj.* престу́пный. —**felony**, *n.* уголо́вное преступле́ние.

felt *n.* во́йлок; фетр. —*adj.* во́йлочный; фе́тровый.

female *adj.* же́нский; же́нского по́ла. —*n.* **1,** (woman) же́нщина. **2,** (female animal) са́мка; ма́тка.

feminine *adj.* **1,** (female) же́нский. **2,** (womanly) же́нственный. **3,** *gram.* же́нского ро́да. *Feminine gender,* же́нский род. —**femininity**, *n.* же́нственность.

feminism *n.* фемини́зм. —**feminist**, *n.* фемини́ст; фемини́стка. —*adj.* фемини́стский; феминисти́ческий.

femur *n.* бе́дренная кость.

fence *n.* забо́р; огра́да. —*v.t.* **1,** *fol. by* **in** (enclose) загора́живать; огора́живать. **2,** *fol. by* **off** (separate) отгора́живать; выгора́живать. —*v.i.* фехтова́ть.

fencer *n.* фехтова́льщик. —**fencing**, *n.* фехтова́ние.

fend *v.t.* [*usu.* **fend off**] отража́ть; отбива́ть. —**fend for oneself,** забо́титься о себе́. *He was left to fend for himself,* он был предоста́влен самому́ себе́.

fender *n.* крыло́.

fennel *n.* фе́нхель.

ferment *n.* **1,** (substance producing fermentation) ферме́нт; заква́ска. **2,** *fig.* (agitation) броже́ние. —*v.i.* броди́ть. —*v.t.* вызыва́ть броже́ние в; заква́шивать.

fermentation *n.* броже́ние.

fermented *adj.* перебро́ди́вший.

fermium *n.* фе́рмий.

fern *n.* па́поротник.

ferocious *adj.* свире́пый; лю́тый. —**ferocity**, *n.* свире́пость; лю́тость.

ferret *n.* хорёк. —*v.t.* [*usu.* **ferret out**] выве́дывать; выпы́тывать.

ferric oxide о́кись желе́за.

Ferris wheel чёртово колесо́.

ferrotype *n.* ферроти́пия.

ferrous *adj.* желе́зистый. —**ferrous metals,** чёрные мета́ллы. —**ferrous oxide,** за́кись желе́за. —**ferrous sulfate,** желе́зный купоро́с.

ferrule *n.* наконе́чник.

ferry *n.* [*also,* **ferryboat**] паро́м. —*v.t.* перевози́ть; переправля́ть. —**ferryman**, *n.* паро́мщик; перево́зчик.

fertile *adj.* плодоро́дный: *fertile soil,* плодоро́дная по́чва. *Fertile imagination,* бога́тое/живо́е/пы́лкое воображе́ние.

fertility *n.* **1,** (of the soil) плодоро́дие. **2,** *biol.* плодови́тость.

fertilization *n.* **1,** (of the soil) удобре́ние. **2,** *biol.* оплодотворе́ние.

fertilize *v.t.* **1,** (spread fertilizer on) удобря́ть. **2,** *biol.* оплодотворя́ть. *Fertilized egg,* оплодотворённое яйцо́.

fertilizer *n.* удобре́ние.

ferule *n.* феру́ла.

fervent *adj.* горя́чий; стра́стный; пы́лкий. —**fervently**, *adv.* горячо́.

fervid *adj.* горя́чий; пы́лкий; пла́менный.

fervor *also,* **fervour** *n.* жар; пыл; задо́р.

fester *v.i.* гно́иться.

festering *n.* гное́ние; нагное́ние. —*adj.* гно́йный.

festival *n.* **1,** (holiday) пра́зднество. **2,** (music, film, youth, etc.) фестива́ль.

festive *adj.* пра́здничный; торже́ственный.

festivity *n.* **1,** (gaiety; mirth) весе́лье. **2,** *pl.* (festive proceedings) пра́зднества; торжества́.

festoon *n.* **1,** (hanging decoration) гирля́нда. **2,** (ornamental carving) фесто́н. —*v.t.* украша́ть.

fetal *adj.* пло́дный.

fetch *v.t.* идти́ за; сходи́ть за; приноси́ть; приводи́ть.

fetching *adj.* привлека́тельный; хоро́шенький; коке́тливый.

fete *n.* пра́зднество. —*v.t.* че́ствовать.

fetid *adj.* злово́нный; воню́чий.

fetish *n.* фети́ш.

fetlock *n.* щётка.

fetter *n., usu. pl.* **1,** (chains) пу́ты; кандалы́. **2,** *fig.* (shackles) око́вы; у́зы; пу́ты. —*v.t.* спу́тывать (ло́шадь).

fettle *n.* состоя́ние; настрое́ние.

fetus *also,* **foetus** *n.* плод; заро́дыш.

feud *n.* вражда́. —*v.i.* вражд ова́ть.

feudal *adj.* феода́льный. —**feudalism,** *n.* феодали́зм.

fever *n.* **1,** (high temperature) жар. **2,** (disease) лихора́дка: *yellow fever,* жёлтая лихора́дка. **3,** (excitement) лихора́дка; горя́чка: *speculative fever,* биржева́я лихора́дка/горя́чка.

feverish *adj.* лихора́дочный. *I feel feverish,* меня́ зноби́т; меня́ лихора́дит.

few *adj.* **1,** (not many) ма́ло; немно́гие. *There were very few people there,* там бы́ло ма́ло наро́ду. *Few people know about it,* ма́ло кто зна́ет об э́том. *With few exceptions,* за немно́гими исключе́ниями. **2,** *usu. preceded by* **a** (a certain small number of) не́сколько: *in a few minutes,* че́рез не́сколько мину́т; *in a few words,* в не́скольких слова́х. *Every few days,* ка́ждые не́сколько дней. *Quite a few,* дово́льно мно́го. —*pron.* немно́гие: *one of the few who...,* оди́н из тех немно́гих, кото́рые... —**few and far between,** о́чень ре́дкие; наперечёт.

fez *n.* фе́ска.

fiancé *n.* жени́х. —**fiancée,** *n.* неве́ста.

fiasco *n.* фиа́ско.

fiat *n.* декре́т; ука́з.

fib *n.* вы́думка; непра́вда. —*v.i.* врать; привира́ть. —**fibber,** *n.* вы́думщик.

fiber *also,* **fibre** *n.* **1,** (filament) волокно́. **2,** *fig.* (inner strength) хара́ктер. —**fiberglass,** *n.* стекловолокно́.

fibrous *adj.* волокни́стый.

fibula *n.* ма́лая берцо́вая кость.

fickle *adj.* непостоя́нный; изме́нчивый.

fiction *n.* **1,** (literature) беллетри́стика; худо́жественная литерату́ра. **2,** (fabrication) фи́кция; вы́мысел. —**fictional,** *adj.* беллетристи́ческий.

fictitious *adj.* **1,** = **fictional. 2,** (false) вы́думанный; вы́мышленный; фикти́вный.

fiddle *n.* скри́пка. —*v.i.* **1,** *colloq.* (play the violin)

игра́ть на скри́пке. **2,** *fol. by* **with** (fidget with) вози́ться с; игра́ть (+ *instr.*). —*v.t.* [*usu.* **fiddle away**] растра́чивать. —**fit as a fiddle,** совсе́м здоро́в; как нельзя́ лу́чше. —**play second fiddle,** игра́ть втору́ю скри́пку.

fiddler *n.* скрипа́ч.

fiddlesticks *interj.* вздор!; чепуха́!

fidelity *n.* **1,** (faithfulness) ве́рность. **2,** (accuracy) то́чность.

fidget *v.i.* **1,** (move restlessly) ёрзать; егози́ть; сует́иться. **2,** *fol. by* **with** (fuss with) игра́ть (+ *instr.*). —*n.* непосе́да; егоза́; юла́. —**fidgety,** *adj.* суетли́вый; егозли́вый; непосе́дливый.

fie *interj.* фи!

fief *n.* фео́д.

field *n.* **1,** (piece of open land) по́ле: *cornfield,* кукуру́зное по́ле. *Playing field,* спорти́вное по́ле. *Landing field,* поса́дочная площа́дка. **2,** (place containing a natural resource) месторожде́ние; про́мысел: *oil fields,* месторожде́ния не́фти; нефтяны́е про́мыслы. **3,** *fig.* (sphere, as of knowledge) о́бласть; о́трасль. —*adj.* полево́й: *field gun,* полево́е ору́дие. —**field of vision,** по́ле зре́ния.

field glasses полево́й бино́кль.

field goal гол с игры́.

field hockey хокке́й на траве́.

field marshal фельдма́ршал.

field mouse полева́я мышь.

fiend *n.* и́зверг; изуве́р. *Dope fiend,* наркома́н.

fiendish *adj.* зве́рский; изуве́рский.

fierce *adj.* **1,** (ferocious) свире́пый; лю́тый. **2,** (violent, as of a storm) нейстовый. **3,** (bitter; intense, as of a struggle) жесто́кий; ожесточённый.

fiery *adj.* **1,** (ablaze) о́гненный. **2,** (impassioned) о́гненный; огнево́й; горя́чий; пла́менный. **3,** (easily provoked) горя́чий; вспы́льчивый.

fife *n.* ду́дка.

fifteen *n. & adj.* пятна́дцать.

fifteenth *adj.* пятна́дцатый. —*n.* **1,** (fifteenth part) пятна́дцатая часть. **2,** (fraction) пятна́дцатая: *one-fifteenth,* одна́ пятна́дцатая.

fifth *adj.* пя́тый. —*n.* **1,** (fifth part) пя́тая часть. **2,** (fraction) пя́тая: *one-fifth,* одна́ пя́тая. —**fifth column,** пя́тая коло́нна. —**fifth wheel,** пя́тое колесо́ в теле́ге; пя́тая спи́ца в колесни́це.

fiftieth *adj.* пятидеся́тый. —*n.* **1,** (fiftieth part) пятидеся́тая часть. **2,** (fraction) пятидеся́тая: *one-fiftieth,* одна́ пятидеся́тая.

fifty *n. & adj.* пятьдеся́т.

fig *n.* **1,** (tree) инжи́р; фи́га; фи́говое де́рево; смоко́вница. **2,** (fruit) инжи́р; фи́га; ви́нная я́года; смо́ква. **3,** (insulting gesture) шиш; ку́киш; фи́га. —**fig leaf,** фи́говый листо́к.

fight *v.i.* **1,** (engage in fisticuffs) дра́ться. **2,** (take part in combat) сража́ться: *fight bravely,* сража́ться хра́бро. **3,** (wage war) воева́ть: *England fought against Germany,* А́нглия воева́ла с Герма́нией. **4,** (wage a campaign) боро́ться: *fight for an idea,* боро́ться за иде́ю; *fight against injustice,* боро́ться про́тив несправедли́вости. —*v.t.* **1,** (combat physically) дра́ться с. **2,** (combat in war) сража́ться с; боро́ться с: *fight the enemy,* сража́ться/боро́ться с враго́м. **3,** (wage; carry on, as a war or battle) вести́. *Fight a duel,* дра́ться на дуэ́ли. **4,** (try to do away with) боро́ться с: *fight crime/poverty,* боро́ться с престу́пностью/нищетой. **5,** *Fight one's way,* пробивать себе дорогу. —*n.* **1,** (fistfight) драка: *start a fight,* затеять драку. *Get into a fight with,* подраться с. **2,** (fighting) бой: *surrender without a fight,* сдаться без боя. **3,** *fig.* (battle; campaign) борьба: *the fight against crime,* борьба с преступностью. —**fight back, 1,** (not yield) оказывать сопротивление. **2,** (try to suppress, as tears) бороться с. —**fight off,** отбиваться от.

fighter *n.* **1,** (combatant) боец. **2,** (pugilist) боксер. **3,** (strong advocate, as of a cause) борец. **4,** (fighter plane) истребитель. —**fighter-bomber,** *n.* истребитель-бомбардировщик. —**fighter-pilot,** *n.* летчик-истребитель.

fighting *n.* бой. *Heavy fighting,* тяжелые *or* упорные бои. —*adj.* **1,** (pert. to combat) боевой. **2,** (militant, as of a speech) воинственный.

figment *n.* вымысел; выдумка. *Figment of the imagination,* плод *or* игра воображения.

figurative *adj.* переносный. —**figuratively,** *adv.* образно: *figuratively speaking,* образно говоря.

figure *n.* **1,** (form; shape; anything visible by its outline) фигура. **2,** (number) цифра: *exact figures,* точные цифры. *Figure eight,* восьмерка. *Bad at figures,* слаб в арифметике. **3,** (representation; picture; design) фигура. **4,** (diagram in a textbook) рисунок. **5,** (personage) фигура; лицо; персона; деятель. **6,** *geom.* фигура. —*v.t.* **1,** *often fol. by out* (calculate) рассчитывать; подсчитывать. **2,** *colloq.* (think; reckon) полагать; считать. **3,** *fol. by out* (solve) разгадывать. **4,** *fol. by out* (understand) сообразить. —*v.i.* **1,** (appear prominently) фигурировать. **2,** *fol. by on* (count on) рассчитывать на. —**figure of speech,** оборот речи.

figured *adj.* фигурный; узорчатый.

figurehead *n.* номинальный глава.

figure skating фигурное катание. —**figure skater,** фигурист.

figurine *n.* фигурка; статуэтка.

filament *n.* **1,** (fine thread or fiber) волокно. **2,** (of a bulb) нить; волосок.

filbert *n.* фундук.

filch *v.t.* стащить; стянуть.

file *n.* **1,** (cabinet) шкаф; (folder) папка; скоросшиватель. **2,** (record) дело; досье. *Card file,* картотека. *Newspaper file,* газетная подшивка. **3,** (line) ряд; шеренга; колонна; вереница. *Single file,* гуськом. **4,** *chess* вертикаль. **5,** (tool) напильник. *Nail file,* пилка для ногтей. —*v.t.* **1,** (smooth with a file) подпиливать. **2,** (store in a file) подшивать (к делу). **3,** (submit; lodge; register) подавать: *file an application/complaint,* подавать заявление/жалобу. *File suit against,* подавать в суд на (+ *acc.*). *File a claim/protest,* заявить претензию/протест. —*v.i.* **1,** (march in file) идти колонной; идти гуськом. *File in,* входить гуськом. *File out,* выходить гуськом. **2,** (make application) подавать заявление. *File for divorce,* возбуждать дело о разводе.

filet *n.* филе.

filial *adj.* сыновний; дочерний.

filigree *n.* филигрань. —*adj.* филигранный.

filing cabinet шкаф (для хранения документов).

filings *n.pl.* опилки.

fill *v.t.* **1,** (make full) наполнять: *fill the pail with water,* наполнить ведро водой. *The room was filled with smoke,* комната наполнилась дымом. **2,** (occupy

the whole of) заполнять. **3,** (plug up; close) затыкать: *fill the cracks,* затыкать щели. **4,** (complete, as an order for merchandise) выполнять (заказ). **5,** (satisfy, as a need) удовлетворять. **6,** (occupy, as an office) занимать. **7,** (put a filling in, as a tooth) пломбировать. —*v.i.* [*usu.* **fill up**] наполняться. —**eat one's fill,** наесться досыта *or* вволю. —**fill in, 1,** (fill, as cracks) затыкать. **2,** (fill up, as a hole) засыпать; закапывать. **3,** (write in) вписывать. **4,** *fol. by for* (be a substitute for) заменять. **5,** *fol. by on* (provide with information about) вводить в курс (+ *gen.*). —**fill out, 1,** (complete, as a questionnaire) заполнять. **2,** (become fuller or more rounded) полнеть; округляться. —**fill up, 1,** (make full) наполнять. **2,** (become full) наполняться.

filler *n.* **1,** (substance to increase bulk) наполнитель. **2,** (substance to fill cracks) шпаклевка. **3,** (filling, as for pies) начинка.

fillet *n.* **1,** (band) лента. **2,** (of meat) филе; вырезка.

filling *n.* **1,** (act of filling) наполнение. **2,** (for pastry, cake, etc.) фарш; начинка. **3,** (for a tooth) пломба. **4,** *textiles* (weft; woof) уток. —*adj.* (of food) сытный. —**filling station,** бензозаправочная станция; автозаправочная станция.

fillip *n.* **1,** (snap of the fingers) щелчок. **2,** *fig.* (stimulus) толчок.

filly *n.* кобылка.

film *n.* **1,** (thin layer) пленка. **2,** *photog.* пленка; фотопленка. **3,** (movie) фильм; картина. —*v.t.* **1,** (photograph) снимать; заснять. **2,** (make a movie of) экранизировать.

filmy *adj.* похожий на пленку; вязкий.

filter *n.* фильтр. —*v.t.* фильтровать; процеживать. —*v.i.* просачиваться.

filth *n.* грязь. —**filthy,** *adj.* грязный.

filtration *n.* фильтрация.

fin *n.* плавник.

final *adj.* **1,** (last) последний; конечный; заключительный. *Final examination,* курсовой экзамен. **2,** (definitive) окончательный: *the decision of the court is final,* решение суда — окончательное. —*n.,* *often pl., sports* финал.

finale *n.* финал.

finalist *n.* финалист.

finality *n.* окончательность. *With an air of finality,* повелительным тоном.

finally *adv.* наконец.

finance *n., often pl.* финансы. —*v.t.* финансировать. —**financial,** *adj.* финансовый. —**financier,** *n.* финансист.

finch *n.* вьюрок. *Bullfinch,* снегирь. *Chaffinch,* зяблик. *Goldfinch,* щегол.

find *v.t.* **1,** (locate; discover) находить. **2,** (discover by chance) заставать: *find someone at home,* застать кого-нибудь дома. **3,** (discover on arrival) находить: *find the door open,* находить дверь открытой. **4,** (consider; think) находить: *find the book interesting,* находить книгу интересной. **5,** (receive, as pleasure, application, etc.) находить. **6,** (reach; attain) попадать в: *find its mark,* попадать в цель. **7,** (adjudge) признавать: *find someone guilty,* признать кого-нибудь виновным. **8,** (recover the use of): *he has found his tongue,* у него язык развязался. **9,** *in* **find fault with,** придираться к. **10,** *in* **find (the) time,** находить время. —*n.* находка: *a real find,* настоящая находка. —**be found,** находиться. *Kangaroos are *found only in Australia*, кенгуру́ во́дятся то́лько в Австра́лии. *He is nowhere to be found*, его́ нигде́ нет. **—find oneself, 1,** (perceive oneself to be somewhere) оказа́ться; очути́ться. **2,** (become aware) лови́ть себя́: *find oneself doing something*, лови́ть себя́ на том, что (+ *verb*). **3,** (discover one's special abilities) найти́ себя́. **—find out,** узнава́ть.

finding *n.* **1,** (verdict) реше́ние. **2,** *usu. pl.* (results of an inquiry) вы́воды. **3,** *pl.* (accessories used in dressmaking) прикла́д.

fine *adj.* **1,** (excellent) хоро́ший; прекра́сный. **2,** (clear; cloudless) я́сный; пого́жий. **3,** (very small, as of print; not coarse, as of sand) ме́лкий. **4,** (very thin, as of thread) то́нкий. **5,** (subtle) то́нкий. *Fine point*, то́нкость. *—adv.* **1,** (into small particles) ме́лко. **2,** (O.K.; swell) хорошо́. *—n.* штраф: *a ten-dollar fine*, штраф в де́сять до́лларов. *—v.t.* штрафова́ть: *he was fined 100 dollars*, его́ оштрафова́ли (*or* он был оштрафо́ван) на сто до́лларов. **—fine arts,** изя́щные *or* изобрази́тельные иску́сства.

finely *adv.* то́нко.

fineness *n.* то́нкость.

finery *n.* наря́ды.

finesse *n.* то́нкость.

finger *n.* па́лец. *—v.t.* перебира́ть. **—not lay a finger on,** па́льцем не тро́гать. **—not lift a finger,** па́лец о па́лец не уда́рить. **—point one's finger at,** пока́зывать *or* ука́зывать па́льцем на (+ *acc.*). **—put the finger on,** *slang* доноси́ть на.

finger board гриф.

fingering *n., music* аппликату́ра.

finger mark пятно́ от па́льца.

fingernail *n.* но́готь.

fingerprint *n.* отпеча́ток па́льца. *—v.t.* снима́ть отпеча́тки па́льцев с (+ *gen.*).

fingertip *n.* ко́нчик па́льца. **—have at one's fingertips,** знать как свои́ пять па́льцев.

finical *adj.* привере́дливый. *Also,* **finicky.**

finish *v.t.* **1,** (complete) конча́ть; зака́нчивать. **2,** (ruin) дока́нчивать; докона́ть. **3,** (give a desired surface to) отде́лывать. *—v.i.* **1,** (complete something being done) конча́ть: *have you finished?,* вы ко́нчили? **2,** (come to an end) конча́ться. *—n.* **1,** (end) коне́ц. *Fight to the finish,* борьба́ не на жизнь, а на смерть. **2,** *sports* фи́ниш. *Finish line,* фи́ниш. **3,** (surface texture) полиро́вка: *dull finish,* ту́склая полиро́вка. **—finish off, 1,** (complete) зака́нчивать. **2,** (eat or drink) прика́нчивать. **3,** (kill; destroy) добива́ть; прика́нчивать; дока́нчивать.

finished *adj.* **1,** (completed) зако́нченный. **2,** (completely processed) гото́вый: *finished goods,* гото́вые изде́лия. **3,** (highly skilled; polished) зако́нченный. **4,** (done for) пропа́вший; поги́бший; *we're finished,* мы пропа́ли; мы поги́бли.

finite *adj.* коне́чный.

Finn *n.* финн; фи́нка. **—Finnish,** *adj.* фи́нский. *—n.* фи́нский язы́к.

Finno-Ugric *adj.* фи́нно-уго́рский.

fiord *n.* фио́рд.

fir *n.* пи́хта. *—adj.* пи́хтовый.

fire *n.* **1,** (flames) ого́нь. *Be on fire,* быть в огне́; горе́ть. **2,** (campfire) костёр: *sit around the fire,* сиде́ть вокру́г костра́. **3,** (conflagration) пожа́р: *forest fire,* лесно́й пожа́р. **4,** (shooting) ого́нь; обстре́л. *Open fire,* откры́ть ого́нь. *Be under fire,* быть под обстре́лом. *—adj.* пожа́рный: *fire hydrant,* пожа́рный кран. *—v.t.* **1,** (shoot, as a gun) стреля́ть из. **2,** (propel) пуска́ть: *fire a bullet,* пуска́ть пу́лю. *Fire a shot,* производи́ть вы́стрел. **3,** (feed the fire of) топи́ть. **4,** (bake in a kiln) обжига́ть. **5,** *fol. by up* (rouse; excite) зажига́ть; воспламеня́ть. **6,** *colloq.* (discharge) увольня́ть; прогоня́ть; выгоня́ть с рабо́ты. *—v.i.* **1,** (shoot) стреля́ть. *Fire on,* стреля́ть в; вести́ ого́нь по. *Fire into a crowd,* стреля́ть в толпу́. **2,** (go off) вы́стрелить. **—be on fire,** горе́ть; быть в огне́. **—catch fire,** загоре́ться. **—come under fire, 1,** (come under gunfire) попа́сть под обстре́л. **2,** (come under criticism) попа́сть под обстре́л кри́тики. **—hang fire,** дать осе́чку. **—play with fire,** игра́ть с огнём. **—set fire to; set on fire,** поджига́ть.

fire alarm пожа́рная трево́га.

firearm *n.* огнестре́льное ору́жие.

fireball *n.* **1,** (large meteor) боли́д. **2,** (cloud formed by a nuclear blast) о́гненный шар.

firebird *n.* жар-пти́ца.

fire bomb зажига́тельная бо́мба.

firebrand *n.* **1,** (piece of smoldering wood) голове́шка. **2,** (one who inflames passions) пла́менный ора́тор.

firecracker *n.* петарда.

fire engine пожа́рная маши́на.

fire escape пожа́рная ле́стница.

fire extinguisher огнетуши́тель.

firefighter *n.* пожа́рный.

firefly *n.* светля́к; светлячо́к.

firehouse *n.* пожа́рное депо́.

fire irons ками́нные щипцы́.

fireman *n.* **1,** (firefighter) пожа́рный. **2,** (stoker) кочега́р.

fireplace *n.* ками́н.

fireplug *n.* пожа́рный кран; гидра́нт.

firepower *n.* огнева́я мощь.

fireproof *adj.* огнесто́йкий; несгора́емый.

fire screen ками́нная решётка.

fireside *n.* оча́г.

fire station пожа́рное депо́.

firewood *n.* дрова́.

fireworks *n.* фейерве́рк.

firing *n.* **1,** (shooting) стрельба́. **2,** (laying off) увольне́ние. **—firing line,** огнево́й рубе́ж; ли́ния огня́. **—firing pin,** уда́рник. **—firing range,** стре́льбище; полиго́н.

firm *adj.* твёрдый; про́чный. *Firm ground,* твёрдая по́чва. *Firm foundation,* про́чный фунда́мент. *Firm tone,* твёрдый тон. *Firm belief,* твёрдое убежде́ние. *—adv.* твёрдо: *stand firm,* держа́ться твёрдо; твёрдо стоя́ть на своём. *—n.* фи́рма: *law firm,* юриди́ческая фи́рма.

firmament *n.* небе́сный свод; небосво́д.

firmly *adv.* твёрдо; про́чно; кре́пко.

firmness *n.* твёрдость.

first *adj.* пе́рвый: *the first time,* пе́рвый раз. *The first thing that comes to mind,* пе́рвое, что прихо́дит в го́лову. *—adv.* **1,** (before all others) пе́рвым: *come in first,* прийти́ пе́рвым. **2,** (before doing something else) снача́ла: *Think first!,* снача́ла поду́май! **3,** (for the first time) впервы́е: *when I first saw her,* когда́ я впервы́е уви́дел(а) её. **4,** (sooner; preferably) скоре́е: *I'd die first,* я скоре́е умру́. *—n.* пе́рвый. *(On) the first of the month,* пе́рвого числа́. *It's the first I've heard*

of it, пéрвый раз слы́шу. —**at first**, снача́ла. —**first of all**, прéжде всего́. —**in the first place**, во-пéрвых.

first aid ско́рая по́мощь; пéрвая по́мощь. —**first-aid kit**, апте́чка; *mil.* санита́рная су́мка. —**first-aid station**, медпу́нкт.

first-born *n.* пéрвенец.

first-class *adj.* **1**, (first-rate) первокла́ссный. **2**, (most expensive, as of accommodations) пéрвого кла́сса. —*adv.* пéрвым кла́ссом.

first cousin двою́родный брат; двою́родная сестра́.

firsthand *adj. & adv.* из пéрвых рук.

firstly *adv.* во-пéрвых.

first name и́мя.

first-rate *adj.* первокла́ссный.

fiscal *adj.* фина́нсовый. —**fiscal year**, фина́нсовый год.

fish *n.* ры́ба. —*adj.* ры́бный: *fish soup*, ры́бный суп. —*v.i.* **1**, (go fishing) лови́ть *or* уди́ть ры́бу; рыба́чить. **2**, *fol. by* **for** (attempt to catch) уди́ть. **3**, *fol. by* **for** (seek indirectly) напра́шиваться на: *fish for compliments*, напра́шиваться на комплиме́нты. —*v.t.* [*usu.* **fish out**] выла́вливать. —**drink like a fish**, пить как бо́чка; пить запо́ем. —**fish in troubled waters**, лови́ть ры́бу в му́тной воде́. —**neither fish nor fowl**, ни ры́ба ни мя́со.

fishbone *n.* ры́бья кость.

fishbowl *n.* аква́риум.

fish cake ры́бная котле́та.

fisher *n.* (animal) и́лька.

fisherman *n.* рыба́к; рыболо́в.

fishery *n.* **1**, (business of fishing) ры́бный про́мысел. **2**, (fishing ground) ры́бные места́.

fishhook *n.* (рыболо́вный) крючо́к.

fishing *n.* ры́бная ло́вля. —*adj.* рыболо́вный. —**fishing boat**, рыба́чья ло́дка. —**fishing line**, леса́. —**fishing rod**, у́дочка; удили́ще. —**fishing tackle**, рыболо́вная снасть.

fish story охо́тничий расска́з.

fish tank аква́риум.

fishy *adj.* **1**, (suggestive of fish) ры́бный. **2**, (expressionless) ры́бий: *fishy eyes*, ры́бьи глаза́. **3**, *colloq.* (questionable; suspicious) сомни́тельный. *Something is fishy here*, тут что́-то нела́дно.

fission *n.* **1**, *physics* расщепле́ние; деле́ние. *Nuclear fission*, я́дерное деле́ние. **2**, *biol.* деле́ние (кле́ток). —**fissionable**, *adj.* расщепля́ющийся.

fissure *n.* тре́щина; рассе́лина; расще́лина.

fist *n.* кула́к. —**fistfight**, *n.* кула́чный бой.

fisticuffs *n.pl.* **1**, (fistfight) кула́чный бой. **2**, (pugilism) бокс.

fistula *n.* фи́стула; свищ.

fit *v.t.* **1**, (be the right size for) быть впо́ру (+ *dat.*); быть в са́мый раз (+ *dat.*). *The key fits the lock*, ключ подхо́дит к замку́. **2**, (be appropriate to) подходи́ть (+ *dat.*); быть подходя́щим для; соотве́тствовать (+ *dat.*). **3**, (find room for; squeeze into) умеща́ть. **4**, (tailor; adjust) пригоня́ть. **5**, *fol. by* **out** (equip) снаряжа́ть; оснаща́ть. —*v.i.* **1**, (be the right size) быть впо́ру; подходи́ть. **2**, (be able to go into something) входи́ть; вмеща́ться; помеща́ться; умеща́ться; укла́дываться. *Fit through the door*, проходи́ть в дверь. *Fit around the table*, умести́ться за столо́м. **3**, *fol. by* **in** (be suitable) подходи́ть. *That*

fits in with my plans, э́то совпада́ет с мои́ми пла́нами. —*adj.* **1**, (suitable) го́дный; приго́дный. *Fit to drink*, го́дный для питья́. *Fit for military service*, го́дный к вое́нной слу́жбе. *Not fit for anything*, ни на что не спосо́бен. **2**, (in good physical condition) здоро́вый; в хоро́шем состоя́нии. **3**, *fol. by passive inf.* (in suitable condition) в состоя́нии (+ *inf.*). *I am not fit to be seen*, я не могу́ показа́ться. —*n.* **1**, (seizure; spell) припа́док; при́ступ. *Epileptic fit*, эпилепти́ческий припа́док. *Fit of coughing*, при́ступ ка́шля. **2**, (outburst) поры́в: *fit of rage*, поры́в гне́ва. **3**, (manner of fitting): *be a good fit*, хорошо́ сиде́ть. —**by fits and starts**, урывками. —**fit to be tied**, вне себя́ от гне́ва.—**see fit**, счита́ть ну́жным (+ *inf.*). *Do as you see fit*, де́лайте, как вы счита́ете ну́жным. *He will do as he sees fit*, он посту́пит так, как ему́ заблагорассу́дится.

fitch *n.* хорёк. **Also, fitchew.**

fitful *adj.* поры́вистый; преры́вистый.

fitness *n.* го́дность; приго́дность. —**physical fitness**, физи́ческая подгото́вка.

fitter *n.* **1**, (of machinery) монтёр; сле́сарь. **2**, (of clothes) портно́й.

fitting *adj.* досто́йный: *fitting reward/rebuke*, досто́йная награ́да/о́тповедь. —*n.* **1**, (trying on) приме́рка: *have a fitting*, сде́лать приме́рку. **2**, *pl.* (fixtures) армату́ра. —**fittingly**, *adv.* досто́йно.

five *adj.* пять. —*n.* **1**, (cardinal number) пять. **2**, (written numeral; school grade) пятёрка. **3**, *cards* пятёрка.

fivefold *adj.* пятикра́тный. —*adv.* впя́теро.

five hundred пятьсо́т. —**five-hundredth**, *adj.* пятисо́тый.

Five-Year Plan пятиле́тка; пятиле́тний план.

fix *v.t.* **1**, (repair) чини́ть; нала́живать. **2**, *fol. by* **up** (decorate, as a room) обставля́ть; отде́лывать. **3**, (fasten securely) укрепля́ть; закрепля́ть. **4**, (direct steadily, as one's gaze) устремля́ть; прико́вывать; фикси́ровать. **5**, (set, as a date) назнача́ть; определя́ть; фикси́ровать. **6**, (prepare, as a meal) гото́вить. **7**, (determine, as blame) устана́вливать (вино́вность). **8**, *photog.* закрепля́ть; фикси́ровать. **9**, *colloq.* (get even with) разде́лываться с. *I'll fix him!*, я ему́ зада́м! —*n.*, *colloq.* переде́лка: *get into a fix*, попа́сть в переде́лку; сесть в лу́жу.

fixation *n.* навя́зчивая иде́я.

fixed *adj.* **1**, (stationary; immobile) неподви́жный: *fixed point*, неподви́жная то́чка. **2**, (not fluctuating) фикси́рованный. **3**, (provided for) обеспе́ченный: *well fixed*, хорошо́ обеспе́ченный. *She is well fixed*, она́ живёт в доста́тке. *How are you fixed for money?*, как у вас с деньга́ми? —**fixed bayonets**, при́мкнутые штыки́. —**fixed idea**, навя́зчивая иде́я.

fixture *n.* прибо́р; дета́ль; *pl.* армату́ра.

fizz *v.i.* шипе́ть. —*n.* шипе́ние.

fizzle *v.i.* **1**, (hiss) шипе́ть. **2**, *colloq.* (peter out) выдыха́ться.

flabbergast *v.t.*, *colloq.* ошара́шивать.

flabby *adj.* дря́блый; вя́лый; обрю́згший; обрю́зглый. *Become flabby*, обрю́згнуть. —**flabbiness**, *n.* дря́блость.

flaccid *adj.* дря́блый; отви́слый.

flag *n.* флаг. —*v.t.* [*usu.* **flag down**] (hail; signal to stop) оклика́ть. —*v.i.* (slacken; wane) слабе́ть; ослабева́ть. *The conversation flagged*, разгово́р (ча́сто) замолка́л.

flagellate v.t. бичевáть. —**flagellation,** n. бичевáние.

flagman n. сигнáльщик.

flag officer флáгман.

flagpole n. флагштóк.

flagrant adj. грýбый; вопиющий.

flagship n. флáгманский корáбль; флáгман.

flagstaff n. флагштóк.

flagstone n. плитá; плитнЯк. —adj. плитнякóвый.

flail n. цеп. —v.t. **1,** (thresh) молотить. **2,** (beat) колотить.

flair n. спосóбности: a flair for music/languages, спосóбности к мýзыке/языкáм.

flak n. зенитная артиллéрия.

flake n., usu. pl. хлóпья. Corn flakes, кукурýзные хлóпья. Soap flakes, мыльная стрýжка. —v.i. [usu. **flake off**] лупиться; шелушиться. —**flaky,** adj. слоéный.

flamboyant adj. цветистый; пышный; показнóй.

flame n. **1,** (fire) плáмя: burst into flame, вспыхнуть плáменем. Be in flames, быть в огнé. **2,** (passion) увлечéние. **3,** colloq. (sweetheart) зазнóба. —v.i. пылáть. —**flame thrower,** огнемёт.

flaming adj. **1,** (ablaze) пылáющий. **2,** (intense; ardent) плáменный.

flamingo n. фламинго.

flammable adj. огнеопáсный.

flange n. **1,** (for a pipe) флáнец. **2,** (for a wheel) ребóрда.

flank n. фланг. —v.t. фланкировать. He was flanked by two bodyguards, у негó по бокáм стояли два телохранителя. —**flanking,** adj. фланговый.

flannel n. фланéль. —adj. фланéлевый.

flap v.t. взмáхивать (крыльями). —v.i. развевáться. —n. **1,** (flapping, as of wings) взмах. **2,** (of a garment or tent) полá; (of a pocket) клáпан. **3,** aero. закрылок.

flare n. **1,** (burst of flame) вспышка. **2,** (signal light) фáкел; сигнáльная ракéта. **3,** (expanding part) раструб; клёш. Flared skirt, юбка клёш. —v.i. [usu. **flare up**] **1,** (flame up brightly) возгорáться. **2,** (suddenly become angry) вспылить. **3,** fig. (break out; erupt) разгорáться; вспыхивать. Tempers flared, стрáсти разгорéлись.

flash n. **1,** (of light) вспышка; прóблеск. Flash of lightning, вспышка мóлнии. **2,** (instant) миг: in a flash, мигом; в один миг. **3,** pl. (sudden manifestations, as of wit) блёстки (остроýмия). —v.i. **1,** (shine brightly or suddenly) сверкáть: lightning flashed, сверкнýла мóлния. A flashing light, мигáющий свет. His eyes flashed with anger, егó глазá сверкáли гнéвом. **2,** fol. by **by, past, across** (pass suddenly and swiftly) мелькнýть; промелькнýть. An idea flashed across my mind, у меня (про)мелькнýла or блеснýла мысль; меня осенила мысль. —v.t. **1,** (shine) светить: flash a light in someone's eyes, светить комý-нибудь в глазá. **2,** (send at great speed) сообщить (с быстротóй мóлнии). Flash a signal, подавáть сигнáл. **3,** colloq. (display ostentatiously) выставлЯть; демонстрировать.

flash bulb лáмпа-вспышка; блиц.

flasher n. мигáлка.

flash gun вспышка.

flashlight n. кармáнный фонáрь.

flashy adj. кричáщий; крикливый.

flask n. **1,** (for carrying liquids) флЯга; флЯжка. **2,** (for use in a laboratory) кóлба.

flat adj. **1,** (level) плóский: flat surface, плóская повéрхность. **2,** (lacking zest, as of a drink) выдохшийся. **3,** (dull; insipid) плóский; прéсный. **4,** (absolute; pointblank) категорический. —adv. **1,** (prostrate) плашмЯ; врастЯжку. Lie flat, ложиться плашмЯ; распластáться. Flat on one's back, нáвзничь; пластóм. **2,** (in full contact) вплотнýю: flat against the wall, вплотнýю к стенé. **3,** (completely) совершéнно: flat broke, совершéнно разорённый. **4,** (exactly) рóвно: in two minutes flat, рóвно за две минýты. **5,** music не в лад. Sing flat, фальшивить. —n. **1,** (apartment) квартира. **2,** music бемóль: E-flat, ми-бемóль. **3,** (low-lying area) бассéйн: salt flats, соляные бассéйны. **4,** pl. (flat-heeled shoes) тýфли без каблукá. **5,** = **flat tire.** —**fall flat,** провáливаться. —**flat tire,** спýщенная шина or покрышка: we had a flat tire, у нас спустила шина/покрышка.

flat-bottomed adj. плоскодóнный.

flatcar n. платфóрма; вагóн-платфóрма.

flat-chested adj. плоскогрýдый.

flatfoot n. плóская стопá; плоскостóпие.

flatfooted adj. страдáющий плоскостóпием. —**catch flatfooted,** colloq. застáть врасплóх.

flatiron n. утюг.

flatly adv. (categorically) наотрéз.

flatness n. плóскость.

flatten v.t. сплющивать; расплющивать. —v.i. [usu. **flatten out**] **1,** (become flat) сплющиваться. **2,** aero. (resume a horizontal line of flight) вырáвниваться.

flatter v.t. льстить. I am flattered, мне лéстно; я польщён. —**flatterer,** n. льстец.

flattering adj. **1,** (intended to flatter) льстивый. **2,** (complimentary) лéстный.

flattery n. лесть.

flatulence n. скоплéние гáзов; метеоризм.

flatware n. столóвые прибóры.

flatworm n. плóский червь.

flaunt v.t. выставлЯть напокáз; афишировать; козырЯть; кокéтничать; щеголЯть (last three with instr.).

flavor also, **flavour** n. **1,** (distinctive taste) вкус. **2,** (distinctive quality) привкус. —v.t. приправлЯть.

flavoring also, **flavouring** n. припрáва.

flavour n. & v. = **flavor.** —**flavouring,** n. = **flavoring.**

flaw n. порóк; брак; изъЯн. —v.t. пóртить. —**flawed,** adj. с изъЯном.

flawless adj. безупрéчный; безукоризненный. —**flawlessly,** adv. безупрéчно; безукоризненно.

flax n. лён. —**flaxen,** adj. льнянóй. Flaxen hair, льняные вóлосы.

flay v.t. **1,** (strip off the skin of) сдирáть кóжу с; обдирáть. **2,** fig. (criticize severely) хлестáть.

flea n. блохá. —**fleabite,** n. блошиный укýс. —**flea market,** толкýчка.

fleck n. пятнó; крáпинка. —v.t. испещрЯть. Hair flecked with gray, вóлосы с прóседью.

fledged adj. оперившийся. Become fully fledged, оперЯться.

fledgling n. птенéц.

flee v.i. бежáть; убегáть; спасáться бéгством. —v.t. бежáть из; убегáть из.

fleece n. рунó. —v.t. (swindle) обирáть; обдирáть.

fleecy adj. **1,** (soft and light) пушистый. **2,** (of clouds) пéристый.

fleet n. **1,** (of warships) флот. **2,** (of boats) флотилия:

whaling fleet, китобо́йная флоти́лия. **3,** (of vehicles) парк. —*adj.* бы́стрый; быстроно́гий. —*v.i.* бежа́ть; лете́ть.

fleeting *adj.* **1,** (momentary) мимолётный. **2,** *phonet.* (of a vowel) бе́глый.

Fleming *n.* флама́ндец. —**Flemish,** *adj.* флама́ндский. —*n.* флама́ндский язы́к.

flesh *n.* **1,** (soft substance of the body) мя́коть; мя́со. *Flesh wound*, пове́рхностная ра́на. **2,** (the body as distinguished from the soul) плоть, во плоти́. —**it makes my flesh creep,** у меня́ мура́шки бе́гают по спине́. —**one's own flesh and blood,** чья́-нибудь плоть и кровь.

flesh-colored *adj.* теле́сный; теле́сного цве́та.

fleshy *adj.* мяси́стый.

flex *v.t.* гнуть; сгиба́ть.

flexible *adj.* ги́бкий. —**flexibility,** *n.* ги́бкость.

flick *n.* щелчо́к. —*v.t.* **1,** (strike deftly) щёлкать. **2,** (remove with a quick snap) сма́хивать.

flicker *v.i.* **1,** (glimmer) мерца́ть; мига́ть; трепета́ть. **2,** *fol. by* **out** (go out) га́снуть; угаса́ть. —*n.* **1,** (wavering light) мерца́ние; мига́ние; тре́пет. **2,** (ray, as of hope) и́скра (наде́жды).

flier *also,* **flyer** *n.* лётчик.

flight *n.* **1,** (act of flying) полёт. *Be in flight*, быть в полёте. **2,** (trip made by air) полёт; перелёт. **3,** (scheduled trip of an airplane) рейс. **4,** (abrupt departure) бе́гство: *put to flight*, обраща́ть в бе́гство; *take flight*, обраща́ться в бе́гство. **5,** (set of stairs) марш. **6,** (flock of birds) ста́я. **7,** (group of airplanes) звено́. **8,** (soaring beyond normal limits) полёт: *flight of fantasy*, полёт фанта́зии. —**flight deck,** полётная па́луба (авиано́сца). —**flight engineer,** бортмеха́ник. —**flight path,** траекто́рия полёта. —**flight recorder,** бортово́й самопи́сец.

flighty *adj.* легкомы́сленный; ве́треный.

flimsy *adj.* **1,** (lacking solidity) непро́чный. **2,** (poor, as of an excuse) сла́бый. —**flimsiness,** *n.* непро́чность.

flinch *v.i.* **1,** (wince, as from pain) вздра́гивать. **2,** (draw back; shrink, as from fear) дро́гнуть.

fling *v.t.* кида́ть; мета́ть; швыря́ть. *Fling open*, распа́хивать. —*n.* **1,** (toss) бросо́к. **2,** *colloq.* (try) попы́тка. *Have a fling at*, попро́бовать.

flint *n.* креме́нь.

flip *v.t.* **1,** (toss) броса́ть. **2,** (toss into the air, as a coin) подбра́сывать. **3,** (flick) сма́хивать. **4,** (turn rapidly, as a dial) верте́ть; крути́ть. **5,** *fol. by* **over** (invert) перевёртывать. —*v.i.* **1,** *fol. by* **over** (turn over) перевёртываться. **2,** *fol. by* **through** (leaf through) перели́стывать.

flippant *adj.* де́рзкий. —**flippancy,** *n.* де́рзость.

flipper *n.* ласт.

flirt *v.i.* коке́тничать; флиртова́ть. —*n.* коке́тка. —**flirtation,** *n.* коке́тство; флирт. —**flirtatious,** *adj.* коке́тливый.

flit *v.i.* порха́ть.

float *v.i.* **1,** (not sink) пла́вать; не тону́ть; держа́ться на воде́. **2,** (drift) плыть; нести́сь. *Float to the surface*, всплыва́ть *or* выпла́ивать на пове́рхность. —*v.t.* **1,** (ship by water, as logs) сплавля́ть. **2,** (arrange for, as a loan) размеща́ть (заём). —*n.* поплаво́к.

floating *adj.* **1,** (on water) пла́вающий; плаву́чий. **2,** *finance* оборо́тный: *floating capital*, оборо́тный капита́л. **3,** *med.* блужда́ющий: *floating kidney*, блужда́ющая по́чка.

flock *n.* **1,** (of sheep, goats, etc.) ста́до. **2,** (of birds) ста́я. **3,** (congregation) па́ства. **4,** (crowd) толпа́. —*v.i.* толпи́ться; стека́ться; (вало́м) вали́ть.

floe *n.* плаву́чая льди́на.

flog *v.t.* сечь; поро́ть; хлеста́ть; стега́ть.

flood *n.* **1,** (deluge) наводне́ние. *The Flood*, всеми́рный пото́п. **2,** *fig.* (huge flow or influx) пото́к. —*v.t.* **1,** (fill with water) затопля́ть; залива́ть. **2,** *fig.* (overwhelm) наводня́ть.

floodgate *n.* шлюз; шлю́зные воро́та.

floodlight *n.* проже́ктор.

flood plain (заливна́я) по́йма.

flood tide прили́в.

floodwaters *n.pl.* по́лая вода́. *The floodwaters are receding*, во́ды убыва́ют.

floor *n.* **1,** (in a room) пол. **2,** (story of a building) эта́ж: *on the sixth floor*, на шесто́м этаже́. **3,** (bottom) дно: *ocean floor*, морско́е дно. **4,** (right to speak) сло́во: *ask for the floor*, проси́ть сло́ва. *Questions from the floor*, вопро́сы с ме́ста. —*v.t.* **1,** (knock to the ground) вали́ть на́ пол. **2,** *colloq.* (stun) оглуши́ть.

floorboard *n.* полови́ца.

flooring *n.* насти́л.

floor lamp торше́р.

floor show варьете́.

floorspace *n.* жила́я пло́щадь; жилпло́щадь.

flop *v.i.* **1,** (fall) плю́хаться; бу́хаться; хло́паться. **2,** *slang* (fail) прова́ливаться. —*n., colloq.* неуда́ча; фиа́ско.

flophouse *n., colloq.* ночле́жка.

flora *n.* фло́ра.

floral *adj.* цвето́чный.

floriculture *n.* цветово́дство.

florid *adj.* цвети́стый; витиева́тый.

florin *n.* флори́н.

florist *n.* торго́вец цвета́ми. *Florist's shop*, цвето́чный магази́н.

flotilla *n.* флоти́лия.

flounce *n.* обо́рка.

flounder *n.* (fish) ка́мбала. —*v.i.* **1,** (move with great difficulty) бара́хтаться. **2,** *fig.* (fare badly) хрома́ть на о́бе ноги́.

flour *n.* мука́. —*adj.* мучно́й: *flour sack*, мучно́й мешо́к.

flourish *v.i.* процвета́ть. —*n.* **1,** (embellishment in writing) ро́счерк; завито́к; завиту́шка. **2,** (use of ornate language) завито́к; завиту́шка: *rhetorical flourishes*, ритори́ческие завиту́шки. **3,** (sound of trumpets) фанфа́ра; туш.

flout *v.t.* бро́сить вы́зов (+ *dat.*); попира́ть.

flow *v.i.* течь; ли́ться. *Flow out to sea*, вытека́ть в мо́ре. *The Volga flows into the Caspian Sea*, Во́лга впада́ет в Каспи́йское мо́ре. *The Danube flows through eight countries*, Дуна́й течёт *or* протека́ет че́рез во́семь стран. —*n.* **1,** (of a fluid) тече́ние. *Flow of blood*, кровотече́ние. **2,** *fig.* (steady movement) пото́к; тече́ние; ход. —**a lot of water has flown under the bridge since then,** мно́го воды́ утекло́ с тех пор.

flower *n.* цвето́к (*pl.* цветы́). —*adj.* цвето́чный: *flower show*, цвето́чная вы́ставка. —*v.i.* цвести́; расцвета́ть. —**flower bed,** клу́мба; цветни́к. —**flower girl,** цвето́чница.

flowering *adj.* цвету́щий; цветко́вый.

flowerpot *n.* цвето́чный горшо́к; вазо́н.

flowery *adj.* цветистый; красочный; витиеватый.

flowing *adj.* **1,** (smooth and continuous) плавный. **2,** (hanging loosely at full length) свисающий.

flu *n.* грипп.

fluctuate *v.i.* колебаться. —**fluctuation,** *n.* колебание.

flue *n.* дымоход.

fluency *n.* плавность; беглость.

fluent *adj.* плавный; беглый; свободный. —**fluently,** *adv.* свободно; бегло.

fluff *n.* пух; пушок. —*v.t.* [*usu.* **fluff up**] взбивать; (рас)пушить. —**fluffy,** *adj.* пушистый; пышный.

fluid *n.* жидкость. —*adj.* жидкий; текучий. —**fluidity,** *n.* текучесть.

fluke *n.* **1,** (fish) камбала. **2,** (part of an anchor) лапа. **3,** *slang* (lucky chance) игра случая.

flunk *v.t., colloq.* **1,** (fail, as an exam) срезаться на (экзамене). **2,** (fail, as a student) срезать. —*v.i., colloq.* срезаться.

flunky *also,* **flunkey** *n.* лакей.

fluoresce *v.i.* флуоресцировать.

fluorescence *n.* свечение; флуоресценция.

fluorescent *adj.* флуоресцирующий. —**fluorescent lamp,** люминесцентная лампа.

fluoride *n.* фторид. ♦ *In combinations* фтористый: *sodium fluoride,* фтористый натрий.

fluorine *n.* фтор.

fluorite *n.* плавиковый шпат. *Also,* **fluorspar.**

flurry *n.* **1,** *pl.* (of snow) снежинки. **2,** (sudden burst) порыв.

flush *v.t.* **1,** (purge) промывать; очищать. *Flush the toilet,* спустить воду в уборной. **2,** (drive from cover) выкуривать. **3,** (redden) румянить. —*v.i.* краснеть; багроветь; румяниться; алеть. —*n.* краска: *flush of anger,* краска гнева. —*adj.* [*usu.* **flush with** or **against**] вровень (с); впритык (к).

fluster *v.t.* конфузить. *Become flustered,* теряться; растеряться; конфузиться.

flute *n.* флейта.

fluted *adj.* рифлёный.

flutist *n.* флейтист.

flutter *v.i.* развеваться; трепетать.

flux *n.* **1,** (continual change): *in a state of flux,* в состоянии изменения; в состоянии неопределённости. **2,** *metall.* флюс; плавень.

fly *v.i.* **1,** (general term) лететь; летать. *The little bird cannot fly,* птичка не может летать. *Fly across the ocean,* лететь через океан. *Sparks flew in all directions,* искры летели во все стороны. *Time flies,* время летит. **2,** (wave, as of a flag) развеваться. **3,** *fol. by* **into** (burst into) приходить в: *fly into a rage,* приходить в ярость. —*v.t.* **1,** (operate, as an aircraft) вести; управлять. **2,** (float, as a kite) пускать (змея). **3,** (transport by aircraft) перевозить (по воздуху); перебрасывать. **4,** (complete, as a sortie or mission) совершать (вылет). —*n.* **1,** (insect) муха. *He wouldn't hurt a fly,* он и мухи не обидит. **2,** (on trousers) ширинка. —**fly across,** перелетать. —**fly away,** улетать. —**fly by,** пролетать. —**fly in, 1,** (arrive by plane) прилетать. **2,** (deliver by air) доставлять (самолётом). —**fly in the face of,** идти вразрез с; противоречить. —**fly in the ointment,** ложка дёгтя в бочке мёда. —**fly off,** улетать. —**fly open,** распахнуться. —**fly past,** пролетать мимо. —**let fly,** пускать. —**on the fly,** на лету.

flycatcher *n.* мухоловка.

flyer *n.* = **flier.**

flying *n.* летание; лётное дело. —*adj.* **1,** (that flies) летающий; летучий. *Flying fish,* летучая рыба. *Flying saucer,* летающая тарелка. **2,** (used for flying) летательный: *flying machine,* летательный аппарат. **3,** (suitable for flying) лётный: *flying weather,* лётная погода. —**with flying colors,** с блеском.

flying squirrel летяга.

flyleaf *n.* форзац.

flypaper *n.* липучая бумага от мух; липучка от мух.

fly swatter хлопушка.

flytrap *n.* мухоловка.

flywheel *n.* маховое колесо; маховик.

foal *n.* жеребёнок. —*v.t.* рожать. —*v.i.* жеребиться.

foam *n.* пена. —*v.i.* пениться. —**foam rubber,** губчатая резина.

foamy *adj.* пенистый.

focal *adj.* фокусный: *focal length,* фокусное расстояние. *Focal point,* фокус; центр; средоточие.

focus *n.* фокус: *be in focus,* быть в фокусе. *Be the focus of attention,* быть в центре внимания. —*v.t.* **1,** (adjust the focus of) фокусировать. **2,** (concentrate) сосредоточивать.

fodder *n.* корм; фураж.

foe *n.* враг.

foetus *n.* = **fetus.**

fog *n.* туман. —*v.t.* туманить; затуманивать. —*v.i.* [*usu.* **fog up**] вспотеть; запотевать.

foggy *adj.* туманный. *It is foggy today,* сегодня туман; сегодня туманно. —**fogginess,** *n.* туманность.

foghorn *n.* наутофон.

foible *n.* слабое место; слабая сторона; слабость.

foil *v.t.* расстраивать; срывать. —*n.* **1,** (thin sheet of metal) фольга. *Tin foil,* станиоль. **2,** (sword) рапира.

foist *v.t.* навязывать; всучать.

fold *v.t.* [*often* **fold up**] складывать. *Fold one's hands,* складывать руки. *Fold up a map,* складывать карту. —*v.i.* **1,** [*often* **fold up**] (be folded) складываться. *A bed that folds up,* складная кровать. **2,** *colloq.* (fail and close down) прогореть. —*n.* **1,** (in paper or cloth; of skin) складка. **2,** (of a tent) пола; (of a screen) створка. **3,** (pen) загон. **4,** (flock; group) паства.

folder *n.* папка; скоросшиватель.

folding *adj.* **1,** (of a chair, table, etc.) складной; раскладной; откидной. **2,** (of doors) (дву)створчатый.

foliage *n.* листва.

folio *n.* **1,** (sheet) лист. **2,** (book) фолиант; фолио.

folk *n.* люди: *simple folk,* простые люди. —*adj.* народный: *folk song,* народная песня.

folklore *n.* фольклор.

follicle *n.* фолликул.

follow *v.t.* **1,** (go after; come after) следовать за. *Follow me!,* идите за мной! **2,** (watch; trail; keep track of) следить за. **3,** (proceed along, as a road) идти по; ехать по. **4,** (heed; obey) следовать (+ *dat.*): *follow advice,* следовать совету. *Follow orders,* выполнять приказания. **5,** (understand the logic of) понимать. —*v.i.* (come next or as a result) следовать. *From this it follows that...,* из этого следует, что... —**as follows,** следующее: *the telegram reads as follows,* телеграмма гласит следующее. *Your duties are as follows,* ваши обязанности заключаются в следующем.

follower *n.* последователь.

following *adj.* следующий. *The following day,* на другой день. *The following morning,* наутро. —*n.* **1,** (group of followers or fans) последователи; поклонники. **2,** *preceded by* **the** (what follows) следующее. —*prep.* после: *following the meeting,* после собрания.

folly *n.* глупость; безумие.

foment *v.t.* раздувать; разжигать.

fond *adj.* **1,** *fol. by* **of** (liking): *be fond of,* любить. **2,** (affectionate) ласковый; нёжный. **3,** (cherished, as of a wish) заветный.

fondle *v.t.* ласкать.

fondness *n.* любовь; увлечение.

font *n.* **1,** (receptacle for holy water) купель. **2,** *printing* комплект шрифта.

food *n.* пища. —*adj.* пищевой: *food poisoning,* пищевое отравление. —**food for thought,** пища для ума; пища для размышления.

foodstuff *n., usu. pl.* пищевые продукты; продовольственные товары.

fool *n.* **1,** (stupid person) дурак. **2,** (court jester) шут. —*adj.* [*usu.* **fool's**] дурацкий; шутовской: *fool's cap,* дурацкий/шутовской колпак. —*v.t.* дурачить; обманывать. —*v.i.* **1,** (jest) шутить: *I'm not fooling,* я не шучу. *Don't fool with him!,* с ним не шути! **2,** *fol. by* **with** (play with carelessly) играть (+ *instr.*). —**fool around,** дурачиться. —**make a fool of,** оставить в дураках; дурачить. —**make a fool of oneself,** остаться в дураках; опростоволоситься. —**nobody's fool,** малый не промах. —**play the fool,** валять дурака.

foolhardy *adj.* безрассудный. —**foolhardiness,** *n.* безрассудство.

foolish *adj.* глупый. —**foolishly,** *adv.* глупо. —**foolishness,** *n.* глупость.

foot *n.* **1,** (of humans) нога. **2,** (of animals) лапа. **3,** (base) подножие. **4,** (lower end; bottom) конец. *At the foot of the stairs,* внизу лестницы. *At the foot of the bed,* в ногах кровати. **5,** (of a mountain, hill, etc.) подножие; подошва. **6,** (measure of length) фут. **7,** *pros.* стопа. —*adj.* ножной: *foot brake,* ножной тормоз. —**get cold feet,** струсить. —**get to one's feet,** вставать на ноги. —**get on one's feet** (*fig.*), стать на ноги. —**on foot,** пешком. —**put one's best foot forward,** показать товар лицом. —**put one's foot in it,** попасть впросак; сесть в лужу. —**set foot on,** ступить на: *set foot on the moon,* ступить на Луну. *I never set foot in there,* нога моя туда не ступает.

footage *n.* **1,** (length expressed in feet) длина (в футах). **2,** *motion pictures* метраж.

foot-and-mouth-disease ящур.

football *n.* **1,** (game) футбол. **2,** (ball) футбольный мяч.

footbridge *n.* мостик; пешеходный мост.

foothill *n.* предгорье.

foothold *n.* точка опоры: *gain a foothold,* найти точку опоры.

footing *n.* **1,** (firm placing of the feet): *keep one's footing,* удержаться на ногах; *lose one's footing,* поскользнуться. **2,** (position; standing): *on an equal footing,* на равных условиях; на равной ноге. *Place on a war footing,* перестроить на военный лад.

footlights *n.pl.* рампа.

footman *n.* лакей; скороход.

footnote *n.* примечание; сноска.

footprint *n.* след; отпечаток ноги.

foot soldier пехотинец.

footstep *n., usu. pl.* **1,** (footprints) следы. **2,** (sound of someone walking) шаги. —**follow in the footsteps of,** идти по стопам (+ *gen.*).

footstool *n.* скамейка для ног.

footwear *n.* обувь.

fop *n.* фат; франт; щёголь; хлыщ. —**foppery,** *n.* фатовство; щегольство. —**foppish,** *adj.* фатоватый; франтоватый.

for *prep.* **1,** (used for; intended for; as regards) для: *a book for children,* книга для детей; *bad for one's health,* вредно для здоровья. ♦ *Less commonly* на: *the lesson for tomorrow,* урок на завтра; *plans for the summer,* планы на лето; *a room for two,* комната на двоих. **2,** (in favor of; in exchange for; in recognition of) за (+ *acc.*): *vote for,* голосовать за; *pay for,* платить за; *fight for,* бороться за. *An award for bravery,* награда за мужество. *Thanks for your help,* спасибо за помощь. **3,** (to fetch) за (+ *instr.*): *send for the doctor,* послать за врачом. **4,** (indicating destination) в (+ *acc.*): *leave for Washington,* уезжать в Вашингтон. **5,** (indicating duration of time) *usu.* omitted in Russian: *wait for two hours,* ждать два часа. *I haven't seen you for ages,* не видел вас целую вечность. ♦ *Also* в течение: *for the last two weeks,* в течение последних двух недель. **6,** (for a period of time begun as action is completed) на (+ *acc.*): *lie down for an hour,* прилечь на час. *Come in for a minute!,* зайдите на минуту! **7,** (in view of the normal character of) для: *very warm for May,* очень тепло для мая. *Not bad for a beginner,* неплохо для начинающего. **8,** (in place of) за (+ *acc.*); вместо. *To sign for the chairman,* расписаться за председателя. *A substitute for sugar,* суррогат сахара. **9,** (from; because of) от: *jump for joy,* прыгать от радости. **10,** (owing to) за (+ *instr.*): *for lack of evidence,* за неимением улик. *For many reasons,* по многим причинам. **11,** (as a cure for) от: *have you anything for a headache?,* у вас есть что-нибудь от головной боли? **12,** (despite) при: *for all his knowledge,* при всех его знаниях. *For all that,* при всём том. —*conj.* (because; inasmuch as) ибо; поскольку.

forage *n.* фураж; корм. —*adj.* кормовой: *forage crops,* кормовые культуры. —*v.i.* [*usu.* **forage for**] разыскивать.

foray *n.* набег; налёт.

forbear *v.t.* (refrain from) удерживаться от; воздерживаться от. —*v.i.* (have patience) терпеть. —*n.* = **forebear.**

forbearance *n.* **1,** (abstinence) воздержание. **2,** (patient endurance) терпеливость.

forbid *v.t.* запрещать; воспрещать. —**God forbid!,** не дай бог!; боже упаси!

forbidden *adj.* **1,** *used predicatively* запрещено: *it is forbidden,* это запрещено. **2,** *modifier* запретный: *forbidden fruit,* запретный плод.

forbidding *adj.* неприступный; неприветливый.

force *n.* **1,** (strength; power) сила: *the force of a blow,* сила удара. **2,** (physical pressure or coercion) сила: *by force,* силой; насильно. *The use of force,* применение силы. **3,** (validity) сила: *remain in force,* оставаться в силе. **4,** *pl., mil.* силы: *armed forces,* вооружённые силы. —*v.t.* **1,** (compel) заставлять;

вынуждáть; принуждáть. *Force oneself,* дéлать над собóй усúлие. **2,** (cause to move against resistance) втáлкивать; вгоня́ть. *Force out of power,* вытесня́ть из правлéния. *Force the crowd back,* осáживать толпý. *Force the enemy back,* оттесня́ть протúвника. *Force one's way into/through,* влáмываться в; пробивáться сквозь. **3,** (break open, as a lock or door) взлáмывать. **4,** (impose, as one's opinions) навя́зывать. **5,** (produce by effort) вы́давить: *force a smile,* вы́давить улы́бку. **6,** (make grow faster, as plants) выгоня́ть. —**by force of arms,** сúлой оружия. —**by force of habit,** в сúлу привы́чки.

forced *adj.* **1,** (compulsory) принудúтельный: *forced labor,* принудúтельный труд. **2,** (emergency, as of a landing) вы́нужденный. **3,** (unnatural, as of a smile) натя́нутый. —**forced march,** *mil.* форсúрованный марш.

forceful *adj.* решúтельный: *forceful measures,* решúтельные мéры.

forceps *n.* хирургúческие щипцы́.

forcible *adj.* насúльственный. —**forcibly,** *adv.* насúльно.

ford *n.* брод. —*v.t.* переходúть вброд.

fore *n.* передний план: *come to the fore,* выдвигáться на передний план.

fore-and-aft *adj.* продóльный. *Fore-and-aft sail,* косóй пáрус.

forearm *n.* предплéчье.

forebear *also,* **forbear** *n.* прéдок.

forebode *v.t.* предвещáть. —**foreboding,** *n.* дурнóе предчýвствие.

forecast *n.* прогнóз; предсказáние. *Weather forecast,* прогнóз *or* свóдка погóды. —*v.t.* предскáзывать. —**forecaster,** *n.* предсказáтель.

forecastle *n.* бак.

forefather *n.* прéдок.

forefinger *n.* указáтельный пáлец.

forefront *n.* авангáрд. *In the forefront,* в авангáрде; в пéрвых ряда́х.

forego *v.* = **forgo.**

foregoing *adj.* предшéствующий; вышеукáзанный. —**the foregoing,** предыдýщее.

foregone *adj.* прошéдший. —**foregone conclusion,** зарáнее извéстный результáт. *The result was a foregone conclusion,* в исхóде нé было сомнéний.

foreground *n.* передний план.

forehand *n., tennis* удáр спрáва. —*adj.* спрáва.

forehead *n.* лоб.

foreign *adj.* **1,** (of another country) инострáнный; чужóй: *foreign language,* инострáнный язы́к; *foreign country,* чужáя странá. **2,** (conducted with other nations) внéшний: *foreign policy,* внéшняя полúтика; *foreign trade,* внéшняя торгóвля. *Foreign aid,* пóмощь инострáнным государствам. **3,** (extraneous) постороний: *foreign body,* постороннее тéло. **4,** (alien; strange) чýждый: *jealousy is foreign to his nature,* рéвность емý чуждá.

foreigner *n.* инострáнец.

foreign minister минúстр инострáнных дел.

foreleg *n.* передняя ногá; передняя лáпа.

forelock *n.* чуб; чёлка; вихóр.

foreman *n.* мáстер; бригадúр.

foremast *n.* фок-мáчта.

foremost *adj.* **1,** (in front) передний; передовóй.

2, (leading; outstanding) выдаю́щийся. —**first and foremost,** прéжде всегó.

forenoon *n.* врéмя до полýдня; ýтро.

forensic *adj.* судéбный.

foreordain *v.t.* предопределя́ть.

forerunner *n.* предшéственник; предвéстник.

foresail *n.* фок.

foresee *v.t.* предвúдеть. —**in the foreseeable future,** в обозрúмом бýдущем.

foreshadow *v.t.* предвещáть.

foreshorten *v.t.* взять в ракýрсе. —**foreshortened,** *adj.* в ракýрсе.

foresight *n.* предусмотрúтельность.

foreskin *n.* крáйняя плоть.

forest *n.* лес. —*adj.* леснóй: *forest fire,* леснóй пожáр. —**not see the forest for the trees,** за дерéвьями лéса не вúдно.

forestall *v.t.* предупреждáть; предвосхищáть.

forester *n.* леснúчий. —**forestry,** *n.* леснóе хозя́йство; лесовóдство.

foretaste *n.* предвкушéние.

foretell *v.t.* предскáзывать.

forethought *n.* предусмотрúтельность.

forever *adv.* **1,** (for all time) вéчно; навсегдá; навéк(и). *Live forever,* жить вéчно. **2,** (constantly) вéчно: *they are forever arguing,* онú вéчно спóрят.

forewarn *v.t.* предостерегáть.

foreword *n.* предислóвие.

forfeit *n.* **1,** (penalty) неустóйка. **2,** *pl.* (game) фáнты. —*v.t.* лишáться; утрáчивать. —**forfeiture,** *n.* потéря; утрáта.

forge *n.* **1,** (smithy) кýзница. **2,** (furnace) горн. —*v.t.* **1,** (shape; fashion) ковáть. **2,** (counterfeit) поддéлывать. —*v.i.* [*usu.* **forge ahead**] продвигáться вперёд; вы́скочить вперёд. —**forged,** *adj.* поддéльный; подлóжный. —**forger,** *n.* фальшивомонéтчик.

forgery *n.* **1,** (act of forging) подлóг; поддéлка. **2,** (something forged) поддéлка.

forget *v.t. & i.* забывáть: *don't forget!,* не забýдьте! *I completely forgot about it,* я совершéнно забы́л(а) об этом. *I forgot to lock the door,* я забы́л(а) заперéть дверь.

forgetful *adj.* забы́вчивый. —**forgetfulness,** *n.* забы́вчивость.

forget-me-not *n.* незабýдка.

forgivable *adj.* простúтельный.

forgive *v.t.* прощáть: *forgive me for being late,* простúте меня́ за опоздáние. *I shall never forgive you for this,* я вам этого никогдá не прощý. —**forgiveness,** *n.* прощéние.

forgo *also,* **forego** *v.t.* отказываться от; воздéрживаться от; поступáться (+ *instr.*).

forgotten *adj.* забы́тый.

fork *n.* **1,** (eating utensil) вúлка. **2,** (in a road) разветвлéние; развúлка. —*v.i.* разветвля́ться; раздвáиваться.

forked *adj.* раздвóенный; разветвлённый. *Forked lightning,* зигзагообрáзная мóлния.

forlorn *adj.* жáлкий: *forlorn appearance,* жáлкий вид. —**forlorn hope,** (очень) слáбая надéжда.

form *n.* **1,** (outward appearance) фóрма: *form and content,* фóрма и содержáние. **2,** (type; variety) фóрма: *form of energy,* фóрма энéргии. *Form of government,* óбраз правлéния. *Low forms of life,* нúзшие фóрмы жúзни. *Familiar form of address,* обращёние на "ты". **3,** (character) фо́рма: *take the form of,* принима́ть фо́рму (+ *gen.*). *In the form of,* в ви́де (+ *gen.*). **4,** (blank document) анке́та. **5,** (fitness) фо́рма: *be in good form,* быть в фо́рме. **6,** (correct social behavior) фо́рма; тон: *for form's sake; as a matter of form,* для фо́рмы; для профо́рмы. *A sign of poor form,* при́знак дурно́го то́на. **7,** *gram.* фо́рма: *short form of adjectives,* кра́ткая фо́рма прилага́тельных. **8,** (mold; dummy) фо́рма: *form for hats,* фо́рма для шляп. —*v.t.* **1,** (make; put together; organize) образо́вывать; составля́ть; формирова́ть. *Form a circle,* образова́ть круг. *Form a group,* образова́ть/составля́ть гру́ппу. *Form a government,* образова́ть/формирова́ть прави́тельство. *Form an alliance with,* заключи́ть сою́з с. **2,** (develop in one's mind) составля́ть: *form an opinion,* соста́вить себе́ мне́ние. **3,** (develop, as a habit) выраба́тывать (в себе́ привы́чку). **4,** (make up; constitute) составля́ть: *form a single whole,* составля́ть еди́ное це́лое. *Form the boundary between,* образова́ть грани́цу ме́жду. *Form the basis of,* лежа́ть в осно́ве (+ *gen.*). —*v.i.* образо́вываться; формирова́ться. *Puddles formed from the rain,* от дождя́ образова́лись лу́жи. *Long lines formed,* вы́строились дли́нные о́череди.

formal *adj.* **1,** (in various meanings) форма́льный: *formal logic,* форма́льная ло́гика. **2,** (official) официа́льный: *formal protest,* официа́льный проте́ст. **3,** (of clothes) пара́дный: *formal attire,* пара́дное пла́тье. **4,** (stiff; constrained) церемо́нный.

formaldehyde *n.* формальдеги́д.

formalism *n.* формали́зм. —**formalist,** *n.* формали́ст. —**formalistic,** *adj.* формалисти́ческий.

formality *n.* форма́льность. *It's a mere formality,* э́то пуста́я форма́льность.

formalize *v.t.* оформля́ть.

formally *adv.* форма́льно.

format *n.* форма́т.

formation *n.* **1,** (process of forming) образова́ние; формирова́ние. **2,** *mil.* строй; построе́ние. **3,** *geol.* форма́ция.

former *adj.* **1,** (earlier) пре́жний: *in former times,* в пре́жнее вре́мя. **2,** (ex-) бы́вший. **3,** (opp. of latter) пе́рвый. —**formerly,** *adv.* ра́ньше; пре́жде.

formic *adj.* муравьи́ный: *formic acid,* муравьи́ная кислота́.

formidable *adj.* **1,** (awesome) гро́зный. **2,** (hard to accomplish, as of a task) тяжёлый. **3,** (strikingly impressive) внуши́тельный.

formless *adj.* бесфо́рменный.

formula *n.* фо́рмула.

formulate *v.t.* формули́ровать. —**formulation,** *n.* формулиро́вка.

fornication *n.* внебра́чная связь.

forsake *v.t.* **1,** (leave; abandon) броса́ть; покида́ть. **2,** (give up; renounce) отка́зываться от; отрека́ться от.

forswear *v.t.* зарека́ться от.

fort *n.* форт.

forte *adj. & adv., music* фо́рте. —*n.* (strong point) си́льная сторона́.

forth *adv.* **1,** (forward) вперёд. *Step forth,* выступа́ть. **2,** (outward) нару́жу. *Spew forth,* изверга́ть. —**and so forth,** и так да́лее; и тому́ подо́бное; и про́чее. —**back and forth,** взад и вперёд.

forthcoming *adj.* **1,** (impending) предстоя́щий. **2,**

(available when needed): *be forthcoming,* поступа́ть; име́ться налицо́.

forthright *adj.* прямоду́шный; прямолине́йный. —**forthrightness,** *n.* прямоду́шие; прямота́.

forthwith *adv.* неме́дленно.

fortieth *adj.* сороково́й. —*n.* **1,** (fortieth part) сорокова́я часть. **2,** (fraction) сорокова́я: *one-fortieth,* одна́ сорокова́я.

fortification *n.* укрепле́ние; фортифика́ция.

fortify *v.t.* **1,** (strengthen; provide with defenses) укрепля́ть. **2,** (reinforce; invigorate) подкрепля́ть.

fortissimo *adj. & adv.* форти́ссимо.

fortitude *n.* сто́йкость.

fortnight *n.* две неде́ли. —**fortnighty,** *adj.* происходя́щий раз в две неде́ли; *(of a publication)* двухнеде́льный. —*adv.* раз в две неде́ли.

fortress *n.* кре́пость.

fortuitous *adj.* случа́йный; неча́янный. —**fortuitousness; fortuity,** *n.* случа́йность.

fortunate *adj.* счастли́вый: *fortunate occurrence,* счастли́вый слу́чай. *It was fortunate that...,* хорошо́, что... —**fortunately,** *adv.* к сча́стью.

fortune *n.* **1,** (fate; lot; destiny) судьба́. **2,** (luck) сча́стье; уда́ча. *Have the good fortune to...,* име́ть сча́стье (+ *inf.*). **3,** (great amount of wealth) состоя́ние: *make a fortune,* нажива́ть состоя́ние. —**tell fortunes,** гада́ть; ворожи́ть.

fortuneteller *n.* гада́лка; ворожея́. —**fortunetelling,** *n.* гада́ние; ворожба́.

forty *n. & adj.* со́рок.

forum *n.* фо́рум.

forward *adv.* вперёд. *Step/come forward,* выступа́ть. —*adj.* **1,** (toward the front) поступа́тельный: *forward motion,* поступа́тельный ход; движе́ние вперед. **2,** (in the front) пере́дний; передово́й. **3,** (presumptuous) развя́зный. —*v.t.* **1,** (send) отправля́ть. **2,** (send to a further destination) пересыла́ть; переправля́ть; переадресо́вывать. **3,** (promote; advance) продвига́ть. —*n.,* *sports* напада́ющий. —**forward march!,** ша́гом марш!

fossil *n.* окамене́лость; ископа́емое. —*adj.* ископа́емый: *fossil remains,* ископа́емые оста́тки; *fossil fuel,* ископа́емое то́пливо. —**fossilized,** *adj.* ископа́емый.

foster *v.t.* **1,** (promote; stimulate) спосо́бствовать. **2,** (cultivate; instill) воспи́тывать. **3,** (cherish) леле́ять. —*adj.* приёмный: *foster father,* приёмный оте́ц.

foul *adj.* га́дкий; скве́рный; мёрзкий. *Foul air,* нечи́стый во́здух. *Foul language,* скверносло́вие. —*v.t.* **1,** (soil; defile) загрязня́ть; зага́живать. **2,** *fol. by up* (bungle) напу́тать. —*n.,* *sports* фол: *personal foul,* персона́льный фол. —**foul the trail,** запу́тывать следы́.

found *v.t.* осно́вывать.

foundation *n.* **1,** (supporting part of a building) фунда́мент. **2,** (basis) основа́ние. *Be without foundation,* не име́ть основа́ния; не име́ть под собо́й по́чвы. **3,** (endowed institution) фонд.

founder *n.* **1,** (one who founds or establishes) основа́тель. **2,** (caster of metals) лите́йщик. —*v.i.* **1,** (sink) тону́ть. **2,** (fail) срыва́ться.

foundling *n.* подки́дыш; найдёныш. *Foundling home,* прию́т; детдо́м.

foundry *n.* лите́йный заво́д. *Iron foundry,* чугуноли́те́йный заво́д *or* цех.

fount *n.* кла́дезь.

fountain *n.* **1,** (large) фонта́н. **2,** (drinking fountain) фонта́нчик. —**fountain pen,** автору́чка.

four *adj.* четы́ре. —*n.* **1,** (cardinal number) четы́ре. **2,** (written numeral; school grade) четвёрка. **3,** *cards* четвёрка. —**on all fours,** ползко́м; на четвере́ньках.

fourfold *adj.* четырёхкра́тный. —*adv.* вче́тверо.

four hundred четы́реста. —**four-hundredth,** *adj.* четырёхсо́тый.

four-legged *adj.* четвероно́гий.

fourteen *n. & adj.* четы́рнадцать. —**fourteenth,** *adj.* четы́рнадцатый.

fourth *adj.* четвёртый. —*n.* **1,** (quarter) че́тверть: *three-fourths,* три че́тверти. **2,** *music* ква́рта. —**in the fourth place,** в-четвёртых.

four-wheel *adj.* четырёхколёсный. *Also,* **four-wheeled.**

fowl *n.* дома́шняя пти́ца. —**fowler,** *n.* птицело́в. —**fowling,** *n.* птицело́вство.

fox *n.* лиса́; лиси́ца. —*adj.* ли́сий: *fox fur,* ли́сий мех.

foxglove *n.* наперстя́нка.

foxhole *n.*, *mil.* яче́йка.

fox terrier фокстерье́р.

fox trot фокстро́т.

foxy *adj.* ли́сий; хи́трый.

foyer *n.* фойе́; вестибю́ль.

fracas *n.* шу́мная ссо́ра; дебо́ш.

fraction *n.* **1,** *math.* дробь. **2,** *fol. by* of (small portion) деся́тая до́ля (+ *gen.*). —**fractional,** *adj.* дро́бный.

fractious *adj.* **1,** (cross) злой. **2,** (unruly) непоко́рный.

fracture *n.* перело́м. —*v.t.* лома́ть; перела́мывать.

fragile *adj.* хру́пкий; ло́мкий. —**fragility,** *n.* хру́пкость; ло́мкость.

fragment *n.* обло́мок; оско́лок. —*v.t.* дроби́ть; раздробля́ть. —**fragmentary,** *adj.* отры́вочный.

fragmentation *n.* **1,** (splitting up) дробле́ние. **2,** (state of being divided) раздро́бленность. —**fragmentation bomb,** оско́лочная бо́мба.

fragrance *n.* арома́т; благоуха́ние.

fragrant *adj.* души́стый; арома́тный; благоуха́нный.

frail *adj.* хру́пкий; тщеду́шный. —**frailty,** *n.* хру́пкость; тщеду́шие.

frame *n.* **1,** (for a picture) ра́ма; ра́мка. **2,** (of a window or door) ра́ма. **3,** (for eyeglasses) опра́ва. **4,** (of a building) карка́с; о́стов; сруб. **5,** (build, as of the human body) (те́ло)сложе́ние. **6,** *motion pictures* кадр. —*v.t.* **1,** (put into a frame) вставля́ть в ра́му; обрамля́ть. **2,** (devise; formulate) составля́ть; формули́ровать. **3,** *colloq.* (falsely incriminate) ло́жно обвиня́ть. —**frame of mind,** настрое́ние; расположе́ние ду́ха.

frame house карка́сный дом.

framework *n.* **1,** (skeleton; structure) карка́с; о́стов; сруб. **2,** *fig.* (basic structure) ра́мки: *within the framework of,* в ра́мках (+ *gen.*).

franc *n.* франк.

franchise *n.* **1,** (suffrage) пра́во го́лоса. **2,** (concession granted by a government) привиле́гия.

francium *n.* фра́нций.

frank *adj.* открове́нный.

frankfurter *n.* соси́ска.

frankincense *n.* ла́дан.

frankly *adv.* **1,** (in a frank manner) открове́нно. **2,** (to be frank; in truth) открове́нно говоря́.

frankness *n.* открове́нность.

frantic *adj.* **1,** (beside oneself with worry) отча́янный. **2,** (hectic; frenetic) лихора́дочный.

fraternal *adj.* бра́тский. —**fraternal twins,** двуя́йцевые близнецы́.

fraternity *n.* **1,** (brotherhood) бра́тство. **2,** (fraternal organization) бра́тия.

fraternize *v.i.* брата́ться. —**fraternization,** *n.* брата́ние.

fratricide *n.* братоуби́йство. —**fratricidal,** *adj.* братоуби́йственный.

fraud *n.* **1,** (criminal deception) обма́н; моше́нничество. **2,** (a cheat) обма́нщик; самозва́нец.

fraudulent *adj.* обма́нный; жу́льнический; моше́ннический. —**fraudulently,** *adv.* обма́ном; обма́нным путём.

fraught *adj.* [*usu.* fraught with] чрева́тый (+ *instr.*).

fray *n.* **1,** (brawl) дра́ка. **2,** (battle) бой. —*v.t.* обтрепа́ть. —*v.i.* обтрепа́ться. —**frayed,** *adj.* обтрёпанный.

freak *n.* уро́д. *Freak of nature,* чу́до *or* игра́ приро́ды. —**freakish,** *adj.* капри́зный; чудакова́тый.

freckle *n.* весну́шка. —**freckled; freckle-faced,** *adj.* весну́шчатый.

free *adj.* **1,** (independent; unrestricted; unburdened; not occupied) свобо́дный: *free country/press,* свобо́дная страна́/печа́ть. *Free from worry,* свобо́дный от забо́т. *Are you free this evening?,* вы свобо́дны сего́дня ве́чером? **2,** *fol. by inf.* (at liberty) во́лен (во́льна): *you are free to leave,* ты во́лен/во́льна уйти́. **3,** (not costing anything) беспла́тный. —*adv.* беспла́тно; да́ром. —*v.t.* освобожда́ть. *Free oneself,* освобожда́ться. —**free city,** во́льный го́род. —**free enterprise,** свобо́дное предпринима́тельство. —**free fall,** свобо́дное паде́ние. —**free hand,** свобо́да де́йствий: *give someone a free hand,* дать кому́-нибудь по́лную свобо́ду де́йствий. —**free love,** свобо́дная любо́вь. —**free port,** откры́тый порт. —**free speech,** свобо́да сло́ва. —**free thought,** вольноду́мство. —**free throw,** *basketball,* штрафно́й бросо́к. —**free trade,** свобо́дная торго́вля. —**free translation,** во́льный перево́д. —**free verse,** во́льный стих. —**set free,** выпуска́ть *or* отпуска́ть на свобо́ду *or* на во́лю.

freedom *n.* свобо́да. —**freedom-loving,** *adj.* свободолюби́вый.

free-for-all *n.* о́бщая сва́лка.

free-lance *adj.* внешта́тный.

freely *adv.* свобо́дно.

Freemason *n.* франкмасо́н. —**Freemasonry,** *n.* франкмасо́нство.

freestyle *n.*, *swimming* во́льный стиль.

freethinker *n.* вольноду́мец; свободомы́слящий. —**freethinking,** *adj.* вольноду́мный; свободомы́слящий.

freeze *v.i.* **1,** (from the cold) мёрзнуть: *I am freezing,* я мёрзну. *The river froze over,* река́ замёрзла. *The pipes froze,* тру́бы замёрзли. *Freeze to death,* поги́бнуть от хо́лода; замёрзнуть. **2,** (from fear, shock, etc.) цепене́ть; ледене́ть; замира́ть: *freeze in horror,* цепене́ть/ледене́ть/замира́ть от у́жаса. *Freeze in one's tracks,* останови́ться как вко́панный. **3,** *impers.* (be very cold) моро́зить: *it is freezing,* морόзит. **4**, *fol. by* **to** (become attached by freezing) примерзάть (к). —*v.t.* заморάживать; морόзить. —*n.* **1**, (freezing weather) морόз. **2**, (of prices, wages, etc.) заморάживание: *price freeze*, заморάживание цен.

freezer *n.* морозήлка.

freezing *adj.* морόзный: *freezing weather*, морόзная погόда. *Freezing cold*, жестόкий хόлод. *Freezing temperature*, температýра нήже нулή (по Цέльсию). *I am freezing*, я мёрзну. —**freezing point**, тόчка замерзάния.

freight *n.* **1**, (goods being transported) товάр; груз. **2**, (transportation of goods) перевόзка. **3**, (charge for such transportation) плάта за провόз. *What will be the freight charges?*, скόлько бýдет стόить перевόзка? —*adj.* товάрный, грузовόй: *freight train*, товάрный пόезд; *freight traffic*, грузовόе движέние.

freighter *n.* грузовόе сýдно.

French *adj.* францýзский. —*n.* **1**, (language) францýзский язык. *Speak French*, говорήть по-францýзски. **2**, *preceded by* **the** (people) францýзы.

French curve лекάло.

French horn валтόрна.

Frenchman *n.* францýз.

frenetic *adj.* лихорάдочный; кипýчий.

frenzy *n.* исступлέние. —**frenzied**, *adj.* исступлённый.

frequency *n.* частотά. —*adj.* частόтный. —**frequency modulation**, частόтная модулήция.

frequent *adj.* чάстый. —*v.t.* чάсто посещάть.

frequentative *adj., gram.* многокрάтный.

frequently *adv.* чάсто.

fresco *n.* фрέска.

fresh *adj.* **1**, (not used, treated, or spoiled) свέжий: *fresh air*, свέжий вόздух; *fresh linen*, свέжее бельё; *fresh eggs/vegetables*, свέжие ήйца/όвощи. *Fresh in one's memory*, свеж (свежό) в пάмяти. **2**, (not salt, as of water) прέсный. **3**, *colloq.* (impudent) нахάльный.

freshen *v.t.* освежάть. —*v.i.* [*usu.* **freshen up**] **1**, (become fresh) свежέть. **2**, (make oneself clean and fresh) освежάться.

freshly *adv.* недάвно; тόлько что: *freshly baked*, тόлько что выпеченный.

freshman *n.* первокýрсник; нόвенький.

freshness *n.* **1**, (newness) свέжесть. **2**, (insolence) дέрзость.

fresh-water *adj.* пресновόдный.

fret *v.i.* мýчиться. —*n., music* лад. —**fretful**, *adj.* раздражήтельный; капрήзный.

fret saw лόбзик.

fretwork *n.* резнάя рабόта.

friable *adj.* рыхлый; рассыпчатый.

friar *n.* монάх; йнок.

fricassee *n.* фрикасέ.

fricative *adj.* фрикатήвный.

friction *n.* **1**, (rubbing together; resistance) трέние. **2**, (conflict; disagreement) трέния.

Friday *n.* пήтница. —**Good Friday**, страстнάя пήтница.

fried *adj.* жάреный. *Fried eggs*, яήчница-глазýнья.

friend *n.* друг. *Be friends*, дружήть. *Become friends*, дружήться.

friendly *adj.* **1**, (outgoing) привέтливый. **2**, (amicable) дрýжеский; дружелюбный. *Friendly countries*,

дрýжественные стрάны. —**friendliness**, *n.* привέтливость; дружелюбие.

friendship *n.* дрýжба.

frieze *n.* фриз.

frigate *n.* фрегάт.

fright *n.* **1**, (sudden fear) испýг. *Give someone (quite) a fright*, напугάть когό-нибудь. **2**, *colloq.* (grotesque person or thing) страшήлище.

frighten *v.t.* пугάть. *Be frightened*, пугάться. —**frighten away** *or* **off**, спугивать.

frightening *adj.* тревόжный: *frightening rumors*, тревόжные слýхи. *It is frightening*, жýтко.

frightful *adj.* ужάсный; стрάшный. —**frightfully**, *adv.* ужάсно: *frightfully expensive*, ужάсно дорогόй.

frigid *adj.* холόдный; ледянόй.

frigidity *n., physiol.* половάя холόдность.

frill *n.* обόрка.

fringe *n.* **1**, (trimming) бахромά. **2**, (edge; margin) край; окрάина. —**fringe benefits**, дополнήтельные льгόты.

frisk *v.i.* (frolic) резвήться. —*v.t., colloq.* (search) обыскивать.

frisky *adj.* рέзвый; игрήвый.

fritter *n.* олάдья. —*v.t.* [*usu.* **fritter away**] растрάчивать.

frivolity *n.* легкомыслие.

frivolous *adj.* легкомысленный.

fro *adv., in* **to and fro**, взад и вперёд.

frock *n.* **1**, (dress) плάтье. **2**, (monk's habit) рήса. —**frock coat**, сюртýк.

frog *n.* лягýшка. —**frog in one's throat**, хрипотά. —**frogs' legs**, лягýшечьи лάпки.

frogman *n.* водолάз-подрывнήк.

frolic *v.i.* резвήться; возήться. —**frolicsome**, *adj.* рέзвый; шаловлήвый.

from *prep.* **1**, (away from; a certain distance from) от: *move away from the window*, отходήть от окнά. *Get up from the table*, вставάть из-за столά. *Far from home*, далекό от дόма. *Three miles from the airport*, в трёх мήлях от аэропόрта. **2**, (from a place) из: *arrive from Paris*, приέхать из Парήжа; *news from America*, нόвости из Амέрики. ♦*With certain nouns* с: *from work*, с рабόты; *from the post office*, с пόчты; *from the south*, с юга. *From head to toe*, с головы до ног. *From all over the world*, со всегό мήра. **3**, (from a person) А, (where the subject initiates the action) у: *buy from*, покупάть у; *take from*, брать у; *find out from*, узнάть у; *get from*, получήть у. В, (where the subject is the recipient of the action) от: *learn/hear from*, узнάть от; *receive a letter from a friend*, получήть письмό от дрýга. **4**, (from out of) из: *drink from a glass*, пить из стакάна; *remove from one's pocket*, вынимάть из кармάна. **5**, (off of; down from) с: *dismount from a horse*, сойтή с лόшади; *take a book from the shelf*, достάть кнήгу с пόлки; *fall from the sky*, пάдать с нέба. *Hang from the ceiling*, висέть на потолкέ. **6**, *with numbers, time, etc.* от; с: *from four to six*, от четырёх до шестή; *from morning till evening*, с утрά до вέчера; *from Monday till Friday*, с понедέльника до пήтницы. *From this moment onward*, с этого момέнта. **7**, (from a source or origin) из: *from the newspapers*, из газέт; *from a good family*, из хорόшей семьή. *Wine is made from grapes*, винό дέлают из виногрάда. *From this it follows that...*, из этого слέдует, что... **8**, (because of) от:

suffer from insomnia, страда́ть от бессо́нницы; *shiver from the cold,* дрожа́ть от хо́лода. **9,** *with various verbs* от: *differ from,* отлича́ться от; *keep from laughing,* удержа́ться от сме́ха; *hide from the police,* пря́таться от поли́ции; *save from disaster,* избавля́ть от катастро́фы; *protect one's eyes from the sun,* защища́ть глаза́ от со́лнца. **10,** *with various verbs* из: *disappear from view,* скрыва́ться из ви́ду; *return from a vacation,* верну́ться из о́тпуска; *strike from the list,* вы́черкнуть из спи́ска; *expel from the party,* исключи́ть из па́ртии; *subtract three from eight,* вычита́ть три из восьми́.

front *n.* **1,** (foremost part or side) пере́дняя часть; пере́дняя сторона́; фаса́д; перёд. *In the front of the book,* в нача́ле кни́ги. **2,** *mil.* фронт: *at the front,* на фро́нте. **3,** *meteorol.* фронт: *cold front,* холо́дный фронт. **4,** (coalition) фронт: *united front,* еди́ный фронт. **5,** *colloq.* (person used as a decoy) подставно́е лицо́. —*adj.* пере́дний: *front wheel,* пере́днее колесо́. *Front door,* пара́дный ход. *Front view,* вид спе́реди. *Front row,* пе́рвый ряд. *Front page,* пе́рвая страни́ца. *Front sight,* му́шка. —*v.t.* (face) выходи́ть в *or* на —**in front,** впереди́. —**in front of,** пе́ред.

frontal *adj.* **1,** (from the front) спе́реди; *frontal view,* вид спе́реди. **2,** *mil.* лобово́й; фронта́льный: *frontal assault,* лобова́я/фронта́льная ата́ка; ата́ка в лоб. **3,** (of the forehead) ло́бный.

frontier *n.* грани́ца.

frontispiece *n.* фронтиспи́с.

frost *n.* **1,** (freezing temperature) моро́з: *ten degrees of frost,* де́сять гра́дусов моро́за. **2,** (hoarfrost) и́ней; и́зморозь.

frostbite *n.* отморо́жение; обморо́жение. *Suffer frostbite,* обмора́живаться. —**frostbitten,** *adj.* отморо́женный; обморо́женный. *My ears are frostbitten,* я отморо́зил/обморо́зил себе́ у́ши.

frosted *adj.* покры́тый и́неем. —**frosted glass,** ма́товое стекло́.

frosting *n.* глазу́рь.

frosty *adj.* **1,** (freezing) моро́зный. **2,** (cold and unfriendly) ледяно́й.

froth *n.* пе́на. —*v.t.* пе́нить. —*v.i.* пе́ниться. —**frothy,** *adj.* пе́нистый.

frown *v.i.* **1,** (contract the brows) хму́риться; хму́рить бро́ви; хму́рить лицо́. **2,** *fol. by* **on** (disapprove of) смотре́ть ко́со (на). —*n.* хму́рое лицо́.

frozen *adj.* **1,** (cold; numb; icebound) замёрзший: *my hands are frozen,* у меня́ замёрзли ру́ки. **2,** (preserved through freezing) моро́женый; заморо́женный.

frugal *adj.* **1,** (thrifty) бережли́вый. **2,** (meager) ску́дный. —**frugality,** *n.* бережли́вость.

fruit *n.* **1,** (juicy edible thing to eat) фрукт; (*in the collective sense*) фру́кты: *I like fruit,* я люблю́ фру́кты. **2,** (yield of a plant or tree) плод: *the acorn is the fruit of the oak tree,* жёлудь – плод ду́ба. **3,** *fig.* (result) плоды́: *bear fruit,* приноси́ть плоды́. *The fruits of one's labor,* плоды́ свои́х трудо́в. —*adj.* фрукто́вый: *fruit juice,* фрукто́вый сок.

fruitful *adj.* плодотво́рный.

fruition *n.* осуществле́ние. *Reach fruition,* осуществля́ться.

fruitless *adj.* беспло́дный.

frustrate *v.t.* расстра́ивать; срыва́ть.

frustration *n.* **1,** (act of frustrating) расстро́йство;

срыв. **2,** (feeling of being frustrated) фрустра́ция.

fry *v.t.* жа́рить. —*v.i.* жа́риться. —*n.,* in **small fry,** мелюзга́; мелкота́.

frying pan сковорода́; сково́родка. —**out of the frying pan into the fire,** из огня́ да в по́лымя.

fuchsia *n.* фу́ксия.

fuchsin *also,* **fuchsine** *n.* фукси́н.

fudge *n.* мя́гкая шокола́дная конфе́та.

fuel *n.* то́пливо; горю́чее. —**add fuel to the fire,** подлива́ть ма́сла в ого́нь.

fuel-efficient *adj.* малолитра́жный.

fuel gauge бензиноме́р.

fuel pump то́пливный насо́с.

fuel tank то́пливный бак; бак горю́чего.

fugitive *n.* бегле́ц. —*adj.* бе́глый.

fugue *n., music* фу́га.

fulcrum *n.* то́чка опо́ры.

fulfill *also,* **fulfil** *v.t.* выполня́ть; исполня́ть. —**fulfillment,** *n.* выполне́ние; исполне́ние.

full *adj.* **1,** (filled; complete; rounded out) по́лный. *Full of water,* по́лон воды́. **2,** (sated) сы́тый. —*v.t.* валя́ть: *to full cloth,* валя́ть сукно́. —**full brother** *or* **sister**), родно́й брат; родна́я сестра́. —**full house,** по́лный зал; по́лный сбор; анилáг. —**full member,** полнопра́вный член. —**full moon,** по́лная луна́; полнолу́ние.—**full of oneself,** поглощён собо́й. —**full professor,** профе́ссор. —**full speed ahead!,** по́лный ход! —**full stop, 1,** (halt; standstill) по́лная остано́вка. **2,** (period) то́чка. —**full well,** прекра́сно: *I know full well,* я прекра́сно зна́ю. —**in full,** по́лностью; сполна́: *paid in full,* по́лностью опла́чено. *Write your name in full,* напиши́те ва́ше и́мя по́лностью.—**to the full** *or* **fullest,** в по́лной ме́ре. *Develop to the full,* разверну́ться во всю ширь.

full-blooded *adj.* полнокро́вный.

fuller *n.* валя́льщик.

full-fledged *adj.* полноце́нный.

full-length *adj.* **1,** (of a portrait) во весь рост. **2,** (unabridged) по́лный. *Full-length film,* полнометра́жный фильм.

fullness *n.* полнота́.

full-scale *adj.* **1,** (the same size as the original) в натура́льную величину́. **2,** (all-out) развёрнутый.

fully *adv.* вполне́; по́лностью; в по́лной ме́ре.

fulmar *n.* глупы́ш.

fulminate *v.i.* мета́ть гро́мы и мо́лнии. *Fulminate against,* громи́ть. —**fulminate of mercury,** грему́чая ртуть.

fulsome *adj.* гру́бый; слаща́вый. *Fulsome flattery,* гру́бая лесть.

fumble *v.i.* **1,** *fol. by* **for** (grope for) нащу́пывать. **2,** *fol. by* **with** (handle clumsily) вози́ться с. —*v.t.* (fail to hold) роня́ть; теря́ть.

fume *n., usu. pl.* чад; испаре́ния. *Exhaust fumes,* выхлопны́е га́зы. —*v.i.* **1,** (emit fumes) чади́ть. **2,** (fret; rage) кипяти́ть.

fumigate *v.t.* оку́ривать. —**fumigation,** *n.* оку́ривание.

fun *n.* заба́ва; поте́ха. —**for the fun of it,** из спорти́вного интере́са. —**have fun, 1,** (live it up) весели́ться. **2,** (have a good time) хорошо́ проводи́ть вре́мя. —**in** (*or* **for**) **fun,** в шу́тку. —**make fun of; poke fun at,** шути́ть над; смея́ться над; подшу́чивать над; подсме́иваться над.

function *n.* **1,** (role) фу́нкция. **2,** (social affair) ве́чер;

приём. **3,** *math.* фу́нкция. —*v.i.* де́йствовать; функциони́ровать. —**functional,** *adj.* фунциона́льный.

functionary *n.* чино́вник.

fund *n.* **1,** (money reserved for a specific purpose) фонд. **2,** *pl.* (money available) сре́дства. **3,** (store; supply) запа́с.

fundamental *adj.* основно́й; коренно́й. —**fundamentally,** *adv.* коренны́м о́бразом. —**fundamentals,** *n.pl.* осно́вы.

funeral *n.* по́хороны. *At the funeral,* на похорона́х. —*adj.* похоро́нный; погреба́льный. *Funeral service,* заупоко́йная слу́жба.

funereal *adj.* гробово́й; тра́урный.

fungous *adj.* грибко́вый. —**fungus,** *n.* грибо́к.

funicular *adj.* кана́тный. *Funicular railway,* фуникуле́р.

funnel *n.* **1,** (conical device) воро́нка. **2,** (smokestack) дымова́я труба́.

funny *adj.* **1,** (amusing) смешно́й; заба́вный. **2,** *colloq.* (strange; odd) стра́нный. —**funny bone,** локтева́я кость.

fur *n.* мех; *pl.* пушни́на; меха́. —*adj.* **1,** (made of fur) мехово́й. **2,** (pert. to fur) пушно́й: *fur auction,* пушно́й аукцио́н. —**fur-bearing,** *adj.* пушно́й. —**fur-lined,** *adj.* на меху́; подби́тый ме́хом.

furious *adj.* **1,** (extremely angry): *be furious,* быть в я́рости; о́чень разозли́ться. **2,** (violent; intense; fierce) нейстовый; я́ростный.

furlough *n.* о́тпуск.

furnace *n.* печь; горн.

furnish *v.t.* **1,** (fit out with furniture) обставля́ть; меблирова́ть. **2,** (provide; give) ока́зывать (по́мощь); дава́ть (информа́цию); представля́ть (доказа́тельства). **3,** (supply) снабжа́ть: *furnish the guests with linen,* снабжа́ть госте́й бельём. —**furnished,** *adj.* меблиро́ванный.

furnishings *n.pl.* меблиро́вка; убра́нство.

furniture *n.* ме́бель; обстано́вка. —*adj.* ме́бельный: *furniture store,* ме́бельный магази́н.

furor *n.* шуми́ха; фуро́р.

furrier *n.* меховщи́к; скорня́к.

furrow *n.* борозда́. —*v.t.* борозди́ть. *Furrowed brow,* изборождённый лоб.

furry *adj.* пуши́стый.

fur seal (морско́й) ко́тик.

further *adj.* дальне́йший. *For further information,* за дальне́йшими све́дениями. *Until further notice,* впредь до распоряже́ния; до осо́бого распоряже́ния. *Without further ado,* без дальне́йших церемо́ний. *I have nothing further to say,* бо́льше мне не́чего сказа́ть. —*adv.* да́льше: *not a step further!,* ни ша́гу да́льше! —*v.t.* спосо́бствовать; продвига́ть.

furtherance *n.* продвиже́ние.

furthermore *adv.* кро́ме того́; сверх того́; к тому́ же.

furthermost *adj.* са́мый да́льний.

furtive *adj.* сде́ланный украдкой; ворова́тый; кра́дущийся. *Cast a furtive glance at,* посмотре́ть украдкой на.—**furtively,** *adv.* украдкой; кра́дучись.

fury *n.* **1,** (rage) я́рость; бе́шенство. **2,** (violence, as of a storm) нейстовство. **3,** *cap., myth.* фу́рия.

furze *n.* дрок.

fuse *n.* **1,** *electricity* про́бка: *a fuse blew,* про́бка перегоре́ла. **2,** (powder wick) запа́л; шнур. **3,** [*also,* **fuze**] (detonating device) взрыва́тель; тру́бка. —*v.t.* **1,** (melt) пла́вить; сплавля́ть. **2,** (blend) слива́ть. —*v.i.* **1,** (melt) пла́виться. **2,** (merge; blend) слива́ться.

fuselage *n.* фюзеля́ж.

fusible *adj.* пла́вкий.

fusillade *n.* стрельба́; обстре́л.

fusion *n.* **1,** (act of fusing; state of being fused) пла́вка. **2,** (union; merger) слия́ние. **3,** *physics* си́нтез. —**fusion bomb,** термоя́дерная бо́мба.

fuss *n.* **1,** (bustle) суета́; возня́; хлопотня́. **2,** (stir; row) шум; сканда́л. *Make/raise a fuss,* поднима́ть шум; сканда́лить. —*v.i.* **1,** (bustle) суети́ться. **2,** *fol. by* **with** (fiddle with) вози́ться с. **3,** *fol. by* **over** (show excessive care or concern) носи́ться с. **4,** *colloq.* (complain) хны́кать.

fussy *adj.* **1,** (exacting) взыска́тельный. **2**́, (finicky) привере́дливый.

futile *adj.* тще́тный; напра́сный; бесполе́зный. —**futility,** *n.* тще́тность.

future *adj.* бу́дущий. —*n.* [*usu.* the future] бу́дущее. *In the future,* в бу́дущем; в дальне́йшем.

futurism *n.* футури́зм. —**futuristic,** *adj.* футури́стический.

fuze *n.* = **fuse** (*in sense #3*).

fuzz *n.* пух.

fuzzy *adj.* **1,** (having fuzz) пуши́стый. **2,** (blurred; vague) сму́тный.

G

G, g седьмáя бýква англи́йского алфави́та. —*n.* (musical note) соль.

gab *n., colloq.* болтовня́. —*v.i., colloq.* болтáть; трепáть языко́м. —**gift of gab,** дар слóва.

gabardine *n.* габарди́н. —*adj.* габарди́новый.

gabby *adj., colloq.* болтли́вый; разговóрчивый.

gable *n.* щипéц. —**gable roof,** двускáтная крыша.

gad *v.i.* [*usu.* **gad about**] шлáться; слоня́ться.

gadfly *n.* **1,** (insect) óвод. **2,** (annoying person) надоéда.

gadget *n.* приспособлéние.

gadolinium *n.* гадоли́ний.

Gaelic *adj.* гэ́льский. —*n.* гэ́льский язык.

gaff *n.* рыболóвный багóр.

gaffe *n.* оплóшность. *Commit a gaffe,* допусти́ть оплóшность; попáсть впросáк.

gag *n.* **1,** (silencer) кляп. **2,** *slang* (joke) шýтка. —*v.t.* засýнуть кляп в рот (+ *dat.*). —*v.i.* (choke) дави́ться.

gaiety *n.* весéлье; весёлость.

gaily *adv.* вéсело.

gain *v.t.* **1,** (get; win; acquire) получáть; завоёвывать. *Gain recognition,* получáть признáние. *Gain one's freedom,* завоёвывать свобóду. *Gain experience,* приобретáть óпыт. *Gain an advantage,* получи́ть преимýщество. **2,** (achieve) доби́ться: *gain one's end,* доби́ться своéй цéли. *What did you gain by that?,* что вы выгадали на э́том? **3,** (increase in) набирáть: *gain altitude,* набирáть высотý. *Gain weight,* прибавля́ть в вéсе. *Gain ten pounds,* прибáвить дéсять фýнтов. **4,** (receive, as an impression) выноси́ть (впечатлéние). *I gained the impression that...,* у меня́ создалóсь впечатлéние, что... —*v.i.* **1,** (benefit) выи́грывать. *Stand to gain,* быть в выигрыше. *Gain in someone's estimation,* выи́грывать в чьём-нибудь мнéнии. **2,** *fol. by* **on** (draw nearer to) догоня́ть; нагоня́ть. —*n.* **1,** (benefit) выгода; выигрыш. **2,** *pl.* (that which is gained) выигрыш; завоевáния. **3,** (increase) увеличéние; прирóст. —**gain ground, 1,** (make progress) дéлать успéхи. **2,** *fol. by* **on** (draw nearer to) догоня́ть; нагоня́ть. —**gain time, 1,** (of a timepiece) идти́ вперёд. **2,** (obtain a delay to one's advantage) выи́грывать врéмя.

gainer *n.* тот, кто выи́грывает. *Be the gainer,* быть в выигрыше.

gainful *adj.* **1,** (profitable) дохóдный; при́быльный. **2,** (paid) опла́чиваемый. —**gainfully,** *adv.* с опла́той. *Be gainfully employed,* имéть опла́чиваемую рабóту; рабóтать за дéньги.

gainsay *v.t.* отрицáть; опровергáть.

gait *n.* **1,** (walk; step) похóдка; пóступь. **2,** (of a horse) аллюр.

gaiters *n.pl.* гéтры.

gal *n., colloq.* дéвушка.

gala *adj.* прáздничный; торжéственный; парáдный.

galactic *adj.* галакти́ческий.

galaxy *n.* **1,** *astron.* галáктика. **2,** (brilliant assemblage) плея́да.

gale *n.* **1,** (strong wind) шторм. *Winds of gale force,* вéтры штормовóй си́лы. **2,** (outburst) раскáт: *gales of laughter,* раскáты смéха.

galena *n.* галени́т; свинцóвый блеск.

gall *n.* **1,** (bile) жёлчь. **2,** (rancor) жёлчь. **3,** *colloq.* (effrontery) нáглость. **4,** *bot.* галл. —*v.t.* раздражáть; обижáть. *It galls me,* мне обóидно.

gallant *adj.* **1,** (brave; daring) хрáбрый; дóблестный. **2,** (chivalrous) галáнтный.

gallantry *n.* **1,** (valor) дóблесть. **2,** (courtly manner) галáнтность.

gall bladder жёлчный пузырь.

gallery *n.* галерéя. *Shooting gallery,* тир.

galley *n.* **1,** (ship) галéра. **2,** (ship's kitchen) кáмбуз. **3,** *printing* (proof) грáнка.

Gallic *adj.* гáлльский. —**Gallicism,** *n.* галлици́зм.

galling *adj.* оби́дный. *It is galling,* оби́дно.

gallinule *n.* водяная кýрочка.

gallium *n.* гáллий.

gallivant *v.i.* шля́ться.

gallnut *n.* черни́льный орéшек.

gallon *n.* галлóн.

galloon *n.* галýн; позумéнт.

gallop *n.* галóп. *At a gallop,* галóпом; вскачь. *Full gallop,* карьéр. —*v.i.* галопи́ровать. *Gallop off,* ускакáть. —*v.t.* пускáть галóпом.

gallows *n.* ви́селица.

gallstone *n.* жёлчный кáмень.

galore *adv.* хоть отбавля́й.

galosh *n.* галóша.

galvanic *adj.* гальвани́ческий.

galvanize *v.t.* **1,** *electricity; metall.* гальванизи́ровать. **2,** *fig.* (rouse to action) возбуждáть; побуждáть.

gambit *n.* гамби́т.

gamble *v.i.* **1,** (play for stakes) игрáть в азáртные и́гры. **2,** (take a chance) рисковáть. —*v.t.* **1,** (risk) рисковáть. **2,** *fol. by* **away** (squander by gambling) прои́грывать. —*n.* рискóванная игрá.

gambler *n.* игрóк; картёжник.

gambling *n.* азáртная игрá. —*adj.* и́горный: *gambling house/parlor/casino,* и́горный дом.

gambol v.i. резви́ться.

game n. **1,** (play; sport) игра́: children's games, де́тские и́гры. Join in the game, включи́ться в игру́. **2,** (single contest) па́ртия: win three games, вы́играть три па́ртии. **3,** (scheme) игра́: play a double game, вести́ двойну́ю игру́. See through someone's game, ви́деть кого́-нибудь наскво́зь. **4,** (animals or birds hunted for food) дичь. Big game, кру́пная дичь; кру́пный зверь. —adj. **1,** (of animals or birds) промысло́вый. Game laws, зако́ны об охо́те. **2,** (plucky; courageous) сме́лый; сто́йкий. **3,** colloq. (ready; willing) гото́вый. **4,** (lame) хромо́й. —**game bag,** ягдта́ш.

gamely adv. сто́йко; отва́жно.

gamete n. гаме́та.

gaming adj. иго́рный: gaming table, иго́рный стол.

gamma globulin га́мма-глобули́н.

gamma rays га́мма-лучи́.

gamut n. га́мма: the whole gamut of emotions, це́лая га́мма ощуще́ний. —**run the gamut,** быть/быва́ть са́мые ра́зные.

gander n. гуса́к. —**take a gander,** slang взгляну́ть.

gang n. **1,** (band, as of thieves) ба́нда; ша́йка. **2,** (crew of workers) брига́да. —v.i. [usu. **gang up on**] обру́шиваться на.

gangling adj. долговя́зый.

ganglion n. не́рвный у́зел; га́нглий.

gangplank n. схо́дни.

gangrene n. гангре́на. —**gangrenous,** adj. гангре́нозный.

gangster n. га́нгстер.

gangway n. **1,** (passageway) прохо́д. **2,** (gangplank) схо́дни. —interj. посторони́тесь!

gannet n. о́луша.

gantlet n. = **gauntlet** (in sense #3).

gaol n. = **jail.**

gap n. **1,** (opening; breach) брешь; проло́м. **2,** (break; lacuna) пробе́л: fill a gap, восполня́ть пробе́л. **3,** (disparity) разры́в: the generation gap, разры́в поколе́ний. **4,** (mountain pass) го́рный прохо́д.

gape v.i. **1,** (stare open-mouthed) глазе́ть; зева́ть. **2,** (open wide) зия́ть: gaping wound, зия́ющая ра́на.

garage n. гара́ж. Public garage, автоба́за.

garb n. наря́д; одея́ние.

garbage n. му́сор; отбро́сы. —**garbage can,** му́сорный я́щик. —**garbage collector,** му́сорщик.

garble v.t. **1,** (make unintelligible) искажа́ть. **2,** (misrepresent) перевира́ть. **3,** (pronounce indistinctly) глота́ть.

garden n. сад. Vegetable garden, огоро́д. —adj. садо́вый; огоро́дный.

gardener n. садо́вник; садово́д.

gardenia n. гарде́ния.

gardening n. садово́дство.

gargantuan adj. гига́нтский.

gargle v.i. полоска́ть го́рло.

garish adj. крича́щий; крикли́вый; бро́ский.

garland n. гирля́нда; вено́к. —v.t. украша́ть гирля́ндами.

garlic n. чесно́к.

garment n. **1,** (article of clothing) предме́т оде́жды. **2,** pl. (clothing) оде́жда. —**garment factory,** швейная фа́брика.

garner v.t. **1,** (store) скла́дывать в амба́р. **2,** (win; obtain) получа́ть: garner first prize, получи́ть пе́рвую пре́мию.

garnet n. грана́т.

garnish v.t. **1,** (embellish) приукра́шивать. **2,** cooking гарни́ровать. —n. гарни́р.

garret n. черда́к; мансарда.

garrison n. гарнизо́н.

garrulous adj. болтли́вый; говорли́вый; разгово́рчивый.

garter n. подвя́зка.

gas n. **1,** (vapor) газ: natural gas, приро́дный газ. Turn on the gas, включи́ть газ. **2,** (gasoline) бензи́н. **3,** physiol. га́зы. —adj. **1,** (pert. to gas) га́зовый. **2,** (pert. to gasoline) бензи́новый. —**step on the gas,** дать газ.

gas burner га́зовый рожо́к.

gas chamber га́зовая ка́мера.

gaseous adj. газообра́зный.

gash n. глубо́кий поре́з. —v.t. си́льно поре́зать.

gasket n. прокла́дка. —**blow a gasket,** slang вы́йти из себя́.

gaslight n. **1,** (light) га́зовое освеще́ние. **2,** (lamp) га́зовая ла́мпа.

gas main га́зовая магистра́ль.

gas mask противога́з.

gas meter га́зовый счётчик; газоме́р.

gasoline n. бензи́н. —adj. бензи́новый.

gasp v.i. задыха́ться. —v.t. [usu. **gasp out**] говори́ть задыха́ющимся го́лосом. —n. вздох. —**to the last gasp,** до после́днего издыха́ния.

gas station бензозапра́вочная ста́нция; автозапра́вочная ста́нция.

gas tank бензоба́к.

gastric adj. желу́дочный. —**gastric juice,** желу́дочный сок. —**gastric ulcer,** я́зва желу́дка.

gastritis n. гастри́т.

gastrointestinal adj. желу́дочно-кише́чный.

gastronome n. гастроно́м. —**gastronomic,** adj. гастрономи́ческий. —**gastronomy,** n. гастроно́мия.

gate n. **1,** (entrance) воро́та. **2,** (swinging door in a picket fence) кали́тка. **3,** pl. (entrance to a city) заста́ва. **4,** (movable barrier) шлагба́ум. **5,** (box-office receipts) сбо́ры.

gatehouse n. сторо́жка (у воро́т).

gatekeeper n. привра́тник.

gateway n. воро́та; вход.

gather v.t. **1,** (pick; collect) собира́ть: gather firewood, собира́ть дрова́; gather data, собира́ть да́нные. Gather in the harvest, собира́ть урожа́й. Gather dust, пыли́ться. **2,** (infer) заключа́ть. **3,** (draw into folds) собира́ть. **4,** (gain, as speed) набира́ть (ско́рость). Gather momentum, разгоня́ться. —v.i. собира́ться; сходи́ться; съезжа́ться. —n., usu. pl. сбо́рки.

gathering n. **1,** (collecting) сбор; собира́ние. Hunting and gathering, охо́та и собира́тельство. **2,** (an assemblage) собра́ние; сбор; сбо́рище.

gaudy adj. крича́щий; пёстрый.

gauge n. **1,** (instrument for measuring) измери́тель. Pressure gauge, мано́метр. Fuel gauge, бензиноме́р. **2,** R.R. колея́: broad gauge, широ́кая колея́. **3,** (standard of measurement) кали́бр. **4,** fig. (standard; yardstick) мери́ло. —v.t. **1,** (measure) измеря́ть. **2,** (estimate; assess) оце́нивать; суди́ть о.

gaunt adj. исхуда́лый; измождённый.

gauntlet n. **1,** (glove) (ла́тная) перча́тка. **2,** fig. (challenge): throw down/take up/the gauntlet, бросать/поднимать перчатку. **3,** [*also,* **gantlet**] (form of punishment): *make someone run the gauntlet,* прогонять кого-нибудь сквозь строй.

gauze *n.* марля. —**gauzy,** *adj.* прозрачный.

gavel *n.* молоток.

gawk *v.i.* глазеть; зевать.

gay *adj.* весёлый.

gaze *n.* пристальный взгляд. —*v.i.* смотреть; вглядываться.

gazelle *n.* газель.

gazette *n.* (официальная) газета.

gazetteer *n.* географический справочник.

gear *n.* **1,** (toothed wheel) шестерня. **2,** (adjustment relative to speed) скорость; передача. *First/second gear,* первая/вторая скорость. *High gear,* высшая скорость *or* передача. *Low gear,* низшая передача. *Reverse gear,* задний ход. *Shift gears,* переключить скорость. **3,** (device; mechanism) устройство: *landing gear,* посадочное устройство; шасси. **4,** (equipment) принадлежности. —*v.t.* (adjust; adapt) приводить в соответствие (с).

gearbox *n.* коробка передач; коробка скоростей.

gearshift *n.* переключение передач.

Geiger counter счётчик Гейгера.

geisha *n.* гейша.

gelatin *n.* желатин. —**gelatinous,** *adj.* желатиновый.

geld *v.t.* холостить; кастрировать.

gelding *n.* мерин.

gem *n.* драгоценный камень.

Gemini *n.* Близнецы.

gemstone *n.* драгоценный камень.

gendarme *n.* жандарм. —**gendarmerie,** *n.* жандармерия.

gender *n.* род: *feminine gender,* женский род.

gene *n.* ген.

genealogy *n.* генеалогия; родословие; родословная. —**genealogical,** *adj.* генеалогический; родословный.

general *n.* **1,** (military officer) генерал. **2,** *preceded by* **the** (that which is applicable to the whole) общее. —*adj.* **1,** (not specific or restricted) общий. *General anesthetic,* общий наркоз. *General practitioner,* врач общей практики. **2,** (widespread; nationwide) всеобщий: *general strike,* всеобщая забастовка. *The general public,* широкая публика. **3,** (chief; highest-ranking) генеральный: *general staff,* генеральный штаб. *Secretary-general,* генеральный секретарь. —**in general,** вообще.

General Assembly Генеральная Ассамблея.

general delivery до востребования.

generalissimo *n.* генералиссимус.

generality *n.* обобщение. *Talk in generalities,* говорить общими словами.

generalization *n.* обобщение.

generalize *v.i.* говорить общими словами; делать общий вывод.

generally *adv.* **1,** (usually) обычно; как правило. **2,** (in general) вообще: *generally speaking,* вообще говоря. **3,** (popularly; commonly) обще-: *generally known,* общеизвестный; *generally accepted,* общепринятый.

generate *v.t.* порождать.

generation *n.* **1,** (stage in natural descent) поколение. **2,** (production, as of electricity) генерация

generator *n.* генератор.

generic *adj.* **1,** (general) общий: *generic term,* общее обозначение. **2,** *biol.* родовой.

generosity *n.* щедрость.

generous *adj.* щедрый. —**generously,** *adv.* щедро.

genesis *n.* **1,** (origin) происхождение; возникновение; генезис. **2,** *cap.* (book of the Bible) Бытие; Книга Бытия.

genetic *adj.* генетический. —**genetic code,** генетический код.

genetics *n.* генетика. —**geneticist,** *n.* генетик.

genial *adj.* сердечный; добродушный. —**geniality,** *n.* сердечность; добродушие.

genie *n.* джин. —**let the genie out of the bottle,** выпустить джина из бутылки.

genital *adj.* половой; детородный. —**genitals,** *n.pl.* половые *or* детородные органы.

genitive *adj.* родительный: *genitive case,* родительный падеж.

genius *n.* **1,** (person) гений. **2,** (extraordinary talent) гениальность. *Man of genius,* гениальный человек.

genocide *n.* геноцид.

genre *n.* жанр. —**genre painting,** жанровая живопись; жанр.

genteel *adj.* **1,** (well-bred) благовоспитанный. **2,** (elegant; polished) изящный.

gentian *n.* горечавка.

gentile *n.* не еврей. —*adj.* не еврейский.

gentility *n.* **1,** (noble birth) родовитость. **2,** (delicacy; refinement) изящество.

gentle *adj.* **1,** (tender) нежный. **2,** (mild; not severe) мягкий: *gentle voice,* мягкий голос. **3,** (not violent) лёгкий: *gentle nudge,* лёгкий толчок; *gentle breeze,* лёгкий ветерок. **4,** (docile) смирный. **5,** (not steep) отлогий.

gentlefolk *n.* дворянство.

gentleman *n.* джентльмен; господин. *Ladies and gentlemen!,* дамы и господа! —**gentlemen's agreement,** джентльменское соглашение.

gentlemanly *adj.* джентльменский.

gentleness *n.* мягкость; нежность.

gently *adv.* мягко; нежно.

gentry *n.* дворянство.

genuflect *v.i.* преклонять колена (колени).

genuine *adj.* **1,** (authentic) подлинный; настоящий. **2,** (sincere) искренний. —**genuinely,** *adv.* искренне.

genus *n.* род.

geocentric *adj.* геоцентрический.

geodesy *n.* геодезия. —**geodetic,** *adj.* геодезический.

geography *n.* география. —**geographer,** *n.* географ. —**geographic; geographical,** *adj.* географический.

geology *n.* геология. —**geological,** *adj.* геологический. —**geologist,** *n.* геолог.

geometry *n.* геометрия. —**geometric; geometrical,** *adj.* геометрический.

geophysics *n.* геофизика. —**geophysical,** *adj.* геофизический.

geopolitics *n.* геополитика.

Georgian *adj.* грузинский. —*n.* **1,** (person) грузин; грузинка. **2,** (language) грузинский язык.

geothermal *adj.* геотермальный; геотермический.

geranium *n.* герань.

gerbil *n.* песчáнка.

geriatrics *n.* гериатрúя. —**geriatric,** *adj.* гериатрúческий.

germ *n.* микрóб. —**germ warfare,** бактериологúческая войнá.

German *adj.* гермáнский; немéцкий. —*n.* **1,** (person) нéмец; нéмка. **2,** (language) немéцкий язык. *Speak German,* говорúть по-немéцки.

germane *adj.* относящийся к дéлу.

Germanic *adj.* гермáнский.

germanium *n.* гермáний.

German measles краснýха.

German shepherd немéцкая овчáрка.

germinal *adj.* зародышевый; зачáточный.

germinate *v.i.* пускáть ростки; прорастáть. —**germination,** *n.* прорастáние.

gerontology *n.* геронтолóгия.

gerund *n.* герýндий.

gestation *n.* берéменность.

gesticulate *v.i.* жестикулúровать. —**gesticulation,** *n.* жестикуляция.

gesture *n.* жест. —*v.i.* дéлать жест.

get *v.t.* **1,** (receive) получáть: *get a letter,* получúть письмó. **2,** (obtain) доставáть; получáть: *get tickets,* достáть билéты; *get permission,* получúть разрешéние. *Where can I get...?,* где я могý достáть/получúть...? **3,** (fetch; bring) приносúть; сходúть за. *Get my shoes,* принесú мне ботúнки. *Get some cigarettes,* сходú за папирóсами. **4,** (deliver quickly or on time) доставлять: *get the manuscript to the printer,* достáвить рýкопись в типогрáфию. **5,** (catch, as an illness) получáть: *get pneumonia,* получúть воспалéние лéгких. **6,** (make; prepare, as a meal) готóвить. **7,** (cause to happen): *get the work done,* закóнчить рабóту. *Get something fixed,* отдавáть чтó-нибудь в починку. *Get one's feet wet,* промочúть нóги. *I can't get the door (to) open,* не могý сдéлать, чтобы дверь открылась. **8,** (induce; prevail upon) застáвить; убедúть; уговорúть. **9,** (apprehend; nab) поймáть; схватúть. **10,** (succeed in shooting or swatting) попáсть в. *I got him!,* попáл! **11,** (be sentenced to): *he got ten years,* емý дáли дéсять лет. **12,** *colloq.* (hear) расслышать. **13,** *colloq.* (understand) понимáть. **14,** *colloq.* (stump) озадáчить. —*v.i.* **1,** (arrive) приходúть; приезжáть: *when I got home,* когдá я пришёл/приéхал домóй. **2,** (reach) попáсть; добрáться до. *How do I get there?,* как мне тудá попáсть? *Get to the end/truth,* добрáться до концá/úстины. **3,** (become) становúться: *get better,* стать лýчше. ♦ *Usu. rendered by individual verbs: get dressed,* одевáться; *get tired,* устáвать; *get sick,* заболевáть; *get well,* оправляться; поправляться; *get lost,* заблудúться; *get wet,* промокáть; *get angry,* сердúться; *get dark,* темнéть; *get married,* женúться; выйти зáмуж; *get ready,* готóвиться; *get stuck,* застревáть; *get used to,* привыкáть к; *get caught in the rain,* попáсть под дождь. **4,** *fol. by* **to** (begin) принимáться за: *get to work,* принимáться за рабóту. *We got to talking,* мы разговорúлись; у нас завязáлся разговóр. **5,** *fol. by* **to** (have the opportunity) приходúться (+ *dat.*): *I don't get to see her often,* мне рéдко приходится встречáться с ней. —**get about,** передвигáться. —**get across, 1,** (reach the opposite side of) перебирáться (чéрез). **2,** (transmit; convey) передавáть.

—**get along, 1,** (fare; progress) поживáть. **2,** (manage) обходúться; устрáиваться. *Get along without,* обходúться без. *Get along on 100 rubles a month,* существовáть на сто рублéй в мéсяц. **3,** (be compatible) лáдить; уживáться. *They could not get along,* онú не лáдили; онú не моглú ужúться; онú не сошлúсь харáктерами. —**get around, 1,** (travel, as of news) распространяться. **2,** (circumvent) обходúть. **3,** (walk) передвигáться. **4,** *fol. by* **to** (find time to) успéть; удосýжиться. —**get at, 1,** (reach) добирáться до. **2,** (imply) клонúть: *what are you getting at?,* к чемý ты клóнишь? —**get away, 1,** (go away) уходúть; уезжáть. *Get away from me!,* прочь от меня! *Get away for a few days,* уезжáть на нéсколько дней. **2,** (escape) убегáть; уходúть. *The fish got away,* рыба ускользнýла. —**get away with, 1,** (make off with) утащúть. **2,** (escape unpunished) сходúть с рук: *he got away with it,* это сошлó емý с рук. —**get back, 1,** (recover) получáть обрáтно. **2,** (return) возвращáться. **3,** (step back) отступáть назáд. —**get behind, 1,** (fall behind) отставáть. **2,** (give support to) поддéрживать. —**get by, 1,** (pass) проходúть. **2,** (sneak past) проскользнýть мúмо. **3,** *colloq.* (manage) устрáиваться. —**get down,** сходúть; спускáться. —**get down to,** брáться за; засéсть за. *Get down to business,* приступúть к дéлу. —**get in, 1,** (enter) входúть; влезáть. **2,** (arrive) приходúть; приезжáть. **3,** (manage to say) ввернýть. **4,** (receive, as a supply of merchandise) получúть. —**get into, 1,** (enter, as a vehicle) садúться в; влезáть в. **2,** (manage to enter) попáсть в: *get into the house,* попáсть в дом. **3,** (arrive in) приезжáть в; прибывáть в. **4,** (put into with difficulty) попáсть (+ *instr.*): *get the key into the lock,* попáсть ключóм в замóк. **5,** (squeeze into) умещáть: *get everything into the suitcase,* умещáть всё в чемодáне. **6,** (fit into) умещáться в; влезáть в. **7,** (penetrate) проникáть в. *Water got into the basement,* водá затеклá в подвáл. *Sand got into my shoes,* песóк засыпал мне в тýфли. **8,** (become involved in) попáсть в: *get into trouble,* попáсть в бедý. *Get into a fight,* подрáться. *Get into an argument,* поспóрить. **9,** (put on) напяливать. **10,** *Get into debt,* влезть в долгú; *get into the habit of,* привыкáть (+ *inf.*). —**get it,** *colloq.* **1,** (understand) понимáть. **2,** (be punished) достáться (+ *dat.*): *he'll get it for doing that,* емý достáнется/попадёт за это. —**get off, 1,** (debark) выходúть; сходúть. **2,** (dismount) сходúть; слезáть. **3,** (remove; take off) снимáть. **4,** (send off) отправлять. **5,** (escape) отдéлываться: *get off cheap,* дёшево отдéлаться. **6,** (help to escape punishment) спастú от наказáния. —**get on, 1,** (mount; board) садúться в *or* на. **2,** (put on) надевáть. **3,** = **get along. 4,** *Get on one's nerves,* дéйствовать на нéрвы (+ *dat.*). **5,** *Get on in years,* быть в годáх *or* в летáх. —**get out, 1,** (leave) уйтú. *Get out!,* вон отсюда! **2,** (become known) выйти нарýжу. —**get out of, 1,** (escape from) выбирáться из. **2,** (depart from) убирáться: *get out of here!,* убирáйтесь; прочь отсюда! *Get out of the way!,* прочь с дорóги! *Get out of my sight!,* прочь с глаз моúх! **3,** (remove) вынимáть: *get the key out of the lock,* вынимáть ключ из замкá. **4,** (evade doing something) избегáть (+ *inf.*). **5,** (elicit from) вырывáть; выведывать. **6,** *Get out of bed,* вставáть с постéли. **7,** *Get out of debt,* выходить из долго́в. **8,** *Get out of the habit of,* отвыка́ть (+ *inf.*). —**get over, 1,** (surmount) преодолева́ть. **2,** (recover from) оправля́ться от. **3,** *with can't or couldn't* (not but wonder) (не мочь) надиви́ться. **4,** = **get across.** —**get through, 1,** (manage to complete) оси́ливать. **2,** (manage to survive) пережива́ть. **3,** *fol. by* to (make oneself understood) доходи́ть до. —**get together,** встреча́ться. —**get up, 1,** (stand up) встава́ть. **2,** *fol. by* to (read as far as) доходи́ть до. *See also* **got.**

get-together *n.* сбо́рище.

getup *n., colloq.* наря́д.

geyser *n.* ге́йзер.

ghastly *adj.* стра́шный; жу́ткий.

gherkin *n.* корнишо́н.

ghetto *n.* ге́тто.

ghost *n.* привиде́ние; при́зрак. —**give up the ghost,** испусти́ть дух. —**not a ghost of a chance,** ни мале́йшего ша́нса.

ghostly *adj.* при́зрачный.

ghoul *n.* вампи́р. —**ghoulish,** *adj.* жу́ткий; чудо́вищный.

giant *n.* гига́нт; велика́н; исполи́н. —*adj.* гига́нтский; исполи́нский.

gibberish *n.* набо́р слов; тарабарщина.

gibbet *n.* ви́селица.

gibbon *n.* гиббо́н.

gibe *v.t. & i.* издева́ться (над); насмеха́ться (над). —*n.* издёвка; насме́шка.

giblets *n.pl.* потроха́; ли́вер.

giddap *interj.* гей!

giddiness *n.* головокруже́ние.

giddy *adj.* **1,** (dizzy) чу́вствующий головокруже́ние. **2,** (causing giddiness, as of a height) головокружи́тельный. **3,** (frivolous) ве́треный; легкомы́сленный.

giddyap *interj.* гей!

gift *n.* **1,** (present) пода́рок. **2,** (talent) дар; спосо́бности. —**gift shop,** магази́н пода́рков.

gifted *adj.* дарови́тый; одарённый.

gig *n.* **1,** (carriage) кабриоле́т; одноко́лка; шараба́н. **2,** (boat) ги́чка.

gigantic *adj.* гига́нтский; исполи́нский.

giggle *v.i.* хихи́кать.

gigolo *n.* сутенёр.

gild *v.t.* золоти́ть.

gilded *adj.* золочёный; позоло́ченный; вы́золоченный. —**gilded cage,** золочёная кле́тка.

gilding *n.* **1,** (process) золоче́ние. **2,** (substance) позоло́та.

gills *n.pl.* жа́бры. —**stuffed to the gills,** сыт по го́рло.

gillyflower *n.* левко́й.

gilt *adj.* золочёный; позоло́ченный; вы́золоченный. —*n.* позоло́та.

gimlet *n.* бура́в; бура́вчик.

gimmick *n., colloq.* уло́вка; трюк; приём.

gin *n.* (liquor) джин. —**cotton gin,** хлопкоочисти́тельная маши́на.

ginger *n.* имби́рь. —*adj.* имби́рный.

gingerbread *n.* имби́рный пря́ник; коври́жка.

gingerly *adj.* осмотри́тельный; осторо́жный. —*adv.* осмотри́тельно; осторо́жно.

gingivitis *n.* воспале́ние дёсен.

ginseng *n.* женьше́нь.

Gipsy *n. & adj.* = **Gypsy.**

giraffe *n.* жира́ф.

gird *v.t.* опоя́сывать; подпоя́сывать.

girder *n.* ба́лка; прого́н.

girdle *n.* по́яс; корсе́т.

girl *n.* **1,** (female child) де́вочка. **2,** (young woman) де́вушка. **3,** (female servant) служа́нка.

girlfriend *n.* **1,** (female friend) подру́га. **2,** (man's steady companion) прия́тельница.

girlhood *n.* де́вичество.

girlish *adj.* де́вичий; деви́ческий.

girth *n.* **1,** (circumference) обхва́т. **2,** (band) подпру́га; чересседе́льник.

gist *n.* суть; су́щность.

give *v.t.* **1,** (hand over; provide; administer) дава́ть: *give me a cigarette,* да́йте мне сигаре́ту. *Give advice/ evidence,* дава́ть сове́т/показа́ния. *Give a concert,* дава́ть конце́рт. *Give a signal,* дава́ть *or* подава́ть сигна́л. **2,** (make a present of) дари́ть; преподноси́ть. *Give someone a present,* де́лать кому́-нибудь пода́рок. **3,** (convey) передава́ть: *give him my regards,* переда́йте ему́ приве́т. **4,** (issue, as an order) отдава́ть. **5,** (deliver, as a lecture; teach, as a course) чита́ть. **6,** (impart) придава́ть (си́лу); доставля́ть (удово́льствие). *He gave us hope,* он всели́л в нас наде́жду. **7,** (hold, as a party) устра́ивать. **8,** (sacrifice, as one's life) отдава́ть (свою́ жизнь). *I'd give anything to...,* всё отда́м, чтобы... **9,** (care to the extent of): *I don't give a damn,* мне наплева́ть на э́то. **10,** *used with various nouns: give one's word,* дава́ть че́стное сло́во; *give birth,* рожа́ть; *give thanks,* благодари́ть; *give a hint,* сде́лать намёк; *give rise to,* порожда́ть. —*v.i.* **1,** (give donations) же́ртвовать. **2,** (yield to physical pressure) подава́ться. —**give away, 1,** (give freely) отдава́ть. **2,** (reveal; betray) выдава́ть. —**give back,** возвраща́ть; отдава́ть. —**give in (to),** уступа́ть (+ *dat.*); поддава́ться (+ *dat.*); склоня́ться (пе́ред). —**give off,** испуска́ть; выделя́ть. —**give out, 1,** (distribute) выдава́ть; раздава́ть. **2,** (be exhausted, as of supplies) иссяка́ть; истоща́ться. —**give to understand,** дать поня́ть. —**give up, 1,** (yield; relinquish) уступа́ть; сдава́ть. **2,** (surrender) сдава́ться. **3,** (abandon, as hope) оставля́ть (наде́жду). **4,** (abandon, as an idea, attempt, etc.) отка́зываться от. **5,** (cease; drop; quit) бро́сить. —**give way,** *see* **way.**

given *adj.* **1,** [*usu.* **the given**] (present) да́нный: *under the given circumstances,* при да́нных обстоя́тельствах. **2,** [*usu.* **a given**] (stated; specified) устано́вленный: *in a given amount of time,* в устано́вленный срок. *At a given signal,* по сигна́лу. **3,** *fol. by* to (prone to) скло́нный (к): *given to exaggeration,* скло́нен к преувеличе́ниям. —*prep.* при: *given the situation,* при тако́м положе́нии дел. —**given name,** и́мя.

glacial *adj.* леднико́вый. —**glacial epoch,** леднико́вый пери́од.

glacier *n.* ледни́к; гле́тчер.

glad *adj.* **1,** (happy; pleased) рад: *I am glad to see you,* я рад (ра́да) вас ви́деть. **2,** (bringing joy) ра́достный: *glad tidings,* ра́достное изве́стие.

gladden *v.t.* ра́довать.

glade *n.* поля́на.

gladiator *n.* гладиа́тор.

gladiolus *n.* гладио́лус.

gladly *adv.* охо́тно; с удово́льствием.

gladness *n.* рáдость.

glamorous *also,* **glamourous** *adj.* чарýющий; очаровáтельный.

glamour *also,* **glamor** *n.* чáры; очаровáние.

glance *n.* (быстрый) взгляд. *Passing glance,* мимолётный взгляд. —*v.i.* **1,** *fol. by* **at** (give a quick look at) взглядывать (на). **2,** *fol. by* **over** *or* **through** (look over quickly) просмáтривать. **3,** *fol. by* **off** (strike and be deflected) скользнýть по; отскочить от. *Glancing blow,* скользящий удáр. —**at a glance,** с пéрвого взгляда. —**at first glance,** на пéрвый взгляд; с пéрвого взгляда.

gland *n.* железá.

glanders *n.* сап.

glandular *adj.* желéзистый.

glandule *n.* желéзка.

glare *n.* **1,** (dazzling light) сверкáние. **2,** (angry stare) свирéпый взгляд. —*v.i.* **1,** (shine very brightly) сверкáть. **2,** (stare fiercely) свирéпо смотрéть.

glaring *adj.* **1,** (dazzlingly bright) яркий; ослепительный. **2,** (flagrant) грýбый; вопиющий.

glass *n.* **1,** (substance) стекло. **2,** (container) стакáн: *a glass of water,* стакáн воды. *Wineglass,* бокáл. *Raise one's glass to,* поднимáть бокáл за (+ *acc.*). **3,** *pl.* (eyeglasses) очки.—*adj.* стеклянный: *glass vase/ door,* стеклянная вáза/дверь.

glass blower стекловдýв.

glassful *n.* стакáн.

glassware *n.* стеклянные издéлия.

glassworks *n.* стекóльный завóд.

glassy *adj.* **1,** (smooth, as of the surface of a lake) зеркáльный. **2,** (blank, as of a stare) стеклянный.

glaucoma *n.* глаукóма.

glaze *n.* глазýрь. —*v.t.* **1,** (fit with glass) застеклять. **2,** (apply a glaze to) глазировáть.

glazed *adj.* глазирóванный. *Glazed paper,* лощёная бумáга.

glazier *n.* стекóльщик.

gleam *n.* прóблеск. *Gleam in one's eye,* огонёк в глазáх. —*v.i.* блестéть.

glean *v.t.* **1,** (collect, as grain) подбирáть (колóсья). **2,** (gather, as information) чéрпать; почерпáть.

glee *n.* рáдость; ликовáние. —**glee club,** хоровóй кружóк.

gleeful *adj.* рáдостный; ликýющий.

glen *n.* лощина; ложбина.

glib *adj.* бóйкий.

glide *v.i.* **1,** (move smoothly) скользить. **2,** *aero.* планировать. —*n.* **1,** (smooth easy movement) скольжéние. **2,** (powerless flight) планировáние.

glider *n.* планёр. *Glider pilot,* планерист.

glimmer *v.i.* мерцáть. —*n.* **1,** (faint light) мерцáние. **2,** *Glimmer of hope,* искра надéжды; прóблеск надéжды.

glimpse *n.* мимолётный взгляд. —*v.t.* увидеть мéльком.

glint *n.* вспышка; блеск.

glisten *v.i.* блестéть.

glitter *v.i.* блестéть; сверкáть. —*n.* блеск. —**glittering,** *adj.* блестящий; блистáтельный.

gloaming *n.* сýмерки.

gloat *v.i.* злорáдствовать.

global *adj.* мировóй; всемирный; глобáльный.

globe *n.* **1,** (sphere) шар. **2,** (the earth) земнóй шар. **3,** (spherical model of the earth) глóбус.

globular *adj.* шаровóй; шаровидный.

globule *n.* **1,** (tiny sphere) шáрик. **2,** (drop) кáпля.

gloom *n.* **1,** (darkness) мрак. **2,** (melancholy feeling) мрáчность; унние.

gloomy *adj.* **1,** (dark; dismal) мрáчный; хмýрый. **2,** (melancholy; morose) мрáчный; угрюмый; хмýрый; пáсмурный. —**gloominess,** *n.* мрáчность; угрюмость.

glorify *v.t.* прославлять. —**glorification,** *n.* прославлéние.

glorious *adj.* **1,** (possessing or deserving glory) слáвный. **2,** *colloq.* (delightful) чудéсный.

glory *n.* слáва. —*v.i.* [*usu.* **glory in**] наслаждáться (+ *instr.*); упивáться (+ *instr.*).

gloss *n.* **1,** (luster) лоск; глянец. **2,** (commentary) глóсса. —*v.t.* [*usu.* **gloss over**] смáзывать; замáзывать.

glossary *n.* глоссáрий.

glossy *adj.* лощёный; глянцевитый; глянцевый.

glottis *n.* голосовáя щель.

glove *n.* перчáтка.

glow *v.i.* **1,** (shine; beam) светиться. **2,** (smolder) тлеть. **3,** *fig.* (radiate, as with emotion) сиять. —*n.* **1,** (luminosity) зáрево. **2,** (flush; redness) румянец.

glower *v.i.* смотрéть исподлóбья; смотрéть вóлком; смотрéть звéрем.

glowing *adj.* **1,** (burning) тлéющий. **2,** (rich and warm, as of colors) яркий. **3,** (ruddy; healthy) румяный. **4,** (highly enthusiastic) востóрженный.

glowworm *n.* светляк.

gloxinia *n.* глоксиния.

glucose *n.* глюкóза.

glue *n.* клей. —*v.t.* клéить; приклéивать. *Glue together,* склéивать. *We sat glued to the TV set,* мы не могли оторвáться от телевизора.

glum *adj.* мрáчный; угрюмый; хмýрый.

glut *n.* избыток. —*v.t.* пресыщáть. *Glut the market,* наводнять рынок товáрами.

glutton *n.* обжóра. —**gluttonous,** *adj.* прожóрливый. —**gluttony,** *n.* обжóрство.

glycerin *also,* **glycerine** *n.* глицерин.

glycogen *n.* гликогéн.

gnarl *n.* сучóк.

gnarled *adj.* **1,** (knotty) сучковáтый. **2,** (twisted, as of fingers) сучковáтый; корявый.

gnash *v.t.* скрежетáть (зубáми).

gnat *n.* мóшка.

gnaw *v.t. & i.* грызть; глодáть. *Gnaw a hole,* выгрызáть дырý. —**gnawing,** *adj.* (of a pain) сверлящий.

gneiss *n.* гнейс.

gnome *n.* гном.

gnu *n.* гну.

go *v.i.* **1,** (proceed on foot) идти. *Go for a walk,* идти гулять. *Who goes there?,* кто идёт? **2,** (travel by vehicle) éхать. *Go for a ride,* éздить на прогýлку. *катáться на машине. Go by plane,* летéть на самолёте. **3,** (leave; depart) уходить. *It's time to go,* порá идти *or* уходить. **4,** (proceed; progress) идти; проходить; сходить. *Things are going well,* делá идýт хорошó. *Everything went well,* всё сошло хорошó. **5,** (function; work) идти; рабóтать. *The car won't go,* машина отказáла. **6,** (be phrased; read) гласить. *As the saying goes,* как говорится. **7,** (engage in an activity): *go swimming,* купáться; *go skiing,* ходить на лы́жах; go shopping, идти́ за поку́пками. **8,** *used with various adjectives:* go mad, сходи́ть с ума́; go broke, прогоря́ть; go blind, осле́пнуть; go bad, испо́ртиться; go hungry, голода́ть; go free, остава́ться на свобо́де. **9,** (fail) пропада́ть; слабе́ть. *His eyesight is going,* он теря́ет зре́ние. **10,** *fol. by* with (be in harmony) гармони́ровать (с); сочета́ться (с). —*v.t.* Used mainly in set expressions: go shares with, войти́ в до́лю с. We are going the same way, нам с ва́ми по пути́. —*n.* Used mainly in set colloquial expressions: on the go, на нога́х; в движе́нии. Have a go at, попыта́ться. From the word "go", с са́мого нача́ла. —**be going to,** собира́ться: *what are you going to do?,* что вы собира́етесь де́лать? —**go about, 1,** (circulate, as of rumors) ходи́ть. **2,** (proceed with) принима́ться за: *I don't know how to go about it,* я не зна́ю, как приня́ться за э́то. —**go against, 1,** (oppose) идти́ про́тив. **2,** (be contrary to) противоре́чить; идти́ вразре́з с. —**go ahead!,** дава́йте! —**go along, 1,** (proceed) идти́. **2,** *fol. by* with (accompany) сопровожда́ть. **3,** (consent) соглаша́ться. **4,** *fol. by* with (agree with) быть согла́сным с. —**go around, 1,** (walk around) обходи́ть. **2,** (revolve around) враща́ться вокру́г. **3,** (enclose; surround) окружа́ть. **4,** (fit around) сходи́ться на (+ *prepl.*). **5,** (suffice for all) хвата́ть: *there is not enough to go around,* на всех не хва́тит. —**go away,** уходи́ть, уезжа́ть. —**go back,** возвраща́ться. —**go back on,** *see* **back.** —**go by, 1,** (pass) проходи́ть. **2,** (be guided by) руково́дствоваться (+ *instr.*). **3,** (be known as): *he goes by the name of..:,* он изве́стен под и́менем... —**go down, 1,** (descend) сходи́ть; спуска́ться. **2,** (set, as of the sun) сади́ться; заходи́ть. **3,** (sink, as of a ship) идти́ ко дну. **4,** (subside, as of swelling) опада́ть. **5,** (fall, as of prices) снижа́ться. **6,** *Go down in history,* войти́ в исто́рию. —**go for, 1,** (fetch) идти́ за (+ *instr.*). **2,** (be used for a purpose) идти́ на (+ *acc.*). **3,** (be sold for) продава́ться за (+ *acc.*). **4,** *slang* (take a fancy to) увлека́ться (+ *instr.*). —**go in, 1,** (enter) входи́ть. **2,** (fit) вмеща́ться. —**go in for,** занима́ться (+ *instr.*). —**go into, 1,** (enter) входи́ть в. *Go into detail,* вдава́ться в подро́бности. *Go into effect,* вступа́ть в си́лу. **2,** (fit into) вмеща́ться в; умеща́ться в; укла́дываться в. **3,** (be invested in) уйти́ на: *a lot of work went into that,* мно́го рабо́ты ушло́ на э́то. —**go off, 1,** (stray) отклоня́ться: *go off course,* отклоня́ться от ку́рса. *The train went off the tracks,* по́езд сошёл с ре́льсов. **2,** (depart) уходи́ть: *go off to war,* уходи́ть на войну́. **3,** (detonate, as of a bomb) взрыва́ться; (discharge, as of a gun) вы́стрелить. —**go on, 1,** (continue) продолжа́ть. *Life goes on,* жизнь продолжа́ется. **2,** (happen) происходи́ть; де́латься. **3,** (appear, as on stage) выходи́ть (на сце́ну). **4,** (be turned on, as of light) зажига́ться. —**go out, 1,** (go outside) выходи́ть на у́лицу. **2,** (stop burning) га́снуть; ту́хнуть. —**go out of, 1,** (leave) выходи́ть из. **2,** *Go out of style,* выходи́ть из мо́ды. **3,** *Go out of control,* потеря́ть управле́ние. —**go over, 1,** (cross over) переходи́ть. **2,** (tumble over) сва́ливаться: *the car went over the cliff,* маши́на свали́лась со скалы́. **3,** (examine) просма́тривать. **4,** (repeat) повторя́ть. —**go round,** враща́ться. —**go through, 1,** (fit through) проходи́ть в; пролеза́ть в. **2,** (pass, as a red light) проскочи́ть. **3,** (search) обша́ривать. **4,** (endure) пережива́ть. **5,**

(repeat) повторя́ть. **6,** (be completed, as of a deal) состоя́ться. **7,** (spend; squander) промота́ть. —**go under, 1,** (sink) тону́ть. **2,** (go bankrupt) прогоре́ть. —**go up, 1,** (ascend) поднима́ться. **2,** (increase) расти́; повыша́ться. —**go without,** обходи́ться без. *See also* **going** *and* **gone.**

goad *v.t.* **1,** (prod, as cattle) подгоня́ть. **2,** (incite) подстрека́ть.

go-ahead *n., colloq.* разреше́ние (сде́лать что́-нибудь). *Give (someone) the go-ahead to...,* дать (кому́-нибудь) добро́ на (+ *acc.*).

goal *n.* **1,** (aim; objective) цель. **2,** *sports* (scoring area) воро́та. **3,** *sports* (point scored) гол.

goalie *n.* врата́рь. *Also,* **goalkeeper.**

goal line ли́ния воро́т.

goal post сто́йка воро́т.

goat *n.* (female) коза́; (male) козёл. —*adj.* [*also,* **goat's**] ко́зий: *goat's milk,* ко́зье молоко́. —**get someone's goat,** *colloq.* разозли́ть; вы́вести из себя́.

goatee *n.* козли́ная боро́дка.

goatskin *n.* ко́зья шку́ра. —*adj.* козло́вый; козли́ный.

goatsucker *n.* козодо́й.

gobble *v.t.* пожира́ть.

go-between *n.* посре́дник.

goblet *n.* бока́л.

goblin *n.* эльф; гном; ле́ший; домово́й.

goby *n.* бычо́к.

god *also,* **God** *n.* бог. —**by God,** кляну́сь бо́гом. —**for God's sake!,** ра́ди бо́га! —**God bless you!** *(after a sneeze),* бу́дьте здоро́вы! —**God forbid!,** не дай бог!; бо́же упаси́! —**God knows!,** бог его́ зна́ет! —**God willing,** е́сли бог даст. —**good God!; my God!,** бо́же мой! —**thank God!,** сла́ва бо́гу!

godchild *n.* кре́стник; кре́стница.

goddaughter *n.* кре́стница; кре́стная дочь.

goddess *n.* боги́ня.

godfather *n.* кре́стный; кре́стный оте́ц.

god-fearing *adj.* богобоя́зненный.

godforsaken *adj.* захолу́стный. *Godforsaken place,* захолу́стье; трущо́ба; медве́жий у́гол.

godless *adj.* безбо́жный. —**godlessness,** *n.* безбо́жие.

godly *adj.* набо́жный; благочести́вый.

godmother *n.* кре́стная; кре́стная мать.

godsend *n.* дар бо́жий.

godson *n.* кре́стник; кре́стный сын.

goggle *v.i.* тара́щить глаза́; де́лать кру́глые глаза́. —**goggle-eyed,** *adj.* пучегла́зый. —**goggles,** *n.pl.* защи́тные очки́.

going *n.* **1,** (act of going) хожде́ние. **2,** (departure) отъе́зд. —*adj.* **1,** (present) теку́щий: *at the going rate,* по теку́щим тари́фам. **2,** (operating and doing well) соли́дный; рента́бельный: *a going concern,* соли́дная компа́ния; рента́бельное предприя́тие.

goiter *also,* **goitre** *n.* зоб. *Exophthalmic goiter,* ба́зедова боле́знь.

gold *n.* зо́лото. —*adj.* золото́й. —**be worth its weight in gold,** быть на вес зо́лота. —**have a heart of gold,** име́ть золото́е се́рдце.

gold dust золото́й песо́к.

golden *adj.* золото́й; золоти́стый. —**golden age,** золото́й век. —**golden eagle,** бе́ркут. —**Golden**

Fleece, золотóе рунó. —**golden mean,** золотáя середи́на.

goldeneye *n.* гóголь.

goldenrod *n.* золотáрник.

goldfinch *n.* щегóл.

goldfish *n.* золотáя ры́бка. *Goldfish bowl,* аквáриум с золоты́ми ры́бками.

gold leaf сусáльное зóлото.

gold mine 1, *often pl.* (mine producing gold ore) золоты́е при́иски. **2,** *fig.* (source of great wealth) золотóе дно.

gold plate накладнóе зóлото. —**gold-plate,** *v.t.* золоти́ть. —**gold-plated,** *adj.* накладнóго зóлота.

goldsmith *n.* золоты́х дел мáстер.

gold standard золотóй стандáрт.

golf *n.* гольф. —**golf club,** клю́шка. —**golf course,** площáдка для гóльфа.

gonad *n.* **1,** (testicle) яи́чко. **2,** (ovary) яи́чник.

gondola *n.* гондóла. —**gondolier,** *n.* гондольéр.

gone *adj.* **1,** (departed; away) ушéдший; в отъéзде. **2,** (missing) пропáвший. **3,** (dead) умéрший.

gong *n.* гонг.

gonococcus *n.* гонокóкк.

gonorrhea *n.* гонорéя; три́ппер.

good *adj.* **1,** (general term) хорóший: *good manners,* хорóшие манéры. *That's good,* э́то хорошó. *Smell good,* хорошó пáхнуть. *Have a good time,* хорошó провести́ врéмя. ♦ *In certain set expressions* дóбрый: *good morning!,* дóброе у́тро! *Good evening!,* дóбрый вéчер! *Good will,* дóбрая вóля. *The good fairy,* дóбрая фéя. **2,** *fol. by at* (having a knack for) спосóбный (к); си́лен (в). **3,** *fol. by for* (of use; helpful) полéзный. *This medicine is good for a cough,* э́то лекáрство полéзно (*or* помогáет) от кáшля. *Not be good for anything,* ни на что не годи́ться. **4,** (honorable) дóбрый. *Good intentions,* дóбрые *or* благи́е намéрения. *One's good name,* своё дóброе и́мя. **5,** (sound) уважи́тельный: *a good reason/excuse,* уважи́тельная причи́на. **6,** (valid) действи́тельный: *good for six months,* действи́телен на шесть мéсяцев. **7,** (considerable) изрядный: *a good distance,* изрядное расстоя́ние. *A good while,* довóльно дóлго. **8,** (not less than) дóбрый: *a good hour,* дóбрый час. —*n.* **1,** (something good; what is right) добрó: *good and evil,* добрó и зло. *Do good,* дéлать добрó. **2,** (benefit; welfare) блáго: *for the good of mankind,* на блáго человéчества. **3,** (gain; advantage) пóльза: *what's the good of it?,* какáя от э́того пóльза? *Do (someone) good,* быть *or* идти́ на пóльзу (+ *dat.*). —**as good as...,** всё равнó, что... —**be up to no good,** замышля́ть недóброе. —**come to no good,** плóхо кóнчить. —**for good,** навсегдá; окончáтельно. —**good and...,** *colloq.* здóрово: *good and tired,* здóрово устáл. —**make good,** преуспевáть. —**to the good,** в вы́игрыше.

goodbye *interj.* до свидáния! —*n.* прощáние. *Say goodbye (to),* прощáться (с).

good-for-nothing *adj.* никчёмный. —*n.* шалопáй.

Good Friday страстнáя пя́тница.

good-hearted *adj.* добросердéчный.

good-looking *adj.* краси́вый; хорóш собóй; хорóшенький; милови́дный.

goodly *adj.* (rather large) порядочный; изрядный.

good-natured *adj.* добродýшный.

good-neighbor *adj.* добрососéдский.

goodness *n.* добротá. —*interj.* гóсподи! —**for goodness' sake!,** рáди бóга! —**thank goodness!,** слáва бóгу!

goods *n.* **1,** (merchandise) изде́лия; товáр(ы). *Leather goods,* кóжаные изде́лия. *Canned goods,* консéрвы. *Consumer goods,* ширпотрéб. *Goods and services,* товáры и услýги. **2,** (personal possessions) вéщи; имýщество. **3,** (fabric) матéрия.

good will дóбрая вóля: *people of good will,* лю́ди дóброй вóли. —**goodwill,** *adj.* дóброй вóли: *goodwill mission,* ми́ссия дóброй вóли.

goose *n.* гусь. —*adj.* гуси́ный: *goose feathers,* гуси́ные пéрья.

gooseberry *n.* крыжóвник.

goose flesh гуси́ная кóжа. *Also,* **goose pimples.**

goose step гуси́ный шаг.

gopher *n.* **1,** (burrowing rodent) гóфер. **2,** (ground squirrel) сýслик.

Gordian knot гóрдиев ýзел.

gore *n.* **1,** (blood) кровь. **2,** (gusset) клин. —*v.t.* забодáть.

gorge *n.* ущéлье. —*v.t.* обкáрмливать. *Gorge oneself,* наéсться дóсыта.

gorgeous *adj.* великолéпный; прекрáсный.

gorilla *n.* гори́лла.

gory *adj.* **1,** (covered with blood) окровáвленный. **2,** (involving bloodshed) кровáвый.

goshawk *n.* тетеревя́тник.

gosling *n.* гусёнок.

gospel *n.* евáнгелие. —**gospel truth,** свята́я и́стина.

gossamer *n.* **1,** (cobweb) паути́на. **2,** (fabric) газ.

gossip *n.* **1,** (talk) сплéтня; пересýды. **2,** (person) сплéтник; сплéтница. —*v.i.* сплéтничать.

got *v.,* past tense of **get.** —**have got, 1,** (having): *have you got a match?,* у вас есть спи́чка? **2,** *fol. by to* (must) нáдо: *I've got to go,* мне нáдо идти́.

Goth *n.* гот.

Gothic *adj.* **1,** (of architecture, script, etc.) готи́ческий. **2,** (of the language) гóтский. —*n.* **1,** (architecture) гóтика. **2,** (language) гóтский язы́к.

gouache *n.* гуáшь.

gouge *v.t.* **1,** (make grooves or holes in) долби́ть. **2,** *fol. by out* (cut out) выдáлбливать. **3,** *fol. by out* (put out, as an eye) выкáпывать. **4,** *colloq.* (cheat; overcharge) обжýливать. —*n.* **1,** (tool) долотó. **2,** (groove) вы́емка.

goulash *n.* гуля́ш.

gourd *n.* **1,** (calabash) горля́нка. **2,** (pumpkin) ты́ква.

gourmand *n.* **1,** (glutton) обжóра. **2,** = **gourmet.**

gourmet *n.* гурмáн; гастронóм.

gout *n.* подáгра.

govern *v.t.* **1,** (rule over) прáвить; управля́ть: *govern a country,* прáвить/управля́ть странóй. **2,** (determine) определя́ть. **3,** *gram.* управля́ть. —*v.i.* прáвить.

governess *n.* гувернáнтка; воспитáтельница.

government *n.* **1,** (governing body of a nation) прави́тельство. *Work for the government,* быть на госудáрственной слýжбе. **2,** (administration; rule) правлéние; управлéние. *Form of government,* óбраз правлéния. *Organs of local government,* óрганы мéстного управлéния.

governmental *adj.* прави́тельственный.

governor *n.* **1,** *polit.* губернáтор. **2,** *mech.* регулятор. —**governorship,** *n.* губерна́торство.

gown *n.* **1,** (long dress) пла́тье: *evening gown,* вече́рнее пла́тье. **2,** (long robe) ма́нтия.

grab *v.t.* **1,** (grasp; snatch) хвата́ть; схва́тывать; выхва́тывать. **2,** (seize; take possession of) захва́тывать.

grace *n.* **1,** (beauty; elegance) гра́ция; изя́щество: *grace of movement,* гра́ция/изя́щество движе́ний. **2,** (proper behavior; sense of what is right): *social graces,* пра́вила хоро́шего то́на. *He conceded defeat with good grace,* он призна́л своё пораже́ние с досто́инством. *At least he had the grace to apologize,* по кра́йней ме́ре, он набра́лся сме́лости извини́ться. **3,** (favor) ми́лость: *by God's grace,* бо́жьей ми́лостью. *Be in someone's good graces,* быть в ми́лости у кого́-нибудь; быть у кого́-нибудь на хоро́шем счету́. *Fall from grace,* впасть в неми́лость. **4,** (extension) отсро́чка: *receive a month's grace,* получи́ть ме́сячную отсро́чку. **5,** (prayer at meals) моли́тва: *say grace,* чита́ть моли́тву. **6,** *cap.* (title of respect) све́тлость: *Your Grace,* ва́ша све́тлость. —*v.t.* украша́ть: *flowers graced the table,* цветы́ украша́ли стол.

graceful *adj.* **1,** (moving with grace) грацио́зный: *graceful dancer,* грацио́зный танцо́р. *Graceful movements,* грацио́зные *or* изя́щные движе́ния. **2,** (well-proportioned) изя́щный; стро́йный.

gracefully *adv.* **1,** (with grace of movement) грацио́зно. **2,** (with good grace) с досто́инством.

grace note форшла́г.

grace period льго́тный срок.

gracious *adj.* любе́зный. —*interj.* бо́же мой! —**graciously,** *adv.* любе́зно. —**graciousness,** *n.* любе́зность.

gradation *n.* града́ция.

grade *n.* **1,** (rank) зва́ние; чин. **2,** (quality) сорт; ка́чество. **3,** (school class or year) класс. **4,** (mark in school) отме́тка; оце́нка; балл. **5,** (slope) склон; укло́н. —*v.t.* **1,** (classify) сортирова́ть. **2,** (give a grade to) ста́вить отме́тку *or* оце́нку (+ *dat.*). **3,** (level) ука́тывать; нивели́ровать. —**make the grade,** быть на до́лжной высоте́.

grader *n.* **1,** (machine for grading) гре́йдер. **2,** (pupil): *third grader,* учени́к тре́тьего кла́сса.

grade school нача́льная шко́ла.

gradient *n.* **1,** (slope) склон; укло́н. **2,** *physics* (rate of change) градие́нт.

gradual *adj.* постепе́нный. —**gradually,** *adv.* постепе́нно.

graduate *v.t. & i.* ко́нчить; око́нчить (шко́лу *or* университе́т). *Graduating class,* выпускно́й класс; вы́пуск. —*n.* выпускни́к. —**graduate school,** аспиранту́ра: *go to graduate school,* пойти́ в аспиранту́ру. —**graduate student,** аспира́нт.

graduated *adj.* **1,** (containing gradations) градуи́рованный. **2,** (of a tax) прогресси́вный.

graduation *n.* **1,** (completion of studies) оконча́ние. **2,** (commencement exercises) выпускно́й акт.

graft *v.t.* **1,** *horticulture* привива́ть. **2,** *surgery* переса́живать. —*n.* **1,** *horticulture* черено́к. **2,** *surgery* переса́женная ткань. **3,** (corruption) по́дкуп.

grain *n.* **1,** (seed; crops) зерно́; хлеб. **2,** (particle) зерно́; крупи́нка; крупи́ца. *Grain of sand,* песчи́нка. *Grain of truth,* зерно́ *or* крупи́ца и́стины. **3,** (arrangement of fibers or layers) волокно́. **4,** (unit of weight) гран. —**against the grain,** про́тив ше́рсти.

grain elevator элева́тор.

grainy *adj.* зерни́стый; крупча́тый.

gram *also,* **gramme** *n.* грамм.

grammar *n.* **1,** (structure of a language) грамма́тика. **2,** (book on grammar) уче́бник грамма́тики. —**grammarian,** *n.* граммати́ст. —**grammatical,** *adj.* граммати́ческий.

gramme *n.* = **gram.**

gramophone *n.* граммофо́н.

granary *n.* **1,** (storehouse for grain) амба́р; зернохрани́лище. **2,** (grain-producing region) жи́тница.

grand *adj.* **1,** (magnificent; luxurious) великоле́пный. *Live in grand style,* жить широко́; жить на широ́кую но́гу. **2,** *colloq.* (fine; splendid) чуде́сный. **3,** (overall) о́бщий: *grand total,* о́бщий ито́г.

grandchild *n.* внук; вну́чка. —**grandchildren,** *n.pl.* вну́ки.

granddaughter *n.* вну́чка.

grand duke вели́кий князь. —**grand duchy,** вели́кое кня́жество.

grandeur *n.* **1,** (splendor) великоле́пие. **2,** (greatness) грандио́зность. —**delusions of grandeur,** ма́ния вели́чия.

grandfather *n.* де́душка; дед.

grandiloquent *adj.* высокопа́рный; напы́щенный. —**grandiloquence,** *n.* высокопа́рность; напы́щенность.

grandiose *adj.* грандио́зный. —**grandiosity,** *n.* грандио́зность.

grand jury большо́е жюри́.

grandmaster *n.* **1,** (of a monastic order) маги́стр. **2,** *chess* гроссме́йстер.

grandmother *n.* ба́бушка.

grandnephew *n.* внуча́тый племя́нник.

grandniece *n.* внуча́тая племя́нница.

grandparent *n.* де́душка; ба́бушка.

grand piano роя́ль.

grand slam большо́й шлем.

grandson *n.* внук.

grandstand *n.* трибу́на.

grange *n.* уса́дьба.

granite *n.* грани́т. —*adj.* грани́тный.

grant *v.t.* **1,** (give; bestow) предоставля́ть; дава́ть: *grant credit,* предоставля́ть креди́т; *grant a delay,* дава́ть отсро́чку. **2,** (agree to fulfill, as a wish or request) исполня́ть; удовлетворя́ть. **3,** (concede; allow) допуска́ть. *Granted she is no beauty,* пусть она́ не краса́вица. —*n.* дота́ция. —**take for granted, 1,** (assume as obvious) счита́ть само́ собо́й разуме́ющимся. **2,** (fail to appreciate) принима́ть как до́лжное.

granular *adj.* зерни́стый.

granulate *v.t.* грануля́ровать. —**granulated sugar,** са́харный песо́к.

granulation *n.* грануля́ция.

granule *n.* зёрнышко.

grape *n.* виногра́дина; *pl.* виногра́д. —*adj.* виногра́дный: *grape wine,* виногра́дное вино́.

grapefruit *n.* гре́йпфрут.

grape sugar виногра́дный са́хар.

grapevine *n.* **1,** (plant) виногра́дная лоза́. **2,** (rumors) слу́хи; то́лки: *the grapevine has it that...,* иду́т то́лки о том, что...

graph *n.* гра́фик; диагра́мма.

graphic *adj.* **1,** (illustrated by graphs) графи́ческий.

2, (vivid) о́бразный; нагля́дный: *graphic description,* о́бразное описа́ние; *graphic example,* нагля́дный приме́р. —**graphic arts,** гра́фика; графи́ческое иску́сство.

graphically *adv.* нагля́дно; воо́чию.

graphite *n.* графи́т. —*adj.* графи́товый.

graph paper бума́га в кле́тку.

grapnel *n.* ко́шка.

grapple *v.t.* зацепля́ть. —*v.i.* **1,** (fight; wrestle) схва́тываться; сцепля́ться. **2,** *fol. by* with (contend with, as a problem) би́ться (над); схва́тываться (с).

grappling iron ко́шка.

grasp *v.t.* **1,** (seize; grab) хвата́ть; схва́тывать. **2,** (understand) схва́тывать; воспринима́ть; постига́ть. —*v.i.* [*usu.* **grasp at**] хвата́ться за; ухвати́ться за: *grasp at a straw,* хвата́ться за соло́минку; *grasp at an opportunity,* ухвати́ться за слу́чай. —*n.* **1,** (firm hold; grip) хва́тка. **2,** (comprehension) понима́ние: *beyond one's grasp,* вы́ше чьего́-нибудь понима́ния.

grasping *adj.* **1,** (prehensile) це́пкий. **2,** (avaricious) жа́дный; а́лчный.

grass *n.* трава́. —*adj.* травяно́й.

grasshopper *n.* кузне́чик.

grassland *n.* травяно́е уго́дье.

grass widow соло́менная вдова́.

grassy *adj.* травяно́й; травяни́стый.

grate *n.* решётка. —*v.t.* тере́ть: *grate carrots,* тере́ть морко́вь. —*v.i.* **1,** (make a harsh grinding sound) скрежета́ть. **2,** *fol. by* on (irritate) коро́бить. *Grate on one's ear,* ре́зать у́хо *or* слух (+ *dat.*).

grateful *adj.* благода́рный; призна́тельный.

grater *n.* тёрка.

gratification *n.* **1,** (act of gratifying) удовлетворе́ние. **2,** (sense of satisfaction) удовлетворе́ние; удово́льствие.

gratify *v.t.* **1,** (give satisfaction to) доставля́ть удово́льствие (+ *dat.*); ра́довать. **2,** (satisfy; indulge, as a desire) удовлетворя́ть. —**gratifying,** *adj.* отра́дный.

grating *n.* решётка. —*adj.* ре́зкий; скрипу́чий.

gratis *adv.* беспла́тно; да́ром.

gratitude *n.* благода́рность; призна́тельность.

gratuitous *adj.* **1,** (freely given) безвозме́здный. **2,** (uncalled-for) неуме́стный: *gratuitous remarks,* неуме́стные замеча́ния. *Gratuitous insult,* ниче́м не вы́званное оскорбле́ние.

gratuity *n.* чаевы́е.

grave *n.* моги́ла. —*adj.* **1,** (serious) серьёзный: *grave matter,* серьёзное де́ло; *grave appearance,* серьёзный вид; *in grave danger,* в серьёзной опа́сности. **2,** (critical) тяжёлый; тя́жкий: *a grave illness,* тяжёлая/тя́жкая боле́знь. *In grave condition,* в тяжёлом состоя́нии. **3,** *phonet.* тупо́й: *grave accent,* тупо́е ударе́ние. —**dig one's own grave,** самому́ себе́ рыть моги́лу. —**have one foot in the grave,** стоя́ть одно́й ного́й в моги́ле. —**turn over in one's grave,** переверну́ться в гробу́.

gravedigger *n.* моги́льщик.

gravel *n.* **1,** (mixture of pebbles and sand) гра́вий. **2,** *med.* мочево́й песо́к.

gravely *adv.* тяжело́: *gravely ill,* тяжело́ бо́лен.

graven *adj.* вы́сеченный. —**graven image,** и́дол; куми́р.

gravestone *n.* моги́льная плита́; моги́льный ка́мень.

graveyard *n.* кла́дбище; пого́ст.

gravitate *v.i.* тяготе́ть. —**gravitation,** *n.* тяготе́ние; гравита́ция.

gravity *n.* **1,** (seriousness) серьёзность; тя́жесть. **2,** *physics* тя́жесть; тяготе́ние. *Center of gravity,* центр тя́жести. *The law of gravity,* зако́н (всеми́рного) тяготе́ния.

gravy *n.* со́ус; подли́вка. —**gravy boat,** со́усник; судо́к.

gray *also,* **grey** *adj.* се́рый; *(of hair)* седо́й; *(of a horse)* си́вый. —*n.* се́рый цвет. *Hair flecked with gray,* во́лосы с про́седью. —**gray matter,** се́рое вещество́ (мо́зга). —**turn gray,** сере́ть; *(of hair)* седе́ть.

gray-haired *adj.* седо́й; седоволо́сый.

graze *v.t.* **1,** (brush lightly, as of a bullet) задева́ть; скользну́ть по. **2,** (put to pasture) пасти́. —*v.i.* пасти́сь. —**grazing land,** па́стбищные уго́дья.

grease *n.* **1,** (melted fat) то́пленое са́ло; жир. *Grease spot,* жи́рное пятно́. **2,** (lubricant) сма́зка. **3,** (ointment) мазь. —*v.t.* сма́зывать. —**grease the palm of,** подма́зывать.

grease monkey *slang* сма́зчик.

grease paint грим.

greasy *adj.* **1,** (smeared with grease) са́льный; жи́рный. **2,** (containing grease, as of food) жи́рный.

great *adj.* **1,** (eminent; outstanding) вели́кий: *a great writer,* вели́кий писа́тель. *Peter the Great,* Пётр Вели́кий. **2,** (large) большо́й: *a great distance,* большо́е расстоя́ние. **3,** (far beyond the ordinary) большо́й; кру́пный: *a great victory,* больша́я/кру́пная побе́да. *A great honor,* больша́я честь. *Great friends,* больши́е друзья́. *With great pleasure,* с больши́м удово́льствием. **4,** *colloq.* (splendid) чуде́сный: *have a great time,* чуде́сно провести́ вре́мя. —*adv., colloq.* прекра́сно; чу́дно. *Feel great,* прекра́сно чу́вствовать себя́.

great-aunt *n.* двою́родная ба́бушка.

great circle большо́й круг.

Great Dane да́тский дог.

great-granddaughter *n.* пра́внучка.

great-grandfather *n.* пра́дед.

great-grandmother *n.* праба́бка; праба́бушка.

great-grandson *n.* пра́внук.

great-great-granddaughter *n.* прапра́внучка.

great-great-grandfather *n.* прапра́дед.

great-great-grandmother *n.* прапраба́бка; прапраба́бушка.

great-great-grandson *n.* прапра́внук.

greatly *adv.* о́чень; си́льно.

greatness *n.* вели́чие.

great-uncle *n.* двою́родный де́душка.

grebe *n.* пога́нка.

greed *n.* жа́дность; а́лчность. —**greedily,** *adv.* жа́дно. —**greediness,** *n.* = greed. —**greedy,** *adj.* жа́дный; а́лчный.

Greek *adj.* гре́ческий. —*n.* **1,** (person) грек; греча́нка. **2,** (language) гре́ческий язы́к.

green *adj.* зелёный. *Be green with envy,* ло́паться от за́висти. —*n.* **1,** (color) зелёный цвет. **2,** *pl.* (leafy vegetables) зе́лень. **3,** (grassy lawn) лужа́йка.

greenery *n.* зе́лень.

green-eyed *adj.* зеленогла́зый.

greengrocer *n.* зеленщи́к.

greenhorn *n.* новичо́к; молокосо́с.

greenhouse *n.* тепли́ца; оранжере́я.

greenish adj. зеленова́тый.

green light зелёный свет. —**give someone the green light,** дать кому́-нибудь зелёную у́лицу.

greet v.t. **1,** (say hello to) здоро́ваться с. **2,** (welcome) приве́тствовать. **3,** (meet in a specified manner) встреча́ть: he was greeted with applause, его́ встре́тили аплодисме́нтами.

greeting n. **1,** (salutation) приве́тствие. **2,** pl. (regards) приве́т.

gregarious adj. **1,** (living in herds) ста́дный. **2,** (fond of company) общи́тельный.

Gregorian adj. григориа́нский. —**Gregorian calendar,** григориа́нский календа́рь.

gremlin n. чертёнок.

grenade n. грана́та. —**grenade launcher,** гранатомет.

grenadier n. гренадёр.

grey adj. & n. = **gray.**

greyhound n. борза́я.

grid n. **1,** (grating) решётка. **2,** (lines dividing a map) се́тка. **3,** electricity се́тка.

griddle n. сковоро́дка.

gridiron n. **1,** (cooking utensil) ра́шпер. **2,** (football field) футбо́льное по́ле.

grief n. го́ре. —**come to grief,** потерпе́ть неуда́чу. —**good grief!,** бо́же мой!

grief-stricken adj. уби́тый го́рем.

grievance n. **1,** (wrong; injustice) оби́да. **2,** (complaint) прете́нзия.

grieve v.t. огорча́ть; печа́лить. —v.i. горева́ть; скорбе́ть; печа́литься; сокруша́ться.

grievous adj. **1,** (distressing) мучи́тельный. **2,** (severe; serious) тяжёлый; тя́жкий. Grievous insult, кро́вная or смерте́льная оби́да.

griffin n. гриф; грифо́н.

griffon n. **1,** (dog) грифо́н. **2,** (griffon vulture) сип.

grill n. **1,** (gridiron) ра́шпер. **2,** (grilled meat) жа́реное (на ра́шпере) мя́со. —v.t. **1,** (broil) жа́рить. **2,** colloq. (interrogate) допра́шивать.

grille n. решётка.

grilled adj. жа́реный.

grim adj. **1,** (ghastly) жу́ткий. **2,** (forbidding; stern) суро́вый. **3,** (resolute; relentless) непоколеби́мый.

grimace n. грима́са; ужи́мка. —v.i. де́лать грима́су; грима́сничать.

grime n. грязь; са́жа. —**grimy,** adj. гря́зный; запа́чканный.

grin v.i. ухмыля́ться; ска́лить зу́бы; расплыва́ться в улы́бке. —n. усме́шка. —**grin and bear it,** де́лать хоро́шую ми́ну при плохо́й игре́.

grind v.t. **1,** (pulverize) моло́ть; размалыва́ть; растира́ть. **2,** (shape by friction) шлифова́ть. **3,** (sharpen) точи́ть. **4,** (grate, as one's teeth) скрежета́ть (зуба́ми). **5,** (press; force) вда́вливать (в зе́млю). —v.i. **1,** (grate) скрежета́ть. **2,** (degree of fineness) помо́л. **2,** colloq. (monotonous routine) колея́. **3,** colloq. (laborious study) зубрёжка. **4,** colloq. (one who so studies) зубри́ла. —**grind away,** colloq. **1,** (work steadily) рабо́тать без у́стали. **2,** (study hard) зубри́ть. —**grind down, 1,** (make smooth) шлифова́ть. **2,** (oppress) заму́чить. —**grind out,** colloq. штампова́ть. —**grind up,** дроби́ть; измельча́ть.

grinder n. **1,** (person) точи́льщик. Organ grinder, шарма́нщик. **2,** (machine for crushing) дроби́лка.

Meat grinder, мясору́бка. **3,** (grindstone) точи́льный стано́к.

grinding n. **1,** (pulverizing) растира́ние. **2,** (sharpening) точе́ние. **3,** (grating, as of wheels) скре́жет. —adj. мучи́тельный. Grinding poverty, кра́йняя нищета́.

grindstone n. точи́льный ка́мень. —**keep one's nose to the grindstone,** рабо́тать, не поклада́я рук.

grip v.t. **1,** (hold tenaciously) зажима́ть. **2,** fig. (seize; engross) завладева́ть; овладева́ть; захва́тывать. —n. **1,** (firm hold) сжа́тие; хва́тка. **2,** colloq. (valise) чемода́н. —**come to grips with,** схва́тываться с.

gripe v.t., colloq. (annoy) раздража́ть. —v.i., colloq. (grouse) ворча́ть. —n., colloq. жа́лоба. —**griper,** n. ворчу́н.

grippe n. грипп.

grisly adj. стра́шный; жу́ткий.

grist n. зерно́ для помо́ла. —**be grist for** (or **bring grist to**) **someone's mill,** лить во́ду на чью-нибудь ме́льницу.

gristle n. хрящ. —**gristly,** adj. хрящева́тый.

grit v.t. сти́скивать: grit one's teeth, сти́скивать зу́бы. —n. (pluck) вы́держка.

grizzly bear гри́зли.

groan n. стон. —v.i. стона́ть.

groats n.pl. крупа́.

grocer n. бакале́йщик.

groceries n.pl. проду́кты; бакале́я; гастроно́мия.

grocery store продукто́вый/продово́льственный/бакале́йный магази́н; гастроно́м.

grog n. грог.

groggy adj. обалде́лый; одуре́лый.

groin n. пах.

groom n. **1,** (stableboy) ко́нюх. **2,** (bridegroom) жени́х. —v.t. **1,** (curry) хо́лить; выхоли́ть: well-groomed, хо́леный; вы́холенный.

groove n. желобо́к.

grope v.i. **1,** (feel one's way) идти́ о́щупью. **2,** fol. by for (search for clumsily) нащу́пывать; иска́ть о́щупью.

grosbeak n. дубоно́с.

gross adj. **1,** (fat; heavy) то́лстый; ту́чный. **2,** (crude; flagrant) гру́бый. **3,** (total; without deductions) валово́й: gross national product, валово́й национа́льный проду́кт. Gross weight, вес бру́тто. —n. (144) гросс.

grotesque adj. **1,** art гроте́скный. **2,** (outlandish) абсу́рдный; карикату́рный.

grotto n. грот.

grouch n., colloq. брюзга́. —v.i. брюзжа́ть. —**grouchy,** adj. брюзгли́вый.

ground n. **1,** (surface of the earth) земля́: lie on the ground, лежа́ть на земле́. **2,** (soil) по́чва: soft ground, мя́гкая по́чва. **3,** (area used for a specific purpose) площа́дка. Parade ground, плац. **4,** pl. (basis; valid reason) основа́ние; по́вод: on what grounds?, на како́м основа́нии? Grounds for divorce, по́вод для разво́да. **5,** pl. (dregs; sediment) гу́ща: coffee grounds, кофе́йная гу́ща. **6,** painting грунт. —adj. **1,** (made fine by grinding) мо́лотый; толчёный. **2,** mil. (operating on the ground) назе́мный: ground troops, назе́мные войска́. —v.t. **1,** (cause to run aground) посади́ть на мель. **2,** (teach; instruct) подко́вывать: well-grounded in mathematics, хорошо́ подко́ван по матема́тике. **3,** (cancel, as a flight) отменя́ть; запреща́ть. **4,** electricity заземля́ть. —**be on firm ground,** стоя́ть на твёрдой по́чве. —**burn to the**

ground, сжечь *or* сгоре́ть дотла́. —**cut the ground from under one's feet,** выбива́ть по́чву из-под ног у кого́-нибудь. —**gain ground,** *see* **gain.** —**give ground, 1,** (retreat) отступа́ть. **2,** (yield) уступа́ть. —**shift one's ground,** перемени́ть пози́цию. —**stand one's ground,** устоя́ть; стоя́ть на своём.

ground floor пе́рвый эта́ж; ни́жний эта́ж.

ground glass притёртое стекло́.

ground hog суро́к.

grounding *n.* подгото́вка: *a good grounding in chemistry,* хоро́шая подгото́вка по хи́мии.

groundless *adj.* необосно́ванный; неоснова́тельный; беспричи́нный; беспо́чвенный; не име́ющий под собо́й по́чвы. *Groundless fears,* беспричи́нные опасе́ния.

ground speed путева́я ско́рость.

ground squirrel су́слик.

groundswell *n.* мёртвая зыбь.

ground water грунто́вые во́ды.

groundwork *n.* фунда́мент. *Lay the groundwork,* закла́дывать фунда́мент; подготавливать по́чву.

group *n.* гру́ппа. *Literary group,* литерату́рный кружо́к. —*adj.* группово́й: *group portrait,* группово́й портре́т. —*v.t.* группирова́ть. —*v.i.* группирова́ться.

grouping *n.* группиро́вка.

grouse *n. Black grouse,* те́терев. *Hazel grouse,* ря́бчик. *Wood grouse,* глуха́рь. —*v.i., colloq.* (grumble) ворча́ть.

grove *n.* ро́ща: *orange grove,* апельси́новая ро́ща.

grovel *v.i.* пресмыка́ться; низкопокло́нничать.

grow *v.i.* **1,** (increase in size) расти́. **2,** (increase) расти́; увели́чиваться; уси́ливаться. **3,** (become) станови́ться. *Grow old,* старе́ть. *Grow tired,* устава́ть. —*v.t.* **1,** (cultivate) выра́щивать. **2,** (develop, as a beard) отра́щивать. —**grow into, 1,** *literally* враста́ть в: *grow into the soil,* враста́ть в по́чву. **2,** (develop into) выраста́ть в. —**grow out of, 1,** (outgrow) выраста́ть из. **2,** (develop from) выраста́ть из. **3,** (result from) вытека́ть из. —**grow up,** расти́; выраста́ть; подраста́ть. *He is quite grown up,* он совсе́м вы́рос.

grower *n. Rendered by the suffix* —во́д: *tobacco grower,* табаково́д; *cotton grower,* хлопково́д.

growing *adj.* расту́щий. —**growing pains,** боле́зни ро́ста.

growl *v.i.* рыча́ть; ворча́ть. —*n.* рыча́ние; ворча́ние.

grown *adj.* взро́слый.

grownup *n.* взро́слый; большо́й.

growth *n.* **1,** (development; increase; expansion) рост: *slow growth,* ме́дленный рост. *Economic growth,* экономи́ческий рост. *Population growth,* рост *or* прирост населе́ния. **2,** (tumor) наро́ст; о́пухоль.

grub *n.* **1,** (larva) личи́нка. **2,** *slang* (food) харчи́. —*v.t.* (clear of roots; root out) выкорчёвывать. —*v.i.* **1,** (rummage) ры́ться. **2,** (toil) труди́ться.

grubby *adj.* неря́шливый; гря́зный.

grudge *n.* зло́ба. *Have/bear a grudge against,* пита́ть *or* (за)та́ить зло́бу к *or* про́тив; (за)та́ить оби́ду на; *colloq.* име́ть зуб про́тив. —*v.t.* = **begrudge.**

grudging *adj.* неохо́тный. —**grudgingly,** *adv.* неохо́тно; не́хотя; с неохо́той; скрепя́ се́рдце.

gruel *n.* ка́шица; размазня́.

grueling *also,* **gruelling** *adj.* изнури́тельный.

gruesome *adj.* ужа́сный; жу́ткий.

gruff *adj.* гру́бый: *gruff voice,* гру́бый го́лос.

grumble *v.i.* брюзжа́ть; ропта́ть; ворча́ть. —**grumbler,** *n.* брюзга́; ворчу́н.

grumpy *adj.* брюзгли́вый; ворчли́вый.

grunt *v.i.* хрю́кать. —*n.* хрю́канье.

guano *n.* гуа́но.

guarantee *n.* гара́нтия; руча́тельство; поручи́тельство. —*v.t.* гаранти́ровать; руча́ться за.

guarantor *n.* поручи́тель.

guard *v.t.* охраня́ть; стере́чь; сторожи́ть; карау́лить. —*v.i.* [*usu.* **guard against**] бере́чься (+ *gen.*). —*n.* **1,** (one who guards) сто́рож; часово́й. *Prison guard,* надзира́тель. **2,** (unit that guards) карау́л; стра́жа; охра́на. *Guard of honor,* почётный карау́л. *Changing of the guard,* сме́на карау́ла. **3,** *often pl.* (special unit of troops) гва́рдия: *red guards,* кра́сная гва́рдия. **4,** (device that protects) щит: *mudguard,* щит от гря́зи. **5,** *sports* защи́тник. —*adj.* карау́льный: *guard duty,* карау́льная слу́жба. —**be on one's guard,** быть насторо́же. —**catch off one's guard,** заста́ть враспло́х. —**put on one's guard,** настора́живать. —**stand guard,** стоя́ть на часа́х/на карау́ле/на стра́же/. —**under guard,** под охра́ной; под конво́ем.

guarded *adj.* **1,** (watched; protected) охраня́емый. **2,** (cautious; restrained) осторо́жный.

guardhouse *n.* **1,** (house used by a guard) карау́льная. **2,** (military prison) гауптва́хта.

guardian *n.* **1,** (protector) блюсти́тель; страж. *Guardian of the law,* блюсти́тель поря́дка. **2,** (one assigned to care for a minor) опеку́н; попечи́тель. —**guardian angel,** а́нгел-храни́тель.

guardianship *n.* опе́ка; опеку́нство; попечи́тельство.

guardsman *n.* гварде́ец.

gubernatorial *adj.* губерна́торский.

gudgeon *n.* песка́рь.

guerrilla *n.* партиза́н. —*adj.* партиза́нский: *guerrilla warfare,* партиза́нская война́.

guess *v.t. & i.* **1,** (make a guess) дога́дываться; уга́дывать; отга́дывать. **2,** *colloq.* (think; suppose) полага́ть. —*n.* дога́дка. —**guesser,** *n.* отга́дчик.

guesswork *n.* дога́дки; гада́ние. *By guesswork,* науга́д.

guest *n.* гость. —**guest conductor,** приглашённый дирижёр. —**guest of honor,** почётный гость. —**guest room,** ко́мната для госте́й.

guffaw *v.i.* хохота́ть. —*n.* хо́хот.

guidance *n.* **1,** (direction) руково́дство. **2,** (advice) консульта́ция. **3,** *aerospace* наведе́ние.

guide *v.t.* **1,** (lead; conduct) вести́. **2,** (direct; manage; govern) руководи́ть. *Be guided by,* руково́дствоваться (+ *instr.*). —*n.* **1,** (person) гид; проводни́к. **2,** (guidebook) путеводи́тель. **3,** (manual; handbook) руково́дство. **4,** (guiding principle) руково́дство.

guidebook *n.* путеводи́тель.

guided missile управля́емая раке́та; управля́емый реакти́вный снаря́д.

guideline *n.* руково́дство.

guidepost *n.* указа́тельный столб.

guild *n.* ги́льдия; цех.

guilder *n.* гу́льден.

guile *n.* хи́трость; кова́рство.

guillemot *n.* чи́стик.

guillotine *n.* гильотина. —*v.t.* гильотинировать.

guilt *n.* вина; виновность.

guiltless *adj.* невинный; невиновный.

guilty *adj.* **1**, (having done wrong) виноватый. **2**, (having committed a crime) виновный. *Guilty party*, виновник. *Guilty of murder*, виновный в убийстве. *He was found guilty*, его признали виновным. **3**, (showing or feeling guilt) виноватый: *guilty look*, виноватый вид. *Guilty conscience*, нечистая совесть. —**plead guilty**, признавать себя виновным. —**plead not guilty**, не признавать себя виновным. —**verdict of "guilty"**, обвинительный приговор. —**verdict of "not guilty"**, оправдательный приговор.

guinea *n.* гинея.

guinea fowl цесарка. *Also,* **guinea hen.**

guinea pig 1, (rodent) морская свинка. **2**, (person used in experiments) подопытный кролик.

guise *n.* вид: *in the guise of*, под видом (+ *gen.*).

guitar *n.* гитара. —**guitarist**, *n.* гитарист.

gulf *n.* **1**, (body of water) залив. **2**, (chasm) пропасть.

gull *n.* чайка.

gullet *n.* **1**, (esophagus) пищевод. **2**, (throat) глотка.

gullible *adj.* легковерный. —**gullibility**, *n.* легковерие.

gully *n.* овраг.

gulp *v.t. & i.* хлебать. —*n.* глоток. *In one gulp*, одним глотком; залпом.

gum *n.* **1**, (substance) камедь; гумми. **2**, (chewing gum) жевательная резинка. **3**, (flesh in which the teeth are set) десна. —*v.t.* **1**, (glue in place) наклеивать. **2**, *fol. by* **up**, *slang* (botch up) напутать. —**gum arabic**, гуммиарабик.

gumbo *n.* бамия; окра.

gumboil *n.* флюс.

gummy *adj.* клейкий; липкий.

gumption *n.*, *colloq.* смелость.

gun *n.* **1**, (portable firearm) ружьё. **2**, (pistol) пистолет. **3**, (heavy weapon) орудие; пушка. *Machine gun*, пулемёт. —*adj.* орудийный: *gun sight*, орудийный прицел. —*v.t.* **1**, (race, as an engine) давать полный газ (+ *dat.*). **2**, *fol. by* **down** (shoot; kill) застрелить. **3**, *fol. by* **for** (seek to catch) охотиться за; (seek to obtain) стремиться к. —**stick to one's guns**, стоять на своём. —**under the gun**, под ударом.

gunboat *n.* канонерская лодка; канонерка. —**gunboat diplomacy**, "дипломатия канонерок".

gun carriage лафет.

gunfire *n.* орудийный огонь. *Exchange of gunfire*, перестрелка.

gunman *n.* бандит.

gunner *n.* артиллерист; пулемётчик; стрелок.

gunnery *n.* артиллерийское дело. *Gunnery school*, артиллерийская школа.

gunpoint *n.*, *in* at gunpoint, под дулом пистолета.

gunpowder *n.* порох.

gunshot *n.* выстрел. *Gunshot wound*, огнестрельная рана.

gunsmith *n.* оружейный мастер; оружейник; ружейник.

gunwale *n.* планшир.

gurgle *v.i.* булькать. —*n.*吅吅 бульканье.

gush *v.i.* хлынуть; брызгать; бить.

gusset *n.* клин.

gust *n.* порыв: *gust of wind*, порыв ветра.

gustatory *adj.* вкусовой.

gusto *n.* смак: *with gusto*, со смаком.

gusty *adj.* **1**, (of wind) порывистый. **2**, (of weather conditions) ветреный.

gut *n.* **1**, (intestine) кишка. **2**, *pl.*, *slang* (courage) дух: *he hasn't got the guts to...*, у него не хватает духа (+ *inf.*). —*adj.*, *colloq.* **1**, (instinctive, as of a reaction) инстинктивный. **2**, (basic, as of an issue) жизненно важный. —*v.t.* **1**, (remove the intestines from) потрошить. **2**, (destroy) опустошать. —**hate someone's guts**, *colloq.* смертельно ненавидеть (кого-нибудь).

gutta-percha *n.* гуттаперча.

gutter *n.* **1**, (of a road) сточная канава. **2**, (of a roof) водосточный жёлоб; водосточная канава.

guttersnipe *n.* беспризорник; уличный мальчишка.

guttural *adj.* гортанный; горловой.

guy *n.*, *colloq.* парень; малый. *Nice guy*, славный малый.

guzzle *v.t.* лакать.

gym *n.*, *colloq.* = **gymnasium.**

gymnasium *n.* гимнастический зал.

gymnast *n.* гимнаст. —**gymnastic**, *adj.* гимнастический. —**gymnastics**, *n.pl.* гимнастика.

gym suit физкультурный костюм.

gynecology *n.* гинекология. —**gynecological**, *adj.* гинекологический. —**gynecologist**, *n.* гинеколог.

gyp *n.*, *slang* **1**, (swindler) жулик; плут. **2**, (swindle) афера. —*v.t.*, *colloq.* обжуливать.

gypsum *n.* гипс.

Gypsy *also,* **Gipsy** *n.* цыган; цыганка. —*adj.* цыганский. —**gypsy moth**, непарный шелкопряд.

gyrate *v.i.* вращаться (по кругу); крутиться. —**gyration**, *n.* вращение.

gyrfalcon *n.* кречет.

gyrocompass *n.* гирокомпас.

gyroscope *n.* гироскоп.

H

H, h восьма́я бу́ква англи́йского алфави́та.

haberdasher *n.* галантере́йщик.

haberdashery *n.* **1,** (goods) галантере́я. **2,** (shop) галантере́йный магази́н.

habit *n.* **1,** (customary practice) привы́чка: *bad habit,* дурна́я привы́чка. *Drug habit,* наркома́ния. *Be in the habit of,* име́ть привы́чку *or* обыкнове́ние (+ *inf.*). **2,** *pl.* (mannerisms) пова́дки: *study the habits of a wolf,* изуча́ть пова́дки во́лка. **3,** (garb): *riding habit,* амазо́нка; *monk's habit,* мона́шеская ря́са.

habitable *adj.* го́дный для жилья́.

habitat *n.* среда́; стихи́я.

habitation *n.* жильё: *unfit for human habitation,* непригодный для жилья́.

habitual *adj.* **1,** (customary) привы́чный; обы́чный. **2,** (inveterate) закорене́лый; отъя́вленный.

habituate *v.t.* приуча́ть.

habitué *n.* завсегда́тай.

hack *n.* **1,** (tool) кайло́. **2,** (banal writer) халту́рщик. —*adj.* халту́рный. —*v.t.* (chop) руби́ть; разруба́ть.

hackneyed *adj.* изби́тый; зата́сканный.

hacksaw *n.* ножо́вка.

hackwork *n.* халту́ра.

haddock *n.* пи́кша.

Hades *n.* ад; преиспо́дняя.

haematite *n.* = **hematite.**

haemoglobin *n.* = **hemoglobin.** —**haemophilia,** *n.* = **hemophilia.** —**haemorrhage,** *n.* = **hemorrhage.** —**haemorrhoid,** *n.* = **hemorrhoid.**

hafnium *n.* га́фний.

haft *n.* черено́к.

hag *n.* ве́дьма; карга́.

haggard *adj.* изможлённый; исхуда́лый.

haggle *v.i.* торгова́ться.

hagiography *n.* агиогра́фия.

hail *n.* град. *Hail of bullets,* град пуль. —*v.t.* **1,** (call) оклика́ть. *Hail a taxi,* подозва́ть такси́. **2,** (greet; welcome) приве́тствовать. **3,** (acclaim) расхва́ливать. —*v.i.* **1,** (be hailing) идти́: *it is hailing,* град идёт. **2,** fol. by **from** (be from) быть ро́дом из: *he hails from California,* он ро́дом из Калифо́рнии.

hailstone *n.* гра́дина.

hailstorm *n.* гроза́ с гра́дом.

hair *n.* **1,** (a single hair) во́лос. **2,** (hair collectively) во́лосы: *red hair,* ры́жие во́лосы. —*adj.* волосяно́й. *Hair net,* се́тка для воло́с. —**split hairs,** спо́рить о мелоча́х; вдава́ться в то́нкости. —**tear one's hair,** рвать на себе́ во́лосы.

hairbreadth *also,* **hairsbreadth** *n., in* **within a hair-**

breadth of, на волосо́к (*or* на волоске́) от.

hairbrush *n.* щётка для воло́с.

haircut *n.* стри́жка. *Get a haircut,* стри́чься; постри́гаться.

hairdo *n.* причёска.

hairdresser *n.* парикма́хер.

hair dryer фен.

hairpiece *n.* пари́к; накла́дка.

hairpin *n.* шпи́лька.

hair-raising *adj.* душераздира́ющий.

hair shirt власяни́ца.

hairspring *n.* волосо́к (в часа́х).

hairstyle *n.* причёска.

hairy *adj.* волоса́тый.

Haitian *adj.* гаитя́нский. —*n.* гаитя́нин; гаитя́нка.

halberd *n.* алеба́рда.

halcyon *n.* зиморо́док. —*adj.* споко́йный; бла́гостный.

hale *adj.* кре́пкий; здоро́вый. —**hale and hearty,** бо́дрый; ядрёный.

half *n.* полови́на: *half of the money,* полови́на де́нег. *One and a half,* полтора́. *Two and a half,* два с полови́ной. *Half past four,* полови́на пя́того. *At half past twelve,* в полови́не пе́рвого. ♦ *Often rendered by the prefixes* пол- *and* полу-: *half an hour,* полчаса́; *a half-turn,* полуоборо́т. —*adj.* полови́нный: *a half share,* полови́нная до́ля. *At half strength,* в полови́нном соста́ве. —*adv.* наполови́ну: *half done,* наполови́ну сде́лано. ♦ *Also with* вдво́е *and comp. adj. of opp. meaning: half as much,* вдво́е ме́ньше. *He is half my age,* он вдво́е моло́же меня́. *Be half the price of,* быть вдво́е деше́вле (+ *gen.*). —**at half price,** за полцены́. —**go halves with,** войти́ в до́лю с. —**half again as much,** в полтора́ ра́за бо́льше. —**in half,** попола́м: *divide in half,* дели́ть попола́м. —**listen with half an ear,** слу́шать кра́ем у́ха. —**that's not the half of it,** э́то далеко́ не всё.

half-asleep *adj.* *Be half-asleep,* быть в полусне́.

halfback *n.* полузащи́тник.

half-baked *adj.* **1,** (incompletely baked) недопечённый. **2,** *fig.* (crude; not well planned) доморо́щенный.

half-blooded *adj.* полукро́вный; нечистокро́вный.

half-breed *n.* полукро́вка.

half brother сво́дный брат.

half-dead *adj.* полумёртвый.

half-dozen *n.* полдю́жины.

halfhearted *adj.* нереши́тельный; неохо́тный.

half-hour *n.* полчаса́.

half-life *n.* пери́од полураспа́да.

half-mast *n.* приспущенный флаг. *Lower a flag to half-mast,* приспускать флаг.

half-moon *n.* полумесяц.

half note половинная нота.

half sister сводная сестра.

half slip нижняя юбка.

half-staff *n.* = half-mast.

half tone *music* полутон.

halftone *n., art* полутон.

half-turn *n.* полуоборот.

halfway *adv.* на полпути: *stop halfway,* останавливаться на полпути. *Turn back halfway,* возвращаться с полпути. *Meet someone halfway,* идти навстречу (+ *dat.*). *Fly halfway around the world,* лететь через половину земного шара. —*adj.* **1,** (midway): *the halfway point,* полпути. **2,** (inadequate; indecisive) половинчатый.

half-wit *n.* дурак; болван. —**half-witted,** *adj.* слабоумный.

halibut *n.* палтус.

hall *n.* **1,** (large public building or room) зал. *Town/city hall,* ратуша. **2,** (vestibule) передняя; прихожая. **3,** (corridor) коридор.

hallelujah *interj.* аллилуйя.

hallmark *n.* **1,** (of precious metals) проба. **2,** (indication of excellence) признак; критерий.

halloo *interj.* ату!; улюлю! —*v.i.* улюлюкать.

hallow *v.t.* освящать.

Halloween *n.* канун дня всех святых (= *Allhallows eve*).

hallucination *n.* галлюцинация.

hallway *n.* **1,** (vestibule) передняя; прихожая. **2,** (corridor) коридор.

halo *n.* ореол.

halogen *n.* галоген.

halt *v.t.* **1,** (bring to a stop) останавливать. **2,** (cease) прекращать. —*v.i.* останавливаться. —*n.* **1,** (stop) остановка. **2,** (cessation) прекращение. —**call a halt to,** прекратить; положить конец (+ *dat.*). —**come to a halt, 1,** (stop moving) останавливаться. **2,** (end) прекращаться.

halter *n.* **1,** (strap for confining an animal) недоуздок. **2,** (woman's garment) лиф.

halting *adj.* связанный: *halting speech,* связанная речь.

halve *v.t.* **1,** (divide in two) делить пополам. **2,** (reduce by half) уменьшать вдвое *or* наполовину.

halyard *n.* фал.

ham *n.* **1,** (meat) ветчина. *Ham sandwich,* бутерброд с ветчиной. **2,** *slang* (one who overacts) позёр. **3,** *colloq.* (amateur radio operator) радиолюбитель.

hamburger *n.* рубленая котлета.

Hamitic *adj.* хамитский.

hamlet *n.* деревушка.

hammer *n.* **1,** (tool) молоток. *Large hammer,* молот. **2,** (of a gun) курок. **3,** *sports* молот: *hammer throw,* метание молота. —*v.t.* **1,** (drive in with a hammer) вбивать; забивать: *hammer a nail into a wall,* вбивать/забивать гвоздь в стену. **2,** (drum in) вбивать в голову. **3,** *fol. by out* (shape with a hammer) выбивать. **4,** *fol. by out* (work out, as an agreement) вырабатывать. —*v.i.* **1,** (use a hammer) работать молотком. **2,** (knock; pound) стучать.

hammerhead *n.* молот-рыба.

hammock *n.* гамак; подвесная койка.

hamper *v.t.* мешать; затруднять; препятствовать. —*n.* корзина.

hamster *n.* хомяк.

hand *n.* **1,** (part of the body) рука: *right hand,* правая рука. **2,** (of a clock) стрелка: *minute hand,* минутная стрелка. **3,** *pl.* (workers) (рабочие) руки. **4,** *pl.* (ship's crew) экипаж; команда. *All hands on deck!,* все наверх! **5,** (help; assistance) помощь: *give/lend someone a helping hand,* подавать руку помощи (+ *dat.*). **6,** (handwriting) почерк; рука. **7,** (permission to marry) рука: *ask for the hand of,* просить руки кого-нибудь. **8,** *colloq.* (round of applause) аплодисменты. **9,** *cards* карты: *a bad hand,* плохие карты. —*adj.* ручной: *hand luggage,* ручной багаж. —*v.t.* передавать: *hand me my hat,* передайте мне шляпу. —**at hand, 1,** (nearby) под рукой. **2,** (about to occur) на носу. —**at the hands of,** от рук (+ *gen.*). —**by hand, 1,** (manually) ручным способом. *This is made by hand,* это ручной работы. *Copy by hand,* писать от руки. **2,** (in person) вручную: *deliver by hand,* доставлять вручную. —**first hand,** из первых рук. —**from hand to hand,** из рук в руки. —**get off one's hands,** сбывать с рук. —**get one's hands on,** добираться до: *wait till I get my hands on him!,* я ещё до него доберусь! *Everything they could get their hands on,* всё, что им попадалось под руку. —**get out of hand,** отбиваться от рук. —**hand down, 1,** (pass on) передавать: *the legend was handed down from generation to generation,* легенда передавалась из поколения в поколение. **2,** (deliver; render, as a verdict) выносить (приговор). —**hand in,** подавать; сдавать. —**hand in hand,** рука в руку; рука об руку. —**hand it to,** *colloq.* отдавать должное (+ *dat.*). —**hand out,** выдавать; раздавать. —**hand over,** передавать; отдавать; сдавать. —**hands down,** легко; без труда. —**hands off!,** руки прочь! —**hands up!,** руки вверх! —**have a hand in,** приложить руку к; участвовать в; играть роль в. —**have one's hands full,** иметь работы по горло. *I have my hands full,* у меня хлопот полон рот. —**live from hand to mouth,** жить сегодняшним днём; жить на птичьих правах; перебиваться с хлеба на квас. —**on hand, 1,** (available) под рукой. **2,** (present) налицо. —**on one's hands,** на руках. —**on the one hand,** с одной стороны. —**on the other hand,** с другой стороны. —**play into the hands of,** играть на руку (+ *dat.*). —**reveal** *or* **tip one's hand,** раскрыть свои карты. —**take in hand,** взять в свои руки.

handbag *n.* сумка; сумочка.

handball *n.* гандбол; ручной мяч.

handbill *n.* рекламный листок.

handbook *n.* руководство.

handcar *n.* дрезина.

handcart *n.* ручная тележка.

handcuff *v.t.* надевать наручники на. —**handcuffs,** *n.pl.* наручники.

handful *n.* горсть; пригоршня.

hand grenade ручная граната.

handgun *n.* ручное огнестрельное оружие.

handicap *n.* **1,** *sports* гандикап. **2,** (disadvantage) недостаток. **3,** (disability) физический недостаток. —*v.t.* **1,** (put a handicap on) давать гандикап (+ *dat.*). **2,** (put at a disadvantage) препятствовать; затруднять.

handicapped *adj.* с физическими недостатками; дефективный.

handicraft *n.* **1,** (craft) ремесло́. **2,** *pl.* (products so made) куста́рные изде́лия. — **handicraftsman,** *n.* реме́сленник; куста́рь.

handily *adv.* **1,** (deftly) ло́вко. **2,** (easily) без труда́.

handiwork *n.* **1,** (manual work) ручна́я рабо́та. **2,** (work; creation) де́ло рук. *It's his handiwork,* э́то его́ рук де́ло.

handkerchief *n.* носово́й плато́к.

handle *n.* ру́чка; рукоя́тка. — *v.t.* **1,** (touch) тро́гать. **2,** (manipulate; treat) обраща́ться с: *handle with care,* обраща́ться с осторо́жностью. **3,** (operate) управля́ть; обраща́ться с. **4,** (deal with) справля́ться с. **5,** (deal in) торгова́ть (+ *instr.*). — *v.i. This car handles easily,* э́той маши́ной легко́ управля́ть. — **fly off the handle,** *colloq.* лезть на́ сте́ну.

handlebar *n.* руль (велосипе́да).

handling *n.* обраще́ние.

handmade *adj.* ручно́й рабо́ты: *this is handmade,* э́то ручно́й рабо́ты.

hand organ шарма́нка.

handout *n.* пода́чка.

handrail *n.* пери́ла; по́ручни.

handsaw *n.* ручна́я пила́; ножо́вка.

handshake *n.* пожа́тие (руки́); рукопожа́тие.

handsome *adj.* **1,** (good-looking) краси́вый. **2,** (considerable) изря́дный: *a handsome sum,* изря́дная су́мма.

handstand *n.* сто́йка. *Do a handstand,* стать на́ руки; де́лать сто́йку на рука́х.

hand-to-hand *adj.* рукопа́шный: *hand-to-hand combat,* рукопа́шный бой.

handwriting *n.* по́черк.

handwritten *adj.* от руки́; руко́й напи́санный; руко́писный; собственнору́чный.

handy *adj.* **1,** (dexterous) ло́вкий; иску́сный. **2,** (within easy reach) под руко́й. **3,** (convenient; useful) удо́бный; поле́зный. — **come in handy,** приходи́ться кста́ти; пригоди́ться.

hang *v.t.* **1,** (fasten from above) ве́шать: *hang a picture,* ве́шать карти́ну. *Hang a door,* наве́шивать дверь. *Hang wallpaper,* кле́ить обо́и. **2,** (execute) ве́шать. *Hang oneself,* ве́шаться. **3,** (let droop, as one's head) ве́шать; поника́ть; пону́рить. **4,** (decorate with hanging things) уве́шивать; обве́шивать; заве́шивать. **5,** *in* **hang fire,** дать осе́чку. — *v.i.* висе́ть. *Hang from the ceiling,* висе́ть на потолке́. *Hang by a thread,* висе́ть на волоске́. — *n.* сноро́вку. *Get the hang of,* напрактикова́ться в; наловчи́ться (+ *inf.*); наби́ть ру́ку на. — **hang around, 1,** (spend time idly) слоня́ться; околачиваться. **2,** *fol. by with* (keep company with) якша́ться с. — **hang down,** свиса́ть. — **hang on, 1,** (hold on) повиса́ть. **2,** (hold the line) не ве́шать тру́бку. **3,** (persist, as of a cold) упо́рствовать. **4,** *Hang on every word,* лови́ть ка́ждое сло́во. — **hang onto,** повиса́ть на. — **hang out, 1,** (hang up, as wash) выве́шивать. **2,** (lean out) высо́вываться. **3,** *colloq.* (spend one's time) крути́ться. — **hang over,** висе́ть над; нависа́ть над. — **hang up, 1,** (place on a hanger or hook) ве́шать. **2,** (a telephone receiver) ве́шать (тру́бку).

hangar *n.* анга́р.

hanger *n.* ве́шалка.

hanger-on *n.* прихлеба́тель; прижива́льщик.

hanging *n.* **1,** (execution) пове́шение: *death by hanging,* казнь че́рез пове́шение. **2,** *usu. pl.* (something hung on a wall) драпиро́вки. — *adj.* вися́чий.

hangman *n.* пала́ч.

hangnail *n.* заусе́ница.

hangover *n.* **1,** (remnant) пережи́ток. **2,** (aftereffect of intoxication) похме́лье.

hank *n.* мото́к.

hanker *v.i.* жа́ждать. — **hankering,** *n.* жела́ние; жа́жда.

haphazard *adj.* беспоря́дочный; бессисте́мный. — **haphazardly,** *adv.* беспоря́дочно; как попа́ло.

hapless *adj.* несча́стный; злополу́чный.

happen *v.i.* **1,** (take place) случа́ться; происходи́ть. *What happened?,* что случи́лось? *Nothing happened,* ничего́ не случи́лось. *As if nothing happened,* как ни в чём не быва́ло. *As often happens,* как э́то ча́сто быва́ет. *It so happens that...,* случи́лось так, что... **2,** *fol. by* **to** (become of; befall) случа́ться с: *what happened to him?,* что случи́лось с ним? **3,** *fol. by inf.* (chance) случи́ться *(impers.)*: *I happened to notice that...,* мне случи́лось заме́тить, что... *I (just) happened to be home,* я случа́йно был (была́) до́ма. *He happens to be my friend,* он, ока́зывается, мой друг. **4,** *fol. by* **on** *or* **upon** (run into) натыка́ться на; ната́лкиваться на.

happening *n.* слу́чай; собы́тие.

happenstance *n.* слу́чай; случа́йность.

happily *adv.* **1,** (in happiness) сча́стливо: *live happily,* жить сча́стливо. **2,** (gladly) с ра́достью. **3,** (luckily) к сча́стью.

happiness *n.* сча́стье.

happy *adj.* **1,** (joyous; contented) счастли́вый. *Make happy,* ра́довать. **2,** (satisfactory, as of an outcome) благополу́чный. **3,** (well-chosen) уда́чный. — **Happy Birthday!,** поздравля́ю вас с днём рожде́ния! — **happy medium,** золота́я середи́на. — **Happy New Year!,** с Но́вым го́дом!

happy-go-lucky *adj.* беззабо́тный; беспе́чный.

hara-kiri *n.* харакири.

harass *v.t.* **1,** (harry) беспоко́ить; пресле́довать; дёргать. **2,** *mil.* беспоко́ить; изма́тывать. — **harassment,** *n.* беспоко́йство; пресле́дование.

harbinger *n.* предве́стник.

harbor *also,* **harbour** *n.* га́вань; порт. — *v.t.* **1,** (shelter) укрыва́ть; приюти́ть. **2,** (entertain in the mind) пита́ть; (за)та́ить. — **harbor pilot,** ло́цман.

hard *adj.* **1,** (not soft) твёрдый; жёсткий: *hard surface,* твёрдая пове́рхность; *hard seat,* жёсткое сиде́нье. **2,** (difficult) тру́дный: *hard problem,* тру́дная зада́ча. *It is hard to say,* тру́дно сказа́ть. **3,** (rigorous; trying) тяжёлый: *hard work/life,* тяжёлая рабо́та/жизнь. *Hard times,* тяжёлые времена́. **4,** (industrious) трудолюби́вый: *hard worker,* трудолюби́вый рабо́тник. **5,** (of or with great force) си́льный: *hard blow,* си́льный уда́р. **6,** (stern; strict) жёсткий; стро́гий. — *adv.* **1,** (with great effort) тяжело́; усиленно. *Work/breathe hard,* тяжело́ рабо́тать/дыша́ть. *Study hard,* приле́жно учи́ться; усиленно занима́ться. *Try hard,* о́чень стара́ться. *Try hard to persuade someone,* усиленно угова́ривать кого́-нибудь. **2,** (with great force) си́льно: *hit hard,* си́льно уда́рить. *It is raining hard,* идёт си́льный дождь. **3,** (with sorrow or distress) тяжело́: *take something hard,* тяжело́ переноси́ть *or* пережива́ть что́-нибудь. — **hard and fast,** жёсткий: *hard and fast rules,* жёсткие пра́вила. — **hard cash,** нали́чные де́ньги. — **hard labor,** ка́торга; каторжные рабо́ты. —**hard line,** жёсткая ли́ния. —**hard liquor,** спиртны́е напи́тки. —**hard luck,** невезе́ние. —**hard of hearing,** туго́й на́ ухо. —**hard palate,** твёрдое не́бо. —**hard up,** не при деньга́х; стеснённый в деньга́х. —**hard water,** жёсткая вода́.

hard-boiled adj. **1,** (of eggs) круто́й: *hard-boiled egg,* круто́е яйцо́; яйцо́ вкруту́ю. **2,** colloq. (unsentimental) чёрствый; твердока́менный.

hardbound adj. в твёрдой обло́жке; в перепле́те. Also, **hard-cover.**

harden v.t. **1,** (make hard) де́лать (бо́лее) твёрдым; закаля́ть. **2,** (toughen) закаля́ть; ожесточа́ть. —v.i. твердеть; затвердева́ть; (of metals) закаля́ться.

hardened adj. **1,** (having become hard) затверде́лый; закалённый. *Hardened steel,* закалённая сталь. **2,** (inveterate) закоренéлый: *hardened criminal,* закорене́лый престу́пник.

hardening n. затвердéние. —**hardening of the arteries,** артериосклеро́з.

hardheaded adj. **1,** (practical; realistic) практи́чный; тре́звый. **2,** (stubborn) упря́мый.

hardhearted adj. жестокосéрдный. —**hardheartedness,** n. жестокосéрдие.

hardiness n. выно́сливость.

hardly adv. **1,** (scarcely) едва́; éле: *we could hardly keep up with him,* мы едва́/éле поспева́ли за ним. **2,** (almost not at all) rendered by ма́ло: *hardly anyone,* ма́ло кто; *hardly ever,* ма́ло когда́; *hardly anywhere,* ма́ло где. **3,** (almost surely not) едва́ ли; вряд ли: *that is hardly possible,* едва́ ли э́то возмо́жно. *He will hardly come now,* вряд ли он уже́ придёт.

hardness n. твёрдость; жёсткость.

hardship n. лишéние: *suffer hardships,* терпéть лишéния.

hardware n. **1,** (tools and household items) скобяно́й това́р; скобяны́е изде́лия. *Hardware store,* скобяно́й магази́н. **2,** (of a computer) техни́ческое обеспéчение.

hard-working adj. трудолюби́вый.

hardy adj. **1,** (robust) кре́пкий; выно́сливый; живу́чий. **2,** (adventuresome) смéлый. **3,** (frost-resistant) морозосто́йкий.

hare n. за́яц.

harebrained adj. легкомы́сленный; безрассу́дный.

harelip n. за́ячья губа́.

harem n. гаре́м.

hark v.i. слу́шать. —interj. слу́шай! —**hark back, 1,** (return) возвраща́ться. **2,** (date back) восходи́ть.

harken v. = **hearken.**

harlequin n. арлеки́н; шут.

harlot n. проститу́тка.

harm n. вред; зло; ущéрб. *She meant no harm,* она́ не хотéла никого́ обидеть. *He wishes you no harm,* он не желáет вам зла. *I see no harm in it,* я не ви́жу в э́том ничего́ плохо́го. *It won't do any harm,* вредá от э́того не бу́дет. *It won't do any harm to...,* не повреди́т, éсли... *What harm is there in asking?,* что стра́шного в том, éсли мы спро́сим? *Do more harm than good,* принести́ бо́льше вредá, чем по́льзы. —v.t. вреди́ть; наноси́ть or причиня́ть вред (+ dat.). *No one was harmed,* никто́ не пострада́л. *Don't harm her!,* не тро́гайте её! —**out of harm's way,** от грехá подáльше.

harmful adj. врéдный.

harmless adj. безврéдный; безоби́дный.

harmonic adj. гармони́ческий. —n., music оберто́н.

harmonica n. губна́я гармо́ника.

harmonious adj. гармони́чный; согла́сный.

harmonium n. фисгармо́ния.

harmonize v.t. гармонизи́ровать. —v.i. гармони́ровать.

harmony n. **1,** music гармо́ния. **2,** (accord) гармо́ния; согла́сие. *Harmony of interests,* гармо́ния интерéсов. *Live in harmony,* жить в согла́сии.

harness n. у́пряжь; сбру́я. —v.t. **1,** (put a harness on) запряга́ть. **2,** fig. (utilize the potential of) испо́льзовать. —**harness races,** бегá.

harp n. а́рфа. —v.i. [usu. **harp on**] тверди́ть (о). —**harp on the same string,** тяну́ть всё ту же пéсню; зала́дить одно́ и то же.

harpist n. арфи́ст; арфи́стка.

harpoon n. острогá; гарпу́н. —v.t. бить острого́й/гарпу́ном; гарпу́нить.

harpsichord n. клавеси́н.

harquebus n. пища́ль.

harridan n. ста́рая каргá.

harrier n. (bird) лунь.

harrow n. боронá. —v.t. борони́ть. —**harrowing,** adj. душераздира́ющий.

harry v.t. му́чить; трави́ть; изводи́ть. *A harried look,* изму́ченный вид.

harsh adj. **1,** (grating) рéзкий; жёсткий. **2,** (severe; grim; cruel) рéзкий; суро́вый; жесто́кий. —**harshly,** adv. рéзко; жесто́ко. —**harshness,** n. рéзкость; суро́вость.

hart n. рогáч.

harum-scarum adv. как попáло; очертá го́лову.

harvest n. **1,** (crop) урожáй. *Poor harvest,* неурожáй; недоро́д. **2,** (gathering in of a crop) жáтва; сбор or убо́рка урожáя. *Harvest time,* врéмя жáтвы. —v.t. собирáть: *harvest the crops,* собирáть урожáй.

harvester n. убо́рочная маши́на; жáтвенная маши́на; жнéйка; жáтка.

hash n. **1,** (food) ру́бленое мя́со. **2,** (mishmash) меша́нина.

hashish n. гаши́ш.

hasp n. пробо́й.

hassle n., colloq. перебрáнка; препирáтельство.

hassock n. пуф.

haste n. поспéшность; торопли́вость. *In haste,* поспéшно; нáспех; второпя́х. *In my haste,* второпя́х; впопыхáх. —**haste makes waste,** поспеши́шь — людéй насмеши́шь. —**make haste,** спеши́ть; торопи́ться.

hasten v.i. спеши́ть; торопи́ться. *He hastened to add that...,* он поспеши́л добáвить, что... —v.t. торопи́ть; ускоря́ть.

hastily adv. поспéшно; нáскоро; нáспех; второпя́х.

hasty adj. поспéшный; торопли́вый.

hat n. шля́па. —adj. шля́пный: *hat shop,* шля́пный магази́н. —**at the drop of a hat,** по малéйшему по́воду; чуть что. —**keep under one's hat,** помáлкивать о. —**take off one's hat to,** снимáть шля́пу пéред; преклоня́ться пéред. —**talk through one's hat,** нести́ чушь.

hatband n. око́лыш.

hatbox n. карто́нка для шля́пы.

hatch *v.t.* **1,** (bring forth, as young) высиживать; выводить. **2,** (incubate, as an egg) насиживать. **3,** (devise, as plans) вынашивать. **4,** (mark with lines) штриховать.—*v.i.* выводиться; вылупляться. —*n.* люк: *escape hatch,* спасательный люк.

hatchet *n.* топорик.

hate *v.t.* **1,** (detest) ненавидеть: *hate onions/liars/war,* ненавидеть лук/лгунов/войну. **2,** (dislike doing) очень не любить *or* хотеть. *Hate writing letters,* очень не любить (*or* ненавидеть) писать письма. *I hate to interrupt, but...,* очень не хочу перебить, но... *I hate to spend money for that,* мне жаль тратить деньги на это. —*n.* ненависть.

hated *adj.* ненавистный.

hateful *adj.* ненавистный.

hatpin *n.* булавка для шляпы; шляпная булавка.

hatrack *n.* вешалка для шляп.

hatred *n.* ненависть.

hatter *n.* шляпный мастер; шляпник; шапочник.

haughty *adj.* надменный; высокомерный. —**haughtiness,** *n.* надменность; высокомерие.

haul *v.t.* **1,** (drag) тянуть; тащить. **2,** (transport) перевозить. **3,** *fol. by* **in** (pull in, as a fish) вытаскивать. **4,** *fol. by* **down** (pull down) спускать. —*n.* **1,** (distance covered) рейс. **2,** (of fish) улов. **3,** (of loot) добыча. —**haul off,** *colloq.* размахнуться: *haul off and strike,* размахнуться и ударить. —**over the long haul,** в долгосрочном плане.

haulage *n.* перевозка.

haunch *n.* бедро; ляжка.

haunt *v.t.* **1,** (dwell in, as of a ghost) обитать. *Haunted house,* заколдованный дом. **2,** (obsess, as of a thought) преследовать. *Haunting melody,* навязчивый мотив. —*n.* любимое место.

have *v.t.* **1,** (possess) иметь: *have the right/opportunity/misfortune,* иметь право/возможность/несчастье. ♦ *Most commonly rendered, however, by* у: *do you have a match?,* у вас есть спичка? *I have no time,* у меня нет времени. **2,** (receive) получать: *I've had no news from him,* я не получал о нём известий. **3,** (do; perform; carry on) *rendered by various verbs: have a look,* посмотреть; *have a talk with,* поговорить с; *have an argument,* поспорить. **4,** (cause to do or be done): *have him come in,* попросите его войти. *Have one's picture taken,* сниматься. **5,** (cause to be treated) отдавать: *have fixed,* отдавать в ремонт; *have cleaned,* отдавать в чистку; *have washed,* отдавать в стирку. **6,** (experience) *rendered by* у: *she has a cold,* у неё насморк; *he had a heart attack,* у него был сердечный припадок. *Have a dream,* видеть сон. *Have a good time,* хорошо проводить время. **7,** (harbor) питать: *have an aversion to,* питать отвращение к. **8,** (feel and show): *have mercy on,* щадить; *have pity on,* сжалиться над. **9,** (eat; drink): *have tea,* пить чай. *Have supper,* ужинать. *What will you have?,* что вы будете пить? **10,** (bear; beget) родить: *she had a son,* у неё родился сын. **11,** (permit; tolerate) потерпеть: *I won't have such conduct,* я не потерплю такого поведения. **12,** (declare; state) гласить: *legend has it that...,* легенда гласит, что... *Rumor has it,* ходят слухи, что... —*v.aux.* **1,** *used to form perfect tenses: I have already eaten,* я уже поел. **2,** *in contrary-to-fact sentences* если бы: *had I only known!,* если бы я только знал! ♦ *Also rendered by the imperative: had the blast occur-*

red ten minutes earlier, произойди взрыв на десять минут раньше. **3,** (*fol. by inf.*) *expressing obligation* надо; нужно; должен: *I have to go,* мне надо/нужно идти; я должен (должна) идти. —**have it in for,** иметь зуб на. —**have it out with,** объясняться с. —**have on,** быть в (+ *prepl.*); быть одетым в (+ *acc.*): *have a raincoat on,* быть в плаще. *What else did she have on?,* что ещё на ней было надето? —**have to do with, 1,** (have a connection with) иметь отношение к: *what has this to do with me?,* какое это имеет отношение ко мне?; при чём я тут? *Money has nothing to do with it,* деньги тут ни при чём. **2,** (associate with) иметь дело с: *he refused to have anything to do with me,* он отказался иметь дело со мной.

haven *n.* **1,** (harbor) гавань. **2,** (shelter) убежище; приют.

haversack *n.* вещевой мешок; ранец.

havoc *n.* опустошение. —**play havoc with,** приводить в расстройство.

hawk *n.* ястреб. —*v.t. & i.* (peddle) торговать вразнос. —*v.i.* (clear one's throat) отхаркиваться. —**hawker,** *n.* разносчик.

hawk-eyed *adj.* зоркий.

hawser *n.* перлинь.

hawthorn *n.* боярышник.

hay *n.* сено. —*adj.* сенной. —**hit the hay,** *colloq.* отправиться на боковую. —**make hay while the sun shines,** куй железо, пока горячо.

haycock *n.* копна.

hay fever сенная лихорадка.

hayfield *n.* сенокос.

hayloft *n.* сеновал.

haystack *n.* стог сена; скирд; скирда.

hazard *n.* опасность; риск. —*v.t.* **1,** (risk) рисковать. **2,** (venture) осмеливаться: *hazard a guess,* осмелиться догадаться. —**hazardous,** *adj.* опасный; рискованный.

haze *n.* дымка; мгла; марево.

hazel *n.* **1,** (tree) орешник; лещина. **2,** (nut) лесной орех. —*adj.* светло-коричневый.

hazel grouse рябчик. *Also,* **hazel hen.**

hazelnut *n.* лесной орех.

hazy *adj.* **1,** (misty) туманный; мглистый. **2,** (vague) смутный; туманный.

he *pers.pron.* он: *he is ill,* он болен; *he left,* он ушёл. *He is not here,* его нет. *He who,* тот, кто... *See also* **him.**

head *n.* **1,** (part of the body) голова. **2,** (top part; head end) глава: *at the head of the table,* во главе стола. **3,** (of a pin, match, etc.) головка; (of a nail) шляпка. **4,** (of cabbage) кочан. **5,** (of a bed) изголовье. **6,** (unit, as of cattle) голова. **7,** (chief) глава: *head of the family,* глава семьи. **8,** (mind; brain) голова; ум: *clear head,* ясная голова; ясный ум. *Do figures in one's head,* считать в уме. **9,** *Ten dollars a/per head,* десять долларов с головы *or* с носа. —*adj.* **1,** (of or for the head) головной. **2,** (chief) главный; старший: *head physician,* главный/старший врач. —*v.t.* **1,** (set the course of) направлять. **2,** (be the head of) возглавлять. **3,** *fol. by* **off** (intercept; avert) пресекать. —*v.i.* (move in a specified direction) направляться. *Head north,* направляться (*or* брать курс) на север. —**come into one's head,** взбрести в голову. —**come to a head,** назреть.

—**from head to toe**, с головы до ног. —**get it into one's head**, вбивать/забивать/забирать себе в голову. —**get it through someone's head**, вбивать в голову (+ *dat.*). —**go to one's head, 1,** (intoxicate) ударять в голову (+ *dat.*). **2,** (make vain) вскружить голову (+ *dat.*). —**head and shoulders above**, на голову выше (+ *gen.*). —**head over heels, 1,** (tumbling) кубарем; кувырком; вверх тормашками. **2,** (completely) по уши (влюблён, в долгах, *etc.*). —**heads or tails?**, орёл или решка? —**lose one's head**, потерять голову. —**make head or tail of**, разбираться в. —**over one's head, 1,** (too difficult for) выше (чьего-нибудь) понимания. **2,** (bypassing) через (чью-нибудь) голову. —**take it into one's head**, вздумать (+ *inf.*). —**talk someone's head off**, заговаривать. —**turn one's head**, вскружить голову (+ *dat.*). —**two heads are better than one**, ум хорошо, а два лучше. —**use one's head**, шевелить мозгами.

headache *n.* головная боль. *I have a headache*, у меня болит голова.

head cold насморк.

headdress *n.* головной убор.

headfirst *adv.* головой вперёд.

heading *n.* рубрика.

headland *n.* мыс.

headless *adj.* безголовый.

headlight *n.* фара.

headline *n.* заголовок.

headlong *adv.* **1,** (headfirst) головой вперёд. **2,** (at breakneck speed) опрометью; стремглав. **3,** (rashly) очертя голову; напропалую. —*adj.* стремительный; безоглядный.

headmaster *n.* директор (школы).

head-on *adv.* в лоб; носом. —*adj.* прямой: *head-on collision*, прямое столкновение.

headphone *n.* наушник.

headquarters *n.pl.* **1,** (place of command) штаб. **2,** (main building) штаб-квартира.

headset *n.* головной телефон.

head start фора.

headstone *n.* **1,** (tombstone) надгробный камень. **2,** *obs.* (cornerstone) краеугольный камень.

headstrong *adj.* упрямый; своевольный.

headwaiter *n.* метрдотель.

headwaters *n.pl.* истоки; верховье.

headway *n.* **1,** (motion forward) продвижение. **2,** (progress) прогресс. *Make headway*, сдвигаться с места.

head wind встречный ветер.

heady *adj.* опьяняющий.

heal *v.t.* залечивать. —*v.i.* заживать. —**healer**, *n.* исцелитель.

health *n.* здоровье. *Public health*, здравоохранение. *He is in good health*, он здоров; он обладает хорошим здоровьем. *She is in poor health*, у неё слабое здоровье. —**to your health!**, за ваше здоровье!

healthful *adj.* здоровый; целебный.

healthy *adj.* здоровый.

heap *n.* куча; груда. —*v.t.* **1,** *often fol. by* **up** (pile up) нагромождать. **2,** (shower) осыпать: *heap ridicule on*, осыпать (кого-нибудь) насмешками.

hear *v.t.* **1,** (perceive; learn) слышать: *hear the music/news*, слышать музыку/новость. *I can't hear you*, не слышу вас. *I can't hear a thing*, мне ничего не слыш-

но. *You can hear the sound of the waves*, слышен шум волн. *I heard someone approaching from behind*, я слышал, как кто-то подходил сзади. **2,** *law* слушать: *hear a case*, слушать дело. —*v.i.* **1,** (be able to perceive sound) слышать: *he can't hear*, он не слышит. **2,** *fol. by* **of** *or* **about** (learn of) слышать (о). *It's the first I've heard of it*, первый раз слышу. **3,** *fol. by* **from** (get mail or a call from) получить известие от. *Let us hear from you*, дайте нам знать о вас. **4,** *fol. by* **of** (consider; consent) слышать (о): *I won't hear of it*, я об этом и слышать не хочу. —**hear out**, выслушивать.

hearing *n.* **1,** (sense) слух. *Hard of hearing*, тугой на ухо. *Lose one's hearing*, (о)глохнуть. **2,** *law* слушание. **3,** (earshot) слышимость: *within hearing*, в пределах слышимости. —**hearing aid**, слуховой аппарат.

hearken *also*, **harken** *v.i.* слушать. *Hearken to*, внимать (+ *dat.*).

hearsay *n.* слухи; молва. *Through hearsay*, по слухам; понаслышке.

hearse *n.* похоронные дроги; погребальная колесница; катафалк.

heart *n.* **1,** (organ of the body) сердце. **2,** (center) центр; сердце. *In the heart of Europe*, в самом центре (*or* в сердце) Европы. **3,** (essence; crux) суть; сущность: *get to the heart of the matter*, добраться до сути дела. **4,** *pl.*, *cards* черви. —*adj.* сердечный: *heart muscle*, сердечная мышца. —**at heart**, в глубине души. —**by heart**, наизусть. —**lose heart**, падать духом; унывать. —**not have the heart to**, не хватать духу (*with* у): *I haven't the heart to...*, у меня не хватает духу (+ *inf.*). —**take heart**, ободряться; воспрянуть духом. —**take to heart**, принимать близко к сердцу. —**with a heavy heart**, с тяжёлым сердцем; с болью на душе. —**with all one's heart**, всем сердцем; всей душой. —**with one's heart in one's mouth**, с замиранием сердца.

heartache *n.* душевная боль.

heart attack сердечный припадок; инфаркт.

heartbeat *n.* биение сердца; сердцебиение.

heartbreaking *adj.* (душе)раздирающий.

heartbroken *adj.* убитый горем.

heartburn *n.* изжога.

heart disease заболевание сердца.

hearten *v.t.* ободрять; подбодрять.

heart failure паралич сердца.

heartfelt *adj.* сердечный; душевный; задушевный.

hearth *n.* очаг.

heartily *adv.* **1,** (warmly; cordially) сердечно. **2,** (with a hearty appetite) с аппетитом; плотно. **3,** (completely) вполне: *I heartily agree/approve*, я вполне согласен/одобряю.

heartless *adj.* бессердечный; бездушный. —**heartlessness**, *n.* бессердечие; бессердечность; бездушие.

heart-rending *adj.* (душе)раздирающий.

heart-shaped *adj.* сердцевидный.

heartsick *adj.* (очень) огорчён; (очень) расстроен.

heart-to-heart *adj.* интимный; сердечный. *Heart-to-heart talk*, разговор по душам.

heartwarming *adj.* радостный.

hearty *adj.* **1,** (cordial, as of a welcome) сердечный; радушный. **2,** (solid, as of a meal) плотный; сытный. **3,** (big, as of one's appetite) хороший; отличный.

heat *n.* **1,** (hotness) жара́. **2,** *physics* теплота́; тепло́. **3,** (heating system) отопле́ние: *steam heat,* парово́е отопле́ние. **4,** (excitement; strong feelings) жар; пыл. *In the heat of battle,* в пылу́ сраже́ния. **5,** (sexual excitement) те́чка: *be in heat,* быть в те́чке. **6,** *sports* забе́г; *swimming* заплы́в. —*v.t.* **1,** (provide with heat) топи́ть. **2,** (make warm) нагрева́ть; согрева́ть. —*v.i.* [*usu.* **heat up**] нагрева́ться; согрева́ться.

heated *adj.* **1,** (warmed) нагре́тый. **2,** (vehement, as of an argument) горя́чий. —**heatedly,** *adv.* горячо́.

heater *n.* нагрева́тельный прибо́р; нагрева́тель. *Electric heater,* электри́ческий ками́н.

heath *n.* **1,** (uncultivated land) пу́стошь. **2,** (shrub) э́рика.

heathen *n.* язы́чник. —*adj.* язы́ческий.

heather *n.* ве́реск.

heating *n.* **1,** (providing with heat) отопле́ние. **2,** (making warm) нагрева́ние. —*adj.* отопи́тельный; нагрева́тельный. —**heating oil,** отопи́тельная нефть. —**heating pad,** электри́ческая гре́лка.

heat lightning зарни́ца.

heat rash потни́ца.

heat-resistant *adj.* теплосто́йкий.

heat shield теплово́й экра́н.

heatstroke *n.* теплово́й уда́р.

heat wave полоса́ си́льной жары́.

heave *v.t.* **1,** (hurl) броса́ть; швыря́ть. **2,** *Heave a sigh,* испусти́ть вздох. —*v.i.* **1,** (rise and fall rhythmically) вздыма́ться. **2,** *colloq.* (retch) рвать.—*n.* бросо́к. —**heave ho!,** раз, два, дру́жно!

heaven *n.* не́бо. —**be in seventh heaven,** быть на седьмо́м не́бе. —**for heaven's sake!,** ра́ди бо́га! —**heaven forbid!,** не дай бог!; бо́же упаси́! —**heavens!,** бо́же мой! —**thank heaven!,** сла́ва бо́гу! —**move heaven and earth,** пусти́ть в ход все сре́дства.

heavenly *adj.* **1,** (of the heavens) небе́сный: *heavenly body,* небе́сное те́ло. **2,** (divine; sublime) боже́ственный.

heaves *n.pl.* запа́л.

heavily *adv.* тяжело́. *Heavily armed,* си́льно вооружённый. *Heavily in debt,* в большо́м долгу́; круго́м в долгу́.

heaviness *n.* тя́жесть.

heavy *adj.* **1,** (weighty) тяжёлый. **2,** (difficult; arduous) тяжёлый: *heavy work,* тяжёлая рабо́та; *heavy breathing,* тяжёлое дыха́ние. **3,** (intense) си́льный: *heavy rain,* си́льный дождь; *a heavy cold,* си́льный на́сморк. *Under heavy guard,* под си́льной охра́ной. *Heavy traffic,* интенси́вное движе́ние. *Heavy fighting,* тяжёлые *or* упо́рные бои́. *He is a heavy drinker,* он си́льно пьёт. **4,** (severe, as of losses) тяжёлый; большо́й; кру́пный; серьёзный. *Pay a heavy price for,* заплати́ть дорого́й цено́й за. **5,** (large, as of industry, artillery, etc.) тяжёлый. **6,** (ponderous, as of writing) тяжёлый; тяжелове́сный. **7,** (hard to digest) тяжёлый. **8,** (choppy, as of the sea) бу́рный. **9,** (gloomy, as of the sky) мра́чный; хму́рый. —*adv.* тяжело́. —**hang heavy,** ме́дленно тяну́ться.

heavy-handed *adj.* неуклю́жий; нело́вкий.

heavyset *adj.* призе́мистый; корена́стый.

heavy water тяжёлая вода́.

heavyweight *n.* тяжелове́с. —*adj.* тяжёлого ве́са.

Hebrew *adj.* (дре́вне)евре́йский. —*n.* **1,** (person) евре́й. **2,** (ancient language) древнееврейский

язы́к. **3,** (modern language) иври́т.

heckle *v.t.* прерыва́ть кри́ками.

hectare *n.* гекта́р.

hectic *adj.* сумато́шный; бу́рный; горя́чий.

hedge *n.* жива́я и́згородь. —*v.t.* [*usu.* **hedge in**] обноси́ть и́згородью. —*v.i.* (equivocate) виля́ть.

hedgehog *n.* ёж.

hedonism *n.* гедони́зм. —**hedonist,** *n.* гедони́ст. —**hedonistic,** *adj.* гедонисти́ческий.

heed *v.t.* слу́шать; прислу́шиваться к. *Heed someone's advice,* прислу́шиваться к чьему́-нибудь сове́ту. *Heed a warning,* обрати́ть внима́ние на предупрежде́ние. —*n.* внима́ние: *pay no need to,* не обраща́ть (никако́го) внима́ния на. —**heedful,** *adj.* обраща́ющий внима́ние. —**heedless,** *adj.* не обраща́ющий внима́ния.

heel *n.* **1,** (part of the foot) пя́тка; пята́. **2,** (part of a shoe) каблу́к. **3,** (part of a stocking) пя́тка. —**head over heels,** *see* **head.** —**on the heels of,** вслед за. —**take to one's heels,** показа́ть пя́тки; улепётывать; дать тя́гу; пусти́ться наутёк; смота́ть у́дочки. —**under the heel of,** под пято́й (+ *gen.*).

hefty *adj.* **1,** (burly) ро́слый; дю́жий. **2,** (substantial) поря́дочный; изря́дный.

hegemony *n.* гегемо́ния.

heifer *n.* тёлка.

height *n.* **1,** (size; altitude) высота́. **2,** (of a person) рост. **3,** *often pl.* (high point) высо́ты. **4,** *fol. by* **of** (greatest degree) верх: *the height of folly,* верх глу́пости. *At the height of its glory,* на верши́не его́ сла́вы. **5,** (time of greatest activity) разга́р: *at the height of the season,* в разга́ре сезо́на. *Be at its height,* быть в разга́ре.

heighten *v.t.* **1,** (raise) повыша́ть. **2,** (intensify) повыша́ть; уси́ливать. —*v.i.* повыша́ться; уси́ливаться.

heinous *adj.* гну́сный. —**heinousness,** *n.* гну́сность.

heir *n.* насле́дник. *Heir to the throne,* насле́дник престо́ла. —**heiress,** *n.* насле́дница.

heirloom *n.* фами́льное сокро́вище.

helicopter *n.* вертолёт.

heliograph *n.* гелио́граф.

heliotrope *n.* гелиотро́п.

heliport *n.* площа́дка для вертолётов.

helium *n.* ге́лий.

hell *n.* ад. —*interj.* чёрт возьми́! —**a hell of a...,** а́дский; чёртовский. *A hell of a long way,* чёртовски далеко́. —**as hell,** чёртовски: *mad as hell,* чёрт се́рдит. —**catch hell,** *slang* получи́ть по ша́пке. —**come hell or high water,** во что бы то ни ста́ло. —**for the hell of it,** про́сто так. —**give someone hell,** *colloq.* распека́ть. —**go through hell,** переноси́ть му́ки а́да. —**go to hell!,** иди́те к чёрту! —**like hell, 1,** (with all one's might) как чёрт: *work like hell,* рабо́тать как чёрт. **2,** *as an exclamation* чёрта с два!; как бы не так! —**raise hell,** *colloq.* поднима́ть шум. —**to hell with,** а ну (+ *gen.*): *to hell with him!,* а ну его́! *To hell with it!,* к чёрту! —**what the hell...?,** како́го чёрта: *what the hell is he doing there?,* како́го чёрта он там де́лает?

hellebore *n.* чемери́ца.

Hellenic *adj.* э́ллинский.

hellish *adj.* а́дский.

hello *interj.* здра́вствуйте! ♦*When answering the telephone* алло́!; слу́шаю!

helm *n.* руль; штурва́л. *Be at the helm,* стоя́ть у руля́.

helmet *n.* шлем; ка́ска.

helmsman *n.* рулево́й; штурва́льный.

help *v.t.* **1,** (aid; assist) помога́ть. *Help someone up,* помо́чь кому́-нибудь встать. *Help someone on with his coat,* подава́ть кому́-нибудь пальто́. **2,** (assist in accomplishing) спосо́бствовать: *help to achieve our goal,* спосо́бствовать достиже́нию на́шей це́ли. **3,** (wait on) обслу́живать. **4,** (serve) класть: *help oneself to,* класть себе́ на таре́лку (+ *gen.*). *May I help you to some meat?,* мо́жно вам положи́ть мя́са? *Help yourself!,* угоща́йтесь, пожа́луйста! **5,** (prevent; change) *I can't help it,* ничего́ не поде́лаешь. *It can't be helped,* ничего́ не поде́лаешь. —*v.i.* помога́ть. —*n.* **1,** (aid; assistance) по́мощь. *You were a big help,* вы нам о́чень помогли́. **2,** (workers) рабо́чие ру́ки. **3,** (household help) слу́ги. —*interj.* на по́мощь! —**not help** (**doing something**), не мочь не (+ *inf.*): *I could not help noticing that...,* я не мог не заме́тить, что... *I couldn't help laughing,* я не мог удержа́ться от сме́ха. *I can't help thinking that...,* я не могу́ освободи́ться от мы́сли, что... —**so help me God,** да помо́жет мне бог.

helper *n.* помо́щник.

helpful *adj.* **1,** (useful) поле́зный. **2,** (accommodating) услу́жливый.

helping *n.* по́рция. —*adj., in* **lend a helping hand,** подава́ть ру́ку по́мощи.

helpless *adj.* беспо́мощный; бесси́льный. —**helplessness,** *n.* беспо́мощность; бесси́лие.

helter-skelter *adv.* как попа́ло; врассыпну́ю.

hem *n.* рубе́ц. —*v.t.* **1,** (sew a hem in) подруба́ть. **2,** *fol. by* in (encircle) сти́скивать. —*v.i., in* **hem and haw,** тяну́ть и мя́млить; ни шьёт ни по́рет.

he-man *n., colloq.* настоя́щий мужчи́на.

hematite *also,* **haematite** *n.* кра́сный железня́к; желе́зный блеск.

hemisphere *n.* полуша́рие.

hemlock *n.* **1,** (poisonous plant) болиголо́в. *Water hemlock,* цику́та. **2,** (evergreen tree) тсу́га.

hemoglobin *also,* **haemoglobin** *n.* гемоглоби́н.

hemophilia *also,* **haemophilia** *n.* гемофили́я; кровоточи́вость.

hemorrhage *also,* **haemorrhage** *n.* кровоизлия́ние. —*v.i.* кровоточи́ть.

hemorrhoid *also,* **haemorrhoid** *n., usu. pl.* гемо́ррой.

hemp *n.* **1,** (plant) конопля́. **2,** (fiber) пенька́. —*adj.* конопля́ный; пенько́вый.

hemstitch *n.* ажу́рная стро́чка.

hen *n.* ку́рица.

henbane *n.* белена́.

hence *adv.* **1,** (therefore) сле́довательно; отсю́да. **2,** (from now) че́рез: *a week hence,* че́рез неде́лю.

henceforth *adv.* впредь; отны́не; с э́того вре́мени. *Also,* **henceforward.**

henchman *n.* приспе́шник.

henhouse *n.* куря́тник.

henna *n.* хна.

henpecked *adj.* под башмако́м (у жены́).

hepatic *adj.* печёночный.

hepatica *n.* печёночница; переле́ска.

hepatitis *n.* воспале́ние пе́чени; гепати́т.

heptagon *n.* семиуго́льник. —**heptagonal,** *adj.* семиуго́льный.

her *pers.pron.* **1,** *used as dir. obj. of a verb* её: *ask her,* спроси́ её. **2,** *used as indir. obj. of a verb* ей: *give her the keys,* дай ей ключи́. **3,** *used as obj. of a prep.* неё; ней: *from her,* от неё; *with her,* с ней. —*poss.adj.* её: *her brother,* её брат. ♦*When the possessor is the subject of the sentence* свой: *she took her purse with her,* она́ взяла́ с собо́й свою́ су́мку.

herald *n.* **1,** *hist.* геро́льд. **2,** (messenger) ве́стник. —*v.t.* возвеща́ть. —**heraldic,** *adj.* геральди́ческий. —**heraldry,** *n.* гера́льдика.

herb *n.* трава́. —**herbaceous,** *adj.* травяно́й; травяни́стый. —**herbarium,** *n.* герба́рий. —**herbicide,** *n.* гербици́д. —**herbivorous,** *adj.* травоя́дный.

Hercules *n.* геркуле́с.

herd *n.* ста́до: *herd of elephants,* ста́до слоно́в. —*v.t.* **1,** (tend) пасти́. **2,** (drive as if in a herd) гнать. *Herd into a pen,* загоня́ть в заго́н. *Herd together,* сгоня́ть. —**herd instinct,** ста́дный инсти́нкт.

herdsman *n.* гуртовщи́к.

here *adv.* **1,** (in this place) здесь; тут. *From here,* отсю́да. **2,** (to this place) сюда́: *come here!,* иди́ сюда́! **3,** *used in presenting something* вот: *here are your glasses,* вот ва́ши очки́. —**here and now,** сейча́с же. —**here and there,** ко́е-где; места́ми; там и тут. —**here's to...,** за (+ *acc.*): *here's to our hosts!,* за на́ших хозя́ев!

hereabout *also,* **hereabouts** *adv.* поблизости.

hereafter *adv.* впредь; отны́не; в дальне́йшем.

hereby *adv.* сим; настоя́щим.

hereditary *adj.* насле́дственный.

heredity *n.* насле́дственность.

herein *adv.* в э́том; здесь.

hereinafter *adv.* в дальне́йшем: *hereinafter referred to as...,* в дальне́йшем имену́емый...

heresy *n.* е́ресь.

heretic *n.* ерети́к. —**heretical,** *adj.* ерети́ческий.

hereto *adv.* при сём: *attached hereto,* при сём прилага́ется.

heretofore *adv.* до э́того; до сих пор; до сего́ вре́мени.

herewith *adv.* при сём: *enclosed herewith,* при сём прилага́ется.

heritage *n.* насле́дие.

hermaphrodite *n.* гермафроди́т.

hermetic *adj.* гермети́ческий. —**hermetically,** *adv.* гермети́чески.

hermit *n.* отше́льник; затво́рник; пусты́нник.

hernia *n.* гры́жа. —**hernial,** *adj.* грыжево́й.

hero *n.* геро́й. *He received a hero's welcome,* его́ приве́тствовали как геро́я.

heroic *adj.* герои́ческий; геро́йский. —**heroically,** *adv.* герои́чески; геро́йски.

heroin *n.* герои́н.

heroine *n.* герои́ня.

heroism *n.* герои́зм; геро́йство.

heron *n.* ца́пля.

herpes *n.* лиша́й.

herring *n.* сельдь; селёдка.

herringbone *n.* ёлочка: *in herringbone style,* ёлочкой; в ёлочку.

hers *poss.pron.* её: *this umbrella is hers,* э́тот зо́нтик её. *An uncle of hers,* оди́н её дя́дя. *My dress is red, hers is blue,* моё пла́тье кра́сное, её – си́нее.

herself *pers.pron.* **1,** *used for emphasis* (она́) сама́: *she did it herself,* она́ сама́ э́то сде́лала. **2,** *used* *reflexively* себя: *she bought it for herself,* она купила это для себя. *She hurt herself,* она ушиблась. —**by herself,** одна. —**she is not herself,** она сама не своя.

hesitancy *n.* колебание.

hesitant *adj.* колеблющийся. *She is hesitant to ask,* она стесняется попросить.

hesitate *v.i.* 1, (waver) колебаться. 2, (be reluctant) стесняться.

hesitation *n.* колебание. *Without (a moment's) hesitation,* без колебаний; не раздумывая; недолго думая.

heterodox *adj.* не ортодоксальный; еретический.

heterogeneous *adj.* разнородный. —**heterogeneity,** *n.* разнородность.

hew *v.t.* 1, (chop) рубить; тесать. 2, (carve) высекать; вытёсывать.

hex *n.* дурной глаз. —*v.t.* сглазить.

hexagon *n.* шестиугольник. —**hexagonal,** *adj.* шестиугольный.

hey *interj.* эй!; гей!

heyday *n.* зенит; расцвет.

hi *interj.* привет!

hiatus *n.* 1, (gap) пробел. 2, (break) перерыв. 3, *ling.* зияние.

hibernate *v.i.* залегать в зимнюю спячку. —**hibernation,** *n.* зимняя спячка.

hibiscus *n.* гибискус.

hiccup *also,* **hiccough** *v.i.* икать. —**hiccups,** *n.pl.* икота.

hick *n.* провинциал; деревенщина. —*adj., colloq.* провинциальный.

hickory *n.* гикори.

hidden *adj.* скрытый; тайный.

hide *v.t.* прятать; скрывать. *Hide something in the drawer,* прятать что-нибудь в ящик(е) стола. —*v.i.* прятаться; скрываться: *hide in the basement/under the bed/behind a tree/,* прятаться/скрываться в подвал(е)/под кроватью(ю)/за дерево(м)/. —*n.* шкура: *cowhide,* коровья шкура.

hide-and-seek *n.* прятки.

hideaway *n.* тайник.

hidebound *adj.* ограниченный; узколобый.

hideous *adj.* отвратительный; уродливый. —**hideousness,** *n.* уродство; безобразие.

hideout *n.* тайник.

hiding *n.* скрытие. *In hiding,* в бегах. *Go into hiding,* скрываться. —**hiding place,** тайник.

hierarchy *n.* иерархия. —**hierarchical,** *adj.* иерархический.

hieroglyph *also,* **hieroglyphic** *n.* иероглиф. —**hieroglyphic,** *adj.* иероглифический.

high *adj.* 1, (lofty) высокий: *a high mountain,* высокая гора. *On a high level,* на высоком уровне. 2, (having a specified height): *that building is 100 meters high,* это здание в сто метров высотой. 3, (above average) высокий: *high temperature,* высокая температура; *high quality,* высокое качество. *High prices,* высокие *or* дорогие цены. *High speed,* большая скорость. *High hopes,* радужные надежды. *A high honor,* высокая честь. *Have a high opinion of,* быть высокого мнения о. *Play for high stakes,* играть по большой. 4, (high-pitched) высокий: *high notes,* высокие ноты. 5, (of high rank) высокопоставленный; старший. 6, (gay) весёлый:

high spirits, весёлое настроение. 7, *colloq.* (tipsy) под хмельком. 8, *High winds,* сильный ветер. 9, *The high seas,* открытое море. 10, *High crimes,* государственные преступления. —*adv.* высоко: *aim high,* метить высоко. —*n.* высшая точка. *Prices reached a new high,* цены повысились до нового предела. —**high and dry,** на мели. *Leave high and dry,* оставить с носом. —**high and mighty,** высокомерный. —**it is high time,** давно уже пора. —**look high and low,** искать всюду и везде. —**on high,** в высоте; в вышине. *From on high,* с высоты. *See also* **higher.**

highbrow *n.* интеллигент.

highchair *n.* высокий детский стульчик.

high-class *adj.* фешенебельный.

high command высшее *or* главное командование.

higher *adj., comp. of* **high.** —**higher education,** высшее образование. —**higher mathematics,** высшая математика.

high-flown *adj.* высокопарный; напыщенный.

high-handed *adj.* самовольный; властный. —**high-handedness,** *n.* своеволие; самоволие; самодурство.

high-heeled *adj.* на высоких каблуках.

high jump прыжок в высоту.

highland *n.* нагорье. —**highlander,** *n.* горец.

highlight *n.* 1, *art; photog.* световой эффект. 2, *fig.* (high point; feature) гвоздь. —*v.t.* обрисовывать; обозначать.

highly *adv.* 1, (to a high degree) высоко. *Highly developed,* высокоразвитый. *Highly seasoned,* остро приправленный. 2, (extremely) весьма: *highly probable/successful,* весьма вероятно/успешный. 3, (with admiration) высоко: *value highly,* высоко ценить. *Think highly of,* быть высокого мнения о. 4, (with praise) лестно: *speak highly of,* лестно отозваться о.

high-minded *adj.* идейный. —**high-mindedness,** *n.* идейность.

Highness *n.* высочество: *Your Highness,* ваше высочество.

high-paid *adj.* высокооплачиваемый.

high-pitched *adj.* высокий.

high-powered *adj.* (of a weapon) крупного калибра; (of a telescope or microscope) сильный.

high-priced *adj.* дорогостоящий.

high priest первосвященник.

high-ranking *adj.* высокопоставленный.

high-rise *adj.* многоэтажный; высотный.

high school средняя школа.

high sign условленный знак.

high society высшее общество; высший свет.

high-sounding *adj.* громкий; высокопарный.

high-speed *adj.* быстроходный; скоростной.

high-strung *adj.* нервный; нервозный.

high-tension *adj.* высокого напряжения.

high tide высшая точка прилива.

high treason государственная измена.

highway *n.* шоссе; магистраль.

highwayman *n.* разбойник.

hijack *v.t.* угонять; похищать (самолёт). —**highjacker,** *n.* похититель (самолёта). —**hijacking,** *n.* угон (самолёта); похищение (самолёта); нападение (на самолёт).

hike *v.i.* ходи́ть пешко́м. —*v.t., colloq.* (raise) повыша́ть. —*n.* **1,** (long walk) похо́д. **2,** (increase) повыше́ние: *price/wage hike,* повыше́ние цен/зарпла́ты.

hilarious *adj.* **1,** (gay) весёлый. **2,** (screamingly funny) умори́тельный. —**hilarity,** *n.* весе́лье.

hill *n.* холм.

hillock *n.* хо́лмик; го́рка; буго́р.

hillside *n.* склон горы́; склон холма́; косого́р.

hilltop *n.* верши́на холма́.

hilly *adj.* холми́стый.

hilt *n.* рукоя́тка; эфе́с. —**to the hilt,** по́лностью; до конца́.

him *pers.pron.* **1,** *used as dir. obj. of a verb* его́: *ask him,* спроси́те его́. **2,** *used as indir. obj. of a verb* ему́: *give him a dollar,* дай ему́ до́ллар. **3,** *used as obj. of a prep.* него́; нему́; нём; ним.

himself *pers.pron.* **1,** *used for emphasis* (он) сам: *he did it himself,* он сам э́то сде́лал. **2,** *used reflexively* себя́: *he bought himself a coat,* он купи́л себе́ пальто́. *He hurt himself,* он уши́бся. —**by himself,** оди́н. —**he is not himself,** он сам не свой.

hind *adj.* за́дний.

hinder *v.t.* меша́ть; препя́тствовать.

Hindi *n.* хи́нди.

hindrance *n.* препя́тствие; поме́ха.

hindsight *n.* ретроспе́кция.

Hindu *n.* инду́с. —*adj.* инду́сский. —**Hinduism,** *n.* индуи́зм.

hinge *n.* **1,** (joint) пе́тля; шарни́р. **2,** (for a postage stamp) накле́йка. —*v.i.* [*usu.* **hinge on**] (depend on) зави́сеть (от).

hinny *n.* лоша́к.

hint *n.* намёк. —*v.t.* намека́ть. —*v.i.* [*usu.* **hint at**] намека́ть (на).

hinterland *n.* глушь; захолу́стье.

hip *n.* бедро́. —**shoot from the hip,** *colloq.* руби́ть сплеча́.

hipbone *n.* та́зовая кость.

hippopotamus *n.* бегемо́т; гиппопота́м.

hire *v.t.* **1,** (employ) нанима́ть. **2,** (rent) брать напрока́т. —*n.* наём. *Be for hire,* сдава́ться напрока́т.

hired *adj.* наёмный. *Hired hand,* наёмный рабо́чий.

hireling *n.* наёмник; найми́т.

his *poss.adj. & pron.* его́: *his aunt,* его́ тётя. *An aunt of his,* одна́ его́ тётя. ♦*When the possessor is the subject of the sentence* свой: *he sold his house,* он про́дал свой дом.

hiss *v.i.* **1,** (give off a hissing sound) шипе́ть. **2,** (whistle disapproval) свисте́ть; ши́кать. —*v.t.* освисты́вать (+ *acc.*); ши́кать (+ *dat.*). —*n.* = **hissing.**

hissing *n.* **1,** (sound of escaping air) шипе́ние. **2,** (sound of disapproval) свист. —*adj.* шипя́щий.

histology *n.* гистоло́гия.

historian *n.* исто́рик.

historic *adj.* истори́ческий.

historical *adj.* истори́ческий. —**historically,** *adv.* истори́чески.

historiography *n.* историогра́фия. —**historiographer,** *n.* историо́граф.

history *n.* исто́рия. *History lesson,* уро́к исто́рии. *History teacher,* учи́тель исто́рии.

histrionic *adj.* театра́льный. —**histrionics,** *n.pl.* театра́льность.

hit *v.t.* **1,** (deal a blow to) ударя́ть. **2,** (strike against) ударя́ться о *or* в. *The car hit a tree,* маши́на нас-

кочи́ла *or* налете́ла на де́рево. **3,** (strike, as a target) попада́ть в. **4,** (reach; attain) достига́ть: *the temperature hit 100°,* температу́ра дости́гла ста гра́дусов. *Hit a high note,* взять высо́кую но́ту. **5,** *usu. passive* (affect severely): *be hard hit by the flood,* си́льно пострада́ть от наводне́ния. —*v.i.* **1,** (strike, as of a storm) обру́шиваться. **2,** *fol. by on or upon* (come up with, as an idea) напада́ть (на); набрести́ (на); доду́маться (до). —*n.* **1,** (blow) уда́р. **2,** (striking of a target) попада́ние: *direct hit,* прямо́е попада́ние. **3,** (success) успе́х: *be a big hit,* име́ть большо́й успе́х. **4,** (film) боеви́к. —**hit back,** дава́ть сда́чи (+ *dat.*). —**hit it off,** сойти́сь хара́ктерами. *Hit it off with,* ла́дить с. —**hit or miss,** как попа́ло; науда́чу; наобу́м. —**hit the road,** *slang* отпра́виться в путь.

hitch *v.t.* **1,** (tie; fasten) привя́зывать; прикрепля́ть. *Hitch a horse to a wagon,* запряга́ть *or* впряга́ть ло́шадь в теле́гу. *Hitch a car onto a train,* прицепля́ть ваго́н к по́езду. **2,** (pull up with a jerk) подтя́гивать: *hitch up one's trousers,* подтя́гивать брю́ки. —*n.* **1,** (tug; jerk) рыво́к. **2,** (delay; complication) зами́нка: *without a hitch,* без зами́нки. **3,** *colloq.* (period of service) срок (слу́жбы).

hitchhike *v.i.* е́хать на попу́тной маши́не; "голосова́ть" на доро́ге.

hitching post ко́новязь.

hither *adv.* сюда́.

hitherto *adv.* до сих пор.

Hittite *adj.* хе́ттский. —**Hittites,** *n.pl.* хе́тты.

hive *n.* **1,** (beehive) у́лей. **2,** *pl.* (skin condition) крапи́вница.

hoard *n.* запа́с. —*v.t.* запаса́ть; накопля́ть; припря́тывать.

hoarfrost *n.* и́ней; и́зморозь.

hoarse *adj.* хри́плый; си́плый. *Be hoarse,* хрипе́ть. *Become hoarse,* (о)хри́пнуть. *Talk oneself hoarse,* договори́ться до хрипоты́. —**hoarsely,** *adv.* хри́пло.

hoarseness *n.* хрипота́.

hoary *adj.* **1,** (gray or white with age) седо́й. **2,** (ancient; venerable) почте́нный.

hoax *n.* шу́тка; мистифика́ция.

hobble *v.i.* ковыля́ть. *Hobble along,* идти́ прихра́мывая. —*v.t.* (fetter) трено́жить; спу́тывать.

hobby *n.* хо́бби.

hobbyhorse *n.* конь-кача́лка.

hobgoblin *n.* **1,** (elf) домово́й. **2,** (bugaboo) жу́пел.

hobnob *v.i.* води́ть компа́нию; якша́ться.

hobo *n.* бродя́га; бося́к.

hock *v.t., colloq.* закла́дывать. —*n., colloq., usu. in* **in hock,** в закла́де.

hockey *n.* хокке́й. —*adj.* хокке́йный: *hockey match,* хокке́йный матч. —**hockey player,** хоккеи́ст. —**hockey stick,** клю́шка.

hockshop *n.* ломба́рд.

hocus-pocus *n.* фо́кус-по́кус.

hodgepodge *n.* меша́нина; ерала́ш.

hoe *n.* моты́га. —*v.t.* моты́жить.

hog *n.* бо́ров; свинья́.

hogwash *n.* **1,** (swill) по́йло (для свине́й). **2,** (nonsense) чепуха́.

hoi polloi плебс; простонаро́дье.

hoist *v.t.* поднима́ть. *Hoist a flag,* поднима́ть/выбра́сывать/вы́кинуть флаг. —*n.* **1,** (act of hoisting) подъём. **2,** (hoisting device) подъёмник.

hold *v.t.* **1,** (grip) держа́ть: *hold in one's hand,* держа́ть в руке́. *Hold hands,* держа́ться за́ руки. *Hold* one's nose, зажима́ть нос. **2,** (keep in a certain position) держа́ть: *hold one's head high,* держа́ть го́лову высоко́. **3,** (bear the weight of) уде́рживать: *the hook will not hold the mirror,* крючо́к не уде́ржит зе́ркала. **4,** (detain) держа́ть: *hold prisoner,* держа́ть в плену́. **5,** (delay the departure of, as a train) заде́рживать. **6,** (set aside until needed or requested) оставля́ть. **7,** (prevent from being captured) уде́рживать. **8,** (have; organize; carry on) проводи́ть; устра́ивать. *Hold a meeting,* проводи́ть собра́ние. *Hold elections,* проводи́ть вы́боры. **9,** (occupy, as a job or office) занима́ть. **10,** (have room for; accommodate) вмеща́ть. **11,** (own) владе́ть. **12,** (maintain, as an opinion) приде́рживаться. **13,** (command, as attention) владе́ть. **14,** (consider; regard): *hold in high esteem,* высоко́ цени́ть; *hold sacred,* свя́то чтить; *hold in contempt,* относи́ться с презре́нием к. **15,** (believe; maintain) утвержда́ть. **16,** (rule) постановля́ть: *the court held that...,* суд постанови́л, что... —*v.i.* **1,** (retain a hold) держа́ться: *hold tight,* держа́ться кре́пко. **2,** (not break or collapse) выде́рживать: *the rope held,* верёвка вы́держала. **3,** (be true or valid) остава́ться в си́ле. —*n.* **1,** (grip) сжа́тие; хва́тка. *Take/catch/grab hold of,* ухвати́ться за. *Lose hold of,* упуска́ть. **2,** (of a ship) трюм. **3,** (sway; control) власть; влия́ние. —**get (a) hold of, 1,** (get a grip on) ухвати́ться за. **2,** *colloq.* (obtain) раздобы́ть. **3,** *colloq.* (reach, as by telephone) связа́ться с; дозвони́ться к. **4,** *Get hold of oneself,* взять себя́ в ру́ки. —**hold against,** ста́вить в упрёк (+ *dat.*). —**hold back, 1,**(restrain) уде́рживать; сде́рживать. **2,** (withhold) уде́рживать; заде́рживать. **3,** (not reveal) ута́ивать. **4,** (retard) заде́рживать. —**hold down, 1,** (pin down) прижима́ть к земле́. **2,** (keep down, as prices) уде́рживать. **3,** *colloq.* (have; keep, as a job) уде́рживаться на (рабо́те). *Hold down two jobs,* рабо́тать на двух рабо́тах; рабо́тать по совмести́тельству. —**hold forth,** разглаго́льствовать. —**hold good,** остава́ться в си́ле. —**hold it!,** стой!; стоп! —**hold off, 1,** (check the advance of) уде́рживать. **2,** (delay in doing something) повремени́ть. —**hold on,** держа́ться. —**hold on to, 1,** (hold so as not to fall) держа́ться за: *hold on to the banister,* держа́ться за пери́ла. **2,** (hold in place) приде́рживать: *hold on to one's hat,* приде́рживать шля́пу. —**hold out, 1,** (proffer) протя́гивать. **2,** (offer, as hope) подава́ть (наде́жду). **3,** (stand firm) держа́ться; продержа́ться; устоя́ть; вы́стоять. **4,** (last; suffice) хвата́ть. —**hold still,** не шевели́ться. —**hold up, 1,** (raise) подноси́ть: *hold up to the light,* подноси́ть к све́ту. **2,** (support; keep from falling) подде́рживать; уде́рживать. **3,** (delay) заде́рживать. **4,** (expose; exhibit): *hold up as an example,* ста́вить в приме́р. *Hold up to ridicule,* поднима́ть на́ смех. **5,** (last; continue to function) выде́рживать. **6,** (rob) гра́бить.

holder *n.* **1,** (possessor) держа́тель; облада́тель. *Holder of an order,* кавале́р о́рдена. **2,** (device) держа́тель. *Cigarette holder,* мундшту́к.

holding *n.* **1,** (having, as elections) проведе́ние. **2,** *usu. pl.* (property) владе́ния; (money) вкла́ды. —**holding pattern,** маршру́т ожида́ния.

holdover *n.* пережи́ток.

holdup *n., colloq.* **1,** (delay) заде́ржка. **2,** (robbery) налёт.

hole *n.* **1,** (opening; tear) дыра́; ды́рка. **2,** (in the ground) я́ма. **3,** (animal's burrow) нора́; но́рка. **4,**

golf лу́нка. **5,** *colloq.* (small dingy quarters) конура́. —*v.i.* [*usu.* **hole up**] скрыва́ться.

holiday *n.* **1,** (commemorative day) пра́здник. **2,** *Brit.* (vacation) о́тпуск. —*adj.* пра́здничный.

holiness *n.* **1,** (sanctity) свя́тость. **2,** *cap.* (papal title) святе́йшество: *His Holiness,* его́ святе́йшество.

holler *v.i., colloq.* ора́ть.

hollow *adj.* **1,** (having a cavity within) по́лый. **2,** (sunken, as of cheeks) впа́лый. **3,** (muffled, as of a sound) глухо́й. **4,** (meaningless; shallow) пусто́й. —*n.* **1,** (cavity) дупло́. **2,** (depression) углубле́ние; впа́дина; вы́емка. —*v.t.* [*usu.* **hollow out**] долби́ть; выда́лбливать.

holly *n.* па́дуб; остроли́ст.

hollyhock *n.* штокро́за.

holmium *n.* го́льмий.

holocaust *n.* катастро́фа; уничтоже́ние.

holography *n.* гологра́фия.

holster *n.* кобура́.

holy *adj.* свято́й; свяще́нный. —**Holy Alliance,** Свяще́нный сою́з. —**Holy Ghost,** свято́й дух. —**holy of holies,** свята́я святы́х. —**Holy Scripture,** свяще́нное писа́ние. —**Holy Thursday,** страстно́й четве́рг. —**holy water,** свята́я вода́. —**Holy Week,** свята́я *or* страстна́я неде́ля.

homage *n.* по́чести: *pay homage to,* оказывать *or* воздава́ть по́чести (+ *dat.*).

home *n.* дом. —*adj.* дома́шний: *home address,* дома́шний а́дрес. *The home team,* хозя́ева по́ля. —*adv.* **1,** (to one's home) домо́й: *go home,* идти́ домо́й. **2,** (at one's home) до́ма: *he is not home,* его́ нет до́ма. —**at home, 1,** (in one's house) до́ма. **2,** *sports* на своём по́ле. **3,** (comfortable; at ease) как до́ма: *feel at home,* чу́вствовать себя́ как до́ма. *Make yourself at home!,* бу́дьте как до́ма! —**bring home to,** внуша́ть; втолкова́ть. —**from home,** из до́ма; от до́ма: *mail from home,* пи́сьма из до́ма; *far from home,* далеко́ от до́ма. *I'm calling from home,* я звоню́ из до́ма. —**strike home,** попа́сть не в бровь, а в глаз.

homebody *n.* домосе́д.

homebred *adj.* доморо́щенный.

home-brew *n.* самого́н.

homecoming *n.* возвраще́ние домо́й.

home economics домово́дство.

home front вну́тренний фронт.

homeland *n.* ро́дина; оте́чество.

homeless *adj.* бездо́мный; бесприю́тный; беспризо́рный.

homely *adj.* **1,** (unpretentious) просто́й. **2,** (unattractive) некраси́вый; невзра́чный.

homemade *adj.* дома́шний; самоде́льный.

homemaker *n.* дома́шняя хозя́йка.

homeopathy *n.* гомеопа́тия. —**homeopath,** *n.* гомеопа́т. —**homeopathic,** *adj.* гомеопати́ческий.

homeowner *n.* домовладе́лец.

home rule самоуправле́ние.

homesick *adj.* тоску́ющий по до́му *or* по ро́дине. *Be homesick,* тоскова́ть по до́му/по ро́дине/.

homespun *adj.* **1,** (woven at home) домотка́ный. **2,** (simple; unpretentious) доморо́щенный.

homestead *n.* уса́дьба.

home town родно́й го́род.

homeward *adv.* домо́й; к до́му. —**homeward-bound,** *adj.* возвраща́ющийся домо́й.

homework *n.* дома́шнее зада́ние; дома́шняя рабо́та. *Do one's homework,* (при)гото́вить уро́ки *or* дома́шние зада́ния.

homicide *n.* убийство.

homily *n.* поуче́ние.

homing pigeon почто́вый го́лубь.

hominy *n.* мамалы́га.

homogeneous *adj.* одноро́дный. **—homogeneity,** *n.* одноро́дность.

homogenize *v.t.* гомогенизи́ровать.

homonym *n.* омо́ним.

homosexual *n.* гомосексуали́ст. **—***adj.* гомосексуа́льный. **—homosexuality,** *n.* гомосексуали́зм.

hone *v.t.* точи́ть. **—***n.* точи́льный ка́мень.

honest *adj.* че́стный. *To be honest...,* че́стно говоря́... **—honest to goodness!,** че́стное сло́во!

honestly *adv.* **1,** (in an honest manner) че́стно. **2,** (really; truly) че́стное сло́во.

honesty *n.* че́стность. **—in all honesty,** че́стно говоря́; по со́вести (говоря́).

honey *n.* **1,** (sweet substance) мёд. **2,** *colloq.* (term of endearment) ми́лый; голу́бчик. **—***adj.* медо́вый.

honeybee *n.* медоно́сная пчела́.

honeycomb *n.* со́ты.

honeydew *n.* медвя́ная роса́. **—honeydew melon,** зи́мняя ды́ня.

honeyed *adj.* медо́вый; слаща́вый; прито́рный.

honeymoon *n.* медо́вый ме́сяц.

honeysuckle *n.* жи́молость.

honk *n.* **1,** (call of the goose) клик. **2,** (sound of an automobile horn) гудо́к. **—***v.i.* **1,** (of a goose) кли́кать. **2,** (blow the horn) гуде́ть. **—***v.t.* дать (гудо́к).

honor *also,* **honour** *n.* **1,** (integrity; reputation; privilege) честь. *Consider it an honor,* счита́ть за честь. **2,** (esteem) почёт. *Place of honor,* почётное ме́сто. **3,** *pl.* (ceremonies of respect) по́чести: *with military honors,* с во́инскими по́честями. **4,** *cap.* (title of respect) честь: *Your Honor,* ва́ша честь. **5,** *pl.* (credit awarded to outstanding students) отли́чие: *graduate with honors,* око́нчить с отли́чием. **6,** *pl., cards* онеры. **—***v.t.* **1,** (show special respect for) почита́ть. **2,** (bring honor or distinction to) ока́зывать честь (+ *dat.*). **3,** (pay tribute to) че́ствовать. **4,** (observe, as one's commitments) выполня́ть. **—do honor to,** де́лать честь (+ *dat.*). **—in honor of,** в честь (+ *gen.*). **—on my honor; word of honor,** че́стное сло́во.

honorable *also,* **honourable** *adj.* **1,** (honest; upright) че́стный. **2,** (deserving of respect) почётный.

honorarium *n.* гонора́р.

honorary *adj.* почётный.

honored *also,* **honoured** *adj.* почётный: *honored guest,* почётный гость. *I am honored to...,* счита́ю за честь (+ *inf.*).

honor guard почётный карау́л.

honor roll кра́сная доска́.

honour *n. & v.* = **honor. —honourable,** *adj.* = **honorable. —honoured,** *adj.* = **honored.**

hood *n.* **1,** (head covering) капюшо́н. **2,** (cover of an engine) капо́т.

hooded *adj.* **1,** (wearing a hood) в капюшо́не. **2,** (containing a hood) с капюшо́ном. **—hooded seal,** хохла́ч.

hoodlum *n.* хулига́н.

hoodwink *v.t.* обма́нывать; провести́; объжу́ливать.

hoof *n.* копы́то. **—hoofed,** *adj.* копы́тный.

hook *n.* крюк; крючо́к. **—***v.t.* **1,** (fasten) застёгивать (на крючо́к). **2,** (attach; hitch) прицепля́ть. **3,** *fol. by* **up** (connect) подключа́ть. **4,** (catch, as a fish) выу́живать. **—***v.i.* **1,** (fasten) застёгиваться:.*the dress hooks in back,* пла́тье застёгивается сза́ди. **2,** *fol. by* **onto** (be attached to) пристёгиваться к; прицепля́ться к. **—by hook or by crook,** каки́м бы то ни́ было спо́собом; все́ми пра́вдами и непра́вдами; не мытьём, так ка́таньем. **—hook, line, and sinker,** по́лностью; цели́ком.

hooked *adj.* **1,** (curved like a hook) крючкова́тый. *Hooked nose,* горба́тый нос; нос с горби́нкой. **2,** *fol. by* **on,** *slang* (addicted to) поме́шанный (на).

hookup *n.* **1,** (network) сеть. **2,** *colloq.* (connection) связь.

hookworm *n.* глист.

hooky *n., in* **play hooky,** прогу́ливать уро́ки.

hooligan *n.* хулига́н. **—hooliganism,** *n.* хулига́нство.

hoop *n.* о́бруч.

hoopla *n.* шум; шуми́ха.

hoopoe *n.* удо́д.

hoop skirt криноли́н.

hooray *interj.* ура́!

hoosegow *n., colloq.* куту́зка.

hoot *n.* **1,** (cry of an owl) крик (совы́). **2,** (toot) гудо́к. **—***v.i.* (of an owl) у́хать. **—***v.t.* (jeer) освистывать.

hop *v.i.* **1,** (leap, as of a frog) пры́гать. **2,** (jump on one foot) пры́гать *or* скака́ть на одно́й ноге́. **—***v.t.* вска́кивать: *hop a train,* вскочи́ть на по́езд. **—***n.* **1,** (jump) прыжо́к; скачо́к. **2,** *colloq.* (short flight) рейс. **3,** (plant) хмель. **4,** *pl.* (flavoring for beer) хмель.

hope *n.* наде́жда. **—***v.t. & i.* наде́яться: *I hope so,* наде́юсь, что да; *I hope not,* наде́юсь, что нет. *Hope for the best,* наде́яться на лу́чшее. *I hope to see you again soon,* наде́юсь ско́ро вас сно́ва уви́деть.

hopeful *adj.* **1,** (having hope): *be hopeful,* наде́яться; пита́ть наде́жды. **2,** (giving hope) обнаде́живающий; подаю́щий наде́жды.

hopefully *adv.* **1,** (with hope) с наде́ждой. **2,** (if all goes well) на́до наде́яться, что...

hopeless *adj.* **1,** (offering no hope) безнадёжный; безвы́ходный. **2,** *colloq.* (worthless; without merit) беспо́мощный. **—hopelessness,** *n.* безнадёжность.

hopper *n.* бу́нкер.

hopscotch *n.* кла́ссы.

horde *n.* по́лчище; орда́.

horizon *n.* **1,** (line between earth and sky) горизо́нт. **2,** *fig.* (intellect) кругозо́р; горизо́нт.

horizontal *adj.* горизонта́льный. **—***n.* горизонта́ль. **—horizontal bar,** *sports* перекла́дина; турни́к.

horizontally *adv.* горизонта́льно.

hormone *n.* гормо́н.

horn *n.* **1,** (bonelike growth) рог. **2,** (instrument sounded by blowing) рог. **3,** (brass-wind instrument) рожо́к. **4,** (of an automobile) гудо́к. **—***v.i.* [*usu.* **horn in**] *slang* вме́шиваться; сова́ться. **—blow one's own horn,** труби́ть о себе́. **—draw/pull in one's horns,** бить отбо́й. **—horn of plenty,** рог изоби́лия. **—take the bull by the horns,** брать быка́ за рога́.

hornbeam *n.* граб.

hornblende *n.* рогова́я обма́нка.

horned *adj.* рога́тый.

hornet n. шéршень. —**hornets' nest**, осúное гнездó.

hornless adj. безрóгий; комóлый.

horn-rimmed adj. роговóй: horn-rimmed glasses, роговые очкú.

horny adj. **1,** (made of a hornlike substance) роговóй. **2,** (calloused; tough) мозóлистый.

horoscope n. гороскóп.

horrendous adj. = **horrible.**

horrible adj. стрáшный; ужáсный.

horrid adj. ужáсный; протúвный.

horrify v.t. ужасáть; приводúть в ýжас. Be horrified, ужасáться; приходúть в ýжас. —**horrifying,** adj. ужасáющий.

horror n. **1,** (terror) ýжас. **2,** pl. (that which horrifies) ýжасы: the horrors of war, ýжасы войны. —**horror movie,** фильм ýжасов.

hors d'oeuvre закýска.

horse n. **1,** (animal) лóшадь; конь. **2,** (frame) рáма. Sawhorse, кóзлы. **3,** gymnastics конь; кобыла. —adj. лошадúный; кóнный. —v.i. (usu. **horse around**] colloq. озорничáть; проказничать; дурúть. —**back the wrong horse,** постáвить не на ту лóшадь. —**change horses in midstream,** менять лошадéй во врéмя перепрáвы. —**horse of a different color,** совсéм другóй коленкóр. —**look a gift horse in the mouth,** смотрéть в зýбы дарёному коню. —**play the horses,** игрáть на скáчках. —**work like a horse,** рабóтать как вол.

horseback adv. верхóм: ride horseback, éздить верхóм. Be on horseback, быть верхóм. —**horseback riding,** верховáя ездá. Go horseback riding, катáться верхóм.

horse breeder коневóд. —**horse breeding,** коневóдство; коннозавóдство.

horsecar n. кóнка.

horse chestnut кóнский каштáн.

horsecloth n. попóна.

horse doctor коновáл.

horse-drawn adj. кóнный.

horseflesh n. конúна.

horsefly n. слепéнь.

horsehair n. кóнский вóлос. —adj. волосянóй: horsehair mattress, волосянóй матрáц.

horsehide n. кóнская шкýра.

horselaugh n. хóхот.

horseman n. всáдник; наéздник. —**horsemanship,** n. искýсство верховóй езды; наéздничество.

horsemeat n. конúна.

horseplay n. баловствó; озорствó.

horsepower n. лошадúная сúла.

horse racing скáчки.

horseradish n. хрен.

horseshoe n. подкóва.

horsetail n. (plant) хвощ.

horse thief конокрáд.

horsetrader n. барышник.

horsewhip n. хлыст. —v.t. отхлестáть.

horsewoman n. всáдница; наéздница; амазóнка.

horticulture n. садовóдство. —**horticultural,** adj. садовóдческий. —**horticulturist,** n. садовóд.

hosanna n. осáнна.

hose n. **1,** (device for squirting water) шланг; кишкá; рукáв. **2,** (stockings) чулкú. —v.t. поливáть из шлáнга.

hosiery n. чулóчные издéлия.

hospitable adj. гостеприúмный.

hospital n. больнúца; mil. гóспиталь. —adj. больнúчный; госпитáльный. —**hospital ship,** госпитáльное or санитáрное сýдно.

hospitality n. гостеприúмство.

hospitalization n. **1,** (being hospitalized) госпитализáция. **2,** (insurance) страховáние на слýчай госпитализáции.

hospitalize v.t. помещáть в больнúцу; госпитализúровать.

host n. **1,** (one who entertains) хозяин. **2,** (multitude) мнóжество; тьма. —**play host to,** sports принимáть на своём пóле.

hostage n. залóжник.

hostel n. турбáза. Youth hostel, молодёжная турбáза.

hostelry n. постоялый двор.

hostess n. хозяйка.

hostile adj. **1,** (antagonistic) враждéбный; неприязненный. **2,** (being or belonging to an enemy) врáжеский.

hostility n. **1,** (antagonism) враждá; враждéбность; неприязнь. With hostility, враждéбно. **2,** pl. (warfare) воéнные дéйствия.

hot adj. **1,** (of the weather, temperature, etc.) жáркий: a hot day, жáркий день. I am hot, мне жáрко. **2,** (of an object, liquid, etc.) горячий. **3,** (highly spiced) óстрый. **4,** (impassioned; fiery) горячий. —**get into hot water,** попáсть в бедý; попáсть как кур вó щи. —**hot on the trail of,** по горячим следáм (+ gen.). —**not so hot,** так себé.

hot air 1, literally нагрéтый вóздух. **2,** colloq. (empty talk) пустослóвие.

hotbed n. **1,** (glass-covered bed of soil) парнúк. **2,** fig. (breeding ground) очáг.

hot-blooded adj. горячий; пылкий; стрáстный.

hot cake блин. —**sell like hot cakes,** продавáться нарасхвáт.

hot dog colloq. сосúска.

hotel n. гостúница. Hotel room, нóмер гостúницы.

hothead n. горячая головá; кипятóк. —**hotheaded,** adj. горячий; вспыльчивый.

hothouse n. теплúца; оранжерéя. —adj. теплúчный; оранжерéйный; парникóвый.

hotly adv. горячó.

hot-tempered adj. горячий; вспыльчивый; запáльчивый.

hot-water bottle грéлка.

hound n. охóтничья собáка; гóнчая. —v.t. **1,** (pursue relentlessly) преслéдовать; травúть. **2,** colloq. (nag; pester) приставáть к.

hour n. час: two hours, два часá. Hour after hour, час за чáсом. Hour by hour, час óт часу.

hourglass n. песóчные часы.

hour hand часовáя стрéлка.

hourly adj. **1,** (occurring every hour) ежечáсный. **2,** (per hour) часовóй. —adv. ежечáсно.

house n. **1,** (dwelling place) дом. At my house, у меня. To my house, ко мне. **2,** (building) здáние; дом. Schoolhouse, шкóльное здáние. Rooming house, пансиóн. Movie house, кинó. Opera house, óперный теáтр. House of worship, молúтвенный дом. **3,** (institution) дом: house of correction, исправúтельный дом. **4,** (business establishment) фúрма. Publishing *house*, издательство. **5,** (theater; audience) зал: *full house*, полный зал. **6,** (legislative body) палата: *House of Representatives*, палата представителей. *House of Commons*, палата общин. *House of Lords*, палата лордов. **7,** (dynasty) дом: *House of Tudor*, дом Тюдоров. —*adj.* домашний: *house arrest*, домашний арест. *House plant*, комнатное растение. —*v.t.* **1,** (provide quarters for) помещать. **2,** (serve as the home of) вмещать. —**house of cards,** карточный домик. —**keep house,** вести (домашнее) хозяйство. —**on the house,** за счёт предприятия.

houseboat *n.* плавучий дом.

housebreaker *n.* взломщик.

housecoat *n.* капот.

household *n.* семья; домочадцы. —*adj.* домашний; хозяйственный. *Household goods*, хозяйственные товары. *Household items*, предметы домашнего обихода. *Household appliances*, бытовые приборы. *Household chores*, хлопоты по хозяйству.

housekeeper *n.* **1,** (housewife) хозяйка. **2,** (woman hired to run a house) экономка.

housekeeping *n.* ведение хозяйства; домашнее хозяйство; домоводство.

housemaid *n.* горничная; домработница.

housetop *n., in* **from the housetops,** во всеуслышание; на всех перекрёстках.

housewarming *n.* новоселье.

housewife *n.* домашняя хозяйка; домхозяйка.

housework *n.* работа по хозяйству. *Help with the housework*, помогать по хозяйству.

housing *n.* **1,** (living quarters) жилище; жилое помещение. *Poor housing*, неудовлетворительные жилищные условия. *Provide with housing*, обеспечивать жилищем. *Shortage of housing*, нехватка жилплощади. **2,** (casing) кожух. —*adj.* жилищный: *housing conditions*, жилищные условия. *Housing allowance*, квартирное довольствие.

hovel *n.* лачуга; хибарка.

hover *v.i.* **1,** (remain suspended in the air) реять. **2,** *fol. by* **over** (stick close to) стоять над (чьей-нибудь) душой. **3,** (waver) колебаться. *Hover between life and death*, быть между жизнью и смертью.

hovercraft *n.* судно на воздушной подушке.

how *adv.* **1,** (in what manner; in what state) как: *how is this done?*, как это делается? *How are you?*, как вы поживаете? *How does the story end?*, чем кончается рассказ? **2,** (to what extent) насколько: *how true is this?*, насколько это верно? *How tall are you?*, какого вы роста? *How high is this building?*, какой высоты это здание? **3,** *in exclamations* как: *how strange!*, как странно! —**and how!,** ещё бы! —**how about...?,** как насчёт...? —**how come?,** почему же? *How come you're not asleep?*, что же ты не спишь? —**how do you do?, 1,** (hello) здравствуйте! **2,** *on being introduced* очень приятно! —**how far?,** *see* **far.** —**how long?,** *see* **long.** —**how many?; how much?,** сколько? —**how so?,** как же так?

however *conj.* однако. —*adv.* как (бы) ни: *however hard he tried*, как он ни старался.

howitzer *n.* гаубица.

howl *v.i.* **1,** (of an animal or the wind) выть; завывать. **2,** (cry out) реветь; вопить. **3,** (laugh loudly) хохотать. —*n.* вой; рёв. —**howling monkey,** ревун.

hub *n.* **1,** (of a wheel) ступица. **2,** (center; focal point) узел; средоточие.

hubbub *n.* гам; гвалт; галдёж.

hubcap *n.* колпак (ступицы).

huckleberry *n.* черника.

huckster *n.* торгаш; барышник.

huddle *v.i.* **1,** (crowd together) жаться; тесниться; ютиться. **2,** *fol. by* **up** (hunch up, as from the cold) ёжиться; жаться.

hue *n.* **1,** (color) цвет; краска. **2,** (shade) оттенок. —**hue and cry,** шум: *raise a hue and cry*, поднимать шум.

huff *n.* вспышка гнева. *Get into a huff*, удариться в амбицию. —*v.i.* (blow) дуть; фукать. *Huff and puff*, задыхаться.

huffy *adj.* обидчивый.

hug *v.t.* **1,** (embrace) обнимать. **2,** (stick close to) держаться (+ *gen.*): *hug the shore*, держаться берега. —*v.i.* обниматься. —*n.* объятие.

huge *adj.* огромный; громадный.

Huguenot *n.* гугенот.

hulk *n.* **1,** (remains of an old ship) корпус корабля. **2,** (huge bulky thing) громада. —**hulking,** *adj.* неуклюжий; медвежий.

hull *n.* **1,** (shell; husk) шелуха. **2,** (body of a ship) корпус (корабля). —*v.t.* шелушить; лущить.

hullabaloo *n.* шумиха; тарарам.

hum *v.i.* **1,** (sing without words) напевать. **2,** (buzz) жужжать. **3,** *colloq.* (be full of activity) кипеть. —*v.t.* напевать. —*n.* **1,** (of insects) жужжание. **2,** (of voices) гул; гомон.

human *adj.* человеческий; людской. —**human being,** человек. —**human nature,** человеческая природа. —**human race,** человеческий род. —**human rights,** права человека.

humane *adj.* гуманный; человечный. —**humanely,** *adv.* гуманно. —**humaneness,** *n.* гуманность; человечность.

humanism *n.* гуманизм.

humanist *n.* гуманист. —**humanistic,** *adj.* гуманистический.

humanitarian *adj.* гуманный; гуманитарный. —*n.* благотворитель; филантроп.

humanity *n.* **1,** (mankind) человечество. **2,** (humaneness) гуманность; человечность. **3,** *pl.* (literature, fine arts, etc.) гуманитарные науки.

humanize *v.t.* очеловечивать.

humankind *n.* человечество.

humanly *adv. Everything that is/was humanly possible*, всё, что в человеческих силах. *Not humanly possible*, выше человеческих сил.

humble *adj.* **1,** (not proud or self-assertive) смиренный; покорный. *Your humble servant*, ваш покорный слуга. *Humble request*, покорная просьба. **2,** (of low social rank) низкий: *of humble origin*, низкого происхождения. **3,** (unpretentious) скромный: *humble abode*, скромное жилище. —*v.t.* унижать; принижать. *Humble oneself*, унижаться. —**humbly,** *adv.* смиренно; покорно.

humdrum *adj.* однообразный; будничный.

humid *adj.* влажный.

humidify *v.t.* увлажнять.

humidity *n.* влажность.

humiliate *v.t.* унижать. —**humiliating,** *adj.* унизительный. —**humiliation,** *n.* унижение.

humility *n.* смирение; смиренность.

hummingbird *n.* колибри.

hummock *n.* **1,** (low mound) кóчка. **2,** (ridge in an ice field) торóс.

humor *also,* **humour** *n.* **1,** (drollery; sense or use of same) ю́мор: *sense of humor,* чýвство ю́мора. **2,** (mood) настроéние: *in good humor,* в хорóшем настроéнии. *Out of humor,* не в дýхе. —*v.t.* ублажáть; увáжить.

humoresque *n.* юморéска.

humorist *n.* юморúст.

humorous *adj.* **1,** (amusing) забáвный; смешнóй. **2,** (containing humor) юмористúческий.

humour *n. & v.* = **humor.**

hump *n.* горб.

humpback *n.* **1,** (hump) горб. **2,** (person so afflicted) горбýн; горбáтый. —**humpbacked,** *adj.* горбáтый.

humus *n.* перегнóй; гýмус.

Hun *n.* гунн.

hunch *n.* **1,** (hump) горб. **2,** *colloq.* (feeling) предчýвствие. —*v.t.* гóрбить; сутýлить. —*v.i.* гóрбиться.

hunchback *n.* = **humpback.** —**hunchbacked,** *adj.* = **humpbacked.**

hundred *adj.* стo. —*n.* **1,** (cardinal number) стo. **2,** *pl.* (groups of 100) сóтни (+ *gen.*): *hundreds of people,* сóтни людéй.

hundredfold *adj.* стокрáтный. —*adv.* вó стo крат.

hundredth *adj.* сóтый. *See also* **one-hundredth.**

Hungarian *adj.* венгéрский. —*n.* **1,** (person) венгр; венгéрка. **2,** (language) венгéрский язы́к.

hunger *n.* **1,** (craving for food) гóлод. **2,** *fig.* (craving) жáжда. —*adj.* голóдный: *hunger pangs,* голóдные бóли. —*v.i.* [*usu.* **hunger for**] жáждать (+ *gen.*). —**die of hunger,** умирáть с гóлоду; умирáть голóдной смéртью. *I am dying of hunger (i.e. very hungry),* я умирáю от гóлода; я стрáшно проголодáлся.

hunger strike голодóвка.

hungry *adj.* **1,** (wanting or needing food) голóдный. *I am hungry,* я гóлоден (голоднá); мне хóчется есть. *Go hungry,* голодáть. **2,** *fol. by* **for** (craving) жáждущий: *be hungry for,* жáждать (+ *gen.*).

hunk *n.* ломóть.

hunky-dory *adj., slang, in* **everything is hunky-dory,** всё идёт как по мáслу.

hunt *v.t.* **1,** (try to kill, as game) охóтиться на. **2,** (chase; pursue) преслéдовать. **3,** *fol. by* **down** (track down) затравúть; вы́следить. —*v.i.* **1,** (go hunting) охóтиться. **2,** *fol. by* **for** (search for) разы́скивать. —*n.* **1,** (hunting) охóта. **2,** (search) пóиски.

hunter *n.* охóтник.

hunting *n.* охóта: *duck hunting,* охóта на ýток. *Go hunting,* идтú на охóту. —*adj.* охóтничий: *hunting season,* охóтничий сезóн.

huntsman *n.* = **hunter.**

hurdle *n.* **1,** (barrier) барьéр; препя́тствие. **2,** *pl.* (hurdle race) барьéрный бег; бег с препя́тствиями. —*v.t.* **1,** (clear, as a barrier) брать (барьéр). **2,** (overcome) преодолевáть.

hurl *v.t.* **1,** (throw; fling) метáть; швыря́ть. **2,** (utter vehemently) осыпáть: *hurl insults at,* осыпáть (когó-нибудь) оскорблéниями. —**hurl back,** отбивáть.

hurly-burly *n.* суматóха; переполóх.

hurrah *interj.* урá! *Also,* **hurray.**

hurricane *n.* урагáн.

hurried *adj.* тороплúвый; поспéшный. —**hurriedly,** *adv.* тороплúво; поспéшно; нáскоро; нáспех; второпя́х.

hurry *v.i.* [*also,* **hurry up**] спешúть; торопúться. *Hurry up!,* скорéй!; быстрéе!; поторáпливайтесь! —*v.t.* торопúть. —*n.* спéшка; тороплúвость; поспéшность. *Be in a hurry,* спешúть; торопúться. *There is no hurry,* не нáдо спешúть; э́то не к спéху.

hurt *v.t.* **1,** (cause pain or discomfort to) причиня́ть боль (+ *dat.*). *It hurts me to walk,* мне бóльно ходúть. *The sun hurts my eyes,* от сóлнца глазáм бóльно. **2,** (injure) поврежда́ть; ушибáть. *Hurt oneself,* ушибáться. **3,** (be detrimental to; damage) вредúть; пóртить. *It wouldn't hurt you to...,* вам не мешáло бы (+ *inf.*). **4,** (wound the feelings of) задевáть; обижáть. —*v.i.* **1,** (be painful) болéть: *my stomach hurts,* у меня́ болúт живóт. *Does it hurt?,* вам бóльно? *It hurts to lie on my back,* бóльно лечь нá спину. **2,** (cause harm) мешáть: *excessive caution never hurts,* чрезмéрная осторóжность никогдá не мешáет.

hurtle *v.i.* **1,** (rush violently) нестúсь; мчáться. **2,** *fol. by* **against** (collide with) врезáться в.

husband *n.* муж. —*v.t.* (conserve) эконóмить.

husbandry *n.* землядéлие. —**animal husbandry,** животновóдство.

hush *v.i.* молчáть. —*v.t.* **1,** (call upon to be silent) шúкать на. **2,** [*usu.* **hush up**] (suppress) замáлчивать; замя́ть. —*n.* тишинá; молчáние. —*interj.* тúше!; тсс!; шш!

husk *n.* шелухá. —*v.t.* шелушúть; лущúть.

husky *adj.* **1,** (hoarse) сúплый; хрúплый. **2,** (burly) рóслый; дю́жий. —*n.* (dog) лáйка.

hussar *n.* гусáр.

hussy *n.* жéнщина лёгкого поведéния.

hustle *v.t.* затолкáть. —*v.i.* торопúться; суетúться. —*n.* [*often* **hustle and bustle**] суетá; суматóха.

hustler *n.* **1,** (petty racketeer) живодёр. **2,** (go-getter) хлопотýн.

hut *n.* хúжина.

hyacinth *n.* гиацúнт.

hybrid *n.* пóмесь; гибрúд. —*adj.* гибрúдный; разнорóдный; смéшанный.

hydra *n.* гúдра.

hydrangea *n.* гортéнзия.

hydrant *n.* водоразбóрный кран; водоразбóрная колóнка; гидрáнт. *Fire hydrant,* пожáрный кран/гидрáнт.

hydrate *n.* гидрáт.

hydraulic *adj.* гидравлúческий. —**hydraulics,** *n.* гидрáвлика.

hydrocarbon *n.* углеводорóд.

hydrochloric acid соля́ная кислотá.

hydrodynamics *n.* гидродинáмика.

hydroelectric *adj.* гидроэлектрúческий. *Hydroelectric station,* гидроэлектростáнция.

hydrofluoric acid плавикóвая кислотá.

hydrofoil *n.* **1,** (winglike structure) подвóдное крылó. **2,** (craft) сýдно на подвóдных кры́льях.

hydrogen *n.* водорóд. —*adj.* водорóдный. —**hydrogen bomb,** водорóдная бóмба. —**hydrogen peroxide,** пéрекись водорóда. —**hydrogen sulfide,** сероводорóд.

hydrology *n.* гидролóгия.

hydrolysis *n.* гидрóлиз.

hydrometer *n.* гидрóметр.

hydrophobia *n.* водобоя́знь; бéшенство.

hydroplane *n.* **1,** (boat) глиссер. **2,** (seaplane) гидросамолёт.

hydrostatics *n.* гидростатика.

hydroxide *n.* гидроокись.

hyena *n.* гиена.

hygiene *n.* гигиена.

hygienic *adj.* **1,** (pert. to hygiene) гигиенический. **2,** (clean; sanitary) гигиеничный.

hymen *n.* девственная плева.

hymn *n.* гимн. —**hymnal,** *n.* сборник гимнов.

hyperbola *n.* гипербола.

hyperbole *n.* гипербола.

hyperbolic *adj.* гиперболический.

hypercritical *adj.* придирчивый.

hypertension *n.* гипертония.

hyphen *n.* дефис; чёрточка.

hyphenate *v.t.* писать через дефис *or* через чёрточку.

hypnosis *n.* гипноз. —**hypnotic,** *adj.* гипнотический. —**hypnotism,** *n.* гипнотизм. —**hypnotist,** *n.* гипнотизёр. —**hypnotize,** *v.t.* гипнотизировать.

hypo *n., photog.* фиксаж.

hypochondria *n.* ипохондрия. —**hypochondriac,** *n.* ипохондрик.

hypocrisy *n.* лицемерие.

hypocrite *n.* лицемер. —**hypocritical,** *adj.* лицемерный.

hypodermic *adj.* подкожный. *Hypodermic needle,* игла для подкожных впрыскиваний.

hypotenuse *n.* гипотенуза.

hypothesis *n.* гипотеза.

hypothesize *v.i.* строить гипотезу. —*v.t.* предполагать.

hypothetical *adj.* предположительный; гадательный; гипотетический.

hyrax *n.* даман.

hyssop *n.* иссоп.

hysterectomy *n.* удаление матки.

hysteria *n.* истерия. —**hysterical,** *adj.* истерический. *Become hysterical,* впадать в истерику. —**hysterics,** *n.pl.* истерика.

I

I, i девятая буква английского алфавита. —**dot the "i's" and cross the "t's",** ставить точки над "и".

I *pers.pron.* я: *I don't know,* я не знаю. *You and I,* мы с вами. *See also* **me.**

iamb *n.* ямб. —**iambic,** *adj.* ямбический. *Iambic pentameter,* пятистопный ямб. *Iambic tetrameter,* четырёхстопный ямб.

ibex *n.* **1,** (alpine) козерог. **2,** (Asiatic) сибирский горный козел.

ibidem *adv.* [*usu. abbreviated to* **ibid.**] там же.

ibis *n.* ибис.

ice *n.* лёд. —*adj.* ледяной. —*v.t.* замораживать. —*v.i.* [*usu.* **ice up**] обледенеть. —**break the ice,** разбить *or* сломать лёд.

ice age ледниковый период.

ice bag пузырь со льдом.

iceberg *n.* айсберг.

iceboat *n.* буер.

icebound *adj.* **1,** (held fast by ice) затёртый льдами: *the ship is icebound,* судно затёрло льдами. **2,** (blocked by ice, as of a river) скованный льдами.

icebox *n.* холодильник.

icebreaker *n.* ледокол.

icecap *n.* ледниковый покров.

ice-cold *adj.* ледяной; холодный как лёд.

ice cream мороженое.

iced tea чай со льдом.

ice field плавучая льдина. *Also,* **ice floe.**

ice hockey хоккей с шайбой.

Icelander *n.* исландец. —**Icelandic,** *adj.* исландский. —*n.* исландский язык.

ice skate конёк. —**ice-skate,** *v.i.* кататься на коньках.

ice water вода со льдом.

ichneumon *n.* ихневмон.

ichthyology *n.* ихтиология.

icicle *n.* сосулька.

icing *n.* **1,** (frosting, as for a cake) глазурь. **2,** *aero.* обледенение.

icon *n.* икона. —*adj.* иконный. —**icon case,** киот. —**icon lamp,** лампада.

iconoclasm *n.* иконобор(че)ство. —**iconoclast,** *n.* иконоборец. —**iconoclastic,** *adj.* иконоборческий.

iconostasis *n.* иконостас.

icy *adj.* ледяной.

idea *n.* идея; мысль. *Not have the slightest idea,* иметь ни малейшего понятия *or* представления.

ideal *n.* идеал. —*adj.* идеальный.

idealism *n.* идеализм. —**idealist,** *n.* идеалист. —**idealistic,** *adj.* идеалистический.

idealize *v.t.* идеализировать.

identical *adj.* одинаковый; тождественный; идентичный. —**identically,** *adv.* одинаково.

identification *n.* **1,** (act of identifying) опознание. **2,** (that which serves to identify) удостоверение личности.

identify *v.t.* опознавать. *Identify oneself,* назвать себя; назваться. —**identifying,** *adj.* опознавательный.

identity *n.* **1,** (sameness) тождество; тождественность. **2,** (fact of being someone) личность. —**identity card,** удостоверение личности.

ideogram *n.* идеогра́мма. *Also,* **ideograph.**

ideology *n.* идеоло́гия. —**ideological,** *adj.* идеологи́ческий; иде́йный. —**ideologist,** *n.* идео́лог.

ides *n.pl.* и́ды: *the ides of March,* и́ды ма́рта.

idiocy *n.* **1,** (mental deficiency) идиоти́зм. **2,** (extreme foolishness) идио́тство.

idiom *n.* **1,** (idiomatic expression) идиомати́ческое выраже́ние; идио́ма. **2,** (language; dialect) язы́к; го́вор; наре́чие. —**idiomatic,** *adj.* идиомати́ческий.

idiosyncrasy *n.* стра́нность; причу́да; вы́верт; заско́к.

idiot *n.* идио́т. —**idiotic,** *adj.* идио́тский; дура́цкий.

idle *adj.* **1,** (doing nothing; not occupied) без де́ла; пра́здный. **2,** (not in operation) безде́йствующий. *Stand idle,* проста́ивать. **3,** (casual) пра́здный: *idle curiosity,* пра́здное любопы́тство. *Idle fantasy,* досу́жая фанта́зия. **4,** (meaningless) пусто́й: *idle chatter,* пуста́я болтовня́. —*v.i.* **1,** (loaf) безде́льничать. **2,** (of a motor) рабо́тать вхолосту́ю. —*v.t.* **1,** (make idle) оставля́ть без рабо́ты. **2,** *fol. by* **away** (while away) корота́ть.

idleness *n.* безде́лье; пра́здность.

idler *n.* безде́льник.

idly *adv.* пра́здно.

idol *n.* **1,** (image of a god) йдол; истука́н. **2,** (object of infatuation) йдол; куми́р.

idolater *n.* идолопокло́нник. —**idolatrous,** *adj.* идолопокло́ннический. —**idolatry,** *n.* идолопокло́нство.

idolize *v.t.* обожа́ть; боготвори́ть.

idyll *also,* **idyl** *n.* иди́ллия. —**idyllic,** *adj.* идилли́ческий.

if *conj.* **1,** (in the event that; on condition that) е́сли: *if I had known,* е́сли бы я знал. **2,** (whether) ли: *I don't know if she's coming,* я не зна́ю, придёт ли она́ (и́ли нет). —**as if,** *see* **as.** —**even if,** да́же е́сли; хотя́ бы. —**if it were not for...,** е́сли бы не (+ *nom.*). —**if not, 1,** (if that is not the case) е́сли нет. **2,** (not to say) е́сли не сказа́ть: *difficult if not impossible,* тру́дно, е́сли не сказа́ть невозмо́жно. —**if only, 1,** (be it only) хотя́ бы: *if only for a few minutes,* хотя́ бы на не́сколько мину́т. **2,** to express a profound wish е́сли (бы) то́лько; о, е́сли бы; лишь бы.

igloo *n.* и́глу.

igneous *adj.* **1,** (of fire) о́гненный. **2,** *geol.* изве́рженный.

ignite *v.t.* зажига́ть; воспламеня́ть. —*v.i.* загора́ться; воспламеня́ться.

ignition *n.* зажига́ние; воспламене́ние. *Turn on the ignition,* включи́ть зажига́ние. —**ignition key,** ключ зажига́ния. —**ignition switch,** выключа́тель зажига́ния.

ignoble *adj.* неблагоро́дный.

ignominious *adj.* позо́рный; бессла́вный. —**ignominy,** *n.* позо́р; бессла́вие.

ignoramus *n.* неве́жда; не́уч.

ignorance *n.* **1,** (lack of education) неве́жество. **2,** (lack of knowledge or information) незна́ние; неве́дение.

ignorant *adj.* **1,** (knowing very little; uninformed) неве́жественный. **2,** (lacking knowledge of a certain field) несве́дущий: *ignorant of physics,* несве́дущий в фи́зике. **3,** (unaware) неосведомлённый.

ignore *v.t.* не обраща́ть внима́ния на; игнори́ровать.

iguana *n.* игуа́на.

ilk *n.* род: *of that ilk,* тако́го ро́да.

ill *adj.* **1,** (sick) больно́й. *Become ill,* заболева́ть. **2,** (bad) дурно́й. *Ill health,* сла́бое здоро́вье. *Ill will,* недоброжела́тельство. —*adv.* **1,** (badly) ду́рно: *speak ill of,* ду́рно говори́ть о. **2,** (hardly) едва́ ли: *we can ill afford to lose him,* едва́ ли мы обойдёмся без него́. —*n.* **1,** (evil; harm) зло; вред. **2,** (malady) неду́г. —**ill at ease,** нело́вко: *feel ill at ease,* чу́вствовать себя́ нело́вко.

ill-advised *adj.* неблагоразу́мный.

ill-bred *adj.* невоспи́танный.

ill-considered *adj.* неблагоразу́мный; неразу́мный.

ill-disposed *adj.* не располо́жен (к).

illegal *adj.* незако́нный; нелега́льный; противозако́нный. —**illegality,** *n.* незако́нность; нелега́льность; противозако́нность. —**illegally,** *adv.* незако́нно; нелега́льно.

illegible *adj.* неразбо́рчивый. —**illegibility,** *n.* неразбо́рчивость.

illegitimate *adj.* **1,** (unlawful) незако́нный. **2,** (born out of wedlock) внебра́чный; незаконнорождённый. —**illegitimacy,** *n.* незако́нность.

ill-fated *adj.* злополу́чный.

illicit *adj.* незако́нный; недозво́ленный.

illiteracy *n.* негра́мотность. —**illiterate,** *adj.* негра́мотный; безгра́мотный.

ill-mannered *adj.* невоспи́танный.

illness *n.* боле́знь.

illogical *adj.* нелоги́чный.

ill-starred *adj.* злополу́чный.

ill-tempered *adj.* злой; раздражи́тельный.

ill-timed *adj.* несвоевре́менный.

illuminate *v.t.* освеща́ть. —**illuminated manuscript,** лицева́я ру́копись.

illuminating *adj.* **1,** (providing light) освети́тельный. **2,** *fig.* (enlightening) поучи́тельный.

illumination *n.* освеще́ние.

illusion *n.* иллю́зия.

illusory *adj.* иллюзо́рный; обма́нчивый; при́зрачный. *Also,* **illusive.**

illustrate *v.t.* иллюстри́ровать. —**illustration,** *n.* иллюстра́ция. —**illustrative,** *adj.* иллюстрати́вный. —**illustrator,** *n.* иллюстра́тор.

illustrious *adj.* знамени́тый; выдаю́щийся; просла́вленный.

image *n.* о́браз; изображе́ние. *He is the image of his father,* он вы́литый оте́ц; он весь в отца́.

imagery *n.* о́бразность.

imaginary *adj.* вообража́емый; мни́мый. *Imaginary line,* вообража́емая *or* усло́вная ли́ния.

imagination *n.* воображе́ние. *It's just your imagination,* э́то вам то́лько показа́лось.

imaginative *adj.* име́ющий большу́ю си́лу воображе́ния.

imagine *v.t. & i.* **1,** (visualize in the mind) вообража́ть; представля́ть себе́. **2,** (suppose) ду́мать; полага́ть.

imbalance *n.* несоотве́тствие.

imbecile *n.* слабоу́мный; идио́т; глупе́ц. —**imbecilic,** *adj.* идио́тский; дура́цкий. —**imbecility,** *n.* слабоу́мие; идиоти́зм.

imbed *v.* = **embed.**

imbibe *v.t.* **1,** (drink) пить. **2,** (absorb) впи́тывать.

imbue *v.t.* внуша́ть; вселя́ть; привива́ть.

imitate *v.t.* подражáть; имити́ровать.

imitation *n.* **1,** (act of imitating) подражáние; имитáция. **2,** (fake) имитáция. —*adj.* искýсственный. *Imitation pearl,* имитáция жéмчуга. —**imitative,** *adj.* подражáтельный. —**imitator,** *n.* подражáтель; имитáтор.

immaculate *adj.* безукори́зненно чи́стый. —**Immaculate Conception,** непорóчное зачáтие.

immaterial *adj.* **1,** (not consisting of matter) невещéственный. **2,** (inconsequential) безразли́чный. *It's immaterial to me,* мне э́то безразли́чно.

immature *adj.* незрéлый. —**immaturity,** *n.* незрéлость.

immeasurable *adj.* неизмери́мый. —**immeasurably,** *adv.* неизмери́мо.

immediacy *n.* неотлóжность.

immediate *adj.* **1,** (instant) немéдленный: *an immediate reply,* немéдленный отвéт. **2,** (nearest; next) ближáйший: *in the immediate future,* в ближáйшем бýдущем. **3,** (direct) непосрéдственный: *immediate threat,* непосрéдственная угрóза.

immediately *adv.* **1,** (right away) немéдленно; срáзу; сейчáс же; тóтчас же. **2,** (right now) сейчáс; тóтчас; немéдленно.

immemorial *adj.* незапáмятный. —**since time immemorial,** с незапáмятных времён.

immense *adj.* огрóмный. —**immensity,** *n.* огрóмность.

immerse *v.t.* погружáть. —**immersion,** *n.* погружéние.

immigrant *n.* иммигрáнт. —**immigrate,** *v.i.* иммигри́ровать.

immigration *n.* иммигрáция. —*adj.* иммиграциóнный.

imminent *adj.* надвигáющийся. *Be imminent,* надвигáться.

immobile *adj.* неподви́жный. —**immobility,** *n.* неподви́жность. —**immobilize,** *v.t.* дéлать неподви́жным; лишáть подви́жности.

immoderate *adj.* неумéренный. —**immoderation,** *n.* неумéренность; невоздéржанность.

immodest *adj.* нескрóмный. —**immodesty,** *n.* нескрóмность.

immolate *v.t.* приноси́ть в жéртву. —**immolation,** *n.* жертвоприношéние.

immoral *adj.* безнрáвственный. —**immorality,** *n.* безнрáвственность.

immortal *adj.* бессмéртный. —**immortality,** *n.* бессмéртие.

immortalize *v.t.* обессмéртить; увековéчивать. —**immortalization,** *n.* увековéчение.

immovable *adj.* неподви́жный; недви́жимый.

immune *adj.* **1,** (protected from a certain disease) невосприи́мчивый. *She is immune to the mumps,* у неё иммунитéт прóтив сви́нки. **2,** (exempt) свобóдный.

immunity *n.* иммунитéт; невосприи́мчивость. —**diplomatic immunity,** дипломати́ческая неприкоснóвенность; дипломати́ческий иммунитéт.

immunize *v.t.* иммунизи́ровать. —**immunization,** *n.* иммунизáция.

immutable *adj.* непрелóжный.

imp *n.* чертёнок; бесёнок; пострéл.

impact *n.* **1,** (force of a collision) удáр; толчóк. **2,** *fig.* (effect) влия́ние; воздéйствие; эффéкт. *Have a*

deep impact upon, оказáть глубóкое влия́ние на.

impair *v.t.* пóртить; вреди́ть. —**impairment,** *n.* пóрча; вред.

impale *v.t.* **1,** (pierce) пронзáть. **2,** (kill or torture) сажáть нá кол.

impart *v.t.* **1,** (transmit, as a quality) придавáть. **2,** (reveal; pass along) сообщáть.

impartial *adj.* беспристрáстный. —**impartiality,** *n.* беспристрáстие.

impassable *adj.* непроходи́мый; непроéзжий. —**impassability,** *n.* непроходи́мость.

impasse *n.* тупи́к.

impassioned *adj.* стрáстный; пы́лкий; горя́чий.

impassive *adj.* бесстрáстный. —**impassivity,** *n.* бесстрáстие.

impatience *n.* нетерпéние. —**impatient,** *adj.* нетерпели́вый. —**impatiently,** *adv.* нетерпели́во.

impeachment *n.* импи́чмент.

impeccable *adj.* безупрéчный; безукори́зненный.

impecunious *adj.* бездéнежный.

impede *v.t.* препя́тствовать; мешáть.

impediment *n.* **1,** (obstruction) препя́тствие. **2,** (defect) дефéкт: *speech impediment,* дефéкт рéчи.

impel *v.t.* побуждáть; заставля́ть.

impending *adj.* предстоя́щий; надвигáющийся.

impenetrability *n.* непроница́емость; непроходи́мость.

impenetrable *adj.* **1,** (impossible to pierce or break through) непроница́емый; непробивáемый. **2,** (impossible to walk or travel across) непроходи́мый. **3,** (impossible to see through) непрогля́дный.

impenitent *adj.* нераскáянный.

imperative *adj.* **1,** (essential) необходи́мый: *it is imperative that we be on time,* нам необходи́мо приéхать вóвремя. **2,** *gram.* повели́тельный. —*n.,* *gram.* повели́тельное наклонéние.

imperceptible *adj.* незамéтный; неощути́мый. —**imperceptibly,** *adv.* незамéтно.

imperfect *adj.* несовершéнный.

imperfection *n.* **1,** (state of being imperfect) несовершéнство. **2,** (defect; flaw) недостáток; дефéкт; несовершéнство.

imperfective *adj., gram.* несовершéнный: *imperfective aspect,* несовершéнный вид.

imperforate *adj.* беззубцóвый.

imperial *adj.* импéрский; императóрский. —**imperialism,** *n.* империали́зм. —**imperialist,** *n.* империали́ст. —**imperialistic,** *adj.* империалисти́ческий.

imperil *v.t.* подвергáть опáсности; стáвить под угрóзу.

imperious *adj.* повели́тельный; влáстный; императи́вный.

imperishable *adj.* **1,** (not subject to decay) непóртящийся. **2,** (enduring; everlasting) неруши́мый; нетлéнный.

impermanent *adj.* непостоя́нный. —**impermanence,** *n.* непостоя́нство.

impermeable *adj.* непроница́емый. —**impermeability,** *n.* непроница́емость.

impermissible *adj.* недопусти́мый; непозволи́тельный.

impersonal *adj.* безли́чный.

impersonate *v.t.* подражáть; выдавáть себя́ за.

impertinent *adj.* дéрзкий; нáглый; нахáльный. —**impertinence,** *n.* дéрзость; нáглость; нахáльство.

imperturbable *adj.* невозмутимый. —**imperturbability,** *n.* невозмутимость.

impervious *adj.* **1,** (impenetrable) непроницаемый. **2,** *fol. by* **to** (not open to; not influenced by) глух (к).

impetuosity *n.* опрометчивость.

impetuous *adj.* опрометчивый; порывистый. —**impetuously,** *adv.* опрометчиво.

impetus *n.* **1,** (motive force) импульс. **2,** (stimulus) толчок; побуждение.

impiety *n.* непочтительность.

impinge *v.i.* [*usu.* **impinge upon**] посягать на; покушаться на.

impish *adj.* проказливый; шаловливый.

implacable *adj.* неумолимый.

implant *v.t.* **1,** (set firmly in the ground) вкапывать. **2,** *med.* вживлять. **3,** *fig.* (instill; inculcate) прививать; укоренять; насаждать.

implausible *adj.* невероятный; неправдоподобный.

implement *n.* орудие; инструмент. —*v.t.* осуществлять. —**implementation,** *n.* осуществление.

implicate *v.t.* вовлекать; замешивать; впутывать.

implication *n.* **1,** (act of involving) вовлечение. **2,** (inference) намёк. **3,** (application; significance) значение.

implicit *adj.* **1,** (understood; implied) подразумеваемый. *Be implicit,* подразумеваться. *Implicit agreement,* молчаливое соглашение. **2,** (unreserved; absolute) беспрекословный. *Implicit faith,* слепая вера.

implore *v.t.* умолять.

imply *v.t.* **1,** (intimate; suggest) намекать. **2,** (presuppose) предполагать.

impolite *adj.* невежливый. —**impoliteness,** *n.* невежливость.

impolitic *adj.* неблагоразумный; нетактичный; бестактный.

imponderable *adj.* неясный; неопределённый; неизвестный.

import *v.t.* ввозить; импортировать. —*n.* **1,** *pl.* (goods imported) ввоз; импорт. **2,** (significance; importance) значение; важность. —*adj.* импортный; ввозный: *import duty,* импортная/ввозная пошлина.

importance *n.* важность: *of particular importance,* особой важности. *Assume an air of importance,* напускать на себя важность.

important *adj.* важный: *important person/event/discovery,* важное лицо/событие/открытие. *It's not important,* это не важно.

importation *n.* ввоз; импорт.

imported *adj.* ввозный; импортный.

importer *n.* импортёр.

importunate *adj.* навязчивый; назойливый; неотвязный.

importune *v.t.* докучать; надоедать.

impose *v.t.* **1,** (place; levy) налагать; облагать. *Impose sanctions,* применять санкции. **2,** (force) навязывать: *impose one's will on someone,* навязывать кому-нибудь свою волю. —*v.i.* [*usu.* **impose on** *or* **upon**] эксплуатировать.

imposing *adj.* внушительный; представительный; импозантный.

imposition *n.* **1,** (levying) наложение; обложение. **2,** (taking advantage) эксплуатация.

impossibility *n.* невозможность.

impossible *adj.* невозможный: *it/that is impossible,* это невозможно. *It is impossible to...,* нельзя (+ *inf.*). *Impossible task,* невыполнимая задача. *Impossible dream,* неисполнимая мечта. —*n., preceded by* **the** невозможное.

impost *n.* налог; подать.

impostor *n.* самозванец.

impotence *n.* **1,** (helplessness) бессилие. **2,** *med.* импотенция; половое бессилие.

impotent *adj.* **1,** (helpless) бессильный. **2,** *med.* импотентный.

impound *v.t.* **1,** (shut up in a pound) загонять. **2,** (take into legal custody) конфисковать.

impoverish *v.t.* **1,** (reduce to poverty) доводить до нищеты. **2,** (exhaust, as soil) истощать. —**impoverished,** *adj.* обеднёвший; обнищалый. —**impoverishment,** *n.* обеднение; обнищание.

impracticable *adj.* невыполнимый; неисполнимый; неосуществимый. —**impracticability,** *n.* невыполнимость; неисполнимость; неосуществимость.

impractical *adj.* непрактичный. —**impracticality,** *n.* непрактичность.

imprecate *v.t.* призывать на чью-нибудь голову. —**imprecation,** *n.* проклятие.

imprecise *adj.* неточный. —**imprecision,** *n.* неточность.

impregnable *adj.* неприступный.

impregnate *v.t.* **1,** (make pregnant) оплодотворять. **2,** (saturate) пропитывать. —**impregnation,** *n.* оплодотворение.

impresario *n.* антрепренёр; импресарио.

impress *v.t.* **1,** (imprint) отпечатывать. **2,** (produce a marked effect upon) производить впечатление на; импонировать. **3,** (establish firmly in one's mind) внушать: *impress upon someone the fact that...,* внушать кому-нибудь, что... **4,** (force into military service) насильно вербовать.

impression *n.* **1,** (imprint) оттиск; отпечаток. **2,** (effect produced on the mind) впечатление: *what are your impressions?,* какие у вас впечатления? *Make a good/deep impression on,* производить хорошее/глубокое впечатление на (+ *acc.*). *I was under the impression that...,* я думал(а), что... —**impressionable,** *adj.* впечатлительный.

impressionism *n.* импрессионизм. —**impressionist,** *n.* импрессионист. —*adj.* [*also,* **impressionistic**] импрессионистический; импрессионистский.

impressive *adj.* впечатляющий; внушительный; представительный.

impressment *n.* насильственная вербовка.

imprint *n.* отпечаток. —*v.t.* отпечатывать.

imprison *v.t.* заключать (в тюрьму); сажать (в тюрьму). —**imprisonment,** *n.* (тюремное) заключение. *Life imprisonment,* пожизненное заключение.

improbable *adj.* маловероятный; неправдоподобный. —**improbability,** *n.* невероятность; неправдоподобие.

impromptu *adj.* импровизированный. —*adv.* экспромтом.

improper *adj.* **1,** (incorrect) неправильный: *improper use of a word,* неправильное употребление слова. **2,** (unseemly) неприличный: *improper behavior,* неприличное поведение. **3,** (inappropriate) неподходя́щий: *improper dress,* неподходя́щая одёжда. —**improper fraction,** непра́вильная дробь.

improperly *adv.* **1,** (incorrectly) непра́вильно. **2,** (in an unseemly manner) неприли́чно.

impropriety *n.* **1,** (being improper or inappropriate) неприли́чие; неуме́стность. **2,** (improper act) просту́пок.

improve *v.t.* улучша́ть. —*v.i.* улучша́ться.

improvement *n.* улучше́ние. *Land improvement,* мелиора́ция.

improvident *adj.* непредусмотри́тельный; нерасчётливый. —**improvidence,** *n.* непредусмотри́тельность; нерасчётливость.

improvise *v.t. & i.* импровизи́ровать. —**improvisation,** *n.* импровиза́ция. —**improviser,** *n.* импровиза́тор.

imprudent *adj.* неблагоразу́мный; неосмотри́тельный. —**imprudence,** *n.* неблагоразу́мие; неосмотри́тельность.

impudent *adj.* де́рзкий; на́глый. —**impudence,** *n.* де́рзость; на́глость.

impugn *v.t.* оспа́ривать; подверга́ть сомне́нию.

impulse *n.* **1,** (impelling force; impetus) толчо́к; и́мпульс. **2,** (sudden inclination) поры́в; и́мпульс. *Yield to a sudden impulse,* подчиня́ться внеза́пному и́мпульсу.

impulsive *adj.* импульси́вный.

impunity *n.* безнака́занность. *With impunity,* безнака́занно.

impure *adj.* нечи́стый.

impurity *n.* **1,** (state of being impure) нечистота́. **2,** *pl.* (foreign matter) нечисто́ты.

impute *v.t.* **1,** (charge, as a crime) вменя́ть (что́-нибудь) в вину́ (+ *dat.*). **2,** (attribute) припи́сывать.

in *prep.* **1,** (in a certain place or condition) в (+ *prepl.*): *in Moscow,* в Москве́; *in the room,* в ко́мнате; *in the car,* в маши́не; *in one's hand,* в руке́; *in order,* в поря́дке; *in good condition,* в хоро́шем состоя́нии. ♦*With certain nouns* на: *in one's arms,* на рука́х; *in the sun,* на со́лнце; *in the sky,* на не́бе; *in the south,* на ю́ге; *in orbit,* на орби́те. **2,** (into; arriving in) в (+ *acc.*): *arrive in Moscow,* прие́хать в Москву́. *Dip a pen in ink,* обмакну́ть перо́ в черни́ла. *Put something in a box,* положи́ть что́-нибудь в я́щик. *Put someone in prison,* посади́ть кого́-нибудь в тюрьму́. **3,** (with months, years, centuries) в (+ *prepl.*): *in August,* в а́вгусте; *in 1900,* в ты́сяча девятисо́том году́. **4,** (with seasons, parts of the day) *rendered by the instr. case: in the morning,* у́тром; *in the evening,* ве́чером; *in the fall,* о́сенью. **5,** (with expressions of time, indicating how long it takes or took to complete a task) в; за: *read a book in two days,* проче́сть кни́гу в/за два дня. **6,** (indicating a certain amount of time from now) че́рез: *he will be here in ten minutes,* он придёт че́рез де́сять мину́т. **7,** (with languages) по-; на (+ *prepl.*): *in Russian,* по-ру́сски; на ру́сском языке́. **8,** (with weather conditions) в (+ *acc.*): *in such weather/heat,* в таку́ю пого́ду/жару́. **9,** (in the person of) в лице́ (+ *gen.*): *a true friend in him,* ве́рный друг в его́ лице́. **10,** *expressing various relationships:* в (+ *prepl.*): *in any case,* во вся́ком слу́чае; *in the light of,* в све́те (+ *gen.*); *poor in arithmetic,* слаб в арифме́тике; *fall in battle,* пасть в бою́. **11,** *expressing various relationships, rendered by the instr. case: rich in vitamins,* бога́т витами́нами; *paint in oils,* писа́ть мас-

лом; *end in disaster,* ко́нчиться катастро́фой. **12,** *in various miscellaneous expressions: in fact,* факти́чески; на са́мом де́ле; *in jest,* в шу́тку; *in passing,* мимохо́дом; вскользь; *in short,* коро́че говоря́. —*adj.* **1,** (at home) до́ма. **2,** (in one's office) у себя́. **3,** (having arrived) прибы́вший: *the train is in,* по́езд прибы́л *or* пришёл. —*adv. Usu. rendered by a prefixed verb: come in,* входи́ть; *drop in,* заходи́ть; *cave in,* обвали́ться. —**in for,** *rendered by* ждать *or* предстоя́ть: *I know what I'm in for,* я зна́ю, что меня́ ждёт. *We are in for a cold winter,* нам предстои́т холо́дная зима́. —**in on, 1,** (having a part in) прича́стный к. **2,** (having knowledge of) посвящён в: *in on the secret,* посвящён в та́йну. —**in that,** тем, что... —**know all the ins and outs,** знать все хо́ды и вы́ходы.

inability *n.* неспосо́бность; неуме́ние.

in absentia зао́чно: *be tried in absentia,* суди́ться зао́чно.

inaccessible *adj.* недосту́пный. —**inaccessibility,** *n.* недосту́пность.

inaccurate *adj.* нето́чный. —**inaccuracy,** *n.* нето́чность.

inaction *n.* безде́йствие.

inactive *adj.* безде́йственный; безде́ятельный. —**inactivity,** *n.* безде́йствие; безде́ятельность.

inadequacy *n.* **1,** (state of being inadequate) недоста́точность. **2,** (failing; lack) недоста́ток.

inadequate *adj.* недоста́точный; не отвеча́ющий тре́бованиям.

inadmissible *adj.* недопусти́мый.

inadvertence *n.* **1,** (carelessness) невнима́тельность; небре́жность. **2,** (oversight) недосмо́тр; опло́шность.

inadvertent *adj.* **1,** (not duly attentive) невнима́тельный; небре́жный. **2,** (unintentional) неча́янный. —**inadvertently,** *adv.* неча́янно; не́хотя.

inadvisable *adj.* нецелесообра́зный.

inalienable *adj.* неотъе́млемый.

inane *adj.* глу́пый; ну́дный.

inanimate *adj.* неодушевлённый.

inanity *n.* глу́пость.

inapplicable *adj.* неприме́ни́мый.

inappropriate *adj.* неуме́стный; неподходя́щий.

inarticulate *adj.* нечленоразде́льный; невня́тный.

inasmuch as так как; поско́льку; ввиду́ того́, что.

inattention *n.* невнима́ние. —**inattentive,** *adj.* невнима́тельный.

inaudible *adj.* неслы́шный.

inaugural *adj.* вступи́тельный. *Inaugural address,* речь при вступле́нии в до́лжность.

inaugurate *v.t.* **1,** (induct into office) вводи́ть в до́лжность. **2,** (introduce; launch) вводи́ть. —**inauguration,** *n.* инаугура́ция.

inauspicious *adj.* неблагоприя́тный; неутеши́тельный.

inborn *adj.* врождённый; прирождённый. *Also,* **inbred.**

incalculable *adj.* несме́тный; неисчисли́мый.

incandescence *n.* нака́л; кале́ние.

incandescent *adj.* накалённый. —**incandescent lamp,** ла́мпа нака́ливания.

incantation *n.* заклина́ние; за́говор.

incapable *adj.* неспосо́бный: *incapable of telling a lie,* неспосо́бный на ложь.

incapacitate *v.t.* де́лать нетрудоспосо́бным. —**in-**

capacitated, *adj.* нетрудоспособный. —**incapacity,** *n.* нетрудоспособность.

incarcerate *v.t.* заключать (в тюрьму); заточать (в тюрьму). —**incarceration,** *n.* (тюремное) заключение; заточение.

incarnate *adj.* воплощённый. —*v.t.* воплощать. —**incarnation,** *n.* воплощение.

incautious *adj.* неосторожный.

incendiary *adj.* зажигательный: *incendiary bomb,* зажигательная бомба. *Incendiary speeches,* зажигательные речи.

incense *n.* фимиам; ладан. —*v.t.* приводить в ярость; разгневать. —**incensed,** *adj.* разгневанный. *Become incensed,* приходить в ярость.

incentive *n.* побуждение; толчок; стимул.

inception *n.* начало.

inceptive *adj.* начальный. —**inceptive verb,** начинательный глагол.

incertitude *n.* неуверенность.

incessant *adj.* беспрестанный; бесконечный; непрестанный. —**incessantly,** *adv.* беспрестанно; бесконечно.

incest *n.* кровосмешение. —**incestuous,** *adj.* кровосмесительный.

inch *n.* дюйм. —*v.i.* ползти: *inch forward,* ползти вперёд. —**every inch a...,** с головы до ног; до мозга костей. —**inch by inch,** пядь за пядью. —**not yield** (or **budge) an inch,** не уступить ни пяди *or* ни на йоту. —**with an inch of,** на волосок (*or* на волоске) от. *Beat within an inch of one's life,* избивать до полусмерти; бить смертным боем.

inchoate *adj.* **1,** (in a rudimentary stage) зачаточный. **2,** (lacking order; shapeless) бесформенный.

incidence *n.* **1,** (prevalence) распространение. *Incidence of a disease,* заболеваемость. **2,** *physics* падение: *angle of incidence,* угол падения.

incident *n.* происшествие; инцидент. *Without incident,* без происшествий. *Border incident,* пограничный инцидент. —*adj.* [*usu.* **incident to**] связанный с.

incidental *adj.* **1,** *fol. by* **to** (associated with) связанный (с). **2,** (minor; secondary) побочный. *Incidental expenses,* случайные расходы.

incidentally *adv.* между прочим; кстати.

incinerate *v.t.* испепелять; сжигать дотла. —**incinerator,** *n.* мусоросжигательная печь.

incipient *adj.* начальный.

incise *v.t.* **1,** (cut into) надрезать. **2,** (carve; engrave) вырезать; насекать.

incision *n.* разрез; надрез.

incisive *adj.* **1,** (trenchant) тонкий. **2,** (keen; penetrating) проницательный.

incisor *n.* резец.

incite *v.t.* возбуждать; подстрекать. —**incitement,** *n.* подстрекательство.

inclement *adj.* ненастный. *Inclement weather,* ненастье; непогода.

inclination *n.* **1,** (slant; slope) наклон; наклонение. *Angle of inclination,* угол наклона. **2,** (tendency; disposition) склонность; наклонность.

incline *v.t.* наклонять; склонять. —*v.i.* наклоняться; склоняться. —*n.* наклон; склон; уклон; скат.

inclined *adj.* **1,** (sloping) наклонный. **2,** *fol. by* **to** (tending toward) склонный (к). *I am inclined to think that...,* я склонен думать, что...

include *v.t.* включать. —**including,** *prep.* включая; в том числе.

inclusion *n.* включение.

inclusive *adj.* **1,** *fol. by* **of** (including) включая. **2,** (within the limits mentioned) включительно.

incognito *adv.* инкогнито.

incoherent *adj.* бессвязный; несвязный. —**incoherence,** *n.* бессвязность; несвязность.

incombustible *adj.* невоспламеняемый.

income *n.* доход. —**income tax,** подоходный налог.

incoming *adj.* входящий; вступающий.

incommensurable *adj.* несоизмеримый. —**incommensurability,** *n.* несоизмеримость.

incommensurate *adj.* несоразмерный.

incommode *v.t.* затруднять; мешать; беспокоить. —**incommodious,** *adj.* неудобный.

incommunicado *adj. & adv.* лишённый права сообщения.

incomparable *adj.* **1,** (not comparable) несравнимый. **2,** (matchless; unsurpassed) несравнённый. —**incomparably,** *adv.* несравнённо.

incompatible *adj.* несовместимый. —**incompatibility,** *n.* несовместимость.

incompetence *n.* **1,** (lack of ability) некомпетентность. **2,** *law* неправомочность; недееспособность.

incompetent *adj.* **1,** (lacking ability) некомпетентный. **2,** *law* неправомочный; недееспособный.

incomplete *adj.* неполный; незаконченный. —**incompleteness,** *n.* неполнота.

incomprehensible *adj.* непонятный; непостижимый. —**incomprehensibility,** *n.* непонятность; непостижимость. —**incomprehensibly,** *adv.* непонятно.

incomprehension *n.* непонимание.

inconceivable *adj.* невообразимый.

inconclusive *adj.* неокончательный.

incongruous *adj.* несообразный. —**incongruity,** *n.* несообразность.

inconsequential *adj.* несущественный; не имеющий значения.

inconsiderate *adj.* невнимательный.

inconsistent *adj.* непоследовательный. —**inconsistency,** *n.* непоследовательность.

inconsolable *adj.* безутешный; неутешный.

inconspicuous *adj.* незаметный; неприметный.

inconstant *adj.* непостоянный. —**inconstancy,** *n.* непостоянство.

incontestable *adj.* неоспоримый; бесспорный.

incontinence *n.* **1,** (immoderate behavior) невоздержанность. **2,** *med.* недержание (мочи). —**incontinent,** *adj.* невоздержанный.

incontrovertible *adj.* неопровержимый.

inconvenience *n.* неудобство. —*v.t.* затруднять. —**inconvenient,** *adj.* неудобный.

incorporate *v.t.* **1,** (combine) объединять. **2,** *fol. by* **into** (make part of) включать (в); вводить (в); сводить (в). **3,** (form into a corporation) инкорпорировать. —*v.i.* объединяться. —**incorporation,** *n.* инкорпорация.

incorporeal *adj.* бестелесный.

incorrect *adj.* неправильный; неверный. —**incorrectly,** *adv.* неправильно; неверно.

incorrigible *adj.* неисправимый.

incorruptible *adj.* неподку́пный. —**incorruptibility**, *n.* неподку́пность.

increase *v.t.* увели́чивать. —*v.i.* увели́чиваться; возраста́ть. —*n.* увеличе́ние; приро́ст.

increasing *adj.* возраста́ющий. *An ever increasing number of people*, всё бо́льшее коли́чество люде́й.

increasingly *adv.* всё бо́лее: *the work is becoming increasingly difficult*, рабо́та стано́вится всё бо́лее тру́дной.

incredible *adj.* невероя́тный. —**incredibly**, *adv.* невероя́тно; до невероя́тности.

incredulity *n.* недове́рие. —**incredulous**, *adj.* недове́рчивый.

increment *n.* прираще́ние.

incriminate *v.t.* изоблича́ть. —**incriminating**, *adj.* изобличи́тельный.

incubate *v.t.* сиде́ть на (я́йцах). —**incubation**, *n.* инкуба́ция. —**incubator**, *n.* инкуба́тор.

inculcate *v.t.* внуша́ть; вселя́ть; внедря́ть.

incumbent *adj.* **1**, *fol. by on or upon* (obligatory) надлежа́щий: *it is incumbent on us to help*, нам надлежи́т помо́чь. **2**, (in office) стоя́щий у вла́сти. —*n.* тот, кто стои́т у вла́сти.

incur *v.t.* **1**, (bring on oneself) навлека́ть на себя́: *incur suspicion*, навлека́ть на себя́ подозре́ние. **2**, (suffer, as losses) нести́ (убы́тки). **3**, (contract, as debts) де́лать (долги́).

incurable *adj.* неизлечи́мый.

incursion *n.* вторже́ние; наше́ствие; набе́г.

indebted *adj.* [*usu.* **indebted to**] в долгу́ (у *or* пе́ред); обя́зан (+ *dat.*). —**indebtedness**, *n.* задо́лженность.

indecency *n.* неприли́чие.

indecent *adj.* неприли́чный. —**indecently**, *adv.* неприли́чно.

indecipherable *adj.* **1**, (of a coded message) не подда́ющийся расшифро́вке. **2**, (of handwriting) неразбо́рчивый.

indecision *n.* нереши́тельность; нереши́мость.

indecisive *adj.* нереши́тельный. —**indecisiveness**, *n.* нереши́тельность.

indeclinable *adj.* несклоня́емый.

indecorous *adj.* некорре́ктный; неприли́чный.

indeed *adv.* в са́мом де́ле; действи́тельно. *I am very glad indeed*, я действи́тельно о́чень рад. *Yes, indeed!*, о да!; да, да! —*interj.* да ну!; вот ещё!

indefatigable *adj.* неутоми́мый. —**indefatigability**, *n.* неутоми́мость.

indefensible *adj.* **1**, *mil.* неприго́дный для оборо́ны. **2**, (inexcusable) непрости́тельный.

indefinable *adj.* неопредели́мый.

indefinite *adj.* неопределённый: *for an indefinite period*, на неопределённый срок. *Indefinite leave of absence*, бессро́чный о́тпуск. —**indefinite article**, неопределённый арти́кль *or* член.

indefinitely *adv.* на неопределённое вре́мя.

indelible *adj.* **1**, (unable to be erased) несмыва́емый: *indelible ink*, несмыва́емые черни́ла. *Indelible pencil*, хими́ческий каранда́ш. **2**, (permanent; lasting) неизгла́димый.

indelicate *adj.* неделика́тный; некорре́ктный; нескро́мный. —**indelicacy**, *n.* неделика́тность.

indemnify *v.t.* возмеща́ть; компенси́ровать. —**indemnification**, *n.* возмеще́ние.

indemnity *n.* **1**, (compensation) возмеще́ние. **2**,

(protection) гара́нтия.

indent *v.t.* **1**, (space in from the margin) писа́ть с абза́ца; писа́ть с о́тступом. **2**, (notch) зазу́бривать. —*v.i.* отступа́ть: *indent slightly*, отступа́ть немно́го.

indentation *n.* **1**, (notch) зазу́брина. **2**, [*also*, **indention**] (spacing in from the margin) абза́ц; о́тступ.

independence *n.* **1**, (freedom from foreign rule) незави́симость. **2**, (self-sufficiency) самостоя́тельность.

independent *adj.* **1**, (autonomous) незави́симый. **2**, (self-sufficient; done on one's own) самостоя́тельный. —**independently**, *adv.* незави́симо; самостоя́тельно.

in-depth *adj.* глубо́кий; углублённый.

indescribable *adj.* неопису́емый.

indestructible *adj.* неразруши́мый.

indeterminate *adj.* неопределённый.

index *n.* **1**, (alphabetical list) указа́тель. **2**, *math.*; *econ.* показа́тель; и́ндекс: *price index*, и́ндекс цен. —*v.t.* **1**, (provide with an index) снабжа́ть указа́телем. **2**, (make an index of) заноси́ть в указа́тель. —**index finger**, указа́тельный па́лец.

India ink тушь.

Indian *n.* **1**, (American) инде́ец. **2**, (of India) инди́ец. —*adj.* **1**, (of America) инде́йский. **2**, (of India) инди́йский. —**Indian Ocean**, Инди́йский океа́н. —**Indian summer**, ба́бье ле́то.

indicate *v.t.* **1**, (point out) ука́зывать. **2**, (be a sign of) ука́зывать на; означа́ть.

indication *n.* указа́ние; при́знак.

indicative *adj.* **1**, (revealing) показа́тельный. *Be indicative of*, ука́зывать на; говори́ть о. **2**, *gram.* изъяви́тельный: *indicative mood*, изъяви́тельное наклоне́ние.

indicator *n.* **1**, (needle, dial, etc.) указа́тель; индика́тор. **2**, *fig.* (general indication) показа́тель.

indict *v.t.* обвиня́ть; предъявля́ть обвине́ние (+ *dat.*); привлека́ть к уголо́вной отве́тственности.

indictment *n.* **1**, (act of indicting) обвине́ние. **2**, (formal written accusation) обвини́тельный акт; обвини́тельное заключе́ние.

indifference *n.* равноду́шие; безразли́чие. *With indifference*, равноду́шно; безразли́чно.

indifferent *adj.* **1**, (unconcerned; apathetic) безразли́чный; равноду́шный. **2**, (mediocre) посре́дственный.

indigence *n.* нужда́; нищета́.

indigenous *adj.* коренно́й; тузе́мный.

indigent *adj.* неиму́щий; обездо́ленный.

indigestible *adj.* неудобовари́мый.

indigestion *n.* несваре́ние желу́дка; расстро́йство пищеваре́ния.

indignant *adj.* негоду́ющий; возмущённый. *Be indignant*, негодова́ть; возмуща́ться.

indignation *n.* негодова́ние; возмуще́ние.

indignity *n.* оскорбле́ние; униже́ние: *suffer indignities*, подверга́ться оскорбле́ниям/униже́ниям.

indigo *n.* инди́го. —*adj.* цве́та инди́го.

indirect *adj.* **1**, (roundabout) непрямо́й. **2**, (not pertaining to or following directly) ко́свенный; побо́чный. *Indirect evidence*, ко́свенные ули́ки. —**indirect object**, ко́свенное дополне́ние.

indirectly *adv.* ко́свенно.

indiscernible *adj.* неразличи́мый.

indiscreet *adj.* нескро́мный; беста́ктный. —**indis-**

cretion, *n.* бестáктность: *commit an indiscretion,* совершúть бестáктность.

indiscriminate *adj.* **1,** (not discriminating) неразбóрчивый. **2,** (random; haphazard) огýльный. —**indiscriminately,** *adv.* без разбóра; без вúбора.

indispensable *adj.* незаменúмый.

indisposed *adj.* **1,** (unwell) нездорóвый. **2,** (disinclined) не расположён.

indisposition *n.* **1,** (ailment) недомогáние. **2,** (disinclination) нерасположéние.

indisputable *adj.* неоспорúмый; бесспóрный.

indissoluble *adj.* **1,** (incapable of being dissolved) нерастворúмый. **2,** (lasting; permanent) неразрúвный; нерасторжúмый; нерушúмый.

indistinct *adj.* неотчётливый; неáсный.

indistinguishable *adj.* неразличúмый.

indium *n.* úндий.

individual *adj.* отдéльный; индивидуáльный. —*n.* индивúдуум; лицó; лúчность; осóба; óсобь.

individualism *n.* индивидуалúзм. —**individualist,** *n.* индивидуалúст. —**individuality,** *n.* индивидуáльность.

individually *adv.* отдéльно; в отдéльности.

indivisible *adj.* неделúмый; неразделúмый; нераздéльный. —**indivisibility,** *n.* делúмость.

indoctrinate *v.t.* обрабáтывать. —**indoctrination,** *n.* обрабóтка.

Indo-European *adj.* индоевропéйский.

indolent *adj.* ленúвый; вáлый. —**indolence,** *n.* лень; вáлость.

indomitable *adj.* неукротúмый.

Indonesian *adj.* индонезúйский. —*n.* индонезúец.

indoor *adj.* **1,** (situated inside) внýтренний. *Indoor pool,* закрúтый бассéйн. **2,** (taking place inside) кóмнатный: *indoor games,* кóмнатные úгры.

indoors *adv.* в дóме; внутрú дóма; в закрúтом помещéнии. *Stay indoors,* не выходúть на ýлицу.

indorse *v.* = **endorse.**

indubitable *adj.* несомнéнный. —**indubitably,** *adv.* несомнéнно.

induce *v.t.* **1,** (cause; prompt) побуждáть. **2,** (persuade; prevail upon) уговорúть. **3,** (cause; bring on) вызывáть.

inducement *n.* побуждéние; примáнка.

induct *v.t.* **1,** (install in office) вводúть в дóлжность. **2,** *mil.* зачислáть на воéнную слýжбу.

inductee *n.* призывнúк.

induction *n.* **1,** (installation in office) введéние в дóлжность. **2,** *mil.* зачислéние на воéнную слýжбу. **3,** *electricity; logic* индýкция. —**induction center,** призывнóй пункт. —**induction coil,** индукциóнная катýшка.

inductive *adj.* индуктúвный.

indulge *v.t.* потвóрствовать; потакáть. —*v.i.* [*usu.* **indulge in**] предавáться (+ *dat.*); баловáться (+ *instr.*). *Indulge in a cigar,* баловáться сигáрой. *Indulge in fantasy,* предавáться фантáзиям.

indulgence *n.* потвóрство; потакáние; поблáжка; снисходúтельность.

indulgent *adj.* снисходúтельный.

industrial *adj.* промúшленный; индустриáльный.

industrialist *n.* промúшленник.

industrialize *v.t.* индустриализúровать. —**industrialization,** *n.* индустриализáция.

industrious *adj.* трудолюбúвый; прилéжный. —**in-**

dustriousness, *n.* трудолюбúе; прилежáние.

industry *n.* **1,** (branch of the economy) промúшленность; индýстрия. **2,** (diligence) трудолюбúе.

inebriate *v.t.* опьянáть. —**inebriated,** *adj.* пьáный; опьянéвший.

inedible *adj.* несъедóбный.

ineffable *adj.* невыразúмый; несказáнный; неописýемый.

ineffective *adj.* неэффектúвный; безрезультáтный. *Also,* **ineffectual.**

inefficacy *n.* неэффектúвность.

inefficient *adj.* неэффектúвный. —**inefficiency,** *n.* неэффектúвность.

ineligible *adj.* не имéющий прáва; не могýщий быть úзбранным.

inept *adj.* **1,** (incompetent) неумéлый; бездáрный. **2,** (inappropriate) неумéстный. —**ineptitude,** *n.* неумéние; бездáрность.

inequality *n.* нерáвенство.

inequitable *adj.* несправедлúвый. —**inequity,** *n.* несправедлúвость.

ineradicable *adj.* **1,** (indelible, as of ink) несмывáемый. **2,** (ingrained) неискоренúмый.

inert *adj.* **1,** *chem.* инéртный: *inert gases,* инéртные гáзы. **2,** (sluggish) инéртный.

inertia *n.* **1,** *physics* инéрция. **2,** *fig.* (disinclination to move or act) инéрция; инéртность.

inescapable *adj.* неизбéжный; неминýемый.

inestimable *adj.* неоценúмый.

inevitable *adj.* неизбéжный. —**inevitability,** *n.* неизбéжность. —**inevitably,** *adv.* неизбéжно.

inexact *adj.* нетóчный. —**inexactness; inexactitude,** *n.* нетóчность.

inexcusable *adj.* непростúтельный.

inexhaustible *adj.* неистощúмый; неисчерпáемый; неиссякáемый.

inexorable *adj.* неумолúмый; непреклóнный.

inexpensive *adj.* дешёвый; недорогóй. —**inexpensively,** *adv.* дёшево; недóрого.

inexperience *n.* неóпытность. —**inexperienced,** *adj.* неóпытный.

inexplicable *adj.* необъяснúмый.

inexpressible *adj.* невыразúмый.

inexpressive *adj.* невыразúтельный.

infallible *adj.* непогрешúмый. —**infallibility,** *n.* непогрешúмость.

infamous *adj.* позóрный; гнýсный.

infamy *n.* **1,** (shame) позóр. **2,** (infamous character) гнýсность.

infancy *n.* младéнчество. *Since infancy,* с рáннего дéтства.

infant *n.* младéнец. —*adj.* дéтский: *infant mortality,* дéтская смéртность.

infanticide *n.* детоубúйство.

infantile *adj.* дéтский; младéнческий. —**infantile paralysis,** дéтский паралúч.

infantry *n.* пехóта. —*adj.* пехóтный: *infantry regiment,* пехóтный полк. —**infantryman,** *n.* пехотúнец.

infatuated *adj.* Be infatuated with, безýмно увлéчься (+ *instr.*). —**infatuation,** *n.* увлечéние.

infeasible *adj.* невыполнúмый; неисполнúмый; неосуществúмый.

infect *v.t.* заражáть. —**infection,** *n.* зарáза; заражéние; инфéкция.

infectious *adj.* **1,** *med.* заразный; инфекционный. **2,** *fig.* (of a smile, laughter, etc.) заразительный.

infer *v.t.* **1,** (deduce) заключать; выводить. **2,** (imply) намекать. **—inference,** *n.* вывод; заключение.

inferior *adj.* **1,** (lower in rank) низший. **2,** (of poor or poorer quality) неполноценный; недоброкачественный. **—** *n.* подчинённый.

inferiority *n.* неполноценность; недоброкачественность. **—inferiority complex,** комплекс неполноценности.

infernal *adj.* **1,** (hellish) адский. **2,** *colloq.* (damnable) проклятый.

inferno *n.* ад.

infertile *adj.* **1,** (unable to produce offspring) бесплодный. **2,** (barren, as of soil) неплодородный; бесплодный. **—infertility,** *n.* бесплодие; неплодородность.

infest *v.t.* наводнять. *Be infested with,* кишеть (+ *instr.*). *Lice-infested,* вшивый.

infidel *n.* неверный.

infidelity *n.* неверность; измена.

infighting *n.* ближний бой.

infiltrate *v.t.* просачиваться в; проникать в. **—infiltration,** *n.* просачивание; проникновение.

infinite *adj.* бесконечный; безграничный. **—infinitely,** *adv.* бесконечно; *(with comp. adjectives)* неизмеримо.

infinitesimal *adj.* бесконечно малый.

infinitive *n.* неопределённая форма глагола; инфинитив.

infinity *n.* бесконечность.

infirm *adj.* немощный.

infirmary *n.* небольшая больница; лазарет.

infirmity *n.* немощь.

inflame *v.t.* **1,** (fire up) зажигать. **2,** (arouse, as passions) разжигать. **—inflamed,** *adj.* воспалённый. *Become inflamed,* воспаляться.

inflammable *adj.* горючий; огнеопасный. **—inflammability,** *n.* воспламеняемость.

inflammation *n.* воспаление.

inflammatory *adj.* **1,** *med.* воспалительный. **2,** (tending to incite) зажигательный.

inflatable *adj.* надувной.

inflate *v.t.* **1,** (fill with air) надувать; накачивать. **2,** (raise or increase unduly) вздувать; раздувать. *Inflated figures/prices,* дутые цифры/цены.

inflation *n.* **1,** (act of inflating) надувание. **2,** *econ.* инфляция. **—inflationary,** *adj.* инфляционный.

inflect *v.t.* **1,** (change the pitch of, as one's voice) модулировать. **2,** *gram.* склонять; спрягать. *Inflected language,* флективный язык.

inflection *also,* **inflexion** *n.* **1,** (of the voice) модуляция. **2,** *gram.* флексия.

inflexible *adj.* **1,** (stiff; rigid) негибкий; несгибаемый. **2,** (intransigent) непреклонный; несгибаемый. **—inflexibility,** *n.* непреклонность.

inflexion *n.* = **inflection.**

inflict *v.t.* наносить: *inflict losses on,* наносить потери (+ *dat.*). *Inflict punishment on,* подвергать (кого-нибудь) наказанию.

inflow *n.* приток; наплыв.

influence *n.* **1,** (impact; effect) влияние; воздействие. **2,** (connections; pull) блат. **—** *v.t.* влиять на; воздействовать на. **—influential,** *adj.* влиятельный.

influenza *n.* грипп.

influx *n.* наплыв; прилив; приток.

inform *v.t.* сообщать; извещать; осведомлять; уведомлять; информировать. **—** *v.i.* [*usu.* **inform on** or **against**] доносить (на).

informal *adj.* **1,** (casual) без формальностей. **2,** (unofficial) неофициальный. **—informality,** *n.* отсутствие формальностей.

informant *n.* осведомитель; информатор.

information *n.* сведения; информация. *For your information,* к вашему сведению. **—** *adj.* справочный: *information bureau,* справочное бюро.

informative *adj.* поучительный; содержательный.

informed *adj.* осведомлённый. *Keep someone informed,* держать кого-нибудь в курсе.

informer *n.* осведомитель; доносчик.

infraction *n.* нарушение.

infrared *adj.* инфракрасный.

infrequent *adj.* редкий. **—infrequently,** *adv.* редко.

infringe *v.t.* нарушать. **—** *v.i.* [*usu.* **infringe on** or **upon**] посягать (на); вторгаться (в).

infringement *n.* **1,** (violation) нарушение. **2,** (encroachment) посягательство.

infuriate *v.t.* приводить в ярость; разъярять; бесить.

infuse *v.t.* вливать; вселять; внушать. **—infusion,** *n.* вливание.

ingenious *adj.* **1,** (of an idea, solution, etc.) остроумный; блестящий. **2,** (of a device) замысловатый; затейливый. **3,** (of a person) изобретательный; хитроумный. **—ingenuity,** *n.* изобретательность.

ingenuous *adj.* бесхитростный; простодушный.

ingest *v.t.* глотать; проглатывать.

inglorious *adj.* бесславный.

ingot *n.* слиток.

ingrain *v.t.* укоренять. **—ingrained,** *adj.* укоренившийся; закоренелый; закоснелый. *Become ingrained,* закоренеть; укореняться. *Become ingrained in one's memory,* запечатлеться в памяти.

ingratiate *v.t. Ingratiate oneself with,* заискивать перед; снискать (чью-нибудь) милость.

ingratiating *adj.* **1,** (pleasing) подкупающий. **2,** (meant to gain favor) заискивающий; вкрадчивый; льстивый.

ingratitude *n.* неблагодарность.

ingredient *n.* составная часть; ингредиент.

ingrown *adj.* **1,** (grown into the flesh) вросший. **2,** (inborn) врождённый.

inhabit *v.t.* обитать в *or* на. **—inhabitant,** *n.* житель; обитатель. **—inhabited,** *adj.* обитаемый.

inhalation *n.* вдыхание.

inhalator *n.* ингалятор.

inhale *v.t. & i.* вдыхать. **—** *v.i.* (draw in tobacco smoke) затягиваться.

inhaler *n.* ингалятор.

inherent *adj.* **1,** (intrinsic) присущий. **2,** (inborn) врождённый. **—inherently,** *adv.* по своему существу.

inherit *v.t.* наследовать; получить в наследство.

inheritance *n.* **1,** (act of inheriting) наследование. **2,** (something inherited) наследство. **—inheritance tax,** налог на наследство.

inherited *adj.* унаследованный.

inhibit *v.t.* стеснять; тормозить. **—inhibited,** *adj.* стеснительный. **—inhibition,** *n.* стеснение.

inhospitable *adj.* негостеприймный; неприветливый.

inhuman *adj.* бесчеловечный. —**inhumanity,** *n.* бесчеловечность.

inimical *adj.* **1,** *fol. by* **to** (detrimental) вредный (для). **2,** (hostile) враждебный.

inimitable *adj.* неподражаемый; неповторимый.

iniquitous *adj.* гнусный; порочный.

iniquity *n.* **1,** (wickedness) гнусность; порочность. **2,** *usu. pl.* (transgression) грех; проступок; прегрешение. —**den of iniquity,** притон разврата.

initial *adj.* начальный; первоначальный. —*n.* инициал. —*v.t.* **1,** (place one's initials on) ставить инициалы на; подписывать инициалами. **2,** (tentatively approve, as a treaty or document) парафировать.

initially *adv.* сначала; вначале.

initiate *v.t.* **1,** (begin; launch) вводить; быть инициатором (+ *gen.*). **2,** (introduce to a subject) знакомить. **3,** (admit; induct) вводить; посвящать.

initiation *n.* посвящение. *Initiation fee,* вступительный взнос.

initiative *n.* инициатива; почин. *Take the initiative,* взять инициативу в свои руки.

initiator *n.* инициатор; зачинатель.

inject *v.t.* **1,** *med.* впрыскивать; вводить. **2,** (introduce, as a new element) вводить. **3,** (interject) вставлять.

injection *n.* инъекция; впрыскивание; вливание; укол. *Give an injection to,* сделать инъекцию/укол (+ *dat.*).

injector *n.* форсунка: *fuel injector,* форсунка горючего.

injudicious *adj.* неблагоразумный; неразумный.

injunction *n.* **1,** (order) предписание. **2,** *law* судебный запрет.

injure *v.t.* **1,** (cause physical harm to) повреждать; ушибать. *Be injured,* пострадать; получить повреждение *or* ранение. *No one was injured,* никто не пострадал. **2,** (be injurious to) вредить.

injured *adj.* **1,** (damaged; hurt) ушибленный; раненый; поврежденный. **2,** (offended) обиженный.

injurious *adj.* вредный. *Smoking is injurious to health,* курение вредит здоровью.

injury *n.* **1,** (physical harm) повреждение; ранение; травма. **2,** (damage) вред.

injustice *n.* несправедливость. *Do someone an injustice,* быть несправедливым к кому-нибудь.

ink *n.* чернила: *write in ink,* писать чернилами. *Printer's ink,* типографская краска. —*adj.* чернильный: *ink spot,* чернильное пятно.

inkblot *n.* клякса.

inkling *n.* **1,** (hint; suggestion) намёк. **2,** (vague idea) представление.

ink pad подушка для штемпелей; штемпельная подушка.

inkstand *n.* чернильный прибор.

inkwell *n.* чернильница.

inky *adj.* покрытый чернилами; в чернилах.

inlaid *adj.* инкрустированный; мозаичный. *Inlaid table,* столик с инкрустацией.

inland *adj.* внутренний: *inland waterways,* внутренние водные пути. *Inland sea,* внутреннее *or* закрытое море. —*adv.* внутрь страны; в глубь страны.

in-law *n.* свойственник.

inlay *v.t.* **1,** (set flush into a surface) вкладывать. **2,** (decorate by inserting such designs) инкрустировать. —*n.* **1,** (inlaid work) мозаика; инкрустация. **2,** *dent.* пломба.

inlet *n.* **1,** (bay) бухта. **2,** (creek) заводь; затон.

inmate *n.* **1,** (in a prison) заключённый. **2,** (in an asylum) больной.

inn *n.* постоялый двор; трактир.

innards *n.pl.* внутренности.

innate *adj.* врождённый; прирождённый; природный.

inner *adj.* внутренний. —**inner ear,** внутреннее ухо. —**inner sole,** стелька. —**inner tube,** камера.

innermost *adj.* **1,** (farthest in) самый глубокий. **2,** (most intimate, as of feelings) сокровенный.

innkeeper *n.* трактирщик.

innocence *n.* **1,** (absence of guilt) невиновность. **2,** (lack of sophistication) невинность.

innocent *adj.* **1,** (not guilty) невиновный. **2,** (naïve; harmless) невинный.

innocuous *adj.* безвредный; безобидный.

innovate *v.i.* вводить новшества. —**innovation,** *n.* новшество; нововведение. —**innovative,** *adj.* новаторский. —**innovator,** *n.* новатор.

innuendo *n.* инсинуация.

innumerable *adj.* бесчисленный; несчётный.

inoculate *v.t.* прививать: *inoculate someone for typhus,* прививать кому-нибудь тиф. —**inoculation,** *n.* прививка.

inoffensive *adj.* безобидный.

inoperable *adj.* неоперабельный.

inoperative *adj.* бездействующий.

inopportune *adj.* несвоевременный.

inordinate *adj.* чрезмерный; непомерный.

inorganic *adj.* неорганический.

input *n.* ввод.

inquest *n.* следствие; дознание.

inquire *v.i.* **1,** (ask; seek information) спрашивать; справляться; осведомляться. **2,** *fol. by* **into** (investigate; study) расследовать; исследовать.

inquiry *n.* **1,** (request for information) запрос. *Make inquiries about,* наводить справки о. **2,** (investigation) расследование; следствие. *Committee of inquiry,* следственная комиссия.

inquisition *n.* инквизиция.

inquisitive *adj.* пытливый; любознательный. —**inquisitiveness,** *n.* пытливость; любознательность.

inquisitor *n.* инквизитор.

inroad *n.* **1,** (incursion) набег. **2,** *usu. pl.* (encroachment) посягательство.

insane *adj.* сумасшедший; душевнобольной; умалишённый. —**insane asylum,** сумасшедший дом; дом умалишённых; психиатрическая больница.

insanity *n.* **1,** (mental condition) сумасшествие; умопомешательство. **2,** (folly) безумие.

insatiable *adj.* ненасытный.

inscribe *v.t.* **1,** (write) надписывать. **2,** (engrave; carve) вырезать. **3,** *geom.* вписывать.

inscription *n.* надпись.

inscrutable *adj.* непостижимый; неисповедимый.

insect *n.* насекомое.

insecticide *n.* средство от насекомых; инсектицид.

insecure *adj.* **1,** (not safe) небезопасный. **2,** (lacking confidence or assurance) неуверенный в себе. —**insecurity,** *n.* неуверенность в себе.

insemination *n.* оплодотворе́ние; осемене́ние. *Artificial insemination,* иску́сственное оплодотворе́ние/осемене́ние.

insensate *adj.* бесчу́вственный.

insensible *adj.* бесчу́вственный; нечувстви́тельный. —**insensibility,** *n.* бесчу́вствие; нечувстви́тельность.

insensitive *adj.* нечувстви́тельный; бесчу́вственный; нечу́ткий. —**insensitivity,** *n.* нечувстви́тельность; бесчу́вствие.

inseparable *adj.* **1,** (of two people) неразлу́чный. **2,** (of objects, concepts, etc.) неотдели́мый. —**inseparability,** *n.* неразлу́чность; неотдели́мость.

insert *v.t.* **1,** (place inside) вкла́дывать; вставля́ть; опуска́ть. **2,** (add; enter) вноси́ть. —*n.* вкла́дка.

insertion *n.* **1,** (act of inserting) вкла́дывание; внесе́ние. **2,** (something inserted) вста́вка.

inset *n.* **1,** (in a book) вкле́йка. **2,** (in a dress) вста́вка.

inside *prep.* внутри́: *inside the house,* внутри́ до́ма. —*adv.* **1,** (motion) внутрь. **2,** (location) внутри́. —*adj.* **1,** (interior) вну́тренний. **2,** *colloq.* (known to only a few) секре́тный: *inside information,* секре́тные све́дения. —*n.* **1,** (interior) вну́тренняя часть; вну́тренность. *From/on the inside,* изнутри́. **2,** *pl., colloq.* (innards) вну́тренности. —**inside out, 1,** (reversed) наизна́нку. *Turn inside out,* вы́вернуть (наизна́нку). **2,** *colloq.* (thoroughly) вдоль и поперёк.

insidious *adj.* кова́рный. —**insidiousness,** *n.* кова́рство.

insight *n.* **1,** (discernment) зо́ркость; проница́тельность. **2,** (illuminating glimpse) понима́ние.

insignia *n.pl.* зна́ки разли́чия.

insignificant *adj.* незначи́тельный. —**insignificance,** *n.* незначи́тельность.

insincere *adj.* нейскренний. —**insincerity,** *n.* нейскренность.

insinuate *v.t.* **1,** (introduce gradually) незаме́тно внуша́ть. *Insinuate oneself into someone's confidence,* втира́ться в чье-нибудь дове́рие. **2,** (hint; suggest) намека́ть; подразумева́ть.

insinuation *n.* намёк; инсину́ация.

insipid *adj.* **1,** (tasteless) невку́сный. **2,** (dull) бесцве́тный; пре́сный.

insist *v.t. & i.* наста́ивать. —**insistence,** *n.* настоя́ние. —**insistent,** *adj.* насто́йчивый; настоя́тельный.

insofar as 1, (as far as) наско́лько. **2,** (to the full extent that) посто́льку, поско́льку.

insole *n.* стелька.

insolent *adj.* на́глый; де́рзкий. —**insolence,** *n.* на́глость; наха́льство; де́рзость.

insoluble *adj.* **1,** (not soluble) нераствори́мый. **2,** (not solvable) неразреши́мый.

insolvent *adj.* несостоя́тельный; неплатёжеспосо́бный. —**insolvency,** *n.* несостоя́тельность; неплатёжеспосо́бность.

insomnia *n.* бессо́нница.

inspect *v.t.* **1,** (examine) осма́тривать; обсле́довать. **2,** (conduct an inspection of) обсле́довать; инспекти́ровать. **3,** (review, as troops) производи́ть смотр (+ *dat.*).

inspection *n.* **1,** (examination) обсле́дование; осмо́тр; досмо́тр; инспе́кция; реви́зия. **2,** *mil.* смотр.

inspector *n.* инспе́ктор; контролёр; ревизо́р; обсле́дователь.

inspiration *n.* **1,** (feeling of being inspired) вдохно-

ве́ние. **2,** (one who inspires) вдохнови́тель. **3,** (inspired idea) блестя́щая мысль.

inspire *v.t.* **1,** (animate; stir) вдохновля́ть; воодушевля́ть. **2,** (arouse; produce, as an emotion) внуша́ть; вселя́ть. —**inspired,** *adj.* вдохнове́нный.

instability *n.* неусто́йчивость.

install *v.t.* **1,** (fix in position for use) устана́вливать; ста́вить; проводи́ть. **2,** (induct) вводи́ть в до́лжность.

installation *n.* **1,** (act of installing) устано́вка; проведе́ние. **2,** (something installed) устано́вка. **3,** (induction) введе́ние в до́лжность. **4,** *mil.* ба́за; объе́кт.

installment *also,* **instalment** *n.* **1,** (payment) взнос. *On the installment plan,* в рассро́чку. **2,** (of a published article) вы́пуск.

instance *n.* **1,** (example) приме́р: *for instance,* наприме́р. **2,** (case) слу́чай: *in this instance,* в да́нном слу́чае. **3,** *law* инста́нция: *court of first instance,* суд пе́рвой инста́нции.

instant *n.* мгнове́ние; миг; мину́та; моме́нт. *This instant,* сию́ мину́ту. —*adj.* момента́льный; мгнове́нный. —**instant coffee,** быстрораствори́мый ко́фе.

instantaneous *adj.* момента́льный; мгнове́нный.

instantly *adv.* момента́льно; мгнове́нно.

instead *adv.* вме́сто *(must be followed by a word in in the genitive case): he is ill, so I came instead,* он заболе́л, и я пришёл вме́сто него́. —**instead of,** вме́сто (+ *gen.*): *drink beer instead of wine,* пить пи́во вме́сто вина́. ♦*When followed by -ing form of a verb* вме́сто того́, что́бы (+ *inf.*): *instead of going to the theater,* вме́сто того́, что́бы пойти́ в теа́тр.

instep *n.* подъём.

instigate *v.t.* **1,** (foment; provoke) провоци́ровать. **2,** (spur; goad) подстрека́ть. —**instigation,** *n.* подстрека́тельство. —**instigator,** *n.* подстрека́тель; зачи́нщик.

instill *also,* **instil** *v.t.* внуша́ть; вселя́ть; влива́ть.

instinct *n.* инсти́нкт.

instinctive *adj.* инстинкти́вный. —**instinctively,** *adv.* нево́льно; инстинкти́вно.

institute *n.* институ́т. —*v.t.* **1,** (establish) устана́вливать; учрежда́ть. **2,** (initiate) вводи́ть; заводи́ть. *Institute reforms,* проводи́ть рефо́рмы.

institution *n.* **1,** (organization) учрежде́ние; заведе́ние. *Institution of higher learning,* вы́сшее уче́бное заведе́ние. **2,** (established custom) учрежде́ние; институ́т: *the institution of marriage,* учрежде́ние/институ́т бра́ка. **3,** (place of confinement) дом: *mental institution,* дом умалишённых.

instruct *v.t.* **1,** (teach) обуча́ть. **2,** (order; direct) поруча́ть.

instruction *n.* **1,** (teaching) обуче́ние. **2,** *pl.* (directions) указа́ния; наставле́ние; инстру́кция. —**instructional,** *adj.* уче́бный; инструкти́вный.

instructive *adj.* поучи́тельный.

instructor *n.* инстру́ктор.

instrument *n.* **1,** (implement) инструме́нт; ору́дие: *surgical instruments,* хирурги́ческие инструме́нты; *instrument of torture,* ору́дие пы́тки. **2,** (means; agency) ору́дие. **3,** (musical instrument) инструме́нт. **4,** (gauge) прибо́р: *instrument landing,* поса́дка по прибо́рам. *Instrument panel,* прибо́рная доска́. **5,** (legal document) гра́мота: *instruments of ratification,* ратификацио́нные гра́моты.

instrumental adj. **1,** (serving to achieve an end): be instrumental in, сыгра́ть реша́ющую роль в. **2,** music инструмента́льный. **3,** gram. твори́тельный: instrumental case, твори́тельный паде́ж.

instrumentalist n. инструмента́лист.

instrumentality n. Through the instrumentality of, при посре́дстве (+ gen.); че́рез посре́дство (+ gen.).

insubordinate adj. самово́льный. —**insubordination,** n. неподчине́ние; неповинове́ние.

insufferable adj. невыноси́мый; нестерпи́мый; несно́сный.

insufficiency n. недоста́точность.

insufficient adj. недоста́точный. —**insufficiently,** adv. недоста́точно.

insular adj. островно́й.

insulate v.t. изоли́ровать. —**insulation,** n. изоля́ция. —**insulator,** n. изоля́тор.

insulin n. инсули́н.

insult v.t. оскорбля́ть. —n. оскорбле́ние; оби́да. —**insulting,** adj. оскорби́тельный; оби́дный.

insuperable adj. непреодоли́мый.

insurance n. страхова́ние. —adj. страхово́й: insurance company, страхова́я компа́ния. Insurance policy/agent, страхово́й по́лис/аге́нт.

insure v.t. **1,** (guarantee) обеспе́чивать. **2,** (take out insurance for) страхова́ть. —**insurer,** n. страхо́вщик.

insurgency n. восста́ние; мяте́ж.

insurgent n. повста́нец; мяте́жник. —adj. повста́нческий; мяте́жный.

insurmountable adj. непреодоли́мый.

insurrection n. восста́ние; мяте́ж.

intact adj. це́лый; в це́лости; в сохра́нности.

intake n. впуск.

intangible adj. неосяза́емый.

integer n. це́лое число́; це́лое.

integral adj. **1,** (essential) неотъе́млемый: integral part, неотъе́млемая часть. **2,** math. интегра́льный: integral calculus, интегра́льное исчисле́ние. —n., math. интегра́л.

integrate v.t. **1,** (combine into a whole) интегри́ровать. **2,** (desegregate) десегреги́ровать. —**integrated circuit,** интегра́льная схе́ма.

integration n. **1,** (combining into a whole) интегра́ция. **2,** (desegregation) десегрега́ция.

integrity n. **1,** (uprightness; honesty) че́стность. **2,** (entirety) це́лостность: territorial integrity, территориа́льная це́лостность.

integument n. покро́в.

intellect n. ум; ра́зум; интелле́кт.

intellectual adj. у́мственный; интеллектуа́льный. —n. интеллиге́нт; интеллектуа́л.

intelligence n. **1,** (mental ability) ум; у́мственные спосо́бности. **2,** (collection of secret information; organization engaged in same) разве́дка. **3,** (information so collected) разве́дывательные да́нные. —adj. разве́дывательный; разве́дочный. —**intelligence quotient,** показа́тель у́мственных спосо́бностей. —**intelligence test,** испыта́ние у́мственных спосо́бностей.

intelligent adj. **1,** (endowed with intellect) разу́мный. **2,** (smart; clever) у́мный.

intelligentsia n. интеллиге́нция.

intelligible adj. поня́тный; толко́вый; вразуми́тельный. —**intelligibility,** n. поня́тность.

intemperance n. невоздержа́нность; невоздержа́ние.

intemperate adj. **1,** (given to excesses; excessive) неуме́ренный; невоздержа́нный. **2,** (improper; rude) невоздержа́нный: intemperate language, невоздержа́нный язы́к.

intend v.t. **1,** (have in mind; plan) собира́ться; намерева́ться. What do you intend to do?, что вы наме́рены де́лать? **2,** (design for a specific purpose) предназнача́ть: intended for children, предназна́чен для дете́й.

intense adj. **1,** (keenly felt) си́льный; о́стрый. Intense heat/hatred, си́льная жара́/не́нависть. Intense pain, си́льная or о́страя боль. **2,** (strenuous; heated) напряжённый.

intensify v.t. **1,** (increase; step up) уси́ливать; усугубля́ть. Intensify one's efforts, усугубля́ть уси́лия. **2,** (make more acute) обостря́ть. —v.i. обостря́ться. —**intensification,** n. усиле́ние; обостре́ние.

intensity n. интенси́вность.

intensive adj. интенси́вный. —**intensive care,** интенси́вная терапи́я.

intent n. **1,** (intention) наме́рение. **2,** law у́мысел: malicious intent, злой у́мысел. —adj. **1,** (firmly fixed or directed) пристальный. **2,** fol. by on (determined) по́лный реши́мости. —**to all intents and purposes,** факти́чески.

intention n. наме́рение. Have no intention of, отню́дь не собира́ться (+ inf.).

intentional adj. наме́ренный; преднаме́ренный; умы́шленный. —**intentionally,** adv. наме́ренно; наро́чно; умы́шленно.

intently adv. при́стально.

inter v.t. хорони́ть; погреба́ть.

interact v.i. взаимоде́йствовать. —**interaction,** n. взаимоде́йствие.

intercede v.i. **1,** (plead in behalf of another) хлопота́ть; хода́тайствовать; вступа́ться; заступа́ться. **2,** (mediate) посре́дничать.

intercept v.t. перехва́тывать. —**interception,** n. перехва́т. —**interceptor,** n. истреби́тель-перехва́тчик.

intercession n. засту́пничество; хода́тайство. —**intercessor,** n. засту́пник; хода́тай.

interchange v.t. меня́ться (+ instr.); обме́ниваться (+ instr.). —v.i. меня́ться места́ми. —n. (взаи́мный) обме́н.

interchangeable adj. взаимозаменя́емый.

intercity adj. междугоро́дный.

interconnect v.i. соедина́ться. The bedrooms interconnect, спа́льни соединены́ ме́жду собо́й. —**interconnected,** adj. взаимосвя́занный.

intercontinental adj. межконтинента́льный.

intercourse n. **1,** (dealings) обще́ние; сноше́ния. **2,** (copulation) полова́я связь.

interdependence n. взаимозави́симость. —**interdependent,** adj. взаимозави́симый.

interdict v.t. **1,** (forbid) запреща́ть. **2,** mil. воспреща́ть.

interdiction n. **1,** (act of forbidding) запре́т; запреще́ние. **2,** mil. воспреще́ние.

interest n. **1,** (curiosity) интере́с: interest in music, интере́с к му́зыке. Be of interest, представля́ть интере́с. **2,** (advantage; benefit) интере́сы: it is in your interest, э́то в ва́ших интере́сах. In the public interest, в общественных интересах. *Protect one's interests,* защищать свой интересы. **3,** (payment for the use of money) проценты. **4,** (legal share) доля: *a half interest,* половинная доля. —*v.t.* интересовать. —**in the interest of,** в интересах (+ *gen.*); ради. —**with interest,** с лихвой: *repay with interest,* отплатить с лихвой.

interested *adj.* заинтересованный. *Be interested in,* интересоваться (+ *instr.*); быть заинтересованным в (+ *prepl.*). *He is not interested,* ему не интересно.

interest-free *adj.* беспроцентный.

interesting *adj.* интересный.

interfere *v.i.* **1,** (meddle; intervene) вмешиваться. **2,** *fol. by* with (hinder; obstruct) мешать.

interference *n.* **1,** (act of interfering) вмешательство. **2,** (static) помехи.

interim *n.* промежуток. *In the interim,* тем временем. —*adj.* временный; предварительный; промежуточный.

interior *adj.* внутренний. —*n.* внутренность; внутренняя часть. —**interior decorator,** декоратор.

interject *v.t.* вставлять; ввёртывать.

interjection *n.* междометие.

interlace *v.t.* **1,** (intertwine) сплетать; переплетать. **2,** (intersperse) пересыпать.

interlard *v.t.* пересыпать.

interlay *v.t.* перекладывать; прокладывать.

interlock *v.t.* сцеплять. —*v.i.* сцепляться.

interloper *n.* незваный гость; пришлый человек.

interlude *n.* **1,** (interval) промежуток. **2,** *music* интерлюдия.

intermarriage *n.* смешанный брак; брак между людьми различной расы. —**intermarry,** *v.i.* вступить в смешанный брак.

intermediary *n.* посредник. —*adj.* **1,** (intermediate) промежуточный. **2,** (acting as a mediator) посреднический.

intermediate *adj.* **1,** (situated in between) промежуточный. **2,** (between elementary and advanced) средний.

interment *n.* погребение.

intermezzo *n.* интермеццо.

interminable *adj.* бесконечный; нескончаемый.

intermingle *v.t.* смешивать; перемешивать. —*v.i.* смешиваться.

intermission *n.* **1,** (recess) перерыв. **2,** *theat.* антракт.

intermittent *adj.* перемежающийся; прерывистый. —**intermittently,** *adv.* с перерывами.

intern *n.* интерн. —*v.i.* служить интерном. —*v.t.* (confine) интернировать.

internal *adj.* внутренний. —**internal-combustion engine,** двигатель внутреннего сгорания. —**internal medicine,** терапия.

internally *adv.* внутренне. *Take medicine internally,* принимать лекарство внутрь.

international *adj.* международный. —**International Date Line,** Линия перемены даты.

Internationale *n.* Интернационал.

internationalism *n.* интернационализм.

internecine *adj.* **1,** (marked by great slaughter) истребительный. **2,** (internal) междоусобный.

internist *n.* терапевт.

internment *n.* интернирование. —**internment camp,** лагерь для интернированных.

interplanetary *adj.* межпланетный.

interplay *n.* взаимодействие.

interpolate *v.t.* **1,** (interject; interpose) вставлять. **2,** *math.* интерполировать. —**interpolation,** *n.* интерполяция.

interpose *v.t.* **1,** (place between) ставить (между). **2,** (inject, as a comment) вставлять.

interpret *v.t.* **1,** (translate orally) переводить. **2,** (explain; construe) толковать; истолковывать; трактовать; интерпретировать.

interpretation *n.* **1,** (translation) перевод. **2,** (explanation) толкование; истолкование; трактовка; интерпретация.

interpreter *n.* **1,** (translator) переводчик. **2,** (commentator) толкователь; истолкователь; интерпретатор.

interregnum *n.* междуцарствие.

interrelated *adj.* взаимодействующий; взаимосвязанный.

interrelation *n.* взаимоотношение. —**interrelationship,** *n.* взаимная связь.

interrogate *v.t.* допрашивать. —**interrogation,** *n.* допрос.

interrogative *adj.* вопросительный.

interrupt *v.t.* прерывать; перебивать; обрывать. —*v.i.* перебивать: *don't interrupt!,* не перебивай(те)!

interruption *n.* **1,** (act of interrupting) прерывание. *Interruption of telephone service,* нарушение телефонной связи. *Interruption of pregnancy,* прерывание беременности. **2,** (instance of interrupting) помеха: *without any interruptions,* без всяких помех. *Excuse the interruption!,* извините за беспокойство! **3,** (break) перерыв: *without interruption,* без перерыва.

intersect *v.t.* пересекать. —*v.i.* пересекаться.

intersection *n.* **1,** (of lines) пересечение. **2,** (of streets, roads, etc.) перекрёсток.

intersperse *v.t.* **1,** (place at intervals) разбрасывать; рассыпать. **2,** (interlace, as with comments) пересыпать; пестрить.

interstellar *adj.* межзвёздный.

intertwine *v.t.* сплетать; переплетать. —*v.i.* сплетаться; переплетаться.

interval *n.* **1,** (space; gap; break) промежуток; интервал. **2,** *Brit.* (intermission) антракт.

intervene *v.i.* **1,** (intercede) вмешиваться. **2,** (occur in the meantime) происходить (тем временем). *In the intervening period,* тем временем.

intervention *n.* вмешательство; интервенция.

interview *n.* **1,** (meeting to evaluate) встреча. **2,** (for a publication, on TV, etc.) интервью. —*v.t.* брать интервью у; интервьюировать. —**interviewer,** *n.* интервьюёр.

interweave *v.t.* сплетать; переплетать *(lit. & fig.).*

intestate *adj.* без завещания; не оставив завещания.

intestine *n.* кишка; *pl.* кишки; кишечник. —**intestinal,** *adj.* кишечный.

intimacy *n.* интимность; близость.

intimate[1] (in-ti-mit) *adj.* интимный: *intimate friend/ circle,* интимный друг/круг. *Become intimate with,* сойтись с.

intimate[2] (in-ti-mate) *v.t.* намекать.

intimately *adv.* интимно. *Intimately connected with,* тесно связанный с.

intimation *n.* намёк.

intimidate *v.t.* запугивать. —**intimidation**, *n.* запугивание.

into *prep.* в (+ *acc.*): *walk into a room,* входить в комнату; *fall into a trap,* попасть в ловушку. *Put into operation,* вводить в действие. *Get into trouble,* попасть в беду. ♦ *With certain verbs* на: *divide into parts,* делить на части. *Run into an acquaintance,* наталкиваться на друга. *Translate into Russian,* переводить на русский язык.

intolerable *adj.* нетерпимый.

intolerant *adj.* нетерпимый. —**intolerance**, *n.* нетерпимость.

intonation *n.* интонация.

intone *v.i.* говорить нараспёв *or* речитативом. —*v.t.* читать *or* произносить нараспёв/речитативом.

intoxicate *v.t.* пьянить; опьянять. —**intoxicated**, *adj.* пьяный; хмельной; опьяневший. —**intoxicating**, *adj.* опьяняющий; хмельной. —**intoxication**, *n.* опьянёние.

intractable *adj.* несговорчивый; неподатливый.

intransigent *adj.* непреклонный. —**intransigence**, *n.* непреклонность.

intransitive *adj.* непереходный.

intravenous *adj.* внутривённый.

intrepid *adj.* неустрашимый; бесстрашный. —**intrepidity**, *n.* неустрашимость.

intricacy *n.* **1,** (complexity) запутанность; сложность. **2,** *pl.* (intricate details) сложности.

intricate *adj.* запутанный; замысловатый; сложный.

intrigue *n.* интрига; *pl.* интриги; происки. —*v.t.* (fascinate) интриговать. —*v.i.* (engage in intrigue) интриговать.

intrinsic *adj.* существенный. *Intrinsic value,* внутренняя *or* действительная ценность. —**intrinsically**, *adv.* в сущности своёй; по своему существу.

introduce *v.t.* **1,** (present so as to make acquainted) знакомить; представлять. *Introduce someone to someone,* (по)знакомить кого-нибудь с кём-нибудь. *Allow me to introduce…,* разрешите мне представить… **2,** (present to an audience) представлять. **3,** (institute) вводить; заводить. **4,** (offer, as a bill) вносить. —**introduce oneself,** представляться; (от)рекомендоваться.

introduction *n.* **1,** (presentation) представлёние: *introduction of a speaker,* представлёние оратора. *A flowery introduction,* красочное представлёние. **2,** (opening portion, as of a book) введёние; вступлёние. **3,** (instituting) введёние. **4,** (elementary phase of study) введёние: *introduction to philosophy,* введёние в философию. **5,** *music* интродукция.

introductory *adj.* вступительный; вводный.

introspection *n.* самонаблюдёние; самоанализ; интроспёкция. —**introspective**, *adj.* интроспективный.

intrude *v.i.* вторгаться; навязываться. —*v.t.* навязывать.

intruder *n.* **1,** (interloper) незваный гость. **2,** (housebreaker) взломщик.

intrusion *n.* **1,** (encroachment) вторжёние: *intrusion of (a country's) airspace,* вторжёние в воздушное пространство. **2,** (interruption) беспокойство: *pardon the intrusion,* простите за беспокойство.

intrusive *adj.* навязчивый.

intuition *n.* интуиция.

intuitive *adj.* интуитивный. —**intuitively**, *adv.* интуитивно; по наитию.

inundate *v.t.* **1,** (flood) затоплять. **2,** *fig.* (overwhelm) наводнять. —**inundation**, *n.* наводнёние.

inure *v.t.* приучать; закалять.

invade *v.t. & i.* вторгаться (в) —**invader**, *n.* захватчик.

invalid[1] (in-va-lid) *n.* инвалид.

invalid[2] (in-val-id) *adj.* **1,** (null; void) недействительный. **2,** (unsound, as of an argument) необоснованный. **3,** (illegitimate, as of an excuse) неуважительный.

invalidate *v.t.* делать недействительным; аннулировать.

invaluable *adj.* неоценимый; бесцённый.

invariable *adj.* неизмённый. —**invariably**, *adv.* неизмённо.

invasion *n.* вторжёние; нашёствие. *Invasion of,* вторжёние в (+ *acc.*); нашёствие на (+ *acc.*).

invective *n.* брань; ругань.

inveigh *v.i.* [*usu.* **inveigh against**] ратовать (против).

inveigle *v.t.* **1,** (talk into) уламывать. **2,** (wangle) выпрашивать.

invent *v.t.* **1,** (devise; create) изобретать. **2,** (fabricate; concoct) выдумывать; сочинять; измышлять.

invention *n.* **1,** (device conceived by original effort) изобретёние. **2,** (fabrication) выдумка; измышлёние.

inventive *adj.* изобретательный. —**inventiveness**, *n.* изобретательность.

inventor *n.* изобретатель.

inventory *n.* **1,** (stock-taking) опись; инвентарь; учёт; переучёт. *Take inventory,* делать опись; составлять инвентарь. *Closed for inventory,* закрыт на учёт. **2,** (stock on hand) инвентарь; запас. —*v.t.* описывать; инвентаризировать.

inverse *adj.* обратный; противоположный. —*n.* противоположность. —**inversely**, *adv.* обратно: *inversely proportional to,* обратно пропорциональный (+ *dat.*).

inversion *n.* **1,** (act of inverting) перевёртывание. **2,** (reversal of order) перестановка. **3,** *gram.; chem.; meteorol.* инвёрсия.

invert *v.t.* **1,** (turn upside down) перевёртывать. **2,** (reverse the order of) переставлять. *Inverted order,* обратный порядок.

invertebrate *adj.* беспозвоночный. —*n.* беспозвоночное. *The invertebrates,* беспозвоночные.

invest *v.t.* **1,** (put, as money, effort, etc.) вкладывать. **2,** (give power to) облекать. —*v.i.* [*usu.* **invest in**] вкладывать дёньги в (+ *acc.*).

investigate *v.t.* **1,** (subject to an official probe) расследовать. **2,** (explore scientifically) исследовать.

investigation *n.* **1,** (official probe) расследование; слёдствие. *Federal Bureau of Investigation,* Федеральное бюро расслёдований. **2,** (scientific study) исследование.

investigator *n.* слёдователь. —**investigatory**, *adj.* слёдственный.

investiture *n.* инвеститура.

investment *n.* вложе́ние; капиталовложе́ние. —**investor,** *n.* вкла́дчик.

inveterate *adj.* закоренélый; застарélый; зайдлый.

invidious *adj.* **1,** (odious) гну́сный. **2,** (giving offense) оскорби́тельный.

invigorate *v.t.* бодри́ть; оживля́ть. —**invigorating,** *adj.* бодря́щий; живи́тельный.

invincible *adj.* непобеди́мый. —**invincibility,** *n.* непобеди́мость.

inviolable *adj.* неруши́мый; неприкоснове́нный. —**inviolability,** *n.* неруши́мость; неприкосновéнность.

inviolate *adj.* **1,** (not violated) не нару́шенный. *Keep inviolate,* свя́то храни́ть. **2,** (not profaned) нетро́нутый.

invisible *adj.* неви́димый. —**invisible ink,** симпати́ческие черни́ла.

invitation *n.* приглаше́ние.

invite *v.t.* **1,** (request the presence of) приглаша́ть. **2,** (tend to bring on; lay oneself open to) накликáть.

inviting *adj.* привлекáтельный; заманчивый; соблазни́тельный.

invocation *n.* **1,** (appeal to a higher power) обраще́ние. **2,** (opening prayer) моли́тва.

invoice *n.* факту́ра; накладна́я.

invoke *v.t.* **1,** (call on for help) обращáться к. **2,** (resort to; put into force) вводи́ть в де́йствие. **3,** (summon by incantation) заклина́ть.

involuntary *adj.* нево́льный; непроизво́льный.

involve *v.t.* **1,** (entail) влечь за собо́й; быть свя́занным с. **2,** (implicate; embroil) вовлека́ть. **3,** (absorb; engross) поглоща́ть.

involved *adj.* **1,** (concerned) заинтересо́ванный. **2,** *fol. by* in (a party to) причáстный (к). **3,** (complex) запу́танный.

involvement *n.* **1,** (act of involving) вовлече́ние. **2,** (state of being involved) учáстие; причáстность.

invulnerable *adj.* неуязви́мый. —**invulnerability,** *n.* неуязви́мость.

inward *adj.* вну́тренний. —*adv.* [*also,* **inwards**] внутрь. —**inwardly,** *adv.* вну́тренне; в душе́.

iodine *n.* йод.

ion *n.* ио́н. —**ionic,** *adj.* ио́нный.

ionize *v.t.* ионизи́ровать. —**ionization,** *n.* иониза́ция.

ionosphere *n.* ионосфéра.

iota *n.* йо́та. *Not one iota,* ни на йо́ту.

Iranian *adj.* ира́нский. —*n.* ира́нец; ира́нка.

Iraqi *adj.* ира́кский.

irascible *adj.* вспы́льчивый.

irate *adj.* гне́вный; разгне́ванный.

ire *n.* гнев.

iridescent *adj.* ра́дужный; перели́вчатый. —**iridescence,** *n.* ра́дужность.

iridium *n.* ири́дий.

iris *n.* **1,** (of the eye) ра́дужная оболо́чка. **2,** (flower) и́рис; каса́тик.

Irish *adj.* ирла́ндский. —*n., preceded by* the ирла́ндцы. —**Irishman,** *n.* ирла́ндец.

irk *v.t.* раздража́ть; досажда́ть; надоеда́ть. —**irksome,** *adj.* доса́дный; надое́дливый.

iron *n.* **1,** (metal) желе́зо. **2,** (flatiron) утю́г. **3,** (instrument of iron): *soldering iron,* па́яльник. *Fire irons,* ками́нные щипцы́. **4,** *pl.* (shackles) кандалы́: *in irons,*

в кандала́х. —*adj.* желе́зный: *iron ore,* желе́зная руда́. —*v.t.* **1,** (press) утю́жить; гла́дить. **2,** *fol. by* out (smooth over, as differences) сгла́живать; ула́живать. —**Iron Age,** желе́зный век. —**iron curtain,** желе́зный за́навес.

ironic *also,* **ironical** *adj.* ирони́ческий. —**ironically,** *adv.* ирони́чески; по иро́нии судьбы́.

ironing *n.* утю́жка; гла́женье. —**ironing board,** глади́льная доска́.

ironworks *n.* чугунолите́йный заво́д.

irony *n.* иро́ния.

irradiate *v.t.* **1,** (illuminate) освеща́ть; озаря́ть. **2,** (expose to rays or radiation) облуча́ть. —**irradiation,** *n.* иррадиáция; облуче́ние.

irrational *adj.* **1,** (not reasoning; senseless) неразу́мный; нерассуди́тельный. **2,** *math.* иррациона́льный. —**irrationality,** *n.* неразу́мность; нерассуди́тельность.

irreconcilable *adj.* непримири́мый. —**irreconcilability,** *n.* непримири́мость.

irrecoverable *adj.* непоправи́мый; невозврáтный.

irrefutable *adj.* неопровержи́мый.

irregular *adj.* **1,** (not symmetrical) непра́вильный: *irregular features,* непра́вильные черты́. **2,** (uneven in occurrence) нерегуля́рный. **3,** (spasmodic) неро́вный: *irregular heartbeat,* неро́вное бие́ние се́рдца. **4,** *gram.* непра́вильный: *irregular verb,* непра́вильный глаго́л. **5,** *mil.* нерегуля́рный.

irregularity *n.* непра́вильность; нерегуля́рность.

irrelevance *also,* **irrelevancy** *n.* неуме́стность. *That is an irrelevance,* э́то не отно́сится к де́лу.

irrelevant *adj.* неуме́стный; не относя́щийся к де́лу.

irreligious *adj.* неве́рующий.

irremovable *adj.* неустрани́мый.

irreparable *adj.* непоправи́мый; невозврáтный; невознагради́мый. *Irreparable damage,* непоправи́мый уще́рб. *Irreparable loss,* невозврáтная/невознагради́мая поте́ря *or* утрáта.

irreplaceable *adj.* незамени́мый.

irrepressible *adj.* **1,** (impossible to hold back) неудержи́мый. **2,** (impossible to discourage) неугомо́нный.

irreproachable *adj.* безукори́зненный; безупре́чный.

irresistible *adj.* неотрази́мый; непреодоли́мый. —**irresistibility,** *n.* неотрази́мость.

irresolute *adj.* нереши́тельный.

irrespective *adj., in* **irrespective of,** незави́симо от; безотноси́тельно к.

irresponsible *adj.* безотве́тственный. —**irresponsibility,** *n.* безотве́тственность.

irretrievable *adj.* непоправи́мый; невозврáтный.

irreverence *n.* непочте́ние. —**irreverent,** *adj.* непочти́тельный.

irreversible *adj.* необрати́мый.

irrevocable *adj.* бесповоро́тный.

irrigate *v.t.* ороша́ть. —**irrigation,** *n.* ороше́ние; иррига́ция.

irritable *adj.* раздражи́тельный. —**irritability,** *n.* раздражи́тельность.

irritant *n.* раздражи́тель.

irritate *v.t.* раздража́ть. —**irritation,** *n.* раздраже́ние.

is *v. see* **be.**

isinglass *n.* **1,** (gelatin) рыбий клей. **2,** (mica) слюда.

Islam *n.* ислам. —**Islamic,** *adj.* мусульманский.

island *n.* остров. —**islander,** *n.* островитянин.

isle *n.* островок.

isobar *n.* изобара.

isolate *v.t.* изолировать; обособлять. —**isolated,** *adj.* изолированный; обособленный. *Isolated cases,* единичные случаи.

isolation *n.* изоляция; обособление. —**isolation ward,** изолятор.

isolationism *n.* изоляционизм.

isolationist *n.* изоляционист. —*adj.* изоляционистский.

isomer *n.* изомер.

isosceles *adj.* равнобедренный.

isotope *n.* изотоп.

Israeli *adj.* израильский. —*n.* израильтянин; израильтянка.

issuance *n.* **1,** (handing out) выдача. **2,** (putting out) выпуск. **3,** (promulgation) издание.

issue *n.* **1,** = **issuance. 2,** (something issued, as of bonds, stamps, etc.) выпуск. **3,** (single number of a periodical) номер. **4,** (point in question) вопрос. *At issue,* под вопросом. **5,** (progeny) потомки; потомство. —*v.t.* **1,** (give; grant; hand out) выдавать: *issue a visa,* выдавать визу. **2,** (put out, as stamps, money, etc.) выпускать. **3,** (promulgate, as an order) издавать. *Issue an ultimatum,* предъявить ультиматум. —*v.i.* исходить; вытекать. —**take issue with,** оспаривать.

isthmus *n.* перешеек.

it *pron.* **1,** *pers.* он; она; оно: *I don't know how good it is,* я не знаю насколько он хорош. *Where did you put it?,* куда вы его положили? ♦ *Frequently omitted in*

Russian: give it to me, дайте мне. *Did you find it?,* нашли? *Would you like to see it?,* хотите посмотреть? **2,** *indef.* это: *it is I,* это я. *I already knew about it,* я уже знал об этом. **3,** *impers.: it seems,* кажется. *It is raining,* идёт дождь. *It is cold,* холодно. *It's hard to say,* трудно сказать. *It's time to go,* пора идти.

Italian *adj.* итальянский. —*n.* **1,** (person) итальянец; итальянка. **2,** (language) итальянский язык. *Speak Italian,* говорить по-итальянски.

italic *n., usu. pl.* курсив; курсивный шрифт. *In italics,* курсивом. —*adj.* курсивный. —**italicize,** *v.t.* выделять курсивом.

itch *n.* зуд. —*v.i.* **1,** (have or produce an itch) чесаться; зудеть. **2,** (cause itching, as of rough material) шерстить. **3,** (have an urge): *I am itching to* (+ *inf.*), у меня руки чешутся *or* зудят; мне не терпится; меня так и подмывает.

itchy *adj.* зудящий; колючий.

item *n.* **1,** (article) предмет. **2,** (unit) статья: *item of export/expense,* статья экспорта/расхода. **3,** (on an agenda) пункт; вопрос. **4,** (in a newspaper) заметка; сообщение. **5,** (on a program) номер.

itemize *v.t.* перечислять по пунктам; указывать в отдельности.

itinerant *adj.* странствующий; бродячий.

itinerary *n.* маршрут.

its *poss.adj.* **1,** (its own) свой. **2,** (something else's) его; её.

itself *pron.* **1,** used for emphasis сам: *the room itself was not large,* сама комната была небольшая. **2,** used reflexively себя; сам себя: *it speaks for itself,* это говорит само за себя. —**in and of itself,** сам по себе.

ivory *n.* слоновая кость.

ivy *n.* плющ.

J

J, j десятая буква английского алфавита.

jab *v.t. & i.* тыкать. —*n.* тычок.

jabber *v.i.* болтать; тараторить.

jack *n.* **1,** (lever) домкрат. **2,** (socket) гнездо. **3,** *cards* валет. —*v.t.* [*usu.* **jack up**] **1,** (hoist with a jack) поднимать домкратом. **2,** (raise, as prices) набивать; взвинчивать.

jackal *n.* шакал.

jackass *n.* осёл.

jackdaw *n.* галка.

jacket *n.* **1,** (man's sport coat) пиджак. **2,** (man's outer garment, as a lumberjacket) куртка. **3,** (woman's garment) жакет; кофта. **4,** (casing; covering) кожух. **5,** (dust jacket) суперобложка. **6,** (skin of a potato) кожура. *Potatoes boiled in their jackets,* картофель в мундире.

jackhammer *n.* пневматический отбойный молоток.

jack-of-all-trades *n.* мастер на все руки.

jackpot *n.* банк. —**hit the jackpot,** сорвать банк.

jack rabbit заяц.

jacksnipe *n.* гаршнеп.

jackstraws *n. pl.* бирюльки.

jade *n.* **1,** (mineral) нефрит. **2,** (old horse) кляча; одёр.

jaded *adj.* **1,** (worn out) измученный. **2,** (satiated) пресыщенный.

jag *n.* зубец.

jagged *adj.* зубчатый; зазубренный. *Jagged coastline,* изрезанный берег.

jaguar *n.* ягуар.

jail *n.* тюрьма. —*adj.* тюремный: *jail term,* срок

jailbreak *n.* побёг *or* бёгство из тюрьмы́.

jailer *also,* **jailor** *n.* тюрёмщик.

jalopy *n.* драндулёт; колыма́га.

jalousie *n.* жалюзи́.

jam *v.t.* **1,** (force; wedge) впи́хивать; вкли́нивать. **2,** (catch, as one's fingers in a door) защемля́ть; ущемля́ть; прищемля́ть. **3,** (cause to become unworkable) закли́нивать. **4,** (crowd; pack) запру́живать: *people jammed the streets,* лю́ди запруди́ли у́лицы. *The aisles were jammed,* прохо́ды бы́ли заби́ты. *The place was jammed,* наро́ду бы́ло битко́м наби́то. **5,** (interfere with, as a broadcast) глуши́ть; заглуша́ть. **6,** *Jam on the brakes,* ре́зко затормози́ть. —*v.i.* **1,** (fail to operate; stick) заеда́ть *(impers.):* *the wheels jammed,* колёса зае́ло. **2,** (crowd) набива́ться: *jam into the elevator,* набива́ться в ли́фте. —*n.* **1,** (congestion) зато́р: *traffic jam,* зато́р у́личного движе́ния; про́бка. **2,** (fruit preserve) варе́нье; джем; повидло. **3,** *colloq.* (predicament) переде́лка; переплёт.

jamb *n.* кося́к.

jangle *v.i.* звя́кать. —*v.t.* **1,** (cause to jangle) звя́кать (+ *instr.*). **2,** (irritate, as nerves) трепа́ть (не́рвы). —*n.* звя́канье.

janitor *n.* убо́рщик.

January *n.* янва́рь. —*adj.* янва́рский.

Japanese *adj.* япо́нский. *He (she) is Japanese,* он япо́нец; она́ япо́нка. —*n.* **1,** (language) япо́нский язы́к. *Speak Japanese,* говори́ть по-япо́нски. **2,** *preceded by* **the** (people) япо́нцы.

jar *n.* **1,** (container) ба́нка. **2,** (jolt) толчо́к. —*v.t.* потряса́ть. —*v.i.* **1,** *fol. by* **on** (grate on) коро́бить. **2,** *fol. by* **with** (clash) дисгармони́ровать (с).

jargon *n.* жарго́н.

jasmine *n.* жасми́н. —*adj.* жасми́нный; жасми́новый.

jasper *n.* я́шма. —*adj.* я́шмовый.

jaundice *n.* желту́ха.

jaundiced *adj.* **1,** (having jaundice) поражённый желту́хой. **2,** (prejudiced) предвзя́тый; предубеждённый.

jaunt *n.* прогу́лка.

jaunty *adj.* **1,** (sprightly) бо́йкий; задо́рный. **2,** (stylish) мо́дный; шика́рный.

javelin *n.* копьё; дро́тик. —**javelin throw,** мета́ние копья́.

jaw *n.* че́люсть. *In the jaws of death,* в когтя́х сме́рти.

jawbone *n.* че́люсть; челюстна́я кость.

jay *n.* со́йка.

jazz *n.* джаз. —*adj.* джа́зовый.

jealous *adj.* ревни́вый. *Be jealous of,* ревнова́ть; зави́довать. —**jealously,** *adv.* ревни́во.

jealousy *n.* ре́вность.

jeans *n.pl.* джи́нсы.

jeep *n.* джип; ви́ллис.

jeer *v.t.* издева́ться над; насмеха́ться над. —*v.i.* издева́тельски крича́ть. —*n.* издёвка.

jejune *adj.* сухо́й; бесцве́тный.

jell *v.i.* **1,** (congeal) застыва́ть. **2,** *fig.* (take definite form) определя́ться.

jelly *n.* желе́.

jellyfish *n.* меду́за.

jeopardize *v.t.* ста́вить под угро́зу.

jeopardy *n.* опа́сность. *Be in jeopardy,* находи́ться под угро́зой. *Place in jeopardy,* ста́вить под угро́зу.

jerboa *n.* тушка́нчик.

jerk *v.t.* дёргать. —*v.i.* дёрнуться. —*n.* **1,** (tug) рыво́к. **2,** *slang* (dope) болва́н.

jerky *adj.* поры́вистый.

jersey *n.* фуфа́йка.

jest *n.* шу́тка: *in jest,* в шу́тку. —*v.i.* шути́ть.

jester *n.* шут: *court jester,* придво́рный шут.

Jesuit *n.* иезуи́т. —*adj.* иезуи́тский.

Jesus *n.* Иису́с.

jet *n.* **1,** (spurt; gush) струя́. **2,** (spout; nozzle) жикле́р. **3,** (mineral) гага́т. **4,** (plane) реакти́вный самолёт. —*adj.* реакти́вный: *jet propulsion,* реакти́вное движе́ние. —*v.i.* бить струёй.

jet-black *adj.* чёрный как смоль.

jet-propelled *adj.* реакти́вный.

jet stream стру́йное тече́ние.

jettison *v.t.* выбра́сывать за́ борт.

jetty *n.* **1,** (breakwater) мол. **2,** (wharf) при́стань.

Jew *n.* евре́й.

jewel *n.* драгоце́нный ка́мень; драгоце́нность.

jeweler *also,* **jeweller** *n.* ювели́р.

jewelry *also.* **jewellery** *n.* драгоце́нности. *Jewelry store,* ювели́рный магази́н.

Jewish *adj.* евре́йский. —**Jewry,** *n.* евре́йство.

jib *n.* **1,** (sail) кли́вер. **2,** (boom of a derrick) стрела́.

jib boom утлега́рь.

jibe *v.i.* **1,** = **gibe.** **2,** *colloq.* (agree; square) сходи́ться.

jiffy *n., colloq.* миг; мгнове́ние. *In a jiffy,* ми́гом; в два счёта.

jig *n.* джи́га: *dance a jig,* танцева́ть джи́гу. —**in jig time,** *colloq.* в два счёта. —**the jig is up,** *colloq.* игра́ ко́нчена.

jigger *n.* рю́мочка.

jiggle *v.t.* шевели́ть.

jigsaw puzzle составна́я карти́нка.

jilt *v.t.* броса́ть; оставля́ть.

jimmy *n.* отмы́чка; воровско́й лом. —*v.t.* [*usu.* **jimmy open**] взла́мывать.

jimsonweed *n.* дурма́н.

jingle *v.t. & i.* звене́ть. —*n.* **1,** (sound) звон. **2,** (humorous verse) часту́шка.

jinks *n.pl.* [*usu.* **high jinks**] шу́мное весе́лье.

jinx *n., colloq.* дурно́й глаз. —*v.t.* сгла́зить.

jitters *n.pl., colloq.* не́рвность. *Have the jitters,* не́рвничать. —**jittery,** *adj., colloq.* не́рвный.

job *n.* **1,** (piece of work) рабо́та; труд. *Odd jobs,* случа́йная рабо́та. *By the job,* сде́льно; поуро́чно. **2,** (position of employment) рабо́та; слу́жба; ме́сто. *Change jobs,* меня́ть рабо́ту. *Soft job,* тёплое месте́чко. **3,** (task; chore) рабо́та; зада́ние. —**give up as a bad job,** *colloq.* махну́ть руко́й на (+ *acc.*); поста́вить крест на (+ *acc. or prepl.*). —**lie down on the job,** *colloq.* рабо́тать спустя́ рукава́. —**on the job, 1,** (at work) на слу́жбе. **2,** (while at work) в рабо́чем поря́дке.

jobber *n.* оптови́к; торго́вый посре́дник.

jobless *adj.* безрабо́тный.

jockey *n.* жоке́й.

jocose *adj.* шутли́вый; игри́вый.

jocular *adj.* шутли́вый; шу́точный.

jocund *adj.* весёлый.

jog *v.i.* **1,** (of a person) бе́гать. **2,** (of a horse) идти́ трусцо́й; труси́ть. —*v.t.* (nudge) подта́лкивать. —**jogger,** *n.* бегу́н.

join *v.t.* **1,** (bring together; link; unite) соединя́ть; свя́зывать. *Join hands,* бра́ться за́ руки. *Join forces,* соединя́ть *or* объединя́ть си́лы. **2,** (attach) присоединя́ть. **3,** (meet and accompany) присоединя́ться к. *Join the crowd,* присоединя́ться *or* примыка́ть к толпе́. **4,** (become a member of) вступа́ть в: *join the party,* вступи́ть в па́ртию. **5,** (enlist in, as a branch of military service) поступа́ть в *or* на. **6,** (enroll in, as a library) запи́сываться в. **7,** (connect with) соединя́ться с. —*v.i.* **1,** (come together) соединя́ться; сходи́ться. **2,** (become a member) присоединя́ться. **3,** *fol. by* in (take part with others) присоединя́ться. *Join in the conversation,* вступи́ть в разгово́р. *Join in singing,* подхва́тывать пе́сню; подпева́ть. **4,** *fol. by* up (enlist) поступа́ть на вое́нную слу́жбу.

joiner *n.* (carpenter) столя́р.

joint *n.* **1,** *anat.* суста́в. **2,** (juncture, as of two pipes) стык. **3,** (coupling) шарни́р: *universal joint,* универса́льный шарни́р. **4,** *slang* (cheap restaurant) кабачо́к. —*adj.* **1,** (done or executed in common) совме́стный. **2,** (shared with another) о́бщий; со—: *joint account,* о́бщий счёт; *joint owner,* совладе́лец. —**out of joint,** вы́вихнутый.

jointly *adv.* совме́стно; сообща́.

joint-stock company акционе́рное о́бщество.

joke *n.* шу́тка; остро́та. *Practical joke,* мистифика́ция. —*v.i.* шути́ть: *you're joking!,* вы шу́тите! *Joking aside,* шу́тки в сто́рону.

joker *n.* **1,** (one who jokes) шу́тник. **2,** *cards* джо́кер.

jokester *n.* шутни́к.

jokingly *adv.* шутя́; в шу́тку.

jolly *adj.* весёлый. —*adv., Brit., colloq.* о́чень.

jolt *n.* толчо́к. —*v.t.* трясти́; встря́хивать.

jonquil *n.* жонки́ль.

Jordanian *adj.* иорда́нский.

josh *v.i., colloq.* шути́ть.

jostle *v.t.* толка́ть; пиха́ть. —*v.i.* толка́ться.

jot *v.t.* [*usu.* jot down] запи́сывать; набра́сывать.

joule *n.* джо́уль.

journal *n.* **1,** (daily record) дневни́к. **2,** (publication) газе́та; журна́л.

journalism *n.* журнали́стика. —**journalist,** *n.* журнали́ст. —**journalistic,** *adj.* журнали́стский.

journey *n.* пое́здка; путеше́ствие. —*v.i.* путеше́ствовать.

joust *n.* ры́царский поеди́нок. —*v.i.* би́ться на поеди́нке.

jovial *adj.* весёлый. —**joviality,** *n.* весёлость.

jowl *n.* **1,** (jaw) че́люсть. **2,** (cheek) щека́. **3,** (dewlap of cattle) подгру́док.

joy *n.* ра́дость; отра́да. —**joyful,** *adj.* ра́достный. —**joyless,** *adj.* безра́достный. —**joyous,** *adj.* ра́достный.

jubilant *adj.* лику́ющий. —**jubilation,** *n.* ликова́ние.

jubilee *n.* юбиле́й.

Judaic *adj.* иуде́йский.

Judaism *n.* иудаи́зм; иуде́йство.

Judas *n.* Иу́да.

judge *n.* **1,** (one who judges; magistrate) судья́. **2,** (connoisseur) цени́тель; знато́к. *Be a good judge of,* быть знатоко́м (+ *gen.*); знать толк в. *I am no judge of such matters,* я не судья́ в э́том де́ле. —*v.t. & i.*

судить. *Judging by,* су́дя по. *Judge for yourself,* посуди́те са́ми.

judgment *n.* **1,** (legal decision) реше́ние: *pronounce judgment,* выноси́ть реше́ние; *defer judgment,* откла́дывать реше́ние. *Pass judgment on,* суди́ть. **2,** (faculty of judging wisely) рассуди́тельность; благоразу́мие. *Show good judgment,* суди́ть здра́во. **3,** (opinion) мне́ние; взгляд; сужде́ние. *In my judgment,* на мой взгляд. —**Judgment Day,** Су́дный день; Стра́шный суд.

judicial *adj.* суде́бный; юриди́ческий.

judiciary *adj.* суде́бный; юриди́ческий. —*n.* судоустро́йство.

judicious *adj.* благоразу́мный; рассуди́тельный. —**judiciously,** *adv.* благоразу́мно.

judo *n.* дзюдо́.

jug *n.* **1,** (vessel) кувши́н; жбан. **2,** *slang* (jail) кутузка.

juggle *v.t.* **1,** (toss and catch) жонгли́ровать. **2,** *fig.* (manipulate, as facts) подтасо́вывать; жонгли́ровать; передёргивать. —**juggler,** *n.* жонглёр. —**juggling,** *n.* жонглёрство.

jugular vein яре́мная ве́на.

juice *n.* сок. —**juicer,** *n.* соковыжима́лка.

juicy *adj.* со́чный. —**juiciness,** *n.* со́чность.

jujitsu *n.* джи́у-джи́тсу; япо́нская борьба́.

Julian calendar юлиа́нский календа́рь.

July *n.* ию́ль. —*adj.* ию́льский.

jumble *v.t.* пу́тать; перепу́тывать. —*n.* пу́таница.

jumbo *adj.* большо́й; гига́нтский.

jump *v.i.* **1,** (leap) пры́гать; скака́ть. *Jump to one's feet,* вскочи́ть на́ ноги. **2,** (start in astonishment) вздра́гивать. **3,** (rise abruptly in amount) подска́кивать. **4,** *in* jump to a conclusion, поспеши́ть с вы́водом. —*v.t.* **1,** (jump over) перепры́гивать. *Jump rope,* пры́гать че́рез скака́лку. **2,** (leave, as a track) сходи́ть с (ре́льсов). **3,** *colloq.* (attack suddenly) набра́сываться на. —*n.* прыжо́к; скачо́к. —**jump at,** ухвати́ться за. —**jump into,** впры́гивать в; вска́кивать в. —**jump off,** спры́гивать; соска́кивать. —**jump on,** **1,** (board quickly) вскочи́ть в. **2,** *colloq.* (rebuke; assail) набра́сываться на. —**jump out of,** выпры́гивать из; выбра́сываться из; выска́кивать из. *Jump out of bed,* вскочи́ть *or* соскочи́ть с посте́ли. —**jump over,** перепры́гивать; переска́кивать. —**jump up,** вска́кивать.

jumper *n.* **1,** (one who jumps) прыгу́н. **2,** (dress) пла́тье (без рукаво́в). **3,** (loose smock) блу́за.

jump rope скака́лка.

jumpy *adj.* не́рвный.

junction *n.* **1,** (of roads) у́зел; перекрёсток. *Railway junction,* железнодоро́жный у́зел. **2,** (of rivers) слия́ние.

juncture *n.* **1,** (joint) соедине́ние. **2,** (point in time) моме́нт: *at this juncture,* в э́тот моме́нт.

June *n.* ию́нь. —*adj.* ию́ньский.

jungle *n.* джу́нгли. —**jungle fever,** тропи́ческая лихора́дка; тропи́ческая маля́рия.

junior *adj.* мла́дший: *junior partner,* мла́дший партнёр. *John Smith, Jr.,* Джон Смит мла́дший. —*n.* **1,** (younger person): *he is ten years my junior,* он моло́же меня́ на де́сять лет. **2,** (third-year student) студе́нт тре́тьего ку́рса.

juniper *n.* можжеве́льник.

junk *n.* **1,** (rubbish; trash) старьё; рухлядь. *Junk dealer,* старьёвщик. **2,** (boat) джонка.

Junker *n.* юнкер.

junket *n.* молочный кисель.

junkman *n.* старьёвщик.

junta *n.* хунта.

Jupiter *n.* Юпитер.

Jurassic *adj.* юрский.

juridical *adj.* юридический.

jurisdiction *n.* **1,** (right to exercise official authority) юрисдикция. **2,** (domain over which such authority extends) ведение; компетенция.

jurisprudence *n.* юриспруденция; законоведение.

jurist *n.* юрист.

juror *n.* присяжный.

jury *n.* **1,** (in a court of law) присяжные. **2,** (in a contest) жюри.

just *adj.* **1,** (fair; right; proper) справедливый: *just decision,* справедливое решение; *just war,* справедливая война. *Just cause,* правое дело. **2,** (deserved) заслуженный: *just reward,* заслуженная награда. *Get one's just reward/deserts,* получить по заслугам. **3,** (upright; righteous) праведный. —*adv.* **1,** (precisely) как раз; именно. *Just in time,* как раз вовремя. *Just what I need,* как раз то, что мне нужно. **2,** (barely) едва. **3,** (merely) просто. **4,** (only a moment ago) только что: *he just left,* он только что ушел. —*particle* только: *just think!,* подумать только! *Just you try!,* только попробуйте! *Just look at him!,* вы только посмотрите на него! *Just what do you mean by that?,* что вы, собственно, хотите этим сказать? —**just about, 1,** (almost; very nearly) почти: *just about*

everything, почти всё. **2,** (on the point of) вот–вот: *he is just about to leave,* он вот–вот уйдет. *I was just about to call you,* я как раз собирался вам звонить. —**just a minute!,** одну минутку! —**just as, 1,** *with adjectives* столько же. **2,** (at the moment when) в тот момент, когда... **3,** (in the same way that) подобно тому, как... —**just as soon,** скорее. —**just as well,** с тем же успехом. *It's just as well,* ну что же. —**just in case,** на всякий случай. —**just now, 1,** (at this instant) сейчас. **2,** (a moment ago) только сейчас. —**just the same,** всё равно.

justice *n.* **1,** (administration of law) правосудие; юстиция. **2,** (fairness) справедливость. **3,** (judge) судья: *justice of the peace,* мировой судья. *Supreme Court justice,* член верховного суда. —**bring to justice,** привлекать к ответственности. —**do justice (to),** отдавать должное (+ *dat.*). *The picture doesn't do her justice,* фотография не делает ей комплимента.

justifiable *adj.* законный; позволительный. —**justifiably,** *adv.* по праву.

justification *n.* оправдание.

justify *v.t.* оправдывать.

justly *adv.* **1,** (fairly) справедливо. **2,** (rightly; deservedly) по праву.

jut *v.i.* [*usu.* jut out] выдаваться; выступать; торчать.

jute *n.* джут.

juvenile *adj.* юный; юношеский. —*n.* юноша; подросток; малолетний. —**juvenile delinquency,** детская преступность.

juxtapose *v.t.* **1,** (place side by side) помещать бок о бок. **2,** (contrast) сопоставлять.

K

K, k одиннадцатая буква английского алфавита.

Kaiser *n.* кайзер.

kaleidoscope *n.* калейдоскоп. —**kaleidoscopic,** *adj.* калейдоскопический.

kangaroo *n.* кенгуру.

kaolin *n.* каолин.

kapok *n.* капок.

karakul *n.* = caracul.

karat *n.* **1,** (24th part of pure gold) проба. ♦ *The Russian system, however, is based on 96: 18-karat gold,* золото семьдесят второй пробы. **2,** = carat.

kasha *n.* каша.

kayak *n.* байдарка; каяк.

keel *n.* киль. —*v.i.* [*usu.* keel over] **1,** (capsize) опрокидываться. **2,** (faint away) упасть без чувств. —**be on an even keel,** идти ровным курсом; придерживаться ровного курса.

keen *adj.* **1,** (sharp; acute) острый. **2,** (sensitive;

perceptive) острый; чуткий; меткий; тонкий. **3,** (avid; enthusiastic) страстный. *Be keen on,* увлекаться (+ *instr.*). —**keenness,** *n.* острота; чуткость; меткость; тонкость.

keep *v.t.* **1,** (hold in a specified place or state) держать; хранить. *Keep one's hands in one's pockets,* держать руки в карманах. *Keep money in the bank,* держать/хранить деньги в банке. *Keep something secret,* хранить/держать что-нибудь в секрете *or* в тайне. **2,** (retain for oneself) сохранять; оставлять; удерживать. **3,** (maintain; preserve) сохранять: *keep order,* сохранять порядок. *Keep watch,* сторожить. *Keep a secret,* хранить/сохранять секрет *or* тайну. *Keep in mind,* иметь в виду. *Keep one's seat,* оставаться сидеть. *Keep one's feet,* удерживаться на ногах. **4,** (maintain at home) держать: *keep a dog,* держать собаку; *keep servants,* держать прислугу. **5,** (carry out; fulfill) сдержать: *keep one's word,* сдержать своё сло́во; *keep a promise,* сдержа́ть обеща́ние. **6,** (observe) соблюда́ть: *keep the laws,* соблюда́ть зако́н. *Keep an appointment,* прийти́ на свида́ние. **7,** (maintain; perform) вести́: *keep score,* вести́ счёт; *keep a diary,* вести́ дневни́к; *keep the books,* вести́ кни́ги; *keep count of,* вести́ счет (+ *dat.*); *keep house,* вести́ (дома́шнее) хозя́йство. *Keep company with,* води́ть компа́нию с. **8,** (delay) заде́рживать. *Keep someone waiting,* заставля́ть кого́-нибудь ждать. **9,** *fol. by* **from** (prevent) уде́рживать (от). *Keep from laughing,* удержа́ться от сме́ха. —*v.i.* **1,** (persist; continue) продолжа́ть. *I kept imagining that...,* мне всё каза́лось, что... **2,** (remain) держа́ться: *keep to the right,* держа́ться пра́вой стороны́. *Keep to oneself,* держа́ться особняко́м. *Keep away,* держа́ться на расстоя́нии; не подходи́ть. *Keep off the grass!,* по траве́ не ходи́ть! *Keep quiet,* молча́ть. *Keep warm,* гре́ться. **3,** (not spoil) сохраня́ться. —*n.* **1,** (livelihood; support) содержа́ние. **2,** (stronghold of a castle) гла́вная ба́шня (за́мка). —**for keeps,** навсегда́. —**keep back, 1,** (hold back) уде́рживать. **2,** (not move forward) держа́ться сза́ди. *Keep back!,* наза́д! —**keep on, 1,** (continue) продолжа́ть; не перестава́ть. **2,** (not remove) не снима́ть. —**keep out, 1,** (not let in) не пуска́ть; не пропуска́ть. **2,** (stay outside) не входи́ть. *Keep out!,* вход воспрещён! **3,** *fol. by* **of** (steer clear of) держа́ться в стороне́ (от). —**keep up, 1,** (maintain) подде́рживать: *keep up a correspondence,* подде́рживать перепи́ску. **2,** (maintain the pace) идти́ в но́гу; не отстава́ть. **3,** (continue; not cease) продолжа́ться. **4,** (prevent from sleeping) не дава́ть спать. —**keep up with,** идти́ в но́гу с; не отстава́ть от; поспева́ть за; угна́ться за.

keeper *n.* храни́тель. *Lighthouse keeper,* смотри́тель маяка́.

keeping *n.* хране́ние. —**in keeping with,** соотве́тствующий (+ *dat.*); сообра́зный с.

keepsake *n.* пода́рок на па́мять.

keg *n.* бочо́нок. —**powder keg,** порохова́я бо́чка; порохово́й по́греб.

ken *n.* круг позна́ний. *Beyond one's ken,* вы́ше чьего́-либо понима́ния.

kennel *n.* конура́.

kept woman содержа́нка; коко́тка.

kerchief *n.* плато́к; косы́нка.

kernel *n.* **1,** (grain or seed) зерно́. **2,** (edible part of a nut) ядро́. **3,** *in* **kernel of truth,** зерно́ и́стины.

kerosene *n.* кероси́н. —*adj.* кероси́новый.

kestrel *n.* пустельга́.

ketchup *n.* тома́тный со́ус.

kettle *n.* **1,** (teakettle) ча́йник. **2,** (pot) котело́к. —**kettle of fish,** исто́рия: *that's a pretty kettle of fish!,* вот так исто́рия!

kettledrum *n.* лита́вра.

key *n.* **1,** (for a lock) ключ. **2,** (of a piano, typewriter, etc.) кла́виша. **3,** (code; solution) ключ. **4,** (explanatory table) ключ. **5,** *fig.* (vital element) зало́г: *the key to his success,* зало́г его́ успе́хов. **6,** *music* тона́льность; лад. *Key of B flat,* тона́льность си бемо́ль. *Sing off key,* петь не в тон *or* фальши́во; фальши́вить. **7,** (tone; style; mood) тон. —*adj.* ключево́й; веду́щий. *Key role,* важне́йшая роль. *Key question,* узлово́й *or* стержнево́й вопро́с. —*v.t.* **1,** (adapt) приспособля́ть. **2,** *fol. by* **up** (arouse) взви́нчивать: *keyed up,* взви́нченный.

keyboard *n.* клавиату́ра.

keyhole *n.* замо́чная сква́жина.

key ring кольцо́ для ключе́й.

khaki *n.* защи́тный цвет; ха́ки. —**khaki-colored,** *adj.* защи́тного цве́та; цве́та ха́ки.

khan *n.* хан. —**khanate,** *n.* ха́нство.

kibitzer *n.* непро́шеный зри́тель.

kick *v.t.* **1,** (strike with the foot) ударя́ть ного́й; дава́ть пинка́ (+ *dat.*); пина́ть. **2,** (propel with the foot, as a ball) поддава́ть (ного́й). **3,** *sports* (score, as a goal) забива́ть (гол). **4,** *slang* (overcome, as a habit) избавля́ться от (привы́чки). —*v.i.* **1,** (of a person, esp. a child) дры́гать нога́ми. **2,** (of a horse) брыка́ть(ся); ляга́ть(ся). **3,** *colloq.* (complain; grumble) ворча́ть. —*n.* **1,** (blow with the foot) пино́к. **2,** *sports* уда́р: *free kick,* свобо́дный уда́р. **3,** (recoil of a firearm) отда́ча. **4,** *colloq.* (complaint) жа́лоба. —**kick out,** выгоня́ть; вышиба́ть. —**kick up,** поднима́ть: *kick up dust,* поднима́ть пыль; *kick up a fuss,* поднима́ть шум.

kid *n.* **1,** (young goat) козлёнок. **2,** (leather) ла́йка; шевро́. **3,** *colloq.* (child) ребёнок; малы́ш. —*adj.* **1,** (made of kidskin) ла́йковый; шевро́вый. **2,** *colloq.* (younger) мла́дший. —*v.t., colloq.* **1,** (try to fool) шути́ть с. **2,** (tease) дразни́ть. —*v.i., colloq.* шути́ть: *you're kidding!,* вы шу́тите! —**treat with kid gloves,** делика́тничать с.

kidder *n.* зубоска́л.

kidnap *v.t.* похища́ть. —**kidnaper,** *n.* похити́тель. —**kidnaping,** *n.* похище́ние.

kidney *n.* по́чка. —**kidney bean,** фасо́ль. —**kidney stones,** по́чечные ка́мни.

kidskin *n.* ла́йка; шевро́. —*adj.* ла́йковый; шевро́вый.

kill *v.t.* убива́ть. *Be killed,* поги́бнуть. *Thou shalt not kill,* не убий. *Kill cockroaches,* трави́ть тарака́нов. *Kill time,* убива́ть вре́мя. *Kill a bill,* провали́ть законопрое́кт. *Kill one's hopes,* убива́ть наде́жды. *Frost killed the flowers,* моро́з погуби́л цветы́. *My feet are killing me,* у меня́ стра́шно боля́т но́ги. —**kill two birds with one stone,** уби́ть двух за́йцев одни́м уда́ром.

killer *n.* уби́йца. —**killer whale,** коса́тка.

killing *n.* **1,** (murder) уби́йство. **2,** *colloq.* (sudden large profit) куш. —*adj.* уби́йственный.

kiln *n.* обжига́тельная печь.

kilocycle *n.* килоге́рц.

kilogram *also,* **kilogramme** *n.* килогра́мм.

kilometer *also,* **kilometre** *n.* киломе́тр.

kiloton *n.* килото́нна.

kilowatt *n.* килова́тт. —**kilowatt-hour,** *n.* килова́тт-час.

kilt *n.* шотла́ндская ю́бочка.

kilter *n., in* **out of kilter,** не в поря́дке.

kimono *n.* кимоно́.

kin *n.* родня́; родны́е; ро́дственники. —**next of kin,** ближа́йшие ро́дственники.

kind *n.* род; вид; сорт. *All kinds of,* вся́кого ро́да (+ *nom.*). *A mandarin is a kind of orange,* мандари́н — вид апельси́на. *The first such book of its kind,* пе́рвая тако́го ро́да кни́га. *What kind of books do you like best?,* каки́е кни́ги вы лю́бите бо́льше всего́? *What kind of person is he?,* что он за челове́к? *Something of the kind,* что́-то в э́том ро́де. *Nothing of the kind,* ничего́ подо́бного. —*adj.* **1,** (kindly) до́брый: *kind*

man, добрый человек. *Kind heart/face,* доброе сердце/лицо. **2,** (considerate) любезный; милый: *very kind of you,* очень любезно/мило с вашей стороны. **3,** (cordial) сердечный: *(with) kind regards,* с сердечным приветом. **—be so kind as to...,** будьте добры *or* любезны (+ *imperative*). **—in kind, 1,** (in goods) натурой. **2,** (in like manner) той же монетой. **—kind of,** *colloq.* как-то: *he is acting kind of strange,* он ведёт себя как-то странно.

kindergarten *n.* детский сад.

kindhearted *adj.* добросердечный; отзывчивый. **—kindheartedness,** *n.* добросердечие; отзывчивость.

kindle *v.t.* разжигать; зажигать.

kindling *n.* **1,** (act of kindling) разжигание. **2,** (kindling wood) растопка.

kindly *adj.* добрый; добродушный. **—adv. 1,** (out of kindness) любезно. **2,** (cordially; warmly) добродушно. **3,** (please) будьте добры. **—take kindly to,** относиться благосклонно к.

kindness *n.* **1,** (quality of being kind) доброта. **2,** (kind act; favor) любезность. **3,** (solicitude) внимание.

kindred *adj.* родственный.

kinescope *n.* кинескоп.

kinetic *adj.* кинетический. **—kinetic energy,** кинетическая энергия; живая сила.

kinetics *n.* кинетика.

kinfolk *n.pl.* родные; родня.

king *n.* **1,** (sovereign) король. **2,** (most powerful creature) царь: *the king of beasts/birds,* царь зверей/птиц. **3,** (tycoon) король: *oil king,* нефтяной король. **4,** *cards; chess* король. **5,** *checkers* дамка. **—adj.** [*usu.* **king's**] королевский. *King's bishop, chess* королевский слон. **—live like a king,** жить барином.

kingbolt *n.* шкворень.

kingdom *n.* **1,** (monarchy) королевство: *United Kingdom,* Соединённое Королевство. **2,** *fig.* (realm) царство: *animal kingdom,* животное царство.

kingfisher *n.* зимородок.

kinglet *n.* (bird) королёк.

kingly *adj.* королевский; царственный.

kingpin *n.* **1,** = **kingbolt. 2,** *colloq.* (key figure) главарь.

kink *n.* **1,** (bend; loop; knot) загиб; петля; узел. **2,** (cramp; crick) судорога. **—kinky,** *adj.* кудрявый; курчавый.

kinsfolk *n.pl.* родные; родня.

kinship *n.* родство.

kinsman *n.* родственник.

kiosk *n.* киоск.

kipper *n.* копчёная селёдка.

kiss *v.t.* целовать. **—v.i.** (of two people) целоваться. **—n.** поцелуй.

kisser *n.,* *slang* морда; рыло; харя.

kit *n.* **1,** (set of equipment) набор; комплект. *First-aid kit,* аптечка; *mil.* санитарная сумка. **2,** (container for same; case) сумка; ящик.

kitchen *n.* кухня. **—adj.** кухонный: *kitchen table,* кухонный стол.

kite *n.* **1,** (device that flies) змей. **2,** (bird) коршун.

kitten *n.* котёнок.

kittiwake *n.* моёвка.

kitty *n.* **1,** (kitten) котёнок; киска. **2,** *cards* банк.

kiwi *n.* киви-киви.

kleptomania *n.* клептомания. **—kleptomaniac,** *n.* клептоман.

knack *n.* сноровка. *Get the knack of,* приноравливаться к; наловчиться (+ *inf.*).

knapsack *n.* рюкзак; ранец; котомка; вещевой мешок.

knave *n.* **1,** (rascal) плут; мошенник. **2,** *cards* валёт.

knead *v.t.* месить; замешивать.

knee *n.* колено. *On one's hands and knees,* на четвереньках. **—adj.** коленный: *knee joint,* коленный сустав. **—bring to one's knees,** ставить (кого-нибудь) на колени.

kneecap *n.* коленная чашка; коленная чашечка.

knee-deep *adj.* по колено; по колени.

kneel *v.i.* **1,** (assume a kneeling position) становиться на колени. **2,** (be in a kneeling position) стоять на коленях.

kneepad *n.* наколенник.

knell *n.* похоронный звон. **—sound the death knell for,** предвещать конец (+ *gen.*).

knickers *n.pl.* бриджи.

knickknack *n.* безделушка; вещица; финтифлюшка.

knife *n.* нож. **—adj.** ножевой: *knife wound,* ножевая рана. **—v.t.** резать *or* колоть ножом.

knight *n.* **1,** (medieval warrior) рыцарь. **2,** *chess* конь. **—v.t.** посвящать в рыцари. **—knight-errant,** *n.* странствующий рыцарь. **—knighthood,** *n.* рыцарство. **—knightly,** *adj.* рыцарский.

knit *v.t.* **1,** (weave) вязать. **2,** (contract, as one's eyebrows) хмурить; сдвинуть. **—v.i.** (grow together, as of bones) срастаться.

knitted *adj.* вязаный; трикотажный. *Knitted fabric,* трикотаж.

knitting *n.* вязание. **—adj.** вязальный. **—knitting kneedle,** (вязальная) спица; вязальная игла.

knob *n.* **1,** (handle of a door) (дверная) ручка. **2,** (lump; protuberance) шишка; бугор.

knock *v.i.* стучать (в дверь). **—v.t. 1,** (hit; strike) ударять; бить; колотить. *Knock someone to the ground,* повалить кого-нибудь на землю. *Be knocked unconscious,* лишиться сознания. **2,** (bang) ударяться; стукаться: *knock heads,* стукнуться головами. *Knock one's head on the door,* удариться головой о дверь. **3,** (make by striking) пробивать: *knock a hole in the wall,* пробивать отверстие в стене. **4,** *colloq.* (criticize) придираться к. **—n. 1,** (rap, as on a door) стук. **2,** (blow) удар. **—knock about,** *colloq.* слоняться; шататься. **—knock down,** сбивать с ног; валить; сваливать. **—knock loose,** расшатывать. **—knock off, 1,** (dislodge; topple) сбивать. **2,** *colloq.* (deduct) скидывать. **3,** *colloq.* (compose quickly; dash off) (на)строчить. **4,** *slang* (quit work) шабашить. **—knock out, 1,** (dislodge) выбивать. **2,** (exhaust completely) истомлять. **3,** *boxing* нокаутировать. **4,** *mil.* (destroy) выводить из строя; подбивать. **—knock over,** опрокидывать. **—knock together,** сколачивать; сбивать.

knockdown *n.,* *boxing* нокдаун.

knocker *n.* дверной молоток.

knock-kneed *adj.* кривоногий.

knockout *n.,* *boxing* нокаут.

knoll *n.* холмик; бугор; пригорок.

knot *n.* **1,** (in rope) узел. **2,** (in wood) сук; сучок. **3,** (nautical mile per hour) узел. **—v.t.** завязывать узлом.

knothole *n.* свищ.
knotted *adj.* **1,** (tied with a knot) завя́занный узло́м. **2,** (full of knots) узлова́тый.
knotty *adj.* **1,** (full of knots, as of wood) сучкова́тый. **2,** *fig.* (difficult; intricate) запу́танный.
knout *n.* кнут.
know *v.t. & i.* знать: *I don't know,* я не зна́ю. *Know what's what,* знать что к чему́. *As far as I know,* насколько я зна́ю. *For all one knows,* чего́ до́брого. *How should I know?,* отку́да же я зна́ю? —*n.,* in **in the know,** в ку́рсе де́ла. —**know better,** знать: *I should have known better than to do that,* я до́лжен был знать, что не сле́дует де́лать э́того. —**know how,** уме́ть.
knowing *adj.* **1,** (knowledgeable; astute) зна́ющий; то́нкий. **2,** (of a smile, glance, etc.) многозначи́тельный.
knowingly *adv.* **1,** (deliberately) созна́тельно; наме́ренно; заве́домо. **2,** (as if having secret information) значи́тельно.
know-it-all *n., colloq.* всезна́йка.
knowledge *n.* зна́ние. *With/without the knowledge of,* с/без ве́дома (+ *gen.*). —**to (the best of) my knowledge,** насколько мне изве́стно.
knowledgeable *adj.* зна́ющий; све́дущий; гра́мотный; осведомлённый. —**knowledgeability,** *n.* зна́ния; гра́мотность; осведомлённость.
known *adj.* изве́стный: *a known fact,* изве́стный факт. *As is known,* как изве́стно. *It is known that...,* изве́стно, что... —**make known,** раскрыва́ть; разглаша́ть.
knuckle *n.* **1,** (joint of the finger) костя́шка. **2,** (animal joint used as food) но́жка. —*v.i.* **1,** *fol. by* **down** (apply oneself vigorously) запряга́ться. **2,** *fol. by* **under** (give in; yield) идти́ на поводу́ (у).
kohlrabi *n.* кольра́би.
kolinsky *n.* колоно́к.
kopeck *n.* копе́йка.
Koran *n.* кора́н.
Korean *adj.* коре́йский. —*n.* **1,** (person) коре́ец; коре́янка. **2,** (language) коре́йский язы́к.
kosher *adj.* коше́рный.
kowtow *v.i.* низкопокло́нничать; раболе́пствовать.
Kremlin *n.* кремль. —*adj.* кремлёвский. —**Kremlinologist,** *n.* сове́толог.
krypton *n.* крипто́н.
kulak *n.* кула́к.
Kurd *n.* курд. *The Kurds,* ку́рды. —**Kurdish,** *adj.* ку́рдский. —*n.* ку́рдский язы́к.

L

L, l двена́дцатая бу́ква англи́йского алфави́та.
la *n., music* ля.
label *n.* ярлы́к; этике́тка; би́рка. —*v.t.* накле́ивать ярлы́к на (*also fig.*).
labial *adj.* губно́й.
labor *also,* **labour** *n.* **1,** (work; toil) труд: *manual/child labor,* ручно́й/де́тский труд. *Capital and labor,* капита́л и труд. *Department of Labor,* министе́рство труда́. **2,** (trade unions) профсою́зы. **3,** (childbirth) ро́ды; родовы́е поту́ги. *Be in labor,* быть в ро́дах. —*v.i.* **1,** (toil) труди́ться. **2,** *fol. by* **under** (be afflicted with): *labor under a delusion,* быть в заблужде́нии. —*adj.* **1,** (pert. to work or workers) трудово́й: *labor laws,* трудово́е законода́тельство. **2,** (pert. to trade unions) профсою́зный: *the labor movement,* профсою́зное движе́ние. **3,** (pert. to childbirth) родово́й: *labor pains,* родовы́е поту́ги/схва́тки/му́ки.
laboratory *n.* лаборато́рия. *Language laboratory,* кабине́т иностра́нных языко́в. —*adj.* лаборато́рный: *laboratory experiments,* лаборато́рные о́пыты.
labored *also,* **laboured** *adj.* **1,** (done with difficulty) затруднённый. **2,** (ponderous) вы́мученный.
laborer *also,* **labourer** *n.* рабо́чий.
laborious *adj.* кропотли́вый.
labor union профсою́з.
labour *n. & v.* = **labor.** —**Labour,** *adj.* лейбори́стс-кий: *Labour Party,* лейбори́стская па́ртия. —**Labourite,** *n.* лейбори́ст.
labyrinth *n.* лабири́нт.
lace *n.* **1,** (fabric) кру́жево. **2,** (cord, as for shoes) шнуро́к. —*adj.* кружевно́й. —*v.t.* шнурова́ть. —*v.i.* [*usu.* **lace into**] *colloq.* обру́шиваться на.
lacerate *v.t.* разрыва́ть; раздира́ть. —**laceration,** *n.* разры́в; рва́ная ра́на.
lachrymal *adj.* слёзный. —**lachrymose,** *adj.* слезли́вый.
lack *n.* **1,** (shortage) недоста́ток: *for lack of money,* за недоста́тком де́нег. **2,** (absence) отсу́тствие: *lack of ability,* отсу́тствие спосо́бностей. *For lack of evidence,* за неиме́нием ули́к. —*v.t.* **1,** (be without) не име́ть. *The building lacks an elevator,* в до́ме нет ли́фта. *Lacking the most basic conveniences,* лишённый элемента́рных удо́бств. **2,** (not have enough of) не хвата́ть (*impers.*); недостава́ть (*impers.*). *He lacks the strength to...,* ему́ не хвата́ет сил, что́бы... —*v.i.* не хвата́ть: *there is only one thing lacking,* одного́ то́лько не хвата́ет.
lackadaisical *adj.* хала́тный; неради́вый.
lackey *n.* лаке́й.
lackluster *also,* **lacklustre** *adj.* **1,** (lacking brightness) ту́склый. **2,** *fig.* (uninspired) пре́сный.
laconic *adj.* лакони́ческий; немногосло́вный.

lacquer *n.* лак. —*v.t.* лакировáть. —**lacquerware,** *n.* лакирóванные издéлия.

lacrosse *n.* лякрóсс.

lactation *n.* лактáция.

lacteal *adj.* молóчный.

lactic *adj.* молóчный. —**lactic acid,** молóчная кислотá.

lactose *n.* молóчный сáхар; лактóза.

lacuna *n.* пробéл; прóпуск.

lad *n.* пáрень; юноша.

ladder *n.* лéстница.

laden *adj.* нагрýженный; перегрýженный.

ladies' man волокúта; ловелáс; бáбник. *Also,* **lady's man.**

ladies' room дáмская убóрная; дáмский туалéт.

ladle *n.* разливáтельная лóжка. —*v.t.* разливáть.

lady *n.* **1,** (woman) дáма. *Ladies and gentlemen,* дáмы и господá. **2,** (woman of rank or nobility) лéди. *The First Lady,* пéрвая лéди. —**lady of the house,** хозяйка дóма.

ladybug *n.* бóжья корóвка. *Also,* **ladybird.**

lady in waiting фрéйлина.

lady-killer *n., colloq.* покорúтель сердéц; сердцеéд.

ladylike *adj.* жéнственный; воспúтанный; прилúчный.

ladylove *n.* дáма сéрдца; зазнóба.

lag *v.i.* отставáть: *lag behind the others,* отставáть от остальных. —*n.* отставáние; запáздывание.

lager *n.* лёгкое пúво.

laggard *n. & adj.* отстающий.

lagoon *n.* лагýна.

lair *n.* лóговище; берлóга.

laity *n.* миряне.

lake *n.* óзеро.

lama *n.* лáма. —**Lamaism,** *n.* ламаúзм. —**lamasery,** *n.* ламáйстский монастырь.

lamb *n.* **1,** (animal) ягнёнок; барáшек. **2,** (meat) (молодáя) барáнина. —**lamb chop,** барáнья отбивнáя.

lambaste *v.t., colloq.* **1,** (beat) колотúть. **2,** (berate) хлестáть.

lambskin *n.* барáшек; мерлýшка. —*adj.* барáшковый; мерлýшковый.

lame *adj.* **1,** (crippled) хромóй. **2,** (poor, as of an excuse) слáбый. —**lameness,** *n.* хромотá.

lament *v.t. & i.* сокрушáться (о); сéтовать (на). —**lamentable,** *adj.* плачéвный; прискóрбный. —**lamentation,** *n.* причитáние; сéтование.

laminated *adj.* слóистый.

lamp *n.* лáмпа.

lamplighter *n.* фонáрщик.

lampoon *n.* шарж; пáсквиль. —*v.t.* шаржúровать.

lamppost *n.* фонáрный столб.

lamprey *n.* минóга.

lampshade *n.* абажýр.

lance *n.* **1,** (weapon) пúка. **2,** (surgical knife) ланцéт. —*v.t.* вскрывáть; разрезáть.

lancet *n.* (knife) ланцéт. —**lancet arch,** стрéльчатая áрка. —**lancet window,** стрéльчатое окнó.

land *n.* **1,** (earth; ground) земля. *Dry land,* сýша. **2,** (country) странá; край. *Native land,* рóдина. —*adj.* земéльный. *Land reform,* земéльная рефóрма. —*v.t.* **1,** (set down, as an aircraft) посадúть. **2,** (catch, as a fish) вытащить (рыбу). **3,** (deliver, as a blow) наносúть (удáр). **4,** *colloq.* (obtain) получúть. *Land*

a job, попáсть на рабóту. —*v.i.* **1,** (put into port) высáживаться. **2,** (touch down, as of an aircraft) приземляться. **3,** (fall; strike) попáсть; прийтúсь. **4,** *colloq.* (end up; wind up) попáсть; угодúть: *land in jail,* попáсть/угодúть в тюрьмý.

landed *adj.* **1,** (owning land) помéстный: *the landed gentry,* помéстное дворянство. **2,** (consisting of land) земéльный.

landing *n.* **1,** (of an aircraft) посáдка. **2,** (debarkation) высáдка. **3,** *mil.* высáдка; десáнт; высáдка десáнта. **4,** (platform, as on stairs) площáдка. —**landing craft,** десáнтное сýдно. —**landing field,** посáдочная площáдка. —**landing gear,** шассú. —**landing strip,** взлётно-посáдочная полосá.

landlady *n.* хозяйка.

landless *adj.* безземéльный.

landlocked *adj.* не имéющий выхода к мóрю.

landlord *n.* хозяин.

landmark *n.* **1,** (prominent object to go by) ориентúр. **2,** (major event) вéха.

land mine фугáс.

landowner *n.* помéщик; землевладéлец.

landscape *n.* пейзáж; ландшáфт. —**landscape architecture,** садóво-пáрковое искýсство.

landslide *n.* обвáл; óползень.

lane *n.* **1,** (narrow path) дорóжка. **2,** (narrow street) уличка. **3,** (marked division on a highway) ряд; полосá. **4,** (on a running track or swimming pool) дорóжка. **5,** *naut.* (морскóй) путь.

language *n.* язык: *foreign language,* инострáнный язык. *Bad language,* брань; рýгань. *Strong language,* сúльные выражéния. —*adj.* языковóй: *language barrier,* языковóй барьéр.

languid *adj.* вялый; тóмный.

languish *v.i.* **1,** (lose vigor; droop) вянуть; чáхнуть. **2,** (live under dispiriting conditions) томúться; изнывáть.

languor *n.* вялость. —**languorous,** *adj.* вялый.

lanky *adj.* долговязый.

lanolin *n.* ланолúн.

lantern *n.* фонáрь.

lanthanum *n.* лантáн.

lap *n.* **1,** (area between the waist and knees) колéни: *sit on one's mother's lap,* сидéть у мáтери на колéнях. **2,** (secure place) лóно: *in the lap of nature,* на лóне прирóды. *Live in the lap of luxury,* утопáть в рóскоши. **3,** (front part of skirt for carrying things) подóл. **4,** (one circuit of a racecourse) круг. **5,** *swimming* заплыв. —*v.t.* [*usu.* **lap up**] (lick up) лакáть. —*v.i.* (of waves) плескáть.

lap dog кóмнатная собáчка.

lapel *n.* отворóт; лáцкан.

lapidary *n.* гранúльщик. —*adj.* гранúльный.

lapis lazuli ляпис-лазýрь.

Lapp *n.* [*also,* **Laplander**] саáм. —*adj.* [*also,* **Lappish**] саáмский.

lap robe пóлость; плед.

lapse *n.* **1,** (slip; failure) лáпсус. *Lapse of the tongue,* обмóлвка; оговóрка. *Lapse of memory,* провáл пáмяти. **2,** (interval, as of time) промежýток. —*v.i.* **1,** *fol. by* **into** (slip into; sink into) впадáть (в). **2,** (expire) терять сúлу.

lapwing *n.* чúбис; пúгалица.

larceny *n.* крáжа; воровствó. —**larcenous,** *adj.* воровскóй.

larch *n.* лúственница.

lard *n.* (топлёное свиное) сало; шпик. —*v.t.* **1,** (apply lard to) шпиговать. **2,** *fig.* (sprinkle; intersperse) шпиговать; пересыпать.

larder *n.* кладовая.

large *adj.* большой; крупный. —**at large,** на свободе. —**by and large,** в целом; в основном. —**in large part,** во многом.

large intestine толстая кишка.

largely *adv.* **1,** (to a great extent) во многом. **2,** (for the most part) в основном.

large-scale *adj.* большого *or* крупного масштаба. *Large-scale map,* крупномасштабная карта.

largess *also,* **largesse** *n.* щедрость.

largo *adj. & adv.* ларго.

lariat *n.* аркан; лассо.

lark *n.* жаворонок.

larkspur *n.* живокость; шпорник.

larva *n.* личинка. —**larval,** *adj.* личиночный.

laryngeal *adj.* гортанный. —**laryngitis,** *n.* ларингит.

larynx *n.* гортань.

lascivious *adj.* похотливый. —**lasciviousness,** *n.* похотливость.

laser *n.* лазер. —*adj.* лазерный: *laser beam,* лазерный луч.

lash *n.* **1,** (whip) плеть; бич. **2,** (stroke of a whip) удар плётью. **3,** (eyelash) ресница. —*v.t.* **1,** (flog) хлестать; стегать. **2,** (dash against) хлестать в *or* о (+ *acc.*). **3,** (shake violently, as the tail) махать. **4,** (tie) привязывать. —**lash out against,** обрушиваться на.

lashing *n.* порка.

lass *n.* девушка; девица.

lassitude *n.* вялость; истома.

lasso *n.* лассо; аркан. —*v.t.* арканить.

last *adj.* **1,** (final) последний. *At the last moment,* в самый последний момент. *The last time I was in England,* в последний раз, когда я был (была) в Англии. **2,** (just past) прошлый: *last week,* на прошлой неделе; *last month,* в прошлом месяце; *last year,* в прошлом году; *last Sunday,* в прошлое воскресенье; *last summer,* прошлым летом. *Last night,* вчера вечером. —*adv.* **1,** (after all others) последним: *come in last,* прийти последним. *He spoke last,* он выступил после всех. **2,** (for the last time) в последний раз. **3,** (finally; lastly) наконец. —*n.* **1,** (final one) последний: *the last of the Mohicans,* последний из могикан. *He was the last to leave,* он ушёл последним; он ушёл после всех. *See the last of someone,* видеть кого-нибудь в последний раз. *Breathe one's last,* испустить дух. **2,** (shoe mold) колодка. —*v.i.* **1,** (continue; remain in existence) продолжаться; длиться. **2,** (remain in good condition) сохраняться. **3,** (hold out) выдержать. **4,** (be enough; suffice) хватать. —**at last,** наконец. —**at long last,** наконец-то. —**before last,** позапрошлый: *the year before last,* в позапрошлом году. —**last but not least,** последнее по порядку, но не по важности. —**last name,** фамилия. —**last straw,** последняя капля. —**last word,** последнее слово: *have the last word,* сказать последнее слово. —**next to last,** предпоследний. —**to the last,** до последнего: *fight to the last,* биться до последнего.

lasting *adj.* прочный: *lasting peace,* прочный мир. —*n.* (cloth) ластик.

lastly *adv.* наконец.

latch *n.* щеколда; защёлка. —*v.t.* запирать на щеколду.

late *adj.* **1,** (tardy; at an advanced time) поздний: *late hour/arrival,* поздний час/приход. *In late autumn,* поздней осенью. *In late October,* в конце октября. *Be late,* опаздывать. *You're late,* вы опоздали. **2,** *preceded by* the (deceased) покойный. —*adv.* поздно. —**of late,** в *or* за последнее время. *See also* **later** *and* **latest.**

latecomer *n.* опоздавший.

lately *adv.* в *or* за последнее время.

lateness *n.* опоздание; запоздание; запаздывание.

latent *adj.* скрытый; латентный.

later *adv.* **1,** (comp. degree of late) позже. *A little later,* попозже. **2,** (later on) потом. *A little while later,* немного погодя. —**sooner or later,** рано или поздно.

lateral *adj.* боковой.

latest *adj.* новейший; последний. *The latest news,* последние известия. —**at the latest,** самое позднее.

latex *n.* латекс.

lath *n.* дранка; планка; рейка.

lathe *n.* токарный станок.

lather *n.* (мыльная) пена. —*v.t.* мылить; намыливать.

Latin *adj.* латинский. —*n.* латинский язык; латынь.

latitude *n.* **1,** *geog.* широта. **2,** (freedom to maneuver) свобода действий.

latrine *n.* отхожее место.

latter *adj.* **1,** (second of two) последний (из двух). **2,** (nearer the end) последний: *in the latter part of the year,* в последней части года.

lattice *n.* решётка. —**latticed,** *adj.* решётчатый. —**latticework,** *n.* решётчатая конструкция.

Latvian *adj.* латвийский; латышский. —*n.* **1,** (person) латвиец; латыш. **2,** (language) латышский язык.

laud *v.t.* восхвалять; превозносить. —**laudable,** *adj.* похвальный. —**laudatory,** *adj.* хвалебный.

laugh *v.i.* смеяться. *What are you laughing at?,* чему вы смеётесь? —*n.* смех. —**laugh off,** смеяться над.

laughable *adj.* смехотворный.

laughing *n.* смех. —*adj.* шуточный: *no laughing matter,* не шуточное дело. —**laughing gas,** веселящий газ.

laughingstock *n.* посмешище. *Make a laughingstock of,* выставлять на посмешище; выставлять в смешном виде; делать из (+ *gen.*) посмешище.

laughter *n.* смех.

launch *v.t.* **1,** (set afloat) спускать (на воду). **2,** (set in flight) запускать. **3,** (initiate) открывать; предпринимать; пускать в ход. *Launch a campaign,* развернуть кампанию. *Launch an offensive,* повести наступление. —*v.i.* [*usu.* **launch into**] пускаться в: *launch into an explanation,* пускаться в объяснения. —*n.* **1,** (act of launching) запуск. **2,** (boat) катер.

launcher *n.* (пусковая) установка. *Rocket launcher,* ракетная *or* реактивная установка. *Grenade launcher,* гранатомёт.

launching *n.* запуск. —**launching pad,** пусковая *or* стартовая площадка.

launder *v.t.* стира́ть. —**laundress,** *n.* пра́чка.

laundry *n.* **1,** (items to be laundered) бельё. *Take in laundry,* брать бельё в сти́рку. **2,** (business establishment) пра́чечная.

laureate *n.* лауреа́т.

laurel *n.* **1,** (tree) лавр. **2,** *pl.* (fame; honor) ла́вры. —*adj.* ла́вровый; лавро́вый. *Laurel wreath,* лавро́вый вено́к. —**rest on one's laurels,** почива́ть на ла́врах.

lava *n.* ла́ва.

lavaliere *n.* подве́ска.

lavatory *n.* убо́рная.

lavender *n.* лава́нда. —*adj.* **1,** (pert. to the shrub) лава́ндовый. **2,** (pale purple) бле́дно-лило́вый.

lavish *adj.* **1,** (very generous) ще́дрый: *lavish in one's praise,* ще́дрый на похвалы́. **2,** (sumptuous; grand) пы́шный. —*v.t.* расточа́ть: *lavish praise upon,* расточа́ть похвалы́ (+ *dat.*). *Lavish care upon,* окружа́ть (кого́-нибудь) забо́той.

law *n.* **1,** (rule of conduct; scientific principle) зако́н: *break the law,* наруша́ть зако́н. *The law of gravity,* зако́н (всеми́рного) тяготе́ния. **2,** (jurisprudence) пра́во: *criminal law,* уголо́вное пра́во. *Study law,* изуча́ть пра́во. *Practice law,* занима́ться адвокату́рой. —**take the law into one's own hands,** распра́виться без суда́.

law-abiding *adj.* законопослу́шный.

lawbreaker *n.* правонаруши́тель.

lawful *adj.* зако́нный.

lawless *adj.* беззако́нный. —**lawlessness,** *n.* беззако́ние.

lawmaker *n.* законода́тель.

lawn *n.* лужа́йка; газо́н. —**lawn mower,** газоноко́силка.

law school юриди́ческий факульте́т.

lawsuit *n.* суде́бный проце́сс; иск.

lawyer *n.* юри́ст; адвока́т.

lax *adj.* расхля́банный; распу́щенный. *Lax morals,* лёгкие нра́вы.

laxative *n.* слаби́тельное.

laxity *n.* расхля́банность; распу́щенность. *Also,* **laxness.**

lay *v.t.* **1,** (put or place horizontally) класть: *lay the wounded man on a stretcher,* класть ра́неного на носи́лки. **2,** (install; place in position) прокла́дывать: *lay a pipeline,* прокла́дывать трубопрово́д. *Lay bricks,* класть кирпичи́. *Lay mines,* ста́вить *or* закла́дывать ми́ны. *Lay a foundation,* закла́дывать фунда́мент. **3,** (spread, as a tablecloth, carpet, etc.) стлать. **4,** (produce, as eggs) класть; нести́. **5,** (locate): *the scene is laid in France,* де́йствие происхо́дит во Фра́нции. **6,** *with various abstract nouns: lay plans,* стро́ить пла́ны; *lay the blame on,* возлага́ть *or* вали́ть вину́ на; *lay emphasis on,* де́лать упо́р на; *lay claim to, see* **claim.** **7,** *in fig. expressions involving parts of the body: lay (one's) hands on,* распра́виться с; *lay eyes on,* (у)ви́деть; *lay a finger on,* па́льцем тро́нуть. **8,** (bet) держа́ть пари́ на. —*v.i.* (of a hen) нести́сь. —*adj.* (secular) мирско́й; све́тский. —*n.* (ballad) песнь. *The Lay of Igor's Host,* Сло́во о полку́ И́гореве. —**lay aside/away/by,** откла́дывать в сто́рону. —**lay bare,** обнажа́ть; выкла́дывать. —**lay down, 1,** (place in a horizontal position) класть; укла́дывать. **2,** (give up; surrender) сложи́ть: *lay down one's arms/life,* сложи́ть ору́жие/го́лову. **3,** (state

authoritatively, as rules) устана́вливать. *Lay down the law,* установи́ть твёрдое пра́вило. —**lay low,** свали́ть; повали́ть; срази́ть. —**lay off, 1,** (discharge) увольня́ть; рассчи́тывать. **2,** *colloq.* (stop; give up) бро́сить. —**lay of the land,** положе́ние веще́й. —**lay oneself open to,** подверга́ться (+ *dat.*). —**lay out, 1,** (spread out) раскла́дывать; выкла́дывать. **2,** (design) плани́ровать; разбива́ть. **3,** (spend, as money) тра́тить. —**lay to rest,** хорони́ть. —**lay up, 1,** (store) заготовля́ть впрок. **2,** (confine to bed) укла́дывать. —**lay waste,** опустоша́ть.

layer *n.* **1,** (covering) слой; пласт. *Layer of dust/ fat,* слой пы́ли/жи́ра. *Layer of snow,* пласт сне́га. **2,** (workman who lays something) укла́дчик: *track layer,* укла́дчик путе́й. **3,** (hen as an egg producer) несу́шка. *Good layer,* но́ская ку́рица.

layette *n.* прида́ное.

layman *n.* миря́нин.

layoff *n.* **1,** (dismissal) увольне́ние. **2,** (period of inactivity) переры́в.

layout *n.* **1,** (arrangement) расположе́ние; устро́йство; плани́ровка. **2,** (design; format, as of a newspaper) оформле́ние.

layover *n.* остано́вка (в пути́).

laze *v.i.* не́житься; лента́йничать.

laziness *n.* лень; ле́ность.

lazy *adj.* лени́вый. —**lazybones,** *n., colloq.* лента́й; лежебо́ка.

lead¹ (led) *n.* **1,** (heavy metal) свине́ц. **2,** (graphite, as used in pencils) графи́т. —*adj.* свинцо́вый. —**lead pencil,** просто́й *or* графи́товый каранда́ш. —**lead poisoning,** отравле́ние свинцо́м.

lead² (leed) *v.t.* **1,** (guide) вести́: *lead a blind man,* вести́ слепо́го. *Lead troops into battle,* вести́ войска́ в бой. **2,** (direct) руководи́ть: *lead an expedition,* руководи́ть экспеди́цией. **3,** (induce; prompt) побужда́ть. **4,** (be first among) быть впереди́ (+ *gen.*). **5,** *Lead the way,* идти́ впереди́. **6,** (live, as a certain kind of life) вести́. **7,** *cards* идти́ с: *lead an ace,* идти́ с туза́. —*v.i.* **1,** (serve as a route) вести́: *this road leads to town,* э́та доро́га ведёт к го́роду. **2,** *fol. by* **to** (tend toward a certain result) вести́ (к); привести́ (к): *lead to nothing,* ни к чему́ не вести́ *or* привести́. **3,** (be in the lead) лиди́ровать. **4,** *cards: who leads?,* чей ход? —*n.* **1,** (first place in a contest) ли́дерство. *Be in the lead,* лиди́ровать. **2,** (distance in front): *have a long lead,* быть далеко́ впереди́. **3,** (role of leader) инициати́ва: *take the lead,* взять инициати́ву в свои́ ру́ки. **4,** (example) приме́р: *follow someone's lead,* сле́довать чьему́-нибудь приме́ру. **5,** *theat.* гла́вная роль. **6,** *cards* ход. **7,** *electricity* про́вод. —*adj.* веду́щий: *lead aircraft,* веду́щий самолёт. *Lead role,* гла́вная роль. *Lead article,* передова́я статья́. —**lead away,** уводи́ть. —**lead in,** вводи́ть. —**lead on,** води́ть за́ нос. —**lead out,** выводи́ть.

leaded *adj.* (of gasoline) этили́рованный.

leaden *adj.* свинцо́вый: *leaden skies,* свинцо́вое не́бо.

leader *n.* руководи́тель; вождь; ли́дер. —**leadership,** *n.* руково́дство.

lead-in *n.* ввод.

leading *adj.* веду́щий. —**leading lady,** премье́рша. —**leading light,** свети́ло; све́точ; корифе́й. —**leading man,** премье́р. —**leading question,** наводя́щий вопро́с.

leaf *n.* **1**, (of a tree or plant) лист: *the leaves are falling,* ли́стья па́дают. *Tea/tobacco leaf,* ча́йный/таба́чный лист. **2**, (of a book) лист. **3**, (of a table) доска́. **4**, (of a door or gate) ство́рка; полотни́ще. **5**, *in gold/ silver leaf,* суса́льное зо́лото/серебро́. —*v.t.* [*usu.* **leaf through**] перели́стывать. —**take a leaf from someone's book,** брать приме́р с. —**turn over a new leaf,** испра́виться.

leaflet *n.* листо́вка.

leafy *adj.* ли́ственный.

league *n.* ли́га; сою́з. *In league with,* в сою́зе с; в сго́воре с. —**League of Nations,** Ли́га на́ций.

leak *n.* течь: *spring a leak,* дать течь. —*v.i.* **1**, (admit water) течь; протека́ть. **2**, *fol. by* **into** (seep into) затека́ть (в); протека́ть (в). —**leak out, 1**, (seep out) вытека́ть. **2**, *fig.* (become known) вы́йти нару́жу; проса́чиваться.

leakage *n.* уте́чка.

leaky *adj.* име́ющий течь.

lean *v.i.* **1**, (incline one's body) наклоня́ться: *lean over the cradle,* наклоня́ться над колыбе́лью. *Lean over the railing,* перегиба́ться че́рез пери́ла. *Lean out of the window,* высо́вываться из окна́. *Lean back in the chair,* отки́дываться в кре́сле. **2**, (not be erect; slant) наклоня́ться. **3**, *fol. by* **against** (rest against) прислоня́ться (к). **4**, *fol. by* **on** (support oneself on; depend on) опира́ться (на). **5**, *fol. by* **toward** (favor slightly) склоня́ться (к). —*v.t.* **1**, (tilt) наклоня́ть. **2**, (prop) прислоня́ть; опира́ть. —*adj.* **1**, (thin) худо́й. **2**, (not fatty, as of meat) не жи́рный; по́стный. **3**, *Lean years,* неурожа́йные го́ды.

leaning *n.* скло́нность; накло́нность. —*adj.* накло́нный.

leanness *n.* худоба́.

leap *v.i.* пры́гать; скака́ть. —*n.* прыжо́к; скачо́к. —**by leaps and bounds,** скачка́ми.

leapfrog *n.* чехарда́.

leap year високо́сный год.

learn *v.t.* **1**, (gain knowledge or mastery of) (на)учи́ться: *learn a great deal,* научи́ться мно́гому; *learn how to swim,* научи́ться пла́вать. **2**, (memorize) зау́чивать. **3**, (find out) узнава́ть. —*v.i.* **1**, (gain knowledge) учи́ться: *learn from one's mistakes,* учи́ться на оши́бках. **2**, *fol. by* **of** *or* **about** (find out about) узнава́ть (о). —**learned,** *adj.* зна́ющий; учёный. —**learner,** *n.* учени́к: *slow learner,* сла́бый учени́к.

learning *n.* **1**, (acquiring knowledge) уче́ние. **2**, (erudition) учёность; эруди́ция.

lease *v.t.* **1**, (rent) брать в аре́нду. **2**, (let) сдава́ть в аре́нду. —*n.* аре́ндный догово́р. —**new lease on life,** втора́я мо́лодость.

leaseholder *n.* аренда́тор.

leash *n.* при́вязь; поводо́к.

least *adj.* мале́йший; наиме́ньший: *not the least doubt,* ни мале́йшего сомне́ния; *the line of least resistance,* ли́ния наиме́ньшего сопротивле́ния. —*adv.* **1**, *before adjectives* наиме́нее: *the least important question,* наиме́нее ва́жный вопро́с. **2**, *with verbs* ме́ньше всего́: *what I like least,* что мне нра́вится ме́ньше всего́. —*n.* [*usu.* **the least**] са́мое ме́ньшее; са́мое ма́лое. *That's the least of my worries,* э́то меня́ ме́ньше всего́ беспоко́ит. —**at least,** по кра́йней ме́ре; хоть; хотя́ бы. —**at the least,** са́мое ме́ньшее; са́мое ма́лое. —**not in the least,** ниско́лько; ни в мале́йшей сте́пени. —**not the**

least bit (+ *adj.*), ниско́лько не; совсе́м не. —**to say the least,** е́сли (*or* что́бы) не сказа́ть бо́льше.

leather *n.* ко́жа. —*adj.* ко́жаный.

leave *v.i.* уходи́ть; уезжа́ть: *he left,* он ушёл; *she left for Florida,* она́ уе́хала во Флори́ду. *The train leaves at eight,* по́езд отхо́дит в во́семь часо́в. —*v.t.* **1**, (go out of) выходи́ть из: *leave the room/house,* выходи́ть из ко́мнаты/из до́му/. **2**, (depart from) уходи́ть из; уезжа́ть из: *leave home,* уходи́ть/уезжа́ть из до́ма. **3**, (go without taking; let remain) оставля́ть: *leave the children at home,* оставля́ть дете́й до́ма. *Leave far behind,* оставля́ть далеко́ позади́. *Leave the door open,* оставля́ть дверь откры́той. *Leave in peace,* оставля́ть в поко́е. **4**, (forget) забы́ть; оста́вить: *leave one's notebook home,* забы́ть/оста́вить тетра́дь до́ма. **5**, (forsake) покида́ть; оставля́ть; бро́сить. *Don't leave me!,* не покида́йте меня́! **6**, (entrust) предоставля́ть: *leave it to me to decide,* предоста́вьте реша́ть э́то мне. **7**, (be survived by): *he leaves a wife and two children,* по́сле него́ оста́лись жена́ и дво́е дете́й. **8**, (bequeath) завеща́ть. **9**, *in subtraction: seven minus three leaves four,* семь ми́нус три равня́ется четырём. —*n.* **1**, (permission) разреше́ние. **2**, *mil.* (furlough) о́тпуск; побы́вка. *Sick leave,* о́тпуск по боле́зни. *Absence without leave,* самово́льная отлу́чка. **3**, *in* **take leave of,** проща́ться с; **take one's leave,** уходи́ть. —**be left,** оста́ться: *be left homeless,* оста́ться без кро́ва. *How much time is left?,* ско́лько вре́мени оста́лось? *I have only one pencil left,* у меня́ оста́лся то́лько оди́н каранда́ш. —**leave alone,** *see* **alone.** —**leave aside,** оставля́ть в стороне́: *leaving aside the question of...,* оставля́я в стороне́ вопро́с о... —**leave back,** оста́вить на второ́й год (в шко́ле). —**leave behind,** *see* **behind.** —**leave off, 1**, (omit at the end) пропуска́ть. **2**, (stop) остана́вливаться: *where did we leave off?,* где мы останови́лись? —**leave out,** пропуска́ть.

leaven *n.* заква́ска; опа́ра. —*v.t.* заква́шивать.

leavings *n.pl.* оста́тки.

Lebanese *adj.* лива́нский.

lecher *n.* развра́тник; распу́тник. —**lecherous,** *adj.* развра́тный; распу́тный. —**lechery,** *n.* развра́т; распу́тство.

lectern *n.* **1**, (speaker's stand) пюпи́тр. **2**, (reading desk in a church) анало́й.

lecture *n.* **1**, (discourse) ле́кция. **2**, (reprimand) нота́ция. —*v.i.* чита́ть ле́кции. —*v.t.* поуча́ть. —**lecture hall,** лекцио́нный зал.

lecturer *n.* ле́ктор.

ledge *n.* **1**, (small shelf) по́лочка. **2**, (on the side of a cliff) вы́ступ; усту́п.

ledger *n.* гла́вная кни́га; гроссбу́х.

leech *n.* пия́вка.

leek *n.* поре́й; лук-поре́й.

leer *v.i.* смотре́ть и́скоса. —*n.* косо́й взгляд.

leery *adj., colloq.* подозри́тельный; скепти́ческий. *Be leery of,* относи́ться подозри́тельно/скепти́чески к.

lees *n.pl.* гу́ща; муть.

leeward *adj.* подве́тренный.

leeway *n.* свобо́да де́йствий.

left[1] *adj.* ле́вый: *left hand,* ле́вая рука́. —*adv.* нале́во: *turn left,* повора́чивать нале́во. —*n.* **1**, (side opp. from the right) ле́вая сторона́. *To the left; on the* *left*, налéво; слéва. **2,** *polit.* [*usu.* **the Left**] лéвые.

left² *past tense and past part. of* **leave.** *See* **leave.**

left-hand *adj.* лéвый.

left-handed *adj.* **1,** (favoring the left hand): *I am left-handed*, я левшá. **2,** (backhanded) сомнúтельный: *left-handed compliment*, сомнúтельный комплимéнт.

leftist *n. & adj.* лéвый.

leftovers *n.pl.* объéдки.

left-wing *adj.* лéвый.

leg *n.* **1,** (part of the body) ногá. **2,** (of a piece of furniture) нóжка. **3,** (of a pair of trousers) штанúна. **4,** (piece of meat) ногá: *leg of mutton*, барáнья ногá. **5,** (stage of a journey) этáп. —**be on one's last legs,** доживáть послéдние дни. —**not have a leg to stand on,** не имéть под собóй пóчвы. —**pull someone's leg,** шутúть над кéм-нибудь.

legacy *n.* наслéдие.

legal *adj.* **1,** (pert. to law) правовóй; юридúческий: *legal question*, юридúческий вопрóс; *legal norms*, правовые нóрмы. **2,** (pert. to lawyers or lawsuits) судéбный: *legal costs*, судéбные издéржки. *Take legal action*, начинáть судéбный процéсс. **3,** (lawful; legitimate) закóнный; легáльный. —**legal tender,** закóнное платёжное срéдство.

legality *n.* закóнность; легáльность.

legalize *v.t.* узакóнивать; легализúровать. —**legalization,** *n.* узаконéние; легализáция.

legation *n.* мúссия.

legato *adj. & adv.* легáто.

legend *n.* легéнда; предáние. —**legendary,** *adj.* легендáрный.

legerdemain *n.* лóвкость рук.

leggings *n.pl.* гамáши; крáги.

legibility *n.* разбóрчивость.

legible *adj.* разбóрчивый. —**legibly,** *adv.* разбóрчиво.

legion *n.* легиóн. —**legionnaire,** *n.* легионéр.

legislation *n.* законодáтельство. —**legislative,** *adj.* законодáтельный. —**legislator,** *n.* законодáтель. —**legislature,** *n.* законодáтельное учреждéние.

legitimate *adj.* **1,** (lawful) закóнный. **2,** (valid, as of an excuse) уважúтельный. **3,** (born in wedlock) законнорождённый. —**legitimacy,** *n.* закóнность.

legitimize *v.t.* узакóнивать.

legless *adj.* безнóгий.

legroom *n.* мéсто для ног.

leguminous *adj.* бобóвый; стручкóвый.

leisure *n.* досýг: *at one's leisure*, на досýге. —*adj.* свобóдный: *leisure time*, свобóдное врéмя. *The leisure class*, прáздный класс.

leisurely *adj.* нетороплúвый. —*adv.* нетороплúво.

leitmotif *n.* лейтмотúв.

lemming *n.* лéмминг.

lemon *n.* лимóн. —*adj.* лимóнный. —**lemonade,** *n.* лимонáд.

lemur *n.* лемýр.

lend *v.t.* **1,** (let have temporarily) одолжáть; давáть: *could you lend me a pencil?*, вы не мóжете одолжúть/дать мне карандáш? **2,** (give as a loan) одолжáть; давáть взаймы. **3,** (give; impart) придавáть. **4,** (give; contribute) подавáть: *lend a helping hand*, подавáть рýку пóмощи. **5,** *fol. by* **itself** (be suitable)

поддавáться (+ *dat.*): *not lend itself to translation*, не поддавáться перевóду.

lender *n.* кредитóр.

length *n.* **1,** (distance from end to end) длинá. **2,** (extent) протяжéние. *Walk the length of the street*, проходúть (всю) ýлицу. **3,** (duration) продолжúтельность. **4,** (piece, as of cloth) отрéз; отрéзок. **5,** *horse racing* кóрпус: *win by two lengths*, опередúть другúх на два кóрпуса. —**at length,** подрóбно. —**go to any length,** идтú на всё. —**keep at arm's length,** держáть на почтúтельном расстоянии.

lengthen *v.t.* удлинять. —*v.i.* удлиняться.

lengthwise *adv.* в длинý; вдоль.

lengthy *adj.* длúтельный; продолжúтельный.

lenient *adj.* снисходúтельный. —**leniency,** *n.* снисходúтельность.

Leninism *n.* ленинúзм. —**Leninist,** *n.* лéнинец. —*adj.* лéнинский.

lens *n.* **1,** (glass) лúнза; объектúв. **2,** (of the eye) хрусталик. —**lens cap,** крышка объектúва.

Lent *n.* велúкий пост. —**Lenten,** *adj.* великопóстный.

lentil *n.* чечевúца. —*adj.* чечевúчный.

lento *adj. & adv.* лéнто.

Leo *n.* Лев.

leopard *n.* леопáрд.

leotard *n.* трикó.

leper *n.* прокажённый. —**leper colony,** колóния прокажёных.

leprosy *n.* прокáза. —**leprous,** *adj.* прокажённый.

lesbian *n.* лесбиянка. —*adj.* лесбúйский.

lesion *n.* поврeждéние.

less *adj.* мéньше (+ *gen.*): *less time*, мéньше врéмени. —*adv.* **1,** *before adjectives* мéнее: *less likely*, мéнее верoятно. **2,** *with verbs* мéньше: *smoke less*, мéньше курúть. —*n.* мéньше: *eat less*, мéньше есть. *Less than I expected*, мéньше, чем я ожидáл(а). —*prep.* за вычетом (+ *gen.*). —**less and less,** всё мéньше и мéньше; *(with adjectives)* всё мéнее (+ *adj.*). —**more or less,** бóлее úли мéнее. —**much less, 1,** *literally* горáздо мéньше. **2,** *before adjectives* горáздо мéнее. **3,** (especially not) тем бóлее.

lessee *n.* арендáтор.

lessen *v.t.* уменьшáть. *Lessen international tension*, уменьшáть/ослаблять/разряжáть междунарóдную напряжённость. —*v.i.* уменьшáться.

lesser *adj.* мéньший: *a lesser offense*, мéньший простýпок. *An official of lesser rank*, сотрýдник мéньшего рáнга. —**the lesser of two evils,** мéньшее из двух зол.

lesson *n.* урóк. *Learn one's lesson (fig.)*, получúть хорóший урóк. *Learn a lesson from*, извлéчь урóк из. *Teach someone a lesson*, проучúть когó-нибудь; дать комý-нибудь урóк. *Let this be a lesson to you*, это бýдет тебé урóком.

lest *conj.* **1,** (so that...not) чтóбы не: *lest any doubts remain*, чтóбы не оставáлось сомнéний. **2,** (for fear that) как бы не: *lest something worse should happen*, как бы хýже нé было.

let *v.t.* **1,** (allow) разрешáть; позволять; давáть. *Let him speak*, дай емý говорúть. *Let me think*, дáйте мне подýмать. *Let me help you*, давáйте я вам помогý. *Let an opportunity slip by*, упустúть возмóжность. *Don't let this happen again!*, чтóбы этого бóльше нé было! ♦*Also with* пусть: *let him go*, пусть он идёт. **2,** (rent; give out) сдава́ть внаём *or* в аре́нду. *Let a contract,* сдава́ть подря́д. *House to let,* сдаётся дом. —*v.aux.* **1,** [*usu.* **let's**] *in suggestions, rendered by the 1st person pl.:* let's go!, пойдём(те)! ♦*Also by* дава́й *or* дава́йте: *let's take the bus,* дава́й(те) ся́дем на авто́бус. **2,** *acquiescence* пусть: *let it rain!,* пусть бу́дет дождь. **3,** *assumption* пусть: *let x equal y,* пусть икс ра́вен и́греку. —**let alone,** *see* **alone.** —**let down, 1,** (lower) опуска́ть; спуска́ть. **2,** (undo, as one's hair) распуска́ть. **3,** (fail to keep one's word to) подводи́ть. —**let go (of),** отпуска́ть. —**let in,** пуска́ть; допуска́ть; впуска́ть; пропуска́ть. —**let in on,** посвяща́ть в: *let someone in on a secret,* посвяща́ть кого́-нибудь в та́йну. —**let know,** дать знать. —**let off, 1,** (emit) испуска́ть. **2,** (release; dismiss) отпуска́ть. —**let on,** *colloq. (usu. neg.)* (никому́ не) говори́ть; (не) подава́ть ви́ду. —**let out, 1,** (release) выпуска́ть: *let a bird out of a cage,* выпуска́ть пти́цу из кле́тки. *Let the water out of the bathtub,* спуска́ть во́ду из ва́нны. *Let the air out of a tire,* спуска́ть ши́ну. **2,** (loosen) распуска́ть. **3,** (make longer) выпуска́ть. **4,** (emit) испуска́ть. **5,** (be over) конча́ться. —**let through,** пропуска́ть. —**let up, 1,** (slacken) ослабева́ть. **2,** (abate, as of a storm) затиха́ть.

letdown *n.* разочарова́ние.

lethal *adj.* смертоно́сный; смерте́льный. *Lethal weapon,* смертоно́сное ору́жие. *Lethal dose,* смерте́льная до́за.

lethargic *adj.* летарги́ческий; вя́лый. —**lethargy,** *n.* летарги́я; вя́лость.

Lett *n.* латы́ш.

letter *n.* **1,** (of the alphabet) бу́ква. **2,** (message sent by mail) письмо́. —*v.t.* помеча́ть бу́квами. —**letter of the law,** бу́ква зако́на. —**man of letters,** литера́тор. —**to the letter,** то́чка в то́чку; в то́чности.

letter carrier почтальо́н.

letterhead *n.* на́дпись (на почто́вой бума́ге).

lettering *n.* на́дпись: *hand lettering,* на́дпись от руки́.

letter of credit аккредити́в.

letter-perfect *adj.* соверше́нно то́чный.

Lettish *adj.* латы́шский. —*n.* латы́шский язы́к.

lettuce *n.* сала́т.

letup *n.* переры́в; остано́вка. *Without letup,* безостано́вочно.

leucocyte *n.* = **leukocyte.**

leukemia *n.* белокро́вие; лейкемия́.

leukocyte *also,* **leucocyte** *n.* лейкоци́т.

levee *n.* да́мба.

level *n.* **1,** (elevation; standard) у́ровень: *water level,* у́ровень воды́. *On/at a high level,* на высо́ком у́ровне. *On a level with,* наравне́ с; наряду́ с; вро́вень с. **2,** (instrument) ватерпа́с; нивели́р; у́ровень. —*adj.* ро́вный: *level ground,* ро́вная ме́стность. —*v.t.* **1,** (make level) выра́внивать; сра́внивать (*pfv.* сровня́ть). **2,** (knock down; raze) сра́внивать/сровня́ть с землёй. **3,** (aim) наводи́ть. **4,** (direct, as an accusation) выдвига́ть (про́тив); возводи́ть (на); броса́ть (+ *dat.*). **5,** *surveying* нивели́ровать. —**do one's level best,** сде́лать всё, что в чьих-нибудь си́лах. —**on the level,** *colloq.* че́стно; правди́во.

levelheaded *adj.* уравнове́шенный; здравомы́слящий.

lever *n.* рыча́г.

leverage *n.* **1,** (action of a lever) де́йствие рычага́. **2,** *fig.* (power to influence) рычаги́: *use leverage,* испо́льзовать рычаги́.

leviathan *n.* левиафа́н.

Leviticus *n.* Леви́т.

levity *n.* легкомы́слие.

levy *v.t.* **1,** (impose) облага́ть (нало́гом); налага́ть (штраф). **2,** (collect) взима́ть; взы́скивать. —*n.* сбор; нало́г.

lewd *adj.* **1,** (lascivious) похотли́вый. **2,** (obscene) са́льный. —**lewdness,** *n.* похотли́вость.

lexical *adj.* лекси́ческий; слова́рный.

lexicography *n.* лексикогра́фия. —**lexicographer,** *n.* лексико́граф. —**lexicographic.** *adj.* лексикографи́ческий

lexicon *n.* **1,** (wordbook; dictionary) лексико́н. **2,** (vocabulary) ле́ксика; лексико́н.

liability *n.* **1,** (state of being liable) отве́тственность. **2,** *pl.* (debts; obligations) пасси́в.

liable *adj.* **1,** (legally obligated): *be liable for damages,* нести́ материа́льную отве́тственность за убы́тки. **2,** *fol. by* **to** (subject to) подлежа́щий (+ *dat.*); подве́рженный (+ *dat.*). *Be liable to,* подлежа́ть (+ *dat.*). **3,** (likely) *rendered by* мочь: *you're liable to catch cold,* ты мо́жешь простуди́ться: *He is liable to come at any moment,* он мо́жет прийти́ в любо́й моме́нт. *He is liable to do anything,* он спосо́бен на всё.

liaison *n.* **1,** (means of contact) связь. **2,** (adulterous relationship) (любо́вная) связь. **3,** *phonet.* слия́ние зву́ков.

liar *n.* лгун; лжец.

libation *n.* возлия́ние.

libel *n.* клевета́. *Libel suit,* иск за клевету́. —*v.t.* клевета́ть на. —**libelous,** *adj.* клеветни́ческий.

liberal *adj.* **1,** *polit.* либера́льный. **2,** (generous; ample) ще́дрый. **3,** (of an education) гуманита́рный. *Liberal arts,* гуманита́рные нау́ки. —*n.* либера́л. —**liberalism,** *n.* либерали́зм. —**liberality,** *n.* ще́дрость.

liberalize *v.t.* де́лать бо́лее либера́льным.

liberate *v.t.* освобожда́ть. —**liberation,** *n.* освобожде́ние. —**liberator,** *n.* освободи́тель.

libertine *n.* распу́тник; развра́тник.

liberty *n.* свобо́да. —**at liberty,** на свобо́де. *At liberty to,* во́лен (+ *inf.*). —**take liberties,** позво́лить себе́ во́льности. —**take liberties with,** фамилья́рничать с. —**take the liberty of,** позво́лить себе́ (+ *inf.*); брать на себя́ сме́лость (+ *inf.*).

Libra *n.* Весы́.

librarian *n.* библиоте́карь. —**librarianship,** *n.* библиоте́чное де́ло.

library *n.* библиоте́ка. *Record library,* фоноте́ка. *Film library,* фильмоте́ка. —*adj.* библиоте́чный: *library book,* библиоте́чная кни́га. —**library science,** библиотекове́дение.

libretto *n.* либре́тто. —**librettist,** *n.* либретти́ст.

Libyan *adj.* ливи́йский.

license *n.* **1,** (official permit) разреше́ние; свиде́тельство; лице́нзия. *Marriage license,* бра́чное свиде́тельство. *Driver's license,* води́тельские права́. **2,** (freedom) во́льность: *poetic license,* поэти́ческая во́льность. —*v.t.* разреша́ть; санкциони́ровать. —**license plate,** номерно́й знак.

licentious *adj.* распу́тный; распу́щенный. —**licentiousness,** *n.* распу́тство; распу́щенность.

lichen *n.* лиша́йник; лиша́й.

lick *v.t.* **1,** (pass the tongue over) лиза́ть; обли́зывать. *Lick off*, сли́зывать. **2,** (touch lightly, as of flames) лиза́ть. **3,** *colloq.* (defeat soundly) поби́ть. —**lick one's chops**, обли́зываться. —**lick one's wounds**, зали́зывать ра́ны. —**lick someone's boots**, лиза́ть пя́тки (+ *dat.*).

licking *n.* **1,** (act of licking) лиза́ние. **2,** *colloq.* (thrashing) по́рка; взбу́чка.

lickspittle *n.* лизоблю́д; подхали́м.

licorice *also,* **liquorice** *n.* лакри́ца. —*adj.* лакри́чный.

lid *n.* кры́шка.

lie *v.i.* **1,** (be in a recumbent position) лежа́ть: *she was lying on the ground*, она́ лежа́ла на земле́. **2,** *fol. by* **down** (assume a recumbent position) ложи́ться: *lie down on the ground*, ложи́ться на зе́млю. **3,** (be situated) лежа́ть. **4,** (be in a certain condition) лежа́ть: *lie idle*, лежа́ть без употребле́ния; *lie fallow*, лежа́ть под па́ром. *Lie at anchor*, стоя́ть на я́коре. **5,** (be buried) поко́иться: *here lies...*, здесь поко́ится... **6,** *fol. by* **in** (be) состоя́ть в; заключа́ться в: *the difficulty lies in the fact that...*, тру́дность состои́т/заключа́ется в том, что... **7,** (make false statements) лгать; врать. *You're lying!*, лжёшь! —*n.* ложь: *it's all a lie*, э́то всё ложь. —**lie ahead**, предстоя́ть. —**lie around/about**, валя́ться. —**lie in wait for**, подстерега́ть. —**lie low**, залега́ть; отлёживаться; притаи́ться. —**take lying down**, прогла́тывать (оскорбле́ние).

lie detector детéктор лжи.

lien *n.* пра́во аре́ста: *obtain a lien on someone's property*, получи́ть пра́во аре́ста чьего́-нибудь иму́щества.

lieu *n., in* **in lieu of**, вме́сто (+ *gen.*).

lieutenant *n.* лейтена́нт. *First lieutenant*, ста́рший лейтена́нт. *Second lieutenant*, мла́дший лейтена́нт. —**lieutenant colonel**, подполко́вник. —**lieutenant commander**, капита́н тре́тьего ра́нга. —**lieutenant general**, генера́л-полко́вник. —**lieutenant governor**, ви́це-губерна́тор.

life *n.* жизнь: *all one's life*, всю жизнь. —*adj.* пожи́зненный: *life imprisonment*, пожи́зненное заключе́ние. —**come to life**, ожива́ть; оживля́ться. —**for dear life**, изо всех сил. —**for life**, на всю жизнь. *Be appointed for life*, назнача́ться пожи́зненно. —**for the life of me**, хоть убе́й. —**life-and-death struggle**, борьба́ не на жизнь, а на смерть. —**life of the party**, душа́ о́бщества. —**matter of life and death**, вопро́с жи́зни и сме́рти. —**not on your life**, ни за что на све́те. —**take one's own life**, лиши́ть себя́ жи́зни. —**true to life**, как живо́й.

life belt спаса́тельный по́яс; про́бковый по́яс.

lifeboat *n.* спаса́тельная ло́дка *or* шлю́пка.

life buoy спаса́тельный круг.

lifeguard *n.* спаса́тель.

life insurance страхова́ние жи́зни.

life jacket спаса́тельный жиле́т.

lifeless *adj.* мёртвый; мёртвенный; безжи́зненный; безды́ханный.

lifelike *adj.* жи́зненный.

lifelong *adj.* на всю жизнь: *lifelong friend*, друг на всю жизнь. *Lifelong desire*, заве́тное жела́ние.

life preserver спаса́тельный по́яс.

life raft спаса́тельный плот.

lifesaver *n.* спаси́тель.

life-size *also,* **life-sized** *adj.* в натура́льную величину́.

lifetime *n.* жизнь: *in one's lifetime*, в тече́ние чьей-нибудь жи́зни. *It's the chance of a lifetime*, тако́й слу́чай представля́ется раз в жи́зни.

lifework *n.* де́ло (чьей-нибудь) жи́зни.

lift *v.t.* **1,** (raise) поднима́ть. *Lift someone's spirits*, поднима́ть дух *or* настрое́ние кого́-нибудь. **2,** (remove; withdraw, as a siege, ban, etc.) снима́ть. *Lift sanctions*, отменя́ть са́нкции. **3,** *Lift out of context*, вы́рвать из конте́кста. —*v.i.* (of fog) поднима́ться. —*n.* **1,** (instance of lifting): *give something a lift*, поднима́ть что́-нибудь. **2,** (free ride): *give a lift to*, подвози́ть. **3,** (machine for lifting) подъёмная маши́на; подъёмник. **4,** *Brit.* (elevator) лифт. **5,** (part of the heel of a shoe) набо́йка. **6,** (elevation of one's spirits): *give someone a lift*, подбодря́ть кого́-нибудь.

liftoff *n.* отры́в от земли́.

ligament *n.* свя́зка.

ligature *n.* лигату́ра.

light *n.* **1,** (illumination) свет: *dim light*, ту́склый свет. *Turn out the light*, (по)туши́ть свет. *Read in good light*, чита́ть при хоро́шем све́те. **2,** (source of illumination) фона́рь: *street light*, у́личный фона́рь. *The lights of a city*, огни́ го́рода. **3,** (traffic light) светофо́р. *Red light*, кра́сный свет. **4,** (for a cigarette): *can you give me a light?*, разреши́те прикури́ть? **5,** (aspect) свет: *see something in its true light*, ви́деть что́-нибудь в и́стинном све́те. —*adj.* **1,** (not dark; bright) све́тлый: *light hair/colors*, све́тлые во́лосы/кра́ски. *It is getting light*, света́ет; светле́ет. ♦ *With colors* светло-: *light gray*, светло-се́рый. **2,** (of or pert. to light) светово́й: *light wave*, светова́я волна́. **3,** (not heavy; not serious) лёгкий: *light suitcase/breakfast/breeze*, лёгкий чемода́н/за́втрак/ветеро́к. *Light reading*, лёгкое чте́ние. *Light sentence*, мя́гкий пригово́р. *Be a light sleeper*, чу́тко спать. —*adv.* легко́. *Travel light*, путеше́ствовать налегке́. —*v.t.* **1,** (ignite; turn on, as a lamp, match, etc.) зажига́ть. *Light a fire*, разжига́ть ого́нь *or* костёр. *Light a stove*, зата́пливать плиту́. *Light (up) a cigarette*, заку́ривать папиро́су. **2,** *often fol. by* **up** (illuminate) освеща́ть; озаря́ть. —*v.i.* **1,** (ignite) зажига́ться. **2,** *fol. by* **up** (brighten, as of one's face) освеща́ться; (of one's eyes) загоре́ться; засвети́ться. **3,** (dismount) сходи́ть; слеза́ть. **4,** (come to rest; perch) сади́ться. **5,** *fol. by* **on** *or* **upon** (come upon) ната́лкиваться на. **6,** *fol. by* **into** (attack violently) обру́шиваться на. —**bring to light**, выявля́ть. —**come to light**, обнару́живаться; вскрыва́ться; всплыва́ть. —**in (the) light of**, в све́те (+ *gen.*). —**make light of**, относи́ться легко́ к. —**see the light**, прозре́ть.

light bulb ла́мпочка.

lighted *adj.* зажжённый: *lighted candles*, зажжённые све́чи.

lighten *v.t.* **1,** (make less heavy) облегча́ть. **2,** (make lighter, as colors) де́лать светле́е. —*v.i.* облегча́ться.

lighter *n.* **1,** (igniting device) зажига́лка. **2,** (boat) ли́хтер.

light-fingered *adj.* на́ руку нечи́ст.

light-haired *adj.* световоло́сый.

lightheaded *adj.* **1,** (giddy; dizzy): *I feel lightheaded,*

у меня́ кру́жится голова́. **2,** (frivolous; silly) легко-
мы́сленный.
lighthearted *adj.* беззабо́тный; весёлый.
lighthouse *n.* мая́к.
lighting *n.* **1,** (act of lighting) зажига́ние: *lighting of
candles,* зажига́ние свеч. **2,** (illumination) освеще́-
ние. —*adj.* освети́тельный: *lighting system,* освети́-
тельная сеть.
lightly *adv.* **1,** (gently) легко́. **2,** (slightly) слегка́.
3, (not as a serious matter) несерьёзно. *Take lightly,*
не принима́ть всерьёз. **4,** (with little or no penalty)
дёшево: *get off lightly,* дёшево отде́латься.
light meter экспози́метр; экспоно́метр.
lightness *n.* **1,** (brightness) све́тлость. **2,** (not being
heavy) лёгкость.
lightning *n.* мо́лния. —*adj.* молниено́сный: *with
lightning speed,* с молниено́сной быстрото́й. —*v.i.
It is lightning,* мо́лния сверка́ет. —**lightning bug,**
светля́к. —**lightning rod,** громоотво́д; молние-
отво́д.
lightproof *adj.* светонепроница́емый.
lightweight *adj.* лёгкий; легкове́сный. —*n., sports*
легкове́с.
light year световой год.
lignite *n.* лигни́т.
likable *also,* **likeable** *adj.* ми́лый; симпати́чный.
like *v.t.* **1,** (be fond of) люби́ть. **2,** (enjoy) *rendered
by* нра́виться: *how did you like the movie?,* как вам
понра́вился э́тот фильм? **3,** (wish) хоте́ть: *I would
like a cup of tea,* я бы хоте́л ча́шку ча́ю. —*v.i.* хоте́ть:
do as you like, де́лайте, как хоти́те. *Ask any questions you like,* задава́йте каки́е уго́дно вопро́сы.
—*prep.* **1,** (similar to) похо́жий на: *she is like her
mother,* она́ похо́жа на свою́ мать. *What is he like?,*
что он собо́й представля́ет?; что он за челове́к?
2, (in a manner similar to) как: *act like a madman,*
поступа́ть как безу́мец. *Don't talk like that!,* не
говори́те так! *All Russians are like that,* все ру́сские
таковы́. **3,** (characteristic of) похо́же; типи́чно: *that's
just (or not) like him,* э́то на него́ (не) похо́же; э́то
(не) типи́чно для него́. —*adj.* **1,** (similar) подо́б-
ный: *in like manner,* подо́бным (же) о́бразом. **2,**
(equal) ра́вный: *a like amount,* ра́вная су́мма. —*n.*
1, (anything similar): *and the like,* и тому́ подо́бное.
I have never seen the like of it, я никогда́ не ви́дел
ничего́ подо́бного. **2,** *pl.* (preferences): *likes and
dislikes,* симпа́тии и антипа́тии. —**like it or not,**
хо́чешь не хо́чешь.
likable *also,* **likeable** *adj.* симпати́чный.
likelihood *n.* вероя́тность. *In all likelihood,* по всей
вероя́тности.
likely *adj.* **1,** (probable; credible) вероя́тный; правдо-
подо́бный. *A likely story,* правдоподо́бный расска́з.
He is likely to be late, он, вероя́тно, опозда́ет. **2,**
(suitable) подходя́щий. —*adv.* вероя́тно. *Quite likely,*
вполне́ вероя́тно. *More likely,* скоре́е. *Most likely,*
скоре́е всего́.
liken *v.t.* уподобля́ть.
likeness *n.* **1,** (similarity) схо́дство; подо́бие. **2,**
(image) ко́пия: *a perfect likeness,* то́чная ко́пия. **3,**
(guise) личи́на: *in the likeness of,* под личи́ной
(+ *gen.*).
likewise *adv.* **1,** (in the same manner) подо́бным
о́бразом. **2,** (by the same token) ра́вным о́бразом.
3, (too; also) та́кже.

liking *n.* симпа́тия; расположе́ние. *Take a liking to,*
полюби́ть. *Be to one's liking,* быть по душе́ (+ *dat.*).
lilac *n.* сире́нь. —*adj.* сире́невый.
lilt *n.* ритм. —**lilting,** *adj.* перели́вчатый.
lily *n.* ли́лия. —**lily of the valley,** ла́ндыш.
lima bean фасо́ль ли́мская.
limb *n.* **1,** (branch) сук; ветвь. **2,** (arm; leg) член.
—**out on a limb,** *colloq.* в ша́тком (*or* в ско́льзком)
положе́нии. —**tear from limb to limb,** разорва́ть
(*or* растерза́ть) на ча́сти.
limber *adj.* **1,** (flexible; pliant) ги́бкий. **2,** (agile;
nimble) прово́рный. —*v.t. & i.* [*usu.* **limber up**] раз-
мина́ть(ся).
limbo *n.* неопределённость: *in a state of limbo,* в
состоя́нии неопределённости.
lime *n.* **1,** (citrus fruit; tree that bears it) лайм. **2,**
(European linden tree) ли́па. **3,** (calcium oxide, used
in cement) известь.
limelight *n.* свет ра́мпы. —**in the limelight,** в
це́нтре внима́ния.
limerick *n.* стихотворе́ние из пяти́ строк.
limestone *n.* известня́к. —*adj.* известняко́вый.
limewater *n.* известко́вая вода́.
limit *n.* преде́л; грани́ца. *Speed limit,* преде́льная
ско́рость. *Time limit,* преде́льный срок. *City limits,*
преде́лы *or* черта́ го́рода. *That's the limit!,* э́то уж
сли́шком!; э́то уже́ после́днее де́ло! —*v.t.* ограни́-
чивать. —**off limits,** закры́т: *off limits to foreigners,*
закры́т для иностра́нцев.
limitation *n.* **1,** (restriction) ограниче́ние. **2,** (drawback) недоста́ток.
limited *adj.* ограни́ченный. —**limited edition,** ма-
лотира́жное изда́ние. —**limited monarchy,** кон-
ституцио́нная мона́рхия.
limitless *adj.* безграни́чный; беспреде́льный.
limonite *n.* бу́рый железня́к.
limousine *n.* лимузи́н.
limp *v.i.* хрома́ть. —*n.* хромота́. *Have a limp; walk
with a limp,* хрома́ть. —*adj.* дря́блый; вя́лый.
limpid *adj.* прозра́чный.
linage *n.* число́ строк.
linchpin *n.* **1,** *mech.* чека́. **2,** *fig.* (mainstay) стано-
во́й хребе́т.
linden *n.* ли́па.
line *n.* **1,** (thin, continuous mark) ли́ния; черта́. *Draw
a line,* провести́ черту́. **2,** (line of writing) строка́:
read between the lines, чита́ть ме́жду строк. **3,** (row;
file) ли́ния; ряд. **4,** (queue) о́чередь: *stand in line,*
стоя́ть в о́череди. **5,** (border) грани́ца: *the state line,*
грани́ца шта́та. **6,** *sports* ли́ния: *starting line,* ста́р-
товая ли́ния. **7,** *pl.* (contour) ли́нии; очерта́ния. **8,**
pl. (wrinkles) морщи́ны. **9,** (rope; string) верёвка:
hang the clothes on the line, ве́шать бельё на верёвку.
10, (course of movement or action) ли́ния: *line of
flight,* ли́ния полёта; *line of fire,* ли́ния огня́. **11,**
(system of transportation) ли́ния: *bus line,* авто́бусная
ли́ния. **12,** (wires to conduct electricity) про́вод:
telephone line, телефо́нный про́вод. **13,** (telephone
connection) ли́ния; про́вод. *The line is busy,* ли́ния
занята́. *Direct line,* прямо́й про́вод. *The chief is on
the line,* нача́льник на про́воде. *The voice on the
other end of the line,* го́лос на друго́м конце́ про́-
вода. **14,** *pl.* (actor's part) роль: *memorize one's lines,*
зау́чивать роль. **15,** (attitude; policy) ли́ния: *take a
hard line,* занима́ть жёсткую ли́нию. **16,** (succession

of descendants) ли́ния: *the male line*, мужска́я ли́ния. —*v.t.* **1**, (mark with lines) линова́ть. **2**, *fol. by up* (arrange in a line) выстра́ивать. **3**, (put a lining in) де́лать *or* подшива́ть подкла́дку к; подбива́ть. **4**, (fill; cram) заставля́ть: *the shelves are lined with books*, по́лки заста́влены кни́гами. **5**, (form a line along) вы́строиться вдоль. —*v.i.* [*usu.* **line up**] выстра́иваться. —**all along the line**, во всех отноше́ниях; во всём. —**bring into line**, приводи́ть в соотве́тствие. —**draw the line**, проводи́ть чёткую черту́ (*or* грань). —**drop me a line**, пришли́те мне весто́чку; черкни́те мне не́сколько слов. —**get a line on**, разузна́ть о. —**hold the line, 1**, *mil.* держа́ть оборо́ну. **2**, (stand firm) держа́ться. **3**, (not hang up the telephone) не ве́шать тру́бку. —**in line of duty**, при исполне́нии служе́бных обя́занностей. —**in line with**, в соотве́тствии с. —**lay it on the line**, *colloq.* говори́ть напрями́к. —**line of work**, род заня́тий. —**not in/out of/my line**, не по мое́й ча́сти. —**out of line, 1**, (not aligned) не в ряд. **2**, (improper; uncalled-for) неуме́стный.

lineage *n.* родосло́вная; происхожде́ние.

lineal *adj.* прямо́й: *lineal descendant*, прямо́й пото́мок.

linear *adj.* лине́йный. —**linear equation**, лине́йное уравне́ние. —**linear measure**, лине́йная ме́ра; ме́ра длины́.

lined *adj.* **1**, (ruled) лино́ванный; в лине́йку. **2**, (wrinkled) морщи́нистый. **3**, (having a lining) на подкла́дке.

lineman *n.* лине́йный монтёр.

linen *n.* **1**, (fabric) полотно́; холст. **2**, (articles made of linen or other cloth) бельё: *bed linen*, посте́льное бельё. —*adj.* **1**, (made of linen) льняно́й; полотня́ный; холщёвый. **2**, (for linen) бельево́й: *linen closet*, бельево́й шкаф.

liner *n.* **1**, (ship) ла́йнер. **2**, (plane) возду́шный ла́йнер. **3**, (lining) подкла́дка.

linesman *n.* **1**, *sports* судья́ на ли́нии. **2**, = **lineman**.

line-up *n.* соста́в (кома́нды). *Starting line-up*, ста́ртовый соста́в.

linger *v.i.* **1**, (tarry) заде́рживаться. **2**, (continue to exist; remain alive) протяну́ть.

lingerie *n.* да́мское бельё.

lingo *n.* жарго́н.

linguist *n.* языкове́д; лингви́ст. —**linguistic**, *adj.* языково́й; лингвисти́ческий. —**linguistics**, *n.* языкозна́ние; лингви́стика.

liniment *n.* втира́ние.

lining *n.* подкла́дка: *silk lining*, шёлковая подкла́дка. *Brake lining*, тормозна́я накла́дка. —**every cloud has a silver lining**, нет ху́да без добра́.

link *n.* **1**, (part of a chain) звено́. **2**, (tie; connection) связь. —*v.t.* соединя́ть; свя́зывать. —*v.i.* [*usu.* **link up**] соединя́ться; смыка́ться. —**linking verb**, глаго́л-свя́зка.

linkage *n.* **1**, (act of linking; coupling) сцепле́ние. *Genetic linkage*, сцепле́ние ге́нов. **2**, (connection) связь. **3**, (linking of two issues) увя́зка.

linnet *n.* конопля́нка; репо́лов.

linoleum *n.* лино́леум.

linotype *n.* линоти́п.

linseed *n.* льняно́е се́мя. —**linseed oil**, льняно́е ма́сло.

lint *n.* **1**, (fluff) пушо́к. **2**, (substance formerly used for dressing wounds) ко́рпия.

lintel *n.* перемы́чка; прито́лока.

lion *n.* лев. —*adj.* [*also*, **lion's**] льви́ный: *lion skin*, льви́ная шку́ра. —**lion's share**, льви́ная до́ля.

lioness *n.* льви́ца.

lionize *v.t.* поднима́ть на щит.

lip *n.* губа́. —**be on everyone's lips**, быть у всех на уста́х. —**keep a stiff upper lip**, храбри́ться. —**none of your lip!**, без де́рзостей! —**pay lip service to**, признава́ть то́лько на слова́х.

lip reading чте́ние с губ.

lipstick *n.* губна́я пома́да.

liquefy *v.t.* сжижа́ть. *Liquefied gas*, сжи́женный газ. —**liquefaction**, *n.* сжиже́ние.

liqueur *n.* ликёр.

liquid *n.* жи́дкость. —*adj.* **1**, (fluid) жи́дкий. **2**, *finance* ликви́дный: *liquid assets*, ликви́дные сре́дства. —**liquid measure**, ме́ра жи́дкости.

liquidate *v.t.* ликвиди́ровать. —**liquidation**, *n.* ликвида́ция.

liquidity *n.* ликви́дность.

liquor *n.* спиртны́е напи́тки.

liquorice *n.* = **licorice**.

lira *n.* ли́ра.

lisp *n.* шепеля́вость; сюсю́канье. —*v.i.* шепеля́вить; сюсю́кать.

lissome *adj.* **1**, (supple) ги́бкий. **2**, (agile) прово́рный.

list *n.* **1**, (enumeration) спи́сок. *Price list*, прейскура́нт. **2**, (tilt, as of a ship) крен. —*v.t.* составля́ть спи́сок (+ *gen.*); перечисля́ть. *Be listed*, чи́слиться. —*v.i.* (of a ship) крени́ться.

listen *v.i.* слу́шать. —**listener**, *n.* слу́шатель.

listening post пункт *or* пост подслу́шивания.

listless *adj.* вя́лый; апати́чный. —**listlessly**, *adv.* вя́ло. —**listlessness**, *n.* вя́лость.

list price прейскура́нтная цена́.

litany *n.* лита́ния.

liter *also*, **litre**, *n.* литр.

literacy *n.* гра́мотность.

literal *adj.* **1**, (reflecting the exact meaning) буква́льный. **2**, (word for word) досло́вный. —**literally**, *adv.* буква́льно; досло́вно.

literary *adj.* литерату́рный.

literate *adj.* гра́мотный.

literature *n.* литерату́ра.

lithe *adj.* **1**, (supple) ги́бкий. **2**, (graceful) стро́йный.

lithium *n.* ли́тий.

lithograph *n.* литогра́фия; литогра́фский о́ттиск. —*v.t.* литографи́ровать. —**lithographer**, *n.* лито́граф. —**lithographic**, *adj.* литогра́фский. —**lithography**, *n.* литогра́фия.

lithosphere *n.* литосфе́ра.

Lithuanian *adj.* лито́вский. —*n.* **1**, (person) лито́вец; лито́вка. **2**, (language) лито́вский язы́к.

litigate *v.i.* суди́ться. —**litigation**, *n.* иск; суде́бное де́ло.

litmus *n.* ла́кмус. —**litmus paper**, ла́кмусовая бума́га.

litre *n.* = **liter**.

litter *n.* **1**, (trash) сор; хлам. **2**, (stretcher) носи́лки. **3**, (animals born at one time) помёт; вы́водок. —*v.t.* **1**, (make untidy) засоря́ть. **2**, (scatter about) сори́ть. —*v.i.* сори́ть.

little *adj.* **1**, (small in size) ма́ленький; небольшо́й.

2, (small in amount) ма́ло: *little time/hope,* ма́ло вре́мени/наде́жды. *Little cause for alarm,* ма́ло основа́ний для трево́ги. *Have little effect on,* ма́ло повлия́ть на. —*adv.* ма́ло: *too little,* сли́шком ма́ло. *Things have changed very little,* де́ло о́чень ма́ло измени́лось. *Little did he suspect that...,* он совсе́м не подозрева́л, что... —*n.* ма́ло; ма́лое; ма́ло что. *I ate very little,* я ел о́чень ма́ло. *Be satisfied with little,* дово́льствоваться ма́лым. *Little has changed,* ма́ло что измени́лось. *We see very little of them,* мы ре́дко ви́димся с ни́ми. *I have little to add,* мне почти́ не́чего доба́вить. —**a little,** немно́го: *a little water,* немно́го воды́; *a little tired,* немно́го уста́л; *a little better,* немно́го лу́чше. —**little by little,** понемно́гу; ма́ло-пома́лу. —**make little of,** не придава́ть значе́ния (+ *dat.*). —**think little of,** быть плохо́го мне́ния о. —**what little,** то немно́гое, что: *I did what little I could,* я сде́лал то немно́гое, что мог.

little finger мизи́нец.

liturgy *n.* литурги́я. —**liturgical,** *adj.* литурги́ческий.

livable *also,* **liveable** *adj.* **1,** (habitable) го́дный для жилья́. **2,** (endurable, as of life) сно́сный.

live[1] (liv) *v.i. & t.* жить: *live next door,* жить ря́дом. *Live forever,* жить ве́чно. *Live to a ripe old age,* дожи́ть до ста́рости. *Live a normal life,* жить норма́льной жи́знью. *Live a long life,* прожи́ть до́лгую жизнь. —**live down,** искупа́ть; загла́живать. —**live for,** жить (+ *instr.*): *live for one's son,* жить свои́м сы́ном. —**live it up,** *colloq.* разгу́ливаться. —**live off, 1,** (use to live on) жить на (+ *acc.*): *live off one's savings,* жить на свои́ сбереже́ния. **2,** (sponge off) жить за счёт (кого́-нибудь). —**live on, 1,** (support oneself on) жить на (+ *acc.*): *what are they living on?,* на каки́е сре́дства они́ живу́т? *It's hardly enough to live on,* э́того едва́ хвата́ет на жизнь. **2,** (subsist on) пита́ться (+ *instr.*): *live on fruit,* пита́ться фру́ктами. **3,** (not fade from memory) жить. *His name will live on,* его́ и́мя не умрёт. —**live out,** дожива́ть: *live out one's last days,* дожива́ть после́дние дни. —**live through,** пережива́ть. —**live up to, 1,** (live in accordance with) жить согла́сно (+ *dat.*). **2,** (satisfy, as expectations) опра́вдывать. **3,** (fulfill, as a bargain) выполня́ть. —**live with, 1,** (cohabit with) жить с. **2,** (learn to accept) мири́ться с.

live[2] (laiv) *adj.* **1,** (alive) живо́й: *live fish,* жива́я ры́ба. **2,** (burning) горя́чий: *live coals,* горя́чие у́гли. **3,** (active, as of a volcano) де́йствующий. **4,** (charged with electricity) под напряже́нием. **5,** (not exploded) боево́й: *live ammunition,* боевы́е патро́ны. **6,** (broadcast while being performed) прямо́й: *live broadcasting,* прямо́й эфи́р.

liveable *adj.* = livable.

livelihood *n.* сре́дства к жи́зни. *Earn one's livelihood,* зараба́тывать на жизнь.

liveliness *n.* жи́вость; оживлённость.

lively *adj.* живо́й; оживлённый. —*adv., in* **step lively!,** живе́й!; скоре́й!; побыстре́е!

liven *v.t.* [*usu.* liven up] оживля́ть —*v.i.* [*usu.* liven up] оживля́ться.

liver *n.* **1,** (organ) пе́чень. **2,** (meat) печёнка. —*adj.* печёночный: *liver extract,* печёночный экстра́кт.

liveried *adj.* в ливре́е; ливре́йный.

liverwort *n.* печёночник.

liverwurst *n.* ли́верная колбаса́.

livery *n.* ливре́я. —**livery stable,** пла́тная коню́шня.

livestock *n.* (дома́шний) скот; живо́й инвента́рь.

livid *adj.* **1,** (pale) (мёртвенно) бле́дный. **2,** (incensed) разъярённый; вне себя́ от я́рости.

living *n.* **1,** (manner or means of living) жизнь: *cost of living,* сто́имость жи́зни; *standard of living,* у́ровень жи́зни. *Earn a living,* зараба́тывать на жизнь. **2,** *preceded by* **the** (those that are alive) живы́е. —*adj.* **1,** (alive; in use) живо́й. **2,** (pert. to living) жили́щный: *living conditions,* жили́щные усло́вия. *Living quarters,* жилы́е помеще́ния.

living room гости́ная.

lizard *n.* я́щерица.

llama *n.* ла́ма.

lo *interj.* вот! —**lo and behold!,** и вот!; и вдруг!

load *n.* **1,** (something carried) груз; тя́жесть. *Heavy load,* тяжёлый груз. *Carry a load on one's back,* нести́ груз/тя́жесть на спине́. **2,** (work performed) нагру́зка: *teaching load,* преподава́тельская нагру́зка; *peak load,* максима́льная нагру́зка. **3,** *fig.* (burden) бре́мя; тя́жесть. *Load off one's shoulders* (or *mind*), тя́жесть *or* гора́ с плеч. **4,** *pl., fol. by of, colloq.* (a great deal of) ма́сса (+ *gen.*): *we have loads of time,* у нас ма́сса вре́мени. —*v.t.* **1,** (place on a conveyance; place cargo on) грузи́ть; нагружа́ть. **3,** (put ammunition or film into) заряжа́ть. **3,** *often fol. by* **down** (fill; cover; weigh down) зава́ливать. —*v.i.* **1,** (take on cargo) грузи́ться. **2,** *fol. by* **into** (board in large numbers) погружа́ться (в): *load into a bus,* погружа́ться в автобус.

loaded *adj.* **1,** (carrying a load) загру́женный; нагру́женный; гружёный. **2,** (filled to capacity) перепо́лненный. **3,** (ready to fire) заряжённый: *loaded gun,* заряжённый пистоле́т. **4,** (overburdened) зава́ленный: *loaded with work,* зава́лен рабо́той. **5,** *slang* (rich) при деньга́х. *He is loaded,* он купа́ется в зо́лоте. **6,** *slang* (drunk) пья́ный. *Get loaded,* напива́ться.

loading *n.* погру́зка. —*adj.* погру́зочный: *loading machine,* погру́зочная маши́на.

loaf *n.* буха́нка. *Long loaf,* бато́н. *Round loaf,* карава́й. —*v.i.* безде́льничать; ло́дырничать.

loafer *n.* **1,** (idler) безде́льник; ло́дырь. **2,** (casual shoe) спорти́вная ту́фля.

loam *n.* сугли́нок; су́песь. —**loamy,** *adj.* сугли́нистый.

loan *n.* заём; ссу́да. —*v.t.* одолжа́ть; дава́ть взаймы́. —**loan translation,** ка́лька. —**loanword,** *n.* заи́мствованное сло́во.

loath *adj.* неохо́тный. *Be loath to,* не хоте́ть (+ *inf.*).

loathe *v.t.* ненави́деть. —**loathing,** *n.* отвраще́ние; омерзе́ние. —**loathsome,** *adj.* отврати́тельный; омерзи́тельный.

lob *v.t.* высоко́ подбра́сывать (мяч).

lobby *n.* **1,** (hall) вестибю́ль; фойе́; холл. **2,** *polit.* ло́бби. —**lobbyist,** *n.* лобби́ст.

lobe *n.* до́ля. *Ear lobe,* мо́чка.

lobster *n.* ома́р.

lobule *n.* до́лька.

local *adj.* ме́стный. —*n.* **1,** (local resident) ме́стный жи́тель. **2,** (local train) при́городный по́езд. —**local anesthetic,** ме́стный нарко́з. —**local color,** ме́стный колори́т.

locale *n.* ме́сто де́йствия.

locality *n.* ме́стность; райо́н.

localize *v.t.* локализовáть. —**localization,** *n.* локализáция.

locate *v.t.* **1,** (place; situate) располагáть: *locate a factory near a river,* располагáть фáбрику у рекú. *Be located,* быть; находúться; быть расположенным (гдé-нибудь). **2,** (find; discover) найтú; разыскáть. *Locate a town on a map,* найтú городóк на кáрте.

location *n.* **1,** (place where something is) местонахождéние. **2,** (site) местоположéние. *Move to a new location,* переходúть на нóвое мéсто. **3,** *motion pictures* натýра: *on location,* на натýре.

locative *adj.,* **in locative case,** мéстный падéж.

locator *n.* локáтор: *sound locator,* звуковóй локáтор.

lock *n.* **1,** (on a door or box) замóк. **2,** (of a canal) шлюз. **3,** (curl of hair) лóкон. —*v.t.* **1,** [*also,* **lock up**] (secure with a lock; confine) запирáть; закрывáть: *lock the door,* запирáть/закрывáть дверь. *Lock something in the desk,* запирáть чтó-нибудь в стол. **2,** (interlock) сцеплять (+ *instr.*): *lock horns/bumpers,* сцеплять рогáми/буферáми. *Be locked in mortal combat,* сцепúться в смертéльной схвáтке. —*v.i.* запирáться. —**lock, stock and barrel,** целикóм; пóлностью; "со всéми потрохáми". —**under lock and key,** под замкóм.

locker *n.* (запирáющийся) шкáфчик. —**locker room,** раздевáльня.

locket *n.* медальóн.

lockjaw *n.* тризм; столбняк.

lockout *n.* локáут.

locksmith *n.* слéсарь.

locomotion *n.* передвижéние.

locomotive *n.* локомотúв; паровóз. —*adj.* двúжущий.

locus *n.* геометрúческое мéсто тóчек.

locust *n.* саранчá.

locution *n.* оборóт рéчи; речéние.

lode *n.* (рýдная) жúла.

lodestar *n.* путевóдная звездá.

lodge *n.* **1,** (hut; cabin) дóмик; сторóжка. *Hunting lodge,* охóтничий дóмик. **2,** (base for outdoor activity) бáза: *skiing lodge,* лыжная бáза. **3,** (fraternal society) лóжа. —*v.t.* **1,** (house) помещáть; вселять. **2,** (file, as a complaint) подавáть. —*v.i.* **1,** (be housed) помещáться. **2,** (become embedded, as of a bullet) засéсть.

lodger *n.* жилéц.

lodging *n.* помещéние; жильё. *Lodging for the night,* ночлéг.

loft *n.* **1,** (attic) чердáк. **2,** (hayloft) сеновáл. **3,** (balcony, as for a choir) хóры.

lofty *adj.* высóкий; возвышенный. —**loftiness,** *n.* возвышенность.

log *n.* **1,** (piece of timber) бревнó. **2,** (same used for burning) полéно. **3,** *pl.* (timber floated down a river) лес. **4,** (daily record) формуляр. *Ship's log,* вáхтенный/бортовóй/судовóй журнáл. —*adj.* бревéнчатый. *Log cabin,* бревéнчатый дóмик; избá. —*v.t.* **1,** (enter in a log) вносúть в журнáл. **2,** (cover, as a certain distance) пройтú; проéхать. *Log 2000 flying hours,* налетáть две тысячи часóв. —**sleep like a log,** спать как сурóк.

logarithm *n.* логарúфм. —**logarithmic,** *adj.* логарифмúческий.

loge *n.* лóжа.

logger *n.* лесорýб.

loggerheads *n.pl.,in* **at loggerheads,** не в ладáх; на ножáх.

logic *n.* лóгика. —**logical,** *adj.* логúческий; логúчный. —**logically,** *adv.* логúчески; логúчно. —**logician,** *n.* лóгик.

logistics *n.* тыл и снабжéние; тыловóе обеспéчение; материáльно-технúческое обеспéчение. —**logistical,** *adj.* тыловóй.

loin *n.* **1,** (part of the back) поясница. **2,** *pl.* (region of the thigh and groin) пах. —**loincloth,** *n.* набéдренная повязка.

loiter *v.i.* **1,** (drift about) слоняться. **2,** (dawdle) мéшкать. —**loiterer,** *n.* лóдырь.

loll *v.i.* валяться; нéжиться.

lollipop *n.* леденéц (на пáлочке).

lone *adj.* одинóкий.

loneliness *n.* одинóчество.

lonely *adj.* **1,** (lonesome) одинóкий. **2,** (solitary) уединённый. **3,** (remote) глухóй: *a lonely street,* глухáя улица.

loner *n., colloq.* дикáрь; бирюк.

lonesome *adj.* одинóкий.

lone wolf одинóчка; бирюк.

long *adj.* **1,** (of considerable length) длúнный: *long hair,* длúнные вóлосы. *A long distance,* большóе расстояние. *We (still) have a long way to go,* нам ещё далекó éхать. **2,** (having a specified length): длинóй в: *two meters long,* длинóй в два мéтра. **3,** (of considerable duration) дóлгий: *long life,* дóлгая жизнь; *a long silence,* дóлгое молчáние. *(For) a long time,* давнó; дóлго. **4,** (taking a long time): *I won't be long,* я не дóлго; я не надóлго. *He was not long in answering,* он не замéдлил с отвéтом. **5,** *Long face,* вытянутое лицó. —*adv.* **1,** (for a long time in the past or future) дóлго: *did you have to wait long?,* вам пришлóсь дóлго ждать? *He hasn't long to live,* емý остáлось недóлго жить. **2,** (for a long time up to and including the present) давнó: *have you been waiting long?,* вы давнó ждéте? **3,** (for the duration of) напролéт: *all night long,* всю ночь напролéт. **4,** мнóго врéмени: *it won't take long,* это не займёт мнóго врéмени. —*v.i.* **1,** *fol. by* **for** (miss; yearn for) тосковáть по. **2,** *fol. by inf.* (earnestly desire) óчень хотéть; стремúться. —**any longer; no longer,** бóльше не; ужé не. *It's no longer a joke,* это ужé не шýтка. —**as long as, 1,** (for all the time that) покá: *as long as I live,* покá я бýду жив (живá). *As long as you like,* скóлько хотúте. **2,** (inasmuch as) так как; ввиду тогó, что. **3,** (provided that) éсли тóлько; лишь бы. —**at long last,** наконéц-то. —**before long,** в скóром врéмени. —**how long?, 1,** (in time) скóлько врéмени?; как дóлго? **2,** (in length): *how long is this carpet?,* каковá длинá этого коврá?; какóй длины этот ковёр? —**in the long run,** *see* **run.** —**long after,** дóлгое врéмя пóсле. —**long ago,** давнó. —**long before,** задóлго до. —**long live...,** да здрáвствует... —**so long, 1,** (for such a long time) так дóлго. **2,** (goodbye) до свидáния!; покá! —**the long and the short of it,** корóче говоря.

long-awaited *adj.* долгождáнный.

long-distance *adj.* на дáльнее расстояние: *long-distance flight,* полёт на дáльнее расстояние. *Long-distance train,* пóезд дáльнего слéдования. *Long-distance call,* междугорóдный телефóнный разговóр. *Long-distance race,* бег на длúнную дистáнцию.

longevity *n.* долгове́чность; долголе́тие.
long-haired *adj.* длинноволо́сый.
longhand *n.* по́черк. *Written in longhand,* напи́санный от руки́.
longing *n.* стремле́ние; жа́жда. —*adj.* тоску́ющий: *a longing look,* тоску́ющий взгляд. —**longingly,** *adv.* с тоско́й; тоскли́во.
longitude *n.* долгота́. —**longitudinal,** *adj.* продо́льный.
long-lasting *adj.* про́чный; сто́йкий.
long-legged *adj.* длинноно́гий.
long-lived *adj.* долгове́чный; многоле́тний.
long-playing *adj.* долгоигра́ющий.
long-range *adj.* **1,** (of a weapon or aircraft) да́льнего де́йствия; дальнобо́йный. **2,** (long-term, as of plans) перспекти́вный.
longshoreman *n.* (портóвый) грýзчик; до́кер.
long shot 1, *horse racing* аутса́йдер. **2,** (unpromising venture) риско́ванное де́ло. —**not by a long shot,** нико́им о́бразом; далеко́ не. *Not everyone by a long shot,* далеко́ не все.
long-standing *adj.* да́вний; давни́шний.
long-suffering *adj.* многострада́льный.
long-term *adj.* долгосро́чный.
long wave дли́нная волна́. —**long-wave,** *adj.* длинново́лновый.
long-winded *adj.* многосло́вный.
look *v.i.* **1,** (use one's sense of sight) смотре́ть: *look at one's watch,* (по)смотре́ть на часы́. **2,** (search) иска́ть: *I don't know but I'll look,* не зна́ю, но поищу́. **3,** (appear; seem) вы́глядеть; име́ть (како́й-нибудь) вид: *she looks well,* она́ вы́глядит хорошо́; у неё хоро́ший вид. —*v.t.* **1,** (face squarely) смотре́ть (+ *dat.*): *look someone in the face,* смотре́ть кому́-нибудь в лицо́. **2,** (appear to be a certain age): *he looks about forty,* ему́ на вид лет со́рок. *She doesn't look her age,* она́ вы́глядит моло́же свои́х лет. —*n.* **1,** (glance) взгляд. **2,** (expression) выраже́ние лица́. **3,** (appearance) вид; о́блик; нару́жность; вне́шность. —**look after,** присма́тривать за; уха́живать за; следи́ть за; смотре́ть за. —**look ahead,** смотре́ть *or* загляну́ть вперёд. —**look around, 1,** (turn around and look back) обора́чиваться. **2,** (look all around) смотре́ть круго́м; осма́триваться; огля́дываться. —**look back,** огля́дываться наза́д. —**look down on,** смотре́ть свысока́ на. —**look for, 1,** (search for) иска́ть. **2,** (expect) ожида́ть. —**look forward to,** о́чень ждать; ждать с нетерпе́нием; предвкуша́ть. —**look here!,** послу́шайте! —**look in on,** загляну́ть к. —**look into,** рассма́тривать; рассле́довать. —**look like, 1,** (resemble) быть похо́жим на. **2,** (be of a certain appearance): *what does he look like?,* како́в он собо́й? **3,** *colloq.* (seem as if): *it looks like rain,* похо́же, что бу́дет дождь. —**look out, 1,** *literally* выгля́дывать. *Look out the window,* смотре́ть *or* выгля́дывать в окно́ *or* из окна́. **2,** (be careful) быть осторо́жным; гляде́ть в о́ба. *Look out!,* осторо́жно! **3,** *fol. by* **for** (beware of) бере́чься (+ *gen.*). **4,** *fol. by* **for** (protect) бере́чь. **5,** *fol. by* **on** (face) выходи́ть; смотре́ть (*with* в *or* на). —**look over,** просма́тривать. —**look through, 1,** = **look over. 2,** (peep through) загля́дывать в. —**look to,** рассчи́тывать на. —**look up, 1,** *literally* поднима́ть глаза́. **2,** (seek in a reference book) иска́ть: *look up a word in the dictionary,* иска́ть сло́во в словаре́. **3,** *fol. by* **to** (admire;

respect) смотре́ть на (+ *acc.*) сни́зу вверх. **4,** *colloq.* (call on; visit) заходи́ть к; загляну́ть к. **5,** *colloq.* (get better) поправля́ться: *things are looking up,* дела́ поправля́ются. —**look upon,** счита́ть; рассма́тривать.
looking glass зе́ркало.
lookout *n.* **1,** (act of watching) наблюде́ние: *keep a lookout,* вести́ наблюде́ние. *Be on the lookout,* быть насторо́же. **2,** (place for keeping watch) наблюда́тельный пункт.
loom *n.* тка́цкий стано́к. —*v.i.* **1,** (appear) видне́ться; вырисо́вываться. **2,** (impend) надвига́ться.
loon *n.* гага́ра.
loop *n.* **1,** (doubled cord) пе́тля. **2,** *aero.* мёртвая пе́тля: *loop the loop,* де́лать мёртвую пе́тлю. —*v.t.* обма́тывать.
loophole *n.* **1,** (embrasure) бойни́ца; амбразу́ра. **2,** *fig.* (avenue of escape) лазе́йка.
loose *adj.* **1,** (not tight or taut) сла́бый. **2,** (loose-fitting) свобо́дный. **3,** (not firmly fastened; not firmly in place) шата́ющийся: *I have a loose tooth,* у меня́ зуб шата́ется. **4,** (dissolute) распу́тный. *Loose morals,* лёгкие нра́вы. —*adv.* свобо́дно. —*v.t.* **1,** (loosen) ослабля́ть. **2,** (shoot; let fly) стреля́ть; пуска́ть. —**at loose ends,** без де́ла; не у дел. —**break loose,** вырыва́ться. —**come loose, 1,** (come untied) развя́зываться; отвя́зываться. **2,** (be dislodged from a fixed position) расша́тываться. —**loose bowels,** поно́с. —**loose soil,** ры́хлая по́чва. —**lose talk,** кривото́лки. —**loose tongue,** язы́к без косте́й. —**loose translation,** нето́чный перево́д. —**on the loose,** на свобо́де. —**set/let/turn loose,** отпуска́ть. —**work loose,** выпу́тываться; вывёртываться.
loose-leaf *adj.* с вкладны́ми листа́ми.
loosely *adv.* **1,** (not tightly) свобо́дно: *fit loosely,* сиде́ть свобо́дно. **2,** (not strictly) широко́: *interpret loosely,* широко́ толкова́ть.
loosen *v.t.* **1,** (make less tight) ослабля́ть; отпуска́ть; распуска́ть. *Loosen someone's tongue,* развяза́ть кому́-нибудь язы́к. **2,** (make less dense, as soil) рыхли́ть; разрыхля́ть. —*v.i.* ослабева́ть.
loot *n.* добы́ча. —*v.t.* гра́бить. —**looter,** *n.* граби́тель. —**looting,** *n.* грабёж.
lop *v.t.* [*usu.* **lop off**] отруба́ть; обруба́ть.
lope *v.i.* бежа́ть вприпры́жку.
lop-eared *adj.* лопоу́хий; вислоу́хий.
lopsided *adj.* кривобо́кий; однобо́кий.
loquacious *adj.* болтли́вый; говорли́вый; разгово́рчивый. —**loquaciousness,** *n.* болтли́вость; говорли́вость; разгово́рчивость.
lord *n.* **1,** (ruler; master) влады́ка; господи́н; ба́рин. **2,** (British title) лорд. *House of Lords,* пала́та ло́рдов. **3,** *cap.* (God) бог; госпо́дь: *oh Lord!; Good Lord!,* го́споди!; бо́же мой! —*v.i., usu. in* **lord it over,** кома́ндовать над; вла́ствовать над.
lordly *adj.* ба́рственный.
lordship *n.* све́тлость: *Your Lordship,* ва́ша све́тлость.
lore *n.* зна́ния.
lorgnette *n.* лорне́т.
lorry *n.* грузови́к.
lose *v.t.* **1,** (misplace) теря́ть. **2,** (be unable to maintain) теря́ть: *lose one's balance,* теря́ть равнове́сие. **3,** (fail to win; gamble away) прои́грывать. **4,** (suffer the loss of) теря́ть; утра́чивать; лиша́ться. **5,** (miss,

as an opportunity) упускать; пропускать. **6,** *colloq.* (elude; shake off) ускользать от. —*v.i.* проигрывать. —**lose heart,** падать духом; унывать. —**lose one's head,** потерять голову. —**lose one's mind,** сходить с ума. —**lose one's temper,** выходить из себя. —**lose one's way,** заблудиться; сбиваться с пути *or* с дороги. —**lose patience,** терять терпение; выходить из терпения. —**lose sight of,** *see* sight. —**lose weight,** терять в весе; убавлять в весе. *See also* lost.

loser *n.* проигравший. *He is a poor loser,* он не умеет достойно проигрывать.

losing *adj.* проигрышный.

loss *n.* **1,** (act of losing; that which is lost) потеря; утрата. **2,** (money lost; opp. of profit) убыток. *Sell at a loss,* продавать в убыток/с убытком/невыгодно. **3,** (defeat in a game) проигрыш; поражение. **4,** *pl.* (casualties) потери. **5,** *pl.* (what is lost in gambling) проигрыш. —**be at a loss,** теряться в догадках. *I am at a loss for words,* не нахожу слов. *He is never at a loss for words,* он не лезет за словом в карман. *I was at a loss as to how to answer,* я не нашёлся, что ответить. —**throw for a loss,** озадачивать.

lost *adj.* **1,** (missing; misplaced; gone) потерянный. *The letter was lost,* письмо потерялось. *Make up for lost time,* наверстать потерянное время. **2,** (having lost one's way) заблудший. *Be/get lost,* заблудиться. *Get lost in a crowd,* потеряться *or* замешаться в толпе. **3,** (killed, drowned, sunk, etc.) погибший. *Give up for lost,* считать погибшим. **4,** (engrossed) погружённый: *lost in thought,* погруженный в размышления. **5,** (missed, as of an opportunity) пропущенный; упущенный. **6,** *fol. by* on *or* upon (unheeded): *the lesson was not lost upon him,* урок не прошёл для него даром. —**lost cause,** гиблое дело. —**lost sheep,** заблудшая овца.

lot *n.* **1,** (object used to determine something by chance) жребий; *cast lots,* бросать жребий. *Decide something by lot,* решить что-нибудь по жребию. *The lot fell upon him,* жребий пал на него. **2,** (fate; portion) судьба; участь: *cast one's lot with,* связать свою судьбу с. *Fall to someone's lot,* выпасть на чью-нибудь долю. **3,** (plot of land) участок. *Parking lot,* стоянка (автомобилей). **4,** (batch; quantity) партия. **5,** *colloq.* [*also pl.* **lots**] много: *a lot of money,* много денег. *Read a lot,* много читать. *Have lots to do,* иметь много дел. *I've heard a lot about you,* я много о вас слышал(а). *Your have quite a lot to be proud of,* вам есть чем гордиться. —*adv.* гораздо; намного: *a lot easier,* гораздо/намного легче.

lotion *n.* (косметическая) жидкость. *Hand lotion,* жидкость для рук. *Face lotion,* лосьон.

lottery *n.* лотерея. —*adj.* лотерейный: *lottery ticket,* лотерейный билет.

lotto *n.* лото.

lotus *n.* лотос.

loud *adj.* **1,** (strongly audible) громкий. *Loud noise,* сильный шум. **2,** *colloq.* (garish) кричащий; крикливый; броский. —*adv.* громко. *Out loud,* вслух. —**loudly,** *adv.* громко.

loudmouth *n.* крикун. —**loudmouthed,** *adj.* крикливый.

loudness *n.* громкость.

loudspeaker *n.* громкоговоритель; репродуктор.

lounge *n.* **1,** (public room) салон. **2,** (sofa) кушетка. —*v.i.* [*often* **lounge around**] нежиться; валяться.

lour *v.* = **lower**[2].

louse *n.* **1,** (insect) вошь. **2,** *slang* (contemptible person) подлец. —**louse up,** *slang* напутать.

lousy *adj.* **1,** (infested with lice) вшивый. **2,** *slang* (rotten; miserable) паршивый; дрянной.

lout *n.* хам; невежа; увалень.

lovable *adj.* милый; славный.

love *n.* любовь. *Love of/for music,* любовь к музыке. *In love,* влюблён. *Fall in love (with),* влюбиться (в). *Marry for love,* жениться *or* выйти замуж по любви. —*adj.* любовный: *love letter,* любовное письмо; *love song,* любовная песнь. *Love story,* история о любви. *Love affair,* роман. —*v.t. & i.* любить: *I love you,* я тебя люблю.

lovely *adj.* прекрасный; прелестный; чудесный. —**loveliness,** *n.* красота; прелесть.

lover *n.* **1,** (person in love) влюблённый. **2,** (enthusiast) любитель. **3,** (paramour) любовник.

love seat диван на двоих.

loving *adj.* **1,** (feeling love) любящий. **2,** (tender) любовный. —**loving cup,** круговая чаша.

lovingly *adv.* любовно; с любовью.

low *adj.* **1,** (not high) низкий: *low ceiling,* низкий потолок. *Low prices,* низкие цены. *Low pressure,* низкое давление. *Low gear,* первая передача. *Low tide,* низшая точка отлива. **2,** (poor; inferior) низкий; плохой: *low quality,* низкое качество; *low mark,* плохая отметка. *Have a low opinion of,* быть невысокого *or* плохого мнения о. **3,** (not loud) негромкий; тихий. **4,** (low-pitched; deep) низкий. **5,** (humble in origin) низкий: *of low station,* низкого происхождения. **6,** (base; mean) подлый; низкий. **7,** (dejected) унылый. *Low spirits,* уныние. **8,** *fol. by* on (not well supplied with): *we're low on gas,* бензин кончается. —*adv.* **1,** (at a low level) низко. **2,** (softly) тихо. —*n.* низшая точка. *Prices reached a new low,* цены понизились до нового предела. —*v.i.* (bellow) мычать. —**lay low,** свалить; повалить; сразить. —**lie low,** залегать; отлёживаться; притаиться. —**run low,** кончаться; истощаться; быть на исходе.

low-cut *adj.* с низким вырезом.

lower[1] (lo-er) *v.t.* **1,** (let down) спускать; опускать. **2,** (reduce) снижать; понижать. **3,** (weaken, as one's resistance) ослаблять. **4,** (reduce the volume of) понижать. **5,** in **lower oneself,** унижаться. —*adj.* нижний: *lower berth,* нижняя полка; *lower deck,* нижняя палуба. *Lower House,* нижняя палата. *Lower class,* низший класс.

lower[2] (lau-er) *also,* **lour** *v.i.* смотреть волком; смотреть зверем.

lower case строчные буквы.

low-grade *adj.* недоброкачественный; низкосортный; низкопробный.

lowland *n.* низменность.

lowly *adj.* **1,** (of low rank) низкий. **2,** (humble; meek) скромный; смиренный.

low-lying *adj.* низменный; низинный.

low-necked *adj.* с низким вырезом.

low-paid *adj.* низкооплачиваемый.

low-powered *adj.* маломощный; слабосильный.

low-priced *adj.* дешёвый.

lox *n.* семга.

loyal *adj.* верный; лояльный. —**loyalty,** *n.* верность; лояльность.

lozenge *n.* лепёшка; таблетка.

lubricant *n.* смазочный материал; смазка.

lubricate *v.t.* смазывать. —**lubrication,** *n.* смазка; смазывание. —**lubricator,** *n.* масленка.

lucid *adj.* ясный: *lucid exposition,* ясное изложение. *Lucid mind,* светлый ум. *Lucid intervals,* светлые минуты. —**lucidity,** *n.* ясность.

luck *n.* счастье; удача. *Good luck!,* желаю вам счастья. —**as luck would have it,** как нарочно; как назло; как на беду; как на грех. —**bad luck,** несчастье: *I had the bad luck to...,* я имел(а) несчастье (+ *inf.*). —**be in luck,** повезти (+ *dat.*): *you are in/out of//luck,* вам (не) повезло. —**for (good) luck,** на счастье.

luckily *adv.* к счастью. *Luckily for me,* на мое счастье.

luckless *adj.* несчастливый; незадачливый.

lucky *adj.* счастливый; удачливый. —**be lucky,** везти (+ *dat.*): *he is lucky at cards,* ему везет в картах. *It is lucky for you that...,* вам повезло, что...

lucrative *adj.* прибыльный; доходный.

lucre *n.* нажива. —**filthy lucre,** презренный металл.

ludicrous *adj.* смешной; нелепый; смехотворный.

lug *v.t.* тащить; волочить.

luggage *n.* багаж.

lugubrious *adj.* печальный; грустный; мрачный.

lukewarm *adj.* тепловатый.

lull *v.t.* усыплять; убаюкивать. —*n.* затишье.

lullaby *n.* колыбельная песня.

lumbago *n.* прострел; люмбаго.

lumbar *adj.* поясничный.

lumber *n.* лес; лесоматериал. —*adj.* лесной. —*v.i.* (move heavily) громыхать. —**lumberjack,** *n.* лесоруб. —**lumber jacket,** куртка. —**lumberyard,** *n.* лесной склад.

luminary *n.* светило.

luminescence *n.* свечение; люминесценция. —**luminescent,** *adj.* светящийся; люминесцентный.

luminosity *n.* освещенность.

luminous *adj.* светящийся; световой.

lummox *n., colloq.* увалень; простофиля.

lump *n.* **1,** (shapeless mass) ком; комок: *lump of dirt,* ком грязи. **2,** (piece, as of sugar) кусок. **3,** (swelling; bump) шишка. —*v.t.* [*usu.* **lump together**] валить в одну кучу; стричь под одну гребенку. —**lump in one's throat,** ком/комок/клубок в горле. *I felt a lump in my throat,* ком подступил к горлу. —**lump sugar,** кусковой *or* пиленый сахар; рафинад. —**Pay (out) in a lump sum,** единовременно выплачиваемая сумма. *Pay (out) in a lump sum,* заплатить все сразу; выплачивать единовременно.

lumpy *adj.* с комками.

lunacy *n.* безумие.

lunar *adj.* лунный.

lunatic *n.* душевнобольной; сумасшедший. *Lunatic asylum,* сумасшедший дом.

lunch *n.* обед; ленч. *Have lunch,* обедать. —*adj.* обеденный: *lunch break,* обеденный перерыв.

luncheon *n.* обед. —**luncheonette,** *n.* закусочная.

lung *n.* легкое. —*adj.* легочный. *Lung cancer,* рак легких. —**at the top of one's lungs,** во весь голос; во все горло; во всю глотку.

lunge *v.i.* дернуться. —*n.* наскок; выпад.

lupus *n.* волчанка.

lurch *v.i.* покачнуться. —*n.* толчок. —**leave in the lurch,** покинуть в беде.

lure *n.* приманка. —*v.t.* завлекать; заманивать; приманивать.

lurid *adj.* **1,** (glowing) огненный. **2,** (shocking) жуткий.

lurk *v.i.* таиться; притаиться.

luscious *adj.* лакомый; сочный.

lush *adj.* **1,** (luxuriant, as of foliage) буйный; пышный; тучный. **2,** (succulent) сочный. —*n., slang* (drunkard) пьяница.

lust *n.* **1,** (sexual desire) похоть; вожделение. **2,** (any overwhelming desire) жажда; страсть. —*v.i.* [*usu.* **lust for** *or* **after**] жаждать (+ *gen.*).

luster *also,* **lustre** *n.* блеск; лоск; глянец. *Lose its luster,* тускнеть.

lustful *adj.* похотливый.

lustre *n.* = **luster.**

lustrous *adj.* глянцевитый; глянцевый.

lusty *adj.* крепкий; дюжий.

lute *n.* лютня.

lutetium *n.* лютеций.

Lutheran *adj.* лютеранский. —*n.* лютеранин. —**Lutheranism,** *n.* лютеранство.

luxuriant *adj.* пышный; буйный.

luxuriate *v.i.* [*usu.* **luxuriate in**] нежиться (в *or* на); наслаждаться (+ *instr.*).

luxurious *adj.* роскошный.

luxury *n.* роскошь. —*adj.* люкс: *luxury hotel,* гостиница-люкс. *Luxury item,* предмет роскоши.

lycée *n.* лицей.

lye *n.* щелок.

lying *adj.* **1,** (recumbent) лежащий; лежачий. **2,** (false) лживый; ложный. —*n.* лганье; вранье.

lymph *n.* лимфа. *Lymph nodes,* лимфатические узлы. —**lymphatic,** *adj.* лимфатический.

lynch *v.t.* линчевать. —**lynching,** *n.* линчевание; самосуд.

lynx *n.* рысь.

lyre *n.* лира.

lyric *n.* **1,** (lyric poem) лирика. **2,** *pl.* (words of a song) текст. —*adj.* [*also,* **lyrical**] лирический.

lyricism *n.* лиризм.

M

M, m тринадцатая буква английского алфавита.
ma *n.*, *colloq.* мама
macabre *adj.* жуткий.
macadam *n.* щебень. —*adj.* щебёночный. —*v.t.* мостить щебнем.
macaque *n.* макака.
macaroni *n.* макароны.
macaroon *n.* миндальное печенье.
macaw *n.* ара; арара.
mace *n.* **1,** (club) булава. **2,** (staff of office) жезл. **3,** (spice) мускатный цвет.
Macedonian *adj.* македонский.
Machiavellian *adj.* макиавеллевский.
machination *n.*, *usu. pl.* махинации; козни.
machine *n.* машина; станок. —*adj.* машинный. *Machine shop,* механический цех; механическая мастерская. *Machine tool,* станок. *Machine translation,* машинный перевод.
machine gun пулемёт. —**machine-gun,** *v.t.* обстреливать пулемётным огнём. —**machine gunner,** пулемётчик.
machinery *n.* **1,** (machines collectively) машины. **2,** (system; organization) аппарат.
machinist *n.* машинист.
mackerel *n.* скумбрия; макрель.
mackintosh *n.* макинтош; плащ.
macrocosm *n.* макрокосм.
mad *adj.* **1,** (insane) сумасшедший. *Drive mad,* сводить с ума. *Go mad,* сходить с ума. **2,** (reckless; foolish) безумный. **3,** (rabid) бешеный. **4,** *fol. by* about (infatuated) без ума (от). **5,** *colloq.* (angry) сердитый. *Get mad,* сердиться. —**like mad,** сломя голову; как угорелый.
madam *n.* мадам; сударыня; госпожа.
madcap *n.* сумасброд; сорванец; сорвиголова.
madden *v.t.* **1,** (drive mad) сводить с ума. **2,** (make furious) бесить. —**maddening,** *adj.* досадный.
madder *n.* (plant) марена.
Madeira *n.* (wine) мадера.
mademoiselle *n.* мадемуазель.
made-to-order *adj.* сделанный на заказ.
madhouse *n.* сумасшедший дом.
madly *adv.* безумно. *Madly in love with,* безумно влюблён (влюблена) в; без ума от.
madman *n.* сумасшедший; безумец.
madness *n.* **1,** (insanity) сумасшествие. **2,** (folly) безумие.
Madonna *n.* мадонна.
madrigal *n.* мадригал.
maelstrom *n.* водоворот; вихрь.

maestro *n.* маэстро.
magazine *n.* **1,** (publication) журнал. **2,** (of a firearm) магазин. **3,** (storage place) погреб: *powder magazine,* пороховой погреб. —*adj.* журнальный: *magazine article,* журнальная статья.
magenta *n.* фуксин. —*adj.* красно-лиловый.
maggot *n.* личинка.
Magi *n.pl.* волхвы.
magic *n.* магия; волшебство. *As if by magic,* как будто по волшебству. —*adj.* [*also,* **magical**] магический; волшебный. *Magic lantern,* волшебный фонарь. *Magic wand,* волшебная палочка.
magician *n.* **1,** (sorcerer; wizard) волшебник; чародей. **2,** (entertainer who performs magic tricks) фокусник; иллюзионист.
magisterial *adj.* **1,** (of or pert. to a magistrate) судебный. **2,** (imperious) повелительный.
magistracy *n.* магистратура.
magistrate *n.* мировой судья.
Magna Carta *also,* **Magna Charta** Великая хартия вольностей.
magnanimity *n.* великодушие. —**magnanimous,** *adj.* великодушный.
magnate *n.* магнат.
magnesia *n.* магнезия.
magnesium *n.* магний.
magnet *n.* магнит.
magnetic *adj.* **1,** *physics* магнитный: *magnetic field,* магнитное поле. *Magnetic tape,* магнитная лента. **2,** *fig.* (powerfully attractive) магнетический. —**magnetics,** *n.* магнетизм. —**magnetism,** *n.* магнетизм.
magnetite *n.* магнетит.
magnetize *v.t.* намагничивать.
magneto *n.* магнето.
magnetron *n.* магнетрон.
magnification *n.* увеличение.
magnificence *n.* великолепие.
magnificent *adj.* великолепный. —**magnificently,** *adv.* великолепно.
magnify *v.t.* **1,** (enlarge) увеличивать. **2,** (exaggerate) преувеличивать. —**magnifying glass,** увеличительное стекло; лупа.
magnitude *n.* **1,** (size; brightness) величина. **2,** (significance) важность.
magnolia *n.* магнолия.
magpie *n.* сорока.
Magyar *n.* мадьяр. —*adj.* мадьярский.
maharajah *n.* магараджа.
mahogany *n.* красное дерево. —*adj.* красного дерева.

maid *n.* **1,** (young woman) дѣ́ва; дѣви́ца; дѣ́вушка. **2,** (housemaid) го́рничная; домрабо́тница; (chambermaid) го́рничная; убо́рщица. —**old maid,** ста́рая дѣ́ва.

maiden *n.* дѣ́ва; дѣви́ца; дѣ́вушка. —*adj.* **1,** (unmarried) незаму́жняя. **2,** (initial) пе́рвый: *maiden voyage,* пе́рвый рейс.

maidenhead *n.* дѣ́вственная плева́.

maidenhood *n.* дѣ́вичество.

maidenly *adj.* дѣ́вичий.

maiden name *n.* дѣ́вичья фами́лия.

mail *n.* **1,** (post; letters) по́чта: *by mail,* по по́чте. **2,** (armor) кольчу́га. —*adj.* почто́вый: *mail train,* почто́вый по́езд. —*v.t.* **1,** (deposit in a mailbox) опуска́ть (в почто́вый я́щик). **2,** (send by mail) посыла́ть по по́чте.

mailbag *n.* почто́вый мешо́к. *Also,* **mail pouch.**

mailbox *n.* почто́вый я́щик.

mailed fist брониро́ванный кула́к.

mailman *n.* почтальо́н.

mail-order *adj.* посы́лочный: *mail-order house,* посы́лочная фи́рма.

maim *v.t.* калѣ́чить; увѣ́чить.

main *adj.* гла́вный; основно́й. *The main thing,* (са́мое) гла́вное. *Main floor,* пе́рвый эта́ж. *Main course,* второ́е (блю́до). —*n.* магистра́ль: *water main,* водопрово́дная магистра́ль. —**in the main,** в основно́м. —**with might and main,** изо всех сил; во всю мочь.

mainland *n.* матери́к.

mainly *adv.* в основно́м; гла́вным о́бразом; бо́льшей ча́стью.

mainmast *n.* грот-ма́чта.

mainsail *n.* грот.

mainspring *n.* **1,** (of a watch) ходова́я пружи́на. **2,** *fig.* (chief source or motive) гла́вная пружи́на.

mainstay *n.* станово́й хребе́т.

mainstream *n.* гла́вное ру́сло: *outside the mainstream,* в сторонѣ́ от гла́вного ру́сла.

maintain *v.t.* **1,** (assert; claim) утвержда́ть. **2,** (carry on; keep up) подде́рживать. **3,** (preserve; retain) сохраня́ть. **4,** (have; own; keep) держа́ть. **5,** (support; provide for) содержа́ть. **6,** (keep in good repair) содержа́ть в испра́вности.

maintenance *n.* **1,** (support) содержа́ние. **2,** (servicing) ухо́д.

maître d'hôtel метрдоте́ль.

maize *n.* маи́с.

majestic *adj.* вели́чественный.

majesty *n.* **1,** (grandeur) вели́чие. **2,** *cap.* (title) вели́чество: *Your Majesty,* ва́ше вели́чество.

major *n.* **1,** (military officer) майо́р. **2,** *music* мажо́р: *key of F major,* тона́льность фа мажо́р. **3,** (main field of study) предме́т специализа́ции. —*adj.* **1,** (greater) бо́льший: *the major part,* бо́льшая часть. **2,** (important; significant) ва́жный; значи́тельный. **3,** (prominent) кру́пный: *a major writer,* кру́пный писа́тель. **4,** (broad in scope) капита́льный: *major repairs,* капита́льный ремо́нт. **5,** *music* мажо́рный. —*v.i.* специализи́роваться.

majordomo *n.* мажордо́м.

major general генера́л-лейтена́нт.

majority *n.* **1,** (more than half of a total) большинство́. **2,** (full legal age) совершенноле́тие.

make *v.t.* **1,** (accomplish; carry out; commit) дѣ́лать;

совершать: *make a mistake,* дѣ́лать/соверша́ть оши́бку; *make an attempt,* дѣ́лать попы́тку; *make an offer,* дѣ́лать предложе́ние; *make progress,* дѣ́лать успѣ́хи; *make a deal,* соверша́ть сдѣ́лку. **2,** (produce; manufacture) дѣ́лать; производи́ть; выраба́тывать; изготовля́ть. *What is this made of?,* из чего́ э́то сдѣ́лано? **3,** (produce; cause) производи́ть: *make an impression,* производи́ть впечатлѣ́ние. *Make a noise,* поднима́ть шум. *Make a scene,* устра́ивать сце́ну. **4,** (produce as a result) дѣ́лать: *make no secret of,* не дѣ́лать секре́та из. *Make an example of,* ста́вить в приме́р. *Make a mess of,* напу́тать. **5,** (cause to be) *usu. rendered by a single verb: make happy,* ра́довать; *make shorter,* укора́чивать. *Make public,* предава́ть гла́сности. **6,** (cause to; force to) заставля́ть: *make someone wait,* заставля́ть кого́-нибудь ждать. *Make someone promise,* брать сло́во с. **7,** (prompt to; impel to) побужда́ть: *what made you do it?,* что вас побуди́ло э́то сдѣ́лать? **8,** (amount to; constitute) составля́ть. *Two and two make four,* два и два равно́ четырём. **9,** (turn out to be; become) ока́зываться. *He will make a good teacher,* из него́ вы́йдет хоро́ший учи́тель. **10,** (establish; enact, as laws or rules) устана́вливать. **11,** (appoint) назнача́ть. **12,** (earn) зараба́тывать: *make a living,* зараба́тывать на жизнь. *Make a fortune,* нажи́ть состоя́ние. **13,** (arrive in time for; catch) успева́ть на *or* к. **14,** (cook) гото́вить: *make dinner,* гото́вить обѣ́д. *Make tea,* зава́ривать чай. **15,** *with certain nouns* дава́ть: *make a promise,* дава́ть обеща́ние; *make a recommendation,* дава́ть рекоменда́цию. *Make room for,* дава́ть мѣ́сто (+ *dat.*). **16,** *with certain nouns* идти́ на: *make concessions,* идти́ на усту́пки; *make sacrifices,* идти́ на же́ртвы. **17,** *used with various other nouns: make a bed,* убира́ть посте́ль; *make a speech,* говори́ть *or* произноси́ть речь; *make a request,* обраща́ться с про́сьбой; *make a decision,* принима́ть реше́ние; *make a date,* назнача́ть свида́ние; *make changes,* вноси́ть измене́ния; *make sense,* имѣ́ть смысл. **18,** *Make oneself understood,* объясня́ться; *make oneself at home,* быть как до́ма; *make oneself comfortable,* устро́иться поудо́бнее. —*n.* **1,** (brand) ма́рка. **2,** (manufacture) изде́лие; произво́дство. *Of foreign make,* иностра́нного произво́дства. —**make as if; make as though,** дѣ́лать вид; притворя́ться. —**make do:** *make do with what we have on hand,* обходи́ться имѣ́ющимися запа́сами. —**make for, 1,** (head for) направля́ться к. **2,** (make a dash for) бро́ситься к. **3,** (tend to create) спосо́бствовать; содѣ́йствовать. **4,** *Made for each other,* со́зданы друг для дру́га. —**make good,** преуспева́ть. —**make it, 1,** (achieve a certain thing) попа́сть. **2,** (be on time) успѣ́ть. **3,** (judge; estimate) *I make it twenty miles,* по-мо́ему здесь два́дцать миль. **4,** *Make it a rule to,* взять себѣ́ за пра́вило (+ *inf.*). —**make of,** понима́ть: *what do you make of his action?,* как вы понима́ете его́ посту́пок? *I don't know what to make of it,* я не зна́ю, что об э́том и ду́мать. —**make off with,** уноси́ть; утаски́ть. —**make out, 1,** (discern) различа́ть; разбира́ть; распознава́ть. **2,** (be able to read) разбира́ть. **3,** (comprehend) понима́ть. **4,** (draw up) составля́ть. **5,** (fill out) заполня́ть. **6,** (write out, as a check) выпи́сывать. **7,** *colloq.* (manage; get along) обходи́ться. *How are you making out?,* как у вас дѣла́? —**make over, 1,** (remake) переде́лывать. **2,** (transfer; sign over) переда-ва́ть. —**make up, 1,** (put together; compose; constitute) составля́ть. **2,** (invent; concoct) выду́мывать. **3,** (be reconciled) мири́ться. **4,** *theat.* гримирова́ть. **5,** *printing* верста́ть. **6,** *Make up the difference,* допла́чивать ра́зницу. —**make up for,** восполня́ть; возмеща́ть; навёрстывать. *Make up for lost time,* возмести́ть/наверста́ть поте́рянное вре́мя. —**make way,** *see* **way.**

maker *n.* **1,** (manufacturer) фабрика́нт: *weapons maker,* фабрика́нт ору́жия. ◆*Usu. in combinations: dressmaker,* портни́ха; *peacemaker,* миротво́рец. **2,** *cap.* (God) творе́ц; созда́тель.

makeshift *adj.* вре́менный; подру́чный.

make-up *n.* **1,** (composition) соста́в. **2,** (nature; disposition) нату́ра; хара́ктер. **3,** (cosmetics) косме́тика. *Put on/use/wear make-up,* кра́ситься; ма́заться. **4,** *theat.* грим. *Make-up artist,* гримёр. **5,** *printing* вёрстка.

makeweight *n.* дове́сок.

making *n.* **1,** (creation) созда́ние. **2,** (manufacture) произво́дство. **3,** *pl.* (potential ability) зада́тки; да́нные: *he has the makings of a fine writer,* у него́ зада́тки хоро́шего писа́теля; у него́ все да́нные, что́бы стать хоро́шим писа́телем.

malachite *n.* малахи́т. —*adj.* малахи́товый.

maladjusted *adj.* неприспосо́бленный. —**maladjustment,** *n.* неприспосо́бленность.

maladroit *adj.* неуклю́жий; нело́вкий.

malady *n.* боле́знь.

Malaga *n.* (wine) мала́га.

malaise *n.* недомога́ние.

malapropos *adj.* неуме́стный. —*adv.* некста́ти.

malaria *n.* маляри́я. —**malarial,** *adj.* маляри́йный.

Malay *adj.* мала́йский. —*n.* **1,** (person) мала́ец; мала́йка. **2,** (language) мала́йский язы́к.

malcontent *n. & adj.* недово́льный.

male *adj.* мужско́й; мужско́го по́ла. —*n.* **1,** (man) мужчи́на. **2,** (male animal) саме́ц.

malediction *n.* прокля́тие.

malefactor *n.* престу́пник; правонаруши́тель; злоде́й.

maleficent *adj.* вре́дный; злове́щий.

malevolent *adj.* зло́бный; недоброжела́тельный. —**malevolence,** *n.* зло́ба; недоброжела́тельство.

malfeasance *n.* должностно́е преступле́ние.

malformation *n.* уро́дство. —**malformed,** *adj.* уро́дливый.

malfunction *n.* неиспра́вность; отка́з. —*v.i.* отка́зывать.

malice *n.* зло́ба; злость.

malicious *adj.* **1,** (spiteful) зло́бный; зло́стный. **2,** *law* злой; злонаме́ренный. *Malicious act,* злонаме́ренный посту́пок. *Malicious intent,* злой у́мысел. —**maliciously,** *adv.* зло́бно; зло; со зло́бой.

malign *v.t.* клевета́ть на; поро́чить.

malignancy *n.* злока́чественная о́пухоль.

malignant *adj.* **1,** (malicious) зло́бный. **2,** (pernicious) па́губный. **3,** *med.* злока́чественный.

malinger *v.i.* притворя́ться больны́м; симули́ровать боле́знь. —**malingerer,** *n.* симуля́нт.

mall *n.* алле́я; бульва́р.

mallard *n.* кря́ква.

malleable *adj.* ко́вкий. —**malleability,** *n.* ко́вкость.

mallet *n.* колоту́шка.

mallow *n.* ма́льва.

malnutrition *n.* недоеда́ние.

malodorous *adj.* злово́нный; воню́чий.

malpractice *n.* небре́жное лече́ние.

malt *n.* со́лод.

maltose *n.* мальто́за; солодо́вый са́хар.

maltreat *v.t.* ду́рно *or* пло́хо обраща́ться с. —**maltreatment,** *n.* дурно́е *or* плохо́е обраще́ние.

mama *also,* **mamma** *n.* ма́ма. —**mama's boy,** ма́менькин сыно́к.

mammal *n.* млекопита́ющее.

mammary *adj.* грудно́й; моло́чный.

mammoth *n.* ма́монт. —*adj.* огро́мный; гига́нтский; колосса́льный.

man *n.* **1,** (person) челове́к: *a nice man,* симпати́чный челове́к. *Man in the street,* "челове́к с у́лицы". *Man of letters,* литера́тор. *All men are mortal,* все лю́ди сме́ртны. **2,** (male human being) мужчи́на: *for men only,* то́лько для мужчи́н. **3,** (mankind) челове́к: *primitive man,* первобы́тный челове́к. *Man is a rational being,* челове́к — существо́ разу́мное. —*adj.* [*usu.* **man's** *or* **men's**] мужско́й: *men's clothes,* мужско́е пла́тье. —*v.t.* **1,** (furnish with men) (у)комплектова́ть. **2,** (take stations at) станови́ться к *or* на. —**as one man,** все как оди́н. —**my good man!,** ми́лый мой. —**to a man,** все до одного́.

manacle *n.* нару́чник. —*v.t.* надева́ть нару́чники на;ско́вывать.

manage *v.t.* **1,** (direct; administer) управля́ть; заве́довать; руководи́ть. **2,** *fol. by inf.* (contrive; succeed) суме́ть; ухитря́ться; умудря́ться; изловчи́ться. —*v.i.* (make out; get along) обходи́ться; устра́иваться.

management *n.* **1,** (act of managing) управле́ние; заве́дование. **2,** (those who manage) правле́ние; дире́кция; администра́ция.

manager *n.* заве́дующий; управля́ющий; дире́ктор.

managerial *adj.* дире́кторский; администрати́вный. *Managerial abilities,* организа́торские спосо́бности.

manatee *n.* ламанти́н.

Manchu *adj.* маньчжу́рский. —*n.* **1,** (person) маньчжу́р. **2,** (language) маньчжу́рский язы́к.

mandarin *n.* **1,** (Chinese official) мандари́н. **2,** *cap.* (language) мандари́нский язы́к. **3,** (tangerine) мандари́н.

mandate *n.* **1,** (instruction from constituents) нака́з (избира́телей). **2,** (charge to administer a territory) манда́т.

mandatory *adj.* обяза́тельный.

mandible *n.* ни́жняя че́люсть.

mandolin *n.* мандоли́на.

mandrake *n.* мандраго́ра.

mandrel *also,* **mandril** *n.* опра́вка.

mandrill *n.* мандри́л.

mane *n.* гри́ва.

maneuver *also,* **manoeuvre** *n.* мане́вр. —*v.t. & i.* маневри́ровать. —**maneuverable,** *adj.* мане́вренный. —**maneuverability,** *n.* мане́вренность.

manganese *n.* ма́рганец.

manganite *n.* мангани́т.

mange *n.* чесо́тка; парша́.

manger *n.* я́сли. —**dog in the manger,** соба́ка на се́не.

mangle *v.t.* **1,** (mutilate; disfigure) калечить. **2,** (spoil; ruin) коверкать. **3,** (press in a mangle) катать. —*n.* каток (для белья).

mango *n.* манго.

mangy *adj.* паршивый; шелудивый; облезлый.

manhandle *v.t.* грубо обращаться с.

manhole *n.* люк; лаз.

manhood *n.* возмужалость; зрелость.

man-hour *n.* человеко-час.

manhunt *n.* полицейская облава.

mania *n.* мания. —**maniac,** *n.* маньяк. —**maniacal,** *adj.* маниакальный.

manic *adj.* маниакальный. —**manic-depressive,** *adj.* маниакально-депрессивный.

manicure *n.* маникюр. —*v.t.* делать маникюр (+ *dat.*). —**manicurist,** *n.* маникюрша.

manifest *v.t.* проявлять. *Manifest itself,* проявляться; выражаться. —*adj.* очевидный; явный. —**manifestation,** *n.* проявление.

manifesto *n.* манифест.

manifold *adj.* разнообразный; разносторонний. —*n.* (pipe) трубопровод.

manikin *n.* манекен.

manioc *n.* маниока.

manipulate *v.t.* манипулировать. —**manipulation,** *n.* манипуляция. —**manipulator,** *n.* манипулятор.

mankind *n.* человечество.

manlike *adj.* человекоподобный.

manly *adj.* мужественный. —**manliness,** *n.* мужественность.

man-made *adj.* искусственный.

manna *n.* манна. *Manna from heaven,* манна небесная.

manned *adj.* пилотируемый; с человеком на борту.

mannequin *n.* манекен.

manner *n.* **1,** (way) способ. *In this manner,* таким образом; *in like manner,* подобным образом. **2,** (mode of behavior) манера. **3,** *pl.* (social ways) манеры: *good manners,* хорошие манеры. *Table manners,* этикет. —**all manner of,** всевозможные. —**by no manner of means,** отнюдь не. —**in a manner of speaking,** так сказать; если можно так выразиться. —**in the manner of,** на манер (+ *gen.*).

mannered *adj.* манерный.

mannerism *n.* **1,** (excessive use of an affected style) манерность. **2,** (peculiarity of manner) манера.

mannerly *adj.* вежливый; воспитанный.

mannish *adj.* мужеподобный.

manoeuvre *n. & v.* = **maneuver.**

man-of-war *n.* военный корабль.

manometer *n.* манометр. —**manometric,** *adj.* манометрический.

manor *n.* поместье. —**manor house,** помещичий дом.

manorial *adj.* помещичий.

manpower *n.* **1,** (power supplied by human physical effort) рабочая сила. **2,** (people available for work) живая сила.

mansard *n.* мансардная крыша. *Also,* **mansard roof.**

manservant *n.* слуга.

mansion *n.* особняк.

manslaughter *n.* непредумышленное убийство; убийство по неосторожности.

mantel *n.* каминная полка. *Also,* **mantelpiece.**

mantilla *n.* мантилья.

mantis *n.* богомол.

mantle *n.* **1,** (cloak) мантия. **2,** (incandescent hood) калильная сетка. **3,** *fig.* (cover) покров.

manual *adj.* ручной: *manual labor,* ручной труд. *Manual training,* уроки по труду. —*n.* **1,** (book of instructions) руководство. **2,** *mil.* наставление. *Field manual,* боевой устав. —**manually,** *adv.* вручную.

manufacture *v.t.* производить; изготовлять; вырабатывать; выделывать; фабриковать. *Manufactured goods,* промышленные товары. —*n.* производство; изготовление; выработка; выделка; фабрикация. —**manufacturer,** *n.* фабрикант; промышленник.

manure *n.* навоз; удобрение.

manuscript *n.* рукопись. —*adj.* рукописный.

many *adj.* много: *many times,* много раз; *in many cases,* во многих случаях. —*pron.* многие: *many of them,* многие из них. *Many believe that...,* многие считают, что... —**a great many,** очень много. —**as many,** столько же. *Twice as many,* в два раза (*or* вдвое) больше. —**as many as, 1,** (the same quantity) столько же..., сколько и...: *as many adults as children,* столько же взрослых, сколько и детей. *Take as many as you like,* берите (столько), сколько вам угодно. **2,** (before numbers, emphasizing a large amount) целые; целых; до. —**how many?,** сколько? —**so many,** так много; столько. *I told him in so many words that...,* я так и сказал ему, что... —**the many,** большинство. —**too many,** слишком много.

many-sided *adj.* многосторонний.

map *n.* карта. *City map,* план города. —*v.t.* **1,** (make a map of) наносить на карту; картографировать. **2,** *fol. by* **out** (plan) намечать. —**map maker,** картограф. —**map making,** картография.

maple *n.* клён. —*adj.* кленовый. —**maple sugar,** кленовый сахар. —**maple syrup,** кленовый сироп.

mar *v.t.* **1,** (spoil) портить; отравлять. **2,** (damage) повреждать. *Mar the appearance of,* уродовать; безобразить.

marabou *n.* марабу.

maraschino *n.* мараскин.

marasmus *n.* маразм.

marathon *n.* марафонский бег.

maraud *v.i.* мародёрствовать. —**marauder,** *n.* мародёр. —**marauding,** *n.* мародёрство. —*adj.* мародёрский.

marble *n.* **1,** (mineral) мрамор. **2,** (little ball) шарик: *play marbles,* играть в шарики. —*adj.* мраморный.

march *v.i.* маршировать. —*n.* **1,** *mil.* марш; поход; переход. *A two-day march,* двухдневный переход. **2,** (demonstration) марш: *protest march,* марш протеста. **3,** *music* марш. **4,** (progress) ход: *march of events,* ход событий. —**on the march,** на марше.

March *n.* март. —*adj.* мартовский.

marching *n.* маршировка. —*adj.* походный; маршировочный.

marchioness *n.* маркиза.

marchpane *n.* марципан.

Mardi gras масленица.

mare *n.* кобыла.

margarine *n.* маргарин.

margin *n.* **1,** (edge of a page) поля (страницы): *write in the margin,* писать на полях. **2,** (border; edge) край. **3,** (reserve) запа́с: *margin of safety*, запа́с безопа́сности; запа́с про́чности. **4,** (difference, as in votes) переве́с: *by a narrow margin*, с незначи́тельным переве́сом.

marginal *adj.* **1,** (written in the margin) напи́санный на поля́х: *marginal note*, заме́тка на поля́х. **2,** (border-line) сре́дний. **3,** (barely profitable) малоприбыльный.

marginalia *n.pl.* маргина́лии.

marigold *n.* **1,** (African or French marigold) ба́рхатцы. **2,** (pot marigold) ноготки́.

marijuana *n.* марихуа́на.

marinade *n.* марина́д.

marinate *v.t.* маринова́ть. —**marinated,** *adj.* мари́нованный.

marine *adj.* морско́й. —*n.* **1,** (seagoing soldier) морско́й пехоти́нец. **2,** *pl.* (Marine Corps) морска́я пехо́та. —**merchant marine,** торго́вый флот.

mariner *n.* моря́к; матро́с.

marionette *n.* марионе́тка.

marital *adj.* супру́жеский; бра́чный. *Marital status,* семе́йное положе́ние.

maritime *adj.* морско́й; примо́рский.

marjoram *n.* майора́н.

mark *n.* **1,** (written line or symbol) ме́тка; поме́тка. **2,** (scratch, scar, etc.) след. **3,** (grade) отме́тка; оце́нка; балл. **4,** (sign in lieu of a signature) крест. **5,** (impression) отпеча́ток: *leave its mark*, накла́дывать свой отпеча́ток. **6,** (token; indication) знак: *mark of respect*, знак внима́ния. **7,** (standard): *up to the mark*, на до́лжной высоте́. **8,** (target) цель: *hit the mark*, попа́сть *or* бить в цель. *Be wide of the mark*, бить ми́мо це́ли; *fig.* попа́сть па́льцем в не́бо. **9,** (starting line in a race) старт: *on your mark!*, на старт! **10,** (monetary unit) ма́рка. —*v.t.* **1,** (place a mark on; indicate with a mark) ме́тить; отмеча́ть; помеча́ть; обознача́ть. *Mark the place in a book*, отмеча́ть/помеча́ть ме́сто в кни́ге. *The roads are poorly marked*, доро́ги пло́хо обозна́чены. **2,** (grade) ста́вить отме́тку (отме́тки) на. **3,** (celebrate; commemorate) отмеча́ть. *To mark the anniversary*, в ознаменова́ние юбиле́я. **4,** (signify; represent) знаменова́ть (собо́й). *Mark the beginning of a new era*, знаменова́ть нача́ло но́вой эпо́хи. —**mark down,** уцени́вать. —**mark my words,** попо́мните моё сло́во. —**mark off,** отсчи́тывать: *mark off ten paces*, отсчи́тывать де́сять шаго́в. —**mark time,** топта́ться на ме́сте. —**mark up, 1,** (cover with markings) испещря́ть. **2,** (raise the price of) наце́нивать.

marked *adj.* **1,** (having a mark or marks) ме́ченый. *Marked cards*, краплёные ка́рты. **2,** (strikingly evident) заме́тный: *a marked improvement*, заме́тное улучше́ние.

marker *n.* **1,** (one who marks) ме́тчик. **2,** (device for marking) флома́стер. **3,** (indicator) знак: *boundary marker*, пограни́чный *or* межево́й знак. **4,** (chip; counter) фи́шка.

market *n.* ры́нок. *Black market*, чёрный ры́нок. —*adj.* ры́ночный: *market price*, ры́ночная цена́. *Market basket*, корзи́на для прови́зии. —*v.t.* продава́ть; сбыва́ть.

marketplace *n.* база́рная пло́щадь.

marking *n.* **1,** (mark) ме́тка. **2,** (coloration) окра́ска; расцве́тка.

marksman *n.* (ме́ткий) стрело́к. —**marksmanship,** *n.* ме́ткость.

markup *n.* наце́нка.

marl *n.* ме́ргель.

marmalade *n.* джем; пови́дло.

marmoset *n.* марты́шка.

marmot *n.* суро́к.

maroon *adj.* бордо́; цве́та бордо́; бордо́вый. —*v.t.* выса́живать (на необита́емом о́строве).

marquee *n.* театра́льный наве́с.

marquis *n.* марки́з. —**marquise,** *n.* марки́за.

marriage *n.* брак; жени́тьба; заму́жество.

married *adj.* **1,** (of a man) жена́т; *modifier* жена́тый. **2,** (of a woman) за́мужем; *modifier* заму́жняя. **3,** (of two or many people) жена́ты. *Married people*, жена́тые. *Married couple*, супру́жеская чета́ *or* па́ра. *Married life*, бра́чная жизнь; супру́жеская жизнь. —**get married,** *see* **marry.**

marrow *n.* ко́стный мозг. —**to the marrow,** до мо́зга косте́й.

marry *v.t.* **1,** (get married to) А, (of a man) жени́ться на (*+ prepl.*). В, (of a woman) выходи́ть за́муж за (*+ acc.*). **2,** *usu. fol. by* **off** (give in marriage) А, (a son) жени́ть. В, (a daughter) выдава́ть за́муж. **3,** (perform the marriage ceremony for) венча́ть. —*v.i.* вступа́ть в брак; жени́ться; выходи́ть за́муж; *(of two people)* пожени́ться.

Mars *n.* Марс.

Marsala *n.* (wine) марса́ла.

Marseillaise *n.* Марселье́за.

marsh *n.* боло́то; топь.

marshal *n.* **1,** *mil.* ма́ршал. **2,** (law-enforcement officer) суде́бный исполни́тель. —*v.t.* **1,** (array, as for battle) выстра́ивать. **2,** (assemble, as thoughts, facts, etc.) собира́ть.

marsh gas боло́тный газ.

marshland *n.* боло́тистая ме́стность.

marshmallow *n.* (candy) зефи́р. —**marsh mallow,** (plant) просви́рник; просвирня́к; проскурня́к.

marsh marigold калу́жница.

marshy *adj.* боло́тистый; то́пкий.

marsupial *n. & adj.* су́мчатый.

marten *n.* куни́ца.

martial *adj.* вое́нный; во́инский. —**martial law,** вое́нное положе́ние.

Martian *n.* марсиа́нин. —*adj.* марсиа́нский.

martyr *n.* му́ченик. —*v.t.* подверга́ть му́ченической сме́рти. —**martyrdom,** *n.* му́ченичество.

marvel *n.* чу́до; ди́во. —*v.i.* диви́ться; изумля́ться.

marvelous *also,* **marvellous** *adj.* удиви́тельный; изуми́тельный; чу́дный; чуде́сный. —**marvelously,** *adv.* удиви́тельно; изуми́тельно; чу́дно; чуде́сно.

Marxism *n.* маркси́зм. —**Marxian,** *adj.* маркси́стский. —**Marxist,** *n.* маркси́ст. —*adj.* маркси́стский.

marzipan *n.* марципа́н.

mascara *n.* тушь.

mascot *n.* талисма́н.

masculine *adj.* **1,** (male) мужско́й. **2,** (manly) му́жественный. **3,** *gram.* мужско́го ро́да. *Masculine gender*, мужско́й род. —**masculinity,** *n.* му́жественность.

mash *n.* **1,** (brewing mixture) су́сло. **2,** (feed for livestock) по́йло; ме́сиво. —*v.t.* размина́ть. *Mashed potatoes*, карто́фельное пюре́.

mask *n.* ма́ска; личи́на. —*v.t.* маскирова́ть. —**masked,** *adj.* замаскиро́ванный.

masochism *n.* мазохи́зм. —**masochist,** *n.* мазохи́ст. —**masochistic,** *adj.* мазохи́стский.

mason *n.* **1,** (worker in stone) ка́менщик. **2,** *cap.* (Freemason) масо́н.

Masonic *adj.* масо́нский.

masonry *n.* **1,** (work in stone) ка́менная кла́дка. **2,** *cap.* (Freemasonry) масо́нство.

masquerade *n.* маскара́д. —*v.i.* выдава́ть себя́ (за).

mass *n.* **1,** (body of matter) ма́сса: *a mass of clay,* гли́няная ма́сса. **2,** (great amount) ма́сса: *a mass of information,* ма́сса информа́ции. **3,** *physics* ма́сса: *critical mass,* крити́ческая ма́сса. **4,** *pl., preceded by* **the** (the common people) ма́ссы. **5,** *cap.* (church service) ме́сса; обе́дня. —*adj.* ма́ссовый: *mass production,* ма́ссовое произво́дство; *mass media,* сре́дства ма́ссовой информа́ции. —*v.t.* масси́ровать: *troops massed on the border,* войска́, масси́рованные на грани́це. —*v.i.* масси́роваться.

massacre *n.* резня́; бо́йня; избие́ние. —*v.t.* выреза́ть; изруби́ть.

massage *n.* масса́ж —*v.t.* масси́ровать; растира́ть.

masseur *n.* массажи́ст. —**masseuse,** *n.* массажи́стка.

massive *adj.* **1,** (huge; heavy and solid) масси́вный. **2,** (enormous in scope) огро́мный.

mast *n.* ма́чта.

master *n.* **1,** (one having control over another) хозя́ин; господи́н. *The dog's master,* хозя́ин соба́ки. *Serve two masters,* служи́ть двум господа́м. **2,** (skilled workman or practitioner) ма́стер. *Past master,* иску́сник. **3,** (holder of a master's degree) маги́стр. *Master's degree,* сте́пень маги́стра. **4,** (captain of a merchant ship) капита́н. —*adj.* **1,** (being master) госпо́дствующий. *Master race,* ра́са госпо́д. **2,** (comprehensive): *master plan,* генера́льный план. **3,** (brilliantly executed) мастерско́й: *master stroke,* мастерско́й уда́р. **4,** (original, as of a copy) по́длинный. **5,** *mech.* (of a switch, cylinder, etc.) гла́вный. —*v.t.* **1,** (bring under control) одолева́ть; оси́лить. **2,** (learn thoroughly) усва́ивать; овладева́ть.

masterful *adj.* **1,** (expert) мастерско́й. **2,** (domineering) вла́стный. —**masterfully,** *adv.* мастерски́.

master key отмы́чка.

masterly *adj.* мастерско́й.

mastermind *v.t.* заду́мать; замышля́ть.

master of ceremonies конферансье́.

masterpiece *n.* шеде́вр.

master sergeant старшина́.

mastery *n.* **1,** (control; dominion) госпо́дство. **2,** (command, as of a subject) овладе́ние.

masthead *n.* **1,** *naut.* топ ма́чты. **2,** (of a newspaper) ша́пка.

mastic *n.* масти́ка. —*adj.* масти́ковый.

masticate *v.t. & i.* жева́ть. —**mastication,** *n.* жева́ние.

mastiff *n.* дог.

mastitis *n.* грудни́ца; масти́т.

mastodon *n.* мастодо́нт.

masturbate *v.i.* онани́ровать. —**masturbation,** *n.* онани́зм.

mat *n.* **1,** (small rug) ко́врик; цино́вка. *Doormat,* полови́к. **2,** (something placed under a dish or vase) под-

сти́лка. **3,** *sports* ковёр. **4,** (dull surface) ма́товая пове́рхность. —*adj.* ма́товый. —*v.t.* (tangle) спу́тывать. —*v.i.* спу́тываться.

match *n.* **1,** (device for igniting) спи́чка. **2,** (equal; peer) ро́вня; ровня́. *No match for,* не чета́ (+ *dat.*). *Meet one's match,* найти́ ра́вного проти́вника. **3,** (suitable or possible mate) па́ра; па́ртия: *she is not a good match for him,* она́ ему́ не па́ра/па́ртия. **4,** (combination; marriage) па́ртия: *a good match,* хоро́шая па́ртия. **5,** (contest) состяза́ние; матч. —*v.t.* **1,** (be equal to; rival) равня́ться с. **2,** (correspond to) быть под стать (+ *dat.*). **3,** (go well with) гармони́ровать с; сочета́ться с; подходи́ть к. **4,** (make a match of; choose to suit) сочета́ть. *Choose a tie to match one's suit,* подбира́ть га́лстук под цвет костю́ма. **5,** *fol. by* **up** (pair; mate) сва́тать. **6,** (pit; place in opposition) противопоставля́ть. *Match wits,* состяза́ться в остроу́мии. —*v.i.* гармони́ровать.

matchbox *n.* спи́чечная коро́бка.

matchless *adj.* несравне́нный; бесподо́бный.

matchmaker *n.* сват; сва́ха. —**matchmaking,** *n.* сватовство́.

mate *n.* **1,** (one of a pair) па́ра. **2,** (spouse) супру́г; супру́га. **3,** (associate; buddy) това́рищ; напа́рник. **4,** *naut.* помо́щник капита́на. **5,** *chess* мат. —*v.t.* **1,** (pair for breeding) спа́ривать; случа́ть. **2,** *chess* де́лать мат (+ *dat.*). —*v.i.* спа́риваться.

material *n.* **1,** (that of which something is made) материа́л. *Raw materials,* сырьё. **2,** (textile fabric) мате́рия; материа́л. **3,** *pl.* (implements) принадле́жности: *writing materials,* пи́сьменные принадле́жности. **4,** (data to be worked up) материа́л. —*adj.* **1,** (physical) материа́льный; веще́ственный. *Material well-being,* материа́льное благополу́чие. *Material evidence,* веще́ственные доказа́тельства. **2,** (significant; substantial) суще́ственный. *Material witness,* ва́жный свиде́тель.

materialism *n.* материали́зм. —**materialist,** *n.* материали́ст. —**materialistic,** *adj.* материалисти́ческий.

materialize *v.i.* осуществля́ться; реализова́ться.

materially *adv.* **1,** (in a material sense) материа́льно: *materially well-off,* материа́льно обеспе́ченный. **2,** (significantly) суще́ственным о́бразом.

matériel *n.* материа́льная часть.

maternal *adj.* **1,** (motherly) матери́нский. **2,** (on one's mother's side of the family) со стороны́ ма́тери; с матери́нской стороны́.

maternity *n.* матери́нство. —**maternity clothes,** оде́жда для бере́менной же́нщины. —**maternity leave,** о́тпуск по бере́менности и ро́дам; декре́тный о́тпуск. —**maternity ward,** роди́льное отделе́ние.

mathematics *n.* матема́тика. —**mathematical,** *adj.* матема́тический. —**mathematician,** *n.* матема́тик.

matin *n., usu. pl.* у́треня; зау́треня.

matinee *n.* дневно́й спекта́кль.

mating *n.* спа́ривание. —**mating call,** токова́ние. —**mating season,** бра́чный пери́од.

matins *n., pl. of* **matin.**

matriarch *n.* мать. —**matriarchal,** *adj.* матриарха́льный. —**matriarchy,** *n.* матриарха́т.

matricide *n.* матереуби́йство.

matriculate *v.i.* зачисля́ться (в вы́сшее уче́бное

заведе́ние). —**matriculation,** *n.* зачисле́ние (в вы́сшее уче́бное заведе́ние).

matrimony *n.* супру́жество; брак. —**matrimonial,** *adj.* супру́жеский; бра́чный; матримониа́льный.

matrix *n.* ма́трица.

matron *n.* матро́на.

matted *adj.* спу́танный.

matter *n.* **1,** (substance) мате́рия; вещество́. **2,** (something printed) материа́л: *reading matter,* материа́л для чте́ния. **3,** (affair; question) вопро́с; де́ло. *A matter of taste,* де́ло вку́са. *A matter of life and death,* вопро́с жи́зни и сме́рти. *As matters stand,* при да́нном положе́нии дел. *It is no laughing matter,* э́то не шу́точное де́ло. —*v.i.* име́ть значе́ние. *It doesn't matter,* ничего́; нева́жно; не име́ет значе́ния. —**as a matter of fact, 1,** (in point of fact) на са́мом де́ле; факти́чески. **2,** (now that you mention it) предста́вьте себе́: *as a matter of fact, yes,* предста́вьте себе́, да. **3,** (in this connection) ме́жду про́чим. —**for that matter,** е́сли (уж) на то пошло́. —**no matter how/what/when** *etc.,* как бы ни/что бы ни/когда́ бы ни, *etc. No matter how he tried,* как он ни стара́лся.—**something is the matter,** что́-то не так. —**what is the matter?,** в чём де́ло?; что тако́е? —**what is the matter with you?,** что с ва́ми?

matter-of-fact *adj.* сухо́й; прозаи́чный.

matting *n.* рого́жа.

mattock *n.* моты́га.

mattress *n.* матра́с; матра́ц.

maturation *n.* созрева́ние.

mature *adj.* зре́лый. —*v.i.* созрева́ть. —*v.t.* доводи́ть до зре́лости. —**maturity,** *n.* зре́лость.

matutinal *adj.* у́тренний.

matzo *n.* маца́.

maudlin *adj.* слезли́вый.

maul *n.* колоту́шка; кува́лда. —*v.t.* терза́ть; растерза́ть.

Maundy Thursday страстно́й четве́рг.

Mauser *n.* ма́узер.

mausoleum *n.* мавзоле́й.

mauve *adj.* лило́вый.

maverick *n.* **1,** (unbranded calf) теле́нок без клейма́. **2,** (independent person) индивидуали́ст.

mawkish *adj.* прито́рный; слаща́вый.

maxim *n.* изрече́ние; сенте́нция.

maximal *adj.* максима́льный.

maximize *v.t.* доводи́ть до ма́ксимума.

maximum *n.* ма́ксимум. —*adj.* максима́льный; преде́льный.

may *v.aux.* **1,** *expressing possibility or contingency* мочь: *they may have gone home already,* они́ могли́ уже́ уйти́ домо́й. ♦*Also rendered by* возмо́жно: *it may be true,* возмо́жно, э́то пра́вда. **2,** *requesting or granting permission* мочь; мо́жно: *may I come in?,* мо́жно войти́? *You may go now,* вы мо́жете идти́ тепе́рь. **3,** *expressing wish, hope, or prayer* пусть; да: *may all your dreams come true!,* пусть/да сбу́дутся все ва́ши мечты́! *May he rest in peace,* мир пра́ху его́. —**be that as it may,** как бы то ни́ было. —**come what may,** будь, что бу́дет.

May *n.* май. —*adj.* ма́йский.

maybe *adv.* мо́жет быть.

May Day Пе́рвое ма́я; пра́здник Пе́рвого ма́я. —**May-Day,** *adj.* первома́йский.

mayfly *n.* поде́нка.

mayhem *n.* **1,** *law* нанесе́ние уве́чья. **2,** (havoc) ха́ос.

mayonnaise *n.* майоне́з.

mayor *n.* мэр.

maze *n.* лабири́нт.

mazurka *n.* мазу́рка.

me *pers.pron.* **1,** *used as dir. obj. of a verb* меня́: *he loves me,* он лю́бит меня́. **2,** *used as indir. obj. of a verb* мне: *show me!,* покажи́те мне. **3,** *used as obj. of a prep.* меня́; мне; мной.

mead *n.* мёд.

meadow *n.* луг.

meadowsweet *n.* та́волга.

meager *also,* **meagre** *adj.* **1,** (scanty) ску́дный. **2,** (lean) худо́й; то́щий.

meal *n.* **1,** (repast) еда́. *Eat three meals a day,* есть три ра́за в день. **2,** (ground grain) мука́: *corn meal,* кукуру́зная мука́.

mealy *adj.* мучни́стый.

mean *v.t.* **1,** (signify; denote) зна́чить: *what does this mean?,* что э́то зна́чит? **2,** *fol. by inf.* (intend) предполага́ть. **3,** (intentionally plan or wish) хоте́ть: *I didn't mean to offend you,* я не хоте́л вас оби́деть. *He means you no harm,* он не жела́ет вам зла. **4,** (intend to express) хоте́ть сказа́ть: *what do you mean by that?,* что вы хоти́те э́тим сказа́ть? **5,** (have in mind) име́ть в виду́: *whom do you mean?,* кого́ вы име́ете в виду́? **6,** *fol. by it* (be serious): *do you really mean it?,* вы э́то серьёзно? *I mean it,* я говорю́ серьёзно. *You don't mean it!,* вы шу́тите! **7,** (intend; design) предназнача́ть. *They were meant for each other,* они́ со́зданы друг для дру́га. **8,** (matter) зна́чить: *mean a great deal to,* мно́го зна́чить для. —*v.i. Mean well,* име́ть до́брые наме́рения. —*adj.* **1,** (nasty) злой: *a mean old man,* злой стари́к. *Be mean to someone,* пло́хо *or* гру́бо обраща́ться с кем-нибудь. **2,** (malicious) ни́зкий; по́длый; злой: *mean trick,* ни́зкий/по́длый посту́пок; зла́я шу́тка. **3,** (average) сре́дний: *mean distance,* сре́днее расстоя́ние. —*n.* **1,** (something between extremes) середи́на: *golden mean,* золота́я середи́на. **2,** *math.* сре́днее число́. **3,** *pl.* (method; instrument) сре́дства: *means of production,* сре́дства произво́дства. *The end justifies the means,* цель опра́вдывает сре́дства. **4,** *pl.* (money; wealth) сре́дства: *man of means,* челове́к со сре́дствами. *Live beyond one's means,* жить не по сре́дствам. —**by all means, 1,** (without fail) обяза́тельно. **2,** (of course) коне́чно; пожа́луйста. —**by means of,** посре́дством (+ *gen.*); путём (+ *gen.*); при по́мощи (+ *gen.*). —**by no means, 1,** *fol. by an adj.* (not the least bit) совсе́м не. **2,** *as an exclamation* (not at all) нет, что вы! —**not...by any means,** совсе́м не: *not cheap by any means,* совсе́м не дёшево.

meander *v.i.* **1,** (follow a winding course) извива́ться. **2,** (ramble; wander) броди́ть. —**meandering,** *adj.* изви́листый.

meaning *n.* значе́ние.

meaningful *adj.* **1,** (having meaning) зна́чащий. **2,** (sig: .icant) многозначи́тельный.

meaningless *adj.* бессмы́сленный; не име́ющий смы́сла; ничего́ не зна́чащий.

meanness *n.* зло́ба; ни́зость; по́длость.

meantime *n., usu. in* **in the meantime,** тем вре́ме-

нем; мёжду тем. —*adv.* = **in the meantime.** *Also,*
meanwhile.

measles *n.* корь. *German measles,* краснуха.

measly *adj., colloq.* ничтóжный; мизéрный.

measurable *adj.* **1,** (allowing of measurement) измерúмый. **2,** (appreciable) замéтный; ощутúмый.

measure *n.* **1,** (unit or system of measurement) мéра: *measure of length,* мéра длины; *dry measure,* мéра сыпýчих тел. **2,** (action; step) мéра: *drastic measures,* крутые мéры. **3,** (degree; extent) мéра; стéпень: *in full measure,* в пóлной мéре. *In some measure,* до нéкоторой стéпени; в извéстной мéре. *In great measure,* в большóй *or* значúтельной мéре. **4,** *pros.* (meter) размéр; метр. **5,** *music* размéр; такт. —*v.t.* **1,** (determine the size of) измерять. **2,** (appraise; gauge) оцéнивать. **3,** (bring into comparison) мéриться: *measure one's strength against,* мéриться сúлами с. **4,** *fol. by* **off** (mark off) отмерять. —*v.i.* имéть (размéры): *the room measures ten feet in length,* кóмната имéет дéсять фýтов в длинý. —**beyond measure,** неизмерúмо; чрезвычáйно. —**for good measure,** в придáчу. —**measure one's length,** растянýться во всю длинý. —**measure up,** быть на высотé. *Measure up to expectations,* опрáвдывать ожидáния. —**take one's measure, 1,** (take someone's measurements) снимáть мéрку с (+ *gen.*). **2,** (size up) присмáтриваться к. —**to measure,** по мéрке: *made to measure,* сшúтый по мéрке.

measured *adj.* **1,** (ascertained by measurement) измéренный. **2,** (regular; steady; deliberate) мéрный; размéренный.

measurement *n.* **1,** (measuring) измерéние. **2,** *usu. pl.* (size found by measuring) мéрка: *take someone's measurements,* снимáть мéрку с (+ *gen.*).

meat *n.* мясо. —*adj.* мяснóй. —**meatballs,** *n.pl.* тéфтели; биткú. —**meat grinder,** мясорýбка. —**meat loaf,** мяснóй рулéт. —**meat pie,** пирóг с мясом.

meaty *adj.* **1,** (fleshy) мясúстый. **2,** (full of substance) содержáтельный. ·

mechanic *n.* мехáник.

mechanical *adj.* **1,** (pert. to machinery) механúческий: *mechanical failure,* механúческая неисправность. *Mechanical toy,* заводнáя игрýшка. *Mechanical aptitude,* технúческие спосóбности. **2,** *fig.* (automatic; done without thinking) машинáльный; механúческий. —**mechanical drawing,** технúческое черчéние. —**mechanical engineer,** мехáник; инженéр-мехáник.

mechanics *n.* мехáника.

mechanism *n.* механúзм.

mechanize *v.t.* механизúровать; машинизúровать. —**mechanization,** *n.* механизáция; машинизáция.

medal *n.* медáль. —**medalist,** *n.* медалúст.

medallion *n.* медальóн.

medallist *n.* = **medalist.**

meddle *v.i.* вмéшиваться. —**meddlesome,** *adj.* вмéшивающийся не в свои делá. —**meddling,** *n.* вмешáтельство.

media *n.pl.* срéдства мáссовой информáции.

mediaeval *adj.* = **medieval.**

median *adj.* срéдний. —*n.* медиáна.

mediate *v.i.* посрéдничать. —*v.t.* улáживать. —**mediation,** *n.* посрéдничество. —**mediator,** *n.* посрéдник.

medical *adj.* медицúнский.

medication *n.* медикамéнты; лекáрство.

medicinal *adj.* лекáрственный; целéбный.

medicine *n.* **1,** (the science) медицúна. **2,** (something taken when ill) лекáрство. —**medicine chest/cabinet,** (домáшняя) аптéчка; аптéчный шкаф. —**medicine man,** знáхарь; шамáн.

medieval *also,* **mediaeval** *adj.* средневекóвый.

mediocre *adj.* посрéдственный; заурядный. —**mediocrity,** *n.* посрéдственность.

meditate *v.i.* размышлять; раздýмывать; задýмываться. —**meditation,** *n.* размышлéние; раздýмье. —**meditative,** *adj.* задýмчивый.

medium *n.* **1,** (mean) середúна: *happy medium,* золотáя середúна. **2,** (means) срéдство: *medium of exchange,* срéдство обмéна. *Through the medium of,* посрéдством (+ *gen.*); чéрез посрéдство (+ *gen.*). **3,** *physics* средá. **4,** (culture medium) питáтельная средá. **5,** (spiritualist) мéдиум. —*adj.* срéдний: *of medium height,* срéднего рóста. *Medium bomber,* срéдний бомбардирóвщик. —**medium-range,** *adj.* срéднего рáдиуса дéйствия. —**medium-sized,** *adj.* срéдней величины; срéднего размéра. *See also* **media.**

medlar *n.* мушмулá.

medley *n.* **1,** (hodgepodge) мешанúна; мéсиво. **2,** *music* попуррú.

medulla *n.* **1,** (marrow) кóстный мозг. **2,** (inner part of an organ) мозговóй слой. —**medulla oblongata,** продолговáтый мозг.

medusa *n.* медýза.

meek *adj.* крóткий; смирéнный. —**meekness,** *n.* крóтость; смирéние.

meerschaum *n.* (морскáя) пéнка. —*adj.* пéнковый.

meet *v.t.* **1,** (come upon; join) встречáть: *meet a friend/a train/resistance,* встречáть дрýга/пóезд/сопротивлéние. **2,** (make the acquaintance of) знакóмиться с. *I would like you to meet my wife,* позвóльте познакóмить вас с моéй женóй. **3,** (conform to; satisfy) отвечáть; удовлетворять: *meet the requirements,* отвечáть/удовлетворять трéбованиям. *Meet a demand,* удовлетворúть трéбование. —*v.i.* **1,** (come upon or join each other) встречáться. **2,** (become acquainted) знакóмиться. *Have you met?,* вы знакóмы? **3,** *fol. by* **with** (confer with) встречáться с; совещáться с. **4,** *fol. by* **with** (encounter) встречáть; стáлкиваться с. **5,** (gather; assemble) собирáться; сходúться. **6,** (intersect) сходúться. **7,** (compete) встречáться; сходúться. —*n.* соревновáние: *track meet,* легкоатлетúческие соревновáния.

meeting *n.* **1,** (encounter) встрéча. **2,** (scheduled appointment) встрéча; свидáние. **3,** (gathering; assembly; conference) собрáние.

megacycle *n.* мегагéрц.

megalomania *n.* мáния велúчия.

megaphone *n.* рýпор; мегафóн.

megaton *n.* мегатóнна.

melancholia *n.* меланхóлия. —**melancholic,** *adj.* меланхолúческий.

melancholy *n.* уныние; тоскá; грусть; меланхóлия. —*adj.* унылый; тосклúвый; меланхолúческий.

mélange *n.* смешéние; смесь.

melee *n.* свáлка.

meliorate *v.t.* улучшáть. —*v.i.* улучшáться. —**melioration,** *n.* улучшéние.

mellifluous *adj.* медоточи́вый; сладкозву́чный.

mellow *adj.* **1,** (fully-flavored; full-bodied) со́чный: *mellow voice,* со́чный го́лос. **2,** *colloq.* (genial) добро-ду́шный. *Become mellow with age,* подобре́ть с года́ми. —*v.t.* смягча́ть. —*v.i.* добре́ть.

melodic *adj.* мелоди́ческий. —**melodics,** *n.* мело́дика.

melodious *adj.* мелоди́чный; певу́чий. —**melodiousness,** *n.* мелоди́чность; певу́честь.

melodrama *n.* мелодра́ма. —**melodramatic,** *adj.* мелодрамати́ческий; театра́льный.

melody *n.* мело́дия.

melon *n.* ды́ня. *Melon field,* бахча́.

melt *v.t.* **1,** (reduce to a liquid state) *A,* (butter, ice, etc.) топи́ть; раста́пливать. *B,* (metals) пла́вить; расплавля́ть. **2,** (dissolve) растворя́ть. —*v.i.* **1,** (turn to liquid) *A,* (of snow, ice cream, etc.) та́ять. *B,* (of metals) пла́виться. **2,** (dissolve) растворя́ться. **3,** (fade away; dwindle) улету́чиваться. *Melt into the background,* слива́ться с фо́ном. —**melt in one's mouth,** та́ять во рту.

melted *adj.* (of snow) та́лый; (of butter) топлёный; (of metals) распла́вленный.

melting *n.* плавле́ние; пла́вка. *Melting point,* то́чка плавле́ния. —**melting pot,** плави́льный котёл.

member *n.* член.

membership *n.* **1,** (status of a member) чле́нство. **2,** (members collectively) чле́ны. **3,** (number of members) коли́чество чле́нов. —*adj.* чле́нский: *membership dues,* чле́нские взно́сы.

membrane *n.* плева́; перепо́нка; оболо́чка. —**membranous,** *adj.* перепо́нчатый.

memento *n.* па́мятный пода́рок; сувени́р.

memo *n., colloq.* = **memorandum.**

memoirs *n.pl.* мемуа́ры.

memorable *adj.* па́мятный; знамена́тельный.

memorandum *n.* **1,** (reminder) па́мятная запи́ска; мемора́ндум. **2,** (informal communication) делова́я *or* докладна́я запи́ска; мемора́ндум. **3,** *dipl.* мемора́ндум.

memorial *n.* па́мятник. —*adj.* мемориа́льный. *Memorial plaque,* па́мятная доска́. *Memorial service,* заупоко́йная слу́жба.

memorialize *v.t.* увекове́чивать.

memorize *v.t.* запомина́ть; зау́чивать (наизу́сть).

memory *n.* **1,** (capacity to remember) па́мять. *From memory,* на мое́й па́мяти; по па́мяти. *Within my memory,* на мое́й па́мяти. **2,** (recollection) воспомина́ние: *memories of childhood,* воспомина́ния де́тства. **3,** (commemoration) па́мять: *in memory of,* в па́мять (+ *gen.*). **4,** *computer science* запомина́ющее устро́йство.

menace *n.* угро́за. —*v.t.* угрожа́ть; грози́ть. —**menacing,** *adj.* гро́зный; угрожа́ющий.

menagerie *n.* звери́нец.

mend *v.t.* **1,** (repair) чини́ть. **2,** (darn) што́пать. **3,** *in* **mend one's ways,** исправля́ться. —*v.i.* (of bones) сраста́ться. —**be on the mend,** выздора́вливать. *He is on the mend,* у него́ де́ло идёт на попра́вку.

mendacious *adj.* лжи́вый; ло́жный. —**mendacity,** *n.* лжи́вость.

mendelevium *n.* менделе́вий.

mendicant *n.* ни́щий. —*adj.* ни́щенствующий. —**mendicancy,** *n.* ни́щенство.

menial *adj.* чёрный: *menial tasks,* чёрная рабо́та.

meningitis *n.* менинги́т.

menopause *n.* климакте́рий.

Menshevik *n.* меньшеви́к. —*adj.* меньшеви́стский.

men's room мужска́я убо́рная; мужско́й туале́т.

menstrual *adj.* менструа́льный.

menstruate *v.i.* менструи́ровать. —**menstruation,** *n.* менструа́ция.

mensuration *n.* измере́ние.

mental *adj.* **1,** (pert. to the mind) у́мственный: *mental faculties,* у́мственные спосо́бности. **2,** (taking place in the mind) мы́сленный: *mental image,* мы́сленный о́браз. **3,** (pert. to the mentally ill) душе́вный; психи́ческий: *mental illness,* душе́вная/психи́ческая боле́знь. *Mental case; mental patient,* душевнобольно́й; психи́чески больно́й. *Mental hospital,* психиатри́ческая больни́ца.

mentality *n.* **1,** (intelligence) ум; у́мственные спосо́бности. **2,** (state of mind) склад ума́.

mentally *adv.* **1,** (in one's mind) мы́сленно. **2,** (as regards one's mental faculties) у́мственно; психи́чески. *Mentally ill,* душевнобольно́й; психи́чески больно́й. *Mentally retarded,* у́мственно отста́лый.

menthol *n.* менто́л. —**mentholated,** *adj.* менто́ловый.

mention *v.t.* упомина́ть. —*n.* упомина́ние: *at the mention of,* при упомина́нии (+ *gen.*). —**don't mention it!,** не́ за что!; пожа́луйста; не сто́ит благода́рности. —**not to mention,** не говоря́ уже́ о.

mentor *n.* наста́вник; воспита́тель.

menu *n.* меню́.

meow *v.i.* мяу́кать. —*n.* мяу́канье.

mercantile *adj.* **1,** (commercial) торго́вый; комме́рческий. **2,** (pert. to mercantilism) мерканти́льный. —**mercantilism,** *n.* меркантили́зм.

mercenary *adj.* **1,** (selfish) коры́стный. **2,** (serving for pay) наёмный. —*n.* наёмник.

merchandise *n.* това́р.

merchant *n.* купе́ц; торго́вец. —**merchant marine,** торго́вый флот. —**merchant ship,** торго́вое су́дно.

merciful *adj.* милосе́рдный; сострада́тельный.

merciless *adj.* безжа́лостный; беспоща́дный; неща́дный. —**mercilessly,** *adv.* безжа́лостно; беспоща́дно; неща́дно.

mercurial *adj.* **1,** [*also,* **mercuric**] (of mercury) рту́тный. **2,** (volatile) изме́нчивый; переме́нчивый. —**mercuric chloride,** сулема́. —**mercuric oxide,** о́кись рту́ти. —**mercuric sulfide,** серни́стая ртуть.

mercury *n.* **1,** (element) ртуть. **2,** *cap.* (god; planet) Мерку́рий. —*adj.* рту́тный: *mercury barometer,* рту́тный баро́метр.

mercy *n.* милосе́рдие; ми́лость; поща́да. *Show mercy toward,* проявля́ть милосе́рдие к. *Have/take mercy on,* щади́ть. —*interj.* го́споди! —**at the mercy of,** во вла́сти (+ *gen.*). *Throw oneself at the mercy of,* отда́ться на ми́лость (+ *gen.*).

mere *adj.* просто́й: *mere mortals,* просты́е сме́ртные. *He is a mere child,* да он ещё ребёнок. *At the mere thought of,* при одно́й мы́сли о.

merely *adv.* то́лько; про́сто.

meretricious *adj.* показно́й; мишу́рный.

merganser *n.* кро́халь.

merge *v.t.* объединя́ть. —*v.i.* слива́ться; объединя́ться.

merger *n.* слия́ние; объедине́ние.

meridian *n.* меридиáн.

meringue *n.* мерéнга.

merino *n.* меринóс. —*adj.* меринóсовый.

merit *n.* **1,** (positive quality; virtue) заслýга; достóинство. **2,** *pl.* (intrinsic rights and wrongs) существó: *the merits of a case,* существó дéла. —*v.t.* заслýживать.

meritorious *adj.* похвáльный. *Award for meritorious service,* нагрáда за заслýги.

merlin *n.* (bird) дéрбник.

mermaid *n.* русáлка.

merrily *adv.* вéсело.

merriment *n.* весéлье.

merry *adj.* весёлый. *Merry Christmas!,* с Рождествóм христóвым. —**make merry,** веселúться. —**the more the merrier,** чем бóльше, тем лýчше.

merry-go-round *n.* карусéль.

merrymaker *n.* весельчáк. —**merrymaking,** *n.* весéлье.

mesa *n.* столóвая горá; плоскогóрье.

mesh *n.* очкó; ячéйка. —*v.i.* (engage) сцепляться.

mesmerism *n.* гипнóз; гипнотúзм. —**mesmerist,** *n.* гипнотизёр. —**mesmerize,** *v.t.* гипнотизúровать.

meson *n.* мезóн.

Mesozoic *adj.* мезозóйский.

mess *n.* **1,** (dirty or untidy condition) грязь: *what a mess!,* какáя грязь! **2,** (confused state) пýтаница; неразберúха. *Make a mess of,* напýтать. **3,** (trouble) бедá. *Get into a mess,* попáсть в бедý/переплёт/передéлку. **4,** (group taking meals together; a meal so taken) óбщий стол. —*v.t.* [*usu.* **mess up**] **1,** (soil) (за)пáчкать. **2,** (disarrange) приводúть в беспорядок. **3,** (bungle; botch) напýтать. —*v.i.* **1,** (take meals together) столовáться. **2,** *fol. by* **around** *or* **about** (putter) возúться.

message *n.* **1,** (communication) сообщéние; донесéние. **2,** (written note) запúска. **3,** (verbal communication to be passed on) *rendered idiomatically: is there any message?,* что емý (*or* ей) передáть? *Did he leave a message?,* он просúл чтó-нибудь передáть? **4,** (formal address) послáние.

messenger *n.* **1,** (one bringing a message or news) вéстник. **2,** (errand boy) посыльный; курьéр. *Send something by messenger,* посылáть чтó-нибудь с посыльным.

mess hall столóвая.

Messiah *n.* мессúя. —**Messianic,** *adj.* мессиáнский.

messy *adj.* **1,** (untidy; disorderly) неопрятный. **2,** *fig.* (complicated; unpleasant) неприятный.

mestizo *n.* метúс.

metabolism *n.* обмéн вещéств. —**metabolic,** *adj.* относящийся к обмéну вещéств: *metabolic disease,* болéзнь обмéна вещéств.

metacarpus *n.* пясть.

metal *n.* метáлл. —*adj.* металлúческий. —**metallic,** *adj.* металлúческий.

metalliferous *adj.* металлонóсный.

metalloid *n.* металлóид.

metallurgy *n.* металлýргия. —**metallurgic,** *adj.* металлургúческий. —**metallurgist,** *n.* металлýрг.

metalworker *n.* слéсарь; металлúст.

metamorphosis *n.* **1,** *biol.* метаморфóз. **2,** *fig.* (complete transformation) метаморфóза.

metaphor *n.* метáфора. —**metaphorical,** *adj.* метафорúческий.

metaphysics *n.* метафúзика. —**metaphysical,** *adj.* метафизúческий. —**metaphysician; metaphysicist,** *n.* метафúзик.

metastasis *n.* метастáз.

metatarsus *n.* плюснá. —**metatarsal,** *adj.* плюсневóй.

mete *v.t.* [*usu.* **mete out**] выделять; распределять. *Mete out punishment,* определять наказáние.

meteor *n.* метеóр.

meteoric *adj.* **1,** (of a meteor) метеóрный. **2,** *fig.* (dazzlingly fast) головокружúтельный.

meteorite *n.* метеорúт.

meteorology *n.* метеоролóгия. —**meteorological,** *adj.* метеорологúческий. —**meteorologist,** *n.* метеорóлог.

meter *also,* **metre** *n.* **1,** (unit of length) метр. **2,** (measuring instrument) счéтчик: *gas meter,* гáзовый счéтчик. *Water meter,* водомéр. **3,** *pros.* размéр; метр. **4,** *music* ритм.

methane *n.* метáн.

method *n.* мéтод; спóсоб. —**methodical,** *adj.* методúческий; методúчный.

Methodist *n.* методúст. —*adj.* методúстский. —**Methodism,** *n.* методúзм.

methodology *n.* методолóгия. —**methodological,** *adj.* методологúческий.

methyl *n.* метúл. —**methyl alcohol,** метúловый спирт.

methylene *n.* метилéн.

meticulous *adj.* аккурáтный; дотóшный. —**meticulousness,** *n.* аккурáтность.

metre *n.* = **meter.**

metric *adj.* метрúческий.

metrics *n.* мéтрика.

metronome *n.* метронóм.

metropolis *n.* крýпный гóрод.

metropolitan *adj.* столúчный. —*n.* (archbishop) митрополúт.

mettle *n.* закáлка; выдержка. *Prove one's mettle,* проявúть себя.

Mexican *adj.* мексикáнский. —*n.* мексикáнец; мексикáнка.

mezzanine *n.* бельэтáж.

mezzo-soprano *n.* мéццо-сопрáно.

mi *n., music* ми.

miasma *n.* миáзмы.

mica *n.* слюдá. —*adj.* слюдянóй.

microbe *n.* микрóб.

microbiology *n.* микробиолóгия. —**microbiologist,** *n.* микробиóлог.

microcircuit *n.* микросхéма.

microcosm *n.* микрокóсм.

microfilm *n.* микрофúльм.

micrometer *n.* микрóметр.

micron *n.* микрóн.

microorganism *n.* микроорганúзм.

microphone *n.* микрофóн.

microscope *n.* микроскóп. —**microscopic,** *adj.* микроскопúческий.

mid- *prefix* в середúне (+ *gen.*): *in mid-June,* в середúне ию́ня.

midair *n., in* **in midair,** на летý. *Midair collision,* столкновéние в вóздухе.

midday *n.* по́лдень. —*adj.* полу́денный; полднёвный.

middle *n.* середи́на. —*adj.* сре́дний: *the middle window,* сре́днее окно́; *the middle class,* сре́дний класс. —**in the middle of,** в середи́не (+ *gen.*); посреди́ (+ *gen.*); посереди́не (+ *gen.*). *In the middle of May,* в середи́не (*or* в полови́не) ма́я. *In the middle of the night,* среди́ но́чи.

middle age сре́дний во́зраст. —**middle-aged,** *adj.* сре́дних лет.

Middle Ages сре́дние века́; средневеко́вье.

middle ear сре́днее у́хо.

Middle East Бли́жний Восто́к. *Middle East countries,* ближневосто́чные стра́ны.

Middle English среднеангли́йский язы́к.

middle finger сре́дний па́лец.

middleman *n.* посре́дник.

middle name второ́е и́мя.

middling *adj.* сре́дний; посре́дственный. —**fair to middling,** так себе́; сно́сно; ни ша́тко ни ва́лко.

midge *n.* мо́шка.

midget *n.* ка́рлик. —*adj.* ка́рликовый.

midnight *n.* по́лночь. *Stay up till midnight,* сиде́ть до по́лночи. —*adj.* полно́чный; полу́ночный; полуно́чный. —**burn the midnight oil,** по́здно заси́живаться за рабо́той.

midshipman *n.* курса́нт вое́нно-морско́го учи́лища.

midst *n.* середи́на. *In the midst of,* в середи́не (+ *gen.*); среди́ (+ *gen.*). *In our midst,* среди́ нас.

midway *adj., in* **the midway point,** полпути́; полдоро́ги. —*adv.* на полпути́; на полдоро́ге.

midwife *n.* акуше́рка. —**midwifery,** *n.* акуше́рство.

mien *n.* вид; ми́на.

miff *v.t., colloq.* обижа́ть: *somewhat miffed,* не́сколько оби́жен.

might[1] *v.aux.* мочь: *who might that be?,* кто бы э́то мог быть? *I might have guessed it,* я мог бы об э́том догада́ться. *You might have offered to help,* вы могли́ бы предложи́ть свою́ по́мощь. *You might at least have said something about it,* вы хоть сказа́ли бы об э́том. *I might (just) as well have stayed home,* с тем же успе́хом я мог бы сиде́ть до́ма.

might[2] *n.* мощь; могу́щество. —**with all one's might,** изо всех сил; во всю мочь; со всего́ разма́ху.

mightily *adv.* усе́рдно; изо всех сил.

mighty *adj.* **1,** (powerful) мо́щный; могу́чий; могу́щественный. **2,** (great; huge) грома́дный; колосса́льный. —*adv., colloq.* о́чень.

mignonette *n.* резеда́.

migraine *n.* мигре́нь.

migrant *n.* пересе́ленец. —*adj.* кочу́ющий.

migrate *v.i.* **1,** (of people) мигри́ровать; переселя́ться. **2,** (of birds) соверша́ть перелёт; перелета́ть; кочева́ть.

migration *n.* **1,** (of people) мигра́ция; переселе́ние. **2,** (of birds) перелёт.

migratory *adj.* **1,** (of people) кочу́ющий. **2,** (of birds) перелётный.

milch *adj.* моло́чный; до́йный.

mild *adj.* **1,** (gentle in disposition) мя́гкий: *a mild man,* мя́гкий челове́к. **2,** (moderate; temperate) мя́гкий: *mild weather,* мя́гкая пого́да. **3,** (not severe) мя́гкий; лёгкий: *a mild reproach,* мя́гкий упрёк; *a mild case,*

лёгкий слу́чай (заболева́ния). **4,** (not strong, as of tobacco) лёгкий; некре́пкий.

mildew *n.* **1,** (plant disease) мучни́стая роса́. **2,** (mold) пле́сень. —**mildewed,** *adj.* запле́сневелый.

mildly *adv.* мя́гко. —**to put it mildly,** мя́гко выража́ясь.

mild-mannered *adj.* сми́рный; безро́потный.

mildness *n.* мя́гкость.

mile *n.* ми́ля. *Miss by a mile,* промахну́ться на киломе́тр.

mileage *n.* расстоя́ние в ми́лях.

milepost *n.* верстово́й столб.

milestone *n.* **1,** = **milepost. 2,** (important event) ве́ха.

milieu *n.* среда́; окруже́ние.

militancy *n.* вои́нственность.

militant *adj.* вои́нственный; вою́ющий. —*n.* активи́ст.

militarily *adv.* с вое́нной то́чки зре́ния; в вое́нном отноше́нии.

militarism *n.* милитари́зм. —**militarist,** *n.* милитари́ст. —**militaristic,** *adj.* милитаристи́ческий.

militarize *v.t.* милитаризи́ровать. —**militarization,** *n.* милитариза́ция.

military *adj.* вое́нный. —*n., preceded by* **the** вое́нные.

militate *v.i.* [*usu.* **militate in favor of** *or* **against**] **1,** (work in one's favor or against) спосо́бствовать (+ *dat.*); быть поме́хой (+ *dat.*). **2,** (be an argument for or against) (не) говори́ть в по́льзу (+ *gen.*).

militia *n.* мили́ция; ополче́ние. —**militiaman,** *n.* милиционе́р; ополче́нец.

milk *n.* молоко́. —*adj.* моло́чный: *milk diet,* моло́чная дие́та. —*v.t.* дои́ть: *milk a cow,* дои́ть коро́ву. —**there's no use crying over spilt milk,** что с во́зу упа́ло, то пропа́ло.

milking *n.* дое́ние; до́йка. —**milking machine,** до́йльная маши́на.

milkmaid *n.* доя́рка.

milkman *n.* моло́чник.

milk shake моло́чный кокте́йль.

milksop *n.* ба́ба; тря́пка; мо́края ку́рица.

milky *adj.* моло́чный. —**Milky Way,** Мле́чный Путь.

mill *n.* **1,** (machine or building for grinding) ме́льница. *Coffee mill,* кофе́йница. **2,** (factory) фа́брика; заво́д: *paper mill,* бума́жная фа́брика; *steel mill,* сталелите́йный заво́д. **3,** (machine for rolling metal) (прока́тный) стан. —*v.t.* **1,** (grind) моло́ть. **2,** (roll, as metal) прока́тывать. **3,** (shape, as metal) фрезерова́ть. —*v.i.* [*usu.* **mill around** *or* **about**] толо́чься.

millennium *n.* тысячеле́тие.

millepede *n.* = **millipede.**

miller *n.* ме́льник.

millet *n.* **1,** (cereal grass) про́со. **2,** (food grain) пшено́.

milliard *n., Brit.* миллиа́рд.

milligram *also,* **milligramme** *n.* миллигра́мм.

millimeter *also,* **millimetre** *n.* миллиме́тр.

milliner *n.* моди́стка.

millinery *n.* да́мские шля́пы. —**millinery shop,** шля́пный магази́н.

milling *n.* **1,** (grinding) размо́л. **2,** (shaping, as of metal) фрезерова́ние. —**milling cutter,** фре́за. —**milling machine,** фре́зерный стано́к.

million *n.* миллио́н.

millionaire *n.* миллионе́р.

millionth *adj.* миллио́нный. —*n.* миллио́нная часть.

millipede *also*, **millepede** *n.* многоно́жка.

millrace *n.* ме́льничный лото́к.

millstone *n.* жёрнов. *Millstone about one's neck*, ка́мень на ше́е.

milquetoast *n., slang* тихо́ня.

milt *n.* моло́ки.

mime *n.* **1**, (pantomime) пантоми́ма. **2**, (farce performed in ancient times) мим. **3**, (mimic) мими́ст.

mimeograph *n.* рота́тор. —*v.t.* размножа́ть на рота́торе.

mimic *v.t.* передра́знивать. —*n.* **1**, (one adept at mimicking) имита́тор. **2**, (stage performer) мими́ст.

mimicry *n.* **1**, (imitating) ми́мика. **2**, *biol.* мимикри́я.

mimosa *n.* мимо́за.

minaret *n.* минаре́т.

mince *v.t.* **1**, (chop) кроши́ть; руби́ть. **2**, (lessen the force of): *not mince words*, не стесня́ться в выраже́ниях. —*v.i.* **1**, (speak or behave daintily) жема́ниться. **2**, (walk daintily or affectedly) семени́ть нога́ми.

mincemeat *n.* **1**, *obs.* (chopped meat) ру́бленое мя́со. **2**, (pie filling) фарш. —**make mincemeat of**, стере́ть в порошо́к.

mind *n.* ум. *On one's mind*, на уме́. *To my mind*, по-мо́ему; на мой взгляд. —*v.t.* **1**, (pay attention to) обраща́ть внима́ние на. *Mind one's own business*, не вме́шиваться в чужи́е дела́. **2**, (obey) слу́шаться. **3**, (look after) присма́тривать за (+ *instr.*). **4**, (object to) возража́ть про́тив. *I wouldn't mind a cup of tea*, не откажу́сь от ча́шки ча́я. **5**, (take care not to): *mind you don't slip*, осторо́жно, не оступи́тесь. *Mind you're not late*, смотри́те, не опозда́йте. —*v.i.* **1**, (be obedient) слу́шаться. **2**, (object) возража́ть; име́ть что́-нибудь про́тив: *if you don't mind*, е́сли вы не возража́ете; е́сли вы не име́ете ничего́ про́тив. —**bear, have, keep in mind**, име́ть в виду́. —**be in one's right mind**, быть в своём (*or* в здра́вом) уме́. —**be of one mind**, быть одного́ мне́ния. —**bring, call, recall to mind**, напомина́ть; воскреша́ть в па́мяти. —**change one's mind**, переду́мать; разду́мать. —**come to mind; cross one's mind**, приходи́ть в го́лову (+ *dat.*). —**give someone a piece of one's mind**, сказа́ть кому́-нибудь па́ру тёплых слов. —**go out of** (*or* **lose**) **one's mind**, сходи́ть с ума́. —**keep one's mind on**, сосредото́чиваться на. —**make up one's mind**, реши́ть; реши́ться; собра́ться. *I can't make up my mind*, я не могу́ реши́ть. —**never mind!**, ничего́; нева́жно; всё равно́. —**out of one's mind**, сумасше́дший. *Are you out of your mind?*, вы с ума́ сошли́? —**read someone's mind**, чита́ть чьи-нибудь мы́сли. —**slip one's mind**, вы́скочить из головы́. —**speak one's mind**, выска́зываться.

mindful *adj.* [*usu.* **mindful of**] име́я в виду́; отдава́я себе́ отчёт (в).

mindless *adj.* **1**, (senseless) бессмы́сленный. **2**, *fol. by* **of** (heedless; unmindful) не обраща́я внима́ния (на).

mind's eye духо́вное о́ко.

mine[1] *poss.pron.* мой. *A friend of mine*, оди́н мой друг; оди́н из мои́х друзе́й.

mine[2] *n.* **1**, (pit) рудни́к; ша́хта; при́иск. *Coal mine*, у́гольная ша́хта; *gold mines*, золоты́е при́иски; *cop-*

per mine, ме́дный рудни́к. **2**, (charge of explosives) ми́на. *Land mine*, фуга́с. —*v.t.* **1**, (extract, as ore) добыва́ть (руду́). **2**, (lay explosives under) мини́ровать; закла́дывать ми́ны под. —*v.i.* производи́ть го́рные рабо́ты.

mine detector миноиска́тель.

minefield *n.* ми́нное по́ле.

minelayer *n.* (ми́нный) загради́тель.

miner *n.* шахтёр; горня́к.

mineral *n.* минера́л; *pl.* минера́лы; поле́зные ископа́емые. *Rich in minerals*, бога́т поле́зными ископа́емыми. —*adj.* минера́льный: *mineral oil*, минера́льное ма́сло.

mineralogy *n.* минерало́гия. —**mineralogical**, *adj.* минералоги́ческий. —**mineralogist**, *n.* минерало́г.

minesweeper *n.* тра́льщик.

mingle *v.i.* **1**, (become mixed) сме́шиваться. **2**, (associate) обща́ться; враща́ться.

miniature *n.* миниатю́ра. —*adj.* миниатю́рный.

minimal *adj.* минима́льный.

minimize *v.t.* **1**, (reduce to a minimum) доводи́ть до ми́нимума. **2**, (belittle) преуменьша́ть; умаля́ть.

minimum *n.* ми́нимум. —*adj.* минима́льный. —**minimum wage**, ми́нимум за́работной пла́ты.

mining *n.* го́рное де́ло. —*adj.* го́рный: *mining engineer*, го́рный инжене́р.

minion *n.* **1**, (servile follower) приспе́шник; клевре́т. **2**, (favorite) ба́ловень: *minion of fortune*, ба́ловень судьбы́.

minister *n.* **1**, (officer of state) мини́стр. **2**, (envoy) посла́нник. **3**, (clergyman) па́стор. —*v.i.* [*usu.* **minister to**] служи́ть; помога́ть.

ministerial *adj.* министе́рский. *On the ministerial level*, на у́ровне мини́стров.

ministration *n.* оказа́ние по́мощи.

ministry *n.* **1**, (governmental department) министе́рство. **2**, (clergy) духове́нство.

mink *n.* но́рка. —*adj.* но́рковый.

minnow *n.* голья́н.

minor *adj.* **1**, (unimportant) незначи́тельный: *minor defects*, незначи́тельные недоста́тки. **2**, (of lesser importance) ме́лкий; второстепе́нный. *Minor role*, второстепе́нная роль; *minor repairs*, ме́лкий ремо́нт. **3**, (under legal age) несовершенноле́тний. **4**, *music* мино́рный. —*n.* **1**, (one under legal age) несовершенноле́тний. **2**, *music* мино́р: *key of G-sharp minor*, тона́льность соль-дие́з мино́р. —**minor piece**, *chess* лёгкая фигу́ра.

minority *n.* **1**, (less than half of a total) меньшинство́. **2**, (period of being under legal age) несовершенноле́тие.

minstrel *n.* менестре́ль.

mint *n.* **1**, (plant) мя́та. **2**, (confection) мя́тная конфе́та. **3**, (place where money is coined) моне́тный двор. —*adj.* **1**, (containing mint) мя́тный. **2**, (of a postage stamp) негашёный. —*v.t.* чека́нить: *mint coins*, чека́нить моне́ты.

mintage *n.* чека́нка.

minuend *n.* уменьша́емое.

minuet *n.* менуэ́т.

minus *prep.* **1**, (less) ми́нус. **2**, (lacking) без. —*n.* (drawback) ми́нус. —*adj.* отрица́тельный. —**minus sign**, (знак) ми́нус.

minuscule *adj.* кро́хотный; малю́сенький.

minute[1] (**min**-it) *n.* **1**, (60th part of an hour or degree) минýта. *Any minute,* с минýты на минýту. **2,** *pl.* (record) протокóл. —**minute hand,** минýтная стрéлка.

minute² (mai-noot) *adj.* **1,** (tiny) мéлкий. **2,** (painstaking; detailed) подрóбный. —**minutely,** *adv.* подрóбно; до тóнкостей.

minutiae *n.pl.* мéлочи.

miracle *n.* чýдо. *He escaped by a miracle,* он спáсся какúм-то чýдом.

miraculous *adj.* **1,** (as if by a miracle) чудéсный: *miraculous escape,* чудéсное спасéние. **2,** (seeming to work miracles) чудотвóрный; чудодéйственный. —**miraculously,** *adv.* чудéсно; чýдом.

mirage *n.* мирáж; мáрево.

mire *n.* **1,** (bog) трясúна. **2,** (mud) грязь. —*v.t. Become mired in,* завязáть в; увязáть в; погрязáть в.

mirror *n.* зéркало. —*v.t.* отражáть.

mirth *n.* весéлье. —**mirthful,** *adj.* весéлый.

misadventure *n.* злоключéние.

misanthrope *n.* человеконенавúстник; мизантрóп. —**misanthropic,** *adj.* человеконенавúстнический; мизантропúческий. —**misanthropy,** *n.* человеконенавúстничество; мизантрóпия.

misapply *v.t.* непрáвильно применáть.

misapprehension *n.* заблуждéние. *Be under a misapprehension,* заблуждáться; быть в заблуждéнии.

misappropriate *v.t.* растрáчивать; расхищáть. —**misappropriation,** *n.* растрáта; хищéние; расхищéние.

misbegotten *adj.* внебрáчный; незаконнорождéнный.

misbehave *v.i.* дýрно вестú себя. —**misbehavior,** *n.* дурнóе поведéние.

miscalculate *v.t.* непрáвильно подсчúтывать. —*v.i.* просчúтываться. —**miscalculation,** *n.* просчéт.

miscarriage *n.* вýкидыш. *Have a miscarriage,* выкинуть. —**miscarriage of justice,** судéбная ошúбка.

miscarry *v.i.* **1,** (go wrong; fail) давáть осéчку. **2,** (have a miscarriage) вýкинуть.

miscast *v.t.* дать (актёру) неподходящую роль.

miscegenation *n.* рáсовое смешéние.

miscellaneous *adj.* **1,** (not falling into a single category) рáзные; *(as a heading)* рáзное. **2,** (made up of different elements) разнорóдный.

miscellany *n.* **1,** (miscellaneous collection) смесь. **2,** (collection of writings) сбóрник.

mischance *n.* несчáстье; несчáстный слýчай. *If by some mischance...,* éсли по несчáстной случáйности...

mischief *n.* озорствó; баловствó; шáлости. —**mischief-maker,** *n.* озорнúк; шалýн; прокáзник; бедокýр. —**mischievous,** *adj.* озорнóй; шаловлúвый.

misconception *n.* заблуждéние.

misconduct *n.* дурнóе поведéние.

misconstrue *v.t.* преврáтно истолкóвывать; перетолкóвывать.

miscount *v.t.* просчúтывать. —*v.i.* просчúтываться; обсчúтываться. —*n.* просчёт.

miscreant *n.* злодéй; негодяй.

misdeal *v.t. & i.* ошибáться при сдáче (карт). —*n.* непрáвильная сдáча.

misdeed *n.* прострýпок.

misdemeanor *also,* **misdemeanour** *n.* прострýпок.

misdirect *v.t.* **1,** (give wrong directions to) сбивáть

с дорóги. **2,** (address to the wrong person) отправлять не по áдресу. *Your remarks are misdirected,* вáши замечáния напрáвлены не по áдресу.

miser *n.* скупéц; скряга.

miserable *adj.* **1,** (unhappy; wretched) жáлкий; несчáстный. **2,** (awful; rotten) сквéрный; отвратúтельный. **3,** (despicable) жáлкий; презрéнный. **4,** (squalid) жáлкий; убóгий.

miserly *adj.* скупóй. —**miserliness,** *n.* скýпость.

misery *n.* **1,** (suffering; distress) страдáние. **2,** (poverty) нищетá. —**put out of one's misery,** положúть конéц чьúм-нибудь страдáниям.

misfire *v.i.* давáть осéчку. —*n.* осéчка.

misfortune *n.* несчáстье.

misgiving *n.* **1,** (doubt) сомнéние. **2,** (apprehensions) опасéние.

misguided *adj.* **1,** (mistaken) ошúбочный. **2,** (deluded) заблуждáющийся.

mishandle *v.t.* **1,** (treat roughly) плóхо обращáться с. **2,** (manage badly) напýтать.

mishap *n.* злоключéние; авáрия. *Without mishap,* без происшéствий.

mishmash *n.* мешанúна.

misinform *v.t.* непрáвильно информúровать. —**misinformation,** *n.* непрáвильная информáция.

misinterpret *v.t.* преврáтно истолкóвывать; перетолкóвывать. —**misinterpretation,** *n.* невéрное истолковáние.

misjudge *v.t.* непрáвильно оцéнивать. —**misjudgment,** *n.* ошúбка; просчёт.

mislay *v.t.* затерять; заложúть.

mislead *v.t.* вводúть в заблуждéние. —**misleading,** *adj.* вводящий в заблуждéние; обмáнчивый.

mismanage *v.t.* плóхо вестú *or* управлять. —**mismanagement,** *n.* бесхозяйственное ведéние дел; бесхозяйственность.

mismatch *n.* плохáя пáртия.

misnomer *n.* непрáвильное назвáние.

misogynist *n.* женоненавúстник. —**misogyny,** *n.* женоненавúстничество.

misplace *v.t.* **1,** (put in the wrong place) класть не на мéсто. **2,** (mislay; lose) затерять; заложúть.

misprint *n.* опечáтка.

mispronounce *v.t.* непрáвильно произносúть. —**mispronunciation,** *n.* непрáвильное произношéние.

misquote *v.t.* непрáвильно цитúровать. —**misquotation,** *n.* непрáвильная цитáта.

misread *v.t.* **1,** (read incorrectly) непрáвильно прочéсть. **2,** (interpret incorrectly) непрáвильно истолкóвывать.

misrepresent *v.t.* искажáть; извращáть. —**misrepresentation,** *n.* искажéние; извращéние.

misrule *n.* плохóе правлéние.

miss *v.t.* **1,** (fail to hit) не попáсть в (цель). **2,** (fail to catch) не поймáть. **3,** (fail to attend) пропускáть. **4,** (fail to meet) не застáть. **5,** (fail to understand or appreciate) не понимáть. **6,** (fail to hear) прослýшать. **7,** (let slip by) упускáть; пропускáть. **8,** (be late for, as a train) опáздывать на. **9,** (escape; avoid, as a mishap): *he narrowly missed being killed,* он чуть не погúб. **10,** (overlook) проглядéть; не замéтить. **11,** (feel the absence of) не хватáть *(impers.);* скучáть по. *I miss you,* мне вас не хватáет. *We shall miss you,* мы бýдем скучáть по вас. **12,** (lack) не хватáть *(impers.);* недоставать *(impers.)*. *The book is missing a few pages*, в книге не хватает несколько страниц. *—v.i.* промахнуться; не попасть в цель. *—n.* **1,** (failure to hit) промах; непопадание. **2,** (young lady) мисс.

misshapen *adj.* уродливый.

missile *n.* **1,** (any projectile) снаряд. **2,** *mil.* (rocket) ракета; реактивный снаряд. *—adj.* ракетный: *missile strike*, ракетный удар.

missing *adj.* отсутствующий; недостающий. *Be missing*, отсутствовать; не хватать; недоставать; не оказаться. *Missing in action*, пропавший без вести. **—missing link,** недостающее звено.

mission *n.* **1,** (assignment; trip) миссия: *rescue mission*, спасательная миссия. *Goodwill mission*, миссия доброй воли. **2,** (combat operation) боевая задача. **3,** (military flight) (боевой) вылет. **4,** (legation) миссия. **5,** (delegation) миссия: *trade mission*, торговая миссия. **6,** *relig.* миссия.

missionary *n.* миссионер. *—adj.* миссионерский.

missive *n.* послание.

misspell *v.t.* неправильно писать. **—misspelling,** *n.* орфографическая ошибка. **—misspelt,** *adj.* неправильно написанный.

misspend *v.t.* растрачивать; расточать. *Misspent youth*, растраченная молодость.

misstate *v.t.* ложно излагать; искажать. **—misstatement,** *n.* ложное заявление.

misstep *n.* ложный шаг.

mist *n.* лёгкий туман; дымка.

mistake *n.* ошибка. *By mistake*, по ошибке. *Make a mistake*, ошибаться; делать ошибку. *—v.t.* **1,** (misinterpret) неправильно понимать. **2,** *fol. by for* (take for someone else) принимать за (+ *acc.*).

mistaken *adj.* **1,** (in error): *you are mistaken*, вы ошибаетесь. **2,** (erroneous) ошибочный: *mistaken identity*, ошибочное опознание. **—mistakenly,** *adv.* ошибочно; по ошибке.

mister *n.* мистер; господин.

mistletoe *n.* омела.

mistranslate *v.t.* неправильно переводить. **—mistranslation,** *n.* неправильный перевод.

mistreat *v.t.* дурно обращаться с. **—mistreatment,** *n.* дурное обращение.

mistress *n.* **1,** (lady of the house; owner) хозяйка. **2,** (paramour) любовница.

mistrial *n.* неправильное судебное разбирательство.

mistrust *n.* недоверие. *—v.t.* не доверять. **—mistrustful,** *adj.* недоверчивый.

misty *adj.* **1,** (marked by mist) туманный. **2,** (obscured by mist) затуманенный.

misunderstand *v.t.* неправильно понять. **—misunderstanding,** *n.* недоразумение.

misuse *v.t.* **1,** (use incorrectly) неправильно употреблять. **2,** (abuse) злоупотреблять. *—n.* **1,** (incorrect use) неправильное употребление. **2,** (abuse) злоупотребление.

mite *n.* **1,** (parasite) клещ. **2,** (tiny person) крошка. **3,** (small contribution) лепта. **—a mite,** чуточку: *a mite better*, чуточку лучше.

miter *also,* **mitre** *n.* **1,** (headdress) митра. **2,** (beveled joint) скос. *—v.t.* скашивать.

mitigate *v.t.* смягчать. *Mitigating circumstances*, смягчающие вину обстоятельства.

mitosis *n.* митоз.

mitre *n. & v.* = **miter.**

mitten *n.* рукавица; варежка.

mix *v.t.* **1,** (blend into a single mass) мешать; смешивать: *mix paints*, мешать/смешивать краски. *Rain mixed with snow*, дождь, смешанный со снегом. **2,** (make by mixing) готовить: *mix a salad*, (при)готовить салат. **3,** (combine) сочетать; совмещать. *Mix business with pleasure*, сочетать полезное с приятным. *—v.i.* **1,** (become mixed) смешиваться; соединяться. **2,** (associate; mingle) общаться; вращаться. *—n.* смесь. **—mix up, 1,** (mix thoroughly) смешивать. **2,** (confuse; jumble) путать; спутывать; смешивать. *Get mixed up*, путаться. **3,** (involve) замешивать; впутывать. *Get mixed up in*, замешиваться в; впутываться в.

mixed *adj.* смешанный. **—mixed marriage,** смешанный брак. **—mixed number,** смешанное число.

mixer *n.* мешалка; смеситель.

mixture *n.* смесь.

mix-up *n.* недоразумение; неувязка.

mizzen *n.* бизань. **—mizzenmast,** *n.* бизань-мачта.

mnemonic *adj.* мнемонический. **—mnemonics,** *n.* мнемоника.

moan *n.* стон. *—v.i.* стонать.

moat *n.* крепостной ров.

mob *n.* толпа. *—v.t.* **1,** (crowd around) нападать толпой на. **2,** (jam) набиваться в. *The place was mobbed*, народу было битком набито.

mobile *adj.* подвижной; мобильный; передвижной. *Mobile warfare*, манёвренная война. **—mobility,** *n.* подвижность; мобильность.

mobilize *v.t.* мобилизовать. *—v.i.* мобилизоваться. **—mobilization,** *n.* мобилизация.

mobster *n., colloq.* гангстер.

moccasin *n.* **1,** (shoe) мокасин. **2,** (snake) мокасиновая змея.

mocha *n.* мокко.

mock *v.t.* издеваться над; насмехаться над; высмеивать; осмеивать. *—adj.* инсценированный: *mock trial*, инсценированный судебный процесс. **—mocker,** *n.* насмешник.

mockery *n.* **1,** (ridicule; derision) издевательство; насмешка; осмеяние. **2,** (travesty) пародия.

mocking *adj.* издевательский; насмешливый.

mockingbird *n.* пересмешник.

mock-up *n.* макет.

modal *adj.* модальный.

mode *n.* **1,** (way; manner) способ. *Mode of living*, образ жизни. **2,** (style; fashion) мода: *dress in the latest mode*, одеваться по последней моде.

model *n.* **1,** (small-scale reproduction) образец; модель; макет. **2,** (make; design) модель. **3,** (standard; ideal) образец. **4,** (one who poses) натурщик; натурщица. **5,** (one who displays clothes by wearing them) манекенщик; манекенщица. *—adj.* образцовый; примерный. *Model airplane*, модель самолёта. *—v.t.* **1,** (make figures of) лепить. **2,** (pattern after) делать по образцу (+ *gen.*). *—v.i.* работать манекенщиком (-щицей).

modeler *also,* **modeller** *n.* модельщик.

modeling *also,* **modelling** *n.* **1,** (making of figures) лепка. **2,** (working as a model): *do modeling*, работать манекенщиком (-щицей). **—modeling clay,** глина для лепки.

modeller *n.* = **modeler.**

moderate *adj.* **1**, (not extreme) умеренный. **2**, (medium) средний. **3**, (reasonable, as of prices) доступный. —*v.t.* смягчать; умерять. —*v.i.* **1**, (become less extreme or severe) смягчаться; умеряться. **2**, (act as moderator) председательствовать.

moderately *adv.* **1**, (in moderation) умеренно. **2**, (fairly; more or less) довольно: *moderately well*, довольно хорошо.

moderation *n.* **1**, (act of moderating) смягчение. **2**, (moderateness) умеренность. —**in moderation**, умеренно.

moderator *n.* председатель.

modern *adj.* современный: *modern art*, современное искусство; *modern methods of treatment*, современные методы лечения. *Modern history*, новая история. *Modern languages*, новые языки. *Modern dance*, танец модерн.

modernism *n.* модернизм. —**modernist**, *n.* модернист. —**modernistic**, *adj.* модернистский. —**modernity**, *n.* современность.

modernize *v.t.* модернизировать. —**modernization**, *n.* модернизация.

modest *adj.* скромный. —**modestly**, *adv.* скромно. —**modesty**, *n.* скромность.

modicum *n.* чуточка; капелька.

modification *n.* видоизменение; модификация. *Make modifications in the design*, вносить изменения в конструкцию.

modifier *n., gram.* определение; атрибут.

modify *v.t.* **1**, (alter) видоизменять; модифицировать. **2**, (moderate) смягчать. **3**, *gram.* определять.

modulate *v.t.* модулировать. —*v.i.* переливаться. —**modulation**, *n.* модуляция. —**modulator**, *n.* модулятор.

module *n.* **1**, (unit of measurement) модуль. **2**, (space vehicle) отсек.

modulus *n.* модуль.

Mogul *n.* **1**, *hist.* могол. **2**, *l.c.* (powerful person) магнат.

mohair *n.* мохер. —*adj.* мохеровый.

Mohammedan *n.* магометанин. —*adj.* магометанский. —**Mohammedanism**, *n.* магометанство; мусульманство.

moire *n.* муар. —**moiré**, *adj.* муаровый.

moist *adj.* влажный.

moisten *v.t.* смачивать.

moisture *n.* влажность; влага.

molar *n.* коренной зуб.

molasses *n.* патока.

mold *also*, **mould** *n.* **1**, (fungus) плесень; гниль. **2**, (matrix) форма. **3**, (cast; model) слепок. **4**, *fig.* (distinctive character) закваска. **5**, *fig.* (fixed pattern) шаблон. —*v.t.* **1**, (make) формовать. **2**, *fig.* (shape) формировать.

molder *also*, **moulder** *v.i.* рассыпаться (в пыль).

molding *also*, **moulding** *n.* лепное украшение.

moldy *also*, **mouldy** *adj.* заплесневелый.

mole *n.* **1**, (blemish) родинка. **2**, (rodent) крот.

molecule *n.* молекула. —**molecular**, *adj.* молекулярный.

molehill *n.* кротовая нора. —**make a mountain out of a molehill**, делать из мухи слона.

mole rat слепыш.

moleskin *n.* **1**, (fur) кротовый мех; крот. **2**, (cloth) молескин. —*adj.* кротовый; молескиновый.

molest *v.t.* приставать к; беспокоить.

mollify *v.t.* **1**, (placate) умилостивить. **2**, (make less intense) смягчать.

mollusk *also*, **mollusc** *n.* моллюск.

mollycoddle *v.t., colloq.* изнеживать. —*n., colloq.* неженка.

molt *also*, **moult** *v.i.* линять.

molten *adj.* расплавленный; жидкий. *Molten lava*, жидкая лава.

molybdenum *n.* молибден. —**molybdic**, *adj.* молибденовый.

mom *n., colloq.* мама.

moment *n.* **1**, (instant; point in time) момент. *At the moment*, в данный момент. *At any moment*, в любой момент. *For the moment*, пока. **2**, (importance) важность; значение.

momentarily *adv.* **1**, (for a moment) на минуту. **2**, (very soon) через несколько минут. **3**, (any moment) с минуты на минуту.

momentary *adj.* мгновенный. *Catch a momentary glimpse of*, увидеть мельком.

momentous *adj.* знаменательный.

momentum *n.* инерция; разгон. *Gather momentum*, разгоняться.

mommy *n.* мама; мамаша.

monarch *n.* монарх. —**monarchical**, *adj.* монархический. —**monarchism**, *n.* монархизм.

monarchist *n.* монархист. —*adj.* монархический.

monarchy *n.* монархия.

monastery *n.* монастырь. —**monasterial**, *adj.* монастырский.

monastic *adj.* монашеский. *Monastic vows*, монашеские обеты. —**monasticism**, *n.* монашество.

Monday *n.* понедельник.

monetary *adj.* денежный; монетный.

money *n.* деньги: *a lot of money*, много денег. *Cost a lot of money*, стоить больших денег. *Play for money*, играть на деньги. —*adj.* денежный: *money market*, денежный рынок.

moneybag *n.* **1**, (sack for money) мешок для денег. **2**, *pl., colloq.* (rich man) золотой *or* денежный мешок; толстосум.

money box копилка; кубышка.

moneychanger *n.* меняла.

moneylender *n.* ростовщик.

moneymaking *adj.* доходный; прибыльный.

money order денежный перевод.

Mongol *n.* монгол. —*adj.* монгольский. *Also*, **Mongolian**.

mongoose *n.* мангуста.

mongrel *n.* **1**, (plant or animal of mixed breed) помесь. **2**, (dog of mixed breed) дворняга; дворняжка. —*adj.* нечистокровный.

moniker *also*, **monicker** *n., slang* прозвище; кличка.

monism *n.* монизм. —**monistic**, *adj.* монистический.

monitor *n.* **1**, (in school) классный руководитель; староста. **2**, (TV monitor) контрольный кинескоп. —*v.t.* проверять; контролировать. —**monitor lizard**, варан.

monk *n.* монах.

monkey *n.* обезьяна. —*v.i.* [*usu.* **monkey with**] *slang* возиться с. —**make a monkey out of**, *slang* оставить в дураках.

monkey business *slang* чудачества.

monkey wrench францу́зский ключ. —**throw a monkey wrench into the works,** вставля́ть па́лки в колёса.

monkhood n. мона́шество.

monkshood n. (plant) акони́т.

monochromatic adj. одноцве́тный; монохрома́тический.

monocle n. моно́кль.

monogamy n. единобра́чие; монога́мия. —**monogamous,** adj. единобра́чный; монога́мный.

monogram n. вёнзель; моногра́мма.

monograph n. моногра́фия. —**monographic,** adj. монографи́ческий.

monolith n. моноли́т. —**monolithic,** adj. моноли́тный.

monologue n. моноло́г.

mononucleosis n. мононуклеоз.

monoplane n. моноплан.

monopolist n. монополи́ст. —**monopolistic,** adj. монополисти́ческий.

monopolize v.t. монополизи́ровать. —**monopolization,** n. монополиза́ция.

monopoly n. монопо́лия.

monorail n. однорельсовая желе́зная доро́га.

monosyllabic adj. односло́жный. —**monosyllable,** n. односло́жное сло́во.

monotheism n. монотеи́зм; единобо́жие. —**monotheistic,** adj. монотеисти́ческий.

monotone n. моното́нная речь; моното́нное пе́ние. In a monotone, моното́нно. —adj. моното́нный; одното́нный.

monotonous adj. **1,** (unchanging in tone) моното́нный. **2,** (tedious; repetitious) однообра́зный. —**monotony,** n. однообра́зие.

monotype n. моноти́п.

monsieur n. мосьё.

Monsignor n. монсеньёр.

monsoon n. муссо́н.

monster n. **1,** (fantastic creature) чудо́вище. **2,** (ugly or grotesque creature) чудо́вище; уро́д. **3,** (vicious or depraved person) чудо́вище; и́зверг.

monstrosity n. **1,** (state of being monstrous) чудо́вищность. **2,** (very ugly thing) уро́д.

monstrous adj. чудо́вищный; зве́рский.

montage n. монта́ж.

month n. ме́сяц. A month's vacation, ме́сячный о́тпуск.

monthly adj. ежеме́сячный. —adv. ежеме́сячно. —n. ежеме́сячник.

monument n. па́мятник. —**monumental,** adj. монумента́льный.

moo v.i. мыча́ть. —n. мыча́ние.

mood n. **1,** (frame of mind) настрое́ние: in a bad mood, в плохо́м настрое́нии. **2,** gram. наклоне́ние. —in the mood, располо́жен: I am not in the mood for work today, я не располо́жен (or у меня́ нет расположе́ния) сего́дня рабо́тать. He is not in the mood for jokes, ему́ не до шу́ток.

moody adj. **1,** (gloomy; sullen) угрю́мый. **2,** (subject to changes of mood) капри́зный.

moon n. луна́. To the moon, на Луну́. —once in a blue moon, в ко́и ве́ки.

moonbeam n. луч луны́.

moon landing прилуне́ние.

moonlight n. лу́нный свет. —**moonlit,** adj. лу́нный:

moonlit night, лу́нная ночь.

moonstone n. лу́нный ка́мень.

moor n. (tract of land) пу́стошь. —v.t., naut. прича́ливать; швартова́ть. —v.i., naut. причаливать; швартова́ться.

Moor n. мавр.

moorage n. прича́л.

mooring n. **1,** (tying up) прича́л. **2,** often pl. (lines, cables, etc.) шварто́вы. —**mooring line,** швартов; чал; ча́лка; прича́л; прича́льный кана́т.

Moorish adj. маврита́нский.

moose n. лось.

moot adj. спо́рный.

mop n. **1,** (cleaning tool) шва́бра. **2,** (mass of hair) копна́ (воло́с). —v.t. **1,** (clean) мыть шва́брой. **2,** (wipe) вытира́ть. **3,** fol. by up, mil. очища́ть от проти́вника.

mope v.i. хандри́ть.

moped n. мопе́д.

moraine n. море́на.

moral adj. мора́льный; нра́вственный. Moral code, мора́льный ко́декс. Moral support/victory/duty, мора́льная подде́ржка/побе́да/обя́занность. —n. **1,** pl. (standards of behavior) мора́ль; нра́вственность. Loose morals, лёгкие нра́вы. **2,** (lesson) мора́ль.

morale n. мора́льное состоя́ние.

moralist n. морали́ст. —**moralistic,** adj. нравоучи́тельный.

morality n. мора́ль; нра́вственность.

moralize v.i. морализи́ровать.

morally adv. **1,** (from a moral point of view) мора́льно. **2,** (virtuously) мора́льно; нра́вственно. **3,** (virtually) практи́чески: morally certain, практи́чески уве́рен.

morass n. боло́то; тряси́на.

moratorium n. морато́рий.

moray n. муре́на. Also, **moray eel.**

morbid adj. **1,** (unhealthy) боле́зненный. **2,** (gruesome) жу́ткий. —**morbidity,** n. боле́зненность.

mordant adj. ко́лкий; язви́тельный. —n. протра́ва.

more adj. **1,** (greater in quantity) бо́льше: it will take more time, э́то займёт бо́льше вре́мени. **2,** (additional) ещё: would you like some more tea?, хоти́те ещё ча́ю? —n. **1,** (a greater quantity) бо́льше: it's more than we need, э́то бо́льше, чем нам ну́жно. More than meets the eye, бо́льше, чем ка́жется на пе́рвый взгляд. **2,** (an additional quantity) ещё: would you like some more?, хоти́те ещё? ♦In neg. sentences бо́льше: I will have no more of this, я бо́льше не бу́ду терпе́ть. I have nothing more to say, мне бо́льше не́чего сказа́ть. —adv. **1,** used to form the comp. degree of adjectives and adverbs бо́лее: more interesting, бо́лее интере́сный. **2,** (greater in amount or degree) бо́льше: more than enough, бо́льше чем доста́точно. More than a hundred people, бо́льше ста челове́к. More than ever before, бо́льше, чем когда́-либо ра́ньше. —all the more, всё бо́лее (+ adj.). —(all) the more so because..., тем бо́лее, что... —any more, see any. —more and more, всё бо́льше и бо́льше; (with adjectives) всё бо́лее (+ adj.). —more or less, бо́лее и́ли ме́нее. —once more, ещё раз. —the more..., the more..., чем бо́льше..., тем бо́льше... —what's more, бо́лее того́; бо́льшего того́.

morel n. сморчо́к.

moreover *adv.* кроме того; сверх того; к тому же.

mores *n.pl.* нравы.

morganatic *adj.* морганатический.

morgue *n.* морг; покойницкая; мертвецкая.

moribund *adj.* умирающий.

Mormon *n.* мормон. —*adj.* мормонский.

morning *n.* утро. *This morning,* сегодня утром. *Tomorrow morning,* завтра утром. *The next morning,* наутро. *Monday morning,* в понедельник утром. —*adj.* утренний: *morning newspaper,* утренняя газета. —**good morning!,** доброе утро! —**in the morning,** утром. *Two o'clock in the morning,* два часа ночи. *Eight o'clock in the morning,* восемь часов утра.

morning coat визитка.

morning-glory *n.* ипомея.

morocco *n.* сафьян. —*adj.* сафьянный; сафьяновый.

moron *n.* слабоумный; идиот. —**moronic,** *adj.* слабоумный; идиотский.

morose *adj.* мрачный; угрюмый; пасмурный. —**moroseness,** *n.* мрачность; угрюмость.

morpheme *n.* морфема.

morphine *n.* морфий. *Morphine addict,* морфинист.

morphology *n.* морфология. —**morphological,** *adj.* морфологический.

Morse code азбука Морзе.

morsel *n.* кусочек.

mortal *adj.* **1,** (subject to death) смертный: *man is mortal,* человек – смертен. **2,** (fatal) смертельный: *mortal blow,* смертельный удар. **3,** (fought to the death) смертный: *mortal combat,* смертный бой. **4,** (bitter; grievous) смертельный: *mortal fear/enemy,* смертельный страх/враг. —*n.* смертный: *mere mortal,* простой смертный. —**mortal remains,** бренные останки. —**mortal sin,** смертный грех.

mortality *n.* смертность: *infant mortality,* детская смертность.

mortally *adv.* смертельно; насмерть.

mortar *n.* **1,** (mixing bowl) ступка; ступа. **2,** (cement) строительный раствор. **3,** (military weapon) миномёт; мортира. —*adj., mil.* миномётный: *mortar fire,* миномётный огонь.

mortgage *n.* закладная; ипотека. —*v.t.* закладывать. —**mortgagee,** *n.* залогодержатель. —**mortgagor,** *n.* закладчик.

mortician *n.* директор похоронного бюро.

mortification *n.* **1,** (humiliation) унижение. **2,** (self-denial) умерщвление (плоти).

mortify *v.t.* **1,** (humiliate) унижать. **2,** (discipline, as the body) умерщвлять (плоть). —**mortifying,** *adj.* унизительный.

mortise *n.* паз; гнездо.

mortuary *n.* морг; покойницкая; мертвецкая. —*adj.* похоронный; погребальный.

mosaic *n.* мозаика. —*adj.* мозаичный.

Moslem *n.* мусульманин. —*adj.* мусульманский.

mosque *n.* мечеть.

mosquito *n.* комар. —**mosquito bite,** укус комара.

moss *n.* мох. —**moss-grown,** *adj.* замшелый; обомшелый. —**mossy,** *adj.* мшистый.

most *adj.* **1,** (in the greatest amount) наибольшее количество: *receive the most votes,* получить наибольшее количество голосов. **2,** (in the majority of instances) большинство (+ *gen.*): *in most cases,* в большинстве случаев. —*n.* **1,** (the majority) большинство; большая часть: *most of them,* большинство из них; *most of the time,* большая часть времени. **2,** *preceded by* **the** (the greatest amount) самое большее: *the most I can do,* самое большее, что я могу сделать. —*adv.* **1,** (in or to the greatest extent) больше всего: *what I need most,* что мне больше всего нужно. **2,** *used to form the superl. degree of adjectives* самый: *the most difficult part,* самая трудная часть. *Most likely,* скорее всего. **3,** (very; highly) весьма; в высшей степени. —**at (the) most,** самое большее; от силы; максимум. —**for the most part,** главным образом; большей частью; в большинстве (своём). —**make the most of,** максимально использовать.

mostly *adv.* главным образом; большей частью; в основном.

mote *n.* пылинка; соринка.

motel *n.* мотель.

moth *n.* **1,** (night-flying insect) бабочка; мотылёк. **2,** (clothes moth) моль.

mothball *n.* **1,** *pl.* (substance) нафталин. **2,** (single ball of same) шарик нафталина.

moth-eaten *adj.* изъеденный молью.

mother *n.* мать. —*adj.* **1,** (maternal) материнский. **2,** (native) родной. —**mother country,** родина; отечество. —**mother tongue,** родной язык.

motherhood *n.* материнство.

mother-in-law *n.* **1,** (husband's mother) свекровь. **2,** (wife's mother) тёща.

motherland *n.* родина; отечество.

motherless *adj.* лишённый матери.

motherly *adj.* материнский.

mother-of-pearl *n.* перламутр. —*adj.* перламутровый.

mother superior игуменья.

motif *n.* мотив.

motion *n.* **1,** (movement) движение; ход. *Set in motion,* приводить в движение; дать ход (+ *dat.*). **2,** (gesture) жест. **3,** (proposal to be put to a vote) предложение. **4,** *law* ходатайство. —*v.t.* показывать жестом. *He motioned me to a chair,* он указал мне на стул. —*v.i.* жестикулировать. *He motioned to me to sit down,* он жестом пригласил меня сесть.

motionless *adj.* неподвижный; без движения. *Stand motionless,* стоять неподвижно.

motion picture **1,** (movie) кинофильм; кинокартина. **2,** *pl.* (the art or field of movie-making) кино; кинематография.

motivate *v.t.* побуждать. —**motivation,** *n.* побуждение.

motive *n.* мотив; побуждение. —*adj.* движущий; двигательный.

motley *adj.* пёстрый.

motor *n.* мотор; двигатель. —*adj.* моторный. —*v.i.* ехать *or* кататься на машине.

motorbike *n.* мопед.

motorboat *n.* моторная лодка.

motorbus *n.* автобус.

motorcade *n.* кортеж.

motorcar *n.* автомобиль.

motorcycle *n.* мотоцикл. *Motorcycle races,* мотогонки. —**motorcyclist,** *n.* мотоциклист.

motorist *n.* автомобилист.

motorized *adj.* моторизо́ванный.
motorman *n.* **1,** (tram driver) вагоновожа́тый. **2,** (engineer on a train) машини́ст.
motor nerve дви́гательный нерв.
motor scooter моторо́ллер.
motor ship теплохо́д.
motor vehicle автомаши́на.
mottle *v.t.* испещря́ть. —**mottled,** *adj.* кра́пчатый.
motto *n.* деви́з.
mould *n. & v.* = mold. —**moulder,** *v.* = molder. —**moulding,** *n.* = molding. —**mouldy,** *adj.* = moldy.
moult *v.* = molt.
mound *n.* буго́р. *Burial mound,* курга́н; моги́льный холм.
mount *v.t.* **1,** (go up; climb up) поднима́ться на; взбира́ться на. **2,** (get up on; get on) сади́ться на. **3,** (set, as a jewel) вставля́ть *or* вде́лывать в опра́ву; оправля́ть. **4,** (display, as a picture) вкле́ивать в альбо́м; накле́ивать на карто́н. **5,** (set in position, as a gun) устана́вливать. **6,** (launch, as an attack) предпринима́ть. —*v.i.* **1,** (ascend; climb) поднима́ться. **2,** (increase) возраста́ть. —*n.* **1,** (used in names of mountain peaks) гора́: *Mount Everest,* гора́ Эвере́ст. **2,** (horse) верхова́я ло́шадь; ло́шадь под седло́м. **3,** (setting, as for a jewel) опра́ва. **4,** (stand, as for a weapon) устано́вка. **5,** (supporting structure) крепле́ние. *Engine mount,* у́зел крепле́ния дви́гателя.
mountain *n.* гора́. —*adj.* го́рный: *mountain air,* го́рный во́здух.
mountain ash ряби́на.
mountain climbing альпини́зм. —**mountain climber,** альпини́ст.
mountaineer *n.* **1,** (highlander) го́рец. **2,** (mountain climber) альпини́ст. —**mountaineering,** *n.* альпини́зм.
mountain lion пу́ма; кугуа́р.
mountainous *adj.* гори́стый; го́рный.
mountaintop *n.* верши́на (горы́).
mountebank *n.* зна́харь; шарлата́н.
mounted *adj.* ко́нный: *mounted police,* ко́нная поли́ция.
mounting *n.* устано́вка; крепле́ние.
mourn *v.t.* опла́кивать. —*v.i.* **1,** (grieve) горева́ть; скорбе́ть. **2,** (be in mourning) быть в тра́уре; носи́ть тра́ур.
mourner *n.* горю́ющий; скорбя́щий.
mournful *adj.* ско́рбный; тра́урный; жа́лобный; плаче́вный.
mourning *n.* тра́ур: *in mourning,* в тра́уре. *Be in mourning for,* быть в тра́уре по; носи́ть тра́ур по. *Go into mourning,* наде́ть тра́ур. —*adj.* тра́урный.
mourning cloak (butterfly) тра́урница.
mouse *n.* мышь.
mousetrap *n.* мышело́вка.
mousse *n.* мусс.
moustache *n.* = mustache.
mousy *adj.* мыши́ный.
mouth *n.* **1,** *anat.* рот. *Have five mouths to feed,* име́ть пять рто́в в семье́. **2,** (opening) жерло́; у́стье. **3,** (of a river) у́стье. —*v.t.* произноси́ть. —**by word of mouth,** из уст в уста́. —**down at the mouth,** па́вший ду́хом; в уны́нии. —**live from hand to mouth,** *see* hand. —**put words in someone's mouth,** вложи́ть слова́ в чьи-нибудь уста́. —**you took the**

words right out of my mouth, и́менно э́то я хоте́л сказа́ть.
mouthful *n.* глото́к. *You said a mouthful,* э́тим вы мно́гое сказа́ли.
mouthpiece *n.* **1,** (part that goes in the mouth) мундшту́к. **2,** *colloq.* (spokesman) ру́пор.
mouthwash *n.* полоска́ние.
movable *adj.* **1,** (that can be moved) подвижно́й; передвижно́й. **2,** *law* (of property) дви́жимый. —**movables,** *n.pl., law* дви́жимость.
move *v.t.* **1,** (change the location of) дви́гать: *move furniture,* дви́гать ме́бель. **2,** (move from a certain place) сдвига́ть. **3,** (move from one place to another) передвига́ть; перемеща́ть. **4,** (transfer) переноси́ть; переводи́ть. **5,** (prompt; cause) побужда́ть. **6,** (touch the feelings of) тро́гать; растро́гать. *Move to tears,* тро́гать (кого́-нибудь) до слёз. **7,** (propose) предлага́ть. **8,** *chess* игра́ть (+ *instr.*); идти́ (+ *instr.*). **9,** (evacuate, as the bowels) очища́ть. —*v.i.* **1,** (change location or position) дви́гаться; сдвига́ться; передвига́ться. *Don't move!,* не дви́гайтесь!; не шеве-ли́тесь! **2,** (change residence) переезжа́ть: *move to Chicago,* переезжа́ть в Чика́го. —*n.* **1,** (movement) движе́ние: *the slightest move,* мале́йшее движе́ние. *One (false) move and I'll shoot!,* одно́ движе́ние и я бу́ду стреля́ть! **2,** (step; maneuver) ход; шаг. **3,** (change of residence) перее́зд. **4,** (play, as in games) ход. —**get a move on!,** *colloq.* потора́пливайтесь! —**move aside,** отодвига́ть(ся) наза́д. —**move in/into,** въезжа́ть (в). —**move in on,** переезжа́ть к. —**move out,** съезжа́ть; выезжа́ть. —**move over,** подвига́ться. —**move up, 1,** (advance in rank or status) продвига́ться. **2,** (schedule earlier) переноси́ть на бо́лее ра́нний срок. —**on the move,** в разъе́здах.
movement *n.* **1,** (motion) движе́ние. **2,** (organized campaign) движе́ние: *the trade union movement,* профсою́зное движе́ние. **3,** *music* (portion of a work) часть.
mover *n.* перево́зчик.
movie *n.* **1,** (motion picture) фильм; кинофи́льм. **2,** *pl.* (showing) кино́: *go to the movies,* ходи́ть в кино́. —**movie camera,** киноаппара́т; кинока́мера. —**movie projector,** кинопрое́ктор. —**movie star,** кинозвезда́. —**movie theater,** кинотеа́тр.
moving *adj.* **1,** (that moves; in motion) дви́жущийся: *moving parts,* дви́жущиеся ча́сти. **2,** (stirring the emotions) тро́гательный.
mow *v.t.* коси́ть. —**mow down,** коси́ть.
mower *n.* **1,** (person) коса́рь; косе́ц. **2,** (machine) коси́лка.
Mr. *abbr.* ми́стер; господи́н.
Mrs. *abbr.* ми́ссис; госпожа́.
much *adj.* мно́го: *much time,* мно́го вре́мени. —*adv.* **1,** (to a great extent or degree) о́чень: *much obliged,* о́чень обя́зан. *I want very much to go,* я о́чень хочу́ пойти́. **2,** (by far) гора́здо; намно́го: *much better,* гора́здо/намно́го лу́чше. **3,** (nearly; about) почти́: *much the same,* почти́ тако́й же. —*n.* мно́го; мно́гое: *leave much to be desired,* оставля́ть жела́ть мно́го лу́чше. *There is much we still don't know,* мы мно́гого не зна́ем ещё. —**as much... as,** сто́лько же... ско́ль-ко и. —**how much?,** ско́лько? —**make much of, 1,** (consider important) придава́ть большо́е значе́ние (+ *dat.*). **2,** (fuss over) носи́ть на рука́х. —**much**

as, как ни: *much as I hate to,* как это ни обидно. —**much less,** *see* less. —**much to my surprise,** к моему великому удивлению. —**not much,** мало. —**not much of a...,** неважный: *he is not much of a swimmer,* он неважно плавает. —**so much,** *see* so. —**so much the better/worse,** тем лучше/хуже. —**too much,** слишком много; слишком. —**too much for,** не под силу (+ *dat.*).

mucilage *n.* **1,** (gummy secretion) (растительная) слизь. **2,** (glue) (растительный) клей.

muck *n.* **1,** (filth) грязь. **2,** (manure) навоз.

mucous *adj.* слизистый. —**mucous membrane,** слизистая оболочка.

mucus *n.* слизь.

mud *n.* грязь. —*adj.* грязевой: *mud bath,* грязевая ванна. *Mud hut,* глинобитная землянка. —**drag through the mud,** втоптать в грязь. —**sling mud at,** забрасывать (кого-нибудь) грязью.

muddle *v.t.* **1,** (mix up; confuse) путать; спутывать. **2,** (bungle) напутать. —*v.i.* [*usu.* **muddle through**] кое-как перебиваться. —*n.* путаница; неразбериха.

muddy *adj.* грязный. —*v.t.* **1,** (soil with mud) испачкать грязью. **2,** (make turbid) мутить. —**muddy the waters,** мутить воду.

mudguard *n.* брызговик; щит от грязи.

mudslide *n.* оползень.

mudslinger *n.* клеветник; злопыхатель.

muezzin *n.* муэдзин.

muff *n.* муфта. —*v.t.* **1,** (fail to catch) пропустить. **2,** (bungle) упустить: *muff a chance,* упустить случай. *Muff one's lines,* смазать свою реплику.

muffin *n.* сдобная булка.

muffle *v.t.* **1,** (cover up; wrap) закутывать. **2,** (deaden, as sound) глушить; заглушать.

muffler *n.* **1,** (scarf) кашне. **2,** (silencing device) глушитель.

mufti *n.* **1,** (civilian garb) штатское платье. **2,** (Moslem jurist) муфтий.

mug *n.* **1,** (vessel) кружка. **2,** *slang* (face) морда; рожа; рыло; харя. —*v.t., colloq.* грабить. —**mugger,** *n., colloq.* налётчик.

muggy *adj.* сырой; гнилой.

mulatto *n.* мулат.

mulberry *n.* **1,** (tree) тутовое дерево; шелковица. **2,** (fruit) тутовая ягода.

mulch *n.* мульча.

mule *n.* мул. *Mule team,* упряжка мулов. *Stubborn as a mule,* упрямый как осёл. —**muleteer,** *n.* погонщик мулов.

mull *v.i.* [*usu.* **mull over**] обдумывать.

mullah *n.* мулла.

mullet *n.* **1,** (gray mullet) кефаль. **2,** (red mullet) барабулька; султанка.

multicolored *also,* **multicoloured** *adj.* многоцветный; многокрасочный.

multifaceted *adj.* разносторонний.

multifarious *adj.* разнообразный.

multiform *adj.* многообразный.

multilateral *adj.* многосторонний.

multilingual *adj.* многоязычный.

multimillionaire *n.* мультимиллионер; миллиардер.

multinational *adj.* многонациональный.

multiple *adj.* **1,** (numerous) многочисленный. *Receive multiple injuries,* получить много поврежде-

ний. **2,** (involving more than one element): *multiple warhead,* разделяющаяся боеголовка. —*n.* кратное. *least common multiple,* общее наименьшее кратное. —**multiple sclerosis,** рассеянный склероз.

multiplicand *n.* множимое.

multiplication *n.* умножение. —**multiplication table,** таблица умножения.

multiplicity *n.* множество: *a multiplicity of cases,* множество случаев; многочисленные случаи.

multiplier *n., math.* множитель.

multiply *v.t.* множить; умножать: *multiply six by eight,* множить/умножать шесть на восемь. —*v.i.* **1,** (perform multiplication) множить; умножать. **2,** (increase) множиться; умножаться. **3,** (propagate) размножаться.

multipurpose *adj.* универсальный.

multistage *adj.* многоступенчатый.

multistoried *adj.* многоэтажный. *Also,* **multistory.**

multitude *n.* множество. —**multitudinous,** *adj.* многочисленный.

mum *adj., colloq.* ни гугу. *Keep mum,* помалкивать. —**mum's the word,** (об этом) ни гугу.

mumble *v.t. & i.* бормотать. —*n.* бормотание.

mummy *n.* **1,** (embalmed body) мумия. **2,** *colloq.* (mother) мамочка.

mumps *n.* свинка.

munch *v.t. & i.* чавкать.

mundane *adj.* земной; мирской; житейский.

municipal *adj.* городской; муниципальный. —**municipality,** *n.* муниципалитет.

munificent *adj.* щедрый. —**munificence,** *n.* щедрость.

munition *n., usu. pl.* военные припасы; военное имущество. *Munitions factory,* военный завод.

mural *n.* (стенная) роспись. —*adj.* стенной.

murder *n.* убийство. —*v.t.* **1,** (kill) убивать. **2,** (butcher) коверкать: *murder the English language,* коверкать английский язык. —**murderer,** *n.* убийца. —**murderous,** *adj.* убийственный.

murky *adj.* **1,** (dark; gloomy) мрачный. **2,** (turbid) мутный.

murmur *n.* **1,** (sound) ропот: *murmur of voices,* ропот голосов. *Without a murmur,* безропотно. **2,** *med.* шум (в сердце). —*v.i.* роптать.

murrain *n.* падёж.

murre *n.* кайра.

muscat *n.* мускат. —*adj.* мускатный.

muscatel *n.* мускат.

muscle *n.* мышца; мускул. —*adj.* мышечный: *muscle tone,* мышечный тонус. —*v.i.* [*usu.* **muscle in**] *colloq.* пробиваться.

Muscovite *n.* москвич.

muscular *adj.* **1,** (of or done by the muscles) мышечный; мускульный. **2,** (brawny) мускулистый. —**muscular dystrophy,** мышечная дистрофия.

musculature *n.* мускулатура.

muse *v.i.* размышлять; задумываться. —*n.* муза.

museum *n.* музей. —**museum piece,** музейная редкость.

mush *n.* каша.

mushroom *n.* гриб. —*v.i.* разрастаться. —**mushroom cloud,** грибовидное облако.

mushy *adj.* **1,** (soft; pulpy) мягкий. **2,** *colloq.* (excessively sentimental) слащавый.

music *n.* **1,** (general term) музыка. *Set words to*

music, положи́ть слова́ на му́зыку. **2,** (written score) но́ты: *play from/without music,* игра́ть по но́там/без нот/. —*adj.* музыка́льный; но́тный. *Music stand,* но́тный пюпи́тр.

musical *adj.* музыка́льный: *musical instrument,* музыка́льный инструме́нт. —*n.* мю́зикл. —**musical comedy,** музыка́льная коме́дия.

musicale *n.* музыка́льный ве́чер.

music box музыка́льная шкату́лка; музыка́льный я́щик.

music hall мю́зик-хо́лл.

musician *n.* музыка́нт.

musicology *n.* музыкове́дение. —**musicologist,** *n.* музыкове́д.

musk *n.* му́скус.

musk deer кабарга́.

musket *n.* мушке́т. —**musketeer,** *n.* мушкетёр.

musketry *n.* стрелко́вое де́ло.

musk ox овцебы́к.

muskrat *n.* онда́тра.

Muslim *n. & adj.* = **Moslem.**

muslin *n.* мусли́н; кисея́. —*adj.* мусли́новый; кисе́йный.

muss *v.t.* растрепа́ть; еро́шить; взлохма́чивать.

mussel *n.* ми́дия.

must *v.aux.* **1,** *expressing necessity* до́лжен; на́до: *I must go,* мне на́до идти́; я до́лжен идти́. **2,** *expressing strong probability* должно́ быть: *he must be here,* он, должно́ быть, здесь. *You must have heard about it,* вы, должно́ быть, слы́шали об э́том. **3,** *used negatively, expressing prohibition* нельзя́; не на́до; не до́лжен: *you mustn't say such things,* таки́х веще́й нельзя́ говори́ть. *We must not be seen together,* нас не должны́ ви́деть вме́сте. *This must not happen again!,* что́бы э́того бо́льше не́ было!

mustache *also,* **moustache** *n.* усы́.

mustang *n.* муста́нг.

mustard *n.* горчи́ца. —**mustard gas,** горчи́чный газ; иприт. —**mustard oil,** горчи́чное ма́сло. — **mustard plaster,** горчи́чник.

muster *v.t.* **1,** (assemble) собира́ть. **2,** (summon, as strength, courage, etc.) набира́ться (+ *gen.*); собира́ться с. **3,** *fol. by* **out** (discharge) увольня́ть (с вое́нной слу́жбы); демобилизова́ть. —*v.i.* собира́ться. —*n.* **1,** (assemblage, as of troops) сбор; смотр. **2,** (list; roll) именно́й спи́сок. —**pass muster,** оказа́ться на высоте́.

musty *adj.* за́тхлый.

mutate *v.t.* видоизменя́ть. —*v.i.* видоизменя́ться.

mutation *n.* **1,** *biol.* мута́ция. **2,** *phonet.* перегласо́вка.

mute *adj.* немо́й. —*n.* **1,** (one incapable of speech) немо́й. **2,** *music* сурди́нка. —*v.t.* **1,** *music* надева́ть

сурди́нку на. **2,** (muffle) приглуша́ть.

muted *adj.* приглушённый.

muteness *n.* немота́; онеме́ние.

mutilate *v.t.* уве́чить; кале́чить. —**mutilation,** *n.* уве́чье.

mutineer *n.* мяте́жник; бунтовщи́к.

mutinous *adj.* мяте́жный; бунта́рский.

mutiny *n.* мяте́ж; бунт. —*v.i.* подня́ть мяте́ж; бунтова́ть.

mutter *v.t. & i.* бормота́ть.

mutton *n.* бара́нина. —*adj.* бара́ний: *mutton chop,* бара́нья отбивна́я.

mutual *adj.* **1,** (given and received in kind) взаи́мный; обою́дный. *Mutual assistance,* взаимопо́мощь. **2,** (possessed in common) о́бщий: *mutual acquaintances,* о́бщие знако́мые. —**mutuality,** *n.* взаи́мность; обою́дность. —**mutually,** *adv.* взаи́мно; обою́дно. *Mutually advantageous/beneficial,* взаимовы́годный.

muzhik *n.* мужи́к.

muzzle *n.* **1,** (of a firearm) ду́ло; жерло́. **2,** (snout) мо́рда; ры́ло. **3,** (covering for an animal's mouth) намо́рдник. —*v.t.* **1,** (put a muzzle on) надева́ть намо́рдник на. **2,** (silence; gag) затыка́ть рот (+ *dat.*).

my *poss. adj.* мой (моя́, моё, мой): *my mother,* моя́ мать. ♦*When the possessor is the subject of the sentence* свой: *I finished my work,* я зако́нчил свою́ рабо́ту. —*interj.* бо́же мой!; ну и ну!

myopia *n.* близору́кость. —**myopic,** *adj.* близору́кий.

myriad *n.* мириа́ды. —*adj.* бесчи́сленный; несме́тный.

myriapod *n.* многоно́жка.

myrrh *n.* ми́рра.

myrtle *n.* мирт. —*adj.* ми́ртовый.

myself *pers. pron.* **1,** *used for emphasis* (я) сам: *I don't know myself,* я сам (сама́) не зна́ю. **2,** *used reflexively* себя́: *I bought it for myself,* я купи́л(а) э́то для себя́. *I hurt myself,* я уши́бся (уши́блась). —**by myself,** оди́н (одна́). —**to myself,** себе́; про себя́.

mysterious *adj.* таи́нственный; зага́дочный.

mystery *n.* **1,** (enigma) та́йна; зага́дка. **2,** (mysteriousness) та́йна; таи́нственность. **3,** (mystery story) детекти́вный рома́н.

mystic *adj.* мисти́ческий. —*n.* ми́стик. —**mystical,** *adj.* мисти́ческий.

mysticism *n.* ми́стика; мистици́зм.

mystify *v.t.* озада́чивать. —**mystification,** *n.* озада́ченность.

mystique *n.* таи́нственность.

myth *n.* миф. —**mythical,** *adj.* мифи́ческий.

mythology *n.* мифоло́гия. —**mythological,** *adj.* мифологи́ческий.

N

N, n четы́рнадцатая бу́ква англи́йского алфави́та.

nab *v.t.*, *colloq.* схвати́ть.

nadir *n.* **1,** *astron.* нади́р. **2,** *fig.* (low point) ни́зшая то́чка.

nag *v.t.* придира́ться к; пристава́ть к; пили́ть. —*n.* **1,** (person who nags) приди́ра. **2,** (old horse) кля́ча.

nagging *n.* пристава́ние. —*adj.* **1,** (of a person) надое́дливый. **2,** (of a pain) ною́щий. **3,** (of a thought, question, etc.) назо́йливый; неотвя́зный. *Nagging fear,* тупо́й страх.

naiad *n.* наи́да.

nail *n.* **1,** (of a finger or toe) но́готь. **2,** (metal fastener) гвоздь. —*v.t.* **1,** (fasten with a nail or nails) прибива́ть: *nail a notice to the wall,* прибить объявле́ние к стене́. **2,** *fol. by* **up** (board up) закола́чивать. **3,** *fol. by* **down** (fasten down with nails) прибива́ть. **4,** (fix firmly; rivet) пригвожда́ть. **5,** *fol. by* **down** (clinch) заключи́ть: *nail down an agreement,* заключи́ть соглаше́ние. —**hit the nail on the head,** попа́сть в (са́мую) то́чку; попасть не в бровь, а в глаз.

nail file пи́лка.

nail polish лак для ногте́й.

naïve *adj.* наи́вный. —**naïveté,** *n.* наи́вность.

naked *adj.* го́лый; наго́й; обнажённый. *Run around naked,* пробега́ть в го́лом ви́де *or* нагишо́м. *The naked truth,* го́лая и́стина. *Naked aggression,* непри-кры́тая агре́ссия. —**with the naked eye,** просты́м гла́зом; невооружённым гла́зом.

nakedness *n.* нагота́.

name *n.* **1,** (first name; Christian name) и́мя. *What is your name?,* как вас зову́т? *My name is...,* меня́ зову́т... **2,** (last name; surname) фами́лия: *a man by the name of Smith,* челове́к по фами́лии Смит. *He goes by the name of Sokolov,* он изве́стен под и́менем Соколо́ва. **3,** (appellation) назва́ние: *the name of the city,* назва́ние го́рода. **4,** (reputation) и́мя: *make a name for oneself,* сде́лать себе́ и́мя. **5,** *colloq.* (celebrity) и́мя: *big names,* кру́пные имена́. —*v.t.* **1,** (give a name to; call) называ́ть. **2,** (state) называ́ть: *name your price,* назови́те ва́шу це́ну. **3,** (appoint; designate) назнача́ть. —**by name,** поимённо: *mention by name,* называ́ть поимённо. —**call (someone) names,** руга́ть; обруга́ть. —**in name only,** то́лько номина́льно. —**in the name of,** во и́мя (+ *gen.*). *In the name of the law,* и́менем зако́на. —**name names,** называ́ть имена́: *I don't want to name names,* я не хочу́ называ́ть имён. —**to one's**

name, за душо́й: *he hasn't a penny to his name,* у него́ за душо́й ни гроша́.

name day имени́ны.

nameless *adj.* безымя́нный.

namely *adv.* а и́менно.

nameplate *n.* доще́чка.

namesake *n.* тёзка.

nanny *n.* ня́ня. —**nanny goat,** коза́.

nap *n.* **1,** (brief sleep) сон. *Take a nap,* поспа́ть; вздремну́ть. **2,** (fuzzy surface) ворс; начёс. —*v.i.* **1,** (be asleep) спать. **2,** (be off one's guard) дрема́ть. *Catch someone napping,* заста́ть кого́-нибудь враспло́х.

napalm *n.* напа́лм. —*adj.* напа́лмовый.

nape *n.* загри́вок.

naphtha *n.* лигро́йн.

naphthalene *n.* нафтали́н.

naphthol *n.* нафто́л.

napkin *n.* салфе́тка.

narcissus *n.* нарци́сс.

narcotic *n.* нарко́тик. —*adj.* наркоти́ческий.

nard *n.* нард.

narrate *v.t.* расска́зывать.

narration *n.* **1,** (act of narrating) расска́зывание. **2,** (a narrative) повествова́ние. **3,** (running commentary for a film) коммента́рий.

narrative *n.* повествова́ние. —*adj.* повествова́тельный.

narrator *n.* **1,** (storyteller) расска́зчик. **2,** (of a film) ди́ктор; коммента́тор.

narrow *adj.* **1,** (not wide) у́зкий: *narrow street/bridge/passageway,* у́зкий переу́лок/мост/прохо́д. **2,** (tight) у́зкий; те́сный: *narrow in the waist,* у́зок/те́сен в та́лии. **3,** (limited in scope) у́зкий: *narrow subject,* у́зкая те́ма. *Narrow circle of friends,* у́зкий *or* те́сный круг друзе́й. **4,** (uncomfortably close) незначи́тельный: *score a narrow victory,* победи́ть с незначи́тельным переве́сом. *Have a narrow escape,* едва́ спасти́сь; едва́ но́ги унести́. —*v.t.* сужива́ть. —*v.i.* сужива́ться. —**narrow down to,** своди́ть(ся) к.

narrow-gauge *adj.* узкоколе́йный.

narrowly *adv.* чуть; е́ле-е́ле. *He narrowly missed being killed,* он чуть не поги́б.

narrow-minded *adj.* у́зкий; ограни́ченный; узколо́бый.

narrowness *n.* у́зость.

narwhal *n.* нарва́л.

nary *adj.*, *colloq.* ни оди́н: *nary a person,* ни одного́ челове́ка.

nasal *adj.* **1,** (pert. to the nose; pronounced through the nose) носово́й. **2,** (having a nasal quality) гнуса́вый.

nascent *adj.* молодо́й: *a nascent republic,* молода́я респу́блика.

nasturtium *n.* насту́рция.

nasty *adj.* **1,** (nauseating; disgusting) проти́вный; отврати́тельный: *nasty odor,* проти́вный/отврати́тельный за́пах. **2,** (very unpleasant) скве́рный; отврати́тельный: *nasty weather,* скве́рная/отврати́тельная пого́да. *He is in for a nasty surprise,* его́ ждёт больша́я неприя́тность. **3,** (malicious; mean) злой: *nasty trick,* зла́я шу́тка. **4,** (causing harm or discomfort) серьёзный; доса́дный: *nasty accident,* серьёзная ава́рия; *nasty cough,* доса́дный ка́шель.

natal *adj.* относя́щийся к рожде́нию.

nation *n.* страна́. *The United Nations,* Объединённые На́ции.

national *adj.* национа́льный; госуда́рственный. —*n.* граждани́н; по́дданный.

nationalism *n.* национали́зм.

nationalist *n.* национали́ст. —*adj.* националисти́ческий. —**nationalistic,** *adj.* националисти́ческий.

nationality *n.* **1,** (national origin) национа́льность. **2,** (body of people) национа́льность; наро́дность. *The nationality question,* национа́льный вопро́с.

nationalize *v.t.* национализи́ровать. —**nationalization,** *n.* национализа́ция.

nationwide *adj.* всенаро́дный.

native *adj.* **1,** (of the land of one's birth) родно́й: *one's native land,* родна́я страна́; родно́й край; ро́дина. **2,** (indigenous) тузе́мный; коренно́й. *Native New Yorker,* уроже́нец Нью-Йо́рка. **3,** (inborn; innate) врождённый. —*n.* **1,** (one born in a particular place) уроже́нец. **2,** (original inhabitant; aborigine) тузе́мец.

nativity *n.* **1,** (birth) рожде́ние. **2,** *cap.* (birth of Christ) рождество́ Христо́во.

natty *adj.* наря́дный; щеголева́тый.

natural *adj.* есте́ственный; приро́дный. *Natural disaster,* стихи́йное бе́дствие. *Die a natural death,* умере́ть свое́й сме́ртью. —*n.,* *music* бека́р. —**natural gas,** приро́дный газ. —**natural resources,** есте́ственные *or* приро́дные бога́тства. —**natural selection,** есте́ственный отбо́р.

naturalism *n.* натурали́зм.

naturalist *n.* естествоиспыта́тель; натурали́ст.

naturalize *v.t.* натурализова́ть. —**naturalization,** *n.* натурализа́ция.

naturally *adv.* **1,** (in a natural manner) есте́ственно. **2,** (by nature) по приро́де; по нату́ре; натура́льно. **3,** (as one might expect; of course) коне́чно; разуме́ется; есте́ственно.

nature *n.* **1,** (universe) приро́да: *the beauties of nature,* красо́ты приро́ды. **2,** (temperament; disposition) нату́ра: *by nature,* по нату́ре; по приро́де. **3,** (essential characteristics) хара́ктер: *the nature of the work,* хара́ктер рабо́ты. *By its very nature,* по са́мой свое́й су́щности. **4,** (sort; kind) род: *things of that nature,* тако́го ро́да ве́щи. —**in the nature of things,** в поря́дке веще́й; в приро́де веще́й.

naught *n.* нуль. *All for naught,* всё напра́сно. *Go for naught,* пропа́сть да́ром. *Come to naught,* своди́ться к нулю́ *or* на нет.

naughty *adj.* **1,** (mischievous) шаловли́вый. *Be naughty,* шали́ть. *Naughty child,* шалу́н. **2,** (indecent) риско́ванный; двусмы́сленный.

nausea *n.* тошнота́. —**nauseate,** *v.t.* вызыва́ть тошноту́ у. —**nauseating,** *adj.* тошнотво́рный.

nauseous *adj.* **1,** (nauseating) тошнотво́рный. **2,** (nauseated): *I feel nauseous,* меня́ тошни́т.

nautical *adj.* морско́й. —**nautical mile,** морска́я ми́ля.

nautilus *n.* кора́блик.

naval *adj.* морско́й; вое́нно-морско́й. *Naval academy,* вое́нно-морско́е учи́лище. *Naval warfare,* война́ на мо́ре.

nave *n.* кора́бль.

navel *n.* пупо́к.

navigable *adj.* судохо́дный. —**navigability,** *n.* судохо́дность.

navigate *v.t.* **1,** (sail through) переплыва́ть. **2,** (steer; operate) управля́ть. —*v.i.* **1,** (sail) пла́вать (на су́дне). **2,** *colloq.* (walk) передвига́ться.

navigation *n.* **1,** (sailing; shipping) судохо́дство; навига́ция; морепла́вание. **2,** (the science) навига́ция; кораблевожде́ние. —**navigational,** *adj.* навигацио́нный.

navigator *n.* **1,** (on a ship or aircraft) шту́рман. **2,** (explorer) морепла́ватель.

navy *n.* (вое́нно-морско́й) флот.

navy blue тёмно-си́ний цвет. —**navy-blue,** *adj.* тёмно-си́ний.

navy yard вое́нно-морска́я верфь.

nay *adv.* нет. —*n.* про́тив: *three ayes, two nays,* три за, два про́тив. *The nays have it,* большинство́ про́тив.

Nazi *n.* наци́ст. —*adj.* наци́стский. —**Nazism,** *n.* наци́зм.

Neanderthal *adj.* неандерта́льский. —**Neanderthal man,** неандерта́лец.

near *adj.* бли́зкий: *the end is near,* коне́ц бли́зок. *It's quite near,* э́то совсе́м бли́зко. *In the near future,* в ско́ром *or* в ближа́йшем бу́дущем. *The nearest way to town,* кратча́йший путь в го́род. —*adv.* бли́зко. *Draw near,* бли́зиться; приближа́ться. —*prep.* о́коло; у; во́зле; бли́зко от *or* к; недалеко́ от. *Near here,* недалеко́ отсю́да; поблизости. *Sit near me,* сядь о́коло меня́. *Sit near each other,* сиде́ть бли́зко друг к дру́гу. *The post office is near the station,* по́чта недалеко́ от вокза́ла. *Be near death,* быть при сме́рти. —*v.t. & i.* бли́зиться (к); приближа́ться (к): *be nearing an end,* бли́зиться/приближа́ться к концу́. —**near at hand,** бли́зко; под руко́й; на носу́. —**near miss,** попада́ние близ це́ли.

nearby *adj.* бли́зкий; сосе́дний. *Their house is right nearby,* их дом совсе́м бли́зко *or* совсе́м ря́дом. —*adv.* бли́зко; вблизи́.

Near East Бли́жний Восто́к.

nearly *adv.* почти́; едва́ ли не; чуть ли не. ♦*With verbs* едва́ не; чуть не: *he nearly drowned,* он едва́ не *or* чуть не утону́л. —**not nearly,** совсе́м не: *not nearly ready,* совсе́м не гото́в.

nearness *n.* бли́зость.

nearsighted *adj.* близору́кий. —**nearsightedness,** *n.* близору́кость.

neat *adj.* **1,** (tidy) опря́тный; аккура́тный; чистопло́тный. **2,** *colloq.* (adroit) ло́вкий. —**neatly,** *adv.*

опря́тно; аккура́тно. —**neatness,** *n.* опря́тность; аккура́тность.

nebula *n.* тума́нность.

nebulous *adj.* сму́тный; нея́сный; тума́нный.

necessarily *adv.* обяза́тельно.

necessary *adj.* необходи́мый; ну́жный. *If necessary,* е́сли ну́жно. *That is not necessary,* э́то не ну́жно (*or* не на́до). *It will be necessary to...,* придётся (+ *inf.*).

necessitate *v.t.* де́лать необходи́мым; тре́бовать.

necessity *n.* **1,** (the fact of being necessary) необходи́мость; на́добность. *Out of necessity,* по необходи́мости. **2,** (something that is necessary) необходи́мая вещь. *The barest necessities,* са́мое необходи́мое; предме́ты пе́рвой необходи́мости.

neck *n.* **1,** (part of the body) ше́я. **2,** (of a garment) вы́рез: *V-neck,* треуго́льный вы́рез. **3,** (of a bottle) го́рлышко; го́рло. **4,** (of a violin; of the uterus) ше́йка. **5,** (of land) переше́ек. —*adj.* ше́йный. —**get it in the neck,** получи́ть по ше́е. —**neck and neck,** голова́ в го́лову. —**risk one's neck,** лезть в пе́тлю. —**stick one's neck out,** ста́вить себя́ под уда́р.

neckerchief *n.* ше́йный плато́к.

necklace *n.* ожере́лье.

neckline *n.* вы́рез: *low neckline,* глубо́кий вы́рез.

necktie *n.* га́лстук.

necrosis *n.* некро́з.

nectar *n.* некта́р.

née *adj.* урождённая.

need *n.* **1,** (poverty) нужда́: *live in dire need,* жить в нужде́. **2,** (necessity) на́добность; нужда́: *no need to,* нет на́добности/нужды́ (+ *inf.*). *In case of dire need,* в слу́чае кра́йней нужды́. **3,** *pl.* (wants; requirements) ну́жды; потре́бности. —*v.t.* **1,** (have need of) нужда́ться в. ♦ *More commonly rendered by* ну́жно: *what do you need that for?,* для чего́ э́то вам ну́жно? *I need a pencil,* мне ну́жен каранда́ш. *I need money,* мне нужны́ де́ньги. **2,** (require) тре́бовать. —*v.aux.* (have to) *rendered by* на́до *or* ну́жно: *you need to rest more,* вам на́до бо́льше отдыха́ть. *You need not be afraid,* вам не ну́жно боя́ться. —**be in need of,** нужда́ться в; тре́бовать. —**if need be,** е́сли ну́жно; в слу́чае нужды́.

needle *n.* **1,** (sewing implement) игла́; иго́лка. **2,** (knitting needle) (вяза́льная) спи́ца. **3,** (of a compass) стре́лка. **4,** (hypodermic needle) (для подко́жных впры́скиваний) игла́. **5,** (for a phonograph) (граммофо́нная) игла́. **6,** (used in engraving) (гравирова́льная) игла́. **7,** (needle-shaped leaf) игла́. —*v.t.,* *colloq.* придира́ться к; грызть; подпуска́ть шпи́льки (+ *dat.*). —**be on pins and needles,** быть *or* сиде́ть как на иго́лках. —**needle in a haystack,** иго́лка в сто́ге се́на.

needless *adj.* нену́жный; бесполе́зный. —**needless to say,** разуме́ется; не́чего и говори́ть.

needlessly *adv.* бесполе́зно.

needlework *n.* шитьё; вышива́ние; рукоде́лие. —**needleworker,** *n.* рукоде́льница.

needy *adj.* нужда́ющийся.

ne'er-do-well *n.* никчёмный челове́к; него́дник; шалопа́й.

nefarious *adj.* гну́сный.

negate *v.t.* **1,** (nullify) своди́ть на нет *or* к нулю́. **2,** (contradict; refute) опроверга́ть. —**negation,** *n.* отрица́ние.

negative *adj.* отрица́тельный. —*n.* **1,** *gram.* отрица́ние. **2,** *photog.* негати́в. —**in the negative,** отрица́тельно: *answer in the negative,* отве́тить отрица́тельно.

neglect *v.t.* **1,** (fail to give proper attention to) пренебрега́ть; запуска́ть; забра́сывать. **2,** *fol. by inf.* (fail to) забыва́ть: *neglect to mention,* забы́ть упомяну́ть; не упомяну́ть. —*n.* **1,** (act of neglecting) пренебреже́ние. **2,** (state of neglect) запу́щенность; запусте́ние. *In a state of neglect,* в запу́щенном состоя́нии; в забро́се.

neglectful *adj.* небре́жный; невнима́тельный.

negligee *n.* неглиже́.

negligence *n.* небре́жность. *Criminal negligence,* престу́пная небре́жность *or* хала́тность. —**negligent,** *adj.* небре́жный.

negligible *adj.* незначи́тельный; ничто́жный.

negotiable *adj.* **1,** (capable of being negotiated) подлежа́щий обсужде́нию: *this question is not negotiable,* э́тот вопро́с не подлежи́т обсужде́нию. **2,** *finance* оборо́тный: *negotiable instrument,* оборо́тный докуме́нт.

negotiate *v.i.* вести́ перегово́ры. —*v.t.* **1,** (conclude through negotiations) заключа́ть. **2,** *colloq.* (traverse; surmount) преодолева́ть.

negotiation *n., usu. pl.* перегово́ры. —**negotiator,** *n.* лицо́, веду́щее перегово́ры.

Negro *n.* негр. —*adj.* негритя́нский.

Negroid *adj.* негро́идный.

neigh *v.i.* ржать.

neighbor *also,* **neighbour** *n.* **1,** (person living nearby) сосе́д. **2,** (fellow being) бли́жний.

neighborhood *also,* **neighbourhood** *n.* райо́н; окру́га. —**in the neighborhood of, 1,** (near) по сосе́дству с. **2,** (approximately) о́коло; приблизи́тельно.

neighboring *adj.* сосе́дний.

neighborly *adj.* доброcосе́дский.

neither *adj.* ни тот, ни друго́й: *in neither case,* в том, ни в друго́м слу́чае. —*pron.* **1,** *when standing alone* ни тот, ни друго́й. **2,** *fol. by* **of** ни оди́н из; никто́ из. —*conj.* **1,** *used with* **nor** ни..., ни...: *neither for nor against,* ни за, ни про́тив. **2,** (nor) то́же не: *neither do I,* я то́же не (хочу́, зна́ю, *etc.*). —**neither here nor there,** ни к селу́, ни к го́роду.

Nemesis *n.* Немези́да.

neoclassical *adj.* неокласси́ческий. —**neoclassicism,** *n.* неоклассици́зм.

neodymium *n.* нио́димий.

neolithic *adj.* неолити́ческий.

neologism *n.* неологи́зм.

neon *n.* нео́н. —*adj.* нео́новый.

neophyte *n.* **1,** *eccles.* неофи́т; новообращённый. **2,** (novice) новичо́к; неофи́т.

neoplasm *n.* новообразова́ние.

nephew *n.* племя́нник.

nephrite *n.* нефри́т.

nephritis *n.* нефри́т.

nepotism *n.* кумовство́; семе́йственность; непоти́зм.

Neptune *n.* Непту́н.

neptunium *n.* непту́ний.

nerve *n.* **1,** *physiol.* нерв. *Get on one's nerves,* де́йствовать на не́рвы (+ *dat.*). *Calm one's nerves,* успока́ивать не́рвы. **2,** (courage; daring) му́жество.

Lose one's nerve, стру́сить. **3,** *Strain every nerve,* напряга́ть все си́лы. **4,** *colloq.* (audacity) на́глость; наха́льство. —*adj.* не́рвный: *nerve centers,* не́рвные це́нтры.

nerve-racking *adj.* мучи́тельный.

nervous *adj.* не́рвный. *Be nervous,* волнова́ться; не́рвничать. —**nervous breakdown,** неврастени́я. —**nervous system,** не́рвная систе́ма.

nervousness *n.* не́рвность; нерво́зность.

nest *n.* гнездо́. —*v.i.* гнезди́ться. —**nest egg,** сбере́жения на чёрный день.

nestle *v.i.* **1,** (cuddle) прижима́ться; льну́ть. **2,** (lie sheltered) юти́ться.

nestling *n.* птене́ц.

net *n.* **1,** (for fishing, hunting, etc.) сеть. **2,** (for catching butterflies) сачо́к. **3,** (for the hair) се́тка. **4,** (for tennis, badminton, etc.) се́тка. **5,** (for hockey, soccer, etc.) воро́та. —*adj.* чи́стый: *net profit,* чи́стая при́быль. *The net result,* коне́чный результа́т. —*v.t.* **1,** (ensnare) пойма́ть (се́тью). **2,** (earn) выруча́ть.

nether *adj.* ни́жний. —**nethermost,** *adj.* са́мый ни́жний. —**nether world,** преиспо́дняя.

netting *n.* се́тка.

nettle *n.* крапи́ва. —*v.t.* уязвля́ть; уколо́ть.

network *n.* сеть.

neural *adj.* не́рвный.

neuralgia *n.* невралги́я. —**neuralgic,** *adj.* невралги́ческий.

neuritis *n.* воспале́ние не́рва; неври́т.

neurology *n.* невроло́гия. —**neurological,** *adj.* неврологи́ческий. —**neurologist,** *n.* невро́лог; невропато́лог.

neuron *n.* нейро́н.

neurosis *n.* невро́з.

neurosurgery *n.* нейрохирурги́я. —**neurosurgeon,** *n.* нейрохиру́рг.

neurotic *adj.* невроти́ческий.

neuter *adj.* сре́дний; сре́днего ро́да. —*n.* сре́дний род.

neutral *adj.* нейтра́льный. —*n.* **1,** (country) нейтра́льное госуда́рство. **2,** (gear) нейтра́льная ско́рость. —**neutrality,** *n.* нейтралите́т.

neutralize *v.t.* нейтрализова́ть. —**neutralization,** *n.* нейтрализа́ция.

neutron *n.* нейтро́н. —*adj.* нейтро́нный. —**neutron bomb,** нейтро́нная бо́мба.

never *adv.* никогда́: *he is never at home,* он никогда́ не быва́ет до́ма. ♦*Also rendered by* так и не: *I never found out,* я так и не узна́л(а). *He never regained consciousness,* он так и не пришёл в созна́ние. —**better late than never,** лу́чше по́здно, чем никогда́. —**never again,** никогда́ бо́льше: *I never saw him again,* я его́ бо́льше не ви́дел(а). —**never before,** никогда́ ещё. —**never mind,** *see* mind. —**now or never,** тепе́рь и́ли никогда́.

never-ending *adj.* несконча́емый; непрекраща́ющийся.

nevermore *adv.* никогда́ бо́льше.

nevertheless *adv.* тем не ме́нее.

new *adj.* но́вый. *What's new?,* что но́вого?; что слы́шно? —**New Deal,** Но́вый курс. —**new moon,** новолу́ние; молодо́й ме́сяц. —**new potatoes,** молодо́й карто́фель. —**New Testament,** Но́вый заве́т. —**new wine,** молодо́е вино́. —**New World,** Но́вый свет. —**New Year,** Но́вый год. *Happy New Year!,* с Но́вым го́дом!

newborn *adj.* новорождённый.

newcomer *n.* прише́лец; прие́зжий; новоприбы́вший.

Newfoundland *n.* (dog) водола́з.

newly *adv.* вновь: *the newly elected president,* вновь и́збранный президе́нт.

newlyweds *n.pl.* новобра́чные; молодожёны.

newness *n.* новизна́.

news *n.* но́вости; изве́стия; ве́сти. *Piece of news,* но́вость; изве́стие; весть. *It's news to me,* э́то для меня́ но́вость. —**news agency,** телегра́фное аге́нство.

newsboy *n.* газе́тчик.

newscast *n.* переда́ча после́дних изве́стий.

newsletter *n.* информацио́нный бюллете́нь.

newsman *n.* **1,** (reporter) репортёр; корреспонде́нт. **2,** (dealer) газе́тчик.

newspaper *n.* газе́та. —*adj.* газе́тный: *newspaper clipping,* газе́тная вы́резка. —**newspaperman,** *n.* журнали́ст.

newsprint *n.* газе́тная бума́га.

newsreel *n.* кинохро́ника.

newsstand *n.* газе́тный кио́ск.

newt *n.* трито́н.

next *adj.* **1,** (coming after the present one) сле́дующий: *who is next?,* кто сле́дующий? *The next stop,* сле́дующая остано́вка. *Next time,* в сле́дующий раз. **2,** *with intervals or periods of time* сле́дующий; бу́дущий: *next week,* на сле́дующей/бу́дущей неде́ле; *next year,* в сле́дующем (бу́дущем) году́. *Next summer,* сле́дующим ле́том. *The next day,* на сле́дующий (*or* на друго́й) день. *The next morning,* нау́тро. **3,** (adjacent) сосе́дний: *in the next room,* в сосе́дней ко́мнате. —*adv.* **1,** (after that) пото́м; да́льше: *what happened next?,* что случи́лось пото́м? *What next?,* (а) что же да́льше? **2,** (again) в сле́дующий раз; сно́ва: *when next we meet,* когда́ мы сно́ва встре́тимся. —**next to, 1,** (beside; alongside) у; ря́дом с; по́дле. **2,** (almost; nearly) почти́: *next to impossible,* почти́ невозмо́жно. **3,** (after; indicating that something is second best) по́сле. —**next to last,** предпосле́дний. —**next to nothing,** почти́ ничего́. *I bought it for next to nothing,* я купи́л э́то за гроши́. —**than the next,** оди́н друго́го (+ *comp. adj.*): *one taller than the next,* оди́н друго́го вы́ше.

next door ря́дом; в сосе́днем до́ме. *Next door to,* ря́дом с. *Next-door neighbor,* ближа́йший сосе́д. *The girl next door,* сосе́дская де́вушка.

nib *n.* ко́нчик; острие́.

nibble *v.t. & i.* **1,** (eat in small bites) грызть; обгрыза́ть. **2,** (bite, as of a fish) клева́ть. —*n.* **1,** (little bit) кусо́чек. **2,** (bite, in fishing): *not a nibble,* ни одна́ ры́ба не клю́нула.

nice *adj.* **1,** (fine; pleasant) хоро́ший; прия́тный: *nice weather,* хоро́шая/прия́тная пого́да. *Have a nice time,* хорошо́ провести́ вре́мя. **2,** (kind; gracious) ми́лый; любе́зный: *very nice of you,* о́чень ми́ло/любе́зно с ва́шей стороны́. **3,** (proper) прили́чный; поря́дочный. *A nice girl,* прили́чная де́вушка. *That's not nice,* э́то некраси́во. **4,** (well-executed) ло́вкий; уда́чный. **5,** (subtle) то́нкий: *a nice distinction,* то́нкое разли́чие. —**nice and...,** и краси́во: *it's nice and warm in here!,* здесь так тепло́ и краси́во!

nice-looking adj. миловидный; хорошенький.

nicely adv. хорошо; прилично.

nicety n. **1,** (fine point) тонкость. **2,** pl. (proprieties) приличия.

niche n. ниша.

nick n. щербина; царапина. —v.t. царапать. —**in the nick of time,** как раз вовремя; в самый последний момент.

nickel n. **1,** (element) никель. **2,** (five-cent coin) пяток. —adj. никелевый.

nickel plate никелировка. —**nickel-plate,** v.t. никелировать.

nickname n. прозвище; кличка. —v.t. прозывать; окрестить.

nicotine n. никотин.

niece n. племянница.

nifty adj., colloq. **1,** (splendid; first-rate) чудный. **2,** (stylish) шикарный.

niggardly adj. **1,** (stingy) скупой; скаредный. **2,** (meager) скудный.

niggling adj. мелочный.

nigh adv. **1,** (near) близко. Draw nigh, приближаться. **2,** fol. by onto (nearly) чуть ли не.

night n. ночь. At night, ночью; по ночам. Last night, вчера вечером; вчера ночью. Tomorrow night, завтра вечером. Saturday night, в субботу вечером. Spend the night, ночевать. —adj. ночной: night train, ночной поезд. —**good night!,** спокойной ночи!

night blindness куриная слепота.

nightcap n. **1,** (cap worn in bed) ночной колпак. **2,** colloq. (drink before retiring) стаканчик спиртного на ночь.

nightclothes n.pl. ночное бельё.

night club ночной клуб.

nightfall n. наступление ночи; наступление темноты. Before nightfall, засветло.

nightgown n. ночная рубашка; ночная сорочка.

nightingale n. соловей.

night light ночник.

nightly adj. еженощный. —adv. еженощно; каждую ночь.

nightmare n. кошмар. I had a nightmare, мне приснился кошмар; я видел во сне кошмар. —**nightmarish,** adj. кошмарный.

night owl полуночник.

night school вечерняя школа.

nightshade n. паслён.

nightshirt n. ночная рубашка; ночная сорочка.

nightstick n. дубинка.

night table ночной столик; тумбочка.

nighttime n. ночное время; ночь.

night watch ночной дозор; naval ночная вахта. —**night watchman,** ночной сторож.

nihilism n. нигилизм. —**nihilist,** n. нигилист. —**nihilistic,** adj. нигилистический.

nil n. нуль; ничего.

nimble adj. проворный.

nimbus n. нимб.

nincompoop n. простофиля; дуралей; растяпа.

nine adj. девять. —n. **1,** (cardinal number) девять. **2,** cards девятка.

nine hundred девятьсот. —**nine-hundredth,** adj. девятисотый.

nineteen n. & adj. девятнадцать. —**nineteenth,** adj. девятнадцатый.

ninety n. & adj. девяносто. —**ninetieth,** adj. девяностый.

ninny n. простофиля; дуралей.

ninth adj. девятый. —n. **1,** (ninth part) девятая часть. **2,** (fraction) девятая: one-ninth, одна девятая.

niobium n. ниобий.

nip v.t. **1,** (pinch) щипать; ущипнуть. **2,** fol. by off (snip; cut off) отщипывать. **3,** (damage, as of frost) побить; тронуть. **4,** (check; head off) пресекать. Nip in the bud, подавлять в зародыше; пресекать в корне. —n. **1,** (pinch) щипок. **2,** (cold) морозец: there is a nip in the air, воздух пахнет морозцем. **3,** colloq. (small drink) рюмочка. —**nip and tuck,** голова в голову.

nipper n. **1,** (claw) клешня. **2,** pl. (pincers) клещи.

nipple n. **1,** (on the breast) сосок. **2,** (for a nursing bottle) соска. **3,** (threaded pipe) ниппель.

nippy adj. холодненький.

nirvana n. нирвана.

nit n. гнида.

niter also, **nitre** n. селитра.

nitrate n. соль азотной кислоты; нитрат. ♦In compounds селитра: sodium nitrate, натриевая селитра. Silver nitrate, ляпис.

nitre n. = niter.

nitric adj. азотный. —**nitric acid,** азотная кислота. —**nitric oxide,** окись азота.

nitrite n. соль азотистой кислоты; нитрит.

nitrogen n. азот.

nitroglycerin also, **nitroglycerine** n. нитроглицерин.

nitrous adj. азотистый. —**nitrous acid,** азотистая кислота. —**nitrous oxide,** закись азота.

nitwit n., slang простофиля; балда; балбес.

no adv. **1,** (opp. of yes) нет: yes or no, да или нет. No, thank you, спасибо, нет. Not take no for an answer, не принимать отказа. He doesn't know how to say no, он не умеет отказывать. **2,** with comp. adjectives (not at all) не: no bigger than a postage stamp, не больше почтовой марки. She is no better today, ей сегодня (нисколько) не лучше. —adj. никакой: no comment, никаких комментариев. There can be no doubt, не может быть никакого сомнения. She is no beauty, никакая она не красавица. ♦ Often rendered by не or нет: spare no effort, не щадить усилий. I have no time, у меня нет времени. No smoking!, не курить! —n. отказ: an emphatic "no", решительный отказ. The noes have it, большинство против.

nobelium n. нобелий.

Nobel Prize Нобелевская премия.

nobility n. **1,** (aristocracy) дворянство. **2,** (quality of being noble) благородство.

noble adj. благородный: a noble act, благородный поступок. Of noble birth, родовитый; благородного происхождения. —n. дворянин.

nobleman n. дворянин.

nobody pron. никто: nobody knows, никто не знает. ♦ With infinitives некого: there was nobody to send to the store, послать в магазин было некого. He has nobody to play with, ему не с кем играть. There is nobody to replace him, некого его заменить. —n. ничтожество; пустое место.

nocturnal adj. ночной.

nocturne n. ноктюрн.

nod *n.* кивóк. —*v.t.* кивáть; качáть (головóй). *Nod assent,* утвердительно кивнýть головóй. —*v.i.* **1,** (nod one's head) кивáть; качáть головóй. **2,** (drowse) клевáть нóсом. —**nodding acquaintance,** шáпочное знакóмство.

node *n.* ýзел. *Lymph nodes,* лимфатические узлы.

nodule *n.* узелóк.

Noel *n.* рождествó.

noggin *n., colloq.* башкá.

noise *n.* шум. *Make noise,* шумéть. —**noiseless,** *adj.* бесшýмный. —**noisily,** *adv.* шýмно.

noisome *adj.* **1,** (foul) протИвный. **2,** (harmful) врéдный.

noisy *adj.* шýмный; шумлИвый. *It is very noisy in here,* здесь óчень шýмно.

nomad *n.* кочéвник. —**nomadic,** *adj.* кочевóй; кочýющий.

no man's land ничья земля.

nomenclature *n.* номенклатýра.

nominal *adj.* номинáльный.

nominate *v.t.* выдвигáть (на дóлжность; на прéмию, etc.); выставлять (чью-нибудь) кандидатýру.

nomination *n.* кандидатýра; выдвижéние кандидáтом. *Second the nomination,* поддéрживать кандидатýру (когó-нибудь). *Decline the nomination,* откáзывать в выдвижéнии кандидáтом. *Seek the Presidential nomination,* добивáться выдвижéния кандидáтом на пост президéнта.

nominative *adj.* именительный: *nominative case,* именительный падéж.

nominee *n.* кандидáт.

nonaggression *n.* ненападéние. *Nonaggression pact,* пакт о ненападéнии.

nonalcoholic *adj.* безалкогóльный.

nonaligned *adj.* неприсоединившийся. —**nonalignment,** *n.* неприсоединéние.

nonbeliever *n.* невéрующий.

nonbelligerent *adj.* невоюющий.

nonbreakable *adj.* небьющийся.

nonchalance *n.* беззабóтность; непринуждённость. —**nonchalant,** *adj.* беззабóтный; непринуждённый.

noncombatant *n. & adj.* нестроевóй.

noncommissioned officer сержáнт; ýнтерофицéр.

noncommittal *adj.* уклóнчивый.

nonconductor *n.* непроводник.

noncontagious *adj.* незарáзный.

nondescript *adj.* непримéтный; ни то ни сё.

nondrinker *n.* непьющий.

none *pron.* **1,** (no one) никтó: *none of them answered,* никтó их не отвéтил. *None of us wanted to go,* никтó из нас не хотéл пойти. **2,** (not any) ни один: *none of them were any good,* ни один из них нé был хорóш. *None of this concerns me,* всё это меня не касáется. *He would have none of it,* он об этом и слышать не хотéл. —*adv.* нискóлько; ничýть: *he is none the worse for it,* емý от этого нискóлько не хýже. —**none other than,** не кто инóй, как.

nonentity *n.* ничтóжество; пустóе мéсто.

nonessential *adj. Nonessential items,* вéщи, в котóрых нет абсолютной необходимости.

nonetheless *adv.* тем не мéнее.

nonexistence *n.* небытиé. —**nonexistent,** *adj.* несуществующий.

nonferrous *adj.* цветнóй.

nonflammable *adj.* несгорáемый; невоспламеняемый.

nonfulfillment *n.* невыполнéние.

noninterference *n.* невмешáтельство.

nonintervention *n.* невмешáтельство.

nonpayment *n.* неуплáта; неплатёж.

nonperishable *adj.* непóртящийся.

nonplus *v.t.* стáвить в тупик; озадáчивать.

nonproductive *adj.* непроизводительный.

nonproliferation *n.* нераспространéние.

nonrecognition *n.* непризнáние.

non-Russian *adj.* нерýсский.

nonsense *n.* ерундá; чепухá; глýпости; вздор. —**nonsensical,** *adj.* глýпый; вздóрный.

nonsmoker *n.* некурящий.

nonstop *adj.* безостанóвочный; беспосáдочный. —*adv.* безостанóвочно.

nonvoting *adj. Nonvoting member,* член с совещáтельным гóлосом.

nonworking *adj.* нерабóчий.

noodle *n.* **1,** (food) лапшá. *Noodle pudding,* лапшéвник. *Noodle soup,* лапшá. **2,** *slang* (head) башкá.

nook *n.* уголóк; закоýлок.

noon *n.* пóлдень. —*adj.* [*also,* **noonday**] полýденный; полднéвный.

no one никтó. *See* **nobody.**

noose *n.* пéтля.

nor *conj.* **1,** (neither) тóже: *nor do I; nor am I,* я тóже. *Nor is there any doubt that...,* нет сомнéния и в том, что... **2,** (and besides) да и (вообщé): *I have not seen him, nor do I wish to,* я егó не видел(а), да и вообщé не хочý. —**neither... nor,** ни..., ни...: *neither for nor against,* ни за, ни прóтив.

norm *n.* нóрма; нxорматив.

normal *adj.* нормáльный. —*n.* **1,** (natural condition) нормáльное состояние. *Return to normal,* войти в нормáльную колéю; снóва налáживаться. **2,** *math.* нормáль.

normalcy *n.* нормáльность.

normalize *v.t.* нормализовáть. —**normalization,** *n.* нормализáция.

normally *adv.* **1,** (in a normal manner) нормáльно. **2,** (ordinarily) обычно.

Norman *adj.* нормáндский: *Norman Conquest,* Нормáндское завоевáние Áнглии.

normative *adj.* нормативный.

Norse *adj.* нормáнский. —**Norseman,** *n.* номáнн.

north *n.* сéвер. —*adj.* сéверный: *north wind,* сéверный вéтер. —*adv.* на сéвер; к сéверу. *North of,* к сéверу от; сéвернее (+ *gen.*).

northeast *n.* сéверо-востóк. —*adj.* сéверо-востóчный. —*adv.* к сéверо-востóку; на сéверо-востóк.

northeaster *n.* норд-óст.

northeasterly *adj.* сéверо-востóчный.

northeastern *adj.* сéверо-востóчный.

northerly *adj.* сéверный.

northern *adj.* сéверный.

northerner *n.* северянин.

northern lights сéверное сияние.

northernmost *adj.* сáмый сéверный.

North Pole Сéверный пóлюс.

North Star Полярная звездá.

northward *adv.* к сéверу. —*adj.* сéверный.

northwest *n.* сéверо-зáпад. —*adj.* сéверо-зáпадный. —*adv.* к северо-западу; на северо-запад.

northwester *n.* норд-вест.

northwesterly *adj.* северо-западный.

northwestern *adj.* северо-западный.

Norwegian *adj.* норвежский. —*n.* **1,** (person) норвежец; норвежка. **2,** (language) норвежский язык.

nose *n.* **1,** (of a person) нос. *Speak through one's nose,* говорить в нос. **2,** (of a ship or aircraft) нос. —*v.i.* [*usu.* **nose about** *or* **around**] разнюхивать. —**as plain as the nose on your face,** ясный как божий день. —**follow one's nose,** идти куда глаза глядят. —**have a nose for,** иметь нюх на. —**lead by the nose,** вести на поводу. —**look down one's nose at,** смотреть свысока на. —**not see farther than the end of one's nose,** не видеть дальше своего носа. —**on the nose,** в (самую) точку. —**pay through the nose,** платить бешеные деньги; платить втридорога. —**poke one's nose into someone else's affairs,** совать нос в чужие дела. —**turn up one's nose,** задирать нос. —**under one's (very) nose,** под самым носом; под носом. *From under one's very nose,* из-под самого носа.

nosebleed *n.* кровотечение из носу.

nose cone носовой конус.

nose dive 1, *aero.* пикирование. **2,** (sharp drop) резкое падение.

nose drops капли от насморка.

nosegay *n.* букетик цветов.

nosey *adj.* = **nosy.**

nostalgia *n.* ностальгия. —**nostalgic,** *adj.* ностальгический. *Feel nostalgic,* испытывать ностальгию.

nostril *n.* ноздря.

nosy *also,* **nosey** *adj.* (не в меру) любопытный.

not *adv.* **1,** *expressing negation* не: *not today,* не сегодня. *He did not come,* он не пришёл. *I am not angry,* я не сердит. **2,** *expressing the absence of something* нет: *he is not here,* его нет. **3,** *in replies* нет: *why not?,* почему нет? *Not yet,* нет ещё. *I hope not,* надеюсь, что нет. —**not a ...,** ни; ни один: *not a word,* ни (одного) слова. —**not at all, 1,** (not in the least) совсем не; нисколько не: *not at all tired,* совсем/нисколько не устал. *Am I disturbing you?, No, not at all,* я вам не мешаю? Нет, что вы! **2,** *in reply to an expression of thanks* пожалуйста!; не за что! —**not that,** не то, чтобы: *it's not that I'm ill, I'm just tired,* я не то, что болен, а просто устал. *Not that I know of,* насколько мне известно, нет. —**or not,** или нет: *are you going or not?,* вы идёте или нет? *Like it or not,* хочешь не хочешь.

notable *adj.* **1,** (noteworthy) примечательный. **2,** (distinguished) знатный. —*n., usu. pl.* знатные люди.

notably *adv.* **1,** (strikingly) удивительно. **2,** (particularly) особенно.

notarize *v.t.* засвидетельствовать.

notary *n.* нотариус. *Also,* **notary public.**

notation *n.* **1,** (note) заметка; запись. **2,** (system of signs or symbols) нотация: *chess notation,* шахматная нотация.

notch *n.* **1,** (on a flat surface) зарубка. **2,** (on a cutting edge) зазубрина. **3,** (defile) теснина. —*v.t.* зарубать; зазубривать.

note *n.* **1,** (short informal letter) записка. **2,** (official communication between governments) нота. **3,** *usu. pl.* (something written down for future reference)

записка; заметка; запись: *take/make notes,* делать заметки/записи. *Lecture from notes,* читать лекцию по записям. *Take notes of a lecture,* записывать лекцию. **4,** *pl.* (record of impressions) заметки: *travel notes,* путевые заметки. **5,** (explanatory comment) заметка: *note in the margin,* заметка на полях. *Explanatory note,* примечание. **6,** *music* нота: *high note,* высокая нота. **7,** (negotiable instrument) билет: *bank note,* кредитный билет; *treasury note,* казначейский билет. *Promissory note,* вексель; долговое обязательство. **8,** (trace; touch) нотка: *note of anxiety,* нотка беспокойства. **9,** (notice; attention) внимание: *worthy of note,* достойный внимания. **10,** (distinction) известность. *A writer of note,* небезызвестный писатель. —*v.t.* **1,** (notice) замечать. **2,** (make mention of; point out) отмечать. **3,** *fol. by* **down** (record) записывать. —**compare notes,** обмениваться впечатлениями. —**make a note of,** записывать; отмечать. —**take note of, 1,** (make a mental note of) брать на заметку. **2,** (notice; pay attention to) обращать внимание на.

notebook *n.* тетрадь; записная книжка.

noted *adj.* известный; знаменитый.

notepaper *n.* почтовая бумага.

noteworthy *adj.* примечательный; достопримечательный.

nothing *n.* **1,** (not anything) ничего: *what did you do? Nothing,* что ты сделал? Ничего. *Nothing of the kind,* ничего подобного. *He said nothing,* он ничего не сказал. *Be left with nothing,* остаться ни с чем. ♦*Less commonly* ничто: *nothing bothers him,* ничто не беспокоит его. *That's nothing compared to...,* это ничто по сравнению с... ♦*Before infinitives* нечего: *I have nothing to say,* мне нечего сказать. *You have nothing to fear,* вам нечего бояться. **2,** *preceded by* **a** (nonentity) ничто; ничтожество. —*adv.* совсем не: *nothing like it used to be,* совсем не похож на то, что было. —**for nothing, 1,** (free; at no cost) бесплатно; даром. **2,** (to no avail) напрасно; даром; зря. **3,** (for no reason) зря. —**have nothing to do with, 1,** (bear no relation to) не иметь никакого отношения к; совсем не касаться. **2,** (refuse to associate with) не желать иметь ничего общего с. —**to say nothing of,** не говоря уже о.

notice *v.t.* замечать. —*n.* **1,** (attention) внимание: *take notice of,* обращать внимание на. *Take no notice of,* оставить без внимания. *Bring to someone's notice,* доводить до чьего-нибудь сведения. **2,** (notification) извещение; уведомление; предупреждение. *Dismissal notice,* уведомление об увольнении. *Give notice to,* ставить (кого-нибудь) в известность. *Give notice of,* сделать предупреждение о. *Until further notice,* впредь до дальнейшего уведомления; до особого распоряжения. *I realize this is very short notice,* я понимаю, что даю вам мало времени. **3,** (announcement) объявление. **4,** (review) отзыв: *receive favorable notices,* получить благоприятные отзывы. —**at a moment's notice,** по первому требованию; в любой момент.

noticeable *adj.* заметный. —**noticeably,** *adv.* заметно.

notification *n.* **1,** (act of notifying) извещение; уведомление; осведомление; оповещение. **2,** (notice given or received) извещение; уведомление.

notify v.t. извещать; уведомлять; осведомлять; оповещать.

notion n. **1,** (general idea) понятие; представление. **2,** pl. (small miscellaneous articles) галантерея.

notoriety n. известность.

notorious adj. заведомый; пресловутый.

notwithstanding adv. тем не менее. —prep. несмотря на.

nougat n. нуга.

nought n. = **naught.**

noun n. существительное; имя существительное. Common noun, имя нарицательное. Proper noun, имя собственное.

nourish v.t. питать. —**nourishing,** adj. питательный. —**nourishment,** n. питание.

nova n. новая звезда.

novel n. роман. —adj. новый; необыкновенный. —**novelist,** n. романист.

novella n. новелла.

novelty n. **1,** (quality of being new) новизна; новость. **2,** (something new) новость; новинка; новшество.

November n. ноябрь. —adj. ноябрьский.

novice n. **1,** (beginner) новичок. **2,** eccles. послушник

novocaine n. новокаин.

now adv. **1,** (at the present time) теперь; сейчас. **2,** (at once) сейчас; сейчас же. —particle ну: come now!, ну вот ещё! —**by now,** уже: he should have been here by now, он уже должен быть здесь. —**for now,** пока. —**from now on,** впредь; отныне. —**now and then,** время от времени; кое-когда. —**now that...,** теперь, когда... —**until now,** до сих пор.

nowadays adv. в наше время; в теперешнее время; нынче.

nowhere adv. **1,** (in no place) нигде. **2,** (to no place) никуда. ♦With infinitives негде; некуда: nowhere to sit, негде сесть; nowhere to go, некуда поехать. —**from out of nowhere,** откуда ни возьмись. —**get nowhere,** ничего не добиться. —**in the middle of nowhere,** у чёрта на куличках. —**lead nowhere,** ни к чему не привести. —**nowhere near,** отнюдь не: nowhere near as big as you think, отнюдь не такой большой, как вы думаете.

noxious adj. вредный; пагубный.

nozzle n. сопло; брандспойт.

nth adj. энный: to the nth degree, в энной степени.

nuance n. оттенок; нюанс.

nub n. **1,** (knob; lump) шишка. **2,** colloq. (gist; point) суть.

nuclear adj. ядерный: nuclear energy/war, ядерная энергия/война. Nuclear-free zone, безъядерная зона.

nucleus n. ядро.

nude adj. нагой; голый; обнажённый. —n. обнажённая фигура. —**in the nude,** в голом виде.

nudge v.t. подталкивать локтем. —n. толчок локтем.

nudity n. нагота.

nugget n. самородок.

nuisance n. **1,** (annoying thing) досада: what a nuisance!, какая досада! **2,** (pest) надоеда. Make a nuisance of oneself, проказничать; озорничать.

null adj. [often **null and void**] недействительный; не имеющий законной силы.

nullification n. аннулирование.

nullify v.t. **1,** (make null and void) аннулировать. **2,** (negate) сводить на нет or к нулю.

numb adj. **1,** (from the cold) окоченелый; окоченевший. **2,** (from paralysis) онемелый. **3,** (from emotion) оцепенелый. Become numb, (о)коченеть; (о)неметь; (о)цепенеть. —v.t. сковывать: the cold numbed our hands, холод сковал нам руки.

number n. **1,** (numeral) число: even number, чётное число. Theory of numbers, теория чисел. **2,** (numeral used to identify something) номер: telephone number, номер телефона. **3,** (quantity) число; количество. **4,** (indefinite quantity) ряд: in a number of cases, в ряде случаев. **5,** (item on a musical program) номер. **6,** gram. (singular or plural) число. —v.t. **1,** (assign numbers to) нумеровать. **2,** (amount to; contain) насчитывать: the garrison numbered 300 men, гарнизон насчитывал триста человек. **3,** fol. by **among** (count among) причислять (к); относить к числу (+ gen.). **4,** His days are numbered, его дни сочтены. —v.i. **1,** (reach an amount) исчисляться: number in the thousands, исчисляться тысячами. **2,** fol. by **among** (be one of) принадлежать к числу (+ gen.). —**without number,** без числа; без счёта.

numbered adj. нумерованный; номерной.

numbering n. нумерация. Numbering machine, нумератор.

numberless adj. бесчисленный.

Numbers n., Bib. Числа.

numbness n. онемение.

numeral n. **1,** (number) цифра. Roman numerals, римские цифры. **2,** gram. (Russian part of speech) (имя) числительное.

numeration n. нумерация.

numerator n. числитель.

numerical adj. числовой; численный; цифровой. Numerical superiority, численное превосходство. Numerical data, цифровые данные. —**numerically,** adv. численно.

numerous adj. многочисленный.

numismatics n. нумизматика. —**numismatic,** adj. нумизматический. —**numismatist,** n. нумизмат.

numskull n. олух; тупица; болван.

nun n. монахиня.

nuncio n. нунций.

nunnery n. женский монастырь.

nuptial adj. брачный; свадебный. —**nuptials,** n.pl. свадьба.

nurse n. **1,** (one who tends the sick) медсестра; сиделка. Male nurse, брат милосердия. **2,** (nursemaid) няня. —v.t. **1,** (suckle) кормить. Nursing mother, кормящая мать. **2,** (take care of) ухаживать за; нянчить. **3,** (treat gently) беречь. **4,** (take steps to cure, as a cold) лечить. **5,** (harbor, as a grudge) питать; таить.

nursemaid n. няня; нянька.

nursery n. **1,** (children's room) детская. **2,** (day nursery) ясли. **3,** (place where plants are raised) питомник. —**nursery rhymes,** детские песенки; детские стишки. —**nursery school,** детский сад.

nursing n. **1,** (suckling) кормление (грудью). **2,** (profession) уход за больными. Study nursing, учиться на медсестру. School of nursing, школа медсестёр. —**nursing bottle,** рожок. —**nursing home,** лечебница.

nurture *v.t.* лелеять: *nurture a child/hope,* лелеять ребёнка/надежду.

nut *n.* **1,** (fruit) орех. **2,** (what goes with a bolt) гайка. **3,** *slang* (crazy person) чудак; сумасброд; псих.

nutcracker *n.* щипцы для орехов.

nuthatch *n.* поползень.

nutmeg *n.* **1,** (seed) мускатный орех; мускат. **2,** (tree) мускатник; мускатное дерево. —*adj.* мускатный.

nutria *n.* нутрия.

nutrient *n.* питательное вещество.

nutrition *n.* **1,** (nourishment) питание. **2,** (study of proper diet) диететика. —**nutritional,** *adj.* пищевой;

питательный. —**nutritious,** *adj.* питательный.

nuts *adj., slang* **1,** (crazy) обалделый. **2,** *fol. by* **about** (mad about) без ума (от). —*interj., slang* тьфу!

nutshell *n., in* **in a nutshell,** вкратце; в двух словах; в кратких словах.

nutty *adj.* **1,** (having or made with nuts) ореховый. **2,** *slang* (silly) глупый.

nuzzle *v.t.* тереться носом о.

nylon *n.* **1,** (fabric) нейлон. **2,** *pl.* (stockings) нейлоновые чулки. —*adj.* нейлоновый.

nymph *n.* нимфа.

nymphomania *n.* нимфомания. —**nymphomaniac,** *n.* нимфоманка.

O

O, o пятнадцатая буква английского алфавита. —*n.* (zero) нуль. —*interj.* о!; ах!

oaf *n.* дурень; тупица; олух. —**oafish,** *adj.* придурковатый.

oak *n.* дуб. —*adj.* дубовый.

oakum *n.* пакля.

oar *n.* весло. —**oarlock,** *n.* уключина.

oarsman *n.* гребец.

oasis *n.* оазис.

oat *n., usu. pl.* овёс. —*adj.* овсяный.

oath *n.* **1,** (solemn promise) присяга; клятва. *Take the oath,* приносить *or* принимать присягу. **2,** (swearword) проклятие.

oatmeal *n.* овсяная каша; овсяная крупа; овсянка; толокно; геркулес.

obdurate *adj.* **1,** (obstinate) упрямый. **2,** (hardhearted) чёрствый. —**obduracy,** *n.* упрямство.

obedient *adj.* послушный. —**obedience,** *n.* послушание; повиновение.

obeisance *n.* **1,** (bow) поклон. **2,** (deference) почтение.

obelisk *n.* обелиск.

obese *adj.* полный; тучный; грузный. —**obesity,** *n.* тучность; ожирение; полнота.

obey *v.t.* **1,** (mind; heed) слушаться (+ *gen.*); повиноваться (+ *dat.*). **2,** (observe; carry out) подчиняться (+ *dat.*): *obey an order/the law/,* подчиняться приказу/закону. —*v.i.* слушаться.

obfuscate *v.t.* затемнять. —**obfuscation,** *n.* затемнение.

obituary *n.* некролог.

object[1] (ob-jekt) *n.* **1,** (material thing) предмет. **2,** (that to which something is directed) объект; предмет. **3,** (goal; purpose) цель. **4,** *gram.* дополнение.

object[2] (ub-jekt) *v.i.* возражать: *no one objected,* никто не возражал.

objection *n.* возражение. *Have no objection,* не

возражать; не иметь возражений; ничего не иметь против.

objectionable *adj.* нежелательный; неприятный.

objective *n.* **1,** (goal; purpose) цель. **2,** *mil.* объект. —*adj.* объективный. —**objective case,** объектный падеж.

objectivity *n.* объективность.

object lesson наглядный урок.

obligate *v.t.* обязывать. —**obligated,** *adj.* обязанный.

obligation *n.* обязательство. *Under an obligation,* обязан. *Under no obligation,* нисколько не обязан.

obligatory *adj.* обязательный.

oblige *v.t.* **1,** (compel) обязывать. **2,** (place under a debt of gratitude) обязывать: *you will oblige me greatly,* вы меня очень обяжете. **3,** (do a favor for): *could you oblige me with an answer?,* вы не могли бы дать мне ответ? —**obliged,** *adj.* обязанный.

obliging *adj.* услужливый; предупредительный.

oblique *adj.* **1,** (slanting) косой. **2,** (indirect) косвенный.

obliquely *adv.* **1,** (at an angle) косо; наискось; вкось. **2,** (indirectly) косвенно.

obliterate *v.t.* **1,** (efface) изглаживать. **2,** (wipe out) уничтожать. —**obliteration,** *n.* уничтожение.

oblivion *n.* забвение. *Sink into oblivion,* кануть в вечность.

oblivious *adj.* [*usu.* **oblivious of** *or* **to**] не имеющий понятия о; в полном неведении (относительно).

oblong *adj.* продолговатый. —*n.* продолговатая фигура.

obloquy *n.* **1,** (abusive language) злословие. **2,** (disgrace) позор.

obnoxious *adj.* неприятный; противный.

oboe *n.* гобой. —**oboist,** *n.* гобоист.

obscene *adj.* непристойный. —**obscenity,** *n.* непристойность.

obscurant *n.* мракобес; обскурант. —**obscuran-**

tism, *n.* мракобесие; обскурантизм.

obscure *adj.* **1,** (dark) тёмный. **2,** (unclear; vague) неясный; смутный. **3,** (hardly known) безвестный. —*v.t.* затемнять.

obscurity *n.* **1,** (lack of clarity) неясность. **2,** (state of being unknown) неизвестность; безвестность.

obsequious *adj.* угодливый; раболепный; подобострастный. —**obsequiousness,** *n.* угодливость; раболепие; подобострастие.

observable *adj.* заметный.

observance *n.* **1,** (compliance) соблюдение. **2,** (celebration) празднование.

observant *adj.* **1,** (perceptive) наблюдательный. **2,** (religious) благочестивый. **3,** *fol. by* **of** (strict in observing something) соблюдающий.

observation *n.* **1,** (act of observing) наблюдение: *keep under observation,* держать под наблюдением. **2,** *usu. pl.* (result of observing) наблюдение: *personal observations,* личные наблюдения. **3,** (remark) замечание. —**observation post,** наблюдательный пункт.

observatory *n.* обсерватория.

observe *v.t.* **1,** (watch) наблюдать: *observe the sunrise,* наблюдать восход солнца. **2,** (notice) замечать. **3,** (comply with; obey) соблюдать: *observe the law,* соблюдать закон. *Observe neutrality,* поддерживать нейтралитет. **4,** (remark) замечать. **5,** (celebrate) отмечать; праздновать.

observer *n.* наблюдатель.

obsess *v.t.* преследовать. *Obsessed by,* одержимый (+ *instr.*).

obsession *n.* одержимость. —**obsessive,** *adj.* навязчивый.

obsolescent *adj.* устаревающий; отживающий. —**obsolescence,** *n.* моральный износ.

obsolete *adj.* устарелый; устаревший.

obstacle *n.* препятствие. —**obstacle course,** полоса препятствий.

obstetrics *n.* акушерство. —**obstetric,** *adj.* акушерский. —**obstetrician,** *n.* акушер.

obstinate *adj.* упрямый. —**obstinacy,** *n.* упрямство.

obstreperous *adj.* шумный; буйный; непокорный.

obstruct *v.t.* **1,** (bar; block) преграждать; заграждать; загораживать. **2,** (hinder; impede) препятствовать. **3,** (cut off from sight) заслонять.

obstruction *n.* **1,** (blocking) преграждение. **2,** (impediment) преграда; заграждение. **3,** (delaying tactics) обструкция. **4,** *med.* непроходимость; закупорка.

obstructionism *n.* обструкционизм.

obstructionist *n.* обструкционист. —*adj.* обструкционный.

obtain *v.t.* получать; доставать; добывать. —*v.i.* (be in effect) существовать.

obtrude *v.t.* **1,** (thrust forward) высовывать. **2,** (thrust forward unasked) навязывать. —*v.i.* навязываться; вторгаться. —**obtrusive,** *adj.* навязчивый.

obtuse *adj.* тупой. *Obtuse angle,* тупой угол. —**obtuseness,** *n.* тупость.

obverse *adj.* лицевой. —*n.* лицевая сторона.

obviate *v.t.* устранять; предупреждать.

obvious *adj.* очевидный; явный. —**obviously,** *adv.* очевидно; явно.

ocarina *n.* окарина.

occasion *n.* **1,** (event) событие: *this happy occasion,* это радостное событие. **2,** (time when something occurs) случай: *on the occasion of,* по случаю (+ *gen.*). **3,** (particular time) раз: *on several occasions,* несколько раз. **4,** (opportunity) случай: *take the occasion,* пользоваться случаем. **5,** (cause; grounds) повод: *occasion for a quarrel,* повод для ссоры. —*v.t.* вызывать; обусловливать. —**have occasion to,** приходиться (+ *dat.*): *I frequently had occasion to...,* мне часто приходилось (+ *inf.*). —**on occasion,** от случая к случаю. —**rise to the occasion,** быть на высоте положения.

occasional *adj.* бывающий время от времени. *I receive an occasional letter from her,* время от времени я получаю от неё письмо. —**occasionally,** *adv.* иногда; время от времени.

occident *n.,* *often cap.* Запад. —**occidental,** *adj.* западный.

occlude *v.t.* закупоривать. —**occlusion,** *n.* закупорка.

occult *adj.* таинственный; оккультный. —**occultism,** *n.* оккультизм.

occupancy *n.* занятие; заселение.

occupant *n.* жилец.

occupation *n.* **1,** (act of occupying) занятие. **2,** *mil.* оккупация. *Army of occupation,* оккупационная армия. **3,** (what one does with one's time) занятие. **4,** (type of work) занятие; профессия. *What is your occupation?,* чем вы занимаетесь?; кем вы работаете?

occupational *adj.* профессиональный. —**occupational therapy,** трудовая терапия.

occupy *v.t.* **1,** (fill; take up; inhabit) занимать: *occupy a seat/house/post,* занимать место/дом/пост. *Be occupied with,* заниматься (+ *instr.*); быть занятым (+ *instr.*). **2,** *mil.* оккупировать; занимать.

occur *v.i.* **1,** (happen) случаться; происходить. **2,** (exist; be found) встречаться; водиться. **3,** *fol. by* **to** (come to mind) приходить в голову (+ *dat.*).

occurrence *n.* случай; происшествие; явление.

ocean *n.* океан. —*adj.* океанский: *ocean liner,* океанский пароход. —**oceanic,** *adj.* океанский.

oceanography *n.* океанография. —**oceanographer,** *n.* океанограф. —**oceanographic,** *adj.* океанографический.

ocelot *n.* оцелот.

ocher *also,* **ochre** *n.* охра.

o'clock *adv.,* *in* **one o'clock,** час; **two o'clock,** два часа; **five o'clock,** пять часов, *etc.*

octagon *n.* восьмиугольник. —**octagonal,** *adj.* восьмиугольный.

octahedron *n.* восьмигранник. —**octahedral,** *adj.* восьмигранный.

octane *n.* октан.

octave *n.* октава.

octavo *n.* восьмушка.

octet *n.* октет.

October *n.* октябрь. —*adj.* октябрьский.

octopus *n.* осьминог; восьминог; спрут.

ocular *adj.* глазной.

oculist *n.* окулист.

odd *adj.* **1,** (strange; queer) странный: *odd name/behavior,* странное имя/поведение. **2,** (not even) нечётный: *odd number,* нечётное число. **3,** (not paired) непарный. **4,** (one of an incomplete set) разрозненный. **5,** (about; some) с ли́шним: *forty odd years ago,* со́рок с ли́шним лет тому́ наза́д. **6,** (occasional) случа́йный: *odd jobs,* случа́йная рабо́та.

oddity *n.* **1,** (strangeness) стра́нность. **2,** (strange person or thing) стра́нный челове́к; стра́нное де́ло; чуда́к.

oddly *adv.* стра́нно. *Oddly enough,* как ни стра́нно.

odds *n.pl.* ша́нсы: *the odds are in your favor,* ша́нсы на ва́шей стороне́. *The odds are that...,* скоре́е всего́... *Against overwhelming odds,* про́тив значи́тельно превосходя́щих сил. —**at odds,** в ссо́ре; не в лада́х. —**by all odds,** несомне́нно; бесспо́рно. —**give odds,** дать не́сколько очко́в вперёд. —**odds and ends,** ме́лкие ве́щи; ме́лочь.

ode *n.* о́да.

odious *adj.* гну́сный; ненави́стный; одио́зный.

odometer *n.* одо́метр.

odontology *n.* одонтоло́гия.

odor *also,* **odour** *n.* за́пах.

odoriferous *adj.* души́стый; паху́чий.

odorless *also,* **odourless** *adj.* не име́ющий за́паха.

odorous *adj.* души́стый; паху́чий.

odour *n.* = **odor.** —**odourless,** *adj.* = **odorless.**

odyssey *n.* одиссе́я.

oesophagus *n.* = **esophagus.**

of *prep.* **1,** (denoting possession, relation, a part of something, the contents of something) *rendered by the gen. case: the name of the book,* назва́ние кни́ги; *a glass of water,* стака́н воды́; *a pound of sugar,* фунт са́хару. **2,** (with the names of cities or countries) *not rendered in Russian (nom. case follows): the city of Moscow,* го́род Москва́; *the State of Israel,* Госуда́рство Изра́иль; *the Kingdom of Denmark,* Короле́вство Да́ния; *in the Republic of India,* в Респу́блике И́ндия. **3,** (from; denoting origin or material) из: *a statue of bronze,* ста́туя из бро́нзы. **4,** (out of; out of a total of) из: *some of us,* не́которые из нас. **5,** (on one's part) с (чьей-нибудь) стороны́: *very kind of you,* о́чень любе́зно с ва́шей стороны́. **6,** (indicating direction from) от: *south of the city,* к ю́гу от го́рода. **7,** (indicating cause) от: *die of cancer,* умира́ть от ра́ка. **8,** (about; concerning) о: *news of his arrival,* весть о его́ прие́зде. *Think a great deal of oneself,* мно́го ду́мать о себе́. **9,** (in telling time) без; *twenty of two,* без двадцати́ два. **10,** (with dates) от: *my letter of May 5th,* моё письмо́ от пя́того ма́я. **11,** *with various miscellaneous verbs: smell of onions,* па́хнуть лу́ком; *accuse someone of stealing,* обвиня́ть кого́-нибудь в кра́же. *He was cured of tuberculosis,* он вы́лечился от туберкулёза. *She was robbed of her purse and glasses,* у неё укра́ли су́мку и очки́.

off *adv.* Usu. *rendered by a prefixed verb: take off,* снима́ть; *cut off,* отреза́ть; *jump off,* спры́гивать; *see off,* провожа́ть. —*adj.* **1,** (not turned on) вы́ключенный: *the light is off,* свет вы́ключен. **2,** (canceled): *The wedding is off,* сва́дьба не состои́тся. *The deal is off,* де́ло расстро́илось. **3,** (free from one's job): *I'm off on Friday,* пя́тница у меня́ выходно́й. **4,** (in error): *be off in one's calculations,* ошиби́ться в расчётах. **5,** (away; into the future): *Christmas is two months off,* до рождества́ оста́лось два ме́сяца. **6,** (in a certain state): *well off,* обеспе́ченный. *You'd be better off if you stayed home,* вам бы лу́чше оста́ться до́ма. **7,** (about to go somewhere): *well, I'm off to town,* ну, пошёл (пошла́) в го́род. **8,** (declining): *production is*

off, произво́дство упа́ло. —*prep.* **1,** (away from) с: *the train went off the tracks,* по́езд сошёл с ре́льсов. *Keep off the grass!,* по траве́ не ходи́ть! **2,** (distant from) от: *100 miles off the coast,* в ста ми́лях от бе́рега. *Just off the main square,* в двух шага́х от гла́вной пло́щади. **3,** (deviating from) от: *stray off course,* отклоня́ться от ку́рса. **4,** (below) ни́же: *ten dollars off the usual price,* де́сять до́лларов ни́же обы́чной цены́. **5,** *with various nouns: off duty,* не дежу́рит; *off balance,* потеря́вший равнове́сие; *off limits,* закры́т; *off one's game,* не в фо́рме. —*interj.* вон; прочь! *Off with you!,* убира́йтесь вон! —**off and on,** с переры́вами.

offal *n.* требуха́.

off-color *also,* **off-colour** *adj.* **1,** (imperfect, as of a gem) нечи́стой воды́. **2,** (risqué) риско́ванный; сомни́тельный.

offence *n.* = **offense.**

offend *v.t.* обижа́ть; оскорбля́ть.

offender *n.* **1,** (one who offends) оби́дчик. **2,** (wrongdoer) правонаруши́тель.

offense *also,* **offence** *n.* **1,** (affront) оби́да. *No offense meant,* не в оби́ду будь ска́зано. **2,** (attack) нападе́ние. **3,** (misdeed; transgression) просту́пок. **4,** *law* преступле́ние; правонаруше́ние. —**give offense (to),** обижа́ть кого́-нибудь. —**take offense,** обижа́ться.

offensive *adj.* **1,** (disagreeable) неприя́тный; проти́вный. **2,** (insulting) оби́дный; оскорби́тельный. **3,** *mil.* наступа́тельный: *offensive weapons,* наступа́тельное ору́жие. —*n.* наступле́ние: *take the offensive,* переходи́ть в наступле́ние.

offer *v.t.* **1,** (present; put forward) предлага́ть: *offer one's services,* предлага́ть свои́ услу́ги. *Offer one's apologies,* приноси́ть свои́ извине́ния. *Offer one's condolences,* выража́ть своё соболе́знование. **2,** (provide) предоставля́ть: *offer opportunities,* предоставля́ть возмо́жности. *Offer hope,* подава́ть наде́жду. **3,** *fol. by inf.* (volunteer) предлага́ть; вызыва́ться. **4,** (put up, as resistance) ока́зывать. —*n.* предложе́ние: *make an offer,* де́лать предложе́ние.

offering *n.* **1,** (gift; contribution) приноше́ние. **2,** (sacrifice) жертвоприноше́ние.

offhand *adv.* без подгото́вки; экспро́мтом. —*adj.* **1,** (impromptu) импровизи́рованный. **2,** (casual; brusque) бесцеремо́нный.

office *n.* **1,** (place of business) конто́ра; канцеля́рия. **2,** (private room for work) кабине́т. **3,** (high position) до́лжность. *Term of office,* срок полномо́чий. **4,** (administrative body) бюро́. **5,** (government department) министе́рство; ве́домство; управле́ние. **6,** *pl.* (services) услу́ги: *good offices,* до́брые услу́ги. —*adj.* служе́бный. *Office hours,* служе́бные *or* приёмные часы́. *Office worker,* канцеляри́ст.

office boy рассы́льный; посы́льный.

officeholder *n.* должностно́е лицо́.

officer *n.* **1,** *mil.* офице́р. **2,** (person in authority) должностно́е лицо́. **3,** (policeman) полице́йский. —*adj.* [*also,* **officer's** *or* **officers'**] офице́рский.

official *adj.* **1,** (authorized; formal) официа́льный. *Official language,* госуда́рственный язы́к. **2,** (connected with one's work) служе́бный: *official duties,* служе́бные обя́занности. —*n.* чино́вник; должностно́е лицо́.

officialdom *n.* чино́вничество.

officially *adv.* официа́льно.

officiate *v.i.* **1,** (preside) председа́тельствовать (на собра́нии). **2,** (conduct a service) соверша́ть богослуже́ние.

officious *adj.* назо́йливый; навя́зчивый.

offing *n., in* **be in the offing,** предстоя́ть; гото́виться.

off-season *adj. & adv.* не в сезо́нное вре́мя.

offset *v.t.* возмеща́ть; компенси́ровать. —*n., printing* офсе́т. —**offset printing,** офсе́тная печа́ть.

offshoot *n.* отро́сток; о́тпрыск; ответвле́ние.

offshore *adj.* прибре́жный. —*adj.* недалеко́ от бе́рега.

offside *adj., sports* вне игры́.

offspring *n.* пото́мок; о́тпрыск.

offstage *adj.* закули́сный. —*adv.* за кули́сами; за кули́сы.

off-white *adj.* беле́сый; белова́тый.

off-year *adj. Off-year elections,* промежу́точные вы́боры.

often *adv.* ча́сто. *How often?,* как ча́сто? —**every so often,** вре́мя от вре́мени. —**more often than not,** ча́ще всего́.

ogle *v.i.* де́лать гла́зки; игра́ть глаза́ми.

ogre *n.* великан-людое́д.

oh *interj.* о!; ах!; ох!

ohm *n.* ом.

oho *interj.* ого́!

oil *n.* **1,** (viscous substance) ма́сло. **2,** (petroleum) нефть. **3,** *art* ма́сло: *paint in oils,* писа́ть ма́слом. —*adj.* ма́сляный; нефтяно́й. —*v.t.* сма́зывать.

oilcan *n.* маслёнка.

oilcloth *n.* клеёнка.

oiler *n.* **1,** (device for oiling) маслёнка. **2,** (ship) нефтеналивно́е су́дно.

oil filter ма́сляный фильтр.

oil painting карти́на, напи́санная ма́сляными кра́сками.

oilseed *n.* ма́сличное се́мя.

oil shale нефтено́сный сла́нец.

oil well нефтяна́я сква́жина.

oily *adj.* ма́сленый; масляни́стый. *Oily skin,* жи́рная ко́жа.

ointment *n.* мазь.

O.K. *interj.* хорошо́!; ла́дно! —*adj.* ничего́; норма́льно. *Everything is O.K.,* всё норма́льно.

okapi *n.* ока́пи.

okra *n.* ба́мия; о́кра.

old *adj.* ста́рый. *Old man,* стари́к. *Old woman,* стару́ха. *Get/grow old,* старе́ть; ста́риться. *How old are you?,* ско́лько вам лет? *I am ten years old,* мне де́сять лет. —**in days of old,** в старину́; в бы́лые времена́.

old age ста́рость. *Old age pension,* пе́нсия по ста́рости. —**old age home,** дом для престаре́лых.

Old Believer старове́р; старообря́дец.

olden *adj.* былой; да́вний. *In olden times,* в старину́.

old-fashioned *adj.* старомо́дный.

old hand тёртый кала́ч; стре́ляный воробе́й.

old maid ста́рая де́ва.

oldster *n., colloq.* стари́к.

Old Testament Ве́тхий заве́т. *Old Testament prophet,* ветхозаве́тный проро́к.

old-time *adj.* стари́нный; ста́рых времён.

old-timer *n.* старожи́л.

old wives' tale ба́бья ска́зка.

Old World Ста́рый свет.

oleaginous *adj.* масляни́стый.

oleander *n.* олеа́ндр.

oleomargarine *n.* маргари́н.

olfactory *adj.* обоня́тельный.

oligarchy *n.* олига́рхия. —**oligarch,** *n.* олига́рх. —**oligarchic,** *adj.* олигархи́ческий.

olive *n.* оли́ва; оли́вка; масли́на. —*adj.* оли́вковый; масли́чный. —**olive branch,** оли́вковая *or* масли́чная ветвь. —**olive-green,** *adj.* оли́вковый. —**olive oil,** оли́вковое *or* прова́нское ма́сло. —**olive tree,** оли́ва; масли́на; оли́вковое де́рево.

Olympiad *n.* олимпиа́да.

Olympian *adj.* олимпи́йский.

Olympic *adj.* олимпи́йский. —**Olympic Games,** Олимпи́йские и́гры.

Olympics *n.pl.* олимпиа́да.

omega *n.* оме́га.

omelet *also,* **omelette** *n.* омле́т.

omen *n.* предзнаменова́ние.

ominous *adj.* злове́щий.

omission *n.* упуще́ние; про́пуск.

omit *v.t.* пропуска́ть.

omnibus *n.* **1,** *obs.* (bus) авто́бус. **2,** (anthology) антоло́гия; сбо́рник. —*adj.* о́бщий; всеобъе́млющий.

omnipotent *adj.* всемогу́щий. —**omnipotence,** *n.* всемогу́щество.

omnipresent *adj.* вездесу́щий.

omniscient *adj.* всеве́дущий. —**omniscience,** *n.* всеве́дение.

omnivorous *adj.* всея́дный.

on *prep.* **1,** (indicating position upon) на (+ *prepl.*): *your keys are on the dresser,* ва́ши ключи́ (лежа́т) на комо́де. *The picture is hanging on the wall,* карти́на виси́т на стене́. **2,** (onto) на (+ *acc.*): *put the books on the shelf,* положи́ть кни́ги на по́лку. *Lie down on the floor,* лечь на́ пол. *Set foot on the moon,* ступи́ть на Луну́. **3,** *with various abstract nouns* на: *based on facts,* осно́ванный на фа́ктах; *on the following conditions,* на сле́дующих усло́виях. *Pin one's hopes on,* возлага́ть наде́жды на (+ *acc.*). *Live on one's earnings,* жить на свой за́работок. *Spend money on books,* тра́тить де́ньги на кни́ги. **4,** (on coming in contact with) о (+ *acc.*): *stumble on a stone,* споткну́ться о ка́мень. *Wipe one's hands on one's apron,* вытира́ть ру́ки о передни́к. *Cut one's finger on a piece of glass,* поре́зать себе́ па́лец о стекло́. **5,** (in one's possession) при: *I have no money on me,* у меня́ при себе́ нет де́нег. **6,** (through the medium of) по: *appear on television,* выступа́ть по телеви́дению. **7,** (about; concerning) о: *an essay on war,* о́черк о войне́. *A book on art,* кни́га по иску́сству. *My opinion on this subject,* моё мне́ние по э́тому вопро́су. **8,** (at the time of) по (+ *prepl.*); при: *on his arrival,* по прие́зде; *on entering the room,* при вхо́де в ко́мнату. **9,** (with dates) *expressed by the gen. case: on July 4th,* четвёртого ию́ля. **10,** (with days of the week) в (+ *acc.*): *on Wednesday,* в сре́ду. ♦*In the meaning "each" or "every"* по (+ *dat.pl.*): *on Wednesday(s),* по среда́м. **11,** *colloq.* (at the expense of): *this is on me,* я угоща́ю. *Drinks are on the house,* все напи́тки за счёт заведе́ния. **12,** *in various miscellaneous expressions: on board,* на борту́; *on fire,* в огне́; *on purpose,* наро́чно;

on time, вовремя; *on trial*, под судом. —*adv.* дальше: *go on*, идти дальше. *Read on!*, читайте дальше! ♦*Usu. rendered by a prefixed verb: put on*, надевать; *turn on*, включать. —*adj.* **1**, (being worn) надетый: *your hat is on backwards*, у вас шляпа надета задом наперёд. **2**, (turned on) включён: *the light is on*, свет включён. **3**, (in progress) *expressed by the verb* идти: *the exam is on*, идёт экзамен. **4**, (not canceled) в силе. —**on and off**, попеременно; то..., то... —**on and on**, без конца.

onager *n.* онагр.

on-board *adj.* бортовой.

once *adv.* **1**, (one time) раз; один раз. *Once a month*, раз в месяц. *Once is enough*, один раз – достаточно. *More than once*, не раз. *Not once*, ни разу. **2**, (on a certain occasion in the past) однажды; как-то раз. **3**, (formerly) некогда; когда-то. *The ruins of a once great city*, руины некогда большого города. —*conj.* как только; раз. *Once he finds out about it*, как только он узнает об этом. —**all at once, 1**, (all simultaneously) все *or* всё вместе; сразу. **2**, (suddenly) вдруг. —**at once, 1**, (right now) сейчас; немедленно. **2**, (just then; immediately) сразу; немедленно. —**for once**, на этот раз. —**just this once**, хотя бы на этот раз. —**once again; once more**, ещё раз. —**once and for all**, раз (и) навсегда. —**once in a while**, время от времени. —**once or twice**, раз-другой; раза два. —**once upon a time**, однажды; жил-был.

oncoming *adj.* встречный; надвигающийся.

one *n.* один. ♦*In counting* раз: *one, two, three*, раз, два, три. —*adj.* **1**, (a single) один (одна, одно): *one time*, один раз; *one portion*, одна порция; *one summer*, одно лето. *One o'clock*, час. *Act One*, действие первое. **2**, (only) единственный: *the one man who can do it*, единственный, кто может это сделать. **3**, (united) единый. —*indef.pron.* **1**, (single element in a group) один (одна): *one of them*, один/одна из них. **2**, (a person) *Rendered variously in Russian: one must observe the rules*, надо соблюдать правила. *One is never too old to learn*, век живи – век учись. **3**, (item) *Omitted in Russian: the red one*, красный (красная, красное). *Buy a new one*, купить новый (новую, новое). **4**, *preceded by* **the** (specific person or thing) тот: *not the one I wanted*, не тот, который я хотел. **5**, (the kind of person) такой: *he is not one to back down*, он не такой, чтобы отступать. —**at one with**, заодно с; солидарный с. —**one and all**, все до одного. —**one another**, друг друга. —**one by one, 1**, (one at a time) по одному. **2**, (one after the other) один за другим.

one-armed *adj.* однорукий.

one-celled *adj.* одноклеточный.

one-eyed *adj.* одноглазый.

one hundred сто. —**one-hundredth**, *adj.* сотый. —*n.* сотая: *one one-hundredth*, одна сотая.

one-legged *adj.* одноногий.

oneness *n.* **1**, (unity) единство. **2**, (sameness) тождество.

one-room *adj.* однокомнатный.

onerous *adj.* тягостный; обременительный.

oneself *pers.pron.* **1**, *used reflexively* себя: *underestimate oneself*, недооценивать себя. *Kill oneself*, покончить с собой. ♦*Often rendered by the reflexive verb: hurt oneself*, ушибиться; *shoot oneself*, застре-

литься. **2**, *used for emphasis* сам: *I don't know myself*, я сам (сама) не знаю. —**be oneself**, быть самим собой. —**by oneself**, один. **2**, —**not oneself**, не по себе (+ *dat.*); сам не свой. —**to oneself**, себе; про себя.

one-sided *adj.* односторонний.

one-story *adj.* одноэтажный.

one-time *adj.* **1**, (former) бывший. **2**, (done only once) разовый.

one-volume *adj.* однотомный.

one-way *adj.* **1**, (moving in one direction) односторонний. *One-way street*, улица с односторонним движением. **2**, (not providing for a return, as of a trip or ticket) в один конец.

onion *n.* луковица; головка лука; *pl.* лук.

onlooker *n.* зритель.

only *adv.* **1**, (merely; exclusively) только; лишь. **2**, (as recently as) ещё: *only last year*, ещё в прошлом году. —*adj.* единственный: *the only way out*, единственный выход. *Only child*, единственный ребёнок. *The only one of its kind*, единственный в своём роде. *The only thing I can say*, единственно, что я могу сказать. —*conj.* только; но. *Only be careful!*, только будьте осторожны! —**have only to**, стоит только: *one has only to ask*, стоит только попросить. —**if only**, *see* **if**. —**not only**, не только. —**only too**, только: *I would be only too happy to do it*, мне будет только приятно это сделать.

onomatopoeia *n.* звукоподражание.

onset *n.* начало; наступление.

on-site *adj.* на местах.

onslaught *n.* натиск.

onstage *adv.* на сцену: *walk onstage*, выходить на сцену.

onto *prep.* на (+ *acc.*): *climb onto the roof*, влезть на крышу.

ontology *n.* онтология. —**ontological**, *adj.* онтологический.

onus *n.* бремя; ответственность.

onward *adv.* вперёд. —*adj.* поступательный.

onyx *n.* оникс. —*adj.* ониксовый.

oodles *n.pl., colloq.* уйма.

ooze *v.i.* сочиться.

opacity *n.* непрозрачность.

opal *n.* опал. —*adj.* опаловый.

opalescent *adj.* радужный.

opaline *adj.* опаловый.

opaque *adj.* непрозрачный; светонепроницаемый. —**opaqueness**, *n.* непрозрачность.

open *v.t.* открывать: *open the window/one's eyes*, открывать окно/глаза. *Open fire*, открыть огонь. —*v.i.* **1**, (become open) открываться. **2**, (spread apart, as of buds) распускаться. **3**, *fol. by* **on** *or* **onto** (give access to) выходить в *or* на. —*adj.* открытый: *the door is open*, дверь открыта. *Open wound*, открытая рана. *Open question*, открытый вопрос.—*n.* [*usu.* **the open**]. *Out in the open*, на открытом воздухе. *Come out/bring out/into the open*, выйти/вывести наружу.

open-air *adj.* открытый; на открытом воздухе; под открытым небом.

opener *n. Can opener*, консервный нож. —**for openers**, *colloq.* для начала.

open-hearted *adj.* чистосердечный. —**open-heartedness**, *n.* чистосердечие.

open-hearth *adj.* мартéновский: *open-hearth furnace,* мартéновская печь; мартéн.
opening *n.* **1,** (act of opening) открытие. **2,** (hole; gap) отвéрстие. **3,** (vacancy) вакáнсия. **4,** *theat.* премьéра. **5,** *chess* дебют. —*adj.* **1,** (first; initial) пéрвый; начáльный. **2,** (introductory) вступительный.
openly *adv.* открыто; в открытую.
open-minded *adj.* непредубеждённый.
open-mouthed *adj.* разинув рот.
openness *n.* прямотá; откровéнность.
openwork *n.* ажурная рабóта; ажур; мерéжка.
opera *n.* óпера. —*adj.* óперный. —**opera glasses,** театрáльный бинóкль. —**opera house,** óперный теáтр.
operate *v.i.* **1,** (function) рабóтать; дéйствовать. **2,** (carry on certain activities) дéйствовать; орудовать. **3,** (perform surgery) оперировать. *Operate on someone,* оперировать когó-нибудь. —*v.t.* **1,** (manage, as an enterprise) управлять; завéдовать. **2,** (handle, as a machine) управлять; обращáться с; обслуживать.
operatic *adj.* óперный.
operating *adj.* **1,** *med.* операциóнный: *operating table,* операциóнный стол. *Operating room,* операциóнная. **2,** *econ.* эксплуатациóнный: *operating costs/expenses,* эксплуатациóнные расхóды.
operation *n.* **1,** (functioning) дéйствие. *Put into operation,* вводить в дéйствие; вводить в строй. *Be in operation,* рабóтать; дéйствовать. *Be out of operation,* не рабóтать; не дéйствовать. **2,** *med.* операция: *heart operation,* операция на сéрдце. **3,** (handling) управлéние: *operation of a motor vehicle,* управлéние автомашиной. **4,** *finance* операция. **5,** *mil.* операция; *pl.* дéйствия.
operational *adj.* **1,** (in use; operating) дéйствующий. **2,** *mil.* оперативный.
operative *adj.* **1,** (in operation) дéйствующий. **2,** (in force; valid) дéйствующий; действительный. **3,** *med.* оперативный. —*n.* агéнт; сыщик.
operator *n.* **1,** (one who works a machine) оперáтор. *Lathe operator,* тóкарь. *Radio operator,* радист. **2,** (telephone operator) телефонистка. **3,** (owner; director) владéлец; управляющий.
operetta *n.* оперéтта.
ophthalmology *n.* офтальмолóгия. —**ophthalmologist,** *n.* офтальмóлог.
opiate *n.* **1,** (drug) наркóтик. **2,** (that which dulls the senses) óпиум: *the opiate of the masses,* óпиум нарóдных масс.
opinion *n.* мнéние. *In my opinion,* по моему мнéнию; по-мóему. *Have a high opinion of,* быть высóкого мнéния о.
opinionated *adj.* упрямый; своевóльный.
opium *n.* óпиум; óпий. *Opium den,* курильня óпиума.
opossum *n.* опóссум.
opponent *n.* протвник.
opportune *adj.* **1,** (appropriate; suitable) подходящий. **2,** (timely) своеврéменный.
opportunism *n.* оппортунизм. —**opportunist,** *n.* оппортунист. —**opportunistic,** *adj.* оппортунистический.
opportunity *n.* возмóжность; (удóбный) случай. *At the first convenient opportunity,* при пéрвом удóбном случае.
oppose *v.t.* **1,** (resist) противиться. **2,** (be against)

выступáть прóтив. **3,** (compete against) состязáться с. **4,** (set in opposition) противопоставлять.
opposed *adj.* прóтив: *be strongly opposed to something,* быть решительно прóтив чегó-нибудь. *Nine in favor, five opposed,* дéвять за, пять прóтив. —**as opposed to,** в отличие от.
opposing *adj.* противный: *opposing sides,* противные стóроны. *Opposing views,* противополóжные взгляды.
opposite *adj.* **1,** (facing) противополóжный: *the opposite shore,* противополóжный бéрег. **2,** (reverse) обрáтный: *in the opposite direction,* в обрáтном направлéнии. **3,** (contrary) противополóжный: *opposite views,* противополóжные взгляды. *The opposite sex,* противополóжный пол. —*n.* противополóжность; обрáтное. *He is the exact opposite of his brother,* он пóлная противополóжность своему брáту. *Yesterday you were saying the opposite,* вчерá вы утверждáли обрáтное. —*adv.* напрóтив: *sit opposite,* сидéть напрóтив. —*prep.* прóтив; напрóтив. *Sit opposite each other,* сидéть друг прóтив друга.
opposition *n.* **1,** (state of being opposed) возражéние: *my opposition to this bill,* моё возражéние прóтив э́того законопроéкта. *Announce one's opposition to,* выступить прóтив. **2,** (resistance) противодéйствие; сопротивлéние: *meet with opposition,* встрéтить противодéйствие/сопротивлéние. **3,** *polit.* оппозиция. **4,** *astron.* противостояние. —*adj.* оппозициóнный.
oppress *v.t.* угнетáть; притеснять. —**oppression,** *n.* угнетéние; притеснéние; гнёт.
oppressive *adj.* **1,** (causing distress) гнетущий; угнетáющий; томительный. *Oppressive heat,* томительная жарá. *Oppressive thoughts,* гнетущие мысли. **2,** (tyrannical) деспотический.
oppressor *n.* угнетáтель; притеснитель; насильник.
opprobrious *adj.* **1,** (scurrilous) оскорбительный. **2,** (shameful) позóрный. —**opprobrium,** *n.* позóр.
opt *v.i.* [*usu.* **opt for**] выбирáть; останáвливать свой выбор на.
optic *adj.* глазнóй; зрительный. —**optic nerve,** глазнóй/зрительный нерв.
optical *adj.* зрительный; оптический. —**optical illusion,** оптический обмáн; обмáн зрéния.
optician *n.* óптик.
optics *n.* óптика.
optimism *n.* оптимизм. —**optimist,** *n.* оптимист. —**optimistic,** *adj.* оптимистический. *I am optimistic,* я настрóен оптимистически.
optimum *adj.* наилучший; оптимáльный. —*n.* óптимум.
option *n.* выбор. —**optional,** *adj.* необязáтельный; факультативный.
optometrist *n.* óптик.
opulent *adj.* пышный; роскóшный; богáтый. —**opulence,** *n.* пышность.
opus *n.* óпус.
or *conj.* **1,** (introducing an alternative) или: *yes or no,* да или нет. **2,** (otherwise; lest) а то; инáче. *Careful, or you'll fall,* осторóжно, а то упадéте. —**or so,** óколо: *an hour or so,* óколо чáса. *In a month or so,* приблизительно чéрез мéсяц.
oracle *n.* орáкул.

oral *adj.* **1,** (spoken) у́стный. **2,** (of the mouth) ротово́й.

orally *adv.* **1,** (verbally) у́стно. **2,** (by mouth) в рот.

orange *n.* апельси́н. —*adj.* **1,** (of or pert. to oranges) апельси́новый; апельси́нный. **2,** (color) ора́нжевый. —**orange blossom,** помера́нцевый цвет. —**orange grove,** апельси́новая ро́ща. —**orange juice,** апельси́новый сок. —**orange tree,** апельси́новое де́рево.

orangutan *also,* **orangutang** *n.* орангута́нг.

orate *v.i.* ора́торствовать; разглаго́льствовать.

oration *n.* речь.

orator *n.* ора́тор. —**oratorical,** *adj.* ора́торский.

oratorio *n.* орато́рия.

oratory *n.* **1,** (art of public speaking) ора́торское иску́сство. **2,** (eloquence) красноре́чие.

orb *n.* шар; сфе́ра.

orbit *n.* орби́та. *Be in orbit,* быть на орби́те. *Go into orbit,* вы́йти на орби́ту. —*v.t.* & *i.* дви́гаться по орби́те (вокру́г). —**orbital,** *adj.* орбита́льный.

orchard *n.* фрукто́вый сад. *Apple orchard,* я́блоневый сад.

orchestra *n.* **1,** (large group of musicians) орке́стр. **2,** (main floor of a theater) парте́р. —**orchestral,** *adj.* оркестро́вый.

orchestrate *v.t.* оркестрова́ть; инструментова́ть. —**orchestration,** *n.* оркестро́вка; инструменто́вка.

orchid *n.* орхиде́я.

ordain *v.t.* **1,** (decree) предпи́сывать. **2,** (predestine) предопределя́ть. **3,** (confer holy orders upon) посвяща́ть (в духо́вный сан).

ordeal *n.* тяжёлое испыта́ние; мыта́рство; иску́с.

order *n.* **1,** (sequence; methodical arrangement; proper condition) поря́док: *in alphabetical order,* в алфави́тном поря́дке. *Everything is in order,* всё в поря́дке. **2,** (command) прика́з; распоряже́ние. *By order of,* по прика́зу (+ *gen.*). **3,** (direction to buy or sell) зака́з: *rush order,* сро́чный зака́з. **4,** (restaurant portion) по́рция: *two orders of peas,* две по́рции горо́ха. **5,** (warrant; writ) о́рдер. **6,** (scientific classification) отря́д. **7,** (medal) the *Order of Lenin,* о́рден Ле́нина. **8,** (regime) поря́док; строй. *The old order,* ста́рый поря́док. **9,** *mil.* поря́док; строй. **10,** (society; brotherhood) о́рден. —*v.t.* **1,** (command; direct) прика́зывать: *order the driver to stop,* приказа́ть води́телю останови́ться. *The doctor ordered me to rest,* врач веле́л мне отдыха́ть. **2,** (place an order for) зака́зывать: *order dinner,* зака́зывать обе́д. *Order something by mail,* вы́писать что́-нибудь по по́чте. **3,** (arrange; manage) устра́ивать: *order one's life,* устра́ивать жизнь. —**call to order,** призыва́ть к поря́дку. —**in order that/to,** для того́, что́бы. —**in short order,** в спе́шном поря́дке. —**on order,** зака́зан(ный). —**on the order of, 1,** (resembling) вро́де (+ *gen.*); наподо́бие (+ *gen.*). **2,** (approximately) поря́дка (+ *gen.*). —**order about,** кома́ндовать над; помыка́ть (+ *instr.*). —**order arms!,** *mil.* к ноге́! —**order out,** показа́ть на дверь; вы́ставить за дверь. —**out of order,** не в поря́дке. *The elevator is out of order,* лифт не рабо́тает. —**to order,** на зака́з: *made to order,* сде́ланный на зака́з.

orderly *adj.* **1,** (tidy) аккура́тный. **2,** (without disruption) организо́ванный; упоря́доченный. *Orderly demonstration,* ми́рная демонстра́ция. —*n.* **1,** *mil.* ордина́рец. **2,** (hospital aide) санита́р.

ordinal number поря́дковое числи́тельное.

ordinance *n.* указ; постановле́ние.

ordinarily *adv.* обы́чно.

ordinary *adj.* **1,** (not exceptional) обы́чный; обыкнове́нный. **2,** (somewhat inferior) заура́дный; посре́дственный. —**out of the ordinary,** из ря́да вон выходя́щий.

ordinate *n.,* *math.* ордина́та.

ordination *n.* посвяще́ние (в духо́вный сан); рукоположе́ние.

ordnance *n.* артилле́рия. *Piece of ordnance,* артиллери́йское ору́дие.

ore *n.* руда́: *iron ore,* желе́зная руда́.

organ *n.* **1,** (musical instrument) орга́н. *Barrel organ,* шарма́нка. **2,** (part of the body) о́рган: *organs of speech,* о́рганы ре́чи. **3,** (organization; body) о́рган. **4,** (publication) о́рган: *press organ,* о́рган печа́ти. *House organ,* многотира́жка. —*adj.* орга́нный: *organ music,* орга́нная му́зыка.

organdy *n.* то́нкая кисея́.

organ grinder шарма́нщик.

organic *adj.* органи́ческий.

organism *n.* органи́зм.

organist *n.* органи́ст.

organization *n.* организа́ция. —**organizational,** *adj.* организацио́нный; организа́торский.

organize *v.t.* устра́ивать; организова́ть. —*v.i.* организова́ться. —**organizer,** *n.* организа́тор.

orgasm *n.* орга́зм.

orgy *n.* о́ргия; разгу́л. —**orgiastic,** *adj.* разгу́льный.

orient *v.t.* ориенти́ровать.

Orient *n.* Восто́к.

Oriental *adj.* восто́чный. —*n.* уроже́нец Восто́ка. —**Orientalist,** *n.* востокове́д.

orientation *n.* **1,** (bearings) ориента́ция; ориенти́ровка. **2,** (leaning) ориента́ция.

orifice *n.* отве́рстие.

origin *n.* **1,** (beginning; original source) происхожде́ние; возникнове́ние. *Have its origin in,* вести́ своё нача́ло от. **2,** (ancestry) происхожде́ние: *of Russian origin,* ру́сского происхожде́ния; ру́сский, по происхожде́нию.

original *adj.* **1,** (first; earliest) первонача́льный: *lose its original shape,* теря́ть первонача́льную фо́рму. **2,** (not imitated; creative) оригина́льный. **3,** (being that from which a copy is made) по́длинный. —*n.* по́длинник; оригина́л: *read in the original,* чита́ть в по́длиннике *or* в оригина́ле. —**original sin,** перворо́дный грех.

originality *n.* оригина́льность.

originally *adv.* **1,** (at first) снача́ла; первонача́льно. **2,** (by origin) ро́дом.

originate *v.t.* создава́ть; порожда́ть. —*v.i.* зарожда́ться; брать нача́ло. *The idea originated with him,* э́то у него́ зароди́лась така́я мысль. —**originator,** *n.* а́втор; созда́тель.

oriole *n.* **1,** (European bird) и́волга. **2,** (American bird) трупиа́л.

Orion *n.* Орио́н.

ornament *n.* украше́ние. —*v.t.* украша́ть. —**ornamental,** *adj.* декорати́вный. —**ornamentation,** *n.* украше́ние.

ornate *adj.* витиева́тый; вы́чурный.

ornery *adj., colloq.* злой; упря́мый; сварли́вый.

ornithology *n.* орнитоло́гия. —**ornithological,**

adj. орнитологи́ческий. —**ornithologist,** *n.* орни-
то́лог.

orotund *adj.* **1,** (sonorous) зву́чный. **2,** (pompous)
напы́щенный.

orphan *n.* сирота́. —*adj.* **1,** (for orphans) сиро́тский.
2, (orphaned) осироте́лый. —*v.t.* де́лать сирото́й.
Be orphaned, (о)сироте́ть.

orphanage *n.* сиро́тский дом; сиро́тский прию́т.

orphanhood *n.* сиро́тство.

orthodontia *n.* ортодонти́я.

orthodox *adj.* **1,** (pert. to the Orthodox Church) пра-
восла́вный. **2,** (adhering to traditional practice) пра-
вове́рный; ортодокса́льный. —**Orthodox Church,**
правосла́вная це́рковь.

orthodoxy *n.* **1,** (religion of the Orthodox Church)
правосла́вие. **2,** (conformity) ортодо́ксия.

orthography *n.* орфогра́фия; правописа́ние.
—**orthographic,** *adj.* орфографи́ческий.

orthopedic *adj.* ортопеди́ческий. —**orthopedics,**
n. ортопе́дия. —**orthopedist,** *n.* ортопе́д.

ortolan *n.* садо́вая овся́нка.

oryx *n.* сернобы́к.

oscillate *v.i.* кача́ться; колеба́ться. —**oscillation,**
n. кача́ние; колеба́ние. —**oscillator,** *n.* генера́тор;
осцилля́тор; вибра́тор.

oscillograph *n.* осцилло́граф.

oscilloscope *n.* осцилло́скоп.

osier *n.* и́ва.

osmium *n.* о́смий.

osmosis *n.* о́смос.

osprey *n.* скопа́.

osseous *adj.* ко́стный; кости́стый.

ossify *v.i.* костене́ть. —**ossification,** *n.* окостене́-
ние. —**ossified,** *adj.* окостене́лый.

ostensible *adj.* **1,** (apparent) ви́димый. **2,** (pro-
fessed) официа́льный. —**ostensibly,** *adv.* я́кобы.

ostentation *n.* мишура́. —**ostentatious,** *adj.* по-
казно́й; мишу́рный.

osteology *n.* остеоло́гия. —**osteologist,** *n.* остео́-
лог.

ostracize *v.t.* изгоня́ть. —**ostracism,** *n.* изгна́ние;
остраки́зм.

ostrich *n.* стра́ус. —*adj.* стра́усовый: *ostrich egg/
feather,* стра́усовое яйцо́/перо́.

other *adj.* **1,** *preceded by* **the,** A (being the remaining
one of two) друго́й: *the other hand/room/car,* дру-
га́я рука́/ко́мната/маши́на. B, (being the remaining
ones of many) остальны́е: *the other children,* осталь-
ны́е де́ти. **2,** (different) друго́й; ино́й. *In other countries,* в други́х стра́нах. *In other words,* други́ми
слова́ми; ины́ми слова́ми. *Somehow or other,* так
и́ли ина́че. *For some reason or other,* по той и́ли
ино́й причи́не. **3,** (additional) *rendered by* ещё: *have
you any other brothers?,* у вас есть ещё бра́тья?
4, (opposite; reverse) обра́тный; друго́й. *The other
side of the coin,* обра́тная сторона́ моне́ты. *On the
other side of the river,* по ту сто́рону (*or* на друго́й
стороне́) реки́. —*n. & pron.* [*usu.* **the others**] други́е;
остальны́е. —**each other,** *see* **each.** —**none other
than,** не кто ино́й, как. —**other than,** кро́ме. —
other things being equal, при про́чих ра́вных
усло́виях. —**some other time,** ка́к-нибудь в друго́й
раз. —**the other day,** на днях. —**the other way
round,** как раз наоборо́т.

otherwise *adv.* **1,** (differently) ина́че; по-друго́му.

2, (if not) ина́че; а то; в проти́вном слу́чае. **3,** (in
all other respects) в остально́м.

otter *n.* вы́дра. *Sea otter,* морска́я вы́дра; кала́н.

ottoman *n.* **1,** (divan) оттома́нка; тахта́. **2,** (footstool) скаме́йка для ног.

ouch *interj.* ай!; ой!

ought *v.aux. Generally rendered by* до́лжен, сле́-
довать, *or the subjunctive mood. He ought to be
grateful to you,* он до́лжен быть вам благода́рен.
She ought to be here at any moment, она́ должна́
прийти́ в любо́й моме́нт. *You ought to see a doctor,*
вам сле́дует (*or* вам бы) пойти́ к врачу́.

ounce *n.* **1,** (unit of weight) у́нция. **2,** (small amount;
bit) ка́пля; чу́точка.

our *poss. adj.* наш: *our house,* наш дом; *our street,*
на́ша у́лица; *our friends,* на́ши друзья́.

ours *poss. pron.* наш. *A friend of ours,* оди́н наш
друг; оди́н из на́ших друзе́й. *Their room is on the
first floor and ours is on the second,* их ко́мната
на пе́рвом этаже́, а на́ша — на второ́м.

ourselves *pers. pron.* **1,** *used for emphasis* (мы)
са́ми: *we don't know ourselves,* мы са́ми не зна́ем.
2, *used reflexively* себя́: *we underestimated ourselves,*
мы недооцени́ли себя́. —**by ourselves,** одни́.

oust *v.t.* вытесня́ть; выгоня́ть. —**ouster,** *n.* выте-
сне́ние.

out *adj.* **1,** (not in; away): *he is out,* он вы́шел; его́
нет. *Out to lunch,* ушёл обе́дать. **2,** (not turned on)
вы́ключен: *the light is out,* свет вы́ключен. **3,** (end-
ed): *before the week is out,* до конца́ неде́ли. **4,**
(not to be considered) исключён: *London is out,*
Ло́ндон исключён. **5,** (no longer in style): *narrow ties
are out,* у́зкие га́лстуки вы́шли из мо́ды. **6,** (known)
раскры́т: *the secret is out,* секре́т раскры́т; секре́т
стал всем изве́стен. **7,** (unconscious) без созна́ния.
8, *colloq.* (having lost) в про́игрыше: *I am out 100
dollars,* у меня́ про́игрыш в сто до́лларов. —*adv.*
нару́жу. ♦*Usu. rendered by a prefixed verb: go out,*
выходи́ть; *take out,* вынима́ть; *throw out,* выбра́сы-
вать; *leave out,* пропуска́ть; *start out,* отправля́ться;
break out, вспы́хивать; *fill out,* заполня́ть. —*prep.*
в; из: *look out the window,* смотре́ть в окно́; вы-
гля́дывать из окна́. *Throw something out the window,*
вы́бросить что́-нибудь в окно́. *Walk out the door,*
выходи́ть в дверь. —*interj.* вон! —**on the outs,** в
ссо́ре; в ко́нтрах. —**out for,** жа́ждущий (+ *gen.*):
he is out for blood/revenge, он жа́ждет кро́ви/ме́сти.
—**out of, 1,** (from within) из: *walk out of the room,*
вы́йти из ко́мнаты; *drink out of a glass,* пить из
стака́на. **2,** (through) из: *lean out of the window,*
высо́вываться из окна́. **3,** (beyond the limits of) за;
вне: *out of town,* за́ го́родом; в отъе́зде. *Out of
danger,* вне опа́сности. *Out of turn,* вне о́череди.
Pass out of sight, скрыва́ться из ви́ду. **4,** (from;
made of) из: *made out of wood,* сде́ланный из де́-
рева. **5,** (from; as a result of) из: *out of curiosity,*
из любопы́тства. *Out of spite,* назло́; со зла. **6,**
(from among) из: *in 99 cases out of 100,* в девя-
но́сто девяти́ слу́чаях из ста. **7,** (not having) без:
out of work, без рабо́ты. *We are out of gas,* у нас
вы́шел *or* ко́нчился бензи́н. **8,** (not in a condition
of) не в: *out of order,* не в поря́дке; *out of step,*
не в но́гу; *out of sorts,* не в ду́хе.

out-and-out *adj.* отъя́вленный: *an out-and-out liar,*
отъя́вленный лгун. *Out-and-out lie,* я́вная ложь.

outargue *v.t.* переспо́рить.

outboard motor подвесно́й мото́р.

outbound *adj.* уходя́щий; отбыва́ющий.

outbreak *n.* вспы́шка. *Outbreak of war,* нача́ло *or* возникнове́ние войны́.

outbuilding *n.* надво́рная постро́йка.

outburst *n.* взрыв; вспы́шка.

outcast *n.* изгна́нник; па́рия; отве́рженный. —*adj.* отве́рженный.

outclass *v.t.* превосходи́ть; оставля́ть далеко́ позади́.

outcome *n.* исхо́д; результа́т.

outcry *n.* **1,** (shout) крик; вы́крик. **2,** (public protest) шум.

outdated *adj.* устаре́лый; устаре́вший.

outdistance *v.t.* обгоня́ть; перегоня́ть; опережа́ть.

outdo *v.t.* превосходи́ть. *He was not to be outdone,* он не оста́лся в долгу́. —**outdo oneself,** превосходи́ть (самого́) себя́.

outdoor *adj.* на откры́том во́здухе. —**outdoors,** *adv.* **1,** (location) на дворе́; на (откры́том) во́здухе. **2,** (motion) на у́лицу; нару́жу; на во́здух.

outdrink *v.t.* перепива́ть.

outer *adj.* **1,** (external) вне́шний; нару́жный: *outer covering,* вне́шняя/нару́жная оболо́чка. *Outer garments,* ве́рхняя оде́жда. *Outer Mongolia,* Вне́шняя Монго́лия. **2,** (farther from the center) да́льний; кра́йний. *Outer limits,* кра́йние преде́лы. —**outer space,** ко́смос.

outermost *adj.* са́мый да́льний от середи́ны; кра́йний.

outfit *n.* **1,** (set of equipment) снаряже́ние. **2,** (set of clothing) наря́д. **3,** *colloq.* (group) гру́ппа; па́ртия; компа́ния. —*v.t.* снаряжа́ть; экипирова́ть.

outflank *v.t.* обходи́ть.

outflow *n.* истече́ние; уте́чка.

outfox *v.t.* перехитри́ть.

outgoing *adj.* **1,** (going out; leaving) уходя́щий; исходя́щий. **2,** (extroverted) общи́тельный; компане́йский.

outgrow *v.t.* **1,** (surpass in growth) перераста́ть. **2,** (grow too big to wear) выраста́ть из. **3,** (grow too old for) стать сли́шком больши́м для. **4,** (get rid of in the course of growing up) избавля́ться от; отде́лываться от.

outgrowth *n.* **1,** (excrescence) отро́сток; о́тпрыск. **2,** (consequence) проду́кт; результа́т.

outguess *v.t.* перехитри́ть.

outhouse *n.* отхо́жее ме́сто.

outing *n.* прогу́лка; похо́д; экску́рсия.

outlandish *adj.* дико́винный.

outlast *v.t.* **1,** (remain in existence longer than) пережива́ть. **2,** (overcome after a long struggle) переси́ливать.

outlaw *n.* банди́т; разбо́йник. —*v.t.* запреща́ть; объявля́ть вне зако́на.

outlay *n.* расхо́д; тра́та.

outlet *n.* **1,** (passage for letting something out) выходно́е *or* выпускно́е отве́рстие. *Outlet to the sea,* вы́ход к мо́рю. **2,** (means of release or expression) вы́ход; отду́шина. **3,** (electrical outlet) (штепсельная) розе́тка. **4,** (commercial market) ры́нок.

outline *n.* **1,** (line forming the outer edge) очерта́ния; ко́нтур. **2,** (sketch) набро́сок; эски́з. **3,** (short sum-

mary) схе́ма. —*v.t.* **1,** (sketch) оче́рчивать. **2,** (describe in general terms) намеча́ть. —**in broad outline,** в о́бщих черта́х.

outlive *v.t.* пережива́ть.

outlook *n.* **1,** (prospect) ви́ды; перспекти́вы. **2,** (mental attitude) кругозо́р; воззре́ние.

outlying *adj.* окра́инный; перифери́йный.

outmoded *adj.* устаре́лый; устаре́вший.

outnumber *v.t.* превосходи́ть чи́сленностью.

out-of-date *adj.* устаре́лый.

out-of-the-way *adj.* отдалённый; захолу́стный.

outpace *v.t.* опережа́ть; обгоня́ть.

outpatient *n.* амбулато́рный (*or* приходя́щий) больно́й.

outplay *v.t.* переи́грывать.

outpost *n.* **1,** *mil.* аванпо́ст; форпо́ст. **2,** (outlying settlement) форпо́ст; окра́ина.

outpouring *n.* излия́ние.

output *n.* проду́кция; вы́пуск; вы́работка.

outrage *n.* **1,** (vicious act) безобра́зие; бесчи́нство; надруга́тельство. *It's an outrage!,* (э́то) безобра́зие!; (э́то) возмути́тельно! **2,** (resentful anger) возмуще́ние; негодова́ние. —*v.t.* **1,** (offend) оскорбля́ть. **2,** (infuriate) возмуща́ть. *Be outraged,* возмуща́ться.

outrageous *adj.* **1,** (grossly offensive) возмути́тельный; вопию́щий. **2,** (exorbitant) непоме́рный: *outrageous demands,* непоме́рные тре́бования. *Outrageous prices,* бе́шеные це́ны. —**outrageously,** *adv.* возмути́тельно.

outrank *v.t.* быть ста́рше чем (по зва́нию).

outrigger *n.* утле́гарь.

outright *adj.* **1,** (unqualified) безоговоро́чный. *Outright refusal,* прямо́й отка́з. *Outright grant,* безвозвра́тная ссу́да. **2,** (total) по́лный: *an outright loss,* по́лная ги́бель. **3,** (out-and-out) отъя́вленный. *An outright lie,* я́вная ложь. —*adv.* **1,** (straight to one's face) пря́мо (в лицо́). **2,** (on the spot) на ме́сте; напова́л.

outrun *v.t.* **1,** (run faster than) обгоня́ть; перегоня́ть; опережа́ть. **2,** (elude by running) убежа́ть от. **3,** (exceed) превыша́ть.

outsell *v.t.* продава́ться лу́чше чем.

outset *n.* нача́ло. *At the outset,* снача́ла. *From the outset,* с са́мого нача́ла.

outshine *v.t.* затмева́ть.

outside *adv.* **1,** (location) на у́лице; на дворе́: *it's cold outside,* на у́лице *or* на дворе́ хо́лодно. **2,** (motion) на у́лицу; нару́жу. *Let's go outside,* пойдём на у́лицу; дава́йте вы́йдем на у́лицу. *Come in from outside,* войти́ с у́лицы. —*adj.* **1,** (external) вне́шний; нару́жный. **2,** (coming from without) посторо́нний: *outside help,* посторо́нняя по́мощь. —*n.* нару́жная сторона́. *On the outside,* снару́жи. —*prep.* вне; за преде́лами (+ *gen.*). —**at the outside,** са́мое бо́льшее. —**outside of,** кро́ме.

outsider *n.* **1,** (one not part of a group) посторо́нний. **2,** *sports* аутса́йдер.

outskirts *n.pl.* окра́ина.

outsmart *v.t.* перехитри́ть. *Outsmart oneself,* перехитри́ть самого́ себя́.

outspoken *adj.* прямо́й; открове́нный.

outspread *adj.* распростёртый.

outstanding *adj.* **1,** (distinguished; extraordinary) выдаю́щийся. **2,** (unsettled, as of an issue) спо́рный. **3,** (unpaid) неупла́ченный.

outstretched *adj.* распростёртый.

outstrip *v.t.* обгонять; опережать.

outtalk *v.t.* переговорить.

outward *adj.* внёшний; наружный. —*adv.* [*also*, **outwards**] наружу. —**outwardly**, *adv.* внёшне; снаружи; на вид.

outwear *v.t.* изнашивать.

outweigh *v.t.* перевёшивать.

outwit *v.t.* перехитрить.

ouzel *n.* **1**, (water ouzel) оляпка. **2**, (ring ouzel) белозобый дрозд.

oval *adj.* овальный. —*n.* овал.

ovary *n.* **1**, *anat.* яичник. **2**, *bot.* завязь.

ovate *adj.* яйцевидный.

ovation *n.* овация. *Give an ovation to*, устроить овацию (+ *dat.*).

oven *n.* духовка; печь.

over *prep.* **1**, (above) над: *fly over the city*, пролетёть над городом; *lean over the cradle*, наклоняться над колыбёлью. *Appear over the horizon*, показаться из-за горизонта. **2**, (higher than) выше: *the water was over our heads*, вода была выше головы. **3**, (above and across) чёрез: *jump over the fence*, перепрыгнуть чёрез забор; *lean over the railing*, перегибаться чёрез перила; *look over the edge*, заглянуть чёрез край. **4**, (along the surface of) по: *run one's fingers over the keyboard*, пробежать пальцами по клавиатуре. **5**, (so as to cover) повёрх; на. *Wear a sweater over one's shirt*, надёть свитер повёрх рубашки. *Pull the blanket over oneself*, натянуть на себя одеяло. *Pull one's hat down over one's eyes*, надвинуть шляпу на глаза. **6**, (more than) больше; свыше: *over an hour*, больше часа; *over 2000 dollars*, свыше двух тысяч долларов. *People over forty*, те, кому за сорок. **7**, (on; through the medium of) по: *over the radio*, по радио. **8**, (about) о: *argue over something*, спорить о чём-нибудь. *Fight over a girl*, драться из-за дёвушки. **9**, (while engaged in or partaking of something) за (+ *instr.*): *discuss the question over dinner*, обсуждать вопрос за обёдом. **10**, (during) в течёние: *over the next ten years*, в течёние ближайших десяти лет. **11**, *Victory over someone*, побёда над кём-нибудь; *advantage over someone*, преимущество пёред кём-нибудь. —*adv.* *Usu. rendered by a prefixed verb.* **1**, (once more; again) пере-: *do over*, передёлывать. **2**, (across; transferring) пере-: *cross over*, переходить; *hand over*, передавать. *Walk over to the window*, переходить к окну. *Come over and see us*, зайдите к нам. **3**, (inverting; overturning) пере-: *turn over*, перевёртывать(ся); *roll over*, перевáливаться. *Knock over*, прокидывать. **4**, (thoroughly; through) про-: *talk over*, обсуждать; *think over*, обдумывать; продумывать; *read over*, прочитать. **5**, (cursorily) про-: *look/glance over*, просматривать. **6**, *after numbers* больше; выше. *Children five and over*, дёти от пяти лет и больше. —*adj.* оконченный: *the meeting is over*, собрание окончено. *The war is over*, война окончилась. —**all over**, **1**, (everywhere) всюду. *All over the world*, по всему миру. *From all over the world*, со всех концов мира. *I ache all over*, у меня всё тёло болит. **2**, (finished) кончен: *it's all over*, всё кончено. *It's all over between them*, мёжду ними всё кончено. **3**, *often fol. by* **again** (again completely) заново. *Start all over (again)*, начинать всё сначала. —**over again**,

сначала; снова. —**over against**, против. —**over and above**, сверх; не считая. —**over and over**, снова и снова. —**over here**, здесь; тут. —**over there**, вон там.

overabundance *n.* избыток. —**overabundant**, *adj.* избыточный.

overact *v.i.* переигрывать.

overage[1] (o-ve-rij) *n.* избыток; излишек.

overage[2] (o-ver-**ayj**) *adj.* вышедший из возраста: *he is overage*, он вышел из возраста.

overall *adj.* общий; *overall length*, общая длина. *Overall impression*, общее впечатлёние.

overalls *n.pl.* рабочий халат; комбинезон; спецодёжда; роба.

overbearing *adj.* властный.

overblown *adj.* раздутый.

overboard *adv.* за борт; за бортом. *Toss overboard*, выбросить за борт. —**go overboard**, *colloq.* перегнуть палку. —**man overboard!**, человёк за бортом! —**wash overboard**, смывать (*impers.*): *he was washed overboard*, его смыло волной (с судна).

overburden *v.t.* перегружать; переобременять.

overcast *adj.* облачный; хмурый; пасмурный. —*n.* облачность. —*v.t.*, *sewing* обмётывать.

overcharge *v.t.* **1**, (charge too high a price) брать лишнее с. **2**, (overload, as a battery) перезаряжать.

overcoat *n.* пальто.

overcome *v.t.* **1**, (surmount; get over) преодолевать; превозмогать. **2**, (defeat) одолевать; побороть. **3**, (seize, as of an emotion) одолевать; охватывать.

overconfident *adj.* чрезмёрно увёренный. —**overconfidence**, *n.* чрезмёрная увёренность.

overcook *v.t.* перевáривать; пережáривать.

overcritical *adj.* придирчивый.

overcrowd *v.t.* переполнять. —**overcrowded**, *adj.* тёсный; переполненный; скученный. —**overcrowding**, *n.* теснотá; переполнёние; скученность.

overdo *v.t.* **1**, (carry too far) утрировать. **2**, = **overcook**. —**overdo it**, **1**, (overexert oneself) переутомляться. **2**, (go too far) перебáрщивать; зарывáться; перестарáться; пересáливать.

overdone *adj.* **1**, (done to excess) утрированный. **2**, (overcooked) пережáренный.

overdose *n.* слишком большáя дóза; чрезмéрная дóза.

overdraft *n.* превышёние крéдита (в бáнке).

overdraw *v.t.* превышáть остáток (счёта в бáнке).

overdress *v.t.* одевáть слишком нарядно.

overdue *adj.* **1**, *comm.* просрóченный. **2**, (late): *the train is overdue*, пóезд опáздывает *or* запáздывает.

overeat *v.i.* переедáть; объедáться.

overemphasize *v.t.* преувеличивать.

overestimate *v.t.* переоцéнивать. —**overestimation**, *n.* переоцéнка.

overexert *v.t.* перенапрягáть. —**overexertion**, *n.* перенапряжёние.

overexpenditure *n.* перерасхóд.

overexpose *v.t.*, *photog.* передéрживать. —**overexposure**, *n.*, *photog.* передéржка.

overfeed *v.t.* перекáрмливать; обкáрмливать; закáрмливать.

overfill *v.t.* переполнять.

overflow *v.i.* литься чёрез край; переливáться

чёрез край. *The bathtub overflowed*, водá в вáнне перелилáсь чéрез край. —*v.t.* вы́ступить из: *overflow its banks*, вы́ступить из берегóв. —*n.* **1**, (overflowing) разли́в. **2**, (that which overflows) изли́шек воды́. —*adj. An overflow crowd*, пóлный зал. —**filled to overflowing**, перепóлненный.

overfulfill *v.t.* перевыполня́ть. —**overfulfillment**, *n.* перевыполнéние.

overgrown *adj.* **1**, (covered, as with vegetation) зарóсший: *the field is overgrown with weeds*, пóле заросло́ сóрной травóй. **2**, (grown excessively) перерóсший.

overhand *adj. & adv., sports* свéрху.

overhang *v.t.* нависáть над; висéть над.

overhaul *v.t.* **1**, (examine for possible revision) пересмáтривать. **2**, (renovate) ремонти́ровать. **3**, (overtake) догоня́ть. —*n.* ремóнт.

overhead *adv.* наверху́; над головóй. *Directly overhead*, над сáмой головóй. —*adj.* **1**, (elevated) воздýшный; надзéмный. **2**, (suspended) подвеснóй. **3**, *comm.* (of costs) накладны́е. —*n.* накладны́е расхóды.

overhear *v.t.* подслýшать; услы́шать.

overheat *v.t.* перегревáть. —*v.i.* перегревáться.

overindulge *v.t.* баловáть; потвóрствовать. —*v.i.* переедáть; объедáться.

overindulgence *n.* **1**, (excessive leniency) баловствó. **2**, (immoderation) неумéренность.

overindulgent *adj.* **1**, (too lenient) сли́шком снисходи́тельный. **2**, (immoderate) неумéренный.

overjoyed *adj.* вне себя́ от рáдости.

overkill *n.* многокрáтное уничтожéние.

overland *adj.* сухопýтный; назéмный. —*adv.* по сýше; на сýше.

overlap *v.i.* части́чно совпадáть.

overlay *v.t.* **1**, (place over) наклáдывать. **2**, (coat; cover) покрывáть. —*n.* покры́шка.

overload *v.t.* перегружáть. —*n.* перегрýзка.

overlook *v.t.* **1**, (fail to notice) просмотрéть. **2**, (lose sight of) упускáть из ви́ду. **3**, (ignore) смотрéть сквозь пáльцы на. **4**, (afford a view of) выходи́ть в *or* на. **5**, (rise above) возвышáться над.

overly *adv.* чрезмéрно; сли́шком.

overnight *adv.* **1**, (for the night) нá ночь: *stay overnight*, остáться нá ночь. **2**, (very quickly; suddenly) моментáльно. —*adj.* **1**, (lasting or staying through the night): *overnight stop*, ночлéг. *Overnight guests*, гóсти, остаю́щиеся нá ночь. **2**, (very rapid; instant) моментáльный.

overpass *n.* путепровóд; эстакáда.

overpay *v.t.* переплáчивать. —**overpayment**, *n.* переплáта.

overplay *v.t.* **1**, (overact) переи́грывать. **2**, (exaggerate) преувели́чивать. —**overplay one's hand**, перестарáться; зайти́ сли́шком далекó.

overpopulate *v.t.* перенаселя́ть. —**overpopulated**, *adj.* перенаселённый. —**overpopulation**, *n.* перенаселéние; перенаселённость.

overpower *v.t.* переси́ливать. —**overpowering**, *adj.* подавля́ющий; неотрази́мый.

overproduction *n.* перепроизвóдство.

overrate *v.t.* переоцéнивать.

override *v.t.* **1**, (disregard; wave aside) отмáхиваться от. **2**, (nullify, as a Presidential veto) аннули́ровать.

overriding *adj.* глáвный; важнéйший; решáющий.

overripe *adj.* перезрéлый.

overrule *v.t.* **1**, (set aside) отменя́ть; аннули́ровать. **2**, (disallow) отклоня́ть; отвергáть.

overrun *v.t.* **1**, (invade and conquer) завоёвывать: *overrun a country*, завоевáть странý. *Overrun the enemy's defenses*, прорвáть оборóну проти́вника. **2**, (swarm over) наводня́ть. *Be overrun with mice*, кишéть мышáми. —*n.* превышéние: *cost overrun*, превышéние стóимости.

overseas *adj.* замóрский; заграни́чный. —*adv.* **1**, (location) зá морем; за грани́цей. **2**, (motion) зá море; за грани́цу. —**overseas cap**, *mil.* пилóтка.

oversee *v.t.* надзирáть за; наблюдáть за. —**overseer**, *n.* надзирáтель; надсмóтрщик.

overshadow *v.t.* затмевáть; заслоня́ть.

overshoe *n.* галóша.

overshoot *v.t. Overshoot one's target; overshoot a landing field*, давáть перелёт.

oversight *n.* **1**, (failure to notice something) недосмóтр; просмóтр; упущéние. **2**, (supervision) надзóр.

oversimplify *v.t.* упрощáть. —**oversimplification**, *n.* упрощён(че)ство.

oversize *adj.* бóльше обы́чного размéра. *Also*, **oversized.**

oversleep *v.i.* просыпáть.

overstate *v.t.* преувели́чивать. —**overstatement**, *n.* преувеличéние.

overstay *v.t., in* **overstay one's welcome**, загости́ться.

overstep *v.t.* переступáть.

oversupply *n.* избы́ток.

overt *adj.* откры́тый; неприкры́тый; я́вный.

overtake *v.t.* **1**, (catch up with) догоня́ть. **2**, (pass after catching up with) обгоня́ть. **3**, (befall) постигáть.

overtax *v.t.* **1**, (tax too heavily) обременя́ть сли́шком высóкими налóгами. **2**, (overexert) надрывáть; надламывать.

overthrow *v.t.* свергáть. —*n.* свержéние.

overtime *n.* **1**, (extra time worked) сверхурóчное врéмя. **2**, (extra work) сверхурóчная рабóта. **3**, (payment for same) сверхурóчные. **4**, *sports* дополни́тельное врéмя. —*adj.* сверхурóчный. —*adv.* сверхурóчно.

overtone *n.* **1**, *music* обертóн. **2**, *usu. pl.* (implications) скры́тые намёки.

overture *n.* **1**, *music* увертю́ра. **2**, *usu. pl.* (offer to negotiate) предложéние: *peace overtures*, ми́рные предложéния. **3**, *usu. pl.* (flirtatious advances) заи́грывания; ухáживания.

overturn *v.t.* опроки́дывать. —*v.i.* опроки́дываться; перевёртываться.

overview *n.* обзóр.

overweening *adj.* **1**, (arrogant) высокомéрный. **2**, (excessive) чрезмéрный.

overweight *adj.* вéсящий бóльше (*or* вы́ше) полóженного вéса. *I am ten pounds overweight*, я вéшу на дéсять фýнтов бóльше/вы́ше полóженного.

overwhelm *v.t.* **1**, (overpower; crush) разбивáть; (раз)громи́ть; сокрушáть. **2**, (swamp) завáливать: *overwhelmed with work*, завáлен рабóтой. **3**, (overcome, as with emotion) охвáтывать. *Overwhelmed with grief*, уби́тый гóрем.

overwhelming *adj.* подавля́ющий. *Overwhelming*

majority, подавля́ющее большинство́.

overwind *v.t.* перевёртывать (часы́).

overwork *v.t.* переутомля́ть. —*v.i.* переутомля́ться; перераба́тывать. —*n.* переутомле́ние.

oviduct *n.* яйцево́д.

oviparous *adj.* яйцекладу́щий; яйцеро́дный.

ovulation *n.* овуля́ция.

ovule *n.* 1, *biol.* яйцекле́тка. 2, *bot.* семяпо́чка.

ovum *n.* яйцо́.

owe *v.t.* 1, (be indebted in the sum of) *rendered by* до́лжен: *he owes me five dollars,* он мне до́лжен пять до́лларов. *You owe ten rubles,* с вас (приходи́ться) де́сять рубле́й. *I owe you an apology,* я до́лжен извини́ться пе́ред ва́ми. 2, (be obligated for) *rendered by* обя́зан: *I owe everything to my teacher,* я всем обя́зан моему́ учи́телю.

owing to из-за; благодаря́ (+ *dat.*); всле́дствие (+ *gen.*); по причи́не (+ *gen.*).

owl *n.* сова́. —**owlish,** *adj.* сови́ный.

own *v.t.* владе́ть: *own a house/car,* владе́ть до́мом/маши́ной. —*v.i.* [*usu.* **own up**] призна́ться (во всём). —*adj.* со́бственный: *see with one's own eyes,* ви́деть (что́-нибудь) со́бственными глаза́ми. *A house of one's own,* свой со́бственный дом. *Go one's own way,* идти́ свое́й доро́гой. *She makes all her own clothes,* она́ шьёт себе́ всё сама́. —**come into one's**

own, вступи́ть в свои́ права́. —**hold one's own,** держа́ться. *He can hold his own against the best players,* он мо́жет поспо́рить с лу́чшими игрока́ми. —**on one's own, 1,** (alone; independently) в одино́чку; самостоя́тельно. *Leave on one's own,* предоставля́ть самому́ себе́. **2,** (on one's own initiative) по со́бственному почи́ну *or* побужде́нию. —**to each his own,** ка́ждому свое́.

owner *n.* владе́лец; со́бственник; хозя́ин. —**ownerless,** *adj.* бесхозя́йный. —**ownership,** *n.* владе́ние; со́бственность.

ox *n.* вол.

oxalic acid щаве́левая кислота́.

oxeye daisy нивя́ник.

oxford *n.* полуботи́нок. *Also,* **oxford shoe.**

oxidation *n.* окисле́ние.

oxide *n.* о́кись; о́кисел. *Ferric oxide,* о́кись желе́за. *Ferrous oxide,* за́кись желе́за.

oxidize *v.t.* окисля́ть. —*v.i.* окисля́ться.

oxygen *n.* кислоро́д. —*adj.* кислоро́дный. —**oxygen mask,** кислоро́дная ма́ска. —**oxygen tent,** кислоро́дная пала́тка.

oyster *n.* у́стрица. —*adj.* у́стричный: *oyster shell,* у́стричная ра́ковина.

ozocerite *n.* озокери́т.

ozone *n.* озо́н.

P

P, p шестна́дцатая бу́ква англи́йского алфави́та.

pa *n., colloq.* па́па.

pace *n.* 1, (step) шаг: *step off twenty paces,* отсчи́тывать два́дцать шаго́в. 2, (rate of speed or progress) темп. *At a brisk/snail's pace,* бы́стрым/черепа́шьим ша́гом. 3, (gait of a horse) и́ноходь. —*v.t.* 1, (walk back and forth across) расха́живать по; проха́живаться по. 2, *fol. by* **off** (measure by paces) отмеря́ть. 3, *fol. by* **oneself** (set a pace for oneself) задава́ть себе́ темп. —*v.i.* шага́ть; расха́живать. —**keep pace with,** идти́ в но́гу с; идти́ наравне́ с; поспева́ть за. —**off the pace,** позади́: *keep off the pace,* держа́ться позади́. —**put through one's paces,** подверга́ть испыта́ниям. —**set the pace,** задава́ть темп.

pacemaker *n., med.* стимуля́тор се́рдца.

pacer *n.* иноходе́ц.

pachyderm *n.* толстоко́жее живо́тное.

·····fic *adj.* 1, (peaceful; calm) споко́йный; ти́хий; ¬ot warlike) ми́рный; миролюби́вый. —**Pacific ⸺an,** Ти́хий океа́н.

·⸺fication *n.* умиротворе́ние.

fier *n.* 1, (one who pacifies) миротво́рец. 2, a baby to suck on) со́ска.

·····fism *n.* пацифи́зм. —**pacifist,** *n.* пацифи́ст. *¬j.* пацифи́стский.

pacify *v.t.* 1, (quiet; calm) усмиря́ть. 2, (establish peace in) умиротворя́ть.

pack *n.* 1, (carried by a person) кото́мка; ра́нец. 2, (carried by an animal) вьюк. 3, (of cigarettes) па́чка. 4, (of cards) коло́да. 5, (of dogs, wolves, etc.) ста́я; сво́ра. 6, (gang; band) ша́йка; сво́ра. 7, *med.* обёртывание. 8, *in* **pack of lies,** сплошна́я ложь. —*v.t.* 1, (put in a suitcase; fill, as a suitcase) укла́дывать; упако́вывать. 2, (put in a box, bag, etc.) упако́вывать; запако́вывать. 3, (cram) заполня́ть; набива́ть. *The hall was packed,* зал был битко́м наби́т. *Play to packed houses,* де́лать по́лные сбо́ры; идти́ с аншла́гом. 4, *fol. by* **down** (press down firmly) уплотня́ть. 5, *fol. by* **off** (send off) отсыла́ть. —*v.i.* 1, *often fol. by* **up** (pack one's things) укла́дываться; упако́вываться. 2, (form into a solid mass) уплотня́ться. —**send packing,** спрова́живать; выпрова́живать.

package *n.* 1, (bundle) паке́т. 2, (parcel) посы́лка. —*v.t.* фасова́ть.

packaging *n.* фасо́вка; расфасо́вка.

pack animal вью́чное живо́тное.

packer *n.* упако́вщик.

packet *n.* 1, (small package) паке́т; па́чка. 2, (ship) пакетбо́т.

packing *n.* **1,** (act) упако́вка. **2,** (material) наби́вка. —*adj.* упако́вочный. —**packing case,** упако́вочный я́щик. —**packing house,** консе́рвная фа́брика.

packsaddle *n.* вьючное седло́.

pact *n.* пакт; догово́р.

pad *n.* **1,** (cushionlike object) поду́шечка. **2,** (writing tablet) блокно́т. **3,** (floating leaf, as of a lily) лист. **4,** (stamp pad) поду́шечка для штемпеле́й. —*v.t.* **1,** (line with padding) подбива́ть ва́той *or* волоса́ми. **2,** (expand unduly) раздува́ть; разма́зывать.

padding *n.* наби́вка; прокла́дка.

paddle *n.* **1,** (oar) весло́; гребо́к. **2,** (stick for administering punishment) па́лка. **3,** *sports* (racket) раке́тка. —*v.t.* **1,** (row) грести́. **2,** (spank) бить па́лкой. —**paddle boat,** колёсный парохо́д. —**paddle wheel,** гребно́е колесо́.

paddock *n.* заго́н.

paddy *n.* [*usu.* **rice paddy**] ри́совое по́ле.

padlock *n.* вися́чий замо́к. —*v.t.* запира́ть на вися́чий замо́к.

paean *n.* хвале́бная песнь.

pagan *n.* язы́чник. —*adj.* язы́ческий. —**paganism,** *n.* язы́чество.

page *n.* **1,** (of a book, newspaper, etc.) страни́ца. **2,** (attendant) паж. —*v.t.* (call; summon) вызыва́ть.

pageant *n.* **1,** (dramatic presentation) спекта́кль. **2,** (costumed procession) ше́ствие; пара́д. —**pageantry,** *n.* по́мпа; блеск; великоле́пие.

page proofs вёрстка; корректу́ра в листа́х.

pagination *n.* пагина́ция.

pagoda *n.* па́года.

paid *adj.* опла́чиваемый; пла́тный. *Paid vacation,* опла́чиваемый о́тпуск. *Paid worker,* пла́тный рабо́тник. *Well paid,* хорошо́ опла́чиваемый.

pail *n.* ведро́. *Milk pail,* подо́йник.

pain *n.* **1,** (feeling of discomfort) боль: *pain in one's chest,* боль в груди́. *Cry out in pain,* вскри́кнуть от бо́ли. *Are you in much pain?,* вам о́чень бо́льно? **2,** *pl.* (efforts) стара́ния. *Take pains,* прилага́ть стара́ния; о́чень стара́ться. —*v.t.* огорча́ть. *It pains me to think about it,* мне бо́льно ду́мать об э́том. —**on pain of,** под стра́хом (+ *gen.*): *on pain of death,* под стра́хом сме́рти.

pained *adj.* огорчённый: *pained look,* огорчённый вид.

painful *adj.* **1,** (hurting) больно́й. *Is it painful?,* вам бо́льно? **2,** (causing pain) боле́зненный: *painful bite,* боле́зненный уку́с. **3,** (unpleasant; agonizing) мучи́тельный. *It is painful to watch,* бо́льно смотре́ть на э́то. —**painfully,** *adv.* боле́зненно; мучи́тельно.

painkiller *n.* болеутоля́ющее сре́дство.

painless *adj.* безболе́зненный. —**painlessly,** *adv.* безболе́зненно.

painstaking *adj.* тща́тельный; стара́тельный. —**painstakingly,** *adv.* тща́тельно; стара́тельно.

paint *n.* кра́ска. —*v.t.* **1,** (coat with paint) кра́сить. **2,** (make, as a picture; make a picture of) писа́ть. **3,** (apply cosmetics to) кра́сить. **4,** (swab) сма́зывать. **5,** *fig.* (describe; depict) рисова́ть; изобража́ть. —*v.i.* писа́ть кра́сками. *Paint in oils,* писа́ть ма́слом.

paintbrush *n.* кисть.

painted *adj.* кра́шеный.

painter *n.* **1,** (house painter) маля́р. **2,** (artist) худо́жник.

painting *n.* **1,** (the art) жи́вопись. **2,** (a painted picture) ро́спись; карти́на.

pair *n.* па́ра: *pair of shoes/pants,* па́ра сапо́г/брюк. *Pair of scissors,* но́жницы. *In pairs,* па́рами; попа́рно. —*v.t.* спа́ривать; случа́ть. —*v.i.* [*usu.* **pair off**] разделя́ться попа́рно.

pajamas *also,* **pyjamas** *n.* пижа́ма.

Pakistani *adj.* пакиста́нский. —*n.* пакиста́нец; пакиста́нка.

pal *n.,* *colloq.* прия́тель; това́рищ. —*v.i.,* [*usu.* **pal around**] дружи́ть (с).

palace *n.* дворе́ц. —*adj.* дворцо́вый: *palace guard,* дворцо́вая стра́жа; *palace coup,* дворцо́вый переворо́т.

palatable *adj.* **1,** (fit to be eaten) вку́сный. **2,** (agreeable; acceptable) прия́тный.

palatal *adj.* **1,** (pert. to the palate) нёбный. **2,** *phonet.* палата́льный.

palatalize *v.t.* палатализова́ть. —**palatalization,** *n.* палатализа́ция.

palate *n.* **1,** (roof of the mouth) нёбо. **2,** (sense of taste) вкус.

palatial *adj.* роско́шный; великоле́пный.

palaver *n.* пуста́я болтовня́.

pale *n.* **1,** (pallid; not bright) бле́дный: *pale cheeks/colors,* бле́дные щёки/кра́ски. *Pale moon,* бле́дная луна́. **2,** (denoting a light shade) бле́дно-: *pale blue,* бле́дно-голубо́й. —*n.* **1,** (stake) кол. **2,** (boundary) грани́ца; преде́лы. *The Pale of Settlement,* черта́ осе́длости. —*v.i.* **1,** (turn pale) бледне́ть. **2,** *fol. by* **before** (suffer in comparison with) бледне́ть (пе́ред); тускне́ть (пе́ред).

Paleo-Asiatic *adj.* палеоазиа́тский.

paleography *n.* палеогра́фия. —**paleographer,** *n.* палео́граф. —**paleographic,** *adj.* палеографи́ческий.

paleolithic *adj.* палеолити́ческий.

paleontology *n.* палеонтоло́гия. —**paleontologist,** *n.* палеонто́лог. —**paleontological,** *adj.* палеонтологи́ческий.

Paleozoic *adj.* палеозо́йский.

Palestinian *adj.* палести́нский. —*n.* палести́нец; палести́нка.

palette *n.* пали́тра. —**palette knife,** шпа́тель.

paling *n.* частоко́л; тын.

palisade *n.* палиса́д.

pall *n.* **1,** (covering for a coffin) покро́в. **2,** (gloom) мра́чность. *Cast a pall over,* омрача́ть. —*v.i.* [*usu.* **pall on**] приеда́ться (+ *dat.*); пригля́дываться (+ *dat.*).

palladium *n.* палла́дий.

pallbearer *n.* челове́к, несу́щий гроб.

pallet *n.* **1,** (straw mattress) тюфя́к. **2,** (pawl) соба́чка.

palliate *v.t.* облегча́ть; смягча́ть. —**palliative,** *n.* паллиати́в. —*adj.* паллиати́вный.

pallid *adj.* бле́дный. —**pallor,** *n.* бле́дность.

palm *n.* **1,** (of the hand) ладо́нь. **2,** (tree) па́льма. —*adj.* па́льмовый. —*v.t.* [*usu.* **palm off**] вsuча́ть; подсо́вывать. —**know like the palm of one's hand,** знать как свои́ пять па́льцев.

palmist *n.* хирома́нт. —**palmistry,** *n.* хирома́нтия.

palm oil па́льмовое ма́сло.

Palm Sunday ве́рбное воскресе́нье.

palpable *adj.* **1,** (tangible) осязáемый; ощутúмый. **2,** (obvious) очевúдный; я́вный.

palpitate *v.i.* трепетáть. —**palpitation,** *n.* трéпет; трепетáние.

palsy *n.* паралúч.

paltry *adj.* ничтóжный; пустякóвый.

pampas *n.pl.* пампáсы.

pamper *v.t.* баловáть; нéжить; изнéживать.

pamphlet *n.* **1,** (small unbound book) брошю́ра. **2,** (political article published in same) памфлéт. — **pamphleteer,** *n.* памфлетúст.

pan *n.* **1,** (frying pan) сковородá; (roasting pan) жарóвня; (baking pan) прóтивень. **2,** (dishpan) таз для мытья́ посýды; (dustpan) совóк. —*v.t.* **1,** (separate, as gold) промывáть. **2,** *colloq.* (criticize unfavorably) раскритиковáть; разругáть. —**pan out,** *colloq.* вы́гореть.

panacea *n.* панацéя; универсáльное срéдство.

Panama hat панáма.

pancake *n.* блин; олáдья.

panchromatic *adj.* панхроматúческий.

pancreas *n.* поджелýдочная железá. —**pancreatic,** *adj.* поджелýдочный.

panda *n.* пáнда.

pandemic *n.* пандемúя.

pandemonium *n.* гвалт; хáос; бедлáм.

pander *v.i.* **1,** (act as a pander) своднúчать. **2,** *fol. by* **to** (cater to) потвóрствовать. —*n.* [*also,* **panderer**] свóдник.

pane *n.* (окóнное) стеклó.

panegyric *n.* панегúрик. —**panegyrist,** *n.* панегирúст.

panel *n.* **1,** (section of a wall, door, etc.) панéль; филёнка. **2,** (board with instruments or controls) щит; щитóк. *Instrument panel,* прибóрная доскá. *Control panel,* щит управлéния; пульт. **3,** (committee) комúссия. *Panel of judges,* судéйская коллéгия. —*v.t.* обшивáть панéлями *or* филёнками. —**paneled,** *adj.* филёночный; филёнчатый. —**paneling,** *n.* панéль.

pang *n., usu. pl.* мýки; бóли: *hunger pangs,* мýки гóлода; голóдные бóли. *Pangs of childbirth,* родовы́е мýки *or* потýги. —**pangs of conscience,** угрызéния сóвести.

pangolin *n.* я́щер.

panhandler *n.* попрошáйка.

panic *n.* пáника. —*v.t.* наводúть пáнику на. —*v.i.* впадáть в пáнику; поддавáться пáнике.

panicky *adj.* панúческий. *Get panicky,* впадáть в пáнику.

panicle *n.* метёлка.

panic-stricken *adj.* панúческий; охвáченный пáникой.

panoply *n.* **1,** (suit of armor) доспéхи. **2,** (magnificent array) блеск.

panorama *n.* панорáма. —**panoramic,** *adj.* панорáмный.

pansy *n.* аню́тины глáзки.

pant *v.i.* пыхтéть; задыхáться; запыхáться; отдувáться. —*n.* вздох.

pantheism *n.* пантеúзм. —**pantheist,** *n.* пантеúст. —**pantheistic,** *adj.* пантеистúческий.

pantheon *n.* пантеóн.

panther *n.* пантéра.

panties *n.pl.* трýсики.

pantomime *n.* пантомúма. —*adj.* пантомимúческий; пантомúмный.

pantry *n.* кладовáя.

pants *n.pl.* брю́ки; штаны́.

panty hose колгóтки.

pap *n.* кáшка.

papa *n.* пáпа.

papacy *n.* пáпство. —**papal,** *adj.* пáпский.

papaya *n.* ды́нное дéрево.

paper *n.* **1,** (material) бумáга. **2,** (newspaper) газéта. **3,** (treatise) доклáд: *deliver a paper,* читáть доклáд. **4,** (written work for school) сочинéние. *Term paper,* курсовáя рабóта. **5,** (document) бумáга; докумéнт. —*v.t.* **1,** (cover with wallpaper) оклéивать (обóями). **2,** *fol. by* **over** (cover up) замáзывать. —**on paper, 1,** (in writing) в пúсьменной фóрме. **2,** (in theory) на бумáге.

paperback *n.* кнúга в бумáжной облóжке.

paper clip скрéпка.

paperhanger *n.* обóйщик.

paperweight *n.* пресс-папьé.

paper work делопроизвóдство.

papier-mâché *n.* папьé-машé.

papoose *n.* индéйский ребёнок.

paprika *n.* крáсный пéрец; пáприка.

papule *n.* пáпула.

papyrus *n.* папúрус.

par *n.* **1,** (equal status): *be/rank on a par with,* быть наравнé с; стоя́ть в однóм ряду́ с. **2,** (normal state or level): *up to par,* на дóлжной высотé; *below par,* не на высотé. **3,** *finance* номинáл. —*adj.* **1,** *finance* номинáльный: *par value,* номинáльная ценá. **2,** (normal; up to par) нормáльный.

parable *n.* прúтча.

parabola *n.* парáбола. —**parabolic,** *adj.* параболúческий.

parachute *n.* парашю́т. —*v.i.* пры́гать *or* вы́броситься с парашю́том. —**parachutist,** *n.* парашютúст.

parade *n.* парáд. —*v.i.* шéствовать. —*v.t.* (flaunt) щеголя́ть. —**parade ground,** плац.

paradigm *n.* парадúгма.

paradise *n.* рай.

paradox *n.* парадóкс. —**paradoxical,** *adj.* парадоксáльный.

paraffin *n.* парафúн.

paragon *n.* образéц.

paragraph *n.* абзáц; пáраграф. *Begin a new paragraph,* начинáть с нóвой (*or* с крáсной) строки́.

parakeet *n.* мáленький попугáй.

parallax *n.* параллáкс.

parallel *adj.* параллéльный. —*adv.* параллéльно. —*n.* параллéль: *the 40th parallel,* сороковáя параллéль. *Draw a parallel,* проводúть параллéль. *Without parallel,* не имéющий себé рáвного. —*v.t.* **1,** (run parallel to) идтú параллéльно (+ *dat.*). **2,** (be analogous to) соотвéтствовать (+ *dat.*). —**parallel bars,** параллéльные брýсья.

parallelepiped *n.* параллелепúпед.

parallelism *n.* параллелúзм.

parallelogram *n.* параллелогрáмм.

paralyse *v.t.* = **paralyze.**

paralysis *n.* паралúч. —**paralytic,** *adj.* паралитúческий; паралúчный. —*n.* паралúтик.

paralyze *also,* **paralyse** *v.t.* парализовáть. —**para-**
lyzed, *adj.* парализóван(ный).
paramecium *n.* тýфелька; парамéция.
parameter *n.* парáметр.
paramilitary *adj.* полувоéнный.
paramount *adj.* **1,** (first in rank or title) верхóвный.
2, (overriding) первостепéнный. *Of paramount im-*
portance, величáйшей *or* первостепéнной вáж-
ности.
paramour *n.* любóвник; любóвница.
paranoia *n.* паранóйя. —**paranoiac,** *n.* паранóик.
—**paranoid,** *adj.* паранóйческий.
parapet *n.* **1,** (low wall or railing) парапéт. **2,** *mil.*
(embankment) брýствер.
paraphernalia *n.* принадлéжности.
paraphrase *n.* перефразирóвка. —*v.t.* перефра-
зировáть.
paraplegia *n.* параплегия. —**paraplegic,** *n.* больнóй параплегией.
parasite *n.* **1,** *biol.* паразит. **2,** (sponger) тунеядец;
дармоéд; прихлебáтель; паразит. —**parasitic,** *adj.*
паразитический; паразитный. —**parasitism,** *n.*
паразитизм.
parasol *n.* сóлнечный зóнтик.
parathyroid gland околощитовидная железá;
паращитовидная железá.
paratrooper *n.* парашютист.
paratyphoid *n.* паратиф. *Also,* **paratyphoid fever.**
parcel *n.* **1,** (package sent through the mail) посылка.
2, (package; bundle) пакéт. **3,** (plot of land) учáсток
(земли). —*v.t.* [*usu.* **parcel out**] выделять; распределять. —**part and parcel,** неотъéмлемая часть.
parch *v.t.* иссушáть. *My throat is parched,* у меня
в гóрле пересóхло. *My lips are parched,* мои гýбы
запеклись.
parchment *n.* пергáмент. —*adj.* пергáментный.
pardon *v.t.* **1,** (forgive) прощáть; извинять. **2,** (release from punishment) помиловать. —*n.* **1,** (forgiveness) прощéние. *I beg your pardon, see* **beg. 2,**
(release from punishment) помилование. —**pardon-**
able, *adj.* простительный.
pare *v.t.* **1,** (peel) чистить. **2,** (reduce) урéзывать.
parent *n., usu. pl.* родители. —**parentage,** *n.* происхождéние. —**parental,** *adj.* родительский.
parentheses *n.pl.* скóбки. —**parenthesize,** *v.t.* заключáть в скóбки. —**parenthetic(al),** *adj.* вводный.
—**parenthetically,** *adv.* в скóбках.
parenthood *n.* отцóвство; материнство.
paresis *n.* парéз.
par excellence превосхóдный; замечáтельный.
pariah *n.* пáрия.
pari-mutuel *n., usu. pl.* тотализáтор.
paring knife нож для чистки фрýктов и овощéй;
фруктóвый нож.
parish *n.* (церкóвный) прихóд. —*adj.* прихóдский:
parish priest, прихóдский свящéнник. —**parish-**
ioner, *n.* прихожáнин.
Parisian *adj.* парижский. —*n.* парижáнин.
parity *n.* паритéт.
park *n.* парк. —*v.t.* **1,** (a car) стáвить (машину).
2, *colloq.* (place) оставлять; положить. *Park oneself*
somewhere, расположиться; усéсться.
parka *n.* пáрка.
parking *n.* стоянка. *No parking!,* стоянка запреще-
нá! —**parking lights,** подфáрники. —**parking lot,**

стоянка (для автомобилей). —**parking place/**
space, мéсто (стоянки автомобиля).
parkway *n.* шоссé.
parlance *n.* язык: *legal parlance,* юридический
язык. *In common parlance,* в просторéчии.
parley *n.* переговóры. —*v.i.* вести переговóры.
parliament *n.* парлáмент. —**parliamentarianism,**
n. парламентаризм. —**parliamentary,** *adj.* парлáментский; парламентáрный.
parlor *also,* **parlour** *n.* **1,** (sitting room) гостиная. **2,**
(establishment): *beauty parlor,* косметический каби-
нéт; *ice-cream parlor,* кафé-морóженое. —**parlor**
car, салóн-вагóн. —**parlor games,** кóмнатные
игры.
parochial *adj.* **1,** (of a parish) прихóдский. **2,** (narrow; provincial) ýзкий; ограниченный. —**parochial**
school, прихóдская шкóла.
parody *n.* парóдия. —*v.t.* пародировать. —**paro-**
dist, *n.* пародист.
parole *n.* услóвно-досрóчное освобождéние. —*v.t.*
освобождáть под чéстное слóво.
paroxysm *n.* пароксизм.
parquet *n.* паркéт. —*adj.* паркéтный. —**parquetry,**
n. паркéт.
parrot *n.* попугáй. —*v.t.* **1,** (repeat) повторять как
попугáй. **2,** (say the same thing as) подпевáть.
parry *v.t.* **1,** (ward off) отражáть; отбивáть; парировать. **2,** (evade) уклоняться от: *parry a question,*
уклоняться от отвéта.
parse *v.t.* разбирáть.
parsimonious *adj.* скупóй. —**parsimony,** *n.* скýпость.
parsley *n.* петрýшка.
parsnip *n.* пастернáк.
parson *n.* прихóдский свящéнник.
part *n.* **1,** (portion; element) часть: *part of the whole,*
часть цéлого. *Parts of the body,* чáсти тéла. *Spare*
parts, запасные чáсти. *Part of speech,* часть рéчи.
2, (role) роль: *bit part,* выходнáя роль. **3,** *pl.* (locality) края: *in these parts,* в этих краях. **4,** (in one's
hair) пробóр. **5,** *music* пáртия. —*adj.* частичный:
a part interest in, частичная дóля (+ *gen.*). *Part*
owner, совладéлец. —*adv.* частично: *she is part*
Russian and part French, онá частично рýсская и
частично францýженка. —*v.t.* **1,** (separate) разлу-
чáть. *Till death do us part,* покá смерть нас не раз-
лучит. **2,** (comb with a part): *part one's hair,* дéлать
себé пробóр. *Part one's hair in the middle/on the side/,*
носить вóлосы на прямóй/косóй пробóр. —*v.i.* **1,**
(divide) разделяться; расступáться; раздвигáться.
2, (part company) расставáться; разлучáться. *We*
parted friends, мы расстáлись *or* разошлись друзьями. **3,** *fol. by* **with** (relinquish) расставáться с. —**do**
one's part, дéлать своé дéло. —**for my part,** я,
со своéй стороны; что касáется меня. —**for the**
most part, *see* **most.** —**in large part,** во мнóгом.
—**in part,** чáстью; частично; отчáсти. —**in parts,**
по частям. —**on the part of,** со стороны (+ *gen.*).
—**take part in,** принимáть учáстие в; учáствовать в.
partake *v.i.* **1,** *fol. by* **in** (take part in) принимáть
учáстие (в). **2,** *fol. by* **of** (take, as food) поéсть. —
partake oneself, угощáться.
parthenogenesis *n.* партеногенéз.
Parthenon *n.* Парфенóн.
partial *adj.* **1,** (involving only a part) частичный. **2,**

(biased) пристра́стный. **3,** *fol. by* **to** (particularly fond of) пристра́стный (к).

partiality *n.* пристра́стие; пристра́стность.

partially *adv.* части́чно; отча́сти.

participant *n.* уча́стник.

paticipate *v.i.* уча́ствовать. —**participation,** *n.* уча́стие.

participle *n.* прича́стие. —**participial,** *adj.* прича́стный.

particle *n.* **1,** (speck) части́ца: *particle of dust,* части́ца пы́ли. **2,** (tiny amount) части́ца; крупи́нка; крупи́ца. *Not a particle of difference,* ни мале́йшей ра́зницы. **3,** *physics* части́ца: *elementary particle,* элемента́рная части́ца. **4,** *gram.* части́ца.

particular *adj.* **1,** (special; unusual) осо́бенный; осо́бый. *Nothing in particular,* ничего́ осо́бенного. *For no particular reason,* без осо́бой причи́ны. **2,** (specific; individual) ча́стный. *At this particular time,* в да́нный моме́нт. *Why did you choose this particular color?,* почему́ вы вы́брали и́менно э́тот цвет? **3,** (fussy) разбо́рчивый; привере́дливый. —*n.* подро́бность. —**in particular,** в ча́стности; в осо́бенности.

particularity *n.* осо́бенность.

particularly *adv.* осо́бенно.

parting *n.* расстава́ние; разлу́ка; проща́ние. *At parting,* на проща́ние. —*adj.* проща́льный.

partisan *n.* **1,** (adherent) сторо́нник. **2,** (guerrilla) партиза́н. —*adj.* **1,** (biased) пристра́стный. **2,** (of guerrillas) партиза́нский. —**partisanship,** *n.* пристра́стие.

partition *n.* **1,** (dividing up) разделе́ние; разде́л. **2,** (something that divides) перегоро́дка. —*v.t.* **1,** (divide into parts) разделя́ть. **2,** *fol. by* **off** (separate by a partition) отгора́живать; перегора́живать.

partitive *adj., gram.* раздели́тельный.

partly *adv.* ча́стью; части́чно; отча́сти.

partner *n.* **1,** (in business) компаньо́н; това́рищ; партнёр. **2,** (in a game) партнёр. **3,** (in dancing) кавале́р; да́ма. —**partnership,** *n.* това́рищество.

partridge *n.* куропа́тка.

part-time *adj. & adv.* на полста́вки. *Work part-time,* рабо́тать на полста́вки; рабо́тать непо́лный день.

partway *adv.* полпути́: *I'll walk you partway,* я пройду́ с ва́ми полпути́.

party *n.* **1,** (social gathering) вечери́нка; ве́чер. **2,** (political party) па́ртия. **3,** *law* сторона́: *interested party,* заинтересо́ванная сторона́. *Through a third party,* че́рез тре́тье лицо́. **4,** (participant) уча́стник. *Be a party to,* быть прича́стным к. **5,** (group of people organized for a purpose) гру́ппа: *search party,* по́исковая гру́ппа. **6,** *mil.* (detachment; detail) кома́нда; па́ртия. *Rescue party,* спаса́тельная кома́нда. —*adj.* парти́йный: *party congress,* парти́йный съезд. —**party line, 1,** (of telephones) телефо́н сме́шанного по́льзования. **2,** *polit.* парти́йная ли́ния.

paschal *adj.* пасха́льный. —**paschal lamb,** пасха́льный а́гнец.

pasha *n.* паша́.

pass *v.t.* **1,** (go by; go past) проходи́ть ми́мо; проезжа́ть ми́мо; минова́ть. **2,** (go beyond) проходи́ть; проезжа́ть. **3,** (overtake) обгоня́ть. *No passing!,* не обгоня́ть! обго́н воспрещён! **4,** (hand over, as at the table) передава́ть. **5,** (move in a certain way) проводи́ть: *pass one's hand through one's hair,* проводи́ть руко́й по волоса́м. *Pass something through*

a filter, пропуска́ть что́-нибудь че́рез фильтр. **6,** (complete successfully, as a test) сдать; вы́держать. **7,** (enact, as a bill) принима́ть. **8,** (while away, as time) корота́ть. **9,** (pronounce, as a sentence) выноси́ть. **10,** (excrete; void) испуска́ть. **11,** *sports* пасова́ть. —*v.i.* **1,** (move ahead; move past; extend) проходи́ть. *Let pass,* пропуска́ть. **2,** (go by; be over) проходи́ть; минова́ть: *a whole year passed,* прошёл це́лый год; *the danger has passed,* опа́сность минова́ла. **3,** (be transferred or communicated) переходи́ть. **4,** (be approved or adopted) быть при́нятым. **5,** *cards* пасова́ть. —*n.* **1,** (passage between mountains) перева́л. **2,** (permit) про́пуск; путёвка. **3,** (free ticket) контрама́рка. **4,** *mil.* (leave) о́тпуск; побы́вка. **5,** *sports* пас; переда́ча. **6,** *cards* пас. —**come to pass,** произойти́; случи́ться. —**pass away,** сконча́ться. —**pass by,** проходи́ть ми́мо; проходи́ть стороно́й. —**pass for,** сходи́ть за. —**pass off,** выдава́ть: *pass oneself off as a physician,* выдава́ть себя́ за врача́. —**pass on, 1,** (give to the next person) передава́ть. **2,** (die) умира́ть. —**pass out, 1,** (hand out) раздава́ть. **2,** *colloq.* (faint) потеря́ть созна́ние; упа́сть в о́бморок. —**pass over, 1,** (skip; disregard) пропуска́ть; обходи́ть. *Pass over in silence,* обходи́ть молча́нием. **2,** (fail to promote) обходи́ть. —**pass through,** проезжа́ть че́рез. *I am just passing through,* я здесь прое́здом. —**pass up,** *colloq.* пропуска́ть.

passable *adj.* **1,** (traversable) проходи́мый. **2,** (barely satisfactory) сно́сный.

passage *n.* **1,** (passing) перехо́д; прохожде́ние; прохо́д; прое́зд. **2,** (passageway) прохо́д; перехо́д; прое́зд. **3,** (voyage) перее́зд. *To book passage,* брать биле́т на парохо́д. **4,** (lapse, as of time) тече́ние (вре́мени). **5,** (enactment, as of a law) приня́тие. **6,** (portion of something written) отры́вок. **7,** *music* пасса́ж.

passageway *n.* прохо́д; перехо́д; коридо́р.

passbook *n.* сберега́тельная кни́жка.

passed pawn *chess* проходна́я пе́шка.

passenger *n.* пассажи́р. —*adj.* пассажи́рский. *Passenger car,* легково́й автомоби́ль. —**passenger pigeon,** стра́нствующий го́лубь.

passer-by *n.* прохо́жий; встре́чный.

passing *adj.* **1,** (going by) проходя́щий. *With each passing year,* с ка́ждым го́дом; год от году. **2,** (quick; cursory) бе́глый: *passing glance,* бе́глый взгляд. **3,** (transitory) мимолётный: *passing fancy,* мимолётная при́хоть. **4,** (casual, as of a remark) попу́тный. **5,** (satisfactory, as of a grade) перехо́дный. —*n.* **1,** (act of passing) прохожде́ние. **2,** (death) кончи́на. —**in passing,** мимохо́дом; вскользь.

passion *n.* страсть: *a passion for music,* страсть к му́зыке. *Passions flared,* стра́сти разгоре́лись. *Fit of passion,* поры́в *or* вспы́шка гне́ва.

passionate *adj.* стра́стный. —**passionately,** *adv.* стра́стно.

passive *adj.* **1,** (not active) пасси́вный: *passive role,* пасси́вная роль. *Passive vocabulary,* пасси́вный слова́рь; пасси́вный запа́с слов. **2,** *gram.* страда́тельный: *passive voice,* страда́тельный зало́г.

passivity *n.* пасси́вность.

passkey *n.* отмы́чка.

Passover *n.* па́сха.

passport *n.* па́спорт. —*adj.* па́спортный: *passport department,* па́спортный отде́л.

password *n.* пароль; пропуск.

past *adj.* **1,** (of a former time) прошлый: *past wars,* прошлые войны. **2,** *preceded by* the (just gone by) последний; минувший; истёкший. *During the past year,* за последний/истёкший год. **3,** (former) бывший: *past president,* бывший президент. **4,** *gram.* прошедший: *past tense,* прошедшее время. —*n.* **1,** (past time) прошлое. *In the past,* в прошлом; раньше. *A thing of the past,* дело прошлое. **2,** *gram.* прошедшее время. —*prep.* **1,** (by) мимо: *slip past the guard,* проскользнуть мимо сторожа. **2,** (beyond) за: *past the city limits,* за пределами города. *Just past the station,* сразу после вокзала. *Well past midnight,* далеко за полночь. **3,** *in telling time: half-past six,* половина седьмого; *twenty past one,* двадцать минут второго. —*adv.* мимо. ♦*Often with the prefix* про-: *fly past,* пролетать; *dart past,* промчаться.

paste *n.* **1,** (soft, creamy substance) паста: *toothpaste,* зубная паста; *tomato paste,* томат-паста. **2,** (adhesive) (мучной) клей; клейстер. **3,** (dough) тесто: *puff paste,* слоёное тесто. —*v.t.* **1,** (affix) наклеивать. *Paste together,* склеивать. *Paste stamps in an album,* вклеивать марки в альбом. **2,** (cover with pasted material) оклеивать. **3,** *slang* (smack) треснуть.

pasteboard *n.* картон.

pastel *n.* пастель. —*adj.* пастельный.

pastern *n.* бабка.

pasteurize *v.t.* пастеризовать. —**pasteurization,** *n.* пастеризация.

pastime *n.* времяпрепровождение.

past master искусник.

pastor *n.* пастор; пастырь.

pastoral *adj.* пасторальный. —*n.* пастораль.

pastorale *n.* пастораль.

pastry *n.* кондитерские изделия; пирожное. —**pastry cook; pastry chef,** кондитер. —**pastry shop,** кондитерская.

pasturage *n.* **1,** (grass) подножный корм. **2,** (land) пастбище. **3,** (grazing) пастьба.

pasture *n.* пастбище. —*v.i.* пастись. —**put out to pasture, 1,** *literally* (вы)пускать на подножный корм. **2,** (allow or compel to retire) увольнять в отставку.

pat *v.t.* похлопывать; трепать. *Pat someone on the back,* похлопывать кого-нибудь по плечу. —*n.* **1,** (tap) хлопок. **2,** (small piece, as of butter) кусочек; комок. —*adj.* готовый: *a pat answer for everything,* готовый ответ на всё. —**give (someone) a pat on the back,** гладить по головке. —**have down** (*or* **know**) **pat,** знать назубок. —**stand pat,** стоять на своём.

patch *n.* **1,** (covering, as for mending) заплата. **2,** (bandage) повязка: *eye patch,* повязка на глазу. **3,** (small plot) участок; клочок. **4,** (small piece or area) клочок: *patch of fog,* клочок тумана; *patch of blue,* клочок лазури. *Patch of sunlight,* солнечный блик. —*v.t.* **1,** (mend) латать; накладывать заплату на. **2,** *fol. by* up (settle) улаживать.

patch pocket накладной карман.

patchwork *n.* **1,** (fabric made of patches) лоскутная работа: *patchwork quilt,* лоскутное одеяло. **2,** (jumble) мешанина; ералаш.

pate *n.* башка.

pâté *n.* паштет.

patent *n.* патент. —*adj.* **1,** (of or pert. to patents) патентный. **2,** (patented) патентованный. **3,** (obvious) явный: *a patent lie,* явная ложь. —*v.t.* патентовать. —**patent leather,** лакированная кожа. —**patent medicine,** патентованное лекарство.

paternal *adj.* **1,** (of one's father) отцовский. **2,** (fatherly) отеческий.

paternalistic *adj.* отеческий.

paternity *n.* отцовство.

path *n.* **1,** (footway) тропинка; тропа; дорожка. **2,** (course) путь.

pathetic *adj.* жалкий.

pathology *n.* патология. —**pathological,** *adj.* патологический. —**pathologist,** *n.* патолог.

pathos *n.* трогательность.

pathway *n.* тропинка; тропа; дорожка.

patience *n.* терпение.

patient *adj.* терпеливый. *Be patient!,* имейте терпение! —*n.* больной; пациент. —**patiently,** *adv.* терпеливо.

patio *n.* патио.

patois *n.* местный говор.

patriarch *n.* патриарх. —**patriarchal,** *adj.* патриархальный. —**patriarchate,** *n.* патриархия. —**patriarchy,** *n.* патриархат.

patrician *n.* патриций.

patricide *n.* отцеубийство.

patrimony *n.* отцовское наследие.

patriot *n.* патриот. —**patriotic,** *adj.* патриотический. —**patriotism,** *n.* патриотизм.

patrol *v.t.* патрулировать. —*n.* дозор; патруль. *Be on patrol,* быть в дозоре. —*adj.* дозорный; патрульный. *Patrol boat,* дозорное судно; сторожевой катер. —**patrolman,** *n.* полицейский.

patron *n.* **1,** (benefactor) покровитель. *Patron of the arts,* меценат. **2,** (customer) клиент.

patronage *n.* покровительство; протекция.

patronize *v.t.* **1,** (sponsor) покровительствовать. **2,** (be a regular customer of) покупать в. —**patronizing,** *adj.* покровительственный.

patronymic *n.* отчество. *Also,* **patronymic name.**

patter *n.* **1,** (drumming sound) стук; шум. *The patter of rain,* шум дождя. *The patter of feet,* топот ног. **2,** (rapid-fire speech) скороговорка. **3,** (cant; jargon) жаргон. —*v.i.* барабанить.

pattern *n.* **1,** (decorative design) узор. **2,** (diagram used in making garments) выкройка. **3,** (model; example) образец: *on the pattern of,* по образцу (*+gen.*). *Set the pattern for,* стать образцом для. **4,** *aero.* маршрут: *holding pattern,* маршрут ожидания; *landing pattern,* маршрут захода на посадку. —*v.t.* [*usu.* **pattern after**] делать (что-нибудь) по образцу (*+ gen.*). *Pattern oneself after,* брать пример с.

patty *n.* **1,** (flat piece of chopped meat) котлета. **2,** (small pie) пирожок.

paucity *n.* скудность.

paunch *n.* **1,** (potbelly) брюшко; пузо. **2,** (rumen) рубец. —**paunchy,** *adj.* пузатый.

pauper *n.* бедняк; нищий. *He died a pauper,* он умер в нищете.

pause *n.* пауза; перерыв; передышка. —*v.i.* делать паузу; останавливаться. —**give one pause,** наводить на размышления.

pave *v.t.* мостить. —**pave the way,** прокладывать путь; подготавливать почву.

paved *adj.* мощёный.

pavement *n.* тротуáр; панéль.

pavilion *n.* павильóн.

paving *n.* мощéние. —**paving block/stone,** торéц; *pl.* брусчáтка.

paw *n.* лáпа. —*v.t.* облáпить.

pawl *n.* собáчка.

pawn *n., chess* пéшка. —*v.t.* заклáдывать; отдавáть в залóг. —**pawnbroker,** *n.* залогодержáтель. —**pawnshop,** *n.* ломбáрд. —**pawn ticket,** ломбáрдная квитáнция.

pay *v.t.* **1,** (give in payment; settle) платúть: *pay ten dollars,* платúть дéсять дóлларов; *pay (in) cash,* платúть налúчными. *Pay a fine,* платúть штраф. *Pay a debt,* выплáчивать/уплáчивать/отдавáть долг. **2,** (give money to; remunerate) платúть (+ *dat.*): *pay the doctor,* платúть врачý. *Pay the cashier,* платúть кассúру; платúть в кáссу. **3,** *fol. by inf.* (be worthwhile) стóить: *it doesn't pay to argue with him,* не стóит с ним спóрить. **4,** (offer in wages) *the job pays 10,000 a year,* зарплáта – дéсять тысяч в год. **5,** *used with certain nouns: pay a visit on,* нанестú визúт (+ *dat.*); *pay attention to,* обращáть внимáние на; *pay someone a compliment,* сдéлать комý-нибудь комплимéнт. —*v.i.* **1,** (make payment) платúть. **2,** (offer wages) *the job pays well,* рабóта хорошó оплáчивается. **3,** (be worthwhile) стóить. **4,** (be profitable) окупáться. —*n.* плáта; зарплáта; жáлованье; оклáд. *Receive no pay,* не получáть зарплáты. *Base pay,* основнóй оклáд. *In the pay of,* на жáлованье у. —**pay back, 1,** (a person) отплáчивать (+ *dat.*). **2,** (money) возвращáть. *Pay back a loan,* выплáчивать *or* возвращáть заём. —**pay for, 1,** *literally* платúть за. **2,** (suffer the consequences of) платúться за; отвéтить за; расплáчиваться за. **3,** *Pay for itself,* окупáться. —**pay off, 1,** (pay in full) выплáчивать; расплáчиваться с; рассчúтываться с; погашáть. **2,** *colloq.* (succeed) увенчáться успéхом. **3,** *slang* (bribe) подкупáть. —**pay out, 1,** (disburse, as money) выплáчивать. **2,** *naut.* (let out, as a rope) травúть. —**pay up,** выплáчивать. *See also* **paid.**

payable *adj. Be payable,* подлежáть уплáте.

paycheck *n.* полýчка.

payday *n.* платёжный день.

payee *n.* получáтель (дéнег).

payer *n.* платéльщик.

paying *adj.* **1,** (who pays) плáтный. **2,** (profitable) рентáбельный.

payload *n.* **1,** *comm.* полéзный груз. **2,** *aero.* полéзная нагрýзка.

paymaster *n.* кассúр; казначéй.

payment *n.* **1,** (act of paying) плáта; оплáта; уплáта; платёж. **2,** (something paid) платёж. *Down payment,* задáток. *Balance of payments,* платёжный балáнс.

payoff *n., colloq.* **1,** (bribe) взятка. **2,** (climax) развязка.

pay phone телефóн-автомáт.

payroll *n.* платёжная вéдомость.

pea *n.* горóшина; *pl.* горóх; горóшек. —*adj.* горóховый: *pea soup,* горóховый суп.

peace *n.* **1,** (absence of war) мир: *at peace,* в мúре. *Live in peace,* жить в мúре. *Make peace with,* заключúть мир с. **2,** (peace of mind) покóй: *leave in peace,* оставлять в покóе. *May he rest in peace,* мир прáху

егó. **3,** (public order) порядок: *keep/disturb the peace,* блюстú/нарушáть порядок. —*adj.* мúрный: *peace treaty,* мúрный договóр. —**hold (or keep) one's peace,** придержáть язык.

peaceable *adj.* мúрный.

peaceful *adj.* **1,** (not involving war) мúрный: *for peaceful purposes,* в мúрных цéлях. **2,** (tranquil) спокóйный. —**peacefully,** *adv.* мúрно; спокóйно.

peacekeeping *n.* поддержáние *or* сохранéние мúра. *Peacekeeping force,* войскá по поддержáнию мúра.

peace-loving *adj.* миролюбúвый.

peacemaker *n.* миротвóрец.

peacetime *n.* мúрное врéмя.

peach *n.* пéрсик. —*adj.* пéрсиковый. —**peach tree,** пéрсик; пéрсиковое дéрево.

peacock *n.* павлúн. *Peacock feathers,* павлúньи пéрья.

peahen *n.* пáва.

pea jacket бушлáт.

peak *n.* **1,** (of a cap) козырёк. **2,** (of a mountain) пик; вершúна. **3,** *fig.* (high point; zenith) высшая тóчка; вершúна. *At the peak of one's powers,* в расцвéте (твóрческих) сил. —*adj.* максимáльный: *peak load,* максимáльная нагрýзка.

peal *n.* **1,** (of a bell) звон; трезвóн. **2,** (of thunder, laughter, etc.) раскáт. —*v.i.* гремéть; трезвóнить.

peanut *n.* арáхис; землянóй орéх. —**peanut butter,** пáста из тёртого арáхиса.

pear *n.* грýша. —*adj.* грýшевый.

pearl *n.* жéмчуг. *A single pearl,* жемчýжина. —*adj.* жемчýжный. —**pearl barley,** перлóвая крупá. —**pearl oyster,** жемчýжница.

pearly *adj.* жемчýжный.

peasant *n.* крестьянин. —*adj.* крестьянский. —**peasantry,** *n.* крестьянство.

peat *n.* торф. —*adj.* торфянóй. —**peat moss,** торфянóй мох.

pebble *n.* кáмешек; голыш; гáлька.

pecan *n.* пекáн.

peccadillo *n.* грешóк.

peccary *n.* пéкари.

peck *v.t. & i.* клевáть. —*n.* клевóк.

pectoral *adj.* груднóй: *pectoral muscles,* грудные мышцы. *Pectoral cross,* напéрсный крест.

peculiar *adj.* **1,** (unique; particular) осóбенный; своеобрáзный. **2,** (odd) стрáнный. —**peculiarity,** *n.* стрáнность.

pecuniary *adj.* дéнежный.

pedagogue *n.* педагóг. —**pedagogic(al),** *adj.* педагогúческий. —**pedagogy,** *n.* педагóгика.

pedal *n.* педáль. —*v.t.* вестú (велосипéд). —*v.i.* **1,** (work a pedal) нажимáть педáль. **2,** (ride a bicycle) éхать на велосипéде.

pedant *n.* педáнт. —**pedantic,** *adj.* педантúчный. —**pedantry,** *n.* педантúзм.

peddle *v.t. & i.* торговáть вразнóс. —**peddler,** *n.* коробéйник; разнóсчик.

pederast *n.* педерáст. —**pederasty,** *n.* педерáстия.

pedestal *n.* пьедестáл; постамéнт; поднóжие.

pedestrian *n.* пешехóд. —*adj.* **1,** (of or for pedestrians) пешехóдный. **2,** (commonplace; dull) прозаúческий.

pediatrics *n.* педиатрúя. —**pediatric,** *adj.* педиатрúческий. —**pediatrician,** *n.* педиáтр.

pedicel *n.* цветоно́жка.
pedicure *n.* педикю́р.
pedigree *n.* **1,** (lineage) происхожде́ние. **2,** (list of ancestors) родосло́вная. —**pedigreed,** *adj.* поро́дистый; племенно́й; чистокро́вный.
pediment *n.* фронто́н.
pedlar *n.* = **peddler.**
pedometer *n.* шагоме́р; педо́метр.
peek *n.* бы́стрый взгляд; взгляд укра́дкой. —*v.i.* загля́дывать.
peel *n.* ко́рка; кожура́; ко́жица; шелуха́. —*v.t.* **1,** (pare, as potatoes, fruit, etc.) чи́стить. **2,** *fol. by* **off** (remove) снима́ть (ко́рку); отклеива́ть (ма́рку). —*v.i.* **1,** (shed skin) лупи́ться: *my face is peeling,* у меня́ лу́пится лицо́. **2,** *often fol. by* **off** (come off) сходи́ть; шелуши́ться; осыпа́ться; лупи́ться; облу́пливаться. —**keep an eye peeled,** смотре́ть в о́ба.
peelings *n.pl.* очи́стки.
peep *v.i.* **1,** (look furtively) загля́дывать; подгля́дывать. **2,** (come partly into view) выгля́дывать; прогля́дывать. **3,** (chirp) пища́ть. —*n.* **1,** (glimpse) бы́стрый взгляд. **2,** (chirp) писк. **3,** (sound) звук.
peephole *n.* глазо́к.
peer *n.* **1,** (equal) ра́вный. **2,** (person one's own age) све́рстник. **3,** (nobleman) пэр. —*v.i.* всма́триваться; вгля́дываться. *Peer into a telescope,* смотре́ть в телеско́п. *Peer out the window,* выгля́дывать из окна́.
peerage *n.* **1,** (rank) пэ́рство. **2,** (peers collectively) сосло́вие пэ́ров.
peerless *adj.* несравне́нный; бесподо́бный.
peeve *v.t.* раздража́ть. —*n., usu. in* **pet peeve,** люби́мая мозо́ль; больно́е ме́сто. —**peeved,** *adj.* раздражённый. —**peevish,** *adj.* сварли́вый.
peg *n.* **1,** (conical pin) ко́лышек. **2,** (such a pin on a stringed instrument) коло́к. —**take (someone) down a peg,** сбива́ть спесь с.
peg leg деревя́нная нога́; деревя́шка.
peg top куба́рь.
peignoir *n.* пеньюа́р.
pejorative *adj.* уничижи́тельный.
pelican *n.* пелика́н.
pellagra *n.* пелла́гра.
pellet *n.* **1,** (small round ball) ша́рик. **2,** (small lead shot) дроби́н(к)а.
pellicle *n.* ко́жица; плёнка.
pell-mell *adv.* **1,** (in total disorder) впереме́шку. **2,** (in wild haste) сломя́ го́лову.
pellucid *adj.* прозра́чный.
pelt *n.* шку́ра. —*v.t.* (bombard) забра́сывать; засыпа́ть. —*v.i.* (beat down) бараба́нить.
pelvis *n.* таз. —**pelvic,** *adj.* та́зовый.
pen *n.* **1,** (quill pen) перо́; (fountain pen, ball-point, etc.) ру́чка. *Fountain pen,* авторучка. **2,** (enclosure for animals) заго́н. *Pigpen,* свина́рник. —*v.t.* **1,** (write; compose) писа́ть; сочиня́ть. **2,** (confine in a pen) загоня́ть в заго́н. —**pen name,** псевдони́м.
penal *adj.* **1,** (prescribing punishment) уголо́вный: *penal code,* уголо́вный ко́декс. **2,** (of or for prisoners) штрафно́й: *penal colony,* штрафна́я коло́ния. *Penal battalion,* штрафно́й батальо́н. —**penal servitude,** ка́торга; ка́торжные рабо́ты.
penalize *v.t.* штрафова́ть.
penalty *n.* **1,** (punishment) наказа́ние; взыска́ние; штраф; пе́ня. *Death penalty,* сме́ртная казнь. *Pay the*

penalty, поплати́ться. **2,** *sports* штраф. —*adj.* штрафно́й: *penalty kick,* штрафно́й уда́р.
penance *n.* покая́ние.
pence *n.pl.* пенс: *six pence,* шесть пе́нсов.
penchant *n.* скло́нность; накло́нность. *Have a penchant for neatness,* отлича́ться аккура́тностью.
pencil *n.* каранда́ш. —*adj.* каранда́шный: *pencil drawing,* каранда́шный рису́нок. —*v.t.* писа́ть (карандашо́м). *Pencil one's eyebrows,* подводи́ть бро́ви. —**pencil case,** пена́л. —**pencil sharpener,** точи́лка.
pendant *n.* кулон; подве́ска.
pending *adj.* ожида́ющий реше́ния. —*prep.* в ожида́нии (+ *gen.*).
pendulum *n.* ма́ятник.
penetrate *v.t. & i.* проника́ть (в).
penetrating *adj.* **1,** (of cold, wind, etc.) прони́зывающий. **2,** (keen; discerning) проница́тельный.
penetration *n.* проникнове́ние.
penguin *n.* пингви́н.
penholder *n.* ру́чка (для пера́).
penicillin *n.* пеницилли́н.
peninsula *n.* полуо́стров. —**peninsular,** *adj.* полуостровно́й.
penis *n.* мужско́й полово́й член.
penitence *n.* покая́ние.
penitent *adj.* **1,** (of a person) ка́ющийся. **2,** (of a look, expression, etc.) покая́нный.
penitentiary *n.* ка́торжная тюрьма́.
penknife *n.* перочи́нный нож(ик).
penmanship *n.* каллигра́фия; чистописа́ние.
pennant *n.* вы́мпел.
penniless *adj.* безде́нежный; без копе́йки; без гроша́.
penny *n.* (American coin) моне́та в оди́н цент; (British coin) пе́нни; пенс. —**a penny for your thoughts,** о чём ты заду́мался? —**cost a pretty penny,** обойти́сь в копе́ечку; бить по карма́ну. —**not have a penny to one's name,** не име́ть ни копе́йки (*or* ни гроша́) за душо́й.
penny pincher скопидо́м; скуперда́й.
pension *n.* пе́нсия. —*v.t.* [*usu.* **pension off**] увольня́ть на пе́нсию. —**pensioner,** *n.* пенсионе́р.
pensive *adj.* заду́мчивый; вду́мчивый. —**pensiveness,** *n.* заду́мчивость.
pentagon *n.* **1,** (geometric figure) пятиуго́льник. **2,** *cap.* (headquarters of U.S. Defense Dept.) Пентаго́н. —**pentagonal,** *adj.* пятиуго́льный.
pentahedron *n.* пятигра́нник.
pentameter *n.* пятисто́пный стих; пента́метр. *Iambic pentameter,* пятисто́пный ямб. —*adj.* пятисто́пный.
Pentateuch *n.* пятикни́жие.
pentathlon *n.* пятибо́рье.
Pentecost *n.* пятидеся́тница.
penthouse *n.* кварти́ра на ве́рхнем этаже́.
pent-up *adj.* затаённый.
penultimate *adj.* предпосле́дний.
penumbra *n.* полуте́нь.
penurious *adj.* **1,** (stingy) скупо́й. **2,** (poor) бе́дный.
penury *n.* нужда́; нищета́.
peon *n.* пео́н. —**peonage,** *n.* пеона́ж.
peony *n.* пио́н.
people *n.* **1,** (persons) лю́ди. **2,** (nation) наро́д.

—*v.t.* населя́ть. —**people's,** *adj.* наро́дный: *people's republic,* наро́дная респу́блика.

pep *n., colloq.* эне́ргия; прыть. —*v.t.* [*usu.* **pep up**] оживля́ть.

pepper *n.* пе́рец. —*v.t.* **1,** (season) пе́рчить. **2,** (pelt) осыпа́ть. —**pepper shaker,** пе́речница.

peppermint *n.* **1,** (herb) пе́речная мя́та. **2,** (candy) мя́тный ледене́ц.

pepsin *n.* пепси́н.

peptic ulcer я́звенная боле́знь.

peptone *n.* пепто́н.

per *prep.* **1,** (for each) в; за: *ten miles per hour,* де́сять миль в час; *ten cents per item,* де́сять це́нтов за шту́ку. *Ten dollars per person,* де́сять до́лларов с челове́ка. **2,** [*often,* **as per**] (according to) в соотве́тствии с.

peradventure *adv., archaic* мо́жет быть; возмо́жно.

perambulator *n.* де́тская коля́ска.

per annum в год.

percale *n.* перка́ль.

per capita на ду́шу населе́ния.

perceive *v.t.* **1,** (become aware of through the senses) воспринима́ть; ощуща́ть. **2,** (come to understand) понима́ть; осознава́ть.

percent *n.* проце́нт: *fifty percent,* пятьдеся́т проце́нтов.

percentage *n.* **1,** (percent) проце́нт. **2,** (part; proportion) часть; до́ля. **3,** (fee; commission) проце́нты: *work on percentage,* рабо́тать на проце́нтах.

perceptible *adj.* заме́тный; ощути́мый.

perception *n.* **1,** (act of perceiving) восприя́тие. **2,** (keenness of mind) проница́тельность.

perceptive *adj.* проница́тельный; то́нкий; зо́ркий. *Perceptive comment,* то́нкое замеча́ние.

perch *n.* **1,** (fish) о́кунь. **2,** (roost) насе́ст. —*v.i.* уса́живаться.

perchance *adv.* случа́йно.

perchloric acid хло́рная кислота́.

percolate *v.t.* проце́живать. —*v.i.* **1,** (seep; ooze) проса́чиваться. **2,** (start bubbling up) кипе́ть. —**percolator,** *n.* кофе́йник с си́течком.

percussion *n.* столкнове́ние; уда́р. —**percussion cap,** ка́псюль; писто́н. —**percussion instrument,** уда́рный инструме́нт.

per diem 1, (per day) за день. **2,** (daily allowance) су́точные де́ньги.

perdition *n.* прокля́тие: *condemn to perdition,* предава́ть прокля́тию.

peregrination *n.* стра́нствие.

peregrine falcon сапса́н.

peremptory *adj.* **1,** (barring further action) безапелляцио́нный. **2,** (allowing no room for disagreement) повели́тельный.

perennial *adj.* **1,** (perpetual) ве́чный. **2,** *bot.* многоле́тний. —*n., bot.* многоле́тнее расте́ние.

perfect *adj.* **1,** (complete; exact; utter) соверше́нный. **2,** (flawless) безупре́чный. **3,** (ideal) идеа́льный; образцо́вый; превосхо́дный. —*v.t.* соверше́нствовать; доводи́ть до соверше́нства. —*n., gram.* перфе́кт.

perfection *n.* **1,** (state of being perfect) соверше́нство. *To perfection,* в соверше́нстве. **2,** (act of perfecting) соверше́нствование.

perfective *adj., gram.* соверше́нный. —*n., gram.* соверше́нный вид.

perfectly *adv.* **1,** (to perfection) в соверше́нстве. **2,** (completely; fully) соверше́нно: *perfectly obvious,* соверше́нно очеви́дно. *I know perfectly well that...,* я прекра́сно зна́ю, что... **3,** (without a hitch) безотка́зно: *work perfectly,* рабо́тать безотка́зно.

perfidious *adj.* вероло́мный. —**perfidy,** *n.* вероло́мство.

perforate *v.t.* перфори́ровать. —*adj.* = **perforated.**

perforated *adj.* **1,** (pierced with holes) перфори́рованный. **2,** (of stamps) зубцо́вый. —**perforated ulcer,** прободна́я я́зва.

perforation *n.* **1,** *med.* прободе́ние; перфора́ция. **2,** (on stamps) перфора́ция; зубцо́вка.

perforator *n.* перфора́тор

perforce *adv.* во́лей-нево́лей.

perform *v.t.* **1,** (execute; carry out) выполня́ть; исполня́ть. *Perform an operation,* сде́лать опера́цию. *Perform an experiment,* проводи́ть о́пыт. *Perform a trick,* показа́ть фо́кус. **2,** (give a performance of) исполня́ть. —*v.i.* **1,** (give a performance) игра́ть; выступа́ть. **2,** (function; operate) рабо́тать.

performance *n.* **1,** (carrying out) выполне́ние; исполне́ние. **2,** (rendition) исполне́ние; игра́. **3,** (show) представле́ние; спекта́кль; сеа́нс. **4,** (efficiency of operation) ходовы́е ка́чества. *Performance tests,* ходовы́е испыта́ния.

performer *n.* исполни́тель.

perfume *n.* духи́. *Perfume bottle,* флако́н для духо́в. —*v.t.* души́ть. —**perfumer,** *n.* парфюме́р. —**perfumery,** *n.* парфюме́рия.

perfunctory *adj.* пове́рхностный; механи́ческий. —**perfunctorily,** *adv.* пове́рхностно; ме́льком.

perhaps *adv.* мо́жет быть.

pericardium *n.* околосерде́чная су́мка.

pericarp *n.* околопло́дник.

perigee *n.* периге́й.

perihelion *n.* периге́лий.

peril *n.* опа́сность; риск. *At one's own peril,* на свой страх и риск. —*v.t.* ста́вить под угро́зу. —**perilous,** *adj.* опа́сный; риско́ванный.

perimeter *n.* пери́метр.

period *n.* **1,** (in history) пери́од; эпо́ха. **2,** (interval of time) срок; пери́од. **3,** (dot placed at end of a sentence) то́чка. **4,** (division of a school day) уро́к. **5,** (division of a game) пери́од; тайм. —*adj.* сти́льный: *period furniture,* сти́льная ме́бель.

periodic *adj.* периоди́ческий.

periodical *adj.* периоди́ческий. —*n.* периоди́ческое изда́ние; *pl.* перио́дика.

periodically *adv.* **1,** (at regular intervals) периоди́чески. **2,** (from time to time) вре́мя от вре́мени.

peripatetic *adj.* стра́нствующий.

peripheral *adj.* **1,** (away from the center) перифери́ческий. **2,** *fig.* (incidental; tangential) несуще́ственный; второстепе́нный.

periphery *n.* перифери́я.

periphrasis *n.* перифра́за.

periscope *n.* периско́п.

perish *v.i.* ги́бнуть; погиба́ть. —**perish the thought!,** упаси́ Бог!; Бо́же упаси́!

perishable *adj.* скоропо́ртящийся. —*n., usu. pl.* скоропо́ртящиеся проду́кты.

peristalsis *n.* перистáльтика. —**peristaltic,** *adj.* перистальтíческий.

peristyle *n.* перистíль.

peritoneum *n.* брюшíна. —**peritonitis,** *n.* воспалéние брюшíны; перитонíт.

periwinkle *n.* **1,** (plant) барвíнок. **2,** (mollusk) литорíна.

perjure *v.t.* [*usu.* **perjure oneself**] лжесвидéтельствовать. —**perjurer,** *n.* лжесвидéтель; клятвопрестýпник. —**perjury,** *n.* лжесвидéтельство; клятвопреступлéние.

perk *v.t.* [*usu.* **perk up**] оживлять; ободрять. —*v.i.* [*usu.* **perk up**] оживáть; оживляться; воспрянуть дýхом. —**perky,** *adj.* бóйкий; задóрный.

permafrost *n.* вéчная мерзлотá.

permanence *n.* постоянство.

permanent *adj.* постоянный. —*n.* = **permanent wave.**

permanently *adv.* на дóлгое врéмя; навсегдá. *Permanently damaged,* непоправíмо поврежден.

permanent wave перманéнт; шестимéсячная завíвка.

permeable *adj.* проницáемый. —**permeability,** *n.* проницáемость.

permeate *v.t.* проникáть в; пронíзывать.

permissible *adj.* позволíтельный; допустíмый; дозвóленный.

permission *n.* разрешéние; позволéние.

permissive *adj.* не стрóгий; снисходíтельный.

permit *v.t.* **1,** (give permission to) разрешáть; позволять: *permit me to...,* разрешíте/позвóльте мне (+ *inf.*). **2,** (allow to happen) допускáть. **3,** (enable) позволять: *this will permit me to...,* это позволит мне (+ *inf.*). —*v.i.* позволять: *if time permits,* éсли врéмя позволяет; *weather permitting,* éсли погóда позвóлит. —*n.* прóпуск; разрешéние.

permutation *n.* перестанóвка.

pernicious *adj.* пáгубный. —**pernicious anemia,** злокáчественное малокрóвие.

perorate *v.i.* орáторствовать; разглагóльствовать.

peroxide *n.* **1,** (chemical) пéрекись. **2,** (antiseptic) пéрекись водорóда.

perpendicular *adj.* перпендикулярный. —*n.* перпендикуляр.

perpetrate *v.t.* совершáть: *perpetrate a crime,* совершíть преступлéние. —**perpetration,** *n.* совершéние (преступлéния). —**perpetrator,** *n.* винóвник (преступлéния).

perpetual *adj.* вéчный. *Perpetual motion,* вéчное движéние. —**perpetually,** *adv.* вéчно.

perpetuate *v.t.* увековéчивать. —**perpetuation,** *n.* увековéчение.

perpetuity *n.* вéчность. —**in perpetuity,** навéчно.

perplex *v.t.* приводíть в недоумéние; озадáчивать. —**perplexed,** *adj.* недоумéнный; недоумевáющий; озадáченный. —**perplexing,** *adj.* недоумéнный. —**perplexity,** *n.* недоумéние; озадáченность.

perquisite *n.* льгóта.

per se сам по себé.

persecute *v.t.* преслéдовать. —**persecution,** *n.* преслéдование; гонéние. —**persecutor,** *n.* преслéдователь; гонíтель.

persevere *v.i.* упóрствовать. —**perseverance,** *n.* упóрство; настóйчивость.

Persian *adj.* персíдский. —*n.* **1,** (person) перс; персиáнка. **2,** (language) персíдский язык. —**Persian cat,** сибíрская кóшка. —**Persian lamb,** карáкуль.

persiflage *n.* беззлóбная насмéшка.

persimmon *n.* хурмá.

persist *v.i.* **1,** (refuse to give up) упóрствовать. **2,** (continue to exist) сохраняться.

persistence *n.* упóрство; настóйчивость; настоятельность.

persistent *adj.* **1,** (refusing to relent) упóрный; настóйчивый; настоятельный. *Persistent cough,* упóрный кáшель. **2,** (repeated; continuous) бесконéчный.

person *n.* **1,** (human being) человéк. **2,** *gram.* лицó: *first person,* пéрвое лицó. —**in person,** лíчно; сóбственной персóной. —**in the person of,** в лицé (+ *gen.*). —**on one's person,** при себé.

personable *adj.* симпатíчный; располагáющий.

personage *n.* **1,** (person) лицó: *historic personage,* историческое лицó. **2,** (character in a play, history, etc.) персонáж.

personal *adj.* лíчный: *my personal opinion,* моё лíчное мнéние. *Get personal,* переходíть на лíчности. —**personal pronoun,** лíчное местоимéние.

personality *n.* лíчность.

personally *adv.* лíчно. *Take something personally,* принимáть чтó-нибудь на свой счёт.

persona non grata персóна нон грáта.

personify *v.t.* олицетворять. —**personification,** *n.* олицетворéние.

personnel *n.* кáдры; персонáл; лíчный состáв. *Personnel department,* отдéл кáдров.

perspective *n.* **1,** *art* перспектíва. **2,** (viewpoint) свет: *in a different perspective,* в другóм свéте. *Keep things in perspective,* широкó смотрéть на вéщи. —*adj.* перспектíвный.

perspicacious *adj.* проницáтельный. —**perspicacity,** *n.* проницáтельность.

perspiration *n.* пот; испáрина.

perspire *v.i.* потéть.

persuade *v.t.* **1,** (induce) уговáривать. **2,** (convince) убеждáть.

persuasion *n.* **1,** (act of persuading) убеждéние. *After considerable persuasion,* пóсле дóлгих уговóров. **2,** (religious belief) вероисповéдание.

persuasive *adj.* убедíтельный. —**persuasively,** *adv.* убедíтельно. —**persuasiveness,** *n.* убедíтельность.

pert *adj.* **1,** (impudent) развязный. **2,** (lively) задóрный.

pertain *v.i.* [*usu.* **pertain to**] относíться (к).

pertinacious *adj.* **1,** (stubborn) упрямый. **2,** (persistent) упóрный. —**pertinacity,** *n.* упрямство; упóрство.

pertinent *adj.* умéстный; относящийся к дéлу. —**pertinence,** *n.* умéстность.

perturb *v.t.* смущáть; волновáть.

perturbation *n., astron.* пертурбáция.

peruse *v.t.* **1,** (read carefully) внимáтельно прочитáть. **2,** (read casually; scan) просмáтривать. —**perusal,** *n.* прочтéние.

Peruvian *adj.* перуáнский.

pervade *v.t.* наполнять; насыщáть; пропíтывать; пронíзывать; распространяться по. —**pervasive,** *adj.* распространяющийся повсюду.

perverse *adj.* **1,** (contrary) упрямый. **2,** (perverted) порóчный.

perversion *n.* извращёние.
perversity *n.* **1,** (contrariness) упря́мство. **2,** (depravity) извращённость; поро́чность.
pervert *v.t.* **1,** (distort; twist) извраща́ть. **2,** (lead astray; corrupt) совраща́ть. —*n.* извращённый челове́к.
perverted *adj.* поро́чный; извращённый; противоесте́ственный.
peseta *n.* песе́та; пезе́та.
pesky *adj., colloq.* надое́дливый; доку́чливый.
peso *n.* пе́со; пезо.
pessimism *n.* пессими́зм. —**pessimist,** *n.* пессими́ст. —**pessimistic,** *adj.* пессимисти́ческий. *I am pessimistic,* я настро́ен пессимисти́чески.
pest *n.* **1,** (annoying person) надое́да. **2;** (destructive insect) вреди́тель.
pester *v.t.* надоеда́ть; докуча́ть; пристава́ть к.
pesticide *n.* ядохимика́т.
pestilence *n.* чума́.
pestle *n.* пест; пе́стик.
pet *n.* **1,** (animal) дома́шнее живо́тное. **2,** (favorite) люби́мец; ба́ловень. —*adj.* **1,** (of an animal) ручно́й. **2,** (favorite) люби́мый. —*v.t.* гла́дить. —**pet name,** уменьши́тельное *or* ласка́тельное и́мя.
petal *n.* лепесто́к.
petard *n.* петáрда.
petcock *n.* спускно́й кран.
peter *v.i.* [*usu.* **peter out**] выдыха́ться.
petiole *n.* черешо́к.
petition *n.* пети́ция. —*v.t.* обраща́ться с пети́цией к. —**petitioner,** *n.* проси́тель.
petrel *n.* буреве́стник; качу́рка.
petrified *adj.* **1,** (having turned to stone) окамене́лый. **2,** (terrified) оцепене́вший. *We were petrified,* мы дрожа́ли от стра́ха.
petrify *v.t.* превраща́ть в ка́мень. —*v.i.* (о)камене́ть.
petrochemical *n.* нефтехими́ческий проду́кт. —*adj.* нефтехими́ческий.
petrol *n., Brit.* бензи́н.
petroleum *n.* нефть. —*adj.* нефтяно́й.
petticoat *n.* ни́жняя ю́бка.
pettifoggery *n.* крючкотво́рство.
pettiness *n.* ме́лочность.
petty *adj.* **1,** (minor; trivial) ме́лкий. **2,** (picayune; niggling) ме́лочный. —**petty larceny,** ме́лкая кра́жа. —**petty officer,** старшина́.
petulant *adj.* раздражи́тельный; сварли́вый. —**petulance,** *n.* раздражи́тельность.
petunia *n.* пету́ния.
pew *n.* (церко́вная) скамья́.
pewit *n.* чи́бис; пи́галица.
pewter *n.* сплав на оловя́нной осно́ве. —*adj.* оловя́нный.
phaeton *n.* фаэто́н.
phagocyte *n.* фагоци́т.
phalanx *n.* фала́нга.
phalarope *n.* плавунчик.
phallus *n.* фа́ллос. —**phallic,** *adj.* фалли́ческий.
phantasmagoria *n.* фантасмаго́рия. —**phantasmagoric,** *adj.* фантасмагори́ческий.
phantom *n.* при́зрак; виде́ние; фанто́м.
Pharaoh *n.* фарао́н.
pharisee *n.* фарисе́й. —**pharisaic,** *adj.* фарисе́йский.

pharmaceutical *adj.* апте́карский; фармацевти́ческий. —**pharmaceutics,** *n.* фармаце́втика.
pharmacist *n.* фармаце́вт; апте́карь; прови́зор.
pharmacology *n.* фармаколо́гия. —**pharmacological,** *adj.* фармакологи́ческий. —**pharmacologist,** *n.* фармако́лог.
pharmacopeia *n.* фармакопе́я.
pharmacy *n.* **1,** (the science) фармаце́втика; фарма́ция. **2,** (drugstore) апте́ка.
pharynx *n.* зев.
phase *n.* фа́за; фа́зис. —*v.t.* [*usu.* **phase in** *or* **phase out**] постепе́нно вводи́ть *or* упраздня́ть. —**phased,** *adj.* поэта́пный.
pheasant *n.* фаза́н.
phenobarbital *n.* люмина́л; фенобарбита́л.
phenol *n.* фено́л.
phenomenal *adj.* феномена́льный.
phenomenon *n.* **1,** (observable fact) явле́ние. **2,** (marvel; wonder) фено́мен.
phial *n.* пузырёк; флако́н; скля́нка.
philander *v.i.* флиртова́ть. —**philanderer,** *n.* воло́кита; ухажёр.
philanthropy *n.* филантро́пия. —**philanthropic,** *adj.* филантропи́ческий. —**philanthropist,** *n.* филантро́п.
philately *n.* филателия. —**philatelic,** *adj.* филателисти́ческий. —**philatelist,** *n.* филатели́ст.
philharmonic *adj.* филармони́ческий. —*n.* **1,** (orchestra) симфони́ческий орке́стр. **2,** (group supporting same) филармо́ния.
philippic *n.* фили́ппика.
Philippine *adj.* филиппи́нский.
philodendron *n.* филоде́ндрон.
philology *n.* филоло́гия. —**philological,** *adj.* филологи́ческий. —**philologist,** *n.* фило́лог.
philosopher *n.* фило́соф. —**philosophic(al),** *adj.* филосо́фский. —**philosophize,** *v.i.* филосо́фствовать.
philosophy *n.* филосо́фия.
phlebitis *n.* флеби́т.
phlebotomy *n.* кровопуска́ние.
phlegm *n.* **1,** (mucus) мокро́та. **2,** (apathy) флегма. —**phlegmatic,** *adj.* флегмати́чный.
phloem *n.* флоэ́ма.
phlox *n.* флокс.
phobia *n.* фо́бия.
Phoenician *adj.* финики́йский.
phoenix *n.* фе́никс.
phone *n., colloq.* телефо́н. *Phone call,* вы́зов (по телефо́ну); телефо́нный звоно́к. *Phone number,* но́мер телефо́на. *Pick up the phone!,* возьми́те тру́бку! —*v.t., colloq.* звони́ть.
phoneme *n.* фоне́ма. —**phonemic,** *adj.* фонемати́ческий.
phonetic *adj.* фонети́ческий. —**phonetics,** *n.* фоне́тика.
phoney *adj.* = **phony.**
phonograph *n.* граммофо́н; патефо́н; прои́грыватель. *Phonograph record,* грампласти́нка.
phonology *n.* фоноло́гия.
phony *also,* **phoney** *adj., slang* подде́льный; ли́повый.
phooey *interj.* тьфу!
phosgene *n.* фосге́н.
phosphate *n.* фосфа́т.

phosphorescence *n.* свече́ние; фосфоресце́н-ция. —**phosphorescent,** *adj.* фосфоресци́рующий.

phosphorus *n.* фо́сфор. —**phosphoric; phosphorous,** *adj.* фо́сфорный.

photo *n., colloq.* фотогра́фия; фо́то.

photocopier *n.* копирова́льная маши́на; фото-ста́т. —**photocopy,** *n.* фотоко́пия.

photoelectric *adj.* фотоэлектри́ческий. —**photoelectric cell,** фотоэлеме́нт.

photoengraving *n.* фотогравю́ра.

photogenic *adj.* фотогени́чный.

photograph *n.* фотогра́фия; фотосни́мок. —*v.t.* фотографи́ровать. —*v.i. I do not photograph well,* я пло́хо выхожу́ на фотогра́фии.

photographer *n.* фото́граф.

photography *n.* фотогра́фия. —**photographic,** *adj.* фотографи́ческий.

photogravure *n.* фотогравю́ра.

photometer *n.* фото́метр.

photon *n.* фото́н.

photosphere *n.* фотосфе́ра.

photostat *n.* фотоко́пия.

photosynthesis *n.* фотоси́нтез.

phrase *n.* фра́за; оборо́т. —*v.t.* формули́ровать. —**phrase book,** разгово́рник.

phraseology *n.* фразеоло́гия. —**phraseological,** *adj.* фразеологи́ческий.

phrenology *n.* френоло́гия.

phylactery *n.* филакте́рия.

phylum *n.* тип.

physical *adj.* физи́ческий. —*n., colloq.* медици́н-ский осмо́тр. —**physical education,** физи́ческое воспита́ние; физи́ческая культу́ра; физкульту́ра. —**physical examination,** медици́нский осмо́тр. —**physical exercise,** физи́ческие упражне́ния. —**physical science,** физи́ческие нау́ки. —**physical training = physical education.**

physically *adv.* физи́чески.

physician *n.* врач.

physicist *n.* фи́зик.

physics *n.* фи́зика.

physiognomy *n.* физионо́мия.

physiology *n.* физиоло́гия. —**physiological,** *adj.* физиологи́ческий. —**physiologist,** *n.* физио́лог.

physiotherapy *n.* физиотерапи́я. —**physiotherapist,** *n.* физиотерапе́вт.

physique *n.* телосложе́ние.

pianissimo *adj. & adv.* пиани́ссимо.

pianist *n.* пиани́ст.

piano *n.* роя́ль; фортепья́но. *Upright piano,* пиани́-но. —*adj.* фортепья́нный: *piano concerto,* форте-пья́нный конце́рт. *Piano bench,* скаме́йка для ро-я́ля. *Piano lessons,* уро́ки игры́ на роя́ле. —*adv.* пиа́но.

pianoforte *n.* фортепья́но.

piaster *also,* **piastre** *n.* пиа́стр.

pica *n.* ци́церо.

picaresque *adj.* плутовско́й.

picayune *adj.* пустяко́вый; ерундо́вый; ме́лочный.

piccolo *n.* пи́кколо.

pick *n.* **1,** (tool) кирка́. **2,** (choice) вы́бор. *Take your pick,* выбира́йте. **3,** (choicest part) лу́чшая часть; цвет. —*v.t.* **1,** (select) выбира́ть; подбира́ть. **2,** (ga-ther, as berries) собира́ть. **3,** (pluck) срыва́ть. **4,** (re-move the feathers of, as a chicken) щипа́ть; ощи́пы-

вать. **5,** (pry open, as a lock) взла́мывать. **6,** (provoke, as a fight or quarrel) лезть в (дра́ку); иска́ть (ссо́ры). **7,** *Pick one's nose/teeth,* ковыря́ть в носу́/зуба́х. **8,** *Pick someone's pocket,* залеза́ть в карма́н (+ *dat.*). —*v.i.* (select) выбира́ть. —**pick on,** придира́ться к. —**pick out, 1,** (select) выбира́ть. **2,** (distinguish; dis-cern) различа́ть. **3,** (play by ear) подбира́ть: *pick out a tune on the piano,* подбира́ть моти́в на роя́ле. —**pick up, 1,** (take up from the ground or floor) под-нима́ть; подбира́ть. **2,** (call for) заходи́ть за; заез-жа́ть за. **3,** (go and collect) идти́ за. **4,** (give a lift to on the road) подвози́ть. **5,** (take on, as a passenger or freight) забира́ть. **6,** (acquire casually) приобрета́ть; подцепля́ть. **7,** (learn superficially) нахвата́ться. **8,** (gain, as speed) набира́ть (ско́рость). **9,** (find, as a trail or scent) напада́ть на (след). **10,** (receive, as a radio signal) лови́ть; ула́вливать. **11,** (give added energy to) подбодря́ть. **12,** (take into custody) заде́рживать. **13,** *colloq.* (improve) поправля́ться.

pickax *also,* **pickaxe** *n.* кирка́.

picker *n.* сбо́рщик.

pickerel *n.* щу́ка.

picket *n.* **1,** (stake) кол. **2,** (protester) пике́тчик. **3,** *mil.* пике́т. —*v.t. & i.* пикети́ровать. —**picket fence,** час-токо́л. —**picket line,** пике́т.

pickle *n.* (солёный) огуре́ц. —*v.t.* соли́ть; заса́ли-вать; маринова́ть. —**pickled,** *adj.* солёный. *Pickled herring,* сельдь в рассо́ле.

pickpocket *n.* карма́нный вор.

pickup *n.* **1,** (acceleration): *the car has good pickup,* маши́на хорошо́ (*or* бы́стро) набира́ет ско́рость. **2,** (collection of mail) вы́емка. **3,** *colloq.* (improvement) оживле́ние. —**pickup truck,** пика́п.

picky *adj., colloq.* привере́дливый.

picnic *n.* пикни́к.

pictograph *n.* пиктогра́мма. —**pictographic,** *adj.* пиктографи́ческий. —**pictography,** *n.* пиктогра́-фия.

pictorial *adj.* **1,** (graphic) живопи́сный; изобрази́-тельный; о́бразный. **2,** (containing pictures) иллюс-три́рованный.

picture *n.* **1,** (drawing or painting) карти́на. **2,** (photo-graph) фотогра́фия; сни́мок; ка́рточка. *Take a pic-ture of,* фотографи́ровать; снима́ть. *Take pictures,* фотографи́ровать. *Have one's picture taken,* сни-ма́ться. **3,** (movie) фильм. **4,** (image on a TV screen) изображе́ние. **5,** (vivid description) карти́на: *a picture of life in Ancient Rome,* карти́на жи́зни в дре́внем Ри́ме. **6,** (mental image) представле́ние: *have a clear picture of,* име́ть я́сное представле́ние о. **7,** (general situation) карти́на: *a gloomy picture,* мра́чная карти́-на. *Be out of the picture,* не фигури́ровать. *I get the picture,* я понима́ю в чём де́ло. **8,** (embodiment) воплоще́ние: *the picture of health,* воплоще́ние здо-ро́вья. —*adj.* карти́нный: *picture gallery,* карти́нная галере́я. —*v.t.* **1,** (visualize) представля́ть себе́. **2,** (depict) изобража́ть.

picture postcard откры́тка с ви́дом.

picturesque *adj.* живопи́сный.

picture tube кинеско́п.

piddling *adj.* ничто́жный; пустяко́вый.

pie *n.* пиро́г; пирожо́к.

piebald *adj.* пе́гий.

piece *n.* **1,** (portion) кусо́к: *piece of bread/meat,* кусо́к хле́ба/мя́са. *Piece of paper,* бума́жка. *Piece of candy,* конфета. *Piece of advice,* совет. **2,** *pl.* (fragments) куски; клочки: *tear to pieces,* рвать на куски *or* в клочки. *Smash to pieces,* разбивать вдребезги. **3,** (item) штука. *Piece of furniture,* мебель. *Five pieces of luggage,* пять мест. *Three-piece suit,* костюм-тройка. *Sell by the piece,* продавать поштучно. **4,** (artistic creation) произведение: *piece of art,* произведение искусства. *Museum piece,* музейная редкость. **5,** (coin) монета. **6,** (firearm) орудие: *artillery piece,* артиллерийское орудие. **7,** *chess* фигура. —*v.t.* [*usu.* **piece together**] составлять по кусочкам. —**give someone a piece of one's mind,** сказать кому-нибудь пару тёплых слов. —**go to pieces,** потерять голову. —**speak one's piece,** высказать своё мнение.

piecemeal *adv.* по частям.

piecework *n.* сдельная работа. —**pieceworker,** *n.* сдельщик.

pier *n.* **1,** (wharf) пристань. **2,** (of a bridge) бык. **3,** (between windows) простенок.

pierce *v.t.* пронзать; прокалывать; протыкать. *Have one's ears pierced,* проколоть уши. —**piercing,** *adj.* пронзительный.

pier glass трюмо.

pier table подзеркальник.

piety *n.* набожность; благочестие.

pig *n.* свинья. *Baby pig,* поросёнок.

pigeon *n.* голубь.

pigeonhole *v.t.* класть под сукно.

pigeon-toed *adj.* косолапый.

piggyback *adv.* на спине; на закорках.

piggy bank копилка (в виде поросёнка).

pigheaded *adj.* крепколобый.

pig iron чугун в чушках.

piglet *n.* поросёнок.

pigment *n.* пигмент. —**pigmentation,** *n.* пигментация.

pigpen *n.* свинарник.

pigskin *n.* **1,** (leather) свиная кожа. **2,** *colloq.* (football) футбольный мяч.

pigsty *n.* **1,** (pigpen) свинарник. **2,** (filthy place) хлев.

pigtail *n.* косичка; крысиный хвостик.

pika *n.* пищуха.

pike *n.* **1,** (fish) щука. **2,** (spear) пика.

pilaf *n.* пилав.

pilaster *n.* пилястра.

pile *n.* **1,** (heap) куча; груда; кипа. *A pile of money,* куча денег. **2,** (foundation for a pier) свая. **3,** (soft nap) ворс. —*v.t.* **1,** [*usu.* **pile up**] (make a pile of) складывать; нагромождать. **2,** (load) наваливать. **3,** (cover) заваливать: *the table is piled with books,* стол завален книгами. —*v.i.* [*usu.* **pile up**] **1,** (form a pile) нагромождаться. **2,** (accumulate) накопляться.

pile driver копёр.

piles *n.pl.* геморрой.

pilfer *v.t.* красть; тащить; стянуть. —**pilferage,** *n.* мелкая кража.

pilgrim *n.* паломник; пилигрим. —**pilgrimage,** *n.* паломничество.

pill *n.* пилюля.

pillage *v.t.* грабить. —*v.i.* мародёрствовать. —*n.* грабёж; мародёрство.

pillar *n.* **1,** (column) столб. *Pillar of smoke,* столб дыма. **2,** *fig.* (mainstay) столп: *the pillars of society,* столпы общества.

pillbox *n.* **1,** (box for pills) коробочка для пилюль. **2,** *mil.* дот.

pillory *n.* позорный столб. —*v.t.* пригвождать/ставить/выставлять к позорному столбу.

pillow *n.* подушка. —**pillowcase,** *n.* наволочка.

pilot *n.* **1,** (of an aircraft) пилот; лётчик. **2,** (harbor pilot) лоцман. —*v.t.* вести; управлять; пилотировать. —*adj.* опытный; пробный; экспериментальный. *Pilot program,* экспериментальная программа.

pilot fish лоцман.

pilothouse *n.* рулевая рубка.

pimento *n.* **1,** [*also,* **pimiento**] (variety of pepper) стручковый перец. **2,** = **allspice**.

pimp *n.* сводник.

pimpernel *n.* очный цвет.

pimple *n.* прыщ. —**pimply,** *adj.* прыщавый; угреватый.

pin *n.* **1,** (small metal fastener) булавка: *safety pin,* английская булавка. **2,** (bar or rod that fastens) штифт; шпилька. **3,** (broach) брошка. **4,** (badge) значок. **5,** *bowling* кегля. —*v.t.* **1,** (fasten with a pin) прикалывать. *Pin up,* подкалывать. **2,** (immobilize) прижимать: *pin to the ground/ropes,* прижимать к земле/канатам. *Pinned under the wreckage,* зажат под обломками. **3,** (place, as hopes, blame, etc.) возлагать. —**be on pins and needles,** быть *or* сидеть как на иголках. —**you could have heard a pin drop,** слышно было, как муха пролетит.

pinafore *n.* передник; фартук.

pince-nez *n.* пенсне.

pincers *n.pl.* **1,** (tool) клещи; пинцет. **2,** (claw) клешня. —**pincers movement,** клещи.

pinch *v.t.* **1,** (nip) щипать; ущипнуть. **2,** *colloq.* (steal) красть; тащить. —*v.i.* (of a shoe) жать. —*n.* **1,** (nip) щипок. **2,** (bit, as of salt) щепоть; щепотка. **3,** (emergency) крайний случай: *in a pinch,* в крайнем случае. —**pinch pennies,** жаться; стеснять себя в средствах.

pincushion *n.* подушечка для булавок.

pine *n.* сосна. —*adj.* сосновый; хвойный: *pine cone,* сосновая шишка; *pine tar,* хвойный дёготь. —*v.i.* **1,** *fol. by* **away** (waste away) чахнуть; томиться. **2,** *fol. by* **for** (long for) тосковать по; томиться по.

pineal *adj.* шишковидный.

pineapple *n.* ананас. —*adj.* ананасный: *pineapple juice,* ананасный сок.

ping *n.* звон.

ping-pong *n.* пинг-понг.

pinhole *n.* булавочная дырка.

pinion *n.* шестерня.

pink *adj.* розовый. —*n.* **1,** (flower) гвоздика. **2,** (color) розовый цвет. —**in the pink,** в расцвете сил.

pinkeye *n.* острый заразный конъюнктивит.

pinkie *also,* **pinky** *n.* мизинец.

pin money деньги на булавки.

pinnacle *n.* вершина. *The pinnacle of power,* вершина власти.

pinnate *adj.* перистый.

pinpoint *n.* остриё булавки. —*v.t* точно определять.

pinprick *n.* булавочный укол.

pint *n.* пинта.

pintail *n.* шилохвость.

pinto *n.* пегая лошадь.

pioneer *n.* пионер. —*adj.* пионерский.

pious *adj.* **1,** (devout) набожный; благочестивый. **2,** (sanctimonious) ханжеский.

pip *n.* **1,** (bird disease) типун. **2,** (spot on a playing card) очко.

pipe *n.* **1,** (tube) труба. **2,** (for smoking) трубка. **3,** (musical instrument) свирель. —*adj.* трубочный: *pipe tobacco,* трубочный табак. —*v.t.* передавать через трубу *or* через трубопровод. —**pipe down,** сбавить тон. *Pipe down!,* молчи! —**pipe up,** заговорить.

pipe dream несбыточная мечта.

pipeline *n.* трубопровод. *Oil pipeline,* нефтепровод. *Gas pipeline,* газопровод.

pipe organ орган.

piper *n.* волынщик.

piping *n.* **1,** (tubing) трубы; система труб. **2,** (edging for dresses) кант; выпушка. —**piping hot,** с пылу, с жару.

pipistrelle *n.* нетопырь.

pipsqueak *n., colloq.* мелкая сошка.

piquant *adj.* пикантный. —**piquancy,** *n.* пикантность.

pique *n.* обида; досада. —*v.t.* **1,** (cause resentment in) уязвлять; уколоть. **2,** (arouse; stimulate) возбуждать.

piqué *n.* пике. —*adj.* пикейный.

piquet *n.* (card game) пикет.

piracy *n.* пиратство.

pirate *n.* пират. —*adj.* пиратский: *pirate ship,* пиратский корабль. —**piratical,** *adj.* пиратский.

pirouette *n.* пируэт.

piscatorial *adj.* рыболовный; рыбацкий.

Pisces *n.* рыбы.

pistachio *n.* фисташка. —*adj.* фисташковый.

pistil *n.* пестик.

pistol *n.* пистолет. *Toy pistol,* пугач.

piston *n.* **1,** (of an engine) поршень. **2,** (of a wind instrument) пистон. —*adj.* поршневой: *piston engine,* поршневой двигатель; *piston ring,* поршневое кольцо; *piston rod,* поршневой шток.

pit *n.* **1,** (stone of a fruit) косточка. **2,** (hole) яма. **3,** (mine) шахта. **4,** *anat.* впадина. *Armpit,* подмышка. *In the pit of the stomach,* под ложечкой. **5,** (place where an orchestra sits) оркестр; оркестровая яма. —*v.t.* **1,** (remove the pit from) вынимать косточку из. **2,** (set in competition) противопоставлять.

pitch *v.t.* **1,** (throw) бросать; кидать. *Pitch hay,* ворошить сено. **2,** (erect, as a tent) разбивать; раскидывать. **3,** (cover or treat with pitch) смолить. —*v.i.* **1,** (fall headlong) сваливаться. **2,** (toss, as of a ship) качать; качаться. —*n.* **1,** (resin) смола. **2,** (slope) скат; уклон; наклон. **3,** (tossing of a ship) качка. **4,** *music* высота. *Absolute pitch,* абсолютный слух. **5,** (degree of intensity) накал: *reach a fever pitch,* дойти до накала. —**pitch in,** внести свою лепту.

pitchblende *n.* смоляная обманка.

pitch-dark *adj.* непроглядный. *It is pitch-dark in here,* здесь ни зги не видно.

pitched battle генеральное сражение.

pitcher *n.* **1,** (vessel) кувшин. **2,** *sports* подающий.

pitchfork *n.* вилы.

piteous *adj.* жалкий.

pitfall *n.* подводный камень.

pith *n.* сердцевина. —**pithy,** *adj.* выразительный; содержательный.

pitiable *adj.* = **pitiful.**

pitiful *adj.* жалкий.

pitiless *adj.* безжалостный.

pittance *n.* жалкие гроши.

pituitary gland гипофиз.

pity *n.* **1,** (compassion) жалость. *Have/take pity on,* сжалиться над. **2,** (cause for sorrow) *rendered by* жаль: *It's a pity that...,* жаль, что... *What a pity!,* как жаль! —*v.t.* жалеть. *I pity him,* я жалею его; мне жаль его.

pivot *n.* стержень; шкворень. —*v.i.* вращаться. —**pivotal,** *adj.* центральный; стержневой.

pizzicato *adj.* щипковый. —*adv.* щипком; пиццикато; пиччикато.

placard *n.* плакат; афиша.

placate *v.t.* умиротворять; умилостивить.

place *n.* место: *from place to place,* с места на место. *Come over to my place,* заходите ко мне. *Set a place for Nina,* поставить прибор для Нины. *What would you do in my place?,* что вы сделаете на моём месте? —*v.t.* **1,** (put; set) класть; ставить. **2,** (put in a certain situation or position) помещать: *place a child in school,* помещать ребёнка в школу. **3,** (order; list) помещать: *place an ad,* помещать рекламу; *place an order,* помещать заказ. *Place orders,* размещать заказы. *Place a telephone call,* заказывать разговор по телефону. **4,** (name; identify) *I can't place him,* не могу вспомнить, кто он такой. **5,** (repose; pin) возлагать (надежду); оказывать (доверие). —*v.i.* занимать (какое-нибудь место): *place third,* занять третье место. —**in place of,** вместо (+ *gen.*). —**in places,** местами. —**in the first place,** во-первых. —**in the second place,** во-вторых. —**know one's place,** знать своё место. —**no place,** нигде; никуда. —**out of place, 1,** (not in the proper place) не на (своём) месте; не на тех местах. **2,** (inappropriate) не к месту; неуместный. —**put someone in his place,** поставить кого-нибудь на место. —**take place,** иметь место; происходить; состояться. —**take the place of,** заменять.

placebo *n.* безобидное средство.

placement *n.* **1,** (act of placing) помещение; размещение. **2,** (placing persons in jobs) расстановка.

place name географическое название.

placenta *n.* плацента; детское место.

place setting прибор.

placid *adj.* спокойный; безмятежный; невозмутимый.

plagiarism *n.* литературное воровство; плагиат. —**plagiarist,** *n.* плагиатор.

plagiarize *v.t.* заимствовать (чужое произведение).

plague *n.* **1,** (disease) чума. **2,** (calamity; scourge) бич. —*v.t.* мучить. *Be plagued by doubts,* мучиться сомнениями.

plaice *n.* камбала.

plaid *n.* шотландка. —*adj.* клетчатый; в клетку.

plain *n.* равнина. —*adj.* **1,** (clear; unambiguous) ясный; понятный. *In plain English,* понятным английским языком. *In plain view of everyone,* у всех на виду. *As plain as the nose on your face,* яснее ясного. **2,** (simple; unpretentious) простой: *plain folk,* простые люди; *plain food,* простая пища. **3,** (downright) чистый; сущий: *plain nonsense,* чистый/сущий вздор. **4,** (having no design) одноцветный; гладкий. **5,** (unattractive) некрасивый; невзрачный. **6,** (not encoded) открытый: *plain text,* открытый текст.

plainclothesman *n.* сыщик в штатском платье.
plainly *adv.* **1,** (clearly) ясно. **2,** (simply) просто: *dress plainly,* одеваться просто.
plain-spoken *adj.* откровенный; прямодушный.
plaintiff *n.* истец; предъявитель иска.
plaintive *adj.* жалобный.
plait *n.* коса. —*v.t.* плести; заплетать.
plan *n.* план. —*v.t.* **1,** (draw up plans for) намечать; планировать. **2,** *fol. by inf.* (intend; expect) собираться; намереваться; предполагать. *We stayed longer than planned,* мы остались дольше, чем предполагали. —*v.i.* строить планы.
plane *n.* **1,** (flat surface) плоскость. **2,** (tool) рубанок. **3,** (airplane) самолёт. *Plane ticket,* билет на самолёт. *Plane fare,* стоимость полёта самолётом. *Plane crash,* авиационная катастрофа. **4,** *fig.* (level) уровень: *on a high moral plane,* на высоком нравственном уровне. —*adj.* плоский. —*v.t.* строгать.
plane geometry планиметрия.
planer *n.* строгальщик.
planet *n.* планета. —**planetarium,** *n.* планетарий. —**planetary,** *adj.* планетный.
plane tree платан; чинар(а).
plank *n.* доска; планка. —*v.t.* настилать. —**planking,** *n.* доски; обшивка.
plankton *n.* планктон.
planned *adj.* запланированный. *Planned economy,* плановое хозяйство.
planner *n.* **1,** (economic planner) плановик. **2,** (designer) планировщик: *town planner,* планировщик городов.
planning *n.* планирование; планировка. *Planning department,* плановый отдел.
plant *n.* **1,** (living organism) растение. **2,** (factory) завод. **3,** (complete apparatus) установка: *power plant,* силовая установка. —*v.t.* **1,** (place in the ground) сажать: *plant a tree,* сажать дерево. **2,** (furnish with plants, as a field) засаживать; усаживать. **3,** (place firmly) упираться (+ *instr.*). **4,** (place surreptitiously) подкладывать; подбрасывать. *Plant a bomb,* подложить бомбу.
plantain *n.* подорожник.
plantation *n.* плантация.
planter *n.* **1,** (plantation owner) плантатор. **2,** (machine for planting) сажалка.
plant louse тля.
plaque *n.* доска; дощечка; табличка.
plasma *n.* плазма.
plaster *n.* **1,** (substance for coating walls) штукатурка. **2,** (substance applied to the body) пластырь. **3,** (plaster of Paris) гипс. —*adj.* штукатурный; гипсовый. —*v.t.* **1,** (cover with plaster) штукатурить. **2,** (cover all over) облеплять. —**plaster cast, 1,** (copy of a statue) гипсовый слепок. **2,** *med.* гипс.
plasterer *n.* штукатур.
plastic *n.* пластмасса; пластик. —*adj.* **1,** (made of plastic) пластмассовый. **2,** (pert. to modeling) пластический. **3,** (capable of being molded) пластичный. —**plastic arts,** пластика. —**plastic bomb,** пластиковая бомба. —**plastic surgery,** пластическая хирургия.
plat du jour дежурное блюдо.
plate *n.* **1,** (dish) тарелка. **2,** (sheet of metal) пластинка.
plateau *n.* плоскогорье; плато.

plate glass зеркальное стекло.
platelet *n., usu. pl.* кровяная пластинка.
platen *n.* валик.
platform *n.* **1,** (landing alongside railway tracks) платформа; перрон. **2,** (stage; rostrum) трибуна; помост. **3,** (of a railway car or streetcar) площадка; тамбур. **4,** (of a political party) платформа.
platinum *n.* платина. —*adj.* платиновый.
platitude *n.* общее место; банальность.
platonic *adj.* платонический.
platoon *n.* взвод. *Platoon leader,* взводный.
platter *n.* блюдо.
platypus *n.* утконос.
plaudit *n., usu. pl.* **1,** (applause) аплодисменты. **2,** (praise) восторженные отзывы.
plausible *adj.* правдоподобный. *Plausible excuse,* благовидный предлог. —**plausibility,** *n.* правдоподобие.
play *v.i.* **1,** (engage in recreation or a game) играть: *play with a doll/with dolls/,* играть с куклой/в куклы/. *Play with blocks,* играть кубиками *or* в кубики. *Play with matches/fire,* играть со спичками/с огнём/. **2,** *fol. by* **with** (fiddle with) играть (+ *instr.*): *play with one's keys,* играть ключами. **3,** (of a film, show, etc.) идти. **4,** (pretend to be) притворяться (+ *instr.*): *play dead,* притворяться мёртвым. **5,** *in* **play for time,** оттягивать время; стараться выиграть время. **6,** *in* **play into the hands of,** играть на руку (+ *dat.*). —*v.t.* **1,** (engage in, as a game) играть в (+ *acc.*): *play ball/chess/cards,* играть в мяч/шахматы/карты. **2,** (perform on, as a musical instrument) играть на (+ *prepl.*): *play the violin,* играть на скрипке. **3,** (compete against) играть с. **4,** (perform) играть: *play a role,* играть роль; *play Hamlet,* играть Гамлета. *Play the fool,* валять дурака. **5,** (gamble at) играть на (+ *prepl.*): *play the horses,* играть на скачках; *play the stock market,* играть на бирже. **6,** (lead, as a card) идти с (+ *gen.*); (move, as a chess piece) играть (+ *instr.*); идти (+ *instr.*). **7,** *Play a record,* (по)ставить пластинку. **8,** *Play tricks,* шалить. **9,** *Play a joke/trick on,* сыграть шутку с. —*n.* **1,** (recreation) игра: *at play,* за игрой. **2,** (drama) пьеса. **3,** (maneuver in a game) комбинация. **4,** *in* **out of play,** вне игры; **in play,** в игре. **5,** *in* **play on words,** игра слов. —**bring into play,** пускать в ход. —**come into play,** вступать в действие. —**play around,** шалить. —**play down,** преуменьшать. —**play on** *or* **upon,** играть на: *play on someone's emotions,* играть на чьих-нибудь чувствах. —**play up,** подчёркивать; выпячивать. —**play up to,** заигрывать с; угодничать перед; подмазываться к.
play-acting *n.* актёрство; позёрство. —**play-actor,** *n.* позёр.
playbill *n.* **1,** (poster) афиша. **2,** (printed program) программа.
playboy *n.* повеса; гуляка; жуир.
player *n.* **1,** (contestant) игрок. *Basketball player,* баскетболист. *Chess player,* шахматист. **2,** (actor) актёр. **3,** (musician) музыкант.
player piano пианола.
playful *adj.* игривый; резвый; шаловливый. —**playfulness,** *n.* игривость; резвость; шаловливость.
playgoer *n.* театрал.
playground *n.* площадка для игр.
playhouse *n.* театр.

playing *adj.* игра́ющий. —**playing card,** игра́льная ка́рта. —**playing field,** спорти́вное по́ле; спорти́вная площа́дка. —**playing time,** *sports* игрово́е вре́мя.

playmate *n.* друг де́тства.

playoff *n., sports* ро́зыгрыш.

playpen *n.* мане́ж.

plaything *n.* игру́шка.

playwright *n.* драмату́рг.

plaza *n.* пло́щадь.

plea *n.* **1,** (entreaty) мольба́: *a plea for help,* мольба́ о по́мощи. **2,** *law* заявле́ние: *plea of not guilty,* заявле́ние о свое́й невино́вности.

plead *v.i.* **1,** (beg) умоля́ть; упра́шивать: *plead with someone for help,* умоля́ть/упра́шивать кого́-нибудь о по́мощи. **2,** *law* (put forward a plea): *plead guilty,* признава́ть себя́ вино́вным. *Plead not guilty,* не признава́ть себя́ вино́вным. —*v.t.* **1,** (argue; present, as a case) вести́ (де́ло). **2,** (offer as justification) ссыла́ться на; отгова́риваться (+ *instr.*).

pleasant *adj.* прия́тный.

pleasantly *adv.* прия́тно; *I was pleasantly surprised,* я был прия́тно удивлён.

pleasantry *n.* шутли́вое замеча́ние; шу́тка. *Exchange pleasantries,* обме́ниваться комплиме́нтами.

please *v.t.* нра́виться; угожда́ть. *You can't please everybody,* на всех не угоди́шь. —*v.i.* **1,** (give satisfaction) дава́ть удовлетворе́ние. **2,** (wish) хоте́ть: *do as you please,* де́лайте как хоти́те. —*imperative* **1,** *in polite requests* пожа́луйста; бу́дьте добры́; бу́дьте любе́зны. **2,** *in earnest entreaties* я вас о́чень прошу́! —**if you please, 1,** (if you would be so kind) пожа́луйста; с ва́шего разреше́ния. **2,** *used ironically* предста́вьте себе́!; поду́майте то́лько! —**please God,** дай Бог.

pleased *adj.* рад; дово́лен. *Pleased to meet you!,* о́чень рад познако́миться с ва́ми!

pleasing *adj.* прия́тный; привлека́тельный.

pleasurable *adj.* прия́тный.

pleasure *n.* **1,** (satisfaction) удово́льствие: *with pleasure,* с удово́льствием. **2,** (wish; choice; perference) жела́ние. *What is your pleasure?,* что вам уго́дно? —*adj.* увесели́тельный: *pleasure trip,* увесели́тельная пое́здка.

pleat *n.* скла́дка. —*v.t.* плиссирова́ть. —**pleated,** *adj.* скла́дчатый; в скла́дку; плиссиро́ванный.

plebeian *adj.* плебе́йский. —*n.* плебе́й.

plebiscite *n.* плебисци́т.

plectrum *n.* плектр.

pledge *n.* **1,** (vow) заро́к. *Pledge of allegiance,* кля́тва ве́рности. **2,** (security) зало́г. —*v.t.* **1,** (solemnly promise) обя́зываться (+ *inf.*); кля́сться в (+ *prepl.*). *Pledge allegiance,* кля́сться в ве́рности. **2,** (leave as security) закла́дывать; отдава́ть в зало́г.

Pleiades *n.pl.* плея́ды.

plenary *adj.* **1,** (complete; absolute) по́лный. **2,** (fully attended) плена́рный: *plenary session,* плена́рное заседа́ние.

plenipotentiary *adj.* полномо́чный. —*n.* полномо́чный представи́тель; уполномо́ченный.

plentiful *adj.* оби́льный; изоби́льный.

plenty *n.* изоби́лие: *the horn of plenty,* рог изоби́лия. —*adj., colloq.* о́чень; изря́дно. —**plenty of,** мно́го; мно́жество (+ *gen.*).

plenum *n.* пле́нум.

plethora *n.* **1,** *med.* полнокро́вие. **2,** (superabundance) изоби́лие.

pleura *n.* плевра. —**pleural,** *adj.* плевра́льный.

pleurisy *n.* плеври́т.

plexiglass *n.* плексигла́с.

plexus *n., anat.* сплете́ние: *solar plexus,* со́лнечное сплете́ние.

pliable *adj.* ги́бкий. —**pliability,** *n.* ги́бкость.

pliant *adj.* = **pliable.**

pliers *n.pl.* кле́щи; плоскогу́бцы.

plight *n.* плаче́вное состоя́ние.

plinth *n.* пли́нтус.

plod *v.i.* брести́; тащи́ться; плести́сь.

plop *v.i.* бултыха́ться. —*adv.* булты́х.

plot *n.* **1,** (piece of ground) уча́сток. **2,** (conspiracy) за́говор. **3,** (story line) фа́була; сюже́т; интри́га. —*v.t.* **1,** (trace) наноси́ть (на ка́рту). **2,** (make secret plans for) замышля́ть. —**plotter,** *n.* загово́рщик.

plough *v. & n.* = **plow.** —**ploughing,** *n.* = **plowing.** —**ploughman,** *n.* = **plowman.** —**ploughshare,** *n.* = **plowshare.**

plover *n.* ржа́нка; зуёк. *Golden plover,* си́вка.

plow *also,* **plough** *n.* плуг. —*v.t.* **1,** (use a plow on) паха́ть. **2,** *fol. by up* (turn up) распа́хивать. —*v.i.* **1,** (use a plow) паха́ть. **2,** *fol. by into* (run into) вреза́ться в. **3,** *fol. by through* (work one's way through) оси́ливать: *plow through a book,* оси́лить кни́гу.

plowing *also,* **ploughing** *n.* па́хота; вспа́шка.

plowman *also,* **ploughman** *n.* па́харь.

plowshare *also,* **ploughshare** *n.* ле́мех; сошни́к. —**beat swords into plowshares,** перекова́ть мечи́ на ора́ла.

ploy *n.* прие́м.

pluck *v.t.* **1,** (pick) срыва́ть. **2,** (snatch) выдёргивать. **3,** (pull out the feathers of) щипа́ть; ощи́пывать; обще́ипывать. **4,** (pull at, as the strings of a musical instrument) щипа́ть. —*n.* (courage; fortitude) сме́лость; сто́йкость. —**plucky,** *adj.* сме́лый.

plug *n.* **1,** (stopper) про́бка; заты́чка; втулка. **2,** (two-pronged electrical device) ште́псель; ви́лка. **3,** = **fireplug.** —*v.t.* **1,** [*often plug up*] (stop up) затыка́ть; заку́поривать. **2,** *fol. by in* (connect) вставля́ть (в розе́тку); включа́ть (в сеть).

plum *n.* сли́ва. —*adj.* сли́вовый: *plum brandy,* сли́вовая насто́йка.

plumage *n.* опере́ние.

plumb *n.* **1,** (device for finding the exact perpendicular) отве́с. **2,** (device for determining the depth of water) лот. —*adj.* отве́сный; вертика́льный. —*adv.* **1,** (vertically) отве́сно; по отве́су. **2,** *slang* (utterly) соверше́нно; абсолю́тно. *I plumb forgot,* я так и забы́л. —*v.t.* **1,** (test the depth of) измеря́ть глубину́ (+ *gen.*). **2,** *fig.* (go deep into) проника́ть в.

plumber *n.* водопрово́дчик. —**plumbing,** *n.* водопрово́д.

plume *n.* **1,** (feather) перо́. **2,** (ornament for a hat or helmet) плюма́ж; султа́н.

plummet *v.i.* па́дать (как ка́мень); лете́ть вниз.

plump *adj.* по́лный; пу́хлый. —*v.i.* бу́хаться.

plunder *v.t.* гра́бить. —*n.* **1,** (robbery) грабёж. **2,** (booty) добы́ча.

plunge *v.t.* **1,** (thrust, as a dagger) вонза́ть. **2,** (throw into, as darkness, despair, etc.) погружа́ть; вверга́ть; поверга́ть. *The city was plunged into darkness,* го́род погрузился (*or* был погружён) в темноту. *Plunge a country into war,* ввергать страну в войну. —*v.i.* **1,** (dive; dash headlong) броситься: *plunge into the water,* броситься в воду. *Plunge down an embankment,* свалиться под откос. *The car plunged into the crowd,* машина врезалась в толпу. **2,** *fig.* (plummet) лететь вниз. —*n.* **1,** (dive) нырок. **2,** (sudden decline) резкое падение.

plunger *n.* плунжер.

plunk *v.t.* **1,** (strum) бренчать. **2,** *fol. by* **down** (toss down) бросить: *plunk down a dollar on the counter,* бросить доллар на прилавок.

pluperfect *adj.* давнопрошедший. —*n.* давнопрошедшее время.

plural *adj.* множественный. *Plural noun,* существительное множественного числа. —*n.* множественное число.

plurality *n.* **1,** (largest number of votes but less than 50%) относительное большинство. **2,** (excess of votes over nearest competitor) перевес.

plus *prep. & n.* плюс. —**plus sign,** (знак) плюс.

plush *n.* (fabric) плюш. —*adj.* **1,** (of this fabric) плюшевый. **2,** [*also,* **plushy**] *colloq.* (luxurious) роскошный.

Pluto *n.* Плутон.

plutocracy *n.* плутократия. —**plutocrat,** *n.* плутократ. —**plutocratic,** *adj.* плутократический.

plutonium *n.* плутоний.

ply *v.t.* **1,** (do work with; wield) работать (+ *instr.*). *Ply the oars,* налегать на вёсла. **2,** (practice, as a trade) подвизаться на (каком-нибудь поприще). **3,** (address constantly with, as questions) засыпать (вопросами). **4,** (keep supplying with) потчевать: *ply with wine,* потчевать вином. **5,** (traverse regularly) бороздить: *ply the seas,* бороздить моря. —*v.i.* (travel back and forth) курсировать; сновать. —*n.* слой: *three-ply wood,* трёхслойная фанера.

plywood *n.* фанера. —*adj.* фанерный.

pneumatic *adj.* пневматический. —**pneumatic drill,** пневматическое сверло.

pneumonia *n.* воспаление лёгких.

poach *v.t.* варить (без скорлупы). *Poached egg,* яйцо-пашот. —*v.i.* заниматься браконьерством. *Poach on,* вторгаться в.

poacher *n.* браконьер. —**poaching,** *n.* браконьерство.

pochard *n.* нырок.

pocket *n.* **1,** (of a garment) карман. **2,** *billiards* луза. **3,** (small area) узел; очаг. *Pocket of resistance,* очаг сопротивления. **4,** *in* **air pocket,** воздушная яма. —*adj.* карманный: *pocket comb,* карманная расчёска.—*v.t.* **1,** (put in one's pocket) класть в карман. **2,** (take dishonestly) класть (себе) в карман; прикарманивать. **3,** (endure, as an insult) проглотить. —**out of pocket,** в убытке; в проигрыше.

pocket billiards лузный бильярд.

pocketbook *n.* **1,** (lady's handbag) сумка; сумочка. **2,** = **paperback.** —**put a hole in one's pocketbook,** бить *or* ударять по карману.

pocketknife *n.* карманный нож.

pocket money карманные деньги.

pockmark *n.* оспина; рябина. —**pockmarked,** *adj.* в оспинах; изрытый оспой; рябой.

pod *n.* стручок. *Peas in the pod,* стручковый горох. —**like two peas in a pod,** как две капли воды.

podiatrist *n.* специалист по лечению ног. —**podiatry,** *n.* лечение заболеваний ног.

podium *n.* помост.

podzol *n.* подзол.

poem *n.* стихотворение; поэма.

poet *n.* поэт. —**poetess,** *n.* поэтесса.

poetic *adj.* поэтический. —**poetic license,** поэтическая вольность.

poetical *adj.* поэтический.

poetry *n.* поэзия; стихи.

pogrom *n.* погром.

poignancy *n.* трогательность.

poignant *adj.* **1,** (cutting; harsh) острый. **2,** (touching) трогательный.

point *n.* **1,** (sharp end) кончик; остриё. **2,** (point in space) пункт; точка. *The furthermost point,* самый дальний пункт. *The shortest distance between two points,* наименьшее расстояние между двумя точками. **3,** (stage; juncture) точка; пункт: *starting point,* начальный пункт; *boiling point,* точка кипения; *turning point,* поворотный пункт. *Reach the point where,* дойти до того, что... **4,** (specific moment in time) момент. *At this point I should like to...,* здесь я хотел бы (+ *inf.*). **5,** (item; element) пункт: *the main points of the plan,* основные пункты плана. *Fine point,* тонкость. *Point of interest,* достопримечательность. **6,** (essence; gist) суть; существо: *come to the point,* доходить до сути дела. *Speak to the point,* говорить по существу *or* напрямик. *Miss the point,* не видеть самого главного. *The point is...,* дело в том, что... *That's just the point,* в том-то и дело. *That's not the point,* не в этом дело. **7,** (idea advanced, esp. a valid one): *I don't get your point,* я не понимаю, что вы хотите сказать *or* куда вы гнёте. *He has a point there!,* в этом он прав. **8,** (purpose; use; advantage) смысл: *there is no point in arguing with him,* нет смысла (*or* не стоит) с ним спорить. *There is no point in even trying,* нечего и пытаться. **9,** (unit of scoring) очко. *Win on points,* победить по очкам. **10,** (characteristic) сторона; место: *weak points,* слабые стороны/места. *Have one's good points,* иметь свои хорошие стороны. **11,** (promontory; cape) мыс; нос. **12,** *printing* пункт. —*v.t.* **1,** (direct, as a weapon) направлять; наводить; наставлять. **2,** (show by pointing) указывать: *point the way to someone,* указывать путь кому-нибудь. **3,** *fol. by* **out** (indicate; explain) указывать (на). **4,** *fol. by* **up** (emphasize; make clear) заострять. —*v.i.* **1,** *fol. by* **to** (motion toward) показывать на; указывать на. **2,** (be turned in a given direction) указывать на: *the needle points south,* стрелка указывает на юг. **3,** *fol. by* **to** (indicate; suggest) говорить о: *everything points to the fact that...,* всё говорит о том, что... —**be on the point of,** как раз собираться (+ *inf.*). —**beside the point,** не к делу; некстати; не по существу. —**case in point,** хороший пример этого. —**in point of,** в отношении (+ *gen.*); с точки зрения (+ *gen.*). —**in point of fact,** фактически; на самом деле. —**make a point of; make it a point to,** взять себе за правило (+ *inf.*). —**point of view,** точка зрения.

pointblank *adj.* **1,** (fired straight at the mark) прямой. **2,** (explicit) категорический. —*adv.* **1,** (straight at the mark) в упор. **2,** (without hesitation or equivocation) наотрез; напрямик.

pointed *adj.* **1,** (coming to a point) заострённый; остроконе́чный. **2.** (sharp; incisive) о́стрый; ме́ткий. **3.** (deliberately emphasized) демонстрати́вный.

pointer *n.* **1.** (indicator) стре́лка; указа́тель. **2.** (rod used in classrooms) па́лочка; ука́зка. **3.** (dog) лега́вая соба́ка; по́йнтер. **4.** *colloq.* (tip; advice) сове́т.

pointless *adj.* бессмы́сленный; бесце́льный; беспредме́тный. *It is pointless to...,* нет смы́сла (+ *inf.*).

poise *n.* **1.** (equilibrium) равнове́сие. **2.** (composure) уравнове́шенность. —*v.t.* уравнове́шивать.

poised *adj.* **1.** (composed) уравнове́шенный. **2.** *fol. by* **to** (suspended in readiness) гото́вый (к).

poison *n.* яд; отра́ва. —*adj.* ядови́тый: *poison gas,* ядови́тый газ. —*v.t.* отравля́ть. —**poisoning,** *n.* отравле́ние: *food poisoning,* пищево́е отравле́ние. —**poisonous,** *adj.* ядови́тый.

poke *v.t.* **1.** (jab) ты́кать; толка́ть. *Poke someone in the ribs,* толкну́ть кого́-нибудь в бок. *Poke one's finger at someone,* ты́кать па́льцем на кого́-нибудь. **2.** (thrust) сова́ть: *poke one's nose into,* сова́ть нос в. **3.** (stir, as a fire) меша́ть; перемеша́ть (у́гли). **4.** (make, as a hole) протыка́ть. —*v.i.* **1.** *fol. by* **around** *or* **about** (search leisurely) ры́ться. **2.** *fol. by* **along** (plod along) таска́ться. **3.** *fol. by* **out** (protrude) торча́ть. —*n.* тычо́к. —**buy a pig in a poke,** купи́ть кота́ в мешке́. —**poke fun at,** *see* **fun.**

poker *n.* **1.** (rod for stirring a fire) кочерга́. **2.** (card game) по́кер.

poky *also,* **pokey** *adj.* те́сный. —*n., slang* (jail) куту́зка.

polar *adj.* поля́рный. —**polar bear,** бе́лый *or* поля́рный медве́дь. —**polar fox,** песе́ц.

polarity *n.* поля́рность.

polarize *v.t.* поляризова́ть. —**polarization,** *n.* поляриза́ция.

pole *n.* **1.** (long stick) шест; жердь. **2.** (upright post) столб. **3.** (of the earth) по́люс: *North Pole,* Се́верный по́люс.

Pole *n.* поля́к; по́лька. *The Poles,* поля́ки.

poleax *also,* **poleaxe** *n.* секи́ра.

polecat *n.* хорёк.

polemic *n.* поле́мика. —*adj.* [*also,* **polemical**] полеми́ческий. —**polemicist,** *n.* полеми́ст. —**polemics,** *n.* поле́мика.

pole vault прыжо́к с шесто́м. —**pole-vault,** *v.i.* пры́гать с шесто́м.

police *n.* поли́ция; мили́ция. —*adj.* полице́йский: *police station,* полице́йский уча́сток. —*v.t.* **1.** (keep order in) охраня́ть; патрули́ровать. **2.** (clean up) чи́стить; убира́ть.

policeman *n.* **1.** (in the USSR) милиционе́р. **2.** (elsewhere) полице́йский; полисме́н.

police state полице́йское госуда́рство.

policy *n.* **1.** (course of action) поли́тика. **2.** (contract of insurance) по́лис.

poliomyelitis *n.* полиомиели́т.

polish *v.t.* **1.** (shine) полирова́ть; шлифова́ть. *Polish one's shoes,* чи́стить боти́нки. **2.** (refine; perfect) шлифова́ть. —*n.* **1.** (glossy finish) полиро́вка. **2.** (polishing substance) лак: *nail polish,* лак для ногте́й. *Shoe polish,* гутали́н; ва́кса. **3.** *fig.* (elegance; refinement) лоск. —**polish off,** поко́нчить с.

Polish *n.* по́льский язы́к. —*n.* по́льский язы́к. *Speak Polish,* говори́ть по-по́льски.

polished *adj.* **1.** (shiny) полиро́ванный. **2.** (elegant) изы́сканный; лощёный. **3.** (finished; flawless) зако́нченный.

polisher *n.* полиро́вщик; шлифова́льщик.

Politburo *n.* политбюро́.

polite *adj.* **1.** (courteous) ве́жливый. **2.** (refined) изы́сканный: *polite society,* изы́сканное о́бщество. —**politely,** *adv.* ве́жливо. —**politeness,** *n.* ве́жливость.

politic *adj.* полити́чный.

political *adj.* полити́ческий. —**political prisoner,** политзаключённый.

politician *n.* **1.** (one engaged in politics) полити́ческий де́ятель; поли́тик. **2.** (political opportunist) полити́кан.

politics *n.* поли́тика.

polity *n.* о́браз правле́ния.

polka *n.* по́лька.

polka dots горо́шек: *polka-dot necktie,* га́лстук в горо́шек.

poll *n.* **1.** (vote) голосова́ние. **2.** *pl.* (voting place) избира́тельный уча́сток. *Go to the polls,* (идти́) голосова́ть. **3.** (survey of opinion) опро́с. —*v.t.* **1.** (receive, as votes) получа́ть; собира́ть. **2.** (survey; canvass) опра́шивать.

pollen *n.* пыльца́.

pollinate *v.t.* опыля́ть. —**pollination,** *n.* опыле́ние.

polling booth каби́на для голосова́ния.

polling place избира́тельный уча́сток.

polliwog *n.* голова́стик.

poll tax поду́шный нало́г; избира́тельный нало́г.

pollute *v.t.* загрязня́ть. —**pollutant,** *n.* загрязня́ющее вещество́. —**pollution,** *n.* загрязне́ние.

polo *n.* по́ло.

polonaise *n.* полоне́з.

polonium *n.* поло́ний.

polo shirt те́нниска.

poltroon *n.* трус.

polyandry *n.* полиа́ндрия.

polychromatic *adj.* многоцве́тный; многокра́сочный.

polyclinic *n.* поликли́ника.

polyester *n.* полиэфи́р. —*adj.* полиэфи́рный.

polyethylene *n.* полиэтиле́н. —*adj.* полиэтиле́новый.

polygamy *n.* многобра́чие; многожёнство; полига́мия. —**polygamist,** *n.* многожёнец. —**polygamous,** *adj.* многобра́чный; полига́мный; полигами́ческий.

polyglot *adj.* многоязы́чный. —*n.* полигло́т.

polygon *n.* многоуго́льник. —**polygonal,** *adj.* многоуго́льный.

polyhedron *n.* многогра́нник. —**polyhedral,** *adj.* многогра́нный.

polymer *n.* полиме́р. —**polymeric,** *adj.* полиме́рный.

Polynesian *adj.* полинези́йский. —*n.* полинези́ец.

polynomial *n.* многочле́н. —*adj.* многочле́нный.

polyp *n.* поли́п.

polystyrene *n.* полистиро́л.

polysyllabic *adj.* многосло́жный.

polytechnic *adj.* политехни́ческий.

polytheism *n.* политеи́зм; многобо́жие. —**polytheist,** *n.* политеи́ст. —**polytheistic,** *adj.* политеисти́ческий.

pomade *n.* пома́да. —*v.t.* пома́дить.

pomegranate *n.* грана́т.

pommel *n.* (of a saddle) лука́. —*v.t.* (beat) колоти́ть.

pomp *n.* пы́шность; по́мпа.

pompon *n.* помпо́н.

pompous *adj.* напы́щенный; наду́тый. —**pomposity,** *n.* напы́щенность.

poncho *n.* по́нчо.

pond *n.* пруд.

ponder *v.t.* обду́мывать; соображáть. —*v.i.* размышля́ть; задýмываться; раздýмывать.

ponderous *adj.* тяжёлый; тяжелове́сный.

pond scum ти́на.

pondweed *n.* рдест.

pontiff *n.* **1,** (Pope) пáпа. **2,** (bishop) епи́скоп. —**pontifical,** *adj.* пáпский; епи́скопский.

pontificate *n.* понтификáт. —*v.i.* орáторствовать.

pontoon *n.* (boat) понто́н. —**pontoon bridge,** понто́нный мост.

pony *n.* по́ни.

pooch *n., colloq.* собáчка.

poodle *n.* пýдель.

pool *n.* **1,** (puddle) лýжа. **2,** (swimming pool) бассе́йн для плáвания. **3,** (billiards) (лýзный) билья́рд. **4,** (combination of resources) фонд. —*v.t.* объединя́ть: *pool one's resources,* объединя́ть ресýрсы.

pool table билья́рд.

poop *n., naut.* ют; полуют. —**poop deck,** пáлуба ю́та.

poor *adj.* **1,** (needy) бéдный: *poor family/country,* бéдная семья́/странá. **2,** (unfortunate) бéдный: *poor Nina!,* бéдная Ни́на! *Poor man/woman/creature!,* бедня́га! **3,** (bad) плохо́й; слáбый: *poor memory,* плохáя/слáбая пáмять. *Poor grades,* плохи́е отмéтки. *Poor student,* слáбый учени́к. *Poor quality,* ни́зкое кáчество. *Poor harvest,* плохо́й урожáй; неурожáй. *Read in poor light,* читáть при плохо́м свéте. *She is in poor health,* у неё слáбое здоро́вье. —*n., preceded by* **the** бéдные; беднотá.

poorbox *n.* крýжка.

poorhouse *n.* богадéльня; рабо́тный дом.

poorly *adv.* плóхо; слáбо; невáжно.

pop *n.* **1,** (sound) хлопо́к. **2,** (drink) газиро́ванная водá. **3,** *colloq.* (dad) пáпа; папáша. —*v.i.* **1,** (make a short explosive sound) хло́пать; трéснуть. **2,** *fol. by* **up** *or* **out** (appear suddenly) покáзываться. **3,** *fol. by* **in** (drop in for a moment) загляну́ть. **4,** (of one's eyes) широко́ раскрывáться. *His eyes nearly popped out of his head,* у него́ глазá полезли́ на лоб. —*v.t.* **1,** (put quickly or suddenly) совáть; всо́вывать. *Pop one's head out the window,* высо́вывать гóлову из окнá. **2,** *in* **pop the question** (propose) сдéлать предложéние.

popcorn *n.* воздýшная кукурýза.

Pope *n.* пáпа.

popgun *n.* пугáч.

poplar *n.* то́поль. —*adj.* то́полевый.

poplin *n.* попли́н. —*adj.* попли́новый.

poppy *n.* мак. *Poppy seeds,* мак.

poppycock *n., colloq.* чушь; галиматья́; белибердá.

populace *n.* населéние.

popular *adj.* **1,** (well-liked; enjoyed by many) популя́рный. **2,** (of the people) нарóдный. *By popular demand,* по трéбованию пýблики. **3,** (within the means of most people) достýпный.

popularity *n.* популя́рность.

popularize *v.t.* популяризи́ровать. —**popularization,** *n.* популяризáция.

populate *v.t.* населя́ть; заселя́ть. *Densely/sparsely populated,* гýсто/рéдко населённый.

population *n.* населéние. —**population explosion,** демографи́ческий взрыв.

Populist *n.* нарóдник. —*adj.* нарóднический. — **Populism,** *n.* нарóдничество.

populous *adj.* лю́дный; многолю́дный; густонаселённый.

porcelain *n.* фарфо́р. —*adj.* фарфо́ровый.

porch *n.* крыльцо́.

porcupine *n.* дикобрáз.

pore *n.* по́ра. —*v.i.* [*usu.* **pore over**] корпéть (над); коптéть (над).

pork *n.* свини́на. —*adj.* свино́й: *pork chop,* свинáя котлéта; свинáя отбивнáя.

pornography *n.* порногрáфия. —**pornographic,** *adj.* порнографи́ческий.

porous *adj.* по́ристый; ноздревáтый. —**porosity,** *n.* по́ристость.

porphyry *n.* порфи́р.

porpoise *n.* морскáя свинья́.

porridge *n.* кáша.

port *n.* **1,** (harbor; seaport) порт. **2,** (left side of a vessel) лéвый борт. **3,** (wine) портвéйн. —**port of call,** порт захóда.

portable *adj.* перенóсный; портати́вный.

portage *n.* **1,** (act of carrying) перенóска. **2,** (route over which boats are carried) волóк.

portal *n.* портáл.

portend *v.t.* предвещáть.

portent *n.* **1,** (omen) предзнаменовáние; предвéстие. **2,** (significance) значéние.

portentous *adj.* **1,** (ominous) зловéщий. **2,** (momentous) знаменáтельный.

porter *n.* **1,** (baggage carrier) носи́льщик. **2,** (handyman) убóрщик.

portfolio *n.* портфéль. *Minister without portfolio,* мини́стр без портфéля.

porthole *n.* иллюминáтор.

portico *n.* пóртик.

portion *n.* **1,** (part of a whole) часть; дóля. **2,** (serving of food) пóрция. —*v.t.* [*usu.* **portion out**] распределя́ть; выделя́ть.

portly *adj.* пóлный; дорóдный.

portrait *n.* портрéт. *Portrait gallery,* портрéтная галерéя. *Portrait painter,* портрети́ст.

portray *v.t.* изображáть. —**portrayal,** *n.* изображéние.

Portuguese *adj.* португáльский. *He (she) is Portuguese,* он португáлец; онá португáлка. —*n.* **1,** (language) португáльский язы́к. *Speak Portuguese,* говори́ть по-португáльски. **2,** *preceded by* **the** (people) португáльцы.

portulaca *n.* портулáк.

pose *n.* пóза. —*v.i.* **1,** (assume a position, as for a portrait) пози́ровать. **2,** *fol. by* **as** (represent oneself as) выдавáть себя́ (за). —*v.t.* **1,** (put, as a question) стáвить; задавáть; предлагáть. **2,** (present) представля́ть: *pose difficulties/a threat/,* представля́ть трýдности/угрóзу.

posh *adj., colloq.* роско́шный; шикáрный.

position *n.* **1,** (location; posture; situation; status) положéние: *in a sitting/awkward position,* в сидя́чем/ нело́вком положéнии. *Be in a position to,* быть в состоя́нии (+ *inf.*). *What would you do in my position?,* что бы вы сде́лали на моём ме́сте? **2,** *mil.* пози́ция. **3,** (job) ме́сто. **4,** (point of view; stand) пози́ция. *—v.t.* ста́вить; помеща́ть.

positional *adj.* позицио́нный.

positive *adj.* **1,** (affirmative; favorable) положи́тельный. **2,** (certain) уве́ренный: *I am positive that...*, я (абсолю́тно) уве́рен, что... **3,** *math.; electricity* положи́тельный. **4,** *photog.* позити́вный. *—n., photog.* позити́в. **—positively,** *adv.* положи́тельно.

positivism *n.* позитиви́зм.

positron *n.* позитро́н.

possess *v.t.* **1,** (have; own) облада́ть: *possess talent*, облада́ть тала́нтом. **2,** (come over) овладева́ть: *fear possessed him*, им овладе́л страх. *What possessed you to do that?*, что вас заста́вило сде́лать э́то?

possessed *adj.* **1,** *fol. by of* (having) облада́ющий. **2,** (obsessed) одержи́мый.

possession *n.* **1,** (fact of possessing) облада́ние; владе́ние. *Be in someone's possession*, быть в чьём-нибудь распоряже́нии. *Take possession of*, вступи́ть во владе́ние (*+ instr.*). **2,** (territory belonging to an outside country) владе́ние. **3,** *pl.* (belongings) иму́щество.

possessive *adj.* **1,** (desiring to possess) со́бственнический. **2,** *gram.* притяжа́тельный.

possessor *n.* облада́тель.

possibility *n.* возмо́жность: *the possibility of error*, возмо́жность оши́бки. *There is little possibility of that*, ша́нсов на э́то ма́ло. *There are two possibilities*, существу́ют два вариа́нта.

possible *adj.* возмо́жный. *If possible*, е́сли возмо́жно. *That is not possible*, э́то невозмо́жно. *That's entirely possible*, э́то вполне́ возмо́жно. *Do everything possible*, сде́лать всё возмо́жное. *Make it possible to*, позволя́ть (*+ inf.*). **—as...as possible,** как мо́жно (*+ comparative*): *as soon as possible*, как мо́жно скоре́е.

possibly *adv.* возмо́жно: *I may possibly be late*, я, возмо́жно, опозда́ю. *As soon as I possibly can*, как то́лько я смогу́. *He could not possibly have done it*, не мо́жет быть, что́бы он сде́лал э́то.

possum *n., colloq.* = **opossum. —play possum,** притворя́ться мёртвым.

post *n.* **1,** (upright pole) столб. **2,** (station) пункт; пост: *observation post*, наблюда́тельный пункт; *control post*, контро́льный пост. **3,** (assigned position) пост: *remain at one's post*, остава́ться на своём посту́. **4,** (camp; base) городо́к: *military post*, вое́нный городо́к. **5,** (appointed public office) пост; до́лжность. **6,** (mail) по́чта. *—v.t.* **1,** (put up; hang up) выве́шивать; раскле́ивать. **2,** (announce) объявля́ть: *post a reward*, объяви́ть пре́мию. **3,** (station, as a sentry) ста́вить; выставля́ть (часово́го); расставля́ть; разводи́ть (часовы́х). **4,** (assign) назнача́ть. **5,** (keep informed) держа́ть в ку́рсе. *Well posted on politics*, в ку́рсе поли́тики. **6,** *comm.* (transfer to a ledger) переноси́ть в гроссбу́х. **7,** *chiefly Brit.* (mail) отправля́ть; опуска́ть (в почто́вый я́щик). **8,** *in* **post bond for,** брать на пору́ки.

postage *n.* почто́вые расхо́ды; сто́имость пересы́лки. *Pay the postage*, (у)плати́ть за пересы́лку. **—postage stamp,** почто́вая ма́рка.

postal *adj.* почто́вый: *postal rates*, почто́вый тари́ф.

postcard *n.* почто́вая ка́рточка; откры́тка.

poster *n.* плака́т; афи́ша.

posterior *adj.* **1,** (rear) за́дний. **2,** (subsequent) после́дующий. *—n.* зад.

posterity *n.* пото́мство: *the verdict of posterity*, суд пото́мства.

postgraduate *n.* аспира́нт. *Postgraduate studies*, аспиранту́ра.

posthaste *adv.* сломя́ го́лову; момента́льно.

posthumous *adj.* посме́ртный. **—posthumously,** *adv.* посме́ртно.

postilion *also,* **postillion** *n.* форе́йтор.

postman *n.* почтальо́н.

postmark *n.* почто́вый ште́мпель. *—v.t.* штемпелева́ть.

postmaster *n.* почтме́йстер. **—postmaster general,** мини́стр почт.

post-mortem *n.* **1,** (autopsy) вскры́тие. **2,** *colloq.* (post-game analysis) ана́лиз игры́.

postnatal *adj.* послеродово́й.

post office по́чта.

postoperative *adj.* послеоперацио́нный.

postpaid *adj. & adv.* с опла́ченными почто́выми расхо́дами.

postpone *v.t.* откла́дывать. **—postponement,** *n.* отсро́чка.

postscript *n.* **1,** (to a letter) припи́ска; постскри́птум. **2,** (to a book or article) послесло́вие.

postulate *n.* постула́т. *—v.t.* постули́ровать.

posture *n.* **1,** (position) положе́ние. **2,** (way of standing) оса́нка: *poor posture*, плоха́я оса́нка. **3,** *fig.* (stance) пози́ция.

postwar *adj.* послевое́нный.

posy *n.* **1,** (flower) цвето́к. **2,** (bouquet) буке́т.

pot *n.* **1,** (for cooking) кастрю́ля; котело́к. *Coffeepot*, кофе́йник. **2,** (for plants) горшо́к: *flowerpot*, цвето́чный горшо́к. **—go to pot,** вы́лететь в трубу́.

potable *adj.* го́дный для питья́.

potash *n.* пота́ш.

potassium *n.* ка́лий. **—potassium bromide,** бро́мистый ка́лий. **—potassium carbonate,** углеки́слый ка́лий. **—potassium chloride,** хло́ристый ка́лий. **—potassium cyanide,** циа́нистый ка́лий. **—potassium iodide,** йо́дистый ка́лий. **—potassium nitrate,** ка́лиевая *or* калийная сели́тра.

potato *n.* картофе́лина; *pl.* карто́фель. *—adj.* карто́фельный. **—potato beetle** (*or* **bug**), (колора́дский) карто́фельный жук. **—potato chips,** чи́псы.

potbelly *n., colloq.* пу́зо; брю́хо. **— potbellied,** *adj., colloq.* пуза́тый.

pot cheese творо́г.

Potemkin village потёмкинская дере́вня.

potency *n.* си́ла.

potent *adj.* **1,** (powerful, as of a weapon) мо́щный. **2,** (convincing; cogent) си́льный; убеди́тельный. **3,** (effective, as of a drug or drink) си́льный; кре́пкий.

potentate *n.* властели́н.

potential *adj.* потенциа́льный. *—n.* потенциа́л. **—potentiality,** *n.* возмо́жности.

pothole *n.* уха́б; ры́твина; вы́боина.

potion *n.* зе́лье. *Love potion*, любо́вный напи́ток.

potpourri *n.* мешани́на; винегре́т.

pot shot вы́стрел в упо́р. *Take a pot shot at*, вы́стрелить в (кого́-нибудь) в упо́р.

pottage *n.* похлёбка.

potted *adj.* **1,** (kept in a pot, as of plants) горше́чный. **2,** *slang* (drunk) пья́ный.

potter *n.* гончáр. —*v.i.* = **putter.** —**potter's wheel,** гончáрный круг.

pottery *n.* гончáрные (*or* глúняные) издéлия.

pouch *n.* **1,** (small bag) сýмка; мешóчек. *Tobacco pouch,* кисéт. **2,** (of a kangaroo) сýмка. —**diplomatic pouch,** дипломатúческая пóчта.

poultice *n.* припáрка.

poultry *n.* домáшняя птúца.

pounce *v.i.* [*usu.* **pounce on** *or* **upon**] набрáсываться (на); обрýшиваться (на); налетáть (на).

pound *n.* **1,** (measure of weight; monetary unit) фунт. **2,** (enclosure for stray animals) загóн. —*v.t.* **1,** (bang) удáрять; колотúть: *pound one's fist on the table,* удáрять/колотúть кулакóм пó столу. **2,** [*also intrans.*] **pound on**] (strike heavily) удáрять (по); колотúть (по); стучáть (о). **3,** (crush; pulverize) толóчь; дробúть; размельчáть. —*v.i.* колотúться: *my heart was pounding,* у меня сéрдце колотúлось.

poundage *n.* вес (в фýнтах).

pour *v.t.* **1,** (a liquid) наливáть; лить. *Pour oneself a glass of milk,* наливáть себé стакáн молокá. *Pour tea for the guests,* разливáть гостя́м чай. **2,** (a dry substance) сы́пать: *pour salt in the soup,* сы́пать соль в суп. —*v.i.* лúться; лить. *It is pouring,* идёт сúльный дождь; дождь так и льёт; дождь лив мя́ льёт. *Tears were pouring down her cheeks,* слёзы катúлись у неё по щекáм. —**pour in, 1,** (stream into a place) валúть. **2,** (arrive in great numbers) сы́паться. —**pour out, 1,** *literally* выливáть. **2,** (give vent to, as one's feelings) изливáть. **3,** (come streaming out) выливáться; валúть.

pout *v.i.* дýться; надувáть гýбы.

poverty *n.* бéдность; нищетá. —**poverty-stricken,** *adj.* обеднéвший; обнищáлый.

powder *n.* **1,** (substance of fine particles) порошóк: *tooth powder,* зубнóй порошóк. **2,** (talcum) пýдра: *face powder,* пýдра для лицá. *Baby powder,* дéтская присы́пка. **3,** (gunpowder) пóрох. —*adj.* пороховóй: *powder keg,* пороховáя бóчка. —*v.t.* пýдрить. *Powder one's nose,* пýдриться. —**keep one's powder dry,** держáть пóрох сухúм.

powdered *adj.* напýдренный: *powdered wig,* напýдренный парúк. —**powdered eggs,** яúчный порошóк. —**powdered milk,** молóчный порошóк. —**powdered sugar,** сáхарная пýдра.

powder puff пухóвка.

powder room дáмская убóрная; дáмский туалéт.

powdery *adj.* порошкообрáзный.

power *n.* **1,** (strength; might) мощь; могýщество. *Military/air power,* воéнная/воздýшная мощь. *The power of the printed word,* власть печáтного слóва. **2,** (political control) власть: *be in power,* быть у влáсти. *Seize power,* захватúть власть. **3,** (form of energy) сúла; мóщность; энéргия. *Horsepower,* лошадúная сúла. *Electric power,* электроэнéргия. *Power failure,* откáз электропитáния. *The power is out,* нет электрúчества. **4,** (large nation) держáва. **5,** *pl.* (faculties) сúлы: *mental powers,* ýмственные сúлы. **6,** *pl.* (authority) полномóчия: *broad powers,* ширóкие полномóчия. **7,** *math.* стéпень: *ten to the sixth power,* дéсять в шестóй стéпени. —*adj.* **1,** (generating or transmitting power) силовóй: *power lines,* силовы́е проводá. *Power station,* электростáнция. **2,** (driven by a motor) механúческий: *power tool,* механúческий инструмéнт. *Power saw,* мотопилá. —*v.t.* двú-

гать: *the plane is powered by two large engines,* два больш́их мотóра двúжут самолёт. —**do everything in one's power,** сдéлать всё, что в чьúх-нибудь сúлах. —**the powers that be,** власть имýщие. —**under one's own power,** сóбственными сúлами; своúм хóдом.

powerful *adj.* сúльный; мóщный; могýчий. *Powerful engine/weapon,* мóщный двúгатель; мóщное орýжие. *Powerful army,* сúльная *or* могýчая áрмия. *Powerful nation,* могýчая *or* могýщественная странá. *Powerful argument,* сúльный дóвод. —**powerfully,** *adv.* сúльно.

powerless *adj.* бессúльный.

power of attorney довéренность.

power pack блок питáния.

power plant 1, (source of power) силовáя устанóвка. **2,** (power station) электростáнция.

pox *n.* óспа.

practicable *adj.* осуществúмый; реáльный. —**practicability,** *n.* осуществúмость.

practical *adj.* практúческий; практúчный: *practical person/advice,* практúческий *or* практúчный человéк/совéт. *Practical application,* практúческое применéние. *Practical method,* практúчный мéтод. —**practical joke,** мистификáция.

practicality *n.* практúчность.

practically *adv.* **1,** (in a practical way) практúчески. **2,** (virtually; in effect) практúчески: *practically impossible,* практúчески невозмóжно. **3,** (almost) почтú: *practically all week,* почтú всю недéлю. —**practically speaking,** фактúчески.

practice *also,* **practise** *n.* **1,** (repeated performance; proficiency) прáктика. *In practice,* на прáктике; на дéле. *Be out of practice,* не имéть прáктики. *Put into practice,* проводúть *or* претворя́ть в жизнь. **2,** (habitual way of doing things) привы́чка; обы́чай. *Make it a practice to; make a practice of,* взять себé за прáвило (+ *inf.*). **3,** (professional activity or clientele) прáктика: *legal practice,* адвокáтская прáктика. *He has a large practice,* у негó большáя прáктика. **4,** *pl.* (questionable activities) делá: *shady practices,* тёмные делá. —*adj.* прóбный: *practice shot/jump,* прóбный вы́стрел/прыжóк. —*v.t.* **1,** (observe; exercise) соблюдáть. *Practice thrift,* соблюдáть эконóмию. *Practice one's religion,* исповéдовать свою́ релúгию. **2,** (drill oneself in) упражня́ться в *or* на; практиковáться в. *Practice the piano,* упражня́ться на роя́ле. **3,** (pursue, as a profession): *practice law,* быть адвокáтом. —*v.i.* **1,** (drill) упражня́ться; практиковáться. **2,** (pursue a certain profession) практиковáть.

practiced *adj.* óпытный; умéлый.

practitioner *n. General practitioner,* врач óбщей прáктики.

praetor *n.* прéтор.

pragmatic *adj.* прагматúческий. —**pragmatism,** *n.* прагматúзм. —**pragmatist,** *n.* прагматúст.

prairie *n.* прéрия; степь.

praise *v.t.* хвалúть. —*n.* похвалá. *In praise of,* в похвалý (+ *dat.*). —**praise to the skies,** превозносúть до небéс. —**sing the praises of,** петь дифирáмбы (+ *dat.*).

praiseworthy *adj.* похвáльный.

pram *n., colloq.* = **perambulator.**

prance *v.i.* **1,** (on a horse) гарцевáть. **2,** (swagger; strut) вáжничать; ходúть гóголем.

prank *n.* выходка; проказа; проделка; шалость. *Play pranks,* проказничать. —**prankish,** *adj.* проказливый. —**prankster,** *n.* проказник.

praseodymium *n.* празеодим.

prate *v.i.* болтать; трещать.

prattle *v.i.* лепетать. —*n.* лепет.

prawn *n.* креветка.

pray *v.i.* (offer prayers) молиться: *pray to God,* молиться богу. —*v.t. & i.* (beg; beseech) умолять. *Pray tell me,* да скажите пожалуйста!

prayer *n.* молитва: *say a prayer,* читать молитву. *Call to prayer,* звать к молитве. *Kneel in prayer,* молиться на коленях. —**prayer book,** молитвенник. —**prayer service,** моление.

praying mantis богомол.

preach *v.t.* 1, (espouse) проповедовать. 2, (deliver, as a sermon) произносить. —*v.i.* (deliver a sermon) проповедовать. —**preacher,** *n.* проповедник.

preamble *n.* преамбула.

prearranged *adj.* заранее условленный; условный.

precarious *adj.* опасный; шаткий: *precarious position,* опасное/шаткое положение.

precaution *n.* предосторожность. *Take precautions,* принимать (меры) предосторожности. —**precautionary,** *adj., in precautionary measures,* меры предосторожности.

precede *v.t.* предшествовать.

precedence *n.* предпочтение: *give precedence to,* отдавать предпочтение (+ *dat.*). *This task takes precedence over all others,* эту задачу надо решить в первую очередь.

precedent *n.* прецедент: *set a precedent,* создавать прецедент.

preceding *adj.* предшествующий; предыдущий.

precept *n.* завет; наставление.

precinct *n.* участок; округ.

precious *adj.* 1, (highly valuable) драгоценный: *precious stones,* драгоценные камни. 2, (held dear) дорогой: *precious memories,* дорогие воспоминания. 3, (vitally important) драгоценный; дорогой. *Waste precious time,* терять драгоценное время. *Time was precious,* время было дорого. 4, (delightful) прелестный: *a precious child,* прелестный ребёнок. 5, (affected, as of a style) манерный.

precipice *n.* обрыв.

precipitate *v.t.* приводить к; вызывать. —*adj.* = **precipitous.**

precipitation *n.* осадки.

precipitous *adj.* 1, (steep) крутой; обрывистый. 2, (hasty; rash) опрометчивый.

precise *adj.* 1, (accurate; exact) точный. 2, (punctilious) аккуратный. 3, (particular) как раз: *at that precise moment,* как раз в тот момент.

precisely *adv.* 1, (in a precise manner) точно. 2, (just; exactly) именно: *precisely for this reason,* именно по этой причине.

precision *n.* точность. —*adj.* точный: *precision instruments,* точные приборы.

preclude *v.t.* исключать возможность (+ *gen.*): *preclude escape,* исключать возможность побега. *Preclude someone's attending the meeting,* мешать кому-нибудь присутствовать на собрании.

precocious *adj.* развитой; развит не по годам.

preconceived *adj.* предвзятый.

preconception *n.* предвзятое мнение.

precondition *n.* 1, (prerequisite) предпосылка. 2, (prior stipulation) предварительное условие.

precursor *n.* 1, (predecessor) предшественник. 2, (harbinger) предвестник.

predate *v.t.* 1, (come before) предшествовать. 2, (put an earlier date on) пометить задним числом.

predator *n.* хищник.

predatory *adj.* 1, (characterized by plundering) грабительский. 2, (rapacious, as of a bird) хищный.

predecessor *n.* предшественник.

predestine *v.t.* предопределять. —**predestination,** *n.* предопределение.

predetermine *v.t.* предопределять; предрешать. —**predetermination,** *n.* предопределение.

predicament *n.* затруднительное положение.

predicate *n.* сказуемое; предикат. —*v.t.* основывать: *on what is this predicated?,* на чём это основано? —**predicative,** *adj.* предикативный.

predict *v.t. & i.* предсказывать. —**predictable,** *adj.* предсказуемый. —**prediction,** *n.* предсказание.

predilection *n.* пристрастие; склонность.

predispose *v.t.* предрасполагать. —**predisposed,** *adj.* предрасположенный. —**predisposition,** *n.* предрасположение.

predominance *n.* преобладание. —**predominant,** *adj.* преобладающий. —**predominantly,** *adv.* преимущественно. *The population is predominantly Catholic,* основная часть населения — католики.

predominate *v.i.* преобладать; господствовать.

preeminent *adj.* выдающийся. —**preeminence,** *n.* превосходство.

preempt *v.t.* захватывать (прежде других). —**preemptive,** *adj.* упреждающий: *preemptive strike,* упреждающий удар.

preen *v.t.* 1, (smooth with the beak) чистить клювом. 2, (primp) прихорашивать.

prefabricated *adj.* сборный.

preface *n.* предисловие. —*v.t.* предпосылать: *preface one's report with a story,* предпослать докладу рассказ. —**prefatory,** *adj.* вступительный; вводный.

prefect *n.* префект. —**prefecture,** *n.* префектура.

prefer *v.t.* 1, (like better) предпочитать: *prefer spring to summer,* предпочитать весну лету. 2, (file) предъявлять: *prefer charges against,* предъявить обвинение (+ *dat.*). *See also* **preferred.**

preferable *adj.* предпочтительный. *Plastic is preferable to wood,* пластмасса предпочтительнее дерева. —**preferably,** *adv.* лучше; скорее.

preference *n.* предпочтение: *give preference to,* отдавать *or* оказывать предпочтение (+ *dat.*). *What is your preference?,* что вы предпочитаете?

preferential *adj.* льготный. *Preferential tariff,* предпочтительный тариф.

preferred *adj.* предпочтительный. —**preferred stock,** привилегированные акции.

prefix *n.* приставка; префикс. —*v.t.* присоединять приставку к (слову). —**prefixed,** *adj.* приставочный. —**prefixion,** *n.* префиксация.

pregnancy *n.* беременность.

pregnant *adj.* беременная. *She is pregnant,* она беременна; она в положении. *Become pregnant,* стать беременной; (за)беременеть.

prehensile *adj.* цепкий.

prehistoric *adj.* доистори́ческий.

prejudge *v.t.* предрешáть.

prejudice *n.* **1,** (bias) предрассýдок; предубеждéние; предвзя́тость. **2,** (detriment) ущéрб. —*v.t.* **1,** (bias) предубеждáть. **2,** (damage) наноси́ть ущéрб (+ *dat.*). —**prejudiced,** *adj.* предубеждённый. *I am prejudiced against him,* к немý я отношýсь предубеждённо; прóтив негó я настрóен предубеждённо. —**prejudicial,** *adj.* врéдный.

prelate *n.* прелáт.

preliminary *adj.* предвари́тельный.

prelude *n.* прелю́дия.

premarital *adj.* добрáчный.

premature *adj.* **1,** (occurring earlier than expected) преждеврéменный: *premature birth/death,* преждеврéменные рóды; преждеврéменная смерть. *Premature child,* недонóшенный ребёнок; недонóсок. **2,** (too hasty) поспéшный: *premature conclusion,* поспéшный вы́вод. —**prematurely,** *adv.* преждевремéнно.

premeditated *adj.* преднамéренный; умы́шленный. —**premeditation,** *n.* преднамéренность.

premier *adj.* пéрвый. —*n.* премьéр-мини́стр; премьéр.

première *n.* премьéра.

premise *n.* **1,** (assumption) предпосы́лка. **2,** *pl.* (building and grounds) помещéние.

premium *n.* прéмия. *At a premium,* нарасхвáт. *Put a premium on,* высокó цени́ть.

premonition *n.* предчýвствие: *a premonition of disaster,* предчýвствие несчáстья.

prenatal *adj.* предродовóй. *Prenatal care,* гигиéна берéменной.

preoccupation *n.* **1,** (absorption) одержи́мость. **2,** (something that preoccupies) забóта.

preoccupied *adj.* **1,** (lost in thought) погружённый в мы́сли. **2,** (totally involved) поглощённый.

preoccupy *v.t.* поглощáть.

preordain *v.t.* предопределя́ть.

prepaid *adj.* уплáченный *or* оплáченный зарáнее.

preparation *n.* **1,** (act of preparing something or getting ready) приготовлéние; подготóвка. **2,** *pl.* (steps taken to prepare) приготовлéния. *Make preparations for,* готóвиться к. **3,** (substance) препарáт.

preparatory *adj.* приготови́тельный; подготови́тельный. —**preparatory to,** прéжде чем.

prepare *v.t.* готóвить; приготовля́ть; подготáвливать. —*v.i.* готóвиться; приготовля́ться; подготáвливаться. *Prepare for an exam,* готóвиться к экзáмену. *Prepare to depart,* готóвиться к отъéзду.

prepared *adj.* готóвый. —**preparedness,** *n.* готóвность; подготóвленность.

prepay *v.t.* уплáчивать *or* оплáчивать зарáнее.

preponderance *n.* перевéс; преобладáние. —**preponderant,** *adj.* преобладáющий.

preposition *n.* предлóг. —**prepositional,** *adj.* предлóжный.

prepossessing *adj.* располагáющий; прия́тный; привлекáтельный.

preposterous *adj.* нелéпый; абсýрдный; ди́кий.

prerequisite *n.* предпосы́лка.

prerevolutionary *adj.* дореволюциóнный.

prerogative *n.* прерогати́ва; привилéгия.

presage *v.t.* предвещáть.

presbyter *n.* пресви́тер.

Presbyterian *n.* пресвитериáнин; пресвитериáнец. —*adj.* пресвитериáнскый.

preschool *adj.* дошкóльный.

prescience *n.* предви́дение. —**prescient,** *adj.* проницáтельный.

prescribe *v.t.* **1,** (set down to be followed) предпи́сывать: *prescribe rules,* предпи́сывать прáвила. **2,** (order the use of, as medicine) прописывать.

prescription *n.* **1,** (instruction; directive) предписáние. **2,** *med.* рецéпт. **3,** *law* дáвность.

presence *n.* прису́тствие; нали́чие. *In the presence of,* при; в прису́тствии (+ *gen.*). —**presence of mind,** прису́тствие дýха.

present *adj.* **1,** (now going on; current) настоя́щий; тепéрешний; ны́нешний. **2,** (here; on hand) прису́тствующий. *Be present,* прису́тствовать; быть налицó. **3,** (this; now being discussed) дáнный; настоя́щий. **4,** *gram.* настоя́щий: *the present tense,* настоя́щее врéмя. —*n.* **1,** preceded by *the* (present time) настоя́щее. *At present,* сейчáс; в настоя́щее врéмя. *For the present,* покá. **2,** (gift) подáрок. —*v.t.* **1,** (give; offer) представля́ть: *present facts/evidence/a report/,* представля́ть фáкты/свидéтельство/отчёт. **2,** (produce; show) предъявля́ть; представля́ть. **3,** (hand over; submit) вручáть: *present one's credentials,* вручи́ть свои́ вери́тельные грáмоты. **4,** (give or award formally) вручáть; преподноси́ть. *Present an award,* вручи́ть нагрáду. *She was presented with a bouquet of roses,* ей преподнесли́ букéт роз. **5,** (introduce) представля́ть. **6,** (offer, as problems or difficulties) представля́ть. **7,** (give, as a play) покáзывать; стáвить. —**present arms,** взять на карáул. —**present itself,** явля́ться; представля́ться.

presentable *adj.* прили́чный; презентáбельный.

presentation *n.* **1,** (submitting; introducing) представлéние. **2,** (producing; showing) предъявлéние. **3,** (awarding; bestowing) вручéние. **4,** (a performance) представлéние.

present-day *adj.* совремéнный. *By present-day standards,* по мéркам нáшего врéмени.

presentiment *n.* предчýвствие.

presently *adv.* **1,** (soon) скóро; вскóре. **2,** (at present) сейчáс; в настоя́щее врéмя.

preservation *n.* **1,** (act of preserving) сохранéние. **2,** (state of being preserved) сохрáнность.

preservative *n.* консервáнт.

preserve *v.t.* **1,** (keep; maintain) сохраня́ть. **2,** (prepare, as food, for future use) консерви́ровать. —*n.* **1,** (restricted area) запове́дник. **2,** *pl.* (confection) вáрéнье.

preside *v.i.* председáтельствовать.

president *n.* **1,** (chief executive) президéнт. **2,** (presiding officer) председáтель. **3,** (of a university) рéктор. —**presidency,** *n.* президéнтство. —**presidential,** *adj.* президéнтский.

presidium *n.* прези́диум.

press *v.t.* **1,** (push, as a button) нажимáть на (кнóпку). **2,** (squeeze out the juice from) дави́ть; жать. **3,** (work in a press) прессовáть: *press cotton,* прессовáть хлóпок. **4,** (iron) глáдить. **5,** *fol. by* **to** *or* **against** (embrace closely) прижимáть: *press one's to one's bosom,* прижимáть к груди́. **6,** (urge persistently) уговáривать. *Press someone for an answer,* торопи́ть когó-нибудь с отвéтом. **7,** (be insistent about) настáивать на: *press a matter,* настáивать на чём-нибудь. *I will* *not press the point,* я не бу́ду наста́ивать на э́том. **8,** (bring, as charges) предъявля́ть (обвине́ние). **9,** (straiten) стесня́ть: *pressed for money,* стеснённый в деньга́х. *I am pressed for time,* у меня́ вре́мени в обре́з. **10,** *in* **press one's luck,** искуша́ть *or* испы́тывать судьбу́. —*v.i.* **1,** (push hard) нажима́ть; нада́вливать; прида́вливать. *Press hard!,* нажми́ кре́пко! **2,** *fol. by* **against** (lean hard against) прижима́ться (к); приника́ть (к). **3,** (advance forcibly) пробира́ться; прота́лкиваться. *Press forward,* протолкну́ться впере́д. —*n.* **1,** (device for pressing or crushing) пресс: *hydraulic press,* гидравли́ческий пресс; *wine press,* дави́льный пресс. *Printing press,* печа́тный стано́к. **2,** (newspapers collectively) печа́ть; пре́сса. *Freedom of the press,* свобо́да печа́ти. **3,** (publishing company) изда́тельство. **4,** (printing) печа́ть: *go to press,* поступи́ть в печа́ть. **5,** (crush) да́вка. **6,** *weightlifting* жим. —*adj.* корреспонде́нтский: *press card/corps,* корреспонде́нтский биле́т/ко́рпус.

press conference пресс-конфере́нция.

presser *n.* прессо́вщик.

pressing *n.* гла́женье. —*adj.* неотло́жный; сро́чный.

pressman *n.* **1,** (one who works a press) прессо́вщик. **2,** (operator of a printing press) печа́тник.

pressmark *n., Brit.* шифр.

pressure *n.* давле́ние. —*v.t.* ока́зывать давле́ние на. —**pressure gauge,** мано́метр.

pressurized *adj.* гермети́ческий: *pressurized cabin,* гермети́ческая каби́на.

prestidigitation *n.* ло́вкость рук. —**prestidigitator,** *n.* фо́кусник.

prestige *n.* прести́ж; авторите́т. —**prestigious,** *adj.* прести́жный.

presto *adv., music* пре́сто.

presumably *adv.* предположи́тельно.

presume *v.t.* **1,** (assume) предполага́ть. **2,** *fol. by inf.* (dare; venture) осме́ливаться; бра́ться. *I do not presume to judge,* не беру́сь суди́ть. —*v.i.* [*usu.* **presume on** *or* **upon**] злоупотребля́ть.

presumption *n.* **1,** (supposition) предположе́ние. **2,** *law* презу́мпция: *presumption of innocence,* презу́мпция неви́новности. **3,** (effrontery) самонаде́янность.

presumptive *adj.* предположи́тельный. —**heir presumptive,** вероя́тный насле́дник.

presumptuous *adj.* самонаде́янный.

presuppose *v.t.* предполага́ть.

pretence *n.* = **pretense.**

pretend *v.t. & i.* притворя́ться; де́лать вид. —**pretended,** *adj.* притво́рный.

pretender *n.* претенде́нт.

pretense *also,* **pretence** *n.* **1,** (sham) притво́рство; по́за. **2,** (claim) прете́нзия. *Make no pretense of,* не претендова́ть на. **3,** (pretext) предло́г. *Under false pretenses,* обма́нным путём.

pretension *n.* прете́нзия. *Have pretensions of,* претендова́ть на.

pretentious *adj.* претенцио́зный; с прете́нзиями. —**pretentiousness,** *n.* претенцио́зность.

pretext *n.* предло́г.

prettily *adv.* краси́во; ми́ло.

pretty *adj.* **1,** (pleasing to the eye) хоро́шенький; милови́дный. **2,** (pleasing to the ear, as of a song or voice) прия́тный; краси́вый. **3,** *colloq.* (quite a large) изря́дный: *a pretty sum,* изря́дная су́мма. **4,** *ironic* (fine; nice) хоро́шенький: *a pretty mess,* хоро́шенькая исто́рия. —*adv.* дово́льно; доста́точно. *Pretty good,* неду́рно; так себе́. —*v.t.* [*usu.* **pretty up**] приукра́шивать.

pretzel *n.* кре́ндель.

prevail *v.i.* **1,** *often fol. by* **over** (triumph; win out) (вос)торжествова́ть (над); брать верх (над); преоблада́ть (над). **2,** (be in use; be current) существова́ть. **3,** *fol. by* **upon** (persuade) убеди́ть; уговори́ть; упроси́ть; умоли́ть. —**prevailing,** *adj.* преоблада́ющий; госпо́дствующий.

prevalent *adj.* распространённый. —**prevalence,** *n.* распростране́ние.

prevaricate *v.i.* **1,** (speak evasively) уви́ливать. **2,** (lie) привира́ть.

prevent *v.t.* **1,** (keep from happening) предупрежда́ть; предотвраща́ть. **2,** (stop from doing something) меша́ть: *illness prevented me from coming,* боле́знь помеша́ла мне прийти́.

prevention *n.* предупрежде́ние; предотвраще́ние.

preventive *adj.* предупреди́тельный; предохрани́тельный. —**preventive medicine,** предупреди́тельная медици́на. —**preventive war,** превенти́вная война́.

preview *n.* **1,** (of a film) предвари́тельный просмо́тр. **2,** (advance view) предвари́тельный взгляд (на бу́дущее).

previous *adj.* предыду́щий: *the previous day/issue,* предыду́щий день/но́мер. —**previous to,** до; пре́жде.

previously *adv.* ра́ньше.

prewar *adj.* довое́нный; предвое́нный.

prey *n.* **1,** (animal killed by another) добы́ча. **2,** (victim) же́ртва: *fall prey to,* пасть же́ртвой (+ *gen.*). **3,** *in* **bird of prey,** хи́щная пти́ца; хи́щник. —*v.i.* [*usu.* **prey on** *or* **upon**] **1,** (seek and take for food) охо́титься на; лови́ть; пита́ться (+ *instr.*). **2,** (plunder) гра́бить. **3,** (victimize) эксплуати́ровать. **4,** *Prey on one's mind,* пресле́довать.

price *n.* цена́. *The price of bread,* цена́ хле́ба *or* цена́ на хлеб. *At any price,* любо́й цено́й. —*v.t.* **1,** (set a price on) расце́нивать. **2,** *colloq.* (ask the price of) прице́ниваться к.

priceless *adj.* бесце́нный. *This ring is priceless,* цены́ э́тому кольцу́ нет.

price list прейскура́нт.

price tag ярлы́к с указа́нием цены́.

prick *v.t.* **1,** (pierce accidentally) уколо́ть: *prick one's finger,* уколо́ть себе́ па́лец. **2,** (puncture, as a bubble or balloon) прока́лывать. —*n.* уко́л. —**prick up one's ears,** насторожи́ть *or* навостри́ть у́ши; насторожи́ться.

prickle *n.* шип; колю́чка.

prickly *adj.* колю́чий; ко́лкий. —**prickly heat,** потни́ца. —**prickly pear,** опу́нция.

pride *n.* **1,** (pleasure; satisfaction) го́рдость. *Take pride in,* горди́ться (+ *instr.*). **2,** (conceit; self-esteem) самолю́бие; го́рдость. *Hurt someone's pride,* заде́ть чье-нибудь самолю́бие. **3,** (that of which one is proud) го́рдость. —*v.t.* [*usu.* **pride oneself on**] горди́ться (+ *instr.*).

priest *n.* свяще́нник. *Pagan priest,* жрец. —**priest-**

hood, *n.* свяще́нство; духове́нство. —**priestly,** *adj.* свяще́ннический.

prim *adj.* чо́порный.

primacy *n.* пе́рвенство; прима́т.

prima donna примадо́нна.

primarily *adv.* преиму́щественно; в основно́м; пре́жде всего́.

primary *adj.* **1,** (first) перви́чный. **2,** (chief; basic) основно́й: *the primary purpose,* основна́я цель. —*n.* перви́чные вы́боры. —**primary color,** основно́й цвет. —**primary school,** нача́льная шко́ла. —**primary source,** первоисто́чник.

primate *n.* **1,** *eccles.* прима́с. **2,** *zool.* прима́т.

prime *adj.* **1,** (chief; paramount) основно́й: *prime requisite,* основно́е тре́бование. *A prime example,* я́ркий приме́р. *Of prime concern,* велича́йшей ва́жности. **2,** (of the finest quality) первосо́ртный. —*n.* расцве́т. *In one's prime; in the prime of life,* во цве́те лет; в расцве́те сил. —*v.t.* **1,** (make ready) подгота́вливать. **2,** (set, as a gun) вставля́ть запа́л в. **3,** (fill, as a pump) наполня́ть (водо́й). —**prime cost,** себесто́имость. —**prime minister,** премье́р-мини́стр. —**prime number,** просто́е число́; недели́мое число́.

primer[1] **(prim-er)** *n.* (beginning reading book) буква́рь.

primer[2] **(prai-mer)** *n.* (detonating device) запа́л; ка́псюль.

primeval *adj.* первобы́тный.

priming *n., painting* грунт.

primitive *adj.* **1,** (earliest) первобы́тный: *primitive man,* первобы́тный челове́к. **2,** (plain; crude) примити́вный.

primogeniture *n.* перворо́дство.

primordial *adj.* иско́нный; изнача́льный.

primp *v.i.* прихора́шиваться.

primrose *n.* первоцве́т; при́мула.

prince *n.* **1,** (in prerevolutionary Russia) князь. **2,** (in other countries) принц.

princely *adj.* кня́жеский. *A princely sum,* огро́мная су́мма.

princess *n.* **1,** *pre-rev.* (prince's wife) княги́ня; (prince's daughter) княжна́. **2,** (outside Russia) принце́сса.

principal *adj.* гла́вный; основно́й: *principal reason,* гла́вная/основна́я причи́на. —*n.* **1,** (head of a school) дире́ктор. **2,** *finance* капита́л: *principal and interest,* капита́л и проце́нты.

principality *n.* кня́жество.

principally *adv.* гла́вным о́бразом; преиму́щественно.

principle *n.* при́нцип. *A man of principle,* принципиа́льный челове́к. —**in principle,** в при́нципе. —**on principle,** из при́нципа.

print *n.* **1,** (impression) отпеча́ток: *footprint,* отпеча́ток ноги́. **2,** (type) шрифт; печа́ть. *Large print,* кру́пный шрифт. **3,** *photog.* отпеча́ток. **4,** (engraving, woodcut, etc.) гравю́ра. **5,** (fabric with a printed design) набивно́й си́тец. —*adj.* си́тцевый: *a print dress,* си́тцевое пла́тье. —*v.t.* **1,** (produce from type; publish in print) печа́тать. **2,** (produce from a negative) отпеча́тывать. **3,** (write in block letters) писа́ть печа́тными бу́квами. **4,** *textiles* набива́ть. —**in print,** печа́тается. *See one's name in print,* ви́деть своё и́мя в печа́ти. —**out of print,** бо́льше не печа́тается.

printed *adj.* печа́тный; напеча́танный; отпеча́тан-

ный; *(of fabric)* набивно́й. —**printed matter,** бандеро́ль. —**the printed word,** печа́тное сло́во.

printer *n.* печа́тник; типо́граф. *Send a manuscript to the printer,* посла́ть ру́копись в типогра́фию.

printing *n.* **1,** (act) печа́тание. **2,** (art) печа́тное де́ло; полигра́фия. **3,** (quantity printed at one time) тира́ж. **4,** *textiles* набивка. —**printing press,** печа́тный стано́к.

prior *adj.* предвари́тельный: *prior condition,* предвари́тельное усло́вие. *By prior agreement,* по предвари́тельному соглаше́нию. *We have a prior engagement,* у нас други́е пла́ны; нас уже́ пригласи́ли. —*n.* (of a monastery) прио́р; настоя́тель. —**prior to,** до.

priority *n.* приорите́т.

priory *n.* монасты́рь.

prism *n.* при́зма. —**prismatic,** *adj.* призмати́ческий.

prison *n.* тюрьма́: *put in prison,* сажа́ть в тюрьму́. *Two years in prison,* два го́да тюре́много заключе́ния. —*adj.* тюре́мный: *prison cell,* тюре́мная ка́мера.

prisoner *n.* заключённый. *Take prisoner,* взять в плен. *Be taken prisoner,* попа́сть в плен. *Hold prisoner,* держа́ть в плену́. —**prisoner of war,** военнопле́нный.

pristine *adj.* первобы́тный.

privacy *n.* уедине́ние. *Invasion of privacy,* вторже́ние в ли́чную жизнь.

private *adj.* ча́стный. —*n., mil.* рядово́й. —**in private,** наедине́; с гла́зу на глаз.

privately *adv.* наедине́; ча́стным о́бразом; в ча́стном поря́дке.

privation *n.* лише́ние: *suffer privations,* терпе́ть лише́ния.

privilege *n.* привиле́гия; льго́та. —**privileged,** *adj.* привилегиро́ванный. *I am privileged to...,* име́ю честь (+ *inf.*).

privy *adj.* [*usu.* **privy to**] посвящённый (в). —*n.* отхо́жее ме́сто. —**privy council,** та́йный сове́т.

prize *n.* пре́мия; приз. —*adj.* **1,** (given as a prize) призово́й. **2,** (having won a prize) преми́рованный. —*v.t.* цени́ть; дорожи́ть.

prize fight боксёрское состяза́ние. —**prize fighter,** боксёр.

prizewinner *n.* призёр.

pro *n.* **1,** (argument in favor): *the pros and cons,* до́воды за и про́тив. **2,** *colloq.* (professional) профессиона́л.

pro- *prefix* про-: *pro-American,* проамерика́нский.

probability *n.* вероя́тность. *In all probability,* по всей вероя́тности.

probable *adj.* вероя́тный. *Highly probable,* весьма́ вероя́тно.

probably *adv.* вероя́тно; наве́рно; пожа́луй. *Most probably,* скоре́е всего́.

probate *n.* утвержде́ние (завеща́ния).

probation *n.* усло́вное освобожде́ние. *He was given a year on probation,* он получи́л год усло́вно.

probe *n.* **1,** (instrument) зонд; щуп. **2,** (investigation) рассле́дование. —*v.t.* **1,** *med.* зонди́ровать. **2,** (investigate) вника́ть в; рассле́довать.

probity *n.* че́стность; поря́дочность.

problem *n.* **1,** (difficult question or matter) пробле́ма. **2,** (arithmetical problem) зада́ча. —**problem child,** тру́дный ребёнок.

problematic *adj.* проблематический; проблематичный. *Also,* **problematical.**

proboscis *n.* хóбот.

procedure *n.* процедýра; порядок. —**procedural,** *adj.* процедýрный.

proceed *v.i.* **1,** (go forward) идти; éхать: *proceed with caution,* идти *or* éхать осторóжно. **2,** (begin) приступáть: *proceed with the vote,* приступить к голосовáнию. *I don't know how to proceed,* не знáю, как приступить к этому дéлу. **3,** (continue) продолжáть: *please proceed,* продолжáйте, пожáлуйста. **4,** *fol. by* **on** *or* **from** (begin in one's reasoning) исходить из: *proceed on the assumption that...,* исходить из тогó, что...

proceedings *n.pl.* **1,** (action taking place) происходящее. **2,** (legal action) судопроизвóдство. **3,** (records; minutes) протокóл.

proceeds *n.pl.* выручка.

process *n.* процéсс. *In the process of,* в процéссе (+ *gen.*). —*v.t.* **1,** (treat) обрабáтывать; перерабáтывать. **2,** (handle, as a document) оформлять.

procession *n.* шéствие; процéссия.

proclaim *v.t.* провозглашáть. —**proclamation,** *n.* объявлéние; провозглашéние.

proclivity *n.* склóнность; наклóнность; тендéнция.

proconsul *n.* прокóнсул.

procrastinate *v.i.* мéдлить; мéшкать. —**procrastination,** *n.* промедлéние; проволóчка. —**procrastinator,** *n.* медлитель.

procreate *v.i.* производить потóмство. —**procreation,** *n.* деторождéние.

proctor *n.* **1,** (for supervising an examination) надзирáтель. **2,** *law* (agent; representative) повéренный.

procure *v.t.* доставáть; добывáть.

procurement *n.* **1,** (acquisition) приобретéние. **2,** (purchase by the government) заготóвка.

procurer *n.* свóдник.

prod *v.t.* **1,** (poke) тыкать. **2,** (urge; goad) подгонять. —*n.* тычóк.

prodigal *adj.* расточительный. —**prodigal son,** блýдный сын.

prodigality *n.* расточительность; мотовствó.

prodigious *adj.* огрóмный; колоссáльный.

prodigy *n.* чýдо. *Child prodigy,* вундеркинд.

produce *v.t.* **1,** (manufacture; bring into being) производить. **2,** (show; offer for inspection) предъявлять; покáзывать. **3,** (bring about) приносить; давáть: *produce income,* приносить дохóд; *produce results,* давáть результáты. **4,** (bring to the stage or screen) стáвить. —*n.* сельскохозяйственные продýкты.

producer *n.* **1,** (one who produces) производитель. **2,** *theat.* дирéктор. **3,** (of a film) продюсер.

product *n.* **1,** (something produced) продýкт. **2,** *fig.* (result; outgrowth) плод. **3,** *math.* произведéние.

production *n.* **1,** (act of producing) произвóдство: *go into production,* поступить в произвóдство. **2,** *theat.* постанóвка: *a new production of Swan Lake,* Лебединое óзеро в нóвой постанóвке. —*adj.* произвóдственный: *production plan,* произвóдственный план. —**production line,** потóчная линия.

productive *adj.* **1,** (producing) производительный; продуктивный. **2,** (fruitful) плодотвóрный. —**productivity,** *n.* производительность; продуктивность.

profanation *n.* осквернéние; профанáция.

profane *adj.* **1,** (irreverent; blasphemous) нечестивый; богохýльный. **2,** (vulgar; coarse) вульгáрный; грýбый. **3,** (secular) свéтский. —*v.t.* осквернять.

profanity *n.* брань; рýгань; *pl.* сáльности.

profess *v.t.* **1,** (openly declare or admit) заявлять о; (открыто) признавáть. *Profess one's love,* признáться в любви. **2,** (avow, as a religion) исповéдовать.

profession *n.* **1,** (occupation) профéссия: *a lawyer by profession,* юрист по профéссии. *The medical profession,* врачи. **2,** (open declaration) заявлéние. **3,** (avowal of a religion) исповéдание.

professional *adj.* профессионáльный. *Professional man,* человéк свобóдной профéссии. —*n.* профессионáл.

professor *n.* профéссор. —**professorial,** *adj.* профéссорский. —**professorship,** *n.* профéссорство; профессýра.

proffer *v.t.* предлагáть.

proficiency *n.* умéние; нáвык; сноpóвка. *Proficiency in a language,* знáние языкá.

proficient *adj.* искýсный; умéлый.

profile *n.* прóфиль.

profit *n.* **1,** (monetary gain) прибыль: *sell at a profit,* продавáть с прибылью. **2,** (benefit) пóльза; выгода. —*v.t.* приносить пóльзу (+ *dat.*). —*v.i.* [*usu.* **profit from**] извлекáть пóльзу (из).

profitable *adj.* **1,** (yielding a profit) прибыльный; выгодный; дохóдный. **2,** (beneficial) полéзный.

profiteer *n.* спекулянт. —*v.i.* спекулировать.

profligacy *n.* **1,** (dissoluteness) распýтство. **2,** (reckless extravagance) расточительность.

profligate *adj.* **1,** (dissolute) распýтный; разврáтный. **2,** (recklessly extravagant) расточительный. —*n.* распýтник; разврáтник.

profound *adj.* глубóкий: *profound knowledge/grief,* глубóкие знáния; глубóкое гóре. *Profound difference,* огрóмная рáзница. *Profound consequences,* далекó идýщие послéдствия. *Undergo a profound change,* óчень изменúться. —**profoundly,** *adv.* глубóко.

profundity *n.* глубинá.

profuse *adj.* **1,** (abundant) обильный. **2,** (lavish): *be profuse in one's praise,* рассыпáться в похвалáх. *Apologize profusely,* рассыпáться в извинéниях. —**profusion,** *n.* изобилие.

progenitor *n.* родоначáльник.

progeny *n.* потóмство.

prognosis *n.* прогнóз.

prognosticate *v.t. & i.* предскáзывать. —**prognostication,** *n.* предсказáние. —**prognosticator,** *n.* предскáзатель.

program *also,* **programme** *n.* прогрáмма. —*v.t.* программировать. —**programmed,** *adj.* прогрáммный; программированный. —**programmer,** *n.* программист. —**programming,** *n.* программировáние.

progress *n.* прогрéсс; успéхи. *Make progress,* дéлать успéхи. —*v.i.* **1,** (make progress) прогрессировать; продвигáться. **2,** (get along) идти: *how is your work progressing?,* как идёт вáша рабóта? —**be in progress,** идти.

progression *n.* **1,** (advancement) продвижéние. **2,** *math.* прогрéссия: *geometric progression,* геометрическая прогрéссия.

progressive *adj.* прогрессивный.

prohibit *v.t.* запрещать. *Be prohibited*, запрещаться; воспрещаться. —**prohibition**, *n.* запрещение.

prohibitive *adj.* запретительный. *Prohibitive prices*, недоступные цены.

project *n.* проект. —*v.t.* **1**, (plan) проектировать. **2**, (estimate into the future) исчислять. **3**, (convey; get across) передавать; внушать. **4**, (show on a screen) проектировать. —*v.i.* (protrude) выдаваться; выступать.

projectile *n.* снаряд.

projection *n.* **1**, (something jutting out) выступ. **2**, (system used in mapmaking) проекция. **3**, (screening) проекция. **4**, (advance estimate) оценка; прогноз; исчисление. —**projection booth**, проекционная будка.

projectionist *n.* киномеханик.

projector *n.* проекционный аппарат *or* фонарь; проектор. *Movie projector*, кинопроектор.

prolapse *n.* выпадение; опущение.

proletarian *n.* пролетарий. —*adj.* пролетарский. —**proletariat**, *n.* пролетариат.

proliferate *v.i.* размножаться; распространяться. —**proliferation**, *n.* распространение.

prolific *adj.* плодовитый.

prolix *adj.* многословный; пространный.

prologue *n.* пролог.

prolong *v.t* продлевать. —**prolongation**, *n.* продление. —**prolonged**, *adj.* длительный; продолжительный.

promenade *n.* **1**, (stroll) прогулка. **2**, (mall) бульвар. —*v.i.* прогуливаться. —**promenade deck**, прогулочная палуба.

Prometheus *n.* Прометей.

promethium *n.* прометий.

prominence *n.* **1**, (fame) известность: *come into prominence*, приобретать известность. **2**, (bulge) выступ.

prominent *adj.* **1**, (leading; well-known) видный; известный. **2**, (protruding) выступающий вперёд.

promiscuous *adj.* лёгкого поведения; распутный. —**promiscuity**, *n.* лёгкое поведение.

promise *v.t.* & *i.* обещать: *I promise you I won't be late*, обещаю вам, что не опоздаю. *The movie promises to be interesting*, фильм обещает быть интересным. *Make someone promise*, брать слово с. —*n.* **1**, (pledge) обещание. **2**, (basis for expectation): *show great promise*, подавать большие надежды. *A violinist of great promise*, многообещающий скрипач. —**Promised Land**, обетованная земля.

promising *adj.* многообещающий; перспективный.

promissory note вексель; долговое обязательство.

promontory *n.* мыс.

promote *v.t.* **1**, (foster; further) способствовать; содействовать. **2**, (raise in rank) продвигать; повышать в чине. *He was promoted at work*, он получил повышение по службе. *He was promoted to captain*, ему присвоили звание капитана; его произвели в капитаны. **3**, (move forward a grade in school) переводить в следующий класс. **4**, (publicize) рекламировать. **5**, *chess* превращать (пешку).

promotion *n.* **1**, (advancement in rank) повышение *or* продвижение по службе; *mil.* присвоение зва-

ния; производство. **2**, (furtherance) продвижение; поощрение. **3**, (publicity) реклама. **4**, *chess* превращение (пешки).

promotional *adj.* рекламный.

prompt *adj.* **1**, (done without delay) быстрый; срочный. *Prompt reply*, быстрый ответ. *Take prompt measures*, принимать срочные меры. **2**, (punctual) аккуратный. —*v.t.* **1**, (induce) побуждать. **2**, (give rise to; occasion) вызывать. **3**, (assist with a reminder) подсказывать. **4**, *theat.* суфлировать. —*v.i.* подсказывать: *no prompting!*, не подсказывать! —**prompter**, *n.* суфлёр. —**promptly**, *adv.* быстро; сразу.

promptness *n.* **1**, (speed) быстрота. **2**, (punctuality) аккуратность.

promulgate *v.t.* издавать; опубликовать; обнародовать. —**promulgation**, *n.* издание; опубликование; обнародование.

prone *adj.* **1**, (prostrate) лежащий ничком. *Prone position*, положение лёжа. **2**, *fol. by* to (inclined) склонный (к); подверженный (+ *dat.*). *Prone to error*, подверженный ошибкам. *Prone to violence*, склонный к насилию.

prong *n.* зубец.

pronoun *n.* местоимение. —**pronominal**, *adj.* местоименный.

pronounce *v.t.* **1**, (articulate) произносить. **2**, (declare to be) объявлять; признавать. *I pronounce you man and wife*, объявляю вас мужем и женой. *Pronounce someone guilty/insane*, признать кого-нибудь виновным/душевнобольным. **3**, (announce, as a sentence) объявлять; зачитывать (приговор). *Pronounce judgment*, выносить решение.

pronounced *adj.* заметный; ярко выраженный.

pronouncement *n.* **1**, (act of announcing) объявление. **2**, (formal declaration) (официальное) заявление.

pronunciation *n.* произношение.

proof *n.* **1**, (conclusive evidence) доказательство. **2**, *printing* корректура; гранка; оттиск. *Page proofs*, вёрстка; корректура в листах.

proofread *v.t.* корректировать. —*v.i.* держать *or* править корректуру. —**proofreader**, *n.* корректор. —**proofreading**, *n.* корректура; правка корректуры.

prop *v.t.* **1**, *fol. by* up (hold up; support) подпирать. **2**, *fol. by* **against** (lean against) прислонять (к). —*n.* **1**, (support) подпора; подпорка. **2**, *pl.*, *theat.* реквизит; бутафория.

propaganda *n.* пропаганда. —**propagandist**, *n.* пропагандист. —**propagandistic**, *adj.* пропагандистский. —**propagandize**, *v.t.* пропагандировать.

propagate *v.t.* **1**, (breed) размножать. **2**, (disseminate) распространять; проповедовать. —*v.i.* размножаться.

propagation *n.* **1**, (reproduction) размножение. **2**, (dissemination) распространение; проповедь.

propane *n.* пропан.

propel *v.t.* двигать; приводить в действие.

propellant *also*, **propellent** *n.* **1**, (explosive charge) метательное взрывчатое вещество. **2**, (fuel for a rocket) ракетное топливо.

propeller *n.* **1**, (of an aircraft) (воздушный) винт; пропеллер. **2**, (of a boat) гребной винт. —**propeller-driven**, *adj.* винтовой.

propensity *n.* склонность; наклонность; предрасположение.

proper *adj.* **1,** (appropriate) подходя́щий. **2,** (correct) пра́вильный. **3,** (seemly) прили́чный; присто́йный. **4,** (in the narrow sense) со́бственно: *the city proper,* со́бственно го́род. **5,** *gram.* со́бственный: *proper noun,* и́мя со́бственное. **6,** *math.* пра́вильный: *proper fraction,* пра́вильная дробь.

properly *adv.* как сле́дует; до́лжным о́бразом.

propertied *adj.* иму́щий.

property *n.* **1,** (that which is owned) со́бственность; иму́щество. **2,** (attribute) сво́йство. **3,** *pl., theat.* реквизи́т; бутафо́рия. —**property man,** бутафо́р. —**property tax,** нало́г на недви́жимость.

prophecy *n.* проро́чество; прорица́ние. —**prophesy,** *v.t. & i.* проро́чить; прорица́ть.

prophet *n.* проро́к. —**prophetic,** *adj.* проро́ческий.

prophylactic *adj.* профилакти́ческий. —*n.* профилакти́ческое сре́дство. —**prophylaxis,** *n.* профила́ктика.

propinquity *n.* **1,** (nearness) бли́зость. **2,** (kinship) родство́.

propitiate *v.t.* уми́лостивить.

propitious *adj.* благоприя́тный; подходя́щий.

proponent *n.* сторо́нник; пропове́дник.

proportion *n.* **1,** *math.* пропо́рция. *Direct/inverse proportion,* пряма́я/обра́тная пропорциона́льность. **2,** (balance; symmetry) соразме́рность. *Sense of proportion,* чу́вство ме́ры. **3,** *pl.* (size; scope) разме́ры. —*v.t.* соразмеря́ть. —**in proportion to,** соразме́рно (+ *dat.*); пропорциона́льно (+ *dat.*). —**out of proportion,** чрезме́рно; че́рез ме́ру. *Out of proportion to,* несоразме́рно с.

proportional *also,* **proportionate** *adj.* пропорциона́льный; соразме́рный. —**proportionally; proportionately,** *adv.* пропорциона́льно.

proposal *n.* предложе́ние.

propose *v.t.* **1,** (suggest) предлага́ть. *Propose a toast,* предложи́ть тост. **2,** *fol. by inf.* (intend) предполага́ть. —*v.i.* сде́лать предложе́ние (о бра́ке).

proposition *n.* **1,** (proposal) предложе́ние. **2,** (thesis) положе́ние. **3,** *logic* выска́зывание.

propound *v.t.* выдвига́ть: *propound a theory,* выдвига́ть тео́рию.

proprietary *adj.* со́бственнический; хозя́йский.

proprietor *n.* со́бственник; владе́лец; хозя́ин.

propriety *n.* прили́чие. *Observe the proprieties,* соблюда́ть прили́чия.

propulsion *n.* движе́ние вперёд; приведе́ние в движе́ние. *Jet propulsion,* реакти́вное движе́ние.

pro rata пропорциона́льно.

prorate *v.t.* распределя́ть пропорциона́льно.

prorogue *v.t.* распуска́ть (парла́мент).

prosaic *adj.* прозаи́ческий; прозаи́чный.

proscenium *n.* просце́ниум; авансце́на.

proscribe *v.t.* **1,** (prohibit) запреща́ть. **2,** (outlaw) объявля́ть вне зако́на. **3,** (banish) изгоня́ть. —**proscription,** *n.* запре́т; запреще́ние.

prose *n.* про́за. *Work of prose,* произведе́ние про́зы. —*adj.* прозаи́ческий. *Prose writer,* проза́ик.

prosecute *v.t.* **1,** *law* отдава́ть под суд; предава́ть суду́; пресле́довать (кого́-нибудь) суде́бным поря́дком. **2,** (conduct, as a war) вести́. —*v.i.* возбужда́ть иск *or* де́ло.

prosecution *n.* **1,** (conducting) веде́ние. **2,** *law* (prosecuting) пресле́дование. **3,** (party initiating criminal proceedings) обвине́ние. *Witness for the prosecution,* свиде́тель обвине́ния.

prosecutor *n.* обвини́тель. *Public prosecutor,* проку́рор.

proselyte *n.* новообращённый; прозели́т. —**proselytize,** *v.t.* обраща́ть (в свою́ ве́ру). —*v.i.* иска́ть прозели́тов.

prosody *n.* просо́дия. —**prosodic,** *adj.* просоди́ческий.

prospect *n.* **1,** (outlook; chance) перспекти́ва; *pl.* ви́ды; перспекти́вы. **2,** (likely candidate) кандида́т. —*v.t.* разве́дывать. —*v.i.* [*usu.* **prospect for**] иска́ть: *prospect for gold,* иска́ть зо́лото. —**be in prospect,** быть в перспекти́ве.

prospective *adj.* **1,** (future) бу́дущий. **2,** (potential) возмо́жный.

prospector *n.* разве́дчик; изыска́тель. *Prospector for gold,* золотоиска́тель; стара́тель.

prospectus *n.* проспе́кт.

prosper *v.i.* процвета́ть. —**prosperity,** *n.* процвета́ние. —**prosperous,** *adj.* зажи́точный; состоя́тельный; обеспе́ченный.

prostate *n.* предста́тельная железа́; проста́та.

prosthetic *adj.* проте́зный. *Prosthetic device,* проте́з.

prostitute *n.* проститу́тка. —**prostitution,** *n.* проститу́ция.

prostrate *adj.* **1,** (flat; prone) распростёртый. *Lie prostrate,* лежа́ть ничко́м. **2,** (exhausted) истощённый. —*v.t.* **1,** *fol. by* **oneself** (lie face down in humility) па́дать ниц. **2,** (exhaust) истоща́ть. —**prostration,** *n.* изнеможе́ние; простра́ция.

protactinium *n.* протакти́ний.

protagonist *n.* протагони́ст.

protect *v.t.* защища́ть; охраня́ть; предохраня́ть; огражда́ть; оберега́ть; убере́чь.

protection *n.* защи́та; охра́на; предохране́ние; огражде́ние.

protectionism *n.* протекциони́зм.

protective *adj.* **1,** (serving to protect) защи́тный: *protective helmet,* защи́тный шлем. **2,** (carefully protecting) забо́тливый: *an overly protective mother,* сли́шком забо́тливая мать. *Be protective of,* бе́режно забо́титься о. —**protective coloration,** защи́тная *or* покрови́тельственная окра́ска. —**protective tariff,** покрови́тельственный тари́ф.

protector *n.* защи́тник.

protectorate *n.* протектора́т.

protégé *n.* протеже́; ста́вленник.

protein *n.* бело́к; протеи́н. —*adj.* белко́вый.

protest *n.* проте́ст. —*v.i.* протестова́ть. —*v.t.* протестова́ть про́тив.

Protestant *n.* протеста́нт. —*adj.* протеста́нтский. —**Protestantism,** *n.* протестанти́зм; протеста́нтство.

protestation *n.* (торже́ственное) заявле́ние. *Protestations of one's innocence,* заявле́ния о свое́й неви́новности.

protester *n.* протеста́нт.

protocol *n.* **1,** (etiquette) пра́вила (дипломати́ческого) этике́та. **2,** (agreement between states) протоко́л.

proton *n.* прото́н.

protoplasm *n.* протопла́зма.

prototype *n.* прототи́п; прообраз; первообраз.

protoxide *n.* закись.

protozoa *n.pl.* простейшие.

protract *v.t.* тянуть; затягивать. —**protracted,** *adj.* длительный; затяжной.

protractor *n.* транспортир.

protrude *v.i.* выдаваться; торчать. —*v.t.* высовывать.

protrusion *n.* выступ.

protuberance *n.* бугорок; выпуклость. —**protuberant,** *adj.* выпуклый.

proud *adj.* гордый: *proud man,* гордый человек. *Proud father,* счастливый отец. *Be proud of,* гордиться (+ *instr.*). *He is too proud to...,* он слишком горд, чтобы... —**do someone proud,** делать честь (+ *dat.*).

proud flesh дикое мясо.

proudly *adv.* гордо; с гордостью.

prove *v.t.* доказывать. —*v.i.* (turn out to be) оказаться (+ *instr.*); показать *or* проявить себя (+ *instr.*). —**prove itself,** оправдать себя (на практике). —**prove oneself,** показать себя; проявить себя.

proven *adj.* **1,** (demonstrated) доказанный. **2,** (tested and found valid) испытанный: *proven method,* испытанный метод.

provenance *n.* происхождение.

provender *n.* корм; фураж.

proverb *n.* пословица. —**Book of Proverbs,** Книга притчей Соломоновых.

proverbial *adj.* вошедший в пословицу.

provide *v.t.* **1,** (supply with something useful) снабжать; обеспечивать. **2,** (give; furnish) давать; оказывать. *Provide assistance,* оказывать помощь. **3,** (give; afford, as pleasure) доставлять. **4,** (stipulate) предусматривать. —*v.i.* [*usu.* **provide for**] **1,** (furnish with means of subsistence) содержать; обеспечивать. **2,** (allow for; stipulate) предусматривать.

provided *conj.* при условии, что; если только.

providence *n.* **1,** (foresight) предусмотрительность. **2,** *cap.* (divine care) провидение.

provident *adj.* предусмотрительный; запасливый.

providential *adj.* провиденциальный.

providing *conj.* = **provided.**

province *n.* **1,** (division of a country) провинция. **2,** *pl.* (rural areas) провинция; периферия. **3,** *fig.* (sphere of knowledge or activity) область знаний; сфера; компетенция.

provincial *adj.* провинциальный. —*n.* провинциал. —**provincialism,** *n.* провинциализм.

proving ground испытательный полигон.

provision *n.* **1,** (supplying) снабжение. **2,** (clause in a legal document) положение. **3,** (stipulation; proviso) условие. **4,** *pl.* (victuals) провизия. —**make provision for,** предусматривать.

provisional *adj.* временный.

proviso *n.* условие; оговорка.

provocation *n.* провокация. *Without provocation,* без всякого повода. *At the slightest provocation,* по малейшему поводу.

provocative *adj.* вызывающий; провокационный.

provoke *v.t.* **1,** (excite to a certain action; cause; bring about) провоцировать. **2,** (evoke, as an emotion) вызывать; возбуждать. **3,** (vex) раздражать.

provost *n.* ректор; декан. —**provost marshal,** начальник военной полиции.

prow *n.* нос (судна).

prowess *n.* **1,** (bravery) доблесть; удаль. **2,** (skill) мастерство.

prowl *v.i.* рыскать; красться. —**prowl car,** машина полицейского патруля.

prowler *n.* взломщик.

proximity *n.* близость.

proxy *n.* **1,** (person authorized to act for another) доверенный. **2,** (authority) полномочие. —**by proxy,** по доверенности.

prude *n.* человек строгих нравов.

prudence *n.* благоразумие.

prudent *adj.* благоразумный; расчётливый. —**prudently,** *adv.* благоразумно.

prudish *adj.* чопорный; пуританский.

prune *n.* (dried plum) чернослив. —*v.t.* (trim) обрезать; подрезать.

prurient *adj.* похотливый.

Prussian *adj.* прусский. —*n.* пруссак. —**Prussian blue,** берлинская лазурь.

prussic acid синильная кислота.

pry *v.t.* **1,** (open; loosen) открывать; взламывать (при помощи рычага). **2,** (worm out, as a secret) выведывать; выпытывать. —*v.i.* **1,** (snoop) подглядывать. **2,** *fol.* **by into** (meddle) совать нос (в). —**prying,** *adj.* пытливый.

psalm *n.* псалом.

Psalter *n.* псалтырь.

pseudonym *n.* псевдоним.

pseudoscience *n.* лженаука. —**pseudoscientific,** *adj.* лженаучный.

pshaw *interj.* фи!

psoriasis *n.* псориаз.

psyche *n.* психика.

psychiatry *n.* психиатрия. —**psychiatric,** *adj.* психиатрический. —**psychiatrist,** *n.* психиатр.

psychic *adj.* психический; душевный.

psychoanalysis *n.* психоанализ. —**psychoanalyst,** *n.* специалист по психоанализу. —**psychoanalytic(al),** *adj.* психоаналитический. —**psychoanalyze,** *v.t.* подвергать психоанализу.

psychology *n.* психология. —**psychological,** *adj.* психологический. —**psychologist,** *n.* психолог.

psychopath *n.* психопат. —**psychopathic,** *adj.* психопатический. —**psychopathy,** *n.* психопатия.

psychosis *n.* психоз.

psychosomatic *adj.* психосоматический.

psychotherapy *n.* психотерапия. —**psychotherapist,** *n.* психотерапевт.

psychotic *adj.* психотический.

ptarmigan *n.* белая куропатка.

PT boat торпедный катер.

pterodactyl *n.* птеродактиль.

ptomaine *n.* трупный яд. —**ptomaine poisoning,** отравление трупным ядом.

pub *n.,* *Brit.* пивная; кабак.

puberty *n.* половая зрелость.

public *adj.* **1,** (of or for the community at large) общественный; публичный. *Public opinion,* общественное мнение. *Public library,* публичная библиотека. *Public health,* здравоохранение. **2,** (done or made in public; open) публичный. *Public speaking,* ораторское искусство. **3,** (of the government) государственный; казённый. —*n.* публика: *the general public,* широкая публика. —**in public,** публично; на людях. —**make public,** предавать гласности.

public-address system система звукоусиления.

publication *n*. **1**, (act of publishing) издание; опубликование; публикация. *Year of publication*, год издания. **2**, (something published) издание; публикация.

publicist *n*. публицист.

publicity *n*. **1**, (public notice) гласность; огласка. **2**, (advertising) реклама.

publicize *v.t.* предавать гласности; рекламировать.

publicly *adv.* публично.

publish *v.t.* **1**, (print and issue) издавать. **2**, (print in a certain publication) публиковать. —**publisher**, *n*. издатель.

publishing *n*. издательское дело. —**publishing house**, издательство.

puck *n., hockey* шайба.

pucker *v.t.* морщить. —*v.i.* морщиться. —*n.* **1**, (pleat) складка. **2**, (wrinkle) морщина.

pudding *n*. пудинг.

puddle *n*. лужа.

pudgy *adj.* пухлый.

puerile *adj.* ребяческий. —**puerility**, *n*. ребячество.

puerperal *adj.* родильный. —**puerperal fever**, родильная горячка.

Puerto Rican 1, *used adjectivally* пуэрториканский. **2**, *used as a noun* пуэрториканец; пуэрториканка.

puff *n*. **1**, (of air, wind, etc.) дуновение. **2**, (of smoke) клуб. **3**, (draw at a cigarette) затяжка. **4**, (powder puff) пуховка. **5**, (pastry) слойка. —*v.t.* **1**, (emit forcibly) пускать. **2**, *fol. by* **up** (swell) надувать; раздувать. —*v.i.* **1**, (pant) пыхтеть; отдуваться. **2**, *fol. by* **on** (smoke) попыхивать (+ *instr.*). **3**, *fol. by* **up** (swell up) вздуваться.

puffin *n*. тупик.

puff paste слоёное тесто. —**puff pastry**, слоёный пирог.

puffy *adj.* одутловатый. *Become puffy*, отекать.

pug *n*. (dog) мопс; моська.

pugilism *n*. бокс. —**pugilist**, *n*. боксёр.

pugnacious *adj.* драчливый. —**pugnacity**, *n*. драчливость.

pug nose курносый нос. —**pug-nosed**, *adj.* курносый.

pulchritude *n*. красота.

pull *v.t.* **1**, (draw; drag) тащить: *the horse is pulling the cart*, лошадь тащит телегу. **2**, (tug; yank) тянуть: *pull the rope*, тянуть верёвку. *Pull someone's hair*, дёргать кого-нибудь за волосы. **3**, (draw into a certain position) натягивать: *pull a blanket over oneself*, натянуть на себя одеяло. *Pull one's cap down over one's ears*, надвинуть шапку на уши. **4**, (remove) вырывать: *pull a tooth*, вырвать зуб. *Six bodies were pulled from the water*, из воды извлечены шесть трупов. **5**, (strain, as a muscle) растягивать. —*v.i.* тянуть. *Pull at someone's sleeve*, дёргать кого-нибудь за рукав. *Pull at one's beard*, теребить бороду. —*n.* **1**, (tug; jerk) рывок. **2**, (drawing) тяга; натяжение. **3**, *slang* (influence) блат; заручка. —**pull apart**, разнимать; растаскивать. —**pull back, 1**, (draw back suddenly) отдёргивать. **2**, (step back) отступать. —**pull down, 1**, (lower, as a shade) опускать. **2**, (take down; remove) снимать. **3**, (tear down, as a building) сносить. —**pull**

in, 1, (draw in) втягивать. **2**, (arrive) прибывать. —**pull into, 1**, *literally* втаскивать. **2**, (arrive in *or* at) прибывать в *or* на. **3**, (drive into) въезжать в. —**pull off, 1**, (remove) стягивать; стаскивать; сдёргивать. **2**, (turn off, as from a road) сворачивать с (дороги). **3**, *colloq.* (accomplish; engineer) совершать. —**pull on**, натягивать: *pull on one's shoes*, натянуть сапоги. —**pull oneself together**, взять себя в руки. —**pull out, 1**, (remove) вытаскивать; выдёргивать. **2**, (depart) отходить; уходить. **3**, (withdraw) выходить. **4**, *fol. by* **of** (drive out of in a car) выезжать (из). —**pull over**, подъезжать: *pull over to the curb*, подъехать к тротуару. —**pull together**, действовать сообща. —**pull through**, выживать; выкарабкиваться (из). —**pull up, 1**, (uproot) вырывать. **2**, (move closer) подставлять: *pull up a chair for someone*, подставлять стул кому-нибудь. **3**, *fol. by* **to** (drive up to) подъезжать (к). **4**, *Pull up stakes*, сняться с места.

pullet *n*. курочка; молодая курица.

pulley *n*. шкив; блок.

pullover *n*. пуловер; джемпер.

pulmonary *adj.* лёгочный.

pulp *n*. **1**, (juicy part of a fruit) мякоть. **2**, (material used in making paper) древесная масса. **3**, (part of a tooth) пульпа. —**beat to a pulp**, не оставить живого места на (+ *prepl.*).

pulpit *n*. кафедра.

pulpy *adj.* мясистый.

pulsar *n*. пульсар.

pulsate *v.i.* пульсировать. —**pulsation**, *n*. пульсация.

pulse *n*. пульс. *Pulse rate*, частота пульса.

pulverize *v.t.* измельчать; размельчать; превращать в порошок.

puma *n*. пума.

pumice *n*. пемза.

pummel *v.t.* колотить; дубасить.

pump *n*. **1**, (device) насос. *Gasoline pump*, бензоколонка. *Stomach pump*, желудочный зонд. **2**, (shoe) лодочка. —*v.t.* **1**, (propel by means of a pump) качать: *pump water/oil*, качать воду/нефть. *Pump air*, нагнетать воздух. **2**, *fol. by* **out** (remove by means of a pump) выкачивать; откачивать. **3**, *fol. by* **up** (inflate) накачивать. **4**, (shake vigorously) трясти. **5**, (fire, as bullets) пускать (пули в кого-нибудь). **6**, *colloq.* (question closely) выспрашивать.

pumpernickel *n*. чёрный хлеб.

pumping *n*. качание. —**pumping station**, насосная станция; водокачка.

pumpkin *n*. тыква.

pun *n*. каламбур; игра слов. —*v.i.* каламбурить.

punch *n*. **1**, (blow) удар (кулаком). **2**, (hole puncher) дырокол; (for punching a ticket) компостер. **3**, (beverage) пунш. —*v.t.* **1**, (strike) ударять кулаком. *Punch someone in the nose*, дать (+ *dat.*) по носу. **2**, (make, as a hole) пробивать. **3**, (validate, as a ticket) компостировать. **4**, (form with a machine that punches) штамповать. —**punch card**, перфокарта. —**punch press**, штамповальный *or* штамповочный пресс.

punching bag боксёрский мешок.

punctilious *adj.* щепетильный.

punctual *adj.* аккуратный; пунктуальный. —**punctuality**, *n*. аккуратность; пунктуальность. —**punctually**, *adv.* аккуратно.

punctuate *v.t.* **1**, (insert punctuation marks in) ставить знáки препинáния в. **2,** (intersperse) пересыпáть.

punctuation *n.* пунктуáция. —**punctuation marks,** знáки препинáния.

puncture *v.t.* прокáлывать. —*n.* прокóл.

pundit *n.* учёный; мудрéц.

pungent *adj.* óстрый; пикáнтный. *Pungent odor,* óстрый *or* рéзкий зáпах. —**pungency,** *n.* остротá.

punish *v.t.* накáзывать: *punish a child for disobedience,* наказáть ребёнка за непослушáние.

punishable *adj.* наказýемый. *Be punishable by death,* карáться смéртной кáзнью.

punishment *n.* наказáние. *In/as punishment for,* в наказáние за (+ *acc.*).

punitive *adj.* карáтельный.

punk *n., slang* хулигáн. —*adj., slang* дряннóй; паршúвый.

punster *n.* каламбурúст.

puny *adj.* **1,** (frail; sickly) щýплый. **2,** (insignificant) ничтóжный.

pup *n.* **1,** (puppy) щенóк. **2,** (young of certain animals) детёныш.

pupa *n.* кýколка.

pupil *n.* **1,** (student) ученúк; учáщийся. **2,** (of the eye) зрачóк.

puppet *n.* **1,** (animated figure) кýкла; марионéтка. **2,** *fig.* (person controlled by another) марионéтка. —*adj.* **1,** (pert. to puppets) кýкольный: *puppet show,* кýкольный теáтр. **2,** *fig.* (controlled by someone else) марионéточный.

puppy *n.* щенóк.

purblind *adj.* подслеповáтый.

purchase *v.t.* покупáть. —*n.* **1,** (act of purchasing) кýпля; покýпка. **2,** (something purchased) покýпка. —**purchase price,** покупнáя ценá. —**purchasing power,** покупáтельная спосóбность.

purchaser *n.* покупáтель.

pure *adj.* чúстый: *pure gold,* чúстое зóлото; *pure chance,* чúстая случáйность; *pure nonsense,* чúстый вздор.

purée *n.* пюрé.

purely *adv.* чúсто: *purely by chance,* чúсто случáйно.

purgative *adj.* слабúтельный. —*n.* слабúтельное.

purgatory *n.* чистúлище.

purge *v.t.* **1,** (evacuate, as the bowels) очищáть. **2,** *fig.* (rid of undesirable elements) чúстить. **3,** (remove and do away with) ликвидúровать. —*n.* чúстка.

purify *v.t.* очищáть. —**purification,** *n.* очúстка; очищéние.

purism *n.* пурúзм. —**purist,** *n.* пурúст.

Puritan *n.* пуритáнин. —*adj.* пуритáнский. —**puritanical,** *adj.* пуритáнский.

purity *n.* чистотá.

purl *v.i.* журчáть.

purloin *v.t.* красть; утáскивать.

purple *adj.* фиолéтовый; лилóвый.

purport *v.t.* претендовáть (на). —*n.* смысл.

purpose *n.* цель. *Answer/serve the purpose,* отвечáть цéли. —**on purpose,** нарóчно. —**to all intents and purposes,** фактúчески. —**to no purpose,** напрáсно.

purposeful *adj.* целеустремлённый.

purposely *adv.* нарóчно; намéренно; умышленно.

purr *v.i.* мурлыкать. —*n.* мурлыканье.

purse *n.* **1,** (change purse) кошелёк. **2,** (handbag)

сýмка; сýмочка. **3,** (prize money) приз; прéмия. —*v.t., in* **purse one's lips,** поджимáть *or* мóрщить гýбы.

purser *n.* казначéй.

purslane *n.* портулáк.

pursuance *n.* выполнéние; исполнéние. —**in pursuance of,** во исполнéние (+ *gen.*).

pursuant *adj. & adv.* [*usu.* **pursuant to**] соотвéтственно (+ *dat.*).

pursue *v.t.* **1,** (chase; seek) преслéдовать: *pursue a fugitive/goal,* преслéдовать беглецá/цель. **2,** (proceed along; follow) идтú по. *Pursue a policy,* проводúть полúтику. **3,** (take up; engage in) занимáться (+ *instr.*). *Pursue a career,* дéлать *or* составлять карьéру. **4,** (continue) продолжáть: *pursue one's studies,* продолжáть учёбу.

pursuer *n.* преслéдователь: *elude one's pursuers,* ускользáть от преслéдователей.

pursuit *n.* **1,** (act of pursuing) преслéдование; погóня. *Set out in pursuit of,* пустúться в погóню за. **2,** (act of seeking) погóня; стремлéние: *the pursuit of happiness,* погóня за счáстьем; стремлéние к счáстью. **3,** (activity; avocation) занятие.

purvey *v.t.* поставлять. —**purveyor,** *n.* поставщúк.

purview *n.* сфéра; компетéнция.

pus *n.* гной.

push *v.t.* **1,** (propel; shove) толкáть: *push a baby carriage,* толкáть дéтскую коляску. *Push one's way through a crowd,* протáлкиваться чéрез толпý. **2,** (press, as a button) нажимáть на. **3,** (urge on) подтáлкивать. **4,** (prosecute vigorously) протáлкивать: *push a matter,* протолкнýть дéло. **5,** *colloq.* (be approaching) *rendered by* стýкнуть: *he is pushing fifty,* емý скóро стýкнет пятьдесят. —*v.i.* **1,** (exert force on something) толкáть: *push harder!,* толкнúте посильнéе! **2,** (shove) толкáться: *don't push!,* не толкáйтесь! —*n.* толчóк. —**push away,** оттáлкивать. —**push back,** отбрáсывать; оттеснять. —**push off, 1,** (force off) стáлкивать. **2,** *colloq.* (leave; depart) уходúть; убирáться. —**push on,** продолжáть путь. —**push out,** вытáлкивать. —**push through, 1,** (shove through) протáлкивать. **2,** *fig.* (force through, as a resolution) протáскивать.

push button кнóпка.

pushcart *n.* ручнáя телéжка.

pushy *adj., colloq.* пробивнóй; напóристый.

pusillanimous *adj.* малодýшный. —**pusillanimity,** *n.* малодýшие.

puss *n.* **1,** (cat) кóшечка; кúс(к)а. **2,** *slang* (face) харя.

pussy *n.* кóшечка; кúс(к)а. *Also,* **pussy cat.**

pussy willow вéрба.

pustule *n.* гнóйничóк.

put *v.t.* **1,** (lay) класть: *put the book on the table,* класть кнúгу на стол. **2,** (stand) стáвить: *put the flowers in water,* стáвить цветы в вóду. **3,** (place) помещáть; стáвить. *Put a child in kindergarten,* помещáть ребёнка в дéтский сад. *Put an ad in a newspaper,* помещáть объявлéние в газéте. *Put someone in prison,* посадúть когó-нибудь в тюрьмý. *Put one's signature on,* стáвить свою пóдпись на (+ *prepl.*). *Put a period at the end of a sentence,* стáвить тóчку в концé предложéния. *Put in an awkward position,* стáвить в нелóвкое положéние. *Put yourself in my place,* постáвьте себя на моё мéсто. **4,** (bring to a certain state): *put at ease,* успокáивать. *Put in order,* приводить в порядок. *Put to bed,* укладывать. *Put to death,* предавать смерти. *Put to flight,*обратить в бегство. *Put to shame,* пристыдить. *Put to sleep,* усыплять. *Put to work,* усаживать за работу. **5,** (cause to take effect): *put an end to,* положить конец (+ *dat.*). *Put into effect/operation,* вводить в действие. **6,** (apply; expend) вкладывать: *put a lot of work into,* вкладывать много труда в. *Put one's heart and soul into,* вкладывать всю душу в. **7,** (cause to undergo) подвергать: *put to the test,* подвергать испытанию. *Put on trial,* предавать суду. *Put to expense,* вводить в расход. *Put to a vote,* поставить на голосование. **8,** (exert) оказывать: *put pressure on,* оказывать давление на. **9,** (express) выражать: *put into words,* выражать (что-нибудь) словами. *To put it mildly,* мягко выражаясь. *I don't know how to put it,* я не знаю, как это сказать. **10,** (pose, as a question) ставить; задавать. **11,** (render; set): *put words to music,* положить слова на музыку. **12,** (attach; attribute): *put the blame on,* валить вину на. *Put a wrong interpretation on,* давать неправильное толкование (+ *dat.*). **13,** (invest; deposit) вкладывать; помещать. *Put money in a savings account,* помещать деньги в сберкассу. **14,** (estimate at a certain figure) оценивать. **15,** (bet) ставить. **16,** *sports: put the shot,* толкать ядро. —**put aside,** откладывать (в сторону); сберегать. —**put away, 1,** (remove from sight) убирать. **2,** (save; reserve) откладывать. **3,** *colloq.* (commit, as to jail) сажать. **4,** *colloq.* (consume) съесть; выпить. —**put back, 1,** (restore to its place) ставить на место. **2,** (turn back, as a clock) переводить. —**put down, 1,** (lay down) положить. **2,** (write down) записывать. **3,** (suppress, as a revolt) подавлять. **4,** *fol. by* **to** (attribute to) относить на счёт (+ *gen.*). **5,** (pay in a lump sum) дать в задаток. **6,** (land) приземляться. **7,** *Put down roots,* пускать корни. —**put forth, 1,** (sprout) пускать. **2,** (exert, as effort) напрягать. **3,** (advance, as a proposal) выдвигать. —**put in, 1,** (insert) вкладывать; вставлять. *Put in a good word for,* замолвить словечко за. **2,** (enter, as a claim) предъявлять. **3,** *fol. by* **for** (apply for) подавать заявление о. **4,** *colloq.* (expend, as time) уделять. —**put into, 1,** (insert) вкладывать (в); вставлять (в). **2,** *naut.* заходить: *put into port,* заходить в гавань. —**put off, 1,** (make get off) высаживать; ссаживать. **2,** (postpone) откладывать. **3,** *colloq.* (repel) отталкивать. —**put on, 1,** (don) надевать. **2,** (apply) накладывать. *Put on make-up,* краситься. *Put on the brakes,* тормозить. **3,** (turn on, as a light) включать. **4,** (stage, as a play) ставить. **5,** (assume; affect) напускать на себя. **6,** (gain, as weight) прибавлять в (весе). *Put on ten pounds,* прибавлять десять фунтов. **7,** *Put on a record,* (по)ставить пластинку. **8,** *Put on some tea,* (по)ставить чайник. —**put out, 1,** (extend) протягивать. **2,** (lay out) выкладывать. **3,** (stick out) высовывать. **4,** (extinguish) тушить. **5,** (gouge out, as an eye) выкалы-

вать. **6,** (eject; dismiss) выгонять. **7,** (manufacture; publish) выпускать. **8,** (inconvenience) затруднять. *Put oneself out,* дать себе немало труда. **9,** (vex) обижать. *Be put out,* быть обиженным. **10,** *Put out of action,* выводить из строя; *put out of one's head,* выбрасывать из головы. **11,** *Put out to sea,* выходить в море. —**put over,** (postpone) переносить. —**put right,** налаживать; поправлять. —**put through, 1,** (implement) проводить. **2,** (cause to undergo) подвергать (+ *dat.*). —**put together, 1,** (assemble) собирать. **2,** (place together) составлять. **3,** (amass) накоплять. **4,** (combined) взятые вместе: *more than all the rest put together,* больше чем все остальные взятые вместе. —**put up, 1,** (erect) строить; воздвигать. **2,** (hang; post) вешать; взвешивать. **3,** (preserve; can) консервировать. **4,** (advance; invest, as money) вкладывавть. **5,** (give lodging to) устраивать (на ночь *or* на ночлег). **6,** (offer): *put up for sale,* пускать в продажу. *Put up resistance,* оказывать сопротивление. **7,** *fol. by* **with** (endure; tolerate) терпеть; выносить. **8,** *fol. by* **to** (incite; goad) подбивать; подучивать; подговаривать.

putative *adj.* предполагаемый.

putrefaction *n.* гниение; разложение.

putrefy *v.i.* гнить. —*v.t.* гноить.

putrid *adj.* **1,** (rotten) гнилой. **2,** (stinking) вонючий.

putsch *n.* путч.

puttee *n., usu. pl.* краги; обмотки.

putter *v.i.* возиться.

putty *n.* замазка; шпаклёвка. —*v.t.* замазывать; шпаклевать. —**putty knife,** шпатель.

puzzle *n.* загадка; головоломка. *Jigsaw puzzle,* составная картинка. *Crossword puzzle,* кроссворд. —*v.t.* **1,** (perplex) приводить в недоумение; озадачивать. **2,** *fol. by* **out** (solve) разгадывать; распутывать. —*v.i.* [*usu.* **puzzle over**] биться над; ломать себе голову над.

puzzled *adj.* недоумённый; недоумевающий. *Be puzzled,* недоумевать.

puzzlement *n.* недоумение. —**puzzling,** *adj.* недоумённый.

pygmy *n.* пигмей.

pyjamas *n.* = **pajamas.**

pylon *n.* пилон.

pyorrhea *also,* **pyorrhoea** *n.* пиорея.

pyramid *n.* пирамида. —**pyramidal,** *adj.* пирамидальный.

pyre *n.* погребальный костёр.

pyrite *n.* пирит.

pyrites *n.* колчедан.

pyrography *n.* выжигание.

pyromania *n.* пиромания.

pyrotechnics *n.* пиротехника.

Pyrrhic victory пиррова победа.

Pythagorean theorum пифагорова теорема.

python *n.* питон.

Q

Q, q семнадцатая буква английского алфавита.
quack *n.* **1,** (duck's cry) кряканье. **2,** (false doctor) знахарь; шарлатан. —*adj.* шарлатанский. —*v.i.* крякать.
quackery *n.* знахарство; шарлатанство.
quadrangle *n.* четырёхугольник. —**quadrangular**, *adj.* четырёхугольный.
quadrant *n.* квадрант.
quadratic *adj.* квадратный.
quadrennial *adj.* происходящий раз в четыре года.
quadrilateral *n.* четырёхугольник. —*adj.* четырёхсторонний.
quadrille *n.* кадриль.
quadrillion *n.* квадрильон.
quadruped *n.* четвероногое.
quadruple *adj.* четверной; четырёхкратный. —*v.t.* учетверять. —*v.i.* увеличиваться в четыре раза; учетверяться.
quadruplets *n.pl.* четверня.
quadruplicate *n. In quadruplicate,* в четырёх экземплярах.
quaff *v.t.* пить залпом.
quagmire *n.* трясина.
quail *n.* перепел. —*v.i.* (lose courage) дрогнуть.
quaint *adj.* причудливый; прихотливый.
quake *v.i.* дрожать; трястись. —*n.* = **earthquake.**
Quaker *n.* квакер. —*adj.* квакерский.
qualification *n.* **1,** (ability; competence) квалификация. *He has all the necessary qualifications,* он подходит по всем статьям. **2,** (limitation; reservation) оговорка.
qualified *adj.* **1,** (able; fit) компетентный. *Qualified for a position,* пригодный для должности. **2,** (limited; with reservations) ограниченный; с оговорками.
qualifier *n., gram.* определение; атрибут.
qualify *v.t.* **1,** (make eligible) давать право (+ *dat.*). **2,** (make less categorical): *qualify a statement,* сделать оговорку. **3,** *gram.* (modify) определять. —*v.i.* выслуживать: *qualify for a pension,* выслуживать пенсию. *Qualify for the finals,* выйти в финал. *He qualifies on all counts,* он подходит по всем статьям.
qualitative *adj.* качественный. —**qualitative analysis,** качественный анализ.
quality *n.* качество. —*adj., colloq.* доброкачественный; добротный; высококачественный.
qualm *n., usu. pl.* **1,** (misgivings) сомнение. **2,** (compunctions) угрызения совести.

quandary *n.* затруднительное положение; затруднение.
quantitative *adj.* количественный. —**quantitative analysis,** количественный анализ.
quantity *n.* **1,** (amount) количество: *enormous quantity,* огромное количество. *Buy in quantity,* покупать в большом количестве. **2,** *math.* величина: *unknown quantity,* неизвестная величина.
quantum *n., physics* квант. —*adj.* квантовый: *quantum mechanics/theory,* квантовая механика/теория.
quarantine *n.* карантин; изоляция. —*v.t.* подвергать карантину; изолировать.
quarrel *n.* ссора. —*v.i.* ссориться. —**quarrelsome**, *adj.* вздорный; сварливый.
quarry *n.* **1,** (place of excavation) каменоломня; карьер. **2,** (prey) добыча. —*v.t.* добывать. *Quarry stone,* ломать камень.
quart *n.* кварта.
quarter *n.* **1,** (one-fourth) четверть: *three-quarters,* три четверти. **2,** (25-cent piece) четвертак. **3,** (period of three months) квартал. **4,** (part of an academic year) четверть. **5,** (fifteen minutes) четверть: *a quarter of two,* без четверти два; *a quarter past seven,* четверть восьмого. **6,** (district of a city) квартал. **7,** (direction) сторона: *from every quarter,* со всех сторон. **8,** *pl.* (place of lodging) помещение; *mil.* квартиры. **9,** (part of an animal) часть: *hind quarters,* задняя часть. **10,** (mercy) пощада. *Give someone no quarter,* не давать спуска (+ *dat.*). —*v.t.* **1,** (divide in four) делить на четыре части. **2,** (billet) расквартировать. **3,** *hist.* (execute) четвертовать.
quarterdeck *n.* шканцы; ют.
quarterfinal *n.* четвертьфинал. —*adj.* четвертьфинальный.
quarterly *adj.* квартальный. —*adv.* поквартально. —*n.* журнал, выходящий поквартально.
quartermaster *n.* интендант; квартирмейстер. —**quartermaster corps,** интендантство.
quarter note *music* четвертная нота.
quartet *n.* квартет.
quartz *n.* кварц. —*adj.* кварцевый.
quartzite *n.* кварцит.
quasar *n.* квазар.
quash *v.t.* **1,** (suppress) подавлять. **2,** *law* (set aside) аннулировать.
quasi- *prefix* полу-: *quasi-official,* полуофициальный.
quatrain *n.* четверостишие.

quaver *v.i.* **1,** (tremble; quake) дрожа́ть. **2,** (be tremulous, as of the voice) дро́гнуть. —*n.* трель.

quay *n.* при́стань.

queasiness *n.* **1,** (nausea) тошнота́. **2,** (squeamishness) брезгли́вость.

queasy *adj.* **1,** (sick to one's stomach): *I felt queasy,* меня́ тошни́ло. **2,** (squeamish) брезгли́вый.

queen *n.* **1,** (sovereign) короле́ва. **2,** *cards* да́ма. **3,** *chess* ферзь. —*adj.* [*usu.* **queen's**] **1,** (of a queen) короле́вский. **2,** *chess* фе́рзевый: *queen's bishop/ gambit,* фе́рзевый слон/гамби́т. —**queen bee,** (пчели́ная) ма́тка. —**queen dowager,** вдо́вствующая короле́ва.

queer *adj.* стра́нный; чудакова́тый; эксцентри́чный. —**queerly,** *adv.* стра́нно.

quell *v.t.* **1,** (suppress) подавля́ть. **2,** (allay) успока́ивать.

quench *v.t.* **1,** (extinguish; put out) гаси́ть; туши́ть. **2,** (slake, as thirst) утоля́ть.

querulous *adj.* ворчли́вый; сварли́вый.

query *n.* вопро́с. —*v.t.* **1,** (ask questions of) расспра́шивать. **2,** (express doubt about) сомнева́ться в; ста́вить под вопро́с.

quest *n.* по́иски. *In quest of,* в по́исках (+ *gen.*).

question *n.* **1,** (query) вопро́с. **2,** (subject; problem; issue) вопро́с; пробле́ма. **3,** (doubt) сомне́ние. *Without question,* бесспо́рно. *Beyond question,* вне сомне́ния. *Open to question,* под вопро́сом. *Call into question,* ста́вить под вопро́с. —*v.t.* **1,** (ask questions of) расспра́шивать. **2,** (interrogate) допра́шивать. **3,** (express uncertainty about) сомнева́ться в; ста́вить под вопро́с. **4,** (challenge; dispute) оспа́ривать. —**in question, 1,** (under consideration) о кото́ром идёт речь: *the case in question,* слу́чай, о кото́ром идёт речь. **2,** (in dispute) под вопро́сом. —**it is a question of...,** речь идёт о... —**that is out of the question,** об э́том не мо́жет быть и ре́чи.

questionable *adj.* сомни́тельный.

question mark вопроси́тельный знак.

questionnaire *n.* анке́та; вопро́сник; опро́сный лист.

queue *n.* о́чередь. —*v.i.* [*usu.* **queue up**] стоя́ть в о́череди; станови́ться в о́чередь.

quibble *n.* **1,** (evasion of a point) увёртка. **2,** (minor criticism) приди́рка. —*v.i.* **1,** (cavil) придира́ться. **2,** (bicker) спо́рить. —**quibbler,** *n.* приди́ра.

quick *adj.* **1,** (rapid; swift) бы́стрый; ско́рый. *Be quick!,* скоре́е! **2,** (bright; alert) поня́тливый. *Quick to grasp things,* сообрази́тельный. **3,** (easily aroused) вспы́льчивый: *quick temper,* вспы́льчивый хара́ктер. —*adv.* бы́стро. *Come quick!,* иди́ скоре́й! —*n.,* *in cut to the quick,* заде́ть за живо́е.

quick-change artist трансформа́тор.

quicken *v.t.* **1,** (accelerate) ускоря́ть. *Quickened pulse,* учащённый пульс. **2,** (arouse; stir) оживля́ть. —*v.i.* ускоря́ться.

quicklime *n.* негашёная и́звесть.

quickly *adv.* бы́стро. *Come quickly!,* иди́ скоре́й!

quickness *n.* **1,** (rapidity) быстрота́. **2,** (keenness of mind) сообрази́тельность.

quicksand *n.* сыпу́чий песо́к.

quicksilver *n.* ртуть.

quick-tempered *adj.* вспы́льчивый.

quick-witted *adj.* сообрази́тельный; сме́тливый; догадли́вый.

quiescent *adj.* неподви́жный; споко́йный. —**quiescence,** *n.* поко́й; неподви́жность.

quiet *adj.* **1,** (making no noise) ти́хий. *Be/keep quiet,* молча́ть. *Keep something quiet,* зама́лчивать что-нибудь. **2,** (calm; tranquil) споко́йный. —*n.* тишина́; споко́йствие. —*v.t.* успока́ивать. —*v.i.* [*usu.* **quiet down**] успока́иваться. —*interj.* ти́ше!; не шуме́ть! —**quietly,** *adv.* ти́хо.

quietude *n.* поко́й; споко́йствие.

quill *n.* **1,** (feather) перо́. **2,** (spine, as of a porcupine) игла́. **3,** (quill pen) перо́.

quilt *n.* стёганое одея́ло. —*v.t.* стега́ть. —**quilted,** *adj.* стёганый.

quince *n.* айва́.

quinine *n.* хини́н.

quintessence *n.* квинтэссе́нция.

quintet *n.* квинте́т.

quintuplets *n.pl.* пя́теро близнецо́в.

quip *n.* остро́та. —*v.i.* остри́ть.

quire *n.* (ру́сская) десть.

quirk *n.* причу́да; вы́верт; заско́к. *Quirk of fate,* игра́ судьбы́; игра́ слу́чая.

quit *v.t.* **1,** (cease) перестава́ть. **2,** (give up) бро́сить: *quit smoking,* бро́сить кури́ть. **3,** (leave) покида́ть. **4,** (resign from) уходи́ть от or с. —*v.i.* **1,** (resign) уходи́ть. **2,** (give up; stop trying) сдава́ться.

quite *adv.* **1,** (entirely) совсе́м; вполне́. *Not quite,* не совсе́м. **2,** (rather) дово́льно: *quite far from here,* дово́льно далеко́ отсю́да. *Quite a few,* дово́льно мно́го. *Quite a while,* дово́льно до́лго. **3,** *fol. by* a (considerable) изря́дный: *quite a distance,* изря́дное расстоя́ние. *It was quite a surprise,* э́то бы́ло большо́й неожи́данностью.

quits *adj.* кви́ты. —**call it quits, 1,** (stop work) ко́нчить рабо́ту; шаба́шить. **2,** (retire) вы́йти на пе́нсию; сойти́ со сце́ны.

quiver *v.i.* трепета́ть; дро́гнуть. —*n.* **1,** (tremor) тре́пет. **2,** (case for arrows) колча́н.

quixotic *adj.* донкихо́тский.

quiz *n.* **1,** (short test) опро́с; контро́льная рабо́та. **2,** (game) виктори́на. —*v.t.* **1,** (interrogate) допра́шивать. **2,** (give a short test to) проверя́ть зна́ния (+ *gen.*).

quizzical *adj.* недоуме́нный; недоумева́ющий.

quorum *n.* кво́рум.

quota *n.* кво́та; но́рма.

quotation *n.* **1,** (words or passage quoted) цита́та. **2,** *finance* котиро́вка. —**quotation marks,** кавы́чки.

quote *v.t.* **1,** (cite) ссыла́ться на; цити́ровать. **2,** *finance* коти́ровать. —*n.* **1,** *colloq.* = **quotation. 2,** *pl.* = **quotation marks.**

quotient *n.* ча́стное.

R

R, r восемна́дцатая бу́ква англи́йского алфави́та. —**the three R's,** чте́ние, письмо́, арифме́тика.

rabbi *n.* равви́н. —**rabbinical,** *adj.* равви́нский.

rabbit *n.* кро́лик. —*adj.* кро́личий: *rabbit hole,* кро́личья нора́.

rabble *n.* толпа́. —**the rabble,** сброд; чернь; отре́бье.

rabid *adj.* **1,** (having rabies) бе́шеный. **2,** (fanatical) оголте́лый; махро́вый.

rabies *n.* бе́шенство; водобоя́знь.

raccoon *n.* ено́т. —*adj.* ено́товый.

race *n.* **1,** (contest of speed) бег; пробе́г; го́нки. *Horse race,* зае́зд. *The races,* ска́чки; бега́. **2,** (any contest) го́нка: *the arms race,* го́нка вооруже́ний. **3,** (ethnic group) ра́са. **4,** *in the human race,* челове́ческий род. —*adj.* ра́совый: *race relations,* ра́совые отноше́ния. —*v.i.* **1,** (compete in a race) бежа́ть; *(of a horse)* скака́ть. **2,** (dash) мча́ться. *Race by,* промча́ться. —*v.t.* **1,** (run against) бежа́ть наперего́нки с. **2,** (run at high speed, as an engine) дава́ть по́лный газ (+ *dat.*).

racecourse *n.* скакова́я доро́жка.

racehorse *n.* бегова́я ло́шадь; скакова́я ло́шадь.

raceme *n.* кисть; соцве́тие.

racer *n.* **1,** (racing driver) го́нщик. **2,** (horse) скакова́я ло́шадь; скаку́н. **3,** (auto) го́ночный автомоби́ль.

racetrack *n.* ипподро́м.

racial *adj.* ра́совый.

racing *n.* бега́; ска́чки. —*adj.* **1,** (of racing) беговой; скаковой. **2,** (used in racing) го́ночный: *racing car,* го́ночный автомоби́ль.

racism *n.* раси́зм. —**racist,** *n.* раси́ст. —*adj.* раси́стский.

rack *n.* **1,** (for coats, hats, etc.) ве́шалка. **2,** (for books or other standing objects) стелла́ж. **3,** (for bombs) бомбодержа́тель. **4,** (instrument of torture) дыба. **5,** (toothed bar) зубча́тая ре́йка. —*v.t.* **1,** [*also,* **wrack**] (afflict) изму́чить; (ис)терза́ть. *Racked with disease,* изму́ченный боле́знью. **2,** *fol. by* **up** (score) набира́ть (...очко́в); одержа́ть (побе́ду). **3,** *in* **rack one's brains,** лома́ть себе́ го́лову. —**go to rack and ruin,** пойти́ пра́хом.

racket *n.* **1,** (din) гам; гвалт. **2,** *sports* (webbed bat) раке́тка. **3,** (fraud) ра́кет. —**racketeer,** *n.* га́нгстер; рэкети́р.

raconteur *n.* расска́зчик.

racy *adj.* **1,** (lively) колори́тный. **2,** (risqué) солёный.

radar *n.* **1,** (system) радиолока́ция. **2,** (device) радиолока́тор. —*adj.* радиолокацио́нный.

radial *adj.* лучево́й; радиа́льный.

radiance *n.* сия́ние; блеск.

radiant *adj.* **1,** (sending out or transmitted by rays) лучи́стый: *radiant heat/energy,* лучи́стая теплота́/ эне́ргия. **2,** (beaming, as with joy) сия́ющий; луче-за́рный.

radiate *v.t.* **1,** (emit) излуча́ть. **2,** (manifest in a glowing manner) сия́ть; лучи́ться: *radiate happiness,* сия́ть/лучи́ться сча́стьем. —*v.i.* **1,** (spread out in rays) излуча́ться. **2,** (branch out) расходи́ться.

radiation *n.* излуче́ние; радиа́ция; лучеиспуска́ние. *Radiation treatment,* облуче́ние. —**radiation sickness,** лучева́я боле́знь.

radiator *n.* батаре́я отопле́ния; радиа́тор.

radical *adj.* **1,** *polit.* радика́льный. **2,** (drastic) коренно́й; радика́льный. —*n.* **1,** *polit.* радика́л. **2,** *math.* ко́рень. *Radical sign,* знак ко́рня; радика́л. **3,** *chem.* радика́л. —**radicalism,** *n.* радикали́зм. —**radically,** *adv.* коренны́м о́бразом; радика́льно.

radio *n.* **1,** (receiving set) радиоприёмник. **2,** (small portable receiver and transmitter) ра́ция. **3,** (broadcasting medium) ра́дио. —*v.t. & i.* ради́ровать. —**radio operator,** ради́ст. —**radio station,** радиоста́нция.

radioactive *adj.* радиоакти́вный. —**radioactivity,** *n.* радиоакти́вность.

radiogram *n.* радиогра́мма.

radiology *n.* **1,** (use of X-rays) рентгеноло́гия. **2,** (use of radiation) радиоло́гия. —**radiologist,** *n.* рентгено́лог; радио́лог.

radio-phonograph *n.* радио́ла.

radiotelegraphy *n.* радиотелегра́фия.

radiotelephone *n.* радиотелефо́н. —**radiotelephony,** *n.* радиотелефони́я.

radiotherapy *n.* радиотерапи́я.

radish *n.* реди́ска; ре́дька; *pl.* реди́с; реди́ски.

radium *n.* ра́дий. —*adj.* ра́диевый.

radius *n.* ра́диус. *Within a radius of,* в ра́диусе (+ *gen.*).

radon *n.* радо́н.

raffle *n.* лотере́я. *Raffle ticket,* лотере́йный биле́т. —*v.t.* разы́грывать.

raft *n.* **1,** (float) плот. **2,** *colloq.* (large amout) у́йма; ку́ча.

rafter *n.* стропи́ло.

rag *n.* **1,** (piece of cloth) тря́пка: *dust rag,* пы́льная тря́пка. **2,** *pl.* (scraps of cloth) тряпьё; ве́тошь. **3,** *pl.* (shabby clothes; tatters) лохмо́тья; тряпьё; ру́бище; отре́пья. —*adj.* тряпи́чный: *rag paper,* тряпи́чная бума́га.

ragamuffin *n.* оборвыш.

rag doll тряпичная кукла.

rage *n.* **1,** (fury) ярость; бешенство. *Fly into a rage,* приходить в ярость. **2,** *colloq.* (fad; craze) последний крик моды. —*v.i.* **1,** (be furious) беситься. **2,** (of a storm, fire, etc.) бушевать; свирепствовать.

ragged *adj.* **1,** (tattered) поношенный; изорванный; оборванный. **2,** (rough; jagged) шероховатый; зазубренный. —**run oneself ragged,** избегаться; забегаться.

raglan *n.* реглан.

ragman *n.* тряпичник.

ragout *n.* рагу.

ragweed *n.* амброзия.

raid *n.* **1,** *mil.* налет; набег; рейд. *Air raid,* воздушный налет. **2,** (by the police) облава. —*v.t.* совершать налет/набег на.

rail *n.* **1,** (horizontal bar) поперечина; перекладина. **2,** (handrail; railing) перила; поручни. **3,** (railroad track) рельс. **4,** (railroad) железная дорога: *by rail,* по железной дороге. **5,** (bird) пастушок. —*adj.* железнодорожный: *rail junction,* железнодорожный узел. —*v.i.* [*usu.* **rail at** *or* **against**] бранить. —**thin as a rail,** худой как щепка.

railing *n.* **1,** (fence) ограда. **2,** (banister) перила.

raillery *n.* беззлобная насмешка.

railroad *n.* железная дорога. —*adj.* железнодорожный.

railway *n.* = **railroad.**

raiment *n.* одеяние.

rain *n.* дождь. —*adj.* дождевой: *rain water,* дождевая вода. —*v.i.* **1,** (be raining) идти: *it is raining,* идет дождь. **2,** *fig.* (fall like rain) сыпаться. —*v.t.* обрушивать. *Rain blows on,* обрушивать удары на; осыпать (кого-нибудь) ударами. —**it is raining cats and dogs,** дождь льет как из ведра. —**rain or shine,** в любую погоду; какая бы ни была погода.

rainbow *n.* радуга.

raincoat *n.* плащ; дождевик.

raindrop *n.* дождевая капля.

rainfall *n.* количество осадков.

rain hat шляпа от дождя.

rainstorm *n.* ливень.

rainy *adj.* дождливый. —**put aside for a rainy day,** сберечь на черный день.

raise *v.t.* **1,** (lift) поднимать. **2,** (increase) повышать. **3,** (rear) воспитывать. **4,** (cultivate) выращивать. **5,** (breed) разводить. **6,** (make louder, as one's voice) повышать. **7,** (collect, as money) собирать. **8,** (bring up, as a question) поднимать; ставить; возбуждать. **9,** (evoke, as doubts) вызывать. **10,** (start; cause, as a clamor) поднимать. **11,** (cause to form, as a blister) натирать. **12,** *math.* возводить (в степень). **13,** *in* **raise from the dead,** оживлять; воскрешать. —*n.,* *colloq.* повышение зарплаты; прибавка; надбавка.

raised *adj.* рельефный: *raised design,* рельефный узор.

raisin *n.* изюмина; изюминка; *pl.* изюм.

rajah *n.* раджа.

rake *n.* **1,** (garden tool) грабли. **2,** (roué) повеса; распутник. —*v.t.* **1,** (gather or smooth with a rake) грести; сгребать. *Rake leaves,* сгребать листья. **2,** (cover with gunfire) простреливать. **3,** *fol.* *by* **in** (amass in large quantities) загребать: *rake in money,* загребать деньги лопатой. **4,** *fol.* *by* **up** (dig up from the past) отка-

пывать. —**rake over the coals,** задать жару (+ *dat.*); взять под обстрел.

rakish *adj.* **1,** (jaunty) лихой. **2,** (dissolute) распутный.

rally *v.t.* **1,** (bring together for a common purpose) сплачивать. **2,** (summon; muster) набираться: *rally one's forces,* набраться сил. —*v.i.* **1,** (unite) сплачиваться. **2,** (show a sudden improvement) оправляться. —*n.* **1,** (mass meeting) митинг; слет. **2,** (sudden improvement) улучшение; поправка.

ram *n.* **1,** (male sheep) баран. **2,** (battering-ram) таран. —*v.t.* **1,** (force into a narrow space; jam) забивать; втискивать. **2,** [*also intrans.* **ram into**] (crash or smash into) наскочить на; налететь на.

ramble *v.i.* **1,** (wander) бродить. **2,** (speak aimlessly) заговариваться. *He tends to ramble,* он часто уклоняется от темы.

rambling *adj.* **1,** (wandering) бродячий. **2,** (disconnected) бессвязный. **3,** (spread out) разбросанный.

rambunctious *adj.,* *colloq.* буйный; непокорный.

ramification *n.* **1,** (branch) разветвление. **2,** *pl.* (consequences) последствия.

ramp *n.* **1,** (inclined passageway) скат. **2,** (boarding ramp) трап.

rampage *n.* буйство. —*v.i.* [*also,* **go on a rampage**] буйствовать; буянить.

rampant *adj.* **1,** (growing unchecked, as of plants) буйный. **2,** (spreading unchecked) безудержный: *rampant inflation,* безудержная инфляция.

rampart *n.* крепостной вал.

ramrod *n.* шомпол. —**ramrod straight,** как аршин проглотил.

ramshackle *adj.* ветхий; обветшалый.

ranch *n.* ранчо.

rancid *adj.* прогорклый. *Turn rancid,* (про)горкнуть.

rancor *also,* **rancour** *n.* злоба; озлобление. —**rancorous,** *adj.* злобный; злопамятный.

random *adj.* случайный. —**at random,** наудачу; наугад; наобум.

random access произвольная выборка.

range *n.* **1,** (scope; extent) размах. *Range of interests,* круг интересов. **2,** (of a weapon, transmitter, etc.) дальность; досягаемость. *Within range,* в пределах досягаемости. *Out of range,* вне досягаемости. *The gun has a range of 500 meters,* орудие бьет на пятьсот метров. **3,** (of an aircraft, missile, etc.) радиус действия; дальность полета. **4,** (distance) расстояние: *at close range,* на близком расстоянии. *Fire at close range,* стрелять в упор. **5,** (variety) круг: *a broad range of questions,* широкий круг вопросов. **6,** (limits of variation) пределы: *fluctuate within a narrow range,* колебаться в узких пределах. **7,** *music* диапазон. **8,** (of mountains) хребет; горная цепь. **9,** (place for shooting practice) стрельбище; полигон. **10,** (large stove) плита. **11,** (grazing land) пастбище. —*v.t.* выстраивать в ряд. *They ranged themselves along the sidewalk,* они выстроились вдоль тротуара. *Various groups were ranged against us,* различные группы выступали против нас. —*v.i.* **1,** (wander) рыскать. **2,** (vary within stated limits) колебаться. *The children's ages range from two to six,* возраст детей — от двух до шести. **3,** *fol.* *by* **over** (cover; take in) охватывать: *range over many topics,* охватывать много предметов.

range finder дальномер.

ranger *n.* **1,** (forest guard) леснйк; объёздчик. **2,** *mil.* диверсáнт.

rangy *adj.* долговя́зый.

rank *n.* **1,** (grade; position) звáние; чин; ранг. *The rank of admiral,* адмирáльское звáние; адмирáльский чин. *An official of lesser rank,* сотрýдник мéньшего рáнга. *Persons of rank,* знáтные лю́ди. **2,** (category) *a writer of the first rank,* первоклáссный писáтель. **3,** (column) шерéнга; ряд. *Close ranks,* смыкáть *or* сплáчивать ряды́. *Break ranks,* расходи́ться. **4,** *pl.* (armed forces) ряды́: *serve in the ranks of the army,* служи́ть в рядáх áрмии. **5,** *pl.* (enlisted men) рядовы́е: *rise from the ranks,* выдвигáться (из рядовы́х в офицéры). **6,** *pl.* (body of people) ряды́: *the ranks of the unemployed,* ряды́ безрабóтных. *Take into their ranks,* принимáть в свои́ ряды́. —*v.t.* **1,** (evaluate relative to each other) давáть оцéнку (+ *dat.).* **2,** (consider; number) относи́ть к числý (+ *gen.*); причислять. —*v.i.* Rank first, занимáть пéрвое мéсто. *Rank on a par with,* стоя́ть в однóм ряду́ с; быть наравнé с. *Rank among the finest,* принадлежáть к числý сáмых лýчших. —*adj.* **1,** (luxuriant) роскóшный; бýйный. **2,** (rancid) прогóрклый. **3,** (utter; gross) я́вный; сýщий. *Rank ingratitude,* чёрная неблагодáрность. *Rank injustice,* вопию́щая несправедли́вость. —**rank and file,** *mil.* рядовóй состáв.

ranking *adj.* стáрший.

rankle *v.i.* мýчить; глодáть: *the memory still rankles,* воспоминáние об э́том ещё мýчит/глóжет меня́.

ransack *v.t.* **1,** (search thoroughly) ры́ться в; обшáривать. **2,** (rob and leave in disarray) разгрáбить.

ransom *n.* вы́куп: *hold for ransom,* трéбовать вы́купа за (+ *acc.*). —*v.t.* выкупáть.

rant *v.i.* неистовствовать; беснoвáться; безýмствовать. —**rant and rave,** рвать и метáть; метáть грóмы и мóлнии.

rap *n.* **1,** (quick, sharp blow) удáр. **2,** (tapping sound) стук. **3,** *slang* (blame; punishment) наказáние: *beat the rap,* избежáть наказáния. *Take the rap for,* отдувáться за (когó-нибудь). —*v.t. & i.* ударя́ть (по); стучáть (в). —**not give/care a rap,** *colloq.* наплевáть: *I don't give a rap,* мне наплевáть на э́то.

rapacious *adj.* хи́щный.

rape *n.* **1,** (sexual violation) изнаси́лование. **2,** (plant) рапс; сурéпица. —*v.t.* наси́ловать. —**rape oil,** рáпсовое мáсло; сурéпное мáсло.

rapid *adj.* бы́стрый; стреми́тельный. *Rapid growth,* бýрный рост. —**rapidity,** *n.* быстротá. —**rapidly,** *adv.* бы́стро.

rapids *n.pl.* порóги; стремни́на; быстрина́.

rapier *n.* рапи́ра.

rapist *n.* наси́льник.

rapport *n.* взаимопонимáние; соглáсие.

rapprochement *n.* сближéние.

rapt *adj.* **1,** (enraptured) восхищённый. **2,** (engrossed) поглощённый. *Rapt attention,* напряжённое *or* при́стальное внимáние.

rapture *n.* востóрг; упоéние. —**rapturous,** *adj.* востóрженный.

rara avis бéлая ворóна.

rare *adj.* **1,** (uncommon) рéдкий. **2,** (lightly cooked) кровáвый.

rarefy *v.t.* разрежáть. —**rarefied,** *adj.* разрежённый.

rarely *adv.* рéдко.

rareness *n.* рéдкость.

rarity *n.* рéдкость.

rascal *n.* **1,** (scoundrel) подлéц. **2,** (imp) пострéл.

rash *adj.* опромéтчивый; необдýманный; безрассýдный. —*n.* сыпь. *Heat rash,* потни́ца.

rasher *n.* лóмтик бекóна.

rashly *adv.* опромéтчиво; безрассýдно.

rashness *n.* опромéтчивость; безрассýдство.

rasp *v.t.* скрести́. —*v.i.* скрипéть. —*n.* **1,** (sound) скрéжет. **2,** (tool) рáшпиль.

raspberry *n.* мали́на. —*adj.* мали́новый: *raspberry jam,* мали́новое варéнье.

rasping *adj.* скрипýчий.

rat *n.* **1,** (rodent) кры́са. **2,** (contemptible person) гад. —*adj.* кры́синый: *rat poison,* кры́синый яд. —**smell a rat,** чýять недóброе.

ratchet *n.* храповик; трещóтка. —**ratchet wheel,** храповóе колесó.

rate *n.* **1,** (measurement relative to a standard) стáвка: *rate of interest,* стáвка процéнта; *wage rate,* стáвка зарплáты. *Rate of exchange,* валю́тный курс. *Rate of return,* нóрма при́были. *Birth rate,* рождáемость. *Death rate,* смéртность. **2,** *often pl.* (price; cost) тари́ф; расцéнка. *Postal rates,* почтóвый тари́ф. *Advertising rates,* расцéнка объявлéний. **3,** (pace) темп: *rate of growth,* темп рóста. *Pulse rate,* частотá пýльса. *At this rate we'll never get there,* при такóм тéмпе мы никогдá не доберёмся. —*v.t.* **1,** (evaluate) оцéнивать. **2,** (consider; regard) считáть. **3,** *colloq.* (deserve) заслýживать. —*v.i.* считáться: *he rates among the best,* он считáется одни́м из сáмых лýчших. —**at any rate,** во вся́ком слýчае.

rather *adv.* **1,** (somewhat) довóльно. **2,** (preferably) скорéе; *I would rather...,* я предпочéл бы (+ *inf.*). *Which would you rather have?,* что вы предпочитáете?; чегó вам бóльше хóчется? **3,** (more correctly) вернéе. —**rather than,** вмéсто тогó, чтóбы...

rathole *n.* кры́синая норá.

ratify *v.t.* ратифици́ровать. —**ratification,** *n.* ратификáция.

rating *n.* **1,** (evaluation) оцéнка. **2,** (scolding) нагоня́й.

ratio *n.* отношéние; соотношéние; коэффициéн *The ratio of women to men,* соотношéние жéнщин (мужчи́н.

ration *n.* **1,** (share; portion) паёк; рациóн. **2,** *pl.* (food) продовóльствие. —*v.t.* норми́ровать. *Bread is ra tioned,* хлеб выдаётся по кáрточкам. —**ration car** продовóльственная кáрточка.

rational *adj.* **1,** (able to reason; reasonable) разýмный; рассýдочный; рациóнальный. *Man is a rational being,* человéк – разýмное существó. **2,** *math.* рациóнальный.

rationale *n.* моти́в: *the rationale behind a decision,* моти́в для решéния.

rationalism *n.* рационали́зм. —**rationalist,** *n.* рационали́ст. —**rationalistic,** *adj.* рационалисти́ческий.

rationality *n.* рационáльность.

rationalize *v.t.* **1,** (give plausible excuses for) опрáвдывать. **2,** (apply modern methods of efficiency to) рационализи́ровать.

rationally *adv.* разýмно.

rationing *n.* кáрточная систéма; норми́рование. *Introduce rationing,* вводи́ть кáрточную систéму.

rattan *n.* ротáнг. —*adj.* ротáнговый.

rattle *v.i.* **1,** (shake with quick sharp sounds) дребез-жа́ть. **2,** (move with such sounds) грохота́ть: *rattle along the road,* грохота́ть по доро́ге. —*v.t.* **1,** (shake noisily) греме́ть: *rattle the dishes,* греме́ть посу́дой. *The wind rattled the windows,* стёкла дребезжа́ли от ве́тра. **2,** *colloq.* (fluster) сбива́ть с то́лку. *Get rattled,* (рас)теря́ться. **3,** *fol. by* **off** (recite rapidly) отбара-ба́нить. —*n.* **1,** (sound) дребезжа́ние. **2,** (sound in one's throat) хрип: *death rattle,* предсме́ртный хрип. **3,** (baby's toy) погрему́шка. **4,** (noisemaker) тре-щётка.

rattlesnake *n.* грему́чая змея́.

rattletrap *n.* колыма́га.

rattrap *n.* крысоло́вка.

raucous *adj.* **1,** (loud and harsh) хри́плый; ре́зкий. **2,** (rowdy; disorderly) шумли́вый; бу́йный.

ravage *v.t.* разоря́ть; опустоша́ть. —*n., usu. pl.* опустоши́тельное де́йствие: *the ravages of time,* опустоши́тельное де́йствие вре́мени.

rave *v.i.* **1,** (speak incoherently) бре́дить. **2,** *fol. by* **about** (praise enthusiastically) быть в восто́рге от; расхва́ливать. —*adj., colloq.* восто́рженный. —*n., colloq.* восто́рженный о́тзыв.

ravel *v.t.* **1,** (fray) обтрепа́ть. **2,** (disentangle) распу́-тывать. —*v.i.* обтрепа́ться.

raven *n.* во́рон. —*adj.* чёрный как смоль.

ravenous *adj.* **1,** (voracious; gluttonous) прожо́рли-вый. *Ravenous appetite,* во́лчий аппети́т. **2,** (rapa-cious) хи́щный.

ravine *n.* уще́лье; овра́г.

raving *adj.* **1,** (wild) бу́йный: *raving maniac,* бу́йный сумасше́дший. **2,** (ravishing) восхити́тельный. —*n., often pl.* бред; бре́дни.

ravish *v.t.* **1,** (enrapture) восхища́ть. **2,** (rape) раст-лева́ть. —**ravishing,** *adj.* восхити́тельный.

raw *adj.* **1,** (uncooked) сыро́й. **2,** (untreated; unproces-sed) необрабо́танный. *Raw data,* необрабо́танные да́нные. ♦ *Often rendered by* -сыре́ц: *raw silk,* шёлк-сыре́ц; *raw whiskey,* спирт-сыре́ц. **3,** (cold and damp) сыро́й. **4,** (exposed; irritated) обо́дранный. *Raw wound,* жива́я ра́на. **5,** (untrained) необу́ченный. **6,** (bawdy) са́льный. —**in the raw,** нагишо́м.

rawboned *adj.* костля́вый.

rawhide *n.* сыромя́ть. —*adj.* сыромя́тный.

raw material сырьё.

ray *n.* **1,** (beam, as of light) луч. **2,** (glimmer, as of hope) луч; и́скра; про́блеск (наде́жды). **3,** (fish) скат.

rayon *n.* иску́сственный шёлк; виско́за.

raze *v.t.* сноси́ть; срыва́ть (*pfv.* срыть); сровня́ть с землёй; разруша́ть до основа́ния.

razor *n.* бри́тва. —**razor blade,** ле́звие бри́твы.

re *n., music* ре.

reach *v.t.* **1,** (get to) достига́ть; доходи́ть до; доез-жа́ть до; *(with difficulty)* добира́ться до. *The letter/news did not reach me,* письмо́/изве́стие до меня́ не дошло́. **2,** (extend as far as) доходи́ть до: *her dress reaches the floor,* её пла́тье дохо́дит до по́ла. **3,** *fol. by* **out** (extend, as one's hand) протя́гивать. **4,** (be able to touch) достава́ть до; дотя́гиваться до. **5,** (obtain and hand over) передава́ть: *reach me the salt,* переда́йте, пожа́луйста, соль. **6,** (attain) достига́ть: *reach one's goal,* достига́ть свое́й це́ли. *Reach supersonic speed,* достига́ть сверхзвуково́й ско́рости. **7,** (come to, as a conclusion or agreement) приходи́ть к. **8,** (get in touch with, as by phone) связа́ться с; доз-

вони́ться к. —*v.i.* **1,** *often fol. by* **out** (extend one's hand) протя́гивать ру́ку. *Reach into one's pocket,* тя-ну́ться *or* лезть в карма́н. *A hand reached out from the crowd,* из толпы́ протяну́лась рука́. **2,** *fol. by* **for** (attempt to grasp) тяну́ться за *or* к. —*n.* **1,** (range) досяга́емость: *within reach,* в преде́лах дося-га́емости; *out of reach,* вне досяга́емости. **2,** *pl.* (of a river) тече́ние: *the upper reaches of the Volga,* вер́х-нее тече́ние Во́лги; верхо́вье Во́лги.

react *v.i.* реаги́ровать. —**reaction,** *n.* реа́кция.

reactionary *adj.* реакцио́нный. —*n.* реакционе́р.

reactive *adj.* реакти́вный.

reactor *n.* реа́ктор.

read *v.t. & i.* чита́ть. *Read someone's lips,* чита́ть с чьих-нибудь губ. *Read someone's mind,* чита́ть чьи-нибудь мы́сли. —*v.t.* **1,** (make out) разбира́ть. **2,** (in-terpret) толкова́ть; понима́ть. **3,** (indicate; register) пока́зывать. **4,** *Brit.* (study) изуча́ть: *read law,* изу-ча́ть пра́во. —*v.i.* **1,** (have a particular wording) гла-си́ть: *the telegram reads as follows,* телегра́мма гла-си́т сле́дующее. **2,** (admit of being read) чита́ться: *the book reads easily,* кни́га легко́ чита́ется. —**read between the lines,** чита́ть ме́жду строк. —**read out of,** исключа́ть из. —**read through,** прочита́ть.

readable *adj.* удобочита́емый. *The book is very readable,* кни́га легко́ чита́ется.

readdress *v.t.* переадресо́вывать.

reader *n.* **1,** (person who reads) чита́тель. **2,** (profes-sional reciter) чтец. **3,** *Brit.* (lecturer) ле́ктор. **4,** (text-book) хрестома́тия.

readership *n.* круг чита́телей.

readily *adv.* **1,** (willingly; promptly) охо́тно. **2,** (easily) легко́; без труда́.

readiness *n.* гото́вность. *All is in readiness,* всё го-то́во. *Hold in readiness,* держа́ть наготове.

reading *n.* **1,** (act of reading; recital) чте́ние. **2,** (inter-pretation) толкова́ние. **3,** (indication on a meter) по-каза́ние; отсчёт. —**reading desk,** пюпи́тр. —**read-ing glasses,** очки́ для чте́ния. —**reading room,** чи-та́льный зал; чита́льня.

readjust *v.t.* (сно́ва) регули́ровать. —*v.i.* приспо-собля́ться (к). —**readjustment,** *n.* приспособле́ние.

readout *n.* счи́тывание информа́ции.

ready *adj.* гото́вый: *are you ready?,* вы гото́вы? *Ready for takeoff,* гото́вый к вы́лету. *Ready for use,* гото́вый для употребле́ния. *Get ready,* гото́виться. *Ready cash,* нали́чные де́ньги. —*v.t.* гото́вить. —**at the ready,** на изгото́вку.

ready-made *adj.* гото́вый: *ready-made clothes,* го-то́вая оде́жда.

reaffirm *v.t.* вновь подтвержда́ть.

reagent *n.* реакти́в; реаге́нт.

real *adj.* **1,** (actual; existing) действи́тельный; реа́ль-ный. **2,** (genuine) настоя́щий; натура́льный. **3,** (true, as of a friend) настоя́щий; и́стинный. —*adv., colloq.* о́чень: *get up real early,* встава́ть о́чень ра́но. —**real estate,** недви́жимое иму́щество; недви́жимость. —**real number,** действи́тельное число́. —**real wages,** реа́льная за́работная пла́та.

realign *v.t.* перестра́ивать. —**realignment,** *n.* пе-ресто́йка; перестано́вка.

realism *n.* реали́зм. —**realist,** *n.* реали́ст. —**realis-tic,** *adj.* реалисти́ческий; реа́льный.

reality *n.* действи́тельность; реа́льность. —**in real-ity,** в действи́тельности; на са́мом де́ле.

realization *n.* **1,** (recognition; awareness) понима́ние; осозна́ние. **2,** (becoming a reality) осуществле́ние; созна́ние; реализа́ция.

realize *v.t.* **1,** (be or become aware of) понима́ть; сознава́ть; осознава́ть; отдава́ть себе́ отчёт в. **2,** (achieve; bring about) осуществля́ть; реализова́ть. **3,** (gain; obtain, as a profit) получа́ть.

really *adv.* **1,** (actually; in actual fact) действи́тельно; на са́мом де́ле. *Better than it really is*, лу́чше чем оно́ есть на са́мом де́ле. **2,** (truly; indeed) действи́тельно; на са́мом де́ле. *The meal really turned out well*, еда́ в са́мом де́ле оказа́лась хоро́шей. —**really?**, неужёли? *Did I really say that?*, неуже́ли я э́то говори́л(а)?

realm *n.* **1,** (kingdom) короле́вство; ца́рство. **2,** (sphere) о́бласть; сфе́ра.

realtor *n.* аге́нт по прода́же недви́жимости. —**realty,** *n.* недви́жимое иму́щество.

ream *n.* **1,** (quantity of paper) стопа́. **2,** *usu. pl., colloq.* (large amount) ма́сса; ку́ча; у́йма.

reamer *n.* развёртка.

reanimation *n.* реанима́ция.

reap *v.t.* **1,** (cut; gather) жать. **2,** *fig.* (gain as a reward) пожина́ть.

reaper *n.* **1,** (one who reaps) жнец. **2,** (reaping machine) жа́твенная маши́на; жа́тка; жне́йка.

reappear *v.i.* сно́ва появля́ться.

reapportion *v.t.* перераспределя́ть. —**reapportionment,** *n.* перераспределе́ние.

reappraise *v.t.* переоце́нивать; пересма́тривать. —**reappraisal,** *n.* переоце́нка; пересмо́тр.

rear *n.* **1,** (back part) за́дняя часть; зад. **2,** (tail end) хвост. **3,** *mil.* тыл. —*adj.* **1,** (back) за́дний: *rear wheel*, за́днее колесо́. **2,** (from the back): *rear view*, вид сза́ди. **3,** (located in the back part of a house) чёрный: *rear door*, чёрный ход. **4,** *mil.* тылово́й. —*v.t.* **1,** (elevate) поднима́ть: *rear one's head*, поднима́ть го́лову. **2,** (raise; bring up) воспи́тывать. —*v.i.* (of a horse) станови́ться на дыбы́. —**at/in the rear of, 1,** (behind) позади́; сза́ди. **2,** (in the back part of) в за́дней ча́сти (+ *gen.*). **3,** (at the tail end of) в хвосте́ (+ *gen.*). —**bring up the rear,** замыка́ть ше́ствие. —**rear end, 1,** (tail end) хвост. **2,** (buttocks) зад.

rear admiral контр-адмира́л.

rear guard арьерга́рд. —**rearguard,** *adj.* арьерга́рдный.

rearm *v.t.* перевооружа́ть. —*v.i.* перевооружа́ться. —**rearmament,** *n.* перевооруже́ние.

rearrange *v.t.* **1,** (move around) переставля́ть: *rearrange the furniture*, переставля́ть ме́бель. **2,** *music* перекла́дывать. —**rearrangment,** *n.* перестано́вка.

rear-view mirror зе́ркало за́днего ви́да.

reason *n.* **1,** (cause; motive) причи́на. *By reason of*, по причи́не (+ *gen.*). *For the reason that...*, по той причи́не, что... *For some reason or other*, по той и́ли ино́й причи́не. *For no reason whatsoever*, безо вся́кой причи́ны. **2,** (justification) основа́ние: *with good reason*, с по́лным основа́нием. **3,** (ability to think) ра́зум; рассу́док. **4,** (common sense; sanity) рассу́док: *devoid of reason*, лишён рассу́дка. —*v.i.* **1,** (think logically) рассужда́ть. **2,** *fol. by with* (persuade) урезо́нивать. —*v.t.* [*usu.* **reason out**] проду́мывать. —**bring to reason,** образу́мить; урезо́нить; наводи́ть на ум. —**listen to reason,** прислу́шиваться к го́лосу рассу́дка. —**stand to reason,** само́ собо́й разуме́ться. —**within reason,** разу́мный: *any offer within reason*, вся́кое разу́мное предложе́ние.

reasonable *adj.* **1,** (amenable to reason) разу́мный; рассуди́тельный; благоразу́мный. **2,** (fair) разу́мный: *a reasonable offer*, разу́мное предложе́ние. **3,** (not excessive) досту́пный: *reasonable prices*, досту́пные це́ны. **4,** (not expensive) недорого́й.

reasonably *adv.* **1,** (sensibly) разу́мно. **2,** (fairly) дово́льно: *reasonably good*, дово́льно хорошо́. *Reasonably certain*, бо́лее и́ли ме́нее уве́рен.

reasoning *n.* рассужде́ние. *Sound reasoning*, здра́вое рассужде́ние. *Line of reasoning*, аргумента́ция.

reassess *v.t.* переоце́нивать; пересма́тривать. —**reassessment,** *n.* переоце́нка; пересмо́тр.

reassign *v.t.* назнача́ть (*or* переводи́ть) на другу́ю до́лжность.

reassure *v.t.* ободря́ть; обнадёживать. —**reassurance,** *n.* ободре́ние. —**reassuring,** *adj.* ободри́тельный; ободря́ющий; успокои́тельный.

rebandage *v.t.* перебинтова́ть.

rebate *n.* **1,** (discount) ски́дка. **2,** (refund) возвра́т.

rebel *v.i.* восстава́ть; бунтова́ть. —*n.* повста́нец; бунтовщи́к; мяте́жник. —*adj.* повста́нческий; мяте́жный: *rebel troops*, повста́нческие/мяте́жные войска́.

rebellion *n.* восста́ние; бунт; мяте́ж.

rebellious *adj.* **1,** (inclined to rebel) мяте́жный. **2,** (opposing any control) непоко́рный. —**rebelliousness,** *n.* непоко́рность.

rebirth *n.* возрожде́ние.

reborn *adj.* Be reborn, возрожда́ться.

rebound *v.i.* отска́кивать. —*n.* рикоше́т. *On the rebound*, рикоше́том.

rebuff *n.* отпо́р. —*v.t.* дать отпо́р (+ *dat.*).

rebuild *v.t.* перестра́ивать.

rebuke *n.* упрёк; вы́говор; замеча́ние; о́тповедь. —*v.t.* упрека́ть.

rebus *n.* ре́бус.

rebut *v.t.* опроверга́ть. —**rebuttal,** *n.* опроверже́ние.

recalcitrant *adj.* непоко́рный. —**recalcitrance,** *n.* непоко́рность.

recall *v.t.* **1,** (call back) отзыва́ть. **2,** (remember) по́мнить; вспо́мнить. **3,** (reminisce about) вспомина́ть. **4,** (bring back to mind) напомина́ть. —*n.* **1,** (summons to return) о́тзыв. **2,** (ability to remember) па́мять.

recant *v.t.* отрека́ться от. —*v.i.* (публи́чно) ка́яться.

recapitulate *v.t. & i.* сумми́ровать; резюми́ровать. —**recapitulation,** *n.* сумми́рование; резюме́.

recapture *v.t.* брать обра́тно; сно́ва захва́тывать; отбива́ть.

recast *v.t.* **1,** (remold) перелива́ть. **2,** (rework) переде́лывать.

recede *v.i.* **1,** (move back) отступа́ть: *recede into the background*, отступа́ть на за́дний план. **2,** (subside, as of floodwaters) убыва́ть; сбыва́ть; идти́ на у́быль. —**receding forehead,** пока́тый лоб.

receipt *n.* **1,** (act of receiving) получе́ние: *upon receipt of*, по получе́нии (+ *gen.*). *Acknowledge receipt of*, подтверди́ть получе́ние (+ *gen.*). **2,** (note acknowledging payment) распи́ска; квита́нция. **3,** *pl.* (proceeds; income) вы́ручка; поступле́ния. *Box-office receipts*, сбо́ры.

receivable *adj.* подлежа́щий упла́те.

receive v.t. **1,** (get; have inflicted on one) получа́ть: *receive permission,* получи́ть разреше́ние; *receive a blow,* получи́ть уда́р. **2,** (admit; greet) принима́ть: *receive guests,* принима́ть госте́й. **3,** (pick up, as a signal) принима́ть. **4,** (deal in, as stolen goods) укрыва́ть.

receiver n. **1,** (part of a telephone) тру́бка. **2,** (instrument for receiving signals) приёмник.

recent adj. **1,** (having just occurred) неда́вний: *recent trip/attempt,* неда́вняя пое́здка/попы́тка. **2,** (just past) после́дний: *in recent years,* в or за после́дние го́ды. *The events of recent weeks,* собы́тия после́дних неде́ль.

recently adv. неда́вно; в or за после́днее вре́мя. *Until recently,* до неда́внего вре́мени. —**as recently as,** ещё: *as recently as last year,* ещё в про́шлом году́.

receptacle n. **1,** (container) вмести́лище. **2,** bot. цветоло́же.

reception n. **1,** (social gathering; manner of being received) приём. **2,** radio; television приём. —**reception room,** приёмная.

receptionist n. секрета́рша (в приёмной).

receptive adj. восприи́мчивый. —**receptivity; receptiveness,** n. восприи́мчивость.

recess n. **1,** (short break between sessions) переры́в. *Parliament is in recess,* парла́мент распу́щен. **2,** (break between school terms) кани́кулы. **3,** (hollow place) углубле́ние. **4,** usu. pl. (inner place, as of the heart) тайни́к. —v.t. **1,** (set back into a recess) отодвига́ть наза́д. **2,** (adjourn) закрыва́ть. —v.i. де́лать переры́в.

recession n. спад.

recessive adj. рецесси́вный.

recharge v.t. перезаряжа́ть.

rechristen v.t. перекре́щивать.

recidivism n. рецидиви́зм. —**recidivist,** n. рециди́вист.

recipe n. реце́пт.

recipient n. получа́тель.

reciprocal adj. взаи́мный; обою́дный. —n., math. обра́тная величина́.

reciprocate v.t. отвеча́ть. *Reciprocate someone's feelings,* отвеча́ть на чьи́-нибудь чу́вства; отвеча́ть кому́-нибудь взаи́мностью. —v.i. отпла́чивать: *we would like to reciprocate somehow,* нам бы хоте́лось вам чём-то отплати́ть. —**reciprocating engine,** поршнево́й дви́гатель.

reciprocity n. взаи́мность; обою́дность.

recital n. **1,** (narration) изложе́ние. **2,** music конце́рт.

recitation n. **1,** (public reading) деклама́ция. **2,** (school exercise) отве́т (уро́ка).

recitative n., music речитати́в.

recite v.t. чита́ть; деклами́ровать. *Recite poetry/one's prayers/,* чита́ть стихи́/моли́твы. *Recite one's lesson,* отвеча́ть уро́к. —**reciter,** n. деклама́тор.

reckless adj. безрассу́дный. —**recklessly,** adv. безрассу́дно. —**recklessness,** n. безрассу́дство.

reckon v.t. **1,** (figure; compute) счита́ть; подсчи́тывать. **2,** (regard) счита́ть; рассма́тривать. **3,** colloq. (think; suppose) ду́мать; полага́ть. —**reckon on,** рассчи́тывать на. —**reckon with, 1,** (settle accounts with) распла́чиваться с. **2,** (take into account) счита́ться с.

reckoning n. расчёт; счёт. —**day of reckoning,** день (or час) распла́ты. —**dead reckoning,** счисле́ние пути́.

reclaim v.t. **1,** (claim back) тре́бовать обра́тно. **2,** (cultivate, as land) поднима́ть; осва́ивать.

reclamation n. мелиора́ция.

recline v.i. полулежа́ть.

recluse n. затво́рник; отше́льник.

recognition n. **1,** (identification) узнава́ние. *Beyond recognition,* до неузнава́емости. **2,** (acknowledgment; acclaim) призна́ние: *gain recognition,* получи́ть призна́ние. *In recognition of his services,* в знак призна́ния его́ заслу́г.

recognize v.t. **1,** (identify from previous knowledge) узнава́ть: *I hardly recognize you,* я едва́ узна́л(а) вас. **2,** (formally acknowledge) признава́ть: *recognize a new nation,* признава́ть но́вую страну́. **3,** (realize; be aware of) сознава́ть: *recognize the danger,* сознава́ть опа́сность. **4,** (give the floor to) предоставля́ть сло́во (+ dat.).

recoil v.i. **1,** (shrink back) отска́кивать; отпря́нуть; отшатну́ться. **2,** (of a firearm) отдава́ть; отка́тываться. —n. отда́ча; отка́т. —**recoilless,** adj. безотка́тный.

recollect v.t. & i. вспомина́ть; припомина́ть.

recollection n. **1,** (capacity to remember) па́мять: *within my recollection,* на мое́й па́мяти. *To the best of my recollection,* наско́лько я по́мню. **2,** (something remembered) воспомина́ние.

recommend v.t. рекомендова́ть: *can you recommend a good doctor?,* мо́жете ли вы порекомендова́ть мне хоро́шего врача́? *You were recommended to me by...,* вас мне рекомендова́л(а)... *That is not recommended,* э́то не рекоменду́ется.

recommendation n. рекоменда́ция. —**letter of recommendation,** рекоменда́тельное письмо́.

recompense v.t. вознагражда́ть; компенси́ровать. —n. вознагражде́ние; компенса́ция.

reconcile v.t. **1,** (restore to good terms; make content) мири́ть; примиря́ть. *Become reconciled to; reconcile oneself to,* мири́ться с; примиря́ться с. **2,** (adjust; resolve) ула́живать: *reconcile differences,* ула́живать разногла́сия. *Reconcile contradictions,* примиря́ть противоре́чия.

reconciliation n. **1,** (bringing or coming together) примире́ние. **2,** (adjustment, as of differences) ула́живание.

recondite adj. замыслова́тый; мудрёный.

recondition v.t. ремонти́ровать.

reconnaissance n. разве́дка; рекогносциро́вка. —adj. разве́дывательный.

reconnoiter also, **reconnoitre** v.t. разве́дывать; рекогносци́ровать. —v.i. вести́ разве́дку.

reconsider v.t. пересма́тривать. —**reconsideration,** n. пересмо́тр.

reconstruct v.t. **1,** (rebuild) перестра́ивать; реконструи́ровать. **2,** (put together from clues) восстана́вливать; воссоздава́ть. —**reconstruction,** n. перестро́йка; реконстру́кция.

reconvene v.i. сно́ва собира́ться.

recook v.t. перева́ривать.

record n. **1,** (written account) за́пись; учёт: *keep record of,* вести́ за́пись/учёт (+ gen.). **2,** (official account of proceedings) протоко́л. **3,** (recorded facts about someone) спи́сок: *work record,* трудово́й спи́сок. *Attendance record,* посеща́емость. *Criminal rec-*

ord, уголо́вное про́шлое; суди́мости. **4,** (best achievement) реко́рд: *break/set a record,* поби́ть/поста́вить реко́рд. **5,** (phonograph record) пласти́нка; граммпласти́нка. —*adj.* реко́рдный: *in record time,* с реко́рдным вре́менем; в реко́рдный срок. —*v.t.* **1,** (set down in writing; keep a record of) запи́сывать; регистри́ровать. **2,** (transcribe, as sound) запи́сывать на плёнку *or* на пласти́нку. *Record one's voice,* нагова́ривать пласти́нку. —**a matter of record,** неоспори́мый факт. —**off the record,** неофициа́льно; не для печа́ти. —**on the record,** официа́льно: *go on the record,* заяви́ть официа́льно. —**on record,** зарегистри́рованный: *the worst earthquake on record,* са́мое си́льное из когда́-либо зарегистри́рованных землетрясе́ний.

recorder *n.* **1,** (recording device) самопи́сец: *flight recorder,* бортово́й самопи́сец. *Tape recorder,* магнитофо́н. **2,** (person who takes notes or minutes) протоколи́ст.

record holder рекордсме́н; рекорди́ст.

recording *n.* **1,** (taking down) за́пись; запи́сывание. **2,** (entering) занесе́ние. **3,** (something on a record or tape) за́пись. *Sound recording,* звукоза́пись.

record player граммофо́н; прои́грыватель.

recount *v.t.* **1,** (relate) расска́зывать. **2,** (count again) пересчи́тывать. —*n.* пересчёт.

recoup *v.t.* оты́грывать. *Recoup one's losses,* оты́грываться.

recourse *n. Have recourse to,* прибега́ть к. *Have no other recourse but to..,* не име́ть никако́го друго́го вы́хода, кро́ме...

recover *v.t.* получа́ть обра́тно; возвраща́ть. —*v.i.* **1,** (regain one's health) выздора́вливать; оправля́ться; поправля́ться. **2,** (regain one's composure) овладе́ть собо́й.

re-cover *v.t.* перекрыва́ть.

recovery *n.* **1,** (getting back) возвраще́ние. **2,** (getting well) выздоровле́ние. *He is on the road to recovery,* у него́ де́ло идёт на попра́вку. —**recovery room,** послеоперацио́нная пала́та.

re-create *v.t.* воссоздава́ть; пересоздава́ть.

recreation *n.* развлече́ние.

recrimination *n.* взаи́мное обвине́ние.

recruit *v.t.* вербова́ть; набира́ть. —*n.* новобра́нец. —**recruiter,** *n.* вербо́вщик. —**recruiting; recruitment,** *n.* вербо́вка.

rectal *adj.* относя́щийся к прямо́й кишке́.

rectangle *n.* прямоуго́льник. —**rectangular,** *adj.* прямоуго́льный.

rectify *v.t.* исправля́ть. —**rectifiable,** *adj.* исправи́мый. —**rectification,** *n.* исправле́ние.

rectilinear *adj.* прямолине́йный.

rectitude *n.* пра́ведность.

rector *n.* **1,** (clergyman) прихо́дский свяще́нник. **2,** (university head) ре́ктор.

rectum *n.* пряма́я кишка́.

recumbent *adj.* лежа́чий; лежа́щий.

recuperate *v.i.* восстана́вливать си́лы; поправля́ться; выздора́вливать. —**recuperation,** *n.* выздоровле́ние.

recur *v.i.* возвраща́ться; повторя́ться; происходи́ть вновь. —**recurrence,** *n.* возвра́т; повторе́ние; рециди́в.

recurrent *adj.* повто́рный; повторя́ющийся; периоди́ческий.

recycle *v.t.* втори́чно испо́льзовать; возвраща́ть в оборо́т.

red *adj.* кра́сный: *red banner,* кра́сное зна́мя. *Red hair,* ры́жие во́лосы. *Turn red,* красне́ть. *Paint something red,* кра́сить что́-нибудь в кра́сный цвет. —*n.* **1,** (color) кра́сный цвет. *Red is my favorite color,* мой люби́мый цвет – кра́сный. **2,** *pl.* (communists) кра́сные. —**in the red, 1,** (showing a loss) с убы́тком. **2,** (in debt) в долгу́. —**paint the town red,** *colloq.* кути́ть; гуля́ть —**see red,** *colloq.* приходи́ть в я́рость.

red-blooded *adj.* полнокро́вный.

Red Cross Кра́сный Крест.

red deer благоро́дный оле́нь.

redden *v.t.* румя́нить. —*v.i.* красне́ть.

reddish *adj.* краснова́тый.

redeem *v.t.* **1,** (buy back; pay off) выкупа́ть. **2,** (cash in) реализова́ть. **3,** (rescue; liberate) избавля́ть. **4,** (make amends for) искупа́ть. *Redeem oneself,* оправда́ть себя́. —**redeemer,** *n.* избави́тель.

redemption *n.* **1,** (paying off) вы́куп. **2,** (deliverance) спасе́ние; избавле́ние.

redesign *v.t.* переконструи́ровать.

red-handed *adj.* с поли́чным: *catch red-handed,* пойма́ть с поли́чным.

redhead *n.* ры́жий. —**redheaded,** *adj.* ры́жий; рыжево́лосый.

red-hot *adj.* накалённый *or* раскалённый докрасна́; калёный.

redistribute *v.t.* перераспределя́ть; переделя́ть. —**redistribution,** *n.* перераспределе́ние; переде́л.

red lead (свинцо́вый) су́рик.

red light кра́сный свет. *Go through a red light,* проскочи́ть светофо́р.

redness *n.* краснота́. *Redness in one's cheeks,* румя́нец.

redo *v.t.* переде́лывать.

redolent *adj.* **1,** (fragrant) души́стый; благоуха́нный. **2,** *fol. by* **of** (smelling of) па́хнущий (+ *instr.*). —**redolence,** *n.* благоуха́ние.

redouble *v.t.* **1,** (double again) втори́чно удва́ивать. **2,** (increase greatly) удва́ивать; усугубля́ть.

redoubt *n.* **1,** (small defensive fortification) реду́т. **2,** (earthwork within a fortification) редю́ит.

redoubtable *adj.* **1,** (fearsome) гро́зный. **2,** (estimable) почте́нный.

redound *v.i. Redound to the credit of,* де́лать честь (+ *dat.*). *Redound to the advantage of,* благоприя́тствовать (+ *dat.*).

red pepper кра́сный пе́рец; стручко́вый пе́рец.

redpoll *n.* чечётка.

redress *v.t.* **1,** (set right, as a wrong) загла́живать (вину́). **2,** (restore, as a balance) восстана́вливать (равнове́сие). —*n.* возмеще́ние. *Demand redress,* тре́бовать возмеще́ния убы́тков.

redskin *n.* краснокожий.

redstart *n.* горихво́стка.

red tape волоки́та.

reduce *v.t.* **1,** (lessen) уменьша́ть; сокраща́ть. *Reduce to the minimum,* доводи́ть до ми́нимума. **2,** (lower, as a price) понижа́ть; снижа́ть. **3,** (put in a simpler form) своди́ть: *reduce to a simple formula,* своди́ть к просто́й фо́рмуле. *Reduce to a common denominator,* приводи́ть к о́бщему знамена́телю. **4,** (bring to an extreme state) *rendered by various verbs: reduce to dust,* обрати́ть в прах; *reduce to rubble,* превращáть в развáлины; *reduce to poverty*, доводи́ть до нищеты́; *reduce to naught*, своди́ть на нет *or* к нулю́. —*v.i.* убавля́ть в вéсе.

reduction *n.* **1,** (lessening) уменьшéние; сокращéние. **2,** (lowering) пониже́ние; сниже́ние. **3,** (discount) ски́дка. **4,** *math.* приведéние (к о́бщему знамéнателю). **5,** *in various technical senses* редýкция.

redundancy *n.* **1,** (state of being redundant) ненýжность. **2,** (redundant word or phrase) тавтоло́гия.

redundant *adj.* **1,** (superfluous) изли́шний; ли́шний. **2,** (wordy; verbose) многосло́вный. **3,** (needlessly repeating something) тавтологи́ческий.

reduplicate *v.t.* удвáивать. —**reduplication,** *n.* удвоéние.

redwood *n.* секвóйя.

reed *n.* **1,** (plant) тростни́к; кáмыш. **2,** (primitive musical instrument) свирéль. **3,** *music* (vibrating piece) язычóк. —*adj.* тростникóвый; камышóвый. —**reed instrument,** язычкóвый инструмéнт.

re-educate *v.t.* перевоспи́тывать. —**re-education,** *n.* перевоспитáние.

reedy *adj.* **1,** (full of reeds) тростникóвый. **2,** (of thin, sharp tone) тóнкий.

reef *n.* риф; подвóдный кáмень; подвóдная скалá.

reek *v.i.* воня́ть. —**reek of/with,** воня́ть (+ *instr.*); рази́ть; нести́ (*both impers.* with *instr.*). *He reeks of vodka*, от негó рази́т/несёт вóдкой.

reel *n.* **1,** (for thread, rope, etc.) катýшка. **2,** (for movie film) рóлик. **3,** (for fishing) катýшка. *Rod and reel*, ýдочка со спи́ннингом. —*v.t.* **1,** (wind) намáтывать. **2,** *fol. by* **in** (pull in, as a fish) выя́гивать. **3,** *fol. by* **off** (recite fluently) отбарабáнить. —*v.i.* **1,** (stagger) шатáться. **2,** (whirl) кружи́ться.

re-elect *v.t.* переизбирáть. —**re-election,** *n.* переизбрáние.

re-enlist *v.i.* поступáть на сверхсрóчную слýжбу.

re-enter *v.t.* снóва входи́ть в.

re-equip *v.t.* переоборýдовать.

re-establish *v.t.* восстанáвливать. —**re-establishment,** *n.* восстановлéние.

re-evaluate *v.t.* переоцéнивать.

re-examine *v.t.* **1,** (scrutinize again) снóва осмáтривать *or* рассмáтривать. **2,** (review; reconsider) пересмáтривать.

refashion *v.t.* преобразóвывать; перекрáивать.

refectory *n.* **1,** (in a school) столóвая. **2,** (in a monastery) трáпезная.

refer *v.t.* **1,** (send; direct) посылáть; отсылáть; направля́ть. *Refer a patient to a specialist*, направля́ть больнóго к специали́сту. **2,** (submit for consideration) передавáть. —*v.i.* [*usu.* **refer to**] **1,** (pertain to) относи́ться к. **2,** (allude to) ссылáться на. *To whom are you referring?*, когó вы имéете в видý? **3,** (consult, as a dictionary) обращáться к.

referee *n.* судья́. —*v.t.* & *i.* суди́ть.

reference *n.* **1,** (act of referring to or consulting) спрáвка: *for reference only*, тóлько для спрáвок. **2,** (allusion) ссы́лка; упоминáние. *Make reference to*, ссылáться на; упомина́ть. **3,** (note) ссы́лка: *cross-reference*, перекрёстная ссы́лка. **4,** (recommendation) óтзыв; рекомендáция. *Character reference*, характери́стика; аттестáция. —*adj.* спрáвочный: *reference material*, спрáвочный материáл. —**with reference to,** в связи́ с; в отношéнии (+*gen.*).

reference book спрáвочник.

reference point ориенти́р; ориентирóвочный пункт; тóчка отсчёта.

referendum *n.* референ́дум; всенарóдный опрóс.

refill *v.t.* снóва наполня́ть.

refine *v.t.* **1,** (purify) очищáть. *Refine oil*, перерабáтывать нефть. **2,** (polish, as one's manners) утончáть. **3,** (perfect) совершéнствовать.

refined *adj.* **1,** (purified) очи́щенный. **2,** (cultivated; polished) утончённый; изя́щный; изы́сканный.

refinement *n.* **1,** (elegance of manner) утончённость; изя́щество; изы́сканность. *Lack of refinement*, некультýрность. **2,** (small improvement) усовершéнствование.

refinery *n.* очисти́тельный завóд. *Oil refinery*, нефтеперегóнный завóд. *Sugar refinery*, сáхарный завóд.

reflect *v.t.* отражáть: *reflect light*, отражáть свет. *Reflect someone's views*, отражáть чьи-нибудь взгля́ды. —*v.i.* **1,** (be reflected) отражáться. **2,** (meditate) размышля́ть. **3,** *fol. by* **on** *or* **upon** (tend to discredit) бросáть тень (на). —**reflecting telescope,** зеркáльный телескóп; рефлéктор.

reflection *n.* **1,** (act of reflecting; image reflected) отраже́ние. **2,** (meditation) размышлéние. **3,** (something that discredits) тень.

reflective *adj.* **1,** (reflecting) отражáющий. **2,** (thoughtful) вдýмчивый.

reflector *n.* рефлéктор; отражáтель.

reflex *n.* рефлéкс. —*adj.* рефлектóрный: *reflex reaction*, рефлектóрная реáкция. —**reflex camera,** зеркáльный фотоаппарáт.

reflexive *adj.* возврáтный: *reflexive verb*, возврáтный глагóл.

reforge *v.t.* перекóвывать.

re-form *v.t.* **1,** (form again) вновь формировáть. **2,** *mil.* перестрáивать. —*v.i.*, *mil.* перестрáиваться.

reform *v.t.* **1,** (introduce changes in) реформи́ровать; преобразóвывать. **2,** (cause to mend one's ways) исправля́ть. —*v.i.* исправля́ться. —*n.* рефóрма; преобразовáние. *Land reform*, земéльная рефóрма. *Calendar/spelling reform*, рефóрма календаря́/правописáния.

reformation *n.* **1,** (change; reshaping) преобразовáние. **2,** *cap.*, *hist.* реформáция.

reformatory *n.* исправи́тельный дом; исправи́тельная колóния.

reformed *adj.* испрáвленный. —**Reformed Church,** реформáтская цéрковь.

reformer *n.* реформáтор; преобразовáтель.

reform school = **reformatory.**

refract *v.t.* преломля́ть. —**refracting,** *adj.* преломля́ющий. *Refracting telescope*, рефрáктор. —**refraction,** *n.* преломлéние; рефрáкция. —**refractor,** *n.* рефрáктор.

refractory *adj.* **1,** (obstinate) упря́мый; непокóрный. **2,** (heat-resistant) огнеупóрный.

refrain *v.i.* [*usu.* **refrain from**] воздéрживаться (от); удéрживаться (от). —*n.* припéв; рефрéн.

refresh *v.t.* освежáть. —**refresher course,** повтори́тельный курс; переподготóвка. —**refreshing,** *adj.* освежáющий; освежи́тельный.

refreshment *n.* **1,** (act of refreshing) освежéние. **2,** *pl.* (food, drink, etc.) угощéние.

refrigerate *v.t.* охлаждáть; заморáживать. —**re-**

frigeration, *n.* охлаждёние; замораживание. —**refrigerator,** *n.* холодильник.

refuel *v. t.* дозаправлять. —*v. i.* дозаправляться. *Without refueling,* без дозаправки.

refuge *n.* убёжище; приют; пристанище. *Take refuge in,* найти убёжище в.

refugee *n.* бёженец. *Refugee camp,* лагерь для бёженцев.

refund *v. t.* возвращать (дёньги). —*n.* возврат (дёнег).

refurbish *v. t.* обновлять; ремонтировать.

refusal *n.* отказ.

refuse[1] (ri-**fyooz**) *v. t.* **1,** *fol. by inf.* (decline to) отказываться (+ *inf.*). **2,** (decline to accept) отказываться от: *refuse help,* отказаться от помощи. **3,** (decline to give) отказывать: *refuse help to someone,* отказывать кому-нибудь в помощи. **4,** (turn down the request of) отказывать (+ *dat.*): *she refused him,* она ему отказала. —*v. i.* отказываться: *he flatly refused,* он отказался наотрёз.

refuse[2] (**ref**-yoos) *n.* мусор; сор; отбросы; хлам.

refute *v. t.* опровергать. —**refutation,** *n.* опровержёние.

regain *v. t.* возвращать; вернуть. *Regain consciousness,* приходить в сознание (*or* в себя); очнуться. *Regain one's composure,* овладёть собой. *Regain one's health,* восстанавливать своё здоровье. *Regain one's balance,* сбалансировать. *Regain one's eyesight,* прозрёть. *Regain the use of one's legs,* снова владёть ногами. *Regain the world championship title,* возвратить/вернуть себё звание чемпиона мира.

regal *adj.* **1,** (of a king) королёвский. **2,** *fig.* (magnificent; stately) царственный; царский.

regale *v. t.* угощать; потчевать.

regalia *n.pl.* регалии. *In full regalia,* во всех регалиях.

regard *v. t.* **1,** (contemplate) смотрёть на; разглядывать. **2,** (look upon; consider) считать; рассматривать. *I regard it as nonsense,* я считаю это ерундой. *I regard it as madness,* я рассматриваю это как безумие. *Regard someone highly,* быть высокого мнёния о. *Regard something with favor,* относиться к чему-нибудь благосклонно. **3,** (concern) касаться. *As regards...,* что касается (+ *gen.*).—*n.* **1,** (consideration; esteem) уважёние: *out of regard for,* из уважёния к. *Have no regard for others,* не считаться с другими. *Without regard to,* безотносительно к. *Have a high regard for,* быть высокого мнёния о. **2,** (attention) внимание: *pay no regard to,* не обращать (никакого) внимания на. **3,** *pl.* (greetings) привёт: *best regards,* сердёчный привёт. *Give one's regards to,* кланяться (+ *dat.*); передавать привёт (+ *dat.*). **4,** (relation; connection) отношёние: *in this regard,* в этом отношёнии. *You need not worry in that regard,* на этот счет можете быть спокойны. —*in/ with regard to,* в отношёнии (+ *gen.*); относительно; в связи с; что касается.

regarding *prep.* относительно; касающийся; по поводу.

regardless *adv., colloq.* невзирая ни на что. —**regardless of,** независимо от; вне зависимости от; невзирая на.

regatta *n.* регата.

regency *n.* рёгентство.

regenerate *v. t.* перерождать. —*v. i.* перерождаться.

regeneration *n.* **1,** (renewal) перерождёние. **2,** *mech.; biol.* регенерация. —**regenerative,** *adj.* регенеративный.

regent *n.* рёгент.

regicide *n.* цареубийство.

regime *n.* режим.

regimen *n.* режим.

regiment *n.* полк. —*v. t.* дисциплинировать. —**regimental,** *adj.* полковой. —**regimentation,** *n.* строгая дисциплина.

region *n.* мёстность; область; район. —**regional,** *adj.* областной; региональный.

register *n.* **1,** (record) вёдомость; регистр; реёстр. **2,** (book containing such a record) журнал; регистр; реёстр. *Guest register,* книга для посетителей. **3,** *music* (range) регистр. —*v. t.* **1,** (record; enroll) регистрировать. **2,** (indicate, as by a mechanical device) показывать. **3,** (show, as emotion) проявлять; обнаруживать. **4,** (insure delivery of, as a letter) посылать (письмо) заказным. *Registered letter,* заказное письмо. —*v. i.* **1,** (sign up) регистрироваться; отмечаться. **2,** (make an impression): *the name doesn't register with me,* это имя мне ничего не говорит. —**cash register,** касса.

registrar *n.* регистратор.

registration *n.* регистрация. —*adj.* регистрационный.

registry *n.* **1,** = **registration. 2,** (place of registration) регистратура.

regress *v. i.* регрессировать. —**regression,** *n.* регрёсс. —**regressive,** *adj.* регрессивный.

regret *v. t.* сожалёть; жалёть: *regret one's decision,* сожалёть/жалёть о своем решёнии. —*n.* **1,** (troubled feeling) сожалёние. *I have no regrets,* я не сожалёю об этом. **2,** *pl.* (polite refusal) извинёния.

regretful *adj.* полный сожалёния. *Be regretful,* сожалёть.

regrettable *adj.* досадный: *regrettable incident,* досадный случай. —**regrettably,** *adv.* к сожалёнию.

regroup *v. t.* перегруппировывать. —*v. i.* перегруппировываться. —**regrouping,** *n.* перегруппировка.

regular *adj.* **1,** (recurring at set times) регулярный. **2,** (even, as one's pulse or heartbeat) правильный. **3,** (steady) постоянный: *regular customer,* постоянный клиёнт. **4,** (customary) обычный: *one's regular place,* чье-нибудь обычное мёсто. **5,** (regularly scheduled) очередной. **6,** (symmetrical, as of features) правильный. **7,** *gram.* правильный: *regular verb,* правильный глагол. **8,** *mil.* регулярный; кадровый. **9,** *colloq.* (out-and-out) настоящий. **10,** *slang* (likable) славный: *a regular guy,* славный малый. —**regularity,** *n.* регулярность. —**regularly,** *adv.* регулярно.

regulate *v. t.* регулировать.

regulation *n.* **1,** (act of regulating) регулирование. **2,** (rule) правило. **3,** *pl.* (set of rules) правила; устав. —*adj.* уставный; установленный.

regulator *n.* регулятор.

regurgitate *v. t.* изрыгать; отрыгивать.

rehabilitate *v. t.* реабилитировать. —**rehabilitation,** *n.* реабилитация.

rehash *n.* повторёние; перепёв.

rehearsal *n.* репетиция. *Dress rehearsal,* генеральная репетиция.

rehearse *v.t. & i.* репетировать.

reheat *v.t.* разогревать; подогревать.

reign *n.* **1,** (period of rule) царствование. *During the reign of Peter I,* в царствование Петра Первого; при Петре Первом. **2,** (rule) власть: *reign of law,* власть закона. —*v.i.* **1,** (of a monarch) царствовать. **2,** *fig.* (of silence, etc.) царить; воцаряться. —**reigning,** *adj.* царствующий.

reimburse *v.t.* возмещать. —**reimbursement,** *n.* возмещение.

rein *n.* **1,** (for a horse) повод (*pl.* поводья); вожжа (*pl.* вожжи). **2,** *The reins of government,* бразды правления. —*v.t.* [*usu.* **rein in**] осаживать (лошадь). —**give free rein to,** давать волю (+ *dat.*). —**keep a tight rein on,** держать в узде.

reincarnate *v.t.* перевоплощать. —**reincarnation,** *n.* перевоплощение.

reindeer *n.* северный олень. —**reindeer moss,** олений мох; ягель.

reinforce *v.t.* усиливать; укреплять; подкреплять. —**reinforced concrete,** железобетон.

reinforcement *n.* **1,** (strengthening) усиление; укрепление; подкрепление. **2,** *pl., mil.* подкрепления.

reinstate *v.t.* восстанавливать в (прежней) должности. —**reinstatement,** *n.* восстановление в должности.

reinsure *v.t.* перестраховывать. —**reinsurance,** *n.* перестраховка.

reinvest *v.t.* снова вкладывать (деньги).

reissue *v.t.* переиздавать. —*n.* переиздание.

reiterate *v.t.* повторять; твердить. —**reiteration,** *n.* повторение.

reject *v.t.* **1,** (turn down) отклонять; отвергать. **2,** (discard because of defects) браковать. —*n.* брак; бракованное изделие. —**rejection,** *n.* отказ; отклонение.

rejoice *v.i.* радоваться; ликовать. —**rejoicing,** *n.* ликование.

rejoin *v.t.* **1,** (meet again after an interval) присоединяться к. **2,** (come back to) возвращаться к. **3,** (resume membership in) снова присоединяться к.

rejoinder *n.* возражение; реплика.

rejuvenate *v.t.* омолаживать. —**rejuvenation,** *n.* омоложение.

relapse *v.i.* [*usu.* **relapse into**] (снова) впадать в; (снова) предаваться (+ *dat.*). —*n.* рецидив —**relapsing fever,** возвратный тиф.

relate *v.t.* **1,** (narrate) рассказывать. **2,** (connect) связывать. —*v.i.* [*usu.* **relate to**] относиться к.

related *adj.* **1,** (connected) связанный. **2,** (kindred) родственный. *Be related to,* быть в родстве с; быть сродни (+ *dat.*). *How is he related to you?,* кем он вам приходится?

relation *n.* **1,** (connection) отношение; связь. **2,** (relative; kin) родственник. **3,** *pl.* (dealings; intercourse) отношения: *friendly/international/diplomatic relations,* дружеские/международные/дипломатические отношения. *Sexual relations,* половая связь. —**in relation to,** в отношении (+ *gen.*).

relationship *n.* **1,** (connection) отношение; связь. **2,** (kinship) родство. **3,** (liaison) связь.

relative *n.* родственник: *distant relative,* дальний родственник. —*adj.* **1,** (comparative; not absolute)

относительный: *relative quiet,* относительная тишина. *Everything is relative,* всё относительно. **2,** *fol. by* **to** (pertaining; relevant) относящийся (к). **3,** *gram.* относительный: *relative pronoun,* относительное местоимение.

relatively *adv.* относительно: *relatively happy,* относительно счастлив. *Relatively speaking,* вообще говоря.

relativity *n.* относительность: *theory of relativity,* теория относительности.

relax *v.t.* **1,** (make less tight or strict) ослаблять. *Relax the muscles,* расслаблять мышцы. **2,** *fig.* (make less tense) разряжать. —*v.i.* **1,** (become less tight) ослабевать. **2,** (take one's ease) отдыхать.

relaxation *n.* **1,** (making less tight or strict) ослабление. **2,** (making less tense) разрядка: *relaxation of tension,* разрядка напряжённости. **3,** (rest) отдых. **4,** (recreation) развлечение.

relaxed *adj.* непринуждённый.

re-lay *v.t.* перекладывать. *Re-lay a floor,* перестилать пол.

relay *n.* **1,** (shift) смена. *Work in relays,* работать посменно. **2,** (race) эстафета. **3,** *electricity* реле. —*v.t.* передавать. —**relay race,** эстафета; эстафетный бег.

relearn *v.t.* переучиваться (+ *dat.*).

release *v.t.* **1,** (let out; set free) выпускать; освобождать: *release from prison,* выпускать/освобождать из тюрьмы. *Release a bird from a cage,* выпускать *or* отпускать птицу из клетки. **2,** (let go of) отпускать; пускать. **3,** (let loose against a target) выпускать; пускать: *release bombs,* выпускать бомбы; *release an arrow,* пустить стрелу из лука. **4,** (disengage, as a brake) отпускать (тормоз); (cause to snap, as a shutter) спускать (затвор). **5,** (relieve, as from an obligation) освобождать. **6,** (allow to be known or published) выпускать. —*n.* **1,** (act of releasing) освобождение. **2,** (something issued or produced) выпуск.

relegate *v.t.* **1,** (consign) отсылать. *Relegate to the background,* отодвигать на задний план. **2,** (refer; delegate) передавать.

relent *v.i.* смягчаться.

relentless *adj.* неотступный: *relentless pursuit,* неотступное преследование. —**relentlessness,** *n.* неотступность.

relevance *n.* **1,** (relation) отношение (к делу). **2,** (timeliness) актуальность.

relevant *adj.* **1,** (pertinent) относящийся к делу. **2,** (timely) актуальный.

reliable *adj.* **1,** (of a person) надёжный. **2,** (of information, a source, etc.) достоверный. —**reliability,** *n.* надёжность; достоверность.

reliance *n.* **1,** (dependence) зависимость. *Place one's reliance on,* надеяться на. **2,** (trust) доверие. **3,** (something relied on) надежда; опора.

reliant *adj. Be reliant on,* полагаться на; рассчитывать на.

relic *n.* **1,** (ancient object) реликт. **2,** (memento of the past) реликвия: *relics of the past,* реликвии прошлого. **3,** (object of religious worship) реликвия.

relief *n.* **1,** (easing of pain or anxiety) облегчение. *Sigh with relief,* вздохнуть с облегчением (*or* облегчённо). **2,** (replacement) смена. **3,** (emergency aid) помощь. **4,** (financial assistance) пособие. **5,** (raised decoration) рельеф. *In relief*, рельефно. —**relief map,** рельефная карта.

relieve *v.t.* **1,** (alleviate) облегчать: *relieve pain*, облегчать боль. *Relieve boredom*, развеять скуку. *Relieve the monotony*, вносить разнообразие. **2,** (reduce, as tension or pressure) ослаблять. **3,** (free from anxiety) успокаивать. *Feel relieved*, облегчаться. **4,** (free, as from a burden) освобождать. **5,** (furnish aid to) оказывать помощь (+ *dat.*). **6,** (remove; release) смещать (с должности); снимать (с работы); отстранять; освобождать (от должности). **7,** (replace) сменять. —**relieve oneself,** "облегчаться".

religion *n.* религия. *Freedom of religion*, свобода религии.

religiosity *n.* религиозность.

religious *adj.* религиозный: *religious man/custom*, религиозный человек/обычай. *Religious persecution*, преследование религии.

religiously *adv.* свято: *observe one's diet religiously*, свято соблюдать диету.

relinquish *v.t.* **1,** (give up) отказываться от: *relinquish one's rights*, отказываться от своих прав. *Relinquish one's seat/place to someone*, уступить место (+ *dat.*). **2,** (let go) *relinquish one's hold on*, выпускать из рук.

relish *n.* **1,** (enjoyment; zest) смак. **2,** (condiment) приправа. —*v.t.* наслаждаться; смаковать. *I don't relish the prospect*, перспектива мне не улыбается.

relive *v.t.* снова переживать.

reload *v.t.* **1,** (transfer to another vehicle) перегружать. **2,** (load again, as a vehicle) снова грузить. **3,** (refill, as a camera or gun) перезаряжать.

relocate *v.t.* перемещать; переселять. —*v.i.* переселяться.

reluctance *n.* неохота; нежелание. —**reluctant,** *adj.* неохотный. —**reluctantly,** *adv.* неохотно; с неохотой; нехотя.

rely *v.i.* [*usu.* **rely on** *or* **upon**] полагаться на.

remain *v.i.* оставаться: *remain at home*, оставаться дома. *Nothing remained*, ничего не осталось. *Remain silent*, хранить молчание. *He remained faithful to his principles*, он остался верен своим принципам.

remainder *n.* остаток.

remaining *adj.* остальной.

remains *n.pl.* **1,** (remnants) остатки. **2,** (dead body) останки; прах. *Mortal remains*, бренные останки.

remake *v.t.* переделывать.

remand *v.t.* возвращать: *remand to custody*, возвращать под стражу.

remark *n.* замечание. —*v.t.* замечать: *he remarked to me that...*, он заметил мне, что... —*v.i.* [*usu.* **remark on**] (comment on) делать замечание (о).

remarkable *adj.* замечательный; удивительный. —**remarkably,** *adv.* удивительно.

remarry *v.i.* вступать в новый брак.

rematch *n.* матч-реванш.

remeasure *v.t.* перемеривать.

remediable *adj.* исправимый.

remedial *adj.* коррективный: *remedial reading*, коррективное чтение.

remedy *n.* средство: *remedy for a cough*, средство от кашля. —*v.t.* **1,** (cure) вылечивать. **2,** (correct) исправлять.

remember *v.t.* **1,** (recall) помнить: *what do you re-*member *about him?*, что вы помните о нём? *Remember what I told you*, запомните то, что я вам сказал(а). *I can't remember his name*, я не могу вспомнить его имени. **2,** (mention in sending regards) кланяться: *remember me to your sister*, кланяйтесь вашей сестре. —*v.i.* помнить: *I don't remember*, я не помню. *I'll remember*, я буду помнить. *Try to remember*, постарайтесь вспомнить.

remembrance *n.* **1,** (memory) память: *in remembrance of*, в память (+ *gen.*). **2,** (memento) сувенир: *a remembrance of our trip*, сувенир от нашей поездки.

remind *v.t.* напоминать: *remind someone about a promise*, напомнить кому-нибудь об обещании. *He reminds me of my brother*, он напоминает мне моего брата. —**which reminds me,** а кстати...

reminder *n.* напоминание: *after repeated reminders*, после неоднократных напоминаний.

reminisce *v.i.* вспоминать. —**reminiscence,** *n.* воспоминание. —**reminiscent,** *adj.* напоминающий: *be reminiscent of*, напоминать.

remiss *adj.* небрежный; невнимательный. *Be remiss in one's duties*, пренебрегать своими обязанностями.

remission *n.* **1,** (pardon) отпущение: *remission of sins*, отпущение грехов. **2,** *med.* ремиссия.

remit *v.t.* **1,** (send, as payment) переводить; пересылать. **2,** (pardon; forgive) прощать; отпускать. **3,** (slacken) ослаблять. **4,** (refrain from exacting) прощать; снимать.

remittance *n.* перевод (денег); пересылка.

remnant *n.* **1,** (remainder) остаток. **2,** (vestige) пережиток. **3,** (leftover piece of cloth) остаток.

remodel *v.t.* переделывать.

remold *v.t.* перековывать.

remonstrance *n.* увещание.

remonstrate *v.i.* **1,** *fol. by* **with** (exhort) увещевать. **2,** *fol. by* **against** (protest; object) возражать; протестовать (против).

remorse *n.* раскаяние. —**remorseful,** *adj.* полный раскаяния. —**remorseless,** *adj.* безжалостный.

remote *adj.* отдалённый: *remote place/past/resemblance*, отдалённое место/прошлое/сходство. *The chances of that are remote*, шансы на это незначительные. —**not the remotest,** ни малейшего (понятия, представления, *etc.*). —**remote control,** дистанционное управление.

remoteness *n.* отдалённость.

remount *v.t. & i.* снова сесть (на лошадь).

removable *adj.* съёмный; сменяемый.

removal *n.* **1,** (taking out; taking away) удаление. **2,** (taking down) съёмка. **3,** (moving to another place) перемещение. **4,** (dismissal, as from office) смещение (с должности).

remove *v.t.* **1,** (take away) убирать; удалять. **2,** (take out; draw out) вынимать. **3,** (take out; extract) удалять. **4,** (take off; take down) снимать. **5,** (move to another place) перемещать. **6,** (eradicate, as a stain) выводить. **7,** (eliminate; get rid of) устранять. **8,** (dismiss, as from office) смещать (с должности). —*v.i.* переезжать; переселяться. —**cousin twice removed,** брат (сестра) во втором колене.

remunerate *v.t.* вознаграждать. —**remuneration,** *n.* вознаграждение. —**remunerative,** *adj.* выгодный; доходный.

renaissance *n.* **1,** (rebirth) возрождéние. **2,** *cap.,* *hist.* Возрождéние.

renal *adj.* пóчечный.

rename *v.t.* переименовáть. *The city was renamed in honor of Lenin,* гóроду бы́ло присвóено и́мя Лéнина.

renascence *n.* возрождéние. —**renascent,** *adj.* возрождáющийся.

rend *v.t.* рвать; разрывáть; раздирáть. *Rend the air,* сотрясáть вóздух.

render *v.t.* **1,** (give; provide) окáзывать: *render assistance,* окáзывать содéйствие. *Render homage,* окáзывать *or* воздавáть пóчести. *For services rendered,* за услýги. **2,** (submit, as a bill) предъявля́ть. **3,** (hand down, as a verdict) выноси́ть (пригово́р). **4,** (cause to be or become) *rendered by various verbs: render harmless,* обезврéживать; *render lifeless,* обескрóвливать. **5,** (translate) переводи́ть. **6,** (depict) изобража́ть. **7,** (perform) исполня́ть. **8,** (melt, as fat) топи́ть.

rendezvous *n.* **1,** (meeting) свидáние. **2,** (meeting place) мéсто свидáния. —*v.i.* встречáться.

rendition *n.* **1,** (performance) исполнéние. **2,** (translation) перевóд.

renegade *n.* отщепéнец; ренегáт.

renege *v.i.* **1,** *fol. by* **on** (go back on) нарушáть; не сдéрживать. **2,** *cards* (revoke) дéлать ренóнс. —*n., cards* ренóнс.

renew *v.t.* **1,** (resume; extend) возобновля́ть. **2,** (make new again) обновля́ть. —**renewal,** *n.* возобновлéние; обновлéние.

rennet *n.* сычýг.

rennin *n.* сычýжный фермéнт; сычýжина.

renounce *v.t.* отрекáться от; откáзываться от.

renovate *v.t.* обновля́ть; ремонти́ровать. —**renovation,** *n.* обновлéние; ремóнт.

renown *n.* слáва; извéстность. —**renowned,** *adj.* знамени́тый; прослáвленный.

rent *n.* **1,** (payment for lodgings) кварти́рная плáта. *Pay the rent,* плати́ть за кварти́ру. *How much rent do you pay?,* скóлько у вас кварти́рная плáта? **2,** *econ.* рéнта. —*v.t.* **1,** (obtain the use of, as an apartment) снимáть; брать внаём; (a car, equipment, etc.) брать напрокáт. **2,** (give the use of, as an apartment) сдавáть; давáть внаём; (a car, equipment, etc.) давáть напрокáт. —**for rent,** сдаётся внаём.

rental *n.* **1,** (of an apartment) арéнда; (of a car, equipment, etc.) прокáт. **2,** (money paid for use) арéндная плáта; плáта за прокáт.

renter *n.* арендáтор.

renumber *v.t.* перенумеровáть.

renunciation *n.* отречéние; откáз.

reoccur *v.i.* повторя́ться.

reopen *v.t.* **1,** вновь открывáть: *reopen the discussion,* вновь открывáть дискýссию. *Reopen old wounds,* береди́ть стáрые рáны. —*v.i.* вновь открывáться.

reorder *v.t.* **1,** (order again) снóва закáзывать. **2,** (restructure) перестрáивать. —*v.i.* сдéлать повтóрный закáз. —*n.* повтóрный закáз.

reorganize *v.t.* реорганизовáть; перестрáивать; переустрáивать; преобразóвывать. —**reorganization,** *n.* реорганизáция; перестрóйка; переустрóйство; преобразовáние.

repaint *v.t.* перекрáшивать.

repair *v.t.* чини́ть; исправля́ть; ремонти́ровать. *Repair the damage,* исправля́ть повреждéние. —*v.i.*

(go) направля́ться. —*n.* **1,** (act of repairing) ремóнт; почи́нка. *Closed for repairs,* закры́то на ремóнт. **2,** (working condition) испрáвность: *in good repair,* в испрáвности. —*adj.* ремóнтный: *repair shop,* ремóнтная мастерскáя.

repairable *adj.* исправи́мый. *Is it repairable?,* мóжно э́то испрáвить?

repairman *n.* мáстер: *TV repairman,* мáстер по ремóнту телеви́зоров.

reparable *adj.* исправи́мый.

reparations *n.pl.* репарáции.

repast *n.* едá.

repatriate *v.t.* репатрии́ровать. —*n.* репатриáнт. —**repatriation,** *n.* репатриáция.

repay *v.t.* **1,** (pay off, as a debt, loan, etc.) возвращáть; отдавáть; выплáчивать. **2,** (return a favor on the part of) отплáчивать (+ *dat.*): *how can I ever repay you?,* как я могý отплати́ть вам?

repayment *n.* **1,** (of money) вы́плата: *repayment of a loan,* вы́плата зáйма. **2,** (returning a favor or ill turn) отплáта.

repeal *v.t.* отменя́ть; аннули́ровать. —*n.* отмéна; аннули́рование.

repeat *v.t.* повторя́ть. *Repeat oneself/itself,* повторя́ться. —*n.* повторéние. —*adj.* повтóрный: *repeat order,* повтóрный закáз.

repeated *adj.* неоднокрáтный; многокрáтный. —**repeatedly,** *adv.* неоднокрáтно; многокрáтно.

repeater *n.* **1,** (pupil not promoted) второгóдник. **2,** (person more than once in jail) рецидиви́ст.

repeating *adj.* (of a firearm) магази́нный. —**repeating decimal,** периоди́ческая дробь.

repel *v.t.* **1,** (ward off) отражáть; отбивáть. **2,** (arouse repulsion in) оттáлкивать.

repellent *adj.* оттáлкивающий. —*n. Insect repellent,* срéдство от насекóмых.

repent *v.t. & i.* раскáиваться (в); кáяться (в). —**repentance,** *n.* раскáяние; покая́ние.

repentant *adj.* **1,** (feeling repentance) кáющийся: *repentant sinner,* кáющийся грéшник. **2,** (showing repentance) покая́нный: *repentant look,* покая́нный вид.

repercussion *n., usu. pl.* послéдствия.

repertoire *n.* репертуáр.

repertory *n.* **1,** (repertoire) репертуáр. **2,** (repository) храни́лище. —*adj.* репертуáрный.

repetition *n.* повторéние.

repetitious *adj.* повторя́ющийся. *Become repetitious,* начáть повторя́ться. *Also,* **repetitive.**

rephrase *v.t.* перефрази́ровать.

replace *v.t.* **1,** (put back) класть *or* стáвить обрáтно. **2,** (find a substitute for) заменя́ть: *replace old furniture,* замени́ть стáрую мéбель. *Replace a window pane,* постáвить нóвое стеклó. *He will be hard to replace,* трýдно бýдет егó замени́ть. **3,** (take the place of) заменя́ть; сменя́ть; вытесня́ть. *There is no one to replace him,* нéкому егó замени́ть. *A replaced B as prime minister,* А смени́л Б на постý премьéр-мини́стра. *Electricity replaced gas as a means of illumination,* электри́чество замени́ло/вы́теснило газ как срéдство освещéния.

replaceable *adj.* замени́мый.

replacement *n.* **1,** (act of replacing; one who replaces) замéна. **2,** *mil.* пополнéние; *pl.* пополнéния.

replay *v.t.* переи́грывать.

replenish *v.t.* пополня́ть; обновля́ть. —**replenishment**, *n.* пополне́ние; обновле́ние.

replete *adj.* изобилующий: *be replete with,* изобиловать (+ *instr.*).

replica *n.* ко́пия.

reply *v.t. & i.* отвеча́ть: *reply to an invitation,* отвеча́ть на приглаше́ние. —*n.* отве́т. *In reply to,* в отве́т на.

report *n.* **1,** (formal account) докла́д; отчёт. **2,** (message; communication) сообще́ние. **3,** (assessment) о́тзыв: *a favorable report,* благоприя́тный о́тзыв. **4,** (rumor) слух; молва́. —*v.t.* **1,** (convey; relate) сообща́ть (о): *report the latest news,* сообща́ть после́дние изве́стия. *Report an incident to the police,* сообща́ть о происше́ствии в мили́цию. **2,** (denounce to a person in authority) доноси́ть на. —*v.i.* **1,** (give a report) докла́дывать: *report on the situation,* докла́дывать обстано́вку. **2,** (present oneself; appear) явля́ться: *report for work,* явля́ться на рабо́ту.

report card та́бель (успева́емости).

reportedly *adv.* по слу́хам.

reporter *n.* репортёр.

repose *n.* **1,** (rest) о́тдых; отдохнове́ние. **2,** (tranquillity) поко́й; споко́йствие. —*v.t.* (place, as trust) возлага́ть. —*v.i.* **1,** (lie at rest) лежа́ть. **2,** (rest; relax) отдыха́ть. **3,** (rest in death) поко́иться.

repository *n.* храни́лище.

reprehensible *adj.* предосуди́тельный.

represent *v.t.* **1,** (symbolize; stand for) представля́ть; изобража́ть. *This figure represents good and this one evil,* э́та фигу́ра представля́ет добро́, а э́та — зло. *Phonetic symbols represent sounds,* фонети́ческие зна́ки изобража́ют зву́ки. **2,** (serve as the agent or representative of) представля́ть. **3,** (be; constitute) представля́ть (собо́й). *Represent nothing new,* не представля́ть собо́й ничего́ но́вого. —**represent oneself as,** изобража́ть из себя́ (+ *acc.*); выдава́ть себя́ за.

representation *n.* **1,** (being represented) представи́тельство: *proportional representation,* пропорциона́льное представи́тельство. **2,** (picture; image) изображе́ние. **3,** (formal statement or protest) представле́ние: *make representations to,* де́лать представле́ния (+ *dat.*).

representative *n.* представи́тель. —*adj.* **1,** (based on the principle of representation) представи́тельный. **2,** (typical) характе́рный. —**House of Representatives,** пала́та представи́телей.

repress *v.t.* подавля́ть; сде́рживать.

repression *n.* **1,** (suppression) подавле́ние. **2,** (practice of repressing) репре́ссия. *Political repression,* полити́ческие репре́ссии.

repressive *adj.* репресси́вный.

reprieve *n.* отсро́чка приведе́ния в исполне́ние (сме́ртного) пригово́ра.

reprimand *n.* вы́говор. —*v.t.* де́лать вы́говор (+ *dat.*).

reprint *v.t.* перепеча́тывать. —*n.* перепеча́тка; о́ттиск.

reprisal *n., often pl.* отве́тная ме́ра: *economic reprisals,* отве́тные экономи́ческие ме́ры.

reprise *n.* репри́за.

reproach *v.t.* упрека́ть; укоря́ть. —*n.* упрёк; уко́р. *Beyond reproach,* безупре́чный. —**reproachful,** *adj.* укори́зненный.

reprobate *n.* распу́тник. —*adj.* распу́тный.

reprobation *n.* порица́ние; осужде́ние.

reproduce *v.t.* воспроизводи́ть: *reproduce a picture,* воспроизводи́ть карти́ну. —*v.i.* размножа́ться: *reproduce by cellular division,* размножа́ться кле́точным деле́нием.

reproduction *n.* **1,** (act of reproducing) воспроизведе́ние. **2,** (copy; facsimile) репроду́кция. **3,** (propagation) размноже́ние.

reproductive *adj.* воспроизводи́тельный. *Reproductive organs,* о́рганы размноже́ния.

reproof *n.* вы́говор; замеча́ние; упрёк; отпо́ведь.

reprove *v.t.* упрека́ть; сде́лать вы́говор *or* замеча́ние (+ *dat.*).

reptile *n.* пресмыка́ющееся.

republic *n.* респу́блика.

republican *n.* республика́нец. —*adj.* республика́нский.

republish *v.t.* переиздава́ть. —**republication,** *n.* переизда́ние.

repudiate *v.t.* **1,** (renounce; disavow) отрека́ться от; отка́зываться от. **2,** (reject as untrue) отрица́ть. **3,** (reject with disapproval) отверга́ть.

repudiation *n.* **1,** (disavowal) отрече́ние; отка́з. **2,** (rejection; rebuff) отпо́р.

repugnance *n.* отвраще́ние.

repugnant *adj.* отта́лкивающий; отврати́тельный. *Be repugnant to,* отта́лкивать.

repulse *v.t.* **1,** (repel) отража́ть; отбива́ть. **2,** (rebuff) дать отпо́р (+ *dat.*). —*n.* отпо́р.

repulsion *n.* **1,** (repulsing) отраже́ние. **2,** (repugnance) отвраще́ние.

repulsive *adj.* отта́лкивающий; отврати́тельный.

repurchase *v.t.* перекупа́ть.

reputable *adj.* соли́дный; по́льзующийся хоро́шей репута́цией.

reputation *n.* репута́ция.

repute *n.* репута́ция.

reputed *adj.* предполага́емый. —**be reputed to be,** слыть (+ *instr.*): *he is reputed to be an expert,* он слывёт знатоко́м.

request *n.* про́сьба. *At the request of,* по про́сьбе (+ *gen.*). —*v.t.* проси́ть: *request permission,* проси́ть разреше́ния. —**on/by request,** по про́сьбе; по тре́бованию.

requiem *n.* панихи́да; ре́квием.

require *v.t.* тре́бовать: *require constant care,* тре́бовать постоя́нного ухо́да.

required *adj.* **1,** (needed; necessary) потре́бный. **2,** (compulsory, as of a subject) обяза́тельный. **3,** *fol. by to* (obliged) обя́зан (+ *inf.*).

requirement *n.* **1,** (condition; prerequisite) тре́бование: *meet the requirements,* отвеча́ть тре́бованиям. **2,** (need) потре́бность.

requisite *adj.* необходи́мый; потре́бный.

requisition *v.t.* реквизи́ровать. —*n.* тре́бование; зая́вка.

requital *n.* взаи́мность: *without requital,* без взаи́мности.

requite *v.t.* **1,** (return) отпла́чивать. *Requite someone's love,* отвеча́ть кому́-нибудь взаи́мностью. **2,** (avenge) вымеща́ть (оби́ду).

reread *v.t.* перечи́тывать.

resale *n.* перепрода́жа.

rescind *v.t.* отменя́ть; аннули́ровать. —**rescission,** *n.* отме́на; аннули́рование.

rescue *v.t.* спаса́ть; избавля́ть. —*n.* спасе́ние. *Come to the rescue of,* приходи́ть на по́мощь (+ *dat.*). —*adj.* спаса́тельный: *rescue operations,* спаса́тельные опера́ции; *rescue party,* спаса́тельная кома́нда.

rescuer *n.* спаси́тель.

research *n.* иссле́дование. —*adj.* иссле́довательский: *research work,* иссле́довательская рабо́та. —*v.t.* иссле́довать. —**researcher,** *n.* иссле́дователь.

resection *n., med.* резе́кция.

resell *v.t.* перепродава́ть.

resemblance *n.* схо́дство.

resemble *v.t.* быть похо́жим на: *he resembles his father,* он похо́ж на отца́.

resent *v.t.* обижа́ться на; негодова́ть на. —**resentful,** *adj.* оби́женный. —**resentment,** *n.* оби́да.

reservation *n.* **1,** (limiting condition) огово́рка: *without reservation,* без огово́рок; безогово́рочно. **2,** (advance order) бро́ня: *I have a reservation,* у меня́ бро́ня. *Make a reservation,* брони́ровать ме́сто; сде́лать предвари́тельный зака́з. **3,** (reserve for Indians) резерва́ция.

reserve *v.t.* **1,** (set aside) откла́дывать: *reserve one copy for me,* отложи́те оди́н экземпля́р для меня́. *Reserve a book in the library,* откла́дывать кни́гу в библиоте́ке. *These seats are reserved for tourists,* э́ти места́ предназна́чены для тури́стов. **2,** (secure in advance) брони́ровать; зака́зывать. *Reserve a room in a hotel,* брони́ровать но́мер в гости́нице. *Reserve a table for two,* заказа́ть стол на двои́х. **3,** (retain for oneself, as a right) сохраня́ть *or* оставля́ть за собо́й. **4,** (defer) откла́дывать. *Reserve judgment,* воздержа́ться от сужде́ния. —*n.* **1,** (something kept for future use) запа́с; резе́рв. *Hold in reserve,* держа́ть про запа́с. **2,** (reservation of public land) запове́дник: *forest reserve,* лесно́й запове́дник. **3,** (qualification; reservation) огово́рка: *without reserve,* без огово́рок. **4,** (reticence) сде́ржанность. **5,** *often pl., mil.* запа́с; резе́рв. **6,** *finance* резе́рвный фонд. **7,** *sports* запасно́й игро́к. —*adj.* запасно́й. *Reserve officer,* офице́р запа́са.

reserved *adj.* **1,** (secured in advance) заброни́рованный. *Reserved seat,* нумеро́ванное ме́сто. **2,** (reticent) сде́ржанный.

reservist *n.* резерви́ст; запасно́й.

reservoir *n.* водохрани́лище; резервуа́р.

reset *v.t.* **1,** *med.* вправля́ть. **2,** *printing* перебира́ть.

resettle *v.t.* переселя́ть. —*v.i.* переселя́ться. —**resettlement,** *n.* переселе́ние.

reshoot *v.t.* переснима́ть.

reshuffle *v.t.* перетасо́вывать. —*n.* перетасо́вка. *Cabinet reshuffle,* перемеще́ния в кабине́те.

reside *v.i.* прожива́ть; жить.

residence *n.* **1,** (act of residing) прожива́ние. *Residence permit,* пропи́ска. **2,** (dwelling place) местожи́тельство; местопребыва́ние; резиде́нция.

resident *n.* жи́тель. —**residential,** *adj.* жило́й: *residential area,* жило́й райо́н.

residue *n.* оста́ток. —**residual,** *adj.* оста́точный.

resign *v.i.* **1,** (give up one's office or position) уходи́ть *or* выходи́ть в отста́вку. **2,** *chess* сдава́ться. —*v.t.* отка́зываться от (до́лжности). —**resign oneself to;**

become resigned to, покоря́ться (+ *dat.*); мири́ться с.

resignation *n.* **1,** (act of resigning) отста́вка: *submit one's resignation,* подава́ть в отста́вку. **2,** (being resigned to something) смире́ние.

resilient *adj.* упру́гий. —**resilience,** *n.* упру́гость.

resin *n.* смола́. —**resinous,** *adj.* смоли́стый.

resist *v.t.* **1,** (try to stop) сопротивля́ться: *resist the invaders,* сопротивля́ться захва́тчикам. *Resist someone's advances,* отверга́ть чьи-нибудь уха́живания. **2,** (withstand, as temptation) устоя́ть про́тив *or* пе́ред; удержа́ться от. *The offer is hard to resist,* от э́того предложе́ния тру́дно отказа́ться. **3,** (restrain oneself) выде́рживать: *I couldn't resist teasing him,* я не вы́держал (*or* я не мог удержа́ться от собла́зна), что́бы не подразни́ть его́. —*v.i.* сопротивля́ться; ока́зывать сопротивле́ние.

resistance *n.* **1,** (act of resisting) сопротивле́ние. *Resistance movement,* движе́ние сопротивле́ния. **2,** *med.* сопротивля́емость. —**follow the line of least resistance,** идти́ по ли́нии наиме́ньшего сопротивле́ния.

resistant *adj.* сто́йкий. *Heat-resistant,* теплосто́йкий. *Rust-resistant,* нержаве́ющий.

resolute *adj.* реши́тельный; твёрдый. —**resoluteness,** *n.* реши́тельность; реши́мость; твёрдость.

resolution *n.* **1,** (act of solving or resolving) разреше́ние. **2,** (formal expression of opinion) резолю́ция. **3,** (vow; pledge) заро́к.

resolve *v.t.* **1,** (decide) реша́ть; реша́ться. **2,** (express by resolution) постановля́ть. **3,** (solve; settle) разреша́ть. *Resolve doubts,* разреша́ть сомне́ния. —*n.* **1,** (determination) реши́мость. **2,** (decision; resolution) твёрдое реше́ние.

resonance *n.* резона́нс. —**resonant,** *adj.* зву́чный; гу́лкий.

resonator *n.* резона́тор.

resort *v.i.* [*usu.* **resort to**] прибега́ть к. —*n.* **1,** (vacation spot) куро́рт. **2,** (recourse) ресу́рс: *last resort,* после́дний ресу́рс. *As a last resort,* в кра́йнем слу́чае. *Have resort to,* прибега́ть к. *Without resort to,* не прибега́я к. —*adj.* куро́ртный: *resort area,* куро́ртный райо́н.

resound *v.i.* **1,** (sound; be heard) раздава́ться; резони́ровать. **2,** (be filled with the sound of) оглаша́ться (+ *instr.*).

resounding *adj.* **1,** (reverberating) зво́нкий; зву́чный; зы́чный; гу́лкий. **2,** (decisive) реши́тельный.

resource *n.* **1,** (source of help) ресу́рс. **2,** *pl.* (assets; wealth) ресу́рсы; бога́тства: *natural resources,* приро́дные ресу́рсы; есте́ственные бога́тства. *Pool one's resources,* объединя́ть ресу́рсы.

resourceful *adj.* нахо́дчивый. —**resourcefulness,** *n.* нахо́дчивость.

respect *v.t.* уважа́ть. —*n.* **1,** (esteem) уваже́ние. **2,** *pl.* (expressions of esteem) почте́ние: *pay one's respects to,* (за)свиде́тельствовать почте́ние (+ *dat.*). *Pay one's last respects to,* отдава́ть после́дний долг (+ *dat.*). **3,** (aspect) отноше́ние: *in many respects,* во мно́гих отноше́ниях. —**in/with respect to,** в отноше́нии (+ *gen.*).

respectable *adj.* **1,** (proper; presentable) прили́чный; респекта́бельный. **2,** (fairly good or large) прили́чный; поря́дочный. —**respectability,** *n.* респекта́бельность.

respected *adj.* уважа́емый.

respectful *adj.* почти́тельный; уважи́тельный.

respectfully *adv.* почти́тельно. —**respectfully yours,** с почте́нием.

respecting *prep.* относи́тельно; по отноше́нию к.

respective *adj.* свой: *in their respective places,* ка́ждый на своём ме́сте.

respectively *adv.* соотве́тственно.

respiration *n.* дыха́ние. —**respirator,** *n.* респира́тор. —**respiratory,** *adj.* дыха́тельный.

respire *v.i.* & *t.* дыша́ть.

respite *n.* переды́шка. *Without respite,* без переды́шки.

resplendent *adj.* блиста́тельный. —**resplendence,** *n.* блеск.

respond *v.i.* [*usu.* **respond to**] отвеча́ть (на); отзыва́ться (на); откли́каться (на). *Respond to treatment,* поддава́ться лече́нию.

response *n.* **1,** (answer) отве́т. **2,** (reaction) о́тклик.

responsibility *n.* **1,** (accountability) отве́тственность. *Position of responsibility,* отве́тственный пост. **2,** (duty) обя́занность.

responsible *adj.* **1,** (accountable) отве́тственный. *Be responsible for,* отвеча́ть за; нести́ отве́тственность за. **2,** (being the cause of): *the person responsible for a crime,* вино́вник преступле́ния. *He is responsible for my being here,* благодаря́ ему́ я здесь. **3,** (reliable) надёжный. **4,** (entailing great responsibility) отве́тственный.

responsive *adj.* отзы́вчивый.

rest *n.* **1,** (relaxation) о́тдых. **2,** (peace and quiet) поко́й. **3,** (absence of motion) поко́й: *at rest,* в поко́е. *Come to rest,* сади́ться. **4,** *music* па́уза. **5,** (the remainder) оста́ток; остально́е. *The rest of the time,* остально́е вре́мя. **6,** (the remaining ones) остальны́е. —*v.i.* **1,** (relax) отдыха́ть. **2,** (lean; be supported) опира́ться. **3,** (fall, as of blame, a duty, etc.) лежа́ть. **4,** *fol. by* **upon** (be based upon) осно́вываться (на). —*v.t.* **1,** (place) класть; ста́вить. **2,** (lean) опира́ть. **3,** (allow to rest) дать о́тдохну́ть (+ *dat.*). —**eternal rest,** ве́чный поко́й. *Go to one's eternal rest,* засну́ть ве́чным сном. —**lay to rest,** хорони́ть. —**may he rest in peace,** мир пра́ху его́. —**put to rest,** рассе́ивать (сомне́ния). —**rest!** *(mil. command),* во́льно!

restate *v.t.* вновь заяви́ть.

restaurant *n.* рестора́н.

restful *adj.* споко́йный. *Restful color,* споко́йный цвет.

rest home дом о́тдыха.

restitution *n.* **1,** (restoration) восстановле́ние. **2,** (reimbursement) возмеще́ние убы́тков. *Make restitution,* возмеща́ть убы́тки.

restive *adj.* **1,** (restless) беспоко́йный; непосе́дливый. **2,** (balky, as of a horse) норови́стый.

restless *adj.* беспоко́йный; непосе́дливый. —**restlessness,** *n.* беспоко́йство; непосе́дливость.

restoration *n.* **1,** (bringing back) восстановле́ние. **2,** (repair; rebuilding; restoring of a monarchy) реставра́ция.

restore *v.t.* **1,** (bring back; re-establish) восстана́вливать: *restore order,* восстанови́ть поря́док. *Be restored to health,* восстанови́ть своё здоро́вье. *The king was restored to the throne,* коро́ль был возвращён на престо́л. **2,** (bring back to its original state) реставри́ровать. **3,** (return; give back) возвраща́ть.

restrain *v.t.* сде́рживать; уде́рживать; обу́здывать.

restraint *n.* **1,** (act of restraining) обузда́ние. **2,** (limitation) ограниче́ние: *wage restraints,* ограниче́ния зарабо́тной пла́ты. **3,** (reserve; moderation) сде́ржанность.

restrict *v.t.* ограни́чивать. *Restricted area,* запре́тная зо́на. —**restriction,** *n.* ограниче́ние. —**restrictive,** *adj.* ограничи́тельный.

rest room туале́т; убо́рная.

result *n.* результа́т; сле́дствие. *As a result (of),* в результа́те (+ *gen.*). —*v.i.* **1,** (happen) вытека́ть; происходи́ть; проистека́ть. **2,** *fol. by* **in** (lead to) приводи́ть (к); конча́ться (+ *instr.*).

resultant *adj.* вытека́ющий.

resume *v.t.* **1,** (start again after a break) возобновля́ть. **2,** (assume again) сно́ва принима́ть. *Resume one's seat,* сно́ва сесть. —*v.i.* возобновля́ться.

résumé *n.* резюме́.

resumption *n.* возобновле́ние.

resurgence *n.* возрожде́ние. —**resurgent,** *adj.* возрожда́ющийся.

resurrect *v.t.* воскреша́ть.

resurrection *n.* **1,** (returning to life) воскресе́ние. **2,** *fig.* (revival) возрожде́ние; воскреше́ние.

resuscitate *v.t.* оживля́ть; приводи́ть в созна́ние. —**resuscitation,** *n.* оживле́ние; реанима́ция.

retail *n.* ро́зничная прода́жа. —*adj.* ро́зничный: *retail store,* ро́зничный магази́н. —*adv.* в ро́зницу. —*v.t.* & *i.* продава́ть(ся) в ро́зницу. —**retailer,** *n.* ро́зничный торго́вец.

retain *v.t.* **1,** (keep possession of) уде́рживать: *retain power,* уде́рживать власть. **2,** (maintain; keep) сохраня́ть: *retain control over,* сохраня́ть контро́ль над. **3,** (hold within) заде́рживать: *retain moisture,* заде́рживать вла́гу. **4,** (remember) уде́рживать в па́мяти; запомина́ть. **5,** (hire) нанима́ть.

retainer *n.* **1,** (servant) приближённый. **2,** (fee) (предвари́тельный) гонора́р.

retaining wall подпо́рная сте́нка.

retake *v.t.* **1,** (recapture) отбива́ть; отвоёвывать. **2,** (photograph again) пересн́има́ть. **3,** (take again, as an examination) пересдава́ть; переде́рживать.

retaliate *v.i.* **1,** (repay in kind) отпла́чивать тем же. **2,** *mil.* наноси́ть отве́тный уда́р. —**retaliation,** *n.* отпла́та; отве́тный уда́р. —**retaliatory,** *adj.* отве́тный.

retard *v.t.* заде́рживать; замедля́ть; тормози́ть.

retardation *n.* **1,** (act of retarding) торможе́ние. **2,** (mental deficiency) у́мственная отста́лость *or* нера́звитость.

retarded *adj.* отста́лый.

retch *v.i.* рвать. —**retching,** *n.* рво́та.

retell *v.t.* переска́зывать.

retention *n.* **1,** (keeping for oneself) удержа́ние. **2,** (maintaining; keeping) сохране́ние. **3,** (holding within) задержа́ние. **4,** (ability to remember) па́мять.

retentive *adj.* це́пкий: *retentive memory,* це́пкая па́мять.

reticent *adj.* сде́ржанный; молчали́вый. —**reticence,** *n.* сде́ржанность; молчали́вость.

retie *v.t.* перевя́зывать.

retighten *v.t.* перетя́гивать.

retina *n.* сетча́тка; сетча́тая оболо́чка; рети́на. —**detached retina,** отсло́йка сетча́тки; отсло́йка сетча́той оболо́чки.

retinue *n.* сви́та.

retire *v.i.* **1,** (withdraw) удаля́ться. **2,** (give up one's work or career) вы́йти *or* уйти́ в отста́вку *or* на пе́нсию. **3,** (go to bed) ложи́ться спать. —*v.t.* **1,** (relieve of duty) увольня́ть в отста́вку. **2,** (withdraw from circulation) изыма́ть из обраще́ния. —**retired,** *adj.* на пе́нсии; *mil.* в отста́вке; отставно́й.

retiree *n.* пенсионе́р.

retirement *n.* **1,** (act of retiring) отста́вка. **2,** (seclusion) уедине́ние.

retiring *adj.* скро́мный; засте́нчивый.

retort *v.i.* (ре́зко) отве́тить. —*n.* **1,** (quick, sharp reply) возраже́ние; ре́плика. **2,** (vessel) ко́лба; ре́торта.

retouch *v.t.* **1,** (touch up) подправля́ть. **2,** *photog.* ретуши́ровать. —**retoucher,** *n.* ретушёр. —**retouching,** *n.* ре́тушь.

retrace *v.t.* **1,** (go back over, as one's steps) возвраща́ться по (свои́м следа́м). **2,** (trace the history of) просле́живать.

retract *v.t.* **1,** (pull in) втя́гивать. *Retract the landing gear,* убира́ть шасси́. **2,** (take back; disavow) отка́зываться от; брать наза́д. —**retraction,** *n.* опроверже́ние: *print a retraction,* печа́тать опроверже́ние.

retrain *v.t.* переу́чивать; переквалифици́ровать. —**retraining,** *n.* переквалифика́ция.

retreat *v.i.* отступа́ть: *retreat from danger,* отступа́ть пе́ред опа́сностью. *Retreat a few steps,* отступи́ть на не́сколько шаго́в. —*n.* **1,** (withdrawal) отступле́ние. *Beat a retreat,* бить отбо́й. **2,** (signal to retreat; bugle call at sunset) отбо́й. *Sound retreat,* дава́ть *or* бить отбо́й. **3,** (secluded place) прию́т; приста́нище.

retrench *v.i.* сокраща́ть расхо́ды; эконо́мить.

retrial *n.* повто́рное слу́шание де́ла.

retribution *n.* возме́здие.

retrieval *n.* возвраще́ние. *Retrieval of information,* по́иск информа́ции.

retrieve *v.t.* взять обра́тно. —**retriever,** *n.* охо́тничья соба́ка.

retroactive *adj.* име́ющий обра́тную си́лу (*or* обра́тное де́йствие). *Make retroactive to January 1,* счита́ть вступи́вшим в си́лу с пе́рвого января́.

retrograde *adj.* обра́тный: *retrograde motion,* обра́тное движе́ние.

retrogress *v.i.* регресси́ровать. —**retrogression,** *n.* регре́сс. —**retrogressive,** *adj.* регресси́вный.

retro-rocket *n.* тормозна́я раке́та.

retrospect *n., in* **in retrospect,** огля́дываясь наза́д.

retrospection *n.* ретроспе́кция. —**retrospective,** *adj.* ретроспекти́вный.

retry *v.t.* сно́ва слу́шать (де́ло); сно́ва суди́ть (обвиня́емого).

return *v.i.* возвраща́ться: *return home,* возвраща́ться домо́й. —*v.t.* **1,** (give back) отдава́ть; возвраща́ть. **2,** (put back) класть обра́тно. **3,** (reciprocate) отвеча́ть на: *return the enemy's fire,* отвеча́ть на ого́нь проти́вника. *Return a favor,* отвеча́ть услу́гой за услу́гу. *Return a visit,* нанести́ отве́тный визи́т; прийти́ с отве́тным визи́том. *Have him return my call,* пусть он мне позвони́т; попроси́те его́ мне позвони́ть. **4,** (yield, as a profit) приноси́ть. **5,** (render, as a verdict) выноси́ть. **6,** (elect) избира́ть; (re-elect) переизбира́ть. **7,** *sports* отбива́ть (мяч). —*n.* **1,** (act of returning) возвраще́ние; возвра́т. **2,** (profit; yield) дохо́д. **3,** (report, as on taxes) деклара́ция. **4,** *pl.* (election returns) результа́ты вы́боров. —*adj.* **1,** (in the opposite direction) обра́тный: *return ticket/address,* обра́тный биле́т/а́дрес. *By return mail,* с обра́тной по́чтой. **2,** (done or held in return) отве́тный: *return visit,* отве́тный визи́т. *Return match,* матч-рева́нш. —**in return,** взаме́н: *receive nothing in return,* ничего́ не получи́ть взаме́н. —**in return for,** в отве́т на; в обме́н на; в отпла́ту за. —**many happy returns of the day,** поздравля́ю вас с днём рожде́ния; жела́ю вам до́лгих лет жи́зни.

retype *v.t.* перепеча́тывать.

reunification *n.* воссоедине́ние.

reunion *n.* встре́ча; сбор.

reunite *v.t.* воссоединя́ть. —*v.i.* воссоединя́ться.

reupholster *v.t.* перебива́ть.

reuse *v.t.* повто́рно испо́льзовать.

revamp *v.t.* переде́лывать; перекра́ивать.

revanchism *n.* реванши́зм. —**revanchist,** *n.* реванши́ст. —*adj.* реванши́стский.

reveal *v.t.* **1,** (show; uncover; display) пока́зывать; обнару́живать: *reveal one's face/feelings,* пока́зывать/обнару́живать своё лицо́/свои́ чу́вства/. **2,** (disclose; divulge) раскрыва́ть. *Reveal a secret,* раскры́ть *or* откры́ть секре́т. —**revealing,** *adj.* показа́тельный; знамена́тельный.

reveille *n.* побу́дка; подъём; (у́тренняя) заря́.

revel *v.i.* **1,** (carouse) пирова́ть; кути́ть. **2,** *fol. by* **in** (delight in) наслажда́ться (+ *instr.*); упива́ться (+ *instr.*).

revelation *n.* **1,** (act of revealing) раскры́тие. **2,** (something revealed): *new revelations have come to light,* но́вые све́дения всплы́ли нару́жу. **3,** (striking discovery) открове́ние: *it was quite a revelation to me,* для меня́ э́то бы́ло настоя́щим открове́нием. **4,** *cap., Bib.* апока́липсис.

reveler *also,* **reveller** *n.* кути́ла; гуля́ка.

revelry *n.* весе́лье.

revenge *n.* **1,** (vengeance) месть; мще́ние. *In revenge for,* в отме́стку за. *Take revenge,* мстить. **2,** (reversal of a defeat) рева́нш: *gain revenge,* взять рева́нш. —*v.t.* мстить за; вымеща́ть.

revengeful *adj.* мсти́тельный.

revenue *n.* дохо́д.

reverberate *v.i.* отража́ться; отдава́ться. —**reverberation,** *n.* ревербера́ция.

revere *v.t.* почита́ть; благогове́ть.

reverence *n.* **1,** (veneration) почте́ние; благогове́ние. **2,** *cap.* (title) преподо́бие.

reverend *adj., usu. cap.* его́ преподо́бие (+ *name*).

reverent *adj.* почти́тельный; благогове́йный.

reverie *n.* мечта́ние; мечта́тельность. *Indulge in reverie,* предава́ться мечта́м.

reversal *n.* **1,** (complete change) измене́ние; переме́на. **2,** *law* отме́на; аннули́рование.

reverse *adj.* обра́тный: *in reverse order,* в обра́тном поря́дке. *Reverse gear,* за́дний ход. —*n.* **1,** *preceded by* **the** (opposite) обра́тное; противополо́жное. *Quite the reverse,* совсе́м наоборо́т. **2,** (setback) неуда́ча. **3,** (backward motion) за́дний ход: *put a car in reverse,* дать за́дний ход. —*v.t.* **1,** (turn about) повора́чивать кру́гом. **2,** (turn inside out) вывёртывать. **3,** (turn upside down) перевёртывать. **4,** (change completely) по́лностью изменя́ть: *reverse one's opinion,* по́лностью измени́ть своё мне́ние. **5,** (transpose) переставля́ть: *reverse two chapters in a book,* переставля́ть две главы́ в кни́ге. *Reverse the* *order of something,* изменить порядок чего-нибудь на обратный. **6,** *law* (set aside; overturn) отменять; аннулировать. **—reverse oneself,** давать задний ход.

reversible *adj.* **1,** (that can be reversed) обратимый. **2,** (worn on either side) двусторонний. **—reversibility,** *n.* обратимость.

reversion *n.* возвращение.

revert *v.i.* возвращаться: *revert to one's old habits,* возвращаться к старым привычкам.

revet *v.t.* облицовывать. **—revetment,** *n.* облицовка.

review *n.* **1,** (re-examination) рассмотрение; пересмотр. *The matter is under review,* дело сейчас рассматривается. **2,** (critique) рецензия; отзыв. *Book review,* рецензия на книгу. *Get rave reviews,* получить восторженные отзывы. **3,** (survey) обзор. **4,** (restudying, as of lessons) повторение. **5,** *mil.* смотр: *review of the troops,* смотр войскам. **6,** (journal) обозрение. **—***v.t.* **1,** (reconsider) рассматривать; пересматривать. **2,** (go over, as a lesson) повторять. **3,** (write a review of) рецензировать. **4,** *mil.* принимать (парад); производить смотр (войскам).

reviewer *n.* рецензент.

reviewing stand трибуна.

revile *v.t.* поносить; ругать.

revise *v.t.* **1,** (alter; change) пересматривать. **2,** (re-edit; rework) перерабатывать. *Revised edition,* исправленное издание.

revision *n.* **1,** (act of revising) пересмотр (программы); переработка (книги). **2,** (change; correction) изменение; поправка. **3,** (revised edition) переработка.

revisionism *n.* ревизионизм. **—revisionist,** *n.* ревизионист. **—***adj.* ревизионисткий.

revisit *v.t.* вновь посетить.

revitalize *v.t.* оживлять; обновлять.

revival *n.* **1,** (resuscitation) оживление. **2,** (restoration; renascence) оживление; возрождение. **3,** (restaging) возобновление (постановки).

revive *v.t.* **1,** (resuscitate) оживлять; приводить в себя *or* в сознание. **2,** (bring back; restore) возрождать; воскрешать. **3,** (bring back to mind) воскрешать в памяти. **4,** (produce or exhibit again) возобновлять. **—***v.i.* **1,** (regain consciousness) очнуться. **2,** (regain vigor) оживать: *the flowers revived in water,* цветы в воде ожили. **3,** (come back into existence) воскресать; возрождаться. *Hope revived,* надежда воскресла.

revocation *n.* отмена; аннулирование.

revoke *v.t.* отменять; аннулировать. **—***v.i., cards* делать ренонс. **—***n., cards* ренонс.

revolt *v.i.* (rebel) восставать. **—***v.t.* (disgust) вызывать отвращение у; отталкивать. **—***n.* восстание; мятеж. **—revolting,** *adj.* отвратительный; отталкивающий.

revolution *n.* **1,** (political upheaval; momentous change) революция. **2,** (rotation) оборот: *70 revolutions per minute,* семьдесят оборотов в минуту.

revolutionary *adj.* революционный. **—***n.* [*also,* **revolutionist**] революционер.

revolutionize *v.t.* революционизировать.

revolve *v.i.* вращаться; вертеться: *revolve around the sun,* вращаться/вертеться вокруг Солнца.

revolver *n.* револьвер.

revolving *adj.* вращающийся. **—revolving door,** вращающаяся дверь; вертушка.

revue *n.* обозрение; ревю.

revulsion *n.* отвращение.

reward *n.* награда. *Get one's just reward,* получить по заслугам. **—***v.t.* награждать; вознаграждать. *Our patience has been rewarded,* наше терпение вознаграждено. **—rewarding,** *adj.* выгодный; полезный.

rewind *v.t.* перематывать.

reword *v.t.* переделывать; переписывать; перефразировать.

rework *v.t.* перерабатывать.

rewrite *v.t.* **1,** (write again) переписывать. **2,** (revise) перерабатывать.

rhapsody *n.* рапсодия.

rhenium *n.* рений.

rheostat *n.* реостат.

rhetoric *n.* риторика. **—rhetorical,** *adj.* риторический.

rheumatic *adj.* ревматический. **—***n.* ревматик. **—rheumatic fever,** суставной ревматизм.

rheumatism *n.* ревматизм.

rhinestone *n.* искусственный бриллиант.

rhinoceros *n.* носорог.

rhizome *n.* корневище.

rhodium *n.* родий.

rhododendron *n.* рододендрон.

rhombic *adj.* ромбический.

rhomboid *n.* ромбоид.

rhombus *n.* ромб.

rhubarb *n.* ревень. **—***adj.* ревенный.

rhyme *n.* рифма. **—***v.t.* рифмовать. **—***v.i.* рифмоваться. **—without rhyme or reason,** ни с того ни с сего.

rhymer *n.* рифмач; рифмоплёт. *Also,* **rhymester.**

rhythm *n.* ритм. **—rhythmic; rhythmical,** *adj.* ритмический; ритмичный. **—rhythmics,** *n.* ритмика.

rib *n.* **1,** *anat.* ребро. *Poke someone in the ribs,* толкнуть кого-нибудь в бок. **2,** (raised stripe in cloth) рубчик. **—***v.t., colloq.* (tease) поддразнивать.

ribald *adj.* скабрёзный; неприличный. **—ribaldry,** *n.* скабрёзность.

ribbed *adj.* **1,** (lined with ridges) ребристый; рубчатый. **2,** (fluted; corrugated) рифлёный.

ribbon *n.* **1,** (ornamental band; military decoration) лента. **2,** *pl.* (shreds) клочья.

rice *n.* рис. **—***adj.* рисовый: *rice pudding,* рисовый пудинг.

rich *adj.* **1,** (wealthy) богатый: *rich widow/country,* богатая вдова/страна. *Rich in iron/vitamins,* богат железом/витаминами. *Get rich,* (раз)богатеть. **2,** (fertile) плодородный. **3,** (fattening) жирный. **4,** (deep; vivid; mellow) сочный; густой. **—***n., preceded by the* богатые; богачи.

riches *n.pl.* богатство.

richly *adv.* **1,** (lavishly) богато. **2,** (fully) вполне: *richly deserved,* вполне заслуженный.

richness *n.* **1,** (wealth) богатство. **2,** (fertility) плодородие. **3,** (vividness, as of sound or color) густота.

rick *n.* стог; скирд; скирда.

rickets *n.* рахит.

rickety *adj.* шаткий; расшатанный.

rickshaw *n.* рикша.

ricochet *n.* рикошет. **—***v.i.* рикошетировать.

rid *v.t.* избавля́ть; освобожда́ть; очища́ть. *Rid the house of mice,* очища́ть дом от мыше́й. —**get rid of,** отде́лываться от; избавля́ться от.

riddance *n.* избавле́ние. —**good riddance!,** ска́тертью доро́га!

riddle *n.* зага́дка. —*v.t.* **1,** (pierce with holes or bullets) изреше́чивать. **2,** *fig.* (affect every part of) проника́ть: *riddled with graft,* прони́кнут корру́пцией.

ride *v.i.* **1,** (be conveyed in a vehicle) е́хать; е́здить. **2,** (be borne on horseback) е́здить верхо́м. **3,** (handle, as of a car) идти́; ходи́ть: *the car rides well,* маши́на хорошо́ идёт/хо́дит. **4,** *fol. by* **on** (depend on) зави́сеть от. —*v.t.* **1,** (be transported by or on) е́хать на; е́здить на; ката́ться на: *ride a bicycle,* е́хать/е́здить на велосипе́де; *ride a horse,* е́здить верхо́м; *ride a camel,* е́здить верхо́м на верблю́де; *ride a merry-go-round,* ката́ться на карусе́ли; *ride the waves,* ката́ться на волна́х. **2,** *usu. passive* (beset) му́чить: *be ridden by doubts,* му́читься сомне́ниями. **3,** *colloq.* (tease) высме́ивать. **4,** *fol. by* **out** (weather, as a storm) вы́держивать. —*n.* **1,** (act of riding) езда́: *a ten-minute ride,* де́сять мину́т езды́. **2,** (leisurely drive) прогу́лка: *go for a ride,* е́здить на прогу́лку; ката́ться на маши́не; прокати́ться; прое́хаться. *Take for a ride,* ката́ть; прока́тывать. —**ride at anchor,** стоя́ть на я́коре. —**ride away; ride off,** отъезжа́ть.

rider *n.* **1,** (one who rides horseback) вса́дник; нае́здник; верхово́й; седо́к; ездо́к. **2,** (passenger) седо́к. **3,** (clause added to a document) дополне́ние; добавле́ние.

ridge *n.* **1,** (range of hills) гряда́; кряж. **2,** (strip of earth raised by a plow) гре́бень. **3,** (rib on material) ру́бчик. **4,** (apex of a roof) конёк; гре́бень.

ridicule *n.* осмея́ние; насме́шка. *Hold up to ridicule,* поднима́ть на́ смех. —*v.t.* насмеха́ться над; осме́ивать; высме́ивать.

ridiculous *adj.* смешно́й; неле́пый. *Don't be ridiculous!,* не глупи́те! —**ridiculously,** *adv.* до смешно́го.

riding *n.* езда́: *horseback riding,* верхова́я езда́. —**riding breeches,** рейту́зы; галифе́. —**riding habit,** амазо́нка. —**riding master,** бере́йтор. —**riding school,** мане́ж.

rife *adj.* **1,** (widespread) распространённый. **2,** *fol. by* **with** (full; abounding) по́лный; изоби́лующий. *The country is rife with rumors,* страна́ полна́ слу́хов (*or* слу́хами).

riffraff *n.* сброд; чернь; подо́нки.

rifle *n.* винто́вка. —*adj.* винто́вочный; руже́йный. —*v.t.* (force open) взла́мывать. —**rifleman,** *n.* стрело́к.

rift *n.* **1,** (crack) тре́щина; рассе́лина. **2,** *fig.* (disagreement) тре́щина; раско́л.

rig *v.t.* **1,** (fit out, as a ship) оснаща́ть. **2,** *fol. by* **up** (construct hastily) скола́чивать. **3,** (control fraudulently) манипули́ровать; фальсифици́ровать. —*n.* **1,** (arrangement of sails) осна́стка. **2,** (device) устано́вка: *drilling rig,* бурова́я устано́вка.

rigging *n.* такела́ж; осна́стка.

right *adj.* **1,** (correct) пра́вильный; пра́вый; ве́рный. *You are right,* вы пра́вы. *Quite right,* соверше́нно пра́вильно. **2,** (opposite of left) пра́вый. **3,** (the one wanted or needed) тот: *is this the right train?,* э́то тот по́езд? **4,** (appropriate) подходя́щий: *the right moment,* подходя́щий моме́нт. **5,** (designating the side

to be seen, as of cloth) пра́вый; лицево́й. *Right side up,* лицо́м кве́рху. **6,** *math.* (of an angle) прямо́й; (of a triangle) прямоуго́льный. —*adv.* **1,** (correctly) пра́вильно. **2,** (to the right) напра́во: *turn right,* поверну́ть напра́во. **3,** (immediately) сейча́с: *I'll be right back,* я сейча́с верну́сь. **4,** (directly) пря́мо. **5,** (exactly; just) как раз: *right in the middle,* как раз в середи́не. *He is standing right over there,* вот он там стои́т. **6,** *used for emphasis:* *come right in!,* войди́те, пожа́луйста! *Right to the end,* до са́мого конца́. *The bullet went right through him,* пу́ля прошла́ навы́лет. **7,** *colloq.* (very) о́чень; здо́рово: *right happy,* о́чень рад. *He was right angry,* он здо́рово рассерди́лся. —*n.* **1,** (that which is right) справедли́вость. *Tell right from wrong,* различа́ть ме́жду добро́м и злом. **2,** (just claim) пра́во: *civil rights,* гражда́нские права́. *Have the right to,* име́ть пра́во (+ *inf.*). **3,** (side opp. the left) пра́вая сторона́. *To the right; on the right,* напра́во; спра́ва. **2,** *polit.* [*usu.* **the right**] пра́вые. —*v.t.* **1,** (set straight) выпрямля́ть. **2,** (redress, as a wrong) исправля́ть (зло). —**all right,** *see* **all right.** —**be in one's right mind,** быть в своём (*or* в здра́вом) уме́. —**be in the right,** быть пра́вым. —**by rights,** по справедли́вости. —**in one's own right,** сам; по себе́. —**might makes right,** кто силён, тот и прав. —**put right,** нала́живать; поправля́ть. —**right after,** сра́зу по́сле (+ *gen.*). —**right away, 1,** (right now) сейча́с; сейча́с же. **2,** (right then) сра́зу. —**right itself, 1,** (regain a vertical position) встава́ть. **2,** (correct itself; return to normal) нала́живаться. —**right now, 1,** (at present) сейча́с. **2,** (immediately) сейча́с; сейча́с же. —**right you are!,** соверше́нно ве́рно!

righteous *adj.* пра́ведный. —**righteousness,** *n.* пра́ведность.

rightful *adj.* зако́нный. —**rightfully,** *adv.* по пра́ву.

right-hand *adj.* пра́вый. —**right-hand man,** пра́вая рука́.

right-handed *adj.* по́льзующийся пра́вой руко́й.

rightist *n. & adj.* пра́вый.

rightly *adv.* **1,** (correctly) пра́вильно. **2,** (fairly) справедли́во. **3,** (justly; deservedly) по пра́ву. —**and rightly so,** да и соверше́нно справедли́во.

rightness *n.* пра́вильность; правота́.

right of way пра́во прохо́да; пра́во прое́зда.

right-wing *adj.* пра́вый.

rigid *adj.* **1,** (stiff; not bending) жёсткий; негну́щийся; неги́бкий. **2,** *fig.* (strict; not deviating) жёсткий; стро́гий; неги́бкий.

rigidity *n.* **1,** (immobility) жёсткость. **2,** (inflexibility) непрекло́нность.

rigor *also,* **rigour** *n.* **1,** (strictness) стро́гость. **2,** (severity) суро́вость. **3,** *usu. pl.* (hardships) тя́готы.

rigor mortis тру́пное окочене́ние.

rigorous *adj.* **1,** (rigidly precise) стро́гий. **2,** (full of rigors; harsh) суро́вый.

rigour *n.* = **rigor.**

rile *v.t., colloq.* раздража́ть; досажда́ть.

rill *n.* ручеёк.

rim *n.* **1,** (edge) край: *the rim of a canyon,* край уще́лья. **2,** (of glasses) опра́ва. **3,** (outer part of a wheel) о́бод. **4,** *basketball* кольцо́ (корзи́ны).

rime *n.* **1,** = **rhyme. 2,** (hoarfrost) и́ней.

rind *n.* кожура́; ко́жица; ко́рка.

ring *n.* **1,** (circular band) кольцо́: *engagement ring,* обручáльное кольцó. *Diamond ring,* бриллиáнтовый пéрстень. *The rings of Saturn,* кóльца Сатýрна. **2,** (circle) круг; кольцó: *form a ring,* стать в круг. *Rings under one's eyes,* кругú под глазáми. *Blow smoke rings,* пускáть кóльца дыма. **3,** (arena, as for a circus) арéна; манéж. **4,** (boxing ring) ринг. **5,** (illegal band) шáйка; бáнда. *Smuggling ring,* шáйка контрабандúстов. **6,** (sound of a bell) звон; звонóк. *Give someone a ring,* позвонúть комý-нибудь. —*v.t.* **1,** (cause to sound, as a bell) звонúть в (кóлокол); давáть (звонóк). **2,** [*also, Brit.* **ring up**] (call on the telephone) звонúть (+ *dat.*). **3,** (encircle) окружáть. —*v.i.* **1,** (of a bell or telephone) звонúть. **2,** (ring a bell) давáть звонóк. **3,** *Ring in one's ears,* звучáть в ушáх. *My ears are ringing,* у меня звенúт в ушáх. —**ring a bell,** *see* bell. —**ring for,** вызывáть. —**ring in,** встречáть (Нóвый год). —**ring off,** дать отбóй. —**ring out,** раздавáться; грянуть: *a shot rang out,* раздáлся/грянул выстрел. —**ring true,** звучáть úскренне.

ringer *n.* **1,** (person who rings a bell) звонáрь. **2,** *slang* (person who greatly resembles another) двойнúк.

ring finger безымянный пáлец.

ringing *n.* звон. —*adj.* звóнкий.

ringleader *n.* зачúнщик; главáрь.

ringlet *n.* **1,** (small ring) колéчко. **2,** (of hair) завитóк; кудряшка.

ringworm *n.* стригýщий лишáй.

rink *n.* катóк.

rinse *v.t.* полоскáть. *Rinse out,* выполáскивать. —*n.* полоскáнйе.

riot *n.* **1,** (wild disturbance) бунт. **2,** *colloq.* (something extremely funny) умóра. **3,** *A riot of color,* всевозмóжные цветá. —*v.i.* бунтовáть. —**read the riot act to,** читáть нотáцию (+ *dat.*). —**run riot,** бýйствовать; буянить.

rioter *n.* бунтовщúк.

riotous *adj.* **1,** (rioting) бунтýющий. **2,** (boisterous) бýйный.

rip *v.t.* рвать; разрывáть. *Rip open,* распáрывать. —*v.i.* рвáться; разрывáться. —*n.* прорéха. —**rip into,** обрýшиваться на. —**rip off, 1,** (tear off) срывáть. **2,** *slang* (cheat) содрáть. —**rip up,** разрывáть.

ripcord *n.* вытяжнóй трос (парашюта).

ripe *adj.* спéлый; зрéлый. —**ripen,** *v.i.* спеть; зреть; поспевáть; созревáть. —**ripeness,** *n.* спéлость; зрéлость.

riposte *n.* **1,** *fencing* отвéтный выпад. **2,** (quick rejoinder) рéплика.

ripple *n.* **1,** (small wave) рябь; зыбь. *Ripples on the water,* кругú на водé. **2,** (slight sound): *ripple of laughter/applause,* небольшáя (*or* крáткая) вспышка аплодисмéнтов. —*v.t. & i.* рябúть.

ripsaw *n.* продóльная пилá.

rise *v.i.* **1,** (ascend) поднимáться. **2,** (stand up; get up) вставáть. **3,** (extend upward) возвышáться. **4,** (of the sun, moon, etc.) всходúть; восходúть; вставáть. **5,** (originate, as of a river) брать начáло. **6,** (increase, as of prices, temperature, etc.) поднимáться; повышáться; растú; возрастáть. **7,** [*usu.* **rise up**] (rebel) восставáть. **8,** (return to life) воскресáть. —*n.* **1,** (ascent) восхóд; подъём. **2,** (raised ground) возвышенность. **3,** (increase) повышéние; рост. **4,** (emergence, as of an empire) возвышéние. —**give rise to,** порождáть; вызывáть к жúзни. —**rise above,** быть выше (+ *gen.*).

rising *adj.* **1,** (ascending) восходящий. **2,** (growing, as of a generation) подрастáющий.

risk *n.* риск. *Take a risk,* идтú на риск. *At one's own risk,* на свой страх и риск. —*v.t.* рисковáть (+ *instr.* or *inf.*): *risk one's life,* рисковáть жúзнью; *risk being killed,* рисковáть погúбнуть.

risky *adj.* рискóванный.

risqué *adj.* рискóванный.

rite *n.* обряд.

ritual *n.* ритуáл. —*adj.* ритуáльный; обрядовый.

rival *n.* сопéрник. —*adj.* сопéрничающий. —*v.t.* сопéрничать с. —**rivalry,** *n.* сопéрничество.

river *n.* рекá. —*adj.* речнóй. —**riverbank; riverside,** *n.* речнóй бéрег; бéрег рекú. —**riverboat,** *n.* речнóе сýдно; речнóй парохóд.

rivet *n.* заклёпка. —*v.t.* **1,** (fasten with rivets) клепáть. **2,** *fig.* (fix rigidly in place) прикóвывать; пригвождáть: *riveted to the spot,* прикóванный/пригвождённый к мéсту. —**riveter,** *n.* клепáльщик.

rivulet *n.* ручéй.

roach *n.* **1,** (cockroach) таракáн. **2,** (fish) плотвá; тарáнь.

road *n.* **1,** (path; highway) дорóга. **2,** *fig.* (avenue) путь: *the road to success,* путь к успéху. —*adj.* дорóжный: *road surface,* дорóжное покрытие. —**be on the road, 1,** (be traveling) разъезжáть. **2,** (be on tour) гастролúровать. **3,** *sports* быть на выезде.

roadbed *n.* полотнó.

roadblock *n.* **1,** (barrier) заграждéние *or* засáда на дорóге. *Set up roadblocks,* перекрыть дорóги. **2,** *fig.* (obstacle) завáл на путú.

road map путевáя кáрта.

roadside *adj.* придорóжный.

road sign дорóжный знак.

roadstead *n., naut.* рейд.

roadway *n.* мостовáя.

roam *v.i. & t.* **1,** (walk around aimlessly) бродúть; блуждáть: *roam (about) the streets,* бродúть/блуждáть по ýлицам. **2,** (wander far and wide) странствовать; скитáться: *roam the world,* странствовать/скитáться по свéту *or* пó миру. —*n.* прогýлка: *a roam around town,* прогýлка по гóроду.

roan *adj.* чáлый.

roar *v.i.* ревéть. *Roar with laughter,* покатúться *or* покáтываться сó смеху. —*v.t.* выкрúкивать: *the crowd roared its approval,* толпá выкрúкивала одобрéние. —*n.* рёв.

roast *v.t.* жáрить. —*v.i.* жáриться. —*adj.* жáреный: *roast lamb,* жáреная барáнина. *Roast beef,* рóстбиф. —*n.* жаркóе.

roasted *adj.* жáреный: *roasted coffee,* жáреный кóфе. *Roasted nuts,* калёные орéхи.

roasting pan жарóвня.

rob *v.t.* **1,** (steal from) грáбить; обкрáдывать: *rob a house,* грáбить/обкрáдывать дом. *He was robbed of $200,* у негó укрáли двéсти дóлларов. **2,** (deprive of something) лишáть; отнимáть. *Rob someone of sleep,* отнимáть сон у когó-нибудь.

robber *n.* грабúтель. —**robbery,** *n.* грабёж; ограблéние.

robe *n.* **1,** (long, loose garment) мáнтия. **2,** (bathrobe) халáт. —*v.t.* облачáть.

robin *n.* малúновка; зарянка.

robot *n.* рóбот; автомáт.

robust *adj.* крéпкий; дюжий.

rock *n.* **1,** (large stone) ка́мень. **2,** (cliff) скала́. **3,** (reef) (подво́дная) скала́: *strike a rock,* наскочи́ть на скалу́. **4,** (substance) го́рная поро́да. —*v.t.* **1,** (move gently) кача́ть. *Rock to sleep,* ука́чивать; баю́кать. **2,** (shake violently) потряса́ть; сотряса́ть. —*v.i.* кача́ться. —**on the rocks, 1,** (in difficulty) на мели́. **2,** (of drinks) со льдом. —**rock crusher,** камнедроби́лка. —**rock crystal,** го́рный хруста́ль. —**rock salt,** ка́менная соль.

rocker *n.* **1,** (rocking chair) кача́лка. **2,** (runner of a rocking chair) по́лоз. —**off one's rocker,** *slang* сумасше́дший. *Are you off your rocker?,* ты с ума́ сошёл?

rocket *n.* **1,** (projectile; space vehicle) раке́та. **2,** (firework) шути́ха. —*adj.* раке́тный: *rocket launcher,* раке́тная устано́вка. —*v.i.* взмыва́ть. —**rocketry,** *n.* раке́тная те́хника.

rocking chair кача́лка.

rocking horse конь-кача́лка.

rocky *adj.* **1,** (stony) скали́стый. **2,** (shaky) ша́ткий.

rococo *n.* рококо́. —*adj.* в сти́ле рококо́.

rod *n.* **1,** (slender, straight stick) прут. **2,** (bar) сте́ржень. **3,** (whip; switch) ро́зга. —**curtain rod,** па́лка для гарди́н. —**fishing rod,** у́дочка; уди́лище. —**lightning rod,** громоотво́д; молниеотво́д. —**piston rod,** поршнево́й шток.

rodent *n.* грызу́н.

roe *n.* **1,** (fish eggs; hard roe) икра́. **2,** (milt; soft roe) моло́ки. **3,** (roe deer) косу́ля.

roebuck *n.* саме́ц косу́ли.

roe deer косу́ля.

rogue *n.* плут; жу́лик; моше́нник. —**roguish,** *adj.* жуликова́тый.

roil *v.t.* **1,** (make turbid) мути́ть. **2,** (annoy) раздража́ть.

role *n.* роль.

roll *v.t.* **1,** (cause to roll; move by rolling) кати́ть: *roll the ball,* кати́ть мяч. **2,** (flatten; shape, as dough) ката́ть; раска́тывать. **3,** (smooth the surface of, as a road) ука́тывать. **4,** (turn, as in bread crumbs) валя́ть (в сухаря́х). **5,** (make, as a cigarette) крути́ть; скру́чивать. **6,** (flatten into a sheet, as metal) прока́тывать; вальцева́ть. **7,** (throw, as dice) броса́ть. **8,** (move in circles, as one's eyes) враща́ть (глаза́ми). —*v.i.* **1,** (move by turning over and over) кати́ться. *The ball rolled under the bed,* мяч покати́лся (*or* закати́лся) под крова́ть. *He is rolling in money,* он купа́ется в зо́лоте. **2,** (toss, as of a ship) кача́ть. **3,** (sound, as of a drum) грохота́ть. —*n.* **1,** (anything rolled up) сви́ток; свёрток; руло́н; *(of film)* кату́шка. **2,** (small bread or biscuit) бу́лка; бу́лочка. **3,** (list of names) ве́домость; рее́стр. *Call the roll,* де́лать перекли́чку. **4,** (swaying of a ship) ка́чка. **5,** (sound of drums) гро́хот. —**roll down,** **1,** (move downward by rolling) ска́тывать. *Roll down one's sleeves,* рассучи́ть рука́в. **2,** (slide down) ска́тываться. —**roll out,** расстила́ть: *roll out the red carpet for,* расстила́ть кра́сный ковёр пе́ред. —**roll over,** перева́ливаться. —**roll up, 1,** (form into a roll) свёртывать; ска́тывать. **2,** (turn up, as one's sleeves) засу́чивать. **3,** (arrive by vehicle) подъезжа́ть.

roll call перекли́чка; пове́рка. —**roll-call vote,** поимённое голосова́ние.

roller *n.* **1,** (caster) колёсико; ро́лик. **2,** (heavy cylinder for smoothing roads) като́к. —**roller bearing,** ро́-
ликовый подши́пник. —**roller coaster,** америка́нские го́ры.

roller skate ро́лик; конёк на ро́ликах; ро́ликовый конёк. —**roller-skate,** *v.i.* ката́ться на ро́ликах.

rollick *v.i.* резви́ться; вози́ться.

rolling *n.* **1,** (moving by turning over and over) ката́ние. **2,** (swaying of a ship or vehicle) ка́чка. **3,** (flattening of metal) прока́тка. —*adj.* **1,** (moving on wheels or rollers) на колёсах. **2,** (pert. to the rolling of metal) прока́тный. **3,** (undulating) волни́стый. —**rolling mill,** прока́тный стан; вальцо́вая ме́льница. —**rolling pin,** ска́лка. —**rolling stock,** подвижно́й соста́в.

roly-poly *adj.* пу́хлый.

Roman *adj.* ри́мский. *Roman numerals,* ри́мские ци́фры. —*n.* ри́млянин.

Roman Catholic **1,** *used as a noun* като́лик. **2,** *used adjectively* ри́мско-католи́ческий.

romance *n.* **1,** (romantic tale) рома́н. **2,** (love affair) рома́н. **3,** (fascination; appeal) рома́нтика. **4,** *music* рома́нс. —*adj., cap.* рома́нский: *Romance languages,* рома́нские языки́.

Romanesque *adj.* рома́нский. —*n.* рома́нский стиль.

Romanian *also,* **Rumanian** *adj.* румы́нский. —*n.* **1,** (person) румы́н; румы́нка. **2,** (language) румы́нский язы́к.

romantic *adj.* романти́ческий; романти́чный. —**romanticism,** *n.* романти́зм; рома́нтика. —**romanticist,** *n.* рома́нтик. —**romanticize,** *v.t.* романтизи́ровать.

romp *v.i.* вози́ться; резви́ться.

rondo *n.* ро́ндо.

roof *n.* кры́ша. *Roof of the mouth,* нёбо. —**roofer,** *n.* кро́вельщик. —**roofing,** *n.* кро́вля.

rook *n.* **1,** (bird) грач. **2,** *chess* ладья́. —*v.t., colloq.* (cheat; swindle) обсчи́тывать.

rookery *n.* ле́жбище.

rookie *n.* новичо́к.

room *n.* **1,** (part of a house or building) ко́мната. *Three-room apartment,* трёхко́мнатная кварти́ра. **2,** (in a hotel) но́мер. **3,** (space) ме́сто: *make room for,* дава́ть ме́сто (+ *dat.*). *Take up too much room,* занима́ть сли́шком мно́го ме́ста. **4,** *pl.* (living quarters) помеще́ние. —*adj.* ко́мнатный: *room temperature,* ко́мнатная температу́ра. —*v.i.* жить. —**room and board,** стол и кварти́ра; пансио́н.

roomer *n.* пансионе́р.

roominess *n.* вмести́тельность.

rooming house пансио́н.

roommate *n.* това́рищ по ко́мнате; сожи́тель. *They are roommates,* они́ живу́т в одно́й ко́мнате.

roomy *adj.* просто́рный; вмести́тельный.

roost *n.* насе́ст. —*v.i.* сади́ться на насе́ст; сиде́ть на насе́сте. —**rule the roost,** верте́ть всем до́мом.

rooster *n.* пету́х.

root *n.* ко́рень: *root of a tree/tooth/word,* ко́рень де́рева/зу́ба/сло́ва. *Square root,* квадра́тный ко́рень. *Pull up by the roots,* вы́рвать (что́-нибудь) с ко́рнем. —*adj.* основно́й: *root cause,* основна́я причи́на. —*v.t.* **1,** (implant deeply) укореня́ть. *Be rooted in,* корени́ться в; (быть) укоренён в (+ *prepl.*). *Rooted to the spot,* прико́ванный к ме́сту. **2,** *fol. by* **out** (eliminate completely) вырыва́ть с ко́рнем; искореня́ть. —*v.i.* [*usu.* **root for**] боле́ть (за). —**root and**

branch, в ко́рне; коренны́м о́бразом. —**root of all evil,** ко́рень зла. —**take root,** укореня́ться.

rooter *n.* боле́льщик.

rootlet *n.* корешо́к.

rope *n.* верёвка; кана́т. *Jump rope,* скака́лка. —*adj.* верёвочный: *rope ladder,* верёвочная ле́стница. —*v.t.* **1,** (fasten by a rope) привя́зывать *or* свя́зывать верёвкой. **2,** (lasso) лови́ть арка́ном. **3,** *fol. by* **off** (fence off) оцепля́ть. **4,** *fol. by* **in** (entice) втя́гивать. —**know the ropes,** знать все ходы́ и вы́ходы. —**learn the ropes,** ориенти́роваться. —**reach the end of one's rope,** дойти́ до то́чки.

rorqual *n.* полоса́тик.

rosary *n.* чётки.

rose *n.* **1,** (flower) ро́за. **2,** (color) ро́зовый цвет. —*adj.* ро́зовый.

roseate *adj.* ро́зовый.

rosebud *n.* буто́н ро́зы.

rosebush *n.* ро́за; ро́зовый куст.

rose-colored *adj.* ро́зовый. —**see through rose-colored glasses,** смотре́ть сквозь ро́зовые очки́.

rosemary *n.* розмари́н.

rosette *n.* розе́тка.

rose water ро́зовая вода́.

rosewood *n.* ро́зовое де́рево; палиса́ндр. —*adj.* палиса́ндровый.

rosin *n.* канифо́ль.

roster *n.* **1,** (list of names) спи́сок; рее́стр. **2,** (duty schedule) расписа́ние дежу́рств; расписа́ние наря́дов.

rostrum *n.* трибу́на; ка́федра.

rosy *adj.* **1,** (rose-colored) ро́зовый; румя́ный. **2,** *fig.* (bright; cheerful; optimistic) ро́зовый; ра́дужный. *Paint a rosy picture of,* представля́ть в ро́зовом/ра́дужном све́те. —**rosy-cheeked,** *adj.* розовощёкий.

rot *v.i.* гнить; ту́хнуть. —*v.t.* гнои́ть —*n.* **1,** (decay) гние́ние. **2,** (anything rotten) гниль; прель. **3,** (plant disease) гниль. **4,** *slang* (nonsense) вздор.

rotary *adj.* враща́тельный; поворо́тный; ротацио́нный. —**rotary engine,** ротацио́нный дви́гатель. —**rotary press,** ротацио́нная (печа́тная) маши́на.

rotate *v.i.* **1,** (turn) враща́ться. **2,** (alternate) чередова́ться. —*v.t.* **1,** (cause to turn) враща́ть. **2,** (alternate) чередова́ть. *Rotate crops,* чередова́ть *or* сменя́ть культу́ры. **3,** (interchange, as tires) переставля́ть (ши́ны).

rotation *n.* **1,** (rotary motion) враще́ние. **2,** (alternation) чередова́ние. *In rotation,* по о́череди. —**rotation of crops,** севооборо́т. —**rotation of the seasons,** кругово́рот времён го́да.

rote *adj.* зазу́бренный. *Rote learning,* зубрёжка. —**by rote,** маши́нально. *Learn by rote,* зубри́ть.

rotor *n.* ро́тор.

rotten *adj.* **1,** (decayed) гнило́й; ту́хлый. **2,** *colloq.* (miserable) парши́вый; дрянно́й; отврати́тельный.

rottenness *n.* гни́лость.

rotund *adj.* **1,** (round; plump) пу́хлый. **2,** (sonorous) зву́чный.

rotunda *n.* рото́нда.

roué *n.* распу́тник.

rouge *n.* румя́на. —*v.t.* румя́нить.

rough *adj.* **1,** (not smooth; coarse) гру́бый; шерша́вый; шерохова́тый. *Rough skin/material,* гру́бая/шерша́вая ко́жа/ткань. *Rough surface,* шерохова́тая пове́рхность. *Rough road,* неро́вная доро́га.

Rough terrain, пересечённая ме́стность. **2,** (not gentle) гру́бый: *rough handling/treatment,* гру́бое обраще́ние. **3,** (preliminary, as of something written) черново́й. *Rough draft/copy,* черновик. **4,** (choppy, as of the sea) бу́рный. **5,** (approximate) гру́бый: *a rough estimate,* гру́бый подсчёт. *A rough idea of,* о́бщее представле́ние о. **6,** *colloq.* (difficult; unpleasant) тру́дный; тяжёлый; неприя́тный. —*adv.* гру́бо. —*v.t.* **1,** *fol. by* **up** (beat up) поби́ть. **2,** *fol. by* **out** (sketch) набра́сывать. —**in the rough,** вчерне́; на́черно. —**rough it,** жить без удо́бств.

roughage *n.* гру́бая пи́ща.

roughen *v.t.* де́лать гру́бым. —*v.i.* грубе́ть.

rough-hew *v.t.* обтёсывать. —**rough-hewn,** *adj.* гру́бо обтёсанный.

roughly *adv.* **1,** (not gently) гру́бо. **2,** (approximately) приблизи́тельно: *roughly forty miles,* приблизи́тельно со́рок миль. —**roughly speaking,** гру́бо говоря́.

roughneck *n.* буя́н.

roughness *n.* гру́бость; шерохова́тость.

roughshod *adj.* подко́ванный на шипы́. —**ride roughshod over,** попира́ть.

roulade *n.* **1,** *music* рула́да. **2,** (meat pie) пирожо́к.

roulette *n.* руле́тка. —**roulette wheel,** руле́тка.

round *adj.* кру́глый: *round table,* кру́глый стол. *In round figures,* кру́глым счётом; в кру́глых ци́фрах. —*n.* **1,** (unit of ammunition) вы́стрел; патро́н. **2,** *often pl.* (tour) обхо́д: *make one's rounds,* идти́ в обхо́д. *Make the round of all the stores,* обходи́ть все магази́ны. **3,** (of a tournament, negotiations, etc.) тур. **4,** *boxing* ра́унд. **5,** (burst, as of applause) взрыв. —*v.t.* **1,** (make round) округля́ть; закругля́ть. **2,** (go round, as a bend, turn, etc.) огиба́ть (поворо́т). —*adv.* **1,** (around) вокру́г; круго́м. *Go round,* враща́ться. **2,** (throughout): *the year round,* кру́глый год. —*prep.* вокру́г. —**round off, 1,** (finish into rounded form) округля́ть; закругля́ть. **2,** (state as a round number) округля́ть. —**round out, 1,** (fill out; become round) округля́ться. **2,** (complete) заверша́ть. *Round out a collection,* (у)комплектова́ть колле́кцию. —**round the clock,** кру́глые су́тки. —**round up, 1,** (assemble) собира́ть. **2,** (herd together) сгоня́ть. **3,** (seize and arrest) производи́ть обла́ву на.

roundabout *adj.* око́льный; обхо́дный; кру́жный.

rounded *adj.* закруглённый; округлённый.

roundhouse *n.* парово́зное депо́.

roundish *adj.* кругло́ватый.

roundly *adv.* **1,** (sharply; severely) ре́зко. **2,** (thoroughly; soundly) здо́рово.

round robin кругова́я систе́ма.

round-shouldered *adj.* суту́лый.

round-the-clock *adj.* круглосу́точный.

round trip пое́здка туда́ и обра́тно. *Round-trip ticket,* биле́т туда́ и обра́тно.

roundup *n.* **1,** (of cattle) заго́н. **2,** (raid) обла́ва. **3,** (summary) обзо́р; обозре́ние.

rouse *v.t.* **1,** (waken) буди́ть. **2,** (excite; stimulate) возбужда́ть: *rouse the populace/one's curiosity/,* возбужда́ть населе́ние/любопы́тство.

rousing *adj.* **1,** (stirring) волну́ющий. **2,** (enthusiastic) восто́рженный: *rousing welcome,* восто́рженный прием.

rout *v.t.* **1,** (put to flight) обраща́ть в бе́гство. **2,** (defeat overwhelmingly) громи́ть; разби́ть на́голову.

3, (drive out) выгоня́ть. *Rout out of bed,* поднима́ть с посте́ли. —*n.* разгро́м.

route *n.* **1,** (road; way) путь: *the shortest route to town,* кратча́йший путь в го́род. **2,** (itinerary) маршру́т: *the route of a trip,* маршру́т путеше́ствия. *Bus route,* маршру́т авто́буса. —*v.t.* направля́ть: *route the traffic through the park,* направля́ть движе́ние че́рез парк. —**en route,** по (*or* в) пути́; по (*or* в) доро́ге.

routine *n.* режи́м; распоря́док; колея́. *Daily routine,* распоря́док дня. *Settle into a routine,* войти́ в колею́. —*adj.* обы́чный; устано́вленный.

rove *v.i.* броди́ть; скита́ться; стра́нствовать.

rover *n.* скита́лец. —**land rover,** вездехо́д.

roving *adj.* бродя́чий. —**roving ambassador,** посо́л по осо́бым поруче́ниям.

row[1] (ro) *n.* ряд: *row of houses,* ряд домо́в. *In the third row,* в тре́тьем ряду́. —*v.t. & i.* грести́. *Row a boat,* грести́ на ло́дке. —**in a row, 1,** (in a line) в ряд; в ряду́. **2,** (consecutively) подря́д.

row[2] (rau) *n.* шу́мная ссо́ра; сканда́л; дебо́ш.

rowan *n.* ряби́на. —**rowanberry,** *n.* ряби́на.

rowboat *n.* гребна́я ло́дка; гребна́я шлю́пка.

rowdy *n.* буя́н; хулига́н; скандали́ст; безобра́зник. —*adj.* бу́йный. —**rowdiness,** *n.* хулига́нство.

rower *n.* гребе́ц.

rowing *n.* гре́бля; гребно́й спорт. —*adj.* гребно́й.

rowlock *n.* уклю́чина.

royal *adj.* короле́вский.

royalism *n.* роя́лизм. —**royalist,** *n.* роя́лист. —*adj.* роя́листский.

royalty *n.* **1,** (royal persons) чле́ны короле́вской семьи́. **2,** *pl.* (fees) а́вторский гонора́р.

rub *v.t.* **1,** (stroke hard) тере́ть; потира́ть: *rub one's eyes,* тере́ть глаза́; *rub one's hands,* потира́ть ру́ки. *Rub one's injured knee,* потира́ть уши́бленное коле́но. *Rub two sticks together,* тере́ть две па́лки друг о дру́га. *Rub one's back with alcohol,* натира́ть спи́ну спи́ртом. **2,** (apply with pressure) растира́ть. *Rub cream into one's face,* натира́ть лицо́ кре́мом. **3,** (chafe) тере́ть; натира́ть; стира́ть. *The collar is rubbing my neck,* воротни́к натира́ет мне ше́ю. —*v.i.* **1,** (apply repeated pressure) тере́ть: *keep rubbing!,* продолжа́йте тере́ть! **2,** (chafe) тере́ть: *the shoe rubs,* сапо́г трет. **3,** *fol. by* **against** (scrape) тере́ться о (+ *acc.*). —*n.* **1,** (vigorous stroking) *give something a good rub,* хорошо́нько потере́ть что́-нибудь. **2,** (difficulty; catch) загво́здка: *that's the rub,* вот в чем загво́здка. —**rub down,** обтира́ть. —**rub in,** втира́ть. —**rub it in,** растравля́ть ра́ну; пили́ть кого́-нибудь. —**rub off,** стира́ться. —**rub off on,** передава́ться (+ *dat.*). —**rub out,** стира́ть. —**rub the wrong way,** гла́дить (кого́-нибудь) про́тив ше́рсти.

rubber *n.* **1,** (raw rubber) каучу́к. **2,** (processed rubber) рези́на. **3,** (overshoe) гало́ша. **4,** *cards* ро́ббер. —*adj.* рези́новый. —**rubber band,** рези́нка.

rubberize *v.t.* прорези́нивать.

rubber plant 1, (plant yielding crude rubber) каучуконо́с. **2,** (ornamental house plant) фи́кус.

rubber stamp штамп; штёмпель; гриф.

rubbish *n.* **1,** (refuse) хлам; му́сор; сор. **2,** (nonsense) вздор; чепуха́; глу́пости.

rubble *n.* **1,** (rough broken stones) рва́ный ка́мень. **2,** (ruins) разва́лины: *reduce to rubble,* превраща́ть в разва́лины.

rubdown *n.* обтира́ние; масса́ж.

rube *n., slang* деревёнщина.

rubella *n.* красну́ха.

Rubicon *n., in* **cross the Rubicon,** перейти́ Рубико́н.

rubicund *adj.* румя́ный.

rubidium *n.* руби́дий.

ruble *n.* рубль.

rubric *n.* ру́брика.

ruby *n.* руби́н. —*adj.* руби́новый.

rucksack *n.* рюкза́к.

ruckus *n., colloq.* шум; гвалт; бата́лия.

rudder *n.* руль.

ruddy *adj.* румя́ный.

rude *adj.* гру́бый; неве́жливый. —**rudeness,** *n.* гру́бость; неве́жливость.

rudiment *n.* **1,** *pl.* (fundamentals) осно́вы; элеме́нты; нача́тки. **2,** (incompletely developed organ) рудимента́рный о́рган; рудиме́нт.

rudimentary *adj.* **1,** (elementary) элемента́рный. **2,** (incompletely developed) рудимента́рный; зача́точный.

rue *v.t.* **1,** (feel remorse for) раска́иваться в. **2,** (regret) сожале́ть о. —**rue the day,** проклина́ть тот день, когда́...

rueful *adj.* печа́льный; уны́лый; ско́рбный.

ruff *n.* **1,** (frilled collar) брыжи. **2,** (bird) турухта́н. **3,** (fish) ерш. —*v.t. & i.* = **trump.**

ruffian *n.* хулига́н; буя́н.

ruffle *n.* обо́рка. —*v.t.* **1,** (disturb) ряби́ть: *ruffle the surface of the lake,* ряби́ть пове́рхность о́зера. **2,** (fluster) смуща́ть; конфу́зить. **3,** (erect, as feathers) еро́шить. *The hen ruffled its feathers,* ку́рица нахо́хлилась.

rug *n.* ковёр.

rugby *n.* ре́гби.

rugged *adj.* **1,** (rough, as of terrain) пересечённый; изре́занный. **2,** (wrinkled; furrowed) гру́бый: *rugged features,* гру́бые черты́ лица́. **3,** (trying; severe) тяжёлый; суро́вый. **4,** (robust; sturdy) кре́пкий; дю́жий.

ruin *n.* **1,** (destruction; downfall) ги́бель; круше́ние. **2,** (financial collapse) разоре́ние. **3,** *pl.* (remains of something destroyed) разва́лины; руи́ны. *Lie in ruins,* лежа́ть в разва́линах. —*v.t.* **1,** (destroy) губи́ть. **2,** (bankrupt) разоря́ть. —**ruination,** *n.* ги́бель. —**ruinous,** *adj.* ги́бельный; губи́тельный; па́губный; разори́тельный.

rule *n.* **1,** (regulation) пра́вило: *the rules of the game,* пра́вила игры́. **2,** (act of governing) правле́ние; управле́ние. *Self-rule,* самоуправле́ние. **3,** (domination; sway) власть: *under colonial rule,* под колониа́льной вла́стью. **4,** (measuring stick) лине́йка. —*v.t.* **1,** (govern) пра́вить; управля́ть. **2,** (decide authoritatively) постановля́ть: *the court ruled that...,* суд постанови́л, что... **3,** (mark with lines) линова́ть; графи́ть. **4,** *fol. by* **out** (eliminate from consideration) исключа́ть; сбра́сывать со счето́в. —*v.i.* пра́вить. —**as a rule,** как пра́вило. —**make it a rule,** взять себе́ за пра́вило.

ruled *adj.* лино́ванный; в лине́йку; графлёный; разграфлённый.

ruler *n.* **1,** (one who governs) прави́тель. **2,** (measuring stick) лине́йка.

ruling *n.* постановле́ние. —*adj.* пра́вящий. —**ruling circles,** пра́вящие круги́.

rum *n.* ром.

Rumanian *adj. & n.* = **Romanian.**

rumba *n.* румба.

rumble *v.i.* **1,** (roar) громыхать; грохотать; греметь; рокотать. **2,** (gurgle, as of the stomach) урчать; бурчать. **3,** (move with such a sound) громыхать; грохотать. —*n.* грохот; рокот. —**rumble seat,** откидное сиденье.

rumen *n.* рубец.

ruminant *n.* жвачное животное. —*adj.* жвачный.

ruminate *v.i.* **1,** (chew the cud) жевать жвачку. **2,** (ponder) раздумывать; размышлять.

rummage *v.t. & i.* рыться в; обшаривать.

rumor *also,* **rumour** *n.* слух. —*v.t.* *It is rumored that...,* ходят слухи, что...

rump *n.* **1,** (hind part of an animal) крестец. **2,** (buttocks) зад; ягодицы.

rumple *v.t.* мять. —*v.i.* мяться.

rump steak ромштекс.

rumpus *n.* шум; гам; гвалт.

run *v.i.* **1,** (move swiftly) бежать: *run fast,* бежать быстро. *Run home/upstairs,* побежать домой/наверх. **2,** (go; operate; function) ходить: *the trains aren't running,* поезда не ходят. *The elevator isn't running,* лифт не работает. *Leave the motor running,* не выключать мотора. **3,** (extend) идти; тянуться. *The road runs along the coast,* дорога идет вдоль берега. **4,** (stream; flow) течь; литься. *My nose is running,* у меня из носу течет. **5,** (spread, as of colors or dyes) линять; (of ink) растекаться; расплываться. **6,** (be in force) быть действительным; оставаться в силе. **7,** (be on, as of a play) идти. **8,** (be a candidate) баллотироваться. **9,** (come in; finish) приходить: *run last,* приходить последним. **10,** *used with various adjectives: run dry,* высыхать; *run low,* истощаться. *Feelings ran high,* страсти разгорелись *or* разыгрались. *Run short, see* **short.** —*v.t.* **1,** (cover by running) пробегать: *run five miles,* пробегать пять миль. **2,** (take; drive) отвозить: *I'll run you to the station,* я вас отвезу на вокзал. **3,** (chase) прогонять: *run someone out of town,* прогнать кого-нибудь из города. **4,** (cause to move quickly) пробегать: *run one's fingers over the keyboard,* пробегать пальцами по клавиатуре. **5,** (manage; govern; conduct) вести; руководить; управлять. *Run a meeting,* вести собрание. *Run the country,* руководить *or* управлять страной. **6,** (print; carry, as a story) печатать; помещать. **7,** *used with various nouns: run a risk,* рисковать; *run errands,* быть на посылках; *run a blockade,* прорвать блокаду; *run a red light,* проскочить светофор. *He is running a temperature,* у него жар. —*n.* **1,** (rapid movement) бег; пробег. **2,** (single trip) рейс: *maiden run,* первый рейс. **3,** (streak, as of luck; spell, as of weather) полоса. **4,** (tear in one's stocking) спустившаяся петля: *I have a run in my stocking,* у меня на чулке спустилась петля. **5,** *music* рулада. —**in the long run,** в конечном счете; в конечном итоге. —**on the run, 1,** (while in motion) на ходу. **2,** (hurriedly) второпях. **3,** (fleeing from justice) в бегах. —**run across, 1,** *literally* перебегать. **2,** (encounter) наталкиваться на. —**run after,** бежать за. —**run along,** побежать: *I'll be running along,* ну, я побегу. —**run around with,** водиться с; путаться с. —**run away,** убегать. —**run down, 1,** *literally* сбегать с: *run down the stairs,* сбегать с лестницы. **2,** (run along;

run through) пробегать по: *run down the street,* пробегать по улице. *A chill ran down her back,* дрожь пробежала по ее спине. **3,** *fol. by* **to** (make a short trip to) сходить (в); сбегать (в); съездить (в). **4,** (of a clock) стать; (of a battery) разряжаться. **5,** (pursue and catch) настигать. **6,** (knock over with a vehicle) наехать на. **7,** (read over rapidly) пробегать. **8,** (disparage) порочить. —**run into, 1,** *literally* вбегать в. **2,** (encounter by chance) наталкиваться на. **3,** (collide with) сталкиваться с; наехать на; налететь на. **4,** (add up to) составлять. —**run off, 1,** (run away) убегать. **2,** (flow off; drain) стекать. **3,** (print) печатать; отпечатывать. —**run out, 1,** *literally* выбегать. **2,** (expire) истекать. **3,** (be used up) выходить; кончаться; истощаться. *We ran out of gas,* у нас вышел/кончился бензин. *His luck ran out,* счастье ему изменило. —**run over, 1,** (overflow) переливаться через. *My cup runneth over,* моя чаша переполнена. **2,** (exceed) превышать. **3,** (knock down with a vehicle) задавить. *He was run over by a car,* он попал под машину. **4,** (review again quickly) повторять. —**run through, 1,** *literally* пробегать через. **2,** (review again quickly) повторять. **3,** (pierce) прокалывать. **4,** (squander) проматывать. —**run up, 1,** *literally* взбегать на *or* по. **2,** (hoist, as a flag) выкинуть. **3,** (pile up, as debts) наделать (долгов).

runaway *adj.* бежавший; беглый. *Runaway victory,* легкая победа. *Runaway inflation,* безудержная инфляция.

rundown *n.* краткое изложение; сводка.

run-down *adj.* **1,** (tired; worn out) переутомленный. **2,** (in poor condition) обветшалый.

rune *n.* руна.

rung *n.* ступенька.

runic *adj.* рунический.

run-in *n.* склока; перебранка.

runner *n.* **1,** (one who runs) бегун. **2,** (messenger) посыльный. **3,** (smuggler) контрабандист. **4,** (blade, as of a sled) полоз. **5,** (strip of carpet) дорожка. **6,** (trailing plant stem) ус.

running *n.* **1,** (act of running; jogging) бег. *Take up running,* бегать; начать бегать. **2,** (chances of winning) шансы: *be in the running,* иметь шансы; *be out of the running,* потерять все шансы. —*adj.* **1,** (moving fast) быстрый. **2,** (used for running) беговой: *running track,* беговая дорожка. **3,** (continuous) непрерывный. —*adv.* подряд: *three years running,* три года подряд. —**running board,** подножка. —**running broad jump,** прыжок с разбега. —**running head,** колонтитул. —**running water,** водопровод.

run-of-the-mill *adj.* заурядный.

runt *n.* недоросток; коротыш(ка).

runway *n.* летная дорожка; взлетно-посадочная полоса.

rupee *n.* рупия.

rupture *n.* **1,** (break) разрыв. **2,** (hernia) грыжа. —*v.t.* прорывать. —*v.i.* прорываться.

rural *adj.* сельский; деревенский.

ruse *n.* уловка.

rush *v.i.* **1,** (hurry) спешить. **2,** (dash) броситься; ринуться. **3,** (flow rapidly) хлынуть. *A rushing river,* стремительная река. *Blood rushed to her cheeks,* кровь бросилась ей в щеки; кровь прилила к ее щекам. —*v.t.* **1,** (force to move hastily) торопить:

don't rush me!, не торопи́те меня́! **2,** (whisk) мчать. *He was rushed to the hospital,* его́ сро́чно доста́вили в больни́цу. —*n.* **1,** (hurry) спе́шка: *what's the rush?,* к чему́ така́я спе́шка? *There is no rush,* не на́до спеши́ть. *I'm in a big rush,* я о́чень тороплю́сь. **2,** (dash) бросо́к. *Gold rush,* золота́я лихора́дка. **3,** (heavy flow, as of air) поры́в. **4,** (grasslike plant) тростни́к; камы́ш; си́тник. —*adj.* **1,** (urgent) сро́чный. **2,** (made of rush) тростнико́вый; камы́шовый. —**rush hours,** часы́-пик.

rusk *n.* сла́дкий суха́рь.

russet *adj.* кра́сно-бу́рый.

Russia leather юфть.

Russian *adj.* ру́сский. —*n.* **1,** (person) ру́сский; ру́сская. **2,** (language) ру́сский язы́к. *Do you speak Russian?,* вы говори́те (*or* разгова́риваете) по-ру́сски?

Russify *v.t.* русифици́ровать. *Become Russified,* об-

русе́ть. —**Russification,** *n.* русифика́ция.

Russophile *n.* русофи́л.

Russophobe *n.* русофо́б. —**Russophobia,** *n.* русофо́бство.

rust *n.* ржа́вчина. —*adj.* (rust-colored) ржа́вый. —*v.i.* ржа́веть.

rustic *adj.* дереве́нский.

rustle *v.i.* шелесте́ть; шурша́ть. —*v.t.* шелесте́ть (+ *instr.*). —*n.* ше́лест; шо́рох.

rusty *adj.* ржа́вый; заржа́вленный. *My French is a bit rusty,* я немно́го забы́л(а) свой францу́зский.

rut *n.* колея́.

rutabaga *n.* брю́ква.

ruthenium *n.* руте́ний.

ruthless *adj.* безжа́лостный. —**ruthlessly,** *adv.* безжа́лостно. —**ruthlessness,** *n.* безжа́лостность.

rye *n.* рожь. —*adj.* ржано́й: *rye bread,* ржано́й хлеб.

S

S, s девятна́дцатая бу́ква англи́йского алфави́та.

Sabbath *n.* суббо́та: *observe the Sabbath,* соблюда́ть суббо́ту.

sabbatical *n.* годи́чный о́тпуск.

saber *also,* **sabre** *n.* са́бля; ша́шка. —**saber rattling,** бряца́ние ору́жием.

sable *n.* со́боль. —*adj.* собо́лий; соболи́ный.

sabotage *n.* сабота́ж; диве́рсия; вреди́тельство. —*v.t.* саботи́ровать. —**saboteur,** *n.* сабота́жник; диверса́нт; вреди́тель.

sabre *n.* = **saber.**

sac *n.* мешо́чек.

saccharin *n.* сахари́н.

saccharine *adj.* **1,** (of or like sugar) са́харистый. **2,** (cloyingly sweet) са́харный; слаща́вый; прито́рный.

sacerdotal *adj.* свяще́ннический.

sack *n.* мешо́к. —*v.t.* **1,** (plunder) гра́бить; разгра́бить; громи́ть. **2,** *slang* (fire) выгоня́ть с рабо́ты. —**get the sack,** *slang* вы́лететь с рабо́ты.

sackcloth *n.* **1,** (sacking) мешкови́на; дерю́га; холст. **2,** (symbol of penitence) власяни́ца.

sacking *n.* мешкови́на; дерю́га.

sacrament *n.* та́инство. —**sacramental,** *adj.* относя́щийся к та́инству; свяще́нный.

sacred *adj.* свяще́нный; свято́й.

sacrifice *n.* **1,** (religious offering) жертвоприноше́ние. **2,** (giving up of something) же́ртва: *make sacrifices,* идти́ на же́ртвы. —*v.t.* же́ртвовать; приноси́ть в же́ртву. —**sacrificial,** *adj.* же́ртвенный.

sacrilege *n.* святота́тство; кощу́нство. —**sacrilegious,** *adj.* святота́тственный; кощу́нственный.

sacristy *n.* ри́зница.

sacrosanct *adj.* свяще́нный; неприкоснове́нный.

sacrum *n.* кресте́ц.

sad *adj.* печа́льный; гру́стный. *Why are you so sad?,* почему́ вам так гру́стно?

sadden *v.t.* печа́лить.

saddle *n.* седло́. —*v.t.* **1,** (put a saddle on) седла́ть. **2,** (burden) обременя́ть: *saddled with debts,* обременён долга́ми. *Saddle someone with a job,* взва́ливать рабо́ту на кого́-нибудь. —**saddlebag,** *n.* седе́льная *or* перемётная сума́. —**saddlecloth,** *n.* потни́к. —**saddler,** *n.* седе́льный ма́стер; седе́льник; шо́рник.

sadism *n.* сади́зм. —**sadist,** *n.* сади́ст. —**sadistic,** *adj.* сади́стский.

sadly *adv.* печа́льно; гру́стно. *Be sadly lacking in,* о́чень *or* о́стро нужда́ться в (+ *prepl.*). ♦*As an introductory word* к несча́стью.

sadness *n.* печа́ль; грусть.

safari *n.* охо́тничья экспеди́ция.

safe *adj.* **1,** (free from danger) безопа́сный: *safe place,* безопа́сное ме́сто. *It is safe here,* здесь безопа́сно. **2,** (dependable) надёжный: *in safe hands,* в надёжных рука́х. **3,** (cautious) осторо́жный: *a safe driver,* осторо́жный води́тель. **4,** (without mishap) благополу́чный: *safe return,* благополу́чное возвраще́ние. **5,** (unharmed) невреди́мый: *the boy is safe,* ма́льчик невреди́м. —*n.* сейф. —**play safe,** де́йствовать наверняка́. —**safe and sound,** цел и невреди́м; в це́лости и сохра́нности. —**to be on the safe side,** для бо́льшей ве́рности; для перестрахо́вки; на вся́кий слу́чай.

safe-conduct *n.* осо́бая охра́на. *Safe-conduct pass,* охра́нная гра́мота; охра́нный лист.

safeguard *n.* гара́нтия; ме́ра предосторо́жности. —*v.t.* охраня́ть; защища́ть.

safekeeping *n.* хране́ние; сохране́ние: *turn over*

for safekeeping, отдавáть на хранéние/сохранéние.

safely *adv.* **1**, (without mishap) благополýчно. **2**, (without fear of being wrong) с увéренностью; смéло.

safety *n.* безопáсность. —**safety catch**, предохранѝтель. —**safety pin**, англѝйская булáвка. —**safety razor**, безопáсная брѝтва. —**safety valve**, предохранѝтельный клáпан.

safflower *n.* сафлóр.

saffron *n.* шафрáн.

sag *v.i.* прогибáться; провисáть. —*n.* прогѝб.

saga *n.* сáга.

sagacious *adj.* проницáтельный; прозорлѝвый. —**sagacity**, *n.* проницáтельность; прозорлѝвость.

sage *n.* **1**, (wise man) мудрéц. **2**, (shrub) шалфéй. —*adj.* мýдрый.

sagebrush *n.* полы́нь.

Sagittarius *n.* Стрелéц.

sail *n.* **1**, (piece of canvas to propel a ship) пáрус. **2**, (ride on a sailing vessel) прогýлка под парусáми. *Go for a sail*, идтѝ катáться на пáрусной лóдке. —*v.i.* **1**, (travel by ship or boat) плáвать; плыть. *Sail around the world*, совершѝть кругосвéтное плáвание. **2**, (set sail) отплывáть; отходѝть. **3**, (soar; glide) плыть; парѝть. —*v.t.* **1**, (handle; steer) вестѝ; управля́ть. **2**, (travel on or over) плáвать по *or* в. —**sail into, 1**, *literally* входѝть в; вплывáть в. **2**, (assail) обрýшиваться на. —**set sail**, отплывáть; отходѝть.

sailboat *n.* пáрусная лóдка.

sailfish *n.* пáрусник.

sailing *n.* **1**, (the sport) пáрусный спорт. **2**, (riding in a sailboat) плáвание; катáние на (пáрусной) лóдке. **3**, (departure from port) отплы́тие. —**sailing vessel**, пáрусное сýдно; пáрусник.

sailor *n.* моря́к; матрóс.·—*adj.* [*also,* **sailor's**] матрóсский: *sailor suit*, матрóсский костю́м.

saint *n.* святóй. *St. Peter*, св. Пётр. *St. Patrick's Day*, день св. Пáтрика. *St. Petersburg*, Санкт-Петербýрг. *St. Louis*, Сент-Лýис. *St. Lawrence River*, рекá Святóго Лаврéнтия. *St. Basil's Cathedral*, храм Васѝлия Блажéнного.

Saint Bernard сенбернáр.

sainthood *n.* лик святы́х: *confer sainthood upon*, причѝслить к лѝку святы́х.

saintly *adj.* святóй; подобáющий святóму.

Saint Vitus' dance пля́ска святóго Вѝтта; вѝттова пля́ска.

sake *n.*, *in* **for the sake of**, рáди (+ *gen.*). —**for goodness' sake!**, рáди бóга!

salacious *adj.* сáльный; скабрёзный.

salad *n.* салáт. —**salad bowl**, салáтник. —**salad dressing**, припрáва к салáту.

salamander *n.* саламáндра.

salami *n.* колбасá твёрдого копчéния; саля́ми.

salary *n.* жáлованье; зарплáта; оклáд.

sale *n.* **1**, (selling) продáжа; сбыт. **2**, (clearance sale) распродáжа. **3**, *pl.* (volume of business) объём продáж: *sales are off/down*, объём продáж упáл. —**for sale**, продаётся.

saleslady *n.* продавщѝца. *Also,* **salesgirl; saleswoman**.

salesman *n.* **1**, [*also,* **salesclerk**] (seller in a store) продавéц. **2**, (traveling agent) коммивояжёр.

sales slip квитáнция.

sales tax налóг на покýпки.

salient *adj.* **1**, (protruding) выдаю́щийся. **2**, (note-worthy) примечáтельный. *The salient points of the plan*, основны́е пýнкты плáна. —*n.*, *mil.* вы́ступ; клин.

saline *adj.* солянóй; солевóй. —**salinity**, *n.* солёность.

saliva *n.* слюнá. —**salivary**, *adj.* слю́нный. —**salivate**, *v.i.* выделя́ть слюнý.

sallow *adj.* желтовáтый; землѝстый.

sally *n.* **1**, *mil.* вы́лазка. **2**, (witticism) острóта; рéплика. —*v.i.* [*usu.* **sally forth**] отправля́ться.

salmon *n.* **1**, (fish) лосóсь. **2**, (food) лососѝна. *Smoked salmon*, сёмга. —*adj.* **1**, (of salmon) лососёвый. **2**, (pinkish orange) орáнжево-рóзового цвéта.

salon *n.* салóн.

saloon *n.* бар; пивня́я.

salt *n.* соль. *Smelling salts*, ню́хательная соль. —*adj.* солянóй: *salt mines*, соляны́е кóпи. *Salt water*, солёная водá. *Salt marsh*, солончáк. —*v.t.* солѝть; засáливать. —**rub salt on a wound**, растравля́ть рáну. —**salt away**, откля́дывать; накопля́ть. —**salt of the earth**, соль землѝ. —**take with a grain of salt**, относѝться скептѝчески к.

saltcellar *n.* солóнка.

salted *adj.* солёный.

saltiness *n.* солёность.

saltpeter *also,* **saltpetre** *n.* селѝтра.

salt shaker солóнка.

saltworks *n.* солевáрня; солевáренный завóд.

saltwort *n.* соля́нка.

salty *adj.* солёный.

salubrious *adj.* здорóвый; целéбный.

salutary *adj.* благотвóрный.

salutation *n.* привéтствие. —**salutatory**, *adj.* привéтственный.

salute *n.* **1**, (with the hand) отдáча чéсти; вóинское привéтствие. **2**, (with guns) салю́т. —*v.t.* **1**, *mil.* отдавáть честь (+ *dat.*). **2**, (hail) привéтствовать. —*v.i.* отдавáть честь.

salvage *n.* **1**, (act of saving) спасéние. **2**, (property saved from danger) спасённое имýщество. —*adj.* спасáтельный: *salvage ship*, спасáтельное сýдно. —*v.t.* спасáть.

salvation *n.* спасéние.

salve *n.* (целéбная) мазь.

salvo *n.* залп.

samarium *n.* самáрий.

same *adj.* **1**, (the one just mentioned) тот же; тот сáмый; тот же сáмый: *the same day*, в тот же день; *in the same place*, в *or* на том же сáмом мéсте. *The same thing*, то же сáмое. **2**, (one; applying to both or all) одѝн: *live under the same roof*, жить под однóй кры́шей. *They are the same age*, онѝ одногó вóзраста (*or* однѝх лет). **3**, (alike; identical) одинáковый: *all politicians are the same*, все полѝтики одинáковы. **4**, (unchanged) такóй же: *remain the same*, остáться такѝм же (какѝм был). —*pron.* [*usu.* **the same**] то же сáмое; однó и то же. *The same to you!*, и вам тогó же!; и вас тáкже! —*adv.* [*usu.* **the same**] так же. *They are pronounced the same*, онѝ произнóсятся одинáково. —**all the same, 1**, [*also,* **just the same**] (nevertheless) всё же; всё ещё; всё равнó. *Thank you just the same*, всё же благодарю́ вас. **2**, *fol. by* **to** (making no difference) всё равнó; безразлѝчно: *it's all the same to me*, мне всё равнó; мне безразлѝчно. —**at the same time**, *see* **time**.

sameness *n.* **1,** (identity) тóждество. **2,** (monotony) однообрáзие.

samovar *n.* самовáр.

sample *n.* **1,** (typical example) образéц; обрáзчик; прóба. **2,** *statistics* вы́борка: *random sample,* случáйная вы́борка. —*adj.* прóбный: *sample copy,* прóбный экземпля́р. —*v.t.* прóбовать.

samurai *n.* самурáй.

sanatorium *n.* санатóрий.

sanctify *v.t.* освящáть. —**sanctification,** *n.* освящéние.

sanctimony *n.* хáнжество. —**sanctimonious,** *adj.* хáнжеский.

sanction *n.* **1,** (official permission) сáнкция. **2,** *usu. pl.* (punitive measures) сáнкции: *impose sanctions,* применя́ть сáнкции. —*v.t.* санкциони́ровать.

sanctity *n.* свя́тость.

sanctuary *n.* **1,** (sacred place) святи́лище. **2,** (place of refuge) убéжище.

sanctum *n.* убéжище.

sand *n.* песóк. —*adj.* песóчный; песчáный. —*v.t.* **1,** (sprinkle with sand) посыпáть пескóм. **2,** (sandpaper) натирáть наждáчной бумáгой.

sandal *n.* сандáлия.

sandalwood *n.* сандáл.

sandbag *n.* мешóк с пескóм.

sandbank *n.* песчáная мель *or* óтмель, перекáт; бáнка. *Also,* **sand bar.**

sandbox *n.* песóчница.

sanderling *n.* песчáнка.

sand fly москúт.

sandpaper *n.* наждáчная бумáга; шкýрка.

sandpiper *n.* песóчник; перевóзчик.

sandstone *n.* песчáник.

sandstorm *n.* песчáная бýря.

sandwich *n.* бутербрóд.

sandy *adj.* **1,** (consisting of sand) песчáный. **2,** (of the color of sand) песóчный.

sane *adj.* **1,** (of sound mind) в здрáвом умé; нормáльный. **2,** (sensible) разýмный.

sanguinary *adj.* **1,** (bloody) кровáвый. **2,** (bloodthirsty) кровожáдный.

sanguine *adj.* **1,** (ruddy) румя́ный. **2,** (optimistic) оптимисти́ческий.

sanitarium *n.* санатóрий.

sanitary *adj.* санитáрный; гигиени́ческий; оздоровúтельный.

sanitation *n.* санитáрия.

sanity *n.* рассýдок.

Sanskrit *n.* санскри́т. —*adj.* санскри́тский.

Santa Claus дед-морóз.

sap *n.* **1,** (juice of a plant) сок. **2,** *slang* (fool) простофи́ля. **3,** *mil.* (trench) сáпа. —*v.t.* подтáчивать: *sap someone's strength,* подтáчивать чьи-нибудь си́лы.

sapling *n.* дéревце; деревцó.

sapper *n., mil.* сапёр.

sapphire *n.* сапфи́р. —*adj.* сапфи́рный; сапфи́ровый.

sapwood *n.* зáболонь.

sarcasm *n.* саркáзм. —**sarcastic,** *adj.* саркасти́ческий; язви́тельный. —**sarcastically,** *adv.* саркасти́чески.

sarcophagus *n.* саркофáг.

sardine *n.* сарди́на; сарди́нка. —**like sardines,** как сéльди в бóчке.

sardonic *adj.* сардони́ческий.

sartorial *adj.* портня́жный.

sash *n.* **1,** (band worn around the waist) кушáк. **2,** (window frame) окóнная рáма; окóнный переплёт.

sassy *adj., colloq.* нахáльный.

Satan *n.* сатанá. —**satanic,** *adj.* сатани́нский.

satchel *n.* рáнец; сýмка.

sate *v.t.* пресыщáть.

sateen *n.* сати́н. —*adj.* сати́новый.

satellite *n.* **1,** (moon) спýтник. **2,** *fig.* (nation dominated by another) сателли́т.

satiate *v.t.* **1,** (satisfy) насыщáть. **2,** (surfeit) пресыщáть. —**satiation; satiety,** *n.* насыщéние; пресыщéние; сы́тость.

satin *n.* атлáс. —*adj.* атлáсный.

satire *n.* сати́ра. —**satirical,** *adj.* сатири́ческий. —**satirist,** *n.* сати́рик. —**satirize,** *v.t.* высмéивать; осмéивать.

satisfaction *n.* удовлетворéние; удовлетворённость.

satisfactory *adj.* удовлетвори́тельный. —**satisfactorily,** *adv.* удовлетвори́тельно.

satisfied *adj.* довóльный: *I am satisfied,* я довóлен; я довóльна.

satisfy *v.t.* удовлетворя́ть: *satisfy the teacher,* удовлетворя́ть учи́теля; *satisfy someone's needs,* удовлетворя́ть чьи-нибудь потрéбности.

satrap *n.* сатрáп. —**satrapy,** *n.* сатрáпия.

saturate *v.t.* насыщáть; пропи́тывать.

saturation *n.* насыщéние. —**saturation point,** тóчка насыщéния.

Saturday *n.* суббóта.

Saturn *n.* Сатýрн.

saturnine *adj.* мрáчный; молчали́вый.

satyr *n.* сати́р.

sauce *n.* сóус; подли́вка.

saucepan *n.* кастрю́ля.

saucer *n.* блю́дце; блю́дечко. —**flying saucer,** летáющая тарéлка.

saucy *adj.* дéрзкий; нахáльный.

sauerkraut *n.* ки́слая капýста.

saunter *v.i.* прогýливаться; прохáживаться.

sausage *n.* колбасá.

sauterne *n.* сотéрн.

savage *adj.* **1,** (uncivilized) ди́кий: *savage tribes,* ди́кие племенá. **2,** (ferocious; vicious) свирéпый: *savage beast,* свирéпый зверь. *Savage attack,* я́ростная атáка. —*n.* дикáрь. —**savagery,** *n.* ди́кость.

savanna *also,* **savannah** *n.* савáнна.

savant *n.* учёный.

save *v.t.* **1,** (rescue) спасáть: *save someone's life,* спасáть чью-нибудь жизнь. **2,** (retain; not throw away) хранить; берéчь. **3,** (lay aside for future use) берéчь; сберегáть. **4,** (conserve) берéчь: *save one's strength,* берéчь свои́ си́лы. **5,** (reduce the expenditure of, as time or money) экономить. *Save ten dollars,* экономить дéсять дóлларов. **6,** (spare) избавля́ть: *that will save me a lot of trouble,* э́то избáвит меня́ от мнóгих хлопóт. **7,** (collect as a hobby) собирáть. **8,** *fol. by* **up** (keep and gradually amass) копи́ть. —*v.i.* **1,** (economize) экономить: *save on fuel,* экономить на тóпливе. **2,** *often fol. by* **up** (put money aside) копи́ть дéньги. —*prep.* крóме; за исключéнием (+ *gen.*).

saving *n.* **1,** (rescuing) спасéние. **2,** (reduction in cost) экономия. **3**, *pl.* (money saved up) сбережёния. —*adj.* спасительный.

savings bank сберегательная касса.

savior *also,* **saviour** *n.* спаситель.

savor *also,* **savour** *n.* вкус; смак. —*v.t.* смаковать; наслаждаться.

savory *also,* **savoury** *adj.* **1**, (appetizing) вкусный. **2**, (piquant) пикантный. **3**, *fig.* (respectable) порядочный. —*n.* (plant) чабер.

savvy *n., slang* смётка. —*v.t. & i., slang* понимать; смекать.

saw *n.* **1**, (cutting tool) пила. **2**, (maxim; saying) изречёние. —*v.t. & i.* пилить. *Saw in half,* распиливать пополам. —**saw off,** отпиливать. *Sawed-off rifle,* обрёз.

sawdust *n.* опилки.

sawfish *n.* рыба-пила.

sawhorse *n.* козлы.

sawmill *n.* лесопильный завод; лесопилка.

sawyer *n.* пильщик.

saxifrage *n.* камнеломка.

Saxon *n.* сакс. —*adj.* саксонский.

saxophone *n.* саксофон.

say *v.t.* **1**, (utter; state) говорить (*pfv.* сказать). *They say he's leaving,* говорят, что он уезжает. *I have nothing to say,* мне нечего сказать. **2**, (recite) читать: *say one's prayers,* читать молитвы. **3**, (assert) утверждать: *he says he's innocent,* он утверждает, что он невиновен. **4**, (assume) допускать: *let's say it's true,* допустим, что это так. **5**, (read; go, as of a law or proverb) гласить. —*n.* слово. *Have one's say,* сказать своё слово; высказывать свое мнение; высказываться. —**as they say,** как говорят; что называется. —**if I (one) may say so,** с позволёния сказать; ёсли можно так выразиться. —**I should say so!,** ещё бы! —**it goes without saying,** само собой разумёется. —**that is to say,** то есть. —**when all is said and done,** в концё концов; в конёчном счёте. —**you don't say!,** да что вы говорите! —**you might say,** можно сказать.

saying *n.* поговорка; изречёние. *As the saying goes,* как говорится.

scab *n.* струп.

scabbard *n.* ножны.

scabies *n.* чесотка.

scads *n.pl., colloq.* масса; уйма.

scaffold *n.* **1**, (platform for a gallows) эшафот. **2**, (raised wooden framework) подмостки. —**scaffolding,** *n.* (строительные) леса.

scald *v.t.* обваривать; ошпаривать. *Scald oneself,* обвариваться; ошпариваться.

scale *n.* **1**, (instrument for weighing) весы. **2**, (scope) масштаб: *on a large scale,* в большом масштабе. **3**, (series of marks for measuring) шкала. **4**, (projection on a map) масштаб: *large-scale map,* карта крупного масштаба. **5**, (graded system of classification) шкала; лёстница: *wage scale,* шкала заработной платы; *social scale,* общественная лёстница. **6**, *music* гамма. **7**, *pl.* (of fish and reptiles) чешуя. —*v.t.* **1**, (have a weight of) вёсить. **2**, (climb to the top of) взбираться на. **3**, *fol. by* **down** (reduce) понижать; снижать. **4**, (remove the scales from) снимать чешую с; чистить. —**tip the scales,** склонить чашу весов (*e.g.* в чью-нибудь пользу).

scalene *adj., math.* разносторонний.

scallion *n.* зелёный лук.

scallop *n.* **1**, (mollusk) гребешок. **2**, *pl.* (decorative curves forming an edge) фестоны. —**scalloped,** *adj.* фестонный; фестончатый.

scalp *n.* **1**, (skin on the top of the head) кожа головы. **2**, (portion of this taken in battle) скальп. —*v.t.* скальпировать.

scalpel *n.* скальпель.

scaly *adj.* чешуйчатый.

scamp *n.* негодяй; мерзавец.

scamper *v.i.* **1**, (race; dash) мчаться. **2**, (frolic) резвиться.

scan *v.t.* **1**, (scrutinize) рассматривать. **2**, (glance over) просматривать. **3**, *pros.* скандировать.

scandal *n.* скандал. —**scandalize,** *v.t.* скандализировать. —**scandalous,** *adj.* скандальный.

Scandinavian *adj.* скандинавский. —*n.* скандинав.

scandium *n.* скандий.

scant *adj.* **1**, (hardly any) почти никакой. *Pay scant attention,* ёле обращать внимание. **2**, (just short of) всего на: *miss by a few scant inches,* промахнуться всего на нёсколько дюймов.

scanty *adj.* скудный: *scanty supplies/information,* скудные запасы/свёдения. *Scantily attired,* едва одётый.

scapegoat *n.* козел отпущёния.

scar *n.* **1**, (mark) рубёц; шрам. **2**, *fig.* (lasting effect) след. —*v.t.* оставлять рубцы *or* шрамы на; обезображивать. —*v.i.* рубцеваться.

scarab *n.* скарабёй.

scarce *adj.* **1**, (in short supply) дефицитный. **2**, (rarely seen) рёдкий. —**make oneself scarce,** не показываться; не попадаться на глаза.

scarcely *adv.* едва; ёле; с трудом. *Scarcely enough,* едва достаточно. *He is scarcely breathing,* он ёле дышит. *I could scarcely make out the road,* я с трудом различал дорогу.

scarcity *n.* **1**, (dearth) нехватка; дефицит. **2**, (rarity) рёдкость.

scare *v.t.* **1**, (frighten) пугать. *I'm scared,* мне страшно. *Be scared to death,* испугаться до смерти. **2**, *fol. by* **away** *or* **off** (drive away) спугивать. —*v.i.* пугаться. *He doesn't scare easily,* его не так легко испугать. —*n.* Give *someone a scare,* напугать кого-нибудь. *Have quite a scare,* очень перепугаться.

scarecrow *n.* пугало; чучело.

scarf *n.* шарф.

scarlet *adj.* алый. —*n.* алый цвет. —**scarlet fever,** скарлатина.

scary *adj., colloq.* пугающий; страшный.

scat *interj.* прочь!; поди прочь!; прочь отсюда!

scathing *adj.* хлесткий; разносный; уничтожающий.

scatter *v.t.* **1**, (strew) разбрасывать; рассыпать. **2**, (disperse; rout) рассёивать; разгонять. —*v.i.* рассёиваться; рассыпаться; разбегаться.

scatterbrain *n.* вётреник; разиня. —**scatterbrained,** *adj.* вётреный; безголовый.

scavenge *v.i.* искать отбросы; рыться в мусоре. —**scavenger,** *n.* животное, питающееся падалью.

scenario *n.* сценарий.

scene *n.* **1**, (place where something occurs) мёсто: *scene of the crime,* мёсто преступлёния. *Appear on the scene,* явиться на сцёну. *Pass from the scene,* сойти со сцены. **2,** (division of an act of a play) сцена; явление; картина. *Act One, Scene Two,* действие первое, сцена вторая. **3,** (part or setting of a play, movie or story) сцена: *love scenes,* любовные сцены. *Scenes from a movie,* кадры из фильма. *The scene is laid in Ancient Rome,* действие происходит в древнем Риме. **4,** (sight; spectacle) сцена; зрелище. **5,** (view) вид: *the scene from the window,* вид из окна. **6,** (display of temper) сцена: *make a scene,* устроить сцену. —**behind the scenes,** за кулисами.

scenery *n.* **1,** (landscape) пейзаж. **2,** *theat.* декорации. —**change of scenery, 1,** *theat.* перемена декораций. **2,** *fig.* (change of surroundings) перемена обстановки.

scenic *adj.* **1,** (pert. to stage effects) сценический: *scenic effects,* сценические эффекты. **2,** (having beautiful scenery) живописный.

scent *n.* **1,** (odor) запах; аромат. **2,** (trail of an animal) след: *pick up the scent,* напасть на след. **3,** (sense of smell) чутьё. **4,** (perfume) духи. —*v.t.* **1,** (smell) обонять. **2,** (sense; suspect) чуять. **3,** (perfume) душить.

scepter *also,* **sceptre** *n.* скипетр.

sceptic *n.* = **skeptic.** —**sceptical,** *adj.* = **skeptical.** —**scepticism,** *n.* = **skepticism.**

sceptre *n.* = **scepter.**

schedule *n.* расписание. *On schedule,* по расписанию; в срок. *Ahead of schedule,* до срока; раньше срока. —*v.t.* назначать; намечать: *the meeting is scheduled for May 5th,* собрание назначено/назначается/намечается на пятое мая.

schematic *adj.* схематический.

scheme *n.* **1,** (plan of action) план. **2,** (underhanded plot) махинация; интрига. **3,** (diagram) схема. **4,** (orderly combination) сочетание: *color scheme,* сочетание цветов. —*v.i.* интриговать; вести интригу. —**schemer,** *n.* интриган.

scherzo *n.* скерцо.

schism *n.* раскол; схизма. —**schismatic,** *adj.* раскольнический.

schist *n.* сланец.

schizophrenia *n.* шизофрения. —**schizophrenic,** *adj.* шизофренический. —*n.* шизофреник.

schnitzel *n.* шницель.

scholar *n.* учёный. —**scholarly,** *adj.* учёный.

scholarship *n.* **1,** (learning) учёность. **2,** (grant) стипендия.

scholastic *adj.* школьный; учебный.

school *n.* **1,** (place of learning) школа: *go to school,* ходить в школу. *Law school,* юридический факультет. **2,** (classes) занятия; уроки: *miss school,* пропустить занятия. *Keep in after school,* оставлять после уроков. **3,** (trend in the arts) школа: *the impressionist school,* импрессионистская школа. **4,** (large group of fish) косяк. —*adj.* школьный; учебный. *School age,* школьный возраст. *School year,* учебный год. —*v.t.* **1,** (educate) воспитывать. *He was schooled in England,* он получил образование в Англии. **2,** (train; discipline) приучать. —**a man of the old school,** человек старого закала. —**school of thought,** точка зрения: *there are two schools of thought on this question,* на этот счёт существуют две различных точки зрения. —**tell tales out of school,** выносить сор из избы.

schoolbook *n.* учебник.

schoolboy *n.* школьник. —**schoolchildren,** *n.pl.* школьники. —**schoolgirl,** *n.* школьница.

schoolhouse *n.* школьное здание.

schooling *n.* образование.

schoolteacher *n.* учитель; учительница.

schooner *n.* шхуна.

sciatic *adj.* седалищный: *sciatic nerve,* седалищный нерв.

sciatica *n.* ишиас.

science *n.* наука. —**science fiction,** научная фантастика.

scientific *adj.* научный. —**scientifically,** *adv.* научно.

scientist *n.* **1,** (eminent scientist) учёный. **2,** (person engaged in scientific research) научный работник.

scimitar *n.* ятаган.

scintilla *n.* капелька; крупица; тень. *Not a scintilla of evidence,* ни малейших доказательств.

scintillate *v.i.* искриться. —**scintillating,** *adj.* блестящий.

scion *n.* отпрыск.

scissors *n.* ножницы.

sclerosis *n.* склероз. —**sclerotic,** *adj.* склеротический.

scoff *v.i.* [*usu.* scoff at] смеяться над.

scold *v.t.* бранить. —**scolding,** *n.* выговор; нагоняй.

scoop *n.* совок; ковш; черпак. —*v.t.* **1,** *fol. by* **up** (gather up) черпать; зачёрпывать. **2,** *fol. by* **out** (remove) вычёрпывать.

scoot *v.i., colloq.* бежать; удирать.

scooter *n.* самокат. —**motor scooter,** мотороллер.

scope *n.* **1,** (range; extent) размах; масштаб. **2,** (outlook; intellect) кругозор: *broaden one's scope,* расширять кругозор.

scorch *v.t.* опаливать; подпаливать. —**scorched-earth policy,** стратегия выжженной земли.

scorching *adj.* палящий.

score *n.* **1,** (in sports and games) счёт: *keep score,* вести счёт. *What's the score?,* какой счёт? *By a score of 2-0,* со счётом два-ноль. **2,** (achievement in a test or competition) результат: *achieve the highest score,* показать лучший результат. **3,** (account) счёт: *have no fear on that score,* на этот счёт можете быть спокойны. **4,** *pl.* (grievance demanding satisfaction) счёты: *settle scores with,* сводить счёты с. **5,** (twenty) двадцать; два десятка; *pl.* десятки; несколько десятков; множество. **6,** *music* партитура. **7,** (mark; incision) след; зарубка. —*v.t.* **1,** *sports: score a goal,* забить гол. *Score a point,* получить *or* выиграть очко. *Score ten points,* набрать десять очков. **2,** (achieve) получить; добиться. *Score a victory,* одержать победу. **3,** (denounce) осуждать. **4,** *music* оркестровать. —*v.i.* получить очко; забить гол. *Score first; be the first to score,* открыть счёт. —**know the score,** знать что к чему.

scoreboard *n.* табло.

scorekeeper *n.* судья.

scoreless *adj.* нулевой: *scoreless tie,* нулевая ничья.

scorn *n.* презрение. —*v.t.* презирать. —**scornful,** *adj.* презрительный.

Scorpio *n.* Скорпион.

scorpion *n.* скорпион.

Scotch *adj.* шотландский. —*n.* **1,** *preceded by* **the**

(people) шотла́ндцы. **2,** (whiskey) (шотла́ндское) ви́ски.

scotch *v.t.* опроверга́ть: *scotch a rumor,* опрове́ргнуть слух.

Scotchman *n.* шотла́ндец.

scot-free *adj.* безнака́занный.

Scotsman *n.* шотла́ндец.

Scottish *adj.* шотла́ндский. —**Scottish terrier,** шотла́ндский терье́р.

scoundrel *n.* подле́ц; негодя́й; мерза́вец; прохво́ст.

scour *v.t.* **1,** (clean thoroughly) чи́стить; отчища́ть. **2,** (range over in search of something) ры́скать по: *scour the woods,* ры́скать по ле́су.

scourge *n.* бич. *The scourge of war,* бич войны́.

scout *n.* **1,** (agent) разве́дчик; лазу́тчик. **2,** (boy scout) ска́ут. —*v.t.* разве́дывать.

scow *n.* шала́нда.

scowl *v.i.* хму́риться. —*n.* серди́тый взгляд.

scraggly *adj.* нечёсаный; взъеро́шенный.

scram *v.i., slang* убира́ться.

scramble *v.i.* **1,** (climb hurriedly) кара́бкаться: *scramble up a tree,* кара́бкаться на де́рево. **2,** (dash) бро́ситься: *scramble for cover/safety,* бро́ситься в укры́тие/в безопа́сное ме́сто. *The boys scrambled for the coins,* ма́льчики бро́сились за моне́тами. —*v.t.* (mix up; jumble) переме́шивать. —*n.* сва́лка. —**scrambled eggs,** яи́чница-болту́нья.

scrap *n.* **1,** (fragment) обры́вок; обре́зок; (of paper) клочо́к; (of material) лоску́т; (of bread) кусо́чек. **2,** *pl.* (bits of food) объе́дки. **3,** (waste metal) лом; ути́ль. **4,** *slang* (fight; quarrel) дра́ка; потасо́вка. —*adj.* ути́льный. *Scrap iron,* желе́зный лом; ути́льное желе́зо. *Scrap metal,* металлоло́м. *Scrap heap,* сва́лка. —*v.t.* **1,** (junk) сдава́ть на слом. *Be scrapped,* идти́ на слом. **2,** (drop, as a project) бро́сить. —*v.i., slang* (quarrel) вздо́рить.

scrapbook *n.* альбо́м для вы́резок.

scrape *v.t.* **1,** (rub the surface of) скрести́; скобли́ть. **2,** (injure; abrade) сдира́ть; сса́живать. —*n.* **1,** (abrasion) сса́дина. **2,** (predicament) переде́лка; передря́га. —**scrape along,** ко́е-как перебива́ться. —**scrape off,** соска́бливать; отска́бливать. — **scrape up; scrape together,** наскрести́; скола́чивать; выкра́ивать.

scraper *n.* скребо́к.

scrapper *n., colloq.* драчу́н; задира; забия́ка.

scrappy *adj., slang* драчли́вый.

scratch *n.* цара́пина. —*v.t.* **1,** (tear the skin slightly) цара́пать. **2,** (rub to relieve itching) чеса́ть. **3,** *fol. by* **out** (cross out) вычёркивать. **4,** (withdraw from a contest) снима́ть с состяза́ний. —*v.i.* **1,** (have a tendency to scratch) цара́паться. **2,** (rub to relieve itching) чеса́ться. **3,** (produce a grating sound) скрипе́ть. —**scratch the surface,** скользи́ть по пове́рхности. —**start from scratch,** нача́ть с азо́в. —**up to scratch,** на до́лжной высоте́.

scratch pad блокно́т.

scratch paper бума́га для заме́ток.

scratchy *adj.* скрипу́чий.

scrawl *n.* кара́кули; мара́нье. —*v.t.* (на)цара́пать. *Slogans were scrawled all over the wall,* стена́ была́ испи́сана ло́зунгами.

scrawny *adj.* костля́вый; сухопа́рый.

scream *v.i.* **1,** (yell) крича́ть: *scream from the pain,*

кричать от бо́ли; *scream with delight,* крича́ть от восто́рга. **2,** (whistle; roar) реве́ть: *sirens screamed,* сире́ны реве́ли. —*n.* **1,** (shriek) (пронзи́тельный) крик. **2,** *colloq.* (very funny person or thing) умо́ра.

screech *n.* визг; клёкот. —*v.i.* визжа́ть; клекота́ть.

screen *n.* **1,** (partition; anything that covers or protects) ши́рма. *Smoke screen,* дымова́я заве́са. **2,** (mesh for a window to keep out insects) се́тка. **3,** (surface for projecting pictures) экра́н. **4,** (motion pictures collectively) кино́; экра́н. *Adapt for the screen,* экранизи́ровать. —*v.t.* **1,** (shield) прикрыва́ть. **2,** *fol. by* **off** (separate by a screen) отгора́живать ши́рмой. **3,** (separate and select) фильтрова́ть.

screw *n.* винт. —*v.t.* **1,** *fol. by* **on** *or* **in** (turn tight, as a lid) нави́нчивать; зави́нчивать; приви́нчивать. *Screw in a bulb,* вви́нчивать *or* ввёртывать ла́мпочку. **2,** (attach with a screw) приви́нчивать: *screw a lock onto a door,* приви́нчивать замо́к к две́ри. *Screw something into a wall,* вви́нчивать что́-нибудь в сте́ну. **3,** *fol. by* **up** (contort) мо́рщить. *Screw up one's eyes,* щу́рить глаза́; щу́риться. **4,** *fol. by* **up,** *slang* (botch) напу́тать. —*v.i.* [*usu.* **screw on** *or* **onto**] нави́нчиваться; вви́нчиваться. —**he has a screw loose,** *slang* у него́ ви́нтика не хвата́ет. —**put the screws on,** нажима́ть на. —**tighten the screws,** зави́нчивать га́йки.

screwball *n., slang* сумасбро́д; чуда́к.

screwdriver *n.* отвёртка.

screw propeller гребно́й винт.

screwy *adj., slang* **1,** (crazy) сумасбро́дный. **2,** (odd) чудакова́тый.

scribble *v.t. & i.* строчи́ть; цара́пать; мара́ть. —*n.* кара́кули; мара́нье. —**scribbler,** *n.* писа́ка.

scribe *n.* **1,** (copier of manuscripts) писе́ц. **2,** *Bib.* кни́жник.

scrimmage *n.* **1,** (tussle) сва́лка. **2,** *football* сва́лка вокру́г мяча́.

scrimp *v.i.* скупи́ться.

scrip *n.* бума́жные де́ньги.

script *n.* **1,** (copy of something to be read) текст. **2,** (system of writing) письмо́: *the Arabic script,* ара́бское письмо́.

scriptural *adj.* библе́йский.

Scripture *n., usu. pl.* свяще́нное писа́ние.

scrofula *n.* золоту́ха.

scroll *n.* сви́ток.

scrotum *n.* мошо́нка.

scrub *v.t.* мыть (щёткой с мы́лом).

scruff *n.* загри́вок. —**by the scruff of the neck,** за ши́ворот.

scruffy *adj.* неря́шливый.

scrumptious *adj., colloq.* великоле́пный; о́чень вку́сный.

scruple *n., often pl.* угрызе́ния со́вести. *Have no scruples,* не стесня́ться в сре́дствах. —*v.i.* стесня́ться; со́веститься.

scrupulous *adj.* **1,** (honest) со́вестливый. **2,** (meticulous) добросо́вестный; скрупулёзный. —**scrupulously,** *adv.* свя́то: *scrupulously observe,* свя́то соблюда́ть (что́-нибудь).

scrutinize *v.t.* (при́стально) рассма́тривать. — **scrutiny,** *n.* рассмотре́ние.

scuffle *n.* дра́ка; сва́лка; потасо́вка. —*v.i.* дра́ться.

scull *n.* **1,** (single long oar) кормово́е весло́. **2,** (one

of a pair of short oars) па́рное весло́. **3**, (boat) греб-
на́я ло́дка. —*v.t. & i.* грести́.
scullery *n.* судомо́йня.
sculpt *v.t.* ва́ять; лепи́ть.
sculptor *n.* ску́льптор; вая́тель.
sculptural *adj.* скульпту́рный.
sculpture *n.* **1**, (art) скульпту́ра; вая́ние. **2**, (piece of
sculptured work) скульпту́ра; извая́ние. —*v.t.* ва́ять.
scum *n.* **1**, (extraneous matter on liquid) на́кипь. **2**,
(riffraff) подо́нки.
scurrilous *adj.* гру́бый; оскорби́тельный; непри-
сто́йный.
scurry *v.i.* бежа́ть; мча́ться.
scurvy *n.* цинга́; скорбу́т.
scutch *v.t.* трепа́ть. —*n.* трепа́ло.
scuttle *v.t.* затопля́ть (кора́бль).
scythe *n.* коса́.
Scythian *adj.* ски́фский. —*n.* скиф.
sea *n.* мо́ре. *Put (out) to sea,* выходи́ть в мо́ре. —*adj.*
морско́й: *sea water,* морска́я вода́. —**be all at sea,**
быть как в лесу́.
sea anemone акти́ния.
seabed *n.* морско́е дно.
seaboard *n.* побере́жье.
sea breeze морско́й бриз; примо́рский ве́тер.
seacoast *n.* побере́жье.
sea cow морска́я коро́ва.
sea dog морско́й волк.
sea elephant морско́й слон.
seafarer *n.* морепла́ватель; морехо́д.
seafood *n.* морски́е проду́кты.
seagoing *adj.* океа́нский; да́льнего пла́вания.
sea gull ча́йка.
sea horse морско́й конёк.
sea kale морска́я капу́ста.
seal *n.* **1**, (imprint; stamp for making same) печа́ть:
affix a seal to, ста́вить печа́ть на (+ *acc.*). *The Great
Seal of the United States,* госуда́рственная печа́ть
США. **2**, (wax to secure an envelope) печа́ть: *break the
seal,* взлома́ть печа́ть. **3**, (something that closes tightly) уплотни́тель: *rubber seal,* рези́новый уплотни́-
тель. **4**, (sign; token) знак: *seal of approval,* знак
одобре́ния. **5**, (marine animal) тюле́нь. *Fur seal,* ко́-
тик. —*v.t.* **1**, (close, as an envelope) закле́ивать; за-
печа́тывать. **2**, *often fol. by* **up** (close tightly) за-
де́лывать; забива́ть; зама́зывать; залепля́ть. **3**, *fol.
by* **off** (cordon off) оцепля́ть. **4**, (affix a seal to) скреп-
ля́ть печа́тью: *signed, sealed and delivered,* подпи́са-
но, скреплено́ печа́тью и вручено́. **5**, (settle finally)
реши́ть: *his fate is sealed,* его́ судьба́ решена́.
sealed move *chess* запи́санный ход.
sea level у́ровень мо́ря.
sealing wax сургу́ч.
sea lion морско́й лев.
sealskin *n.* ко́тик. —*adj.* ко́тиковый; тюле́невый.
seam *n.* шов. —*v.t.* сшива́ть. —**come apart at the
seams,** треща́ть по всем швам.
seaman *n.* матро́с; моря́к.
seamless *adj.* **1**, (of stockings) без шва. **2**, (of pipes)
бесшо́вный.
seamstress *n.* швея́; белошве́йка.
seamy *adj.,* *in* **the seamy side,** изна́нка: *the seamy
side of life,* изна́нка жи́зни.
séance *n.* спирити́ческий сеа́нс.
seaplane *n.* гидроплан; гидросамолёт.

seaport *n.* **1**, (harbor) морско́й порт. **2**, (city) порто́-
вый го́род.
sear *v.t.* опа́ливать. *Searing heat,* паля́щая жара́.
search *v.i.* [*usu.* **search for**] иска́ть: *search for one's
keys,* иска́ть свои́ ключи́. *I've searched everywhere,*
я всю́ду иска́л(а). —*v.t.* обы́скивать: *search a house/
suspect,* обы́скивать дом/подозрева́емого. *Search
the woods,* обы́скивать лес. —*n.* **1**, (for something
missing or desired) по́иски: *in search of,* в по́исках
(+ *gen.*). *Set out in search of,* отпра́виться на по́иски
(+ *gen.*). **2**, (of a suspect person or place) о́быск.
—**search party,** поиско́вая гру́ппа. —**search warrant,** о́рдер на о́быск.
searching *adj.* **1**, (extremely thorough) тща́тельный.
2, (penetrating, as of a look) испыту́ющий.
searchlight *n.* прожёктор.
seascape *n.* морско́й пейза́ж; мари́на.
sea shell раку́шка.
seashore *n.* морско́й бе́рег.
seasick *adj.* *Be seasick,* укача́ть (*impers.*): *I got
seasick,* меня́ укача́ло. —**seasickness,** *n.* морска́я
боле́знь.
seaside *n.* бе́рег мо́ря; примо́рье. —*adj.* примо́р-
ский: *seaside resort,* примо́рский куро́рт. *Seaside
cottage,* да́ча на мо́ре.
season *n.* **1**, (quarter of the year) вре́мя го́да: *the
four seasons,* четы́ре вре́мени го́да. **2**, (period of the
year, as for business, sports, etc.) сезо́н. *Strawberries
are out of season,* сейча́с не сезо́н для клубни́ки.
—*adj.* сезо́нный: *season ticket,* сезо́нный биле́т.
—*v.t.* **1**, (flavor) приправля́ть; заправля́ть; сда́бри-
вать. **2**, (inure; harden) закаля́ть. —*v.i.* (become seasoned) созрева́ть.
seasonal *adj.* сезо́нный.
seasoning *n.* припра́ва.
seat *n.* **1**, (place to sit) ме́сто: *reserved seat,* нуме-
ро́ванное ме́сто. *Take a seat,* сади́ться. *Take your
seats,* занима́йте свои́ места́. *Have a seat!,* при-
са́живайтесь! *Seat in parliament,* ме́сто в парла́-
менте. *We sat in the cheap seats,* мы сиде́ли на
дешёвых места́х. **2**, (that on which one sits) сиде́нье:
seat of a chair, сиде́нье сту́ла. *Back seat,* за́днее
сиде́нье. **3**, (back part of trousers) зад; сиде́нье. *Tight
in the seat,* у́зки в шагу́. **4**, (center; site) местопребы-
ва́ние: *seat of government,* местопребыва́ние пра-
ви́тельства. *Seat of learning,* расса́дник просвеще́-
ния. —*v.t.* **1**, (place on a seat) сажа́ть; уса́живать. **2**,
(hold; accommodate) вмеща́ть. —**be seated, 1**, (sit
down) сади́ться. *Please be seated,* прошу́ сади́ться.
2, (be sitting down) сиде́ть.
seat belt привязно́й реме́нь; реме́нь безопа́с-
ности.
seating *n.* сидя́чие места́. —**seating capacity,** чис-
ло́ мест. *The stadium has a seating capacity of
100,000,* стадио́н вмеща́ет сто ты́сяч челове́к.
sea urchin морско́й ёж.
sea wall волноре́з; волноло́м.
seaway *n.* фарва́тер.
seaweed *n.* (морска́я) во́доросль.
seaworthy *adj.* го́дный для пла́вания; морехо́д-
ный.
sebaceous glands са́льные же́лезы.
secant *n.* **1**, *geom.* секу́щая. **2**, *trig.* се́канс.
secede *v.i.* выходи́ть (из сою́за). —**secession,** *n.*
вы́ход.

seclude *v.t.* уединять. —**secluded,** *adj.* уединённый; укромный. —**seclusion,** *n.* уединение.

second *adj.* второй. *Come in second,* прийти вторым. *She married for a second time,* она вышла замуж вторично. *He is second to none,* он никому не уступает. —*n.* **1,** (unit of time or angular measure) секунда. *Just a second!,* одну минут(к)у!; одну секунд(очк)у! **2,** (attendant in boxing, a duel, etc.) секундант. **3,** *music* секунда. **4,** *pl.* (imperfect merchandise) (за)бракованный товар. —*v.t.* поддерживать: *second the motion,* поддерживать предложение. —**in the second place,** во-вторых.

secondary *adj.* **1,** (of less importance) второстепенный. **2,** (of education, school, etc.) средний. —**secondary sex characteristics,** вторичные половые признаки.

second-class *adj.* второклассный; второразрядный. *Second-class passengers,* пассажиры второго класса. *Second-class coach,* жёсткий вагон. —*adv.* вторым классом: *travel second-class,* ехать вторым классом.

second cousin *see* cousin.

second hand секундная стрелка.

secondhand *adj.* (not new) подержанный. *Secondhand bookstore,* букинистический магазин. —*adv.* (not from the original source) из вторых рук.

second lieutenant младший лейтенант.

secondly *adv.* во-вторых.

second nature вторая натура.

second-rate *adj.* второсортный; второразрядный.

second thought раздумье: *he had second thoughts,* его взяло раздумье. —**on second thought,** по зрелом размышлении; пораскинув умом.

second wind второе дыхание.

secrecy *n.* секретность. *In great secrecy,* под большим секретом.

secret *n.* секрет; тайна. *In secret,* тайно; втайне; тайком. —*adj.* **1,** (done or operating in secret) секретный; тайный. *Secret agent,* тайный агент. *Keep (something) secret,* держать *or* хранить в секрете (*or* в тайне). **2,** (hidden) потайной: *secret passage,* потайной ход.

secretarial *adj.* секретарский.

secretariat *n.* секретариат.

secretary *n.* **1,** (clerical assistant) секретарь; секретарша. **2,** (official; officer) секретарь. **3,** (cabinet officer) министр; секретарь. *Secretary of state,* государственный секретарь. *Secretary of the treasury,* министр финансов. *Foreign secretary,* министр иностранных дел. —**secretary-general,** генеральный секретарь.

secrete *v.t.* **1,** (conceal) укрывать; прятать. **2,** *physiol.* выделять. —**secretion,** *n.* секреция; выделение.

secretive *adj.* скрытный. —**secretiveness,** *n.* скрытность.

secretly *adv.* тайно; втайне; тайком.

secretory *adj.* выделительный.

sect *n.* секта.

sectarian *adj.* сектантский. —*n.* сектант. —**sectarianism,** *n.* сектантство.

section *n.* **1,** (portion, as of a road) отрезок. **2,** (part, as of a fence or bookcase) секция. **3,** (view in a given plane) сечение; разрез: *cross section,* поперечное сечение; поперечный разрез. *Conic section,* коническое сечение. **4,** (district; neighborhood) район. **5,** (division of an organization) отдел; секция. **6,** (division of a book or newspaper) отдел; раздел; (of a law) параграф. **7,** (slice, as of an orange) долька. **8,** (slice of something used for microscopic study) срез. **9,** (incision) сечение: *Caesarean section,* кесарево сечение.

sectional *adj.* **1,** (made up of sections) секционный; разборный; составной. **2,** (regional) местный.

sector *n.* **1,** (part of a circle) сектор. **2,** *mil.* участок. **3,** (division) сектор: *the private sector,* частный сектор.

secular *adj.* светский; мирской.

secularize *v.t.* секуляризировать. —**secularization,** *n.* секуляризация.

secure *adj.* **1,** (safe) безопасный: *secure place,* безопасное место. *Feel secure,* чувствовать себя в безопасности. **2,** (firm) прочный; крепкий: *secure foothold,* прочная опора; *secure grip,* крепкая хватка. —*v.t.* **1,** (firmly fasten) закреплять. **2,** (make safe) обезопасить. **3,** (make certain; ensure) обеспечивать. **4,** (gain; obtain) получить; достать. —**securely,** *adv.* прочно: *tie securely,* прочно привязывать.

security *n.* **1,** (safety; protection) безопасность: *national security,* государственная безопасность. *Provide security,* обеспечивать безопасность. **2,** (material well-being) обеспечение; обеспеченность. *Financial security,* материальное обеспечение. **3,** (pledge; deposit) залог: *leave something as security,* оставить что-нибудь под залог. **4,** *pl.* (stocks, bonds, etc.) ценные бумаги. —*adj.* *Security guard,* сторож; охранник. *Security measures,* меры безопасности. —**security clearance, 1,** (check) проверка благонадёжности. **2,** (access) допуск.

Security Council Совет Безопасности.

sedan *n.* легковой автомобиль. —**sedan chair,** портшёз.

sedate *adj.* степенный; чинный. —*v.t.* давать успокоительное средство (+ *dat.*).

sedation *n.* успокоение. *Place under sedation,* давать успокоительное средство (+ *dat.*). —**sedative,** *n.* успокоительное *or* успокаивающее средство; успокоительное.

sedentary *adj.* сидячий.

sedge *n.* осока.

sediment *n.* **1,** (matter that settles at the bottom) осадок. **2,** *geol.* отложение. —**sedimentary,** *adj.* осадочный.

sedition *n.* подстрекательство к мятежу. —**seditious,** *adj.* мятежный; бунтарский.

seduce *v.t.* соблазнять; обольщать. —**seducer,** *n.* соблазнитель; обольститель. —**seduction,** *n.* обольщение. —**seductive,** *adj.* соблазнительный; обольстительный.

sedulous *adj.* прилежный; старательный.

see *v.t. & i.* **1,** (perceive visually; have the power of sight) видеть: *see a man/car/difference,* видеть человека/машину/разницу. *Can you see?,* вам видно? *See in the dark,* видеть в темноте. *I saw him come in,* я видел, как он вошёл. **2,** (view) смотреть: *see a play,* смотреть пьесу. *Would you like to see it?,* хотите посмотреть? *I'll go see,* я пойду посмотрю. **3,** (understand) понимать: *I see,* я понимаю. *I see what you mean,* я понимаю, что вы имеете в виду. —*v.t.* **1,** (consult) обращаться к: *see a doctor,* обращаться к врачу́. **2,** (receive) принима́ть: *he refused to see me,* он отказа́лся приня́ть меня́. **3,** (visit; meet) ви́деть; встреча́ть: *we rarely see each other,* мы ре́дко ви́димся/встреча́емся. *He came to see me last night,* он пришёл ко мне вчера́ ве́чером. **4,** (escort) провожа́ть: *see someone to the door,* провожа́ть кого́-нибудь до двере́й. **5,** (find out; ascertain) смотре́ть; узнава́ть: *see who is at the door,* посмотри́те, кто стучи́т *or* звони́т (в дверь). **6,** (visualize) представля́ть (себе́). *I can't see myself doing that,* не могу́ предста́вить себя́ в э́той ро́ли. **7,** (interpret) рассма́тривать: *his hesitancy is seen as a sign of weakness,* его́ колеба́ние рассма́тривается как при́знак сла́бости. **8,** (admire) находи́ть: *what does she see in him?,* что она́ в нём нашла́? —*n.* престо́л: *holy see,* па́пский престо́л. —**let me see!,** да́йте мне поду́мать. —**see fit,** *see* **fit.** —**see for oneself,** воо́чию убеди́ться. *I want to see for myself,* я хочу́ убеди́ться сам (сама́). —**see here!,** послу́шайте! —**see off,** провожа́ть: *see someone off on the train,* провожа́ть кого́-нибудь на по́езд. —**see things,** каза́ться (+ *dat.*); чу́диться (+ *dat.*): *you're seeing things!,* вам то́лько ка́жется/чу́дится. —**see through, 1,** (not be fooled by) ви́деть наскво́зь. **2,** (carry through to the end) доводи́ть до конца́. **3,** (carry through a difficult time) хвата́ть: *this money should see you through the week,* де́нег должно́ вам хвати́ть до конца́ неде́ли. —**see to,** забо́титься о. —**see (to it) that...,** забо́титься о том, чтобы; доби́ться того́, чтобы.

seed *n.* **1,** (that which can grow into a new plant) се́мя. **2,** (of fruits, sunflowers, etc.) се́мечко. **3,** *fig.* (source) се́мя: *seeds of rebellion,* семена́ бу́нта. —*adj.* семенно́й: *seed coat,* семенна́я оболо́чка. —*v.t.* засева́ть (*e.g.* сад) семена́ми. —**go to seed, 1,** (shed seeds) пойти́ в семена́. **2,** (deteriorate) опуска́ться.

seeder *n.* се́ялка.

seedless *adj.* бессеме́нный.

seedling *n.* се́янец; *pl.* расса́да.

seedy *adj.* потрёпанный; потёртый.

seeing *conj.* [*usu.* **seeing that**] поско́льку; ввиду́ того́, что...

Seeing Eye dog соба́ка-поводы́рь.

seek *v.t.* **1,** (try to find) иска́ть: *seek one's long-lost sister,* иска́ть свою́ давно́ пропа́вшую сестру́. **2,** (try to obtain) иска́ть; добива́ться. *Seek work/help/advice/the cause/,* иска́ть рабо́ту/по́мощи/сове́та/причи́ну. *Seek recognition/an advantage/,* добива́ться призна́ния/преиму́щества. **3,** *fol. by inf.* (endeavor) пыта́ться; стреми́ться.

seeker *n.* иска́тель.

seem *v.i.* каза́ться: *he seems ill,* он ка́жется больны́м. *It seems to me that...,* мне ка́жется, что... *It may seem strange to you,* вам э́то мо́жет показа́ться стра́нным. *I can't seem to get used to it,* я ника́к не могу́ привы́кнуть к э́тому.

seeming *adj.* ка́жущийся; ви́димый. —**seemingly,** *adv.* каза́лось бы: *a seemingly small amount,* каза́лось бы небольша́я су́мма.

seemly *adj.* прили́чный; присто́йный.

seep *v.i.* проса́чиваться. —**seepage,** *n.* проса́чивание.

seer *n.* проро́к; прови́дец.

seesaw *n.* каче́ли.

seethe *v.i.* кипе́ть; бурли́ть.

segment *n.* **1,** (section) отре́зок. **2,** *geom.* сегме́нт.

segregate *v.t.* отделя́ть. —**segregation,** *n.* сегрега́ция.

seismic *adj.* сейсми́ческий.

seismograph *n.* сейсмо́граф.

seismology *n.* сейсмоло́гия. —**seismological,** *adj.* сейсмологи́ческий. —**seismologist,** *n.* сейсмо́лог.

seize *v.t.* **1,** (grasp) хвата́ть; схва́тывать. **2,** (take by force) захва́тывать; завладева́ть. **3,** (confiscate) конфискова́ть. **4,** (take prompt advantage of) ухвати́ться за. **5,** (overwhelm, as of fear) овладева́ть; охва́тывать; обуя́ть.

seizure *n.* **1,** (act of seizing) захва́т. **2,** (confiscation) конфиска́ция. **3,** (fit; attack) припа́док; при́ступ; уда́р.

seldom *adv.* ре́дко.

select *v.t.* отбира́ть; подбира́ть; избира́ть. *Selected works,* и́збранные сочине́ния. —*adj.* отбо́рный; и́збранный.

selection *n.* **1,** (act of selecting) отбо́р; подбо́р. **2,** (assortment) вы́бор; ассортиме́нт. **3,** *biol.* отбо́р: *natural selection,* есте́ственный отбо́р. —**selection committee,** отбо́рочная коми́ссия.

selective *adj.* **1,** (covering only selected items) вы́борочный. **2,** (choosy) разбо́рчивый. —**selective service,** во́инская пови́нность.

selectivity *n.* разбо́рчивость.

selenite *n.* сплени́т.

selenium *n.* селе́н.

self *n.* One's own self, со́бственная персо́на. *My other self,* моё второ́е я. *He is only a shadow of his former self,* от него́ оста́лась одна́ тень.

self-addressed *adj.* адресо́ванный самому́ себе́.

self-assurance *n.* самоуве́ренность; самонаде́янность. —**self-assured,** *adj.* самоуве́ренный; самонаде́янный.

self-centered *also,* **self-centred** *adj.* себялюби́вый.

self-complacent *adj.* самодово́льный. —**self-complacency,** *n.* самодово́льство.

self-confidence *n.* самоуве́ренность. —**self-confident,** *adj.* самоуве́ренный.

self-conscious *adj.* засте́нчивый; стесни́тельный; стыдли́вый.

self-contained *adj.* **1,** (existing on its own) самодовле́ющий. **2,** *mech.* автоно́мный: *self-contained equipment,* автоно́мное обору́дование.

self-control *n.* самооблада́ние. —**self-controlled,** *adj.* вы́держанный.

self-criticism *n.* самокри́тика. —**self-critical,** *adj.* самокрити́чный.

self-deception *n.* самообма́н.

self-defense *also,* **self-defence** *n.* самозащи́та; самооборо́на.

self-denial *n.* самоотрече́ние.

self-designation *n.* самоназва́ние.

self-destruction *n.* самоуничтоже́ние.

self-determination *n.* самоопределе́ние.

self-discipline *n.* самодисципли́на.

self-employed *adj.* самостоя́тельно за́нятый; рабо́тающий на себя́.

self-esteem *n.* самоуваже́ние.

self-evident *adj.* самоочеви́дный.

self-governing *adj.* самоуправля́ющийся. —**self-government,** *n.* самоуправле́ние.

self-immolation *n.* самосожже́ние.

self-importance *n.* ва́жность: *assume an air of self-importance,* напуска́ть на себя́ ва́жность. —**self-important,** *adj.* ва́жный.

self-interest *n.* коры́сть; корыстолю́бие; своекоры́стие.

selfish *adj.* **1,** (of a person) эгоисти́ческий; эгоисти́чный. **2,** (of interests, motives, etc.) коры́стный. —**selfishness,** *n.* эгои́зм.

selfless *adj.* самоотве́рженный. —**selflessness,** *n.* самоотве́рженность.

self-portrait *n.* автопортре́т.

self-possessed *adj.* вы́держанный.

self-preservation *n.* самосохране́ние.

self-propelled *adj.* самохо́дный; самодви́жущийся.

self-reliant *adj.* самостоя́тельный. —**self-reliance,** *n.* самостоя́тельность.

self-respect *n.* чу́вство со́бственного досто́инства; самолю́бие; самоуваже́ние.

self-restraint *n.* сде́ржанность.

self-righteous *adj.* ха́нжеский. —**self-righteousness,** *n.* ха́нжество.

self-sacrifice *n.* самопоже́ртвование.

selfsame *adj.* тот же са́мый.

self-satisfaction *n.* самодово́льство. —**self-satisfied,** *adj.* самодово́льный.

self-seeking *adj.* своекоры́стный.

self-service *n.* самообслу́живание. *Self-service store,* магази́н самообслу́живания.

self-starter *n.* самопу́ск.

self-styled *adj.* самозва́н(н)ый.

self-sufficient *adj.* самостоя́тельный. —**self-sufficiency,** *n.* (экономи́ческая) самостоя́тельность.

self-supporting *adj.* самостоя́тельный.

self-taught *adj. Rendered by* самоу́чка: *self-taught engineer,* инжене́р-самоу́чка.

self-willed *adj.* самово́льный.

sell *v.t.* **1,** (transfer for money) продава́ть: *she was selling flowers,* она́ продава́ла цветы́. *I sold my house,* я про́дал свой дом. **2,** (deal in; carry) торгова́ть (+ *instr.*). *The store sells bicycles,* в магази́не продаю́тся велосипе́ды; магази́н торгу́ет велосипе́дами. —*v.i.* **1,** (engage in selling) продава́ть. **2,** (be sold) продава́ться; расходи́ться: *be selling well,* хорошо́ продава́ться/расходи́ться. *These ties sell for a dollar,* э́ти га́лстуки мо́жно купи́ть за до́ллар. —**sell oneself, 1,** (sell one's services) продава́ться; продава́ть себя́. **2,** *colloq.* (convince others of one's worth) набива́ть себе́ це́ну. —**sell out, 1,** (sell completely) распрода́ть: *the book is sold out,* кни́га распро́дана. *The book sold out immediately,* кни́гу разошла́сь момента́льно; кни́гу неме́дленно раскупи́ли. **2,** *colloq.* (betray one's cause) продава́ться: *sell out to the enemy,* продава́ться врагу́.

seller *n.* продаве́ц.

selling *n.* прода́жа. —**selling price,** прода́жная цена́.

sellout *n. The show is a complete sellout,* пье́са де́лает по́лные сбо́ры.

seltzer *n.* [*usu.* **seltzer water**] се́льтерская вода́.

selvage *n.* кро́мка.

semantic *adj.* семанти́ческий; смыслово́й. —**semantics,** *n.* сема́нтика.

semaphore *n.* семафо́р.

semblance *n.* **1,** (likeness; copy) подо́бие. **2,** (outward appearance) ви́димость: *a semblance of order,* ви́димость поря́дка.

semen *n.* се́мя; спе́рма.

semester *n.* семе́стр.

semiannual *adj.* полугодово́й.

semiautomatic *adj.* полуавтомати́ческий.

semicircle *n.* полукру́г. —**semicircular,** *adj.* полукру́глый.

semicolon *n.* то́чка с запято́й.

semiconductor *n.* полупроводни́к.

semiconscious *adj.* полусозна́тельный; полубессозна́тельный; в полу(бес)созна́тельном состоя́нии.

semidarkness *n.* полумра́к; полутьма́; су́мрак.

semifinal *n.* [*also,* **semifinals**] полуфина́л. —*adj.* полуфина́льный. —**semifinalist,** *n.* полуфинали́ст.

semiliterate *adj.* полугра́мотный; малогра́мотный.

seminal *adj.* **1,** *biol.* семенно́й: *seminal fluid,* семенна́я жи́дкость. **2,** *fig.* (breaking new ground) основополага́ющий.

seminar *n.* семина́р.

seminary *n.* семина́рия.

semiprecious *adj.* самоцве́тный. *Semiprecious stone,* самоцве́т.

Semitic *adj.* семи́тский; семити́ческий.

semitrailer *n.* полуприце́п.

senate *n.* сена́т. —**senator,** *n.* сена́тор. —**senatorial,** *adj.* сена́торский.

send *v.t.* посыла́ть; присыла́ть; отправля́ть: *send a package/messenger,* посыла́ть/присыла́ть/отправля́ть посы́лку/курье́ра. *Send a telegram,* дать/посла́ть/отпра́вить телегра́мму. *Send regards,* посла́ть или передава́ть приве́т. *Send a pupil from the room,* выгоня́ть ученика́ из кла́сса. —**send away,** усыла́ть. —**send away for,** выпи́сывать. —**send for,** посыла́ть за (+ *instr.*). —**send off,** отсыла́ть. —**send out, 1,** (mail out) высыла́ть; рассыла́ть: *send out a package,* высыла́ть посы́лку; *send out invitations,* рассыла́ть приглаше́ния. **2,** (assign; dispatch) засыла́ть: *send out spies,* засыла́ть шпио́нов. **3,** (transmit, as a signal) передава́ть.

sender *n.* отправи́тель.

send-off *n.* про́воды.

senile *adj.* ста́рческий. —**senility,** *n.* ста́рческое слабоу́мие.

senior *adj.* ста́рший: *senior member,* ста́рший член. *John Smith, Sr.,* Джон Смит ста́рший. —*n.* **1,** (elder) ста́рший. *Three years my senior,* ста́рше меня́ на три го́да. **2,** (student) старшеку́рсник. —**seniority,** *n.* старшинство́.

sensation *n.* **1,** (feeling) чу́вство; ощуще́ние. **2,** (great excitement; that which causes it) сенса́ция.

sensational *adj.* **1,** (causing great excitement) сенсацио́нный. **2,** (extraordinary; phenomenal) потряса́ющий.

sense *n.* **1,** (faculty) чу́вство: *the five senses,* пять чувств. *Sense of smell,* обоня́ние. *Sense of touch,* осяза́ние. *Sense of humor,* чу́вство ю́мора. *Sense organs,* о́рганы чувств. **2,** (good judgment; logic; point) смысл. *There is no sense in...,* нет смы́сла (+ *inf.*). *Make no sense at all,* не име́ть никако́го смы́сла. *Talk sense,* говори́ть де́ло. **3,** *pl.* (rationality) ум: *take leave of one's senses,* сойти́ с ума́; *come to one's senses,* бра́ться за ум;

bring to one's senses, наводи́ть на ум. **4,** (meaning) смысл: in the literal sense of the word, в буква́льном смы́сле э́того сло́ва. —v.t. чу́вствовать; ощуща́ть; чу́ять. Sense danger, чу́вствовать опа́сность. I sensed that something was wrong, я почу́вствовал что́-то недо́брое. —**in a sense,** в изве́стном смы́сле.

senseless adj. **1,** (making no sense) бессмы́сленный. **2,** (unconscious) без созна́ния. Beat senseless, бить до бесчу́вствия. —**senselessly,** adv. бессмы́сленно.

senselessness n. **1,** (irrationality) бессмы́сленность. **2,** (unconsciousness) бесчу́вствие.

sensibility n. **1,** (ability to perceive) чувстви́тельность. **2,** pl. (feelings; pride) чу́вства (прили́чия); самолю́бие.

sensible adj. разу́мный; благоразу́мный. —**sensibly,** adv. разу́мно.

sensitive adj. **1,** (perceptive; responsive; tender) чувстви́тельный: sensitive skin/film, чувстви́тельная ко́жа/плёнка. Sensitive to light, чувстви́тельный к све́ту. **2,** (easily offended) оби́дчивый. **3,** (involving secret matters) секре́тный; засекре́ченный. —**sensitivity,** n. чувстви́тельность.

sensor n. да́тчик.

sensory adj. сенсо́рный. Sensory nerve, чувстви́тельный нерв.

sensual adj. чу́вственный; сладостра́стный. —**sensuality,** n. чу́вственность; сладостра́стие.

sensuous adj. чу́вственный.

sentence n. **1,** (group of words) предложе́ние; фра́за. **2,** (penalty pronounced) пригово́р. Death sentence, сме́ртный пригово́р. Serve out a sentence, отбыва́ть срок наказа́ния. —v.t. пригова́ривать: sentence to prison, пригова́ривать к тюре́мному заключе́нию.

sententious adj. сентенцио́зный.

sentiment n. **1,** usu. pl. (feelings) чу́вства: lofty sentiments, высо́кие чу́вства. Pacifist sentiments, паци-фи́стские настрое́ния. **2,** (opinion) мне́ние: public sentiment, обще́ственное мне́ние. **3,** (sentimentality) сентимента́льность.

sentimental adj. сентимента́льный. —**sentimentality,** n. сентимента́льность.

sentinel n. часово́й.

sentry n. часово́й; карау́льный. —**sentry box,** карау́льная or постова́я бу́дка.

sepal n. чашели́стик.

separate v.t. **1,** (set apart) отделя́ть: separate the boys from the girls, отделя́ть ма́льчиков от де́вочек. **2,** (form a barrier or boundary between) разделя́ть. **3,** (pull apart, as two combatants) разнима́ть. **4,** (force to part company) разъединя́ть; разлуча́ть. Be separated from the group, отстава́ть от гру́ппы. Become separated in a crowd, потеря́ть друг дру́га в толпе́. —v.i. **1,** (become divided) отделя́ться. **2,** (part company) разлуча́ться. **3,** (break up without a divorce) расходи́ться; разъезжа́ться. —adj. отде́льный: separate entrance, отде́льный вход. Conclude a separate peace, заключи́ть сепара́тный мир. —**separately,** adv. отде́льно.

separation n. **1,** (dividing) отделе́ние. **2,** (parting company) разлу́ка. —**separation of powers,** разделе́ние вла́сти.

separatism n. сепарати́зм. —**separatist,** n. сепара-ти́ст. —adj. сепарати́стский.

separator n. сепара́тор.

sepia n. се́пия. —adj. кори́чневый.

sepsis n. се́псис.

September n. сентя́брь. —adj. сентя́брьский.

septic adj. септи́ческий.

sepulcher also, **sepulchre** n. моги́ла; склеп. —**sepulchral,** adj. моги́льный; замоги́льный.

sequel n. продолже́ние.

sequence n. поря́док. In sequence, по поря́дку. Sequence of events, ход собы́тий. Sequence of tenses, gram. согласова́ние времён.

sequester v.t. налага́ть секве́стр на; секвестрова́ть. —**sequestration,** n. секве́стр.

sequin n. блёстка.

sequoia n. секво́йя.

seraglio n. сера́ль.

seraph n. серафи́м.

Serb n. серб. —**Serbian,** adj. се́рбский. —n. се́рбский язы́к.

Serbo-Croatian adj. сербохорва́тский; сербско-хорва́тский.

serenade n. серена́да.

serene adj. **1,** (unclouded) безо́блачный. **2,** (tranquil) споко́йный; безмяте́жный. —**serenity,** n. споко́йствие; безмяте́жность.

serf n. крепостно́й. —**serfdom,** n. крепостно́е пра́во; крепостни́чество.

serge n. са́ржа. —adj. са́ржевый.

sergeant n. сержа́нт.

serial adj. сери́йный. —n. по́весть в не́скольких частя́х; фильм в не́скольких се́риях.

serialize v.t. издава́ть се́риями.

serial number 1, (of a serviceman) ли́чный но́мер. **2,** (of a manufactured product) поря́дковый но́мер.

sericulture n. шелково́дство.

series n. **1,** (set) се́рия: series of experiments, се́рия о́пытов. **2,** (number of; succession of) ряд: a whole series of disasters, це́лый ряд катастро́ф. **3,** math. ряд.

serious adj. серьёзный: serious tone/step/student, серьёзный тон/шаг/студе́нт; serious error/illness, серьёзная оши́бка/боле́знь. Are you serious?, вы э́то серьёзно? I'm serious, я говорю́ серьёзно.

seriously adv. **1,** (in earnest) серьёзно: talk seriously, говори́ть серьёзно. Take seriously, принима́ть всерьёз. **2,** (gravely) тяжело́: seriously ill/injured, тяжело́ бо́лен/ра́нен.

seriousness n. серьёзность. In all seriousness, серьёзно; со всей серьёзностью.

sermon n. про́поведь. Sermon on the Mount, Наго́рная про́поведь.

sermonize v.i. пропове́довать. —**sermonizer,** n. пропове́дник; резонёр.

serology n. сероло́гия.

serpent n. змея́. —**serpentine,** adj. змееви́дный.

serrate adj. зу́бчатый; зазу́бренный. Also, **serrated.**

serum n. сы́воротка.

servant n. (man) слуга́; (woman) служа́нка; прислу́га. Servants, слу́ги; прислу́га. —**civil servant,** госуда́рственный служащий.

serve v.t. **1,** (work for; be in the service of) служи́ть (+ dat.): serve one's country, служи́ть свое́й ро́дине. If memory serves me correctly, е́сли па́мять мне не изменя́ет. **2,** (provide with goods or services) обслу́живать: serve a customer/district, обслу́живать покупа́теля/райо́н. **3,** (prepare and offer, as food or a meal) подава́ть; сервирова́ть. *Dinner is served!*, обе́д по́дан! **4,** (set food before): *may I serve you?*, мо́жно вам положи́ть на таре́лку? **5,** (present; deliver, as a legal document) вруча́ть. **6,** (complete, as a prison term) отбыва́ть: *serve one's sentence*, отбыва́ть срок наказа́ния. *Serve five years in prison*, (от)сиде́ть пять лет в тюрьме́. **7,** *sports* подава́ть (мяч). **8,** *Serve the purpose*, отвеча́ть це́ли. —*v.i.* **1,** (perform service) служи́ть: *serve in the navy*, служи́ть во фло́те. **2,** *fol. by* **as** (function as) служи́ть (+ *instr.*): *serve as a judge/bedroom/pretext*, служи́ть судьёй/спа́льней/предло́гом. **3,** (be suitable or usable) годи́ться. **4,** *sports* подава́ть. —*n.*, *sports* пода́ча. —**it serves him right,** так ему́ и на́до; туда́ ему́ и доро́га.

server *n.* **1,** (waiter) подава́льщик. **2,** (tray) подно́с; (utensil) лопа́тка. **3,** *sports* игро́к, подаю́щий мяч.

service *n.* **1,** (act of serving) слу́жба: *military service*, вое́нная слу́жба. **2,** (work professionally performed) обслу́живание: *medical service*, медици́нское обслу́живание. *Poor service*, плохо́е обслу́живание. **3,** (public institution or facility) слу́жба: *weather service*, слу́жба пого́ды. *Rail service*, железнодоро́жное сообще́ние *or* движе́ние. *Telephone service*, телефо́нная связь. **4,** (help given another) услу́га: *offer one's services*, предлага́ть свои́ услу́ги. **5,** *pl.* (deeds performed) заслу́ги: *in recognition of one's services*, в знак призна́ния чьих-нибудь заслу́г. **6,** (armed forces) вое́нная слу́жба: *drafted into the service*, при́зван на вое́нную слу́жбу. **7,** (set of dishes) серви́з: *tea service*, ча́йный серви́з. **8,** (public worship) слу́жба; богослуже́ние. **9,** (religious ceremony) слу́жба: *funeral service(s)*, заупоко́йная слу́жба. **10,** *sports* пода́ча. —*adj.* обслу́живающий: *service personnel*, обслу́живающий персона́л. *Service elevator*, грузово́й лифт. *Service record*, послужно́й спи́сок. —*v.t.* обслу́живать: *service a car*, обслу́живать автомоби́ль. —**at your service,** к ва́шим услу́гам. —**be in service,** рабо́тать; де́йствовать. —**be of service,** быть поле́зным. —**"out of service",** "не рабо́тает".

serviceable *adj.* поле́зный; приго́дный.

service cap фура́жка.

service charge допла́та за обслу́живание.

serviceman *n.* **1,** (member of the armed forces) военнослу́жащий. **2,** (repairman) ма́стер.

service station бензозапра́вочная ста́нция; автозапра́вочная ста́нция.

servile *adj.* рабо́лепный; подобостра́стный. —**servility,** *n.* рабо́лепие; подобостра́стие.

serving *n.* по́рция.

servitude *n.* ра́бство. —**penal servitude,** ка́торга; ка́торжные рабо́ты.

sesame *n.* кунжу́т; сеза́м. —*adj.* кунжу́тный; сеза́мовый. —**open sesame!,** сеза́м, откро́йся!

session *n.* **1,** (meeting) заседа́ние; се́ссия. *Joint session*, совме́стное заседа́ние. *Be in session*, заседа́ть. **2,** (sitting; appointment) сеа́нс. **3,** (school term): *summer session*, ле́тние ку́рсы.

set *v.t.* **1,** (put; place) ста́вить; класть: *set the package on the table*, ста́вить/класть посы́лку на стол. **2,** (arrange, as a table) накрыва́ть. *Set the table for six*, накры́ть стол на шесть прибо́ров. **3,** (adjust to a certain setting) ста́вить: *set the alarm for 6:00*, ста́вить буди́льник на шесть часо́в. *Set one's watch by the radio*, ста́вить *or* установи́ть часы́ по ра́дио. **4,**

(mount, as a gem) оправля́ть; обде́лывать. **5,** (arrange, as one's hair) укла́дывать. **6,** (lay, as a trap) ста́вить. **7,** *med.* вправля́ть: *set a bone*, вправля́ть кость. **8,** (fix, as a date) назнача́ть; намеча́ть (срок); (a price) устана́вливать (це́ну). **9,** (establish) устана́вливать: *set a limit*, устана́вливать преде́л. *Set a record*, устана́вливать *or* ста́вить реко́рд. *Set a precedent*, создава́ть прецеде́нт. *Set an example*, подава́ть приме́р. *Set the tone*, задава́ть тон. **10,** (assign; lay down) ста́вить: *set a task for oneself*, ста́вить себе́ зада́чу. **11,** *printing* набира́ть. **12,** (bring to a certain state) *rendered by various verbs*: *set free*, освобожда́ть; *set in motion*, приводи́ть в движе́ние; *set at ease*, успока́ивать; *set on fire*, поджига́ть; *set to music*, положи́ть на му́зыку. —*v.i.* **1,** (sink below the horizon) заходи́ть; сади́ться. **2,** (solidify; congeal) затвердева́ть; застыва́ть. —*n.* **1,** (group of matching things) набо́р; компле́кт; гарниту́р; прибо́р. *Set of tools*, набо́р/компле́кт инструме́нтов. *Desk set*, пи́сьменный прибо́р. *Set of china*, фарфо́ровый серви́з. *Set of underwear*, гарниту́р белья́. *Chess set*, ша́хматы. *Set of stamps*, се́рия ма́рок. **2,** (transmitting or receiving device) устро́йство. *Television set*, телеви́зор. **3,** (group of people) о́бщество; свет. *The smart set*, мо́дный свет. **4,** *theat.* обстано́вка. **5,** *motion pictures* съёмочная площа́дка. **6,** *tennis* сет. **7,** *math.* мно́жество: *theory of sets*, тео́рия мно́жеств. —*adj.* **1,** (fixed) устано́вленный; определённый. **2,** (rigid; unchanging) неизме́нный. *Set pattern*, шабло́н. *Set expression*, усто́йчивое словосочета́ние. **3,** *colloq.* (ready) гото́вый. *Get set*, гото́виться. **4,** *in dead set against*, категори́чески про́тив. —**set about,** начина́ть; приступа́ть к. —**set against, 1,** (balance; compare) противопоставля́ть. **2,** (prejudice against) восстана́вливать про́тив; настра́ивать про́тив; вооружа́ть про́тив. —**set apart,** выделя́ть. —**set aside, 1,** (lay aside) откла́дывать (в сто́рону); сберега́ть. **2,** (annul) отменя́ть. —**set back, 1,** (move back, as a clock) ста́вить наза́д. **2,** (hinder the progress of) заде́рживать: *the fire set us back six months*, пожа́р задержа́л на́шу рабо́ту на шесть ме́сяцев. **3,** *The house is set back from the road*, дом стои́т в стороне́ от доро́ги. **4,** *colloq.* (cost) сто́ить; обходи́ться. *How much did it set you back?*, ско́лько вы за э́то заплати́ли? —**set down, 1,** (put down) ста́вить; класть. **2,** (land, as an aircraft) посади́ть. **3,** (put in writing) запи́сывать; пи́сьменно излага́ть. —**set forth, 1,** (state; express) излага́ть. **2,** (start out) отправля́ться. —**set in,** устана́вливаться; водворя́ться; воцаря́ться. *Winter has set in*, установи́лась зима́. —**set off, 1,** (start; touch off) вызыва́ть; порожда́ть. *Set off a chain reaction*, вызыва́ть цепну́ю реа́кцию. **2,** (cause to go off or explode) взрыва́ть. **3,** (set in relief; make prominent) оттеня́ть. **4,** (start out) отправля́ться. —**set out, 1,** (display) выставля́ть. **2,** (start out) отправля́ться; дви́гаться в путь. —**set up,** устра́ивать; создава́ть; организова́ть. *Set up house*, обзавести́сь хозя́йством. *Set up camp*, распола́гаться ла́герем. —**set upon, 1,** (attack) напада́ть на. **2,** (cause to attack) натра́вливать (соба́ку) на.

setback *n.* неуда́ча.

settee *n.* небольшо́й дива́н.

setter *n.* лега́вая соба́ка; се́ттер.

setting *n.* **1,** (surroundings; background) окруже́ние; обстано́вка. **2,** (mount, as for a jewel) опра́ва. **3,** (роsition, as on a dial) устано́вка. **4,** (place setting) прибо́р. **5,** *Setting of the sun,* захо́д со́лнца.

settle *v.t.* **1,** (resolve, as a dispute, issue, etc.) реша́ть; разреша́ть; ула́живать; урегули́ровать. *The matter is settled,* вопро́с исче́рпан. **2,** (populate; colonize) заселя́ть; осва́ивать. **3,** (cause to come to rest) прибива́ть: *the rain settled the dust,* дождь приби́л пыль. **4,** (calm, as one's nerves or stomach) успока́ивать. **5,** (dispose of; pay) опла́чивать; упла́чивать: *settle an account,* оплати́ть счёт; уплати́ть по счёту. *Settle one's debts,* распла́чиваться с долга́ми. *Settle scores with,* своди́ть счёты с. —*v.i.* **1,** (establish residence) поселя́ться; обосно́вываться. **2,** (come to rest) сади́ться; оседа́ть. *The dust settled,* пыль улегла́сь. **3,** (become clear, as of liquids) отста́иваться; устоя́ться. —**settle down, 1,** (calm down; quiet down) успока́иваться. **2,** (lead a more settled life) остепени́ться. **3,** *fol. by* **to** (sit down and begin) уса́живаться за (+ *acc.*); располага́ться (+ *inf.*). —**settle for,** дово́льствоваться (+ *instr.*): *settle for a draw,* дово́льствоваться ничье́й. —**settle on/upon, 1,** (decide upon) остана́вливаться на. **2,** (agree upon) догова́риваться о. —**settle up,** рассчи́тываться; распла́чиваться.

settlement *n.* **1,** (resolution, as of a dispute) урегули́рование; разреше́ние. **2,** (agreement) соглаше́ние. **3,** (settling of a new region) заселе́ние. **4,** (small settled area) поселе́ние; селе́ние; посёлок. **5,** (payment) расчёт.

settler *n.* поселе́нец.

setup *n.* организа́ция; структу́ра; устро́йство.

seven *adj.* семь. —*n.* **1,** (cardinal number) семь. **2,** *cards* семёрка.

sevenfold *adj.* семикра́тный. —*adv.* в семь раз.

seven hundred семьсо́т. —**seven-hundredth,** *adj.* семисо́тый.

seventeen *n. & adj.* семна́дцать. —**seventeenth,** *adj.* семна́дцатый.

seventh *adj.* седьмо́й. —*n.* **1,** (seventh part) седьма́я часть. **2,** (fraction) седьма́я: *one-seventh,* одна́ седьма́я. **3,** *music* се́птима. —**be in seventh heaven,** быть на седьмо́м не́бе.

seventy *n. & adj.* се́мьдесят. —**seventieth,** *adj.* семидеся́тый.

sever *v.t.* **1,** (cut off) отреза́ть; отруба́ть; отка́лывать. **2,** (break off, as ties) порыва́ть; разрыва́ть; прерыва́ть.

several *adj.* не́сколько: *several times,* не́сколько раз. —*n.* не́которые: *several of them,* не́которые из них.

severance *n.* разры́в. —**severance pay,** выходно́е посо́бие.

severe *adj.* **1,** (harsh) суро́вый; стро́гий. *Severe winter,* суро́вая зима́. *Severe sentence,* суро́вый/стро́гий пригово́р. **2,** (very great; intense) си́льный: *severe pain,* си́льная боль. *Severe frost,* си́льный *or* жесто́кий моро́з. *Suffer severe damage,* си́льно пострада́ть.

severely *adv.* **1,** (harshly) суро́во; стро́го. **2,** (seriously) си́льно: *severely damaged,* си́льно повреждён.

severity *n.* суро́вость; стро́гость.

sew *v.t. & i.* шить. —**sew on,** пришива́ть. —**sew up,** зашива́ть.

sewage *n.* нечисто́ты; сто́чные во́ды.

sewer *n.* сто́чная труба́. —**sewerage,** *n.* канализа́ция.

sewing *n.* шитьё. —**sewing machine,** швейная маши́на.

sex *n.* **1,** (male or female) пол: *the opposite sex,* противополо́жный пол. **2,** (sexual activity, feelings, etc.) секс: *a book about sex,* кни́га о се́ксе. *Have sex with,* вступи́ть в половую связь с. —*adj.* половой: *the sex act,* половой акт; *sex education,* половое воспита́ние.

sexless *adj.* беспо́лый.

sextant *n.* секста́нт.

sextet *also,* **sextette** *n.* сексте́т.

sexton *n.* церко́вный сто́рож; понома́рь.

sexual *adj.* половой; сексуа́льный. —**sexuality,** *n.* сексуа́льность.

shabbily *adv.* **1,** (poorly) бе́дно: *shabbily dressed,* бе́дно оде́тый. **2,** (meanly) по́дло.

shabbiness *n.* убо́гость.

shabby *adj.* **1,** (threadbare) поно́шенный; потёртый; потрёпанный. **2,** (run-down; dilapidated) ве́тхий; убо́гий. **3,** (mean; unfair) по́длый; ни́зкий.

shack *n.* хижина.

shackle *n., usu. pl.* кандалы́; око́вы. —*v.t.* зако́вывать в кандалы́; ско́вывать.

shade *n.* **1,** (darkness; dark area) тень: *in the shade,* в тени́. **2,** (gradation of color) отте́нок. **3,** (nuance) отте́нок: *shade of meaning,* отте́нок значе́ния. **4,** (blind) што́ра. **5,** (small amount) she is a shade better today, ей немно́го лу́чше сего́дня. —*v.t.* **1,** (screen from light) затеня́ть; заслоня́ть. *Shade one's eyes from the sun,* защища́ть глаза́ от со́лнца. **2,** (add shading to) оттеня́ть; тушева́ть; штрихова́ть.

shading *n.* **1,** (small variation) разли́чие. **2,** *drawing* тушёвка; штрихо́вка.

shadow *n.* тень: *cast a shadow,* отбра́сывать тень. *Shadows are falling,* те́ни ло́жатся. *Not a shadow of doubt,* ни те́ни сомне́ния. *He is only a shadow of his former self,* от него́ оста́лась одна́ тень. —*v.t.* (trail) следи́ть за; высле́живать; просле́живать. —**shadow boxing,** бой с те́нью.

shadowy *adj.* тёмный; сму́тный.

shady *adj.* **1,** (in the shade at a given time) теневой, (generally in the shade) тени́стый. **2,** *colloq.* (dubious; underhanded) тёмный; сомни́тельный; нечи́стый.

shaft *n.* **1,** (long body, as of a spear) дре́вко. **2,** (beam, as of light) сноп (све́та). **3,** (bar transmitting motion) вал: *drive shaft,* приводно́й вал. **4,** (pole to which an animal is hitched) огло́бля; ды́шло. **5,** (passage, as in a mine or for an elevator) ша́хта.

shaggy *adj.* косма́тый; лохма́тый; мохна́тый.

shah *n.* шах.

shake *v.t.* **1,** (agitate) трясти́: *shake a tree,* трясти́ де́рево. *Shake one's watch,* встря́хивать часы́. *Shake well before using,* взба́лтывать пе́ред употребле́нием. **2,** (rock; jolt) потряса́ть; сотряса́ть. **3,** (brandish) потряса́ть: *shake one's fists,* потряса́ть кулака́ми. *Shake one's fist at,* грози́ть кулако́м (+ *dat.*). **4,** (shock; unnerve) потряса́ть. **5,** (weaken; undermine) колеба́ть; пошатну́ть: *shake one's faith in,* колеба́ть/пошатну́ть чью-нибудь ве́ру в (+ *acc.*). **6,** *in* **shake hands,** пожима́ть ру́ки. *Shake hands with,* пожима́ть ру́ку (+ *dat.*). **7,** *in* **shake one's head,** кача́ть голово́й. —*v.i.* **1,** (tremble) дрожа́ть; трясти́сь; сотряса́ться. —*n.* **1,** (an act of shaking) встря́ска. **2,** *pl.* [*usu.* **the shakes**] (trembling) дрожь. **3,** (drink) кокте́йль: *milk shake,* моло́чный кокте́йль. **4,** *colloq.* (jiffy) миг. *In two* *shakes,* в два счёта. —**shake down,** стря́хивать: *shake down a thermometer,* стря́хивать термо́метр. —**shake off, 1,** (brush off) отря́хивать; стря́хивать. **2,** (get rid of, as a feeling) избавля́ться от; отде́лываться от; сбра́сывать; стря́хивать. *Shake off a cold,* изба́виться от просту́ды. **3,** (elude) отрыва́ться от. —**shake out,** вытря́хивать; вытряса́ть. —**shake up, 1,** (shake hard) встря́хивать; взба́лтывать. **2,** (unnerve) потряса́ть. **3,** (shuffle) перетасо́вывать.

shake-up *n.* перетасо́вка.

shaky *adj.* ша́ткий; нетвёрдый; зы́бкий.

shale *n.* (гли́нистый) сла́нец. *Oil shale,* нефтено́сный сла́нец. —**shale oil,** сла́нцевое ма́сло.

shall *v.aux.* **1,** *used to form the future tense: What shall we do?,* что мы бу́дем де́лать? **2,** *used to make a suggestion: Shall we dance?,* потанцу́ем?

shallot *n.* шало́т.

shallow *adj.* **1,** (not deep) ме́лкий. **2,** *fig.* (lacking depth) пове́рхностный.

sham *n.* **1,** (fraudulent imitation) подде́лка. **2,** (pretense) притво́рство.

shaman *n.* шама́н. —**shamanism,** *n.* шама́нство.

shambles *n.* разгро́м: *the room was a shambles,* в ко́мнате был по́лный разгро́м.

shame *n.* **1,** (feeling of guilt) стыд. *Shame on you!,* сты́дно!; как вам не сты́дно! **2,** (disgrace; dishonor) позо́р. *Bring shame upon,* (о)позо́рить. **3,** (a pity) жаль: *what a shame!,* как жаль! *It's a shame that...,* жаль, что... —*v.t.* **1,** (make ashamed) стыди́ть. **2,** (disgrace) позо́рить. —**put to shame, 1,** (make ashamed) пристыди́ть; устыди́ть. **2,** (excel; outshine) затмева́ть; заткну́ть за́ пояс.

shameful *adj.* позо́рный; посты́дный.

shameless *adj.* бессты́дный. —**shamelessness,** *n.* бессты́дство.

shampoo *n.* **1,** (act of washing) мытьё. *Give oneself a shampoo,* помы́ть го́лову. **2,** (soaplike preparation) шампу́нь. —*v.t.* мыть (го́лову).

shamrock *n.* трили́стник.

shank *n., anat.* го́лень.

shanty *n.* хиба́рка; лачу́га.

shape *n.* **1,** (physical form) фо́рма: *oval shape,* ова́льная фо́рма. **2,** *colloq.* (condition) состоя́ние: *in bad shape,* в плохо́м состоя́нии. **3,** *colloq.* (good physical condition) фо́рма: *out of shape,* не в фо́рме. —*v.t.* **1,** (give shape to) формова́ть. **2,** (cause to develop in a certain way) определя́ть. **3,** (adjust; adapt) приспособля́ть. —**shape up,** *colloq.* **1,** (turn out; develop) скла́дываться. **2,** (start behaving or performing properly) исправля́ться. —**take shape,** скла́дываться; оформля́ться; определя́ться.

shapeless *adj.* бесфо́рменный.

shapely *adj.* стро́йный; ста́тный.

share *n.* **1,** (portion) до́ля. *Do one's share,* вноси́ть свою́ до́лю. **2,** (unit of corporate stock) а́кция; пай. —*v.t.* **1,** (use jointly) дели́ть; дели́ться; разделя́ть. *Share a room with,* дели́ть ко́мнату с. *Share everything with,* дели́ть всё (*or* дели́ться всем) с. *Share thoughts,* дели́ться мы́слями. **2,** (hold or experience jointly) разделя́ть: *share someone's opinion/fate,* разделя́ть чьё-нибудь мне́ние (чью-нибудь судьбу́). —*v.i.* [*usu.* **share in**] уча́ствовать в: *share in the expenses,* уча́ствовать в расхо́дах. —**go shares with,** войти́ в до́лю с.

sharecropper *n.* испо́льщик; изде́льщик.

shareholder *n.* акционе́р; па́йщик.

shark *n.* аку́ла.

sharp *adj.* **1,** (having a fine cutting edge) о́стрый: *sharp knife,* о́стрый нож. **2,** (acute; pungent) о́стрый: *sharp pain,* о́страя боль; *sharp cheese,* о́стрый сыр. *He has a sharp tongue,* у него́ о́стрый язы́к. **3,** (keen; acute) зо́ркий: *sharp eyes,* зо́ркие глаза́. **4,** (harsh; biting) ре́зкий: *sharp wind,* ре́зкий ве́тер; *sharp retort,* ре́зкий отве́т. **5,** (abrupt) круто́й: *sharp turn,* круто́й поворо́т. **6,** (sudden; precipitous) ре́зкий: *a sharp drop in prices,* ре́зкое паде́ние цен. **7,** (clever; astute) бо́йкий; шу́стрый. —*adv.* то́чно; ро́вно: *at six o'clock sharp,* ро́вно в шесть часо́в. —*n., music* дие́з: *F sharp,* фа дие́з.

sharpen *v.t.* точи́ть; заостря́ть. *Sharpen a pencil,* точи́ть *or* чини́ть каранда́ш.

sharpener *n.* точи́лка.

sharp-eyed *adj.* зо́ркий; острогла́зый; глаза́стый.

sharply *adv.* о́стро; ре́зко.

sharpness *n.* **1,** (cutting quality) острота́. **2,** (clarity; definition) ре́зкость; чёткость.

sharpshooter *n.* иску́сный стрело́к; сна́йпер.

shashlik *n.* шашлы́к.

shatter *v.t.* **1,** (smash) разбива́ть (вдре́безги). **2,** (ruin, as one's health) разруша́ть; расша́тывать. **3,** (dash, as hopes) разбива́ть; разруша́ть. —*v.i.* разбива́ться (вдре́безги).

shattering *adj.* сокруши́тельный: *shattering blow,* сокруши́тельный уда́р.

shatterproof *adj.* небью́щийся.

shave *v.t.* **1,** (cut, as a beard; cut the beard of) брить. *Shave off,* сбрива́ть. **2,** (plane) строга́ть. —*v.i.* бри́ться: *I haven't shaved for three days,* я три дня не бри́лся. —*n.* бритьё. *I need a shave,* мне на́до побри́ться. —**have a close shave,** едва́ спасти́сь; быть на волосо́к от ги́бели.

shaver *n.* **1,** (razor) (электри́ческая) бри́тва. **2,** *colloq.* (youngster) юне́ц.

shaving *n.* **1,** (act of one who shaves) бритьё. **2,** *pl.* (pieces of thinly sliced wood) стру́жка. —**shaving brush,** помазо́к; ки́сточка для брить́я. —**shaving cream,** крем для брить́я.

shawl *n.* шаль.

she *pers.pron.* она́: *she left,* она́ ушла́. *She is not here,* её нет. *See also* **her.**

she- *combining form, denoting the female of animals* -и́ца; -и́ха: *she-lion,* льви́ца; *she-elephant,* слони́ха.

sheaf *n.* **1,** (of hay, grain, etc.) сноп. **2,** (of papers) свя́зка.

shear *v.t.* **1,** (cut off; cut the fleece from) стричь. **2,** *fol. by* **off** (slice off) отсека́ть. —**shears,** *n.pl.* но́жницы.

sheatfish *n.* сом.

sheath *n.* но́жны. —**sheathe,** *v.t.* вкла́дывать в но́жны.

shed *v.t.* **1,** (pour forth, as blood, tears, light, etc.) пролива́ть. **2,** (cast off, as leaves, feathers, skin, etc.) сбра́сывать; роня́ть; теря́ть. —*v.i.* линя́ть. —*n.* сара́й: *woodshed,* дровяно́й сара́й.

sheen *n.* блеск; лоск.

sheep *n.* **1,** (domesticated) овца́. **2,** (wild) бара́н. —*adj.* ове́чий; бара́ний. —**black sheep,** парши́вая овца́ (в семье́). —**lost sheep,** заблу́дшая овца́.

sheep dog овча́рка.

sheepfold *n.* овча́рня.

sheepish *adj.* застéнчивый; стыдлúвый.
sheepskin *n.* овчúна. —*adj.* овчúнный; барáний.
sheer *adj.* 1, (extremely thin) прозрáчный; сквознóй. 2, (precipitous) отвéсный. 3, (utter; absolute) сплошнóй; чúстый; сýщий.
sheet *n.* 1, (for a bed) простынá. 2, (of paper, metal, etc.) лист. 3, (list) вéдомость: *expense sheet,* вéдомость расхóдов. 4, (continuous expanse) пеленá: *sheet of fog,* пеленá тумáна. *Sheet of ice,* сплошнóй лёд.
sheeting *n.* 1, (material for bedsheets) простынное полотнó. 2, (thin plates, as of metal) обшúвка.
sheet metal листовóй метáлл.
sheik *n.* шейх.
sheldrake *n.* пегáнка.
shelf *n.* 1, (horizontal support) пóлка. 2, (ledge jutting out from a cliff) устýп; вúступ.
shell *n.* 1, (hard covering of a mollusk) рáковина. 2, (of a turtle) пáнцирь; щит. 3, (of a fruit or seed) оболóчка. 4, (of a nut or egg) скорлупá. 5, (sea shell) рáковина; ракýшка. 6, (framework) óстов; сруб. 7, (projectile) снарáд. 8, (cartridge) гúльза. —*v.t.* 1, (remove from a shell) лущúть; шелушúть. *Shell peas,* лущúть горóх. 2, (bombard) обстрéливать. 3, *fol. by* **out,** *colloq.* (spend) трáтить. —**come out of one's shell,** вúйти из своéй скорлупú. —**withdraw into one's shell,** уйтú в свою скорлупý.
shellac *n.* шеллáк. —*v.t.* покрывáть шеллáком.
shellfish *n.* моллюск.
shelter *n.* 1, (refuge) убéжище; приют; пристáнище; кров. *Take shelter,* укрúться. 2, (something affording protection) убéжище; укрúтие. *Bomb shelter,* бомбоубéжище. —*v.t.* 1, (protect) укрывáть. 2, (give refuge to) приютúть.
shelve *v.t.* 1, (put on a shelf) стáвить *or* класть на пóлку. 2, (put off) отклáдывать; класть под сукнó; отклáдывать в дóлгий ящик.
shelving *n.* стеллáж.
shenanigans *n.pl., colloq.* чудáчества.
shepherd *n.* пастýх. —*v.t.* проводúть: *shepherd tourists around town,* проводúть турúстов по гóроду.
sherbet *n.* шербéт.
sheriff *n.* шерúф.
sherry *n.* хéрес.
shh *interj.* шш!
shield *n.* щит. —*v.t.* защищáть; заслонять.
shift *v.t.* 1, (move; transfer) передвигáть; перемещáть; переклáдывать. *Shift the furniture,* передвигáть мéбель. *Shift the blame,* свалúть винý. 2, (change; switch) переменúть; переключáть. *Shift gears,* переключúть скóрость. *Shift one's ground,* переменúть позúцию. —*v.i.* 1, (move) передвигáться; перемещáться. *Shift from foot to foot,* переминáться с ногú нá ногу. 2, (switch) переходúть; переключáться. *Shift to the offensive,* переходúть в наступлéние. *The wind shifted,* вéтер переменúлся. *The scene shifts to London,* дéйствие перехóдит в Лóндон. 3, (get along) обходúться: *shift for oneself,* обходúться без посторóнней пóмощи. —*n.* 1, (movement) перемещéние. 2, (change; switch) сдвиг. 3, (work period) смéна. *Work in shifts,* рабóтать посмéнно. 4, (gearshift) передáча: *automatic shift,* автоматúческая передáча. —**shift work,** смéнная *or* посмéнная рабóта.

shiftless *adj.* ленúвый; нерадúвый.
shifty *adj.* увéртливый; изворóтливый.
shillelagh *n.* дубúнка.
shilling *n.* шúллинг.
shimmer *v.i.* мерцáть.
shin *n.* гóлень. —**shinbone,** *n.* большáя берцóвая кость.
shine *v.i.* 1, (emit light) светúть; светúться. *The sun is shining,* сóлнце свéтит. 2, (gleam) блестéть; сиять. 3, (excel) блистáть. —*v.t.* 1, (polish) полировáть. *Shine shoes,* чúстить ботúнки. 2, (point; direct, as light) светúть (+ *instr.*): *shine the light in the corner,* светúть фонарём в углý. *Don't shine the light in my eyes,* не светúте мне в глазá. —*n.* 1, (luster) лоск; блеск; глянец. 2, (shoeshine): *get a shine,* почúстить ботúнки. —**take a shine to,** *colloq.* полюбúть.
shiner *n.* 1, (fish) гольян. 2, *slang* (black eye) фонáрь.
shingle *n.* 1, (wood tile) дрáнка; *pl.* гонт. 2, (small sign) вúвеска.
shingles *n., med.* опоясывающий лишáй.
shinguard *n.* щитóк.
shining *adj.* сиáющий; блестящий.
Shinto *n.* синтоúзм. *Also,* **Shintoism.**
shiny *adj.* поснящийся.
ship *n.* 1, (large vessel) парохóд; сýдно. *Go by ship,* éхать на парохóде. *Cargo ship,* грузовóе сýдно. 2, (naval vessel) корáбль. *Warship,* воéнный корáбль. —*v.t.* 1, (transport) отправлять; перевозúть; отгружáть. 2, *fol. by* **off** (send away) отсылáть. —*v.i.* [*usu.* **ship out**] отправляться; отплывáть.
shipbuilder *n.* кораблестройтель; судострóитель.
shipbuilding *n.* кораблестроéние; судострóение.
shipment *n.* 1, (shipping of goods) отпрáвка; отгрýзка. 2, (a consignment of goods) пáртия.
shipowner *n.* судовладéлец.
shipper *n.* грузоотправúтель.
shipping *n.* 1, (shipment) отгрýзка; отпрáвка. 2, (movement of ships carrying cargo) судохóдство: *closed to shipping,* закрúт для судохóдства. 3, (ships collectively) судá. —*adj.* судохóдный: *shipping company,* судохóдная компáния.
shipshape *adj.* в пóлном порядке.
shipwreck *n.* кораблекрушéние. *Be shipwrecked,* потерпéть кораблекрушéние.
shipyard *n.* верфь; судовéрфь.
shire *n.* грáфство.
shirk *v.t.* уклоняться от; увúливать от. —**shirker,** *n.* прогýльщик.
shirt *n.* рубáшка; сорóчка. —**keep one's shirt on,** *slang* не горячúться; не кипятúться. —**lose one's shirt,** *slang* проигрáться.
shirtsleeves *n.pl., in* **in one's shirtsleeves,** без пиджакá.
shirttail *n.* низ рубáшки. *Your shirttail is hanging out,* у вас вúлезла рубáшка.
shish kebab шашлúк.
shiver *v.i.* дрожáть; трястúсь. —*n.* дрожь. *It gives one the shivers,* морóз по кóже подирáет.
shoal *n.* мель; óтмель.
shock *n.* 1, (sudden jolt) удáр; толчóк; сотрясéние. 2, (sudden emotional disturbance) потрясéние. 3, *med.* шок. 4, (jolt of electricity) (электрúческий) удáр. 5, (mass, as of hair) копнá; шáпка (волóс). —*v.t.* потрясáть; шокúровать.
shock absorber амортизáтор.

shocking *adj.* **1,** (extremely upsetting) стра́шный; ужаса́ющий. **2,** (outrageous) возмути́тельный; сканда́льный.

shock troops уда́рные войска́.

shock wave уда́рная волна́.

shoddy *adj.* недоброка́чественный.

shoe *n.* **1,** (general term) боти́нок. **2,** (lady's) ту́фля. **3,** (for a horse) подко́ва. **4,** *mech.* башма́к; коло́дка: *brake shoe,* тормозно́й башма́к; тормозна́я коло́дка. —*adj.* обувно́й: *shoe store,* обувно́й магази́н. —*v.t.* обува́ть: *well shod,* хорошо́ обу́тый. *Shoe a horse,* подко́вывать ло́шадь. —**be in someone's shoes,** быть на чьём-нибудь ме́сте; быть в чьей-нибудь шку́ре. —**fill someone's shoes,** занима́ть чьё-нибудь ме́сто.

shoehorn *n.* рожо́к.

shoelace *n.* шнуро́к (для боти́нок).

shoemaker *n.* сапо́жник.

shoe polish гутали́н; ва́кса; сапо́жный крем; сапо́жная мазь.

shoeshine *n.* чи́стка сапо́г. —**shoeshine boy,** чи́стильщик сапо́г.

shoetree *n.* коло́дка.

shoo *interj.* кш!; вон! —*v.t.* [*usu.* **shoo away**] ши́кать на.

shoot *v.t.* **1,** (let forth; discharge) пуска́ть: *shoot an arrow,* пуска́ть стрелу́. **2,** (fire at and hit) стреля́ть в (и ра́нить): *shoot a burglar,* стреля́ть во взло́мщика (и ра́нить его́). *Shoot someone in the leg,* ра́нить кого́-нибудь в но́гу. **3,** (fire at and kill) застрели́ть. *Shoot oneself,* застрели́ться. **4,** (hunt and kill) стреля́ть: *shoot deer,* стреля́ть оле́ней. **5,** (execute) расстре́ливать. **6,** *fol. by* **down** (bring down by shooting) сбива́ть. **7,** (fire, as a gun) стреля́ть из (ружья́). **8,** (propel with great force) запуска́ть. *Shoot forth lava,* изверга́ть ла́ву. **9,** (photograph) снима́ть; засня́ть. **10,** *sports* посыла́ть (мяч). **11,** *games* игра́ть в: *shoot dice/pool/marbles,* игра́ть в ко́сти/в билья́рд/в ша́рики/. **12,** *Shoot rapids,* переправля́ться че́рез поро́ги. —*v.i.* **1,** (fire a weapon) стреля́ть: *don't shoot!,* не стреля́йте! **2,** (flash; dart) мча́ться; нести́сь. *Shoot past,* промча́ться; пронести́ться; промелькну́ть. *Shoot ahead,* вы́рваться вперёд. *The horse shot out of the gate,* ло́шадь вы́летела из-за барье́ра. *Flames shot up into the air,* пла́мя взвило́сь в во́здух. **3,** *fol. by* **up** (soar, as of prices, temperature, etc.) подска́кивать. **4,** *fol. by* **up** (grow rapidly) вы́расти; вы́тянуться. **5,** *fol. by* **for** (aim for; strive for) ме́тить в. —*n.* отро́сток; росто́к; побе́г. —**shoot back,** (return fire) отвеча́ть огнём. **2,** *colloq.* (retort) найти́сь. —**shoot off one's mouth,** *slang* проболта́ться. —**shoot the breeze,** *colloq.* болта́ть. —**shoot the works,** *slang* идти́ ва-ба́нк.

shooting *n.* **1,** (firing of weapons) стрельба́. **2,** (filming) съёмка. —*adj.* **1,** (pert. to shooting) стрелко́вый. **2,** (stabbing, as of pain) стреля́ющий; ко́лющий. —**shooting gallery,** тир. —**shooting star,** па́дающая звезда́.

shop *n.* **1,** (small store) магази́н; ла́вка. **2,** (place where work is done) мастерска́я: *repair shop,* ремо́нтная мастерска́я. **3,** (factory division) цех; мастерска́я: *machine shop,* механи́ческий цех; механи́ческая мастерска́я. —*adj.* цехово́й: *shop foreman,* цехово́й ма́стер. —*v.i.* [*also,* **go shopping**] ходи́ть по магази́нам; де́лать поку́пки. —**talk shop,** говори́ть о служе́бных дела́х.

shopkeeper *n.* ла́вочник.

shoplifter *n.* магази́нный вор.

shopper *n.* покупа́тель.

shopping bag су́мка для поку́пок; хозя́йственная су́мка.

shopping center торго́вый центр.

shore *n.* бе́рег. —*v.t.* [*usu.* **shore up**] подпира́ть.

shoreline *n.* берегова́я ли́ния.

short *adj.* **1,** (not long) коро́ткий: *a short distance,* коро́ткое расстоя́ние; коро́ткая диста́нция. *Short hair/sleeves,* коро́ткие во́лосы/рукава́. *The shortest distance between two points,* наиме́ньшее расстоя́ние ме́жду двумя́ то́чками. **2,** (not tall) ни́зкого ро́ста; ма́ленького ро́ста: *a short man,* челове́к ни́зкого/ма́ленького ро́ста. **3,** (not of long duration) коро́ткий: *short winter/memory,* коро́ткая зима́/па́мять. *A short time ago,* неда́вно. **4,** (brief; concise) коро́ткий; кра́ткий. **5,** (insufficient) недоста́точный. *Be in short supply,* име́ться в недоста́точном коли́честве; быть дефици́тным. **6,** *fol. by* **of** (not having enough of): *we are short of milk,* у нас не хвата́ет молока́. **7,** (brusque; curt) ре́зкий. —*adv.* ко́ротко: *cut one's hair short,* ко́ротко постри́чь во́лосы. —*n.* **1,** (short film) короткометра́жный фильм. **2,** *pl.* (short pants) *see* **shorts. 3,** = **short circuit.** —**cut short,** обрыва́ть. —**fall short of,** не достига́ть: *fall short of the mark,* не достига́ть це́ли. —**for short,** сокращённо; для кра́ткости. —**in short,** коро́че говоря́. —**in short order,** в спе́шном поря́дке. —**run short,** иссяка́ть; истоща́ться: *our supplies are running short,* на́ши запа́сы иссяка́ют/истоща́ются. *Time is running short,* вре́мя истека́ет. —**short of,** кро́ме; поми́мо. —**stop short,** внеза́пно останови́ться; *(in speaking)* останови́ться на полусло́ве. —**to make a long story short,** коро́че говоря́.

shortage *n.* недоста́ток; нехва́тка; дефици́т.

shortbread *n.* песо́чное пече́нье; рассы́пчатое пече́нье.

shortcake *n.* песо́чный торт.

shortchange *v.t., colloq.* обсчи́тывать.

short circuit коро́ткое замыка́ние.

shortcoming *n.* недоста́ток.

shortcut *n.* коро́ткий путь. *Take a shortcut,* сре́зать у́гол.

shorten *v.t.* укора́чивать; сокраща́ть.

shortening *n.* сдо́ба.

shortfall *n.* дефици́т; недобо́р.

shorthand *n.* стеногра́фия. *Take down in shorthand,* стенографи́ровать.

short-lived *adj.* недолгове́чный.

shortly *adv.* ско́ро; вско́ре. *Shortly before,* незадо́лго до. *Shortly after,* вско́ре по́сле. *Shortly thereafter,* вско́ре.

shortness *n.* коро́ткость. —**shortness of breath,** оды́шка.

short-range *adj.* бли́жнего де́йствия; с ма́лым ра́диусом де́йствия.

shorts *n.pl.* трусы́; тру́сики; шо́рты.

shortsighted *adj.* близору́кий; недальнови́дный. —**shortsightedness,** *n.* близору́кость; недальнови́дность.

short story расска́з; новелла.

short-tempered *adj.* вспы́льчивый.

short-term *adj.* краткосро́чный.

short wave коро́ткая волна́. —**short-wave**, *adj.* коротково́лновый.

shot *n.* **1,** (discharge of a firearm) вы́стрел: *I heard a shot,* я услы́шал вы́стрел. **2,** (one who shoots) стрело́к: *a good shot,* хоро́ший стрело́к. **3,** (small pellets) дробь. **4,** (picture) сни́мок. **5,** *sports* бросо́к; уда́р. *Penalty shot,* штрафно́й уда́р. *Take a shot,* де́лать бросо́к. *Put the shot,* толка́ть ядро́. **6,** (inoculation) приви́вка: *rabies shot,* приви́вка от (*or* про́тив) бе́шенства. **7,** *colloq.* (drink of liquor) глото́к (спиртно́го). **8,** *colloq.* (attempt) попы́тка. —*adj.* **1,** (streaked): *shot with gold,* с золоты́м отли́вом. **2,** *colloq.* (worn out) изно́шенный. *These pants are shot,* э́ти брю́ки совсе́м износи́лись. —**big shot,** (ва́жная) ши́шка. —**call the shots,** распоряжа́ться. —**like a shot,** пу́лей: *take off like a shot,* понести́сь пу́лей. —**not by a long shot,** отню́дь нет; далеко́ не.

shotgun *n.* дробови́к. *Sawed-off shotgun,* обре́з.

shot-put *n.* толка́ние ядра́.

should *v.aux.* **1,** *expressing mild obligation or advisability: you should write a book about it,* вы бы об э́том кни́гу написа́ли. *You shouldn't have done it,* вы не должны́ бы́ли де́лать э́того. *It should be borne in mind that...,* сле́дует име́ть в виду́, что... **2,** *expressing expectation* до́лжен: *he should be here soon,* он до́лжен ско́ро прийти́. **3,** *expressing condition or assumption* е́сли: *should the need arise,* е́сли возни́кнет необходи́мость. *Should I be late,* (в слу́чае) е́сли я опозда́ю. **4,** *used in polite requests* бы: *I should like to ask...,* я бы хоте́л(а) спроси́ть...

shoulder *n.* **1,** (part of the body) плечо́. *Wear a coat over one's shoulders,* носи́ть пальто́ внаки́дку. **2,** (side of a road) обо́чина. —*v.t.* **1,** (place on one's shoulders) взва́ливать на пле́чи. **2,** (assume; bear) брать на себя́; брать на пле́чи. **3,** *in* **shoulder one's way,** прота́лкиваться. —**give someone the cold shoulder,** хо́лодно встре́тить. —**have a good head on one's shoulders,** име́ть го́лову на плеча́х. —**shoulder to shoulder,** плечо́м к плечу́. —**straight from the shoulder,** начистоту́.

shoulder blade лопа́тка.

shoulder strap ля́мка; *mil.* пого́н.

shout *v.t. & i.* крича́ть: *don't shout!,* не кричи́(те)! *Shout hurrah,* крича́ть ура́. *Shout someone's name,* вы́крикнуть чьё-нибудь и́мя. *Shout slogans,* выкри́кивать ло́зунги. —*n.* крик; вы́крик; во́зглас. —**shout down,** перекрича́ть.

shove *v.t.* толка́ть; пиха́ть. —*v.i.* толка́ться: *don't shove!,* не толка́йтесь! —*n.* толчо́к. —**shove off, 1,** (push off from shore) отта́лкиваться от бе́рега. **2,** *colloq.* (depart) уходи́ть; отправля́ться.

shovel *n.* лопа́та. —*v.t.* сгреба́ть: *shovel snow from the sidewalk,* сгреба́ть снег с тротуа́ра.

show *v.t.* **1,** (make visible; point out; demonstrate) пока́зывать: *show one's ticket,* пока́зывать биле́т; *show someone the way,* показа́ть кому́-нибудь доро́гу. *I'll show you how to do it,* я вам покажу́ как э́то де́лается. **2,** (display publicly) выставля́ть. **3,** (reveal; evince) проявля́ть; обнару́живать. *Show courage,* проявля́ть му́жество. *Show no signs of life,* не подава́ть при́знаков жи́зни. **4,** (prove; demonstrate) пока́зывать; дока́зывать; устана́вливать. **5,** (guide; escort) провожа́ть: *show someone to the door,* провожа́ть кого́-нибудь до двере́й. **6,** (extend) ока-

зывать: *show kindness to,* ока́зывать любе́зность (+ *dat.*). **7,** (indicate; register) пока́зывать: *the clock shows 3:00,* часы́ пока́зывают три часа́. **8,** *colloq.* (teach a lesson to) показа́ть: *I'll show him!,* я ему́ покажу́! **9,** *Show one's face,* показа́ться. **10,** *Show oneself to be...,* показа́ть себя́ (+ *instr.*). —*v.i.* быть ви́дным; быть заме́тным; видне́ться. *Your slip is showing,* у вас видна́ ни́жняя ю́бка. —*n.* **1,** (piece of entertainment) спекта́кль. **2,** (single performance or presentation) сеа́нс. **3,** (exhibition) вы́ставка: *dog show,* вы́ставка соба́к. **4,** (pointed display) демонстра́ция: *show of strength/force,* демонстра́ция си́лы. **5,** (that which is intended to impress) эффе́кт. *Done for show,* сде́ланный напока́з; рассчи́танный на эффе́кт. **6,** *Show of hands,* подня́тие руки́. —**show in,** вводи́ть. —**show off, 1,** (flaunt) щеголя́ть (+ *instr.*); выставля́ть напока́з. **2,** (make a great display of oneself) рисова́ться; красова́ться. —**show out,** провожа́ть до двере́й. —**show up, 1,** (arrive) явля́ться. **2,** *colloq.* (prove superior to) затмева́ть.

showcase *n.* витри́на.

showdown *n.* развя́зка.

shower *n.* **1,** (shower bath) душ: *take a shower,* принима́ть душ. **2,** (light rain) дождь; до́ждик. **3,** (torrent; profusion) град. —*v.t.* **1,** (cover; pelt) забра́сывать: *shower someone with leaflets,* заброса́ть кого́-нибудь листо́вками. **2,** (spray) обры́згивать. **3,** *fig.* (deluge) засыпа́ть; осыпа́ть; забра́сывать (*e.g.* пода́рками). *Shower with praise,* осыпа́ть похвала́ми. —*v.i.* принима́ть душ. —**shower room,** душева́я.

showing *n.* **1,** (act of showing) пока́з. **2,** (overall performance) результа́т: *make a good showing,* показа́ть хоро́ший результа́т.

showman *n.* антрепренёр.

showroom *n.* вы́ставочный зал; демонстрацио́нный зал; сало́н.

show trial показа́тельный суд.

showy *adj.* показно́й; эффе́ктный.

shrapnel *n.* шрапне́ль. *Shrapnel wound,* оско́лочная ра́на.

shred *n.* клок; клочо́к; лоску́т. *Tear to shreds,* разрыва́ть в кло́чья *or* в клочки́. *Not a shred of evidence,* ни мале́йших доказа́тельств. —*v.t.* измельча́ть; кромса́ть. *Shred cabbage,* шинкова́ть капу́сту. *Shred documents,* уничтожа́ть докуме́нты.

shrew *n.* **1,** (animal) землеро́йка. **2,** (scolding woman) меге́ра; фу́рия.

shrewd *adj.* **1,** (of a person) проница́тельный; расчётливый. **2,** (of an action) ло́вкий. —**shrewdness,** *n.* проница́тельность.

shriek *n.* пронзи́тельный крик. —*v.i.* пронзи́тельно крича́ть.

shrift *n., in* **make short shrift of,** (бы́стро) распра́виться с.

shrike *n.* сорокопу́т.

shrill *adj.* ре́зкий; пронзи́тельный.

shrimp *n.* **1,** (crustacean) креве́тка. **2,** *colloq.* (small person) коро́тыш(ка); недоро́сток.

shrine *n.* **1,** (tomb of a saint) ра́ка. **2,** (revered site) святы́ня.

shrink *v.i.* **1,** (of fabric) сади́ться. **2,** (become smaller) сжима́ться. **3,** (draw back; recoil) отпря́нуть, *fol. by from* (avoid) уклоня́ться от. —*v.t.* **1,** (cause shrinkage in) вызыва́ть уса́дку (+ *gen.*). **2,** (reduce in size) сжима́ть.

shrinkage *n.* усáдка.

shrivel *v.i.* смóрщиваться; съёживаться.

shroud *n.* **1,** (burial cloth) сáван. **2,** (that which covers or envelops) пеленá. —*v.t.* окýтывать: *shrouded in secrecy,* окýтанный тáйной.

Shrovetide *n.* мáсленица.

shrub *n.* куст; кустáрник. —**shrubbery,** *n.* кустáрник.

shrug *v.t. & i.* пожимáть (плечáми). —*n.* пожимáние (плеч). —**shrug off,** не обращáть внимáния на.

shuck *n.* **1,** (husk) шелухá. **2,** (shell) скорлупá. —*v.t.* лущúть; шелушúть.

shucks *interj.* чёрт побери!

shudder *v.i.* содрогáться. —*n.* содрогáние.

shuffle *v.t.* **1,** (drag, as one's feet) шáркать (ногáми); волочúть (нóги). **2,** (mix, as cards) тасовáть. —*v.i.* **1,** *fol. by* **along** (walk by dragging one's feet) волочúться. **2,** (mix the cards) тасовáть. —*n.* **1,** (of feet) шáрканье. **2,** (mixing of cards) тасóвка.

shun *v.t.* избегáть; сторонúться.

shunt *v.t.* **1,** (turn aside) отводúть. **2,** *R.R.* переводúть на запáсный путь.

shut *v.t.* закрывáть. —*v.i.* закрывáться. —**shut down,** закрывáть(ся). —**shut off, 1,** (turn off) отключáть. **2,** (halt, as debate) прекращáть. **3,** (isolate) отгорáживать. —**shut out, 1,** (keep out) не допускáть. **2,** *sports* сдéлать сухýю (+ *dat.*). —**shut up, 1,** (incarcerate) заточáть. **2,** *colloq.* (stop talking) замолчáть. *Shut up!,* заткнúсь!

shutout *n., sports* сухáя.

shutter *n.* **1,** (for a window) стáвень; стáвня. **2,** (of a camera) затвóр. —*v.t.* закрывáть стáвнями.

shuttle *n.* челнóк. *Space shuttle,* космúческий челнóк. —*v.i.* курсúровать; сновáть. —**shuttle diplomacy,** "челнóчная" дипломáтия.

shuttlecock *n.* волáн.

shy *adj.* **1,** (timid) рóбкий; застéнчивый. **2,** *colloq.* (lacking; short): *we are shy a few dollars,* нам не хватáет нéсколько дóлларов. —*v.i.* **1,** (rear, as of a horse) отпрянуть. **2,** [*usu.* **shy away from**] (avoid) уклоняться от. —*v.t.* (throw) бросáть.

shyness *n.* рóбость; застéнчивость.

si *n., music* си.

Siamese *adj.* сиáмский. —**Siamese twins,** сиáмские близнецы́.

Siberian *adj.* сибúрский. —*n.* сибиряк.

sibilant *n. & adj.* **1,** (ж,ч,ш,щ) шипящий. **2,** (с,з) свистящий.

sibling *n.* роднóй брат; роднáя сестрá.

sic *also,* **sick** *v.t.* натрáвливать. —**sic 'im!,** атý егó!

sick *adj.* **1,** (ill) больнóй: *sick child,* больнóй ребёнок. *I was sick,* я был бóлен; я былá больнá. **2,** (nauseous): *I feel sick to my stomach,* меня тошнúт. **3,** (mentally ill) душевнобольнóй. **4,** (perverted) извращённый: *sick mind,* извращённый ум. **5,** (extremely upset) óчень огорчён. *I am sick at heart,* у меня болúт душá. **6,** *fol. by* **of** (fed up with): *I am sick of staying home,* мне надоéло сидéть дóма. —*n., preceded by* **the** больны́е. —**take sick,** заболевáть.

sick bay лазарéт.

sicken *v.t.* претúть. *It sickens me,* мне претúт (*or* меня тошнúт) от этого.

sickening *adj.* тошнотвóрный; отвратúтельный.

sickle *n.* серп.

sick leave óтпуск по болéзни.

sickly *adj.* болéзненный; хúлый. —**sickliness,** *n.* болéзненность.

sickness *n.* болéзнь.

side *n.* **1,** (in most meanings) сторонá: *the right side of the road,* прáвая сторонá дорóги. *The two sides of a coin,* óбе стóроны монéты. *On the other side of the river,* по ту стóрону реки́. *Whose side are you on?,* вы на чьей сторонé? *A relative on his mother's side,* рóдственник со стороны́ мáтери. **2,** (either half of the human body) бок: *lie on one's side,* лежáть на бокý. **3,** (area immediately adjacent) край: *along the side of the road,* по крáю дорóги. *Stand at someone's side,* стоя́ть ря́дом с кéм-нибудь. **4,** (of a geometric figure) грань: *a cube has six sides,* куб имéет шесть грáней. **5,** (vertical surface) стéнка; стенá: *the side of a box/canyon,* стéнка я́щика; стенá каньóна. **6,** *naut.* борт: *starboard side,* прáвый борт. **7,** (of beef) бок: *side of mutton,* барáний бок. —*adj.* **1,** (located on one side) боковóй: *side door,* боковáя дверь. **2,** (from one side) сбóку: *side view,* вид сбóку. **3,** (incidental) побóчный: *side effects,* побóчные эффéкты. —*v.i.* [*usu.* **side with**] становúться *or* вставáть на стóрону (+ *gen.*). —**from side to side,** из стороны́ в стóрону; с бóку нá бок. —**on all sides,** со всех сторóн. —**on the side,** на сторонé: *do work on the side,* подрабáтывать на сторонé. —**side by side,** ря́дом; бок ó бок. —**take sides,** стать на чью́-нибудь стóрону.

sideboard *n.* буфéт; сервáнт.

sideburns *n.pl.* бакенбáрды.

sidecar *n.* коля́ска (мотоцúкла).

sideline *n.* **1,** (additional work) побóчная рабóта. *He does this as a sideline,* он занимáется этим мéжду дéлом. **2,** *sports* боковáя лúния. —**on the sidelines,** в сторонé.

sidelong *adj.* косóй: *sidelong glance,* косóй взгляд.

sidestep *v.t.* обходúть (сторонóй); уклоня́ться от.

side street переýлок; боковáя ýлица.

sidetrack *n.* запáсный путь. —*v.t.* **1,** *R.R.* переводúть на запáсный путь. **2,** (divert; shunt aside): *I got sidetracked on the way,* я задержáлся в дорóге. *The bill got sidetracked in Congress,* обсуждéние законопроéкта в конгрéссе бы́ло отложено.

sidewalk *n.* тротуáр.

sideways *adv.* бóком; бочкóм.

siding *n.* запáсный путь.

sidle *v.i.* ходúть бóком; пробирáться бочкóм. *Sidle up to,* пробрáться бочкóм к.

siege *n.* осáда; блокáда. *Under siege,* в осáде. —**lay siege to,** осаждáть. —**state of siege,** осáдное положéние.

sienna *n.* сиéна.

sieve *n.* решетó; сúто.

sift *v.t.* **1,** (pass through a sieve) просéивать. **2,** (consider carefully) взвéшивать. —*v.i.* [*usu.* **sift through**] ры́ться в.

sigh *v.i.* вздыхáть. —*n.* вздох.

sight *n.* **1,** (vision; eyesight) зрéние: *lose one's sight,* лишúться зрéния. *Lose the sight of one eye,* ослéпнуть на одúн глаз. **2,** (act of seeing) вид: *at the sight of,* при вúде (+ *gen.*). *I can't stand the sight of blood,* я не выношý вúда крóви. **3,** (field of vision) пóле зрéния: *come within sight,* попáсть в пóле зрéния. *The end is in sight,* конéц ужé вúден. *There was not a house in sight,* нé было вúдно ни одногó дóма.

Pass out of sight, скрываться из виду. *Out of my sight!*, с глаз моих долой! **4**, (something seen) зрелище: *a horrible sight*, ужасное зрелище. **5**, *pl.* (places worth seeing) достопримечательности: *see the sights*, осматривать достопримечательности. **6**, (mechanism on a gun) прицел. —*v.t.* увидеть: *sight land*, увидеть землю. —**a darned sight**, *colloq.* гораздо; несравненно (+ *comp.*). —**catch sight of**, увидеть; завидеть. —**from sight**, с листа: *play from sight*, играть с листа. —**know by sight**, знать в лицо. —**lose sight of**, **1**, (see no longer) (по)терять из виду. **2**, (fail to realize) упускать из виду; (по)терять из виду. —**love at first sight**, любовь с первого взгляда. —**out of sight, out of mind**, с глаз долой, из сердца вон. —**shoot on sight**, стрелять без предупреждения. —**sight unseen**, заглазно; за глаза.

sighted *adj.* видящий; зрячий.

sightless *adj.* невидящий; незрячий.

sight-read *v.t. & i.* читать с листа.

sightseeing *n.* осмотр достопримечательностей. *Go sightseeing*, осматривать достопримечательности. *Sightseeing tour of the city*, экскурсия по городу. —**sightseer**, *n.* турист; экскурсант.

sign *n.* **1**, (mark; symbol; gesture; token; omen) знак: *minus sign*, знак минус. *A sign of respect*, знак уважения. *A good sign*, добрый знак. *The signs of the zodiac*, знаки зодиака. **2**, (display board) вывеска. *Road sign*, дорожный знак. *Neon sign*, неоновая реклама. **3**, (evidence; trace; indication) признак: *signs of life*, признаки жизни. *Sign of the times*, знамение времени. —*v.t.* подписывать: *sign a petition*, подписывать петицию. *Sign one's name*, подписываться; расписываться. —*v.i.* расписываться. *Sign for a parcel*, расписываться в получении посылки. —**sign off**, заканчивать радиопередачу. —**sign out**, отмечаться. —**sign up (for)**, записываться (в *or* на).

signal *n.* сигнал: *distress signal*, сигнал бедствия. *Hand signal*, знак рукой. *At a given signal*, по сигналу; по знаку. —*adj.* знаменательный: *a signal achievement*, знаменательное достижение. —*v.t.* **1**, (make a signal to) подавать сигнал *or* знак (+ *dat.*). **2**, (indicate) сигнализировать. —*v.i.* подавать сигнал; сигнализировать.

signalman *n.* сигнальщик; *mil.* связист.

signatory *n.* подписавший.

signature *n.* **1**, (name written by oneself) подпись. **2**, *printing* печатный лист.

signboard *n.* вывеска.

signer *n.* подписавший.

signet *n.* печатка.

significance *n.* значение: *be of great significance*, иметь большое значение.

significant *adj.* значительный: *significant discovery/increase*, значительное открытие/увеличение. *Be significant*, иметь значение. *It is significant that...*, характерно, что...; знаменательно, что... —**significantly**, *adv.* значительно.

signify *v.t.* **1**, (mean; denote) значить; означать. **2**, (make known; indicate) указывать: *signify by raising one's hand*, указывать поднятием руки.

sign language немая азбука; жестикуляция.

sign painter мастер по вывескам; оформитель *or* изготовитель вывесок.

signpost *n.* указательный столб.

silage *n.* силос.

silence *n.* **1**, (absence of sound) тишина. **2**, (failure to speak) молчание. *In silence*, молча. —*interj.* помолчите! —*v.t.* **1**, (make silent) заставить замолчать. **2**, (suppress; still) заглушать.

silencer *n.* глушитель.

silent *adj.* **1**, (making no sound; tacit; taciturn) молчаливый; безмолвный. *Keep silent*, молчать. *Fall silent*, замолкать; умолкать. *Remain silent*, хранить молчание. **2**, (not pronounced): *the "k" is silent*, буква "k" не произносится. **3**, (of a film) немой.

silently *adv.* молча.

silhouette *n.* силуэт.

silica *n.* кремнезём.

silica gel силикагель.

silicate *n.* силикат.

siliceous *adj.* кремнистый.

silicic *adj.* кремниевый: *silicic acid*, кремниевая кислота.

silicon *n.* кремний.

silicone *n.* силикон.

silk *n.* шёлк. *Raw silk*, шёлк-сырец. —*adj.* шёлковый.

silken *adj.* шелковистый.

silkworm *n.* (тутовый) шелкопряд; шелковичный червь.

silky *adj.* шелковистый.

silliness *n.* глупость.

silly *adj.* глупый. *Don't be silly!*, не говорите глупости! *Laugh oneself silly*, смеяться до упаду.

silo *n.* **1**, (for grain) силосная башня. **2**, (for a missile) шахта.

silt *n.* ил. —*v.i.* [*usu.* **silt up**] засоряться илом. —**silty**, *adj.* илистый.

silver *n.* серебро. —*adj.* серебряный. —*v.t.* серебрить. —**be born with a silver spoon in one's mouth**, родиться в сорочке *or* в рубашке.

silver fox черно-бурая лисица.

silver nitrate ляпис.

silver plate **1**, (coating of silver) серебро. **2**, (silverware) столовое серебро; серебряная посуда. —**silver-plate**, *v.t.* серебрить. —**silver-plated**, *adj.* посеребрённый.

silversmith *n.* серебряных дел мастер.

silverware *n.* столовое серебро.

silvery *adj.* серебристый.

similar *adj.* **1**, (alike) подобный; похожий; сходный. *A rabbit is similar to a hare*, кролик подобен зайцу; кролик похож на зайца; кролик сходен с зайцем. **2**, *geom.* подобный.

similarity *n.* сходство: *a great similarity between them*, большое сходство между ними. *The similarity between Victor and his father*, сходство Виктора с отцом.

similarly *adv.* подобным образом.

simile *n.* сравнение.

simmer *v.i.* закипать. —**simmer down**, успокаиваться.

simper *v.i.* ухмыляться.

simple *adj.* простой: *simple woman/task/food/life*, простая женщина/задача/пища/жизнь. *It's not so simple*, это не так просто. —**simple fracture**, простой перелом. —**simple sentence**, простое предложение.

simple-hearted *adj.* простодушный; простосердёчный. —**simple-heartedness**, *n.* простоду́шие; простосерде́чие.

simple-minded *adj.* слабоу́мный.

simpleton *n.* проста́к.

simplicity *n.* простота́.

simplify *v.t.* упроща́ть. —**simplification**, *n.* упроще́ние. —**simplified**, *adj.* упрощённый.

simplistic *adj.* упроще́нческий.

simply *adv.* про́сто: *write/live simply*, писа́ть/жить про́сто. *It's simply outrageous*, э́то про́сто безобра́зие.

simulate *v.t.* симули́ровать; притворя́ться. —**simulation**, *n.* симуля́ция. —**simulator**, *n.* тренажёр.

simultaneity *n.* одновре́менность.

simultaneous *adj.* одновре́менный. *Simultaneous translation*, синхро́нный перево́д. —**simultaneously**, *adv.* одновре́менно.

sin *n.* грех. —*v.i.* греши́ть.

since *adv.* **1,** (between then and now) с тех пор: *I have lived here ever since*, я живу́ здесь с тех пор. *He has since changed his mind*, он пото́м переду́мал. **2,** (ago) уже́: *long since forgotten*, давно́ уже́ забы́т. —*prep.* с (+ *gen.*); со вре́мени (+ *gen.*): *since childhood*, с де́тства; *since yesterday*, со вчера́шнего дня; *since the war*, со вре́мени войны́. ♦*Also* по́сле: *since his return*, по́сле его́ возвраще́ния. *For the first time since last year*, впервы́е по́сле про́шлого го́да. —*conj.* **1,** (during the time after) с тех пор, как: *since he arrived*, с тех пор, как он прие́хал. **2,** (because; inasmuch as) так как; поско́льку. —**since then**, с тех пор. —**since when?**, с каки́х пор?

sincere *adj.* и́скренний.

sincerely *adv.* и́скренне; и́скренно. *I mean that sincerely*, я говорю́ и́скренне; я действи́тельно так ду́маю. —**sincerely yours**, и́скренне ваш.

sincerity *n.* и́скренность. —**in all sincerity**, от чи́стого се́рдца.

sine *n.*, *math.* си́нус.

sinecure *n.* синеку́ра.

sinew *n.* сухожи́лие. —**sinewy**, *adj.* жи́листый.

sinful *adj.* гре́шный.

sing *v.t. & i.* петь: *can you sing?*, вы поёте? *Sing us a song*, спо́йте нам пе́сню.

singe *v.t.* **1,** (burn slightly) подпа́ливать. **2,** (burn off the feathers of) опа́ливать: *singe a goose*, опа́ливать гу́ся.

singer *n.* певе́ц; певи́ца.

singing *n.* пе́ние.

single *adj.* **1,** (only one) оди́н; еди́ный: *a single purpose*, еди́ная цель. *Made from a single piece of material*, сде́ланный из одного́ куска́ мате́рии. *Every single one*, все до одного́; все до еди́ного. *Not a single word*, ни одного́ (*or* ни еди́ного) сло́ва. **2,** (unmarried) A, (of a man) нежена́тый; холосто́й. B, (of a woman) незаму́жняя. *Single mother*, мать-одино́чка. **3,** (for use by one person) одино́чный. *Single room*, ко́мната *or* но́мер на одного́. *Single bed*, односпа́льная крова́ть. —*v.t.* [*usu.* **single out**] выделя́ть; отлича́ть. —*n.* **1,** = **single room**. **2,** *pl.*, *tennis* игры́ в одино́чном разря́де.

single-breasted *adj.* однобо́ртный.

single combat одино́чный бой; единобо́рство.

single file коло́нна по одному́. *Proceed single file*, идти́ гусько́м.

single-handed *adj. & adv.* без посторо́нней по́мощи. *Also*, **single-handedly**, *adv.*

single-minded *adj.* целеустремлённый.

single-track *adj.* одноколе́йный.

singly *adv.* **1,** (separately; alone) оди́н; в одино́чку. **2,** (one at a time) поодино́чке.

singsong *adj.* моното́нный. *In a singsong voice*, напе́вом.

singular *adj.* **1,** (unique) исключи́тельный. **2,** (peculiar; distinctive) своеобра́зный. **3,** *gram.* еди́нственный. —*n.*, *gram.* еди́нственное число́. —**singularity**, *n.* своеобра́зие. —**singularly**, *adv.* необыча́йно.

sinister *adj.* злове́щий.

sink *v.i.* **1,** (go beneath the surface) погружа́ться: *sink into quicksand*, погружа́ться в сыпу́чий песо́к. **2,** (go down in water) тону́ть: *the ship sank*, кора́бль потону́л *or* затону́л. *Sink to the bottom*, идти́ ко дну. **3,** (descend slowly) опуска́ться; сади́ться; оседа́ть: *sink into a chair*, опуска́ться в кре́сло; *sink below the horizon*, сади́ться за горизо́нт. *The foundation is sinking*, фунда́мент оседа́ет. **4,** (pass gradually into a given condition) впада́ть; погружа́ться: *sink into despair*, впада́ть/погружа́ться в отча́яние. **5,** (fall; drop) па́дать. **6,** (be near death) га́снуть. **7,** *My heart sank*, у меня́ се́рдце за́мерло; у меня́ душа́ ушла́ в пя́тки. **8,** *fol. by* **in** (penetrate the mind) запечатлева́ться. —*v.t.* **1,** (cause to sink) топи́ть: *the ship was sunk*, кора́бль был пото́плен. **2,** (drive into something) вонза́ть; втыка́ть; вса́живать. *Sink one's teeth into*, впива́ться зуба́ми в (+ *acc.*). **3,** (dig, as a well) рыть. **4,** *basketball* забра́сывать: *sink a shot*, забро́сить мяч в корзи́ну. **5,** *colloq.* (invest) вса́живать. —*n.* ра́ковина: *kitchen sink*, ку́хонная ра́ковина.

sinker *n.*, *fishing* грузи́ло.

sinking fund амортизацио́нный фонд.

sinner *n.* гре́шник.

sinuous *adj.* изви́листый.

sinus *n.* па́зуха; си́нус. —**sinusitis**, *n.* синуси́т; сину́йт.

sip *v.t.* потя́гивать; отпива́ть; прихлёбывать. *Sip lemonade through a straw*, соса́ть лимона́д че́рез соло́минку. —*n.* ма́ленький глото́к. *Take a sip of*, отпи́ть; прихлебну́ть; пригуби́ть.

siphon *n.* сифо́н. —*v.t.* слива́ть *or* спуска́ть сифо́ном.

sir *n.* сэр; су́дарь.

sire *n.* **1,** (progenitor) производи́тель. **2,** (form of address for a sovereign) госуда́рь. —*v.t.* роди́ть; производи́ть.

siren *n.* сире́на.

sirloin *n.* филе́.

sirocco *n.* сиро́кко.

sisal *n.* сиза́ль.

siskin *n.* чиж.

sissy *n.*, *colloq.* не́женка.

sister *n.* сестра́.

sister-in-law *n.* **1,** (husband's sister) золо́вка. **2,** (wife's sister) своя́чeница. **3,** (brother's wife or spouse's brother's wife) неве́стка.

sit *v.i.* **1,** [*usu.* **sit down**] (take a seat) сади́ться: *sit down!*, сади́тесь! *Sit down to dinner*, сади́ться за обе́д. **2,** (be in a sitting position) сиде́ть: *he was sitting on the floor*, он сиде́л на полу́. **3,** (be located) стоя́ть: *the house sits on a hill,* дом стои́т на холму́. **4,** (remain inactive or unused) сиде́ть: *sit home all day,* весь день сиде́ть до́ма. *Sit idle,* проста́ивать. **5,** (pose) пози́ровать. **6,** (be in session) заседа́ть. —*v.t.* сажа́ть; уса́живать: *sit someone down to work,* сажа́ть/уса́живать кого́-нибудь за рабо́ту. —**sit back,** отки́дываться. —**sit out,** вы́сидеть до конца́. —**sit through,** просиде́ть. —**sit up, 1,** (rise to a sitting position) приподнима́ться. *Sit up in bed,* сесть в посте́ли. **2,** (stay up late) не ложи́ться спать; заси́живаться до по́здней но́чи. *Sit up all night,* просиде́ть всю ночь. —**sit well with,** устра́ивать.

sit-down strike сидя́чая забасто́вка; италья́нская забасто́вка.

site *n.* **1,** (place where something is) местоположе́ние. **2,** (place where something takes place) ме́сто: *crash site,* ме́сто ава́рии. *Building site,* строи́тельная площа́дка.

sitting *n.* **1,** (act of sitting) сиде́ние. **2,** (session) сеа́нс. *At one sitting,* в оди́н присе́ст. —*adj.* сидя́чий: *sitting position,* сидя́чее положе́ние. —**sitting room,** гости́ная.

situate *v.t.* располага́ть. —**situated,** *adj.* располо́женный.

situation *n.* **1,** (state of affairs) положе́ние; обстано́вка; ситуа́ция. **2,** (position of employment) ме́сто; рабо́та.

six *adj.* шесть. —*n.* **1,** (cardinal number) шесть. **2,** *cards* шестёрка.

sixfold *adj.* шестикра́тный. —*adv.* в шесть раз.

six hundred шестьсо́т. —**six-hundredth,** *adj.* шестисо́тый.

six-shooter *n., colloq.* шестизаря́дный револьве́р.

sixteen *n. & adj.* шестна́дцать. —**sixteenth,** *adj.* шестна́дцатый.

sixth *adj.* шесто́й. —*n.* **1,** (sixth part) шеста́я часть. **2,** (fraction) шеста́я: *one-sixth,* одна́ шеста́я. **3,** *music* се́кста. —**sixth sense,** шесто́е чу́вство.

sixty *n. & adj.* шестьдеся́т. —**sixtieth,** *adj.* шестидеся́тый.

sizable *also,* **sizeable** *adj.* значи́тельный; поря́дочный.

size *n.* **1,** (largeness) величина́; разме́р. *Hailstones the size of one's fist,* град величино́й/разме́ром с (*or* в) кула́к. *Be twice/half the size of,* быть в два ра́за (*or* вдво́е) бо́льше/ме́ньше (*+ gen.*). **2,** (standard measure for shoes, clothes, etc.) разме́р; но́мер: *what size shoe do you wear?,* како́й разме́р/но́мер боти́нок вы но́сите? **3,** *colloq.* (state of affairs): *that's about the size of it,* вот как обстои́т де́ло. —*v.t.* [*usu.* **size up**] оце́нивать. *Size up the situation,* уясни́ть себе́ положе́ние.

sizeable *adj.* = **sizable.**

sizzle *v.i.* шипе́ть.

skate *n.* **1,** (ice skate) конёк; (roller skate) ро́лик; конёк на ро́ликах. **2,** (fish) скат. —*v.i.* [*also,* **go skating**] ката́ться на конька́х *or* на ро́ликах. —**skater,** *n.* конькобе́жец.

skating *n.* ката́ние на конька́х; конькобе́жный спорт. *Speed skating,* скоростно́й бег на конька́х. —**skating rink,** като́к.

skedaddle *v.i., slang* улепётывать.

skein *n.* мото́к.

skeletal *adj.* скеле́тный.

skeleton *n.* **1,** *anat.* скеле́т; костя́к. **2,** (inner frame-

work) о́стов; карка́с. —**skeleton key,** отмы́чка.

skeptic *also,* **sceptic** *n.* ске́птик. —**skeptical,** *adj.* скепти́ческий. —**skepticism,** *n.* скептици́зм.

sketch *n.* **1,** (rough drawing) набро́сок; эски́з; зарисо́вка. **2,** (short essay or outline) о́черк. **3,** (short play; skit) скетч. —*v.t.* **1,** (draw in rough outline) набра́сывать; зарисо́вывать. **2,** *fig.* (outline; describe) обрисо́вывать; оче́рчивать.

sketchy *adj.* схемати́ческий; пове́рхностный.

skewer *n.* ве́ртел.

ski *n.* лы́жа. —*adj.* лы́жный: *ski suit,* лы́жный костю́м. —*v.i.* ходи́ть на лы́жах. *Go skiing,* идти́/пойти́ на лы́жах.

skid *v.i.* **1,** (slip because of lack of traction) заноси́ть (*impers.*): *the car skidded,* маши́ну занесло́. **2,** (slide instead of revolving) идти́ ю́зом.

skier *n.* лы́жник.

skiff *n.* скиф; я́лик.

skiing *n.* лы́жный спорт.

ski jump лы́жный трамплин.

skilful *adj.* = **skillful.**

skill *n.* **1,** (expertness) мастерство́; уме́ние; иску́сство. *Chess is a game of skill,* ша́хматы тре́буют мастерства́. **2,** (a specific ability) на́вык; квалифика́ция. *Reading skills,* на́выки чте́ния.

skilled *adj.* квалифици́рованный.

skillet *n.* сковорода́; сковоро́дка.

skillful *also,* **skilful** *adj.* иску́сный; уме́лый. —**skillfully,** *adv.* иску́сно; уме́ло.

skim *v.t.* **1,** (remove from the top of a liquid) снима́ть: *skim the cream from the milk,* снима́ть сли́вки с молока́. **2,** (read superficially) (бе́гло) просма́тривать. **3,** (glide lightly over) скользи́ть по: *skim the surface,* скользи́ть по верха́м *or* по пове́рхности. —*v.i.* **1,** (glide) скользи́ть. **2,** *fol. by* **through** *or* **over** (read superficially) (бе́гло) просма́тривать.

skimmer *n.* шумо́вка.

skim milk снято́е (*or* обезжи́ренное) молоко́.

skimp *v.i.* скупи́ться; эконо́мничать.

skimpy *adj.* **1,** (meager) ску́дный. **2,** (not quite large enough) ку́цый.

skin *n.* **1,** (tissue covering the body) ко́жа. **2,** (hide; pelt) ко́жа; шку́ра. **3,** (thin skin, as of a sausage) ко́жица. **4,** (rind; peel) кожура́; ко́жица; ко́рка. **5,** (vessel for holding liquids) мех. —*adj.* ко́жный: *skin disease,* ко́жная боле́знь. *Skin rash,* нако́жная сыпь. *Skin cancer,* рак ко́жи. —*v.t.* **1,** (remove the skin from) сдира́ть ко́жу с; обдира́ть; свежева́ть. **2,** (scrape; abrade) сса́живать: *skin one's knee,* сса́живать себе́ коле́но. —**by the skin of one's teeth,** с грехо́м попола́м. —**save one's skin,** спасти́ свою́ шку́ру. —**skin and bones,** ко́жа да ко́сти. —**soaked to the skin,** промо́кший до косте́й.

skin-deep *adj.* пове́рхностный.

skin diver аквалангист. —**skin diving,** подво́дное пла́вание (с аквала́нгом).

skinflint *n., colloq.* скря́га; скопидо́м; сквалы́га.

skinny *adj.* то́щий; худо́й; сухоща́вый; сухопа́рый.

skip *v.i.* **1,** (move with light springing steps) бежа́ть вприпры́жку. **2,** (move quickly from point to point) переска́кивать: *skip from place to place,* переска́кивать с одного́ ме́ста на друго́е. **3,** *fol. by* **over** (jump over; omit) переска́кивать: *skip over a puddle/page,* переска́кивать лу́жу/страни́цу. —*v.t.* **1,** (jump over) переска́кивать. *Skip rope,* пры́гать че́рез скака́лку.

2, (omit; bypass; fail to attend) пропускать: *skip a line,* пропускать строчку. *Skip a grade,* перескакивать через класс. *My heart skipped a beat,* у меня сердце ёкнуло. **3,** *colloq.* (depart hurriedly from) удрать от: *skip town,* удрать от города. —*n.* прыжок; скачок.

skipper *n.* шкипер.

skirmish *n.* стычка; схватка; перестрелка. —*v.i.* перестреливаться.

skirt *n.* юбка. —*v.t.* (go around; avoid) огибать; обходить (что-нибудь) стороной.

skit *n.* скетч.

skittish *adj.* норовистый.

skittles *n.* кегли.

skulduggery *also,* **skullduggery** *n.* надувательство.

skulk *v.i.* красться.

skull *n.* череп. *Fracture one's skull,* разбить голову. —**skull and crossbones,** череп и кости.

skullcap *n.* ермолка; тюбетейка; скуфья.

skullduggery *n.* = skulduggery.

skunk *n.* **1,** (animal) скунс; вонючка. **2,** *colloq.* (vile person) гад.

sky *n.* небо. *In the sky,* на небе. *Fall from the sky,* падать с неба. —**out of a clear blue sky,** ни с того ни с сего; как снег на голову. —**praise to the skies,** превозносить до небес.

sky-high *adv.* до небес; высоко-высоко.

skylark *n.* жаворонок.

skylight *n.* застеклённая крыша; световой люк; фонарь.

skyline *n.* очертание небоскрёбов на фоне неба.

skyrocket *v.i.* подскакивать.

skyscraper *n.* небоскрёб.

skyward *adv.* к небу; в небо.

slab *n.* плита.

slack *adj.* **1,** (not taut) слабый; свободный. **2,** (slow; sluggish) медленный: *slack pace,* медленный темп. **3,** (marked by a slowdown in activity) вялый. *Slack period,* глухая пора. —*n.* слабина: *take up the slack,* выбирать слабину. —*v.i.* [*usu.* slack off] ослабевать; спадать.

slacken *v.t.* **1,** (loosen; relax) ослаблять. **2,** (slow down) замедлять. —*v.i.* ослабевать.

slacker *n.* лентяй; прогульщик.

slacks *n.pl.* брюки.

slag *n.* шлак.

slake *v.t.* **1,** (quench, as thirst) утолять. **2,** (treat with water, as lime) гасить.

slalom *n.* слалом.

slam *v.t.* **1,** (shut with force) захлопывать (дверь). **2,** (throw or apply with force) хлопать: *slam the book on the table,* хлопать книгой по столу. *Slam down the telephone,* бросить трубку. *Slam on the brakes,* резко тормозить. —*v.i.* **1,** (shut noisily) захлопываться. **2,** *fol. by into* (run into) врезаться в; налетать на. —*n.* **1,** (act of slamming) хлопанье. **2,** *cards* шлем.

slander *n.* клевета. —*v.t.* клеветать на. —**slanderer,** *n.* клеветник. —**slanderous,** *adj.* клеветнический.

slang *n.* жаргон. —*adj.* жаргонный.

slant *v.t.* **1,** (set at an angle) наклонять. **2,** *colloq.* (write so as to express a bias) искажать. —*v.i.* коситься. —*n.* наклон; уклон; склон. *On a slant,* косо.

slanted *adj.* (biased) пристрастный; тенденциозный.

slanting *adj.* **1,** (oblique) косой; наклонный. **2,** (of eyes) раскосый.

slap *v.t.* шлёпать; хлопать. *Slap someone's face,* ударить кого-нибудь по лицу. —*n.* шлепок. *Slap in the face,* пощёчина.

slapdash *adj.* безалаберный; неряшливый. —*adv.* кое-как; на скорую руку; спустя рукава.

slapstick *n.* фарс. —*adj.* фарсовый.

slash *v.t.* **1,** (cut severely) порезать; рубить. *Slash tires,* вспарывать шины. *Slash one's wrists,* вскрыть себе на руках вены. **2,** (reduce drastically) урезывать. —*n.* **1,** (sweeping stroke) взмах. **2,** (sign [/]) дробь: *8/10,* восемь дробь десять. —**slashing,** *adj.* резкий; хлёсткий.

slat *n.* планка; пластинка.

slate *n.* **1,** (mineral) сланец; шифер. **2,** (writing plate) грифельная доска. **3,** (list of candidates) список кандидатов. —*adj.* **1,** (of slate) сланцевый; шиферный. **2,** (slate-colored) цвета сланца. —**wipe the slate clean,** всё простить.

slattern *n.* **1,** (slob) неряха; грязнуля. **2,** (slut) шлюха.

slaughter *n.* **1,** (of animals) убой: *lead to the slaughter,* вести на убой. **2,** (massacre) резня; бойня; избиение. *The slaughter of thousands of people,* убийство тысяч людей. —*v.t.* **1,** (kill, as animals) резать. **2,** (massacre) уничтожать.

slaughterhouse *n.* бойня; скотобойня.

Slav *n.* славянин.

slave *n.* раб. —*adj.* рабский; невольничий. *Slave labor,* рабский труд. *Slave market,* невольничий рынок. *Slave trade,* работорговля. —*v.i.* трудиться. —**slaveowner,** *n.* рабовладелец.

slaver *n.* слюни. —*v.i.* пускать слюни.

slavery *n.* рабство.

Slavic *adj.* славянский. —**Slavicist,** *n.* славист.

slavish *adj.* рабский.

Slavonic *adj.* славянский.

Slavophile *n.* славянофил.

slaw *n.* = coleslaw.

slay *v.t.* убивать. —**slayer,** *n.* убийца.

sleazy *adj.* **1,** (flimsy) непрочный. **2,** (run-down) убогий.

sled *n.* **1,** (for traveling over distances) сани. *Dog sled,* нарты. **2,** (for children) санки. —*v.i.* [*usu.* go sledding] кататься на санках.

sledge *n.* сани; санки.

sledgehammer *n.* молот; кувалда.

sleek *adj.* прилизанный.

sleep *v.i.* спать. *Go to sleep,* ложиться спать. —*n.* сон. —**put to sleep, 1,** (put to bed) укладывать (в постель). **2,** (make drowsy) усыплять; нагонять сон на. **3,** (put to death, as a sick animal) усыплять. —**sleep it off,** проспаться. —**sleep through,** просыпать. —**sleep with,** спать с.

sleeper *n.* **1,** (one who sleeps): *he is a light/heavy sleeper,* он чутко/крепко спит. **2,** (sleeping car) спальный вагон. **3,** *Brit.* (railroad tie) шпала.

sleepiness *n.* сонливость.

sleeping *adj.* **1,** (asleep) спящий. **2,** (of or for sleep) спальный. —**sleeping bag,** спальный мешок. —**sleeping car,** спальный вагон. —**sleeping pill,** снотворная таблетка. —**sleeping sickness,** сонная болезнь.

sleepless adj. бессо́нный. *Spend a sleepless night,* провести́ ночь без сна.

sleepwalker n. луна́тик. —**sleepwalking,** n. лунати́зм.

sleepy adj. со́нный; сонли́вый. —**be sleepy,** хоте́ть спать: *I am sleepy,* я хочу́ спать.

sleepy-eyed adj. за́спанный.

sleepyhead n. со́ня; со́нная тете́ря.

sleet n. дождь со сне́гом.

sleeve n. рука́в: *short sleeves,* коро́ткие рукава́. —**have something up one's sleeve,** име́ть что́-то на уме́; замышля́ть что́-то.

sleeveless adj. без рукаво́в; безрука́вный. *Sleeveless jacket,* безрука́вка.

sleigh n. са́ни. —v.i. [*usu.* **go sleighing** or **sleigh riding**] ката́ться на саня́х. —**sleigh bells,** бубе́нчики.

sleight of hand ло́вкость рук.

slender adj. **1,** (thin) то́нкий. **2,** (gracefully slim) стро́йный. **3,** (meager) ску́дный. **4,** (slight; feeble, as of hope) сла́бый.

sleuth n. **1,** (detective) сы́щик; шпик; ище́йка. **2,** (bloodhound) ище́йка.

slew n., colloq. ма́сса; у́йма.

slice n. ло́мтик. *Slice of bread,* кусо́к хле́ба. —v.t. **1,** (divide into slices) ре́зать; нареза́ть. **2,** fol. by **off** (cut off) отреза́ть. **3,** sports ре́зать; среза́ть (мяч).

slick adj. **1,** (slippery) ско́льзкий. **2,** (sleek, as of hair) прили́занный. **3,** colloq. (clever; tricky) хи́трый. —v.t. [*usu.* **slick down**] прила́живать. —n. покрыва́ло: *oil slick,* нефтяно́е покрыва́ло.

slide v.i. **1,** (slip; glide) скользи́ть: *slide on the ice,* скользи́ть по льду. *Slide down a pole,* соска́льзывать по шесту́. **2,** (move easily, as of a drawer) задвига́ться; выдвига́ться. **3,** fol. by **off** (slip off) соска́льзывать. —v.t. задвига́ть: *slide the suitcase under the bed,* задвига́ть чемода́н под крова́ть. —n. **1,** (act of sliding) скольже́ние. **2,** (inclined track) скат. **3,** (avalanche) обва́л; о́ползень. **4,** (transparency) диапозити́в. **5,** (specimen holder) предме́тное стекло́.

slide rule логарифми́ческая лине́йка.

sliding adj. скользя́щий; задвижно́й; выдвижно́й; раздвижно́й. *Sliding door,* раздвижна́я дверь. *Sliding scale,* скользя́щая шкала́. —**sliding board,** го́рка.

slight adj. **1,** (not great) небольшо́й: *a slight increase,* небольшо́е увеличе́ние. **2,** (not severe or heavy) лёгкий: *a slight cold,* лёгкий на́сморк. *A slight accent,* лёгкий акце́нт. *A slight temperature,* повы́шенная температу́ра. **3,** (short; brief) небольшо́й: *a slight pause,* небольшо́й переры́в. **4,** (slender; slim) то́нкий. —v.t. **1,** (neglect) пренебрега́ть. **2,** (treat discourteously) обижа́ть; трети́ровать. —n. оби́да; щелчо́к.

slightest adj. мале́йший: *I haven't the slightest idea,* я не име́ю ни мале́йшего представле́ния. *Not in the slightest,* ничу́ть; ни на йо́ту.

slighting adj. оби́дный: *slighting remark,* оби́дное замеча́ние.

slightly adv. слегка́; немно́го. *Slightly wounded,* легко́ ра́неный.

slim adj. **1,** (thin; slender) то́нкий; стро́йный. **2,** (meager) ску́дный. **3,** (poor, as of a chance) сла́бый. —v.i. [*usu.* **slim down**] худе́ть.

slime n. **1,** (mud) грязь. **2,** (animal secretion) слизь.

slimy adj. **1,** (covered with slime) сли́зистый. **2,** (repulsive) га́дкий.

sling n. **1,** (support for an injured arm) пе́ревязь. **2,** (rifle strap) (руже́йный) реме́нь. **3,** (device for shooting stones) праща́. **4,** = **slingshot.** —v.t. броса́ть; швыря́ть. *Sling a gun over one's shoulder,* заки́нуть ружьё за плечо́. *Sling mud at,* забра́сывать (кого́-нибудь) гря́зью.

slingshot n. рога́тка.

slink v.i. кра́сться; идти́ кра́дучись. *Slink away,* ускольза́ть.

slip v.i. **1,** (lose one's footing) поскользну́ться: *slip on the ice,* поскользну́ться на льду. **2,** (slide out of place) скользи́ть. *Slip off,* соска́льзывать; сбива́ться. **3,** (slide from one's grasp) выска́льзывать (из). **4,** (move quickly or furtively) скользну́ть. *Slip in/into,* вкра́дываться (в); прокра́дываться (в). *Slip out (of),* выска́льзывать (из). *Slip away (from),* ускольза́ть (от); улизну́ть (из). *Slip by/past,* скользну́ть (ми́мо); проска́льзывать (ми́мо). **5,** fol. by **over to, down to,** etc. (run a quick errand) сбе́гать (в). **6,** fol. by **into** (put on quickly) наки́нуть. **7,** fol. by **by** (pass imperceptibly, as of time) проноси́ться; промелькну́ть. **8,** (decline in vigor) сдава́ть. —v.t. **1,** fol. by **on** (put on quickly) наки́нуть. **2,** fol. by **off** (take off quickly) сбро́сить. **3,** (thrust quickly) засо́вывать. **4,** (convey stealthily) подбра́сывать; подкла́дывать; подсо́вывать. **5,** (escape, as one's mind) вы́скочить (из головы́). —n. **1,** (mistake; lapse) оши́бка. *Slip of the tongue,* обмо́лвка; огово́рка. **2,** (woman's undergarment) комбина́ция. *Your slip is showing,* у вас видна́ ни́жняя ю́бка. **3,** (pillowcase) на́волочка. **4,** (piece, as of paper) листо́к (бума́ги). *Order slip,* бланк зака́за. *Sales slip,* квита́нция. **5,** (plant cutting) чере́нок. **6,** (docking place) прича́л. —**give someone the slip,** ускольза́ть от кого́-нибудь. —**let slip, 1,** (miss, as an opportunity) упуска́ть. **2,** (utter unintentionally) отпуска́ть. —**slip through someone's fingers,** проскочи́ть (or проскользну́ть) у кого́-нибудь ме́жду па́льцами (па́льцев). —**slip up,** colloq. оплоша́ть.

slip cover чехо́л.

slipknot n. скользя́щий у́зел.

slippage n. скольже́ние; проска́льзывание.

slipper n. (дома́шняя) ту́фля; шлёпанец.

slippery adj. **1,** (smooth; slick) ско́льзкий. **2,** (shifty; elusive) увёртливый; изворо́тливый.

slipshod adj. небре́жный; неря́шливый. *In a slipshod manner,* спустя́ рукава́.

slip-up n., colloq. неувя́зка.

slit n. щель; разре́з; проре́з; про́резь. —v.t. разреза́ть. *Slit someone's throat,* перере́зать го́рло (+ dat.). *Slit open an envelope,* вскрыть конве́рт. —**slit trench,** щель.

slither v.i. **1,** (slide) скользи́ть. **2,** (move like a snake) ползти́.

sliver n. ще́пка.

slob n., slang неря́ха; грязну́ля; растрёпа.

slobber v.i. пуска́ть слю́ни. —n. слю́ни.

sloe n. тёрн.

slogan n. ло́зунг.

sloop n. шлюп.

slop n. помо́и. —v.t. расплёскивать. —**slop basin,** полоска́тельница.

slope n. склон; накло́н; укло́н; отко́с; скат; спуск.

—*v.i.* име́ть накло́н. *Slope downward,* идти́ *or* спус-ка́ться под укло́н. *Slope forty degrees,* име́ть накло́н в со́рок гра́дусов. —**sloping,** *adj.* накло́нный; пока́-тый; поло́гий; отло́гий.

sloppy *adj.* **1,** (muddy) гря́зный. **2,** (untidy; slipshod) неря́шливый. —**sloppiness,** *n.* неря́шливость.

slosh *v.i.* шлёпать (по гря́зи).

slot *n.* **1,** (long opening) щель. **2,** (round opening for a coin) отве́рстие.

sloth *n.* **1,** (animal) лени́вец. **2,** (indolence) ле́ность. —**slothful,** *adj.* лени́вый; ине́ртный.

slot machine иго́рный автома́т.

slouch *v.i.* суту́литься; го́рбиться. —*n.* **1,** (bent posture) суту́лость. **2,** (incompetent person): *he is no slouch,* он не лы́ком шит.

slough *v.t.* **1,** (shed) сбра́сывать. **2,** *cards* сбра́сы-вать. —*v.i.* сходи́ть; шелуши́ться.

Slovak *n.* **1,** (person) слова́к. **2,** (language) слова́ц-кий язы́к. —*adj.* слова́цкий.

Slovene *n.* слове́нец. —**Slovenian,** *adj.* слове́н-ский. —*n.* слове́нский язы́к.

slovenly *adj.* неря́шливый. —**slovenliness,** *n.* не-ря́шливость; неря́шество.

slow *adj.* **1,** (not fast) ме́дленный: *slow pace,* ме́д-ленный ход. *On a slow fire,* на ме́дленном огне́. *Be slow in replying,* заме́длить с отве́том. **2,** (behind time, as of a clock): *my watch is slow,* мои́ часы́ отстаю́т. **3,** (dull-witted) тупо́й. —*adv.* ме́дленно. —*v.t.* [*usu.* **slow down**] замедля́ть. —*v.i.* [*usu.* **slow down**] замедля́ть ход; замедля́ться.

slowdown *n.* замедле́ние.

slowly *adv.* ме́дленно.

slow motion заме́дленная съемка.

slowness *n.* ме́дленность.

slowpoke *n., colloq.* медли́тельный челове́к.

sludge *n.* грязь; ил.

slug *n.* **1,** (bullet) пу́ля. **2,** (object used in place of a coin) жето́н. **3,** *printing* шпон. **4,** (mollusk) слизня́к; сли́зень. —*v.t.* (punch) тузи́ть.

sluggard *n.* ленти́й; лежебо́ка.

sluggish *adj.* вя́лый; ине́ртный. —**sluggishly,** *adv.* вя́ло. —**sluggishness,** *n.* вя́лость.

sluice *n.* шлюз. —**sluice gate,** шлю́зные воро́та.

slum *n.* трущо́ба.

slumber *n.* сон. —*v.i.* спать; дрема́ть.

slump *n.* спад. —*v.i.* **1,** (fall heavily) вали́ться. *Slump into a chair,* опусти́ться в кре́сло. **2,** (decline sud-denly) ре́зко па́дать.

slung shot кисте́нь.

slur *v.t.* **1,** (pronounce indistinctly) глота́ть (слова́). *His speech is slurred,* у него́ язы́к заплета́ется. **2,** [*usu.* **slur over**] (pass over lightly) сма́зывать. **3,** (disparage) поро́чить. —*n.* **1,** (stain) пятно́ (на репу-та́ции). *Cast slurs on someone's reputation,* черни́ть чью-нибудь репута́цию. **2,** (disparaging remark) ин-синуа́ция. **3,** *music* ли́га.

slush *n.* сля́коть; та́лый снег. —**slushy,** *adj.* сля-котный.

slut *n.* **1,** (slovenly woman) неря́ха. **2,** (loose woman) шлю́ха.

sly *adj.* хи́трый. —**on the sly,** тайко́м· потихо́ньку.

slyly *adv.* хи́тро.

smack *v.t.* **1,** (slap) хло́пать; шлёпать. **2,** *Smack one's lips,* чмо́кать губа́ми. —*v.i.* отдава́ть (+ *instr.*): *smack of dishonesty,* отдава́ть нече́стностью. —*n.*

1, (slap) шлепо́к. **2,** (trace; suggestion) при́вкус. —*adv., colloq.* пря́мо: *run smack into a tree,* вре́-заться пря́мо в де́рево.

small *adj.* **1,** (little; not large) ма́ленький; небольшо́й; ме́лкий. *Small child/house/town,* ма́ленький ребе-нок/дом/городо́к. *Small print,* ме́лкий шрифт. *Small income,* небольшо́й дохо́д. *On a small scale,* в небольшо́м масшта́бе. *She is a small eater,* она́ ма́ло ест. *These shoes are too small,* э́ти боти́нки (мне) малы́. **2,** (operating on a limited scale) ме́лкий: *a small business,* ме́лкое предприя́тие; *small deposi-tor,* ме́лкий вкла́дчик. **3,** (petty) ме́лкий; ме́лочный. **4,** *in small letter,* ма́ленькая *or* строчна́я бу́ква. —*n., in small of the back,* поясни́ца.

small arms стрелко́вое ору́жие.

small change ме́лкие де́ньги; ме́лочь.

small fry *colloq.* ме́лкая со́шка; *collective* мелюзга́; мелкота́.

small intestine то́нкая кишка́.

small-minded *adj.* ме́лкий; ме́лочный.

smallpox *n.* (черная) о́спа.

small talk сало́нный разгово́р.

smart *adj.* **1,** (bright; clever) у́мный; спосо́бный. **2,** (brisk; vigorous) бы́стрый: *at a smart pace,* бы́стрым хо́дом. **3,** (stylish) шика́рный; наря́дный. —*v.i.* **1,** (sting; burn) садни́ть. **2,** (suffer keenly) му́читься. —**smart aleck,** *colloq.* у́мник.

smarten *v.t.* [*usu.* **smarten up**] **1,** (improve in ap-pearance) прихора́шивать. **2,** (make more aware) вразумля́ть. —*v.i.* [*usu.* **smarten up**] образу́миться.

smartly *adv.* **1,** (stylishly) шика́рно. **2,** (with brisk and precise movements) че́тко.

smash *v.t.* **1,** (break to pieces) разбива́ть: *smash a vase,* разби́ть ва́зу. *Smash up a car,* разби́ть ма-ши́ну. *Smash down a door,* вы́ломать дверь. *Smash something to the ground,* разби́ть что́-нибудь о зе́млю. **2,** (defeat utterly) разбива́ть; громи́ть. —*v.i.* **1,** (break into pieces) разбива́ться. **2,** *fol. by* **into** (run into) вреза́ться в; налете́ть на. —*n.* гро́хот.

smashing *adj., colloq.* потряса́ющий.

smattering *n.* пове́рхностное зна́ние.

smear *v.t.* **1,** (cover with grease, paint, etc.) ма́зать. **2,** (spread on; apply) нама́зывать; разма́зывать. **3,** (soil) ма́зать; па́чкать. **4,** (smudge, as ink) разма́-зывать. **5,** (defame) черни́ть. —*v.i.* разма́зываться. —*n.* **1,** (spot; smudge) пятно́. **2,** *med.* мазо́к. **3,** (slander) клевета́.

smell *v.i.* **1,** (have a certain odor) па́хнуть: *smell good,* хорошо́ па́хнуть; *smell of fish,* па́хнуть ры́бой. **2,** (be malodorous) воня́ть. —*v.t.* **1,** (catch the smell of) чу́вствовать за́пах (+ *gen.*). *I don't smell anything,* я не чу́вствую никако́го за́паха. **2,** (test by smelling; sniff) ню́хать. **3,** (sense the presence of) чу́ять: *smell a rat,* чу́ять недо́брое. —*n.* **1,** (sense of smell) обо-ня́ние. **2,** (odor; aroma) за́пах. *There is a smell of smoke,* па́хнет ды́мом.

smelling salts нюха́тельная соль.

smelly *adj.* ду́рно па́хнущий; злово́нный.

smelt *n.* (fish) корю́шка. —*v.t.* (fuse; melt) пла́вить; выплавля́ть. —**smelter,** *n.* плави́льщик. —**smelt-ing,** *n.* пла́вка.

smidgen *also,* **smidgeon** *n., colloq.* чу́точка.

smile *v.i.* улыба́ться. *Fortune smiled on him,* сча́стье ему́ улыбну́лось. —*n.* улы́бка.

smirch *v.t.* пятна́ть; мара́ть. —*n.* пятно́.

smirk *n.* усмёшка. —*v.i.* ухмыляться.

smite *v.t.* **1,** (strike; kill; afflict) поражать. **2,** (affect strongly) охватывать: *smitten with love,* охвачённый любовью. **3,** (captivate) увлекать; восхищать.

smith *n.* кузнёц.

smithereens *n.pl., in* **smash to smithereens,** разбивать вдрёбезги.

smithy *n.* кузница.

smock *n.* блуза; халат.

smog *n.* дымная мгла; "смог".

smoke *n.* **1,** (vapor) дым. **2,** (an act of smoking): *have a smoke,* покурить. —*adj.* дымовой: *smoke signal,* дымовой сигнал. —*v.i.* **1,** (indulge in smoking) курить. *No smoking!,* не курить! **2,** (give off smoke) дымить; дымиться. —*v.t.* **1,** (a cigarette, pipe, opium, etc.) курить. **2,** (treat or preserve with smoke) коптить. **3,** *fol. by* **out** (drive out) выкуривать. —**go up in smoke,** взлетёть на воздух.

smoked *adj.* копчёный: *smoked fish,* копчёная рыба. *Smoked salmon,* сёмга.

smokehouse *n.* коптильня.

smoker *n.* курящий; курильщик.

smoke screen дымовая завёса.

smokestack *n.* дымовая труба.

smoking *n.* **1,** (of a cigarette, cigar, etc.) курёние. **2,** (treatment with smoke) копчёние. —**smoking car,** вагон для курящих.

smoky *adj.* дымный.

smolder *also,* **smoulder** *v.i.* **1,** (burn) тлеть. **2,** (exist in a suppressed state) таиться. *Smoldering resentment,* затаённая злоба.

smooth *adj.* **1,** (not rough) гладкий: *smooth surface/skin,* гладкая повёрхность/кожа. **2,** (not jerky) плавный; спокойный. *Smooth gait,* плавная походка. *Smooth trip/flight,* спокойный рейс. —*v.t.* **1,** (make smooth) сглаживать; приглаживать. **2,** *fol. by* **out** (remove the wrinkles from) разглаживать; расправлять. **3,** *fol. by* **over** (mitigate) сглаживать.

smoothbore *adj.* гладкоствольный.

smoothly *adv.* гладко: *go smoothly,* проходить гладко.

smoothness *n.* гладкость.

smooth-spoken *adj.* сладкоречивый.

smorgasbord *n.* швёдская закуска.

smother *v.t.* душить; удушать. —*v.i.* задыхаться.

smoulder *v.* = **smolder.**

smudge *n.* пятно. —*v.t.* размазывать. —*v.i.* размазываться. —**smudge pot,** дымовая шашка.

smug *adj.* самодовольный.

smuggle *v.t.* **1,** (bring into a country illegally) провозить. **2,** (convey surreptitiously) проносить: *smuggle a gun into prison,* проносить пистолёт в тюрьму. —**smuggler,** *n.* контрабандист. —**smuggling,** *n.* контрабанда.

smugness *n.* самодовольство.

smut *n.* **1,** (sooty matter) сажа. **2,** (plant disease) головня. **3,** (obscene writing) непристойность.

snack *n.* закуска. *Have a snack,* закусить. —**snack bar,** закусочная; буфет.

snaffle *n.* трёнзель.

snafu *n., slang* путаница.

snag *n.* **1,** (tree stump sticking out of the water) коряга. **2,** *fig.* (hitch) зацёпка; заминка; загвоздка. *Hit a snag,* наскочить на мель. —*v.t.* зацеплять. —*v.i.*

зацепляться; задевать: *snag on a nail,* зацепляться/задевать за гвоздь.

snail *n.* улитка. —**at a snail's pace,** черепашьим шагом.

snake *n.* змея. —*v.i.* змеиться. —**snake in the grass,** змея подколодная.

snakebite *n.* укус змей.

snake charmer заклинатель змей.

snap *v.i.* **1,** (break suddenly) лопнуть; порваться. **2,** [*usu.* **snap shut**] (close with a sudden sharp sound) защёлкиваться. **3,** *fol. by* **at** (bite suddenly) цапать (за); (lunge at menacingly) огрызаться (на). **4,** (speak or retort sharply) отрёзать; отрубить; огрызаться. *Snap at someone,* огрызаться на кого-нибудь. **5,** *Snap to attention,* вытянуться в стойке "смирно". —*v.t.* **1,** (cause to make a sharp sound) щёлкать: *snap one's fingers,* щёлкать пальцами. **2,** [*usu.* **snap shut**] (fasten with a sharp sound) защёлкивать. **3,** (release, as a shutter) щёлкать (затвором *or* затвор). **4,** (take, as a picture) сдёлать (снимок). **5,** (break) порвать. **6,** *fol. by* **up** (buy quickly) расхватывать. —*n.* **1,** (sharp sound) щёлканье; щёлк. **2,** (fastening device) застёжка; кнопка. **3,** (brief spell) полоса. *Cold snap,* похолодание. **4,** (cookie) пряник: *ginger snap,* имбирный пряник. **5,** *slang* (easy task) пустяки; ерунда. —*adj.* скоропалительный: *snap judgment,* скоропалительное суждёние. —**snap back,** оправляться. —**snap out of,** избавляться от.

snapdragon *n.* львиный зев; львиная пасть.

snappy *adj.* **1,** (brisk) быстрый; живой. **2,** (cold and invigorating) холодненький. **3,** *colloq.* (stylish) броский. —**make it snappy!,** живо!; поскорёе!

snapshot *n.* снимок; фотоснимок.

snare *n.* силок; тенёта. —*v.t.* **1,** (catch; trap) поймать в ловушку. **2,** (entice; inveigle) заманивать; завлекать.

snarl *v.i.* **1,** (growl) рычать; огрызаться **2,** (become entangled) спутываться; запутываться. —*v.t.* спутывать; запутывать. —*n.* **1,** (growl) рычание. **2,** (tangle) путаница.

snatch *v.t.* **1,** (grab) хватать; выхватывать; урывать. **2,** *fol. by* **up** (buy quickly) расхватывать. —*v.i.* [*usu.* **snatch at**] хвататься за; ухватиться за. —*n.* **1,** (act of snatching) хватка. **2,** *weightlifting* рывок. **3,** (bit) обрывок; отрывок. *Snatches of a conversation,* отрывки разговора. **4,** (brief period of time): *work in snatches,* работать урывками.

snazzy *adj., slang* броский; шикарный.

sneak *v.i.* красться. *Sneak into,* вкрадываться в; лезть в. *Sneak out of,* выскользнуть из. *Sneak up to,* подкрадываться к. —*v.t.* проносить; протаскивать. —*adj.* внезапный: *sneak attack,* внезапное нападёние. —*n.* пройдоха.

sneakers *n.pl.* тапочки; кёды.

sneaky *adj.* лукавый; пронырливый.

sneer *n.* усмёшка. —*v.i.* **1,** (make a sneer) насмехаться; насмёшничать. **2,** *fol. by* **at** (scoff at) насмехаться (над).

sneeze *v.i.* чихать. —*n.* чих.

snicker *v.i.* хихикать. —*n.* хихиканье.

snide *adj.* язвительный; ехидный.

sniff *v.i.* сопёть. —*v.t.* **1,** (breathe in forcibly) вдыхать. **2,** (try to smell by sniffing) нюхать. —*n.* вдох носом.

sniffle *v.i.* **1,** (breathe with difficulty) сопёть. **2,**

(cry intermittently) всхлипывать. —**sniffles**, *n.pl.* насморк.

snip *v.t.* **1,** (cut; clip) резать. **2,** *fol. by* **off** (cut off) отрезать; отхватывать.

snipe *n.* кулик; бекас.

sniper *n.* снайпер.

snitch *v.t., slang* (swipe) стащить. —*v.i.* [*usu.* **snitch on**] *slang* (tell on) ябедничать (на).

snivel *v.i.* **1,** (run at the nose) распускать сопли. **2,** (complain; whine) хныкать; распускать нюни.

snob *n.* сноб. —**snobbery**, *n.* снобизм. —**snobbish**, *adj.* чванный; спесивый. —**snobbishness**, *n.* снобизм.

snoop *v.i., colloq.* подглядывать; подслушивать. —**snoop around**, рыскать; шнырять.

snooty *adj., colloq.* чванный; спесивый.

snooze *v.i., colloq.* вздремнуть. —*n., colloq.* коротский сон.

snore *v.i.* храпеть. —*n.* храп. —**snorer**, *n.* храпун.

snorkel *n.* шнёркель.

snort *v.i.* фыркать. —*n.* **1,** (snorting sound) фырканье. **2,** *slang* (short drink) глоток (спиртного); рюмочка.

snot *n.* сопли.

snotty *adj.* **1,** (covered with snot) сопливый. **2,** *slang* (saucy) нахальный.

snout *n.* рыло; морда.

snow *n.* снег. —*adj.* снежный. —*v.i.* снежить. *It is snowing,* идёт снег. —*v.t.* **1,** *fol. by* **in** *or* **under** (cover or obstruct with snow) заваливать снегом. **2,** *fol. by* **under** (overwhelm, as with work) заваливать (работой).

snowball *n.* снежок; снежный ком. *Throw snowballs,* играть в снежки.

snowbank *n.* снежный занос.

snowbound *adj.* заваленный снегом.

snow bunting пуночка.

snow-clad *adj.* заснеженный. *Also,* **snow-covered.**

snowdrift *n.* сугроб; снежный занос; снежный завал.

snowdrop *n.* подснежник.

snowfall *n.* снегопад.

snowflake *n.* снежинка; *pl.* хлопья снега.

snow leopard барс.

snow line снеговая линия.

snow maiden снегурка; снегурочка.

snowman *n.* снежная баба.

snowmobile *n.* снегоход.

snowplow *also,* **snowplough** *n.* снегоочиститель; снеговой плуг.

snowshoe *n.* снегоступ.

snowstorm *n.* метель.

snow-white *adj.* белоснежный.

snowy *adj.* снежный. —**snowy owl,** белая сова.

snub *v.t.* третировать. —*n.* щелчок. —*adj.* (of the nose) вздёрнутый.

snub-nosed *adj.* курносый.

snuff *n.* **1,** (powdered tobacco) нюхательный табак. **2,** (charred end of a candle) нагар. —*v.t.* нюхать. —**snuff out, 1,** (extinguish) тушить. **2,** (suppress; destroy) разрушать. *Snuff out human lives,* погубить человеческие жизни. —**up to snuff,** *colloq.* на должной высоте.

snuffbox *n.* табакерка.

snug *adj.* **1,** (cozy) уютный. **2,** (compact; tight-fitting) тесный.

snuggle *v.i.* [*usu.* **snuggle up to**] прижиматься (к).

so *adv.* **1,** (to the extent indicated; to a high degree) так: *so soon,* так скоро; *so long,* так долго. *I am so sorry!,* мне так жаль! ♦ *Before long-form adjectives* такой: *she is so beautiful!,* она такая красивая! **2,** (thus; in the manner indicated) так. *He said so,* он так сказал. *I think/hope so,* думаю/надеюсь, что да. *I don't think so,* думаю, что нет. *Let us hope so,* будем надеяться. *It so happened that...,* случилось так, что... **3,** (then; it turns out) так; так что: значит. *So you know her!,* так вы её знаете! *So if you want to go...,* так что, если вам хочется пойти... *So you've come after all!,* значит, вы всё равно пришли! **4,** (also; likewise) тоже: *so do I,* я тоже. **5,** *expressing disagreement with a neg. statement:* you don't know how to cook. I do so, вы не умеете готовить. Неправда, умею. —*adj.* так: *isn't that so?,* не так ли? *That is not so,* это не верно. *Is that so!,* да что вы говорите! —*conj.* поэтому: *it was raining, so we stayed home,* шёл дождь, и поэтому мы остались дома. —**and so,** итак. —**and so on; and so forth,** и так далее. —**or so,** *see* **or.** —**so as to,** с тем, чтобы. —**so be it,** так и быть; пусть будет так. —**so far,** *see* **far.** —**so long!,** пока!; до свидания! —**so long as,** если только; лишь бы. —**so many; so much, 1,** (such a large amount or number) так много; столько. **2,** (a specific amount or number) столько-то. —**so much for...,** вот тебе и...: *so much for our trip to Europe!,* вот тебе и поездка в Европу! —**so much the better/worse,** тем лучше/хуже. —**so that,** с тем, чтобы. —**so what?,** ну и что?

soak *v.t.* **1,** (keep in water) мочить; замачивать; вымачивать. **2,** (drench) промачивать. *Get soaked,* промокать. **3,** *fol. by* **up** (absorb) впитывать; всасывать. **4,** *fol. by* **off** (remove, as a stamp) отмачивать. —*v.i.* **1,** (stay immersed in water) пролежать в воде; мокнуть. **2,** *fol. by* **through** (seep through) просачиваться (сквозь). —**soaking wet,** мокрый, хоть выжми.

so-and-so *n.* такой-то: *Mr. So-and-so,* господин такой-то.

soap *n.* мыло. —*adj.* мыльный: *soap bubble,* мыльный пузырь. —*v.t.* мылить; намыливать.

soap dish мыльница.

soap flakes мыльная стружка.

soap powder стиральный порошок.

soapstone *n.* мыльный камень.

soapsuds *n.pl.* мыльная пена.

soapwort *n.* мыльнянка.

soapy *adj.* мыльный.

soar *v.i.* **1,** (fly high into the air) взлетать; взвиваться; взмывать. **2,** (glide) парить; реять. **3,** (shoot up, as of prices) подскакивать.

sob *v.i.* рыдать. —*n.* рыдание.

sober *adj.* трёзвый. —*v.t.* отрезвлять; вытрезвлять. *Have a sobering effect upon,* действовать (на кого-нибудь) отрезвляюще. —*v.i.* [*usu.* **sober up**] трезветь; отрезвляться; вытрезвляться. —**sobering-up station,** вытрезвитель.

sobriety *n.* трёзвость.

sobriquet *n.* прозвище; кличка.

so-called *adj.* так называемый.

soccer *n.* футбо́л.
sociable *adj.* общи́тельный. —**sociability,** *n.* общи́-
тельность.
social *adj.* **1,** (pert. to society) обще́ственный; со-
циа́льный: *social status,* обще́ственное/социа́ль-
ное положе́ние. *Social strata,* слои́ о́бщества. **2,**
(involving relations between people) дру́жеский:
social visit, дру́жеский визи́т. *Social gathering,*
встре́ча друзе́й. —**social security,** социа́льное
обеспе́чение.
socialism *n.* социали́зм. —**socialist,** *n.* социали́ст.
—*adj.* [*also,* **socialistic**] социалисти́ческий.
socialize *v.t.* социализи́ровать; обобществля́ть.
Socialized medicine, госуда́рственное медици́н-
ское обслу́живание. —*v.i.* (associate; consort)
обща́ться. —**socialization,** *n.* социализа́ция; обоб-
ществле́ние.
society *n.* о́бщество: *feudal society,* феода́льное
о́бщество. *High society,* вы́сшее о́бщество; вы́сший
свет. *A scientific society,* нау́чное о́бщество.
sociology *n.* социоло́гия. —**sociological,** *adj.* со-
циологи́ческий. —**sociologist,** *n.* социо́лог.
sock *n.* **1,** (short stocking) носо́к. **2,** *slang* (a punch)
тума́к. —*v.t., slang* тра́хнуть.
socket *n.* **1,** (electric outlet) розе́тка; гнездо́. **2,**
(for an electric bulb) патро́н. **3,** *anat.* впа́дина. *Eye
socket,* глазна́я впа́дина; глазни́ца. *Socket of a
tooth,* яче́йка.
socle *n.* цо́коль.
sod *n.* дёрн. —*v.t.* обкла́дывать дёрном.
soda *n.* **1,** (sodium or sodium compound) со́да. **2,**
= **soda water.** —**soda fountain,** сто́йка. —**soda water,** со́довая вода́; газиро́ванная вода́.
sodden *adj.* промо́кший; пропи́танный вла́гой.
sodium *n.* на́трий. —**sodium bicarbonate,** двуугле-
ки́слый на́трий. —**sodium carbonate,** углеки́слый
на́трий. —**sodium chloride,** хло́ристый на́трий.
—**sodium fluoride,** фто́ристый на́трий. —**sodium
hydroxide,** е́дкий натр. —**sodium nitrate,** на́трие-
вая сели́тра. —**sodium phosphate,** фосфа́т на́трия.
—**sodium sulfate,** серноки́слый на́трий. —**sodium-vapor lamp,** на́триевая ла́мпа.
sodomy *n.* педера́стия; скотоло́жство.
sofa *n.* дива́н; софа́.
soft *adj.* **1,** (not hard) мя́гкий: *soft pillow,* мя́гкая
поду́шка. **2,** (not loud) ти́хий: *soft voice,* ти́хий го́лос.
3, (not bright; subdued) мя́гкий: *soft colors,* мя́гкие
тона́. **4,** (out of condition; flabby) дря́блый; не в
фо́рме. **5,** (easy to digest) лёгкий: *soft foods,* лёгкая
пи́ща. **6,** (nonalcoholic) безалкого́льный. **7,** *colloq.*
(easy): *soft job,* тёплое месте́чко. —*adv.* мя́гко;
ти́хо. —**have a soft spot in one's heart for,** пита́ть
сла́бость к.
soft-boiled egg яйцо́ всмя́тку.
soft coal битумино́зный у́голь.
soften *v.t.* смягча́ть. —*v.i.* смягча́ться.
softhearted *adj.* мягкосерде́чный. —**softheartedness,** *n.* мягкосерде́чие; мягкосерде́чность.
soft landing мя́гкая поса́дка.
softly *adv.* **1,** (gently) мя́гко. **2,** (quietly) ти́хо.
softness *n.* мя́гкость.
soft palate мя́гкое небо.
soft-spoken *adj.* ти́хий; кро́ткий.
software *n.* математи́ческое обеспе́чение (цифровой вычисли́тельной маши́ны).

soggy *adj.* сыро́й; отсыре́лый.
soil *n.* **1,** (top layer of the earth's surface) по́чва. **2,**
fig. (country; land) земля́: *on foreign soil,* на чужо́й
земле́. —*v.t.* (dirty) па́чкать. —*v.i.* па́чкаться. —**soil
science,** почвове́дение. —**soil scientist,** почвове́д.
soirée *n.* ве́чер; вечери́нка.
sojourn *v.i.* жить. —*n.* пребыва́ние.
sol *n., music* соль.
solace *n.* утеше́ние.
solar *adj.* со́лнечный. *Solar system,* со́лнечная сис-
те́ма. *Solar energy,* со́лнечная эне́ргия.
solarium *n.* соля́рий.
solar plexus со́лнечное сплете́ние.
solder *n.* припо́й. —*v.t.* пая́ть. *Solder together,*
спа́ивать. —**solderer,** *n.* пая́льщик. —**soldering
iron,** пая́льник.
soldier *n.* солда́т. *Play soldier,* игра́ть в солда́тики.
—**soldier of fortune,** кондотье́р.
soldierly *adj.* вое́нный; во́инский.
sole *n.* **1,** (of the foot) ступня́; подо́шва. **2,** (of a shoe)
подмётка; подо́шва. *Inner sole,* сте́лька. **3,** (fish)
ка́мбала. —*v.t.* ста́вить подмётку на; подши́вать.
—*adj.* **1,** (only) еди́нственный: *the sole reason,* еди́н-
ственная причи́на. **2,** (exclusive) исключи́тельный:
sole right, исключи́тельное пра́во. *Sole owner,* еди́н-
ственный владе́лец.
solecism *n.* солеци́зм.
solely *adv.* еди́нственно; то́лько; исключи́тельно.
solemn *adj.* торже́ственный: *solemn occasion/oath,*
торже́ственный слу́чай; торже́ственная кля́тва.
solemnity *n.* торже́ственность. *With great solemnity,* торже́ственно.
solemnly *adv.* торже́ственно: *I solemnly swear,*
торже́ственно кляну́сь.
solenoid *n.* солено́ид.
solfeggio *n.* сольфе́джио.
solicit *v.t.* проси́ть; выпра́шивать; хода́тайство-
вать о. *Solicit alms,* проси́ть ми́лостыню. —**solicitation,** *n.* хода́тайство.
solicitor *n.* **1,** (one who solicits) проси́тель. **2,** (lawyer) адвока́т.
solicitous *adj.* забо́тливый. —**solicitude,** *n.* забо́т-
ливость.
solid *adj.* **1,** (of firm structure) твёрдый: *solid body/
state,* твёрдое те́ло/состоя́ние. *Solid food,* твёрдая
пи́ща. **2,** (sturdily built) соли́дный; про́чный: *solid
building,* соли́дное/про́чное зда́ние. **3,** (upstanding;
reliable) соли́дный: *solid person,* соли́дный челове́к;
solid company, соли́дная компа́ния. **4,** (unbroken)
сплошно́й: *solid line/wall,* сплошна́я ли́ния/стена́.
5, (pure; unalloyed) чи́стый: *of solid gold,* из чи́стого
зо́лота. **6,** (plain; without a design) одното́нный: *solid
color,* одното́нная кра́ска. **7,** (three-dimensional) ку-
би́ческий; трёхме́рный. **8,** (uninterrupted) це́лый:
A solid hour, би́тый час. —*n.* твёрдое те́ло.
solidarity *n.* солида́рность; сплочённость.
solid geometry стереоме́трия.
solidify *v.i.* затвердева́ть; отвердева́ть. —*v.t.* **1,**
(harden) де́лать твёрдым. **2,** (consolidate) закреп-
ля́ть.
solidity *n.* твёрдость.
solidly *adv.* про́чно; соли́дно.
soliloquize *v.i.* произноси́ть моноло́г.
soliloquy *n.* моноло́г.

solitaire *n.* **1,** (gem) солитёр. **2,** (card game) пасьянс.

solitary *adj.* **1,** (lone) одиночный; одинокий. **2,** (single; sole) единственный. **3,** (secluded; remote) уединённый; обособленный. —**solitary confinement,** одиночное заключение.

solitude *n.* одиночество; уединение.

solo *n.* соло. —*adj.* сольный. —**soloist,** *n.* солист; солистка.

solstice *n.* солнцестояние.

soluble *adj.* растворимый. —**solubility,** *n.* растворимость.

solution *n.* **1,** (answer to a problem or puzzle) решение. **2,** (resolution of a question or issue) разрешение. **3,** (dissolving) растворение. **4,** (mixture of various substances) раствор.

solvable *adj.* разрешимый.

solve *v.t.* **1,** (find the answer to) решать; разгадывать. **2,** (resolve; settle) разрешать.

solvency *n.* платёжеспособность.

solvent *adj.* **1,** (able to pay one's debts) платёжеспособный. **2,** (dissolving another substance) растворяющий. —*n.* растворитель.

somatic *adj.* соматический.

somber *also,* **sombre** *adj.* **1,** (gloomy) мрачный; хмурый; пасмурный. **2,** (morose) мрачный; угрюмый.

some *adj.* **1,** (of an unspecified quantity) *rendered by the gen. case: would you like some tea?,* хотите чаю? ♦ *With abstract nouns* некоторый: *some time/doubt,* некоторое время/сомнение; *to some extent,* в некоторой степени. **2,** (a few) несколько: *some apples,* несколько яблок. **3,** (rather a lot of) немало: *it took some effort,* понадобилось немало усилий. **4,** (certain ones) некоторые: *some people,* некоторые люди. **5,** (unspecified one of ones) какой-то; какой-нибудь. *Some man was asking for you,* вас спрашивал какой-то человек. **6,** *slang* (quite a) вот это; ну и: *some singer!,* вот это певец! *Some weather!,* ну и погода! —*pron.* **1,** (a certain amount) *not rendered in Russian: would you like some?,* хотите?; хотите попробовать? **2,** (certain ones) некоторые: *some of my friends,* некоторые из моих друзей. *Some believe that...,* некоторые считают, что... **3,** (certain ones as opposed to others) одни: *some want to go, others do not,* одни хотят пойти, другие нет. —*adv.* (approximately) около; до; какой-нибудь. *Some forty miles,* какие-нибудь сорок миль. —**and then some,** *colloq.* и ещё сверх того. —**some other time,** как-нибудь в другой раз.

somebody *pron.* кто-то; кто-нибудь. *Somebody else,* кто-то другой; кто-нибудь другой. *Somebody's,* чей-то; чей-нибудь. —*n., colloq.* важная персона; важная особа.

someday *adv.* когда-то; когда-нибудь.

somehow *adv.* как-то; как-нибудь. —**somehow or other,** так или иначе.

someone *pron.* кто-то; кто-нибудь. *Someone else,* кто-то другой; кто-нибудь другой. *Someone else's,* чужой. *Someone's,* чей-то; чей-нибудь.

someplace *adv.* = **somewhere.**

somersault *n.* сальто; сальто-мортале. —*v.i.* кувыркаться.

something *pron.* что-то; что-нибудь; кое-что. *Something is happening,* что-то происходит. *Would you like something to drink?,* хотите что-нибудь выпить? *I want to ask you something,* я хочу вас кое-что спросить. *Something else,* что-то другое; что-нибудь другое. *Something like that,* что-то в этом роде. *Or something,* или что-то в этом роде.

sometime *adv.* когда-то; когда-нибудь.

sometimes *adv.* иногда.

somewhat *adv.* немного; несколько; слегка.

somewhere *adv.* где-то; где-нибудь; куда-то; куда-нибудь. *Somewhere else,* где-то в другом месте.

somnambulate *v.i.* ходить во сне. —**somnambulism,** *n.* лунатизм. —**somnambulist,** *n.* лунатик.

somnolent *adj.* **1,** (sleepy) сонный; сонливый. **2,** (causing drowsiness) снотворный. —**somnolence,** *n.* сонливость; дремота.

son *n.* сын.

sonar *n.* **1,** (method) гидролокация. **2,** (device) гидролокатор.

sonata *n.* соната.

song *n.* песня. *Break/burst into song,* запеть. —**for a song,** за бесценок; за гроши.

songbird *n.* певчая птица.

songbook *n.* песенник.

songster *n.* певец. —**songstress,** *n.* певица.

songwriter *n.* песенник.

sonic *adj.* звуковой. —**sonic boom,** звуковой удар; сверхзвуковой хлопок.

son-in-law *n.* зять.

sonnet *n.* сонет.

sonny *n.* сынок.

sonorous *adj.* звучный; звонкий.

soon *adv.* скоро. *Soon after,* вскоре после. *Too soon,* слишком рано. —**as soon as,** как только. —**just as soon,** скорее; лучше. *I'd just as soon stay home,* я предпочёл бы остаться дома.

sooner *adv.* **1,** (earlier) скорее; раньше. **2,** (preferably) скорее: *I would sooner die,* я скорее умру. —**no sooner,** едва: *no sooner did we start out than the car broke down,* едва мы отправились в путь, как машина испортилась. —**no sooner said than done,** сказано — сделано. —**sooner or later,** рано или поздно. —**the sooner the better,** чем раньше, тем лучше.

soot *n.* сажа; копоть.

soothe *v.t.* **1,** (calm; mollify) успокаивать. **2,** (alleviate; ease) облегчать.

soothsayer *n.* предсказатель; прорицатель.

sooty *adj.* в саже; закоптелый.

sop *v.t.* **1,** (soak) намачивать. **2,** *fol. by up* (absorb) впитывать. —*n.* подачка.

sophism *n.* софизм. —**sophist,** *n.* софист. —**sophistic,** *adj.* софистический.

sophisticated *adj.* **1,** (urbane) искушённый; утончённый; изысканный. **2,** (technologically advanced) сложный. —**sophistication,** *n.* утончённость; изысканность.

sophistry *n.* софистика.

sophomore *n.* студент-второкурсник.

soporific *adj.* **1,** *med.* снотворный; усыпляющий. **2,** (boring) усыпительный.

sopping *adj.* промокший. —**sopping wet,** мокрый, хоть выжми.

soprano *n.* сопрано. —*adj.* сопрановый; сопранный.

sorcerer *n.* колдун; чародей. —**sorceress,** *n.* колдýнья; чародéйка. **—sorcery,** *n.* колдовствó; чародéйство.

sordid *adj.* грýзный. *A sordid affair,* грýзное дéло; грýзная истóрия.

sore *adj.* **1,** (hurting) больнóй: *sore finger,* больнóй пáлец. *I have a sore throat,* у менý болúт гóрло. **2,** *fig.* (painful; irritating) больнóй: *sore point; sore subject,* больнóй вопрóс. **3,** *colloq.* (offended; angry) обúженный; сердúтый. *—n.* болýчка; ýзва.

sorely *adv.* **1,** (grievously) до бóли: *sorely distressed,* до бóли огорчён. **2,** (greatly) óчень: *you were sorely missed,* вас óчень не хватáло. *I am sorely tempted,* ýто óчень соблазнúтельно.

soreness *n.* болéзненное ощущéние; боль.

sorghum *n.* сóрго.

sorrel *n.* **1,** (plant) щавéль. *Wood sorrel,* кислúца. **2,** (color) крáсно-корúчневый цвет.

sorrow *n.* печáль; скорбь. *To my sorrow,* на своё гóре.

sorrowful *adj.* печáльный; скóрбный. **—sorrowfully,** *adv.* скóрбно; сокрушённо.

sorry *adj.* **1,** (feeling sympathy) жаль: *I am sorry,* мне жаль. *I feel sorry for her,* мне её жаль. **2,** (feeling regret): *be sorry,* сожалéть; жалéть: *I am sorry now that I did it,* тепéрь я сожалýю, что сдéлал ýто. **3,** (expressing one's apologies): *I'm sorry!,* простúте!; прошý извинéния. **4,** (pitiful) жáлкий; плачéвный: *a sorry sight,* жáлкое зрéлище; *in a sorry state,* в плачéвном состоýнии.

sort *n.* род; сорт; вид. *A sort of,* врóде (+ *gen.*); нéчто врóде (+ *gen.*). *All sorts of,* всевозмóжные; всýкого рóда (+ *nom.*). *Something of the sort,*чтó-то врóде ýтого; чтó-то в ýтом рóде. *Nothing of the sort,* ничегó подóбного. *What sort of person is he?,* что он за человéк? *—v.t.* [*also,* **sort out**] разбирáть; сортировáть; перебирáть. **—after a sort; of sorts,** нéкоторым óбразом. **—out of sorts,** не в дýхе. **—sort of,** кáк-то: *I'm sort of glad,* я кáк-то рад.

sorter *n.* **1,** (person) сортирóвщик. **2,** (machine) сортирóвочная машúна.

sortie *n.* вýлазка.

so-so *adj.* невáжный; снóсный. *—adv.* так себé; снóсно.

sot *n.* гóрький пьýница.

soufflé *n.* суфлé.

soul *n.* душá. *A simple soul,* простáя душá. *There was not a soul present,* там нé было ни душú. *Put one's heart and soul into,* вклáдывать всю дýшу в (+ *acc.*). *Don't tell a soul!,* никомý не говорúте!; об ýтом ни гугý!

sound *n.* **1,** (what can be heard) звук: *not a sound,* ни звýка. *The sound of footsteps,* звук *or* шум шагóв. **2,** (inlet) залúв. **3,** (strait) пролúв. *—adj.* **1,** (healthy) здорóвый. *Of sound mind,* в здрáвом умé; *law* вменýемый. **2,** (free from defect or harm) исправный. *In sound condition,* в хорóшем состоýнии; в исправности. *Safe and sound,* цел и невредúм. **3,** (solid; firm; stable) прóчный; основáтельный. *Sound basis,* прóчная оснóва. **4,** (sensible; logical) здрáвый; разýмный; благоразýмный; основáтельный. *Sound advice,* ýмный *or* дéльный совéт; *sound arguments,* основáтельные дóводы. **5,** (of sleep) крéпкий. **6,** (thorough) здорóвый: *sound thrashing,* здорóвая пóрка. **7,** (pert. to sound) звуковóй: *sound barrier,* звуковóй барьéр. *—adv. She is sound asleep,* онá

крéпко спит. *—v.i.* звучáть; раздавáться. *The whistle sounded,* раздáлся гудóк. *It sounds strange somehow,* ýто звучúт кáк-то стрáнно. *—v.t.* **1,** (cause to sound) трубúть в: *sound the trumpets,* трубúть в трýбы. *Sound the bells,* звонúть в колоколá. *Sound the alarm,* бить/забúть/ударýть тревóгу *or* (в) набáт. *Sound retreat,* давáть *or* бить отбóй. **2,** (pronounce; articulate) произносúть. **3,** (fathom; probe) зондúровать. **4,** *fol. by* out (solicit the opinion of) зондúровать; расспрáшивать. **—sound off, 1,** *mil.* откликáться. **2,** *colloq.* (express one's views) выскáзываться.

sound effects шумовые эффéкты.

sounding board дéка.

soundless *adj.* беззвýчный.

soundly *adv.* **1,** (logically) разýмно; толкóво. **2,** (so as not to be awakened) крéпко: *sleep soundly,* крéпко спать. **3,** (thoroughly; decisively) здóрово: *our team was soundly beaten,* нáша комáнда былá здóрово разбúта.

soundness *n.* **1,** (solidity) прóчность. **2,** (logic; validity) основáтельность.

soundproof *adj.* звуконепроницáемый.

sound track звуковáя дорóжка.

soup *n.* суп. *—adj.* суповóй: *soup tureen,* суповáя мúска. **—soupspoon,** *n.* столóвая лóжка.

sour *adj.* **1,** (having a sharp acid taste) кúслый. **2,** (cross; peevish) злой. *In a sour mood,* в дурнóм настроéнии. *—v.i.* **1,** (turn sour) кúснуть; скисáть; прокисáть. **2,** *fol. by* on (become disenchanted with) разочаровáться в. *—v.t.* (disenchant) отталкивать. **—sour grapes!,** зéлен виногрáд!

source *n.* **1,** (beginning of a stream or river) истóк. **2,** (that from which something comes) истóчник: *source of energy,* истóчник энéргии. **3,** (something that provides information) истóчник: *reliable source,* достовéрный истóчник.

sour cream сметáна.

souse *v.t.* **1,** (pickle) мариновáть. **2,** (plunge in a liquid) погружáть; окунáть. **3,** (drench; soak) промáчивать. **4,** *slang* (intoxicate) опьянýть. *—n., slang* (drunkard) пьýница.

south *n.* юг. *—adj.* южный: *the south bank,* южный бéрег. *—adv.* на юг; к югу. *South of,* к югу от; южнéе (+ *gen.*).

southeast *n.* юго-востóк. *—adj.* юго-востóчный. *—adv.* на юго-востóк.

southeaster *n.* зюйд-óст.

southeasterly *adj.* юго-востóчный. *—adv.* к юго-востóку; с юго-востóка.

southeastern *adj.* юго-востóчный.

southerly *adj.* южный.

southern *adj.* южный. **—southerner,** *n.* южáнин. **—southernmost,** *adj.* сáмый южный.

southpaw *n., slang* левшá.

South Pole Южный пóлюс.

southward *adv.* к югу. *—adj.* южный.

southwest *n.* юго-зáпад. *—adj.* юго-зáпадный. *—adv.* на юго-зáпад.

southwester *n.* зюйд-вéст.

southwesterly *adj.* юго-зáпадный. *—adv.* к юго-зáпаду; с юго-зáпада.

southwestern *adj.* юго-зáпадный.

souvenir *n.* сувенúр. *Souvenir shop,* магазúн сувенúров.

sovereign *n.* 1, (ruler) государь; суверён. 2, (British coin) соверён. —*adj.* суверённый. —**sovereignty,** *n.* суверенитёт.

soviet *n.* совёт. *The Supreme Soviet,* Верхóвный Совёт. —**Soviet,** *adj.* совётский: *the Soviet government,* совётское правительство. —**Soviet Union,** Совётский Сою́з.

sow[1] (so) *v.t.* 1, (scatter) сéять: *sow wheat,* сéять пшеницу. 2, (plant seed in) засевáть: *sow a field with rye,* засевáть пóле рóжью. 3, *fig.* (implant) сéять: *sow suspicion,* сéять подозрéние. —*v.i.* сéять: *as you sow so you shall reap,* что посéешь, то и пожнёшь.

sow[2] (sau) *n.* свиномáтка.

sower *n.* сéятель.

sowing *n.* сев; посéв; засéв.

soy *n.* сóя. *Also,* **soya.**

soybean *n.* сóя; сóевый боб. —*adj.* сóевый: *soybean oil,* сóевое мáсло.

soy sauce сóя.

spa *n.* курóрт с минерáльными вóдами.

space *n.* 1, (infinite expanse) прострáнство: *time and space,* врéмя и прострáнство. 2, (place; room) мéсто. *Parking space,* мéсто для стоя́нки машины. *Living space,* жилáя плóщадь. *Take up a lot of space,* занимáть мнóго мéста. 3, (interval) промежýток; интервáл. *Leave a space between,* оставля́ть промежýток мéжду. *Within the space of five years,* в течéние пяти лет. 4, (outer space) кóсмос. —*adj.* космический: *space flight,* космический полёт. —*v.t.* 1, (arrange with spaces between) расставля́ть с промежýтками. 2, *printing* разбивáть на шпáции. —**spacecraft,** *n.* космический аппарáт. —**spaceman,** *n.* космонáвт. —**spaceship,** *n.* космический корáбль. —**space suit,** скафáндр.

spacious *adj.* прострóрный; вместительный. —**spaciousness,** *n.* прострóр; вместительность.

spade *n.* 1, (tool) лопáта; зáступ. 2, *pl., cards* пики. —**call a spade a spade,** называ́ть вéщи своими именáми. —**spade work,** подготовительная рабóта.

spaghetti *n.* тóнкие макарóны; спагéтти.

span *n.* 1, (distance from thumb to little finger) пядь. 2, (distance between vertical supports) пролёт. 3, (spread) размáх: *wingspan,* размáх крыльев. 4, (period of time) отрéзок: *a short span of time,* небольшóй отрéзок врéмени. —*v.t.* 1, (extend across) протя́гиваться чéрез. *The bridge spans the river,* мост соединя́ет берегá рекú. 2, *fig.* (encompass, as a period of time) охвáтывать.

spangle *n.* блёстка.

Spaniard *n.* испáнец; испáнка.

spaniel *n.* спаниéль.

Spanish *adj.* испáнский. —*n.* испáнский язык. *Speak Spanish,* говорить по-испáнски. —**Spanish fly,** шпáнская мýшка; шпáнка. —**Spanish moss,** испáнский *or* луизиáнский мох.

spank *v.t.* шлёпать.

spanking *n.* шлёпка. —*adv., colloq.* совершéнно: *spanking new,* совершéнно нóвый.

spanner *n., Brit.* гáечный ключ.

spar *n.* 1, *naut.* рангóутное дéрево. 2, *aero.* лонжерóн. 3, (mineral) шпат. —*v.i.* 1, (box) дрáться на кулáчках. 2, (argue) препирáться; пререкáться.

spare *v.t.* 1, (show mercy toward) щадить: *spare the*

women and children, щадить жéнщин и детéй. *Spare someone's life/feelings,* щадить чью-нибудь жизнь/чьи-нибудь чýвства/. 2, (use sparingly) щадить; жалéть. *Spare no expense/effort,* не жалéть расхóдов/усилий. 3, (give up conveniently) обходиться без: *I can't spare him,* без негó не могý обходиться. *Spare time for something,* уделя́ть врéмя чемý-нибудь. *Can you spare a dollar?,* вы мóжете дать мне дóллар?; нет ли у вас лишнего дóллара? *We haven't a moment to spare,* у нас нет ни однóй свобóдной минýты. 4, (save) избавля́ть: *spare someone trouble,* избавля́ть когó-нибудь от хлопóт. —*adj.* 1, (extra) лишний. *Spare time,* свобóдное врéмя. 2, (in reserve) запаснóй: *spare parts,* запасны́е чáсти. *Spare tire,* запаснáя шина *or* покрышка. 3, (lean) худóй; худощáвый. 4, (meager; frugal) скýдный.

spareribs *n.pl.* свиные рёбра.

sparing *adj.* скупóй: *sparing with words,* скупóй на словá.

spark *n.* искра. —*v.i.* искриться. —*v.t.* вызывáть; порождáть. *Spark interest,* вызывáть интерéс.

sparkle *v.i.* 1, (glitter) сверкáть. 2, (effervesce) игрáть. —*n.* прóблеск.

sparkler *n.* 1, (firecracker) шутиха. 2, *colloq.* (diamond) солитéр.

sparkling *adj.* 1, (glittering) искря́щийся; искристый. 2, (effervescent) игристый; шипýчий.

spark plug запáльная свечá.

sparrow *n.* воробéй. —*adj.* [*also,* **sparrow's**] воробьиный: *sparrow's nest,* воробьиное гнездó. —**sparrow hawk,** перепеля́тник.

sparse *adj.* рéдкий. —**sparseness; sparsity,** *n.* рéдкость.

Spartan *adj.* спартáнский. —*n.* спартáнец.

spasm *n.* спазм; спáзма.

spasmodic *adj.* 1, (convulsive) спазматический. 2, (uneven; irregular) скачкообрáзный.

spastic *adj.* спастический.

spat *n.* 1, (petty quarrel) перебрáнка; размóлвка. 2, *usu. pl.* (short cloth gaiters) гéтры. —*v.i.* (squabble) препирáться.

spate *n.* потóк.

spatial *adj.* прострáнственный.

spatter *v.t.* 1, (scatter in drops) брызгать; разбрызгивать. 2, (splash; spot; soil) брызгать; забрызгивать; обрызгивать. —*v.i.* разбрызгиваться.

spatula *n.* шпáтель.

spawn *v.i.* метáть икрý. —*v.t.* (give rise to) порождáть.

spawning *n.* метáние икры; нéрест. —**spawning ground,** нерестилище.

spay *v.t.* удаля́ть яичники у.

speak *v.t. & i.* говорить: *speak to someone,* говорить с кéм-нибудь. *Speak the truth,* говорить прáвду. *Speak Russian,* говорить *or* разговáривать по-рýсски. *Frankly speaking,* откровéнно говоря́. *Speak at a meeting,* выступáть на собрáнии. —**it speaks for itself,** э́то говорит самó за себя́. —**so to speak,** так сказáть. —**speak one's mind,** выскáзывать своё мнéние. —**speak out,** выскáзываться. —**speak up,** говорить грóмче. —**speak up for,** заступáться за. —**speak well for,** говорить в пóльзу (+ *gen.*). —**speak well of,** хорошó отзывáться о. —**to speak of,** осóбенный: *nothing to speak of,* ничегó осóбенного.

speaker *n.* **1,** (person speaking) тот, кто говори́т; говоря́щий. **2,** (person giving a speech) выступа́ющий. **3,** (one who speaks a certain language) носи́тель. **4,** (orator) ора́тор. **5,** (presiding officer) спи́кер. **6,** (loudspeaker) громкоговори́тель.

speaking *n.* разгово́р. *Public speaking,* ора́торское иску́сство. —**in a manner of speaking,** *see* **manner.** —**not be on speaking terms,** не говори́ть (*or* не разгова́ривать) друг с дру́гом.

spear *n.* **1,** (weapon) копьё. **2,** (for spearing fish) острога́. —*v.t.* пронза́ть копьём; бить (ры́бу) острого́й.

spearhead *n.* **1,** (head of a spear) острие́. **2,** *fig.* (that which leads) передово́й отря́д. —*v.t.* возглавля́ть; стоя́ть во главе́ (+ *gen.*).

special *adj.* **1,** (distinctive; particular) осо́бенный; осо́бый: *special case,* осо́бенный/осо́бый слу́чай. *Special assignment,* осо́бое зада́ние. *Require special effort,* тре́бовать осо́бых уси́лий. *Nothing special,* ничего́ осо́бенного. **2,** (separate) осо́бый: *special section,* осо́бый разде́л. **3,** (having a particular purpose) специа́льный: *special course/flight/correspondent,* специа́льный курс/рейс/корреспонде́нт. **4,** (extra) э́кстренный: *special edition,* э́кстренный вы́пуск. —**special delivery,** спе́шная по́чта.

specialist *n.* специали́ст.

speciality *n.* = **specialty.**

specialization *n.* специализа́ция.

specialize *v.i.* специализи́роваться. —**specialized,** *adj.* специа́льный: *specialized terms,* специа́льные те́рмины.

specialty *also,* **speciality** *n.* специа́льность. —**specialty of the house,** фи́рменное блю́до.

specie *n.* зво́нкая моне́та.

species *n.* вид.

specific *adj.* **1,** (explicit) конкре́тный: *specific purpose,* конкре́тная цель; *specific proposal,* конкре́тное предложе́ние. **2,** (individual; particular) отде́льный: *in each specific case,* в ка́ждом отде́льном слу́чае. **3,** *physics* уде́льный: *specific gravity,* уде́льный вес. —*n., usu. pl.* подро́бности.

specifically *adv.* в ча́стности.

specification *n.* **1,** (act of specifying) специфика́ция. **2,** *pl.* (detailed description) техни́ческие усло́вия.

specify *v.t.* **1,** (indicate clearly) ука́зывать: *specify the time,* ука́зывать вре́мя. **2,** (stipulate) предусма́тривать: *the law specifies that...,* зако́н предусма́тривает, что...

specimen *n.* образе́ц; экземпля́р.

specious *adj.* благови́дный.

speck *n.* **1,** (spot) пя́тнышко; кра́пинка. **2,** (small particle) части́ца. *Speck of dust,* пыли́нка; сори́нка.

speckle *n.* кра́пинка. —*v.t.* испещря́ть. —**speckled,** *adj.* (of material) в кра́пинку; кра́пчатый; (of animal) рябо́й.

spectacle *n.* **1,** (sight) зре́лище. **2,** *pl.* (glasses) очки́. —**make a spectacle of oneself,** обраща́ть на себя́ внима́ние.

spectacular *adj.* грандио́зный; потряса́ющий.

spectator *n.* зри́тель.

specter *also,* **spectre** *n.* при́зрак.

spectral *adj.* **1,** (ghostly) при́зрачный. **2,** (produced by a spectrum) спектра́льный.

spectre *n.* = **specter.**

spectroscope *n.* спектроско́п. —**spectroscopic,** *adj.* спектроскопи́ческий.

spectrum *n.* спектр.

speculate *v.i.* **1,** (ponder) размышля́ть. **2,** (conjecture) стро́ить дога́дки. **3,** *comm.* спекули́ровать.

speculation *n.* **1,** (conjecture) дога́дка: *a matter of sheer speculation,* чи́стая дога́дка. **2,** *comm.* спекуля́ция.

speculative *adj.* **1,** (based on an assumption) гипотети́ческий. **2,** (involving risk) спекуляти́вный.

speculator *n.* спекуля́нт.

speech *n.* речь: *organs of speech,* о́рганы ре́чи. *Make a speech,* говори́ть *or* произноси́ть речь. *Freedom of speech,* свобо́да сло́ва. —*adj.* речево́й. *Speech defect,* дефе́кт ре́чи.

speechless *adj.* **1,** (incapable of speech) немо́й. **2,** (at a loss for words) онеме́вший: *we were left speechless,* мы онеме́ли от изумле́ния.

speed *n.* ско́рость. *At full speed,* по́лным хо́дом; во весь опо́р. —*v.t.* [*usu.* **speed up**] ускоря́ть. —*v.i.* **1,** (move rapidly; race) мча́ться. *Speed by,* промча́ться. *Speed away/off,* умча́ться; унести́сь. **2,** (go too fast) превыша́ть дозво́ленную ско́рость. **3,** *fol. by* **up** (go faster) ускоря́ть ход. —**speed limit,** дозво́ленная ско́рость.

speedboat *n.* быстрохо́дный ка́тер.

speedometer *n.* спидо́метр.

speed skating скоростно́й бег на конька́х.

speedway *n.* **1,** (racing strip) автодро́м. **2,** (superhighway) автостра́да.

speedy *adj.* бы́стрый; ско́рый.

spell *v.t.* **1,** (write using certain letters) писа́ть: *how is this word spelled?,* как пи́шется э́то сло́во? **2,** (name the letters of) называ́ть по бу́квам: *spell the word "воскресе́нье",* назови́те по бу́квам сло́во "воскресе́нье". **3,** (be the letters of) образо́вывать. **4,** (signify; mean) означа́ть. **5,** (replace temporarily; relieve) сменя́ть. —*v.i. He spells poorly,* у него́ хрома́ет орфогра́фия. —*n.* **1,** (compelling attraction) ча́ры. *Cast a spell over,* заколдо́вывать; околдо́вывать. **2,** (short period) полоса́: *spell of good weather,* полоса́ хоро́шей пого́ды. *Cold spell,* похолода́ние. **3,** (attack; fit) при́ступ: *coughing spell,* при́ступ ка́шля. *Fainting spell,* о́бморок. —**spell out,** уточня́ть; подро́бно излага́ть.

spellbound *adj.* очаро́ванный; зачаро́ванный; заворожённый.

spelling *n.* орфогра́фия; правописа́ние. *Correct spelling,* пра́вильная орфогра́фия. *Correct spelling of a word,* пра́вильное написа́ние сло́ва. —*adj.* орфографи́ческий: *spelling error,* орфографи́ческая оши́бка. *Spelling rules,* пра́вила правописа́ния. *Spelling reform,* орфографи́ческая рефо́рма; рефо́рма правописа́ния.

spend *v.t.* **1,** (expend) тра́тить: *spend money,* тра́тить де́ньги. *Spend two hours fixing something,* тра́тить два часа́ на почи́нку чего́-нибудь. **2,** (pass) проводи́ть: *spend the summer at the seashore,* проводи́ть ле́то на мо́ре. **3,** (use up; exhaust) истоща́ть; исче́рпывать.

spending *n.* расхо́ды: *military spending,* вое́нные расхо́ды. —**spending money,** де́ньги на ме́лкие расхо́ды.

spendthrift *n.* расточи́тель; транжи́р; мот.

spent *adj.* **1,** (physically exhausted) изнурённый;

измученный. **2,** (used up) истощённый; исчёрпанный. **3,** (fired) стрéляный: *spent shell*, стрéляная гильза. *Spent bullet*, пуля на излёте.

sperm *n.* спéрма. —**sperm whale**, кашалóт.

spew *v.t.* извергáть. —*v.i.* извергáться: *lava spewed forth from the volcano*, лáва извергáлась из вулкáна.

sphere *n.* **1,** (round body) шар; сфéра. **2,** *fig.* (area) сфéра: *sphere of influence*, сфéра влияния. *Out of my sphere*, не в моéй сфéре; вне моéй сфéры. —**spherical**, *adj.* шарообрáзный; сферический.

spheroid *n.* сферóид. —**spheroidal**, *adj.* сфероидáльный.

sphinx *n.* сфинкс.

spice *n.* **1,** (seasoning) прáность; спéция. **2,** (zest; piquancy) остротá; пикáнтность. —*v.t.* приправлять. *Spice a story with jokes*, приправлять рассказ острóтами.

spick-and-span *adj.* чисто-нáчисто; безукоризненно чистый.

spicy *adj.* **1,** (highly seasoned) прáный. **2,** *fig.* (titilating) солёный; пикáнтный.

spider *n.* паук. —**spider web**, паутина.

spigot *n.* **1,** (faucet) кран. **2,** (plug) прóбка; затычка.

spike *n.* **1,** (sharp-pointed projection) острие. **2,** (large nail) костыль. **3,** (for athletic shoes) шип. **4,** (ear of grain) кóлос. —*v.t.* **1,** (pierce with a spike) пронзáть; прокáлывать. **2,** (squash, as a rumor) опровергáть.

spikenard *n.* нард.

spill *v.t.* **1,** (a liquid) проливáть; разливáть. **2,** (a dry substance) просыпáть; рассыпáть. —*v.i.* **1,** (of a liquid) проливáться; разливáться. *Spill over the top*, переливáться чéрез край. **2,** (of a dry substance) сыпаться; просыпáться; рассыпáться. **3,** *fol. by* **over** (spread) перекидываться. —**spill the beans**, *see* **bean**.

spillway *n.* водослив.

spin *v.t.* **1,** (make into thread) прясть: *spin flax*, прясть лён. *Spin a web*, плести *or* ткать паутину. **2,** (twirl) кружить; вертéть. *Spin a top*, вертéть *or* пускáть волчóк. **3,** (relate; tell) плести: *spin tales*, плести небылицы. —*v.i.* **1,** (spin thread) прясть. **2,** (whirl) кружиться; вертéться. *My head is spinning*, у меня кружится головá. **3,** (move along smoothly) катиться. —*n.* **1,** (spinning motion) кружéние. **2,** (short ride) прогулка. *Go for a spin*, проéхаться; прокатиться. **3,** *aero.* штóпор: *go into a spin*, входить в штóпор.

spinach *n.* шпинáт.

spinal *adj.* спиннóй; спинномозговóй. —**spinal column**, спиннóй хребéт; позвонóчный столб; позвонóчник. —**spinal cord**, спиннóй мозг. —**spinal fluid**, спинномозговáя жидкость.

spindle *n.* **1,** (rod used in spinning) веретенó. **2,** (axle; shaft) шпиндель.

spindlelegs *n.pl.* журавлиные нóги.

spine *n.* **1,** (backbone) позвонóчник; спиннóй хребéт. **2,** (quill) иглá. **3,** (thorn) шип. **4,** (stiff backing, as of a book) корешóк. —**spineless**, *adj.* бесхребéтный; бесхарáктерный.

spinet *n.* пианино.

spinner *n.* прядильщик; прядильщица; пряха.

spinning *n.* прядéние. —*adj.* прядильный. —**spinning machine**, прядильная машина. —**spinning wheel**, прялка.

spinoff *n.* побóчный продукт.

spinster *n.* стáрая дéва.

spiny *adj.* иглистый. —**spiny anteater**, ехидна. —**spiny lobster**, лангуст.

spiral *n.* спирáль. —*adj.* спирáльный. *Spiral staircase*, витáя *or* винтовáя лéстница.

spire *n.* шпиль.

spirit *n.* **1,** (vital principle in man) дух. **2,** *often pl.* (frame of mind) настроéние: *in low spirits*, в дурнóм настроéнии. **3,** (supernatural being) дух: *evil spirit*, злой дух. **4,** (real meaning or intent) дух: *the spirit of the law*, дух закóна. **5,** *pl.* (alcohol) спиртные напитки; спиртнóе. **6,** *pl.* (distillate) спирт: *spirits of camphor*, камфáрный спирт. —*v.t.* [*usu.* **spirit away** *or* **off**] умчáть.

spirited *adj.* живóй; оживлённый.

spirit lamp спиртовáя лáмпа; спиртóвка.

spirit level ватерпáс.

spiritual *adj.* духóвный. —*n.* негритянская религиóзная песнь.

spiritualism *n.* **1,** (belief in communication with the dead) спиритизм. **2,** *philos.* спиритуализм.

spiritualist *n.* **1,** (medium) спирит. **2,** *philos.* спиритуалист.

spit *v.i.* плевáть: *no spitting!*, не плевáть! *Spit on the floor*, наплевáть нá пол. *Spit in someone's face*, плюнуть комý-нибудь в лицó. —*v.t.* плевáть (+ *instr.*). *Spit blood*, плевáть *or* хáркать крóвью. *Spit out the pits*, выплёвывать кóсточки. —*n.* **1,** (saliva) плевóк. **2,** (rack for roasting meat) вéртел. **3,** (narrow point of land) косá; стрéлка. —**the spit and (** *or* **spitting) image of**, живóй портрéт (+ *gen.*).

spite *n.* злóба. *For/out of/spite*, назлó; со зла. —*v.t.* дéлать назлó (+ *dat.*). *Do something in order to spite someone*, дéлать чтó-нибудь назлó комý-нибудь. —**in spite of**, несмотря на.

spiteful *adj.* злóбный.

spittle *n.* плевóк.

spittoon *n.* плевáтельница.

spitz *n.* шпиц.

splash *v.t.* **1,** (scatter about, as a liquid or mud) брызгать; плескáть. **2,** (spatter, as with water or mud) забрызгивать. —*v.i.* **1,** (fall or strike with a splash) плескáть; плескáться. **2,** (move about with splashes) плескáться; полоскáться. —*n.* **1,** (act or sound of splashing) плеск; всплеск. **2,** (that which is splashed) брызги.

splashdown *n.* приводнéние.

splatter *v.t. & i.* = **spatter**.

splay *n.* скос. —*v.t.* скáшивать.

spleen *n.* **1,** *anat.* селезёнка. **2,** (ill will) злóба. —**vent one's spleen**, сорвáть злóбу.

splendid *adj.* **1,** (magnificent) великолéпный; пышный; роскóшный. **2,** *colloq.* (fine; excellent) великолéпный; чудный; чудéсный.

splendor *also,* **splendour** *n.* великолéпие; пышность; блеск. *In all its splendor*, во всём (своём) блéске.

splenetic *adj.* **1,** *anat.* селезёночный. **2,** (peevish) жёлчный.

splice *v.t.* срáщивать: *splice wires*, срáщивать проводá.

splint *n.* лубóк; шина.

splinter *n.* **1,** (fragment) оскóлок. **2,** (that which gets under the skin) занóза. —*v.t.* раздроблять. —*v.i.* раздробляться.

split *v.t.* **1,** (cleave) раскалывать; расщеплять: *split logs,* раскалывать/расщеплять поленья. *Split the atom,* расщеплять атом. **2,** (disunite) раскалывать. **3,** (divide up and share) делить. **4,** *fol. by up* (divide into smaller units) разбивать. —*v.i.* **1,** (break in two) раскалываться; расщепляться. *The ship split in two,* корабль раскололся надвое. **2,** (burst; rip apart) лопаться; распарываться. **3,** (divide into two or more groups or factions) разбиваться; раскалываться. **4,** *fol. by up* (separate; part company) расходиться. **5,** *fol. by off* (break off or away) откалываться. **6,** *in* **my head is splitting,** у меня трещит голова. —*n.* **1,** (break; tear) трещина. **2,** (division; schism) раскол. **3,** *gymnastics* шпагат. —*adj.* расколотый; расщеплённый. —**split decision,** *boxing* неединогласное решение. —**split hairs,** спорить о мелочах; вдаваться в тонкости. —**split personality,** раздвоение личности. —**split second,** мгновение ока. *Split-second timing,* синхронизация с точностью до секунды. —**split the difference,** поделить разницу пополам.

splitting *n.* расщепление: *splitting of the atom,* расщепление атома. —*adj.* мучительный: *splitting headache,* мучительная головная боль.

splotch *n.* пятно; клякса.

splurge *v.i.* раскошеливаться.

splutter *v.i.* **1,** (make hissing sounds) шипеть. **2,** (speak hurriedly or confusedly) лопотать.

spoil *v.t.* **1,** (damage; mar) портить. **2,** (pamper) баловать. —*v.i.* портиться. —*n., usu. pl.* добыча; трофеи. —**be spoiling for a fight,** лезть в драку.

spoilage *n.* порча.

spoiled *adj.* **1,** (damaged) испорченный. **2,** (pampered) избалованный; балованный.

spoke *n.* спица. —**put a spoke in someone's wheel,** вставлять палки в колёса (+ *dat.*).

spoken *adj.* устный.

spokesman *n.* представитель.

sponge *n.* губка. —*v.t.* вытирать губкой. —*v.i., colloq.* жить на чужой счёт. *Sponge off someone,* жить за счёт кого-нибудь. —**throw/toss in the sponge,** *colloq.* признать себя побеждённым.

sponge cake бисквит.

sponger *n., colloq.* тунеядец; дармоед; прихлебатель; приживальщик.

spongy *adj.* губчатый.

sponsor *n.* **1,** (guarantor) поручитель. **2,** (patron; benefactor) покровитель. —*v.t.* **1,** (act as a sponsor for) ручаться за. **2,** (pay for) финансировать. **3,** (introduce, as a bill or resolution) вносить.

sponsorship *n.* покровительство; поручительство.

spontaneity *n.* стихийность; непосредственность; самопроизвольность.

spontaneous *adj.* **1,** (resulting from a natural impulse) стихийный; непосредственный. *Spontaneous uprising,* стихийное восстание. *Spontaneous laughter,* непосредственный смех. **2,** (self-generated) самопроизвольный; спонтанный. —**spontaneous combustion,** самовоспламенение; самовозгорание. —**spontaneous generation,** самозарождение.

spoof *n.* пародия; сатира. —*v.i.* шутить. —*v.t.* высмеивать.

spook *n., colloq.* **1,** (ghost) привидение; призрак.

2, (secret agent) шпик. —**spooky,** *adj.* призрачный; пугающий.

spool *n.* шпулька; катушка.

spoon *n.* ложка. —*v.t.* черпать ложкой.

spoon bait блесна.

spoonbill *n.* колпица.

spoonful *n.* ложка.

sporadic *adj.* спорадический. —**sporadically,** *adv.* спорадически; время от времени.

spore *n.* спора.

sport *n.* **1,** *usu. pl.* (athletic activity) спорт. **2,** (particular game) вид спорта: *my favorite sport,* мой любимый вид спорта. **3,** (fun; diversion) забава; потеха. **4,** (jest) шутка: *say something in sport,* сказать что-нибудь в шутку. **5,** *colloq.* (good fellow) молодец. *Be a sport!,* будь человеком! —*adj.* [*also,* **sports**] спортивный: *sport shirt,* спортивная рубашка; *sports car,* спортивный автомобиль. —*v.t.* щеголять в: *sport a new suit,* щеголять в новом костюме. —**make sport of,** подшучивать над.

sporting *adj.* **1,** (used in sports) спортивный: *sporting gear,* спортивное оборудование. **2,** (fair) неплохой: *a sporting chance,* неплохие шансы.

sportscaster *n.* спортивный комментатор.

sportsman *n.* спортсмен. —**sportsmanlike,** *adj.* спортсменский. —**sportsmanship,** *n.* поведение, подобающее спортсмену.

sportswear *n.* спортивная одежда.

spot *n.* **1,** (stain; blemish) пятно: *grease spot,* жирное пятно. *Spots on one's face,* пятна на лице. **2,** *usu. pl.* (marking on an animal or bird) пятно; крапинка. **3,** (place; location) место: *a convenient spot,* удобное место. *Sore spot,* больное место. *Weak spot,* слабое место. *Nailed to the spot,* пригвождённый к месту. *Have a soft spot in one's heart for,* питать слабость к. **4,** (set of circumstances) положение: *in a tight spot,* в затруднительном положении. —*v.t.* **1,** (stain) пятнать. **2,** (catch sight of; detect) заметить; увидеть; рассмотреть; разглядеть. **3,** (give, as a certain number of points) давать (несколько очков) вперёд. —*v.i.* пачкаться. —**in spots,** местами. —**on the spot, 1,** (at once) сразу. **2,** (at the scene of action) на месте. **3,** (in a difficult position) в тупике. *Put on the spot,* ставить в тупик.

spot check выборочная проверка.

spotless *adj.* незапятнанный. *Spotlessly clean,* чисто-начисто; безукоризненно чистый.

spotlight *n.* прожектор. —**be in the spotlight,** быть в центре внимания.

spotted *adj.* пятнистый; крапчатый; рябой.

spotter *n., mil.* корректировщик. —**spotter plane,** самолёт-корректировщик.

spouse *n.* супруг; супруга.

spout *v.t.* **1,** (discharge with force) извергать. **2,** (utter profusely) сыпать. —*v.i.* **1,** (shoot out with force) хлынуть; бить струёй. **2,** (speak pompously) разглагольствовать. —*n.* **1,** (projection for pouring a liquid) носик. **2,** (stream of liquid) струя.

sprain *n.* растяжение. —*v.t.* растягивать; подвёртывать. *Sprain one's ankle,* подвернуть себе ногу.

sprat *n.* килька; шпрота.

sprawl *v.i.* растягиваться; разваливаться. *Send someone sprawling,* повалить кого-нибудь с ног.

spray *n.* **1,** (fine liquid particles) брызги. **2,** (atomizer) распылитель; пульверизатор. **3,** (liquid discharged from an atomizer) жи́дкость: *hair spray*, жи́дкость для воло́с. **4**, (branch) ве́точка. —*v.t.* **1**, (direct a spray of) обры́згивать; разбры́згивать. **2**, (treat with a spray) опры́скивать; распыля́ть.

sprayer *n.* распыли́тель; пульвериза́тор.

spray gun краскопу́льт.

spread *v.t.* **1**, (lay; unfurl) расстила́ть: *spread a table-cloth*, расстила́ть ска́терть. *Spread one's wings*, расправля́ть кры́лья. **2**, (lay out in display) выкла́дывать; раскла́дывать; раски́дывать. **3**, (draw or move apart) раздвига́ть; расставля́ть; раски́дывать. **4**, (diffuse; disseminate) распространя́ть: *spread rumors*, распространя́ть слу́хи. *Flies spread disease*, му́хи распространя́ют боле́зни. **5**, (scatter; strew) рассыпа́ть; разбра́сывать. *Spread manure*, разбра́сывать наво́з. **6**, (smear) нама́зывать: *spread butter on bread*, нама́зывать ма́сло на хлеб. **7**, (extend over a period of time, as payments) рассро́чивать. —*v.i.* распространя́ться: *the fire spread quickly*, пожа́р бы́стро распространя́лся. *The news spread all over town*, но́вость обошла́ весь го́род. —*n.* **1**, (diffusion; dissemination) распростране́ние. **2**, (expanse) разма́х: *wingspread*, разма́х кры́льев. **3**, (bedspread) покрыва́ло. **4**, (soft food) па́ста: *cheese spread*, сы́рная па́ста. **5**, (difference, as between prices) разры́в. —**spread oneself thin**, разбра́сываться.

spreading *n.* распростране́ние. —*adj.* **1**, (expanding its range) бы́стро распространя́ющийся. **2**, (of a tree) разве́систый; раски́дистый.

spree *n.* кутёж. *Go on a spree*, кути́ть; устра́ивать кутёж.

sprig *n.* ве́точка; побе́г.

sprightly *adj.* бо́дрый; задо́рный.

spring *v.i.* **1**, (leap) пры́гать; вска́кивать. *Spring to one's feet*, вскочи́ть на́ ноги. **2**, *fol. by* up (come into being) возника́ть; появля́ться. *New towns are springing up everywhere*, но́вые города́ возника́ют повсю́ду. **3**, *fol. by* from (stem from; be due to) происходи́ть (от). **4**, *in* **spring open**, распахну́ться; **spring shut**, захло́пнуться. —*v.t.* **1**, (release; actuate) пуска́ть в ход. **2**, (present or make known suddenly) преподноси́ть: *spring a surprise on*, преподноси́ть сюрпри́з (+ *dat.*). **3**, *in* **spring a leak**, дать течь. —*n.* **1**, (leap) прыжо́к. **2**, (season) весна́. *In spring*, весно́й. **3**, (device for applying tension) пружи́на; *(on vehicles)* рессо́ра. **4**, (elasticity) упру́гость. **5**, (water rising from the ground) исто́чник; ключ; родни́к. —*adj.* **1**, (of springtime) весе́нний: *spring vacation*, весе́нние кани́кулы. **2**, (motivated by tension) пружи́нный: *spring mattress*, пружи́нный матра́с. **3**, (flowing up from the ground) ключево́й; роднико́вый.

springboard *n.* **1**, (used by athletes and acrobats) трампли́н. **2**, *fig.* (avenue to success) трампли́н; плацда́рм.

springtime *n.* весна́; весе́нняя пора́; весе́ннее вре́мя.

springy *adj.* упру́гий; пружи́нистый.

sprinkle *v.t.* **1**, (scatter in drops) бры́згать: *sprinkle water on*, бры́згать водо́й на (+ *acc.*). **2**, (scatter drops of something on) обры́згивать; кропи́ть; окропля́ть; опры́скивать (*e.g.* что́-нибудь водо́й). **3**, (scatter in particles) сы́пать: *sprinkle salt in the soup*, сы́пать соль в суп. **4**, (scatter particles of something

on) посыпа́ть: *sprinkle the road with sand*, посыпа́ть доро́гу песко́м. —*v.i.* (rain lightly) мороси́ть; накра́пывать. —*n.* до́ждик; и́зморось.

sprinkler *n.* пульвериза́тор. —**sprinkler system**, дождева́льная устано́вка.

sprinkling *n.* **1**, (spraying of water) дождева́ние. **2**, (small admixture) при́месь. —**sprinkling can**, ле́йка.

sprint *n.* **1**, (short race) спринт. **2**, (extra burst of speed) рыво́к; бросо́к. —*v.i.* бро́ситься; помча́ться; бежа́ть во весь опо́р. —**sprinter**, *n.* спри́нтер.

sprite *n.* эльф. *Water sprite*, водяно́й.

sprocket *n.* зуб; зубе́ц. —**sprocket wheel**, цепно́е колесо́.

sprout *v.i.* пуска́ть ростки́; прораста́ть. —*v.t.* отра́щивать. —*n.* отро́сток; росто́к; побе́г.

spruce *n.* (tree) ель. —*v.t. & i.* [*usu.* **spruce up**] наряжа́ть(ся); прихора́шивать(ся).

spry *adj.* живо́й; бо́йкий; ю́ркий. —**spryness**, *n.* жи́вость; бо́йкость.

spud *n., colloq.* карто́фелина.

spume *n.* пе́на; на́кипь.

spun *adj.* пря́деный.

spunk *n., colloq.* сме́лость. —**spunky**, *adj., colloq.* сме́лый.

spur *n.* **1**, (of a horseman) шпо́ра. **2**, (of a gamecock) (петуши́ная) шпо́ра. **3**, (of a mountain) отро́г. **4**, (branch line) подъездно́й путь. **5**, *fig.* (stimulus) толчо́к. —*v.t.* **1**, (urge on with spurs) пришпо́ривать. **2**, (goad; impel) побужда́ть; подстрека́ть. —**on the spur of the moment**, под влия́нием мину́ты. —**win one's spurs**, сде́лать себе́ и́мя.

spurious *adj.* **1**, (counterfeit) подло́жный; подде́льный. **2**, (false; not true) ло́жный: *spurious charges*, ло́жные обвине́ния.

spurn *v.t.* отверга́ть; отта́лкивать.

spurt *n.* **1**, (gush of liquid) струя́. **2**, (sudden burst of speed) рыво́к; бросо́к. —*v.i.* **1**, (gush) бить струёй; бры́згать. **2**, (put on a burst of speed) сде́лать рыво́к *or* бросо́к.

sputter *v.i.* **1**, (make hissing sounds) шипе́ть. **2**, (speak hurriedly or confusedly) лопота́ть.

sputum *n.* плево́к.

spy *n.* шпио́н. —*adj.* шпио́нский: *spy ring*, шпио́нская организа́ция *or* сеть. —*v.i.* **1**, (engage in espionage) шпио́нить. **2**, *fol. by* on (watch furtively) подсма́тривать за. —*v.t.* (see; catch sight of) рассмотре́ть; разгляде́ть.

spyglass *n.* подзо́рная труба́.

squab *n.* (неопери́вшийся) го́лубь.

squabble *n.* перебра́нка; пререќа́ния. —*v.i.* вздо́рить; препира́ться; пререка́ться.

squad *n.* **1**, (smallest army unit) отделе́ние. **2**, (small organized group) отря́д; наря́д; кома́нда; брига́да. *Rescue squad*, спаса́тельная кома́нда.

squadron *n.* **1**, *naval* эска́дра. **2**, (of cavalry) эскадро́н. **3**, *aero.* эскадри́лья.

squalid *adj.* убо́гий.

squall *n.* **1**, (yell) вопль. **2**, (storm) шквал. —*v.i.* ора́ть; вопи́ть.

squalor *n.* убо́жество; убо́гость. *Live in squalor*, жить в убо́жестве.

squander *v.t.* растра́чивать; расточа́ть; прома́тывать. —**squanderer**, *n.* расточи́тель.

square *n.* **1**, (equilateral rectangle) квадра́т. **2**, (open area in a city) пло́щадь: *Red Square,* Кра́сная пло́щадь. **3,** *math.* квадра́т: *the square of three is nine,* три в квадра́те равно́ девяти́. **4,** (T-shaped or L-shaped instrument) уго́льник; науго́льник; рейсши́на. **5,** (space on a checkerboard) кле́тка. —*adj.* **1,** (square in shape) квадра́тный. **2,** (expressing surface measures) квадра́тный: *square meter,* квадра́тный метр. *Ten meters square,* де́сять ме́тров в длину́ и в ширину́. **3,** (honest; fair; equitable) че́стный: *square deal,* че́стная сде́лка. **4,** (paid-up; even) в расчёте; кви́ты: *we're all square,* мы с ва́ми в расчёте; мы с ва́ми кви́ты. **5,** *Square meal,* пло́тный обе́д. —*v.t.* **1,** (cut into a square shape) обтёсывать. **2,** (straighten, as one's shoulders) расправля́ть; распрямля́ть. **3,** (multiply by itself) возводи́ть в квадра́т. *Ten squared equals 100,* де́сять в квадра́те равня́ется ста. **4,** (settle, as accounts) своди́ть (счёты). **5,** (reconcile, as one statement with another) увя́зывать. —*v.i.* (conform) соотве́тствовать; вяза́ться. —*adv.* **1,** (at right angles) под прямы́м угло́м. **2,** (fairly) че́стно. **3,** (directly) пря́мо.

squarely *adv.* пря́мо. *Face the facts squarely,* смотре́ть фа́ктам пря́мо в лицо́.

square root квадра́тный ко́рень.

squash *n.* **1,** (vegetable) кабачо́к. **2,** (beverage) лимона́д. —*v.t.* **1,** (crush) расплю́щивать; (раз)дави́ть. **2,** (suppress) подавля́ть.

squat *v.i.* приседа́ть; сиде́ть на ко́рточках; сесть на ко́рточки. —*n.* приседа́ние. —*adj.* призе́мистый. —**squatter,** *n.* сква́ттер.

squaw *n.* индиа́нка.

squawk *v.i.* **1,** (cry hoarsely) клекота́ть. **2,** *slang* (complain) ворча́ть. —*n.* **1,** (hoarse cry) клёкот. **2,** *slang* (complaint) жа́лоба.

squeak *v.i.* скрипе́ть. —*n.* скрип. —**squeaky,** *adj.* скрипу́чий.

squeal *v.i.* **1,** (utter a loud, sharp sound) визжа́ть. **2,** *slang* (inform) доноси́ть. —*n.* визг. —**squealer,** *n., slang* (informer) доно́счик; стука́ч.

squeamish *adj.* брезгли́вый. —**squeamishness,** *n.* брезгли́вость.

squeeze *v.t.* **1,** (compress) сжима́ть; сда́вливать; сти́скивать. *Squeeze a lemon,* дави́ть *or* жать лимо́н. **2,** (extract by squeezing) выжима́ть. **3,** (cram) вти́скивать. —*v.i.* **1,** (apply pressure) жать; сжима́ть. **2,** *fol. by* **in, into** *or* **through** (force one's way) вти́скиваться (в); проти́скиваться (в). —*n.* **1,** (act of squeezing) сжа́тие. *Give someone's hand a squeeze,* кре́пко пожа́ть ру́ку (+ *dat.*). **2,** (embrace) объя́тие. **3,** (cramming; crowding) да́вка. *It was something of a squeeze,* бы́ло тесно́вато.

squeezer *n.* соковыжима́лка.

squelch *v.t.* пресека́ть; подавля́ть. *Squelch a rumor,* развея́ть слух.

squid *n.* кальма́р.

squiggle *n.* закорю́чка.

squint *v.i.* **1,** (screw up one's eyes) жму́риться; щу́риться. **2,** (be cross-eyed) коси́ть. **3,** (look sideways) коси́ть глаза́ми. —*n.* косогла́зие.

squire *n.* **1,** (title) сквайр. **2,** (lady's escort) кавале́р. —*v.t.* сопровожда́ть.

squirm *v.i.* **1,** (wriggle) извива́ться; ко́рчиться. *Squirm out of,* вывёртываться из. **2,** (fret; worry) му́читься.

squirrel *n.* бе́лка. —*adj.* бе́личий: *squirrel coat,* бе́личья шу́ба.

squirt *v.t.* пуска́ть струёй. *Squirt water in someone's face,* пуска́ть стру́йку воды́ в лицо́ (+ *dat.*). —*v.i.* бить струёй. —*n.* струя́; стру́йка.

stab *v.t.* коло́ть. *Stab to death,* заколо́ть. *Stab in the back,* наноси́ть (+ *dat.*) преда́тельский уда́р. —*n.* уда́р (ножо́м). *Stab in the back,* нож в спи́ну. —**stabbing pain,** ко́лющая боль.

stability *n.* усто́йчивость; стаби́льность.

stabilize *v.t.* стабилизи́ровать. —*v.i.* стабилизи́роваться. —**stabilization,** *n.* стабилиза́ция. —**stabilizer,** *n.* стабилиза́тор.

stable *adj.* **1,** (steady; firm) усто́йчивый; стаби́льный. *Stable currency,* усто́йчивая валю́та. *Stable prices,* усто́йчивые *or* стаби́льные це́ны. **2,** *chem.* сто́йкий. —*n.* коню́шня. —*v.t.* ста́вить в коню́шню; держа́ть в коню́шне. —**stable hand,** ко́нюх.

staccato *adj.* отры́вистый. —*adv.* стакка́то.

stack *n.* **1,** (orderly pile) ки́па: *stack of papers,* ки́па бума́г. *Stack of logs,* поле́нница. **2,** (pile of hay or straw) стог; скирд; скирда́. **3,** (chimney) дымова́я труба́. **4,** (set of shelves) стелла́ж. —*v.t.* [*often* **stack up**] скла́дывать. —**stack the cards** *or* **deck,** подтасо́вывать ка́рты.

stadium *n.* стадио́н.

staff *n.* **1,** (long stick) по́сох. **2,** (flagpole) дре́вко. **3,** (rod as a symbol of authority) жезл. **4,** (personnel) штат; соста́в. *Be on the staff,* быть *or* состоя́ть в шта́те. *Teaching staff,* преподава́тельский соста́в. *Staff reduction,* сокраще́ние шта́тов. **5,** *mil.* штаб: *the general staff,* генера́льный штаб. *Chief of staff,* нача́льник шта́ба. **6,** *music* но́тный стан; нотоно́сец. —*adj.* **1,** (permanent) шта́тный: *staff position,* шта́тная до́лжность. **2,** *mil.* штабно́й: *staff officer,* штабно́й офице́р. —*v.t.* обеспе́чивать персона́лом; *mil.* укомплекто́вывать ли́чным соста́вом.

stag *n.* (male deer) рога́ч. —*adj., colloq.* (for men only) холостя́цкий. —**stag beetle,** рога́ч.

stage *n.* **1,** (theater platform) сце́на: *appear on the stage,* выступа́ть на сце́не. **2,** (dais) помо́ст. **3,** (theatrical profession) сце́на: *retire from the stage,* уходи́ть со сце́ны. **4,** (step; phase) ста́дия; эта́п. *In stages,* по ста́диям. **5,** (leg of a journey) перего́н. —*v.t.* **1,** (put on) ста́вить: *stage a play,* ста́вить пье́су. **2,** (adapt for the stage) инсцени́ровать. **3,** (carry out; hold) устра́ивать; проводи́ть; организова́ть. **4,** (make appear spontaneous) инсцени́ровать. —**set the stage for,** подгота́вливать по́чву для.

stagecoach *n.* дилижа́нс.

stage fright стесне́ние пе́ред пу́бликой. *Suffer from stage fright,* стесня́ться пу́блики.

stagehand *n.* рабо́чий сце́ны.

stage manager режиссёр.

stage props реквизи́т; бутафо́рия.

stagger *v.i.* шата́ться; пошатну́ться. —*v.t.* **1,** (overwhelm; stun) потряса́ть; ошеломля́ть. **2,** (alternate) чередова́ть. —**staggering,** *adj.* потряса́ющий; ошеломля́ющий.

staging *n.* постано́вка (пье́сы). —**staging area,** *mil.* плацда́рм.

stagnant *adj.* **1,** (foul; polluted) стоя́чий; засто́йный. *Become stagnant,* заста́иваться. **2,** *fig.* (sluggish) вя́лый; ко́сный.

stagnate *v.i.* **1,** (become foul) заста́иваться. **2,** (become sluggish) коснѐть. —**stagnation**, *n.* застóй.

staid *adj.* степѐнный; положѝтельный.

stain *n.* **1,** (spot; blemish) пятнó. **2,** (coloring substance) морѝлка. —*v.t.* **1,** (spot; soil) пятнáть; пáчкать. **2,** (color; tint) морѝть: *stain wood*, морѝть дéрево. —*v.i.* пáчкаться.

stained *adj.* морѐный: *stained oak*, морѐный дуб. —**stained glass**, цветнóе стеклó. *Stained-glass window*, витрáж.

stainless steel нержавѐющая сталь.

stair *n.* **1,** (step) ступѐнька. **2,** [*usu.* **stairs**] (staircase) лéстница.

staircase *n.* лéстница. *Also*, **stairway.**

stairwell *n.* лéстничная клѐтка; пролѐт; прогóн.

stake *n.* **1,** (pointed stick) кол. **2,** (boundary mark) вѐха. **3,** (post for execution): *be burned at the stake*, погѝбнуть на кострѐ. **4,** (money wagered) стáвка. *Play for high stakes*, игрáть по большóй. **5,** (share; interest) дóля. *Have a stake in the outcome*, быть заинтересóванным в исхóде дéла. —*v.t.* **1,** *fol. by* **out** *or* **off** (delineate) отмечáть вѐхами. *Stake out a claim*, заявлять претѐнзию. **2,** *fol. by* **out** (put under surveillance) установѝть слѐжку за. **3,** (bet; risk) стáвить; стáвить на кáрту. *Stake one's all*, постáвить всё на кáрту. *Stake one's life on it*, ручáться за чтó-нибудь головóй; давáть рýку (*or* гóлову) на отсечѐние. **4,** (provide with money or resources) финансѝровать. —**at stake**, постáвлен на кáрту. *The fate of the country was at stake*, решáлась судьбá нарóда. —**pull up stakes**, снять́ся с мéста.

Stakhanovite *n.* стахáновец.

stalactite *n.* сталактѝт.

stalagmite *n.* сталагмѝт.

stale *adj.* **1,** (no longer fresh) чѐрствый: *stale bread*, чѐрствый хлеб. *Stale air*, спѐртый вóздух. *Become stale*, черствѐть. **2,** (trite; hackneyed) избѝтый. *Stale news*, устарѐвшие нóвости.

stalemate *n.* **1,** *chess* пат. **2,** (deadlock) мёртвая тóчка; тупѝк. —*v.t.* заводѝть в тупѝк. *Be stalemated*, заходѝть в тупѝк.

stalk *n.* стѐбель. —*v.i.* шагáть. *Stalk out of the room*, демонстратѝвно уйтѝ из кóмнаты. —*v.t.* **1,** (pursue stealthily) выслѐживать. **2,** (advance grimly across) бродѝть по: *hunger stalked the land*, гóлод бродѝл по странѐ.

stall *n.* **1,** (for an animal) стóйло. **2,** (market booth) ларѐк; палáтка. **3,** *Brit.* (orchestra seat) крѐсло в партѐре. —*v.t.* **1,** (put or lodge in a stall) стáвить в стóйло. **2,** (delay; check) задѐрживать; тормозѝть. *Negotiations are stalled*, переговóры зашлѝ в тупѝк. **3,** *fol. by* **off** (delay; divert) задѐрживать. —*v.i.* **1,** (stop running, as of an engine) глóхнуть; захлёбываться. **2,** (get stuck) застревáть. **3,** (use delaying tactics) увилѝвать. *Stall for time*, оття́гивать врѐмя.

stallion *n.* жеребѐц.

stalwart *adj.* **1,** (robust) дю́жий; рóслый. **2,** (loyal; staunch) вѐрный; стóйкий. **3,** (brave; valiant) отвáжный; дóблестный. —*n.* стóйкий сторóнник.

stamen *n.* тычѝнка.

stamina *n.* вынóсливость.

stammer *v.i.* заикáться. —*n.* заикáние. —**stammerer**, *n.* зáика. —**stammering**, *n.* заикáние.

stamp *n.* **1,** (marking device; impression so made) печáть; штамп; штѐмпель. **2,** (postage stamp) мáрка. **3,** (a stamping of the foot) тóпот. **4,** *fig.* (mark) пе-

чáть: *the stamp of genius*, печáть гѐния. **5,** (kind; ilk) склад: *people of that stamp*, лю́ди такóго склáда. —*v.t.* **1,** (bring down forcibly) тóпать: *stamp one's feet*, тóпать ногáми. **2,** (impress with a mark) штамповáть; штемпелевáть. *Stamp a passport*, штамповáть пáспорт; стáвить штамп на пáспорт. **3,** (imprint permanently, as in one's memory) запечатлевáть. **4,** *fol. by* **out** (extinguish by stamping on) затáптывать. **5,** *fol. by* **out** (eradicate) искоренять. —*v.i.* тóпать ногáми. —**stamp album**, альбóм для мáрок. —**stamp collecting**, собирáние мáрок. —**stamp collection**, коллѐкция мáрок. —**stamp collector**, филателѝст. —**stamp pad**, подýшка для штемпелѐй; штѐмпельная подýшка.

stampede *n.* панѝческое бѐгство. —*v.i.* бросáться врассыпнýю; обращáться в панѝческое бѐгство.

stance *n.* пóза; положѐние.

stanch *v.t.* останáвливать (кровотечѐние). —*adj.* = **staunch.**

stanchion *n.* стóйка; *naut.* пѝллерс.

stand *v.i.* **1,** (be in an upright position) стоя́ть: *she was standing in the doorway*, онá стоя́ла в дверя́х. *Stand (i.e. wait) in line*, стоя́ть в óчереди. **2,** (station oneself somewhere standing) становѝться (*pfv.* стать): *stand in the corner*, стать в ýгол. *Stand (i.e. get) in line*, стать в óчередь. **3,** *often fol. by* **up** (get up; rise) вставáть. **4,** (be placed or situated) стоя́ть: *the house stands on a hill*, дом стоѝт на холмѐ. **5,** (be a certain height) быть рóстом: *he stands six feet tall*, он рóстом шесть фýтов. **6,** (be; remain) стоя́ть. *The door stood open*, дверь былá нáстежь. *That is how matters stand*, вот как обстоѝт дѐло. *Stand accused of*, обвиня́ться в. *The thermometer stands at zero*, термóметр покáзывает нуль. **7,** (remain in effect) оставáться в сѝле: *the decision stands*, решѐние остаётся в сѝле. *The record did not stand for long*, рекóрд продержáлся недóлго. **8,** *Brit.* (be a candidate) баллотѝроваться. —*v.t.* **1,** (set upright) стáвить: *stand the vase on the table*, стáвить вáзу на стол. **2,** (endure) терпѐть; выносѝть. *I can't stand it*, я э́того терпѐть не могý. **3,** *Stand guard*, стоя́ть на часáх/на карáуле/на стрáже. **4,** *Stand trial*, идтѝ под суд. **5,** *Stand a chance*, имѐть шáнсы. —*n.* **1,** (instance of standing) стоя́ние: *a long stand in line*, дóлгое стоя́ние в óчереди. **2,** (small table, rack, etc.) стенд; стóлик; этажѐрка. **3,** (support; base) подстáвка. **4,** (platform) эстрáда. **5,** (market stall) ларѐк; киóск. **6,** (parking place for taxis) стоя́нка. **7,** *pl.* (grandstand) трибýна. **8,** (defensive effort) сопротивлѐние: *make a stand*, окáзывать сопротивлѐние. **9,** (view; opinion; position) позѝция. *Take a stand*, занимáть определённую позѝцию. **10,** *One-night stand*, однодневные гастрóли. —**stand aside**, **1,** (of a person) отходѝть в стóрону. **2,** (of a crowd) расступáться. —**stand back**, отступáть; держáться на расстоя́нии. —**stand by**, **1,** (remain aloof) держáться в сторонѐ. **2,** (stand ready) быть наготóве. **3,** (stand firmly behind) оставáться вѐрным (+ *dat.*). **4,** (not depart from) придѐрживаться (+ *gen.*). —**stand for**, **1,** (represent; signify) означáть. **2,** (tolerate) терпѐть. **3,** (advocate; favor) стоя́ть за. —**stand in for**, замещáть. —**stand out**, выделя́ться: *stand out in a crowd*, выделя́ться в толпѐ. —**stand over**, стоя́ть над (чьей-нибудь) душóй. —**stand up**, **1,** (rise) вставáть. *Stand up straight*, держáться прямо. **2,** (set upright) стáвить стоймя́. **3,** *slang* (disappoint) подводи́ть. —**stand up for,** стоя́ть за; заступа́ться за. —**stand up to,** вы́стоять про́тив. —**stand up under,** выде́рживать.

standard *n.* **1,** (norm) станда́рт; но́рма; мери́ло; ме́рка. *Double standard,* двойна́я ме́рка. **2,** (degree; level) у́ровень: *standard of living,* жи́зненный у́ровень. **3,** (basis of a monetary system) станда́рт: *gold standard,* золото́й станда́рт. **4,** (banner) зна́мя; шта́ндарт. —*adj.* станда́ртный; типово́й. —**standard-bearer,** *n.* знамёносец.

standardize *v.t.* стандартизи́ровать; нормиро́вать; унифици́ровать. —**standardization,** *n.* стандартиза́ция; нормирова́ние; унифика́ция.

standee *n., colloq.* стоя́щий зри́тель; стоя́щий пасса́жир.

stand-in *n.* дублёр.

standing *n.* **1,** (act of standing) стоя́ние. **2,** (status) положе́ние. *Be in good standing,* быть на хоро́шем счету́. **3,** *pl., sports* положе́ние: *team standings,* положе́ние кома́нд. —*adj.* **1,** (upright; on one's feet) стоя́чий; стоя́щий. *Standing position,* стоя́чее положе́ние. **2,** *sports* (from a standing position) с ме́ста: *standing broad jump,* прыжо́к с ме́ста. **3,** (permanent) постоя́нный: *standing army,* постоя́нная а́рмия; *standing invitation,* постоя́нное приглаше́ние. —**of long standing,** да́вний: *a friendship of long standing,* да́вняя дру́жба.

standing room стоя́чие места́: *standing room only,* биле́ты то́лько на стоя́чие места́.

stand-off *n.* ничья́. —**standoffish,** *adj.* необщи́тельный; холо́дный.

standpoint *n.* то́чка зре́ния.

standstill *n.* мёртвая то́чка. *Be at a standstill,* проста́ивать; быть на мёртвой то́чке. *Come to a standstill,* замира́ть.

stanza *n.* строфа́.

staple *n.* **1,** (wire clamp) скоба́; ско́бка. **2,** (clip) скре́пка. **3,** (principal commodity) основно́й проду́кт. **4,** (raw material) сырьё. —*adj.* основно́й; гла́вный. —*v.t.* скрепля́ть.

star *n.* звезда́. *Movie star,* кинозвезда́. —*adj.* **1,** (of stars) звёздный: *star map,* звёздная ка́рта. **2,** (outstanding) выдаю́щийся. —*v.t.* **1,** (mark with an asterisk) помеча́ть звёздочкой. **2,** (feature): *the film stars...,* в фи́льме...игра́ет гла́вную роль. —**see stars,** *colloq.* све́та невзви́деть. *He saw stars,* у него́ и́скры из глаз посы́пались. —**thank one's lucky stars,** благодари́ть судьбу́.

starboard *adj.* пра́вый. —*n.* пра́вый борт.

starch *n.* крахма́л. —*v.t.* крахма́лить. —**starched,** *adj.* накрахма́ленный; крахма́льный.

starchy *adj.* **1,** (containing starch) крахма́листый. **2,** (stiffened with starch) накрахма́ленный.

stare *v.i.* смотре́ть при́стально. *Stare at,* уста́виться на. —*n.* при́стальный взгляд.

starfish *n.* морска́я звезда́.

stark *adj.* **1,** (bleak; desolate) пусты́нный. **2,** (blunt; grim) жесто́кий. **3,** (pure; sheer; utter) сплошно́й. *Stark contrast,* ре́зкий контра́ст. —*adv.* соверше́нно: *stark naked,* соверше́нно го́лый; *stark raving mad,* соверше́нно сумасше́дший.

starless *adj.* беззвёздный.

starlight *n.* свет звёзд.

starling *n.* скворе́ц.

starry *adj.* звёздный.

start *v.t.* **1,** (begin) начина́ть: *start work,* начина́ть рабо́ту. *She started to cry,* она́ начала́ пла́кать; она́ запла́кала. **2,** (initiate) заводи́ть; завя́зывать; затея́ть. *Start an argument,* затея́ть спор. *Start a fight,* завяза́ть бой. *Start a rumor,* пусти́ть слух. *Start a war,* развяза́ть войну́. **3,** (organize, as a business) заводи́ть (де́ло). **4,** (set going, as an engine) запуска́ть (мото́р). *Start the car,* заводи́ть маши́ну. —*v.i.* **1,** (begin) начина́ть: *start from the beginning,* начина́ть снача́ла. *Starting 1 April,* начина́я с пе́рвого апре́ля. **2,** (commence) начина́ться: *the meeting starts at 10:00,* собра́ние начина́ется в де́сять часо́в. **3,** (begin to move) тро́нуться: *the train started,* по́езд тро́нулся. **4,** (begin to function, as of an engine) заводи́ться. **5,** *fol. by* **out** (set out) отправля́ться в путь. **6,** (be a starter in a race) стартова́ть. **7,** (jump from fright) вздра́гивать. —*n.* **1,** (beginning) нача́ло. *From start to finish,* снача́ла до конца́. **2,** (beginning of a race) старт: *false start,* неве́рный старт. **3,** (edge; advantage) фо́ра. **4,** (sudden movement): *give a start,* вздра́гивать. *Give someone a start,* испуга́ть *or* напуга́ть кого́-нибудь. **5,** *in* **by fits and starts,** уры́вками.

starter *n.* **1,** *mech.* ста́ртер. **2,** (one who starts in a race) уча́стник (состяза́ния). **3,** (one who gives the signal to start in a race) ста́ртер. **4,** (dispatcher) диспе́тчер. —**for starters,** *colloq.* для нача́ла.

starting line старт; ста́ртовая ли́ния.

starting point нача́льный пункт; отправно́й пункт; исхо́дная то́чка.

startle *v.t.* **1,** (frighten) испуга́ть. **2,** (shock) поража́ть. —**startling,** *adj.* порази́тельный; потряса́ющий.

starvation *n.* го́лод; голода́ние. *Die of starvation,* умира́ть с го́лоду; умира́ть голо́дной сме́ртью.

starve *v.i.* **1,** (go continually hungry) голода́ть. *Starve to death,* умира́ть с го́лоду; умира́ть голо́дной сме́ртью. **2,** *colloq.* (be very hungry) быть о́чень голо́дным. *I'm starving,* я умира́ю от го́лода; я стра́шно проголода́лся. —*v.t.* мори́ть го́лодом: *starve oneself,* мори́ть себя́ го́лодом. *Starve into submission,* взять измо́ром.

starveling *n.* замо́рыш.

starving *adj.* голода́ющий.

stash *v.t., colloq.* [*usu.* **stash away**] припря́тывать.

state *n.* **1,** (condition) состоя́ние; положе́ние. *State of affairs,* положе́ние дел *or* веще́й. *State of mind,* душе́вное состоя́ние. *State of emergency,* чрезвыча́йное положе́ние. *State of siege,* оса́дное положе́ние. *In a drunken state,* в пья́ном ви́де. **2,** (nation; government) госуда́рство: *sovereign state,* суверённое госуда́рство. *The State of Israel,* Госуда́рство Изра́иль. *Affairs of state,* госуда́рственные дела́. *Separation of church and state,* отделе́ние це́ркви от госуда́рства. **3,** (unit of a republic) штат: *United States,* Соединённые Шта́ты. —*adj.* **1,** (of a nation) госуда́рственный: *state secret,* госуда́рственная та́йна. *(The U.S.) State Department,* госуда́рственный департа́мент. **2,** (of a U.S. state) rendered by шта́та: *state law,* зако́н шта́та. **3,** (marked by ceremony) торже́ственный: *state dinner,* торже́ственный обе́д. —*v.t.* **1,** (set forth) излага́ть: *state one's case,* излага́ть своё де́ло. *State one's opinion,* вы́сказать своё мне́ние. **2,** (announce; assert) заявлять: *he stated that...,* он заявил, что... —**lie in state,** покоиться в открытом гробу.

stated *adj.* **1,** (announced) изложенный; высказанный. **2,** (fixed) установленный; определённый.

stateless *adj.* не имеющий гражданства.

stately *adj.* величественный; величавый.

statement *n.* **1,** (act of stating) изложение. **2,** (something stated; a declaration) заявление. **3,** *comm.* отчёт.

stateroom *n.* каюта.

statesman *n.* государственный деятель.

static *adj.* **1,** *physics* статический: *static pressure,* статическое давление. **2,** (not moving or progressing) статичный. —*n.* помехи. —**static electricity,** статическое электричество.

statics *n.* статика.

station *n.* **1,** (terminal) вокзал; станция. **2,** (establishment) станция: *gas station,* бензозаправочная станция; *tracking station,* станция слежения. *Fire station,* пожарное депо. *Police station,* полицейский участок; отделение милиции. *First-aid station,* медицинский пункт. **3,** (duty post) пост: *battle station,* боевой пост. **4,** (status) общественное положение. **5,** *radio* радиостанция. **6,** *mil.; naval* база. —*v.t.* размещать; дислоцировать (войска). *Station a guard at the door,* ставить часового у двери. *Station oneself at the window,* стать у окна. *He is stationed in Texas,* он служит в Техасе.

stationary *adj.* неподвижный.

stationer *n.* торговец канцелярскими принадлежностями.

stationery *n.* **1,** (paper) почтовая бумага. **2,** (supplies) канцелярские *or* писчебумажные принадлежности. —**stationery store,** писчебумажный магазин.

station house полицейский участок.

stationmaster *n.* начальник станции.

statistical *adj.* статистический.

statistician *n.* статистик.

statistics *n.* **1,** (science) статистика. **2,** (figures) статистические данные.

statue *n.* статуя.

statuesque *adj.* скульптурный; статный.

statuette *n.* статуэтка.

stature *n.* **1,** (height) рост. **2,** *fig.* (reputation) престиж.

status *n.* состояние; положение; статус. —**status quo,** статус-кво.

statute *n.* статут; закон. —**statute law,** писаный закон. —**statute mile,** английская миля. —**statute of limitations,** срок давности.

statutory *adj.* установленный законом.

staunch *adj.* верный; стойкий.

stave *n.* клёпка. —*v.t.* [*usu.* **stave off**] предотвращать.

stay *v.i.* **1,** (remain) оставаться: *stay home,* оставаться дома. **2,** (reside temporarily) останавливаться: *stay at a hotel,* останавливаться в гостинице. *Stay with friends,* останавливаться *or* гостить у друзей. *Where are you staying?,* где вы остановились? —*v.t.* **1,** (stop; halt) останавливать; приостанавливать. *Stay the hand of,* остановить руку (+ *gen.*). **2,** (appease, as hunger) утолять. —*n.* **1,** (sojourn) пребывание. **2,** (delay) приостановление: *stay of execution,* приостановление исполнения приго-

вора. **3,** (collar support) косточка. —**stay away,** отсутствовать; не приходить. —**stay in,** оставаться дома. —**stay out,** прогуливать: *stay out all night,* прогуливать всю ночь. —**stay put,** *colloq.* оставаться на месте. —**stay up,** не ложиться спать. *Stay up all night,* просидеть всю ночь.

stay-at-home *n.* домосед.

staying power выносливость.

staysail *n.* стаксель.

stead *n.* место. *In someone's stead,* вместо (+ *gen.*). —**stand (someone) in good stead,** пригодиться (+ *dat.*); сослужить (+ *dat.*) хорошую службу.

steadfast *adj.* стойкий; непоколебимый. —**steadfastness,** *n.* стойкость; непоколебимость.

steady *adj.* **1,** (stable; firm) устойчивый: *steady ladder,* устойчивая лестница. *Steady on one's feet,* твёрдый на ногах. *Sew with a steady hand,* шить твёрдой рукой. **2,** (regular) постоянный: *steady job,* постоянная работа; *steady customer,* постоянный клиент. **3,** (uninterrupted) непрерывный; неуклонный. *Steady downpour,* беспрерывные дожди. *Steady growth,* неуклонный рост. **4,** (even) равномерный: *steady speed,* равномерная скорость. **5,** (reliable; not frivolous) степенный. —*v.t.* **1,** (prevent from rocking) приводить в равновесие. **2,** (calm) успокаивать: *steady one's nerves,* успокаивать нервы. —*v.i.* приходить в равновесие.

steak *n.* бифштекс; антрекот.

steal *v.t.* **1,** (rob) красть. *His bicycle was stolen,* у него украли велосипед. **2,** *fig.* (take furtively): *steal a glance at,* украдкой посмотреть на; *steal a kiss,* сорвать поцелуй. —*v.i.* **1,** (commit theft) красть. **2,** (move furtively) красться; подкрадываться. *Steal into,* вкрадываться в; прокрадываться в. *Steal away,* ускользать.

stealth *n., usu. in* **by stealth,** украдкой. —**stealthily,** *adv.* украдкой; крадучись. —**stealthy,** *adj.* сделанный украдкой: *stealthy glance,* взгляд украдкой.

steam *n.* пар. —*adj.* паровой: *steam heat,* паровое отопление. —*v.t.* парить. *Steamed oysters,* паровые устрицы. —*v.i.* **1,** (emit vapor) выпускать пар. **2,** *fol. by* **up** (become covered with vapor) запотевать. **3,** (move by steam) плыть. *The ship steamed into port,* пароход вошёл в гавань. —**let/blow off steam,** давать выход своим чувствам. —**under a full head of steam,** на всех парах. —**under one's own steam,** собственными силами; своим ходом.

steamboat *n.* пароход.

steam engine паровая машина.

steamer *n.* (steamship) пароход. —**steamer rug,** плед. —**steamer trunk,** баул.

steamroller *n.* паровой каток.

steam room парильня.

steamship *n.* пароход.

steam shovel землеройная машина; экскаватор.

steamy *adj.* **1,** (filled with steam) наполненный паром. **2,** (hot and humid) знойный; влажный. *Steamy jungle,* влажные джунгли.

stearin *n.* стеарин.

steatite *n.* стеатит.

steed *n.* конь.

steel *n.* сталь. —*adj.* стальной. *Steel mill,* сталелитейный завод. —*v.t.* **1,** (plate with steel) покрывать сталью. **2,** *fig.* (harden; make tough) закалять.

steelworker *n.* сталелитéйщик; сталевáр. —**steel- works**, *n.* сталелитéйный завóд.

steelyard *n.* безмéн.

steep *adj.* **1,** (precipitous) крутóй. **2,** *colloq.* (high, as of a price) высóкий; (expensive) дорогóй. —*v.t.* **1,** (soak) вымáчивать; замáчивать. **2,** *fig.* (immerse; saturate): *steep oneself in a subject,* глубокó изучáть какóй-нибудь предмéт. *Be steeped in ignorance,* погрязáть в невéжестве.

steepen *v.t.* дéлать бóлее круты́м.

steeple *n.* шпиль.

steeplechase *n.* скáчки с препя́тствиями.

steeplejack *n.* верхолáз.

steeply *adv.* крýто.

steepness *n.* крýтость; крутизнá.

steer *v.t.* **1,** (guide) прáвить; управля́ть. **2,** (set and follow) держáться: *steer a middle course,* держáться срéднего кýрса. —*v.i., in* **steer clear of,** избегáть; сторони́ться. —*n.* (ox) вол.

steerage *n.* **1,** (part of a ship) ни́зший класс. **2,** (steering) управлéние.

steering *n.* рулевóе управлéние. —**steering co- lumn,** рулевáя колóнка. —**steering committee,** руководя́щий комитéт. —**steering wheel,** руль; рулевóе колесó; штурвáл.

stein *n.* пивнáя крýжка.

stellar *adj.* **1,** (consisting of stars) звёздный. **2,** (outstanding) превосхóдный.

stem *n.* **1,** (of a plant) стéбель. **2,** (of a glass) нóжка. **3,** (of a pipe) черенóк. **4,** (of a ship) форштéвень. **5,** *ling.* оснóва. —*v.t.* останáвливать. —*v.i.* [*usu.* **stem from**] вытекáть из; происходи́ть от; проистекáть из.

stench *n.* вонь; смрад; зловóние.

stencil *n.* шаблóн; трафарéт. —*v.t.* наноси́ть по трафарéту.

stenography *n.* стеногрáфия. —**stenographer,** *n.* стенóграф; стенографи́ст; стенографи́стка. —**sten- ographic,** *adj.* стенографи́ческий.

stentorian *adj.* громовóй; зы́чный.

step *n.* **1,** (movement of the foot) шаг: *take a step,* сдéлать шаг. **2,** (gait) шаг; похóдка; пóступь. *Smooth step,* плáвный шаг; плáвная похóдка. **3,** (in dancing) па. **4,** (stair) ступéнь; ступéнька. *Flight of steps,* марш. **5,** (action) шаг; мероприя́тие. *Take steps,* предпринимáть шаги́. *In taking this step,* пойдя́ на такóй шаг. **6,** (degree of progress or retrogression) шаг: *a big step forward,* большóй шаг вперёд; *a step backward,* шаг назáд. —*v.i.* шагáть; ступáть. *Step this way please!,* сюдá, пожáлуйста! —**in step,** в нóгу. —**keep in step,** идти́ в нóгу. —**out of step,** не в нóгу. —**step aside,** сторони́ться. *Step aside for,* уступáть дорóгу (+ *dat.*). —**step back,** отступáть. —**step by step,** шаг за шáгом. —**step down,** уйти́ с постá. —**step in, 1,** (enter) входи́ть. *Won't you step in?,* зайди́те, пожáлуйста! **2,** (step into) ступáть в: *step in a puddle,* ступи́ть в лýжу. —**step off, 1,** *literally* сходи́ть с. **2,** (mark off) отсчи́тывать: *step off ten paces,* отсчи́тывать дéсять шагóв. —**step on,** наступáть на. *Step on the gas,* дать газ. —**step on it,** поторáпливаться. *Step on it!,* живéй!; скорéй! —**step out,** выходи́ть. —**step over,** переступáть; перешáгивать. —**step up, 1,** (step forward) проходи́ть. **2,** (increase) повышáть; нарáщивать.

stepbrother *n.* свóдный брат.

stepchild *n.* пáсынок.

stepdaughter *n.* пáдчерица.

stepfather *n.* óтчим.

stepladder *n.* стремя́нка.

stepmother *n.* мáчеха.

stepparent *n.* óтчим; мáчеха.

steppe *n.* степь.

stepping stone ступéнька на пути́: *stepping stone to success,* ступéнька на пути́ к успéху.

stepsister *n.* свóдная сестрá.

stepson *n.* пáсынок.

stereophonic *adj.* стереофони́ческий.

stereoscope *n.* стереоскóп. —**stereoscopic,** *adj.* стереоскопи́ческий. —**stereoscopy,** *n.* стереоскопи́я.

stereotype *n.* **1,** *printing* стереоти́п. **2,** (conventional notion) шаблóн; трафарéт; стандáрт; стереоти́п. —*v.t.* **1,** *printing* стереотипи́ровать. **2,** (represent in a conventional way) превращáть в стандáрт. —**ster- eotyped,** *adj.* шаблóнный; трафарéтный.

sterile *adj.* **1,** (germ-free) стери́льный. **2,** (incapable of producing offspring) бесплóдный. **3,** *fig.* (devoid of substance) пустóй.

sterility *n.* **1,** (absence of germs) стери́льность. **2,** (inability to produce offspring) бесплóдие.

sterilize *v.t.* стерилизовáть. —**sterilization,** *n.* стерилизáция. —**sterilizer,** *n.* стерилизáтор.

sterlet *n.* стéрлядь.

sterling *n.* **1,** (standard for British coins) стéрлинг. *Pound sterling,* фунт стéрлингов. **2,** (silver) серебрó. —*adj.* **1,** (pert. to the pound sterling) стéрлинговый. **2,** (silver) серéбряный. **3,** (excellent; outstanding) превосхóдный.

stern *adj.* стрóгий; сурóвый. *Stern judge,* стрóгий судья́. *Stern look,* стрóгий *or* сурóвый взгляд. *Stern measures,* стрóгие *or* сурóвые мéры. —*n.* (of a ship) кормá. —**sternness,** *n.* стрóгость; сурóвость.

sternpost *n.* ахтерштéвень.

sternum *n.* груди́на.

steroid *n.* стерóид.

stethoscope *n.* стетоскóп.

stevedore *n.* грýзчик.

stew *n.* тушёное мя́со; рагý. —*v.t.* туши́ть; пáрить. —*v.i.* туши́ться; пáриться.

steward *n.* **1,** (manager of a household) завхóз; эконóм. **2,** (on a ship or plane) бортпроводни́к; стю́ард. —**stewardess,** *n.* бортпроводни́ца; стюардéсса.

stewed *adj.* **1,** (cooked by stewing) тушёный; пáреный. **2,** *slang* (drunk) под хмелькóм. —**stewed fruit,** компóт.

stewpan *n.* кастрю́ля.

stick *n.* **1,** (long slender piece of wood) пáлка; пáлочка. *Walking stick,* трость; пáлка. *Hockey stick,* клю́шка. **2,** (sticklike piece, as of chewing gum) пли́тка. *Stick of dynamite,* шáшка динами́та. **3,** *aero.* рычáг. **4,** *pl., colloq.* (rural districts) глушь. —*v.t.* **1,** (prick) колóть. **2,** (insert; pin) втыкáть; вкáлывать. *Stick a pin into something,* воткнýть булáвку во чтó-нибудь. *Stick a flower in one's lapel,* воткнýть цветóк в петли́цу. **3,** (thrust) совáть: *stick a pie in the oven,* сýнуть пирóг в духóвку. *Stick one's head in the door,* просýнуть гóлову в дверь. *Stick one's head out the window,* вы́сунуться из окнá. **4,** (glue) приклéивать; наклéивать. —*v.i.* **1,** (adhere) клéиться; заклéиваться; приставáть. *The envelope doesn't stick,* конвёрт не заклёивается. **2**, *fol. by* **to** (adhere to) лйпнуть (к); прилипа́ть (к); пристава́ть (к). **3**, (become embedded) застрева́ть. *The words stuck in her throat,* слова́ застря́ли у неё в го́рле. **4**, (fail to operate; jam) заеда́ть *(impers.): the door stuck,* дверь зае́ло. **5**, (become permanent, as of a nickname) пристава́ть; прикле́иваться. **6**, *fol. by* **to** (not deviate from) не отклоня́ться от; приде́рживаться. **7**, *fol. by* **to** (persevere in) упо́рствовать в. —**stick around,** *colloq.* остава́ться поблйзости. —**stick by,** остава́ться ве́рным (+ *dat.*); не покида́ть. —**stick out, 1,** (protrude) торча́ть. **2**, (put out) высо́вывать; выставля́ть. *Stick out one's tongue,* вы́сунуть язы́к. **3**, (be conspicuous) отлича́ться; выдава́ться. —**stick together, 1,** (adhere) скле́иваться; слипа́ться. **2**, (remain united) держа́ться вме́сте. —**stick up, 1,** (protrude upward) торча́ть; выдава́ться. **2**, *slang* (rob) гра́бить. **3**, *Stick 'em up!,* ру́ки вверх! —**stick up for,** заступа́ться за. *See also* **stuck.**

sticker *n.* накле́йка.

stickiness *n.* кле́йкость.

sticking plaster лйпкий пла́стырь.

sticking point загво́здка; заце́пка.

stickleback *n.* колю́шка.

stickup *n., slang* налёт; грабёж; ограбле́ние.

sticky *adj.* **1**, (adhesive; gummy) лйпкий; кле́йкий. **2**, (humid) вла́жный. **3**, *colloq.* (ticklish) щекотлйвый.

stiff *adj.* **1**, (rigid; unbending) жёсткий; негну́щийся. *Stiff brush,* жёсткая щётка. *Stiff cardboard,* твёрдый *or* негну́щийся карто́н. **2**, (sore and not moving easily) онеме́вший: *stiff joints,* онеме́вшие суста́вы. *I have a stiff neck,* мне наду́ло (в) ше́ю; у меня́ ше́я не повора́чивается. *My hands are stiff from the cold,* ру́ки мой окочене́ли от хо́лода. **3**, (hard to move or operate) туго́й: *stiff door,* туга́я дверь. **4**, (awkward; constrained) натя́нутый; принуждённый. **5**, (moving with great force) сйльный. *Stiff wind,* сйльный/ жесто́кий ве́тер. *Stiff current,* бы́строе тече́ние. **6**, (stout; resolute) упо́рный. *Stiff resistance,* упо́рное *or* жесто́кое сопротивле́ние. **7**, (harsh; severe) суро́вый: *stiff sentence,* суро́вый пригово́р. **8**, (difficult; demanding) тру́дный: *stiff exam,* тру́дный экза́мен. *Stiff requirements,* высо́кие тре́бования. *Stiff competition,* о́страя конкуре́нция. **9**, (potent) кре́пкий: *stiff drink,* кре́пкий напи́ток. **10**, *colloq.* (high, as of a price) ду́тый. —*adv.* **1**, (so as to be stiff): *be frozen stiff,* окочене́ть от хо́лода. **2**, *colloq.* (to an extreme degree) до́ смерти: *be scared stiff,* перепуга́ться до́ смерти.

stiffen *v.t.* **1**, (make stiff) де́лать жёстким. **2**, (make more resolute) укрепля́ть: *stiffen someone's will,* укрепля́ть чью-нибудь во́лю. —*v.i.* станови́ться неподвйжным; кочене́ть.

stiffness *n.* **1**, (firmness) жёсткость. **2**, *med.* неподвйжность. **3**, (awkwardness) натя́нутость; принуждённость.

stifle *v.t.* **1**, (suffocate; smother) души́ть; удуша́ть. **2**, (suppress, as a yawn) подавля́ть. **3**, (suppress, as criticism or initiative) подавля́ть; глуши́ть; души́ть; зажима́ть. —**stifling,** *adj.* уду́шливый.

stigma *n.* **1**, (mark of shame) клеймо́. **2**, *bot.* ры́льце. —**stigmatize,** *v.t.* клейми́ть.

stiletto *n.* стиле́т.

still *adj.* **1**, (motionless) неподвйжный. **2**, (tranquil)

тйхий: *still water,* тйхая вода́. **3**, (silent) безмо́лвный. *Be still!,* молчи́! —*n.* **1**, (distilling apparatus) перего́нный куб. **2**, (distillery) винокуренный заво́д. **3**, (silence; quiet) тишина́. *In the still of the night,* в ночно́й тишй. —*adv.* **1**, (yet) ещё; всё ещё: *she is still young,* она́ (всё) ещё молода́я. **2**, (all the same) всё же; всё-таки; всё равно́: *I still love him,* я все же/всё-таки/всё равно́/люблю́ его́. **3**, *with comp. adjectives* ещё: *still further,* ещё да́льше. **4**, (motionless) неподвйжно. *Sit still!,* сиди́те смйрно! —*v.t.* **1**, (silence) унима́ть. **2**, (calm) успока́ивать. —*v.i.* успока́иваться. —*conj.* всё же; всё-таки; тем не ме́нее. *Still, you ought to go,* всё же/тем не ме́нее/ вам сле́дует пойтй. —**still and all,** несмотря́ на всё э́то; тем не ме́нее.

stillborn *adj.* мертворождённый.

still life натюрмо́рт.

stillness *n.* **1**, (motionlessness) неподвйжность. **2**, (calm; quiet) тишина́.

stilt *n.* **1**, (tall pole) ходу́ля: *walk on stilts,* ходи́ть на ходу́лях. **2**, (post; support) сва́я. **3**, (wading bird) ходу́лочник.

stilted *adj.* ходу́льный: *stilted phrases,* ходу́льные фра́зы.

stimulant *adj.* возбужда́ющий. —*n.* возбужда́ющее сре́дство.

stimulate *v.t.* возбужда́ть; поощря́ть; стимулйровать. —**stimulation,** *n.* возбужде́ние; поощре́ние; стимулйрование.

stimulus *n.* стймул; побужде́ние; толчо́к.

sting *v.t.* **1**, (wound, as of a bee) жа́лить. **2**, (cause severe pain to; burn) щипа́ть; жечь. **3**, *fig.* (hurt; distress) уязвля́ть. —*v.i.* **1**, (of a bee) жа́лить. **2**, (hurt) жечь. —*n.* **1**, (wound caused by stinging) уку́с. **2**, (stinger) жа́ло.

stinger *n.* (stinging organ) жа́ло.

stingily *adv.* скупо.

stinginess *n.* скупость.

stinging *adj.* язвйтельный: *stinging rebuke,* язвйтельный упре́к.

stingray *n.* морско́й кот.

stingy *adj.* скупо́й. *Don't be (so) stingy!,* не скупйтесь!

stink *v.i.* воня́ть; смерде́ть. —*v.t.* [*usu.* **stink up**] прово́нивать; вонь; смрад.

stinking *adj.* воню́чий; злово́нный; смра́дный.

stint *v.t. & i.* скупй́ться (на); уре́зывать себя́ (в). *Not stint one's praise,* не скупй́ться на похвалы́. *He does not stint himself,* он не стесня́ет себя́ в сре́дствах. *She stints herself in everything,* она́ уре́зывает себя́ во всём. —*n.* **1**, (limitation; restriction) ограниче́ние. **2**, (short period of service) срок.

stipend *n.* **1**, (salary) жа́лованье. **2**, (scholarship) стипе́ндия.

stipple *v.t.* рисова́ть *or* гравирова́ть пункти́ром.

stipulate *v.t.* обусло́вливать; огова́ривать; предусма́тривать. —**stipulation,** *n.* усло́вие; огово́рка.

stir *v.t.* **1**, (agitate) меша́ть: *stir the coffee/fire,* меша́ть ко́фе/у́гли. **2**, (move slightly) шевелй́ть: *the wind stirred the leaves,* ве́тер шевелй́л лйстья. **3**, (arouse, as an emotion) возбужда́ть; вызыва́ть. **4**, *fol. by* **up** (incite; foment) возбужда́ть; разжига́ть: *stir up the crowd,* возбужда́ть толпу́; *stir up hatred,* разжига́ть не́нависть. *Stir up trouble,* мутйть во́ду. **5**, (affect strongly) волнова́ть. —*v.i.* двйгаться; сдви гáться; шевелúться. —n. **1,** (act of stirring): *give the soup a stir,* помешáть суп. **2,** (movement) движéние. **3,** (excited reaction) резонáнс: *create quite a stir,* вы́звать широ́кий резонáнс.

stirring *adj.* волнýющий.

stirrup *n.* стрéмя. —**stirrup cup,** прощáльный кýбок.

stitch *n.* **1,** *sewing* стежóк. **2,** *knitting* пéтля. **3,** *surgery* шов. **4,** (sudden sharp pain) резь. *I have a stitch in my side,* у меня́ кóлет в бокý. **5,** (article of clothing): *without a stitch of clothing,* в чём мать родилá. —*v.t.* **1,** *sewing* строчи́ть; прострáчивать. **2,** *surgery* наклáдывать швы на (рáну). —**be in stitches,** *colloq.* надрывáть животы́ (со́ смеху).

St.-John's-wort *n.* зверобóй.

stock *n.* **1,** (supply of merchandise) инвентáрь; ассортимéнт. *In stock,* в налúчии. *Out of stock,* нет в продáже; рáспродан. **2,** (reserve supply) запáс. **3,** (corporate shares) áкции; фóнды. **4,** (lineage) род: *of good stock,* хорóшего рóда. **5,** (part of a firearm) лóжа. **6,** (raw material) сырьё: *paper stock,* бумáжное сырьё. **7,** (broth from boiled meat) мяснóй отвáр. **8,** (livestock) скот. **9,** *Summer stock,* лéтний теáтр. **10,** *pl.* (instrument of punishment) колóдки. —*adj.* **1,** (of the stock market) биржевóй. *Stock prices,* курс áкций. **2,** (regularly on sale) основнóй. *Stock sizes,* стандáртные размéры. **3,** (regularly used) шаблóнный: *stock phrases,* шаблóнные фрáзы. —*v.t.* **1,** (supply with merchandise) снабжáть (товáрами). *Well-stocked stores,* хорошó снабжáемые магазúны. **2,** (have on hand) держáть. **3,** *Stock a pond with fish,* запустúть ры́бу в пруд. —*v.i.* **1,** [*usu.* **stock up**] запасáться. *Stock up on food,* запасáться продовóльствием; запасáть продовóльствие. —**take stock, 1,** (take inventory) составля́ть инвентáрь. **2,** *fol. by* **of** (inventory) инвентаризовáть; переучúтывать. **3,** *fig.* (evaluate a situation) подводúть итóги.

stockade *n.* **1,** (fence) частокóл. **2,** (fort) форт. **3,** (prison) гауптвáхта.

stockbroker *n.* (биржевóй) мáклер.

stock car гóночный автомобúль.

stock company 1, *comm.* акционéрная компáния. **2,** *theat.* театрáльная трýппа.

stock exchange фóндовая бúржа.

stockfish *n.* вя́леная ры́ба.

stockholder *n.* акционéр.

stocking *n.* чулóк. *In one's stocking feet,* в одни́х чулкáх.

stock market фóндовая бúржа.

stockpile *n.* запáс; резéрв. —*v.t.* накопля́ть; запасáть.

stocky *adj.* призéмистый; коренáстый.

stockyard *n.* скóтный двор; скотопригóнный двор.

stodgy *adj.* скýчный; нýдный.

stoic *n.* стóик. —**stoical,** *adj.* стои́ческий. —**stoically,** *adv.* стои́чески; стóйко. —**stoicism,** *n.* стоицúзм.

stoke *v.t.* **1,** (stir, as a fire) расшевелúть (ýгли). **2,** (tend, as a furnace) топи́ть.

stoker *n.* **1,** (person) кочегáр; истопни́к. **2,** (device) стóкер.

stole *n.* палантúн.

stolen *adj.* крáденый.

stolid *adj.* бесстрáстный.

stomach *n.* **1,** (digestive organ) желýдок. *On an*

empty stomach, натощáк. **2,** (abdomen; belly) живóт. —*v.t.* (tolerate) перевáривать. —**stomach ache,** боль в животé. *I have a stomach ache,* у меня́ болúт живóт. —**stomach pump,** желýдочный зонд.

stomatology *n.* стоматолóгия. —**stomatologist,** *n.* стоматóлог.

stomp *v.t. & i.* тóпать (ногáми). *Stomp on,* топтáть.

stone *n.* **1,** (substance) кáмень: *pave with stone,* мостúть кáмнем. *Heart of stone,* кáменное сéрдце. **2,** (small rock) кáмень. *Precious stone,* драгоцéнный кáмень. *Throw stones at,* забросáть (когó-нибудь) камня́ми. **3,** (pit of fruits) кóсточка. **4,** *med.* кáмень: *kidney stone,* пóчечный кáмень. —*adj.* кáменный: *stone wall,* кáменная стенá. —*v.t.* забивáть камня́ми. —**leave no stone unturned,** сдéлать всё возмóжное; пустúть в ход все срéдства. —**not to leave a stone standing,** кáмня на кáмне не остáвить. —**within a stone's throw,** в двух шагáх; рукóй подáть.

Stone Age кáменный век.

stone-broke *adj.* без грошá.

stonecutter *n.* камнерéз.

stone-deaf *adj.* совершéнно глухóй.

stonemason *n.* кáменщик; каменотёс.

stonework *n.* кáменная клáдка.

stony *adj.* **1,** (of or like stone) кáменный. **2,** (full of stones) камени́стый. **3,** *fig.* (unfeeling) кáменный; окаменéлый. *Stony gaze,* кáменный взгляд. **4,** *Stony silence,* гробовóе молчáние.

stooge *n., colloq.* **1,** *theat.* посмéшище. **2,** (underling) приспéшник.

stool *n.* **1,** (seat) табурéтка; табурéт. **2,** (excrement) стул. —**fall between two stools,** сидéть мéжду двух стýльев.

stool pigeon стукáч.

stoop *v.i.* **1,** (bend the body) наклоня́ться; нагибáться. **2,** (slouch) сутýлиться. **3,** *fol. by* **to** (lower or degrade oneself) унижáться до; снисходúть до. —*n.* **1,** (slouch) сутýлость. **2,** (front steps) крыльцó. —**stooped,** *adj.* сутýлый.

stop *v.t.* **1,** (bring to a halt) остáнавливать: *stop a car/traffic/pain,* остановúть маши́ну/ýличное движéние/боль. **2,** (terminate) прекращáть: *stop a war/payments/assistance,* прекратúть войнý/платежú/пóмощь. *Stop that noise!,* прекратú э́тот шум! **3,** (cease) переставáть: *stop crying,* перестáть плáкать. **4,** (prevent) мешáть; удéрживать. *Stop someone from speaking,* мешáть комý-нибудь говорúть. *Stop someone from committing suicide,* удержáть когó-нибудь от самоубúйства. **5,** *fol. by* **up** (block; plug) затыкáть; закýпоривать. —*v.i.* **1,** (come to a halt) остáнавливаться. *My watch has stopped,* у меня́ часы́ стáли *or* остановúлись. **2,** (cease) прекращáться; переставáть. *The rain has stopped,* дождь кóнчился/перестáл/прошёл/прекратúлся. **3,** (stay, as at a hotel) остáнавливаться. —*n.* **1,** (halt; place to stop) остановка: *bus stop,* автóбусная остановка. *Get off at the next stop,* сойти́ на слéдующей остановке. **2,** *music* (of a fretted instrument) лад; (of an organ) регúстр. —**pull out all the stops,** нажáть на все пружúны. —**put a stop to,** положúть конéц (+ *dat.*). —**stop at nothing,** ни пéред чем не остáнавливаться. —**stop by; stop in,** зайтú; заглянýть. —**stop off,** остановúться в путú. —**stop short,** *see* **short.**

stopgap *n.* паллиатúв. —*adj.* паллиати́вный.

stoplight *n.* **1,** (traffic light) светофо́р. **2,** (brake light) стоп-сигна́л.

stopover *n.* остано́вка в пути́.

stoppage *n.* прекраще́ние: *work stoppage*, прекраще́ние рабо́ты.

stopper *n.* про́бка.

stopwatch *n.* секундоме́р.

storage *n.* хране́ние: *put in storage*, отдава́ть *or* сдава́ть на хране́ние. —**storage battery**, аккумуля́торная батаре́я.

store *n.* **1,** (shop) магази́н: *shoe/furniture store*, обувно́й/ме́бельный магази́н. **2,** (supply) запа́с: *stores of food*, запа́сы продово́льствия; *store of knowledge*, запа́с зна́ний. —*v.t.* **1,** *often fol. by* **up** (put aside for future use) запаса́ть; заготовля́ть (впрок). **2,** (put away for safekeeping) отдава́ть *or* сдава́ть на хране́ние. —**be in store**, предстоя́ть; ждать впереди́. *What is in store for him?*, что его́ ждёт? —**hold in store**, держа́ть про запа́с. *Who knows what the future holds in store?*, кто зна́ет, что ждёт нас впереди́? —**set store by**, придава́ть значе́ние (+ *dat.*).

storehouse *n.* **1,** (warehouse) склад. **2,** *fig.* (abundant source) сокро́вищница: *storehouse of knowledge*, сокро́вищница зна́ний.

storekeeper *n.* **1,** (shopkeeper) ла́вочник. **2,** (keeper of supplies) кладовщи́к.

storeroom *n.* кладова́я; чула́н.

storey *n.* = **story** (*in sense* #5).

storied *adj.* легенда́рный; басносло́вный.

stork *n.* а́ист.

storm *n.* **1,** (windstorm) бу́ря; (thunderstorm) гроза́. **2,** *naut.* шторм. **3,** *fig.* (outburst) бу́ря; взрыв. **4,** *mil.* штурм: *take by storm*, взять шту́рмом. —*v.i.* **1,** (rage) бушева́ть: *it is storming*, бушу́ет гроза́. **2,** (move with great force) проноси́ться. *Storm into the room*, ворва́ться в ко́мнату. —*v.t.* штурмова́ть: *storm the town*, штурмова́ть го́род. —**take by storm**, *fig.* захвати́ть; увле́чь; покори́ть.

storm cloud (грозова́я) ту́ча.

storm trooper штурмови́к.

storm windows двойны́е ра́мы; вставны́е ра́мы.

stormy *adj.* бу́рный.

story *n.* **1,** (short literary work) расска́з; по́весть. *Short story*, нове́лла. *Detective story*, детекти́в. **2,** (something related; account) исто́рия; расска́з. *Tell someone a story*, рассказа́ть кому́-нибудь исто́рию. *The story of one's life*, исто́рия свое́й жи́зни. *Get ahead of one's story*, забега́ть вперёд в расска́зе. **3,** (news event) собы́тие; (report on same) сообще́ние. **4,** *colloq.* (lie) ска́зка: *don't tell me stories!*, ска́зки мне не расска́зывай! **5,** [*also,* **storey**] (floor of a building) эта́ж. —**a long story**, до́лгая пе́сня. —**to make a long story short**, коро́че говоря́. —**that's a different story**, э́то друго́е де́ло.

storyteller *n.* **1,** (narrator) расска́зчик. **2,** *colloq.* (fibber) вы́думщик.

stout *adj.* **1,** (corpulent) по́лный; ту́чный. **2,** (sturdy) кре́пкий; про́чный. *On his stout back*, на его́ кре́пкой спине́. **3,** (resolute) сто́йкий: *stout defense*, сто́йкая оборо́на. *Stout resistance*, упо́рное сопротивле́ние.

stouthearted *adj.* сто́йкий; отва́жный.

stove *n.* **1,** (coal or wood stove) печь. **2,** (electric or gas range) плита́.

stovepipe *n.* дымохо́д.

stow *v.t.* укла́дывать. —**stow away**, **1,** (store) убира́ть; пря́тать. **2,** (hide aboard a ship) е́хать за́йцем.

stowaway *n.* безбиле́тный пассажи́р; "за́яц".

strabismus *n.* косогла́зие.

straddle *v.t.* сиде́ть верхо́м на.

strafe *v.t.* обстре́ливать.

straggle *v.i.* **1,** (move along separately) идти́ вразбро́д. **2,** (fall behind) отстава́ть. **3,** (stray) отбива́ться. —**straggler,** *n.* отста́вший.

straight *adj.* **1,** (not crooked; not curly) прямо́й: *straight line*, пряма́я ли́ния; *straight hair*, прямы́е во́лосы. **2,** (properly arranged) в поря́дке. *Put things straight*, приводи́ть дела́ в поря́док. **3,** (direct and candid) прямо́й; открове́нный. **4,** (consecutive) подря́д: *five straight days*, пять дней подря́д. **5,** *colloq.* (undiluted) чи́стый: *straight alcohol*, чи́стый спирт. **6,** *in* **straight razor**, опа́сная бри́тва. —*adv.* пря́мо: *straight to the airport*, пря́мо в аэропо́рт. *Go straight home*, пойти́ домо́й пря́мо. *Stand up straight*, держа́ться пря́мо. *Is my hat on straight?*, у меня́ шля́па пра́вильно наде́та? —**get (something) straight**, вспо́мнить: *I can't get their names straight*, не могу́ вспо́мнить их имена́. *Get this straight!*, заруби́те э́то на носу́. —**set (someone) straight**, наставля́ть на путь и́стинный. —**straight ahead**, пря́мо. —**straight face**, бесстра́стное лицо́. *With a straight face*, не рассмея́вшись. —**straight away**; **straight off**, сра́зу.

straightedge *n.* лине́йка.

straighten *v.t.* **1,** (make straight) выпрямля́ть; распрямля́ть; расправля́ть. **2,** (adjust, as one's tie) поправля́ть. **3,** *fol. by* **up** (tidy up) убира́ть. **4,** *fol. by* **out** (set right) нала́живать. —*v.i.* **1,** *fol. by* **up** (stand up straight) выпрямля́ться; распрямля́ться; разгиба́ться. **2,** *fol. by* **out** (become straight) распрямля́ться. **3,** *fol. by* **out** (return to normal) нала́живаться; образо́вываться.

straightforward *adj.* прямо́й; прямоду́шный. —**straightforwardness**, *n.* прямота́; прямоду́шие.

straightness *n.* прямизна́.

strain *v.t.* **1,** (exert to the utmost) напряга́ть: *strain every nerve*, напряга́ть все си́лы. **2,** (overtax) надрыва́ть. *Strain one's voice*, сорва́ть го́лос. *Strain one's eyes*, по́ртить себе́ глаза́; по́ртить зре́ние. **3,** (injure; sprain) растя́гивать. **4,** (filter) цеди́ть; проце́живать. —*v.i.* напряга́ться. *Strain at the leash*, рва́ться с при́вязи. —*n.* **1,** (tension; pressure) напряже́ние: *nervous strain*, не́рвное напряже́ние. *Withstand the strain*, выде́рживать напряже́ние. **2,** (sprain) растяже́ние. **3,** (species) поро́да: *a new strain of cattle*, но́вая поро́да скота́. **4,** *pl.* (sounds of music) зву́ки: *the strains of a waltz*, зву́ки ва́льса.

strained *adj.* **1,** (aggravated) натя́нутый; напряжённый. **2,** (passed through a strainer) проце́женный.

strainer *n.* си́то; решето́.

strait *n.* **1,** (channel) проли́в. **2,** *pl.* (difficulty) затрудни́тельное положе́ние; стеснённые обстоя́тельства.

straiten *v.t.* стесня́ть. *In straitened circumstances*, в стеснённых обстоя́тельствах.

strait jacket смири́тельная руба́шка.

strait-laced *adj.* чо́порный; пурита́нский.

strand *v.t.* **1,** (drive or run aground) посади́ть на мель. **2,** (leave in a helpless position) поки́нуть в бедé. —n. **1,** (of hair, rope, etc.) прядь. **2,** (string, as of beads) нитка.

strange adj. **1,** (queer; odd) стрáнный: strange man, стрáнный человéк; strange occurrence, стрáнное явлéние. It is strange, стрáнно. Strange as it seems, как ни стрáнно. **2,** (unfamiliar) незнакóмый: strange place, незнакóмое мéсто. **3,** (foreign) чужóй: in a strange country, в чужóй странé. —**strangely,** adv. стрáнно. —**strangeness,** n. стрáнность.

stranger n. **1,** (person not known) незнакóмец. **2,** (outsider) посторóнний. **3,** (newcomer) приéзжий.

strangle v.t. душить; удавить. —v.i. задыхáться.

stranglehold n. Have a stranglehold on, держáть в тискáх.

strangulation n. **1,** (strangling) удавлéние. **2,** med. ущемлéние.

strap n. **1,** (general term) ремéнь. **2,** (of an undergarment) бретéль(ка). —v.t. связывать or скреплять ремнём.

strapped adj., colloq. стеснённый в деньгáх.

strapping adj. рóслый; дюжий.

stratagem n. воéнная хитрость; улóвка.

strategy n. стратéгия. —**strategic,** adj. стратегический. —**strategist,** n. стратéг.

stratification n. **1,** geol. напластовáние; стратификáция. **2,** fig. (division into strata) расслоéние: stratification of society, расслоéние óбщества.

stratified adj. слóистый. Stratified society, расслоёное óбщество.

stratify v.t. расслáивать.

stratosphere n. стратосфéра.

stratum n. **1,** (layer) слой; пласт; прослóйка. **2,** fig.(class; division) слой; прослóйка.

stratus n. слóистое óблако.

straw n. **1,** (stalk of grain) солóма. **2,** (sipping tube) солóминка. —adj. солóменный: straw hat, солóменная шляпа. —**grasp at a straw,** хватáться за солóминку. —**the last straw,** послéдняя кáпля; предéл терпéния.

strawberry n. (wild) земляника; (cultivated) клубника. —adj. земляничный; клубничный.

stray v.i. **1,** (wander off) отбивáться: stray from the flock, отбивáться от стáда. **2,** (deviate) отклоняться; уклоняться: stray off course, отклоняться/уклоняться от кýрса. —adj. **1,** (lost) заблудившийся; бездóмный. Stray dog, бродячая or бездóмная собáка. **2,** (random; chance) случáйный. Stray bullet, шальнáя пýля.

streak n. **1,** (thin line, as in marble) прожилка. **2,** (mark; smear) потёк; подтёк; pl. разводы. **3,** (trace of a certain characteristic) жилка. Person with a lazy streak, человéк с ленцóй. **4,** (spell; run) полосá. **5,** sports шéствие: winning streak, победóное шéствие. —v.t., usu. passive: hair streaked with gray, вóлосы с прóседью. The wallpaper is all streaked, обóи все в потёках. —v.i. **1,** (form streaks) растекáться. **2,** (dash; flash) проноситься; промелькнýть. —**talk a blue streak,** colloq. говорить без ýмолку.

stream n. **1,** (small river) ручéй. **2,** (current) течéние. **3,** (steady flow) потóк. —v.i. **1,** (flow rapidly) течь; литься; хлынуть; струиться. Tears were streaming down her cheeks, слёзы катились у неё по щекáм. **2,** (move in large numbers) валить.

streamer n. серпантин.

streamline v.t. **1,** (shape so as to offer little wind resistance) придавáть (+ dat.) обтекáемую фóрму. **2,** (modernize) рационализировать. —**streamlined,** adj. обтекáемый.

street n. ýлица. Gorky Street, ýлица Гóрького. —adj. ýличный: street scene, ýличная сцéна. —**man in the street,** рядовóй человéк; "человéк с ýлицы".

streetcar n. трамвáй.

street lamp ýличный фонáрь. Also, **street light.**

streetwalker n. ýличная дéвка/девица/жéнщина.

strength n. **1,** (force; power) сила: physical strength, физическая сила. **2,** (durability) прóчность: tensile strength, прóчность на разрыв. **3,** (potency) крéпость. **4,** (complement of personnel) числéнность. At full strength, в пóлном состáве. —**on the strength of,** в силу (+ gen.); на основáнии (+ gen.).

strengthen v.t. усиливать; укреплять.

strenuous adj. **1,** (requiring great exertion) напряжённый. **2,** (emphatic) решительный: strenuous objection, решительное возражéние.

streptococcus n. стрептокóкк.

streptomycin n. стрептомицин.

stress n. **1,** (physical pressure exerted) напряжéние. **2,** (mental strain) стресс: be under great stress, быть под большим стрéссом. **3,** (accent) ударéние: the stress is on the first syllable, ударéние пáдает на пéрвый слог. **4,** (emphasis) ударéние. Lay stress on, дéлать ударéние/акцéнт/упóр на. —v.t. **1,** (emphasize) подчёркивать. **2,** (pronounce with emphasis) дéлать ударéние на. Stressed syllable, удáрный слог.

stretch v.t. **1,** (expand; extend) растягивать; вытягивать. Stretch one's legs, разминáть нóги. Stretch a canvas over a frame, натягивать холст на рáмку. Stretch a rope across the yard, протягивать верёвку чéрез двор. Have one's shoes stretched, отдáть тýфли на растяжку. **2,** (put forth; hold out) протягивать. **3,** in stretch one's luck, искушáть судьбý; stretch a point, допустить натяжку. —v.i. **1,** (be capable of being stretched) тянýться; растягиваться. **2,** (take a stretch) потягиваться. **3,** fol. by out (lie flat) растягиваться; вытягиваться. **4,** (extend) тянýться; простирáться. Stretch for many miles, тянýться на мнóго миль. —n. **1,** (act of stretching): take a stretch, потягиваться. **2,** (expanse) отрéзок: stretch of land, отрéзок земли. **3,** (interval of time) срок: three-month stretch, трёхмéсячный срок. —adj. эластичный; безразмéрный: stretch socks, эластичные/безразмéрные носки. —**at a stretch,** подряд; за один присéст.

stretchable adj. растяжимый; тягýчий. —**stretchability,** n. растяжимость; тягýчесть.

stretcher n. носилки: carry on a stretcher, нести (когó-нибудь) на носилках. —**stretcher-bearer,** n. санитáр; санитáр-носильщик.

strew v.t. **1,** (scatter) разбрáсывать; рассыпáть. Papers were strewn all over the floor, бумáги были разбрóсаны по всемý пóлу. **2,** (cover with scattered things) засыпáть; усыпáть.

stricken adj. поражённый; пострадáвший. ♦ Often as a combining form: grief-stricken, убитый гóрем; poverty-stricken, обеднéвший; обнищáлый.

strict adj. стрóгий: strict teacher/diet, стрóгая учительница/диéта; strict rules, стрóгие прáвила. In strict confidence, под большим секрéтом.

strictly adv. стрóго: strictly forbidden, стрóго запрещается. —**strictly speaking,** стро́го говоря́; со́бственно говоря́.

strictness *n.* стро́гость.

stricture *n.* стро́гая кри́тика; осужде́ние.

stride *v.i.* шага́ть. —*n.* **1,** (long step) большо́й шаг. **2,** *pl.* (progress) успе́хи: *make great strides,* де́лать больши́е успе́хи; далеко́ шагну́ть вперёд.

strident *adj.* ре́зкий. *Strident criticism,* ре́зкая кри́тика.

strife *n.* ра́спря; раздо́р.

strike *v.t.* **1,** (deal a blow to; hit) ударя́ть: *strike someone in the face,* уда́рить кого́-нибудь по лицу́ *or* в лицо́. **2,** (deliver, as a blow) наноси́ть (уда́р). **3,** (bang; knock) ударя́ться: *strike one's head on the door,* уда́риться голово́й о дверь. **4,** (make impact against) уда́риться о; попа́сть в (+ *acc.*). *The boat struck a rock,* ло́дка уда́рилась о скалу́. *The bullet struck him in the shoulder,* пу́ля попа́ла ему́ в плечо́. *Two bullets struck the general,* две пу́ли попа́ли в генера́ла. *He was struck by a car,* его́ сбил автомоби́ль. *A hurricane struck the island,* урага́н обру́шился на о́стров. **5,** (cause to ignite, as a match) чи́ркнуть (спи́чкой). **6,** (mint, as a coin or medal) чека́нить. **7,** (announce by striking) бить; проби́ть; ударя́ть. *The clock struck ten,* часы́ проби́ли де́сять часо́в. **8,** (discover) находи́ть: *strike oil,* найти́ нефть. **9,** (attack; afflict) поража́ть. *Strike dead,* сража́ть на́смерть. *Be struck dumb,* онеме́ть. *The disease strikes mainly young people,* боле́знь поража́ет в основно́м молодёжь. **10,** (impress; appear to; seem to) каза́ться: *he strikes me as an honest man,* он мне ка́жется че́стным челове́ком. *How does this strike you?,* как вам э́то нра́вится? **11,** (impress strongly) поража́ть; броса́ться в глаза́ (+ *dat.*). **12,** (implant, as an emotion) нагоня́ть: *strike fear into the heart of,* нагоня́ть страх на. **13,** (occur to; come to mind) приходи́ть (+ *dat.*) в го́лову; осени́ть; озаря́ть. **14,** *often fol. by* **off** *or* **from** (delete; drop) исключа́ть; вычёркивать. **15,** (assume, as a pose or attitude) стать (в по́зу). **16,** (sound, as a note) взять (но́ту). **17,** (conclude, as an agreement) заключа́ть. *Strike a bargain,* пойти́ на сде́лку; уда́рить по рука́м. **18,** (achieve, as a balance) подводи́ть (бала́нс). —*v.i.* **1,** (deliver a blow) наноси́ть уда́р. *Strike while the iron is hot,* куй желе́зо, пока́ горячо́. **2,** (attack) ударя́ть. *The enemy struck at dawn,* враг уда́рил на рассве́те. **3,** (refuse to work) бастова́ть. —*n.* **1,** (attack) уда́р: *air strike,* уда́р с во́здуха. **2,** (work stoppage) забасто́вка: *go (out) on strike,* объяви́ть забасто́вку. —*adj.* забасто́вочный: *strike fund,* забасто́вочный фонд. —**strike down, 1,** (knock down; afflict) сража́ть. **2,** (overrule; annul) отменя́ть. —**strike home,** *see* **home.** —**strike it rich,** напа́сть на золоту́ю жи́лу. —**strike off,** вычёркивать (из спи́ска). —**strike out, 1,** (cross out) зачёркивать. **2,** (fail) потерпе́ть неуда́чу. —**strike up, 1,** (initiate, as a conversation) завя́зывать; заводи́ть. **2,** (begin to play) заигра́ть.

strikebreaker *n.* штрейкбре́хер.

striker *n.* забасто́вщик; басту́ющий.

striking *adj.* **1,** (remarkable) порази́тельный. **2,** (refusing to work) басту́ющий. —**within striking distance,** в преде́лах досяга́емости.

strikingly *adv.* порази́тельно.

string *n.* **1,** (cord) верёвка; бечёвка. **2,** (on clothes) завя́зка: *apron string,* завя́зка пере́дника. **3,** (of

pearls, beads, etc.) ни́тка. **4,** (of a musical instrument) струна́. **5,** *pl.* (musical instruments) стру́нные инструме́нты. **6,** (of a tennis racket) струна́. **7,** (bowstring) тетива́. **8,** (succession; series) ряд. **9,** *sports* соста́в: *first string,* пе́рвый соста́в. **10,** *pl.* (limiting condition) усло́вия: *with no strings attached,* без каки́х-либо усло́вий. —*adj.* стру́нный: *string quartet,* стру́нный кварте́т. —*v.t.* **1,** (provide with strings) снабжа́ть стру́нами. **2,** (arrange on a string) нани́зывать. **3,** (extend; stretch) протя́гивать: *string a rope across the yard,* протя́гивать верёвку че́рез двор. **4,** *fol. by* **up,** *colloq.* (hang) ве́шать; вздёргивать. —**pull strings,** нажима́ть на та́йные пружи́ны. —**string (someone) along,** води́ть за́ нос.

string bean стручко́вая фасо́ль; фасо́ль в стручка́х.

stringed instrument стру́нный инструме́нт.

stringent *adj.* стро́гий. —**stringency,** *n.* стро́гость.

stringy *adj.* волокни́стый; жи́листый.

strip *n.* **1,** (undress) раздева́ть. **2,** *fol. by* **off** (take off; remove) снима́ть; срыва́ть (с себя́). **3,** (tear off) сдира́ть: *strip the bark from a tree,* сдира́ть кору́ с де́рева. **4,** (deprive; divest) лиша́ть. **5,** (dismantle) разбира́ть. —*v.i.* раздева́ться; обнажа́ться. —*n.* **1,** (long narrow piece or area) полоса́; поло́ска. **2,** (airstrip) (взлётно-поса́дочная) полоса́.

stripe *n.* **1,** (band of different color) полоса́. **2,** (insignia) наши́вка. **3,** (kind; ilk) род; тип. *Of every stripe,* всех масте́й. —**striped,** *adj.* полоса́тый; в поло́ску.

stripling *n.* ю́ноша; подро́сток.

strip mining откры́тая добы́ча угля́.

striptease *n.* стрипти́з.

strive *v.i.* стреми́ться: *strive for success,* стреми́ться к успе́ху. *Strive to become independent,* стреми́ться стать самостоя́тельным.

stroboscope *n.* стробоско́п.

stroke *n.* **1,** (single movement) уда́р; взмах; мах: *with one stroke,* одни́м уда́ром/взма́хом/ма́хом. *Deft stroke,* ло́вкий уда́р. **2,** (of a brush in painting) штрих. *With a stroke of the pen,* одни́м ро́счерком пера́. **3,** (of an oar) гребо́к; взмах весла́. **4,** *swimming* стиль. **5,** (gentle caress) ла́ска. **6,** *mech.* ход: *stroke of a piston,* ход по́ршня. **7,** (sounding of a bell or chime) уда́р. *At the stroke of ten,* ро́вно в де́сять часо́в. **8,** *med.* уда́р; инсу́льт. **9,** *in* **stroke of luck,** уда́ча; **stroke of bad luck,** уда́р судьбы́. **10,** (effective or inspired action) ход; приём. *Master stroke,* мастерско́й уда́р. *Stroke of genius,* гениа́льная иде́я. —*v.t.* гла́дить: *stroke one's beard,* гла́дить бо́роду.

stroll *v.i.* прогу́ливаться. —*n.* прогу́лка. *Go for a stroll,* идти́ гуля́ть; погуля́ть.

strong *adj.* **1,** (powerful; intense; forceful) си́льный: *strong swimmer,* си́льный плове́ц; *strong medicine,* си́льное лека́рство. *Strong language,* си́льные выраже́ния. *Strong measures,* жёсткие *or* круты́е ме́ры. **2,** (capable of enduring stress) кре́пкий; про́чный. *Strong rope,* кре́пкая верёвка. **3,** (concentrated, as of coffee) кре́пкий. **4,** (deeply held) твёрдый; глубо́кий. *Strong beliefs,* твёрдые/глубо́кие убежде́ния. **5,** (clearly noticeable) си́льный: *a strong accent,* си́льный акце́нт. *Strong resemblance,* большо́е схо́дство. **6,** (numbering): *one hundred strong,* чи́сленностью в сто челове́к; в коли́честве ста челове́к.

strongbox *n.* несгораемый ящик.

stronghold *n.* крепость; твердыня.

strongly *adv.* решительно: *strongly condemn*, решительно осуждать. *Be strongly opposed to*, быть решительно против. *He feels very strongly about it*, он твёрдо убеждён в этом.

strong point *n.* 1, *mil.* опорный пункт. 2, *fig.* (asset) сильная сторона.

strong-willed *adj.* волевой; своевольный.

strontium *n.* стронций.

strop *n.* точильный ремень.

structural *adj.* структурный. *Structural changes*, изменения в конструкции. —**structural engineer**, инженер-строитель. —**structural linguistics**, структурная лингвистика. —**structural steel**, строительная сталь.

structure *n.* 1, (arrangement of parts) структура; строение; устройство. 2, (something built) строение; сооружение.

struggle *n.* борьба: *the struggle for survival*, борьба за существование. —*v.i.* бороться: *struggle with an assailant*, бороться с налётчиком. *Struggle to one's feet*, с трудом подняться на ноги. *Struggle to break loose*, вырываться.

strum *v.t. & i.* тренькать; бренчать.

strumpet *n.* потаскуха.

strut *v.i.* выступать; ходить гоголем. —*n.* 1, (swagger) важная походка. 2, (brace) стойка; подкос.

strychnine *n.* стрихнин.

stub *n.* 1, (fragment; end) огрызок; *(of a cigar)* окурок. 2, (counterfoil) корешок. —*v.t.* расшибать: *stub one's toe*, расшибить палец ноги.

stubble *n.* 1, (stubs of grain) жнивьё; стерня. 2, (rough growth, as of beard) щетина.

stubborn *adj.* 1, (obstinate) упрямый: *stubborn as a mule*, упрямый как осёл. 2, (persistent) упорный: *stubborn cough*, упорный кашель; *stubborn resistance*, упорное сопротивление.

stubbornness *n.* 1, (obstinacy) упрямство. 2, (persistence) упорство.

stubby *adj.* 1, (short and thickset) толстый. 2, (bristly, as of a beard) щетинистый.

stucco *n.* штукатурка. —*adj.* штукатурный. —*v.t.* штукатурить.

stuck *adj.* 1, (mired): *get stuck in the mud*, застрять *or* завязнуть в грязи. 2, (jammed): *the door is stuck*, дверь заело. 3, *colloq.* (stumped) в тупике.

stud *n.* 1, (shirt front ornament) запонка. 2, (projecting pin or spike) штифт. 3, (breeding) развод; завод. *Purchase for stud*, купить на развод. —*v.t.* усыпать; усеивать; унизывать. *Studded with diamonds*, усыпан алмазами.

student *n.* 1, (pupil) ученик; учащийся. 2, (university student) студент. —*adj.* студенческий: *student unrest*, студенческие волнения.

stud farm конный завод; коневодческая ферма.

stud horse заводская лошадь; жеребец-производитель.

studied *adj.* 1, (not natural; affected) заученный. 2, (carefully considered) обдуманный.

studio *n.* 1, (workroom) студия; мастерская; ателье. 2, *motion pictures* киностудия; павильон. 3, (for broadcasting) студия; радиостудия; телестудия.

studious *adj.* прилежный; старательный. —**stu-**

diously, *adv.* старательно: *studiously avoid*, старательно избегать.

study *n.* 1, (studying) изучение: *the study of history*, изучение истории. *Make a study of*, тщательно изучать. 2, *pl.* (academic pursuits) занятия; учение; учёба. *Continue one's studies*, продолжать учёбу. 3, (a work on a particular subject) исследование. 4, (deep thought) раздумье. 5, (room reserved for study) кабинет. —*v.t.* 1, (take a course in) изучать; учиться (+ *dat.*): *study Russian*, изучать русский язык; учиться русскому языку. *Study music/drawing*, учиться музыке/рисованию. 2, (make a study of) изучать: *study a problem*, изучать проблему. *Study the origin/behavior of*, изучать происхождение/поведение (+ *gen.*). —*v.i.* 1, (take courses) учиться: *he is studying to be a doctor*, он учится чтобы быть врачом; он учится на врача. 2, (do one's lessons) заниматься. 3, *fol. by* **for** (prepare for) готовиться (к).

stuff *n.* 1, (material) материал. 2, *colloq.* (things; effects) вещи. 3, (basic elements; character) закваска. *He is made of different stuff*, он из другого теста. 4, (anything eaten or drunk): *sweet stuff*, сласти. *I don't touch the stuff*, капли в рот не беру. 5, (rubbish; junk) хлам; дрянь. 6, (nonsense) дрянь. 7, *in* **kid stuff**, пустяковое дело; чудачества. 8, *in* **know/do one's stuff**, *colloq.* знать/делать своё дело. —*v.t.* 1, (fill; pack) набивать: *stuff one's briefcase with papers*, набивать портфель бумагами. 2, (cram in) втискивать; запихивать: *stuff one's things in a suitcase*, втискивать/запихивать вещи в чемодан. 3, (thrust in) засовывать. 4, *cookery* начинять; фаршировать. 5, (glut with food) закармливать; кормить как на убой. *I'm stuffed*, я сыт по горло. *Stuff oneself*, объедаться. 6, (plug; block) затыкать. *My nose is stuffed up*, мне заложило нос.

stuffed *adj.* фаршированный: *stuffed peppers*, фаршированный перец. *Stuffed animal*, чучело.

stuffiness *n.* духота.

stuffing *n.* 1, (act of stuffing) набивка. 2, (material for stuffing) вата; набивка. 3, *cookery* начинка; фарш.

stuffy *adj.* душный; спёртый.

stultify *v.t.* сковывать; стеснять.

stumble *v.i.* 1, (trip) спотыкаться; оступаться. 2, (stagger) шататься; пошатнуться. 3, (falter in speech) запинаться. 4, *fol. by* **on, upon,** *or* **across** (chance to meet) наталкиваться на; натыкаться на; набрести на.

stumbling block камень преткновения.

stump *n.* 1, (tree trunk) пень. 2, (remaining part; stub) обрубок; *(of an amputated limb)* культя. —*v.t.* (baffle) ставить в тупик.

stun *v.t.* ошеломлять; оглушать; потрясать.

stunning *adj.* 1, (staggering, as of a blow) сокрушительный. 2, (shocking, as of news) ошеломляющий; сногсшибательный. 3, *colloq.* (gorgeous) великолепный.

stunt *n.* трюк: *acrobatic stunt*, акробатический трюк. —*v.t.* останавливать: *stunt the growth of*, останавливать рост (+ *gen.*).

stupefaction *n.* отупение; оцепенение; остолбенение.

stupefy *v.t.* 1, (dull the senses of) дурманить. 2, (astound) ошеломлять.

stupendous *adj.* колоссáльный; потрясáющий.

stupid *adj.* глýпый. —**stupidity**, *n.* глýпость. —**stupidly**, *adv.* глýпо.

stupor *n.* отупéние; оцепенéние; остолбенéние; стýпор. *In a stupor*, в состоя́нии отупéния/оцепенéния.

sturdy *adj.* **1**, (strong; stout) крéпкий: *of sturdy build*, крéпкого сложéния. **2**, (firm; steady) прóчный: *sturdy table/foundation*, прóчный стол/фундáмент.

sturgeon *n.* **1**, (fish) осётр. *White sturgeon*, белýга. **2**, (food) осетрина.

stutter *v.i.* заикáться. —*n.* заикáние. —**stutterer**, *n.* зáйка.

sty *n.* **1**, (pigpen) свинáрник. **2**, (inflammation of the eyelid) ячмéнь.

style *n.* **1**, (fashion) мóда; фасóн. *Be in style*, быть в мóде. *The latest style*, послéдняя мóда. **2**, (manner of expression or design) стиль: *writing style*, стиль письмá. *Lofty style*, возвы́шенный стиль. *Byzantine style*, византийский стиль. **3**, (way of doing things) стиль: *that's not my style*, э́то не в моём стиле. **4**, (way of reckoning dates) стиль: *Old/New Style*, по стáрому/нóвому стилю. **5**, (elegance; grace) шик: *do something with style*, дéлать чтó-нибудь с шиком. *Live in style*, жить на широкую нóгу. **6**, *bot.* стóлбик. —*v.t.* моделировать: *style dresses*, моделировать плáтья.

stylish *adj.* мóдный. —**stylishly**, *adv.* мóдно.

stylist *n.* **1**, (master of literary style) стилист. **2**, (designer) модельéр. **3**, *Hair stylist*, парикмáхер.

stylistic *adj.* стилистический. —**stylistics**, *n.* стилистика.

stylize *v.t.* стилизовáть. —**stylization**, *n.* стилизáция.

stylus *n.* гравировáльная иглá.

stymie *v.t.* срывáть. *Be stymied*, зайти в тупик.

styptic *adj.* кровоостанáвливающий.

styrene *n.* стирóл.

suave *adj.* обходительный. —**suavity**, *n.* обходительность.

subclass *n.* подклáсс.

subcommittee *n.* подкомиссия; подкомитéт.

subconscious *adj.* подсознáтельный. —*n.*, *preceded by* **the** подсознáние.

subcontinent *n.* субконтинéнт.

subcontract *n.* субподря́д. —**subcontractor**, *n.* субподря́дчик.

subdivide *v.t.* подразделя́ть. —*v.i.* подразделя́ться. —**subdivision**, *n.* подразделéние.

subdue *v.t.* покоря́ть; подчиня́ть.

subdued *adj.* **1**, (less noisy or aggressive) подáвленный. **2**, (less bright) мя́гкий; нея́ркий.

subgroup *n.* подгрýппа.

subheading *n.* подзаголóвок. *Also*, **subhead**.

subject *n.* **1**, (topic) тéма; предмéт. *Change the subject*, переменить разговóр. **2**, (academic course) предмéт. **3**, (recipient of treatment, examination, etc.) субъéкт. **4**, (one who owes allegiance) пóдданный: *British subject*, британский пóдданный. **5**, *gram.* подлежáщее. —*adj.* **1**, (under the power of another) подчинённый. **2**, *fol. by* **to** (open to) подлежáщий (+ *dat.*); подвéрженный (+ *dat.*). *Be subject to arrest*, подлежáть арéсту. *The treaty is subject to revision*, договóр подлежит пересмóтру. **3**, *fol. by* **to** (prone to) подвéрженный (+ *dat.*); предрасполóженный

(+ *dat.*). *He is subject to nervous fits*, он подвéржен нéрвным припáдкам. **4**, *fol.* **by** to (contingent on) завися́щий (от). *All this is subject to the chief's approval*, всё э́то зависит от одобрéния начáльника. —*v.t.* **1**, (expose) подвергáть. *He was subjected to harsh criticism*, он подвéргся рéзкой критике. **2**, (subjugate) подчиня́ть; покоря́ть. —**subject matter**, содержáние; сюжéт.

subjection *n.* подчинéние.

subjective *adj.* субъективный. —**subjectivism**, *n.* субъективизм. —**subjectivity**, *n.* субъективность.

subjugate *v.t.* покоря́ть; подчиня́ть. —**subjugation**, *n.* покорéние; подчинéние.

subjunctive *adj.* сослагáтельный. —*n.* сослагáтельное наклонéние.

sublease *n.* субарéнда. —*v.t.* [*also*, **sublet**] пересдавáть.

sublimate *v.t.*, *chem.* возгоня́ть; сублимировать. —*n.* сублимáт. —**corrosive sublimate**, сулемá.

sublimation *n.* возгóнка; сублимáция.

sublime *adj.* величественный; возвы́шенный. —**from the sublime to the ridiculous**, от великого до смешнóго.

submachine gun пистолéт-пулемёт; автомáт.

submarine *n.* подвóдная лóдка. —*adj.* подвóдный: *submarine warfare*, подвóдная войнá.

submerge *v.t.* погружáть (в вóду). —*v.i.* погружáться (в вóду).

submersion *n.* погружéние (в вóду).

submission *n.* **1**, (presentation) представлéние; подáча: *submission of evidence*, представлéние доказáтельств; *submission of an application*, подáча заявлéния. **2**, (yielding) подчинéние. *Starve into submission*, взять измóром.

submissive *adj.* покóрный. —**submissiveness**, *n.* покóрность.

submit *v.t.* **1**, (present for consideration) представля́ть; выдвигáть; вносить; подавáть. *Submit a list of names*, представля́ть список имён. *Submit a proposal*, вносить *or* выдвигáть предложéние. *Submit an application*, подавáть заявлéние. **2**, (contend) утверждáть: *I submit that...*, смéю утверждáть, что... —*v.i.* уступáть; подчиня́ться; покоря́ться. *Submit to someone's demands*, уступáть чьим-нибудь трéбованиям.

subnormal *adj.* **1**, (below normal) ниже нормáльного. **2**, (of low intelligence) слабоýмный.

subordinate *adj.* **1**, (lower-ranking) подчинённый. *Be subordinate to*, быть в подчинéнии у. **2**, *gram.* придáточный: *subordinate clause*, придáточное предложéние. —*n.* подчинённый. —*v.t.* подчиня́ть.

subordination *n.* подчинённость; подчинéние.

suborn *v.t.* подкупáть.

subpoena *n.* повéстка в суд. —*v.t.* вызывáть в суд.

subscribe *v.i.* [*usu.* **subscribe to**] **1**, (take out a subscription to) подписываться на. **2**, (receive regularly by subscription) выписывать. **3**, (endorse; support) присоединя́ться к.

subscriber *n.* подписчик.

subscription *n.* (to a magazine or newspaper) подписка; (to a series of cultural events) абонемéнт.

subsequent *adj.* послéдующий; дальнéйший. —**subsequently**, *adv.* впослéдствии.

subservience *n.* подчинéние. *Position of subservience*, подчинённое положéние.

subservient *adj.* **1,** (subordinate) подчинённый. **2,** (servile) раболе́пный.

subside *v.i.* **1,** (abate; wane) утиха́ть; затиха́ть; стиха́ть; уле́чься. **2,** (ease, as of pain) стиха́ть; смягча́ться; успока́иваться. **3,** (go down, as of fever or swelling) спада́ть. **4,** (recede, as of floodwaters) спада́ть; убыва́ть; идти́ на у́быль.

subsidiary *adj.* вспомога́тельный; подсо́бный. —*n.* доче́рняя компа́ния; филиа́л.

subsidize *v.t.* субсиди́ровать.

subsidy *n.* субси́дия; дота́ция.

subsist *v.i.* **1,** (continue to exist) просуществова́ть. **2,** *fol. by* **on** (sustain oneself) пита́ться (+ *instr.*); корми́ться (+ *instr.*).

subsistence *n.* существова́ние; пропита́ние. *Means of subsistence,* сре́дства к существова́нию; сре́дства пропита́ния.

subsoil *n.* подпо́чва; матери́к.

subsonic *adj.* дозвуково́й.

subspecies *n.* подви́д.

substance *n.* **1,** (material) вещество́: *a hard substance,* твёрдое вещество́. **2,** (essence; gist) су́щность; существо́; суть. *In substance,* в су́щности. **3,** (wealth): *a man of substance,* состоя́тельный челове́к. **4,** (density; body) твёрдость; пло́тность. **5,** *fig.* (solid quality) содержа́ние: *lacking substance,* бе́ден содержа́нием. *A report lacking in substance,* бессодержа́тельный докла́д. **6,** *philos.* субста́нция.

substandard *adj.* ни́зкого ка́чества; ни́же устано́вленного станда́рта.

substantial *adj.* **1,** (firm; solid) соли́дный: *a substantial building,* соли́дное зда́ние. *A substantial breakfast,* пло́тный за́втрак. **2,** (considerable; significant) суще́ственный; значи́тельный: *substantial improvement,* суще́ственное/значи́тельное улучше́ние. *A substantial difference,* суще́ственная ра́зница. *Substantial income,* соли́дный дохо́д. **3,** (in essentials) основно́й. *We are in substantial agreement,* в основно́м мы схо́димся во взгля́дах; в основно́м мы договори́лись. —**substantially,** *adv.* суще́ственно; значи́тельно.

substantiate *v.t.* обосно́вывать. —**substantiation,** *n.* обоснова́ние.

substantive *adj.* суще́ственный. —*n., gram.* и́мя существи́тельное.

substation *n.* подста́нция.

substitute *n.* **1,** (replacement) заме́на; замести́тель. **2,** *sports* запасно́й (игро́к). **3,** (synthetic product) замени́тель; суррога́т. —*adj.* **1,** (of a product) суррога́тный. **2,** (of a person): *substitute teacher,* замести́тель. —*v.t.* подставля́ть: *substitute one word for another,* подставля́ть одно́ сло́во вме́сто друго́го. —*v.i.* [*usu.* **substitute for**] заменя́ть; замеща́ть.

substitution *n.* **1,** (act of substituting) заме́на; замеще́ние. **2,** *math.* подстано́вка.

substratum *n.* субстра́т.

subsume *v.t.* подводи́ть: *subsume under a certain category,* подводи́ть под катего́рию.

subterfuge *n.* уве́ртка; уло́вка.

subterranean *adj.* подзе́мный.

subtitle *n.* **1,** (secondary title) подзаголо́вок. **2,** *motion pictures* субти́тр.

subtle *adj.* то́нкий: *subtle hint,* то́нкий намёк; *subtle distinction,* то́нкое разли́чие. —**subtlety,** *n.* то́нкость. —**subtly,** *adv.* то́нко.

subtotal *n.* ча́стный ито́г.

subtract *v.t. & i.* вычита́ть. —**subtraction,** *n.* вычита́ние.

subtrahend *n.* вычита́емое.

subtropics *n. pl.* субтро́пики. —**subtropical,** *adj.* субтропи́ческий.

subunit *n., mil.* подразделе́ние.

suburb *n.* при́город; предме́стье; *pl.* при́городы; предме́стья; окре́стности. —**suburban,** *adj.* при́городный; да́чный. —**suburbanite,** *n.* жи́тель при́города.

subversion *n.* **1,** (subversive activities) подрывна́я де́ятельность. **2,** (overthrow) сверже́ние; ниспроверже́ние. —**subversive,** *adj.* подрывно́й.

subvert *v.t.* **1,** (destroy; overthrow) сверга́ть; ниспроверга́ть. **2,** (corrupt) развраща́ть.

subway *n.* метро́; метрополите́н.

subzero *adj.* ни́же нуля́.

succeed *v.i.* **1,** (achieve one's purpose) доби́ться успе́ха. **2,** (achieve a specified purpose) удава́ться (*impers., with dat.*): *he succeeded in obtaining a loan,* ему́ удало́сь получи́ть заём. **3,** (achieve success) преуспева́ть: *succeed in life,* преуспева́ть в жи́зни. **4,** (turn out successfully) удава́ться; увенча́ться успе́хом. **5,** *fol. by* **to** (inherit) насле́довать: *succeed to the throne,* насле́довать престо́л. —*v.t.* **1,** (come after) сле́довать за; сменя́ть; приходи́ть на сме́ну (+ *dat.*).

succeeding *adj.* после́дующий.

success *n.* успе́х: *achieve success,* доби́ться успе́ха. —**be a success, 1,** (succeed in life) преуспева́ть. **2,** (turn out well) удава́ться: *the experiment was a success,* о́пыт уда́лся. *The play was a huge success,* пье́са име́ла огро́мный успе́х.

successful *adj.* успе́шный; уда́чный. —**be successful, 1,** (achieve one's purpose) доби́ться успе́ха. **2,** (turn out successfully) удава́ться: *the operation was successful,* опера́ция удала́сь.

successfully *adv.* успе́шно; уда́чно.

succession *n.* **1,** (following in order) прее́мственность. **2,** (transfer of power) прее́мственность; перехо́д вла́сти. **3,** (succeeding by descent) пра́во насле́дования. *Succession to the throne,* престолонасле́дие. *War of the Austrian Succession,* война́ за Австри́йское насле́дство. **4,** (series) ряд; цепь. —**in succession, 1,** (one after another) по поря́дку. **2,** (in a row; consecutively) подря́д.

successive *adj.* после́довательный. *Three successive years,* три го́да подря́д.

successor *n.* прее́мник.

succinct *adj.* сжа́тый; кра́ткий.

succor *also,* **succour** *n.* по́мощь; соде́йствие.

succotash *n.* блю́до из кукуру́зы и бобо́в.

succour *n.* = **succor.**

succulent *adj.* со́чный. —**succulence,** *n.* со́чность.

succumb *v.i.* **1,** (yield) уступа́ть; поддава́ться. *Succumb to pressure,* уступа́ть давле́нию. *Succumb to temptation,* поддава́ться собла́зну *or* искуше́нию. **2,** (die) умере́ть.

such *adj. & adv.* тако́й: *in such cases,* в таки́х слу́чаях; *such a large house,* тако́й большо́й дом; *such tall buildings,* таки́е высо́кие зда́ния. *Such a long time ago,* так давно́. *In such a way that,* так, что... —*pron.* тако́в: *such is life,* такова́ жизнь. —**and such,** и тому́ подо́бное. —**as such,** как таково́й; сам по себе́. —**no such thing,** ничего́ тако́го; ничего́ подóбного. *I said no such thing*, я не сказáл(а) ничегó такóго/подóбного. —**such a thing**, такóе: *how could you say such a thing?*, как вы моглú сказáть такóе? —**such and such**, такóй-то. —**such as**, как напримéр.

suck *v.t.* сосáть. —**give suck**, кормúть грýдью. —**suck in**, всáсывать; засáсывать.

sucker *n.* **1**, (person or thing that sucks) сосýн; сосунóк. **2**, *bot.; zool.* присóсок. **3**, *slang* (dupe) простáк.

suckle *v.t.* кормúть (грýдью). —*v.i.* сосáть.

suckling *n.* сосýн; сосунóк. —*adj.* груднóй; молóчный. *Suckling pig*, поросёнок.

sucrose *n.* сахарóза.

suction *n.* всáсывание. —**suction pump**, всáсывающий насóс.

sudden *adj.* внезáпный; неожúданный. *Sudden departure/downpour*, внезáпный отъéзд/лúвень. *Sudden death*, внезáпная *or* скоропостúжная смерть. *This is so sudden*, это так неожúданно. —**all of a sudden**, вдруг; внезáпно; ни с тогó ни с сегó.

suddenly *adv.* вдруг; внезáпно. —**suddenness**, *n.* внезáпность.

suds *n. pl.* **1**, (soapy water) мыльная водá. **2**, (lather) мыльная пéна.

sue *v.t. & i.* подавáть в суд (на); предъявлять иск (к); возбуждáть дéло *or* иск (о *or* прóтив). *Sue for damages*, предъявлять иск о возмещéнии убытков. *Sue for libel*, возбуждáть дéло о клеветé. *Sue for peace*, добивáться мúра. *He sued to get his job back*, он пóдал в суд, чтóбы егó восстановúли на рабóту.

suede *n.* зáмша. —*adj.* зáмшевый.

suffer *v.i.* страдáть: *suffer from the cold*, страдáть от хóлода; *suffer from a rare disease*, страдáть рéдкой болéзнью. *Suffer in translation*, терять в перевóде. —*v.t.* **1**, (sustain) потерпéть; понестú; получúть. *Suffer a defeat*, потерпéть пораженúе. *Suffer losses*, понестú потéри. *Suffer an injury*, получúть повреждéние. *He suffered the same fate*, егó постúгла та же ýчасть. **2**, (put up with) терпéть; выносúть. *Suffer fools*, терпéть дуракóв.

sufferance *n.* **1**, (passive permission) мúлость: *at the sufferance of*, по мúлости (+ *gen.*). **2**, (endurance) терпéние; терпелúвость.

sufferer *n.* страдáлец.

suffering *n.* страдáние. —*adj.* страдáющий.

suffice *v.i.* быть достáточным; хватáть. —**suffice (it) to say**, достáточно сказáть.

sufficiency *n.* достáточность.

sufficient *adj.* достáточно: *sufficient fuel*, достáточно тóплива. *Three gallons are sufficient*, три галлóна — достáточно. —**sufficiently**, *adv.* достáточно.

suffix *n.* сýффикс.

suffocate *v.t.* душúть; удушáть. —*v.i.* задыхáться. —**suffocation**, *n.* удушéние.

suffrage *n.* прáво гóлоса; избирáтельное прáво.

suffragette *n.* суфражúстка.

suffuse *v.t.* заливáть: *the room is suffused with light*, кóмната залитá свéтом.

sugar *n.* сáхар. —*adj.* сáхарный. —**sugar beet**, сáхарная свёкла. —**sugar bowl**, сáхарница. —**sugar cane**, сáхарный тростнúк. —**sugar loaf**, головá (*or* голóвка) сáхару. —**sugar refinery**, сáхарный завóд.

sugar-coat *v.t.* покрывáть сáхаром; *fig.* подслáщивать.

sugary *adj.* **1**, (of or containing sugar) сáхарный; сáхаристый. **2**, *fig.* (cloyingly sweet) слащáвый; сáхарный; прúторный.

suggest *v.t.* **1**, (advise; recommend) предлагáть: *he suggested that I see a doctor*, он предложúл мне обратúться к врачý. **2**, (offer, as an idea) подавáть; наводúть на (мысль). **3**, (indicate; lead to believe) говорúть о: *the evidence suggests that...*, улúки говорят о том, что... **4**, (imply) намекáть: *are you suggesting that...?*, вы намекáете, что...?

suggestion *n.* **1**, (something suggested) предложéние. **2**, (faint hint; trace) намёк; нóтка. **3**, *psychol.* внушéние.

suggestive *adj.* **1**, *fol. by of* (recalling; resembling) напоминáющий. **2**, (suggesting something indecent) двусмысленный.

suicidal *adj.* самоубúйственный.

suicide *n.* самоубúйство. —**commit suicide**, покóнчить жизнь самоубúйством; покóнчить с собóй.

suit *n.* **1**, (outfit) костюм: *three-piece suit*, костюм-трóйка. *Bathing suit*, купáльный костюм. *Space suit*, космúческий костюм. *Suit of armor*, лáтные доспéхи. **2**, *law* иск; дéло; процéсс. *Divorce suit*, бракоразвóдный процéсс. *Bring/file suit against*, подавáть в суд на (+ *acc.*); предъявлять иск к. **3**, *cards* масть. *Follow suit*, ходúть в масть. —*v.t.* **1**, (be right for) подходúть: *the job doesn't suit him*, рабóта емý не подхóдит. **2**, (please; be to one's liking) устрáивать: *it suits me fine*, это меня вполнé устрáивает. *Nothing suits him*, на негó (*or* емý) не угодúшь. **3**, (adapt) приспособлять. —**suit yourself**, дéлайте как хотúте. *See also* **suited**.

suitability *n.* гóдность; пригóдность.

suitable *adj.* **1**, (appropriate) подходящий. **2**, (usable) гóдный; пригóдный: *suitable for drinking*, гóдный для питья. —**suitably**, *adv.* как слéдует; дóлжным óбразом.

suitcase *n.* чемодáн.

suite *n.* **1**, (of rooms) анфилáда. **2**, (of furniture) гарнитýр. **3**, (retinue) свúта. **4**, *music* сюúта.

suited *adj. Be suited for/to*, годúться в: *he is not suited to be a teacher*, он не годúтся в учителя. *He is not suited for this type of work*, такáя рабóта емý не подхóдит.

suiting *n.* костюмный материáл.

suitor *n.* поклóнник.

sulfa drugs *also*, **sulpha drugs** сульфаниламúдные препарáты.

sulfate *also*, **sulphate** *n.* сульфáт; сернокúслая соль. *See also* **ammonium/barium/copper/sodium sulfate**.

sulfide *also*, **sulphide** *n.* сульфúд. ♦*In compounds* сéрнистый: *hydrogen sulfide*, сéрнистый водорóд.

sulfur *also*, **sulphur** *n.* сéра. —*adj.* сéрный: *sulfur springs*, сéрные истóчники. —**sulfur dioxide**, двуóкись сéры.

sulfuric *also*, **sulphuric** *adj.* сéрный. —**sulfuric acid**, сéрная кислотá.

sulfurous *also*, **sulphurous** *adj.* сернúстый.

sulk *v.i.* дýться.

sulky *adj.* надýтый. —*n.* (carriage) одномéстная двукóлка.

sullen *adj.* угрюмый; хмурый; пасмурный. —**sullenness**, *n.* угрюмость.

sully *v.t.* **1**, (soil) пачкать; пятнать. **2**, (tarnish, as someone's reputation) пятнать.

sulphate *n.* = sulfate. —**sulphide**, *n.* = sulfide. —**sulphur**, *n.* = sulfur. —**sulphuric**, *adj.* = sulfuric. —**sulphurous**, *adj.* = sulfurous.

sultan *n.* султан. —**sultanate**, *n.* султанат.

sultry *adj.* знойный. *It is sultry,* парит.

sum *n.* **1**, (total) сумма; итог. **2**, (amount) сумма: *a healthy sum of money,* изрядная сумма денег. —*v.t.* [*usu.* **sum up**] суммировать; резюмировать; подытоживать; подводить итог (+ *dat.*). —*v.i.* [*usu.* **sum up**] подводить итоги. *To sum up,* в итоге; короче говоря. —**sum total**, общий итог. —**the sum and substance of,** самая суть (+ *gen.*).

sumac *n.* сумах.

summarily *adv.* бесцеремонно.

summarize *v.t.* суммировать; резюмировать.

summary *n.* сводка; резюме; конспект. —*adj.* **1**, (brief; general) суммарный. **2**, (without observing the formalities) бесцеремонный.

summation *n.* резюме. —**in summation,** в итоге; подводя итоги.

summer *n.* лето. *In summer,* летом. —*adj.* летний: *summer day,* летний день. —*v.i.* проводить лето.

summerhouse *n.* беседка.

summer lightning зарница.

summertime *n.* лето; летнее время.

summery *adj.* летний.

summit *n.* вершина: *reach the summit,* добраться до вершины. —**summit conference,** встреча на высшем уровне; встреча в верхах.

summon *v.t.* **1**, (order to appear) вызывать. **2**, (convene) созывать. **3**, *fol. by* **up** (muster) собраться с; набраться (+ *gen.*): *summon up courage,* собраться с духом; набраться храбрости.

summons *n.* вызов; повестка (в суд).

sumptuous *adj.* роскошный; пышный. —**sumptuousness**, *n.* пышность.

sun *n.* солнце. —*adj.* солнечный. —*v.t.* [*usu.* **sun oneself**] греться на солнце. —**sun bath,** солнечная ванна.

sun-bathe *v.i.* принимать солнечную ванну; загорать.

sunbeam *n.* солнечный луч.

sunburn *n.* загар. —**sunburned; sunburnt,** *adj.* загорелый. *Get/become sunburned,* загорать.

sundae *n.* пломбир.

Sunday *n.* воскресенье. —*adj.* воскресный: *Sunday issue,* воскресный номер.

sunder *v.t.* раскалывать; разбивать.

sundew *n.* росянка.

sundial *n.* солнечные часы.

sundown *n.* закат. *At sundown,* на закате.

sundries *n. pl.* разное; всякая всячина.

sundry *adj.* различный; разный.

sunfish *n.* луна-рыба.

sunflower *n.* подсолнечник. *Sunflower oil,* подсолнечное масло. *Sunflower seeds,* семечки.

sunglasses *n.* очки от солнца.

sunken *adj.* **1**, (under water) затопленный; затонувший. **2**, (hollow, as of cheeks, eyes, etc.) впалый; запавший; углублённый.

sun lamp лампа солнечного света.

sunlight *n.* солнечный свет.

sunlit *adj.* освещённый солнцем.

sunny *adj.* **1**, (bright with sunshine) солнечный. *It is sunny,* солнечно. **2**, *fig.* (cheerful) весёлый; радостный.

sunrise *n.* восход солнца. *At sunrise,* на заре.

sunset *n.* заход солнца; закат. *At sunset,* на закате.

sunshade *n.* **1**, (parasol) зонтик. **2**, (awning) навес. **3**, (visor) козырёк.

sunshine *n.* **1**, (sunlight) солнечный свет. *In the sunshine,* на солнце. **2**, *fig.* (good cheer) веселье.

sunspot *n.* солнечное пятно.

sunstroke *n.* солнечный удар.

sun tan загар. —**suntanned,** *adj.* загорелый.

super *n., colloq.* = superintendent *(in sense #1).* —*adj., colloq.* чудный; превосходный.

superabundance *n.* чрезмерный избыток.

superannuated *adj.* **1**, (retired) в отставке. **2**, (past one's point of usefulness) отживший свой век.

superb *adj.* превосходный; великолепный.

supercharger *n.* нагнетатель.

supercilious *adj.* высокомерный; надменный.

superficial *adj.* поверхностный. —**superficiality,** *n.* поверхностность. —**superficially,** *adv.* поверхностно.

superfluous *adj.* излишний; лишний.

superhighway *n.* автострада; автомагистраль.

superhuman *adj.* сверхчеловеческий. *Superhuman efforts,* нечеловеческие усилия.

superimpose *v.t.* накладывать.

superintend *v.t.* надзирать (за); заведовать; управлять.

superintendent *n.* **1**, (of a building) смотритель; комендант. **2**, (of a military academy) начальник.

superior *adj.* **1**, (higher in quality) лучший: *far superior to,* намного лучше (+ *gen.*). **2**, (higher in rank) старший. **3**, (greater; preponderant) превосходящий: *superior forces,* превосходящие силы. **4**, (excellent) отличный; отменный. *Of superior quality,* высшего качества. **5**, (haughty) высокомерный; надменный. —*n.* **1**, (one superior in rank) старший; начальник. **2**, (head of a monastery) настоятель. *Mother superior,* игуменья; настоятельница.

superiority *n.* превосходство.

superlative *adj.* превосходный. —*n., gram.* превосходная степень.

superman *n.* сверхчеловек.

supermarket *n.* супермаркет.

supernatural *adj.* сверхъестественный.

supernumerary *adj.* сверхштатный. —*n., theat.* статист.

superpower *n.* сверхдержава.

superscript *n.* надстрочный знак.

supersede *v.t.* заменять; идти на смену (+ *dat.*).

supersensitive *adj.* сверхчувствительный.

supersonic *adj.* сверхзвуковой.

superstition *n.* суеверие. —**superstitious,** *adj.* суеверный.

superstructure *n.* надстройка.

supertanker *n.* супертанкер.

supervise *v.t.* наблюдать за; надзирать за. —**supervision,** *n.* наблюдение; надзор; присмотр; надсмотр.

supervisor *n.* **1**, (overseer) надзиратель; надсмотрщик. **2,** (immediate superior) нача́льник. —**supervisory,** adj. руководя́щий: *supervisory personnel,* руководя́щие рабо́тники.

supine adj. **1,** (on one's back) лежа́щий на́взничь. **2,** (inactive; passive) безуча́стный.

supper n. у́жин. *Have supper,* у́жинать. —**the Last Supper,** та́йная ве́черя.

suppertime n. вре́мя у́жина.

supplant v.t. вытесня́ть; идти́ на сме́ну (+ dat.).

supple adj. ги́бкий.

supplement n. **1,** (anything added) дополне́ние. **2,** (addition to a publication) приложе́ние. —v.t. дополня́ть. —**supplemental; supplementary,** adj. дополни́тельный; доба́вочный.

suppliant n. проси́тель. —adj. умоля́ющий; проси́тельный. *Also,* **supplicant.**

supplicate v.t. моли́ть; умоля́ть. —**supplication,** n. мольба́.

supplier n. поставщи́к.

supply v.t. **1,** (provide with what is needed) снабжа́ть; обеспе́чивать. *Supply a factory with raw materials,* снабжа́ть фа́брику сырьём. **2,** (make available) поставля́ть. *Supply merchandise to a store,* поставля́ть това́р магази́ну; снабжа́ть магази́н това́ром. —n. **1,** (act of supplying) снабже́ние. **2,** (stock) запа́с. **3,** econ. предложе́ние: *supply and demand,* спрос и предложе́ние. **4,** pl. (provisions) припа́сы.

support v.t. **1,** (hold up) подде́рживать; держа́ть: *beams support the ceiling,* ба́лки подде́рживают/держа́т потоло́к. **2,** (back) подде́рживать: *support a proposal/candidate,* подде́рживать предложе́ние/кандида́та. **3,** (provide for) содержа́ть: *support a family,* содержа́ть семью́. **4,** (confirm, as a theory) подтвержда́ть. **5,** (tolerate) терпе́ть; выноси́ть. —n. **1,** (backing) подде́ржка: *moral support,* мора́льная подде́ржка. **2,** (base; prop) опо́ра; подпо́рка; подста́вка. **3,** (maintenance) содержа́ние. *Child support,* де́ньги на содержа́ние ребёнка. *Be left without visible means of support,* оста́ться без подде́ржки. **4,** mil. обеспе́чение; подде́ржка: *air support,* авиацио́нное обеспе́чение; авиацио́нная подде́ржка.

supporter n. сторо́нник.

supporting adj. опо́рный: *supporting beam,* опо́рная ба́лка. —**supporting cast,** исполни́тели второстепе́нных роле́й.

supportive adj. отзы́вчивый; уча́стливый.

suppose v.t. **1,** (think; imagine) полага́ть: *I suppose so,* полага́ю, что да. *What do you suppose this means?,* что э́то, по-ва́шему, зна́чит? **2,** (assume) предполага́ть. **3,** *used to make a suggestion: suppose we do it this way,* дава́йте сде́лаем э́то так.

supposed adj. **1,** (assumed) предполага́емый: *the supposed cause of the crash,* предполага́емая причи́на ава́рии. **2,** (expected) до́лжен; поло́жено. *He is supposed to be here at noon,* он до́лжен прийти́ в по́лдень. *You are supposed to obey,* тебе́ поло́жено слу́шаться. *I am not supposed to drink,* мне пить не полага́ется.

supposedly adv. предположи́тельно; я́кобы. *The money which he supposedly took,* де́ньги, кото́рые он я́кобы забра́л. *Supposedly, he will be there already,* предполага́ется, что он уже́ бу́дет там.

supposition n. предположе́ние.

suppository n. свеча́; све́чка.

suppress v.t. **1,** (quell; crush) подавля́ть; усмиря́ть.

2, (repress, as a yawn, one's feelings, etc.) подавля́ть; сде́рживать. **3,** (hush up) зама́лчивать; замя́ть. **4,** (keep from being published) запреща́ть. —**suppression,** n. подавле́ние.

suppurate v.i. гнои́ться. —**suppuration,** n. нагное́ние.

supremacy n. **1,** (supreme power) госпо́дство; главе́нство. **2,** (superiority) превосхо́дство: *military supremacy,* вое́нное превосхо́дство.

supreme adj. верхо́вный. *The Supreme Court,* верхо́вный суд. *The supreme penalty,* вы́сшая ме́ра наказа́ния. *Make the supreme sacrifice,* же́ртвовать жи́знью.

supremely adv. в вы́сшей сте́пени. *Supremely confident of victory,* соверше́нно уве́ренный в побе́де.

surcease n. прекраще́ние; остано́вка.

surcharge n. припла́та; допла́та.

surcingle n. подпру́га.

sure adj. **1,** (certain; confident) уве́ренный: *you may be sure,* бу́дьте уве́рены. *You may be sure of that,* вы мо́жете не сомнева́ться в э́том. **2,** (reliable; unfailing; inevitable) ве́рный: *sure sign,* ве́рный при́знак; *sure death,* ве́рная смерть. **3,** (not disputed) несомне́нный: *one thing is sure,* одно́ несомне́нно. **4,** fol. by inf. (bound to) обяза́тельно: *he is sure to be there,* он обяза́тельно там бу́дет. **5,** (confident; steady) уве́ренный: *sure hand,* уве́ренная рука́; *sure step,* уве́ренный шаг. —adv., colloq. коне́чно! —**be sure to,** не забы́ть (+ inf.). *Be sure not to...,* смотри́(те), не (+ inf.). —**for sure, 1,** (without fail) обяза́тельно. **2,** (for a certainty) наверняка́: *no one knows for sure,* никто́ не зна́ет наверняка́. —**make sure, 1,** (see to it) постара́ться (что́бы); доби́ться (что́бы). **2,** (ascertain for certain) убеди́ться. —**sure enough,** действи́тельно; на са́мом де́ле. —**to be sure, 1,** (certainly) что и говори́ть. **2,** (admittedly) пра́вда.

sure-footed adj. твёрдо стоя́щий на нога́х.

surely adv. несомне́нно; наверняка́; коне́чно. *Surely you don't believe that,* вы, коне́чно, э́тому не ве́рите. —**slowly but surely,** ме́дленно, но ве́рно.

sureness n. уве́ренность.

surety n. **1,** (certainty) уве́ренность. **2,** (guarantee) пору́ка. **3,** (guarantor) поручи́тель.

surf n. прибо́й; буруны́.

surface n. пове́рхность. *smooth surface,* гла́дкая пове́рхность. *Road surface,* доро́жное покры́тие. *Float to the surface,* всплыва́ть на пове́рхность. —adj. **1,** (moving over land or water) назе́мный; надво́дный: *surface forces,* назе́мные си́лы; *surface ship,* надво́дный кора́бль. **2,** (superficial) пове́рхностный: *surface judgments,* пове́рхностные сужде́ния. —v.t. (pave) мости́ть; замаши́вать. —v.i. (come to the surface) всплыва́ть. —**on the surface,** вне́шне.

surfeit n. **1,** (overindulgence) пресыще́ние. **2,** (excess) изли́шек. —v.t. пресыща́ть.

surge n. волна́; прито́к; прили́в. —v.i. **1,** (billow) вздыма́ться. **2,** (move in large numbers) хлы́нуть; нахлы́нуть. *The crowd surged forward,* толпа́ подала́сь вперёд.

surgeon n. хиру́рг.

surgery n. хирурги́я. *Undergo surgery,* подве́ргнуться опера́ции. —**surgical,** adj. хирурги́ческий.

surly adj. злой; ворчли́вый.

surmise *v.t. & i.* предполагáть. —*n.* предположéние; догáдка.

surmount *v.t.* **1,** (overcome) преодолевáть: *surmount difficulties,* преодолевáть трýдности. **2,** *usu. passive* (place on top of) увéнчивать: *surmounted by a dome,* увéнчан кýполом. —**surmountable,** *adj.* преодолúмый.

surname *n.* фамúлия.

surpass *v.t.* **1,** (exceed) превосходúть: *surpass all expectations,* превосходúть все ожидáния. **2,** (overtake and pass) перегонáть. —**surpassing,** *adj.* исключúтельный; несравнéнный.

surplice *n.* стихáрь.

surplus *n.* избыток; излúшек. —*adj.* избыточный. —**surplus value,** прибáвочная стóимость.

surprise *v.t.* **1,** (astonish) удивлять. *Be surprised,* удивляться. *I'm surprised at you,* я тебé удивляюсь. **2,** (catch unawares) застáть врасплóх. —*n.* **1,** (astonishment) удивлéние. *In surprise,* удивлённо. **2,** (unexpected development) неожúданность; сюрпрúз. —*adj.* неожúданный; внезáпный. *Surprise attack,* внезáпное нападéние. —**take by surprise,** застáть врасплóх.

surprising *adj.* удивúтельный. —**surprisingly,** *adv.* удивúтельно; на удивлéние.

surrealism *n.* сюрреалúзм. —**surrealist,** *n.* сюрреалúст. —**surrealistic,** *adj.* сюрреалистúческий.

surrender *v.t.* **1,** ⟨yield; give up⟩ сдавáть: *surrender a fortress,* сдавáть крéпость. **2,** (relinquish) откáзываться: *surrender a right,* отказáться от прáва. —*v.i.* сдавáться: *I surrender!,* я сдаюсь! *Surrender to the enemy,* сдавáться врагý. —*n.* сдáча; капитуляция.

surreptitious *adj.* тáйный. —**surreptitiously,** *adv.* тайкóм; исподтишкá.

surrey *n.* пролётка.

surrogate *n.* **1,** (substitute; deputy) заместúтель. **2,** *law* судья по наслéдственным делáм. —**surrogate court,** суд по наслéдственным делáм.

surround *v.t.* окружáть. *Surrounded on all sides,* окружён со всех сторóн. *Surround oneself with,* окружáть себя (+ *instr.*).

surrounding *adj.* окружáющий. —**surroundings,** *n. pl.* окружéние; средá; окружáющая обстанóвка.

surtax *n.* добáвочный налóг.

surveillance *n.* надзóр; наблюдéние; слéжка.

survey *v.t.* **1,** (view; review) обозревáть. *Survey the situation,* уяснúть себé положéние. **2,** (poll) опрáшивать. **3,** (measure, as land) межевáть. —*n.* **1,** (review) обзóр; обозрéние. **2,** (poll) опрóс. **3,** (measurement) съёмка. —**surveying,** *n.* межевáние. —**surveyor,** *n.* землемéр.

survival *n.* **1,** (fact of surviving) выживáние. *Survival of the fittest,* выживáние наиболее приспособленных. **2,** (vestige) пережúток.

survive *v.i.* **1,** (remain alive) выживáть; уцелéть; оставáться в живых. **2,** (continue in existence) сохраняться. —*v.t.* **1,** (come through alive) уцелéть от; пережúвать. **2,** (outlive) пережúвáть.

survivor *n.* остáвшийся в живых; уцелéвший. *There were no survivors,* никтó не уцелéл.

susceptibility *n.* подвéрженность; воспрúимчивость.

susceptible *adj.* [*usu.* **susceptible to**] подвéрженный (+ *dat.*); воспрúимчивый (к). *Susceptible to colds,* подвéрженный простýде. *Susceptible to flattery,* пáдкий на лесть.

suspect *v.t.* **1,** (believe possibly guilty; sense the existence of) подозревáть: *he is suspected of murder,* егó подозревáют в убúйстве. *Suspect arson/cancer,* подозревáть поджóг/рак. **2,** (believe to be the case; surmise) полагáть. —*n.* подозревáемый. —*adj.* вызывáющий подозрéние.

suspend *v.t.* **1,** (hang from above) подвéшивать. **2,** (halt temporarily) приостанáвливать; прекращáть. **3,** (debar temporarily) врéменно отстранять (от дóлжности, занятий, *etc.*). **4,** (revoke temporarily, as a rule) врéменно отменять. *His driver's licence was suspended,* он был врéменно лишён водúтельских прав. **5,** (defer) отклáдывать. *Suspend judgment,* воздержáться от суждéний.

suspended *adj.* подвеснóй. *Be suspended from the ceiling,* висéть на потолкé. —**suspended animation,** бесчýвствие. —**suspended sentence,** услóвный приговóр.

suspenders *n. pl.* подтяжки; пóмочи.

suspense *n.* неизвéстность; неопределённость. *Keep in suspense,* держáть в неизвéстности. *The suspense is killing me,* неопределённость мýчит меня.

suspension *n.* **1,** (temporary halt) приостанóвка; прекращéние. **2,** (temporary debarment) врéменное отстранéние (от дóлжности). **3,** (temporary revocation) врéменная отмéна. **4,** *mech.* подвéска. —**suspension bridge,** висячий мост. —**suspension points,** многотóчие.

suspicion *n.* подозрéние.

suspicious *adj.* подозрúтельный: *suspicious person/noise/look,* подозрúтельный человéк/шум/взгляд. *Be suspicious of,* относúться подозрúтельно к. —**suspiciously,** *adv.* подозрúтельно.

sustain *v.t.* **1,** (hold up; support) поддéрживать; держáть. **2,** (support; maintain) поддéрживать: *sustain life,* поддéрживать жизнь. **3,** (experience; suffer) потерпéть; понестú. *Sustain losses,* понестú потéри. *Sustain injuries,* получúть увéчье. **4,** (strengthen the spirits of) подкреплять. **5,** (uphold, as an objection) принимáть: *objection sustained,* возражéние принимáется. **6,** (prolong, as a note) тянýть; протягивать.

sustenance *n.* пропитáние.

suture *n.* шов; нить. —*v.t.* сшивáть.

suzerain *n.* сюзерéн. —*adj.* сюзерéнный. —**suzerainty,** *n.* сюзеренитéт.

svelte *adj.* стрóйный; гúбкий.

swab *v.t.* **1,** (mop; scrub) дрáить. **2,** *med.* (paint) смáзывать: *swab with iodine,* смáзывать йóдом.

swaddle *v.t.* свивáть; пеленáть. —**swaddling clothes,** свивáльник.

swag *n., slang* добыча.

swagger *v.i.* идтú вáжной пóступью; выступáть. —*n.* вáжная пóступь.

Swahili *n.* суахúли.

swallow *v.i.* глотáть. —*v.t.* **1,** (pass into the stomach) глотáть; проглáтывать. **2,** (pronounce indistinctly) глотáть; проглáтывать (словá). **3,** (endure, as an insult) проглáтывать (обúду). **4,** (suppress) подавлять: *swallow one's pride,* подавúть самолюбие. **5,** *fol. by* **up** (engulf) поглощáть; засáсывать. **6,** *colloq.* (believe credulously) вéрить; принимáть на вéру. *Swallow the bait,* попáсться на ýдочку. —*n.* **1,** (gulp) глотóк. **2,** (bird) лáсточка.

swallowtail *n.* (butterfly) парусник; махаон. — **swallow-tailed coat,** фрак.

swamp *n.* болото. —*v.t.* завалить: *swamped with work,* завален работой.

swampland *n.* болото.

swampy *adj.* болотистый; топкий.

swan *n.* лебедь. —*adj.* [*also,* **swan's**] лебяжий; лебединый. *Swan's-down,* лебяжий пух. *Swan's neck,* лебединая шея. —**swan dive,** прыжок в воду ласточкой. —**swan song,** лебединая песня.

swank *n., slang* шик; форс. —*adj.* [*also,* **swanky**] *colloq.* шикарный; роскошный.

swap *v.t.* **1,** (exchange for something different) обменивать; менять (что на что). **2,** (exchange like things) меняться; обмениваться (+ *instr.*). —*v.i.* обмениваться. —*n.* обмен.

swarm *n.* рой: *swarm of bees,* рой пчел. —*v.i.* **1,** (move about in great numbers) роиться; кишеть; копошиться. **2,** *fol. by* **with** (teem with) кишеть (+ *instr.*).

swarthy *adj.* смуглый.

swashbuckler *n.* сорвиголова.

swastika *n.* свастика.

swat *v.t., colloq.* **1,** (slap) шлёпать. **2,** (crush, as a fly) раздавить. —*n., colloq.* шлепок.

swatch *n.* образчик.

swath *n.* прокос. —**cut a wide swath, 1,** *mil.* действовать на широком фронте. **2,** *fig.* (attract notice) наделать много шума; привлекать всеобщее внимание.

swathe *v.t.* закутывать; обматывать. *Swathed in bandages,* обмотанный бинтами.

sway *v.i.* качаться; колебаться; колыхаться. *Sway in the breeze,* колыхаться на ветру *or* от ветра. —*v.t.* **1,** (cause to sway) качать; колыхать. **2,** (influence; persuade) склонять. —*n.* **1,** (swaying movement) качание; колебание; колыхание. **2,** (power; dominion) власть. *Hold sway over,* властвовать над; господствовать над.

swear *v.i.* **1,** (make an oath) клясться; присягать; давать клятву *or* присягу. *I swear to God!,* клянусь богом! *Make someone swear that...,* взять с кого-нибудь клятву, что... **2,** (use profanity) ругаться. *Swear at someone,* обругать кого-нибудь. —*v.t.* клясться. *Swear an oath,* давать клятву *or* присягу. *Swear allegiance to,* клясться *or* присягать в верности (+ *dat.*). *Swear someone to secrecy,* взять с кого-нибудь клятву молчать. —**swear by, 1,** (name in taking an oath) клясться (+ *instr.*). **2,** (have great faith in) питать полное доверие к. —**swear in,** приводить к присяге. —**swear off,** зарекаться (+ *instr.*); дать зарок не (+ *inf.*). *See also* **sworn.**

swearword *n.* бранное слово; ругательство.

sweat *v.i.* потеть. —*v.t.* [*usu.* **sweat up**] *My shirt is all sweated up,* моя рубашка намокла (*or* промокла) от пота; моя рубашка пропиталась потом. —*n.* пот: *in a sweat,* в поту. —**by the sweat of one's brow,** в поте лица.

sweater *n.* свитер.

sweat gland потовая железа.

sweat shirt фуфайка.

sweatshop *n.* потогонная фабрика.

sweaty *adj.* потный.

Swede *n.* швед; шведка.

Swedish *adj.* шведский. —*n.* шведский язык.

sweep *v.t.* **1,** (clean or remove with a broom) мести; подметать. **2,** (carry with force) мчать; проносить. **3,** (move quickly throughout) охватывать: *flames swept the building,* пламя охватило здание. *A wave of strikes swept the country,* волна забастовок прокатилась по стране. —*v.i.* **1,** (use a broom) мести. **2,** (move swiftly) мчаться; проноситься. *A murmur swept through the crowd,* ропот пронёсся по толпе. —*n.* **1,** (motion; stroke) взмах; размах. **2,** (scope; extent) размах; охват. —**sweep away,** уносить: *the boat was swept away by the current,* лодку унесло течением. —**sweep off,** сметать. —**sweep out,** выметать. *Sweep out the basement,* выметать *or* подметать подвал.

sweeper *n.* подметальщик.

sweeping *adj.* **1,** (extending in a wide curve) широкий; размашистый. **2,** (wide-ranging) огульный. *Sweeping generalization,* широкое обобщение. *Sweeping changes,* радикальные изменения. —*n.* **1,** (act of sweeping) подметание. **2,** *pl.* (litter) мусор; сор.

sweepstakes *n.* лотерея.

sweet *adj.* **1,** (having a sugary taste) сладкий: *sweet wine,* сладкое вино. **2,** (pleasant) сладкий; приятный. *Smell sweet,* приятно пахнуть. **3,** (likable) милый: *sweet girl,* милая девушка. *Very sweet of you,* очень мило с вашей стороны. **4,** (not saline) пресный. —*n.* **1,** *pl.* (confections) сласти; сладости; сладкое. **2,** *Brit.* (piece of candy) конфета. **3,** *Brit.* (dessert) сладкое. **4,** (beloved person) дорогой.

sweet-and-sour *adj.* кисло-сладкий.

sweetbread *n.* сладкое мясо.

sweeten *v.t.* подслащивать. —**sweeten the pill,** золотить *or* подслащивать пилюлю.

sweetener *n.* сладкое вещество. *Also,* **sweetening.**

sweetheart *n.* возлюбленный; возлюбленная.

sweetly *adv.* сладко.

sweetmeat *n.* конфета; сласть.

sweetness *n.* сладость.

sweet pea душистый горошек.

sweet potato сладкий картофель; батат.

sweet-smelling *adj.* душистый; ароматный.

sweet tooth *colloq.* пристрастие к сластям. *Have a sweet tooth,* быть падким до сладкого. *Person with a sweet tooth,* сластена; лакомка.

sweet william турецкая (*or* бородатая) гвоздика.

swell *v.i.* пухнуть; набухать; вздуваться. —*v.t.* надувать; раздувать. *Swell the ranks,* увеличивать ряды. —*n.* **1,** (bulge in the ground) возвышение. **2,** (rise of the sea) зыбь. **3,** *colloq.* (dandy) франт; щеголь. —*adj., colloq.* **1,** (fine; excellent) чудный. **2,** (stylish) щегольской. —**get a swelled head,** зазнаваться; надуваться; заноситься; возомнить о себе. *See also* **swollen.**

swelling *n.* опухоль; припухлость; вздутие.

swelter *v.i.* изнемогать от жары. —**sweltering,** *adj.* знойный; душный.

sweptback *adj.* стреловидный.

swerve *v.t. & i.* сворачивать (в сторону).

swift *adj.* быстрый: *swift current,* быстрое течение. —*n.* (bird) стриж. —**swiftly,** *adv.* быстро. —**swiftness,** *n.* быстрота.

swig *n., colloq.* большой глоток.

swill *n.* **1,** (garbage; slop) помо́и. **2,** (food for animals) пойло́. —*v.t.* жа́дно пить; лака́ть.

swim *v.i.* пла́вать, плыть. *Go swimming,* купа́ться. —*v.t.* переплыва́ть: *swim the English Channel,* переплы́ть Ла-Ма́нш. —*n. Go for a swim,* попла́вать.

swimmer *n.* плове́ц; пловчи́ха.

swimming *n.* пла́вание. —*adj.* **1,** (that swims) пла́вающий. **2,** (of or for swimming) пла́вательный. —**swimming pool,** бассе́йн для пла́вания.

swimsuit *n.* купа́льный костю́м.

swindle *v.t.* обжу́ливать. —*n.* афе́ра. —**swindler,** *n.* моше́нник; плут; жу́лик; афери́ст.

swine *n.* свинья́.

swineherd *n.* свинопа́с.

swing *v.i.* **1,** (move back and forth) кача́ться. **2,** (turn on a pivot) верте́ться. *Swing open,* распа́хиваться. **3,** *fol. by* **around** (turn around quickly) повора́чиваться. **4,** (move laterally) свора́чивать: *swing over to the right,* сверну́ть напра́во. **5,** (shift) переходи́ть: *swing over to our side,* переходи́ть на на́шу сто́рону. **6,** (aim or deliver a blow) разма́хиваться. **7,** *colloq.* (be executed by hanging) быть пове́шенным: *he'll swing for it,* его́ пове́сят за э́то. —*v.t.* **1,** (cause to oscillate) кача́ть; раска́чивать. **2,** (wave; brandish) разма́хивать. **3,** (turn) развора́чивать: *swing the car around,* развора́чивать маши́ну. **4,** *Swing an election,* реши́ть исхо́д вы́боров. —*n.* **1,** (movement back and forth) кача́ние: *swing of the pendulum,* кача́ние ма́ятника. **2,** (stroke; sweep) разма́х; взмах. **3,** (shift) сдвиг. **4,** (playground device) каче́ли. **5,** (short trip) пое́здка; объе́зд. —**in full swing,** в (по́лном) разга́ре; в по́лном ходу́.

swingle *n.* трепа́ло; трепа́лка.

swingletree *n.* валёк.

swinish *adj.* сви́нский.

swipe *v.t., slang* (steal) стяну́ть; стащи́ть —*n., colloq.* (blow) тума́к.

swirl *v.t.* крути́ть; кружи́ть; клуби́ть; взвива́ть. —*v.i.* кружи́ться; клуби́ться. —*n.* вихрь: *swirl of dust,* вихрь пы́ли.

swish *v.t.* разма́хивать. *Swish one's tail,* пома́хивать *or* бить хвосто́м. —*v.i.* рассека́ть во́здух (со сви́стом). —*n.* **1,** (whistling sound) свист. **2,** (movement producing such a sound) взмах.

Swiss *adj.* швейца́рский. —*n., preceded by* **the,** швейца́рцы. —**Swiss cheese,** швейца́рский сыр.

switch *n.* **1,** (flexible rod) прут. **2,** *electricity* выключа́тель; переключа́тель. **3,** *R.R.* стре́лка. **4,** (change; shift) поворо́т; переме́на. —*v.t.* **1,** (change; shift) перемени́ть; переключа́ть. **2,** (exchange) меня́ться: *switch places,* меня́ться места́ми. —*v.i.* переключа́ться. —**switch off,** выключа́ть. —**switch on,** включа́ть.

switchboard *n.* коммута́тор; распредели́тельный щит.

switchman *n.* стре́лочник.

switchyard *n.* сортиро́вочная ста́нция.

swivel *n.* вертлю́г. —*v.i.* враща́ться. —**swivel chair,** стул с враща́ющимся сиде́ньем.

swollen *adj.* **1,** (of a part of one's body) взду́тый; разду́тый; опу́хший; вспу́хший. **2,** (of a river or stream) взду́тый; разду́тый; набу́хший; взбу́хший.

swoon *n.* о́бморок. —*v.i.* па́дать в о́бморок.

swoop *v.i.* [*usu.* **swoop down upon**] устремля́ться

(на); налета́ть (на); броса́ться (на). —*n.* налёт. —**in one fell swoop,** одни́м уда́ром; одни́м ма́хом.

sword *n.* меч; шпа́га. —**at swords' points,** на ножа́х. —**cross swords,** скрести́ть мечи́ *or* шпа́ги. —**put to the sword,** предава́ть мечу́. —**sword of Damocles,** дамо́клов меч.

swordfish *n.* меч-ры́ба.

swordplay *n.* фехтова́ние.

swordsman *n.* фехтова́льщик.

sworn *adj.* под прися́гой: *sworn testimony,* показа́ния под прися́гой. *Sworn enemy,* закля́тый враг.

sybarite *n.* сибари́т. —**sybaritic,** *adj.* сибари́тский.

sycamore *n.* **1,** (fig tree of the Middle East) сикомо́р. **2,** (maple tree of Eurasia) я́вор. **3,** (plane tree of America) за́падный плата́н; сикомо́р.

sycophant *n.* льстец; подхали́м.

syllable *n.* слог. —**syllabic,** *adj.* слогово́й.

syllabus *n.* програ́мма (ку́рса).

syllogism *n.* силлоги́зм. —**syllogistic,** *adj.* силлогисти́ческий.

sylph *n.* сильф. —**sylphid,** *n.* сильфи́да.

sylvan *adj.* лесно́й; леси́стый.

symbiosis *n.* симбио́з.

symbol *n.* си́мвол. —**symbolic,** *adj.* символи́ческий; символи́чный.

symbolism *n.* символи́зм.

symbolize *v.t.* символизи́ровать.

symmetry *n.* симме́трия. —**symmetrical,** *adj.* симметри́чный; симметри́ческий.

sympathetic *adj.* сочу́вственный; отзы́вчивый; чу́ткий. *Be sympathetic to,* сочу́вствовать (+ *dat.*). —**sympathetic nervous system,** симпати́ческая не́рвная систе́ма.

sympathetically *adv.* сочу́вственно; чу́тко.

sympathize *v.i.* [*usu.* **sympathize with**] сочу́вствовать (+ *dat.*).

sympathy *n.* **1,** (pity; compassion) сочу́вствие; сострада́ние. *My sincere sympathy,* моё и́скреннее соболе́знование. **2,** (sameness of feeling) симпа́тия: *the sympathies of the crowd,* симпа́тии толпы́. *Be in sympathy with,* симпатизи́ровать (+ *dat.*). —**sympathy strike,** ста́чка солида́рности.

symphonic *adj.* симфони́ческий.

symphony *n.* симфо́ния. *Symphony orchestra,* симфони́ческий орке́стр.

symposium *n.* симпо́зиум.

symptom *n.* симпто́м; при́знак.

symptomatic *adj.* **1,** *med.* симптомати́ческий. **2,** (indicative of something) симптомати́чный.

synagogue *n.* синаго́га.

synchronic *adj.* синхрони́ческий.

synchronize *v.t.* синхронизи́ровать. —**synchronization,** *n.* синхрониза́ция.

synchronous *adj.* синхро́нный.

syncopate *v.t.* синкопи́ровать. —**syncopation,** *n.* синко́па.

syncope *n.* **1,** *med.* о́бморок. **2,** *gram.* синко́па.

syndicate *n.* синдика́т —*v.t.* объединя́ть в синдика́т.

syndrome *n.* синдро́м.

synod *n.* сино́д. —**synodal,** *adj.* синода́льный.

synonym *n.* сино́ним. —**synonymous,** *adj.* синоними́ческий; однозна́чный.

synopsis *n.* конспе́кт; аннота́ция; рефера́т.

syntax *n.* си́нтаксис. —**syntactical,** *adj.* синтакси́-
ческий.
synthesis *n.* си́нтез.
synthesize *v.t.* обобща́ть; синтези́ровать.
synthetic *adj.* синтети́ческий.
syphilis *n.* си́филис. —**syphilitic,** *adj.* сифилити́-
ческий. —*n.* сифили́тик.
Syrian *adj.* сири́йский. —*n.* сири́ец; сири́йка.
syringe *n.* **1,** (bulb-shaped device) спринцо́вка. **2,**
(hypodermic syringe) шприц. —*v.t.* спринцева́ть.
syrup *n.* сиро́п.
system *n.* **1,** (set arrangement or method) систе́ма.
The solar system, со́лнечная систе́ма. *The nervous*
system, не́рвная систе́ма. **2,** (political, social, economic) систе́ма; строй; устро́йство. **3,** (the human
body) органи́зм: *bad for one's system,* вре́дно для
органи́зма. **4,** *mech.* систе́ма: *ignition system,* си-
сте́ма зажига́ния. **5,** *aerospace* систе́ма; ко́мплекс.
Missile system, раке́тный ко́мплекс. *Delivery system,*
сре́дство доста́вки. **6,** (network) систе́ма; сеть.
Highway system, доро́жная сеть. *Early-warning system,* систе́ма да́льнего обнаруже́ния.
systematic *adj.* математи́ческий. —**systematically,** *adv.* математи́чески.
systematize *v.t.* систематизи́ровать.
systole *n.* си́стола. —**systolic,** *adj.* систоли́ческий.

T

T, t двадца́тая бу́ква англи́йского алфави́та. —**to
a T,** вполне́; точь-в-точь.
tab *n.* **1,** (flap to aid in handling) ушко́. **2,** *colloq.* (bill)
счёт. —**keep tab (*or* tabs) on,** следи́ть за.
tabernacle *n.* **1,** (portable sanctuary) ски́ния. **2,**
(house of worship) моле́льня.
table *n.* **1,** (article of furniture) стол. *Night table,* ноч-
но́й сто́лик; ту́мбочка. *Operating table,* операцио́н-
ный стол. **2,** (chart with rows and columns) табли́ца.
Multiplication table, табли́ца умноже́ния. **3,** (list; roster) та́бель. *Table of contents,* оглавле́ние. —*adj.* сто-
ло́вый: *table linen,* столо́вое бельё. —*v.t.* **1,** (postpone) откла́дывать. **2,** *Brit.* (submit for discussion)
ста́вить на обсужде́ние. —**turn the tables on,** бить
(кого́-нибудь) его́ же ору́жием. —**under the table,**
из-под полы́.
tableau *n.* **1,** (dramatic scene) карти́на. **2,** (tableau vivant) жива́я карти́на.
tablecloth *n.* ска́терть.
table d'hôte табльдо́т.
tableland *n.* плоского́рье; столо́вая гора́.
tablespoon *n.* столо́вая ло́жка.
tablet *n.* **1,** (writing pad) блокно́т. **2,** (pill) табле́тка. **3,**
(slab with writing) табли́чка.
table tennis насто́льный те́ннис.
tableware *n.* столо́вые прибо́ры.
taboo *also,* **tabu** *n.* табу́. —*adj.* запрещённый.
tabular *adj.* табли́чный. *In tabular form,* в ви́де
табли́цы.
tabulate *v.t.* своди́ть в табли́цу. —**tabulator,** *n.* та-
буля́тор.
tachometer *n.* тахо́метр.
tacit *adj.* молчали́вый: *tacit consent,* молчали́вое
согла́сие.
taciturn *adj.* молчали́вый; неразгово́рчивый. —**taciturnity,** *n.* молчали́вость; неразгово́рчивость.
tack *n.* **1,** (nail) гво́здик; кно́пка. **2,** *naut.* галс. **3,**
(course of action) путь; курс. —*v.t.* **1,** (fasten) при-
крепля́ть (гво́здиками). **2,** *fol. by* **on** (add on) при-
бавля́ть. —*v.i.,* *naut.* лави́ровать. —**get down to
brass tacks,** добра́ться до су́ти де́ла.
tackle *n.* снасть: *fishing tackle,* рыболо́вная снасть.
—*v.t.* **1,** (jump on and pin down) схва́тывать. **2,** (undertake) бра́ться за.
tacky *adj.* **1,** (sticky) кле́йкий; ли́пкий. **2,** *colloq.* (gaudy; showy) мишу́рный.
tact *n.* такт; такти́чность. —**tactful,** *adj.* такти́чный.
—**tactfully,** *adv.* такти́чно; с та́ктом.
tactic *n.* та́ктика. —**tactical,** *adj.* такти́ческий.
—**tactician,** *n.* та́ктик.
tactics *n.* та́ктика.
tactile *adj.* осяза́тельный.
tactless *adj.* беста́ктный; нетакти́чный. —**tactlessness,** *n.* беста́ктность; нетакти́чность.
tadpole *n.* голова́стик.
taffeta *n.* тафта́. —*adj.* тафтяно́й.
taffy *n.* тяну́чка; ири́с.
tag *n.* **1,** (label) ярлы́к; ярлычо́к; этике́тка; би́рка. **2,**
(game) пятна́шки; са́лки. —*v.t.* накле́ивать ярлычо́к
на. —*v.i.* [*usu.* **tag along**] идти́ вслед. —**tag end,**
са́мый коне́ц.
taiga *n.* тайга́.
tail *n.* **1,** (of an animal or bird) хвост. **2,** (of an aircraft,
kite, comet, etc.) хвост. **3,** (of a coat) фа́лда. **4,** *pl.*
(tailcoat) фрак. **5,** *pl.* (reverse side of a coin) ре́шка:
heads or tails?, орёл и́ли ре́шка? —*adj.* хвостово́й:
tail section, хвостова́я часть. —*v.t.,* *colloq.* (shadow)
высле́живать. —*v.i.* [*usu.* **tail along**] идти́ вслед.
—**tail end,** са́мый коне́ц. —**turn tail,** пусти́ться на-
уте́к.
tailcoat *n.* фрак.
taillight *n.* за́дний фона́рь.
tailor *n.* портно́й. —*v.t.* **1,** (fit) подгоня́ть. **2,** *fig.*
(adapt) приспособля́ть. —**tailor-made,** *adj.* сши́тый
на зака́з.
tailpipe *n.* выхлопна́я труба́.

tailspin *n., aero.* штопор на хвост.

tail wind попутный ветер.

taint *v.t.* **1,** (infect; contaminate) портить. **2,** (tarnish, as one's reputation) пятнать. —*n.* **1,** (blemish) пятно. **2,** (trace of decay) душок. —**tainted,** *adj.* тухлый; испорченный; с душком.

take *v.t.* **1,** (grasp; get possession of) брать (*pfv.* взять): *who took my umbrella?,* кто взял мой зонтик? *Take by the hand,* брать за руку. *Take a book from the shelf,* достать книгу с полки. **2,** (seize; capture) брать; захватывать. **3,** (bring along) брать с собой. **4,** (carry; deliver) относить: *take a letter to the post office,* относить письмо на почту. **5,** (escort) отводить: *take a child to school,* отводить ребёнка в школу. **6,** (drive) отвозить: *take to the airport,* отвозить в аэропорт. **7,** (require) требовать. **8,** (use up, as time) занимать; отнимать. **9,** (travel by means of) брать; поехать на; сесть в *or* на. **10,** (follow, as a street or road) идти по; ехать по. **11,** (follow, as advice) следовать; слушаться. *Take the hint,* понять намёк. **12,** (win) получать: *take first prize,* получить первую премию. **13,** (rent temporarily) снимать. **14,** (choose) выбирать. **15,** (measure, as temperature, pulse, etc.) измерять. *Take someone's measurements,* снимать мерку с. **16,** (subtract) вычитать. **17,** (study) изучать: *take French,* изучать французский язык. **18,** (be subjected to; absorb) подвергаться (+ *dat.*). **19,** (endure, as a joke, criticism, etc.) терпеть. **20,** (assume) принимать; брать на себя. *Take command,* принимать командование. *Take the offensive,* переходить в наступление. *Take the blame,* брать на себя вину. *Take the name Smith,* принимать фамилию Смит. **21,** (charm) увлекать: *be taken with,* увлекаться (+ *instr.*). **22,** (receive or regard in a certain way) принимать; воспринимать. *Take seriously,* принимать всерьёз. *Take something hard,* тяжело перенести что-нибудь. *Take life as it is,* воспринимать жизнь такой, какая она есть. **23,** *gram.* требовать: *take the dative case,* требовать дательного падежа. **24,** *chess* (capture) брать: взять. **25,** *colloq.* (cheat; dupe) надувать: *I was taken for ten rubles,* меня надули на десять рублей. **26,** *with certain nouns* брать: *take lessons,* брать уроки; *take a vacation,* брать отпуск; *take a bribe,* брать взятку; *take prisoner,* взять в плен. **27,** *with certain nouns* принимать: *take food,* принимать пищу; *take medicine,* принимать лекарство; *take poison,* принимать яд; *take a bath,* принимать ванну; *take measures,* принимать меры; *take part,* принимать участие; *take someone's side,* принимать чью-нибудь сторону. **28,** *with certain nouns* делать: *take a step,* делать шаг; *take a picture,* делать фотографию; *take notes,* делать заметки. **29,** *used with various other nouns: take aim,* прицеливаться; *take a course,* (про)слушать курс; *take an examination,* сдавать экзамен; *take a look,* посмотреть; *take a nap,* поспать; вздремнуть; *take a poll,* производить опрос; *take a seat,* присаживаться; *take a certain size,* носить (какой-нибудь) размер; *take a trip,* совершать поездку; *take a walk,* погулять; *take cover/shelter,* укрыться; *take offense,* обижаться; *take office,* вступить в должность; *take pity,* сжалиться; *take pride in,* гордиться (+ *instr.*); *take revenge,* мстить; *take turns,* чередоваться. **30,** *used in various set expressions: take place,* происходить; состояться; иметь место;

take the trouble to, дать себе труд (+ *inf.*); *take by surprise,* застать врасплох; *take one's own life,* лишить себя жизни. —*v.i.* **1,** (have the intended effect) действовать. *The vaccination didn't take,* оспа не привилась *or* не принялась. **2,** (become) *take sick/ill,* заболеть. **3,** *fol. by* **to** (go to; leave for) отправляться в: *take to the road,* отправляться в путь. *Take to one's bed,* слечь в постель. **4,** *Take to drink,* спиться. **5,** *Take to one's heels,* показать пятки. —**take aback,** озадачить; огорошить. —**take after, 1,** (pursue) погнаться за. **2,** (resemble) быть похожим на; уродиться в. —**take along,** брать с собой. —**take apart,** разбирать. —**take aside,** отводить в сторону; отзывать. —**take away, 1,** (carry off) уносить; увозить. **2,** (remove) убирать. **3,** (seize) отбирать; отнимать. —**take back, 1,** (return) возвращать. **2,** (retract) брать назад. —**take down, 1,** (carry down) сносить. **2,** (pull down) снимать. **3,** (write down) записывать. —**take for,** принимать за: *I took him for a German,* я его принял за немца. —**take in, 1,** (accept) брать. *Take in lodgers,* брать *or* пускать жильцов. *Take in laundry,* брать бельё в стирку. **2,** (shorten; narrow) собирать; забирать; ушивать; суживать. **3,** (include) охватывать. **4,** (trick) надувать. **5,** (visit; tour) осматривать. *Take in a movie,* пойти в кино. —**take it, 1,** (assume) полагать. **2,** (withstand difficulty) терпеть. —**take it out on,** сорвать злобу на. —**take off, 1,** (remove) снимать. **2,** (lose, as weight or so many pounds) сгонять. **3,** (deduct) вычитать. **4,** (of an airplane) взлетать. **5,** *colloq.* (depart) уходить; уезжать. —**take on, 1,** (take on board) нагружаться (+ *instr.*). **2,** (undertake; assume) брать *or* принимать на себя. **3,** (hire) нанимать. **4,** (compete with) состязаться с. —**take out, 1,** (remove) вынимать. *Take out a tooth,* удалять зуб. *Take out stains,* выводить пятна. **2,** (escort) повести: *take out to dinner,* повести (в ресторан) обедать. **3,** (obtain by application) получать: *take out a patent,* получить патент. *Take out insurance,* застраховываться. **4,** (vent) сорвать; вымещать: *take out one's anger on,* сорвать/вымещать злобу на (+ *prepl.*). —**take over, 1,** (assume direction) принимать дела. *Take over someone's duties,* принимать дела от. **2,** (assume direction of) принимать: *take over the class,* принимать класс. —**take up, 1,** (carry up) поднимать. **2,** (occupy, as space) занимать. **3,** (consume, as time) занимать; отнимать. **4,** (go in for) заниматься (+ *instr.*). **5,** (assume; begin, as an assignment) принимать. **6,** (discuss) рассматривать. **7,** (quickly accept or adopt) подхватывать. **8,** (remove the slack from) натягивать. **9,** *Take up arms,* браться за оружие. —**take upon oneself,** брать на себя. —**take up with,** гулять с.

takeoff *n.* **1,** *aero.* взлёт; вылет; отрыв от земли. **2,** *colloq.* (imitation) подражание; карикатура.

taking *n.* **1,** (act of taking) взятие. **2,** *pl.* выручка; сбор.

talc *n.* тальк.

talcum *n.* тальк. —*adj.* тальковый. —**talcum powder,** тальковый порошок; тальк.

tale *n.* **1,** (story) рассказ; повесть. **2,** (folk tale; fairy tale) сказка. **3,** (falsehood) сказка.

talebearer *n.* сплетник; ябедник.

talent *n.* талант. —**talented,** *adj.* талантливый.

talisman *n.* талисман.

talk *v.i.* **1,** (speak) говори́ть. **2,** (converse) разгова́ривать. *What is there to talk about?,* како́й мо́жет быть разгово́р? **3,** (chat) бесе́довать. **4,** (gossip) погова́ривать. *People are starting to talk,* уже́ пошли́ то́лки. **5,** (yield information under stress) заговори́ть. —*v.t.* говори́ть; болта́ть. *Talk nonsense,* говори́ть чепуху́; болта́ть глу́пости; нести́ вздор. *Talk oneself hoarse,* договори́ться до хрипоты́. —*n.* **1,** (conversation) разгово́р. *Have a talk with,* поговори́ть с. *Small talk,* сало́нный разгово́р. **2,** (chat) бесе́да. **3,** *pl.* (high-level discussions) перегово́ры. **4,** (informal speech or lecture) бесе́да; ле́кция. **5,** (type of speech) речь. *Baby talk,* де́тский ле́пет. **6,** (meaningless conversation) пусто́й разгово́р. *It's just talk,* э́то одни́ слова́. **7,** (rumors) разгово́ры; то́лки; молва́. *There is talk that...,* погова́ривают, что... —**talk back,** груби́ть; дерзи́ть. —**talk into,** уговори́ть. —**talk out of,** отговори́ть от. —**talk over,** обсужда́ть.

talkative *adj.* болтли́вый; разгово́рчивый; говорли́вый. —**talkativenes,** *n.* разгово́рчивость; говорли́вость.

talking-to *n., colloq.* взбу́чка; нагоня́й.

tall *adj.* **1,** (of considerable height) высо́кий: *a tall man,* высо́кий челове́к. *He is tall,* он высо́кого ро́ста. **2,** (having a specified height) ро́стом в: *six feet tall,* ро́стом в шесть фу́тов. *I am six feet tall,* мой рост шесть фу́тов. *How tall are you?,* како́й ваш рост?; како́го вы ро́ста? —**tall story,** небыли́ца.

tallow *n.* са́ло. —*adj.* са́льный: *tallow candle,* са́льная свеча́.

tally *n.* **1,** *obs.* (notched stick) би́рка. **2,** (score) счёт. —*v.t.* (calculate) подсчи́тывать. —*v.i.* (agree) совпада́ть; сходи́ться; вяза́ться.

tallyho *interj.* ату́!

Talmud *n.* талму́д. —**Talmudic,** *adj.* талмуди́ческий.

talon *n.* ко́готь.

tamarind *n.* тамари́нд.

tamarisk *n.* тамари́ск.

tambour *n.* пя́льцы.

tambourine *n.* бу́бен; тамбури́н.

tame *adj.* **1,** (domesticated) ручно́й; приручённый. **2,** (docile) поко́рный. **3,** (lacking excitement) пре́сный. —*v.t.* **1,** (domesticate) прируча́ть; укроща́ть. **2,** (control, as passions) укроща́ть; смиря́ть.

tamer *n.* укроти́тель.

tamper *v.i.* [*usu.* **tamper with**] **1,** (meddle with) тро́гать. **2,** (fraudulently alter) фальсифици́ровать. **3,** (bribe) подкупа́ть.

tampon *n.* тампо́н.

tan *adj.* **1,** (light brown) светло-кори́чневый. **2,** (bronzed by the sun) загоре́лый. —*n.* **1,** (color) светло-кори́чневый цвет. **2,** (sun tan) зага́р. —*v.t.* **1,** (cure, as leather) дуби́ть. **2,** *usu. passive* (give a sun tan to): *well tanned,* загоре́лый. **3,** *in* **tan one's hide,** сечь; драть.

tanager *n.* тана́гра.

tandem *n.* та́ндем. —**in tandem,** цу́гом.

tang *n.* привку́с.

tangent *n.* **1,** *geom.* каса́тельная. **2,** *trig.* та́нгенс. —**go off on a tangent,** отклоня́ться от те́мы.

tangential *adj.* **1,** *math.* тангенциа́льный. **2,** (not directly related) не име́ющий прямо́го отноше́ния.

tangerine *n.* мандари́н.

tangible *adj.* осяза́емый; осяза́тельный; ощути́мый.

tangle *v.t.* запу́тывать. —*v.i.* **1,** (become entangled) запу́тываться. **2,** *fol. by* **with** (come into conflict with) ста́лкиваться (с). —*n.* **1,** (snarled or intricate mass) сплете́ние. **2,** (confused state) пу́таница. —**tangled,** *adj.* запу́танный.

tango *n.* та́нго.

tangy *adj.* о́стрый; с ре́зким при́вкусом.

tank *n.* **1,** (container) бак. *Gas tank,* бензоба́к. *Fish tank,* садо́к. *Oil storage tank,* нефтехрани́лище. **2,** (military vehicle) танк. —*adj.* та́нковый: *tank army,* та́нковая а́рмия.

tankard *n.* кру́жка.

tank car цисте́рна.

tanker *n.* наливно́е су́дно; та́нкер. *Oil tanker,* нефтеналивно́е су́дно.

tanned *adj.* **1,** (treated by tanning) дублёный. **2,** (sunburned) загоре́лый.

tanner *n.* дуби́льщик. —**tannery,** *n.* коже́венный заво́д; дуби́льня.

tannic *adj.* тани́нный. —**tannic acid,** дуби́льная кислота́.

tannin *n.* тани́н.

tanning *n.* **1,** (process of tanning hides) дубле́ние. **2,** *colloq.* (thrashing) взбу́чка.

tantalize *v.t.* му́чить; дразни́ть.

tantalum *n.* танта́л.

tantamount *adj.* [*usu.* **tantamount to**] равноси́льный (+ *dat.*).

tantrum *n.* при́ступ гне́ва.

tap *v.t.* **1,** (strike gently) сту́кнуть: *tap someone on the shoulder,* сту́кнуть кого́-нибудь по плечу́. **2,** (strike repeatedly against something) посту́кивать: *tap a pencil on the table,* посту́кивать карандашо́м по́ столу. **3,** *fol. by* **out** (produce by tapping, as a message) выстукивать. **4,** (wiretap) перехва́тывать. **5,** (draw upon, as resources) испо́льзовать. —*v.i.* **1,** (make repeated sounds by striking something) посту́кивать. **2,** *fol. by* **on** (rap gently) ти́хо сту́кать в. —*n.* **1,** (light blow) стук. **2,** (faucet) кран. *Tap water,* вода́ из-под кра́на; водопрово́дная вода́. **3,** (leather affixed to a shoe) набо́йка. —**on tap, 1,** (served from a tap) разливно́й. **2,** *colloq.* (ready for action or use) гото́вый; под руко́й.

tap dance чечётка. —**tap-dance,** *v.i.* отбива́ть чечётку.

tape *n.* **1,** (strip of material) ле́нта. *Adhesive tape,* ли́пкий пла́стырь. **2,** (material used for recording) плёнка. *Magnetic tape,* магнитофо́нная ле́нта. **3,** (strip across the finish line) фи́нишная ле́нта. —*v.t.* **1,** (fasten with tape) прикрепля́ть: *tape something to the wall,* прикрепля́ть что́-нибудь к стене́. **2,** *fol. by* **up** (bind with tape) перевя́зывать. **3,** (record on tape) запи́сывать на плёнку.

tape deck магнитофо́нная приста́вка.

tape measure руле́тка; сантиме́тр.

taper *n.* то́нкая свеча́. —*v.t.* заостря́ть. —*v.i.* [*usu.* **taper off**] **1,** (narrow toward one end) заостря́ться. **2,** *fig.* (diminish; subside) убыва́ть.

tape-record *v.t.* запи́сывать на плёнку. —**tape recorder,** магнитофо́н. —**tape recording,** магнитофо́нная за́пись.

tapestry *n.* гобеле́н.

tapeworm *n.* ле́нточный червь; солитёр.

tapioca *n.* тапио́ка.

tapir *n.* тапи́р.

taproom *n.* пивна́я.

taproot *n.* стержнево́й ко́рень.

taps *n.* (вече́рняя) заря́.

tar *n.* дёготь; смола́. —*v.t.* смоли́ть.

tarantula *n.* таранту́л.

tardy *adj.* **1,** (late) запозда́лый. **2,** (slow) медли́тельный. —**tardiness,** *n.* опозда́ние; запозда́ние; запа́здывание.

tare *n.* **1,** (vetch) ви́ка. **2,** *comm.* та́ра.

target *n.* **1,** (object fired at in practice) мише́нь. **2,** (something aimed or fired at) цель: *moving target,* дви́жущаяся цель. **3,** *mil.* цель; объе́кт: *Hit the target,* поража́ть цель. **4,** *fig.* (object, as of criticism or ridicule) мише́нь; предме́т. **5,** (goal) цель; план. —**target date,** наме́ченная да́та. —**target practice,** уче́бная стрельба́.

tariff *n.* тари́ф. —*adj.* тари́фный: *tariff barriers,* тари́фные барье́ры.

tarnish *v.t.* **1,** (dim the luster of) лиша́ть бле́ска. **2,** (detract from, as one's reputation) пятна́ть. —*v.i.* тускне́ть. —*n.* ту́склость.

tarpaulin *n.* брезе́нт.

tarragon *n.* эстраго́н.

tarred *adj.* смолёный.

tarry *v.i.* **1,** (delay) ме́длить. **2,** (stay) остава́ться.

tarsus *n.* предплюсна́. —**tarsal,** *adj.* предплюснево́й.

tart *adj.* **1,** (sour) ки́слый; тёрпкий. **2,** *fig.* (caustic) е́дкий; ко́лкий. —*n.* **1,** (pie) пиро́г. **2,** (loose woman) потаску́ха.

tartan *n.* шотла́ндка.

tartar *n.* ви́нный ка́мень. —**tartaric,** *adj.* виннока́менный.

Tartar *n.* тата́рин. —*adj.* тата́рский.

task *n.* зада́ча; зада́ние. —**take to task,** взять в рабо́ту; взять в оборо́т.

task force операти́вная гру́ппа.

taskmaster *n.* надсмо́трщик. *Hard taskmaster,* стро́гий нача́льник.

tassel *n.* кисть; ки́сточка.

taste *n.* вкус. *A matter of taste,* де́ло вку́са. *Take a taste of,* попро́бовать (что́-нибудь) на вкус. —*v.t.* **1,** (test the flavor of) про́бовать. **2,** (detect the flavor of) чу́вствовать вкус (+ *gen.*). **3,** (experience) вкуша́ть; изве́дывать; отве́дывать. —*v.i.* име́ть (како́й-нибудь) вкус: *taste sour,* име́ть ки́слый вкус. —**in bad taste,** безвку́сно; беста́ктно. —**in good taste,** со вку́сом. —**to one's taste,** по вку́су (+ *dat.*); в чьём-нибудь вку́се.

taste bud вкусова́я по́чка.

tasteful *adj.* сде́ланный со вку́сом. —**tastefully,** *adv.* со вку́сом.

tasteless *adj.* безвку́сный. —**tastelessness,** *n.* безвку́сие.

taster *n.* дегуста́тор.

tasty *adj.* вку́сный.

Tatar *n.* тата́рин. —*adj.* тата́рский.

tatter *n.,* *usu. pl.* лохмо́тья; тряпьё; ру́бище; отре́пья. —*v.t.* растрепа́ть.

tatterdemalion *n.* оборва́нец; обо́рвыш.

tattered *adj.* разо́рванный; обо́рванный; потре́панный; растрёпанный.

tattle *v.i.* [*often* **tattle on**] я́бедничать (на).

tattler *n.* я́бедник; фиска́л. *Also,* **tattletale.**

tattoo *n.* татуиро́вка. —*v.t.* татуи́ровать.

taunt *v.t.* насмеха́ться над; издева́ться над. —*n.* насме́шка.

Taurus *n.* Теле́ц.

taut *adj.* туго́й; ту́го натя́нутый.

tautology *n.* тавтоло́гия. —**tautological,** *adj.* тавтологи́ческий.

tavern *n.* тракти́р; каба́к; бар. —**tavern keeper,** тракти́рщик.

tawdry *adj.* мишу́рный.

tawny *adj.* светло-кори́чневый. —**tawny owl,** нея́сыть.

tax *n.* нало́г. —*adj.* нало́говый: *tax revenues,* нало́говые дохо́ды. —*v.t.* **1,** (impose a tax on) облага́ть (+ *acc.*) нало́гом. **2,** (put a strain on) надрыва́ть. **3,** (try, as someone's patience) испы́тывать. —**tax collector,** сбо́рщик нало́гов.

taxable *adj.* облага́емый нало́гом; подлежа́щий обложе́нию нало́гом.

taxation *n.* обложе́ние (нало́гом); налогообложе́ние.

tax-exempt *adj.* освобождённый от нало́гов.

taxi *n.* такси́. —*v.i.* **1,** (travel by taxi) е́хать на такси́. **2,** *aero.* рули́ть. *Taxi up to,* подру́ливать к.

taxicab *n.* такси́.

taxidermy *n.* наби́вка чу́чел. —**taxidermist,** *n.* наби́вщик чу́чел.

taxi driver шофёр такси́.

taximeter *n.* таксо́метр.

taxonomy *n.* таксоно́мия. —**taxonomic,** *adj.* таксономи́ческий.

taxpayer *n.* налогоплате́льщик.

tea *n.* чай: *a cup of tea,* ча́шка ча́ю. *I'll put on some tea,* я поста́влю ча́йник. —*adj.* ча́йный: *tea service,* ча́йный серви́з.

tea bag мешо́чек *or* паке́тик с ча́ем.

tea caddy ча́йница.

teach *v.t.* **1,** (be a teacher of or in) преподава́ть: *teach Russian,* преподава́ть ру́сский язы́к. *Teach a course,* чита́ть курс. *Teach school,* преподава́ть в шко́ле. *Teach first grade,* преподава́ть в пе́рвом кла́ссе. **2,** (give instruction to) учи́ть; обуча́ть: *teach someone Russian,* учи́ть/обуча́ть кого́-нибудь ру́сскому языку́. *Teach someone how to swim,* (на)учи́ть кого́-нибудь пла́вать. **3,** (show by experience) учи́ть: *history teaches that...,* исто́рия у́чит, что... *Teach someone a lesson,* проучи́ть кого́-нибудь. —*v.i.* преподава́ть.

teacher *n.* учи́тель; учи́тельница.

teaching *n.* **1,** (act of teaching) преподава́ние. **2,** (profession of teaching) учи́тельство. **3,** *usu. pl.* (precepts) уче́ние: *the teachings of Christ,* уче́ние Христа́. —*adj.* преподава́тельский; педагоги́ческий: *teaching experience,* преподава́тельский о́пыт; *teaching load,* педагоги́ческая нагру́зка.

teacup *n.* ча́йная ча́шка.

teahouse *n.* ча́йный до́мик.

teak *n.* тик. —*adj.* ти́ковый.

teakettle *n.* ча́йник.

teal *n.* чиро́к.

tea leaf ча́йный лист.

team *n.* **1,** *sports* кома́нда. **2,** (working group) брига́да. **3,** (horses harnessed to a vehicle) упря́жка. —*v.i.* [*usu.* **team up**] объединя́ться.

teammate *n.* член той же кома́нды.

teamster *n.* **1,** *obs.* (driver of a team) пого́нщик. **2,** (truck driver) води́тель грузовика́.

teamwork *n.* сыгранность.

teapot *n.* чайник.

tear[1] (teer) *n.* слеза. *Be in tears,* быть в слезах. *Tears of joy,* слёзы радости. —*v.i.* слезиться: *my eyes are tearing,* мои глаза слезятся.

tear[2] (tayr) *v.t.* **1,** (rip accidentally) рвать; разрывать: *tear one's stocking,* рвать/разрывать чулок. *Tear one's dress on a nail,* порвать/разорвать платье о гвоздь. *Your trousers are torn in the back,* брюки у вас порваны/разорваны сзади. **2,** *fol. by* **up** (rip up) разрывать; рвать: *tear up a letter,* разрывать/рвать письмо. **3,** (make; open, as a hole) пробивать (отверстие). *Tear a hole in the wall,* пробить стену. *Tear a hole in one's stocking,* протирать дырку в чулке. **4,** (snatch) вырывать; выхватывать: *tear something out of someone's hands,* вырвать/выхватить что-нибудь из чьих-нибудь рук. **5,** (plague; rack) мучить; терзать. **6,** *in* **tear one's hair,** рвать на себе волосы. —*v.i.* **1,** (rip) рваться: *this material tears easily,* эта материя легко рвётся. **2,** (move swiftly) нестись; мчаться: *tear along the road,* нестись/мчаться по дороге. —*n.* прореха; дыра; дырка. —**tear apart, 1,** (tear to pieces; kill) растерзать. **2,** *colloq.* (criticize severely) разругать. —**tear away,** отрывать: *I couldn't tear myself away from the book,* я не мог оторваться от книги. —**tear down,** сносить. —**tear off,** отрывать; срывать. —**tear open,** разрывать. —**tear out,** вырывать. —**tear to pieces, 1,** (rip up) рвать *or* разрывать на куски *or* на клочки. **2,** (kill) терзать; растерзать.

teardrop *n.* слеза; слезинка.

tear duct слёзный проток.

tearful *adj.* слезливый.

tear gas слезоточивый газ.

tearoom *n.* чайная.

tear-stained *adj.* заплаканный.

teary *adj.* слезоточивый.

tease *v.t.* дразнить; поддразнивать.

teaspoon *n.* чайная ложка.

teat *n.* сосок.

technetium *n.* технеций.

technical *adj.* технический.

technicality *n.* **1,** (technical term) техническая деталь. **2,** (minute point) формальность.

technically *adv.* **1,** (from a technical point of view) технически. **2,** (strictly speaking) формально: *technically you're correct,* формально вы правы.

technician *n.* техник.

technique *n.* **1,** (sophisticated method) приём. **2,** (technical skill) техника.

technology *n.* технология; техника. —**technological,** *adj.* технологический. —**technologist,** *n.* технолог.

teddy bear мишка.

tedious *adj.* скучный; утомительный; кропотливый.

tedium *n.* скука.

teem *v.i.* **1,** *fol. by* **with** (swarm; abound) кишеть (+ *instr.*). **2,** (of rain) ливмя лить.

teen-age *adj.* отроческий. —**teenager,** *n.* подросток.

teeny *adj., colloq.* крохотный; крошечный.

teeter *v.i.* качаться; колебаться.

teethe *v.i. The child is teething,* у ребёнка прорезаются зубы.

teetotaler *also,* **teetotaller** *n.* трезвенник; непьющий.

telecast *n.* телепередача. —*v.t.* передавать по телевидению.

telegram *n.* телеграмма.

telegraph *n.* телеграф. —*adj.* телеграфный. *Telegraph office,* телеграф. *Telegraph operator,* телеграфист. —*v.t.* телеграфировать.

telegrapher *n.* телеграфист.

telegraphic *adj.* телеграфный.

telegraphy *n.* телеграфия.

telemeter *n.* телеметр. —**telemetry,** *n.* телеметрия.

teleology *n.* телеология. —**teleological,** *adj.* телеологический.

telepathy *n.* телепатия. —**telepathic,** *adj.* телепатический.

telephone *n.* телефон. *Just a minute, I'm on the telephone!,* одну минуту, я разговариваю по телефону. —*adj.* телефонный: *telephone book,* телефонная книга. *Telephone number,* номер телефона. *Telephone call,* вызов по телефону. *Telephone bill,* счёт за телефон. *Telephone operator,* телефонист(ка). —*v.t.* звонить по телефону; телефонировать.

telephonic *adj.* телефонный.

telephony *n.* телефония.

telephoto lens телеобъектив.

telescope *n.* телескоп. —**telescopic,** *adj.* телескопический.

teletype *n.* телетайп.

televise *v.t.* показывать по телевидению.

television *n.* телевидение. *Watch television,* смотреть телевизор. *What's on television?,* что идёт по телевизору? —*adj.* телевизионный. —**television set,** телевизор.

tell *v.t.* **1,** (utter) говорить (*pfv.* сказать): *tell the truth,* говорить правду; *tell a lie,* сказать неправду. **2,** (relate) рассказывать: *tell a story,* рассказать историю. **3,** (inform) говорить; сказать (+ *dat.*): *can you tell me how to...?,* вы не скажете, как...? *I told you so!,* я тебе и говорил. *I can't tell you how sorry I am,* не могу даже сказать, насколько мне жаль. **4,** (order) сказать; велеть. *Tell him to go away,* скажите ему, чтобы он ушёл. *Do as you are told,* делайте, как вам велено. **5,** (determine; decide; know) сказать: *know how to tell time,* уметь сказать, который час. *Tell the difference,* различать. **6,** (distinguish) отличать: *tell one from the other,* отличать один от другого. **7,** (indicate) указывать. *The clock tells time,* часы показывают время. —*v.i.* **1,** (say) сказать: *it's hard to tell,* трудно сказать. *Time will tell,* время покажет. **2,** *fol. by* **of** (give an account of) рассказывать (о). **3,** (have force or effect) сказываться. —**tell apart,** различать. —**tell off,** *colloq.* бранить; отчитывать. —**tell on, 1,** [*also,* **tell upon**] (have an effect upon) сказываться на. **2,** *colloq.* (tattle on) ябедничать на.

teller *n.* **1,** (narrator) рассказчик. **2,** (bank clerk) кассир. **3,** (one who counts votes) счётчик.

telling *adj.* **1,** (having great force) сильный. *A telling blow,* тяжёлый удар. **2,** (revealing) многозначительный.

telltale *adj.* показательный: *telltale sign,* показательный признак.

tellurium *n.* теллур.

temerity *n.* смелость.

temper *n.* **1,** (composure; equanimity): *keep one's temper,* владе́ть собо́й; *lose one's temper,* выходи́ть из себя́. **2,** (disposition) нрав; хара́ктер: *bad temper,* дурно́й нрав/хара́ктер. *Hot temper,* вспы́льчивость. **3,** (mood) настрое́ние. **4,** (anger; rage) гнев: *fit of temper,* при́ступ гне́ва. *Tempers flared,* стра́сти разгоре́лись. —*v.t.* **1,** *metall.* закаля́ть. **2,** *fig.* (moderate) умеря́ть; смягча́ть.

tempera *n.* те́мпера. *In tempera,* те́мперой.

temperament *n.* темпера́мент; нрав.

temperamental *adj.* капри́зный; темпера́ментный.

temperance *n.* **1,** (moderation) уме́ренность. **2,** (abstinence) возде́ржанность.

temperate *adj.* уме́ренный. *Temperate Zone,* уме́ренный по́яс.

temperature *n.* **1,** (degree of heat or cold) температу́ра. **2,** (fever) температу́ра; жар. *He has a temperature,* у него́ повы́шенная температу́ра; у него́ жар.

tempest *n.* бу́ря. —**tempest in a teapot,** бу́ря в стака́не воды́.

tempestuous *adj.* бу́рный.

template *n.* шабло́н.

temple *n.* **1,** (church) храм. **2,** (side of the head) висо́к.

templet *n.* = **template.**

tempo *n.* темп.

temporal *adj.* **1,** (pert. to time) временно́й. **2,** (temporary; transient) вре́менный; преходя́щий. **3,** (worldly; secular) мирско́й; све́тский.

temporary *adj.* вре́менный. *Be temporary,* носи́ть вре́менный хара́ктер. —**temporarily,** *adv.* вре́менно.

temporize *v.i.* оття́гивать вре́мя.

tempt *v.t.* соблазня́ть; искуша́ть. *I am tempted,* меня́ э́то соблазня́ет. *Tempt fate,* искуша́ть *or* испы́тывать судьбу́. —**temptation,** *n.* собла́зн; искуше́ние. —**tempter,** *n.* соблазни́тель; искуси́тель. —**tempting,** *adj.* соблазни́тельный; зама́нчивый.

ten *adj.* де́сять. —*n.* **1,** (cardinal number) де́сять. **2,** (written numeral) деся́тка. **3,** *cards* деся́тка. **4,** *pl.* (quantities of 10) деся́тки (+ *gen.*): *tens of thousands,* деся́тки ты́сяч.

tenacious *adj.* це́пкий.

tenacity *n.* **1,** (firmness of hold) це́пкость. **2,** (persistence) упо́рство.

tenant *n.* **1,** (one who rents) нанима́тель; аренда́тор; квартира́нт. **2,** (occupant) жиле́ц. —**tenant farmer,** фе́рмер-аренда́тор.

tend *v.t.* **1,** (care for) уха́живать за: *tend the sick,* уха́живать за больны́ми. **2,** (look after) присма́тривать за. *Tend sheep,* пасти́ ове́ц. *Tend the fire,* подде́рживать ого́нь. —*v.i.* **1,** (lead in a certain direction) направля́ться. **2,** *fol. by* **to** (have a tendency) име́ть тенде́нцию (к). *He tends to exaggerate,* он скло́нен преувели́чивать. **3,** *fol. by* **to** (mind) обраща́ть внима́ние на.

tendency *n.* тенде́нция; скло́нность; накло́нность.

tendentious *adj.* тенденцио́зный. —**tendentiousness,** *n.* тенденцио́зность.

tender *adj.* **1,** (gentle; delicate) не́жный: *tender caress,* не́жная ла́ска; *tender skin,* не́жная ко́жа. *Tender age,* не́жный во́зраст. **2,** (sensitive; painful) чувстви́тельный: *tender spot,* чувстви́тельное ме́сто.

3, (soft, as of meat) мя́гкий. —*n.* **1,** (offer) предложе́ние. **2,** (money) платёжное сре́дство: *legal tender,* зако́нное платёжное сре́дство. **3,** *R.R.* те́ндер. **4,** *naut.* плаву́чая ба́за. —*v.t.* предлага́ть. *Tender one's resignation,* подава́ть в отста́вку.

tenderhearted *adj.* мягкосерде́чный. —**tenderheartedness,** *n.* мягкосерде́чие; мягкосерде́чность.

tenderloin *n.* вы́резка.

tenderly *adv.* не́жно.

tenderness *n.* не́жность.

tendon *n.* сухожи́лие.

tendril *n.* у́сик.

tenement *n.* (убо́гий) жило́й дом.

tenet *n.* положе́ние; устано́вка.

tenfold *adj.* десятикра́тный. —*adv.* в де́сять раз; вдеся́теро.

tennis *n.* те́ннис. —*adj.* те́ннисный: *tennis court,* те́ннисный корт; *tennis racket,* те́ннисная раке́тка. *Tennis player,* тенниси́ст; тенниси́стка. —**tennis shoes,** та́почки.

tenon *n.* шип.

tenor *n.* **1,** *music* те́нор. **2,** (purport; thrust) смысл. —*adj.* теноро́вый. —**tenor clef,** теноро́вый ключ.

tenpins *n.* ке́гли.

tense *adj.* напряжённый: *tense atmosphere,* напряжённая атмосфе́ра. —*v.t.* напряга́ть. —*v.i.* напряга́ться. —*n., gram.* вре́мя: *present tense,* настоя́щее вре́мя.

tensile *adj.* растяжи́мый. —**tensile strength,** растяжи́мость; про́чность на разры́в.

tension *n.* **1,** (strain; strained relations) напряже́ние; напряжённость. *International tension,* междунаро́дная напряжённость. **2,** *electricity* напряже́ние.

tent *n.* пала́тка; шатёр.

tentacle *n.* щу́пальце.

tentative *adj.* предвари́тельный; усло́вный. —**tentatively,** *adv.* усло́вно.

tenterhook *n., in* be on tenterhooks, быть *or* сиде́ть как на иго́лках *or* как на у́гольях.

tenth *adj.* деся́тый. —*n.* **1,** (tenth part) деся́тая часть. **2,** (fraction) деся́тая: *one-tenth,* одна́ деся́тая.

tenuous *adj.* **1,** (thin) то́нкий. **2,** (not firm or strong) непро́чный.

tenure *n.* **1,** (holding of a position) пребыва́ние: *one's tenure in office,* пребыва́ние у вла́сти (*or* в до́лжности). **2,** (permanence of a position) несменя́емость.

tepid *adj.* теплова́тый.

terbium *n.* те́рбий.

tercentenary *adj.* трёхсотле́тний. —*n.* трёхсотле́тие.

term *n.* **1,** (period of time) срок: *term of office,* срок полномо́чий. *Prison term,* срок тюре́много заключе́ния. *Be elected for a four-year term,* избира́ться сро́ком на четы́ре го́да. **2,** (semester) семе́стр. **3,** (word or phrase) те́рмин: *technical term,* техни́ческий те́рмин. **4,** *pl.* (manner of expression) выраже́ния: *in flattering terms,* в ле́стных выраже́ниях. **5,** *pl.* (provisions, as of a contract) усло́вия. **6,** *pl.* (relations) отноше́ния. *Be on good terms with,* быть в хоро́ших отноше́ниях с; быть на дру́жеской (*or* на коро́ткой) ноге́ с. **7,** *math.* член. —*v.t.* называ́ть; характеризова́ть. —**come to terms,** прийти́ к заключе́нию; догова́риваться. —**come to terms with,** мириться с (чём-нибудь). —**in terms of,** с тóчки зрéния (+ *gen.*).

termagant *n.* мегéра; фýрия.

terminal *n.* **1,** (terminus; station) вокзáл. *Air terminal,* аэровокзáл. **2,** *electricity* зажúм. **3,** (for a computer) терминáл. —*adj.* **1,** (last; final) конéчный. **2,** *med.* смертéльный: *terminal illness,* смертéльная болéзнь.

terminate *v.t.* прекращáть. —*v.i.* кончáться; оканчиваться. —**termination,** *n.* прекращéние.

terminology *n.* терминолóгия.

terminus *n.* конéчная стáнция.

termite *n.* термúт.

term paper курсовáя рабóта.

tern *n.* крáчка.

terrace *n.* террáса. —**terraced,** *adj.* террáсный.

terra cotta терракóта. —**terra-cotta,** *adj.* терракóтовый.

terrain *n.* мéстность.

terrapin *n.* черепáха.

terrestrial *adj.* земнóй.

terrible *adj.* ужáсный; стрáшный. —**terribly,** *adv.* ужáсно; стрáшно.

terrier *n.* терьéр.

terrific *adj.* **1,** (very great; tremendous) огрóмный: *terrific speed,* огрóмная скóрость. *Terrific noise,* стрáшный шум. **2,** *colloq.* (marvelous) чýдный; потрясáющий.

terrified *adj. Be terrified,* ужасáться. *Be terrified of,* ужáсно *or* безýмно боя́ться (+ *gen.*). *Terrified look,* выражéние ýжаса.

terrify *v.t.* ужасáть; приводúть в ýжас. —**terrifying,** *adj.* ужасáющий.

territorial *adj.* территориáльный. —**territorial waters,** территориáльные вóды.

territory *n.* территóрия.

terror *n.* **1,** (intense fear) ýжас. **2,** (use of violence as a political weapon) террóр.

terrorism *n.* террорúзм. —**terrorist,** *n.* террорúст. —*adj.* террористúческий.

terrorize *v.t.* терроризúровать.

terror-stricken *adj.* объя́тый *or* охвáченный ýжасом.

terry cloth махрóвая ткань.

terse *adj.* крáткий; сжáтый. —**terseness,** *n.* крáткость; сжáтость.

tertiary *adj.* третúчный.

test *n.* **1,** (trial) испытáние; прóба. *Test of strength,* прóба сил. *Put to the test,* подвергáть испытáнию. **2,** (school examination) зачёт; экзáмен. **3,** *med.* анáлиз: *blood test,* анáлиз крóви. —*adj.* испытáтельный; прóбный: *test flight,* испытáтельный/прóбный полёт. —*v.t.* испы́тывать; проверя́ть; испрóбовать.

testament *n.* завещáние. *Last will and testament,* духóвное завещáние; послéдняя вóля. —**New Testament,** Нóвый завéт. —**Old Testament,** Вéтхий завéт.

testator *n.* завещáтель. —**testatrix,** *n.* завещáтельница.

tester *n.* испытáтель.

testes *n. pl.* я́ички.

testicle *n.* я́ичко.

testify *v.t. & i.* давáть показáния; покáзывать; свидéтельствовать. *He testified that...,* он показáл, что...

testimonial *n.* рекомендáция; характерúстика.

—*adj.* рекомендáтельный. *Testimonial dinner,* обéд в честь когó-нибудь.

testimony *n.* **1,** (statement made under oath) показáние; свидéтельство. **2,** (proof) свидéтельство.

test pilot лётчик-испытáтель.

test tube пробúрка.

testy *adj.* раздражúтельный; брюзглúвый.

tetanus *n.* столбня́к.

tête-à-tête *n.* бесéда с глáзу на глаз.

tether *n.* прúвязь. —*v.t.* привя́зывать. —**reach the end of one's tether,** дойтú до тóчки.

tetragon *n.* четырёхугóльник. —**tetragonal,** *adj.* четырёхугóльный.

tetrahedron *n.* четырёхгрáнник. —**tetrahedral,** *adj.* четырёхгрáнный.

tetrameter *n.* четырёхстóпный стих. *Iambic tetrameter,* четырёхстóпный ямб. —*adj.* четырёхстóпный.

Teuton *n.* тевтóн. —**Teutonic,** *adj.* тевтóнский.

text *n.* текст.

textbook *n.* учéбник.

textile *n., usu. pl.* текстúль. —*adj.* текстúльный.

textual *adj.* **1,** (pert. to a text) текстовóй; текстуáльный. **2,** (literal) текстуáльный.

texture *n.* строéние; переплетéние (ткáни).

Thai *adj.* тáйский. —*n.* тáйский язы́к.

thallium *n.* тáллий.

than *conj.* чем: *less strict than you,* мéнее стрóгий (стрóгая), чем вы. *More than ever before,* бóльше чем когдá-либо рáньше. ♦*Also rendered by the genitive case: he is taller than you,* он вы́ше вас.

thank *v.t.* благодарúть. —**thank God!,** слáва бóгу! —**thank you,** спасúбо; благодарю́ вас. *Thank you very much!,* большóе (вам) спасúбо!

thankful *adj.* благодáрный. —**thankfulness,** *n.* благодáрность.

thankless *adj.* неблагодáрный.

thanks *n.pl.* благодáрность. —*interj.* спасúбо. —**thanks to,** благодаря́ (+ *dat.*).

thanksgiving *n.* **1,** (giving of thanks) благодарéние. *A prayer of thanksgiving,* благодáрственная молúтва. **2,** *cap.* (American holiday) День Благодарéния.

that *adj.* тот: *that house,* тот дом; *at that time,* в то врéмя. —*dem.pron.* э́то: *that's all,* э́то всё; *that's not the point,* дéло не в э́том. *Is that you, Nina?,* э́то ты, Нúна? —*rel.pron.* котóрый; что: *the book that was lying on the table,* кнúга, котóрая лежáла на столé. *Everything that happened,* всё, что случúлось. —*conj.* что: *I admit that I was wrong,* я признаю́, что был непрáв. *He demanded that we apologize,* он потрéбовал, чтóбы мы извинúлись. —*adv.* так; такóй. *I can't walk that far,* я не могý идтú так далекó. —**and all that,** и всё такóе. —**at that,** *see at.* —**by that,** э́тим. —**for all that,** при всём том. —**in that,** тем, что. —**like that,** так. —**so that,** с тем, чтóбы. —**that is,** то есть. —**that much,** так мнóго; стóлько. —**that which,** то, что... —**this and that,** *see this.*

thatch *n.* крóвельная солóма. —*v.t.* крыть солóмой. *Thatched roof,* солóменная крыша.

thaw *n.* óттепель. —*v.i.* тáять; оттáивать. —*v.t.* растáпливать; оттáивать.

the *def.art. Not rendered in Russian: the end of the road,* конéц дорóги; *the 20th century,* двадцáтый век. —**the..., the...,** чем..., тем...: *the sooner the better,* чем рáньше, тем лýчше.

theater *n.* **1,** (playhouse) театр. *Theater tickets,* билéты в теáтр. **2,** *mil.* теáтр: *theater of operations,* теáтр воéнных дéйствий. *Theater nuclear weapons,* я́дерное орýжие срéдней дáльности. —**theatergoer,** *n.* теáтрáл. —**theatrical,** *adj.* театрáльный.

theatrics *n.pl.* **1,** (art of the theater) театрáльное искýсство. **2,** (histrionics) театрáльность.

thee *pers.pron., archaic* тебя́; тебé; тобóй.

theft *n.* воровствó; крáжа.

their *poss.adj.* их: *their mother,* их мать. ♦*When the possessor is the subject of the sentence* свой: *they sold their house,* они́ прóдали свой дом.

theirs *poss.pron.* их: *a friend of theirs,* оди́н из их друзéй. *Is this our luggage or theirs?,* э́тот багáж наш и́ли их?

theism *n.* теи́зм. —**theist,** *n.* теи́ст. —**theistic,** *adj.* теисти́ческий.

them *pers.pron.* **1,** *used as dir. obj. of a verb* их: *I saw them,* я ви́дел их. **2,** *used as indir. obj. of a verb* им: *give them the money,* дáйте им дéньги. **3,** *used as obj. of a prep.* них; ним; ни́ми.

thematic *adj.* темати́ческий.

theme *n.* тéма.

themselves *pers.pron.* **1,** *used for emphasis* (они́) сáми: *they don't know themselves,* они́ сáми не знáют. **2,** *used reflexively* себя́: *they behaved themselves badly,* они́ плóхо вели́ себя́. *They hurt themselves,* они́ уши́блись. —**by themselves,** одни́.

then *adv.* **1,** (at that time) тогдá; в то врéмя. *We were young then,* тогдá мы бы́ли молоды́ми. *Where were you living then?,* где вы жи́ли в то врéмя? **2,** (afterward; next) потóм; затéм: *first we go to London, and then to Paris,* снача́ла мы поéдем в Лóндон, а потóм/затéм в Пари́ж. **3,** (in that case) тогдá; то. *What will you do then?,* что вы бýдете дéлать тогдá? *If he is ill, then we shouldn't go there,* éсли он бóлен, то не нáдо идти́ тудá. **4,** (so) знáчит: *then you're not going,* знáчит, вы не идёте. —*adj., preceded by* the тогдáшний. —**but then,** затó; впрóчем. —**by then,** к томý врéмени. —**now and then,** врéмя от врéмени; кóекогдá. —**since then,** с тех пор. —**then and there,** тут же. —**till then,** до тех пор.

thence *adv.* **1,** (from there) оттýда. **2,** (from that time) с тех пор. **3,** (therefore) отсю́да; поэ́тому.

thenceforth *adv.* с тех пор; с тогó врéмени. *Also,* **thenceforward.**

theocracy *n.* теокрáтия. —**theocratic,** *adj.* теократи́ческий.

theologian *n.* богослóв.

theological *adj.* богослóвский; теологи́ческий. *Theological seminary,* духóвная семинáрия.

theology *n.* богослóвие; теолóгия.

theorem *n.* теорéма.

theoretical *adj.* теорети́ческий. —**theoretically,** *adv.* теорети́чески; в теóрии.

theoretician *n.* теорéтик. *Also,* **theorist.**

theorize *v.i.* теоретизи́ровать.

theory *n.* теóрия.

theosophy *n.* теосóфия. —**theosophical,** *adj.* теосóфский; теософи́ческий. —**theosophist,** *n.* теосóф.

therapeutic *adj.* терапевти́ческий.

therapist *n.* физиотерапéвт. *Speech therapist,* логопéд.

therapy *n.* терапи́я. *Physical therapy,* физиотерапи́я. *Speech therapy,* логопéдия.

there *adv.* **1,** (in that place) там. *From there,* оттýда. **2,** (to that place) тудá: *there and back,* тудá и обрáтно. **3,** (from that place) оттýда: *he left there,* он уéхал оттýда. **4,** *used to call attention* вон: *there he goes!,* вон он идёт! **5,** (in that matter) здесь: *I disagree with you there,* здесь я с вáми не соглáсен. *You've got me there!,* здесь я попáлся. **6,** (at that point) в (*or* на) э́том; э́тим. *He didn't stop there,* он на э́том не останови́лся. *The matter didn't end there,* э́тим дéло не кóнчилось. —*interj.* **1,** *to express satisfaction* ну вот! **2,** *to express sympathy* ну ну! —**not all there,** *colloq.* (у негó/неё) не все дóма. —**over there,** вон там. —**there and then,** тут же. —**there is; there are,** есть; имéется (имéются). *There is reason to believe that...,* есть основáние полагáть, что... *There is nothing/no one/here,* здесь ничегó/никогó нет. *There is no telling when...,* нельзя́ сказáть, когдá... *There is no stopping him,* егó не останóвишь. *There is nothing you can do about it,* ничегó не подéлаешь. —**there was; there were,** был; бы́ло: *there was no one there,* там никогó нé было. *There were three of them,* их бы́ло трóе.

thereabout *adv.* **1,** (near that place) поблизости. **2,** (approximately) óколо э́того: *ten miles or thereabout,* дéсять миль и́ли чтó-нибудь óколо э́того. *Also,* **thereabouts.**

thereafter *adv.* с э́того (*or* с тогó) врéмени.

thereby *adv.* тем сáмым.

therefore *adv.* поэ́тому.

therein *adv.* в э́том.

thereupon *adv.* **1,** (following that) вслед за тем. **2,** (because of that) вслéдствие тогó.

thermal *adj.* теплово́й; терми́ческий.

Thermit *also,* **Thermite** *n.* терми́т.

thermocouple *n.* термопáра.

thermodynamics *n.* термодинáмика. —**thermodynamic,** *adj.* термодинами́ческий.

thermometer *n.* термóметр; грáдусник.

thermonuclear *adj.* термоя́дерный.

thermos *n.* тéрмос. *Also,* **thermos bottle.**

thermostat *n.* термостáт.

thesaurus *n.* тезáурус.

these *dem.adj. & pron.* э́ти: *these houses,* э́ти домá. *I'll take these,* я возьмý э́ти. *These are my children,* э́то мои́ дéти. *One of these days,* на днях.

thesis *n.* **1,** (proposition) тéзис; положéние. **2,** (dissertation) диссертáция.

Thespian *adj.* траги́ческий; драмати́ческий. —*n.* траги́ческий актёр.

they *pers.pron.* они́. *They say that...,* говоря́т, что... *See also* **them.**

thick *adj.* **1,** (not thin) тóлстый: *thick book/board/neck,* тóлстая кни́га/доскá/шéя. **2,** (having a specified thickness) толщинóй в: *six inches thick,* толщинóй в шесть дю́ймов. **3,** (dense; not watery) густóй: *thick fog/soup/syrup,* густóй тумáн/суп/сирóп. **4,** (heavy, as of an accent) си́льный. —*adv.* *Slice the bread thick,* нарéжьте хлеб тóлстыми ломтя́ми. —**lay it on thick,** сгущáть крáски. —**thick and fast,** грáдом.

thicken *v.t.* **1,** (make thicker or broader) утолщáть. **2,** (make more dense) сгущáть: *thicken a solution,* сгущáть раствóр. —*v.i.* густéть; сгущáться. *The plot* *thickens,* интрига становится всё сложнее.

thicket *n.* чаща; чащоба.

thickheaded *adj.* тупоголовый; тупоумный; твердолобый.

thick-lipped *adj.* толстогубый; губастый.

thickness *n.* **1,** (size) толщина. **2,** (density) густота. **3,** (layer) слой.

thickset *adj.* коренастый; приземистый; кряжистый.

thick-skinned *adj.* толстокожий.

thief *n.* вор.

thieve *v.i.* воровать. —**thievery,** *n.* воровство. —**thievish,** *adj.* вороватый.

thigh *n.* бедро. —**thighbone,** *n.* бедренная кость.

thimble *n.* напёрсток.

thin *adj.* **1,** (not thick) тонкий: *thin line/waist/shirt,* тонкая линия/талия/рубашка. **2,** (not fat) худой. *She has gotten very thin,* она очень похудела. **3,** (not dense) редкий. *His hair is getting thin,* волосы у него редеют. **4,** (watery) жидкий: *thin soup,* жидкий суп. —*adv. Slice the bread thin,* нарезать хлеб тонкими ломтями. —*v.t.* **1,** *often fol. by* **down** (make thinner) утончать. **2,** *fol. by* **out** (make less dense) разрежать. —*v.i.* **1,** *fol. by* **out** (become less dense) редеть. **2,** *fol. by* **down** (slim down) худеть. —**wear thin, 1,** (become worn) изнашиваться; стираться. **2,** *fig.* (of patience) истощаться; иссякать.

thine *poss.pron. & adj., archaic* твой.

thing *n.* **1,** (object) вещь. *The same thing,* то же самое. *I haven't a thing to wear,* мне нечего надеть. **2,** *pl.* (clothes; belongings) вещи. **3,** (matter; factor; circumstance) дело: *it's a strange thing,* странное дело! *Other things being equal,* при прочих равных условиях. ♦*Often omitted in Russian: the first thing (that)...,* первое, что... *The main thing is to...,* самое главное, чтобы... *It's a good thing (that)...,* хорошо, что... *Only one thing bothers me,* меня беспокоит лишь одно. *Such a thing could not happen here,* такое не может случиться здесь. *It comes to the same thing,* это всё равно. **4,** (act; task) дело: *I have a number of things to do,* у меня много дел; мне много надо сделать. *You did the right thing,* вы правильно поступили. **5,** *pl.* (state of affairs) дела: *how are things?,* как дела? **6,** (creature) существо. *Poor thing!,* бедняжка! —**a thing or two,** кое-что.

think *v.i.* **1,** (exercise one's mind) думать: *let me think,* дайте мне подумать. *I don't think so,* думаю, что нет. **2,** (reason) мыслить: *think logically,* логически мыслить. *The ability to think,* способность мыслить. —*v.t.* **1,** (have in mind; imagine): *who would have thought it?,* кто бы мог подумать? *How could you think such things?,* как у вас могли появиться такие мысли? **2,** (believe; suppose) полагать; считать: *I think he's wrong,* я считаю, что он неправ. *There is no reason to think that...,* нет оснований полагать, что... —**think better of it,** одуматься. —**think nothing of,** *rendered by* хоть бы что (+ *dat.*): *he thinks nothing of running five miles,* ему хоть бы что пробежать пять миль. *He thinks nothing of hurting a person's feelings,* ему ничего не стоит обидеть человека. —**think of, 1,** (have an opinion about) думать о. **2,** (choose) задумать: *think of a number,* задумать какое-нибудь число. **3,** (be concerned about) думать о: *she thinks only of herself,* она думает

только о себе. **4,** (recall) припомнить. **5,** (intend) думать: *she is thinking of getting married,* она думает выйти замуж. —**think out** *or* **through,** продумывать. —**think over,** обдумывать. —**think twice (before),** подумать хорошенько (прежде чем...). —**think up, 1,** (devise) придумывать. **2,** (concoct) выдумывать.

thinkable *adj.* мыслимый.

thinker *n.* мыслитель.

thinking *adj.* мыслящий. —*n.* мышление. —**to my way of thinking,** по моему мнению; на мой взгляд.

thinly *adv.* тонко. *Thinly veiled threat,* едва скрываемая угроза.

thinness *n.* тонкость; худоба.

thin-skinned *adj.* **1,** (having a thin skin) тонкокожий. **2,** (sensitive) обидчивый; чувствительный.

third *adj.* третий. *The third world,* третий мир. —*n.* **1,** (fraction) треть: *two-thirds,* две трети. **2,** *music* терция. —**in the third place,** в-третьих.

third-rate *adj.* третьесортный; третьестепенный.

thirst *n.* жажда. —*v.i.* [*usu.* **thirst for**] жаждать (+ *gen.*).

thirsty *adj.* жаждущий. *I am thirsty,* я хочу пить.

thirteen *n. & adj.* тринадцать. —**thirteenth,** *adj.* тринадцатый.

thirty *n. & adj.* тридцать. —**thirtieth,** *adj.* тридцатый.

this *adj.* этот: *this house,* этот дом; *this book,* эта книга; *this place,* это место; *this one,* этот; *this time,* на этот раз; *this week,* на этой неделе; *this month,* в этом месяце; *this year,* в этом году.—*dem.pron.* это: *what does this mean?,* что это значит? —*adv.* так: *this quiet,* так тихо; *this soon,* так скоро. —**like this,** так. —**this and that,** то и сё; то да сё. *Talk about this and that,* поговорить о том, о сём. —**this is,** это: *this is my sister,* это моя сестра. —**this is how, where,** *etc.,* вот как; вот где, *etc.*

thistle *n.* чертополох.

thither *adv.* туда.

thong *n.* **1,** (strap) ремень. **2,** (lash of a whip) плеть.

thoracic *adj.* грудной. —**thoracic duct,** грудной проток.

thorax *n.* грудная клетка.

thorium *n.* торий.

thorn *n.* шип; колючка. —**thorn in one's flesh (or side),** бельмо на глазу.

thorn apple дурман.

thorny *adj.* **1,** (full of thorns) колючий. **2,** (controversial) спорный: *thorny question,* спорный вопрос. **3,** *fig.* (full of pitfalls) тернистый: *thorny path,* тернистый путь.

thorough *adj.* **1,** (painstaking; complete) основательный; доскональный. **2,** (utter; out-and-out) совершённый; отъявленный.

thoroughbred *adj.* чистокровный; породистый. —*n.* чистокровная/породистая лошадь.

thoroughfare *n.* **1,** (main road) магистраль. **2,** (passage) проезд: *no thoroughfare,* нет проезда.

thoroughgoing *adj.* = **thorough.**

thoroughly *adv.* **1,** (carefully) основательно. **2,** (completely; utterly) совершённо.

thoroughness *n.* основательность; доскональность.

those *dem.adj. & pron.* те: *those buildings,* те здания. *Those wishing to go,* те, кто желает идти. *Those were my children,* то были мои дети.

thou *pers.pron., archaic* ты.

though *conj.* **1,** (in spite of the fact that) хотя́: *though it is late,* хотя́ уже́ по́здно. **2,** (while) хотя́ и; хоть и: *our house, though small, is very cozy,* наш дом, хотя́/хоть и небольшо́й, но о́чень ую́тный. —*adv.* всё же; всё-таки; впро́чем. *Do as you like, though,* впро́чем, де́лайте как хоти́те. —**as though,** бу́дто; как бу́дто; сло́вно.

thought *n.* **1,** (idea) мысль. *At the thought of,* при мы́сли о. **2,** (thinking) мышле́ние. **3,** (reflection; meditation) размышле́ние. *Lost in thought,* погружён в размышле́ния. **4,** (intention) наме́рение. *Have no thought of,* отню́дь не собира́ться (+ *inf.*). —**give thought to,** обду́мывать. —**on second thought,** по зре́лом размышле́нии; пораски́нув умо́м.

thoughtful *adj.* **1,** (pensive) заду́мчивый; вду́мчивый. **2,** (considerate) забо́тливый; внима́тельный. —**thoughtfulness,** *n.* забо́тливость; внима́тельность.

thoughtless *adj.* **1,** (ill-considered) необду́манный. **2,** (inconsiderate) невнима́тельный.

thousand *n. & adj.* ты́сяча.

thousandfold *adj.* тысячекра́тный. —*adv.* в ты́сячу раз.

thousandth *adj.* ты́сячный. —*n.* **1,** (thousandth part) ты́сячная часть. **2,** (fraction) ты́сячная: *one thousandth,* одна́ ты́сячная.

Thracian *adj.* фраки́йский.

thrash *v.t.* поро́ть; колоти́ть. —*v.i.* [*usu.* **thrash about**] мета́ться; бара́хтаться. —**thrash out,** подро́бно обсужда́ть.

thrashing *n.* трёпка; взбу́чка; по́рка.

thread *n.* **1,** (thin cord; fiber) ни́тка. **2,** (spiral ridge of a screw) наре́зка; резьба́. **3,** *fig.* (sequence) нить: *lose the thread of the conversation,* потеря́ть нить разгово́ра. —*v.t.* **1,** (pass through the eye of a needle) продева́ть; вдева́ть (ни́тку в иго́лку). **2,** (string) нани́зывать. **3,** (cut grooves in, as a screw) нареза́ть. **4,** *in* thread one's way, пробира́ться (сквозь). —**hang by a thread,** висе́ть на волоске́.

threadbare *adj.* потёртый; потрёпанный; изно́шенный.

threat *n.* угро́за. *The threat of war,* угро́за войны́. *A threat to peace,* угро́за ми́ру. *He is always making threats,* он всегда́ угрожа́ет.

threaten *v.t.* грози́ть; угрожа́ть. *Don't threaten me!,* вы мне не грози́те! *Threaten to resign,* грози́ть вы́йти в отста́вку. *He threatened to kill me,* он грози́л уби́ть меня́. *Threaten the very existence of,* грози́ть са́мому существова́нию (+ *gen.*).

threatening *adj.* угрожа́ющий: *threatening gesture,* угрожа́ющий жест. *Threatening weather,* мра́чная пого́да.

three *adj.* три. —*n.* **1,** (cardinal number) три. **2,** (written number; school grade) тро́йка. **3,** *cards* тро́йка.

three-colored *adj.* трёхцве́тный.

three-dimensional *adj.* трёхме́рный; *(optics; photog.)* объёмный.

threefold *adj.* тройно́й. —*adv.* втро́е; втройне́.

three hundred три́ста. —**three-hundredth,** *adj.* трёхсо́тый.

three-legged *adj.* трено́гий.

three-quarter time трёхдо́льный разме́р.

three-room *adj.* трёхко́мнатный.

three-sided *adj.* трёхсторо́нний.

three-story *adj.* трёхэта́жный.

three-time *adj.* троекра́тный: *three-time champion,* троекра́тный чемпио́н.

three-way *adj.* тройно́й: *three-way exchange,* тройно́й обме́н.

three-wheel *adj.* трёхколёсный. *Also,* **three-wheeled.**

thresh *v.t.* молоти́ть.

thresher *n.* **1,** (one who threshes) молоти́льщик. **2,** (threshing machine) молоти́лка. **3,** (variety of shark) морска́я лиси́ца.

threshing *n.* молотьба́. *Threshing floor,* гумно́; ток.

threshold *n.* **1,** (doorstep) поро́г. **2,** *fig.* (beginning) поро́г; преддве́рие.

thrice *adv.* три́жды.

thrift *n.* бережли́вость; расчётливость; эконо́мность. —**thrifty,** *adj.* бережли́вый; расчётливый; эконо́мный.

thrill *v.t.* захва́тывать. —*n.* о́строе ощуще́ние. —**thriller,** *n.* захва́тывающий рома́н, фильм, *etc.* —**thrilling,** *adj.* захва́тывающий.

thrive *v.i.* процвета́ть.

throat *n.* го́рло. *Clear one's throat,* отка́шливаться. *Cut someone's throat,* перере́зать го́рло (+ *dat.*). —**cut one's own throat,** рыть самому́ себе́ я́му. —**jump down someone's throat,** набра́сываться на кого́-нибудь.

throaty *adj.* горлово́й; горта́нный.

throb *v.i.* си́льно би́ться; стуча́ть; пульси́ровать. *Throbbing pain,* ко́лющая боль. —*n.* бие́ние; стук; пульса́ция.

throe *n., usu. pl.* му́ки. *Throes of death,* (предсме́ртная) аго́ния.

thrombosis *n.* тромбо́з.

throne *n.* престо́л; трон. —*adj.* тро́нный: *throne room,* тро́нный зал.

throng *n.* толпа́. —*v.i.* толпи́ться; стека́ться. —*v.t.* заполня́ть: *people thronged the square,* лю́ди запо́лнили пло́щадь.

throttle *n.* дро́ссель. —*v.t.* души́ть.

through *prep.* **1,** (in and out of) че́рез; сквозь: *through a tunnel,* че́рез тунне́ль; *through the crowd,* сквозь толпу́. *Breathe through one's mouth,* дыша́ть ртом. ♦*With certain nouns* в: *through a window,* в окно́; *look through a telescope,* смотре́ть в телеско́п; *speak through one's nose,* говори́ть в нос. **2,** (in the midst of) по: *walk through the mud,* идти́ по гря́зи; *fly through the air,* лете́ть по во́здуху. **3,** (to various places in) по: *travel through France,* е́здить по Фра́нции. **4,** (up to and including) по (+ *acc.*): *from May through September,* с ма́я по сентя́брь. *I'm staying through Sunday,* я бу́ду здесь по воскресе́нье. **5,** [*usu.* **all through**] (throughout) в тече́ние всего́: *all through dinner,* в тече́ние всего́ обе́да. *All through the night,* всю ночь напролёт. **6,** (because of) по: *through no fault of mine,* не по мое́й вине́. **7,** (through the medium of) че́рез: *speak through an interpreter,* говори́ть че́рез перево́дчика. **8,** (by means of) путём; посре́дством. *Achieve one's goals through revolution,* дости́гнуть це́лей путём револю́ции. ♦*Often with the prefix* про-: *look through a report,* просмотре́ть докла́д; *go through a red light,* проскочи́ть кра́сный свет. *Pass through three stages of development,* проходи́ть три ста́дии разви́тия. *Less commonly* пере-: *leaf through a book,* перели́стывать книгу; *live through a crisis*, пережи́ть кри́зис. —*adj.* **1**, (direct) беспереса́дочный: *through flight*, беспереса́дочный полёт. **2**, (finished): *are you through?*, вы ко́нчили? —*adv.* **1**, (in space) наскво́зь: *soaked through*, промо́кший наскво́зь. *Let him through*, -пропусти́те его́. **2**, (in time) напролёт: *the whole night through*, всю ночь напролёт. —**through and through, 1**, (thoroughly; throughout) наскво́зь: *soaked through and through*, промо́кший наскво́зь. **2**, (completely; in every respect) соверше́нно; до конца́.

throughout *prep.* **1**, (in every part of) по всему́; по всей (+ *dat*): *throughout the country*, по всей стране́. **2**, (from the beginning to the end of) в тече́ние всего́/всей (+ *gen.*); в продолже́ние всего́/всей (+ *gen.*); на протяже́нии всего́/всей (+ *gen.*). —*adv.* повсю́ду; во всех отноше́ниях.

throw *v.t.* **1**, (toss) броса́ть; кида́ть. *Throw stones at*, забра́сывать камня́ми (+ *acc.*). *Throw into prison*, бро́сить в тюрьму́. *Throw troops into battle*, броса́ть войска́ в бой. **2**, *fol. by* **oneself** (lunge) бро́ситься; набро́ситься. *Throw oneself at*, набро́ситься на (+ *acc.*). *Throw oneself into someone's arms*, бро́ситься в чьи-нибудь объя́тия. **3**, (put on; lay over) набро́сить; наки́нуть: *throw a shawl over one's shoulders*, набро́сить/накину́ть шаль на пле́чи. **4**, (unseat, as a rider) сбра́сывать. **5**, (put into a certain condition) приводи́ть: *throw into confusion*, приводи́ть в замеша́тельство. **6**, *colloq.* (give, as a big party) задава́ть. —*v.i.* броса́ть; кида́ть. —*n.* **1**, (single act) бросо́к. **2**, (general act) мета́ние: *discus throw*, мета́ние ди́ска. —**throw away, 1**, (discard) выбра́сывать. **2**, (waste) расточа́ть. **3**, (lose; miss) пропуска́ть. —**throw back**, отбра́сывать; отки́дывать. —**throw off, 1**, (cast off) сбра́сывать. **2**, (disconcert) сбива́ть. **3**, (shake off; elude) отрыва́ться от. **4**, (emit) испуска́ть. —**throw open**, распа́хивать. —**throw out, 1**, (discard) выбра́сывать. **2**, (evict; eject) выгоня́ть. **3**, (put forth) предлага́ть. —**throw up, 1**, (construct) стро́ить; возводи́ть. *Throw up a bridge*, наводи́ть мост. **2**, (vomit) рвать: *he threw up*, его́ вы́рвало. **3**, *Throw up one's hands*, развести́ рука́ми.

throwaway *adj.* бро́совый.
thrower *n.* мета́тель.
throw-weight *n.* забра́сываемый вес.
thru *prep., adj. & adv.* = **through.**
thrush *n.* **1**, (bird) дрозд. **2**, (disease) моло́чница.
thrust *v.t.* **1**, (stick, as one's hands in one's pockets) сова́ть; засо́вывать. **2**, (plunge, as a dagger) вонза́ть. —*n.* **1**, (shove) толчо́к. **2**, (lunge) вы́пад. **3**, (of an engine, propeller, etc.) тя́га. **4**, *mil.* уда́р.
thruway *n.* автостра́да.
thud *n.* глухо́й звук. —*v.i.* па́дать с глухи́м зву́ком.
thug *n.* громи́ла; головоре́з.
thulium *n.* ту́лий.
thumb *n.* большо́й па́лец. —*v.t.* **1**, (soil by handling) захва́тывать (*pfv.* захвата́ть). **2**, *fol. by* **through** (leaf through) перели́стывать. **3**, *in* **thumb a ride**, *colloq.* "голосова́ть" на доро́ге. —**he is all thumbs**, у него́ всё из рук ва́лится. —**thumb one's nose at**, показа́ть нос (+ *dat.*). —**turn thumbs down on**, реши́тельно отклоня́ть. —**under the thumb of**, под башмако́м *or* под каблуко́м у.
thumbnail *n.* но́готь большо́го па́льца. —**thumbnail sketch**, кра́ткое описа́ние.

thumbscrew *n.* **1**, (screw turned by hand) бара́шек. **2**, (instrument of torture) тиски́ для больши́х па́льцев.
thumbtack *n.* кно́пка.
thump *n.* тяжёлый уда́р; тума́к. —*v.t.* колоти́ть. —*v.i.* колоти́ться: *my heart was thumping*, у меня́ се́рдце колоти́лось.
thunder *n.* гром. —*v.i.* **1**, (produce thunder) греме́ть. *It is thundering*, гром греми́т. **2**, (make or move with a loud noise) грохота́ть.
thunderbolt *n.* уда́р мо́лнии.
thunderclap *n.* уда́р гро́ма.
thundercloud *n.* грозова́я ту́ча.
thunderous *adj.* громово́й.
thundershower *n.* ли́вень.
thunderstorm *n.* гроза́.
thunderstruck *adj.* как гро́мом поражённый.
Thursday *n.* четве́рг.
thus *adv.* **1**, (in this manner) так; таки́м о́бразом. **2**, (hence) так; поэ́тому. **3**, (thereby) тем са́мым. —**thus far**, пока́ что; пока́ ещё.
thwart *v.t.* расстра́ивать; срыва́ть.
thy *poss.adj., archaic* твой.
thyme *n.* тимья́н; чабре́ц.
thymus *n.* зо́бная железа́.
thyroid *n.* [*also,* **thyroid gland**] щитови́дная железа́. —*adj.* щитови́дный.
ti *n., music* си.
tiara *n.* тиа́ра.
Tibetan *adj.* тибе́тский. —*n.* тибе́тский язы́к.
tibia *n.* больша́я берцо́вая кость.
tic *n.* тик: *nervous tic*, не́рвный тик.
tick *n.* **1**, (sound) ти́канье. **2**, (parasite) клещ. **3**, (mark) пти́чка; га́лочка. —*v.i.* ти́кать. —*v.t.* [*usu.* **tick off**] **1**, (check off) отмеча́ть пти́чкой/га́лочкой. **2**, (rattle off) отбараба́нить. **3**, *slang* (anger; annoy) разозли́ть.
ticker *n.* ти́ккер.
ticket *n.* **1**, (token of admission) биле́т: *theater tickets*, биле́ты в теа́тр. *Plane ticket*, биле́т на самолёт. *Tickets to a show/match*, биле́ты на спекта́кль/матч. **2**, (check; receipt) номеро́к; квита́нция. *Pawn ticket*, зало́говая квита́нция. **3**, (label; tag) этике́тка; ярлы́к. **4**, (notification of a violation) штраф. **5**, (electoral slate) спи́сок кандида́тов (како́й-нибудь па́ртии). —*v.t.* прикле́ивать этике́тку *or* ярлы́к к. —**ticket collector**, билетёр; контролёр. —**ticket office; ticket window**, биле́тная ка́сса.
ticking *n.* **1**, (sound) ти́канье. **2**, (material) тик.
tickle *v.t. & i.* щекота́ть: *don't tickle!*, не щекочи́! *My throat tickles*, у меня́ в го́рле перши́т. —*n.* щеко́тка; щекота́ние. —**be tickled to death**, захлёбываться от удово́льствия.
ticklish *adj.* **1**, (sensitive to tickling): *be ticklish*, боя́ться щеко́тки. **2**, (delicate; tricky) щекотли́вый. —**ticklishness**, *n.* щекотли́вость.
tick-tack-toe *n.* (игра́ в) кре́стики и но́лики.
tidal *adj.* прили́вный. —**tidal wave**, прили́вная волна́; волна́ прили́ва.
tidbit *n.* ла́комый кусо́чек.
tiddlywinks *n.* блёшки.
tide *n.* **1**, (rise and fall of waters) прили́вы и отли́вы. *Flood tide*, прили́в. *Ebb tide*, отли́в. *High tide*, вы́сшая то́чка прили́ва. *Low tide*, ни́зшая то́чка отли́ва. *The tide is in/out*, сейча́с прили́в/отли́в. **2**, (drift of

events) делá; ход собы́тий. *The tide has turned,* делá при́няли ино́й оборóт. *Turn the tide,* измени́ть ход собы́тий. *Go against the tide,* идти́ прóтив течéния. —*v.t.* [*usu.* **tide over**] подкрепля́ть. *This will tide us over till spring,* э́того нам хвáтит до весны́.

tidewater *n.* прили́вная водá.

tidiness *n.* опря́тность; аккурáтность.

tidings *n.pl.* вéсти; нóвости; извéстия.

tidy *adj.* **1,** (neat) опря́тный; аккурáтный. **2,** *colloq.* (considerable) поря́дочный; изря́дный; крýгленький. —*v.t.* [*usu.* **tidy up**] убирáть; прибирáть; приводи́ть в поря́док.

tie *v.t.* **1,** (fasten) завя́зывать: *tie one's shoelaces,* завя́зывать шнурки́. *Tie one's shoes,* шнуровáть боти́нки. *Tie one's tie,* повя́зывать гáлстук. *Tie a knot,* завя́зывать у́зел. *Tie a horse to a post,* привязáть лóшадь к столбý. *Tie a rope around something,* обвязáть чтó-нибудь верёвкой. *Tie someone's hands (fig.),* связáть комý-нибудь рýки. **2,** *fol. by* **to** (confine; restrict) привя́зывать (к): *she is tied to the kitchen,* онá привя́зана к кýхне. **3,** (link) свя́зывать: *closely tied to,* тéсно свя́занный с. **4,** *sports* сыгрáть вничью́ с; сдéлать ничью́ с. *Tie the score,* сравня́ть счёт. *Tie a record,* повторя́ть рекóрд. —*v.i.* **1,** (be tied) завя́зываться: *the apron ties in front,* передник завя́зывается спéреди. **2,** *sports:* **tie for first place,** подели́ть пéрвое и вторóе мéсто. —*n.* **1,** (necktie) гáлстук. **2,** (bond) связь; *pl.* у́зы. *Ties of friendship,* у́зы дрýжбы. **3,** (draw; stalemate) ничья́. **4,** *R.R.* шпáла. —**tie down,** привя́зывать. —**tie up, 1,** (tie securely) привя́зывать: *the dog is tied up,* собáка привя́зана. **2,** (tie with a string) перевя́зывать. **3,** (bind hand and foot) связáть по рукáм и ногáм. **4,** (moor) причáливать; швартовáться. **5,** (obstruct; halt) тормози́ть: *tie up traffic,* тормози́ть у́личное движéние. **6,** (keep busy) занимáть: *I'm tied up right now,* я сейчáс зáнят.

tiepin *n.* закóлка. *Also,* **tie clasp.**

tier *n.* я́рус. —**tiered,** *adj.* я́русный.

tie-up *n.* **1,** (stoppage) останóвка. **2,** (jam, as of traffic) затóр (у́личного движéния); прóбка.

tiff *n.* размóлвка; перебрáнка.

tiger *n.* тигр. —*adj.* тигрóвый: *tiger skin,* тигрóвая шкýра.

tiger lily тигрóвая ли́лия.

tight *adj.* **1,** (taut; fast) тугóй: *tight spring,* тугáя пружи́на. **2,** (fitting closely) тéсный; ýзкий. *These shoes are tight,* э́ти тýфли жмут. **3,** (crowded; cramped) тéсный: *tight quarters,* тéсное помещéние. **4,** (strict; rigid) стрóгий: *tight control,* стрóгий контрóль. **5,** (affording little leeway) жёсткий: *tight schedule,* жёсткий грáфик; жёсткое расписáние. **6,** (difficult) пи́ковый: *a tight spot,* пи́ковое положéние. **7,** *colloq.* (stingy) скупóй. **8,** *slang* (drunk) подвы́пивший. —*adv.* **1,** (taut) тýго. **2,** (firmly) крéпко: *hold tight!,* держи́тесь крéпко! **3,** (with no openings) нáглухо: *sealed up tight,* нáглухо закры́т. —**sit tight,** выжидáть. —**sleep tight!,** спи́те спокóйно!

tighten *v.t.* **1,** (pull tight; make taut) натя́гивать; затя́гивать; стя́гивать. *Tighten a rope/spring,* натя́гивать верёвку/пружи́ну. *Tighten the strings on a violin,* натя́гивать стрýны на скри́пке. *Tighten a knot,* затя́гивать *or* стя́гивать у́зел. **2,** (turn to a tight position) зави́нчивать; завёртывать: *tighten a screw,* зави́нчивать/завёртывать гáйку. *Tighten a faucet,* завёр-

тывать крáн. **3,** (compress; close) сжимáть; смыкáть: *tighten the ring around,* сжимáть/смыкáть кольцó вокрýг. *Tighten one's grip,* сжимáть крéпче. —*v.i.* **1,** (become taut) натя́гиваться. **2,** (tense up) напрягáться. **3,** (become smaller; close in) сжимáться; смыкáться. —**tighten one's belt, 1,** *literally* затянýться пóясом. **2,** (be more frugal) класть зýбы на пóлку. —**tighten the screws,** зави́нчивать гáйки.

tight-fisted *adj.* скупóй; скáредный; прижи́мистый.

tight-lipped *adj.* зáмкнутый.

tightly *adv.* **1,** (tight) тýго. **2,** (firmly) прóчно. **3,** (with no openings) нáглухо.

tightness *n.* теснотá. *I feel a tightness in my chest,* мне тесни́т грудь.

tightrope *n.* канáт. —**tightrope walker,** канатохóдец; эквилибри́ст.

tights *n.pl.* трикó.

tightwad *n.,* *slang* скопидóм; скупердя́й.

tigress *n.* тигри́ца.

tilde *n.* ти́льда.

tile *n.* **1,** (glazed slab) кáфель; изразéц. **2,** (roof tile) черепи́ца; (floor tile) пли́тка. —*v.t.* крыть черепи́цей.

tiled *adj.* **1,** (of a stove) кáфельный; изразцóвый; (of a roof) черепи́чный; (of a floor) пли́точный.

till *prep.* до: *till now,* до сих пор; *till then,* до тех пор; *till tomorrow,* до зáвтра. *From morning till night,* с утрá до вéчера. *Till then!,* покá! *Till we meet again!,* до слéдующей встрéчи. —*conj.* покá не: *till he arrives,* покá он не придёт. *She is not coming till Sunday,* онá придёт тóлько в воскресéнье. —*n.* (cash box) кáсса. —*v.t.* обрáбатывать; возделывать (зéмлю).

tillage *n.* обрабóтка.

tiller *n.* земледéлец.

tilt *v.t.* наклоня́ть: *tilt one's head to one side,* наклоня́ть гóлову нáбок. *Tilt a chair backward,* наклоня́ть стул назáд. —*v.i.* **1,** (slant) наклоня́ться. **2,** *fol. by* **over** (tip over) опроки́дываться. —*n.* **1,** (slant) наклóн. **2,** (joust) поеди́нок. —**full tilt,** пóлным хóдом; во весь опóр.

timber *n.* лес; лесоматериáл; древеси́на. —**timber line,** грани́ца распространéния лéса.

timbre *n.* тембр.

time *n.* **1,** (general term) врéмя: *all the time,* всё врéмя; *in time,* вó-время; *any time,* в любóе врéмя. *Dinner time,* обéденное врéмя. *I have no time,* у меня́ нет врéмени; мне нéкогда. **2,** (occasion) раз: *three times,* три рáза; *this time,* на э́тот раз. **3,** (period; interval) срок: *in a short time,* в корóткий срок. **4,** *often pl.* (historical period or conditions) временá: *hard times,* тяжёлые временá. *In Dante's time,* во временá Дáнте. *Since ancient times,* с дáвних времён. *Times have changed,* временá измени́лись. **5,** *music* такт: *keep time,* отбивáть такт. *Three-quarter time,* трёхдóльный размéр. **6,** *pl., in multiplication,* rendered by двáжды, три́жды, пя́тью, шéстью, *etc.:* *three times seven is twenty-one,* три́жды семь — двáдцать оди́н. —*v.t.* **1,** (set for a certain time; set to coincide with) приурóчивать (к). **2,** (measure the time of) хронометри́ровать. —**ahead of time,** заблаговрéменно. —**at no time,** никогдá; ни рáзу. —**at one time, 1,** (simultaneously) одноврéменно; рáзом. **2,** (at a certain time in the past) однó врéмя. —**at the same time, 1,** (simultaneously) в то же врéмя; однóвре́менно. **2,** (besides) вме́сте с тем. —**at times,** иногда́; времена́ми. —**do time,** *colloq.* отбыва́ть срок. —**for the time being,** пока́; до поры́ до вре́мени. —**from time to time,** вре́мя от вре́мени; по времена́м. —**have a good time,** хорошо́ провести́ вре́мя. —**in due time,** в своё вре́мя. —**in good time,** своевре́менно. —**in no time,** в два счёта. —**in one's time,** в своё вре́мя. *I have seen a lot in my time,* я мно́го повида́л на своём веку́. —**in time, 1,** (on time) во́время. **2,** (eventually) со вре́менем. —**it is time,** пора́: *it is time to go,* пора́ идти́. —**many a time,** мно́го раз. —**once upon a time,** одна́жды; жил-был. —**one at a time,** по одному́; поодино́чке. —**on time, 1,** (punctually) во́время. **2,** (on installment) в рассро́чку. —**take one's time,** не спеши́ть; не торопи́ться. —**time after time; time and time again,** раз за ра́зом. —**what time is it?,** кото́рый тепе́рь час?; ско́лько вре́мени сейча́с?

time bomb бо́мба заме́дленного де́йствия.

time clock та́бельные часы́.

time-consuming *adj.* отнима́ющий мно́го вре́мени.

time exposure больша́я вы́держка.

time-honored *adj.* освящённый века́ми.

timekeeper *n.* **1,** (one who records the hours worked by employees) та́бельщик. **2,** *sports* хронометри́ст.

timeless *adj.* вневре́менный.

timely *adj.* своевре́менный; уме́стный. —**timeliness,** *n.* своевре́менность; уме́стность.

time-out *n.* переры́в.

timepiece *n.* часы́; хроно́метр.

timer *n.* **1,** (timepiece) хроно́метр. **2,** (timekeeper) хронометри́ст.

time study хронометра́ж.

timetable *n.* расписа́ние; гра́фик.

time trouble *chess* цейтно́т.

time zone часово́й по́яс.

timid *adj.* ро́бкий; засте́нчивый; боязли́вый. —**timidity,** *n.* ро́бость; засте́нчивость. —**timidly,** *adv.* ро́бко.

timing *n.* расчёт вре́мени; синхрониза́ция.

timorous *adj.* боязли́вый; пугли́вый.

timothy *n., bot.* тимофе́евка. *Also,* **timothy grass.**

timpani *also,* **tympani** *n. pl.* тимпа́н.

tin *n.* **1,** (metal) о́лово. **2,** (tin plate) жесть. **3,** [*also,* **tin can**] (container) ба́нка; жестя́нка. —*adj.* оловя́нный; жестяно́й. —*v.t.* луди́ть.

tincture *n.* тинкту́ра; насто́йка.

tinder *n.* трут. —**tinderbox,** *n.* порохова́я бо́чка (*fig.*).

tine *n.* зубе́ц.

tin foil стани́оль.

tinge *n.* оттёнок; при́месь; налёт. —*v.t.* **1,** (tint) подкра́шивать. *Tinged with blue,* с голубова́тым отте́нком. **2,** (give a slight trace to) придава́ть отте́нок: *her voice was tinged with sadness,* в её го́лосе чу́вствовался отте́нок гру́сти. *Admiration tinged with envy,* восхище́ние с при́месью за́висти.

tingle *v.i.* пощи́пывать (*impers.*): *my cheeks are tingling,* щёки у меня́ пощи́пывает. *Tingle with excitement,* трепета́ть от возбужде́ния.

tinker *n.* ме́дник. —*v.i.* (putter) вози́ться.

tinkle *v.i.* звя́кать. —*v.t.* звя́кать (+ *instr.*). —*n.* звя́канье.

tinny *adj.* оловя́нный. *Tinny sound,* металли́ческий звук.

tin plate жесть. —**tin-plate,** *v.t.* луди́ть. —**tin-plated,** *adj.* лужёный.

tinsel *n.* **1,** (thin strips of something shiny) блёстки. **2,** (something superficially showy) мишура́.

tinsmith *n.* луди́льщик; жестя́нщик.

tint *n.* отте́нок. —*v.t.* подкра́шивать.

tintype *n.* ферроти́пия.

tiny *adj.* кро́хотный; кро́шечный; малю́сенький.

tip *n.* **1,** (point; end) ко́нчик. **2,** (piece attached to the end of something) наконе́чник. **3,** (gratuity) чаевы́е. *Give someone a tip,* дава́ть (+ *dat.*) на чай. **4,** (piece of advice) сове́т. —*v.t.* **1,** (tilt) наклоня́ть. **2,** *fol. by* **over** (overturn) опроки́дывать. **3,** (give a gratuity to) дава́ть (+ *dat.*) на чай. **4,** *fol. by* **off** (notify; warn) сообща́ть; предупрежда́ть. —*v.i.* **1,** (tilt) наклоня́ться. **2,** *fol. by* **over** (overturn) опроки́дываться. —**it is on the tip of my tongue,** э́то ве́ртится у меня́ на языке́. —**tip one's hand,** раскры́ть свои́ ка́рты. —**tip the scales (at),** ве́сить.

tipoff *n., colloq.* намёк; предупрежде́ние.

tipple *v.i.* выпива́ть. —**tippler,** *n.* пья́ница.

tipsy *adj.* подвы́пивший; под хмелько́м; навеселе́.

tiptoe *n.* цы́почки: *on tiptoe; on one's tiptoes,* на цы́почках; на цы́почки. —*v.i.* ходи́ть на цы́почках.

tiptop *adj.* отли́чный: *in tiptop shape,* в отли́чном состоя́нии.

tirade *n.* тира́да.

tire[1] *v.i.* **1,** (become weary) устава́ть; утомля́ться: *tire easily,* бы́стро устава́ть/утомля́ться. **2,** *fol. by* **of** (lose interest in) устава́ть (+ *inf.*). *I never tire of looking at...,* не могу́ насмотре́ться *or* налюбова́ться на (+ *acc.*). —*v.t.* утомля́ть.

tire[2] *also,* **tyre** *n.* ши́на; покры́шка.

tired *adj.* **1,** (fatigued) уста́лый. *I am tired,* я уста́л(а). *Get tired,* устава́ть. **2,** *fol. by* **of** (impatient; no longer willing) *I am tired of always waiting for him,* мне надое́ло всегда́ ждать его́.

tireless *adj.* неутоми́мый. —**tirelessly,** *adv.* не уставая́; без у́стали.

tiresome *adj.* **1,** (tiring) утоми́тельный. **2,** (annoying) надое́дливый.

tiring *adj.* утоми́тельный.

tissue *n.* **1,** (structural material) ткань: *nerve tissue,* не́рвная ткань. **2,** (piece of soft absorbent paper) бума́га: *toilet tissue,* туале́тная бума́га. **3,** *fig.* (web, as of lies) сплете́ние (лжи). —**tissue paper,** папиро́сная бума́га.

tit *n.* (titmouse) сини́ца. —**tit for tat,** той же моне́той.

titan *n.* тита́н. —**titanic,** *adj.* титани́ческий.

titanium *n.* тита́н.

tithe *n.* десяти́на.

titillate *v.t.* щекота́ть. —**titillation,** *n.* щекота́ние; щеко́тка.

title *n.* **1,** (name, as of a book) загла́вие; назва́ние. **2,** (designation of rank or profession) зва́ние. **3,** (designation of nobility) ти́тул. **4,** *law* пра́во. **5,** *sports* чемпио́нское зва́ние. *The heavyweight title,* зва́ние чемпио́на по тяжёлому ве́су. **6,** (subtitle) титр. —*v.t.* озагла́вливать. —**title page,** загла́вный лист; ти́тульный лист. —**title role,** загла́вная роль.

titled *adj.* титуло́ванный.

titmouse *n.* сини́ца.

titter *v.i.* хихи́кать. —*n.* хихи́канье.

tittle-tattle *n.* тáры-бáры.

titular *adj.* номинáльный.

TNT тол; тротúл; тринитротолуóл.

to *prep.* **1,** (indicating destination) в (+ *acc.*): *go to the store/theater,* идтú в магазúн/теáтр; *go to London/ England,* поéхать в Лóндон/Áнглию. ♦ *With certain nouns* на: *go to the post office,* идтú на пóчту; *go to work,* éхать на рабóту. **2,** (toward) к: *come to me,* идú ко мне; *walk to the river,* идтú к рекé. **3,** (as far as; till) до: *to the end of the street,* до концá ýлицы; *soaked to the skin,* промóкший до костéй; *to a certain extent,* до нéкоторой стéпени; *from four to six o'clock,* от четырёх до шестú часóв. *To this day,* по сей день. **4,** *introducing the indirect object, rendered by the dative case: it seems to me,* мне кáжется; *I gave the letter to him,* я дал емý письмó. **5,** *used to form the infinitive: to read,* читáть; *to dance,* танцевáть. *An operation to remove a bullet,* операция по удалéнию пýли. **6,** (in one's behavior toward) к: *he is very kind to her,* он óчень добр к ней. *Polite to one's relatives,* вéжлив со своúми рóдственниками. **7,** (producing or resulting in) к: *to my surprise,* к моемý удивлéнию. **8,** (belonging to) от: *the key to the room,* ключ от кóмнаты. **9,** *in toasts* за (+ *acc.*): *drink to someone's health,* пить за здорóвье кого-нибудь. **10,** (to the accompaniment of) под (+ *acc.*): *dance to the music,* танцевáть под мýзыку. **11,** *used in telling time: a quarter to three,* без чéтверти три. **12,** *with various nouns and verbs* в: *introduction to physics,* введéние в фúзику; *shift to the offensive,* переходúть в наступлéние. **13,** *with various nouns and verbs* на: *spring to one's feet,* вскочúть нá ноги; *tear to pieces,* разорвáть на кускú; *come to someone's aid,* прийтú на пóмощь (+ *dat.*); *from Russian to English,* с рýсского на англúйский. **14,** *in various constructions* к: *face to face,* лицóм к лицý; *deaf to our pleas,* глух к нáшим прóсьбам; *come to an end,* приходúть к концý; *tie to a post,* привязáть к столбý; *sentence to death,* приговорúть к смéртной кáзни. **15,** *in certain combinations* для: *open to the public,* открýт для пýблики; *be of interest to all,* представлять интерéс для всех; *mean a great deal to,* мнóго знáчить для. —**as to,** что касáется. —**to and fro,** взад и вперёд.

toad *n.* жáба.

toadstool *n.* погáнка.

toady *n.* подхалúм. —*v.i.* подхалúмничать (пéред). —**toadyism,** *n.* подхалúмство.

toast *n.* **1,** (toasted bread) поджáренный хлеб. **2,** (drink in honor of someone) тост. —*v.t.* **1,** (brown) поджáривать. **2,** (pay tribute to) провозглашáть тост за (+ *acc.*).

toaster *n.* тóстер.

toastmaster *n.* тамадá.

tobacco *n.* табáк. —*adj.* табáчный: *tobacco leaves,* табáчные лúстья. —**tobacco grower,** табаковóд. —**tobacco pouch,** кисéт.

toboggan *n.* салáзки. —*v.i.* катáться на салáзках.

tocsin *n.* набáт.

today *n. & adv.* сегóдня. *What is today's date?,* какóе сегóдня числó? *Today's lesson,* сегóдняшний урóк.

toddle *v.i.* ковылять. —**toddler,** *n.* ребёнок, начинáющий ходúть.

toe *n.* **1,** (digit of the foot) пáлец ногú; пáлец на ногé. **2,** (tip of a stocking or shoe) носóк. —**on one's toes,**

начекý; насторожé. —**toe the line** (*or* **mark**), **1,** *sports* встать на стáртовую лúнию. **2,** (conform to the rules) ходúть по стрýнке.

toenail *n.* нóготь на пáльце ногú.

toffee *also,* **toffy** *n.* тянýчка; ирúс.

toga *n.* тóга.

together *adv.* вмéсте: *go together,* идтú вмéсте. *Tie together,* связывать. *Paste together,* склéивать. *Rub two sticks together,* терéть две пáлки друг о дрýга. —**together with,** вмéсте с.

toil *n.* (тяжёлый) труд. —*v.i.* трудúться. —**toiler,** *n.* трýженик.

toilet *n.* **1,** (receptacle) унитáз. **2,** (washroom) убóрная; туалéт. **3,** (personal appearance) туалéт. —*adj.* туалéтный. —**toilet paper,** туалéтная бумáга. —**toilet seat,** стульчáк. —**toilet water,** туалéтная водá.

toiletries *n. pl.* туалéтные принадлéжности.

token *n.* **1,** (sign; symbol) знак; залóг: *as a token of,* в знак *or* в залóг (+ *gen.*). **2,** (keepsake) сувенúр. **3,** (coin; counter) жетóн. —*adj.* символúческий: *token payment,* символúческий взнос. —**by the same token,** рáвным óбразом.

tolerable *adj.* **1,** (endurable) терпúмый; снóсный. **2,** (passable) снóсный; прилúчный. —**tolerably,** *adv.* [*also,* **tolerably well**] снóсно.

tolerance *n.* **1,** (toleration) терпúмость. **2,** *mech.* дóпуск.

tolerant *adj.* терпúмый. *Be tolerant of,* относúться терпúмо к.

tolerate *v.t.* **1,** (bear; endure) терпéть. **2,** (allow; permit) допускáть. —**toleration,** *n.* терпúмость.

toll *n.* **1,** (fee) сбор. **2,** (peal of a bell) звон. **3,** (extent of losses) потéри. *The hurricane took a heavy toll of lives,* урагáн унёс мнóго человéческих жúзней. —*adj.* плáтный: *toll bridge,* плáтный мост. *Toll call,* междугорóдный телефóнный разговóр. *Toll collector,* сбóрщик. —*v.t.* звонúть в. —*v.i.* звонúть: *for whom the bell tolls,* по ком звонúт кóлокол. —**take its toll,** брать своё: *time had taken its toll,* врéмя брáло своё.

tollgate *n.* застáва (где взимáется сбор).

toluene *n.* толуóл.

tomahawk *n.* томагáвк.

tomato *n.* помидóр; томáт. —*adj.* томáтный: *tomato juice,* томáтный сок. *Tomato paste,* томáт-пáста.

tomb *n.* гробнúца. —**Tomb of the Unknown Soldier,** могúла Неизвéстного солдáта.

tomboy *n.* сорванéц.

tombstone *n.* надгрóбный кáмень; надгрóбная плитá.

tomcat *n.* кот.

tome *n.* том.

tomfoolery *n.* **1,** (foolish behavior) дурáчества. **2,** (nonsense) чепухá.

Tommy gun автомáт.

tommyrot *n., slang* вздор; галиматья.

tomorrow *n. & adv.* зáвтра. *Beginning tomorrow,* начинáя с зáвтрашнего дня. —*adj.* [*usu.* **tomorrow's**] зáвтрашний: *tomorrow's date,* зáвтрашнее числó. —**the day after tomorrow,** послезáвтра. —**tomorrow morning,** зáвтра ýтром. —**tomorrow evening; tomorrow night,** зáвтра вéчером.

tomtit *n.* синúца.

tom-tom *n.* тамтáм.

ton *n.* тóнна.

tonal *adj.* тонáльный. —**tonality**, *n.* тонáльность.

tone *n.* **1,** (quality of sound or color) тон: *light tones,* свéтлые тонá. *Tone of voice,* тон гóлоса. **2,** *physiol.* тóнус: *muscle tone,* мышечный тóнус. **3,** *fig.* (general tenor) тон: *set the tone,* задáть тон. —*v.t.* **1,** *fol. by* **down** (moderate; soften) смягчáть; тушевáть. **2,** *fol. by* **up,** *physiol.* тонизировать.

tone poem симфоническая поэма.

tongs *n. pl.* щипцы; клéщи.

tongue *n.* язык. *Loose tongue,* язык без костéй. *Mother tongue,* роднóй язык. *Smoked tongue,* копчёный язык. *Tongue of a shoe,* язычóк ботинка. *Tongues of flame,* языки плáмени. —**hold one's tongue,** придержáть язык; проглотить язык; держáть язык за зубáми. —**with tongue in cheek,** в шýтку.

tongue-lashing *n.* нагонáй; разнóс.

tongue-tie *n.* косноязычие. —*v.t.* связáть язык (+ *dat.*). —**tongue-tied,** *adj.* косноязычный.

tongue twister скороговóрка.

tonic *n.* укрепляющее срéдство. —*adj.* тонический.

tonight *n. & adv.* сегóдня вéчером.

tonnage *n.* тоннáж.

tonsil *n.* миндáлина; миндалевидная железá; глáнда.

tonsillectomy *n.* удалéние миндáлин.

tonsillitis *n.* воспалéние миндáлин.

tonsorial *adj.* парикмáхерский.

tonsure *n.* тонзýра.

too *adv.* **1,** (also; as well) тóже; тáкже. *I'm sorry too,* мне тóже жаль. **2,** (excessively) слишком: *too far,* слишком далекó. —**not too,** не óчень: *not too clever,* не óчень умён. —**only too,** тóлько: *I will be only too happy to...,* я бýду тóлько рад (+ *inf.*). —**too bad,** *see* **bad.** —**too much,** слишком мнóго; слишком. —**too much for,** не под силу (+ *dat.*).

tool *n.* **1,** (hand-held implement) инструмéнт: *carpenter's tools,* плóтничьи инструмéнты. **2,** (anything that serves as a tool) орýдие: *tools of production,* орýдия произвóдства. **3,** (stooge) орýдие; марионéтка. —*v.t.* **1,** (shape with a tool) обрабáтывать. **2,** *fol. by* **up** (provide with tools) оборýдовать инструмéнтами. —*v.i.* [*usu.* **tool along**] (ride; drive) éхать; катиться. —**toolbox,** *n.* ящик для инструмéнтов. —**toolmaker,** *n.* инструментáльщик.

toot *n.* гудóк. —*v.t. & i.* гудéть.

tooth *n.* **1,** (in the mouth) зуб (*pl.* зýбы). **2,** (projecting point, as of a saw) зуб (*pl.* зýбья); зубéц. —**armed to the teeth,** вооружённый до зубóв. —**in the teeth of,** вопреки; наперекóр. *In the teeth of the wind,* прямо прóтив вéтра. —**show one's teeth,** покáзывать кóгти. —**tooth and nail,** изо всех сил; всéми силами.

toothache *n.* зубнáя боль. *I have a toothache,* у меня болят зýбы.

toothbrush *n.* зубнáя щётка.

toothed *adj.* зубчáтый.

toothless *adj.* беззýбый.

toothpaste *n.* зубнáя пáста.

toothpick *n.* зубочистка.

tooth powder зубнóй порошóк.

toothy *adj.* зубáстый.

top *n.* **1,** (highest part) верхýшка; вершина; верх; макýшка. *At the top of,* на верхý (+ *gen.*). *At the top of the page,* вверхý страницы. *From the top,* свéрху.

2, (lid; cover) крышка. **3,** (toy) волчóк. **4,** *pl.* (aboveground part of a plant) ботвá. —*adj.* **1,** (highest) вéрхний: *on the top shelf,* на вéрхней пóлке. **2,** (best) лýчший; пéрвый: *top pupil,* лýчший/пéрвый ученик. —*v.t.* **1,** (be at the top of) стоять пéрвым в списке. **2,** (place something on top of) покрывáть. *Top fruit with whipped cream,* покрывáть фрýкты взбитыми сливками. **3,** (exceed; surpass) превышáть; превосходить. **4,** *fol. by* **off** (climax) закáнчивать. —**at top speed,** во весь опóр. —**blow one's top,** *colloq.* взорвáться. —**from top to bottom,** свéрху дóнизу. *Come out on top,* прийти пéрвым; взять верх. —**on top,** наверхý. —**on top of,** **1,** (on) на. **2,** (in addition to) крóме; сверх. *On top of everything (else),* сверх всегó. **3,** (following upon) вслед за. **4,** (in control of) на высотé (+ *gen.*): *on top of the situation,* на высотé положéния. —**on top of the world,** *colloq.* на седьмóм нéбе; на верхý блажéнства. —**sleep like a top,** спать как сурóк. —**to top it off,** в довершéние всегó.

topaz *n.* топáз. —*adj.* топáзовый.

topcoat *n.* пальтó.

topflight *adj.* первоклáссный; превосхóдный.

topgallant *n.* [*also,* **topgallant sail**] брáмсель. —**topgallant mast,** брам-стéньга.

top hat цилиндр.

topic *n.* тéма; предмéт.

topical *adj.* **1,** (pert. to a topic) тематический. **2,** (of current interest) актуáльный.

topknot *n.* хохóл.

topmast *n.* стéньга.

topnotch *adj., colloq.* первоклáссный.

topography *n.* топогрáфия. —**topographer**, *n.* топóграф. —**topographical,** *adj.* топографический.

topology *n.* тополóгия.

topple *v.t.* **1,** (overturn) валить; опрокидывать. **2,** (overthrow) свергáть. —*v.i.* [*usu.* **topple over**] валиться; опрокидываться.

topsail *n.* тóпсель; мáрсель.

top-secret *adj.* совершéнно секрéтный.

topside *adv.* на пáлубе. —**topsides,** *n. pl.* надвóдная часть.

topsoil *n.* вéрхний слой пóчвы; пóчвенный покрóв.

topsy-turvy *adv.* вверх дном; шиворот-навыворот.

toque *n.* ток.

Torah *n.* тóра.

torch *n.* **1,** (flaming light) фáкел. **2,** (device used in welding and soldering) горéлка: *acetylene torch,* ацетилéновая горéлка. **3,** *Brit.* (flashlight) кармáнный фонáрь. **4,** *fig.* (source of enlightenment) фáкел; свéточ: *the torch of knowledge,* фáкел/свéточ знáния. —**torchbearer,** *n.* фáкельщик.

torchlight *n.* свет фáкела. *Torchlight procession,* фáкельное шéствие.

toreador *n.* тореадóр.

torment *v.t.* мýчить. —*n.* мýка; мучéние. —**tormentor,** *n.* мучитель.

tornado *n.* смерч.

torpedo *n.* торпéда. —*v.t.* торпедировать. —**torpedo boat,** миноносец.

torpid *adj.* **1,** (sluggish) вялый. **2,** (numb) онемéлый.

torpor *n.* оцепенéние; отупéние.

torrent *n.* потóк. —**torrential,** *adj.* проливнóй.

torrid *adj.* **1,** (scorching) палящий. **2,** *fig.* (heated; ardent) горячий. —**Torrid Zone,** тропический пóяс.

torsion *n.* кручёние.

torso *n.* **1,** (of the human body) тýловище. **2,** (statue) торс.

tort *n.* правонарушёние.

tortoise *n.* черепáха.

tortoise shell черепáха. —**tortoise-shell,** *adj.* черепáховый.

tortuous *adj.* извúлистый.

torture *n.* **1,** (inflicting of pain) пы́тка; истязáние. **2,** *fig.* (agony) мýка: *sheer/pure torture,* настоя́щая мýка. —*v.t.* подвергáть пы́тке; пытáть; истязáть. —**torture chamber,** застёнок.

torturer *n.* истязáтель.

Tory *n.* тóри.

toss *v.t.* **1,** (throw) бросáть; кидáть; метáть. *Toss one's hat in the air,* брóсить шля́пу в вóздух. **2,** (flip, as a coin) подбрáсывать (монéту). **3,** (jerk upward, as the head) вскúдывать. **4,** (fling about) подбрáсывать: *the waves tossed the ship,* вóлны подбрáсывали сýдно. **5,** *fol. by* **off** (drink down) вы́пить зáлпом. —*v.i.* **1,** (be thrown about) качáть; бросáть; швыря́ть *(impers): the boat is tossing,* лóдку качáет/бросáет/ швыря́ет. **2,** (shift about restlessly) метáться: *toss in one's sleep,* метáться во сне. —*n.* бросóк. *Toss of a coin,* жеребьёвка. —**toss aside,** отбрáсывать. —**toss out,** выбрáсывать; вышвы́ривать.

tot *n.* малы́ш.

total *n.* сýмма; итóг; *(at the bottom of a column of figures)* итогó. *A total of...,* в óбщей слóжности. —*adj.* **1,** (overall) óбщий: *the total amount/cost,* óбщая сýмма/стóимость. **2,** (complete; utter) пóлный: *total victory,* пóлная побéда. *Total eclipse,* пóлное затмéние. *The house is a total loss,* от дóма ничегó не остáлось. **3,** (all-out, as of war) тотáльный. —*v.t.* **1,** (add up) суммúровать; подытóживать; подводúть итóг (+ *dat.*). **2,** (amount to) составля́ть. **3,** *slang* (demolish) разбúть вдрéбезги.

totalitarian *adj.* тоталитáрный. —**totalitarianism,** *n.* тоталитарúзм.

totality *n.* совокýпность.

totalizator *n.* тотализáтор.

totally *adv.* пóлностью; целикóм; совершéнно.

tote *v.t., colloq.* нестú; тащúть. *Tote a gun,* имéть при себé оружие.

totem *n.* тотéм. —**totemism,** *n.* тотемúзм.

totter *v.i.* шатáться; ковыля́ть.

toucan *n.* тукáн.

touch *v.t.* **1,** (place one's hand on) трóгать: *don't touch me!,* не трóгай меня́! **2,** (come into contact with) касáться: *touch bottom,* коснýться дна. **3,** *usu. neg.* (eat some of) притрáгиваться к; прикасáться к. **4,** (border) соприкасáться с. **5,** (injure slightly) трóнуть *(impers.): frost touched the plants,* морóзом трóнуло растéния. **6,** (move emotionally) трóгать; растрóгать. *Touch someone's heart,* брать зá сердце *or* зá душу. —*v.i.* трóгать: *"do not touch",* не трóгать! —*n.* **1,** (act of touching; feeling of being touched) прикосновéние. **2,** (sense of touch) осязáние. *To the touch,* на óщупь. **3,** (tinge; dash) прúмесь; налёт. **4,** (slight attack, as of illness) лёгкий прúступ. **5,** *music* тушé. **6,** *in* **finishing touches,** послéдние штрихú. —**in touch with, 1,** (in communication with) в контáкте с. *Get in touch with,* связáться с. *Keep in touch with,* поддéрживать связь с. **2,** (informed about) в кýрсе (+ *gen.*). —**lose touch with,** потеря́ть связь с; оторвáться от.

—**touch down,** приземля́ться. —**touch off, 1,** (detonate) взрывáть. **2,** (initiate; trigger) вызывáть. —**touch on** *or* **upon,** затрáгивать; касáться. —**touch up,** подкрáшивать.

touched *adj.* **1,** (affected with emotion) трóнут; растрóганный. **2,** *colloq.* (unbalanced) трóнутый.

touchiness *n.* обúдчивость.

touching *adj.* трóгательный.

touch-me-not *n.* недотрóга.

touchstone *n.* **1,** (testing stone) пробúрный кáмень; оселóк. **2,** *fig.* (criterion; standard) прóбный кáмень; оселóк.

touch-type *v.i.* печáтать на машúнке вслепýю. —**touch-typing,** *n.* слепóй мéтод печáтания на машúнке.

touchy *adj.* **1,** (easily offended) обúдчивый. **2,** (delicate) щекотлúвый.

tough *adj.* **1,** (firm; durable) прóчный: *tough leather,* прóчная кóжа. **2,** (hard to chew) жёсткий: *tough meat,* жёсткое мя́со. **3,** (difficult) трýдный: *tough job,* трýдная задáча. **4,** (robust; rugged) вынóсливый. **5,** *colloq.* (unfortunate): *tough luck; a tough break,* незадáча; невезéние.

toughen *v.t.* закаля́ть.

toughness *n.* **1,** (durability) прóчность. **2,** (strength of character) закáл; закáлка.

toupee *n.* парúк.

tour *n.* **1,** (organized trip) турнé; поéздка. *Sightseeing tour of the city,* экскýрсия по гóроду. **2,** (round of public appearances) гастрóли. *Be on tour,* гастролúровать. **3,** *mil.* срок: *tour of duty,* срок слýжбы. —*v.i.* **1,** (travel) путешéствовать. **2,** (give public appearances) гастролúровать. —*v.t.* совершáть турнé по; объезжáть.

touring *adj.* гастрóльный: *touring company,* гастрóльная трýппа.

tourism *n.* турúзм.

tourist *n.* турúст. —*adj.* турúстский. —**tourist class,** трéтий класс.

tourmaline *n.* турмалúн.

tournament *n.* турнúр.

tourniquet *n.* жгут.

tousle *v.t.* ерóшить; взлохмáчивать.

tow *v.t.* тянýть (на буксúре); тащúть; буксúровать. —*n.* **1,** (act of towing) буксирóвка. **2,** (fiber) пáкля; кудéль. —**take in tow,** брать на буксúр.

towage *n.* буксирóвка.

toward *prep.* **1,** (in the direction of) к: *walk toward the house,* идтú к дóму. **2,** (with respect to) к: *animosity toward someone,* враждá к комý-нибудь. *America's policy toward the USSR,* полúтика США в отношéнии СССР. **3,** (near in point of time) к; под: *toward evening,* к вéчеру; под вéчер. *Toward the end of his life,* под конéц жúзни. **4,** (in furtherance of) для: *money toward one's education,* дéньги для получéния образовáния. *Also,* **towards.**

towboat *n.* буксúр.

towel *n.* полотéнце.

tower *n.* бáшня; вы́шка. —*v.i.* [*usu.* **tower over** *or* **above**] вы́ситься (над); возвышáться (над). —**tower of strength,** надёжная опóра.

towering *adj.* **1,** (very high) высóкий; возвышáющийся. **2,** (outstanding) выдаю́щийся. **3,** (intense, as of rage) нейстовый.

towheaded *adj.* белобры́сый.

towing *n.* букси́ровка.
towline *n.* букси́р; бечева́.
town *n.* го́род. *Small town,* (ма́ленький) городо́к. *Out of town,* в отъе́зде. —**town crier,** глаша́тай. —**town hall,** ра́туша. —**town planning,** плани́рование го́рода; градострои́тельство.
townsfolk *n. pl.* горожа́не; городски́е жи́тели.
townsman *n.* горожа́нин.
towpath *n.* бечевни́к.
towrope *n.* букси́р; бечева́.
tow truck авари́йная маши́на.
toxemia *n.* токсеми́я.
toxic *adj.* токси́ческий; ядови́тый; отравля́ющий.
toxicology *n.* токсиколо́гия. —**toxicological,** *adj.* токсикологи́ческий. —**toxicologist,** *n.* токсико́лог.
toxin *n.* токси́н.
toy *n.* игру́шка. —*adj.* игру́шечный: *toy pistol,* игру́шечный пистоле́т. —*v.i.* [*usu.* **toy with**] игра́ть (+ *instr.*). *Toy with the idea of,* носи́ться с иде́ей (+ *inf.*).
trace *n.* **1,** (mark; track) след. *Disappear without a trace,* исче́знуть бессле́дно. **2,** (barely perceptible display) тень: *a trace of sadness,* тень печа́ли. *Not a trace of evidence,* ни мале́йших доказа́тельств. **3,** (part of a harness) постро́мка. —*v.t.* **1,** (sketch) черти́ть. **2,** (make a tracing of) кальки́ровать. **3,** (track down) высле́живать. **4,** (outline the development of) просле́живать. *Trace one's ancestry back to...,* вести́ свой род от...
tracer *n.* запро́с (о пропа́вшей посы́лке). —**tracer bullet,** трасси́рующая пу́ля.
trachea *n.* трахе́я. —**tracheal,** *adj.* трахе́йный.
trachoma *n.* трахо́ма.
tracing *n.* ка́лька. —**tracing paper,** бума́жная ка́лька.
track *n.* **1,** (mark; trace) след: *tracks in the snow,* следы́ на снегу́. **2,** *R.R.* (single rail) рельс: *go off the tracks,* сходи́ть с ре́льсов. **3,** *R.R.* (set of rails) путь; коле́я. *Sidetrack,* запа́сный путь. *What track does the train leave on?,* с како́й платфо́рмы отхо́дит по́езд? **4,** *sports* доро́жка; трек. *Running track,* бегова́я доро́жка. **5,** (track and field) лёгкая атле́тика. **6,** (method of proceeding) путь: *on the right/wrong track,* на ве́рном/ло́жном пути́. —*v.t.* **1,** (follow the tracks of) высле́живать. **2,** *fol. by* **down** (pursue and capture) вы́следить. **3,** (monitor the course of) следи́ть за. **4,** *fol. by* **up** (leave footprints in or on) следи́ть (*pfv.* насле́дить) в *or* на (+ *prepl.*). —**in one's tracks,** на ме́сте. *Stop dead in one's tracks,* останови́ться, как вко́панный. —**keep track of, 1,** (keep a record of) запи́сывать. **2,** (remain informed about) быть в ку́рсе (+ *gen.*); следи́ть за. —**lose track of, 1,** (lose touch with) (по)теря́ть и́з виду. *We lost track of each other,* мы потеря́ли друг дру́га и́з виду. **2,** (lose count of) (по)теря́ть счёт (+ *dat.*). —**make tracks,** *colloq.* дать тя́гу. —**throw (someone) off the track,** сбива́ть (кого́-нибудь) с пути́.
tracking station ста́нция слеже́ния.
trackman *n.* укла́дчик путе́й. *Also,* **track layer.**
track meet состяза́ние по лёгкой атле́тике.
tract *n.* **1,** (expanse) масси́в. **2,** *anat.* тракт; путь: *digestive tract,* пищевари́тельный тракт; *respiratory tract,* дыха́тельные пути́. **3,** (brief treatise) тракта́т.
tractable *adj.* **1,** (docile) сгово́рчивый. **2,** (malleable) ко́вкий.

tractile *adj.* тягу́чий; ко́вкий.
traction *n.* **1,** (pulling power) тя́га. **2,** (friction that prevents skidding) сцепле́ние (с гру́нтом). **3,** *med.* вытяже́ние.
tractive *adj.* тя́говый.
tractor *n.* **1,** (farm vehicle) тра́ктор. **2,** (truck for pulling trailers) тяга́ч. —**tractor-trailer,** *n.* тяга́ч с прице́пом.
trackwalker *n.* путево́й обхо́дчик.
trade *n.* **1,** (commerce) торго́вля: *foreign trade,* вне́шняя торго́вля. **2,** (craft) ремесло́: *learn a trade,* учи́ться ремеслу́. **3,** (exchange) обме́н. *Make a trade,* соверши́ть обме́н; обменя́ться. —*adj.* торго́вый: *trade relations,* торго́вые отноше́ния. —*v.t.* **1,** (swap) меня́ться: *trade places,* меня́ться места́ми. **2,** (give in exchange for) обме́нивать: *trade cigarettes for vodka,* обме́нивать папиро́сы на во́дку. —*v.i.* **1,** (swap) обме́ниваться: *let's trade,* дава́йте обменя́емся. **2,** (engage in trade) торгова́ть: *trade with other countries,* торгова́ть с други́ми стра́нами.
trademark *n.* фабри́чная ма́рка.
trader *n.* торго́вец.
trade school ремёсленное учи́лище.
tradesman *n.* торго́вец.
trade union профсою́з.
trade wind пасса́т.
trading *n.* торго́вля. —*adj.* торго́вый; торгу́ющий. —**trading post,** факто́рия.
tradition *n.* тради́ция. —**traditional,** *adj.* традицио́нный.
traduce *v.t.* клевета́ть на; черни́ть; поро́чить.
traffic *n.* **1,** (movement of vehicles) движе́ние: *heavy traffic,* интенси́вное движе́ние. **2,** (trade) торго́вля: *drug traffic,* торго́вля нарко́тиками. —*v.i.* [*usu.* **traffic in**] торгова́ть (+ *instr.*). —**traffic circle,** пло́щадь с кругово́ым движе́нием. —**traffic jam,** зато́р у́личного движе́ния; про́бка. —**traffic light,** светофо́р. —**traffic manager,** диспе́тчер. —**traffic sign,** доро́жный знак. —**traffic signal,** доро́жный сигна́л.
tragedian *n.* тра́гик. —**tragedienne,** *n.* траги́ческая актри́са.
tragedy *n.* **1,** (form of drama; calamity) траге́дия. **2,** (tragic nature) траги́чность; траги́зм.
tragic *adj.* траги́ческий; траги́чный. —**tragically,** *adv.* траги́чески; траги́чно.
tragicomedy *n.* трагикоме́дия. —**tragicomic,** *adj.* трагикоми́ческий.
trail *n.* **1,** (tracks) след: *pick up the trail,* найти́ след. *Leave a trail behind,* оставля́ть за собо́й след. *Be hot on the trail of,* идти́ по горя́чим следа́м (+ *gen.*). **2,** (stream) след: *trail of blood,* крова́вый след. *Leave behind a trail of dust,* оставля́ть за собо́й столб пы́ли. **3,** (path) тропа́; тропи́нка. *Blaze a trail,* прокла́дывать путь. —*v.t.* **1,** (drag loosely) тащи́ть; волочи́ть. **2,** (follow; shadow) высле́живать; просле́живать. **3,** (lag behind, as in a contest) отстава́ть от. —*v.i.* **1,** (be dragged) тащи́ться; волочи́ться. **2,** (move slowly along) тащи́ться; плести́сь. **3,** *sports* (be behind) прои́грывать: *trail by a score of 3-2,* прои́грывать со счётом три-два. **4,** *fol. by* **off** (fade away) замира́ть.
trailblazer *n.* пионе́р; нова́тор; следопы́т.
trailer *n.* прице́п.
train *n.* **1,** *R.R.* по́езд. **2,** (long line of vehicles) цепь; верени́ца. *Wagon train,* обо́з. **3,** (sequence) ход: *train*

of thought, ход мы́слей. **4,** (of a dress) шлейф. —*adj.* поездно́й: *train crew,* поездна́я брига́да. *Train service,* железнодоро́жное сообще́ние. *Train schedule,* расписа́ние поездо́в. *Train wreck,* круше́ние по́езда. —*v.t.* **1,** (instruct systematically) обуча́ть; гото́вить. **2,** (teach to act properly or in a certain way) воспи́тывать; приуча́ть. **3,** (make physically sound; prepare for an athletic contest) трениро́вать. *Train one's ear,* трениро́вать слух. **4,** (teach to perform tricks, as an animal) дрессирова́ть. **5,** (aim) наводи́ть. —*v.i.* тренирова́ться.

trained *adj.* **1,** (of a person) подгото́вленный; трениро́ванный. *Trained nurse,* медсестра́. **2,** (of an animal) дрессиро́ванный.

trainee *n.* практика́нт.

trainer *n.* **1,** (of athletes) тре́нер. **2,** (of animals) дресси́ровщик. **3,** (training device) тренажёр.

training *n.* **1,** (of people) обуче́ние; подгото́вка; трениро́вка. *Voice training,* постано́вка го́лоса. **2,** (of animals) дрессиро́вка. —*adj.* уче́бный; трениро́вочный. *Training program,* курс обуче́ния/подгото́вки.

trait *n.* черта́: *character trait,* черта́ хара́ктера.

traitor *n.* преда́тель; изме́нник. —**traitorous,** *adj.* преда́тельский; изме́ннический.

trajectory *n.* траекто́рия.

tram *n.* трамва́й.

trammel *n., usu. pl.* **1,** (shackles) пу́ты. **2,** (hindrance) око́вы. —*v.t.* ско́вывать.

tramp *v.i.* то́пать; топота́ть. *Tramp all over town,* исходи́ть весь го́род. —*n.* (vagabond) бродя́га; бося́к.

trample *v.t. & i.* **1,** [*also,* **trample on** *or* **down**] (press down; mash) топта́ть; раста́птывать; вы́таптывать. **2,** (crush and injure severely) зата́птывать: *trample to death,* зата́птывать на́смерть. **3,** *fig.* (flout, as someone's rights) попира́ть.

trampoline *n.* бату́т.

trance *n.* транс: *in a trance,* в тра́нсе.

tranquil *adj.* споко́йный. —**tranquilize,** *v.t.* успока́ивать. —**tranquilizer,** *n.* успокои́тельное сре́дство. —**tranquillity,** *n.* споко́йствие.

transact *v.t.* **1,** (carry on) вести́: *transact business,* вести́ дела́. **2,** (complete) заключа́ть: *transact a deal,* заключи́ть сде́лку.

transaction *n.* **1,** (act of transacting) веде́ние (дел). **2,** (business deal) сде́лка.

transatlantic *adj.* трансатланти́ческий.

transcend *v.t.* **1,** (go beyond the range of) выходи́ть за преде́лы (+ *gen.*). **2,** (rise above; excel) превосходи́ть.

transcendent *adj.* **1,** (surpassing) исключи́тельный; непревзойдённый. **2,** *philos.* трансценде́нтный.

transcendental *adj.* **1,** *philos.* трансцендента́льный. **2,** *math.* трансценде́нтный.

transcontinental *adj.* трансконтинента́льный.

transcribe *v.t.* **1,** (make a written copy of) перепи́сывать. **2,** (record) запи́сывать на плёнку.

transcript *n.* ко́пия. *Stenographic transcript,* стеногра́мма. *Academic transcript,* академи́ческая спра́вка.

transcription *n.* **1,** *ling.* транскри́пция: *phonetic transcription,* фонети́ческая транскри́пция. **2,** (recording) звукоза́пись. **3,** *music* транскри́пция.

transfer *v.t.* **1,** (move to another place) переноси́ть;

перемеща́ть. **2,** (move to a different job, school, etc.) переводи́ть; перемеща́ть. **3,** (shift; remit, as funds) переводи́ть. **4,** (make over possession of) передава́ть. —*v.i.* **1,** (change affiliation) переходи́ть. **2,** (change trains, buses, etc.) переса́живаться. —*n.* **1,** (carrying; conveying) перено́с; перенесе́ние; переме́ще́ние. **2,** (change of jobs or affiliation) перево́д; перемеще́ние. **3,** (shift or remittal of funds) перево́д. **4,** (making over possession) переда́ча. **5,** (change of trains, buses, etc.) переса́дка. **6,** (ticket for same) переса́дочный *or* транзи́тный биле́т.

transferable *adj.* могу́щий быть пе́реданным. —"not transferable", без пра́ва переда́чи.

transference *n.* перенесе́ние; перемеще́ние. *Thought transference,* переда́ча мы́слей.

Transfiguration *n., relig.* преображе́ние.

transfigure *v.t.* преображáть.

transfix *v.t.* **1,** (impale) пронза́ть. **2,** (make motionless) прико́вывать к ме́сту.

transform *v.t.* **1,** (change the appearance of) преображáть. **2,** (change the basic nature of) преобразо́вывать. **3,** (turn into something else) превраща́ть. **4,** *electricity; physics* преобразо́вывать.

transformation *n.* превраще́ние; преобразова́ние; преображе́ние.

transformer *n.* преобразова́тель; трансформа́тор.

transfuse *v.t.* перелива́ть. —**transfusion,** *n.* перелива́ние: *blood transfusion,* перелива́ние кро́ви.

transgress *v.t.* наруша́ть; переступа́ть. —*v.i.* греши́ть. —**transgression,** *n.* грех; прегреше́ние; правонаруше́ние. —**transgressor,** *n.* гре́шник; правонаруши́тель.

transient *adj.* **1,** (fleeting) преходя́щий; мимолётный; скороте́чный. **2,** (staying for a short time) проéзжий. —*n.* проéзжий.

transistor *n.* транзи́стор.

transit *n.* **1,** (passage) перее́зд. *Be in transit,* быть в пути́. **2,** (conveyance) транзи́т; перево́зка. *Damaged in transit,* испо́рчен при перево́зке. —*adj.* транзи́тный.

transition *n.* перехо́д. —*adj.* [*also,* **transitional**] перехо́дный: *transition period,* перехо́дный пери́од.

transitive *adj.* перехо́дный: *transitive verb,* перехо́дный глаго́л.

transitory *adj.* преходя́щий; мимолётный; скороте́чный.

translate *v.t. & i.* переводи́ть: *translate from Russian to English,* переводи́ть с ру́сского (языка́) на англи́йский.

translation *n.* перево́д. *Read something in translation,* чита́ть что-нибудь в перево́де.

translator *n.* перево́дчик.

transliterate *v.t.* транслитери́ровать. —**transliteration,** *n.* транслитера́ция.

translucent *adj.* полупрозра́чный. *Be translucent,* просве́чивать.

transmigration *n.* **1,** (migration) переселе́ние. **2,** *relig.* переселе́ние душ.

transmission *n.* переда́ча.

transmit *v.t.* передава́ть. —**transmittal,** *n.* переда́ча. —**transmitter,** *n.* (ра́дио)переда́тчик.

transoceanic *adj.* трансокеа́нский; заокеа́нский.

transom *n.* **1,** (small window above a door) фрамýга. **2,** (crossbeam) перекла́дина.

transparency *n.* 1, (quality of being transparent) прозрáчность. 2, (slide) диапозитѝв.

transparent *adj.* 1, (not opaque) прозрáчный. 2, (easily detected) я́вный.

transpire *v.i.* 1, (become known) обнарýживаться. 2, (occur) происходѝть.

transplant *v.t.* переса́живать. —*n.* переса́дка. —**transplantation**, *n.* переса́дка.

transport *v.t.* 1, (convey) перевозѝть; транспортѝровать. 2, (carry away with emotion) охва́тывать: *transported with joy,* охва́чен ра́достью; вне себя́ (*or* не пóмня себя́) от ра́дости. —*n.* 1, (act of transporting) тра́нспорт; перевóзка. *Public transport,* общéственный тра́нспорт. 2, (ship) тра́нспорт: *troop transport,* войсковóй тра́нспорт.

transportable *adj.* транспортáбельный.

transportation *n.* перевóзка; тра́нспорт.

transporter *n.* транспортёр: *tank transporter,* та́нковый транспортёр.

transpose *v.t.* 1, (interchange) переставля́ть. 2, *music* транспонѝровать.

transposition *n.* 1, (act of transposing) перестанóвка. 2, *music* транспонирóвка. 3, *chess* перестанóвка ходóв.

transship *v.t.* перегружа́ть; перева́ливать. —**transshipment,** *n.* перегрýзка; перева́лка. *Transshipment point,* перегрýзочный *or* перева́лочный пункт; перева́лка.

trans-Siberian *adj.* транссибѝрский.

transverse *adj.* поперéчный.

trap *n.* западня́; ловýшка. —*v.t.* пойма́ть в западню́. *People were trapped in the building,* лю́ди, находя́щиеся в дóме, оказа́лись в ловýшке.

trap door люк.

trapeze *n.* трапéция.

trapezoid *n.* трапéция.

trapper *n.* зверолóв.

trappings *n. pl.* 1, (adornments) украшéния; декорáции. 2, (items associated with something) сѝмволы: *the trappings of monarchy,* сѝмволы монáрхии.

trapshooting *n.* стрельба́ по тарéлочкам; стéндовая стрельба́.

trash *n.* 1, (refuse) отбрóсы; мýсор; хлам; сор. 2, (worthless literature) макулатýра. —**trash can,** мýсорный я́щик.

trashy *adj.* 1, (like junk) дрянно́й. 2, (of literature) бульва́рный.

trauma *n.* 1, (bodily injury) тра́вма. 2, (emotional shock) психѝческая тра́вма. —**traumatic,** *adj.* травматѝческий. —**traumatize,** *v.t.* травмѝровать. —**traumatology,** *n.* травматолóгия.

travail *n.* 1, (hard work) тяжёлый труд. 2, (anguish) мýка.

travel *v.i.* путешéствовать; разъезжа́ть. *Travel abroad,* éхать за гранѝцу; путешéствовать за гранѝцей. *The news traveled fast,* нóвость бы́стро распространя́лась. *Light travels at 186,000 miles per second,* скóрость свéта – 186,000 миль в секýнду. —*n.* 1, (traveling) путешéствие. 2, *pl.* (series of trips) разъéзды. —*adj.* дорóжный: *travel expenses,* дорóжные расхóды. *Travel allowance,* командирóвочные дéньги. —**travel agency,** бюрó путешéствий.

traveler *also,* **traveller** *n.* путешéственник; пýтник. —**traveler's check,** дорóжный чек.

traveling *also,* **travelling** *adj.* 1, (journeying) путешéствующий. 2, (of or for travel) дорóжный: *traveling clothes,* дорóжный костю́м. —**traveling bag,** саквоя́ж. —**traveling companion,** спýтник; попýтчик. —**traveling salesman,** коммивояжéр.

traverse *v.t.* пересека́ть. —*n.* поперéчина. —*adj.* поперéчный.

travesty *n.* парóдия.

trawl *n.* трал. —*v.t.* тра́лить. —**trawler,** *n.* тра́улер.

tray *n.* 1, (for food or utensils) поднóс. 2, (of a street peddler) лотóк.

treacherous *adj.* 1, (perfidious) предáтельский; веролóмный; кова́рный. 2, (unsafe) опáсный; ненадёжный. —**treachery,** *n.* предáтельство; веролóмство; кова́рство.

treacle *n.* пáтока.

tread *v.i.* 1, (step; walk) ступáть: *tread lightly,* ступáть легкó. 2, *fol. by* **on** (step on) наступáть на. —*v.t.* идтѝ по (какóму-нибудь) путѝ. —*n.* 1, (stepping; footsteps) шаги́. 2, (surface of a tire) протéктор. —**tread water,** плыть стóя.

treadle *n.* педáль.

treadmill *n.* топчáк. *Be on a treadmill,* вертéться, как бéлка в колесé.

treason *n.* измéна.

treasonable *adj.* измéннический; предáтельский. *Also,* **treasonous.**

treasure *n.* сокрóвище. *Buried treasure,* клад. —*v.t.* дорожѝть.

treasure house сокрóвищница.

treasurer *n.* казначéй.

treasury *n.* казначéйство. *Secretary of the Treasury,* минѝстр финáнсов. —*adj.* казначéйский: *treasury note,* казначéйский билéт.

treat *v.t.* 1, (behave in a certain manner toward) обраща́ться с; обходѝться с; поступáть с. 2, (deal with, as a subject) трактова́ть. 3, (regard and act accordingly) относѝться к: *treat as a joke,* относѝться (к чемý-нибудь) как к шýтке. 4, (subject to a process) обраба́тывать. 5, (give medical attention to) лечѝть. 6, (entertain at one's own expense) угоща́ть. —*v.i.* угоща́ть. —*n.* 1, (something paid for by someone else) *it's my treat; the treat's on me,* я угоща́ю. 2, *colloq.* (something very enjoyable) удовóльствие.

treatise *n.* тракта́т.

treatment *n.* 1, (way in which one treats another) обраще́ние; обхожде́ние. 2, (medical treatment) лече́ние. *Undergo treatment,* лечѝться; проходѝть курс лече́ния. 3, (processing) обрабóтка. 4, (handling of a subject) трактóвка.

treaty *n.* договóр. *Treaty obligations,* договóрные обяза́тельства.

treble *adj.* 1, (threefold) тройнóй. 2, *music* дискантóвый. —*n.,* *music* дѝскант. —*v.t.* утра́ивать. —*v.i.* утра́иваться. —**treble clef,** скрипѝчный ключ.

tree *n.* дéрево. *Christmas tree,* рождéственская ёлка. *Family tree,* родослóвное дéрево.

tree frog древéсница; ква́кша.

treeless *adj.* безлéсный.

treetops *n. pl.* верхýшки дерéвьев.

trefoil *n.* трилѝстник.

trek *v.i.* тащѝться; переселя́ться. —*n.* путешéствие; переселéние.

trellis *n.* шпалéры; трелья́ж.

tremble *v.i.* дрожáть: *tremble with fear,* дрожáть от стрáха. —*n.* дрожь.

tremendous *adj.* огро́мный; грома́дный.

tremolo *n.* тре́моло; вибра́ция.

tremor *n.* дрожь; тре́пет. *Earth tremor,* подзе́мный толчо́к.

tremulous *adj.* дрожа́щий; тре́петный.

trench *n.* **1,** (ditch) ров; кана́ва. **2,** *mil.* око́п; транше́я. —**trench coat,** плащ. —**trench fever,** транше́йная лихора́дка. —**trench foot,** транше́йная стопа́. —**trench warfare,** око́пная война́.

trenchant *adj.* о́стрый; ко́лкий.

trend *n.* направле́ние; тенде́нция; тече́ние. *Trend of thought,* ход мы́слей.

trepak *n.* трепа́к.

trepidation *n.* тре́пет: *fear and trepidation,* страх и тре́пет.

trespass *v.i.* **1,** (enter another's property unlawfully) наруша́ть грани́цу. **2,** *fol. by* **on** (encroach upon) посяга́ть (на). —**trespasser,** *n.* наруши́тель.

tress *n.* **1,** (lock; ringlet) ло́кон. **2,** *pl.* (hair) во́лосы.

trestle *n.* **1,** (wooden frame) ко́злы. **2,** (bridge) эстака́да.

trey *n.* тро́йка.

triad *n.* **1,** (group of three) триа́да. **2,** *music* трезву́чие.

trial *n.* **1,** *law* суд; (суде́бный) проце́сс. *The trial of...,* суд над... *Be on trial,* быть под судо́м. *Put on trial,* предава́ть суду́. **2,** (test) про́ба; испыта́ние. *Take on trial,* взять (что́-нибудь) на про́бу. *Method of trial and error,* ме́тод проб и оши́бок. **3,** (hardship) испыта́ние. —*adj.* про́бный; испыта́тельный. *Trial period/run,* испыта́тельный срок/пробе́г. —**trial balance,** про́бный бала́нс. —**trial balloon,** про́бный шар.

triangle *n.* **1,** (figure) треуго́льник. **2,** (drawing instrument) уго́льник. —**triangular,** *adj.* треуго́льный.

triangulation *n.* триангуля́ция.

Triassic *adj.* триа́совый.

tribal *adj.* племенно́й; родово́й.

tribe *n.* пле́мя. *The ten lost tribes of Israel,* де́сять исче́знувших коле́н Изра́илевых.

tribesman *n.* член пле́мени.

tribulation *n.* **1,** (suffering) страда́ние. **2,** (misfortune) несча́стье.

tribunal *n.* трибуна́л.

tribune *n.* трибу́н.

tributary *n.* прито́к.

tribute *n.* **1,** (enforced payment) дань. **2,** (testimonial) дань; до́лжное: *pay tribute to,* отда́ть дань/до́лжное (+ *dat.*).

tricentennial *adj. & n.* = **tercentenary.**

triceps *n.* трёхгла́вая мы́шца.

trichina *n.* трихи́на.

trichinosis *n.* трихинеллёз.

trick *n.* **1,** (ruse) обма́н; хи́трость; подво́х. *I suspect a trick,* мне ка́жется, здесь како́й-то подво́х (*or* что́-то нечи́сто). **2,** (prank; practical joke) шу́тка; проде́лка; прока́за; вы́ходка. *Play a trick on,* сыгра́ть шу́тку с. *Dirty/mean trick,* зла́я шу́тка; по́длость. *Play a dirty trick on,* подложи́ть свинью́ (+ *dat.*). *None of your tricks!,* без фо́кусов! **3,** (stunt; feat) трюк; фо́кус. *Card trick,* ка́рточный фо́кус. **4,** (knack) сноро́вка: *there's a trick to it,* тут сноро́вка нужна́. **5,** *cards* взя́тка. —*adj.* трю́ковый: *trick photography,* трю́ковая съёмка. *Trick lock,* замо́к с секре́том. —*v.t.* обма́нывать; надува́ть. —**he doesn't miss a**

trick, от него́ ничто́ не укро́ется. —**that'll do the trick,** вот так э́то полу́чится.

trickery *n.* обма́н; надува́тельство.

trickle *v.i.* сочи́ться: *blood trickled from the wound,* кровь сочи́лась из ра́ны. *Tears trickled down her cheeks,* слёзы ползли́ у неё по щека́м. —*n.* стру́йка: *a trickle of perspiration,* стру́йка по́та.

trickster *n.* обма́нщик; плут.

tricky *adj.* **1,** (deceptive; sly) хи́трый: *tricky methods,* хи́трые приёмы. **2,** (intricate) хи́трый; сло́жный; мудрёный. *A tricky game,* хи́трая игра́. **3,** (delicate) щекотли́вый: *a tricky situation,* щекотли́вое положе́ние.

tricolor *also,* **tricolour** *adj.* трёхцве́тный. —*n.* трёхцве́тный флаг.

tricot *n.* трико́.

tricycle *n.* трёхколёсный велосипе́д.

trident *n.* трезу́бец.

tried *adj.* испы́танный.

trifle *n.* пустя́к; ме́лочь. —*v.i.* [*usu.* **trifle with**] шути́ть с. *He is not to be trifled with,* с ним шу́тки пло́хи. —*v.t.* [*usu.* **trifle away**] растра́чивать. —**a trifle,** немно́жко: *a trifle annoyed,* немно́жко раздражён.

trifler *n.* безде́льник; лени́вец.

trifling *adj.* ничто́жный; пустяко́вый. *A trifling amount,* ничто́жная су́мма. *No trifling matter,* не шу́точное де́ло.

trigger *n.* соба́чка; гашётка; спусково́й крючо́к. *Pull the trigger,* спуска́ть куро́к. —*v.t.* порожда́ть; пусти́ть в ход.

trigonometry *n.* тригономе́трия. —**trigonometric,** *adj.* тригонометри́ческий.

trihedron *n.* трёхгра́нник. —**trihedral,** *adj.* трёхгра́нный.

trilateral *adj.* трёхсторо́нний.

trill *n.* трель. —*v.i.* пуска́ть *or* выводи́ть трель.

trillion *n.* (*U.S.*) триллио́н; (*Brit.*) миллио́н триллио́нов.

trilogy *n.* трило́гия.

trim *v.t.* **1,** (clip; prune) подстрига́ть; подреза́ть; обреза́ть; подра́внивать. **2,** (adorn) отде́лывать: *trim with lace,* отде́лывать кружева́ми. **3,** (reduce; pare) уре́зывать. —*n.* **1,** (haircut): *give someone a trim,* подра́внивать во́лосы (+ *dat.*). **2,** (trimming) отде́лка: *lace trim,* кружевна́я отде́лка. **3,** (proper condition) гото́вность; фо́рма. *In fighting trim,* в боево́й гото́вности. —*adj.* **1,** (neat; tidy) опря́тный; аккура́тный. **2,** (well-proportioned) стро́йный.

trimester *n.* триме́стр.

trimming *n.* **1,** (decoration; ornament) отде́лка; обши́вка; бордю́р. **2,** *pl.* (side dishes) гарни́р.

trinitrotoluene *n.* тринитротолуо́л; троти́л.

Trinity *n.* тро́ица.

trinket *n.* безделу́шка.

trinomial *n.* трёхчле́н. —*adj.* трёхчле́нный.

trio *n.* три́о.

triode *n.* трио́д.

trip *n.* пое́здка; путеше́ствие. *Go on a trip,* соверши́ть пое́здку. —*v.i.* **1,** (stumble) спотыка́ться; оступа́ться. **2,** (run lightly; skip) семени́ть нога́ми; бежа́ть вприпры́жку. —*v.t.* **1,** (release, as a mechanism) спуска́ть. **2,** (cause to stumble) подставля́ть но́жку (+ *dat.*); дава́ть подно́жку (+ *dat.*). **3,** *fol. by* **up** (cause to make a mistake) запу́тывать.

tripartite *adj.* трёхсторо́нний; тро́йственный.

tripe *n.* **1,** (food) рубе́ц. **2,** *colloq.* (rubbish) чушь.

triphammer *n.* па́дающий мо́лот.

triple *adj.* тройно́й; тро́йкий; тро́йственный. —*v.t.* утра́ивать. —*v.i.* утра́иваться.

triplet *n.* **1,** *pl.* (three offspring born together) тро́йня. **2,** *music* трио́ль.

triplicate *n.* In triplicate, в трёх экземпля́рах.

tripod *n.* трено́га; трено́жник; штати́в.

triptych *n.* три́птих.

trisect *v.t.* дели́ть на три ра́вные ча́сти.

trisyllabic *adj.* трёхсло́жный.

trite *adj.* бана́льный; изби́тый.

tritium *n.* три́тий.

triton *n.* трито́н.

triumph *n.* **1,** (victory) побе́да; торжество́; триу́мф. **2,** (exultation over victory) торжество́; ликова́ние. —*v.i.* побежда́ть; торжествова́ть. —**triumphal,** *adj.* торже́ственный; триумфа́льный.

triumphant *adj.* **1,** (victorious) победоно́сный. **2,** (exultant in triumph) торжеству́ющий.

triumvir *n.* триумви́р. —**triumvirate,** *n.* триумвира́т.

trivalent *adj.* трёхвале́нтный.

trivet *n.* **1,** (for holding pots over a fire) тага́н. **2,** (for holding hot dishes) подста́вка.

trivia *n.pl.* ме́лочи. —**trivial,** *adj.* ничто́жный; пустяко́вый. —**triviality,** *n.* ме́лочь.

trochaic *adj.* хорее́ческий; трохеи́ческий.

troche *n.* табле́тка.

trochee *n.* хоре́й; трохе́й.

troika *n.* тро́йка.

Trojan *adj.* троя́нский. —**Trojan horse,** троя́нский конь. —**Trojan War,** Троя́нская война́.

troll *n., folklore* тролль. —*v.t. & i.* (sing) распева́ть.

trolley *n.* **1,** (streetcar) трамва́й. **2,** (small truck) ваго́нетка. **3,** (device for conducting current) токоприёмник. —**trolley bus,** тролле́йбус. —**trolley car,** трамва́й.

trollop *n.* **1,** (slovenly woman) неря́ха; грязну́ля. **2,** (prostitute) потаску́ха.

trombone *n.* тромбо́н. —**trombonist,** *n.* тромбони́ст.

troop *n.* **1,** (group) гру́ппа; отря́д. **2,** *pl.* (soldiers collectively) войска́. —*adj.* войсково́й. Troop train, во́инский эшело́н. —*v.i.* идти́ стро́ем.

trooper *n.* **1,** (cavalryman) кавалери́ст. **2,** (policeman) полице́йский. —**swear like a trooper,** руга́ться как изво́зчик.

troopship *n.* войсково́й тра́нспорт.

trope *n.* троп.

trophy *n.* **1,** (prize) приз; ку́бок. **2,** (memento of war) трофе́й.

tropic *n.* тро́пик. —**Tropic of Cancer,** тро́пик Ра́ка. —**Tropic of Capricorn,** тро́пик Козеро́га.

tropical *adj.* тропи́ческий.

tropics *n.pl.* тро́пики.

troposphere *n.* тропосфе́ра.

trot *n.* **1,** (gait of a horse) рысь. At a trot, ры́сью; на рыся́х. **2,** (jogging gait of a person) рысца́. —*v.i.* **1,** (of a horse) идти́ ры́сью. **2,** (of a person) труси́ть.

trotter *n.* рыси́стая ло́шадь; рыса́к.

trotting races рыси́стые бега́.

troubadour *n.* трубаду́р; менестре́ль.

trouble *n.* **1,** (difficult or distressing situation) беда́; неприя́тности. Get into trouble, попа́сть в беду́. Ask for trouble, напра́шиваться на неприя́тности. **2,** (problem) беда́: the trouble is..., беда́ в том, что... What's the trouble?, в чём де́ло? That's just the trouble!, в том-то и беда́. **3,** (difficulty) труд. I'm having trouble opening the safe, я ника́к не могу́ откры́ть сейф. **4,** (extra effort; bother) труд; хло́поты. Take the trouble to, дать себе́ or взять на себя́ труд (+ inf.); потруди́ться (+ inf.). Will it be much trouble?, э́то вас не затрудни́т? It will be no trouble, э́то не не соста́вит труда́. It's not worth the trouble, э́то не сто́ит труда́. Give someone a lot of trouble, доставля́ть кому́-нибудь мно́го хлопо́т. **5,** (malfunction) неиспра́вность: engine trouble, неиспра́вность дви́гателя. Stomach trouble, расстро́йство желу́дка. Heart trouble, больно́е се́рдце. —*v.t.* **1,** (worry; bother; upset) беспоко́ить: what's troubling you?, что вас беспоко́ит? **2,** (bother; inconvenience) беспоко́ить; затрудня́ть. Don't trouble yourself!, не беспоко́йтесь! May I trouble you for a match?, мо́жно попроси́ть у вас спи́чку?

troubled *adj.* беспоко́йный; трево́жный.

troublemaker *n.* смутья́н.

troublesome *adj.* беспоко́йный.

trough *n.* **1,** (container) коры́то. Feeding trough, корму́шка. Kneading trough, квашня́. **2,** (long narrow depression) впа́дина; котлови́на.

trounce *v.t.* **1,** (thrash) колоти́ть. **2,** *colloq.* (defeat decisively) разбива́ть.

troupe *n.* тру́ппа.

trousers *n.pl.* брю́ки; штаны́.

trousseau *n.* прида́ное.

trout *n.* форе́ль.

trowel *n.* лопа́тка; садо́вый сово́к.

truancy *n.* прогу́л.

truant *n.* прогу́льщик. —**play truant,** прогу́ливать уро́ки; стать прогу́льщиком.

truce *n.* переми́рие.

truck *n.* **1,** (motor vehicle) грузови́к. **2,** (cart) теле́жка; ваго́нетка. —*v.t.* перевози́ть на грузовике́. —**trucker,** *n.* води́тель грузовика́.

truck farm огоро́дное хозя́йство. —**truck farmer,** огоро́дник. —**truck farming,** огоро́дничество.

truckle *v.i.* [*usu.* **truckle to**] раболе́пствовать (пе́ред); уго́дничать (пе́ред).

truculent *adj.* **1,** (fierce) свире́пый. **2,** (pugnacious) драчли́вый. **3,** (scathing) хлёсткий.

trudge *v.i.* брести́; тащи́ться; плести́сь.

true *adj.* **1,** (accurate; correct) и́стинный. It/that is true, э́то пра́вда; э́то ве́рно. Is it true that...?, пра́вда ли, что...? **2,** (factual) правди́вый: a true story, правди́вая исто́рия; правди́вый расска́з. **3,** (actual) действи́тельный: the true state of affairs, действи́тельное положе́ние веще́й. **4,** (genuine) настоя́щий: true gold, настоя́щее зо́лото. **5,** (rightful) зако́нный: its true owner, зако́нный владе́лец. **6,** (faithful) ве́рный: remain true to, остава́ться ве́рным (+ dat.). **7,** *astron.* и́стинный: true north, и́стинный се́вер. —**come true,** осуществля́ться; сбыва́ться.

truffle *n.* трю́фель.

truism *n.* изби́тая/прописна́я/а́збучная и́стина; трюи́зм.

truly *adv.* **1,** (indeed) и́стинно; пои́стине. **2,** (sincerely) и́скренне. —**yours truly,** пре́данный вам.

trump *n.* ко́зырь. Play one's trump card, пусти́ть в ход после́дний ко́зырь. —*v.i.* козыря́ть. —*v.t.* бить *or* крыть кóзырем. —**trump up,** фабриковáть: *trumped-up charges,* сфабрикóванные обвинéния.

trumpet *n.* трубá. —*v.i.* (of an elephant) ревéть. —*v.t.* (proclaim loudly) трубить о. —**trumpeter,** *n.* трубáч.

truncate *v.t.* усекáть. —**truncated,** *adj.* усечённый.

truncheon *n.* **1,** (cudgel) дубина. **2,** (staff) жезл.

trundle *n.* колéсико. —*v.t.* катить. —*v.i.* катиться. —**trundle bed,** кровáть на колёсиках.

trunk *n.* **1,** (of a tree) ствол. **2,** (of an elephant) хóбот. **3,** (torso) тýловище. **4,** (large box or case) сундýк. **5,** (of an automobile) багáжник. **6,** *pl.* (for swimming) плáвки.

truss *n.* **1,** (support, as for a bridge) фéрма. **2,** (device worn to support a hernia) грыжевóй бандáж.

trust *n.* **1,** (confidence in another's honesty) довéрие. **2,** (monopoly) трест. —*v.t.* **1,** (have confidence in) доверять: *he is not to be trusted,* емý нельзя доверять. **2,** (rely on) полагáться на: *Trust one's memory,* полагáться на свою пáмять. *Trust someone's judgment,* полагáться на чьё-нибудь мнéние. **3,** (assume confidently) надéяться. —*v.i., in* **trust to luck,** полагáться на слýчай.

trustee *n.* опекýн; попечитель. —**trusteeship,** *n.* опéка; попечительство.

trustful *adj.* довéрчивый. *Also,* **trusting.**

trust territory подопéчная территóрия.

trustworthy *adj.* заслýживающий довéрия; надёжный. —**trustworthiness,** *n.* надёжность.

trusty *adj.* вéрный.

truth *n.* прáвда. —**in truth,** на сáмом дéле. —**to tell the truth...,** по прáвде говоря; по прáвде сказáть...

truthful *adj.* правдивый. —**truthfulness,** *n.* правдивость.

try *v.t.* **1,** *fol. by inf.* (attempt) пытáться; старáться. **2,** (taste) прóбовать. **3,** (test) прóбовать: *try a new remedy,* прóбовать нóвое срéдство. *Try one's luck,* попытáть счáстья. *Try one's hand at,* прóбовать силы в (+ *prepl.*). **4,** (strain) испытывать: *try one's patience,* испытывать чьё-нибудь терпéние. **5,** (put on trial) судить: *he was tried for murder,* его судили за убийство. *He was tried and executed,* он был судим и казнён. **6,** (hear, as a case) слýшать (дéло). —*v.i.* старáться: *I'll try,* я постарáюсь. —*n.* попытка: *on the first try,* с пéрвой попытки. —**try on,** примерять. —**try out,** испытывать; прóбовать.

trying *adj.* трýдный; тяжёлый.

tryout *n.* прóба (на роль).

try square угóльник.

tryst *n.* любóвное свидáние.

tsar *n.* царь. —**tsarevitch,** *n.* царéвич. —**tsarevna,** *n.* царéвна. —**tsarina,** *n.* царица. —**tsarism,** *n.* царизм. —**tsarist,** *adj.* цáрский.

tsetse fly (мýха) цеце.

T-shirt *n.* мáйка.

T square рейсшина.

tub *n.* **1,** (large container) кáдка; лохáнь; ушáт. **2,** (bathtub) вáнна. **3,** *colloq.* (old boat) посýдина.

tuba *n.* тýба.

tubby *adj.* пýхлый; тýчный.

tube *n.* **1,** (hollow cylinder) трýбка. **2,** (inner tube for a tire) кáмера. **3,** (radio component) лáмпа. **4,** (container for glue, toothpaste, etc.) тýбик. **5,** *anat.* трубá.

tubeless *adj.* бескáмерный.

tuber *n.* клýбень.

tubercle *n.* бугорóк. —**tubercle bacillus,** туберкулёзная пáлочка.

tubercular *adj.* туберкулёзный.

tuberculosis *n.* туберкулёз. —**tuberculous,** *adj.* туберкулёзный.

tuberose *n.* туберóза.

tuberous *adj.* клубневóй; бугóрчатый.

tubing *n.* тюбинг.

tubular *adj.* трýбчатый.

tuck *v.t.* **1,** (place so as to be held firmly) заправлять: *tuck one's shirt into one's trousers,* заправлять рубáшку в штаны. **2,** (fold under something) подбирáть; подгибáть; подвёртывать; подтыкáть. *Tuck in a blanket,* подвёртывать *or* подтыкáть одеяло. **3,** (place snugly) засóвывать: *tuck something into one's pocket,* засóвывать чтó-нибудь в кармáн. *Tuck a child into bed,* уложить ребёнка в постéль. —*n.* вытачка.

tucker *v.t., colloq.* [*usu.* **tucker out**] изнурять. *Be tuckered out,* измáяться; быть без ног.

Tuesday *n.* втóрник.

tuft *n.* **1,** (of hair) вихóр; клок волóс. **2,** (of grass) пук; пучóк.

tug *v.t. & i.* тянýть; дёргать. —*n.* **1,** (strong pull): *give a tug,* потянýть; дёрнуть. **2,** (tugboat) буксир.

tugboat *n.* буксир.

tuition *n.* **1,** (fee) плáта за обучéние. **2,** (teaching) обучéние: *free tuition,* бесплáтное обучéние.

tulip *n.* тюльпáн. —*adj.* тюльпáнный.

tulle *n.* тюль. —*adj.* тюлевый.

tumble *v.i.* **1,** (fall; drop) пáдать; валиться. *Tumble down the stairs,* упáсть с лéстницы. *Tumble over a cliff,* свалиться со скалы. *Come tumbling down,* рýхнуть; обрýшиваться; свáливаться; обвáливаться. *Prices tumbled,* цéны упáли. **2,** (do somersaults) кувыркáться. —*n.* падéние.

tumble-down *adj.* вéтхий; обветшáлый; полуразрýшенный.

tumbler *n.* **1,** (glass) стакáн. **2,** (of a lock) сувáльда. **3,** (gymnast) акробáт. **4,** (pigeon) тýрман.

tumbleweed *n.* перекати-пóле.

tumid *adj.* распýхший.

tummy *n., colloq.* живóтик.

tumor *also,* **tumour** *n.* óпухоль.

tumult *n.* суматóха. —**tumultuous,** *adj.* шýмный; бýйный.

tuna *n.* тунéц.

tundra *n.* тýндра.

tune *n.* **1,** (melody) мотив; напéв. **2,** (proper pitch or key) лад: *sing in tune,* петь в лад. *The piano is out of tune,* рояль расстрóен. —*v.t.* **1,** (a musical instrument) настрáивать. **2,** (an engine) (от)регулировать. **3,** *fol. by in* (adjust a radio to receive) настрáиваться на. —**be in tune with the times,** идти в нóгу со врéменем. —**call the tune,** распоряжáться. —**change one's tune,** запéть другóе; запéть на другóй лад. —**dance to someone's tune,** плясáть под чью-нибудь дýдку. —**to the tune of,** на сýмму (+ *gen.*).

tuneful *adj.* мелодичный.

tuner *n.* настрóйщик: *piano tuner,* настрóйщик роялей.

tune-up *n.* регулирóвка: *engine tune-up,* регулирóвка двигателя.

tung oil тýнговое мáсло.

tungsten *n.* вольфрáм. —*adj.* вольфрáмовый.

tung tree тунг; тýнговое дéрево.

tunic *n.* **1,** (garment worn in ancient times) туни́ка. **2,** (uniform coat) ки́тель.

tuning fork камерто́н.

tunnel *n.* тунне́ль. —*v.i.* **1,** (build a tunnel) прокла́дывать тунне́ль: *tunnel through a mountain,* прокла́дывать тунне́ль че́рез го́ру. **2,** *fol.* **by under** (dig one's way) подка́пывать; подка́пываться под.

tunny *n., Brit.* = **tuna.**

turban *n.* тюрба́н; чалма́.

turbid *adj.* му́тный. —**turbidity,** *n.* му́тность.

turbine *n.* турби́на.

turbojet *adj.* турбореакти́вный. —*n.* турбореакти́вный самолёт.

turboprop *adj.* турбовинтово́й. —*n.* турбовинтово́й самолёт.

turbot *n.* тюрбо́.

turbulent *adj.* бу́рный; бу́йный; бурли́вый. —**turbulence,** *n.* волне́ние; *aero.* болта́нка.

tureen *n.* ми́ска. *Soup tureen,* супова́я ми́ска; су́пник.

turf *n.* **1,** (matted grass) дёрн. **2,** (grass part of a racetrack) трава́. **3,** (horse racing) ска́чки.

turgid *adj.* **1,** (swollen) опу́хший. **2,** (bombastic) напы́щенный.

Turk *n.* ту́рок. *The Turks,* ту́рки.

turkey *n.* инде́йка. —**talk turkey,** *colloq.* говори́ть без обиняко́в.

Turkic *adj.* тю́ркский.

Turkish *adj.* туре́цкий. —*n.* туре́цкий язы́к. —**Turkish bath,** туре́цкая ба́ня. —**Turkish delight,** раха́т-луку́м. —**Turkish towel,** мохна́тое полоте́нце.

turmeric *n.* куркума́.

turmoil *n.* беспоря́док; сумато́ха.

turn *v.t.* **1,** (change the position or direction of) повора́чивать: *turn one's head,* повора́чивать го́лову; *turn a key in a lock,* повора́чивать ключ в замке́. **2,** (cause to revolve) враща́ть: *turn a wheel,* враща́ть колесо́. **3,** (aim; direct) направля́ть; обраща́ть. *Turn a hose on someone,* напра́вить струю́ на кого́-нибудь. *Turn a gun on oneself,* обрати́ть ору́жие про́тив себя́. *Turn one's attention to,* направля́ть внима́ние на. **4,** (shape in a lathe) точи́ть. **5,** *in various combinations: turn the page,* перевёртывать страни́цу; *turn the corner,* заверну́ть за́ угол; *turn one's back on,* отвора́чиваться от; *turn somersaults,* кувырка́ться; *turn one's ankle,* подверну́ть себе́ но́гу. **6,** *in various idiomatic expressions: turn a deaf ear to,* пропуска́ть ми́мо уше́й; *turn one's stomach,* прети́ть; *turn the other cheek,* подставля́ть другу́ю щёку; *turn someone's head,* кружи́ть го́лову (+ *dat.*); *turn to one's advantage,* обраща́ть в свою́ по́льзу. *He turned forty,* ему́ испо́лнилось со́рок лет. —*v.i.* **1,** (change direction) повора́чивать: *turn (to the) right,* повора́чивать напра́во. **2,** (face in a different direction) повора́чиваться: *turn toward someone,* повора́чиваться к кому́-нибудь. **3,** (be able to be turned) повора́чиваться: *the key won't turn,* ключ не повора́чивается. **4,** (rotate) враща́ться. **5,** (become) станови́ться: *turn cold,* станови́ться хо́лодно. *Turn traitor,* стать преда́телем. ♦*Also rendered by various verbs: turn sour,* ки́снуть; *turn gray,* седе́ть; *turn pale,* побледне́ть. **6,** (shift) переходи́ть: *the conversation turned to politics,* разгово́р перешёл к поли́тике. **7,** (change color) желте́ть: *the leaves are turning,* ли́стья желте́ют. **8,** (become sour or rancid) проки́снуть. —*n.* **1,** (change

of direction) поворо́т: *turn to the right,* поворо́т напра́во. *Make a turn,* де́лать поворо́т. **2,** (revolution) оборо́т: *turn of a wheel,* оборо́т колеса́. **3,** (turning, as in a road) поворо́т. **4,** (occasion; chance) о́чередь: *wait one's turn,* ждать свое́й о́череди. *In turn,* по о́череди; поочерёдно; попереме́нно. *Out of turn,* вне о́череди. *Take turns,* чередова́ться. **5,** (action; deed) услу́га: *ill turn,* плоха́я услу́га. *One good turn deserves another,* долг платежо́м кра́сен. **6,** (change in trend) поворо́т; оборо́т. *Turn of events,* поворо́т де́ла. *Take a turn for the worse,* принима́ть дурно́й оборо́т. *Things took a turn for the better,* де́ло поверну́лось к лу́чшему. **7,** *in various expressions: turn of mind,* склад ума́; *turn of speech,* оборо́т ре́чи; *turn of the century,* нача́ло ве́ка. —**at every turn,** на ка́ждом шагу́. —**to a turn,** как раз в ме́ру. —**turn against, 1,** (set against) восстана́вливать *or* настра́ивать про́тив. **2,** (rise up against) восстава́ть про́тив. —**turn around, 1,** (face in the opposite direction) повора́чиваться (круго́м); обора́чиваться. **2,** (reverse the direction of) развора́чивать. —**turn aside, 1,** (turn to one side) развора́чивать. **2,** (turn and face a different way) сверну́ть в сто́рону. **3,** (reject) отклоня́ть. —**turn away, 1,** (turn so as not to be visible) отвора́чивать. *Turn away one's eyes,* отвора́чивать *or* отводи́ть (свои́) глаза́. **2,** (send away) прогоня́ть. **3,** (turn one's back) отвора́чиваться. —**turn back, 1,** (fold back) отгиба́ть. **2,** (set back, as a clock) поверну́ть *or* перевести́ наза́д. **3,** (turn around and return) поверну́ть наза́д *or* обра́тно. **4,** (force to turn around and return) завора́чивать. **5,** (repulse) отража́ть. —**turn down, 1,** (fold down) отвора́чивать; загиба́ть. **2,** (turn into, as a narrow street) свора́чивать в *or* на; повора́чивать в. *Turn down a path,* свора́чивать на тропи́нку. **3,** (reject) отклоня́ть; отверга́ть; отка́зываться от. *Turn down an invitation,* отклони́ть приглаше́ние; отказа́ться от приглаше́ния. *Turn down a part,* отказа́ться от ро́ли. *Turn down someone's request,* отказа́ть кому́-нибудь в про́сьбе. *They turned him down,* ему́ отказа́ли. **4,** (reduce) уменьша́ть: *turn down the volume,* уменьша́ть звук. —**turn in, 1,** (hand in) сдава́ть; предъявля́ть. **2,** (inform on) доноси́ть на. **3,** *colloq.* (go to bed) ложи́ться спать. —**turn into, 1,** (make a turn into) свора́чивать в; повора́чивать в. **2,** (transform into) превраща́ть в; обраща́ть в. **3,** (be transformed into) превраща́ться в; обраща́ться в. —**turn loose,** отпуска́ть; выпуска́ть. —**turn off, 1,** (leave, as a road) свора́чивать с. **2,** (extinguish) туши́ть; выключа́ть. **3,** (switch off) выключа́ть. *Turn off the water,* закрыва́ть кран. —**turn on, 1,** (switch on) включа́ть; зажига́ть. *Turn on the water,* открыва́ть кран. **2,** (attack) набро́ситься на. —**turn out, 1,** (extinguish) туши́ть; выключа́ть. **2,** (eject) выгоня́ть. **3,** (produce) выпуска́ть. **4,** (come; appear) приходи́ть; явля́ться. **5,** (prove to be) ока́зываться (+*instr.*). **6,** (end up) оберну́ться. *It turned out that...,* оказа́лось *or* вы́яснилось, что... *Turn out well,* ко́нчиться благополу́чно. —**turn over, 1,** (invert) перевёртывать. **2,** (topple) опроки́дывать. **3,** (roll over, as when lying down) перевёртываться. **4,** (capsize) перевёртываться. **5,** (start, as of an engine) заводи́ться. **6,** (hand over) передава́ть; отдава́ть; сдава́ть. **7,** *comm.* име́ть оборо́т в. **8,** *Turn over in one's mind,* перебира́ть. —**turn to, 1,** (appeal to; refer to) обраща́ться к. **2,** (open to a certain page) открыва́ть на (како́й-нибудь страни́це). **3,** (begin; take up) бра́ться за; принима́ться за. **4,** (change into) превраща́ться в. —**turn up, 1,** (fold up) подвёртывать. **2,** (loosen, as soil) взрыхля́ть. **3,** (uncover; discover) раскрыва́ть; обнару́живать. **4,** (increase) увели́чивать: *turn up the volume,* увели́чивать звук. **5,** (arrive; appear) явля́ться; пока́зываться; ока́зываться; подверну́ться. **6,** *Turn up one's nose,* задира́ть нос. —**turn upon, 1,** (attack) набро́ситься на. **2,** (hinge on) зави́сеть от.

turnabout *n.* **1,** (turn) поворо́т круго́м. **2,** *fig.* (reversal) поворо́т на сто во́семьдесят гра́дусов.

turncoat *n.* перебе́жчик; ренега́т.

turndown *adj. (of a collar)* отложно́й.

turner *n.* то́карь.

turning *n.* поворо́т. —*adj.* враща́ющийся. —**turning point,** поворо́тный пункт; перело́м.

turnip *n.* ре́па.

turnout *n.* **1,** (gathering) собра́ние. **2,** (number of people assembled): *a large turnout,* мно́го наро́ду.

turnover *n.* оборо́т. *Turnover of personnel,* теку́честь ка́дров.

turnpike *n.* автомагистра́ль; автостра́да.

turnstile *n.* турнике́т.

turntable *n.* **1,** *R.R.* поворо́тный круг. **2,** (of a phonograph) диск.

turpentine *n.* скипида́р.

turpitude *n.* разврат; развращённость: *moral turpitude,* нра́вственный разврат; нра́вственная развращённость.

turquoise *n.* бирюза́. —*adj.* бирюзо́вый.

turret *n.* **1,** (small tower) ба́шенка. **2,** (revolving structure for a gun) оруди́йная ба́шня. —**turret lathe,** револьве́рный стано́к.

turtle *n.* черепа́ха. —*adj.* черепа́ховый: *turtle soup,* черепа́ховый суп.

turtledove *n.* го́рлица.

tusk *n.* клык; би́вень.

tussle *n.* дра́ка; сва́лка. —*v.i.* дра́ться.

tut *interj.* фи!; цыц!

tutelage *n.* **1,** (guardianship) опе́ка. **2,** (instruction) обуче́ние.

tutelary *adj.* опеку́нский.

tutor *n.* репети́тор; гувернёр. —*v.t.* репети́ровать. —*v.i.* дава́ть ча́стные уро́ки. —**tutorial,** *adj.* репети́торский.

tutu *n.* па́чка.

tuxedo *n.* смо́кинг.

twaddle *v.i.* пустосло́вить. —*n.* пустосло́вие. —**twaddler,** *n.* пустосло́в; пустомеля.

twang *n.* гнуса́вость. *Nasal twang,* гнуса́вый го́лос.

tweak *v.t.* ущипну́ть. —*n.* щипо́к.

tweed *n.* твид.

tweet *n.* щебет. —*v.i.* щебета́ть; чири́кать.

tweezers *n.pl.* пинце́т; щи́пчики.

twelfth *adj.* двена́дцатый. —*n.* **1,** (twelfth part) двена́дцатая часть. **2,** (fraction) двена́дцатая: *one-twelfth,* одна́ двена́дцатая.

twelve *n. & adj.* двена́дцать.

twentieth *adj.* двадца́тый. —*n.* **1,** (twentieth part) двадца́тая часть. **2,** (fraction) двадца́тая: *one-twentieth,* одна́ двадца́тая.

twenty *n. & adj.* два́дцать.

twice *adv.* **1,** (two times) два́жды; два ра́за. **2,** (doubly) вдво́е; в два ра́за: *twice as much,* вдво́е *or* в два

ра́за бо́льше. *He is twice her age,* он вдво́е ста́рше её. —**once or twice,** раз-друго́й; ра́за два.

twiddle *v.t.* игра́ть (+ *instr.*); верте́ть. —**twiddle one's thumbs,** бить баклу́ши.

twig *n.* прут; ве́тка; ве́точка.

twilight *n.* су́мерки.

twin *n.* близне́ц; *pl.* близнецы́; дво́йня. —*adj.* **1,** (being a twin or twins): *twin brothers,* бра́тья-близнецы́. **2,** (forming an identical pair) спа́ренный: *twin engines,* спа́ренные мото́ры. *Twin beds,* две односпа́льные крова́ти.

twine *n.* бечёвка; шпага́т. —*v.t.* обвива́ть. —*v.i.* ви́ться. *Twine around,* обвива́ться вокру́г.

twin-engine *adj.* двухмото́рный. *Also,* **twin-engined.**

twinge *n.* при́ступ бо́ли. *Twinge of conscience,* угрызе́ние со́вести.

twinkle *v.i.* мерца́ть; мига́ть. —*n.* мерца́ние; мига́ние.

twinkling *n.* **1,** (gleam) мерца́ние; мига́ние. **2,** (instant) мгнове́ние. —**in the twinkling of an eye,** в мгнове́ние о́ка.

twirl *v.t.* кружи́ть; верте́ть. *Twirl a baton,* верте́ть па́лочкой. *Twirl one's mustache,* крути́ть усы́.

twist *v.t.* **1,** (turn; wind) крути́ть; закру́чивать: *twist the handle,* крути́ть руко́ятку. *The rope became twisted,* верёвка закрути́лась. **2,** (make by twisting) вить; крути́ть; скру́чивать; сучи́ть. **3,** (wrench; sprain) подверну́ть; вы́вернуть. **4,** (warp; distort) искажа́ть. —*v.i.* **1,** (squirm; writhe) ко́рчиться. **2,** (wind, as of a road) ви́ться; извива́ться. **3,** *fol. by* **around** (twine around) ви́ться; обвива́ться (вокру́г). —*n.* **1,** (twisting motion) круче́ние. *Give something a twist,* закрути́ть что́-нибудь. **2,** (bend; curve) поворо́т; изги́б. **3,** *fig.* unexpected turn or change) поворо́т; оборо́т. **4,** (loaf of bread) вито́й хлеб; вита́я бу́лка; плетёнка. —**twist around one's little finger,** обвести́ вокру́г па́льца; вить верёвки из. —**twist someone's arm,** вы́вернуть *or* вы́крутить кому́-нибудь ру́ку. *Twist someone's arms behind his back,* закрути́ть кому́-нибудь ру́ки.

twit *v.t.* поддева́ть; подка́лывать.

twitch *v.t.* дёргать; подёргивать. —*v.i.,* дёргаться; подёргиваться. —*n.* подёргивание.

twitter *v.i.* щебета́ть; чири́кать. —*n.* ще́бет; чири́канье.

two *adj.* два; две. —*n.* **1,** (cardinal number) два. **2,** (written number; school grade) дво́йка. **3,** *cards* дво́йка. —**in two,** на́двое; попола́м. —**two by two,** по́ два; по́ двое; попа́рно.

two-faced *adj.* двули́чный; двули́кий.

twofold *adj.* двойно́й; двоя́кий; двукра́тный. —*adv.* вдво́е; вдвойне́.

two-headed *adj.* двугла́вый.

two hundred две́сти. —**two-hundredth,** *adj.* двухсо́тый.

two-legged *adj.* двуно́гий.

two-party *adj.* двухпарти́йный.

two-room *adj.* двухко́мнатный.

two-sided *adj.* двусторо́нний.

twosome *n.* па́ра.

two-story *adj.* двухэта́жный.

two-syllable *adj.* дву(х)сло́жный.

two-time *adj.* двукра́тный: *two-time champion,* двукра́тный чемпио́н.

two-way *adj.* двусторо́нний. *Two-way street,* у́лица с двусторо́нним движе́нием.

two-wheel *adj.* двухколёсный. *Also,* **two-wheeled.**

tycoon *n., colloq.* магна́т.

tyke *n.* малы́ш.

tympani *n.pl.* = **timpani.**

type *n.* **1,** (kind; class) тип; род. **2,** (print) печа́ть; шрифт. *Set in type,* набира́ть. —*v.t.* (categorize) классифици́ровать. —*v.t. & i.* (typewrite) писа́ть на маши́нке.

typeface *n.* шрифт.

typescript *n.* машинопи́сный текст.

typesetter *n.* набо́рщик.

typewriter *n.* пи́шущая маши́нка.

typewritten *adj.* машинопи́сный. *Eight typewritten pages,* во́семь страни́ц машинопи́си.

typhoid *n.* (брюшно́й) тиф. —*adj.* тифо́зный. —**typhoid fever,** тифо́зная лихора́дка; брюшно́й тиф.

typhoon *n.* тайфу́н.

typhus *n.* (сыпно́й) тиф.

typical *adj.* типи́чный; характе́рный. *Typical of,* типи́чно для; характе́рно для. —**typically,** *adv.* типи́чно.

typify *v.t.* служи́ть типи́чным приме́ром (+ *gen.*).

typing *n.* машинопись.

typist *n.* машини́стка.

typographer *n.* типо́граф; печа́тник. —**typographic; typographical,** *adj.* типогра́фский.

typography *n.* типогра́фское де́ло; типогра́фское иску́сство.

tyrannical *adj.* тирани́ческий. —**tyrannize,** *v.t.* тира́нить.

tyranny *n.* тирани́я; тира́нство.

tyrant *n.* тира́н; наси́льник.

tyre *n.* = **tire**².

tyro *n.* новичо́к.

U

U, u два́дцать пе́рвая бу́ква англи́йского алфави́та.

ubiquitous *adj.* вездесу́щий.

udder *n.* вы́мя.

ugh *interj.* фу!

ugliness *n.* уро́дство; уро́дливость; безобра́зие.

ugly *adj.* **1,** (unsightly) некраси́вый; безобра́зный. **2,** (nasty; unpleasant) неприя́тный; скве́рный; ме́рзкий. —**ugly duckling,** га́дкий утёнок.

ukase *n.* ука́з.

Ukrainian *adj.* украи́нский. —*n.* **1,** (person) украи́нец; украи́нка. **2,** (language) украи́нский язы́к.

ukulele *n.* гава́йская гита́ра.

ulcer *n.* я́зва.

ulcerate *v.t.* изъязвля́ть. —*v.i.* изъязвля́ться.

ulcerous *adj.* я́звенный.

ulterior *adj.* скры́тый. —**ulterior motive,** за́дняя мысль; скры́тый моти́в.

ultimate *adj.* коне́чный; оконча́тельный. *The ultimate purpose of something,* коне́чная цель чего́-нибудь. *The ultimate weapon,* абсолю́тное ору́жие. —*n.* [*usu.* **the ultimate in**] вы́сшая сте́пень (+ *gen.*). —**ultimately,** *adv.* в конце́ концо́в; в коне́чном ито́ге; в коне́чном счёте.

ultimatum *n.* ультима́тум.

ultra- *prefix* ультра-.

ultramarine *n.* ультрамари́н. —*adj.* ультрамари́новый.

ultramodern *adj.* ультрасовреме́нный.

ultrasonic *adj.* ультразвуково́й.

ultraviolet *adj.* ультрафиоле́товый.

umber *n.* у́мбра.

umbilical *adj.* пупо́чный. —**umbilical cord,** пупови́на.

umbilicus *n.* пупо́к.

umbra *n.* тень.

umbrage *n.* оби́да. *Take umbrage,* обижа́ться; уда́риться в амби́цию.

umbrella *n.* зо́нтик; зонт.

umlaut *n.* умля́ут.

umpire *n.* **1,** *sports* судья́. **2,** (one empowered to settle a dispute) арби́тр. —*v.t.* суди́ть.

umpteen *adj., colloq.* мно́го; бесчи́сленные. *Umpteen reasons,* ты́сяча причи́н. —**umpteenth,** *adj., colloq. For the umpteenth time,* в кото́рый раз.

unable *adj.* не в состоя́нии. *I am unable to come today,* не могу́ прийти́ сего́дня.

unabridged *adj.* по́лный; несокращённый.

unaccented *adj.* безуда́рный.

unacceptable *adj.* неприе́млемый. —**unacceptability,** *n.* неприе́млемость.

unaccompanied *adj.* без сопровожде́ния.

unaccountable *adj.* **1,** (inexplicable) необъясни́мый. **2,** (not responsible) безотве́тственный.

unaccounted-for *adj.* пропа́вший бе́з вести.

unaccustomed *adj.* **1,** *fol. by* **to** (unused to): *be/become unaccustomed to,* не привыка́ть к; отвыка́ть от. **2,** (unfamiliar) непривы́чный.

unacquainted *adj.* незнако́мый.

unadorned *adj.* неприкра́шенный: *the unadorned truth,* неприкра́шенная и́стина.

unadulterated *adj.* **1,** (undiluted) чи́стый; це́льный. **2,** *fig.* (sheer; utter) чи́стый; сплошно́й.

unaffected *adj.* **1,** (not affected): *I am unaffected by the decision,* реше́ние меня́ не каса́ется. **2,** (without affectation) непринуждённый; есте́ственный.

unafraid *adj. Be unafraid,* не бояться; не страшиться.

unaided *adj.* без (посторонней) помощи. *With the unaided eye,* невооружённым глазом.

unalike *adj.* непохожий; несходный.

unalterable *adj.* неизменный; неизменяемый. — **unalterably,** *adv.* категорически: *unalterably opposed,* категорически против.

unambiguous *adj.* недвусмысленный.

unanimity *n.* единодушие; единогласие.

unanimous *adj.* единодушный; единогласный. —**unanimously,** *adv.* единодушно; единогласно.

unannounced *adj.* без доклада: *walk in unannounced,* входить без доклада.

unanswered *adj.* без ответа: *go unanswered,* оставаться без ответа.

unappealing *adj.* непривлекательный; неаппетитный.

unappetizing *adj.* неаппетитный.

unapproachable *adj.* недоступный.

unarmed *adj.* невооружённый; безоружный.

unassailable *adj.* **1,** (impregnable) неприступный. **2,** (incontrovertible) неоспоримый; неопровержимый.

unassisted *adj.* без (посторонней) помощи.

unassuming *adj.* непритязательный; скромный.

unattached *adj.* **1,** (not connected) неприкреплённый. **2,** (unmarried) неженатый; незамужняя.

unattainable *adj.* недостижимый.

unattended *adj.* без ухода; без присмотра.

unattractive *adj.* непривлекательный; некрасивый.

unauthorized *adj.* самовольный; недозволенный.

unavailable *adj.* не имеющийся в наличии. *Further information is unavailable at this time,* никаких больше сведений сейчас нет.

unavailing *adj.* тщетный; напрасный; бесполезный; безрезультатный; безуспешный.

unavoidable *adj.* неизбежный; неминуемый. — **unavoidably,** *adv.* неизбежно; неминуемо.

unaware *adj. Be unaware (of),* не знать (о); не отдавать себе отчёта (в).

unawares *adv.* врасплох: *catch unawares,* застать врасплох.

unbalanced *adj.* неуравновешенный.

unbandage *v.t.* разбинтовывать.

unbearable *adj.* невыносимый; непереносимый; нестерпимый; несносный. —**unbearably,** *adv.* невыносимо.

unbeaten *adj.* не потерпевший поражения.

unbecoming *adj.* **1,** (not attractive or flattering) не к лицу. **2,** (unseemly; indecorous) неприличный; неподобающий.

unbeknown *adj.* неведомый. *Unbeknown to me,* без моего ведома. *Also,* **unbeknownst.**

unbelievability *n.* невероятность.

unbelievable *adj.* невероятный. —**unbelievably,** *adv.* невероятно; до невероятности.

unbeliever *n.* неверующий. —**unbelieving,** *adj.* неверующий.

unbend *v.t.* распрямлять; выпрямлять; разгибать; отгибать. —**unbending,** *adj.* несгибаемый; непреклонный.

unbiased *adj.* беспристрастный.

unbind *v.t.* развязывать; отвязывать.

unbleached *adj.* небелёный; суровый.

unblemished *adj.* незапятнанный.

unboiled *adj.* сырой: *drink unboiled water,* пить сырую воду.

unborn *adj.* (ещё) не рождённый (*or* родившийся).

unbosom *v.t. Unbosom oneself,* изливать душу.

unbound *adj.* без переплёта.

unbounded *adj.* неограниченный; безмерный.

unbraid *v.t.* расплетать.

unbreakable *adj.* небьющийся.

unbridle *v.t.* разнуздывать.

unbridled *adj.* **1,** (having no bridle) разнузданный. **2,** *fig.* (unrestrained) необузданный.

unbroken *adj.* **1,** (intact) целый. **2,** (continuous) сплошной.

unbuckle *v.t.* расстёгивать.

unburden *v.t.* снимать бремя с. —**unburden oneself,** отводить душу.

unbutton *v.t.* расстёгивать.

uncalled-for *adj.* **1,** (unnecessary) ненужный. **2,** (out of place) неуместный.

uncanceled *also,* **uncancelled** *adj.* (of stamps) негашёный.

uncanny *adj.* необъяснимый.

uncared-for *adj.* безнадзорный; заброшенный.

unceasing *adj.* непрестанный; беспрестанный.

unceremonious *adj.* бесцеремонный. —**unceremoniously,** *adv.* бесцеремонно.

uncertain *adj.* **1,** (unsure) неуверенный. **2,** (indefinite) неопределённый. —**in no uncertain terms,** недвусмысленно.

uncertainty *n.* **1,** (lack of confidence) неуверенность. **2,** (lack of definite information) неизвестность; неопределённость.

unchain *v.t.* **1,** (release from a chain) спускать с цепи. **2,** *fig.* (set free) расковывать.

unchallengeable *adj.* неоспоримый.

unchallenged *adj.* **1,** (having no rivals) не имеющий соперников. **2,** (not answered or disputed) без возражений: *allow to go unchallenged,* пропускать без возражений; ничего не говорить в ответ.

unchanging *adj.* неизменный; неизменяемый.

uncharted *adj.* неисследованный.

unchecked *adj.* беспрепятственный.

uncivil *adj.* невежливый; неучтивый.

uncivilized *adj.* **1,** (barbarous) нецивилизованный. **2,** (crude) некультурный.

unclaimed *adj.* невостребованный.

unclassified *adj.* несекретный.

uncle *n.* дядя.

unclean *adj.* нечистый. —**uncleanliness,** *n.* нечистота. —**uncleanly,** *adj.* нечистый.

unclear *adj.* неясный.

unclench *v.t.* разжимать.

uncoil *v.t.* разматывать; раскручивать.

uncomfortable *adj.* неудобный: *uncomfortable chair,* неудобный стул; *uncomfortable situation,* неудобное положение. *I am uncomfortable,* мне неудобно. —**uncomfortably,** *adv.* неудобно.

uncommitted *adj.* неприсоединившийся.

uncommon *adj.* редкий; необыкновенный. —**uncommonly,** *adv.* необыкновенно.

uncommunicative *adj.* молчаливый; неразговорчивый.

uncomplaining *adj.* безропотный.

uncompleted *adj.* незаконченный; незавершенный.

uncomplicated *adj.* несложный.

uncomplimentary *adj.* нелестный.

uncompromising *adj.* бескомпромиссный.

unconcealed *adj.* нескрываемый.

unconcern *n.* **1,** (lack of worry) беззаботность; беспечность. **2,** (indifference) безразличие; равнодушие.

unconcerned *adj.* **1,** (unworried) беззаботный; беспечный. **2,** (indifferent) безразличный; равнодушный.

unconditional *adj.* безоговорочный; безусловный. —**unconditional surrender,** безоговорочная капитуляция.

unconfirmed *adj.* неподтвержденный.

unconnected *adj.* **1,** (not related) не связанный: *the two events are unconnected,* эти два события не связаны друг с другом. **2,** (incoherent) бессвязный.

unconquerable *adj.* непобедимый.

unconscientious *adj.* недобросовестный.

unconscionable *adj.* бессовестный.

unconscious *adj.* **1,** (having lost consciousness): *he is unconscious,* он без сознания; он в бессознательном состоянии. *The blow knocked him unconscious,* удар лишил его сознания. **2,** (involuntary) бессознательный; безотчётный. —**unconsciousness,** *n.* бессознательное состояние; беспамятство; бесчувствие.

unconstitutional *adj.* неконституционный.

uncontrollable *adj.* неукротимый; неудержимый; безудержный. *Uncontrollable anger,* неукротимый гнев. *Uncontrollable desire,* неудержимое желание. *Uncontrollable laughter,* безудержный смех.

uncontrolled *adj.* бесконтрольный.

unconventional *adj.* необычный; оригинальный.

unconvinced *adj.* не убеждён. *I remain unconvinced,* я остаюсь при своём мнении.

unconvincing *adj.* неубедительный.

uncooked *adj.* сырой.

uncooperative *adj.* несговорчивый.

uncoordinated *adj.* несогласованный.

uncork *v.t.* откупоривать; раскупоривать.

uncountable *adj.* неисчислимый. —**uncounted,** *adj.* несчётный; бесчисленный.

uncouple *v.t.* расцеплять; отцеплять.

uncouth *adj.* грубый; неотёсанный.

uncover *v.t.* раскрывать; открывать. —**uncovered,** *adj.* непокрытый; неприкрытый.

uncritical *adj.* некритический.

uncrowned *adj.* некоронованный.

unction *n.* **1,** (act of anointing) миропомазание. *Extreme unction,* соборование. **2,** (oil; ointment) елей; мазь.

unctuous *adj.* елейный.

uncultivated *adj.* **1,** (untilled) необработанный; невозделанный. **2,** (unrefined) некультурный.

uncultured *adj.* некультурный.

uncut *adj.* **1,** (not sliced) неразрезанный. **2,** (not abridged) полный; несокращённый. **3,** (not ground or polished) неотшлифованный.

undamaged *adj.* невредимый.

undaunted *adj.* неустрашимый; бесстрашный.

undecided *adj.* **1,** (not settled) под вопросом. **2,** (not having reached a decision) в нерешительности; в нерешимости. *I am still undecided as to what to do,* я ещё не решил(а), что сделать.

undecipherable *adj.* неразборчивый.

undeclared *adj.* необъявленный: *undeclared war,* необъявленная война.

undefeated *adj.* не потерпевший поражения.

undefended *adj.* незащищенный.

undemanding *adj.* нетребовательный; невзыскательный.

undemocratic *adj.* антидемократический.

undeniable *adj.* неоспоримый; бесспорный.

undependable *adj.* ненадёжный.

under *prep.* **1,** (below) под (+ *instr.*): *under the table/ tree,* под столом/деревом. *Under water,* под водой. *From under the table,* из-под стола. *Live under the same roof,* жить под одной крышей. ♦*With verbs of motion* под (+ *acc.*): *the ball rolled under the bed,* мяч закатился под кровать. *Slip something under the door,* подсунуть что-нибудь под дверь. **2,** (less than) меньше чем: *under two dollars,* меньше чем два доллара; меньше двух долларов. *Children under five,* дети до пяти лет. **3,** (according to) по; согласно: *under the terms of the treaty,* по условиям договора. **4,** (in view of) при: *under the circumstances,* при таких обстоятельствах. **5,** (in the time of) при: *under the old regime,* при старом режиме. **6,** *with various nouns* под: *under oath,* под присягой; *under arrest,* под арестом; *under arms,* под ружьём; *under lock and key,* под замком; *under the leadership of,* под руководством (+ *gen.*); *under an assumed name,* под чужим именем. *Be under repair/siege,* быть в ремонте/осаде. ♦*Also with the refl. verb:* be under construction, строиться; be under discussion, обсуждаться; be under consideration, рассматриваться. —*adv.* **1,** (to a place below) вниз. *The swimmer went under,* пловец утонул. *The business went under,* дело прогорело. **2,** (less) меньше: *five dollars or under,* пять долларов или (даже) меньше. *Children six and under,* дети от шести лет и моложе. —**under way,** *see* **way.**

underage *adj.* несовершеннолетний; малолетний.

underbodice *n.* лифчик.

underbrush *n.* подлесок.

undercarriage *n.* шасси.

undercharge *v.t.* брать слишком дёшево с.

underclothes *n.pl.* нижнее бельё.

undercook *v.t.* недоваривать; недожарить.

undercover *adj.* тайный; секретный.

undercurrent *n.* **1,** (lower current) подводное течение. **2,** (latent manifestation): *undercurrent of discontent,* скрытое недовольство.

undercut *v.t.* **1,** = **undersell. 2,** (undermine) подрывать.

underdeveloped *adj.* недоразвитый. *Underdeveloped countries,* слаборазвитые страны.

underdone *adj.* недожаренный; кровавый.

underdrawers *n.pl.* кальсоны.

underestimate *v.t.* недооценивать; преуменьшать. —**underestimation,** *n.* недооценка; преуменьшение.

underexpose *v.t., photog.* недодерживать. —**underexposure,** *n.* недодержка.

underfed *adj.* Be *underfed*, недоедáть.
underfoot *adv.* под ногáми. *Trample underfoot*, затáптывать.
undergarment *n.* предмéт нúжнего белья.
undergo *v.t.* проходúть: *undergo tests/training*, проходúть испытáния/подготóвку. *Undergo changes*, претерпéть изменéния. *Undergo an operation*, подвéргнуться опéрации.
undergraduate *n.* студéнт университéта.
underground *n.* **1,** (clandestine movement) подпóлье. *Go underground*, уйтú в подпóлье. **2,** *Brit.* = **subway.** —*adj.* **1,** (subterranean) подзéмный. **2,** (clandestine) подпóльный. —*adv.* под землéй.
undergrowth *n.* подлéсок; зáросли.
underhand *adj.* = **underhanded.** —*adj. & adv., sports* снúзу.
underhanded *adj.* тáйный; надувáтельский.
underlie *v.t.* **1,** (lie under) лежáть под. **2,** (be the basis of) лежáть в оснóве (+ *gen.*).
underline *v.t.* подчёркивать.
underling *n.* прислýжник.
underlying *adj.* лежáщий в оснóве; основнóй.
undermine *v.t.* подрывáть.
underneath *adv.* внизý; нúже. —*prep.* под: *underneath the rug*, под коврóм.
undernourished *adj.* Be *undernourished*, недоедáть.
underpaid *adj.* низкооплáчиваемый.
underpants *n.pl.* **1,** (shorts; panties) трусы́; трýсики. **2,** (long drawers) кальсóны.
underpass *n.* подзéмный перехóд.
underpay *v.t.* оплáчивать (когó-нибудь) слúшком нúзко. —*v.i.* недоплáчивать: *underpay by ten dollars*, недоплáчивать дéсять дóлларов.
underpopulated *adj.* малонаселённый.
underprivileged *adj.* неимýщий.
underproduction *n.* недопроизвóдство.
underrate *v.t.* недооцéнивать; преуменьшáть.
underripe *adj.* недоспéлый; недозрéлый.
underscore *v.t.* подчёркивать.
undersea *adj.* подвóдный.
undersecretary *n.* заместúтель минúстра.
undersell *v.t.* продавáть дешéвле чем.
undershirt *n.* нúжняя рубáшка.
undershorts *n.pl.* трусы́.
underside *n.* изнáнка.
undersigned *n., preceded by* **the** нижеподписáвшийся.
undersized *adj.* малорóслый; низкорóслый.
underskirt *n.* нúжняя юбка.
understand *v.t. & i.* понимáть: *understand Russian*, понимáть по-рýсски. *I don't understand*, я не понимáю. —*v.t.* **1,** (hear) слы́шать: *I understand that...*, я слы́шал(а), что... **2,** (assume without stating) подразумевáть: *the subject (of the sentence) is understood*, подлежáщее подразумевáется. —**give to understand**, дать понять. —**make oneself understood**, объяснáться.
understandable *adj.* понятный. —**understandably**, *adv.* понятно; понятное дéло.
understanding *n.* **1,** (comprehension) понимáние. **2,** (an agreement) договорённость; соглашéние. —*adj.* **1,** (comprehending) понимáющий. **2,** (sympathetic) отзы́вчивый.
understate *v.t.* преуменьшáть. —**understatement,**

n. преуменьшéние. *That's an understatement!,* это слúшком мягкое выражéние; так сказáть — ничегó не сказáть.
understudy *n.* дублёр. —*v.t.* дублúровать.
undertake *v.t.* **1,** (take upon oneself; agree to do) предпринимáть; брáться за. *Undertake a trip*, предпринимáть поéздку. *Undertake a job/an assignment/,* брáться за рабóту/поручéние. **2,** *fol. by inf.* (pledge) обязываться.
undertaker *n.* владéлец похорóнного бюрó.
undertaking *n.* предприятие.
undertone *n. In an undertone*, вполгóлоса.
undertow *n.* подвóдное течéние.
undervalue *v.t.* недооцéнивать.
underwater *adj.* подвóдный.
underwear *n.* нúжнее бельё.
underweight *adj.* вéсящий мéньше (*or* нúже) полóженного вéса. *I am ten pounds underweight*, я вéшу на дéсять фýнтов мéньше/нúже полóженного.
underworld *n.* **1,** (criminal element) престýпный мир; уголóвщина. **2,** (hell) преиспóдняя.
underwrite *v.t.* гарантúровать: *underwrite a loan*, гарантúровать размещéние зáйма.
underwriter *n.* страхóвщик.
undeserved *adj.* незаслýженный.
undesirable *adj.* нежелáтельный. —*n., usu.pl.* сомнúтельные элемéнты.
undetermined *adj.* неопределённый.
undeveloped *adj.* неразвитóй.
undignified *adj.* недостóйный.
undisciplined *adj.* недисциплинúрованный.
undiscriminating *adj.* неразбóрчивый.
undisguised *adj.* неприкрытый; нескрывáемый.
undismayed *adj.* необескурáженный.
undisputed *adj.* неоспорúмый.
undistinguished *adj.* заурядный; непримечáтельный.
undisturbed *adj.* спокóйный; необеспокóенный.
undivided *adj.* безраздéльный. *One's undivided attention*, пóлное внимáние.
undo *v.t.* **1,** (reverse the doing of) сводúть на нет. *Undo an error*, исправлять ошúбку. *Undo what has been done*, уничтожáть сдéланное. **2,** (unfasten) расстёгивать; отстёгивать; развязывать.
undoing *n. Be (or prove) the undoing of*, (по)губúть когó-нибудь.
undone *adj.* **1,** (not done) незакóнченный. **2,** (unfastened) *come undone*, расстёгиваться; отстёгиваться; развязываться.
undoubted *adj.* несомнéнный; бесспóрный. —**undoubtedly,** *adv.* несомнéнно; бесспóрно.
undreamed-of *adj.* во сне не снúвшийся; невообразúмый.
undress *v.t.* раздевáть. —*v.i.* раздевáться. —**undressed,** *adj.* раздéтый.
undue *adj.* чрезмéрный: *undue haste*, чрезмéрная поспéшность.
undulate *v.i.* **1,** (ripple) рябúть. **2,** (flutter) колыхáться. —**undulating,** *adj.* волнúстый; волнообрáзный.
unduly *adv.* чрезмéрно.
undying *adj.* неугасúмый; неувядáемый; немéркнущий.
unearned *adj.* **1,** (not earned) нетрудовóй: *unearned*

income, нетрудовы́е дохо́ды. **2,** (not deserved) незаслу́женный.

unearth *v.t.* **1,** (dig up from the earth) выка́пывать; вырыва́ть; отка́пывать; отрыва́ть. **2,** (find; discover) выка́пывать; отка́пывать; раска́пывать.

unearthly *adj.* неземно́й; нездѐшний. *At this unearthly hour,* в таку́ю рань.

uneasy *adj.* беспоко́йный; неспоко́йный. —**uneasiness,** *n.* беспоко́йство.

uneatable *adj.* несъедо́бный.

uneconomical *adj.* неэконо́мный; бесхозя́йственный.

uneducated *adj.* необразо́ванный.

unemployed *adj.* безрабо́тный. —*n., preceded by* **the** безрабо́тные.

unemployment *n.* безрабо́тица. *Unemployment insurance/benefits,* посо́бие по безрабо́тице.

unencouraging *adj.* неутеши́тельный.

unending *adj.* несконча́емый.

unendurable *adj.* невыноси́мый; непереноси́мый; несно́сный; нестерпи́мый.

unenforceable *adj.* неосуществи́мый.

unenlightened *adj.* непросвещённый.

unenterprising *adj.* непредприи́мчивый; безынициати́вный.

unenthusiastic *adj.* лишённый энтузиа́зма. *The critics were unenthusiastic,* кри́тики нѐ бы́ли в восто́рге; кри́тики относи́лись хо́лодно (к чему́-нибудь)

unenviable *adj.* незави́дный.

unequal *adj.* **1,** (not equal in amount; not equitable) нера́вный. *Unequal battle,* нера́вный бой. *Unequal treaty,* неравнопра́вный догово́р. **2,** *fol. by* **to** (not up to): *he proved unequal to the task,* зада́ча оказа́лась ему́ не по си́лу.

unequaled *also,* **unequalled** *adj.* непревзойдённый.

unequivocal *adj.* недвусмы́сленный. —**unequivocally,** *adv.* недвусмы́сленно.

unerring *adj.* безоши́бочный.

unethical *adj.* неэти́чный.

uneven *adj.* **1,** (not level or straight) неро́вный. **2,** (not uniform or consistent) неравноме́рный. **3,** (odd, as of a number) нечётный. —**unevenly,** *adv.* неро́вно; неравноме́рно. —**unevenness,** *n.* неро́вность; неравноме́рность.

uneventful *adj.* без происше́ствий: *the trip was uneventful,* путь прошёл без происше́ствий.

unexampled *adj.* бесприме́рный.

unexcelled *adj.* непревзойдённый.

unexceptionable *adj.* безупре́чный.

unexceptional *adj.* ниче́м не выделя́ющийся; зауря́дный.

unexpected *adj.* неожи́данный. —**unexpectedly,** *adv.* неожи́данно.

unexplainable *adj.* необъясни́мый.

unexplored *adj.* неиссле́дованный; неизвѐданный; неразвѐданный.

unexposed *adj., photog.* неэкспони́рованый.

unexpressed *adj.* невы́сказанный.

unexpressive *adj.* невырази́тельный.

unfailing *adj.* **1,** (constant; unflagging) неосла́бный. **2,** (devoted; staunch) неизме́нный. —**unfailingly,** *adv.* неукосни́тельно.

unfair *adj.* **1,** (inequitable) несправедли́вый. **2,** (un-

ethical) нече́стный. —**unfairly,** *adv.* несправедли́во. —**unfairness,** *n.* несправедли́вость.

unfaithful *adj.* неве́рный. *Be unfaithful to,* изменя́ть; обма́нывать.

unfamiliar *adj.* незнако́мый. —**unfamiliarity,** *n.* незнако́мство.

unfasten *v.t.* **1,** (detach) открепля́ть. **2,** (unbutton; untie) расстёгивать; отстёгивать; отвя́зывать.

unfathomable *adj.* **1,** (impossible to measure) неизмери́мый. **2,** (impossible to understand) непостижи́мый.

unfavorable *also,* **unfavourable** *adj.* неблагоприя́тный. *Unfavorable balance of trade,* пасси́вный торго́вый бала́нс.

unfeasible *adj.* невыполни́мый; неосуществи́мый.

unfeeling *adj.* бесчу́вственный.

unfeigned *adj.* непритво́рный; неподде́льный.

unfetter *v.t.* расковывать.

unfilled *adj.* **1,** (vacant) вака́нтный. *Unfilled position,* вака́нсия. **2,** (not executed) невы́полненный: *unfilled orders,* невы́полненные зака́зы.

unfinished *adj.* незако́нченный.

unfit *adj.* него́дный; неприго́дный.

unflagging *adj.* неосла́бный.

unflappable *adj., colloq.* невозмути́мый.

unflattering *adj.* нелѐстный.

unfledged *adj.* неопери́вшийся.

unflinching *adj.* непоколеби́мый; неукло́нный.

unfold *v.t.* развёртывать. —*v.i.* **1,** (open out) развёртываться. **2,** (gradually become known) раскрыва́ться; развёртываться.

unforeseen *adj.* непредви́денный.

unforgettable *adj.* незабыва́емый; незабве́нный.

unforgivable *adj.* непрости́тельный.

unfortunate *adj.* **1,** (unlucky; hapless) несча́стный. **2,** (regrettable; inappropriate) неуда́чный. —**unfortunately,** *adv.* к сожале́нию; к несча́стью.

unfounded *adj.* необосно́ванный; неоснова́тельный; беспо́чвенный.

unfreeze *v.t.* размора́живать.

unfriendly *adj.* недружелю́бный; неприве́тливый. —**unfriendliness,** *n.* недружелю́бие; неприве́тливость.

unfrock *v.t.* расстрига́ть; лиша́ть духо́вного са́на.

unfulfilled *adj.* **1,** (not realized) невы́полненный. **2,** (broken; unkept) несде́ржанный.

unfurl *v.t.* развёртывать; распуска́ть.

unfurnished *adj.* немеблиро́ванный.

ungainly *adj.* неуклю́жий; нескла́дный.

ungird *v.t.* распоя́сывать.

unglue *v.t.* откле́ивать; раскле́ивать. *Come unglued,* откле́иваться; раскле́иваться.

ungodly *adj.* **1,** (not believing in God) безбо́жный. **2,** *colloq.* (horrible) ди́кий. *At this ungodly hour,* в таку́ю рань.

ungraceful *adj.* нестро́йный; нескла́дный.

ungracious *adj.* нелюбе́зный; неприве́тливый. —**ungraciousness,** *n.* неприве́тливость.

ungrammatical *adj.* негра́мотный; безгра́мотный.

ungrateful *adj.* неблагода́рный.

ungrounded *adj.* **1,** (unfounded) необосно́ванный; неоснова́тельный; беспо́чвенный. **2,** (unversed) несве́дущий.

unguarded *adj.* **1,** (unprotected) незащищённый. **2,** (indiscreet) неосторожный; неосмотрительный.

unguent *n.* мазь.

ungulate *adj.* копытный. —*n.* копытное животное.

unhampered *adj.* беспрепятственный.

unhand *v.t.* отнимать руки от.

unhandy *adj.* **1,** (inconvenient) неудобный. **2,** (clumsy) безрукий.

unhappiness *n.* недовольство; неудовольствие.

unhappy *adj.* **1,** (sad) грустный: *why are you so unhappy?,* почему вам так грустно? *You look unhappy,* у вас несчастный вид. **2,** (unfortunate; miserable) несчастливый; несчастный: *unhappy life,* несчастливая/несчастная жизнь. **3,** (not successful; unsatisfactory) несчастливый; неблагополучный. *Unhappy ending,* несчастливый конец. *Unhappy outcome,* неблагополучный исход. **4,** (dissatisfied) недоволен: *unhappy with the results,* недоволен результатами. **5,** (inappropriate) неудачный: *an unhappy choice,* неудачный выбор.

unharmed *adj.* невредимый.

unharness *v.t.* распрягать; отпрягать; выпрягать.

unhealthy *adj.* нездоровый.

unheard-of *adj.* неслыханный.

unheated *adj.* не имеющий отопления; холодный.

unheeded *adj. His advice went unheeded,* его советы остались без внимания.

unhelpful *adj.* бесполезный: *unhelpful advice,* бесполезный совет. *He was completely unhelpful,* он совсем не помог.

unhesitatingly *adv.* без колебаний.

unhindered *adj.* беспрепятственный.

unhinge *v.t.* **1,** (remove from its hinges) снимать с петель. **2,** (unbalance; upset) расшатывать. *His mind became unhinged,* он тронулся умом.

unhitch *v.t.* отцеплять; расцеплять.

unholy *adj.* **1,** (wicked) нечестивый. **2,** *colloq.* (dreadful) сущий: *unholy hell,* сущий ад.

unhook *v.t.* **1,** (detach) отцеплять; расцеплять. **2,** (unbutton) расстёгивать.

unhurried *adj.* неторопливый.

unhurt *adj.* невредимый.

Uniat *n.* униат. —*adj.* униатский.

unicameral *adj.* однопалатный.

unicorn *n.* единорог.

unidentified *adj.* неопознанный.

unification *n.* объединение.

uniform *n.* форма; обмундирование. *In uniform,* в форме. —*adj.* **1,** (of a uniform) форменный: *uniform dress,* форменная одежда. **2,** (regular; unchanging) ровный; равномерный. *Uniform temperature,* ровная температура. **3,** (the same everywhere) единообразный: *a uniform system,* единообразная система. —**uniformed,** *adj.* одетый в форму.

uniformity *n.* единообразие.

unify *v.t.* объединять.

unilateral *adj.* односторонний.

unimaginable *adj.* невообразимый.

unimpeachable *adj.* безукоризненный; безупречный.

unimpeded *adj.* беспрепятственный.

unimportant *adj.* неважный.

unimpressed *adj. I was unimpressed,* это на меня не произвело никакого впечатления.

uninformed *adj.* неосведомленный; несведущий.

uninhabitable *adj.* непригодный для жилья.

uninhabited *adj.* необитаемый; безлюдный.

uninhibited *adj.* нестесненный; раскованный.

uninitiated *adj.* непосвященный.

uninjured *adj.* невредимый.

uninspired *adj.* бездушный; бескрылый.

unintelligent *adj.* неумный.

unintelligible *adj.* непонятный; невразумительный. —**unintelligibility,** *n.* непонятность.

unintentional *adj.* ненамеренный; невольный; неумышленный. —**unintentionally,** *adv.* ненамеренно; невольно.

uninteresting *adj.* неинтересный.

uninterrupted *adj.* непрерывный; беспрерывный; бесперебойный.

uninvited *adj.* незваный; непрошеный.

uninviting *adj.* неприветливый.

union *n.* **1,** (joining together) соединение; объединение; слияние. *Marital union,* брачный союз. **2,** (a confederation) союз; объединение. *Universal Postal Union,* Всемирный почтовый союз. **3,** (labor union) профсоюз. —*adj.* **1,** *USSR* союзный: *union republic,* союзная республика. **2,** (pert. to a trade union) профсоюзный.

unionize *v.t. & i.* объединять(ся) в профсоюз.

unique *adj.* единственный в своем роде; уникальный; исключительный; неповторимый. *Unique opportunity,* исключительная возможность.

unisexual *adj.* однополый.

unison *n.* унисон. —**in unison,** в унисон.

unit *n.* **1,** (basic element or amount) единица: *monetary unit,* денежная единица. **2,** *mil.* часть. **3,** (apparatus) установка; блок; узел.

unite *v.t.* соединять; объединять. —*v.i.* соединяться; объединяться. *"Workers of the world unite!",* Пролетарии всех стран, соединяйтесь!

united *adj.* соединенный; объединенный. *United front,* единый фронт. —**United Kingdom,** Соединенное Королевство. —**United Nations,** Объединенные Нации. —**United States,** Соединенные Штаты.

unity *n.* **1,** (oneness; sameness) единство. **2,** (quality of being united) единство; единение; сплоченность.

universal *adj.* **1,** (worldwide) всеобщий; всемирный. *Universal suffrage,* всеобщее избирательное право. *Universal language,* всемирный язык. **2,** (touching everything) универсальный. —**universal joint,** универсальный шарнир.

universality *n.* универсальность.

universally *adv.* во всем мире; всеми. *Universally recognized,* всеми признанный.

universe *n.* вселенная.

university *n.* университет. —*adj.* университетский.

unjust *adj.* несправедливый.

unjustified *adj.* неоправданный.

unjustly *adv.* несправедливо.

unkempt *adj.* **1,** (uncombed) нечесаный. **2,** (untidy) неопрятный; неряшливый; нечистоплотный.

unkept *adj.* несдержанный.

unkind *adj.* недобрый.

unknown *adj.* **1,** (not known) неизвестный; безвестный. **2,** *math.* неизвестный. —*n., math.* неизвестное; искомое. —**fear of the unknown,** страх перед неизвестностью.

unlace *v.t.* расшнуро́вывать.

unlawful *adj.* незако́нный; противозако́нный. **—unlawfully,** *adv.* незако́нно.

unleaded *adj.* (of gasoline) неэтили́рованный.

unleash *v.t.* спуска́ть с при́вязи. *Unleash a war,* развяза́ть *or* разжига́ть войну́.

unleavened *adj.* пре́сный. *Unleavened bread,* пре́сный хлеб; маца́.

unless *conj.* е́сли не: *unless I am mistaken,* е́сли я не ошиба́юсь. *Unless I hear to the contrary,* е́сли я не услы́шу чего́-нибудь ино́го.

unlighted *adj.* неосвещённый.

unlike *adj.* непохо́жий; несхо́дный. **—prep. 1,** (differing from) непохо́жий на. ♦*When introducing a contrasting situation* в отли́чие от; не в приме́р (+ *dat.*). **2,** (not typical of) нетипи́чно (для); нехара́ктерно (для).

unlikelihood *n.* маловероя́тность.

unlikely *adj.* маловероя́тный. *It is unlikely that he will come,* вряд ли он придёт.

unlikeness *n.* несхо́дство.

unlimited *adj.* неограни́ченный.

unlisted *adj.* не включённый в спи́сок. *We have an unlisted number,* наш но́мер не внесён в телефо́нную кни́гу.

unlit *adj.* неосвещённый.

unload *v.t.* **1,** (remove cargo from, as a ship) разгружа́ть. **2,** (remove, as cargo) выгружа́ть. **3,** (remove the ammunition from) разряжа́ть. **4,** *colloq.* (sell; get rid of) спуска́ть. **—v.i.** разгружа́ться. **—unloaded,** *adj.* незаря́женный. **—unloading,** *n.* разгру́зка; вы́грузка.

unlock *v.t.* отпира́ть. **—v.i.** отпира́ться. **—unlocked,** *adj.* неза́пертый.

unloose *v.t.* **1,** (relax, as a grip) ослабля́ть. **2,** (release) выпуска́ть. *Also,* **unloosen.**

unloved *adj.* нелюби́мый.

unlucky *adj.* **1,** (having no luck) неуда́чливый; незада́чливый. **2,** (bringing bad luck) несчастли́вый: *unlucky number,* несчастли́вая ци́фра.

unmanned *adj.* беспило́тный.

unmannerly *adj.* невоспи́танный; некульту́рный.

unmarried *adj.* (of a man) нежена́тый; (of a woman) незаму́жняя.

unmask *v.t.* разоблача́ть.

unmentionable *adj.* нецензу́рный. **—unmentionables,** *n.pl., colloq.* "невырази́мые".

unmerciful *adj.* немилосе́рдный; беспоща́дный.

unmindful *adj.* [*usu.* **unmindful of**] не обраща́я внима́ния на.

unmistakable *adj.* **1,** (that cannot be confused) ве́рный: *unmistakable sign,* ве́рный при́знак. **2,** (allowing no misunderstanding) недвусмы́сленный.

unmitigated *adj.* **1,** (thoroughgoing; out-and-out) отъя́вленный. **2,** (total; utter) по́лный.

unmoved *adj.* нетро́нутый; нерастро́ганный.

unnamed *adj.* нена́званный.

unnatural *adj.* неесте́ственный.

unnavigable *adj.* несудохо́дный.

unnecessary *adj.* нену́жный.

unnerve *v.t.* нерви́ровать; расстра́ивать; лиша́ть прису́тствия ду́ха. **—unnerved,** *adj.* расстро́енный; развинченный.

unnoticed *adj.* незаме́ченный: *go unnoticed,* пройти́ незаме́ченным.

unobservant *adj.* ненаблюда́тельный.

unobtainable *adj.* недосту́пный.

unoccupied *adj.* неза́нятый.

unofficial *adj.* неофициа́льный.

unorganized *adj.* неорганизо́ванный.

unorthodox *adj.* необы́чный; оригина́льный.

unpack *v.t.* распако́вывать. **—v.i.** распако́вываться.

unpaid *adj.* **1,** (not yet paid) неопла́ченный; неупла́ченный. **2,** (receiving no pay) не получа́ющий пла́ты.

unpainted *adj.* некра́шеный.

unpalatable *adj.* невку́сный.

unparalleled *adj.* беспри́ме́рный; беспрецеде́нтный.

unpardonable *adj.* непрости́тельный.

unpaved *adj.* немощёный.

unpin *v.t.* отка́лывать.

unplanned *adj.* беспла́новый.

unpleasant *adj.* неприя́тный. **—unpleasantness,** *n.* неприя́тность.

unplug *v.t.* отключа́ть.

unpolished *adj.* неотполиро́ванный; неотшлифо́ванный.

unpopular *adj.* непопуля́рный. **—unpopularity,** *n.* непопуля́рность.

unprecedented *adj.* беспрецеде́нтный; небыва́лый.

unpredictable *adj.* непредсказу́емый.

unprejudiced *adj.* непредубеждённый.

unpremeditated *adj.* непреднаме́ренный; непредумы́шленный.

unprepared *adj.* неподгото́вленный. *Catch unprepared,* заста́ть враспло́х.

unpretentious *adj.* непритяза́тельный; неприхотли́вый.

unpreventable *adj.* неотврати́мый; неизбе́жный; немину́емый.

unprincipled *adj.* беспринци́пный.

unprintable *adj.* непеча́тный; нецензу́рный.

unproductive *adj.* непродукти́вный; непроизводи́тельный. **—unproductiveness,** *n.* непродукти́вность; непроизводи́тельность.

unprofitable *adj.* **1,** (not yielding a profit) невы́годный; бесприбыльный; нерента́бельный. **2,** (not accomplishing anything) безрезульта́тный.

unpromising *adj.* не подаю́щий наде́жды; неперспекти́вный.

unpronounceable *adj.* не(удо́бо)произноси́мый.

unpropitious *adj.* неблагоприя́тный.

unprotected *adj.* незащищённый; беззащи́тный.

unproved *adj.* недока́занный. *Also,* **unproven.**

unprovoked *adj.* неспровоци́рованный.

unpublished *adj.* неопублико́ванный; нейзда́нный.

unpunished *adj.* безнака́занный. *Go unpunished,* оста́ться безнака́занным.

unqualified *adj.* **1,** (not fit) не име́ющий (соотве́тствующей) квалифика́ции. **2,** (unreserved) безогово́рочный: *unqualified support,* безогово́рочная подде́ржка.

unquenchable *adj.* **1,** (inextinguishable) неугаси́мый. **2,** (insatiable) неутоли́мый.

unquestionable *adj.* неоспори́мый; бесспо́рный. **—unquestionably,** *adv.* бесспо́рно.

unquestioned *adj.* несомне́нный; неоспори́мый.

unquestioning *adj.* беспрекословный.

unravel *v.t.* **1,** (untangle) распутывать. **2,** (solve) распутывать; разгадывать.

unreadable *adj.* неудобочитаемый.

unready *adj.* неготовый.

unreal *adj.* нереальный.

unrealistic *adj.* нереальный.

unrealizable *adj.* неосуществимый; несбыточный.

unreasonable *adj.* **1,** (impossible to reason with) неразумный. **2,** (excessive; unfair) непомерный. —**unreasonableness,** *n.* неразумность.

unreasoning *adj.* неразумный; нерассудительный.

unreceptive *adj.* невосприимчивый.

unrecognizable *adj.* неузнаваемый.

unrecognized *adj.* непризнанный.

unreel *v.t.* разматывать.

unrefined *adj.* **1,** (raw) неочищенный. **2,** (lacking refinement) невоспитанный.

unrehearsed *adj.* неподготовленный.

unrelated *adj.* [*usu.* unrelated to] не имеющий отношения к.

unrelenting *adj.* **1,** (relentless) неотступный. **2,** (not relaxing or slackening) неослабный.

unreliable *adj.* ненадёжный. —**unreliability,** *n.* ненадёжность.

unrelieved *adj.* беспросветный: *unrelieved misery,* беспросветная тоска.

unremitting *adj.* неослабный.

unremunerative *adj.* невыгодный; бесприбыльный.

unrepentant *adj.* нераскаянный.

unrequited *adj.* без взаимности; безответный.

unreserved *adj.* **1,** (not reserved, as of a seat) незабронированный; (of a car on a train) бесплацкартный. **2,** (unqualified; unconditional) безоговорочный.

unresolved *adj.* неразрешённый; нерешённый.

unresponsive *adj.* неотзывчивый.

unrest *n.* **1,** (worry; concern) беспокойство; волнение. **2,** (disturbances; agitation) волнения; беспорядки.

unrestrained *adj.* несдержанный; необузданный; безудержный.

unrestricted *adj.* неограниченный.

unripe *adj.* незрелый; неспелый.

unrivaled *also,* **unrivalled** *adj.* не имеющий себе равных; непревзойдённый.

unroll *v.t.* развёртывать; раскатывать.

unruffled *adj.* безмятежный.

unruly *adj.* непокорный; буйный.

unsaddle *v.t.* расседлывать.

unsafe *adj.* опасный. *Unsafe bridge,* ненадёжный мост.

unsanitary *adj.* антисанитарный.

unsatisfactory *adj.* неудовлетворительный. —**unsatisfactorily,** *adv.* неудовлетворительно.

unsaturated *adj.* ненасыщенный.

unsavory *also,* **unsavoury** *adj.* **1,** (having an unpleasant taste) невкусный. **2,** (disreputable) сомнительный; тёмный.

unscathed *adj.* невредимый. *Emerge unscathed,* выйти сухим из воды.

unscientific *adj.* ненаучный.

unscramble *v.t.* **1,** (unravel) распутывать. **2,** (decipher) расшифровывать.

unscrew *v.t.* отвинчивать; развинчивать; вывинчивать; вывёртывать; отвёртывать.

unscrupulous *adj.* бессовестный; недобросовестный; беспринципный; неразборчивый в средствах. —**unscrupulousness,** *n.* неразборчивость в средствах.

unseal *v.t.* распечатывать; вскрывать.

unseat *v.t.* **1,** (throw from the saddle) сбрасывать с седла. **2,** (remove from office) смещать с должности.

unseeing *adj.* невидящий; незрячий.

unseemly *adj.* неподобающий; неблаговидный.

unseen *adj.* невидимый. —**sight unseen,** за глаза; заглазно.

unselfish *adj.* бескорыстный. —**unselfishness,** *n.* бескорыстие.

unsettle *v.t.* **1,** (make unstable) подрывать; расшатывать. **2,** (disconcert) расстраивать; смущать.

unsettled *adj.* **1,** (disordered) неустроенный. **2,** (unresolved) неразрешённый; неурегулированный. **3,** (unpaid) неоплаченный. **4,** (not populated) незаселённый.

unshackle *v.t.* расковывать.

unshakable *also,* **unshakeable** *adj.* непоколебимый.

unshaven *adj.* небритый.

unsheathe *v.t.* обнажать; вынимать из ножен.

unshoe *v.t.* расковывать (лошадь).

unsightly *adj.* некрасивый; неприглядный.

unsinkable *adj.* непотопляемый.

unskilled *adj.* неквалифицированный.

unskillful *also,* **unskilful** *adj.* неискусный; неумелый.

unsnarl *v.t.* распутывать.

unsociable *adj.* необщительный; нелюдимый. —**unsociability,** *n.* необщительность; нелюдимость.

unsold *adj.* залежалый: *unsold merchandise,* залежалый товар. *Remain unsold,* не находить сбыта.

unsolder *v.t.* распаивать.

unsolicited *adj.* непрошеный.

unsolved *adj.* нерешённый; неразрешённый; неразгаданный.

unsophisticated *adj.* неискушённый; бесхитростный; безыскусственный.

unsought *adj.* непрошеный.

unsound *adj.* **1,** (not healthy) нездоровый. **2,** (not solid or firm) непрочный. **3,** (not valid; fallacious) необоснованный.

unspeakable *adj.* невыразимый; несказанный.

unspecified *adj.* неуказанный.

unspoiled *adj.* неиспорченный.

unspoken *adj.* невысказанный.

unsportsmanlike *adj.* недостойный спортсмена; неспортивный.

unstable *adj.* **1,** (not stable) неустойчивый; непрочный. **2,** *chem.* нестойкий.

unstained *adj.* незапятнанный.

unsteady *adj.* неустойчивый; нетвёрдый; шаткий. *Be unsteady on one's feet,* нетвёрдо держаться на ногах.

unstinting *adj.* *Be unstinting in,* не скупиться на (+ *acc.*).

unstitch *v.t.* распарывать; пороть.

unstressed *adj.* безударный.

unstuck *adj., in* come unstuck, **1,** (come loose) откле́иваться; раскле́иваться. **2,** *colloq.* (go awry) раскле́иваться.

unsubstantiated *adj.* бездоказа́тельный; беспо́чвенный.

unsuccessful *adj.* неуда́чный; безуспе́шный. *Be unsuccessful,* не уда́ться. —**unsuccessfully,** *adv.* безуспе́шно.

unsuitable *adj.* неподходя́щий.

unsuited *adj.* непригодный: *unsuited for this type of work,* непригодный к э́той рабо́те.

unsullied *adj.* незапя́танный.

unsung *adj.* невоспе́тый: *unsung hero,* невоспе́тый геро́й.

unsupervised *adj.* безнадзо́рный; бесконтро́льный.

unsupported *adj.* **1,** (not buttressed) не име́ющий опо́ры. **2,** (unsubstantiated) бездоказа́тельный.

unsure *adj.* неуве́ренный.

unsurpassed *adj.* непревзойдённый.

unsuspecting *adj.* ни о чём не подозрева́ющий.

unsympathetic *adj.* несочу́вствующий. *Be unsympathetic to,* не сочу́вствовать (+ *dat.*).

unsystematic *adj.* бесsystéмный; беспоря́дочный.

untalented *adj.* неталáнтливый; бесталáнный; безда́рный.

untamable *adj.* неукроти́мый.

untangle *v.t.* распу́тывать.

untapped *adj.* нетро́нутый.

untarnished *adj.* незапя́танный.

untenable *adj.* **1,** (unsound, as of an argument) несостоя́тельный. **2,** (that cannot be defended or saved) безвы́ходный: *in an untenable position,* в безвы́ходном положе́нии.

untested *adj.* неиспы́танный.

unthinkable *adj.* немы́слимый.

unthinking *adj.* безду́мный.

untidy *adj.* неопря́тный; неаккура́тный. —**untidiness,** *n.* неопря́тность.

untie *v.t.* развя́зывать; отвя́зывать.

until *prep.* до: *until spring,* до весны́. *Until tomorrow!,* до за́втра! —*conj.* пока́ не: *wait until he comes,* подожди́те, пока́ он не придёт. —**not until,** то́лько: *not until ten o'clock,* то́лько в де́сять часо́в. *He did not return until the next morning,* он верну́лся то́лько на сле́дующее у́тро.

untilled *adj.* невозде́ланный; необрабо́танный.

untimely *adj.* **1,** (ill-timed) несвоевре́менный; неуме́стный. **2,** (premature, as of a death) преждевре́менный; безвре́менный.

untiring *adj.* неуста́нный; неутоми́мый.

unto *prep., poetic & archaic* = **to.**

untold *adj.* **1,** (not told) нерасска́занный. **2,** (incalculable) несчётный; несме́тный.

untouchable *n., usu. pl.* неприкаса́емые.

untouched *adj.* нетро́нутый.

untoward *adj.* **1,** (unfavorable) неблагоприя́тный. **2,** (unfortunate) несча́стный: *untoward incident,* несча́стный слу́чай. **3,** (improper; inappropriate) неподходя́щий; неуме́стный.

untrained *adj.* неподгото́вленный; необу́ченный.

untranslatable *adj.* непереводи́мый.

untried *adj.* неиспы́танный.

untroubled *adj.* безмяте́жный.

untrue *adj.* неве́рный. *That is untrue,* э́то неве́рно. *Be untrue to,* быть неве́рным (+ *dat.*).

untrustworthy *adj.* ненадёжный.

untruth *n.* непра́вда. —**untruthful,** *adj.* ло́жный; лжи́вый.

untwist *v.t.* раскру́чивать; откру́чивать.

unusable *adj.* непригодный.

unused *adj.* **1,** (not made use of) неиспо́льзованный. **2,** *fol. by* to (unaccustomed) не привы́кший (к). **3,** *philately* негашёный.

unusual *adj.* необы́чный; необыкнове́нный.

unusually *adv.* необыкнове́нно: *unusually large,* необыкнове́нно большо́й.

unutterable *adj.* невырази́мый; несказа́нный.

unvarnished *adj.* **1,** (not varnished) нелакиро́ванный. **2,** (undisguised) неприкра́шенный: *the unvarnished truth,* неприкра́шенная и́стина.

unvarying *adj.* неизме́нный.

unveil *v.t.* открыва́ть; раскрыва́ть.

unverified *adj.* непрове́ренный.

unversed *adj.* несве́дущий.

unvoiced *adj., phonet.* глухо́й.

unwanted *adj.* нежела́тельный.

unwarranted *adj.* неопра́вданный.

unwary *adj.* неосторо́жный.

unwavering *adj.* непоколеби́мый; незы́блемый.

unwed *adj.* незаму́жняя. —**unwed mother,** мать-одино́чка.

unwelcome *adj.* нежела́тельный.

unwell *adj.* нездоро́вый. *He is unwell,* ему́ нездоро́вится.

unwholesome *adj.* нездоро́вый.

unwieldy *adj.* громо́здкий.

unwilling *adj.* неохо́тный. *Be unwilling to,* не хоте́ть (+ *inf.*). —**unwillingly,** *adv.* неохо́тно; не́хотя. —**unwillingness,** *n.* неохо́та; нежела́ние.

unwind *v.t.* разма́тывать. —*v.i.* разма́тываться.

unwise *adj.* неу́мный; неразу́мный; неблагоразу́мный.

unwitting *adj.* нево́льный; непреднаме́ренный. —**unwittingly,** *adv.* нево́льно; непреднаме́ренно.

unworkable *adj.* непракти́чный; неосуществи́мый.

unworried *adj.* необеспоко́енный.

unworthy *adj.* недосто́йный. *Unworthy of respect,* недосто́ин уваже́ния. *He is unworthy of her,* он её недосто́ин.

unwrap *v.t.* развёртывать.

unwritten *adj.* непи́саный: *unwritten law,* непи́саный зако́н.

unyielding *adj.* неусту́пчивый; неподатливый.

up *adv.* **1,** (to a higher level) вверх; наве́рх: *hands up!,* ру́ки вверх! ♦*Usu. rendered by a prefixed verb: go up,* поднима́ться; *stand up,* встава́ть; *climb up,* влеза́ть. **2,** (at a high or higher level) наверху́: *what are you doing up there?,* что ты де́лаешь там наверху́? *They live three floors up,* они́ живу́т тремя́ этажа́ми вы́ше. **3,** *used as an intensifier: eat up,* съесть; *tear up,* разорва́ть; *dry up,* вы́сохнуть. —*adj.* **1,** (having risen): *prices are up,* це́ны подняли́сь; *the sun is up,* со́лнце уже́ встало. **2,** (awake; out of bed) на нога́х. *The children are already up,* де́ти уже́ встали. *I was up all night,* я не спал всю ночь. **3,** (over; finished) ко́нчено: *your time is up,* вре́мя ко́нчилось *or* истекло́. *The game* (or *jig*) *is up,* игра́ ко́нчена. **4,** *colloq.* (going on): *what's* *up?,* в чём дело? *Something is up,* что-то происходит. —*prep.* **1,** (to a high or higher place on) вверх по: *up the stairs,* вверх по лестнице. *The dog chased the cat up a tree,* собака загнала кошку на дерево. **2,** (farther along) дальше по: *just up the road,* чуть дальше по этой дороге. —*v.t.* повышать: *up the price,* повышать цену. —*v.i.* взять: *he up and left,* он взял и ушёл. —*n., in* **ups and downs,** превратности судьбы. —**up against,** лицом к лицу с (+ *instr.*). —**up against it,** *colloq.* туго: *he is up against it,* ему туго приходится. —**up and about,** на ногах. —**up and down,** **1,** *literally* вверх и вниз. *Jump up and down,* подпрыгивать. **2,** (back and forth) взад и вперёд: *walk up and down the room,* ходить взад и вперёд по комнате. —**up on,** в курсе (+ *gen.*). —**up to, 1,** (to; as far as) по (+ *acc.*); до: *up to one's waist,* по пояс; *up to the ceiling,* до потолка. *Up to one's ears in debt,* по уши в долгах. **2,** (until) до: *up to now,* до сих пор. **3,** (approaching) к: *walk up to someone,* подходить к кому-нибудь. **4,** (incumbent upon) за: *it's up to you,* дело за вами. **5,** (equal to): *up to the mark,* на должной высоте. *I am not up to the task,* эта задача мне не под силу. **6,** *colloq.* (plotting): *what is he up to?,* что он замышляет/выделывает/вытворяет? *He is up to something,* он что-то затевает.

up-and-coming *adj., colloq.* многообещающий.

upas *n.* анчар.

upbraid *v.t.* упрекать; порицать.

upbringing *n.* воспитание.

upcoming *adj.* предстоящий.

update *v.t.* дополнять; включить (самые) последние данные в.

upend *v.t.* опрокидывать.

upgrade *n.* подъём. —*v.t.* **1,** (raise to a higher rank) возводить. **2,** (raise to a higher standard) повышать качество (+ *gen.*).

upheaval *n.* переворот; потрясение.

uphill *adv.* в гору. —*adj.* **1,** (upward) идущий в гору. **2,** (difficult) трудный; тяжёлый.

uphold *v.t.* **1,** (maintain; defend) отстаивать: *uphold a principle,* отстаивать принцип. **2,** (approve) утверждать: *uphold a sentence,* утверждать приговор.

upholster *v.t.* обивать. *Upholstered chair,* обитый стул. —**upholsterer,** *n.* обойщик; драпировщик. —**upholstery,** *n.* обивка.

upkeep *n.* содержание.

upland *n.* нагорье.

uplift *v.t.* поднимать. *Uplift someone's spirits,* поднимать чьё-нибудь настроение.

upon *prep.* **1,** (resting on) на: *high upon the hill,* высоко на холме. **2,** (at the time of) по: *upon (his/her) arrival,* по приезде. **3,** (after) за: *row upon row,* ряд за рядом. **4,** *fol. by* **us** (having arrived): *winter is upon us,* наступила зима. **5,** *in verbal combinations: come upon,* набрести на; *look upon,* рассматривать; *rely upon,* полагаться на. —**once upon a time,** однажды; жил-был. —**upon my word!,** честное слово!

upper *adj.* верхний: *upper berth,* верхняя полка; *upper house,* верхняя палата. *Upper class,* высший класс. *Upper Volta,* Верхняя Вольта. *The Upper Nile,* верхнее течение Нила. —**gain the upper hand,** брать *or* одержать верх.

upper case прописные буквы.

upper crust верхушка общества.

uppermost *adj.* самый верхний. *Uppermost in one's mind,* в центре чьего-нибудь внимания.

upright *adj.* **1,** (erect) прямой; стоячий. **2,** (honorable) честный; праведный. —*adv.* прямо; стоймя. —*n.* стойка. —**upright piano,** пианино.

uprising *n.* восстание.

uproar *n.* шум; гам; гвалт.

uproarious *adj.* шумный; бурный; буйный.

uproot *v.t.* **1,** (remove from the ground) вырывать с корнем; корчевать; выкорчёвывать. **2,** (force to leave a familiar place) срывать с места. *Uproot oneself,* сниматься с места. *Uproot people from their homes,* выгонять людей из своих домов.

upset *v.t.* **1,** (tip over) опрокидывать. **2,** (distress; unnerve) расстраивать; смущать. **3,** (disrupt) нарушать; расстраивать: *upset the balance,* нарушать равновесие; *upset someone's plans,* расстраивать чьи-нибудь планы. **4,** *Upset one's stomach,* расстраивать желудок. —*adj.* **1,** (overturned) опрокинутый. **2,** (distressed) расстроенный: *she is very upset,* она очень расстроена. —*n., sports* неожиданный результат. —**upset stomach,** расстройство желудка.

upsetting *adj.* тревожный: *upsetting news,* тревожные вести.

upshot *n.* исход; развязка.

upside down вверх дном; вверх ногами. *Turn upside down,* перевернуть вверх дном/ногами.

upstage *v.t.* затмевать.

upstairs *adv.* **1,** (location) наверху. **2,** (direction) наверх. —*n.* верхняя часть (дома).

upstanding *adj.* **1,** (erect) прямой; стоячий. **2,** (honorable) честный; прямой.

upstart *n.* выскочка.

upstream *adv.* вверх по течению; против течения.

upsurge *n.* рост; подъём.

up-to-date *adj.* современный.

upturn *n.* оживление.

upward *also,* **upwards** *adv.* наверх; вверх. —**upwards of,** свыше (+ *gen.*).

uranium *n.* уран. —*adj.* урановый.

Uranus *n.* Уран.

urban *adj.* городской. *Urban planning/development,* градостроительство. *Urban renewal,* перестройка городов.

urbane *adj.* вежливый; обходительный.

urchin *n.* мальчишка. —**sea urchin,** морской ёж.

Urdu *n.* урду.

urea *n.* мочевина.

uremia *n.* уремия. —**uremic,** *adj.* уремический.

urethra *n.* мочеиспускательный канал; уретра.

urge *v.t.* **1,** (try hard to persuade) убеждать. **2,** *usu. fol. by* **on** (drive onward) подгонять; погонять; понукать. **3,** (advocate strongly) призывать к. —*n.* побуждение; стремление; позыв.

urgency *n.* срочность; неотложность. *A matter of great urgency,* срочное *or* неотложное дело.

urgent *adj.* **1,** (requiring immediate action) срочный; неотложный; спешный; настоятельный; безотлагательный. **2,** (conveying a sense of urgency) настоятельный: *urgent request,* настоятельная просьба.

urgently *adv.* срочно; безотлагательно. *Urgently request,* настоятельно просить.

uric *adj.* мочевой. —**uric acid,** мочевая кислота.

urinal *n.* писсуар.

urinalysis *n.* анализ мочи.

urinary *adj.* мочевой.

urinate *v.i.* мочиться. —**urination,** *n.* мочеиспускание.

urine *n.* моча.

urn *n.* **1,** (vase) урна. **2,** (container for brewing coffee or tea) самовар.

urology *n.* урология. —**urological,** *adj.* урологический. —**urologist,** *n.* уролог.

Ursa Major Большая Медведица. —**Ursa Minor,** Малая Медведица.

us *pers.pron.* **1,** *used as dir. obj. of a verb* нас: *they drove us home,* нас отвезли домой. **2,** *used as indir. obj. of a verb* нам: *tell us a story,* расскажи нам историю. **3,** *used as obj. of a prep.* нас; нам; нами.

usable *also,* **useable** *adj.* годный к употреблению.

usage *n.* употребление. *Proper usage,* правильное употребление слов.

use *v.t.* **1,** (employ; utilize) употреблять; пользоваться; использовать; применять. *Use an expression,* употреблять выражение. *Use salt in one's food,* употреблять соль в пищу. *Use a pencil/dictionary,* пользоваться карандашом/словарём. *Use a method,* использовать *or* применять метод. *Use force,* применять силу. **2,** (consume) использовать; потреблять; расходовать. *Use raw materials,* использовать сырьё. **3,** *fol. by* **up** (consume completely; exhaust) расходовать; тратить. —*v.i., fol. by* **to 1,** (do customarily) *rendered by the imperfective aspect in Russian: we used to visit them every week,* мы их посещали каждую неделю. **2,** (formerly) раньше: *they used to live in Kiev,* раньше они жили в Киеве. —*n.* **1,** (employment; utilization) употребление; использование; применение. *Be in use,* быть в употреблении; употребляться. *Go out of use,* выйти из употребления. *Have many uses,* применяться для различных целей. **2,** (control, as of one's limbs): *have the use of one's legs,* владеть ногами. *He has lost the use of his right arm,* у него не действует правая рука. **3,** (benefit; advantage) польза: *be of use,* приносить пользу. *Be of no use,* быть бесполезным. *There is no use asking him,* нет смысла (*or* не стоит) его спрашивать. *What's the use of arguing?,* какой смысл (*or* к чему) спорить? —**have no use for, 1,** (have no need for) не нуждаться в. *I have no use for it,* это мне совершенно не нужно. **2,** (dislike strongly) не выносить: *I have no use for him,* я не выношу его. —**make use of,** пользоваться; использовать. —**put to use,** применять.

useable *adj.* = **usable.**

used *adj.* **1,** (having been used) использованный. **2,** (secondhand) подержанный. **3,** (cancelled, as of a stamp) гашёный. **4,** *fol. by* **to** (accustomed) привыкший (к). *Get used to,* привыкать к.

useful *adj.* полезный. *Be useful to,* пригодиться (+ *dat.*). —**usefulness,** *n.* полезность.

useless *adj.* бесполезный. —**uselessly,** *adv.* бесполезно; даром. —**uselessness,** *n.* бесполезность.

user *n.* потребитель.

usher *n.* билетёр. —*v.t.* **1,** (escort) провожать. *Usher someone into a room,* вводить кого-нибудь в комнату. **2,** *fol. by* **in** (herald) возвещать: *usher in a new era,* возвещать новую эру.

usherette *n.* билетёрша.

usual *adj.* обыкновенный; обычный. —**as usual,** как обычно. —**than usual,** чем обычно; обычного.

usually *adv.* обычно; обыкновенно.

usurer *n.* ростовщик. —**usurious,** *adj.* ростовщический.

usurp *v.t.* узурпировать. —**usurpation,** *n.* узурпация. —**usurper,** *n.* узурпатор.

usury *n.* ростовщичество.

utensil *n.* посуда; *pl.* утварь; посуда. *Kitchen utensils,* кухонная посуда/утварь.

uterus *n.* матка. —**uterine,** *adj.* маточный; утробный.

utilitarian *adj.* утилитарный. —**utilitarianism,** *n.* утилитаризм.

utility *n.* **1,** (usefulness) полезность. **2,** (public service company) предприятие общественного пользования. **3,** *pl.* (gas, electricity, etc.) (домашние)* удобства.

utilize *v.t.* использовать; утилизировать. —**utilization,** *n.* использование; утилизация.

utmost *adj.* крайний; предельный; максимальный; величайший. *Of the utmost importance,* величайшей важности. —*n.* **1,** (greatest possible degree) высшая степень. *To the utmost,* до последнего. **2,** (best of one's abilities) всё возможное: *do one's utmost,* делать всё возможное.

utopia *n.* утопия. —**utopian,** *adj.* утопический. —**utopianism,** *n.* утопизм.

utter *v.t.* **1,** (make, as a sound) издавать (звук). **2,** (say, as a word) произносить. *Not utter a word,* не проронить ни слова. —*adj.* полный; чистый; сплошной. *Utter nonsense,* сплошная ерунда; чистый вздор.

utterance *n.* высказывание. *Give utterance to,* высказывать; дать выход (+ *dat.*).

utterly *adv.* совершенно.

uttermost *adj.* **1,** (outermost) самый отдалённый. **2,** (extreme; utmost) крайний; предельный.

U-turn *n.* разворот.

uvula *n.* язычок; нёбная занавеска. —**uvular,** *adj.* язычковый.

Uzbek *n.* **1,** (person) узбек. **2,** (language) узбекский язык. —*adj.* узбекский.

V

V, v двадцать вторая буква английского алфавита.
vacancy *n.* **1,** (emptiness) пустота. **2,** (unfilled position) вакансия. **3,** (untenanted quarters) свободная комната *or* квартира; (in a hotel) свободный номер.
vacant *adj.* **1,** (empty) пустой. **2,** (unoccupied) свободный. **3,** (not filled, as of a position) вакантный. **4,** (blank, as of a stare) отсутствующий.
vacate *v.t.* освобождать.
vacation *n.* отпуск; *(from school)* каникулы. *Be on vacation,* быть в отпуске. —*adj.* отпускной: *vacation time,* отпускное время. —*v.i.* отдыхать.
vaccinate *v.t.* прививать оспу (+ *dat.*); вакцинировать. —**vaccination,** *n.* прививка оспы; оспопрививание; вакцинация.
vaccine *n.* вакцина.
vacillate *v.i.* колебаться. —**vacillation,** *n.* колебание.
vacuity *n.* пустота.
vacuole *n.* вакуоля.
vacuous *adj.* пустой.
vacuum *n.* безвоздушное пространство; вакуум; пустота. —*v.t.* чистить пылесосом. —**vacuum cleaner,** пылесос. —**vacuum pump,** вакуум-насос. —**vacuum tube,** электронная лампа.
vagabond *n.* бродяга; босяк.
vagary *n.* каприз; причуда.
vagina *n.* влагалище. —**vaginal,** *adj.* влагалищный.
vagrant *n.* бродяга. —*adj.* бродячий. —**vagrancy,** *n.* бродяжничество.
vague *adj.* смутный; неясный; туманный; неопределённый. *Vague resemblance,* отдалённое сходство. *I haven't the vaguest notion,* не имею ни малейшего понятитя. —**vaguely,** *adv.* смутно: *I vaguely remember,* я смутно помню. —**vagueness,** *n.* неясность; неопределённость.
vain *adj.* **1,** (futile) тщетный; напрасный. **2,** (conceited) тщеславный. —**in vain,** напрасно; тщетно; даром. *It was all in vain,* всё было напрасно.
vainglorious *adj.* тщеславный; хвастливый. —**vainglory,** *n.* тщеславие; хвастливость.
vainly *adv.* напрасно; тщетно.
valance *n.* **1,** (for a bed) полог. **2,** (across the top of a window) карниз.
vale *n.* долина; дол.
valedictory *adj.* прощальный. —*n.* прощальная речь.
valence *n.* валентность.
valerian *n.* валерьяна.
valet *n.* камердинер.

valiant *adj.* храбрый; доблестный.
valid *adj.* **1,** (having legal force) действительный. **2,** (sound; well-founded) обоснованный. **3,** (legitimate, as of a reason or excuse) уважительный.
validate *v.t.* оформлять: *validate a passport,* оформить паспорт.
validity *n.* **1,** (legal force) действительность; законная сила. **2,** (sound basis) обоснованность. *Have no validity,* не иметь под собой почвы.
valise *n.* чемодан.
valley *n.* долина.
valor *also,* **valour** *n.* доблесть. —**valorous,** *adj.* доблестный.
valuable *adj.* ценный. —**valuables,** *n.pl.* ценные вещи; ценности; драгоценности.
valuation *n.* оценка.
value *n.* **1,** (worth) ценность. *Be of great value,* представлять большую ценность. **2,** *econ.* стоимость: *surplus value,* прибавочная стоимость. **3,** (numerical quantity) величина; значение. **4,** *pl.* (principles; standards) ценности. —*v.t.* **1,** (estimate the value of) оценивать. **2,** (prize; treasure) ценить; дорожить.
valued *adj.* ценный.
valve *n.* **1,** *mech.; anat.* клапан. **2,** (of a mollusk) створка.
vamoose *v.i.,* *slang* убираться; удирать.
vamp *n.* передок (ботинка).
vampire *n.* **1,** *folklore* вампир; упырь; вурдалак. **2,** = **vampire bat.**
vampire bat (true bloodsucker) кровосос; (non-bloodsucker) вампир.
van *n.* фургон: *moving van,* мебельный фургон.
vanadium *n.* ванадий.
vandal *n.* хулиган. —**vandalism,** *n.* хулиганство. —**vandalize,** *v.t.* наносить ущерб (+ *dat.*).
vane *n.* **1,** (weathercock) флюгер. **2,** (revolving blade of a windmill) крыло.
vanguard *n.* авангард; передовой отряд.
vanilla *n.* ваниль. —*adj.* ванильный.
vanish *v.i.* исчезать. *All hope vanished,* все надежды разлетелись. *Vanish into thin air,* как в воду кануть.
vanity *n.* **1,** (pride; conceit) тщеславие. **2,** (triviality) суета: *vanity of vanities,* суета сует. **3,** (dressing table) туалетный столик; туалет. —**vanity case,** несессер.
vanquish *v.t.* побеждать.
vantage point 1, (position with a commanding view) командная позиция; командная высота. **2,** *fig.* (perspective; viewpoint) точка зрения.
vapid *adj.* пустой; пресный; бессодержательный; бесцветный.

vapor *also,* **vapour** *n.* пар. —**vapor trail,** конденсационный след.

vaporize *v.t.* испаря́ть. —*v.i.* испаря́ться. —**vaporization,** *n.* парообразова́ние. —**vaporizer,** *n.* испари́тель.

vaporous *adj.* парообра́зный.

vapour *n.* = **vapor.**

variable *adj.* переме́нный. —*n.* переме́нная величина́.

variance *n.* 1, (difference) расхожде́ние. *Be at variance with,* противоре́чить. 2, (variation; fluctuation) измене́ние.

variant *n.* вариа́нт. —*adj.* ра́зный; разли́чный.

variation *n.* 1, (change; fluctuation) измене́ние; колеба́ние. 2, (anything somewhat different) вариа́нт; вариа́ция. 3, *music* вариа́ция.

varicolored *also,* **varicoloured** *adj.* разноцве́тный.

varicose *adj.* варико́зный. —**varicose veins,** расшире́ние вен.

varied *adj.* 1, (assorted) разли́чный. 2, (diverse) разнообра́зный.

variegate *v.t.* 1, (mark with different colors) испестря́ть. 2, (diversify) разнообра́зить.

variegated *adj.* 1, (having diverse colors) пёстрый. 2, (having different forms) разнообра́зный.

variety *n.* 1, (diversity) разнообра́зие. 2, (number) ряд: *for a variety of reasons,* по (це́лому) ря́ду причи́н. 3, (type) род; сорт: *items of every variety,* вся́кого ро́да това́ры. 4, (subspecies) разнови́дность: *varieties of wheat,* разнови́дности пшени́цы. —**variety show,** варьете́. —**variety store,** галантере́йный магази́н.

various *adj.* ра́зный; разли́чный: *various kinds of,* ра́зного/разли́чного ро́да (+ *nom.*). *For various reasons,* по ра́зным причи́нам.

varnish *n.* лак. —*v.t.* лакирова́ть.

vary *v.t.* 1, (modify) изменя́ть. 2, (make diverse) разнообра́зить. —*v.i.* 1, (change) меня́ться; изменя́ться. 2, (fluctuate) колеба́ться. *With varying (degrees of) success,* с переме́нным успе́хом. 3, (differ) расходи́ться: *opinions vary,* мне́ния расхо́дятся.

vascular *adj.* сосу́дистый.

vase *n.* ва́за.

vaseline *n.* вазели́н.

vassal *n.* васса́л. —*adj.* васса́льный.

vast *adj.* 1, (of great extent or size) обши́рный; грома́дный; необозри́мый. 2, (great in number or degree) огро́мный. —**vastly,** *adv.* значи́тельно; в огро́мной сте́пени. —**vastness,** *n.* необозри́мость.

vat *n.* чан.

Vatican *n.* Ватика́н.

vaudeville *n.* эстра́да; варьете́; водеви́ль. —*adj.* эстра́дный.

vault *n.* 1, (arched roof or chamber) свод. 2, (safe storage place) храни́лище; сейф. 3, (burial vault) склеп. 4, (leap) прыжо́к. *Pole vault,* прыжо́к с шесто́м. —*v.i.* пры́гать. *Vault over a fence,* перепры́гнуть (че́рез) забо́р. —**vaulted,** *adj.* сво́дчатый.

vaunted *adj.* хвалёный.

veal *n.* теля́тина. —*adj.* теля́чий: *veal cutlet,* теля́чья отбивна́я.

vector *n.* ве́ктор. —*adj.* ве́кторный: *vector analysis,* ве́кторный ана́лиз.

veer *v.t. & i.* свора́чивать (в сто́рону). *Veer around,* ре́зко повора́чиваться круго́м.

vegetable *n.* о́вощ. —*adj.* овощно́й; расти́тельный. *Vegetable garden,* огоро́д. —**vegetable kingdom,** расти́тельный мир. —**vegetable oil,** расти́тельное ма́сло.

vegetarian *n.* вегетариа́нец. —*adj.* вегетариа́нский.

vegetate *v.i.* 1, (grow) расти́. 2, (live an inactive life) прозяба́ть.

vegetation *n.* 1, (plant life) расти́тельность. 2, (process of vegetating) вегета́ция.

vehement *adj.* бу́рный; горя́чий: *vehement argument/protest,* бу́рный/горя́чий спор/проте́ст. —**vehemence,** *n.* горя́чность.

vehicle *n.* 1, (conveyance) маши́на. *Motor vehicle,* автомаши́на. *Space vehicle,* косми́ческий кора́бль. 2, *fig.* (means) сре́дство: *vehicle to success,* сре́дство (для) достиже́ния успе́ха.

veil *n.* 1, (light fabric worn over the face) вуа́ль. 2, (bridal veil) фата́. 3, (face-covering worn by Moslem women) чадра́. 4, (anything that covers or conceals) заве́са. —*v.t.* 1, (cover with a veil) закрыва́ть вуа́лью *or* чадро́й. 2, *fig.* (conceal; hold back) скрыва́ть; завуали́ровать: *veiled threat,* скры́тая/завуали́рованная угро́за. —**take the veil,** постри́чься в мона́хини.

vein *n.* 1, (blood vessel) ве́на; жи́ла; жи́лка. 2, (when showing through the skin) прожи́лка. 3, (of a leaf) жи́лка. 4, (in marble) жи́лка; прожи́лка. 5, (lode) жи́ла. 6, *fig.* (mood; tone; style) дух; тон; стиль. *In the same vein,* в том же ду́хе. 7, *fig.* (streak; tendency) жи́лка.

velar *adj.* веля́рный; задненёбный.

vellum *n.* 1, (parchment) (то́нкий) перга́мент. 2, (paper) веле́невая бума́га.

velocity *n.* ско́рость.

velodrome *n.* велодро́м.

velour *also,* **velours** *n.* велю́р. —*adj.* велю́ровый.

velvet *n.* ба́рхат. —*adj.* ба́рхатный.

velveteen *n.* вельве́т. —*adj.* вельве́товый.

velvety *adj.* бархати́стый.

venal *adj.* прода́жный. —**venality,** *n.* прода́жность.

vend *v.t & i.* продава́ть.

vender *n.* = **vendor.**

vendetta *n.* кро́вная месть.

vending machine автома́т.

vendor *also,* **vender** *n.* продаве́ц; торго́вец. *Street vendor,* у́личный торго́вец.

veneer *n.* 1, (thin layer of wood) фане́ра. 2, *fig.* (superficial display) (вне́шний) лоск.

venerable *adj.* почте́нный; масти́тый.

venerate *v.t.* благогове́ть. —**veneration,** *n.* благогове́ние.

venereal *adj.* венери́ческий: *venereal disease,* венери́ческая боле́знь.

Venetian *adj.* венециа́нский. —**Venetian blinds,** подъёмные жалюзи́.

Venezuelan *adj.* венесуэ́льский.

vengeance *n.* месть; мще́ние. *Take vengeance,* мстить. —**with a vengeance,** с лихво́й.

vengeful *adj.* мсти́тельный.

venial *adj.* прости́тельный.

venison *n.* оле́нина.

venom *n.* яд. —**venomous,** *adj.* ядови́тый.

venous *adj.* вено́зный.

vent *n.* отду́шина. —*v.t.* [*also,* **give vent to**] изливáть; срывáть; вымещáть; дать вы́ход (+ *dat.*).

ventilate *v.t.* проветривать; вентилировать. —**ventilation**, *n.* проветривание; вентиляция. —**ventilator**, *n.* вентилятор.

ventral *adj.* брюшной.

ventricle *n.* желудочек.

ventriloquism *n.* чревовещáние. —**ventriloquist**, *n.* чревовещáтель.

venture *n.* затея; предприятие. —*v.t.* **1**, (risk) рисковáть. **2**, (bet; stake) стáвить. **3**, (express at the risk of criticism) выскáзывать (мнéние). **4**, *fol. by inf.* (dare) сметь; осмéливаться; отвáживаться; позволить себé. —*v.i.* осмéливаться: *venture out on the street at night*, осмéливаться выходить на у́лицу ночью.

venturesome *adj.* смéлый; отвáжный.

Venus *n.* Венéра.

veracious *adj.* правдивый. —**veracity**, *n.* правдивость.

veranda *n.* верáнда.

verb *n.* глагол. —*adj.* глагольный: *verb endings*, глагольные окончáния.

verbal *adj.* **1**, (oral) у́стный: *verbal agreement*, у́стное соглашéние. **2**, (pert. to words) словéсный: *verbal battle*, словéсная войнá. **3**, *gram.* глагольный; отглагольный. —**verbal adverb**, деепричáстие. — **verbal noun**, отглагольное существительное.

verbalize *v.t.* выражáть словáми.

verbally *adv.* у́стно.

verbatim *adj.* дословный. —*adv.* дословно; слово в слово.

verbena *n.* вербéна.

verbiage *n.* пусты́е словá; пустословие.

verbose *adj.* многословный. —**verbosity**, *n.* многословие.

verdant *adj.* зелёный.

verdict *n.* приговор; вердикт. *Verdict of "guilty"*, обвинительный приговор. *Verdict of "not guilty"*, оправдáтельный приговор. *The verdict of history*, суд истории.

verdigris *n.* медянка; ярь-медянка.

verdure *n.* зéлень.

verge *n.* грань: *on the verge of*, на грáни (+ *gen.*). —*v.i.* [*usu.* **verge on**] граничить с.

verify *v.t.* проверять. —**verifiable**, *adj.* поддающийся контролю. —**verification**, *n.* проверка; контроль.

verily *adv.*, *archaic* поистине; воистину.

verisimilitude *n.* правдоподобие.

veritable *adj.* настоящий; истинный.

vermicelli *n.* вермишéль.

vermiform *adj.* червеобрáзный. —**vermiform appendix**, червеобрáзный отросток.

vermilion *n.* **1**, (pigment) киноварь. **2**, (color) яркокрáсный цвет. —*adj.* ярко-крáсный.

vermin *n.* вредители; паразиты.

vermouth *n.* вéрмут.

vernacular *n.* просторéчие. —*adj.* просторéчный.

vernal *adj.* весéнний. —**vernal equinox**, весéннее равноденствие.

vernalize *v.t.* яровизировать. —**vernalization**, *n.* яровизáция.

versatile *adj.* многосторонний; разносторонний. —**versatility**, *n.* многосторонность; разносторонность.

verse *n.* **1**, (line of poetry) стих. **2**, (stanza) строфá. **3**, (poetry) стихи: *in verse*, в стихáх.

versed *adj.* [*usu.* **versed in**] свéдущий (в).

versification *n.* стихосложéние.

version *n.* вéрсия; вариáнт.

versus *prep.* против.

vertebra *n.* позвонок. —**vertebral**, *adj.* позвоночный.

vertebrate *adj.* позвоночный. —*n.* позвоночное животное.

vertex *n.* вершина.

vertical *adj.* вертикáльный. —*n.* вертикáль. —**vertically**, *adv.* вертикáльно.

vertigo *n.* головокружéние. —**vertiginous**, *adj.* головокружительный.

verve *n.* живость; подъём; огонёк.

very *adv.* **1**, (to a high degree) очень: *very glad*, очень рад. **2**, (precisely) же: *the very same day*, на слéдующий же день; *the very same place*, то же сáмое мéсто. **3**, *before superlatives* сáмый: *the very best*, сáмый лу́чший. —*adj.* **1**, (absolute) сáмый: *from the very beginning*, с сáмого начáла; *in the very center of town*, в сáмом цéнтре города. **2**, (precise) тот сáмый: *at that very moment*, в тот сáмый момéнт. *This very minute*, сию́ же мину́ту. **3**, (identical) тот сáмый: *the very man we read about*, тот сáмый человéк, о котором мы читáли. **4**, (precisely) именно тот: *you're the very person I wanted to see*, вы именно тот, кого́ я хотéл видеть. **5**, (mere) один: *at the very thought of it*, при одной мы́сли об этом. —**very much**, очень: *want very much to go*, очень хотéть идти. *Thank you very much!*, большое (вам) спасибо! —**very well!**, хорошо́!; лáдно!

vespers *n.pl.* вечéрня; всéнощная.

vessel *n.* **1**, (container) сосу́д. **2**, *anat.* сосу́д: *blood vessel*, кровеносный сосу́д. **3**, (ship) су́дно; корáбль. *Fishing vessel*, рыболовное су́дно.

vest *n.* жилéт; жилéтка. —*adj.* жилéтный: *vest pocket*, жилéтный кармáн. —*v.t.* **1**, (clothe) облачáть. **2**, (endow, as with power) облекáть.

vestibule *n.* передняя; прихожая.

vestige *n.* остáток; пережиток. —**vestigial**, *adj.* остáточный; рудиментáрный.

vestment *n.* облачéние.

vestry *n.* ризница.

vetch *n.* вика.

veteran *n.* ветерáн. —*adj.* стáрый; бывáлый; матёрый.

veterinarian *n.* ветеринáр.

veterinary *adj.* ветеринáрный. —**veterinary medicine**, ветеринáрия.

veto *n.* вéто. *Veto power*, прáво вéто. —*v.t.* налож+ить вéто на.

vex *v.t.* досаждáть; раздражáть. —**vexation**, *n.* досáда; раздражéние. —**vexatious**, *adj.* досáдный.

via *prep.* чéрез.

viable *adj.* жизнеспособный. —**viability**, *n.* жизнеспособность.

viaduct *n.* виаду́к.

vial *n.* пузырёк; флакон; склянка.

vibrant *adj.* **1**, (vibrating) вибрирующий. **2**, (lively; pulsating) живой; оживлённый.

vibrate *v.i.* вибрировать. —**vibration**, *n.* вибрáция. —**vibrator**, *n.* вибрáтор.

viburnum *n.* калина.

vicar *n.* викáрий.

vicarious *adj.* чужой.

vice *n.* **1.** (immoral behavior; personal failing) порок. **2.** (vise) тиски.

vice-admiral *n.* вице-адмирал.

vice-consul *n.* вице-консул.

vice-president *n.* вице-президент.

viceroy *n.* вице-король.

vice versa наоборот; обратно.

vicinity *n.* **1.** (proximity) соседство; близость. *In the vicinity of,* по соседству с. **2.** (neighborhood) округа; район.

vicious *adj.* **1.** (malicious) злостный: *vicious remark,* злостное замечание. **2.** (heinous; depraved) гнусный: *vicious act/criminal,* гнусный поступок/преступник. **3.** (savage; fierce) злой; свирепый: *vicious dog,* злая собака; *vicious shark,* свирепая акула.

vicissitude *n.* превратность; перипетия.

victim *n.* жертва; пострадавший. *Flood victims,* пострадавшие от наводнения. *Fall victim to,* пасть *or* стать жертвой (+ *gen.*).

victimize *v.t.* надувать; обдирать.

victor *n.* победитель. —**victorious,** *adj.* победоносный. *Be victorious,* побеждать.

victory *n.* победа.

victuals *n. pl.* пища; яства; съестные припасы.

vicuna *n.* вигонь. —*adj.* вигоневый.

video *n.* телевидение. —*adj.* телевизионный. —**video tape,** видеозапись.

vie *v.i.* соперничать; тягаться. *Vie with one another,* соперничать друг с другом. *Vie for the championship,* соревноваться за (*or* оспаривать) звание чемпиона. *Vie for the honor of...,* добиваться чести (+ *inf.*).

Viennese *adj.* венский.

Vietnamese *adj.* вьетнамский.

view *n.* **1.** (sight) вид: *disappear from view,* скрыться из виду. *Come into view,* показаться. **2.** (scene; vista) вид: *room with a view of the mountains,* комната с видом на горы. **3.** (opinion) взгляд; мнение: *exchange of views,* обмен взглядами/мнениями. — *v.t.* **1.** (look at; examine) осматривать. **2.** (regard) смотреть на: *how do you view the situation?,* как вы смотрите на положение дел? —**in view,** видно. —**in view of,** ввиду (+ *gen.*). —**on view,** у всех на виду. —**with a view to,** с целью (+ *inf. or gen.*); в целях (+ *gen.*).

viewer *n.* телезритель.

view finder видоискатель; визир.

viewpoint *n.* точка зрения.

vigil *n.* бдение. *Keep vigil,* дежурить; бодрствовать.

vigilant *adj.* бдительный. —**vigilance,** *n.* бдительность.

vignette *n.* **1.** (ornamental design) виньетка. **2.** (literary piece) очерк.

vigor *also,* **vigour** *n.* сила; бодрость. —**vigorous,** *adj.* бодрый; энергичный. —**vigorously,** *adv.* энергично.

Viking *n.* викинг.

vile *adj.* гадкий; мерзкий; противный; гнусный.

vilify *v.t.* поносить; порочить; чернить. —**vilification,** *n.* поношение.

villa *n.* вилла.

village *n.* деревня; село. —*adj.* деревенский; сельский. —**villager,** *n.* сельский житель.

villain *n.* злодей. —**villainous,** *adj.* злодейский. —**villainy,** *n.* злодейство.

vim *n.* прыть.

vindicate *v.t.* оправдывать. —**vindication,** *n.* оправдание.

vindictive *adj.* мстительный. —**vindictiveness,** *n.* мстительность.

vine *n.* **1.** (climbing or trailing plant) вьющееся *or* ползучее растение. **2.** (grapevine) лоза.

vinegar *n.* уксус. —*adj.* уксусный.

vineyard *n.* виноградник.

viniculture *n.* виноградарство.

vintage *n.* урожай; *this wine is vintage 1960,* это вино урожая 1960-го года. —*adj.* высшего качества. *Vintage wine,* марочное вино.

vinyl *n.* винил.

viol *n.* виола. —**bass viol,** контрабас.

viola *n.* альт; виола.

violate *v.t.* **1.** (break) нарушать: *violate a law/an oath/,* нарушать закон/клятву. **2.** (rape) насиловать.

violate *v.t.* **1.** (break) нарушать: *violate a law/an oath/,* нарушать закон/клятву. **2.** (rape) растлевать.

violation *n.* **1.** (breaking) нарушение. **2.** (rape) растление. —**violator,** *n.* нарушитель; коверкать.

violent *adj.* **1.** (fierce; powerful) неистовый; яростный; свирепый; бурный. *Violent storm,* неистовая/яростная/свирепая буря. *Violent argument,* яростный/бурный спор. *Violent passions,* неистовые/бурные страсти. **2.** (marked or caused by violence) насильственный: *violent death,* насильственная смерть.

violet *n.* фиалка. —*adj.* фиолетовый.

violin *n.* скрипка. —*adj.* скрипичный: *violin concerto,* скрипичный концерт. —**violinist,** *n.* скрипач.

violoncello *n.* виолончель.

VIP *colloq.* важное лицо; важная персона; высокопоставленное лицо.

viper *n.* **1.** (snake) гадюка. **2.** (vicious person) гадюка; ехидна.

virago *n.* мегера.

viral *adj.* вирусный.

virgin *n.* девственница. *The Virgin Mary,* богородица. —*adj.* **1.** (chaste) девственный. **2.** *fig.* (unexploited) девственный; целинный. *Virgin forest,* девственный лес. *Virgin lands,* целинные земли. *Virgin soil,* целина.

virginal *adj.* девственный; непорочный.

virginity *n.* девственность.

Virgo *n.* Дева.

virile *adj.* возмужалый. —**virility,** *n.* возмужалость.

virtual *adj.* фактический. —**virtually,** *adv.* практически; почти.

virtue *n.* **1.** (moral excellence; admirable quality) добродетель. **2.** (merit; advantage) достоинство. —**by virtue of,** в силу (+ *gen.*).

virtuoso *n.* виртуоз. —**virtuosity,** *n.* виртуозность.

virtuous *adj.* добродетельный.

virulence *n.* **1.** *med.* вирулентность. **2.** (bitterness) ярость.

virulent *adj.* **1.** (noxious; deadly) вирулентный. **2.** (bitterly hostile) яростный; злостный: *virulent attacks,* яростные/злостные нападки.

virus *n.* вирус.

visa *n.* виза.

visage *n.* **1,** (face) лицо. **2,** (countenance) вид; выражёние лица.

vis-à-vis *prep.* по отношёнию к; в отношёнии (+ *gen.*).

viscera *n.pl.* внутренности.

viscose *n.* вискоза.

viscosity *n.* вязкость; тягучесть.

viscount *n.* виконт.

viscous *adj.* вязкий; тягучий.

vise *n.* тиски: *grip in a vise,* зажимать в тиски.

visibility *n.* видимость.

visible *adj.* **1,** (in sight) видимый; видный. *The lake is not visible from here,* отсюда озера не видно. *The moon is hardly visible behind the clouds,* луна чуть видна из-за туч. **2,** (noticeable; marked) видимый; заметный: *visible improvement,* видимое/заметное улучшёние. *With no visible means of support,* без определённых средств к существованию.

visibly *adv.* заметно; явно: *he was visibly shaken,* он был заметно/явно потрясён.

vision *n.* **1,** (sense of sight) зрёние. *Field of vision,* поле зрёния. **2,** (foresight) проницательность. *A man of vision,* дальновидный человёк. **3,** (mental image) мечта: *visions of glory,* мечты о славе. **4,** (revelation) видёние.

visionary *adj.* несбыточный; непрактичный. —*n.* мечтатель; фантазёр.

visit *v.t.* **1,** (call on) навещать; посещать. **2,** (go to) посещать: *visit a museum,* посещать музёй. —*n.* посещёние; визит. *Pay a visit on,* наносить визит (+ *dat.*).

visitation *n.* посещёние.

visiting *adj.* приёзжий. —**visiting hours,** часы посещёния. —**visiting professor,** приглашённый профёссор.

visitor *n.* посетитель.

visor *also,* **vizor** *n.* **1,** (of a cap) козырёк. **2,** (of a helmet) забрало.

vista *n.* вид; перспектива.

visual *adj.* **1,** (produced by sight) зрительный: *visual impressions,* зрительные впечатлёния. **2,** (serving to instruct) наглядный: *visual aids,* наглядные пособия.

visualize *v.t.* представлять себё.

vital *adj.* **1,** (basic to survival) жизненный; насущный: *vital interests,* жизненные/насущные интерёсы. *Vital necessity,* жизненная необходимость. *Vital organs,* жизненно важные органы. **2,** *fol. by* **to** (essential) необходимый (для): *vital to the success of,* абсолютно необходим для успёха (+ *gen.*). **3,** (utmost) первостепённый: *of vital importance,* первостепённой важности.

vitality *n.* **1,** (ability to sustain life) жизненность. **2,** (vigor; energy) энёргия; энергичность.

vitally *adv.* жизненно: *vitally important,* жизненно важный. *Vitally interested,* кровно заинтересованный.

vitamin *n.* витамин. —**vitamin B**[1], витамин В[1] (*pronouced* бэ один). —**vitamin C,** витамин С (*pronounced* цэ).

vitiate *v.t.* **1,** (spoil) портить. **2,** (invalidate) дёлать недействительным.

viticulture *n.* виноградарство.

vitreous *adj.* стеклянный; стекольный.

vitriol *n.* купорос. *Blue/green/white vitriol,* мёдный/желёзный/цинковый купорос. —**oil of vitriol,** сёрная кислота.

vitriolic *adj.* ёдкий; ехидный.

vituperation *n.* брань; ругань. —**vituperative,** *adj.* бранный; ругательный.

vivacious *adj.* живой; оживлённый. —**vivaciousness; vivacity** *n.* живость; оживлённость.

vivid *adj.* **1,** (intense, as of a color) яркий. **2,** (lively; striking) живой; яркий. *Vivid description,* яркое описание. *Vivid memories,* живые/яркие воспоминания. *Vivid imagination,* живое *or* пылкое воображёние.

vividly *adv.* ярко; живо. *Vividly remember,* живо помнить.

vividness *n.* яркость; живость.

viviparous *adj.* живородящий.

vivisection *n.* вивисёкция.

vixen *n.* **1,** (female fox) самка лисицы. **2,** (ill-tempered woman) мегёра.

vizier *n.* визирь.

vizor *n.* = **visor.**

V-neck *n.* треугольный вырез.

vocabulary *n.* словарь; запас слов. *Vocabulary building,* накоплёние словаря.

vocal *adj.* **1,** (pert. to the voice) голосовой. **2,** (meant to be sung) вокальный. **3,** (vociferous) громкий; шумный. —**vocal cords,** голосовые связки.

vocalist *n.* певёц; певица.

vocation *n.* призвание.

vocational *adj.* профессиональный: *vocational training,* профессиональное образование. *Vocational school,* ремёсленное училище.

vocative *adj.* звательный: *vocative case,* звательный падёж.

vociferous *adj.* громкий; шумный.

vodka *n.* водка.

vogue *n.* мода. *Be in vogue,* быть в моде.

voice *n.* **1,** (sound made when speaking) голос: *in a loud voice,* громким голосом. *Be in good voice,* быть в голосе. **2,** *gram.* залог: *passive voice,* страдательный залог. —*v.t.* высказывать: *voice one's opinion,* высказать своё мнёние. —**give voice to,** выражать. —**with one voice,** в один голос.

voice box гортань.

voiced *adj., phonet.* звонкий.

voiceless *adj.* **1,** (having no voice) безголосый. **2,** *phonet.* глухой.

void *adj.* **1,** (invalid) недействительный: *declare null and void,* объявить недействительным. **2,** *fol. by* **of** (utterly lacking) лишённый (+ *gen.*): *void of sense,* лишён смысла. **3,** (empty) пустой. —*n.* пустота: *a void in one's life,* пустота в жизни. *Fill a void,* заполнить пустоту. —*v.t.* (nullify) дёлать недействительным; аннулировать. —*v.i., physiol.* опорожнять мочевой пузырь; мочиться.

voile *n.* газ.

volatile *adj.* **1,** (evaporating rapidly) летучий. **2,** (changeable; fickle) изменчивый. **3,** (unstable; explosive) неустойчивый.

volatility *n.* **1,** *chem.* летучесть. **2,** (changeability) изменчивость.

volcanic *adj.* вулканический.

volcano *n.* вулкан.

vole *n.* полёвка.

volition *n.* воля. *Of one own's volition,* по собственному желанию; по доброй воле. —**volitional,** *adj.* волевой.

volley *n.* **1,** (salvo) залп. **2,** *fig.* (torrent) град.

volleyball *n.* волейбо́л.

volt *n.* вольт. —**voltage,** *n.* напряже́ние; вольта́ж. —**voltmeter,** *n.* вольтме́тр.

voluble *adj.* говорли́вый; разгово́рчивый. —**volubility,** *n.* говорли́вость; разгово́рчивость.

volume *n.* **1,** (size; amount) объём: *the volume of a sphere,* объём ша́ра; *volume of trade,* объём торго́вли. **2,** (book) том: *in two volumes,* в двух тома́х. **3,** (loudness) си́ла зву́ка; гро́мкость. *Turn down the volume,* уме́ньшить звук. —**speak volumes,** говори́ть о мно́гом.

volumetric *adj.* объёмный.

voluminous *adj.* обши́рный: *voluminous correspondence,* обши́рная перепи́ска.

voluntary *adj.* **1,** (done by free choice) доброво́льный. **2,** *physiol.* произво́льный. —**voluntarily,** *adv.* доброво́льно.

volunteer *n.* доброво́лец. *Are there any volunteers?,* есть жела́ющие?; есть охо́тники? —*adj.* доброво́льческий: *volunteer army,* доброво́льческая а́рмия. —*v.t.* предлага́ть: *volunteer one's services,* предлага́ть свои́ услу́ги. —*v.i.* вызыва́ться: *volunteer to help,* вы́зваться помо́чь.

voluptuous *adj.* чу́вственный.

vomit *v.i.* рвать *(impers.):* *he is vomiting,* его́ рвёт; *she vomited,* её вы́рвало. —*n.* рво́тная ма́сса. —**vomiting,** *n.* рво́та.

voodoo *n.* колдовство́.

voracious *adj.* прожо́рливый. *Voracious appetite,* во́лчий аппети́т. *He is a voracious reader,* он чита́ет запо́ем.

vortex *n.* вихрь; водоворо́т.

vote *n.* **1,** (choice expressed) го́лос: *win by ten votes,* вы́играть с переве́сом в де́сять голосо́в. **2,** (act of voting) голосова́ние: *put to a vote,* поста́вить на голосова́ние. *Vote of confidence,* во́тум дове́рия. *By a majority vote,* большинство́м голосо́в. *By a 5-4 vote,* пятью́ голоса́ми про́тив четырёх. —*v.i.* голосова́ть: *vote for a candidate,* голосова́ть за кандида́та. *The right to vote,* пра́во го́лоса. —*v.t.* **1,** (authorize by vote) одобря́ть; ассигнова́ть. **2,** *fol.* by **in** (elect) избира́ть. **3,** *fol.* by **down** (defeat; reject) прова́ливать.

voter *n.* избира́тель.

voting *n.* голосова́ние. —**voting booth,** каби́на для голосова́ния. —**voting member,** член с реша́ющим го́лосом.

vouch *v.i.* [*usu.* **vouch for**] руча́ться (за).

voucher *n.* о́рдер: *expense voucher,* расхо́дный о́рдер.

vouchsafe *v.t.* удоста́ивать; соизволя́ть.

vow *n.* обе́т; кля́тва; заро́к. —*v.t. & i.* кля́сться (в). *Vow loyalty,* кля́сться в ве́рности.

vowel *n.* **1,** (sound) гла́сный звук. **2,** (letter) гла́сная бу́ква.

voyage *n.* путеше́ствие; пла́вание. —*v.i.* путеше́ствовать.

vulcanite *n.* эбони́т.

vulcanize *v.t.* вулканизи́ровать. —**vulcanization,** *n.* вулканиза́ция.

vulgar *adj.* гру́бый; по́шлый; вульга́рный. —**vulgarism,** *n.* вульгари́зм. —**vulgarity,** *n.* вульга́рность.

vulgarize *v.t.* опошля́ть; вульгаризи́ровать.

vulnerable *adj.* уязви́мый. —**vulnerability,** *n.* уязви́мость.

vulture *n.* гриф.

W

W, w два́дцать тре́тья бу́ква англи́йского алфави́та.

wacky *adj., slang* чудакова́тый; эксцентри́чный.

wad *n.* **1,** (small lump or mass) комо́к; кусо́чек. *Wad of cotton,* комо́к ва́ты. **2,** (bunch; roll) па́чка: *wad of money,* па́чка де́нег. **3,** (for a firearm) пыж.

wadding *n.* ва́та; наби́вка.

waddle *v.i.* перева́ливаться (с бо́ку на́ бок); ходи́ть вперева́лку; ходи́ть вразва́лку; ходи́ть у́точкой. —*n.* перева́лка.

wade *v.i.* идти́ вброд. *Wade into the water,* входи́ть в во́ду. *Wade across a river,* переходи́ть ре́ку вброд. —**wade through, 1,** (walk through) пробира́ться сквозь. **2,** *fig.* (plow through; work one's way through) оси́ливать (*e.g.* кни́гу).

wading bird боло́тная пти́ца.

wafer *n.* **1,** (biscuit) сухо́е пече́нье. **2,** (bread used in the Eucharist) обла́тка.

waffle *n.* ва́фля. —**waffle iron,** ва́фельница.

waft *v.t.* навева́ть. —*v.i.* тяну́ть *(impers.):* *cool air wafted in from the sea,* с мо́ря тяну́ло све́жим во́здухом. —*n.* дунове́ние (во́здуха).

wag *v.t.* виля́ть; маха́ть (хвосто́м). *Wag one's tongue,* болта́ть языко́м; чеса́ть язы́к. —*v.i.* виля́ть. —*n.* шутни́к; остря́к; балагу́р.

wage *n., often pl.* зарабо́тная пла́та; жа́лованье. —*v.t.* вести́ (войну́); проводи́ть (кампа́нию). —**wage earner,** рабо́чий. —**wage scale,** шкала́ зарабо́тной пла́ты.

wager *n.* пари́. —*v.i.* держа́ть пари́; би́ться об закла́д. —*v.t.* ста́вить.

wagon *also,* **waggon** *n.* пово́зка; теле́га; подво́да. *Covered wagon,* фурго́н.

wagtail *n.* трясогу́зка.

waif *n.* у́личный мальчи́шка; беспризо́рник.

wail *v.i.* выть; вопи́ть. —*n.* вой; вопль.

wainscot *n.* панéль.

waist *n.* тáлия. ♦*In idioms* пóяс: *bow from the waist,* клáняться в пóяс. *Strip to the waist,* раздéться до пóяса. *In water up to one's waist,* по пóяс в водé.

waistband *n.* пóяс.

waistcoat *n.* жилéт.

waistline *n.* тáлия.

wait *v.i.* ждать. *Wait for the train,* ждать пóезда. *Wait for the rain to stop,* ждать, когдá (*or* покá) перестáнет дождь. *I can't wait!,* жду не дождýсь!; я не могý дождáться! —*n.* **1,** (time spent waiting) ожидáние: *a long wait,* дóлгое ожидáние. **2,** *in* **lie in wait for,** подстерегáть. —**wait on,** обслýживать. *Wait on a table,* обслýживать стол. —**wait out,** выжидáть; пережидáть.

waiter *n.* официáнт.

waiting *n.* ожидáние. *Waiting period,* срок ожидáния. —*adj.* выжидáтельный: *play a waiting game,* занимáть выжидáтельную позицию.

waiting list óчередь: *a long waiting list,* большáя óчередь. *Be on the waiting list,* быть *or* стоять на óчереди. *Put someone on the waiting list,* постáвить когó-нибудь на óчередь.

waiting room 1, (in a railroad station) зал ожидáния. **2,** (in a doctor's office) приёмная.

waitress *n.* официáнтка.

waive *v.t.* **1,** (give up; forgo) отказываться от; поступáться (+ *instr.*). **2,** (set aside; dispense with) воздéрживаться от. *Waive a rule,* не применять прáвила.

waiver *n.* откáз.

wake *v.t.* будить: *wake me at seven o'clock,* разбудите меня в семь часóв. —*v.i.* [*usu.* **wake up**] просыпáться. —*n.* **1,** (for a dead person) помúнки. **2,** (track of a ship) кильвáтер. **3,** (route passed over): *leave in its wake,* оставлять за собóй. *Bring in its wake,* влечь за собóй. —**in the wake of,** по следáм (+ *gen.*); по пятáм (+ *gen.*).

waken *v.t.* будить. —*v.i.* просыпáться.

walk *v.i.* **1,** (take steps; proceed on foot) ходить; идти (пешкóм). *Walk slowly,* ходить/идти мéдленно. *Learn to walk,* учиться ходить. *Don't run, walk!,* не бегúте, идите шáгом! *It's not far — I'll walk,* это недалекó – я пойдý пешкóм. **2,** (stroll) ходить; гулять; прогýливаться; прохáживаться. *Walk in the park,* ходить/гулять в пáрке *or* по пáрку. —*v.t.* **1,** (pace) расхáживать по: *walk the floors,* расхáживать по кóмнате. **2,** (take for a walk) прогýливать: *walk the dog,* прогýливать собáку. **3,** (accompany) провожáть: *walk someone home,* провожáть когó-нибудь домóй. —*n.* **1,** (act of walking; distance walked) ходьбá: *ten minute walk,* дéсять минýт ходьбы. *20-km. walk,* sports ходьбá на двáдцать киломéтров. **2,** (stroll) прогýлка. *Go for a walk,* идти гулять. *Take for a walk,* водить гулять. **3,** (manner of walking; gait) похóдка. **4,** (slow pace) шаг: *slow a horse to a walk,* сводить лóшадь на шаг. **5,** (path; promenade) аллéя; дорóжка. **6,** *in* **from all walks of life,** всех слоёв óбщества. —**walk off,** уходить. *Walk off the job,* объявить забастóвку. —**walk off with, 1,** (steal) утащить. **2,** (win) взять; завоевáть. —**walk out,** выходить. *Walk out of a meeting,* (демонстративно) уйти с собрáния. —**walk out on,** брóсить; уйти от. —**walk up to,** подходить к.

walker *n.* **1,** (person) ходóк. **2,** (device to aid in walking) ходункú.

walkie-talkie *n.* (портативная) рáция.

walking *adj.* ходячий. *It is within walking distance,* тудá мóжно дойти пешкóм. —*n.* ходьбá. —**get one's walking papers,** быть увóленным; вылететь.

walking stick пáлка; трость.

walkout *n.* **1,** (abrupt departure) демонстративный ухóд. **2,** (strike) забастóвка.

wall *n.* стенá. —*adj.* стеннóй; настéнный. *Wall newspaper,* стеннáя газéта. —*v.t.* **1,** fol. by **in** (enclose) обносить стенóй. **2,** fol. by **up** (board up) задéлывать; замурóвывать. **3,** fol. by **off** (partition off) отгорáживать. —**drive up a wall,** colloq. сводить с умá; доводить до сумасшéствия. —**up against** (*or* with one's back to) the wall, припёртый к стенé.

wallet *n.* бумáжник.

walleye *n.* бельмó.

wallflower *n.* **1,** (plant) лакфиóль; желтофиóль. **2,** colloq. (girl without a partner at a dance) дéвушка без кавалéра.

wallop *n.* тумáк. —*v.t.* дать тумакá (+ *dat.*).

wallow *v.i.* [*usu.* **wallow in**] **1,** (roll about in) валяться (в). **2,** fig. (indulge oneself to excess) погрязнуть (в); утопáть (в).

wallpaper *n.* обóи. —*v.t.* оклéивать (кóмнату) обóями.

walnut *n.* **1,** (tree; wood) орéх; орéховое дéрево. **2,** (nut) грéцкий орéх. —*adj.* орéховый.

walrus *n.* морж.

waltz *n.* вальс. —*v.i.* вальсировать.

wan *adj.* блéдный.

wand *n.* пáлочка: *magic wand,* волшéбная пáлочка.

wander *v.i.* **1,** (walk or stroll aimlessly) бродить; блуждáть. **2,** (roam about the world) странствовать; скитáться. **3,** (fail to concentrate) блуждáть: *his mind tends to wander,* егó мысли чáсто блуждáют. —**wander into,** забрести в. —**wander off, 1,** [*also,* **wander away**] (stray) забрести. *Wander off/away from the group,* отставáть от грýппы. **2,** [*also,* **wander from**] (digress) отходить от.

wanderer *n.* стрáнник; скитáлец.

wandering *n.* стрáнствие; скитáние. —*adj.* бродячий; блуждáющий.

wanderlust *n.* страсть к путешéствиям.

wane *v.i.* **1,** (of the moon) убывáть. **2,** fig. (fade; ebb) угасáть; идти на ýбыль. —*n.,* *in* **on the wane,** на ущéрбе.

wangle *v.t.* выпрáшивать; раздобывáть. *Wangle a ticket/an invitation/,* выпросить/раздобыть билéт/приглашéние. *Wangle a secret from someone,* вывéдывать секрéт у когó-нибудь.

want *v.t.* хотéть: *what do you want?,* что вы хотите? *What do you want me to do?,* что вы хотите, чтобы я сдéлал(а)? *You are wanted on the phone,* вас прóсят к телефóну. *He is wanted by the authorities,* он разыскивается властями. —*n.* **1,** (lack) недостáток. *For want of something better,* за неимéнием лýчшего. **2,** (poverty; need) нуждá: *freedom from want,* свобóда от нужды. *Be in want of,* нуждáться в. **3,** *pl.* (needs) потрéбности.

want ad colloq. объявлéние (в газéте).

wanton *adj.* **1,** (vicious; unprovoked) бессмысленный. **2,** (dissolute) распýтный.

war *n.* войнá. *Be at war,* быть в состоянии войны; воевáть. —*adj.* воéнный: *war game,* воéнная игрá. —*v.i.* воевáть: *warring parties,* воюющие стóроны.

warble *v.i.* щёлкать. —*n.* трель.

warbler *n.* славка.

war crime воённое преступлéние. —**war criminal**, воённый престýпник.

war cry боевóй клич.

ward *n.* **1**, (dependent) опекáемый; подопéчный. **2**, (of a hospital) палáта. *Maternity ward*, родúльное отделéние. **3**, (district) райóн. —*v.t.* [*usu.* **ward off**] отражáть; отводúть.

warden *n.* стóрож; объéздчик: *forest warden*, леснóй стóрож/объéздчик. *Prison warden*, тюрéмщик. *Game warden*, инспéктор по охрáне дúчи.

warder *n.* **1**, (guard; watchman) стóрож. **2**, *Brit.* = **prison warden.**

wardrobe *n.* **1**, (clothes closet) гардерóб; платянóй шкаф. **2**, (supply of clothes) гардерóб.

ware *n.* **1**, *pl.* (merchandise) товáры. **2**, *used in compounds* издéлия; посýда: *hardware*, скобянýе издéлия; *earthenware*, глúняная посýда.

warehouse *n.* склад.

warfare *n.* войнá: *guerrilla warfare*, партизáнская войнá.

warhead *n.* **1**, (section of a missile) боевáя часть; боевáя голóвка. **2**, (explosive charge contained therein) заря́д; боеприпáс: *nuclear warhead*, я́дерный заря́д/боеприпáс.

warhorse *n.* боевóй конь.

warily *adv.* осторóжно.

wariness *n.* осторóжность.

warlike *adj.* воúнственный.

warm *adj.* тёплый: *warm milk/summer/coat/letter*, тёплое молокó/лéто/пальтó/письмó. *It is warm*, теплó. *Are you warm?*, вам теплó? *The sun is warm*, сóлнце грéет. *Get warm*, согревáться. —*v.t.* [*also*, **warm up**] греть; нагревáть; согревáть: *warm up the food*, греть/нагревáть/согревáть пúщу. *Warm one's feet by the fire*, греть нóги у огня́. *Warm one's heart*, рáдовать сéрдце; согревáть дýшу. —*v.i.* **1**, *fol. by* **up** (of the weather, temperature, etc.) теплéть. **2**, *fol. by* **up** (of a heating device, food on the stove, etc.) согревáться; нагревáться; (of an engine) прогревáться. **3**, *fol. by* **to** (get into the swing of) войтú во вкус (+ *gen.*). *Warm to one's subject*, разговорúться. —**warm oneself**, грéться. —**warm over**, разогревáть; подогревáть: *warmed-over dinner*, разогрéтый обéд. —**warm up**, (exercise; limber up) дéлать размúнку; разминáться. —**warm up to**, (бóлее) теплó относúться к.

warm-blooded *adj.* теплокрóвный.

warmhearted *adj.* тёплый; сердéчный.

warmly *adv.* **1**, (so as to be warm) теплó: *dress warmly*, теплó одевáться. **2**, (cordially) теплó; сердéчно.

warmonger *n.* поджигáтель войны́.

warmth *n.* теплó; теплотá. *Give off warmth*, излучáть теплó. *Warmth of feeling*, теплотá чýвства. *With great warmth*, с большóй теплотóй.

warm-up *n.* размúнка.

warn *v.t.* предупреждáть: *I'm warning you!*, предупреждáю (вас)! *I warned you not to do it*, я предупреждáл(а) вас не дéлать э́того. *Don't say I didn't warn you!*, не говорúте, что я вас не предупреждáл(а).

warning *n.* предупреждéние; предостережéние. *Fire without warning*, стреля́ть без предупреждéния. *Get off with a warning*, отдéлаться предупреж-

дéнием. —*adj.* предупредúтельный: *warning shot*, предупредúтельный вы́стрел.

warp *v.t.* **1**, (twist; bend) корóбить. **2**, (pervert) извращáть; ковéркать. *Warped mind*, извращённый ум. —*v.i.* корóбиться. —*n.* **1**, (bend) корóбление. **2**, *textiles* оснóва.

warplane *n.* воённый самолёт.

warrant *n.* óрдер; мандáт; наря́д. *Search warrant*, óрдер на обы́ск. —*v.t.* **1**, (justify) опрáвдывать. **2**, (merit) заслýживать.

warrant officer (in the army) прáпорщик; (in the navy) мúчман.

warranty *n.* гарáнтия; ручáтельство.

warren *n.* крóличья норá; крóличий садóк.

warrior *n.* боéц; вóин.

warship *n.* воённый корáбль.

wart *n.* бородáвка.

wart hog бородáвочник.

wartime *n.* воённое врéмя.

wary *adj.* осторóжный; осмотрúтельный. *Be wary of*, остерегáться (+ *gen.*).

wash *v.t.* **1**, (clean; scrub) мыть; умывáть. *Wash one's hands*, мыть рýки. *Wash the dishes*, мыть посýду. **2**, (launder) стирáть: *wash clothes*, стирáть бельё. **3**, (flow over) омывáть: *waves wash the shore*, вóлны омывáют бéрег. —*v.i.* **1**, [*often* **wash up**] (get washed) мы́ться; умывáться. **2**, (do laundry) стирáть. **3**, (be capable of being washed) стирáться. **4**, *colloq.* (stand up to scrutiny): *the story won't wash*, э́та истóрия никогó не убедúт. —*n.* **1**, (act of washing) мытьё. **2**, (laundering) стúрка: *fade in the wash*, линя́ть от стúрки. *The stains came out in the wash*, пя́тна вы́вились при стúрке. **3**, (things to be washed) бельё: *hang out the wash*, вывéшивать бельё. **4**, (liquid refuse) жúжа. **5**, (liquid used for cleansing) примóчка: *eyewash*, примóчка для глаз. —**wash away**, размывáть; сносúть (*impers.*): *the road was washed away*, дорóгу размы́ло. *The bridge was washed away by the flood*, мост снеслó водóй. —**wash down**, запивáть: *wash down medicine with water*, запивáть лекáрство водóй. —**wash off**, смывáть. —**wash one's hands of something**, умывáть рýки. —**wash out**, **1**, (wash) стирáть (*pfv.* вы́стирать). *Wash out one's socks*, вы́стирать носкú. **2**, (rinse out) сполáскивать. **3**, (remove) смывáть: *wash out a stain*, смывáть пятнó. **4**, (wash away) размывáть: *the flood washed out the road*, водá размы́ла дорóгу. —**wash overboard**, *see* **overboard.** —**wash up**, **1**, (wash one's hands and face) умывáться. **2**, (deposit on the shore) наносúть на бéрег.

washbasin *n.* умывáльник.

washboard *n.* стирáльная доскá.

washbowl *n.* умывáльник.

washcloth *n.* тря́пка для мытья́.

washed-out *adj.* **1**, (faded) полиня́вший. **2**, *colloq.* (tired; weak) лишён сил. **3**, *colloq.* (wan) блéдный.

washer *n.* **1**, (person who washes) мóйщик: *window washer*, мóйщик óкон. **2**, (washing machine) стирáльная машúна. **3**, *mech.* шáйба; проклáдка.

washerwoman *n.* прáчка.

washing *n.* мытьё; мóйка; умывáние; *(of clothes)* стúрка. —**washing machine**, стирáльная машúна.

washrag *n.* = **washcloth.**

washroom *n.* убóрная; туалéт.

washstand *n.* умывáльник.

washtub *n.* лоха́нь; коры́то.

wasp *n.* оса́.

waste *v.t.* **1,** (spend needlessly) тра́тить; да́ром/попусту/зря тра́тить. *Waste time,* теря́ть вре́мя. *Waste one's breath,* тра́тить слова́ да́ром. *His efforts were wasted,* его́ уси́лия пропа́ли да́ром. **2,** (fail to take advantage of) упуска́ть; прозева́ть (удо́бный случай). —*v.i.* [*usu.* **waste away**] ча́хнуть. —*n.* **1,** (unnecessary expenditure) растра́та. *Waste of time,* потеря́ *or* растра́та вре́мени; пуста́я тра́та вре́мени. **2,** (superfluous matter) отхо́ды; отбро́сы. *Industrial wastes,* отхо́ды произво́дства. **3,** *physiol.* выделе́ния. —**go to waste,** пропада́ть да́ром. —**lay waste,** опустоша́ть. —**waste products,** отхо́ды. *See also* **wasted.**

wastebasket *n.* корзи́на для бума́ги.

wasted *adj.* **1,** (squandered) растра́ченный. **2,** (fruitless; gone for naught) напра́сный; пропа́вший да́ром. **3,** (emaciated) истощённый: *wasted by disease,* истощённый боле́знью.

wasteful *adj.* расточи́тельный. —**wastefulness,** *n.* расточи́тельность.

wasteland *n.* пусты́ня.

wastrel *n.* **1,** (spendthrift) транжи́р. **2,** (good-for-nothing) шалопа́й.

watch *v.t.* **1,** (look at; observe) смотре́ть; наблюда́ть. *Watch television,* смотре́ть телеви́зор. *Watch the sun rise,* наблюда́ть восхо́д со́лнца. **2,** (guard; keep an eye on; look after) смотре́ть за; следи́ть за; наблюда́ть за. —*v.i.* смотре́ть: *watch how it's done,* посмотри́те, как э́то де́лается. *Watch that he doesn't fall,* смотри́те, что́бы он не упа́л. —*n.* **1,** (timepiece) часы́. **2,** (observation) наблюде́ние. *Keep watch over,* наблюда́ть за. *Be on the watch for,* подстерега́ть. **3,** (guarding) стра́жа; *naval* ва́хта: *stand watch,* стоя́ть на стра́же *or* на ва́хте. **4,** (those who guard) стра́жа; дозо́р. *Night watch,* ночно́й дозо́р. —*adj.* часово́й: *watch spring,* часова́я пружи́на. —**watch for,** ждать; стере́чь; подстерега́ть. —**watch it!,** осторо́жно! —**watch oneself,** бере́чься. —**watch one's step, 1,** (be careful not to fall) стара́ться не оступи́ться: *watch your step!,* осторо́жно, не оступи́тесь! **2,** (be prudent) бере́чься; быть осторо́жным; соблюда́ть осторо́жность. —**watch out,** бере́чься. *Watch out!,* осторо́жно! —**watch out for,** бере́чься (+ *gen.*); остерега́ться (+ *gen.*).

watchband *n.* ремешо́к для часо́в.

watch chain цепо́чка для часо́в.

watchdog *n.* дворо́вая соба́ка; сторожево́й пёс.

watchful *adj.* насторо́женный. *Keep a watchful eye on,* внима́тельно следи́ть за.

watchmaker *n.* часовщи́к.

watchman *n.* сто́рож.

watchtower *n.* сторожева́я ба́шня/вы́шка.

watchword *n.* **1,** (password) паро́ль. **2,** (motto) ло́зунг; деви́з.

water *n.* вода́: *be under water,* быть под водо́й. *Mineral/territorial waters,* минера́льные/территориа́льные во́ды. *Ship something by water,* отправля́ть что́-нибудь во́дным путём. *Land a plane on the water,* посади́ть самолёт на́ воду. —*adj.* во́дный; водяно́й: *water sports,* во́дный спорт; *water vapor,* водяно́й пар. *Water glass,* стака́н для воды́. —*v.t.* **1,** (pour water on) полива́ть: *water the flowers,* полива́ть цветы́. **2,** (provide with water, as animals) пои́ть. **3,** *fol. by*

down (dilute; weaken) разбавля́ть; разжижа́ть; *fig.* смягча́ть. —*v.i.* **1,** (of one's eyes) слези́ться. **2,** (of one's mouth): *my mouth is watering,* у меня́ слю́нки теку́т. —**of the first water,** чи́стой *or* чисте́йшей воды́. —**not hold water,** не выде́рживать кри́тики. —**throw cold water on,** облива́ть (+ *acc.*) холо́дной водо́й.

water buffalo инди́йский (*or* водяно́й) бу́йвол.

water carrier водоно́с; водово́з.

water closet убо́рная.

watercolor *also,* **watercolour** *n., often pl.* акваре́ль. —*adj.* акваре́льный. —**watercolorist,** *n.* акварели́ст.

water-cooled *adj.* с водяны́м охлажде́нием.

watercress *n.* водяно́й кресс.

waterfall *n.* водопа́д.

waterfowl *n.* водопла́вающая пти́ца.

waterfront *n.* порт; райо́н по́рта.

watering *n.* **1,** (of plants) поли́вка. **2,** (of livestock) водопо́й. —**watering can,** ле́йка. —**watering place,** водопо́й.

waterless *adj.* безво́дный.

water lily водяна́я ли́лия; кувши́нка.

waterline *n.* ватерли́ния.

waterlogged *adj.* пропи́танный водо́й.

water main водопрово́дная магистра́ль.

watermark *n.* водяно́й знак.

watermelon *n.* арбу́з. —*adj.* арбу́зный: *watermelon seeds,* арбу́зные ко́сточки.

water meter водоме́р.

water pipe водопрово́дная труба́.

water polo во́дное по́ло; ватерпо́ло.

water power во́дная эне́ргия.

waterproof *adj.* непромока́емый; водонепроница́емый. *Be waterproof,* не пропуска́ть воды́.

watershed *n.* водоразде́л.

water ski во́дная лы́жа. —**water-ski,** *v.i.* ката́ться на во́дных лы́жах. —**water-skiing,** *n.* воднолы́жный спорт.

waterspout *n.* **1,** (outlet for water) водосто́чная труба́. **2,** (tornado) смерч.

water sprite водяно́й.

water table у́ровень грунтовы́х вод.

watertight *adj.* **1,** (waterproof) водонепроница́емый; непромока́емый. **2,** (impossible to refute) неопроверж́и́мый.

water tower водонапо́рная ба́шня.

waterway *n.* во́дный путь; во́дная арте́рия.

water wheel водяно́е колесо́.

watery *adj.* водяни́стый; жи́дкий.

watt *n.* ватт: *100-watt bulb,* ла́мпочка в сто ватт. —**wattage,** *n.* мо́щность (в ва́ттах).

wattle *n.* **1,** (interlaced twigs forming a fence) плете́нь. **2,** (fleshy skin hanging from the throat of certain fowl) борода́; серёжка. —**wattled,** *adj.* плетёный.

wave *n.* **1,** (of water) волна́. **2,** (in one's hair) зави́вка. **3,** *physics* волна́: *sound wave,* звукова́я волна́. **4,** (motion with the hand) взмах. **5,** *fig.* (surge) волна́: *a wave of discontent,* волна́ недово́льства. **6,** (period of cold or heat) полоса́. —*v.t.* **1,** (move back and forth; swing) маха́ть; помаха́ть. *Wave goodbye,* маха́ть/ помаха́ть на проща́ние. *Wave a flag,* разма́хивать флаѓом. **2,** (curl, as hair) завива́ть. —*v.i.* **1,** (flutter) развева́ться. **2,** (wave one's hand) маха́ть/помаха́ть руко́й. *Wave to someone*, маха́ть руко́й (+ *dat.*). —**wave aside**, отма́хиваться от.

wavelength *n.* длина́ волны́.

waver *v.i.* **1.** (sway; flutter) колыха́ться; развева́ться. **2,** (show hesitation) дро́гнуть; колеба́ться.

wavy *adj.* волни́стый.

wax *n.* воск. —*adj.* восково́й. —*v.t.* вощи́ть. *Wax the floor*, натира́ть пол. —*v.i.* **1,** (of the moon) прибыва́ть; прибавля́ться. **2,** (become): *wax angry*, рассерди́ться; *wax calm*, успоко́иться.

waxen *adj.* восково́й.

wax museum пано́птикум.

wax paper вощёная бума́га; вощёнка.

waxwing *n.* свиристе́ль.

waxy *adj.* восково́й.

way *n.* **1,** (route) путь; доро́га: *on the way home*, по пути́/по доро́ге/домо́й. *All the way*, всю доро́гу. *Part of the way*, часть пути́. *The shortest way to town*, кратча́йший путь в го́род. *Lose one's way*, заблуди́ться; сби́ться с пути́/с доро́ги. *Are you going my way?*, нам по пути́? вам со мной по пути́? **2,** (direction) сторона́: *he went that way*, он пошёл в ту сто́рону. *Which way are you going?*, вам в каку́ю сто́рону? *This way, please!*, сюда́, пожа́луйста! **3,** (position such as to be an obstacle): *be in the way*, меша́ть. *Get out of the way!*, не меша́йте!; прочь с доро́ги! *Keep out of the way*, держа́ться в стороне́. *Stand in someone's way*, стоя́ть на чьём-нибудь пути́; стоя́ть у кого́-нибудь поперёк доро́ги. **4,** (manner; method) спо́соб; путь: *this way*, таки́м спо́собом; таки́м о́бразом. *The same way*, так же. *In what way?*, каки́м о́бразом?; каки́м путём? *One's own way*, на свой лад; по-сво́ему. *Don't do it that way*, не де́лайте так. *There is no other way to do it*, э́то нельзя́ сде́лать ина́че. *Try in every way*, все́ми си́лами стара́ться. **5,** (respect) отноше́ние: *in a way*, в не́котором отноше́нии; в не́котором ро́де; в изве́стном смы́сле. *In many ways*, во мно́гих отноше́ниях. **6,** (distance): *a long way from here*, далеко́ отсю́да. *We have a way to go*, нам ещё далеко́ е́хать. *We've come a long way*, мы прие́хали издалека́; мы проде́лали большо́й путь; *fig.* мы доби́лись мно́гого. **7,** (wish; will): *have one's way*, настоя́ть на своём. *Get one's way*, доби́ться своего́. *Have it your way*, пусть бу́дет по-ва́шему. **8,** *colloq.* (condition) положе́ние: *in a bad way*, в плохо́м положе́нии. **9,** *colloq.* (locality; region) райо́н: *out our way*, в на́шем райо́не. **10,** *pl.* (customs; manners) нра́вы. *Mend one's ways*, исправля́ться. —*adv.* далеко́: *way behind*, далеко́ позади́. —**by the way**, ме́жду про́чим; кста́ти. —**by way of, 1,** (via) че́рез. **2,** (as) в ка́честве (+ *gen.*): *by way of example*, в ка́честве приме́ра. *By way of proof*, в ви́де доказа́тельства. —**come one's way**, попада́ться (+ *dat.*). —**give way, 1,** (yield to physical pressure) подава́ться: *the door gave way*, дверь подала́сь. *The rope gave way*, верёвка порвала́сь. *The roof gave way*, кры́ша обвали́лась. *His legs gave way under him*, у него́ но́ги подкоси́лись. **2,** *fol. by* **to** (succumb to) поддава́ться (+ *dat.*); предава́ться (+ *dat.*). *Give way to despair*, предава́ться отча́янию. **3,** *fol. by* **to** (be replaced or succeeded by) сменя́ться (+ *instr.*); уступа́ть ме́сто (+ *dat.*). —**go out of one's way, 1,** (make a detour) сде́лать крюк. **2,** (put oneself out) прилага́ть осо́бые уси́лия. —**have a way with**, уме́ть обраща́ться с. —**in one's way; in its way**, в

своём ро́де. —**in the way of, 1,** (hindering): *stand in the way of progress*, тормози́ть прогре́сс. **2,** (in; by way of) в ка́честве (+ *gen.*). *What have you got in the way of fabrics?*, что у вас есть из материа́лов? —**lead the way**, идти́ впереди́. —**make one's way**, пробира́ться. —**make way**, сторони́ться; расступа́ться. *Make way for*, дать *or* уступи́ть доро́гу (+ *dat.*). —**out of the way, 1,** (not on one's route) не по пути́. **2,** (not blocking anything; aside) в стороне́. **3,** (finished; disposed of) зако́нчен. **4,** *Put (someone) out of the way, colloq.* (kill) ликвиди́ровать; уложи́ть. —**under way**, *rendered by various verbs: talks are under way*, перегово́ры начали́сь/иду́т/веду́тся. *Get under way*, начина́ть(ся); отправля́ться в путь. —**way of life**, о́браз *or* укла́д жи́зни. —**ways and means**, пути́ и сре́дства. —**way out**, вы́ход.

waybill *n.* накладна́я.

wayfarer *n.* пу́тник. —**wayfaring**, *adj.* стра́нствующий.

waylay *v.t.* напада́ть на; устра́ивать заса́ду на.

wayside *adj.* придоро́жный. *Wayside inn*, постоя́лый двор. —**fall by the wayside**, выбыва́ть из стро́я.

way station попу́тная ста́нция; полуста́нок.

wayward *adj.* заблу́дший; беспу́тный. *Wayward son*, заблу́дший сын. *Wayward existence*, беспу́тная жизнь.

we *pers.pron.* мы. *See also* **us.**

weak *adj.* сла́бый: *weak from hunger*, сла́бый от го́лода. *Weak link*, сла́бое звено́. *Weak tea*, сла́бый чай. *Weak point*, сла́бое ме́сто. *Grow weak*, слабе́ть; ослабева́ть. *Feel weak*, чу́вствовать каку́ю-то сла́бость. *Have a weak spot in one's heart for*, име́ть *or* пита́ть сла́бость к.

weaken *v.t.* ослабля́ть. —*v.i.* слабе́ть.

weakling *n.* тря́пка.

weakly *adj.* хи́лый. —*adv.* сла́бо.

weakness *n.* сла́бость. *Have a weakness for*, име́ть *or* пита́ть сла́бость к.

weak-willed *adj.* безво́льный; слабово́льный; бесхара́ктерный.

weal *n.* **1,** (welt) рубе́ц; полоса́. **2,** *archaic* (welfare) бла́го; благосостоя́ние.

wealth *n.* **1,** (riches; prosperity) бога́тство. **2,** *fol. by* **of** (abundance) бога́тство; оби́лие (+ *gen.*). *A wealth of information*, ма́сса информа́ции. *A wealth of material*, бога́тый материа́л.

wealthy *adj.* бога́тый; зажи́точный; состоя́тельный.

wean *v.t.* **1,** (a child) отнима́ть от груди́. **2,** (break, as of a habit) отуча́ть (от).

weapon *n.* ору́жие *(always sing.)*: *secret weapon*, секре́тное ору́жие; *nuclear weapons*, я́дерное ору́жие. *Weapons of mass destruction*, ору́жие ма́ссового уничтоже́ния. —**weaponry**, *n.* вооруже́ние.

wear *v.t.* **1,** (have on) надева́ть: *what are you going to wear to the party?*, что ты собира́ешься наде́ть на ве́чер? *I have nothing to wear*, мне не́чего наде́ть. *He is wearing a new suit*, на нем но́вый костю́м. **2,** (wear habitually) носи́ть: *wear glasses/a beard/*, носи́ть очки́/бо́роду. *Wear one's hair short*, носи́ть коро́ткие во́лосы. *He always wears a tie*, он всегда́ но́сит га́лстук. *What size shoe do you wear?*, како́й но́мер боти́нок вы но́сите? **3,** (bring to a state by wearing) изна́шивать: *wear a coat to shreds*, изна́-

шивать пальто́ до дыр. *Wear a hole in one's pocket,* продыря́вить карма́н. **4**, (have; exhibit) име́ть: *wear a dejected look,* име́ть мра́чный вид. —*v.i.* **1**, (hold up) носи́ться: *this skirt wears well,* э́та ю́бка хорошо́ но́сится. **2**, (show the effects of wear) изна́шиваться. —*n.* **1**, (act of wearing) но́ска: *from long wear,* от до́лгой но́ски. **2**, (effect of wearing) изно́с. *Show signs of wear,* обтрепа́ться. **3**, (clothes) оде́жда: *men's wear,* мужска́я оде́жда. —**wear and tear,** изно́с. —**wear away,** стира́ть. *The inscription is worn away,* на́дпись стёрлась. —**wear down, 1,** (wear out, as footwear) ста́птывать. **2**, (overcome, as resistance) преодолева́ть; сломи́ть. —**wear off,** проходи́ть: *the pain wore off,* боль прошла́. —**wear out, 1,** (wear until no longer usable) изна́шивать. **2**, (be no longer usable) изна́шиваться. **3**, (exhaust) изнуря́ть; изму́чить. —**wear thin,** *see* thin.

weariness *n.* уста́лость; утомле́ние.

wearing *adj.* утоми́тельный. —**wearing apparel,** оде́жда.

wearisome *adj.* томи́тельный.

weary *adj.* уста́лый; утомлённый. —*v.t.* утомля́ть. —*v.i.* устава́ть; утомля́ться.

weasel *n.* ла́ска.

weather *n.* пого́да. *Weather forecast,* прогно́з пого́ды. —*v.t.* **1**, (wear away by exposure to the elements) выве́тривать. **2**, (survive) выде́рживать: *weather a storm,* вы́держать бу́рю. —**keep one's weather eye open,** держа́ть у́хо востро́. —**under the weather, 1,** (ill) нездоро́в. **2**, (drunk) под хмелько́м.

weather-beaten *adj.* обве́тренный.

weathercock *n.* флю́гер.

weatherman *n.* сино́птик; метеоро́лог.

weather map синопти́ческая ка́рта.

weather satellite метеорологи́ческий спу́тник; метеоспу́тник.

weather vane флю́гер.

weave *v.t.* **1**, (form into fabric) ткать: *weave cloth,* ткать сукно́. **2**, (make by weaving) плести́: *weave a basket,* плести́ корзи́ну. **3**, (spin, as a tale) плести́. —*v.i.* **1**, (do weaving) ткать. **2**, (zigzag) петля́ть; виля́ть. —*n.* переплете́ние: *close weave,* ча́стое переплете́ние.

weaver *n.* ткач.

weaving *n.* тканьё.

web *n.* **1**, (spider's web) паути́на. **2**, *fig.* (tangle) сплете́ние; паути́на: *web of lies,* сплете́ние/паути́на лжи. **3**, *zool.* (membrane) перепо́нка.

webbed *adj.* перепо́нчатый: *webbed feet,* перепо́нчатые ла́пы.

web-footed *adj.* с перепо́нчатыми ла́пами.

wed *v.t.* жени́ться на; выходи́ть за́муж за. —*v.i.* жени́ться; выходи́ть за́муж; вступи́ть в брак.

wedded *adj.* **1**, (married): *my lawfully wedded wife,* моя́ зако́нная супру́га. **2**, *fol. by* to (bound) привя́занный: *I am not wedded to this job,* я не привя́зан(а) к э́той рабо́те.

wedding *n.* сва́дьба. —*adj.* сва́дебный: *wedding cake/present,* сва́дебный торт/пода́рок. *Wedding day,* день сва́дьбы. *Wedding dress,* сва́дебное *or* подвене́чное пла́тье. *Wedding palace,* дворе́ц бракосочета́ния. *Wedding ring,* обруча́льное кольцо́.

wedge *n.* клин. —*v.t.* закли́нивать. *Become wedged,* закли́ниваться. —**wedge-shaped,** *adj.* клинови́дный; клинообра́зный.

wedlock *n.* брак. *Born out of wedlock,* рождённый вне бра́ка.

Wednesday *n.* среда́.

wee *adj.* кро́шечный; малю́сенький. —**a wee bit,** чуть-чуть.

weed *n.* со́рная трава́; сорня́к. —*v.t.* **1**, (clear of weeds) поло́ть; пропа́лывать. **2**, *fol. by out* (eliminate) отсе́ивать. —**weed-killer,** *n.* гербици́д.

week *n.* неде́ля. *A week's vacation,* неде́льный о́тпуск. *A week from Wednesday,* в сре́ду на сле́дующей неде́ле; че́рез неде́лю в сре́ду.

weekday *n.* бу́дний *or* бу́дничный день.

weekend *n.* суббо́та и воскресе́нье.

weekly *adj.* еженеде́льный. —*adv.* еженеде́льно —*n.* еженеде́льник.

weep *v.i.* **1**, (cry) пла́кать. **2**, *fol. by for* (mourn) опла́кивать. —*v.t.* (shed, as tears) пролива́ть.

weeping *n.* плач. —**weeping willow,** плаку́чая и́ва.

weevil *n.* долгоно́сик.

weft *n.*, *textiles* уто́к.

weigh *v.t.* взве́шивать. *Weigh oneself,* взве́шиваться. *Weigh one's words,* взве́шивать свои́ слова́. —*v.i.* **1**, (have a certain weight) ве́сить. *How much do you weigh?,* како́й у вас вес?; ско́лько вы ве́сите? *I weigh 140 pounds,* мой вес (*or* я ве́шу) сто со́рок фу́нтов. **2**, (carry weight) име́ть вес: *weigh heavily,* име́ть большо́й вес. **3**, *Weigh on one's mind,* тяготи́ть (кого́-нибудь). —**weigh anchor,** снима́ться с я́коря. —**weigh down,** отягоща́ть; оття́гивать. —**weigh out,** отве́шивать; разве́шивать.

weight *n.* **1**, (heaviness) вес. *Gain/lose weight,* прибавля́ть/теря́ть в ве́се. **2**, *fig.* (influence; importance) вес: *carry weight,* име́ть вес. *Attach great weight to,* придава́ть большо́е значе́ние (+ *dat.*). **3**, *fig.* (burden) тя́жесть: *the weight of cares,* тя́жесть забо́т. *The weight of evidence,* тя́жесть ули́к. **4**, (anything heavy, used for its weight) ги́ря. *Paperweight,* пресс-папье́. **5**, *sports* ги́ря; штанга; тя́жесть: *lift weights,* поднима́ть ги́ри/тя́жести. —*v.t.* утяжеля́ть: *weight sacks with lead,* утяжеля́ть мешки́ свинцо́м. —**throw one's weight around,** распоряжа́ться; хозя́йничать. —**worth its weight in gold,** на вес зо́лота.

weightless *adj.* невесо́мый. —**weightlessness,** *n.* невесо́мость.

weightlifter *n.* гиреви́к; штанги́ст; тяжелоатле́т. —**weightlifting,** *n.* подня́тие тя́жестей; тяжёлая атле́тика.

weighty *adj.* ве́ский; весо́мый.

weir *n.* запру́да.

weird *adj.* **1**, (eerie) таи́нственный. **2**, (odd) стра́нный.

welcome *adj.* **1**, (gladly received) прия́тный: *welcome news,* прия́тное изве́стие. *A welcome guest,* жела́нный гость. **2**, *fol. by* to (gladly invited): *you are always welcome to come,* ми́лости про́сим. *You are welcome to use my car,* моя́ маши́на к ва́шим услу́гам. —*n.* приём; встре́ча: *hearty welcome,* раду́шный приём; раду́шная встре́ча. *Speech of welcome,* приве́тственная речь. —*v.t.* приве́тствовать: *welcome a delegation/proposal,* приве́тствовать делега́цию/предложе́ние. —*interj.* добро́ пожа́ловать!: *welcome to Moscow!,* добро́ пожа́ловать в Москву́! —**you are welcome!,** пожа́луйста!

weld *v.t.* **1**, (join by heating and fusing) сва́ривать. **2**, *fig.* (bring into close union) спла́чивать. —**welder,** *n.* сва́рщик.

welding *n.* сва́рка. —*adj.* сва́рочный: *welding torch,* сва́рочная горе́лка.

welfare *n.* **1,** (well-being) благосостоя́ние; благополу́чие. **2,** (support of the needy) социа́льное обеспе́чение. *Be on welfare,* получа́ть посо́бие.

well[1] *n.* коло́дец. *Oil well,* нефтяна́я сква́жина. —*adj.* коло́дезный: *well water,* коло́дезная вода́. —*v.i.* [*usu.* **well up**] (of emotions) вскипа́ть. *Tears welled up in her eyes,* слёзы наверну́лись на её глаза́.

well[2] *adv.* **1,** (satisfactorily; properly; excellently) хорошо́: *well said!,* хорошо́ ска́зано! *Turn out well,* ко́нчиться благополу́чно. *Shake well before using,* взба́лтывать пе́ред употребле́нием. *All's well that ends well,* всё хорошо́, что хорошо́ конча́ется. **2,** (fully; entirely) вполне́: *it may well be that...,* вполне́ возмо́жно, что... *Be well aware of,* отдава́ть себе́ по́лный отчёт в. **3,** (considerably; far) далеко́: *well past midnight,* далеко́ за́ полночь. —*adj.* **1,** (in good health) здоро́вый. *Get well,* выздора́вливать. *He looks well,* он хорошо́ вы́глядит. **2,** (satisfactory) хорошо́; в поря́дке: *all is well,* всё в поря́дке. —*interj.* **1,** used to introduce a statement ну. **2,** expressing surprise вот как; вот тебе́ и на. —**as well,** а та́кже: *and in Paris as well,* а та́кже в Пари́же. —**as well as, 1,** (in addition) а та́кже: *as well as in a number of other countries,* а та́кже в ря́де други́х стран. **2,** (equally with) как..., так...: *women as well as men,* как же́нщины, так и мужчи́ны. —**wish someone well,** жела́ть кому́-нибудь добра́.

well-behaved *adj.* благовоспи́танный. *The children were well-behaved,* де́ти вели́ себя́ хорошо́.

well-being *n.* благополу́чие; благосостоя́ние.

well-bred *adj.* (благо)воспи́танный.

well-done *adj.* **1,** (capably done) хорошо́ сде́ланный. **2,** (thoroughly cooked) (хорошо́) прожа́ренный.

well-dressed *adj.* хорошо́ оде́тый; наря́дный.

well-earned *adj.* заслу́женный.

well-fed *adj.* отко́рмленный; упи́танный.

well-founded *adj.* обосно́ванный; состоя́тельный.

well-groomed *adj.* хо́леный.

well-grounded *adj.* **1,** (well-founded) обосно́ванный. **2,** (knowledgeable) хорошо́ подко́ван (*e.g.* в хи́мии).

well-informed *adj.* (хорошо́) осведомлённый.

well-intentioned *adj.* име́ющий до́брые наме́рения; благонаме́ренный.

well-known *adj.* изве́стный.

well-mannered *adj.* (благо)воспи́танный.

well-meaning *adj.* име́ющий до́брые наме́рения; благонаме́ренный.

well-nigh *adv.* почти́; чуть ли не.

well-off *adj.* зажи́точный; состоя́тельный; обеспе́ченный.

well-paid *adj.* хорошо́ опла́чиваемый.

well-preserved *adj.* хорошо́ сохрани́вшийся.

well-read *adj.* начи́танный.

well sweep жура́вль.

well-to-do *adj.* зажи́точный; состоя́тельный; обеспе́ченный.

well-versed *adj.* све́дущий.

well-wisher *n.* доброжела́тель. —**well-wishing,** *adj.* доброжела́тельный.

Welsh *adj.* уэ́льский; валли́йский. —*n.* уэ́льский/валли́йский язы́к. —**Welshman,** *n.* валли́ец.

welt *n.* **1,** (part of a shoe) рант. **2,** (cord trimming) обши́вка. **3,** (mark left by a whip or stick) полоса́.

welter *n.* пу́таница: *welter of ideas,* пу́таница мы́слей.

welting *n.* обши́вка.

wench *n.* де́вка.

wend *v.t.,* in **wend one's way,** направля́ть свой шаги́ *or* стопы́.

were *v.,* past tense of **be.** —*subjunctive* будь: *were he alive today,* будь он сейча́с жив. —**as it were,** так сказа́ть.

werewolf *n.* о́боротень.

west *n.* за́пад. *The West,* За́пад. —*adj.* за́падный: *the West Coast,* за́падное побере́жье. —*adv.* на за́пад; к за́паду. *West of,* к за́паду от; за́паднее (+ *gen.*).

westerly *adj.* за́падный.

western *adj.* за́падный. —*n.* ковбо́йский фильм. —**westernmost,** *adj.* са́мый за́падный.

westward *adv.* к за́паду. —*adj.* за́падный.

wet *adj.* мо́крый: *wet hands//shoes,* мо́крые ру́ки/ту́фли. *Wet pavement,* мо́крый тротуа́р. *"Wet paint!",* осторо́жно! окра́шено! *Get wet,* промока́ть. *Get one's feet wet,* промочи́ть но́ги. —*v.t.* мочи́ть; сма́чивать. *Wet one's bed,* де́лать под себя́. —**he is still wet behind the ears,** у него́ молоко́ на губа́х не обсо́хло.

wet nurse корми́лица.

whack *n., colloq.* тума́к. —*v.t., colloq.* тра́хнуть; тре́снуть. —**out of whack,** *slang* не в поря́дке.

whale *n.* кит. —*adj.* кито́вый: *whale oil,* кито́вый жир.

whalebone *n.* кито́вый ус.

whaler *n.* **1,** (person) китобо́й. **2,** (ship) китобо́й; китобо́ец; китобо́йное су́дно.

whaling *n.* китобо́йный про́мысел. —*adj.* китобо́йный: *whaling ship,* китобо́йное су́дно; китобо́й; китобо́ец.

whammy *n., slang* дурно́й глаз. *Put the whammy on,* сгла́зить (кого́-нибудь).

wharf *n.* при́стань.

what *pron.* **1,** *interr.* что?: *what is this?,* что э́то тако́е? *What do you want?,* что вы хоти́те? *What else do you need?,* что ещё вам ну́жно? *What is that building?,* что э́то за зда́ние? ♦*Often rendered by* как *and* како́й: *what is your name?,* как вас зову́т? *What is this called?,* как э́то называ́ется? *What's the score?,* како́й счёт? *What is your phone number?,* како́й у вас но́мер телефо́на? *What's the difference between...?,* кака́я ра́зница ме́жду...? **2,** *rel.* то, что: *just what I need,* как раз то, что мне ну́жно. *What he says is true,* то, что он говори́т – пра́вда. *Say what you will,* что ни говори́те. *And what is worse,* а что ещё ху́же. *Come what may,* будь, что бу́дет. *Did you find what you were looking for?,* вы нашли́, что иска́ли? —*adj.* **1,** *interr.* како́й: *what clothes should I take?,* каку́ю оде́жду мне с собо́й взять? *What good will it do?,* кака́я от э́того по́льза? *What time is it?,* кото́рый тепе́рь час? **2,** used in exclamations како́й: *what nonsense!,* кака́я чепуха́! *What a surprise!,* како́й сюрпри́з! **3,** (as much; whatever) тот: *I forgot what little I knew,* я забы́л то немно́гое, что знал. *I gave him what money I had,* я дал ему́ все де́ньги, каки́е у меня́ бы́ли. —*adv.* **1,** *interr.: what does it matter?,* како́е э́то име́ет значе́ние? **2,** *used in exclamations* како́й: *what lovely weather!,* кака́я чу́дная пого́да! —**what about...?,** а что с...?; как насчёт...? —**what for?,** заче́м? —**what if...?,** а что е́сли...? —**what of it?,** ну, что?; ма́ло ли что! —**what's more,** *see* **more.** —**what's what,** что к чему́. —**what with,** из-за; ввиду́.

whatever *pron.* **1,** (no matter what) что ни; что бы ни: *whatever happens,* что бы ни случи́лось. *Whatever the outcome,* незави́симо от исхо́да. **2,** (anything) что уго́дно: *take whatever you like,* возьми́те что вам уго́дно. **3,** *expressing perplexity or wonderment* что же: *whatever can he want?,* что же он хо́чет? —*adj.* **1,** (no matter which) како́й бы ни: *whatever city you come to,* в како́й бы го́род вы ни прие́хали. **2,** (absolutely) абсолю́тно; реши́тельно. *No doubt whatever,* абсолю́тно никако́го сомне́ния. *I know nothing whatever about it,* я реши́тельно ничего́ не зна́ю об э́том.

whatsoever *adv.* абсолю́тно; реши́тельно. *No plans whatsoever,* абсолю́тно никаки́х пла́нов.

wheat *n.* пшени́ца. —*adj.* пшени́чный: *wheat flour,* пшени́чная мука́. *Wheat crop,* урожа́й пшени́цы.

wheedle *v.t.* **1,** (cajole; coax) обжа́живать. **2,** (get by cajolery) выпра́шивать; выма́нивать; выкля́нчивать.

wheel *n.* **1,** (circular device) колесо́: *rear wheel,* за́днее колесо́. *Potter's wheel,* гонча́рный круг. *Spinning wheel,* пря́лка. **2,** (steering wheel) руль: *be at the wheel,* быть за рулём. **3,** *slang* (big shot) ши́шка; туз. —*v.t.* кати́ть: *wheel a baby carriage,* кати́ть де́тскую коля́ску. —*v.i.* [*usu.* **wheel around** *or* **about**] кру́то поверну́ться. —**break on the wheel,** колесова́ть.

wheelbarrow *n.* та́чка.

wheelbase *n.* колёсная ба́за.

wheelchair *n.* инвали́дное кре́сло.

wheeled *adj.* колёсный.

wheel horse коренни́к; коренна́я ло́шадь.

wheeze *v.i.* дыша́ть с при́свистом; сопе́ть. —*n.* свистя́щее дыха́ние.

whelp *n.* щено́к. —*v.i.* щени́ться.

when *adv. & conj.* когда́: *when will you be ready?,* когда́ вы бу́дете гото́вы? *When she comes I'll ask her,* когда́ она́ придёт, я её спрошу́. ♦*With the -ing form of the verb* при: *when crossing the border,* при перее́зде че́рез грани́цу. —*conj.* (considering that; since) е́сли: *why ask him when he's bound to say no?,* заче́м его́ проси́ть, е́сли он обяза́тельно отка́жет? —**since when?,** с каки́х пор?

whence *adv.* отку́да. *From whence he came,* отку́да он пришёл.

whenever *adv. & conj.* когда́ (бы) ни; вся́кий раз, когда́. *Whenever you like,* когда́ хоти́те; когда́ вам уго́дно.

where *adv. & conj.* **1,** (in what or that place) где: *where is he right now?,* где он сейча́с? *This is where I live,* вот где я живу́. *Stay where you are!,* остава́йтесь там, где вы сейча́с! *There have been cases where...,* быва́ли слу́чаи, когда́... **2,** (to what or that place) куда́: *where are you going?,* куда́ вы идёте? *Let's go where there are not so many people,* пойдём туда́, где не так мно́го наро́ду. **3,** (from what place) отку́да: *where are you from?,* отку́да вы? *Where shall we begin?,* с чего́ мы начнём?

whereabouts *n.* местонахожде́ние. —*adv.* где?; о́коло како́го ме́ста?

whereas *conj.* **1,** (in view of the fact that) поско́льку; ввиду́ того́, что. **2,** (while on the one hand) в то вре́мя как; е́сли. **3,** (while on the other hand) тогда́ как; в то вре́мя как; ме́жду тем как.

whereby *adv.* при кото́ром: *a new method whereby...,* но́вый ме́тод, при кото́ром...

wherefore *adv., archaic* почему́? —*conj., archaic* почему́.

wherein *adv.* (in what way) в чём? —*conj.* (in which) в кото́ром.

whereof *adv. & conj.* о кото́ром; о чём. *In witness whereof,* в удостовере́ние чего́.

whereupon *conj.* по́сле чего́.

wherever *adv. & conj.* где бы ни; куда́ бы ни; везде́, где. *Wherever possible,* везде́, где мо́жно. *Wherever you like,* где *or* куда́ хоти́те; где *or* куда́ вам уго́дно.

wherewithal *n.* необходи́мые сре́дства.

wherry *n.* я́лик.

whet *v.t.* **1,** (sharpen) точи́ть; отта́чивать. **2,** (stimulate, as the appetite) возбужда́ть; (раз)дразни́ть.

whether *conj.* ли: *tell me whether you like it,* скажи́те мне, нра́вится ли э́то вам. *Whether you want to or not,* хоти́те вы и́ли нет; хо́чешь не хо́чешь.

whetstone *n.* точи́льный ка́мень; осело́к; брусо́к.

whew *interj.* фу!

whey *n.* сы́воротка.

which *pron. & adj.* **1,** *interr.* како́й?: *which newspapers do you read?,* каки́е газе́ты вы чита́ете? *Which way did he go?,* в каку́ю сто́рону он пошёл? *Which is your house?,* како́й дом ваш? *Which (one) of you?,* кто из вас? *Which one of these umbrellas is yours?,* кото́рый из э́тих зо́нтиков ваш? *Which is worse — drugs or alcohol?,* что ху́же — нарко́тики и́ли алкого́ль? **2,** *rel.* кото́рый: *the book which you lent me,* кни́га, кото́рую вы мне одолжи́ли. *The play which you told me about,* пье́са, о кото́рой вы мне говори́ли. *The first case in which...,* пе́рвый слу́чай, когда́... ♦*When referring to a fact or circumstance* что: *I did not answer, which made him even angrier,* я не отве́тил, что рассерди́ло его́ ещё бо́льше. **3,** (just mentioned) *rendered by* чего́: *in which case,* в слу́чае чего́; *after which,* по́сле чего́.

whichever *pron. & adj.* како́й бы ни: *whichever country you go to,* в каку́ю бы страну́ вы ни пое́хали. *Take whichever one you want,* возьми́те како́й вам уго́дно.

whiff *n.* **1,** (puff; gust) дунове́ние. **2,** (slight odor) лёгкий за́пах: *a whiff of onions,* лёгкий за́пах лу́ка. **3,** (inhalation): *take a whiff of,* поню́хать (что́-нибудь).

while *conj.* **1,** (at the time that) пока́; когда́; в то вре́мя как. *While I was waiting for her,* пока́/когда́ я её ждал. *While in London,* бу́дучи в Ло́ндоне. *While on vacation,* во вре́мя о́тпуска. *While sitting by the fireplace,* си́дя у ками́на. **2,** (during all the time that; as long as) пока́: *while she is here,* пока́ она́ здесь. *Make hay while the sun shines,* куй желе́зо, пока́ горячо́. **3,** (whereas by contrast) тогда́ как. **4,** (whereas on the one hand) в то вре́мя как: *while I was in favor, some are opposed,* в то вре́мя как большинство́ за, не́которые выступа́ют про́тив. **5,** (although) хотя́: *while many disagree...,* хотя́ мно́гие несогла́сны... —*n.* не́которое вре́мя: *a while ago,* не́которое вре́мя наза́д. *For a while,* не́которое вре́-

мя. *A short while,* недо́лго. *In a little while,* ско́ро. *After a while,* че́рез не́которое вре́мя. *All the while,* всё вре́мя. —*v.t.* [*usu.* **while away**] корота́ть (вре́мя). —**be worth one's while,** сто́ить труда́. —**once in a while,** вре́мя от вре́мени.

whilst *conj.* = **while.**

whim *n.* при́хоть; причу́да; капри́з.

whimper *v.i.* **1,** (of a person, esp. a child) хны́кать. **2,** (of a dog) скули́ть. —*n.* хны́канье.

whimsical *adj.* причу́дливый; прихотли́вый.

whimsy *n.* при́хоть; причу́да.

whine *v.i.* хны́кать; ныть. —*n.* хны́канье. —**whiner,** *n.* ны́тик.

whinny *v.i.* ржать. —*n.* ржа́ние.

whip *n.* кнут; хлыст. —*v.t.* **1,** (thrash; flog) хлеста́ть; сечь; поро́ть; стега́ть. **2,** (beat, as eggs, cream, etc.) сбива́ть; взбива́ть. **3,** *fol. by* **out** (take out suddenly) выхва́тывать. —**whip up, 1,** (stir up; foment) разду́вать. **2,** *colloq.* (cook in a hurry) состря́пать.

whipped cream взби́тые сли́вки.

whippet *n.* борза́я.

whipping *n.* по́рка; трёпка. —**whipping boy,** козёл отпуще́ния.

whippoorwill *n.* козодо́й.

whipsaw *n.* лучко́вая пила́.

whir *also,* **whirr** *v.i.* жужжа́ть. —*n.* жужжа́ние.

whirl *v.i.* **1,** (spin) кружи́ться. **2,** *fol. by* **around** (turn quickly around) кру́то поверну́ться. —*v.t.* **1,** (spin) верте́ть; кружи́ть. **2,** (swirl, as dust) крути́ть. —*n.* **1,** (rapid gyration) круже́ние. *My head is in a whirl,* у меня́ кру́жится голова́. **2,** *colloq.* (brief try): *give it a whirl,* попро́бовать.

whirligig *n.* юла́.

whirlpool *n.* водоворо́т.

whirlwind *n.* вихрь; смерч.

whirr *v. & n.* = **whir.**

whisk *v.t.* **1,** (carry swiftly) мчать; нести́; проноси́ть. *Whisk away,* уноси́ть. **2,** *fol. by* **off** (brush away) сма́хивать.

whisk broom метёлка.

whisker *n., usu. pl.* **1,** (on a man's face) бакенба́рды. **2,** (of an animal) усы́.

whiskey *also,* **whisky** *n.* ви́ски.

whisper *v.t. & i.* шепта́ть. —*n.* шёпот. *In a whisper,* шёпотом. —**whisperer,** *n.* шепту́н.

whist *n.* вист.

whistle *v.i.* свисте́ть. *Whistle for a taxi,* сви́стом подозва́ть такси́. *The wind whistled through the trees,* ве́тер свисте́л в дере́вьях. *Bullets whistled past our ears,* пу́ли просви́стывали ми́мо на́ших уше́й. —*v.t.* насви́стывать: *whistle a tune,* насви́стывать моти́в. —*n.* **1,** (sound) свист. **2,** (device to be blown) свисто́к. **3,** (of a factory, train, etc.) гудо́к. —**wet one's whistle,** промочи́ть го́рло.

whistler *n.* свисту́н.

whit *n.* йо́та; *not a whit,* ни на йо́ту.

white *adj.* бе́лый. *White meat/wine,* бе́лое мя́со/вино́. *White hair,* седы́е во́лосы. *The White House,* Бе́лый дом. —*n.* **1,** (color) бе́лый цвет. *All in white,* весь (вся) в бе́лом. **2,** (of an egg; of the eye) бело́к. **3,** (Caucasian) бе́лый. **4,** *chess* бе́лые: *white resigned,* бе́лые сда́лись. —**turn white, 1,** (become white) беле́ть. **2,** (turn pale) побледне́ть; побеле́ть.

white bread бе́лый хлеб.

whitecap *n., usu. pl.* бара́шки; беля́ки.

whitefish *n.* сиг.

white-haired *adj.* белоголо́вый.

white heat бе́лое кале́ние; бе́лый нака́л.

white-hot *adj.* раскалённый добела́.

white lead свинцо́вые бели́ла.

white lie неви́нная ложь.

whiten *v.t.* бели́ть.

whiteness *n.* белизна́.

whitewash *v.t.* **1,** (whiten with whitewash) бели́ть. **2,** *fig.* (gloss over) сма́зывать. —*n.* известко́вый раство́р. —**whitewashing,** *n.* побе́лка.

white whale белу́ха.

whither *adv.* куда́.

whiting *n.* бели́ла.

whitish *adj.* белёсый; белова́тый.

Whitmonday *n.* ду́хов день.

Whitsunday *n.* тро́ицын день; тро́ица.

whittle *v.t.* **1,** (carve) строга́ть. **2,** *fol. by* **down** (reduce) урезывать.

whiz *also,* **whizz** *v.i.* **1,** (whir; hiss) свисте́ть. **2,** (rush past) промча́ться. —*n., slang* (marvel) феноме́н.

who *pron.* **1,** *interr.* кто?: *who are you?,* кто вы? *Who is there?,* кто там? *Who knows?,* кто зна́ет? *Do you know who he is?,* вы зна́ете, кто он? **2,** *rel.* кото́рый: *the man who was just here,* челове́к, кото́рый то́лько сейча́с был здесь. ♦*After* тот (та, те) *and* все — кто: *those who came late,* те, кто опозда́л. *Everyone who was at the meeting,* все, кто был на собра́нии. *See also* **whom.**

whoa *interj.* тпру!

whoever *pron.* **1,** (no matter who) кто ни; кто бы ни: *whoever you are,* кто бы вы ни́ бы́ли. **2,** (whatever person) кто; тот, кто. *Whoever says that is mistaken,* кто говори́т э́то, ошиба́ется. **3,** *expressing perplexity or bewilderment* кто?: *whoever heard of such a thing?,* кто слыха́л подо́бное? *See also* **whomever.**

whole *adj.* **1,** (entire; complete) це́лый: *a whole piece,* це́лый кусо́к; *a whole year,* це́лый год. *A whole series of,* це́лый ряд (+ *gen.*). *Swallow something whole,* проглоти́ть что́-нибудь целико́м. **2,** *preceded by* **the** (all) весь: *the whole world,* весь мир. **3,** (with none of the elements removed) це́льный: *whole milk,* це́льное молоко́; *whole blood,* це́льная кровь. —*n.* це́лое: *into a single whole,* в еди́ное це́лое. —**as a whole,** в це́лом. —**on the whole,** в о́бщем; в о́бщем и це́лом.

wholehearted *adj.* беззаве́тный. *Wholehearted support,* горя́чая подде́ржка.

wholeness *n.* це́льность; це́лость.

whole note *music* це́лая но́та.

whole number це́лое число́; це́лое.

wholesale *adj.* **1,** *comm.* опто́вый. **2,** *fig.* (blanket; sweeping) огу́льный. —*adv.* о́птом. —**wholesaler,** *n.* опто́вик.

wholesome *adj.* здоро́вый; поле́зный: *wholesome food,* здоро́вая/поле́зная пи́ща. *Wholesome influence,* благотво́рное влия́ние.

wholly *adv.* целико́м; по́лностью.

whom *pron., objective case of* **who,** кого́; кому́; кем; ком: *whom do you have in mind?,* кого́ вы име́ете в виду́? *To whom did you give the money?,* кому́ вы да́ли де́ньги? *With whom were you speaking?,* с кем вы говори́ли?

whomever *pron., objective case of* **whoever.** *Invite whomever you like,* пригласи́те кого́ вам уго́дно.

whoop *v.i.* выкри́кивать; ги́кать. —*n.* вы́крик; во́зглас.

whooping cough коклю́ш.

whooping crane америка́нский жура́вль.

whopping *adj., colloq.* огро́мный. *A whopping 100 rubles,* це́лых сто рубле́й.

whore *n.* проститу́тка. —**whorehouse,** *n.* публи́чный дом.

whorl *n.* **1,** (curve) вито́к; завито́к. **2,** *bot.* муто́вка.

whortleberry *n.* черни́ка.

whose *pron.* **1,** *interr.* чей?: *whose hat is this?,* чья э́та шля́па? *Whose side are you on?,* вы на чьей стороне́? **2,** *rel.* кото́рого; кото́рой: *the girl whose book I borrowed,* де́вушка, кни́гу кото́рой я за́нял.

whosever *pron.* чей бы ни.

whosoever *pron.* кто бы ни.

why *adv.* почему́: *why didn't you answer my letter?,* почему́ вы не отве́тили на моё письмо́? *I don't understand why he objects,* не понима́ю, почему́ он возража́ет. *The reason why he came,* причи́на, по кото́рой он пришёл. *I see no reason why you can't go,* я не зна́ю, почему́ бы тебе́ не пойти́. —*interj.* ведь: *why everyone knows that!,* ведь э́то изве́стно всем! *Why it's Nina!,* да ведь э́то Ни́на! —**that's why,** вот почему́; потому́ и. *That's why I asked,* потому́ я и спроси́л(а). —**which is why,** потому́. —**why not?,** почему́ нет? *Why not ask him?,* почему́ бы не спроси́ть его́? —**why so?,** почему́ же?

wick *n.* фити́ль.

wicked *adj.* **1,** (evil) злой; дурно́й. *Wicked man,* дурно́й челове́к. *Wicked deed,* злой *or* дурно́й посту́пок. *Wicked thoughts,* дурны́е мы́сли. **2,** (harmful; grievous) жесто́кий: *a wicked blow,* жесто́кий уда́р. —**wickedness,** *n.* зло.

wicker *n.* плете́ние. —*adj.* плетёный: *wicker basket,* плетёная корзи́на.

wickerwork *n.* плете́ние; плетёные изде́лия.

wicket *n.* **1,** (small door or gate) кали́тка. **2,** *croquet* воро́та. **3,** *cricket* кали́тка.

wide *adj.* **1,** (broad; extensive) широ́кий: *wide street,* широ́кая у́лица; *wide assortment,* широ́кий ассортиме́нт. **2,** (having a specified width) ширино́й в: *three feet wide,* ширино́й в три фу́та. **3,** (astray) ми́мо це́ли. *Be wide of the mark,* бить *or* попада́ть ми́мо це́ли; *fig.* попа́сть па́льцем в не́бо. —*adv.* **1,** (to the full extent of opening) настежь: *the windows were wide open,* о́кна бы́ли широко́ откры́ты; о́кна бы́ли на́стежь. **2,** (over a large area) широко́. *Far and wide,* вдоль и поперёк. **3,** (astray) в сто́рону; ми́мо це́ли.

wide-angle *adj.* широкоуго́льный.

wide-eyed *adj.* с широко́ раскры́тыми глаза́ми. *Stare wide-eyed at,* смотре́ть на (+ *acc.*) больши́ми глаза́ми.

widely *adv.* широко́. *Widely scattered,* широко́ разбро́санный. *Vary widely,* широко́ расходи́ться. *Travel widely,* мно́го путеше́ствовать.

widen *v.t.* расширя́ть. —*v.i.* расширя́ться.

widespread *adj.* распространённый.

widgeon *n.* свия́зь.

widow *n.* вдова́. —**widowed,** *adj.* вдо́вый; овдове́вший. *Be/become widowed,* овдове́ть.

widower *n.* вдове́ц.

widowhood *n.* вдовство́.

width *n.* **1,** (breadth) ширина́. **2,** (piece of material of a certain width) полотни́ще.

wield *v.t.* **1,** (brandish) маха́ть; разма́хивать. **2,** (handle) рабо́тать; ору́довать (*both with instr.*). **3,** (exercise, as power, influence, etc.) облада́ть; по́льзоваться.

wife *n.* жена́. *Take (someone) for a wife,* взять кого́-нибудь) в жёны.

wig *n.* пари́к.

wiggle *v.t.* шевели́ть: *wiggle one's toes,* шевели́ть па́льцами ног. —*v.i.* ёрзать.

wigwam *n.* вигва́м.

wild *adj.* **1,** (uncivilized; uncultivated; undomesticated) ди́кий: *wild duck/rose/region,* ди́кая у́тка/ро́за/ме́стность. **2,** (boisterous; unruly) ди́кий; бу́йный. **3,** (fantastically impractical) ди́кий; сумасбро́дный; бредово́й. **4,** (random; erratic) науга́д: *make a wild guess,* сказа́ть науга́д; *fire a wild shot,* стреля́ть науга́д. **5,** *colloq., fol. by* **about** (mad about) без ума́ (от). —*adv.* ди́ко: *grow wild,* расти́ ди́ко. —*n., often pl.* глушь; де́бри. *Call of the wild,* зов приро́ды. —**run wild,** бу́йствовать; бу́йнить.

wild boar каба́н.

wildcat *n.* ди́кая ко́шка.

wilderness *n.* пусты́ня; глушь. —**voice in the wilderness,** глас вопию́щего в пусты́не.

wildfire *n., in* **spread like wildfire,** распространя́ться с молниено́сной быстрото́й *or* со ско́ростью лесно́го пожа́ра.

wildflower *n.* дикорасту́щее расте́ние; *pl.* полевы́е цветы́.

wildlife *n.* ди́кие живо́тные.

wildly *adv.* ди́ко.

wile *n., usu. pl.* хи́трости; уло́вки.

wilful *adj.* = **willful.**

will *n.* **1,** (in most meanings) во́ля: *the will of the people,* во́ля наро́да. *God's will,* бо́жья *or* бо́жия во́ля. *Good will,* до́брая во́ля. *Ill will,* недоброжела́тельство. *The will to win/live,* во́ля к побе́де/жи́зни. *At will,* по жела́нию. *Of one's own free will,* по до́брой во́ле. *Against one's will,* не по свое́й во́ле; про́тив во́ли; понево́ле. *Where there's a will there's a way,* при жела́нии мо́жно всего́ доби́ться. **2,** (testament) завеща́ние. —*v.t.* **1,** (wish) хоте́ть: *do what you will,* де́лай, что хо́чешь. **2,** (decree; ordain) суди́ть: *fate willed otherwise,* судьба́ суди́ла ина́че. *God has willed that...,* бо́жья во́ля (*or* бо́гу уго́дно), что... **3,** (bequeath) завеща́ть. —*v. aux.* **1,** *used to form the future tense:* *you will be sorry,* вы бу́дете сожале́ть об э́том. *The window won't open,* окно́ не открыва́ется. *Accidents will happen,* всегда́ быва́ют несча́стные слу́чаи. **2,** *in requests:* *will you have a cup of tea?,* мо́жно вам предложи́ть ча́шку ча́ю? *Won't you sit down?,* сади́тесь, пожа́луйста! *Will you please be quiet!,* да замолчи́те же! **3,** *expressing probability:* *that will be Vera,* э́то, наве́рно, Ве́ра. —**if you will,** е́сли хоти́те.

willful *also,* **wilful** *adj.* **1,** (deliberate) преднаме́ренный; умы́шленный. **2,** (headstrong) самово́льный; своево́льный.

willing *adj.* **1,** (ready; disposed) гото́вый: *I'm willing to help,* я гото́в(а) помо́чь. **2,** (acting or performing gladly) услу́жливый; стара́тельный. **3,** (readily given) доброво́льный. —**willingly,** *adv.* охо́тно. —**willingness,** *n.* гото́вность.

will-o'-the-wisp *n.* блужда́ющий огонёк.

willow *n.* и́ва. —*adj.* и́вовый.

willowy *adj.* стро́йный.

will power сила воли.

willy-nilly *adv.* волей-неволей.

wilt *v.i.* **1.** (wither) вянуть; чахнуть. **2.** (lose strength or vigor) изнемогать: *wilt from the heat,* изнемогать от жары. —*v.t.* губить: *the heat wilted the flowers,* жара погубила цветы.

wily *adj.* хитрый; лукавый.

win *v.i.* выигрывать; побеждать: *who won?,* кто выиграл/победил? —*v.t.* **1.** (gain victory in) выигрывать: *win a game/bet/war,* выиграть игру/пари/войну. **2.** (gain in competition) завоёвывать: *win first place/a gold medal/,* завоевать первое место/золотую медаль/. *Win a prize,* взять *or* получить приз. **3.** (gain; earn) завоёвывать: *win one's freedom,* завоевать свободу. *Win recognition,* завоевать *or* снискать признание. *Win applause,* срывать аплодисменты. *Win someone's heart,* покорить чьё-нибудь сердце. —*n.* победа: *six wins and two losses,* шесть побед и два поражения. —**win back,** отыгрывать. —**win over, 1,** (charm) располагать к себе; привязывать к себе. **2,** (prevail upon) склонять в свою пользу. *Win over to one's side,* склонять *or* привлекать на свою сторону.

wince *v.i.* вздрагивать; морщиться (от боли).

winch *n.* лебёдка; ворот.

wind[1] (wind) *n.* **1.** (air in motion) ветер. **2.** (breath) дыхание: *second wind,* второе дыхание. *Get one's wind,* отдышаться. —**get wind of,** пронюхивать. —**see which way the wind blows,** узнать куда ветер дует. —**something is in the wind,** что-то затевается. *See also* **winded.**

wind[2] (waind) *v.t.* **1.** (turn) вертеть: *wind a crank,* вертеть рукоятку. **2.** (set going) заводить: *wind a watch/toy,* заводить часы/игрушку. **3.** (coil onto or around something) мотать. *Wind thread onto a spool,* намотать нитки на катушку. *Wind a scarf around one's head,* обмотать/обернуть/обвить шарф вокруг головы. —*v.i.* **1.** (move in a curving or twisting path) виться; извиваться. *The road winds through the mountains,* дорога вьётся по горам. **2.** *fol. by* **around** (twine around) обвиваться; обматываться (вокруг). —*n.* оборот; поворот. —**wind up, 1,** (wind onto a spool) сматывать. **2,** (tighten the spring of) заводить. **3,** (finish; conclude) заканчивать. **4,** (end up; find oneself) очутиться. **5,** *usu. passive* (make tense) взвинчивать. *All wound up,* взвинченный.

windbag *n., slang* пустозвон; пустослов; пустомеля; краснобай.

winded *adj.* запыхавшийся.

windfall *n.* золотой дождь; непредвиденный доход. *Windfall profits,* непредвиденная прибыль; сверхприбыль.

winding *adj.* **1.** (serving to wind) заводной; мотальный: *winding mechanism,* заводной/мотальный механизм. **2.** (twisting, as of a road) извилистый. *Winding staircase,* витая лестница.

wind instrument духовой инструмент.

windlass *n.* лебёдка; ворот; *naut.* брашпиль.

windless *adj.* безветренный.

windmill *n.* ветряная мельница. —**tilt at windmills,** сражаться с ветряными мельницами.

window *n.* **1.** (opening to let in light) окно. **2.** (display window of a store) витрина. —*adj.* оконный: *window curtain,* оконная занавеска.

window dressing мишура; декорации; показуха.

windowpane *n.* оконное стекло.

window shade штора.

window-shop *v.i.* рассматривать витрины.

window sill подоконник.

windpipe *n.* дыхательное горло.

windshield *n.* переднее стекло; ветровое стекло. —**windshield wiper,** стеклоочиститель; дворник.

windstorm *n.* буря.

wind tunnel аэродинамическая труба.

windward *adj.* наветренный.

windy *adj.* ветреный. *It is windy,* ветрено.

wine *n.* вино. —*adj.* винный: *wine bottle,* винная бутылка. —**wine cellar,** винный погреб.

wineglass *n.* бокал.

winegrower *n.* винодел. —**winegrowing,** *n.* виноделие.

wine list карта (*or* карточка) вин.

wine press давильный пресс.

wineskin *n.* бурдюк; мех для вина.

wing *n.* **1.** (of a bird; of a plane) крыло. **2.** (of fowl, when eaten) крылышко. **3.** (extension of a building) флигель; крыло. **4.** (side of a stage) кулиса: *in the wings,* за кулисами. **5.** (political faction) крыло. **6,** *Brit.* (fender) крыло. —*v.t.* **1,** (shoot; wound) подстреливать. **2,** *in wing one's way,* пролетать. —**on the wing,** на лету. —**take under one's wing,** брать под своё крылышко *or* покровительство; брать под защиту. —**take wing,** вспорхнуть.

winged *adj.* крылатый.

wingless *adj.* бескрылый.

wingspan *n.* размах крыльев. *Also,* **wingspread.**

wink *v.i.* мигать; моргать. —*n.* мигание. *Not sleep a wink,* совсем не спать; не смыкать глаз. —**wink at, 1,** (signal with a wink) мигать (+ *dat.*); моргать (+ *dat.*); подмигивать (+ *dat.*). **2,** (pretend not to notice) смотреть сквозь пальцы на.

winner *n.* победитель.

winning *adj.* **1.** (victorious) победивший. *Winning streak,* победное шествие. **2,** (leading to victory) выигрышный: *winning ticket/move,* выигрышный билет/ход. **3,** (captivating) подкупающий; обезоруживающий. —*n.* **1,** (victory) победа. **2,** *pl.* (money won) выигрыш.

winnow *v.t.* **1,** (blow the chaff from) веять. **2,** *fol. by* **out** (sift or separate out) отсеивать.

winnowing *n.* веяние. *Winnowing machine,* веялка.

winsome *adj.* привлекательный; располагающий.

winter *n.* зима. *In winter,* зимой. —*adj.* зимний: *winter clothes,* зимняя одежда. *Winter crops,* озимые культуры. —*v.i.* зимовать.

winterize *v.t.* утеплять; отеплять.

wintertime *n.* зима; зимнее время.

wintry *adj.* зимний.

wipe *v.t.* вытирать: *wipe the sweat from one's brow,* вытирать пот со лба; *wipe one's feet on the mat,* вытирать ноги о половик. *Wipe one's eyes,* осушать слёзы. *Wipe one's nose,* утереть (себе) нос. *Wipe from the face of the earth,* стирать с лица земли. —**wipe away,** вытирать; утирать: *wipe away the tears,* вытирать/утирать слёзы. —**wipe off,** стирать. —**wipe out,** уничтожать. —**wipe up,** подтирать.

wire *n.* **1.** (metal strand) проволока: *barbed wire,* колючая проволока. **2,** (electric, telegraph, etc.) провод. **3,** (telegram) телеграмма. —*adj.* проволочный:

wire netting, проволочная сеть. —*v.t.* **1,** (fasten with wire) скреплять проволокой. **2,** (install wiring in) прокладывать провода в. **3,** (send a telegram to) телеграфировать.

wire cutter кусачки.

wireless *n., Brit.* = **radio.** —*adj.* беспроволочный.

wire service телеграфное агентство.

wiretap *v.t.* перехватывать. —**wiretapping,** *n.* перехват телефонных сообщений.

wiring *n.* проводка.

wiry *adj.* жилистый.

wisdom *n.* мудрость. —**wisdom tooth,** зуб мудрости.

wise *adj.* **1,** (sagacious) мудрый. **2,** (prudent) умный; благоразумный. **3,** *fol. by* **to** (aware of) в курсе: *wise to what is going on,* в курсе дела. **4,** *slang* (impudent; fresh) нахальный. —**put wise,** *slang* вводить в курс дела. —**wise up,** *slang* образумиться.

wisecrack *n.* острота.

wisely *adv.* благоразумно.

wish *v.t.* **1,** (want; desire) хотеть; желать: *I do not wish to see him,* не хочу/желаю его видеть. *I wish I could stay longer,* я хотел бы дольше остаться. *I wish you would stop bothering me!,* нельзя ли не беспокоить меня? **2,** (bid) желать: *I wish you luck,* желаю вам счастья. **3,** *fol. by* **on** (impose) навязывать: *who wished this job on us?,* кто навязал нам эту работу? —*n.* **1,** (desire) желание; охота. *Act against someone's wishes,* поступить вопреки чьим-нибудь желаниям. *She got her wish,* она добилась чего хотела. **2,** *pl.* (expressed desire for someone's well-being) пожелание: *best wishes,* наилучшие пожелания.

wishful *adj. A wishful expression on one's face,* выражение желания на лице. *Indulge in wishful thinking,* принимать желаемое за действительное.

wishy-washy *adj.* бесхарактерный; слабовольный.

wisp *n.* **1,** (of hay, straw, etc.) пучок; клок. **2,** (of smoke, vapor, etc.) струйка.

wisteria *n.* глициния.

wistful *adj.* **1,** (melancholy) тоскливый. **2,** (pensive) задумчивый.

wit *n.* **1,** (wittiness) остроумие. *Man of great wit,* остроумный человек. **2,** (witty person) остряк. **3,** *pl.* (innate intelligence) ум; мозги. *Battle of wits,* игра ума. *Use one's wits,* шевелить мозгами. *Live by one's wits,* жить хитростью. **4,** *pl.* (sanity) рассудок: *lose one's wits,* терять рассудок. —**be at one's wits' end,** дойти до точки. *I am at my wits' end,* у меня ум за разум заходит. —**frighten out of one's wits,** напугать до смерти. —**keep one's wits about one,** не терять головы. —**to wit,** а именно.

witch *n.* ведьма.

witchcraft *n.* колдовство.

witch doctor знахарь.

witch hunt охота за ведьмами.

with *prep.* **1,** (in most meanings) с (+ *instr.*): *come with me,* идите со мной; *a house with a fireplace,* дом с камином; *read with difficulty,* читать с трудом; *I agree with you,* я согласен с вами. *Play/argue/cope/part with,* играть/спорить/справляться/расставаться с. **2,** (by means of; using) *rendered by the instr. case: write with a pencil,* писать карандашом; *work with one's hands,* работать руками; *cut the meat with a knife,* резать мясо ножом. **3,** (at the home of) у:

stay with friends, жить *or* гостить у друзей. **4,** (in the possession or care of) у: *leave the keys with the watchman,* оставить ключи у сторожа. **5,** (in regard to): *satisfied with something,* доволен чём-нибудь; *angry with someone,* сердит на кого-нибудь. **6,** (involving a material or substance) *rendered by the instr. case: covered with dust,* покрыт пылью; *be filled with smoke,* наполниться дымом. *Line a coat with silk,* подбивать пальто шёлком. **7,** (from) от: *tremble with fear,* дрожать от холода; *be green with envy,* лопаться от зависти. **8,** (beginning with) с (+ *gen.*): *let's start with you,* начнём с вас. *In German all nouns are written with a capital letter,* в немецком языке все существительные пишутся с большой буквы. **9,** (having received) с (+ *gen.*): *with your permission,* с вашего разрешения.

withdraw *v.t.* **1,** (draw back; remove) отнимать; отдёргивать. **2,** (remove; evacuate, as troops) выводить. **3,** (retract) снимать: *withdraw one's offer/motion,* снимать своё предложение. **4,** (retire) изымать: *withdraw from circulation,* изымать из обращения. **5,** (take out, as money from a bank) снимать со счёта. —*v.i.* **1,** (leave; retire) удаляться. **2,** (drop out) выходить; выбывать. **3,** *mil.* (retreat) отходить; отступать. **4,** *in* **withdraw into oneself,** уходить в себя; замыкаться в себе.

withdrawal *n.* **1,** (retreat) отход. **2,** (dropping out) выход. **3,** (removal, as of troops) вывод. **4,** (removal, as from circulation) изъятие. **5,** (retraction of a motion) снятие. **6,** (removal, as of funds) снятие со счёта. *Make a withdrawal,* снимать деньги со счёта. **7,** *med.* воздержание от наркотиков.

withdrawn *adj.* (retiring; reticent) сдержанный; замкнутый.

wither *v.i.* **1,** (shrivel) вянуть; увядать; сохнуть; блёкнуть. **2,** *fol. by* **away** (gradually cease to exist) отмирать: *"The state will wither away",* государство отмирает. —*v.t.* иссушать. —**withered,** *adj.* вялый; увядший; высохший; блёклый. —**withering,** *adj.* уничтожающий: *withering glance/crossfire,* уничтожающий взгляд/перекрёстный огонь/.

withers *n. pl.* холка; загривок.

withhold *v.t.* **1,** (hold back, as money) удерживать; задерживать. *Withhold payment,* задерживать выплату. **2,** (refrain from giving) воздерживаться от: *withhold comment,* воздерживаться от комментариев. **3,** (refuse to grant) не давать: *withhold permission,* не давать разрешения. **4,** (not divulge) утаивать: *withhold information,* утаивать сведения.

within *prep.* **1,** (inside) в; внутри. **2,** (not beyond) в; в пределах (+ *gen.*). *Within a radius of,* в радиусе (+ *gen.*); *within the framework of,* в рамках (+ *gen.*). *Within ten paces of,* в десяти шагах от. *Within the city limits,* в пределах города. *Within reach/earshot,* в пределах досягаемости/слышимости. ♦*Also rendered by various other combinations: within my recollection,* на моей памяти. *Live within one's means,* жить по своим средствам. *Is it within walking distance?,* туда можно дойти пешком? *Guess someone's age within a year,* угадать чей-нибудь возраст с точностью до года. **3,** (not later than) в; в течение (+ *gen.*): *within a year,* в течение года; *within 24 hours,* в двадцать четыре часа. —*adv.* внутри. *From within,* изнутри.

without *prep.* **1,** (lacking; free from) без: *without* *exception,* без исключе́ния. **2,** (failing to) без того́, что́бы (+ *inf.*); не (+ *verbal adverb*). *Without saying a word,* не говоря́ (*or* сказа́в) ни сло́ва. *Without saying goodbye to anyone,* ни с кем не прости́сь. **3,** (outside of) вне. —*adv.* снару́жи. *From without,* извне́. —**do** (*or* **go**) **without,** обходи́ться без.

withstand *v.t.* выде́рживать; устоя́ть про́тив; противостоя́ть. *Withstand the test of time,* выде́рживать прове́рку вре́менем.

witless *adj.* безмо́зглый.

witness *n.* свиде́тель. *Eyewitness,* очеви́дец. —*v.t.* **1,** (be present at; see) быть свиде́телем/очеви́дцем (+ *gen.*). **2,** (certify, as a signature) заверя́ть; удостоверя́ть. —**bear witness to,** свиде́тельствовать о. —**in witness whereof,** в удостовере́ние чего́.

witticism *n.* остро́та.

wittiness *n.* остроу́мие.

wittingly *adv.* созна́тельно; заве́домо.

witty *adj.* остроу́мный.

wizard *n.* **1,** (sorcerer) колду́н; чароде́й. **2,** *colloq.* (whiz) ге́ний.

wizardry *n.* колдовство́.

wizened *adj.* вы́сохший: *wizened old man,* вы́сохший стари́к.

wobble *v.i.* шата́ться; пошатыва́ться. —*n.* шата́ние. —**wobbly,** *adj.* ша́ткий.

woe *n.* го́ре. *Tale of woe,* печа́льный расска́з. *Woe (be it) to him who...,* го́ре тому́, кто... —**woe is me!,** го́ре мне!; бе́дная моя́ голо́вушка!

woebegone *adj.* удручённый; го́рестный.

woeful *adj.* **1,** (sad) го́рестный. **2,** (wretched) жа́лкий. —**knight of the woeful countenance,** ры́царь печа́льного о́браза.

wolf *n.* волк. —*adj.* [*also,* **wolf's**] во́лчий. —**wolf in sheep's clothing,** волк в ове́чьей шку́ре.

wolfhound *n.* (Irish) волкода́в; (Russian) борза́я.

wolverine *n.* росома́ха.

woman *n.* же́нщина. *Old woman,* стару́ха. —*adj.* **1,** (being a woman) же́нщина-: *woman doctor,* же́нщина-врач. **2,** [*usu.* **woman's** *or* **women's**] (of women) же́нский: *women's rights,* же́нские права́.

woman-hater *n.* женонави́стник.

womanhood *n.* **1,** (maturity) зре́лость. **2,** (women collectively) же́нщины.

womanizer *n., colloq.* ба́бник; женолю́б.

womankind *n.* же́нщины; же́нский пол.

womanly *adj.* же́нственный.

womb *n.* ма́тка.

wonder *v.t.* хоте́ть знать. *I wonder what he wants / where she went /,* интере́сно, что он хо́чет/куда́ она́ пошла́/. *I wonder what's wrong with my watch,* не понима́ю, что с мои́ми часа́ми. —*v.i.* **1,** *fol. by* **at** (marvel) удивля́ться (+ *dat.*). **2,** (have doubts) сомнева́ться: *I wonder,* я в э́том сомнева́юсь; я не уве́рен(а). *I wonder about his sincerity,* я сомнева́юсь в его́ и́скренности. *I wonder if she'll ever get married,* задаю́ себе́ вопро́с, вы́йдет ли она́ за́муж? —*n.* **1,** (awe) удивле́ние; изумле́ние: *watch in / with wonder,* смотре́ть с удивле́нием/изумле́нием. **2,** (a marvel; miracle) чу́до: *work wonders,* твори́ть чудеса́. *It's a wonder that...,* удиви́тельно, что... —**no wonder,** не удиви́тельно; не ди́во; не мудрено́: *no wonder he's angry!,* не удиви́тельно/ди́во/мудрено́, что он рассерди́лся. *And no wonder!,* и не удиви́тельно!; и немудрено́!

wonderful *adj.* чуде́сный; чу́дный; замеча́тельный. —**wonderfully,** *adv.* чуде́сно; чу́дно; замеча́тельно.

wonderland *n.* страна́ чуде́с.

wonderment *n.* удивле́ние; изумле́ние.

wonder-working *adj.* чудоде́йственный; чудотво́рный.

wondrous *adj.* чу́дный; ди́вный.

wont *adj., used predicatively:* **be wont to,** име́ть привы́чку (+ *inf.*). —*n.* привы́чка; обыкнове́ние: *as was his wont,* по свое́й привы́чке; по своему́ обыкнове́нию.

woo *v.t.* уха́живать за.

wood *n.* **1,** (material) де́рево; древеси́на. **2,** (firewood) дрова́: *chop wood,* руби́ть/коло́ть дрова́. **3,** *usu. pl.* (forest) лес: *in the woods,* в лесу́. —*adj.* деревя́нный. —**out of the woods,** вне опа́сности.

wood alcohol древе́сный спирт.

wood block лубо́к.

woodchuck *n.* суро́к.

woodcock *n.* ва́льдшнеп.

woodcut *n.* гравю́ра на де́реве; лубо́к.

woodcutter *n.* лесору́б; дровосе́к.

wooded *adj.* леси́стый.

wooden *adj.* деревя́нный. *Wooden leg,* деревя́шка.

woodland *n.* леси́стая ме́стность.

wood louse мокри́ца.

woodman *n.* = **woodsman.**

woodpecker *n.* дя́тел.

wood pulp древе́сная ма́сса.

woods *see* **wood.**

woodshed *n.* дровяно́й сара́й.

woodsman *n.* лесору́б; лесни́к.

wood sorrel кисли́ца.

wood tar древе́сный дёготь.

woodwinds *n.pl.* деревя́нные духовы́е инструме́нты.

woodwork *n.* деревя́нные ча́сти (до́ма). —**woodworker,** *n.* деревообде́лочник. —**woodworking,** *adj.* деревообде́лочный.

woody *adj.* древе́сный; деревяни́стый.

woof *n., textiles* уто́к.

wool *n.* шерсть. —*adj.* шерстяно́й. —**pull the wool over someone's eyes,** втира́ть очки́ (+ *dat.*).

woolen *also,* **woollen** *adj.* шерстяно́й. —**woolens,** *n. pl.* шерстяны́е ве́щи.

woolly *adj.* шерсти́стый.

woozy *adj., slang* одуре́лый.

word *n.* **1,** (unit of speech) сло́во: *a rare word,* ре́дкое сло́во. *Harsh words,* ре́зкие слова́. *Just say the word!,* скажи́те то́лько сло́во! *Set words to music,* класть слова́ на му́зыку. **2,** (promise) сло́во: *give one's word,* дава́ть (че́стное) сло́во; *keep one's word,* сдержа́ть (своё) сло́во. **3,** (news; information) весть; изве́стие. *There hasn't been a word from him,* о нём (*or* от него́) ни слу́ху ни ду́ху. —*v.t.* выража́ть слова́ми; формули́ровать. —**by word of mouth,** у́стно; из уст в уста́. —**have a word with,** поговори́ть с. *May I have a word with you?,* мо́жно вас на полсло́ва? —**have words with,** име́ть кру́пный разгово́р с. —**in a word,** одни́м сло́вом. —**in other words,** други́ми слова́ми; ина́че говоря́. —**in so many words,** недвусмы́сленно. *I told her in so many words that...,* я так и сказа́л(а) ей, что... —**leave word,** оставля́ть запи́ску. —**man of his word,** челове́к сло́ва; хозя́ин своего́ сло́ва. —**of few words,**

немногосло́вный. —**take at one's word**, лови́ть на сло́ве. —**take one's word for it**, ве́рить (+ dat.) на́ сло́во. —**word for word**, сло́во в сло́во; досло́вно. —**word of honor**, че́стное сло́во.

wording n. формулиро́вка; реда́кция.

wordy adj. многосло́вный.

work n. **1**, (labor) рабо́та: hard work, тяжёлая рабо́та. **2**, (employment) рабо́та; слу́жба. Out of work, без рабо́ты; безрабо́тный. What sort of work do you do?, кем вы рабо́таете? **3**, (something done or produced) рабо́та: stucco work, лепна́я рабо́та. Public works, обще́ственные рабо́ты. That's his work, э́то его́ рабо́та; э́то его́ рук де́ло. The blast was the work of terrorists, взрыв – де́ло рук террори́стов. **4**, (literary or artistic creation) произведе́ние; сочине́ние; вещь. Work of art, произведе́ние иску́сства. The complete works of Chekhov, по́лное собра́ние сочине́ний Че́хова. Two works by Glinka, две ве́щи Гли́нки. **5**, pl. (factory) заво́д: glassworks, стеко́льный заво́д. **6**, pl., mil. сооруже́ния: defensive works, оборони́тельные сооруже́ния. **7**, [usu. **the works**] slang (everything) всё: shoot the works, идти́ на всё; идти́ ва-ба́нк. —v.i. **1**, (do work) рабо́тать: work as a draftsman, рабо́тать чертёжником. **2**, (function) рабо́тать: the radio doesn't work, радиоприёмник не рабо́тает. **3**, (prove effective, as of medicine) де́йствовать; возыме́ть де́йствие. **4**, (accomplish its purpose) удава́ться: his idea didn't work, его́ за́мысел не уда́лся. —v.t. **1**, (perform; accomplish) твори́ть: work miracles, твори́ть чудеса́. **2**, (operate) обраща́ться с: know how to work a lathe, уме́ть обраща́ться с тока́рным станко́м. **3**, (till, as the soil; treat, as metal) обраба́тывать: Work a mine, разраба́тывать рудни́к. **4**, (make work, as subordinates) заставля́ть рабо́тать. **5**, in **work one's way**, прокла́дывать себе́ доро́гу. Work one's way out of debt, вы́биться из долго́в. —**do its work**, сде́лать своё де́ло. —**go to work**, **1**, (leave for work) идти́ на рабо́ту. **2**, (set to work) бра́ться за рабо́ту. —**work loose**, выпу́тываться; выве́ртываться. —**work off**, **1**, (pay off by working) отраба́тывать. **2**, (shed, as excess weight) сгоня́ть. —**work on**, **1**, (do work on) рабо́тать над. **2**, (try to persuade) угова́ривать; склоня́ть. —**work out**, **1**, (develop, as a plan) разраба́тывать; выраба́тывать. **2**, (solve) разга́дывать. **3**, (turn out) оберну́ться. **4**, (end successfully) устро́иться; обойти́сь. **5**, sports тренирова́ться; размина́ться. —**work up**, **1**, (develop) разраба́тывать. **2**, (arouse) возбужда́ть. Work up an appetite, нагуля́ть себе́ аппети́т.

workable adj. выполни́мый; осуществи́мый.

workaday adj. бу́дничный; повседне́вный.

workbench n. верста́к.

workbook n. тетра́дь.

workday n. **1**, (day on which one works) бу́дний день. **2**, (time normally worked in one day) рабо́чий день.

worker n. **1**, (one who works) рабо́тник: conscientious worker, добросо́вестный рабо́тник. **2**, (member of the working class) рабо́чий; трудя́щийся.

workhouse n. **1**, (prison) исправи́тельный дом. **2**, Brit. (poorhouse) рабо́тный дом.

working adj. рабо́чий: working class, рабо́чий класс; working clothes, рабо́чая оде́жда. Working conditions, усло́вия труда́. Working mothers, рабо́тающие ма́тери. In working order, испра́вный; в испра́вности. Working capital, оборо́тный капита́л.

workingman n. рабо́чий.

workload n. нагру́зка.

workman n. рабо́тник.

workmanlike adj. иску́сный.

workmanship n. рабо́та; мастерство́; вы́делка; вы́работка. Of marvelous workmanship, великоле́пной рабо́ты.

workout n. трениро́вка.

workroom n. рабо́чая ко́мната.

workshop n. мастерска́я.

workweek n. рабо́чая неде́ля.

world n. мир; свет. The ancient world, дре́вний мир. The Old/New World, Ста́рый/Но́вый свет. The next world, тот свет. —adj. мирово́й: a world record, мирово́й реко́рд. —**be dead to the world**, спать мёртвым сном. —**bring/come into the world**, произвести́/появи́ться на свет. —**do someone a world of good**, о́чень идти́ на по́льзу (+ dat.). —**for all the world**, точь-в-то́чь. —**in the world**, **1**, literally в ми́ре; на све́те. **2**, used for emphasis: where in the world have you been?, Куда́ же э́то вы пропа́ли? Where in the world did you find it?, где то́лько вы э́то нашли́? —**not for all the world**, ни за что на све́те. —**not long for this world**, не жиле́ц на э́том све́те. —**on top of the world**, на седьмо́м не́бе; на верху́ блаже́нства. —**out of this world**, из ря́да вон выходя́щий. —**think the world of**, быть о́чень высо́кого мне́ния о.

worldly adj. **1**, (earthly; mundane) мирско́й; жите́йский. **2**, (worldly-wise) быва́лый.

worldly-wise adj. вида́вший ви́ды; быва́лый.

world's fair всеми́рная вы́ставка.

world war мирова́я война́. World War II, втора́я мирова́я война́.

worldwide adj. мирово́й; всеми́рный.

worm n. червь; червя́к. Intestinal worm, глист. —v.t. **1**, often fol. by out (elicit, as a secret) выве́дывать. **2**, in **worm one's way into**, вкра́дываться в; втира́ться в. —v.i. [usu. **worm out of**] выве́ртываться (из); выпу́тываться (из).

worm-eaten adj. черви́вый.

worm gear червя́чная шестерня́.

wormhole n. червото́чина.

worm wheel червя́чное колесо́.

wormwood n. полы́нь.

wormy adj. черви́вый.

worn adj. **1**, (showing the effects of wear) поно́шенный. **2**, (haggard) изму́ченный; заму́ченный.

worn-out also, **worn out** adj. **1**, (no longer fit for wear) изно́шенный. **2**, (exhausted) изнурённый. I am worn out, я смерте́льно уста́л; я соверше́нно изму́чился.

worried adj. **1**, (experiencing worry) обеспоко́енный: I am very worried, я о́чень обеспоко́ен(а). **2**, (showing worry) беспоко́йный: a worried look, беспоко́йный вид.

worrisome adj. беспоко́йный.

worry v.t. беспоко́ить. —v.i. беспоко́иться. —n. **1**, (anxiety) беспоко́йство. **2**, (cause of anxiety) забо́та. That's the least of my worries, э́то меня́ ме́ньше всего́ беспоко́ит. See also **worried**.

worse adj. **1**, modifier ху́дший: in worse shape, в ху́дшем состоя́нии. **2**, predicate ху́же: worse than I expected, ху́же чем я ожида́л. It could have been worse, могло́ бы быть и ху́же. Make worse, уху́дшить. Get/grow worse, стать ху́же; ухудша́ться. —adv. ху́же. —n. ху́дшее: change for the worse, переме́на к ху́дшему. Take a turn for the worse, принима́ть дурно́й

оборо́т. —**be none the worse for,** ничу́ть не стра́-
да́ть от. —**for better or worse,** что бы ни случи́-
лось. —**go from bad to worse,** станови́ться всё
ху́же и ху́же. —**so much the worse,** тем ху́же. —
what is worse; to make matters worse, (и) что ещё
ху́же. —**worse off,** в ху́дшем состоя́нии.

worsen *v.t.* ухудша́ть. —*v.i.* ухудша́ться.

worship *v.t.* **1,** (venerate, as a deity) поклоня́ться:
worship God, поклоня́ться бо́гу. **2,** (idolize) обожа́ть;
боготвори́ть. —*v.i.* моли́ться. —*n.* поклоне́ние. *Freedom of worship,* свобо́да вероиспове́дания. *House
of worship,* храм.

worshiper *also,* **worshipper** *n.* **1,** (person at prayer)
моля́щийся. **2,** (fervent admirer) покло́нник.

worst *adj.* са́мый плохо́й; са́мый ху́дший; наиху́д-
ший. *One's worst enemy,* злейший враг. *My worst
mistake,* са́мая больша́я моя́ оши́бка. —*adv.* ху́же
всего́; ху́же всех. —*n.* (са́мое) ху́дшее: *prepare for
the worst,* гото́виться к ху́дшему. *Assume the worst,*
предполага́ть са́мое ху́дшее. —**at worst,** в ху́дшем
слу́чае. —**get the worst of it, 1,** (lose) быть в про́-
игрыше. **2,** (suffer most) страда́ть бо́льше всех.
—**if worst comes to worst,** в кра́йнем слу́чае; на
худо́й коне́ц. —**in the worst way,** *colloq.* о́чень;
си́льно; стра́стно. —**the worst of it is that...,** ху́же
всего́ то, что...

worsted *n.* камво́льная пря́жа; га́рус. —*adj.* кам-
во́льный; га́русный.

worth *n.* **1,** (value) цена́; це́нность. *Know one's worth,*
знать себе́ це́ну. *Show one's worth,* показа́ть себя́;
прояви́ть себя́. **2,** *fol. by* of (amount to be had for a
given sum) *rendered by* на: *a dollar's worth of stamps,*
на до́ллар ма́рок. —*adj., used predicatively: rendered
by the verb* сто́ить: *this painting is worth a thousand
dollars,* эта карти́на сто́ит ты́сячу до́лларов. *It is not
worth the trouble,* не сто́ит труда́. *The play is worth
seeing,* пье́су сто́ит посмотре́ть. *He is worth 100,000
dollars,* он име́ет капита́л в сто ты́сяч до́лларов.
—**for all one is worth,** изо всех сил; что есть сил.

worthiness *n.* досто́инство.

worthless *adj.* **1,** (valueless) ничего́ не сто́ящий. *Be
worthless,* ничего́ не сто́ить. **2,** (useless; good-for-
nothing) него́дный; никчёмный. —**worthlessness,** *n.*
него́дность.

worthwhile *adj.* сто́ящий. *Be worthwhile,* сто́ить;
име́ть смысл.

worthy *adj.* досто́йный: *a worthy adversary,* досто́й-
ный проти́вник. *Worthy of attention,* досто́йный
внима́ния. *He is not worthy of her,* он не сто́ит её; он
недосто́ин её.

would *v. aux.* **1,** *used to express futurity: he said he
would be here by six,* он сказа́л, что придёт к шести́
часа́м. **2,** *used to form the conditional mood* бы: *I
would go if I could,* я пошёл бы, е́сли б мог. **3,** *used
to express a polite request or desire* бы: *I would like a
glass of milk,* я бы хоте́л(а) стака́н молока́. *I would
rather stay home,* я бы предпочёл оста́ться до́ма.
Would you like to see it?, хоти́те посмотре́ть? *Would
you be so kind,* бу́дьте добры́. **4,** *used to express
customary action: he would often drop in to say hello,*
он ча́сто заходи́л, чтобы поздоро́ваться с на́ми.
She would sit for hours in front of the fireplace, она́,
быва́ло, сиде́ла це́лыми часа́ми пе́ред ками́ном.
5, *used to express a strong wish: would that he were
here!,* о, е́сли бы он был здесь!

would-be *adj.* претенду́ющий на; с прете́нзией на.

wound *n.* ра́на; ране́ние. —*v.t.* ра́нить. *He was*
wounded in the chest, он был ра́нен в грудь. *Wounded in action,* ра́нен в бою́.

wounded *adj.* ра́неный. *The wounded,* ра́неные.

woven *adj.* тка́ный.

wrack *v.t.* = **rack.** —**go to wrack and ruin,** пойти́
пра́хом.

wraith *n.* привиде́ние; при́зрак.

wrangle *v.i.* пререка́ться. —*n.* пререка́ния; пере-
бра́нка.

wrap *v.t.* **1,** [*often* **wrap up**] (make a package of)
завёртывать: *wrap a gift,* заверну́ть пода́рок. *Wrap
something in paper,* заверну́ть *or* оберну́ть что́-
нибудь в бума́гу. **2,** (enclose snugly) заку́тывать; уку́-
тывать; завёртывать: *wrap a child in a blanket,* заку́-
тывать/уку́тывать/завёртывать ребёнка одея́лом
(*or* в одея́ло). **3,** *fol. by* **around** (wind around) обма́-
тывать; обёртывать: *wrap a towel around one's head,*
обма́тывать/обёртывать полоте́нце вокру́г голо-
вы́. **4,** *fol. by* **up,** *colloq.* (finish; conclude) зака́нчи-
вать, заключа́ть. —*v.i.* [*usu.* **wrap around**] обвива́ть-
ся (вокру́г). —*n.* шаль; наки́дка. —**under wraps,**
под спу́дом. —**wrapped up in,** поглощён (+ *instr.*);
погружён в; углублён в.

wrapper *n.* обёртка.

wrapping *n.* обёртка.—**wrapping paper,** обёрточная бума́га.

wrath *n.* гнев. —**wrathful,** *adj.* гне́вный.

wreak *v.t.* наноси́ть. *Wreak havoc on,* разоря́ть;
опустоша́ть.

wreath *n.* **1,** (garland; crown) вено́к. **2,** (puff, as of
smoke) кольцо́.

wreathe *v.t.* свива́ть. *His face was wreathed in smiles,*
его́ лицо́ расплыло́сь в улы́бке.

wreck *v.t.* разбива́ть: *wreck a car,* разби́ть маши́ну.
Wreck someone's hopes, разби́ть чьи-нибудь наде́ж-
ды. —*n.* **1,** (crash) круше́ние: *train wreck,* круше́ние
по́езда. **2,** (anything badly damaged; person in bad
shape) разва́лина.

wreckage *n.* обло́мки.

wrecker *n.* **1,** (one who wrecks) разруши́тель. **2,**
(truck) авари́йная маши́на.

wren *n.* крапи́вник.

wrench *n.* **1,** (tool) (га́ечный) ключ. *Monkey wrenc[h]*
францу́зский ключ. **2,** (sudden pull; yank) рыво́к. [3]
(sprain) вы́вих. **4,** (emotional shock) потрясе́ние. —*v.[t.]*
1, (twist; sprain) вы́вихнуть; вы́вернуть. **2,** (wrest)
вырыва́ть.

wrest *v.t.* вырыва́ть: *wrest a gun from one's assailan[t]*
вырыва́ть пистоле́т у налётчика.

wrestle *v.i.* **1,** *sports* боро́ться. **2,** *fol. by* **with** (struggle with, as a problem) би́ться (над). —**wrestler,** *n.*
боре́ц.

wrestling *n.* борьба́. *Wrestling match,* встре́ча по
борьбе́.

wretch *n.* **1,** (unfortunate person) несча́стный. **2,**
(despicable person) негодя́й.

wretched *adj.* **1,** (miserable) жа́лкий: *wretched existence,* жа́лкое существова́ние. **2,** (squalid) убо́гий:
жа́лкий: *wretched hovel,* убо́гая/жа́лкая лачу́га. **3,**
(awful) отврати́тельный: *wretched performance,* от-
врати́тельное исполне́ние.

wriggle *v.i.* **1,** (squirm) извива́ться. **2,** *fol. by* **out**
(extricate oneself) выпу́тываться; вывёртываться:
wriggle out of a predicament, выпу́тываться/вывёр-
тываться из затрудни́тельного положе́ния. *Wriggle out of a commitment,* увили́вать от обяза́тель-
ства.

wring *v.t.* **1,** (twist) скручивать. *Wring one's hands,* ломать себе руки. *Wring someone's neck,* свернуть шею (+ *dat.*). **2,** *fol. by* **out** (squeeze the water from) выжимать; отжимать. **3,** (obtain by pressure or coercion) вырывать; исторгать. —**wringing wet,** мокрый, хоть выжми.

wringer *n.* пресс.

wrinkle *n.* морщина. —*v.t.* **1,** (crease) мять. **2,** (draw up; pucker) морщить. —*v.i.* мяться; морщиться.

wrinkled *adj.* **1,** (of one's face) морщинистый; сморщенный. *Become wrinkled,* морщиться. **2,** (of fabric) мятый; измятый. *Become wrinkled,* мяться.

wrist *n.* запястье.

wristband *n.* напульсник.

wrist watch ручные *or* наручные часы.

writ *n.* приказ *or* распоряжение суда; исполнительный лист. —**Holy Writ,** священное писание.

write *v.t. & i.* писать: *write a letter,* писать письмо. *Write a check,* выписать чек. *Know how to write,* уметь писать. *This pen writes well,* эта ручка хорошо пишет. —**write down,** записывать. —**write in,** вписывать. —**write off, 1,** *bookkeeping* списывать. **2,** *fig.* (acknowledge as a failure) махнуть рукой на. —**write out,** выписывать. —**write up,** описывать; писать отчёт о. *See also* **written.**

writer *n.* писатель.

writhe *v.i.* корчиться: *he was writhing in pain,* он корчился (*or* его корчило) от боли.

writing *n.* **1,** (act of writing; ability to write) писание; письмо. *Reading, writing, arithmetic,* чтение, письмо, арифметика. *He is good at writing,* он хорошо пишет. *Take up writing,* стать писателем. **2,** (something written on a surface): *read the writing on the blackboard,* читать то, что написано на доске. **3,** *pl.* (written works) произведения; сочинения: *the writings of Plato,* произведения/сочинения Платона. **4,** (characters of a language) письмо: *hieroglyphic writing,* иероглифическое письмо. *The language was only recently reduced to writing,* язык только недавно стал письменным. —*adj.* писчий; письменный: *writing paper,* писчая бумага; *writing table,* письменный стол. —**in writing,** письменно; в письменной форме; в письменном виде.

written *adj.* **1,** (having been written) написанный: *well written,* хорошо написанный. **2,** (in writing) письменный: *written exam,* письменный экзамен. *In*

written form, в письменном виде; в письменной форме.

wrong *adj.* **1,** (incorrect) неправильный; неверный: *wrong answer,* неправильный/неверный ответ. *You are wrong,* вы неправы; вы ошибаетесь. *My watch is wrong,* мои часы идут неверно. *Be on the wrong track,* быть на ложном пути. **2,** *preceded by* **the** (not the one intended) не тот: *I took the wrong train,* я сел не на тот поезд. *You have the wrong number,* вы не туда попали. *You've come to the wrong place,* вы попали не по адресу. **3,** (inappropriate) неподходящий: *at the wrong time,* в неподходящее время. *That was the wrong thing to say,* это не надо было говорить. *Did I say something wrong?,* я что-то не так сказал? **4,** (amiss) неладный: *something is wrong,* что-то неладно. *Something is wrong with the phone,* что-то случилось с телефоном. *What's wrong with you?,* что с вами? *What's wrong with it?,* чем это плохо? **5,** (immoral) дурной; грешный. *It is wrong to kill,* грешно убивать. **6,** (not intended to be seen) левый: *the wrong side,* левая сторона; изнанка. *Wrong side out,* наизнанку. —*adv.* **1,** (incorrectly) неправильно; неверно. **2,** (inside out) наизнанку: *you've got your shirt on wrong,* у вас рубашка надета наизнанку. —*n.* зло: *right a wrong,* исправить зло. *Two wrongs don't make a right,* злом зла не поправишь. —*v.t.* обижать: *wrong a friend,* обижать друга. —**do wrong,** грешить. —**get (something) wrong,** путать; перепутывать. —**go wrong, 1,** (go astray) заблудиться. **2,** (go awry) не выйти; не получиться. **3,** (degenerate) опускаться. —**in the wrong,** виноватый.

wrongdoer *n.* правонарушитель. —**wrongdoing,** *n.* правонарушение.

wrongful *adj.* **1,** (improper; illegal) незаконный. **2,** (unjust) несправедливый; ложный. —**wrongfully,** *adv.* несправедливо; ложно.

wrongly *adv.* **1,** (incorrectly; improperly) неправильно. **2,** (unjustly) несправедливо; ложно.

wrought *adj.* отделанный: *finely wrought,* тонко отделанный. —**wrought iron,** сварочное железо.

wrought-up *adj.* взвинченный.

wry *adj.* **1,** (twisted) кривой. *Make a wry face,* кривиться; морщиться. **2,** (ironic; perverse) тонкий: *wry humor,* тонкий юмор.

X

X, x двадцать четвёртая буква английского алфавита; икс. —*n.* **1,** *math.* икс: *let x equal y,* пусть икс равен игреку. **2,** (mark in lieu of a signature) крест.

xenon *n.* ксенон.

X-ray *n.* **1,** (picture) рентген; рентгенограмма; рентгеновский снимок. *Have X-rays taken,* идти на рентген. **2,** *pl.* (rays) рентгеновы лучи; рентген. —*adj.* рентгеновский. —*v.t.* просвечивать.

xylophone *n.* ксилофон.

Y

Y, y двадцать пятая буква английского алфавита; игрек.

yacht *n.* яхта. —**yachtsman,** *n.* яхтсмен.

yak *n.* як.

yam *n.* **1,** (tropical plant) ямс. **2,** (sweet potato) батат.

yammer *v.i., colloq.* **1,** (whine; complain) ныть. **2,** (talk loudly) орать.

yank *v.t., colloq.* дёргать. *Yank the covers off someone,* стащить одеяла с кого-нибудь. —*n.* рывок.

Yankee *n.* янки.

yap *v.i.* **1,** (bark) тявкать. **2,** *slang* (jabber) тараторить.

yard *n.* **1,** (unit of length) ярд. **2,** (area surrounded by buildings) двор. *Barnyard,* птичий двор. *Lumber yard,* лесной склад. **3,** *R.R.* парк. *Freight yard,* товарная станция.

yardstick *n.* **1,** (measuring stick) мерка. **2,** *fig.* (standard) мерка; мерило.

yarn *n.* **1,** (spun fiber) пряжа. **2,** *colloq.* (story) россказни.

yawl *n.* ял.

yawn *v.i.* **1,** (open the mouth, when sleepy) зевать. **2,** (gape, as of an opening) зиять: *yawning abyss,* зияющая пропасть. —*n.* зевок.

yaws *n.* фрамбезия.

ye *pers. pron., archaic* вы. —*def. art., archaic* = **the.**

yea *adv., archaic* да. —*n.* за: *ten yeas, two nays,* десять за, два против.

year *n.* год. *Three years,* три года. *Five years,* пять лет. *Year after year,* из года в год.

yearbook *n.* ежегодник.

yearling *n.* годовалое животное.

yearly *adj.* ежегодный; годовой. —*adv.* ежегодно; раз в год.

yearn *v.i.* [*usu.* **yearn for**] **1,** (crave) жаждать. **2,** (long to see) тосковать по. —**yearning,** *n.* тоска: *yearning for one's homeland,* тоска по родине.

year-old *adj.* годовалый.

yeast *n.* дрожжи.

yell *v.i.* кричать. —*n.* крик.

yellow *adj.* жёлтый. —*n.* жёлтый цвет. —*v.i.* желтеть. —**yellowed,** *adj.* пожелтелый.

yellow fever жёлтая лихорадка.

yellowhammer *n.* (обыкновенная) овсянка.

yellowish *adj.* желтоватый.

yellowjacket *n.* оса.

yelp *v.i.* тявкать; визжать; взвизгивать. —*n.* визг; взвизг.

yen *n.* **1,** (monetary unit) иена. **2,** *colloq.* (longing) жажда; страсть.

yes *adv.* да: *yes or no,* да или нет. *Yes, sir!, mil.* так точно!; есть! —**yes man,** *colloq.* подпевала; подголосок.

yesterday *n. & adv.* вчера: *yesterday was Tuesday,* вчера был вторник. *Since yesterday,* со вчерашнего дня. —*adj.* [*usu.* **yesterday's**] вчерашний: *yesterday's weather,* вчерашняя погода. —**the day before yesterday,** позавчера. —**yesterday morning,** вчера утром.

yet *adv.* ещё: *not yet,* нет ещё. *He hasn't come yet,* он ещё не пришёл. *I'll beat you yet!,* я его ещё (когда-нибудь) побью! *Don't take your coat off yet,* не снимайте пока пальто. *Yet another example,* ещё один пример. ♦*In interr. sentences* уже: *have you eaten yet?,* вы уже поели? *Has the mail come yet?,* почта уже прибыла? —*conj.* но; однако: *yet he keeps trying,* но он всё старается. —**as yet,** пока что; пока ещё; до сих пор.

yew *n.* тис.

Yiddish *n.* идиш: *speak Yiddish,* говорить на идише. —*adj.* на идише: *a Yiddish newspaper,* газета на идише.

yield *v.t.* **1,** (bear; produce) приносить: *yield fruit/a profit/,* приносить плоды/прибыль. **2,** (give up; surrender) сдавать; уступать. *Yield the right of way,* уступать дорогу. *Yield the floor to,* давать *or* предоставлять слово (+ *dat.*). —*v.i.* **1,** (surrender) сдаваться. **2,** *fol. by* **to** (give in; succumb) уступать (+ *dat.*); поддаваться (+ *dat.*): *yield to pressure,* уступать/поддаваться давлению. **3,** (give way) сдаваться: *the door yielded,* дверь подалась. —*n.* **1,** (amount yielded) урожай; урожайность. *Yield of milk,* удой; надой. **2,** (return, as on an investment) доход.

yoga *n.* йога. —**yogi** *n.* йог.

yogurt *n.* кефир.

yoke *n.* **1,** (device for coupling draft animals) ярмо. **2,** (for carrying buckets) коромысло. **3,** (of a dress) кокетка. **4,** *fig.* (oppressive force) иго; гнет; ярмо. —*v.t.* впрягать в ярмо. *Yoke to a plow,* впрягать (*e.g.* волов) в плуг.

yokel *n.* деревенщина.

yolk *n.* желток.

yonder *adj.* вон тот. —*adv.* вон там.

yore *n., in* **in days of yore,** во время оно; *since days of yore,* издавна.

you *pers. pron.* **1,** *sing. (familiar)* ты; *(polite)* вы. *You are right,* ты прав/права; вы правы. *You are very funny,* ты/вы очень смешной/смешная. **2,** *pl.* вы: *the three of you,* вы втроём.

young adj. молодóй. —n. **1,** preceded by the (young people) молодёжь. **2,** (offspring) детёныши. —**young and old alike,** от мáла до велúка; стар и млад.

youngster n. мáльчик; юноша.

your poss. adj. **1,** sing. (familiar) твой; polite ваш: your sisters, твои/вáши сёстры. Wash your hands!, вымой рýки! **2,** pl. ваш: where are your bicycles?, где вáши велосипéды?

yours poss. pron. твой; ваш: is this coat yours?, это твоё/вáше пальтó? A friend of yours, одúн ваш друг; одúн из вáших друзéй.

yourself pers. pron. **1,** used for emphasis (ты) сам (самá); (вы) сáми. **2,** used reflexively себя. Did you hurt youself?, вы ушúблись? You ought to be ashamed of yourself!, как вам не стыдно! —**by yourself,** одúн (однá).

youth n. **1,** (quality of being young; one's early years) мóлодость; юность. In my youth, в мóлодости/юности. **2,** (young man) юноша. **3,** (young people collectively) молодёжь. Youth festival, фестивáль молодёжи.

youthful adj. юный; молодóй. Youthful appearance, моложáвый вид.

ytterbium n. иттéрбий.

yttrium n. úттрий.

yucca n. юкка.

Yugoslav adj. [also, **Yugoslavian**] югослáвский. —n. югослáв; югослáвка.

Yule n. святки. Also, **Yuletide.**

Z

Z, z двáдцать шестáя бýква англúйского алфавúта. —**from A to Z,** от А до Я.

zeal n. усéрдие; рвéние. —**zealot,** n. фанáтик. —**zealous,** adj. усéрдный; ретúвый; рьяный. —**zealously,** adv. усéрдно; ретúво.

zebra n. зéбра.

zebu n. зéбу.

zenith n. зенúт.

zephyr n. зефúр.

zeppelin n. цеппелúн.

zero n. нуль. —adj. нулевóй. —v.t. [usu. **zero in**] пристрéливать. —v.i. [usu. **zero in on**] пристрéливать; пристрéливаться по.

zest n. **1,** (keen enjoyment) смак. Zest for life, жизнерáдостность. **2,** (flavor) пикáнтность; изюминка.

Zeus n. Зевс.

zigzag n. зигзáг. —adj. зигзагообрáзный. —v.i. дéлать зигзáги; петлять.

zinc n. цинк. —adj. цúнковый. —**zinc oxide,** óкись цúнка. —**zinc white,** цúнковые белúла.

zinnia n. цúнния.

Zionism n. сионúзм. —**Zionist,** n. сионúст. —adj. сионúстский.

zip n. **1,** (whizzing sound) свист. **2,** colloq. (vim; pep) прыть.—v.t. [usu. **zip up**] застёгивать (на мóлнию). —v.i. **1,** colloq. (move rapidly) мчáться. **2,** slang (make a quick errand) сбéгать.

zipper n. мóлния.

zircon n. цирóн.

zirconium n. циркóний.

zither n. цúтра.

zloty n. злóтый.

zodiac n. зодиáк.

zonal adj. зонáльный.

zone n. зóна; пояс; полосá. —v.t. разделять на зóны.

zoo n. зоопáрк.

zoology n. зоолóгия. —**zoological,** adj. зоологúческий. —**zoologist,** n. зоóлог.

zoom v.i. **1,** (fly suddenly upwards) взмывáть. **2,** fig. (rise rapidly) подскáкивать. **3,** (move rapidly) мчáться.

Zulu n. зулýс. —adj. зулýсский.

zwieback n. сухáрь.

zygote n. зигóта.

Russian-English Section

A

А, а *n.neut.* first letter of the Russian alphabet. —**от А до Я,** from A to Z.

а *conj.* **1,** and: хорошо́!, а вы?, fine!, and you? Сего́дня гу́сто, а за́втра пу́сто, feast today and fast tomorrow. **2,** but: я приду́, а он нет, I'll come but he won't. —*particle* and; so: а что случи́лось с Бори́сом?, and what ever happened to Boris? А что он сказа́л?, and/ so what did he say? —*interj., expressing various emotions* oh!; ah!: а!, что я наде́лал!, oh!, what have I done! А, вот молоде́ц!, ah, that's a fine fellow!

абажу́р *n.* lampshade.

абба́т *n.* abbot. —**аббати́са,** *n.* abbess. —**абба́тство,** *n.* abbey.

аббревиату́ра *n.* abbreviation.

аберра́ция *n.* aberration.

абза́ц *n.* **1,** indentation; indention. **2,** paragraph.

абитурие́нт *n.* **1,** *obs.* person graduating secondary school. **2,** applicant/candidate for admission to a university.

абонеме́нт *n.* subscription *(to a series of concerts, lectures, etc.).*

абоне́нт *n.* **1,** user *(of a telephone).* **2,** member; cardholder *(of a library).* **3,** subscriber *(to a series of cultural events).*

аборда́ж *n.,* naval boarding *(of an enemy vessel).* —**брать на аборда́ж,** to board (an enemy vessel).

абориге́н *n.* aborigine.

або́рт *n.* abortion. —**аборти́вный,** *adj., med.* abortive.

абрази́в *n.* abrasive. —**абрази́вный,** *adj.* abrasive.

абракада́бра *n.* abracadabra.

абрико́с *n.* **1,** apricot. **2,** apricot tree. —**абрико́совый,** *adj.* apricot.

абсе́нт (сэ) *n.* absinthe.

абсолю́т *n.* absolute.

абсолюти́зм *n.* absolutism. —**абсолюти́ст,** *n.* absolutist. —**абсолюти́стский,** *adj.* absolutist.

абсолю́тно *adv.* absolutely.

абсолю́тный *adj.* absolute. —**абсолю́тный нуль, 1,** absolute zero. **2,** an absolute nothing *(said of a person).* —**абсолю́тный слух,** absolute (*or* perfect) pitch.

абсорби́ровать *v. impfv. & pfv. [pres.* -рую, -руешь] to absorb.

абсо́рбция *n.* absorption.

абстраги́ровать *v. impfv. & pfv. [pres.* -рую, -руешь] to abstract.

абстра́ктный *adj.* abstract. —**абстра́ктно,** *adv.* in an abstract manner; in the abstract.

абстракциони́зм *n.* abstract art. —**абстракциони́ст,** *n.* abstract artist.

абстра́кция *n.* abstraction.

абсу́рд *n.* absurdity. —**доводи́ть до абсу́рда,** to carry to the point of absurdity.

абсу́рдный *adj.* absurd; preposterous. —**абсу́рдность,** *n.f.* absurdity.

абсце́сс *n.* abscess.

абсци́сса *n.* abscissa.

абха́з *n.m. [fem.* абха́зка] Abkhaz *(one of a people inhabiting the Caucasus).* —**абха́зский,** *adj.* Abkhazian.

аванга́рд *n.* **1,** *mil.* advance guard. **2,** *fig.* vanguard: в аванга́рде, in the vanguard; in the forefront.

авангарди́зм *n.* avant-gardism. —**авангарди́ст,** *n.* member of the avant-garde. —**авангарди́стский,** *adj.* avant-garde.

аванза́л *n.* anteroom; antechamber.

аванпо́ст *n., mil.* outpost.

ава́нс *n.* **1,** advance *(of money).* **2,** *pl., obs.* advances; overtures.

аванси́ровать *v. impfv. & pfv. [pres.* -рую, -руешь] to advance money to (an enterprise, organization, etc.).

ава́нсом *adv.* in advance.

авансце́на *n.* proscenium.

авантю́ра *n.* adventure; (risky) venture.

авантюри́зм *n.* adventurism.

авантюри́ст *n.* **1,** *obs.* adventurer. **2,** adventurist. —**авантюристи́ческий,** *adj.* adventuristic.

авантю́рный *adj.* **1,** speculative; risky. **2,** shady. **3,** *(of a story, novel, etc.)* adventure *(attrib.).*

ава́рец [*gen.* -рца] *n.m. [fem.* -рка] Avar *(one of a people inhabiting the Caucasus).* —**ава́рский,** *adj.* Avar.

авари́йность *n.f.* accident rate.

авари́йный *adj.* **1,** salvage *(attrib.);* wrecking *(attrib.):* авари́йная маши́на, wrecker; tow truck. **2,** emergency *(attrib.):* авари́йная поса́дка, emergency landing; crash landing.

ава́рия *n.* **1,** accident; crash; wreck. **2,** breakdown. **3,** mishap.

ава́ры *n.pl. [sing.* ава́р] Avars *(powerful Turkic people of the 6th-9th centuries).*

а́вгиев *adj., in* а́вгиевы коню́шни, Augean stables.

авгу́р *n.* augur.

а́вгуст *n.* August. —**а́вгустовский,** *adj.* August *(attrib.).*

авеню́ *n.f. indecl.* avenue.

авиа- *prefix* air-: авиаба́за, air base.

авиакомпа́ния *n.* **1,** aircraft company. **2,** airline.

авиаконстру́ктор *n.* aircraft designer.

авиакосми́ческий *adj.* aerospace *(attrib.).*

авиамоде́ль (дэ) *n.f.* model airplane.

авиано́сец [*gen.* -сца] *n.* aircraft carrier.

авиапо́чта *n.* air mail.

авиа́тор *n.* aviator.

авиатра́сса *n.* air route.

авиацио́нный *adj.* **1,** aviation *(attrib.).* **2,** aeronautical. **3,** aircraft *(attrib.);* airplane *(attrib.).*

авиа́ция *n.* **1,** aviation. **2,** airplanes; aircraft.

авока́до *n. indecl.* avocado.

аво́сь *particle, colloq.* maybe; perhaps. —**на аво́сь,** hit or miss; by guesswork.

аво́ська [*gen. pl.* -сек] *n., colloq.* string bag.

авра́л *n.* **1,** naval job involving all hands. **2,** *colloq.* rush job.

авро́ра *n.* aurora.

австрали́ец [*gen.* -и́йца] *n.m.* [*fem.* -и́йка] Australian. —**австрали́йский,** *adj.* Australian.

австри́ец [*gen.* -и́йца] *n.m.* [*fem.* -и́йка] Austrian. —**австри́йский,** *adj.* Austrian.

авто- *prefix* **1,** self-; auto-: автопортре́т, self-portrait; автобиогра́фия, autobiography. **2,** automatic: автопило́т, automatic pilot. **3,** automobile: автозаво́д, automobile factory.

автоба́за *n.* motor transport depot.

автобиогра́фия *n.* autobiography. —**автобиографи́ческий; автобиографи́чный,** *adj.* autobiographical.

авто́бус *n.* bus. —**авто́бусный,** *adj.* bus *(attrib.).*

авто́граф *n.* **1,** autograph. **2,** original handwritten manuscript.

автодро́м *n.* speedway.

автожи́р *n.* autogiro.

автозаво́д *n.* automobile factory.

автозапра́вочный *adj., in* автозапра́вочная ста́нция, gas station; service station.

автока́р *n.* self-propelled cart.

автокра́т *n.* autocrat. —**автокра́тия,** *n.* autocracy. —**автократи́ческий,** *adj.* autocratic.

авто́л *n.* motor oil.

автомагистра́ль *n.f.* superhighway; expressway; thruway.

автома́т *n.* **1,** any automatic device: телефо́н-автома́т, pay telephone. **2,** vending machine. **3,** automaton; robot. **4,** submachine gun; Tommy gun.

автоматиза́ция *n.* automation: автоматиза́ция произво́дства, automation of production.

автоматизи́ровать *v. impfv. & pfv.* [*pres.* -рую, -руешь] to automate.

автома́тика *n.* automation: век автома́тики, the age of automation.

автомати́чески *adv.* automatically.

автомати́ческий *adj.* **1,** automatic; automatically operated. **2,** automatic; mechanical; involuntary.

автома́тчик *n.* submachine gunner.

автомаши́на *n.* motor vehicle.

автомобили́ст *n.* motorist.

автомоби́ль *n.m.* automobile. —**автомоби́льный,** *adj.* automobile *(attrib.);* vehicle *(attrib.);* automotive.

автоно́мия *n.* autonomy.

автоно́мный *adj.* **1,** autonomous. **2,** *mech.* self-contained.

автопило́т *n.* automatic pilot.

автопортре́т *n.* self-portrait.

а́втор *n.* author.

авторефера́т *n.* abstract *(by the author).*

авторизова́ть *v. impfv. & pfv.* [*pres.* -зу́ю, -зу́ешь] to authorize (the translation, reproduction, etc. of a literary work).

авторита́рный *adj.* authoritarian.

авторите́т *n.* **1,** authority; prestige. **2,** an authority. —**авторите́тный,** *adj.* authoritative.

а́вторский *adj.* author's. —**а́вторское пра́во,** copyright.

а́вторство *n.* authorship.

автору́чка [*gen. pl.* -чек] *n.* fountain pen.

автостра́да *n.* superhighway; expressway; thruway.

автотра́нспорт *n.* motor transport.

ага́ *interj.* aha!

ага́ва *n.* agave.

ага́т *n.* agate. —**ага́товый,** *adj.* agate.

агглютинати́вный *adj.* agglutinative. —**агглютина́ция,** *n.* agglutination.

аге́нт *n.* agent. —**аге́нтство,** *n.* agency.

агенту́ра *n.* **1,** intelligence agency; secret service. **2,** secret agents. —**агенту́рный,** *adj.* intelligence *(attrib.).*

агиогра́фия *n.* hagiography.

агита́тор *n.* political agitator.

агита́ция *n.* political agitation; propaganda work. —**агитацио́нный,** *adj.* agitation *(attrib.);* propaganda *(attrib.).*

агити́ровать *v. impfv.* [*pres.* -рую, -руешь] **1,** to agitate *(politically);* carry on propaganda work. **2,** [*pfv.* сагити́ровать] *colloq.* to try to win over; try to persuade.

аги́тка *n., colloq.* piece of art propaganda; propaganda play, novel, etc.

агитпу́нкт *n.* local agitation and propaganda headquarters.

а́гнец [*gen.* а́гнца] *n., obs.* lamb.

агностици́зм *n.* agnosticism. —**агно́стик,** *n.* agnostic. —**агности́ческий,** *adj.* agnostic.

аго́ния *n.* agony; throes of death.

агра́рный *adj.* agrarian.

агрега́т *n.* unit: силово́й агрега́т, power unit.

агре́ссия *n.* aggression. —**агресси́вный,** *adj.* aggressive. —**агре́ссор,** *n.* aggressor.

агроно́мия *n.* agronomy. —**агроно́м,** *n.* agronomist. —**агрономи́ческий,** *adj.* agronomic.

ад [*2nd loc.* аду́] *n.* hell.

ада́жио *adv. & n. indecl.* adagio.

ада́мов *adj.* Adam's. —**ада́мово я́блоко,** Adam's apple.

адапта́ция *n., biol.* adaptation.

ада́птер (тэ) *n., mech.* adapter.

адвока́т *n.* lawyer; attorney. —**адвока́тский,** *adj.* lawyer's; lawyers'; legal.

адвокату́ра *n.* **1,** the practice of law. **2,** lawyers collectively; the bar.

адеква́тный (дэ) *adj.* **1,** identical. **2,** adequate.

адено́ид (дэ) *n.* adenoid.

аде́пт (дэ) *n.* adherent; follower.

администрати́вный *adj.* administrative.

администра́тор *n.* administrator; manager.

администра́ция *n.* administration; management; managing officials.

администри́ровать *v. impfv.* [*pres.* -рую, -руешь] to administer; manage.

адмира́л *n.* admiral.

адмиралте́йство *n.* **1,** admiralty. **2,** the Admiralty (building).

адмира́льский *adj.* admiral's.

адренали́н *n.* adrenalin.

а́дрес [*pl.* адреса́] *n.* address. —**по а́дресу** (+ *gen.);* по (чьему́-нибудь) а́дресу, about; regarding; concerning; directed at/toward/against: по моему́ а́дресу, about me; directed against me. —**не по а́дресу,** to the wrong quarter, place, or party.

адреса́т *n.* addressee.

а́дресный *adj.* address *(attrib.).* —**а́дресная кни́га,** directory. —**а́дресный стол; а́дресное бюро́,** address bureau.

адресова́ть *v.impfv. & pfv.* [*pres.* -су́ю, -су́ешь] to address (a letter, question, etc.). —**адресова́ться,** *refl.* **1,** to be addressed. **2,** *(with* к*)* to address (someone); apply (to).

а́дский *adj.* **1,** of hell. **2,** hellish. **3,** fiendish; diabolical. **4,** *colloq.* colossal; stupendous.

адсорби́ровать *v. impfv. & pfv.* [*pres.* -рую, -руешь] to adsorb.

адсо́рбция *n.* adsorption.

адъюта́нт *n.* aide-de-camp; adjutant.

адыге́ец [*gen.* -е́йца] *n.m.* [*fem.* -е́йка] Adygei *(one of a people inhabiting the Caucasus).* —**адыге́йский,** *adj.* Adygei.

ажиота́ж *n.* **1,** price fixing. **2,** *fig.* hullabaloo.

ажу́р *n.* **1,** *obs.* openwork. **2,** *bookkeeping* current basis. —**в ажу́ре,** *colloq.* in perfect order; shipshape.

ажу́рный *adj.* **1,** openwork *(attrib.).* **2,** finely wrought; delicate. —**ажу́рная стро́чка,** hemstitch.

аз [*gen.* аза́] *n.* **1,** old name of the letter A. **2,** *pl.* letters. **3,** *pl., fig.* rudiments; elements; fundamentals. —**начина́ть с азо́в,** to start from the beginning. —**ни аза́ не знать,** not to know a thing.

аза́лия *n.* azalea.

аза́рт *n.* zeal; ardor; fervor. —**войти́ в аза́рт,** to get carried away.

аза́ртный *adj.* **1,** ardent; zealous; fervent. **2,** heated; impassioned. —**аза́ртная игра́,** game of chance.

а́збука *n.* **1,** alphabet. **2,** alphabet book; primer. **3,** rudiments; ABC's.

а́збучный *adj.* **1,** alphabet *(attrib.).* **2,** alphabetical. —**а́збучная и́стина,** truism; obvious truth.

азербайджа́нец [*gen.* -нца] *n.m.* [*fem.* -нка] Azerbaijani. —**азербайджа́нский,** *adj.* Azerbaijani.

азиа́т *n.m.* [*fem.* -а́тка] Asian; Asiatic. —**азиа́тский,** *adj.* Asian; Asiatic.

а́зимут *n.* azimuth.

азо́т *n.* nitrogen. —**азо́тистый,** *adj.* nitrous. —**азо́тный,** *adj.* nitric; nitrogen *(attrib.).*

а́ист *n.* stork.

ай *interj.* **1,** oh! **2,** ouch!

айва́ *n.* **1,** quince. **2,** quince tree. —**айво́вый,** *adj.* quince.

айда́ *interj., colloq.* go!; let's go!

а́йсберг (бэ) *n.* iceberg.

акаде́мия *n.* academy. —**акаде́мик,** *n.* academician. —**академи́ческий,** *adj.* academic.

ака́нт *also,* **ака́нф** *n.* acanthus.

а́канье *n.* pronunciation of unstressed о as а in standard Russian.

а́кать *v. impfv.* to pronounce unstressed о as а in standard Russian.

ака́ция *n.* acacia.

аквала́нг *n.* aqualung. —**акваланги́ст,** *n.* skin diver.

аквамари́н *n.* aquamarine. —**аквамари́новый,** *adj.* aquamarine.

акваре́ль *n.f.* watercolors; watercolor painting. —**акваре́льный,** *adj.* watercolor *(attrib.).* —**акварели́ст,** *n.* watercolorist.

аква́риум *n.* **1,** aquarium. **2,** fishbowl; fish tank.

аквати́нта *n.* aquatint.

аквато́рия *n.* area of water *(on the globe).*

акведу́к *n.* aqueduct.

акклиматиза́ция *n.* acclimatization; acclimation.

акклиматизи́ровать *v. impfv. & pfv.* [*pres.* -рую, -руешь] to acclimatize; acclimate. —**акклиматизи́роваться,** *refl.* to become acclimatized; become acclimated.

аккомпанеме́нт *n., music* accompaniment.

аккомпаниа́тор *n.* accompanist.

аккомпани́ровать *v. impfv.* [*pres.* -рую, -руешь] *(with dat.) music* to accompany.

акко́рд *n.* **1,** *music* chord. **2,** *obs.* agreement; accord.

аккордео́н *n.* accordion. —**аккордеони́ст,** *n.* accordionist.

акко́рдный *adj.* by the piece: акко́рдная рабо́та, piecework.

аккредити́в *n.* letter of credit.

аккредитова́ть *v. impfv. & pfv.* [*pres.* -ту́ю, -ту́ешь] *dipl.* to accredit.

аккумуля́тор *n.* battery. —**аккумуля́торный,** *adj., in* аккумуля́торная батаре́я, storage battery.

аккура́тно *adv.* **1,** neatly. **2,** punctually. **3,** efficiently. **4,** *colloq.* regularly. **5,** *colloq.* cautiously.

аккура́тность *n.f.* **1,** meticulousness; care. **2,** tidiness; neatness. **3,** punctuality; promptness.

аккура́тный *adj.* **1,** neat; tidy. **2,** punctual; prompt. **3,** efficient; thorough.

акони́т *n.* aconite; monkshood.

акр *n.* acre.

акроба́т *n.* acrobat. —**акроба́тика,** *n.* acrobatics. —**акробати́ческий,** *adj.* acrobatic.

акро́поль *n.m.* acropolis.

акрости́х *n.* acrostic.

акселера́тор *n.* accelerator.

аксельба́нт *n.* aiguillette; aglet.

аксессуа́р *n.* **1,** accessory. **2,** *pl.* secondary features; background details *(of a painting, literary work, etc.).* **3,** *pl.* stage props.

аксио́ма *n.* axiom. —**аксиомати́ческий,** *adj.* axiomatic.

акт *n.* **1,** act: престу́пный акт, criminal act. **2,** document; deed. **3,** *law* act. **4,** *theat.* act. **5,** graduation exercise; commencement.

актёр *n.* actor. —**актёрский,** *adj.* actor's; actors'.

актёрство *n.* **1,** acting *(as a profession).* **2,** affected behavior; play-acting.

акти́в *n.* **1,** most active members of an organization. **2,** *finance* assets. **3,** *bookkeeping & fig.* credit side of the ledger.

активизи́ровать *v. impfv. & pfv.* [*pres.* -рую, -руешь] to step up.

активи́ст *n.* political or social activist.

акти́вно *adv.* actively.

акти́вность *n.f.* activity; participation; involvement.

акти́вный *adj.* **1,** active. **2,** *econ.* favorable.

акти́ний *n.* actinium.

акти́ния *n.* sea anemone.

а́ктовый *adj., in* а́ктовый зал, assembly hall.

актри́са *n.* actress.

актуа́льность *n.f.* **1,** timeliness; relevance. **2,** urgency.

актуа́льный *adj.* current; timely; relevant.

аку́ла *n.* shark.

акупункту́ра *n.* acupuncture.

аку́стика *n.* acoustics. —акусти́ческий, *adj.* acoustic; acoustical.

акушёр *n.* obstetrician. —акуше́рка, *n.* midwife. —акуше́рский, *adj.* obstetric.

акуше́рство *n.* **1,** obstetrics. **2,** midwifery.

акце́нт *n.* accent: говори́ть с акце́нтом, to speak with an accent. —де́лать акце́нт на (+ *prepl.*), to accentuate; emphasize; place the emphasis on.

акценти́ровать *v. impfv. & pfv.* [*pres.* -рую, -руешь] **1,** *phonet.* to accent; stress. **2,** *fig.* to accentuate.

акци́з *n.* excise; excise tax. —акци́зный, *adj.* excise (*attrib.*).

акционе́р *n.* stockholder; shareholder.

акционе́рный *adj.* stockholder'; joint-stock (*attrib.*): акционе́рное о́бщество, joint-stock company.

а́кция *n.* **1,** share of stock. **2,** *pl., fig.* stock: его́ а́кции повыша́ются, his stock is rising. **3,** action.

алба́нец [*gen.* -нца] *n.m.* [*fem.* -нка] Albanian. —алба́нский, *adj.* Albanian.

а́лгебра *n.* algebra. —алгебраи́ческий, *adj.* algebraic.

алгори́тм *n.* algorithm.

алеба́рда *n.* halberd.

алеба́стр *n.* alabaster. —алеба́стровый, *adj.* alabaster.

александри́т *n.* alexandrite.

але́ть *v. impfv.* [*pfv.* заале́ть] **1,** to turn red; turn scarlet; blush. **2,** (*of anything red*) to glow; gleam.

алжи́рец [*gen.* -рца] *n.m.* [*fem.* -рка] Algerian. —алжи́рский, *adj.* Algerian.

а́либи *n. neut. indecl., law* alibi.

алиме́нты [*gen.* -тов] *n. pl.* alimony. —алиме́нтный, *adj.* alimony (*attrib.*).

алкало́ид *n.* alkaloid.

алка́ть *v. impfv.* [*pres.* а́лчу, а́лчешь] (*with gen.*) *obs.* to crave; hunger (for).

алка́ш [*gen.* -каша́] *n., colloq.* drunkard.

алкоголи́зм *n.* alcoholism. —алкого́лик, *n.* alcoholic.

алкого́ль *n.m.* alcohol. —алкого́льный, *adj.* alcohol (*attrib.*).

алла́х *n.* Allah.

аллего́рия *n.* allegory. —аллегори́ческий, *adj.* allegorical.

аллегре́тто *adv. & n. indecl.* allegretto.

алле́гро *adv. & n. indecl.* allegro.

аллерги́я *n.* allergy. —аллерги́ческий, *adj.* allergic.

алле́я *n.* tree-lined walk.

аллига́тор *n.* alligator.

аллилу́йя *interj.* hallelujah!

аллитера́ция *n.* alliteration.

алло́ *interj., used when answering the telephone* hello!

аллопа́тия *n.* allopathy. —аллопа́т, *n.* allopath. —аллопати́ческий, *adj.* allopathic.

аллю́вий *n.* alluvium. —аллювиа́льный, *adj.* alluvial.

аллю́р *n.* gait (*of a horse*).

алма́з *n.* diamond. —алма́зный, *adj.* diamond.

ало́э *n. neut. indecl.* **1,** aloe (*plant*). **2,** aloes (*drug*).

алта́ец [*gen.* -а́йца] *n.m.* [*fem.* -а́йка] Altai (*one of a people inhabiting southern Siberia*).

алта́йский *adj.* **1,** Altai. **2,** Altaic.

алта́рь [*gen.* -таря́] *n.m.* altar.

алты́н [*gen. pl.* -ты́н] *n.* old Russian coin worth three kopecks; altyn.

алфави́т *n.* alphabet. —алфави́тный, *adj.* alphabetical.

алхи́мия *n.* alchemy. —алхи́мик, *n.* alchemist.

а́лчный *adj.* greedy. —а́лчность, *n.f.* greed.

а́лый *adj.* scarlet.

алыча́ *n.* a variety of plum.

альбатро́с *n.* albatross.

альбини́зм *n.* albinism. —альбино́с, *n.* albino.

альбо́м *n.* album.

альбуми́н *n.* albumin.

альвео́ла *n.* alveolus. —альвеоля́рный, *adj.* alveolar.

алько́в *n.* alcove.

альмана́х *n.* **1,** literary miscellany. **2,** *obs.* almanac.

альпака́ *n. neut. indecl.* alpaca.

альпи́йский *adj.* Alpine.

альпини́зм *n.* mountain climbing. —альпини́ст, *n.* mountain climber. —альпини́стский, *adj.* mountain-climbing (*attrib.*).

альт [*gen.* альта́] *n.* **1,** alto (*voice or part*). **2,** viola.

альтернати́ва (тэ) *n.* alternative. —альтернати́вный, *adj.* alternative; alternate.

альтерна́тор (тэ) *n.* alternator.

альтиме́тр *n.* altimeter.

альто́вый *adj.* alto.

альтруи́зм *n.* altruism. —альтруи́ст, *n.* altruist. —альтруисти́ческий, *adj.* altruistic.

а́льфа *n.* alpha. —а́льфа-лучи́, alpha rays. —а́льфа-части́ца, alpha particle.

алья́нс *n.* alliance.

алюми́ний *n.* aluminum. —алюми́ниевый, *adj.* aluminum.

аляпова́тый *adj.* **1,** crude; crudely made. **2,** ugly.

амазо́нка [*gen. pl.* -нок] *n.* **1,** *myth.* Amazon. **2,** horsewoman. **3,** *obs.* riding habit.

амальга́ма *n.* **1,** amalgam. **2,** *fig.* amalgamation; mixture; blend.

амальгама́ция *n., chem.* amalgamation.

амальгами́ровать *v. impfv. & pfv.* [*pres.* -рую, -руешь] **1,** to amalgamate; alloy with mercury. **2,** to coat with an amalgam.

амара́нт *n.* amaranth.

амари́ллис *n.* amaryllis.

амба́р *n.* **1,** barn; granary. **2,** storehouse; warehouse. —амба́рный, *adj.* barn (*attrib.*).

амбицио́зный *adj.* ambitious.

амби́ция *n.* **1,** pride; self-respect. **2,** arrogance; conceit. —уда́риться в амби́цию, to take umbrage; get into a huff.

а́мбра *n.* ambergris.

амбразу́ра *n.* embrasure; loophole.

амбро́зия *n.* **1,** ambrosia. **2,** ragweed.

амбулато́рия *n.* outpatient clinic; dispensary.

амбулато́рный *adj.* dispensary (*attrib.*). —амбулато́рный больно́й, outpatient.

амёба *n.* ameba.

америка́нец [*gen.* -нца] *n.m.* [*fem.* -нка] American.

америка́нский *adj.* American.

аме́риций *n.* americium.

амети́ст *n.* amethyst. —амети́стовый, *adj.* amethyst.

аминокислота [*pl.* -лоты] *n.* amino acid.

аминь *particle & interj.* amen!

аммиак *n.* ammonia.

аммиачный *adj.* ammonia *(attrib.)*; ammonium *(attrib.)*. —**аммиачная селитра,** ammonium nitrate.

аммоний *n.* ammonium. —**аммониевый,** *adj.* ammonium *(attrib.)*.

амнистировать *v. impfv. & pfv.* [*pres.* -рую, -руешь] to grant amnesty to.

амнистия *n.* amnesty.

аморальный *adj.* amoral; immoral. —**аморальность,** *n.f.* amorality; immorality.

амортизатор *n.* shock absorber.

амортизационный *adj.* **1,** shock-absorbing. **2,** *finance* amortization *(attrib.)*.

амортизация *n.* **1,** amortization; depreciation. **2,** shock absorption.

амортизировать *v. impfv. & pfv.* [*pres.* -рую, -руешь] to amortize.

аморфный *adj.* amorphous.

ампер [*gen. pl.* ампер] *n.* ampere. —**амперметр,** *n.* ammeter.

амплитуда *n., physics* amplitude.

амплуа *n. neut. indecl., theat.* (one's) kind of role.

ампула *n.* ampule.

ампутация *n.* amputation.

ампутировать *v. impfv. & pfv.* [*pres.* -рую, -руешь] to amputate.

амулет *n.* amulet; charm.

амур *n.* **1,** Cupid. **2,** *pl., obs., colloq.* love affairs.

амфибия *n.* **1,** amphibian. **2,** amphibious plane or vehicle.

амфитеатр *n.* **1,** amphitheater. **2,** *theat.* raised back rows of the orchestra.

анабаптизм *n.* Anabaptism. —**анабаптист,** *n.* Anabaptist.

анаграмма *n.* anagram.

анаконда *n.* anaconda.

анализ *n.* **1,** analysis. **2,** *med.* test: анализ крови, blood test.

анализировать *v. impfv. & pfv.* [*pfv. also* проанализировать; *pres.* -рую, -руешь] to analyze.

аналитик *n.* analyst. —**аналитический,** *adj.* analytic; analytical.

аналогичный *adj.* analogous.

аналогия *n.* analogy.

аналой *n.* lectern *(in a church)*.

анальный *adj.* anal.

ананас *n.* pineapple. —**ананасный,** *adj.* pineapple.

анапест *n.* anapest.

анархизм *n.* anarchism. —**анархист,** *n.* anarchist. —**анархистский,** *adj.* anarchist *(attrib.)*. —**анархический,** *adj.* anarchistic. —**анархичный,** *adj.* anarchic; chaotic.

анархия *n.* **1,** anarchy. **2,** *colloq.* chaos.

анатом *n.* anatomist.

анатомировать *v. impfv. & pfv.* [*pres.* -рую, -руешь] to anatomize; dissect.

анатомия *n.* anatomy. —**анатомический,** *adj.* anatomical.

анафема *n.* anathema.

анахронизм *n.* anachronism. —**анахронический,** *adj.* anachronistic.

анаэроб *n.* anaerobe. —**анаэробный,** *adj.* anaerobic.

ангар *n.* hangar.

ангел *n.* angel. —**ангельский,** *adj.* angelic.

ангина *n.* angina.

англизировать *v. impfv. & pfv.* [*pres.* -рую, -руешь] to Anglicize.

английский *adj.* **1,** English. **2,** British. —**английская булавка,** safety pin. —**английская миля,** statute mile. —**английская соль,** Epsom salt(s).

англиканский *adj.* Anglican.

англицизм *n.* Anglicism.

англичанин [*pl.* -чане, -чан] *n.* **1,** Englishman. **2,** *pl.* the English; the British.

англичанка [*gen. pl.* -нок] *n.* Englishwoman.

англосаксонский *adj.* Anglo-Saxon.

англофил *n.* Anglophile.

анданте (тэ) *adv. & n. neut. indecl.* andante.

анекдот *n.* **1,** anecdote; joke. **2,** amusing incident; funny thing.

анекдотический *adj.* **1,** anecdotal. **2,** [*also,* анекдотичный] improbable; incredible.

анемия *n.* anemia. —**анемичный,** *adj.* anemic.

анемометр *n.* anemometer.

анемон *n.* anemone. *Also,* **анемона.**

анероид *n.* aneroid barometer.

анестезиолог (нэстэ) *n.* anesthesiologist.

анестезировать (нэстэ) *v. impfv. & pfv.* [*pres.* -рую, -руешь] to anesthetize.

анестезирующий (нэстэ) *adj.* anesthetic. —**анестезирующее средство,** anesthetic.

анестезия (нэстэ) *n.* anesthesia.

анилин *n.* aniline. —**анилиновый,** *adj.* aniline.

анимизм *n.* animism. —**анимист,** *n.* animist. —**анимистический,** *adj.* animistic.

анис *n.* anise.

анисовка *n.* anisette.

анисовый *adj.* anise.

анкета *n.* **1,** questionnaire; form; blank. **2,** survey.

анкетный *adj.* questionnaire *(attrib.)*. —**анкетные данные,** biographical data.

анклав *n.* enclave.

анналы [*gen.* -лов] *n. pl.* annals.

аннексировать *v. impfv. & pfv.* [*pres.* -рую, -руешь] to annex.

аннексия *n.* annexation.

аннотация *n.* synopsis.

аннулирование *n.* annulment; cancellation; abrogation.

аннулировать *v. impfv. & pfv.* [*pres.* -рую, -руешь] to annul; cancel; abrogate.

анод *n.* anode.

аномалия *n.* anomaly. —**аномальный,** *adj.* anomalous.

аноним *n.* **1,** anonymous author. **2,** anonymous work; anonymous letter.

анонимный *adj.* anonymous. —**анонимно,** *adv.* anonymously. —**анонимность,** *n.f.* anonymity.

анонс *n.* announcement; notice *(of a performance)*.

анонсировать *v. impfv. & pfv.* [*pres.* -рую, -руешь] to announce; advertise (a performance).

анормальный *adj.* abnormal.

анофелес *n.* anopheles.

ансамбль *n.m.* ensemble.

антагонизм *n.* antagonism. —**антагонист,** *n.* antagonist. —**антагонистический,** *adj.* antagonistic.

антарктический *adj.* antarctic.

антенна (тэ) *n.* aerial; antenna.

антиамериканизм *n.* anti-Americanism. —**антиамериканский**, *adj.* anti-American.

антибиотик *n.* antibiotic.

антивещество *n.* antimatter.

антивоенный *adj.* antiwar.

антиген *n.* antigen.

антидемократический *adj.* undemocratic.

антиквар *n.* antique dealer; antiquary. —**антикварный**, *adj.* antique.

антикоммунизм *n.* anticommunism. —**антикоммунист**, *n.* anticommunist. —**антикоммунистический**, *adj.* anticommunist.

антилопа *n.* antelope.

антиобщественный *adj.* antisocial; harmful to society.

антипартийный *adj.* anti-party.

антипатичный *adj.* unpleasant; disagreeable; antipathetic.

антипатия *n.* antipathy; aversion.

антиракета *n.* anti-missile missile; anti-ballistic missile.

антирелигиозный *adj.* antireligious.

антисанитарный *adj.* unsanitary.

антисемитизм *n.* anti-Semitism. —**антисемит**, *n.* anti-Semite. —**антисемитский**, *adj.* anti-Semitic.

антисептика (сэ) *n.* **1,** antisepsis. **2,** antiseptics. —**антисептический**, *adj.* antiseptic.

антисоветский *adj.* anti-Soviet.

антитеза (тэ) *n.* antithesis; opposite.

антитезис (тэ) *n.*, *logic* antithesis.

антитело [*pl.* -**тела**] *n.* antibody.

антитетический (тэ) *adj.* antithetical.

антитоксин *n.* antitoxin. —**антитоксический**, *adj.* antitoxic.

антифриз *n.* antifreeze.

антихрист *n.* Antichrist.

античный *adj.* ancient. —**античность**, *n.f.* antiquity.

антология *n.* anthology.

антоним *n.* antonym.

антоновка *n.* a variety of apple.

антракт *n.* **1,** *theat.* intermission. **2,** musical interlude.

антрацит *n.* anthracite. —**антрацитный**; **антрацитовый**, *adj.* anthracite *(attrib.)*.

антрекот *n.* rib steak.

антрепренёр *n.* **1,** impresario. **2,** *obs.* entrepreneur.

антресоли [*gen.* -**лей**] *n. pl.* **1,** attic. **2,** mezzanine.

антропоид *n.* anthropoid.

антропология *n.* anthropology. —**антрополог**, *n.* anthropologist. —**антропологический**, *adj.* anthropological.

антропоморфизм *n.* anthropomorphism. —**антропоморфический**, *adj.* anthropomorphic.

анфас *adv.* full-face: сняться анфас, to be photographed full-face.

анфилада *n.* suite of rooms.

анчар *n.* upas *(tree)*.

анчоус *n.* anchovy.

аншлаг *n.*, *theat.* "sold out" sign. —**идти** (*or* **проходить**) **с аншлагом**, to be sold out; play to packed houses.

анютин *adj.*, *in* **анютины глазки**, pansy.

аорта *n.* aorta.

апартамент *also*, **апартамент** *n.*, *usu. pl.* luxurious living quarters.

апартеид (тэ) *n.* apartheid.

апатичный *adj.* apathetic.

апатия *n.* apathy.

апеллировать *v. impfv. & pfv.* [*pres.* -**рую**, -**руешь**] **1,** *law* to appeal. **2,** (*with* к) to appeal (to).

апелляционный *adj.*, *law* of appeal; appellate.

апелляция *n.* **1,** *law* appeal. **2,** (*with* к) plea; appeal.

апельсин *n.* **1,** orange. **2,** orange tree. —**апельсинный; апельсиновый**, *adj.* orange *(attrib.)*.

апертура *n.* aperture.

аплодировать *v. impfv.* [*pres.* -**рую**, -**руешь**] (*with dat.*) to applaud.

аплодисменты [*gen.* -**тов**] *n. pl.* applause.

апломб *n.* self-assurance; aplomb.

апогей *n.* **1,** *astron.* apogee. **2,** *fig.* high point; pinnacle; acme.

апокалипсис *n.* **1,** apocalypse. **2,** *cap.* (book of) Revelation. —**апокалипсический**, *adj.* apocalyptic.

апокрифы [*gen.* -**фов**] *n. pl.* Apocrypha. —**апокрифический**, *adj.* Apocryphal.

аполитичный *adj.* apolitical. —**аполитичность**, *n.f.* indifference to politics.

Аполлон *n.* Apollo.

апологет *n.* apologist.

апологетика *n.* apologetics.

апология *n.* apologia.

апоплексический *adj.* apoplectic.

апоплексия *n.* apoplexy; apoplectic stroke.

апостериори (тэ) *adv.* a posteori. —**апостериорный**, *adj.* a posteriori.

апостол *n.* apostle. —**апостольский**, *adj.* apostolic.

апостроф *n.* apostrophe.

апофеоз *n.* apotheosis.

аппарат *n.* **1,** apparatus; device. **2,** *physiol.* system: дыхательный аппарат, respiratory system. **3,** administrative machinery: государственный аппарат, machinery of government. —**фотографический аппарат**, camera.

аппаратура *n.* apparatus; equipment.

аппаратчик *n.* **1,** maintenance man. **2,** party functionary.

аппендикс *n.*, *anat.* appendix. —**аппендицит**, *n.* appendicitis.

апперцепция *n.*, *psychol.* apperception.

аппетит *n.* appetite. —**приятного аппетита!**, hearty appetite!

аппетитный *adj.* appetizing.

аппликатура *n.*, *music* fingering.

аппликация *n.* appliqué work.

апрель *n.m.* April. —**апрельский**, *adj.* April *(attrib.)*.

априори *adv.* a priori. —**априорный**, *adj.* a priori.

апробация *n.* approbation; approval.

апробировать *v. impfv. & pfv.* [*pres.* -**рую**, -**руешь**] to approve.

апсида *n.*, *archit.* apse; apsis.

аптека *n.* drugstore; pharmacy. —**как в аптеке**, *colloq.* exactly.

аптекарь *n.m.*, *obs.* druggist. —**аптекарский**, *adj.* pharmaceutical.

аптечка [*gen. pl.* -**чек**] *n.* **1,** medicine chest; medicine cabinet. **2,** first-aid kit.

аптечный *adj.* of or for drugs. —**аптечный шкаф**, medicine chest; medicine cabinet.

ар *n.* are *(100 sq. meters)*.

ара *n.* macaw.

араб *n.m.* [*fem.* **арабка**] Arab.

арабеска [*gen. pl.* -**сок**] *n.* arabesque. *Also*, **арабеск**.

ара́бский *adj.* **1,** Arab. **2,** Arabic.

арави́йский *adj.* Arabian.

араме́йский *adj.* Aramaic.

аранжи́ровать *v. impfv. & pfv.* [*pres.* -ру́ю, -ру́ешь] *music* to arrange.

аранжиро́вка *n., music* arrangement.

ара́п *n.* **1,** *obs.* Negro. **2,** *colloq.* cheat; crook.

ара́пник *n.* hunting whip.

ара́ра *n.* macaw.

ара́хис *n.* **1,** peanut plant. **2,** peanuts. —**ара́хисовый,** *adj.* peanut *(attrib.).*

арба́ [*pl.* а́рбы] *n.* a kind of cart used in the Crimea and the Caucasus.

арби́тр *n.* arbitrator; arbiter.

арбитра́ж *n.* arbitration. —**арбитра́жный,** *adj.* of arbitration: арбитра́жный суд, court of arbitration.

арбу́з *n.* watermelon. —**арбу́зный,** *adj.* watermelon *(attrib.).*

аргенти́нец [*gen.* -нца] *n.m.* [*fem.* -нка] Argentinean. —**аргенти́нский,** *adj.* Argentinean; Argentine.

арго́ *n. indecl.* jargon; argo; cant.

арго́н *n.* argon.

аргуме́нт *n.* argument.

аргумента́ция *n.* argumentation; line of reasoning.

аргументи́ровать *v. impfv. & pfv.* [*pres.* -ру́ю, -ру́ешь] to argue; adduce arguments.

аре́на *n.* **1,** arena. **2,** *fig.* field; sphere; arena.

аре́нда *n.* **1,** rental. **2,** rent. —**брать в аре́нду,** to take a lease on; rent. —**сдава́ть в аре́нду,** to rent out.

аренда́тор *n.* renter; tenant; lessee; leaseholder.

аре́ндный *adj.* rent *(attrib.);* rental *(attrib.):* аре́ндная пла́та, rent. —**аре́ндный догово́р,** lease.

арендова́ть *v. impfv. & pfv.* [*pres.* -ду́ю, -ду́ешь] to rent; take a lease on.

аре́ст *n.* **1,** arrest; custody: брать под аре́ст, to place under arrest; take into custody. **2,** *law* attachment.

аресто́ванный *n.,* decl. as an *adj.* person arrested; prisoner.

арестова́ть [*infl.* -ту́ю, -ту́ешь] *v., pfv.* of **аресто́вывать.**

аресто́вывать *v. impfv.* [*pfv.* **арестова́ть**] to arrest.

ари́ец [*gen.* ари́йца] *n.m.* [*fem.* ари́йка] Aryan. —**ари́йский,** *adj.* Aryan.

аристокра́т *n.* aristocrat. —**аристократи́ческий; аристократи́чный,** *adj.* aristocratic. —**аристокра́тия,** *n.* aristocracy.

арифме́тика *n.* arithmetic. —**арифмети́ческий,** *adj.* arithmetic; arithmetical.

арифмо́метр *n.* automatic calculating machine; calculator.

а́рия *n.* aria.

а́рка [*gen. pl.* а́рок] *n.* arch.

арка́да *n., archit.* arcade.

арка́н *n.* lasso.

арка́нить *v. impfv.* [*pfv.* заарка́нить] to lasso.

аркти́ческий *adj.* arctic.

арлеки́н *n.* harlequin.

арма́да *n.* armada.

армату́ра *n.* **1,** steel framework. **2,** fittings; fixtures. **3,** armature.

арме́ец [*gen.* -е́йца] *n.* army man; serviceman.

арме́йский *adj.* army *(attrib.).*

а́рмия *n.* army.

армяни́н [*pl.* -мя́не, -мя́н] *n.m.* [*fem.* -мя́нка] Armenian. —**армя́нский,** *adj.* Armenian.

арома́т *n.* aroma; fragrance. —**арома́тный; арома-ти́чный; аромати́ческий,** *adj.* aromatic; fragrant.

а́рочный *adj.* arched: а́рочный мост, arched bridge.

арпе́джио *adv. & n. indecl.* arpeggio.

арсена́л *n.* arsenal; armory.

арта́читься *v.r. impfv.* to balk.

артезиа́нский *adj.* artesian: артезиа́нский коло́дец, artesian well.

арте́ль *n.f.* workers' cooperative; artel. —**арте́льный,** *adj.* artel *(attrib.).* —**арте́льщик,** *n.* member of an artel.

артериа́льный *adj.* arterial.

артериосклеро́з *n.* arteriosclerosis.

арте́рия *n.* **1,** *anat.* artery. **2,** main route; artery. —**во́дная арте́рия,** waterway.

арти́кль *n.m., gram.* article.

артикули́ровать *v. impfv.* [*pres.* -ру́ю, -ру́ешь] to articulate.

артикуля́ция *n.* articulation.

артилле́рия *n.* artillery. —**артиллери́йский,** *adj.* artillery *(attrib.);* gunnery *(attrib.);* ordnance *(attrib.).* —**артиллери́ст,** *n.* artilleryman; gunner.

арти́ст *n.m.* [*fem.* -ти́стка] performing artist; performer.

артисти́ческий *adj.* **1,** artist's; performer's. **2,** artistic; masterly; masterful.

артисти́чность *n.f.* artistic talent; artistry.

арти́стка [*gen. pl.* -ток] *n., fem.* of **арти́ст.**

артишо́к *n.* artichoke.

артри́т *n.* arthritis. —**артрити́ческий,** *adj.* arthritic.

а́рфа *n.* harp. —**арфи́ст; арфи́стка,** *n.* harpist.

архаи́зм *n.* archaism. —**архаи́ческий; арха́йчный,** *adj.* archaic.

арха́нгел *n.* archangel.

археоло́гия *n.* archeology. —**архео́лог,** *n.* archeologist. —**археологи́ческий,** *adj.* archeological.

архи́в *n.* archives. —**сдать в архи́в,** to put away for good; consign to oblivion.

архива́риус *n.* archivist.

архи́вный *adj.* archive *(attrib.).*

архидья́кон *n.* archdeacon.

архиепи́скоп *n.* archbishop.

архиере́й *n., Orth. Ch.* bishop; archbishop; metropolitan.

архимандри́т *n., Orth. Ch.* archimandrite.

архипела́г *n.* archipelago.

архите́ктор *n.* architect. —**архите́кторский,** *adj.* architect's.

архитекту́ра *n.* architecture. —**архитекту́рный,** *adj.* architectural.

арши́н *n.* **1,** [*gen. pl.* арши́н] old Russian unit of length equal to approx. 28 inches; arshin. **2,** [*gen. pl.* арши́нов] ruler measuring an arshin in length. —**как арши́н проглоти́л,** ramrod straight. —**ме́рить на свой арши́н,** to measure by one's own yardstick.

арши́нный *adj.* **1,** of the length of an arshin. **2,** *(of writing, headlines, etc.)* huge.

арьерга́рд *n.* rear guard. —**арьерга́рдный,** *adj.* rear-guard *(attrib.).*

ас *n.* ace (pilot).

асбе́ст *n.* asbestos. —**асбе́стовый,** *adj.* asbestos.

асе́птика (сэ) *n.* asepsis. —**асепти́ческий,** *adj.* aseptic.

асимметри́я *n.* asymmetry. —**асимметри́ческий; асимметри́чный,** *adj.* asymmetric; asymmetrical.

аскéт *n.* ascetic. —**аскетúзм**, *n.* asceticism. —**аскетúческий**, *adj.* ascetic.

аскорбúновый *adj., in* **аскорбúновая кислотá**, ascorbic acid.

аспéкт *n.* aspect; viewpoint; perspective.

áспид *n.* **1**, asp *(snake)*. **2**, *obs.* slate.

áспидный *adj.* **1**, slate. **2**, slate-black. —**áспидный слáнец**, slate.

аспирáнт *n.* graduate student. —**аспирантýра**, *n.* postgraduate course.

аспирúн *n.* aspirin.

ассамблéя *n.* assembly.

ассенизáция *n.* sewage disposal.

ассигновáние *n.* **1**, allocation; appropriation. **2**, allocated sum; appropriation.

ассигновáть *v. impfv. & pfv. [pres.* -нýю, -нýешь] to allocate; appropriate *(funds)*.

ассимилúровать *v. impfv. & pfv. [pres.* -рую, -руешь] to assimilate. —**ассимилúроваться**, *refl.* to assimilate; become assimilated.

ассимиляция *n.* assimilation.

ассирúец [*gen.* -úйца] *n.m.* [*fem.* -úйка] Assyrian. —**ассирúйский**, *adj.* Assyrian.

ассистéнт *n.* **1**, assistant. **2**, lecturer; assistant professor.

ассистúровать *v. impfv. [pres.* -рую, -руешь] *(with dat.)* to assist.

ассонáнс *n.* assonance.

ассортимéнт *n.* selection; assortment.

ассоциáция *n.* **1**, association; society. **2**, association *(in one's mind)*.

ассоциúровать *v. impfv. & pfv. [pres.* -рую, -руешь] to associate *(in one's mind)*; make an association between.

астатúн *n.* astatine.

астерóид (тэ) *n.* asteroid.

астигматúзм *n.* astigmatism. —**астигматúческий**, *adj.* astigmatic.

áстма *n.* asthma. —**асмáтик**, *n., colloq.* asthmatic. —**астматúческий**, *adj.* asthmatic.

áстра *n.* aster.

астролóгия *n.* astrology. —**астрóлог**, *n.* astrologer. —**астрологúческий**, *adj.* astrological.

астролябия *n.* astrolabe.

астронавигáция *n.* celestial navigation.

астронóмия *n.* astronomy. —**астронóм**, *n.* astronomer. —**астрономúческий**, *adj.* astronomic(al).

астрофúзика *n.* astrophysics. —**астрофúзик**, *n.* astrophysicist. —**астрофизúческий**, *adj.* astrophysical.

асфáльт *n.* asphalt.

асфальтúровать *v. impfv. & pfv. [pres.* -рую, -руешь] to asphalt.

асфáльтовый *adj.* asphalt.

асфúксия *n.* asphyxia; asphyxiation.

атавúзм *n.* atavism. —**атавистúческий**, *adj.* atavistic.

атáка *n.* attack.

атаковáть *v. impfv. & pfv. [pres.* -кýю, -кýешь] to attack.

атаксúя *n.* ataxia.

атамáн *n.* Cossack chieftain; ataman.

атеúзм (тэ) *n.* atheism. —**атеúст**, *n.* atheist. —**атеистúческий**, *adj.* atheistic.

ательé (тэ) *n. neut. indecl.* **1**, studio. **2**, dress shop; tailor shop.

атипúческий *adj.* atypical.

атлантúческий *adj.* Atlantic.

áтлас *n.* atlas.

атлáс *n.* satin. —**атлáсный**, *adj.* satin.

атлéт *n.* athlete.

атлéтика *n.* athletics. —**лёгкая атлéтика**, track and field. —**тяжёлая атлéтика**, weightlifting.

атлетúческий *adj.* athletic.

атмосфéра *n.* atmosphere. —**атмосфéрный**, *adj.* atmospheric.

атóлл *n.* atoll.

áтом *n.* atom.

áтомный *adj.* atomic. —**áтомная бóмба**, atomic bomb.

атонáльный *adj.* atonal. —**атонáльность**, *n.f.* atonality.

атрибýт *n.* **1**, attribute; characteristic. **2**, *gram.* modifier; qualifier; attribute; attributive. —**атрибутúвный**, *adj.* attributive.

атропúн *n.* atropine.

атрофúроваться *v.r. impfv. & pfv. [pres.* -руется] to atrophy; become atrophied.

атрофúя *n.* atrophy.

атташé *n.m. indecl.* attaché.

аттестáт *n.* certificate; diploma. —**аттестáт зрéлости**, secondary-school diploma.

аттестáция *n.* written recommendation; character reference.

аттестовáть *v. impfv. & pfv. [pres.* -тýю, -тýешь] **1**, to recommend. **2**, to promote.

аттракциóн *n.* **1**, number; act. **2**, *pl.* amusements; attractions *(in a park)*.

атý *interj., used in hunting with hounds* tallyho!; halloo! —**атý егó!**, sic 'im!

аý *interj., shouted to another from a distance* hello there!

аудиéнция *n.* audience; formal interview.

аудитóрия *n.* **1**, auditorium; lecture hall. **2**, audience.

аýкать *v. impfv. [pfv.* аýкнуть] *colloq.* to shout "аý!" —**аýкаться**, *refl.* to exchange shouts of "аý!"

аукциóн *n.* auction. —**аукционúст**, *n.* auctioneer. —**аукциóнный**, *adj.* auction *(attrib.)*.

аýл *n.* village in the Caucasus or Central Asia; aul.

аутентúчный (тэ) *adj.* authentic; genuine. —**аутентúчность**, *n.f.* authenticity.

аутсáйдер (дэ) *n., sports* outsider; long shot.

афáзия *n.* aphasia.

афгáнец [*gen.* -нца] *n.m.* [*fem.* -нка] Afghan. —**афгáнский**, *adj.* Afghan; Afghanistani.

афéлий *n.* aphelion.

афéра *n.* swindle; fraud. —**аферúст**, *n.* swindler; crook.

афúнский *adj.* Athenian.

афúша *n.* poster; bill.

афишúровать *v. impfv. & pfv. [pres.* -рую, -руешь] to flaunt; parade; advertise.

афорúзм *n.* aphorism. —**афористúческий; афористúчный**, *adj.* aphoristic.

африкáнец [*gen.* -нца] *n.m.* [*fem.* -нка] African. —**африкáнский**, *adj.* African.

афрóнт *n., obs.* affront; insult.

аффéкт *n.* fit; paroxysm *(of rage, terror, despair, etc.)*.

аффектáция *n.* affectation.

аффектúрованный *adj.* affected.

ах *interj.* ah!; oh!

áхать *v. impfv. [pfv.* áхнуть] to shout "ах!"

ахиллéсов *adj., in* **ахиллéсова пятá**, Achilles' heel.

ахинéя *n., colloq.* nonsense: **нестú ахинéю,** to talk nonsense.

áхнуть *v., pfv. of* **áхать.**

ахтерштéвень (тэ) [*gen.* **-вня**] *n.m.* sternpost.

ахтú *interj., obs.* oh! —**не ахтú как,** *colloq.* not particularly. —**не ахтú какóй,** *colloq.* no great shakes; nothing to rave about.

ацетилéн *n.* acetylene. —**ацетилéновый,** *adj.* acetylene.

ацетóн *n.* acetone.

аэрáрий *n.* terrace for sunbathing.

аэрáция *n.* aeration.

аэровокзáл *n.* air terminal.

аэродинáмика *n.* aerodynamics.

аэродинамúческий *adj.* aerodynamic. —**аэродинамúческая трубá** wind tunnel.

аэродрóм *n.* airdrome; airfield.

аэрозóль *n.m.* aerosol.

аэронáвт *n.* balloonist; aeronaut. —**аэронáвтика,** *n.* aeronautics.

аэроплáн *n., obs.* airplane. —**аэроплáнный,** *adj., obs.* airplane *(attrib.).*

аэропóрт [*2nd loc.* **аэропортý**] *n.* airport.

аэроснúмок [*gen.* **-мка**] *n.* aerial photograph.

аэростáт *n.* balloon; aerostat. —**аэростáтика,** *n.* aerostatics.

аэрофотоаппарáт *n.* aerial camera.

аэрофотосъёмка *n.* aerial photography.

аятóлла *n.m.* ayatollah.

Б

Б, б *n. neut.* second letter of the Russian alphabet.

б *particle* = **бы.**

ба *interj., colloq., expressing surprise* well!

бáба *n.* **1,** *colloq.* woman. **2,** *colloq.* milksop; sissy. **3,** *mech.* ram. **4,** tall round cake. —**рóмовая бáба,** baba au rhum. —**снéжная бáба,** snowman.

бáбий [*fem.* **-бья**] *adj., colloq.* woman's. —**бáбье лéто,** Indian summer. —**бáбьи скáзки,** old wives' tales. —**бáбье цáрство,** petticoat government.

бáбка [*gen. pl.* **-бок**] *n.* **1,** *colloq.* grandmother. **2,** *colloq.* old woman. **3,** [*often,* **повивáльная бáбка**] *obs.* midwife. **4,** *anat.* pastern.

бáбник *n., colloq.* ladies' man.

бáбочка [*gen. pl.* **-чек**] *n.* **1,** butterfly. **2,** moth. **3,** *colloq.* bow tie.

бáбушка [*gen. pl.* **-шек**] *n.* grandmother.

бавáрский *adj.* Bavarian.

багáж [*gen.* **-гажá**] *n.* baggage; luggage.

багáжник *n.* **1,** luggage rack. **2,** trunk *(of an automobile).*

багáжный *adj.* baggage *(attrib.).*

багóр [*gen.* **-грá**] *n.* hook; boat hook. —**рыболóвный багóр,** gaff.

багровéть *v. impfv.* [*pfv.* **побагровéть**] to turn crimson; flush.

багрóвый *adj.* crimson.

багрянец [*gen.* **-нца**] *n.* crimson.

бадминтóн *n.* badminton.

бадья́ *n.* bucket; pail.

бáза *n.* **1,** base, basis; foundation. **3,** depot. **4,** camp; lodge.

базáльт *n.* basalt. —**базáльтовый,** *adj.* basalt.

базáр *n.* **1,** market; marketplace; bazaar. **2,** sale; fair; bazaar. **3,** *colloq.* clamor; hullabaloo. —**птúчий базáр,** seashore colony of birds.

базáрный *adj.* market *(attrib.);* of the marketplace.

базéдов (зэ) *adj., in* **базéдова болéзнь,** exophthalmic goiter.

базилúк *n.* basil.

базилúка *n.* basilica.

базúровать *v. impfv.* [*pres.* **-рую, -руешь**] to base. —**базúроваться,** *refl. (with* **на** + *prepl.)* to be based (on).

бáзис *n.* base; basis.

бáзисный *adj.* base: **бáзисная ценá,** base price.

бáзовый *adj.* base *(attrib.);* of a base.

бай-бáй *interj.* bye-bye.

байбáк [*gen.* **-бакá**] *n.* a species of marmot; bobac.

байдáрка [*gen. pl.* **-рок**] *n.* kayak; canoe.

бáйка *n.* baize; flannel. —**бáйковый,** *adj.* baize; flannel.

бак *n.* **1,** tank; cistern. **2,** forecastle.

бакалáвр *n.* bachelor *(holder of a bachelor's degree).* —**стéпень бакалáвра,** bachelor's degree; baccalaureate.

бакалéя *n.* groceries. —**бакалéйный,** *adj.* grocery *(attrib.).* —**бакалéйщик,** *n.* grocer.

бакелúт *n.* bakelite.

бáкен *n.* buoy.

бакенбáрды [*gen.* **-бáрд**] *n. pl.* whiskers.

бáки [*gen.* **бак**] *n.pl.* = **бакенбáрды.**

баккарá *n. neut. indecl.* baccarat.

баклáга *n.* flask; canteen.

баклажáн *n.* eggplant. —**баклажáнный,** *adj.* eggplant *(attrib.).*

баклáн *n.* cormorant *(bird).*

баклýши *n. pl., in* **бить баклýши,** to twiddle one's thumbs.

бактериáльный *adj.* bacterial; bacteria *(attrib.).*

бактериолóгия *n.* bacteriology. —**бактериóлог,** *n.* bacteriologist. —**бактериологúческий,** *adj.* bacteriological.

бактéрия *n.* bacterium.

бал [*2nd loc.* балу́; *pl.* балы́] *n.* ball; formal dance. —**ко́нчен бал**, it's all over.

балага́н *n., obs.* **1,** carnival booth. **2,** side show. **3,** *fig.* farce.

балага́нить *v. impfv., colloq.* to play the buffoon; clown (around).

балага́нный *adj.* farcical.

балагу́р *n., colloq.* joker; jester.

балагу́рить *v. impfv., colloq.* to jest; joke.

балагу́рство *n.* witty talk; joking.

балала́ечник *n.* balalaika player.

балала́йка [*gen. pl.* -**ла́ек**] *n.* balalaika.

бала́нс *n.* **1,** balance; equilibrium. **2,** *econ.; finance* balance: платёжный/торго́вый бала́нс, balance of payments/trade. —**подводи́ть бала́нс, 1,** to balance the books. **2,** *fig.* to strike a balance.

балансёр *n.* balancer; tightrope walker.

банси́р *n.* **1,** balancing pole. **2,** *mech.* balance beam. **3,** balance wheel.

баланси́ровать *v. impfv.* [*pfv.* **сбаланси́ровать**; *pres.* -**рую,** -**руешь**] **1,** [*impfv. only*] to balance oneself; remain balanced. **2,** [*impfv. only*] (*with instr.*) to balance (something precariously). **3,** to balance; bring into balance. **4,** *bookkeeping* to balance.

бала́нсовый *adj.* balance (*attrib.*): бала́нсовый отчёт, balance sheet.

балбе́с *n., colloq.* booby; nitwit.

балда́ *n.m. & f., colloq.* blockhead.

балдахи́н *n.* canopy.

балери́на *n.* ballerina.

бале́т *n.* ballet.

балетме́йстер *n.* ballet master.

бале́тный *adj.* ballet (*attrib.*).

балетома́н *n.* ballet lover.

ба́лка [*gen. pl.* -**лок**] *n.* **1,** beam; girder. **2,** ravine; gully.

балка́нский *adj.* Balkan.

балка́р [*gen. pl.* -**ка́р**] *n.m.* [*fem.* -**ка́рка**] Balkar (*one of a people inhabiting the Caucasus*). *Also,* **балка́рец** [*gen.* -**рца**].

балка́рский *adj.* Balkar.

балко́н *n.* balcony.

балл *n.* **1,** unit of measure of the intensity of winds, earthquakes, etc. **2,** mark (*in school*). **3,** *sports* point.

балла́да *n.* **1,** ballad. **2,** *music* ballade.

балла́ст *n.* ballast.

балли́стика *n.* ballistics. —**баллисти́ческий,** *adj.* ballistic.

балло́н *n.* **1,** cylinder; bottle. **2,** rubber tire.

баллоти́ровать *v. impfv.* [*pres.* -**рую,** -**руешь**] to vote on; vote for. —**баллоти́роваться,** *refl.* (*with* **в** *or* **на** + *acc.*) to run (for); be a candidate (for).

баллотиро́вка *n.* voting; balloting.

бало́ванный *adj., colloq.* spoiled; pampered.

балова́ть *v. impfv.* [*pfv.* **избалова́ть**; *pres.* -**лу́ю,** -**лу́ешь**] to spoil; pamper. —**балова́ться,** *refl.* [*impfv. only*] *colloq.* **1,** to be naughty; be mischievous. **2,** (*with* **с** + *instr.*) to play with (something dangerous). **3,** (*with instr.*) to dabble (in); indulge (in).

ба́ловень [*gen.* -**вня**] *n.m.* **1,** pet; favorite. **2,** mischievous child. —**ба́ловень судьбы́,** child of fortune; lucky person.

баловни́к [*gen.* -**ника́**] *n., colloq.* naughty child; mischievous child.

баловство́ *n., colloq.* **1,** spoiling. **2,** mischief.

балти́йский *adj.* Baltic.

бальза́м *n.* **1,** balsam. **2,** *fig.* balm.

бальзами́ровать *v. impfv.* [*pfv.* **набальзами́ровать**; *pres.* -**рую,** -**руешь**] to embalm.

бальзамиро́вщик *n.* embalmer.

ба́льный *adj.* of or for a ball; ball (*attrib.*).

балюстра́да *n.* balustrade.

баля́сина *n.* baluster.

баля́сы *n. pl., in* **баля́сы точи́ть,** *colloq.* to joke; jest; talk nonsense.

бамбу́к *n.* bamboo. —**бамбу́ковый,** *adj.* bamboo.

ба́мия *n.* okra; gumbo.

ба́мпер *n.* bumper.

бана́льность *n.f.* **1,** banality. **2,** platitude.

бана́льный *adj.* trite; banal.

бана́н *n.* banana. —**бана́новый,** *adj.* banana (*attrib.*).

ба́нда *n.* gang; band.

банда́ж [*gen.* -**дажа́**] *n.* **1,** abdominal support: грыжево́й банда́ж, truss. **2,** *mech.* tire; rim.

бандеро́ль *n.f.* **1,** wrapping for mailing printed matter. **2,** printed matter sent through the mail: отправля́ть бандеро́лью, to send as printed matter.

ба́нджо *n. indecl.* banjo.

банди́т *n.* bandit; thug. —**бандити́зм,** *n.* banditry. —**банди́тский,** *adj.* bandit (*attrib.*).

банк *n.* **1,** bank. **2,** faro (*card game*).

ба́нка [*gen. pl.* -**нок**] *n.* **1,** jar; can. **2,** *usu. pl.* cupping glass. **3,** shoal; sandbank. —**у́стричная ба́нка,** oyster bed.

банке́т *n.* banquet. —**банке́тный,** *adj.* banquet (*attrib.*).

банки́р *n.* banker. —**банки́рский,** *adj.* banking (*attrib.*).

банкно́т *n.* bank note.

ба́нковский *adj.* bank (*attrib.*): ба́нковская кни́жка, bankbook.

ба́нковый *adj.* bank (*attrib.*); banking (*attrib.*).

банкомёт *n.* banker (*in a game*).

банкро́т *n.* one who is bankrupt. —**банкро́тство,** *n.* bankruptcy.

ба́нный *adj.* bath (*attrib.*): ба́нное полоте́нце, bath towel.

бант *n.* bow: завяза́ть ба́нтом, to tie in a bow. —**ба́нтик,** *n.* small bow.

ба́нщик *n.* bathhouse attendant.

ба́ня *n.* **1,** public bath. **2,** *colloq.* steam bath. **3,** *colloq.* tongue-lashing; dressing-down. —**крова́вая ба́ня,** blood bath.

баоба́б *n.* baobab.

бапти́ст *n.* Baptist. —**бапти́стский,** *adj.* Baptist.

баптисте́рий *n.* baptistery.

бар *n.* **1,** bar; barroom. **2,** bar (*unit of pressure*).

бараба́н *n.* **1,** drum. **2,** cylinder (*of a revolver*).

бараба́нить *v. impfv.* **1,** to drum: бараба́нить па́льцами по́ столу, to drum on the table. **2,** (*of rain*) to patter.

бараба́нный *adj.* drum (*attrib.*); of drums. —**бараба́нная перепо́нка,** eardrum.

бараба́нщик *n.* drummer.

барабу́лька [*gen. pl.* -**лек**] *n.* red mullet.

бара́к *n.* hut.

бара́н *n.* **1,** ram. **2,** (wild) sheep. —**сне́жный бара́н,** bighorn sheep.

бара́ний [*fem.* -**нья**] *adj.* **1,** sheep's; sheep (*attrib.*);

ram's; ram *(attrib.)*. **2,** sheepskin. **3,** mutton *(attrib.)*. —в бара́ний рог согну́ть, to bend to one's will.

бара́нина *n.* **1,** mutton. **2,** lamb.

бара́нка [*gen. pl.* -нок] *n.* **1,** bagel. **2,** *colloq.* steering wheel.

барахло́ *n., colloq.* **1,** old things; old clothes. **2,** junk; trash.

бара́хтаться *v.r. impfv.* to flounder; thrash around.

бара́чный *adj.* like barracks.

бара́шек [*gen.* -шка] *n.* **1,** lamb. **2,** lambskin. **3,** *mech.* thumbscrew. **4,** *pl.* fleecy clouds. **5,** whitecaps *(on the sea)*.

бара́шковый *adj.* lamb *(attrib.)*; lambskin *(attrib.)*.

барба́рис *n.* **1,** barberries. **2,** a (single) barberry.

барбитура́т *n.* barbiturate.

барбо́с *n.* watchdog.

барви́нок [*gen.* -нка] *n.* periwinkle.

бард *n.* bard.

барелье́ф *n.* bas-relief. —**барелье́фный,** *adj.* bas-relief *(attrib.)*.

ба́ржа *also,* **баржа́** *n.* barge.

ба́рий *n.* barium.

ба́рин *n., pre-rev.* gentleman; nobleman; aristocrat. —**жить ба́рином,** to live like a king.

бари́т *n.* barite; heavy spar.

барито́н *n.* baritone.

баритона́льный *adj.* baritone. —**баритона́льный бас,** bass baritone.

барито́нный *adj.* baritone.

барк *n.* bark *(sailing vessel)*.

ба́рка [*gen. pl.* -рок] *n.* barge.

баркаро́ла *n.* barcarole.

барка́с *n.* **1,** large rowboat. **2,** harbor vessel; launch.

баро́кко *n. indecl.* baroque.

баро́метр *n.* barometer. —**барометри́ческий,** *adj.* barometric.

баро́н *n.* baron.

бароне́сса *n.* baroness.

бароне́т *n.* baronet.

баро́нство *n.* barony. —**баро́нский,** *adj.* baron's; baronial.

баро́чный *adj.* baroque.

ба́ррель *n.m.* barrel *(measure)*.

баррика́да *n.* barricade.

баррикади́ровать *v. impfv.* [*pfv.* забаррикади́ровать; *pres.* -рую, -руешь] to barricade.

барс *n.* snow leopard.

ба́рский *adj.* **1,** gentleman's; master's. **2,** haughty; supercilious.

ба́рственный *adj.* lordly.

ба́рство *n., pre-rev.* **1,** gentry; nobility. **2,** haughtiness. **3,** idle luxury.

барсу́к [*gen.* -сука́] *n.* badger.

барха́н *n.* sand dune.

ба́рхат *n.* velvet.

бархати́стый *adj.* velvety.

ба́рхатка [*gen. pl.* -ток] *n.* velvet ribbon.

ба́рхатный *adj.* velvet. —**ба́рхатный сезо́н,** warm months of early autumn in the south of Russia.

ба́рхатцы [*gen.* -цев] *n. pl.* (French *or* African) marigold.

ба́рыня *n., pre-rev.* wife of a **ба́рин.**

барьіш [*gen.* -рыша́] *n., usu. pl.* profit.

барыщник *n., obs.* **1,** horsetrader. **2,** profiteer. —**ба́рышничество,** *n.* profiteering.

ба́рышня [*gen. pl.* -шень] *n., pre-rev.* **1,** unmarried daughter of a nobleman. **2,** young lady; miss.

барье́р *n.* **1,** barrier; bar. **2,** *sports* hurdle. —**барье́рный,** *adj.* hurdle *(attrib.)*: барье́рный бег, hurdle race; hurdles.

бас [*pl.* басы́] *n., music* bass.

баси́стый *adj., colloq.* deep; low *(in sound)*; bass.

баси́ть *v. impfv.* [*pres.* башу́, баси́шь] *colloq.* to speak *(or* sing*)* in a bass voice.

баск *n.m.* [*fem.* -ко́нка] Basque.

баскетбо́л *n.* basketball. —**баскетболи́ст,** *n.* basketball player. —**баскетбо́льный,** *adj.* basketball *(attrib.)*.

ба́скский *adj.* Basque.

баснопи́сец [*gen.* -сца] *n.* fabulist.

баснослóвный *adj.* **1,** fabled; legendary. **2,** fabulous; fantastic.

ба́сня [*gen. pl.* ба́сен] *n.* fable.

ба́совый *adj., music* bass.

бассе́йн *n.* **1,** pool: бассе́йн для пла́вания, swimming pool. **2,** *geol.* basin: бассе́йн реки́, river basin; у́гольный бассе́йн, coal basin.

ба́ста *interj., colloq.* enough!; that'll do!

бастио́н *n.* bastion.

бастова́ть *v. impfv.* [*pres.* -сту́ю, -сту́ешь] to strike; be on strike; go on strike.

батали́ст *n.* painter of battle scenes.

бата́лия *n.* **1,** *obs.* battle; fray. **2,** *colloq.* row; ruckus.

батальо́н *n.* battalion. —**батальо́нный,** *adj.* battalion.

батаре́йка [*gen. pl.* -ре́ек] *n.* small battery.

батаре́йный *adj.* **1,** battery *(attrib.)*; battery-operated. **2,** *mil.* battery *(attrib.)*.

батаре́я *n.* **1,** *mil.* battery. **2,** *electricity* battery. —**батаре́я отопле́ния,** radiator.

бата́т *n.* sweet potato; yam.

ба́тенька *n.m., obs. familiar form of address* my friend; old boy.

бати́ст *n.* cambric; batiste. —**бати́стовый,** *adj.* made of this fabric.

бато́н *n.* **1,** long loaf of bread. **2,** stick of candy.

батра́к [*gen.* -трака́] *n.* farm worker; farm hand. —**батра́цкий,** *adj.* farm worker's.

батра́чество *n.* **1,** farm work. **2,** farm laborers; farmhands.

батра́чить *v. impfv.* to work as a farm laborer.

бату́т *n.* trampoline.

ба́тюшка *n.m.* **1,** *obs.* father. **2,** *(used in addresing a priest)* father. **3,** *obs., colloq.* old boy!; my dear fellow! **4,** *colloq.* father's name; patronymic. —**ба́тюшки (мои)!,** good gracious!; dear me!

бау́л *n.* steamer trunk.

бах *interj.* bang!

бахва́л *n., colloq.* braggart.

бахва́литься *v.r. impfv., colloq.* to brag.

бахва́льство *n., colloq.* bragging; boasting.

бахрома́ *n.* fringe. —**бахро́мчатый,** *adj.* fringed.

бахча́ *n.* melon field.

бац *interj.* bang!; smack!; crack!

баци́лла *n.* bacillus.

ба́шенка [*gen. pl.* -нок] *n.* small tower; turret.

ба́шенный *adj.* tower *(attrib.)*.

башка́ *n., colloq.* head; noggin.

башки́р [*gen. pl.* -ки́р] *n.m.* [*fem.* -ки́рка] Bashkir *(one of a people inhabiting central European Russia).* —**башки́рский,** *adj.* Bashkir.

башкови́тый *adj., colloq.* brainy.

башма́к [gen. -мака́] n. shoe. —под башмако́м у, under the thumb of.

башма́чник n., obs. shoemaker; cobbler.

башма́чный adj. shoe (attrib.).

ба́шня [gen. pl. ба́шен] n. tower. —оруди́йная ба́шня, turret (for a gun).

баю́кать v. impvf. [pfv. убаю́кать] to lull/sing/rock to sleep.

ба́н n. accordion.

бде́ние n., obs. vigil; watch.

бди́тельный adj. vigilant. —бди́тельность, n.f. vigilance.

бег n. 1, run; running. 2, race. —бег на ме́сте, sports running in place. —в бега́х, on the run. —на бегу́, on the double.

бега́ [gen. бего́в] n. pl. harness racing; harness races.

бе́гать v. impvf. 1, indeterm. of бежа́ть. 2, to move rapidly; flit; dart. 3, (with от) colloq. to avoid; get away from. 4, (with за + instr.) colloq. to chase (after).

бегемо́т n. 1, hippopotamus. 2, Bib. behemoth.

бегле́ц [gen. -леца́] n.m. [fem. -ля́нка] fugitive; escaped convict.

бе́гло adv. 1, fluently. 2, with facility. 3, in a cursory manner.

бе́глость n.f. 1, fluency. 2, facility.

бе́глый adj. 1, fluent. 2, facile. 3, cursory. 4, phonet. (of a vowel) fleeting. 5, in бе́глый ого́нь, rapid fire. 6, fugitive; runaway. —n. fugitive.

бегля́нка [gen. pl. -нок] n., fem. of бегле́ц.

бегово́й adj. running (attrib.); racing (attrib.); race (attrib.). —бегова́я доро́жка, running track. —бегова́я ло́шадь, racehorse.

бего́м adv. running; on the double.

бего́ния n. begonia.

беготня́ n., colloq. running about; scurrying about.

бе́гство n. 1, flight: обраща́ть в бе́гство, to put to flight. 2, escape.

бегу́н [gen. -гуна́] n.m. [fem. -гу́нья] sports runner.

беда́ [pl. бе́ды] n. 1, trouble; misfortune. —беда́ в том, что..., the trouble is... —беда́ как, colloq. very much. —в то́м-то и беда́, that's just the trouble. —как на беду́, as luck would have it. —на беду́, unfortunately. —на свою́ беду́, to one's cost. —не беда́, it doesn't matter; no harm done. —что за беда́!, what does it matter?

бедла́м n. bedlam; chaos.

бедне́ть v. impvf. [pfv. обедне́ть] to become poor.

бе́дно adv. 1, in poor circumstances: они́ живу́т ужа́сно бе́дно, they live in utter poverty. 2, shabbily: бе́дно оде́тый, shabbily dressed.

бе́дность n.f. poverty.

беднота́ n. 1, the poor. 2, colloq. poverty.

бе́дный adj. [short form бе́ден, бедна́, бе́дно] 1, poor. 2, meager.

бедня́га n.m. & f., colloq. poor fellow; poor devil. Also, бедня́жка.

бедня́к [gen. -няка́] n. poor person; pauper.

бедо́вый adj., colloq. 1, daring. 2, mischievous.

бедоку́р n.m. [fem. -ку́рка] colloq. mischief-maker.

бедоку́рить v. impvf. [pfv. набедоку́рить] colloq. to make mischief.

бе́дренный adj. hip (attrib.); thigh (attrib.). —бе́дренная кость, thighbone; femur.

бедро́ [pl. бёдра, бёдер] n. hip; thigh.

бе́дственный adj. calamitous; disastrous.

бе́дствие n. calamity; disaster. —сигна́л бе́дствия, distress signal.

бе́дствовать v. impvf. [pres. -ствую, -ствуешь] to live in poverty.

бедуи́н n. Bedouin.

беж adj. indecl. beige: пла́тье цве́та беж, beige dress.

бежа́ть v. impvf. [pfv. побежа́ть; pres. бегу́, бежи́шь, ...бегу́т] 1, to run. 2, to race. 3, fig. to fly; flow; fleet. —v. impvf. & pfv. to escape; flee: бежа́ть из тюрьмы́, to escape from prison. See also бе́гать.

бе́жевый adj., colloq. beige.

бе́женец [gen. -нца] n.m. [fem. -нка] refugee.

без also, before весь and вся́кий, безо prep., with gen. 1, without: идти́ без шля́пы, to go without a hat. 2, used to express minutes before the hour to; before; of: без десяти́ семь, ten minutes to seven; без че́тверти три, a quarter to three. —и без того́, already: и без того́ сло́жное положе́ние, an already complicated situation.

без- also, бес-, безъ- prefix not; without; lacking; often equivalent to English un-; in-; ir-; im-; il-; -less: безалкого́льный, nonalcoholic; бесце́льный, aimless.

безала́берный adj. disorderly; slipshod.

безалкого́льный adj. nonalcoholic.

безапелляцио́нный adj. 1, law not subject to appeal. 2, categorical; peremptory.

безато́мный adj. atom-free.

безбе́дный adj. materially secure; comfortable. —безбе́дно, adv. comfortably: жить безбе́дно, to live comfortably.

безбиле́тный adj. having no ticket.

безбо́жие n. atheism. —безбо́жник, n. atheist.

безбо́жный adj. 1, obs. godless. 2, colloq. shameless; outrageous. —безбо́жно, adv., colloq. outrageously; something awful.

безболе́зненный adj. painless. —безболе́зненно, adv. painlessly.

безборо́дый adj. beardless.

безбоя́зненный adj. fearless; dauntless.

безбра́чие n. celibacy. —безбра́чный, adj. celibate.

безбре́жный adj. boundless; limitless.

безве́стный adj. unknown; obscure. —безве́стность, n.f. obscurity.

безве́тренный adj. 1, windless. 2, still; calm.

безве́трие n. absence of wind; calm.

безви́нный adj. innocent; guiltless.

безвку́сие n. poor taste; lack of taste; tastelessness. Also, colloq. безвку́сица.

безвку́сный adj. 1, tasteless. 2, in poor taste. 3, lacking good taste. —безвку́сно, adv. without taste.

безвла́стие n. anarchy.

безво́дный adj. arid; waterless. —безво́дье, n. lack (or shortage) of water.

безвозвра́тный adj. 1, irretrievable. 2, not requiring repayment: безвозвра́тная ссу́да, outright grant. —безвозвра́тно, adv. for good; forever.

безвозду́шный adj., in безвозду́шное простра́нство, vacuum.

безвозме́здный adj. free (of charge). —безвозме́здно, adv. free of charge; gratis.

безво́лие n. lack of will.

безволо́сый adj. having no hair.

безво́льный adj. weak-willed.

безвре́дный adj. harmless; innocuous.

безвре́менный adj. (of someone's death) untimely.

безвы́ездно *adv.* **1,** without a break. **2,** all one's life.

безвы́ездный *adj. (of a stay or residence)* permanent.

безвы́ходный *adj.* hopeless; untenable.

безгла́зый *adj.* **1,** having no eyes. **2,** one-eyed.

безгла́сный *adj., obs.* **1,** mute. **2,** timid; reticent.

безголо́вый *adj.* **1,** headless. **2,** *colloq.* brainless; scatterbrained.

безголо́сый *adj.* **1,** voiceless; without a voice. **2,** having a poor voice.

безгра́мотный *adj.* **1,** illiterate. **2,** ungrammatical; full of mistakes. —**безгра́мотно,** *adv.* like an illiterate person. —**безгра́мотность,** *n.f.* illiteracy.

безграни́чный *adj.* boundless; limitless; infinite.

безда́рность *n.f.* **1,** lack of talent. **2,** *fig.* person without talent.

безда́рный *adj.* **1,** lacking (*or* without) talent. **2,** incompetent; inept. **3,** without merit; without a redeeming feature.

безде́йственный *adj.* inactive; idle.

безде́йствие *n.* inaction; inactivity; idleness.

безде́йствовать *v. impfv.* [*pres.* -ствую, -ствуешь] **1,** to do nothing; take no action. **2,** to be idle; be inoperative.

безде́лица *n., colloq.* trifle.

безделу́шка [*gen. pl.* -шек] *n.* trinket; knickknack.

безде́лье *n.* idleness.

безде́льник *n., colloq.* idler; loafer.

безде́льничать *v. impfv.* to idle; loaf; do nothing.

безде́нежный *adj.* **1,** not involving cash. **2,** *colloq.* penniless.

безде́нежье *n.* lack of money.

безде́тный *adj.* childless. —**безде́тность,** *n.f.* childlessness.

безде́ятельный *adj.* inactive; lethargic. —**безде́ятельность,** *n.f.* inactivity; lethargy.

бе́здна *n.* **1,** chasm; abyss. **2,** *colloq.* huge amount; endless number.

бездоказа́тельный *adj.* unsubstantiated; unsupported.

бездо́мный *adj.* homeless; stray.

бездо́нный *adj.* bottomless: бездо́нная про́пасть, bottomless pit.

бездоро́жье *n.* **1,** absence of passable roads; bad roads. **2,** time of year when roads are impassable.

безду́мный *adj.* thoughtless; unthinking.

безду́мье *n.* inability to think clearly; daze.

безду́шие *n.* heartlessness; callousness.

безду́шный *adj.* **1,** *obs.* dead; lifeless. **2,** *fig.* heartless; without a soul. **3,** *fig. (of a performance)* uninspired.

бездыха́нный *adj.* lifeless.

безжа́лостный *adj.* ruthless; merciless; pitiless. —**безжа́лостно,** *adv.* ruthlessly; mercilessly. —**безжа́лостность,** *n.f.* ruthlessness.

безжи́зненный *adj.* **1,** dead; lifeless. **2,** *fig.* without expression; blank.

беззабо́тный *adj.* carefree; happy-go-lucky. —**беззабо́тно,** *adv.* in a carefree manner; without a care. —**беззабо́тность,** *n.f.* unconcern.

беззаве́тный *adj.* selfless.

беззако́ние *n.* **1,** lawlessness. **2,** unlawful act.

беззако́нный *adj.* lawless; unlawful.

беззасте́нчивый *adj.* shameless; brazen.

беззащи́тный *adj.* defenseless; unprotected.

беззвёздный *adj.* starless.

беззву́чный *adj.* soundless; silent.

безземе́лье *n.* lack of land. —**безземе́льный,** *adj.* landless.

беззло́бие *n.* good nature. —**беззло́бный,** *adj.* good-natured.

беззубцо́вый *adj. (of postage stamps)* imperforate.

беззу́бый *adj.* toothless.

безле́сный *adj.* treeless.

безле́сье *n.* lack of forests.

безли́кий *adj.* faceless.

безли́чный *adj.* **1,** faceless. **2,** impersonal.

безлю́дный *adj.* **1,** uninhabited; sparsely populated. **2,** *(of streets, public places, etc.)* empty; deserted.

безлю́дье *n.* absence of people.

безме́н *n.* steelyard.

безме́рный *adj.* boundless; immeasurable. —**безме́рно,** *adv.* beyond measure; extraordinarily.

безмо́зглый *adj., colloq.* brainless; witless.

безмо́лвие *n.* silence.

безмо́лвный *adj.* silent; hushed; mute; speechless.

безмо́лвствовать *v. impfv.* [*pres.* -ствую, -ствуешь] to be silent; keep silent.

безмяте́жный *adj.* serene; tranquil. —**безмяте́жность,** *n.f.* serenity; tranquillity.

безнадёжный *adj.* hopeless. —**безнадёжность,** *n.f.* hopelessness.

безнадзо́рный *adj.* unsupervised; neglected.

безнака́занный *adj.* unpunished. —**безнака́занно,** *adv.* with impunity. —**безнака́занность,** *n.f.* impunity.

безнали́чный *adj.* not involving cash.

безнача́лие *n.* anarchy.

безно́гий *adj.* **1,** legless. **2,** having only one leg.

безнра́вственный *adj.* immoral. —**безнра́вственность,** *n.f.* immorality.

безо *prep., var. of* без, *used before* весь *and* вся́кий.

безоби́дный *adj.* inoffensive; innocuous; harmless.

безо́блачный *adj.* **1,** cloudless. **2,** *fig.* serene.

безобра́зие *n.* **1,** ugliness. **2,** outrage; scandal; disgrace.

безобра́зить *v. impfv.* [*pres.* -жу, -зишь] to mar the appearance of.

безобра́зник *n., colloq.* **1,** hooligan; rowdy. **2,** naughty child.

безобра́зничать *v. impfv., colloq.* to carry on; behave disgracefully.

безобра́зный *adj.* **1,** formless; shapeless. **2,** *(of writing)* lacking imagery.

безобра́зный *adj.* **1,** ugly; hideous; deformed. **2,** outrageous; scandalous; disgraceful.

безогля́дный *adj.* headlong.

безоговоро́чный *adj.* unconditional; unreserved; unqualified.

безопа́сно *adv.* safely. —*adj., used predicatively* safe: здесь безопа́сно, it is safe here.

безопа́сность *n.f.* safety; security. —**Сове́т Безопа́сности,** Security Council. —**те́хника безопа́сности,** accident prevention; safety procedures.

безопа́сный *adj.* **1,** safe; secure. **2,** safety *(attrib.)*; security *(attrib.)*: безопа́сная бри́тва, safety razor.

безору́жный *adj.* **1,** unarmed. **2,** *fig.* defenseless.

безоснова́тельный *adj.* groundless; baseless.

безостано́вочный *adj.* **1,** ceaseless; uninterrupted. **2,** nonstop. —**безостано́вочно,** *adv.* nonstop.

безотве́тный *adj.* **1,** unrequited. **2,** silent. **3,** meek.

безотве́тственный *adj.* irresponsible. —**безотве́тственность**, *n.f.* irresponsibility.

безотка́зный *adj., colloq.* smooth; steady. —**безотка́зно**, *adv.* smoothly; perfectly.

безотка́тный *adj.* recoilless.

безотлага́тельный *adj.* urgent. —**безотлага́тельно**, *adv.* urgently.

безотлу́чный *adj.* 1, ever-present. 2, continual.

безотноси́тельно *adv. (with к)* irrespective of; regardless of; without regard to.

безотра́дный *adj.* bleak; dismal; cheerless.

безотчётный *adj.* 1, instinctive; unconscious. 2, not accountable; not subject to control.

безоши́бочный *adj.* 1, without error; perfect. 2, unerring; infallible.

безрабо́тица *n.* unemployment.

безрабо́тный *adj.* unemployed. —*n.* unemployed person.

безра́достный *adj.* joyless; cheerless.

безразде́льный *adj.* undivided; absolute; complete.

безразли́чие *n.* indifference.

безразли́чно *adv.* with indifference. —*adj., used predicatively* immaterial: мне э́то безразли́чно, it's immaterial to me.

безразли́чный *adj.* 1, indifferent. 2, inconsequential; immaterial.

безразме́рный *adj. (of socks, stockings, etc.)* stretch.

безрассу́дный *adj.* rash; reckless; foolhardy. —**безрассу́дно**, *adv.* rashly; recklessly.

безрассу́дство *n.* 1, recklessness; foolhardiness. 2, rash act; reckless act.

безрезульта́тный *adj.* futile; unsuccessful. —**безрезульта́тно**, *adv.* without results; in vain.

безро́гий *adj.* hornless.

безро́дный *adj.* having no relatives; without kith or kin.

безро́потный *adj.* uncomplaining; mild-mannered. —**безро́потно**, *adv.* without complaining; without a murmur.

безрука́вка [*gen. pl.* -вок] *n.* sleeveless jacket. —**безрука́вный**, *adj.* sleeveless.

безру́кий *adj.* 1, lacking one or both arms; lacking one or both hands. 2, *colloq.* unhandy; clumsy.

безуда́рный *adj., phonet.* unaccented; unstressed.

безуде́ржный *adj.* unrestrained; unchecked; uncontrollable. —**безуде́ржная инфля́ция**, rampant (*or* runaway) inflation.

безукори́зненно *adv.* flawlessly; perfectly. —**безукори́зненно чи́стый**, spotlessly clean.

безукори́зненный *adj.* irreproachable; unimpeachable; flawless; impeccable.

безу́мец [*gen.* -мца] *n.* madman; lunatic.

безу́мие *n.* 1, *obs.* madness; insanity. 2, madness; folly. —**до безу́мия**, to distraction.

безу́мно *adv.* 1, madly. 2, *colloq.* terribly: безу́мно уста́л, terribly tired.

безу́мный *adj.* 1, *obs.* mad; insane. 2, *colloq.* crazy. 3, *colloq.* extreme.

безумо́лчный *adj. (of noise)* incessant.

безу́мство *n.* madness; folly.

безу́мствовать *v. impfv.* [*pres.* -ствую, -ствуешь] to rant; rave; behave like a madman.

безупре́чный *adj.* irreproachable; unimpeachable; flawless; impeccable. —**безупре́чно**, *adv.* flawlessly; perfectly.

безусло́вно *adv.* certainly; absolutely; positively.

безусло́вный *adj.* absolute; unconditional.

безуспе́шный *adj.* unsuccessful; unavailing. —**безуспе́шно**, *adv.* without success; unsuccessfully.

безуста́нный *adj., obs.* 1, tireless; untiring. 2, ceaseless; endless.

безу́сый *adj.* 1, having no mustache. 2, *fig.* callow; beardless.

безуте́шный *adj.* inconsolable.

безуча́стие *n.* indifference; apathy.

безуча́стный *adj.* indifferent; apathetic. —**безуча́стность**, *n.f.* indifference; apathy.

безъя́дерный *adj.* nuclear-free.

безыде́йный *adj.* lacking proper ideological orientation. —**безыде́йность**, *n.f.* lack of proper ideological orientation.

безызве́стный *adj.* obscure; unknown. —**безызве́стность**, *n.f.* obscurity.

безымя́нный *adj.* nameless; anonymous. —**безымя́нный па́лец**, ring finger; fourth finger.

безынициати́вный *adj.* lacking initiative; unenterprising.

безыску́сственный *adj.* artless; ingenuous.

безысхо́дный *adj.* 1, hopeless. 2, endless.

бейсбо́л *n.* baseball. —**бейсбо́льный**, *adj.* baseball *(attrib.).*

бека́р *n., music* natural sign; natural.

бека́с *n.* snipe.

беко́н *n.* bacon.

белена́ *n.* henbane.

беле́ние *n.* bleaching.

белёный *adj.* bleached.

белёсый *adj.* whitish; off-white.

беле́ть *v. impfv.* [*pfv.* **побеле́ть**] 1, to turn white. 2, [*impfv. only*] *(of anything white)* to be visible; appear; shine; gleam.

белиберда́ *n., colloq.* nonsense; rubbish.

белизна́ *n.* whiteness.

бели́ла [*gen.* -ли́л] *n. pl.* 1, whiting. 2, ceruse *(cosmetic).* —**свинцо́вые бели́ла**, white lead; ceruse. —**ци́нковые бели́ла**, zinc white.

бели́льный *adj.* bleaching *(attrib.).*

бели́ть *v. impfv.* [*pres.* белю́, бе́лишь *or* бели́шь] 1, [*pfv.* **побели́ть**] to whitewash; whiten. 2, [*pfv.* **набели́ть**] to whiten (one's face) with ceruse. 3, [*pfv.* **вы́белить**] to bleach. —**бели́ться**, *refl.* [*pfv.* **набели́ться**] to put on white makeup; whiten one's face with ceruse.

бе́личий [*fem.* -чья] *adj.* squirrel *(attrib.);* squirrel's.

бе́лка [*gen. pl.* -лок] *n.* squirrel. —**верте́ться как бе́лка в колесе́**, to be on a treadmill; go around in circles.

белко́вый *adj.* protein *(attrib.).*

беллодо́нна *n.* belladonna.

беллетри́стика *n.* fiction. —**беллетри́ст**, *n.* fiction writer. —**беллетристи́ческий**, *adj.* fictional.

белобры́сый *adj., colloq.* towheaded.

белова́тый *adj.* whitish; off-white.

белови́к [*gen.* -вика́] *n.* clean copy.

белово́й *adj. (of a copy, manuscript, etc.)* clean; in final form.

белогварде́ец [*gen.* -е́йца] *n.* White Guard; counter-revolutionary. —**белогварде́йский**, *adj.* White-Guard *(attrib.).*

белоголо́вый *adj.* 1, white-haired. 2, fair-haired.

белóк [*gen.* -лкá] *n.* **1,** white of an egg; albumen. **2,** protein. **3,** white of the eye.

белокрóвие *n.* leukemia.

белокýрый *adj.* blond; fair-haired.

белолúцый *adj.* white-faced.

белорýс *n.m.* [*fem.* -рýска] Byelorussian. —**белорýсский,** *adj.* Byelorussian.

белорýчка *n.m & f., colloq.* one who disdains manual labor; one not wishing to dirty his hands.

белоснéжный *adj.* snow-white.

белошвéйка [*gen. pl.* -éек] *n.* seamstress.

белоэмигрáнт *n.* early emigrant from the Soviet Union.

белýга *n.* white sturgeon; beluga. —**ревéть белýгой,** to howl like a stuck pig.

белýха *n.* white whale; beluga.

бéлый *adj.* white. —*n.* **1,** white man; white. **2,** *neut.* white (clothes): одéт(а) в бéлое, dressed in white. **3,** *pl.* whites (*in the Russian Civil War*). **4,** *pl., chess* white: игрáть бéлыми, to be white; play the white pieces. —**бéлая ворóна,** rara avis. —**бéлый медвéдь,** polar bear. —**бéлые пятна,** unexplored areas; blank spaces. —**бéлая совá,** snowy owl. —**бéлые стихú,** blank verse.

бельгúец [*gen.* -úйца] *n.m.* [*fem.* -úйка] Belgian. —**бельгúйский,** *adj.* Belgian.

бельё *n.* **1,** linen: столóвое бельё, table linen. **2,** laundry; wash. —**нúжнее бельё,** underwear.

бельевóй *adj.* linen *(attrib.).*

бельмéс *n., colloq., in* не знать (*or* не понимáть) ни бельмéса о, not to know the first thing about.

бельмó *n.* walleye. —**бельмó на глазý,** thorn in one's side.

бельэтáж *n.* **1,** second floor. **2,** *theat.* mezzanine.

белýк [*gen.* -якá] *n.* **1,** white hare. **2,** *pl.* whitecaps.

бемóль *n.m., music* flat sign; flat.

бенгáлец [*gen.* -льца] *n.m.* [*fem.* -лка] Bengali. —**бенгáльский,** *adj.* Bengali.

бенефúс *n., theat.* benefit performance.

бензúн *n.* **1,** benzine. **2,** gasoline. —**бензúновый,** *adj.* gasoline *(attrib.).*

бензиномéр *n.* gasoline gauge; fuel gauge.

бензобáк *n.* gas tank.

бензозапрáвочный *adj., in* бензозапрáвочная колóнка, gasoline pump; бензозапрáвочная стáнция, gas station; service station.

бензоúн *n.* benzoin.

бензоколóнка [*gen. pl.* -нок] *n.* gas (*or* gasoline) pump.

бензóл *n.* benzene; benzol.

бенуáр *n., theat.* boxes (*at orchestra level*).

бéрег [*2nd loc.* берегý; *pl.* берегá] *n.* **1,** coast: плыть вдоль бéрега, to sail along the coast. **2,** bank (*of a river*): выступить из берегóв, to overflow its banks. **3,** shore: достигáть бéрега, to reach the shore. Сойтú на бéрег, to go ashore. —**бéрег мóря,** sea-shore.

береговóй *adj.* coastal; shore *(attrib.).* —**береговáя лúния,** coastline. —**береговáя охрáна,** coast guard.

бередúть *v. impfv.* [*pfv.* разбередúть; *pres.* -жý, -дúшь] to irritate; aggravate (a wound). —**бередúть стáрые рáны,** to reopen old wounds.

бережлúвость *n.f.* **1,** thrift. **2,** *obs.* care.

бережлúвый *adj.* **1,** thrifty; economical. **2,** = бéрежный.

бéрежный *adj.* **1,** careful; gentle. **2,** solicitous; considerate. —**бéрежно,** *adv.* carefully; gently. —**бéрежность,** *n.f.* care.

берёза *n.* birch.

березняк [*gen.* -някá] *n.* birch forest.

берёзовый *adj.* birch *(attrib.).*

берéйтор *n.* riding master.

берéменеть *v. impfv.* [*pfv.* заберéменеть] to become pregnant.

берéменная *adj.* pregnant. —*n.* pregnant woman.

берéменность *n.f.* pregnancy.

берёста *n.* birch bark.

берестянóй *adj.* birch-bark *(attrib.).* Also, **берёстовый.**

берéт *n.* beret.

берéчь *v. impfv.* [*pres.* берегý, бережёшь, ...берегýт; *past* берёг, береглá, береглó] **1,** to save; keep. **2,** to save; conserve. **3,** to guard; protect. —**берéчься,** *refl.* (*with gen.*) to watch out (for); beware (of).

бéри-бéри *n.f. indecl.* beriberi.

берúлл *n.* beryl.

берúллий *n.* beryllium.

беркéлий *n.* berkelium.

бéркут *n.* golden eagle.

берлóга *n.* den; lair (*of a bear*).

берцóвый *adj., in* большáя берцóвая кость, shinbone; tibia; мáлая берцóвая кость, fibula.

бес *n.* demon; evil spirit. —**рассыпáться мéлким бéсом пéред,** *colloq.* to curry favor with; play up to.

бес- *prefix, var. of* без- (*used before voiceless consonants*).

бесéда *n.* **1,** conversation; talk; chat. **2,** discussion. **3,** interview.

бесéдка [*gen. pl.* -док] *n.* summerhouse.

бесéдовать *v. impfv.* [*pres.* -дую, -дуешь] to talk; chat; converse.

бесёнок [*gen.* -нка; *pl.* бесенáта, -нят] *n., colloq.* imp; little devil.

бесúть *v. impfv.* [*pfv.* взбесúть; *pres.* бешý, бéсишь] to enrage; infuriate. —**бесúться,** *refl.* **1,** to become enraged. **2,** (*of animals*) to become rabid.

бескáмерный *adj.* (*of a tire*) tubeless.

бесклáссовый *adj.* classless.

бескозырка [*gen. pl.* -рок] *n.* peakless cap.

бескомпромúссный *adj.* uncompromising.

бесконéчно *adv.* infinitely; endlessly. —**бесконéчно мáлый,** infinitesimal.

бесконéчность *n.f.* infinity. —**до бесконéчности,** endlessly; ad infinitum.

бесконéчный *adj.* **1,** endless; interminable. **2,** infinite.

бесконтрóльный *adj.* uncontrolled; unsupervised. —**бесконтрóльно,** *adv.* uncontrolled; without control.

бескорыстие *n.* unselfishness. —**бескорыстный,** *adj.* unselfish; disinterested.

бескрáйний *adj.* endless; boundless.

бескрúзисный *adj.* crisis-free.

бескрóвный *adj.* **1,** pallid; anemic. **2,** bloodless; without bloodshed. **3,** *obs.* homeless.

бескрылый *adj.* **1,** wingless. **2,** *fig.* uninspired.

бескультýрье *n., colloq.* lack of culture.

беснóватый *adj., obs.* mad; deranged.

беснóваться *v.r. impfv.* [*pres.* -нýюсь, -нýешься] to rant; rage.

бесóвский *adj.* diabolical; devilish.

беспáлый *adj.* **1,** having no fingers. **2,** having no toes.

беспамятный *adj., colloq.* forgetful.

беспамятство *n.* unconsciousness.

беспардонный *adj., colloq.* shameless; brazen.

беспартийный *adj.* non-party. —*n.* person not a member of the party.

бесперебойный *adj.* uninterrupted; regular; smooth. —**бесперебойно**, *adv.* without interruption; without a hitch.

беспересадочный *adj.* through; without transfer to another vehicle: беспересадочное сообщение, through connection.

бесперспективный *adj.* having no prospects; hopeless.

беспечный *adj.* carefree; happy-go-lucky. —**беспечно**, *adv.* in a carefree manner; without a care. —**беспечность**, *n.f.* unconcern.

беспилотный *adj.* not piloted; *(of a spacecraft)* unmanned.

бесписьменный *adj.* **1,** having no written language. **2,** *(of a language)* unwritten.

беспланный *adj.* unplanned.

бесплатный *adj.* free (of charge): бесплатное обучение, free education. —**бесплатно**, *adv.* free of charge; gratis.

бесплацкартный *adj.* **1,** *(of a car on a train)* unreserved; with unreserved seats. **2,** *(of a passenger)* having no reserved seat.

бесплодие *n.* **1,** sterility; infertility. **2,** barrenness; infertility *(of soil)*.

бесплодность *n.f.* **1,** barrenness; infertility *(of soil)*. **2,** futility.

бесплодный *adj.* **1,** barren; sterile. **2,** futile; fruitless.

бесплотный *adj.* incorporeal.

бесповоротный *adj.* irrevocable.

бесподобный *adj., colloq.* incomparable; matchless; peerless.

беспозвоночный *adj.* invertebrate. —**беспозвоночные**, *n. pl.* invertebrates.

беспокоить *v. impfv.* to worry; trouble; bother; disturb. —**беспокоиться**, *refl.* **1,** to worry. **2,** to trouble oneself; bother.

беспокойный *adj.* **1,** worried; troubled; anxious; uneasy. **2,** worrisome; disturbing. **3,** restless; uneasy.

беспокойство *n.* **1,** worry; anxiety; uneasiness; concern. **2,** trouble; disturbance; bother.

бесполезно *adv.* uselessly. —*adj., used predicatively* useless: спорить с ним бесполезно, it's useless to argue with him.

бесполезность *n.f.* uselessness.

бесполезный *adj.* **1,** useless. **2,** futile.

беспольцй *adj.* sexless; asexual.

беспомощный *adj.* **1,** helpless. **2,** utterly without merit; hopeless. —**беспомощность**, *n.f.* helplessness.

беспорочный *adj.* faultless; irreproachable.

беспорядок [*gen.* -дка] *n.* **1,** disorder; disarray; confusion. **2,** *pl.* disorders; disturbances; riots.

беспорядочный *adj.* **1,** disorderly; untidy. **2,** unsystematic; disorganized. —**беспорядочно**, *adv.* in disorder; haphazardly.

беспосадочный *adj. (of a flight)* nonstop.

беспочвенный *adj.* groundless; unfounded.

беспошлинный *adj.* duty-free.

беспощадный *adj.* merciless. —**беспощадно**, *adv.* mercilessly.

бесправие *n.* absence of rights.

бесправный *adj.* without rights.

беспредельный *adj.* boundless; limitless; infinite.

беспредметный *adj.* pointless; aimless.

беспрекословный *adj.* unquestioning; absolute; implicit. —**беспрекословно**, *adv.* without question; blindly; implicitly.

беспрепятственный *adj.* unhampered; unimpeded. —**беспрепятственно**, *adv.* without hindrance; unimpeded.

беспрерывный *adj.* continuous; uninterrupted. —**беспрерывно**, *adv.* continuously.

беспрестанный *adj.* continual; incessant. —**беспрестанно**, *adv.* continually; incessantly.

беспрецедентный *adj.* unprecedented.

бесприбыльный *adj.* unprofitable; unremunerative.

бесприданница *n., obs.* girl without a dowry.

беспризорник *n.* street urchin; waif.

беспризорничать *v. impfv., colloq.* to live on the streets; be a waif.

беспризорный *adj.* **1,** neglected; uncared-for. **2,** homeless; stray. —*n.* = **беспризорник**.

беспримерный *adj.* unexampled; unparalleled.

беспринципный *adj.* unprincipled; unscrupulous.

беспристрастие *n.* impartiality. —**беспристрастный**, *adj.* impartial; unbiased.

беспричинный *adj.* lacking any visible cause; groundless. —**беспричинно**, *adv.* for no (apparent) reason.

бесприютный *adj.* homeless; lacking a roof over one's head.

беспробудный *adj.* **1,** *(of sleep)* deep. **2,** *colloq. (of drinking)* unrestrained.

беспроволочный *adj.* wireless: беспроволочный телеграф, wireless.

беспроигрышный *adj.* risk-free; safe.

беспросветный *adj.* **1,** pitch black; pitch dark. **2,** *(of darkness)* absolute. **3,** *fig.* hopeless; unrelieved.

беспроцентный *adj.* interest-free.

беспутный *adj.* dissolute. —**беспутство**, *n.* dissoluteness.

бессвязный *adj.* rambling; disconnected; incoherent; disjointed. —**бессвязность**, *n.f.* incoherence.

бессемейный *adj.* having no family.

бессемянный *adj.* seedless.

бессердечие *n.* heartlessness; callousness. *Also,* **бессердечность**, *n.f.*

бессердечный *adj.* heartless; callous.

бессилие *n.* **1,** weakness; debility. **2,** helplessness; impotence. —половое бессилие, *med.* impotence.

бессильный *adj.* **1,** week; feeble. **2,** powerless; helpless; impotent.

бессистемный *adj.* unsystematic.

бесславие *n.* ignominy. —**бесславный**, *adj.* inglorious; ignominious.

бесследный *adj.* without a trace. —**бесследно**, *adv.* without a trace; completely.

бессловесный *adj.* **1,** mute; dumb. **2,** quiet; meek. —бессловесная роль, non-speaking part.

бессменный *adj.* **1,** permanent. **2,** continuous.

бессмертие *n.* immortality.

бессмертный *adj.* immortal.

бессмысленно *adv.* senselessly. —*adj., used predicatively* making no sense: сделать это — совершенно бессмысленно, it makes no sense whatever to do that.

бессмысленность *n.f.* senselessness.

бессмы́сленный *adj.* **1,** meaningless. **2,** senseless; irrational; wanton. **3,** inane. **4,** blank; vacant.

бессмы́слица *n., colloq.* foolishness; nonsense.

бессо́вестный *adj.* unscrupulous; unconscionable.

бессодержа́тельный *adj.* empty; shallow; insipid; dull.

бессозна́тельный *adj.* **1,** unconscious. **2,** involuntary; instinctive.

бессо́нница *n.* insomnia.

бессо́нный *adj.* sleepless.

бесспо́рный *adj.* indisputable; incontrovertible. —**бесспо́рно,** *adv.* unquestionably; without question.

бессро́чный *adj.* for an indefinite period; for an unlimited time.

бесстра́стие *n.* impassivity. —**бесстра́стный,** *adj.* impassive.

бесстра́шие *n.* fearlessness. —**бесстра́шный,** *adj.* fearless; intrepid.

бессты́дник *n.m.* [*fem.* **-ница**] *colloq.* shameless person.

бессты́дный *adj.* shameless; brazen. —**бессты́дство,** *n.* shamelessness.

бессчётный *adj.* countless; innumerable.

беста́ктность *n.f.* **1,** tactlessness. **2,** indiscretion: соверши́ть беста́ктность, to commit an indiscretion.

беста́ктный *adj.* tactless.

бестала́нный *adj.* **1,** lacking talent; untalented. **2,** luckless; ill-starred.

бестеле́сный *adj.* incorporeal.

бе́стия *n.* rogue; knave.

бестолко́вый *adj.* **1,** obtuse; stupid. **2,** incoherent; confused.

бестсе́ллер (сэ) *n.* best seller.

бесфо́рменный *adj.* formless; shapeless; amorphous.

бесхара́ктерный *adj.* lacking in character; weak-willed.

бесхи́тростный *adj.* artless; ingenuous.

бесхо́зный *adj., colloq.* = бесхозя́йный.

бесхозя́йный *adj.* without an owner; ownerless.

бесхозя́йственный *adj.* **1,** incompetent; inefficient. **2,** uneconomical; wasteful. —**бесхозя́йственность,** *n.f.* mismanagement.

бесхребе́тный *adj.* spineless; weak-willed.

бесцве́тный *adj.* **1,** colorless. **2,** *fig.* colorless; insipid; dull; drab. —**бесцве́тность,** *n.f.* dullness; drabness; monotony.

бесце́льный *adj.* **1,** aimless. **2,** pointless. —**бесце́льно,** *adv.* aimlessly.

бесце́нный *adj.* priceless; invaluable.

бесцено́к *n., in* за бесце́нок, for next to nothing; for a song.

бесцеремо́нный *adj.* unceremonious; familiar. —**бесцеремо́нно,** *adv.* unceremoniously. —**бесцеремо́нность,** *n.f.* familiarity.

бесчелове́чный *adj.* inhuman. —**бесчелове́чность,** *n.f.* inhumanity.

бесче́стить *v. impfv.* [*pfv.* обесче́стить; *pres.* **-щу, -стишь**] to disgrace; dishonor.

бесче́стный *adj.* dishonorable. —**бесче́стье,** *n.* disgrace; dishonor.

бесчи́нство *n.* outrage.

бесчи́нствовать *v. impfv.* [*pres.* **-ствую, -ствуешь**] to commit outrages.

бесчи́сленный *adj.* countless; innumerable.

бесчу́вственный *adj.* **1,** insensible; unconscious. **2,** insensitive; unfeeling.

бесчу́вствие *n.* **1,** insensibility; unconsciousness. **2,** insensitivity; indifference.

бесшаба́шный *adj., colloq.* reckless; devil-may-care.

бесшо́вный *adj. (of pipes)* seamless.

бесшу́мный *adj.* noiseless.

бе́та (бэ) *n.* beta. —**бе́та-лучи́,** beta rays. —**бе́та-части́ца,** beta particle.

бе́тель *n.m.* betel.

бето́н *n.* concrete.

бетони́ровать *v. impfv.* [*pfv.* забетони́ровать; *pres.* **-рую, -руешь**] to pave with concrete.

бето́нный *adj.* concrete.

беф-стро́ганов *n.* beef stroganoff.

бечева́ *n.* towline; towrope.

бечёвка [*gen. pl.* **-вок**] *n.* string; twine.

бечевни́к [*gen.* **-ника́**] *n.* towpath. *Also,* **бечёвник.**

бечево́й *adj.* towing *(attrib.)*; tow *(attrib.)*.

бе́шенство *n.* **1,** rabies; hydrophobia. **2,** rage; fury.

бе́шеный *adj.* **1,** *(of an animal)* rabid; mad. **2,** violent; furious. —**бе́шеные де́ньги, 1,** *obs.* quick *(or easy)* money. **2,** exorbitant price: плати́ть бе́шеные де́ньги, to pay through the nose.

библе́йский *adj.* Biblical.

библиогра́фия *n.* bibliography. —**библио́граф,** *n.* bibliographer. —**библиографи́ческий,** *adj.* bibliographic.

библиоте́ка *n.* library.

библиоте́карь *n.m.* [*fem.* **-арша**] librarian.

библиотекове́дение *n.* library science.

библиоте́чный *adj.* library *(attrib.)*. —**библиоте́чное де́ло,** librarianship.

библиофи́л *n.* bibliophile.

би́блия *n.* the Bible; bible.

бива́к *also,* **бивуа́к** *n.* bivouac. —**жить (как) на бива́ках,** to camp out.

би́вень [*gen.* **-вня**] *n.m.* tusk.

бивуа́к *n.* = бива́к.

бигуди́ *n. pl. indecl.* (hair) curlers.

бидо́н *n.* large can: бидо́н для молока́, milk can.

бие́ние *n.* beating *(of the heart or pulse)*.

биза́нь *n.f.* mizzen *(sail)*.

би́знес (нэ) *n.* business. —**бизнесме́н,** *n.* businessman.

бизо́н *n.* bison.

биле́т *n.* **1,** ticket: биле́ты в теа́тр, theater tickets; биле́т на самолёт, plane ticket. **2,** membership card; identity card. —**креди́тный биле́т,** bank note. —**экзаменацио́нный биле́т,** question selected at random during an oral examination.

билетёр *n.m.* [*fem.* **-тёрша**] ticket collector; usher.

биле́тный *adj.* ticket *(attrib.)*.

биллио́н *n.* billion.

билль *n.m.* bill *(draft of a proposed law)*. —**билль о права́х,** Bill of Rights.

би́ло *n.* striking part *(of various mechanisms)*.

билья́рд *n.* **1,** billiards. **2,** billiard table; pool table. —**билья́рдная,** *n.* billiard room. —**билья́рдный,** *adj.* billiard.

биметалли́зм *n.* bimetallism. —**биметалли́ческий,** *adj.* bimetallic.

бина́рный *adj.* binary.

бино́кль *n.m.* binoculars. —**полево́й бино́кль,** field glasses. —**театра́льный бино́кль,** opera glasses.

бино́м *n., math.* binomial.

бинт [*gen.* **бинта́**] *n.* bandage.

бинтова́ть *v. impfv.* [*pfv.* **забинтова́ть;** *pres.* **-ту́ю, -ту́ешь**] to bandage.

биогра́фия *n.* biography. —**био́граф,** *n.* biographer. —**биографи́ческий,** *adj.* biographical.

биоло́гия *n.* biology. —**био́лог,** *n.* biologist. —**биологи́ческий,** *adj.* biological.

био́ника *n.* bionics.

биопси́я *n.* biopsy.

биофи́зика *n.* biophysics.

биохи́мия *n.* biochemistry. —**биохи́мик,** *n.* biochemist. —**биохими́ческий,** *adj.* biochemical.

бипла́н *n.* biplane.

би́ржа *n.* exchange; market: **фо́ндовая би́ржа,** stock exchange; stock market. —**би́ржа труда́, 1,** state employment agency. **2,** labor exchange.

биржеви́к [*gen.* **-вика́**] *n.* trader in stocks.

биржево́й *adj.* stock *(attrib.);* stock market *(attrib.).*

би́рка [*gen. pl.* **-рок**] *n.* **1,** tally *(notched stick).* **2,** tag; marker; label.

бирма́нец [*gen.* **-нца**] *n.m.* [*fem.* **-нка**] Burmese: **он бирма́нец,** he is Burmese. —**бирма́нский,** *adj.* Burmese.

бирюза́ *n.* turquoise. —**бирюзо́вый,** *adj.* turquoise.

бирю́к [*gen.* **-юка́**] *n.* lone wolf *(lit. & fig.).* —**бирюко́м смотре́ть,** to look sullen; scowl.

бирю́льки [*gen.* **-лек**] *n. pl.* jackstraws. —**игра́ть в бирю́льки, 1,** to play jackstraws. **2,** *fig.* to trifle away one's time.

бис *interj.* encore! —**испо́лнить (что́-нибудь) на бис,** to perform (something) as an encore.

би́сер *n.* beads. —**мета́ть би́сер пе́ред сви́ньями,** to cast pearls before swine.

би́серина *n.* bead. *Also,* **би́серинка.**

би́серный *adj.* **1,** bead *(attrib.);* beaded. **2,** *(of handwriting)* tiny; minute.

биси́ровать *v. impfv.& pfv.* [*pres.* **-рую, -руешь**] to give an encore.

бискви́т *n.* sponge cake.

бита́ *n.* bat *(used in various games).*

би́тва *n.* battle.

битко́м *adv., in* **битко́м наби́ть,** to pack; jam; fill to capacity.

бито́к [*gen.* **-тка́**] *n.* meatball.

биту́м *n.* bitumen. —**битумино́зный; биту́мный,** *adj.* bituminous.

би́тый *adj.* **1,** beaten. **2,** broken. —**би́тый час,** a whole *(or* good) hour.

бить *v. impfv.* [*pres.* **бью, бьёшь**] **1,** to beat; strike; hit. **2,** [*pfv.* **поби́ть**] to give a beating to; thrash. **3,** [*pfv.* **поби́ть**] to defeat; conquer; subdue. **4,** [*pfv.* **разби́ть**] to break; shatter; smash. **5,** [*pfv.* **проби́ть**] *(of clocks)* to strike; chime; *(of drums)* beat. **6,** [*pfv.* **проби́ть**] to sound (an alarm, retreat, etc.). **7,** [*pfv.* **проби́ть**] *(with* **в** + *acc.)* to beat (a drum); strike (a bell); clap (one's hands). **8,** to kill; shoot (game). **9,** to shoot; *(with* **из**) fire (a weapon). **10,** to gush; spurt. —**бить в глаза́,** to be striking; catch the eye. —**бить в цель,** to hit the mark. —**бить ми́мо це́ли,** to be wide of the mark.

битьё *n.* **1,** *colloq.* beating; thrashing. **2,** breaking; smashing.

би́ться *v.r. impfv.* [*pres.* **бьюсь, бьёшься**] **1,** to fight; struggle. **2,** *(with* **над**) *fig.* to struggle with; strug-gle over. **3,** *(with* **о** + *acc.)* to beat (against); strike (against); batter. **4,** *(of the heart, pulse, etc.)* to beat; pulsate. **5,** to writhe; toss about. **6,** to be fragile; be breakable. —**би́ться об закла́д,** to bet; wager. —**би́ться как ры́ба об лёд,** to struggle to keep body and soul together.

битю́г [*gen.* **-тюга́**] *n.* a type of dray horse.

бифште́кс (тэ) *n.* steak; beefsteak.

бихевиори́зм *n.* behaviorism.

би́цепс *n.* biceps.

бич [*gen.* **бича́**] *n.* **1,** whip; lash. **2,** *fig. (with gen.)* scourge (of).

бичева́ние *n.* flagellation.

бичева́ть *v. impfv.* [*pres.* **-чу́ю, -чу́ешь**] **1,** to whip; flog. **2,** *fig.* to castigate; excoriate.

бишь *particle, colloq.,* used when one has forgotten something: **о чём бишь мы говори́ли?,** what is it we were talking about? —**то бишь,** *colloq.* or rather.

бла́го[1] *n.* **1,** good: **на бла́го челове́чества,** for the good of mankind. **2,** *pl.* benefits; blessings. —**всех благ,** best wishes; all the best! —**ни за каки́е бла́га,** not for anything in the world.

бла́го[2] *conj., colloq.* since; inasmuch as.

бла́говест *n.* ringing of church bells; call to prayer.

бла́говестить *v. impfv.* [*pres.* **-щу, -стишь**] *obs.* to ring church bells.

благове́щение *n., relig.* Annunciation. —**благове́щенский,** *adj.* Annunciation *(attrib.):* **Благове́щенский собо́р,** Cathedral of the Annunciation *(in the Kremlin).*

благови́дный *adj.* **1,** *obs.* attractive; good-looking. **2,** proper; suitable. **3,** *(of an excuse)* plausible; specious.

благоволе́ние *n., obs.* favor; good graces.

благоволи́ть *v. impfv.* **1,** *(with* **к**) to like; regard with favor; be favorably disposed (toward). **2,** *(with inf.) obs.* to be so kind as to: **благоволи́те отве́тить,** kindly favor us with a reply.

благовоспи́танный *adj.* well-mannered; well-bred.

благове́йный *adj.* reverent.

благогове́ние *n. (with* **пе́ред)** reverence (for); veneration (of).

благогове́ть *v. impfv. (with* **пе́ред)** to revere; venerate.

благодаре́ние *n., obs.* expression of gratitude; thanksgiving.

благодари́ть *v. impfv.* [*pfv.* **поблагодари́ть**] to thank. —**благодарю́ вас!,** thank you!

благода́рность *n.f.* **1,** gratitude. **2,** (expression of) thanks. —**не сто́ит благода́рности,** don't mention it!

благода́рный *adj.* [*short form* **-рен, -рна**] **1,** grateful; thankful; appreciative. **2,** worthy; worthwhile.

благода́рственный *adj., obs.* of thanks; of gratitude.

благодаря́ *prep., with dat.* thanks to; owing to. —**благодаря́ тому́, что...,** owing to *(or* due to) the fact that...

благода́тный *adj.* **1,** bringing joy or happiness; blessed. **2,** fertile; abundant.

благода́ть *n.f.* **1,** *obs.* blessing; divine gift. **2,** abundance; plenty. **3,** *colloq.* a delight.

благоде́нствие *n., obs.* prosperity.

благоде́нствовать *v. impfv.* [*pres.* **-ствую, -ству-ешь**] to prosper; thrive.

благоде́тель *n.m., obs.* benefactor.

благоде́тельный *adj.* **1,** beneficial. **2,** *obs.* benevolent.

благодея́ние *n.* **1,** good deed. **2,** blessing; boon.

благоду́шие *n.* good nature. —**благоду́шный,** *adj.* good-natured.

благожела́тельный *adj.* **1,** good-natured; kindly. **2,** favorable. —**благожела́тельность,** *n.f.* good will; benevolence.

благозву́чие *n.* harmony; euphony. *Also,* **благозву́чность,** *n.f.*

благозву́чный *adj.* euphonious; harmonious; melodious.

благо́й *adj., obs.* good. —**крича́ть благи́м ма́том,** *colloq.* to yell one's head off.

благонадёжный *adj.* reliable; trustworthy. —**благонадёжность,** *n.f.* reliability; trustworthiness.

благонаме́ренный *adj., obs.* well-intentioned; well-meaning.

благообра́зный *adj.* good-looking; handsome.

благополу́чие *n.* welfare; well-being.

благополу́чный *adj.* successful; happy; satisfactory. —**благополу́чно,** *adv.* all right; safely; without mishap.

благопристо́йный *adj., obs.* decorous; seemly.

благоприя́тный *adj.* favorable; propitious.

благоприя́тствовать *v. impfv.* [*pres.* -ствую, -ствуешь] *(with dat.)* to favor; work to the advantage of.

благоразу́мие *n.* prudence; discretion; good sense.

благоразу́мный *adj.* **1,** reasonable; prudent; judicious; discreet. **2,** *(of advice)* sensible. —**благоразу́мно,** *adv.* prudently; judiciously; wisely.

благоро́дный *adj.* noble. —**благоро́дные мета́ллы,** precious metals. —**благоро́дный оле́нь,** red deer.

благоро́дство *n.* nobility.

благоскло́нный *adj.* favorable; kindly. —**благоскло́нно,** *adv.* with favor; favorably. —**благоскло́нность,** *n.f.* favor; good graces.

благослове́ние *n.* blessing.

благослове́нный *adj., poetic* blessed.

благословля́ть *v. impfv.* [*pfv.* **благослови́ть**] to bless.

благосостоя́ние *n.* welfare; well-being.

бла́гостный *adj.* **1,** lovely. **2,** serene.

благотвори́тель *n.m.* philanthropist. —**благотвори́тельность,** *n.f.* charity; philanthropy. —**благотвори́тельный,** *adj.* charitable; philanthropic.

благотво́рный *adj.* beneficial; wholesome; salutary.

благоустро́енный *adj.* well-designed; well-equipped; with all the modern conveniences.

благоустро́йство *n.* providing of public services and amenities.

благоуха́ние *n.* fragrance; sweet smell; redolence. —**благоуха́нный,** *adj.* fragrant; sweet-smelling; redolent.

благоуха́ть *v. impfv.* to smell sweet; be fragrant.

благочести́вый *adj.* pious; devout. —**благоче́стие,** *n.* piety.

блаже́нный *adj.* **1,** blissful. **2,** blessed. **3,** *colloq.* wacky. —**блаже́нной па́мяти,** of blessed memory. —**в блаже́нном неве́дении,** in blissful ignorance. —**блаже́нство** *n.* bliss.

блаже́нствовать *v. impfv.* [*pres.* -ствую, -ствуешь] **1,** to be blissfully happy; be in a state of bliss. **2,** to enjoy oneself.

блажь *n.f., colloq.* whim; fancy.

бланк *n.* form; blank.

блат *n.* **1,** thieves' jargon. **2,** *colloq.* pull; connections; influence: по бла́ту, by pulling strings.

блатно́й *adj.* thieves': блатно́й язы́к, thieves' jargon.

бледне́ть *v. impfv.* [*pfv.* **побледне́ть**] **1,** to turn pale; turn white. **2,** [*impfv. only*] *(with* **перед***)* *fig.* to pale (before); suffer in comparison (with).

бледно- *prefix, used with colors* pale: бледно-зелё-ный, pale green.

бле́дность *n.f.* pallor.

бле́дный *adj.* [*short form* -ден, -дна́, -дно] **1,** pale. **2,** *fig.* dull; colorless; insipid.

блёклый *adj.* faded; withered.

блёкнуть *v. impfv.* [*pfv.* **поблёкнуть**; *past* блёк, -ла] **1,** to fade. **2,** to wither.

блеск *n.* **1,** brilliance; luster. **2,** *fig.* magnificence; splendor: во всём бле́ске, in all its splendor. **3,** *(with gen.)* brilliance (*of wit, talent, etc.*). —**с бле́ском,** with flying colors.

блесна́ [*pl.* бле́сны, блёсен] *n.* spoon bait.

блесну́ть *v. pfv.* **1,** *pfv. of* блесте́ть. **2,** to flash across one's mind: у меня́ блесну́ла мысль, the thought flashed across my mind.

блесте́ть *v. impfv.* [*pfv.* блесну́ть; *pres.* блещу́, блести́шь *or* бле́щешь] **1,** to shine; sparkle; glitter; gleam. **2,** *fig. (with instr.)* to be blessed with: он не бле́щет умо́м, he is not the smartest person in the world.

блёстки *n. pl.* [*sing.* блёстка] **1,** spangles; sequins. **2,** *fig. (with gen.)* flashes (*of wit, talent, etc.*).

блестя́щий *adj.* brilliant. —**блестя́ще,** *adv.* brilliantly.

блеф *n.* bluff.

блефова́ть *v. impfv.* [*pres.* -фу́ю, -фу́ешь] *colloq.* to bluff.

бле́яние *n.* bleat; bleating.

бле́ять *v. impfv.* [*pres.* бле́ет] to bleat. .

ближа́йший *adj.* **1,** nearest. **2,** next: в ближа́йшие дни, in the next few days. **3,** immediate: ближа́йший нача́льник, immediate superior. **4,** *in* ближа́йший ро́дственник, nearest relative; next of kin. —**в ближа́йшем бу́дущем; в ближа́йшее вре́мя,** in the near (*or* immediate) future.

бли́же *adj., comp. of* бли́зкий.

ближневосто́чный *adj.* Middle East (*attrib.*); Middle Eastern.

бли́жний *adj.* near; nearby. —*n., obs.* neighbor; fellow human being. —**бли́жний бой,** close combat. —**Бли́жний Восто́к,** Middle East.

близ *prep., with gen.* near; close to.

бли́зиться *v.r. impfv.* to approach; draw near.

бли́зкий *adj.* [*short form* -зок, -зка́, -зко; *comp.* бли́же] **1,** near; close (*in space or time*). **2,** close; intimate. —**бли́зкие,** *n.pl.* one's relatives.

бли́зко *adv.* near; close; nearby. —*adj., used predicatively* nearby; close to here: по́чта совсе́м бли́зко, the post office is right nearby. —**бли́зко от** *or* **к,** near; close to.

близлежа́щий *adj.* nearby; neighboring.

близне́ц [*gen.* -неца́] *n.* **1,** twin. **2,** *pl., cap.* Gemini.

близору́кий *adj.* **1,** nearsighted; myopic. **2,** *fig.* shortsighted.

близору́кость *n.f.* **1,** nearsightedness; myopia. **2,** *fig.* shortsightedness.

бли́зость *n.f.* nearness; closeness; proximity.

блик *n.* patch of light.

блин [*gen.* блина́] *n.* pancake.

блиндаж [*gen.* -дажа́] *n.*, *mil.* dugout; bunker.

бли́нчатый *adj.* pancake *(attrib.).*

бли́нчик *n.* small pancake.

блиста́тельный *adj.* brilliant; glittering; resplendent.

блиста́ть *v. impfv.* to shine; sparkle; glitter. —**блиста́ть свои́м отсу́тствием**, to be conspicuous by one's absence.

блиц *n.* flash bulb.

блок *n.* **1,** bloc. **2,** block *(pulley).* **3,** *mech.* block: блок цили́ндров, cylinder block. **4,** (cement) block. **5,** *philately* block; souvenir sheet.

блока́да *n.* blockade.

блокга́уз *n.*, *mil.* blockhouse.

блоки́ровать *v. impfv. & pfv.* [*pres.* -рую, -руешь] **1,** to blockade. **2,** *sports* to block. —**блоки́роваться**, *refl. (with* с + *instr.)* to form an alliance (with).

блокно́т *n.* writing pad; note pad; tablet.

блонди́н *n.* blond (man). —**блонди́нка**, *n.* blonde.

блоха́ [*pl.* бло́хи, блох, блоха́м] *n.* flea. —**блоши́ный**, *adj.* flea *(attrib.).*

бло́шки [*gen. pl.* -шек] *n. pl.* tiddlywinks.

блуд *n.*, *obs.* lechery; debauchery.

блуди́ть *v. impfv.* [*pres.* блужу́, блу́дишь] *colloq.* to wander.

блу́дный *adj.*, *in* блу́дный сын, prodigal son.

блужда́ть *v. impfv.* to roam; wander. —**блужда́ть в потёмках**, to feel one's way.

блужда́ющий *adj.* roaming; wandering. —**блужда́ющий огонёк**, will-o'-the wisp.

блу́за *n.* **1,** smock. **2,** *obs.* blouse.

блу́зка [*gen. pl.* -зок] *n.* (lady's) blouse.

блю́дечко [*gen. pl.* -чек] *n.* saucer.

блю́до *n.* **1,** platter. **2,** dish; food: моё люби́мое блю́до, my favorite dish/food. **3,** course: обе́д из трёх блюд, three-course dinner.

блю́дце [*gen. pl.* -дец] *n.* saucer.

блюз *n.*, *music* blues.

блюсти́ *v. impfv.* [*pfv.* соблюсти́; *pres.* блюду́, блюдёшь; *past* блюл, блюла́, блюло́] **1,** to guard; watch over. **2,** to maintain; keep. **3,** to observe; abide by.

блюсти́тель *n.m.*, *obs.* keeper; guardian. —**блюсти́тель поря́дка**, keeper of order; guardian of the law.

бля́ха *n.* name plate; badge. *Also,* **бля́шка.**

боа́ *n.m. indecl.* boa constrictor. —*n. neut. indecl.*, *obs.* boa *(lady's scarf).*

боб [*gen.* боба́] *n.* bean. —**оста́ться на боба́х**, *colloq.* to be left with nothing.

бобёр [*gen.* -бра́] *n.* beaver fur.

бобо́вый *adj.* **1,** bean *(attrib.).* **2,** leguminous.

бобр [*gen.* бобра́] *n.* beaver.

бо́брик *n.* castor *(cloth).*

бобро́вый *adj.* beaver *(attrib.).*

бо́бслей *n.* bobsled.

бобы́ль [*gen.* -была́] *n.m.* **1,** *obs.* poor landless peasant. **2,** *colloq.* lonely unmarried man.

бог *n.*, *often cap.* God; god. —**бог его́ зна́ет!**, God knows! —**бог с** (+ *instr.*), to hell with...; forget about... —**дай бог!**, God grant. —**ей бо́гу!**, really!; truly! —**не дай бог!**, God forbid!; heaven forbid! —**ра́ди бо́га!**, for God's sake!; for goodness' sake!; for heaven's sake —**сла́ва бо́гу!**, thank God!; thank goodness!; thank heaven!

богаде́льня [*gen. pl.* -лен] *n.* poorhouse; almshouse.

богате́ть *v. impfv.* [*pfv.* разбогате́ть] to get rich.

бога́то *adv.* richly.

бога́тство *n.* **1,** wealth; riches. **2,** richness. **3,** *pl.* (natural) resources. **4,** *(with gen.)* fig. wealth (of); profusion (of).

бога́тый *adj.* [*comp.* бога́че] **1,** rich; wealthy. **2,** abundant. **3,** *(of a collection)* large; *(of experience)* broad; *(of one's imagination)* fertile. **4,** luxurious; sumptuous. —*n.* rich man. —**чем бога́ты, тем и ра́ды**, you are welcome to what we have.

богаты́рь [*gen.* -тыря́] *n.m.* **1,** Russian epic hero. **2,** *fig.* big strapping man. —**богаты́рский**, *adj.* of a богаты́рь.

бога́ч [*gen.* -гача́] *n.* rich man.

бога́че *adj.*, *comp. of* бога́тый.

боге́ма *n.* **1,** Bohemians. **2,** *colloq.* Bohemian way of life. —**боге́мный**, *adj.*, *colloq.* Bohemian.

боге́мский *adj.* Bohemian; of or from Bohemia.

боги́ня *n.* goddess.

богобоя́зненный *adj.* god-fearing.

богома́терь *n.f.*, *usu. cap.* Mother of God *(the Virgin Mary).*

богомо́л *n.* **1,** pilgrim. **2,** *zool.* (praying) mantis.

богомо́лец [*gen.* -льца] *n.m.* [*fem.* -лка] **1,** devout person. **2,** pilgrim. —**богомо́лье**, *n.* pilgrimage. —**богомо́льный**, *adj.* devout.

богоро́дица *n.*, *usu. cap.* the Virgin Mary.

богосло́вие *n.* theology. —**богосло́в**, *n.* theologian. —**богосло́вский**, *adj.* theological.

богослуже́ние *n.* religious service.

боготвори́ть *v. impfv.* to idolize; worship.

богоху́льство *n.* blasphemy. —**богоху́льный**, *adj.* blasphemous.

богоху́льствовать *v. impfv.* [*pres.* -ствую, -ствуешь] to blaspheme; engage in blasphemy.

богоявле́ние *n.*, *usu. cap.* Epiphany.

бода́ть *v. impfv.* to butt. —**бода́ться**, *refl.* **1,** to butt *(generally).* **2,** to butt each other.

бодли́вый *adj. (of an animal)* that butts a lot.

бодри́ть *v. impfv.* to invigorate. —**бодри́ться**, *refl.* to try to keep one's spirits up.

бо́дрость *n.f.* **1,** vigor. **2,** cheerfulness; good spirits.

бо́дрствовать *v. impfv.* [*pres.* -ствую, -ствуешь] to stay awake; keep vigil.

бо́дрый *adj.* **1,** cheerful; buoyant; jaunty. **2,** vigorous; sprightly; hale and hearty.

бодря́щий *adj.* invigorating; bracing.

боеви́к [*gen.* -вика́] *n.* **1,** *hist.* worker taking part in the 1905 Revolution. **2,** *colloq.* hit *(movie).*

боеви́тость *n.f.* fighting spirit; enthusiasm. —**боеви́тый**, *adj.* active; energetic; lively; enthusiastic.

боево́й *adj.* **1,** fighting; battle *(attrib.);* combat *(attrib.).* **2,** *mil.* live: боевы́е патро́ны, live ammunition. **3,** militant; belligerent. **4,** urgent. —**боева́я часть**; боева́я голо́вка, warhead.

боеголо́вка [*gen. pl.* -вок] *n.* warhead.

боегото́вность *n.f.* combat readiness.

боеприпа́сы [*gen.* -сов] *n. pl.* ammunition.

боеспосо́бность *n.f.*, *mil.* fighting efficiency; combat effectiveness. —**боеспосо́бный**, *adj.* battleworthy.

бое́ц [*gen.* бойца́] *n.* soldier; fighting man.

бо́же *n.*, *vocative case of* бог. —*interj.* God! —**бо́же мой!**, God!; my God!

боже́ственный *adj.* **1,** divine. **2,** *colloq.* divine; idyllic; sublime. —**боже́ственность**, *n.f.* divinity.

божество́ *n.* deity.

бо́жий [*fem.* -жья] *adj.* God's. —**бо́жья коро́вка**, ladybug; ladybird. —**каждый божий день**, every blessed day. —**ясно как божий день**, as clear as day.

божиться *v.r. impfv.* [*pfv.* **побожиться**] to swear.

божок [*gen.* -**жка**] *n.* **1**, figurine or statuette of a god. **2**, idol; one who is idolized.

бой [*2nd loc.* **бою**; *pl.* **бои, боёв**] *n.* **1**, combat; battle: **пасть в бою**, to fall/be killed/in combat/battle/action. **2**, fight: **кулачный бой**, fistfight; **бой быков**, bullfight. Без боя, without a fight. **3**, *pl.* fighting: **тяжелые бои**, heavy fighting. **4**, breaking; breakage. **5**, striking (of a clock); beating (of drums). **6**, killing; slaughter (of fish, whales, etc.). —**взять с бою**, to take by force.

бойкий *adj.* [*short form* **боек, бойка, бойко**; *comp.* **бойче**] **1**, sharp; clever. **2**, lively; brisk. **3**, glib; facile.

бойкот *n.* boycott.

бойкотировать *v. impfv.* [*pres.* -**рую, -руешь**] to boycott.

бойница *n.* loophole; embrasure.

бойня [*gen. pl.* **боен**] *n.* **1**, slaughterhouse. **2**, massacre; slaughter; carnage.

бок [*2nd loc.* **боку**; *pl.* **бока**] *n.* side. —**бок о бок**, side by side. —**под боком**, nearby; close at hand. —**с боку на бок**, from side to side. *See also* **боком**.

бокал *n.* wineglass; goblet.

боковой *adj.* side (attrib.); lateral. —**отправиться на боковую**, *colloq.* to turn in; hit the hay.

боком *adv.* sideways.

бокс *n.* boxing.

боксёр *n.* boxer. —**боксёрский**, *adj.* boxing (attrib.).

боксировать *v. impfv.* [*pres.* -**рую, -руешь**] *sports* to box.

боксит *n.* bauxite. —**бокситовый**, *adj.* bauxite (attrib.).

болван *n.* **1**, *colloq.* dolt; blockhead. **2**, block (for shaping hats). **3**, *cards* dummy.

болгарин [*pl.* -**гары, -гар**] *n.m.* [*fem.* -**гарка**] Bulgarian. —**болгарский**, *adj.* Bulgarian.

более *adv.* **1**, more: я более чем доволен, I am more than satisfied. Более полугода тому назад, more than half a year ago. **2**, *used in forming compound comparatives* more: более интересный, more interesting. —**более или менее**, more or less. —**более того**, what is more. —**всё более** (+ *adj.*), more and more. —**тем более**, all the more; the more so. —**тем более, что...**, especially since; all the more so because...

болезненно *adv.* **1**, painfully. **2**, with difficulty; hard.

болезненность *n.f.* **1**, sickliness. **2**, morbidity.

болезненный *adj.* **1**, sickly. **2**, painful; causing pain. **3**, of pain: болезненный крик, a cry of pain. **4**, abnormal; morbid: болезненное любопытство, morbid curiosity.

болезнь *n.f.* illness; disease. —**болезни роста**, growing pains. —**морская болезнь**, seasickness. —**отпуск по болезни**, sick leave.

болельщик *n.*, *colloq.*, *sports* fan.

болен *see* **больной**.

болеть[1] *v. impfv.* [*pres.* **болею, болеешь**] **1**, to be ill. **2**, (with за + *acc.* or o) *colloq.* to agonize (over). **3**, (with за + *acc.*) *colloq.* to be a fan (of); root (for). —**болеть душой** (with за+ *acc.* or o), to feel for; take to heart.

болеть[2] *v. impfv.* [*pres.* **болит, болят**] to ache; hurt: у меня болит голова, I have a headache. —**у меня душа болит за** (+ *acc.*), my heart aches for...

болеутоляющий *adj.* pain-relieving; analgesic. —**болеутоляющее средство**, analgesic.

болиголов *n.* (poison) hemlock.

болид *n.* fireball (meteor).

болонка [*gen. pl.* -**нок**] *n.* small white poodle.

болото *n.* swamp; marsh. —**болотистый**, *adj.* swampy; marshy. —**болотный**, *adj.* marsh (attrib.).

болт [*gen.* **болта**] *n.*, *mech.* bolt.

болтанка *n.*, *aero.*, *colloq.* bumpiness; turbulence.

болтать *v. impfv.* **1**, *colloq.* to talk; chatter. **2**, [*pfv.* **взболтать**] to shake; stir (a liquid). **3**, (with *instr.*) to dangle; swing. **4**, *in* болтать языком, *colloq.* to babble; prattle. —**болтаться**, *refl.* **1**, to dangle. **2**, *colloq.* to hang around; loiter.

болтливый *adj.* talkative; loquacious; garrulous. —**болтливость**, *n.f.* loquaciousness.

болтовня *n.*, *colloq.* chatter.

болтун [*gen.* -**туна**] *n.m.* [*fem.* -**тунья**] chatterbox.

болтунья *n.* **1**, *fem. of* **болтун**. **2**, *in* яичница-болтунья, scrambled eggs.

боль *n.f.* pain; ache. —**с болью в душе** *or* в сердце, with a heavy heart.

больница *n.* hospital.

больничный *adj.* hospital (attrib.). —**больничный лист** *or* листок, medical/doctor's certificate (certifying inability to work).

больно *adv.* **1**, badly: больно ушибиться, to hurt oneself badly. **2**, *colloq.* terribly; a bit too. —*adj.*, *used predicatively (with dat.)* painful: мне больно, it is painful; it hurts. Мне больно видеть..., it pains me to see... —**сделать больно** (+ *dat.*), to hurt.

больной *adj.* [*short form* **болен, больна**] **1**, sick; ill. **2**, sore: больной зуб, a sore tooth. **3**, bad: больное сердце, a bad heart. —*n.* patient; sick person. —**больной вопрос**, sore subject. —**больное место**, sore spot; tender spot.

больше *adj.*, *comp. of* **большой**, bigger; larger; greater. —*adv.*, *comp. of* **много**, more. —**больше всего**, most of all. —**больше не**, no more; anymore; any longer. —**больше нигде**, nowhere else. —**больше никогда**, never again. —**больше никого**, no one else. —**больше ничего**, nothing else. —**больше того**, what is more.

большевик [*gen.* -**вика**] *n.* Bolshevik. —**большевистский**, *adj.* Bolshevik (attrib.).

больший *adj.*, *used only as a modifier*, *comp. of* **большой** *and* **великий**, larger; greater. —**большая часть** (+ *gen.*), most (of). —**большей частью**; по большей части, for the most part; mostly. —**самое большее**, **1**, at (the) most. **2**, (fol. by что) the most (that).

большинство *n.* **1**, majority. **2**, (with *gen. or* из) most: в большинстве случаев, in most cases; большинство из нас, most of us. —**в большинстве**; в большинстве своём, for the most part; mainly.

большой *adj.* [*comp.* **больше** *and* **больший**] **1**, big; large. **2**, great. **3**, *colloq.* grownup. —*n.*, usu. *pl.*, *colloq.* grownup. —**большая буква**, capital letter. —**большой палец**, thumb. —**большое (вам) спасибо!**, thank you very much! *See also* **больше** *and* **больший**.

большущий *adj.*, *colloq.* huge; tremendous.

болячка [*gen. pl.* -**чек**] *n.*, *colloq.* sore.

бомба *n.* bomb.

бомбардир *n.* bombardier.

бомбардировать *v. impfv.* [*pres.* -**рую, -руешь**] to bombard; bomb.

бомбардиро́вка *n.* bombardment; bombing. —**бомбардиро́вочный**, *adj.* bombing *(attrib.).*

бомбардиро́вщик *n.* bomber.

бомбёжка *n., colloq.* bombing.

бомби́ть *v. impfv.* [*pres.* -блю́, -би́шь] *colloq.* to bomb.

бо́мбовый *adj.* bomb *(attrib.).*

бомбодержа́тель *n.m.* bomb rack.

бомбомета́ние *n.* bombing.

бомбоубе́жище *n.* bomb shelter; air-raid shelter.

бо́ндарь *n.m.* cooper. *Also,* **бонда́рь** [*gen.* -даря́].

бо́нза *n.m., colloq.* bigwig; member of the elite.

бор[1] [*2nd loc.* бору́; *pl.* боры́] *n.* pine forest.

бор[2] *n.* boron.

бордо́ *n. indecl.* claret *(wine).* —*adj. indecl.* wine-colored; claret; maroon. —**бордо́вый**, *adj.* = бордо́.

бордю́р *n.* border; trimming.

боре́ц [*gen.* -рца́] *n.* **1,** *(often with* за + *acc.)* fighter (for). **2,** wrestler.

борза́я *n., decl. as an adj.* **1,** borzoi; Russian wolfhound. **2,** greyhound; whippet.

бо́рзый *adj., archaic (of a horse)* fleet; swift.

бормаши́на *n.* (dentist's) drill.

бормота́нье *n.* muttering; mumbling.

бормота́ть *v. impfv.* [*pfv.* пробормота́ть; *pres.* -мочу́, -мо́чешь] to mutter; mumble.

бо́рный *adj.* boric: бо́рная кислота́, boric acid.

бо́ров *n.* **1,** [*pl.* бо́ровы, -во́в] gelded hog. **2,** [*pl.* борова́, -во́в] chimney flue.

борода́ [*acc.* бо́роду; *pl.* бо́роды, боро́д, -да́м] *n.* **1,** beard. **2,** wattle *(of a bird).*

борода́вка [*gen. pl.* -вок] *n.* wart.

борода́вочник *n.* wart hog.

борода́вчатый *adj.* covered with warts.

борода́тый *adj.* bearded.

борода́ч [*gen.* -дача́] *n.* **1,** *colloq.* man with a beard. **2,** bearded vulture.

боро́дка [*gen. pl.* -док] *n.* small beard. —**козли́ная боро́дка**, goatee.

борозда́ [*pl.* бо́розды, боро́зд, -да́м] *n.* furrow.

борозди́ть *v. impfv.* [*pfv.* избоpозди́ть; *pres.* -зжу́, -зди́шь] **1,** to furrow. **2,** *in* борозди́ть моря́ *or* океа́ны, to ply the seas.

борона́ [*acc.* бо́рону; *pl.* бо́роны, боро́н, -на́м] *n.* harrow.

борони́ть *v. impfv.* [*pfv.* взборони́ть] to harrow. *Also,* **боронова́ть** [*pres.* -ну́ю, -ну́ешь].

боро́ться *v.r. impfv.* [*pres.* борю́сь, бо́решься] **1,** to fight. **2,** *(with* с + *instr.)* to combat; fight; battle. **3,** to wrestle.

борт [*2nd loc.* борту́; *pl.* борта́] *n.* **1,** side *(of a ship).* **2,** breast *(of a coat).* **3,** cushion *(of a billiard table).* —**за́ борт; за бо́ртом**, overboard. —**на́ борт; на борту́**, aboard; on board. —**оста́вить/оста́ться за бо́ртом**, to leave/be left/out in the cold. —**челове́к за бо́ртом!**, man overboard!

бортмеха́ник *n.* flight engineer.

бортово́й *adj.* **1,** on-board. **2,** side *(attrib.).* —**борто́вая ка́чка**, rolling *(of a ship).*

бортпроводни́к [*gen.* -ника́] *n.* steward. —**бортпроводни́ца**, *n.* stewardess.

борщ [*gen.* борща́] *n.* borsch.

борьба́ *n.* **1,** struggle; fight. **2,** wrestling. —**япо́нская борьба́**, jujitsu.

босико́м *adv., colloq.* barefoot; in one's bare feet.

босо́й *adj.* **1,** barefoot. **2,** *(of feet)* bare. —**(надева́ть ту́фли) на босу́ но́гу**, (to put on one's shoes) without socks.

босоно́гий *adj.* barefoot.

босоно́жка [*gen. pl.* -жек] *n.* **1,** barefoot girl or woman. **2,** *usu. pl.* sandals.

босс *n.* (political) boss.

боса́к [*gen.* -сяка́] *n.* vagabond; tramp.

бот *n.* **1,** boat. **2,** boot.

бота́ника *n.* botany. —**бота́ник**, *n.* botanist. —**ботани́ческий**, *adj.* botanical.

ботва́ *n.* vegetable tops.

ботви́нья *n.* cold soup made of kvass, cooked vegetables, and fish.

бо́тик *n.* **1,** small boat. **2,** lady's boot.

боти́нок [*gen.* -нка; *gen. pl.* -нок] *n.* shoe.

бо́цман *n.* boatswain.

боча́р [*gen.* -чара́] *n.* cooper.

бо́чка [*gen. pl.* -чек] *n.* barrel; keg. —**де́ньги на бо́чку**, cash on the barrel.

бочко́м *adv.* sideways.

бочо́нок [*gen.* -нка] *n.* small barrel; keg.

боязли́вый *adj.* timid; timorous. —**боязли́вость**, *n.f.* timidity.

боя́зно *adj., used predicatively (with dat.) colloq.* afraid.

боя́знь *n.f.* fear; dread.

боя́рин [*pl.* боя́ре, боя́р] *n., hist.* boyar. —**боя́рский**, *adj.* boyar *(attrib.);* boyars'. —**боя́рство**, *n.* the boyars.

боя́рышник *n.* hawthorn.

боя́ться *v.r. impfv.* [*pres.* бою́сь, бои́шься] **1,** *(with gen.)* to be afraid of; fear. **2,** *(with a dependent clause)* to be afraid; fear: бою́сь, что..., I'm afraid/I fear/that... **3,** *(with gen.)* to be sensitive to. —**бою́сь сказа́ть**, I cannot say for sure.

бра *n. neut. indecl.* candlestick or lamp bracket mounted on a wall.

брава́да *n.* bravado.

брави́ровать *v. impfv.* [*pres.* -рую, -руешь] *(with instr.)* **1,** to flaunt; parade. **2,** to brave; defy.

брави́ссимо *interj.* bravissimo!

бра́во *interj.* bravo!

брабу́рный *adj. (of music)* stirring. —**бравурная му́зыка**, bravura.

бра́вый *adj.* dashing.

бра́га *n.* home-brewed beer.

бразды́ *n. pl., obs.* bridle; bit. —**бразды́ правле́ния**, the reins of government.

брази́лец [*gen.* -льца] *n.m.* [*fem.* -ля́нка] Brazilian. —**брази́льский**, *adj.* Brazilian.

брак *n.* **1,** marriage. **2,** defect; flaw. **3,** defective merchandise.

брако́ванный *adj. (of merchandise)* defective.

бракова́ть *v. impfv.* [*pfv.* забракова́ть; *pres.* -ку́ю, -ку́ешь] to reject as defective.

брако́вщик *n.* quality control inspector.

бракоде́л *n.* slipshod worker.

браконье́р *n.* poacher. —**браконье́рство**, *n.* poaching.

бракоразво́дный *adj.* divorce *(attrib.).*

бракосочета́ние *n.* wedding ceremony. —**дворе́ц бракосочета́ния**, wedding palace.

брами́н *n.* = брахма́н.

бра́мсель *n.m.* topgallant sail.

брам-сте́ньга *n.* topgallant mast.

брандспо́йт *n.* **1,** nozzle *(of a fire hose).* **2,** portable pump.

брани́ть *v. impfv.* to scold; berate. —**брани́ться,** *refl.* **1,** to quarrel. **2,** to swear; curse.

бра́нный *adj.* **1,** abusive: бра́нное сло́во, swearword. **2,** *archaic* martial.

брань *n.f.* **1,** swearing; profanity. **2,** *archaic* battle.

брасле́т *n.* bracelet.

брасс *n., swimming* breast stroke.

брат *[pl.* бра́тья, бра́тьев] *n.* brother.

брата́ние *n.* fraternization.

брата́ться *v.r. impfv.* *[pfv.* побрата́ться] to fraternize.

бра́тец *[gen.* -тца] *n.* **1,** *dim., endearing form of* брат. **2,** *in direct address* old man; old chap.

брати́шка *[gen. pl.* -шек] *n.m., dim. of* брат.

бра́тия *n.* fraternity: литерату́рная бра́тия, literary fraternity.

братоуби́йство *n.* fratricide. —**братоуби́йствен-ный,** *adj.* fratricidal.

бра́тский *adj.* brotherly; fraternal. —**бра́тская моги́ла,** common grave.

бра́тство *n.* brotherhood; fraternity.

брать *v. impfv.* *[pfv.* взять; *pres.* беру́, берёшь; *past fem.* брала́] **1,** to take. **2,** to seize. **3,** to buy; get. **4,** to levy; exact. **5,** to charge (a certain price). **6,** to clear (a hurdle, height, etc.). **7,** *(with instr.)* to succeed (by means of). **8,** *colloq.* to work; be effective: нож не берёт, the knife doesn't cut. —**брать верх,** *see* верх. —**брать за́ сердце** *(or* за́ душу), to touch someone's heart. —**брать курс на,** to make for; head for. —**брать на себя́,** to take upon oneself; assume. —**брать но́ту,** to strike *or* hit a note. —**брать приме́р с** (+ *gen.*), to follow someone's example. —**брать своё,** *see* свой. —**брать себя́ в ру́ки,** to pull oneself together. —**брать сло́во с** (+ *gen.*), to make someone promise. *See also* взять.

бра́ться *v.r. impfv.* *[pfv.* взя́ться; *pres.* беру́сь, берёшься; *past* бра́лся, брала́сь, брало́сь] **1,** *(with за* + *acc.)* to take hold of; grasp. **2,** *(with за* + *acc.)* to begin; take up; undertake. **3,** *(with inf.)* to take it upon oneself (to); dare (to); presume (to). **4,** to come (from): отку́да же они́ беру́тся?, where on earth do they come from? —**бра́ться за́ руки,** to join hands. —**бра́ться за ору́жие,** to take up arms. —**бра́ться за ум,** *colloq.* to come to one's senses. *See also* взя́ться.

брахма́н *also,* брами́н *n.* Brahman. —**брахмани́зм;** браман́изм, *n.* Brahmanism.

бра́чный *adj.* marriage *(attrib.);* marital; matrimonial; conjugal; nuptial. —**бра́чный пери́од,** mating period; mating season.

бра́шпиль *n.m.* windlass.

бреве́нчатый *adj.* log *(attrib.);* made of logs.

бревно́ *[pl.* брёвна, брёвен] *n.* log.

бред *[2nd loc.* бреду́] *n.* **1,** delirium: быть в бреду́, to be delirious. **2,** ravings.

бре́день *[gen.* -дня] *n.m.* dragnet.

бре́дить *v. impfv.* *[pres.* бре́жу, бре́дишь] **1,** to be delirious; rave. **2,** *(with instr.)* colloq. to be crazy (about); be mad (about).

бре́дни *[gen.* -ней] *n. pl.* ravings; wild fantasy.

бредово́й *adj.* **1,** delirious. **2,** *fig.* nonsensical.

бре́згать *v. impfv.* *[pfv.* побре́згать] *(with instr. or inf.)* **1,** to be squeamish about; have an aversion to. **2,** to disdain; shrink from: не бре́згать никаки́ми сре́дствами, to stop at nothing.

брезгли́вый *adj.* squeamish. —**брезгли́вость,** *n.f.* squeamishness.

брезе́нт *n.* tarpaulin. —**брезе́нтовый,** *adj.* tarpaulin.

бре́зжить *v. impfv.* **1,** to glimmer; gleam faintly. **2,** *impers.* to dawn; get light. *Also,* бре́зжиться, *refl.*

брело́к *n.* charm *(on a chain or bracelet).*

бре́мя *[gen., dat., & prepl.* бре́мени; *instr.* бре́менем] *n. neut.* burden.

бре́нный *adj., obs.* perishable. —**бре́нные оста́нки,** mortal remains.

бренча́ть *v. impfv.* *[pres.* -чу́, -чи́шь] **1,** *v.i. (of inanimate objects)* to jingle; clink. **2,** *v.t. (with instr.)* to jingle; clink (something). **3,** *(with на* + *prepl.)* colloq. to strum.

брести́ *v. impfv.* *[pres.* бреду́, бредёшь; *past* брёл, брела́, брело́] to trudge along; drag oneself along.

брете́лька (тэ) *[gen. pl.* -лек] *n.* strap *(of an undergarment).*

бреха́ть *v. impfv.* *[pfv.* брехну́ть; *pres.* брешу́, бре́шешь] *colloq.* **1,** to bark. **2,** to tell lies.

бреху́н *[gen.* -хуна́] *n.m.* *[fem.* -ху́нья] *colloq.* liar.

брешь *n.f.* breach; gap.

бре́ющий *pres. active part. of* брить. —*adj., in* бре́ющий полёт, low-altitude flight.

бриг *n.* brig *(ship).*

брига́да *n.* **1,** *mil.* brigade. **2,** team; crew; brigade *(of workers).* —**бригади́р,** *n.* foreman.

бридж *n., cards* bridge.

бри́джи *[gen.* -жей] *n. pl.* breeches.

бриз *n.* sea breeze.

брике́т *n.* briquette.

бриллиа́нт *also,* брилья́нт *n.* (cut) diamond. —**бриллиа́нтовый,** брилья́нтовый, *adj.* diamond.

брита́нский *adj.* British.

бри́тва *n.* razor.

бри́твенный *adj.* shaving *(attrib.):* бри́твенные принадле́жности, shaving equipment.

бри́тый *adj.* clean-shaven.

брить *v. impfv.* *[pfv.* побри́ть; *pres.* бре́ю, бре́ешь] to shave.

бритьё *n.* shaving; shave.

бри́ться *v.r.impfv.* *[pfv.* побри́ться; *pres.* бре́юсь, бре́ешься] to shave (oneself); get a shave.

бри́чка *[gen. pl.* -чек] *n.* light cart or carriage.

бровь *[pl.* бро́ви, -ве́й, -вя́м] *n.f.* eyebrow. —**попа́сть не в бровь, а в глаз,** to hit the nail on the head.

брод *n.* ford.

броди́льный *adj.* fermenting *(attrib.).*

броди́ть *v. impfv.* *[pres.* брожу́, бро́дишь] **1,** to wander; roam. **2,** to ferment.

бродя́га *n.m.* tramp; vagrant; vagabond; hobo.

бродя́жничать *v. impfv., colloq.* **1,** to lead the life of a tramp. **2,** to wander; roam. *Also,* бродя́жить.

бродя́жничество *n.* **1,** vagrancy. **2,** wandering.

бродя́чий *adj.* **1,** wandering; itinerant. **2,** *(of a dog or cat)* stray. **3,** nomadic.

броже́ние *n.* **1,** fermentation. **2,** *fig.* ferment.

бро́кколи *n.f. indecl.* broccoli.

бром *n.* **1,** bromine. **2,** *med.* bromide. —**броми́д,** *n., chem.* bromide. —**бро́мистый,** *adj.* bromide: бро́мистый ка́лий, potassium bromide.

бронеавтомоби́ль *n.m.* armored car.

бронебо́йный *adj.* armor-piercing.

броневи́к *[gen.* -вика́] *n.* = **бронеавтомоби́ль.**

бронево́й *adj.* armored. —**бронева́я плита́;** бронево́й лист, armor plate; armor plating.

бронемашина *n.* armored car.

броненосец [*gen.* -сца] *n.* **1**, *hist.* battleship. **2**, armadillo.

броненосный *adj.* armored: броненосный крейсер, armored cruiser.

бронепоезд *n.* armored train.

бронетанковый *adj.* armored: бронетанковые войска, armored troops.

бронетранспортёр *n.* armored personnel carrier.

бронза *n.* bronze.

бронзировать *v. impfv. & pfv.* [*pres.* -рую, -руешь] to bronze.

бронзовый *adj.* **1**, bronze; made of bronze. **2**, bronze (*in color*).

бронированный *adj.* armored. **—бронированный кулак**, mailed fist.

бронировать *v. impfv. & pfv.* [*pfv. also* забронировать; *pres.* -рую, -руешь] to reserve; book.

бронировать *v. impfv. & pfv.* [*pfv. also* забронировать; *pres.* -рую, -руешь] to armor; cover with armor.

бронтозавр *n.* brontosaurus.

бронхи *n. pl.* [*sing.* бронх] bronchi; bronchial tubes. **—бронхиальный**, *adj.* bronchial.

бронхит *n.* bronchitis.

броня *n.* reservation (*advance order*).

броня *n.* armor.

бросать *v. impfv.* [*pfv.* бросить] **1**, to throw; toss. **2**, to cast (a shadow, glance, etc.). **3**, to throw away. **4**, to abandon; forsake; desert. **5**, to give up; quit: бросить курить, to give up/quit smoking. **6**, *impers.* to careen: машину бросало из стороны в сторону, the car careened from side to side. **7**, *impers.* to break into: его бросило в пот, he broke into a sweat. **—бросать деньги на ветер**, to throw money away. **—бросать жребий**, to cast lots; decide something by chance. **—бросать оружие**, to throw down one's weapons. **—бросать якорь**, to cast *or* drop anchor. **—брось!; бросьте!**, stop!; stop it!

бросаться *v.r. impfv.* [*pfv.* броситься] **1**, to rush; dash; fall; jump. **2**, (with *inf.*) to hasten (to). **3**, [*impfv. only*] (*with instr.*) to throw (something) at each other. **—бросаться в глаза**, to be striking; catch the eye. **—бросаться деньгами**, to toss money around. **—бросаться словами**, to make irresponsible statements; make idle promises.

бросить [*infl.* брошу, бросишь] *v., pfv. of* бросать. **—броситься**, *refl., pfv. of* бросаться.

броский *adj., colloq.* **1**, garish; loud. **2**, striking.

бросовый *adj., colloq.* **1**, cheap; trashy; worthless. **2**, throwaway; disposable. **—бросовые цены**, prices below cost; giveaway prices.

бросок [*gen.* -ска] *n.* **1**, throw. **2**, *sports* shot. **3**, spurt; burst of speed.

брошь *n.f.* brooch. *Also,* брошка.

брошюра (шу) *n.* pamphlet; brochure.

брус [*pl.* брусья, брусьев] *n.* **1**, beam. **2**, *pl., sports* bars: параллельные брусья, parallel bars.

брусника *n.* **1**, cowberries. **2**, a (single) cowberry.

брусок [*gen.* -ска] *n.* **1**, bar. **2**, whetstone.

бруствер *n.* breastwork; parapet.

брусчатка *n.* **1**, paving stones; paving blocks. **2**, *colloq.* paved road.

брусчатый *adj.* made of paving blocks.

брутто *adj. & adv. indecl.* gross: вес брутто, gross weight; цена брутто, gross price.

брыжи [*gen.* -жей] *n. pl., obs.* frilled collar; ruff.

брызгать *v. impfv.* [*pfv.* брызнуть; *pres.* брызжу, брызжешь *or* брызгаю, брызгаешь] **1**, (*with instr.*) to sprinkle; splash (a liquid). **2**, to sprinkle (something with a liquid). **3**, to spurt; gush; shoot forth; shoot out. **—брызгаться**, *refl.* [*impfv. only*] **1**, (*with instr.*) to sprinkle; splash (a liquid); spray oneself (with a liquid). **2**, to splash each other.

брызги [*gen.* брызг] *n. pl.* spray.

брызговик [*gen.* -вика] *n.* mudguard.

брызнуть *v., pfv. of* брызгать.

брыкать *v. impfv.* [*pfv.* брыкнуть] to kick. *Also,* брыкаться, *refl.*

брынза *n.* cheese made from sheep's milk.

брюзга *n.m. & f.* grouch.

брюзгливый *adj.* grouchy; grumpy.

брюзжать *v. impfv.* [*pres.* -зжу, -зжишь] to grumble; grouch.

брюква *n.* rutabaga.

брюки [*gen.* брюк] *n. pl.* trousers; pants.

брюнет *n.m.* [*fem.* -нетка] brunette.

брюссельский (сэ) *adj., in* брюссельская капуста, Brussels sprouts.

брюхо *n.* **1**, belly (*of an animal*). **2**, *colloq.* paunch.

брюшина *n.* peritoneum. **—воспаление брюшины**, peritonitis.

брюшко [*pl.* -ки, -ков] *n.* paunch; potbelly.

брюшной *adj.* abdominal. **—брюшной тиф**, typhoid.

брякать *v. impfv.* [*pfv.* брякнуть] *colloq.* **1**, *v.i.* to rattle; clang; clatter; jingle. **2**, *v.t.* (*with instr.*) to rattle; jingle. **3**, to slam down. **4**, to blurt out. **—брякаться**, *refl., colloq.* to fall heavily; come crashing down.

бряцание *n.* clank; jingling; jangling. **—бряцание оружием**, saber rattling.

бряцать *v. impfv.* **1**, *v.i.* to clank; jingle; jangle. **2**, *v.i.* (*with на* + *prepl.*) to strum. **3**, to jingle; jangle. **—бряцать оружием**, to brandish weapons; indulge in saber rattling.

бубен [*gen.* -бна] *n.* tambourine.

бубенцы *n. pl.* [*sing.* бубенец] small bells; sleigh bells.

бубенчики *n. pl.* [*sing.* бубенчик] = бубенцы.

бублик *n.* thick bagel.

бубнить *v. impfv.* [*pfv.* пробубнить] *colloq.* **1**, to mumble; mutter. **2**, [*impfv. only*] to drone (on and on).

бубновый *adj., cards* of diamonds: бубновый король, king of diamonds.

бубны [*gen.* бубён; *dat.* бубнам] *n. pl., cards* diamonds.

бубон *n.* bubo.

бубонный *adj.* bubonic. **—бубонная чума**, bubonic plague.

бугор [*gen.* -гра] *n.* **1**, mound; knoll. **2**, bump; lump.

бугорок [*gen.* -рка] *n.* **1**, *dim. of* бугор. **2**, protuberance. **3**, *med.* tubercle.

бугорчатый *adj.* **1**, covered with lumps. **2**, tuberous.

бугристый *adj.* **1**, hilly; uneven. **2**, bumpy.

буддизм *n.* Buddhism. **—буддийский**, *adj.* Buddhist.

буддист *n.m.* [*fem.* -дистка] Buddhist.

будет *v.*, *3rd person sing. of* быть. **—interj., colloq.** enough!; that'll do! **—что будет, то будет**, what will be will be.

будильник *n.* alarm clock.

будить *v. impfv.* [*pres.* бужу, будишь] **1**, [*pfv.* разбуди́ть] to waken; awaken. **2**, [*pfv.* пробуди́ть] *fig.* to arouse; evoke.

бу́дка [*gen. pl.* -док] *n.* booth. —**карау́льная бу́дка**, sentry box. —**телефо́нная бу́дка**, telephone booth.

бу́дни [*gen.* -ней] *n. pl.* **1**, weekdays. **2**, *fig.* humdrum existence.

бу́дний *adj., in* бу́дний день, weekday.

бу́дничный *also,* бу́днишний *adj.* **1**, = бу́дний. **2**, everyday; ordinary. **3**, *fig.* humdrum; routine.

будора́жить *v. impfv.* [*pfv.* взбудора́жить] *colloq.* to stir up; rouse; excite.

бу́дто *conj.* **1**, that *(implying doubt as to the truth of a statement):* говоря́т, бу́дто она́ за́мужем, they say she's married. **2**, [*also,* как бу́дто] as if: как бу́дто по волшебству́, as if by magic. У вас тако́й вид, бу́дто вы не по́няли, you look as if you did not understand. —*particle, colloq.* **1**, [*also,* как бу́дто] apparently: дождь как бу́дто ко́нчился, the rain appears to have stopped. **2**, really?: уж бу́дто ты так спеши́шь домо́й?, are you really in such a hurry to get home?

будуа́р *n.* boudoir.

бу́дучи *verbal adv. of* быть, being: бу́дучи в Ми́нске, being in Minsk; while in Minsk.

бу́дущее *n., decl. as an adj.* the future.

бу́дущий *adj.* **1**, future. **2**, next: в бу́дущем году́, next year.

бу́дущность *n.f.* future.

будь *v., imperative of* быть. ♦*Also, in contrary-to-fact constructions,* were: будь он сейча́с жив, were he alive today; будь я на её ме́сте, if I were in her place. —**будь то...**, be it... —**будь, что бу́дет**, come what may. —**не будь** (+ *gen.*), were it not for...

бу́ер [*pl.* буера́] *n.* iceboat.

бужени́на *n.* boiled pork.

бузина́ *n.* elder *(shrub).*

буй [*pl.* буи́, буёв] *n.* buoy.

бу́йвол *n.* buffalo. —**бу́йволовый**, *adj.* buffalo *(attrib.).*

бу́йный *adj.* **1**, wild; boisterous; unruly; rambunctious. **2**, *(of natural phenomena)* violent; stormy. **3**, *(of vegetation)* lush; luxuriant.

бу́йство *n.* unruly behavior.

бу́йствовать *v. impfv.* [*pres.* -ствую, -ствуешь] to run wild; run riot; go on a rampage; run amuck.

бук *n.* beech (tree).

бу́ка *n.m. & f., colloq.* **1**, bogeyman. **2**, surly, unfriendly person. —**смотре́ть бу́кой**, to look surly.

бука́шка [*gen. pl.* -шек] *n.* insect; bug.

бу́ква *n.* **1**, letter *(of the alphabet).* **2**, *fig. (with gen.)* the letter (of): бу́ква зако́на, the letter of the law. —**бу́ква в бу́кву**, word for word; literally.

буква́льный *adj.* literal. —**буква́льно**, *adv.* literally.

буква́рь [*gen.* -варя́] *n.m.* primer; book of ABC's.

бу́квенный *adj.* letter *(attrib.).*

буквое́д *n.* pedant.

буке́т *n.* bouquet. —**буке́тик**, *n.* small bouquet.

букини́ст *n.* secondhand book dealer. —**букинисти́ческий**, *adj.* secondhand-book *(attrib.).*

букле́т *n.* booklet.

букме́кер *n.* bookmaker.

бу́ковый *adj.* **1**, beech *(attrib.).* **2**, beechwood *(attrib.).*

букси́р *n.* **1**, tugboat. **2**, towline; towrope. —**брать на букси́р**, to take in tow *(lit. & fig.).*

букси́ровать *v. impfv.* [*pres.* -рую, -руешь] to tow.

букси́ровка *n.* towing.

буксова́ть *v. impfv.* [*pres.* -су́ет] *(of wheels)* to spin around *(without gaining traction).*

булава́ *n.* mace *(weapon).*

була́вка [*gen. pl.* -вок] *n.* pin. —**англи́йская була́вка**, safety pin. —**де́ньги на була́вки**, pin money.

була́вочный *adj.* pin *(attrib.).*

бу́лка [*gen. pl.* -лок] *n.* roll; bun.

бу́лла *n.* (papal) bull.

бу́лочка [*gen. pl.* -чек] *n.* small roll; bun.

бу́лочная *n., decl. as an adj.* bakery.

бу́лочник *n.* baker.

бултьίх *interj., colloq.* plop!; splash!

бултыха́ться *v.r. impfv.* [*pfv.* бултьίхнуться *or* бултыхну́ться] *colloq.* **1**, to plunge; flop; plop *(into water).* **2**, [*impfv. only*] to flop about; thrash about.

булы́жник *n.* cobblestone. —**булы́жный**, *adj.* cobbled; cobblestone *(attrib.).*

бульва́р *n.* public walk; promenade; mall.

бульва́рный *adj.* **1**, of a бульва́р. **2**, *fig. (of literature, a newspaper, etc.)* trashy.

бульдо́г *n.* bulldog.

бульдо́зер *n.* bulldozer.

бу́льканье *n.* gurgling; gurgle.

бу́лькать *v. impfv.* to gurgle.

бульо́н *n.* clear soup; broth; consommé; bouillon.

бум *n.* **1**, *econ.* boom. **2**, (media) sensation. —*interj.* boom!

бума́га *n.* **1**, paper. **2**, *pl.* papers; documents. **3**, *archaic* cotton. —**це́нные бума́ги**, securities.

бума́жка [*gen. pl.* -жек] *n.* **1**, piece of paper. **2**, *colloq.* bill; bank note: бума́жка в пять до́лларов, five-dollar bill.

бума́жник *n.* wallet; billfold.

бума́жный *adj.* **1**, paper. **2**, cotton.

бумера́нг *n.* boomerang.

бу́нкер [*pl.* бункера́] *n.* bunker; storage bin.

бунт *n.* **1**, [*gen.* бу́нта; *pl.* бу́нты] riot; uprising; rebellion; mutiny. **2**, [*gen.* бунта́; *pl.* бунты́] bundle; bale.

бунта́рский *adj.* rebellious; mutinous. —**бунта́рство**, *n.* rebelliousness.

бунта́рь [*gen.* -таря́] *n.m.* **1**, rioter. **2**, rebel.

бунтова́ть *v. impfv.* [*pres.* -ту́ю, -ту́ешь] **1**, [*pfv.* взбунтова́ться] to rebel; revolt; mutiny. **2**, [*pfv.* взбунтова́ть] *archaic* to incite to rebellion.

бунтовщи́к [*gen.* -щика́] *n.* rioter; rebel.

бур *n.* **1**, drill; auger. **2**, Boer.

бура́ *n.* borax.

бура́в [*gen.* -рава́] *n.* auger; gimlet.

бура́вить *v. impfv.* [*pfv.* пробура́вить; *pres.* -влю, -вишь] to bore; drill.

бура́вчик *n.* auger; gimlet.

бура́к [*gen.* -рака́] *n., colloq.* beet.

бура́н *n.* blizzard.

бургоми́стр *n.* burgomaster.

бурда́ *n., colloq.* slop.

бурдю́к [*gen.* -дюка́] *n.* wineskin.

буреве́стник *n.* petrel *(bird).*

буре́лом *n.* fallen trees.

буре́ние *n.* boring; drilling.

буре́ть *v. impfv.* [*pfv.* побуре́ть] to become brown; turn brown.

буржуа́ *n.m. indecl.* bourgeois.

буржуази́я *n.* bourgeoisie. —**буржуа́зный**, *adj.* bourgeois.

бури́льный *adj.* boring *(attrib.);* drilling *(attrib.).*

бури́ть v. impfv. [pfv. **пробури́ть**] to bore; drill.

бу́рка [gen. pl. -рок] n. **1**, felt cloak (worn in the Caucasus). **2**, usu. pl. felt boot with a leather sole.

бу́ркать v. impfv. [pfv. **бу́ркнуть**] colloq. to mutter; growl.

бурла́к [gen. -лака́] n. bargeman.

бурле́ск n. burlesque.

бурли́вый adj. turbulent.

бурли́ть v. impfv. to seethe.

бу́рный adj. **1**, stormy. **2**, violent; wild. **3**, hectic; frantic. **4**, rapid.

бурово́й adj. boring (attrib.); drilling (attrib.). —**бурова́я вы́шка**, oil derrick.

бу́рский adj. Boer.

буру́н [gen. -руна́] n. breaker (wave).

бурунду́к [gen. -дука́] n. chipmunk.

бурча́ть v. impfv. [pfv. **пробурча́ть**; pres. -чу́, -чи́шь] colloq. **1**, to mumble; mutter. **2**, (of one's stomach) to rumble.

бу́рый adj. brown.

бурья́н n. (tall) weeds.

бу́ря n. storm. —**бу́ря в стака́не воды́**, tempest in a teapot.

буря́т [gen. pl. буря́т] n.m. [fem. -ря́тка] Buryat (one of a people inhabiting southern Siberia). —**буря́тский**, adj. Buryat.

бу́сина n. bead. Also, **бу́синка**.

буссо́ль n.f. surveyor's compass.

бу́сы [gen. бус] n. pl. beads.

бута́н n. butane.

бутафо́рия n., theat. properties; stage props. —**бутафо́р**, n. property man. —**бутафо́рский**, adj. of or for stage props.

бутербро́д (тэ) n. sandwich.

бути́л n. butyl.

бутиле́н n. butylene.

буто́н n. bud.

бутонье́рка [gen. pl. -рок] n. boutonniere.

буту́з n., colloq. roly-poly child.

буты́лка [gen. pl. -лок] n. bottle. —**буты́лочка**, n. small bottle.

буты́лочный adj. **1**, bottle (attrib.). **2**, bottled. —**буты́лочный цвет**, bottle green.

буты́ль n.f. large bottle.

бу́фер [pl. буфера́] n. **1**, bumper. **2**, fig. buffer. —**бу́ферный**, adj. buffer (attrib.).

буфе́т n. **1**, buffet; sideboard. **2**, snack bar.

буфе́тная n., decl. as an adj. pantry.

буфе́тчик n.m. [fem. -чица] **1**, person who works behind a counter. **2**, bartender; fem. barmaid.

буффо́н n. buffoon. —**буффона́да**, n. buffoonery.

буха́нка [gen. pl. -нок] n. loaf of bread.

бу́хать v. impfv. [pfv. **бу́хнуть**] colloq. **1**, to bang: бу́хнуть кулако́м в or по, to bang one's fist on. **2**, to drop (something) with a thud. **3**, (of a door) to slam; (of a shot) be heard. —**бу́хаться**, refl., colloq. to throw oneself; plop.

бухга́лтер n. bookkeeper; accountant.

бухгалте́рия n. **1**, bookkeeping; accounting. **2**, bookkeeping department; accounting department. —**бухга́лтерский**, adj. bookkeeping (attrib.); accounting (attrib.).

бу́хнуть[1] v. impfv. [pfv. **разбу́хнуть**; past бух, -ла] to swell; swell up.

бу́хнуть[2] [past бу́хнул] v., pfv. of **бу́хать**. —**бу́хнуться**, refl., pfv. of **бу́хаться**.

бу́хта n. small bay.

бу́хточка [gen. pl. -чек] n. cove; inlet.

бу́ча n., colloq. row; fuss.

бушева́ть v. impfv. [pres. -шу́ю, -шу́ешь] (of a fire, storm, etc.) to rage.

бу́шель n.m. bushel.

бушла́т n. pea jacket.

бушпри́т n. bowsprit.

буя́н n. rowdy; ruffian; roughneck.

буя́нить v. impfv. to run wild; run riot; go on a rampage; run amuck.

бы also, **б** particle, used only with the inf. or past tense of a verb **1**, would; should: я бы хоте́л(а) спроси́ть..., I would/should like to ask... Я бы сказа́л(а) вам е́сли бы вы спроси́ли, I would have told you if you had asked. **2**, used to express a polite suggestion: ты бы бро́сил кури́ть, you should give up smoking. Вам лу́чше бы пойти́ самому́, you had better go yourself. **3**, used to express a profound wish: был бы он здесь!, if only he were here!

быва́ло particle, colloq. would (often): он, быва́ло, ча́сто заходи́л к нам, he would often come to see us.

быва́лый adj. **1**, obs. former; olden; bygone. **2**, colloq. experienced; worldly-wise. —**э́то де́ло быва́лое**, it's nothing new; it has happened before.

быва́ть v. impfv. **1**, to be (regularly or customarily): он быва́ет в магази́не ка́ждый день, he is in the store every day. Он ча́сто быва́ет у нас, he is often over at our house. **2**, to happen: как э́то ча́сто быва́ет, as often happens. **3**, to take place; be held: заседа́ния быва́ют раз в ме́сяц, meetings are held once a month. —**как ни в чём не быва́ло**, as if nothing happened.

бы́вший adj. former; ex-.

бык [gen. быка́] n. **1**, bull. **2**, pier (of a bridge). —**бой быко́в**, bullfight; bullfighting. —**взять быка́ за рога́**, to take the bull by the horns.

были́на n. Russian epic poem.

были́нка [gen. pl. -нок] n. blade of grass.

бы́ло particle (without stress) just about to; on the point of: он встал бы́ло из-за стола́, когда́..., he was about to get up from the table when...

было́й adj. former; bygone. —**было́е**, n. the past.

быль n.f. **1**, archaic fact; event. **2**, true story.

былье́ n., obs. weeds. —**былье́м поросло́**, lost in oblivion.

быстрина́ [pl. -три́ны] n. rapids.

бы́стро adv. fast; quickly; rapidly.

быстроно́гий adj. fleet-footed.

быстрораствори́мый adj. dissolving quickly. —**быстрораствори́мый ко́фе**, instant coffee.

быстрота́ n. speed; rapidity.

быстрохо́дный adj. fast-moving; high-speed.

бы́стрый adj. fast; quick; rapid; swift.

быт [2nd loc. быту́] n. **1**, way of life; life. **2**, daily life.

бытие́ n. **1**, being; existence. **2**, cap., Bib. Genesis: Кни́га Бытия́, the book of Genesis.

бы́тность n.f., in **в бы́тность** (мою́, его́, etc.), during one's stay (in); (with instr.) when one was (in a certain capacity).

бытова́ть v. impfv. [pres. -ту́ет] to exist.

бытово́й adj. pert. to daily life; everyday.

быть v., used only in the future [бу́ду, бу́дешь] and the past [был, была́, бы́ло, бы́ли; neg. не́ был, не была́, не́ было, не́ были] to be. —**не́ было** (with gen.), *expressing the absence of something in the past:* там никогó нé было, there was no one there. —былá не былá!, come what may; whatever the risk. —как бы то ни было, be that as it may. —как быть?, what are we to do?; what is to be done? —так и быть, so be it. *See also* бýдет, бýдь, было.

бытьё *n., archaic* life; existence.

бычáчий [*fem.* -чья] *adj.* ox (attrib.); bovine. *Also,* **бычий** [*fem.* -чья].

бычóк [*gen.* -чкá] *n.* **1,** young bull; young ox. **2,** goby (fish). **3,** *colloq.* cigarette butt.

бювáр *n.* letter case with leaves of blotting paper.

бюджéт *n.* budget. —**бюджéтный,** *adj.* budget (attrib.); budgetary.

бюллетéнь *n.m.* **1,** bulletin. **2,** ballot. **3,** *colloq.* doctor's certificate (stating that one is ill).

бюргер *n.* burgher.

бюрó *n. indecl.* **1,** office; bureau. **2,** writing desk. —бюрó нахóдок, lost and found department. —спрáвочное бюрó, information office.

бюрокрáт *n.* bureaucrat.

бюрократи́зм *n.* **1,** bureaucracy. **2,** red tape.

бюрокрáтия *n.* bureaucracy. —**бюрократи́ческий,** *adj.* bureaucratic.

бюст *n.* **1,** *sculpture* bust. **2,** bosom; bust.

бюстгáльтер (тэ) *n.* brassiere.

бязь *n.f.* heavy cloth; sheeting.

В

В, в *n. neut.* third letter of the Russian alphabet.

в *also,* **во** *prep.* A, *with acc.* **1,** to: ходи́ть в шкóлу, to go to school. **2,** into: попáсть в ловýшку, to fall into a trap; вложи́ть письмó в конвéрт, to put the letter into an envelope. **3,** for (a destination): уйти́ в шкóлу, to leave for school. **4,** in (a certain amount of time): одéться в однý минýту, to get dressed in one minute. **5,** (with the time of day) at: в три часá, at three o'clock. **6,** (with days of the week) on: в срéду, on Wednesday. **7,** a; per: два рáза в недéлю, twice a week. **8,** in numerical comparisons: в два рáза бóльше, twice as much. B, with prepl. **1,** in; at: в шкóле, in/at school. **2,** (with months, years, centuries) in: в апрéле, in April; в 1941-ом годý, in 1941; в 17-ом вéке, in the 17th century. **3,** at a distance of: в двух киломéтрах от гости́ницы, two kilometers from the hotel.

в- *also,* **во-, въ-** *prefix, indicating motion into:* входи́ть, to enter; вклáдывать, to insert.

ва-бáнк *adv., in* идти́ ва-бáнк, to go for broke; shoot the works.

вавилóнский *adj.* Babylonian. —**вавилóнская бáшня,** Tower of Babel.

вáга *n.* **1,** weighing machine. **2,** lever; crowbar.

вагóн *n.* (railroad) car; (trolley) car. —**вагóн-ресторáн,** dining car; diner.

вагонéтка [*gen. pl.* -ток] *n.* trolley; truck; car. —**подвеснáя вагонéтка,** cable car.

вагóнный *adj.* car (attrib.); wagon (attrib.).

вагоновожáтый *n., decl. as an adj.* motorman (on a streetcar).

важнéйший *adj.* most important; paramount.

важнéцкий *adj., colloq.* excellent; first-rate.

вáжничать *v. impfv., colloq.* to put on airs; give oneself airs.

вáжно *adv.* proudly; with an air of importance. —*adj., used predicatively* important: э́то не вáжно, it's not important; мне вáжно знать, it is important for me to know.

вáжность *n.f.* **1,** importance. **2,** self-importance; pomposity.

вáжный *adj.* [*short form* вáжен, важнá, вáжно] **1,** important. **2,** self-important; pompous.

вáза *n.* vase; bowl.

вазели́н *n.* vaseline.

вазóн *n.* flowerpot.

вакáнсия *n.* vacancy; opening. —**вакáнтный,** *adj.* vacant; unfilled.

вáкса *n.* black shoe polish.

вáксить *v. impfv.* [*pfv.* навáксить; *pres.* вáкшу, вáксишь] *colloq.* to shine; polish (shoes).

вакуóля [*gen. pl.* -лей] *n.* vacuole.

вáкуум *n.* vacuum. —**вáкуум-насóс,** vacuum pump.

вакци́на *n.* vaccine. —**вакцинáция,** *n.* vaccination.

вакцини́ровать *v. impfv. & pfv.* [*pres.* -рую, -руешь] to vaccinate.

вал [*pl.* валы́] *n.* **1,** earthen wall; bank; embankment. **2,** large wave; billow. **3,** shaft: колéнчатый вал, crankshaft. —**крепостнóй вал,** rampart.

валéжник *n.* windfallen branches.

валёк [*gen.* -лькá] *n.* **1,** roller. **2,** swingletree.

вáленок [*gen.* -нка; *gen. pl.* -нок] *n.* felt boot.

валéнтность *n.f.* valence.

валерьяна *also,* **валериáна** *n.* valerian. —**валерья́нка,** *n., colloq.* valerian drops. —**валерья́новый,** *adj.* valerian.

валéт *n., cards* jack.

вáлик *n.* **1,** roller. **2,** platen (on a typewriter). **3,** bolster (pillow).

вали́ть[1] *v. impfv.* [*pfv.* свали́ть; *pres.* валю́, вáлишь] **1,** [*pfv. also* повали́ть] to knock down; fell; overturn; topple. **2,** (with в + *acc.*) to throw (into); toss (into); dump (into): вали́ть в кýчу, to toss into a pile. **3,** (with на + *acc.*) *colloq.* to blame: вали́ть (винý) на когó-нибудь, to put the blame on someone. —**вали́ть с**

больно́й головы́ на здоро́вую, to lay the blame at someone else's doorstep.

вали́ть² *v. impfv.* [*pres.* вали́т] **1,** *(of people)* to flock; throng. **2,** *(of snow)* to fall heavily; *(of smoke)* to pour out.

вали́ться *v. r. impfv.* [*pfv.* повали́ться *or* свали́ться; *pres.* валю́сь, ва́лишься] to fall. —**вали́ться с ног,** to be exhausted; be falling off one's feet.

ва́лка *n.* chopping down; felling *(of trees).*

ва́лкий *adj.* [*short form* ва́лок, валка́, ва́лко] unsteady; shaky; wobbly. —**ни ша́тко ни ва́лко,** fair to middling; so-so.

валли́ец [*gen.* -и́йца] *n.* Welshman. —**вали́йский,** *adj.* Welsh.

валово́й *adj., econ.* gross: валово́й дохо́д, gross income.

вало́м *adv., colloq., in* вало́м вали́ть, to flock; throng.

валто́рна *n.* French horn.

валу́н [*gen.* -луна́] *n.* boulder.

ва́льдшнеп (нэ) *n.* woodcock.

вальс *n.* waltz.

вальси́ровать *v. impfv.* [*pres.* -рую, -руешь] to waltz.

вальцева́ть *v. impfv.* [*pres.* -цу́ю, -цу́ешь] to roll; mill (metal).

вальцо́вка *n.* rolling; milling. —**вальцо́вый,** *adj.* rolling: вальцо́вая ме́льница, rolling mill.

валю́та *n.* currency.

валю́тный *adj.* currency *(attrib.).* —**валю́тный курс,** rate of exchange.

валя́льщик *n.* fuller *(of cloth).*

ва́ляный *adj. (of boots)* made of felt.

валя́ть *v. impfv.* **1,** [*pfv.* повала́ть] *cooking* to roll *(e.g.* in bread crumbs). **2,** *(with* по) to drag (along). **3,** [*pfv.* сваля́ть] to full (cloth). **4,** *in* валя́ть дурака́, to play the fool. —**валя́ться,** *refl.* [*pfv.* повала́ться] **1,** to roll; wallow. **2,** [*impfv. only*] to lie (scattered) about. **3,** to lie around; lounge; loll.

вам *pron., dat. of* вы.

ва́ми *pron., instr. of* вы.

вампи́р *n.* **1,** vampire. **2,** vampire bat.

вана́дий *n.* vanadium.

вани́ль *n.f.* vanilla. —**вани́льный,** *adj.* vanilla.

ва́нна *n.* **1,** bath. **2,** bathtub.

ва́нная *n., decl. as an adj.* bathroom.

ва́нночка [*gen. pl.* -чек] *n., dim. of* ва́нна (bath). —**глазна́я ва́нночка,** eyecup.

ва́нный *adj.* bath *(attrib.):* ва́нная ко́мната, bathroom.

ва́нька-вста́нька *n.m.* self-righting toy doll.

вар *n.* pitch. —**сапо́жный вар,** cobbler's wax.

вара́н *n.* monitor lizard.

ва́рвар *n.* barbarian. —**варвари́зм,** *n.* (literary) barbarism. —**ва́рварский,** *adj.* barbarian; barbarous; barbaric. —**ва́рварство,** *n.* barbarity.

ва́режка [*gen. pl.* -жек] *n.* mitten.

варене́ц [*gen.* -нца́] *n.* fermented boiled milk.

варе́ние *n.* boiling.

варе́ник *n.* dumpling filled with cheese or fruit.

варёный *adj.* boiled.

варе́нье *n.* jam.

вариа́нт *n.* **1,** version. **2,** possibility; alternative.

вариа́ция *n.* variation.

варико́зный *adj.* varicose.

вари́ть *v. impfv.* [*pfv.* свари́ть; *pres.* варю́, ва́ришь]

1, to boil; cook. **2,** to brew (beer); make (soap); weld (metals). —**вари́ться,** *refl.* to boil; be boiling; cook; be cooking.

ва́рка *n.* boiling.

варьете́ (тэ) *n. neut. indecl.* variety show; floor show.

варьи́ровать *v. impfv.* [*pres.* -рую, -руешь] to vary; modify. —**варьи́роваться,** *refl.* to vary.

варя́г *n.* Varangian. —**варя́жский,** *adj.* Varangian.

вас *pron., gen., acc., & prepl. of* вы.

василёк [*gen.* -лька́] *n.* cornflower.

васса́л *n.* vassal. —**васса́льный,** *adj.* vassal *(attrib.).*

ва́та *n.* **1,** absorbent cotton. **2,** wadding; padding; stuffing.

вата́га *n., colloq.* crowd; throng; gang.

ватерли́ния (тэ) *n.* waterline.

ватерпа́с (тэ) *n.* spirit level.

ватерпо́ло (тэ) *n. indecl.* water polo.

Ватика́н *n.* Vatican.

вати́н *n.* batting *(sewn into a garment for extra warmth).*

ва́тник *n., colloq.* quilted jacket.

ва́тный *adj.* wadded; quilted.

ватру́шка [*gen. pl.* -шек] *n.* pastry containing cheese or jam.

ватт [*gen. pl.* ватт] *n.* watt.

ва́фля [*gen. pl.* -фель] *n.* waffle. —**ва́фельница,** *n.* waffle iron.

ва́хта *n., naut.* watch: стоя́ть на ва́хте, to stand watch.

ва́хтенный *adj., naut.* watch *(attrib.).* —**ва́хтенный журна́л,** (ship's) log.

вахтёр *n.* (security) guard.

ваш [*fem.* ва́ша; *neut.* ва́ше; *pl.* ва́ши] *poss. adj. & pron.* your; yours.

вая́ние *n., obs.* sculpture. —**вая́тель,** *n.m., obs.* sculptor.

вая́ть *v. impfv.* [*pfv.* извая́ть] *obs.* to sculpture; chisel; carve; model.

вбега́ть *v. impfv.* [*pfv.* вбежа́ть] **1,** to run in. **2,** *(with* в + *acc.)* to run into. **3,** *(with* на + *acc.)* to run up (a hill, stairs, etc.).

вбежа́ть [*infl. like* бежа́ть] *v., pfv. of* вбега́ть.

вбива́ть *v. impfv.* [*pfv.* вбить] to hammer in; drive in. —**вбива́ть в го́лову** (+ *dat.),* to get it through someone's head. —**вбива́ть себе́ в го́лову,** to get it into one's head.

вбира́ть *v. impfv.* [*pfv.* вобра́ть] to absorb; take in; draw in.

вбить [*infl.* вобью́, вобьёшь] *v., pfv. of* вбива́ть.

вблизи́ *adv.* **1,** near; nearby; close by. **2,** up close. —*prep., with gen.* near. —**вблизи́ от,** not far from.

вбок *adv.* to the side; to one side.

вброд *adv.* by wading: переходи́ть вброд, to wade across; ford.

вва́ливать *v. impfv.* [*pfv.* ввали́ть] *(with* в + *acc.) colloq.* to throw (into); toss (into). —**вва́ливаться,** *refl.* **1,** *(of one's cheeks)* to become sunken; become hollow. **2,** *(with* в + *acc.) colloq.* to fall into; plunge into. **3,** *(with* в + *acc.) colloq.* to burst into.

ввали́ть [*inf.* ввалю́, вва́лишь] *v., pfv. of* вва́ливать. —**ввали́ться,** *refl., pfv. of* вва́ливаться.

введе́ние *n.* introduction.

ввезти́ [*infl. like* везти́] *v., pfv. of* ввози́ть.

ввек *adv., colloq.* never.

вверга́ть *v. impfv.* [*pfv.* вве́ргнуть] **1,** *obs.* to hurl; toss. **2,** *fig.* to plunge; throw (into despair, confusion, etc.).

вве́ргнуть [*past* вверг, -ла] *v., pfv. of* вверга́ть.

вве́рить *v., pfv. of* вверя́ть. —**вве́риться,** *refl., pfv. of* вверя́ться.

вве́ртывать *v. impfv.* [*pfv.* вверну́ть] **1,** to screw in. **2,** *colloq.* to interject; interpose; put in (a word, remark, etc.).

вверх *adv., expressing motion or direction* up; upward(s). —**вверх дном; вверх нога́ми,** upside down; topsy-turvy. —**вверх по,** up: вверх по тече́нию, upstream.

вверху́ *adv., expressing location* **1,** above; overhead. **2,** at the top. —*prep., with gen.* at the top of.

вверя́ть *v. impfv.* [*pfv.* вве́рить] to entrust; confide. —**вверя́ться,** *refl. (with dat.)* to entrust oneself to; place oneself in the hands of.

ввести́ [*infl. like* вести́] *v., pfv. of* вводи́ть.

вви́ду *prep., with gen.* in view of.

вви́нчивать *v. impfv.* [*pfv.* ввинти́ть] to screw in. —**вви́нчиваться,** *refl.* to screw in.

ввод *n.* **1,** *mech.* lead-in. **2,** bringing in(to). **3,** putting into: ввод в де́йствие, putting into operation. **4,** input.

вводи́ть *v. impfv.* [*pfv.* ввести́; *pres.* ввожу́, вво́дишь] **1,** to bring in; bring into. **2,** to lead in; lead into. *Also fig.:* вводи́ть в собла́зн, to lead into temptation. **3,** to introduce; institute; initiate. **4,** to include; incorporate. **5,** *med.* to inject. —**вводи́ть в бой,** to commit to battle. —**вводи́ть в де́йствие, 1,** to put into effect. **2,** to put into operation. —**вводи́ть в курс де́ла,** to brief; bring up to date. —**вводи́ть в расхо́д,** to put to expense. —**вводи́ть в строй,** to put into service; put into operation.

вво́дный *adj.* introductory. —**вво́дное сло́во,** *gram.* parenthetic word; introductory particle.

ввоз *n.* **1,** importing; importation. **2,** total imports.

ввози́ть *v. impfv.* [*pfv.* ввезти́; *pres.* ввожу́, вво́зишь] **1,** to import. **2,** *(with* в + *acc.)* to convey into; transport into. **3,** *(with* на + *acc.)* to convey up; convey to the top of.

вво́зный *adj.* **1,** import *(attrib.).* **2,** imported.

вво́лю *adv., colloq.* = вдо́воль.

ввысь *adv.* upward; high into the air.

ввяза́ть [*infl.* вяжу́, вя́жешь] *v., pfv. of* ввя́зывать. —**ввяза́ться,** *refl., pfv. of* ввя́зываться.

ввя́зывать *v. impfv.* [*pfv.* ввяза́ть] *(with* в + *acc.)* **1,** to knit in. **2,** *colloq.* to involve in; get (someone) mixed up in. —**ввя́зываться,** *refl. (with* в + *acc.) colloq.* to meddle (in); get mixed up (in); become involved (in).

вгиба́ть *v. impfv.* [*pfv.* вогну́ть] to bend inwards; curve inwards.

вглубь *adv.* deep inside; deep into the interior. —*prep., with gen.* deep into; far into.

вгляде́ться [*infl.* -жу́сь, -ди́шься] *v.r., pfv. of* вгля́дываться.

вгля́дываться *v.r. impfv.* [*pfv.* вгляде́ться] **1,** to look closely; take a good look. **2,** *(with* в + *acc.)* to peer into.

вгоня́ть *v. impfv.* [*pfv.* вогна́ть] *(with* в + *acc.)* **1,** to drive into; herd into. **2,** *colloq.* to hammer in; drive in. —**вгоня́ть в кра́ску,** to make (someone) blush. —**вгоня́ть в пот,** to make (someone) sweat *(from hard work).*

вдава́ться *v.r. impfv.* [*pfv.* вда́ться; *pres.* вдаю́сь, вдаёшься] *(with* в + *acc.)* **1,** to protrude into; jut out into. **2,** *fig.* to sink into; lapse into. **3,** *fig.* to go into; delve into. —**вдава́ться в кра́йности,** to go to extremes. —**вдава́ться в подро́бности,** to go into detail.

вдави́ть [*infl.* вдавлю́, вда́вишь] *v., pfv. of* вда́вливать.

вда́вливать *v. impfv.* [*pfv.* вдави́ть] **1,** to press in; force in. **2,** to batter in; dent.

вда́лбливать *v. impfv.* [*pfv.* вдолби́ть] *colloq.* to drum in; drill in: вдолби́ть что́-нибудь в го́лову (+ *dat.*), to drum/drill something into someone's head.

вдалеке́ *adv.* in the distance. —**вдалеке́ от,** far from; a long way from.

вдали́ *adv.* in the distance. —**вдали́ от,** far from; a long way from.

вдаль *adv.* into the distance.

вда́ться [*infl. like* да́ться] *v.r., pfv. of* вдава́ться.

вдвига́ть *v. impfv.* [*pfv.* вдви́нуть] *(with* в + *acc.)* to push into; thrust into.

вдво́е *adv.* **1,** twice as; double the: вдво́е бо́льше, twice as much; double the amount. **2,** (in) half: вдво́е ме́ньше, half as much; вдво́е сократи́ть, to reduce in half; halve. —**сложи́ть вдво́е,** to fold in half *or* in two.

вдвоём *adv.* **1,** two together: они́ вдвоём, the two of them. **2,** together with one another.

вдвойне́ *adv.* **1,** double; twice as much. **2,** *(with adjectives)* doubly.

вдева́ть *v. impfv.* [*pfv.* вдеть] *(with* в + *acc.)* to put in; put into. —**вдеть ни́тку в иго́лку,** to thread a needle.

вде́лывать *v. impfv.* [*pfv.* вде́лать] *(with* в + *acc.)* **1,** to set (a gem, stone, etc.) into. **2,** to embed (in).

вдёргивать *v. impfv.* [*pfv.* вдёрнуть] to draw through; thread.

вде́сятеро *adv.* ten times; tenfold.

вдесятеро́м *adv.* ten together: они́ вдесятеро́м, the ten of them.

вдеть [*infl.* вде́ну, вде́нешь] *v., pfv. of* вдева́ть.

вдоба́вок *adv., colloq.* besides; in addition; to boot.

вдова́ [*pl.* вдо́вы] *n.* widow.

вдове́ть *v. impfv.* to be a widow *or* widower.

вдове́ц [*gen.* -вца́] *n.* widower.

вдо́воль *adv., colloq.* **1,** in abundance; as much as one could wish for. **2,** to one's heart's content: нае́сться вдо́воль, to eat one's fill.

вдовство́ *n.* widowhood.

вдо́вый *adj.* widowed.

вдого́нку *adv., colloq.* after; right behind; in pursuit of: бро́ситься вдого́нку за (+ *instr.*), to take off after. Кри́кнуть вдого́нку (+ *dat.*), to call after (someone).

вдолби́ть [*infl.* -блю́, -би́шь] *v., pfv. of* вда́лбливать.

вдоль *prep., with gen.* along: идти́ вдоль доро́ги, to walk along (the side of) the road. —*adv.* lengthwise. —**вдоль и поперёк, 1,** far and wide. **2,** *colloq.* thoroughly; inside out; backwards and forwards.

вдо́сталь *adv., colloq.* **1,** in abundance; as much as one could wish for. **2,** to one's heart's content.

вдох *n.* (a single) breath.

вдохнове́ние *n.* inspiration. —**вдохнове́нно,** *adv.* with inspiration; in an inspired manner. —**вдохнове́нный,** *adj.* inspired.

вдохнови́тель *n.m.* moving spirit; inspiration.

вдохновля́ть *v. impfv.* [*pfv.* вдохнови́ть] to inspire.

вдохну́ть *v. pfv.* **1,** *pfv. of* вдыха́ть. **2,** *(with* в + *acc.)* to breathe (into): вдохну́ть жизнь в кого́-нибудь, to breathe new life into someone.

вдре́безги *adv.* **1,** to pieces; to smithereens. **2,** *colloq.* completely; utterly: вдре́безги пьян, dead drunk.

вдруг *adv.* **1,** suddenly; all of a sudden. **2,** *colloq.*

together; at once: не говори́те все вдруг, don't talk all at once. 3, *colloq.* suppose...?; what if...?

вдува́ть v. impfv. [pfv. **вдуть**] (with в + acc.) to blow (e.g. air) into (something).

вду́маться v.r., pfv. of **вду́мываться**.

вду́мчивый adj. thoughtful; pensive.

вду́мываться v.r. impfv. [pfv. **вду́маться**] 1, to reflect; ponder. 2, (with в + acc.) to consider; go into.

вдуть [infl. **вду́ю**, **вду́ешь**] v., pfv. of **вдува́ть**.

вдыха́ние n. inhalation.

вдыха́тельный adj. 1, respiratory. 2, intake (attrib.): вдыха́тельный кла́пан, intake valve.

вдыха́ть v. impfv. [pfv. **вдохну́ть**] to inhale; breathe in. See also **вдохну́ть**.

вегетариа́нец [gen. -нца] n. vegetarian. —**вегетариа́нский**, adj. vegetarian.

вегета́ция n. (process of) vegetation.

ве́дать v. impfv. 1, (with instr.) to manage; be in charge of. 2, obs. to know.

ве́дение n. authority; jurisdiction.

веде́ние n. (with gen.) keeping (of); conduct (of); handling (of); management (of).

ве́домо n., in с/без ве́дома (+ gen.), with/without the knowledge of.

ве́домость [pl. ве́домости, -сте́й] n.f. 1, register; roll. 2, pl. official bulletin. —**платёжная ве́домость**, payroll.

ве́домственный adj. departmental.

ве́домство n. (government) department.

ве́домый pres. passive part. of **вести́**. —**ве́домый самолёт**, supporting aircraft.

ведро́ [pl. вёдра, вёдер] n. bucket; pail. —**дождь льёт как из ведра́**, it is raining cats and dogs.

веду́щий adj. 1, leading: веду́щий самолёт, lead aircraft. 2, fig. leading; chief. 3, mech. drive (attrib.); transmission (attrib.).

ведь particle 1, why; after all; you know: ведь э́то всем изве́стно, why everyone knows that! Он ведь ребёнок, after all, he is only a child. 2, isn't that so?: ведь он до́ма?, he is home, isn't he?

ве́дьма n. witch; hag.

ве́ер [pl. веера́] n. fan.

веерообра́зный adj. fan-shaped.

ве́жливый adj. polite; courteous. —**ве́жливо**, adv. politely; courteously. —**ве́жливость**, n.f. politeness; courtesy.

везде́ adv. everywhere. —**везде́, где...**, everywhere; wherever. —**везде́ и всю́ду**, absolutely everywhere.

вездесу́щий adj. omnipresent; ubiquitous.

вездехо́д n. cross-country vehicle; land rover. —**вездехо́дный**, adj. cross-country.

везе́ние n., colloq. luck.

везти́ v. impfv. [pfv. **повезти́**; pres. везу́, везёшь; past вёз, везла́, везло́] 1, to carry; convey (in a vehicle). 2, (with dat.) impers., colloq. to be lucky; have luck: ему́ всегда́ везёт, he is always lucky. Вам повезло́, что..., you are lucky that...

век [pl. века́] n. 1, century. 2, age: ка́менный век, the Stone Age; сре́дние века́, the Middle Ages. 3, colloq. life; lifetime: я мно́го повида́л на своём веку́, I have seen a lot in my life/lifetime. —**во ве́ки веко́в**, archaic for all time; for all eternity. —**в ко́и ве́ки; в ко́и-то ве́ки**, once in a blue moon. —**на ве́ки ве́чные**, forever. —**от ве́ка (веко́в); испоко́н веко́в**, since time immemorial.

ве́ко [pl. ве́ки, век] n. eyelid.

веково́й adj. age-old.

ве́ксель [pl. векселя́] n.m. promissory note; bill of exchange.

ве́ктор n. vector. —**ве́кторный**, adj. vector (attrib.).

веле́невый adj. (of paper) vellum.

веле́ние n. command; prescription; dictates.

веле́ть v. impfv. & pfv. [pres. велю́, вели́шь] (with dat.) 1, to order; tell. 2, used negatively not to allow; forbid.

велика́н n. giant.

вели́кий adj. 1, great. 2, [short form only] (of clothes) too big; too large: боти́нки мне велики́, the shoes are too big for me. —**от ма́ла до вели́ка**, young and old alike.

великоду́шие n. magnanimity. —**великоду́шный**, adj. magnanimous.

великоле́пие n. splendor; magnificence.

великоле́пно adv. 1, magnificently. 2, marvelously. 3, as an interj. splendid!

великоле́пный adj. 1, magnificent; splendid. 2, colloq. wonderful; marvelous.

великопо́стный adj. Lenten.

велича́вый adj. stately; majestic.

велича́йший adj., superl. of **вели́кий**, greatest; utmost: де́ло велича́йшей ва́жности, a matter of the greatest/utmost importance.

велича́ть v. impfv., obs. 1, to call (by a certain name). 2, to extol; sing the praises of.

вели́чественный adj. majestic; stately.

вели́чество n. Majesty: его́ вели́чество, His Majesty.

вели́чие n. greatness; grandeur. —**ма́ния вели́чия**, megalomania; delusions of grandeur.

величина́ [pl. -чи́ны] n. 1, size. 2, math. value; quantity. 3, magnitude (of a star). 4, fig. eminent figure.

велого́нка [gen. pl. -нок] n. bicycle race. —**велого́нщик**, n. bicycle racer.

велодро́м n. velodrome.

велосипе́д n. bicycle. —**велосипеди́ст**, n. cyclist. —**велосипе́дный**, adj. bicycle (attrib.).

вельве́т n. velveteen. —**вельве́товый**, adj. velveteen.

вельмо́жа n.m. 1, archaic aristocrat. 2, ironic bigwig.

велю́р n. velour. —**велю́ровый**, adj. velour.

веля́рный adj. velar.

ве́на n. vein.

венге́рка [gen. pl. -рок] n. 1, Hungarian woman. 2, Hungarian dance. 3, Hungarian-style jacket.

венге́рский adj. Hungarian.

венгр n.m. [fem. -ге́рка] Hungarian.

Вене́ра n. Venus.

венери́ческий adj. venereal.

венесуэ́льский adj. Venezuelan.

вене́ц [gen. -нца́] n. 1, crown. 2, poetic wreath. 3, astron. corona. 4, (with gen.) crowning achievement (of). 5, row of crossbeams. —**идти́ под вене́ц**, obs. to wed.

венециа́нский adj. Venetian.

вене́чный adj. coronary.

ве́нзель [pl. вензеля́] n.m. monogram.

ве́ник n. broom made of twigs.

вено́зный adj. venous.

вено́к [gen. -нка́] n. wreath.

ве́нский adj. of Vienna; Viennese.

вентили́ровать v. impfv. [pfv. провентили́ровать; pres. -рую, -руешь] to ventilate.

ве́нтиль *n.m.* valve.

вентиля́тор *n.* fan; blower.

вентиля́ция *n.* ventilation.

венча́льный *adj.* wedding *(attrib.).*

венча́ние *n.* **1,** (religious) wedding ceremony. **2,** coronation.

венча́ть *v. impfv.* **1,** [*pfv.* увенча́ть] to crown. **2,** [*pfv.* повенча́ть *or* обвенча́ть] to marry. —**венча́ться**, *refl.* **1,** to be crowned. **2,** to be married.

ве́нчик *n.* **1,** *dim. of* венец. **2,** corolla.

вепрь *n.m.* wild boar.

ве́ра *n.* faith; belief. —**дава́ть ве́ру** (+ *dat.*), to give credence to. —**принима́ть на ве́ру**, to take on faith. —**служи́ть ве́рой и пра́вдой**, to serve faithfully.

вера́нда *n.* veranda.

ве́рба *n.* pussy willow.

вербе́на *n.* verbena.

верблю́д *n.* camel.

верблю́жий [*fem.* -жья] *adj.* **1,** camel *(attrib.).* **2,** camel's-hair.

ве́рбный *adj.* pussy-willow *(attrib.).* —**ве́рбное воскресе́нье**, Palm Sunday.

вербова́ть *v. impfv.* [*pfv.* завербова́ть; *pres.* -бу́ю, -бу́ешь] to recruit.

вербо́вка *n.* recruitment. —**вербо́вщик**, *n.* recruiter.

ве́рбовый *adj.* pussy-willow *(attrib.).*

верди́кт *n.* verdict.

верёвка [*gen. pl.* -вок] *n.* rope; cord; string; line: верёвка для белья́, clothesline. —**вить верёвки из**, to twist around one's little finger.

верёвочный *adj.* rope *(attrib.);* string *(attrib.).*

верени́ца *n.* file; row; line.

ве́реск *n.* heather.

веретено́ [*pl.* -тёна, -тён] *n.* spindle.

вереща́ть *v. impfv.* [*pres.* -щу́, -щи́шь] to chirp.

верзи́ла *n.m. & f., colloq.* tall, ungainly person.

вери́ги *n.pl.* [*sing.* вери́га] chains worn by religious ascetics.

вери́тельный *adj., in* вери́тельные гра́моты, credentials *(of a diplomat).*

ве́рить *v. impfv.* [*pfv.* пове́рить] **1,** *(with dat.)* to believe. **2,** *(with* в + *acc.)* to believe in. **3,** [*impfv. only*] to believe (in God). **4,** *in* ве́рить (+ *dat.*) на́ слово, to take at one's word; take one's word for it. —**ве́риться**, *refl.* [*impfv. only*] *impers. (with dat.)* to believe: мне не ве́рится, I can't believe it.

вермише́ль *n.f.* vermicelli.

ве́рмут *n.* vermouth.

верне́е *adj., comp. of* ве́рный. —*particle* or rather; or to be more precise.

верниса́ж *n.* **1,** opening day *(of an art exhibit).* **2,** preview; advance showing *(of an art exhibit).*

ве́рно *adv.* **1,** faithfully. **2,** correctly. —*adj., used predicatively* **1,** true: э́то не ве́рно, that is not true. **2,** correct; right: соверше́нно ве́рно, absolutely right. —*particle, colloq.* probably; most likely.

ве́рность *n.f.* **1,** fidelity; faithfulness; loyalty. **2,** correctness; accuracy.

верну́ть *v., pfv. of* возвраща́ть. —**верну́ться**, *refl., pfv. of* возвраща́ться.

ве́рный *adj.* [*short form* ве́рен, верна́, ве́рно] **1,** faithful; loyal; true. **2,** correct; right; true. **3,** reliable; sure; safe. **4,** sure; certain; inevitable.

ве́рование *n.* **1,** belief; conviction. **2,** *pl.* religious beliefs.

ве́ровать *v. impfv.* [*pres.* -рую, -руешь] **1,** *(with* в + *acc.)* to believe (in). **2,** to believe in God.

вероиспове́дание *n.* faith; religion; creed; denomination.

вероло́мный *adj.* perfidious. —**вероло́мство**, *n.* perfidy.

вероуче́ние *n., relig.* teachings; dogma.

вероя́тно *adv.* probably.

вероя́тность *n.f.* probability; likelihood. —**по всей вероя́тности**, in all probability.

вероя́тный *adj.* probable; likely.

ве́рсия *n.* version.

верста́ [*pl.* вёрсты] *n.* old Russian unit of length equal to approx. one kilometer; verst. —**за́ версту**, from far off.

верста́к [*gen.* -ста́ка] *n.* carpenter's bench.

верста́ть *v. impfv.* [*pfv.* сверста́ть] *printing* to make up; make into pages.

вёрстка *n., printing* **1,** page make-up. **2,** page proofs.

верстово́й *adj., in* верстово́й столб, milepost; milestone.

ве́ртел [*pl.* вертела́] *n.* spit; skewer.

верте́п *n.* den *(of criminals, vice, etc.).*

верте́ть *v. impfv.* [*pres.* верчу́, ве́ртишь] **1,** to turn. **2,** to twirl. **3,** *(with instr.) colloq.* to boss about; twist around one's little finger. —**как ни верти́**, no matter what you do; like it or not.

верте́ться *v.r. impfv.* [*pres.* верчу́сь, ве́ртишься] **1,** to turn; spin; revolve; rotate. **2,** to fidget. **3,** *colloq.* to hang around. **4,** *colloq.* to beat around the bush. —**верте́ться на языке́** *or* **на ко́нчике языка́**, to be on the tip of one's tongue. —**верте́ться пе́ред глаза́ми** *(with* у*),* to pester. —**верте́ться под нога́ми** *(with* у*),* to be (*or* keep getting) in someone's way. —**как ни верти́сь** = **как ни верти́**.

вертика́ль *n.f.* **1,** vertical line. **2,** *chess* file.

вертика́льный *adj.* vertical. —**вертика́льно**, *adv.* vertically.

вёрткий *adj., colloq.* agile; nimble; spry.

вертлю́г [*gen.* -люга́] *n.* swivel.

вертля́вый *adj., colloq.* fidgety; frisky.

вертолёт *n.* helicopter.

верту́шка [*gen. pl.* -шек] *n., colloq.* **1,** any of a number of revolving devices; revolving door; revolving bookcase. **2,** flighty woman.

ве́рующий *n., decl. as an adj.* believer.

верфь *n.f.* shipyard.

верх [*2nd loc.* верху́; *pl.* верхи́] *n.* **1,** top. **2,** folding top *(of a carriage, automobile, etc.).* **3,** right side *(of material);* outer side *(of a garment).* **4,** *pl., colloq.* the leadership; the upper strata. **5,** *(with gen.)* the height (of); the acme (of). **6,** *pl., music* upper register; high notes. **7,** *pl.* superficial aspects: скользи́ть по верха́м, to skim the surface. —**брать** *or* **одержа́ть верх, 1,** to prevail; gain the upper hand; come out on top. **2,** *(with* над*)* to prevail over; get the better (*or* best) of. —**совеща́ние в** *(or* на*)* **верха́х**, summit conference. *See also* ве́рхом *and* верхо́м.

ве́рхний *adj.* upper; top. —**ве́рхняя оде́жда**; **ве́рхнее пла́тье**, outer clothing; outdoor clothes.

верхо́вный *adj.* supreme.

верхово́д *n., colloq.* boss.

верхово́дить *v. impfv.* [*pres.* -жу, -дишь] *colloq.* to be the boss; *(with instr.)* boss around.

верхово́й *adj.* **1,** horseback: верхова́я езда́, horseback riding. **2,** up-river: **верхо́вые се́ла,** towns located up-river. —*n.* horseman; rider.

верхо́вье *n.* upper reaches *(of a river);* headwaters.

верхола́з *n.* steeplejack.

ве́рхом *adv.* **1,** along the top; taking the high ground. **2,** to the brim; to overflowing.

верхо́м *adv.* (on) horseback: **е́здить верхо́м,** to ride horseback; ride a horse; **ката́ться верхо́м,** to go (horseback) riding. —**верхо́м на** (+ *prepl.),* astride.

верху́шка [*gen. pl.* **-шек**] *n.* **1,** peak; top. **2,** *colloq.* the leaders; the elite.

ве́рша *n.* creel.

верши́на *n.* **1,** top; peak; summit. **2,** *math.* apex *(of a triangle);* vertex *(of an angle).* **3,** *fig.* (with gen.) the acme (of); the pinnacle (of).

верши́ть *v. impfv.* **1,** to decide. **2,** *(with instr.)* to direct; control.

вершо́к [*gen.* **-шка́**] *n.* old Russian unit of length equal to approx. 1 3/4 inches.

вес *n.* weight. —**держа́ть(ся) на весу́,** to hold/remain suspended in midair. —**на вес зо́лота,** worth its weight in gold. See also **весы́.**

весел́еть *v. impfv.* [*pfv.* **повеселе́ть**] to cheer up; become cheerful.

весели́ть *v. impfv.* **1,** to gladden; cheer. **2,** to amuse. —**весели́ться,** *refl.* to enjoy oneself; make merry; have fun.

ве́село *adv.* gaily; merrily. —*adj.,* used predicatively gay; merry: **на вечери́нке бы́ло о́чень ве́село,** it was a very gay party.

весёлость *n.f.* gaiety; cheerfulness.

весёлый *adj.* [*short form* **ве́сел, весела́, ве́село**] gay; merry; cheerful.

весе́лье *n.* gaiety; merriment.

весельча́к [*gen.* **-чака́**] *n., colloq.* jolly fellow.

веселя́щий *adj., in* **веселя́щий газ,** laughing gas.

весе́нний *adj.* spring *(attrib.).* —**весе́ннее равноде́нствие,** vernal equinox.

ве́сить *v. impfv.* [*pres.* **ве́шу, ве́сишь**] to weigh (so many pounds).

ве́ский *adj.* weighty.

весло́ [*pl.* **вёсла, вёсел**] *n.* oar; paddle.

весна́ [*pl.* **вёсны, вёсен**] *n.* spring *(season).*

весно́й *also,* **весно́ю** *adv.* in (the) spring.

весну́шка [*gen. pl.* **-шек**] *n.* freckle. —**весну́шчатый,** *adj.* freckled; freckle-faced.

весо́мый *adj.* **1,** having weight; not weightless. **2,** *fig.* weighty.

вест *n., naut.* **1,** west. **2,** west wind.

вести́ *v. impfv.* [*pres.* **веду́, ведёшь;** *past* **вёл, вела́, вело́**] **1,** [*pfv.* **повести́**] to lead. **2,** *(of a road, path, etc.)* to lead (somewhere). **3,** to drive; steer; pilot. **4,** to conduct (a meeting, seminar, etc.). **5,** to carry on (a conversation, correspondence, etc.). **6,** to keep (a diary, the books, etc.). **7,** to wage (war, a struggle, etc.). **8,** to lead (a certain kind of life). **9,** [*pfv.* **повести́**] *(with к)* to lead (to a certain result). **10,** *(with instr. and по)* to pass; run (something over something). —**вести́ себя́,** to behave. See also **води́ть.**

вестибю́ль *n.m.* lobby; foyer.

вести́сь *v.r. impfv.* [*pres.* **ведётся**] **1,** to be conducted; be carried out. **2,** *impers., colloq.* to be the custom: так у нас не ведётся, that is not the way we do things.

ве́стник *n.* **1,** messenger; herald. **2,** bulletin *(title of a publication).*

вестово́й *n., decl. as an adj., obs.* orderly.

ве́сточка [*gen. pl.* **-чек**] *n., dim. of* **весть.** —**пришли́те мне ве́сточку,** drop me a line.

весть[1] [*pl.* **ве́сти, -сте́й, -стя́м**] *n.f.* (piece of) news. —**пропа́сть без вести,** to be missing; disappear without a trace.

весть[2] *v., obs. 3rd person sing. of* **ве́дать.** —**бог весть,** God knows! —**не бог весть,** not particularly: не бог весть как далеко́, not particularly far; не бог весть кака́я кру́пная фигу́ра, not a particularly prominent figure.

весы́ [*gen.* **весо́в**] *n. pl.* **1,** scale(s). **2,** *cap.* Libra.

весь [*fem.* **вся;** *neut.* **всё;** *pl.* **все;** *gen.* **всего́, всей, всех;** *acc. fem.* **всю;** *dat.* **всему́, всей, всем;** *instr.* **всем, всей, все́ми;** *prepl.* **всём, всей, всех**] *adj.* all; the whole: весь день, all day; весь мир, the whole world; всё вре́мя, all the time; все стра́ны, all nations. —**весь в** (+ *acc.*), the image of: он весь в отца́, he is the image of his father. See also **всё, все, всего́.**

весьма́ *adv.* highly; extremely.

ветви́стый *adj.* having many branches.

ветвь [*pl.* **ве́тви, -ве́й, -вя́м**] *n.f.* branch; limb.

ве́тер [*gen.* **-тра**] *n.* wind. —**броса́ть де́ньги на ве́тер,** to toss money to the winds. —**броса́ть слова́ на ве́тер,** to waste words. —**держа́ть нос по ве́тру,** to follow the prevailing winds. —**ищи́ ве́тра в по́ле,** you'll never find it (him, her, *etc.*). —**куда́** *or* **отку́да ве́тер ду́ет,** which way the wind blows. —**у него́ ве́тер в голове́,** he hasn't got a brain in his head.

ветера́н *n.* veteran.

ветерина́р *n.* veterinarian. —**ветерина́рия,** *n.* veterinary medicine. —**ветерина́рный,** *adj.* veterinary.

ветеро́к [*gen.* **-рка́**] *n.* breeze.

ве́тка [*gen. pl.* **-ток**] *n.* branch; twig.

ветла́ [*pl.* **вётлы, вётел**] *n.* white willow.

ве́то *n. indecl.* veto.

ве́точка [*gen. pl.* **-чек**] *n.* twig; sprig.

ве́тошь *n.f.* tattered clothes; rags.

ве́треник *n., colloq.* frivolous person; flighty person; scatterbrain.

ве́треница *n.* **1,** *fem. of* **ве́треник. 2,** anemone.

ве́трено *adv.* frivolously. —*adj.,* used predicatively windy: сего́дня ве́трено, it is windy today.

ве́треный *adj.* **1,** windy. **2,** *colloq.* frivolous.

ветрово́й *adj.* wind *(attrib.).* —**ветрово́е стекло́,** windshield.

ветроме́р *n.* anemometer.

ветря́нка *n., colloq.* chicken pox.

ветряно́й *adj.* wind *(attrib.).* —**ветряна́я ме́льница,** windmill.

ве́тряный *adj., in* **ве́тряная о́спа,** chicken pox.

ве́тхий *adj.* ramshackle; dilapidated. —**Ве́тхий заве́т,** the Old Testament.

ветхозаве́тный *adj.* Old Testament *(attrib.).*

ве́тхость *n.f.* disrepair; decay: приходи́ть в ве́тхость, to fall into disrepair.

ветчина́ *n.* ham.

ветша́ть *v. impfv.* [*pfv.* **обветша́ть**] to deteriorate; become dilapidated; fall into decay.

ве́ха *n.* **1,** signpost. **2,** *usu. pl., fig.* landmark; milestone.

ве́че *n., hist.* popular assembly in old Russia; veche.

ве́чер [*pl.* **вечера́**] *n.* **1,** evening. **2,** (evening) party; soirée. See also **ве́чером.**

вечере́ть *v. impfv., impers.* to grow dark: вечере́ет, dusk is falling; evening is coming on.

вечери́нка [*gen. pl.* -нок] *n.* (evening) party.

вече́рний *adj.* evening *(attrib.).* —вече́рняя шко́ла, night school.

вече́рня *n.* vespers.

ве́чером *adv.* in the evening. —вчера́ ве́чером, last evening; last night. —за́втра ве́чером, tomorrow evening; tomorrow night. —сего́дня ве́чером, this evening; tonight.

ве́черя *n., in* та́йная ве́черя, the Last Supper.

ве́чно *adv.* 1, eternally; forever. 2, *colloq.* constantly; always; forever.

вечнозелёный *adj.* evergreen.

ве́чность *n.f.* 1, eternity. 2, *in* це́лая ве́чность, ages: не ви́дел(а) вас це́лую ве́чность, I haven't seen you for ages. —ка́нуть в ве́чность, to sink into oblivion. —отойти́ в ве́чность, to pass into eternity.

ве́чный *adj.* 1, eternal; everlasting; perpetual. 2, *colloq.* endless; constant; continual. —ве́чная па́мять (+ *dat.*), may (someone's) memory live forever. —ве́чное перо́, *obs.* fountain pen. —на ве́ки ве́чные, forever. —на ве́чные времена́, for all time. —засну́ть ве́чным сном, to go to one's eternal rest.

ве́шалка [*gen. pl.* -лок] *n.* 1, rack. 2, hanger. 3, *colloq.* cloakroom.

ве́шать *v. impfv.* 1, [*pfv.* пове́сить] to hang; hang up. 2, *in* ве́шать нос *or* го́лову, to be/become discouraged; lose heart. 3, [*pfv.* све́шать] to weigh. —ве́шаться, *refl.* [*pfv.* пове́ситься] to hang oneself.

веща́ние *n.* 1, broadcasting. 2, prophesying. 3, prophecy.

веща́ть *v. impfv.* 1, *obs.* to prophesy. 2, *colloq.* to preach; expound. 3, to broadcast.

вещево́й *adj.* clothing *(attrib.).* —вещево́й мешо́к, knapsack. —вещево́й склад, warehouse.

веще́ственный *adj.* material. —веще́ственные доказа́тельства, material evidence.

вещество́ *n.* matter; substance. —обме́н веще́ств, metabolism.

ве́щий *adj., obs.* 1, wise. 2, prophetic.

вещи́ца *n.* 1, *dim. of* вещь. 2, knickknack.

вещь [*pl.* ве́щи, веще́й, веща́м] *n.f.* 1, thing. 2, *pl.* things; belongings; clothes. 3, work; piece *(of art, literature, music, etc.):* три ве́щи Проко́фьева, three works by Prokofiev.

ве́ялка [*gen. pl.* -лок] *n.* winnowing machine.

ве́яние *n.* 1, winnowing. 2, blowing *(of the wind).* 3, sign; portent. 4, trend; tendency.

ве́ять *v. impfv.* [*pres.* ве́ю, ве́ешь] 1, to blow gently. 2, *(with instr.) fig.* to be in the air: ве́ет весно́й, spring is in the air. 3, to wave; flutter. 4, *v.t.* [*pfv.* прове́ять] to winnow.

вжива́ться *v.r. impfv.* [*pfv.* вжи́ться] (with в + *acc.*) to get used to. —вжива́ться в свою́ роль, to get the feel of one's part.

вживля́ть *v. impfv.* [*pfv.* вживи́ть] *med.* to implant.

вжи́ться [*infl. like* жить] *v.r., pfv. of* вжива́ться.

взад *adv., colloq.* back. —взад и вперёд, back and forth; to and fro; up and down.

взаи́мный *adj.* mutual; reciprocal. —взаи́мно, *adv.* mutually. —взаи́мность, *n.f.* mutuality; reciprocity.

взаимовы́годный *adj.* mutually beneficial/advantageous.

взаимоде́йствие *n.* 1, interaction; interplay. 2, *mil.* cooperation; coordination.

взаимоде́йствовать *v. impfv.* [*pres.* -ствую, -ствуешь] 1, to interact. 2, *mil.* to cooperate.

взаимозави́симый *adj.* interdependent. —взаимозави́симость, *n.f.* interdependence.

взаимозаменя́емый *adj.* interchangeable.

взаимоотноше́ние *n.* relation; interrelation.

взаимопо́мощь *n.f.* mutual aid/assistance.

взаимопонима́ние *n.* mutual understanding.

взаимосвя́занный *adj.* interconnected; interrelated.

взаймы́ *adv.* on loan. —дава́ть взаймы́, to lend; loan. —брать *or* получа́ть взаймы́, to borrow.

взаме́н *adv.* 1, instead. 2, in return; in exchange. —*prep., with gen.* 1, in return for; in exchange for. 2, in place of.

взаперти́ *adv.* 1, locked up; under lock and key. 2, *fig.* in seclusion.

вза́пуски *adv., colloq.* racing (with) one another: бе́гать вза́пуски, to race each other.

взахлёб *adv., colloq.* avidly; with gusto.

взба́лмошный *adj., colloq.* eccentric; erratic; unbalanced.

взба́лтывать *v. impfv.* [*pfv.* взболта́ть] to shake (up).

взбега́ть *v. impfv.* [*pfv.* взбежа́ть] *(with на* + *acc. or* по*)* to run up.

взбежа́ть [*infl. like* бежа́ть] *v., pfv. of* взбега́ть.

взбелени́ться *v.r. pfv., colloq.* to fly into a rage.

взбеси́ть *v., pfv. of* беси́ть. —взбеси́ться, *refl., pfv. of* беси́ться.

взбива́ть *v. impfv.* [*pfv.* взбить] 1, to fluff (up). 2, to whip (cream); beat (egg whites); churn up (water).

взбира́ться *v.r. impfv.* [*pfv.* взобра́ться] *(with на* + *acc. or* по*)* to climb; climb up.

взби́тый *adj.* beaten; whipped: взби́тые сли́вки, whipped cream.

взбить [*infl.* взобью́, взобьёшь] *v., pfv. of* взбива́ть.

взбодри́ть *v. pfv., colloq.* to cheer up; hearten.

взболта́ть *v., pfv. of* болта́ть *(in sense #2)* and взба́лтывать.

взборони́ть *v., pfv. of* борони́ть.

взбреда́ть *v. impfv.* [*pfv.* взбрести́] *(with на* + *acc.) colloq.* to mount with difficulty. —взбрести́ в го́лову *or* на ум (+ *dat.*), to come into one's head.

взбрести́ [*infl. like* брести́] *v., pfv. of* взбреда́ть.

взбудора́жить *v., pfv. of* будора́жить.

взбунтова́ть *v., pfv. of* бунтова́ть *(in sense #2).* —взбунтова́ться, *refl., pfv. of* бунтова́ть *(in sense #1).*

взбуха́ть *v. impfv.* [*pfv.* взбу́хнуть] to swell out; bulge.

взбу́хнуть [*past* взбух, -ла] *v., pfv. of* взбуха́ть.

взбу́чка *n., colloq.* 1, beating; thrashing. 2, scolding; dressing-down.

взва́ливать *v. impfv.* [*pfv.* взвали́ть] *(with на* + *acc.)* 1, to load (onto). 2, *fig.* to load (work on someone). 3, *fig.* to lay; place (blame).

взвали́ть [*infl.* взвалю́, взва́лишь] *v., pfv. of* взва́ливать.

взве́сить [*infl.* -шу, -сишь] *v., pfv. of* взве́шивать. —взве́ситься, *refl., pfv. of* взве́шиваться.

взвести́ [*infl. like* вести́] *v., pfv. of* взводи́ть.

взве́шивать *v. impfv.* [*pfv.* взве́сить] 1, to weigh. 2, *fig.* to weigh; ponder. —взве́шиваться, *refl.* to weigh oneself.

взвива́ть *v. impfv.* [*pfv.* взвить] to blow up; swirl.

—**взвива́ться**, *refl.* **1,** to fly up; soar. **2,** *(of a flag, curtain, etc.)* to go up.

взвизг *n., colloq.* screech; yelp.

взви́згивать *v. impfv.* [*pfv.* **взви́згнуть**] to screech; yelp.

взви́нчивать *v. impfv.* [*pfv.* **взвинти́ть**] *colloq.* **1,** to excite; arouse. **2,** to jack up (prices).

взви́ть [*infl.* **взовью́, взовьёшь**] *v., pfv. of* **взвива́ть.** —**взви́ться**, *refl., pfv. of* **взвива́ться.**

взвод *n.* **1,** platoon. **2,** cocking recess *(of a firearm):* на боево́м взво́де, cocked; ready to fire; на предохрани́тельном взво́де, at half cock. —**на взво́де,** *colloq.* tipsy.

взводи́ть *v. impfv.* [*pfv.* **взвести́**; *pres.* **-вожу́, -во́дишь**] **1,** to lead up. **2,** to level (an accusation). **3,** *in* взводи́ть куро́к, to cock a gun.

взво́дный *adj.* platoon *(attrib.).* —*n.* platoon leader.

взволно́ванный *adj.* agitated; anxious; uneasy.

взволнова́ть *v., pfv. of* **волнова́ть.** —**взволнова́ться,** *refl., pfv. of* **волнова́ться.**

взвы́ть *v. pfv.* [*infl.* **взво́ю, взво́ешь**] to howl.

взгляд *n.* **1,** look; glance. **2,** opinion; view: на мой взгляд, in my opinion. —**на пе́рвый взгляд,** at first glance; on the face of it. —**с пе́рвого взгля́да, 1,** at first glance. **2,** at a glance; from the first.

взгля́дывать *v. impfv.* [*pfv.* **взгляну́ть**] *(with* на + *acc.)* to glance (at); take a look (at).

взго́рье *n., colloq.* hill.

взгроможда́ть *v. impfv.* [*pfv.* **взгромозди́ть**] *(with* на + *acc.) colloq.* to pile (onto); load (onto); hoist (onto). —**взгроможда́ться,** *refl. (with* на + *acc.) colloq.* to clamber up (on).

вздёргивать *v. impfv.* [*pfv.* **вздёрнуть**] *colloq.* **1,** to raise; hoist up; jerk up. **2,** to execute by hanging; string up.

вздёрнутый *adj., in* вздёрнутый нос, snub nose.

вздёрнуть *v., pfv. of* **вздёргивать.**

вздор *n.* nonsense.

вздо́рить *v. impfv.* [*pfv.* **повздо́рить**] *colloq.* to argue; squabble; bicker.

вздо́рный *adj., colloq.* **1,** absurd; preposterous. **2,** quarrelsome; cantankerous.

вздорожа́ть *v., pfv. of* **дорожа́ть.**

вздох *n.* deep breath; sigh.

вздохну́ть *v. pfv.* **1,** *pfv. of* **вздыха́ть. 2,** *colloq.* to take a short rest; take a breath.

вздра́гивать *v. impfv.* [*pfv.* **вздро́гнуть**] to give a start; jump; wince.

вздремну́ть *v. pfv., colloq.* to take a nap.

вздро́гнуть *v., pfv. of* **вздра́гивать.**

вздува́ть *v. impfv.* [*pfv.* **вздуть**] **1,** to blow up *(into the air).* **2,** to bloat. **3,** *fig., colloq.* to inflate (prices). —**вздува́ться,** *refl.* to swell up; puff up.

взду́мать *v. pfv., colloq.* to take a notion (to); take it into one's head (to). —**взду́маться,** *refl., impers., colloq.* = **взду́мать:** мне взду́малось, I took it into my head (to).

взду́тие *n.* swelling.

взду́тый *adj.* **1,** swollen. **2,** *fig.* inflated.

взду́ть [*infl.* **взду́ю, взду́ешь**] *v., pfv. of* **вздува́ть.** —**взду́ться,** *refl., pfv. of* **вздува́ться.**

вздыбли́ваться *v.r. impfv.* [*pfv.* **вздыбиться**] *(of a horse)* to rear.

вздыма́ть *v. impfv.* to raise. —**вздыма́ться,** *refl.* **1,** to rise. **2,** *(of the chest)* to heave.

вздыха́ть *v. impfv.* [*pfv.* **вздохну́ть**] **1,** to sigh. **2,** [*impfv. only*] *(with* по + *prepl.)* to yearn (for); pine (for).

взима́ть *v. impfv.* to levy; collect. Взима́ть пла́ту, to charge a fee.

взира́ть *v. impfv., obs.* to look; gaze.

взла́мывать *v. impfv.* [*pfv.* **взлома́ть**] to break open; force open.

взлеза́ть *v. impfv.* [*pfv.* **взлезть**] *colloq.* to climb up.

взлезть [*infl. like* **лезть**] *v., pfv. of* **взлеза́ть.**

взлёт *n.* **1,** upward flight. **2,** *aero.* takeoff. **3,** *fig. (with gen.)* upsurge (of).

взлета́ть *v. impfv.* [*pfv.* **взлете́ть**] to fly up; soar; *(of an airplane)* take off. —**взлете́ть на во́здух,** to go up in smoke.

взлете́ть [*infl.* **-чу́, -ти́шь**] *v., pfv. of* **взлета́ть.**

взлётный *adj.* take-off *(attrib.).* —**взлётно-поса́дочная полоса́,** runway.

взлом *n.* breaking in. —**кра́жа со взло́мом,** burglary.

взлома́ть *v., pfv. of* **взла́мывать.**

взло́мщик *n.* burglar.

взлохма́тить [*infl.* **-чу, -тишь**] *v., pfv. of* **взлохма́чивать.**

взлохма́ченный *adj.* disheveled.

взлохма́чивать *v. impfv.* [*pfv.* **взлохма́тить**] to muss; tousle.

взмах *n.* wave; sweep *(of the hand);* stroke *(of an oar);* flap *(of wings).*

взма́хивать *v. impfv.* [*pfv.* **взмахну́ть**] *(with instr.)* to flap; wave.

взметну́ть *v. pfv.* **1,** to throw up into the air; send flying. **2,** *(with instr.)* to flap (one's wings); throw up (one's hands). —**взметну́ться,** *refl.* to shoot up; fly up into the air.

взмоли́ться *v.r. pfv.* [*infl.* **-молю́сь, -мо́лишься**] to implore; *(with* о*)* beg (for).

взмо́рье *n.* seashore.

взмыва́ть *v. impfv.* [*pfv.* **взмыть**] to soar.

взмы́ленный *adj. (of a horse)* foaming.

взмыть [*infl.* **взмо́ю, взмо́ешь**] *v., pfv. of* **взмыва́ть.**

взнос *n.* **1,** deposit; payment. **2,** fee; dues.

взну́здывать *v. impfv.* [*pfv.* **взнузда́ть**] to bridle (a horse).

взобра́ться [*infl. like* **брать**] *v.r., pfv. of* **взбира́ться.**

взойти́ [*infl.* **взойду́, взойдёшь**; *past* **взошёл, взошла́**] *v., pfv. of* **всходи́ть** *and* **восходи́ть.**

взор *n.* look; glance; gaze.

взорва́ть [*infl. like* **рвать**] *v., pfv. of* **взрыва́ть¹.** —**взорва́ться,** *refl., pfv. of* **взрыва́ться.**

взрасти́ть [*infl.* **-щу́, -сти́шь**] *v., pfv. of* **взра́щивать.**

взра́щивать *v. impfv.* [*pfv.* **взрасти́ть**] **1,** to grow; cultivate. **2,** to raise; rear; bring up.

взреве́ть *v. pfv.* [*infl.* **-ву́, -вёшь**] to roar; let out a roar.

взро́слый *adj.* adult; grown. —*n.* adult; grownup.

взрыв *n.* **1,** explosion; blast. **2,** *fig. (with gen.)* burst: взрыв аплодисме́нтов, burst of applause.

взрыва́тель *n.m.* fuse.

взрыва́ть¹ *v. impfv.* [*pfv.* **взорва́ть**] **1,** to blow up (a bridge, building, etc.); set off (a charge). **2,** *fig., colloq.* to infuriate; send into a rage. —**взрыва́ться,** *refl.* **1,** to explode; burst; blow up; *(of a charge, grenade, etc.)* go off. **2,** *fig., colloq.* to blow up; become infuriated.

взрыва́ть² *v. impfv.* [*pfv.* **взрыть**] to dig up.

взрывно́й *adj.* blasting *(attrib.):* взрывны́е рабо́ты, blasting operations.

взрывчáтка *n., colloq.* explosives.

взры́вчатый *adj.* explosive.

взрыть [*infl.* взрóю, взрóешь] *v., pfv. of* взрывáть[2].

взрыхли́ть *v., pfv. of* рыхли́ть *and* взрыхля́ть.

взрыхля́ть *v. impfv.* [*pfv.* взрыхли́ть] to loosen; turn up (soil, dirt, etc.).

взъедáться *v.r. impfv.* [*pfv.* взъéсться] *colloq.* 1, to rant and rave. 2, *(with* на + *acc.)* to lace into.

взъезжáть *v. impfv.* [*pfv.* взъéхать] *(with* на + *acc.)* to drive up; ascend.

взъерóшенный *adj.* disheveled.

взъерóшить *v., pfv. of* ерóшить.

взъéсться [*infl. like* есть] *v.r., pfv. of* взъедáться.

взъéхать [*infl. like* éхать] *v., pfv. of* взъезжáть.

взывáть *v. impfv.* [*pfv.* воззвáть] to appeal.

взыгрáть *v. pfv.* 1, to become playful; act up. 2, *(of the sea)* to become choppy. —**сéрдце во мне взыгрáло,** my heart leaped for joy.

взыскáние *n.* penalty.

взыскáтельный *adj.* exacting; demanding.

взыскáть [*infl.* взыщу́, взы́щешь] *v., pfv. of* взы́скивать.

взы́скивать *v. impfv.* [*pfv.* взыскáть] 1, to exact; force payment of. 2, *(with* с + *gen.)* to call to account; make answer.

взя́тие *n.* taking; capture; seizure.

взя́тка [*gen. pl.* -ток] *n.* 1, bribe. 2, *cards* trick.

взя́точник *n.* bribe taker. —**взя́точничество,** *n.* bribery.

взять *v. pfv.* [*infl.* возьму́, возьмёшь; *past fem.* взяла́] 1, *pfv. of* брать. 2, to seize; arrest. 3, *(with* и, да *or* да и*) denoting an unexpected action:* он взял и ушёл, he up and left. —**с чегó вы взя́ли, что...?,** what made you think that...?; where did you get the idea that...?

взя́ться [*infl.* возьму́сь, возьмёшься; *past* взя́лся, -лáсь, -лóсь, -ли́сь] *v.r., pfv. of* брáться. —**откудá ни возьми́сь,** from out of nowhere; from out of the blue.

виадýк *n.* viaduct.

вибрáтор *n.* vibrator.

вибрáция *n.* 1, vibration. 2, *music* tremolo.

вибри́ровать *v. impfv.* [*pres.* -рует] to vibrate.

виве́рра *n.* civet.

вивисéкция *n.* vivisection.

вигвáм *n.* wigwam.

вигóнь *n.f.* vicuna. —**вигóневый,** *adj.* vicuna.

вид *n.* 1, look; appearance. 2, [*with* в + *an adj.)* state; condition: в пья́ном ви́де, drunk; in a drunken state. 3, view: вид на мóре, view of the sea. 4, sight: при ви́де (+ *gen.),* at the sight of. 5, *pl.* prospects. 6, kind; sort. 7, species. 8, *gram.* aspect. 9, *mil.* branch (of the armed forces). —**в ви́де** (+ *gen.*), in the form of. —**для ви́да,** for the sake of appearance. —**из ви́да; из ви́ду,** from view. —**на вид; по ви́ду; с ви́ду,** in appearance. —**на виду́,** in the public eye. —**ни под каки́м ви́дом,** under no circumstances. —**под ви́дом** (+ *gen.*), under the guise of. —**у всех на виду́,** on view; in full view of everyone. —**дéлать вид,** to pretend. —**имéть в виду́,** 1, to have in mind. 2, to bear in mind; keep in mind. —**имéть ви́ды на** (+ *acc.*), 1, to have an eye on; have designs on. 2, to count on. —**постáвить на вид** (+ *dat.*), to reprimand (someone).

ви́данный *adj., in* ви́данное ли это дéло?, *colloq.* did you ever see such a thing?

видáть[1] *v. impfv.* [*pfv.* повидáть] *colloq.* 1, to see. 2, *in* видáть ви́ды, to have seen a lot; have been through a lot. —**видáться,** *refl.* *(with* с + *instr.)* to see; visit.

видáть[2] *particle, colloq.* apparently; it seems.

ви́дение *n.* sight; vision.

виде́ние *n.* apparition; vision.

видеозáпись *n.f.* video tape.

ви́деть *v. impfv.* [*pfv.* уви́деть; *pres.* ви́жу, ви́дишь] to see. —**ви́деться,** *refl.* 1, [*impfv. only*] to be visible. 2, *(with* с + *instr.)* to see; meet with. 3, to see each other.

ви́димо *adv.* apparently; evidently.

ви́димость *n.f.* 1, visibility. 2, semblance; appearance. —**по всей ви́димости,** from all appearances.

ви́димый *adj.* 1, visible. 2, apparent; evident. 3, *colloq.* seeming; apparent.

видне́ться *v.r. impfv.* to be seen; be visible.

ви́дно *adj., used predicatively* 1, visible: мостá ещё не ви́дно, the bridge cannot be seen as yet. 2, clear; obvious: ви́дно, что он не придёт, it is clear/obvious that he is not coming. —*adv., colloq.* apparently; evidently.

ви́дный *adj.* [*short form* ви́ден, виднá, ви́дно, ви́дны *or* видны́] 1, visible; in sight. 2, noticeable; conspicuous. 3, *(of a person)* prominent.

видовóй *adj.* 1, *biol.* pert. to a species. 2, *gram.* aspectual. —**видовóй фильм,** travel film.

видоизмене́ние *n.* 1, modification; alteration. 2, type; variety.

видоизменя́ть *v. impfv.* [*pfv.* видоизмени́ть] to modify; alter.

видоискáтель *n.m., photog.* view finder.

ви́за *n.* visa.

визави́ *adv.* face to face. —*n.m. & f.indecl.* person opposite; person facing.

византи́йский *adj.* Byzantine.

визг *n.* squeal; screech; yelp.

визгли́вый *adj.* 1, shrill. 2, squealing; screeching.

визжáть *v. impfv.* [*pfv.* ви́згнуть; *pres.* визжу́, визжи́шь] to squeal; screech; yelp.

визи́р *n.* 1, sight *(sighting device).* 2, *photog.* view finder.

визи́ровать *v. impfv. & pfv.* [*pres.* -рую, -руешь] 1, to enter a visa in (a passport). 2, to sight; aim.

визи́рь *n.m.* vizier.

визи́т *n.* visit; call. —**визитёр,** *n., obs.* visitor; caller.

визи́тка [*gen. pl.* -ток] *n.* morning coat.

визи́тный *adj.* of or for visiting. —**визи́тная кáрточка,** business card; calling card.

ви́ка *n.* vetch.

викáрий *n.* vicar.

ви́кинг *n.* Viking.

виконт *n.* viscount.

виктори́на *n.* quiz.

ви́лка [*gen. pl.* -лок] *n.* 1, fork. 2, plug *(for a socket).*

ви́лла *n.* villa.

ви́ллис *n.* jeep.

вилóк [*gen. pl.* -лкá] *n., colloq.* head of cabbage.

ви́лы [*gen.* вил] *n. pl.* pitchfork.

виля́ть *v. impfv.* [*pfv.* вильнýть] 1, *(with instr.)* to wag (one's tail). 2, *(of one's tail)* to wag. 3, to weave; zigzag. 4, *colloq.* to equivocate; hedge.

винá *n.* 1, fault; blame. 2, guilt. 3, misdeed; transgression: заглáживать винý, to redress a wrong. —**всемý винóй** (+ *nom.),* it's all because of; it's all due to.

—**не по мое́й вине́**, through no fault of mine. —**по вине́** (+ *gen.),* because of; on account of.

винегре́т *n.* **1**, Russian salad. **2,** *fig., colloq.* hodge-podge; potpourri.

вини́л *n.* vinyl.

вини́тельный *adj., in* вини́тельный паде́ж, accusative case.

вини́ть *v. impfv.* to blame.

виннока́менный *adj.* tartaric.

ви́нный *adj.* wine *(attrib.).* —**ви́нный ка́мень**, tartar; cream of tartar. —**ви́нный спирт**, ethyl alcohol. —**ви́нная я́года,** fig.

вино́ [*pl.* ви́на] *n.* wine.

винова́тый *adj.* **1,** guilty; at fault; to blame: я винова́т, it's my fault. **2,** *(of a look or expression)* guilty; apologetic. —**винова́т!**, I'm sorry!; I beg your pardon!

вино́вник *n.* **1,** culprit; guilty party. **2,** *(with gen.)* perpetrator (of); cause (of). —**вино́вник торжества́**, guest of honor; hero of the occasion.

вино́вность *n.f.* guilt; culpability.

вино́вный *adj.* [*short form* -**вен, -вна**] guilty.

виногра́д *n.* grapes. —**виногра́дарство**, *n.* viniculture; viticulture. —**виногра́дина**, *n.* a (single) grape. —**виногра́дник**, *n.* vineyard.

виногра́дный *adj.* grape *(attrib.).* —**виногра́дный са́хар**, grape sugar.

виноде́л *n.* winegrower. —**виноде́лие**, *n.* winegrowing. —**виноде́льческий**, *adj.* wine-growing *(attrib.).*

винокýр *n.* distiller. —**винокуре́ние**, *n.* distilling. —**винокýренный**, *adj.* distilling *(attrib.).*

винт [*gen.* винта́] *n.* **1,** screw. **2,** propeller.

ви́нтик *n., dim. of* винт. —**у него́ ви́нтика не хвата́ет**, *colloq.* he has a screw loose.

винто́вка [*gen. pl.* -**вок**] *n.* rifle.

винтово́й *adj.* **1,** spiral: винтова́я ле́стница, spiral staircase. **2,** propeller-driven.

винто́вочный *adj.* rifle *(attrib.).*

винтообра́зный *adj.* spiral.

виньéтка [*gen. pl.* -**ток**] *n.* vignette.

вио́ла *n.* **1,** viol. **2,** viola.

виолончели́ст *n.* cellist.

виолончéль *n.f.* cello.

вира́ж *n.* **1,** [*gen.* -**ража́**] turn. **2,** [*gen.* -**ра́жа**] *photog.* toning agent.

виртуо́з *n.* virtuoso.

виртуо́зный *adj.* masterful; masterly. —**виртуо́зно**, *adv.* masterfully. —**виртуо́зность**, *n.f.* virtuosity.

вирулéнтный *adj.* virulent; deadly. —**вирулéнтность**, *n.f.* virulence.

ви́рус *n.* virus. —**ви́русный**, *adj.* viral.

ви́рши [*gen.* -**шей**] *n.pl.* poetry; doggerel.

ви́селица *n.* gallows.

висéть *v. impfv.* [*pres.* виси́т, вися́т] to hang. —**висéть в во́здухе**, to be up in the air; be undecided.

ви́ски *n. neut. indecl.* whiskey.

виско́за *n.* **1,** viscose. **2,** rayon. —**виско́зный**, *adj.* viscose.

вислоýхий *adj.* lop-eared.

ви́смут *n.* bismuth.

ви́снуть *v. impfv.* [*past* вис *or* ви́снул] *colloq.* **1,** to hang. **2,** to droop.

висо́к [*gen.* -**ска́**] *n., anat.* temple.

високо́сный *adj., in* високо́сный год, leap year.

вист *n.* whist.

висю́лька [*gen. pl.* -**лек**] *n., colloq.* pendant.

вися́чий *adj.* hanging; suspended. —**вися́чий замо́к**, padlock. —**вися́чий мост**, suspension bridge.

витами́н *n.* vitamin. —**витами́нный**, *adj.* vitamin *(attrib.).* —**витамино́зный**, *adj.* rich in vitamins.

вита́ть *v. impfv.* **1,** *obs.* to be; live. **2,** *(with над)* to hang (over); hover (over). —**вита́ть в облака́х**, to be up in the clouds.

витиева́тый *adj.* flowery; ornate.

вито́й *adj.* **1,** twisted: витая бýлка, twist *(of bread).* **2,** winding; spiral.

вито́к [*gen.* -**тка́**] *n.* **1,** turn; loop; coil. **2,** strand. **3,** circuit *(of a planet by a space vehicle).*

витра́ж [*gen.* -**ража́**] *n.* stained-glass window.

витри́на *n.* **1,** store window. **2,** showcase.

вить *v. impfv.* [*pfv.* свить; *pres.* вью, вьёшь; *past fem.* вила́] **1,** to make *(by twisting).* **2,** *in* вить/свить гнездо́, to build a nest. —**ви́ться**, *refl.* [*past* ви́лся, вила́сь, вило́сь, вили́сь] [*impfv. only*] **1,** *(of hair)* to curl; *(of vines)* to twine. **2,** *(of a road)* to wind; *(of a snake)* to twist. **3,** *(of a bird)* to hover; *(of dust)* to swirl.

ви́тязь *n.m., obs., folk poetry* warrior; hero.

вихо́р [*gen.* -**хра́**] *n.* tuft *(of hair).*

вихрь *n.m.* **1,** whirlwind; vortex. **2,** swirl *(of dust);* eddy *(of snow).*

ви́це- *prefix* vice-: ви́це-президéнт, vice-president; ви́це-адмира́л, vice-admiral. —**ви́це-коро́ль**, viceroy.

вишнёвка *n.* cherry brandy.

вишнёвый *adj.* **1,** cherry *(attrib.).* **2,** cherry-colored; cerise.

ви́шня [*gen. pl.* -**шен**] *n.* **1,** cherries. **2,** a (single) cherry. **3,** cherry tree.

вка́лывать *v. impfv.* [*pfv.* вколо́ть] *(with в + acc.)* to stick in; stick into.

вка́пывать *v. impfv.* [*pfv.* вкопа́ть] *(with в + acc.)* to implant; set (in the ground).

вкати́ть [*infl.* вкачý, вка́тишь] *v., pfv. of* вка́тывать. —**вкати́ться**, *refl., pfv. of* вка́тываться.

вка́тывать *v. impfv.* [*pfv.* вкати́ть] **1,** *(with в + acc.)* to roll into; wheel into. **2,** *colloq.* to give; administer. —**вка́тываться**, *refl. (with в + acc.)* to roll into.

вклад *n.* **1,** deposit. **2,** *fig.* contribution.

вкла́дка [*gen. pl.* -**док**] *n.* supplement; insert *(in a publication).*

вкладно́й *adj.* **1,** deposit *(attrib.).* **2,** deposited. **3,** *in* вкладно́й лист, page insert.

вкла́дчик *n.* depositor.

вкла́дывание *n.* inserting; insertion.

вкла́дывать *v. impfv.* [*pfv.* вложи́ть] *(with в + acc.)* **1,** to put into; insert. **2,** to invest (money) in.

вклéивать *v. impfv.* [*pfv.* вклéить] *(with в + acc.)* to paste in.

вклéйка [*gen. pl.* -**éек**] *n.* **1,** pasting in. **2,** inset.

вкли́нивать *v. impfv.* [*pfv.* вкли́нить *or* вклини́ть] *(with в + acc.)* to wedge (into). —**вкли́ниваться**, *refl.* **1,** to be wedged in. **2,** *(with в + acc.)* to drive a wedge (into).

включа́ть *v. impfv.* [*pfv.* включи́ть] **1,** to include. **2,** to turn on; switch on. —**включа́ться**, *refl. (with в + acc.)* to join in.

включа́я *prep., with acc.* including.

включéние *n.* **1,** inclusion. **2,** turning on; switching on.

включи́тельно *adv.* inclusive.

включи́ть *v., pfv. of* включа́ть. —**включи́ться**, *refl., pfv. of* включа́ться.

вкола́чивать *v. impfv.* [*pfv.* вколоти́ть] *colloq.* to hammer in; drive in.

вколоти́ть [*infl.* -лочý, -ло́тишь] *v., pfv. of* вкола́чивать.

вколо́ть [*infl.* вколю́, вко́лешь] *v., pfv. of* вка́лывать.

вконе́ц *adv., colloq.* completely; entirely; utterly.

вкопа́ть *v., pfv. of* вка́пывать. —**как вко́панный**, dead in one's tracks.

вкореня́ть *v. impfv.* [*pfv.* вкорени́ть] to implant; inculcate. —**вкореня́ться**, *refl.* to take root.

вкось *adv.* at an angle; diagonally; catty-corner.

вкра́дчивый *adj.* ingratiating.

вкра́дываться *v.r. impfv.* [*pfv.* вкра́сться] *(with* в + *acc.)* **1,** to creep in(to); steal in(to). **2,** *(of errors, misprints, etc.)* to creep in. —**вкра́дываться в дове́рие к,** to worm one's way into the confidence of.

вкра́пить *v. pfv.* [*infl.* -плю́, -пишь] to sprinkle *(usu. fig.):* в докла́д бы́ли вкра́плены анекдо́ты, the report was sprinkled with (*or* contained numerous) anecdotes.

вкра́сться [*infl. like* красть] *v.r., pfv. of* вкра́дываться.

вкра́тце *adv.* in brief; briefly.

вкривь *adv., colloq.* aslant. —**вкривь и вкось, 1,** in all directions. **2,** without direction; aimlessly.

вкругову́ю *adv., colloq.* around; in a circle.

вкруту́ю *adv., in* яйцо́ вкруту́ю, hard-boiled egg.

вку́пе *adv., obs.* together.

вкус *n.* taste. —**быть по вку́су** (+ *dat.*); **быть в (чьём-нибудь) вкусе**, to be to someone's taste.

вкуси́ть [*infl.* вкушу́, вку́сишь] *v., pfv. of* вкуша́ть.

вку́сно *adv.* (*with verbs of eating, cooking, etc.*) well: вку́сно есть, eat well; вку́сно гото́вить, be a good cook. —*adj., used predicatively* tasty; delicious: о́чень вку́сно!, delicious!

вку́сный *adj.* tasty; delicious; good.

вкусово́й *adj.* taste (*attrib.*); gustatory.

вкуша́ть *v. impfv.* [*pfv.* вкуси́ть] to taste; savor.

вла́га *n.* moisture.

влага́лище *n.* vagina. —**влага́лищный,** *adj.* vaginal.

владе́лец [*gen.* -льца] *n.m.* [*fem.* -лица] owner.

владе́ние *n.* **1,** ownership; possession. **2,** *obs.* property. **3,** *pl.* territories; possessions.

владе́ть *v. impfv.* (*with. instr.*) **1,** to own. **2,** to control (a territory). **3,** to hold (an audience, someone's attention, etc.). **4,** to know how to use; use with skill: владе́ть перо́м, to be a talented writer; владе́ть иностра́нным языко́м, to speak a foreign language. **5,** (*usu. neg.*) (not) to have the use of (a part of one's body). —**владе́ть собо́й,** to control oneself; keep one's temper.

влады́ка *n.m., obs.* ruler; sovereign. —**влады́чество,** *n., obs.* dominion; sway.

вла́жность *n.f.* **1,** humidity. **2,** moisture; dampness.

вла́жный *adj.* **1,** humid. **2,** moist; damp.

вла́мываться *v.r. impfv.* [*pfv.* вломи́ться] (*with* в + *acc.*) **1,** to burst into. **2,** to break into.

вла́ствовать *v. impfv.* [*pres.* -ствую, -ствуешь] (*with* над) to rule; wield power (over).

властели́н *n.* **1,** absolute ruler. **2,** *fig.* (*with gen.*) master (of).

власти́тель *n.m., obs.* ruler. —**власти́тель дум,** major figure; major influence.

вла́стный *adj.* **1,** [*short form only; masc.* вла́стен] having power; (*with inf.*) having the power to. **2,** overpowering. **3,** overbearing; domineering. **4,** (*of one's tone of voice*) peremptory.

властолюби́вый *adj.* power-seeking; power-hungry. —**властолю́бие,** *n.* love of power.

власть *n.f.* **1,** power. **2,** rule: сове́тская власть, Soviet

rule; the Soviet regime. **3,** *pl.* [*gen.* власте́й; *dat.* -стя́м] the authorities. —**ва́ша власть,** *colloq.* as you wish; please yourself. —**во вла́сти** (+ *gen.*), at the mercy of.

власяни́ца *n.* hair shirt.

влачи́ть *v. impfv.* **1,** *obs.* to drag. **2,** *fig.* to lead; live: влачи́ть жа́лкое существова́ние, to lead a miserable existence.

вле́во *adv.* to the left.

влеза́ть *v. impfv.* [*pfv.* влезть] **1,** (*with* на + *acc.*) to climb (a tree, wall, etc.); climb onto. **2,** (*with* в + *acc.*) to climb into; get into (a car, bathtub, etc.). **3,** (*with* в + *acc.*) *colloq.* to fit (into). —**влезть в дове́рие к,** to gain the confidence of. —**влезть в долги́,** to get into debt. —**влезть в ду́шу** (*with gen., dat., or* к), **1,** to win over; gain the confidence of. **2,** to intrude into the personal life of.

влезть [*infl. like* лезть] *v., pfv. of* влеза́ть.

влепи́ть [*infl.* влеплю́, вле́пишь] *v., pfv. of* влепля́ть.

влепля́ть *v. impfv.* [*pfv.* влепи́ть] **1,** to inlay. **2,** *colloq.* to give; let one have: влепи́ть пощёчину (+ *dat.*), to give someone a slap in the face.

влета́ть *v. impfv.* [*pfv.* влете́ть] (*with* в + *acc.*) **1,** to fly into. **2,** *colloq.* to burst into; dash into. **3,** *impers.* (*with dat.*) *colloq.* to get into trouble: ему́ опя́ть влете́ло, he is in trouble again.

влете́ть [*infl.* -чу́, -ти́шь] *v., pfv. of* влета́ть.

влече́ние *n.* (*with* к) **1,** bent (for); penchant (for). **2,** desire (for); lust (for): полово́е влече́ние, sexual desire/drive/appetite.

влечь *v. impfv.* [*pfv.* повле́чь; *pres.* влеку́, влечёшь, ...влеку́т; *past* влёк, влекла́, влекло́] **1,** to draw. **2,** to attract. —**влечь за собо́й, 1,** to involve; entail. **2,** to lead to; bring in its wake.

влива́ние *n.* injection; infusion.

влива́ть *v. impfv.* [*pfv.* влить] (*with* в + *acc.*) **1,** to pour in; pour into. **2,** *fig.* to infuse; instill. —**влива́ться,** *refl.* (*with* в + *acc.*) **1,** to flow into. **2,** to be added to; join.

влипа́ть *v. impfv.* [*pfv.* вли́пнуть] (*with* в + *acc.*) **1,** to stick (to); get stuck (to); get stuck (in). **2,** *colloq.* to get into (trouble, a mess, etc.).

вли́пнуть [*past* влип, -ла] *v., pfv. of* влипа́ть.

влить [*infl.* волью́, вольёшь; *past fem.* влила́] *v., pfv. of* влива́ть. —**вли́ться,** *refl., pfv. of* влива́ться.

влия́ние *n.* influence.

влия́тельный *adj.* influential.

влия́ть *v. impfv.* [*pfv.* повлия́ть] (*with* на + *acc.*) to influence; affect; have an effect upon.

вложе́ние *n.* **1,** enclosure. **2,** investment.

вложи́ть [*infl.* вложу́, вло́жишь] *v., pfv. of* вкла́дывать.

вломи́ться [*infl.* вломлю́сь, вло́мишься] *v.r., pfv. of* вла́мываться.

влюби́ть [*infl.* влюблю́, влю́бишь] *v., pfv. of* влюбля́ть. —**влюби́ться,** *refl., pfv. of* влюбля́ться.

влюблённый *adj.* **1,** (*with* в + *acc.*) in love (with). **2,** loving; amorous. —*n., usu. pl.* lover(s).

влюбля́ть *v. impfv.* [*pfv.* влюби́ть] (*with* в + *acc.*) to make (someone) fall in love (with). —**влюбля́ться,** *refl.* (*with* в + *acc.*) to fall in love (with).

влю́бчивый *adj.* amorous. —**влю́бчивость,** *n.f.* amorousness.

вмени́ть [*infl.* вменю́, вмени́шь] *v., pfv. of* вменя́ть.

вменя́емый *adj., law* of sound mind. —**вменя́емость,** *n.f.* responsibility.

вменя́ть *v. impfv.* [*pfv.* **вмени́ть**] (*with* в + *acc.*) to regard; consider: вменя́ть что́-нибудь в недоста́ток (+ *gen.*), to regard something as a shortcoming of. —**вменя́ть (что́-нибудь) в вину́** (+ *dat.*), to impute something to someone; accuse of. —**вменя́ть себе́ в обя́занность** (+ *inf.*), to take upon oneself the job of.

вме́сте *adv.* together. —**вме́сте с**, together with; along with. —**вме́сте с тем**, at the same time.

вмести́лище *n.* container; receptacle.

вмести́мость *n.f.* capacity.

вмести́тельный *adj.* spacious; roomy. —**вмести́-тельность**, *n.f.* spaciousness; roominess.

вмести́ть [*infl.* -щу́, -сти́шь] *v.*, *pfv. of* вмеща́ть. —**вмести́ться**, *refl.*, *pfv. of* вмеща́ться.

вме́сто *prep.*, *with gen.* instead of; in place of: вме́сто меня́, instead of me; in my place. Вме́сто того́, чтобы оста́ться здесь, instead of remaining here.

вмеша́тельство *n.* (*with* в + *acc.*) interference (in); intervention (in); meddling (in).

вме́шиваться *v.r. impfv.* [*pfv.* **вмеша́ться**] (*with* в + *acc.*) to interfere (in); intervene (in); meddle (in).

вмеща́ть *v. impfv.* [*pfv.* **вмести́ть**] **1,** to hold; seat; accommodate; have a capacity of. **2,** (*with* в + *acc.*) to fit (into); get (into). —**вмеща́ться**, *refl.* (*with* в + *acc.*) to fit (into); go (into).

вмиг *adv.* in an instant; in a flash.

вмина́ть *v. impfv.* [*pfv.* **вмять**] **1,** to press in. **2,** to dent.

вмя́тина *n.* dent.

вмять [*infl.* вомну́, вомнёшь] *v.*, *pfv. of* вмина́ть.

внаём *also*, **внаймы́** *adv.*, *in* брать внаём, to rent; hire; сдава́ть *or* отдава́ть внаём, to rent (out).

внаки́дку *adv.* over one's shoulders: носи́ть пальто́ внаки́дку, to wear a coat over one's shoulders.

внакла́де *adv.*, *colloq.*, *in* оста́ться внакла́де, to be the loser; end up losing.

внакла́дку *adv.*, *in* пить чай внакла́дку, to drink tea with sugar.

внача́ле *adv.* at first; in the beginning.

вне *prep.*, *with gen.* **1,** outside: вне го́рода, outside the city. **2,** out of: вне о́череди, out of turn. **3,** *in* вне сомне́ния, beyond doubt; вне подозре́ний, above suspicion. —**вне себя́ (от)**, beside oneself (with joy, grief, etc.). —**челове́к вне зако́на**, outlaw.

внебра́чный *adj.* **1,** extramarital. **2,** (*of a child*) illegitimate.

вневре́менный *adj.* timeless.

внедре́ние *n.* introduction; incorporation; adoption.

внедря́ть *v. impfv.* [*pfv.* **внедри́ть**] **1,** (*with* в + *acc.*) to instill (in); inculcate (in). **2,** to introduce: внедря́ть но́вую те́хнику, to introduce new equipment.

внеза́пно *adv.* suddenly.

внеза́пность *n.f.* **1,** suddenness. **2,** *mil.* (element of) surprise.

внеза́пный *adj.* **1,** sudden. **2,** *mil.* surprise: внеза́пное нападе́ние, surprise attack.

внекла́ссный *adj.* extracurricular.

внеочередно́й *adj.* **1,** out of turn; out of order. **2,** (*of a meeting, session, etc.*) extraordinary; special.

внесе́ние *n.* **1,** bringing in; carrying in. **2,** entering; insertion. **3,** putting forward; submission.

внести́ [*infl. like* нести́] *v.*, *pfv. of* вноси́ть.

вне́шне *adv.* outwardly; on the surface.

вне́шний *adj.* **1,** outward; outer; outside; external. **2,** foreign: вне́шняя поли́тика, foreign policy.

вне́шность *n.f.* appearance; exterior.

внешта́тный *adj.* not on the permanent staff.

вниз *adv.*, *expressing motion or direction* **1,** down; downward. **2,** downstairs. —**вниз по**, down: вниз по тече́нию, downstream.

внизу́ *adv.*, *expressing location* **1,** below. **2,** downstairs. —*prep.*, *with gen.* at the bottom of.

вника́ть *v. impfv.* [*pfv.* **вни́кнуть**] (*with* в + *acc.*) to go deeply into; delve into; probe.

вни́кнуть [*past* вник *or* вни́кнул, вни́кла] *v.*, *pfv. of* вника́ть.

внима́ние *n.* **1,** attention: обраща́ть внима́ние на, to pay attention to. **2,** kindness; consideration. —**принима́ть во внима́ние**, to consider; take into account; take account of.

внима́тельно *adv.* **1,** attentively; closely. **2,** with consideration.

внима́тельность *n.f.* **1,** attentiveness. **2,** kindness; consideration.

внима́тельный *adj.* **1,** attentive. **2,** considerate; thoughtful.

внима́ть *v. impfv.* [*pfv.* **внять**] (*with* dat.) *poetic* to hearken (to); heed.

вничью́ *adv.*, *sports; games* in a draw; in a tie: зако́н-читься вничью́, to end in a draw/tie. Сыгра́ть вничью́, to play to a draw/tie.

вновь *adv.* **1,** once again; once more. **2,** newly.

вноси́ть *v. impfv.* [*pfv.* **внести́**; *pres.* вношу́, вно́сишь] **1,** to bring in; carry in. **2,** to introduce; bring about. **3,** to cause; create: вноси́ть разла́д в семью́, to cause dissension in the family. **4,** to enter; insert. **5,** to put forward; submit. **6,** to contribute (one's share). Вноси́ть свой вклад (*with* в + *acc.*), to make one's contribution (to).

внук *n.* grandson; grandchild.

вну́тренний *adj.* **1,** internal; inner; interior; inside. **2,** domestic (*as opposed to foreign*). —**вну́тренне**, *adv.* inwardly.

вну́тренность *n.f.* **1,** interior; inside. **2,** *pl.* internal organs; innards.

внутри́ *adv.* inside. —*prep.*, *with gen.* inside; within.

внутриве́нный *adj.* intravenous.

внутрь *adv.*, *expressing direction* inside. —*prep.*, *with gen.* into; inside.

внуча́та [*gen.* -ча́т] *n. pl.*, *colloq.* grandchildren.

внуча́тый *adj.*, *in* внуча́тый племя́нник, grand-nephew; **внуча́тая племя́нница**, grandniece. *Also*, **внуча́тный**.

вну́чка [*gen. pl.* -чек] *n.* granddaughter.

внуша́ть *v. impfv.* [*pfv.* **внуши́ть**] **1,** to instill (respect, confidence, etc.); arouse (fear, envy, etc.): внуша́ть кому́-нибудь страх, to arouse fear in someone. **2,** to suggest (a thought, idea, etc.). **3,** (*with a dependent clause*) to convince; bring home to: он нам внуши́л, что..., he convinced us (of the fact) that...

внуше́ние *n.* **1,** *psychol.* suggestion. **2,** hypnosis. **3,** reprimand.

внуши́тельный *adj.* imposing; impressive.

внуши́ть *v.*, *pfv. of* внуша́ть.

вня́тный *adj.* **1,** distinct; clear. **2,** intelligible.

внять *v.pfv.*, used only in the past [*fem.* вняла́] *pfv. of* внима́ть.

во *prep.* = в.

вобра́ть [*infl.* вберу́, вберёшь; *past fem.* вобрала́] *v.*, *pfv. of* вбира́ть.

вове́к *also*, **вове́ки** *adv.* **1**, forever. **2**, *with a neg. verb* never.

вовлека́ть *v. impfv.* [*pfv.* **вовле́чь**] (*with* **в** + *acc.*) to draw (into); involve (in).

вовлече́ние *n.* involvement.

вовле́чь [*infl. like* **влечь**] *v.*, *pfv. of* **вовлека́ть**.

вовне́ *adv.* outside; without.

во́время *adv.* in time; on time. —**не во́время**, at the wrong time.

во́все *adv.*, *colloq.* **1**, completely. **2**, (*with* **не**) not at all. —**во́все нет!**, not at all!

вовсю́ *adv.*, *colloq.* with all one's might; as fast (*or* hard) as one can.

во-вторы́х secondly; in the second place.

вогна́ть [*infl.* **вгоню́**, **вго́нишь**; *past fem.* **вогнала́**] *v.*, *pfv. of* **вгоня́ть**.

во́гнутый *adj.* concave. —**во́гнутость**, *n.f.* concavity.

вогну́ть *v.*, *pfv. of* **вгиба́ть**.

вода́ [*acc.* **во́ду**; *pl.* **во́ды**] *n.* water.

водворе́ние *n.* **1**, settlement. **2**, establishment.

водворя́ть *v. impfv.* [*pfv.* **водвори́ть**] **1**, to settle; install (people somewhere). **2**, to put back (in its former place). **3**, *fig.* to establish; restore. —**водворя́ться**, *refl.* **1**, to settle. **2**, *fig.* to be established; set in.

водеви́ль *n.m.* vaudeville.

води́тель *n.m.* driver (*of a vehicle*).

води́тельский *adj.* driver (*attrib.*); driver's. —**води́тельские права́**, driver's license.

води́тельство *n.*, *obs.* leadership.

води́ть *v. impfv.* [*pres.* **вожу́**, **во́дишь**] **1**, *indeterm. of* **вести́**. **2**, *colloq.* to keep (animals, birds, etc.). —**води́ть дру́жбу с**, to keep up a friendship with. —**води́ть компа́нию с**, to keep company with.

води́ться *v.r. impfv.* [*pres.* **вожу́сь**, **во́дишься**] **1**, (*of animals, birds, etc.*) to be found (*in a certain area*). **2**, (*with* **с** + *instr.*) *colloq.* to associate (with); consort (with). **3**, (*with* **за** + *instr.*) (*of traits of character*) to be noticed; be observed: за ним никаки́х стра́нностей не води́лось, no peculiarities were observed in his behavior. —**как во́дится**, as usual.

во́дка *n.* vodka.

воднолы́жный *adj.*, *in* **воднолы́жный спорт**, waterskiing.

во́дный *adj.* water (*attrib.*).

водобоя́знь *n.f.* rabies; hydrophobia.

водово́з *n.* water carrier.

водоворо́т *n.* **1**, whirlpool; eddy. **2**, *fig.* vortex; maelstrom.

водоём *n.* reservoir.

водоизмеще́ние *n.*, *naut.* displacement; tonnage.

водока́чка [*gen. pl.* **-чек**] *n.* pumping station.

водола́з *n.* **1**, diver. **2**, Newfoundland dog. —**водола́зный**, *adj.* diving (*attrib.*).

Водоле́й *n.* Aquarius.

водоме́р *n.* water meter.

водонапо́рный *adj.*, *in* **водонапо́рная ба́шня**, water tower.

водонепроница́емый *adj.* waterproof; watertight.

водоно́с *n.* water carrier.

водоотво́д *n.* drainage system. —**водоотво́дный**, *adj.* drain (*attrib.*); drainage (*attrib.*).

водопа́д *n.* waterfall.

водопла́вающий *adj.*, *in* **водопла́вающая пти́ца**, water bird; waterfowl.

водопо́й *n.* **1**, watering place. **2**, watering (*of livestock*).

водопрово́д *n.* indoor plumbing; running water.

водопрово́дный *adj.* pert. to the carrying or supplying of water: водопрово́дная магистра́ль, water main. —**водопрово́дная вода́**, tap water.

водопрово́дчик *n.* plumber.

водоразбо́рный *adj.*, *in* **водоразбо́рная коло́нка** *and* **водоразбо́рный кран**, hydrant.

водоразде́л *n.* watershed.

водоро́д *n.* hydrogen.

водоро́дный *adj.* hydrogen. —**водоро́дная бо́мба**, hydrogen bomb.

во́доросль *n.f.* algae; seaweed. *Often,* **морска́я во́доросль**.

водосви́нка [*gen. pl.* **-нок**] *n.* capybara.

водосли́в *n.* spillway.

водосто́к *n.* drain; gutter.

водосто́чный *adj.*, *in* **водосто́чный жёлоб** *and* **водосто́чная кана́ва**, gutter; **водосто́чная труба́**, drainpipe.

водохрани́лище *n.* reservoir.

во́дочный *adj.* vodka (*attrib.*).

водружа́ть *v. impfv.* [*pfv.* **водрузи́ть**] to place firmly; plant; implant.

водяни́стый *adj.* **1**, watery. **2**, *fig.* colorless; insipid.

водя́нка *n.* dropsy.

водяно́й *adj.* water (*attrib.*); aquatic. —*n.* water sprite. —**водяно́й знак**, watermark. —**водяно́е колесо́**, water wheel. —**водяна́я ли́лия**, water lily.

воева́ть *v. impfv.* [*pres.* **вою́ю**, **вою́ешь**] **1**, (*with* **с** + *instr. or* **про́тив**) to be at war (with); fight (against). **2**, (*of a soldier*) to fight; see action.

воево́да *n.m.*, *hist.* military governor in Old Russia (*from the 16th to the end of the 18th century*).

воеди́но *adv.* into one; together.

военача́льник *n.* commander (*of a large military or naval unit*).

вое́нно-возду́шный *adj.*, *in* **вое́нно-возду́шные си́лы**, air force.

вое́нно-морско́й *adj.*, *in* **вое́нно-морско́й флот**, navy.

военнообя́занный *n.*, *decl. as an adj.* person subject to call-up; person subject to the draft.

военнопле́нный *n.*, *decl. as an adj.* prisoner of war.

военнослу́жащий *n.*, *decl. as an adj.* soldier; serviceman.

вое́нный *adj.* **1**, war (*attrib.*): вое́нное вре́мя, wartime. **2**, military. **3**, martial. —*n.* military man; serviceman. —**вое́нные де́йствия**, military operations; hostilities. —**вое́нный заво́д**, munitions factory. —**вое́нное положе́ние**, martial law. —**вое́нная промы́шленность**, the armaments industry. —**вое́нный суд**, court-martial.

вое́нщина *n.* the military; militarists.

вожа́к [*gen.* **-жака́**] *n.* **1**, leader. **2**, guide.

вожа́тый *n.*, *decl. as an adj.* **1**, *obs.* guide. **2**, young pioneer leader. **3**, streetcar driver.

вожделе́ние *n.* **1**, longing; craving. **2**, desire; lust.

вожде́ние *n.* driving; steering; piloting.

вождь [*gen.* **вождя́**] *n.m.* leader.

во́жжи [*gen.* **вожже́й**] *n. pl.* [*sing.* **вожжа́**] reins.

воз [*2nd loc.* **возу́**; *pl.* **возы́**] *n.* **1**, cart. **2**, cartload. —**а воз и ны́не там**, things are right where they started. —что с во́зу упа́ло, то пропа́ло, there's no use crying over spilt milk.

воз- *also*, вос- *prefix*, **1**, *indicating upward direction*: возводи́ть, to erect; elevate; raise. **2**, *indicating repetition of an action*: воссоединя́ть, to reunite; воспроизводи́ть, to reproduce.

возбраня́ть *v. impfv.* [*pfv.* возбрани́ть] *obs.* to forbid. —возбраня́ться, *refl.* [*impfv. only*] *obs.* to be forbidden.

возбуди́мый *adj.* excitable. —возбуди́мость, *n.f.* excitability.

возбуди́тель *n.m.* agent; cause; stimulus.

возбуди́ть [*infl.* -жу́, -ди́шь] *v., pfv. of* возбужда́ть.

возбужда́ть *v. impfv.* [*pfv.* возбуди́ть] **1**, to arouse; rouse; excite. **2**, to stir up; incite. **3**, to raise (a question); bring (a lawsuit).

возбужда́ющий *adj.* rousing; stirring. —возбужда́ющее сре́дство, stimulant.

возбужде́ние *n.* **1**, excitation; stimulation. **2**, excitement.

возбуждённый *adj.* excited.

возведе́ние *n.* **1**, erection. **2**, leveling (*of an accusation*). **3**, *math.* raising (*to a certain power*).

возвели́чивать *v. impfv.* [*pfv.* возвели́чить] *obs.* to extol; exalt.

возвести́ [*infl. like* вести́] *v., pfv. of* возводи́ть.

возвеща́ть *v. impfv.* [*pfv.* возвести́ть] **1**, to announce. **2**, to herald; usher in.

возводи́ть *v. impfv.* [*pfv.* возвести́; *pres.* -вожу́, -во́дишь] **1**, to erect. **2**, to elevate (to a certain rank): возводи́ть на престо́л, to raise to the throne. **3**, to level (an accusation). **4**, to trace back (*in time*). **5**, *math.* to raise (to a certain power).

возвра́т *n.* **1**, return. **2**, recurrence. **3**, repayment.

возврати́ть [*infl.* -щу́, -ти́шь] *v., pfv. of* возвраща́ть. —возврати́ться, *refl., pfv. of* возвраща́ться.

возвра́тный *adj.* **1**, *obs.* return (*attrib.*): на возвра́тном пути́, on the way back. **2**, *gram.* reflexive: возвра́тный глаго́л, reflexive verb. —возвра́тный тиф, relapsing fever.

возвраща́ть *v. impfv.* [*pfv.* верну́ть *and* возврати́ть] **1**, to return; give back. **2**, to pay (a debt); repay (a loan). **3**, to restore. **4**, to recover; regain; get back. —возвраща́ться, *refl.* to return; come back; go back.

возвраще́ние *n.* **1**, return: по возвраще́нии домо́й, on returning home. **2**, return; giving back. **3**, repayment.

возвыша́ть *v. impfv.* [*pfv.* возвы́сить] **1**, to raise. **2**, [*impfv. only*] to uplift; ennoble. —возвыша́ться, *refl.* **1**, to rise. **2**, [*impfv. only*] (with над) to tower (over *or* above).

возвыше́ние *n.* **1**, rise; rising. **2**, platform; dais. **3**, elevation; hill.

возвы́шенность *n.f.* **1**, height; hill. **2**, loftiness.

возвы́шенный *adj.* **1**, high; elevated. **2**, *fig.* lofty.

возглавля́ть *v. impfv.* [*pfv.* возгла́вить] to head; be the head of.

во́зглас *n.* shout; cry; exclamation.

возглаша́ть *v. impfv.* [*pfv.* возгласи́ть] to proclaim.

возго́нка *n., chem.* sublimation.

возгоня́ть *v. impfv., chem.* to sublimate.

возгора́ться *v.r. impfv.* [*pfv.* возгоре́ться] **1**, to flare up. **2**, *fig.* (with instr.) to be stirred (with); be inflamed (with).

возгорди́ться *v.r. pfv.* [*infl.* -жу́сь, -ди́шься] (with instr.) to get a swelled head (over).

возгоре́ться *v.r., pfv. of* возгора́ться.

воздава́ть *v. impfv.* [*pfv.* возда́ть; *pres.* -даю́, -даёшь] **1**, to render. **2**, (with instr.) to repay (with). —воздава́ть до́лжное, *see* до́лжное.

возда́ть [*infl. like* дать; *past* возда́л, -ла́, -да́ло] *v., pfv. of* воздава́ть.

воздвига́ть *v. impfv.* [*pfv.* воздви́гнуть] to erect.

воздви́гнуть [*past* -дви́г *or* -дви́гнул, -дви́гла] *v., pfv. of* воздвига́ть.

возде́йствие *n.* influence; effect.

возде́йствовать *v. impfv. & pfv.* [*pres.* -ствую, -ствуешь] (with на + acc.) to influence; bring pressure to bear (on).

возде́лать *v., pfv. of* возде́лывать.

возде́лывать *v. impfv.* [*pfv.* возде́лать] to till; cultivate.

воздержа́вшийся *n., decl. as an adj.* abstention: при двух воздержа́вшихся, with two abstentions.

воздержа́ние *n.* **1**, (with от) abstention; abstinence. **2**, (with в + prepl.) moderation; temperance.

возде́ржанность *n.f.* moderation; temperance. —возде́ржанный, *adj.* observing moderation.

воздержа́ться [*infl.* -держу́сь, -де́ржишься] *v.r., pfv. of* возде́рживаться.

возде́рживаться *v.r. impfv.* [*pfv.* воздержа́ться] (with от) **1**, to refrain (from). **2**, to abstain (from).

возде́ть *v. pfv.* [*infl.* -де́ну, -де́нешь], *in* возде́ть ру́ки, *obs.* to lift up (*or* raise) one's hands.

во́здух *n.* air. —на во́здух (*with verbs of motion*), outdoors. —на (откры́том) во́здухе, outdoors; out of doors.

воздухопла́вание *n.* aeronautics. —воздухопла́ватель, *n.m.* aeronaut. —воздухопла́вательный, *adj.* aeronautic; aeronautical.

воздушнодеса́нтный *adj., mil.* airborne: воздушнодеса́нтные войска́, airborne troops.

возду́шный *adj.* **1**, air (*attrib.*); aerial. **2**, airy. —возду́шный шар, balloon.

воззва́ние *n.* appeal.

воззва́ть [*infl. like* звать] *v., pfv. of* взыва́ть.

воззре́ние *n.* outlook; view.

вози́ть *v. impfv.* [*pres.* вожу́, во́зишь] *indeterm. of* везти́. —вози́ться, *refl.* **1**, to play; romp; frolic. **2**, *colloq.* to putter (about). **3**, (with с + instr.) *colloq.* to fiddle (with); tinker (with).

возлага́ть *v. impfv.* [*pfv.* возложи́ть] (with на + acc.) **1**, to place (on); lay (on): возложи́ть вено́к на моги́лу, to place/lay a wreath on a grave. **2**, to give; assign; turn over (work, a task, etc.) to. **3**, to place; pin (hopes, blame, responsibility, etc.) on.

во́зле *prep., with gen.* **1**, by; near. **2**, beside; alongside; next to. —*adv.* nearby.

возложи́ть [*infl.* -ложу́, -ло́жишь] *v., pfv. of* возлага́ть.

возлю́бленный *n., decl. as an adj.* loved one; sweetheart.

возме́здие *n.* retribution; requital.

возмеща́ть *v. impfv.* [*pfv.* возмести́ть] **1**, to refund (expenses); make up; recover (losses); make up for (lost time). **2**, (with dat.) to compensate; reimburse: возмеща́ть кому́-нибудь расхо́ды, to reimburse someone for his expenses.

возмещёние *n.* compensation; reimbursement.

возмо́жно *adv.* **1,** possibly. **2,** (*with comp. adjectives & adverbs*) as ... as possible: возмо́жно скоре́е, as soon as possible. —*adj., used predicatively* possible: э́то вполне́ возмо́жно, it/that is entirely possible.

возмо́жность *n.f.* **1,** possibility. **2,** opportunity; chance. **3,** *pl.* means; resources. **4,** *pl., mil.* capabilities. —до после́дней возмо́жности, to the utmost. —по (ме́ре) возмо́жности, as far as possible.

возмо́жный *adj.* possible. —де́лать всё возмо́жное, to do everything possible; do everything in one's power; do one's utmost.

возмужа́лый *adj.* mature; virile. —**возмужа́лость,** *n.f.* maturity; virility.

возмужа́ть *v. pfv.* (*of a young boy or girl*) to mature; develop.

возмути́тельно *adv.* outrageously. —*adj., used predicatively* outrageous: э́то возмути́тельно!, it's outrageous!; it's an outrage!

возмути́тельный *adj.* outrageous; disgraceful.

возмуща́ть *v. impfv.* [*pfv.* **возмути́ть**] to rouse the indignation of; outrage. —**возмуща́ться,** *refl.* to be indignant; be outraged.

возмуще́ние *n.* indignation; outrage.

возмущённый *adj.* indignant; outraged.

вознагражда́ть *v. impfv.* [*pfv.* **вознагради́ть**] to reward; compensate; remunerate; recompense.

вознагражде́ние *n.* reward; compensation; remuneration; recompense.

вознаме́риться *v.r. pfv.* (*with inf.*) *obs.* to decide (to); make up one's mind (to).

возненави́деть *v. pfv.* [*infl.* -жу, -дишь] to develop a hatred for.

вознесе́ние *n., relig.* **1,** the Ascension. **2,** Ascension Day.

вознести́ [*infl. like* нести́] *v., pfv. of* возноси́ть. —**вознести́сь,** *refl., pfv. of* возноси́ться.

возника́ть *v. impfv.* [*pfv.* **возни́кнуть**] to arise; spring up; crop up.

возникнове́ние *n.* origin; rise; beginning.

возни́кнуть [*past* -ни́к, -ла] *v., pfv. of* возника́ть.

возни́ца *n.m.* coachman.

возноси́ть *v. impfv.* [*pfv.* **вознести́;** *pres.* -ношу́, -но́сишь] **1,** to raise; lift up. **2,** to offer up (a prayer). —**возноси́ться,** *refl.* to loom up.

возня́ *n., colloq.* **1,** bustle; scurrying. **2,** trouble; bother. —мыши́ная возня́, petty cares.

возоблада́ть *v. pfv., obs.* to prevail.

возобнови́ть [*infl.* -влю́, -ви́шь] *v., pfv. of* возобновля́ть.

возобновле́ние *n.* renewal; resumption.

возобновля́ть *v. impfv.* [*pfv.* **возобнови́ть**] to renew; resume. —**возобновля́ться,** *refl.* to start again; resume.

возомни́ть *v. pfv.* [*usu. with* себя́ *and instr.*] *colloq.* to to imagine oneself to be. —**возомни́ть о себе́,** to get a swelled head.

возража́ть *v. impfv.* [*pfv.* **возрази́ть**] to object; have an objection.

возраже́ние *n.* objection.

возрази́ть [*infl.* -жу́, -зи́шь] *v., pfv. of* возража́ть.

во́зраст *n.* age.

возраста́ние *n.* growth; increase.

возраста́ть *v. impfv.* [*pfv.* **возрасти́**] **1,** *obs.* to grow. **2,** to increase.

возрасти́ [*infl. like* расти́] *v., pfv. of* возраста́ть.

возрастно́й *adj.* age (*attrib.*).

возрожда́ть *v. impfv.* [*pfv.* **возроди́ть**] to revive; restore. —**возрожда́ться,** *refl.* **1,** to be revived. **2,** to be reborn.

возрожде́ние *n.* **1,** revival; rebirth; renaissance. **2,** *cap.* the Renaissance.

во́зчик *n.* carter.

возыме́ть *v. pfv.* **1,** *obs.* to acquire; achieve. **2,** to develop (a feeling, liking, etc.). —**возыме́ть де́йствие,** to have an effect; achieve the desired effect. —**возыме́ть обра́тное де́йствие,** to have the reverse effect. —**возыме́ть си́лу,** to go into effect; come into force.

во́ин *n.* warrior; soldier.

во́инский *adj.* military. —**во́инский эшело́н,** troop train.

во́инственный *adj.* militant; warlike; belligerent; bellicose. —**во́инственность,** *n.f.* militancy; belligerence; bellicosity.

во́инствующий *adj.* militant.

вои́стину *adv., archaic* truly; verily.

вой *n.* howl; howling; wail; wailing.

во́йлок *n.* felt. —**во́йлочный,** *adj.* felt.

война́ [*pl.* во́йны] *n.* war.

войска́ [*gen.* войск] *n., pl. of* во́йско, troops.

во́йско *n.* army.

войсково́й *adj.* troop (*attrib.*).

войти́ [*infl.* войду́, войдёшь; *past* вошёл, вошла́, вошло́] *v., pfv. of* входи́ть.

вокали́ст *n.* voice teacher.

вока́льный *adj.* vocal.

вокза́л *n.* (railroad) station. —**вокза́льный,** *adj.* station (*attrib.*).

вокру́г *prep., with gen.* around. —*adv.* around; about. —ходи́ть вокру́г да о́коло, to beat around the bush.

вол [*gen.* вола́] *n.* ox.

вола́н *n.* **1,** flounce (*on a dress*). **2,** shuttlecock.

волды́рь [*gen.* -дыря́] *n.m.* blister.

волево́й *adj.* **1,** volitional. **2,** strong-willed.

волейбо́л *n.* volleyball. —**волейболи́ст,** *n.* volleyball player. —**волейбо́льный,** *adj.* volleyball (*attrib.*).

во́лей-нево́лей *adv.* having no other choice; perforce; willy-nilly.

волк [*pl.* во́лки, волко́в, волка́м] *n.* wolf. —**волк в ове́чьей шку́ре,** wolf in sheep's clothing. —**во́лком смотре́ть,** to scowl; glower. —**морско́й волк,** *colloq.* old sailor; sea dog.

волкода́в *n.* wolfhound.

волна́ [*pl.* во́лны, волн, волна́м *or* во́лнам] *n.* wave.

волне́ние *n.* **1,** rough seas; choppy seas. **2,** agitation; nervousness. **3,** *pl.* unrest; disturbances (*civil, political, etc.*).

волни́стый *adj.* **1,** wavy. **2,** rolling; undulating.

волнова́ть *v. impfv.* [*pfv.* **взволнова́ть;** *pres.* -ну́ю, -ну́ешь] **1,** to agitate; ruffle; stir. **2,** to excite; disturb; upset. —**волнова́ться,** *refl.* **1,** (*of the sea*) to be agitated; be choppy. **2,** to be excited; be disturbed; be nervous; be upset.

волноло́м *n.* breakwater.

волнообра́зный *adj.* undulating.

волноре́з *n.* breakwater.

волну́ющий *adj.* **1,** stirring; exciting; thrilling. **2,** disturbing; troubling; upsetting.

воло́вий [*fem.* -вья] *adj.* ox (*attrib.*).

во́лок *n.* (place of) portage.

ВОЛОКИ́ТА *n.f.* red tape. —*n.m.*, *obs.* ladies' man.

ВОЛОКНИ́СТЫЙ *adj.* fibrous; stringy.

ВОЛОКНО́ [*pl.* -о́кна, -о́кон] *n.* fiber; filament.

ВОЛОНТЁР *n.*, *obs.* volunteer.

ВО́ЛОС [*pl.* во́лосы, воло́с, -са́м] *n.* **1**, a single hair. **2**, *pl.* hair. —**ни на́ волос**, not in the least; not a bit.

ВОЛОСА́ТЫЙ *adj.* hairy.

ВОЛОСО́К [*gen.* -ска́] *n.* **1**, *dim. of* во́лос. **2**, filament (*of a bulb*); hairspring (*of a watch*). —**висе́ть на волоске́**, to hang by a thread. —**на волосо́к (волоске́) от**, within a hairbreadth of.

ВО́ЛОСТЬ *n.f.*, *obs.* small administrative district.

ВОЛОСЯНО́Й *adj.* hair (*attrib.*).

ВОЛОЧИ́ТЬ *v. impfv.* [*pres.* -очу́, -о́чишь] to drag. —**волочи́ться**, *refl.* **1**, to drag; trail. **2**, to drag oneself along; shuffle along.

ВОЛО́ЧЬ *v. impfv.* [*pres.* -оку́, -очёшь, ...-оку́т; *past* воло́к, -локла́, -локло́] *colloq.* = воло́чить. —воло́чься, *refl.* = волочи́ться.

ВОЛХВ [*gen.* волхва́] *n.* **1**, sorcerer. **2**, *pl.* the Magi.

ВОЛЧА́НКА *n.* lupus (*skin disease*).

ВО́ЛЧИЙ [*fem.* -чья] *adj.* wolf (*attrib.*); wolf's. —**во́лчий аппети́т**, voracious appetite. —**во́лчья пасть**, cleft palate.

ВОЛЧО́К [*gen.* -чка́] *n.* top (*toy*).

ВОЛЧО́НОК [*gen.* -нка; *pl.* -ча́та, -ча́т] *n.* wolf cub.

ВОЛШЕ́БНИК *n.* magician; wizard; sorcerer.

ВОЛШЕ́БНЫЙ *adj.* **1**, magic; magical. **2**, *fig.* enchanting; captivating. —**волше́бная ска́зка**, fairy tale.

волшебство́ *n.* magic.

ВОЛЫ́НКА *n.* **1**, bagpipe; bagpipes. **2**, *colloq.* delay; dawdling; procrastination. —**волы́нщик**, *n.* piper.

ВОЛЬГО́ТНЫЙ *adj.*, *colloq.* free; free and easy.

ВОЛЬЕ́Р *also*, **вольера** *n.* enclosure (*for animals or birds*).

ВО́ЛЬНИЧАТЬ *v. impfv.*, *colloq.* to take liberties.

ВО́ЛЬНО *adv.* **1**, freely; voluntarily. **2**, loosely. **3**, *mil.* at ease. —*interj.*, *mil.* at ease!; as you were!

ВОЛЬНОДУ́МЕЦ [*gen.* -мца] *n.*, *obs.* freethinker. —**вольноду́мный**, *adj.*, *obs.* freethinking. —**вольноду́мство**, *n.*, *obs.* free thought.

ВОЛЬНОЛЮБИ́ВЫЙ *adj.* freedom-loving.

ВОЛЬНОНАЁМНЫЙ *adj.* civilian.

ВОЛЬНОСЛУ́ШАТЕЛЬ *n.m.*, *obs.* non-matriculated student.

ВО́ЛЬНОСТЬ *n.f.* **1**, freedom; liberty; license. **2**, undue familiarity; liberties. —**поэти́ческая во́льность**, poetic license.

ВО́ЛЬНЫЙ *adj.* **1**, free. **2**, unrestricted. **3**, unduly familiar. **4**, [*short form only* — во́лен, вольна́] (*with inf.*) free (to); at liberty (to).

ВОЛЬТ [*gen. pl.* вольт] *n.* volt.

ВОЛЬТА́Ж [*gen.* -тажа́] *n.* voltage.

ВОЛЬТМЕ́ТР *n.* voltmeter.

ВОЛЬФРА́М *n.* tungsten. —**вольфра́мовый**, *adj.* tungsten.

ВО́ЛЯ *n.* **1**, will. **2**, freedom. **3**, *hist.* emancipation. —**во́ля ва́ша**, as you please. —**дава́ть во́лю** (+ *dat.*), to give free rein to. —**до́брая во́ля**, good will. —**отпуска́ть на во́лю**, to set free. —**по до́брой во́ле**, of one's own free will. —**после́дняя во́ля**, last will and testament. —**си́ла во́ли**, will power.

ВОН *adv.*, *colloq.* out; away: **он вы́шел вон**, he went out; **пошёл вон!**, away with you! **У меня́ э́то из ума́ вон**, it completely slipped my mind. —*particle* there;

over there: **вон там**, over there. **Вон он идёт**, there he goes. —*interj.* be off!; get out!

ВОНЗА́ТЬ *v. impfv.* [*pfv.* вонзи́ть] (*with* в + *acc.*) to thrust (into); plunge (into). —**вонза́ться**, *refl.* (*with* в + *acc.*) to pierce; enter.

ВОНЗИ́ТЬ [*infl.* вонжу́, вонзи́шь] *v.*, *pfv. of* вонза́ть. —**вонзи́ться**, *refl.*, *pfv. of* вонза́ться.

ВОНЬ *n.f.*, *colloq.* stink; stench.

ВОНЮ́ЧИЙ *adj.*, *colloq.* stinking.

ВОНЮ́ЧКА [*gen. pl.* -чек] *n.* skunk.

ВОНЯ́ТЬ *v. impfv.*, *colloq.* **1**, to stink. **2**, (*with* от) to reek (of).

вообража́емый *adj.* imaginary.

вообража́ть *v. impfv.* [*pfv.* вообрази́ть] to imagine.

воображе́ние *n.* imagination.

вообрази́мый *adj.* imaginable.

вообрази́ть [*infl.* -жу́, -зи́шь] *v.*, *pfv. of* вообража́ть.

вообще́ *adv.* **1**, in general. **2**, always. **3**, *fol. by* не (not) at all. —**вообще́ говоря́**, generally speaking.

воодушеви́ть [*infl.* -влю́, -ви́шь] *v.*, *pfv. of* воодушевля́ть.

воодушевле́ние *n.* enthusiasm; animation.

воодушевля́ть *v. impfv.* [*pfv.* воодушеви́ть] to inspire; fill with enthusiasm.

вооружа́ть *v. impfv.* [*pfv.* вооружи́ть] **1**, to arm. **2**, to equip; supply. **3**, (*with* про́тив) to set against. —**вооружа́ться**, *refl.* to arm (oneself).

вооруже́ние *n.* **1**, arming; armament. **2**, *often pl.* armaments; arms: го́нка вооруже́ний, arms race. —**брать** *or* **принима́ть (что-нибудь) на вооруже́ние**, to add to one's arsenal; place in service.

вооружённый *adj.* armed. —**вооружённые си́лы**, armed forces.

вооружи́ть *v.*, *pfv. of* вооружа́ть. —**вооружи́ться**, *refl.*, *pfv. of* вооружа́ться.

воо́чию *adv.* **1**, with one's own eyes: воо́чию убеди́ться, to see for oneself. **2**, clearly; graphically.

во-пе́рвых in the first place; to begin with.

ВОПИ́ТЬ *v. impfv.* [*pres.* воплю́, вопи́шь] *colloq.* to cry out.

вопию́щий *adj.* **1**, outrageous; appalling. **2**, glaring; flagrant. —**глас вопию́щего в пусты́не**, voice in the wilderness.

воплоща́ть *v. impfv.* [*pfv.* воплоти́ть] to embody; personify. —**воплоща́ть в жизнь**, to make a reality of.

воплоще́ние *n.* embodiment.

ВОПЛЬ *n.m.* cry; howl; wail.

ВОПРЕКИ́ *prep.*, *with dat.* contrary to; in defiance of.

ВОПРО́С *n.* **1**, question. **2**, problem; matter. —**под вопро́сом**, open to question; undecided. —**ста́вить под вопро́с**, to question; call into question.

ВОПРОСИ́ТЕЛЬНЫЙ *adj.* **1**, questioning; inquiring. **2**, *gram.* interrogative. —**вопроси́тельный знак**, question mark.

ВОПРО́СНИК *n.* questionnaire.

ВОР [*pl.* во́ры, воро́в, вора́м] *n.* thief. —**карма́нный вор**, pickpocket. —**магази́нный вор**, shoplifter.

ВО́РВАНЬ *n.f.* blubber.

ВОРВА́ТЬСЯ [*infl. like* рвать] *v.r.*, *pfv. of* врыва́ться.

ВОРИ́ШКА [*gen. pl.* -шек] *n.m.* petty thief.

ВОРКОВА́ТЬ *v. impfv.* [*pres.* -ку́ю, -ку́ешь] **1**, to coo. **2**, *fig.* to bill and coo.

ВОРКОТНЯ́ *n.*, *colloq.* grumbling; griping.

ВОРОБЕ́Й [*gen.* -бья́] *n.* sparrow. —**стре́ляный воробе́й**, *colloq.* old hand.

воробьи́ный *adj.* sparrow's.

воро́ванный *adj.* stolen.

ворова́тый *adj.* **1,** thievish. **2,** furtive.

ворова́ть *v. impfv.* [*pres.* -ру́ю, -ру́ешь] to steal.

воро́вка [*gen. pl.* -вок] *n., fem. of* вор.

воровски́ *adv., colloq.* **1,** dishonestly. **2,** furtively.

воровско́й *adj.* thieves'.

воровство́ *n.* stealing; theft; larceny.

ворожба́ *n.* fortunetelling. —ворожея́, *n.* fortuneteller.

ворожи́ть *v. impfv.* [*pfv.* поворожи́ть] to tell fortunes.

во́рон *n.* raven.

воро́на *n.* crow.

воро́ний [*fem.* -нья] *adj.* **1,** crow's. **2,** of crows: воро́нья ста́я, flock of crows.

ворони́ть *v. impfv.* to burnish.

воро́нка [*gen. pl.* -нок] *n.* **1,** funnel. **2,** bomb crater.

вороно́й *adj.* (*of a horse*) black. —*n.* black horse.

во́рот *n.* **1,** collar. **2,** winch.

воро́та [*gen.* воро́т] *n. pl.* **1,** gate. **2,** *sports* goal; net.

вороти́ла *n.m., colloq.* bigwig.

вороти́ть *v. pfv.* [*infl.* -рочу́, -ро́тишь] *colloq.* to bring back. —вороти́ться, *refl., colloq.* to return; come back.

воротни́к [*gen.* -ника́] *n.* collar.

воротничо́к [*gen.* -чка́] *n., dim. of* воротни́к.

во́рох [*pl.* вороха́] *n.* pile; heap.

воро́чать *v. impfv.* **1,** to move; shift; roll; turn. **2,** (*with instr.*) *colloq.* to boss; manage; manipulate. —воро́чаться, *refl., colloq.* to turn from side to side; toss and turn.

вороши́ть *v. impfv.* **1,** to stir. **2,** to pitch (hay). —вороши́ться, *refl.* to stir; move about.

ворс *n.* nap; pile (*on cloth*).

ворси́нка [*gen. pl.* -нок] *n.* hair; fiber.

ворча́ние *n.* **1,** growling. **2,** *colloq.* grumbling; griping.

ворча́ть *v. impfv.* [*pres.* -чу́, -чи́шь] **1,** (*with* на + *acc.*) to growl (at). **2,** *colloq.* to grumble; gripe.

ворчли́вый *adj.* grumbling; grouchy; grumpy; surly.

ворчу́н [*gen.* -чуна́] *n.m.* [*fem.* -чу́нья] grumbler; griper.

вос- *prefix, var. of* воз- (*used before voiceless consonants*).

восвоя́си *adv., colloq.* home: пойти́ восвоя́си, to go home.

восемна́дцать *numeral* eighteen. —восемна́дцатый, *ordinal numeral* eighteenth.

во́семь [*gen., dat., & prepl.* восьми́; *instr.* восьмью́ *or* восемью́] *numeral* eight.

во́семьдесят [*gen., dat., & prepl.* восьми́десяти; *instr.* восьмью́десятью *or* восемью́десятью] *numeral* eighty.

восемьсо́т [*gen.* восьмисо́т; *dat.* восьмиста́м; *instr.* восьмьюста́ми *or* восемьюста́ми; *prepl.* восьмиста́х] *numeral* eight hundred.

во́семью *adv.* eight times: во́семью де́сять — во́семьдесят, eight times ten is eighty.

воск *n.* wax.

воскли́кнуть *v., pfv. of* восклица́ть.

восклица́ние *n.* exclamation.

восклица́тельный *adj.* exclamatory; exclamation (*attrib.*). —восклица́тельный знак, exclamation point.

восклица́ть *v. impfv.* [*pfv.* воскли́кнуть] to exclaim.

восково́й *adj.* **1,** wax (*attrib.*). **2,** waxy; waxen.

воскреса́ть *v. impfv.* [*pfv.* воскре́снуть] **1,** to rise from the dead; come back to life. **2,** to regain one's strength; revive. **3,** to come back to mind.

воскресе́ние *n.* **1,** resurrection. **2,** *fig.* revival.

воскресе́нье *n.* Sunday.

воскреси́ть [*infl.* -шу́, -си́шь] *v., pfv. of* воскреша́ть.

воскре́снуть [*past* -кре́с, -ла] *v., pfv. of* воскреса́ть.

воскре́сный *adj.* Sunday (*attrib.*).

воскреша́ть *v. impfv.* [*pfv.* воскреси́ть] **1,** to resurrect; raise from the dead; bring back to life. **2,** to revive; resurrect (a custom, hopes, etc.). **3,** to revitalize. **4,** *in* воскреша́ть в па́мяти, to (re)call to mind.

воскреше́ние *n.* resurrection; revival.

воспале́ние *n.* inflammation. —воспале́ние лёгких, pneumonia. —воспале́ние не́рвов, neuritis.

воспалённый *adj.* inflamed.

воспали́тельный *adj.* inflammatory; inflammation (*attrib.*).

воспаля́ть *v. impfv.* [*pfv.* воспали́ть] *obs.* to inflame. —воспаля́ться, *refl.* to become inflamed.

воспева́ть *v. impfv.* [*pfv.* воспе́ть] to praise; extol (*in verse or song*).

воспе́ть [*infl.* -пою́, -поёшь] *v., pfv. of* воспева́ть.

воспита́ние *n.* **1,** raising; rearing; bringing up. **2,** upbringing. **3,** education. **4,** (good) breeding. **5,** fostering; cultivating.

воспи́танник *n.* **1,** pupil. **2,** adopted child; ward. **3,** (*with gen.*) graduate (of); alumnus (of).

воспи́танность *n.f.* (good) breeding.

воспи́танный *adj.* well-bred; well-mannered.

воспита́тель *n.m.* educator; teacher; mentor. —воспита́тельница, *n.* teacher; governess.

воспита́тельный *adj.* educational. —воспита́тельный дом, *pre-rev.* foundling home.

воспи́тывать *v. impfv.* [*pfv.* воспита́ть] **1,** to raise; bring up; rear. **2,** to educate; train. **3,** to foster; cultivate.

воспламене́ние *n.* **1,** combustion. **2,** ignition.

воспламени́ть *v., pfv. of* воспламеня́ть. —воспламени́ться, *refl., pfv. of* воспламеня́ться.

воспламеня́емость *n.f.* inflammability.

воспламеня́ть *v. impfv.* [*pfv.* воспламени́ть] **1,** to ignite; kindle. **2,** *fig.* to rouse; fire (up). —воспламеня́ться, *refl.* **1,** to flare up; burst into flames. **2,** *fig.* (*with instr.*) to become fired (with).

восполня́ть *v. impfv.* [*pfv.* воспо́лнить] to fill (a gap); make up for (a deficiency).

воспо́льзоваться *v.r., pfv. of* по́льзоваться.

воспомина́ние *n.* **1,** memory; recollection. **2,** *pl.* memoirs; reminiscences.

воспрепя́тствовать *v., pfv. of* препя́тствовать.

воспрети́ть [*infl.* -щу́, -ти́шь] *v., pfv. of* воспреща́ть.

воспреща́ть *v. impfv.* [*pfv.* воспрети́ть] **1,** to prohibit; forbid. **2,** *mil.* to interdict. —воспреща́ться, *refl.* [*impfv. only*] to be prohibited; be forbidden.

воспреще́ние *n.* **1,** prohibition. **2,** *mil.* interdiction.

восприи́мчивость *n.f.* **1,** receptivity. **2,** susceptibility.

восприи́мчивый *adj.* **1,** keen; receptive. **2,** (*with* к) susceptible (to).

воспринима́ть *v. impfv.* [*pfv.* восприня́ть] **1,** to perceive. **2,** to take in; assimilate; absorb (*mentally*). **3,** (*with* как) to take (as).

восприня́ть [*infl. like* приня́ть] *v., pfv. of* воспринима́ть.

восприя́тие *n.* perception.

воспроизведе́ние *n.* reproduction.

воспроизвести́ [*infl. like* вести́] *v., pfv. of* воспроизводи́ть.

воспроизводи́тельный *adj.* reproductive.

воспроизводи́ть *v. impfv.* [*pfv.* воспроизвести́; *pres.* -вожу́, -во́дишь] to reproduce.

воспроти́виться *v.r., pfv. of* проти́виться.

воспря́нуть *v. pfv., obs.* to leap up. —воспря́нуть ду́хом, to cheer up; perk up; take heart.

воспыла́ть *v. pfv.* 1, *obs.* to flare up; burst into flame. 2, *fig.* (*with instr.*) to become fired (with).

воссоедине́ние *n.* reunification.

воссоединя́ть *v. impfv.* [*pfv.* воссоедини́ть] to re-unite. —воссоединя́ться, *refl.* to be reunited.

воссоздава́ть *v. impfv.* [*pfv.* воссозда́ть; *pres.* -даю́, -даёшь] 1, to re-create. 2, to (mentally) reconstruct.

воссозда́ть [*infl. like* дать; *past* -да́л, -ла́, -да́ло] *v., pfv. of* воссоздава́ть.

восстава́ть *v. impfv.* [*pfv.* восста́ть; *pres.* -стаю́, -стаёшь] to revolt; rebel.

восстана́вливать *v. impfv.* [*pfv.* восстанови́ть] 1, to restore; re-establish. 2, to recover; regain (one's health, strength, etc.). 3, (*with* про́тив) to set against. —восстана́вливать про́тив себя́, to antagonize.

восста́ние *n.* revolt; rebellion; uprising; insurrection.

восстанови́ть [*infl.* -новлю́, -но́вишь] *v., pfv. of* восстана́вливать.

восстановле́ние *n.* 1, restoration. 2, recovery (*of one's health*).

восста́ть [*infl.* -ста́ну, -ста́нешь] *v., pfv. of* восстава́ть.

восто́к *n.* 1, east. 2, *cap.* the East.

востокове́д *n.* Orientalist. —востокове́дение, *n.* Oriental studies.

восто́рг *n.* ecstasy: быть в восто́рге от, to be in ecstasy over; be ecstatic about.

восторга́ть *v. impfv.* to delight; enchant; enrapture. —восторга́ться, *refl.* (*with instr.*) to be in ecstasy (over); be enchanted (with).

восто́рженность *n.f.* ecstasy; delight.

восто́рженный *adj.* ecstatic; rapturous.

восторжествова́ть *v., pfv. of* торжествова́ть.

восто́чный *adj.* 1, eastern; East; easterly. 2, oriental.

востре́бование *n.* claiming. —до востре́бования, general delivery.

востре́бовать *v. pfv.* [*infl.* -бую, -буешь] to claim.

востро́ *adv., in* держа́ть у́хо востро́, *colloq.* to be on one's guard.

восхвале́ние *n.* 1, extolling. 2, acclaim.

восхвали́ть [*infl.* -хвалю́, -хва́лишь] *v., pfv. of* восхваля́ть.

восхваля́ть *v. impfv.* [*pfv.* восхвали́ть] to laud; extol; eulogize.

восхити́тельный *adj.* captivating; enchanting.

восхити́ть [*infl.* -щу́, -ти́шь] *v., pfv. of* восхища́ть. —восхити́ться, *refl., pfv. of* восхища́ться.

восхища́ть *v. impfv.* [*pfv.* восхити́ть] to captivate; enchant. —восхища́ться, *refl.* (*with instr.*) to be captivated (by); be enchanted (with).

восхище́ние *n.* delight; enchantment; admiration.

восхо́д *n.* rise. —восхо́д со́лнца, sunrise.

восходи́ть *v. impfv.* [*pfv.* взойти́; *pres.* -хожу́, -хо-

дишь] 1, = всходи́ть. 2, [*impfv. only*] (*with* к) to go back to; date back to.

восходя́щий *adj.* rising. —восходя́щая звезда́, *fig.* rising star.

восхожде́ние *n.* ascent.

восше́ствие *n., obs.* ascent. —восше́ствие на престо́л, accession to the throne.

восьма́я *n., decl. as an adj.* eighth: одна́ восьма́я, one-eighth.

восьмёрка *n.* 1, the numeral 8. 2, *colloq.* anything numbered 8. 3, figure eight (*in skating, flying, etc.*). 4, *cards* eight.

во́сьмеро *collective numeral* eight.

восьмигра́нник *n.* octahedron. —восьмигра́нный, *adj.* octahedral.

восьмидеся́тый *ordinal numeral* eightieth.

восьмиле́тний *adj.* 1, eight-year (*attrib.*). 2, eight-year-old.

восьмино́г *n.* octopus.

восьмисо́тый *ordinal numeral* eight-hundredth.

восьмиуго́льник *n.* octagon. —восьмиуго́льный, *adj.* octagonal.

восьмичасово́й *adj.* eight-hour (*attrib.*).

восьмо́й *ordinal numeral* eighth.

восьму́шка [*gen. pl.* -шек] *n.* 1, eighth of a pound. 2, octavo.

вот *particle* 1, here (is): вот ва́ша кни́га, here is your book; вот он идёт, here he comes. 2, (*with* где, как, что) this is; that is: вот где я живу́, this is where I live. 3, *used for emphasis:* вот э́то на́до посмотре́ть!, you really must see it! —вот как!; вот что!, really!; you don't say! —вот так так!, well, I never!; well, I'll be! —вот тебе́ и..., so much for... —вот э́то да!, now that's something like it!

вот-во́т *adv., colloq., used with future tense of verbs* (just) about to: он вот-во́т уйдёт, he is (just) about to leave.

воткну́ть *v., pfv. of* втыка́ть.

во́тум *n.* vote. —во́тум (не)дове́рия, vote of (no) confidence.

во́тчина *n., hist.* ancestral lands; estate; patrimony.

воцаря́ться *v.r. impfv.* [*pfv.* воцари́ться] 1, *obs.* to ascend the throne. 2, *fig.* to set in; be established: воцари́лась тишина́, silence reigned.

вошь [*gen., dat., & prepl.* вши; *instr.* во́шью] *n.f.* louse.

вощанка *n.* wax paper.

вощёный *adj.* waxed.

вощи́ть *v. impfv.* [*pfv.* навощи́ть] to wax.

вою́ющий *adj.* warring; belligerent.

воя́ка *n.m., colloq., ironic* warrior.

впада́ть *v. impfv.* [*pfv.* впасть] 1, [*impfv. only*] (*with* в + *acc.*) to flow (into); empty (into). 2, to become hollow; become sunken. 3, *fig.* (*with* в + *acc.*) to fall (into); sink (into); lapse (into).

впаде́ние *n.* 1, emptying (*of a river into a larger body of water*). 2, confluence: при впаде́нии (*or* у впаде́ния) реки́ Оки́ в Во́лгу, at the confluence of the Oka and Volga; where the Oka flows into the Volga.

впа́дина *n.* 1, hollow; depression; cavity. 2, *anat.* socket: глазна́я впа́дина, eye socket.

впа́лый *adj.* hollow; sunken.

впасть [*infl. like* пасть] *v., pfv. of* впада́ть.

впервы́е *adv.* first; for the first time.

вперевáлку *adv., colloq., in* **ходи́ть вперевáлку,** to waddle.

вперёд *adv.* **1,** forward; ahead. **2,** *colloq.* henceforth; from now on. **3,** *colloq.* ahead of time; beforehand; in advance.

впереди́ *adv.* **1,** in front; ahead. **2,** ahead; yet to occur: что нас ждёт впереди́?, what lies ahead for us? Развя́зка ещё впереди́, the climax is yet to come. —*prep., with gen.* in front of; ahead of.

вперемéжку *adv., colloq.* alternately.

вперемéшку *adv., colloq.* pell-mell; every which way.

впечатлéние *n.* impression.

впечатли́тельный *adj.* impressionable.

впечатля́ющий *adj.* impressive.

впивáть *v. impfv.* [*pfv.* **впить**] to absorb; imbibe. —**впивáться,** *refl.* (*with* в + *acc.*) **1,** (*of something sharp*) to stick (in). **2,** (*with instr.*) to sink (one's teeth, claws, etc.) into. **3,** *fig.* (*with instr.*) to fix (one's eyes, gaze, etc.) on.

вписáть [*infl.* **впишу́, впи́шешь**] *v., pfv. of* **впи́сывать.** —**вписáться,** *refl., pfv. of* **впи́сываться.**

впи́сывать *v. impfv.* [*pfv.* **вписáть**] (*with* в + *acc.*) **1,** to write in; enter; insert. **2,** *math.* to inscribe. —**впи́сываться,** *refl.* (*with* в + *acc.*) **1,** *colloq.* to enroll (in); join. **2,** to blend in (with).

впи́тывать *v. impfv.* [*pfv.* **впитáть**] to absorb; soak up.

впить [*infl.* **вопью́, вопьёшь;** *past fem.* **впилá**] *v., pfv. of* **впивáть.** —**впи́ться,** *refl., pfv. of* **впивáться.**

впи́хивать *v. impfv.* [*pfv.* **впихну́ть**] *colloq.* **1,** to stuff in; cram in; force in. **2,** to push in; shove in.

вплáвь *adv.* by swimming.

вплести́ [*infl. like* **плести́**] *v., pfv. of* **вплетáть.**

вплетáть *v. impfv.* [*pfv.* **вплести́**] to entwine; intertwine.

вплотну́ю *adv.* **1,** closely; tightly. **2,** (*with* к) right up to; right up against. **3,** *fig., colloq.* in earnest.

вплоть *adv., usu. in* **вплоть до** (+ *gen.*), **1,** right up to. **2,** down to.

вплывáть *v. impfv.* [*pfv.* **вплы́ть**] **1,** to swim in. **2,** to sail in.

вплы́ть [*infl. like* **плы́ть**] *v., pfv. of* **вплывáть.**

вповáлку *adv., colloq.* side by side: лежáть/спать вповáлку, to lie/sleep side by side.

вполго́лоса *adv.* in a low voice; under one's breath; in an undertone.

вползáть *v. impfv.* [*pfv.* **вползти́**] (*with* в + *acc.*) **1,** to crawl into; creep into. **2,** to crawl up; creep up.

вползти́ [*infl. like* **ползти́**] *v., pfv. of* **вползáть.**

вполнé *adv.* fully; entirely; completely; quite.

вполоборо́та *adv.* (*with* к) half-turned (toward).

впопáд *adv., colloq.* to the point.

впопыхáх *adv.* **1,** hastily; hurriedly. **2,** in one's haste.

впо́ру *adv., colloq.* of the right size: плáтье вам впо́ру, the dress is the right size for you.

впорхну́ть *v. pfv.* to fly in; flit in.

впослéдствии *adv.* afterwards; subsequently; later on.

впотьмáх *adv.* in the dark.

впрáвду *adv., colloq.* really.

вправе *adv.* having a right: онá впрáве горди́ться, she has a right to be proud.

впрáвить [*infl.* -влю, -вишь] *v., pfv. of* **вправля́ть.**

вправля́ть *v. impfv.* [*pfv.* **впрáвить**] **1,** to set (a bone, joint, etc.). **2,** (*with* в + *acc.*) *colloq.* to tuck into.

впрáво *adv.* to the right.

впредь *adv.* hereafter; henceforth; from now on. —**впредь до,** until; pending.

вприку́ску *adv., in* **пить чай вприку́ску,** to drink tea holding a lump of sugar in one's mouth.

вприпры́жку *adv., in* **бежáть вприпры́жку,** to skip along.

вприся́дку *adv.* in a squatting position (*while dancing*).

впри́тык *adv.* (*with* к) *colloq.* flush (against).

впро́голодь *adv.* hungry: жить/питáться впро́голодь, to go hungry.

впрок *adv.* **1,** in store; for future use: заготовля́ть впрок, to store up; stock up on. **2,** (*usu. with* идти́) to one's advantage: э́то вам не пойдёт впрок, it won't do you any good. Ему́ всё (идёт) впрок, everything goes right for him.

впросáк *adv., in* **попáсть впросáк,** *colloq.* to commit a gaffe; put one's foot in it.

впросо́нках *adv., colloq.* while half-asleep.

впро́чем *conj.* **1,** however; but; though. **2,** but then; but then again.

впры́гивать *v. impfv.* [*pfv.* **впры́гнуть**] **1,** (*with* в + *acc.*) to jump into. **2,** (*with* на + *acc.*) to jump onto.

впры́скивание *n.* injection.

впры́скивать *v. impfv.* [*pfv.* **впры́снуть**] to inject.

впрягáть *v. impfv.* [*pfv.* **впрячь**] (*with* в + *acc.*) to harness (to); hitch (to).

впряму́ю *adv., colloq.* directly.

впрямь *adv., colloq.* really; indeed.

впрячь [*infl.* **впрягу́, впряжёшь, ...впрягу́т;** *past* **впряг, -лá, -ло́**] *v., pfv. of* **впрягáть.**

впуск *n.* **1,** admission; admittance. **2,** intake.

впускáть *v. impfv.* [*pfv.* **впусти́ть**] to admit; let in.

впусти́ть [*infl.* **впущу́, впу́стишь**] *v., pfv. of* **впускáть.**

впусту́ю *adv., colloq.* in vain; for nothing.

впу́тать *v., pfv. of* **пу́тать** (*in sense #6*) *and* **впу́тывать.** —**впу́таться,** *refl., pfv. of* **пу́таться** (*in sense #3*) *and* **впу́тываться.**

впу́тывать *v. impfv.* [*pfv.* **впу́тать**] (*with* в + *acc.*) *colloq.* to involve (in); embroil (in). —**впу́тываться,** *refl.* (*with* в + *acc.*) *colloq.* to get mixed up (in).

впя́теро *adv.* five times: впя́теро бо́льше, five times as much.

впятеро́м *adv.* five together: они́ впятеро́м, the five of them.

враг [*gen.* **врагá**] *n.* enemy.

враждá *n.* hostility; animosity; enmity.

враждéбный *adj.* hostile. —**враждéбно,** *adv.* with hostility; with animosity. —**враждéбность,** *n.f.* hostility; animosity.

враждовáть *v. impfv.* [*pres.* -ду́ю, -ду́ешь] (*with* с + *instr.*) to feud (with); be at odds (with).

врáжеский *adj.* enemy (*attrib.*); hostile.

вразби́вку *adv., colloq.* at random; in no particular order.

вразбро́д *adv., colloq.* **1,** separately; not together. **2,** without coordination.

вразбро́с *adv., colloq.* scattered about; every which way.

вразвáлку *adv., colloq., in* **ходи́ть вразвáлку,** to waddle.

вразно́с *adv., colloq., in* **торговáть вразно́с,** to peddle.

вразрéз *adv., in* **идти́ вразрéз с** (+ *instr.*), to run counter to; go against.

вразуми́тельный *adj.* clear; intelligible; understandable.

вразумля́ть *v. impfv.* [*pfv.* **вразуми́ть**] to make (someone) understand; bring to reason.

вра́ки [*gen.* **врак**] *n. pl., colloq.* **1,** nonsense. **2,** lies.

враль [*gen.* **враля́**] *n.m., colloq.* **1,** liar. **2,** chatterbox.

враньё *n., colloq.* **1,** lying. **2,** lies.

врасплóх *adv., in* заста́ть *or* засти́гнуть врасплóх, to take by surprise; catch unawares.

врассыпну́ю *adv.* in all directions; helter-skelter; every which way.

враста́ть *v. impfv.* [*pfv.* **врасти́**] (*with* в + *acc.*) **1,** to grow into. **2,** to become embedded (in).

врасти́ [*infl. like* расти́] *v., pfv. of* враста́ть.

врастя́жку *adv., colloq.* **1,** flat; stretched out. **2,** in a drawl.

врата́рь [*gen.* **-таря́**] *n.m.* **1,** *obs.* gatekeeper. **2,** *sports* goalkeeper; goalie.

врать *v. impfv.* [*pfv.* **совра́ть**; *pres.* **вру, врёшь;** *past fem.* **врала́**] *colloq.* to lie; tell lies.

врач [*gen.* **врача́**] *n.* doctor; physician. —**зубнóй врач**, dentist.

враче́бный *adj.* medical.

враща́тельный *adj.* rotary.

враща́ть *v. impfv.* to revolve; turn (*trans. verb*). —**враща́ться**, *refl.* **1,** to revolve; rotate; turn (*intrans.*). **2,** (*with* в + *prepl.*) *fig.* to move (*in certain circles*).

враще́ние *n.* rotation.

вред [*gen.* **вреда́**] *n.* harm; injury; damage. —**во вред** (+ *dat.*), to the detriment of.

вреди́тель *n.m.* **1,** pest; *pl.* vermin. **2,** economic saboteur. —**вреди́тельство**, *n.* economic sabotage.

вреди́ть *v. impfv.* [*pfv.* **повреди́ть**; *pres.* **врежу́, вреди́шь**] (*with dat.*) to harm; damage; be injurious to.

вре́дно *adv.* in a harmful manner: вре́дно де́йствовать на, to have a harmful effect on. —*adj., used predicatively* harmful; bad: вре́дно для зре́ния, bad for one's eyesight.

вре́дный *adj.* harmful; damaging; detrimental; injurious.

вредонóсный *adj.* harmful.

вре́зать [*infl.* **вре́жу, вре́жешь**] *v., pfv. of* вреза́ть *and* вре́зывать. —**вре́заться**, *refl., pfv. of* вреза́ться *and* вре́зываться.

вреза́ть *v. impfv.* [*pfv.* **вре́зать**] (*with* в + *acc.*) **1,** to cut into; fit into. **2,** *fig.* to embed (in one's memory). —**вреза́ться**, *refl.* (*with* в + *acc.*) **1,** to cut into. **2,** (*of a vehicle, airplane, etc.*) to crash (into); slam (into); plunge (into). **3,** *fig.* to become ingrained (in one's memory).

вре́зывать *v. impfv.* = вреза́ть. —**вре́зываться**, *refl.* = вреза́ться.

вре́менно *adv.* temporarily.

временнóй *adj.* time (*attrib.*); temporal.

вре́менный *adj.* **1,** temporary. **2,** provisional.

вре́мя [*gen., dat., & prepl.* **вре́мени;** *instr.* **вре́менем;** *pl.* **времена́, времён, времена́м**] *n. neut.* **1,** time. **2,** *gram.* tense. **3,** *in* вре́мя гóда, season. —**во вре́мя** (+ *gen.*), during. —**во времена́** (+ *gen.*), in (someone's) time. —**во все времена́**, at all times. —**в** (*or* за) **послéднее вре́мя**, recently; of late. —**времена́ми**, at times; now and then. —**вре́мя от вре́мени**, from time to time. —**в своё вре́мя, 1,** in one's time. **2,** in due time; in due course. —**всё вре́мя**, all the time. —**в скóром вре́мени**, before long; shortly. —**в то вре́мя как**, while; whereas. —**в то же вре́мя**, at the same time.

—**на вре́мя**, for a while; for a time. —**на вре́мя** (+ *gen.*), for the duration of. —**однó вре́мя**, at one time. —**пéрвое вре́мя**, at first. —**по времена́м**, from time to time. —**скóлько вре́мени?, 1,** how long? **2,** what time?: скóлько вре́мени сейча́с/у вас?/, what time is it/have you got? —**со вре́менем**, in time. —**со вре́мени** (+ *gen.*), since. —**тем вре́менем**, meanwhile.

время́нка [*gen. pl.* **-нок**] *n., colloq.* temporary structure.

времяпрепровожде́ние *n.* way of spending time; pastime. *Also,* времяпровожде́ние.

врóвень *adv.* (*with* с + *instr.*) on a level (with); even (with); flush (with).

врóде *prep., with gen.* **1,** like; not unlike. **2,** a sort of. —*particle, colloq.* **1,** (*with nouns*) such as; like. **2,** (*with verbs*) seems to (have).

врождённый *adj.* innate; inborn; inherent; congenital.

врозь *adv.* apart: жить врозь, to live apart.

вруба́ть *v. impfv.* [*pfv.* **вруби́ть**] (*with* в + *acc.*) to place; set (in an opening that has been cut out). —**вруба́ться**, *refl.* (*with* в + *acc.*) to cut one's way (into *or* through).

вруби́ть [*infl.* **врублю́, вру́бишь**] *v., pfv. of* вруба́ть. —**вруби́ться**, *refl., pfv. of* вруба́ться.

врукопа́шную *adv.* in hand-to-hand combat: би́ться врукопа́шную, to engage in hand-to-hand combat.

врун [*gen.* **вруна́**] *n.m.* [*fem.* **вру́нья**] *colloq.* liar.

вруча́ть *v. impfv.* [*pfv.* **вручи́ть**] **1,** to hand over; deliver; present. **2,** *fig.* to entrust.

вруче́ние *n.* delivery; presentation.

вручи́ть *v., pfv. of* вруча́ть.

вручну́ю *adv.* by hand; manually.

врыва́ть *v. impfv.* [*pfv.* **врыть**] (*with* в + *acc.*) to implant; set (in the ground).

врыва́ться *v.r. impfv.* [*pfv.* **ворва́ться**] (*with* в + *acc.*) **1,** to burst into. **2,** to break into.

врыть [*infl.* **врою, врóешь**] *v., pfv. of* врыва́ть.

вряд ли *particle* hardly; it is unlikely; I doubt whether...: вряд ли он придёт, I doubt whether he is coming.

всади́ть [*infl.* **всажу́, вса́дишь**] *v., pfv. of* вса́живать.

вса́дник *n.* rider; horseman.

вса́живать *v. impfv.* [*pfv.* **всади́ть**] (*with* в + *acc.*) **1,** to plunge (a knife) into; put (a bullet) in. **2,** *colloq.* to sink (money) into.

вса́сывание *n.* **1,** suction. **2,** absorption.

вса́сывать *v. impfv.* [*pfv.* **всоса́ть**] to suck in; absorb. —**вса́сываться**, *refl.* (*with* в + *acc.*) **1,** to be absorbed in. **2,** to be sucked into (a swamp, morass, etc.).

все *adj., pl. of* весь. —*indef. pron.* everybody; everyone. —**все и вся**, *colloq.* [*acc.* всех и вся] everybody and everything. *See also* весь.

всё *adj., neut. of* весь: всё вре́мя, all the time. —*indef. pron.* everything; all: э́то всё, that's all; всё в поря́дке, everything is all right. —*adv., colloq.* **1,** constantly; all the time: телефóн всё звони́т, the phone keeps ringing (all the time). **2,** still. **3,** (*with comp. adjectives and some verbs*) more and more; -er and -er: всё лу́чше и лу́чше, better and better; все бóлее интере́сный, more and more interesting. Он все слабе́ет, he keeps getting weaker and weaker. —**всё ещё; всё же**, still; all the same. —**всё равнó**, *see* равнó. —**при всём том**, for all that. *See also* весь.

всеве́дение *n.* omniscience.

всеве́дущий *adj.* omniscient.

всевозмо́жный *adj.* all sorts of; all kinds of; every possible.

всегда́ *adv.* always. —**как всегда́**, as always; as usual.

всегда́шний *adj., colloq.* regular; usual; customary.

всего́ *adj., gen. of* **весь**. —*adv.* **1,** in all. **2,** only. —*interj.* so long! —**всего́ хоро́шего!**, **всего́ до́брого!**, all the best! —**всего́-на́всего**, only; nothing but.

всезна́йка *n.m. & f., colloq.* know-it-all.

вселе́ние *n.* moving in: вселе́ние в но́вый дом, moving into a new house.

вселе́нная *n., decl. as an adj.* universe.

вселе́нский *adj.* ecumenical.

вселя́ть *v. impfv.* [*pfv.* **всели́ть**] (*with* в + *acc.*) **1,** to move; settle (people) into. **2,** *fig.* to instill (hope, confidence, etc.) into; strike (fear) into. —**вселя́ться**, *refl.* (*with* в + *acc.*) **1,** to move into; settle in. **2,** *fig.* (*of an emotion*) to fill; seize.

всеме́рный *adj.* all possible: всеме́рная подде́ржка, all possible support. —**всеме́рно**, *adv.* in every (possible) way.

всеми́рный *adj.* world (*attrib.*); worldwide; universal. —**всеми́рная вы́ставка**, world's fair.

всемогу́щество *n.* omnipotence. —**всемогу́щий**, *adj.* all-powerful; almighty; omnipotent.

всенаро́дный *adj.* nationwide; national.

всено́щная *n., decl. as an adj.* vespers.

всео́бщий *adj.* universal; general.

всеобъе́млющий *adj.* all-embracing; comprehensive.

всеору́жие *n., in* **во всеору́жии**, fully armed. —**во всеору́жии зна́ний**, fully versed in one's subject.

всепобежда́ющий *adj.* all-conquering.

всепоглоща́ющий *adj.* all-consuming.

всеросси́йский *adj.* All-Russian.

всерьёз *adv.* seriously; in earnest. —**принима́ть всерьёз**, to take seriously.

всеси́льный *adj.* all-powerful; omnipotent.

всесою́зный *adj.* All-Union.

всесторо́нний *adj.* all-round; thorough; comprehensive.

всё-таки *conj.* still; all the same.

всеуслы́шание *n., in* **во всеуслы́шание**, publicly; for everyone to hear.

всеце́ло *adv.* completely.

всея́дный *adj.* omnivorous.

вска́кивать *v. impfv.* [*pfv.* **вскочи́ть**] **1,** (*with* в + *acc.*) to jump into; leap into. **2,** to jump up; (*with* на + *acc.*) jump onto. Вскочи́ть на́ ноги, to leap (*or* spring) to one's feet. **3,** *colloq.* (*of a bruise, pimple, etc.*) to appear.

вска́пывать *v. impfv.* [*pfv.* **вскопа́ть**] to dig; dig up.

вскара́бкиваться *v.r. impfv.* [*pfv.* **вскара́бкаться**] (*with* на + *acc.*) *colloq.* to climb (onto); scramble (up); clamber (up).

вска́рмливать *v. impfv.* [*pfv.* **вскорми́ть**] to raise (animals, birds, etc.). —**вскорми́ть и вспои́ть**, to raise; nurture (a child).

вскачь *adv.* at a gallop.

вски́дывать *v. impfv.* [*pfv.* **вски́нуть**] **1,** to throw up; toss up. **2,** (*with* на + *acc.*) to toss (onto). —**вски́нуть глаза́**, to look up suddenly. —**вски́нуть го́лову**, to toss one's head.

вскипа́ть *v. impfv.* [*pfv.* **вскипе́ть**] **1,** to boil up; come

to a boil. **2,** (*of emotions*) to well up; flare up. **3,** [*also,* **вскипе́ть гне́вом**] to fly into a rage.

вскипе́ть [*infl.* -плю́, -пи́шь] *v., pfv. of* **вскипа́ть**.

вскипяти́ть *v., pfv. of* **кипяти́ть**. — **вскипяти́ться**, *refl., pfv. of* **кипяти́ться**.

всклоко́ченный *adj., colloq.* disheveled.

всколыхну́ть *v. pfv.* **1,** to stir. **2,** *fig.* to stir up; agitate.

вско́льзь *adv.* casually; in passing: упомяну́ть вско́льзь, to mention in passing.

вскопа́ть *v., pfv. of* **вска́пывать**.

вско́ре *adv.* soon; shortly; presently.

вскорми́ть [*infl.* вскормлю́, вско́рмишь] *v., pfv. of* **вска́рмливать**.

вскочи́ть [*infl.* вскочу́, вско́чишь] *v., pfv. of* **вска́кивать**.

вскри́кивать *v. impfv.* [*pfv.* **вскри́кнуть**] to cry out; scream; shriek.

вскрича́ть *v. pfv.* [*infl.* -чу́, -чи́шь] to exclaim; cry.

вскружи́ть *v. pfv., in* **вскружи́ть го́лову** (+ *dat.*), to turn someone's head; go to one's head.

вскрыва́ть *v. impfv.* [*pfv.* **вскрыть**] **1,** to open up; unseal. **2,** to expose; uncover; reveal. **3,** *med.* to lance. **4,** *med.* to dissect; perform an autopsy on. —**вскрыва́ться**, *refl.* **1,** to be revealed; come to light. **2,** (*of a river*) to become free of ice.

вскры́тие *n.* **1,** opening; unsealing. **2,** revelation; disclosure. **3,** thawing; breaking up (*of a frozen river*). **4,** *med.* autopsy; dissection. **5,** *med.* lancing.

вскрыть [*infl.* вскро́ю, вскро́ешь] *v., pfv. of* **вскрыва́ть**. —**вскры́ться**, *refl., pfv. of* **вскрыва́ться**.

всласть *adv., colloq.* to one's heart's content.

вслед *adv.* after; behind: идти́ вслед, to follow after; walk behind. —*prep., with dat.* after; following. Смотре́ть вслед (+ *dat.*), to follow with one's eyes. —**вслед за** (+ *instr.*), **1,** after; in pursuit of. **2,** right after; on the heels of. —**вслед за тем,** after that.

всле́дствие *prep., with gen.* as a result of; on account of; owing to.

вслепу́ю *adv., colloq.* blind; blindly; blindfolded.

вслух *adv.* aloud; out loud.

вслу́шиваться *v.r. impfv.* [*pfv.* **вслу́шаться**] (*with* в + *acc.*) to listen carefully (to); strain one's ears to hear.

всма́триваться *v.r. impfv.* [*pfv.* **всмотре́ться**] (*with* в + *acc.*) to peer into; take a good look at.

всмотре́ться [*infl.* всмотрю́сь, всмо́тришься] *v.r., pfv. of* **всма́триваться**.

всмя́тку *adv., in* яйцо́ всмя́тку, soft-boiled egg.

всо́вывать *v. impfv.* [*pfv.* **всу́нуть**] (*with* в + *acc.*) to stick (into); slip (into); thrust (into).

всоса́ть [*infl.* -су́, -сёшь] *v., pfv. of* **вса́сывать**. —**всоса́ться**, *refl., pfv. of* **вса́сываться**.

вспа́ивать *v. impfv.* [*pfv.* **вспои́ть**] *colloq.* to raise; rear; bring up.

вспа́рывать *v. impfv.* [*pfv.* **вспоро́ть**] *colloq.* to cut open; rip open.

вспаха́ть [*infl.* вспашу́, вспа́шешь] *v., pfv. of* **паха́ть** *and* **вспа́хивать**.

вспа́хивать *v. impfv.* [*pfv.* **вспаха́ть**] to plow.

вспа́шка *n.* plowing.

вспе́нить *v., pfv. of* **пе́нить**. —**вспе́ниться**, *refl., pfv. of* **пе́ниться**.

всплакну́ть *v. pfv., colloq.* to have a little cry; shed a few tears.

всплеск *n.* splash; splashing.

всплёскивать *v. impfv.* [*pfv.* **всплесну́ть**] to splash.

—**всплесну́ть рука́ми**, to clasp one's hands (*in astonishment, dismay, etc.*).

всплыва́ть *v. impfv.* [*pfv.* всплыть] **1,** to float to the surface; (*of a submarine*) to surface. **2,** *fig.* to come to light.

всплыть [*infl. like* плыть] *v., pfv. of* всплыва́ть.

вспои́ть [*infl.* вспою́, вспои́шь *or* вспо́ишь] *v., pfv. of* вспа́ивать.

всполоши́ть *v. pfv., colloq.* to startle; alarm. —**всполоши́ться**, *refl., colloq.* to be startled; be alarmed.

вспомина́ть *v. impfv.* [*pfv.* вспо́мнить] **1,** to remember; recall; recollect. **2,** [*impfv. only*] to try to remember. **3,** [*impfv. only*] to recall; reminisce about. —**вспомина́ться**, *refl.* (*with dat.*) to come back to (someone); come back to (one's) mind.

вспомога́тельный *adj.* **1,** auxiliary; subsidiary. **2,** *gram.* auxiliary: вспомога́тельный глаго́л, auxiliary verb.

вспоро́ть [*infl.* вспорю́, вспо́решь] *v., pfv. of* вспа́рывать.

вспорхну́ть *v. pfv.* to take wing.

вспоте́ть *v. pfv.* **1,** *pfv. of* поте́ть. **2,** to become fogged; fog up.

вспры́гивать *v. impfv.* [*pfv.* вспры́гнуть] (*with* на + *acc.*) to jump onto; jump up on.

вспры́скивание *n.* sprinkling.

вспры́скивать *v. impfv.* [*pfv.* вспры́снуть] to sprinkle.

вспу́гивать *v. impfv.* [*pfv.* вспугну́ть] to frighten away; scare away.

вспуха́ть *v. impfv.* [*pfv.* вспу́хнуть] to swell up.

вспу́хнуть [*past* вспух, -ла] *v., pfv. of* вспуха́ть.

вспыли́ть *v. pfv., colloq.* to flare up; fly into a rage.

вспы́льчивый *adj.* hot-tempered; quick-tempered; irascible.

вспы́хивать *v. impfv.* [*pfv.* вспы́хнуть] **1,** to blaze up; suddenly catch fire. Вспы́хнуть пла́менем, to burst into flames. **2,** (*of fire, war, panic, etc.*) to break out. **3,** to blush; flush. **4,** to flare up (*in anger*).

вспы́шка [*gen. pl.* шек] *n.* **1,** flash. **2,** *fig.* (*with gen.*) burst (of); outburst (of); outbreak (of). **3,** (*angry*) outburst. **4,** *photog.* flash gun.

вспять *adv.* back; in the opposite direction.

встава́ние *n.* standing up; rising.

встава́ть *v. impfv.* [*pfv.* встать; *pres.* встаю́, встаёшь] **1,** to stand up; get up; rise. **2,** (*of the sun*) to rise. **3,** *fig.* (*of a question, difficulty, etc.*) to arise; come up. **4,** to stand (*in a certain place*). **5,** *colloq.* (*of a machine or device*) to stop (working). —**встать на сто́рону** (+ *gen.*), to side with; take the side of.

вста́вить [*infl.* -влю, -вишь] *v., pfv. of* вставля́ть.

вста́вка [*gen. pl.* -вок] *n.* **1,** mounting; setting. **2,** an insertion. **3,** inset; front (*of a dress*).

вставля́ть *v. impfv.* [*pfv.* вста́вить] **1,** to put in; insert. **2,** to interject; interpose; put in (a word, remark, etc.).

вставно́й *adj.* that can be inserted and later removed. —**вставны́е зу́бы**, false teeth. —**вставны́е ра́мы**, storm windows.

встарь *adv.* in the old days; in olden times.

встать [*infl.* вста́ну, вста́нешь] *v., pfv. of* встава́ть.

встрево́женный *adj.* alarmed.

встрево́жить *v., pfv. of* трево́жить. —**встрево́житься**, *refl., pfv. of* трево́житься.

встрёпанный *adj., colloq.* disheveled.

встрепену́ться *v.r. pfv.* **1,** (*of a bird*) to ruffle its feathers. **2,** to give a start (and be aroused). **3,** (*of the heart*) to palpitate; begin to beat faster.

встре́тить [*infl.* встре́чу, встре́тишь] *v., pfv. of* встреча́ть. —**встре́титься**, *refl., pfv. of* встреча́ться.

встре́ча *n.* **1,** meeting; encounter. **2,** welcome; reception. **3,** *sports* match; contest. **4,** *in* встре́ча Но́вого го́да, New Year's Eve party. —**до (ско́рой) встре́чи!**, see you soon! До встре́чи в два часа́!, see you at two o'clock!

встреча́ть *v. impfv.* [*pfv.* встре́тить] **1,** to meet. **2,** to encounter; meet with; be met with. **3,** to greet; welcome; receive. **4,** to celebrate (a holiday, esp. New Year's Eve). —**встреча́ться**, *refl.* **1,** to meet (each other). **2,** to get together; see each other. **3,** (*with* с + *instr.*) to meet; encounter; come across. **4,** to be found; occur.

встре́чный *adj.* **1,** oncoming; approaching. **2,** counter-: встре́чный уда́р, counterblow. —*n.* passer-by. —**встре́чный ве́тер**, head wind. —**ка́ждый встре́чный и попере́чный**, *adj.* any (*or* every) Tom, Dick, or Harry. —**пе́рвый встре́чный**, the first person to come along; anyone.

встря́ска *n., colloq.* **1,** shaking. **2,** shock. **3,** dressing-down.

встря́хивать *v. impfv.* [*pfv.* встряхну́ть] to shake; shake out; shake up. —**встря́хиваться**, *refl.* **1,** to shake oneself off. **2,** *fig., colloq.* to cheer up; pull oneself together.

вступа́ть *v. impfv.* [*pfv.* вступи́ть] (*with* в + *acc.*) **1,** to enter; enter into: вступи́ть в но́вую э́ру, to enter a new era; вступи́ть в перепи́ску, to enter into correspondence. **2,** to join: вступи́ть в па́ртию, to join the party. —**вступи́ть в брак**, to marry; get married. —**вступи́ть в де́йствие** *or* **в строй**, to go into operation. —**вступи́ть в до́лжность**, to assume office. —**вступи́ть в свои́ права́**, to come into one's own. —**вступи́ть в си́лу**, to go into effect. —**вступи́ть на престо́л**, to assume *or* ascend the throne.

вступа́ться *v.r. impfv.* [*pfv.* вступи́ться] (*with* за + *acc.*) to come to the defense of; stand up for; stick up for.

вступи́тельный *adj.* **1,** introductory; opening. **2,** entrance (*attrib.*): вступи́тельный экза́мен, entrance examination.

вступи́ть [*infl.* вступлю́, всту́пишь] *v., pfv. of* вступа́ть. —**вступи́ться**, *refl., pfv. of* вступа́ться.

вступле́ние *n.* **1,** (*with* в + *acc.*) entry (*into a place*); joining (*an organization*); assumption (*of office*). **2,** introduction (*to a book, musical work, etc.*).

всу́е *adv., obs.* in vain.

всу́нуть *v., pfv. of* всо́вывать.

всухомя́тку *adv., colloq., in* есть всухомя́тку, to eat food dry (*without an accompanying beverage*).

всуху́ю *adv., colloq.* **1,** without grease. **2,** without having anything to drink. **3,** *sports* being shut out: проигра́ть всуху́ю, to be shut out.

всу́чивать *v. impfv.* [*pfv.* всучи́ть] (*with dat.*) *colloq.* to foist (on); palm off (on). *Also,* всу́чивать.

всучи́ть [*infl.* всучу́, всу́чишь] *v., pfv. of* всуча́ть *and* всу́чивать.

всхли́пывать *v. impfv.* [*pfv.* всхли́пнуть] to sniffle (*when crying*).

всходи́ть *v. impfv.* [*pfv.* взойти́; *pres.* всхожу́, всхо́дишь] **1,** (*with* на + *acc.*) to go up; mount; ascend; climb. **2,** (*of the sun, moon, etc.*) to rise. **3,** (*of plants, crops, etc.*) to sprout; come up.

ВСХÓДЫ [gen. -дов] n. pl. shoots; sprouts.

ВСХРÁПЫВАТЬ v. impfv. to snore.

ВСЫ́ПАТЬ [infl. всы́плю, всы́плешь] v., pfv. of всыпáть.

ВСЫПÁТЬ v. impfv. [pfv. всы́пать] 1, (with в + acc.) to pour into. 2, (with dat.) colloq. to give (someone) a good licking.

ВСЮ́ДУ adv. everywhere.

ВСЯ adj., fem. of весь.

ВСЯ́КИЙ adj. 1, any. 2, all sorts of; all kinds of. —n. anyone; anybody. —во вся́ком слу́чае, in any case; at any rate. —на вся́кий слу́чай, just in case.

ВСЯ́КОЕ n., decl. as an adj. anything: вся́кое мóжет случи́ться, anything can happen.

ВСЯ́ЧЕСКИ adv., colloq. in every way.

ВСЯ́ЧЕСКИЙ adj., colloq. of every kind; of all kinds.

ВСЯ́ЧИНА n., colloq., in вся́кая вся́чина, all sorts of things.

ВТÁЙНЕ adv. secretly; in secret.

ВТÁЛКИВАТЬ v. impfv. [pfv. втолкну́ть] (with в + acc.) to push in; shove in; force in.

ВТÁПТЫВАТЬ v. impfv. [pfv. втоптáть] (with в + acc.) to trample into. —втоптáть в грязь, to drag through the mud; vilify.

ВТÁСКИВАТЬ v. impfv. [pfv. втащи́ть] 1, (with в + acc.) to drag in. 2, (with на + acc.) to drag up.

ВТАЩИ́ТЬ [infl. втащу́, втáщишь] v., pfv. of втáскивать.

ВТЕКÁТЬ v. impfv. [pfv. втечь] (with в + acc.) to flow into.

ВТЕРÉТЬ [infl. вотру́, вотрёшь; past втёр, -ла] v., pfv. of втирáть. —втерéться, refl., pfv. of втирáться.

ВТИРÁНИЕ n. 1, rubbing in. 2, liniment.

ВТИРÁТЬ v. impfv. [pfv. втерéть] 1, (with в + acc.) to rub in. 2, in втирáть очки́ (+ dat.), to pull the wool over someone's eyes. —втирáться, refl. 1, to be absorbed through rubbing. 2, (with в + acc.) colloq. to make one's way (through); force one's way (into). 3, (with в + acc.) fig. to worm one's way (into): втирáться в довéрие к, to worm one's way into the confidence of.

ВТИ́СКИВАТЬ v. impfv. [pfv. вти́снуть] (with в + acc.) to squeeze (into); stuff (into); cram (into). —вти́скиваться, refl. (with в + acc.) colloq. to squeeze (into); crowd (into); jam (into).

ВТИХОМÓЛКУ adv., colloq. secretly; stealthily; on the sly.

ВТОЛКНУ́ТЬ v., pfv. of втáлкивать.

ВТОЛКОВÁТЬ [infl. -ку́ю, -ку́ешь] v., pfv. of втолкóвывать.

ВТОЛКÓВЫВАТЬ v. impfv. [pfv. втолковáть] (with dat.) colloq. to make (someone) understand; drive home the point (to).

ВТОПТÁТЬ [infl. втопчу́, втóпчешь] v., pfv. of втáптывать.

ВТОРГÁТЬСЯ v.r. impfv. [pfv. втóргнуться] (with в + acc.) 1, to invade. 2, fig. to intrude (into). 3, fig. to encroach (upon); infringe (upon).

ВТÓРГНУТЬСЯ [past втóргся or втóргнулся, втóрглась] v.r., pfv. of вторгáться.

ВТОРЖÉНИЕ n. invasion.

ВТÓРИТЬ v. impfv. (with dat.) 1, music to sing second part (to). 2, to echo; repeat.

ВТОРИ́ЧНО adv. a second time; for the second time.

ВТОРИ́ЧНЫЙ adj. 1, second. 2, secondary.

ВТÓРНИК n. Tuesday.

ВТОРОГÓДНИК n. pupil left back in school.

ВТОРÓЕ n., decl. as an adj. 1, (with dates) second: сегóдня — вторóе апрéля, today is April 2nd. 2, main course; entrée.

ВТОРОЗАКÓНИЕ n. Deuteronomy.

ВТОРÓЙ ordinal numeral & adj. second. —из вторы́х рук, second hand; through an intermediary. See also вторóе.

ВТОРОКЛÁССНИК n. second-grade pupil.

ВТОРОКУ́РСНИК n. second-year student; sophomore.

ВТОРОПЯ́Х adv. 1, hastily; hurriedly. 2, in one's haste.

ВТОРОРАЗРЯ́ДНЫЙ adj. second-rate.

ВТОРОСÓРТНЫЙ adj. second-rate.

ВТОРОСТЕПÉННЫЙ adj. 1, secondary. 2, minor.

В-ТРÉТЬИХ thirdly; in the third place.

ВТРИ́ДОРОГА adv., colloq. triple the price; three times as much. —плати́ть втри́дорога, to pay through the nose.

ВТРÓЕ adv. 1, three times; triple: втрóе бóльше, three times as much. 2, in three: сложи́ть втрóе, to fold in three.

ВТРОЁМ adv. three together: они́ втроём, the three of them.

ВТРОЙНÉ adv. triple; three times as much.

ВТУ́ЛКА [gen. pl. -лок] n. 1, mech. bushing. 2, plug; stopper.

ВТУ́НЕ adv., obs. for nothing; in vain.

ВТЫКÁТЬ v. impfv. [pfv. воткну́ть] (with в + acc.) to drive in; drive into; stick in; stick into.

ВТЯ́ГИВАТЬ v. impfv. [pfv. втяну́ть] 1, to draw in; pull in. 2, to breathe in; absorb. 3, colloq. to draw into; involve. —втя́гиваться, refl. (with в + acc.) colloq. 1, to make one's way into. 2, (of one's cheeks) to become drawn. 3, to become involved in; be drawn into. 4, to get used to; come to enjoy.

ВТЯНУ́ТЬ [infl. втяну́, втя́нешь] v., pfv. of втя́гивать. —втяну́ться, refl., pfv. of втя́гиваться.

ВУÁЛЬ n.f. veil.

ВУЗ n., abbr. of вы́сшее учéбное заведéние, institution of higher learning.

ВУ́ЗОВЕЦ [gen. -вца] n.m. [fem. -вка] colloq. student in a вуз.

ВУЛКÁН n. volcano.

ВУЛКАНИЗÁЦИЯ n. vulcanization.

ВУЛКАНИЗИ́РОВАТЬ v. impfv. & pfv. [pres. -рую, -руешь] to vulcanize.

ВУЛКАНИ́ЧЕСКИЙ adj. volcanic; volcano (attrib.).

ВУЛЬГАРИЗИ́РОВАТЬ v. impfv. & pfv. [pres. -рую, -руешь] to vulgarize.

ВУЛЬГАРИ́ЗМ n. vulgarism.

ВУЛЬГÁРНЫЙ adj. vulgar. —вульгáрность, n.f. vulgarity.

ВУНДЕРКИ́НД (дэ) n. child prodigy.

ВУРДАЛÁК n., folklore vampire.

ВХОД n. 1, entry. 2, admission. 3, entrance.

ВХОДИ́ТЬ v. impfv. [pfv. войти́; pres. вхожу́, вхóдишь] (with в + acc.) 1, to enter; come in; go in; walk in. 2, to go into; be a part of. 3, to fit into. 4, to join. —входи́ть во вкус (+ gen.), to begin to enjoy. —входи́ть в довéрие к, to gain the confidence of. —входи́ть в истóрию, to go down in history. —входи́ть в привы́чку, to become a habit. —входи́ть в роль, to grow into a role. —входи́ть в дóлю/мóду/обихóд/послóвицу/состáв, see entry under noun.

входно́й *adj.* entrance (*attrib.*); admission (*attrib.*): входна́я пла́та, admission/entrance fee.

входя́щий *adj.* incoming.

вхожде́ние *n.* (*with* в + *acc.*) entering; joining.

вхо́жий *adj., colloq.* having entrée: он вхож в лу́чшие дома́, he has entrée into the best homes.

вхолосту́ю *adv., in* рабо́тать вхолосту́ю, (*of a motor*) to idle.

вцепи́ться [*infl.* вцеплю́сь, вце́пишься] *v.r., pfv. of* вцепля́ться.

вцепля́ться *v.r. impfv.* [*pfv.* вцепи́ться] (*with* в + *acc.*) to seize; grab hold of.

вчера́ *adv.* yesterday.

вчера́шний *adj.* yesterday's; of yesterday. —**вчера́шний день**, yesterday.

вчерне́ *adv.* in the rough: докла́д напи́сан вчерне́, the report is written in the rough.

вче́тверо *adv.* **1**, four times; quadruple: вче́тверо бо́льше, four times as much. **2**, in four parts; in quarters.

вчетверо́м *adv.* four together: они́ вчетверо́м, the four of them.

в-четвёртых in the fourth place.

вчи́тываться *v.r. impfv.* [*pfv.* вчита́ться] (*with* в + *acc.*) *colloq.* **1**, to read carefully. **2**, to be thoroughly familiar with (*by reading*).

вшива́ть *v. impfv.* [*pfv.* вшить] (*with* в + *acc.*) to sew in; sew into.

вшивно́й *adj.* sewn in.

вши́вый *adj.* infested with lice.

вширь *adv.* **1**, in breadth. **2**, over a great distance.

вшить [*infl.* вошью́, вошьёшь] *v., pfv. of* вшива́ть.

въеда́ться *v.r. impfv.* [*pfv.* въе́сться] (*with* в + *acc.*) **1**, to eat into. **2**, (*of something sharp*) to sink into.

въе́дливый *adj., colloq.* **1**, corrosive. **2**, meticulous.

въезд *n.* **1**, entry. **2**, entrance. —**въездно́й**, *adj.* entry (*attrib.*); entrance (*attrib.*).

въезжа́ть *v. impfv.* [*pfv.* въе́хать] (*with* в + *acc.*) **1**, to enter (*in a conveyance*); drive into. **2**, to move in; move into (a house, apartment, etc.). **3**, (*with* на + *acc.*) to ride up; drive up.

въе́сться [*infl. like* есть] *v.r., pfv. of* въеда́ться.

въе́хать [*infl.* въе́ду, въе́дешь] *v., pfv. of* въезжа́ть.

вы [*gen., acc., & prepl.* вас; *dat.* вам; *instr.* ва́ми] *pers. pron.*, 2nd person pl. and polite 2nd person sing. you. —**быть с** (+ *instr.*) **на вы**, to address each other as ''вы'' (*as opposed to* ''ты'').

вы- *prefix* **1**, *indicating motion to the outside:* вы́бежать, to run out. **2**, *indicating thoroughness of an action or process:* вы́мокнуть, to get soaked. **3**, *indicating attainment of a goal:* вы́требовать, to demand and obtain. **4**, (*with* -ся) *indicating indulgence to the point of complete satisfaction:* вы́спаться, to have a good sleep; вы́плакаться, have a good cry.

выба́лтывать *v. impfv.* [*pfv.* вы́болтать] *colloq.* to blab; let out: вы́болтать секре́т, to let the cat out of the bag.

выбега́ть *v. impfv.* [*pfv.* вы́бежать] to run out.

вы́бежать [*infl. like* бежа́ть] *v., pfv. of* выбега́ть.

вы́белить *v., pfv. of* бели́ть (*in sense #3*).

выбива́ть *v. impfv.* [*pfv.* вы́бить] **1**, to knock out. **2**, to dislodge (an enemy). **3**, to beat down. **4**, to beat (a carpet). **5**, to strike (a medal); hammer out (metals). —**выбива́ться**, *refl.* **1**, *colloq.* to get out; work one's way out. **2**, to come out; appear. **3**, *in* вы́биться из сил, to be exhausted.

выбира́ть *v. impfv.* [*pfv.* вы́брать] **1**, to choose; select. **2**, to elect. **3**, to take out; remove (all of something). **4**, to haul in (a net); pull up (an anchor). **5**, *colloq.* to find (time, a spare moment, etc.). —**выбира́ться**, *refl.* **1**, to be chosen. **2**, (*with* из) to get out (of); find one's way out (of). **3**, *colloq.* to move (*change one's residence*). **4**, (*with* в + *acc.*) *colloq.* to find time to go to.

вы́бить [*infl.* вы́бью, вы́бьешь] *v., pfv. of* выбива́ть. —**вы́биться**, *refl., pfv. of* выбива́ться.

вы́боина *n.* **1**, dent; hole. **2**, pothole.

вы́болтать *v., pfv. of* выба́лтывать.

вы́бор *n.* **1**, choice. **2**, assortment. —**без вы́бора**, indiscriminately. —**на вы́бор** (*with* предлага́ть), one's choice; of one's choice *See also* вы́боры.

вы́борка *n.* **1**, choice; selection. **2**, sample; sampling: случа́йная вы́борка, random sample/sampling. **3**, *pl.* excerpts. —**произво́льная вы́борка**, random access.

вы́борность *n.f.* election; electing.

вы́борный *adj.* **1**, election (*attrib.*). **2**, elective; electoral. **3**, elected. —*n.* elected representative.

вы́борочный *adj.* selective. —**вы́борочная прове́рка**, spot check.

вы́борщик *n.* elector.

вы́боры [*gen.* -ров] *n. pl.* election; elections.

вы́бранить *v. pfv., colloq.* to chew out; give (someone) the devil.

выбра́сывание *n.* throwing out; ejection.

выбра́сывать *v. impfv.* [*pfv.* вы́бросить] **1**, to throw out: вы́бросить что́-нибудь в окно́, to throw something out the window. **2**, to throw away; throw out; discard. **3**, to hoist (a flag). **4**, *colloq.* to delete. **5**, *colloq.* to proclaim (a slogan). —**выбра́сывать из головы́**, to put out of one's head; dismiss from one's mind. —**выбра́сывать на у́лицу**, to put out (*or* turn out) on the street.

выбра́сываться *v.r. impfv.* [*pfv.* вы́броситься] to jump out.

вы́брать [*infl.* -беру́, -берёшь] *v., pfv. of* выбира́ть. —**вы́браться**, *refl.* **1**, *pfv. of* выбира́ться. **2**, *colloq.* (*of time*) to become available.

выбрива́ть *v. impfv.* [*pfv.* вы́брить] to shave off; shave clean. —**выбрива́ться**, *refl.* to shave (oneself).

вы́брить [*infl.* -бре́ю, -бре́ешь] *v., pfv. of* выбрива́ть. —**вы́бриться**, *refl., pfv. of* выбрива́ться.

вы́бросить [*infl.* -шу, -сишь] *v., pfv. of* выбра́сывать. —**вы́броситься**, *refl., pfv. of* выбра́сываться.

выбыва́ть *v. impfv.* [*pfv.* вы́быть] **1**, to leave; depart. **2**, (*with* из) to quit; drop out (of). **3**, *sports* to be eliminated. —**выбыва́ть из стро́я**, **1**, to quit the ranks. **2**, to be put out of action.

вы́быть [*infl.* -буду, -будешь] *v., pfv. of* выбыва́ть.

выва́ливать *v. impfv.* [*pfv.* вы́валить] *colloq.* to throw out; dump out. —**выва́ливаться**, *refl., colloq.* to fall out.

выва́ривать *v. impfv.* [*pfv.* вы́варить] **1**, to remove by boiling. **2**, to overcook.

выве́дывать *v. impfv.* [*pfv.* вы́ведать] *colloq.* to worm (out); wangle; ferret out (a secret, information, etc.).

вы́везти [*infl. like* везти́] *v., pfv. of* вывози́ть.

вы́верить *v., pfv. of* выверя́ть.

вы́верка *n.* adjustment.

вы́вернуть *v., pfv. of* вывёртывать. —**вы́вернуться**, *refl., pfv. of* вывёртываться.

вы́верт *n., colloq.* **1**, turn; twist. **2**, quirk; eccentricity; idiosyncrasy.

вывёртывать v. impfv. [pfv. **вывернуть**] **1,** to unscrew. **2,** to turn inside out. **3,** colloq. to twist; wrench. —**вывёртываться,** refl. **1,** colloq. to come unscrewed. **2,** to be turned inside out. **3,** to wriggle out; slip away.

выверя́ть v. impfv. [pfv. **вы́верить**] **1,** to adjust. **2,** to check.

вы́весить [infl. -шу, -сишь] v., pfv. of **вывешивать.**

вы́веска [gen. pl. -сок] n. sign; signboard.

вы́вести [infl. like вести́] v., pfv. of **выводи́ть.** —**вы́вестись,** refl., pfv. of **выводи́ться.**

выве́тривание n. **1,** ventilating; ventilation. **2,** erosion; decay.

выве́тривать v. impfv. [pfv. **вы́ветрить**] **1,** to get rid of (an odor) by ventilation. **2,** to erode; wear away. —**выве́триваться,** refl. **1,** (of something in the air) to disappear; be blown away. **2,** to erode; become eroded.

выве́шивать v. impfv. [pfv. **вы́весить**] **1,** to hang out. **2,** to put up; post. **3,** to weigh.

выви́нчивать v. impfv. [pfv. **вы́винтить**] to unscrew. —**выви́нчиваться,** refl. to come unscrewed.

вы́вих n., med. dislocation.

вы́вихнуть v. pfv., med. to dislocate.

вы́вод n. **1,** conclusion. **2,** derivation. **3,** withdrawal.

выводи́ть v. impfv. [pfv. **вы́вести;** pres. -вожу́, -во́дишь] **1,** to bring out; take out; lead out. **2,** to remove; withdraw. **3,** to remove; expel. **4,** to conclude; deduce; infer. **5,** to derive (a formula); draw (a conclusion). **6,** to grow; raise. **7,** to hatch. **8,** to construct; put up. **9,** to write carefully; trace. **10,** to give (a grade). **11,** to remove; take out (a stain). **12,** to exterminate (insects). —**выводи́ть из равнове́сия,** to disconcert; rattle. —**выводи́ть из себя́,** to drive (someone) crazy. —**выводи́ть из стро́я,** to put out of operation (or commission). —**выводи́ть из терпе́ния,** to make (someone) lose patience. —**выводи́ть на чи́стую во́ду,** to bring out into the open.

выводи́ться v.r. impfv. [pfv. **вы́вестись;** pres. -вожу́сь, -во́дишься] **1,** to disappear; become extinct. **2,** (of a stain) to come out. **3,** to hatch; be hatched; be born.

выводно́й adj. **1,** discharge (attrib.). **2,** anat. excretory.

вы́водок [gen. -дка] n. brood; litter.

вы́воз n. **1,** removal. **2,** exporting. **3,** exports.

вывози́ть v. impfv. [pfv. **вы́везти;** pres. -вожу́, -во́зишь] **1,** to take out; take away; cart out; cart away. **2,** to take; bring; deliver. **3,** to bring back (a souvenir). **4,** to export. **5,** colloq. to save; rescue.

вы́возка n. carting out; removal.

вывозно́й adj. export (attrib.).

вывола́кивать v. impfv. [pfv. **вы́волочь**] colloq. to drag out.

вы́волочь [infl. -локу, -лочешь, ...-локут; past -лок, -локла] v., pfv. of **вывола́кивать.**

вывора́чивать v. impfv. [pfv. **вы́воротить**] colloq. **1,** to pull out; extract. **2,** to wrench; twist. **3,** to turn inside out.

вы́воротить [infl. -чу, -тишь] v., pfv. of **вывора́чивать.**

выга́дывать v. impfv. [pfv. **вы́гадать**] **1,** to gain. **2,** to save (time, money, etc.).

вы́гиб n. bend; curve.

выгиба́ть v. impfv. [pfv. **вы́гнуть**] to bend; arch. —**выгиба́ться,** refl. to bend; curve.

вы́гладить v. pfv. of **гла́дить** (in sense #1).

вы́глядеть v. impfv. [pres. -жу, -дишь] (with an adv. or instr. case) to look: она́ хорошо́ вы́глядит, she looks well. Он вы́глядит здоро́вым/старико́м, he looks healthy/like an old man/.

выгля́дывать v. impfv. [pfv. **вы́глянуть**] **1,** to look out. **2,** to appear; come into view.

вы́гнать [infl. -гоню, -гонишь] v., pfv. of **выгоня́ть.**

вы́гнутый adj. curved; bent.

вы́гнуть v., pfv. of **выгиба́ть.** —**вы́гнуться,** refl., pfv. of **выгиба́ться.**

выгова́ривать v. impfv. [pfv. **вы́говорить**] **1,** to pronounce; enunciate; articulate. **2,** (with себе́) colloq. to reserve for oneself. **3,** [impfv. only] (with dat.) to scold; berate.

вы́говор n. **1,** pronunciation. **2,** reprimand; rebuke.

вы́говорить v., pfv. of **выгова́ривать.** —**вы́говориться,** refl., colloq. to speak one's mind; sound off.

вы́года n. **1,** profit; gain. **2,** benefit; advantage.

вы́годно adv. **1,** to advantage; favorably. **2,** at a profit. —adj., used predicatively advantageous; profitable: кому́ это вы́годно?, whom is this good for?; who stands to gain from this?

вы́годный adj. **1,** profitable. **2,** favorable; advantageous.

вы́гон n. pasture.

выгоня́ть v. impfv. [pfv. **вы́гнать**] **1,** to drive out; chase out. **2,** colloq. to expel. **3,** in выгоня́ть с рабо́ты, colloq. to fire; give (someone) the sack. **4,** to force (plants).

выгора́живать v. impfv. [pfv. **вы́городить**] **1,** to fence off. **2,** colloq. to shield (from blame, responsibility, etc.).

выгора́ть v. impfv. [pfv. **вы́гореть**] **1,** to burn down. **2,** (of colors) to fade. **3,** colloq. to work out; pan out.

вы́городить [infl. -жу, -дишь] v., pfv. of **выгора́живать.**

вы́гравировать v., pfv. of **гравирова́ть.**

выгреба́ть v. impfv. [pfv. **вы́грести**] **1,** v.t. to rake out; scoop out; shovel out. **2,** v.i. to row: выгреба́ть к бе́регу, to row toward shore.

выгребно́й adj., in выгребна́я я́ма, cesspool.

вы́грести [infl. like грести́] v., pfv. of **выгреба́ть.**

выгружа́ть v. impfv. [pfv. **вы́грузить**] to unload (cargo). —**выгружа́ться,** refl. to disembark.

вы́грузка n. unloading.

выгрыза́ть v. impfv. [pfv. **вы́грызть**] to gnaw (a hole).

вы́грызть [infl. like грызть] v., pfv. of **выгрыза́ть.**

выдава́ть v. impfv. [pfv. **вы́дать;** pres. -даю́, -даёшь] **1,** to give out; issue. **2,** to deliver up; extradite. **3,** to give away; betray. **4,** (with за + acc.) to pass (someone) off as; (with себя́ and за + acc.) pose as. —**выдава́ться,** refl. **1,** to stick out; jut out; protrude. **2,** to stand out; be distinguished. **3,** colloq. to turn out to be: вы́дался хоро́ший денёк, it turned out to be a nice day.

вы́давить [infl. -влю, -вишь] v., pfv. of **выда́вливать.**

выда́вливать v. impfv. [pfv. **вы́давить**] **1,** to press out; squeeze out. **2,** to break; knock out (e.g. a pane of glass). **3,** fig. to force (a smile, laugh, etc.).

выда́лбливать v. impfv. [pfv. **вы́долбить**] to hollow out.

вы́дать [infl. like дать] v., pfv. of **выдава́ть.** —**вы́даться,** refl., pfv. of **выдава́ться.**

вы́дача n. **1,** giving out; issuing; distribution. **2,** extradition.

выдаю́щийся *adj.* outstanding; distinguished; eminent; illustrious.

выдвига́ть *v. impfv.* [*pfv.* вы́двинуть] **1,** to pull out; draw out; move out. **2,** to advance; put forward (an idea, proposal, etc.). **3,** to nominate. **4,** to promote (*in rank*). —**выдвига́ться,** *refl.* **1,** to advance; move forward. **2,** to rise (*in rank*); work one's way up. **3,** [*impfv. only*] (*of a drawer*) to slide.

выдвиже́нец [*gen.* -нца] *n.m.* [*fem.* -нка] worker promoted to a position of responsibility.

выдвиже́ние *n.* **1,** moving forward. **2,** nomination. **3,** promotion.

выдвижно́й *adj.* sliding.

вы́двинуть *v., pfv. of* выдвига́ть. —**вы́двинуться,** *refl., pfv. of* выдвига́ться.

выдворя́ть *v. impfv.* [*pfv.* вы́дворить] **1,** to expel (from a country). **2,** *colloq.* to throw out; kick out.

вы́делать *v., pfv. of* выде́лывать.

выделе́ние *n.* **1,** allocation; allotment; apportionment. **2,** excretion; secretion; discharge. **3,** *pl.* (bodily) secretions.

выдели́тельный *adj.* secretory; excretory.

вы́делить *v., pfv. of* выделя́ть. —**вы́делиться,** *refl., pfv. of* выделя́ться.

вы́делка *n.* **1,** manufacturing. **2,** workmanship.

выде́лывать *v. impfv.* [*pfv.* вы́делать] **1,** to manufacture; make; fashion. **2,** to curry; dress (leather, hides, etc.). **3,** *colloq.* to do; perform.

выделя́ть *v. impfv.* [*pfv.* вы́делить] **1,** to single out. **2,** to set apart. **3,** to allot; allocate; apportion; earmark. **4,** to give off; excrete; secrete. **5,** *in* выделя́ть курси́вом, to italicize; set off in italics. —**выделя́ться,** *refl.* **1,** to stand out. **2,** to ooze; exude. **3,** to take one's inheritance and separate from the family.

выде́ргивать *v. impfv.* [*pfv.* вы́дернуть] to pull out.

вы́держанность *n.f.* **1,** consistency. **2,** steadfastness. **3,** self-control.

вы́держанный *adj.* **1,** consistent. **2,** self-controlled; self-possessed. **3,** (*of wine, cheese, etc.*) aged; mellowed.

вы́держать [*infl.* -держу, -держишь] *v., pfv. of* выде́рживать.

выде́рживать *v. impfv.* [*pfv.* вы́держать] **1,** to bear; support. **2,** to endure; withstand. **3,** *v.i.* to control oneself; contain oneself. **4,** to maintain; keep up. **5,** to pass (an examination). **6,** to age (wine, cheese, etc.). —**выде́рживать хара́ктер,** to stand firm. —**не выде́рживать кри́тики,** not stand up (to criticism); not hold water.

вы́держка *n.* **1,** endurance; self-control. **2,** extract; excerpt. **3,** *photog.* exposure. —**на вы́держку,** picked at random.

вы́дернуть *v., pfv. of* выде́ргивать.

выдира́ть *v. impfv.* [*pfv.* вы́драть] *colloq.* to tear out.

вы́долбить [*infl.* -блю, -бишь] *v., pfv. of* выда́лбливать.

вы́дох *n.* an outward breath; exhalation.

вы́дохнуть [*past* -нул, -нула] *v., pfv. of* выдыха́ть. —**вы́дохнуться,** *refl.* [*past* -дохся, -дохлась] *pfv. of* выдыха́ться.

вы́дра *n.* otter.

вы́драть [*infl.* -деру -дерешь] *v., pfv. of* драть (*in sense #3*) *and* выдира́ть.

вы́дрессировать *v., pfv. of* дрессирова́ть.

вы́дубить *v., pfv. of* дуби́ть.

выдува́ть *v. impfv.* [*pfv.* вы́дуть] to blow out.

вы́думанный *adj.* fictitious; made-up.

вы́думать *v., pfv. of* выду́мывать.

вы́думка *n.* **1,** *colloq.* inventiveness; imagination. **2,** invention. **3,** fabrication; fib.

вы́думщик *n., colloq.* **1,** one who thinks up anything. **2,** liar.

выду́мывать *v. impfv.* [*pfv.* вы́думать] **1,** to think up; invent. **2,** to make up; concoct.

вы́дуть [*infl.* -дую, -дуешь] *v., pfv. of* выдува́ть.

выдыха́ние *n.* exhalation.

выдыха́ть *v. impfv.* [*pfv.* вы́дохнуть] to exhale; breathe out. —**выдыха́ться,** *refl.* **1,** to lose its fragrance/taste/zest. **2,** *fig., colloq.* to fizzle; bog down; peter out.

выеда́ть *v. impfv.* [*pfv.* вы́есть] to eat away; corrode. —**вы́еденного яйца́ не сто́ит,** not worth a hill of beans.

вы́езд *n.* **1,** departure. **2,** exit; road leading out. **3,** horse and carriage. —**на вы́езде,** *sports* on the road.

вы́ездить [*infl.* -езжу, -ездишь] *v., pfv. of* выезжа́ть (*in sense #4*).

выездно́й *adj.* **1,** exit (*attrib.*). **2,** (*of a horse*) for riding.

выезжа́ть *v. impfv.* [*pfv.* вы́ехать] **1,** to drive out; depart; leave (*by conveyance*). **2,** to move out. **3,** (*with* на + *prepl.*) *colloq.* to exploit; make capital of. **4,** [*pfv.* вы́ездить] to break in (a horse).

вы́емка *n.* **1,** taking out; removing. **2,** hollow; depression. —**вы́емка пи́сем,** collection (*of mail*).

вы́есть [*infl. like* есть] *v., pfv. of* выеда́ть.

вы́ехать [*infl.* -еду, -едешь] *v., pfv. of* выезжа́ть.

вы́жать [*infl.* -жму, -жмешь] *v., pfv. of* выжима́ть.

вы́ждать [*infl.* вы́жду, вы́ждешь] *v., pfv. of* выжида́ть.

вы́жечь [*infl. like* жечь] *v., pfv. of* выжига́ть.

вы́жженный *past passive part. of* вы́жечь. —**страте́гия вы́жженной земли́,** scorched-earth policy.

выжива́ние *n.* survival. —**выжива́ние наибо́лее приспосо́бленных,** survival of the fittest.

выжива́ть *v. impfv.* [*pfv.* вы́жить] **1,** *v.i.* to survive; live; pull through. **2,** *v.t., colloq.* to drive out (by making life impossible). —**вы́жить из ума́,** to lose possession of one's faculties.

выжига́ние *n.* **1,** burning out. **2,** pyrography. **3,** cauterization.

выжига́ть *v. impfv.* [*pfv.* вы́жечь] **1,** to burn down; burn out. **2,** to burn in; trace by burning. **3,** to cauterize.

выжида́ние *n.* **1,** waiting. **2,** expectancy.

выжида́тельный *adj.* waiting; temporizing.

выжида́ть *v. impfv.* [*pfv.* вы́ждать] **1,** to wait for (the right moment): выжида́ть удо́бный слу́чай, to wait for an opportunity. **2,** to wait out; wait till the end of. **3,** to bide one's time; sit tight.

выжима́ть *v. impfv.* [*pfv.* вы́жать] to squeeze out; wring out. —**мо́крый, хоть вы́жми,** wringing/soaking/sopping wet.

вы́жить [*infl.* -живу, -живешь] *v., pfv. of* выжива́ть.

вы́звать [*infl.* -зову, -зовешь] *v., pfv. of* вызыва́ть. —**вы́зваться,** *refl., pfv. of* вызыва́ться.

вызволя́ть *v. impfv.* [*pfv.* вы́зволить] *colloq.* to help out (of trouble).

выздора́вливать *v. impfv.* [*pfv.* вы́здороветь] to get well; recover; recuperate.

вы́здороветь [*infl.* -ею, -еешь] *v., pfv. of* выздора́вливать.

выздоровле́ние *n.* recovery.

вы́зов *n.* **1,** call: вы́зов по телефо́ну, telephone call. **2,** summons. **3,** challenge. **4,** invitation; affidavit (*from someone abroad to emigrate from the USSR*). —бро́сить вы́зов (+ *dat.*), to challenge.

вы́золотить *v., pfv. of* золоти́ть.

вы́золоченный *adj.* gilded; gilt.

вызрева́ть *v. impfv.* [*pfv.* вы́зреть] to ripen.

вызу́бривать *v. impfv.* [*pfv.* вы́зубрить] **1,** to notch; make notches in. **2,** *colloq.* to learn by rote.

вызыва́ть *v. impfv.* [*pfv.* вы́звать] **1,** to call. **2,** to summon. **3,** to challenge. **4,** to cause. **5,** to arouse; evoke. **6,** *in* вызыва́ть к жи́зни, to give rise to. —вызыва́ться, *refl.* to volunteer.

вызыва́ющий *adj.* defiant.

выи́грывать *v. impfv.* [*pfv.* вы́играть] **1,** to win. **2,** (*with* у) to defeat; beat. **3,** to gain.

вы́игрыш *n.* **1,** winnings. **2,** win; winning: игра́ть на вы́игрыш, to play to win; play for a win. **3,** gain; advantage. —быть в вы́игрыше, to be winning; be ahead of the game.

вы́игрышный *adj.* **1,** winning. **2,** advantageous.

вы́искать *v. pfv.* [*infl.* -ищу, -ищешь] *colloq.* to find; locate; turn up. —вы́искаться, *refl., colloq.* to turn up; appear.

выи́скивать *v. impfv., colloq.* to seek; try to find.

вы́йти [*infl.* вы́йду, вы́йдешь; *past* вы́шел, вы́шла] *v., pfv. of* выходи́ть.

вы́казать [*infl.* -кажу, -кажешь] *v., pfv. of* выка́зывать.

выка́зывать *v. impfv.* [*pfv.* вы́казать] *colloq.* to show; display; evince.

выка́лывать *v. impfv.* [*pfv.* вы́колоть] to put out; gouge out (someone's eye). —темно́, хоть глаз вы́коли, so dark you can't see your hand in front of your face.

выка́пывать *v. impfv.* [*pfv.* вы́копать] **1,** to dig (a hole, well, etc.). **2,** to dig up; dig out. **3,** to exhume; disinter. **4,** *fig.* to unearth.

выкара́бкиваться *v.r. impfv.* [*pfv.* вы́карабкаться] *colloq.* **1,** to scramble out; extricate oneself. **2,** *fig.* to pull through (an illness).

выка́рмливать *v. impfv.* [*pfv.* вы́кормить] to bring up; rear.

вы́катать *v., pfv. of* ката́ть (*in sense #4*).

вы́катить [*infl.* -чу, -тишь] *v., pfv. of* выка́тывать. —вы́катиться, *refl., pfv. of* выка́тываться.

выка́тывать *v. impfv.* [*pfv.* вы́катить] to roll out; wheel out. —выка́тываться, *refl.* to roll out.

выка́чивать *v. impfv.* [*pfv.* вы́качать] to pump; pump out.

выка́шливать *v. impfv.* [*pfv.* вы́кашлять] *colloq.* to cough up. —выка́шливаться, *refl., colloq.* to clear one's throat.

выки́дывать *v. impfv.* [*pfv.* вы́кинуть] **1,** to throw out. **2,** to delete. **3,** to raise; hoist (a flag). **4,** *v.i.* to have a miscarriage. **5,** *colloq.* to play (a trick).

вы́кидыш *n.* **1,** miscarriage; abortion. **2,** stillborn fetus.

вы́кинуть *v., pfv. of* выки́дывать.

выкипа́ть *v. impfv.* [*pfv.* вы́кипеть] to boil away.

вы́кладка *n.* **1,** *colloq.* laying out; spreading out. **2,** *usu. pl.* calculations. **3,** *mil.* kit: с по́лной вы́кладкой, with full kit.

выкла́дывать *v. impfv.* [*pfv.* вы́ложить] **1,** to lay out; spread out. **2,** *fig., colloq.* to tell; reveal; lay bare. **3,**

(*with instr.*) to face (with); line (with); pave (with). —выкла́дываться, *refl., colloq.* to go all out. Он осо́бенно не выкла́дывался, he did not try especially hard.

вы́клевать [*infl.* -клюю, -клюешь] *v., pfv. of* выклё́вывать.

выклё́вывать *v. impfv.* [*pfv.* вы́клевать] to peck out.

выклика́ть *v. impfv.* [*pfv.* вы́кликнуть] to call out by name.

выключа́тель *n.m.* switch (*for turning something on or off*).

выключа́ть *v. impfv.* [*pfv.* вы́ключить] to turn off; switch off; shut off (a device); turn out (the light).

выкля́нчивать *v. impfv.* [*pfv.* вы́клянчить] *colloq.* to coax out of.

вы́ковать [*infl.* -кую, -куешь] *v., pfv. of* выко́вывать.

выко́вывать *v. impfv.* [*pfv.* вы́ковать] to forge.

выкола́чивать *v. impfv.* [*pfv.* вы́колотить] **1,** to knock out; beat out; hammer out. **2,** to beat (*in order to clean*).

вы́колоть [*infl.* -колю, -колешь] *v., pfv. of* выка́лывать.

вы́копать *v., pfv. of* копа́ть (*in sense #2*) *and* выка́пывать.

вы́кормить [*infl.* -млю, -мишь] *v., pfv. of* выка́рмливать.

вы́корчевать [*infl.* -чую, -чуешь] *v., pfv. of* выкорчё́вывать.

выкорчё́вывать *v. impfv.* [*pfv.* вы́корчевать] **1,** to uproot. **2,** to root out; eradicate.

выкра́дывать *v. impfv.* [*pfv.* вы́красть] to steal.

выкра́ивать *v. impfv.* [*pfv.* вы́кроить] **1,** to cut out the material for: вы́кроить пла́тье, to cut out (the material for) a dress. **2,** *fig., colloq.* to scrape up (money); find (time).

вы́красить [*infl.* -шу, -сишь] *v., pfv. of* выкра́шивать.

вы́красть [*infl. like* красть] *v., pfv. of* выкра́дывать.

выкра́шивать *v. impfv.* [*pfv.* вы́красить] to paint; dye.

вы́крик *n.* shout; cry; yell.

выкри́кивать *v. impfv.* [*pfv.* вы́крикнуть] **1,** *v.i.* to cry out; shout; yell. **2,** *v.t.* to shout (an order, slogan, etc.).

вы́кроить *v., pfv. of* выкра́ивать.

вы́кройка [*gen. pl.* -кроек] *n.* pattern (*for sewing*).

выкрута́сы [*gen.* -сов] *n. pl., colloq.* **1,** twists and turns. **2,** *fig.* flourishes.

вы́крутить [*infl.* -чу, -тишь] *v., pfv. of* выкру́чивать. —вы́крутиться, *refl., pfv. of* выкру́чиваться.

выкру́чивать *v. impfv.* [*pfv.* вы́крутить] **1,** to twist; make by twisting. **2,** *colloq.* to twist: вы́крутить кому́-нибудь ру́ку, to twist someone's arm. **3,** *colloq.* to unscrew. —выкру́чиваться, *refl., colloq.* **1,** to come unscrewed. **2,** *fig.* to wiggle out (of a situation).

вы́куп *n.* **1,** redeeming; redemption. **2,** ransom.

вы́купать *v., pfv. of* купа́ть. —вы́купаться, *refl., pfv. of* купа́ться.

выкупа́ть *v. impfv.* [*pfv.* вы́купить] **1,** to redeem. **2,** to ransom.

выку́ривать *v. impfv.* [*pfv.* вы́курить] **1,** to finish smoking; smoke completely. **2,** to smoke out; flush out.

выла́вливать *v. impfv.* [*pfv.* вы́ловить] to fish out.

вы́лазка [*gen. pl.* -зок] *n.* **1,** *mil.* sortie; sally. **2,** excursion; outing.

вы́лакать *v., pfv. of* лака́ть.

выла́мывать *v. impfv.* [*pfv.* **вы́ломать**] to break open; break down (a door).

вы́лежать *v. pfv.* [*infl.* -лежу, -лежишь] *colloq.* (of a sick person) to remain in bed (for a certain length of time). —**вы́лежаться**, *refl.* **1,** *colloq.* to have a complete rest. **2,** to ripen; mature.

вылеза́ть *v. impfv.* [*pfv.* **вы́лезть** *or* **вы́лезти**] **1,** to crawl out; climb out. **2,** (of hair) to fall out.

вы́лезть *also,* **вы́лезти** [*infl. like* лезть] *v., pfv. of* вылеза́ть.

вы́лепить *v., pfv. of* лепи́ть (*in sense #1*).

вы́лет *n.* **1,** flight. **2,** takeoff. **3,** *mil.* mission.

вылета́ть *v. impfv.* [*pfv.* **вы́лететь**] **1,** to fly out. **2,** to leave; depart (by plane). **3,** (of a plane) to leave; take off. **4,** *fig.* to dash out; rush out. **5,** *colloq.* to be fired (from a job); be eliminated (from a tournament). —**вы́лететь из головы́,** to slip one's mind; go right out of one's mind.

вы́лететь [*infl.* -чу, -тишь] *v., pfv. of* вылета́ть.

вылечивать *v. impfv.* [*pfv.* **вы́лечить**] (with от) to cure (of). —**вылечиваться**, *refl.* (with от) to be cured (of).

вылива́ть *v. impfv.* [*pfv.* **вы́лить**] **1,** to pour out. **2,** *fig.* to vent (feelings). **3,** to cast; mold. —**вылива́ться**, *refl.* **1,** to run out; flow out. **2,** (with в + *acc.*) to take the form of; develop into; end up being.

вы́лизать [*infl.* -лижу, -лижешь] *v., pfv. of* вылизывать.

вылизывать *v. impfv.* [*pfv.* **вы́лизать**] to lick clean.

вы́линять *v., pfv. of* линя́ть (*in sense #2*).

вы́литый *adj., colloq.,* in вы́литый оте́ц *and* вы́литая мать, the very image of one's father *or* mother.

вы́лить [*infl.* вылью, вы́льешь] *v., pfv. of* вылива́ть. —**вы́литься**, *refl., pfv. of* вылива́ться.

вы́ловить [*infl.* -влю, -вишь] *v., pfv. of* выла́вливать.

вы́ложить *v., pfv. of* выкла́дывать. —**вы́ложиться**, *refl., pfv. of* выкла́дываться.

вы́ломать *v., pfv. of* выла́мывать.

вы́лощить *v. pfv.* to polish.

вылупля́ться *v.r. impfv.* [*pfv.* **вы́лупиться**] to hatch.

вы́мазать [*infl.* -мажу, -мажешь] *v., pfv. of* ма́зать (*in senses #2 & #4*) *and* выма́зывать. —**вы́мазаться**, *refl., pfv. of* ма́заться (*in sense #2*).

выма́зывать *v. impfv.* [*pfv.* **вы́мазать**] (*with instr.*) to coat (with); cover (with).

выма́ливать *v. impfv.* [*pfv.* **вы́молить**] **1,** [*impfv.* only] to beg for; plead for. **2,** to get by begging or pleading.

выма́нивать *v. impfv.* [*pfv.* **вы́манить**] *colloq.* **1,** (with из) to lure out of. **2,** (with у) to coax out of. **3,** (with у) to cheat out of.

вы́марать *v., pfv. of* мара́ть (*in sense #3*) *and* выма́рывать.

выма́рывать *v. impfv.* [*pfv.* **вы́марать**] *colloq.* **1,** to soil; dirty. **2,** to cross out.

выма́тывать *v. impfv.* [*pfv.* **вы́мотать**] *colloq.* to exhaust; drain; use up.

выма́чивать *v. impfv.* [*pfv.* **вы́мочить**] **1,** (of rain) to soak; drench. **2,** to soak; steep.

выма́щивать *v. impfv.* [*pfv.* **вы́мостить**] to pave.

выме́нивать *v. impfv.* [*pfv.* **вы́менять**] to exchange; swap.

вы́мереть [*infl.* вы́мрет; *past* вы́мер, -ла] *v., pfv. of* вымира́ть.

вымерза́ть *v. impfv.* [*pfv.* **вы́мерзнуть**] **1,** to freeze; be destroyed by frost. **2,** to freeze solid.

вы́мерзнуть [*past* вы́мерз, -ла] *v., pfv. of* вымерза́ть.

вы́мерить *v., pfv. of* вымеря́ть *and* вымеривать.

вы́мерший *adj.* extinct.

вымеря́ть *v. impfv.* [*pfv.* **вы́мерить**] to measure. *Also,* вымеривать.

вы́мести [*infl. like* мести́] *v., pfv. of* вымета́ть.

вы́местить [*infl.* -щу, -стишь] *v., pfv. of* вымеща́ть.

вы́метать *v. pfv.* **1,** [*infl.* -мечу, -мечешь] *pfv. of* вымётывать (*in senses #1 & #2*). **2,** [*infl.* -таю, -таешь] *pfv. of* вымётывать (*in sense #3*).

вымета́ть *v. impfv.* [*pfv.* **вы́мести**] **1,** to sweep up; sweep out (refuse). **2,** to sweep (a surface).

вымётывать *v. impfv.* [*pfv.* **вы́метать**] **1,** to throw out. **2,** in вымётывать икру́, to spawn. **3,** to make (buttonholes).

вымеща́ть *v. impfv.* [*pfv.* **вы́местить**] **1,** to avenge. **2,** to vent (one's feelings): вымеща́ть свою́ доса́ду на ко́м-нибудь, to take out one's anger on someone.

вымира́ние *n.* dying out; extinction.

вымира́ть *v. impfv.* [*pfv.* **вы́мереть**] **1,** to die out; become extinct. **2,** to become depopulated; become desolate.

вымога́тель *n.m.* extortionist. —**вымога́тельство**, *n.* extortion.

вымога́ть *v. impfv.* to extort.

вы́мокнуть *v. pfv.* [*past* вы́мок, -ла] to get drenched; get soaked.

вы́молвить *v. impfv.* [*infl.* -влю, -вишь] *colloq.* to utter.

вы́молить *v., pfv. of* выма́ливать.

вымора́живать *v. impfv.* [*pfv.* **вы́морозить**] **1,** to air out. **2,** to kill by freezing.

вы́морить *v., pfv. of* мори́ть (*in sense #1*).

вы́морозить [*infl.* -жу, -зишь] *v., pfv. of* вымора́живать.

вы́мостить [*infl.* -щу, -стишь] *v., pfv. of* мости́ть *and* выма́щивать.

вы́мотать *v., pfv. of* выма́тывать.

вы́мочить *v., pfv. of* выма́чивать.

вы́мпел *n.* pennant.

вы́мученный *adj., colloq.* labored; forced; unnatural.

вы́мучивать *v. impfv.* [*pfv.* **вы́мучить**] *colloq.* **1,** to force; wrest; wring. **2,** to force; produce only with great effort.

вы́муштровать *v., pfv. of* муштрова́ть.

вымыва́ть *v. impfv.* [*pfv.* **вы́мыть**] to wash. —**вымыва́ться**, *refl.* to wash; get washed.

вы́мысел [*gen.* -сла] *n.* **1,** fantasy; figment of the imagination. **2,** untruth; fiction; falsehood.

вы́мыть [*infl.* -мою, -моешь] *v., pfv. of* мыть *and* вымыва́ть. —**вы́мыться**, *refl., pfv. of* мы́ться *and* вымыва́ться.

вы́мышленный *adj.* fictitious; imaginary.

вы́мя [*gen., dat., & prepl.* вы́мени; *instr.* вы́менем] *n. neut.* udder.

вына́шивать *v. impfv.* [*pfv.* **вы́носить**] **1,** to carry; be pregnant with. **2,** to nurture (an idea); hatch (plans). **3,** *colloq.* to wear out.

вы́нести [*infl. like* нести́] *v., pfv. of* выноси́ть. —**вы́нестись**, *refl., pfv. of* выноси́ться.

вынима́ть *v. impfv.* [*pfv.* **вы́нуть**] to take out. —**вынь да поло́жь,** *colloq.* here and now; on the spot.

вы́нос *n.* **1,** carrying out. На вы́нос, (*of food*) to take out; "to go". **2,** funeral procession.

выноси́ть [*infl.* -ношу́, -носишь] *v., pfv. of* вына́шивать.

выноси́ть *v. impfv.* [*pfv.* вы́нести; *pres.* -ношу́, -но́сишь] **1,** to carry out; take out; bring out. **2,** to carry away. **3,** to get; come away with. **4,** to pass; render; pronounce; hand down (a decision, verdict, etc.). **5,** *in* вы́нести благода́рность (+ *dat.*), to thank. **6,** to stand; bear; endure: я его́ не выношу́, I can't stand him. —**выноси́ться,** *refl.* to dash out; dart out.

выно́сливый *adj.* sturdy; hardy; possessing great powers of endurance. —**вы́носливость,** *n.f.* endurance; staying power.

вынужда́ть *v. impfv.* [*pfv.* вы́нудить] **1,** to force; compel. **2,** to extract (a promise, confession, etc.).

вы́нужденный *adj.* forced: вы́нужденная поса́дка, forced landing; emergency landing.

вы́нуть *v., pfv. of* вынима́ть.

вы́нырнуть *v. pfv.* **1,** to come to the surface. **2,** *fig., colloq.* to emerge.

выня́нчивать *v. impfv.* [*pfv.* вы́нянчить] *colloq.* to bring up; raise; nurse.

вы́пад *n.* **1,** *sports* lunge; thrust. **2,** (verbal) attack.

выпада́ть *v. impfv.* [*pfv.* вы́пасть] **1,** to fall out. **2,** (*of rain, snow, etc.*) to fall. **3,** (*with dat.*) to fall to; befall. Выпада́ть на до́лю (+ *dat.*), to fall to someone's lot. **4,** to turn out to be: день вы́пал хоро́ший, it turned out to be a nice day.

выпаде́ние *n.* **1,** falling out (*of hair, teeth, etc.*). **2,** falling (*of rain, snow, etc.*). **3,** *med.* prolapse.

выпа́ливать *v. impfv.* [*pfv.* вы́палить] *colloq.* **1,** to fire; shoot. **2,** *fig.* to blurt out.

вы́палить *v., pfv. of* пали́ть (*in sense #4*) *and* выпа́ливать.

выпа́ривать *v. impfv.* [*pfv.* вы́парить] to steam; steam-clean.

выпа́рывать *v. impfv.* [*pfv.* вы́пороть] to rip out.

вы́пасть [*infl. like* пасть] *v., pfv. of* выпада́ть.

вы́пачкать *v. pfv., colloq.* to soil; get (something) dirty. —**вы́пачкаться,** *refl., colloq.* to get (oneself) dirty.

выпека́ть *v. impfv.* [*pfv.* вы́печь] to bake.

вы́переть [*infl.* -пру, -прешь; *past* вы́пер, -ла] *v., pfv. of* выпира́ть.

вы́пестовать *v., pfv. of* пе́стовать.

вы́печка *n.* **1,** baking. **2,** batch (*of baked goods*).

вы́печь [*infl. like* печь] *v., pfv. of* выпека́ть.

выпива́ть *v. impfv., colloq.* to drink; like to drink; hit the bottle.

вы́пивка *n., colloq.* **1,** drinking spree; binge. **2,** drinks.

выпи́ливать *v. impfv.* [*pfv.* вы́пилить] to cut; cut out (*with a saw*).

выпира́ть *v. impfv.* [*pfv.* вы́переть] *colloq.* **1,** to push out; shove out; force out. **2,** [*impfv. only*] to stick out; jut out; protrude.

вы́писать [*infl.* -пишу, -пишешь] *v., pfv. of* выпи́сывать. —**вы́писаться,** *refl., pfv. of* выпи́сываться.

вы́писка *n.* **1,** writing out; copying out. **2,** (*with gen.*) subscription (to). **3,** discharge; release. **4,** excerpt.

выпи́сывать *v. impfv.* [*pfv.* вы́писать] **1,** to write out; make out. **2,** to copy out. **3,** to order (*by mail*). **4,** to subscribe to. **5,** to send for (*in writing*); summon; call home. **6,** to discharge. —**выпи́сываться,** *refl.* to be discharged (from a hospital).

вы́пить [*infl.* вы́пью, вы́пьешь] *v., pfv. of* пить.

выпи́хивать *v. impfv.* [*pfv.* вы́пихнуть] *colloq.* to push out; shove out.

вы́плавить [*infl.* -влю, -вишь] *v., pfv. of* выплавля́ть.

вы́плавка *n.* **1,** smelting. **2,** smelted metal; output of smelted metal.

выплавля́ть *v. impfv.* [*pfv.* вы́плавить] to smelt.

вы́плакать *v. pfv.* [*infl.* -плачу, -плачешь] **1,** to cry out; alleviate (sorrow, disappointment, etc.) by crying. **2,** *colloq.* to obtain by crying. **3,** *in* вы́плакать все глаза́, to cry one's eyes out. —**вы́плакаться,** *refl.* to have a good cry.

вы́плата *n.* payment.

вы́платить [*infl.* -чу, -тишь] *v., pfv. of* выпла́чивать.

выпла́чивать *v. impfv.* [*pfv.* вы́платить] **1,** to pay out; disburse. **2,** to pay; pay off; pay in full.

выплёвывать *v. impfv.* [*pfv.* вы́плюнуть] to spit out.

выплёскивать *v. impfv.* [*pfv.* вы́плеснуть] to splash out.

выплыва́ть *v. impfv.* [*pfv.* вы́плыть] **1,** to swim out. **2,** to sail out. **3,** to come to the surface. **4,** *fig.* to emerge; come up; come to light.

вы́плыть [*infl.* -плыву, -плывешь] *v., pfv. of* выплыва́ть.

вы́плюнуть *v., pfv. of* выплёвывать.

выпола́скивать *v. impfv.* [*pfv.* вы́полоскать] to rinse; rinse out.

выполза́ть *v. impfv.* [*pfv.* вы́ползти] to crawl out; creep out.

вы́ползти [*infl. like* ползти́] *v., pfv. of* выполза́ть.

выполне́ние *n.* **1,** fulfillment; execution. **2,** discharge; performance (*of one's duties*).

выполни́мый *adj.* feasible.

выполня́ть *v. impfv.* [*pfv.* вы́полнить] **1,** to fulfill; carry out; execute. **2,** to discharge; perform (one's duties).

вы́полоскать [*infl.* -лощу, -лощешь] *v., pfv. of* полоска́ть *and* выпола́скивать.

вы́полоть [*infl.* -полю, -полешь] *v., pfv. of* полоть.

вы́пороть [*infl.* -порю, -порешь] *v., pfv. of* пороть (*in sense #1*) *and* выпа́рывать.

выпорхну́ть *v. pfv.* **1,** to fly out; flit out. **2,** *colloq.* to dash out; dart out.

вы́потрошить *v., pfv. of* потроши́ть.

вы́править [*infl.* -влю, -вишь] *v., pfv. of* выправля́ть. —**вы́правиться,** *refl., pfv. of* выправля́ться.

вы́правка *n.* bearing; carriage.

выправля́ть *v. impfv.* [*pfv.* вы́править] **1,** to straighten. **2,** *fig.* to rectify; straighten out. **3,** to correct; make corrections in (a manuscript, proofs, etc.). —**выправля́ться,** *refl.* to get straightened out; straighten oneself out.

выпра́шивать *v. impfv.* [*pfv.* вы́просить] **1,** to obtain by persistent asking; coax out of; wheedle. **2,** [*impfv. only*] to try hard to get; keep asking for.

выпрова́живать *v. impfv.* [*pfv.* вы́проводить] *colloq.* to send on one's way; send packing.

вы́просить [*infl.* -шу, -сишь] *v., pfv. of* выпра́шивать.

выпры́гивать *v. impfv.* [*pfv.* вы́прыгнуть] to jump out; leap out.

выпряга́ть *v. impfv.* [*pfv.* вы́прячь] to unharness.

выпрямля́ть *v. impfv.* [*pfv.* вы́прямить] to straighten. —**выпрямля́ться,** *refl.* to stand erect; stand up straight.

выпрячь [*infl.* вы́прягу, вы́пряжешь, ...вы́прягут; *past* вы́пряг, -ла] *v., pfv. of* выпряга́ть.

вы́пуклость *n.f.* **1,** convexity. **2,** bulge; protuberance.

вы́пуклый *adj.* **1,** convex. **2,** prominent; bulging.

вы́пуск *n.* **1,** issue; issuance. **2,** output. **3,** an issue; number; installment; edition. **4,** graduates; graduating class.

выпуска́ть *v. impfv.* [*pfv.* вы́пустить] **1,** to let out. **2,** to release; set free. **3,** to produce; turn out. **4,** to publish; put out. **5,** to issue (stamps, money, etc.). **6,** to graduate; turn out. **7,** to delete. **8,** to put out; let stick out. **9,** to let out (clothing). **10,** fire (a bullet, shell, etc.). —**выпуска́ть в свет,** to bring out; publish. —**выпуска́ть из рук, 1,** to let go of. **2,** *fig.* to let slip; miss.

выпускни́к [*gen.* -ника́] *n.* **1,** senior. **2,** graduate.

выпускно́й *adj.* **1,** *mech.* exhaust (*attrib.*). **2,** graduation (*attrib.*); final.

вы́пустить [*infl.* -щу, -стишь] *v., pfv. of* выпуска́ть.

выпу́тывать *v. impfv.* [*pfv.* вы́путать] to extricate; disentangle. —**выпу́тываться,** *refl.* to extricate oneself; disentangle oneself.

вы́пучить *v. pfv., in* вы́пучить глаза́, to stare wide-eyed.

вы́пушка [*gen. pl.* -шек] *n.* edging; piping.

выпы́тывать *v. impfv.* [*pfv.* вы́пытать] *colloq.* to elicit; find out (information, a secret, etc.).

выпь *n.f.* bittern.

выпя́чивать *v. impfv.* [*pfv.* вы́пятить] *colloq.* **1,** to stick out; throw out (one's stomach, chest, etc.). **2,** *fig.* to emphasize; play up. —**выпя́чиваться,** *refl., colloq.* to stick out; jut out; protrude.

выраба́тывать *v. impfv.* [*pfv.* вы́работать] **1,** to make; produce; manufacture. **2,** to work out; draw up. **3,** to develop; cultivate. **4,** *colloq.* to earn. —**выраба́тываться,** *refl.* to develop. У него́ вы́работалась привы́чка (+ *inf.*), he has developed the habit of...

вы́работка *n.* **1,** making; manufacture. **2,** working out; drawing up. **3,** production; output. **4,** *colloq.* workmanship.

выра́внивание *n.* **1,** smoothing; leveling. **2,** alignment.

выра́внивать *v. impfv.* [*pfv.* вы́ровнять] **1,** to even; level; smooth out. **2,** to align; dress (a file, column, etc.). **3,** to straighten out (an airplane). **4,** *in* вы́ровнять шаг, to get in step; regain one's stride. —**выра́вниваться,** *refl.* **1,** to even out. **2,** to line up; dress. **3,** to develop (*physically*). **4,** to improve; get better.

выража́ть *v. impfv.* [*pfv.* вы́разить] to express. *See also* вы́раженный.

выража́ться *v.r. impfv.* [*pfv.* вы́разиться] **1,** to be expressed. **2,** to express oneself. Е́сли мо́жно так вы́разиться, if I (one) may say so. **3,** (*with* в + *prepl.*) to manifest itself (in). **4,** *in* выража́ться в су́мме (+ *gen.*), to amount to; come to. —**мя́гко выража́ясь,** to put it mildly.

выраже́ние *n.* **1,** expression; act of expressing. **2,** expression (*on one's face*). **3,** expression; feeling: чита́ть с выраже́нием, to read with expression. **4,** expression; phrase: идиомати́ческое выраже́ние, idiomatic expression.

вы́раженный *adj., usu. preceded by an adverb,* pronounced; marked. —**я́рко вы́раженная фо́рма боле́зни,** acute form of a disease.

вырази́тельный *adj.* expressive. —**вырази́тельность,** *n.f.* expressiveness.

вы́разить [*infl.* -жу, -зишь] *v., pfv. of* выража́ть. —**вы́разиться,** *refl., pfv. of* выража́ться.

выраста́ть *v. impfv.* [*pfv.* вы́расти] **1,** to grow; grow up. **2,** (*with* из) *colloq.* to outgrow; grow out of. **3,** (*with* в + *acc.*) to grow into; develop into. **4,** to appear; loom up. —**вы́расти в (чьи́х-нибудь) глаза́х,** to go up in someone's estimation.

вы́расти [*infl. like* расти́] *v., pfv. of* расти́ *and* выраста́ть.

вы́растить [*infl.* -щу, -стишь] *v., pfv. of* расти́ть *and* выра́щивать.

выра́щивать *v. impfv.* [*pfv.* вы́растить] **1,** to raise; grow; cultivate (plants). **2,** to raise; breed (animals).

вы́рвать *v. pfv.* [*infl.* вы́рву, вы́рвешь] **1,** *pfv. of* вырыва́ть. **2,** *pfv. of* рвать (*in sense #8*). —**вы́рваться,** *refl., pfv. of* вырыва́ться.

вы́рез *n.* cut; cut-out section: пла́тье с ни́зким/больши́м/глубо́ким вы́резом, low-cut dress; low-necked dress. —**треуго́льный вы́рез,** V-neck.

вы́резать [*infl.* -режу, -режешь] *v., pfv. of* выреза́ть *and* вырезывать.

выреза́ть *v. impfv.* [*pfv.* вы́резать] **1,** to cut out; excise. **2,** to carve; engrave. **3,** to massacre; slaughter. *Also,* вырезывать.

вы́резка [*gen. pl.* -зок] *n.* **1,** cutting out. **2,** clipping (*from a newspaper, magazine, etc.*). **3,** fillet; tenderloin (*of beef*).

вырезно́й *adj.* **1,** carved. **2,** to be cut out: вырезны́е карти́нки, pictures to be cut out.

вы́резывать *v. impfv.* = выреза́ть.

вырисова́ть [*infl.* -сую, -суешь] *v., pfv. of* вырисо́вывать. —**вырисова́ться,** *refl., pfv. of* вырисо́вываться.

вырисо́вывать *v. impfv.* [*pfv.* вырисова́ть] to draw carefully; draw in great detail. —**вырисо́вываться,** *refl.* to loom; appear; be etched (*against a background*).

вы́ровнять *v., pfv. of* выра́внивать. —**вы́ровняться,** *refl., pfv. of* выра́вниваться.

вы́родиться *v.r., pfv. of* вырожда́ться.

вы́родок [*gen.* -дка] *n., colloq.* outcast.

вырожда́ться *v.r. impfv.* [*pfv.* вы́родиться] to degenerate.

вырожде́нец [*gen.* -нца] *n.* degenerate. —**вырожде́ние,** *n.* degeneration; degeneracy. —**вырожде́нческий,** *adj.* degenerative.

вы́ронить *v. pfv.* to drop.

выруба́ть *v. impfv.* [*pfv.* вы́рубить] **1,** to chop down; cut down. **2,** to cut out; hack out. **3,** to carve; carve out.

вы́рубка *n.* **1,** chopping down; cutting down. **2,** clearing; glade.

вы́ругать *v., pfv. of* руга́ть. —**вы́ругаться,** *refl., colloq.* to swear; curse.

выруча́ть *v. impfv.* [*pfv.* вы́ручить] **1,** to rescue; help out; come to the aid of. **2,** to make (money, a profit, etc.).

вы́ручка *n.* **1,** *colloq.* rescue: прийти́ на вы́ручку (+ *dat.*), to come to the rescue of. **2,** receipts; proceeds; takings.

вырыва́ть *v. impfv.* [*pfv.* вы́рвать] **1,** to tear out. **2,** to pull up (*from the ground*). **3,** to pull; extract (a tooth). **4,** to grab; snatch; wrest (something from someone). **5,** *fig.* to wring (a confession, concession, etc.); wrest (the initiative). **6,** *in* вырыва́ть из конте́кста, to take (*or* lift) out of context. **7,** [*pfv.* вы́рыть] to dig; dig up; exhume; unearth. —**вырыва́ться,** *refl.* [*pfv.* вы́рваться] **1**, to break away; break out; break loose. **2**, (*of pages*) to come out; come loose. **3**, to shoot forward; shoot ahead. **4**, (*of fire*) to shoot up; shoot out. **5**, (*of a sigh, groan, etc.*) to escape.

вы́рыть [*infl.* -рою, -роешь] *v.*, *pfv. of* рыть *and* вырыва́ть (*in sense #7*).

выряжа́ть *v. impfv.* [*pfv.* вы́рядить] *colloq.* to dress up. —**выряжа́ться**, *refl.*, *colloq.* to get dressed up.

вы́садить [*infl.* -жу, -дишь] *v.*, *pfv. of* выса́живать. —**вы́садиться**, *refl.*, *pfv. of* выса́живаться.

вы́садка *n.* **1**, debarkation; disembarkation. **2**, *mil.* landing. **3**, transplanting.

выса́живать *v. impfv.* [*pfv.* вы́садить] **1**, to drop off; let off; discharge (a passenger). **2**, to help out; help off (of or from a vehicle). **3**, to make (a passenger) get off; put off. **4**, *mil.* to land (troops); put ashore. **5**, to transplant. —**выса́живаться**, *refl.* to get off; disembark.

выса́сывать *v. impfv.* [*pfv.* вы́сосать] to suck out. —**вы́сосать из па́льца**, to fabricate; concoct.

высве́рливать *v. impfv.* [*pfv.* вы́сверлить] to drill; bore.

высвобожда́ть *v. impfv.* [*pfv.* вы́свободить] to free; release.

высева́ть *v. impfv.* [*pfv.* вы́сеять] to sow.

высека́ть *v. impfv.* [*pfv.* вы́сечь] to carve; carve out; hew.

выселе́ние *n.* **1**, eviction. **2**, resettlement.

выселя́ть *v. impfv.* [*pfv.* вы́селить] **1**, to evict. **2**, to resettle. —**выселя́ться**, *refl.* to move.

вы́сечь [*infl.* -секу, -сечешь; *past* -сек, -ла] *v.*, *pfv. of* сечь (*in sense #2*) *and* высека́ть.

вы́сеять [*infl.* -сею, -сеешь] *v.*, *pfv. of* высева́ть.

выси́живать *v. impfv.* [*pfv.* вы́сидеть] **1**, *colloq.* to sit; stay (for a certain length of time). **2**, *in* вы́сидеть до конца́ (+ *gen.*), to sit (something) out to the end. **3**, to hatch.

вы́ситься *v.r. impfv.* to tower; rise; loom.

выска́бливать *v. impfv.* [*pfv.* вы́скоблить] **1**, to scrape off; scrape clean. **2**, to scrape out; erase.

вы́сказать [*infl.* -скажу, -скажешь] *v.*, *pfv. of* выска́зывать. —**вы́сказаться**, *refl.*, *pfv. of* выска́зываться.

выска́зывание *n.* **1**, expression; utterance. **2**, statement; pronouncement. **3**, *logic* proposition.

выска́зывать *v. impfv.* [*pfv.* вы́сказать] to express. —**выска́зываться**, *refl.* **1**, to state one's opinion; have one's say. **2**, (*with* за *or* про́тив) to come out (in favor of or against).

выска́кивать *v. impfv.* [*pfv.* вы́скочить] **1**, to jump out. **2**, *colloq.* to dart out. **3**, *colloq.* (*of a sore, boil, etc.*) to appear. **4**, *colloq.* to fall out; slip out. —**вы́скочить из головы́**, to slip one's mind; go right out of one's mind.

выска́льзывать *v. impfv.* [*pfv.* вы́скользнуть] **1**, to slip out. **2**, to sneak out.

вы́скоблить *v.*, *pfv. of* выска́бливать.

вы́скользнуть *v.*, *pfv. of* выска́льзывать.

вы́скочить *v.*, *pfv. of* выска́кивать.

вы́скочка *n.m. & f.*, *colloq.* upstart.

вы́слать [*infl.* вы́шлю, вы́шлешь] *v.*, *pfv. of* высыла́ть.

вы́следить *v. pfv.* [*infl.* -жу, -дишь] **1**, *pfv. of* высле́живать. **2**, to track down; hunt down.

высле́живать *v. impfv.* [*pfv.* вы́следить] to follow; trail; track; shadow.

вы́слуга *n.*, *in* за вы́слугу лет, by virtue of long service.

вы́служивать *v. impfv.* [*pfv.* вы́служить] **1**, to qualify for; receive (*through service*). **2**, *colloq.* to serve; serve out (a designated period). —**вы́служиваться**, *refl.* (*with* пе́ред) *colloq.* to curry favor (with).

вы́слушать *v.*, *pfv. of* выслу́шивать.

выслу́шивание *n.* auscultation.

выслу́шивать *v. impfv.* [*pfv.* вы́слушать] **1**, to listen (to); hear out. **2**, *med.* to listen to; examine.

высма́тривать *v. impfv.* [*pfv.* вы́смотреть] **1**, to spot; spy; detect. **2**, (*with* все *or* всё) to look over; examine. **3**, [*impfv. only*] to look out.

высме́ивать *v. impfv.* [*pfv.* вы́смеять] to mock; deride; ridicule; make fun of.

вы́смеять [*infl.* -смею, -смеешь] *v.*, *pfv. of* высме́ивать.

вы́смолить *v.*, *pfv. of* смоли́ть.

высмо́ркать *v.*, *pfv. of* сморка́ть. —**вы́сморкаться**, *refl.*, *pfv. of* сморка́ться.

вы́смотреть [*infl.* -трю, -тришь] *v.*, *pfv. of* высма́тривать.

высо́вывать *v. impfv.* [*pfv.* вы́сунуть] to stick out. —**высо́вываться**, *refl.* **1**, to stick out; jut out. **2**, to lean out.

высо́кий *adj.* [*short form* высо́к, высока́, высоко́ *or* высо́ко, высоки́ *or* высо́ки; *comp.* вы́ше] **1**, high. **2**, tall. **3**, *fig.* lofty; elevated. **4**, high; high-pitched.

высоко́ *also*, **высо́ко** *adv.* high: держа́ть го́лову высоко́, to hold one's head high. —*adj.*, *used predicatively* **1**, high: о́кна бы́ли высоко́ от земли́, the windows were high off the ground. **2**, too high: э́то мне высоко́, it is too high for me.

высокока́чественный *adj.* high-quality; quality (*attrib.*).

высокоме́рие *n.* haughtiness; arrogance.

высокоме́рный *adj.* haughty; arrogant; supercilious.

высокоопла́чиваемый *adj.* high-paid.

высокопа́рный *adj.* high-flown; bombastic; grandiloquent. —**высокопа́рность**, *n.f.* grandiloquence; bombast.

высокопоста́вленный *adj.* high-ranking: высокопоста́вленное лицо́, V.I.P.

высокоразви́тый *adj.* highly developed.

вы́сосать *v.*, *pfv. of* выса́сывать.

высота́ [*pl.* высо́ты] *n.* **1**, height. **2**, altitude. **3**, height(s): кома́ндные высо́ты, commanding heights. **4**, *music* pitch. —**быть на высоте́ (положе́ния)**, to be equal to (*or* rise to) the occasion. —**на до́лжной высоте́**, up to the mark; up to par.

высо́тный *adj.* **1**, (*of a flight*) high-altitude. **2**, (*of a building*) very tall.

высотоме́р *n.* altimeter.

вы́сохнуть [*past* вы́сох, -ла] *v.*, *pfv. of* со́хнуть *and* высыха́ть.

высоча́йший *adj.* **1**, *superl. of* высо́кий. **2**, *pre-rev.* royal; imperial.

высо́ченный *adj.*, *colloq.* very high; very tall.

высо́чество *n.* Highness (*title*).

вы́спаться [*infl.* -сплюсь, -спишься] *v.r.*, *pfv. of* высыпа́ться (*in sense #2*).

выспра́шивать *v. impfv.* [*pfv.* вы́спросить] *colloq.* **1**, (*with acc. or* у) to ply with questions; pump. **2**, to find out (*by asking a lot of questions*).

вы́ставить [*infl.* -влю, -вишь] *v., pfv. of* выставля́ть. —вы́ставиться, *refl., pfv. of* выставля́ться.

вы́ставка [*gen. pl.* -вок] *n.* **1,** exhibition; show. **2,** display. —всеми́рная вы́ставка, world's fair.

выставля́ть *v. impfv.* [*pfv.* вы́ставить] **1,** to put out; move out. **2,** to stick out. **3,** to exhibit; display. **4,** *colloq.* to send out; order out. **5,** to post (a guard). **6,** to put forth (demands, arguments, etc.). **7,** *colloq.* to present (in a certain light). **8,** to put down; enter (grades, a date, etc.). —выставля́ть на свет, to expose to the light. —выставля́ть себя́ (*instr.*), *colloq.* to make oneself out to be.

выставля́ться *v.r. impfv.* [*pfv.* вы́ставиться] *colloq.* **1,** to stick out; lean out. **2,** *fig.* to show off.

вы́ставочный *adj.* exhibition (*attrib.*).

выста́ивать *v. impfv.* [*pfv.* вы́стоять] **1,** to stand; remain standing. **2,** *fig.* to hold out. —выста́иваться, *refl.* (*of wine*) to mature.

вы́стегать *v., pfv. of* стега́ть (*in sense #1*).

выстила́ть *v. impfv.* [*pfv.* вы́стлать] **1,** to cover. **2,** to pave.

вы́стирать *v., pfv. of* стира́ть (*in sense #4*).

вы́стлать [*infl.* -стелю, -стелешь] *v., pfv. of* выстила́ть.

вы́стоять [*infl.* -стою, -стоишь] *v., pfv. of* выста́ивать. —вы́стояться, *refl., pfv. of* выста́иваться.

вы́страдать *v. pfv.* **1,** to suffer; endure; have been (*or* gone) through. **2,** to achieve through suffering.

выстра́ивать *v. impfv.* [*pfv.* вы́строить] *mil.* to form up. —выстра́иваться, *refl.* **1,** *mil.* to form; line up. **2,** (*of a line*) to form.

вы́стрел *n.* shot: произвести́ вы́стрел, to fire a shot. —без вы́стрела, without firing a shot. —на вы́стрел, within gunshot.

вы́стрелить *v. pfv.* **1,** *pfv. of* стреля́ть. **2,** (*of a gun*) to go off.

выстрига́ть *v. impfv.* [*pfv.* вы́стричь] **1,** to cut off. **2,** to cut (one's hair in a certain style).

вы́стричь [*infl. like* стричь] *v., pfv. of* выстрига́ть.

вы́строгать *v., pfv. of* строга́ть.

вы́строить *v. pfv.* **1,** *pfv. of* выстра́ивать. **2,** to build. —вы́строиться, *refl.* **1,** *pfv. of* выстра́иваться. **2,** to be built; go up.

вы́стукивать *v. impfv.* [*pfv.* вы́стукать] *colloq.* to tap out.

вы́ступ *n.* **1,** projection. **2,** ledge.

выступа́ть *v. impfv.* [*pfv.* вы́ступить] **1,** to come forward; step forward. **2,** to appear (publicly): выступа́ть на сце́не, to appear on stage; выступа́ть по телеви́дению, to appear on television; выступа́ть на собра́нии, to address a meeting; выступа́ть на соревнова́ниях, to appear (*or* take part) in a competition; выступа́ть с ре́чью, to give *or* deliver a speech. **3,** (*with* за + *acc.*) to come out in favor of; favor; advocate. **4,** (*with* про́тив) to come out against; oppose. **5,** to appear (*on one's face or body*). **6,** (*of a river*) to overflow. **7,** [*impfv. only*] to jut out. **8,** [*impfv. only*] to strut; swagger.

вы́ступить [*infl.* -плю, -пишь] *v., pfv. of* выступа́ть.

выступле́ние *n.* **1,** performance; appearance. **2,** speech; address.

вы́сунуть *v., pfv. of* высо́вывать. —вы́сунуться, *refl., pfv. of* высо́вываться.

высу́шивать *v. impfv.* [*pfv.* вы́сушить] to dry; dry out. —высу́шиваться, *refl.* to dry out; become dry.

вы́сушить *v., pfv. of* суши́ть *and* высу́шивать. —вы́сушиться, *refl., pfv. of* суши́ться *and* высу́шиваться.

высчи́тывать *v. impfv.* [*pfv.* вы́считать] to calculate; compute.

вы́сший *adj., used only as a modifier* **1,** highest: вы́сшего ка́чества, of the highest quality. **2,** higher: вы́сшее уче́бное заведе́ние, institution of higher learning. **3,** *with certain nouns* high: вы́сшее кома́ндование, high command; вы́сшая то́чка, the high point; climax. —в вы́сшей сте́пени (+ *adj.*), extraordinarily; most. —вы́сшая ме́ра наказа́ния, the supreme penalty.

высыла́ть *v. impfv.* [*pfv.* вы́слать] **1,** to send (out); mail (out). **2,** to send out; order out. **3,** to banish; exile; deport.

вы́сылка *n.* **1,** sending; dispatch. **2,** banishment; deportation.

вы́сыпать [*infl.* -сыплю, -сыплешь] *v., pfv. of* высыпа́ть. —вы́сыпаться, *refl., pfv. of* высыпа́ться (*in sense #1*).

высыпа́ть *v. impfv.* [*pfv.* вы́сыпать] **1,** to pour; empty (out of, into, onto). **2,** *colloq.* (*of many people*) to pour out; throng. **3,** *impers.* to break out (*in a rash*): у него́ вы́сыпало на лице́, his face is broken out.

высыпа́ться *v.r. impfv.* **1,** [*pfv.* вы́сыпаться] to pour out; spill out. **2,** [*pfv.* вы́спаться] to have a good (night's) sleep.

высыха́ть *v. impfv.* [*pfv.* вы́сохнуть] **1,** to dry out; dry up. **2,** to wither. **3,** to waste away.

высь *n.f.* **1,** height. **2,** *pl.* mountain tops.

выта́лкивать *v. impfv.* [*pfv.* вы́толкнуть] to push out; throw out.

выта́пливать *v. impfv.* [*pfv.* вы́топить] **1,** to heat. **2,** to melt.

выта́птывать *v. impfv.* [*pfv.* вы́топтать] to trample down.

вы́таращить *v., pfv. of* тара́щить.

выта́скивать *v. impfv.* [*pfv.* вы́тащить] **1,** to pull out; drag out. **2,** to pull out; extract. **3,** to haul in (a fish). **4,** *colloq.* to drag (someone) somewhere against his will.

вы́тачать *v., pfv. of* тача́ть.

выта́чивать *v. impfv.* [*pfv.* вы́точить] to make; fashion (*in a lathe*).

вы́тачка [*gen. pl.* -чек] *n.* tuck (*on a garment*).

вы́тащить *v., pfv. of* тащи́ть (*in senses #3, 4, 5*) *and* выта́скивать.

вы́твердить *v., pfv. of* тверди́ть (*in sense #2*).

вытворя́ть *v. impfv., colloq.* to do (something odd or foolish).

вытека́ть *v. impfv.* [*pfv.* вы́течь] **1,** to flow out; run out; leak out. **2,** [*impfv. only*] to follow; result; ensue.

вы́тереть [*infl.* вы́тру, вы́трешь; *past* вы́тер, -ла] *v., pfv. of* вытира́ть. —вы́тереться, *refl., pfv. of* вытира́ться.

вы́терпеть *v. pfv.* [*infl.* -плю, -пишь] **1,** to endure. **2,** (*usu. neg.*) to stand it: наконе́ц он не вы́терпел, finally he could stand it no longer.

вы́тертый *adj., colloq.* threadbare.

выте́сать [*infl.* -тешу, -тешешь] *v., pfv. of* вытёсывать.

вытесне́ние *n.* ouster; exclusion.

вытесня́ть *v. impfv.* [*pfv.* вы́теснить] **1,** to crowd out; force out; oust. **2,** to replace; displace; supplant.

вытёсывать *v. impfv.* [*pfv.* вы́тесать] to hew.

вы́течь [*infl. like* течь] *v., pfv. of* вытека́ть.

выти́рáть v. impfv. [pfv. **вы́тереть**] to wipe. —**выти́ра́ться**, refl. 1, to dry oneself. 2, colloq. to wear thin.

вы́тисня́ть v. impfv. [pfv. **вы́тиснить**] to imprint.

вы́ткать v. pfv. [infl. **вы́тку, вы́ткешь**] to weave.

вы́топить [infl. -плю, -пишь] v., pfv. of **вытáпливать**.

вы́топтать [infl. -топчу, -топчешь] v., pfv. of **вытáптывать**.

вы́торговать [infl. -гую, -гуешь] v., pfv. of **выторгóвывать**.

выторгóвывать v. impfv. [pfv. **вы́торговать**] colloq. 1, to make; earn; clear; net. 2, to get (a reduction in price) by bargaining.

вы́точить v., pfv. of **точи́ть** (in sense #2) and **вытáчивать**.

вы́травить [infl. -влю, -вишь] v., pfv. of **трави́ть** (in senses #1,4, & 5) and **вытравля́ть**.

вытравля́ть v. impfv. [pfv. **вы́травить**] 1, to remove (a spot, mark, etc.). 2, to exterminate. 3, (of cattle) to trample down.

вы́требовать v. pfv. [infl. -бую, -буешь] 1, to demand and obtain. 2, to summon; send for.

вытрезви́тель n.m. sobering-up station.

вытрезвля́ть v. impfv. [pfv. **вы́трезвить**] to sober; sober up. —**вытрезвля́ться**, refl. to sober up; become sober.

вытряса́ть v. impfv. [pfv. **вы́трясти**] to shake out.

вы́трясти [infl. like **трясти́**] v., pfv. of **вытряса́ть**.

вытря́хивать v. impfv. [pfv. **вы́тряхнуть**] to shake out.

выть v. impfv. [pres. **вóю, вóешь**] to howl; wail.

вытьё n., colloq. howling; wailing.

вытя́гивать v. impfv. [pfv. **вы́тянуть**] 1, to stretch. 2, to draw out (air, smoke, etc.). 3, colloq. to extract. 4, v.i., colloq. to hold out; last. —**вытя́гиваться**, refl. 1, to stretch; expand. 2, to stretch; extend. 3, to stretch out. 4, colloq. to straighten up; stand up straight. 5, colloq. to grow; shoot up. 6, (of one's face) to fall.

вытяжéние n. 1, stretching. 2, med. traction.

вы́тяжка n. 1, drawing out. 2, stretching. 3, chem. extract.

вытяжнóй adj. exhaust (attrib.): **вытяжнóй вентилятор**, exhaust fan. —**вытяжнóй трос**, ripcord.

вы́тянутый adj. outstretched. —**вы́тянутое лицó**, long face.

вы́тянуть v., pfv. of **вытя́гивать**. —**вы́тянуться**, refl., pfv. of **вытя́гиваться**.

выу́живать v. impfv. [pfv. **вы́удить**] 1, to hook; catch (a fish). 2, fig., colloq. to coax out; worm out.

вы́утюжить v., pfv. of **утюжить**.

выу́чивать v. impfv. [pfv. **вы́учить**] 1, to learn. 2, to teach. —**выу́чиваться**, refl. (with dat.) to learn.

вы́учить [infl. -учу, -учишь] v., pfv. of **учи́ть** and **выу́чивать**. —**вы́учиться**, refl., pfv. of **учи́ться** (in sense #2) and **выу́чиваться**.

вы́учка n. 1, training. 2, level of training; skill.

выхáживать v. impfv. [pfv. **вы́ходить**] colloq. 1, to nurse back to health. 2, to bring up; raise.

выхвáтывать v. impfv. [pfv. **вы́хватить**] 1, to grab; snatch. 2, to pull out; whip out. 3, to pick out (at random).

вы́хлоп n., mech. exhaust. —**выхлопнóй**, adj. exhaust (attrib.).

вы́хлопотать v. pfv. [infl. -почу, -почешь] to manage to obtain (after much effort).

вы́ход n. 1, going out; coming out. 2, theat. entrance (onstage). 3, exit. 4, in **вы́ход к мóрю**, outlet to the sea. 5, fig. way out. 6, appearance; publication. 7, output; yield. —**дать вы́ход** (+ dat.), to give vent to.

вы́ходец [gen. -дца] n. (with из) 1, person originally from; émigré (from). 2, person originally of a different social class. —**вы́ходец с тогó свéта**, apparition.

вы́ходить v. pfv. [infl. -хожу, -ходишь] colloq. 1, pfv. of **выхáживать**. 2, to walk all over or around.

выходи́ть v. impfv. [pfv. **вы́йти**; pres. -хожу́, -хóдишь] 1, to go out; come out; walk out; get out. 2, to leave. 3, to run out; be used up. 4, [often **выходи́ть в свет**] to appear; come out; be published. 5, (of a photograph or subject) to come out. 6, (with instr.) to come out; emerge: **вы́йти победи́телем**, to emerge the victor. 7, (of something unfortunate) to occur. 8, to work out; come off. 9, to turn out: **вы́шло, что...**, it turned out that... 10, (with из) to come of: **из э́того ничегó не вы́йдет**, nothing will come of it. 11, (with из) to make: **из негó вы́йдет хорóший врач**, he will make a good doctor. 12, [impfv. only] (with в or на + acc.) (of a window) to look out on; face. —**выходи́ть в мóре**, to put out to sea. —**выходи́ть из себя́**, to lose one's temper.

вы́ходка [gen. pl. -док] n. trick; prank; escapade.

выходнóй adj. 1, serving as an exit. 2, worn on social occasions: **выходнóе плáтье**, party dress; cocktail dress. —n., colloq. day off. —**выходнóй день**, day off. —**выходнóе посóбие**, severance pay. —**выходнáя роль**, bit part.

выхолáщивать v. impfv. [pfv. **вы́холостить**] 1, to castrate. 2, fig. to emasculate.

вы́холенный adj. well-groomed; trim; dapper.

вы́холостить [infl. -щу, -стишь] v., pfv. of **холости́ть** and **выхолáщивать**.

вы́хухоль n.m. desman.

выцáрапывать v. impfv. [pfv. **вы́царапать**] 1, to scratch out. 2, colloq. to get; obtain; wangle.

вы́цвести [infl. like **цвести́**] v., pfv. of **выцветáть**.

выцветáть v. impfv. [pfv. **вы́цвести**] to fade.

вы́цветший adj. faded.

вычекáнивать v. impfv. [pfv. **вы́чеканить**] to mint.

вычёркивание n. deleting; deletion.

вычёркивать v. impfv. [pfv. **вы́черкнуть**] to cross out; cross off; delete. —**вы́черкнуть из пáмяти**, to erase from one's memory. —**вы́черкнуть из свое́й жи́зни**, to put out of one's life.

вычéрпывать v. impfv. [pfv. **вы́черпать**] to scoop out; bail out.

вычéрчивать v. impfv. [pfv. **вы́чертить**] to draw; trace.

вы́чесать [infl. -чешу, -чешешь] v., pfv. of **вычёсывать**.

вы́честь [infl. **вы́чту, вы́чтешь**; past **вы́чел, вы́чла**] v., pfv. of **вычитáть**.

вычёсывать v. impfv. [pfv. **вы́чесать**] to comb out.

вы́чет n. deduction. —**за вы́четом** (+ gen.), less; minus; after deducting.

вычислéние n. calculation; computation.

вычисли́тель n.m. 1, calculator. 2, computer. 3, computer specialist.

вычисли́тельный adj. 1, computing. 2, computer (attrib.). —**вычисли́тельная маши́на**, computer.

вычисля́ть v. impfv. [pfv. **вы́числить**] to calculate; compute.

вы́чистить [*infl.* -щу, -стишь] *v., pfv. of* чи́стить *and* вычища́ть.

вычита́емое *n., decl. as an adj.* subtrahend.

вычита́ние *n.* subtraction.

вы́читать *v., pfv. of* вычи́тывать.

вычита́ть *v. impfv.* [*pfv.* вы́честь] **1**, to subtract. **2**, to deduct.

вычи́тывать *v. impfv.* [*pfv.* вы́читать] **1**, *colloq.* to learn; find out (*by reading*). **2**, to read; proofread.

вычища́ть *v. impfv.* [*pfv.* вы́чистить] to clean; clean out.

вы́чурный *adj.* fancy; elaborate.

вышвы́ривать *v. impfv.* [*pfv.* вы́швырнуть] *colloq.* to hurl out; toss out.

вы́ше *adj., comp. of* высо́кий. —*adv.* **1**, *comp. of* высоко́. **2**, above. —*prep., with gen.* **1**, above; over. **2**, beyond: вы́ше моего́ понима́ния, beyond my comprehension.

вышеприведённый *adj.* cited above.

вышеска́занный *adj.* aforesaid.

вышестоя́щий *adj.* higher: вышестоя́щий о́рган, higher body.

вышеука́занный *adj.* foregoing.

вышеупомя́нутый *adj.* above-mentioned; aforementioned. —**вышеупомя́нутое**, *n.* the above.

вышиба́ла *n.m., colloq.* bouncer.

вышиба́ть *v. impfv.* [*pfv.* вы́шибить] *colloq.* **1**, to knock out; dislodge. **2**, to throw out; kick out.

вы́шибить [*infl.* -бу, -бешь; *past* вы́шиб, -ла] *v., pfv. of* вышиба́ть.

вышива́ние *n.* embroidery.

вышива́ть *v. impfv.* [*pfv.* вы́шить] to embroider.

вы́шивка *n.* embroidery.

вышина́ *n.* height. —**в вышине́**, **1**, on high. **2**, in the sky.

вы́шитый *adj.* embroidered.

вы́шить [*infl.* вы́шью, вы́шьешь] *v., pfv. of* вышива́ть.

вы́шка [*gen. pl.* -шек] *n.* tower. —**бурова́я вы́шка**, oil derrick.

вы́школить *v., pfv. of* шко́лить.

выштукату́ривать *v. impfv.* [*pfv.* вы́штукатурить] to plaster; stucco.

вы́щипать [*infl.* -плю, -плешь] *v., pfv. of* выщи́пывать.

выщи́пывать *v. impfv.* [*pfv.* вы́щипать] to pull out; pluck.

вы́явить [*infl.* -влю, -вишь] *v., pfv. of* выявля́ть.

выявле́ние *n.* **1**, revelation. **2**, discovery.

выявля́ть *v. impfv.* [*pfv.* вы́явить] **1**, to reveal; display. **2**, to discover; bring to light.

выясне́ние *n.* clarification.

выясня́ть *v. impfv.* [*pfv.* вы́яснить] **1**, to clarify; clear up. **2**, to find out; ascertain. —**выясня́ться**, *refl.* **1**, to be discovered; become clear. **2**, to turn out: вы́яснилось, что..., it turned out that...

вьетна́мец [*gen.* -мца] *n.m.* [*fem.* -мка] Vietnamese. —**вьетна́мский**, *adj.* Vietnamese.

вьюга *n.* snowstorm; blizzard.

вьюк *n.* pack; load.

вьюно́к [*gen.* -нка́] *n.* bindweed.

вьюро́к [*gen.* -рка́] *n.* **1**, brambling. **2**, (*in combinations*) finch: го́рный вьюро́к, rosy finch.

вью́чить *v. impfv.* [*pfv.* навью́чить] to load (an animal).

вью́чный *adj.* pack (*attrib.*): вью́чное живо́тное, pack animal; beast of burden. —**вью́чное седло́**, packsaddle. —**вью́чная тропа́**, bridle path.

вью́шка [*gen. pl.* -шек] *n.* damper.

вью́щийся *adj.* **1**, (*of hair*) curly. **2**, (*of a plant*) climbing.

вя́жущий *adj.* astringent.

вяз *n.* elm.

вяза́льный *adj.* knitting (*attrib.*): вяза́льная спи́ца, knitting needle.

вяза́ние *n.* **1**, binding; tying. **2**, knitting; crocheting.

вяза́нка [*gen. pl.* -нок] *n.* bundle.

вя́заный *adj.* knitted.

вяза́ть *v. impfv.* [*pfv.* связа́ть; *pres.* вяжу́, вя́жешь] **1**, to bind; tie up. **2**, to knit; crochet. **3**, [*impfv. only*] *impers.* to be astringent: у меня́ вя́жет во рту, my mouth feels drawn. —**вяза́ться**, *refl.* [*impfv. only*] **1**, (*with* с + *instr.*) to accord (with); tally (with); square (with). **2**, (*usu. neg.*) (not) work out well: де́ло не вя́жется, things are not working out well.

вя́зка *n.* **1**, binding; tying. **2**, knitting; crocheting. **3**, *colloq.* bunch.

вя́зкий *adj.* [*short form* -зок, -зка́, -зко; *comp.* вя́зче] **1**, sticky; viscous. **2**, muddy; swampy. —**вя́зкость**, *n.f.* viscosity.

вя́знуть *v. impfv.* [*pfv.* завя́знуть *or* увя́знуть; *past* вяз *or* вя́знул, вя́зла] to get stuck.

вя́леный *adj.* dried; cured by drying.

вя́лить *v. impfv.* [*pfv.* провя́лить] to cure (meat) by drying.

вя́лый *adj.* **1**, faded; withered. **2**, flabby; limp. **3**, sluggish; listless. —**вя́ло**, *adv.* sluggishly; listlessly. —**вя́лость**, *n.f.* sluggishness; languor; lethargy.

вя́нуть *v. impfv.* [*pfv.* завя́нуть *or* увя́нуть; *past* вял *or* вя́нул, вя́ла] **1**, to wilt; wither. **2**, (*of a person*) to fade; decline. —**у́ши вя́нут**, one gets sick of hearing it.

вя́щий *adj., obs.* greater: для вя́щей убеди́тельности, in order to be more convincing.

Г

Г, г *n. neut.* fourth letter of the Russian alphabet.

габарди́н *n.* gabardine. —**габарди́новый,** *adj.* gabardine.

габари́т *n.* size; dimensions.

га́вань *n.f.* harbor.

га́га *n.* eider.

гага́ра *n.* loon (*bird*).

гага́рка [*gen. pl.* -ро́к] *n.* auk.

гага́т *n.* jet (*mineral*).

гага́чий [*fem.* -**чья**] *adj.* eider (*attrib.*). —**гага́чий пух,** eiderdown.

гад *n.* **1,** reptile. **2,** *colloq.* skunk; rat; louse.

гада́лка [*gen. pl.* -**лок**] *n.* fortuneteller.

гада́ние *n.* **1,** fortunetelling. **2,** guessing; guesswork; conjecture.

гада́тельный *adj.* doubtful; problematic; hypothetical; conjectural.

гада́ть *v. impfv.* **1,** to guess; speculate; conjecture. **2,** to tell fortunes.

га́дина *n., colloq.* = **гад.**

га́дкий *adj.* [*comp.* **га́же**] nasty; foul; vile. —**га́дкий утёнок,** ugly duckling.

гадли́вый *adj.* of disgust; of revulsion: гадли́вое чу́вство, feeling of disgust/revulsion. —**гадли́вость,** *n.f.* disgust; revulsion.

гадоли́ний *n.* gadolinium.

га́дость *n.f.* **1,** filth; muck. **2,** dirty trick; foul deed. **3,** *pl.* ugly/nasty remarks.

гадю́ка *n.* adder; viper.

га́ечный *adj., in* **га́ечный ключ,** wrench.

газ *n.* **1,** gas. **2,** *pl.* gas (*in one's stomach*). **3,** sheer silk; voile. —**дать газ,** *colloq.* to step on the gas. —**сба́вить газ,** *colloq.* to slow down.

газе́ль *n.f.* gazelle.

газе́та *n.* newspaper.

газе́тный *adj.* newspaper (*attrib.*). —**газе́тная бума́га,** newsprint. —**газе́тный кио́ск,** newsstand.

газе́тчик *n.* **1,** news vendor; newsboy. **2,** *colloq.* newsman; journalist.

газиро́ванный *adj.* carbonated.

газирова́ть *v. impfv.* [*pres.* -ру́ю, -ру́ешь] to carbonate.

га́зовый *adj.* **1,** gas (*attrib.*): га́зовый рожо́к, gas burner. **2,** made of sheer silk.

газоли́н *n.* gasoline.

газоме́р *n.* gas meter.

газо́н *n.* lawn. —**газонокоси́лка,** *n.* lawn mower.

газообра́зный *adj.* gaseous.

газопрово́д *n.* gas pipeline.

гаитя́нин [*pl.* -тя́не, -тя́н] *n.m.* [*fem.* -тя́нка] Haitian. —**гаитя́нский,** *adj.* Haitian.

га́ичка [*gen. pl.* -чек] *n.* chickadee.

га́йка [*gen. pl.* га́ек] *n.* nut (*for a bolt*).

гала́ктика *n.* galaxy. —**галакти́ческий,** *adj.* galactic.

галантере́я *n.* dry goods; haberdashery. —**галантере́йный,** *adj.* haberdashery (*attrib.*); haberdasher's. —**галантере́йщик,** *n.* haberdasher.

гала́нтный *adj.* gallant (*toward women*); chivalrous. —**гала́нтность,** *n.f.* gallantry; chivalry.

галдёж [*gen.* -дежа́] *n., colloq.* uproar; hubbub.

галде́ть *v. impfv.* [*pres.* -ди́шь; *1st person sing. not used*] *colloq.* to make a racket.

галени́т *n.* galena.

гале́ра *n.* galley (*ship*).

галере́я *n.* gallery.

галёрка [*gen. pl.* -ро́к] *n., colloq.* gallery (*in a theater*).

гале́та *n.* cracker; biscuit.

галиматья́ *n., colloq.* nonsense; rubbish.

галифе́ (фэ) *n. pl. or neut. indecl.* riding breeches.

га́лка [*gen. pl.* -лок] *n.* jackdaw. —**счита́ть га́лок, 1,** to gape. **2,** to loaf.

галл *n., bot.* gall.

га́ллий *n.* gallium.

галлици́зм *n.* Gallicism.

галло́н *n.* gallon.

га́лльский *adj.* Gallic.

галлюцина́ция *n.* hallucination.

галоге́н *n.* halogen.

гало́п *n.* gallop. —**гало́пом,** at a gallop.

галопи́ровать *v. impfv.* [*pres.* -рую, руешь] to gallop.

га́лочка [*gen. pl.* -чек] *n., colloq.* mark; check; tick.

гало́ши *n. pl.* [*sing.* **гало́ша**] rubbers; overshoes; galoshes.

галс *n., naut.* tack.

га́лстук *n.* tie; necktie.

галу́н [*gen.* -луна́] *n.* galloon.

галу́шки *n. pl.* [*sing.* **галу́шка**] dumplings.

гальванизи́ровать *v. impfv. & pfv.* [*pres.* -рую, -руешь] to galvanize.

гальвани́ческий *adj.* galvanic.

га́лька [*gen. pl.* -лек] *n.* **1,** pebble. **2,** pebbles.

гам *n., colloq.* racket; din; hubbub.

гама́к [*gen.* -мака́] *n.* hammock.

гама́ши [*gen.* -ма́ш] *n. pl.* leggings.

гамби́т *n.* gambit.

гаме́та *n.* gamete.

га́мма *n.* **1,** *music* scale. **2,** *fig.* gamut. —**га́мма-**

глобулúн, *n.* gamma globulin. —гáмма-лучú, *n. pl.* gamma rays.

гáнглий *n.* ganglion.

гангрéна *n.* gangrene. —гангренóзный, *adj.* gangrenous.

гáнгстер *n.* gangster.

гандбóл *n.* team handball.

гандикáп *n., sports* handicap.

гантéль (тэ) *n.f., often pl.* dumbbell.

гарáж [*gen.* -ражá] *n.* garage.

гарантúровать *v. impfv. & pfv.* [*pres.* -рую, -руешь] to guarantee.

гарáнтия *n.* guarantee.

гардéния *n.* gardenia.

гардерóб *n.* 1, cloakroom. 2, wardrobe.

гардерóбщик *n.m.* [*fem.* -щица] cloakroom attendant.

гардúна *n.* window curtain.

гаревóй *also,* гáревый *adj.* cinder (*attrib.*): гаревáя дорóжка, cinder path/track.

гарéм *n.* harem.

гáркать *v. impfv.* [*pfv.* гáркнуть] *colloq.* to shout; bark.

гармонизúровать *v. impfv. & pfv.* [*pres.* -рую, -руешь] *music* to harmonize. *Also,* гармонизовáть [*pres.* -зýю, -зýешь]

гармóника *n.* accordion. —губнáя гармóника, harmonica.

гармонúровать *v. impfv.* [*pres.* -рую, -руешь] (*with* с + *instr.*) to harmonize (with); go well (with).

гармонúст *n.* accordionist.

гармонúческий *adj.* 1, harmonic. 2, harmonious.

гармонúчный *adj.* harmonious.

гармóния *n.* harmony.

гармóнь *n.f., colloq.* = гармóника. *Also,* гармóшка.

гарнизóн *n.* garrison.

гарнúр *n.* garnish; trimmings.

гарнúровать *v. impfv. & pfv.* [*pres.* -рую, -руешь] to garnish.

гарнитýр *n.* 1, complete set. 2, suite (*of furniture*).

гарпýн [*gen.* -пунá] *n.* harpoon.

гарпýнить *v. impfv.* to harpoon.

гáрус *n.* worsted. —гáрусный, *adj.* worsted.

гарцевáть *v. impfv.* [*pres.* -цýю, -цýешь] to prance (*on a horse*).

гáршнеп (нэ) *n.* jacksnipe.

гарь *n.f.* 1, something burning: пáхнет гáрью, there is a smell of something burning. 2, cinders.

гасúть *v. impfv.* [*pfv.* погасúть; *pres.* гашý, гáсишь] 1, to extinguish; put out. 2, cancel (a stamp); liquidate (a debt). 3, *fig.* to suppress; stifle. 4, to slake (lime).

гáснуть *v. impfv.* [*pfv.* погáснуть *or* угáснуть; *past* гас *or* гáснул, гáсла] 1, (*of a light, fire, etc.*) to go out. 2, (*of emotions*) to fade; wane. 3, (*of a person*) to be failing; sink.

гастрúт *n.* gastritis.

гастролёр *n.* guest performer.

гастролúровать *v. impfv.* [*pres.* -рую, -руешь] (*of a performer*) to tour; be on tour.

гастрóль *n.f., usu. pl.* tour: выезжáть на гастрóли, to go on tour. —гастрóльный, *adj.* touring; on tour.

гастронóм *n.* 1, gourmet. 2, grocery store; delicatessen. —гастрономúческий, *adj.* gastronomic.

гастронóмия *n.* 1, gastronomy. 2, groceries.

гать *n.f.* road of logs laid across a marshy area.

гáубица *n.* howitzer.

гауптвáхта *n., mil.* guardhouse; stockade.

гáфний *n.* hafnium.

гашéние *n.* 1, extinguishing; extinction. 2, cancellation (*on a postage stamp*).

гашёный *adj.* 1, (*of a postage stamp*) used; canceled. 2, *in* гашёная úзвесть, slaked lime.

гашéтка [*gen. pl.* -ток] *n.* trigger.

гашúш *n.* hashish.

гвалт *n., colloq.* racket; hubbub.

гвардéец [*gen.* -дéйца] *n.* guardsman. —гвардéйский, *adj.* guards (*attrib.*); of guards.

гвáрдия *n.* Guards: Крáсная гвáрдия, Red Guards. —стáрая гвáрдия, the old guard.

гвóздик *n.* small nail; tack.

гвоздúка *n.* 1, pink (*flower*); carnation. 2, cloves. —турéцкая *or* бородáтая гвоздúка, sweet william.

гвоздúчный *adj.* clove (*attrib.*). —гвоздúчный пéрец, allspice; pimento.

гвоздь [*gen.* -здя́; *pl.* гвóзди, -здéй, -здя́м] *n.m.* 1, nail. 2, *colloq.* highlight; hit.

где *adv.* 1, *interr.* where?: где вы рабóтаете?, where do you work? 2, *rel.* where: я не знáю, где онá живёт, I don't know where she lives. —где бы ни, wherever; no matter where.

гдé-либо *adv.* = гдé-нибудь.

гдé-нибудь *adv.* somewhere; anywhere.

гдé-то *adv.* somewhere; someplace.

гегемóния *n.* hegemony.

гедонúзм *n.* hedonism. —гедонúст, *n.* hedonist. —гедонистúческий, *adj.* hedonistic.

гей *interj., colloq.* 1, hey! 2, gidd(y)ap!

гéйзер *n.* geyser.

гéйша *n.* geisha.

гектáр *n.* hectare.

гéлий *n.* helium.

гелиóграф *n.* heliograph.

гелиотрóп *n.* heliotrope.

гемоглобúн *n.* hemoglobin.

геморрóй *n.* hemorrhoids; piles.

гемофилúя *n.* hemophilia.

ген *n.* gene.

генеалóгия *n.* genealogy. —генеалогúческий, *adj.* genealogical.

гéнезис (нэ) *n.* genesis; origin.

генерáл *n.* general. —генерáл-майóр, major general (*equivalent to U.S. brigadier general*). —генерáл-лейтенáнт, lieutenant general (*equivalent to U.S. major general*). —генерáл-полкóвник, colonel general (*equivalent to U.S. lieutenant general*). —генерáл áрмии, general of the army (*equivalent to U.S. full general*).

генералúссимус *n.* generalissimo.

генералитéт *n.* the generals.

генерáльный *adj.* general. —Генерáльная Ассамблéя, General Assembly. —генерáльный прокурóр, prosecutor general (*of the USSR*). —генерáльная репетúция, dress rehearsal. —генерáльный секретáрь, 1, secretary-general (*e.g. of the United Nations*). 2, general secretary (*of a communist party*). —генерáльное сражéние, decisive battle; pitched battle. —генерáльный штаб, general staff.

генерáльский *adj.* of or for a general; general's.

генерáтор *n.* generator; oscillator.

генéтика (нэ) *n.* genetics. —генéтик, *n.* geneticist. —генети́ческий, *adj.* genetic.

гениáльный *adj.* of genius. —гениáльность, *n.f.* genius.

гéний *n.* genius.

геноци́д *n.* genocide.

геогрáфия *n.* geography. —геóграф, *n.* geographer. —географи́ческий, *adj.* geographic.

геодéзия (дэ) *n.* geodesy. —геодези́ческий, *adj.* geodetic.

геолóгия *n.* geology. —геóлог, *n.* geologist. —геологи́ческий, *adj.* geologic.

геомéтрия *n.* geometry. —геометри́ческий, *adj.* geometric; geometrical.

геополи́тика *n.* geopolitics.

георги́н *n.* dahlia. *Also,* георги́на.

геотермáльный *adj.* geothermal. *Also,* геотерми́ческий.

геофи́зика *n.* geophysics. —геофизи́ческий, *adj.* geophysical.

геоцентри́ческий *adj.* geocentric.

гепáрд *n.* cheetah.

гепати́т *n.* hepatitis.

герáльдика *n.* heraldry. —геральди́ческий, *adj.* heraldic.

герáнь *n.f.* geranium.

герб [*gen.* гербá] *n.* coat of arms.

гербáрий *n.* herbarium.

гербици́д *n.* herbicide; weed-killer.

гéрбовый *adj.* bearing the coat of arms.

гериатри́я *n.* geriatrics. —гериатри́ческий, *adj.* geriatric.

Геркулéс *n.* 1, hercules. 2, *l.c.* oatmeal.

гермáнец [*gen.* -нца] *n.m.* [*fem.* -нка] German.

гермáний *n.* germanium.

гермáнский *adj.* 1, German. 2, Germanic.

гермафроди́т *n.* hermaphrodite.

гермет

и́чески *adv.* hermetically. —гермети́ческий, *adj.* airtight; pressurized.

геро

и́зм *n.* heroism. —герóика, *n.* heroic spirit.

герои́н *n.* heroin.

герои́ня *n.* heroine.

герои́ческий *adj.* heroic. —герои́чески, *adv.* heroically.

герóй *n.* hero.

герóйский *adj.* heroic. —герóйски, *adv.* heroically.

герóйство *n.* heroism.

герóльд *n.,* *hist.* herald.

геронтолóгия *n.* gerontology.

герýндий *n.* gerund.

герц [*gen. pl.* герц] *n., electricity* cycle per second.

гéрцог *n.* duke. —герцоги́ня, *n.* duchess. —гéрцогский, *adj.* ducal.

гéрцогство *n.* 1, dukedom. 2, duchy.

гéтман *n., hist.* Ukrainian Cossack leader in the 17th and 18th centuries; hetman.

гéтры *n. pl.* [*sing.* гéтра] gaiters; spats.

гéтто *n. indecl.* ghetto.

гиаци́нт *n.* hyacinth.

гиббóн *n.* gibbon.

ги́бель *n.f.* 1, destruction; death. 2, wreck; crash. 3, ruin; ruination. —ги́бельный, *adj.* disastrous; ruinous; fatal.

гиби́скус *n.* hibiscus.

ги́бкий *adj.* [*comp.* ги́бче] 1, flexible. 2, supple. —ги́бкость, *n.f.* flexibility.

ги́блый *adj., colloq.* hopeless; worthless. —ги́блое дéло, hopeless case; lost cause.

ги́бнуть *v. impfv.* [*pfv.* поги́бнуть; *past* гиб *or* ги́бнул, ги́бла] to be killed; perish.

гибри́д *n.* hybrid. —гибри́дный, *adj.* hybrid.

гигáнт *n.* giant. —гигáнтский, *adj.* giant; gigantic.

гигиéна *n.* hygiene. —гигиени́ческий, *adj.* of or pert. to hygiene; hygienic. —гигиени́чный, *adj.* hygienic; clean; sanitary.

гид *n.* 1, guide (*person*). 2, *obs.* guidebook.

ги́дра *n.* hydra.

гидрáвлика *n.* hydraulics. —гидравли́ческий, *adj.* hydraulic.

гидрáнт *n.* (fire) hydrant.

гидрáт *n.* hydrate.

гидродинáмика *n.* hydrodynamics.

гидрóлиз *n.* hydrolysis.

гидролóгия *n.* hydrology.

гидролокáтор *n.* sonar (*device*). —гидролокáция, *n.* sonar (*method*).

гидрóметр *n.* hydrometer.

гидроóкись *n.f.* hydroxide.

гидроплáн *n.* seaplane.

гидросамолёт *n.* seaplane.

гидростáтика *n.* hydrostatics.

гидроэлектри́ческий *adj.* hydroelectric.

гидроэлектростáнция *n.* hydroelectric station.

гиéна *n.* hyena.

ги́кать *v. impfv.* [*pfv.* ги́кнуть] *colloq.* to shout; whoop.

гикóри *n.m. indecl.* hickory.

ги́льдия *n., hist.* guild.

ги́льза *n.* 1, shell; cartridge case. 2, cigarette wrapper.

гильоти́на *n.* guillotine.

гильотини́ровать *v. impfv. & pfv.* [*pres.* -рую, -руешь] to guillotine.

гимн *n.* hymn. —госудáрственный гимн, national anthem.

гимнáзия *n., pre-rev.* high school. —гимнази́ст, *n., pre-rev.* high school student.

гимнáст *n.* gymnast.

гимнастёрка [*gen. pl.* -рок] *n.* soldier's blouse.

гимнáстика *n.* gymnastics.

гимнасти́ческий *adj.* gymnastic. —гимнасти́ческий зал, gymnasium.

гинеколóгия *n.* gynecology. —гинекóлог, *n.* gynecologist. —гинекологи́ческий, *adj.* gynecological.

гинéя *n.* guinea.

гипéрбола *n.* 1, hyperbola. 2, hyperbole. —гиперболи́ческий, *adj.* hyperbolic.

гипертони́я *n.* hypertension; high blood pressure.

гипнóз *n.* hypnosis. —гипнотизёр, *n.* hypnotist.

гипнотизи́ровать *v. impfv.* [*pfv.* загипнотизи́ровать; *pres.* -рую, -руешь] to hypnotize.

гипноти́зм *n.* hypnotism. —гипноти́ческий, *adj.* hypnotic.

гипóтеза *n.* hypothesis.

гипотенýза *n.* hypotenuse.

гипотети́ческий *also,* гипотети́чный *adj.* hypothetical.

гипóфиз *also,* гипофи́з *n.* pituitary gland.

гиппопотáм *n.* hippopotamus.

гипс *n.* 1, gypsum. 2, plaster of Paris. 3, cast. —ги́псовый, *adj.* gypsum (*attrib.*); plaster.

гиреви́к [*gen.* -вика́] *n.* weightlifter.

гирля́нда *n.* garland.

гироко́мпас *n.* gyrocompass.

гироско́п *n.* gyroscope.

ги́ря *n.* **1,** weight. **2,** *sports* weight; dumbbell.

гистоло́гия *n.* histology.

гита́ра *n.* guitar. —**гитари́ст,** *n.* guitarist.

ги́чка [*gen. pl.* -чек] *n.* gig (*boat*).

глава́ [*pl.* гла́вы] *n.* **1,** *m. or f.* (*with gen.*) head (of): глава́ семьи́, head of the family. **2,** chapter. **3,** cupola; dome. **4,** *poetic* = голова́. —**во главе́** (+ *gen.*), at the head of. —**во главе́ с** (+ *instr.*), headed by; led by. —**ста́вить во главу́ угла́,** to put at the head of the list.

глава́рь [*gen.* -варя́] *n.m.* leader; ringleader.

главе́нство *n.* supremacy.

главе́нствовать *v. impfv.* [*pres.* -ствую, -ствуешь] **1,** to be dominant. **2,** (*with* над) to dominate; hold sway over.

главнокома́ндующий *n., decl. as an adj.* commander in chief.

гла́вный *adj.* **1,** main; chief; principal. **2,** head; chief. —**гла́вное,** *n.* the main thing. —**гла́вным о́бразом,** mainly; chiefly; for the most part.

глаго́л *n.* verb.

глаго́лица *n., hist.* one of the two original Slavonic alphabets; Glagolitic alphabet.

глаго́льный *adj.* verbal.

гладиа́тор *n.* gladiator.

глади́льный *adj.* ironing (*attrib.*): глади́льная доска́, ironing board.

гладио́лус *n.* gladiolus.

гла́дить *v. impfv.* [*pres.* гла́жу, гла́дишь] **1,** [*pfv.* вы́гладить] to iron; press. **2,** [*pfv.* погла́дить] to stroke; pet. —**гла́дить по голо́вке,** to give (someone) a pat on the back.

гла́дкий *adj.* [*short form* -док, -дка́, -дко; *comp.* гла́же] **1,** smooth. **2,** (*of material*) plain. —**гла́дко,** *adv.* smoothly.

гладкоство́льный *adj.* smoothbore.

гла́дкость *n.f.* smoothness.

гладь *n.f.* **1,** smooth surface. **2,** satin stitch.

гла́же *adj., comp. of* гла́дкий.

гла́женье *n.* ironing; pressing.

глаз [*2nd loc.* глазу́; *pl.* глаза́, глаз] *n.* eye. —**в глаза́ не ви́деть,** to have never seen (someone or something). —**в глаза́х** (+ *gen.*), in the eyes of. —**за глаза́, 1,** behind one's back. **2,** sight unseen. **3,** quite enough; more than enough. —**на глаза́х** (+ *gen. or* у), in plain view of; before the very eyes of. —**с гла́зу на глаз,** alone with one another; in private. —**с глаз доло́й, из се́рдца вон,** out of sight, out of mind.

глаза́стый *adj., colloq.* **1,** big-eyed. **2,** sharp-eyed.

глазе́ть *v. impfv., colloq.* to stare; gawk; gape.

глази́рованный *adj.* **1,** glazed. **2,** with icing. **3,** (*of paper*) glossy.

глазирова́ть *v. impfv. & pfv.* [*pres.* -рую, -руешь] **1,** to glaze (pottery). **2,** to put icing on. **3,** to give a glossy finish to.

глазни́к [*gen.* -ника́] *n., colloq.* eye doctor.

глазни́ца *n.* eye socket.

глазно́й *adj.* eye (*attrib.*).

глазо́к [*gen.* -зка́] *n.* **1,** [*pl.* гла́зки] *dim. of* глаз. **2,** [*pl.* глазки́] *colloq.* peephole. —**де́лать** *or* **стро́ить гла́зки** (+ *dat.*), to make eyes (at). —**одни́м глазко́м,** with half an eye.

глазоме́р *n.* **1,** measurment with the naked eye. **2,** ability to so measure.

глазу́нья *n.* fried eggs. *Also,* яи́чница-глазу́нья.

глазу́рь *n.f.* **1,** glaze (*on pottery*). **2,** icing.

гла́нды *n. pl.* [*sing.* гла́нда] **1,** tonsils. **2,** *colloq.* swollen glands.

глас *n., archaic* voice. —**глас вопию́щего в пусты́не,** voice in the wilderness.

гласи́ть *v. impfv.* (*of a text, saying, etc.*) to read; say; go: как гласи́т погово́рка, as the saying goes.

гла́сность *n.f.* publicity. —**предава́ть (что́-нибудь) гла́сности,** to make public; publicize.

гла́сный *adj.* **1,** vowel (*attrib.*). **2,** open; public. —*n.* vowel.

глауко́ма *n.* glaucoma.

глаша́тай *n.* **1,** town crier. **2,** messenger; herald.

гле́тчер *n.* glacier.

гликоге́н *n.* glycogen.

гли́на *n.* clay.

гли́нистый *adj.* clay (*attrib.*); clayey. —**гли́нистый сла́нец,** shale.

глиноби́тный *adj.* clay (*attrib.*); mud (*attrib.*); adobe (*attrib.*).

гли́няный *adj.* **1,** clay (*attrib.*). **2,** earthenware (*attrib.*).

гли́ссер *n.* hydroplane (*boat*).

глист [*gen.* глиста́] *n.* (intestinal) worm.

глицери́н *n.* glycerine. —**глицери́новый,** *adj.* glycerine.

глици́ния *n.* wisteria.

глоба́льный *adj.* global.

гло́бус *n.* globe.

глода́ть *v. impfv.* [*pres.* гложу́, гло́жешь] to gnaw.

глокси́ния *n.* gloxinia.

гло́сса *n.* gloss (*commentary*).

глосса́рий *n.* glossary.

глота́ние *n.* swallowing.

глота́ть *v. impfv.* [*pfv.* глотну́ть] to swallow.

гло́тка [*gen. pl.* -ток] *n.* **1,** gullet. **2,** *colloq.* throat. —**во всю гло́тку,** at the top of one's lungs.

глотну́ть *v., pfv. of* глота́ть.

глото́к [*gen.* -тка́] *n.* **1,** swallow; gulp. **2,** mouthful.

гло́хнуть *v. impfv.* [*past* глох *or* гло́хнул, гло́хла] **1,** [*pfv.* огло́хнуть] to become deaf. **2,** [*pfv.* загло́хнуть] to die down; (*of an engine*) stall. **3,** [*pfv.* загло́хнуть] to become overgrown with weeds.

глу́бже *adj., comp. of* глубо́кий.

глубина́ [*pl.* -би́ны] *n.* **1,** depth. **2,** *pl.* depths: морски́е глуби́ны, ocean depths. —**в глубине́ души́,** in one's heart; deep down.

глуби́нный *adj.* **1,** deep; deep-water (*attrib.*). **2,** remote; out-of-the-way. —**глуби́нная бо́мба,** depth charge.

глубо́кий *adj.* [*short form* -бо́к, -бока́, -боко́ *or* -бо́ко, -боки́ *or* -бо́ки; *comp.* глу́бже] **1,** deep. **2,** profound. **3,** in-depth; thorough. —**глубо́кой но́чью,** in the dead of night. —**глубо́кая о́сень,** late autumn. —**глубо́кая ста́рость,** extreme old age.

глубоко́ *adv.* deeply; profoundly. —*adj., used predicatively* deep: здесь глубоко́, it is deep here.

глубоково́дный *adj.* deep-water; deep-sea.

глубокомы́сленный *adj.* profound. —**глубокомы́слие,** *n.* depth of thought; profundity.

глубокоуважа́емый *adj., used in salutations* honored; dear.

глубь *n.f.* depth; depths. —**в глубь** (+ *gen.*), deep into; far into.

глуми́ться *v.r. impfv.* [*pres.* -млю́сь, -ми́шься] (*with* над) to mock; deride.

глумле́ние *n.* mocking; derision.

глумли́вый *adj.* mocking; derisive.

глупе́ть *v. impfv.* [*pfv.* поглупе́ть] to become foolish; become stupid.

глупе́ц [*gen.* -пца́] *n.* dolt; oaf; dunce.

глупи́ть *v. impfv.* [*pres.* -плю́, -пи́шь] *colloq.* to be foolish; behave foolishly.

глу́по *adv.* foolishly; stupidly. —*adj., used predicatively* foolish; silly: глу́по волнова́ться из-за э́того, it is silly to get upset over that.

глупова́тый *adj.* dull; not very bright.

глу́пость *n.f.* **1,** foolishness; stupidity. **2,** foolish action; foolish thing. **3,** *usu. pl., colloq.* nonsense.

глу́пый *adj.* foolish; dumb; silly; stupid.

глупы́ш [*gen.* -пыша́] *n.* **1,** fulmar (*bird*). **2,** *colloq.* silly person.

глуха́рь [*gen.* -харя́] *n.m.* **1,** wood grouse. **2,** *colloq.* deaf person.

глу́хо *adv.* **1,** softly. **2,** vaguely. **3,** thickly. **4,** *colloq.* tight(ly). —*adj., used predicatively* quiet: в лесу́ бы́ло глу́хо, it was quiet in the woods.

глухо́й *adj.* **1,** deaf. **2,** (*of a sound*) muted; muffled; hollow. **3,** *phonet.* voiceless. **4,** closed up; having no openings. Глуха́я стена́, blank wall. **5,** latent; suppressed. **6,** (*of a forest*) dense. **7,** remote; desolate. Глуха́я у́лица, lonely street. **8,** *in* глуха́я о́сень, late autumn; глуха́я ночь, the dead of night. —*n.* deaf person.

глухома́нь *n.f.* remote corner; out-of-the-way place.

глухонемо́й *adj.* deaf-and-dumb. —*n.* deaf-mute.

глухота́ *n.* deafness.

глуши́тель *n.m.* muffler; silencer.

глуши́ть *v. impfv.* [*pfv.* заглуши́ть] **1,** to muffle; drown out. **2,** to deaden (pain). **3,** (*of weeds*) to choke. **4,** to turn off (the motor). **5,** to jam (a radio broadcast). **6,** *fig.* to stifle; suppress. **7,** *colloq.* [*pfv.* оглуши́ть] to stun (*with a blow*).

глушь [*gen., dat., & prepl.* глуши́; *instr.* глу́шью] *n.f.* **1,** wilderness; wilds. **2,** out-of-the-way place.

глы́ба *n.* **1,** block (*of ice, granite, etc.*). **2,** clod (*of earth*).

глюко́за *n.* glucose.

гляде́ть *v. impfv.* [*pfv.* погляде́ть; *pres.* гляжу́, гляди́шь] **1,** to look. **2,** (*with* на + *acc.*) to look at. **3,** (*with* за + *instr.*) *colloq.* to look after; keep an eye on. **4,** [*impfv. only*] (with на + *acc.*) to look out on. **5,** [*impfv. only*] *colloq.* (*with an adv.*) to look; appear; (*with instr.*) look like. —**гля́дя по** (+ *dat.*), depending on. —**идти́ куда́ глаза́ глядя́т,** to wander aimlessly; follow one's nose. —**того́ и гляди́,** one would expect (at any moment).

гляде́ться *v.r. impfv.* [*pfv.* погляде́ться; *pres.* -жу́сь, -ди́шься] to look at oneself: гляде́ться в зе́ркало, to look at oneself in the mirror.

гля́нец [*gen.* -нца] *n.* luster; gloss.

гля́нуть *v. pfv.* (*with* на + *acc.*) to glance (at).

гля́нцевый *adj.* glossy; lustrous. *Also,* **глянцеви́тый.**

гм *interj.* ahem!, hm!

гнать *v. impfv.* [*pres.* гоню́, го́нишь; *past fem.* гнала́] **1,** to drive (cattle). **2,** to urge on; ride *or* drive hard. **3,** *v.i.* to race; tear along. **4,** to hunt; chase (an animal). **5,** (*of the wind*) to blow (leaves, snow, etc.). **6,** to drive out. **7,** *colloq.* to drive (a car, truck, etc.). **8,** to distill.

—**гна́ться,** *refl.* (*with* за + *instr.*) to chase; pursue.

гнев *n.* anger. —**гне́вный,** *adj.* angry; irate.

гнедо́й *adj.* (*of a horse*) bay.

гнезди́ться *v.r. impfv.* **1,** to nest. **2,** *fig.* to be lodged.

гнездо́ [*pl.* гнёзда] *n.* **1,** nest. **2,** socket. **3,** mortise.

гнёздышко [*pl.* -шки, -шек] *n., dim. of* гнездо́.

гнейс *n.* gneiss.

гнести́ *v. impfv.* [*pres.* гнету́, гнетёшь] to weigh on; oppress.

гнёт *n.* **1,** burden; weight; yoke. **2,** oppression.

гнету́щий *adj.* oppressive.

гни́да *n.* nit.

гние́ние *n.* rotting; decay.

гнило́й *adj.* **1,** rotten; decayed. **2,** (*of weather*) damp; muggy.

гни́лостный *adj.* putrid.

гни́лость *n.f.* rottenness.

гниль *n.f.* **1,** something rotten or decayed. **2,** mold. **3,** rot (*plant disease*).

гнить *v. impfv.* [*pfv.* сгнить; *pres.* гнию́, гниёшь; *past fem.* гнила́] to rot; decay.

гное́ние *n.* festering.

гнои́ть *v. impfv.* [*pfv.* сгнои́ть] **1,** to let rot; leave to rot. **2,** to cause to rot. —**гнои́ться,** *refl.* [*impfv. only*] to fester.

гной *n.* pus.

гнойни́к [*gen.* -ника́] *n.* abscess.

гнойничо́к [*gen.* -чка́] *n.* pustule.

гно́йный *adj.* festering.

гном *n.* gnome.

гну *n.m. indecl.* gnu.

гнус *n.* bloodsucking insects (*mosquitoes, gnats, etc.*).

гнуса́вить *v. impfv.* [*pres.* -влю, -вишь] to speak with a nasal twang.

гнуса́вый *adj.* **1,** (*of one's voice*) nasal. **2,** (*of a person*) speaking with a nasal twang.

гну́сность *n.f.* **1,** heinousness; infamy. **2,** heinous act; rotten thing.

гну́сный *adj.* vile; heinous; odious; infamous.

гнуть *v. impfv.* [*pfv.* согну́ть] **1,** to bend. **2,** [*impfv. only*] *colloq.* to drive at: куда́ ты гнёшь?, what are you driving at? —**гнуть спи́ну, 1,** to break one's back (*i.e.* work hard). **2,** (*with* пе́ред) to kowtow (to).

гну́ться *v.r. impfv.* [*pfv.* согну́ться] to bend.

гнуша́ться *v.r. impfv.* [*pfv.* погнуша́ться] **1,** (*with gen. or instr.*) to disdain; have an aversion to. **2,** (*with inf.*) to disdain (to); be averse (to).

гобеле́н *n.* tapestry.

гобо́й *n.* oboe. —**гобои́ст,** *n.* oboist.

гове́ть *v. impfv.* to prepare for Communion (*by worship and fasting*).

го́вор *n.* **1,** sound of voices. **2,** manner of speaking; accent. **3,** dialect.

говори́ть *v. impfv.* [*pfv.* сказа́ть] **1,** [*impfv. only*] to speak; talk. **2,** to say; tell. **3,** to make; deliver (a speech, sermon, etc.). **4,** [*impfv. only*] (with о) to indicate; suggest: говори́ть о мно́гом, to say a lot; speak volumes. —**говори́ть само́ за себя́,** to speak for itself. —**да что вы говори́те!,** you don't say! —**и не говори́!,** you can say that again! —**как говоря́т,** as they say. —**не говоря́ уже́ о,** not to mention; to say nothing of. —**не́чего и говори́ть,** it goes without saying. —**об э́том и говори́ть не́чего,** it is not even worth talking about; forget it. —**что и говори́ть,** to be sure; it cannot be denied. *See also* сказа́ть.

говори́ться *v.r. impfv.* to be said; be stated. —**как говори́тся**, as the saying goes; as they say.

говорли́вый *adj.* talkative; loquacious. —**говорли́вость**, *n.f.* loquaciousness.

говору́н [*gen.* -руна́] *n.m.* [*fem.* -ру́нья] *colloq.* habitual talker; chatterbox.

говя́дина *n.* beef.

говя́жий [*fem.* -жья] *adj.* beef (*attrib.*).

го́голь *n.m.* goldeneye (*duck*). —**ходи́ть го́голем**, to strut.

го́гот *n.* cackle (*of a goose*).

гогота́нье *n.* cackling (*of geese*).

гогота́ть *v. impfv.* [*pres.* -гочу́, -го́чешь] (*of geese*) to cackle.

год [*2nd loc.* году́; *nom. pl.* го́ды *and sometimes* года́; *gen. pl.* лет *and sometimes* годо́в; *other plural forms* года́м, года́ми, года́х] *n.* year. —**бе́з году неде́ля**, *colloq.* a very short time; only a few days. —**быть в года́х**, to be getting on in years. —**в мои́ го́ды**, at my age. —**год о́т году; год от го́да**, with each passing year. —**из го́да в год**, year after year; year in and year out. —**не по года́м**, beyond one's years: у́мный не по года́м, smart beyond one's years. —**с года́ми**, over the years. —**с Но́вым го́дом!**, Happy New Year! *See also* ле́та.

годи́ться *v.r. impfv.* [*pres.* -жу́сь, -ди́шься] **1**, to do; be all right; fill the bill. **2**, (*with* на + *acc.*) to be good (for); do (for). **3**, (*with* в + *nom. pl.*) to be fit to be; be qualified to be: он не годи́тся в учителя́, he is not qualified to be a teacher. **4**, (*with* в + *nom. pl.*) to be old enough to be: я вам в отцы́ гожу́сь, I'm old enough to be your father. —**никуда́ не годи́ться**, to be of no use; be no good at all.

годи́чный *adj.* **1**, a year's; lasting a year. **2**, annual; yearly.

го́дность *n.f.* fitness; suitability.

го́дный *adj.* [*short form* го́ден, годна́, го́дно, го́дны *or* годны́] (*with* к *or* для) fit (for *or* to); suitable (for).

годова́лый *adj.* year-old.

годово́й *adj.* annual; yearly.

годовщи́на *n.* anniversary.

гол [*pl.* голы́] *n.*, *sports* goal.

Голго́фа *n.* Calvary.

голени́ще *n.* boot top.

го́лень *n.f.* shin.

голла́ндец [*gen.* -дца] *n.m.* [*fem.* -дка] Dutchman.

голла́ндский *adj.* Dutch. —**голла́ндская печь**, tiled stove.

голова́ [*acc.* го́лову; *pl.* го́ловы, голо́в, -ва́м] *n.* head. —**в пе́рвую го́лову**, *colloq.* first of all. —**голова́ в го́лову**, neck and neck. —**на́ голову вы́ше** (+ *gen.*), head and shoulders above. —**над голово́й**, overhead. —**на све́жую го́лову**, with a fresh mind. —**на свою́ го́лову**, to one's detriment; to one's cost. —**с голово́й**, **1**, smart; bright; clever. **2**, *in* окуну́ться *or* уйти́ с голово́й в (+ *acc.*), to plunge into; become completely absorbed in. —**с головы́**, a/per head. —**с головы́ до ног**, from head to toe. —**че́рез го́лову** (+ *gen.*), over the head of; without letting someone know.

голова́стик *n.* tadpole.

голове́шка [*gen. pl.* -шек] *n.* smoldering piece of wood.

голо́вка [*gen. pl.* -вок] *n.* **1**, *dim. of* голова́. **2**, head (*of a pin, match, etc.*). **3**, *colloq.* the people on top; the brass. —**боева́я голо́вка**, warhead.

головно́й *adj.* **1**, head (*attrib.*). **2**, *mil.* leading; advance.

головня́ [*gen. pl.* -не́й] *n.* **1**, charred log. **2**, smut (*plant disease*).

головокруже́ние *n.* dizziness. —**головокружи́тельный**, *adj.* dizzying; causing one's head to spin.

головоло́мка [*gen. pl.* -мок] *n.* puzzle; brain-twister. —**головоло́мный**, *adj.* baffling.

головомо́йка *n.*, *colloq.* scolding; dressing-down.

головоре́з *n.*, *colloq.* **1**, daredevil. **2**, bandit; cutthroat; desperado.

голо́вушка [*gen. pl.* -шек] *n.*, *colloq. dim. of* голова́. —**бе́дная моя́ голо́вушка!**, woe is me!

гологра́фия *n.* holography.

го́лод *n.* **1**, hunger. **2**, starvation. **3**, famine. **4**, *fig.* dearth.

голода́ние *n.* starvation.

голода́ть *v. impfv.* to starve; go hungry.

голода́ющий *adj.* starving; hungry. —*n.* starving person; hungry person.

голо́дный *adj.* [*short form* го́лоден, -дна́, го́лодны] **1**, hungry. **2**, hunger (*attrib.*): голо́дные бо́ли, hunger pangs. **3**, *colloq.* (*of a meal*) meager. —*n.* hungry person. —**умира́ть голо́дной сме́ртью**, to die of hunger/starvation; starve to death.

голодо́вка *n.* **1**, *colloq.* starvation. **2**, hunger strike.

гололе́дица *n.* **1**, icy surface. **2**, icy conditions.

го́лос [*pl.* голоса́] *n.* **1**, voice. **2**, vote. —**во весь го́лос**, at the top of one's lungs. —**в оди́н го́лос**, with one voice.

голоси́стый *adj.* having a loud voice.

голоси́ть *v. impfv.* [*pres.* -лошу́, -лоси́шь] *colloq.* to wail.

голосло́вно *adv.* without (furnishing) any evidence.

голосло́вный *adj.* groundless; unfounded; unsubstantiated. —**чтобы не быть голосло́вным**, by way of evidence; to back up my statement.

голосова́ние *n.* voting; vote. —**ста́вить** (*e.g.* вопро́с) **на голосова́ние**, to put to the vote.

голосова́ть *v. impfv.* [*pfv.* проголосова́ть; *pres.* -су́ю, -су́ешь] **1**, (*with* за *or* про́тив) to vote (for *or* against). **2**, (*with a dir. obj.*) to vote on. **3**, *colloq.* to hitchhike; thumb a ride.

голосово́й *adj.* vocal.

голубе́ть *v. impfv.* [*pfv.* поголубе́ть] **1**, to turn blue; become blue. **2**, [*impfv. only*] (*of anything blue*) to shine; gleam.

голубизна́ *n.* bright blue color.

голуби́ный *adj.* pigeon (*attrib.*).

голу́бка [*gen. pl.* -бок] *n.* **1**, female pigeon. **2**, (*in direct address*) darling; sweetheart.

голубова́тый *adj.* bluish.

голубо́й *adj.* light blue; sky-blue.

голубо́к [*gen.* -бка́] *n.*, *dim. of* го́лубь.

голубцы́ *n. pl.* [*sing.* голубе́ц] stuffed cabbage.

голу́бчик *n.*, used in direct address, my dear fellow; my friend.

го́лубь [*pl.* го́луби, -бе́й, -бя́м] *n.m.* pigeon; dove.

голубя́тник *n.* pigeon lover.

голубя́тня [*gen. pl.* -тен] *n.* dovecote; pigeon house.

го́лый *adj.* naked; bare.

голы́ш [*gen.* -ша́] *n.* **1**, *colloq.* naked child. **2**, *obs.* pauper. **3**, pebble.

голышо́м *adv.*, *colloq.* stark naked; in the nude.

голь *n.f.*, *obs.* **1**, the poor. **2**, wasteland.

го́льмий *n.* holmium.

гольф *n.* golf.

гольян *n.* minnow.

гомеопатия *n.* homeopathy. —**гомеопат**, *n.* homeopath. —**гомеопатический**, *adj.* homeopathic.

гомогенизировать *v. impfv. & pfv.* [*pres.* -рую, -руешь] to homogenize.

гомогенный *adj.* homogenous.

гомон *n., colloq.* hum (*of voices*); hubbub.

гомосексуализм *n.* homosexuality. —**гомосексуалист**, *n.* homosexual. —**гомосексуальный**, *adj.* homosexual.

гонг *n.* gong.

гондола *n.* gondola. —**гондольёр**, *n.* gondolier.

гонение *n.* persecution.

гонец [*gen.* -нца] *n.* messenger.

гонитель *n.m.* persecutor.

гонка [*gen. pl.* -нок] *n.* **1**, *usu. pl.* race: автомобильные гонки, automobile race. **2**, *colloq.* rush; hurry. **3**, *obs.* dressing-down. —**гонка вооружений**, arms race.

гонококк *n.* gonococcus.

гонор *n.* arrogance; conceit.

гонорар *n.* fee; royalty; honorarium.

гонорея *n.* gonorrhea.

гоночный *adj.* racing (*attrib.*).

гонт *n.* shingles (*for roofing*).

гончар [*gen.* -чара] *n.* potter. —**гончарный**, *adj.* pottery (*attrib.*); potter's.

гончая *n., decl. as an adj.* hound; beagle.

гонщик *n.* racing driver.

гонять *v. impfv., indeterm. of* гнать. —**гоняться**, *refl., indeterm. of* гнаться.

гопак [*gen.* -пака] *n.* gopak (*Ukrainian dance*).

гора [*acc.* гору; *pl.* горы, гор, горам] *n.* mountain. —**в гору**, uphill. —**гора с плеч**, a load off one's shoulders. —**идти в гору**, to come up in the world. —**надеяться на кого-нибудь как на каменную гору**, to rely fully on; put implicit faith in. —**не за горами**, not far off. —**под гору**, downhill. —**стоять за кого-нибудь горой**, to stand behind (someone) completely.

горазд *adj.* (*with* на + *acc. or* в + *prepl.*) *colloq.* good (at). —**кто во что горазд**, each in his own way.

гораздо *adv., used only with comparative adjectives* much; far.

горб [*gen.* горба; *2nd loc.* горбу] *n.* hump.

горбатый *adj.* **1**, hunchbacked; humpbacked. **2**, (*of one's nose*) hooked. —*n.* hunchback; humpback.

горбина *n.* bump; rise.

горбить *v. impfv.* [*pfv.* сгорбить; *pres.* -блю, -бишь] to hunch. —**горбиться**, *refl.* to hunch one's back; be hunched over.

горбун [*gen.* -буна] *n.m.* [*fem.* -бунья] hunchback; humpback.

горбушка [*gen. pl.* -шек] *n.* end crust.

горделивый *adj.* proud; haughty.

гордец [*gen.* -деца] *n.* proud man; haughty man.

гордиев *adj., in* гордиев узел, Gordian knot.

гордиться *v.r. impfv.* [*pres.* -жусь, -дишься] (*with instr.*) to be proud (of).

гордо *adv.* proudly.

гордость *n.f.* pride.

гордый *adj.* proud.

горе *n.* **1**, grief. Убитый горем, grief-stricken. **2**, misfortune. —**горе мне!**, woe is me! —**на своё горе**, to one's grief; to one's sorrow.

горевать *v. impfv.* [*pres.* -рюю, -рюешь] to mourn; grieve.

горелка [*gen. pl.* -лок] *n.* **1**, burner: газовая горелка, gas burner. **2**, torch: сварочная горелка, welding torch.

горелки [*gen.* -лок] *n. pl.* children's game similar to tag.

горелый *adj.* burnt.

горемыка *n.m. & f., colloq.* hapless creature; unlucky soul.

горение *n.* **1**, burning; combustion. **2**, *fig.* ardor; enthusiasm.

горестный *adj.* sorrowful; mournful.

горесть *n.f.* **1**, sorrow; grief. **2**, *pl.* misfortunes; sorrows.

гореть *v. impfv.* [*pres.* -рю, -ришь] **1**, to burn; be on fire. **2**, to be on; be burning. **3**, to shine; sparkle. **4**, *fig.* (*with instr.*) to burn; seethe (with an emotion).

горец [*gen.* -рца] *n.* mountaineer; highlander.

горечавка *n.* gentian.

горечь *n.f.* **1**, bitter taste. **2**, something bitter. **3**, *fig.* bitterness.

горжет *n.* fur neckpiece. *Also,* горжетка.

горизонт *n.* horizon.

горизонталь *n.f.* **1**, horizontal line; horizontal. **2**, contour line.

горизонтальный *adj.* horizontal. —**горизонтально**, *adv.* horizontally.

горилла *n.* gorilla.

гористый *adj.* mountainous.

горихвостка [*gen. pl.* -ток] *n.* redstart.

горка [*gen. pl.* -рок] *n.* **1**, hill; hillock. **2**, (glass) cabinet. **3**, *aero.* vertical climb. **4**, sliding board.

горкнуть *v. impfv.* [*pfv.* прогоркнуть; *past* горкнул *or* горк, горкла] to turn rancid.

горланить *v. impfv., colloq.* to bellow.

горлица *n.* turtledove. *Also,* горлинка.

горло *n.* **1**, throat. **2**, neck (*of a bottle*). —**во всё горло**, at the top of one's lungs.

горловой *adj.* **1**, throat (*attrib.*). **2**, guttural.

горлышко [*pl.* -шки, -шек] *n., dim. of* горло.

горлянка *n.* calabash; gourd.

гормон *n.* hormone.

горн *n.* **1**, furnace; forge. **2**, bugle.

горнило *n.* crucible.

горнист *n.* bugler.

горничная *n., decl. as an adj.* maid; housemaid; chambermaid.

горнопромышленный *adj.* mining (*attrib.*).

горнорабочий *n., decl. as an adj.* miner.

горностай *n.* ermine. —**горностаевый**, *adj.* ermine.

горный *adj.* **1**, mountain (*attrib.*). **2**, mountainous. **3**, mining (*attrib.*). **4**, mineral (*attrib.*). —**горное дело**, mining. —**горная порода**, *geol.* rock. —**горное солнце**, artificial sunlight. —**горный хрусталь**, rock crystal.

горняк [*gen.* -няка] *n.* **1**, miner. **2**, mining engineer. **3**, mining student.

город [*pl.* города] *n.* city; town. —**за город**, to the country; out of town. —**за городом**, in the country; out of town.

городить *v. impfv.* [*pres.* -рожу, -родишь *or* -родишь] *colloq.* to talk (nonsense).

городки́ [*gen.* -ко́в] *n. pl.* game similar to skittles.

городо́к [*gen.* -дка́] *n.* **1,** small town. **2,** premises of an institution: медици́нский городо́к, medical center; вое́нный городо́к, military post; университе́тский городо́к, campus.

городско́й *adj.* city (*attrib.*); town (*attrib.*); municipal; urban.

горожа́нин [*pl.* -жа́не, -жа́н] *n.* city dweller; townsman.

гороско́п *n.* horoscope.

горо́х *n.* peas. —как об сте́нку горо́х, like talking to a stone wall.

горо́ховый *adj.* pea (*attrib.*).

горо́шек [*gen.* -шка] *n.* **1,** *dim. of* горо́х. **2,** polka dots. —души́стый горо́шек, sweet peas.

горо́шина *n.* pea.

горсове́т *n.* municipal council (*contr. of* городско́й сове́т).

го́рсточка [*gen. pl.* -чек] *n.* handful.

горсть [*gen.* го́рсти, -сте́й, -стя́м] *n.f.* **1,** hollow of the hand. **2,** (*with gen.*) handful (of).

горта́нный *adj.* **1,** laryngeal. **2,** guttural.

горта́нь *n.f.* larynx.

горте́нзия (тэ) *n.* hydrangea.

горчи́ть *v. impfv.* to taste bitter; have a bitter taste.

горчи́ца *n.* mustard. —горчи́чник, *n.* mustard plaster. —горчи́чница, *n.* mustard pot. —горчи́чный, *adj.* mustard (*attrib.*).

горше́чник *n.* master potter.

горше́чный *adj.* **1,** pottery (*attrib.*); potter's. **2,** (*of plants*) potted.

горшо́к [*gen.* -шка́] *n.* (earthenware) pot. —ночно́й горшо́к, chamber pot.

го́рькая *n., decl. as an adj.* **1,** vodka. **2,** bitters.

го́рький *adj.* [*short form* го́рек, горька́, го́рько; *comp.* го́рче] bitter. —го́рький пья́ница, heavy drinker. —пить го́рькую, to drink hard; hit the bottle.

го́рько *adv.* bitterly. —*adj., used predicatively* **1,** bitter: у меня́ го́рько во рту, I have a bitter taste in my mouth. **2,** (*with inf.*) distressing: мне го́рько слы́шать таки́е слова́, it distresses me to hear such words.

горю́чее *n., decl. as an adj.* (motor) fuel. —горю́честь, *n.f.* combustibility. —горю́чий, *adj.* combustible; inflammable.

горя́чий *adj.* [*short form* горя́ч, -ча́, -чо́] **1,** hot. **2,** ardent; passionate. **3,** heated; intense. **4,** warm; hearty. **5,** hot-tempered. **6,** busy; hectic. —по горя́чим следа́м, **1,** hot on the trail. **2,** without delay.

горячи́ть *v. impfv.* [*pfv.* разгорячи́ть] **1,** to heat; make hot. **2,** to excite; arouse. —горячи́ться, *refl.* to become excited; get hot under the collar.

горя́чка *n., colloq.* **1,** fever. **2,** fever; panic: биржева́я горя́чка, speculative fever. **3,** bustle; rush. **4,** *m. & f.* hothead.

горя́чность *n.f.* **1,** ardor; fervor. **2,** hot temper.

горячо́ *adv.* **1,** hotly; heatedly. **2,** ardently; fervently. —*adj., used predicatively* hot: куй желе́зо, пока́ горячо́, strike while the iron is hot.

госба́нк *n.* State Bank (*contr. of* Госуда́рственный банк).

госпитализа́ция *n.* hospitalization.

госпитализи́ровать *v. impfv. & pfv.* [*pres.* -рую, -руешь] to hospitalize.

го́спиталь *n.m.* (military) hospital. —госпита́льный, *adj.* hospital (*attrib.*).

госпо́день [*fem.* -дня] *adj.* the Lord's. —гроб госпо́день, the Holy Sepulcher. —ле́та госпо́дня, (*with dates*) of the year of our Lord. —моли́тва госпо́дня, the Lord's Prayer.

го́споди *interj.* good Lord!; good heavens! —го́споди поми́луй!, Lord have mercy!

господи́н [*pl.* господа́, -по́д, -пода́м] *n.* **1,** master. **2,** gentleman. **3,** (*in direct address to foreigners*) Mister; Mr.

госпо́дство *n.* **1,** domination; dominion. **2,** dominance; supremacy.

госпо́дствовать *v. impfv.* [*pres.* -ствую, -ствуешь] **1,** (*with над, в or на*) to dominate. **2,** to predominate. **3,** (*with над*) to dominate; tower over.

госпо́дствующий *adj.* **1,** ruling; dominant. **2,** prevailing.

госпо́дь *n.m., often cap.* Lord; God. *See also* го́споди.

госпожа́ *n., fem. of* господи́н, Mrs.; madam.

гостеприи́мный *adj.* hospitable. —гостеприи́мство, *n.* hospitality.

гости́ная *n., decl. as an adj.* living room; drawing room; sitting room; parlor.

гости́ница *n.* hotel.

гости́ный *adj., in* гости́ный двор, *pre-rev.* arcade.

гости́ть *v. impfv.* [*pres.* гощу́, гости́шь] (*with y*) to be a guest (of); stay (with).

гость [*pl.* го́сти, -сте́й, -стя́м] *n.m.* [*fem.* го́стья] guest. —быть в гостя́х (*with y*), to be a guest (of); be visiting. —идти́ в го́сти, to go visiting.

госуда́рственный *adj.* **1,** state (*attrib.*); government (*attrib.*). **2,** national: госуда́рственный гимн, national anthem. —госуда́рственные дела́, affairs of state. —госуда́рственный де́ятель, statesman. —госуда́рственная изме́на, high treason. —госуда́рственный переворо́т, coup d'état. —госуда́рственное пра́во, constitutional law. —госуда́рственный слу́жащий, civil servant. —госуда́рственная слу́жба, government service; civil service. —госуда́рственный язы́к, official language.

госуда́рство *n.* **1,** state. **2,** the State.

госуда́рь *n.m.* **1,** sovereign. **2,** (*in direct address*) Your Majesty; Sire.

гот *n.* Goth. —го́тика, *n.* Gothic architecture. —готи́ческий, *adj.* Gothic.

гото́вить *v. impfv.* [*pfv.* пригото́вить; *pres.* -влю, -вишь] **1,** to prepare. **2,** to cook. **3,** [*impfv. only*] to train. —гото́виться, *refl.* **1,** (*with к*) to prepare (for); get ready (for). **2,** [*impfv. only*] to be in the offing.

гото́вность *n.f.* **1,** readiness; preparedness. **2,** readiness; willingness.

гото́вый *adj.* **1,** ready. **2,** prepared. **3,** willing. **4,** (*of goods*) finished; (*of clothes*) ready-made; ready-to-wear; (*of a dish*) ready to serve.

го́тский *adj.* Gothic: го́тский язы́к, Gothic.

го́фер *n.* gopher.

гофрирова́ть *v. impfv. & pfv.* [*pres.* -ру́ю, -ру́ешь] **1,** to corrugate. **2,** to emboss.

граб *n.* hornbeam.

грабёж [*gen.* -бежа́] *n.* **1,** robbery. **2,** pillage. —грабёж на большо́й доро́ге, highway robbery.

граби́тель *n.m.* robber.

граби́тельский *adj.* **1,** predatory. **2,** (*of prices*) exorbitant; prohibitive.

гра́бить *v. impfv.* [*pfv.* огра́бить; *pres.* -блю, -бишь] **1,** to rob. **2,** to sack; plunder; pillage.

грáбли [gen. -бель or -блей] n. pl. rake.

гравёр n. engraver; etcher.

грáвий n. gravel.

гравировáльный adj. engraving (attrib.).

гравировáние n. engraving.

гравировáть v. impvf. [pfv. вы́гравировать; pres. -рую, -руешь] to engrave; etch.

гравирóвка n. engraving.

гравитáция n. gravitation.

гравю́ра n. engraving; etching; print. —гравю́ра на дéреве, woodcut.

град n. 1, hail: град идёт, it is hailing. 2, fig. hail; flurry; shower; volley: град пуль, hail of bullets. 3, archaic city.

градáция n. gradation.

градиéнт n., physics gradient.

грáдина n., colloq. hailstone.

градúрня [gen. pl. -рен] n. 1, salt pan. 2, cooling tower.

грáдом adv. thick and fast.

градострóительство n. town planning; urban planning; urban development.

градуúровать v. impvf. & pfv. [pres. -рую, -руешь] to calibrate. —градуúрованная шкалá, graduated scale.

грáдус n. degree: сóрок грáдусов, 40°.

грáдусник n., colloq. thermometer.

граждани́н [pl. грáждане, -дан] n.m. [fem. -дáнка] 1, citizen. 2, man.

граждáнский adj. 1, civil: граждáнская войнá, civil war. 2, civilian: граждáнское плáтье, civilian clothes. 3, civic: граждáнский долг, civic duty.

граждáнство n. citizenship.

грамзáпись n.f. recording.

грамм n. gram.

граммáтика n. grammar. —граммати́ст, n. grammarian. —граммати́ческий, adj. grammatical.

граммофóн n. phonograph. —граммофóнный, adj. phonograph (attrib.).

грáмота n. 1, ability to read and write. 2, document; deed. —вери́тельные грáмоты, credentials. —ратификацио́нные грáмоты, instruments of ratification.

грáмотно adv. 1, grammatically. 2, competently.

грáмотность n.f. 1, literacy. 2, grammatical correctness. 3, knowledgeability.

грáмотный adj. 1, literate; educated. 2, grammatically correct. 3, knowledgeable; competent.

грампласти́нка [gen. pl. -нок] n. phonograph record (contr. of граммофóнная пласти́нка).

гран [gen. pl. гран] n. grain (unit of weight).

гранáт n. 1, pomegranate. 2, garnet.

гранáта n. grenade. —гранáтный, adj. grenade (attrib.).

гранáтовый adj. 1, pomegranate (attrib.). 2, garnet (attrib.).

гранатомёт n. grenade launcher.

грандио́зный adj. grandiose; vast; huge; tremendous. —грандио́зность, n.f. grandeur; immensity.

гранёный adj. (of glass, gems, etc.) cut.

грани́льный adj. lapidary. —грани́льщик, n. lapidary; diamond cutter.

грани́т n. granite. —грани́тный, adj. granite.

грани́ть v. impvf. to cut (glass, gems, etc.).

грани́ца n. 1, border; boundary; frontier. 2, usu. pl. limits; bounds: не знать грани́ц, to know no bounds. —за грани́цей, abroad (location). —за грани́цу,

abroad (direction). —из-за грани́цы, from abroad.

грани́чить v. impvf. (with с + instr.) 1, to border (on). 2, fig. to border (on); verge (on).

грáнка n. [gen. pl. -нок] n. (galley) proof.

грануáли́ровать v. impvf. & pfv. [pres. -рую, -руешь] to granulate.

грануля́ция n. granulation.

грань n.f. 1, boundary. 2, verge; brink: на грáни вымирáния, on the verge of extinction. 3, side; surface (of a geometric figure). 4, line (i.e. distinction); провести́ грань мéжду, to draw a line/distinction between. 5, facet (of a gem).

граф n. count; earl.

графá n. column (of a page).

грáфик n. 1, graph; chart. 2, schedule; timetable. 3, graphic artist.

грáфика n. graphic arts.

графи́н n. carafe; decanter.

графи́ня n. countess.

графи́т n. 1, graphite. 2, lead (for a pencil). —графи́товый, adj. graphite (attrib.).

графи́ть v. impvf. [pfv. разграфи́ть; pres. -флю́, -фи́шь] to rule (paper).

графи́ческий adj. graphic.

графлёный adj. (of paper) ruled.

грáфство n. county; shire.

грацио́зный adj. graceful. —грацио́зно, adv. gracefully.

грáция n. grace.

грач [gen. грачá] n. rook (bird).

гребёнка [gen. pl. -нок] n. comb. —стричь когó-нибудь под гребёнку, to crop someone's hair. —стричь под одну́ гребёнку, to lump together.

грéбень [gen. -бня] n.m. 1, comb. 2, comb (of fowl); crest (of a bird). 3, crest (of a wave, mountain, etc.). 4, ridge (of a roof). 5, ridge (of plowed land).

гребéц [gen. -бцá] n. rower; oarsman.

гребешóк [gen. -шкá] n. 1, dim. of грéбень. 2, scallop.

грéбля n. rowing.

гребнóй adj. rowing (attrib.). —гребнóй винт, screw propeller. —гребнóе колесó, paddle wheel. —гребнáя лóдка/шлю́пка, rowboat.

гребóк [gen. -бкá] n. 1, stroke (of an oar). 2, paddle.

грёза n. dream; vision. —мир грёз; цáрство грёз, dreamworld; dreamland.

грéзить v. impvf. [pres. грéжу, грéзишь] to dream; daydream. —грéзиться, refl. [pfv. пригрéзиться] (with dat.) to appear in one's dreams: онá ему́ чáсто грéзилась, he often dreamt about her.

грéйдер (дэ) n. 1, mech. grader. 2, colloq. graded road.

грéйпфрут n. grapefruit.

грек n.m. [fem. гречáнка] Greek.

грéлка [gen. pl. -лок] n. hot-water bottle. —электри́ческая грéлка, heating pad.

греметь v. impvf. [pres. -млю́, -ми́шь] 1, to thunder; rumble. 2, to ring out; resound. 3, to clank; rattle; jingle. 4, (with instr.) to rattle; jingle. 5, fig. to be famous.

грему́чий adj. 1, thundering. 2, rattling. —грему́чая змея́, rattlesnake. —грему́чая ртуть, fulminate of mercury.

гренадёр [gen. pl. -дéр] n. grenadier.

гренки́ n. pl. [sing. гренóк] croutons.

грести v. impfv. [pres. **гребу́, гребёшь;** past **грёб, гребла́, гребло́**] **1,** to row; paddle. **2,** to rake.

греть v. impfv. **1,** to warm. **2,** to provide warmth: со́лнце гре́ет, the sun is warm; шу́ба гре́ет, the coat keeps one warm. **3,** to heat; heat up. —**гре́ться,** refl. **1,** to warm oneself. **2,** to warm up; get warm. **3,** to bask (in the sun).

грех [gen. **греха́**] n. sin. —**как на грех,** as luck would have it. —**нечего греха́ тайть,** we might as well admit it. —**от греха́ пода́льше,** out of harm's way. —**с грехо́м попола́м,** barely; by the skin of one's teeth.

гре́цкий adj., in гре́цкий оре́х, walnut.

греча́нка [gen. pl. **-нок**] n. Greek woman.

гре́ческий adj. Greek.

гречи́ха n. buckwheat.

гре́чневый adj. buckwheat (attrib.).

греши́ть v. impfv. **1,** [pfv. **согреши́ть**] to sin. **2,** [pfv. **погреши́ть**] (with **про́тив**) to go against: греши́ть про́тив ло́гики, to go against logic.

гре́шник n. sinner.

грешно́ adv., used predicatively with inf. it's a sin (to); it is wrong (to).

гре́шный adj. **1,** sinful. **2,** [short form only — гре́шен, грешна́] colloq. guilty. —**гре́шным де́лом,** I must admit; sad to say.

грешо́к [gen. **-шка́**] n. sin; peccadillo.

гриб [gen. **гриба́**] n. mushroom.

грибко́вый adj. fungous; fungus (attrib.).

грибно́й adj. mushroom (attrib.). —**грибно́й дождь,** rain that falls while the sun is shining.

грибо́к [gen. **-бка́**] n. **1,** dim. of гриб. **2,** fungus.

гри́ва n. mane.

гри́венник n., colloq. ten-kopeck piece.

григориа́нский adj. Gregorian. —**григориа́нский календа́рь,** Gregorian calendar.

гри́зли n.m. indecl. grizzly bear.

грим n. make-up; grease paint.

грима́са n. grimace.

грима́сничать v. impfv. to make faces; grimace.

гример n. make-up artist.

гримирова́ть v. impfv. [pres. **-ру́ю, -ру́ешь**] theat. **1,** [pfv. **нагримирова́ть**] to make up; put make-up on. **2,** [pfv. **загримирова́ть**] (with instr. or **под** + acc.) to make (someone) up to look like. —**гримирова́ться,** refl. **1,** [pfv. **нагримирова́ться**] to put on one's make-up. **2,** [pfv. **загримирова́ться**] (with instr. or **под** + acc.) to make oneself up (as).

грипп n. grippe; influenza.

гриф n. **1,** vulture. **2,** myth. griffin. **3,** music finger board. **4,** rubber stamp. **5,** security classification (stamped on a document).

гри́фель n.m. slate pencil.

гри́фельный adj. slate (attrib.). —**гри́фельная доска́,** writing slate.

грифо́н n. **1,** myth. griffin. **2,** griffon (dog).

гроб [2nd loc. **гробу́;** pl. **гробы́**] n. coffin; casket. —**до гро́ба; по гроб жи́зни,** till the end of one's days; to one's dying day.

гробни́ца n. tomb.

гробово́й adj. **1,** coffin (attrib.). **2,** deathly; funereal: гробово́е молча́ние, deathly silence. —**до гробово́й доски́,** to the end of one's days.

гробовщи́к [gen. **-щика́**] n. coffin maker.

грог n. grog.

гроза́ [pl. **гро́зы**] n. storm; thunderstorm.

гроздь [pl. **гро́зди, -де́й, -дя́м** or **гро́здья, -дьев, -дьям**] n.f. cluster; bunch.

грози́ть v. impfv. [pres. **грожу́, -зи́шь**] (with dat.) to threaten.

гро́зный adj. **1,** threatening; menacing. **2,** fearsome; awesome; dread. —**Ива́н Гро́зный,** Ivan the Terrible.

грозово́й adj. storm (attrib.). —**грозова́я ту́ча,** storm cloud; thundercloud.

гром n. thunder. —**гром среди́ я́сного не́ба,** bolt from the blue.

грома́да n. huge mass; hulk: грома́да горы́, the great hulk of a mountain.

грома́дный adj. huge; enormous; tremendous; immense.

громи́ла n.m., colloq. **1,** burglar. **2,** thug.

громи́ть v. impfv. [pfv. **разгроми́ть;** pres. **-млю́, -ми́шь**] **1,** to smash; wreck. **2,** to rout; crush. **3,** colloq. to assail; fulminate against.

гро́мкий adj. [short form **-мок, -мка́, -мко;** comp. **гро́мче**] **1,** loud. **2,** famous; notorious. **3,** high-sounding; fine-sounding. —**гро́мко,** adv. loud; loudly.

громкоговори́тель n.m. loudspeaker.

гро́мкость n.f. loudness; volume.

громово́й adj. **1,** thunder (attrib.). **2,** thunderous. **3,** devastating; crushing.

громогла́сный adj. **1,** loud. **2,** loud-voiced.

громозди́ть v. impfv. [pfv. **нагромозди́ть;** pres. **-зжу́, -зди́шь**] to pile up. —**громозди́ться,** refl. [impfv. only] **1,** to tower; rise. **2,** (with **на** + acc.) colloq. to climb up on.

громо́здкий adj. bulky; cumbersome; unwieldy.

громоотво́д n. lightning rod.

громоподо́бный adj. thunderous.

гро́мче adj., comp. of **гро́мкий.**

громыха́ние n., colloq. rumble; rumbling.

громыха́ть v. impfv., colloq. to rumble; clatter.

гросс n. gross (12 dozen).

гроссбу́х also, **гро́ссбух** n. ledger.

гроссме́йстер n., chess grandmaster.

грот n. **1,** grotto. **2,** mainsail.

гроте́ск (тэ) n., art grotesque style. —**гроте́скный,** adj. art grotesque.

грот-ма́чта n. mainmast.

гро́хать v. impfv. [pfv. **гро́хнуть**] colloq. **1,** to come crashing down. **2,** to bang down; slam down.

гро́хнуть v., pfv. of **гро́хать.** —**гро́хнуться,** refl., colloq. to fall with a bang; come crashing down.

гро́хот n. **1,** crash; din. **2,** screen; sieve.

грохота́ть v. impfv. [pres. **-хочу́, -хо́чешь**] **1,** to rumble. **2,** colloq. to howl (with laughter).

грош [gen. **гроша́**] n. **1,** pre-rev. half a kopeck. **2,** colloq. red cent; plug nickel. —**грош цена́** (+ dat.); ни гроша́ не сто́ит; гроша́ ме́дного (or ло́маного) не сто́ит, worthless; not worth two cents. —**ни в грош не ста́вить,** not give two cents for. —**ни за грош,** for nothing; completely in vain. —**ни на грош** (+ gen.), not a bit (or drop) of (some admirable quality).

грошо́вый adj., colloq. **1,** cheap (in quality). **2,** petty; paltry; insignificant.

грубе́ть v. impfv. [pfv. **огрубе́ть**] to become rough; become coarse.

груби́ть v. impfv. [pfv. **нагруби́ть;** pres. **-блю́, -би́шь**] (with dat.) **1,** to make rude or offensive remarks (to); be insulting (to). **2,** to talk back (to); answer back. Also, **грубия́нить** [pfv. **нагрубия́нить**].

грубия́н *n., colloq.* rude person; boor.

гру́бо *adv.* **1,** roughly. **2,** crudely. **3,** rudely. **4,** *in* гру́бо ошиби́ться, to make a gross mistake. —**гру́бо говоря́, 1,** roughly speaking. **2,** to put it rather crudely.

гру́бость *n.f.* **1,** rudeness. **2,** coarseness; crudity. **3,** rude remark; coarse remark.

гру́бый *adj.* **1,** rough. **2,** coarse; crude; rude. **3,** gross; flagrant.

гру́да *n.* heap; pile.

гру́дина *n.* breastbone; sternum.

груди́нка *n.* brisket. —**копчёная груди́нка,** bacon.

грудни́ца *n.* mastitis.

грудно́й *adj.* **1,** chest (*attrib.*); thoracic; pectoral. **2,** (*of an infant*) suckling. —**грудна́я жа́ба,** angina pectoris. —**грудна́я железа́,** mammary gland. —**грудна́я кле́тка,** thorax.

грудобрю́шный *adj., in* грудобрю́шная прегра́да, *anat.* diaphragm.

грудь [*gen.* гру́ди *or* груди́; *2nd loc.* груди́; *pl.* гру́ди, -де́й, -дя́м] *n.f.* **1,** chest. **2,** breast. —**отнима́ть от груди́,** to wean. —**стоя́ть** *or* **встать гру́дью за** (+ *acc.*), to stand firmly behind.

гружёный *adj.* loaded.

груз *n.* **1,** load. **2,** freight; cargo.

груздь [*gen.* -здя́; *pl.* гру́зди, -здей, -здя́м] *n.m.* a variety of mushroom.

грузи́ло *n., fishing* sinker.

грузи́н [*gen. pl.* -зи́н] *n.m.* [*fem.* -зи́нка] Georgian. —**грузи́нский,** *adj.* Georgian.

грузи́ть *v. impfv.* [*pres.* гружу́, гру́зишь *or* грузи́шь] **1,** [*pfv.* нагрузи́ть *or* загрузи́ть] to load (a vehicle, vessel, etc.). **2,** [*pfv.* погрузи́ть] to load (cargo). —**грузи́ться,** *refl.* [*pfv.* погрузи́ться] **1,** to take on cargo. **2,** to get on board; (*with* в *or* на + *acc.*) to board.

гру́зный *adj.* **1,** heavy; weighty. **2,** stout; corpulent.

грузови́к [*gen.* -вика́] *n.* truck.

грузово́й *adj.* freight (*attrib.*); cargo (*attrib.*).

грузоотправи́тель *n.m.* shipper.

грузоподъёмный *adj., in* грузоподъёмный кран, (loading) crane.

гру́зчик *n.* longshoreman; stevedore.

грунт *n.* **1,** soil; ground. **2,** *painting* ground; priming.

грунтово́й *adj., in* грунтова́я доро́га, dirt road; грунтовы́е во́ды, ground water.

гру́ппа *n.* group. —**гру́ппа кро́ви,** blood type.

группирова́ть *v. impfv.* [*pfv.* сгруппирова́ть; *pres.* -ру́ю, -ру́ешь] to group; classify. —**группирова́ться,** *refl.* to group; form groups.

группиро́вка [*gen. pl.* -вок] *n.* **1,** grouping; classification. **2,** group; grouping.

группово́й *adj.* group (*attrib.*).

грусти́ть *v. impfv.* [*pres.* грущу́, -сти́шь] **1,** to be melancholy. **2,** (*with* по *or* о) to yearn for; mourn the loss of.

гру́стно *adv.* sadly. —*adj., used predicatively with dat.* sad: почему́ вам так гру́стно?, why are you so sad?

гру́стный *adj.* sad; melancholy.

грусть *n.f.* melancholy; sadness.

гру́ша *n.* **1,** pear. **2,** pear tree. —**земляна́я гру́ша,** Jerusalem artichoke.

гру́шевый *also,* грушо́вый *adj.* pear (*attrib.*).

гры́жа *n.* hernia; rupture.

грыжево́й *also,* гры́жевый *adj.* of or for a hernia; hernial. —**грыжево́й мешо́к,** hernial sac. —**грыжево́й банда́ж,** truss.

грызня́ *n., colloq.* **1,** fight (*between animals*). **2,** *fig.* squabble.

грызть *v. impfv.* [*pres.* грызу́, грызёшь; *past* грыз, -ла] **1,** to gnaw. **2,** to nibble (at). **3,** *colloq.* to nag; badger. **4,** to torment; beset. —**гры́зться,** *refl.* **1,** (*of animals*) to fight. **2,** *colloq.* to squabble; bicker.

грызу́н [*gen.* -зуна́] *n.* rodent.

гряда́ [*pl.* гря́ды, гряд, гряда́м] *n.* **1,** ridge (*of mountains*). **2,** bed (*for flowers or vegetables*). **3,** row; series. **4,** bank (*of clouds*).

гря́дка [*gen. pl.* -док] *n.* bed (*for flowers, vegetables, etc.*).

гряду́щий *adj.* coming; future. —**на сон гряду́щий,** *colloq.* at bedtime.

грязево́й *adj.* mud (*attrib.*).

грязни́ть *v. impfv.* [*pfv.* загрязни́ть] **1,** to soil; dirty. **2,** [*impfv. only*] to sully; besmirch. —**грязни́ться,** *refl.* to get dirty.

гря́зно *adv.* sloppily. —*adj., used predicatively* **1,** dirty; messy: здесь гря́зно, it is dirty/messy in here. **2,** muddy.

грязну́ля *n.m. & f., colloq.* slob. *Also,* грязну́ха.

гря́зный *adj.* [*short form* -зен, -зна́, -зно] dirty; filthy; muddy.

грязь [*2nd loc.* грязи́] *n.f.* **1,** mud. **2,** dirt; filth. **3,** *pl.* mud; mud baths. —**броса́ть** *or* **забра́сывать гря́зью** (+ *acc.*), to throw mud at.

гря́нуть *v. pfv.* **1,** to sound; ring out. **2,** to break out; erupt.

гуа́но *n. indecl.* guano.

гуа́шь *n.f.* gouache.

губа́ [*pl.* гу́бы, губ, губа́м] *n.* **1,** lip. **2,** inlet; bay (*in Northern Russia*).

губа́стый *adj., colloq.* thick-lipped.

губерна́тор *n.* governor. —**губерна́торский,** *adj.* governor's; gubernatorial. —**губерна́торство,** *n.* governorship.

губе́рния *n., pre-rev.* province.

губи́тельный *adj.* disastrous; devastating; pernicious; ruinous.

губи́ть *v. impfv.* [*pfv.* погуби́ть; *pres.* гублю́, гу́бишь] to ruin; destroy; kill.

гу́бка [*gen. pl.* -бок] *n.* **1,** *dim. of* губа́. **2,** sponge.

губно́й *adj.* **1,** lip (*attrib.*). **2,** *phonet.* labial. —**губна́я пома́да,** lipstick.

гу́бчатый *adj.* spongy. —**гу́бчатая рези́на,** foam rubber.

гуверна́нтка [*gen. pl.* -ток] *n.* governess.

гуверне́р *n.* tutor.

гугено́т *n.m.* [*fem.* -но́тка] Huguenot.

гугу́ *adv., in* ни гугу́, silent; mum. —**ни гугу́!,** mum's the word!

гуде́ние *n.* **1,** buzzing; droning; hum. **2,** honking (*of horns*).

гуде́ть *v. impfv.* [*pres.* гужу́, гуди́шь] **1,** to buzz; hum; drone. **2,** (*of a horn or factory whistle*) to sound; blow. **3,** *colloq.* to blow the horn (*of a car*).

гудо́к [*gen.* -дка́] *n.* **1,** (car) horn; (factory) whistle. **2,** hoot; toot; honk.

гудро́н *n.* petroleum tar.

гул *n.* hum; rumble; drone; din.

гу́лкий *adj.* **1,** resounding; booming. **2,** resonant.

гу́льден (дэ) *n.* guilder (*monetary unit of the Netherlands*).

гуля́ка *n.m. & f., colloq.* playboy; reveler.

гуля́нье *n.* **1,** walking; strolling. **2,** outdoor party. **3,** festival; celebration.

гуля́ть *v. impfv.* **1,** to walk; stroll. **2,** *colloq.* to make merry; live it up. **3,** *colloq.* to be off from work; have the day off. **4,** (*with* с + *instr.*) *colloq.* to run around (with); take up (with). —**води́ть гуля́ть,** to take for a walk. —**идти́ гуля́ть,** to go for a walk.

гуля́ш [*gen.* -яша́] *n.* goulash.

ГУМ *n., abbr. of* Госуда́рственный универса́льный магази́н, State Department Store (*on Red Square, Moscow*).

гумани́зм *n.* humanism. —**гумани́ст,** *n.* humanist. —**гуманисти́ческий,** *adj.* humanistic.

гуманита́рный *adj.* humanitarian. —**гуманита́рные нау́ки,** liberal arts; the humanities.

гума́нный *adj.* humane; humanitarian. —**гума́нно,** *adv.* humanely. —**гума́нность,** *n.f.* humaneness; humanity.

гу́мми *n. neut. indecl.* gum.

гуммиара́бик *n.* gum arabic.

гумно́ [*pl.* гу́мна, гу́мен *or* гумён] *n.* threshing floor.

гу́мус *n.* humus.

гунн *n., hist.* Hun.

гурма́н *n.* gourmet.

гурт [*gen.* гурта́] *n.* herd; flock.

гуртовщи́к [*gen.* -щика́] *n.* herdsman; drover.

гурто́м *adv., colloq.* **1,** wholesale; in bulk. **2,** in a group; as one group.

гурьба́ *n., colloq.* crowd; throng.

гуса́к [*gen.* -сака́] *n.* gander.

гуса́р [*gen. pl.* гуса́р] *n.* hussar.

гу́сеница *n.* **1,** caterpillar. **2,** *mech.* caterpillar track.

гу́сеничный *adj.* **1,** caterpillar (*attrib.*). **2,** (*of a vehicle*) tracked.

гусёнок [*gen.* -нка; *pl.* -ся́та, -ся́т] *n.* gosling.

гуси́ный *adj.* goose (*attrib.*). —**гуси́ная ко́жа,** goose flesh; goose pimples. —**гуси́ный шаг,** goose step.

гу́сли [*gen.* -лей] *n. pl.* old Russian stringed instrument; gusli.

густе́ть *v. impfv.* [*pfv.* **загусте́ть** *or* **погусте́ть**] to thicken.

гу́сто *adv.* **1,** densely. **2,** *colloq.* in abundance. —**то гу́сто, то пу́сто,** it's feast or famine.

густо́й *adj.* [*comp.* гу́ще] **1,** thick; dense. **2,** (*of a sound, voice, etc.*) deep; rich.

густонаселённый *adj.* densely populated.

густота́ *n.* **1,** thickness; density. **2,** richness (*of color, voice, etc.*).

гусы́ня *n.* female goose.

гусь [*pl.* гу́си, гусе́й, гуся́м] *n.m.* goose. —**как с гу́ся вода́,** like water off a duck's back.

гусько́м *adv.* (in) single file.

гуся́тина *n.* goose (*prepared as food*).

гуся́тник *n.* goose pen.

гутали́н *n.* shoe polish.

гуттапе́рча *n.* gutta-percha.

гу́ща *n.* **1,** dregs; grounds; lees. **2,** (*with gen.*) the thick of: в гу́ще ле́са, in the thick of the forest. —**гада́ть на кофе́йной гу́ще,** to guess in the dark.

гэ́льский *adj.* Gaelic.

Д

Д, д *n. neut.* fifth letter of the Russian alphabet.

да *particle* **1,** yes. **2,** right?; isn't that so? **3,** really?; indeed? **4,** *used for emphasis:* да замолчи́те же!, do be quiet! **5,** let; may: да бу́дет изве́стно, что..., let it be known that... Да испо́лнится ва́ше жела́ние!, may your wish be fulfilled! —*conj.* **1,** and: хлеб да вода́, bread and water. **2,** but: я и пошёл бы, да не могу́, I would like to go, but I can't. —**да и,** and; and besides. —**да ещё,** and besides; and what is more. —**да и то,** and even; at that: то́лько одна́ руба́шка, да и то потрёпанная, only one shirt and a tattered one at that. —**да и то́лько,** and nothing else: он смея́лся, да и то́лько, all he did was laugh; he just laughed and laughed.

дабы́ *conj., archaic* in order to; in order that.

дава́й *also,* **дава́йте** *verbal particle* **1,** *fol. by inf. or 1st person pl.* let's: дава́й чита́ть вме́сте, let's read together; дава́й ся́дем на авто́бус, let's take the bus. **2,** start!; go ahead!: ну, дава́йте!, O.K., go ahead!

дава́ть *v. impfv.* [*pfv.* **дать;** *pres.* **даю́, даёшь**] **1,** to give. **2,** to let: дай ему́ говори́ть, let him speak. **3,** *with certain nouns* to make: дава́ть обеща́ние/рекоменда́цию, to make a promise/recommendation. **4,** to yield; produce; provide. **5,** *in* дать звоно́к, to ring the bell; дать свисто́к, to blow a whistle. **6,** *in* дать течь, to spring a leak; дать тре́щину, to crack; дать осе́чку, misfire. **7,** *in* дать телегра́мму, to send a telegram. **8,** (*with dat.*) *colloq.* to hit; strike; clip: дать кому́-нибудь в зу́бы, to give someone a smack in the teeth. —**дать знать** (+ *dat.*), to let (someone) know. —**дать поня́ть,** to give to understand. —**дать себя́ знать** *or* **чу́вствовать,** to make itself felt. —**ни дать ни взять,** exactly alike.

дава́ться *v.r. impfv.* [*pfv.* **да́ться;** *pres.* **даю́сь, даёшься**] *colloq.* **1,** (*with* в + *acc.*) to allow oneself (to be): не дава́ться в оби́ду, not to allow oneself to be pushed around. **2,** (*usually with* легко́ *and dat.*) to come easy (to): языки́ ему́ легко́ даю́тся, languages come easy to him.

дави́льный *adj.* for pressing: дави́льный пресс, wine press.

дави́льня [*gen. pl.* **-лен**] *n.* wine press.

дави́ть *v. impfv.* [*pres.* **давлю́, да́вишь**] **1,** to press down on; weigh heavily on. **2,** to squeeze. **3,** to pinch; be tight. **4,** [*pfv.* **раздави́ть**] to crush. **5,** [*pfv.* **раздави́ть** *or* **задави́ть**] to run over; kill. **6,** [*pfv.* **задави́ть**] *fig.* to suppress; stifle. —**дави́ться,** *refl.* [*pfv.* **подави́ться**] to choke.

да́вка *n.* crowding together; crush; jam.

давле́ние *n.* pressure.

да́вний *adj.* **1,** old; olden; ancient. **2,** long-standing; of long standing. —**с да́вних пор,** for a long time; for ages.

давни́шний *adj., colloq.* = **да́вний.**

давно́ *adv.* **1,** long ago; a long time ago: э́то случи́лось давно́, it happened long ago. **2,** a long time (*up to and including the present moment*): вы давно́ жде́те?, have you been waiting long? —**давны́м-давно́,** *colloq.* long long ago; ages ago.

давнопроше́дший *adj.* of long ago; that happened long ago. —**давнопроше́дшее вре́мя,** *gram.* pluperfect tense.

да́вность *n.f.* **1,** distance back in time: собы́тия сорокале́тней да́вности, events which took place forty years ago. **2,** long history; long standing. **3,** *law* prescription. —**срок да́вности,** statute of limitations.

да́же *particle* even.

да́ктиль *n.m.* dactyl. —**дактили́ческий,** *adj.* dactylic.

да́лее *adv.* farther; further. —**и так да́лее,** and so on; and so forth; et cetera.

далёкий *adj.* [*short form* **далёк, далека́, далеко́** *or* **далеко́, далеки́** *or* **дале́ки;** *comp.* **да́льше**] **1,** far; far away; faraway; distant. **2,** (*of a distance, journey, etc.*) long. **3,** [*short form only*] (*with* **от**) *fig.* far from: он не далек от и́стины, he is not far wrong.

далеко́ *adv.* far: оста́вить далеко́ позади́, to leave far behind. Он пойдет далеко́, he will go far. —*adj., used predicatively* far; far away: Москва́ далеко́, Moscow is far away. Туда́ ещё далеко́, it is still a long way to there. —**далеко́ до,** far beneath; not in the same class as: ему́ далеко́ до нее, he can't compare to her. —**далеко́ за** (+ *acc.*), well past: далеко́ за́ полночь, well past midnight. —**далеко́ иду́щий,** far-reaching. —**далеко́ не,** far from; by no means: далеко́ не уве́рен, far from/by no means/certain.

даль [*2nd loc.* **дали́**] *n.f.* **1,** distance: в таку́ю даль, such a great distance; expanse: бесконе́чная даль, endless expanse.

дальневосто́чный *adj.* Far Eastern.

дальне́йший *adj.* further. —**в дальне́йшем, 1,** in the future; hereafter. **2,** hereinafter.

да́льний *adj.* **1,** far-off; distant. **2,** (*of a trip, distance, etc.*) long. **3,** *in* да́льний ро́дственник, distant relative. —**без да́льних слов,** without wasting words; wasting no time on talk. —**Да́льний Восто́к,** Far East. —**да́льнего де́йствия,** *mil.* long-range.

дальнобо́йный *adj., mil.* long-range.

дальнови́дный *adj.* farsighted; having or showing foresight. —**дальнови́дность,** *n.f.* foresight.

дальнозо́ркий *adj., med.* farsighted. —**дальнозо́ркость,** *n.f., med.* farsightedness.

дальноме́р *n.* range finder.

да́льность *n.f.* **1,** distance. **2,** range. —**за да́льностью расстоя́ния,** because of the great distance.

дальтони́зм *n.* color blindness. —**дальто́ник,** *n., colloq.* color-blind person.

да́льше *adj., comp. of* **далёкий** *and* **далеко́.** —*adv.* **1,** *comp. of* **далеко́. 2,** then; next. **3,** further; on: чита́йте да́льше!, read on! **4,** continue!; go on! **5,** any longer: молча́ть да́льше бы́ло нельзя́, it was impossible to remain silent any longer. —*prep., with gen.* beyond: его́ не́ было слы́шно да́льше тре́тьего ря́да, he could not be heard beyond the third row.

да́ма *n.* **1,** lady. **2,** *cards* queen. **3,** partner (*in dancing*).

дама́н *n.* hyrax.

да́мба *n.* dike; levee.

да́мка [*gen. pl.* **-мок**] *n., checkers* king.

дамо́клов *adj., in* дамо́клов меч, sword of Damocles.

да́мский *adj.* lady's; ladies'.

да́нник *n.* one forced to pay tribute.

да́нные *n. pl., decl. as an adj.* **1,** data; facts. **2,** gifts; talent; ability.

да́нный *adj.* this; the given; the present. —**в да́нный моме́нт,** at the present moment. —**в да́нном слу́чае,** in the present case.

данти́ст *n., obs.* dentist.

дань *n.f.* **1,** *hist.* tribute (*exacted from the population*). **2,** *fig.* tribute; due: плати́ть *or* отдава́ть дань (+ *dat.*), to give someone (*or something*) his/its due.

дар [*pl.* **дары́**] *n.* **1,** gift. **2,** gift; talent: дар красноре́чия, the gift of eloquence.

дарёный *adj., colloq.* received as a gift. —**дарёному коню́ в зу́бы не смо́трят,** don't look a gift horse in the mouth.

дари́ть *v. impfv.* [*pfv.* **подари́ть;** *pres.* **дарю́, да́ришь**] to give (*as a gift*).

дармое́д *n., colloq.* sponger; parasite.

дарова́ние *n.* gift; talent.

дарова́ть *v. impfv. & pfv.* [*pres.* **-ру́ю, -ру́ешь**] *obs.* to grant; bestow.

дарови́тый *adj.* gifted.

даровой *adj., colloq.* free; given away free.

да́ром *adv.* **1,** gratis; free of charge. **2,** *colloq.* for next to nothing; for a song. **3,** in vain; for nothing; to no purpose. —**пропада́ть да́ром,** to go to waste; go for naught. —**не пройти́ да́ром, 1,** (*with dat.*) to have serious consequences for: э́то ему́ да́ром не пройдёт, he won't get away with that. **2,** (*with для*) (*of a lesson*) not to be lost upon.

да́та *n.* date.

да́тельный *adj., in* да́тельный паде́ж, dative case.

дати́ровать *v. impfv. & pfv.* [*pres.* **-рую, руешь**] to date.

да́тский *adj.* Danish.

датча́нин [*pl.* **-ча́не, -ча́н**] *n.m.* [*fem.* **-ча́нка**] Dane.

да́тчик *n.* sensor: теплово́й да́тчик, heat sensor.

дать [*infl.* **дам, дашь, даст, дади́м, дади́те, даду́т;** *past fem.* **дала́**] *v., pfv. of* **дава́ть.** —**да́ться,** *refl.* [*past* **да́лся, дала́сь, -лось, -ли́сь**] *pfv. of* **дава́ться.**

да́ча *n.* **1,** country house; summer cottage; dacha. **2,** the country: жить на да́че, to live in the country. **3,** giving: да́ча ло́жных показа́ний, giving false evidence.

да́чник *n.* person spending the summer in the country.

да́чный *adj.* **1,** of or pert. to a dacha. **2,** suburban. **3,** *in* да́чный сезо́н, summer season.

два [*fem.* **две;** *gen. & prepl.* **двух;** *dat.* **двум;** *instr.* **двумя́**] *numeral* two. —**два-три** [*fem.* **две-три**], a couple; two or three.

двадцатиле́тие *n.* **1,** twentieth anniversary; twentieth birthday. **2,** twenty-year period.

двадцатиле́тний *adj.* **1**, twenty-year (*attrib.*). **2**, twenty-year-old.

двадцатипятиле́тие *n.* **1**, twenty-fifth anniversary; twenty-fifth birthday. **2**, twenty-five-year period.

двадцатипятиле́тний *adj.* **1**, twenty-five-year (*attrib.*). **2**, twenty-five-year-old.

двадца́тый *ordinal numeral* twentieth.

два́дцать [*gen., dat., & prepl.* -цати́; *instr.* -цатью́] *numeral* twenty.

два́жды *adv.* twice; two times. —**как два́жды два четы́ре**, as plain as day.

две *numeral, fem. of* два.

двенадцатипе́рстный *adj., in* двенадцатипе́рстная кишка́, duodenum.

двена́дцатый *ordinal numeral* twelfth.

двена́дцать [*gen., dat., & prepl.* -цати; *instr.* -цатью] *numeral* twelve.

две́рка [*gen. pl.* -рок] *n., dim. of* дверь.

дверно́й *adj.* door (*attrib.*).

две́рца [*gen. pl.* -рец] *n.* door.

дверь [*2nd loc.* двери́; *pl.* две́ри, -ре́й, -ря́м, дверя́ми *or* дверьми́, -ря́х] *n.f.* door. —**в дверя́х**, in the doorway. —**при закры́тых дверя́х**, behind closed doors.

две́сти [*gen.* двухсо́т; *dat.* двумста́м; *instr.* двумя́ста́ми; *prepl.* двухста́х] *numeral* two hundred.

дви́гатель *n.m.* motor; engine.

дви́гательный *adj.* motive. —**дви́гательный нерв**, motor nerve.

дви́гать *v. impfv.* [*pfv.* дви́нуть; *pres.* -гаю, -гаешь *or* дви́жу, дви́жешь] **1**, to move. **2**, (*with instr.*) to move (a part of one's body). **3**, [*impfv. only*] to drive: мото́р дви́гает колесо́, a motor drives the wheel. **4**, *fig.* to promote; further; advance. —**дви́гаться**, *refl.* **1**, to move. **2**, to stir; budge. **3**, *colloq.* to start out.

движе́ние *n.* **1**, motion; movement. **2**, traffic. **3**, *fig.* movement: освободи́тельное движе́ние, liberation movement.

дви́жимость *n.f., law* movable property; personal property.

дви́жимый *adj.* movable. —**дви́жимое иму́щество**, = дви́жимость.

дви́жущий *adj.* **1**, *in* дви́жущая си́ла, motive force. **2**, *in* дви́жущие си́лы (+ *gen.*), *fig.* the driving force (of); the forces which drive.

дви́нуть *v., pfv. of* дви́гать. —**дви́нуться**, *refl., pfv. of* дви́гаться.

дво́е [*gen. & prepl.* двои́х; *dat.* двои́м; *instr.* двои́ми] *collective numeral* two.

двоебра́чие *n.* bigamy.

двоевла́стие *n.* diarchy.

двоеже́нец [*gen.* -нца] *n.* bigamist. —**двоеже́нство**, *n.* bigamy.

двоето́чие *n.* colon (*punctuation mark*).

двои́ться *v.r. impfv.* **1**, to divide in two. **2**, *impers.* to see double: у меня́ двои́тся в глаза́х, I am seeing double.

дво́йка *n.* **1**, the numeral 2. **2**, *colloq.* anything numbered 2. **3**, a grade of "two", signifying "poor". **4**, *cards* two; deuce.

двойни́к [*gen.* -ника́] *n.* **1**, (a person's) double. **2**, *colloq.* twin.

двойно́й *adj.* double; dual.

дво́йня [*gen. pl.* дво́ен] *n.* (set of) twins.

дво́йственность *n.f.* **1**, duality. **2**, ambivalence. **3**, duplicity.

дво́йственный *adj.* **1**, dual. **2**, bipartite. **3**, ambivalent. **4**, two-faced.

двор [*gen.* двора́] *n.* **1**, court (*of a sovereign*). **2**, yard; courtyard. **3**, peasant homestead. —**на дворе́**, out of doors; outdoors. —**не ко двору́**, not right; ill-suited.

дворе́ц [*gen.* -рца́] *n.* palace. —**дворе́ц съе́здов**, the Palace of Congresses (*in the Kremlin*).

дворе́цкий *n., decl. as an adj.* butler.

дво́рник *n.* **1**, caretaker. **2**, *colloq.* windshield wiper.

дво́рницкая *n., decl. as an adj., obs.* caretaker's house or quarters.

дворня́га *n., colloq.* mongrel. *Also*, **дворня́жка**.

дворо́вый *adj.* yard (*attrib.*). —**дворо́вая соба́ка**, watchdog.

дворцо́вый *adj.* palace (*attrib.*).

дворяни́н [*pl.* -я́не, -я́н] *n.m.* [*fem.* -я́нка] nobleman; noble. —**дворя́нский**, *adj.* nobleman's. —**дворя́нство**, *n.* the nobility; the gentry.

двою́родный *adj., denoting relationships of cousins:* двою́родный брат; двою́родная сестра́, first cousin. Двою́родный дя́дя; двою́родная тётка, cousin of one's father or mother. Двою́родный племя́нник; двою́родная племя́нница, child of one's first cousin. ♦*Also denoting other relationships:* двою́родная ба́бушка, great-aunt; двою́родный де́душка, great-uncle. Двою́родный внук, grandnephew; двою́родная вну́чка, grandniece.

двоя́кий *adj.* double; dual.

двоя́ко *adv.* in two ways.

двубо́ртный *adj.* double-breasted.

двугла́вый *adj.* two-headed. —**двугла́вая мы́шца**, biceps.

двугла́сный *adj., in* двугла́сный звук, diphthong. —*n.* diphthong.

двугра́нный *adj.* dihedral.

двугри́венный *n., decl. as an adj., colloq.* twenty-kopeck piece.

двудо́льный *adj.* dicotyledonous.

двузна́чный *adj.* two-digit.

двуко́лка [*gen. pl.* -лок] *n.* two-wheeled cart.

двукра́тный *adj.* **1**, twofold; double. **2**, second. **3**, two-time (*attrib.*).

двули́кий *adj.* **1**, having a dual nature. **2**, two-faced; double-dealing.

двули́чие *n.* duplicity. *Also*, **двули́чность**, *n.f.*

двули́чный *adj.* two-faced; double-dealing.

двуно́гий *adj.* two-legged.

двуо́кись *n.f.* dioxide.

двупо́лый *adj.* bisexual.

двуру́шник *n.* double-dealer. —**двуру́шнический**, *adj.* double-dealing. —**двуру́шничество**, *n.* double-dealing.

двуска́тный *adj., in* двуска́тная кры́ша, gable roof.

двусло́жный *adj.* two-syllable. *Also*, **двухсло́жный**.

двусмы́сленность *n.f.* **1**, ambiguity. **2**, double entendre.

двусмы́сленный *adj.* **1**, ambiguous. **2**, suggestive.

двуспа́льный *adj.* (*of a bed*) double. *Also*, **двухспа́льный**.

двуство́лка *also*, **двухстство́лка** [*gen. pl.* -лок] *n., colloq.* double-barreled gun. —**двуство́льный**, *adj.* double-barreled.

двуство́рчатый *adj.* **1**, bivalve. **2**, (*of doors*) folding. *Also*, **двухство́рчатый**.

двусторо́нний *adj.* **1,** two-sided. **2,** bilateral; bipartite. **3,** two-way. **4,** (*of a garment*) reversible.

двууглеки́слый *adj., chem.* bicarbonate (of): двууглеки́слый на́трий, sodium bicarbonate; двууглеки́слая со́да, bicarbonate of soda.

двухвале́нтный *adj.* bivalent.

двухгоди́чный *adj.* two-year (*attrib.*).

двухдне́вный *adj.* two-day (*attrib.*).

двухколёсный *adj.* two-wheel(ed).

двухко́мнатный *adj.* two-room.

двухле́тний *adj.* **1,** two-year (*attrib.*). **2,** two-year-old. **3,** *bot.* biennial.

двухме́стный *adj.* accommodating two persons; for two.

двухме́сячник *n.* bimonthly (*publication*).

двухме́сячный *adj.* **1,** two-month (*attrib.*). **2,** two-month-old. **3,** bimonthly.

двухмото́рный *adj.* twin-engine.

двухнеде́льник *n.* biweekly (*publication*).

двухнеде́льный *adj.* **1,** two-week (*attrib.*). **2,** two-week-old. **3,** (*of a publication*) biweekly; fortnightly.

двухпала́тный *adj.* bicameral.

двухпарти́йный *adj.* **1,** two-party (*attrib.*). **2,** bipartisan.

двухсоле́тие *n.* bicentennial; bicentenary. —**двух-соле́тний,** *adj.* bicentennial.

двухсо́тый *ordinal numeral* two-hundredth.

двухфо́кусный *adj.* bifocal.

двухчасово́й *adj.* **1,** two-hour (*attrib.*). **2,** *colloq.* two-o'clock (*attrib.*).

двухэта́жный *adj.* two-story.

двучле́н *n.* binomial. —**двучле́нный,** *adj.* binomial.

двуязы́чие *n.* bilingualism. —**двуязы́чный,** *adj.* bilingual.

двуяйцево́й *adj., in* двуяйцевы́е близнецы́, fraternal twins.

дебарка́дер (дэ, дэ) *n.* pier; wharf; landing stage.

дебати́ровать *v. impfv.* [*pres.* -рую, -руешь] to debate.

деба́ты [*gen.* -тов] *n.pl.* debate; discussion.

дебе́лый *adj., colloq.* plump; buxom.

де́бет *n.* debit.

дебетова́ть *v. impfv. & pfv.* [*pres.* -ту́ю, -ту́ешь] to debit.

дебо́ш *n.* row; fracas; brawl.

дебоши́рить *v. impfv.* to carry on; run wild; kick up a row.

де́бри [*gen.* -рей] *n. pl.* **1,** jungle; wilderness; wilds. **2,** backwoods; sticks. **3,** maze; labyrinth.

дебю́т *n.* **1,** debut. **2,** *chess* opening.

дебюта́нт *n.m.* [*fem.* -та́нтка] person making his or her debut.

дебюти́ровать *v. impfv. & pfv.* [*pres.* -рую, -руешь] to make one's debut.

де́ва *n.* **1,** *archaic* maid; maiden. **2,** *relig.* the virgin. **3,** *cap.* Virgo. —**ста́рая де́ва,** old maid.

девальва́ция (дэ) *n.* devaluation.

девальви́ровать (дэ) *v. impfv. & pfv.* [*pres.* -рую, -руешь] to devalue.

дева́ть *v. impfv.* [*pfv.* деть] *colloq.* to put; do with: куда́ я дел мои́ очки́?, where did I put my glasses?; what did I do with my glasses? —**дева́ться,** *refl., colloq.* **1,** (*usu. with* куда́) to get (to); disappear (to): куда́ де́лась моя́ шля́па?, where has my hat gotten/disappeared to? **2,** (*with* куда́ *or* не́куда) to go; hide:

мне не́куда дева́ться, I have no place to go/hide.

де́верь [*pl.* -рья́, -рей] *n.m.* brother-in-law (*husband's brother*).

деви́з *n.* motto.

деви́ца *also,* де́вица *n., obs., poetic* maiden; damsel.

деви́ческий *adj.* = де́вичий. —**деви́чество,** *n.* girlhood; maidenhood.

де́вичий *also,* деви́чий [*fem.* -чья] *adj.* girlish; maidenly. —**де́вичья фами́лия,** maiden name.

де́вка [*gen. pl.* -вок] *n., colloq.* girl; wench.

де́вочка [*gen. pl.* -чек] *n.* (little) girl.

де́вственник *n.m.* [*fem.* -ица] virgin.

де́вственный *adj.* **1,** virgin; virginal. **2,** (*of a forest*) virgin; primeval. —**де́вственность,** *n.f.* virginity.

де́вушка [*gen. pl.* -шек] *n.* (teenage) girl; young lady.

девчо́нка [*gen. pl.* -нок] *n., colloq.* girl.

девяно́сто [*gen., dat., instr., & prepl.* девяно́ста] *numeral* ninety. —**девяно́стый,** *ordinal numeral* ninetieth.

девя́тая *n., decl. as an adj.* ninth: одна́ девя́тая, one-ninth.

де́вятеро *collective numeral* nine.

девятиле́тний *adj.* **1,** nine-year (*attrib.*). **2,** nine-year-old.

девятисо́тый *ordinal numeral* nine-hundredth.

девя́тка *n.* **1,** the numeral 9. **2,** *colloq.* anything numbered 9. **3,** *cards* nine.

девятна́дцатый *ordinal numeral* nineteenth.

девятна́дцать *numeral* nineteen.

девя́тый *ordinal numeral* ninth.

де́вять [*gen., dat., & prepl.* девяти́; *instr.* девятью́] *numeral* nine.

девятьсо́т [*gen.* девятисо́т; *dat.* девятиста́м; *instr.* девятьюста́ми; *prepl.* девятиста́х] *numeral* nine hundred.

де́вятью *adv.* nine times: де́вятью де́сять — девяно́сто, nine times ten is ninety.

дегаза́ция (дэ) *n.* decontamination.

дегази́ровать (дэ) *v. impfv. & pfv.* [*pres.* -рую, -руешь] to decontaminate.

дегенера́т *n.* degenerate.

дегенера́ция *n.* degeneration.

дёготь [*gen.* дёгтя] *n.m.* tar. —**ло́жка дёгтя в бо́чке мёда,** fly in the ointment.

деграда́ция (дэ) *n.* degeneration.

дегради́ровать (дэ) *v. impfv. & pfv.* [*pres.* -рую, -руешь] to degenerate.

дегтя́рный *adj.* tar (*attrib.*).

дегуста́тор (дэ) *n.* taster. —**дегуста́ция,** *n.* tasting: дегуста́ция вина́, wine-tasting.

дед *n.* grandfather. —**дед-моро́з,** Santa Claus; Grandfather Frost.

де́дов *adj.* belonging to one's grandfather; grandfather's.

де́довский *adj.* **1,** grandfather's. **2,** old-fashioned.

деду́кция *n., logic* deduction. —**дедукти́вный,** *adj., logic* deductive.

де́душка [*gen. pl.* -шек] *n.* grandfather.

дееприча́стие *n.* verbal adverb.

дееспосо́бность *n.f.* **1,** efficiency; energy; vitality. **2,** *law* competence.

дееспосо́бный *adj.* **1,** able to function. **2,** effective. **3,** *law* competent.

дежу́рить *v. impfv.* **1,** to be on duty. **2,** to keep vigil.

дежу́рный *adj.* **1,** on duty. **2,** (*of a store*) open extra hours. **3,** *fig.* everyday; ordinary. —*n.* person on duty. —**дежу́рное блю́до,** plat du jour.

дежу́рство *n.* duty: расписа́ние дежу́рств, duty roster.

дезерти́р *n.* deserter.

дезерти́ровать *v. impfv. & pfv.* [*pres.* -ру́ю, -ру́ешь] *mil.* to desert.

дезерти́рство *n., mil.* desertion.

дезинфе́кция *n.* disinfection.

дезинфици́ровать *v. impfv. & pfv.* [*pres.* -ру́ю, -ру́ешь] to disinfect.

дезинформа́ция (дэ) *n.* disinformation.

дезинформи́ровать (дэ) *v. impfv. & pfv.* [*pres.* -ру́ю, -ру́ешь] to misinform.

дезодора́тор (дэ) *n.* deodorant.

дезорганиза́ция *n.* disorganization; disruption.

дезорганизова́ть *v. impfv. & pfv.* [*pres.* -зу́ю, -зу́ешь] to disorganize; disrupt.

дезориента́ция *n.* disorientation.

дезориенти́ровать *v. impfv. & pfv.* [*pres.* -ру́ю, руешь] to disorient.

деи́зм (дэ) *n.* deism. —**дейст,** *n.* deist. —**деисти́ческий,** *adj.* deistic.

де́йственный *adj.* effective; efficacious. —**де́йственность,** *n.f.* effectiveness; efficacy.

де́йствие *n.* **1,** action. **2,** *pl.* acts: незако́нные де́йствия, illegal acts. **3,** operation: вводи́ть в де́йствие, to put into operation. Приводи́ть в де́йствие, to start (*e.g.* a machine) going. **4,** effect: оказа́ть де́йствие на, to have an effect on. **5,** (legal) force; effect: вводи́ть зако́н в де́йствие, to put a law into effect; invoke a law. Продли́ть де́йствие догово́ра, to extend a treaty. **6,** act (*of a play*). —**вое́нные де́йствия,** military operations; hostilities. —**свобо́да де́йствий,** freedom of action.

действи́тельно *adv.* really; actually; truly; indeed.

действи́тельность *n.f.* **1,** reality: в действи́тельности, in reality. **2,** validity.

действи́тельный *adj.* **1,** real; actual; true. **2,** valid. **3,** effective. **4,** *mil.* active: действи́тельная слу́жба, active duty. —**действи́тельный зало́г,** *gram.* active voice. —**действи́тельное число́,** real number. —**действи́тельный член,** full member.

де́йствовать *v. impfv.* [*pres.* -ствую, -ствуешь] **1,** to act. **2,** to operate; function; work. **3,** (*with instr.*) *colloq.* to use; employ; operate; handle. **4,** [*pfv.* **поде́йствовать**] to take effect; work; (*with* на + *acc.*) have an effect (on). —**де́йствовать на не́рвы** (+ *dat.*), to get on someone's nerves.

де́йствующий *adj.* active; operating; functioning. —**де́йствующая а́рмия,** army in the field; front-line army. —**де́йствующее лицо́,** character (*in a play or story*).

дейте́рий (дэ,тэ) *n.* deuterium.

де́ка (дэ) *n., music* sounding board.

декабри́ст *n., hist.* Decembrist. —**декабри́стский,** *adj.* Decembrist.

дека́брь [*gen.* -бря́] *n.m.* December. —**дека́брьский,** *adj.* December (*attrib.*).

дека́да *n.* ten days; ten-day period.

декаде́нт *n.* decadent. —**декаде́нтский,** *adj.* decadent. —**декаде́нтство,** *n.* decadence.

дека́дный *adj.* ten-day (*attrib.*).

дека́н *n.* dean (*at a university*). —**декана́т,** *n.* dean's office.

деклама́тор *n.* reciter.

деклама́ция *n.* declamation; recitation. —**деклама-цио́нный,** *adj.* declamatory.

деклами́ровать *v. impfv.* [*pfv.* **продеклами́ровать;** *pres.* -ру́ю, -ру́ешь] to recite; declaim.

декларати́вный *adj.* **1,** declarative. **2,** solemn.

деклара́ция *n.* (solemn) declaration.

деклари́ровать *v. impfv. & pfv.* [*pres.* -ру́ю, -ру́ешь] to declare; proclaim.

декольте́ (дэ, тэ) *n. neut. indecl.* décolletage. —*adj. indecl.* low-necked; décolleté. —**декольти́рованный,** *adj.* = **декольте́.**

декорати́вный *adj.* **1,** decorative; ornamental. **2,** picturesque.

декора́тор *n.* **1,** stage designer. **2,** interior decorator.

декора́ция *n., usu. pl.* **1,** *theat.* scenery. **2,** *fig.* trappings; window dressing. —**переме́на декора́ций, 1,** *theat.* change of scenery. **2,** *fig.* change in the situation.

декори́ровать *v. impfv. & pfv.* [*pres.* -ру́ю, -ру́ешь] to decorate.

деко́рум (дэ) *n.* decorum.

декре́т *n.* decree.

декре́тный *adj.* established by decree. —**декре́тный о́тпуск,** maternity leave.

декстро́за (дэ) *n.* dextrose.

де́ланный *adj.* affected; unnatural. —**де́ланность,** *n.f.* affectation.

де́лать *v. impfv.* [*pfv.* **сде́лать**] **1,** to do. **2,** to make. **3,** *rendered by various English verbs depending on the noun:* де́лать опера́цию, to perform an operation; де́лать шаг, to take a step; де́лать комплиме́нт, to pay a compliment; де́лать пода́рок, to give a present; де́лать вы́вод, to draw a conclusion; де́лать уко́л, to give an injection; де́лать упо́р, to lay *or* place (the) emphasis. —**де́латься,** *refl.* **1,** [*impfv. only*] to be done (*in a certain way*). **2,** [*impfv. only*] (*with* из) to be made (of *or* from). **3,** (*with instr.*) to become. **4,** to happen; take place; be going on.

делега́т *n.* delegate. —**делега́ция,** *n.* delegation.

делеги́ровать *v. impfv. & pfv.* [*pres.* -ру́ю, -ру́ешь] to send as a delegate.

дележ́ [*gen.* -лежа́] *n., colloq.* dividing up; parceling out. *Also,* **делёжка.**

деле́ние *n.* **1,** division. **2,** fission. **3,** *math.* division. **4,** unit; point; notch (*on a scale, thermometer, etc.*).

деле́ц [*gen.* -льца́] *n.* shrewd businessman; smart operator.

деликате́с *n.* delicacy (*choice item of food*).

делика́тничать *v. impfv., colloq.* to be overly delicate; (*with* с + *instr.*) treat with kid gloves.

делика́тный *adj.* **1,** delicate; tactful. **2,** *colloq.* delicate; ticklish. **3,** *colloq.* delicate; frail. —**делика́тность,** *n.f.* delicacy; tact.

дели́мое *n., decl. as an adj., math.* dividend.

дели́мый *adj.* divisible. —**дели́мость,** *n.f.* divisibility.

дели́тель *n.m., math.* divisor.

дели́ть *v. impfv.* [*pfv.* **раздели́ть** *or* **поде́ли́ть;** *pres.* делю́, де́лишь] **1,** to divide. **2,** to share. —**дели́ться,** *refl.* **1,** [*pfv.* **раздели́ться**] to divide; be divided. **2,** [*pfv.* **поде́ли́ться**] (*with instr.*) to share: дели́ться с ке́м-нибудь куско́м хле́ба, to share a piece of bread with someone. **3,** [*pfv.* **поде́ли́ться**] (*with* с + *instr.*)

to confide in. **4,** [*impfv. only*] (*with* **на** + *acc.*) *math.* to be divisible (by).

делишко *n., colloq., dim. of* **дело**: как ваши делишки?, how are you getting along?

дело [*pl.* **дела, дел, делам**] *n.* **1,** matter; affair; business. **2,** deed; act. **3,** cause: **дело мира**, the cause of peace. **4,** *law* case. **5,** file. **6,** *pl., colloq.* things; matters: **как дела?**, how are things? **7,** *in* **горное дело**, mining; **печатное дело**, printing; **переплётное дело**, bookbinding, etc. —**в самом деле**, really; truly; indeed. —**в том-то и дело**, that's just the point. —**в чём дело?**, what's the matter? —**говорить дело**, to talk sense. —**дело в том, что...**, the point is... —**дело рук** (+ *gen.*), one's doing; the work of; one's handiwork. —**иметь дело с**, to deal with. —**между делом**, at odd moments; in between times. —**на деле**, in practice. —**на самом деле**, actually; in point of fact. —**не в этом дело**, that is not the point. —**нет дела** (+ *dat.*), not to care about. —**первым делом**, *colloq.* first of all. —**сделать своё дело, 1,** to do one's job; do one's part. **2,** to do its work; have its effect. —**то и дело**, continually; constantly.

деловитый *adj.* businesslike. —**деловитость**, *n.f.* businesslike manner; efficiency.

деловой *adj.* **1,** business (*attrib.*). **2,** businesslike. —**деловые качества**, professional qualities.

делопроизводство *n.* office work; paper work.

дельный *adj.* **1,** able; efficient. **2,** (*of advice, an idea, etc.*) practical; sensible; sound.

дельта (дэ) *n.* delta.

дельтовидный (дэ) *adj.* deltoid.

дельфин *n.* dolphin.

демагог *n.* demagogue. —**демагогический**, *adj.* demagogic. —**демагогия**, *n.* demagoguery; demagogy.

демаркационный *adj., in* **демаркационная линия**, line of demarcation.

демаркация *n.* demarcation.

демарш (дэ) *n.* démarche.

демилитаризация *n.* demilitarization.

демилитаризовать (дэ) *v. impfv. & pfv.* [*pres.* **-зую, -зуешь**] to demilitarize.

демисезонный *adj.* (*of a coat*) worn in the spring or fall.

демобилизация *n.* demobilization.

демобилизовать *v. impfv. & pfv.* [*pres.* **-зую, -зуешь**] *mil.* **1,** to demobilize. **2,** to discharge. —**демобилизоваться**, *refl.* to be discharged; receive one's discharge.

демография (дэ) *n.* demography. —**демограф**, *n.* demographer. —**демографический**, *adj.* demographic.

демократ *n.* democrat.

демократизация *n.* democratization.

демократизировать *v. impfv. & pfv.* [*pres.* **-рую, -руешь**] to democratize.

демократия *n.* democracy. —**демократический**, *adj.* democratic.

демон *n.* demon. —**демонический**, *adj.* demonic; demoniac.

демонстрант *n.* demonstrator (*one who takes part in a demonstration*).

демонстративно *adv.* in a pointed or emphatic manner: **демонстративно покинуть собрание**, to stalk out of the meeting.

демонстративный *adj.* **1,** pointed; emphatic. **2,** employing visual aids. **3,** *mil.* diversionary.

демонстратор *n.* demonstrator (*one who demonstrates something*).

демонстрационный *adj.* used for demonstrations.

демонстрация *n.* **1,** demonstration; march. **2,** demonstration; show. **3,** *mil.* diversionary action.

демонстрировать *v. impfv. & pfv.* [*pres.* **-рую, -руешь**] **1,** to demonstrate; participate in a demonstration. **2,** to demonstrate; show.

демонтаж (дэ) *n.* dismantling.

демонтировать (дэ) *v. impfv. & pfv.* [*pres.* **-рую, -руешь**] to dismantle.

деморализация (дэ) *n.* demoralization.

деморализовать (дэ) *v. impfv. & pfv.* [*pres.* **-зую, -зуешь**] to demoralize.

демпинг (дэ) *n., econ.* dumping.

денатурат *n.* denatured alcohol.

денатурировать *v. impfv. & pfv.* [*pres.* **-рую, -руешь**] to denature (alcohol).

дендрарий (дэ) *n.* arboretum.

дендрит (дэ) *n.* dendrite.

денежный *adj.* **1,** monetary; money (*attrib.*). **2,** *colloq.* affluent; well-to-do.

денёк [*gen.* **-нька**] *n., dim. of* **день**. Выдался хороший денёк, it turned out to be a nice day.

денно *adv., colloq., in* **денно и нощно**, day and night.

денонсировать (дэ) *v. impfv. & pfv.* [*pres.* **-рую, -руешь**] to repudiate; renounce (a treaty, agreement, etc.).

дентин (дэ) *n.* dentine.

день [*gen.* **дня**] *n.m.* day. —**день деньской**, all day long. —**день ото дня**, day by day; with each passing day. —**изо дня в день**, day after day; day in and day out. —**на днях, 1,** the other day. **2,** one of these days; some day soon. —**по сей день**, to this day. —**со дня на день, 1,** any day (now). **2,** from one day to the next. —**средь бела дня**, in broad daylight.

деньги [*gen.* **денег**; *dat.* **деньгам**] *n. pl.* money. —**быть при деньгах**, to be in the chips. —**быть не при деньгах**, to be short of cash.

департамент *n.* (governmental) department.

депеша *n.* **1,** dispatch. **2,** *obs.* telegram.

депо *n. indecl., R.R.* repair shop. —**пожарное депо**, firehouse; fire station.

депрессия (дэ) *n.* **1,** depression; dejection. **2,** *econ.* depression.

депутат *n.* deputy (*in a legislative body*). —**палата депутатов**, Chamber of Deputies.

депутация *n.* deputation.

дерби (дэ) *n. neut. indecl., horse racing* derby.

дербник *n.* merlin (*bird*).

дервиш *n.* dervish.

дёргать *v. impfv.* [*pfv.* **дёрнуть**] **1,** to pull; jerk; yank; tug at. **2,** (*with instr.*) to jerk (a part of one's body). **3,** [*impfv. only*] *impers.* to twitch: **его всего дёргает**, he is twitching all over. **4,** [*impfv. only*] *colloq.* to pull out; extract. **5,** [*impfv. only*] *colloq.* to harass. —**дёргаться**, *refl.* **1,** to quiver. **2,** to twitch. *See also* **дёрнуть** *and* **дёрнуться**.

дергач [*gen.* **-гача**] *n.* corn crake (*bird*).

деревенеть *v. impfv.* [*pfv.* **одеревенеть**] to become stiff; become numb.

деревенский *adj.* **1,** village (*attrib.*). **2,** country (*attrib.*); rural.

деревéнщина *n.m. & f., colloq.* country bumpkin; hick; yokel.

деревня [*pl.* деревни, -вéнь, -вням] *n.* **1,** village. **2,** the country (*as opposed to the city*).

дéрево *n.* **1,** [*pl.* дерéвья, -вьев] tree. **2,** wood. —за дерéвьями лéса не видно, (one) cannot see the forest for the trees.

деревообдéлочник *n.* woodworker. —**деревообдéлочный,** *adj.* woodworking.

деревýшка [*gen. pl.* -шек] *n.* small village; hamlet.

дéревце *also,* деревцó, [*pl.* -вцá, -вéц, -вцáм] *n.* sapling.

деревянистый *adj.* woody.

деревянный *adj.* **1,** wooden; wood. **2,** *fig.* wooden; dull.

деревяшка [*gen. pl.* -шек] *n.* **1,** piece of wood. **2,** *colloq.* wooden leg; peg leg.

держáва *n.* power: мировáя держáва, a world power.

держáтель *n.m.* holder.

держáть *v. impfv.* [*pres.* держý, дéржишь] **1,** to hold. **2,** to keep. **3,** to support; hold up. —**держáть курс** *or* **путь на** (+ *acc.*), to head for. —**держáть пари,** to bet. —**держáть речь,** to make a speech. —**держáть себя,** to behave. —**держáть чью-нибудь стóрону,** to take someone's side. —**держáть экзáмен,** to take an examination. —**держите вóра!,** stop thief!

держáться *v.r. impfv.* [*pres.* держýсь, дéржишься] **1,** (*with* за + *acc.*) to hold on to. **2,** (*with* на + *prepl.*) to be held up (by); be supported (by). **3,** to stay; remain: держáться на водé, to remain afloat. **4,** (*with gen.*) to keep to: держáться прáвой стороны, to keep to the right. **5,** (*with gen.*) to adhere to. **6,** to hold together; remain in one piece. **7,** to hold out; stand firm. **8,** to behave. **9,** to last; persist. —**держáться бéрега,** to hug the shore. —**держáться вмéсте,** to stick together. —**держáться прямо,** to stand up straight.

дерзáние *n.* **1,** daring. **2,** *pl.* bold initiatives.

дерзáть *v. impfv.* [*pfv.* дерзнýть] **1,** [*impfv. only*] to be daring. **2,** to dare.

дерзить *v. impfv.* [*pfv.* надерзить] (*with dat.*) *colloq.* to be rude (to); be insolent (to).

дéрзкий *adj.* [*short form* -зок, -зкá, -зко] **1,** impudent; impertinent; insolent. **2,** daring; bold; audacious.

дерзнýть *v., pfv. of* дерзáть (*in sense* #2).

дéрзость *n.f.* **1,** impudence; impertinence; insolence. **2,** daring; audacity.

деривáт (дэ) *n., chem.* derivative.

дерматолóгия (дэ) *n.* dermatology. —**дерматóлог,** *n.* dermatologist.

дёрн *n.* turf; sod.

дёрнуть *v. pfv.* **1,** *pfv. of* дёргать. **2,** to lurch forward. —**дёрнуться,** *refl.* **1,** *pfv. of* дёргаться. **2,** to lurch forward. **3,** to lunge.

дéррик (дэ) *n.* derrick. *Also,* дéррик-крáн.

дерюгá *n.* sackcloth; burlap. —**дерюжный,** *adj.* burlap.

десáнт *n., mil.* **1,** landing (*of troops*). **2,** landing party. —**десáнтник,** *n.* member of a landing party; commando. —**десáнтный,** *adj.* landing (*attrib.*).

десегрегáция (дэ) *n.* desegregation.

десегрегировать (дэ) *v. impfv. & pfv.* [*pres.* -рую, -руешь] to desegregate.

десéрт *n.* dessert. —**десéртный,** *adj.* dessert (*attrib.*).

дéскать *particle, colloq.* they say; he/she says.

деснá [*pl.* дёсны, дёсен] *n.* gum (*in the mouth*).

десница *n., poetic* right hand.

дéспот *n.* despot. —**деспотизм,** *n.* depotism. —**деспотический; деспотичный,** *adj.* despotic.

десть [*pl.* дéсти, дестéй, дестям] *n.f.* unit of quantity for sheets of paper: рýсская десть, quire; метрическая десть, fifty sheets.

десятая *n., decl. as an adj.* tenth: однá десятая, one-tenth.

дéсятеро *collective numeral* ten.

десятибóрье *n., sports* decathlon.

десятигрáнник *n.* decahedron. —**десятигрáнный,** *adj.* decahedral.

десятиднéвный *adj.* ten-day (*attrib.*).

десятикрáтный *adj.* tenfold.

десятилéтие *n.* **1,** tenth anniversary; tenth birthday. **2,** decade.

десятилéтка [*gen. pl.* -ток] *n.* ten-year secondary school.

десятилéтний *adj.* **1,** ten-year (*attrib.*). **2,** ten-year-old.

десятина *n.* **1,** *hist.* tithe. **2,** old Russian measure equal to approx. 2.7 acres.

десятирублёвка [*gen. pl.* -вок] *n., colloq.* ten-ruble note.

десятиугóльник *n.* decagon.

десятичный *adj.* decimal (*attrib.*).

десятка *n.* **1,** the numeral 10. **2,** *colloq.* anything numbered 10. **3,** *colloq.* group of ten. **4,** *cards* ten. **5,** *colloq.* ten-ruble note.

десяток [*gen.* -тка] *n.* (*with gen. pl.*) **1,** ten: десяток яблок, ten apples. **2,** decade (*of one's life*): емý идёт шестóй десяток, he is in his sixties. **3,** *pl.* tens of; десятки раз, dozens of times; десятки тысяч рублéй, tens of thousands of rubles.

десятый *ordinal numeral* tenth.

дéсять [*gen., dat., & prepl.* десяти; *instr.* десятью] *numeral* ten.

дéсятью *adv.* ten times: десятью дéсять — сто, ten times ten is a hundred.

детализáция *n.* working out in detail.

детализировать *v. impfv. & pfv.* [*pres.* -рую, -руешь] to work out in detail.

детáль *n.f.* **1,** detail. **2,** part; component.

детáльный *adj.* detailed. —**детáльно,** *adv.* in detail.

детворá *n., colloq.* children; kids.

детдóм *n.* children's home (*contr. of* дéтский дом).

детектив (дэ, тэ) *n.* **1,** detective. **2,** detective story. —**детективный,** *adj.* detective (*attrib.*).

детéктор (дэ, тэ) *n.* detector. —**детéктор лжи,** lie detector.

детёныш *n.* young animal; cub; calf.

детерминизм (дэ, тэ) *n.* determinism.

дéти [*gen.* детéй; *dat.* дéтям; *instr.* детьми; *prepl.* дéтях] *n.pl.* children.

детишки [*gen.*-шек] *n. pl., colloq.* children; kids.

дéтище *n.* **1,** *obs.* child; offspring. **2,** *fig.* brainchild.

детонáтор *n.* detonator.

детонáция *n.* detonation.

детонировать *v. impfv.* [*pres.* -рую, -руешь] **1,** to detonate; go off. **2,** to be out of tune; be off key.

детородный *adj.* genital.

деторождéние *n.* **1,** childbearing. **2,** procreation.

детоубийство *n.* infanticide.

детса́д *n.* kindergarten; nursery school (*contr. of* де́тский сад).

де́тская *n., decl. as an adj.* nursery; room for children.

де́тский *adj.* **1,** children's; child's. **2,** childish; childlike. —**де́тское ме́сто**, afterbirth; placenta. —**де́тский сад**, kindergarten. —**де́тская сме́ртность**, infant mortality. —**де́тский труд**, child labor.

де́тство *n.* childhood. —**впада́ть в де́тство**, to be in one's second childhood; be in one's dotage.

деть [*infl.* де́ну, де́нешь] *v., pfv. of* дева́ть. —**де́ться**, *refl., pfv. of* дева́ться.

де-фа́кто *adv.* de facto.

дефе́кт *n.* defect. —**дефекти́вный**, *adj.* handicapped. —**дефе́ктый**, *adj.* defective.

дефи́с *n.* hyphen.

дефици́т *n.* **1,** deficit. **2,** shortage: дефици́т в то́пливе, fuel shortage.

дефици́тный *adj.* **1,** operating at a loss; unprofitable. **2,** (*of goods*) scarce; in short supply.

дефля́ция (дэ) *n., econ.* deflation.

деформа́ция (дэ) *n.* deformation.

деформи́ровать (дэ) *v. impfv. & pfv.* [*pres.* -ру́ю, -ру́ешь] to change the shape of.

децентрализа́ция (дэ) *n.* decentralization.

децентрализова́ть (дэ) *v. impfv. & pfv.* [*pres.* -зу́ю, -зу́ешь] to decentralize.

децибе́л (дэ) *n.* decibel.

дециграмм (дэ) *n.* decigram.

децили́тр (дэ) *n.* deciliter.

дециме́тр (дэ) *n.* decimeter.

дешеве́ть *v. impfv.* [*pfv.* подешеве́ть] to go down in price; become cheaper.

дешиви́зна *n.* (*with gen.*) low price level (of); low prices (for).

дешёвка *n., colloq.* **1,** low price. **2,** something low in price. —**по дешёвке**, dirt-cheap.

деше́вле *adj., comp. of* дешёвый.

дёшево *adv.* cheap; cheaply. —**дёшево и серди́то**, good and inexpensive. —**дёшево отде́латься**, to get off cheap.

дешёвый *adj.* [*short form* дёшев, дешева́, дёшево; *comp.* деше́вле] **1,** inexpensive; cheap. **2,** (*of a price*) low. **3,** *fig.* cheap; worthless; vulgar.

дешифри́ровать (дэ) *v. impfv. & pfv.* [*pres.* -ру́ю, -ру́ешь] to decipher. *Also,* дешифрова́ть [*pres.* -ру́ю, -ру́ешь].

дешифро́вка (дэ) *n.* decipherment; deciphering.

де-ю́ре (дэ) *adv.* de jure.

дея́ние *n.* deed; act.

де́ятель *n.m.* figure: обще́ственный де́ятель, public figure. —**госуда́рственный де́ятель**, statesman.

де́ятельность *n.f.* **1,** activity; activities. **2,** functioning; action.

де́ятельный *adj.* active.

джаз *n.* jazz. —**джа́зовый**, *adj.* jazz.

джем *n.* jam.

дже́мпер *n.* pullover; jersey.

джентльме́н *n.* gentleman.

джентльме́нский *adj.* gentlemanly. —**джентльме́нское соглаше́ние**, gentlemen's agreement.

джи́га *n.* jig (*dance*).

джиги́т *n.* skillful horseman.

джин *n.* **1,** gin. **2,** [*also*, джинн] genie.

джи́нсы [*gen.* -ов] *n. pl.* jeans.

джип *n.* jeep.

джи́у-джи́тсу *n. neut. indecl.* jujitsu.

джо́кер *n., cards* joker.

джо́нка [*gen. pl.* -нок] *n.* junk (*boat*).

джо́уль *n.m.* joule.

джу́нгли [*gen.* -лей] *n. pl.* jungle.

джут *n.* jute. —**джу́товый**, *adj.* jute.

дзюдо́ *n. indecl.* judo.

диабе́т *n.* diabetes. —**диабе́тик**, *n.* diabetic. —**диабети́ческий**, *adj.* diabetic.

диа́гноз *n.* diagnosis.

диагно́ст *n.* diagnostician. —**диагности́ческий**, *adj.* diagnostic.

диагона́ль *n.f.* diagonal. —**диагона́льный**, *adj.* diagonal.

диагра́мма *n.* diagram; chart; graph.

диаде́ма (дэ) *n.* diadem.

диакрити́ческий *adj.* diacritical.

диале́кт *n.* dialect.

диале́ктика *n.* dialectics. —**диалекти́ческий**, *adj.* dialectical.

диале́ктный *adj.* dialectal.

диало́г *n.* dialogue.

диа́метр *n.* diameter.

диаметра́льно *adv.* diametrically: диаметра́льно противополо́жный, diametrically opposite. —**диаметра́льный**, *adj.* diametrical.

диапазо́н *n.* **1,** *music* range. **2,** *radio* band. **3,** *fig.* range; scope.

диапозити́в *n., photog.* slide; transparency.

диатерми́я (тэ) *n.* diathermy.

диатони́ческий *adj.* diatonic.

диафра́гма *n., anat.; optics; photog.* diaphragm.

дива́н *n.* sofa; couch. —**дива́нный**, *adj.* sofa (*attrib.*); couch (*attrib.*).

диверса́нт *n.* saboteur.

диверсио́нный *adj.* **1,** *mil.* diversionary. **2,** of sabotage.

диверсифика́ция *n.* diversification.

диве́рсия *n.* **1,** *mil.* diversion. **2,** sabotage.

дивиде́нд *n.* dividend.

дивизио́н *n.* (artillery) battalion.

дивизио́нный *adj., mil.* division (*attrib.*); divisional.

диви́зия *n., mil.* division.

диви́ть *v. impfv.* [*pres.* дивлю́, диви́шь] *colloq.* to surprise; startle. —**диви́ться**, *refl.* [*pfv.* подиви́ться] (*with dat.*) *colloq.* to wonder (at); marvel (at).

ди́вный *adj.* **1,** wonderful; marvelous. **2,** *obs.* amazing; remarkable.

ди́во *n.* wonder: ди́во, что..., it's a wonder that... —**ди́ву дава́ться**, to wonder; marvel. —**на ди́во**, wonderfully; marvelously.

дида́ктика *n.* didactics. —**дидакти́ческий**, *adj.* didactic.

дие́з *n., music* sharp: ля дие́з, A sharp.

дие́та *n.* diet.

диетвра́ч [*gen.* -ча́] *n.* dietitian.

диете́тика (тэ) *n.* dietetics; nutrition. —**диетети́ческий**, *adj.* dietetic.

диети́ческий *adj.* dietary.

диза́йн *n.* (industrial) design.

ди́зель *n.m.* diesel engine. —**ди́зельный**, *adj.* diesel.

дизентери́я *n.* dysentery.

дика́рь [*gen.* -каря́] *n.m.* [*fem.* -ка́рка] **1,** savage. **2,** *colloq.* unsociable person; loner.

ди́кий *adj.* **1,** wild. **2,** absurd; preposterous. **3,** shy;

retiring. —**ди́кое мя́со**, proud flesh. —**ди́кое я́блоко**, crab apple.

ди́ко *adv.* **1,** wild: расти́ ди́ко, to grow wild. **2,** wildly. —*adj., used predicatively* **1,** desolate: вокру́г бы́ло ди́ко, it was desolate all around. **2,** absurd: ди́ко да́же ду́мать об э́том, it is absurd even to think about it.

дикобра́з *n.* porcupine.

дико́вина *also,* **дико́винка** *n., colloq.* strange thing; wonder; novelty. —**быть в дико́вин(к)у** (+ *dat.*), to be amazing to.

дико́винный *adj., colloq.* odd; strange; bizarre.

дикорасту́щий *adj.* wild; growing wild.

ди́кость *n.f.* **1,** wild state; uncivilized state. **2,** savagery. **3,** lack of sociability. **4,** *colloq.* folly.

дикта́нт *n.* dictation (*classroom exercise*).

дикта́т *n.* imposed settlement. —**поли́тика дикта́та**, policy of dictating to others.

дикта́тор *n.* dictator. —**дикта́торский**, *adj.* dictatorial.

диктату́ра *n.* dictatorship.

диктова́ть *v. impfv.* [*pfv.* **продиктова́ть**; *pres.* **-ту́ю, -ту́ешь**] **1,** to dictate. **2,** *usu. passive* to prompt: реше́ние диктова́лось (*or* бы́ло продикто́вано) двумя́ фа́кторами, the decision was prompted by two factors.

дикто́вка *n.* dictation: писа́ть под дикто́вку, to take dictation. —**под дикто́вку** (+ *gen.*), at the urging of; at the behest of.

ди́ктор *n.* (radio) announcer.

диктофо́н *n.* dictaphone.

ди́кция *n.* diction; enunciation.

диле́мма *n.* dilemma.

дилета́нт *n.* amateur; dilettante. —**дилетанти́зм; дилета́нтство,** *n.* dilettantism. —**дилета́нтский**, *adj.* amateurish.

дилижа́нс *n.* stagecoach.

диминуэ́ндо *adv.* diminuendo.

ди́на *n.* dyne.

динами́зм *n.* dynamism.

дина́мика *n.* dynamics.

динами́т *n.* dynamite. —**динами́тный**, *adj.* dynamite (*attrib.*).

динами́ческий *adj.* **1,** of dynamics. **2,** dynamic.

динами́чный *adj.* dynamic. —**динами́чность**, *n.f.* dynamic quality.

дина́мо *n. indecl.* dynamo.

динамо́метр *n.* dynamometer.

дина́стия *n.* dynasty. —**династи́ческий**, *adj.* dynastic.

диноза́вр *n.* dinosaur.

дио́д *n.* diode.

дипло́м *n.* diploma; degree.

диплома́т *n.* diplomat.

дипломати́ческий *adj.* **1,** diplomatic. **2,** *fig.* diplomatic; tactful.

дипломати́чный *adj.* diplomatic; tactful. —**дипломати́чность**, *n.f.* diplomacy; tact.

диплома́тия *n.* diplomacy.

диплома́тия *n.* diplomacy.

дипломи́рованный *adj.* having a degree: дипломи́рованный инжене́р, person with a degree in engineering.

дипло́мный *adj.* done toward a degree: дипло́мный прое́кт, project for one's degree.

директи́ва *n.* directive. —**директи́вный**, *adj.* containing instructions.

дире́ктор [*pl.* **директора́**] *n.* **1,** director; manager. **2,** *theat.* producer.

директора́т *n.* board of directors; directorate.

дире́кторский *adj.* director's; directorial.

дире́кция *n.* **1,** (top) management. **2,** director's office.

дирижа́бль *n.m.* dirigible.

дирижёр *n., music* conductor. —**дирижёрский**, *adj.* conductor's.

дирижи́ровать *v. impfv.* [*pres.* -**рую**, -**руешь**] *music* (*with instr.*) to conduct.

дисгармони́ровать *v. impfv.* [*pres.* -**рую**, -**руешь**] (*with* **с**) to clash (with).

дисгармо́ния *n.* disharmony.

диск *n.* **1,** disk. **2,** dial (*of a telephone*). **3,** turntable (*of a phonograph*). **4,** *sports* discus.

ди́скант *n., music* treble. —**дисканто́вый**, *adj.* treble.

дисквалифика́ция *n.* disqualification.

дисквалифици́ровать *v. impfv. & pfv.* [*pres.* -**рую**, -**руешь**] to disqualify.

ди́сковый *adj.* disk-shaped. —**ди́сковая борона́**, disk harrow. —**ди́сковый то́рмоз**, disk brake.

дискредити́ровать *v. impfv. & pfv.* [*pres.* -**рую**, -**руешь**] to discredit.

дискрецио́нный *adj.* discretionary.

дискримина́ция *n.* discrimination. —**дискриминацио́нный**, *adj.* discriminatory.

дискримини́ровать *v. impfv. & pfv.* [*pres.* -**рую**, -**руешь**] to discriminate (against).

дискуссио́нный *adj.* **1,** discussion (*attrib.*): в дискуссио́нном поря́дке, as a basis for discussion. **2,** debatable; controversial.

диску́ссия *n.* discussion; debate.

дискути́ровать *v. impfv.* [*pres.* -**рую**, -**руешь**] to discuss; debate.

дислока́ция *n., mil.* disposition (*of troops*).

дислоци́ровать *v. impfv. & pfv.* [*pres.* -**рую**, -**руешь**] *mil.* to deploy (troops).

диспансе́р (сэ) *n.* sanitarium; health center.

диспепси́я *n.* dyspepsia.

дисперсия *n., physics* dispersion.

диспе́тчер *n.* **1,** traffic manager. **2,** air traffic controller.

диспе́тчерская *n., decl. as an adj.* control tower. Also, **диспе́тчерская вы́шка**.

диспро́зий *n.* dysprosium.

диспропо́рция *n.* disproportion.

ди́спут *n.* (public) debate.

диссерта́ция *n.* dissertation; thesis.

диссона́нс *n.* **1,** *music* dissonance; discord. **2,** *fig.* disharmony; incongruity.

дистанцио́нный *adj.* controlled from a distance. —**дистанцио́нное управле́ние**, remote control.

диста́нция *n.* distance. —**сойти́ с диста́нции**, to drop out of a race; fail to go the distance.

дистилли́ровать *v. impfv. & pfv.* [*pres.* -**рую**, -**руешь**] to distill.

дистилля́ция *n.* distillation.

дистрофи́я *n.* dystrophy.

дисципли́на *n.* **1,** discipline. **2,** discipline (*branch of knowledge*).

дисциплина́рный *adj.* disciplinary. —**дисциплина́рное взыска́ние**, summary punishment.

дисциплини́ровать *v. impfv. & pfv.* [*pres.* -ру́ю, -ру́ешь] to discipline.

дитя́ *n. neut.* [*other cases rarely used*] child.

дифира́мб *n., in* петь дифира́мбы (+ *dat.*), to sing the praises of.

дифтери́я *also,* **дифтери́т** *n.* diphtheria. —**дифтери́йный**, *adj.* diphtheria (*attrib.*); diphtherial.

дифто́нг *n.* diphthong.

диффама́ция *n.* defamation.

дифференциа́л *n., math.; mech.* differential. —**дифференциа́льный**, *adj.* differential.

дифференциа́ция *n.* differentiation.

дифференци́ровать *v. impfv. & pfv.* [*pres.* -ру́ю, -ру́ешь] to differentiate.

диффу́зия *n., physics* diffusion.

дича́ть *v. impfv.* [*pfv.* **одича́ть**] **1,** to become wild. **2,** to become shy; become unsociable.

дичи́ться *v.r. impfv., colloq.* **1,** to be shy; avoid people. **2,** (*with gen.*) to avoid.

дичь *n.f.* **1,** game (*animals, birds, etc.*): кру́пная дичь, big game. **2,** *colloq.* wilderness. **3,** *colloq.* nonsense.

длина́ *n.* length. —**в длину́**, lengthwise. —**длина́ волны́**, wavelength.

длинново́лновый *adj.* long-wave.

длинноволо́сый *adj.* long-haired.

длинноно́гий *adj.* long-legged.

длиннота́ [*pl.* **длинно́ты**] *n.* **1,** *obs.* (great) length. **2,** *pl.* long drawn-out passages.

дли́нный *adj.* [*short form* дли́нен, длинна́, дли́нно] long.

дли́тельный *adj.* long; lengthy; protracted; prolonged. —**дли́тельность**, *n.f.* length; duration.

дли́ться *v.r. impfv.* [*pfv.* **продли́ться**] to last.

для *prep., with gen.* for: кни́га для дете́й, a book for children. Корзи́на для бума́ги, a wastebasket. Хорошо́ вы́глядеть для своего́ во́зраста, to look well for one's age. —**для того́, что́бы,** *see* что́бы.

днева́льный *n., decl. as an adj., mil.* man on duty.

днева́ть *v. impfv.* [*pres.* **дню́ю, дню́ешь**] to spend the day (*in a certain place*). —**днева́ть и ночева́ть,** to spend all one's time; "live" (*in a certain place*).

дневни́к [*gen.* -ника́] *n.* diary.

дневно́й *adj.* **1,** day (*attrib.*). **2,** daytime (*attrib.*). **3,** a day's; one day's.

днём *adv.* during the day; in the daytime.

дни́ще *n.* bottom (*of a vessel or barrel*).

дно *n.* bottom. Морско́е дно, ocean floor; seabed. —**вверх дном,** upside down; topsy-turvy. —**идти́ ко дну,** (*of a ship*) to sink; go down. —**пить до дна,** to empty one's glass. —**пуска́ть ко дну,** to sink; send to the bottom.

до¹ *prep., with gen.* **1,** to; up to; as far as: дойти́ до ста́нции, to walk as far as the station. От Балти́йского до Чёрного мо́ря, from the Baltic to the Black Sea. **2,** before: до войны́, before the war. **3,** until: рабо́тать до двух часо́в но́чи, to work until two o'clock in the morning. **4,** to the point of: рабо́тать до изнеможе́ния, to work to the point of exhaustion. **5,** up to; as many as: зал вмеща́ет до ты́сячи челове́к, the hall accommodates up to a thousand people. —**до сих/тех пор; до тех пор пока́ (не),** *see* пора́. —**до того́,** so: до того́ уста́л, что..., so tired that... —**до того́, что,** until. —**не до,** not in the mood for: ему́ не до шу́ток, he is not in the mood for jokes. —**что до,** as for.

до² *n. neut., music* do; C.

до- *prefix* **1,** *indicating action or motion up to a point:* дойти́ до моста́, to walk as far as the bridge. **2,** *indicating completion of an action:* договори́ть, to finish speaking. **3,** *indicating something additional:* дополучи́ть, to receive in addition. **4,** (*with -ся*) *indicating attainment after persistent effort:* дозвони́ться, to ring until someone answers. **5,** (*with -ся*) *indicating an action to some extreme:* докрича́ться до хрипоты́, to shout oneself hoarse. **6,** *with adjectives* pre-: дошко́льный, preschool. **7,** *with adverbs* completely: до́суха, completely dry.

доба́вить [*infl.* -влю, -вишь] *v., pfv. of* **добавля́ть**.

доба́вка *n., colloq.* **1,** addition. **2,** second helping (*of food*).

добавле́ние *n.* **1,** addition (*act of adding*). **2,** an addition: примеча́ния и добавле́ния, notes and additions. —**в добавле́ние к,** in addition to.

добавля́ть *v. impfv.* [*pfv.* **доба́вить**] to add.

доба́вочный *adj.* **1,** additional; extra. **2,** (*with telephone numbers*) extension: доба́вочный со́рок два, extension 42. —**доба́вочный нало́г,** surtax.

добега́ть *v. impfv.* [*pfv.* **добежа́ть**] (*with* до) to run to; run up to; run as far as.

добежа́ть [*infl. like* **бежа́ть**] *v., pfv. of* **добега́ть**.

добела́ *adv.* **1,** until something is spotlessly clean. **2,** *in* раскали́ть добела́, to make white-hot; **раскалённый добела́,** white-hot.

добива́ть *v. impfv.* [*pfv.* **доби́ть**] **1,** to kill; finish off; deal the finishing blow to. **2,** to crush; rout; smite. **3,** (*with* до) to beat to a certain point or state.

добива́ться *v.r. impfv.* [*pfv.* **доби́ться**] (*with gen.*) **1,** to achieve; obtain; get. **2,** [*impfv. only*] to seek; strive for. —**добива́ться своего́,** to gain one's objective; get one's way.

добира́ться *v.r. impfv.* [*pfv.* **добра́ться**] (*with* до) *colloq.* **1,** to reach; get to. **2,** to get one's hands on (someone).

доби́ть [*infl.* -бью́, -бьёшь] *v., pfv. of* **добива́ть**. —**доби́ться,** *refl., pfv. of* **добива́ться**.

до́блестный *adj.* valiant; valorous.

до́блесть *n.f.* valor.

добра́сывать *v. impfv.* [*pfv.* **добро́сить**] (*with* до) to throw as far as.

добра́ться [*infl. like* **брать**] *v.r., pfv. of* **добира́ться**.

добра́чный *adj.* before one is/was married; premarital.

добрести́ *v.pfv.* [*infl. like* **брести́**] (*with* до) to manage to reach; finally make it to.

добре́ть *v. impfv.* **1,** [*pfv.* **подобре́ть**] to become kind; become kinder. **2,** [*pfv.* **раздобре́ть**] *colloq.* to get fat; put on weight.

добро́ *n.* **1,** good: добро́ и зло, good and evil. Жела́ть кому́-нибудь добра́, to wish someone well. **2,** *colloq.* goods; property. —*adv., colloq.* good; all right. —**дать добро́ на** (+ *acc.*), *colloq.* to give the go-ahead for. —**добро́ бы,** *colloq.* it would be all right if; it would be one thing if. —**добро́ пожа́ловать!,** welcome! —**э́то не к добру́,** it's a bad omen.

доброво́лец [*gen.* -льца] *n.* volunteer.

доброво́льный *adj.* voluntary. —**доброво́льно,** *adv.* voluntarily.

доброво́льческий *adj.* volunteer (*attrib.*).

доброде́тель *n.f.* virtue. —**доброде́тельный**, *adj.* virtuous.

добродушие *n.* good nature. —**добродушный**, *adj.* good-natured.

доброжелатель *n.m.* well-wisher. —**доброжелательный**, *adj.* good-natured; friendly. —**доброжелательство**, *n.* good will.

доброкачественный *adj.* 1, of good quality. 2, *med.* benign; non-malignant.

добром *adv.*, *colloq.* of one's own free will.

добросердечие *n.* kindheartedness. —**добросердечный**, *adj.* kindhearted; good-hearted.

добросить [*infl.* -шу, -сишь] *v.*, *pfv. of* **добрасывать**.

добросовестный *adj.* conscientious. —**добросовестность**, *n.f.* conscientiousness.

добрососедский *adj.* neighborly; good-neighbor.

доброта *n.* kindness.

добротный *adj.* of high quality; sound; durable.

добрый *adj.* [*short form* добр, добра, добро] 1, kind. 2, good: доброе дело, good deed; добрая воля, good will. 3, *in greetings* good: доброе утро!, good morning!; добрый вечер!, good evening! 4, *colloq.* a good; at least: добрый час, a good hour. —**будьте добры** (+*imperative*), be so kind as to... —**в добрый час!**, the best of luck (in your new venture)! —**всего доброго!**, all the best! —**чего доброго**, for all one knows.

добряк [*gen.* -бряка] *n.*, *colloq.* good-natured person; good soul.

добудиться *v.r.* *pfv.* [*infl.* -бужусь, -будишься] (*with gen.*) *colloq.* to succeed in waking.

добывать *v. impfv.* [*pfv.* **добыть**] 1, to obtain. 2, to extract; mine.

добыть [*infl. like* быть; *past* добыл *or* добыл, добыла, добыло *or* добыло] *v.*, *pfv. of* **добывать**.

добыча *n.* 1, extraction; mining. 2, anything mined from the earth. 3, booty; loot; plunder; spoils. 4, prey.

доваривать *v. impfv.* [*pfv.* **доварить**] to finish cooking; finish making.

доварить [*infl.* -варю, -варишь] *v.*, *pfv. of* **доваривать**.

довезти [*infl. like* везти] *v.*, *pfv. of* **довозить**.

доверенность *n.f.* power of attorney. —**по доверенности**, by proxy.

доверенный *adj.* authorized. —*n.* proxy; agent.

доверие *n.* confidence; trust.

доверительный *adj.* 1, trusting. 2, *obs.* secret; classified.

доверить *v.*, *pfv. of* **доверять**. —**довериться**, *refl.*, *pfv. of* **доверяться**.

доверху *adv.* to the top; to the brim. —**снизу доверху**, from top to bottom.

доверчивый *adj.* trusting. —**доверчивость**, *n.f.* trusting nature.

довершать *v. impfv.* [*pfv.* **довершить**] to complete.

довершение *n.* completion. —**в довершение всего**, to top it off.

довершить *v.*, *pfv. of* **довершать**.

доверять *v. impfv.* [*pfv.* **доверить**] 1, [*impfv. only*] (*with dat.*) to trust. 2, to entrust; confide. —**доверяться**, *refl.* (*with dat.*) to trust (in).

довесок [*gen.* -ска] *n.* makeweight.

довести [*infl. like* вести] *v.*, *pfv. of* **доводить**. —**довестись**, *refl.*, *pfv. of* **доводиться**.

довлеть *v. impfv.* 1, *obs.* to suffice. 2, (*with* над) to hold sway over (*a usage generally considered incorrect*).

довод *n.* argument: доводы за и против, the arguments for and against; the pros and cons.

доводить *v. impfv.* [*pfv.* довести; *pres.* -вожу, -водишь] (*with* до) 1, to take to; bring to; accompany to. 2, to drive; carry; reduce (*to a certain point or state*): доводить до отчаяния/крайности/нищеты, to drive to despair/carry to an extreme/reduce to poverty/. 3, to convey (news, information, etc.). —**доводить до конца**, to see through to the end. —**доводить до (чьего-нибудь) сведения**, *see* **сведение**.

доводиться *v.r impfv.* [*pfv.* довестись; *pres.* -вожусь, -водишься] 1, *impers.* (*with dat. and inf.*) *colloq.* to happen (to); have occasion (to): нам не довелось встретиться, we did not have occasion to meet. 2, [*impfv. only*] (*with dat. and instr.*) *colloq.* to be related in a certain way: он доводится мне дядей, he is my uncle.

довоенный *adj.* prewar.

довозить *v. impfv.* [*pfv.* довезти; *pres.* -вожу, -возишь] (*with* до) to take to; bring to.

довольно *adv.* 1, rather; fairly; pretty: довольно часто, fairly often. 2, enough: довольно кричать!, enough shouting! С меня довольно, I've had enough. 3, contentedly.

довольный *adj.* 1, [*short form* -лен, -льна, -льно] (*with instr.*) pleased (with); satisfied (with); contented (with). 2, contented: довольный вид, contented look.

довольствие *n.*, *mil.* allowance.

довольство *n.* 1, satisfaction; contentment. 2, *colloq.* comfortable circumstances.

довольствоваться *v.r. impfv.* [*pfv.* удовольствоваться; *pres.* -ствуюсь, -ствуешься] (*with instr.*) to be content (with); be satisfied (with).

дог *n.* mastiff. —**датский дог**, Great Dane.

догадаться *v.r.*, *pfv. of* **догадываться**.

догадка [*gen. pl.* -док] *n.* 1, guess; conjecture. 2, *pl.* guesswork. —**строить догадки**, to conjecture; speculate. —**теряться в догадках**, to be at a loss.

догадливый *adj.* bright; clever; quick-witted.

догадываться *v.r. impfv.* [*pfv.* догадаться] 1, to guess. 2, to figure out. 3, to have the good sense to.

догма *n.* dogma. —**догматизм**, *n.* dogmatism. —**догматик**, *n.* dogmatist. —**догматический**, *adj.* dogmatic.

догнать [*infl. like* гнать] *v.*, *pfv. of* **догонять**.

договаривать *v. impfv.* [*pfv.* договорить] to finish speaking; have one's say. —**договариваться**, *refl.* 1, to make arrangements: договорились!, it's all arranged/settled. 2, (*with inf.*) to agree (to); arrange (to). 3, (*with* до) to talk to some extreme: договориться до хрипоты, to talk oneself hoarse. Договариваться до того, что..., to go so far as to say.

договор *also*, **договор** *n.* 1, treaty. 2, contract. —**арендный договор**, lease.

договорённость *n.f.* agreement; understanding.

договорить *v.*, *pfv. of* **договаривать**. —**договориться**, *refl.*, *pfv. of* **договариваться**.

договорный *adj.* 1, treaty (*attrib.*). 2, contractual.

догола *adv.* (*with verbs of undressing*) naked; to the skin.

догонять *v. impfv.* [*pfv.* догнать] to overtake; catch up with.

догорать *v. impfv.* [*pfv.* догореть] to burn down; burn out.

додавать *v. impfv.* [*pfv.* додать; *pres.* -даю, -даёшь] to pay the remainder: он додáст вам дéсять рублéй, he will pay you the remaining ten rubles.

додáть [*infl. like* дать; *past* дóдал, додалá, дóдало] *v., pfv. of* **додавáть**.

додéлывать *v. impfv.* [*pfv.* **додéлать**] to finish; complete.

додýмываться *v.r. impfv.* [*pfv.* **додýматься**] (*with* до) to think of; hit upon; come up with (an idea, solution, etc.).

доедáть *v. impfv.* [*pfv.* **доéсть**] to finish eating; eat up.

доезжáть *v. impfv.* [*pfv.* **доéхать**] (*with* до) **1**, to reach; arrive at. **2**, to go/drive/ride as far as.

доéние *n.* milking.

доéсть [*infl. like* есть] *v., pfv. of* **доедáть**.

доéхать [*infl.* -éду, -éдешь] *v., pfv. of* **доезжáть**.

дож *n.* doge.

дождáться *v.r. pfv.* [*infl. like* ждать] **1**, to wait (*as long as necessary*): я не могý дождáться, I can't wait. **2**, (*with gen.*) to wait (*until someone comes or something happens*): дождáться врачá, to wait till the doctor comes. Я éле дождáлся вас, I almost didn't wait for you. Он не дождáлся нас, he did not wait for us; he left before we came. —**ждать не дождáться**, *colloq.* to anxiously await.

дождевáльный *adj.* sprinkling (*attrib.*); sprinkler (*attrib.*): дождевáльная устанóвка, sprinkler system.

дождевáние *n.* sprinkling (*of a lawn, crops, etc.*).

дождевúк [*gen.* -вика́] *n., colloq.* raincoat.

дождевóй *adj.* rain (*attrib.*): дождевáя водá, rain water.

дóждик *n.* light rain; shower.

дождлúвый *adj.* rainy.

дождь [*gen.* дождя́] *n.m.* rain. —**дождь идёт; идёт дождь**, it is raining.

доживáть *v. impfv.* [*pfv.* **дожúть**] **1**, (*with* до) to live to; live to see. **2**, [*impfv. only*] to live out: доживáть послéдние дни, to be living out one's last days; be nearing the end of one's life. **3**, *colloq.* to spend the rest of: дожúть лéто на дáче, to spend the rest of the summer in the country.

дожúть [*infl.* -живý, -живёшь; *past* дóжил, дожилá, дóжило] *v., pfv. of* **доживáть**.

дóза *n.* dose.

дозапрáвить [*infl.* -влю, -вишь] *v., pfv. of* **дозаправля́ть**. —**дозапрáвиться**, *refl., pfv. of* **дозаправля́ться**.

дозапрáвка *n.* refueling.

дозаправля́ть *v. impfv.* [*pfv.* **дозапрáвить**] to refuel. —**дозаправля́ться**, *refl.* (*of a plane*) to refuel.

дозвáться *v.r. pfv.* [*infl. like* звать] (*with gen.*) *colloq.* (*usu. neg.*) to reach on the telephone: егó никáк не дозовёшься, you can't reach/get him on the phone.

дозвóленный *adj.* permitted; permissible.

дозволя́ть *v. impfv.* [*pfv.* **дозвóлить**] *obs.* to permit; allow.

дозвонúться *v.r. pfv.* (*with* к) *colloq.* to ring until one receives an answer; reach (*by telephone*).

дозвуковóй *adj.* subsonic.

дозирóвка *n.* dosage.

дознавáться *v.r. impfv.* [*pfv.* **дознáться**; *pres.* -знаю́сь, -знаёшься] *colloq.* **1**, to find out. **2**, [*impfv. only*] to inquire.

дознáние *n., law* inquest; inquiry.

дознáться *v.r., pfv. of* **дознавáться**.

дозóр *n.* patrol. —**дозóрный**, *adj.* patrol (*attrib.*).

дозревáть *v. impfv.* [*pfv.* **дозрéть**] to become fully ripe.

доúгрывать *v. impfv.* [*pfv.* **доигрáть**] to finish playing; play to the end.

доúльный *adj.* used for milking: доúльная машúна, milking machine.

доискáться [*infl.* -ищýсь, -úщешься] *v.r., pfv. of* **доúскиваться**.

доúскиваться *v.r. impfv.* [*pfv.* **доискáться**] (*with gen.*) *colloq.* **1**, to try to find; search for (*something*) until it is found. **2**, to inquire into; try to find out; seek.

доисторúческий *adj.* prehistoric.

доúть *v. impfv.* [*pfv.* **подоúть**; *pres.* дою́, дóишь *or* доúшь] to milk. —**доúться**, *refl.* [*impfv. only*] to give milk.

дóйка *n.* milking.

дóйный *adj.* milch.

дойтú [*infl.* дойдý, дойдёшь; *past* дошёл, дошлá, дошлó] *v., pfv. of* **доходúть**.

док *n.* dock.

доказáтельный *adj.* demonstrative; conclusive.

доказáтельство *n.* proof; evidence.

доказáть [*infl.* -кажý, -кáжешь] *v., pfv. of* **доказывать**.

доказýемый *adj.* demonstrable.

докáзывать *v. impfv.* [*pfv.* **доказáть**] **1**, to prove. **2**, [*impfv. only*] to try to prove; argue.

докáнчивать *v. impfv.* [*pfv.* **докóнчить**] **1**, to finish. **2**, *colloq.* to finish off (*i.e. eating or drinking*).

докáпывать *v. impfv.* [*pfv.* **докопáть**] to finish digging. —**докáпываться**, *refl.* (*with* до) **1**, to dig as far as. **2**, *fig., colloq.* to get to: докопáться до úстины, to get to the truth.

докатúться [*infl.* -качýсь, -кáтишься] *v.r., pfv. of* **докáтываться**.

докáтываться *v.r. impfv.* [*pfv.* **докатúться**] **1**, (*with* до) to roll to; roll as far as. **2**, *colloq.* (*of loud noises*) to thunder; resound. **3**, (*with* до) *fig., colloq.* to sink to.

дóкер *n.* dock worker; longshoreman.

доклáд *n.* **1**, report. **2**, lecture; paper. **3**, announcement (*of a visitor*): входúть без доклáда, to walk in unannounced.

докладнóй *adj., in* докладнáя запúска, report; memorandum.

доклáдчик *n.* person delivering a report; speaker.

доклáдывать *v. impfv.* [*pfv.* **доложúть**] **1**, to report. **2**, (*with* о) to announce (*a visitor*). **3**, *colloq.* to add.

докóле *adv., obs.* **1**, how long? **2**, as long as.

доконáть *v. pfv., colloq.* to finish; be the end of.

докóнчить *v., pfv. of* **докáнчивать**.

докопáть *v., pfv. of* **докáпывать**. —**докопáться**, *refl., pfv. of* **докáпываться**.

докраснá *also*, **дóкраснá** *adv.* **1**, until something is red. **2**, *in* раскаля́ть докраснá, to make red-hot; раскалённый докраснá, red-hot.

докричáться *v.r. pfv.* [*infl.* -чýсь, -чúшься] **1**, *colloq.* to shout until one is heard. **2**, (*with* до) to shout to some extreme: докричáться до хрипоты́, to shout oneself hoarse.

дóктор [*pl.* докторá] *n.* **1**, doctor (*holder of a doctoral degree*): дóктор наýк, Doctor of Science; Ph.D. **2**, *colloq.* doctor; physician. —**дóкторский**, *adj.* doctor's; doctoral.

доктри́на *n.* doctrine. —**доктринёрский**, *adj.* doctrinaire.

докуме́нт *n.* document. —**документа́льный**, *adj.* documentary. —**документа́ция**, *n.* documentation.

документи́ровать *v. impfv. & pfv.* [*pres.* -ру́ю, -ру́ешь] to document.

докупа́ть *v. impfv.* [*pfv.* **докупи́ть**] to buy in addition.

докупи́ть [*infl.* -куплю́, -ку́пишь] *v., pfv. of* **докупа́ть**.

доку́ривать *v. impfv.* [*pfv.* **докури́ть**] to finish smoking.

докури́ть [*infl.* -курю́, -ку́ришь] *v., pfv. of* **доку́ривать**.

докуча́ть *v. impfv.* (*with dat.*) *colloq.* to bother; annoy; pester.

доку́чливый *adj., colloq.* annoying; bothersome.

дол *n., poetic* valley; vale; dale.

долби́ть *v. impfv.* [*pres.* -блю́, -би́шь] **1**, [*pfv.* **продолби́ть**] to gouge; hollow out. **2**, *colloq.* to bang (*repeatedly*). **3**, *colloq.* to memorize; learn by rote.

долг *n.* **1**, duty. **2**, [*2nd loc.* долгу́; *pl.* долги́] debt. —**в долгу́ пе́ред** *or* **у**, indebted to; in someone's debt. —**брать в долг**, to borrow. —**дава́ть в долг**, to lend. —**долг платежо́м кра́сен**, one good turn deserves another. —**не остава́ться в долгу́**, to reply in kind; (one was) not to be outdone. —**отда́ть после́дний долг** (+ *dat.*), to pay one's last respects to. —**по до́лгу слу́жбы**, in one's official capacity.

до́лгий *adj.* [*comp.* **до́льше** and **до́лее**] long (*in time*). —**до́лгие го́ды**, many long years.

до́лго *adv.* long; (for) a long time. —**как до́лго?**, how long?

долгове́чный *adj.* long-lasting; long-lived. —**долгове́чность**, *n.f.* longevity.

долгово́й *adj.* of or for a debt. —**долгово́е обяза́тельство**, promissory note. —**долгова́я тюрьма́**; **долгова́я я́ма**, debtor's prison.

долговре́менный *adj.* of long duration; lasting a long time.

долговя́зый *adj., colloq.* lanky; gangling.

долгожда́нный *adj.* long-awaited.

долгоигра́ющий *adj., in* **долгоигра́ющая пласти́нка**, long-playing record.

долголе́тие *n.* longevity. —**долголе́тний**, *adj.* of many years.

долгоно́жка [*gen. pl.* -жек] *n.* crane fly.

долгоно́сик *n.* weevil. —**хло́пковый долгоно́сик**, boll weevil.

долгосро́чный *adj.* long-term.

долгота́ *n.* **1**, length: долгота́ дня, the length of a day. **2**, [*pl.* -го́ты] longitude.

до́лее *adj., comp. of* **до́лгий**. —*adv., comp. of* **до́лго**.

долеза́ть *v. impfv.* [*pfv.* **доле́зть**] (*with* **до**) **1**, to climb as far as. **2**, to reach by climbing.

доле́зть [*infl. like* **лезть**] *v., pfv. of* **долеза́ть**.

долета́ть *v. impfv.* [*pfv.* **долете́ть**] (*with* **до**) **1**, to fly as far as. **2**, to reach by flying. **3**, (*of sounds, news, etc.*) to reach.

долете́ть [*infl.* -чу́, -ти́шь] *v., pfv. of* **долета́ть**.

до́лжен *adj., used predicatively* [*fem.* -жна́; *neut.* -жно́; *pl.* -жны́] **1**, must; have to: я до́лжен (должна́) идти́, I must go. **2**, should; ought to: она́ должна́ ско́ро прийти́, she should be here soon. **3**, due to; supposed to; scheduled to: по́езд до́лжен прибы́ть в семь часо́в, the train is due/scheduled to arrive at

seven o'clock. **4**, to owe: он мне до́лжен два рубля́, he owes me two rubles. —**должно́ быть**, probably; must: он, должно́ быть, уже́ ушёл, he must have left already.

должни́к [*gen.* -ника́] *n.* debtor.

до́лжное *n., decl. as an adj.* one's due. —**отдава́ть/воздава́ть до́лжное** (+ *dat.*), to give someone his/her due; give someone credit. —**принима́ть как до́лжное**, to take as a matter of course; take for granted.

должностно́й *adj.* official. —**должностно́е лицо́**, official; officeholder. —**должностно́е преступле́ние**, malfeasance in office.

до́лжность [*pl.* до́лжности, -сте́й, -стя́м] *n.f.* post; position; office.

до́лжный *adj.* due; proper. —**до́лжным о́бразом**, properly. *See also* **до́лжное**.

долива́ть *v. impfv.* [*pfv.* **доли́ть**] **1**, to fill (*by pouring*). **2**, (*with gen.*) to pour more (of).

доли́на *n.* valley.

доли́ть [*infl.* долью́, дольёшь; *past* до́лил *or* доли́л, долила́, до́лило *or* доли́ло *v., pfv. of* **долива́ть**.

до́ллар *n.* dollar. —**до́лларовый**, *adj.* dollar (*attrib.*).

доложи́ть [*infl.* -ложу́, -ло́жишь] *v., pfv. of* **докла́дывать**.

доло́й *adv.* **1**, (*with acc.*) down with...! **2**, off: ша́пки доло́й!, hats off! —**с глаз мои́х доло́й!**, out of my sight! —**с плеч доло́й**, (a load) off one's shoulders.

доломи́т *n.* dolomite.

долото́ [*pl.* доло́та] *n.* chisel.

до́лька [*gen. pl.* -лек] *n.* **1**, lobule. **2**, section (*of a citrus fruit*).

до́льше *adj., comp. of* **до́лгий**. —*adv., comp. of* **до́лго**.

до́ля [*pl.* до́ли, доле́й, доля́м] *n.* **1**, share; portion. **2**, lot: вы́пасть на до́лю (+ *dat.*), to fall to someone's lot. **3**, *anat.* lobe. **4**, *in* до́ля и́стины, grain of truth. —**войти́ в до́лю с** (+ *instr.*), to go shares with.

дом [*pl.* дома́] *n.* **1**, house; home. **2**, building. —**из до́ма**, from home. —**из дому**, out of the house. —**на́ дом**, to one's home. —**на дому́**, at home (*as opposed to one's place of work*). *See also* **до́ма** and **домо́й**.

до́ма *adv.* at home. —**бу́дьте как до́ма**, make yourself at home. —**у него́ не все до́ма**, he is not all there.

дома́шние *n.pl., decl. as an adj.* members of one's family.

дома́шний *adj.* **1**, home (*attrib.*); house (*attrib.*); household (*attrib.*). **2**, domestic. **3**, homemade; (*of a meal*) home-cooked. —**дома́шнее зада́ние**, homework. —**дома́шняя пти́ца**, poultry. —**дома́шняя хозя́йка**, housewife. —**дома́шнее хозя́йство**, housekeeping.

до́менный *adj., in* до́менная печь, blast furnace.

до́мик *n.* small house; cottage.

доминио́н *n.* dominion.

домини́ровать *v. impfv.* [*pres.* -ру́ю, -ру́ешь] **1**, (*of a thought, idea, etc.*) to be (pre)dominant. **2**, (*with* над) to dominate; tower over.

домини́рующий *adj.* dominant.

домино́ *n. indecl.* **1**, domino (*costume*). **2**, dominoes (*game*).

доми́шко [*pl.* -шки, -шек] *n.m.* **1**, tiny house. **2**, shack; hovel.

домкра́т *n.* jack (*for lifting*).

до́мна [*gen. pl.* -мен] *n.* blast furnace.

домови́тый *adj.* **1,** thrifty; economical. **2,** capable; efficient.

домовладе́лец [*gen.* **-льца**] *n.* homeowner.

домово́дство *n.* **1,** housekeeping. **2,** home economics.

домово́й *n., decl. as an adj.* elf; goblin.

домо́вый *adj.* house (*attrib.*). —**домо́вая кни́га,** register of tenants.

домога́тельство *n.* solicitation; *pl.* overtures.

домога́ться *v.r. impfv.* (*with gen.*) to seek; strive to obtain.

домо́й *adv.* home: идти́ домо́й, to go home.

доморо́щенный *adj.* **1,** homebred. **2,** *fig.* homespun; half-baked.

домосе́д *n.* stay-at-home; homebody.

домотка́ный *adj.* homespun.

домоуправле́ние *n.* **1,** building management. **2,** *colloq.* building manager's office.

домохозя́йка [*gen. pl.* **-я́ек**] *n.* housewife.

домоча́дцы [*gen.* **-цев**] *n. pl., obs.* household.

до́мра *n.* old Russian musical instrument resembling a mandolin.

домрабо́тница *n.* maid; housemaid.

домча́ть *v. pfv.* [*infl.* **-чу́, -чи́шь**] *colloq.* to deliver in a hurry; rush; whisk. —**домча́ться,** *refl.* (*with* **до**) *colloq.* to race to; rush to; dash to.

до́мысел [*gen.* **-сла**] *n.* conjecture; supposition.

донага́ *adv., colloq.* (*with verbs of undressing*) naked; to the skin.

дона́шивать *v. impfv.* [*pfv.* **доноси́ть**] **1,** to wear out. **2,** to carry (a baby) to full term.

доне́льзя *adv., colloq.* completely; utterly: доне́льзя уста́л, utterly exhausted.

донесе́ние *n.* message; dispatch.

донести́ [*infl. like* **нести́**] *v., pfv. of* **доноси́ть**[1]. —**донести́сь,** *refl., pfv. of* **доноси́ться.**

до́низу *adv.* to the bottom. —**све́рху до́низу,** from top to bottom.

донима́ть *v. impfv.* [*pfv.* **доня́ть**] *colloq.* to exasperate.

донкихо́тский *adj.* quixotic.

до́нор *n.* blood donor.

доно́с *n.* denunciation; accusation; report to the authorities.

доноси́ть[1] *v. impfv.* [*pfv.* **донести́**; *pres.* **-ношу́, -но́сишь**] **1,** (*with* **до**) to carry to; deliver to. **2,** to report. **3,** (*with* **на** + *acc.*) to report; inform against; squeal on. —**доноси́ться,** *refl.* **1,** to be heard; be sensed. **2,** (*with* **до**) to reach.

доноси́ть[2] [*infl.* **-ношу́, -но́сишь**] *v., pfv. of* **дона́шивать.**

доно́счик *n.* informer; stool pigeon.

донско́й *adj.* of the Don River. —**донско́й каза́к,** Don Cossack.

доны́не *adv., poetic* to this day.

доня́ть [*infl. like* **поня́ть**] *v., pfv. of* **донима́ть.**

допека́ть *v. impfv.* [*pfv.* **допе́чь**] **1,** to finish baking. **2,** *colloq.* to plague.

допе́чь [*infl. like* **пе́чь**] *v., pfv. of* **допека́ть.**

допива́ть *v. impfv.* [*pfv.* **допи́ть**] to drink (up); finish drinking. —**допива́ться,** *refl.* (*with* **до**) *colloq.* to drink oneself into a state of.

дописа́ть [*infl.* **-пишу́, -пи́шешь**] *v., pfv. of* **допи́сывать.**

допи́сывать *v. impfv.* [*pfv.* **дописа́ть**] **1,** to finish writing. **2,** (*with* **до**) to write as far as. **3,** to write additionally; add (*by writing*).

допи́ть [*infl.* **-пью́, -пьёшь;** *past* **до́пил** *or* **допи́л, допила́, до́пило** *or* **допи́ло**] *v., pfv. of* **допива́ть.** —**допи́ться,** *refl.* [*past* **допи́лся** *or* **допился́, допила́сь, допи́лось** *or* **допило́сь**] *pfv. of* **допива́ться.**

допла́та *n.* additional charge; surcharge.

доплати́ть [*infl.* **-плачу́, -пла́тишь**] *v., pfv. of* **допла́чивать.**

допла́чивать *v. impfv.* [*pfv.* **доплати́ть**] **1,** to pay in addition; pay the remainder: доплати́ть два рубля́, to pay an additional (*or* the remaining) two rubles. **2,** to pay in full.

доплести́сь [*infl. like* **плести́**] *v.r., pfv. of* **доплета́ться.**

доплета́ться *v.r. impfv.* [*pfv.* **доплести́сь**] (*with* **до**) *colloq.* to drag oneself (to).

доплыва́ть *v. impfv.* [*pfv.* **доплы́ть**] (*with* **до**) to swim as far as.

доплы́ть [*infl. like* **плы́ть**] *v., pfv. of* **доплыва́ть.**

допо́длинный *adj., colloq.* true; authentic. —**допо́длинно,** *adv., colloq.* for certain.

допоздна́ *adv., colloq.* till late at night.

доползáть *v. impfv.* [*pfv.* **доползти́**] (*with* **до**) to crawl up to; crawl as far as.

доползти́ [*infl. like* **ползти́**] *v., pfv. of* **доползáть.**

дополна́ *adv., colloq.* to the brim.

дополне́ние *n.* **1,** addition. **2,** supplement. **3,** *gram.* object. —**в дополне́ние к,** in addition to.

дополни́тельно *adv.* in addition.

дополни́тельный *adj.* **1,** additional; supplementary. **2,** (*of colors*) complementary. —**дополни́тельное вре́мя,** *sports* overtime.

дополня́ть *v. impfv.* [*pfv.* **допо́лнить**] to enlarge; expand; supplement; amplify; add to. —**дополня́ть друг дру́га,** to complement each other.

дополуча́ть *v. impfv.* [*pfv.* **дополучи́ть**] to receive in addition; receive the remainder.

дополучи́ть [*infl.* **-лучу́, -лу́чишь**] *v., pfv. of* **дополуча́ть.**

допото́пный *adj.* antediluvian.

допра́шивать *v. impfv.* [*pfv.* **допроси́ть**] to interrogate; question.

допро́с *n.* interrogation; questioning.

допроси́ть [*infl.* **-прошу́, -про́сишь**] *v., pfv. of* **допра́шивать.**

до́пуск *n.* **1,** admission; admittance. **2,** *mech.* tolerance.

допуска́ть *v. impfv.* [*pfv.* **допусти́ть**] **1,** to admit; let in. **2,** to allow; permit; tolerate. **3,** to commit (an error, indiscretion, etc.). **4,** to assume. **5,** to grant; concede.

допусти́мый *adj.* **1,** permissible. **2,** conceivable; possible.

допусти́ть [*infl.* **-пущу́, -пу́стишь**] *v., pfv. of* **допуска́ть.** —**допу́стим,** let us assume.

допуще́ние *n.* **1,** admission. **2,** assumption.

допы́тываться *v.r. impfv.* [*pfv.* **допыта́ться**] *colloq.* **1,** to find out. **2,** [*impfv. only*] to try to find out.

допьяна́ *also,* **до́пьяна** *adv., colloq.* till one is completely drunk.

дораба́тывать *v. impfv.* [*pfv.* **дорабо́тать**] **1,** *v.t.* to finish; put the finishing touches on. **2,** *v.i.* (*with* **до**) to work until. —**дораба́тываться,** *refl.* (*with* **до**) *colloq.* to work to some extreme: дорабо́таться до изнеможе́ния, to work to the point of exhaustion.

дорастáть v. impfv. [pfv. **дорастú**] (with до) **1**, to grow to (a certain height). **2**, to reach the age of. **3**, (with не) not be old enough: он ещё не дорóс, чтобы (+ inf.), he is not old enough to...

дорастú [infl. like растú] v., pfv. of **дорастáть**.

дореволюциóнный adj. prerevolutionary.

дорóга n. **1**, road. **2**, way. **3**, trip: устáть с дорóги, to be tired from the trip. —**по** (or **в**) **дорóге**, on the way; en route. —**дать дорóгу** (+ dat.), to make way for. —**идтú своéй дорóгой**, to go one's own way. —**стать поперёк дорóги** (+ dat.), to stand in someone's way. —**тудá емý и дорóга**, it serves him right.

дóрого adv. **1**, a lot (of money): заплатúть/брать дóрого, to pay/charge a lot of money. **2**, dearly: это емý дóрого обошлóсь, it cost him dearly. —adj., used predicatively **1**, expensive: это не дóрого, that's not expensive. **2**, dear; precious: врéмя бы́ло дóрого, time was precious.

дороговúзна n. **1**, high prices. **2**, (with gen.) the high cost of.

дорогóй adj. [short form **дóрог, дорогá, дóрого**; comp. **дорóже**] **1**, dear: дорогóй друг, a dear friend. **2**, expensive. **3**, (of a price) high. **4**, precious. —n. dear; my dear.

дорогостóящий adj. high-priced; expensive; costly.

дорóдный adj. stout; corpulent. —**дорóдность**; дорóдство, n. corpulence.

дорожáть v. impfv. [pfv. **вздорожáть** or **подорожáть**] to go up in price; become more expensive.

дорóже adj., comp. of **дорогóй**.

дорожúть v. impfv. (with instr.) to value; prize; treasure.

дорóжка [gen. pl. -жек] n. **1**, path; walk. **2**, track: беговáя дорóжка, running track. **3**, lane (on a running track). **4**, strip of carpet. —**звуковáя дорóжка**, sound track. —**лётная дорóжка**, runway.

дорóжный adj. **1**, road (attrib.): дорóжный знак, road sign. **2**, travel (attrib.); traveling (attrib.).

дортуáр n., obs. dormitory.

досáда n. annoyance; vexation. —**какáя досáда!**, how annoying!

досадúть [infl. -жý, -дúшь] v., pfv. of **досаждáть**.

досáдливый adj. expressing annoyance; of annoyance.

досáдный adj. **1**, annoying; maddening. **2**, regrettable. —**досáдно**, adj., used predicatively annoying: как досáдно!, how annoying!

досáдовать v. impfv. [pres. -дую, -дуешь] (with на + acc.) to be annoyed (with).

досаждáть v. impfv. [pfv. **досадúть**] (with dat.) to annoy; vex.

досидéть [infl. -жý, -дúшь] v., pfv. of **досúживать**.

досúживать v. impfv. [pfv. **досидéть**] (with до) to sit (until); stay (until).

доскá [acc. дóску; pl. дóски, досóк, доскáм] n. **1**, board. **2**, blackboard. **3**, plaque. —**от доскú до доскú**, from cover to cover. —**стáвить на однý дóску**, to equate; place on a par.

досказáть v. pfv. [infl. -скажý, -скáжешь] **1**, to finish telling. **2**, (with до) to tell as far as.

досконáльный adj. thorough. —**досконáльно**, adv. thoroughly. —**досконáльность**, n.f. thoroughness.

дослóвный adj. literal; verbatim. —**дослóвно**, adv. literally; verbatim; word for word.

дослýживать v. impfv. [pfv. **дослужúть**] (with до

to serve (until). —**дослýживаться**, refl. (with до) to serve (until one reaches a certain rank): дослужúться до майóра, to rise to the rank of major.

дослужúть [infl. -служý, -слýжишь] v., pfv. of **дослýживать**. —**дослужúться**, refl., pfv. of **дослýживаться**.

дослýшать v. pfv. to listen (to something) till the end.

досмáтривать v. impfv. [pfv. **досмотрéть**] **1**, to watch to the end. **2**, to watch (until): досмотрéть пьéсу до трéтьего дéйствия, to watch a play till the third act.

досмóтр n. examination; inspection: тамóженный досмóтр, customs inspection.

досмотрéть [infl. -смотрю́, -смóтришь] v., pfv. of **досмáтривать**.

досмóтрщик n. customs inspector.

доспáть [infl. like спать] v., pfv. of **досыпáть**.

доспевáть v. impfv. [pfv. **доспéть**] to become fully ripe.

доспéхи [gen. -хов] n. pl. armor.

досрóчно adv. ahead of schedule. —**досрóчный**, adj. ahead of schedule; early.

доставáть v. impfv. [pfv. **достáть**; pres. -стаю́, -стаёшь] **1**, (with до) to reach; be able to touch. **2**, to take (from a certain place): достáть кнúгу с пóлки, to take a book from the shelf. **3**, to obtain; get. **4**, impers. (with gen.) colloq. to suffice: дéнег у нас достáнет, we have enough money. —**доставáться**, refl., impers. (with dat.) **1**, to pass into the possession of. **2**, to fall one's lot. **3**, colloq. to get it; catch it; catch hell.

достáвить [infl. -влю, -вишь] v., pfv. of **доставля́ть**.

достáвка n. delivery.

доставля́ть v. impfv. [pfv. **достáвить**] **1**, to deliver. **2**, to give; provide; afford (pleasure, an opportunity, etc.). **3**, to give; cause (trouble, anxiety, etc.).

достáток [gen. -тка] n. **1**, circumstances; means: лю́ди срéднего достáтка, people of moderate means. **2**, comfortable circumstances. **3**, colloq. sufficiency; plenty. **4**, pl., colloq. income.

достáточно adv. enough; sufficiently: достáточно ширóкий, wide enough. —adj. **1**, (with gen.) enough; sufficient: достáточно сил, enough strength. **2**, (with inf.) it is sufficient to: достáточно сказáть, suffice it to say. —interj. enough!

достáточность n.f. sufficiency.

достáточный adj. sufficient; ample.

достáть [infl. -стáну, -стáнешь] v., pfv. of доставáть. —**достáться**, refl., pfv. of доставáться.

достигáть v. impfv. [pfv. **достúгнуть** or **достúчь**] (with gen.) **1**, to reach. **2**, to achieve; attain.

достúгнуть [past -стúг, -ла] v., pfv. of **достигáть**.

достижéние n. achievement.

достижúмый adj. attainable.

достúчь [infl. like достúгнуть] v., pfv. of достигáть.

достовéрно adv. for certain; for sure.

достовéрность n.f. **1**, reliability. **2**, authenticity.

достовéрный adj. (of information or a source) reliable.

достóинство n. **1**, dignity. **2**, merit; virtue; advantage. **3**, value; denomination (of a bill or coin). —**оценúть по достóинству**, see **оцéнивать**.

достóйно adv. **1**, in a worthy or fitting manner. **2**, obs. with dignity.

достóйный adj. [short form -стóин, -стóйна] **1**, (with

достопримеча́тельность *n.f.* sight; point of interest.

достопримеча́тельный *adj.* noteworthy.

достоя́ние *n.* **1,** property. **2,** *fig.* common property: стать достоя́нием наро́да, to become the common property of the people.

достра́ивать *v. impfv.* [*pfv.* **достро́ить**] to finish building.

до́ступ *n.* access.

досту́пность *n.f.* **1,** accessibility. **2,** availability.

досту́пный *adj.* **1,** accessible. **2,** (*of a person*) approachable. **3,** available. **4,** easily understood; understandable. **5,** (*of prices*) moderate; reasonable.

достуча́ться *v.r. pfv.* [*infl.* -чу́сь, -чи́шься] *colloq.* to knock until someone answers.

досу́г *n.* leisure. —**на досу́ге**, in one's spare time.

досу́жий *adj., colloq.* **1,** (*of time*) leisure. **2,** idle.

до́суха *adv.* dry; until thoroughly dry.

досыпа́ть *v. impfv.* [*pfv.* **доспа́ть**] *colloq.* **1,** to get enough sleep. **2,** (*with* до) to sleep until. **3,** to sleep through.

до́сыта *also,* **досы́та** *adv.* **1,** one's fill: нае́сться до́сыта, to eat one's fill. **2,** to one's heart's content.

досье́ *n. neut. indecl.* dossier.

досю́да *adv., colloq.* up to here; up to this point.

досяга́емость *n.f.* range; reach: вне досяга́емости, out of range.

дот *n.* pillbox (*abbr. of* долговре́менная огнева́я то́чка).

дота́скивать *v. impfv.* [*pfv.* **дотащи́ть**] (*with* до) to drag to; drag as far as. —**дота́скиваться**, *refl.* (*with* до) *colloq.* to drag oneself to.

дота́ция *n.* subsidy; grant.

дотащи́ть [*infl.* -тащу́, -та́щишь] *v., pfv. of* **дота́скивать**. —**дотащи́ться**, *refl., pfv. of* **дота́скиваться**.

дотемна́ *adv.* until dark; until nightfall.

дотла́ *adv.* to the ground: сгоре́ть дотла́, to burn to the ground.

дото́ле *adv., obs.* hitherto.

дото́шный *adj., colloq.* meticulous.

дотра́гиваться *v.r. impfv.* [*pfv.* **дотро́нуться**] (*with* до) to touch.

дотя́гивать *v. impfv.* [*pfv.* **дотяну́ть**] (*with* до) **1,** to drag as far as. **2,** to stretch as far as. **3,** *colloq.* to bring in (a disabled ship, aircraft, etc.). **4,** *colloq.* to make it to (a place). **5,** *colloq.* to live until; hold out until. —**дотя́гиваться**, *refl.* (*with* до) **1,** to reach; be able to touch. **2,** *colloq.* to stretch; extend (as far as). **3,** *colloq.* to make it (to a place).

дотяну́ть [*infl.* -тяну́, -тя́нешь] *v., pfv. of* **дотя́гивать.** —**дотяну́ться**, *refl., pfv. of* **дотя́гиваться.**

доу́чивать *v. impfv.* [*pfv.* **доучи́ть**] **1,** to finish teaching; (*with* до) teach up to. **2,** to finish learning; (*with* до) learn up to. —**доу́чиваться**, *refl.* **1,** to finish one's studies. **2,** (*with* до) to study up to a certain point: доучи́ться до восьмо́го кла́сса, to go through the eighth grade.

доучи́ть [*infl.* -учу́, -у́чишь] *v., pfv. of* **доу́чивать.** —**доучи́ться**, *refl., pfv. of* **доу́чиваться.**

дофи́н *n.* dauphin.

доха́ [*pl.* до́хи] *n.* heavy fur coat (*with fur both outside and inside*).

до́хлый *adj.* **1,** (*of animals, insects, fish, etc.*) dead. **2,** *colloq.* sickly.

дохля́тина *n., colloq.* carrion.

до́хнуть *v. impfv.* [*pfv.* **подо́хнуть**; *past* дох *or* до́хнул, до́хла] (*of animals*) to die.

дохну́ть *v. pfv.* to breathe; take a breath.

дохо́д *n.* income; revenue.

доходи́ть *v. impfv.* [*pfv.* **дойти́**; *pres.* -хожу́, -хо́дишь] (*with* до) **1,** to walk as far as. **2,** to reach. **3,** *colloq.* (*of a speech, play, etc.*) to come across (to). **4,** to reach the point of: дойти́ до отча́яния, to be on the point of despair; become desperate. Де́ло дошло́ до того́, что..., things got to the point where... —**дойти́ свои́м умо́м**, to figure it out by oneself. —**ру́ки не дохо́дят**, there is no time.

дохо́дный *adj.* lucrative; profitable; remunerative.

дохо́дчивый *adj.* lucid; easy to understand.

доце́нт *n.* associate professor.

доче́рний *adj.* **1,** one's daughter's. **2,** filial.

до́чиста *adv.* clean; till something is spotless. —**всё до́чиста**, absolutely everything; so that nothing is left.

дочи́тывать *v. impfv.* [*pfv.* **дочита́ть**] **1,** to finish reading. **2,** (*with* до) to read as far as.

до́чка [*gen. pl.* -чек] *n., dim. of* **дочь.**

дочь [*gen., dat., & prepl.* до́чери; *instr.* до́черью; *pl.* до́чери, -ре́й, -ря́м, -рьми́, -ря́х] *n.f.* daughter.

дошко́льник *n.* child of preschool age. —**дошко́льный**, *adj.* preschool.

до́шлый *adj., colloq.* clever; shrewd.

доща́тый *adj.* made of boards or planks.

доще́чка [*gen. pl.* -чек] *n.* **1,** small board. **2,** nameplate; plaque.

доя́рка [*gen. pl.* -рок] *n.* milkmaid.

дра́га *n.* dredge.

драгоце́нность *n.f.* **1,** jewel; gem. **2,** *pl.* jewelry. **3,** *pl.* valuables.

драгоце́нный *adj.* precious. —**драгоце́нный ка́мень**, **1,** precious stone; gemstone. **2,** jewel; gem.

драгу́н [*gen. pl.* -гу́н] *n.* dragoon.

драже́ *n. neut. indecl.* drops (*candy*).

дразни́ть *v. impfv.* [*pres.* дразню́, дра́знишь] **1,** to tease. **2,** to whet; arouse (one's appetite, curiosity, etc.).

дра́ить *v. impfv.* to scrub; swab.

дра́ка *n.* fight: затея́ть дра́ку, to start a fight. —**дойти́ до дра́ки**, to come to blows.

драко́н *n.* dragon.

драко́новский *adj.* draconian: драко́новские ме́ры, draconian measures.

дра́ма *n.* **1,** drama. **2,** *fig.* tragedy; calamity.

драматизи́ровать *v. impfv. & pfv.* [*pres.* -рую, -руешь] to dramatize.

драмати́зм *n.* dramatic effect; drama.

драмати́ческий *adj.* dramatic.

драмату́рг *n.* playwright.

драматурги́я *n.* **1,** dramaturgy. **2,** plays; works.

драмкружо́к [*gen.* -жка́] *n.* dramatic circle (*contr. of* драмати́ческий кружо́к).

драндуле́т *n., colloq.* jalopy.

дра́нка [*gen. pl.* -нок] *n.* **1,** lath. **2,** shingle.

дра́ный *adj., colloq.* ragged; tattered.

драп *n.* heavy woolen cloth.

драпирова́ть *v. impfv.* [*pfv.* **задрапирова́ть**; *pres.* -ру́ю, -ру́ешь] to drape.

драпиро́вка [*gen. pl.* -вок] *n.* drapery.

драпиро́вщик *n.* upholsterer.

дра́повый *adj.* made of heavy woolen cloth.

драть *v. impfv.* [*pres.* деру́, дерёшь; *past fem.* драла́] **1,** *colloq.* to tear to pieces. **2,** to strip off. **3,** [*pfv.* вы́драть] to whip; thrash; flog. **4,** [*pfv.* содра́ть] *colloq.* to charge (an exorbitant price): драть вдво́е доро́же, чем..., to charge twice as much as. —дра́ться, *refl.* to fight.

дра́хма *n.* drachma (*monetary unit of Greece*).

драчли́вый *adj.* pugnacious; combative. —драчли́вость, *n.f.* pugnacity.

драчу́н [*gen.* -чуна́] *n., colloq.* scrapper; brawler.

дребеде́нь *n.f., colloq.* **1,** nonsense. **2,** junk.

дребезжа́ние *n.* rattling; rattle.

дребезжа́ть *v. impfv.* [*pres.* -жи́т] **1,** to rattle. **2,** to jingle.

древеси́на *n.* **1,** wood. **2,** timber.

древе́сница *n.* tree frog.

древе́сный *adj.* **1,** arboreal. **2,** wood (*attrib.*). —древе́сная ма́сса, wood pulp. —древе́сный спирт, wood alcohol. —древе́сный у́голь, charcoal.

дре́вко [*pl.* -вки, -вков] *n.* **1,** pole; staff (*for a flag or banner*). **2,** shaft (*of a spear*).

древнеангли́йский *adj.* Old English.

древнегре́ческий *adj.* ancient Greek.

древнееврейский *adj.* Hebrew.

древнеру́сский *adj.* Old Russian.

дре́вний *adj.* ancient. —дре́вние, *n. pl.* the ancients.

дре́вность *n.f.* **1,** antiquity; ancient times. **2,** *pl.* antiquities.

дре́во [*pl.* древеса́, -ве́с, -веса́м] *n., archaic & poetic* tree.

дредно́ут *n.* dreadnought.

дрези́на *n., R.R.* handcar.

дрейф *n., naut.* drift.

дрейфова́ть *v. impfv.* [*pres.* -фу́ет] *naut.* to drift.

дрель *n.f.* drill (*tool*).

дрема́ть *v. impfv.* [*pres.* дремлю́, дре́млешь] to doze; slumber.

дремо́та *n.* drowsiness.

дремо́тный *adj.* drowsy.

дрему́чий *adj.* (*of a forest*) thick; dense.

дрена́ж *n.* drainage. —дрена́жный, *adj.* drainage (*attrib.*); drain (*attrib.*).

дрени́ровать *v. impfv. & pfv.* [*pres.* -рую, -руешь] to drain.

дрессиро́ванный *adj.* (*of an animal*) trained.

дрессирова́ть *v. impfv.* [*pfv.* вы́дрессировать; *pres.* -рую, -руешь] to train (animals).

дрессиро́вка *n.* training (*of animals*). —дрессиро́вщик, *n.* animal trainer.

дроби́лка [*gen. pl.* -лок] *n.* crusher; crushing machine.

дроби́льный *adj.* crushing (*attrib.*). —дроби́льная маши́на, = дроби́лка.

дроби́на *n.* pellet. *Also,* дроби́нка.

дроби́ть *v. impfv.* [*pfv.* раздроби́ть; *pres.* -блю́, -би́шь] **1,** to crush; shatter; splinter. **2,** to divide up; split up; fragment. —дроби́ться, *refl.* **1,** to break into pieces; splinter. **2,** to split up.

дробле́ние *n.* **1,** crushing; grinding. **2,** splitting up; fragmentation.

дроблёный *adj.* crushed.

дро́бный *adj.* **1,** separate; fragmented. **2,** (*of sounds*) rhythmic; steady. **3,** *math.* fractional.

дробови́к [*gen.* -вика́] *n.* shotgun.

дробь *n.f.* **1,** shot: кру́пная дробь, buckshot. **2,** steady sound; beating; patter. **3,** [*pl.* дро́би, -бе́й] *math.* fraction. **4,** oblique stroke; slash.

дрова́ [*gen.* дров] *n. pl.* firewood.

дро́вни [*gen.* -ней] *n. pl.* sledge.

дровосе́к *n., obs.* woodcutter.

дровяно́й *adj.* wood (*attrib.*): дровяно́й сара́й, woodshed.

дро́ги [*gen.* дрог] *n. pl.* wagon; cart. —похоро́нные дро́ги, hearse.

дро́гнуть[1] *v. impfv.* [*past* дрог, -ла] to freeze; be chilled to the bone.

дро́гнуть[2] *v. pfv.* [*past* дро́гнул] **1,** to shake; tremble; quiver. **2,** to waver; falter; flinch.

дрожа́ние *n.* trembling; shivering; shaking.

дрожа́ть *v. impfv.* [*pres.* -жу́, -жи́шь] to tremble; shiver; shake.

дро́жжи [*gen.* -ей] *n. pl.* yeast.

дро́жки [*gen.* -жек] *n. pl.* open carriage; droshky.

дрожь *n.f.* tremor; trembling. —меня́ бро́сило в дрожь, I began to tremble/shiver.

дрозд [*gen.* -зда́] *n.* thrush. —чёрный дрозд, blackbird.

дромаде́р (дэ) *n.* dromedary.

дро́ссель *n.m.* throttle; choke.

дро́тик *n.* javelin.

дрофа́ [*pl.* дро́фы] *n.* bustard.

друг [*pl.* друзья́, -зе́й, -зья́м] *n.* friend. —друг дру́га, each other; one another. —друг за дру́гом, one after another; one after the other. —друг с дру́гом, with each other.

друго́й *adj.* **1,** other; another: друго́е де́ло, another matter; други́е стра́ны, other countries. **2,** else: кто́-то друго́й, someone else; что́-то друго́е, something else. —*n.* **1,** the other (one). **2,** another person. **3,** *neut.* another thing; something else. **4,** *pl.* others. —на друго́й день, the next day. —тот и́ли друго́й, one...or another. —и тот и друго́й, both. —ни тот ни друго́й, neither (one).

дру́жба *n.* friendship.

дружелю́бие *n.* friendliness. —дружелю́бный, *adj.* friendly; amicable.

дру́жеский *adj.* friendly; amicable.

дру́жественный *adj.* friendly; amicable.

дружи́на *n.* **1,** *hist.* military retinue of a medieval Russian prince. **2,** *pre-rev.* militia unit; detachment. **3,** squad; brigade.

дружи́ть *v. impfv.* [*pres.* дружу́, дру́жишь *or* дружи́шь] (with с + *instr.*) to be friends (with). —дружи́ться, *refl.* [*pfv.* подружи́ться] (with с + *instr.*) to become friends (with); become friendly (with).

дру́жно *adv.* **1,** amicably. **2,** (all) together; in concert.

дру́жный *adj.* [*short form* дру́жен, дружна́, дру́жны] **1,** friendly; amicable; harmonious. **2,** [*short form only*] friendly; friends: он дру́жен с мои́м сы́ном, he is friendly with my son; he and my son are friends. **3,** on the part of everyone; concerted.

дружо́к [*gen.* -жка́] *n., colloq.* friend; pal.

дры́гать *v. impfv.* (with *instr.*) *colloq.* to kick (one's feet).

дря́блый *adj.* flabby; flaccid. —дря́блость, *n.f.* flabbiness.

дря́зги [*gen.* дрязг] *n. pl., colloq.* petty quarrels; squabbles.

дрянно́й *adj., colloq.* miserable; rotten; lousy.

дрянь *n.f., colloq.* **1,** rubbish; trash. **2,** nonsense. **3,** good-for-nothing. **4,** something that is no good: де́ло дрянь, things are lousy.

дряхле́ть *v. impfv.* [*pfv.* одряхле́ть] to become decrepit; become enfeebled.

дря́хлый *adj.* decrepit; enfeebled. —дря́хлость, *n.f.* decrepitude.

дуали́зм *n.* dualism. —дуалисти́ческий, *adj.* dualistic.

дуб [*pl.* дубы́] *n.* oak (*tree & wood*).

дуба́сить *v. impfv.* [*pres.* -шу, -сишь] *colloq.* **1,** to beat; thrash. **2,** (*with* по *or* в) to bang on.

дуби́льный *adj.* tanning (*attrib.*). —дуби́льная кислота́, tannic acid.

дуби́льня [*gen. pl.* -лен] *n.* tannery.

дуби́льщик *n.* tanner.

дуби́на *n.* club; cudgel; bludgeon; truncheon. *Also,* дуби́нка.

дуби́ть *v. impfv.* [*pfv.* вы́дубить; *pres.* -блю, -би́шь] to tan (leather).

дубле́ние *n.* tanning.

дублёнка [*gen. pl.* -нок] *n., colloq.* sheepskin coat.

дублёный *adj.* tanned. —дублёный полушу́бок, sheepskin coat.

дублёр *n.* **1,** *theat.* understudy. **2,** *motion pictures* one who dubs in a part.

дубле́т *n.* duplicate.

дублика́т *n.* duplicate. —дублика́тный, *adj.* duplicate.

дубли́рование *n.* **1,** duplication. **2,** understudying. **3,** dubbing.

дубли́ровать *v. impfv.* [*pres.* -рую, -руешь] **1,** to duplicate. **2,** to understudy. **3,** to dub.

дубня́к [*gen.* -няка́] *n.* oak forest.

дубова́тый *adj., colloq.* clumsy; coarse.

дубо́вый *adj.* oak (*attrib.*).

дубо́к [*gen.* -бка́] *n.* young oak.

дубоно́с *n.* grosbeak.

дубра́ва *n.* oak forest.

дуга́ [*pl.* ду́ги] *n.* **1,** arc. **2,** shaft bow (*of a harness*).

дугообра́зный *adj.* arched.

дуде́ть *v. impfv., colloq.* **1,** *in* дуде́ть в ду́дку, to play a fife. **2,** to drone (on and on). —дуде́ть в одну́ ду́дку, to sing the same song.

ду́дка [*gen. pl.* -док] *n.* fife. —пляса́ть под чью́-нибудь ду́дку, to dance to someone's tune.

ду́дник *n.* angelica.

ду́жка [*gen. pl.* -жек] *n.* **1,** hoop. **2,** handle.

дука́т *n.* ducat.

ду́ло *n.* muzzle (*of a gun*). —под ду́лом пистоле́та, at gunpoint.

ду́ма *n.* **1,** thought. **2,** *hist.* Duma.

ду́мать *v. impfv.* [*pfv.* поду́мать] to think. —ду́маю, что нет, I don't think so. —мно́го ду́мать о себе́, to have an exalted opinion of oneself. —не ду́маю!, I hardly think so; I doubt it. —я ду́маю!, I should think so! —я так и ду́мал!, I thought so!

ду́маться *v.r. impfv., impers.* (*with dat.*) to seem: мне ду́мается, it seems to me; I think.

ду́мка [*gen. pl.* -мок] *n., colloq.* small pillow.

дунове́ние *n.* puff; breath (*of wind, air, etc.*).

ду́нуть *v. pfv.* to blow.

ду́пель [*pl.* дупеля́] *n.m.* double snipe (*bird*).

дупле́т *n., billiards* bank shot.

дупли́стый *adj.* (*of a tree*) hollow.

дупло́ [*pl.* ду́пла, ду́пел] *n.* **1,** hollow (*in a tree*). **2,** cavity (*in a tooth*).

дура́к [*gen.* -рака́] *n.m.* [*fem.* ду́ра] fool. —остава́ться в дурака́х, to make a fool of oneself; look like a fool.

дурале́й *n., colloq.* fool; jerk; dope.

дура́цкий *adj., colloq.* **1,** fool's. **2,** ridiculous; idiotic.

дура́чество *n., colloq.* **1,** prank. **2,** *pl.* horseplay; tomfoolery.

дура́чить *v. impfv.* [*pfv.* одура́чить] to fool; make a fool of. —дура́читься, *refl.* [*impfv. only*] to fool around.

дурачо́к [*gen.* -чка́] *n., colloq.* **1,** little fool. **2,** idiot.

дура́шливый *adj., colloq.* **1,** silly. **2,** mischievous.

ду́рень [*gen.* -рня] *n.m., colloq.* dope; dolt.

дуре́ть *v. impfv.* [*pfv.* одуре́ть] *colloq.* to go crazy; lose one's wits.

дури́ть *v. impfv., colloq.* to play around; horse around.

дурма́н *n.* **1,** thorn apple; jimsonweed. **2,** narcotic; drug.

дурма́нить *v. impfv.* [*pfv.* одурма́нить] to dull one's mind; cloud one's mind.

дурне́ть *v. impfv.* [*pfv.* подурне́ть] to lose one's beauty; become less attractive.

ду́рно *adv.* badly. —*adj., used predicatively* faint; ill: мне ду́рно, I feel faint.

дурно́й *adj.* **1,** bad. **2,** evil; wicked. —ду́рен (дурна́) собо́й, homely; unattractive.

дурнота́ *n.* (feeling of) faintness: чу́вствовать дурноту́, to feel faint.

дурну́шка [*gen. pl.* -шек] *n., colloq.* plain girl; homely girl.

дуршла́г *n.* colander.

дурь *n.f., colloq.* foolishness; nonsense.

ду́тый *adj.* **1,** hollow. **2,** *fig.* inflated; exaggerated.

дуть *v. impfv.* [*pfv.* поду́ть; *pres.* ду́ю, ду́ешь] to blow.

дутьё *n.* **1,** blowing. **2,** blast.

ду́ться *v.r. impfv.* [*pres.* ду́юсь, ду́ешься] *colloq.* to pout; sulk.

дух *n.* spirit. —быть в ду́хе, to be in good spirits. —быть не в ду́хе, to be out of sorts. —во весь дух, full tilt. —в том же ду́хе, in the same vein; along the same lines. —одни́м ду́хом, **1,** in one breath. **2,** all at once. —что есть ду́ху, **1,** full tilt. **2,** at the top of one's lungs. —что́-то в э́том ду́хе, something of the sort.

духи́ [*gen.* духо́в] *n. pl.* perfume.

ду́хов *adj., in* ду́хов день, Whitmonday.

духове́нство *n.* clergy.

духо́вка [*gen. pl.* -вок] *n.* oven.

духовни́к [*gen.* -ника́] *n.* confessor.

духо́вный *adj.* **1,** spiritual. **2,** ecclesiastical. **3,** (*of a seminary, academy, etc.*) theological. —духо́вное завеща́ние, last will and testament. —духо́вное о́ко, mind's eye.

духово́й *adj.* **1,** *music,* духово́й инструме́нт, wind instrument; духово́й орке́стр, brass band. **2,** operated by heat: духова́я печь, oven. —духово́е ружьё, **1,** air gun. **2,** blowgun.

духота́ *n.* **1,** stuffiness; closeness. **2,** sweltering heat.

душ *n.* **1,** shower. **2,** douche.

душа́ [*acc.* ду́шу; *pl.* ду́ши] *n.* soul. —в душе́, **1,** inwardly; in one's heart. **2,** at heart. —всей душо́й, with all one's heart. —**для души́**, for one's own pleasure. —**душа́ в ду́шу**, in perfect harmony. —**душа́ о́бщества**, the life of the party. —**душо́й и те́лом**, heart and soul. —**за душо́й**, to one's name. —**на ду́шу населе́ния**, per capita. —**ни души́**, not a soul. —**от всей души́**, from the bottom of one's heart. —**по душе́** (+ *dat.*), to one's liking. —**разгово́р по душа́м**, heart-to-heart talk. —**с бо́лью на душе́**, with a heavy heart. —**с душо́й**, with feeling. —**ско́лько душе́ уго́дно**, to one's heart's content. —**стоя́ть над чьей-либо душо́й**, to stand over; breathe down someone's neck.

душева́я *n., decl. as an adj.* shower room.

душевнобольно́й *adj.* mentally ill. —*n.* mental patient; mental case.

душе́вный *adj.* **1,** mental; emotional: душе́вное состоя́ние, state of mind; душе́вная боле́знь, mental illness. **2,** sincere; heartfelt.

душево́й *adj.* **1,** per capita. **2,** shower (*attrib.*).

душегу́б *n., obs., colloq.* killer; murderer.

душегу́бка [*gen. pl.* -**бок**] *n.* **1,** canoe. **2,** mobile gas chamber.

ду́шенька *n.f.* (*used in direct address*) dear; darling; sweetheart.

душеприка́зчик *n., obs.* executor (*of a will*).

душераздира́ющий *adj.* heart-rending; harrowing; bloodcurdling.

ду́шечка *n.* = ду́шенька.

души́стый *adj.* fragrant; aromatic; sweet-smelling. —**души́стый горо́шек**, sweet peas. —**души́стый пе́рец**, allspice; pimento.

души́ть *v. impfv.* [*pfv.* **задуши́ть**; *pres.* **душу́, ду́шишь**] **1,** to strangle. **2,** *fig.* to stifle. **3,** [*impfv. only*] to choke: его́ ду́шит ка́шель, he is choking from a cough. **4,** [*pfv.* **надуши́ть**] to perfume. —**души́ться,** *refl.* [*pfv.* **надуши́ться**] to use perfume; put on perfume.

ду́шка [*gen. pl.* -**шек**] *n.m. & f., colloq.* **1,** dear person; lovely person. **2,** dear; darling.

ду́шно *adj., used predicatively* stuffy: здесь ду́шно, it is stuffy in here; мне ду́шно, I am suffocating.

ду́шный *adj.* stuffy; close.

душо́к [*gen.* -**шка́**] *n., colloq.* **1,** smell of something beginning to decay. **2,** *fig.* taint; tinge.

дуэ́ль *n.f.* duel. —**дуэли́ст; дуэля́нт,** *n.* duelist.

дуэ́нья *n., obs.* chaperon.

дуэ́т *n.* duet.

ды́ба *n.* rack (*instrument of torture*).

ды́бом *adv., in* станови́ться/стать ды́бом, (*of hair*) to stand on end.

дыбы́ *adv., in* станови́ться на дыбы́, **1,** (*of a horse*) to rear. **2,** to stand straight up in the air. **3,** *colloq.* to raise objections.

ды́лда *n.m. & f., colloq.* tall, ungainly person.

дым [*2nd loc.* дыму́] *n.* smoke.

дыми́ть *v. impfv.* [*pfv.* **надыми́ть**] **1,** to smoke; give off smoke. **2,** [*impfv. only*] (*with instr.*) to smoke (a cigarette, cigar, etc.). —**дыми́ться,** *refl.* [*impfv. only*] to give off smoke.

ды́мка *n.* haze.

ды́мный *adj.* smoky.

дымово́й *adj.* smoke (*attrib.*). —**дымова́я заве́са,** smoke screen. —**дымова́я труба́,** chimney; smokestack.

дымо́к [*gen.* -**мка́**] *n.* thin column of smoke.

дымохо́д *n.* flue; stovepipe.

ды́мчатый *adj.* smoky; smoke-colored.

ды́нный *adj.* melon (*attrib.*). —**ды́нное де́рево,** papaya.

ды́ня *n.* melon.

дыра́ [*pl.* ды́ры] *n.* **1,** hole. **2,** *colloq.* out-of-the-way place.

ды́рка [*gen. pl.* -**рок**] *n.* (small) hole.

дыроко́л *n., colloq.* punch; hole punch.

дыря́вый *adj.* having a hole; full of holes. —**дыря́вая па́мять,** memory like a sieve.

дыха́ние *n.* breath; breathing; respiration. —**второе дыха́ние,** second wind.

дыха́тельный *adj.* respiratory. —**дыха́тельное го́рло,** windpipe.

дыша́ть *v. impfv.* [*pres.* дышу́, ды́шишь] to breathe.

ды́шло *n.* pole; beam; shaft (*on a carriage*).

дья́вол *n.* devil. —**дья́вольский,** *adj.* devilish; diabolical.

дья́кон [*pl.* дьякона́] *n.* deacon.

дю́жий *adj., colloq.* hefty; robust; strapping.

дю́жина *n.* dozen.

дю́жинный *adj.* ordinary; run-of-the-mill.

дюйм *n.* inch. —**дюймо́вый,** *adj.* one-inch; inch-long.

дю́на *n.* dune.

дюралюми́ний *n.* duralumin.

дя́гиль *n.m.* angelica.

дя́денька *n.m., colloq.* uncle. *Also,* дя́дюшка.

дя́дя [*gen. pl.* дя́дей] *n.m.* uncle.

дя́тел [*gen.* -**тла**] *n.* woodpecker.

Е

Е, е *n. neut.* sixth letter of the Russian alphabet.

Ё, ё *n. neut.* not considered a separate letter of the Russian alphabet. Usually written Е and е except in dictionaries and textbooks.

ева́нгелие *n.* gospel. —**евангели́ст,** *n., Bib.* Evangelist. —**евангели́ческий,** *adj.* evangelical. —**ева́нгельский,** *adj.* in *or* of the gospel.

евге́ника *n.* eugenics. —**евгени́ческий,** *adj.* eugenic.

е́внух *n.* eunuch.

евразий́ский *adj.* Eurasian.

евре́й *n.m.* [*fem.* -ре́йка] Jew. —**евре́йский,** *adj.* Jewish; Hebrew. —**евре́йство,** *n.* Jewry.

европе́ец [*gen.* -е́йца] *n.m.* [*fem.* -е́йка] European. —**европе́йский,** *adj.* European.

европео́ид *n.* Caucasoid; Caucasian. —**европео́идный,** *adj.* Caucasoid; Caucasian.

евро́пий *n.* europium.

евста́хиев *adj., in* **евста́хиева труба́,** Eustachian tube.

евхари́стия *n.* Eucharist.

е́герь [*pl.* егеря́] *n.m.* professional hunter.

еги́петский *adj.* Egyptian.

египтоло́гия *n.* Egyptology. —**египто́лог,** *n.* Egyptologist.

египтя́нин [*pl.* -тя́не, -тя́н] *n.m.* [*fem.* -тя́нка] Egyptian.

его́ (vo) *pron., gen. & acc. of* **он** *and* **оно́.** —*poss. adj. & pron.* his; its.

егоза́ *n.m. & f., colloq.* fidgety person; fidget.

егози́ть *v. impfv.* [*pres.* -жу́, -зи́шь] *colloq.* **1,** to fidget. **2,** (*with* **пе́ред**) to fawn (upon).

егозли́вый *adj., colloq.* fidgety.

еда́ *n.* **1,** meal. **2,** food.

едва́ *adv.* **1,** hardly; scarcely. **2,** just; barely. —**едва́..., как...,** hardly/scarcely..., when.... он едва́ ко́нчил говори́ть, как..., he had hardly finished speaking, when...—**едва́ ли,** hardly; it is unlikely (that). —**едва́ ли не,** nearly; almost; practically: едва́ ли не ка́ждый день, nearly every day. —**едва́ не,** almost; nearly: он едва́ не утону́л, he nearly drowned.

едине́ние *n.* unity.

едини́ца *n.* **1,** the numeral 1. **2,** a grade of "one", signifying "very poor". **3,** unit. **4,** *pl.* (only) a few individuals.

едини́чный *adj.* individual; isolated; unique.

едино- *prefix* **1,** one; single: единобо́жие, monotheism. **2,** same; of the same: единове́рный, of the same religion.

единобо́жие *n.* monotheism.

единобо́рство *n.* single combat.

единобра́чие *n.* monogamy. —**единобра́чный,** *adj.* monogamous.

единове́рец [*gen.* -рца] *n.* coreligionist.

единове́рный *adj.* of the same religion; of the same faith.

единовла́стие *n.* autocracy; absolute rule. —**единовла́стный,** *adj.* autocratic; having absolute power.

единовре́менный *adj.* one-time; given only once. —**единовре́менно,** *adv.* all at once; in a lump sum.

единогла́сие *n.* unanimity.

единогла́сный *adj.* unanimous. —**единогла́сно,** *adv.* unanimously.

единоду́шие *n.* unanimity.

единоду́шный *adj.* unanimous. —**единоду́шно,** *adv.* unanimously.

единокро́вный *adj., obs.* **1,** having the same father. **2,** kindred; consanguineous.

единоли́чный *adj.* individual. —**единоли́чно,** *adv.* alone; on one's own; single-handedly.

единомы́слие *n.* harmony of views; agreement.

единомы́шленник *n.* **1,** person holding similar views. **2,** confederate; accomplice.

единообра́зие *n.* uniformity. —**единообра́зный,** *adj.* uniform.

единоро́г *n.* unicorn.

единоутро́бный *adj., obs.* having the same mother.

еди́нственно *adv.* only; solely. —**еди́нственно, что...,** the only thing that...: еди́нственно, что я могу́ сказа́ть, the only thing I can say is...; all I can say is...

еди́нственный *adj.* only; sole. —*n., fol. by* **кто,** the only one (who); the only person (who). —**еди́нственный в своём ро́де,** unique; the only one of its kind. —**еди́нственное число́,** *gram.* the singular.

еди́нство *n.* unity.

еди́ный *adj.* **1,** (*with* **ни** *or* **без**) (not) a single. **2,** united; unified. **3,** common; single. —**все до еди́ного,** everyone without exception; one and all.

е́дкий *adj.* **1,** caustic; corrosive. **2,** acrid; pungent. **3,** *fig.* cutting; sarcastic.

е́дкость *n.f.* **1,** corrosiveness; causticity. **2,** *fig.* cutting remark.

едо́к [*gen.* едока́] *n.* **1,** mouth to feed: пять едоко́в в семье́, five mouths to feed. **2,** *colloq.* eater: хоро́ший едо́к, good eater.

её *pron., gen. & acc. of* **она́.** —*poss. adj. & pron.* her; hers; its.

ёж [*gen.* ежа́] *n.* hedgehog. —**морско́й ёж,** sea urchin.

еже- *prefix* -ly; once a: ежеме́сячный, monthly; еже-ме́сячно, once a month.

ежеви́ка *n.* **1,** blackberries. **2,** a (single) blackberry. **3,** blackberry bush.

ежего́дник *n.* yearbook; annual.

ежего́дный *adj.* yearly; annual. —**ежего́дно,** *adv.* annually.

ежедне́вный *adj.* daily. —**ежедне́вно,** *adv.* daily.

е́жели *conj., obs., colloq.* = **е́сли.**

ежеме́сячник *n.* monthly publication; monthly.

ежеме́сячный *adj.* monthly. —**ежеме́сячно,** *adv.* monthly; once a month.

ежемину́тный *adj.* **1,** occurring once a minute. **2,** constant; incessant.

еженеде́льник *n.* weekly publication; weekly.

еженеде́льный *adj.* weekly. —**еженеде́льно,** *adv.* weekly; once a week.

ежено́щный *adj.* nightly. —**ежено́щно,** *adv.* nightly.

ежеча́сный *adj.* hourly.

ёжик *n., dim. of* **ёж.** —**ёжиком,** *adv.* in a crew cut: постри́чься ёжиком, to get a crew cut.

ёжиться *v.r. impfv.* [*pfv.* **съёжиться**] **1,** to huddle up (*from the cold*). **2,** *fig.* colloq. to hesitate; waver.

ежо́вый *adj.* hedgehog (*attrib.*). —**держа́ть в ежо́-вых рукави́цах,** to rule with an iron hand.

езда́ *n.* ride; riding; drive; driving: два часа́ езды́, a two-hour ride/drive.

е́здить *v. impfv.* [*pres.* **е́зжу, е́здишь**] **1,** *indeterm. of* **е́хать. 2,** to ride: е́здить на велосипе́де, to ride a bicycle. Е́здить верхо́м, to ride a horse; ride horse-back.

ездово́й *adj.* **1,** for riding. **2,** *in* **ездова́я соба́ка,** draft dog; harness dog. —*n., mil.* driver (*of a team of horses*).

ездо́к [*gen.* -дока́] *n.* rider; horseman. —**туда́ я бо́льше не ездо́к,** you won't catch me going there again.

е́зженый *adj., colloq.* (*of a road*) well-worn; well-trodden.

ей *pron., dat. & instr. of* **она́.**

ей-бо́гу *interj., colloq.* really; really and truly.

ёкать *v. impfv.* [*pfv.* **ёкнуть**] (*of one's heart*) to skip a beat: у меня́ се́рдце ёкнуло, my heart skipped a beat.

éле *adv.* **1,** hardly; scarcely. **2,** just; barely. *Also,* **éле-éле.**

елéй *n.* **1,** holy oil; unction. **2,** *fig.* balm; solace.

елéйный *adj.* unctuous.

ёлка [*gen. pl.* **ёлок**] *n.* **1,** spruce. **2,** Christmas tree. **3,** children's New Year's party.

ёловый *adj.* spruce (*attrib.*).

ёлочка *n., dim. of* **ёлка.** —**ёлочкой; в ёлочку,** herringbone style.

ёлочный *adj.* of or for a Christmas tree.

ель *n.f.* spruce.

éльник *n.* spruce grove.

ёмкий *adj.* capacious. —**ёмкость,** *n.f.* capacity; cubic content.

ему́ *pron., dat. of* **он** *and* **оно́.**

енóт *n.* raccoon. —**енóтовый,** *adj.* raccoon (*attrib.*).

епáрхия *n.* diocese.

епи́скоп *n.* bishop. —**епископáльный,** *adj.* Episco-palian. —**епи́скопский,** *adj.* Episcopal.

ералáш *n., colloq.* muddle; jumble; confusion.

éресь *n.f.* heresy.

еретúк [*gen.* -тикá] *n.m.* [*fem.* -тúчка] heretic. —**еретúческий,** *adj.* heretical.

ёрзать *v. impfv., colloq.* to fidget.

ермóлка [*gen. pl.* -лок] *n.* skullcap.

ерóшить *v. impfv.* [*pfv.* **взъерóшить**] *colloq.* to muss; tousle.

ерундá *n., colloq.* **1,** nonsense. **2,** trifling amount: пять рублéй — ерундá, five rubles is nothing. **3,** a cinch; a snap; child's play.

ерундóвый *adj., colloq.* **1,** nonsensical. **2,** trifling; petty.

ёрш [*gen.* ершá] *n.* **1,** ruff (*fish*). **2,** brush; lamp brush.

ершúться *v.r. impfv., colloq.* **1,** (*of one's hair*) to bristle. **2,** *fig.* to flare up; get excited.

есаýл *n., pre-rev.* Cossack captain.

éсли *conj.* **1,** if: éсли он прав, if he is right. **2,** when (*considering that*): зачéм убеждáть егó, éсли он и слýшать не хóчет?, why try to persuade him when he won't even listen? **3,** whereas: éсли в 1970..., то сегóдня..., whereas in 1970..., today...—**éсли бы не,** if it were not for; were it not for. —**éсли бы тóлько,** if only. —**éсли не...,** **1,** if not... **2,** unless. —**éсли тóлько,** only if; provided; on condition that.

естéственник *n.* natural scientist; naturalist.

естéственно *adv.* **1,** naturally. **2,** naturally; of course. —*adj., used predicatively* natural: естéственно полагáть, что..., it is natural to suppose that...

естéственный *adj.* natural.

естествó *n.* essence.

естествовéд *n., obs.* natural scientist; naturalist.

естествовéдение *n., obs.* = **естествознáние.**

естествознáние *n.* natural sciences.

естествоиспытáтель *n.m.* naturalist.

есть[1] *v. impfv.* [*pres.* **ем, ешь, ест, едúм, едúте, едя́т**] **1,** [*pfv.* **съесть**] to eat. **2,** [*pfv.* **поéсть**] to eat; have something to eat.

есть[2] *v.,* *3rd person sing. pres. of* **быть. 1,** (he, she, it) is: закóн есть закóн, the law is the law. Рáзница мáленькая, но всё-таки есть, it is a small difference but it exists nevertheless. **2,** there is; there are: есть такúе лю́ди, there are such people. **3,** (*with* **у**) *indicating possession:* у вас есть спúчка?, do you have a match? —*interj., mil.; naval* yes, sir!; aye aye, sir! —**есть когдá!,** *colloq.* there is still time. —**есть такóе дéло!,** *colloq.* agreed! —**ни на есть, 1,** any at all: кто ни на есть, anyone at all. **2,** (*with superl. adjectives*) the most: сáмый ни на есть обыкновéн-ный человéк, the most ordinary kind of person. —**так и есть,** and so it is.

ефрéйтор *n., mil.* private first class.

éхать *v. impfv.* [*pfv.* **поéхать;** *pres.* **éду, éдешь**] to go (*by riding*); ride; drive. *See also* **éздить.**

ехúдна *n.* **1,** spiny anteater; echidna. **2,** *colloq.* vicious person; viper.

ехúдный *adj.* malicious.

ехúдство *n.* malice; spite.

ещё *adv.* **1,** still: он ещё мáльчик, he is still a boy. **2,** yet: я ещё не ел, I haven't eaten yet. **3,** else: кудá вы ещё éздили?, where else did you go? **4,** more: хотúте ещё хлéба?, would you like some more bread? **5,** another: хотúте ещё чáшку чáю?, would you like another cup of tea? **6,** (*before comp. adjectives*) still; even: ещё бóльше, still more; even greater. **7,** as long ago as; as far back as: Москва́ была́ осно́вана ещё в 12-ом ве́ке, Moscow was founded as far back as the 12th century. **8,** as recently as: ещё в 1960-ом году́, as recently as 1960. —**всё ещё,** still; all the same. —**ещё бы!,** and how!; you can say that again! —**ещё раз,** again; once again. —**нет ещё,** not yet. —**никогда́ ещё,** never before.

ёю *pron., instr. of* она́.

Ж

Ж, ж *n. neut.* seventh letter of the Russian alphabet.

ж *conj. & particle* = же.

жа́ба *n.* **1,** toad. **2,** *obs.* angina. —**грудна́я жа́ба,** angina pectoris.

жа́бры *n. pl.* [*sing.* жа́бра] gills.

жа́воронок [*gen.* -нка] *n.* lark.

жа́дничать *v. impfv., colloq.* to be greedy; be stingy.

жа́дно *adv.* **1,** greedily. **2,** avidly; eagerly.

жа́дность *n.f.* **1,** greed; avarice. **2,** stinginess. —**с жа́дностью,** eagerly; avidly.

жа́дный *adj.* [*short form* жа́ден, жадна́, жа́дно] **1,** greedy. **2,** (*with* на, до, к) hungry (for). **3,** (*of desire, curiosity, etc.*) avid. **4,** stingy.

жа́жда *n.* **1,** thirst. **2,** (*with gen.*) thirst (for); craving (for).

жа́ждать *v. impfv.* [*pres.* -ду, -дешь] **1,** (*with gen.*) to thirst for; crave. **2,** (*with inf.*) to long (to); be dying (to).

жаке́т *n.* woman's jacket. *Also,* **жаке́тка.**

жале́ть *v. impfv.* [*pfv.* пожале́ть] **1,** to feel sorry for; pity. **2,** to regret. **3,** to spare. **4,** to begrudge.

жа́лить *v. impfv.* [*pfv.* ужа́лить] to sting.

жа́лкий *adj.* [*short form* жа́лок, жалка́, жа́лко] **1,** pitiful; pathetic. **2,** wretched; miserable.

жа́лко *adv.* pitifully; pathetically. —*adj., used predicatively* = жаль.

жа́ло *n.* stinger.

жа́лоба *n.* complaint. —**кассацио́нная** *or* **апелляцио́нная жа́лоба,** *law* appeal.

жа́лобный *adj.* plaintive; mournful. —**жа́лобная кни́га,** complaints book.

жа́лобщик *n.* person registering a complaint.

жа́лованье *n.* wage(s); salary.

жа́ловать *v. impfv.* [*pfv.* пожа́ловать; *pres.* -лую, -луешь] **1,** *obs.* to grant; confer; award; bestow. **2,** [*impfv. only*] *colloq.* to like; favor. **3,** (*with* к) *obs.* to visit. **4,** *in* добро́ пожа́ловать!, welcome! —**жа́ловаться,** *refl.* (*with* на + *acc.*) to complain (about).

жа́лостливый *adj., colloq.* **1,** sympathetic; compassionate. **2,** sad; mournful.

жа́лостный *adj., colloq.* **1,** plaintive. **2,** sympathetic.

жа́лость *n.f.* pity.

жаль *predicate* **1,** it is a pity; it is a shame: жаль!, it's a shame! Жаль сиде́ть до́ма сего́дня, it's a shame/pity to have to sit home today. **2,** (*with dat.*) sorry for: мне жаль его́, I feel sorry for him. **3,** (*with dat.*) sorry about: мне жаль вас беспоко́ить, I am sorry to bother you. **4,** (*with dat.*) to hate to: мне жаль тра́тить де́ньги на э́то, I hate to spend money for that.

жалюзи́ *n. pl. indecl.* jalousie. —**подъёмные жалюзи́,** Venetian blinds.

жанда́рм *n.* gendarme. —**жандарме́рия,** *n.* gendarmerie.

жанр *n.* **1,** genre. **2,** genre painting. —**жа́нровый,** *adj.* genre (*attrib.*): жа́нровая жи́вопись, genre painting.

жар *n.* **1,** heat. **2,** fever; high temperature. **3,** *fig.* ardor; fervor. **4,** *colloq.* embers. —**в жару́,** running a high temperature. —**зада́ть жа́ру** (+ *dat.*), to rake over the coals.

жара́ *n.* heat.

жарго́н *n.* jargon; slang. —**жарго́нный,** *adj.* slang.

жа́реный *adj.* fried; roast; broiled.

жа́рить *v. impfv.* [*pfv.* **зажа́рить** *or* **изжа́рить**] **1,** to fry; roast; broil. **2,** [*impfv. only*] *colloq.* (*of the sun*) to beat down (on). —**жа́риться,** *refl.* **1,** (*of meat, coffee, etc.*) to fry; roast. **2,** [*impfv. only*] *colloq.* to bake (in the sun).

жа́ркий *adj.* [*comp.* жа́рче] **1,** hot. **2,** *fig.* heated; passionate; intense.

жа́рко *adj., used predicatively* hot: сего́дня жа́рко, it is hot today; мне жа́рко, I am hot.

жарко́е *n., decl. as an adj.* roast meat.

жаро́вня [*gen. pl.* -вен] *n.* roasting pan; brazier.

жар-пти́ца *n.* firebird.

жа́рче *adv., comp. of* жа́ркий *and* жа́рко.

жасми́н *n.* jasmine. —**жасми́нный; жасми́новый,** *adj.* jasmine.

жа́тва *n.* **1,** harvesting; reaping. **2,** harvest. **3,** harvest time.

жа́твенный *adj.* harvesting (*attrib.*). —**жа́твенная маши́на,** harvester; reaper.

жа́тка [*gen. pl.* -ток] *n.* harvester; reaper.

жать[1] *v. impfv.* [*pres.* жму, жмёшь] **1,** to squeeze; press. **2,** [*pfv.* пожа́ть] (*with* ру́ку + *dat.*) to shake (someone's hand). **3,** (*of clothes, shoes, etc.*) to pinch; be tight.

жать[2] *v. impfv.* [*pfv.* сжать; *pres.* жну, жнёшь] to reap.

жа́ться *v.r. impfv.* [*pres.* жмусь, жмёшься] **1,** to huddle up. **2,** (*with* к) to press close against. **3,** to crowd together; squeeze together. **4,** *colloq.* to hesitate; waver. **5,** *colloq.* to economize; watch one's pocketbook.

жбан *n.* jug.

жвáчка *n.* cud.

жвáчный *adj. & n.* ruminant.

жгут [*gen.* **жгутá**] *n.* **1,** twisted strand; braid. **2,** tourniquet.

жгýчий *adj.* burning.

ждать *v. impfv.* [*pfv.* **подождáть**; *pres.* **жду, ждёшь**; *past fem.* **ждалá**] **1,** to wait; wait for; await. **2,** [*impfv. only*] to expect. —**тогó и жди,** at any moment.

же *also,* **ж** *conj., expressing contrast:* я уезжáю, он же остаётся, I am leaving but he is staying. —*particle* **1,** *used for emphasis:* говорúте же!, speak up! Откýда же я знáю?, how should I know? Вам лýчше слýшаться егó, он же ваш отéц, you had better obey him — after all, he is your father. **2,** *expressing sameness or identity:* тот же; такóй же, the same; так же, in the same way; тогдá же, at the same time; там же, in the same place.

жевáние *n.* chewing; mastication.

жёваный *adj.* **1,** chewed. **2,** *colloq.* crumpled.

жевáтельный *adj.* chewing (*attrib.*): жевáтельный табáк, chewing tobacco. —**жевáтельная резúнка,** chewing gum.

жевáть *v. impfv.* [*pres.* **жую, жуёшь**] to chew.

жезл [*gen.* **жезлá**] *n.* rod; staff (*carried as a symbol of authority*).

желáние *n.* wish; desire. —**при всём моём желáнии,** much as I would like to.

желáнный *adj.* **1,** desired. **2,** welcome. **3,** *obs.* dearest.

желáтельно *adj., used predicatively* desirable: желáтельно, чтóбы..., it is desirable that...

желáтельный *adj.* **1,** desirable. **2,** desired. —**желáтельность,** *n.f.* desirability.

желатúн *n.* gelatin. —**желатúновый,** *adj.* gelatinous; gelatin (*attrib.*).

желáть *v. impfv.* [*pfv.* **пожелáть**] **1,** (*with gen.*) to wish for; desire. **2,** (*with inf.*) to wish (to); (*with чтóбы*) wish (that). **3,** (*with dat. and gen.*) to wish (someone something): желáю вам всегó хорóшего, I wish you the best of everything. —**оставлять желáть лýчшего,** to leave something to be desired.

желáющие *n. pl., decl. as an adj.* those wishing; those who wish.

желвáк [*gen.* **-вакá**] *n.* lump; swelling; tumor.

желé *n. neut. indecl.* jelly.

железá [*pl.* **жéлезы, желёз, железáм**] *n.* gland.

желéзистый *adj.* **1,** glandular. **2,** containing iron; ferrous.

желéзка [*gen. pl.* **-зок**] *n.* **1,** *colloq.* piece of iron; iron bar. **2,** *obs., colloq.* railroad.

желёзка [*gen. pl.* **-зок**] *n.* glandule.

железнодорóжник *n.* railway worker.

железнодорóжный *adj.* railroad (*attrib.*); railway (*attrib.*).

желéзный *adj.* iron. —**желéзный блеск,** hematite. —**желéзная дорóга,** railroad.

железняк [*gen.* **-няка**] *n.* iron ore. —**бýрый железняк,** limonite. —**крáсный железняк,** hematite. —**хрóмистый железняк,** chromite.

желéзо *n.* iron.

железобетóн *n.* reinforced concrete. —**железобетóнный,** *adj.* of reinforced concrete.

жёлоб [*pl.* **желобá**] *n.* chute. —**водостóчный жёлоб,** gutter.

желобóк [*gen.* **-бкá**] *n.* groove.

желтéть *v. impfv.* [*pfv.* **пожелтéть**] **1,** to become yellow; turn yellow. **2,** (*of leaves*) to turn. **3,** [*impfv. only*] (*of anything yellow*) to appear; gleam.

желтизнá *n.* yellow color; yellow hue.

желтовáтый *adj.* **1,** yellowish. **2,** sallow.

желтóк [*gen.* **-ткá**] *n.* yolk.

желторóтый *adj.* **1,** yellow-beaked. **2,** *colloq.* immature; inexperienced; green.

желтофиóль *n.f.* wallflower.

желтýха *n.* (yellow) jaundice.

жёлтый *adj.* yellow.

желудёвый *adj.* acorn (*attrib.*).

желýдок [*gen.* **-дка**] *n.* stomach.

желýдочек [*gen.* **-чка**] *n.* ventricle.

желýдочный *adj.* stomach (*attrib.*); gastric.

жёлудь [*pl.* **жёлуди, -дéй, -дям**] *n.m.* acorn.

жёлчный *adj.* **1,** bilious. **2,** *fig.* ill-tempered; peevish. —**жёлчные кáмни,** gallstones. —**жёлчный протóк,** bile duct. —**жёлчный пузы́рь,** gall bladder.

жёлчь *n.f.* **1,** bile. **2,** *fig.* bitterness; rancor.

жемáниться *v.r. impfv., colloq.* to put on airs.

жемáнный *adj.* unnatural; affected. —**жемáнство,** *n.* affectation.

жéмчуг [*pl.* **жемчугá**] *n.* pearl; pearls.

жемчýжина *n.* a (single) pearl. —**жемчýжница,** *n.* pearl oyster. —**жемчýжный,** *adj.* pearl (*attrib.*); pearly.

женá [*pl.* **жёны**] *n.* wife.

женáтый *adj.* (*with* на + *prepl.*) (*of a man*) married (to): он женáт на англичáнке, he is married to an Englishwoman.

женúть *v. impfv. & pfv.* [*pres.* **женю, жéнишь**] to marry off (a son). —**женúться,** *refl.* (*with* на + *prepl.*) (*of a man*) to marry; get married (to).

женúтьба *n.* marriage (*of a man*).

женúх [*gen.* **-нихá**] *n.* **1,** fiancé. **2,** groom; bridegroom. **3,** eligible bachelor.

женолюб *n.* ladies' man; womanizer. —**женолюбúвый,** *adj.* having a fondness for women. —**женолюбие,** *n.* fondness for women.

женоненавúстник *n.* woman-hater; misogynist. —**женоненавúстничество,** *n.* misogyny.

женоподóбный *adj.* effeminate.

жéнский *adj.* **1,** feminine; female. **2,** woman's; women's.

жéнственный *adj.* feminine; womanly. —**жéнственность** *n.f.* femininity.

жéнщина *n.* woman.

женьшéнь *n.m.* ginseng.

жердь [*pl.* **жéрди, -дéй, -дям**] *n.f.* pole; long stick.

жеребёнок [*gen.* **-нка;** *pl.* **-бята, -бят**] *n.* **1,** colt. **2,** foal.

жеребéц [*gen.* **-бцá**] *n.* stallion.

жеребúться *v.r. impfv.* [*pfv.* **ожеребúться**] to foal.

жеребьёвка *n.* casting of lots.

жерлó [*pl.* **жéрла**] *n.* **1,** mouth (*of a volcano*). **2,** muzzle (*of a gun*).

жёрнов [*pl.* **жерновá**] *n.* millstone.

жéртва *n.* **1,** victim: пасть жéртвой (+ *gen.*), to fall victim to. Жертв нé было, there were no casualties. **2,** sacrifice: идтú на жéртвы, to make sacrifices. Принестú (чтó-нибудь) в жéртву, to sacrifice (something).

жéртвенник *n.* altar.

жéртвенный *adj.* **1,** sacrificial. **2,** selfless.

жéртвователь *n.m.* contributor; donor.

жéртвовать *v. impfv.* [*pfv.* **пожéртвовать;** *pres.*

-твую, -твуешь] 1, (with instr.) to sacrifice. **2,** to contribute; donate.

жертвоприношéние n. sacrifice; (burnt) offering.

жест n. gesture.

жестикули́ровать v. impfv. [pres. **-рую, -руешь]** to gesticulate.

жестикуля́ция n. gesticulation.

жёсткий adj. [short form **жёсток, жестка́, жёстко;** comp. **жёстче] 1,** hard. **2,** stiff; rigid. **3,** harsh. **4,** fig. rigid; strict. **—жёсткий вагóн,** coach with hard (unupholstered) seats.

жёстко adv. **1,** harshly. **2,** abruptly. **3,** decisively. **—**adj., used predicatively hard: мне жёстко сидéть, this seat is too hard for me.

жёсткость n.f. **1,** hardness; toughness. **2,** stiffness; rigidity.

жестóкий adj. [short form **жестóк, -токá, -тóко] 1,** cruel; brutal. **2,** bitter; fierce. **3,** severe; harsh.

жестóко adv. **1,** cruelly. **2,** severely; harshly.

жестокосéрдие n. hardheartedness. **—жестокосéрдный,** adj. hardhearted.

жестóкость n.f. **1,** cruelty. **2,** atrocity. **3,** severity.

жёстче adj., comp. of **жёсткий.**

жесть n.f. tin.

жестя́нка [gen. pl. **-нок]** n. tin can.

жестянóй adj. tin.

жестя́нщик n. tinsmith.

жетóн n. **1,** token; counter. **2,** badge; medal.

жечь v. impfv. [pfv. **сжечь;** pres. **жгу, жжёшь,...** жгут;** past **жёг, жгла, жгло] 1,** to burn. **2,** [impfv. only] to burn; sting. **—жечь свой корáбли** (or мостóы), to burn one's bridges.

жéчься v.r. impfv. [pres. **жгусь, жжёшься, ...жгутся]** colloq. **1,** (of an object) to get very hot; burn. **2,** to sting. **3,** to burn oneself.

жжéние n. burning sensation.

жжёнка n. hot beverage made of rum or brandy with burnt sugar and spices.

жжёный adj. burnt.

живéй interj. hurry!; speed it up!

живéц [gen. **-вцá]** n. small fish used for bait.

живи́тельный adj. **1,** life-giving. **2,** invigorating; bracing.

жи́вность n.f., colloq. **1,** living things. **2,** poultry; livestock.

жи́во adv. **1,** vividly. **2,** keenly. **3,** with great animation. **4,** colloq. quickly.

живодёр n., colloq. hustler.

живóй adj. [short form **жив, живá, жи́во] 1,** living; alive; live. **2,** lively; active. **3,** vivacious; animated. **4,** real. **5,** vivid; expressive. **6,** (of flowers) real; natural. **7,** (of a wound) raw. **—живáя си́ла, 1,** manpower. **2,** kinetic energy. **—задевáть за живóе,** to cut to the quick. **—на живýю рýку,** hastily; on the run. **—остáваться в живых,** to survive; remain alive.

жи́вокость n.f. delphinium; larkspur.

живопи́сец [gen. **-сца]** n. painter.

живопи́сный adj. picturesque.

жи́вопись n.f. **1,** painting (as an art). **2,** paintings.

живородя́щий adj. viviparous.

жи́вость n.f. **1,** agility. **2,** liveliness; vivacity. **3,** vividness; intensity. **4,** clarity.

живóт [gen. **-вотá]** n. **1,** stomach; belly; abdomen. **2,** obs. life. **—надрывáть животы́ (сó смеху),** to laugh oneself silly; be in stitches.

животвóрный adj. life-giving. Also, **животворя́щий.**

живóтик n., colloq. tummy.

животновóдство n. livestock breeding; cattle raising; animal husbandry.

живóтное n., decl. as an adj. animal.

живóтный adj. **1,** animal (attrib.). **2,** fig. bestial.

животрепéщущий adj. timely; vital.

живýчесть n.f. ability to survive; hardiness.

живýчий adj. **1,** hardy. **2,** fig. hard to change: предрассýдки живýчи, prejudices die hard.

жи́вчик n., colloq. **1,** lively person. **2,** noticeable pulsation of an artery in one's temple.

живьём adv., colloq. alive: брать когó-нибудь живьём, to take someone alive.

жид [gen. **жидá]** n. Jew (derogatory term).

жи́дкий adj. [comp. **жи́же] 1,** liquid; fluid. **2,** thin; watery; weak. **3,** (of hair, a beard, etc.) thin; scanty. **4,** (of metal, lava, etc.) molten. **5,** colloq. puny.

жи́дкость n.f. liquid; fluid.

жи́жа n. liquid; wash; swill. Also, **жи́жица.**

жи́же adj., comp. of **жи́дкий.**

жи́зненно adv. **1,** true to life. **2,** vitally.

жи́зненность n.f. **1,** vitality. **2,** closeness to life. **3,** lifelike quality.

жи́зненный adj. **1,** of life. **2,** lifelike. **3,** vital. **—жи́зненный ýровень,** standard of living.

жизнеописáние n. biography.

жизнерáдостный adj. buoyant; bubbling with life. **—жизнерáдостность,** n.f. zest for life.

жизнеспосóбный adj. viable. **—жизнеспосóбность,** n.f. viability.

жизнь n.f. life. **—в жи́зни не** (+ verb), never in one's life. **—как жизнь?,** colloq. how are you?; how are things?; how is life (treating you)? **—на всю жизнь,** for life. **—не на жизнь, а на смерть,** to the death. **—никогдá в жи́зни,** never. **—при жи́зни,** in/during one's lifetime.

жиклёр n. jet; nozzle.

жи́ла n. **1,** anat. vein. **2,** tendon; sinew. **3,** mining lode; vein.

жилéт n. vest.

жилéтка [gen. pl. **-ток]** n., colloq. vest.

жилéтный adj. vest (attrib.).

жилéц [gen. **-льцá]** n.m. [fem. **-ли́ца]** tenant; lodger.**—не жилéц (на э́том свéте),** not long for this world.

жи́листый adj. **1,** sinewy; wiry. **2,** (of meat) stringy.

жили́ще n. dwelling; abode; living quarters. **—жили́щный,** adj. housing (attrib.).

жи́лка [gen. pl. **-лок]** n. **1,** vein. **2,** fig. bent: артисти́ческая жи́лка, artistic bent.

жилóй adj. **1,** living (attrib.); dwelling (attrib.): жилóе помещéние, living quarters; жилáя плóщадь, floorspace. **2,** residential: жилы́е квартáлы, residential districts; жилóй дом, apartment house. **3,** in жилóй вид, lived-in look.

жилплóщадь n.f. floorspace (contr. of жилáя плóщадь).

жильё n. **1,** habitation. **2,** colloq. living quarters; place to live.

жим n., weightlifting press.

жи́молость n.f. honeysuckle.

жир [2nd loc. **жирý;** pl. **жиры́]** n. fat; grease. **—ры́бий жир,** cod-liver oil.

жирáф n. giraffe. Also, **жирáфа.**

жире́ть *v. impfv.* [*pfv.* **ожире́ть** *or* **разжире́ть**] to get fat.

жи́рно *adv.* **1,** with a lot of butter or fat. Есть жи́рно, to eat a lot of rich (*or* fatty) food. **2,** *colloq.* too much.

жи́рный *adj.* **1,** fatty. **2,** (*of foods*) fattening; rich. **3,** greasy; oily. **4,** fat; plump. **5,** (*of a line*) thick; (*of type*) boldface; bold-faced. —**жи́рное пятно́,** grease spot.

жи́ро *n. indecl.* endorsement (*on a check*).

жирови́к [*gen.* -вика́] *n.* fatty tumor.

жирово́й *adj.* fatty.

жите́йский *adj.* worldly; mundane.

жи́тель *n.m.* inhabitant; resident.

жи́тельство *n.* residence. —**вид на жи́тельство,** residence permit.

жи́тница *n.* **1,** *obs.* granary. **2,** grain-producing region; granary; breadbasket.

жи́то *n., regional* grain; rye; barley.

жить *v. impfv.* [*pres.* **живу́, живёшь;** *past fem.* **жила́**] to live. —**как живёшь?; как живёте?,** how are you?; how are things?; how are you getting along?

житьё *n., colloq.* **1,** life; existence. **2,** habitation; occupancy.

жи́ться *v.r. impfv.* [*pres.* **живётся**] *colloq., used impersonally with the dat. case,* to live: им непло́хо живётся, they don't live badly.

жму́рить *v. impfv.* [*pfv.* **зажму́рить**] *in* **жму́рить глаза́** to squint. —**жму́риться,** *refl.* to squint.

жму́рки [*gen.* -рок] *n. pl.* blindman's bluff.

жне́йка [*gen. pl.* **жне́ек**] *n.* harvester; reaper.

жнец [*gen.* **жнеца́**] *n.m.* [*fem.* **жни́ца**] harvest hand.

жнивьё *n.* stubs of cut grain; stubble.

жоке́й *n.* jockey.

жонглёр *n.* juggler. —**жонглёрство,** *n.* juggling (*lit. & fig.*).

жонгли́ровать *v. impfv.* [*pres.* -рую, -руешь] (*with instr.*) to juggle (*lit. & fig.*).

жонки́ль *n.m. or f.* jonquil.

жрать *v. impfv.* [*pfv.* **сожра́ть;** *pres.* **жру, жрёшь;** *past fem.* **жрала́**] *vulg.* to eat; gobble up.

жре́бий *n.* **1,** lot: по жре́бию, by lot. **2,** lots: бро-

са́ть/тяну́ть жре́бий, to cast/draw lots. —**жре́бий бро́шен,** the die is cast.

жрец [*gen.* **жреца́**] *n.* pagan priest.

жужжа́ние *n.* hum; buzz.

жужжа́ть *v. impfv.* [*pres.* -жжу́, -жжи́шь] to hum; buzz; drone.

жуи́р *n.* playboy.

жук [*gen.* жука́] *n.* beetle. —**ма́йский жук,** cockchafer.

жу́лик *n.* crook; swindler; cheat. —**жуликова́тый,** *adj.* roguish.

жу́льничать *v. impfv., colloq.* to cheat.

жу́льнический *adj., colloq.* crooked; underhand. —**жу́льничество,** *n., colloq.* cheating; trickery.

жу́пел *n.* bugaboo; bugbear.

жура́вль [*gen.* -вля́] *n.m.* **1,** crane (*bird*). **2,** well sweep.

жури́ть *v. impfv.* [*pfv.* **пожури́ть**] *colloq.* to chide.

журна́л *n.* **1,** magazine; journal. **2,** log: ва́хтенный журна́л, ship's log.

журнали́ст *n.* journalist; newspaperman.

журнали́стика *n.* **1,** journalism. **2,** periodic literature.

журнали́стский *adj.* journalist's; journalistic.

журна́льный *adj.* magazine (*attrib.*).

журча́ние *n.* babble; babbling (*of a stream, brook, etc.*).

журча́ть *v. impfv.* [*pres.* -чи́т] **1,** (*of water*) to rumble; (*of a brook*) to babble. **2,** (*of a speech, conversation, etc.*) to drone on.

жу́ткий *adj.* frightful; ghastly; gruesome; grim.

жу́тко *adv.* **1,** frighteningly. **2,** *colloq.* terribly. —*adj., used predicatively* **1,** terrified: мне бы́ло жу́тко, I was terrified. **2,** frightening: но́чью в лесу́ бы́ло жу́тко, it was frightening in the woods at night.

жуть *n.f., colloq.* horror.

жу́хлый *adj.* **1,** withered; dried up. **2,** (*of colors*) faded.

жу́хнуть *v. impfv.* [*past* жух *or* жу́хнул, жу́хла] **1,** to wither; dry up. **2,** (*of colors*) to fade.

жучо́к [*gen.* -чка́] *n., dim. of* жук.

жюри́ (жу) *n. neut. indecl.* **1,** judges; jury (*in a contest*). **2,** *law* jury: большо́е жюри́, grand jury.

З

З, з *n. neut.* eighth letter of the Russian alphabet.

за *prep.* A, *with acc.* **1,** behind (*with verbs of motion*): со́лнце зашло́ за ту́чи, the sun went behind the clouds. **2,** beyond (*with verbs of motion*): вы́йти за преде́лы (+ *gen.*), to go beyond the bounds of... **3,** (*with ages*) past; over: ему́ за со́рок, he is past/over forty. **4,** for; in exchange for: купи́ть за три рубля́, to buy for three rubles. **5,** for; in place of: расписа́ться за председа́теля, to sign for the chair-

man. **6,** for; in favor of: голосова́ть за кандида́та, to vote for a candidate. **7,** during: за э́то вре́мя, during that time. **8,** in (*a certain amount of time*): покры́ть расстоя́ние за три дня, to cover the distance in three days. **9,** (*with* до) before: за час до его́ отъе́зда, an hour before his departure. **10,** (*with verbs of sitting*) at; to: сесть за стол, to sit down at the table. **11,** (*with verbs of taking, grasping, holding*) by; on to: взять за́ руку, to take by the hand. **12,** (*with verbs* and nouns expressing fear, joy, struggle, death, for-giveness, gratitude, punishment, reward, and many others) for: боя́ться за свою́ жизнь, to fear for one's life; умере́ть за ро́дину, to die for one's country. B, with instr. **1,** behind: за мое́й спино́й, behind my back. **2,** beyond: за преде́лами го́рода, beyond the city limits. **3,** (following) after: оди́н за други́м, one after the other; one by one. **4,** for; to fetch: идти́ за папиро́сами, to go for some cigarettes; заходи́ть за това́рищем, to call for one's friend. **5,** after; in pursuit of: бежа́ть за ке́м-нибудь, to run after someone. **6,** at; occupied with; doing something: обсужда́ть вопро́с за обе́дом, to discuss a question at (or over) dinner; проводи́ть вре́мя за чте́нием, to spend time reading. **7,** (with verbs of sitting) at: сиде́ть за столо́м, to be sitting at the table. **8,** (with verbs of watching, caring, etc.) for: присма́тривать за детьми́, to look after the children. **9,** owing to; for: за неиме́-нием ули́к, for lack of evidence. **10,** indicating someone's turn: сло́во за ва́ми, you have the floor; де́ло за ва́ми, it's up to you.

за- prefix **1,** indicating the beginning of an action: засмея́ться, to (begin to) laugh. **2,** indicating motion behind or beyond: заходи́ть, to go behind. **3,** indicating action taken en route: заходи́ть к кому́-нибудь, to drop in on someone. **4,** (with **-ся**) indicating absorption to the point of forgetfulness: засмотре́ться, to be lost in contemplation. **5,** (with nouns and adjectives) outside of: за́городный, out-of-town. **6,** (with proper nouns and adjectives) Trans-: Закавка́зье, Transcaucasia.

заале́ть v., pfv. of **але́ть.**

заарка́нить v., pfv. of **арка́нить.**

заатланти́ческий adj. transatlantic; located across the Atlantic.

заба́ва n. **1,** amusement; fun. **2,** pastime.

забавля́ть v. impfv. to amuse; entertain. —**забавля́ться,** refl. to amuse oneself.

заба́вник n., colloq. funny person; amusing fellow.

заба́вно adv. in an amusing way. —adj., used predicatively funny: заба́вно!, that's funny! Мне заба́вно, что..., I find it funny that...

заба́вный adj. funny; amusing.

забаллоти́ровать v. pfv. [infl. -рую, -руешь] to fail to elect; reject; blackball.

забаррикади́ровать v., pfv. of **баррикади́ровать.**

забастова́ть v. pfv. [infl. -сту́ю, -сту́ешь] to strike; go on strike.

забасто́вка [gen. pl. -вок] n. strike. —**забасто́воч-ный,** adj. strike (attrib.).

забасто́вщик n. striker.

забве́ние n. **1,** oblivion: предава́ть забве́нию, to consign to oblivion. **2,** (with gen.) neglect (of); disregard (of).

забе́г n., sports heat; race.

забега́ловка n., colloq. eating house.

забе́гать v. pfv. to start running. —**забе́гаться,** refl., colloq. to run oneself ragged.

забега́ть v. impfv. [pfv. забежа́ть] **1,** (with в or на + acc.) to run into. **2,** (with к) colloq. to drop in on. **3,** to run (far) away. —**забега́ть вперёд, 1,** to run ahead. **2,** to anticipate events; act in advance.

забежа́ть [infl. like бежа́ть] v., pfv. of **забега́ть.**

забели́ть v. pfv. [infl. -белю́, -бе́лишь or -бели́шь]

1, to whiten; paint white. **2,** colloq. to add milk or sour cream to.

забере́менеть v., pfv. of **бере́менеть.**

забеспоко́иться v.r. pfv. to become anxious; become uneasy; begin to worry.

забетони́ровать v., pfv. of **бетони́ровать.**

забива́ть v. impfv. [pfv. заби́ть] **1,** to drive in; hammer in. **2,** to seal up; board up. **3,** to block up; clog. **4,** to beat to death; beat into submission. **5,** colloq. to outdo; surpass. **6,** sports to drive in (a ball); score (a goal). **7,** in забива́ть чью́-нибудь го́лову (+ instr.), to fill or stuff someone's head (with). **8,** in забива́ть себе́ в го́лову, to get it into one's head; develop a fixed idea. —**забива́ться,** refl. **1,** colloq. to hide; huddle. **2,** to become blocked; become clogged.

забинтова́ть v., pfv. of **бинтова́ть.**

забира́ть v. impfv. [pfv. забра́ть] **1,** to take. **2,** to take away. **3,** to arrest. **4,** to take in; shorten. **5,** colloq. (of a feeling) to come over (someone). **6,** to seal up; close up. **7,** to bear: забра́ть впра́во, to bear (to the) right. **8,** in забира́ть в ру́ки, to take over. **9,** in забира́ть себе́ в го́лову, to get it into one's head; develop a fixed idea. —**забира́ться,** refl. **1,** (with на, в or под + acc.) to climb. **2,** (with в + acc.) to get into; steal into. **3,** to get to: куда́ он забра́лся?, where has he gotten to? **4,** to hide.

заби́тый adj. downtrodden; cowed.

заби́ть v. pfv. [infl. -бью́, -бьёшь] **1,** pfv. of **забива́ть. 2,** to begin to strike. **3,** to sound (an alarm, retreat, etc.). —**заби́ться,** refl. **1,** pfv. of **забива́ться. 2,** to begin to beat.

забия́ка n.m. & f., colloq. roughneck; bully.

забла́говре́менно adv. beforehand; in advance; ahead of time.

заблагорассу́диться v.r. pfv., impers. (with dat.) to see fit: я сде́лаю, что мне заблагорассу́дится, I shall do as I see fit.

заблесте́ть v. pfv. [infl. like блесте́ть] to begin to shine; begin to sparkle.

заблуди́ться v.r. pfv. [infl. -блужу́сь, -блу́дишься] to lose one's way; get lost. —**заблуди́ться в трёх со́снах,** to be confounded by the simplest problem.

заблу́дший adj. **1,** lost; stray. **2,** fig. wayward; gone astray. —**заблу́дшая овца́,** lost sheep.

заблужда́ться v.r. impfv. to be mistaken.

заблужде́ние n. error; delusion; misconception. —**вводи́ть в заблужде́ние,** to mislead; delude; lead astray.

забода́ть v. pfv. to gore.

заболева́емость n.f. incidence; prevalence; rate; number of cases (of a disease).

заболева́ние n. illness; disease.

заболева́ть v. impfv. [pfv. заболе́ть] to become ill; fall ill; be taken ill.

заболе́ть v. pfv. **1,** [infl. -е́ю, -е́ешь] pfv. of **заболева́ть. 2,** [infl. -и́т] to begin to hurt; begin to ache.

за́болонь n.f. alburnum; sapwood.

заболта́ться v.r. pfv., colloq. to become engrossed in conversation.

забо́р n. fence.

забо́ристый adj., colloq. **1,** strong; pungent. **2,** racy; risqué.

забо́рный adj. **1,** fence (attrib.). **2,** coarse; vulgar.

забо́та n. **1,** care; concern: забо́та о челове́ке, concern for people. **2,** care; worry: без забо́т, without a care.

забо́титься *v.r. impfv.* [*pfv.* позабо́титься; *pres.* -чусь, -тишься] (*with* о) **1,** to take care of; care for; look after. **2,** to care about; be concerned about.

забо́тливый *adj.* thoughtful; solicitous; considerate. —**забо́тливость,** *n.f.* thoughtfulness; solicitude.

забракова́ть *v., pfv. of* бракова́ть.

забра́ло *n.* visor (*of a helmet*). —**с откры́тым забра́лом,** openly; frankly; boldly.

забра́сывать[1] *v. impfv.* [*pfv.* заброса́ть] (*with instr.*) **1,** to fill (with). **2,** to pelt (with): заброса́ть кого́-нибудь камня́ми, to throw stones at. **3,** *fig.* to shower (with); bombard (with): заброса́ть кого́-нибудь вопро́сами, to shower/bombard with questions.

забра́сывать[2] *v. impfv.* [*pfv.* забро́сить] **1,** to throw (*with force or over a distance*). **2,** to throw; toss (a part of one's body): забро́сить го́лову наза́д, to toss one's head back. **3,** to give up; drop; abandon. **4,** *colloq.* to deliver; drop off.

забра́ть [*infl. like* брать] *v., pfv. of* забира́ть. —**забра́ться,** *refl., pfv. of* забира́ться.

забрести́ *v. pfv.* [*infl. like* брести́] *colloq.* **1,** (*with* в + *acc.*) to wander into. **2,** to wander off.

заброни́ровать *v., pfv. of* брони́ровать.

забронирова́ть *v., pfv. of* бронирова́ть.

забро́с *n., colloq.* neglect: быть в забро́се, to be in a state of neglect.

заброса́ть *v., pfv. of* забра́сывать[1].

забро́сить [*infl.* -шу, -сишь] *v., pfv. of* забра́сывать[2].

забро́шенный *adj.* **1,** neglected. **2,** deserted; desolate.

забры́згивать *v. impfv.* [*pfv.* забры́згать] (*with instr.*) to splash (with); spatter (with); splatter (with).

забыва́ть *v. impfv.* [*pfv.* забы́ть] **1,** to forget: не забу́дьте!, don't forget! **2,** to leave (*accidentally*): забы́ть зо́нтик на рабо́те, to leave one's umbrella at work. —**забыва́ться,** *refl.* **1,** to doze off. **2,** to be lost in thought. **3,** to forget oneself. **4,** to be forgotten.

забы́вчивый *adj.* forgetful. —**забы́вчивость,** *n.f.* forgetfulness.

забы́тый *adj.* forgotten.

забы́ть [*infl.* -бу́ду, -бу́дешь] *v., pfv. of* забыва́ть. —**забы́ться,** *refl., pfv. of* забыва́ться.

забытьё [*prepl.* в забытьи́] *n.* **1,** drowsiness. **2,** semiconsciousness. **3,** (state of) distraction.

зава́л *n.* **1,** pile; accumulation: снёжный зава́л, snowdrift. **2,** obstruction; barrier.

зава́ливать *v. impfv.* [*pfv.* завали́ть] **1,** to block up. **2,** (*with instr.*) *colloq.* to pile high (with); *fig.* overload (with); flood (with); swamp (with). —**зава́ливаться,** *refl.* **1,** to fall. **2,** *colloq.* to fall down; come tumbling down; collapse. **3,** *colloq.* to tilt to one side. **4,** *colloq.* to lie down; flop down.

завали́ть [*infl.* -валю́, -ва́лишь] *v., pfv. of* зава́ливать. —**завали́ться,** *refl., pfv. of* зава́ливаться.

за́валь *n.f., colloq.* unsold or unsalable merchandise; junk.

заваля́ться *v.r. pfv., colloq.* to lie unused; lie unsold; lie unattended to.

зава́ривать *v. impfv.* [*pfv.* завари́ть] to make; brew (coffee, tea, etc.). —**завари́ть ка́шу,** to stir up trouble.

завари́ть [*infl.* -варю́, -ва́ришь] *v., pfv. of* зава́ривать.

заварно́й *adj.* boiled. —**заварно́й крем,** custard. —**заварно́е пиро́жное,** pastry filled with custard.

заведе́ние *n.* institution; establishment. —**вы́сшее учё́бное заведе́ние,** institution of higher learning.

заве́дование *n.* management; supervision.

заве́довать *v. impfv.* [*pres.* -дую, -дуешь] (*with instr.*) to manage.

заве́домо *adv.* **1,** obviously; known to be. **2,** knowingly; wittingly.

заве́домый *adj.* **1,** notorious. **2,** obvious.

заве́дующий *n., decl. as an adj.* manager.

завезти́ [*infl. like* везти́] *v., pfv. of* завози́ть.

завербова́ть *v., pfv. of* вербова́ть.

завере́ние *n.* assurance.

заве́рить *v., pfv. of* заверя́ть.

заверну́ть *v., pfv. of* завё́ртывать. —**заверну́ться,** *refl., pfv. of* завё́ртываться.

заверте́ть *v. pfv.* [*infl.* -верчу́, -ве́ртишь] **1,** (*with instr.*) to begin to twirl. **2,** *fig., colloq.* to carry away. —**заверте́ться,** *refl.* **1,** to begin to spin; begin to whirl. **2,** *fig., colloq.* to be in a whirl.

завё́ртывать *v. impfv.* [*pfv.* заверну́ть] **1,** to wrap; wrap up; (*with* в + *acc.*) wrap in. **2,** to turn: заверну́ть за́ угол, to turn the corner. **3,** to turn up; roll up; tuck up. **4,** to screw tight; tighten. **5,** *colloq.* to turn off. **6,** (*with* к) *colloq.* to drop in (on). —**завё́ртываться,** *refl.* **1,** (*with* в + *acc.*) to wrap oneself (in). **2,** to be turned up; be folded *or* rolled back.

заверша́ть *v. impfv.* [*pfv.* заверши́ть] to complete. —**заверша́ться,** *refl.* **1,** to be completed. **2,** (*with instr.*) to be concluded (with *or* by).

заверша́ющий *adj.* concluding; closing. —**заверша́ющий уда́р,** crowning blow.

заверше́ние *n.* completion; conclusion; consummation.

заверши́ть *v., pfv. of* заверша́ть. —**заверши́ться,** *refl., pfv. of* заверша́ться.

заверя́ть *v. impfv.* [*pfv.* заве́рить] **1,** to assure. **2,** to witness; certify.

заве́са *n.* **1,** curtain. **2,** *fig.* veil; screen. —**дымова́я заве́са,** smoke screen.

заве́сить [*infl.* -шу, -сишь] *v., pfv. of* заве́шивать (*in sense #1*).

завести́ [*infl. like* вести́] *v., pfv. of* заводи́ть. —**завести́сь,** *refl., pfv. of* заводи́ться.

заве́т *n.* **1,** precept. **2,** *relig.* covenant. **3,** *obs.* vow. —**Ве́тхий заве́т,** Old Testament. —**Но́вый заве́т,** New Testament.

заве́тный *adj.* **1,** (*of a dream, desire, etc.*) fondest; lifelong. **2,** secret; hidden.

заве́шивать *v. impfv.* **1,** [*pfv.* заве́сить] to cover; curtain off. **2,** [*pfv.* заве́шать] to hang with: сте́ны бы́ли заве́шаны карти́нами, the walls were hung with paintings.

завеща́ние *n.* will. —**духо́вное завеща́ние,** last will and testament.

завеща́тель *n.m.* testator. —**завеща́тельница,** *n.* testatrix.

завеща́ть *v. impfv. & pfv.* to bequeath; will; leave.

завзя́тый *adj., colloq.* **1,** inveterate. **2,** avid; ardent.

завива́ть *v. impfv.* [*pfv.* зави́ть] to curl; wave. —**завива́ться,** *refl.* **1,** (*of hair*) to curl; become curly. **2,** to have one's hair curled.

зави́вка [*gen. pl.* вок] *n.* wave. —**шестиме́сячная зави́вка,** permanent wave.

завидеть *v. pfv.* [*infl.* -жу, -дишь] *colloq.* to catch sight of (*from afar*).

завидно *adj., used predicatively* (*with dat.*) envious: ему завидно смотреть на неё, he is envious when he looks at her.

завидный *adj.* enviable.

завидовать *v. impfv.* [*pfv.* позавидовать; *pres.* -дую, -дуешь] (*with dat.*) to envy; be jealous of.

завидущий *adj., colloq.* envious; covetous.

завинчивать *v. impfv.* [*pfv.* завинтить] to tighten (a screw, nut, etc.).

завираться *v.r. impfv.* [*pfv.* завраться] *colloq.* to become tangled in lies.

зависеть *v. impfv.* [*pres.* -шу, -сишь] (*with* от) to depend (on).

зависимость *n.f.* dependence. —в зависимости от, depending on. —вне зависимости от, regardless of.

зависимый *adj.* dependent.

завистливый *adj.* envious.

завистник *n.* envious person.

зависть *n.f.* envy.

завитой *adj.* (*of hair*) curled; waved.

завиток [*gen.* -ткá] *n.* **1,** lock; ringlet. **2,** flourish (*in handwriting or oratory*).

завитушка [*gen. pl.* -шек] *n., colloq.* = завиток.

завить [*infl. like* вить] *v., pfv. of* завивать. —завиться, *refl., pfv. of* завиваться.

завком *n.* factory committee (*contr. of* заводской комитет).

завладевать *v. impfv.* [*pfv.* завладеть] (*with instr.*) **1,** to seize; take possession of; capture. **2,** *fig.* to grip: завладеть чьим-нибудь вниманием, to grip someone's attention. **3,** *fig.* to captivate.

завлекательный *adj.* enticing; alluring.

завлекать *v. impfv.* [*pfv.* завлечь] **1,** to entice; lure. **2,** to captivate; enthrall.

завлечь [*infl. like* влечь] *v., pfv. of* завлекать.

завод *n.* **1,** factory; plant; mill; works. ♦*Used with various adjectives:* конный завод, stud farm; пивоваренный завод, brewery; сахарный завод, sugar refinery. **2,** winding mechanism.

заводить *v. impfv.* [*pfv.* завести; *pres.* -вожу, -водишь] **1,** to take to; bring to. **2,** (*with* в +*acc.*) to bring into; lead into. **3,** to take out of one's way; take far away: куда ты нас завёл?, where have you taken us? **4,** to start; launch. **5,** to introduce; institute. **6,** to strike up (a conversation, acquaintance, etc.). **7,** to get; acquire. **8,** to wind (a watch); start (a car or motor). —заводиться, *refl.* **1,** to appear; turn up. **2,** to be established; start up. **3,** (*of an engine*) to start.

заводский *also,* **заводской** *adj.* **1,** factory (*attrib.*). **2,** *in* заводская лошадь, stud horse.

заводчик *n.* factory owner.

заводь *n.f.* inlet; creek.

завоевание *n.* **1,** conquest. **2,** *pl.* conquests. **3,** *pl.* achievements. —завоеватель, *n.m.* conqueror.

завоевать [*infl.* -воюю, -воюешь] *v., pfv. of* завоёвывать.

завоёвывать *v. impfv.* [*pfv.* завоевать] **1,** to conquer. **2,** to gain; win.

завоз *n.* delivery.

завозить *v. impfv.* [*pfv.* завезти; *pres.* -вожу, -возишь] **1,** to deliver; drop off. **2,** to take far away; take out of one's way. **3,** to bring into (a country).

заволакивать *v. impfv.* [*pfv.* заволочь] to cloud; obscure: тучи заволокли солнце, clouds obscured the sun. *Also impers.:* её глаза заволокло слезами, her eyes were clouded with tears.

заволноваться *v.r. pfv.* [*infl.* -нуюсь, -нуешься] to become agitated.

заволочь [*infl. like* волочь] *v., pfv. of* заволакивать.

завораживать *v. impfv.* [*pfv.* заворожить] **1,** to bewitch; cast a spell over. **2,** *fig.* to bewitch; captivate.

заворачивать *v. impfv.* [*pfv.* заворотить] *colloq.* **1,** *v.i.* to turn; make a turn. **2,** *v.t.* to turn around; turn back. **3,** to turn up (an edge, sleeve, etc.). **4,** to drop in. **5,** [*impfv. only*] (*with instr.*) to be in charge of.

заворожённый *adj.* spellbound; bewitched.

заворожить *v., pfv. of* завораживать.

заворот *n., colloq.* **1,** sharp turn. **2,** bend (*in a road, river, etc.*).

заворотить [*infl.* -рочу, -ротишь] *v., pfv. of* заворачивать.

завраться [*infl. like* врать] *v.r., pfv. of* завираться.

завсегдатай *n.* habitué.

завтра *adv.* tomorrow.

завтрак *n.* **1,** breakfast. **2,** lunch. **3,** luncheon.

завтракать *v. impfv.* [*pfv.* позавтракать] to have breakfast; have lunch.

завтрашний *adj.* tomorrow's. —завтрашний день, **1,** tomorrow. **2,** the future.

завуалировать *v. pfv.* [*infl.* -рую, -руешь] to veil; conceal.

завуч *n., colloq.* director of studies (*contr. of* заведующий учебной частью).

завхоз *n., colloq.* steward; household manager (*contr. of* заведующий хозяйством).

завывать *v. impfv.* to howl; wail.

завышать *v. impfv.* [*pfv.* завысить] to set (goals, norms, etc.) too high; give too high (a grade).

завязать[1] [*infl.* -вяжу, -вяжешь] *v., pfv. of* завязывать. —завязаться, *refl., pfv. of* завязываться.

завязать[2] *v. impfv.* [*pfv.* завязнуть; *pres.* -заю, -заешь] **1,** to get stuck. **2,** *fig., colloq.* to become mired.

завязка [*gen. pl.* -зок] *n.* **1,** string; lace; band. **2,** beginning; starting point.

завязнуть [*past* -вяз, -ла] *v., pfv. of* вязнуть and завязать[2].

завязывать *v. impfv.* [*pfv.* завязать] **1,** to tie; tie up. **2,** to bind; bind up. **3,** *in* завязать глаза (+*dat.*), to blindfold. **4,** to start; strike up (a conversation, acquaintance, etc.). —завязываться, *refl.* **1,** to be tied; tie. **2,** to begin; develop; spring up.

завязь *n.f., bot.* ovary.

завянуть [*past* -вял, -вяла] *v., pfv. of* вянуть.

загадать *v., pfv. of* загадывать.

загадить [*infl.* -жу, -дишь] *v., pfv. of* загаживать.

загадка [*gen. pl.* -док] *n.* **1,** riddle; puzzle. **2,** mystery; enigma.

загадочный *adj.* enigmatic; mysterious.

загадывать *v. impfv.* [*pfv.* загадать] **1,** to pose (a riddle). **2,** to think of; pick (*as part of a riddle*). **3,** to think ahead; look ahead.

загаживать *v. impfv.* [*pfv.* загадить] *colloq.* to foul; dirty; pollute.

загáр *n.* sunburn; sun tan.

загаси́ть v. pfv. [infl. -гашу́, -га́сишь] colloq. to put out; extinguish.

загво́здка [gen. pl. -док] n., colloq. hitch; catch; snag; rub.

заги́б n. 1, bend. 2, crease (in a page). 3, fig. deviation.

загиба́ть v. impfv. [pfv. загну́ть] 1, to turn up; turn down; fold down; fold over. 2, v.i., colloq. to turn: загну́ть за́ угол, to turn the corner. 3, colloq. to utter; come out with. —**загиба́ться**, refl. 1, to turn up. 2, to bend.

загипнотизи́ровать v., pfv. of гипнотизи́ровать.

загла́вие n. title.

загла́вный adj. title (attrib.). —**загла́вная бу́ква**, capital letter. —**загла́вный лист**, title page. —**загла́вная роль**, title role.

загла́дить [infl. -жу, -дишь] v., pfv. of загла́живать.

загла́живать v. impfv. [pfv. загла́дить] 1, to smooth out; iron out. 2, to redress; make amends for.

загла́зно adv., colloq. 1, behind one's back. 2, sight unseen.

загла́зный adj., colloq. said or done behind one's back.

заглóхнуть [past -гло́х, -ла] v., pfv. of гло́хнуть (in senses #2 and #3).

заглуша́ть v. impfv. [pfv. заглуши́ть] 1, to muffle; drown out (sound); jam (radio broadcasts). 2, to deaden (pain). 3, (of weeds) to choke. 4, fig. to stifle.

заглуши́ть v., pfv. of глуши́ть and заглуша́ть.

загляде́нье n., colloq. lovely sight; sight for sore eyes.

загляде́ться [infl. -жу́сь, -ди́шься] v.r., pfv. of загля́дываться.

загля́дывать v. impfv. [pfv. загляну́ть] 1, (with в + acc.) to look (into); peep (into); (with под + acc.) look under. 2, colloq. to drop in; drop by; (with к) drop in on; look in on. 3, in загля́дывать вперёд, to look ahead. —**загля́дываться**, refl. [pfv. загляде́ться] to stare at (longingly); eye.

загляну́ть [infl. -гляну́, -гля́нешь] v., pfv. of загля́дывать.

загна́ивать v. impfv. [pfv. загнои́ть] colloq. to allow to fester; allow to rot. —**загна́иваться**, refl. to fester.

за́гнанный adj. 1, (of an animal) exhausted (from being chased). 2, fig. downtrodden; persecuted.

загна́ть [infl. like гнать] v., pfv. of загоня́ть.

загнива́ние n. 1, rotting. 2, fig. decay.

загнива́ть v. impfv. [pfv. загни́ть] to rot; decay.

загни́ть [infl. like гнить] v., pfv. of загнива́ть.

загнои́ть v., pfv. of загна́ивать. —**загнои́ться**, refl., pfv. of загна́иваться.

загну́ть v., pfv. of загиба́ть. —**загну́ться**, refl., pfv. of загиба́ться.

загова́ривать v. impfv. [pfv. заговори́ть] 1, [impfv. only] (with с + instr.) to start a conversation (with). 2, colloq. to talk (someone's) head off. 3, to cast a spell over. 4, in загова́ривать зу́бы (+ dat.), colloq. to fool (someone) with fine words. —**загова́риваться**, refl. 1, [impfv. only] to ramble (when speaking). 2, to become engrossed in conversation.

за́говор n. 1, plot; conspiracy. 2, incantation.

заговори́ть v. pfv. 1, pfv. of загова́ривать. 2, to learn to speak. 3, to begin to speak. —**заговори́ться**, refl., pfv. of загова́риваться (in sense #2).

загово́рщик n. conspirator; plotter. —**загово́рщический**, adj. conspiratorial.

за́годя adv., colloq. ahead of time; in advance.

заголо́вок [gen. -вка] n. 1, headline. 2, heading.

заго́н n. 1, pen (for cattle). 2, herding; rounding up. 3, strip of land. —**быть в заго́не**, to be neglected; be in a state of neglect.

загоня́ть v. impfv. [pfv. загна́ть] 1, (with в + acc.) to herd into; drive into. 2, colloq. to drive in; hammer in. 3, to drive away. 4, to drive to exhaustion. 5, to bring (an animal) to bay.

загора́живать v. impfv. [pfv. загороди́ть] 1, to enclose; fence in. 2, to bar; block; obstruct.

загора́ть v. impfv. [pfv. загоре́ть] 1, to become (or get) sunburned. 2, [impfv. only] to sun-bathe. —**загора́ться**, refl. 1, to catch fire. 2, (of one's eyes) to light up; (of one's face) be flushed. 3, (of an argument, fight, etc.) to break out. 4, (with instr.) to be consumed with (an emotion, idea, etc.). 5, impers. (with dat.) colloq. to have a burning desire.

загоре́лый adj. sunburned; suntanned.

загоре́ть [infl. -горю́, -гори́шь] v., pfv. of загора́ть. —**загоре́ться**, refl., pfv. of загора́ться.

загороди́ть [infl. -рожу́, -ро́дишь or -роди́шь] v., pfv. of загора́живать.

загоро́дка [gen. pl. -док] n., colloq. 1, fence. 2, partition. 3, enclosure.

за́городный adj. out-of-town; country (attrib.).

загости́ться v.r. pfv. [infl. -гощу́сь, -сти́шься] colloq. to overstay one's welcome.

загота́вливать v. impfv. = заготовля́ть.

загото́вить [infl. -влю, -вишь] v., pfv. of загота́вливать and заготовля́ть.

загото́вка n. 1, storing up; stocking up. 2, often pl. purchase(s) (by the state).

заготовля́ть v. impfv. [pfv. загото́вить] 1, to prepare in advance. 2, (often fol. by впрок) to store up; stock up on.

загради́тель n.m. minelayer. Also, ми́нный загради́тель.

загради́тельный adj., mil. protecting; covering. —**загради́тельный ого́нь**, covering fire; barrage.

загради́ть [infl. -жу́, -ди́шь] v., pfv. of загражда́ть.

загражда́ть v. impfv. [pfv. загради́ть] to bar; block; obstruct.

загражде́ние n. obstacle; barrier; obstruction.

заграни́ца n., colloq. foreign countries. —**по заграни́цам**, abroad.

заграни́чный adj. foreign.

загреба́ть v. impfv. [pfv. загрести́] 1, to rake together; rake up. 2, in загреба́ть жар, to bank the fire (in a furnace). 3, colloq. to rake in (money). —**чужи́ми рука́ми жар загреба́ть**, to make someone else do one's dirty work.

загреме́ть v. pfv. [infl. -млю́, -ми́шь] 1, to begin to sound, clank, thunder, etc.; resound. 2, (with instr.) to rattle. 3, colloq. to come crashing down.

загрести́ [infl. like грести́] v., pfv. of загреба́ть.

загри́вок [gen. -вка] n. 1, withers. 2, colloq. nape of the neck.

загримирова́ть v., pfv. of гримирова́ть (in sense #2). —**загримирова́ться**, refl., pfv. of гримирова́ться (in sense #2).

загро́бный adj. occurring after death: загро́бный мир, the next world; загро́бная жизнь, life after death; afterlife.

загромождать *v. impfv.* [*pfv.* загромоздить] to clutter (up); jam.

загромоздить [*infl.* -зжу́, -зди́шь] *v., pfv. of* загромождать.

загрубе́лый *adj.* calloused.

загрубе́ть *v. pfv.* **1,** to become calloused. **2,** *fig.* to become callous.

загружа́ть *v. impfv.* [*pfv.* загрузи́ть] **1,** to load (a vehicle, vessel, etc.). **2,** *fig.* to assign a full load of work to (someone); fill out (a period of time) with work. —**загружа́ться,** *refl.* to load up.

загрузи́ть [*infl.* -гружу́, -гру́зишь *or* -грузи́шь] *v., pfv. of* грузи́ть (*in sense #1*) *and* загружа́ть. —**загрузи́ться,** *refl., pfv. of* загружа́ться.

загру́зка *n.* **1,** loading. **2,** *colloq.* workload; capacity.

загрусти́ть *v. pfv.* [*infl.* -щу́, -сти́шь] to become sad.

загрыза́ть *v. impfv.* [*pfv.* загры́зть] **1,** to kill; bite to death; tear to pieces. **2,** *colloq.* to nag; hound; badger.

загры́зть [*infl. like* грызть] *v., pfv. of* загрыза́ть.

загрязне́ние *n.* **1,** soiling. **2,** pollution; contamination.

загрязни́ть *v., pfv. of* грязни́ть *and* загрязня́ть. —**загрязни́ться,** *refl., pfv. of* грязни́ться *and* загрязня́ться.

загрязня́ть *v. impfv.* [*pfv.* загрязни́ть] **1,** to soil; dirty. **2,** to pollute; contaminate. —**загрязня́ться,** *refl.* to get dirty.

загс *n.* civilian registry office (*abbr. of* за́пись а́ктов гражда́нского состоя́ния).

загуби́ть *v. pfv.* [*infl.* -гублю́, -гу́бишь] *colloq.* **1,** to ruin. **2,** to squander.

загуля́ть *v. pfv., colloq.* to go on a spree. —**загуля́ться,** *refl., colloq.* **1,** to walk for too long a time. **2,** to carouse till one forgets the time.

загусте́ть *v., pfv. of* густе́ть.

зад [*2nd loc.* заду́; *pl.* зады́] *n.* **1,** back; rear. **2,** behind; backside. **3,** rump; buttocks. **4,** *pl., colloq.* old stuff: повторя́ть зады́, to repeat old stuff; say what has been said many times before. *See also* за́дом.

задо́бривать *v. impfv.* [*pfv.* задо́брить] **1,** to bring around; win over. **2,** to cajole; coax.

задава́ть *v. impfv.* [*pfv.* зада́ть; *pres.* -даю́, -даёшь] **1,** to ask (a question); pose (a problem). **2,** to assign (a lesson, task, etc.). **3,** to set (the tone, fashion, etc.). **4,** *colloq.* to give; throw (a party, banquet, etc.). **5,** *colloq.* to give; administer (a scolding, punishment, etc.). —**задава́ться,** *refl.* **1,** *in* задава́ться це́лью (+ *inf.*), to set as one's goal. **2,** *in* зада́ться вопро́сом, to ask oneself a question. **3,** *colloq.* (*usu. neg.*) (not) turn out well. **4,** [*impfv. only*] *colloq.* to put on airs.

задави́ть *v., pfv. of* дави́ть (*in senses #5 & #6*).

зада́ние *n.* task; assignment. —**дома́шнее зада́ние,** homework.

задаривать *v. impfv.* [*pfv.* задари́ть] **1,** to lavish gifts upon. **2,** *obs.* to bribe; ''buy off''.

задари́ть [*infl.* -дарю́, -да́ришь] *v., pfv. of* зада́ривать.

зада́ром *adv., colloq.* = да́ром.

зада́ток [*gen.* -тка] *n.* **1,** deposit; down payment. **2,** *pl.* makings: зада́тки хоро́шего писа́теля, the makings of a good writer.

зада́ть [*infl. like* дать; *past* за́дал, задала́, за́дало] *v., pfv. of* задава́ть. —**зада́ться,** *refl.* [*past* зада́лся, задала́сь, задало́сь] *pfv. of* задава́ться.

зада́ча *n.* **1,** task. **2,** (arithmetical) problem.

зада́чник *n.* book of arithmetical problems.

задвига́ть *v. impfv.* [*pfv.* задви́нуть] **1,** to push; slide (in, under, *or* behind). **2,** to close; slide shut. **3,** to close off. **4,** to draw (a curtain). **5,** to bolt (a door). —**задвига́ться,** *refl.* **1,** to slide into place. **2,** [*impfv. only*] to be movable; slide.

задви́жка [*gen. pl.* -жек] *n.* bolt; catch (*for a door, gate, etc.*).

задвижно́й *adj.* sliding.

задви́нуть *v., pfv. of* задвига́ть. —**задви́нуться,** *refl., pfv. of* задвига́ться.

задво́рки [*gen.* -рок] *n. pl.* area behind a house. —**на задво́рках,** in the background.

задева́ть *v. impfv.* [*pfv.* заде́ть] **1,** to brush against; graze. **2,** *v.i.* (*with* за + *acc.*) catch (on); snag (on). **3,** to affect. **4,** to touch; affect (*emotionally*). **5,** to arouse; whet (one's curiosity); hurt; wound (one's pride). **6,** *colloq.* to hurt; offend. —**задева́ть за живо́е,** to cut to the quick.

заде́л *n., colloq.* **1,** beginning; start. **2,** reserve; margin.

заде́лывать *v. impfv.* [*pfv.* заде́лать] to close; seal up (a hole, crack, breach, etc.).

задёргать *v. pfv.* **1,** (*with instr.*) to tug at; give a tug. **2,** *colloq.* to wear out (a horse) by continually tugging at the reins. **3,** *colloq.* to harass.

задёргивать *v. impfv.* [*pfv.* задёрнуть] **1,** to draw (a curtain). **2,** to cover with a curtain.

задеревене́лый *adj., colloq.* stiff; numb.

задеревене́ть *v. pfv., colloq.* to become numb; become stiff.

задержа́ние *n.* **1,** detention; arrest. **2,** retention (*of moisture, urine, etc.*).

задержа́ть [*infl.* -держу́, -де́ржишь] *v., pfv. of* заде́рживать. —**задержа́ться,** *refl., pfv. of* заде́рживаться.

заде́рживать *v. impfv.* [*pfv.* задержа́ть] **1,** to delay; detain; hold up. **2,** to withhold; hold back. **3,** to arrest; detain. **4,** to retain (moisture). —**заде́рживаться,** *refl.* **1,** to be delayed. **2,** to linger.

заде́ржка [*gen. pl.* -жек] *n.* delay. —**без заде́ржек,** without interruption.

задёрнуть *v., pfv. of* задёргивать.

заде́ть [*infl.* -де́ну, -де́нешь] *v., pfv. of* задева́ть.

задира *n.m. & f., colloq.* roughneck; bully.

задира́ть *v. impfv.* [*pfv.* задра́ть] *colloq.* **1,** to lift up; stick up. **2,** [*impfv. only*] to tease; pick on. **3,** *in* задира́ть нос, to turn up one's nose; put on airs. —**задира́ться,** *refl.* [*impfv. only*] *colloq.* to pick a fight. *See also* задра́ть.

задненёбный *adj.* velar.

заднепроходный *adj.* anal.

за́дний *adj.* rear; back; hind. —**за́дняя мысль,** ulterior motive. —**за́дний план,** background. —**за́дний прохо́д,** anus. —**за́дним умо́м кре́пок,** wise after the event. —**за́дний ход,** reverse motion: дать за́дний ход, to go into reverse; back up; *fig.* reverse oneself. —**за́дним число́м,** later; afterwards; after the fact. —**поме́тить за́дним число́м,** to backdate.

за́дник *n.* **1,** back (*of a shoe*). **2,** *theat.* backdrop.

задо́брить *v., pfv. of* задо́бривать.

задо́к [*gen.* -дка́] *n.* back (*of a vehicle, piece of furniture, or shoe*).

задо́лго *adv.* [*usu.* задо́лго до] long before.

задолжа́ть *v. pfv., colloq.* **1,** to borrow. **2,** to owe.

задо́лженность *n.f.* indebtedness; debts.

за́дом *adv.* **1,** backward; backwards. **2,** (*with* к) with one's back to. —**за́дом наперёд,** *see* наперёд.

задо́р *n.* ardor; zeal; fervor.

задо́ринка *n., in* ни/без сучка́, ни/без задо́ринки, without a hitch.

задо́рный *adj.* **1,** ardent; passionate. **2,** lively; sprightly.

задохну́ться *v.r., pfv. of* задыха́ться.

задра́ивать *v. impfv.* [*pfv.* задра́ить] to batten down.

задрапирова́ть *v., pfv. of* драпирова́ть.

задра́ть *v. pfv.* [*infl. like* драть] **1,** *pfv. of* задира́ть. **2,** to tear (the skin); break (a nail). **3,** to tear to pieces; kill. **4,** to whip; flog.

задрема́ть *v. pfv.* [*infl.* -дремлю́, -дре́млешь] to doze off.

задрожа́ть *v. pfv.* [*infl.* -жу́, -жи́шь] to begin to tremble; begin to shiver.

задува́ть *v. impfv.* [*pfv.* заду́ть] **1,** (*of the wind*) to begin to blow. **2,** [*impfv. only*] (*of the wind*) (*with a prep.*) A, *v.i.* to blow (into, through, etc.). B, *v.t.* to blow (something somewhere). **3,** to blow out (a candle).

заду́мать *v., pfv. of* заду́мывать. —**заду́маться,** *refl., pfv. of* заду́мываться.

заду́мчивый *adj.* thoughtful; pensive. —**заду́мчивость,** *n.f.* pensiveness; deep thought.

заду́мывать *v. impfv.* [*pfv.* заду́мать] **1,** to plan; conceive. **2,** to decide on; (*with inf.*) decide to. **3,** to think of; choose (*e.g.* a number in a game). —**заду́мываться,** *refl.* **1,** (*with* над *or* о) to ponder; meditate (over). **2,** to be lost in thought. **3,** to hesitate.

заду́ть [*infl.* -ду́ю, -ду́ешь] *v., pfv. of* задува́ть.

задуше́вный *adj.* **1,** sincere; heartfelt. **2,** intimate; innermost.

задуши́ть *v., pfv. of* души́ть.

задыми́ть *v. pfv.* [*infl.* -млю́, -ми́шь] **1,** to begin to emit smoke. **2,** to blacken with smoke.

задымлённый *adj.* smoky.

задыха́ться *v.r. impfv.* [*pfv.* задохну́ться] **1,** to gasp for breath; pant. **2,** to choke (*with anger, tears, etc.*). **3,** to suffocate.

заеда́ть *v. impfv.* [*pfv.* зае́сть] **1,** to chew to death; nibble to death. **2,** to take away the taste of (something) by eating something else: зае́сть лека́рство са́харом, to take sugar with the medicine. **3,** *fig.* to torment; harass. **4,** *fig.* to corrupt. **5,** *impers.* to stick; jam: ключ в замке́ зае́ло, the key stuck in the lock.

зае́зд *n.* **1,** visit; call. **2,** horse race.

зае́здить *v. pfv.* [*infl.* -е́зжу, -е́здишь] *colloq.* to overwork; wear out.

заезжа́ть *v. impfv.* [*pfv.* зае́хать] **1,** (*with* в + *acc. or* к) to stop in at; drop in on. **2,** (*with* за + *instr.*) to pick up; call for. **3,** (*with* в + *acc.*) to drive into (*accidentally*). **4,** to approach (from a certain direction).

зае́зженный *adj., colloq.* **1,** (*of a horse*) worn out. **2,** *fig.* hackneyed; trite.

зае́зжий *adj.* visiting; touring. —*n.* person passing through.

заём [*gen.* за́йма] *n.* loan. —**заёмщик,** *n.* borrower.

зае́сть [*infl. like* есть] *v., pfv. of* заеда́ть.

зае́хать [*infl.* -е́ду, -е́дешь] *v., pfv. of* заезжа́ть.

зажа́рить *v., pfv. of* жа́рить. —**зажа́риться,** *refl., pfv. of* жа́риться.

зажа́ть [*infl.* -жму́, -жмёшь] *v., pfv. of* зажима́ть.

зажда́ться *v.r. pfv.* [*infl. like* ждать] (*with gen.*) *colloq.* to get tired of waiting (for).

заже́чь [*infl. like* жечь] *v., pfv. of* зажига́ть. —**заже́чься,** *refl., pfv. of* зажига́ться.

зажива́ть *v. impfv.* [*pfv.* зажи́ть] to heal. —**зажива́ться,** *refl., colloq.* to live too long.

заживля́ть *v. impfv.* [*pfv.* заживи́ть] *colloq.* to heal (a wound).

за́живо *adv., used only with verbs of burying,* alive: хорони́ть за́живо, to bury alive.

зажига́лка [*gen. pl.* -лок] *n.* cigarette lighter.

зажига́ние *n.* **1,** lighting; act of lighting. **2,** *mech.* ignition.

зажига́тельный *adj.* **1,** incendiary. **2,** *fig.* fiery; inflammatory; incendiary.

зажига́ть *v. impfv.* [*pfv.* заже́чь] **1,** to light (a lamp or match); turn on (a light). **2,** *fig.* to fire up. **3,** *fig.* to kindle; spark; ignite (emotions). —**зажига́ться,** *refl.* **1,** (*of a match*) to light; (*of lights*) go on; (*of stars*) come out. **2,** (*with instr.*) (*of one's eyes*) to light up; blaze (with an emotion). **3,** (*of emotions*) to be aroused.

зажи́м *n.* **1,** clamp. **2,** *electricity* terminal.

зажима́ть *v. impfv.* [*pfv.* зажа́ть] **1,** to squeeze; clutch; grip. **2,** to stop up; block up; plug up. **3,** to hold (one's nose). **4,** *fig., colloq.* to stifle; suppress.

зажи́точный *adj.* prosperous; affluent; well-to-do. —**зажи́точность,** *n.f.* prosperity; affluence.

зажи́ть *v. pfv.* [*infl.* -живу́, -живёшь; *past* за́жил, зажила́, за́жило] **1,** *pfv. of* зажива́ть. **2,** to begin to live: зажи́ть споко́йной жи́знью, to begin to live a quiet life. —**зажи́ться,** *refl.* [*past* зажи́лся, -ла́сь, -ло́сь] *pfv. of* зажива́ться.

зажму́рить *v., pfv. of* жму́рить. —**зажму́риться,** *refl., pfv. of* жму́риться.

зазва́ть [*infl. like* звать] *v., pfv. of* зазыва́ть.

зазвони́ть *v. pfv.* to begin to ring.

заздра́вный *adj., in* заздра́вный тост, toast to someone's health.

зазева́ться *v.r. pfv.* (*with* на + *acc.*) *colloq.* to stare (at); gape (at).

зазелене́ть *v. pfv.* to turn green.

заземле́ние *n., electricity* ground connection.

заземля́ть *v. impfv.* [*pfv.* заземли́ть] *electricity* to ground.

зазимова́ть *v. pfv.* [*infl.* -му́ю, -му́ешь] to winter; spend the winter.

зазнава́ться *v.r. impfv.* [*pfv.* зазна́ться; *pres.* -зна́юсь, -знаёшься] *colloq.* to get a swelled head.

зазна́йство *n., colloq.* conceit.

зазна́ться *v.r., pfv. of* зазнава́ться.

зазно́ба *n., colloq.* ladylove.

зазо́р *n., mech.* clearance.

зазо́рный *adj., colloq.* shameful.

зазре́ние *n., in* без зазре́ния со́вести, without any pangs of conscience; without compunction.

зазу́бренный *adj.* **1,** jagged; notched. **2,** *bot.* serrate(d). **3,** *colloq.* memorized; rote.

зазу́бривать *v. impfv.* [*pfv.* зазубри́ть] **1,** to notch; make notches in. **2,** *colloq.* to learn by rote.

зазу́брина *n.* notch.

зазубри́ть *v. pfv. of* зубри́ть *and* зазу́бривать.

зазыва́ть *v. impfv.* [*pfv.* зазва́ть] *colloq.* to invite repeatedly; urge to come.

заигра́ть *v. pfv.* **1,** *pfv. of* заи́грывать. **2,** to begin to play.

зайгрывание *n.* flirting; *pl.* advances.

зайгрывать *v. impfv.* [*pfv.* **заигра́ть**] **1,** to wear out (cards, records, etc.) by playing. **2,** to make trite by repetition; play to death. **3,** [*impfv. only*] (*with* **с** + *instr.*) *colloq.* to flirt (with); play up to. —**зайгрываться**, *refl.* to become absorbed in playing.

зайка *n.m. & f.* stutterer.

заика́ние *n.* stutter; stuttering.

заика́ться *v.r. impfv.* [*pfv.* **заикну́ться**] **1,** [*impfv. only*] to stammer; stutter. **2,** (*with* **о**) *colloq.* to mention; breathe a word of.

заимода́вец [*gen.* **-вца**] *n., obs.* moneylender.

займствование *n.* borrowing.

займствовать *v. impfv. & pfv.* [*pfv. also* **позайимствовать**; *pres.* **-ствую, -ствуешь**] to borrow; adopt; incorporate.

за́йндеветь *v., pfv. of* **и́ндеветь**.

заинтересо́ванность *n.f.* interest.

заинтересо́ванный *adj.* **1,** (*with* **в** + *prepl.*) interested (in). **2,** interested; concerned: заинтересо́ванные сто́роны, the interested parties the parties concerned.

заинтересова́ть *v. pfv.* [*infl.* **-су́ю, -су́ешь**] to interest; arouse the interest of. —**заинтересова́ться**, *refl.* (*with instr.*) to become interested (in).

заинтригова́ть *v., pfv. of* **интригова́ть**.

зайскивать *v. impfv.* (*with* **пе́ред**) to try to ingratiate oneself (with); curry favor (with).

зайти́ [*infl.* **зайду́, зайдёшь;** *past* **зашёл, зашла́, зашло́**] *v., pfv. of* **заходи́ть**.

за́йчик *n.* **1,** *dim. of* **за́яц. 2,** *colloq.* spot of reflected light.

закабаля́ть *v. impfv.* [*pfv.* **закабали́ть**] to enslave.

закавка́зский *adj.* Transcaucasian.

закады́чный *adj., in* закады́чный друг, *colloq.* bosom friend.

зака́з *n.* order. —**на зака́з**, (made) to order.

заказа́ть [*infl.* **-кажу́, -ка́жешь**] *v., pfv. of* **зака́зывать.**

заказно́й *adj., in* заказно́е письмо́, registered letter.

зака́зчик *n.* customer.

зака́зывать *v. impfv.* [*pfv.* **заказа́ть**] to order; place an order for.

зака́л *n.* **1,** tempering; hardening. **2,** toughness. **3,** *fig.* cast; stamp; breed: челове́к ста́рого зака́ла, man of the old school.

закалённый *adj.* tempered; hardened. —**закалённый в боя́х**, battle-hardened.

закали́ть *v., pfv. of* **закаля́ть**. —**закали́ться**, *refl., pfv. of* **закаля́ться**.

зака́лка *n.* **1,** hardening; tempering. **2,** *fig.* toughness.

зака́лывать *v. impfv.* [*pfv.* **заколо́ть**] **1,** to stab to death. **2,** to slaughter (an animal). **3,** to fasten with a pin.

закаля́ть *v. impfv.* [*pfv.* **закали́ть**] **1,** to temper; harden. **2,** *fig.* to steel; inure. —**закаля́ться**, *refl.* **1,** to harden; become hard. **2,** *fig.* to become strong; become inured.

зака́нчивать *v. impfv.* [*pfv.* **зако́нчить**] to finish. —**зака́нчиваться**, *refl.* to end; be over.

зака́пать *v. pfv.* **1,** to spot; stain. **2,** to begin to drip.

зака́пывать *v. impfv.* [*pfv.* **закопа́ть**] **1,** to bury. **2,** to fill in (a hole).

зака́рмливать *v. impfv.* [*pfv.* **закорми́ть**] to overfeed; stuff.

зака́т *n.* **1,** sunset. **2,** *fig.* decline. —**на зака́те дней**,

in one's declining years; in the twilight of one's life.

заката́ть *v., pfv. of* **зака́тывать**[1].

закати́ть [*infl.* **-качу́, -ка́тишь**] *v., pfv. of* **зака́тывать**[2]. —**закати́ться**, *refl., pfv. of* **зака́тываться**.

зака́тывать[1] *v. impfv.* [*pfv.* **заката́ть**] **1,** (*with* **в** + *acc.*) to roll (in); roll up (in). **2,** *colloq.* to roll up (one's sleeves).

зака́тывать[2] *v. impfv.* [*pfv.* **закати́ть**] **1,** to roll; wheel (into, under, behind, etc.). **2,** *colloq.* to cause; create (a scandal); make (a scene). —**закати́ть глаза́**, to roll up one's eyes. —**закати́ть исте́рику**, *colloq.* to go into hysterics.

зака́тываться *v.r. impfv.* [*pfv.* **закати́ться**] **1,** to roll (into, under, behind, etc.). **2,** (*of the sun*) to set; go down.

закача́ть *v. pfv.* **1,** to rock to sleep. **2,** *impers.* to feel sick; feel nauseous (*from rocking or swaying*); меня́ закача́ло, I feel sick. **3,** to begin to shake.

зака́шлять *v. pfv.* to begin to cough. —**зака́шляться**, *refl.* to have a fit of coughing.

зака́яться, *v.r. pfv.* [*infl.* **-ка́юсь, -ка́ешься**] (*with inf.*) *colloq.* to swear off; swear never to do again.

закваси́ть [*infl.* **-шу, -сишь**] *v., pfv. of* **заква́шивать**.

заква́ска *n.* **1,** leaven; ferment. **2,** *fig.* mold: одно́й заква́ски, of the same mold. **3,** *fig.* stuff: у него́ хоро́шая заква́ска, he is made of good stuff.

заква́шивать *v. impfv.* [*pfv.* **закваси́ть**] to leaven; ferment.

заки́дывать[1] *v. impfv.* [*pfv.* **закида́ть**] = **забра́сывать**.[1] —**ша́пками закида́ем**, *colloq.* we'll win easily; we've got it won.

заки́дывать[2] *v. impfv.* [*pfv.* **заки́нуть**] = **забра́сывать**.[2] —**заки́нуть слове́чко за** (+ *acc.*), to put in a word for. —**заки́нуть у́дочку**, to drop a hint; put out a feeler.

закипа́ть *v. impfv.* [*pfv.* **закипе́ть**] **1,** to begin to boil; simmer. **2,** *fig.* (*with instr.*) to be seething (with). **3,** *fig.* to become agitated; become wrought up. **4,** *fig.* to get rolling; move into high gear.

закиса́ть *v. impfv.* [*pfv.* **заки́снуть**] **1,** to turn sour. **2,** *fig., colloq.* to become apathetic; become listless.

заки́снуть [*past* **-ки́с, -ла**] *v., pfv. of* **закиса́ть**.

за́кись *n.f.* protoxide. ♦*In compounds* —ous oxide: за́кись желе́за, ferrous oxide.

закла́д *n., obs.* **1,** pawning: в закла́де, in hock. **2,** bet; wager. —**би́ться об закла́д**, to bet; wager.

закла́дка [*gen. pl.* **-док**] *n.* **1,** laying. **2,** bookmark.

закладна́я *n., decl. as an adj.* mortgage.

закла́дчик *n., obs.* **1,** mortgagor. **2,** one who has pawned something. **3,** pawnbroker.

закла́дывать *v. impfv.* [*pfv.* **заложи́ть**] **1,** to put; place (*usually deep into something*). **2,** (*with* **за** + *acc.*) to put behind; place behind. **3,** to lay (mines, a foundation, etc.). **4,** to mark (a place in a book). **5,** to pawn; mortgage. **6,** to harness. **7,** (*with instr.*) to load (with); pile (with). **8,** to stop up; block. *See also* **заложи́ть**.

заклева́ть [*infl.* **-клюю́, -клюёшь**] *v., pfv. of* **заклёвывать**.

заклёвывать *v. impfv.* [*pfv.* **заклева́ть**] **1,** to peck to death. **2,** *fig., colloq.* to nag; harass.

закле́ивать *v. impfv.* [*pfv.* **закле́ить**] **1,** to seal up. **2,** to seal (an envelope). —**закле́иваться**, *refl.* to stick: конве́рт не закле́ивается, the envelope doesn't stick.

заклейми́ть *v., pfv. of* **клейми́ть**.

заклепа́ть *v., pfv. of* **заклёпывать**.

заклёпка [*gen. pl.* -пок] *n.* rivet.

заклёпывать *v. impfv.* [*pfv.* **заклепа́ть**] to rivet.

заклина́ние *n.* **1,** incantation. **2,** entreaty.

заклина́тель *n.m.* conjurer. —**заклина́тель змей,** snake charmer.

заклина́ть *v. impfv.* **1,** to bewitch; cast a spell over. **2,** to entreat; implore.

закли́нивать *v. impfv.* [*pfv.* **заклини́ть**] **1,** to wedge. **2,** to jam (a device, machine, etc.). **3,** *impers.* to jam; become jammed: дверь заклини́ло, the door jammed. —**закли́ниваться,** *refl.* **1,** to become wedged. **2,** to jam; become jammed.

заключа́ть *v. impfv.* [*pfv.* **заключи́ть**] **1,** to conclude; close; end. **2,** to conclude (a deal, peace, etc.); sign (a treaty, agreement, etc.); form (an alliance). **3,** to enclose: заключи́ть в ско́бки, to enclose in brackets. **4,** [*impfv. only*] (*often with* в себе́) to contain. **5,** to conclude; infer; gather. **6,** to imprison; confine; incarcerate. —**заключа́ться,** *refl.* [*impfv. only*] **1,** to conclude; close; end. **2,** (*of an agreement*) to be concluded; be signed. **3,** to be enclosed. **4,** (*with* в + *prepl.*) to be; consist of; lie in.

заключе́ние *n.* **1,** conclusion: прийти́ к заключе́нию, to come to/arrive at/ a conclusion. **2,** conclusion; end. **3,** signing (*of a treaty, agreement, etc.*). **4,** imprisonment; confinement. —**в заключе́ние,** in conclusion; in closing.

заключённый *n., decl. as an adj.* prisoner.

заключи́тельный *adj.* concluding; closing; final.

заключи́ть *v., pfv. of* **заключа́ть.**

закля́тие *n., obs.* **1,** incantation. **2,** oath; pledge.

закля́тый *adj.* (*of an enemy*) sworn: закля́тый враг, sworn enemy; archenemy.

закова́ть [*infl.* -кую́, -куёшь] *v., pfv. of* **зако́вывать.**

зако́вывать *v. impfv.* [*pfv.* **закова́ть**] to chain; shackle.

закола́чивать *v. impfv.* [*pfv.* **заколоти́ть**] *colloq.* **1,** to board up; seal up. **2,** to hammer in; drive in. **3,** to beat up; beat the life out of.

заколдо́ванный *adj.* charmed; bewitched; enchanted. —**заколдо́ванный круг,** vicious circle.

заколдова́ть [*infl.* -ду́ю, -ду́ешь] *v., pfv. of* **заколдо́вывать.**

заколдо́вывать *v. impfv.* [*pfv.* **заколдова́ть**] **1,** to cast a spell over. **2,** *fig.* to bewitch; charm.

зако́лка [*gen. pl.* -лок] *n., colloq.* **1,** bobby pin. **2,** tiepin.

заколоти́ть *v. pfv.* [*infl.* -лочу́, -ло́тишь] **1,** *pfv. of* **закола́чивать. 2,** to begin to knock.

заколо́ть [*infl.* -колю́, -ко́лешь] *v., pfv. of* **коло́ть** (*in sense #5*) *and* **зака́лывать.**

зако́н *n.* law. —**объяви́ть вне зако́на,** to outlaw.

зако́нник *n., colloq.* **1,** expert in law. **2,** one who strictly observes the law.

законнорождённый *adj.* (*of a child*) legitimate.

зако́нность *n.f.* legality; legitimacy.

зако́нный *adj.* **1,** legal; lawful; legitimate. **2,** legitimate; justifiable. **3,** rightful.

законове́д *n.* specialist in law; jurist. —**законове́дение,** *n.* jurisprudence.

законода́тель *n.m.* **1,** legislator; lawmaker. **2,** arbiter: законода́тель мод, arbiter of fashions.

законода́тельный *adj.* legislative. —**законода́тельство,** *n.* legislation.

закономе́рный *adj.* natural; regular; in accordance with the laws of nature. —**закономе́рность,** *n.f.* regularity; pattern; rule.

законопа́тить *v., pfv. of* **конопа́тить.**

законоположе́ние *n.* statute.

законопослу́шный *adj.* law-abiding.

законопрое́кт *n.* (legislative) bill.

законсерви́ровать *v., pfv. of* **консерви́ровать.**

законтрактова́ть *v., pfv. of* **контрактова́ть.**

зако́нченность *n.f.* completeness.

зако́нченный *adj.* **1,** complete; finished. **2,** (*of an artist, musician, etc.*) finished; accomplished; consummate.

зако́нчить *v., pfv. of* **зака́нчивать.** —**зако́нчиться,** *refl., pfv. of* **зака́нчиваться.**

закопа́ть *v., pfv. of* **зака́пывать.**

закопте́лый *adj.* sooty.

закопте́ть *v. pfv., colloq.* to become covered with soot.

закопти́ть *v., pfv. of* **копти́ть** (*in sense #1*). —**закопти́ться,** *refl.* to become covered with soot.

закорене́лый *adj.* **1,** chronic; ingrained; deep-rooted. **2,** inveterate; hardened; confirmed.

закорене́ть *v. pfv.* **1,** to become ingrained. **2,** (*with* в + *prepl.*) to become steeped in (prejudice, sin, etc.).

зако́рки *n. pl., colloq., in* на зако́рки; на зако́рках, on one's back; on one's shoulders; piggyback.

закорми́ть [*infl.* -кормлю́, -ко́рмишь] *v., pfv. of* **зака́рмливать.**

закорю́чка [*gen. pl.* -чек] *n., colloq.* **1,** hook; squiggle. **2,** trick; ploy. **3,** hitch; snag.

закосне́лый *adj.* **1,** inveterate; confirmed. **2,** ingrained; deep-seated.

закостене́лый *adj.* numb; stiff.

закостене́ть *v. pfv.* to become numb; become stiff.

закоу́лок [*gen.* -у́лка] *n.* **1,** back street. **2,** nook: все закоу́лки, every nook and cranny.

закочене́лый *adj.* frozen stiff; numb.

закочене́ть *v., pfv. of* **коченеть.**

закра́дываться *v.r. impfv.* [*pfv.* **закра́сться**] (*of feelings, doubts, etc.*) to creep in.

закра́сить [*infl.* -шу, -сишь] *v., pfv. of* **закра́шивать.**

закра́сться [*infl. like* красть] *v.r., pfv. of* **закра́дываться.**

закра́шивать *v. impfv.* [*pfv.* **закра́сить**] to paint over; cover over.

закрепи́тель *n.m., photog.* fixing agent.

закрепи́ть [*infl.* -плю́, -пи́шь] *v., pfv. of* **закрепля́ть.**

закрепле́ние *n.* **1,** fastening; securing. **2,** consolidation. **3,** *photog.* fixing.

закрепля́ть *v. impfv.* [*pfv.* **закрепи́ть**] **1,** to fasten; secure. **2,** to consolidate. **3,** (*with* за + *instr.*) to assign (to); set aside (for). Закрепи́ть за собо́й (+ *acc.*), to get; obtain; secure for oneself. **4,** *photog.* to fix.

закрепоща́ть *v. impfv.* [*pfv.* **закрепости́ть**] to enslave.

закрепоще́ние *n.* enslavement.

закрича́ть *v. pfv.* [*infl.* -чу́, -чи́шь] to cry out; shout; scream; yell.

закро́йщик *n.* cutter (*of cloth*).

за́кром [*pl.* закрома́] *n.* (grain) bin.

закругле́ние *n.* **1,** rounding; curving. **2,** curve.

закругля́ть *v. impfv.* [*pfv.* **закругли́ть**] to round off.

закружи́ть *v. pfv.* [*infl.* -кружу́, -кру́жишь *or* -кру́жишь] **1,** to begin to twirl/swirl/whirl; set spinning. **2,** to make dizzy. —**закружи́ться,** *refl.* **1,** to begin to whirl/swirl. **2,** to be dizzy; be in a whirl.

закрути́ть [*infl.* -кручу́, -кру́тишь] *v., pfv. of* крути́ть (*in sense #1*) *and* закру́чивать. —**закрути́ться**, *refl., pfv. of* закру́чиваться.

закру́чивать *v. impfv.* [*pfv.* закрути́ть] **1,** to twist. **2,** to twirl (one's mustache). **3,** (*with* на + *acc.*) to wind (around *or* onto). —**закру́чиваться**, *refl.* to become twisted.

закрыва́ть *v. impfv.* [*pfv.* закры́ть] **1,** to close; shut. **2,** to lock. **3,** to turn off; shut off (water, gas, etc.). **4,** to close down. **5,** to adjourn (a meeting). **6,** to cover. —**закрыва́ться**, *refl.* **1,** to close; shut; be closed; be shut. **2,** to lock: чемода́н закрыва́ется на ключ, the suitcase locks with a key. **3,** to cover oneself. **4,** (*of a meeting*) to adjourn.

закры́лок [*gen.* -лка] *n.* flap (*of an aircraft wing*).

закры́тие *n.* **1,** closing; shutting. **2,** close; end.

закры́тый *adj.* closed. —**закры́тый бассе́йн**, indoor pool. —**закры́тое голосова́ние**, secret ballot. —**закры́тое мо́ре**, inland sea. —**закры́тое пла́тье**, high-necked dress.

закры́ть [*infl.* -кро́ю, -кро́ешь] *v., pfv. of* закрыва́ть. —**закры́ться**, *refl., pfv. of* закрыва́ться.

закули́сный *adj.* occurring behind the scenes; backstage; offstage.

закупа́ть *v. impfv.* [*pfv.* закупи́ть] to buy up.

закупи́ть [*infl.* -куплю́, -ку́пишь] *v., pfv. of* закупа́ть.

заку́пка *n.* purchase.

заку́поривать *v. impfv.* [*pfv.* заку́порить] to plug up; stop up; cork.

заку́порка *n.* **1,** plugging up; stopping up. **2,** *med.* embolism; thrombosis; occlusion.

заку́почный *adj.* purchase (*attrib.*); purchasing.

заку́пщик *n.* (wholesale) buyer.

заку́ривать *v. impfv.* [*pfv.* закури́ть] **1,** *v.t.* to light (a cigarette, cigar, etc.). **2,** *v.i.* to light up; light a cigarette.

закури́ть *v. pfv.* [*infl.* -курю́, -ку́ришь] **1,** *pfv. of* заку́ривать. **2,** to begin to smoke; take up smoking.

закуси́ть [*infl.* -кушу́, -ку́сишь] *v., pfv. of* заку́сывать.

заку́ска [*gen. pl.* -сок] *n.* **1,** snack; bite. **2,** hors d'oeuvre; appetizer.

заку́сочная *n., decl. as an adj.* snack bar.

заку́сывать *v. impfv.* [*pfv.* закуси́ть] **1,** to have a snack; have a bite to eat. **2,** (*with instr.*) to have (with); eat *or* drink (with): закуси́ть во́дку селёдкой, to have some vodka with one's herring. **3,** to bite. —**закуси́ть губу́** *or* **гу́бы**, to bite one's lip. —**закуси́ть язы́к**, to hold one's tongue. —**закуси́ть удила́**, to take the bit in one's teeth.

заку́тать *v., pfv. of* ку́тать *and* заку́тывать. —**заку́таться**, *refl., pfv. of* ку́таться *and* заку́тываться.

заку́тывать *v. impfv.* [*pfv.* заку́тать] (*with instr. or* в + *acc.*) to wrap (in); bundle (in). —**заку́тываться**, *refl.* (*with instr. or* в + *acc.*) to wrap/bundle oneself (in).

зал *n.* hall. —**а́ктовый зал**, assembly hall. —**гимнасти́ческий зал**, gymnasium. —**зал ожида́ния**, waiting room. —**зри́тельный зал**, auditorium. —**по́лный зал**, full house; packed house. —**чита́льный зал**, reading room.

за́ла *n., obs.* = зал.

зала́дить *v. pfv.* [*infl.* -жу, -дишь] *colloq.* **1,** to keep repeating. **2,** (*with inf.*) to take to (doing something). —**зала́дить одно́ и то же**, to harp on the same string.

зала́мывать *v. impfv.* [*pfv.* заломи́ть] **1,** to break (*by bending*). **2,** *colloq.* to charge (an exorbitant price).

—**зала́мывать ру́ки**, to bend one's arms; twist one's arms. —**зала́мывать ша́пку**, to cock one's hat.

залата́ть *v., pfv. of* лата́ть.

зала́ять *v. pfv.* [*infl.* -ла́ю, -ла́ешь] to begin to bark.

залега́ть *v. impfv.* [*pfv.* зале́чь] **1,** to lie down (*for a long rest*). **2,** to lie low. **3,** to lie; be located (*in a low place*). **4,** *fig.* to become ingrained.

заледене́лый *adj.* **1,** covered with ice; icy. **2,** frozen; icy.

заледене́ть *v., pfv. of* ледене́ть.

залежа́лый *adj., colloq.* **1,** lying unused *or* unsold. **2,** stale.

залёживаться *v.r. impfv.* [*pfv.* залежа́ться] **1,** to lie around (unused *or* unsold). **2,** to become stale.

за́лежный *adj.* (*of land*) long fallow.

за́лежь *n.f.* **1,** (mineral) deposit. **2,** *pl.* accumulation. **3,** fallow land. **4,** *colloq.* unsold or unsalable merchandise.

залеза́ть *v. impfv.* [*pfv.* зале́зть] **1,** (*with* на + *acc.*) to climb; climb onto. **2,** (*with* в + *acc.*) to climb in; climb into. **3,** (*with* под + *acc.*) to climb under. **4,** (*with* в + *acc.*) *colloq.* to get into. —**зале́зть в долги́**, to get into debt. —**зале́зть в ду́шу**, *see* влезть в ду́шу. —**зале́зть в карма́н** (+ *dat.*), to pick the pocket of; rob.

зале́зть [*infl. like* лезть] *v., pfv. of* залеза́ть.

залени́ться *v.r. pfv.* [*infl.* -еню́сь, -е́нишься] *colloq.* to become lazy.

залепи́ть [*infl.* -леплю́, -ле́пишь] *v., pfv. of* залепля́ть.

залепля́ть *v. impfv.* [*pfv.* залепи́ть] **1,** to seal up. **2,** to cover; plaster.

залета́ть *v. impfv.* [*pfv.* залете́ть] **1,** (*with* в + *acc.*) to fly into. **2,** (*with* в + *acc.*) to stop briefly (in); land briefly (in). **3,** (*with* за + *acc.*) to fly over; fly beyond.

залете́ть [*infl.* -чу́, -ти́шь] *v., pfv. of* залета́ть.

залётный *adj.* stray: залётная пу́ля, stray bullet. —**залётная пти́ца**, migratory bird.

зале́чивать *v. impfv.* [*pfv.* залечи́ть] **1,** to heal (a wound, sore, etc.). **2,** *colloq.* to doctor (someone) to death. —**зале́чиваться**, *refl.* (*of a wound*) to heal.

залечи́ть [*infl.* -лечу́, -ле́чишь] *v., pfv. of* зале́чивать. —**залечи́ться**, *refl., pfv. of* зале́чиваться.

зале́чь [*infl. like* лечь] *v., pfv. of* залега́ть.

зали́в *n.* bay; gulf.

залива́ть *v. impfv.* [*pfv.* зали́ть] **1,** (*of water, a river, etc.*) to flood. **2,** to stain (*by spilling something*): зали́ть ска́терть вино́м, to spill wine on the tablecloth. **3,** to douse (a fire). **4,** (*with instr.*) to cover (with); pave (with). **5,** *colloq.* to pour in; put in (gas, oil, etc.). **6,** *fig.* (*with instr.*) to suffuse (in); bathe (in): зали́тый со́лнцем, bathed in sunlight. —**залива́ться**, *refl.* **1,** (*with instr.*) to be filled; be covered (with a liquid). **2,** *fig.* (*with instr.*) to burst into; break into (tears, laughter, song, etc.). **3,** (*with* в + *acc.*) (*of liquids*) to run into; get into.

заливно́е *n., decl. as an adj.* aspic.

заливно́й *adj.* **1,** flood (*attrib.*): заливны́е по́ймы, flood plains; заливно́й луг, water meadow. **2,** jellied: заливна́я осетри́на, jellied sturgeon.

зализа́ть [*infl.* -лижу́, -ли́жешь] *v., pfv. of* зали́зывать.

зали́зывать *v. impfv.* [*pfv.* зализа́ть] **1,** to lick (a wound). **2,** *colloq.* to slick down (one's hair).

зали́ть [*infl. like* лить; *past* за́лил *or* зали́л, залила́, за́лило *or* зали́ло] *v., pfv. of* залива́ть. —**зали́ться**, *refl.* [*past* зали́лся, залила́сь, залило́сь *or* зали́лось] *pfv. of* залива́ться.

залихва́тский *adj., colloq.* rollicking; devil-may-care.

зало́г *n.* **1,** pawning: отдава́ть в зало́г, to pawn. **2,** deposit; security. **3,** (*with gen.*) pledge (of): token (of). **4,** (*with gen.*) guarantee (of); key (to). **5,** *gram.* voice.

зало́говый *adj.* pawn (*attrib.*); mortgage (*attrib.*): зало́говая квита́нция, pawn ticket.

залогода́тель *n.m.* one who pawns or mortgages something.

залогодержа́тель *n.m.* pawnbroker.

заложи́ть *v. pfv.* [*infl.* -ложу́, -ло́жишь] **1,** *pfv. of* закла́дывать. **2,** *colloq.* to mislay. **3,** *impers.* (*with dat.*) *colloq., indicating a stuffy or heavy feeling:* мне заложи́ло нос/грудь, my nose is stuffed up; I feel a heaviness in my chest.

зало́жник *n.* hostage.

заломи́ть [*infl.* -ломлю́, -ло́мишь] *v., pfv. of* зала́мывать.

залп *n.* volley; salvo.

за́лпом *adv.* **1,** in one volley. **2,** *colloq.* without stopping; without pausing for breath; (*with verbs of drinking*) in one gulp; (*with verbs of reading*) in one stretch.

залуча́ть *v. impfv.* [*pfv.* залучи́ть] *colloq.* to entice; lure.

залюбова́ться *v.r. pfv.* [*infl.* -бу́юсь, -бу́ешься] (*with instr.*) to gaze with admiration (at); be lost in contemplation (of).

зама́зать [*infl.* -ма́жу, -ма́жешь] *v., pfv. of* зама́зывать.

зама́зка *n.* putty.

зама́зывать *v. impfv.* [*pfv.* зама́зать] **1,** to paint over. **2,** *fig., colloq.* to cover up; conceal. **3,** to seal up; putty. **4,** to smear; soil; dirty.

зама́лчивать *v. impfv.* [*pfv.* замолча́ть] *colloq.* to keep (something) quiet; keep quiet about; hush up.

зама́нивание *n.* enticing; enticement.

зама́нивать *v. impfv.* [*pfv.* замани́ть] to entice; lure; decoy.

замани́ть [*infl.* -маню́, -ма́нишь] *v., pfv. of* зама́нивать.

зама́нчивый *adj.* tempting; enticing; alluring.

замара́ть *v., pfv. of* мара́ть (*in sense #1*). —зама́ра́ться, *refl., pfv. of* мара́ться.

замара́шка [*gen. pl.* -шек] *n., colloq.* slob.

замаринова́ть *v., pfv. of* маринова́ть.

замаскиро́ванный *adj.* **1,** masked. **2,** disguised; camouflaged.

замаскирова́ть *v., pfv. of* маскирова́ть. —замаскирова́ться, *refl., pfv. of* маскирова́ться.

зама́сливать *v. impfv.* [*pfv.* зама́слить] **1,** to spill oil or grease on. **2,** to treat with oil. **3,** *fig., colloq.* to butter up. —зама́сливаться, *refl.* to become soiled with oil or grease.

зама́тывать *v. impfv.* [*pfv.* замота́ть] *colloq.* **1,** to wind around *or* onto. **2,** (*with instr.*) to wrap (in *or* with). **3,** to wear out; tire out. —зама́тываться, *refl., colloq.* **1,** (*with* вокру́г) to be wound around. **2,** (*with instr.*) to wrap oneself (in). **3,** to be worn out.

зама́хиваться *v.r. impfv.* [*pfv.* замахну́ться] (*with instr. and* на + *acc.*) to threaten (with); brandish; wave: замахну́ться ножо́м на кого́-нибудь, to threaten someone with a knife.

зама́чивать *v. impfv.* [*pfv.* замочи́ть] **1,** to get (something) wet. **2,** to soak.

зама́шки *n. pl.* [*sing.* -ма́шка] *colloq.* ways; manner.

зама́щивать *v. impfv.* [*pfv.* замости́ть] to pave.

замедле́ние *n.* **1,** slowing down; deceleration. **2,** *obs.* delay.

заме́дленный *adj.* slow; slowed; slowed-down. —заме́дленного де́йствия, delayed-action (*attrib.*): бо́мба заме́дленного де́йствия, time bomb.

замедля́ть *v. impfv.* [*pfv.* заме́длить] **1,** to slow down. **2,** to delay. **3,** (*with inf. or* с + *instr.*) to be slow (in); be long (in). —замедля́ться, *refl.* to slow down; become slower.

заме́на *n.* **1,** substitution; replacement. **2,** substitute.

замени́мый *adj.* replaceable.

замени́тель *n.m.* substitute: замени́тель ко́жи, leather substitute.

замени́ть [*infl.* -меню́, -ме́нишь] *v., pfv. of* заменя́ть.

заменя́ть *v. impfv.* [*pfv.* замени́ть] **1,** (*with instr.*) to replace (with). **2,** to replace; take the place of; substitute for.

замере́ть [*infl.* -мру́, -мрёшь; *past* за́мер, замерла́, за́мерло] *v., pfv. of* замира́ть.

замерза́ние *n.* freezing.

замерза́ть *v. impfv.* [*pfv.* замёрзнуть] **1,** to freeze; become frozen. **2,** (*of a person*) to be freezing (cold); be frozen. **3,** to freeze to death; perish from the frost.

замёрзнуть [*past* -мёрз, -ла] *v., pfv. of* мёрзнуть *and* замерза́ть.

за́мертво *adv.* unconscious; in a dead faint.

замеси́ть [*infl.* -мешу́, -ме́сишь] *v., pfv. of* заме́шивать (*in sense #2*).

замести́ [*infl. like* мести́] *v., pfv. of* замета́ть[1].

замести́тель *n.m.* **1,** substitute; replacement. **2,** deputy: замести́тель дире́ктора, deputy director.

замести́ть [*infl.* -щу́, -сти́шь] *v., pfv. of* замеща́ть.

замета́ть[1] *v. impfv.* [*pfv.* замести́] **1,** (*with* в + *acc.*) to sweep; sweep into. **2,** (*of snow*) to cover. *Also impers.:* доро́гу замело́ сне́гом, the road is covered/blocked with snow. —замета́ть следы́, to cover up one's tracks; cover up the traces.

замета́ть[2] *v., pfv. of* замётывать.

замета́ться *v.r. pfv.* [*infl.* -мечу́сь, -ме́чешься] **1,** to begin rushing about. **2,** to begin tossing about (*in bed*). **3,** to become confused; become flustered.

заме́тить [*infl.* -чу, -тишь] *v., pfv. of* замеча́ть.

заме́тка [*gen. pl.* -ток] *n.* **1,** mark. **2,** note: путевы́е заме́тки, travel notes. **3,** notice; item (*in a newspaper*). —брать на заме́тку, to take/make note of.

заме́тно *adv.* noticeably; visibly: он заме́тно постаре́л, he has aged visibly. —*adj., used predicatively* noticeable: э́то едва́ заме́тно, it is hardly noticeable.

заме́тный *adj.* noticeable; visible; appreciable; marked.

замётывать *v. impfv.* [*pfv.* замета́ть] to baste.

замеча́ние *n.* **1,** remark; observation; comment. **2,** reprimand; rebuke.

замеча́тельно *adv.* **1,** remarkably. **2,** marvelously. —*adj., used predicatively* wonderful; marvelous: э́то замеча́тельно, that's wonderful.

замеча́тельный *adj.* remarkable; wonderful; marvelous.

замеча́ть *v. impfv.* [*pfv.* заме́тить] **1,** to notice. **2,** to note; make note of. **3,** to remark; comment; observe.

замечта́ться *v.r. pfv.* to fall to thinking; lapse into daydreaming.

замеша́тельство *n.* confusion; embarrassment.

замеша́ть *v., pfv. of* замешивать (*in sense #1*). —замеша́ться, *refl., pfv. of* замешиваться.

заме́шивать *v. impfv.* 1, [*pfv.* замеша́ть] (*with* в + *acc.*) to mix up (in); implicate (in). 2, [*pfv.* замеси́ть] to knead. —замеша́ться, *refl.* [*pfv.* замеша́ться] 1, to get lost: замеша́ться в толпе́/толпу́, to get lost in the crowd. 2, (*with* в + *acc.*) to get mixed up (in); become implicated (in).

заме́шкаться *v.r. pfv., colloq.* to tarry; linger.

замеща́ть *v. impfv.* [*pfv.* замести́ть] 1, to replace. 2, to fill (a position). 3, [*impfv. only*] to substitute for; fill in for.

замеще́ние *n.* 1, substitution; replacement. 2, filling (*of a position*).

замини́ровать *v., pfv. of* мини́ровать.

зами́нка [*gen. pl.* -нок] *n., colloq.* 1, hitch; delay. 2, hesitation (*in speech*).

замира́ние *n.* dying down. —с замира́нием се́рдца, with a sinking heart; with one's heart in one's mouth.

замира́ть *v. impfv.* [*pfv.* замере́ть] 1, to freeze; stand motionless. 2, *fig.* to come to a standstill. 3, (*of a sound*) to die down. 4, (*of one's heart*) to sink. 5, [*impfv. only*] (*of one's voice*) to falter.

за́мкнутый *adj.* 1, withdrawn; tight-lipped; close-mouthed. 2, exclusive. 3, secluded.

замкну́ть *v., pfv. of* замыка́ть. —замкну́ться, *refl., pfv. of* замыка́ться.

замоги́льный *adj.* 1, *obs.* occurring after death. 2, *colloq.* (*of a voice*) sepulchral.

за́мок [*gen.* за́мка] *n.* castle.

замо́к [*gen.* -мка́] *n.* lock. —за семью́ замка́ми, 1, guarded day and night. 2, a deep dark secret. —под замко́м, under lock and key.

замо́лвить *v. pfv.* [*infl.* -влю, -вишь] *colloq., in* замо́лвить сло́во (*or* слове́чко) за (+ *acc.*), to put in a word for.

замолка́ть *v. impfv.* [*pfv.* замо́лкнуть] 1, to fall silent. 2, (*of noise, sounds, conversation, etc.*) to die away; stop; cease.

замо́лкнуть [*past* -мо́лк, -ла] *v., pfv. of* замолка́ть.

замолча́ть *v. [infl.* -чу́, -чи́шь] 1, to stop talking; fall silent. 2, *pfv. of* зама́лчивать.

замора́живание *n.* freezing.

замора́живать *v. impfv.* [*pfv.* заморо́зить] to freeze.

замори́ть *v. pfv., colloq.* 1, *pfv. of* мори́ть (*in sense #2*). 2, to starve. 3, to assuage (one's hunger, appetite, etc.). —замори́ть червяка́, *colloq.* to have a bite to eat.

заморо́женный *adj.* 1, frozen. 2, icy; iced-up. 3, *fig.* (*of a person, one's face, etc.*) cold; icy.

заморо́зить [*infl.* -жу, -зишь] *v., pfv. of* замора́живать.

за́морозки [*gen.* -ков] *n.pl.* light frost (*in spring or autumn*).

замо́рский *adj., obs.* foreign; from overseas.

замо́рыш *n., colloq.* puny creature; starveling.

замости́ть [*infl.* -щу́, -сти́шь] *v., pfv. of* зама́щивать.

замота́ть *v., pfv. of* зама́тывать. —замота́ться, *refl., pfv. of* зама́тываться.

замочи́ть [*infl.* -мочу́, -мо́чишь] *v., pfv. of* мочи́ть *and* зама́чивать.

замо́чный *adj.* of a lock. —замо́чная сква́жина, keyhole.

замполи́т *n.* deputy chief for political indoctrination.

за́муж *adv.* 1, *in* выходи́ть за́муж за (+ *acc.*), (*of a woman*) to marry; get married (to). 2, *in* выдава́ть (+ *acc.*) за́муж за (+ *acc.*), to marry off (a daughter) to.

за́мужем *adv.* (*with* за + *instr.*) (*of a woman*) married (to).

заму́жество *n.* marriage (*of a woman*).

заму́жняя *adj.* (*of a woman*) married.

замурова́ть [*infl.* -ру́ю, -ру́ешь] *v., pfv. of* замуро́вывать.

замуро́вывать *v. impfv.* [*pfv.* замурова́ть] to wall up.

замусо́ливать *v. impfv.* [*pfv.* замусо́лить] *colloq.* to soil.

замути́ть *v., pfv. of* мути́ть (*in sense #1*). —замути́ться, *refl., pfv. of* мути́ться.

заму́чить *v. pfv.* 1, to torture to death. 2, to torment; rack; wear out. —заму́читься, *refl.* to be exhausted.

за́мша *n.* suede; chamois. —за́мшевый, *adj.* suede.

замше́лый *adj.* moss-grown.

замыва́ть *v. impfv.* [*pfv.* замы́ть] to wash off; wash out.

замыка́ние *n.* locking; closing. —коро́ткое замыка́ние, short circuit.

замыка́ть *v. impfv.* [*pfv.* замкну́ть] 1, *obs.* to lock. 2, to close. 3, to ring; surround. 4, [*impfv. only*] *in* замыка́ть ше́ствие, to bring up the rear. —замыка́ться, *refl.* 1, *obs.* to lock; be locked; lock oneself in. 2, to close. 3, *fig.* (*with* в + *acc. or prepl.*) to withdraw (into): замыка́ться в себе́, to withdraw into oneself.

за́мысел [*gen.* -сла] *n.* 1, design; intention. 2, idea; conception.

замы́слить *v., pfv. of* замышля́ть.

замыслова́тый *adj.* 1, intricate; ingenious. 2, abstruse; recondite. 3, elaborate; fancy.

замы́ть [*infl.* -мо́ю, -мо́ешь] *v., pfv. of* замыва́ть.

замышля́ть *v. impfv.* [*pfv.* замы́слить] to plan; contemplate.

замя́ть *v. pfv.* [*infl.* -мну́, -мнёшь] *colloq.* to hush up; suppress. —замя́ться, *refl., colloq.* 1, to become flustered. 2, to stumble (*in speech*).

за́навес *n.* curtain.

занаве́сить [*infl.* -шу, -сишь] *v., pfv. of* занаве́шивать.

занаве́ска [*gen. pl.* -сок] *n.* (window) curtain.

занаве́шивать *v. impfv.* [*pfv.* занаве́сить] to curtain.

зана́шивать *v. impfv.* [*pfv.* заноси́ть] to wear out.

занемо́чь *v. pfv.* [*infl. like* мочь] *obs.* to be taken ill.

занесе́ние *n.* entering; recording.

занести́ [*infl. like* нести́] *v., pfv. of* заноси́ть[1]. —занести́сь, *refl., pfv. of* заноси́ться.

занижа́ть *v. impfv.* [*pfv.* зани́зить] to set (goals, norms, etc.) too low.

занима́тельный *adj.* entertaining; diverting.

занима́ть *v. impfv.* [*pfv.* заня́ть] 1, to occupy. 2, to take; take up (time, space, etc.). 3, to entertain; keep amused. 4, to borrow. —занима́ться, *refl.* 1, (*with instr.*) to be occupied (with); be engaged (in). 2, (*with instr.*) to go in for; take up. 3, [*impfv. only*] to study: он меша́ет мне занима́ться, he is preventing me from studying. 4, [*impfv. only*] (*with instr.*) to study (a certain subject). 5, [*impfv. only*] (*with* с + *instr.*) to give special instruction to. 6, to catch fire.

за́ново *adv.* all over again; anew.

занóза *n.* splinter.

занóзистый *adj., colloq.* **1,** rough; jagged. **2,** *fig.* abrasive.

занозить *v. pfv.* [*infl.* -жý, -зишь] (*usu. with* себé) to get a splinter in: занозить себé пáлец, to get a splinter in one's finger.

занóс *n.* drift: снéжный занóс, snowdrift.

заносить[1] *v. impfv.* [*pfv.* занести; *pres.* -ношý, -нóсишь] **1,** to bring; carry. **2,** to drop off; deliver (*on one's way*). **3,** (*with* в + *acc.*) to enter (on a list, in the minutes, etc.). **4,** to raise (*in order to strike with or put somewhere*). **5,** *impers.* to become covered with: дорóгу занеслó снéгом, the road is covered with snow. **6,** *impers.* to skid: машину занеслó, the car skidded. —**заноситься**, *refl., colloq.* **1,** to get carried away. **2,** to get a swelled head.

заносить[2] [*infl.* -ношý, -нóсишь] *v., pfv. of* занáшивать.

заносчивый *adj.* arrogant. —**заносчивость**, *n.f.* arrogance.

занóшенный *adj.* worn; threadbare.

занумеровáть *v., pfv. of* нумеровáть.

занятие *n.* **1,** occupation (*act of occupying*). **2,** occupation; work. **3,** *pl.* studies; lessons. **4,** pastime.

занятный *adj., colloq.* amusing; entertaining.

занятóй *adj.* busy.

зáнятость *n.f.* **1,** being busy; pressure of work. **2,** *econ.* employment: пóлная зáнятость, full employment.

зáнятый *adj.* [*short form* зáнят, занятá, зáнято] **1,** busy. **2,** occupied.

заня́ть [*infl.* займý, займёшь; *past* зáнял, занялá, зáняло] *v., pfv. of* занимáть. —**заня́ться**, *refl.* [*past* заня́лся, -лáсь, -лóсь] *pfv. of* занимáться.

заоднó *adv.* **1,** jointly; together; in concert. **2,** *colloq.* at the same time. —**быть заоднó с**, to be in agreement with; be at one with.

заокеáнский *adj.* located across the ocean; transoceanic.

заострённый *adj.* sharp; pointed.

заостря́ть *v. impfv.* [*pfv.* заострить] **1,** to sharpen. **2,** *fig.* to emphasize; point up. **3,** *fig.* to make more pointed. **4,** *in* заостря́ть внимáние, to focus attention. —**заостря́ться**, *refl.* **1,** to come to a point; taper off. **2,** *fig.* to become more acute.

заóчник *n.* student taking correspondence courses.

заóчно *adv.* **1,** in absentia: судиться заóчно, to be tried in absentia. **2,** by correspondence.

заóчный *adj.* **1,** in absentia. **2,** by correspondence: заóчные кýрсы, correspondence courses.

зáпад *n.* **1,** west. **2,** *cap.* the West.

западáть *v. impfv.* [*pfv.* запáсть] **1,** to become hollow; become sunken. **2,** (*of piano keys*) to stick. **3,** (*with* в + *acc.*) *colloq.* to fall into. **4,** (*with* в + *acc.*) *fig.* to become ingrained in (one's memory, heart, etc.).

зáпадный *adj.* western; West; westerly.

западня́ [*gen. pl.* -нéй] *n.* trap.

запáздывание *n.* **1,** tardiness; lateness. **2,** time lag.

запáздывать *v. impfv.* [*pfv.* запоздáть] to be late.

запáивать *v. impfv.* [*pfv.* запая́ть] to solder.

запáйка *n.* soldering.

запаковáть [*infl.* -кýю, -кýешь] *v., pfv. of* запакóвывать.

запакóвывать *v. impfv.* [*pfv.* запаковáть] to pack; pack up.

запáл *n.* **1,** primer; fuse. **2,** *colloq.* ardor. **3,** heaves (*disease of horses*).

запалить *v. pfv., colloq.* to set fire to.

запáльный *adj., in* запáльная свечá, spark plug.

запáльчивый *adj.* hot-tempered; quick-tempered; explosive. —**запáльчивость**, *n.f.* quick temper.

запанибрáта *adv., colloq.* as equals; on equal terms.

запáривать *v. impfv.* [*pfv.* запáрить] to steam.

запаршиветь *v., pfv. of* паршиветь.

запáрывать *v. impfv.* [*pfv.* запорóть] to whip to death; flog to death.

запáс *n.* **1,** supply; stock; reserve. Запáс знáний, fund of knowledge. Запáс слов, stock of words; vocabulary. Запáс прóчности, margin of safety. **2,** *mil.* reserve. **3,** *colloq.* hem. —**про запáс**, as a reserve; in case of need. Держáть *or* оставля́ть про запáс, to hold/keep in reserve.

запасáть *v. impfv.* [*pfv.* запасти] to store up. —**запасáться**, *refl.* (*with instr.*) **1,** to stock up on. **2,** *in* запасáться терпéнием, to steel oneself.

запáсливый *adj.* provident.

запáсник *n., mil., colloq.* reservist.

запаснóй *adj.* spare; reserve. —*n., mil.* reservist.

запáсный *adj.* = запаснóй. —запáсный вы́ход, emergency exit. —запáсный путь, sidetrack; siding.

запасти [*infl. like* пасти] *v., pfv. of* запасáть. —**запастись**, *refl., pfv. of* запасáться.

запáсть [*infl. like* пасть] *v., pfv. of* западáть.

зáпах *n.* smell; odor.

запахáть [*infl.* -пашý, -пáшешь] *v., pfv. of* запáхивать (*in sense #1*).

запáхивать *v. impfv.* **1,** [*pfv.* запахáть] to plow. **2,** [*pfv.* запахнýть] to wrap around oneself.

запáхнуть *v. pfv.* [*past* -пáх, -ла] *pfv.* to begin to smell.

запахнýть *v., pfv. of* запáхивать (*in sense #2*).

запáчкать *v., pfv. of* пáчкать. —**запáчкаться**, *refl., pfv. of* пáчкаться.

запая́ть *v., pfv. of* запáивать.

запевáла *n.m. & f.* **1,** leading singer in a choir. **2,** *fig.* guiding spirit.

запевáть *v. impfv.* to be the first to sing; lead the singing.

запекáнка *n.* **1,** baked pudding. **2,** spiced brandy.

запекáть *v. impfv.* [*pfv.* запéчь] to bake. —**запекáться**, *refl.* **1,** to bake; be baked. **2,** to clot; coagulate. **3,** (*of lips*) to become parched.

запеленáть *v., pfv. of* пеленáть.

запениться *v.r. pfv.* to begin to foam.

заперéть [*infl.* -прý, -прёшь; *past* зáпер, заперлá, зáперло] *v., pfv. of* запирáть. —**заперéться**, *refl.* [*past* заперся́ *or* зáперся, заперлáсь, заперлóсь *or* зáперлось] *pfv. of* запирáться.

запéть *v. pfv.* [*infl.* -пою́, -поёшь] to begin to sing; break (*or* burst) into song. —**запéть другóе**; **запéть на другóй лад**, to change one's tune; sing a different tune.

запечáтать *v., pfv. of* запечáтывать.

запечатлевáть *v. impfv.* [*pfv.* запечатлéть] **1,** to set down; record; capture (*in writing, painting, on film, etc.*). **2,** to ingrain (in one's memory). **3,** to mark; commemorate. —**запечатлевáться**, *refl.* to be stamped; be ingrained.

запечáтывать *v. impfv.* [*pfv.* запечáтать] to seal.

запéчь [*infl. like* печь] *v., pfv. of* запекáть. —**запéчься**, *refl., pfv. of* запекáться.

запива́ть v. impfv. [pfv. **запи́ть**] **1,** [past pfv. запи́л] (with instr.) to wash down (with). **2,** [past pfv. за́пил] colloq. to take to drink.

запина́ться v.r. impfv. [pfv. **запну́ться**] **1,** (with за or о + acc.) to stumble (on). **2,** to stumble (in speech).

запи́нка n. stumbling (in speech). —**без запи́нки**, without stumbling once.

запира́тельство n. refusal to confess one's guilt.

запира́ть v. impfv. [pfv. **запере́ть**] **1,** to lock (a door, room, etc.). **2,** to lock; lock up; lock in (someone or something). **3,** to block. —**запира́ться**, refl. **1,** to lock oneself in. **2,** (of a door, lock, etc.) to lock. **3,** [impfv. only] colloq. to refuse to admit one's guilt.

записа́ть [infl. -пишу́, -пи́шешь] v., pfv. of **запи́сывать.** —**записа́ться**, refl., pfv. of **запи́сываться.**

запи́ска [gen. pl. -сок] n. **1,** note; short letter: оставля́ть запи́ску, to leave a note. **2,** memorandum. **3,** pl. notes.

записно́й adj. **1,** intended for notes: записна́я кни́жка, notebook. **2,** colloq. a true; real; out-and-out.

запи́сывание n. writing down; recording.

запи́сывать v. impfv. [pfv. **записа́ть**] **1,** to write down; record. **2,** to take notes of. **3,** (with в + acc.) to enter (in); enroll (in). **4,** (with на + acc.) to record (on film, tape, a phonograph record, etc.). —**запи́сываться**, refl. **1,** (with в or на + acc.) to sign up for; enroll in; join. **2,** (with к) to make an appointment (with).

за́пись n.f. **1,** writing down; recording. **2,** entry; notation. **3,** recording (on a record, tape, etc.). **4,** pl. notes.

запи́ть [infl. like пить] v., pfv. of **запива́ть.**

запи́хивать v. impfv. [pfv. **запиха́ть** or **запихну́ть**] (with в + acc.) colloq. to stuff (into); cram (into).

запла́канный adj. full of tears; tear-stained.

запла́кать v. pfv. [infl. -пла́чу, -пла́чешь] to begin to cry.

заплани́ровать v., pfv. of **плани́ровать** (in sense #1).

запла́та n. patch.

заплати́ть v., pfv. of **плати́ть.**

заплева́ть [infl. -плюю́, -плюёшь] v., pfv. of **заплёвывать.**

заплёвывать v. impfv. [pfv. **заплева́ть**] to spit on.

заплесневе́лый adj. moldy; mildewed.

заплесневе́ть v., pfv. of **пле́сневеть.**

заплести́ [infl. like плести́] v., pfv. of **заплета́ть.**

заплета́ть v. impfv. [pfv. **заплести́**] to braid; plait. —**заплета́ться**, refl. [impfv. only] **1,** (of one's legs) to wobble. **2,** (with язы́к): у него́ язы́к заплета́ется, his speech is slurred.

запломбирова́ть v., pfv. of **пломбирова́ть.**

заплута́ться v.r. pfv., colloq. to lose one's way.

заплы́в n., swimming heat; lap.

заплыва́ть v. impfv. [pfv. **заплы́ть**] **1,** to swim (to a distant point). **2,** to be swollen; be bloated.

заплы́ть [infl. like плыть] v., pfv. of **заплыва́ть.**

запну́ться v.r., pfv. of **запина́ться.**

запове́дник n. reserve; preserve.

запове́дный adj. **1,** closed; off-limits. **2,** secret. **3,** cherished.

за́поведь n.f. **1,** relig. commandment. **2,** precept.

заподо́зрить v. pfv. (with в + prepl.) to (begin to) suspect (of).

запо́ем adv., colloq. avidly; nonstop: чита́ть запо́ем, to read avidly; пить запо́ем, to drink like a fish; кури́ть запо́ем, to chain-smoke.

запозда́лый adj. belated; tardy.

запозда́ние n. lateness; tardiness.

запозда́ть v., pfv. of **запа́здывать.**

запо́й n. **1,** addiction to alcohol. **2,** drinking bout.

заполза́ть v. impfv. [pfv. **заползти́**] **1,** (with в + acc.) to crawl into. **2,** (with под + acc.) to crawl under.

заползти́ [infl. like ползти́] v., pfv. of **заполза́ть.**

заполня́ть v. impfv. [pfv. **запо́лнить**] **1,** to fill. **2,** to fill out (a form).

запомина́ть v. impfv. [pfv. **запо́мнить**] **1,** to remember; make it a point to remember. **2,** to memorize. —**запомина́ться**, refl., impers. (with dat.) to remain in one's memory.

за́понка [gen. pl. -нок] n. cuff link; stud.

запо́р n. **1,** bolt; lock. **2,** constipation.

запоро́ть [infl. -порю́, -по́решь] v., pfv. of **запа́рывать.**

запороши́ть v. pfv. (of snow, dust, etc.) to cover lightly.

запотева́ть v. impfv. [pfv. **запоте́ть**] to become misty; steam up.

запоте́лый adj. steamed up; misted up.

запоте́ть v., pfv. of **поте́ть** (in sense #2) and **запотева́ть.**

запра́вила n.m., colloq. **1,** boss; bigwig. **2,** ringleader; instigator.

запра́вить [infl. -влю, -вишь] v., pfv. of **заправля́ть.** —**запра́виться**, refl., pfv. of **заправля́ться.**

запра́вка n. **1,** seasoning. **2,** refueling.

заправля́ть v. impfv. [pfv. **запра́вить**] **1,** to tuck in; tuck under. **2,** (with instr.) to season (with). **3,** to put fuel in; put gas in. **4,** [impfv. only] (with instr.) colloq. to boss; run. —**заправля́ться**, refl., colloq. to take on fuel; refuel.

запра́вочный adj. (re)fueling (attrib.): запра́вочная ста́нция, filling station.

запра́вский adj., colloq. real; true; regular.

запра́шивать v. impfv. [pfv. **запроси́ть**] **1,** (with о) to inquire (about). **2,** to question (someone). **3,** to charge (a high price).

запре́т n. prohibition; ban.

запрети́тельный adj. prohibitive.

запрети́ть [infl. -щу́, -ти́шь] v., pfv. of **запреща́ть.**

запре́тный adj. forbidden. —**запре́тная зо́на**, forbidden zone; restricted area.

запреща́ть v. impfv. [pfv. **запрети́ть**] **1,** (with dat.) to forbid (someone to do something). **2,** to forbid; prohibit; ban; outlaw. **3,** to suppress (a publication). —**запреща́ться**, refl. [impfv. only] to be forbidden; be prohibited.

запреще́ние n. prohibition; ban.

заприхо́довать v., pfv. of **прихо́довать.**

запрограмми́ровать v., pfv. of **программи́ровать.**

запроки́дывать v. impfv. [pfv. **запроки́нуть**] colloq. to throw back (one's head).

запро́с n. **1,** inquiry. **2,** demand. **3,** pl. needs; requirements. **4,** pl. aspirations; pretensions. **5,** colloq. overcharging.

запроси́ть [infl. -прошу́, -про́сишь] v., pfv. of **запра́шивать.**

за́просто adv., colloq. without ceremony; on an informal basis.

запру́да n. **1,** weir; dam. **2,** pond; reservoir (formed by dammed-up water).

запруди́ть [*infl.* -пружу́, -пру́дишь *or* -пруди́шь] *v., pfv. of* пруди́ть *and* запру́живать.

запру́живать *v. impfv.* [*pfv.* запруди́ть] **1**, to dam up. **2**, to jam; pack; throng.

запряга́ть *v. impfv.* [*pfv.* запря́чь] to harness; hitch up. —**запряга́ться**, *refl.* (*with* в + *acc.*) *colloq.* to buckle down to.

запря́жка *n.* **1**, harnessing. **2**, team of horses in harness.

запря́тать [*infl.* -пря́чу, -пря́чешь] *v., pfv. of* запря́тывать.

запря́тывать *v. impfv.* [*pfv.* запря́тать] *colloq.* to hide away; secrete.

запря́чь [*infl.* -прягу́, -пряжёшь, ...-прягу́т; *past* -пря́г, -прягла́, -прягло́] *v., pfv. of* запряга́ть. —**запря́чься**, *refl., pfv. of* запряга́ться.

запу́гивание *n.* intimidation.

запу́гивать *v. impfv.* [*pfv.* запуга́ть] to intimidate; cow; browbeat.

за́пуск *n.* **1**, starting. **2**, launching.

запуска́ть *v. impfv.* [*pfv.* запусти́ть] **1**, to launch; send up; fly (a rocket, balloon, kite, etc.). **2**, (*usu. with instr.*) *colloq.* to throw; hurl: запусти́ть ка́мнем в кого́-нибудь, to throw a stone at someone. **3**, to start; start up (a machine, motor, etc.). **4**, (*with* в + *acc.*) *colloq.* to thrust (into); plunge (into). **5**, to neglect.

запусте́лый *adj., obs.* neglected; deserted; abandoned.

запусте́ние *n.* **1**, desolation. **2**, (state of) neglect.

запусти́ть [*infl.* -пущу́, -пу́стишь] *v., pfv. of* запуска́ть.

запу́танный *adj.* **1**, tangled. **2**, *fig.* intricate; involved: запу́танный вопро́с, knotty problem. —**запу́танность**, *n.f.* confusion.

запу́тать *v., pfv. of* пу́тать *and* запу́тывать. —**запу́таться**, *refl., pfv. of* пу́таться (*in sense #1*) *and* запу́тываться.

запу́тывать *v. impfv.* [*pfv.* запу́тать] **1**, to tangle. **2**, to muddle; complicate. **3**, *colloq.* to confuse; mix up. **4**, (*with* в + *acc.*) *colloq.* to involve (in); embroil (in). —**запу́тываться**, *refl.* **1**, to become (en)tangled. **2**, *fig., colloq.* to become confused; get mixed up.

запуши́ть *v. pfv.* (*of snow, frost, etc.*) to cover lightly.

запу́щенный *adj.* neglected. —**запу́щенность**, *n.f.* neglect.

запыла́ть *v. pfv.* to flare up; burst into flame.

запыли́ть *v., pfv. of* пыли́ть (*in sense #2*). —**запыли́ться**, *refl., pfv. of* пыли́ться.

запыха́ться *v.r. impfv. & pfv., colloq.* to be out of breath; pant.

запя́стье *n.* **1**, wrist. **2**, *obs.* bracelet.

запята́я *n., decl. as an adj.* comma. —**то́чка с запято́й**, semicolon.

запятна́ть *v., pfv. of* пятна́ть.

зараба́тывать *v. impfv.* [*pfv.* зарабо́тать] to earn. Хорошо́ зараба́тывать, to earn good money. Зараба́тывать на жизнь, to earn a living; earn one's livelihood. —**зараба́тываться**, *refl., colloq.* to overwork.

зарабо́тать *v. pfv.* **1**, *pfv. of* зараба́тывать. **2**, to start working. —**зарабо́таться**, *refl., pfv. of* зараба́тываться.

за́работный *adj., in* за́работная пла́та, wages; pay; salary.

за́работок [*gen.* -тка] *n.* earnings; wages; pay.

зара́внивать *v. impfv.* [*pfv.* заровня́ть] to fill; even up (a hole).

заража́ть *v. impfv.* [*pfv.* зарази́ть] **1**, to infect. **2**, to contaminate; pollute. **3**, *fig.* (*with instr.*) to infect (with); inspire (with). —**заража́ться**, *refl.* (*with instr.*) to become infected (with); catch.

зараже́ние *n.* infection. —**зараже́ние кро́ви**, blood poisoning.

зара́з *adv., colloq.* all at once; at one sitting; in one fell swoop.

зара́за *n.* infection.

зарази́тельный *adj.* infectious; contagious.

зарази́ть [*infl.* -жу́, -зи́шь] *v., pfv. of* заража́ть. —**зарази́ться**, *refl., pfv. of* заража́ться.

зара́зный *adj.* infectious; contagious; communicable.

зара́нее *adv.* beforehand; in advance.

зарапортова́ться *v.r. impfv.* [*infl.* -ту́юсь, -ту́ешься] *colloq.* to talk too much; run off at the mouth.

зараста́ть *v. impfv.* [*pfv.* зарасти́] **1**, (*with instr.*) to be overgrown (with). **2**, *colloq.* (*of a wound*) to heal.

зарасти́ [*infl. like* расти́] *v., pfv. of* зараста́ть.

зарва́ться [*infl. like* рвать] *v.r., pfv. of* зарыва́ться (*in sense #2*).

зарде́ться *v.r. pfv.* to flush with color; blush.

за́рево *n.* glow.

зарегистри́ровать *v., pfv. of* регистри́ровать. —**зарегистри́роваться**, *refl., pfv. of* регистри́роваться.

заре́з *n., in* до заре́зу, urgently; desperately.

заре́зать *v., pfv. of* ре́зать (*in sense #5*). —**заре́заться**, *refl., colloq.* to cut one's throat.

зарека́ться *v.r. impfv.* [*pfv.* заре́чься] (*with inf.*) *colloq.* to swear off.

зарекомендова́ть *v. pfv.* [*infl.* -ду́ю, -ду́ешь] (*with* себя́ *and instr.*) to prove to be. —**хорошо́ зарекомендова́ть себя́**, to make a good showing; give a good account of oneself.

заре́чный *adj.* located on the other side of the river.

заре́чье *n.* area on the other side of a river.

заре́чься [*infl. like* отре́чься] *v.r., pfv. of* зарека́ться.

заржа́веть *v., pfv. of* ржа́веть.

заржа́вленный *adj.* rusty.

зарисова́ть [*infl.* -су́ю, -су́ешь] *v., pfv. of* зарисо́вывать.

зарисо́вка [*gen. pl.* -вок] *n.* **1**, sketching. **2**, sketch.

зарисо́вывать *v. impfv.* [*pfv.* зарисова́ть] to sketch.

за́риться *v.r. impfv.* [*pfv.* поза́риться] (*with* на + *acc.*) *colloq.* to covet.

зарни́ца *n.* summer lightning; heat lightning.

заровня́ть *v., pfv. of* зара́внивать.

зароди́ть [*infl.* -жу́ -ди́шь] *v., pfv. of* зарожда́ть. —**зароди́ться**, *refl., pfv. of* зарожда́ться.

заро́дыш *n.* embryo; fetus. —**подавля́ть в заро́дыше**, to nip in the bud.

заро́дышевый *adj.* embryonic.

зарожда́ть *v. impfv.* [*pfv.* зароди́ть] to generate; engender. —**зарожда́ться**, *refl.* to arise; originate; come into being.

зарожде́ние *n.* **1**, generation; engendering. **2**, *fig.* origin.

заро́к *n.* pledge; vow; resolution.

зарони́ть *v. pfv.* [*infl.* -роню́, -ро́нишь] **1**, *colloq.* to drop. **2**, *fig.* to arouse; inspire (feelings, thoughts, etc.).

за́росль *n.f., usu. pl.* undergrowth; brushwood.

зарпла́та *n.* wages; pay; salary (*contr. of* за́работная пла́та).

заруба́ть *v. impfv.* [*pfv.* заруби́ть] **1,** to slash to death; hack to death. **2,** to notch; make a notch in. —**заруби́те себе́ на носу́,** remember for the next time; don't you dare forget.

зарубе́жный *adj.* foreign.

заруби́ть [*infl.* -рублю́, -ру́бишь] *v., pfv. of* заруба́ть.

зару́бка [*gen. pl.* -бок] *n.* notch.

зарубцева́ться *v.r., pfv. of* рубцева́ться.

зарумя́нить *v., pfv. of* румя́нить (*in sense #2*). —**зарумя́ниться,** *refl., pfv. of* румя́ниться (*in sense #2*).

заручи́ться *v.r. pfv.* (*with instr.*) to enlist; secure; obtain (one's support, services, etc.).

зару́чка *n., colloq.* influence; pull.

зарыва́ть *v. impfv.* [*pfv.* зары́ть] to bury. —**зарыва́ться,** *refl.* [*pfv.* зары́ться] to bury oneself. **2,** [*pfv.* зарва́ться] *colloq.* to go too far; go to extremes; overdo things.

зары́ть [*infl.* -ро́ю, -ро́ешь] *v., pfv. of* зарыва́ть. —**зары́ться,** *refl., pfv. of* зарыва́ться.

заря́ *n.* **1,** glow on the horizon before sunrise or after sunset. **2,** (*often with* у́тренняя) dawn; daybreak: на заре́, at dawn. **3,** (*often with* вече́рняя) dusk; nightfall. **4,** *fig.* dawn; beginning. **5,** [*acc.* зо́рю] *mil.* reveille; taps. —**ни свет ни заря́,** before dawn; at the crack of dawn. —**от зари́ до зари́, 1,** from dawn to dusk. **2,** from night to morn.

заря́д *n.* **1,** (powder) charge. **2,** *electricity* charge. **3,** cartridge. **4,** warhead. **5,** *fig.* (*with gen.*) fund; supply; store.

заряди́ть *v. pfv.* [*infl.* -ряжу́, -ряди́шь] **1,** *pfv. of* заряжа́ть. **2,** *colloq.* to keep repeating. **3,** *colloq.* (*of rain*) to keep coming down.

заря́дка *n.* **1,** loading (*of a gun*); charging (*of a battery*). **2,** exercise(s); calisthenics.

заря́дный *adj.* charging (*attrib.*): заря́дный агрега́т, battery charger. —**заря́дный я́щик,** caisson; ammunition wagon.

заряжа́ние *n.* loading (*of a gun or camera*); charging (*of a battery*).

заряжа́ть *v. impfv.* [*pfv.* заряди́ть] to load (a gun, camera, etc.); charge (a battery).

заря́нка [*gen. pl.* -нок] *n.* robin.

заса́да *n.* ambush.

засади́ть [*infl.* -сажу́, -са́дишь] *v., pfv. of* заса́живать.

заса́живать *v. impfv.* [*pfv.* засади́ть] **1,** to plant: заса́живать сад цвета́ми, to plant a garden with flowers. **2,** *colloq.* to confine; keep confined (at home, in/to prison, etc.). **3,** (*with* за + *acc.*) *colloq.* to sit down (to): заса́живать кого́-нибудь за кни́гу, to sit someone down to a book. **4,** (*with* в + *acc.*) *colloq.* to stick; thrust; plunge (something into something).

заса́ливать *v. impfv.* **1,** [*pfv.* заса́лить] to soil; get grease on. **2,** [*pfv.* засоли́ть] to salt; pickle.

заса́сывать *v. impfv.* [*pfv.* засоса́ть] to suck in; swallow up.

заса́харенный *adj.* candied.

засвети́ть *v. pfv.* [*infl.* -свечу́, -све́тишь] **1,** to light (a candle, lamp, etc.). **2,** *photog.* to spoil (a roll of film) by exposing it to light. —**засвети́ться,** *refl.* **1,** to (begin to) shine; sparkle. **2,** (*of one's eyes*) to light up. **3,** (*of film*) to be spoiled.

за́светло *adv.* before dark.

засвиде́тельствовать *v. pfv.* [*infl.* -ствую, -ствуешь] **1,** to attest (to). **2,** to certify; notarize. —**засвиде́тельствовать почте́ние** (+ *dat.*), *obs.* to pay one's respects to.

засе́в *n.* **1,** sowing. **2,** sown area.

засева́ть *v. impfv.* [*pfv.* засе́ять] to sow.

заседа́ние *n.* session; meeting.

заседа́тель *n.m.* (people's) representative.

заседа́ть *v. impfv.* to be in session; meet.

засе́ивать *v. impfv.* = засева́ть.

засе́ка *n.* barricade of felled trees.

засека́ть *v. impfv.* [*pfv.* засе́чь] **1,** [*past pfv.* -се́к, -секла́, -секло́] to notch. **2,** [-се́к, -секла́, -секло́] to locate; plot (*on a map*). **3,** [-се́к, -се́кла, -се́кло] to whip brutally; flog to death. —**засе́чь вре́мя** [*past fem.* -секла́], to note the time.

засекре́ченный *adj.* **1,** secret. **2,** (*of documents*) classified.

засекре́чивать *v. impfv.* [*pfv.* засекре́тить] **1,** to classify (as secret). **2,** *colloq.* to give (someone) access to classified documents; clear.

заселе́ние *n.* **1,** settlement (*of an area*). **2,** occupancy (*of a building*).

заселя́ть *v. impfv.* [*pfv.* засели́ть] **1,** to populate; settle. **2,** to settle (in); occupy.

засе́сть *v. pfv.* [*infl. like* сесть] *colloq.* **1,** (*with* за + *acc.*) to sit down (to); settle down to: засе́сть за рабо́ту, to sit down to work. **2,** to ensconce oneself. **3,** (*with* в + *prepl.*) (*of a bullet*) to lodge (in).

засе́чка [*gen. pl.* -чек] *n.* notch.

засе́чь [*infl. like* сечь] *v., pfv. of* засека́ть.

засе́ять [*infl.* -се́ю, -се́ешь] *v., pfv. of* засева́ть *and* засе́ивать.

засиде́ться [*infl.* -жу́сь, -ди́шься] *v.r., pfv. of* заси́живаться.

заси́живаться *v.r. impfv.* [*pfv.* засиде́ться] *colloq.* **1,** to sit a long time; sit up late. **2,** *fig.* to remain for a long time.

заси́лье *n.* domination; dominance.

засия́ть *v. pfv.* **1,** to begin to shine. **2,** (*of something bright*) to appear.

заско́к *n., colloq.* quirk; idiosyncrasy.

заскору́злый *adj.* **1,** hardened; calloused. **2,** *fig.* callous.

засла́ть [*infl.* -шлю́, -шлёшь] *v., pfv. of* засыла́ть.

засло́н *n.* **1,** barrier; screen. **2,** *mil.* covering force.

заслони́ть *v., pfv. of* заслоня́ть.

засло́нка [*gen. pl.* -нок] *n.* **1,** oven door. **2,** damper.

заслоня́ть *v. impfv.* [*pfv.* заслони́ть] **1,** to shield. **2,** *fig.* to overshadow. —**заслоня́ть свет** (+ *dat.*), to stand in someone's light.

заслу́га *n.* **1,** *usu. pl.* services; contribution; accomplishments; achievements. **2,** merit; virtue. —**по заслу́гам,** according to one's deserts; as one deserves. —**получи́ть по заслу́гам,** to get what one deserves; get one's just deserts/reward. —**ста́вить что́-нибудь в заслу́гу** (+ *dat.*), to give (someone) credit for something.

заслу́женно *adv.* deservedly.

заслу́женный *adj.* **1,** deserved; well-earned. **2,** distinguished. **3,** (*in titles*) Honored.

заслу́живать *v. impfv.* (*with gen.*) to deserve; merit; be worthy of.

заслужи́ть *v. pfv.* [*infl.* -служу́, -слу́жишь] to deserve; earn; win; gain.

заслу́шивать v. impfv. [pfv. **заслу́шать**] to listen to; hear (a report, speech, etc.). —**заслу́шиваться**, refl. (with gen.) to listen (to) with rapt attention.

заслы́шать v. pfv. [infl. -шу, -шишь] to hear; catch the sound of.

засма́тривать v. impfv. (with в + acc.) colloq. to peep into; peer into.

засма́триваться v.r. impfv. [pfv. **засмотре́ться**] (with на + acc.) 1, to be lost in contemplation of. 2, [impfv. only] colloq. to stare at; eye.

засмея́ться v.r. pfv. [infl. -смею́сь, -смеёшься] to laugh; begin to laugh.

засмотре́ться [infl. -смотрю́сь, -смо́тришься] v.r., pfv. of **засма́триваться**.

засне́женный also, **заснежённый** adj. snow-clad; snow-covered.

засну́ть v., pfv. of **засыпа́ть**¹.

засня́ть v. pfv. [infl. like **снять**] to photograph; film; shoot.

засо́в n. bolt; bar.

засо́вывать v. impfv. [pfv. **засу́нуть**] 1, to stick; thrust. 2, colloq. to put (somewhere and be unable to find).

засо́л n. salting; pickling.

засоли́ть [infl. -солю́, -со́лишь or -соли́шь] v., pfv. of **заса́ливать** (in sense #2).

засоре́ние n. clogging up. —**засоре́ние желу́дка**, constipation.

засоря́ть v. impfv. [pfv. **засори́ть**] 1, to litter. 2, to clog (up). 3, to choke (with weeds). 4, to clutter up. —**засоря́ться**, refl. to become clogged.

засоса́ть [infl. -сосу́, -сосёшь] v., pfv. of **заса́сывать**.

засо́хнуть [past -со́х, -ла] v., pfv. of **засыха́ть**.

за́спанный adj. sleepy; sleepy-eyed.

заспа́ться v.r. impfv. [infl. like **спать**] colloq. to oversleep.

заста́ва n. 1, gate; gates (to a city). 2, mil. security detachment. Пограни́чная заста́ва, frontier post.

застава́ть v. impfv. [pfv. **заста́ть**; pres. -стаю́, -стаёшь] to find; catch (at a certain moment): заста́ть кого́-нибудь до́ма, to find someone at home. заста́ть кого́-нибудь враспло́х, to catch someone unawares.

заста́вить [infl. -влю, -вишь] v., pfv. of **заставля́ть**.

заставля́ть v. impfv. [pfv. **заста́вить**] 1, to make; force; compel. 2, to cram; jam; clutter. 3, to block off; close off.

заста́иваться v.r. impfv. [pfv. **застоя́ться**] 1, to stand too long. 2, to become stale; become stagnant.

застаре́лый adj. chronic; inveterate.

заста́ть [infl. -ста́ну, -ста́нешь] v., pfv. of **застава́ть**.

застёгивать v. impfv. [pfv. **застегну́ть**] to button (up); fasten; hook. —**застёгиваться**, refl. 1, to button; hook. 2, to button oneself up.

застёжка [gen. pl. -жек] n. clasp; fastener. —за-стёжка-мо́лния, zipper.

застекля́ть v. impfv. [pfv. **застекли́ть**] to glaze; fit with glass.

засте́нок [gen. -нка] n. torture chamber.

засте́нчивый adj. shy; timid; bashful; diffident. —засте́нчивость, n.f. shyness; timidity; bashfulness; diffidence.

застига́ть v. impfv. [pfv. **засти́гнуть** or **засти́чь**] to catch (unawares); take by surprise.

засти́гнуть [past -сти́г, -ла] v., pfv. of **застига́ть**.

застила́ть v. impfv. [pfv. **застла́ть**] 1, to cover. 2, to cloud; obscure.

засти́рывать v. impfv. [pfv. **застира́ть**] colloq. 1, to wash out (a spot, stain, etc.). 2, to ruin in the wash.

засти́чь [infl. like **засти́гнуть**] v., pfv. of **застига́ть**.

застла́ть [infl. -стелю́, -сте́лешь] v., pfv. of **застила́ть**.

засто́й n. 1, standing still; immobility. 2, fig. stagnation. 3, in засто́й кро́ви, med. congestion. —**засто́йный**, adj. stagnant.

засто́лье n., colloq. meal; repast.

засто́льный adj. occurring at the table: засто́льная бесе́да, table talk.

засто́порить v., pfv. of **сто́порить**. —**засто́пориться**, refl., pfv. of **сто́пориться**.

застоя́ться v.r., pfv. of **заста́иваться**.

застра́ивать v. impfv. [pfv. **застро́ить**] to build up (an area).

застрахова́ть [infl. -ху́ю, -ху́ешь] v., pfv. of **страхова́ть** and **застрахо́вывать**. —**застрахова́ться**, refl., pfv. of **страхова́ться** and **застрахо́вываться**.

застрахо́вывать v. impfv. [pfv. **застрахова́ть**] to insure. —**застрахо́вываться**, refl. to insure oneself; take out insurance.

застра́чивать v. impfv. [pfv. **застрочи́ть**] to sew up; stitch up.

застра́щивать v. impfv. [pfv. **застраща́ть**] colloq. to intimidate; frighten.

застрева́ть v. impfv. [pfv. **застря́ть**] to stick; get stuck.

застрели́ть v. pfv. [infl. -стрелю́, -стре́лишь] to shoot; kill. —**застрели́ться**, refl. to shoot oneself; kill oneself.

застре́льщик n. leader; initiator; pioneer.

застро́ить v., pfv. of **застра́ивать**.

застро́йка n. building up; development. —**застро́йщик**, n. builder; developer.

застрочи́ть v. pfv. [infl. -строчу́, -строчи́шь or -стро́чишь] 1, pfv. of **застра́чивать**. 2, (of a machine gun) to blaze away.

застря́ть [infl. -стря́ну, -стря́нешь] v., pfv. of **застрева́ть**.

застуди́ться v.r. pfv. [infl. -стужу́сь, -сту́дишься] colloq. to catch cold.

за́ступ n. spade.

заступа́ться v.r. impfv. [pfv. **заступи́ться**] (with за + acc.) to come to the defense of; stand up for; stick up for.

заступи́ться [infl. -ступлю́сь, -сту́пишься] v.r., pfv. of **заступа́ться**.

засту́пник n. defender; intercessor. —**засту́пничество**, n. intercession.

застыва́ть v. impfv. [pfv. **засты́ть**] 1, to thicken; harden; congeal. 2, colloq. to freeze; be frozen. 3, fig. to freeze: засты́ть от у́жаса, to freeze in horror.

застыди́ть v. pfv. [infl. -жу́, -ди́шь] colloq. to shame. —**застыди́ться**, refl. to become embarrassed.

засты́ть [infl. -сты́ну, -сты́нешь] v., pfv. of **застыва́ть**.

засу́нуть v., pfv. of **засо́вывать**.

за́суха n. drought.

засу́чивать v. impfv. [pfv. **засучи́ть**] to roll up (one's sleeves).

засучи́ть [infl. -сучу́, -су́чишь] v., pfv. of **засу́чивать**.

засу́шивать *v. impfv.* [*pfv.* **засуши́ть**] to dry; press (flowers).

засуши́ть [*infl.* **-сушу́, -су́шишь**] *v., pfv. of* **засу́шивать.**

засу́шливый *adj.* drought-afflicted; arid.

засчи́тывать *v. impfv.* [*pfv.* **засчита́ть**] (*with* в + *acc.*) to count (toward); apply (toward). —**засчи́тываться,** *refl.* [*impfv. only*] (*with* в + *acc.*) to count (toward); be counted (toward).

засыла́ть *v. impfv.* [*pfv.* **засла́ть**] *colloq.* **1,** to send out (*on a secret mission*). **2,** to send (*far away or to the wrong place*).

засыпа́ть [*infl.* **-сы́плю, -сы́плешь**] *v., pfv. of* **засыпа́ть.²** —**засыпа́ться,** *refl., pfv. of* **засыпа́ться.**

засыпа́ть¹ *v. impfv.* [*pfv.* **засну́ть**] to fall asleep.

засыпа́ть² *v. impfv.* [*pfv.* **засы́пать**] (*with instr.*) **1,** to fill up (with dirt, sand, etc.). **2,** to cover; strew (with dust, papers, etc.). **3,** *fig.* to shower; deluge; bombard (with questions, gifts, etc.).—**засыпа́ться,** *refl.* **1,** (*with* в + *acc.*) (*of sand, snow, etc.*) to get into. **2,** (*with instr.*) to be covered (with).

засыха́ть *v. impfv.* [*pfv.* **засо́хнуть**] **1,** to dry up. **2,** to wither.

зата́ивать *v. impfv.* [*pfv.* **затаи́ть**] **1,** *colloq.* to hide; conceal. **2,** to bear; harbor; nurse (a grudge). **3,** to hold (one's breath): затаи́в дыха́ние; с затаённым дыха́нием, with bated breath.

зата́лкивать *v. impfv.* [*pfv.* **затолкну́ть**] *colloq.* to push; shove (into, under, etc.).

зата́пливать *v. impfv.* [*pfv.* **затопи́ть**] to light (a stove).

зата́птывать *v. impfv.* [*pfv.* **затопта́ть**] **1,** to trample down; trample upon. **2,** (*with* в + *acc.*) to press into (the ground). **3,** to stamp out (a fire, cigarette, etc.). **4,** *colloq.* to leave footmarks on; track up. —**зата́птывать в грязь,** to drag through the mud.

зата́сканный *adj., colloq.* **1,** worn; worn out; threadbare. **2,** *fig.* trite; hackneyed.

зата́скивать *v. impfv.* **1,** [*pfv.* **затащи́ть**] to drag away; drag off. **2,** [*pfv.* **затаска́ть**] *colloq.* to wear out; *fig.* make trite.

зата́чивать *v. impfv.* [*pfv.* **заточи́ть**] to sharpen.

затащи́ть [*infl.* **-тащу́, -та́щишь**] *v., pfv. of* **зата́скивать** (*in sense #1*).

затвердева́ть *v. impfv.* [*pfv.* **затверде́ть**] to harden; become hard.

затверде́лый *adj.* hardened.

затверде́ние *n.* **1,** hardening. **2,** hard lump.

затверде́ть *v., pfv. of* **тверде́ть** *and* **затвердева́ть.**

затверди́ть *v., pfv. of* **тверди́ть** (*in sense #2*).

затво́р *n.* **1,** *colloq.* bolt (*of a door*). **2,** bolt (*of a gun*); shutter (*of a camera*).

затвори́ть [*infl.* **-творю́, -тво́ришь**] *v., pfv. of* **затворя́ть.** —**затвори́ться,** *refl., pfv. of* **затворя́ться.**

затво́рник *n.* hermit; recluse. —**затво́рнический,** *adj.* of a hermit; solitary. —**затво́рничество,** *n.* solitary life.

затворя́ть *v. impfv.* [*pfv.* **затвори́ть**] to close; shut. —**затворя́ться,** *refl.* **1,** to close; be closed. **2,** to shut oneself in.

затева́ть *v. impfv.* [*pfv.* **зате́ять**] *colloq.* **1,** to start; undertake; launch. **2,** (*with inf.*) to decide (to); make up one's mind (to). **3,** *in* затева́ть недо́брое, to be up to something; be up to no good. —**затева́ться,** *refl., colloq.* **1,** to start. **2,** [*impfv. only*] to be afoot.

зате́йливый *adj.* **1,** elaborate; fancy. **2,** intricate. **3,** clever; ingenious.

зате́йник *n.* **1,** amusing fellow; jokester. **2,** organizer of social activities; social director.

затека́ть *v. impfv.* [*pfv.* **зате́чь**] (*with* в + *acc.*) **1,** to leak (into); get (into). **2,** to swell; swell up. **3,** to become numb.

зате́м *adv.* **1,** then; next. **2,** that is why. —**зате́м, что́бы,** to; in order to.

затемне́ние *n.* **1,** darkening. **2,** blackout. **3,** *fig.* obscuring.

затемни́ть *v., pfv. of* **затемня́ть.**

за́темно *adv., colloq.* before dawn; before daybreak; before daylight.

затемня́ть *v. impfv.* [*pfv.* **затемни́ть**] **1,** to darken; black out. **2,** *fig.* to obscure; cloud; blur.

затеня́ть *v. impfv.* [*pfv.* **затени́ть**] to shade; shield.

затере́ть [*infl. like* **тере́ть**] *v., pfv. of* **затира́ть.**

затеря́нный *adj.* lost; forgotten.

затеря́ть *v. pfv., colloq.* to lose; mislay. —**затеря́ться,** *refl., colloq.* **1,** to be lost. **2,** to disappear.

затеса́ться *v.r. pfv.* [*infl.* **-тешу́сь, -те́шешься**] (*with* в *or* на + *acc.*) *colloq.* to get into; worm one's way into.

зате́чь [*infl. like* **течь**] *v., pfv. of* **затека́ть.**

зате́я *n.* **1,** undertaking; venture. **2,** game; amusement. —**без зате́й** [*often,* **по́просту, без зате́й**], simply; without fanfare.

зате́ять [*infl.* **-те́ю, -те́ешь**] *v., pfv. of* **затева́ть.** —**зате́яться,** *refl., pfv. of* **затева́ться.**

затира́ть *v. impfv.* [*pfv.* **затере́ть**] **1,** to rub out; efface. **2,** to hem in; trap; hold fast. —**затёртый льда́ми,** icebound.

зати́скивать *v. impfv.* [*pfv.* **зати́снуть**] *colloq.* to squeeze in.

затиха́ть *v. impfv.* [*pfv.* **зати́хнуть**] to subside; abate; die down.

зати́хнуть [*past* **-ти́х, -ла**] *v., pfv. of* **затиха́ть.**

зати́шье *n.* calm; lull. —**зати́шье пе́ред грозо́й,** the calm before the storm.

заткну́ть *v., pfv. of* **затыка́ть.** —**заткну́ться,** *refl., colloq.* to shut up: заткни́сь!, shut up!

затмева́ть *v. impfv.* [*pfv.* **затми́ть**] **1,** to obscure. **2,** *fig.* to outshine; overshadow.

затме́ние *n.* eclipse.

затми́ть *v., pfv. of* **затмева́ть.**

зато́ *conj.* but; but then; but on the other hand.

затолка́ть *v. pfv.* **1,** to push; shove. **2,** to jostle; elbow.

затолкну́ть *v., pfv. of* **зата́лкивать.**

зато́н *n.* inlet; creek.

затону́ть *v. pfv.* [*infl.* **-тону́, -то́нешь**] to sink.

затопи́ть [*infl.* **-топлю́, -то́пишь**] *v., pfv. of* **зата́пливать** *and* **затопля́ть.**

затопле́ние *n.* **1,** sinking. **2,** flooding.

затопля́ть *v. impfv.* [*pfv.* **затопи́ть**] **1,** to flood; inundate. **2,** to sink.

затопта́ть [*infl.* **-топчу́, -то́пчешь**] *v., pfv. of* **зата́птывать.**

зато́р *n.* jam (*of people, traffic, etc.*).

затормози́ть *v., pfv. of* **тормози́ть.**

заточа́ть *v. impfv.* [*pfv.* **заточи́ть**] *obs.* to imprison; incarcerate.

заточе́ние *n., obs.* imprisonment; incarceration.

заточи́ть *v. pfv.* **1,** [*infl.* **-точу́, -то́чишь**] *pfv. of* **зата́чивать.** **2,** [*infl.* **-точу́, -точи́шь**] *pfv. of* **заточа́ть.**

затрави́ть v., pfv. of **трави́ть** (in sense #3).

затра́гивать v. impfv. [pfv. **затро́нуть**] **1**, (of a bullet) to touch; graze. **2**, to affect. **3**, fig. to wound (someone's pride). **4**, to touch upon; broach.

затра́та n. **1**, expenditure. **2**, usu. pl. expenses.

затра́тить [infl. -чу, -тишь] v., pfv. of **затра́чивать**.

затра́чивать v. impfv. [pfv. **затра́тить**] to spend; expend.

затре́бовать v. pfv. [infl. -бую, -буешь] to request; demand; require; order.

затрепа́ть v. pfv. [infl. -треплю́, -тре́плешь] colloq. to wear out.

затре́щина n., colloq. box on the ears.

затро́нуть v., pfv. of **затра́гивать**.

затрудне́ние n. **1**, difficulty. **2**, predicament.

затруднённый adj. difficult; labored.

затрудни́тельный adj. difficult; awkward; embarrassing.

затрудня́ть v. impfv. [pfv. **затрудни́ть**] **1**, to bother; trouble; inconvenience. **2**, to hamper; make difficult. —**затрудня́ться**, refl. to have difficulty; find it difficult.

затума́нивать v. impfv. [pfv. **затума́нить**] to cloud; obscure. —**затума́ниваться**, refl. **1**, to cloud up; become clouded. **2**, (of the senses) to become muddled.

затума́нить v., pfv. of **тума́нить** and **затума́нивать**. —**затума́ниться**, refl., pfv. of **тума́ниться** and **затума́ниваться**.

затупи́ть v., pfv. of **тупи́ть**. —**затупи́ться**, refl., pfv. of **тупи́ться**.

затуха́ть v. impfv. [pfv. **зату́хнуть**] colloq. (of something burning) to go out.

зату́хнуть [past -ту́х, -ла] v., pfv. of **затуха́ть**.

затушева́ть [infl. -шу́ю, -шу́ешь] v., pfv. of **тушева́ть** and **затушёвывать**.

затушёвывать v. impfv. [pfv. **затушева́ть**] **1**, to shade; add shading to. **2**, fig. to veil; obscure.

затуши́ть v. pfv. [infl. -тушу́, -ту́шишь] colloq. **1**, to put out; extinguish. **2**, to suppress.

за́тхлый adj. musty.

затыка́ть v. impfv. [pfv. **заткну́ть**] **1**, to stop up; plug up; cork up. **2**, to stick; thrust. —**заткну́ть за́ пояс**, colloq. to outdo; outshine; put to shame.

заты́лок [gen. -лка] n. back of the head. —**в заты́лок**, single file; one behind the other.

заты́лочный adj. cervical.

заты́чка [gen. pl. -чек] n., colloq. stopper; plug.

затя́гивать v. impfv. [pfv. **затяну́ть**] **1**, to tighten; pull tight; draw tight. **2**, (with instr.) to cover (with); clothe (in). **3**, to delay; drag out. **4**, to suck in. **5**, (with в + acc.) to draw (into); involve (in). **6**, colloq. to strike up (a song). —**затя́гиваться**, refl. **1**, to tighten something around oneself: затяну́ться по́ясом, to tighten one's belt. **2**, (of a wound) to heal over. **3**, (of the sky) to become obscured. **4**, to drag out; last a long time. **5**, to inhale (when smoking).

затя́жка [gen. pl. -жек] n. **1**, tightening; drawing. **2**, delay; dragging out. **3**, puff; drag (on a cigarette).

затяжно́й adj. lengthy; protracted.

затяну́ть [infl. -тяну́, -тя́нешь] v., pfv. of **затя́гивать**. —**затяну́ться**, refl., pfv. of **затя́гиваться**.

зау́мный adj. abstruse; esoteric; arcane.

зауны́вный adj. mournful; plaintive.

заупоко́йный adj. for the repose of the dead. Заупоко́йная слу́жба, funeral service.

заупря́миться v.r., pfv. of **упря́миться**.

заря́дный adj. ordinary; mediocre.

заусе́ница n. **1**, hangnail. **2**, burr (on metal).

зау́треня n. matins; Morning Prayer.

зау́ченный adj. **1**, studied; affected. **2**, mechanical; automatic.

зау́чивать v. impfv. [pfv. **заучи́ть**] to memorize; learn by heart. —**зау́чиваться**, refl., colloq. to study too hard; study too much.

заучи́ть [infl. -учу́, -у́чишь] v., pfv. of **зау́чивать**. —**заучи́ться**, refl., pfv. of **зау́чиваться**.

зауша́тельский adj. vicious; abusive. —**зауша́тельство**, n. vicious criticism; abuse.

зафикси́ровать v., pfv. of **фикси́ровать**.

зафрахтова́ть v., pfv. of **фрахтова́ть**.

заха́живать v. impfv., colloq. to drop in; stop in.

захва́ливать v. impfv. [pfv. **захвали́ть**] colloq. to praise excessively.

захвали́ть [infl. -хвалю́, -хва́лишь] v., pfv. of **захва́ливать**.

захва́т n. seizure; capture.

захва́танный adj., colloq. soiled by fingering; full of finger marks.

захвата́ть v., pfv. of **захва́тывать** (in sense #6).

захвати́ть [infl. -хвачу́, -хва́тишь] v., pfv. of **захва́тывать**.

захва́тнический adj. (of a policy) expansionist; (of wars) of conquest.

захва́тчик n. invader.

захва́тывать v. impfv. [pfv. **захвати́ть**] **1**, to seize; capture. **2**, to take (along). **3**, to carry away; thrill; engross. **4**, colloq. to catch; take by surprise. **5**, colloq. to stop; check (in time). **6**, [pfv. **захвата́ть**] to soil (by fingering). —**от э́того дух захва́тывает**, it takes one's breath away.

захва́тывающий adj. exciting; thrilling; gripping; engrossing; absorbing.

захвора́ть v. pfv., colloq. **1**, to be taken ill. **2**, (with instr.) to come down with.

захире́ть v., pfv. of **хире́ть**.

захлёбываться v.r. impfv. [pfv. **захлебну́ться**] **1**, to choke. **2**, fig. (with от) to be breathless (with an emotion). **3**, to bog down; peter out. **4**, (of an engine) to stall.

захлёстывать v. impfv. [pfv. **захлестну́ть**] **1**, (with за + acc.) to wind around. **2**, (with instr.) to secure (with a rope, lasso, etc.). **3**, (of water) to sweep over.

захло́пывать v. impfv. [pfv. **захло́пнуть**] to slam; slam shut. —**захло́пываться**, refl. (of a door) to slam shut; close with a bang.

захо́д n. stop; call. —**захо́д со́лнца**, sunset.

заходи́ть[1] v. impfv. [pfv. **зайти́**; pres. -хожу́, -хо́дишь] **1**, (with в + acc.) to stop (in) at; (with к) to call on; drop in on. **2**, (with за + instr.) to call for. **3**, (with за + acc.) to go behind. **4**, to go (far). **5**, (of the sun) to set. **6**, (with о) (of an argument) to arise (over); (of a conversation) to turn (to).

заходи́ть[2] v. pfv. [infl. -хожу́, -хо́дишь] **1**, to begin to walk. **2**, to circulate. **3**, (of an object) to begin to shake.

захолу́стный adj. **1**, remote; out-of-the-way. **2**, provincial.

захолу́стье n. out-of-the-way place.

захорони́ть v. pfv. [infl. -роню́, -ро́нишь] to bury.

захоте́ть v. pfv. [infl. like **хоте́ть**] to want. —**захоте́ться**, refl., impers. (with dat.) to want.

захуда́лый *adj.* **1,** impoverished. **2,** insignificant. **3,** *colloq.* (*of a child*) frail; (*of a horse*) run-down.

зацвести́ *v. pfv.* [*infl. like* цвести́] to begin to bloom.

зацелова́ть *v. pfv.* [*infl.* -лу́ю, -лу́ешь] *colloq.* to smother with kisses.

зацепи́ть [*infl.* -цеплю́, -це́пишь] *v., pfv. of* зацепля́ть. —зацепи́ться, *refl., pfv. of* зацепля́ться.

заце́пка [*gen. pl.* -пок] *n., colloq.* **1,** hook; peg. **2,** pull; influence; connections. **3,** hitch; catch; snag.

зацепля́ть *v. impfv.* [*pfv.* зацепи́ть] **1,** to hook. **2,** (*with* за + *acc.*) to catch (on); snag (on). —зацепля́ться, *refl.* (*with* за + *acc.*) to get caught (on); get snagged (on).

зачаро́ванный *adj.* **1,** enchanted. **2,** bewitched. **3,** spellbound.

зачарова́ть [*infl.* -ру́ю, -ру́ешь] *v., pfv. of* зачаро́вывать.

зачаро́вывать *v. impfv.* [*pfv.* зачарова́ть] to bewitch; charm; enchant; captivate.

зачасти́ть *v. pfv.* [*infl.* -щу́, -сти́шь] *colloq.* **1,** to increase in intensity. **2,** to begin to speak rapidly. **3,** (*with* к) to begin to visit frequently.

зачасту́ю *adv., colloq.* often; frequently.

зача́тие *n., physiol.* conception.

зача́ток [*gen.* -тка] *n.* **1,** embryo. **2,** *usu. pl.* beginning; early stages.

зача́точный *adj.* rudimentary.

зача́ть *v. pfv.* [*infl.* -чну́, -чнёшь; *past fem.* зачала́] to conceive (a child).

зача́хнуть *v., pfv. of* ча́хнуть.

зачём *adv.* **1,** why?; what for? **2,** why; what ...for: он забы́л, зачём пришел, he forgot what he came for. —вот зачём, that's why.

зачём-то *adv.* for some reason or other.

заче́ркивать *v. impfv.* [*pfv.* зачеркну́ть] to cross out.

заче́рпывать *v. impfv.* [*pfv.* зачерпну́ть] to scoop up; ladle.

зачерстве́лый *adj.* **1,** stale; hard. **2,** *fig.* callous.

зачерстве́ть *v., pfv. of* черстве́ть (*in sense #1*).

зачеса́ть *v. pfv.* [*infl.* -чешу́, -че́шешь] **1,** *pfv. of* заче́сывать. **2,** *colloq.* to scratch; begin to scratch (an itch). —зачеса́ться, *refl.* to itch; begin to itch.

заче́сть [*infl.* -чту́, -чтёшь; *past* -чёл, -чла́] *v., pfv. of* зачи́тывать². —заче́сться, *refl., pfv. of* зачи́тываться.

заче́сывать *v. impfv.* [*pfv.* зачеса́ть] to comb.

зачёт *n.* test (*in school*).

зачётный *adj.* **1,** test (*attrib.*). **2,** record (*attrib.*): зачётная кни́жка, (student's) record book.

зачина́тель *n.m.* founder; initiator; pioneer.

зачи́нивать *v. impfv.* [*pfv.* зачини́ть] *colloq.* **1,** to mend; repair. **2,** to sharpen (a pencil).

зачини́ть [*infl.* -чиню́, -чи́нишь] *v., pfv. of* зачи́нивать.

зачи́нщик *n.* instigator; ringleader.

зачисле́ние *n.* enrollment.

зачисля́ть *v. impfv.* [*pfv.* зачи́слить] **1,** to enroll; take in (a student); hire; take on (an employee). **2,** to enter; record. —зачисля́ться, *refl.* to enroll; join.

зачи́тывать¹ *v. impfv.* [*pfv.* зачита́ть] **1,** to read out. **2,** *colloq.* to read (a book) until it is tattered. **3,** *colloq.* to fail to return (a borrowed book). —зачи́тываться, *refl.* (*with instr.*) *colloq.* to become engrossed in reading (a book, novel, etc.).

зачи́тывать² *v. impfv.* [*pfv.* заче́сть] **1,** (*with* в + *acc.*) to apply (toward). **2,** to accept; pass (academic work). —зачи́тываться, *refl.* to count; be counted.

зашага́ть *v. pfv.* to set out on foot.

зашевели́ть *v. pfv.* (*with acc. or instr.*) to (begin to) stir. —зашевели́ться, *refl.* **1,** to move slightly; begin to stir. **2,** *colloq.* to begin to take action; begin to move.

зашива́ть *v. impfv.* [*pfv.* заши́ть] to sew up; mend.

заши́ть [*infl.* -шью́, -шьёшь] *v., pfv. of* зашива́ть.

зашифрова́ть *v., pfv. of* шифрова́ть.

зашнурова́ть *v., pfv. of* шнурова́ть.

зашпаклева́ть *v., pfv. of* шпаклева́ть.

зашпи́ливать *v. impfv.* [*pfv.* зашпи́лить] to pin; fasten with a pin.

заштемпелева́ть *v., pfv. of* штемпелева́ть.

зашто́пать *v., pfv. of* што́пать.

заштрихова́ть *v., pfv. of* штрихова́ть.

защёлка [*gen. pl.* -лок] *n.* latch; catch.

защёлкивать *v. impfv.* [*pfv.* защёлкнуть] to snap; snap shut. —защёлкиваться, *refl.* to snap shut.

защеми́ть *v. pfv.* [*infl.* -млю́, -ми́шь] **1,** *pfv. of* защемля́ть. **2,** (*of one's heart*) to ache.

защемля́ть *v. impfv.* [*pfv.* защеми́ть] **1,** to squeeze; crush. **2,** *colloq.* to catch; jam.

защи́та *n.* defense; protection. —брать (кого́-нибудь) под защи́ту, to take under one's wing.

защити́тельный *adj., in* защити́тельная речь, speech for the defense.

защити́ть [*infl.* -щу́, -ти́шь] *v., pfv. of* защища́ть. —защити́ться, *refl., pfv. of* защища́ться.

защи́тник *n.* **1,** defender; protector. **2,** defense attorney. **3,** *sports* defenseman; back.

защи́тный *adj.* protective. —защи́тная окра́ска, protective coloration. —защи́тный цвет, khaki.

защища́ть *v. impfv.* [*pfv.* защити́ть] **1,** to defend. **2,** to protect. —защища́ться, *refl.* to defend oneself; protect oneself.

заяви́ть [*infl.* -явлю́, -я́вишь] *v., pfv. of* заявля́ть.

зая́вка [*gen. pl.* -вок] *n.* **1,** claim. **2,** order; application; requisition.

заявле́ние *n.* **1,** announcement; statement. **2,** application.

заявля́ть *v. impfv.* [*pfv.* заяви́ть] **1,** (*with* о) to announce: заяви́ть о своём реше́нии, to announce one's decision. **2,** (*with a dependent clause*) to state (that)...; declare (that)... **3,** to file; lodge (a protest, complaint, etc.). **4,** to report: заяви́ть о происше́ствии в мили́цию, to report an incident to the police.

зая́длый *adj., colloq.* inveterate; avid.

за́яц [*gen.* за́йца] *n.* **1,** hare. **2,** *colloq.* stowaway: е́хать за́йцем, to stow away.

за́ячий [*fem.* -чья] *adj.* hare (*attrib.*); hare's. —за́ячья губа́, harelip.

зва́ние *n.* **1,** rank: во́инское зва́ние, military rank. **2,** title: зва́ние чемпио́на, championship title.

зва́ный *adj.* **1,** invited: зва́ный гость, invited guest. **2,** with invited guests: зва́ный обе́д, dinner party.

зва́тельный *adj., in* зва́тельный паде́ж, vocative case.

звать *v. impfv.* [*pfv.* позва́ть; *pres.* зову́, зовёшь; *past fem.* звала́] **1,** to call. **2,** to invite. **3,** [*impfv. only*] to name; call: как вас зову́т?, what is your name? Меня́ зову́т Ири́на, my name is Irina. —зва́ться, *refl.* [*impfv. only*] to be called.

звезда́ [*pl.* звёзды] *n.* star. —морска́я звезда́, starfish. —но́вая звезда́, nova.

звёздный *adj.* **1**, star (*attrib.*); stellar. **2**, starry.

звездочёт *n., obs.* astrologer.

звёздочка [*gen. pl.* **-чек**] *n.* **1**, little star. **2**, asterisk.

звене́ть *v. impfv.* [*pres.* **-ню́, -ни́шь**] **1**, *v.i.* to ring; jingle: колоко́льчики звеня́т, sleighbells are ringing. **2**, *v.t.* (*with instr.*) to jingle: звене́ть моне́тами, to jingle coins.

звено́ [*pl.* **зве́нья, зве́ньев**] *n.* **1**, link. **2**, unit; section (*of a device or structure*). **3**, team; group; unit. **4**, flight (*of aircraft*). **5**, *mil.* level; echelon.

зверёк [*gen.* **-рька́**] *n.* small animal.

звере́ныш *n., colloq.* cub.

звере́ть *v. impfv.* [*pfv.* **озвере́ть**] to become like an animal.

звери́нец [*gen.* **-нца**] *n., obs., colloq.* menagerie.

звери́ный *adj.* **1**, animal (*attrib.*). **2**, brutal; savage.

зверобо́й *n.* **1**, hunter (*of aquatic mammals*). **2**, St.-John's-wort.

звероло́в *n.* trapper.

зве́рский *adj.* **1**, brutal; savage. **2**, *colloq.* beastly; frightful. **—зве́рски,** *adv.* brutally.

зве́рство *n.* **1**, brutality; bestiality. **2**, *usu. pl.* atrocities.

зверь [*pl.* **зве́ри, звере́й, зверя́м**] *n.m.* (wild) animal; beast. **—смотре́ть зве́рем,** to glare; glower.

зверьё *n., colloq.* wild animals.

звон *n.* **1**, ringing; pealing; tolling. **2**, jingling; tinkling.

звона́рь [*gen.* **-наря́**] *n.m.* bell ringer.

звони́ть *v. impfv.* [*pfv.* **позвони́ть**] **1**, (*of a bell, phone, alarm clock, etc.*) to ring. **2**, (*with* в + *acc.*) to ring: звони́ть в ко́локол, to ring a bell. **3**, (*with dat.*) to call; phone: я вам позвоню́, I'll call/phone you. Звони́ть на вокза́л, to call/phone the station.

зво́нкий *adj.* **1**, clear; ringing; resounding. **2**, *phonet.* voiced. **—зво́нкая моне́та,** specie; coin. **—зво́нкая фра́за,** high-sounding phrase.

зво́нница *n.* bell tower; belfry.

звоно́к [*gen.* **-нка́**] *n.* **1**, bell. **2**, ring. **3**, *colloq.* phone call.

звук *n.* sound.

звуково́й *adj.* sound (*attrib.*). **—звуково́й фильм,** talking film.

звукоза́пись *n.f.* sound recording.

звуконепроница́емый *adj.* soundproof.

звукоопера́тор *n.* sound technician.

звукоподража́ние *n.* onomatopoeia.

звукоусиле́ние *n.* amplification. **—систе́ма звукоусиле́ния,** amplification system; public-address system.

звуча́ние *n.* **1**, sound. **2**, *fig.* significance: пье́са огро́много звуча́ния, play of enormous significance.

звуча́ть *v. impfv.* [*pfv.* **прозвуча́ть**; *pres.* **-чу́, -чи́шь**] to sound; be heard.

зву́чный *adj.* **1**, ringing; resounding. **2**, resonant.

звя́канье *n.* tinkling; jingling; jangling.

звя́кать *v. impfv.* [*pfv.* **звя́кнуть**] to tinkle; jingle; jangle.

зги *n., in* ни зги не ви́дно, it is pitch dark.

зда́ние *n.* building.

здесь *adv.* here.

зде́шний *adj., colloq.* of this place; local.

здоро́ваться *v.r. impfv.* [*pfv.* **поздоро́ваться**] (*with* с + *instr.*) to say hello (to); greet.

здорове́нный *adj., colloq.* robust; healthy.

здорове́ть *v. impfv.* [*pfv.* **поздорове́ть**] *colloq.* to grow healthy.

здо́рово *adv., colloq.* **1**, very; awfully; terribly. **2**, marvelously; splendidly. **—adj.**, *used predicatively* nice; wonderful: как здо́рово бы́ло бы (+ *inf.*), how nice/wonderful it would be to...

здоро́во *adv. & adj.* healthy: вы́глядеть здоро́во, to look healthy. **—(за) здоро́во живёшь,** *colloq.* just like that.

здоро́вый *adj.* healthy. **—бу́дьте здоро́вы!, 1**, stay well! **2**, (*after a sneeze*) bless you! **— жив и здоро́в,** alive and well; safe and sound.

здоро́вье *n.* health. **—за ва́ше здоро́вье!,** to your health! to good health! **—как ва́ше здоро́вье?,** how are you? **—на здоро́вье,** help yourself; take as much as you like.

здорови́к [*gen.* **-яка́**] *n., colloq.* healthy person; robust person.

здра́вица *n.* toast to one's health.

здра́вница *n.* health resort.

здра́во *adv.* **1**, soundly. **2**, sensibly.

здравомы́слящий *adj.* sensible; of sound judgment.

здравоохране́ние *n.* public health.

здра́вствовать *v. impfv.* [*pres.* **-ствую, -ствуешь**] to be well; be healthy; thrive. **—здра́вствуйте!,** *interj.* hello! **—да здра́вствует...!,** long live...!

здра́вый *adj.* sensible; sound. **—в здра́вом уме́,** of sound mind; sane. **—здра́вый смысл,** common sense.

зе́бра *n.* zebra.

зе́бу *n.m. indecl.* zebu.

зев *n.* pharynx. **—льви́ный зев,** snapdragon.

зева́ка *n.m. & f., colloq.* idle onlooker.

зева́ть *v. impfv.* **1**, [*pfv.* **зевну́ть**] to yawn. **2**, [*impfv. only*] *colloq.* to gape. **3**, [*pfv.* **прозева́ть**] *colloq.* to let an opportunity slip by.

зево́к [*gen.* **-вка́**] *n.* yawn.

зево́та *n.* yawning.

Зевс *n.* Zeus.

зелене́ть *v. impfv.* [*pfv.* **позелене́ть**] **1**, to become green; turn green. **2**, [*impfv. only*] (*of anything green*) to loom; appear.

зеленщи́к [*gen.* **-щика́**] *n.* greengrocer.

зелёный *adj.* green. **—зелёная ску́ка** *or* **тоска́,** utter boredom. **—зелёная у́лица,** the green light.

зе́лень *n.f.* **1**, greenery; verdure. **2**, greens; vegetables.

зе́лье *n., obs.* **1**, poison. **2**, potion: любо́вное зе́лье, love potion.

земе́льный *adj.* land (*attrib.*).

землеве́дение *n.* physical geography.

землевладе́лец [*gen.* **-льца**] *n.* landowner. **—землевладе́льческий,** *adj.* landowner's. **—землевладе́ние,** *n.* ownership of land.

земледе́лец [*gen.* **-льца**] *n.* farmer.

земледе́лие *n.* farming. **—земледе́льческий,** *adj.* farming (*attrib.*).

землеко́п *n.* digger.

землеме́р *n., obs.* surveyor. **—землеме́рный,** *adj.* surveying (*attrib.*).

землеро́йка [*gen. pl.* **-ро́ек**] *n.* shrew.

землеро́йный *adj.* excavation (*attrib.*). **—землеро́йная маши́на,** steam shovel.

землетрясе́ние *n.* earthquake.

земли́стый *adj.* **1**, earthy. **2**, (*of one's complexion*) sallow.

земля́ [*acc.* **зе́млю;** *pl.* **зе́мли, земе́ль, зе́млям**] *n.* **1**, land; ground; earth. **2**, *cap.* the earth.

земля́к [gen. -ляка́] n.m. [fem. -ля́чка] compatriot; fellow countryman.

земляни́ка n. 1, (wild) strawberries. 2, a (single) strawberry. —земляни́чный, adj. strawberry (attrib.).

земля́нка [gen. pl. -нок] n. dugout; mud hut.

земляно́й adj. earthen. —земляно́й оре́х, peanut. —земляно́й червь, earthworm.

земново́дный adj. amphibious. —земново́дные, n. pl. amphibia; amphibians.

земно́й adj. 1, of the earth; the earth's; terrestrial. 2, earthly; mundane.

зе́мский adj. 1, hist. national; people's: зе́мский собо́р, zemski sobor (legislative assembly in old Russia). 2, of or pert. to the zemstvos.

зе́мство n., hist. zemstvo (local assembly in 19th-cent. Russia).

зени́т n. zenith.

зени́тка [gen. pl. -ток] n., colloq. antiaircraft gun.

зени́тный adj. 1, astron. zenith (attrib.). 2, mil. antiaircraft.

зени́ца n., obs. pupil of the eye. —бере́чь как зени́цу о́ка, to guard like the apple of one's eye.

зе́ркало [pl. -кала́, -ка́л] n. mirror.

зерка́льный adj. 1, mirror (attrib.). 2, having a mirror. 3, mirror-like. 4, (of a telescope) reflecting; (of a camera) reflex. —зерка́льное стекло́, plate glass.

зе́ркальце [gen. pl. -лец] n. small mirror.

зерни́стый adj. 1, grainy. 2, granular. —зерни́стая икра́, soft caviar.

зерно́ [pl. зёрна, зёрен] n. 1, grain: произво́дства зерна́, grain production. 2, fig. grain; particle: зерно́ и́стины, grain of truth. —жемчу́жное зерно́, a pearl. —кофе́йные зёрна, coffee beans.

зернрво́й adj. grain (attrib.); cereal (attrib.).

зернохрани́лище n. granary.

зёрнышко [gen. pl. -шек] n. grain; granule.

зефи́р n. 1, obs. zephyr (gentle breeze). 2, zephyr (lightweight cloth). 3, a kind of candy; marshmallow.

зигза́г n. zigzag. —зигзагообра́зный, adj. zigzag.

зиго́та n. zygote.

зи́ждиться v.r. impfv. [pres. -ждется] (with на + prepl.) to be based (upon).

зима́ [acc. зи́му; pl. зи́мы] n. winter.

зи́мний adj. 1, winter (attrib.). 2, wintry.

зимова́ть v. impfv. [pfv. прозимова́ть; pres. -му́ю, -му́ешь] to spend the winter.

зимо́вка n. 1, wintering; spending the winter. 2, winter camp; winter quarters.

зимо́вье n. winter camp; winter quarters.

зимо́й adv. in (the) winter. Also, зимо́ю.

зиморо́док [gen. -дка] n. halcyon; kingfisher.

зимосто́йкий adj. winter (attrib.); winter-hardy.

зипу́н [gen. -пуна́] n. homespun peasant's coat worn in old Russia.

зия́ние n., ling. hiatus.

зия́ть v. impfv. (of a wound, abyss, etc.) to gape; yawn.

зла́ки n. pl. [sing. злак] cereals. —зла́ковый, adj. cereal (attrib.).

зла́то n., poetic gold.

злейший adj. worst; bitterest.

злить v. impfv. [pfv. обозли́ть or разозли́ть] to anger. —зли́ться, refl. to become angry.

зло¹ [gen. pl. зол] n. 1, evil. 2, wrong. 3, harm. 4, colloq. spite: со зла, out of spite. —из двух зол выбира́ть ме́ньшее, to choose the lesser of two evils.

зло² adv. maliciously. Зло подшути́ть (над), to play a mean trick (on).

зло́ба n. 1, spite; malice. 2, grudge: таи́ть зло́бу, to bear a grudge. —зло́ба дня, topic of the day.

зло́бный adj. malicious; spiteful. —зло́бно, adv. maliciously.

злободне́вный adj. (of a question, issue, etc.) timely; vital.

зло́бствовать v. impfv. [pres. -ствую, -ствуешь] (with на + acc.) to bear malice (towards).

злове́щий adj. ominous; sinister.

злово́ние n. stench. —злово́нный, adj. stinking; fetid.

зловре́дный adj. harmful; pernicious.

злоде́й n. evildoer; villain; scoundrel.

злоде́йский adj. 1, vicious; heinous. 2, insidious.

злоде́йство n. 1, villainy. 2, evil deed.

злодея́ние n. evil deed; crime; outrage.

злой adj. [short form зол, зла, зло] 1, wicked; evil. 2, cross; ill-tempered. 3, [short form only] (with на + acc.) angry (at); cross (with). 4, mean; malicious. 5, (of animals) mean; ferocious. 6, biting; acerbic. 7, colloq. severe.

злока́чественный adj., med. malignant. —злока́чественное малокро́вие, pernicious anemia.

злоключе́ние n. misadventure; mishap.

злонаме́ренный adj. malicious.

злопа́мятный adj. bearing a grudge; rancorous.

злополу́чный adj. ill-fated; ill-starred; hapless.

злопыха́тель n.m. malicious critic; mudslinger. —злопыха́тельский, adj. malicious. —злопыха́тельство, n. maliciousness.

злора́дный adj. gloating.

злора́дство n. malicious pleasure.

злора́дствовать v. impfv. [pres. -ствую, -ствуешь] to gloat.

злосло́вие n. malicious gossip.

злосло́вить v. impfv. [pres. -влю, -вишь] to utter malicious gossip.

зло́стный adj. 1, malicious. 2, (of an offender, defaulter, etc.) persistent; habitual.

злость n.f. 1, malice. 2, rage; fury.

зло́тый n., decl. as an adj. zloty (monetary unit of Poland).

злоупотреби́ть [infl. -блю́ -би́шь] v., pfv. of злоупотребля́ть.

злоупотребле́ние n. 1, (with instr.) misuse (of); abuse (of): злоупотребле́ние вла́стью, abuse of power. 2, abuse; instance of wrongdoing.

злоупотребля́ть v. impfv. [pfv. злоупотреби́ть] (with instr.) to misuse; abuse.

злю́ка n.m. & f., colloq. ill-tempered person; grouch.

змееви́дный adj. like a serpent; serpentine.

змеи́ный adj. snake (attrib.); snake's.

змеи́ться v.r. impfv. to wind; snake.

змей [gen. & acc. зме́я] n. 1, dragon. 2, kite.

змея́ [pl. зме́и, змей, зме́ям] n. snake.

знава́ть v. impfv., colloq., used only in the past tense to have known: он знава́л лу́чшие времена́, he has known better times.

знак n. 1, sign. 2, signal. 3, mark; point: зна́ки препина́ния, punctuation marks; восклица́тельный знак, exclamation point. 4, (in денежный знак, (piece of) paper money. —в знак (+ gen.), as a sign, token, or gesture of. —под зна́ком (+ gen.), under the banner (of).

знако́мить v. impfv. [pfv. познако́мить; pres. -млю,

-мишь] (with с + instr.) **1**, to introduce (to). **2**, to acquaint (with); familiarize (with). —**знако́миться**, refl. (with с + instr.) **1**, to make the acquaintance (of); become acquainted (with). **2**, to familiarize oneself (with); become familiar (with).

знако́мство n. **1**, acquaintance. **2**, (circle of) acquaintances. **3**, familiarity; knowledge.

знако́мый adj. **1**, acquainted: вы знако́мы?, are you acquainted?; do you know each other? **2**, familiar: знако́мый звук, a familiar sound. Я знако́м с э́тим вопро́сом, I am familiar with the matter. —n. acquaintance.

знамена́тель n.m. denominator. —**приводи́ть к одному́** (or **к о́бщему**) **знамена́телю**, to reduce to a common denominator.

знамена́тельный adj. **1**, momentous; memorable. **2**, significant; revealing.

зна́мение n., obs. sign. —**зна́мение вре́мени**, sign of the times. —**кре́стное зна́мение**, sign of the cross.

знамени́тость n.f. **1**, fame; eminence; celebrity. **2**, a celebrity.

знамени́тый adj. famous; celebrated.

знаменова́ть v. impfv. [pfv. **ознаменова́ть**; pres. **-ну́ю, -ну́ешь**] (often with **собо́й**) to mark; signify; represent.

знамено́сец [gen. -сца] n. standard-bearer.

зна́мя [gen., dat. & prepl. зна́мени; instr. зна́менем; pl. знамёна, знамён] n. neut. banner.

зна́ние n., often pl. knowledge. —**со зна́нием де́ла**, **1**, knowledgeably. **2**, with great skill.

зна́тный adj. **1**, from among the nobility or elite. **2**, prominent; noted: зна́тные лю́ди, notables. **3**, colloq. sizable. **4**, colloq. splendid.

знато́к [gen. -тока́] n. expert; connoisseur.

знать[1] v. impfv. to know. —**как зна́ешь**, as you wish. —**как знать?**, how is one to know? —**кто его́ зна́ет?**, who knows? —**то и знай**, colloq. continually.

знать[2] n.f. aristocracy; nobility.

зна́ться v.r. impfv. (with с + instr.) colloq. to associate (with); have to do with.

зна́харь n.m. [fem. зна́харка] medicine man; witch doctor; quack. —**зна́харство**, n. quackery.

зна́чащий adj. meaningful; significant.

значе́ние n. **1**, meaning; sense: двойно́е значе́ние, dual meaning. **2**, significance; importance: не име́ть значе́ния, to be of no significance. Име́ть большо́е значе́ние для, to be of great importance to. **3**, value: коне́чное значе́ние, finite value.

значи́мый adj. significant. —**зна́чимость**, n.f. significance.

зна́чит particle, colloq. so; then.

значи́тельно adv. considerably; significantly; substantially.

значи́тельность n.f. significance; importance.

значи́тельный adj. **1**, considerable. **2**, significant.

зна́чить v. impfv. to mean; signify. —**зна́читься**, refl. to be listed.

значо́к [gen. -чка́] n. **1**, badge. **2**, mark.

зна́ющий adj. knowledgeable.

зноби́ть v. impfv., impers. to have a chill; be chilled: меня́ зноби́т, I have a chill.

зной n. intense heat.

зно́йный adj. burning hot; sultry.

зоб n. **1**, craw; crop (of a bird). **2**, med. goiter.

зо́бный adj., in зо́бная железа́, thymus.

зов n. **1**, call. **2**, colloq. invitation.

зодиа́к n. zodiac.

зо́дчество n. architecture. —**зо́дческий**, adj. architectural.

зо́дчий n., decl. as an adj. architect.

зол adj., short form of **злой**. —n., gen. pl. of **зло**.

зола́ n. **1**, ashes. **2**, ash: вулкани́ческая зола́, volcanic ash.

золо́вка [gen. pl. -вок] n. sister-in-law (husband's sister).

золота́рник n. goldenrod.

золоти́стый adj. golden.

золоти́ть v. impfv. [pfv. **позолоти́ть** or **вы́золотить**; pres. -чу́, -ти́шь] to gild. —**золоти́ть пилю́лю**, to sweeten the pill.

золотни́к [gen. -ника́] n. old Russian measure of weight equal to about 1/6 of an ounce. —**мал золотни́к, да до́рог**, good things come in small packages.

зо́лото n. gold. —**на вес зо́лота**, worth its weight in gold.

золотоиска́тель n.m. prospector (for gold).

золото́й adj. gold; golden. —**золоты́х дел ма́стер**, goldsmith. —**золото́е дно**, gold mine (fig.). —**золото́й дождь**, windfall. —**золото́й мешо́к**, rich man; moneybags.

золотоно́сный adj. containing gold.

золоту́ха n., obs. scrofula.

золоче́ние n. gilding.

золочёный adj. gilded; gilt.

Зо́лушка n. Cinderella.

зо́на n. zone. —**зона́льный**, adj. zone (attrib.); zonal.

зонд n. **1**, med. probing device: желу́дочный зонд, stomach pump. **2**, weather balloon.

зонди́ровать v. impfv. [pres. -рую, -руешь] **1**, to probe; sound. **2**, fig. to sound out. —**зонди́ровать по́чву**, to get the lay of the land.

зонт [gen. зонта́] n. **1**, umbrella. **2**, awning.

зо́нтик n. umbrella.

зооло́гия n. zoology. —**зоо́лог**, n. zoologist. —**зоологи́ческий**, adj. zoological.

зоопа́рк n. zoo.

зо́ркий adj. **1**, sharp-eyed. **2**, perceptive. —**зо́рко**, adv. with a watchful eye. —**зо́ркость**, n.f. keen vision.

зра́зы [gen. зраз] n.pl. meat patties stuffed with rice, kasha, etc.

зрачо́к [gen. -чка́] n. pupil (of the eye).

зре́лище n. **1**, sight; spectacle. **2**, show.

зре́лость n.f. **1**, ripeness; maturity. —**полова́я зре́лость**, puberty.

зре́лый adj. **1**, ripe. **2**, mature.

зре́ние n. sight; eyesight; vision. —**по́ле зре́ния**, field of vision. —**то́чка зре́ния**, point of view; viewpoint. —**у́гол зре́ния**, viewpoint; standpoint.

зреть[1] v. impfv. [pfv. **созре́ть**; pres. зре́ю, зре́ешь] to ripen; mature.

зреть[2] v. impfv. [pfv. **узре́ть**; pres. зрю, зришь] archaic to behold.

зри́тель n.m. **1**, spectator. **2**, pl. audience.

зри́тельный adj. **1**, visual. **2**, optic. —**зри́тельный зал**, auditorium.

зря adv., colloq. in vain; for nothing; to no purpose.

зря́чий adj. able to see; sighted. —n. sighted person.

зуб n. **1**, [pl. зу́бы, зубо́в, зуба́м] tooth. **2**, [pl. зу́бья, зу́бьев] tooth (of a saw, gear, etc.). —**име́ть зуб на** or **про́тив**, to have a grudge against. —**класть зу́бы на по́лку**, to go hungry; suffer hard times. —**не**

по зуба́м (+ *dat.*), *colloq.* too much for; beyond one.

зуба́стый *adj., colloq.* **1,** having large teeth; toothy. **2,** *fig.* sharp-tongued.

зубе́ц [*gen.* -бца́] *n.* tooth; cog; prong.

зуби́ло *n.* cutting tool; chisel.

зубно́й *adj.* tooth (*attrib.*); dental. —**зубно́й врач,** dentist. —**зубна́я па́ста,** toothpaste. —**зубна́я щётка,** toothbrush.

зубоврачёбный *adj.* of or pert. to dentistry; dental.

зубо́к [*gen.* -бка́] *n., colloq., dim. of* зуб. —**на зубо́к,** *colloq.* **1,** as a present for a new-born child. **2,** (*with verbs of knowing or learning*) thoroughly; inside out. —**попа́сть на зубо́к** (+ *dat.*), to be subjected to (someone's) criticism or ridicule; be the target of someone's tongue.

зубоска́л *n., colloq.* joker; kidder. —**зубоска́льство,** *n., colloq.* scoffing; kidding.

зубочи́стка [*gen. pl.* -ток] *n.* toothpick.

зубр *n.* European bison.

зубрёжка *n., colloq.* cramming.

зубри́ла *n.m. & f., colloq.* crammer; grind. *Also,* зубри́лка.

зубри́ть *v. impfv.* [*pfv.* зазубри́ть; *pres.* зубрю́, зубри́шь *or* зу́бришь] **1,** to notch; make notches in. **2,** *colloq.* to cram (*study hard*). **3,** *colloq.* to learn by rote.

зубцо́вка *n.* perforation (*on stamps*). —**зубцо́вый,** *adj.* perforate; perforated.

зубча́тый *adj.* **1,** toothed. **2,** jagged. **3,** (*of a wall of a fortress*) crenelated. —**зубча́тое колесо́,** cogwheel.

зуд *n.* itch.

зуде́ть *v. impfv.* [*pres.* -ди́т] *colloq.* to itch.

зуёк [*gen.* зуйка́] *n.* plover.

зулу́с *n.m.* [*fem.* -ка] Zulu. —**зулу́сский,** *adj.* Zulu.

зу́ммер *n.* buzzer.

зы́бкий *adj.* **1,** unsteady; unstable. **2,** shifting; rippling. **3,** *fig.* vacillating.

зыбу́чий *adj.* shifting: зыбу́чий песо́к, shifting sands.

зыбь *n.f.* rippling; undulating (*of water*). —**лёгкая зыбь,** ripples. —**мёртвая зыбь,** groundswell.

зы́чный *adj.* loud; resounding.

зюйд *n., naut.* **1,** south. **2,** south wind.

зя́бкий *adj., colloq.* sensitive to cold.

зя́блик *n.* chaffinch.

зя́бнуть *v. impfv.* [*past* зяб, -ла] to be frozen; be chilled to the bone.

зябь *n.f.* **1,** autumn plowing. **2,** land plowed in autumn for spring sowing.

зять [*pl.* зятья́, зятьёв] *n.m.* **1,** son-in-law. **2,** brother-in-law (*sister's husband or husband's sister's husband*).

И

И, и *n. neut.* ninth letter of the Russian alphabet.

и *conj.* **1,** and: причи́на и сле́дствие, cause and effect. **2,** *used for emphasis:* вы себе́ и предста́вить не мо́жете!, you just can't imagine! **3,** also; as well: он опозда́л и на второ́й по́езд, he missed the second train as well. **4,** (*with negatives*) either: э́то не легко́ и для меня́, it is not easy for me either. **5,** even: он и спаси́бо не сказа́л, he didn't even say thank you. —**и ... и,** both: и мужчи́ны и же́нщины, both men and women.

и́бис *n.* ibis.

и́бо *conj.* for; as.

и́ва *n.* willow. —**плаку́чая и́ва,** weeping willow.

ива́новский *adj., in* во всю ива́новскую, at the top of one's lungs.

ивня́к [*gen.* -няка́] *n.* **1,** willow bed. **2,** willow branches.

и́вовый *adj.* willow (*attrib.*).

и́волга *n.* European oriole.

иври́т *n.* (modern) Hebrew.

игла́ [*pl.* и́глы, игл] *n.* **1,** needle. **2,** quill (*of an animal*).

игли́стый *adj.* covered with needles or quills.

иглова́тый *adj.* **1,** needle-like. **2,** *colloq.* prickly.

иглови́дный *adj.* needle-shaped. *Also,* иглообра́зный.

иглотерапи́я *n.* acupuncture. *Also,* иглоука́лывание.

и́глу *n. neut. indecl.* igloo.

игнори́ровать *v. impfv. & pfv.* [*pres.* -рую, -руешь] to ignore; disregard.

и́го *n.* yoke (*of oppression*).

иго́лка [*gen. pl.* -лок] *n.* needle. —**быть** *or* **сиде́ть как на иго́лках,** to be on pins and needles; be on tenterhooks.

иго́лочка [*gen. pl.* -чек] *n., dim. of* игла́ *and* иго́лка. —**с иго́лочки,** brand-new. —**оде́т с иго́лочки,** impeccably dressed.

иго́лочный *adj.* needle (*attrib.*).

иго́льник *n.* needle cushion; needle case.

иго́льный *adj.* of a needle; needle (*attrib.*): иго́льное ушко́, eye of a needle.

иго́льчатый *adj.* needle-shaped.

иго́рный *adj.* gambling (*attrib.*); gaming (*attrib.*).

игра́ [*pl.* и́гры, игр] *n.* **1,** game. **2,** play; playing: игра́ на ро́яле, playing (of) the piano. **3,** performance; acting. —**игра́ воображе́ния,** figment of the imagination. —**игра́ приро́ды, 1,** extraordinary natural phenomenon. **2,** freak of nature. —**игра́ слов,** play on words. —**игра́ судьбы́** *or* **слу́чая,** quirk of fate. —**игра́ ума́,** battle of wits.

игра́льный *adj.* playing (*attrib.*). —**игра́льные ко́сти,** dice.

игра́ть *v. impfv.* [*pfv.* сыгра́ть] **1,** to play. **2,** (*with* в + *acc.*) to play (a game). **3,** (*with* на + *prepl.*) to play (an instrument). **4,** to act; perform. **5,** [*impfv. only*] (*with instr.*) to play (with); toy (with); trifle (with). **6,** [*impfv. only*] (*with instr.*) to play (with); fiddle (with); twiddle. **7,** [*impfv. only*] (*of beverages*) to sparkle. **8,** (*with instr.*) *chess* to move (a pawn or piece). —игра́ть в зага́дки, to talk in riddles. —игра́ть глаза́ми, to ogle. —игра́ть на́ руку (+ *dat.*), to play into the hands of. —игра́ть слова́ми, to make plays on words; pun. —игра́ть с огнём, to play with fire.

игра́ючи *adv., colloq.* effortlessly; as if it were child's play.

и́грек *n.* the letter y.

игри́вый *adj.* playful. —игри́вость, *n.f.* playfulness.

игри́стый *adj.* (*of wine, champagne, etc.*) sparkling.

игрово́й *adj.* **1,** playing (*attrib.*). **2,** acting (*attrib.*). **3,** (*of a film, play, etc.*) full of action.

игро́к [*gen.* игрока́] *n.* **1,** player. **2,** gambler.

игру́шечный *adj.* **1,** toy (*attrib.*). **2,** miniature.

игру́шка [*gen. pl.* шек] *n.* **1,** toy. **2,** *fig.* plaything.

игуа́на *n.* iguana.

игу́мен *n.* abbot; father superior (*of a Russian Orthodox monastery*). —игу́менья, *n.* abbess; mother superior (*of a Russian Orthodox convent*).

идеа́л *n.* ideal.

идеализи́ровать *v. impfv. & pfv.* [*pres.* -рую, -руешь] to idealize.

идеали́зм *n.* idealism. —идеали́ст, *n.* idealist. —идеалисти́ческий, *adj.* idealistic.

идеа́льный *adj.* **1,** ideal; sublime. **2,** ideal; perfect.

иде́йность *n.f.* **1,** ideological content. **2,** progressive character. **3,** high-mindedness.

иде́йный *adj.* **1,** ideological. **2,** progressive; high-minded. **3,** *in* иде́йный за́мысел, the basic idea; the point (*of a novel, play, etc.*).

иденти́чный (дэ) *adj.* identical. —иденти́чность, *n.f.* identity.

идеогра́мма *n.* ideogram; ideograph.

идеоло́гия *n.* ideology. —идео́лог, *n.* ideologist. —идеологи́ческий, *adj.* ideological.

иде́я *n.* idea.

иди́ллия *n.* idyll. —идилли́ческий, *adj.* idyllic.

идио́ма *n.* idiom. —идиомати́ческий, *adj.* idiomatic.

идио́т *n.* idiot; imbecile. —идиоти́зм, *n.* idiocy; imbecility. —идио́тский, *adj.* idiotic; imbecilic. —идио́тство, *n., colloq.* idiocy; nonsense.

и́диш *n.* Yiddish.

и́дол *n.* idol. —(сиде́ть *or* стоя́ть) и́долом, motionless; like a statue.

идолопокло́нник *n.* idolater. —идолопокло́ннический, *adj.* idolatrous. —идолопокло́нство, *n.* idolatry.

идти́ *v. impfv.* [*pfv.* пойти́; *pres.* иду́, идёшь; *past* шёл, шла, шло] **1,** to go. **2,** to come: вот они́ иду́т, here they come. **3,** to come out: дым идёт из трубы́, smoke is coming out of the chimney. **4,** to go; proceed; progress: рабо́та идёт хорошо́, the work is going well. **5,** to be in progress: иду́т экза́мены, exams are in progress. **6,** (*of time*) to pass; go by: вре́мя бы́стро идет, time passes quickly. **7,** (*of mail*) to take a certain amout of time to reach: письма́ сюда́ иду́т о́чень до́лго, the mail takes a long time to get here. **8,** (*of rain, snow, etc.*): идёт дождь, it is raining. **9,** (*of a road, mountain range, etc.*) to run; extend. **10,** (*of a device*) to work: мои́ часы́ не иду́т, my watch is not working. **11,** (*of a film or play*) to be playing. **12,** (*with* на + *acc.*)

to be used for; go into the making of: де́рево идёт на изготовле́ние бума́ги, wood is used in making paper. **13,** (*with dat.*) to become: шля́па вам идёт, the hat is becoming to you. **14,** (*with* на + *acc.*) to make (*with certain nouns*): идти́ на усту́пки/же́ртвы, to make concessions/sacrifices. **15,** *cards* to play; lead: идти́ с туза́, to play/lead an ace; идти́ ко́зырем, to play/lead a trump. **16,** (*with instr.*) *chess* to move: идти́ пе́шкой, to move a pawn. **17,** *colloq.* to sell: това́р хорошо́ идёт, the merchandise is selling well. **18,** (*with* в *or* на + *acc.*) *colloq.* to go into; go onto: гвоздь не идёт в сте́ну, the nail will not go into the wall; боти́нок не идёт на́ ногу, the shoe will not go onto my foot. *See also* ходи́ть *and* пойти́.

и́ды [*gen.* ид.] *n. pl.* ides: и́ды ма́рта, the ides of March.

иезуи́т *n.* Jesuit. —иезуи́тский, *adj.* Jesuit.

иена *n.* yen (*monetary unit of Japan*).

иера́рхия *n.* hierarchy. —иерархи́ческий, *adj.* hierarchical.

иеро́глифы *n. pl.* [*sing.* иеро́глиф] (Egyptian) hieroglyph(ic)s; (Chinese) characters. —иероглифи́ческий, *adj.* hieroglyphic.

иждиве́нец [*gen.* -нца] *n.m.* [*fem.* -нка] dependent.

иждиве́ние *n.* maintenance; support. —на иждиве́нии кого́-нибудь, dependent on someone for support.

из *also,* изо *prep., with gen.* **1,** from: прие́хать из Пари́жа, to arrive from Paris. Из достове́рных исто́чников, from reliable sources. **2,** out of: вы́йти из ко́мнаты, to go out of the room. **3,** of; made of: стол из де́рева, a table made of wood. **4,** of; consisting of: буке́т из роз, a bouquet of roses. **5,** of (*a group*): оди́н из них, one of them. **6,** (*with emotions*) out of: из жа́лости, out of pity.

из- *also,* ис-, изо-, изъ- *prefix* **1,** out of; ex-: извлека́ть, to extract; исключа́ть, to exclude. **2,** covering a surface: исписа́ть лист бума́ги, to fill up a sheet of paper with writing. **3,** entirely; all over: изъе́здить всю страну́, to travel all over the country. **4,** thoroughly; severely: измока́ть, to get soaked; исцара́пывать, to scratch severely. **5,** (*with* -ся) to the point of exhaustion: избе́гаться, to run oneself ragged.

изба́ [*pl.* и́збы] *n.* peasant's hut; log cabin.

избави́тель *n.m.* deliverer; savior; redeemer.

изба́вить [*infl.* -влю, -вишь] *v., pfv. of* избавля́ть. —изба́виться, *refl., pfv. of* избавля́ться.

избавле́ние *n.* deliverance.

избавля́ть *v. impfv.* [*pfv.* изба́вить] (*with* от) to save (from); rescue (from); deliver (from); spare. —избавля́ться, *refl.* (*with* от) **1,** to get rid of; rid oneself of. **2,** to avoid; escape.

избало́ванный *adj.* spoiled.

избалова́ть [*infl.* -лу́ю, -лу́ешь] *v., pfv. of* балова́ть *and* избало́вывать. —избалова́ться, *refl., pfv. of* избало́вываться.

избало́вывать *v. impfv.* [*pfv.* избалова́ть] to spoil; pamper. —избало́вываться, *refl.* to become spoiled.

избе́гать *v. pfv., colloq.* to run all over (a place).

избега́ть *v. impfv.* [*pfv.* избежа́ть *or* избе́гнуть] (*with gen.*) to avoid; evade.

избе́гаться *v.r. pfv., colloq.* to run oneself ragged.

избе́гнуть [*past* -бег *or* -бегнул, -бегла] *v., pfv. of* избега́ть.

избежа́ние *n., in* во избежа́ние (+ *gen.*), in order to avoid.

избежа́ть [*infl. like* бежа́ть] *v., pfv. of* избега́ть.

избива́ть v. impfv. [pfv. **изби́ть**] **1,** to beat up. **2,** obs. to slaughter; massacre.

избие́ние n. **1,** beating. **2,** slaughter; massacre. **3,** law assault and battery.

избира́тель n.m. voter.

избира́тельный adj. electoral; election (attrib.). —**избира́тельный бюллете́нь,** ballot. —**избира́тельное пра́во,** suffrage. —**избира́тельная у́рна,** ballot box. —**избира́тельный уча́сток, 1,** voting district. **2,** polling place.

избира́ть v. impfv. [pfv. **избра́ть**] **1,** to select. **2,** to elect.

изби́тый adj. **1,** beaten up. **2,** fig. (of a road, path, etc.) familiar; well-trodden. **3,** trite; hackneyed. —**изби́тая и́стина,** truism.

изби́ть [infl. **изобью́, изобьёшь**] v., pfv. of **избива́ть.**

изборозд́ить v., pfv. of **борозди́ть.**

избра́ние n. election.

избра́нник n. chosen one.

и́збранные n. pl., decl. as an adj. select people.

и́збранный adj. **1,** elected. **2,** select. —**и́збранные сочине́ния,** selected works.

избра́ть [infl. like **брать**] v., pfv. of **избира́ть.**

избу́шка [gen. pl. **-шек**] n. hut; log cabin.

избы́ток [gen. **-тка**] n. **1,** surplus; excess. **2,** abundance. —**в избы́тке; с избы́тком,** in abundance.

избы́точный adj. surplus; excess.

изваяние n. piece of sculpture; sculptured figure.

изваять v., pfv. of **ваять.**

изве́дывать v. impfv. [pfv. **изве́дать**] to experience.

и́зверг n. fiend; monster.

изверга́ть v. impfv. [pfv. **изве́ргнуть**] to spew forth. —**изверга́ться,** refl. **1,** (of a volcano) to erupt. **2,** (of lava) to spew forth.

изве́ргнуть [past **-ве́рг** or **-ве́ргнул, -ве́ргла**] v., pfv. of **изверга́ть.** —**изве́ргнуться,** refl., pfv. of **изверга́ться.**

изверже́ние n. **1,** eruption. **2,** ejection; expulsion. **3,** fig. outpouring; torrent (of words, abuse, etc.).

изве́рженный adj., geol. igneous.

изве́риться v.r. pfv. (with **в** + prepl. or acc.) colloq. to lose faith (in); lose confidence (in).

изверну́ться v.r., pfv. of **извора́чиваться.**

извести́ [infl. like **вести́**] v., pfv. of **изводи́ть.** —**извести́сь,** refl., pfv. of **изводи́ться.**

изве́стие n. **1,** piece of news. **2,** pl. news.

извести́ть [infl. **-щу́, -сти́шь**] v., pfv. of **извеща́ть.**

извёстка n., colloq. = **и́звесть.**

известко́вый adj. lime. —**известко́вая вода́,** limewater.

изве́стно adj., used predicatively known: как изве́стно, as is known. Изве́стно, что..., it is known that... Наско́лько мне изве́стно, as far as I know. —**одному́ бо́гу изве́стно,** God alone knows.

изве́стность n.f. **1,** fame; notoriety; renown. **2,** colloq. a celebrity. —**поста́вить в изве́стность,** to inform; notify.

изве́стный adj. [short form **-стен, -стна**] **1,** known. **2,** well-known. **3,** notorious. **4,** a certain: до изве́стной сте́пени, to a certain degree. —**изве́стное де́ло,** naturally; of course.

известня́к [gen. **-няка́**] n. limestone. —**известняко́вый,** adj. limestone.

и́звесть n.f. lime. —**хло́рная и́звесть,** bleaching powder.

изве́чный adj. primeval; age-old; ancient.

извеща́ть v. impfv. [pfv. **извести́ть**] to inform; notify.

извеще́ние n. notice; notification.

изви́в n. bend (in a river); curve (in a road).

извива́ться v.r. impfv. **1,** to wriggle; squirm. **2,** (of a river, road, etc.) to wind; meander.

изви́лина n. bend (in a river); curve (in a road).

изви́листый adj. winding.

извине́ние n. **1,** apology. **2,** pardon: проси́ть извине́ния у, to beg someone's pardon. **3,** excuse: э́то не мо́жет служи́ть извине́нием, that's no excuse.

извини́тельный adj. **1,** pardonable; excusable. **2,** apologetic.

извиня́ть v. impfv. [pfv. **извини́ть**] to excuse; pardon: извини́те!, excuse me!; pardon me! —**извиня́ться,** refl. (with **пе́ред**) to apologize (to).

извиня́ющийся adj. apologetic.

извлека́ть v. impfv. [pfv. **извле́чь**] **1,** to extract. **2,** to derive.

извлече́ние n. **1,** extraction. **2,** excerpt; extract.

извле́чь [infl. like **влечь**] v., pfv. of **извлека́ть.**

извне́ adv. from without; from the outside.

изводи́ть v. impfv. [pfv. **извести́;** pres. **-вожу́, -во́дишь**] colloq. **1,** to use up; waste; exhaust. **2,** to destroy; exterminate. **3,** to torment; exasperate. —**изводи́ться,** refl., colloq. **1,** to tire oneself out. **2,** to eat one's heart out. **3,** to waste away. **4,** to be used up.

изво́зчик n. **1,** driver; coachman (of a hired carriage). **2,** carriage for hire.

изво́лить v. impfv., obs. to wish; desire. —**изво́льте,** (with inf.) please; be so kind as to...

извора́чиваться v.r. impfv. [pfv. **изверну́ться**] **1,** to twist and turn. **2,** fig., colloq. to use cunning; resort to trickery.

изворо́т n. **1,** obs. bend. **2,** usu. pl. twist. **3,** fig. trick.

изворо́тливый adj. **1,** (of a person) shifty; clever; resourceful. **2,** (of an animal) elusive; slippery.

извраща́ть v. impfv. [pfv. **изврати́ть**] **1,** to distort; misrepresent. **2,** to corrupt; pervert.

извраще́ние n. **1,** distortion; misrepresentation. **2,** corruption; perversion. —**извращённость,** n.f. perversity.

изги́б n. bend; curve.

изгиба́ть v. impfv. [pfv. **изогну́ть**] to bend; curve; arch. —**изгиба́ться,** refl. **1,** to bend; become bent. **2,** (of a path, river, etc.) to curve; wind.

изгла́живать v. impfv. [pfv. **изгла́дить**] to efface; blot out; obliterate.

изгна́ние n. **1,** banishment; expulsion; ostracism. **2,** exile: жить в изгна́нии, to live in exile. —**изгна́нник,** n. exile; outcast.

изгна́ть [infl. like **гнать**] v., pfv. of **изгоня́ть.**

изго́й n. outcast.

изголо́вье n. head of a bed.

изголода́ться v.r. pfv. **1,** to starve; be starving. **2,** (with **по** + dat.) to yearn (for).

изгоня́ть v. impfv. [pfv. **изгна́ть**] to drive out; banish; exile; ostracize.

и́згородь n.f. fence. —**жива́я и́згородь,** hedge.

изгота́вливать v. = **изготовля́ть.**

изгото́вить [infl. **-влю, -вишь**] v., pfv. of **изготовля́ть** and **изгота́вливать.**

изгото́вка n., in **на изгото́вку,** (of a gun) at the ready.

изготовле́ние n. manufacture.

изготовля́ть v. impfv. [pfv. **изгото́вить**] to make; manufacture.

издава́ть v. impfv. [pfv. **изда́ть**; pres. **-даю́, -даёшь**] **1,** to publish. **2,** to issue; promulgate. **3,** to emit; utter. **4,** to emit; give off (an odor).

и́здавна adv. **1,** since olden times; since days of yore. **2,** for a very long time; for as long as one can remember.

издалека́ also, **издалёка** adv. from a distance; from afar.

и́здали adv. from a distance; from afar.

изда́ние n. **1,** issuance; promulgation. **2,** publication. **3,** a publication. **4,** edition.

изда́тель n.m. publisher. **—изда́тельский**, adj. publishing (attrib.). **—изда́тельство**, n. publishing house.

изда́ть [infl. like **дать**; past **изда́л, издала́, изда́ло**] v., pfv. of **издава́ть**.

издева́тельский adj. mocking; derisive.

издева́тельство n. (usu. with **над**) **1,** mockery; derision. **2,** harassment; persecution; violation of one's dignity. **3,** usu. pl. malicious insults.

издева́ться v.r. impfv. (with **над**) to mock; taunt.

издёвка [gen. pl. **-вок**] n., colloq. **1,** gibe. **2,** mockery. Говори́ть с издёвкой, to speak in a mocking tone.

изде́лие n. **1,** make; manufacture. **2,** manufactured article. **3,** pl. goods: ко́жаные изде́лия, leather goods.

издёргать v. pfv., colloq. to harry; harass; unnerve. **—издёргаться**, refl., colloq. to be unnerved.

издержа́ть [infl. **-держу́, -де́ржишь**] v., pfv. of **изде́рживать**. **—издержа́ться**, refl., pfv. of **изде́рживаться**.

изде́рживать v. impfv. [pfv. **издержа́ть**] to spend; expend. **—изде́рживаться**, refl., colloq. to spend all one's money.

изде́ржки [gen. **-жек**] n. pl. expenses; costs.

издо́льщик n. sharecropper. Also, **издо́льник**.

издо́хнуть [past **-до́х, -ла**] v., pfv. of **издыха́ть**.

издре́вле adv. from time immemorial.

издыха́ние n. last breath; dying gasp. **—до после́днего издыха́ния**, to one's last breath; to the death. **—при после́днем издыха́нии**, breathing one's last; near death.

издыха́ть v. impfv. [pfv. **издо́хнуть**] (of animals) to die.

изжа́рить v., pfv. of **жа́рить**. **—изжа́риться**, refl., pfv. of **жа́риться**.

изжива́ть v. impfv. [pfv. **изжи́ть**] to rid oneself of; eliminate. **—изжи́ть себя́**, to become obsolete.

изжи́ть [infl. like **жить**] v., pfv. of **изжива́ть**.

изжо́га n. heartburn.

из-за prep., with gen. **1,** from behind. **2,** because of; on account of.

иззя́бнуть v. pfv. [past **-зя́б, -ла**] colloq. to be chilled to the bone.

излага́ть v. impfv. [pfv. **изложи́ть**] to state; set forth; expound.

изла́мывать v. impfv. [pfv. **изломать**] **1,** to smash; shatter. **2,** colloq. to warp; pervert. **—изла́мываться**, refl. to be broken; be smashed.

излени́ться v.r. pfv. [infl. **-леню́сь, -ле́нишься**] colloq. to become incorrigibly lazy.

излёт n., in **на излёте**, (of a bullet) spent.

излече́ние n. **1,** medical treatment. **2,** recovery.

изле́чивать v. impfv. [pfv. **излечи́ть**] to cure. **—изле́чиваться**, refl. (with **от**) to be cured (of).

излечи́мый adj. curable.

излечи́ть [infl. **-лечу́, -ле́чишь**] v., pfv. of **изле́чивать**. **—излечи́ться**, refl., pfv. of **изле́чиваться**.

излива́ть v. impfv. [pfv. **изли́ть**] **1,** obs. to pour out. **2,** fig. to pour out; give vent to. **3,** in **излива́ть ду́шу**, to pour out one's heart/soul. **—излива́ться**, refl. to give vent to one's feelings.

изли́ть [infl. **изолью́, изольёшь**; past **изли́л, излила́, изли́ло**] v., pfv. of **излива́ть**. **—изли́ться**, refl., pfv. of **излива́ться**.

изли́шек [gen. **-шка**] n. **1,** surplus. **2,** excess. **—с изли́шком**, with something to spare.

изли́шество n. **1,** obs. excess; overabundance. **2,** excess; immoderation; pl. excesses. **—до изли́шества**, to excess.

изли́шне adv. excessively. **—adj.**, used predicatively superfluous; unnecessary: изли́шне сказа́ть, что..., it is superfluous/unnecessary to say that...

изли́шний adj. **1,** excessive. **2,** superfluous; unnecessary.

излия́ние n., usu. pl. outpouring (of emotion).

излови́ть v. pfv. [infl. **-ловлю́, -ло́вишь**] colloq. to catch.

изловчи́ться v.r. pfv., colloq. to manage; contrive.

изложе́ние n. exposition; presentation.

изложи́ть [infl. **-ложу́, -ло́жишь**] v., pfv. of **излага́ть**.

изло́м n. **1,** break; fracture. **2,** sharp turn; sharp curve.

изло́манный adj. **1,** broken; fractured. **2,** crooked; winding. **3,** fig. warped; perverted.

изломать v., pfv. of **изла́мывать**. **—изломаться**, refl., pfv. of **изла́мываться**.

излуча́ть v. impfv. to radiate. **—излуча́ться**, refl. to radiate; emanate.

излуче́ние n. radiation.

излу́чина n. bend; curve.

излю́бленный adj. favorite; pet.

изма́зать [infl. **-ма́жу, -ма́жешь**] v., pfv. of **изма́зывать**. **—изма́заться**, refl., pfv. of **изма́зываться**.

изма́зывать v. impfv. [pfv. **изма́зать**] colloq. to smear; get dirty. **—изма́зываться**, refl. (with instr.) colloq. to get (dirt, paint, ink, etc.) all over oneself.

изма́тывать v. impfv. [pfv. **измота́ть**] colloq. to exhaust; wear out. **—изма́тываться**, refl., colloq. to be exhausted; be worn out.

изма́яться v.r. pfv., colloq. to be exhausted.

измельча́ть[1] v., pfv. of **мельча́ть**.

измельча́ть[2] v. impfv. [pfv. **измельчи́ть**] to grind down; reduce to fine particles.

изме́на n. **1,** treason. **2,** betrayal. **3,** infidelity.

измене́ние n. change; alteration.

измени́ть [infl. **-меню́, -ме́нишь**] v., pfv. of **изменя́ть**. **—измени́ться**, refl., pfv. of **изменя́ться**.

изме́нник n. traitor. **—изме́ннический**, adj. traitorous; treasonable.

изме́нчивый adj. changeable; fickle. **—изме́нчивость**, n.f. changeability.

изменя́ть v. impfv. [pfv. **измени́ть**] **1,** to change; alter. **2,** (with dat.) to betray; be unfaithful to. **3,** (with dat.) to fail: си́лы ему́ измени́ли, his strength failed him.

изменя́ться v.r. impfv. [pfv. **измени́ться**] to change: времена́ измени́лись, times have changed. **—измени́ться в лице́**, to change the expression on one's face.

измере́ние n. **1,** measurement; measuring. **2,** taking (of temperature). **3,** dimension.

измери́мый *adj.* measurable.

измери́тель *n.m.* **1,** measuring device; gauge. **2,** indicator; index. —**измери́тельный,** *adj.* (for) measuring.

измеря́ть *v. impfv.* [*pfv.* **изме́рить**] to measure. —**измеря́ть температу́ру** (+ *dat.*), to take someone's temperature.

измождённый *adj.* haggard; gaunt; emaciated.

измока́ть *v. impfv.* [*pfv.* **измо́кнуть**] *colloq.* to get drenched; get soaked.

измо́кнуть [*past* -мо́к, -ла] *v., pfv. of* **измока́ть.**

измо́р *n., in* **взять изм́ором, 1,** to starve into submission. **2,** *fig.* to wear down; wear down the resistance of.

измори́ть *v.t., colloq.* to wear out; exhaust.

и́зморозь *n.f.* frost; hoarfrost.

и́зморось *n.f.* drizzle.

измота́ть *v., pfv. of* **изма́тывать.** —**измота́ться,** *refl., pfv. of* **изма́тываться.**

изму́ченный *adj.* worn out; exhausted.

изму́чить *v. pfv.* **1,** to wear out; exhaust. **2,** to torment; rack. —**изму́читься,** *refl.* to be worn out; be exhausted.

измыва́ться *v.r. impfv.* (*with* **над**) *colloq.* to make fun of; poke fun at.

измы́слить *v., pfv. of* **измышля́ть.**

измышле́ние *n.* fabrication; falsehood; invention.

измышля́ть *v. impfv.* [*pfv.* **измы́слить**] **1,** to invent; fabricate. **2,** to think up; devise.

измя́тый *adj.* **1,** crumpled; creased. **2,** battered. **3,** haggard.

измя́ть *v. pfv.* [*infl.* **изомну́, изомнёшь**] **1,** *pfv. of* **мять** (*in sense #2*). **2,** to batter. —**измя́ться,** *refl., pfv. of* **мя́ться** (*in sense #1*).

изна́нка *n.* **1,** wrong side; reverse side. **2,** *fig.* seamy side.

изнаси́лование *n.* rape.

изнаси́ловать *v., pfv. of* **наси́ловать.**

изнача́льный *adj.* primordial.

изна́шивание *n.* wearing out.

изна́шивать *v. impfv.* [*pfv.* **износи́ть**] to wear out (clothing, machinery, etc.). —**изна́шиваться,** *refl.* to wear out; be worn out.

изне́женный *adj.* soft; spoiled.

изне́живать *v. impfv.* [*pfv.* **изне́жить**] to spoil; pamper.

изнемога́ть *v. impfv.* [*pfv.* **изнемо́чь**] to be exhausted; be worn out.

изнеможе́ние *n.* utter exhaustion.

изнеможённый *adj.* utterly exhausted.

изнемо́чь [*infl. like* **мочь**] *v., pfv. of* **изнемога́ть.**

изне́рвничаться *v.r. pfv., colloq.* to be a nervous wreck.

изно́с *n.* wear; wear and tear. —**нет изно́су** (+ *dat.*), immune to wear: э́тим боти́нкам нет изно́су, these shoes will never wear out.

износи́ть [*infl.* -ношу́, -но́сишь] *v., pfv. of* **изна́шивать.** —**износи́ться,** *refl., pfv. of* **изна́шиваться.**

изно́шенный *adj.* worn out; threadbare.

изнуре́ние *n.* exhaustion.

изнури́тельный *adj.* **1,** exhausting; grueling. **2,** enervating; debilitating.

изнуря́ть *v. impfv.* [*pfv.* **изнури́ть**] to exhaust.

изнутри́ *adv.* **1,** from inside; from within. **2,** on the inside.

изныва́ть *v. impfv.* [*pfv.* **изны́ть**] to languish.

изны́ть [*infl.* -но́ю, -но́ешь] *v., pfv. of* **изныва́ть.**

изо *prep.* = **из.**

изоба́ра *n.* isobar.

изоби́лие *n.* abundance; plenty. —**рог изоби́лия,** horn of plenty; cornucopia.

изоби́ловать *v. impfv.* [*pfv.* -лует] (*with instr.*) to abound (in).

изоби́льный *adj.* abundant.

изоблича́ть *v. impfv.* [*pfv.* **изобличи́ть**] **1,** to expose; convict. **2,** [*impfv. only*] to reveal; give away: акце́нт изоблича́л в нём иностра́нца, his accent gave him away as a foreigner.

изобличе́ние *n.* exposure.

изобличи́тель *n.m.* exposer. —**изобличи́тельный,** *adj.* incriminating.

изобличи́ть *v., pfv. of* **изоблича́ть.**

изобража́ть *v. impfv.* [*pfv.* **изобрази́ть**] to depict; portray; represent. —**изобража́ть из себя́** (+ *acc.*), *colloq.* to make oneself out to be.

изображе́ние *n.* **1,** portrayal; representation. **2,** image; picture.

изобрази́тельный *adj.* graphic. —**изобрази́тельные иску́сства,** fine arts.

изобрази́ть [*infl.* -жу́, -зи́шь] *v., pfv. of* **изобража́ть.**

изобрести́ [*infl.* -брету́, -брете́шь; *past* -брёл, -брела́, -брело́] *v., pfv. of* **изобрета́ть.**

изобрета́тель *n.m.* inventor. —**изобрета́тельность,** *n.f.* inventiveness. —**изобрета́тельный,** *adj.* inventive.

изобрета́ть *v. impfv.* [*pfv.* **изобрести́**] to invent.

изобрете́ние *n.* invention.

изо́гнутый *adj.* bent; curved.

изогну́ть *v., pfv. of* **изгиба́ть.** —**изогну́ться,** *refl., pfv. of* **изгиба́ться.**

изодра́ть *v. pfv.* [*infl.* издеру́, издерёшь; *past fem.* изодрала́] *colloq.* to tear up; tear to shreds.

изойти́ [*infl.* изойду́, изойдёшь; *past* изошёл, изошла́] *v., pfv. of* **исходи́ть**[1] (*in sense #4*).

изолга́ться *v.r. pfv.* [*infl. like* **лгать**] to become a habitual liar.

изоли́ровать *v. impfv. & pfv.* [*pres.* -рую, -руешь] **1,** to isolate. **2,** to quarantine. **3,** to insulate.

изоля́тор *n.* **1,** insulator. **2,** isolation ward.

изоляциони́зм *n.* isolationism. —**изоляциони́ст,** *r.* isolationist. —**изоляциони́стский,** *adj.* isolationist.

изоляцио́нный *adj.* **1,** isolation (*attrib.*). **2,** quarantin (*attrib.*). **3,** insulation (*attrib.*).

изоля́ция *n.* **1,** isolation. **2,** quarantine. **3,** insulatio

изоме́р *n.* isomer.

изо́рванный *adj.* torn; tattered.

изорва́ть *v. pfv.* [*infl. like* **рвать**] to tear up; tear to shreds. —**изорва́ться,** *refl.* **1,** to be torn to shreds. **2,** *colloq.* to be in shreds; become full of holes.

изото́п *n.* isotope.

изощре́ние *n.* refinement; perfection.

изощрённый *adj.* acute; keen.

изощря́ть *v. impfv.* [*pfv.* **изощри́ть**] to sharpen (one's hearing, mind, etc.); refine; cultivate (one's taste); perfect (one's skills). —**изощря́ться,** *refl.* **1,** to become refined. **2,** (*with* **в** + *prepl.*) to excel (in); be a master of.

из-под *prep., with gen.* **1,** from under: из-под стола́, from under the table. Вода́ из-под кра́на, water from the tap; tap water. **2,** from somewhere near. **3,** (*of a container*) for holding: буты́лка из-под вина́, a wine bottle.

изразе́ц [*gen.* -зца́] *n.* (glazed) tile. —**изразцо́вый,** *adj.* tile (*attrib.*); tiled.

изра́ильский *adj.* Israeli.

израильтя́нин [*pl.* -тя́не, -тя́н] *n.m.* [*fem.* -тя́нка] **1,** *hist.* Israelite. **2,** Israeli.

изра́нить *v. pfv.* to wound severely; wound in many places.

израсхо́довать *v., pfv. of* **расхо́довать.** —**израс-хо́довать,** *refl.* to be used up; be consumed.

и́зредка *adv.* now and then; from time to time.

изре́занный *adj.* **1,** cut up; sliced up. **2,** (*of a coastline*) irregular; indented; jagged. **3,** (*of a region*) rugged.

изре́зать [*infl.* -ре́жу, -ре́жешь] *v., pfv. of* **изре́зы-вать.**

изре́зывать *v. impfv.* [*pfv.* изре́зать] **1,** to cut up; cut to pieces. **2,** to gash; slash. **3,** to cut across; crisscross.

изрека́ть *v. impfv.* [*pfv.* изре́чь] *obs.* to utter; state.

изрече́ние *n.* saying; maxim; adage; dictum.

изре́чь [*infl.* -реку́, -речёшь, ...-реку́т; *past* -рёк, -рекла́, рекло́] *v., pfv. of* **изрека́ть.**

изреше́чивать *v. impfv.* [*pfv.* изрешети́ть] to riddle (with bullets, shrapnel, etc.).

изрисова́ть *v. pfv.* [*inf.* -су́ю, -су́ешь] to cover with drawings.

изруби́ть *v. pfv.* [*infl.* -рублю́, -ру́бишь] **1,** to chop up; hack to pieces. **2,** to massacre (*by sword*).

изруга́ть *v. pfv., colloq.* to curse (someone) roundly; heap abuse on.

изрыва́ть *v. impfv.* [*pfv.* изры́ть] to dig up; tear up; churn up.

изрыга́ть *v. impfv.* [*pfv.* изры́гнуть] **1,** to belch up; regurgitate. **2,** to belch forth (flames, smoke, etc.). **3,** *fig.* to utter (profanities).

изры́тый *adj.* **1,** dug up. **2,** rough; bumpy; uneven. —**изры́тый о́спой,** pockmarked.

изры́ть [*infl.* -ро́ю, -ро́ешь] *v., pfv. of* **изрыва́ть.**

изря́дно *adv., colloq.* **1,** (*with adjectives*) rather; pretty. **2,** (*with verbs*) quite a lot.

изря́дный *adj., colloq.* quite a; a pretty fair; a handsome; a goodly.

изуве́р *n.* **1,** fanatic. **2,** *fig.* monster; fiend.

изуве́рский *adj.* **1,** fanatical. **2,** *fig.* savage; barbaric.

изуве́рство *n.* **1,** fanaticism. **2,** *fig.* barbarity.

изуве́чивать *v. impfv.* [*pfv.* изуве́чить] to maim.

изукра́шивать *v. impfv.* [*pfv.* изукра́сить] to decorate lavishly; bedeck.

изуми́тельно *adv.* **1,** amazingly. **2,** marvelously.

изуми́тельный *adj.* **1,** amazing; astonishing. **2,** wonderful; marvelous.

изуми́ть [*infl.* -млю́, -ми́шь] *v., pfv. of* изумля́ть. —**изуми́ться,** *refl., pfv. of* изумля́ться.

изумле́ние *n.* amazement; astonishment.

изумля́ть *v. impfv.* [*pfv.* изуми́ть] to amaze; astonish. —**изумля́ться,** *refl.* (*with dat.*) to be amazed (at); be astonished (at).

изумру́д *n.* emerald. —**изумру́дный,** *adj.* emerald.

изуро́дованный *adj.* disfigured.

изуро́довать *v., pfv. of* **уро́довать.**

изуча́ть *v. impfv.* [*pfv.* изучи́ть] to study.

изуче́ние *n.* study; studying.

изучи́ть *v. pfv.* [*infl.* -учу́, -у́чишь] **1,** *pfv. of* изуча́ть. **2,** to learn. **3,** to get to know.

изъеда́ть *v. impfv.* [*pfv.* изъе́сть] **1,** to eat away. **2,** to eat into.

изъе́здить *v. pfv.* [*infl.* -е́зжу, -е́здишь] *colloq.* to travel all over (an area).

изъе́сть [*infl. like* есть] *v., pfv. of* изъеда́ть.

изъяви́тельный *adj., in* **изъяви́тельное наклоне́-ние,** *gram.* indicative mood.

изъяви́ть [*infl.* -явлю́, -я́вишь] *v., pfv. of* изъявля́ть.

изъявле́ние *n.* expression; declaration.

изъявля́ть *v. impfv.* [*pfv.* изъяви́ть] to express.

изъязвля́ть *v. impfv.* [*pfv.* изъязви́ть] to ulcerate. —**изъязвля́ться,** *refl.* to ulcerate; become ulcerated.

изъя́н *n.* defect; flaw (*in merchandise*).

изъясня́ться *v.r. impfv.* [*pfv.* изъясни́ться] **1,** *obs.* to express oneself. **2,** [*impfv. only*] to speak.

изъя́тие *n.* **1,** withdrawal; removal. **2,** exception.

изъя́ть [*infl.* изыму́, изы́мешь] *v., pfv. of* изыма́ть.

изыма́ть *v. impfv.* [*pfv.* изъя́ть] **1,** to withdraw; remove. **2,** to seize; confiscate.

изыска́ние *n.* **1,** seeking. **2,** *usu. pl.* research. **3,** *usu. pl.* surveying; prospecting.

изы́сканный *adj.* refined; exquisite. —**изы́скан-ность,** *n.f.* refinement.

изыска́тель *n.m.* prospector.

изыска́ть [*infl.* изыщу́, изы́щешь] *v., pfv. of* изы́с-кивать.

изы́скивать *v. impfv.* [*pfv.* изыска́ть] **1,** to find; obtain. **2,** [*impfv. only*] to seek; look for.

изю́бр *also,* **изю́брь** *n.m.* a variety of red deer; Altai wapiti.

изю́м *n.* raisins. —**не фунт изю́му,** nothing to be sneezed at.

изю́мина *n.* a (single) raisin.

изю́минка [*gen. pl.* -нок] *n.* **1,** a (single) raisin. **2,** *fig.* spark; sparkle (*in a person*).

изя́щество *n.* elegance; grace.

изя́щно *adv.* elegantly.

изя́щный *adj.* elegant; graceful. —**изя́щные иску́с-ства,** fine arts.

Иису́с *n.* Jesus.

ика́ть *v. impfv.* [*pfv.* икну́ть] to hiccup.

ико́на *n.* icon. —**ико́нный,** *adj.* icon (*attrib.*).

иконобо́рец [*gen.* -рца] *n.* iconoclast. —**иконобо́р-(че)ство,** *n.* iconoclasm. —**иконобо́рческий,** *adj.* iconoclastic.

иконопи́сец [*gen.* -сца] *n.* icon painter. —**и́коно-пись,** *n.f.* icon painting.

иконоста́с *n.* iconostasis.

ико́та *n.* hiccups.

икра́ *n.* **1,** fish eggs; roe. **2,** caviar. **3,** [*pl.* и́кры] calf (*of the leg*).

икромета́ние *n.* spawning.

икс *n.* the letter x.

ил *n.* silt.

и́ли *conj.* or. —**и́ли..., и́ли...,** either..., or...

и́листый *adj.* silty; slimy; muddy.

иллюзиони́ст *n.* magician.

иллю́зия *n.* illusion.

иллюзо́рный *adj.* illusory.

иллюмина́тор *n.* porthole.

иллюмина́ция *n.* illumination; decorative lighting.

иллюминова́ть *v. impfv. & pfv.* [*pres.* -ну́ю, -ну́ешь] to decorate with lights. *Also,* **иллюмини́ровать** [*pres.* -рую, -руешь].

иллюстра́ция *n.* illustration. —**иллюстрати́вный,** *adj.* illustrative. —**иллюстра́тор,** *n.* illustrator.

иллюстри́ровать v. impfv. & pfv. [pfv. also **проил-люстри́ровать**; pres. -рую, -руешь] to illustrate.

и́лька [gen. pl. и́лек] n. fisher (animal).

ильм n. elm.

им pron. **1,** instr. of он and оно́. **2,** dat. of они́.

имби́рь [gen. -ря́] n.m. ginger. —**имби́рный,** adj. ginger.

име́ние n. estate.

имени́ны [gen. -ни́н] n. pl. name day; one's saint's day. —**имени́нник,** n. person celebrating his name day. —**имени́нный,** adj. of or pert. to one's name day.

имени́тельный adj., in **имени́тельный паде́ж,** nominative case.

имени́тый adj. prominent; distinguished; eminent.

и́менно particle **1,** just; exactly; precisely. Вот и́менно!, exactly!; precisely! **2,** [often **а и́менно**] namely; to wit.

именно́й adj. inscribed with the owner's name. —**именно́й спи́сок,** roll; list of names.

имено́ванный adj., in **имено́ванное число́,** math. concrete number.

именова́ть v. impfv. [pfv. **наименова́ть;** pres. -ну́ю, -ну́ешь] to name. —**именова́ться,** refl. [impfv. only] to be called.

име́ть v. impfv. **1,** to have: име́ть возмо́жность (+ inf.), to have the opportunity to. **2,** rendered by various English verbs according to the noun: име́ть вес, to carry weight; име́ть успе́х, to be successful; име́ть схо́дство с, to bear a resemblance to; не име́ть смы́сла, to make no sense; не име́ть значе́ния, to be of no significance. —**ничего́ не име́ть про́тив,** to have no objection.

име́ться v.r. impfv. to be; exist; be available. В го́роде име́ется мно́го кни́жных магази́нов, there are many bookstores in town. Возраже́ний не име́ется, there are no objections.

име́ющийся adj. available; on hand.

и́ми pron., instr. of они́.

имита́тор n. imitator; mimic.

имита́ция n. **1,** imitation; mimicry. **2,** imitation; fake.

имити́ровать v. impfv. [pres. -рую, -руешь] to imitate.

иммигра́нт n.m. [fem. -ка] immigrant.

иммигра́ция n. immigration. —**иммиграцио́нный,** adj. immigration (attrib.).

иммигри́ровать v. impfv. & pfv. [pres. -рую, -руешь] to immigrate.

иммуниза́ция n. immunization.

иммунизи́ровать v. impfv. & pfv. [pres. -рую, -руешь] to immunize.

иммуните́т n. immunity.

императи́вный adj. **1,** imperative; obligatory. **2,** imperious; peremptory.

импера́тор n. emperor. —**импера́торский,** adj. emperor's; imperial.

императри́ца n. empress.

империали́зм n. imperialism. —**империали́ст,** n. imperialist. —**империалисти́ческий,** adj. imperialist; imperialistic.

импе́рия n. empire. —**импе́рский,** adj. imperial.

импи́чмент n. impeachment.

импоза́нтный adj. imposing; impressive.

импони́ровать v. impfv. [pres. -рую, -руешь] (with dat.) to impress; make an impression on.

и́мпорт n. **1,** import; importation. **2,** imports. —**импортёр,** n. importer.

импорти́ровать v. impfv. & pfv. [pres. -рую, -руешь] to import.

и́мпортный adj. **1,** import (attrib.). **2,** imported.

импоте́нтный adj., med. impotent. —**импоте́нция,** n., med. impotence.

импреса́рио n.m. indecl. impresario.

импрессиони́зм n. impressionism. —**импрессиони́ст,** n. impressionist. —**импрессионисти́ческий; импрессиони́стский,** adj. impressionist(ic).

импровиза́ция n. improvisation. —**импровиза́тор,** n. improviser.

импровизи́рованный adj. improvised; extemporaneous; impromptu.

импровизи́ровать v. impfv. & pfv. [pres. -рую, -руешь] to improvise.

и́мпульс n. impulse; impetus. —**импульси́вный,** adj. impulsive.

иму́щественный adj. property (attrib.).

иму́щество n. **1,** property. **2,** mil. equipment. **3,** colloq. belongings. —**недви́жимое иму́щество,** real estate.

иму́щий adj. propertied. —**власть иму́щие,** those in power; the powers that be.

и́мя [gen., dat., & prepl. и́мени; instr. и́менем; pl. имена́, имён, имена́м] n. neut. **1,** name; first name. **2,** name; reputation: сде́лать себе́ и́мя, to make a name for oneself. **3,** noun: и́мя со́бственное, proper noun. **4,** in **и́мя существи́тельное,** noun; **и́мя прилага́тельное,** adjective; **и́мя числи́тельное,** numeral. —**во и́мя** (+ gen.), in the name of; for the sake of. —**на и́мя** (+ gen.), addressed to. —**от и́мени** (+ gen.), on behalf of. —**по и́мени, 1,** by name. **2,** (fol. by a name) by the name of. —**и́менем** (+ gen.), in the name of: и́менем зако́на, in the name of the law. —**и́мени** (+ gen.), named in honor of: институ́т и́мени Па́влова, the Pavlov Institute.

инакомы́слие n. dissent; dissidence. —**инакомы́слящий,** adj. & n. dissident.

инаугура́ция n. inauguration.

ина́че also, **и́наче** adv. differently; otherwise. Сде́лать что-нибудь ина́че, to do something differently. Вышло ина́че, it turned out otherwise. —conj., colloq. or; or else; otherwise. Спеши́те, ина́че вы опозда́ете, hurry, or you'll be late. —**ина́че говоря́,** in other words. —**так и́ли ина́че,** somehow or other; one way or another.

инвали́д n. invalid. —**инвали́дность,** n.f. disability.

инвали́дный adj. invalid (attrib.); invalid's. —**инвали́дное кре́сло,** wheelchair.

инвентариза́ция n. (taking of) inventory.

инвентаризи́ровать v. impfv. & pfv. [pres. -рую, -руешь] to take inventory of. Also, **инвентаризова́ть** [pres. -зу́ю, -зу́ешь].

инвента́рный adj. inventory (attrib.).

инвента́рь [gen. -ря́] n.m. inventory. —**живо́й инвента́рь,** livestock. —**мёртвый инвента́рь,** farm tools and equipment.

инве́рсия n., gram.; chem.; meteorol. inversion.

инвенсти́тура n. investiture.

ингаля́тор n., med. inhaler.

ингредие́нт n. ingredient.

ингу́ш [gen. -ша́] n.m. [fem. -гу́шка] Ingush (one of a

people inhabiting the Caucasus). —**ингýшский**, *adj.* Ingush.

йндеветь *v. impfv.* [*pfv.* **зайндеветь**] to become covered with frost.

индéец [*gen.* -**дéйца**] *n.m.* [*fem.* -**диáнка**] American Indian.

индéйка [*gen. pl.* -**дéек**] *n.* turkey.

индéйский *adj.* (American) Indian.

йндекс (дэ) *n.* index: йндекс цен, price index.

индиáнка [*gen. pl.* -**нок**] *n.* **1**, Indian woman; woman of India. **2**, American Indian woman; squaw.

индивúд *n.* individual.

индивидуалúзм *n.* individualism. —**индивидуалúст**, *n.* individualist.

индивидуáльный *adj.* individual. —**индивидуáльность**, *n.f.* individuality.

индивúдуум *n.* individual.

индúго *n. indecl.* indigo.

индúец [*gen.* -**дúйца**] *n.m.* [*fem.* -**диáнка**] Indian; native of India.

йндий *n.* indium.

индúйский *adj.* Indian; of India.

индикáтор *n.* indicator.

индифферéнтный *adj.* indifferent. —**индифферéнтность**, *n.f.* indifference.

индоевропéйский *adj.* Indo-European.

индонезúец [*gen.* -**úйца**] *n.m.* [*fem.* -**úйка**] Indonesian. —**индонезúйский**, *adj.* Indonesian.

индоссамéнт *n., comm.* endorsement.

индоссúровать *v. impfv. & pfv.* [*pres.* -**рую**, -**руешь**] *comm.* to endorse.

индуúзм *n.* Hinduism.

индуктúвный *adj.* inductive.

индýктор *n.* inductor.

индукциóнный *adj.* induction (*attrib.*): индукциóнная катýшка, induction coil.

индýкция *n., logic; electricity* induction.

индýс *n.m.* [*fem.* -**дýска**] Hindu. —**индýсский**, *adj.* Hindu.

индустриализáция *n.* industrialization.

индустриализúровать *v. impfv. & pfv.* [*pres.* -**рую**, -**руешь**] to industrialize.

индустриáльный *adj.* industrial.

индýстрия *also,* **индустрúя** *n.* industry.

индюк [*gen.* -**дюкá**] *n.* turkey cock.

индюшка [*gen. pl.* -**шек**] *n., colloq.* turkey.

йней *n.* frost; hoarfrost.

инéртный *adj.* **1**, *chem.* inert. **2**, inert; sluggish. —**инéртность**, *n.f.* inertia; sluggishness.

инéрция *n.* **1**, inertia. **2**, momentum. **3**, *fig.* inertia; sluggishness.

инженéр *n.* engineer. —**инженéр-механик**, mechanical engineer. —**инженéр-строúтель**, civil engineer. —**инженéр-хúмик**, chemical engineer. —**инженéр-электрик**, electrical engineer.

инженéрный *adj.* **1**, engineering (*attrib.*). **2**, *mil.* engineer (*attrib.*): инженéрные войскá, engineer troops.

инжúр *n.* **1**, fig. **2**, fig tree.

инициáлы [*gen.* -**лов**] *n. pl.* initials.

инициатúва *n.* initiative. —**инициатúвный**, *adj.* with initiative; possessing intiative.

инициáтор *n.* initiator.

инквизúция *n.* inquisition. —**инквизúтор**, *n.* inquisitor.

инкóгнито *adv.* incognito.

инкорпорáция *n.* incorporation.

инкорпорúровать *v. impfv. & pfv.* [*pres.* -**рую**, -**руешь**] to incorporate.

инкриминúровать *v. impfv. & pfv.* [*pres.* -**рую**, -**руешь**] (*with dat.*) to charge; accuse.

инкрустáция *n.* inlaid work; inlay.

инкрустúровать *v. impfv. & pfv.* [*pres.* -**рую**, -**руешь**] to inlay; encrust.

инкубáтор *n.* incubator.

инкубáция *n.* incubation. —**инкубациóнный**, *adj.* incubation (*attrib.*).

иногдá *adv.* sometimes.

иногорóдний *adj.* from another city; out-of-town.

иноземец [*gen.* -**мца**] *n.m.* [*fem.* -**мка**] *obs.* foreigner. —**иноземный**, *adj.* foreign.

инóй *adj.* **1**, other; another. **2**, else: никтó инóй, no one else. **3**, some; certain. —**инóй раз**, sometimes. —**не кто инóй, как**, none other than. —**не что инóе, как**, nothing but; nothing less than. —**тот úли инóй**, some ... or other; one ... or another.

йнок *n., obs.* monk.

инорóдный *adj.* foreign: инорóдное тéло, foreign body.

иносказáние *n.* allegory. —**иносказáтельный**, *adj.* allegorical.

иностранец [*gen.* -**нца**] *n.m.* [*fem.* -**нка**] foreigner.

иностранный *adj.* foreign.

иноходец [*gen.* -**дца**] *n.* pacer (*horse*).

йноходь *n.f.* amble; pace: идтú йноходью, to amble; pace.

иноязычный *adj.* **1**, speaking another language. **2**, belonging to another language; foreign.

инсектицúд *n.* insecticide.

инсинуáция *n.* insinuation; innuendo.

инспектúровать *v. impfv.* [*pres.* -**рую**, -**руешь**] to inspect.

инспéктор [*pl.* инспекторá] *n.* inspector. —**инспéкторский**, *adj.* inspector's.

инспéкция *n.* **1**, inspection. **2**, inspectors. —**инспекциóнный**, *adj.* inspection (*attrib.*).

инспирúровать *v. impfv. & pfv.* [*pres.* -**рую**, -**руешь**] **1**, to influence. **2**, to inspire; instigate.

инстáнция *n.* **1**, level of authority; echelon. **2**, *law* instance: суд пéрвой инстáнции, court of first instance. —**комáндные инстáнции**, *mil.* chain of command.

инстúнкт *n.* instinct.

инстинктúвный *adj.* instinctive. —**инстинктúвно**, *adv.* instinctively.

институт *n.* **1**, institute. **2**, institution: институт брáка, the institution of marriage.

инструктáж *n., colloq.* **1**, instructing. **2**, instructions; *mil.* briefing.

инструктúвный *adj.* instructional.

инструктúрование *n.* instructing; instruction.

инструктúровать *v. impfv. & pfv.* [*pres.* -**рую**, -**руешь**] **1**, to instruct. **2**, to brief.

инстрýктор *n.* instructor.

инстрýкция *n.* instructions; directions.

инструмéнт *n.* **1**, tool; instrument. **2**, *music* instrument.

инструменталúст *n.* instrumentalist.

инструментáльный *adj.* **1**, tool (*attrib.*); used in making tools. **2**, *music* instrumental.

инструментáльщик *n.* toolmaker.

инструментáрий *n.* tools; instruments.

инструментова́ть v. impfv. & pfv. [pres. -ту́ю, -ту́-ешь] to orchestrate.

инструменто́вка n. orchestration.

инсули́н n. insulin.

инсу́льт n., med. stroke.

инсцени́ровать v. impfv. & pfv. [pres. -ру́ю, -ру́ешь] **1**, to stage; adapt for the stage. **2**, fig. to feign.

инсцениро́вка n. staging.

интегра́л (тэ) n., math. integral.

интегра́льный (тэ) adj. **1**, math. integral. **2**, electronics integrated: интегра́льная схе́ма, integrated circuit.

интегра́ция (тэ) n. integration. Also, **интегри́рование**.

интегри́ровать (тэ) v. impfv. & pfv. [pres. -ру́ю, -ру́ешь] to integrate.

интелле́кт n. intellect.

интеллектуа́л n. intellectual. —**интеллектуа́льный**, adj. intellectual.

интеллиге́нт n. intellectual.

интеллиге́нтный adj. cultured; educated.

интеллиге́нция n. intelligentsia.

интенда́нт n., mil. quartermaster. —**интенда́нтство**, n. quartermaster corps; commissariat.

интенси́вный (тэ) adj. intensive. —**интенси́вность**, n.f. intensity.

интерва́л n. interval; space. —**че́рез два интерва́ла**, double-spaced.

интерве́нция n. intervention.

интервью́ (тэ) n. neut. indecl. interview. —**интервью́ер**, n. interviewer.

интервьюи́ровать (тэ) v. impfv. & pfv. [pres. -ру́ю, -ру́ешь] to interview.

интере́с n. interest. —**в интере́сах** (+ gen.), in the interest of; for the sake of.

интере́сно adv. in an interesting manner. —adj., used predicatively **1**, interesting: интере́сно знать, кто э́то сказа́л, it would be interesting to know who said that. **2**, (with dat.) interested: е́сли вам интере́сно знать, in case you're interested; if it is of any interest to you. **3**, I wonder: интере́сно, куда́ он пошёл, I wonder where he went.

интере́сный adj. [short form -сен, -сна] **1**, interesting. **2**, colloq. attractive; good-looking; cute. —**в инте-ре́сном положе́нии**, in the family way.

интересова́ть v. impfv. [pres. -су́ю, -су́ешь] to interest. —**интересова́ться**, refl. (with instr.) to be interested (in).

интерлю́дия (тэ) n., music interlude.

интерме́ццо (тэ) n. indecl. intermezzo.

интерн (тэ) n. intern.

интерна́т (тэ) n. dormitory. —**шко́ла-интерна́т**, boarding school.

Интернациона́л (тэ) n. **1**, International (socialist organization). **2**, the Internationale (revolutionary hymn).

интернационали́зм (тэ) n. internationalism.

интернациона́льный (тэ) adj. international.

интерни́рование (тэ) n. internment.

интерни́ровать (тэ) v. impfv. & pfv. [pres. -ру́ю, -ру́ешь] to intern.

интерполи́ровать (тэ) v. impfv. & pfv. [pres. -ру́ю, -ру́ешь] to interpolate.

интерполя́ция (тэ) n. interpolation.

интерпрета́тор (тэ) n. interpreter.

интерпрета́ция (тэ) n. interpretation.

интерпрети́ровать (тэ) v. impfv. & pfv. [pres. -ру́ю, -ру́ешь] to interpret.

интерье́р (тэ) n. interior (of a building).

инти́мный adj. intimate. —**инти́мно**, adv. intimately. —**инти́мность**, n.f. intimacy.

интона́ция n. intonation.

интри́га n. **1**, intrigue. **2**, plot (of a novel). **3**, obs. love affair.

интрига́н n. schemer.

интригова́ть v. impfv. [pfv. заинтригова́ть; pres. -гу́ю, -гу́ешь] **1**, to intrigue; fascinate. **2**, [impfv. only] to engage in intrigue; scheme.

интроду́кция n., music introduction.

интроспе́кция n. introspection. —**интроспекти́в-ный**, adj. introspective.

интуити́вный adj. intuitive. —**интуити́вно**, adv. intuitively.

интуи́ция n. intuition.

инфа́ркт n. heart attack.

инфе́кция n. infection. —**инфекцио́нный**, adj. infectious.

инфинити́в n. infinitive.

инфля́ция n. inflation. —**инфляцио́нный**, adj. inflation (attrib.); inflationary.

информа́тор n. informant.

информа́ция n. information. —**информацио́нный**, adj. information (attrib.).

информи́ровать v. impfv. & pfv. [pfv. also проин-форми́ровать; pres. -ру́ю, -ру́ешь] to inform.

инфракра́сный adj. infrared.

инциде́нт n. incident.

инъе́кция n. injection.

ио́н n. ion.

иониза́ция n. ionization.

иони́зировать v. impfv. & pfv. [pres. -ру́ю, -ру́ешь] to ionize. Also, **ионизова́ть** [pres. -зу́ю, -зу́ешь].

ио́нный adj. ionic; ion (attrib.).

ионосфе́ра n. ionosphere.

иорда́нский adj. Jordanian.

ипоме́я n. morning-glory.

ипоте́ка n. mortgage.

ипохо́ндрия n. hypochondria. —**ипохо́ндрик**, n. hypochondriac.

ипподро́м n. racetrack.

ипри́т n. mustard gas.

ира́кский adj. Iraqi.

ира́нец [gen. -нца] n.m. [fem. -нка] Iranian. —**ира́н-ский**, adj. Iranian.

ири́дий n. iridium.

и́рис n. iris (flower).

ири́с n. taffy.

ирла́ндец [gen. -дца] n.m. [fem. -дка] Irishman. —**ирла́ндский**, adj. Irish.

иронизи́ровать v. impfv. [pres. -ру́ю, -ру́ешь] to speak ironically; be ironic.

ирони́ческий adj. ironic; ironical. —**ирони́чески**, adv. ironically.

иро́ния n. irony. —**по иро́нии судьбы́**, by an irony of fate; ironically.

иррадиа́ция n. irradiation.

иррациона́льный adj., math. irrational.

иррига́ция n. irrigation. —**ирригацио́нный**, adj. irrigation (attrib.).

ис- prefix, var. of **из-** (used before voiceless consonants).

иск n. suit; lawsuit.

искажа́ть v. impfv. [pfv. искази́ть] **1**, to distort; contort. **2**, to distort; misrepresent.

искажéние *n.* distortion.

исказить [*infl.* -жý, -зи́шь] *v.*, *pfv. of* искажáть.

искалéчить *v.*, *pfv. of* калéчить.

искáлывать *v. impfv.* [*pfv.* исколóть] to prick all over.

искáние *n.*, *often pl.* search; quest.

искáпывать *v. impfv.* [*pfv.* ископáть] to dig up.

искáтель *n.m.* seeker. —**искáтель приключéний,** adventure-seeker; adventurer.

искáть *v. impfv.* [*pres.* ищý, и́щешь] **1,** (*with acc.*) to look for; search for. **2,** (*with gen. or acc.*) to seek; try to obtain.

исключáть *v. impfv.* [*pfv.* исключи́ть] **1,** to expel; dismiss; remove. **2,** to eliminate. **3,** to exclude; preclude; rule out: э́то исключенó, that is out of the question. **4,** to delete; drop; strike off *or* from.

исключáя *prep.*, *with acc.* except; excepting; excluding; barring.

исключéние *n.* **1,** exception: за исключéнием (+ *gen.*), with the exception of. **2,** elimination; exclusion. **3,** expulsion.

исключи́тельно *adv.* **1,** exceptionally. **2,** exclusively; only; solely.

исключи́тельность *n.f.* **1,** exceptional nature. **2,** superiority: рáсовая исключи́тельность, racial superiority.

исключи́тельный *adj.* **1,** exceptional. **2,** exclusive.

исключи́ть *v.*, *pfv. of* исключáть.

исковéркать *v.*, *pfv. of* ковéркать.

исколеси́ть *v. pfv.* [*infl.* -шý, -си́шь] *colloq.* to travel all over (an area).

исколоти́ть *v. pfv.* [*infl.* -лочý, -лóтишь] *colloq.* to beat up.

исколóть [*infl.* -колю́, -кóлешь] *v.*, *pfv. of* искáлывать.

иско́мый *adj.* **1,** sought after. **2,** *math.* sought; to be found. —**иско́мое,** *n.*, *math.* unknown.

искони́ *adv.*, *obs.* from time immemorial.

иско́нный *adj.* **1,** age-old; long-standing. **2,** native.

ископáемое *n.*, *decl. as an adj.* fossil. —**полéзные ископáемые,** minerals.

ископáемый *adj.* **1,** extracted from the earth. **2,** fossil (*attrib.*); fossilized.

ископáть *v.*, *pfv. of* искáпывать.

искоренéние *n.* eradication; rooting out.

искореня́ть *v. impfv.* [*pfv.* искорени́ть] to eradicate; stamp out; root out.

и́скорка [*gen. pl.* -рок] *n.*, *dim. of* и́скра.

искóса *adv.* askance; out of the corner of one's eye.

и́скра *n.* **1,** spark. **2,** *fig.* (*with gen.*) ray; glimmer (*of* hope); seed (*of doubt, suspicion, etc.*). —**у негó и́скры из глаз посы́пались,** he saw stars.

и́скренний *adj.* sincere. —**и́скренне; и́скренно,** *adv.* sincerely. —**и́скренность,** *n.f.* sincerity.

искриви́ть [*infl.* -влю́, -ви́шь] *v.*, *pfv. of* искривля́ть.

искривлéние *n.* curvature.

искривля́ть *v. impfv.* [*pfv.* искриви́ть] **1,** to bend out of shape. **2,** to distort; contort.

искри́стый *adj.* sparkling.

и́скриться *also,* искри́ться *v.r. impfv.* to sparkle.

искромётный *adj.* sparkling; flashing; dazzling.

искромсáть *v.*, *pfv. of* кромсáть.

искроши́ть *v.*, *pfv. of* кроши́ть. —**искроши́ться,** *refl.*, *pfv. of* кроши́ться.

искупáть *v. impfv.* [*pfv.* искупи́ть] **1,** to atone for; expiate. **2,** to make up for; make amends for.

искупи́тельный *adj.* expiatory.

искупи́ть [*infl.* -куплю́, -кýпишь] *v.*, *pfv. of* искупáть.

искуплéние *n.* (*with gen.*) expiation (of); atonement (for).

искýс *n.* **1,** ordeal. **2,** test.

искусáть *v. pfv.* to sting; bite (*in many places*).

искуси́тель *n.m.* tempter.

искуси́ть [*infl.* -кушý, -куси́шь] *v.*, *pfv. of* искушáть. —**искуси́ться,** *refl.* (*with* в + *prepl.*) *obs.* to become experienced in; become an expert at.

искýсник *n.*, *colloq.* master craftsman; past master.

искýсный *adj.* skillful. —**искýсно,** *adv.* skillfully.

искýсственный *adj.* **1,** artificial; imitation. **2,** artificial; unnatural. —**искýсственно,** *adv.* artificially. —**искýсственность,** *n.f.* artificiality.

искýсство *n.* **1,** art: изя́щные искýсства, fine arts; произведéние искýсства, work of art; искýсство шитья́, the art of sewing. **2,** skill: с больши́м искýсством, with great skill.

искусствовéд *n.* art critic. —**искусствовéдение,** *n.* art criticism; study of art.

искушáть *v. impfv.* [*pfv.* искуси́ть] to tempt. —**искушáть судьбý,** to tempt fate; press *or* stretch one's luck.

искушéние *n.* temptation.

искушённый *adj.* experienced; knowledgeable.

ислáм *n.* Islam.

ислáндец [*gen.* -дца] *n.m.* [*fem.* -дка] Icelander. —**ислáндский,** *adj.* Icelandic.

испáнец [*gen.* -нца] *n.m.* [*fem.* -нка] Spaniard.

испáнка [*gen. pl.* -нок] *n.* **1,** Spanish woman. **2,** *colloq.* influenza; flu.

испáнский *adj.* Spanish.

испарéние *n.* **1,** evaporation. **2,** *pl.* vapor; fumes.

испáрина *n.* perspiration.

испари́тель *n.m.* vaporizer.

испаря́ть *v. impfv.* [*pfv.* испари́ть] to evaporate; convert to vapor. —**испаря́ться,** *refl.* **1,** to evaporate; turn into vapor. **2,** *colloq.* to vanish; evaporate.

испáчкать *v.*, *pfv. of* пáчкать. —**испáчкаться,** *refl.*, *pfv. of* пáчкаться.

испепеля́ть *v. impfv.* [*pfv.* испепели́ть] to incinerate; reduce to ashes.

испестря́ть *v. impfv.* [*pfv.* испестри́ть] to color; make colorful.

испéчь *v.*, *pfv. of* печь. —**испéчься,** *refl.*, *pfv. of* пéчься (*in sense #1*).

испещря́ть *v. impfv.* [*pfv.* испещри́ть] **1,** to dot with color. **2,** to mark up.

исписáть [*infl.* -пишý, -пи́шешь] *v.*, *pfv. of* испи́сывать. —**исписáться,** *refl.*, *pfv. of* испи́сываться.

испи́сывать *v. impfv.* [*pfv.* исписáть] **1,** to cover with writing. **2,** to use up (paper, a pencil, etc.). —**испи́сываться,** *refl.* **1,** (*of a pencil*) to be used up; be worn to a stump. **2,** *colloq.* (*of a writer*) to lose one's creativity; become stale.

испито́й *adj.*, *colloq.* haggard; gaunt; drawn.

исповедáльня [*gen. pl.* -лен] *n.* confessional.

исповéдание *n.* **1,** profession (*of a certain faith*). **2,** *obs.* faith; creed.

исповéдник *n.* confessor.

исповéдовать *v. impfv. & pfv.* [*pres.* -дую, -дуешь] *relig.* **1,** to hear the confession of. **2,** to profess (a religion). —**исповéдоваться,** *refl.* to confess; confess one's sins.

и́споведь *n.f.* confession.

и́сподволь *adv., colloq.* gradually; slowly; little by little.

исподло́бья *adv., in* смотре́ть исподло́бья (на), to glower (at).

исподтишка́ *adv., colloq.* secretly; stealthily; on the sly.

испоко́н *adv., in* испоко́н веко́в (*or* ве́ку), since time immemorial.

исполи́н *n.* giant. —**исполи́нский,** *adj.* giant; gigantic.

исполко́м *n.* executive committee (*contr. of* исполни́тельный комите́т).

исполне́ние *n.* 1, execution; fulfillment; performance. 2, performance; rendition. —приводи́ть в исполне́ние, to carry out.

испо́лненный *adj.* (*with gen.*) full (of).

исполни́мый *adj.* feasible.

исполни́тель *n.m.* 1, executor. 2, performer. —соста́в исполни́телей, cast. —суде́бный исполни́тель, bailiff.

исполни́тельный *adj.* 1, executive. 2, efficient; industrious. —исполни́тельный комите́т, executive committee. —исполни́тельный лист, writ.

исполня́ть *v. impfv.* [*pfv.* испо́лнить] 1, to fulfill; execute; carry out. 2, to perform (a song, dance, role, etc.). —исполня́ться, *refl.* 1, to be fulfilled. 2, (*of an anniversary*) to occur; be. 3, *impers.* (*with dat.*) indicating attainment of a certain age: за́втра мне испо́лнится два́дцать оди́н год, tomorrow I will be twenty-one.

испо́льзование *n.* utilization; use.

испо́льзовать *v. impfv. & pfv.* [*pres.* -зую, -зуешь] to use; utilize; make use of; exploit.

испо́льщик *n.* sharecropper.

испо́ртить *v., pfv. of* по́ртить. —испо́ртиться, *refl., pfv. of* по́ртиться.

испо́рченный *adj.* 1, spoiled; rotten; tainted. 2, damaged. 3, depraved; perverted.

исправи́мый *adj.* 1, reparable; rectifiable; remediable. 2, repairable.

исправи́тельный *adj.* corrective; remedial. —исправи́тельный дом, reformatory; reform school; house of correction.

испра́вить [*infl.* -влю, -вишь] *v., pfv. of* исправля́ть. —испра́виться, *refl., pfv. of* исправля́ться.

исправле́ние *n.* 1, repairing; correcting. 2, correction.

исправля́ть *v. impfv.* [*pfv.* испра́вить] 1, to correct. 2, to repair. 3, to reform. —исправля́ться, *refl.* to reform; mend one's ways.

испра́вность *n.f.* good condition; good working order.

испра́вный *adj.* 1, in good condition; in good working order. 2, conscientious; industrious.

испражне́ние *n.* 1, defecation. 2, *pl.* excrement; feces.

испражня́ться *v.r. impfv.* [*pfv.* испражни́ться] to defecate.

испра́шивать *v. impfv.* [*pfv.* испроси́ть] *obs.* to solicit; formally request.

испро́бовать *v. pfv.* [*infl.* -бую, -буешь] 1, to test; try out. 2, to experience.

испроси́ть *v. pfv.* [*infl.* -прошу́, -про́сишь] 1, *pfv. of* испра́шивать. 2, to obtain; receive (*by asking*).

испу́г *n.* fright.

испу́ганный *adj.* frightened; scared.

испуга́ть *v., pfv. of* пуга́ть. —испуга́ться, *refl., pfv. of* пуга́ться.

испуска́ние *n.* emission.

испуска́ть *v. impfv.* [*pfv.* испусти́ть] 1, to emit; give off. 2, to emit; utter. —испусти́ть дух *or* после́дний вздох, to breathe one's last.

испусти́ть [*infl.* -пущу́, -пу́стишь] *v., pfv. of* испуска́ть.

испыта́ние *n.* 1, test; trial. 2, examination. 3, trial; ordeal.

испы́танный *adj.* tried; tested; proven.

испыта́тель *n.m.* tester. —лётчик-испыта́тель, test pilot.

испыта́тельный *adj.* test (*attrib.*); trial (*attrib.*).

испыта́ть *v., pfv. of* испы́тывать.

испыту́ющий *adj.* searching; penetrating.

испы́тывать *v. impfv.* [*pfv.* испыта́ть] 1, to test; try out. 2, to experience; feel. 3, to try; tax (someone's patience). 4, *in* испы́тывать судьбу́, to tempt fate; press one's luck.

иссека́ть *v. impfv.* [*pfv.* иссе́чь] 1, to carve. 2, *med.* to excise. 3, to slash in many places. 4, *obs.* to flog.

иссече́ние *n., med.* excision.

иссе́чь *v. pfv.* [*infl. like* сечь] 1, [*past* -се́к, -секла́, секло́] *pfv. of* иссека́ть (*in senses #1 & #2*). 2, [*past* -се́к, -се́кла, се́кло] *pfv. of* иссека́ть (*in senses #3 & #4*).

иссле́дование *n.* 1, research. 2, a study (*piece of research*). 3, exploration.

иссле́дователь *n.m.* 1, researcher. 2, explorer.

иссле́довательский *adj.* research (*attrib.*).

иссле́довать *v. impfv. & pfv.* [*pres.* -дую, -дуешь] 1, to explore. 2, to examine. 3, to study; do research in.

иссо́п *n.* hyssop.

иссо́хнуть [*past* -со́х, -ла] *v., pfv. of* иссыха́ть.

и́сстари *adv.* since ancient times.

исстрада́ться *v.r. pfv.* to be worn out with suffering.

исступле́ние *n.* frenzy.

исступлённый *adj.* frenzied.

иссуша́ть *v. impfv.* [*pfv.* иссуши́ть] 1, to dry thoroughly; dry completely. 2, *fig.* to drain; exhaust (someone).

иссуши́ть [*infl.* -сушу́, -су́шишь] *v., pfv. of* иссуша́ть.

иссыха́ть *v. impfv.* [*pfv.* иссо́хнуть] 1, to dry up. 2, *fig.* to shrink away to nothing.

иссяка́ть *v. impfv.* [*pfv.* исся́кнуть] 1, to dry up; run dry. 2, to give out; run out; be used up; be exhausted.

исся́кнуть [*past* -ся́к, -ла] *v., pfv. of* иссяка́ть.

иста́пливать *v. impfv.* [*pfv.* истопи́ть] 1, to heat; heat up (a stove). 2, *colloq.* to use; consume (firewood). 3, *colloq.* to melt completely; melt all of.

иста́птывать *v. impfv.* [*pfv.* истопта́ть] 1, to trample. 2, *colloq.* to track up (a clean floor). 3, *colloq.* to wear out (shoes).

иста́скивать *v. impfv.* [*pfv.* истаска́ть] *colloq.* to wear out.

иста́чивать *v. impfv.* [*pfv.* источи́ть] 1, to wear down (*by repeated rubbing*). 2, to eat away.

истека́ть *v. impfv.* [*pfv.* исте́чь] 1, *obs.* to flow out. 2, *in* истека́ть кро́вью, to bleed profusely. 3, (*of time*) to elapse; expire; run out; be up. 4, [*impfv. only*] (*with* от *or* из) to emanate (from); stem (from).

исте́кший *adj.* past: за исте́кший год, during the past year.

истере́ть [*infl.* изотру́, изотрёшь *past* истёр, -ла] *v., pfv. of* истира́ть.

исте́рзанный *adj.* 1, slashed to bits. 2, bedraggled. 3, tormented.

истерза́ть *v. pfv.* **1,** to tear to pieces. **2,** *fig.* to beset; torment; wrack.

исте́рик *n., colloq.* person often going into fits of hysteria.

исте́рика *n.* hysterics.

истери́ческий *adj.* hysterical.

истери́чка [*gen. pl.* **-чек**] *n., colloq.* hysterical woman.

истери́чный *adj.* hysterical.

истери́я *n.* hysteria.

истёртый *adj.* **1,** worn out; worn down. **2,** *fig.* trite; overused.

исте́ц [*gen.* **истца́**] *n.* plaintiff.

истече́ние *n.* **1,** outflow. **2,** expiration.

исте́чь [*infl. like* **течь**] *v., pfv. of* **истека́ть.**

и́стина *n.* truth.

и́стинный *adj.* true; veritable. **—и́стинно,** *adv.* truly.

истира́ние *n.* abrasion; wear.

истира́ть *v. impfv.* [*pfv.* **истере́ть**] **1,** to grate; shred. **2,** to wear away (a surface); wear out (clothes or furniture); wear down (an eraser).

истлева́ть *v. impfv.* [*pfv.* **истле́ть**] **1,** to rot; decay. **2,** to burn to ashes.

и́стовый *adj., obs.* **1,** real; true. **2,** energetic; vigorous. **3,** proper; sedate.

исто́к *n.* **1,** source (*of a river*); *pl.* headwaters. **2,** *usu. pl.* source; origin.

истолкова́ние *n.* interpretation.

истолкова́тель *n.m.* interpreter; commentator.

истолкова́ть [*infl.* **-ку́ю, -ку́ешь**] *v., pfv. of* **истолко́вывать.**

истолко́вывать *v. impfv.* [*pfv.* **истолкова́ть**] to interpret; construe.

истоло́чь *v., pfv. of* **толо́чь.**

исто́ма *n.* languor; lassitude.

истоми́ть [*infl.* **-млю́, -ми́шь**] *v., pfv. of* **томи́ть** *and* **истомля́ть.**

истомля́ть *v. impfv.* [*pfv.* **истоми́ть**] to tire; weary; fatigue; exhaust.

истопи́ть [*infl.* **-топлю́, -то́пишь**] *v., pfv. of* **иста́пливать.**

истопни́к [*gen.* **-ника́**] *n.* boilerman; stoker.

истопта́ть [*infl.* **-топчу́, -то́пчешь**] *v., pfv. of* **иста́птывать.**

исторга́ть *v. impfv.* [*pfv.* **исто́ргнуть**] *obs.* **1,** to banish. **2,** to wrest; grab. **3,** to rescue; deliver. **4,** to elicit; evoke. **5,** to extract; extort.

исто́ргнуть [*past* **-то́рг** *or* **-то́ргнул, -то́ргла**] *v., pfv. of* **исторга́ть.**

истори́зм *n.* historical method.

исто́рик *n.* historian.

историогра́фия *n.* historiography. **—исто́риограф,** *n.* historiographer.

истори́ческий *adj.* **1,** historical. **2,** historic. **—истори́чески,** *adv.* historically.

исто́рия *n.* **1,** history. **2,** story. **3,** *colloq.* incident; untoward event: **попа́сть** *or* **вли́пнуть в исто́рию,** to get into an unpleasant situation. **—исто́рия боле́зни,** case history.

истоскова́ться *v.r. pfv.* [*infl.* **-ку́юсь, -ку́ешься**] (*with* **по** + *dat.*) *colloq.* to miss greatly; yearn for.

источа́ть *v. impfv.* **1,** *obs.* to shed (tears). **2,** to give off; emit.

источи́ть [*infl.* **-точу́, -то́чишь**] *v., pfv. of* **иста́чивать.**

исто́чник *n.* **1,** spring. **2,** *fig.* source.

исто́шный *adj., colloq.* heart-rending; blood-curdling.

истоща́ть *v. impfv.* [*pfv.* **истощи́ть**] **1,** to exhaust; tire out. **2,** to exhaust; deplete; use up. **—истоща́ться,** *refl.* **1,** to be exhausted (*physically*). **2,** to be used up; run out.

истоще́ние *n.* **1,** exhaustion: **не́рвное истоще́ние,** nervous exhaustion. **2,** exhaustion; depletion. **—война́ на истоще́ние,** war of attrition.

истощённый *adj.* **1,** exhausted. **2,** emaciated.

истощи́ть *v., pfv. of* **истоща́ть. —истощи́ться,** *refl., pfv. of* **истоща́ться.**

истра́тить *v., pfv. of* **тра́тить. —истра́титься,** *refl., pfv. of* **тра́титься.**

истреби́тель *n.m.* **1,** (*with gen.*) destroyer (of). **2,** fighter (*aircraft*).

истреби́тельный *adj.* **1,** destructive. Истреби́тельная война́, war of annihilation. **2,** *aero.* fighter (*attrib.*).

истреби́ть [*infl.* **-блю́, би́шь**] *v., pfv. of* **истребля́ть.**

истребле́ние *n.* destruction; extermination.

истребля́ть *v. impfv.* [*pfv.* **истреби́ть**] to destroy; annihilate; exterminate; wipe out.

истрепа́ть [*infl.* **-треплю́, -тре́плешь**] *v., pfv. of* **трепа́ть** (*in sense #4*) *and* **истрёпывать. —истрепа́ться,** *refl., pfv. of* **трепа́ться** (*in sense #2*) *and* **истрёпываться.**

истрёпывать *v. impfv.* [*pfv.* **истрепа́ть**] *colloq.* to wear out. **—истрёпываться,** *refl., colloq.* to be worn out.

истука́н *n.* idol. **—(сиде́ть** *or* **стоя́ть) истука́ном,** motionless; like a statue.

иступи́ть *v., pfv. of* **тупи́ть. —иступи́ться,** *refl., pfv. of* **тупи́ться.**

и́стый *adj.* true; real.

истяза́ние *n.* torture. **—истяза́тель,** *n.m.* torturer.

истяза́ть *v. impfv.* to torture.

исхо́д *n.* **1,** end; close. **2,** outcome. **3,** way out (*of a situation*). **4,** outlet (*for one's emotions*). **5,** *Bib.* exodus; *cap.* (book of) Exodus. **—на исхо́де, 1,** drawing to a close. **2,** (*with gen.*) at the end (of). **3,** running low; running out.

исходи́ть[1] *v. impfv.* [*pres.* **-хожу́, -хо́дишь**] **1,** (*with* **из** *or* **от**) (*of smoke, an odor, etc.*) to come (from); issue (from). **2,** (*with* **из** *or* **от**) to originate (from); emanate (from). **3,** (*with* **из**) to proceed on (an assumption, premise, etc.). **4,** [*pfv.* **изойти́**] (*with instr.*) *colloq.* to be drained of (tears, blood, etc.).

исходи́ть[2] *v. pfv.* [*infl.* **-хожу́, -хо́дишь**] *colloq.* to walk all over (a place).

исхо́дный *adj.* initial; starting.

исходя́щий *adj.* (*of mail, documents, etc.*) outgoing.

исхуда́лый *adj.* emaciated; haggard; gaunt.

исхуда́ть *v. pfv.* to become emaciated.

исцара́пывать *v. impfv.* [*pfv.* **исцара́пать**] to scratch severely; scratch in many places.

исцеле́ние *n.* **1,** cure; healing. **2,** recovery. **—исцели́тель,** *n.m.* healer.

исцеля́ть *v. impfv.* [*pfv.* **исцели́ть**] to cure; heal.

исча́дие *n., obs.* child; offspring. **—исча́дие а́да,** the devil incarnate.

исча́хнуть *v. pfv.* [*past* **-ча́х, -ла**] to waste away.

исчеза́ть *v. impfv.* [*pfv.* **исче́знуть**] to disappear; vanish.

исчезнове́ние *n.* disappearance.

исче́знуть [*past* **-че́з, -ла**] *v., pfv. of* **исчеза́ть.**

исче́рпывать *v. impfv.* [*pfv.* **исче́рпать**] **1,** to exhaust. **2,** to settle; close (a matter).

исчёрпывающий *adj.* exhaustive.

исчерти́ть [*infl.* -черчу́, -че́ртишь] *v., pfv. of* исче́р-
чивать.

исче́рчивать *v. impfv.* [*pfv.* исчерти́ть] to cover with
lines.

исчисле́ние *n.* **1,** calculation. **2,** calculus.

исчисля́ть *v. impfv.* [*pfv.* исчи́слить] to calculate;
estimate. —**исчисля́ться**, *refl.* [*impfv. only*] (*with instr.
or* в + *acc.*) to number in; amount to.

ита́к *conj.* so; and so; thus.

италья́нец [*gen.* -нца] *n.m.* [*fem.* -нка] Italian.

италья́нский *adj.* Italian. —**италья́нская забасто́в-
ка**, sit-down strike.

и т.д. *abbr. of* **и так да́лее**, and so forth; et cetera.

ито́г *n.* **1,** sum; total. **2,** result. —**в ито́ге**, as a result.
—**в коне́чном ито́ге**, in the final analysis. —**подво-
ди́ть ито́г** *or* **ито́ги** (+ *dat.*), to total; add up; *fig.* sum
up.

итого́ *adv.* **1,** in all; altogether. **2,** (*at the bottom of a
column of figures*) total.

ито́говый *adj.* **1,** total. **2,** final.

итте́рбий *n.* ytterbium.

и́ттрий *n.* yttrium.

Иу́да *n.* Judas.

иудаи́зм *n.* Judaism.

иуде́й *n.* Jew. —**иуде́йский**, *adj.* Judaic. —**иуде́й-
ство**, *n.* Judaism.

их *pron., gen. & acc. of* **они́**. —*poss. adj. & pron.* their;
theirs.

ихневмо́н *n.* ichneumon.

и́хний *adj., colloq.* their; theirs.

ихтиоло́гия *n.* ichthyology.

иша́к [*gen.* ишака́] *n.* donkey.

и́шиас *n.* sciatica.

ишь *particle, colloq.* see!; look!; oh! —**ишь ты, 1,** =
ишь. **2,** oh come on!; what are you talking about!

ище́йка [*gen. pl.* ище́ек] *n.* **1,** bloodhound. **2,** *colloq.*
sleuth.

ию́ль *n.m.* July. —**ию́льский**, *adj.* July (*attrib.*).

ию́нь *n.m.* June. —**ию́ньский**, *adj.* June (*attrib.*).

Й

Й, й *n. neut., called* **и кра́ткое**, tenth letter of the Russian alphabet.

йог *n.* yogi. —**йо́га**, *n.* yoga.

йод *n.* iodine.

йо́дистый *adj.* **1,** containing iodine. **2,** iodide (of):
йо́дистый ка́лий, potassium iodide.

йо́дный *adj.* iodine (*attrib.*).

йо́та *n.* iota. —**ни на йо́ту**, not a bit; not one iota.

К

К, к *n. neut.* eleventh letter of the Russian alphabet.

к *also,* **ко** *prep., with dat.* **1,** to; toward; in the direction
of: идти́ к доске́, to go to the blackboard; подходи́ть
к концу́, to draw to a close. **2,** to; to the home or
place of business of: идти́ к врачу́, to go to the doctor.
Он ча́сто приходи́л к нам, he often came to visit us.
3, *with emotions* of; for; toward: любо́вь к ро́дине,
love of one's country; мои́ чу́вства к ней, my feelings
toward her. **4,** *in introductory expressions* to: к мо-
ему́ удивле́нию, to my surprise. К сча́стью, fortunately; к сожале́нию, unfortunately. **5,** *with expressions of time* by: к тому́ вре́мени, by that time; by then.
—**к тому́ же**, moreover; besides.

-ка *particle, colloq.,* used to lessen the force of a suggestion, request, command, etc.: ну́-ка, well?; вста-
ва́й-ка!, get up, now!; закро́й-ка окно́!, close the
window, will you?

каба́к [*gen.* -бака́] *n.* **1,** *pre-rev.* tavern. **2,** *colloq.* mess.

кабала́ *n.* servitude; bondage.

каба́льный *adj.* **1,** serving to enslave. **2,** (*of a treaty,
provisions, etc.*) one-sided.

каба́н [*gen.* -бана́] *n.* **1,** wild boar. **2,** male hog.

кабарга́ [*gen. pl.* -ро́г] *n.* musk deer.

кабарди́нец [*gen.* -нца] *n.m.* [*fem.* -нка] Kabardian
(*one of a people inhabiting the Caucasus*). —**кабар-
ди́нский**, *adj.* Kabardian.

кабаре́ (рэ) *n. neut. indecl.* cabaret.

кабачо́к [*gen.* -чка́] *n.* **1,** cheap restaurant. **2,** squash (*vegetable*).

ка́бель *n.m.* cable. —**ка́бельный,** *adj.* cable (*attrib.*).

кабеста́н *n.* capstan.

каби́на *n.* **1,** booth; cubicle. **2,** cab (*of a truck*). **3,** *aero.* cabin; cockpit.

кабине́т *n.* **1,** private office; study. **2,** (specially equipped) room: рентге́новский кабине́т, X-ray room. **3,** set of office furniture. **4,** private room in a restaurant. **5,** *polit.* cabinet.

кабине́тный *adj.* office (*attrib.*). —**кабине́тный роя́ль,** baby grand piano. —**кабине́тный страте́г,** armchair strategist.

каби́нка [*gen. pl.* -нок] *n., dim. of* каби́на.

каблогра́мма *n.* cablegram.

каблу́к [*gen.* -блука́] *n.* heel (*of a shoe*). —**под каблуко́м у,** under the thumb of.

каблучо́к [*gen.* -чка́] *n., dim. of* каблу́к.

кабриоле́т *n.* cabriolet; gig.

кабы́ *conj., colloq.* **1,** if. **2,** if only. —е́сли бы да кабы́, (то во рту росли́ б грибы́), if wishes were horses (beggars would ride).

кавале́р *n.* **1,** escort; dancing partner. **2,** holder (*of an order or award*). **3,** *colloq.* admirer.

кавале́рия *n.* cavalry. —**кавалери́йский,** *adj.* cavalry (*attrib.*). —**кавалери́ст,** *n.* cavalryman.

кавалька́да *n.* cavalcade.

каварда́к [*gen.* -дака́] *n., colloq.* confusion; disorder; mess.

ка́верза *n., colloq.* **1,** intrigue; chicanery. **2,** mean trick.

ка́верзный *adj., colloq.* **1,** scheming. **2,** tricky; intricate.

каве́рна *n., med.* cavity.

кавака́зец [*gen.* -зца] *n.m.* [*fem.* -зка] native of the Caucasus. —**кавка́зский,** *adj.* Caucasian; Caucasus (*attrib.*).

кавы́чки [*gen.* -чек] *n. pl.* quotation marks.

каде́нция (дэ) *n., music* **1,** cadence. **2,** cadenza.

каде́т *n.* **1,** *pre-rev.* (military) cadet. **2,** *hist.* member of the Constitutional Democrat party; Cadet.

каде́тский *adj.* **1,** *pre-rev.* cadet (*attrib.*). **2,** *hist.* of or pert. to the Constitutional Democrats.

кади́ло *n.* censer.

кади́ть *v. impfv.* [*pres.* кажу́, кади́шь] to gently wave a container of burning incense.

ка́дка [*gen. pl.* -док] *n.* tub.

ка́дмий *n.* cadmium.

кадр *n., motion pictures* **1,** frame. **2,** shot; scene.

кадри́ль *n.f.* quadrille.

ка́дровый *adj.* **1,** (*of a worker*) trained; skilled. **2,** *mil.* regular.

ка́дры [*gen.* -ров] *n. pl.* **1,** personnel. **2,** cadres.

кады́к [*gen.* -дыка́] *n.* Adam's apple.

каёмка [*gen. pl.* -мок] *n.* border; edging.

каждодне́вный *adj.* daily; everyday.

ка́ждый *adj.* every; each: ка́ждый день, every day. —*indef. pron.* **1,** each one. **2,** everyone; everybody. **3,** anyone; anybody. —**ка́ждому своё,** to each his own.

ка́жущийся *adj.* apparent; seeming; imaginary.

каза́к [*gen.* -зака́] *n.* Cossack.

каза́рка [*gen. pl.* -рок] *n.* brant goose. —**белощё-**

кая каза́рка, barnacle goose. —**кана́дская каза́рка,** Canada goose.

каза́рма *n.* **1,** *usu. pl.* barracks. **2,** *colloq.* ugly building. —**каза́рменный,** *adj.* barracks (*attrib.*).

каза́ться *v.r. impfv.* [*pfv.* показа́ться; *pres.* кажу́сь, ка́жешься] (*with instr.*) to seem: каза́ться стра́нным, to seem strange. *Also impers.:* ка́жется, it seems. Мне ка́жется, что..., it seems to me that... —**каза́лось бы, 1,** it would seem. **2,** seemingly.

каза́х *n.m.* [*fem.* -за́шка] Kazakh (*one of a people living mainly in the Kazakh S.S.R.*). —**каза́хский,** *adj.* Kazakh.

каза́цкий *adj.* Cossack (*attrib.*).

каза́чество *n.* the Cossacks.

каза́чий [*fem.* -чья] *adj.* Cossack (*attrib.*).

казачо́к [*gen.* -чка́] *n.* **1,** a lively Ukrainian dance. **2,** *obs.* boy servant; page.

казеи́н *n.* casein.

каземат *n.* **1,** casemate. **2,** cell for solitary confinement.

казённый *adj.* **1,** public; belonging to, issued by, or paid for by the government. **2,** *fig.* bureaucratic; formal. —**казённая часть,** breech (*of a firearm*).

казино́ *n. indecl.* casino.

казна́ *n., obs.* **1,** treasury. **2,** the State. **3,** money.

казначе́й *n.* **1,** treasurer. **2,** purser; paymaster. —**казначе́йский,** *adj.* treasury (*attrib.*): казначе́йский биле́т, treasury note. —**казначе́йство,** *n., pre-rev.* treasury.

казни́ть *v. impfv. & pfv.* to execute; put to death. —**казни́ться,** *refl.* to suffer acute remorse; blame oneself bitterly.

казнокра́д *n.* embezzler of public funds.

казнь *n.f.* execution. —**сме́ртная казнь,** the death penalty; capital punishment.

казуи́стика *n.* casuistry. —**казуи́ст,** *n.* casuist. —**казуисти́ческий,** *adj.* casuistic.

ка́зус *n.* **1,** complex legal case. **2,** *colloq.* incident.

ка́зусный *adj.* involved; complex.

ка́йзер (зэ) *n.* Kaiser.

кайло́ [*pl.* ка́йла] *n.* pick; hack. *Also,* кайла́.

кайма́ [*gen. pl.* каём] *n.* border; edging.

ка́йра *n.* murre (*bird*).

как *adv.* **1,** how: как дела́?, how are things?; как краси́во!, how beautiful! Я забы́л, как туда́ пройти́, I forgot how to get there. **2,** *in certain expressions* what?: как ва́ше и́мя?, what is your name?; как э́то называ́ется?, what is this called? —*conj.* **1,** as; like: как обы́чно, as usual; бе́лый как снег, white as snow; рабо́тать как вол, to work like a horse. **2,** *following verbs of perceiving:* я ви́дел, как он ушёл, I saw him leave. **3,** (*with* не) but; besides: кто мо́жет э́то сде́лать, как не вы?, who can do it but/besides you? **4,** *when preceded and followed by the same word like any other:* го́род как го́род, a city like any other city. —**как бы, 1,** as if. **2,** seeming to. **3,** a sort of. —**как бы не,** that (*something might happen*). —**как бы то ни́ было,** *see* быть. —**как быть?,** *see* быть. —**как же!,** why, of course! —**как ни,** however; no matter how: как он ни стара́лся, no matter how he tried. —**как раз,** *see* раз. —**как..., так и,** both..., and. —**как то́лько,** as soon as.

какаду́ *n.m. indecl.* cockatoo.

кака́о *n. indecl.* **1,** cacao. **2,** cocoa.

ка́к-либо *adv.* somehow.

ка́к-нибудь *adv.* **1,** somehow. **2,** *colloq.* haphazardly; any which way. **3,** *colloq.* sometime; someday.

как-ника́к *adv., colloq.* **1,** despite all; still and all. **2,** after all; in the end.

како́в [*fem.* какова́; *pl.* каковы́] *pron.* **1,** *interr.* what is?; what are?: каковы́ фа́кты?, what are the facts? **2,** *interr.* what is... like?; what kind of... is...?: како́в он?, what is he like?; како́в он собо́й?, what does he look like? **3,** *rel.* what kind of; the sort of: я тебе́ расскажу́, каковы́ э́ти лю́ди, I'll tell you what kind of people they are. **4,** *rel.* such as: како́в он есть, such as he is. —**како́в..., тако́в и...,** like..., like...: како́в оте́ц, тако́в и сын, like father, like son.

каково́ *pron., neut. of* **како́в.** —*interr. & rel. adv., colloq.* how: каково́ ей живётся?, how is she getting along?

каково́й *rel. pron., obs.* which.

како́й *adj.* **1,** which?; what?: в каку́ю сто́рону он пошёл?, which way did he go? До како́й сте́пени?, to what extent? **2,** what is...?: како́й счет?, what's the score? Како́е сего́дня число́?, what is today's date? **3,** what sort of; what kind of: кака́я сего́дня пого́да?, what sort of weather is it today?; what is the weather like today? **4,** *in exclamations* what...!: како́е чу́дное ме́сто!, what a delightful place! —*rel. pron.* such as; the kind of: он не тако́й знато́к, како́й ты ду́мал, he is not the expert you thought he was. —**како́й (бы) ни,** whatever; whichever. —**како́й бы то ни́ бы́ло,** any whatsoever. —**ни** (+ *prep.*) **како́й,** not any; no: ни под каки́м ви́дом, under no circumstances. Он не отвеча́л ни на каки́е вопро́сы, he did not answer any questions.

како́й-либо *adj.* = **како́й-нибудь.**

како́й-нибудь *adj.* **1,** some; a: да́йте мне како́й-нибудь приме́р, give me an example. **2,** (*with numerals*) *colloq.* about; some.

како́й-то *adj.* **1,** some: вас спра́шивает како́й-то челове́к, some man is asking for you. **2,** a kind of; a sort of.

какофо́ния *n.* cacophony. —**какофони́ческий,** *adj.* cacophonous.

ка́к-то *adv.* **1,** somehow. **2,** *colloq.* once; one day. **3,** *colloq.* I wonder how. **4,** *colloq.* namely. —**ка́к-то раз,** once.

ка́ктус *n.* cactus.

кал *n.* excrement.

каламбу́р *n.* pun. —**каламбури́ст,** *n.* punster.

каламбу́рить *v. impfv.* to pun; make puns.

кала́н *n.* sea otter.

кала́ндр *n.* calender.

каланча́ *n.* **1,** watch tower (*of a fire station*). **2,** *colloq.* beanpole (*tall person*).

кала́ч [*gen.* -лача́] *n.* a kind of roll with a distinctive shape. —**тёртый кала́ч,** old hand; person who has been around.

кала́чик *n., dim. of* **кала́ч.** —**сверну́ться кала́чиком,** to curl up into a ball.

калейдоско́п *n.* kaleidoscope. —**калейдоскопи́ческий,** *adj.* kaleidoscopic.

кале́ка *n.m. & f.* cripple.

календа́рь [*gen.* -даря́] *n.m.* calendar. —**календа́рный,** *adj.* calendar (*attrib.*).

кале́ние *n.* incandescence. —**бе́лое кале́ние,** white heat.

калёный *adj.* **1,** red-hot. **2,** (*of nuts*) roasted.

кале́чить *v. impfv.* [*pfv.* искале́чить] **1,** to maim; cripple. **2,** *fig.* to pervert; warp.

кали́бр *n.* **1,** caliber (*of a gun or bullet*). **2,** gauge.

калиброва́ние *n.* calibration.

калиброва́ть *v. impfv.* [*pres.* -ру́ю, -ру́ешь] to calibrate.

ка́лий *n.* potassium. —**ка́лиевый; кали́йный,** *adj.* potassium (*attrib.*).

кали́льный *adj.* used for heating or smelting metals. —**кали́льная се́тка,** (incandescent) mantle.

кали́на *n.* viburnum.

кали́тка [*gen. pl.* -ток] *n.* gate in a fence.

кали́ть *v. impfv.* **1,** to make red-hot. **2,** to roast.

кали́ф *n.* caliph.

калифо́рний *n.* californium.

каллигра́фия *n.* calligraphy. —**каллиграфи́ческий,** *adj.* calligraphic.

калмы́к *n.m.* [*fem.* -мы́чка] Kalmyk; Kalmuck (*one of a Mongol people inhabiting the Volga delta*). —**калмы́цкий,** *adj.* Kalmyk; Kalmuck.

кало́рия *n.* calorie. —**калори́йность,** *n.f.* caloric content. —**калори́метр,** *n.* calorimeter.

кало́ши *n. pl.* [*sing.* кало́ша] rubbers. —**сесть в кало́шу,** *colloq.* to make a fool of oneself; put one's foot in it. *Also,* **гало́ши.**

калу́жница *n.* marsh marigold.

ка́лька [*gen. pl.* -лек] *n.* **1,** [*usu.* бума́жная ка́лька] tracing paper. **2,** a tracing. **3,** *ling.* loan translation; calque.

кальки́ровать *v. impfv.* [*pfv.* скальки́ровать; *pres.* -рую, -руешь] to trace.

калькули́ровать *v. impfv.* [*pfv.* скалькули́ровать; *pres.* -рую, -руешь] to calculate.

калькуля́тор *n.* calculator.

кальма́р *n.* squid.

кальсо́ны [*gen.* -со́н] *n. pl.* men's drawers; long underpants.

ка́льций *n.* calcium. —**ка́льциевый,** *adj.* calcium (*attrib.*).

каля́кать *v. impfv., colloq.* to chatter.

кама́ринская *n., decl. as an adj.* Russian folk dance.

ка́мбала *n.* flounder; plaice; sole.

ка́мбий *n.* cambium.

ка́мбуз *n.* **1,** ship's galley. **2,** ship's boiler.

камво́льный *adj.* worsted.

каме́дь *n.f.* gum.

камелёк [*gen.* -лька́] *n.* small fireplace.

каме́лия *n.* camellia.

камене́ть *v. impfv.* [*pfv.* окамене́ть] **1,** to turn to stone; become petrified; petrify. **2,** to stiffen; freeze. **3,** *fig.* to harden; become callous.

камени́стый *adj.* stony; rocky.

каменноу́гольный *also,* **каменноуго́льный** *adj.* coal (*attrib.*).

ка́менный *adj.* **1,** stone. **2,** *fig.* stony. —**ка́менный век,** the Stone Age. —**ка́менная соль,** rock salt. —**ка́менный у́голь,** (anthracite or bituminous) coal.

каменоло́мня [*gen. pl.* -мен] *n.* quarry.

каменотёс *n.* stonemason.

ка́менщик *n.* mason; bricklayer.

ка́мень [*gen.* -мня; *pl.* ка́мни, -не́й, -ня́м] *n.m.* stone; rock. —**ка́мня на ка́мне не оста́вить,** not to leave a stone standing.

ка́мера *n.* **1,** chamber. **2,** cell (*of a prison*). **3,** inner tube. **4,** camera. —**ка́мера хране́ния (багажа́),** baggage room.

камерге́р *n.* chamberlain.

камердинер *n.* valet.

камеристка [*gen. pl.* -ток] *n.* lady's maid.

камерный *adj.* **1**, *mech.* having chambers. **2**, *music* chamber (*attrib.*): камерная музыка, chamber music.

камертон *n.* tuning fork.

камешек [*gen.* -шка] *n.* small stone; pebble. —бросать камешки в чей-нибудь огород, to make snide remarks about someone.

камея *n.* cameo.

камин *n.* fireplace. —электрический камин, electric heater.

каминный *adj.* fireplace (*attrib.*). —каминная полка, mantel; mantelpiece. —каминная решётка, fire screen. —каминные щипцы, fire irons.

камнедробилка *n.* stone crusher; rock crusher.

камнеломка *n.* saxifrage.

камнерез *n.* stonecutter.

каморка [*gen. pl.* -рок] *n.* tiny room; closet.

кампания *n.* campaign.

камуфлировать *v. impfv. & pfv.* [*pres.* -рую, -руешь] to camouflage.

камуфляж *n.* camouflage.

камушек [*gen.* -шка] *n.* = камешек.

камфара *also,* камфора *n.* camphor. —камфарный; камфорный, *adj.* camphor.

камыш [*gen.* -мыша] *n.* reed; rush; cane. —камышовый, *adj.* made of reed/rush/cane.

канава *n.* ditch. —сточная *or* водосточная канава, gutter.

канадец [*gen.* -дца] *n.m.* [*fem.* -дка] Canadian. —канадский, *adj.* Canadian.

канал *n.* **1**, canal. **2**, *anat.* duct. **3**, bore (*of a firearm*). **4**, *television* channel. **5**, *fig.* channel: дипломатические каналы, diplomatic channels.

канализация *n.* sewage system. —канализационный, *adj.* sewage (*attrib.*).

канареечный *adj.* **1**, canary (*attrib.*). **2**, canary-yellow.

канарейка [*gen. pl.* -реек] *n.* canary.

канат *n.* **1**, rope. **2**, cable. —канатный, *adj.* rope (*attrib.*); cable (*attrib.*).

канатоходец [*gen.* -дца] *n.* tightrope walker.

канва *n.* **1**, canvas (*for needlework*). **2**, *fig.* background.

кандалы [*gen.* -лов] *n. pl.* shackles; fetters.

канделябр *n.* candelabrum.

кандидат *n.* **1**, candidate. **2**, holder of an academic degree roughly equivalent to a master's degree; candidate: кандидат наук, candidate of science. —кандидат в члены (+ *gen.*), candidate (*or* alternate) member (of).

кандидатский *adj.* candidate's.

кандидатура *n.* candidacy. —выдвигать *or* выставлять чью-нибудь кандидатуру, to nominate someone. —выдвигать *or* выставлять свою кандидатуру, to announce one's candidacy; run.

каникулы [*gen.* -кул] *n. pl.* vacation (*from school*). —каникулярный, *adj.* vacation (*attrib.*).

канителиться *v.r. impfv.* [*pfv.* проканителиться] *colloq.* to dawdle.

канитель *n.f.* **1**, gold or silver thread. **2**, *colloq.* long drawn-out affair; waste of time. —канительный, *adj.*, *colloq.* long drawn-out.

канифоль *n.f.* rosin.

канкан *n.* cancan.

каннибал *n.* cannibal. —каннибализм, *n.* canniba-

lism. —каннибальский, *adj.* cannibalistic. —каннибальство, *n.* cannibalism.

каноист *n.* canoeist.

канон *n.* canon.

каннонада *n.* cannonade.

канонерка [*gen. pl.* -рок] *n.* gunboat. —канонерский, *adj.*, *in* канонерская лодка, gunboat.

канонизировать *v. impfv. & pfv.* [*pres.* -рую, -руешь] to canonize.

каноник *n.* canon (*clergyman*).

канонический *adj.* canonical. —каноническое право, canon law.

каноэ *n. neut. indecl.* canoe.

кант *n.* edging; piping. *Also,* кантик.

канталупа *n.* cantaloupe.

кантата *n.* cantata.

кантовать *v. impfv.* [*pfv.* окантовать; *pres.* -тую, -туешь] **1**, to mount (a picture). **2**, [*impfv. only*] to invert; turn over: "не кантовать", "do not invert".

кантон *n.* canton. —кантональный, *adj.* cantonal.

кантор *n.* cantor.

канун *n.* eve. —в канун (+ *gen.*), on the eve of.

кануть *v. pfv.* **1**, *obs.* to drip; drop. **2**, *obs.* to sink. **3**, to disappear; fade from memory. —как в воду кануть, to vanish into thin air. —кануть в вечность, to sink into oblivion.

канцелярист *n.* **1**, *obs.* clerk. **2**, *fig.* bureaucrat.

канцелярия *n.* **1**, office. **2**, chancellery.

канцелярский *adj.* **1**, office (*attrib.*). **2**, *fig.* (*of language*) bureaucratic.

канцелярщина *n.* **1**, routine office work. **2**, bureaucracy; red tape.

канцероген *n.* carcinogen. —канцерогенный, *adj.* carcinogenic.

канцлер *n.* chancellor.

каньон *n.* canyon.

канюк [*gen.* -нюка] *n.* buzzard.

каолин *n.* kaolin.

капанье *n.* dripping; drip.

капать *v. impfv.* [*pfv.* капнуть] **1**, to drip; fall in drops. **2**, to pour a drop at a time. **3**, to drip; spill: капать себе на галстук, to spill something on one's tie; капать вином на скатерть, to drip wine on the tablecloth. —над нами не каплет (*old conjugation*), there's no rush.

капелла *n.* **1**, choir. **2**, chapel.

капеллан *n.* chaplain.

капелька [*gen. pl.* -лек] *n.* **1**, *dim. of* капля. **2**, *fig.* drop; grain; ounce; particle; modicum. —до капельки, **1**, to the last drop. **2**, completely; absolutely. —ни капельки, not a bit.

капельку *adv.*, *colloq.* a little; just a bit.

капельмейстер *n.* conductor; bandmaster.

капельница *n.* dropper; eye dropper; medicine dropper.

каперсы [*gen.* -сов] *n. pl.* capers (*condiment*).

капилляр *n.* capillary. —капиллярный, *adj.* capillary.

капитал *n.* capital.

капитализация *n.* capitalization.

капитализировать *v. impfv. & pfv.* [*pres.* -рую, -руешь] to capitalize; convert into capital.

капитализм *n.* capitalism. —капиталист, *n.* capitalist. —капиталистический, *adj.* capitalist.

капиталовложения *n. pl.* [*sing.* -ние] capital investment.

капита́льный *adj.* **1,** *econ.* capital (*attrib.*). **2,** major: капита́льный ремо́нт, major repairs.

капита́н *n.* captain. —капита́н пе́рвого ра́нга, *naval* captain. —капита́н второ́го ра́нга, *naval* commander. —капита́н тре́тьего ра́нга, *naval* lieutenant commander.

капита́нский *adj.* captain's.

капито́лий *n.* capitol.

капитули́ровать *v. impfv. & pfv.* [*pres.* -рую, -руешь] to capitulate.

капитуля́ция *n.* surrender; capitulation.

ка́пище *n.* pagan temple.

капка́н *n.* trap; snare.

каплу́н [*gen.* -луна́] *n.* capon.

ка́пля [*gen. pl.* -пель] *n.* **1,** drop: ка́пля воды́, a drop of water. Ка́пли по́та, beads of perspiration. **2,** *pl.* drops: глазны́е ка́пли, eye drops. —ка́пля в мо́ре, a drop in the bucket. —ка́пля за ка́плей; ка́пля по ка́пле, bit by bit. —ни ка́пли, not a bit. —по ка́пле, a drop at a time. —после́дняя ка́пля, the last straw. —похо́жи как две ка́пли воды́, like two peas in a pod.

ка́пнуть *v., pfv. of* ка́пать.

капо́к [*gen.* -пка́] *n.* kapok.

ка́пор *n.* bonnet.

капо́т *n.* **1,** *obs.* housecoat. **2,** *mech.* hood.

капра́л *n.* corporal.

капри́з *n.* whim; caprice.

капри́зничать *v. impfv.* to be capricious.

капри́зный *adj.* capricious.

капро́н *n.* kapron (*a kind of nylon*). —капро́новый, *adj.* kapron.

ка́псула *n.* **1,** capsule. **2,** space capsule.

ка́псюль *n.m.* percussion cap; primer.

капу́ста *n.* cabbage. —брюссе́льская капу́ста, Brussels sprouts. —ки́слая капу́ста, sauerkraut. —морска́я капу́ста, sea kale. —спа́ржевая капу́ста, broccoli. —цветна́я капу́ста, cauliflower.

капу́стница *n.* cabbage butterfly.

капу́стный *adj.* cabbage (*attrib.*).

капу́т *adv.* (*with dat.*) *colloq.* done for: ему́ капу́т, he's done for.

капуци́н *n.* **1,** Capuchin (*monk*). **2,** capuchin (*monkey*).

капюшо́н *n.* hood.

ка́ра *n.* punishment; retribution.

караби́н *n.* carbine.

кара́бкаться *v.r. impfv.* to clamber; scramble.

карава́й *n.* round loaf of bread.

карава́н *n.* **1,** caravan. **2,** convoy (*of ships*).

караве́лла *n.* caravel.

карака́тица *n.* cuttlefish.

кара́ковый *adj.* (*of a horse*) dark bay.

кара́куль *n.m.* Persian lamb; astrakhan; caracul. —кара́кулевый, *adj.* Persian lamb (*attrib.*).

караку́льский *adj., in* караку́льская овца́, caracul sheep.

каракульча́ *n.* broadtail.

кара́куля *n., usu. pl.* scrawl; scribble.

карамбо́ль *n.m.* billiards carom (shot).

караме́ль *n.f.* **1,** caramels. **2,** a (single) caramel.

караме́лька [*gen. pl.* -лек] *n., colloq.* a (single) caramel.

караме́льный *adj.* caramel.

каранда́ш [*gen.* -даша́] *n.* pencil. —каранда́шный, *adj.* pencil (*attrib.*).

каранти́н *n.* quarantine.

кара́сь [*gen.* -ся́] *n.m.* European carp.

кара́т *n.* carat.

кара́тельный *adj.* punitive.

кара́ть *v. impfv.* [*pfv.* покара́ть] to punish. —кара́ться, *refl.* [*impfv. only*] (*with instr.*) to be punishable (by).

карау́л *n.* **1,** guard: почётный карау́л, honor guard. **2,** guard duty; sentry duty. —брать (взять) на карау́л, to present arms.

карау́лить *v. impfv.* **1,** to guard; watch over. **2,** *colloq.* to watch for; lie in wait for.

карау́льный *adj.* guard (*attrib.*); sentry (*attrib.*). —*n.* sentry. —карау́льная, *n.f.* guardhouse.

карау́льня [*gen. pl.* -лен] *n.* guardhouse.

карау́льщик *n., colloq.* watchman.

кара́чки *n. pl., colloq., in* на кара́чки *and* на кара́чках, on one's hands and knees; on all fours.

карби́д *n.* carbide.

карбо́лка *n., colloq.* carbolic acid.

карбо́ловый *adj.* carbolic.

карбона́т *n.* carbonate.

карбору́нд *n.* carborundum.

карбу́нкул *n.* carbuncle.

карбюра́тор *n.* carburetor.

карга́ *n., colloq.* hag.

кардина́л *n.* **1,** cardinal (*prelate*). **2,** cardinal (*bird*).

кардина́льный *adj.* cardinal; fundamental.

кардиогра́мма *n.* cardiogram.

кардио́граф *n.* cardiograph.

кардиоло́гия *n.* cardiology. —кардио́лог, *n.* cardiologist.

каре́та *n.* coach; carriage. —каре́та ско́рой по́мощи, *obs.* ambulance.

каре́тка [*gen. pl.* -ток] *n.* **1,** *dim. of* каре́та. **2,** carriage (*of a typewriter*).

каре́тный *adj.* of or for a coach. —каре́тный сара́й, coach house.

кариати́да *n.* caryatid.

ка́риес *n.* caries. —ка́риес зубо́в, tooth decay.

ка́рий *adj.* (*of one's eyes*) brown.

карикату́ра *n.* **1,** cartoon. **2,** caricature. —карикатури́ст, *n.* cartoonist.

карикату́рный *adj.* **1,** of or like a cartoon. **2,** *fig.* grotesque; ludicrous.

карильо́н *n.* carillon.

карио́з *n.* = ка́риес. —карио́зный, *adj.* carious.

ка́рканье *n.* caw; cawing.

карка́с *n.* frame; framework. —карка́сный, *adj.* frame (*attrib.*): карка́сный дом, frame house.

ка́ркать *v. impfv.* [*pfv.* ка́ркнуть] (*of a bird*) to caw.

ка́рлик *n.m.* [*fem.* ка́рлица] midget; dwarf. —ка́рликовый, *adj.* midget; tiny.

карма́н *n.* pocket. —бить *or* ударя́ть по карма́ну, to put a hole in one's pocketbook. —э́то мне не по карма́ну, I can't afford it.

карма́нный *adj.* pocket (*attrib.*). —карма́нный вор, pickpocket.

карми́н *n.* carmine. —карми́нный; карми́новый, *adj.* carmine.

карнава́л *n.* carnival.

карни́з *n.* cornice.

карп *n.* carp.

ка́рта *n.* **1,** map. **2,** playing card. —(с)пу́тать чьи́-нибудь ка́рты, to upset someone's plans. —(с)пу́тать все ка́рты, to upset the applecart. —ста́вить (что́-нибудь) на ка́рту, to stake.

картавить v. impfv. [pres. -влю, -вишь] to have difficulty pronouncing the sounds "R" and "L".

картавость n.f. improper pronunciation of the letters "L" and "R"; burr.

картёжник n., colloq. inveterate cardplayer.

картёжный adj., colloq. of or pert. to card playing.

картель (тэ) n.m. cartel.

картер n. crankcase.

картечь n.f. 1, canister shot. 2, buckshot.

картина n. 1, picture. 2, painting. 3, theat. scene (part of an act of a play). 4, colloq. movie.

картинка [gen. pl. -нок] n., dim. of картина. —модная картинка, fashion plate. —составная картинка, jigsaw puzzle.

картинный adj. 1, picture (attrib.). 2, picturesque.

картограф n. cartographer.

картографировать v. impfv. [pres. -рую, -руешь] to map; draw a map of.

картография n. cartography. —картографический, adj. cartographic.

картон n. cardboard.

картонаж n. article made of cardboard. —картонажный, adj. cardboard.

картонка [gen. pl. -нок] n. cardboard box; carton. —картонка для шляпы, hatbox; bandbox.

картонный adj. cardboard.

картотека n. card index; card file. —картотечный, adj. of or for a card file.

картофелина n., colloq. a (single) potato.

картофель n.m. potatoes.

картофельный adj. potato (attrib.). —картофельный жук, potato beetle (or bug). —картофельное пюре, mashed potatoes.

карточка [gen. pl. -чек] n. 1, card. 2, small photograph.

карточный adj. card (attrib.). —карточный домик, house of cards. —карточная система, rationing.

картошка [gen. pl. -шек] n., colloq. 1, potatoes. 2, a (single) potato.

картуз [gen. -туза] n. peaked cap.

карусель n.f. merry-go-round; carousel.

карцер n. prison cell (usu. dark and cold) used for special punishment.

карциноген n. carcinogen.

карьер n. 1, full gallop. 2, quarry. —с места в карьер, right away; at once.

карьера n. career. —быстро сделать карьеру, to rise (very) rapidly.

карьерист n. careerist.

касание n. touch; contact.

касательная n., decl. as an adj., geom. tangent.

касательно prep., with gen. regarding; concerning.

касательство n. relation; connection.

касатик n. iris (flower).

касатка [gen. pl. -ток] n. barn swallow.

касаться v.r. impfv. [pfv. коснуться] (with gen.) 1, to touch. 2, to touch upon. 3, to concern; have to do with. —что касается (+ gen.), as to; as for; as far as... is concerned.

касающийся prep., with gen. regarding; concerning.

каска [gen. pl. -сок] n. helmet.

каскад n. cascade.

касса n. 1, cashier's office; cashier's desk: платить в кассу, to pay the cashier. 2, box office; ticket office. 3, cash register. 4, cash box; till. 5, ticket machine

(on a bus or trolley). 6, cash. 7, typography case. —несгораемая касса, safe; strongbox. —сберегательная касса, savings bank.

кассация n., law appeal. —кассационный, adj. appeal (attrib.); of appeal.

кассета n. cassette.

кассир n.m. [fem. -ирша] n. 1, cashier. 2, (bank) teller. 3, ticket seller.

кассировать v. impfv. & pfv. [pres. -рую, -руешь] law to annul; set aside.

кассовый adj. cash (attrib.): кассовая книга, cashbook.

каста n. caste.

кастаньеты n. pl. [sing. -ньета] castanets.

кастелянша n. woman in charge of linen (in a hotel, hospital, etc.).

кастет n. brass knuckles.

кастовый adj. caste (attrib.).

кастор n. castor (heavy woolen cloth).

касторка n., colloq. castor oil.

касторовый adj. 1, made of castor or beaver fur. 2, in касторовое масло, castor oil.

кастрат n. castrated man or boy. —кастрация, n. castration.

кастрировать v. impfv. & pfv. [pres. -рую, -руешь] to castrate.

кастрюля n. pot; saucepan. Also, кастрюлька.

катаклизм n. cataclysm.

катакомбы n. pl. [sing. -комба] catacombs.

каталанский adj. = каталонский.

каталепсия n. catalepsy. —каталептический; каталепсический, adj. cataleptic.

катализ n. catalysis.

катализатор n. catalyst. —каталитический, adj. catalytic.

каталог n. catalogue.

каталогизатор n. cataloguer.

каталогизировать v. impfv. & pfv. [pres. -рую, -руешь] to catalogue.

каталожный adj. catalogue (attrib.). —каталожная, n. catalogue room (in a library).

каталонский adj. Catalan. Also, каталанский.

катание n. 1, rolling. 2, riding; driving. —катание на велосипеде/коньках/лодке, bicycling/skating/boating.

катанье n. = катание. —не мытьём, так катаньем (with different stress), by hook or by crook.

катапульта n. 1, catapult. 2, aero. ejection seat.

катар n. catarrh.

катаракт n. cataract (waterfall).

катаракта n. cataract (of the eye).

катастрофа n. 1, catastrophe; disaster; calamity. 2, accident; crash. —катастрофический, adj. catastrophic; disastrous.

катать v. impfv. 1, indeterm. of катить. 2, [pfv. покатать] to take for a ride or drive. 3, to roll (dough); make (little balls). 4, [pfv. выкатать] to mangle; press in a mangle.

кататься v.r. impfv. 1, indeterm. of катиться. 2, [pfv. покататься] to ride; go riding: кататься на машине, to go for a drive; кататься верхом, to go horseback riding; кататься на велосипеде, to go bicycle riding. Кататься на коньках, to go skating. Кататься на лодке, to go boating. —кататься как сыр в масле, to be in clover. **—ката́ться со́ смеху,** to roar with laughter.

катафа́лк *n.* **1,** hearse. **2,** bier; catafalque.

категори́ческий *adj.* categorical. **—категори́чески,** *adv.* categorically.

катего́рия *n.* category.

ка́тер [*pl.* катера́] *n.* cutter; launch. ♦*In combinations* boat: сторожево́й ка́тер, patrol boat; торпе́дный ка́тер, PT boat.

кате́тер (тэтэ) *n.* catheter.

катехи́зис *n.* catechism.

кати́ть *v. impfv.* [*pfv.* покати́ть; *pres.* качу́, ка́тишь] **1,** to roll; wheel. **2,** *v.i., colloq.* (*of a vehicle*) to roll along. **3,** to stir; cause to move slightly. **—кати́ться,** *refl.* **1,** to roll. **2,** (*of a vehicle*) to roll along. **3,** to slide down. **4,** to flow; stream. **5,** (*of a sound*) to roll; resound. *See also* **ката́ть** *and* **ката́ться.**

като́д *n.* cathode. **—като́дный,** *adj.* cathode (*attrib.*): като́дные лучи́, cathode rays.

като́к [*gen.* -тка́] *n.* **1,** skating rink. **2,** roller: парово́й като́к, steamroller. **3,** mangle; rolling press.

като́лик *n.m.* [*fem.* -ли́чка] Catholic. **—католици́зм,** *n.* Catholicism. **—католи́ческий,** *adj.* Catholic. **—католи́чество,** *n.* Catholicism.

ка́торга *n.* penal servitude; hard labor.

ка́торжник *n.* convict.

ка́торжный *adj.* **1,** of or pert. to penal servitude. **2,** *fig.* backbreaking. **—ка́торжные рабо́ты,** penal servitude; hard labor.

кату́шка [*gen. pl.* -шек] *n.* **1,** spool; reel; bobbin. **2,** roll (*of film*). **3,** *electricity* coil.

катю́ша *n.* rocket launcher mounted on a vehicle; Katyusha.

каусти́ческий *adj.* caustic.

каучу́к *n.* rubber. **—каучу́ковый,** *adj.* rubber. **—каучуконо́с,** *n.* rubber plant.

кафе́ *n. neut. indecl.* café.

ка́федра *n.* **1,** pulpit; rostrum. **2,** department (*of a university*). **3,** chair; professorship.

кафедра́льный *adj., in* **кафедра́льный собо́р,** cathedral.

ка́фель *n.m.* (glazed) tile. **—ка́фельный,** *adj.* tiled; tile (*attrib.*).

кафете́рий (тэ) *n.* cafeteria.

кафта́н *n.* caftan.

кача́лка [*gen. pl.* -лок] *n.* rocking chair.

кача́ние *n.* **1,** rocking; swinging. **2,** pumping.

кача́ть *v. impfv.* [*pfv.* качну́ть] **1,** to rock; swing. **2,** *impers.* (*of a boat*) to toss; pitch; roll: ло́дку кача́ет, the boat is tossing. **3,** to pump. **4,** *in* кача́ть голово́й, to shake one's head; nod one's head. **—кача́ться,** *refl.* **1,** to swing; rock. **2,** to reel; stagger.

каче́ли [*gen.* -лей] *n. pl.* (child's) swing.

ка́чественный *adj.* **1,** qualitative. **2,** high-quality; high-grade.

ка́чество *n.* quality. **—в ка́честве** (+ *gen.*), as; by way of; in the capacity of.

ка́чка *n.* tossing; pitching; rolling (*of a ship*).

качну́ть *v., pfv. of* **кача́ть. —качну́ться,** *refl., pfv. of* **кача́ться.**

качу́рка [*gen. pl.* -рок] *n.* petrel (*bird*).

ка́ша *n.* cooked cereal; porridge; kasha. **—овся́ная ка́ша,** oatmeal.

кашало́т *n.* sperm whale.

кашева́р *n., mil.* cook.

ка́шель [*gen.* -шля] *n.m.* cough.

кашеми́р *n.* cashmere. **—кашеми́ровый,** *adj.* cashmere.

каши́ца *also,* **ка́шица** *n.* gruel.

ка́шка *n.* pap.

ка́шлять *v. impfv.* [*pfv.* ка́шлянуть] to cough.

кашне́ (нэ) *n. neut. indecl.* muffler; scarf.

кашта́н *n.* **1,** chestnut. **2,** chestnut tree.

кашта́новый *adj.* **1,** (of) chestnut. **2,** chestnut-colored; brown.

каю́та *n.* cabin; stateroom.

ка́ющийся *adj.* repentant; penitent.

кая́к *n.* kayak.

ка́яться *v.r. impfv.* [*pfv.* пока́яться; *pres.* ка́юсь, ка́ешься] **1,** to repent; be sorry. **2,** to confess. Публи́чно ка́яться, to publicly recant.

квадра́нт *n.* quadrant.

квадра́т *n.* **1,** square (*figure*). **2,** *math.* square (*second power*): возводи́ть в квадра́т, to square.

квадра́тный *adj.* square. **—квадра́тный ко́рень,** square root. **—квадра́тные ско́бки,** brackets. **—квадра́тное уравне́ние,** quadratic equation.

квадрату́ра *n.* squaring. **—квадрату́ра кру́га,** squaring the circle.

квадрильо́н *also,* **квадриллио́н** *n.* quadrillion.

кваза́р *n.* quasar.

ква́канье *n.* croaking.

ква́кать *v. impfv.* [*pfv.* ква́кнуть] to croak.

ква́кер *n.* Quaker. **—ква́керский,** *adj.* Quaker.

ква́кша *n.* tree frog.

квалифика́ция *n.* qualification; skill.

квалифици́рованный *adj.* skilled.

квалифици́ровать *v. impfv. & pfv.* [*pres.* -рую, -руешь] to characterize; categorize.

квант *n., physics* quantum. **—ква́нтовый,** *adj.* quantum (*attrib.*).

ква́рта *n.* **1,** quart. **2,** *music* fourth.

кварта́л *n.* **1,** quarter; section (*of a city*). **2,** block (*in a city*). **3,** quarter (*of a year*). **—кварта́льный,** *adj.* quarterly.

кварте́т *n., music* quartet.

кварти́ра *n.* **1,** apartment. **2,** *pl., mil.* quarters; billets. **—квартира́нт,** *n., colloq.* lodger; tenant.

квартирме́йстер *n.* quartermaster.

кварти́рный *adj.* housing (*attrib.*); billeting (*attrib.*). **—кварти́рная пла́та,** rent.

квартирова́ть *v. impfv.* [*pres.* -рую, -руешь] **1,** *colloq.* to lodge; live. **2,** *mil.* to be quartered; be billeted.

квартпла́та *n., colloq.* rent (*contr. of* **кварти́рная пла́та**).

кварц *n.* quartz. **—ква́рцевый,** *adj.* quartz.

кварци́т *n.* quartzite.

квас *n.* kvass (*fermented drink*).

ква́сить *v. impfv.* [*pres.* -шу, -сишь] to pickle; make sour.

квасно́й *adj.* kvass (*attrib.*).

квасцы́ [*gen.* -цо́в] *n. pl.* alum.

ква́шеный *adj.* pickled; sour.

квашня́ [*gen. pl.* -не́й] *n.* kneading trough.

кве́рху *adv.* up; upward(s). **—лицо́м кве́рху,** face up; right side up.

квинте́т *n.* quintet.

квинтэссе́нция *n.* quintessence.

квит *also,* **кви́ты** *adj., colloq.* all even: мы (с ва́ми) кви́ты, we are all even.

квита́нция *n.* **1,** receipt. **2,** sales slip.

кво́рум *n.* quorum.

кво́та *n.* quota.

КГБ *abbr. of* Комите́т госуда́рственной безопа́сности, Committee of State Security; the KGB.

кегельба́н *n.* bowling alley.

ке́гля [*gen. pl.* **-лей**] *n.* **1,** bowling pin. **2,** *pl.* bowling (*game*).

кедр *n.* cedar. —**кедро́вый,** *adj.* cedar.

ке́ды [*gen.* **ке́дов** *or* **кед**] *n. pl.* sneakers.

кекс *n.* fruit cake.

келе́йный *adj.* **1,** like that in a monastic cell. **2,** *fig.* secret; private.

ке́льнер *n.* waiter, esp. in Germany. —**ке́льнерша,** *n.* waitress.

кельт *n.* Celt. —**ке́льтский,** *adj.* Celtic.

ке́лья *n.* monastic cell.

кем *pron., instr. of* кто.

ке́мпинг (кэ) *n.* campsite.

кенгуру́ *n.m. indecl.* kangaroo.

кента́вр *n.* centaur.

ке́пка [*gen. pl.* **-пок**] *n.* cap.

кера́мика *n.* ceramics. —**керами́ческий,** *adj.* ceramic.

керога́з *n.* kerosene stove.

кероси́н *n.* kerosene.

кероси́нка [*gen. pl.* **-нок**] *n.* kerosene stove.

кероси́новый *adj.* kerosene (*attrib.*).

ке́сарев *adj., in* **ке́сарево сече́ние,** Caesarean section.

кессо́н *n.* caisson.

кессо́нный *adj.* caisson (*attrib.*). —**кессо́нная боле́знь,** the bends.

ке́та *n.* Siberian salmon.

кетгу́т *n.* catgut.

ке́товый *adj., in* **ке́товая икра́,** red caviar.

кефа́ль *n.f.* (gray) mullet.

кефи́р *n.* yogurt.

киберне́тика (нэ) *n.* cybernetics.

киби́тка [*gen. pl.* **-ток**] *n.* **1,** covered wagon. **2,** nomad's tent. **3,** mud house (*found in Central Asia*).

кива́ть *v. impfv.* [*pfv.* **кивну́ть**] **1,** (*with instr.*) to nod (one's head). **2,** (*with* на + *acc.*) to nod (to). **3,** (*with* на + *acc.*) *colloq.* to try to put the blame on.

ки́ви-ки́ви *n.f. or neut. indecl.* kiwi.

кивну́ть *v., pfv. of* кива́ть.

киво́к [*gen.* **-вка́**] *n.* nod.

кида́ть *v. impfv.* [*pfv.* **ки́нуть**] **1,** to throw; toss; cast. **2,** *in* **куда́ не кинь,** wherever you look. —**кида́ться,** *refl.* **1,** to throw oneself; rush; dash. **2,** [*impfv. only*] (*with instr.*) to throw (something) at each other.

кизи́л *n.* dogwood. *Also,* **кизи́ль,** *n.m.* [*gen.* **кизиля́**].

кий [*gen.* **кия́** *or* **кия;** *pl.* **кии́; киёв**] *n.* billiard cue.

кики́мора *n., folklore* female hobgoblin.

кило́ *n. indecl.* = килогра́мм.

килова́тт [*gen. pl.* **-ва́тт**] *n.* kilowatt. —**килова́тт-ча́с,** *n.* kilowatt-hour.

килоге́рц [*gen. pl.* **-ге́рц**] *n.* kilocycle.

килогра́мм *n.* kilogram.

киломе́тр *n.* kilometer.

килото́нна *n.* kiloton.

киль *n.m.* keel.

кильва́тер (тэ) *n., naut.* wake.

ки́лька [*gen. pl.* **-лек**] *n.* sprat.

кимоно́ *n. indecl.* kimono.

кинемато́граф *n.* **1,** motion-picture camera; movie camera. **2,** *obs.* movie theater.

кинематогра́фия *n.* cinematography.

кинеско́п *n.* kinescope; picture tube.

кине́тика (нэ) *n.* kinetics. —**кинети́ческий,** *adj.* kinetic.

кинжа́л *n.* dagger.

кино́ *n. indecl.* **1,** motion pictures; films; movies; the cinema. Немо́е кино́, silent pictures/films. Ходи́ть в кино́, to go to the movies. **2,** movie theater.

киноактёр *n.* movie actor. —**киноактри́са,** *n.* movie actress.

киноаппара́т *n.* motion-picture camera; movie camera.

киноарти́ст *n.* movie actor. —**киноарти́стка,** *n.* movie actress.

ки́новарь *n.f.* cinnabar; vermilion.

киножурна́л *n.* short subject.

кинозвезда́ [*pl.* **-звёзды**] *n., colloq.* movie star.

кинока́мера *n.* movie camera.

кинокарти́на *n., colloq.* film; picture; movie.

кинокри́тик *n.* film critic.

кинолента *n.* film.

киномеха́ник *n.* projectionist.

кинооператор *n.* cameraman.

киноплёнка *n.* movie film.

кинопроектор *n.* movie projector.

кинорежиссёр *n.* film director.

киносту́дия *n.* movie studio.

кинотеа́тр *n.* movie theater.

кинофестива́ль *n.m.* film festival.

кинофи́льм *n.* film; picture; movie.

кинохро́ника *n.* newsreel.

ки́нуть *v., pfv. of* кида́ть. —**ки́нуться,** *refl., pfv. of* кида́ться.

кио́ск *n.* kiosk; booth; stand.

кио́т *n.* icon case.

ки́па *n.* **1,** pile; stack. **2,** bale (*measure*).

кипари́с *n.* cypress. —**кипари́сный; кипари́совый,** *adj.* cypress (*attrib.*).

кипе́ние *n.* boiling. —**то́чка кипе́ния,** boiling point.

кипе́ть *v. impfv.* [*pres.* **-плю́, -пи́шь**] **1,** to boil. **2,** to seethe. **3,** (*of emotions*) to boil; rage. **4,** (*of activity*) to be in full swing. **5,** (*with instr.*) to boil; seethe; burn (with anger, indignation, etc.).

кипу́чий *adj.* **1,** seething. **2,** ebullient. **3,** frenetic.

кипяти́ть *v. impfv.* [*pfv.* **вскипяти́ть;** *pres.* **-чу́, -ти́шь**] to boil. —**кипяти́ться,** *refl.* **1,** to boil. **2,** *colloq.* to get excited; flare up.

кипято́к [*gen.* **-тка́**] *n.* **1,** boiling water. **2,** *colloq.* hothead.

кипяче́ние *n.* boiling.

кипячёный *adj.* boiled.

кира́са *n.* cuirass.

кирги́з *n.m.* (*fem.* **-ка**) Kirghiz (*one of a people living mainly in the Kirghiz S.S.R.*). —**кирги́зский,** *adj.* Kirghiz.

кири́ллица *n.* the Cyrillic alphabet.

ки́рка [*gen. pl.* **-рок**] *n.* Protestant church. *Also,* **ки́рха.**

кирка́ [*pl.* **ки́рки, ки́рок**] *n.* pick (*tool*).

кирпи́ч [*gen.* **-пича́**] *n.* brick.

кирпи́чный *adj.* **1,** brick (*attrib.*). **2,** brick-red.

ки́са *n., colloq.* pussy cat.

кисе́йный *adj.* muslin.

кисéль [*gen.* -селя́] *n.m.* dessert made of fruit, berries and potato- (or corn-) starch and served with milk.

кисéт *n.* tobacco pouch.

кисея́ *n.* muslin.

кúска [*gen. pl.* -сок] *n.* pussy cat.

кислúца *n.* wood sorrel.

кислорóд *n.* oxygen. —кислорóдный, *adj.* oxygen (*attrib.*).

кúсло-слáдкий *adj.* sweet-and-sour.

кислотá *n.* 1, [*pl.* кислóты] acid. 2, acidity.

кислóтный *adj.* acid (*attrib.*). —кислóтность, *n.f.* acidity.

кúслый *adj.* [*short form* кúсел, кислá, кúсло] sour.

кúснуть *v. impfv.* [*pfv.* прокúснуть; *past* кис *or* кúснул, кúсла] 1, to turn sour. 2, *fig., colloq.* (*of a person*) A, to stagnate; vegetate. B, to mope.

кистá *n.* cyst.

кистéнь [*gen.* -теня́] *n.m.* slung shot.

кúсточка [*gen. pl.* -чек] *n.*, *dim. of* кисть. —кúсточка для бритья́, shaving brush.

кисть [*pl.* кúсти, -стéй, -стя́м] *n.f.* 1, hand. 2, cluster; bunch. 3, *bot.* raceme. 4, tassel. 5, paintbrush. 6, painting; brushwork.

кит [*gen.* китá] *n.* whale.

китáец [*gen.* -áйца] *n.m.* [*fem.* -áянка] Chinese (man): он китáец, he is Chinese. —китáйский, *adj.* Chinese.

кúтель [*pl.* кителя́] *n.m.* tunic.

китобóец [*gen.* -бóйца] *n.* whaling ship.

китобóй *n.* 1, whaler (*person*). 2, whaling ship. —китобóйный, *adj.* whaling (*attrib.*).

кúтовый *adj.* whale (*attrib.*). —кúтовый жир, whale oil. —кúтовый ус, whalebone.

кичúться *v.r. impfv.* 1, to boast; sing one's own praises. 2, (*with instr.*) to brag about; trumpet.

кичлúвый *adj.* conceited; arrogant. —кичлúвость, *n.f.* conceit.

кишéть *v. impfv.* [*pres.* кишúт] 1, to swarm. 2, (*with instr.*) to swarm (with); teem (with).

кишéчник *n.* bowels; intestines.

кишéчный *adj.* intestinal.

кишкá [*gen. pl.* -шóк] *n.* 1, intestine. 2, hose. —прямáя кишкá, rectum. —слепáя кишкá, cecum.

кишмя́ *adv.*, *in* кишмя́ кишéть, to swarm.

клавесúн *n.* harpsichord.

клавиатýра *n.* keyboard.

клавикóрды [*gen.* -дов] *n. pl.* clavichord.

клáвиша *n.* key (*of a piano, organ, typewriter, etc.*).

клад *n.* 1, buried treasure. 2, *colloq.* treasure.

клáдбище *n.* cemetery; graveyard. —кладбúщенский, *adj.* cemetery (*attrib.*).

клáдезь *n.m.*, *archaic* = колóдец. —клáдезь премýдрости, fountain of information.

клáдка *n.* laying (*of stone or brick*). —кáменная клáдка, masonry. —кирпúчная клáдка, brickwork.

кладовáя *n.*, *decl. as an adj.* pantry; larder; storeroom.

кладóвка [*gen. pl.* -вок] *n.*, *colloq.* small pantry.

кладовщúк [*gen.* -щикá] *n.* storekeeper; keeper of supplies.

кладь *n.f.* load. —ручнáя кладь, hand luggage.

клáка *n.* claque. —клакёр, *n.* claqueur.

клан *n.* clan.

клáняться *v.r. impfv.* [*pfv.* поклонúться] 1, to bow. 2, (*with dat.*) to give one's regards (to).

клáпан *n.* 1, valve. 2, flap (*of a pocket*).

кларнéт *n.* clarinet. —кларнетúст, *n.* clarinetist.

класс *n.* 1, (social) class: рабóчий класс, the working class. 2, class (*category*): éхать пéрвым клáссом, to travel first class. 3, class; classroom: идтú/войтú в класс, to go to/enter the/class. Класс оживúлся, the class came alive. 4, grade: быть в трéтьем клáссе, to be in the third grade.

клáссик *n.* 1, classical writer. 2, classicist.

клáссика *n.* the classics.

классификáция *n.* classification.

классифицúровать *v. impfv. & pfv.* [*pres.* -рую, -руешь] to classify.

классицúзм *n.* classicism.

классúческий *adj.* 1, classical. 2, classic: классúческий примéр, classic example.

клáссный *adj.* 1, class (*attrib.*); classroom (*attrib.*). 2, *sports* first-class; top-level. —клáссный вагóн, railway passenger car. —клáссная доскá, blackboard.

клáссовый *adj.* class (*attrib.*): клáссовая борьбá, class struggle.

клáссы [*gen.* -сов] *n. pl.* hopscotch.

класть *v. impfv.* [*pfv.* положúть; *pres.* кладý, кладёшь; *past* клал, клáла] 1, to lay; put; place. 2, to apply (*to a surface*). 3, [*impfv. only*] to build; erect. 4, [*impfv. only*] to lay (eggs). 5, to put (work, effort, etc.) into. 6, *colloq.* to set aside; lay aside; put aside. —класть не на мéсто, to put in the wrong place; misplace. —класть нóгу нá ногу, to cross one's legs. *See also* положúть.

клаустрофóбия *n.* claustrophobia.

клевáть *v. impfv.* [*pfv.* клю́нуть; *pres.* клюю́, клюёшь] 1, to peck. 2, to bite; take the bait. —клевáть нóсом, to nod; be drowsy. —у негó дéнег кýры не клюю́т, he has money to burn.

клéвер *n.* clover. —клéверный, *adj.* of clover.

клеветá *n.* slander; libel.

клеветáть *v. impfv.* [*pfv.* наклеветáть; *pres.* -вещý, -вéщешь] (*with* на + *acc.*) to slander.

клеветнúк [*gen.* -никá] *n.* slanderer.

клеветнúческий *adj.* slanderous; libelous.

клевóк [*gen.* -вкá] *n.* peck.

клеврéт *n.* follower; supporter; minion.

клеёнка *n.* oilcloth. —клеёнчатый, *adj.* oilcloth (*attrib.*).

клéить *v. impfv.* [*pfv.* склéить] 1, to glue; paste. 2, to hang (wallpaper). 3, to make (*by gluing or pasting something together*). —клéиться, *refl.* 1, *colloq.* to get sticky. 2, to stick. 3, *colloq.* (*usu. neg.*) to go well: дéло не клéится, things are not going well.

клей [*2nd loc.* на клею́] *n.* glue. —птúчий клей, birdlime. —ры́бий клей, isinglass.

клéйкий *adj.* sticky; gummy. —клéйкость, *n.f.* stickiness.

клеймúть *v. impfv.* [*pfv.* заклеймúть; *pres.* -млю́, -мúшь] 1, to stamp; mark. 2, to brand (cattle). 3, *fig.* to brand; stigmatize.

клеймó [*pl.* клéйма, клейм] *n.* 1, mark; stamp. 2, brand (*on cattle*). 3, branding iron. —клеймó позóра, stigma.

клéйстер *n.* paste.

клёкот *n.* screech.

клекотáть *v. impfv.* [*pres.* -кóчет] to screech.

клён *n.* maple (tree). —кленóвый, *adj.* maple.

клепáльщик *n.* riveter.

клепáть *v. impfv.* to rivet.

клёпка [*gen. pl.* -пок] *n.* 1, riveting. 2, barrel stave.

клептома́н *n.* kleptomaniac. —клептома́ния, *n.* kleptomania.

клерк *n.* clerk.

клёст [*gen.* клеста́] *n.* crossbill.

кле́тка [*gen. pl.* -ток] *n.* **1,** cage. **2,** check; square. **3,** *biol.* cell. —грудна́я кле́тка, thorax. —ле́стничная кле́тка, stairwell.

кле́точка *n., dim. of* кле́тка.

кле́точный *adj.* cellular.

клету́шка [*gen. pl.* -шек] *n., colloq.* tiny room; cubicle.

клетча́тка *n.* cellulose.

кле́тчатый *adj.* checked.

клёцки [*gen.* -цек] *n. pl.* [*sing.* клёцка] dumplings.

клёш *n.* flare (*in a skirt or trousers*): ю́бка клёш, flared skirt; брю́ки клёш, bell-bottom trousers.

клешня́ [*gen. pl.* -не́й] *n.* claw; nipper.

клещ [*gen.* клеща́] *n.* tick; mite.

кле́щи [*gen.* -ще́й] *n. pl.* pincers; tongs.

клещи́ [*gen.* -ще́й] *n. pl.* **1,** = кле́щи. **2,** *mil.* pincers movement.

кли́вер [*pl.* кливера́] *n., naut.* jib.

клие́нт *n.* client; customer.

клиенту́ра *n.* clientele.

кли́зма *n.* enema.

клик *n.* **1,** call. **2,** honk (*of geese*).

кли́ка *n.* clique.

кли́кать *v. impfv.* [*pfv.* кли́кнуть; *pres.* кли́чу, кли́чешь] **1,** *colloq.* to call. **2,** (*of swans and geese*) to honk.

климакте́рий *n.* menopause.

кли́мат *n.* climate. —климати́ческий, *adj.* climatic.

клин [*pl.* кли́нья, кли́ньев] *n.* **1,** wedge. **2,** gore; gusset.

кли́ника *n.* clinic. —клини́ческий, *adj.* clinical.

клиновидный *adj.* wedge-shaped.

клино́к [*gen.* -нка́] *n.* blade (*of a sword, knife, etc.*).

клинообра́зный *adj.* wedge-shped.

кли́нопись *n.f.* cuneiform.

кли́пер [*pl.* клипера́] *n., naut.* clipper.

кли́пс *n.* earring (*for an unpierced ear*).

кли́ринг *n., comm.* clearing.

кли́рос *n.* choir (*part of a church*).

кли́тор *n.* clitoris.

клич *n.* call; appeal. —боево́й клич, war cry; battle cry.

кли́чка [*gen. pl.* -чек] *n.* **1,** name of a household pet. **2,** nickname.

клише́ *n. neut. indecl.* cliché.

клоа́ка *n.* **1,** sewer; cesspool. **2,** *fig.* foul place; sewer.

клок [*gen.* клока́; *pl.* кло́чья, кло́чьев *or* клоки́, клоко́в] *n.* **1,** shred. **2,** tuft (*of hair*); wisp (*of hay*).

клокота́ть *v. impfv.* [*pres.* -кочу́, -ко́чешь] **1,** (*of liquids*) to bubble. **2,** *fig.* (*of emotions*) to bubble; seethe.

клони́ть *v. impfv.* [*pres.* клоню́, кло́нишь] **1,** to bend; incline. *Also impers.:* ло́дку клони́ло на́ бок, the boat was listing. **2,** (*of sleep*) to overcome. *Also impers.:* его́ кло́нит ко сну, he is drowsy. **3,** (*with* к) *fig.* to incline (toward); predispose (toward). **4,** *fig.* to guide; steer (a conversation, affair, etc.). **5,** (*with* к) *colloq.* to get at; drive at: к чему́ ты кло́нишь?, what are you getting/driving at? —клони́ться, *refl.* **1,** to bow; bend. **2,** (*with* к) to be nearing. **3,** (*with* к) *fig.* to be leading to: к чему́ всё э́то кло́нится?, what is all this leading to?

клоп [*gen.* клопа́] *n.* bedbug.

кло́ун *n.* clown.

кло́унский *adj.* **1,** clown (*attrib.*); clown's. **2,** clownish.

клохта́нье *n.* cluck; clucking.

клохта́ть *v. impfv.* [*pres.* клохчу́, кло́хчешь] to cluck.

клочо́к [*gen.* -чка́] *n.* **1,** scrap (*of paper*). **2,** shred. **3,** wisp (*of hay*). **4,** small plot; patch. **5,** patch (*of fog, blue sky, etc.*).

клуб *n.* **1,** [*pl.* клу́бы] club. **2,** [*pl.* клубы́] puff (*of smoke*); cloud (*of dust*).

клу́бень [*gen.* -бня] *n.m.* tuber.

клуби́ть *v. impfv.* [*pres.* клублю́, клуби́шь; blow into the air. —клуби́ться, *refl.* **1,** to swirl (*in the wind*). **2,** (*of smoke*) to curl.

клубнево́й *adj.* tuberous.

клубни́ка *n.* **1,** strawberries. **2,** a (single) strawberry. —клубни́чный, *adj.* strawberry (*attrib.*).

клу́бный *adj.* club (*attrib.*).

клубо́к [*gen.* бка́] *n.* **1,** ball (*of thread or yarn*). **2,** *fig.* (*with gen.*) tangle (of); maze (of). —клубо́к в го́рле, lump in one's throat.

клу́мба *n.* flower bed.

клык [*gen.* клыка́] *n.* **1,** fang. **2,** tusk. **3,** canine tooth.

клюв *n.* beak; bill.

клюка́ *n.* cane; walking stick.

клю́ква *n.* **1,** cranberries. **2,** a (single) cranberry. **3,** cranberry bush. —клю́квенный, *adj.* cranberry (*attrib.*).

клю́нуть *v., pfv. of* клева́ть.

ключ [*gen.* ключа́] *n.* **1,** key. **2,** [*also,* га́ечный ключ] wrench: францу́зский ключ, monkey wrench. **3,** *music* clef; key. **4,** spring: го́рные ключи́, mountain springs. —бить ключо́м, **1,** to spurt; spout. **2,** *fig.* to throb; be bursting (with life, energy, etc.).

ключево́й *adj.* **1,** key (*attrib.*). **2,** *fig.* key; vital. **3,** coming from underground: ключева́я вода́, spring water.

клю́чик *n., dim. of* ключ.

ключи́ца *n.* collarbone; clavicle.

клю́шка [*gen. pl.* -шек] *n.* **1,** hockey stick. **2,** golf club.

кля́кса *n.* inkblot.

кля́нчить *v. impfv., colloq.* to beg; pester.

кляп *n.* gag.

кля́сть *v. impfv.* [*pres.* кляну́, кляне́шь; *past* клял, кляла́, кля́ло] to curse. —кля́сться, *refl.* [*pfv.* покля́сться] to swear; vow.

кля́тва *n.* oath; vow. —дава́ть кля́тву, to take an oath; swear.

кля́твенный *adj.* (*of a promise, oath, etc.*) solemn; sworn.

клятвопреступле́ние *n.* perjury. —клятвопресту́пник, *n.* perjurer.

кля́уза *n.* **1,** petty lie; petty complaint. **2,** *obs.* petty lawsuit.

кля́узничать *v. impfv., colloq.* to tell petty lies; spread malicious gossip.

кля́ча *n.* old horse; nag; jade.

кни́га *n.* book.

книголю́б *n.* bibliophile.

кни́жка [*gen. pl.* -жек] *n., dim. of* кни́га. —сберега́тельная кни́жка, bankbook; passbook. —трудова́я кни́жка, work-record book. —че́ковая кни́жка, checkbook.

кни́жник *n.* **1,** lover of books; bibliophile. **2,** one who has only book knowledge. **3**, *colloq*. bookseller. **4**, *Bib*. scribe.

кни́жный *adj*. **1**, book (*attrib*.). **2**, *fig*. bookish.

кни́зу *adv*. down; downward(s).

кни́ксен (сэ) *n*. curtsy.

кно́пка [*gen. pl*. -пок] *n*. **1**, button; push button. **2**, thumbtack. **3**, snap; snap fastener.

кнут [*gen*. кнута́] *n*. whip; knout.

кнутови́ще *n*. whip handle.

княги́ня *n*. princess (*wife of a prince*).

кня́жеский *adj*. **1**, prince's. **2**, princely.

кня́жество *n*. principality. —**вели́кое кня́жество**, grand duchy.

кня́жить *v. impfv*. to reign (*as prince*).

княжна́ [*gen. pl*. -жо́н] *n*. princess (*daughter of a prince*).

князь [*pl*. князья́, -зе́й, -зья́м] *n.m.*, pre-rev. prince. —**вели́кий князь**, grand duke.

ко *prep*. = **к**.

коагуля́нт *n*. coagulant. —**коагуля́ция**, *n*. coagulation.

коаксиа́льный *adj.*, in **коаксиа́льный ка́бель**, coaxial cable.

коали́ция *n*. coalition. —**коалицио́нный**, *adj*. coalition (*attrib*.).

ко́бальт *n*. cobalt. —**ко́бальтовый**, *adj*. cobalt.

кобе́ль [*gen*. -беля́] *n.m.* male dog.

ко́бра *n*. cobra.

кобура́ *n*. holster.

кобы́ла *n*. **1**, mare. **2**, *gymnastics* horse.

кобы́лка [*gen. pl*. -лок] *n*. **1**, filly. **2**, bridge (*of a stringed instrument*).

ко́ваный *adj*. **1**, forged; hammered. **2**, *fig*. terse; concise.

кова́рный *adj*. insidious; treacherous. —**кова́рство**, *n*. treachery.

кова́ть *v. impfv*. [*pres*. кую́, куёшь] **1**, to forge. **2**, to shoe (a horse). **3**, *fig*. to forge; carve out (a victory). —**куй желе́зо, пока́ горячо́**, strike while the iron is hot; make hay while the sun shines.

ковбо́й *n*. cowboy.

ковбо́йка [*gen. pl*. -бо́ек] *n., colloq*. man's checked shirt.

ковбо́йский *adj*. cowboy (*attrib*.); cowboy's.

ковёр [*gen*. -вра́] *n*. carpet; rug.

кове́ркать *v. impfv*. [*pfv*. исковеркать] **1**, to break; damage; wreck; mangle. **2**, to warp; distort. **3**, to mispronounce (a word, name, etc.); murder; butcher (a language).

ко́вка *n*. **1**, forging. **2**, shoeing.

ко́вкий *adj*. [*short form* -вок, -вка́, -вко] malleable; ductile. —**ко́вкость**, *n.f.* malleability.

коври́га *n*. large round loaf of bread.

коври́жка [*gen. pl*. -жек] *n*.**1**, *dim. of* **коври́га**. **2**, honey cake; gingerbread. —**ни за каки́е коври́жки**, *colloq*. not for the world.

ко́врик *n*. **1**, small rug. **2**, mat.

ковро́вый *adj*. carpet (*attrib*.); rug (*attrib*.).

ковче́г *n*. ark: Но́ев ковче́г, Noah's ark. —**ковче́г заве́та**, ark of the covenant.

ковш [*gen*. ковша́] *n*. scoop; dipper.

ковы́ль [*gen*. -выля́] *n.m.* feather grass.

ковыля́ть *v. impfv*. **1**, to hobble. **2**, (*of a child*) to toddle.

ковыря́ть *v. impfv., colloq*. **1**, to dig up (earth, soil,

etc.). **2**, (*with* в + *prepl*.) to pick (one's teeth, nose, etc.). —**ковыря́ться**, *refl*. (*with* в + *prepl*.) *colloq*. to rummage (in).

когда́ *adv*. **1**, *interr*. when?: когда́ он придёт?, when is he coming? **2**, *rel*. when: быва́ли дни, когда́..., there were days when... —*conj*. **1**, when: когда́ я был (была́) в Москве́, when I was in Moscow. **2**, while; as: когда́ мы обе́дали, while/as we were having dinner. —**вот когда́...**, that was when... —**есть когда́!**, *colloq*. there is no time. —**когда́ бы ни**, whenever; no matter when. —**когда́ как; как когда́**, *colloq*. it depends. —**тепе́рь, когда́...**, now that... —**тогда́, когда́...**, when...

когда́-либо *adv*. **1**, sometime. **2**, ever: бо́льше чем когда́-либо ра́ньше, more than ever before.

когда́-нибудь *adv*. **1**, sometime. **2**, (*in interr. sentences*) ever: вы когда́-нибудь быва́ли там?, have you ever been there?

когда́-то *adv*. **1**, at one time; once. **2**, someday; sometime.

кого́ (во) *pron., gen. & acc. of* **кто**.

ко́готь [*gen*. -гтя; *pl*. -гти, -гтей, -гтя́м] *n.m.* claw. —**в когтя́х сме́рти**, in the jaws of death. —**пока́зывать ко́гти**, to show one's teeth. —**попа́сть в ко́гти** (*with* к), to fall into the clutches of.

когти́стый *adj*. having sharp claws.

когти́ть *v. impfv*. to claw.

код *n*. code.

кодеи́н *n*. codeine.

ко́декс (дэ) *n*. code (*of law, principles, etc*.).

коди́ровать *v. impfv. & pfv*. [*pres*. -рую, -руешь] to encode.

кодифика́ция *n*. codification.

кодифици́ровать *v. impfv. & pfv*. [*pres*. -рую, -руешь] to codify.

ко́довый *adj*. code (*attrib*.).

ко́е-где́ *adv*. in some places; here and there.

ко́е-ка́к *adv*. **1**, carelessly; any which way. **2**, somehow; with great difficulty.

ко́е-како́й *adj*. some.

ко́е-когда́ *adv*. now and then.

ко́е-кто́ *indef. pron*. someone; some people.

ко́е-куда́ *adv*. somewhere.

ко́е-что́ *indef. pron*. something.

ко́жа *n*. **1**, skin. **2**, leather. —**гуси́ная ко́жа**, goose flesh; goose pimples.

ко́жаный *adj*. leather.

коже́венный *adj*. leather (*attrib*.). —**коже́венный заво́д**, tannery.

коже́вник *n*. currier.

кожими́т *n*. imitation leather.

ко́жица *n*. **1**, *dim. of* **ко́жа**. **2**, thin skin (*e.g. of a sausage*). **3**, skin; peel; rind.

ко́жный *adj*. skin (*attrib*.).

кожура́ *n*. rind; skin; peel.

кожу́х [*gen*. -жуха́] *n*. **1**, sheepskin coat. **2**, housing; casing.

коза́ [*pl*. ко́зы] *n*. (nanny) goat.

козёл [*gen*. -зла́] *n*. goat; billy goat. —**козёл отпуще́ния**, scapegoat.

козеро́г *n*. **1**, ibex. **2**, *cap*. Capricorn: тро́пик Козеро́га, Tropic of Capricorn.

ко́зий [*fem*. -зья] *adj*. goat (*attrib*.); goat's.

козлёнок [*gen*. -нка; *pl*. -ля́та, -ля́т] *n*. young goat; kid.

ко́злик *n.*, *dim. of* козёл.

козли́ный *adj.* **1,** goat (*attrib.*); goat's. **2,** goatskin (*attrib.*). —козли́ная боро́дка, goatee.

козло́вый *adj.* goatskin (*attrib.*).

ко́злы [*gen.* -зел] *n. pl.* **1,** coachman's seat. **2,** trestle. **3,** sawhorse.

козля́тина *n.* goat meat.

ко́зни [*gen.* -ней] *n. pl.* intrigues; machinations.

козодо́й *n.* goatsucker (*bird*).

ко́зочка [*gen. pl.* -чек] *n.*, *dim. of* коза́.

козырёк [*gen.* -рька́] *n.* peak; visor. —взять *or* сде́лать под козырёк, to salute.

козырно́й *also*, **козы́рный** *adj.* trump (*attrib.*); of trump: козырно́й/козы́рный туз, ace of trump.

козырну́ть *v.*, *pfv. of* козыря́ть.

ко́зырь [*pl.* ко́зыри, -рей, -ря́м] *n.m.* **1,** trump. **2,** *fig.* trump card. —пусти́ть в ход после́дний ко́зырь, to play one's trump card.

козыря́ть *v. impfv.* [*pfv.* козырну́ть] *colloq.* **1,** to play a trump. **2,** (*with instr.*) to flaunt. **3,** to salute.

козя́вка [*gen. pl.* -вок] *n.*, *colloq.* insect; bug.

кой *adj.*, *archaic* = како́й *and* кото́рый. —в ко́и ве́ки, once in a blue moon. —ни в ко́ем слу́чае, under no circumstances.

ко́йка [*gen. pl.* ко́ек] *n.* **1,** berth; bunk. **2,** hospital bed. —подвесна́я ко́йка, hammock.

койо́т *n.* coyote.

кок *n.* cook (*on board a ship*).

ко́ка *n.* coca.

кока́ин *n.* cocaine.

кока́рда *n.* cockade.

коке́тка [*gen. pl.* -ток] *n.* **1,** coquette; flirt. **2,** yoke (*of a dress*).

коке́тливый *adj.* **1,** coquettish; flirtatious. **2,** attractive; fetching.

коке́тничать *v. impfv.* **1,** to flirt. **2,** (*with instr.*) to flaunt.

коке́тство *n.* coquetry; flirting.

кокк *n.* coccus.

коклю́ш *n.* whooping cough.

ко́кон *n.* cocoon.

коко́с *n.* **1,** coconut. **2,** coconut palm; coconut tree. —коко́совый, *adj.* coconut (*attrib.*).

коко́тка [*gen. pl.* -ток] *n.* kept woman.

коко́шник *n.* woman's headdress worn in old Russia.

кокс *n.* coke. —ко́ксовый; коксова́льный, *adj.* coke (*attrib.*). —коксу́ющийся, *adj.*, *in* коксу́ющийся у́голь, coking coal.

кокте́йль (тэ) *n.m.* cocktail. —моло́чный кокте́йль, milk shake.

кол [*gen.* кола́] *n.* **1,** [*pl.* ко́лья, ко́льев] stake; picket. Посади́ть на́ кол, to impale on a stake. **2,** [*pl.* колы́, коло́в] *colloq.* one (*lowest grade in school*).

ко́лба *n.* flask; retort.

колбаса́ [*pl.* -ба́сы] *n.* sausage.

колба́сник *n.* sausage maker.

колба́сный *adj.* sausage (*attrib.*).

колго́тки [*gen.* -ток] *n. pl.* panty hose.

колдо́бина *n.*, *colloq.* rut; pothole.

колдова́ть *v. impfv.* [*pres.* -ду́ю, -ду́ешь] to practice witchcraft.

колдовство́ *n.* sorcery; witchcraft.

колду́н [*gen.* -дуна́] *n.* sorcerer.

колду́нья *n.* sorceress.

колеба́ние *n.* **1,** swaying. **2,** oscillation; vibration. **3,** fluctuation; variation. **4,** *often pl.* hesitation; hesitancy; vacillation: без колеба́ний, without hesitation.

колеба́ть *v. impfv.* [*pfv.* поколеба́ть; *pres.* -ле́блю, -ле́блешь] to shake. —колеба́ться, *refl.* **1,** to sway; swing to and fro. **2,** to oscillate. **3,** to fluctuate; vary. **4,** to hesitate; waver; vacillate.

коле́нка [*gen. pl.* -нок] *n.*, *colloq.* knee.

коленко́р *n.* buckram. —э́то совсе́м друго́й коленко́р, that's a horse of a different color.

коле́нный *adj.* knee (*attrib.*). —коле́нная ча́шка *or* ча́шечка, kneecap.

коле́но *n.* **1,** [*pl.* коле́ни, -ней *or* -лён] knee; *pl.* lap. **2,** [*pl.* коле́нья, -ьев] bend (*in a pipe, river, road, etc.*). **3,** [*pl.* -ья, -ьев] section (*of a pipe, river, road, etc.*). **4,** [*pl.* коле́на, -лён] *colloq., music* part; *dance* figure. **5,** [*pl.* -на, -лён] generation. Брат (сестра́) во второ́м коле́не, cousin twice removed. **6,** [*pl.* -на, -лён] *Bib.* tribe: коле́на Изра́илевы, the tribes of Israel. —ему́ мо́ре по коле́но, *colloq.* he doesn't care about anything.

коле́нчатый *adj.* consisting of several branches. —коле́нчатый вал, crankshaft.

колёсико *n.* **1,** *dim. of* колесо́. **2,** caster.

колеси́ть *v. impfv.* [*pres.* -шу́, -си́шь] *colloq.* **1,** to travel in a roundabout way; zigzag. **2,** to travel about (*a place*); travel all over.

колесни́ца *n.* chariot. —погреба́льная колесни́ца, hearse.

колёсный *adj.* **1,** wheel (*attrib.*). **2,** wheeled.

колесо́ [*pl.* колёса] *n.* wheel. —вставля́ть па́лки в колёса, **1,** to throw a monkey wrench into the works. **2,** (*with dat.*) to put a spoke in someone's wheel.

колесова́ть *v. impfv. & pfv.* [*pres.* -су́ю, -су́ешь] to break on the wheel.

коле́чко [*gen. pl.* -чек] *n.*, *dim. of* кольцо́.

колея́ *n.* **1,** rut. **2,** *R.R.* track; gauge. **3,** *fig.* normal routine. —войти́ в колею́, to settle into one's normal routine. —вы́бить из колеи́, to unsettle; upset someone's routine.

ко́ли *also*, **коли́** *and* **коль** *conj.*, *obs.* if.

коли́бри *n.m. or f. indecl.* hummingbird.

колизе́й *n.* coliseum.

ко́лики [*gen.* -лик] *n. pl.* colic.

коли́т *n.* colitis.

коли́чественный *adj.* quantitative. —коли́чественное числи́тельное, cardinal number.

коли́чество *n.* quantity; number; amount.

ко́лкий *adj.* **1,** prickly. **2,** *fig.* biting; mordant; caustic.

ко́лкость *n.f.* **1,** causticity; mordancy. **2,** caustic remark.

коллаборациони́ст *n.* collaborator.

колле́га *n.m. & f.* colleague.

коллегиа́льный *adj.* collective; joint.

колле́гия *n.* **1,** board: редакцио́нная колле́гия, editorial board. **2,** collegium; college. **3,** *in* суде́йская колле́гия, panel of judges.

колле́дж *n.* college.

коллекти́в *n.* collective; body; group.

коллективиза́ция *n.* collectivization.

коллективизи́ровать *v. impfv. & pfv.* [*pres.* -рую, -руешь] to collectivize.

коллективи́зм *n.* collectivism.

коллекти́вный *adj.* collective. —коллекти́вное хозя́йство, collective farm(ing).

коллекционе́р *n.* collector.

коллекциони́ровать *v. impfv.* [*pres.* -ру́ю, -ру́ешь] to collect.

колле́кция *n.* collection.

ко́лли *n.m. indecl.* collie.

колло́дий *n.* collodion. *Also,* **колло́диум.**

колло́ид *n.* colloid. —**колло́идный,** *adj.* colloidal.

колло́квиум *n.* oral examination.

колобро́дить *v. impfv.* [*pres.* -жу, -дишь] *colloq.* **1,** to wander; drift; loiter. **2,** to carouse; live it up.

коловоро́т *n.* drill brace.

коло́да *n.* **1,** log. **2,** chopping block. **3,** deck (*of cards*). —**че́рез пень коло́ду,** in a slipshod manner.

коло́дезный *adj.* well (*attrib.*): коло́дезная вода́, well water.

коло́дец [*gen.* -дца] *n.* well.

коло́дка [*gen. pl.* -док] *n.* **1,** shoetree. **2,** last (*for a shoe*). **3,** shoe (*of a brake*). **4,** *pl.* stocks (*instrument of punishment*).

коло́к [*gen.* -лка́] *n.* peg (*of a musical instrument*).

ко́локол [*pl.* колокола́] *n.* bell.

колоко́льный *adj.* of bells: колоко́льный звон, ringing/tolling of bells.

колоко́льня [*gen. pl.* -лен] *n.* bell tower. —**смотре́ть (на что-нибудь) со свое́й колоко́льни,** to look at (solely) from one's own point of view.

колоко́льчик *n.* **1,** small bell. **2,** bluebell; bellflower; campanula.

колониали́зм *n.* colonialism.

колониа́льный *adj.* colonial.

колониза́тор *n.* **1,** colonialist; colonizer. **2,** colonist. —**колониза́ция,** *n.* colonization.

колонизи́ровать *v. impfv. & pfv.* [*pres.* -ру́ю, -ру́ешь] to colonize. *Also,* **колонизова́ть** [*pres.* -зу́ю, -зу́ешь].

колони́ст *n.* colonist; settler.

коло́ния *n.* colony.

коло́нка [*gen. pl.* -нок] *n.* **1,** *dim. of* коло́нна. **2,** column (*of print, figures, etc.*). **3,** any of a number of devices dispensing liquid: бензи́новая коло́нка, gasoline pump. **4,** hot-water heater. —**рулева́я коло́нка,** steering column.

коло́нна *n.* **1,** column; pillar. **2,** column; file: коло́нна демонстра́нтов, column of demonstrators/marchers. **3,** column (*of print, figures, etc.*).

колонна́да *n.* colonnade.

коло́нный *adj.* columned.

колоно́к [*gen.* -нка́] *n.* kolinsky (*Russian mink*).

колонти́тул *n.* running head.

колорату́ра *n.* coloratura. —**колорату́рный,** *adj.* coloratura.

колори́т *n.* coloring; color. —**ме́стный колори́т,** local color.

колори́тный *adj.* colorful.

ко́лос [*pl.* коло́сья, коло́сьев] *n.* ear (*of a cereal plant*).

колосовы́е *n. pl., decl. as an adj.* cereals.

коло́сс *n.* colossus.

колосса́льный *adj.* colossal; huge; tremendous.

колоти́ть *v. impfv.* [*pres.* -лочу́, -ло́тишь] **1,** (*with* в + *acc. or* по) to strike; bang; pound. **2,** *colloq.* to beat; whip; thrash. **3,** *colloq.* to break; smash. —**колоти́ться,** *refl., colloq.* **1,** (*with* о + *acc.*) to beat (against); strike (against). **2,** (*of the heart*) to thump; pound.

колоту́шка [*gen. pl.* -шек] *n.* **1,** wooden hammer; mallet. **2,** watchman's stick.

коло́ть *v. impfv.* [*pfv.* кольну́ть; *pres.* колю́, ко́лешь] **1,** to prick. **2,** to stab. **3,** *impers.* to have a sharp pain: у меня́ ко́лет в боку́, I have a sharp pain in my side. **4,** [*pfv.* расколо́ть] to crack (nuts); chop (wood). **5,** [*pfv.* заколо́ть] to slaughter (an animal). **6,** to taunt. —**коло́ться,** *refl.* [*impfv. only*] **1,** to be prickly. **2,** to split. **3,** to slash each other.

колпа́к [*gen.* -пака́] *n.* **1,** tall pointed cap. **2,** cone-shaped cover. **3,** hubcap. **4,** cowl.

колпачо́к [*gen.* -чка́] *n.* **1,** *dim. of* колпа́к. **2,** cap: буты́лочный колпачо́к, bottle cap.

ко́лпица *n.* spoonbill.

колумби́йский *adj.* **1,** Colombian. **2,** Columbia (*attrib.*): колумби́йский университе́т, Columbia University.

колу́н [*gen.* -луна́] *n.* heavy ax.

колхо́з *n.* collective farm (*contr. of* коллекти́вное хозя́йство). —**колхо́зник,** *n.* collective farmer; member of a collective farm. —**колхо́зный,** *adj.* of or pert. to a collective farm.

колча́н *n.* quiver.

колчеда́н *n.* pyrites.

колчено́гий *adj., colloq.* having one leg shorter than the other.

колыбе́ль *n.f.* cradle.

колыбе́льный *adj.* cradle (*attrib.*). —**колыбе́льная пе́сня,** lullaby.

колыма́га *n.* **1,** old-fashioned coach. **2,** *colloq.* rattletrap; jalopy.

колыха́ние *n.* swaying.

колыха́ть *v. impfv.* [*pfv.* колыхну́ть; *pres.* -лы́шу, -лы́шешь] to sway. —**колыха́ться,** *refl.* to sway; wave; flutter.

ко́лышек [*gen.* -шка] *n.* peg.

коль *conj.* = коли. —**коль ско́ро, 1,** if. **2,** as soon as.

кольдкре́м *n.* cold cream.

колье́ *n. neut. indecl.* necklace.

кольну́ть *v., pfv. of* коло́ть.

кольра́би *n.f. indecl.* kohlrabi.

кольцево́й *adj.* circular.

кольцо́ [*pl.* ко́льца, коле́ц, ко́льцам] *n.* ring.

ко́льчатый *adj.* **1,** made of rings. **2,** ring-shaped.

кольчу́га *n.* mail; chain mail.

колю́чий *adj.* **1,** prickly. **2,** itchy. **3,** *fig.* biting; cutting; sarcastic. —**колю́чая про́волока,** barbed wire.

колю́чка [*gen. pl.* -чек] *n.* thorn; barb.

ко́люшка [*gen. pl.* -шек] *n.* stickleback.

ко́лющий *adj.* stabbing: ко́лющая боль, stabbing pain.

коля́дка [*gen. pl.* -док] *n.* Christmas carol.

коля́ска [*gen. pl.* -сок] *n.* carriage. —**де́тская коля́ска,** baby carriage.

ком¹ [*pl.* ко́мья, ко́мьев] *n.* lump; clod. Сне́жный ком, snowball. —**ком в го́рле,** lump in one's throat.

ком² *pron., prepl. of* кто.

ко́ма *n.* coma.

кома́нда *n.* **1,** command; order. **2,** command: под кома́ндой (+ *gen.*), under the command of. **3,** crew (*of a ship*). **4,** *sports* team. **5,** *mil.* party; team. —**пожа́рная кома́нда,** fire brigade. —**спаса́тельная кома́нда,** rescue party.

команди́р *n.* **1,** commander. **2,** (ship's) captain.

командирова́ть *v. impfv. & pfv.* [*pres.* -ру́ю, -ру́ешь] to send on an assignment; dispatch.

командиро́вка [*gen. pl.* -вок] *n.* assignment; business trip.

командиро́вочный *adj.* connected with an assignment or business trip. — *n.* **1,** person on an assignment or business trip. **2,** *pl., colloq.* travel allowance.

кома́ндный *adj.* **1,** command (*attrib.*). **2,** team (*attrib.*). **3,** *fig.* commanding: кома́ндная высота́, commanding heights.

кома́ндование *n.* **1,** command: принима́ть кома́ндование, to assume command. **2,** command; commanding officers: верхо́вное кома́ндование, high command.

кома́ндовать *v. impfv.* [*pres.* -дую, -дуешь] **1,** to command; give orders. **2,** (*with instr.*) to command; be in command of. **3,** (*with* над) *colloq.* to order about.

кома́ндующий *n., decl. as an adj.* commander.

кома́р [*gen.* -мара́] *n.* mosquito. — **комари́ный,** *adj.* mosquito (*attrib.*).

комато́зный *adj.* comatose.

комба́йн *n.* combine (*harvesting machine*).

комбина́т *n.* **1,** (industrial) combine. **2,** center: комбина́т бытово́го обслу́живания, service center. — **уче́бный комбина́т,** training center.

комбина́ция *n.* **1,** combination. **2,** *sports* maneuver. **3,** *fig.* scheme. **4,** (lady's) slip.

комбинезо́н *n.* overalls.

комбини́ровать *v. impfv.* [*pfv.* скомбини́ровать; *pres.* -рую, -руешь] to combine.

коме́дийный *adj.* comedy (*attrib.*).

коме́дия *n.* comedy. — **разы́грывать** *or* **лома́ть коме́дию,** to put on an act.

ко́мель [*gen.* -мля] *n.m.* thick end; stump; base.

комеда́нт *n.* **1,** commandant. **2,** superintendent.

комеда́нтский *adj., in* комеда́нтский час, curfew.

комендату́ра *n.* commandant's headquarters.

коме́та *n.* comet.

коми́зм *n.* comedy; humor.

ко́мик *n.* comedian; comic actor.

ко́микс *n., usu. pl.* comics.

Коминте́рн (тэ) *n.* the Comintern (*contr. of* Коммунисти́ческий Интернациона́л).

комисса́р *n.* **1,** commissar. **2,** commissioner. — **комиссариа́т,** *n.* commissariat.

комиссионе́р *n.* broker; agent.

комиссио́нный *adj.* commission (*attrib.*). — **комиссио́нные,** *n. pl.* commission; fee.

коми́ссия *n.* **1,** commission; committee; board. **2,** commission: брать ве́щи на коми́ссию, to accept items for sale on a commission basis.

комите́т *n.* committee.

коми́ческий *adj.* **1,** comic. **2,** comical.

коми́чный *adj.* comical; funny.

ко́мкать *v. impfv.* [*pfv.* ско́мкать] **1,** to crumple. **2,** *colloq.* to rush through; cut short.

комкова́тый *adj.* bumpy; uneven.

коммента́рий *n.* **1,** commentary. **2,** *pl.* comment: никаки́х коммента́риев, no comment.

коммента́тор *n.* commentator.

комменти́ровать *v. impfv. & pfv.* [*pres.* -рую, -руешь] **1,** to annotate. **2,** to comment on; interpret.

коммерса́нт *n.* merchant.

комме́рция *n.* commerce. — **комме́рческий,** *adj.* commercial.

коммивояжёр *n.* traveling salesman.

комму́на *n.* commune.

коммуна́льный *adj.* **1,** public; municipal. **2,** (*of an apartment*) communal.

коммуни́зм *n.* communism.

коммуника́бельный *adj.* communicative; approachable; easy to talk to.

коммуника́ция *n., mil., often pl.* communications. — **коммуникацио́нный,** *adj.* of communication.

коммуни́ст *n.* communist. — **коммунисти́ческий,** *adj.* communist.

коммута́тор *n.* switchboard.

коммюнике́ *n. neut. indecl.* communiqué.

ко́мната *n.* room.

ко́мнатный *adj.* **1,** room (*attrib.*). **2,** indoor: ко́мнатные расте́ния, indoor plants. — **ко́мнатные и́гры,** indoor games; parlor games. — **ко́мнатная соба́чка,** lap dog.

комо́д *n.* bureau; dresser.

комо́к [*gen.* -мка́] *n.* lump. — **комо́к в го́рле,** lump in one's throat. — **комо́к не́рвов,** bundle of nerves.

комо́лый *adj.* hornless.

компа́ктный *adj.* compact; solid.

компане́йский *adj., colloq.* sociable; companionable; outgoing.

компа́ния *n.* **1,** company: води́ть компа́нию с, to keep company with. Он тебе́ не компа́ния, he is not the proper company for you. **2,** group: отдели́ться от компа́нии, to become separated from the group. Пойти́ всей компа́нией, to go in a group. **3,** *comm.* company: нефтяна́я компа́ния, oil company.

компаньо́н *n.* **1,** (male) companion. **2,** partner. — **компаньо́нка,** *n.* (female) companion.

компа́ртия *n.* Communist Party (*contr. of* коммунисти́ческая па́ртия).

ко́мпас *n.* compass. — **ко́мпасный,** *adj.* compass (*attrib.*).

компе́ндиум *also,* **компе́ндий** *n.* compendium; digest.

компенса́ция *n.* compensation. — **компенсацио́нный,** *adj.* compensatory.

компенси́ровать *v. impfv. & pfv.* [*pres.* -рую, -руешь] **1,** to compensate. **2,** to compensate for; make up for; offset.

компете́нтный *adj.* **1,** competent; qualified. **2,** competent; having jurisdiction. — **компете́нтность,** *n.f.* competence.

компете́нция *n.* jurisdiction.

компили́ровать *v. impfv.* [*pfv.* скомпили́ровать; *pres.* -рую, -руешь] to compile.

компиля́ция *n.* compilation. — **компиля́тор,** *n.* compiler.

ко́мплекс *n.* **1,** complex. **2,** series. **3,** system. **4,** *psychoanalysis* complex: ко́мплекс неполноце́нности, inferiority complex.

ко́мплексный *adj.* **1,** complex; composite; multiple. **2,** integrated. **3,** all-round; comprehensive.

компле́кт *n.* **1,** (complete) set. **2,** complement (*of personnel*). — **компле́ктный,** *adj.* (*of a set*) complete.

комплектова́ть *v. impfv.* [*pfv.* укомплектова́ть; *pres.* -ту́ю, -ту́ешь] **1,** to complete (a set); acquire a complete set of. **2,** to bring up to full strength.

компле́кция *n.* build; figure; frame.

комплиме́нт *n.* compliment.

компози́тор *n.* composer.

компози́ция *n.* composition.

компоне́нт *n.* component.

компонова́ть *v. impfv.* [*pfv.* скомпонова́ть; *pres.* -ну́ю, -ну́ешь] to arrange; put together.

компоно́вка *n.* arrangement; layout.

компо́ст *n.* compost.

компо́стер *n.* punch (*for punching tickets*).

компости́ровать *v. impfv.* [*pfv.* прокомпости́ровать; *pres.* -рую, -руешь] to punch (a ticket).

компо́т *n.* fruit compote; stewed fruit.

компре́сс *n.* compress.

компре́ссор *n.* compressor.

компрома́ция *n.* compromising (*of someone or something*).

компромети́ровать *v. impfv.* [*pfv.* скомпромети́ровать; *pres.* -рую, -руешь] to compromise; place in a compromising position.

компроми́сс *n.* compromise. —**компроми́ссный,** *adj.* compromise (*attrib.*).

компью́тер *n.* computer.

комсомо́л *n.* Komsomol; Communist Youth League (*contr. of* Коммунисти́ческий Сою́з Молодёжи).

комсомо́лец [*gen.* -льца] *n.m.* [*fem.* -лка] member of the Komsomol.

комсомо́льский *adj.* Komsomol (*attrib.*).

кому́ *pron., dat. of* кто.

комфо́рт *n.* comfort.

комфорта́бельный *adj.* comfortable.

конве́йер *n.* conveyer. —**сбо́рочный конве́йер,** assembly line.

конве́йерный *adj.* conveyer (*attrib.*): конве́йерная ле́нта, conveyer belt.

конве́нт *n., hist.* convention.

конве́нция *n.* convention; compact.

конве́рт *n.* envelope.

конве́ртер (тэ) *n.* converter. *Also,* конве́ртор.

конверти́ровать *v. impfv. & pfv.* [*pres.* -рую, -руешь] *finance* to convert.

конвои́р *n.* **1,** armed guard; escort. **2,** escort (*for ships*).

конвои́ровать *v. impfv.* [*pres.* -рую, -руешь] *mil.* to escort.

конво́й *n.* (armed) escort: под конво́ем, under escort; under guard.

конво́йный *adj.* escort (*attrib.*). —*n.* armed guard; escort.

конву́льсия *n.* convulsion. —**конвульси́вный,** *adj.* convulsive.

конгломера́т *n.* **1,** conglomeration. **2,** conglomerate.

конгре́сс *n.* **1,** congress: Ве́нский конгре́сс, Congress of Vienna. **2,** Congress (*of the U.S.*). —**конгрессме́н,** *n.* (U.S.) congressman.

конгруэ́нтный *adj., math.* congruent. —**конгруэ́нция,** *n., math.* congruence.

конденса́тор (дэ) *n.* **1,** *chem.* condenser. **2,** *electricity* capacitator; condenser.

конденса́ция (дэ) *n., physics* condensation. —**конденсацио́нный,** *adj.* obtained by condensation.

конденси́ровать (дэ) *v. impfv. & pfv.* [*pres.* -рую, -руешь] *physics* to condense.

конди́тер *n.* pastry cook; pastry chef; confectioner.

конди́терская *n., decl. as an adj.* pastry shop; confectionery. —**конди́терский,** *adj.* pastry (*attrib.*); confectionery (*attrib.*).

кондиционе́р *n.* air conditioner.

кондициони́рование *n.* conditioning. —**кондициони́рование во́здуха,** air conditioning.

кондициони́ровать *v. impfv. & pfv.* [*pres.* -рую, -руешь] to air-condition.

кондоми́ниум *n.* condominium.

ко́ндор *n.* condor.

кондотье́р *n.* soldier of fortune.

конду́ктор [*pl.* кондуктора́] *n.* conductor (*on a train, bus, etc.*). —**конду́кторский,** *adj.* conductor's.

конево́дство *n.* horse breeding. —**конево́д,** *n.* horse breeder. —**конево́дческий,** *adj.* of or pert. to breeding horses: конево́дческая фе́рма, stud farm.

конёк [*gen.* -нька́] *n.* **1,** *dim. of* конь. **2,** *pl.* skates (*esp.* ice skates). **3,** *fig.* one's chief interest; one's favorite topic of conversation. **4,** ridge (*of a roof*). **5,** carved horse's head used as a decoration for a roof. —**морско́й конёк,** sea horse.

коне́ц [*gen.* -нца́] *n.* end. —**без конца́,** endlessly. —**в конце́ концо́в,** in the end; after all; when all is said and done. —**в оди́н коне́ц,** (*of a trip*) one-way. —**до конца́, 1,** to the end. **2,** completely; totally. —**и де́ло с концо́м,** *colloq.* and that will be the end of it. —**и концы́ в во́ду,** and no one will know the difference; and none will be the wiser. —**на худо́й коне́ц,** *colloq.* if worst comes to worst. —**со всех концо́в** (+ *gen.*), from every corner of.

коне́чно *adv.* of course; certainly.

коне́чность *n.f.* extremity (*of the body*).

коне́чный *adj.* **1,** final; last. **2,** ultimate; eventual. **3,** finite. —**в коне́чном ито́ге** *or* **счёте,** ultimately; in the final analysis.

кони́на *n.* horsemeat.

кони́ческий *adj.* conic; conical.

ко́нка [*gen. pl.* -нок] *n.* horsecar.

конкла́в *n., relig.* conclave.

конкорда́т *n.* concordat.

конкретизи́ровать *v. impfv. & pfv.* [*pres.* -рую, -руешь] to make specific; spell out.

конкре́тный *adj.* concrete; specific.

конкуре́нт *n.* (business) competitor. —**конкурентоспосо́бный,** *adj.* able to compete; competitive. —**конкуре́нция,** *n.* (business) competition.

конкури́ровать *v. impfv.* [*pres.* -рую, -руешь] to compete.

ко́нкурс *n.* competition; contest. —**ко́нкурсный,** *adj.* competitive.

ко́нник *n.* cavalryman.

ко́нница *n.* cavalry.

коннозаво́дство *n.* horse breeding.

ко́нный *adj.* **1,** horse (*attrib.*). **2,** horse-drawn. **3,** mounted. **4,** (*of a statue*) equestrian. —**ко́нный двор,** stable. —**ко́нный заво́д,** stud farm.

конова́л *n.* horse doctor.

ко́новязь *n.f.* hitching post.

конокра́д *n.* horse thief. —**конокра́дство,** *n.* horse stealing.

конопа́тить *v. impfv.* [*pfv.* законопа́тить; *pres.* -чу, -тишь] to caulk.

конопля́ *n.* hemp.

конопля́нка [*gen. pl.* -нок] *n.* linnet.

конопля́ный *adj.* hemp (*attrib.*).

коносаме́нт *n.* bill of lading.

консерва́нт *n.* preservative.

консервати́вный *adj.* conservative. —**консервати́зм**, *n.* conservatism. —**консерва́тор**, *n.* conservative.

консервато́рия *n.* conservatory (*of music*).

консерва́ция *n.* 1, preservation. 2, temporary closing.

консерви́ровать *v. impfv. & pfv.* [*pfv. also* законсерви́ровать; *pres.* -рую, -руешь] 1, to can; preserve. 2, to close down temporarily.

консе́рвный *adj.* canning (*attrib.*). —**консе́рвная ба́нка**, tin can. —**консе́рвный нож**, can opener. —**консе́рвная фа́брика**, cannery.

консе́рвы [*gen.* -вов] *n.pl.* canned food; canned goods: мясны́е консе́рвы, canned meat; овощны́е консе́рвы, canned vegetables.

конси́лиум *n.* consultation (*between doctors*).

консисте́нция *n.* consistency (*firmness*).

ко́нский *adj.* horse (*attrib.*). —**ко́нский во́лос**, horsehair.

консолида́ция *n.* consolidation.

консо́ль *n.f.* 1, console (*bracket*). 2, pedestal; stand. —**консо́льный**, *adj.* cantilever (*attrib.*): консо́льный мост, cantilever bridge.

консона́нс *n.* consonance.

консо́рциум *n.* consortium.

конспе́кт *n.* synopsis; outline; abstract.

конспекти́вный *adj.* concise; brief.

конспекти́ровать *v. impfv.* [*pfv.* проконспекти́ровать; *pres.* -рую, -руешь] to abstract; make an abstract of.

конспирати́вный *adj.* secret. —**конспира́тор**, *n.* conspirator. —**конспира́ция**, *n.* secrecy.

конста́нта *n., physics; math.* constant.

констата́ция *n.* establishment; certification.

констати́ровать *v. impfv. & pfv.* [*pres.* -рую, -руешь] to establish; certify.

консте́бль *n.m.* constable.

конститу́ция *n.* constitution. —**конституцио́нный**, *adj.* constitutional.

констру́ировать *v. impfv.* [*pfv.* сконструи́ровать; *pres.* -рую, -руешь] 1, to construct; design. 2, to organize.

конструкти́вный *adj.* 1, structural. 2, *fig.* constructive.

констру́ктор *n.* designer.

констру́кторский *adj.* design (*attrib.*). —**констру́кторское бюро́**, design office (*in a factory*).

констру́кция *n.* 1, construction; design. 2, a structure. 3, *gram.* construction.

ко́нсул *n.* consul. —**ко́нсульский**, *adj.* consular. —**ко́нсульство**, *n.* consulate.

консульта́нт *n.* 1, consultant. 2, consulting physician.

консультати́вный *adj.* consultative; advisory.

консульта́ция *n.* 1, consultation. 2, expert advice; expert opinion. 3, guidance center; clinic.

консульти́ровать *v. impfv.* [*pfv.* проконсульти́ровать; *pres.* -рую, -руешь] 1, to advise; give advice to. 2, [*impfv. only*] (*with* с + *instr.*) to consult. —**консульти́роваться**, *refl.* (*with* с + *instr.*) to consult.

конта́кт *n.* contact.

конта́ктный *adj.* contact (*attrib.*). —**конта́ктные ли́нзы**, contact lenses.

конте́йнер (тэ) *n.* container (*for shipping goods*). —**конте́йнерный**, *adj.* container (*attrib.*).

конте́кст *n.* context: вырыва́ть из конте́кста, to take out of context.

континге́нт *n.* 1, contingent. 2, quota.

контине́нт *n.* continent. —**континента́льный**, *adj.* continental.

конто́ра *n.* office.

конто́рка [*gen. pl.* -рок] *n.* 1, small office. 2, high old-fashioned writing desk.

конто́рский *adj.* office (*attrib.*).

ко́нтра *n., colloq.* 1, rebel; counterrevolutionary. 2, *pl.* quarrel; falling-out. —**быть в ко́нтрах с** (+ *instr.*), to be on the outs with.

контраба́нда *n.* 1, smuggling. 2, contraband goods. —**контрабанди́ст**, *n.* smuggler. —**контраба́ндный**, *adj.* contraband.

контраба́с *n.* bass viol; double bass; contrabass.

контраге́нт *n.* contractor.

контр-адмира́л *n.* rear admiral.

контра́кт *n.* contract.

контрактова́ть *v. impfv.* [*pfv.* законтрактова́ть; *pres.* -ту́ю, ту́ешь] to contract (for).

контра́льто *n. neut. indecl.* contralto (*voice*). — *n. fem. indecl.* contralto (*singer*). —**контра́льтовый**, *adj.* contralto.

контрама́рка [*gen. pl.* -рок] *n.* free pass; complimentary ticket.

контрапу́нкт *n., music* counterpoint. —**контрапункти́ческий**, *adj.* contrapuntal.

контра́ст *n.* contrast.

контрасти́ровать *v. impfv.* [*pres.* -рую, -руешь] to contrast; form a contrast.

контра́стный *adj.* contrasting.

контрата́ка *n.* counterattack.

контратакова́ть *v. impfv. & pfv.* [*pres.* -ку́ю, -ку́ешь] to counterattack.

контрафаго́т *n.* double bassoon; contrabassoon.

контрибу́ция *n.* levy; tribute.

контрме́ра *n.* countermeasure.

контрнаступле́ние *n.* counteroffensive.

контролёр *n.* 1, controller. 2, inspector; examiner. 3, ticket collector. —**фина́нсовый контролёр**, auditor.

контроли́ровать *v. impfv.* [*pfv.* проконтроли́ровать; *pres.* -рую, -руешь] 1, to check. 2, [*impfv. only*] to control.

контро́ль *n.m.* 1, control. 2, inspection; verificaton; monitoring.

контро́льный *adj.* 1, control (*attrib.*). 2, check (*attrib.*): контро́льный пункт, checkpoint. 3, monitoring: контро́льный аппара́т/прибо́р, monitoring device. —**контро́льный о́пыт**, control experiment. —**контро́льная рабо́та**, test (*in school*). —**контро́льные ци́фры**, control figures (*in a planned economy*).

контрпредложе́ние *n.* counteroffer; counterproposal.

контрразве́дка *n.* counterintelligence; counterespionage. —**контрразве́дчик**, *n.* counterintelligence agent.

контрреволю́ция *n.* counterrevolution. —**контрреволюционе́р**, *n.* counterrevolutionary. —**контрреволюцио́нный**, *adj.* counterrevolutionary.

контруда́р *n.* counterblow.

контрфо́рс *n.* buttress.

конту́зить *v. impfv.* [*pres.* -жу, -зишь] to contuse.

конту́зия *n.* contusion.

ко́нтур *n.* 1, contour. 2, *electricity* circuit. —**ко́нтурный**, *adj.* contour (*attrib.*).

конура́ *n.* **1,** kennel; doghouse. **2,** *colloq.* hovel; dump.

ко́нус *n., geom.* cone.

конусообра́зный *adj.* cone-shaped.

конфедера́ция (дэ) *n.* confederation; confederacy. —**конфедерати́вный,** *adj.* confederate.

конферансье́ *n.m. indecl.* master of ceremonies.

конфере́нц-за́л *n.* conference hall.

конфере́нция *n.* conference.

конфе́та *also,* **конфе́тка** *n.* **1,** piece of candy. **2,** *pl.* candy. —**конфе́тный,** *adj.* candy (*attrib.*).

конфетти́ *n. neut. indecl.* confetti.

конфигура́ция *n.* configuration.

конфиденциа́льный *adj.* confidential. —**конфиденциа́льно,** *adv.* confidentially.

конфирма́ция *n., relig.* confirmation.

конфирмова́ть *v. impfv. & pfv.* [*pres.* -му́ю, -му́ешь] *relig.* to confirm.

конфиска́ция *n.* confiscation.

конфискова́ть *v. impfv. & pfv.* [*pres.* -ку́ю, -ку́ешь] to confiscate.

конфли́кт *n.* conflict.

конфо́рка [*gen. pl.* -рок] *n.* burner (*on a stove*).

конформи́зм *n.* conformism.

конфронта́ция *n.* confrontation.

конфу́з *n.* embarrassment.

конфу́зить *v. impfv.* [*pfv.* сконфу́зить; *pres.* -жу, -зишь] to embarrass. —**конфу́зиться,** *refl.* **1,** to be embarrassed. **2,** (*with gen.*) to be shy (in the presence of).

конфу́зливый *adj.* bashful; shy.

конфу́зный *adj., colloq.* embarrassing; awkward.

концентра́т *n.* concentrate.

концентрацио́нный *adj., in* **концентрацио́нный ла́герь,** concentration camp.

концентра́ция *n.* concentration.

концентри́ровать *v. impfv.* [*pfv.* сконцентри́ровать; *pres.* -рую, -руешь] to concentrate. —**концентри́роваться,** *refl.* **1,** to concentrate; mass. **2,** [*impfv. only*] (*with* на + *prepl.*) to concentrate (on).

концентри́ческий *adj.* concentric.

конце́пция *n.* conception.

конце́рн *n.* (business) concern.

конце́рт *n.* **1,** concert; recital. **2,** concerto.

концерта́нт *n.m.* [*fem.* -та́нтка] concert performer.

концерти́но *n. indecl.* concertina.

концерти́ровать *v. impfv.* [*pres.* -рую, -руешь] to give concerts.

концертме́йстер *n.* concertmaster.

конце́ртный *adj.* concert (*attrib.*).

конце́ссия *n., comm.* concession. —**концессионе́р,** *n.* concessionaire.

концла́герь [*pl.* -лагеря́] *n.m.* concentration camp (*contr. of* **концентрацио́нный ла́герь**).

конча́ть *v. impfv.* [*pfv.* ко́нчить] **1,** to finish. **2,** to close; conclude. **3,** to stop. **4,** to graduate from. **5,** *in* **пло́хо ко́нчить,** to end up badly; come to a bad end. —**конча́ться,** *refl.* **1,** to end; come to an end; be over. **2,** to be used up; run out.

ко́нченый *adj., colloq.* hopeless. —**ко́нченый челове́к,** failure; has-been.

ко́нчик *n.* tip; point.

кончи́на *n.* death; passing; demise.

ко́нчить *v., pfv. of* **конча́ть.** —**ко́нчиться,** *refl., pfv. of* **конча́ться.**

конъюнктиви́т *n.* conjunctivitis.

конъюнкту́ра *n.* situation; state of affairs.

конъюнкту́рный *adj.* temporary; of the moment: конъюнкту́рные соображе́ния, considerations of the moment.

конь [*gen.* коня́; *pl.* ко́ни, коне́й, коня́м] *n.m.* **1,** horse. **2,** *chess* knight. **3,** *gymnastics* horse. —**ко́нь-кача́лка,** hobbyhorse.

конько́вый *n. pl.* See **конёк.**

конькобе́жец [*gen.* -жца] *n.* skater. —**конькобе́жный,** *adj.* skating.

коньа́к [*gen.* -яка́] *n.* cognac; brandy.

ко́нюх *n.* stable hand; groom.

коню́шня [*gen. pl.* -шен] *n.* stable.

кооперати́в *n.* **1,** cooperative. **2,** *colloq.* cooperative store. —**кооперати́вный,** *adj.* cooperative.

коопера́ция *n.* **1,** *econ.* cooperation. **2,** cooperative.

координа́та *n.* **1,** *math.* coordinate. **2,** *pl., colloq.* whereabouts.

координа́ция *n.* coordination.

координи́ровать *v. impfv. & pfv.* [*pres.* -рую, -руешь] to coordinate.

копа́л *n.* copal.

копа́ние *n.* digging.

копа́тель *n.m., obs.* digger.

копа́ть *v. impfv.* **1,** [*pfv.* копну́ть] to dig. **2,** [*pfv.* вы́копать] to dig; dig up; dig out. —**копа́ться,** *refl.* [*impfv. only*] (*with* в + *prepl.*) **1,** to dig in (the sand, dirt, etc.). **2,** to rummage through. **3,** to delve (into); probe. **4,** (*with* с + *instr.*) *colloq.* to dawdle (over).

копе́ечка [*gen. pl.* -чек] *n., dim. of* **копе́йка.** —**обойти́сь** (*or* **влете́ть**) **в копе́ечку,** to cost a fortune.

копе́ечный *adj.* **1,** worth one kopeck; one-kopeck (*attrib.*). **2,** (*of expenses*) minor; trifling. **3,** *fig.* petty.

копе́йка [*gen. pl.* -пе́ек] *n.* **1,** kopeck. **2,** *in idiomatic expressions* penny: копе́йка в копе́йку, penny for penny; до после́дней копе́йки, to the last penny. —**без копе́йки,** penniless.

копёр [*gen.* -пра́] *n.* pile driver.

ко́пи [*gen.* ко́пей] *n. pl.* mines.

копи́лка [*gen. pl.* -лок] *n.* money box; piggy bank.

копи́рка *n., colloq.* carbon paper.

копирова́льный *adj.* copying (*attrib.*). —**копирова́льная бума́га,** carbon paper.

копи́рование *n.* copying.

копи́ровать *v. impfv.* [*pfv.* скопи́ровать; *pres.* -рую, -руешь] **1,** to copy; make a copy of. **2,** to copy; imitate.

копиро́вка *n., colloq.* copying. —**копиро́вщик,** *n.* copier; copyist.

копи́ть *v. impfv.* [*pfv.* накопи́ть; *pres.* коплю́, ко́пишь] to accumulate; amass. —**копи́ться,** *refl.* to accumulate; pile up.

ко́пия *n.* **1,** copy. **2,** (*with gen.*) *colloq.* the image of: то́чная (*or* жива́я) ко́пия своего́ отца́, the living image of his father.

копна́ [*pl.* ко́пны, копён, копна́м] *n.* **1,** haycock. **2,** shock (*of hair*).

копну́ть *v., pfv. of* **копа́ть.**

ко́поть *n.f.* soot.

копоши́ться *v.r. impfv.* **1,** (*of insects*) to swarm about; (*of fish*) to swim about. **2,** *colloq.* (*of a person*) to putter about.

ко́пра *n.* copra.

копте́ть *v. impfv.* [*pres.* -пчу́, -пти́шь] **1,** to smoke; emit smoke. **2,** *colloq.* to vegetate; stagnate. **3,** (*with* над) *colloq.* to pore over.

копти́лка [*gen. pl.* -лок] *n.* wick lamp.

копти́льня [*gen. pl.* -лен] *n.* smokehouse.

копти́ть *v. impfv.* [*pres.* -пчу́, -пти́шь] **1,** [*pfv.* закопти́ть] to smoke (ham, fish, glass, etc.). **2,** [*pfv.* накопти́ть] (*of a lamp, candle, etc.*) to smoke; emit smoke. —**не́бо копти́ть,** to sit around doing nothing.

ко́птский *adj.* Coptic.

копче́ние *n.* smoking (*of meat*).

копчёности *n. pl.* [*sing.* -ность] smoked products.

копчёный *adj.* smoked.

ко́пчик *n.* coccух.

копы́тный *adj.* **1,** hoof (*attrib.*). **2,** hoofed; ungulate.

копы́то *n.* hoof.

копьё [*pl.* ко́пья, ко́пий] *n.* spear.

кора́ *n.* **1,** bark. **2,** *bot.* cortex. **3,** crust: земна́я кора́, the earth's crust. —**кора́ головно́го мо́зга,** *anat.* cortex.

корабе́льный *adj.* ship (*attrib.*); ship's.

кораблевожде́ние *n.* navigation.

кораблекруше́ние *n.* shipwreck.

кораблестрое́ние *n.* shipbuilding. —**кораблестро́итель,** *n.m.* shipbuilder.

кора́блик *n.* **1,** *dim. of* кора́бль. **2,** nautilus.

кора́бль [*gen.* -бля́] *n.m.* **1,** ship. **2,** *archit.* nave. —**косми́ческий кора́бль,** spaceship.

кора́лл *n.* coral. —**кора́лловый,** *adj.* coral.

кора́н *n.* the Koran.

корве́т *n.* corvette.

кордебале́т (дэ) *n.* corps de ballet.

кордо́н *n.* **1,** cordon. **2,** post; station.

коре́ец [*gen.* -е́йца] *n.m.* [*fem.* -е́янка] Korean. —**коре́йский,** *adj.* Korean.

коре́йка *n.* brisket (*of pork or veal*).

корена́стый *adj.* stocky; thickset; heavyset.

корени́ться *v.r. impfv.* (*with* в + *prepl.*) to be rooted (in).

коренни́к [*gen.* -ника́] *n.* wheel horse.

коренно́й *adj.* **1,** native; indigenous. **2,** fundamental; radical. —**коренно́й зуб,** molar. —**коренна́я ло́шадь,** = коренни́к. —**коренны́м о́бразом,** radically.

ко́рень [*gen.* ко́рня; *pl.* ко́рни, -не́й, -ня́м] *n.m.* root. —**в ко́рне,** radically. —**вырыва́ть с ко́рнем,** to uproot. —**знак ко́рня,** *math.* radical sign. —**ко́рень зла,** the root of all evil. —**на корню́,** (*of timber, crops, etc.*) standing; not (yet) cut down. —**пресека́ть в ко́рне,** to nip in the bud. —**пуска́ть ко́рни, 1,** to develop roots; put down roots. **2,** to take root. —**смотре́ть в ко́рень** (+ *gen.*), to get to the root (*or* heart) of.

коре́нья [*gen.* -ньев] *n. pl.,* cooking roots.

корешо́к [*gen.* -шка́] *n.* **1,** *dim. of* ко́рень. **2,** spine (*of a book*). **3,** counterfoil; stub.

ко́ржик *n.* cookie.

корзи́на *n.* basket. —**корзи́на для бума́ги,** wastebasket.

корзи́нка [*gen. pl.* -нок] *n.* small basket.

кориа́ндр *n.* coriander. —**кориа́ндровый,** *adj.* coriander (*attrib.*).

коридо́р *n.* corridor; hall.

коридо́рный *adj.* corridor (*attrib.*); hall (*attrib.*). —*n.* bellboy.

кори́нка *n.* currants (*seedless raisins*).

кори́нфский *adj.* Corinthian.

кори́ть *v. impfv.,* *colloq.* to scold; rebuke; upbraid.

корифе́й *n.* leading light; luminary.

кори́ца *n.* cinnamon.

кори́чневый *adj.* brown.

ко́рка *n.* **1,** crust. **2,** rind; peel. —**от ко́рки до ко́рки,** from cover to cover.

корм [*pl.* корма́] *n.* **1,** forage; feed; fodder. **2,** feeding. —**пти́чий корм,** birdseed.

корма́ *n.,* *naut.* stern.

кормёжка *n., colloq.* feeding.

корми́лец [*gen.* -льца] *n.* breadwinner.

корми́лица *n.* **1,** wet nurse. **2,** (female) breadwinner.

корми́ло *n., archaic* helm. —**стоя́ть у корми́ла вла́сти** (*or* правле́ния), to be at the helm of state.

корми́ть *v. impfv.* [*pfv.* накорми́ть *or* покорми́ть; *pres.* кормлю́, ко́рмишь] **1,** to feed. **2,** to suckle; nurse. —**корми́ться,** *refl.* [*impfv. only*] (*with instr.*). to eat; live on; live by.

кормле́ние *n.* **1,** feeding. **2,** suckling; nursing.

кормово́й *adj.* **1,** *naut.* stern (*attrib.*). **2,** fodder (*attrib.*); forage (*attrib.*).

корму́шка [*gen. pl.* -шек] *n.* feeding trough.

ко́рмчий *n., decl. as an adj.* helmsman.

корневи́ще *n.* rhizome.

корнево́й *adj.* root (*attrib.*).

корне́т *n.* cornet.

корнишо́н *n.* gherkin.

ко́роб [*pl.* короба́] *n.* basket. —**це́лый ко́роб новосте́й,** all sorts of news; loads of news.

коробе́йник *n.* peddler.

коро́бить *v. impfv.* [*pfv.* покоро́бить] **1,** to warp: жар коро́бил де́рево, the heat warped the wood. *Also impers. & intrans.* до́ски покоро́било, the boards have warped. **2,** *fig., colloq.* to irk; grate on: его́ э́то покоро́било (*or impers.* его́ покоро́било от э́того), it irked/grated on/him. —**коро́биться,** *refl.* to warp; buckle.

коро́бка [*gen. pl.* -бок] *n.* **1,** box. **2,** frame (*of a building, door, etc.*). —**коро́бка переда́ч/скоросте́й,** gearbox. —**черепна́я коро́бка,** cranium.

коро́бление *n.* warping.

коробо́к [*gen.* -бка́] *n.* small box.

коро́бочка [*gen. pl.* -чек] *n.* **1,** small box. **2,** *bot.* boll.

коро́ва *n.* cow. Ста́до коро́в, herd of cattle. —**морска́я коро́ва,** sea cow.

коро́вий [*fem.* -вья] *adj.* cow (*attrib.*); cow's. —**коро́вья о́спа,** cowpox.

коро́вка [*gen. pl.* -вок] *n., dim. of* коро́ва. —**бо́жья коро́вка,** ladybug; ladybird.

коро́вник *n.* cowshed.

короле́ва *n.* queen.

короле́вский *adj.* **1,** king's; queen's. **2,** royal. **3,** *chess* king's.

короле́вство *n.* kingdom.

короле́к [*gen.* -лька́] *n.* **1,** kinglet (*bird*). **2,** blood orange.

коро́ль [*gen.* -ля́] *n.m.* **1,** king. **2,** *cards; chess* king.

коромы́сло [*gen. pl.* -сел] *n.* yoke (*for carrying buckets*).

коро́на *n.* **1,** crown. **2,** *astron.* corona.

корона́ция *n.* coronation.

коро́нка [*gen. pl.* -нок] *n.* **1,** *dim. of* коро́на. **2,** crown (*of or for a tooth*).

коро́нный *adj.* crown (*attrib.*). —**коро́нный но́мер, 1,** best-known number (*of a performer*). **2,** *colloq.* one's usual trick: э́то его́ коро́нный но́мер, that's his usual trick; he's always doing that. —**коро́нная роль,** best-known role (*of an actor*).

коронова́ть *v. impfv. & pfv.* [*pres.* -ну́ю, -ну́ешь] to crown.

коро́ста *n.* sores; pustules.

коросте́ль [*gen.* -стеля́] *n.m.* corn crake (*bird*).

корота́ть *v. impfv.* [*pfv.* скорота́ть] *colloq.* to while away (the time).

коро́тенький *adj., colloq.* short.

коро́ткий *adj.* [*short form* ко́роток, -тка́, ко́ротко́, ко́ротки́; *comp.* коро́че] short.

ко́ротко *adv.* **1,** short. **2,** briefly. **3,** intimately.

коротково́лновый *adj.* short-wave.

короткометра́жный *adj., in* короткометра́жный фильм, short.

коро́ткость *n.f.* **1,** shortness. **2,** intimacy; familiarity.

короты́ш [*gen.* -тыша́] *n., colloq.* shrimp; runt. *Also,* короты́шка.

коро́че *adj., comp. of* коро́ткий. —коро́че говоря́, in short.

корпе́ть *v. impfv.* [*pres.* -плю́, -пи́шь] (*with* над) *colloq.* to pore over.

ко́рпия *n.* lint (*for surgical dressings*).

корпора́ция *n.* corporation. —корпорати́вный, *adj.* corporate; corporative.

ко́рпус *n.* **1,** [*pl.* -ы] body; trunk; torso. **2,** [*pl.* -á] body; casing; frame. **3,** [*pl.* -á] hull (*of a ship*). **4,** [*pl.* -á] building (*one of several in a complex*). **5,** [*no pl.*] corps: дипломати́ческий ко́рпус, diplomatic corps. **6,** [*pl.* -á] *mil.* corps. **7,** [*pl.* -ы] horse racing length. —ко́рпусный; корпусно́й, *adj.* corps (*attrib.*).

корректи́в *n.* correction; modification; change.

корректи́вный *adj.* remedial: корректи́вное чте́ние, remedial reading.

корректи́ровать *v. impfv.* [*pfv.* прокорректи́ровать; *pres.* -рую, -руешь] **1,** to correct; adjust. **2,** to proofread.

корректиро́вщик *n., mil.* **1,** spotter. **2,** spotter plane.

корре́ктный *adj.* correct; proper. —корре́ктность, *n.f.* proper behavior.

корре́ктор *n.* proofreader.

корректу́ра *n.* **1,** proofreading. **2,** proofs. —держа́ть *or* пра́вить корректу́ру, to read proofs; proofread.

корреспонде́нт *n.* correspondent. —корреспонде́нтский, *adj.* correspondent's; press (*attrib.*).

корреспонде́нция *n.* **1,** correspondence; mail. **2,** report; dispatch.

корро́зия *n.* corrosion.

корру́пция *n.* corruption.

корса́ж *n.* bodice.

корса́р *n.* corsair.

корсе́т *n.* corset.

корт *n.* tennis court.

корте́ж (тэ) *n.* **1,** cortege; procession. **2,** motorcade.

кортизо́н *n.* cortisone.

ко́ртик *n.* dagger.

ко́рточки *n. pl., in* сиде́ть на ко́рточках; сесть (*or* присе́сть) на ко́рточки, to squat.

кору́нд *n.* corundum.

корчева́ть *v. impfv.* [*pres.* -чу́ю, -чу́ешь] to uproot; tear up by the roots.

ко́рчи [*gen.* -чей] *n. pl.* [*sing.* ко́рча] *colloq.* cramps; convulsions.

ко́рчить *v. impfv.* [*pfv.* ско́рчить] **1,** *impers.* to writhe: его́ ко́рчит от бо́ли, he is writhing in pain. **2,** [*impfv. only*] (*with* из себя́ + *acc.*) *colloq.* to pose (as): ко́рчить из себя́ знатока́ му́зыки, to pose as an expert

on music. **3,** *in* ко́рчить ро́жи *or* грима́сы, to make faces. —ко́рчиться, *refl.* to writhe.

корчма́ [*gen. pl.* -че́м] *n.,* pre-rev. tavern; inn.

ко́ршун *n.* kite (*bird*).

коры́стный *adj.* mercenary; selfish.

корыстолюби́вый *adj.* mercenary. —корыстолю́бие, *n.* self-interest.

коры́сть *n.f.* **1,** profit; advantage; gain. **2,** self-interest.

коры́то *n.* washtub; trough. —оста́ться (*or* оказа́ться) у разби́того коры́та, to be left with nothing.

корь *n.f.* measles.

ко́рюшка [*gen. pl.* -шек] *n.* smelt (*fish*).

коря́вый *adj.* **1,** twisted; gnarled. **2,** *colloq.* clumsy; maladroit. **3,** *colloq.* pockmarked.

коря́га *n.* snag (*tree or branch lying in the water*).

коса́ [*acc.* ко́су; *pl.* ко́сы] *n.* **1,** scythe. **2,** braid; plait. **3,** spit (*of land*). —нашла́ коса́ на ка́мень, stone cutting stone; a clash of wills.

коса́рь [*gen.* -ря́] *n.m.* **1,** one who mows grass, cuts hay, etc. **2,** chopping knife.

коса́тка [*gen. pl.* -ток] *n.* killer whale.

ко́свенно *adv.* indirectly; obliquely.

ко́свенный *adj.* indirect; oblique. —ко́свенные ули́ки, circumstantial evidence.

косе́канс (сэ) *n.* cosecant.

косе́ц [*gen.* -сца́] *n.* one who mows grass, cuts hay, etc.

коси́лка [*gen. pl.* -лок] *n.* mower.

ко́синус *n.* cosine.

коси́ть[1] *v. impfv.* [*pfv.* скоси́ть; *pres.* кошу́, ко́сишь] **1,** to mow; cut. **2,** *fig.* to mow down; wipe out; decimate.

коси́ть[2] *v. impfv.* [*pfv.* скоси́ть; *pres.* кошу́, коси́шь] **1,** to twist; contort. **2,** (*with acc. or instr.*) to cock (one's eye). **3,** *v.i.* [*impfv. only*] to be cross-eyed; (*of one's eyes*) be crossed. —коси́ться, *refl.* [*pfv.* покоси́ться] **1,** to slant. **2,** to look sideways. **3,** [*impfv. only*] *fig.* to look askance.

коси́чка [*gen. pl.* -чек] *n.* pigtail.

косма́тый *adj.* shaggy.

косме́тика *n.* **1,** make-up; cosmetics. **2,** cosmetology.

космети́ческий *adj.* cosmetic. —космети́ческий кабине́т, beauty parlor.

космети́чка [*gen. pl.* -чек] *n., colloq.* beautician.

косми́ческий *adj.* **1,** space (*attrib.*): косми́ческий кора́бль, spaceship. **2,** cosmic.

космого́ния *n.* cosmogony.

космодро́м *n.* space center.

космоло́гия *n.* cosmology.

космона́вт *n.* cosmonaut; astronaut; spaceman.

космополи́т *n.* cosmopolite; cosmopolitan. —космополити́зм, *n.* cosmopolitanism. —космополити́ческий, *adj.* cosmopolitan.

ко́смос *n.* (outer) space; the cosmos.

ко́смы [*gen.* косм] *n. pl., colloq.* long disheveled locks of hair.

косне́ть *v. impfv.* **1,** to stagnate. **2,** *fig.* (*with* в + *prepl.*) to wallow (in). **3,** (*of the tongue*) to become stiff.

ко́сность *n.f.* lethargy; indolence; resistance to change.

косноязы́чие *n.* tongue-tie. —косноязы́чный, *adj.* tongue-tied.

косну́ться *v.r., pfv. of* каса́ться.

ко́сный *adj.* negative; unreceptive to new ideas.

ко́со *adv.* obliquely; aslant; askew. —смотре́ть ко́со, to look askance.

кособо́кий *adj.* lopsided; crooked.

косоворо́тка [*gen. pl.* -ток] *n.* man's blouse (*with the collar fastening at the side*).

косогла́зие *n.* strabismus; cross-eye. —**косогла́зый**, *adj.* cross-eyed.

косого́р *n.* **1,** hillside. **2,** slope.

косо́й *adj.* **1,** slanting; oblique. **2,** (*of eyes*) slanting. **3,** crooked. —**косо́й взгляд, 1,** glance to one side. **2,** suspicious look. —**косо́й па́рус**, fore-and-aft sail.

косола́пый *adj.* **1,** pigeon-toed. **2,** *colloq.* clumsy; awkward.

костёл *n.* Roman Catholic church, esp. in Poland.

костене́ть *v. impfv.* [*pfv.* **окостене́ть**] **1,** to become numb (*from the cold*). **2,** (*of a corpse*) to become stiff; ossify.

костёр [*gen.* -стра́] *n.* fire; campfire; bonfire.

кости́стый *adj.* bony (*full of bones*).

костля́вый *adj.* bony (*skinny*).

ко́стный *adj.* bone (*attrib.*). —**ко́стный мозг**, marrow.

костое́да *n.* bone decay; caries.

ко́сточка [*gen. pl.* -чек] *n.* **1,** *dim. of* **кость. 2,** pit; stone (*of fruit*). **3,** stay (*for a corset, collar, etc.*).

косты́ль [*gen.* -ля́] *n.m.* **1,** crutch. **2,** large nail; spike.

кость [*pl.* ко́сти, -сте́й, -стя́м] *n.f.* **1,** bone. **2,** *pl.* dice. **3,** *in* слоно́вая кость, ivory. —**до мо́зга косте́й**, to the marrow of one's bones; through and through. —**лечь костьми́**, to be killed (*in battle*). —**продрогнуть до мо́зга косте́й**, to be chilled to the bone. —**промо́кнуть до косте́й**, to be soaked to the skin. —**язы́к без косте́й**, loose tongue.

костю́м *n.* **1,** suit. **2,** outfit; attire. **3,** costume.

костюме́р *n.m.* [*fem.* -ме́рша] costume designer.

костюмиро́ванный *adj.* costumed. —**костюмиро́ванный бал**, costume party; masquerade.

костю́мный *adj.* of or for a suit.

костя́к [*gen.* -яка́] *n.* **1,** skeleton. **2,** *fig.* backbone.

костяно́й *adj.* made of bone; bone (*attrib.*). —**костяна́я мука́**, bone meal.

костя́шка [*gen. pl.* -шек] *n.*, *colloq.* **1,** knuckle. **2,** ball; bead; button.

косу́ля *n.* roe deer.

косы́нка [*gen. pl.* -нок] *n.* triangular kerchief or scarf.

косьба́ *n.* mowing.

кося́к [*gen.* -яка́] *n.* **1,** doorpost; jamb. **2,** school (*of fish*); flock (*of birds*); herd (*of horses*).

кот [*gen.* кота́] *n.* **1,** male cat; tomcat. **2,** *in* морско́й кот, stingray. —**кот напла́кал**, *colloq.* practically none: де́нег у меня́ кот напла́кал, I have practically no money. —**купи́ть кота́ в мешке́**, to buy a pig in a poke.

кота́нгенс *n.* contangent.

коте́л [*gen.* -тла́] *n.* **1,** caldron. **2,** boiler.

котело́к [*gen.* -лка́] *n.* **1,** pot. **2,** mess tin. **3,** bowler (*hat*); derby.

коте́льная *n.*, *decl. as an adj.* boiler room.

коте́льный *adj.* boiler (*attrib.*).

котёнок [*gen.* -нка; *pl.* -тя́та, -тя́т] *n.* kitten.

ко́тик *n.* **1,** *dim. of* кот. **2,** [*also*, морско́й ко́тик] fur seal. **3,** sealskin. —**ко́тиковый**, *adj.* sealskin.

котильо́н *n.* cotillion.

коти́ровать *v. impfv. & pfv.* [*pres.* -рую, -руешь] *finance* to quote.

котиро́вка *n.*, *finance* quotation.

коти́ться *v.r. impfv.* [*pfv.* **окоти́ться**] to have kittens.

котле́та *n.* chop; cutlet: свина́я котле́та, pork chop;

теля́чья котле́та, veal cutlet. —**отбивна́я котле́та**, chop; cutlet. —**ру́бленая котле́та**, hamburger.

котлова́н *n.* foundation pit.

котлови́на *n.* hollow; depression.

кото́мка [*gen. pl.* -мок] *n.* knapsack; shoulder pack.

кото́рый *pron.* **1,** *interr.* what?; which?: в кото́ром часу́?, at what time? Кото́рый из них ста́рше?, which (one) of them is older? **2,** *rel.* who; that; which: челове́к, кото́рый то́лько что ушёл, the man who just left. Кни́га, кото́рую вы мне одолжи́ли, the book that/which you lent me.—**в кото́рый раз**, once again; for the umpteenth time. —**кото́рый раз?**, how many times?: кото́рый раз я тебе́ говорю́?, how many times have I told you?

котте́дж (тэ) *n.* cottage.

ко́фе *n.m. indecl.* coffee.

кофеи́н *n.* caffeine.

кофе́йник *n.* coffeepot.

кофе́йница *n.* coffee mill.

кофе́йный *adj.* **1,** coffee (*attrib.*). **2,** coffee-colored.

ко́фта *n.* woman's jacket.

ко́фточка [*gen. pl.* -чек] *n.* blouse.

коча́н [*gen.* -чана́] *n.* head of cabbage.

кочева́ть *v. impfv.* [*pres.* -чу́ю, -чу́ешь] **1,** to lead a nomadic life; be a nomad. **2,** (*of animals, birds, etc.*) to migrate.

коче́вник *n.* nomad.

кочево́й *adj.* nomadic; nomad's.

коче́вье *n.* **1,** migration. **2,** nomads' encampment. **3,** territory where nomads roam.

кочега́р *n.* stoker; fireman (*on a locomotive*).

кочене́ть *v. impfv.* [*pfv.* **окочене́ть** *or* **закочене́ть**] to become numb (*from the cold*).

кочерга́ [*gen. pl.* -рёг] *n.* poker (*for a fire*).

кочеры́жка [*gen. pl.* -жек] *n.* cabbage stump.

ко́чка [*gen. pl.* -чек] *n.* hummock.

коша́чий [*fem.* -чья] *adj.* cat (*attrib.*); cat's; feline.

кошелёк [*gen.* -лька́] *n.* purse.

коше́лка [*gen. pl.* -лок] *n.*, *colloq.* basket.

кошени́ль *n.f.* cochineal.

коше́рный *adj.* kosher.

ко́шечка [*gen. pl.* -чек] *n.* pussy cat.

ко́шка [*gen. pl.* -шек] *n.* **1,** cat. **2,** *pl.* cat-o'-nine-tails. **3,** grapnel; grappling iron. **4,** *pl.* climbing irons. —**жить как ко́шка с соба́кой**, to be at each other's throat. —**ме́жду ни́ми пробежа́ла чёрная ко́шка**, they have had a falling-out; something has come between them.

кошма́р *n.* nightmare. —**кошма́рный**, *adj.* nightmarish.

Коще́й *n.*, *folklore* a bony old man who knows the secret of eternal life.

кощу́нство *n.* sacrilege; blasphemy. —**кощу́нственный**, *adj.* sacrilegious; blasphemous.

кощу́нствовать *v. impfv.* [*pres.* -ствую, -ствуешь] to blaspheme; commit a sacrilege.

коэффицие́нт *n.* coefficient; factor; ratio. —**коэффицие́нт поле́зного де́йствия**, efficiency (*of a machine in transmitting energy*).

краб *n.* crab. —**кра́бовый**, *adj.* crab (*attrib.*).

кра́ги [*gen.* краг] *n. pl.* leggings; puttees.

кра́деное *n.*, *decl. as an adj.* stolen goods; loot.

кра́деный *adj.* stolen.

кра́дучись *adv.* stealthily.

кра́дущийся *adj.* stealthy; furtive.

краеве́дение *n.* the study of a particular region. —**краеве́дческий**, *adj., in* **краеве́дческий музе́й**, regional museum.

краево́й *adj.* of or pert. to a **край**; regional.

краеуго́льный *adj., in* **краеуго́льный ка́мень**, cornerstone.

кра́ешек [*gen.* **-шка**] *n., colloq.* edge.

кра́жа *n.* theft; larceny. —**кра́жа со взло́мом**, burglary.

край [*2nd loc.* **краю́**; *pl.* **края́, краёв**] *n.* **1**, edge; rim; brim; brink. **2**, land; country; *pl.* places; parts: в э́тих края́х, in these places/parts. **3**, large administrative division of the USSR; krai. —**кра́ем у́ха**, **1**, (*with* слу́шать) to listen with half an ear. **2**, (*with* слы́шать) to happen to hear. —**на край све́та** (*or* земли́), to the ends of the earth. —**по́лный до краёв**, filled to the brim.—**че́рез край**, **1**, over the edge: ли́ться че́рез край, to overflow. **2**, *fig.* in abundance. **3**, *in* хвати́ть че́рез край, *see* хвати́ть. **4**, *in* хлебну́ть че́рез край, *colloq.* to have had a bit too much to drink.

кра́йне *adv.* extremely.

кра́йний *adj.* **1**, extreme. **2**, last: кра́йняя ко́мната спра́ва, the last room on the right. **3**, *fig.* (*of surprise, exhaustion, etc.*) complete; utter. **4**, *fig.* dire. **5**, *in* кра́йний срок, deadline. **6**, *in* кра́йний Се́вер, the Far North. **7**, *in* кра́йняя цена́, lowest price; rock-bottom price. —**в кра́йнем слу́чае**, if worst comes to worst; as a last resort. —**по кра́йней ме́ре**, at least.

кра́йность *n.f.* **1**, extreme. **2**, extreme situation. —**до кра́йности**, to an extreme.

крамо́ла *n., obs.* uprising; revolt. —**крамо́льный**, *adj., obs.* seditious; rebellious.

кран *n.* **1**, faucet; spigot; tap. **2**, [*also,* **подъёмный кран**] crane. —**водоразбо́рный кран**, hydrant. —**пожа́рный кран**, fire hydrant.

крап *n.* spots; specks.

кра́пать *v. impfv.* [*pres.* **кра́плет** *or* **кра́пает**] (*of rain*) to drizzle; fall in drops.

крапи́ва *n.* nettle.

крапи́вник *n.* wren.

крапи́вница *n.* hives.

кра́пинка [*gen. pl.* **-нок**] *n.* dot; spot; speckle. —**в кра́пинку**, dotted; speckled. —**в кра́сную кра́пинку**, with red dots. *Also,* **кра́пина**.

краплёный *adj.* (*of cards*) marked.

кра́пчатый *adj.* spotted; speckled.

краса́ *n.* **1**, *archaic* beauty. **2**, (*with gen.*) the pride (of).

краса́вец [*gen.* **-вца**] *n.* **1**, very handsome man. **2**, a beauty.

краса́вица *n.* **1**, beautiful woman. **2**, a beauty.

краси́вый *adj.* beautiful; handsome; good-looking. —**краси́во**, *adv.* beautifully.

краси́льный *adj.* dye (*attrib.*); dyeing (*attrib.*).

краси́льня [*gen. pl.* **-лен**] *n.* dye works. —**краси́льщик**, *n.* dyer.

краси́тель *n.m.* dye.

кра́сить *v. impfv.* [*pfv.* **покра́сить**; *pres.* **кра́шу, кра́сишь**] **1**, to paint; dye. **2**, [*impfv. only*] to become; make (someone) look pretty. —**кра́ситься**, *refl.* [*pfv.* **накра́ситься**] *colloq.* to put on make-up.

кра́ска [*gen. pl.* **-сок**] *n.* **1**, paint. **2**, dye. **3**, *pl.* colors. **4**, flush (*of anger, embarrassment, etc.*). —**ма́сляная кра́ска**, oil (*for painting*). —**типогра́фская кра́ска**, printer's ink.

краскопу́льт *n.* spray gun.

красне́ть *v. impfv.* [*pfv.* **покрасне́ть**] **1**, to turn red; redden; flush. **2**, to blush. **3**, [*impfv. only*] (*of anything red*) to appear prominently; shine; gleam.

краснобай *n.* windbag; big talker.

краснова́тый *adj.* reddish.

красногварде́ец [*gen.* **-де́йца**] *n.* Red Guard. —**красногварде́йский**, *adj.* Red Guard (*attrib.*).

красноко́жий *adj.* red-skinned. —*n.* redskin; American Indian.

краснола́сье *n.* pine forest.

красноли́цый *adj.* ruddy-faced.

красноречи́вый *adj.* eloquent.

красноре́чие *n.* eloquence.

краснота́ *n.* redness.

краснота́л *n.* red willow.

красну́ха *n.* German measles.

кра́сный *adj.* **1**, red. **2**, *obs., poetic* beautiful. —*n.* **1**, the red one. **2**, *pl.* reds (*communists*). —**кра́сное де́рево**, mahogany. —**кра́сная доска́**, roll of honor. —**кра́сная строка́**, new paragraph. —**кра́сный уголо́к**, recreation and reading room.

красова́ться *v.r. impfv.* [*pres.* **-су́юсь, -су́ешься**] **1**, to stand out (in all its splendor). **2**, to show off.

красота́ *n.* **1**, beauty. **2**, [*pl.* **-со́ты**] beauty: красо́ты приро́ды, the beauties of nature.

красо́тка [*gen. pl.* **-ток**] *n.,' colloq.* pretty girl.

кра́сочный *adj.* **1**, paint (*attrib.*); dye (*attrib.*). **2**, colorful.

красть *v. impfv.* [*pfv.* **укра́сть**; *pres.* **краду́, краде́шь**; *past* **крал, кра́ла**] to steal. —**кра́сться**, *refl.* [*impfv. only*] to sneak; creep; steal.

кра́сящий *adj.* dye (*attrib.*); dyeing (*attrib.*). —**кра́сящее вещество́**, dyestuff.

крат *n., in* **во́ сто крат**, a hundredfold.

кра́тер *n.* crater.

кра́ткий *adj.* [*short form* **-ток, -тка́, -тко**] short; brief; concise. —**в кра́тких слова́х**, briefly; in a few words.

кра́тко *adv.* briefly.

кратковре́менный *adj.* brief; of short duration.

краткосро́чный *adj.* short-term.

кра́ткость *n.f.* brevity. —**для кра́ткости**, for short.

кра́тный *adj.* (*of a number*) divisible by another number. —**кра́тное**, *n.* multiple.

кратча́йший *adj., superl.* of **кра́ткий**.

крах *n.* **1**, (financial) crash. Крах ба́нка, bank failure. **2**, *fig.* collapse.

крахма́л *n.* starch. —**крахма́листый**, *adj.* starchy.

крахма́лить *v. impfv.* [*pfv.* **накрахма́лить**] to starch.

крахма́льный *adj.* starched.

кра́чка [*gen. pl.* **-чек**] *n.* tern.

кра́ше *adj., colloq.* more beautiful.

кра́шение *n.* dyeing.

кра́шеный *adj.* **1**, painted. **2**, dyed. **3**, wearing make-up; made up.

краю́ха *n., colloq.* hunk (*of bread*).

креве́тка [*gen. pl.* **-ток**] *n.* shrimp.

кре́дит *n., bookkeeping* credit.

креди́т *n.* credit: в креди́т, on credit. —**креди́тный**, *adj.* credit (*attrib.*).

кредитова́ть *v. impfv. & pfv.* [*pres.* **-ту́ю, -ту́ешь**] **1**, to extend credit (to). **2**, to extend credit for; finance.

кредито́р *n.* creditor.

кре́до *n. indecl.* credo.

кре́йсер *n.* cruiser.

крейсерский adj. cruiser (attrib.). —**крейсерская скорость,** cruising speed.

крейси́ровать v. impfv. [pres. -рую, -руешь] to cruise.

крем n. 1, cream; lotion. 2, cream (used in desserts). 3, in сапо́жный крем, shoe polish.

кремато́рий n. crematorium.

крема́ция n. cremation.

креме́нь [gen. -мня́] n.m. flint.

креми́ровать v. impfv. & pfv. [pres. -рую, -руешь] to cremate.

кремлёвский adj. of the Kremlin; Kremlin (attrib.).

Кремль [gen. -мля́] n.m. 1, the Kremlin (in Moscow). 2, l.c. fortress or citadel in old Russian towns; kremlin.

кремнёвый adj. made of flint; flint (attrib.).

кремнезём n. silica.

кре́мниевый adj. silicic: кре́мниевая кислота́, silicic acid.

кре́мний n. silicon.

кремни́стый adj. 1, siliceous. 2, stony.

кре́мовый adj. 1, cream (attrib.). 2, cream-colored.

крен n. 1, naut. list. 2, aero. bank.

кре́ндель [pl. кре́ндели, -лей, -ля́м] n.m. pretzel.

крени́ть v. impfv. [pfv. накрени́ть] to tip; tilt. —**крени́ться,** refl. to tilt; list.

креозо́т n. creosote.

крео́л n. Creole. —**крео́льский,** adj. Creole.

креп n. crepe.

крепи́тельный adj. 1, obs. invigorating; refreshing. 2, med. binding.

крепи́ть v. impfv. [pres. -плю́, -пи́шь] 1, to fasten. 2, to strengthen. 3, to constipate. Also impers.: его́ крепи́т, he is constipated. —**крепи́ться,** refl. to hold out; stand firm; bear up.

кре́пкий adj. [short form -пок, -пка́, -пко; comp. кре́пче] 1, strong; durable. 2, strong; sturdy; robust. 3, (of tea, wine, etc.) strong. 4, (of frost) hard. 5, (of sleep) sound.

кре́пко adv. 1, firmly. 2, sturdily: кре́пко сло́жённый, sturdily built. 3, tight(ly): держа́ться кре́пко, to hold tight. —**кре́пко спать,** to be sound/fast asleep.

крепколо́бый adj., colloq. stubborn; pigheaded.

крепле́ние n. 1, strengthening; fastening. 2, mount; mounting. —**у́зел крепле́ния дви́гателя,** engine mount.

кре́пнуть v. impfv. [pfv. окре́пнуть; past креп or кре́пнул, кре́пла] to grow stronger; regain one's strength.

крепостни́чество n. serfdom.

крепостно́й adj. 1, serf (attrib.). 2, of a fortress. —n. serf. —**крепостно́е пра́во,** serfdom.

кре́пость n.f. 1, strength. 2, [pl. кре́пости, -сте́й, -стя́м] fortress.

крепча́ть v. impfv. 1, to increase in intensity; (of the wind) blow harder. 2, colloq. (of a person) to grow stronger; gain strength.

кре́пче adj., comp. of кре́пкий.

крепы́ш [gen. -пыша́] n., colloq. robust man; sturdy youngster.

кре́сло [gen. pl. -сел] n. armchair; easy chair. —**инвали́дное кре́сло,** wheelchair.

кресс n. cress. —**водяно́й кресс,** watercress. —**кресс-сала́т,** garden cress.

крест [gen. креста́] n. 1, cross. 2, the sign of the cross. —**ста́вить крест на** (+ prepl.), to give up on; give up as hopeless.

крестец [gen. -тца́] n. 1, anat. sacrum. 2, rump (of an animal).

кре́стик n. 1, dim. of крест. 2, printing dagger (†).

крести́льный adj. baptismal.

крести́ны [gen. -ти́н] n. pl. christening.

крести́ть v. impfv. [pres. крещу́, кре́стишь] 1, [pfv. окрести́ть] to baptize; christen. 2, [impfv. only] to be a godfather or godmother to. 3, [pfv. перекрести́ть] to make the sign of the cross over. —**крести́ться,** refl. 1, [pfv. окрести́ться] to be baptized. 2, [pfv. перекрести́ться] to cross oneself.

крест-на́крест adv. crosswise; crisscross.

кре́стная n., decl. as an adj., colloq. godmother.

кре́стник n. godson; godchild. —**кре́стница,** n. goddaughter; godchild.

кре́стный adj., in 1, кре́стное зна́мение, the sign of the cross. 2, кре́стный ход religious procession.

крёстный adj., in крёстный оте́ц, godfather; крёстная мать, godmother; крёстный сын, godson; крёстная дочь, goddaughter. —n. godfather.

крестови́на n. crosspiece.

кресто́вый adj., in кресто́вый похо́д, hist. crusade.

крестоно́сец [gen. -сца] n., hist. crusader.

крестообра́зный adj. in the shape of a cross; cruciform. —**крестообра́зно,** adv. crosswise.

крестья́нин [pl. -я́не, -я́н] n.m. [fem. -я́нка] peasant. —**крестья́нский,** adj. peasant (attrib.). —**крестья́нство,** n. peasantry.

крети́н n. cretin. —**кретини́зм,** n. cretinism.

крето́н n. cretonne. —**крето́нный; крето́новый.** adj. cretonne.

кре́чет n. gyrfalcon.

креще́ндо adv. & n. indecl. crescendo.

креще́ние n. 1, baptism; christening. 2, Epiphany.

крещёный adj. baptized.

крива́я n., decl. as an adj., math. curve.

кривизна́ n. 1, curvature. 2, crookedness.

криви́ть v. impfv. [pfv. покриви́ть or скриви́ть; pres. -влю́, -ви́шь] 1, to twist; contort. 2, in (по)криви́ть душо́й, to play the hypocrite. —**криви́ться,** refl. 1, to become bent; get out of shape. 2, colloq. to make a face; grimace.

кривля́ка n.m. & f., colloq. affected person.

кривля́нье n. affectation; artificiality.

кривля́ться v.r. impfv. 1, to make faces. 2, to put on airs.

кри́во adv. 1, in a crooked line. 2, askew; awry.

кривобо́кий adj. lopsided.

криво́й adj. 1, crooked. 2, colloq. one-eyed; blind in one eye. —**криво́е зе́ркало,** distorting mirror. —**кривы́е пути́,** crooked ways. —**крива́я улы́бка,** wry smile.

криволине́йный adj. curvilinear.

кривоно́гий adj. bowlegged; bandy-legged; knock-kneed.

кривото́лки [gen. -ков] n. pl. false rumors; idle gossip; loose talk.

кривоши́п n., mech. crank.

кри́зис n. crisis. —**кри́зисный,** adj. crisis (attrib.); critical.

крик n. cry; shout; scream; yell. —**после́дний крик мо́ды,** the latest thing in fashion.

кри́кет n., sports cricket.

крикли́вый *adj.* **1,** loud; noisy. **2,** *fig.* loud; flashy; garish.

кри́кнуть *v., pfv. of* **крича́ть.**

крику́н [*gen.* -куна́] *n.m.* [*fem.* -ку́нья] *colloq.* noisy person; loudmouth.

кримина́л *n., colloq.* a crime.

криминали́ст *n.* criminal lawyer. —**криминали́сти-ка,** *n.* criminal law. —**криминалисти́ческий,** *adj.* of or pert. to criminal law.

кримина́льный *adj.* criminal.

криминоло́гия *n.* criminology. —**кримино́лог,** *n.* criminologist.

кри́нка [*gen. pl.* -нок] *n.* = **кры́нка.**

кринoли́н *n.* hoop skirt.

криптогра́мма *n.* cryptogram.

криптогра́фия *n.* cryptography. —**криптографи́-ческий,** *adj.* cryptographic.

крипто́н *n.* krypton.

криста́лл *n.* crystal.

кристаллиза́ция *n.* crystallization.

кристаллизова́ть *v. impfv. & pfv.* [*pres.* -зу́ю, -зу́ешь] to crystallize. —**кристаллизова́ться,** *refl.* to crystallize; take shape.

кристалли́ческий *adj.* crystalline.

криста́льный *adj.* **1,** crystal-clear. **2,** pure; perfect.

крите́рий *n.* criterion.

кри́тик *n.* critic.

кри́тика *n.* criticism.

критика́н *n.* faultfinder. —**критика́нство,** *n.* carping; faultfinding.

критикова́ть *v. impfv.* [*pres.* -ку́ю, -ку́ешь] to criticize.

крити́ческий *adj.* **1,** critical; containing criticism. **2,** critical; crucial.

крича́ть *v. impfv.* [*pfv.* **кри́кнуть**; *pres.* -чу́, -чи́шь] to shout; yell; scream.

крича́щий *adj.* loud; flashy; garish.

кров *n.* shelter. —**оста́ться без кро́ва,** to be left without a roof over one's head.

крова́вый *adj.* **1,** bloody. **2,** blood-red. **3,** (*of meat*) rare; underdone. —**крова́вая ба́ня,** blood bath. —**крова́вое пятно́,** bloodstain.

крова́тка [*gen. pl.* -ток] *n.* small bed; child's bed.

крова́ть *n.f.* bed. —**де́тская крова́ть,** crib.

кро́вельный *adj.* roofing (*attrib.*).

кро́вельщик *n.* roofer.

кровено́сный *adj.* of the circulatory system. —**кровено́сная систе́ма,** circulatory system. —**кровено́с-ный сосу́д,** blood vessel.

крови́нка [*gen. pl.* -нок] *n., colloq.* drop of blood. —**ни крови́нки в лице́,** white as a sheet.

кро́вля [*gen. pl.* -вель] *n.* **1,** roof. **2,** roofing.

кро́вно *adv.* **1,** by blood: кро́вно свя́занный, bound by ties of blood. **2,** vitally: кро́вно заинтересо́ван-ный, vitally interested. **3,** grievously: кро́вно оби́деть кого́-нибудь, to grievously offend someone.

кро́вный *adj.* **1,** blood (*attrib.*); related by blood. **2,** thoroughbred. **3,** *fig.* vital. —**кро́вный враг,** mortal enemy. —**кро́вные де́ньги,** hard-earned money. —**кро́вная месть,** vendetta. —**кро́вная оби́да,** grievous insult.

кровожа́дный *adj.* bloodthirsty.

кровоизлия́ние *n.* hemorrhage.

кровообраще́ние *n.* circulation (*of the blood*).

кровоостана́вливающий *adj.* styptic. —**крово-остана́вливающее сре́дство,** styptic agent.

кровопи́йца *n.m. & f.* bloodsucker.

кровоподтёк *n.* bruise.

кровопроли́тие *n.* bloodshed.

кровопуска́ние *n.* bloodletting; phlebotomy.

кровосмеше́ние *n.* incest. —**кровосмеси́тельный,** *adj.* incestuous.

кровосо́с *n.* vampire bat.

кровотече́ние *n.* bleeding; hemorrhaging.

кровоточи́вость *n.f.* **1,** bleeding: кровоточи́вость дёсен, bleeding gums. **2,** hemophilia.

кровоточи́ть *v. impfv.* to bleed.

кровь [*2nd loc.* крови́] *n.f.* blood. —**в кровь** (*with verbs of beating*), till one bleeds. —**в крови́,** bloody; covered with blood. —**э́то у него́ в крови́,** it's in his blood.

кровяно́й *adj.* blood (*attrib.*). —**кровяно́е давле́ние,** blood pressure. —**кровяны́е ша́рики,** corpuscles.

кро́ить *v. impfv.* [*pfv.* **скро́ить**] to cut; cut out (material or a garment).

кро́йка *n.* cutting.

кроке́т *n.* croquet.

крокоди́л *n.* crocodile. —**крокоди́лов,** *adj., in* крокоди́ловы слёзы, crocodile tears. —**крокоди́ловый,** *adj.* made of crocodile skin; crocodile (*attrib.*).

кро́кус *n.* crocus.

кро́лик *n.* rabbit. —**кро́личий,** *adj.* [*fem.* -чья] rabbit (*attrib.*).

кроль *n.m., swimming* crawl.

кро́ме *prep., with gen.* **1,** except (for); but. **2,** besides; in addition to. —**кро́ме как,** except. —**кро́ме того́,** besides; moreover; furthermore; in addition.

кроме́шный *adj., in* ад кроме́шный, sheer hell; тьма кроме́шная, absolute darkness.

кро́мка [*gen. pl.* -мок] *n.* **1,** selvage. **2,** edge.

кромса́ть *v. impfv.* [*pfv.* **искромса́ть**] *colloq.* to cut up; hack.

кро́на *n.* **1,** crown (*of a tree*). **2,** crown (*monetary unit*).

кронци́ркуль *n.m.* calipers.

кро́ншнеп (нэ) *n.m.* curlew (*bird*).

кроншта́йн (тэ) *n.* bracket; holder.

кропи́ть *v. impfv.* [*pres.* -плю́, -пи́шь] **1,** to sprinkle. **2,** (*of rain*) to fall lightly.

кропотли́вый *adj.* laborious; painstaking.

кросс *n.* cross-country race.

кроссво́рд *n.* crossword puzzle.

крот [*gen.* крота́] *n.* **1,** mole. **2,** moleskin.

кро́ткий [*short form* -ток, -тка́, -тко] *adj.* meek.

крото́вый *adj.* **1,** mole (*attrib.*); mole's. **2,** moleskin.

кро́тость *n.f.* meekness.

кроха́ [*acc.* кро́ху; *pl.* кро́хи, крох, -ха́м] *n.* **1,** *obs.* crumb. **2,** *pl.* crumbs: кро́хи зна́ний, crumbs of knowledge.

кроха́ль [*gen.* -халя́] *n.m.* merganser.

кро́хотный *adj., colloq.* tiny. *Also,* **кро́шечный.**

кроши́ть *v. impfv.* [*pfv.* **искроши́ть**; *pres.* крошу́, кро́шишь] **1,** to chop up. **2,** to crumble. **3,** [*impfv. only*] to spill crumbs. —**кроши́ться,** *refl.* to crumble; disintegrate.

кро́шка [*gen. pl.* -шек] *n.* crumb. —**ни кро́шки,** not a bit.

круг [*2nd loc.* кру́ге *or* кругу́; *pl.* круги́] *n.* **1,** circle. **2,** *fig.* (*with gen.*) circle (*of people*); sphere; range (*of activities*). **3,** detour: сде́лать круг, to make a detour. **4,** *sports* lap. —**гонча́рный круг,** potter's wheel. —**поворо́тный круг,** turntable. —**спаса́тельный круг,** life buoy.

кру́гленький *adj.* **1,** round. **2,** chubby; plump. —**кру́гленькая су́мма,** a tidy sum.

кругле́ть *v. impfv.* to become round.

круглоли́цый *adj.* round-faced.

круглосу́точный *adj.* twenty-four-hour (*attrib.*); round-the-clock.

кру́глый *adj.* **1,** round. **2,** (*with periods of time*) all: кру́глые су́тки, day and night; round the clock. **3,** *colloq.* utter. —**кру́глый** (*or* **кру́глая**) **сирота́,** child who has lost both parents. —**кру́глая су́мма,** a tidy sum. —**кру́глым счётом,** in round figures.

кругово́й *adj.* circular. —**кругова́я доро́га,** roundabout route. —**кругова́я систе́ма,** *sports* round robin. —**кругова́я ча́ша,** loving cup.

кругово́рот *n.* **1,** rotation. **2,** *fig.* constant flow (*of events, life, etc.*).

кругозо́р *n.* **1,** range of vision. **2,** *fig.* outlook; range of interests.

круго́м *adv.* **1,** (all) around. **2,** *colloq.* entirely. —*prep.,* with *gen., colloq.* around. —*interj., mil.* about face!

кругообра́зный *adj.* circular.

кругосве́тный *adj.* round-the-world.

кружевно́й *adj.* lace (*attrib.*).

кру́жево [*often pl.* -жева́, кру́жев, -жева́м] *n.* lace.

круже́ние *n.* whirling; swirling.

кружи́ть *v. impfv.* [*pres.* кружу́, кру́жишь *or* кру-жи́шь] **1,** *v.t.* to twirl; whirl; swirl. **2,** *v.i.* to spin; circle; swirl. **3,** *colloq.* to wander. —**кружи́ть го́лову** (+ *dat.*), **1,** to make (someone) dizzy. **2,** [*pfv.* вскружи́ть] to turn someone's head; go to one's head.

кружи́ться *v.r. impfv.* [*pres.* кружу́сь, кру́жишься *or* кружи́шься] **1,** to spin; whirl; go round: у меня́ кру́жится голова́, my head is spinning. **2,** (*of a bird, plane, etc.*) to circle. **3,** (*of dust, snow, etc.*) to swirl. **4,** *colloq.* to wander.

кру́жка [*gen. pl.* -жек] *n.* **1,** mug; tankard. **2,** poorbox.

кру́жный *adj., colloq.* roundabout; circuitous.

кружо́к [*gen.* -жка́] *n.* **1,** *dim. of* круг. **2,** circle; group; club.

круи́з *n.* cruise.

круп *n.* **1,** *med.* croup. **2,** croup (*of a horse*).

крупа́ *n.* **1,** groats. **2,** sleet. —**гре́чневая крупа́,** buckwheat. —**ма́нная крупа́,** farina. —**овся́ная крупа́,** oatmeal. —**перло́вая крупа́,** pearl barley.

крупи́нка [*gen. pl.* -нок] *n.* grain.

крупи́ца *n.* **1,** grain. **2,** *fig.* grain; ounce; particle.

кру́пно *adv.* **1,** into large pieces. **2,** with large strides or strokes. **3,** using strong language: кру́пно погово-ри́ть с, to use strong language with.

крупномасшта́бный *adj.* (*of a map*) large-scale.

кру́пный *adj.* **1,** large. **2,** major; prominent; important. **3,** (*of sand*) coarse. —**кру́пный план,** close-up. —**кру́пный разгово́р,** sharp words; sharp exchange.

крупча́тый *adj.* grainy; coarse.

крупье́ *n.m. indecl.* croupier.

крупяно́й *adj.* groats (*attrib.*).

крутизна́ *n.* **1,** steepness. **2,** steep slope.

крути́ть *v. impfv.* [*pres.* кручу́, кру́тишь] **1,** [*pfv.* зак-рути́ть] to turn; twist; twirl. **2,** [*pfv.* скрути́ть] to twist (cloth, rope, etc.); roll (a cigarette). **3,** [*impfv. only*] to whirl; swirl (dust, snow, etc.). **4,** *v.i.* [*impfv. only*] (*of a snowstorm*) to swirl. —**крути́ться,** *refl.* [*impfv. only*]

1, to turn; spin; gyrate; whirl. **2,** *fig., colloq.* to hang around.

кру́то *adv.* **1,** steeply. **2,** abruptly; sharply. **3,** tightly. **4,** harshly.

круто́й *adj.* [*comp.* кру́че] **1,** steep. **2,** sharp; abrupt. **3,** drastic. **4,** stern. **5,** (*of foods*) thick. —**круто́е яйцо́,** hard-boiled egg.

кру́тость *n.f.* **1,** steepness; slope. **2,** sternness.

кру́ча *n.* steep slope.

кру́че *adj., comp. of* круто́й.

круче́ние *n.* **1,** twisting. **2,** torsion.

кручи́на *n., poetic* sorrow; grief.

круше́ние *n.* **1,** crash; wreck. **2,** *fig.* downfall; collapse.

круши́на *n.* buckthorn.

круши́ть *v. impfv.* to destroy; shatter; smite.

крыжо́вник *n.* **1,** gooseberries. **2,** a (single) gooseber-ry. **3,** gooseberry shrub.

крыла́тый *adj.* winged. —**крыла́тая раке́та,** cruise missile. —**крыла́тые слова́,** pithy saying; popular expression.

крыле́чко [*gen. pl.* -чек] *n., dim. of* крыльцо́.

крыло́ [*pl.* кры́лья, -льев, -льям] *n.* **1,** wing. **2,** fender. **3,** blade; vane.

кры́лышко [*gen. pl.* -шек] *n., dim. of* крыло́. —**взять под своё кры́лышко,** to take under one's wing.

крыльцо́ [*pl.* кры́льца, -ле́ц, -льца́м] *n.* porch.

кры́мский *adj.* Crimean.

кры́нка [*gen. pl.* -нок] *n.* milk jug.

кры́са *n.* rat. —**крыси́ный,** *adj.* rat (*attrib.*).

крысоло́вка [*gen. pl.* -вок] *n.* rattrap.

кры́тый *adj.* covered; sheltered.

крыть *v. impfv.* [*pfv.* покры́ть; *pres.* кро́ю, кро́ешь] to cover. —**кры́ться,** *refl.* [*impfv. only*] to lie (beneath the surface): что за э́тим кро́ется?, what's behind it all?

кры́ша *n.* roof. —**застеклённая кры́ша,** skylight.

кры́шка [*gen. pl.* -шек] *n.* lid; cover.

крюк [*gen.* крюка́; *pl.* крю́чья, -чьев *or* крюки́, -ко́в] *n.* **1,** hook. **2,** *colloq.* detour.

крючкова́тый *adj.* hooked.

крючкотво́рство *n., obs.* pettifoggery; chicanery.

крючо́к [*gen.* -чка́] *n.* **1,** hook. **2,** curlicue. —**рыбо-ло́вный крючо́к,** fishhook. —**спусково́й крючо́к,** trigger.

крюшо́н *n.* punch made of white wine, liqueur, and fruit.

кря́ду *adv., colloq.* in a row; running.

кряж *n.* **1,** ridge (*of mountains*). **2,** block; stump (*of wood*).

кря́жистый *adj.* **1,** (*of a tree*) sturdy. **2,** *fig.* stocky; thickset.

кря́канье *n.* **1,** quacking. **2,** grunting.

кря́кать *v. impfv.* [*pfv.* кря́кнуть] **1,** to quack. **2,** *colloq.* to grunt.

кря́ква *n.* wild duck; mallard.

кря́кнуть *v., pfv. of* кря́кать.

кряхте́ть *v. impfv.* [*pres.* -хчу́, -хти́шь] *colloq.* to groan.

ксено́н *n.* xenon.

ксилогра́фия *n.* wood engraving.

ксилофо́н *n.* xylophone.

кста́ти *adv.* **1,** incidentally; by the way. **2,** timely; apro-pos; to the point. **3,** at the same time; while you're at it. —**приходи́ться кста́ти,** to come in handy.

кто [*gen. & acc.* кого́; *dat.* кому́; *instr.* кем; *prepl.*

ком] *pron.* **1,** *interr.* who?; whom?: кто зна́ет?, who knows? **2,** *rel.* who; whom: те, кто хо́чет идти́..., those wishing to go... Он тот, кого́ никто́ не лю́бит, he is the one (whom) no one likes. **3,** *indef., colloq.* anyone; someone: е́сли кто спро́сит, if anyone asks. —**кто (бы) ни,** whoever. —**кто бы то ни́ был,** whoever it may be. —**кто где,** in various places. —**кто как,** in various ways. —**кто куда́,** in various directions.

кто́-либо *indef. pron.* = **кто́-нибудь.**

кто́-нибудь *indef. pron.* someone; somebody; anyone; anybody.

кто́-то *indef. pron.* someone; somebody.

куб [*pl.* кубы́] *n.* **1,** cube (*figure*). **2,** *math.* cube (*third power*). **3,** *colloq.* cubic meter. **4,** boiler. —**перего́нный куб,** still (*for distilling liquids*).

ку́барем *adv., colloq.,* in **кати́ться ку́барем,** to roll head over heels.

куба́рь [*gen.* -баря́] *n.m.* peg top.

кубату́ра *n.* cubic capacity.

куби́зм *n., art* cubism.

ку́бик *n.* **1,** *dim. of* куб. **2,** *pl.* (children's) blocks. **3,** *colloq.* cubic centimeter.

куби́нец [*gen.* -нца] *n.m.* [*fem.* -нка] Cuban. —**куби́нский,** *adj.* Cuban.

куби́ческий *adj.* cubic. —**куби́ческий ко́рень,** cube root.

ку́бовый *adj.* deep blue.

ку́бок [*gen.* -бка] *n.* **1,** goblet. **2,** *sports* trophy; cup.

кубоме́тр *n.* cubic meter.

ку́брик *n., naut.* crew's quarters.

кубы́шка [*gen. pl.* -шек] *n.* **1,** money box. **2,** *colloq.* plump woman.

кува́лда *n.* sledgehammer.

кувши́н *n.* pitcher; jug.

кувши́нка [*gen. pl.* -нок] *n.* water lily.

кувырка́ться *v.r. impfv.* [*pfv.* кувыркну́ться *or* кувырну́ться] to somersault; turn somersaults; tumble.

кувырко́м *adv., colloq.* head over heels.

кугуа́р *n.* cougar.

куда́ *adv.* **1,** *interr.* (*with verbs of motion*) where?; which way?: куда́ ты идёшь?, where are you going? Куда́ мне э́то положи́ть?, where should I put it? **2,** *rel.* (*with verbs of motion*) where; to which: я не зна́ю, куда́ мы идём, I don't know where we're going. Го́род, куда́ его́ сосла́ли, the city to which he was exiled. **3,** *colloq.* what for?: куда́ вам сто́лько де́нег?, what do you need all that money for? **4,** *colloq.* much; much more: куда́ лу́чше, much better. —**куда́ (бы) ни,** wherever. —**куда́ ни шло,** all right; very well.

куда́-либо *adv.* = **куда́-нибудь.**

куда́-нибудь *adv.* somewhere; anywhere.

куда́-то *adv.* somewhere; to some place.

куда́хтанье *n.* cackle.

куда́хтать *v. impfv.* [*pres.* -хчу, -хчешь] to cackle.

куде́ль *n.f.* tow (*fiber*).

куде́сник *n.* sorcerer.

кудла́тый *adj., colloq.* shaggy.

ку́дри [*gen.* -дре́й] *n. pl.* curls.

кудря́вый *adj.* **1,** (*of hair*) curly. **2,** curly-headed. **3,** leafy; lush. **4,** *fig.* flowery.

кудря́шки *n. pl.* [*sing.* -шка] ringlets (*of hair*).

кузе́н (зэ) *n.* (male) cousin.

кузи́на *n.* (female) cousin.

кузне́ц [*gen.* -неца́] *n.* blacksmith.

кузне́чик *n.* grasshopper.

кузне́чный *adj.* blacksmith's.

ку́зница *n.* blacksmith's shop; smithy; forge.

ку́зов [*pl.* кузова́] *n.* **1,** basket. **2,** body (*of a car or carriage*).

кукаре́канье *n.* crowing; crow (*of a rooster*).

кукаре́кать *v. impfv.* (*of a rooster*) to crow.

ку́киш *n., colloq.* fig (*insulting gesture*).

ку́кла [*gen. pl.* -кол] *n.* **1,** doll. **2,** puppet.

кукова́ть *v. impfv.* [*pres.* -ку́ет] to cuckoo; cry "cuckoo".

ку́колка [*gen. pl.* -лок] *n.* **1,** *dim. of* ку́кла. **2,** *zool.* chrysalis; pupa.

ку́коль *n.m.* cockle (*weed*).

ку́кольный *adj.* **1,** doll (*attrib.*). **2,** puppet (*attrib.*).

ку́кситься *v.r. impfv.* [*pres.* -шусь, -сишься] *colloq.* to sulk; mope.

кукуру́за *n.* corn. —**кукуру́зный,** *adj.* corn (*attrib.*).

куку́шка [*gen. pl.* -шек] *n.* cuckoo.

кула́к [*gen.* -лака́] *n.* **1,** fist. **2,** kulak. **3,** *mech.* cam. —**держа́ть в кулаке́,** to keep under one's thumb. —**смея́ться в кула́к,** to laugh up one's sleeve.

кула́цкий *adj.* of the kulaks; kulak (*attrib.*).

кула́чество *n.* the kulaks.

кула́чки *n. pl.,* in **би́ться** *or* **дра́ться на кула́чках,** to engage in fisticuffs; spar.

кулачко́вый *adj.,* in **кулачко́вый вал,** camshaft.

кула́чный *adj.* with fists: кула́чный бой, fisticuffs.

кулачо́к [*gen.* -чка́] *n.* **1,** *dim. of* кула́к. **2,** *mech.* cam.

кулебя́ка *n.* pie with meat, fish, or cabbage filling.

кулёк [*gen.* -лька́] *n.* small bag.

ку́ли *n.m. indecl.* coolie.

кули́к [*gen.* -лика́] *n.* snipe.

кулина́рия *n.* **1,** (the art of) cooking; cookery. **2,** delicatessen: отде́л кулина́рии, delicatessen department. —**кулина́рный,** *adj.* culinary.

кули́сы *n. pl.* [*sing.* кули́са] *theat.* wings. —**за кули́сами,** backstage; behind the scenes.

кули́ч [*gen.* -лича́] *n.* Easter cake.

кули́чки *n. pl.,* in **у чёрта на кули́чках,** in the middle of nowhere; at the ends of the earth.

куло́н *n.* **1,** pendant. **2,** coulomb (*unit of electricity*).

кулуа́ры [*gen. pl.* -ров] *n. pl.* corridors. —**кулуа́рный,** *adj.* in the corridors: кулуа́рные разгово́ры, talk in the corridors.

куль [*gen.* куля́] *n.m.* sack.

кульмина́ция *n.* culmination. —**кульминацио́нный,** *adj.* climactic: кульминацио́нный пункт, climax; culmination.

культ *n.* cult.

культиви́ровать *v. impfv.* [*pres.* -рую, -руешь] to cultivate.

культу́ра *n.* **1,** culture. **2,** (*with gen.*) standard (of); level (of). **3,** (*with gen.*) *agric.* cultivation (of). **4,** crop: кормовы́е культу́ры, forage crops. **5,** *bacteriology* culture.

культу́рность *n.f.* level of culture; high degree of culture.

культу́рный *adj.* **1,** cultural. **2,** cultured. **3,** refined; gracious.

культя́ *n.* stump (*of an amputated limb*).

кум [*pl.* кумовья́, -вёв] *n.* **1,** godfather of one's child. **2,** father of one's godchild. **3,** (*with respect to a godmother*) co-sponsor; godparent in common.

кума́ *n.* **1,** godmother of one's child. **2,** mother of one's godchild. **3,** (*with respect to a godfather*) co-sponsor; godparent in common.

кумани́ка *n.* bramble (*shrub*).

кума́ч [*gen.* **-мача́**] *n.* bright red cotton cloth. —**кума́чный,** *adj.* made of this material.

куми́р *n.* idol.

кумовство́ *n., colloq.* nepotism.

ку́мушка [*gen. pl.* **-шек**] *n.* **1,** *dim. of* **кума́. 2,** gossipmonger.

кумы́к *n.m.* [*fem.* **-мы́чка**] Kumyk (*one of a people inhabiting the Caucasus*). —**кумы́кский,** *adj.* Kumyk.

кумы́с *n.* fermented mare's milk; kumiss.

кунжу́т *n.* sesame. —**кунжу́тный,** *adj.* sesame (*attrib.*).

куни́ца *n.* marten.

ку́па *n.* clump (*of trees, bushes, etc.*).

купа́льник *n., colloq.* bathing suit.

купа́льный *adj.* bathing (*attrib.*): купа́льный костю́м, bathing suit.

купа́льня [*gen. pl.* **-лен**] *n.* bathhouse.

купа́льщик *n.* bather.

купа́ние *n.* bathing.

купа́ть *v. impfv.* [*pfv.* **вы́купать**] to bathe; give a bath to. —**купа́ться,** *refl.* **1,** to bathe; take a bath. **2,** to go bathing; go swimming.

купе́ (пэ) *n. neut. indecl.* compartment (*on a train*).

купе́ль *n.f., eccles.* font; baptistery.

купе́ц [*gen.* **-пца́**] *n.* merchant. —**купе́ческий,** *adj.* merchants'. —**купе́чество,** *n.* the merchants (*as an economic class*).

Купидо́н *n.* Cupid.

купи́ть [*infl.* **куплю́, ку́пишь**] *v., pfv. of* **покупа́ть.**

купле́т *n.* **1,** verse; stanza. **2,** *pl.* satiric songs.

ку́пля *n.* purchase.

ку́пол [*pl.* **купола́**] *n.* dome; cupola.

купо́н *n.* coupon.

купоро́с *n.* vitriol. —**желе́зный купоро́с,** green vitriol; ferrous sulfate. —**ме́дный купоро́с,** blue vitriol; copper sulfate. —**ци́нковый купоро́с,** white vitriol; zinc sulfate.

купчи́ха *n.* **1,** woman merchant. **2,** merchant's wife.

купю́ра *n.* **1,** cut; deletion. **2,** bill (*paper money*).

курага́ *n.* dried apricots.

кура́житься *v.r. impfv., colloq.* **1,** to swagger; boast. **2,** (*with* **над**) to lord it over. **3,** to act coy.

кура́нты [*gen.* **-тов**] *n. pl.* chimes.

курга́н *n.* burial mound.

курд *n.m.* [*fem.* **-дя́нка**] Kurd. —**ку́рдский,** *adj.* Kurdish.

ку́рево *n., colloq.* something to smoke.

куре́ние *n.* **1,** smoking. **2,** incense.

кури́льница *n.* censer.

кури́льня [*gen. pl.* **-лен**] *n.* place where narcotics are smoked: кури́льня о́пиума, opium den.

кури́льщик *n.* smoker; one who smokes.

кури́ный *adj.* chicken (*attrib.*); chicken's; hen's. —**кури́ная слепота́,** night blindness.

кури́тельный *adj.* smoking (*attrib.*).

кури́ть *v. impfv.* [*pres.* **курю́, ку́ришь**] to smoke. —**кури́ться,** *refl.* to smoke; give off smoke.

ку́рица [*pl.* **ку́ры, кур**] *n.* hen; chicken. —**мо́края ку́рица,** milksop.

ку́рия *n.* curia.

куркума́ *n.* turmeric.

курно́сый *adj.* **1,** *in* курно́сый нос, pug nose. **2,** pug-nosed; snub-nosed.

курово́дство *n.* poultry breeding.

куро́к [*gen.* **-рка́**] *n.* cock; hammer (*of a firearm*). —**спуска́ть куро́к,** to pull the trigger.

куропа́тка [*gen. pl.* **ток**] *n.* partridge. —**бе́лая куропа́тка,** ptarmigan.

куро́рт *n.* resort. —**куро́ртник,** *n., colloq.* person staying at a resort. —**куро́ртный,** *adj.* resort (*attrib.*).

курослеп *n.* buttercup.

ку́рочка [*gen. pl.* **-чек**] *n.* **1,** pullet. **2,** crake. —**водяна́я ку́рочка,** gallinule.

курс *n.* **1,** course: измени́ть курс, to change course. **2,** policy: ми́рный курс, peaceful policy. **3,** course (*of instruction*): (про)слу́шать курс, to take a course. **4,** year (*in school*). **5,** rate: курс валю́ты, rate of exchange. **6,** *in* курс лече́ния, course of treatment. —**быть в ку́рсе** (+ *gen.*), to be up on. —**в ку́рсе де́ла,** aware of what is going on. —**вводи́ть (кого-нибудь) в курс (де́ла),** to bring someone up to date. —**держа́ть (кого-нибудь) в ку́рсе,** to keep someone informed.

курса́нт *n.* **1,** student. **2,** cadet.

курси́в *n.* italics. —**курси́вный,** *adj.* italic.

курси́ровать *v. impfv.* [*pres.* **-рую, -руешь**] to ply; travel back and forth.

курсо́вка *n.* document entitling the bearer to treatment and meals (but not accommodations) at a sanitarium.

курсово́й *adj.* course (*attrib.*). —**курсова́я рабо́та,** term paper. —**курсово́й экза́мен,** final examination.

куртиза́нка [*gen. pl.* **-нок**] *n.* courtesan.

ку́ртка [*gen. pl.* **-ток**] *n.* (man's) jacket.

курча́вый *adj.* **1,** (*of hair*) curly. **2,** curly-headed.

ку́ры *n., pl. of* **ку́рица.**

курьёз *n.* funny thing; queer thing. —**курьёзный,** *adj.* strange; odd; queer; curious.

курье́р *n.* **1,** courier. **2,** messenger; errand boy.

курье́рский *adj.* courier's. —**курье́рский по́езд,** express train.

куря́тина *n., colloq.* chicken (*as food*).

куря́тник *n.* henhouse; chicken coop.

куря́щий *n., decl. as an adj.* smoker. —**ваго́н для куря́щих,** smoking car.

куса́ть *v. impfv.* [*pfv.* **укуси́ть**] to bite. —**куса́ться,** *refl.* [*impfv. only*] **1,** to bite; have a tendency to bite. **2,** to bite each other.

куса́чки [*gen.* **-чек**] *n. pl.* cutting pliers; wire cutter.

кусково́й *adj.* lump (*attrib.*): кусково́й са́хар, lump sugar.

кусо́к [*gen.* **-ска́**] *n.* **1,** piece; bit. **2,** slice (*of bread*); lump (*of sugar*); bar (*of soap*).

кусо́чек [*gen.* **-чка**] *n., dim. of* **кусо́к.**

куст [*gen.* **куста́**] *n.* bush; shrub.

куста́рник *n.* bushes; shrubs; shrubbery.

куста́рный *adj.* **1,** handicraft (*attrib.*). **2,** *fig.* crude; primitive.

куста́рь [*gen.* **-старя́**] *n.m.* handicraftsman.

ку́тать *v. impfv.* [*pfv.* **заку́тать**] to wrap; bundle. —**ку́таться,** *refl.* (*with* **в** + *acc.*) to wrap/bundle oneself in.

кутёж [*gen.* **-тежа́**] *n.* drinking spree; binge.

кутерьма́ *n., colloq.* commotion.

кути́ла *n.m., colloq.* reveler; carouser.

кути́ть *v. impfv.* [*pres.* **кучу́, ку́тишь**] to carouse.

куту́зка [*gen. pl.* **-зок**] *n., obs., colloq.* jail; hoosegow.

куха́рка [*gen. pl.* **-рок**] *n.* cook.

ку́хня [*gen. pl.* -хонь] *n.* **1,** kitchen. **2,** cooking; cuisine; cookery. —**ку́хонный,** *adj.* kitchen (*attrib.*).

ку́цый *adj.* **1,** (*of a tail*) short. **2,** short-tailed. **3,** (*of clothes*) skimpy. **4,** *fig.* limited; reduced; incomplete.

ку́ча *n.* **1,** pile; heap. **2,** (*with gen.*) *colloq.* heaps (of); lots (of). —**вали́ть в одну́ ку́чу,** to lump together.

кучево́й *adj.* (*of clouds*) cumulous.

ку́чер [*pl.* кучера́] *n.* coachman.

ку́чка [*gen. pl.* -чек] *n.* **1,** *dim. of* ку́ча. **2,** small circle (*of people*).

куш *n.* **1,** bet (*in a card game*). **2,** *colloq.* large sum of money. —**сорва́ть куш,** to clean up; make a killing.

куша́к [*gen.* -шака́] *n.* sash.

ку́шанье *n.* food.

ку́шать *v. impfv.* [*pfv.* поку́шать] to eat.

куше́тка [*gen. pl.* -ток] *n.* couch.

кш *interj.* shoo! Also, кыш.

кюве́т *n.* ditch (*along the side of a road*).

кю́рий *n.* curium.

Л

Л, л *n. neut.* twelfth letter of the Russian alphabet.

лабири́нт *n.* labyrinth; maze.

лабора́нт *n.* laboratory assistant.

лаборато́рия *n.* laboratory. —**лаборато́рный,** *adj.* laboratory (*attrib.*).

ла́ва *n.* lava.

лава́нда *n.* lavender. —**лава́ндовый,** *adj.* lavender (*attrib.*).

лави́на *n.* avalanche.

лави́ровать *v. impfv.* [*pres.* -рую, -руешь] **1,** *naut.* to tack with the wind. **2,** *fig.* to maneuver.

ла́вка [*gen. pl.* -вок] *n.* **1,** bench. **2,** shop; store.

ла́вочка [*gen. pl.* -чек] *n.* **1,** small bench. **2,** small shop; small store. —**закры́ть ла́вочку,** to close up shop.

ла́вочник *n.,* *obs.* shopkeeper.

лавр *n.* **1,** laurel. **2,** laurel wreath. **3,** *pl.,* *fig.* laurels: почива́ть на ла́врах, to rest on one's laurels.

ла́вра *n.* large monastery: Пече́рская ла́вра, Monastery of the Caves (*in Kiev*).

лавро́вый *also,* **ла́вровый** *adj.* laurel (*attrib.*). —**лавро́вый лист,** bay leaf.

лавса́н *n.* a polyester fiber similar to dacron; lavsan.

ла́герный *adj.* camp (*attrib.*).

ла́герь *n.m.* **1,** [*pl.* лагеря́] camp. **2,** [*pl.* ла́гери] *fig.* camp; side; faction.

лагу́на *n.* lagoon.

лад [*2nd loc.* ладу́; *pl.* лады́] *n.* **1,** *colloq.* harmony (*between people*). **2,** way: на друго́й лад, a different way. **3,** *music* key; tone. **4,** *usu. pl.* fret (*of a stringed instrument*); key (*of an accordion*). —**в лад, 1,** in harmony; in tune. **2,** (*with dat.*) in time to. —**в ладу́; в лада́х,** on good terms. —**на все лады́,** thoroughly; from all angles. —**не в ладу́; не в лада́х,** on the outs. —**де́ло идёт на лад,** *colloq.* things are going well. —**запе́ть на друго́й лад,** to change one's tune; sing a different tune. —**перестро́ить на вое́нный лад,** to place on a war footing.

ла́дан *n.* **1,** incense. **2,** *in* ро́сный ла́дан, benzoin. —**дыша́ть на ла́дан,** to be near death; have one foot in the grave. —**как чёрт от ла́дана,** (*with verbs of shunning, fearing, etc.*) like the plague.

ла́данка [*gen. pl.* -нок] *n.* amulet.

ла́дить *v. impfv.* [*pres.* ла́жу, ла́дишь] (*with* с + *instr.*) to get along (with); be on good terms (with). —**ла́диться,** *refl.* to get on well; proceed satisfactorily: де́ло не ла́дится, things are not working out well.

ла́дно *particle, colloq.* all right; O.K. —*adv., colloq.* **1,** harmoniously. **2,** well.

ла́дный *adj., colloq.* **1,** graceful. **2,** harmonious. **3,** well-built; well-made.

ладо́нь *n.f.* palm of the hand. —**ви́дно как на ладо́ни,** clearly visible.

ладо́ши *n. pl., in* хло́пать *or* бить в ладо́ши, to clap one's hands.

ладья́ *n., chess* rook; castle.

лаз *n.* manhole.

ла́занье *n.* climbing.

лазаре́т *n.* **1,** field hospital. **2,** infirmary.

лазе́йка [*gen. pl.* -зе́ек] *n.* **1,** small opening. **2,** *fig.* loophole: оста́вить себе́ лазе́йку, to leave oneself a loophole.

ла́зер *n.* laser. —**ла́зерный,** *adj.* laser (*attrib.*).

ла́зить *v. impfv.* [*pres.* ла́жу, ла́зишь] *indeterm. of* лезть.

лазу́рный *adj.* light-blue; azure.

лазу́рь *n.f.* light blue; azure. —**берли́нская лазу́рь,** Prussian blue.

лазу́тчик *n., obs.* **1,** scout. **2,** spy.

лай *n.* bark; barking.

ла́йка [*gen. pl.* ла́ек] *n.* **1,** husky (*dog*). **2,** kidskin. —**ла́йковый,** *adj.* kid (*attrib.*); kidskin (*attrib.*): ла́йковые перча́тки, kid gloves.

лайм *n.* lime (*fruit & tree*).

ла́йнер *n.* ocean liner. —**возду́шный ла́йнер,** airliner.

лак *n.* lacquer; varnish; polish. —**лак для ногте́й,** nail polish.

лака́ть *v. impfv.* [*pfv.* вы́лакать] to lap; lap up.

лаке́й *n.* **1,** footman. **2,** *fig.* lackey.

лаке́йский *adj.* **1,** of a footman. **2,** *fig.* servile.

лакиро́ванный *adj.* **1,** lacquered. Лакиро́ванные

изде́лия, lacquerware. **2,** gleaming; lustrous. —**лаки-ро́ванная ко́жа,** patent leather. —**лакиро́ванные ту́фли,** patent-leather shoes.

лакирова́ть *v. impfv.* [*pfv.* **отлакирова́ть**; *pres.* -ру́ю, -ру́ешь] **1,** to lacquer; varnish. **2,** [*impfv. only*] *fig.* to varnish; embellish.

лакиро́вка *n.* lacquering; varnishing.

ла́кмус *n.* litmus. —**ла́кмусовый,** *adj.* litmus (*attrib.*): ла́кмусовая бума́га, litmus paper.

ла́ковый *adj.* **1,** lacquer (*attrib.*). **2,** lacquered.

ла́комиться *v.r. impfv.* [*pfv.* **пола́комиться**; *pres.* -млюсь, -мишься] (*with instr.*) to feast on.

ла́комка [*gen. pl.* **-мок**] *n.m. & f., colloq.* person with a sweet tooth.

ла́комство *n.* **1,** *usu. pl.* sweets. **2,** delicacy.

ла́комый *adj.* **1,** tasty; luscious. **2,** [*short form only*] (*with* **до**) *colloq.* fond (of); having a weakness (for). —**ла́комый кусо́чек,** tempting morsel; prize catch.

лакони́зм *n.* terseness; brevity.

лакони́ческий *adj.* laconic.

лакони́чный *adj.* laconic. —**лакони́чность,** *n.f.* terseness; brevity.

лакри́ца *n.* licorice. —**лакри́чный,** *adj.* licorice.

лакта́ция *n.* lactation.

лакто́за *n.* lactose.

лакфио́ль *n.f.* wallflower.

ла́ма¹ *n.* llama.

ла́ма² *n.* lama. —**ламаи́зм,** *n.* Lamaism. —**ламаи́ст-ский,** *adj.* of or pert. to Lamaism.

ламанти́н *n.* manatee.

ла́мпа *n.* **1,** lamp. **2,** *radio tube:* электро́нная ла́мпа, vacuum tube. —**ла́мпа дневно́го све́та,** daylight lamp.

лампа́да *n.* icon lamp.

лампа́с *n.* stripe (*on the side of uniform trousers*).

ла́мповый *adj.* lamp (*attrib.*).

ла́мпочка [*gen. pl.* **-чек**] *n.* **1,** *dim. of* ла́мпа. **2,** (electric light) bulb.

ланге́т *n.* sliced steak.

лангу́ст *also,* **лангу́ста** *n.* spiny lobster.

ландша́фт *n.* landscape.

ла́ндыш *n.* lily of the valley. ·

ланоли́н *n.* lanolin.

ланта́н *n.* lanthanum.

ланце́т *n.* lancet.

лань *n.f.* fallow deer.

ла́па *n.* **1,** paw. **2,** claw (*of a hammer*); fluke (*of an anchor*). —**попа́сть в ла́пы** (+ *dat. or with* **к**), to fall into the clutches of.

ла́пка [*gen. pl.* **-пок**] *n.* **1,** paw. **2,** *in* гуси́ные ла́пки, crow's-feet (*near the eye*). —**ходи́ть на за́дних ла́пках пе́ред,** to kowtow to; bow and scrape to.

ла́поть [*gen.* **-птя**; *pl.* ла́пти, -пте́й, -птя́м] *n.m.* sandal made of bark.

лапта́ *n.* **1,** Russian game, somewhat like baseball. **2,** wooden bat used in this game.

лапша́ *n.* **1,** noodles. **2,** noodle soup.

лапше́вник *n.* noodle pudding.

ла́рго *n. neut. & adv., music* largo.

ларёк [*gen.* **-рька́**] *n.* stall; booth.

ларе́ц [*gen.* **-рца́**] *n.* small box or case (*for valuables*).

ларинги́т *n.* laryngitis.

ла́рчик *n.* small box. —а ла́рчик про́сто открыва́лся, the explanation was quite simple.

ларь [*gen.* **ларя́**] *n.m.* bin.

ла́ска *n.* **1,** [*gen. pl.* **ласк**] caress. **2,** [*sing. only*] kindness. **3,** [*gen. pl.* **ла́сок**] weasel.

ласка́тельный *adj.* **1,** tender. **2,** *gram.* of endearment: ласка́тельное и́мя, endearing form of a name.

ласка́ть *v. impfv.* **1,** to caress; fondle; pet. **2,** *fig.* to please; delight (the senses). —**ласка́ться,** *refl.* (*with* **к**) **1,** to snuggle up (to). **2,** *obs.* to play up to.

ла́сковый *adj.* **1,** affectionate; tender. **2,** *fig.* (*of a breeze, sound, etc.*) gentle.

лассо́ *n. indecl.* lasso; lariat.

ласт *n.* flipper (*of a seal, walrus, etc.*).

ла́стик *n.* **1,** lasting. **2,** *colloq.* eraser.

ла́сточка [*gen. pl.* **-чек**] *n.* swallow (*bird*). —**пе́рвая ла́сточка,** first sign. —**прыжо́к в во́ду ла́сточкой,** swan dive.

ла́сточкин *adj.* of a swallow; swallows': ла́сточкино гнездо́, swallows' nest. —**ла́сточкин хвост,** dovetail.

лата́ть *v. impfv.* [*pfv.* **залата́ть**] *colloq.* to patch; patch up.

латви́йский *adj.* Latvian.

ла́текс *n.* latex.

лате́нтный *adj.* latent.

лати́нский *adj.* **1,** Latin. **2,** (*of the alphabet, characters, etc.*) Roman.

ла́тный *adj.* armor (*attrib.*). —**ла́тные доспе́хи,** suit of armor.

лату́к *n.* lettuce.

лату́нь *n.f.* brass. —**лату́нный,** *adj.* brass.

ла́ты [*gen.* **лат**] *n. pl.* armor.

латы́нь *n.f., colloq.* Latin.

латы́ш [*gen.* **-тыша́**] *n.m.* [*fem.* **-ты́шка**] Latvian; Lett. —**латы́шский,** *adj.* Latvian; Lettish.

лауреа́т *n.* laureate.

лафе́т *n.* gun carriage.

ла́цкан *n.* lapel.

лачу́га *n.* shanty; hovel.

ла́ять *v. impfv.* [*pres.* **ла́ю, ла́ешь**] to bark.

лганьё *n.* **1,** lying. **2,** lies.

лгать *v. impfv.* [*pfv.* **солга́ть**; *pres.* **лгу, лжёшь, ... лгут;** *past fem.* **лгала́**] to lie; tell lies.

лгун [*gen.* **лгуна́**] *n.m.* [*fem.* **лгу́нья**] liar.

лебеди́ный *adj.* **1,** swan (*attrib.*); of swans. **2,** like that of a swan; graceful. —**лебеди́ная пе́сня,** swan song.

лебёдка [*gen. pl.* **-док**] *n.* **1,** female swan. **2,** *mech.* winch.

ле́бедь [*pl.* **ле́беди, -де́й, -дя́м**] *n.m.* swan.

лебези́ть *v. impfv.* [*pres.* **-жу́, -зи́шь**] (*with* **пе́ред**) *colloq.* to be obsequious (to); kowtow (to).

лебя́жий [*fem.* **-жья**] *adj.* swan (*attrib.*); swan's.

лев [*gen.* **льва**] *n.* **1,** lion. **2,** *cap.* Leo. —**морско́й лев,** sea lion.

леве́ть *v. impfv.* [*pfv.* **полеве́ть**] to move to the left (*politically*).

левиафа́н *n.* leviathan.

Леви́т *n.* Leviticus.

левко́й *n.* gillyflower.

левре́тка [*gen. pl.* **-ток**] *n.* Italian greyhound.

левша́ *n.m. & f.* left-handed person.

ле́вый *adj.* **1,** left; lefthand. **2,** *polit.* left; left-wing. **3,** (*of a side of material*) wrong. **4,** *naut.* port. —*n.* left-winger; leftist. —**встать с ле́вой ноги́,** to get up on the wrong side of the bed.

лега́вый *adj., in* лега́вая соба́ка, pointer; setter.

легализа́ция *n.* legalization.

легализи́ровать *v. impfv. & pfv.* [*pres.* -ру́ю, -ру́-ешь] to legalize. *Also,* **легализова́ть** [*pres.* -зу́ю, -зу́-ешь].

лега́льный *adj.* legal. —**лега́льность,** *n.f.* legality.

лега́то *n. neut. & adv., music* legato.

леге́нда *n.* legend. —**легенда́рный,** *adj.* legendary.

легио́н *n.* legion. —**легионе́р,** *n.* legionnaire.

лёгкий *adj.* [*short form* лёгок, легка́, легко́; *comp.* ле́гче] **1,** light (*in weight*). **2,** easy. **3,** not severe; light; slight; mild. **4,** graceful; light. **5,** (*of a breeze, nudge, etc.*) slight; gentle. **6,** (*of foods*) light; soft; bland; (*of a meal*) light. **7,** (*of music, reading, etc.*) light. **8,** easygoing. **9,** (*of behavior*) lax; loose. **10,** (*of industry, artillery, etc.*) light. —**лёгкая атле́тика,** track and field. —**лёгкая фигу́ра,** *chess* minor piece. —**лёгок на подъём,** always ready and willing. —**лё-гок на поми́не!,** talk of the devil! —**с лёгкой руки́** (+ *gen.*), thanks to; at the initiative of. —**у него́ лёгкая рука́,** he brings luck; he has a magic touch. *See also* **ле́гче.**

легко́ *adv.* **1,** easily. **2,** lightly. **3,** *in* легко́ ра́неный, slightly wounded. —*adj., used predicatively* easy: легко́ ошиба́ться, it is easy to make a mistake.

легкоатле́т *n.* (track and field) athlete; one taking part in any track or field event. —**легкоатлети́ческий,** *adj.* track-and-field.

легкове́рие *n.* credulity; gullibility. —**легкове́рный,** *adj.* credulous; gullible.

легкове́с *n., sports* lightweight.

легкове́сный *adj.* **1,** lightweight. **2,** *fig.* frivolous.

легково́й *adj., in* легково́й автомоби́ль, passenger car.

лёгкое *n., decl. as an adj.* lung.

легкомы́сленный *adj.* frivolous; flighty. —**легко-мы́слие,** *n.* frivolity.

лёгкость *n.f.* **1,** lightness. **2,** ease; facility.

лёгочный *adj.* lung (*attrib.*); pulmonary.

легча́ть *v. impfv.* [*pfv.* полегча́ть] *colloq.* **1,** to abate; moderate. **2,** *impers.* (*with dat.*) to feel better.

ле́гче *adj., comp. of* лёгкий. —**ле́гче на поворо́тах!,** *colloq.* take it easy!; watch what you're saying! —**ста́ло ле́гче** (*with dat.*), one is feeling somewhat better. —**час от часу не ле́гче!,** things are getting worse by the minute.

лёд [*gen.* льда; *2nd loc.* льду] *n.* ice.

ледене́ть *v. impfv.* [*pfv.* заледене́ть *or* оледене́ть] to freeze; become numb.

ледене́ц [*gen.* -нца́] *n.* piece of hard candy.

ледени́ть *v. impfv.* [*pfv.* оледени́ть] to freeze; cause to freeze.

ле́ди *n.f. indecl.* lady.

ле́дник *n.* **1,** ice house; ice cellar. **2,** icebox; refrigerator.

ледни́к [*gen.* -ника́] *n.* glacier. —**леднико́вый,** *adj.* glacial.

ледо́вый *adj.* **1,** ice (*attrib.*). **2,** (*of a voyage*) made through icy regions.

ледоко́л *n.* icebreaker (*ship*).

ледоста́в *n.* freeze-up (*of a river*).

ледохо́д *n.* drifting of ice.

леды́шка [*gen. pl.* -шек] *n., colloq.* piece of ice.

ледяно́й *adj.* **1,** of ice; ice (*attrib.*). **2,** icy; ice-cold. **3,** *fig.* icy: ледяно́й взгляд, icy look.

лёжа *adv.* in a reclining position; lying down.

лежа́лый *adj.* stale; old.

лежа́нка [*gen. pl.* -нок] *n.* sleeping ledge over a Russian chimney stove.

лежа́ть *v. impfv.* [*pres.* лежу́, лежи́шь] **1,** to lie. **2,** to be; be situated; lie. **3,** (*of responsibility, duties, etc.*) to lie; rest. —**лежа́ть на боку́,** *colloq.* to loaf. —**всё, что пло́хо лежи́т,** everything in sight; everything that is not tied down. —**у него́ душа́ не лежи́т к э́тому,** his heart isn't in it; he has no appetite for it.

лежа́чий *adj.* **1,** lying; recumbent. **2,** *colloq.* confined to bed. —*n., in* бить лежа́чего, to hit a man when he is down.

ле́жбище *n.* breeding ground (*of seals, walruses, etc.*).

лежебо́ка *n.m. & f., colloq.* loafer; lazybones.

лежмя́ *adv., colloq., in* лежмя́ лежа́ть, to lie prostrate.

ле́звие *n.* blade (*of a knife, axe, etc.*). —**ле́звие бри́т-вы,** razor blade.

лезги́н [*gen. pl.* -ги́н] *n.m.* [*fem.* -ги́нка] Lezgin (*one of a people inhabiting the Caucasus*). —**лезги́нский,** *adj.* Lezgin.

лезть *v. impfv.* [*pfv.* поле́зть; *pres.* ле́зу, ле́зешь; *past* лез, ле́зла] **1,** to climb. **2,** (*with в* + *acc.*) to sneak (into). **3,** (*with в* + *acc.*) *colloq.* to reach (into). **4,** [*impfv. only*] *usu. neg.* to fit: ша́пка тебе́ не ле́зет, the hat doesn't fit you. **5,** (*of hair, fur, etc.*) to fall out. **6,** to stick out. —**лезть в буты́лку,** *colloq.* to fly off the handle. —**лезть в го́лову,** (*of thoughts*) to pop into one's head. —**лезть в дра́ку,** to be spoiling for a fight. —**лезть в ду́шу** (+ *dat.*), to worm one's way into someone's confidence. —**лезть в карма́н** (+ *dat.*), to pick someone's pocket. —**лезть в пе́тлю,** to risk one's neck. —**лезть из ко́жи вон,** to try in every way. —**лезть на глаза́** (+ *dat.*), *colloq.* to (try to) catch one's eye. —**лезть (поле́зть) на лоб,** (*of one's eyes*) to pop out of one's head. —**лезть на́ стену,** *colloq.* to fly off the handle; hit the ceiling. —**не лезть в карма́н за сло́вом,** never to be at a loss for words.

лейбори́ст *n.* Labourite. —**лейбори́стский,** *adj.* Labour (*attrib.*).

ле́йка [*gen. pl.* -ле́ек] *n.* **1,** watering can; sprinkling can. **2,** *colloq.* funnel.

лейкеми́я *n.* leukemia.

лейкоци́т *n.* leukocyte.

лейтена́нт *n.* lieutenant.

лейтмоти́в *n.* leitmotiv.

лека́ло *n.* French curve.

лека́рственный *adj.* medicinal.

лека́рство *n.* medicine.

ле́карь [*pl.* ле́кари, -ре́й, -ря́м] *n.m., obs.* doctor.

ле́ксика *n.* vocabulary; lexicon.

лексикогра́фия *n.* lexicography. —**лексико́граф,** *n.* lexicographer. —**лексикографи́ческий,** *adj.* lexicographic.

лексико́н *n.* lexicon.

лекси́ческий *adj.* lexical.

ле́ктор *n.* lecturer.

ле́кция *n.* lecture. —**лекцио́нный,** *adj.* lecture (*attrib.*).

леле́ять *v. impfv.* [*pres.* леле́ю, леле́ешь] **1,** to care for lovingly. **2,** *fig.* to cherish; nurture (a dream, hope, etc.).

ле́мех *also,* леме́х [*pl.* лемеха́] *n.* plowshare.

ле́мминг *n.* lemming.

лему́р *n.* lemur.

лён [*gen.* льна] *n.* flax.

лени́вец [*gen.* -вца] *n.* **1,** lazy person. **2,** *zool.* sloth.

лени́вый *adj.* **1,** lazy. **2,** sluggish.

ле́нинец [*gen.* -нца] *n.* Leninist. —ленини́зм, *n.* Leninism. —ле́нинский, *adj.* Leninist.

лени́ться *v.r. impfv.* [*pres.* леню́сь, ле́нишься] 1, to be lazy. 2, (*with inf.*) to be too lazy (to).

ле́ность *n.f.* laziness.

ле́нта *n.* 1, ribbon. 2, tape. 3, band. 4, film. —конве́йерная ле́нта, conveyer belt. —патро́нная ле́нта, cartridge belt.

ле́нто *n. neut. & adv., music* lento.

ле́нточный *adj.* tape (*attrib.*); band (*attrib.*). —ле́нточная пила́, band saw. —ле́нточный транспортёр, conveyer belt. —ле́нточный червь, tapeworm.

лентя́й *n.m.* [*fem.* -тя́йка] *colloq.* lazy person; lazybones.

лентя́йничать *v. impfv., colloq.* to loaf; idle.

ленца́ *n., colloq.* lazy streak: челове́к с ленцо́й, person with a lazy streak.

ленч *n.* lunch.

лень *n.f.* laziness. —*predicate* (*with dat.*) *colloq.* too lazy: мне лень идти́, I am too lazy to go.

леопа́рд *n.* leopard. —леопа́рдовый, *adj.* leopard (*attrib.*); leopard's.

лепесто́к [*gen.* -стка́] *n.* petal.

ле́пет *n.* babble; prattle.

лепета́ние *n.* babbling; prattling.

лепета́ть *v. impfv.* [*pres.* -печу́, -пе́чешь] to babble; prattle.

лепёшка [*gen. pl.* -шек] *n.* 1, small cake; crumpet. 2, tablet; lozenge. 3, (*with gen.*) clod (*of dirt*).

лепи́ть *v. impfv.* [*pres.* леплю́, ле́пишь] 1, [*pfv.* вы́лепить] to model; fashion; sculpture. 2, [*pfv.* слепи́ть] to make; build (a nest, hive, etc.). —лепи́ться, *refl.* [*impfv. only*] to nestle.

ле́пка *n.* modeling.

лепно́й *adj.* sculptured. —лепно́е украше́ние, molding.

ле́пта *n.* small contribution; mite: вноси́ть свою́ ле́пту, to contribute one's (small) share; do one's bit.

лес [*2nd loc.* лесу́; *pl.* леса́] *n.* 1, forest; woods. 2, timber; lumber. —быть как в лесу́, to be all at sea.

леса́[1] *also,* ле́са [*pl.* лёсы] *n.* fishing line.

леса́[2] [*gen.* лесо́в] *n. pl.* scaffolding.

лесбия́нка [*gen. pl.* -нок] *n.* lesbian. —лесби́йский, *adj.* lesbian.

ле́сенка [*gen. pl.* -нок] *n.* 1, small ladder. 2, short flight of stairs.

леси́стый *adj.* wooded.

ле́ска [*gen. pl.* -сок] *n.* fishing line.

лесни́к [*gen.* -ника́] *n.* forest ranger.

лесни́чество *n.* forest district.

лесни́чий *n., decl. as an adj.* forester.

лесно́й *adj.* 1, forest (*attrib.*). 2, timber (*attrib.*); lumber (*attrib.*). 3, of forestry. —лесна́я земляни́ка, wild strawberries. —лесно́й оре́х, hazelnut.

лесово́д *n.* specialist in forestry. —лесово́дство, *n.* forestry.

лесозаво́д *n.* lumber mill.

лесоматериа́л *n., usu. pl.* timber; lumber.

лесопи́лка [*gen. pl.* -лок] *n., colloq.* sawmill.

лесопи́льный *adj.* sawing; saw (*attrib.*). —лесопи́льный заво́д, sawmill.

лесору́б *n.* woodcutter; lumberjack.

ле́стница *n.* 1, stairs; staircase; stairway. 2, ladder. —пожа́рная ле́стница, fire escape.

ле́стничный *adj.* stair (*attrib.*).

ле́стно *adv.* in flattering terms. —*adj.,* used predicatively flattering: мне бы́ло ле́стно, что..., it was flattering to me that...; I was flattered that...

ле́стный *adj.* flattering; complimentary.

лесть *n.f.* flattery.

лёт *n.* flight; flying. —на лету́, in midair; on the fly; on the wing. —лови́ть на лету́, *fig.* to be quick to grasp.

лета́ [*gen.* лет] *n. pl.* years: пять лет, five years. Мне два́дцать лет, I am twenty years old. —быть в лета́х, to be getting on in years. —мно́гая ле́та (*with different stress*), here's to long life! —одни́х лет, the same age. —с де́тских (*or* с ма́лых) лет, since childhood. —ско́лько вам лет?, how old are you? —сре́дних лет, middle-aged.

летарги́я *n.* lethargy. —летарги́ческий, *adj.* lethargic.

лета́тельный *adj.* flying (*attrib.*).

лета́ть *v. impfv., indeterm. of* лете́ть.

лете́ть *v. impfv.* [*pfv.* полете́ть; *pres.* лечу́, лети́шь] to fly. —лете́ть вверх, *colloq.* to soar. —лете́ть вниз, *colloq.* to plummet.

ле́тний *adj.* summer (*attrib.*).

лётный *adj.* flying (*attrib.*). —лётная доро́жка, runway. —лётное по́ле, airfield. —лётный соста́в, flight personnel.

ле́то *n.* summer. —ле́том, *adv.* in (the) summer.

летоисчисле́ние *n.* method of numbering the years.

летопи́сец [*gen.* -сца] *n.* chronicler.

ле́топись *n.f.* chronicle.

летосчисле́ние *n.* = летоисчисле́ние.

лету́н [*gen.* -туна́] *n., colloq.* 1, flier. 2, person continually changing jobs.

лету́честь *n.f.* volatility.

лету́чий *adj.* 1, flying. 2, fleeting; momentary. 3, *chem.* volatile. —лету́чая мышь, *zool.* bat. —лету́чая ры́ба, flying fish.

лету́чка [*gen. pl.* -чек] *n., colloq.* 1, leaflet. 2, quick meeting. 3, mobile unit.

лётчик *n.* pilot. —лётчик-испыта́тель, test pilot. —лётчик-истреби́тель, fighter-pilot.

летя́га *n.* flying squirrel.

лече́бница *n.* hospital; nursing home.

лече́бный *adj.* 1, medical. 2, medicinal; curative.

лече́ние *n.* (medical) treatment.

лечи́ть *v. impfv.* [*pres.* лечу́, ле́чишь] to treat (*medically*). —лечи́ться, *refl.* 1, to undergo (medical) treatment. 2, to treat oneself.

лечь [*infl.* ля́гу, ля́жешь, ...ля́гут; *past* лёг, легла́, легло́] *v., pfv. of* ложи́ться.

ле́ший *n., decl. as an adj.* wood goblin.

лещ [*gen.* леща́] *n.* bream (*fish*).

лещи́на *n.* hazel (*tree*).

лженау́ка *n.* pseudoscience. —лженау́чный, *adj.* pseudoscientific.

лжесвиде́тель *n.m.* false witness; perjurer. —лжесвиде́тельство, *n.* false evidence; perjury.

лжесвиде́тельствовать *v. impfv.* [*pres.* -ствую, -ствуешь] to give false evidence; commit perjury; perjure oneself.

лжец [*gen.* лжеца́] *n.* liar.

лжи́вый *adj.* lying; untruthful; false. —лжи́вость, *n.f.* falsity.

ли *conj.* if; whether: я не зна́ю, смогу́ ли я пойти́, I don't know if I'll be able to go. Он попро́бовал, хорошо́ ли вино́, he tasted the wine to see if it was good. —*interr. particle:* есть ли у вас спи́чка?, do you have a match?; have you a match? Нра́вится ли вам э́то?, do you like it?

либера́л *n.* liberal. —**либерали́зм**, *n.* liberalism.

либера́льничать *v. impfv., colloq.* to be overly tolerant.

либера́льный *adj.* liberal.

ли́бо *conj.* or. —**ли́бо..., ли́бо...,** either..., or...

либре́тто *n. indecl.* libretto. —**либретти́ст,** *n.* librettist.

лива́нский *adj.* Lebanese.

ли́вень [*gen.* ли́вня] *n.m.* rainstorm; downpour; cloudburst; thundershower.

ли́вер *n.* giblets.

ли́верный *adj., in* ли́верная колбаса́, liverwurst.

ливи́йский *adj.* Libyan.

ливмя́ *adv., colloq., in* ливмя́ лить, (*of rain*) to come down in torrents.

ливре́я *n.* livery. —**ливре́йный,** *adj.* livery (*attrib.*); liveried; in livery.

ли́га *n.* **1,** league: Ли́га на́ций, League of Nations. **2,** *music* slur.

лигату́ра *n.* ligature.

лигни́т *n.* lignite.

лигрои́н *n.* naphtha.

ли́дер *n.* leader.

ли́дерство *n.* **1,** leadership. **2,** *sports* lead (*in a race, contest, etc.*).

лиди́ровать *v. impfv. & pfv.* [*pres.* -рую, -руешь] *sports* to lead; be in the lead.

лиза́ние *n.* licking.

лиза́ть *v. impfv.* [*pfv.* лизну́ть; *pres.* лижу́, ли́жешь] to lick.

лизоблю́д *n., colloq.* bootlicker.

лик *n.* **1,** *archaic* face; countenance. **2,** face (*of the moon, sun, etc.*). **3,** *eccles.* assembly. —**причи́слить к ли́ку святы́х,** to canonize.

ликвида́ция *n.* liquidation.

ликвиди́ровать *v. impfv. & pfv.* [*pres.* -рую, -руешь] **1,** to liquidate. **2,** to eliminate.

ликви́дный *adj., finance* liquid: ликви́дные сре́дства, liquid assets. —**ликви́дность,** *n.f.* liquidity.

ликёр *n.* liqueur; cordial.

likováние *n.* rejoicing; jubilation; exultation.

ликова́ть *v. impfv.* [*pres.* -ку́ю, -ку́ешь] to rejoice; exult.

ликующий *adj.* jubilant; exultant.

ли́лия *n.* lily. —**водяна́я ли́лия,** water lily.

лилове́ть *v. impfv.* to turn purple.

лило́вый *adj.* purple.

лима́н *n.* estuary.

лими́т *n.* limit; quota.

лимити́ровать *v. impfv. & pfv.* [*pres.* -рую, -руешь] to limit.

лимо́н *n.* **1,** lemon. **2,** lemon tree.

лимона́д *n.* **1,** lemonade. **2,** carbonated fruit drink; squash.

лимо́нный *adj.* lemon. —**лимо́нная кислота́,** citric acid.

лимузи́н *n.* limousine.

ли́мфа *n.* lymph. —**лимфати́ческий,** *adj.* lymph (*attrib.*); lymphatic.

лингви́ст *n.* linguist. —**лингви́стика,** *n.* linguistics. —**лингвисти́ческий,** *adj.* linguistic.

лине́йка [*gen. pl.* -не́ек] *n.* **1,** ruled line (*on paper*). В лине́йку, (*of paper*) lined; ruled. **2,** ruler; straight edge. **3,** line; file: вы́строиться в лине́йку, to form a line. **4,** line-up; assembly (*in a camp*). —**логарифми́ческая лине́йка,** slide rule.

лине́йный *adj.* linear. —**лине́йный кора́бль,** battleship.

ли́нза *n.* lens.

ли́ния *n.* line. —**по ли́нии** (+ *gen.*), through; under the auspices of.

линко́р *n.* battleship (*contr. of* лине́йный кора́бль).

лино́ванный *adj.* lined; ruled.

линова́ть *v. impfv.* [*pfv.* налинова́ть; *pres.* -ну́ю, -ну́ешь] to rule; draw lines on.

лино́леум *n.* linoleum.

линоти́п *n.* linotype.

линчева́ние *n.* lynching.

линчева́ть *v. impfv. & pfv.* [*pres.* -чу́ю, -чу́ешь] to lynch.

ли́нька *n.* molting.

линю́чий *adj., colloq.* (*of material*) that fades easily.

линя́лый *adj., colloq.* faded; discolored.

линя́ть *v. impfv.* **1,** [*pfv.* полиня́ть] (*of material*) to fade; (*of colors*) to run. **2,** [*pfv.* вы́линять] (*of animals*) to shed hair; (*of birds*) to molt.

ли́па *n.* linden tree; lime tree.

ли́пкий *adj.* sticky; adhesive. —**ли́пкий пла́стырь,** sticking plaster.

ли́пнуть *v. impfv.* [*past* лип *or* ли́пнул, ли́пла] (*with* к) to stick (to).

ли́повый *adj.* **1,** linden (*attrib.*); lime (*attrib.*). **2,** *colloq.* false; fake; phony.

липу́чий *adj., colloq.* sticky.

липу́чка *n., colloq.* **1,** sticky paper: липу́чка от мух, flypaper. **2,** sticking plaster.

ли́ра *n.* **1,** lyre. **2,** lira (*monetary unit of Italy and Turkey*).

лири́зм *n.* lyricism.

ли́рик *n.* lyric poet.

ли́рика *n.* **1,** lyric poetry. **2,** lyric poem. —**лири́ческий,** *adj.* lyric; lyrical.

лиса́ [*pl.* ли́сы] *n.* fox.

ли́сий [*fem.* -сья] *adj.* **1,** fox (*attrib.*). **2,** *fig.* foxy.

лиси́ца *n.* fox. —**морска́я лиси́ца,** thresher shark.

лиси́чка [*gen. pl.* -чек] *n.* a kind of edible mushroom; chanterelle.

лист [*gen.* листа́] *n.* **1,** [*pl.* ли́стья, ли́стьев] leaf. **2,** [*pl.* листы́, листо́в] sheet (*of paper, metal, etc.*). **3,** [*pl.* листы́, листо́в] any of various official documents: опро́сный лист, questionnaire; исполни́тельный лист, writ. —**с листа́,** from sight: чита́ть с листа́, to sight-read. Перево́д с листа́, sight translation.

листа́ть *v. impfv., colloq.* to leaf through.

листва́ *n.* foliage.

ли́ственница *n.* larch (*tree*).

ли́ственный *adj.* leafy; leaf-bearing.

листо́вка [*gen. pl.* -вок] *n.* leaflet.

листово́й *adj.* **1,** sheet (*attrib.*): листово́й мета́лл, sheet metal. **2,** leaf (*attrib.*).

листо́к [*gen.* -стка́] *n.* **1,** leaf. **2,** sheet (*of paper*).

листопа́д *n.* falling of leaves. —**листопа́дный,** *adj.* deciduous.

лита́вры *n. pl.* [*sing.* лита́вра] kettledrums.

лита́ния *n.* litany.

литéйный *adj.* founding; casting. —**литéйный завóд,** foundry.

литéйщик *n.* founder; caster.

литерáтор *n.* man of letters.

литератýра *n.* literature. —**литератýрный,** *adj.* literary.

ли́терный *adj.* **1,** designated by a letter. **2,** (*of a seat*) reserved.

ли́тий *n.* lithium.

литóвец [*gen.* -вца] *n.m.* [*fem.* -вка] Lithuanian. —**литóвский,** *adj.* Lithuanian.

литóграф *n.* lithographer.

литографи́ровать *v. impfv. & pfv.* [*pres.* -рую, -руешь] to lithograph.

литогрáфия *n.* **1,** lithography. **2,** lithograph. —**литогрáфский,** *adj.* lithographic.

литóй *adj.* (*of metals*) cast.

литори́на *n.* periwinkle (*mollusk*).

литосфéра *n.* lithosphere.

литр *n.* liter. —**литрóвый,** *adj.* with a capacity of one liter.

литурги́я *n.* liturgy. —**литурги́ческий,** *adj.* liturgical.

лить *v. impfv.* [*pres.* лью, льёшь; *past fem.* лилá] **1,** to pour. **2,** to emit (sound, light, etc.). **3,** to shed (tears, blood, etc.). **4,** to cast; form; make. **5,** *v.i., colloq.* (*of liquids*) to flow; stream; run; (*of rain*) to come down.

литьё *n.* **1,** casting (*process*). **2,** castings.

ли́ться *v.r. impfv.* [*pres.* льётся; *past* ли́лся, лилáсь, ли́лось *or* лилóсь, ли́лись *or* лили́сь] to flow; stream; pour.

лиф *n.* bodice.

лифт *n.* elevator.

лифтёр *n.* elevator operator. —**лифтёрша,** *n., colloq.* (female) elevator operator.

ли́фчик *n.* underbodice.

лихáч [*gen.* -хачá] *n.* **1,** daredevil. **2,** reckless driver. **3,** *obs.* coachman (*equipped with a good horse and carriage*).

лихáчество *n.* recklessness; foolhardiness.

лихвá *n., obs.* interest (*on a loan*). —**с лихвóй,** with something to spare: окупáться с лихвóй, to more than pay for itself.

ли́хо *n., colloq.* evil; misfortune. —*adv., colloq.* **1,** dashingly; jauntily. **2,** *colloq.* at a brisk pace. —**не поминáйте ли́хом,** don't think badly of me. —**почём фунт ли́ха,** what misfortune is all about.

лихóй *adj.* **1,** *obs.* evil; hard. **2,** *colloq.* daring; dashing; jaunty. **3,** *colloq.* rapid; fast; brisk. **4,** *colloq.* deft.

лихорáдить *v. impfv., impers.* to have a fever: егó лихорáдит, he has a fever; he is feverish.

лихорáдка *n.* fever. —**лихорáдочный,** *adj.* feverish.

ли́хость *n.f.* daring; audacity; bravado.

ли́хтер *n., naut.* lighter.

лицевóй *adj.* **1,** facial. **2,** *in* лицевáя сторонá, the right side (*of material, a coin, etc.*). —**лицевáя рýкопись,** illuminated manuscript. —**лицевóй счёт,** personal account.

лицезрéть *v. impfv., obs.* to behold.

лицéй *n.* lycée.

лицемéр *n.* hypocrite. —**лицемéрие,** *n.* hypocrisy.

лицемéрить *v. impfv.* to be hypocritical; play the hypocrite.

лицемéрный *adj.* hypocritical.

лицéнзия *n.* (commercial) license.

лицó [*pl.* ли́ца] *n.* **1,** face. **2,** person; individual; personage. **3,** face; right side (*of an object, fabric, etc.*). **4,** *gram.* person. —**в лицé** (+ *gen.*), in the person of. —**в лицó** (+ *dat.*), to one's face. —**знать в лицó,** to know (someone) by sight. —**к лицý** (+ *dat.*), becoming: плáтье вам к лицý, the dress is becoming to you. —**лицóм к,** facing. —**лицóм квéрху,** face up; right side up. —**лицóм к лицý,** face to face. —**на нём (ней) нет лицá,** he (she) looks awful. —**на однó лицó,** all alike; exactly alike. —**от лицá** (+ *gen.*), on behalf of. —**пéред лицóм** (+ *gen.*), in the face of. —**показáть своё настоя́щее лицó,** to show one's true colors. —**показáть товáр лицóм,** to show something in its best light; put one's best foot forward. —**с лицá земли́,** from the face of the earth. —**смотрéть** (+ *dat.*) **в лицó,** to face (squarely): смотрéть фáктам в лицó, to face facts.

ли́чико *n., dim. of* лицó.

личи́на *n.* mask.

личи́нка *n.* **1,** larva. **2,** maggot. —**личи́ночный,** *adj.* larval.

ли́чно *adv.* **1,** personally. **2,** in person.

личнóй *adj.* face (*attrib.*).

ли́чность *n.f.* **1,** person; figure; individual; character. **2,** personality; identity. —**переходи́ть на ли́чности,** to get personal.

ли́чный *adj.* **1,** personal. **2,** private. —**ли́чный состáв,** personnel; staff.

лишáй [*gen.* -шáя] *n.* **1,** [*also,* лишáйник] lichen. **2,** *med.* herpes. —**опоя́сывающий лишáй,** shingles. —**стри́гущий лишáй,** ringworm.

лишáть *v. impfv.* [*pfv.* лиши́ть] (*with gen.*) to deprive (of); rob (of). —**лишáться,** *refl.* (*with gen.*) to be deprived (of); lose.

лишéние *n.* **1,** deprivation. **2,** *pl.* privations; hardships.

лишённый *adj.* (*with gen.*) devoid (of); void (of); lacking; without.

лиши́ть *v., pfv. of* лишáть. —**лиши́ться,** *refl., pfv. of* лишáться.

ли́шнее *n., decl. as an adj.* too much: брать ли́шнее, to overcharge. —**с ли́шним,** *colloq.* a little over: три дóллара с ли́шним, three dollars and change.

ли́шний *adj.* **1,** superfluous; excess. **2,** spare; extra. —**ли́шний раз,** once again; once more. —**не ли́шнее,** worthwhile; not a bad idea.

лишь *adv.* only. —**лишь бы, 1,** if only. **2,** as long as. —**лишь тóлько,** as soon as.

лоб [*gen.* лба; *2nd loc.* лбу] *n.* forehead; brow. —**в лоб,** frontally; head-on. —**пусти́ть себé пýлю в лоб,** to blow one's brains out. —**что в лоб, что пó лбу,** it's as broad as it is long.

лóбби *n. neut. indecl., polit.* lobby. —**лоббизм,** *n.* lobbying. —**лоббист,** *n.* lobbyist.

лобзáть *v. impfv., archaic* to kiss.

лóбзик *n.* fret saw.

лóбный *adj., anat.* frontal. —**лóбное мéсто,** *hist.* place of execution (*in a public square*).

лобовóй *adj.* **1,** *mil.* frontal. **2,** front.

лоботря́с *n., colloq.* lazybones; loafer.

лобызáть *v. impfv.* =**лобзáть.**

лов *n.* catch (*of fish*).

ловелáс *n.* ladies' man.

ловéц [*gen.* -вцá] *n.* **1,** fisherman. **2,** hunter.

лови́ть *v. impfv.* [*pfv.* поймáть; *pres.* ловлю́, лóвишь] **1,** to (try to) catch. **2,** *colloq.* to pick up (a radio signal). —ловить кáждое слóво, to devour (*or* hang on) every word. —ловить на слóве, to take at one's word. —ловить момéнт *or* слýчай, to seize the opportunity. —ловить рь́бу в мýтной водé, to fish in troubled waters. —ловить себя на (+ *prepl.*), to catch oneself doing something. —ловить чей-нибудь взгляд, to catch someone's eye.

ловкáч [*gen.* -качá] *n., colloq.* clever fellow.

лóвкий *adj.* [*short form* лóвок, ловкá, лóвко; *comp.* лóвче] **1,** adroit; deft. **2,** *colloq.* clever; shrewd.

лóвко *adv.* **1,** adroitly. **2,** *colloq.* well: лóвко сдéлано!, well done!

лóвкость *n.f.* **1,** adroitness; dexterity. **2,** *colloq.* ingenuity. —лóвкость рук, sleight of hand; legerdemain.

лóвля *n.* catching (*of fish*); trapping (*of animals*). —рь́бная лóвля, fishing.

ловýшка [*gen. pl.* -шек] *n.* trap.

лóвчий *adj.* hunting (*attrib.*).

лог [*2nd loc.* лóге *or* логý; *pl.* логá] *n.* ravine.

логарифм *n.* logarithm. —логарифмúческий, *adj.* logarithmic.

лóгик *n.* logician.

лóгика *n.* logic.

логúческий *adj.* logical. —логúчески, *adv.* logically.

логúчный *adj.* logical. —логúчно, *adv.* logically. —логúчность, *n.f.* logic.

лóговище *n.* lair; den. *Also,* лóгово.

логопéдия *n.* speech therapy. —логопéд, *n.* speech therapist.

лóдка [*gen. pl.* -док] *n.* boat. —подвóдная лóдка, submarine.

лóдочка [*gen. pl.* -чек] *n.* **1,** small boat. **2,** pump (*shoe*).

лóдочник *n.* boatman.

лóдочный *adj.* boat (*attrib.*); boating (*attrib.*).

лодь́жка [*gen. pl.* -жек] *n.* ankle.

лóдырничать *v. impfv., colloq.* to loaf.

лóдырь *n.m., colloq.* loafer; idler.

лóжа *n.* **1,** *theat.* box. **2,** *obs.* (masonic) lodge. **3,** rifle stock.

ложбúна *n.* dale; glen.

лóже *n.* **1,** *archaic; poetic* bed. **2,** river bed.

лóжечка [*gen. pl.* -чек] *n., dim. of* лóжка. —под лóжечкой, in the pit of one's stomach.

ложúться *v.r. impfv.* [*pfv.* лечь] **1,** to lie down. **2,** (*of shadows, light, etc.*) to fall. **3,** (*with* в + *acc.*) to go into; enter (a hospital, clinic, etc.). **4,** *fig.* (*of responsibility, suspicion, etc.*) to lie; fall. —лечь в могúлу *or* в гроб, to die. —лечь на курс, (*of an aircraft or ship*) to embark (*or* set off) on a certain course. —лечь/ложúться спать, to go to sleep; go to bed.

лóжка [*gen. pl.* -жек] *n.* **1,** spoon. **2,** spoonful. **3,** ladle: разливáтельная лóжка, soup ladle. —чéрез час по чáйной лóжке, in dribs and drabs.

лóжно *adv.* **1,** falsely; wrongfully. **2,** incorrectly; wrongly.

лóжный *adj.* **1,** false. **2,** erroneous; fallacious. —лóжность, *n.f.* falsity.

ложь [*gen., dat., & prepl.* лжи; *instr.* лóжью] *n.f.* **1,** lie; falsehood. **2,** lying; lies.

лозá [*pl.* лóзы] *n.* **1,** vine: виногрáдная лозá, grapevine. **2,** twig: úвовая лозá, willow twig.

лознýк [*gen.* -някá] *n.* willow shrub.

лóзунг *n.* slogan.

локализáция *n.* localization.

локализовáть *v. impfv. & pfv.* [*pres.* -зýю, -зýешь] to localize. —локализовáться, *refl.* to become localized.

локáльный *adj.* local.

локáтор *n.* locator; detector; radar.

локáут *n.* lockout.

локомотúв *n.* locomotive.

лóкон *n.* lock; curl.

лóкоть [*gen.* лóктя; *pl.* лóкти, локтéй, локтя́м] *n.m.* **1,** elbow. Толкнýть лóктем, to nudge. **2,** elbow (*of a garment*): потéртый на локтя́х, worn at the elbows. **3,** cubit (*ancient measure*). —блúзок лóкоть, да не укýсишь, so near and yet so far. —чýвство лóктя, feeling of comradeship.

локтевóй *adj.* elbow (*attrib.*). —локтевáя кость, funny bone.

лом *n.* **1,** [*pl.* лóмы, ломóв, ломáм] crowbar. **2,** scrap: желéзный лом, scrap iron.

ломáка *n.m. & f., colloq.* affected person.

лóманый *adj.* broken.

ломáть *v. impfv.* [*pfv.* сломáть] **1,** to break. **2,** to tear down. **3,** [*impfv. only*] to quarry. **4,** to break down (old beliefs or customs). **5,** [*pfv.* поломáть] to alter; transform. **6,** to ruin; wreck. —ломáть себé гóлову, to rack one's brains. —ломáть себé рýки, to wring one's hands.

ломáться *v.r. impfv.* [*pfv.* сломáться] **1,** to break. **2,** [*impfv. only*] to be breakable. **3,** [*impfv. only*] (*of one's voice*) to break; crack; (*of a young man's voice*) to change. **4,** (*of something well-established*) to break down; collapse; crumble. **5,** [*pfv.* поломáться] to be coy; put on airs.

ломбáрд *n.* pawnshop; hockshop. —ломбáрдный, *adj.* of or pert. to a pawnshop: ломбáрдная квитáнция, pawn ticket.

лóмберный *adj., in* лóмберный стол, card table.

ломúть *v. impfv.* [*pres.* ломлю́, лóмишь] **1,** *colloq.* to break. **2,** *impers.* to ache: у меня́ лóмит спúну, my back aches; I have a pain in my back. —ломúться, *refl.* **1,** to break; snap. **2,** (*with* от) to be loaded (with); be weighed down (with). **3,** (*with* в + *acc.*) *colloq.* to break through; force one's way into. **4,** *in* ломúться в открь́тую дверь, to belabor the obvious.

лóмка *n.* breaking; breakup.

лóмкий *adj.* fragile; brittle. —лóмкость, *n.f.* fragility.

ломовúк [*gen.* -викá] *n., colloq.* carter.

ломовóй *adj.* dray (*attrib.*): ломовáя лóшадь, dray horse. *n.* [*also,* ломовóй извóзчик] carter.

ломонóс *n.* clematis.

ломóта *n.* dull ache (*in the joints, muscles, etc.*).

ломóть [*gen.* -мтя́] *n.m.* hunk; chunk (*of bread, meat, etc.*).

лóмтик *n.* slice.

лонжерóн *n., aero.* spar.

лóно *n., poetic* **1,** bosom. **2,** lap: на лóне прирóды, in the lap of nature.

лóпасть [*pl.* лóпасти, -стéй, -стя́м] *n.f.* blade (*of an oar, propeller, etc.*).

лопáта *n.* shovel.

лопáтка [*gen. pl.* -ток] *n.* **1,** small shovel; trowel. **2,** blade. **3,** shoulder blade. **4,** chuck (*cut of beef*). —бежáть во все лопáтки, *colloq.* to run for all one is worth. —положúть на óбе лопáтки, **1,** *wrestling* to pin down. **2,** *fig.* to beat; get the best (*or* better) of.

ло́пать *v. impfv.* [*pfv.* сло́пать] *colloq.* to eat; gobble.

ло́паться *v.r. impfv.* [*pfv.* ло́пнуть] **1,** to burst; break; snap. **2,** (*of one's patience*) to be at an end. **3,** *colloq.* to fail; go broke.

лопота́ть *v. impfv.* [*pres.* -почу́, -по́чешь] *colloq.* to mumble; mutter.

лопоу́хий *adj., colloq.* lop-eared.

лопу́х [*gen.* -пуха́] *n.* burdock.

лорд *n.* lord.

лорне́т *n.* lorgnette.

лоси́на *n.* **1,** elk skin. **2,** elk meat. **3,** *pl.* buckskin breeches.

лоси́ный *adj.* **1,** elk (*attrib.*); elk's. **2,** made of elk skin.

лоск *n.* **1,** luster; gloss; sheen. **2,** *fig.* polish; refinement.

лоску́т [*gen.* -кута́; *pl.* -куты́, -куто́в *or* -кутья́, -ку́тьев] *n.* shred; scrap of cloth.

лоску́тный *adj.* made of patches; patchwork (*attrib.*): лоску́тное одея́ло, patchwork quilt.

лосни́ться *v.r. impfv.* to be glossy; shine.

лососёвый *adj.* salmon (*attrib.*).

лососи́на *n.* salmon (*prepared as food*).

лосо́сь *also,* ло́сось *n.m.* salmon.

лось [*pl.* ло́си, -се́й, -ся́м] *n.m.* elk; moose.

лосьо́н *n.* face lotion.

лот *n.* **1,** *naut.* plumb line. **2,** old Russian unit of weight equal to 12.8 grams.

лотере́я *n.* lottery; raffle. —лотере́йный, *adj.* lottery (*attrib.*).

лото́ *n. indecl.* lotto; bingo.

лото́к [*gen.* -тка́] *n.* **1,** tray (*of a street peddler*). **2,** chute: ме́льничный лото́к, millrace.

ло́тос *n.* lotus.

лото́чник *n.* street vendor.

лоха́нь *n.f.* washtub. *Also,* лоха́нка.

лохма́тый *adj.* **1,** shaggy. **2,** disheveled.

лохмо́тья [*gen.* -тьев] *n. pl.* tatters.

ло́ция *n.* book of navigational information for a certain body of water.

ло́цман *n.* **1,** harbor pilot. **2,** pilot fish.

лошади́ный *adj.* horse (*attrib.*). —лошади́ная си́ла, horsepower.

лоша́дка [*gen. pl.* -док] *n., dim. of* ло́шадь.

ло́шадь [*pl.* ло́шади, -де́й, -дя́м, -дьми́, -дя́х] *n.f.* horse.

лоша́к [*gen.* -шака́] *n.* hinny.

лощёный *adj.* **1,** glossy. **2,** *fig.* polished.

лощи́на *n.* dale; glen.

лощи́ть *v. impfv.* [*pfv.* налощи́ть] to buff; polish.

лоя́льный *adj.* loyal. —лоя́льность, *n.f.* loyalty.

луб *n.* bast.

лубо́к [*gen.* -бка́] *n.* **1,** strip of bast. **2,** splint. **3,** wood block; woodcut.

лубяно́й *adj.* bast (*attrib.*).

луг [*2nd loc.* лугу́; *pl.* луга́] *n.* meadow.

лугови́на *n., colloq.* small meadow.

лугово́й *adj.* meadow (*attrib.*).

луди́льщик *n.* tinsmith.

луди́ть *v. impfv.* [*pfv.* полуди́ть; *pres.* лужу́, лу́дишь *or* луди́шь] to tin; tin-plate.

лу́жа *n.* puddle. —сесть в лу́жу, *colloq.* to make a fool of oneself; put one's foot in it.

лужа́йка [*gen. pl.* -а́ек] *n.* **1,** clearing (*in a forest*). **2,** lawn.

лужёный *adj.* tin-plated. —лужёный желу́док, cast-iron stomach.

лу́жица *n., dim. of* лу́жа.

лужо́к [*gen.* -жка́] *n., dim. of* луг.

лу́за *n.* pocket (*of a billiard table*). —лу́зный, *adj.,* in лу́зный билья́рд, pocket billiards.

луизиа́нский мох Spanish moss.

лук *n.* **1,** onions. **2,** bow (*for shooting arrows*). —лук-поре́й, leek.

лука́ [*pl.* лу́ки] *n.* **1,** bend (*in a road or river*). **2,** pommel (*of a saddle*).

лука́вить *v. impfv.* [*pres.* -влю, -вишь] to be cunning.

лука́вство *n.* cunning.

лука́вый *adj.* cunning; sly; crafty.

лу́ковица *n.* **1,** an onion. **2,** *bot.* bulb. **3,** onion dome (*of a Russian church*). —лу́ковичный, *adj.* bulbous.

лу́ковый *adj.* onion (*attrib.*).

луна́ [*pl.* лу́ны] *n.* moon.

луна́-па́рк *n.* amusement park.

луна́-ры́ба [*pl.* лу́ны-ры́бы] *n.* sunfish.

лунати́зм *n.* sleepwalking; somnambulism. —луна́тик, *n.* sleepwalker; somnambulist.

лу́нка [*gen.* -нок] *n.* **1,** small hole. **2,** alveolus.

лу́нный *adj.* **1,** moon (*attrib.*); lunar. **2,** moonlit.

лунь [*gen.* луня́] *n.m.* harrier (*bird*).

лу́па *n.* magnifying glass.

лупи́ть *v. impfv.* [*pres.* луплю́, лу́пишь] *colloq.* **1,** [*pfv.* облупи́ть *or* слупи́ть] to peel off. **2,** [*pfv.* слупи́ть] to charge (*an exorbitant price*). **3,** [*pfv.* отлупи́ть] to beat; thrash. —лупи́ться, *refl.* [*pfv.* облупи́ться] *colloq.* **1,** to peel off; come off. **2,** (*of one's face*) to peel.

луфа́рь [*gen.* -фаря́] *n.m.* bluefish.

луч [*gen.* луча́] *n.* ray; beam.

лучево́й *adj.* radial. —лучева́я боле́знь, radiation sickness.

лучеза́рный *adj.* radiant; effulgent.

лучеиспуска́ние *n.* radiation.

лучи́на *n.* thin stick; sliver (*of kindling wood*).

лучи́стый *adj.* radiant.

лучи́ться *v.r. impfv.* **1,** to shine; sparkle. **2,** *fig.* (*with instr.*) to radiate.

лучко́вый *adj.,* in лучко́вая пила́, whipsaw.

лу́чше *adj. & adv., comp. of* хоро́ший *and* хорошо́, better. —лу́чше всего́, best of all. —тем лу́чше, so much the better.

лу́чшее *n., decl. as an adj.* something better: я ожида́л лу́чшего, I expected something better. —жела́ю вам всего́ (са́мого) лу́чшего, I wish you all the best. —оставля́ть жела́ть мно́го лу́чшего, to leave much to be desired. —переме́на к лу́чшему, change for the better.

лу́чший *adj., used only as a modifier, comp. and superl. of* хоро́ший **1,** (a) better. **2,** (the) best. —в лу́чшем слу́чае, at best. —измени́ться в лу́чшую сто́рону, to change for the better.

лущи́ть *v. impfv.* [*pfv.* облущи́ть] to shell; husk; hull.

лы́жа *n.* ski. —лы́жник, *n.* skier. —лы́жный, *adj.* ski (*attrib.*); skiing (*attrib.*).

лыжня́ [*gen. pl.* -не́й] *n.* track left by skis.

лы́ко *n.* bast. —не лы́ком шит, *colloq.* no slouch.

лы́ковый *adj.* made of bast.

лысе́ть *v. impfv.* [*pfv.* облысе́ть *or* полысе́ть] to become bald.

лы́сина *n.* bald spot.

лысу́ха *n.* coot.

лы́сый *adj.* bald.

ль *conj.* = **ли.**

львёнок [*gen.* -нка; *pl.* **льви́та, львят**] *n.* lion cub.

льви́ный *adj.* lion's. —**льви́ная до́ля,** the lion's share. —**льви́ный зев; льви́ная пасть,** snapdragon.

льви́ца *n.* lioness.

льго́та *n.* privilege; benefit.

льго́тный *adj.* **1,** favorable; preferential: на льго́тных усло́виях, on favorable terms. **2,** (*of a price, fare, etc.*) reduced; (*of a ticket*) cut-rate. —**льго́тный срок,** grace period. Три́дцать льго́тных дней, 30-day grace period.

льди́на *n.* block of ice. —**плаву́чая льди́на,** ice field.

льнуть *v. impfv.* [*pfv.* **прильну́ть**] (*with* **к**) **1,** to cling (to). **2,** [*impfv. only*] *fig.* to feel drawn toward.

льняно́й *adj.* **1,** flax (*attrib.*). **2,** linen (*attrib.*). **3,** (*of hair*) flaxen. —**льняно́е ма́сло,** linseed oil.

льстец [*gen.* **льстеца́**] *n.* flatterer.

льсти́вый *adj.* flattering; ingratiating.

льстить *v. impfv.* [*pfv.* **польсти́ть;** *pres.* **льщу, льстишь**] (*with dat.*) to flatter.

любвеоби́льный *adj.* loving; full of love.

любе́зничать *v. impfv.* (*with* **с** + *instr.*) *colloq.* to exchange pleasantries with; say nice things to.

любе́зно *adv.* kindly; graciously. —*adj., used predicatively* kind; gracious: о́чень любе́зно с ва́шей стороны́, very kind/gracious of you.

любе́зность *n.f.* **1,** courtesy; graciousness. **2,** *pl.* kind words; compliments. **3,** favor; kindness; good turn.

любе́зный *adj.* [*short form* -**зен,** -**зна**] kind; gracious. —**бу́дьте любе́зны** (+ *imperative*), be so kind as to...

люби́мец [*gen.* -**мца**] *n.m.* [*fem.* -**мица**] favorite; pet.

люби́мчик *n., colloq.* favorite; pet.

люби́мый *adj.* **1,** loved. **2,** favorite; pet.

люби́тель *n.m.* **1,** lover: люби́тель му́зыки, music lover. **2,** amateur; dilettante. —**люби́тельский,** *adj.* amateur.

люби́ть *v. impfv.* [*pres.* **люблю́, лю́бишь**] **1,** to love. **2,** to like; be fond of.

лю́бо *predicate, used with inf., colloq.* it is a pleasure (to).

любова́ться *v.r. impfv.* [*pfv.* **полюбова́ться;** *pres.* -**бу́юсь,** -**бу́ешься**] (*with instr. or* **на** + *acc.*) to admire; watch with pleasure.

любо́вник *n.* lover; paramour.

любо́вница *n.* lover; mistress.

любо́вный *adj.* **1,** love (*attrib.*). **2,** loving; tender. **3,** amorous. —**любо́вно,** *adv.* lovingly.

любо́вь [*gen., dat., & prepl.* **любви́;** *instr.* **любо́вью**] *n.f.* love.

любозна́тельный *adj.* curious; inquisitive; thirsty for knowledge. —**любозна́тельность,** *n.f.* (intellectual) curiosity; inquisitiveness.

любо́й *adj.* **1,** any. **2,** either. —*n.* **1,** anyone; anybody. **2,** either one. —**в любо́м слу́чае,** in either case; either way.

любопы́тно *adv.* curiously; with curiosity. —*adj.,* *used predicatively* curious: мне любопы́тно знать, куда́ они́ пое́хали, I am curious to know where they went.

любопы́тный *adj.* curious. —**любопы́тство,** *n.* curiosity.

любопы́тствовать *v. impfv.* [*pfv.* **полюбопы́тствовать;** *pres.* -**ствую,** -**ствуешь**] to be curious.

лю́бящий *adj.* loving.

люд *n., colloq.* people.

лю́ди [*gen.* **люде́й;** *dat.* **лю́дям;** *instr.* **людьми́;** *prepl.* **лю́дях**] *n. pl.* people. —**вы́вести в лю́ди,** to put (someone) on his feet. —**вы́йти** *or* **вы́биться в лю́ди,** to make one's way in the world. —**на лю́дях,** in public.

лю́дный *adj.* **1,** populous. **2,** crowded.

людое́д *n.* cannibal. —**людое́дский,** *adj.* cannibalistic. —**людое́дство,** *n.* cannibalism.

людска́я *n., decl. as an adj.* servants' quarters.

людско́й *adj.* human.

люк *n.* hatch; manhole; trap door. —**светово́й люк,** skylight.

люкс *adj. indecl.* de luxe: гости́ница-люкс, de luxe hotel.

лю́лька [*gen. pl.* -**лек**] *n.* cradle.

люмба́го *n. indecl.* lumbago.

люмина́л *n.* phenobarbital.

люминесце́нтный *adj.* luminescent. —**люминесце́нтная ла́мпа,** fluorescent lamp.

люминесце́нция *n.* luminescence.

лю́стра *n.* chandelier.

лютера́нин [*pl.* -**ра́не,** -**ра́н**] *n.m.* [*fem.* -**ра́нка**] Lutheran. —**лютера́нский,** *adj.* Lutheran. —**лютера́нство,** *n.* Lutheranism.

люте́ций (тэ) *n.* lutetium.

лю́тик *n.* buttercup.

лю́тня [*gen. pl.* -**тен**] *n.* lute.

лю́тый *adj.* **1,** fierce; ferocious. **2,** (*of cold, hatred, etc.*) bitter. **3,** (*of pain*) excruciating. —**лю́тость,** *n.f.* ferocity.

люце́рна *n.* alfalfa.

ля *n. neut., music* la; A.

ляга́ть *v. impfv.* [*pfv.* **лягну́ть**] (*of a horse*) to kick. *Also,* **ляга́ться** [*impfv. only*].

лягу́шечий *also,* **лягуша́чий** [*fem.* -**чья**] *adj.* frog's; frogs'.

лягу́шка [*gen. pl.* -**шек**] *n.* frog.

ля́жка [*gen. pl.* -**жек**] *n., colloq.* thigh; haunch.

лязг *n.* clang; clank.

ля́згать *v. impfv.* [*pfv.* **ля́згнуть**] **1,** to clang; clank; make a clanking sound. **2,** (*with instr.*) to rattle; clank.

лякро́сс *n.* lacrosse.

ля́мка [*gen. pl.* -**мок**] *n.* shoulder strap. —**тяну́ть ля́мку,** *colloq.* to slave; toil.

ля́пис *n.* silver nitrate.

ля́пис-лазу́рь *n.f.* lapis-lazuli.

ля́пнуть *v. pfv., colloq.* to blurt out.

ля́псус *n.* blunder.

M

M, м *n. neut.* thirteenth letter of the Russian alphabet.

мавзоле́й *n.* mausoleum.

мавр *n.* Moor. —**маврита́нский,** *adj.* Moorish.

маг *n.* magician; wizard.

магази́н *n.* **1,** store; shop. **2,** magazine (*of a firearm, camera, etc.*).

магази́нный *adj.* **1,** store (*attrib.*); shop (*attrib.*). **2,** *mil.* magazine (*attrib.*). —**магази́нная винто́вка,** repeating rifle. —**магази́нный вор,** shoplifter.

магара́джа *n.m.* maharajah.

маги́стр *n.* **1,** holder of a master's degree. **2,** master's degree. **3,** grandmaster (*of a monastic or knightly order*).

магистра́ль *n.f.* **1,** highway; thoroughfare. **2,** *R.R.* main line. **3,** main: га́зовая магистра́ль, gas main. —**магистра́льный,** *adj.* main; arterial.

магистра́т *n.* city council. —**магистрату́ра,** *n.* magistracy.

маги́ческий *adj.* magic; magical.

ма́гия *n.* magic.

магна́т *n.* magnate; tycoon.

магне́зия *n.* magnesia.

магнети́зм *n.* **1,** magnetism. **2,** magnetics.

магнети́т *n.* magnetite.

магнети́ческий *adj.* magnetic.

магне́то *n. indecl.* magneto.

магнетро́н *n.* magnetron.

ма́гниевый *adj.* magnesium (*attrib.*).

ма́гний *n.* magnesium.

магни́т *n.* magnet. —**магни́тный,** *adj.* magnetic.

магнитофо́н *n.* tape recorder. —**магнитофо́нный,** *adj.* of a tape recorder: магнитофо́нная за́пись, tape recording.

магно́лия *n.* magnolia.

магомета́нин [*pl.* -та́не, -та́н] *n.m.* [*fem.* -та́нка] Mohammedan. —**магомета́нский,** *adj.* Mohammedan. —**магомета́нство,** *n.* Mohammedanism.

мада́м *n.f. indecl.* madam.

мадемуазе́ль (дмуазэ) *n.f. indecl.* mademoiselle.

маде́ра *n.* Madeira wine.

мадо́нна *n.* madonna.

мадрига́л *n.* madrigal.

мадья́р *n.m.* [*fem.* -ка] Magyar. —**мадья́рский,** *adj.* Magyar.

мае́вка [*gen. pl.* -вок] *n.* **1,** illegal May-day meeting (*in pre-rev. Russia*). **2,** spring outing; picnic.

мажо́р *n.* **1,** *music* major key: тона́льность до мажо́р, key of C major. **2,** *colloq.* good/high spirits.

мажордо́м *n.* majordomo.

мажо́рный *adj.* **1,** *music* major. **2,** *fig.* buoyant; exuberant.

ма́занка [*gen. pl.* -нок] *n.* clay-walled hut.

ма́зать *v. impfv.* [*pres.* ма́жу, ма́жешь] **1,** [*pfv.* нама́зать *or* пома́зать] (*with instr.*) to smear (with): ма́зать хлеб ма́слом, to smear butter on bread; butter one's bread. **2,** [*pfv.* вы́мазать] (*with instr.*) to coat (with): ма́зать сте́ны кра́ской, to paint the walls. **3,** [*pfv.* нама́зать] *colloq.* to paint (one's lips); put make-up on (one's face). **4,** [*pfv.* вы́мазать] *colloq.* to soil. **5,** [*pfv.* нама́зать] *colloq.* to paint poorly; daub. **6,** [*pfv.* прома́зать] *colloq.* to miss (*in shooting or games*). —**ма́заться,** *refl.* **1,** [*pfv.* нама́заться] to put on make-up; (*with instr.*) put on (salve, make-up, etc.). **2,** [*pfv.* вы́мазаться] *colloq.* to soil; get dirty.

мазня́ *n., colloq.* poor painting.

мазо́к [*gen.* -зка́] *n.* **1,** dab; stroke (*with a paintbrush*). **2,** *med.* smear.

мазохи́зм *n.* masochism. —**мазохи́ст,** *n.* masochist. —**мазохи́стский,** *adj.* masochistic.

мазу́рка *n.* mazurka.

мазу́т *n.* fuel oil.

мазь *n.f.* **1,** ointment. **2,** grease. **3,** *in* сапо́жная мазь, shoe polish. —**де́ло на мази́,** *colloq.* things are moving right along.

ма́ис *n.* maize.

май *n.* May.

ма́йка [*gen. pl.* ма́ек] *n.* T-shirt.

майоне́з *n.* mayonnaise.

майо́р *n.* major.

майора́н *n.* marjoram.

майо́рский *adj.* major's.

ма́йский *adj.* May (*attrib.*).

мак *n.* **1,** poppy. **2,** poppy seeds.

мака́ка *n.* macaque.

макаро́ны [*gen.* -ро́н] *n. pl.* macaroni.

мака́ть *v. impfv.* [*pfv.* макну́ть] to dip; dunk.

македо́нский *adj.* Macedonian.

маке́т *n.* **1,** model; mock-up. **2,** *printing* dummy.

макиаве́ллевский *adj.* Machiavellian.

макинто́ш *n.* mackintosh.

ма́клер *n.* stockbroker. —**ма́клерский,** *adj.* of a broker; brokerage (*attrib.*). —**ма́клерство,** *n.* brokerage.

макну́ть *v., pfv. of* мака́ть.

ма́ковка [*gen. pl.* -вок] *n.* **1,** poppy head. **2,** dome; cupola (*of a church*). **3,** *colloq.* top.

ма́ковый *adj.* poppy (*attrib.*).

макре́ль *n.f.* mackerel.

макрокосм *n.* macrocosm.

максима́льный *adj.* maximum. —**максима́льно,** *adv.* to the maximum.

ма́ксимум *n.* maximum. —*adv.* a maximum of; at (the) most.

макулату́ра *n.* **1,** pages spoiled in printing. **2,** literary trash.

маку́шка [*gen. pl.* -шек] *n.* **1,** top. **2,** crown of the head.

мала́га *n.* Malaga wine.

мала́ец [*gen.* -а́йца] *n.m.* [*fem.* -а́йка] Malay. —**мала́йский,** *adj.* Malay.

малахи́т *n.* malachite. —**малахи́товый,** *adj.* malachite.

малева́ть *v. impfv.* [*pfv.* **намалева́ть;** *pres.* **малю́ю,** `малю́ешь]` *colloq.* to paint.

мале́йший *adj., superl. of* **ма́лый,** the least; the slightest; the faintest. —**ни в мале́йшей сте́пени,** not in the least.

малёк [*gen.* -лька́] *n.* young fish; newly-hatched fish.

ма́ленький *adj.* [*comp.* **ме́ньше**] little; small. —*n.* the little one; the baby. *See also* **ме́ньше.**

мале́нько *adv., colloq.* a little; a bit; somewhat.

мали́на *n.* **1,** raspberries. **2,** a (single) raspberry.

мали́новка [*gen. pl.* -вок] *n.* robin (redbreast).

мали́новый *adj.* **1,** raspberry (*attrib.*). **2,** crimson.

ма́ло *adv.* **1,** little; not much: ма́ло сде́лать, to do little; not do much; ма́ло вре́мени, little time; not much time. **2,** few; not many: ма́ло наро́ду, few people; not many people. **3,** hardly: ма́ло кто, hardly anyone; ма́ло что, hardly anything. **4,** (*with* ли) many; lots of: all kinds of: ма́ло ли что, all kinds of things; anything. —**ма́ло (ли) что** (+ *past tense verb*), what of it!; what if I (you, *etc.*) did...? —**ма́ло того́,** moreover. —**ма́ло того́, что...,** not only...; it is not enough that...

малова́жный *adj.* of little importance; of little significance.

малова́то *adv., colloq.* not quite enough.

малове́р *n.* skeptic.

малоvеро́ятный *adj.* not likely; unlikely; improbable. —**маловеро́ятность,** *n.f.* unlikelihood.

малово́дный *adj.* **1,** shallow. **2,** arid.

малово́дье *n.* **1,** shortage of water. **2,** low level of water (*in a river, lake, etc.*).

малогабари́тный *adj.* small-size; compact.

малогра́мотный *adj.* semiliterate.

малодосту́пный *adj.* **1,** inaccessible. **2,** *fig.* esoteric.

малоду́шие *n.* faintheartedness; cowardice. —**малоду́шный,** *adj.* fainthearted; craven; cowardly.

малозаме́тный *adj.* **1,** hardly noticeable. **2,** ordinary; undistinguished.

малознако́мый *adj.* unfamiliar.

малоизве́стный *adj.* little-known.

малоинтере́сный *adj.* of little interest; uninteresting.

малокро́вие *n.* anemia. —**малокро́вный,** *adj.* anemic.

малоле́тний *adj.* underage. —*n.* juvenile. —**малоле́тство,** *n., colloq.* childhood.

малолитра́жный *adj.* fuel-efficient.

малолю́дный *adj.* **1,** sparsely populated. **2,** with few people to be seen. **3,** (*of a meeting*) poorly attended.

мало-ма́льски *adv., colloq.* the least bit; the slightest bit: ка́ждый, кто мало-ма́льски знако́м с..., anyone who is the least acquainted with...

маломо́щный *adj.* not powerful; low-powered.

малонадёжный *adj.* not very reliable.

малонаселённый *adj.* sparsely populated.

ма́ло-пома́лу *adv., colloq.* little by little; bit by bit.

малопоня́тный *adj.* difficult to understand.

малоприбыльный *adj.* showing little profit.

малора́звитый *adj.* **1,** undeveloped; underdeveloped. **2,** limited (*in intellect*).

малоро́слый *adj.* undersized.

малосве́дущий *adj.* poorly informed.

малосеме́йный *adj.* having a small family.

малоси́льный *adj.* **1,** weak. **2,** low-powered.

малосодержа́тельный *adj.* containing little of interest; lacking substance.

малосо́льный *adj.* lightly salted.

ма́лость *n.f.* **1,** *obs.* small size. **2,** tiny bit. **3,** *colloq.* trifle. —*adv., colloq.* a little; a bit.

малотира́жный *adj.* **1,** having a small circulation. **2,** (*of an edition*) limited.

малоупотреби́тельный *adj.* little used; rarely used.

малоце́нный *adj.* of little value.

малочи́сленный *adj.* small in number; not numerous. —**малочи́сленность,** *n.f.* small number.

ма́лый *adj.* **1,** small. **2,** [*short form only* — **мал, мала́, мало́, малы́**] (too) small: боти́нки мне малы́, the shoes are too small for me. —*n.* **1,** *colloq.* fellow; chap; guy: до́брый ма́лый, a decent fellow. **2,** *neut.* little: дово́льствоваться ма́лым, to be satisfied with little. **3,** *pl.* little ones; children. —**без ма́ла; без ма́лого,** *colloq.* almost; nearly. —**за ма́лым де́ло ста́ло,** only one small matter is holding things up. —**от ма́ла до вели́ка,** young and old alike. —**са́мое ма́лое,** the least. **2,** at (the) least. —**с ма́лых лет,** since childhood.

малы́ш [*gen.* -лыша́] *n.* small child; tot.

ма́льва *n.* mallow.

мальто́за *n.* maltose.

ма́льчик *n.* boy.

мальчи́шеский *adj.* **1,** boy's. **2,** childish. —**мальчи́шество,** *n.* childish behavior.

мальчи́шка [*gen. pl.* -шек] *n.m., colloq.* (little) boy.

мальчуга́н *n., colloq.* little boy; little fellow.

малю́сенький *adj., colloq.* tiny; wee; minuscule.

малю́тка [*gen. pl.* -ток] *n.m. & f.* little one.

маля́р [*gen.* -яра́] *n.* house painter.

маляри́йный *adj.* malarial.

маля́рия *n.* malaria.

маля́рный *adj.* painting (*attrib.*); paint (*attrib.*). —**маля́рная кисть,** paintbrush. —**маля́рный цех,** paint shop (*in a factory*).

ма́ма *n.* mama; mommy.

мамалы́га *n.* hominy.

ма́маша *n., colloq.* = ма́ма.

ма́менька *n., obs.* = ма́ма.

ма́менькин *adj., colloq.* mother's. —**ма́менькин сынок,** mother's boy; mama's boy.

ма́мин *adj.* mother's.

ма́монт *n.* mammoth.

ма́мочка *n.* mother dear.

мана́тки [*gen.* -ток] *n. pl., colloq.* (one's) things; belongings.

мангани́т *n.* manganite.

ма́нго *n. indecl.* **1,** mango. **2,** mango tree.

мангу́ста *n.* mongoose.

мандари́н *n.* **1,** tangerine; mandarin. **2,** mandarin (*Chinese official*). —**мандари́нный; мандари́новый,**

adj. tangerine (*attrib.*). —**мандари́нский,** *adj.* Mandarin: мандари́нский язы́к, Mandarin.

манда́т *n.* **1,** mandate. **2,** warrant.

манда́тный *adj.* mandate (*attrib.*); mandated. —**манда́тная коми́ссия,** credentials committee.

мандоли́на *n.* mandolin.

мандраго́ра *n.* mandrake.

мандри́л *n.* mandrill.

мане́вр *n.* maneuver.

манёвренный *adj.* **1,** *mil.* mobile: манёвренная война́, mobile warfare. **2,** maneuverable. —**манёвренность,** *n.f.* mobility; maneuverability.

маневри́ровать *v. impfv.* [*pres.* -рую, -руешь] **1,** to maneuver. **2,** *fig.* (*with instr.*) to manipulate.

мане́ж *n.* **1,** riding academy; riding school. **2,** circus arena; ring. **3,** playpen.

манеке́н *n.* mannequin; dummy.

манеке́нщик *n.m.* [*fem.* -щица] model.

мане́р *n., colloq.* manner; way. —**на мане́р** (+ *gen.*), in the manner of. На ру́сский мане́р, in the Russian manner; Russian-style.

мане́ра *n.* **1,** manner. **2,** *pl.* manners.

мане́рный *adj.* affected; mannered. —**мане́рность,** *n.f.* affectation.

манже́та *n.* cuff.

маниака́льный *adj.* maniacal; manic. —**маниака́льно-депресси́вный,** *adj.* manic-depressive.

маникю́р *n.* manicure. —**маникю́рный,** *adj.* manicure (*attrib.*). —**маникю́рша,** *n.* manicurist.

мани́ока *n.* manioc; cassava.

манипули́ровать *v. impfv.* [*pres.* -рую, -руешь] (*with instr.*) to manipulate.

манипуля́тор *n.* manipulator.

манипуля́ция *n.* manipulation.

мани́ть *v. impfv.* [*pfv.* помани́ть; *pres.* маню́, ма́нишь] **1,** to beckon. **2,** *fig.* to draw; attract: его́ ма́нит мо́ре, he feels drawn to the sea.

манифе́ст *n.* manifesto.

манифеста́ция *n.* demonstration; march.

мани́шка [*gen. pl.* -шек] *n.* shirt front; dickey.

ма́ния *n.* mania. —**ма́ния вели́чия,** delusions of grandeur; megalomania. —**ма́ния пресле́дования,** persecution complex.

манки́ровать *v. impfv. & pfv.* [*pres.* -рую, -руешь] **1,** (*with instr.*) to neglect. **2,** *obs.* to be absent.

ма́нна *n.* manna.

ма́нный *adj.* **1,** *in* ма́нная крупа́, farina. **2,** *in* ма́нная ка́ша, cereal made from farina.

манове́ние *n., obs.* wave (*of the hand*); nod (*of the head*). —**как по манове́нию волше́бного жезла́,** instantly; as if by magic.

мано́метр *n.* pressure gauge; manometer. —**манометри́ческий,** *adj.* manometric.

манса́рда *n.* garret.

манса́рдный *adj.* of a garret; garret (*attrib.*). —**манса́рдная кры́ша,** mansard roof.

манти́лья *n.* mantilla.

ма́нтия *n.* mantle; cloak; robe; gown.

манто́ *n. indecl.* (woman's) fur coat.

мануфакту́ра *n.* **1,** *hist.* manufacturing. **2,** *obs.* textile mill. **3,** textiles; soft goods.

мануфакту́рный *adj.* **1,** manufacturing (*attrib.*). **2,** textile (*attrib.*); soft-goods (*attrib.*).

маньчжу́р *n.* Manchu. —**маньчжу́рский,** *adj.* Manchu.

манья́к *n.* maniac.

маня́щий *adj.* alluring.

марабу́ *n.m. indecl.* marabou.

мара́зм *n.* marasmus.

мара́л *n.* a variety of red deer; maral.

мара́нье *n., colloq.* **1,** soiling. **2,** scribble; scrawl.

мараски́н *n.* maraschino.

мара́ть *v. impfv., colloq.* **1,** [*pfv.* замара́ть] to soil; dirty. **2,** [*pfv.* намара́ть] to scribble. **3,** [*pfv.* вы́марать] to cross out. —**мара́ться,** *refl.* [*pfv.* замара́ться] *colloq.* to get oneself dirty.

марафо́нский *adj., in* марафо́нский бег, marathon (race).

ма́рганец [*gen.* -нца] *n.* manganese. —**ма́рганцевый,** *adj.* manganese (*attrib.*).

маргари́н *n.* margarine.

маргари́тка [*gen. pl.* -ток] *n.* daisy; English daisy.

маргина́лии *n. pl.* [*sing.* маргина́лия] marginalia.

ма́рево *n.* **1,** mirage. **2,** haze.

маре́на *n.* madder (*plant*).

мари́ец [*gen.* -и́йца] *n.m.* [*fem.* -и́йка] *n.* Mari (*one of a people inhabiting central European Russia*). —**мари́йский,** *adj.* Mari.

мари́на *n.* seascape.

марина́д *n.* marinade.

марини́ст *n.* painter of seascapes.

марино́ванный *adj.* pickled; marinated.

маринова́ть *v. impfv.* [*pfv.* замаринова́ть; *pres.* -ну́ю, -ну́ешь] **1,** to pickle; marinate. **2,** *colloq.* to delay; shelve; put off.

марионе́тка [*gen. pl.* -ток] *n.* **1,** puppet; marionette. **2,** *fig.* puppet. —**марионе́точный,** *adj., fig.* puppet (*attrib.*): марионе́точное прави́тельство, puppet government.

марихуа́на *n.* marijuana.

ма́рка [*gen. pl.* -рок] *n.* **1,** (postage) stamp. **2,** make; model; brand. **3,** mark: фабри́чная ма́рка, trademark. **4,** counter; token (*used as payment*). **5,** chip (*used in games*). **6,** mark (*German monetary unit*). **7,** *fig.* reputation: держа́ть ма́рку, to uphold one's reputation. —**всех ма́рок,** of every stamp. —**вы́сшей ма́рки, 1,** of the highest quality. **2,** (*of a type of person*) of the worst type. —**под ма́ркой** (+ *gen.*), under the guise of.

марки́з *n.* marquis.

марки́за *n.* **1,** marquise; marchioness. **2,** sun blind.

ма́ркий *adj.* [*short form* ма́рок, -рка, -рко] that soils easily.

маркирова́ть *v. impfv. & pfv.* [*pres.* -ру́ю, -ру́ешь] to mark.

маркси́зм *n.* Marxism. —**маркси́ст,** *n.* Marxist. —**маркси́стский,** *adj.* Marxist; Marxian.

ма́рля *n.* gauze. —**ма́рлевый,** *adj.* gauze (*attrib.*).

мармела́д *n.* fruit jellies (*candy*).

мароде́р *n.* **1,** marauder. **2,** *colloq.* profiteer. —**мароде́рский,** *adj.* marauding. —**мароде́рство,** *n.* marauding.

мароде́рствовать *v. impfv.* [*pres.* -ствую, -ствуешь] to maraud.

ма́рочный *adj., in* ма́рочные ви́на, fine wines; vintage wines.

Марс *n.* Mars.

марса́ла *n.* Marsala wine.

ма́рсель *n.m.* topsail.

Марсельеза *n.* Marseillaise.

марсиа́нин [*pl.* -а́не, -а́н] *n.* Martian. —**марсиа́нский**, *adj.* Martian.

март *n.* March (*month*).

марте́н (тэ) *n.* open-hearth furnace. —**марте́новский**, *adj.* open-hearth (*attrib.*): марте́новская печь, open-hearth furnace.

ма́ртовский *adj.* March (*attrib.*).

марты́шка [*gen. pl.* -шек] *n.* marmoset.

марципа́н *n.* marchpane; marzipan.

марш *n.* **1,** march. **2,** (*as a military command*) forward, march! **3,** flight of stairs.

ма́ршал *n.* marshal. —**ма́ршальский**, *adj.* marshal's.

марширова́ть *v. impfv.* [*pres.* -ру́ю, -ру́ешь] to march.

марширо́вка *n.* marching. —**марширо́вочный**, *adj.* marching (*attrib.*).

маршру́т *n.* route; itinerary.

ма́ска [*gen. pl.* -сок] *n.* **1,** mask. **2,** *fig.* mask; guise.

маскара́д *n.* masquerade. —**маскара́дный**, *adj.* masquerade (*attrib.*).

маскирова́ть *v. impfv.* [*pfv.* замаскирова́ть; *pres.* -ру́ю, -ру́ешь] **1,** to disguise. **2,** *fig.* to mask; conceal. **3,** to camouflage. —**маскирова́ться**, *refl.* **1,** (*with instr.*) to dress up (as); come disguised (as). **2,** to camouflage oneself.

маскиро́вка *n.* **1,** masking; disguising; concealment. **2,** *mil.* camouflage.

маскиро́вочный *adj.* camouflage (*attrib.*).

ма́сленица *n.* Shrovetide; Mardi gras.

масле́нка [*gen. pl.* -нок] *n.* **1,** butter dish. **2,** lubricator; oilcan.

маслёнок [*gen.* -нка] *n.* a variety of edible mushroom.

ма́сленый *adj.* **1,** buttered. **2,** oily. **3,** *fig.* unctuous.

масли́на *n.* **1,** olive. **2,** olive tree.

ма́слить *v. impfv.* [*pfv.* нама́слить] *colloq.* **1,** to butter. **2,** to oil; grease.

масли́чный *adj.* yielding edible oil; oil-bearing. —**ма́сличное се́мя**, oilseed.

масли́чный *adj.* olive (*attrib.*).

ма́сло *n.* **1,** butter. **2,** oil. **3,** *art* oil; oils: писа́ть ма́слом, to paint in oils. —**всё идёт как по ма́слу**, everything is hunky-dory. —**подлива́ть ма́сла в огóнь**, to add fuel to the fire.

маслобо́йка [*gen. pl.* -бо́ек] *n.* churn.

маслобо́йня [*gen. pl.* -бо́ен] *n.* creamery.

маслоде́лие *n.* butter making. —**маслоде́льный**, *adj.* butter-making.

маслозаво́д *n.* creamery.

масляни́стый *adj.* oily.

ма́сляный *adj.* oil (*attrib.*); grease (*attrib.*).

масо́н *n.* Mason; Freemason. —**масо́нский**, *adj.* Masonic; Mason's; Freemason's. —**масо́нство**, *n.* Masonry; Freemasonry.

ма́сса *n.* **1,** mass. **2,** *pl.* the masses. **3,** pulp: древе́сная ма́сса, wood pulp. **4,** (*with gen.*) *colloq.* a lot (of); heaps (of). —**в (о́бщей) ма́ссе**, on the whole; for the most part. —**основна́я ма́сса** (+ *gen.*), the bulk (of).

масса́ж *n.* massage. —**массажи́ст**, *n.* masseur. —**массажи́стка**, *n.* masseuse.

масси́в *n.* **1,** mountain range. **2,** tract of land.

масси́вный *adj.* massive.

масси́ровать *v. impfv. & pfv.* [*pres.* -рую, -руешь] **1,** to massage. **2,** *mil.* to mass. —**масси́роваться**, *refl., mil.* to mass.

массо́вка *n., colloq.* **1,** secret meeting. **2,** group excursion. **3,** *theat.; motion pictures* crowd scene.

ма́ссовый *adj.* **1,** mass (*attrib.*). **2,** for the masses; popular. —**ма́ссовое произво́дство**, mass production.

ма́стер [*pl.* мастера́] *n.* **1,** skilled craftsman. Сапо́жный ма́стер, shoemaker. Ма́стер по ремо́нту (+ *gen.*), repairman (*TV, washing machine, etc.*). **2,** master: ма́стер расска́за, master storyteller. **3,** foreman. —**ма́стер на все ру́ки**, jack-of-all-trades.

мастери́ть *v. impfv.* [*pfv.* смастери́ть] *colloq.* to make; fashion; build.

мастерска́я *n., decl. as an adj.* **1,** shop; repair shop; workshop: пошиво́чная мастерска́я, tailor's/dressmaker's shop; обувна́я мастерска́я, shoe repair shop; железнодоро́жные мастерски́е, railroad workshops. **2,** shop (*in a factory*). **3,** (artist's) studio.

мастерски́ *adv.* in a masterful fashion; like an expert.

мастерско́й *adj.* masterly; masterful.

мастерство́ *n.* **1,** skill. **2,** handicraft; trade.

масти́ка *n.* **1,** mastic. **2,** floor polish. —**масти́ковый**, *adj.* mastic.

масти́т *n.* mastitis.

масти́тый *adj.* venerable.

мастодо́нт *n.* mastodon.

масть [*pl.* ма́сти, -сте́й, -стя́м] *n.f.* **1,** color (*of an animal*). **2,** *cards* suit. —**всех масте́й**, of every stripe. —**ходи́ть в масть**, to follow suit.

масшта́б *n.* **1,** scale (*of a map*). **2,** *fig.* scale: в большо́м масшта́бе, on a large scale.

мат *n.* **1,** *chess* mate; checkmate. **2,** floor mat. **3,** *obs.* mat (*dull surface*). **4,** obscene language. —**крича́ть благи́м ма́том**, *colloq.* to yell one's head off.

матема́тика *n.* mathematics. —**матема́тик**, *n.* mathematician. —**математи́ческий**, *adj.* mathematical.

матереуби́йство *n.* matricide.

материа́л *n.* **1,** material: строи́тельные материа́лы, building materials; материа́л для докла́да, material for a report. **2,** material; fabric.

материали́зм *n.* materialism.

материализова́ть *v. impfv. & pfv.* [*pres.* -зу́ю, -зу́ешь] to give material form to. —**материализова́ться**, *refl.* to assume material form.

материали́ст *n.* materialist. —**материалисти́ческий**, *adj.* materialistic.

материа́льно *adv.* materially.

материа́льный *adj.* **1,** material. **2,** financial: материа́льные затрудне́ния, financial difficulties. —**материа́льная часть**, matériel.

матери́к [*gen.* -рика́] *n.* **1,** continent; mainland. **2,** subsoil.

материко́вый *adj.* continental. —**материко́вая поро́да**, bedrock.

матери́нский *adj.* maternal.

матери́нство *n.* motherhood; maternity.

мате́рия *n.* **1,** matter. **2,** material; fabric. **3,** *colloq.* subject; topic.

ма́терный *adj., colloq.* obscene.

мате́рчатый *adj.* cloth (*attrib.*); made of cloth.

матёрый *adj.* **1,** (*of an animal*) full-grown. **2,** *colloq.* experienced; veteran. **3,** inveterate.

ма́тка [*gen. pl.* -ток] *n.* **1,** uterus; womb. **2,** female (*of animals*). **3,** queen bee.

ма́товый *adj.* mat; dull. —**ма́товое стекло́**, frosted glass.

ма́точный *adj.* uterine.

матра́с *also*, **матра́ц** *n.* mattress. —**матра́сный**, *adj.* mattress (*attrib.*).

матре́шка [*gen. pl.* -шек] *n.* set of nesting dolls.

матриарха́льный *adj.* matriarchal. —**матриарха́т**, *n.* matriarchy.

матримониа́льный *adj., obs.* matrimonial.

ма́трица *n.* matrix.

матро́на *n.* matron.

матро́с *n.* sailor; seaman.

матро́ска [*gen. pl.* -сок] *n.* sailor's jacket.

матро́сский *adj.* sailor's; sailor (*attrib.*).

ма́тушка *n., archaic* mother.

матч *n., sports* match. —**матч-рева́нш**, return match.

мать [*gen., dat., & prepl.* **ма́тери**; *instr.* **ма́терью**; *pl.* **ма́тери**, -ре́й, -ря́м] *n.f.* mother.

ма́узер (зэ) *n.* Mauser.

мах *n., colloq.* stroke. —**дать ма́ху**, to commit a blunder. —**одни́м ма́хом, 1,** with one stroke. **2,** at a single bound. —**с ма́ху, 1,** with all one's might. **2,** rashly; without thinking.

махао́н *n.* swallowtail (*butterfly*).

маха́ть *v. impfv.* [*pfv.* **махну́ть**; *pres.* **машу́, ма́шешь**] (*with instr.*) **1,** to wave: маха́ть руко́й (+ *dat.*), to wave to someone. **2,** to wag (one's tail); flap (one's wings). —**махну́ть руко́й на** (+ *acc.*), to give up on; give up as hopeless.

махи́на *n., colloq.* large cumbersome object.

махина́ция *n.* machination.

махну́ть *v., pfv. of* **маха́ть.**

махови́к [*gen.* -вика́] *n.* flywheel.

махово́й *adj., in* махово́е колесо́, flywheel.

махо́рка *n.* **1,** a kind of low-grade tobacco. **2,** the plant from which it comes.

махро́вый *adj.* **1,** made of terry cloth: махро́вая ткань, terry cloth. **2,** *bot.* double: махро́вая ро́за, double rose. **3,** *fig.* blatant; out-and-out. **4,** *fig.* rabid; fanatical.

маца́ *n.* matzo.

ма́чеха *n.* stepmother.

ма́чта *n.* mast (*of a ship*).

маши́на *n.* **1,** machine: стира́льная маши́на, washing machine. **2,** car. **3,** vehicle: боева́я маши́на, combat vehicle. **4,** engine: парова́я маши́на, steam engine.

машина́льный *adj.* mechanical; automatic; subconscious.

машиниза́ция *n.* mechanization.

машинизи́ровать *v. impfv. & pfv.* [*pres.* -рую, -руешь] to mechanize.

машини́ст *n.* **1,** machinist. **2,** engineer; motorman.

машини́стка [*gen. pl.* -ток] *n.* (female) typist.

маши́нка [*gen. pl.* -нок] *n.* **1,** machine. **2,** device. —**пи́шущая маши́нка,** typewriter.

маши́нный *adj.* machine (*attrib.*).

машинопи́сный *adj.* typewritten.

маши́нопись *n.f.* typing.

машинострое́ние *n.* machine building. —**машиностро́ительный**, *adj.* machine-building.

мае́стро *n.m. indecl.* maestro.

мая́к [*gen.* маяка́] *n.* lighthouse.

ма́ятник *n.* **1,** pendulum. **2,** balance wheel.

ма́яться *v.r. impfv., colloq.* **1,** to toil; slave. **2,** to suffer.

ма́ячить *v. impfv., colloq.* to loom up; appear in the distance.

мгла *n.* **1,** haze. **2,** gloom; darkness. —**мгли́стый**, *adj.* hazy.

мгнове́ние *n.* instant; moment. —**в мгнове́ние о́ка,** in the twinkling of an eye.

мгнове́нный *adj.* **1,** instantaneous. **2,** momentary. —**мгнове́нно**, *adv.* instantly.

ме́бель *n.f.* furniture. —**ме́бельный**, *adj.* furniture (*attrib.*). —**ме́бельщик**, *n.* furniture maker.

меблиро́ванный *adj.* furnished.

меблирова́ть *v. impfv. & pfv.* [*pres.* -ру́ю, -ру́ешь] to furnish.

меблиро́вка *n.* **1,** furnishing. **2,** furniture; furnishings.

мегаге́рц [*gen. pl.* -ге́рц] *n.* megacycle.

мегато́нна *n.* megaton.

мегафо́н *n.* megaphone.

меге́ра *n.* shrew; termagant; virago.

мёд [*2nd loc.* меду́] *n.* **1,** honey. **2,** mead.

медали́ст *n.m.* [*fem.* -ли́стка] medal winner; medalist.

меда́ль *n.f.* medal. —**оборо́тная сторона́ меда́ли,** the other side of the coin.

медальо́н *n.* medallion; locket.

медве́дица *n.* female bear. —**Больша́я Медве́дица,** Big Dipper; Ursa Major. —**Ма́лая Медве́дица,** Little Dipper; Ursa Minor.

медве́дь *n.m.* bear. —**бе́лый** *or* **поля́рный медве́дь,** polar bear.

медве́жий [*fem.* -жья] *adj.* **1,** bear (*attrib.*); bear's. **2,** bearskin. —**медве́жий у́гол,** godforsaken place. —**медве́жья услу́га,** a well-meaning gesture that backfires.

медвежо́нок [*gen.* -нка; *pl.* -жа́та, -жа́т] *n.* bear cub.

медвя́ный *adj.* smelling of honey. —**медвя́ная роса́,** honeydew.

медиа́на *n.* median.

ме́дик *n.* **1,** *obs.* physician; doctor. **2,** *colloq.* medical student.

медикаме́нты [*gen.* -тов] *n. pl.* medicines.

ме́диум *n.* medium; spiritualist.

медици́на *n.* medicine (*the science*).

медици́нский *adj.* medical. —**медици́нский осмо́тр,** physical examination. —**медици́нская сестра́,** (hospital) nurse.

ме́дленный *adj.* slow. —**ме́дленно**, *adv.* slowly. —**ме́дленность**, *n.f.* slowness.

медли́тельный *adj.* slow; slow-moving; sluggish. —**медли́тельность**, *n.f.* slowness; sluggishness.

ме́длить *v. impfv.* to be slow; delay; tarry.

ме́дник *n.* coppersmith.

ме́дный *adj.* copper. —**ме́дный лоб,** *colloq.* blockhead.

медо́вый *adj.* **1,** honey (*attrib.*). **2,** sweet-smelling. **3,** *fig.* honeyed; sugary. —**медо́вый ме́сяц,** honeymoon.

медоно́сный *adj.* yielding or producing honey. —**медоно́сная пчела́,** honeybee.

медосмо́тр *n.* physical examination (*contr. of* медици́нский осмо́тр).

медпу́нкт *n.* first-aid station (*contr. of* медици́нский пункт).

медсестра́ *n.* (hospital) nurse (*contr. of* медици́нская сестра́).

меду́за *n.* jellyfish; medusa.

медь *n.f.* copper.

медя́к [*gen.* -дяка́] *n., colloq.* copper coin.

медя́нка *n.* **1,** a species of non-poisonous snake. **2,** verdigris.

меж *prep.* = **ме́жду.**

межа́ [*pl.* ме́жи, меж, межа́м] *n.* boundary (*between property*).

междоме́тие *n.*, *gram.* interjection.

междоусо́бие *also,* **междоусо́бица** *n.* civil strife. —**междоусо́бный,** *adj.* internecine.

ме́жду *prep., with instr.* **1,** between: ме́жду окно́м и две́рью, between the window and the door; ме́жду пятью́ и шестью́ часа́ми, between five and six o'clock. **2,** among: ме́жду собо́й, among oneselves. ♦ *Also with gen. in certain set expressions:* чита́ть ме́жду строк, to read between the lines. —**ме́жду на́ми,** between you and me; confidentially. —**ме́жду про́чим,** by the way. —**ме́жду тем,** meanwhile; in the meantime. —**ме́жду тем как,** while; whereas.

междугоро́дный *adj.* **1,** intercity; interurban. **2,** (*of a phone call*) long-distance.

междунаро́дный *adj.* international.

междуца́рствие *n.* interregnum.

межева́ние *n.* surveying.

межева́ть *v. impfv.* [*pres.* -жу́ю -жу́ешь] to survey; set boundaries to.

межево́й *adj.* **1,** boundary (*attrib.*): межево́й знак, boundary marker. **2,** surveying (*attrib.*).

ме́жень *n.f.* lowest water level (*of a river or lake*).

межзвёздный *adj.* interstellar.

межконтинента́льный *adj.* intercontinental.

межплане́тный *adj.* interplanetary.

межсезо́нье *n.* off-season.

мезозо́йский *adj.* Mesozoic.

мезо́н *n.* meson.

мезони́н *n.* attic.

мексика́нец [*gen.* -нца] *n.m.* [*fem.* -нка] Mexican. —**мексика́нский,** *adj.* Mexican.

мел *n.* chalk.

меланхо́лия *n.* **1,** melancholy. **2,** *med.* melancholia. —**меланхо́лик,** *n.* melancholic person. —**меланхоли́ческий; меланхоли́чный,** *adj.* melancholic; melancholy.

меле́ть *v. impfv.* [*pfv.* обмеле́ть] to become shallow.

мелиора́ция *n.* land reclamation.

ме́лкий *adj.* [*short form* ме́лок, мелка́, ме́лко; *comp.* ме́льче; *superl.* мельча́йший] **1,** small; minute. **2,** (*of rain, sand, etc.*) fine. **3,** shallow. **4,** minor: ме́лкий чино́вник/ремо́нт, minor official/repairs. **5,** petty: ме́лкие забо́ты, petty cares. **6,** *fig.* petty; small-minded. —**ме́лкая буржуази́я,** petty bourgeoisie. —**ме́лкие де́ньги,** small change. —**ме́лкая кра́жа,** petty larceny. —**ме́лкая таре́лка,** (flat) plate; dinner plate.

ме́лко *adv.* fine; into small particles.

мелкобуржуа́зный *adj.* petty-bourgeois.

мелково́дный *adj.* shallow.

мелково́дье *n.* shallow water.

мелкота́ *n.*, *colloq.* **1,** small size. **2,** small fry.

мелово́й *adj.* **1,** chalk (*attrib.*); chalky. **2,** *geol.* cretaceous.

мело́дика *n.* melodics.

мелоди́ческий *adj.* **1,** melodic. **2,** melodious.

мелоди́чный *adj.* melodious. —**мелоди́чность,** *n.f.* melodiousness.

мело́дия *n.* melody; tune.

мелодра́ма *n.* melodrama. —**мелодрамати́ческий,** *adj.* melodramatic.

мело́к [*gen.* -лка́] *n.* piece of chalk. —**игра́ть на мело́к,** *cards* to play on credit.

мелома́н *n.* music lover.

ме́лочный *also,* **мелочно́й** *adj.* petty; picayune. —**ме́лочность,** *n.f.* pettiness.

ме́лочь [*pl.* ме́лочи, -че́й, -ча́м] *n.f.* **1,** small things; small items. **2,** (small) change. **3,** trifle.

мель [*2nd loc.* мели́] *n.f.* **1,** shoal. **2,** *in* песча́ная мель, sandbank. —**на мели́, 1,** aground. **2,** *fig.* high and dry; on the rocks. —**сесть на мель,** to run aground.

мелька́ть *v. impfv.* [*pfv.* мелькну́ть] **1,** to flash; flash by: у меня́ мелькну́ла мысль, the thought flashed across my mind. **2,** (*of stars*) to glimmer.

ме́льком *adv.* **1,** for a moment; briefly; quickly: ви́деть ме́льком, to catch a glimpse of; слы́шать ме́льком, chance to hear. **2,** cursorily; perfunctorily.

ме́льник *n.* miller.

ме́льница *n.* mill. —**лить во́ду на чью́-нибудь ме́льницу,** to be grist for (*or* bring grist to) someone's mill.

мельхио́р *n.* nickel silver.

мельча́ть *v. impfv.* [*pfv.* измельча́ть] **1,** to become smaller. **2,** to become shallow. **3,** *fig.* to deteriorate; degenerate.

ме́льче *adj.*, *comp. of* **ме́лкий.**

мельчи́ть *v. impfv.* to crush; grind.

мелюзга́ *n.*, *colloq.* small fry.

мембра́на *n.* diaphragm (*in an earphone, microphone, etc.*).

мемора́ндум *n.* memorandum.

мемориа́льный *adj.* memorial.

мемуа́ры [*gen.* -ров] *n. pl.* memoirs.

менделе́вий *n.* mendelevium.

ме́нее *adv.*, *used in forming compound comparatives* less: ме́нее интере́сный, less interesting. —**бо́лее и́ли ме́нее,** more or less. —**тем не ме́нее,** nevertheless.

менестре́ль *n.m.* minstrel; troubadour.

мензу́рка [*gen. pl.* -рок] *n.* measuring glass.

менинги́т *n.* meningitis.

меново́й *adj.* of exchange: менова́я едини́ца, unit of exchange. —**менова́я торго́вля,** barter.

менструа́ция *n.* menstruation. —**менструа́льный,** *adj.* menstrual.

менструи́ровать *v. impfv.* [*pres.* -рую, -руешь] to menstruate.

менто́л *n.* menthol. —**менто́ловый,** *adj.* menthol (*attrib.*); mentholated.

ме́нтор *n.*, *obs.* mentor.

менуэ́т *n.* minuet.

ме́ньше *adj.*, *comp. of* **ма́лый** *and* **ма́ленький,** smaller. —*adv.*, *comp. of* **ма́ло,** less. —**ме́ньше всего́,** least of all.

меньшеви́к [*gen.* -вика́] *n.* Menshevik. —**меньшеви́стский,** *adj.* Menshevik (*attrib.*).

ме́ньший *adj.*, *used only as a modifier, comp. of* **ма́лый** *and* **ма́ленький,** smaller; lesser. —**по ме́ньшей ме́ре, 1,** at least. **2,** to say the least. —**са́мое ме́ньшее, 1,** the least. **2,** at least.

меньшинство́ *n.* minority.

меню́ *n. neut. indecl.* menu.

меня́ *pron.*, *gen. & acc. of* **я.**

меня́ла *n.m.* moneychanger.

меня́ть *v. impfv.* [*pfv.* поменя́ть] **1,** to change. **2,** to exchange. —**меня́ться,** *refl.* **1,** [*impfv. only*] to change. **2,** (*with instr.*) to exchange; trade: меня́ться роля́ми, to exchange roles; **меня́ться места́ми**, to trade places.

ме́ра *n.* **1,** measure: **ме́ра жи́дкости**, liquid measure. **2,** extent; degree; measure: **в большо́й ме́ре**, to a great extent/degree; in large measure. **3,** measure (*action*): **кру́тые ме́ры**, drastic measures. —**в ме́ру, 1,** sufficiently; in the right amount. **2,** (*with gen.*) to the extent of. —**в по́лной ме́ре**, fully; in full measure. —**знать ме́ру**, to know one's limits; know when to stop. —**не в ме́ру**, excessively. —**по кра́йней ме́ре**, at least. —**по ме́ньшей ме́ре, 1,** at least. **2,** to say the least. —**по ме́ре** (+ *gen.*), in proportion to; to the extent of: **по ме́ре возмо́жности**, to the fullest extent possible. —**по ме́ре того́, как**, as. —**сверх ме́ры; че́рез ме́ру**, excessively. —**чу́вство ме́ры**, sense of proportion.

ме́ргель *n.m., geol.* marl.

ме́режка *n.* openwork.

мере́нга *n.* meringue.

мере́ть *v. impfv.* [*pres.* **мрёт, мрут;** *past* **мёр, -ла**] *colloq.* to die (*in large numbers*).

мере́щиться *v.r. impfv.* [*pfv.* **помере́щиться**] (*with dat.*) *colloq.* to seem (to).

мерза́вец [*gen.* -**вца**] *n.* scoundrel.

ме́рзкий *adj.* [*short form* -**зок, -зка́, -зко**] **1,** loathsome; vile. **2,** *colloq.* rotten; foul.

мерзлота́ *n.* frozen earth. —**ве́чная мерзлота́**, permafrost.

мёрзлый *adj.* frozen.

мёрзнуть *v. impfv.* [*pfv.* **замёрзнуть;** *past* **мёрз, -ла**] **1,** to freeze; become frozen. **2,** (*of a person*) to be freezing (cold); be frozen. **3,** to freeze to death; perish from the frost.

ме́рзость *n.f.* vile thing; abomination.

меридиа́н *n.* meridian.

мери́ло *n.* standard; criterion; yardstick; gauge.

ме́рин *n.* gelding. —**врать как си́вый ме́рин**, to be a habitual liar.

мерино́с *n.* **1,** merino sheep. **2,** merino wool. —**мерино́совый**, *adj.* merino.

ме́рить *v.impfv.* **1,** to measure. **2,** to try on. —**ме́риться**, *refl.* [*pfv.* **поме́риться**] (*with instr.*) to measure: **ме́риться си́лами с**, to measure one's strength against.

ме́рка [*gen. pl.* -**рок**] *n.* **1,** measurements. **2,** measuring rod; yardstick. **3,** *fig.* yardstick; criterion. —**по ме́рке**, to measure.

меркантили́зм *n.* mercantilism. —**мерканти́льный**, *adj.* mercantile.

ме́ркнуть *v. impfv.* [*pfv.* **поме́ркнуть;** *past* **мерк, -ла**] **1,** to grow dim. **2,** *fig.* to fade; wane.

Мерку́рий *n.* Mercury (*the planet*).

мерлу́шка *n.* lambskin (*attrib.*). —**мерлу́шковый**, *adj.* lambskin (*attrib.*).

ме́рный *adj.* measured; rhythmical.

мероприя́тие *n.* measure; step.

ме́ртвенный *adj.* **1,** lifeless; dead. **2,** *fig.* deathly.

мертве́ть *v. impfv.* [*pfv.* **омертве́ть** *or* **помертве́ть**] **1,** to become numb. **2,** *fig.* to be paralyzed (*with fear, terror, etc.*).

мертве́ц [*gen. & acc.* -**веца́**] *n.* dead person.

мертве́цкая *n., decl. as an adj., colloq.* mortuary; morgue.

мертве́цки *adv., colloq., in* **мертве́цки пьян**, dead drunk; **спать мертве́цки**, be dead to the world.

мертвечи́на *n.* carrion.

мертви́ть *v. impfv.* [*pres.* -**влю́, -ви́шь**] **1,** to kill; destroy. **2,** *fig.* to deaden.

мертворождённый *adj.* stillborn.

мёртвый *adj.* dead. —*n.* **1,** dead person. **2,** *pl.* the dead. —**мёртвая бу́ква**, dead letter. —**мёртвый груз**, dead weight. —**мёртвая то́чка**, dead center: **сдви́нуть(ся) с мёртвой то́чки**, to move off dead center. —**на мёртвой то́чке**, deadlocked; at a standstill. —**ни жив ни мёртв**, in a state of shock. —**спать мёртвым сном**, to be dead to the world.

мерца́ние *n.* glimmer; twinkling; flickering.

мерца́ть *v. impfv.* to twinkle; flicker; glimmer; shimmer.

ме́сиво *n., colloq.* **1,** liquid refuse; slop. **2,** mud; mire. **3,** swill; mash (*fed to livestock*).

меси́ть *v. impfv.* [*pres.* **мешу́, ме́сишь**] to knead. —**меси́ть грязь**, to slosh through the mud.

ме́сса *n., relig.* Mass.

месси́я *n.* Messiah. —**мессиа́нский**, *adj.* Messianic.

месте́чко [*pl.* -**чки, -чек**] *n.* **1,** *dim. of* **ме́сто. 2,** small town. —**тёплое месте́чко**, soft job.

мести́ *v. impfv.* [*pres.* **мету́, метёшь;** *past* **мёл, мела́, мело́**] **1,** to sweep. **2,** to scatter; swirl. **3,** (*of a snowstorm*) to be raging. **4,** *impers.* to be snowing: **сего́дня си́льно метёт**, it is snowing hard today.

ме́стность *n.f.* **1,** area; region; district: **се́льская/боло́тистая ме́стность**, rural/marshy area. **2,** country; terrain: **холми́стая ме́стность**, hilly country; **пересечённая ме́стность**, rugged terrain.

ме́стный *adj.* local. —**ме́стный паде́ж**, locative case.

ме́сто [*pl.* **места́**] *n.* **1,** place. **2,** (*with gen.*) site (of); scene (of). **3,** space; room. **4,** seat; place. **5,** (*with gen.*) part; place (*of/in a book, story, etc.*). **6,** berth. **7,** job; position. **8,** piece (*of luggage*). **9,** *pl.* provinces; outlying areas. —**знать своё ме́сто**, to know one's place. —**име́ть ме́сто, 1,** to take place. **2,** to exist; be found. —**класть не на ме́сто**, to misplace. —**места́ми**, in places; in spots; here and there. —**на ва́шем ме́сте**, in your place; if I were you. —**на ме́сте, 1,** in place: **стоя́ть на ме́сте**, to stand in place; stand still. **2,** on the spot: **уби́ть кого́-нибудь на ме́сте**, to kill someone on the spot. —**на своём ме́сте**, in one's proper place; doing what one should be doing. —**не к ме́сту; не у ме́ста**, inappropriate; out of place. —**не ме́сто, 1,** (*with dat.*) not to belong: **здесь вам не ме́сто**, you don't belong here. **2,** not the place to: **здесь не ме́сто говори́ть об э́том**, this is not the place to talk about it. —**ни с ме́ста, 1,** (*as a command*) don't move!; stay put! **2,** making no progress; getting nowhere. —**поста́вить кого́-нибудь на (своё) ме́сто**, to put someone in his place.

местожи́тельство *n.* (place of) residence.

местоиме́ние *n.* pronoun. —**местоиме́нный**, *adj.* pronominal.

местонахожде́ние *n.* location; whereabouts.

местоположе́ние *n.* location; site.

местопребыва́ние *n.* residence; abode. —**местопребыва́ние прави́тельства**, the seat of government.

месторожде́ние *n.* **1,** deposit; field: **месторожде́ние не́фти**, oil field. **2,** *obs.* place of birth.

месть *n.f.* revenge; vengeance. —**кро́вная месть**, vendetta.

ме́сяц *n.* **1,** month. **2,** moon. —**медо́вый ме́сяц**, honeymoon.

ме́сячник *n.* month (*devoted to a special cause*): ме́сячник де́тской кни́ги, children's book month.

ме́сячный *adj.* **1,** lasting a month; a month's. **2,** monthly.

ме́та *n.* **1,** mark. **2,** *obs.* target.

мета́лл *n.* metal. —**металли́ст**, *n.* metalworker. —**металли́ческий**, *adj.* metal (*attrib.*); metallic.

металло́ид *n.* metalloid.

металлоло́м *n.* scrap metal.

металлоно́сный *adj.* metalliferous.

металлоплави́льный *adj.* smelting (*attrib.*).

металлу́ргия *also*, **металлурги́я** *n.* metallurgy. —**металлу́рг**, *n.* metallurgist. —**металлурги́ческий**, *adj.* metallurgic.

метаморфо́з *n.*, *biol.* metamorphosis. —**метаморфо́за**, *n.*, *fig.* metamorphosis; complete transformation.

мета́н *n.* methane.

мета́ние *n.* **1,** throwing: мета́ние ди́ска, discus throw. **2,** *in* мета́ние икры́, spawning.

метаста́з *n.* metastasis.

мета́тель *n.m.*, *sports* thrower: мета́тель ди́ска, discus thrower.

мета́тельный *adj.* to be thrown or launched: мета́тельный снаря́д, missile; projectile.

мета́ть[1] *v. impfv.* [*pfv.* **метну́ть**; *pres.* **мечу́, ме́чешь**] to throw; hurl; fling; cast. —**мета́ть банк**, *cards* to keep the bank. —**мета́ть гро́мы и мо́лнии**, to fulminate; rant and rave. —**мета́ть икру́**, to spawn. —**мета́ть се́но**, to stack hay.

мета́ть[2] *v. impfv.* [*pfv.* **смета́ть**; *pres.* **-та́ю, -та́ешь**] to baste. —**мета́ть пе́тли**, **1,** to make buttonholes. **2,** to foul the trail. **3,** to confuse the issue.

мета́ться *v.r. impfv.* [*pres.* **мечу́сь, ме́чешься**] **1,** to rush about. **2,** to toss about (*in bed*); toss (*in one's sleep*).

метафи́зика *n.* metaphysics. —**метафи́зик**, *n.* metaphysician; metaphysicist. —**метафизи́ческий**, *adj.* metaphysical.

мета́фора *n.* metaphor. —**метафори́ческий**, *adj.* metaphorical.

мете́лица *n.* = **мете́ль.**

мете́лка [*gen. pl.* **-лок**] *n.* **1,** whisk broom. **2,** *bot.* panicle.

мете́ль *n.f.* snowstorm; blizzard.

метео́р *n.* meteor.

метеори́зм *n.*, *med.* flatulence.

метеори́т *n.* meteorite.

метео́рный *adj.* meteor (*attrib.*); meteoric.

метеороло́гия *n.* meteorology. —**метеоро́лог**, *n.* meteorologist. —**метеорологи́ческий**, *adj.* meteorological.

метеоспу́тник *n.* weather satellite.

метиза́ция *n.* crossbreeding.

мети́л *n.* methyl.

метиле́н *n.* methylene.

мети́ловый *adj.* methyl (*attrib.*).

мети́с *n.* **1,** mongrel. **2,** mestizo.

ме́тить *v. impfv.* [*pres.* **ме́чу, ме́тишь**] **1,** [*pfv.* **наме́тить** *or* **поме́тить**] to mark. **2,** (*with* в + *acc.*) to aim (at). **3,** (*with* в + *nom. pl.*) *colloq.* to aim (to become); aspire (to).

ме́тка [*gen. pl.* **-ток**] *n.* **1,** marking. **2,** mark. **3,** name tape containing one's initials.

ме́ткий *adj.* [*short form* **-ток, -тка́, -тко**] **1,** (*of a* marksman, weapon, etc.) accurate. **2,** (*of a blow, bullet, etc.*) well-aimed. **3,** (*of one's eye*) keen. **4,** *fig.* (*of a comment, remark, etc.*) pointed; apt.

ме́ткость *n.f.* **1,** accuracy; marksmanship. **2,** keenness (*of eyesight*).

метла́ [*pl.* **ме́тлы, мётел**] *n.* broom.

метну́ть *v.*, *pfv. of* **мета́ть**[1].

ме́тод *n.* method.

методи́зм *n.* Methodism.

мето́дика *n.* methods.

методи́ст *n.* **1,** Methodist. **2,** specialist in the methodology of teaching. —**методи́стский**, *adj.* Methodist.

методи́ческий *adj.* **1,** [*also*, **методи́чный**] methodical; systematic. **2,** pert. to the methodology of teaching.

методоло́гия *n.* methodology. —**методологи́ческий**, *adj.* methodological.

метр *n.* **1,** meter (*unit of length*). **2,** measuring rod *or* tape (*one meter in length*). **3,** *pros.* meter.

метра́ж [*gen.* **-жа́**] *n.* **1,** length (*in meters*). **2,** *motion pictures* footage. **3,** area (*in square meters*).

метрдоте́ль (тэ) *n.m.* maître d'hotel; headwaiter.

ме́трика *n.* **1,** birth certificate. **2,** *pros.* metrics.

метри́ческий *adj.* **1,** metric. **2,** pert. to the registration of births, marriages, and deaths: метри́ческое свиде́тельство, birth certificate.

метро́ *n. indecl.* subway.

метроно́м *n.* metronome.

метрополите́н (тэ) *n.* subway.

метрополи́я *n.* parent state; home country (*of an empire*).

ме́тчик *n.* marker; one who marks.

мех *n.* **1,** [*pl.* **меха́**] fur. **2,** [*pl.* **мехи́**] skin (*vessel*); wineskin. —**на меху́**, fur-lined. *See also* **мехи́.**

механиза́тор *n.* **1,** specialist in mechanization. **2,** machine operator; machine servicer (*in agriculture*).

механиза́ция *n.* mechanization.

механизи́ровать *v. impfv. & pfv.* [*pres.* **-рую, -руешь**] to mechanize.

механи́зм *n.* mechanism.

меха́ник *n.* **1,** mechanical engineer. **2,** mechanic.

меха́ника *n.* mechanics.

механи́ческий *adj.* **1,** mechanical. **2,** power-driven; power (*attrib.*). **3,** *fig.* mechanical; automatic. —**механи́ческий цех; механи́ческая мастерска́я**, machine shop.

мехи́ [*gen.* **мехо́в**] *n. pl.* bellows.

мехово́й *adj.* fur.

меховщи́к [*gen.* **-щика́**] *n.* furrier.

мецена́т *n.* patron of the arts.

ме́ццо-сопра́но *n. neut. indecl.* mezzo-soprano (*voice*). —*n.f. indecl.* mezzo-soprano (*singer*).

меч [*gen.* **меча́**] *n.* sword.

мечено́сец [*gen.* **-сца**] *n.* **1,** sword-bearer. **2,** *hist.* Teutonic knight.

ме́ченый *adj.* marked.

мече́ть *n.f.* mosque.

меч-ры́ба *n.* swordfish.

мечта́ *n.* **1,** dream: заве́тная мечта́, lifelong dream. **2,** daydreaming: предава́ться мечта́м, to give way to daydreaming.

мечта́ние *n.* daydreaming; reverie.

мечта́тель *n.m.* dreamer; visionary.

мечта́тельный *adj.* **1,** given to dreaming. **2,** dreamy. **3,** visionary. —**мечта́тельность**, *n.f.* reverie.

мечта́ть *v. impfv.* **1,** to dream. **2,** to daydream.

мешáлка [*gen. pl.* -лок] *n.* mixer.

мешанúна *n.*, *colloq.* mishmash; hodgepodge.

мешáть *v. impfv.* [*pfv.* помешáть] **1**, (*with dat.*) to bother; disturb; hinder; impede; prevent. **2**, to stir. **3**, [*pfv.* смешáть] to mix; blend. —**мешáться**, *refl.* [*pfv.* смешáться] **1**, to mix; blend; mingle. **2**, to become confused. **3**, [*impfv. only*] (*with* в + *acc.*) *colloq.* to interfere (in). **4**, [*impfv. only*] *colloq.* to be a hindrance; get in the way.

мéшкать *v. impfv.*, *colloq.* to tarry; dally; dawdle.

мешковáтый *adj.* **1**, (*of clothing*) baggy. **2**, clumsy; awkward.

мешковúна *n.* sacking; sackcloth.

мéшкотный *adj.*, *colloq.* **1**, sluggish. **2**, laborious.

мешóк [*gen.* -шкá] *n.* bag; sack. —**дéнежный мешóк**, moneybags; rich man. —**мешкú под глазáми**, bags under one's eyes. —**сидéть мешкóм**, (*of a garment*) to be too big; be baggy.

мешóчек [*gen.* -чка] *n.* **1**, *dim. of* мешóк. **2**, sac. —**яйцó в мешóчек**, medium-boiled egg.

мещанúн [*pl.* -щáне, -щáн] *n.m.* [*fem.* -щáнка] **1**, petty bourgeois. **2**, *fig.* person of narrow or petty interests.

мещáнский *adj.* **1**, petty-bourgeois. **2**, *fig.* narrow-minded.

мещáнство *n.* **1**, lower middle class; petty bourgeoisie. **2**, *fig.* narrow-mindedness.

мздá *n.*, *obs.* **1**, payment. **2**, bribe.

ми *n. neut.*, *music* mi; E.

миáзмы *n. pl.* [*sing.* миáзма] miasma.

миг *n.* moment; instant. —**в одúн миг**, in a flash; in a jiffy.

мигáлка [*gen. pl.* -лок] *n.*, *colloq.* **1**, wick lamp. **2**, blinking light; blinker; flasher.

мигáние *n.* **1**, wink (*of the eye*). **2**, blinking (*of a light*).

мигáть *v. impfv.* [*pfv.* мигнýть] **1**, to blink. **2**, (*with instr.*) to blink (one's eyes). **3**, (*with dat.*) to wink (at). **4**, to twinkle; flicker.

мúгом *adv.*, *colloq.* in a flash; in a jiffy.

миграция *n.* migration.

мигрéнь *n.f.* migraine.

мигрúровать *v. impfv.* [*pres.* -рую, -руешь] to migrate.

мúдия *n.* mussel.

мизансцéна *n.*, *theat.* staging.

мизантрóпия *n.* misanthropy. —**мизантрóп**, *n.* misanthrope. —**мизантропúческий**, *adj.* misanthropic.

мизéрный *adj.* **1**, wretched. **2**, paltry; meager; measly.

мизúнец [*gen.* -нца] *n.* **1**, little finger. **2**, little toe.

микрóб *n.* microbe; germ.

микробиолóгия *n.* microbiology. —**микробиóлог**, *n.* microbiologist.

микрокóсм *n.* microcosm.

микрóметр *n.* micrometer.

микрóн [*gen. pl.* -крóн] *n.* micron.

микроорганúзм *n.* microorganism.

микроскóп *n.* microscope. —**микроскопúческий**, *adj.* microscopic.

микросхéма *n.* microcircuit.

микрофúльм *n.* microfilm.

микрофóн *n.* microphone.

микстýра *n.* mixture; medicine.

мúлая *n.*, *decl. as an adj.* sweetheart; darling.

мúленький *adj.*, *colloq.* **1**, pretty; cute. **2**, dear; sweet. **3**, (*in direct address*) darling.

милитаризáция *n.* militarization.

милитаризúровать *v. impfv. & pfv.* [*pres.* -рую, -руешь] to militarize. *Also*, **милитаризовáть** [*pres.* -зýю, -зýешь].

милитарúзм *n.* militarism. —**милитарúст**, *n.* militarist. —**милитаристúческий**, *adj.* militaristic.

милицéйский *adj.* **1**, militia (*attrib.*). **2**, police (*attrib.*).

милиционéр *n.* **1**, policeman. **2**, militiaman.

милúция *n.* **1**, the police. **2**, militia.

миллиáрд *n.* (*U.S.*) billion; (*Brit.*) milliard. —**миллиардéр**, (дэ) *n.* multimillionaire.

миллиáрдный *ordinal numeral* billionth. —*adj.* **1**, containing or consisting of billions. **2**, worth billions.

миллигрáмм *n.* milligram.

миллимéтр *n.* millimeter.

миллиóн *n.* million. —**миллионéр**, *n.* millionaire.

миллиóнный *ordinal numeral* millionth. —*adj.* **1**, containing or consisting of millions. **2**, worth millions.

мúло *adv.* **1**, nicely. **2**, prettily. —*adj.*, *used predicatively* nice; kind: **как мúло, что вы пришлú**, how nice; kind of you to come!

мúловать *v. impfv.* [*pres.* -лую, -луешь] *obs.* to show mercy to; pardon.

миловúдный *adj.* pretty; good-looking.

милосéрдие *n.* **1**, mercy. **2**, clemency. —**милосéрдный**, *adj.* merciful; charitable.

мúлостивый *adj.*, *obs.* kind; gracious.

мúлостыня *n.* alms.

мúлость *n.f.* **1**, favor; good graces: **быть в мúлости у**, to be in the good graces of. **2**, favor; good turn: **сдéлать мúлость** (+ *dat.*), to do (someone) a favor. **3**, mercy. —**мúлости прóсим**!, you are always welcome! —**по мúлости** (+ *gen.*), **1**, thanks to. **2**, through the fault of. —**сдавáться на мúлость** (+ *gen.*), to surrender unconditionally to. —**скажú(те) на мúлость**, **1**, would you please tell (*or* mind telling) me. **2**, you don't say!

мúлый *adj.* **1**, nice; sweet. **2**, dear: **мúлый друг**, dear friend. —*n.* darling; sweetheart.

мúля *n.* mile. —**англúйская мúля**, statute mile.

мим *n.* mime (*farce performed in ancient times*).

мúмика *n.* **1**, facial expressions. **2**, mimicry.

мимикрúя *n.*, *biol.* mimicry.

мúмст *n.* mimic. —**мимúческий**, *adj.* mimic.

мúмо *prep.*, *with gen.* past; by: **проходúть мúмо дóма**, to walk past/by the house. —*adv.* past; by: **солдáты прошлú мúмо**, the soldiers walked past (*or* passed by). —**мúмо цéли**, wide of the mark.

мимóза *n.* mimosa.

мимолётный *adj.* passing; fleeting.

мимохóдом *adv.* **1**, while passing by; on the way. **2**, *colloq.* in passing: **упомянýть мимохóдом**, to mention in passing.

мúна *n.* **1**, *mil.* mine. **2**, mortar shell. **3**, facial expression; countenance. —**дéлать хорóшую (вéселую) мúну при плохóй игрé**, to put up a bold front. —**подклáдывать** (*or* **подводúть**) **мúну** (+ *dat. or with* под + *acc.*), to play a dirty trick on.

минарéт *n.* minaret.

миндалевúдный *adj.* almond-shaped. —**миндалевúдная железá**, tonsil.

миндáлина *n.* tonsil.

миндáль [*gen.* -далá] *n.m.* **1**, almonds. **2**, almond tree. —**миндáльный**, *adj.* almond (*attrib.*).

минёр *n.* specialist in mine-laying.

минера́л *n.* mineral.

минерало́гия *n.* mineralogy. —**минерало́г,** *n.* mineralogist. —**минералоги́ческий,** *adj.* mineralogical.

минера́льный *adj.* mineral.

миниатю́ра *n.* miniature.

миниатю́рный *adj.* **1,** miniature. **2,** tiny.

минима́льный *adj.* minimum; minimal.

ми́нимум *n.* minimum. —*adv.* a minimum of; at least.

мини́ровать *v. impfv. & pfv.* [*pfv. also* **замини́ровать;** *pres.* -ру́ю, -ру́ешь] *mil.* to mine.

министе́рский *adj.* ministerial.

министе́рство *n.* ministry.

мини́стр *n.* minister. —**мини́стр иностра́нных дел,** foreign minister. —**мини́стр фина́нсов,** finance minister; (*U.S.*) Secretary of the Treasury. —**мини́стр юсти́ции,** Minister of Justice; (*U.S.*) Attorney General.

ми́нный *adj., mil.* mine (*attrib.*). —**ми́нное по́ле,** minefield. —**ми́нный по́рох,** blasting powder.

минова́ть *v. pfv.* [*infl.* -ну́ю, -ну́ешь] **1,** [*also impfv.*] *v.t.* to pass; pass by. **2,** *v.i.* to pass; be over. **3,** (*usu. neg.*) to avoid; escape. —**мину́я подро́бности,** omitting details.

мино́га *n.* lamprey.

миноиска́тель *n.m.* mine detector.

миномёт *n., mil.* mortar. —**миномётный,** *adj.* mortar (*attrib.*).

минoно́сец [*gen.* -сца] *n.* torpedo boat. —**эска́дренный минoно́сец,** destroyer.

мино́р *n.* **1,** *music* minor key: сона́та си мино́р, sonata in B minor. **2,** *colloq.* melancholy; the blues; the dumps: быть в мино́ре, to be in the dumps.

мино́рный *adj.* **1,** *music* minor. **2,** *colloq.* melancholy; gloomy.

мину́вший *adj.* past; bygone.

ми́нус *n.* **1,** *math.* minus. **2,** minus sign. **3,** *fig., colloq.* minus; drawback. —*adv.* minus: пять ми́нус два равно́ трём, five minus two equals three; ми́нус де́сять гра́дусов, ten degrees below freezing.

мину́та *n.* **1,** minute. **2,** moment: незабыва́емая мину́та, unforgettable moment. —**мину́та в мину́ту,** on the dot. —**с мину́ты на мину́ту,** any minute.

мину́тка [*gen. pl.* -ток] *n., dim. of* **мину́та.**

мину́тный *adj.* **1,** minute (*attrib.*): мину́тная стре́лка, minute hand. **2,** lasting a moment; momentary.

мину́точка [*gen. pl.* -чек] *n., colloq., dim. of* **мину́тка.**

мину́ть *v. pfv.* [*infl.* ми́нет] **1,** [*past* мину́л] to pass. **2,** [*past* ми́нуло] *impers.* (*with dat.*) *indicating attainment of a certain age:* ему́ ми́нуло со́рок лет, he has turned forty.

мир [*pl.* миры́] *n.* **1,** world. **2,** peace: мир во всём ми́ре, peace throughout the world. **3,** *hist.* village community; mir. —**не от ми́ра сего́,** (*of a person*) from (*or* living in) a different world. —**пусти́ть по́ миру,** to bankrupt; make a beggar out of (someone). —**ходи́ть по́ миру,** to live by begging.

мира́ж *n.* mirage.

мириа́ды [*gen.* -а́д] *n. pl.* myriads.

мири́ть *v. impfv.* [*pfv.* **помири́ть** *or* **примири́ть**] to reconcile. —**мири́ться,** *refl.* **1,** to become reconciled (*after a quarrel*); make up. **2,** (*with* с + *instr.*) to reconcile oneself (to); resign oneself (to); (learn to) accept.

ми́рный *adj.* **1,** peace (*attrib.*). **2,** peaceful. —**ми́рно,** *adv.* peacefully.

мирова́я *n., decl. as an adj., colloq.* amicable agree-

ment: пойти́ на мирову́ю, to reach an amicable agreement.

мировоззре́ние *n.* world outlook; world view.

мирово́й *adj.* **1,** world (*attrib.*). Втора́я мирова́я война́, World War II. **2,** *law* of arbitration: мирово́й суд, court of arbitration. Мирово́й судья́, justice of the peace.

мирозда́ние *n.* the universe.

миролюби́вый *adj.* peace-loving; peaceful. —**миролю́бие,** *n.* peaceful nature.

миропома́зание *n.* anointing; unction.

миротво́рец [*gen.* -рца] *n.* peacemaker.

ми́рра *n.* myrrh.

мирско́й *adj.* **1,** worldly; mundane. **2,** secular; lay. **3,** *hist.* pert. to a **мир.**

мирт *n.* myrtle. —**ми́ртовый,** *adj.* myrtle.

миря́нин [*pl.* -я́не, -я́н] *n.* **1,** *obs.* layman. **2,** *hist.* member of a **мир.**

ми́ска [*gen. pl.* -сок] *n.* bowl; tureen.

мисс *n.f. indecl.* miss; Miss.

миссионе́р *n.* missionary. —**миссионе́рский,** *adj.* missionary. —**миссионе́рство,** *n.* missionary work.

ми́ссис *n.f. indecl.* Mrs.

ми́ссия *n.* **1,** mission (*assignment*). **2,** delegation; mission. **3,** legation; diplomatic mission. **4,** *relig.* mission.

ми́стер *n.* mister; Mr.

ми́стик *n.* mystic.

ми́стика *n.* mysticism.

мистифика́ция *n.* hoax; practical joke.

мистици́зм *n.* mysticism.

мисти́ческий *adj.* mystical.

ми́тинг *n.* mass meeting; rally.

митка́ль [*gen.* -каля́] *n.m.* calico (*plain unfinished cloth*). —**миткалёвый; митка́левый,** *adj.* calico.

мито́з *n.* mitosis.

ми́тра *n.* miter (*worn by a bishop*).

митрополи́т *n., Orth. Ch.* metropolitan.

миф *n.* myth. —**мифи́ческий,** *adj.* mythical.

мифоло́гия *n.* mythology. —**мифологи́ческий,** *adj.* mythological.

ми́чман *n., naval* warrant officer.

мише́нь *n.f.* target. —**я́блоко мише́ни,** bull's-eye.

ми́шка [*gen. pl.* -шек] *n.* teddy bear.

мишура́ *n.* **1,** tinsel. **2,** *fig.* ostentation.

мишу́рный *adj.* **1,** tinsel (*attrib.*). **2,** *fig.* showy; tawdry; ostentatious.

младе́нец [*gen.* -нца] *n.* infant; baby. —**младе́нческий,** *adj.* infantile. —**младе́нчество,** *n.* infancy.

младо́й *adj., archaic* young. —**стар и млад,** young and old (alike).

мла́дший *adj., used only as a modifier* **1,** younger. **2,** youngest. **3,** junior. —**мла́дший лейтена́нт,** second lieutenant.

млекопита́ющее *n., decl. as an adj.* mammal.

млеть *v. impfv.* **1,** (*with* от) to be overcome (*with an emotion*). **2,** to languish. **3,** *colloq.* to become numb.

мле́чный *adj., archaic* = **моло́чный.** —**Мле́чный Путь,** the Milky Way.

мне *pron., dat. & prepl. of* **я.**

мнемо́ника *n.* mnemonics. —**мнемони́ческий,** *adj.* mnemonics.

мне́ние *n.* opinion. —**быть высо́кого мне́ния о,** have a high opinion of. —**быть одного́ мне́ния,** to be of one mind. —**по моему́ мне́нию,** in my opinion. —**я того́ мне́ния, что...,** I am of the opinion that...

мни́мый *adj.* **1,** imaginary. **2,** false; feigned.

мни́тельный *adj.* **1,** forever worrying about one's health. **2,** suspicious; distrustful.

мни́ть *v. impfv., obs.* to imagine. —**мнить себя́** (+ *instr.*), to imagine oneself to be; see oneself as; like to think of oneself as. —**мно́го** (*or* **высоко́) мнить о себе́,** to have a high opinion of oneself.

мно́гие *adj.* many: мно́гие дома́, many houses; со мно́гими друзья́ми, with many friends. —*indef. pron.* many; many people: мно́гие счита́ют, что..., many people believe that...

мно́го *adv.* much; a lot; a great deal: я мно́го о вас слы́шал(а), I've heard a lot about you. Ви́деть и слы́шать мно́го, to see and hear a great deal. —*adj.* (*with gen.*) many; much; a lot of; a great deal of: мно́го рабо́ты, a lot of work; мно́го друзе́й, many friends. —**ни мно́го ни ма́ло,** as much as; no less than. *See also* **мно́гое.**

многобо́жие *n.* polytheism.

многобра́чие *n.* polygamy. —**многобра́чный,** *adj.* polygamous.

многова́то *adv., colloq.* a bit too much.

многогра́нник *n.* polyhedron. —**многогра́нный,** *adj.* polyhedral; many-sided.

мно́гое [*gen.* мно́гого; *dat.* мно́гому; *instr.* мно́гим; *prepl.* мно́гом] *n., decl. as an adj.* much; a great deal: о́пыт нас у́чит мно́гому, experience teaches us a great deal. Я мно́гим ему́ обя́зан, I am much indebted to him. —**во мно́гом,** in many respects; largely; in large part.

многоже́нец [*gen.* -нца] *n.* polygamist. —**много-же́нство,** *n.* polygamy.

многозначи́тельный *adj.* **1,** significant. **2,** (*of a look, smile, etc.*) knowing.

многокра́сочный *adj.* multicolored; polychromatic.

многокра́тный *adj.* **1,** repeated; frequent. **2,** *gram.* frequentative: многокра́тный вид, frequentative aspect. —**многокра́тно,** *adv.* repeatedly.

многоле́тний *adj.* **1,** of many years. **2,** long-lived. **3,** *bot.* perennial.

многолю́дный *adj.* **1,** populous. **2,** crowded.

многомиллио́нный *adj.* consisting of many millions.

многонациона́льный *adj.* multinational.

многоно́жка [*gen. pl.* -жек] *n.* myriapod; centipede; millipede.

многообеща́ющий *adj.* promising; up-and-coming.

многообра́зие *n.* variety; diversity.

многообра́зный *adj.* varied; diverse.

многоречи́вый *adj.* loquacious; verbose; long-winded.

многосеме́йный *adj.* having a large family.

многосло́вие *n.* verbosity. —**многосло́вный,** *adj.* long-winded; verbose.

многосло́жный *adj.* polysyllabic.

многосторо́нний *adj.* **1,** multilateral. **2,** *fig.* versatile. —**многосторо́нность,** *n.f.* versatility.

многострада́льный *adj.* long-suffering.

многоступе́нчатый *adj.* multistage.

многотира́жка [*gen. pl.* -жек] *n., colloq.* company newspaper; house organ.

многотира́жный *adj.* (*of a publication*) having a large circulation.

многото́мный *adj.* multivolume.

многото́чие *n.* suspension points (......).

многоуважа́емый *adj.* (*in salutations of letters*) dear:

многоуважа́емый Ива́н Петро́вич, Dear Ivan Petrovich.

многоуго́льник *n.* polygon. —**многоуго́льный,** *adj.* polygonal.

многоцве́тный *adj.* multicolored; polychromatic.

многочи́сленность *n.f.* **1,** great number. **2,** large size (*of a family, army, etc.*).

многочи́сленный *adj.* **1,** numerous. **2,** consisting of many people; large.

многочле́н *n.* polynomial. —**многочле́нный,** *adj.* polynomial.

многоэта́жный *adj.* multistoried.

многоязы́чный *adj.* multilingual; polyglot.

мно́жественность *n.f.* multiplicity.

мно́жественный *adj.* plural. —**мно́жественное число́,** *gram.* the plural.

мно́жество *n.* **1,** (*with gen.*) a great number (of); a multitude (of). **2,** *math.* set: тео́рия мно́жеств, theory of sets. —**во мно́жестве,** in great numbers.

мно́жимое *n., decl. as an adj., math.* multiplicand.

мно́житель *n.m., math.* **1,** multiplier. **2,** factor.

мно́жить *v. impfv.* [*pfv.* помно́жить *or* умно́жить] **1,** *math.* to multiply. **2,** *fig.* to increase; augment. —**мно́житься,** *refl.* [*pfv.* умно́житься] to multiply; increase in number.

мной *also,* **мно́ю** *pron., instr. of* **я.**

мобилиза́ция *n.* mobilization. —**мобилизацио́н-ный,** *adj.* mobilization (*attrib.*).

мобилизова́ть *v. impfv. & pfv.* [*pres.* -зу́ю, -зу́ешь] **1,** to mobilize. **2,** *fig.* to mobilize; muster; rally. —**мо-билизова́ться,** *refl.* **1,** to mobilize; be mobilized. **2,** *fig.* to brace oneself; buckle down.

моби́льный *adj.* mobile. —**моби́льность,** *n.f.* mobility.

моги́ла *n.* grave. —**своди́ть в моги́лу,** to be the death of. —**стоя́ть одно́й ного́й в моги́ле,** to have one foot in the grave.

моги́льный *adj.* **1,** grave (*attrib.*); burial (*attrib.*). **2,** deathly; sepulchral. —**моги́льная плита́,** gravestone.

моги́льщик *n.* gravedigger.

мого́л *n.* Mogul.

могу́чий *adj.* powerful; mighty.

могу́щественный *adj.* powerful; mighty.

могу́щество *n.* power; might.

мо́да *n.* fashion; style; vogue: быть в мо́де, to be in style. —**войти́ в мо́ду,** to come into fashion. —**вы́йти из мо́ды,** to go out of style.

мода́льный *adj.* modal.

модели́ровать (дэ) *v. impfv. & pfv.* [*pres.* -рую, -руешь] to design (clothes).

моде́ль (дэ) *n.f.* model.

модельё́р (дэ) *n.* designer (*of clothes*).

моде́льный (дэ) *adj.* **1,** model (*attrib.*); pattern (*attrib.*): моде́льный цех, pattern shop. **2,** fashionable.

мо́де́льщик (дэ) *n.* modeler.

моде́рн (дэ) *n.* modernist style. —*adj. indecl.* modern: та́нец моде́рн, modern dance.

модерниза́ция (дэ) *n.* modernization.

модернизи́ровать (дэ) *v. impfv. & pfv.* [*pres.* -рую, -руешь] to modernize.

модерни́зм (дэ) *n.* modernism. —**модерни́ст,** *n.* modernist. —**модерни́стский,** *adj.* modernistic.

моди́стка [*gen. pl.* -сток] *n.* milliner.

модифика́ция *n.* modification.

модифици́ровать v. impfv. & pfv. [pres. -ру́ю, -ру́ешь] to modify.

мо́дник n.m. [fem. -ница] colloq. fashion plate.

мо́дничать v. impfv., colloq. to dress fashionably; dress in the latest fashions.

мо́дно adv. stylishly; fashionably. —adj., used predicatively fashionable: стать мо́дно, to become fashionable.

мо́дный adj. 1, fashionable; stylish. 2, fashion (attrib.): мо́дный журна́л, fashion magazine.

модули́ровать v. impfv. [pres. -ру́ю, -ру́ешь] to modulate.

мо́дуль n.m. module; modulus.

модуля́тор n. modulator.

модуля́ция n. modulation. —часто́тная модуля́ция, frequency modulation.

мое́вка [gen. pl. -вок] n. kittiwake.

можжеве́льник n. juniper. —можжеве́ловый, adj. juniper (attrib.).

мо́жно predicate may; can; it is permitted: мо́жно войти́?, may I come in? Здесь мо́жно кури́ть, you may smoke here; you are allowed to smoke here. —как мо́жно (+ comp.), as ... as possible: как мо́жно бо́льше, as much as possible; как мо́жно скоре́е, as soon as possible.

моза́ика n. mosaic; inlay. —моза́ичный, adj. mosaic; inlaid.

мозг [2nd loc. мозгу́; pl. мозги́] n. 1, brain. 2, pl. brains (food). —головно́й мозг, cerebrum. —ко́стный мозг, marrow. —продолгова́тый мозг, medulla oblongata. —спинно́й мозг, spinal cord.

мозго́витый adj., colloq. brainy.

мозгово́й adj. brain (attrib.); cerebral.

мозжечо́к [gen. -чка́] n. cerebellum.

мозо́листый adj. calloused.

мозо́ль n.f. callus; corn. —мозо́льный, adj. for removing corns: мозо́льный пла́стырь, corn plaster.

мой [fem. моя́; neut. моё; pl. мои́; gen. моего́, мое́й, мои́х; acc. fem. мою́; dat. моему́, мое́й, мои́м; instr. мои́м, мое́й, мои́ми; prepl. моём, мое́й, мои́х] poss. adj. & pron. my; mine.

мо́йка n. 1, colloq. washing. 2, washer (machine).

мо́йщик n. washer (one who washes).

мокаси́н [gen. pl. -си́н] n. moccasin.

мокаси́новый adj., in мокаси́новая змея́, moccasin (snake).

мо́кко n.indecl. mocha.

мо́кнуть v. impfv. [past мок, -ла] 1, to become wet; get wet. 2, to soak.

мокри́ца n. wood louse.

мокрова́тый adj. moist; damp.

мокро́та n. phlegm.

мокрота́ n., colloq. 1, dampness; humidity. 2, light rain; wet snow.

мо́крый adj. wet. —у неё глаза́ на мо́кром ме́сте, she is easily moved to tears.

мол[1] n. breakwater; jetty.

мол[2] particle, colloq. he says; they say.

молва́ n. rumors; talk.

мо́лвить v. impfv. & pfv. [pres. -влю, -вишь] obs., poetic to say.

молдава́нин [pl. -ва́не, -ва́н] n.m. [fem. -ва́нка] Moldavian. —молда́вский, adj. Moldavian.

моле́бен [gen. -бна] n. short church service.

моле́кула n. molecule. —молекуля́рный, adj. molecular.

моле́льня [gen. pl. -лен] n. prayer house; meeting house.

моле́ние n. 1, prayer service: соверши́ть моле́ние, to hold a prayer service. 2, entreaty; supplication.

молески́н n. moleskin (cloth). —молески́новый, adj. moleskin.

молибде́н (дэ) n. molybdenum. —молибде́новый, adj. molybdic.

моли́тва n. prayer. —моли́твенник, n. prayer book. —моли́твенный, adj. of prayer.

моли́ть v. impfv. [pres. молю́, мо́лишь] (with о) to beg (for); plead (for). —моли́ться, refl. 1, [pfv. помоли́ться] to pray. 2, (with на + acc.) colloq. to idolize.

моллю́ск n. mollusk.

молниено́сный adj. quick as lightning; lightning-fast. —молниено́сная война́, blitzkrieg.

молниеотво́д n. lightning rod.

мо́лния n. 1, lightning. 2, [also, засте́жка-мо́лния] zipper. 3, express telegram. 4, special edition (of a newspaper).

молодёжный adj. youth (attrib.).

молодёжь n.f. youth; young people.

моло́денький adj., colloq. young; very young.

молоде́ть v. impfv. [pfv. помолоде́ть] to get younger; become young again.

молоде́ц [gen. -дца́] n. good boy; fine fellow. —interj. well done!

молоде́цкий adj. bold; dashing.

молоде́чество n. daring; bravado.

молоди́ть v. impfv. [pres. -ложу́, -ло́дишь] to make (someone) look younger; give a youthful appearance (to).

молодня́к [gen. -няка́] n. 1, saplings. 2, young animals. 3, colloq. youth; the younger generation.

молодожёны [gen. -жёнов] n. pl. newlyweds.

молодо́й adj. [short form мо́лод, молода́, мо́лодо; comp. моло́же] 1, young. 2, (of qualities or emotions) youthful: молодо́й задо́р, youthful enthusiasm. 3, (of potatoes, wine, etc.) new. —молоды́е, n. pl. 1, young people. 2, young couple; newlyweds. 3, (of animals) newly-born; (their) young.

мо́лодость n.f. youth. —втора́я мо́лодость, new lease on life. —не пе́рвой мо́лодости, getting on in years; no spring chicken. —по мо́лодости лет, through inexperience.

молодцева́тый adj. dashing.

моло́дчик n., colloq. punk; thug.

молодчи́на n.m., colloq. = молоде́ц.

моложа́вый adj. young-looking; youthful.

моло́же adj., comp. of молодо́й.

моло́ки [gen. -лок] n. pl. milt; soft roe.

молоко́ n. milk. —кровь с молоко́м, the picture of health.

молокосо́с n., colloq. greenhorn; neophyte.

мо́лот n. (large) hammer; sledgehammer.

молоти́лка [gen. pl. -лок] n. thresher; threshing machine.

молоти́льщик n. thresher (one who threshes).

молоти́ть v. impfv. [pres. -лочу́, -ло́тишь] 1, to thresh. 2, colloq. to thrash.

молото́к [gen. -тка́] n. hammer. —продава́ть с молотка́, to auction (off).

мо́лот-ры́ба n. hammerhead (fish).

МÓЛОТЫЙ *adj.* ground.

МОЛÓТЬ *v. impfv.* [*pfv.* смолÓть; *pres.* мелЮ, мÉлешь] **1,** to grind. **2,** [*impfv. only*] *colloq.* to talk (nonsense).

молотьбÁ *n.* **1,** threshing. **2,** threshing season.

молÓчная *n., decl. as an adj.* dairy.

молÓчник *n.* **1,** milk pitcher. **2,** milkman; dairyman.

молÓчница *n.* **1,** dairymaid. **2,** thrush (*disease*).

молÓчный *adj.* **1,** milk (*attrib.*). **2,** dairy (*attrib.*). **3,** milky. **4,** suckling. **5,** lactic. —молÓчные жÉлезы, mammary glands. —молÓчный зуб, baby tooth. —молÓчная корÓва, milch cow. —молÓчный сÁхар, milk sugar; lactose. —молÓчный скот, dairy cattle.

мÓлча *adv.* silently; in silence.

молчалИвый *adj.* **1,** taciturn; reticent. **2,** tacit. —молчалИвость, *n.f.* taciturnity; reticence.

молчÁние *n.* silence. —обойтИ (чтÓ-нибудь) молчÁнием, to pass over in silence. —хранИть молчÁние, to maintain silence; keep/remain silent.

молчÁть *v. impfv.* [*pres.* -чУ, -чИшь] to be quiet; keep quiet; be silent.

моль *n.f.* moth; clothes moth.

мольбÁ *n.* entreaty; supplication.

мольбÉрт *n.* easel.

молЯщийся *n., decl. as an adj.* worshiper.

момÉнт *n.* **1,** moment; instant: в дÁнный момÉнт, at the present moment. **2,** feature; element; factor; aspect.

моментÁльно *adv.* instantly; instantaneously; immediately. —моментÁльный, *adj.* instantaneous.

монÁрх *n.* monarch. —монархИзм, *n.* monarchism. —монархИст, *n.* monarchist. —монархИческий, *adj.* monarchist; monarchical. —монÁрхия, *n.* monarchy.

монастЫрь [*gen.* -рЯ] *n.m.* monastery; convent; cloister. —монастЫрский, *adj.* of a monastery; monasterial.

монÁх *n.* monk. —пострИчься в монÁхи, to take the monastic vows.

монÁхиня *n.* nun. —пострИчься в монÁхини, to take the veil.

монÁшенка [*gen. pl.* -нок] *n., colloq.* nun.

монÁшеский *adj.* monastic.

монÁшество *n.* **1,** monasticism; monkhood. **2,** monks.

монгÓл *n.m.* [*fem.* -гÓлка] Mongol. —монгÓльский, *adj.* Mongol; Mongolian.

монÉта *n.* coin. МÉлкая *or* размÉнная монÉта, small change. —платИть той же монÉтой, to repay in kind. —принимÁть за чИстую монÉту, to take in good faith; take at face value.

монÉтный *adj.* monetary. —монÉтный двор, mint.

монИзм *n.* monism. —монистИческий, *adj.* monistic.

монИсто *n.* necklace (*of beads or coins*).

моногÁмия *n.* monogamy. —моногÁмный, *adj.* monogamous.

моногрÁмма *n.* monogram.

моногрÁфия *n.* monograph. —монографИческий, *adj.* monographic.

монÓкль *n.m.* monocle.

монолИт *n.* monolith.

монолИтный *adj.* monolithic. —монолИтность, *n.f.* monolithic nature.

монолÓг *n.* monologue.

мононуклеÓз *n.* mononucleosis.

моноплÁн *n.* monoplane.

монополизÁция *n.* monopolization.

монополизИровать *v. impfv. & pfv.* [*pres.* -рую, -руешь] to monopolize.

монополИст *n.* monopolist. —монополистИческий, *adj.* monopolistic.

монопÓлия *n.* monopoly.

монопÓльный *adj.* **1,** monopoly (*attrib.*). **2,** exclusive.

монотеИзм (тэ) *n.* monotheism. —монотеистИческий, *adj.* monotheistic.

монотИп *n.* monotype.

монотÓнный *adj.* **1,** monotone. **2,** monotonous. —монотÓнность, *n.f.* monotony.

монохроматИческий *adj.* monochromatic.

монсеньёр *n.* Monsignor.

монтÁж [*gen.* -жÁ] *n.* **1,** assembling; installing (*of machinery*). **2,** editing (*of a film or literary work*); arrangement (*of a musical composition*). **3,** montage.

монтёр *n.* **1,** fitter. **2,** electrician.

монтИровать *v. impfv.* [*pfv.* смонтИровать; *pres.* -рую, -руешь] **1,** to assemble. **2,** to edit (a film).

монумÉнт *n.* monument. —монументÁльный, *adj.* monumental.

мопÉд *n.* motorbike; moped.

мопс *n.* pug (*dog*).

морализИровать *v. impfv.* [*pres.* -рую, -руешь] to moralize.

моралИст *n.* moralist.

морÁль *n.f.* **1,** morals; morality. **2,** moral; moral lesson. **3,** *colloq.* moralizing. —читÁть морÁль (+ *dat.*), to lecture; preach (to).

морÁльно *adv.* morally.

морÁльный *adj.* moral. —морÁльное состоЯние, morale. —морÁльный изнÓс, obsolescence.

моратÓрий *n.* moratorium.

морг *n.* morgue; mortuary.

морганатИческий *adj.* morganatic.

моргÁть *v. impfv.* [*pfv.* моргнУть] **1,** to blink. **2,** (*with instr.*) to blink (one's eyes). **3,** (*with dat.*) to wink (at). **4,** to twinkle; flicker. —глÁзом не моргнУв, without batting an eye.

мÓрда *n.* **1,** snout; muzzle. **2,** *colloq.* face; mug.

мордвИн *n.m.* [*fem.* -вИнка] Mordvin (*one of a people inhabiting central European Russia*). —мордÓвский, *adj.* Mordvinian; Mordovian.

мÓре [*pl.* морЯ, морÉй] *n.* sea. —вЫйти в мÓре, to put (out) to sea.

морÉна *n.* moraine.

морёный *adj.* stained: морёный дуб, stained oak.

мореплÁвание *n.* navigation. —мореплÁватель, *n.m.* navigator.

морехÓд *n.* = мореплÁватель.

морехÓдный *adj.* **1,** nautical; navigational. **2,** seaworthy.

морж [*gen.* моржÁ] *n.* walrus.

Мóрзе (зэ) *n. indecl., in* Áзбука Мóрзе, Morse code.

морИлка *n.* stain (*for wood*).

морИть *v. impfv.* **1,** [*pfv.* вЫморить] to exterminate; poison (insects, rodents, etc.). **2,** [*pfv.* заморИть] *colloq.* to wear out; exhaust. **3,** [*impfv. only*] to stain (wood). —морИть гÓлодом, to starve.

мор-кÓвь *n.f.* **1,** carrots. **2,** a (single) carrot. —моркÓвный, *adj.* carrot (*attrib.*).

мормÓн *n.* Mormon. —мормÓнский, *adj.* Mormon.

морÓженое *n., decl. as an adj.* ice cream.

морÓженщик *n.* ice-cream vendor.

моро́женый *adj.* frozen.

моро́з *n.* **1,** frost: де́сять гра́дусов моро́за, ten degrees of frost. **2,** freezing weather.

моро́зец [*gen.* -зца] *n., colloq.* slight frost.

морози́лка [*gen. pl.* -лок] *n.* freezing compartment; freezer.

моро́зить *v. impfv.* [*pres.* -жу, -зишь] **1,** to freeze. **2,** *impers.* to be freezing: на дворе́ моро́зит, it is freezing outside.

моро́зный *adj.* frosty; freezing.

морозосто́йкий *adj.* frost-resistant; hardy.

мороси́ть *v. impfv.* to drizzle.

моро́чить *v. impfv.* [*pfv.* обморо́чить] *colloq.* to trick; fool. —моро́чить го́лову (+ *dat.*), to mislead; deceive.

моро́шка *n.* **1,** cloudberries. **2,** a (single) cloudberry.

морс *n.* fruit drink.

морско́й *adj.* sea (*attrib.*); maritime; marine; naval; nautical. —морска́я боле́знь, seasickness. —морска́я пехо́та, the marines. —морско́й флот, navy.

морти́ра *n., mil.* mortar.

морфе́ма *n.* morpheme.

мо́рфий *n.* morphine.

морфини́ст *n.* morphine addict.

морфоло́гия *n.* morphology. —морфологи́ческий, *adj.* morphological.

морщи́на *n.* wrinkle. —морщи́нистый, *adj.* wrinkled.

мо́рщить *v. impfv.* [*pfv.* намо́рщить *or* смо́рщить] to wrinkle; pucker. —мо́рщиться, *refl.* **1,** [*pfv.* намо́рщиться] (*of one's skin, eyebrows, etc.*) to become wrinkled; contract; pucker. **2,** [*pfv.* смо́рщиться *or* помо́рщиться] to make a face; wince. **3,** [*pfv.* смо́рщиться] *colloq.* (*of material*) to crease; become creased.

морщи́ть *v. impfv., colloq.* (*of material*) to become creased; pucker.

моря́к [*gen.* -яка́] *n.* sailor; seaman.

москате́ль *n.f.* paint supplies. —москате́льный, *adj.* pert. to paint supplies: москате́льный магази́н, store selling paint supplies.

москви́ч [*gen.* -вича́] *n.* Muscovite; native of Moscow.

моски́т *n.* sand fly.

моско́вский *adj.* Moscow (*attrib.*).

мост [*gen.* мо́ста *or* моста́; *2nd loc.* мосту́; *pl.* мосты́] *n.* bridge.

мо́стик *n.* **1,** small bridge; footbridge. **2,** bridge (*of a ship*).

мости́ть *v. impfv.* [*pfv.* вы́мостить; *pres.* мощу́, мости́шь] to pave.

мостки́ [*gen.* -ко́в] *n. pl.* **1,** planked walkway; footbridge. **2,** wooden platform (*extending out over water*).

мостова́я *n., decl. as an adj.* roadway.

мостово́й *adj.* bridge (*attrib.*).

мосье́ *n.m. indecl.* monsieur.

мо́ська *n., colloq.* pug (*dog*).

мот *n., colloq.* spendthrift.

мота́льный *adj., mech.* winding.

мота́ть *v. impfv.* [*pfv.* намота́ть] **1,** to wind. **2,** [*impfv. only*] (*with instr.*) *colloq.* to shake (one's head). —мота́ть себе́ на ус, *colloq.* to make a mental note of.

мота́ться *v.r. impfv., colloq.* to dangle; bob.

моте́ль (тэ) *n.m.* motel.

моти́в *n.* **1,** motive; reason. **2,** motif; theme. **3,** tune; melody.

мотиви́ровать *v. impfv. & pfv.* [*pres.* -рую, -руешь] to explain; justify; give reasons for; show just cause for.

мотивиро́вка *n.* reasons; justification.

мотобо́л *n.* football (soccer) played on motorcycles.

мотовство́ *n.* extravagance; prodigality.

мотого́нки [*gen.* -нок] *n. pl.* motorcycle races/racing.

мото́к [*gen.* -тка́] *n.* skein; hank (*of thread*).

мотопехо́та *n.* motorized infantry.

мотопила́ *n.* power saw.

мото́р *n.* motor; engine.

моторизо́ванный *adj.* motorized.

мото́рный *adj.* motor (*attrib.*).

моторо́ллер *n.* motor scooter.

мотоци́кл *also,* мотоцикле́т *n.* motorcycle. —мотоцикли́ст, *n.* motorcyclist.

моты́га *n.* hoe.

моты́жить *v. impfv.* to hoe.

мотылёк [*gen.* -лька́] *n.* moth.

мох [*gen.* мха *or* мо́ха] *n.* moss.

мохе́р *n.* mohair. —мохе́ровый, *adj.* mohair.

мохна́тый *adj.* shaggy; hairy. —мохна́тое полоте́нце, Turkish towel.

моцио́н *n.* exercise.

моча́ *n.* urine.

моча́лка [*gen. pl.* -лок] *n.* piece of bast used as a bath sponge.

моча́ло *n.* bast.

мочеви́на *n.* urea.

мочево́й *adj.* **1,** urinary. **2,** uric. —мочева́я кислота́, uric acid. —мочево́й песо́к, *med.* gravel.

мочего́нный *adj.* diuretic. —мочего́нное сре́дство, diuretic.

мочеиспуска́ние *n.* urination.

мочеиспуска́тельный *adj.* urinary. —мочеиспуска́тельный кана́л, urethra.

мочёный *adj.* (*of foods*) soaked.

мочи́ть *v. impfv.* [*pfv.* намочи́ть *or* замочи́ть; *pres.* мочу́, мо́чишь] **1,** to wet. **2,** to get (something) wet. **3,** to soak. —мочи́ться, *refl.* [*pfv.* помочи́ться] to urinate.

мо́чка [*gen. pl.* -чек] *n.* **1,** wetting; soaking. **2,** ear lobe.

мочь¹ *v. impfv.* [*pfv.* смочь; *pres.* могу́, мо́жешь, ...мо́гут; *past* мог, могла́, могло́] to be able. —мо́жет быть, perhaps; maybe. —не мо́жет быть!, impossible!; it can't be! —не мочь не (+ *inf.*), one can't help: я не могу́ не ду́мать об э́том, I can't help thinking about it.

мочь² *n.f., colloq.* power; might. —во всю мочь, with all one's might.

моше́нник *n.* swindler.

моше́нничать *v. impfv.* [*pfv.* смоше́нничать] to practice fraud.

моше́ннический *adj.* fraudulent. —моше́нничество, *n.* swindle; swindling; fraud.

мо́шка [*gen. pl.* -шек] *n.* gnat; midge. —мошкара́, *n.* gnats.

мошо́нка *n.* scrotum.

моще́ние *n.* paving.

мощёный *adj.* paved.

мо́щи [*gen.* мощей] *n. pl.* earthly remains (*of a saint*).

мо́щность *n.f.* **1,** power. **2,** output; capacity: рабо́тать на по́лную мо́щность, to operate at full capacity.

мо́щный *adj.* powerful.

мощь *n.f.* power; might.

мо́ющий *adj., in* мо́ющее сре́дство, cleanser; detergent.

мрак *n.* darkness; gloom.

мракобе́с *n.* obscurantist. —**мракобе́сие,** *n.* obscurantism.

мра́мор *n.* marble. —**мра́морный,** *adj.* marble.

мрачне́ть *v. impfv.* [*pfv.* помрачне́ть] to grow dark; become gloomy.

мра́чный *adj.* **1,** gloomy; dismal; dreary. **2,** somber; morose; glum. —**мра́чность,** *n.f.* gloominess; dreariness; moroseness.

мсти́тель *n.m.* avenger.

мсти́тельный *adj.* vindictive. —**мсти́тельность,** *n.f.* vindictiveness.

мстить *v. impfv.* [*pfv.* отомсти́ть; *pres.* мщу, мстишь] **1,** (*with dat.*) to take revenge on. **2,** (*with* за + *acc.*) to avenge.

муа́р *n.* moire. —**муа́ровый,** *adj.* moiré.

мудрено́ *adj., used predicatively* difficult; next to impossible: мудрено́ поня́ть его́, there is no making him out. —**не мудрено́,** it is no wonder.

мудрёный *adj., colloq.* **1,** difficult; hard to understand; esoteric. **2,** (*of a task*) difficult; formidable. **3,** intricate; fancy. **4,** odd; queer.

мудре́ц [*gen.* -реца́] *n.* wise man; sage.

мудри́ть *v. impfv., colloq.* to (try to) be clever.

му́дрость *n.f.* wisdom.

му́дрствовать *v. impfv.* [*pres.* -ствую, -ствуешь] *colloq.* to philosophize. —**не му́дрствуя лука́во,** without equivocation; without beating around the bush.

му́дрый *adj.* wise.

муж [*pl.* мужья́, муже́й, мужья́м] *n.* husband.

мужа́ть *v. impfv.* to mature; become a man. —**мужа́ться,** *refl.* (*usu. imperative*) to be brave.

мужеподо́бный *adj.* mannish.

му́жественно *adv.* bravely; courageously.

му́жественность *n.f.* **1,** courageousness. **2,** manliness; masculinity.

му́жественный *adj.* **1,** brave; courageous. **2,** manly.

му́жество *n.* courage.

мужи́к [*gen.* -ика́] *n., pre-rev.* Russian peasant; muzhik.

мужско́й *adj.* **1,** masculine; male. **2,** man's; men's.

мужчи́на *n.m.* man.

му́за *n.* muse.

музе́й *n.* museum.

музе́йный *adj.* museum (*attrib.*). —**музе́йная ре́дкость,** museum piece.

му́зыка *n.* music. —**испо́ртить всю му́зыку,** *colloq.* to upset the applecart.

музыка́льный *adj.* **1,** music (*attrib.*). **2,** musical. —**музыка́льный ве́чер,** musicale. —**музыка́льный слух,** ear for music. —**музыка́льная шкату́лка; музыка́льный я́щик,** music box.

музыка́нт *n.* musician.

музыкове́д *n.* musicologist. —**музыкове́дение,** *n.* musicology.

му́ка *n.* **1,** torment; torture. **2,** *pl.* pangs; throes.

мука́ *n.* **1,** flour. **2,** meal.

мукомо́льный *adj.* flour-milling (*attrib.*).

мул *n.* mule.

мула́т *n.m.* [*fem.* -ка] mulatto.

мулла́ *n.m.* mullah.

мультимиллионе́р *n.* multimillionaire.

мультипликацио́нный *adj., in* **мультипликацио́нный фильм,** animated cartoon.

мультиплика́ция *n.* **1,** making of animated cartoons. **2,** cartoon.

му́льча *n.* mulch.

му́мия *n.* mummy.

мунди́р *n.* uniform dress coat. —**карто́фель в мунди́ре,** potatoes boiled in their skins.

мундшту́к [*gen.* -штука́] *n.* **1,** mouthpiece. **2,** cigarette holder; cigar holder.

муниципалите́т *n.* municipality.

муниципа́льный *adj.* municipal.

мура́ *n., colloq.* rubbish; nonsense.

мураве́й [*gen.* -вья́] *n.* ant.

мураве́йник *n.* anthill.

мураве́д *n.* anteater.

муравьи́ный *adj.* **1,** ant (*attrib.*); ants'. **2,** *chem.* formic.

мура́шки *n. pl., colloq., in* мура́шки бе́гают (забе́гали, поползли́) по спине́ (*with* у), to get the creeps; get chills up and down one's spine.

муре́на *n.* moray (eel).

мурлы́канье *n.* purr; purring.

мурлы́кать *v. impfv.* [*pres.* -лы́чу, -лы́чешь] **1,** to purr. **2,** *colloq.* to hum.

муска́т *n.* **1,** nutmeg. **2,** muscat (*grape*). **3,** muscatel (*wine*). —**муска́тник,** *n.* nutmeg (*tree*).

муска́тный *adj.* nutmeg. —**муска́тное вино́,** muscatel wine. —**муска́тный оре́х,** nutmeg. —**муска́тный цвет,** mace (*spice*).

му́скул *n.* muscle. —**мускулату́ра,** *n.* muscles; musculature. —**му́скулистый,** *adj.* muscular; brawny. —**му́скульный,** *adj.* muscle (*attrib.*); muscular.

му́скус *n.* musk. —**му́скусный,** *adj.* musk (*attrib.*).

мусли́н *n.* muslin. —**мусли́новый,** *adj.* muslin.

му́сор *n.* garbage; rubbish; refuse; trash.

му́сорный *adj.* garbage (*attrib.*); rubbish (*attrib.*); refuse (*attrib.*); trash (*attrib.*). —**му́сорный я́щик,** garbage can; trash can.

мусоропрово́д *n.* garbage chute; refuse chute.

мусоросжига́тельный *adj., in* **мусоросжига́тельная печь,** incinerator.

му́сорщик *n.* garbage collector.

мусс *n.* mousse.

мусси́ровать *v. impfv.* [*pres.* -рую, -руешь] to spread; fan (rumors, fears, etc.).

муссо́н *n.* monsoon.

муста́нг *n.* mustang.

мусульма́нин [*pl.* -ма́не, -ма́н] *n.m.* [*fem.* -ма́нка] Moslem. —**мусульма́нский,** *adj.* Moslem. —**мусульма́нство,** *n.* Mohammedanism; Islam.

мута́ция *n.* mutation.

мути́ть *v. impfv.* [*pres.* мучу́, мути́шь *or* му́тишь] **1,** [*pfv.* замути́ть] to make turbid; muddy (water). **2,** [*pfv.* помути́ть] to dull; cloud (the senses). **3,** *in* мути́ть во́ду, *fig.* to muddy the waters. **4,** *impers., colloq.* to feel nauseous: его́ мути́т, he feels nauseous. —**мути́ться,** *refl.* [*pfv.* замути́ться *or* помути́ться] **1,** to become cloudy. **2,** to be dulled.

мутне́ть *v. impfv.* [*pfv.* помутне́ть] to become cloudy; become muddy.

му́тный *adj.* **1,** turbid; murky. **2,** clouded; misty. **3,** dull; dim. —**му́тность,** *n.f.* turbidity.

муто́вка [*gen. pl.* -вок] *n.* **1,** *bot.* whorl. **2,** stick for churning or whipping.

муть *n.f.* **1,** dregs; lees. **2,** haze; mist.

му́фта *n.* **1,** muff. **2,** *mech.* coupling; clutch.

му́фтий *n.* mufti (*interpreter of Moslem law*).

му́ха *n.* fly (*insect*). —**де́лать из му́хи слона́,** to make a mountain out of a molehill. —**кака́я му́ха его́ укуси́ла?,** what's eating him? —**он и му́хи не оби́дит,** he wouldn't hurt a fly. —**слы́шно, как му́ха пролети́т,** you could have heard a pin drop.

мухоло́вка [*gen. pl.* -вок] *n.* **1,** flytrap; flycatcher. **2,** flycatcher (*bird*). **3,** flytrap (*plant*).

мухомо́р *n.* a variety of poisonous mushroom; fly agaric.

муче́ние *n.* torment; torture.

му́ченик *n.* martyr. —**му́ченический**, *adj.* martyr's. —**му́ченичество**, *n.* martyrdom.

мучи́тель *n.m.* tormentor.

мучи́тельно *adv.* 1, painfully. 2, terribly. —*adj., used predicatively* agonizing: мучи́тельно смотре́ть на них, it is an agony/ordeal to look at them.

мучи́тельный *adj.* 1, painful; agonizing; excruciating. 2, of anguish; anguished.

му́чить *v. impfv.* [*pfv.* му́чу, му́чишь *or* му́чаю, му́чаешь] to torment; harass; plague. —**му́читься**, *refl.* 1, to suffer. 2, (*with instr.*) to be plagued (with). 3, (*with* с *or* над) to slave (over).

мучни́стый *adj.* farinaceous. —**мучни́стая роса́**, mildew.

мучно́й *adj.* flour (*attrib.*).

му́шка [*gen. pl.* -шек] *n.* 1, *dim. of* му́ха. 2, beauty spot. 3, front sight (*on a firearm*). —**взять на му́шку**, to draw a bead on.

мушке́т *n.* musket. —**мушкете́р**, *n.* musketeer.

мушмула́ *n.* medlar.

муштра́ *n.* 1, drill; drilling. 2, strict discipline; regimentation.

муштрова́ть *v. impfv.* [*pfv.* вы́муштровать; *pres.* -тру́ю, -тру́ешь] to drill.

муштро́вка *n.* drilling.

муэдзи́н *n.* muezzin.

мчать *v. impfv.* [*pfv.* помча́ть; *pres.* мчу, мчишь] to rush; whisk. —**мча́ться**, *refl.* to race; speed along; tear along.

мши́стый *adj.* mossy.

мще́ние *n.* revenge; vengeance.

мы [*gen., acc., & prepl.* нас; *dat.* нам; *instr.* на́ми] *pers. pron.*, 1st person pl. 1, we. 2, (*with* с + *instr.*) and I: мы с ва́ми, you and I.

мы́лить *v. impfv.* [*pfv.* намы́лить] to soap; lather. —**мы́литься**, *refl.* to soap oneself.

мы́лкий *adj.* (*of soap*) soft; easily lathering.

мы́ло *n.* soap.

мылова́ре́ние *n.* soap making.

мылова́ренный *adj., in* мылова́ренный заво́д, soap works.

мы́льница *n.* soap dish.

мы́льный *adj.* 1, soap (*attrib.*). 2, soapy.

мыльня́нка *n.* soapwort.

мыс *n., geog.* cape.

мы́сленный *adj.* mental. —**мы́сленно**, *adv.* mentally; in one's mind.

мысли́мый *adj.* conceivable.

мысли́тель *n.m.* thinker.

мы́слить *v. impfv.* to think; reason.

мысль *n.f.* 1, thought; idea. —**за́дняя мысль**, ulterior motive. —**о́браз мы́слей**, way of thinking. —**ход мы́слей**, train of thought.

мы́слящий *adj.* thinking; capable of thinking.

мыта́рить *v. impfv., colloq.* to torment. —**мыта́риться**, *refl., colloq.* to suffer; have a hard time of it; go through hell.

мыта́рство *n., usu. pl.* ordeal; tribulation.

мыть *v. impfv.* [*pfv.* помы́ть *or* вы́мыть; *pres.* мо́ю, мо́ешь] to wash.

мытьё *n.* washing.

мы́ться *v.r. impfv.* [*pfv.* помы́ться *or* вы́мыться; *pres.* мо́юсь, мо́ешься] to wash; wash oneself.

мыча́ние *n.* 1, moo; mooing. 2, *colloq.* mumbling.

мыча́ть *v. impfv.* [*pres.* -чу́, -чи́шь] 1, to moo; bellow. 2, *colloq.* to mumble.

мышело́вка [*gen. pl.* -вок] *n.* mousetrap.

мы́шечный *adj.* muscle (*attrib.*); muscular.

мыши́ный *adj.* 1, mouse (*attrib.*). 2, like that of a mouse. —**мыши́ная возня́**, fuss over nothing.

мы́шка [*gen. pl.* -шек] *n.* 1, *dim. of* мышь. 2, *in* под мы́шкой *and* под мы́шку, under one's arm: нести́ под мы́шкой, to carry under one's arm. —**игра́ в ко́шки-мы́шки**, cat-and-mouse game.

мышле́ние *also,* **мы́шление** *n.* thinking; thought.

мышо́нок [*gen.* -нка; *pl.* -ша́та, -ша́т] *n.* baby mouse.

мы́шца *n.* muscle.

мышь [*pl.* мы́ши, мыше́й, мыша́м] *n.f.* mouse. —**лету́чая мышь**, bat.

мышья́к [*gen.* -яка́] *n.* arsenic. —**мышьяко́вый**, *adj.* arsenic (*attrib.*).

мэр *n.* mayor.

мэ́рия *n.* 1, city administration. 2, city hall.

мю́зикл *n.* musical.

мю́зик-хо́лл *n.* music hall.

мя́гкий *adj.* [*short form* мя́гок, мягка́, мя́гко; *comp.* мя́гче] 1, soft. 2, mild. 3, gentle. 4, (*of punishment, a sentence, etc.*) light. —**мя́гкий ваго́н**, coach with soft (upholstered) seats. —**мя́гкий знак**, soft sign (ь).

мя́гко *adv.* 1, softly. 2, mildly. —**мя́гко выража́ясь**, to put it mildly.

мягкосерде́чие *n.* softheartedness; tenderheartedness. *Also,* **мягкосерде́чность**, *n.f.*

мягкосерде́чный *adj.* softhearted; tenderhearted.

мя́гкость *n.f.* softness; mildness; gentleness.

мягкоте́лый *adj.* 1, flabby; soft. 2, *fig.* spineless.

мя́гче *adj., comp. of* мя́гкий.

мягчи́ть *v. impfv.* to soften (*the skin*).

мяки́на *n.* chaff.

мя́киш *n.* the soft part of bread.

мя́кнуть *v. impfv.* [*pfv.* размя́кнуть; *past* мяк, -ла] to become soft; become flabby.

мя́коть *n.f.* 1, flesh. 2, pulp (*of fruit*).

мя́млить *v. impfv.* [*pfv.* промя́млить] *colloq.* 1, to mumble. 2, [*impfv. only*] to procrastinate. —**тяну́ть и мя́млить**, to hem and haw.

мя́мля *n.m. & f., colloq.* wishy-washy person.

мяси́стый *adj.* meaty; fleshy.

мясна́я *n., decl. as an adj., colloq.* butcher shop.

мясни́к [*gen.* -ника́] *n.* butcher.

мясно́й *adj.* meat (*attrib.*); beef (*attrib.*). —**мясна́я ла́вка**, butcher shop.

мя́со *n.* 1, meat. 2, flesh. —**сла́дкое мя́со**, sweetbread.

мясокомбина́т *n.* meat-packing plant.

мясору́бка [*gen. pl.* -бок] *n.* meat grinder.

мя́та *n., bot.* mint.

мяте́ж [*gen.* -тежа́] *n.* mutiny; revolt; rebellion. —**мяте́жник**, *n.* mutineer; rebel; insurgent.

мяте́жный *adj.* 1, mutinous; rebellious. 2, stormy; restless.

мя́тный *adj.* 1, mint (*attrib.*). 2, mint-flavored; peppermint.

мя́тый *adj.* crushed; crumpled; creased.

мять *v. impfv.* [*pres.* мну, мнёшь] 1, [*pfv.* размя́ть] to knead. 2, [*pfvs.* измя́ть, помя́ть, смять] to rumple; crease; wrinkle; crush. 3, [*pfv.* смять] to crush; crumble. 4, [*pfv.* помя́ть] *colloq.* to press; squeeze. —**мя́ться**, *refl.* 1, [*pfv.* из-, по-, с-] to become rumpled; become creased. 2, [*pfv.* по-] *colloq.* to hesitate; waver.

мяу́канье *n.* meow; meowing.

мяу́кать *v. impfv.* to meow.

мяч [*gen.* мяча́] *n.* ball.

мя́чик *n., dim. of* мяч.

Н

Н, н *n. neut.* fourteenth letter of the Russian alphabet.

на[1] *prep.* A, *with acc.* **1,** on; onto: положи́ть кни́гу на стол, to put the book on the table. **2,** to (*used in place of* **в** *with certain nouns denoting a large building, an open place, an event, or direction*): идти́ на по́чту, на вокза́л, на фа́брику, на пло́щадь, на рабо́ту, на собра́ние, to go to the post office, station, factory, square, work, meeting. **3,** for: уро́к на за́втра, the lesson for tomorrow; обе́д на двои́х, dinner for two. Он прие́хал на три дня, he has come to stay for three days. **4,** *expressing the degree of difference, as in comparisons:* он на три го́да ста́рше меня́, he is three years older than I. Населе́ние увели́чилось на три миллио́на, the population has increased by three million. **5,** by: продава́ть на фунт, to sell by the pound; шесть ме́тров на три, six meters by three; помно́жить семь на пять, to multiply seven by five. **6,** (*with dates*) as of: на пе́рвое ию́ля 1980, as of July 1, 1980. **7,** worth of: на рубль ма́рок, a ruble's worth of stamps. В, *with prepl.* **1,** on: кни́га лежи́т на столе́, the book is (lying) on the table. **2,** in; at (*used in place of* **в** *as above*): на пло́щади, in the square; на конце́рте, at the concert. **3,** by (*with modes of travel*): е́хать на по́езде, to go by train.

на[2] *particle, colloq.* here!: на, возьми́те!, here, take it! Да́йте мне, пожа́луйста, кни́гу! На!, Give me the book, please! Here! —**вот тебе́ и на!**, look what happened!; see what happened!

на- *prefix* **1,** on; onto: наплева́ть, to spit on. **2,** *indicating accidental meeting or collision:* нае́хать, to run over; run down. **3,** (*with pfv. verbs only*) a quantity of: накупи́ть, to buy a quantity of. **4,** (*with* **-ся**) to one's heart's content: наигра́ться, to play to one's heart's content.

наба́вить [*infl.* **-влю, -вишь**] *v., pfv. of* **набавля́ть.**

набавля́ть *v. impfv.* [*pfv.* **наба́вить**] **1,** to add on (a certain amount to the price of something). **2,** to raise (a price).

набалда́шник *n.* handle; knob (*of a walking stick*).

набальзами́ровать *v., pfv. of* **бальзами́ровать.**

наба́т *n.* alarm: бить (в) наба́т, to sound the alarm.

наба́тный *adj.* alarm (*attrib.*): наба́тный ко́локол, alarm bell.

набе́г *n.* raid; foray; incursion.

набега́ть *v. impfv.* [*pfv.* **набежа́ть**] **1,** (*with* **на** + *acc.*) to run into; smash into; dash against. **2,** to appear suddenly; gather suddenly.

набе́гаться *v.r. pfv., colloq.* **1,** to run to one's heart's content. **2,** to tire oneself out by running.

набедоку́рить *v., pfv. of* **бедоку́рить.**

набе́дренный *adj., in* **набе́дренная повя́зка,** loincloth.

набежа́ть [*infl. like* **бежа́ть**] *v., pfv. of* **набега́ть.**

набекре́нь *adv., colloq.* cocked; at an angle; on one side.

набели́ть *v., pfv. of* **бели́ть** (*in sense #2*). —**набели́ться,** *refl., pfv. of* **бели́ться.**

на́бело *adv.* (*of something written*) in final form; without corrections or erasures.

на́бережная *n., decl. as an adj.* embankment.

набива́ть *v. impfv.* [*pfv.* **наби́ть**] **1,** to stuff; fill; cram; pack. **2,** to nail; attach. **3,** *textiles* to print. —**наби́ть ру́ку на** (+ *prepl.*), *colloq.* to become experienced at. —**наби́ть це́ну,** to jack up the price. —**наби́ть себе́ це́ну,** to build oneself up.

набива́ться *v.r. impfv.* [*pfv.* **наби́ться**] **1,** (*with* **в** + *acc.*) to crowd into. **2,** (*with instr.*) to be crammed (with); be jammed (with). **3,** *colloq.* to force; impose (oneself): набива́ться в друзья́, to force one's friendship on someone; набива́ться в го́сти, invite oneself somewhere.

наби́вка *n.* **1,** (act of) stuffing. **2,** stuffing; filling; packing; padding. **3,** *textiles* printing. —**наби́вка чу́чел,** taxidermy.

набивно́й *adj.* (*of fabric*) printed.

наби́вщик *n.* one who stuffs anything. —**наби́вщик чу́чел,** taxidermist.

набира́ть *v. impfv.* [*pfv.* **набра́ть**] **1,** (*with gen. or acc.*) to gather; collect (a quantity of something). **2,** to gain (strength, experience, altitude, etc.). **3,** to recruit; enlist. **4,** to form; make up (a group, team, etc.). **5,** *printing* to compose; set in type. **6,** to dial (a telephone number). **7,** *sports* to score (points). —**набира́ться,** *refl.* **1,** to collect; gather; accumulate. **2,** to amount to; add up to. **3,** (*with gen.*) *colloq.* to summon up; muster (courage, strength, etc.). **4,** (*with gen.*) *colloq.* to pick up; acquire. **5,** *in* набра́ться ума́, to get smart. **6,** *colloq.* to get drunk.

наби́тый *adj.* stuffed; tightly packed; crammed. —**наби́тый дура́к,** *colloq.* utter fool.

наби́ть [*infl.* **-бью, -бьёшь**] *v., pfv. of* **набива́ть.** —**наби́ться,** *refl., pfv. of* **набива́ться.**

наблюда́тель *n.m.* observer.

наблюда́тельный *adj.* **1,** observant. **2,** observation (*attrib.*). —**наблюда́тельность,** *n.f.* keenness of observation; powers of observation.

наблюда́ть *v. impfv.* **1,** (*with acc. or* **за** + *instr.*) to observe; watch. **2,** (*with* **за** + *instr.*) to look after;

keep an eye on. **3,** (*with* за + *instr.*) to see that (order, cleanliness, etc.) is maintained. —**наблюда́ться,** *refl.* to exist; be seen: наблюда́ются определённые тру́дности, certain difficulties exist (*or* are to be seen).

наблюде́ние *n.* **1,** observation. **2,** supervision. **3,** surveillance. —**вести́ наблюде́ние,** to keep a lookout.

на́божный *adj.* pious; devout. —**на́божность,** *n.f.* piety.

набо́йка [*gen. pl.* -бо́ек] *n.* **1,** printed fabric. **2,** lift; tap (*on a heel*).

на́бок *adv.* to one side.

наболе́вший *adj.* painful; sore. —**наболе́вший вопро́с,** sore subject; sore point.

наболе́ть *v. pfv.* [*infl.* -éет *or* -и́т] to become painful.

наболта́ть *v. pfv., colloq.* to talk (a lot of).

набо́р *n.* **1,** recruitment; enrollment. **2,** set; collection. **3,** *printing* composition. —**набо́р высоты́,** *aero.* climb. —**набо́р слов,** gibberish.

набо́рный *adj.* typesetting (*attrib.*); composition (*attrib.*).

набо́рщик *n.* typesetter; compositor.

набра́сывать[1] *v. impfv.* [*pfv.* наброса́ть] **1,** to toss (a quantity of something). **2,** to sketch; outline. **3,** to jot down; dash off.

набра́сывать[2] *v. impfv.* [*pfv.* набро́сить] to throw on; throw over: набро́сить что́-нибудь на́ пол/на плечи/, to throw something on the floor/over one's shoulders/. —**набра́сываться,** *refl.* (*with* на + *acc.*) **1,** to attack; pounce on. **2,** *colloq.* to jump on; jump down someone's throat.

набра́ть [*infl. like* брать] *v., pfv. of* набира́ть. —**набра́ться,** *refl., pfv. of* набира́ться.

набрести́ *v. pfv.* [*infl. like* брести́] **1,** (*with* на + *acc.*) to come upon; wander upon; *fig.* hit upon (an idea). **2,** (*neut. past tense only*) to gather: набрело́ мно́го наро́ду, a large crowd gathered.

наброса́ть *v., pfv. of* набра́сывать[1].

набро́сить [*infl.* -шу, -сишь] *v., pfv. of* набра́сывать[2]. —**набро́ситься,** *refl., pfv. of* набра́сываться.

набро́сок [*gen.* -ска] *n.* sketch; draft; outline.

набры́згать *v. pfv.* (*with instr. or gen.*) to spill; splash.

набрю́шник *n.* abdominal band.

набуха́ть *v. impfv.* [*pfv.* набу́хнуть] to swell.

набу́хнуть [*past* -бу́х, -ла] *v., pfv. of* набуха́ть.

нава́га *n.* a variety of codfish found in northern waters.

наважде́ние *n.* delusion; hallucination.

нава́ксить *v., pfv. of* ва́ксить.

нава́ливать *v. impfv.* [*pfv.* навали́ть] **1,** (*with* на + *acc.*) to load on; pile on. **2,** *colloq.* to toss into a pile; pile up. **3,** *impers.* (*of snow*) to pile up. —**нава́ливаться,** *refl.* (*with* на + *acc.*) **1,** to lean heavily on; put all one's weight on. **2,** *colloq.* to attack; pounce on; tear into.

навали́ть [*infl.* -валю́, -ва́лишь] *v., pfv. of* нава́ливать. —**навали́ться,** *refl., pfv. of* нава́ливаться.

нава́лом *adv., colloq.* **1,** in a pile; in a heap. **2,** (*with gen.*) piles of; tons of: рабо́ты у меня́ нава́лом, I have piles/tons of work.

нава́р *n.* fat (*forming on the surface of soup*).

нава́ривать *v. impfv.* [*pfv.* навари́ть] to weld on.

нава́ристый *adj.* (*of soup*) rich; concentrated.

навари́ть [*infl.* -варю́, -ва́ришь] **1,** *pfv. of* нава́ривать. **2,** to cook (a quantity of something).

наварно́й *adj.* welded.

навева́ть *v. impfv.* [*pfv.* наве́ять] **1,** (*of the wind*) to bring on; waft. **2,** *fig.* to bring on; induce.

наве́даться *v.r., pfv. of* наве́дываться.

наведе́ние *n.* **1,** aiming (*of a gun*). **2,** applying; application (*of a polish*). **3,** *aerospace* guidance. **4,** *in* наведе́ние спра́вок, making of inquiries.

наве́дываться *v.r. impfv.* [*pfv.* наве́даться] (*with* к) *colloq.* to drop in on; call on.

навезти́ *v. pfv.* [*infl. like* везти́] to bring (a quantity of something).

наве́к *also,* **наве́ки** *adv.* forever.

навербова́ть *v. pfv.* [*infl.* -бу́ю, -бу́ешь] to recruit (a quantity of people).

наве́рно *adv.* **1,** probably; most likely. **2,** *obs.* certainly; for sure. *Also,* **наве́рное.**

наверну́ть *v., pfv. of* наве́ртывать. —**наверну́ться,** *refl., pfv. of* наве́ртываться.

наверняка́ *adv., colloq.* **1,** for sure. **2,** when one is sure of success.

наве́рстывать *v. impfv.* [*pfv.* наверста́ть] to make up for: наверста́ть поте́рянное вре́мя, to make up for lost time.

наверте́ть *v. pfv.* [*infl.* -верчу́, -ве́ртишь] **1,** *pfv. of* наве́ртывать (*in sense* #1). **2,** (*with gen.*) to make (*by spinning or drilling*).

наве́ртывать *v. impfv.* [*pfv.* наверну́ть] (*with* в + *acc.*) **1,** [*pfv. also* наверте́ть] to wind onto; wind around. **2,** to screw onto. —**наве́ртываться,** *refl.* [*pfv.* наверну́ться] (*of tears*) to well up: у неё навернули́сь слёзы, tears came to her eyes.

наве́рх *adv., expressing motion or direction* **1,** up; upward(s). **2,** upstairs.

наверху́ *adv., expressing location* **1,** above. **2,** upstairs.

наве́с *n.* **1,** awning. **2,** *fig.* cover: под наве́сом (+ *gen.*), under a cover of.

навеселе́ *adv., colloq.* tipsy; high.

наве́сить [*infl.* -шу, -сишь] *v., pfv. of* наве́шивать.

навесно́й *adj.* hanging.

навести́ [*infl. like* вести́] *v., pfv. of* наводи́ть.

навести́ть [*infl.* -щу́, -сти́шь] *v., pfv. of* навеща́ть.

наве́т *n., obs.* slander; calumny.

наве́тренный *adj.* windward.

наве́чно *adv.* forever; for all time.

наве́шать *v. pfv.* **1,** to hang up; hang out (a quantity of something). **2,** to weigh; weigh out (a quantity of something).

наве́шивать *v. impfv.* [*pfv.* наве́сить] to hang; install by hanging.

навеща́ть *v. impfv.* [*pfv.* навести́ть] to visit.

наве́ять *v. pfv.* [*infl.* -ве́ю, -ве́ешь] **1,** *pfv. of* навева́ть. **2,** to winnow (a quantity of something).

на́взничь *adv.* flat on one's back: упа́сть на́взничь, to fall flat on one's back.

навзры́д *adv., in* пла́кать навзры́д, to sob uncontrollably.

навига́тор *n.* navigator.

навига́ция *n.* navigation. —**навигацио́нный,** *adj.* navigation (*attrib.*); navigational.

навида́ться *v.r. pfv.* (*with gen.*) *colloq.* to have seen a lot (*or* enough) of.

навинчивать *v. impfv.* [*pfv.* навинти́ть] to screw on. —**навинчиваться,** *refl.* (*of an object*) to screw on.

нависа́ть *v. impfv.* [*pfv.* нави́снуть] **1,** (*with* на + *acc. or* над) to hang over; overhang. **2,** (*with* над) *fig.* (*of danger, a threat, etc.*) to hang over.

нави́снуть [*past* -ви́с, -ла] *v., pfv. of* нависа́ть.

нави́сший *adj.* overhanging. —**с нави́сшими бровя́ми**, beetle-browed.

навлека́ть *v. impfv.* [*pfv.* навле́чь] (*with* на себя́) to incur.

навле́чь [*infl. like* влечь] *v., pfv. of* навлека́ть.

наводи́ть *v. impfv.* [*pfv.* навести́; *pres.* -вожу́, -во́дишь] **1,** (*with* на + *acc.*) to lead (to); guide (to). **2,** to aim; point; train; direct. **3,** (*with* на + *acc.*) to suggest (a thought); give rise to (doubts). **4,** to cause; arouse; inspire (sadness, fear, etc.). **5,** to apply; apply a coat of. —**наводи́ть блеск** *or* **лоск на** (+ *acc.*), to give a luster/sheen to. —**наводи́ть (на себя́) красоту́**, to make oneself beautiful. —**наводи́ть кри́тику на** (+ *acc.*), to level criticism at. —**наводи́ть мост**, to throw up a bridge. —**наводи́ть (кого́-нибудь) на ум**, to bring to one's senses; bring to reason. —**наводи́ть поря́док**, to establish *or* restore order. —**наводи́ть спра́вки**, to make inquiries. —**наводи́ть чистоту́ в** (+ *prepl.*), to bring an air of cleanliness to.

наво́дка *n.* **1,** aiming (*of a weapon*). **2,** application (*of a coat or layer of something*). **3,** throwing up (*of a bridge*).

наводне́ние *n.* flood.

наводня́ть *v. impfv.* [*pfv.* наводни́ть] **1,** *obs.* to flood; inundate. **2,** *fig.* to flood: наводня́ть ры́нок, to flood the market.

наво́дчик *n., mil.* one who aims a gun.

наводя́щий *adj., in* наводя́щий вопро́с, leading question.

наво́з *n.* manure; dung.

наво́зить *v. impfv.* [*pfv.* унаво́зить; *pres.* -во́жу, -во́зишь] to treat with manure.

навози́ть *v. pfv.* [*infl.* -вожу́, -во́зишь] to bring in (a supply of something).

наво́зник *n.* dung beetle.

наво́зный *adj.* manure (*attrib.*); dung (*attrib.*). —**наво́зный жук**, dung beetle.

на́волочка *n.* [*gen. pl.* -чек] *n.* pillowcase.

навора́чивать *v. impfv.* [*pfv.* навороти́ть] *colloq.* **1,** to pile up. **2,** [*impfv. only*] (*with* на + *acc.*) to wind onto.

наворова́ть *v. pfv.* [*infl.* -ру́ю, -ру́ешь] to steal (a quantity of something).

навороти́ть [*infl.* -рочу́, -ро́тишь] *v., pfv. of* навора́чивать.

навостри́ть *v. pfv., colloq.* to sharpen. —**навостри́ть лы́жи**, *colloq.* to take to one's heels. —**навостри́ть у́ши**, *colloq.* to prick up one's ears.

навощи́ть *v., pfv. of* вощи́ть.

навра́ть *v. pfv.* [*infl. like* врать] *colloq.* **1,** to tell lies. **2,** (*with* на + *acc.*) to tell lies about. **3,** (*with* в + *prepl.*) to make a mistake (in).

навреди́ть *v. pfv.* [*infl.* -жу́, -ди́шь] (*with* dat.) *colloq.* to harm; do a great deal of harm to.

навря́д ли *particle, colloq.* = вряд ли.

навсегда́ *adv.* forever; for good. —**раз (и) навсегда́**, once and for all.

навстре́чу *adv.* in someone's direction. —*prep., with dat.* toward; to meet: вы́йти навстре́чу гостя́м, to go out to meet the guests. —**идти́ навстре́чу** (+ *dat.*), to meet halfway; cooperate with; accommodate.

навы́ворот *adv., colloq.* **1,** inside out. **2,** *fig.* upside down; backwards: все получи́лось навы́ворот, everything turned out backwards.

на́вык *n.* skill; ability: на́выки чте́ния/письма́, reading/writing skills.

навы́кат *also,* **навы́кате** *adv., in* глаза́ навы́кат(е), bulging eyes.

навы́лет *adv.* (*of a bullet, wound, etc.*) going right through (one's body).

навы́нос *adv., colloq.* for comsumption off the premises.

навы́пуск *adv., in* брю́ки навы́пуск, trousers worn over one's boots.

навы́рез *adv., in* купи́ть арбу́з навы́рез, to buy watermelon with the right to sample a piece.

навы́тяжку *adv., in* стоя́ть навы́тяжку, to stand at attention.

навью́чить *v., pfv. of* вью́чить.

навяза́ть[1] *v. impfv.* [*pfv.* навя́знуть; *pres.* -за́ю, -за́ешь] to stick; get stuck. —**навя́знуть у** (+ *gen.*) **в зуба́х**, *colloq.* to bore to death; make sick and tired.

навяза́ть[2] *v. pfv.* [*infl.* -вяжу́, -вя́жешь] **1,** *pfv. of* навя́зывать. **2,** to knit (a quantity of something). —**навяза́ться**, *refl., pfv. of* навя́зываться.

навя́знуть [*past* -вя́з, -ла] *v., pfv. of* навяза́ть[1].

навя́зчивый *adj.* **1,** obtrusive; irksome; pesky. **2,** (*of an idea, thought, etc.*) fixed; obsessive. **3,** (*of a melody*) haunting.

навя́зывать *v. impfv.* [*pfv.* навяза́ть] **1,** (*with* на + *acc.*) to tie (to); attach (to); fasten (to). **2,** (*with* dat.) to impose (upon); force (upon); foist (upon): навяза́ть свою́ во́лю кому́-нибудь, to impose one's will on someone. —**навя́зываться**, *refl.* to intrude; obtrude.

нага́йка [*gen. pl.* -га́ек] *n.* whip.

нага́н *n.* revolver.

нага́р *n.* snuff (*of a candle*).

нагиба́ть *v. impfv.* [*pfv.* нагну́ть] to bend. —**нагиба́ться**, *refl.* to bend over; bend down; stoop.

нагишо́м *adv., colloq.* stark naked.

нагла́живать *v. impfv.* [*pfv.* нагла́дить] *colloq.* **1,** to iron. **2,** to smooth out.

нагла́зник *n.* **1,** eyeshade. **2,** blinker; blinder.

нагле́ть *v. impfv.* [*pfv.* обнагле́ть] to become insolent.

нагле́ц [*gen.* -леца́] *n.* insolent person; impudent person.

на́глость *n.f.* **1,** insolence; impudence; impertinence. **2,** effrontery; gall.

наглота́ться *v.r. pfv.* (*with gen.*) to swallow (a quantity of something).

на́глухо *adv.* (*with verbs of closing*) tightly; tight.

на́глый *adj.* insolent; impudent; impertinent.

нагляде́ться *v.r. pfv.* [*infl.* -жу́сь, -ди́шься] (*with* на + *acc.*) to see a lot (of); see enough (of).

нагля́дно *adv.* graphically.

нагля́дность *n.f.* **1,** clarity. Для нагля́дности, for clarity; for visual effect; to demonstrate one's point. **2,** use of visual aids.

нагля́дный *adj.* **1,** graphic: нагля́дный приме́р, graphic example. **2,** employing visual aids: нагля́дное обуче́ние, instruction using visual aids. —**нагля́дные посо́бия**, visual aids. —**нагля́дный уро́к**, object lesson.

нагна́ть [*infl. like* гнать] *v., pfv. of* нагоня́ть.

нагнести́ [*infl. like* гнести́] *v., pfv. of* нагнета́ть.

нагнета́тель *n.m.* supercharger.

нагнета́ть *v. impfv.* [*pfv.* нагнести́] to force; pump (liquid, air, etc.).

нагное́ние *n.* festering; suppuration.

нагнои́ться *v.r. pfv.* to fester.

нагну́ть *v., pfv. of* нагиба́ть. —**нагну́ться**, *refl., pfv. of* нагиба́ться.

нагова́ривать *v. impfv.* [*pfv.* наговори́ть] **1,** (*with* на + *acc.*) *colloq.* to slander. **2,** *in* нагова́ривать пластúнку, to record one's voice. —**наговáриваться**, *refl.* to have a long talk; say all one wishes to say.

наговóр *n., colloq.* slander; calumny.

наговорúть *v. pfv.* **1**, *pfv. of* **наговáривать**. **2**, to say; utter (a lot of things). —**наговорúться**, *refl., pfv. of* **наговáриваться**.

нагóй *adj.* naked; nude; bare.

нáголо *adv., in* **стричь нáголо**, to cut off all of someone's hair; shave someone's head.

наголó *adv. (of a sword, saber, etc.)* drawn.

нáголову *adv., in* **разбúть нáголову**, to rout; defeat utterly.

наголодáться *v.r. pfv., colloq.* to go hungry; be half-starved.

нагоняй *n., colloq.* scolding; bawling out; dressing-down; tongue-lashing.

нагонять *v. impfv.* [*pfv.* **нагнáть**] **1**, to overtake; catch up to. **2**, to make up for. **3**, to drive together; gather together. **4**, *colloq.* to cause; arouse; evoke (fear; boredom, drowsiness, etc.).

нагорáть *v. impfv.* [*pfv.* **нагорéть**] **1**, *(of a candle)* to be covered with snuff. **2**, *impers., colloq. (of fuel or electricity)* to be consumed. **3**, *impers., colloq.* to get it; catch it; catch hell.

нагóрный *adj.* **1**, situated in the mountains; mountain *(attrib.)*. **2**, *(of a river bank)* high. —**Нагóрная прóповедь**, the Sermon on the Mount.

нагородúть *v. pfv.* [*infl.* -**рожý**, -**рóдишь** *or* -**родúшь**] **1**, to erect; put up. **2**, *colloq.* to heap up. **3**, *colloq.* to talk (nonsense).

нагóрье *n.* upland.

наготá *n.* nakedness; nudity.

наготóве *adv.* in readiness.

наготóвить *v. pfv.* [*infl.* -**влю**, -**вишь**] *colloq.* **1**, to lay in (a supply of something). **2**, to cook (a large quantity of something).

награбить *v. pfv.* [*infl.* -**блю**, -**бишь**] to rob (a quantity of something); amass by robbing.

награ́да *n.* **1**, reward. **2**, award; decoration.

наградúть [*infl.* -**жý**, -**дúшь**] *v., pfv. of* **награждáть**.

наградной *adj.* reward *(attrib.)*. —**наградны́е**, *n. pl.* bonus.

награждáть *v. impfv.* [*pfv.* **наградúть**] **1**, to reward. **2**, to award. **3**, *fig.* to endow.

награждéние *n.* **1**, rewarding; awarding. **2**, *obs.* reward; award.

награждённый *n., decl. as an adj.* recipient of an award.

нагрéв *n.* heat; heating.

нагревáние *n.* heating.

нагревáтель *n.m.* heater. —**нагревáтельный**, *adj.* heating *(attrib.)*.

нагревáть *v. impfv.* [*pfv.* **нагрéть**] **1**, to warm; heat. **2**, *in* **нагрéть рýки**, to line one's pocket; feather one's nest. —**нагревáться**, *refl.* to become warm; get warm.

нагримировáть *v., pfv. of* **гримировáть** *(in sense #1)*. —**нагримировáться**, *refl., pfv. of* **гримировáться** *(in sense #1)*.

нагромождáть *v. impfv.* [*pfv.* **нагромоздúть**] to pile up. —**нагромождáться**, *refl.* to pile up; accumulate.

нагромождéние *n.* **1**, piling up. **2**, disorderly pile.

нагромоздúть [*infl.* -**зжý**, -**здúшь**] *v., pfv. of* **громоздúть** *and* **нагромождáть**. —**нагромоздúться**, *refl., pfv. of* **нагромождáться**.

нагрубить *v., pfv. of* **грубúть**.

нагрубиянить *v., pfv. of* **грубиянить**.

нагрýдник *n.* **1**, bib. **2**, breastplate.

нагрýдный *adj.* breast *(attrib.)*; worn over the breast.

нагружáть *v. impfv.* [*pfv.* **нагрузúть**] **1**, to load (a vehicle, vessel, etc.). **2**, *fig., colloq.* to burden. —**нагружáться**, *refl. (with instr.)* to load up (with); take on.

нагрузúть [*infl.* -**гружý**, -**грýзишь** *or* -**грузúшь**] *v., pfv. of* **грузúть** *(in sense #1)* and **нагружáть**. —**нагрузúться**, *refl., pfv. of* **нагружáться**.

нагрýзка *n.* **1**, loading. **2**, load. **3**, workload. —**полéзная нагрýзка**, payload.

нагрянуть *v. pfv.* **1**, to arrive unexpectedly. **2**, *(with* **к***)* to descend on.

нагýливать *v. impfv.* [*pfv.* **нагулять**] *colloq.* to develop; work up *(as the result of walking)*: **нагулять аппетúт**, to work up an appetite.

нагулять *v., pfv. of* **нагýливать**. —**нагуляться**, *refl.* to have had a long walk; have walked enough.

над *also,* **надо** *prep., with instr.* **1**, over: **кры́ша над головóй**, a roof over one's head; **побéда над врагóм**, victory over the enemy. **2**, above: **над ýровнем мóря**, above sea level. **3**, *used with certain verbs and nouns*: **рабóтать над**, to work on; **смеяться над**, to laugh at. **Суд над кéм-нибудь**, the trial of someone.

над- *also,* **надо-** *prefix* **1**, adding on: **надстрáивать**, to build on; **надставлять**, to lengthen. **2**, supervision: **надзирáть**; **надсмáтривать**, to supervise. **3**, *indicating partial or superficial action*: **надрывáть**, to tear slightly; **надкусúть**, to take a bite of.

надавáть *v. pfv.* [*infl.* -**даю́**, -**даёшь**] *colloq.* to give (a quantity of something).

надавúть [*infl.* -**давлю́**, -**дáвишь**] *v., pfv. of* **надáвливать**.

надáвливать *v. impfv.* [*pfv.* **надавúть**] *(with acc. or* **на** + *acc.)* to press (on).

надарúть *v. pfv.* [*infl.* -**дарю́**, -**дáришь**] *colloq.* to give (a quantity of gifts).

надбáвить [*infl.* -**влю**, -**вишь**] *v., pfv. of* **надбавлять**.

надбáвка *n.* **1**, increase. **2**, raise *(in pay)*.

надбавлять *v. impfv.* = **набавлять**.

надбивáть *v. impfv.* [*pfv.* **надбúть**] *colloq.* to chip (a glass, cup, etc.).

надбúть [*infl.* -**добью́**, -**добьёшь**] *v., pfv. of* **надбивáть**.

надвигáть *v. impfv.* [*pfv.* **надвúнуть**] *(with* **на** + *acc.)* to pull; pull down (over one's ears, forehead, etc.). —**надвигáться**, *refl.* **1**, to approach; come on. **2**, to be impending; be imminent.

надвигáющийся *adj.* imminent; impending.

надвúнуть *v., pfv. of* **надвигáть**. —**надвúнуться**, *refl., pfv. of* **надвигáться**.

надвóдный *adj.* surface *(attrib.)*: **надвóдный корáбль**, surface vessel. —**надвóдная часть**, topsides.

нáдвое *adv.* in two; in half. —**бáбушка нáдвое сказáла**, it *(or* that) remains to be seen.

надвóрный *adj.* situated outside: **надвóрная пострóйка**, outbuilding.

надгортáнник *n.* epiglottis.

надгрóбие *n.* **1**, tombstone. **2**, *obs.* epitaph.

надгрóбный *adj.* **1**, grave *(attrib.)*; tomb *(attrib.)*: **надгрóбный кáмень**; **надгрóбная плитá**, gravestone; tombstone. **Надгрóбная нáдпись**, epitaph. **2**, funeral *(attrib.)*: **надгрóбная речь**, funeral oration.

надгрызáть *v. impfv.* [*pfv.* **надгры́зть**] to nibble at; nibble on.

надгры́зть [*infl. like* грызть] *v., pfv. of* надгрыза́ть.

надева́ние *n.* putting on; donning.

надева́ть *v. impfv.* [*pfv.* наде́ть] **1,** to put on. **2,** to wear: что мне наде́ть?, what should I wear?

наде́жда *n.* hope.

наде́жный *adj.* **1,** reliable; dependable; trustworthy. **2,** safe: в надёжных рука́х, in safe hands. **3,** firm; steady. —**наде́жность,** *n.f.* reliability; dependability.

наде́л *n., hist.* parcel of land (*given to a peasant*).

наде́лать *v. pfv.* **1,** to make (a quantity of something). **2,** (*with gen.*) to do (damage); make (mistakes); cause (trouble). —что ты наде́лал?, what have you done?

наделе́ние *n.* allotment.

наделя́ть *v. impfv.* [*pfv.* надели́ть] (*with instr.*) **1,** to allot; provide with. **2,** *fig.* to endow (with).

надерзи́ть *v., pfv. of* дерзи́ть.

наде́ть [*infl.* -де́ну, -де́нешь] *v., pfv. of* надева́ть.

наде́яться *v.r. impfv.* [*pres.* наде́юсь, наде́ешься] **1,** to hope; (*with* на + *acc.*) hope for. **2,** (*with* на + *acc.*) to rely on; count on.

надзе́мный *adj.* above-ground; overhead; elevated.

надзира́тель *n.m.* **1,** supervisor; overseer. **2,** (prison) guard. —**надзира́тельский,** *adj.* supervisory.

надзира́ть *v. impfv.* (*with* за + *instr.*) **1,** to supervise; oversee. **2,** to look after; keep an eye on. **3,** to see that (something) is maintained.

надзо́р *n.* **1,** supervision. **2,** surveillance.

надиви́ться *v.r. pfv., colloq., in* не мочь надиви́ться, to not but wonder; not get over; never cease to be amazed.

нади́р *n., astron.* nadir.

надка́лывать *v. impfv.* [*pfv.* надколо́ть] to split (slightly).

надколо́ть [*infl.* -колю́, -ко́лешь] *v., pfv. of* надка́лывать.

надкуси́ть [*infl.* -кушу́, -ку́сишь] *v., pfv. of* надку́сывать.

надку́сывать *v. impfv.* [*pfv.* надкуси́ть] to bite into; take a bite (out) of.

надла́мывать *v. impfv.* [*pfv.* надломи́ть] **1,** to break partly; fracture; crack. **2,** *fig.* to overtax; undermine. —**надла́мываться,** *refl.* **1,** to crack. **2,** to break down.

надлежа́ть *v. impfv.* [*pres.* -жи́т] *impers.* to be required: э́то надлежи́т сде́лать в ука́занный срок, this must (*or* is to) be done within the period indicated. Вам надлежи́т яви́ться в де́вять часо́в, you are to appear at nine o'clock.

надлежа́щий *adj.* proper; appropriate. —**надлежа́щим о́бразом,** properly.

надло́м *n.* **1,** break; crack. **2,** *fig.* breakdown.

надломи́ть [*infl.* -ломлю́, -ло́мишь] *v., pfv. of* надла́мывать. —**надломи́ться,** *refl., pfv. of* надла́мываться.

надло́мленный *adj.* **1,** broken; cracked. **2,** *fig.* shattered; broken (*in spirit*).

надме́нный *adj.* haughty; arrogant; supercilious. —**надме́нность,** *n.f.* haughtiness; arrogance.

надо *prep.* = над (*used mainly in the combination* надо мной).

на́до *adv.* (one) must; (one) has to: на́до соблюда́ть пра́вила, one must observe the rules; мне на́до идти́, I have to go. —**не на́до, 1,** (one) must not: не на́до так говори́ть, you must not talk like that. **2,** (one) does not have to; (one) need not: не на́до боя́ться, you need not be afraid. —**так ему́ и на́до,** it serves him right.

на́добно *adv., obs.* = на́до.

на́добность *n.f.* necessity; need.

на́добный *adj., obs.* necessary; needed.

надое́да *n.m. & f., colloq.* pest; nuisance. *Also,* надое́дала.

надоеда́ть *v. impfv.* [*pfv.* надое́сть] (*with dat.*) **1,** to pester; bother; bore. **2,** *impers.* to be tired of; be sick of: мне надое́ло безде́льничать, I am tired of doing nothing.

надое́дливый *adj.* **1,** annoying; irksome. **2,** tiresome; boring.

надое́сть [*infl. like* есть] *v., pfv. of* надоеда́ть.

надои́ть *v. pfv.* [*infl.* -дою́, -до́ишь *or* -дои́шь] to draw (a quantity of milk).

надо́й *n.* yield (*of milk*).

надо́лго *adv.* for a long time (*subsequent to the action expressed in the verb*): он уе́хал надо́лго, he went away (*or* has gone away) for a long time.

надо́мник *n.* person who works at home.

надорва́ть [*infl. like* рвать] *v., pfv. of* надрыва́ть. —**надорва́ться,** *refl.* **1,** *pfv. of* надрыва́ться. **2,** *colloq.* to strain oneself. **3,** *fig.* to break down; crack up.

надоу́мить *v. pfv.* [*infl.* -млю, -мишь] *colloq.* to suggest; give someone the idea (to *or* that).

надпа́рывать *v. impfv.* [*pfv.* надпоро́ть] to rip partly open; remove a few stitches from.

надпи́ливать *v. impfv.* [*pfv.* надпили́ть] to saw a little; saw partially.

надпили́ть [*infl.* -пилю́, -пи́лишь] *v., pfv. of* надпи́ливать.

надписа́ть [*infl.* -пишу́, -пи́шешь] *v., pfv. of* надпи́сывать.

надпи́сывать *v. impfv.* [*pfv.* надписа́ть] **1,** to inscribe; autograph. **2,** *obs.* to address (a letter).

на́дпись *n.f.* inscription.

надпоро́ть [*infl.* -порю́, -по́решь] *v., pfv. of* надпа́рывать.

надпо́чечник *n.* adrenal gland.

надпо́чечный *adj.* adrenal.

надра́ть *v. pfv.* [*infl. like* драть] to tear off (a quantity of something). —**надра́ть у́ши** (+ *dat.*), *colloq.* to pull someone's ears.

надре́з *n.* cut; incision.

надре́зать [*infl.* -ре́жу, -ре́жешь] *v., pfv. of* надреза́ть *and* надре́зывать.

надреза́ть *v. impfv.* [*pfv.* надре́зать] to cut slightly; make an incision in. *Also,* надре́зывать.

надруга́тельство *n.* an outrage.

надруга́ться *v.r. pfv.* (*with* над) to commit an outrage (against).

надры́в *n.* **1,** (slight) tear. **2,** *fig.* great effort. **3,** *fig.* breakdown. **4,** *fig.* emotional outburst.

надрыва́ть *v. impfv.* [*pfv.* надорва́ть] **1,** to tear slightly. **2,** to strain; overtax. —**надрыва́ться,** *refl.* **1,** to have a slight tear; be slightly torn. **2,** [*impfv. only*] to overexert oneself. **3,** [*impfv. only*] to yell at the top of one's lungs. **4,** [*impfv. only*] (*with* от) to suffer grievously. **5,** *in* се́рдце надрыва́ется, one's heart aches.

надры́вный *adj.* heart-rending; (*of laughter*) hysterical.

надсма́тривать *v. impfv.* (*with* над *or* за + *instr.*) to supervise; oversee; watch over.

надсмо́тр *n.* supervision.

надсмо́трщик *n.* overseer; supervisor.

надста́вить [*infl.* -влю, -вишь] *v., pfv. of* надставля́ть.

надста́вка [*gen. pl.* -вок] *n.* **1,** lengthening. **2,** extra piece.

надставля́ть *v. impfv.* [*pfv.* **надста́вить**] to lengthen (a garment).

надстра́ивать *v. impfv.* [*pfv.* **надстро́ить**] **1,** to build on (*at the top*). **2,** to increase the height of; make taller.

надстро́йка [*gen. pl.* -стро́ек] *n.* **1,** building on(to). **2,** superstructure.

надстро́чный *adj.* written above the line. —**надстро́чный знак,** superscript.

надтре́снутый *adj.* cracked.

надува́ла *n.m. & f., colloq.* swindler; cheat.

надува́ние *n.* inflation; blowing up.

надува́тельство *n., colloq.* cheating; trickery; deceit. —**надува́тельский,** *adj., colloq.* deceitful; underhand.

надува́ть *v. impfv.* [*pfv.* **наду́ть**] **1,** to inflate; blow up. **2,** *in* **надува́ть гу́бы,** to pout; show displeasure. **3,** *colloq.* to swindle; cheat; dupe. —**надува́ться,** *refl.* **1,** to become filled with air. **2,** to puff up one's cheeks. **3,** *colloq.* to swell; become swollen. **4,** *fig., colloq.* to get a swelled head. **5,** *fig., colloq.* to pout; sulk.

надувно́й *adj.* inflatable.

наду́манный *adj.* farfetched; artificial; forced.

наду́мать *v. pfv., colloq.* **1,** to decide. **2,** to think up; devise.

наду́тый *adj.* **1,** inflated. **2,** swollen. **3,** *colloq.* haughty; puffed up. **4,** (*of a style of writing*) pompous. **5,** *colloq.* peeved.

наду́ть *v. pfv.* [*infl.* -ду́ю, -ду́ешь] **1,** *pfv. of* **надува́ть. 2,** *impers., colloq.* to be affected (*by sitting in a draft*): мне наду́ло (в) ше́ю, I have a stiff neck. —**наду́ться,** *refl., pfv. of* **надува́ться.**

надуши́ть *v., pfv. of* **души́ть** (*in sense #4*). —**надуши́ться,** *refl., pfv. of* **души́ться.**

надшива́ть *v. impfv.* [*pfv.* **надши́ть**] **1,** to lengthen (*by sewing*). **2,** (*with* к *or* на) to sew onto.

надши́ть [*infl.* надошью́, надошьёшь] *v., pfv. of* **надшива́ть.**

надыми́ть *v., pfv. of* **дыми́ть.**

наеда́ться *v.r. impfv.* [*pfv.* **нае́сться**] to eat one's fill.

наедине́ *adv.* **1,** in private; privately. **2,** (*with* с + *instr.*) alone (with).

нае́зд *n.* quick visit: он быва́ет там то́лько нае́здом (*or* нае́здами), he goes there only on quick visits.

нае́здить *v. pfv.* [*infl.* -е́зжу, -е́здишь] **1,** *pfv. of* **наезжа́ть** (*in sense #3*) *and* **нае́зживать. 2,** to travel (a certain distance *or* amount of time).

нае́здник *n.* horseman; rider. —**нае́здничество,** *n.* horsemanship.

наезжа́ть *v. impfv.* **1,** [*pfv.* **нае́хать**] (*with* на + *acc.*) to run into; strike: на него́ нае́хала маши́на, he was struck by a car. **2,** [*pfv.* **нае́хать**] *colloq.* to arrive in large numbers. **3,** [*pfv.* **нае́здить**] to smooth down (a road). **4,** [*impfv. only*] (*with* в + *acc.*) *colloq.* to make periodic visits (to).

нае́зженный *adj.* (*of a road*) worn; well-trodden.

нае́зживать *v. impfv.* [*pfv.* **нае́здить**] to smooth down (a road).

наём [*gen.* на́йма] *n.* **1,** hiring. **2,** renting. —**рабо́тать по на́йму,** to work as a hired hand.

наёмник *n.* **1,** hireling. **2,** mercenary (*soldier*).

наёмный *adj.* **1,** hired. **2,** mercenary.

нае́сться [*infl. like* есть] *v.r., pfv. of* **наеда́ться.**

нае́хать [*infl.* -е́ду, -е́дешь] *v., pfv. of* **наезжа́ть.**

нажа́рить *v. pfv.* to roast; fry (a quantity of something).

нажа́ть[1] *v.pfv.* [*infl.* -жму́, -жмёшь] **1,** *pfv. of* **нажима́ть. 2,** to squeeze (a quantity of something).

нажа́ть[2] *v.pfv.* [*infl.* -жну́, -жнёшь] to harvest (a quantity of something).

наждак [*gen.* -дака́] *n.* emery.

наждачный *adj.* emery (*attrib.*). —**наждачная бума́га,** sandpaper.

наже́чь *v. pfv.* [*infl. like* жечь] to burn (a quantity of something).

нажи́ва *n.* **1,** making money. **2,** bait.

нажива́ть *v. impfv.* [*pfv.* **нажи́ть**] **1,** to make; amass (a fortune). **2,** to contract (a disease). **3,** (*with gen.*) to make (trouble, enemies, etc.) for oneself. —**нажива́ться,** *refl.* (*with* на + *prepl.*) to get rich (on).

наживи́ть [*infl.* -влю́, -ви́шь] *v., pfv. of* **наживля́ть.**

нажи́вка *n.* bait.

наживля́ть *v. impfv.* [*pfv.* **наживи́ть**] to bait.

нажи́м *n.* pressure.

нажима́ть *v. impfv.* [*pfv.* **нажа́ть**] **1,** (*with acc. or* на + *acc.*) to press (on). **2,** (*with* на + *acc.*) *colloq.* to put pressure on.

нажи́ть [*infl.* -живу́, -живёшь; *past* на́жил, нажила́, на́жило] *v., pfv. of* **нажива́ть.** —**нажи́ться,** *refl.* [*past* нажи́лся, -ла́сь, -ло́сь] *pfv. of* **нажива́ться.**

наза́втра *adv., colloq.* the next day.

наза́д *adv.* back; backwards. —*interj.* stand back! —**тому́ наза́д,** ago.

назва́ние *n.* **1,** name; appellation. **2,** title (*of a book, film, etc.*).

назва́ть [*infl. like* звать] *v., pfv. of* **называ́ть.** —**назва́ться,** *refl., pfv. of* **называ́ться.**

назе́мный *adj.* ground (*attrib.*); surface (*attrib.*); overland.

на́земь *adv., colloq.* to the ground.

назида́ние *n.* edification. —**в назида́ние** (+ *dat.*), for the edification of.

назида́тельный *adj.* **1,** edifying; instructive. **2,** didactic: назида́тельный тон, didactic tone.

назло́ *also,* **на́зло** *adv.* for spite; out of spite. —*prep., with dat.* to spite (someone). —**как назло́,** as luck would have it.

назнача́ть *v. impfv.* [*pfv.* **назна́чить**] **1,** to set; schedule. **2,** to appoint; name. **3,** to assign. **4,** to designate; earmark. **5,** to award; grant. **6,** *colloq.* to prescribe.

назначе́ние *n.* **1,** setting (of a date); awarding (of a pension or scholarship); prescribing (of medicine). **2,** assignment; appointment. **3,** function; purpose. —**ме́сто назначе́ния,** destination.

назна́чить *v., pfv. of* **назнача́ть.**

назо́йливый *adj.* obtrusive; officious.

назрева́ть *v. impfv.* [*pfv.* **назре́ть**] **1,** to ripen; mature. **2,** *fig.* to come to a head.

назре́вший *adj.* (*of a problem or question*) urgent.

назубо́к *adv., colloq.* (*with verbs of knowing, learning, etc.*) thoroughly; by heart.

называ́емый *adj., in* так называ́емый, the so-called.

называ́ть *v. impfv.* [*pfv.* **назва́ть**] **1,** to call; name. **2,** *in* наз(ы)ва́ть себя́, to identify oneself; give one's name. —**называ́ть ве́щи свои́ми имена́ми,** to call a spade a spade.

называ́ться *v.r. impfv.* [*pfv.* **назва́ться**] **1,** to call oneself. **2,** [*impfv. only*] to be called. **3,** to identify oneself; give one's name. **4,** *colloq.* to invite oneself. —**что называ́ется,** as they say.

наибо́лее *adv.,* used in forming compound superla-

tives the most: наибо́лее уда́чный спо́соб, the most successful method.

наибо́льший *adj.* the greatest; the largest.

наи́вный *adj.* naïve. —**наи́вность**, *n.f.* naïveté.

наивы́сший *adj.* the highest; the greatest.

наи́гранный *adj.* affected; pretended.

наигра́ть *v., pfv. of* наи́грывать. —**наигра́ться**, *refl.* to play to one's heart's content; play as much as one wishes.

наи́грывать *v. impfv.* [*pfv.* наигра́ть] **1,** *colloq.* to win (money) in a game. **2,** to make (a record); record. **3,** [*impfv. only*] to play softly.

наизна́нку *adv.* inside out.

наизу́сть *adv.* by heart.

наилу́чший *adj.* the best: наилу́чшим о́бразом, in the best possible manner. —**наилу́чшие пожела́ния,** best wishes.

наиме́нее *adv., used in forming compound superlatives* the least: наиме́нее вероя́тный слу́чай, the least probable case.

наименова́ние *n.* name; appellation.

наименова́ть *v., pfv. of* именова́ть.

наиме́ньший *adj.* the least; the least amount.

наискосо́к *adv., colloq.* = на́искось.

на́искось *adv.* at an angle; diagonally; catty-corner.

на́йтие *n.* inspiration. —**по на́йтию,** instinctively; intuitively.

наиху́дший *adj.* the worst.

найдёныш *n.* foundling.

найми́т *n.* hireling.

найти́ [*infl.* найду́, найдёшь; *past* нашёл, нашла́, нашло́] *v., pfv. of* находи́ть. —**найти́сь,** *refl., pfv. of* находи́ться.

нака́з *n.* **1,** *obs.* order; instructions. **2,** mandate (*from the voters*). **3,** *hist.* set of instructions issued by Catherine II.

наказа́ние *n.* punishment.

наказа́ть [*infl.* -кажу́, -ка́жешь] *v., pfv. of* нака́зывать.

наказу́емый *adj., law* punishable.

нака́зывать *v. impfv.* [*pfv.* наказа́ть] to punish.

нака́л *n.* **1,** incandescence. **2,** *fig.* fever pitch. —**бе́лый/кра́сный нака́л,** white/red heat.

накалённый *adj.* **1,** burning hot; incandescent. **2,** *fig.* tense; charged; explosive.

нака́ливание *n., in* ла́мпа нака́ливания, incandescent lamp.

нака́ливать *v. impfv.* [*pfv.* накали́ть] **1,** to make red hot. **2,** *fig.* to inflame. —**нака́ливаться,** *refl.* **1,** to become red hot. **2,** *fig.* to heat up.

накали́ть *v., pfv. of* нака́ливать *and* накаля́ть. —**накали́ться,** *refl., pfv. of* нака́ливаться *and* накаля́ться.

нака́лывать *v. impfv.* [*pfv.* наколо́ть] **1,** to prick. **2,** (*with* на + *acc.*) to pin on. —**нака́лываться,** *refl.* to prick oneself.

накаля́ть *v. impfv.* = нака́ливать. —**накаля́ться,** *refl.* = нака́ливаться.

накану́не *adv.* the day before. —*prep., with gen.* on the eve of.

нака́пливать *v. impfv.* = накопля́ть. —**нака́пливаться,** *refl.* = накопля́ться.

наката́ть *v. pfv.* **1,** *pfv. of* нака́тывать (*in sense #1*). **2,** to roll (a quantity of something).

накати́ть [*infl.* -качу́, -ка́тишь] *v., pfv. of* нака́тывать (*in sense #2*).

нака́тывать *v. impfv.* **1,** [*pfv.* наката́ть] to wear down; smooth down (a road). **2,** [*pfv.* накати́ть] (*with* на + *acc.*) to roll onto.

нака́чивать *v. impfv.* [*pfv.* накача́ть] **1,** to pump. **2,** to pump up; inflate.

наки́дка [*gen. pl.* -док] *n.* **1,** cape. **2,** pillow cover. **3,** *colloq.* extra charge.

наки́дывать *v. impfv.* [*pfv.* наки́нуть] **1,** to throw on; throw over. **2,** *colloq.* to add on (a certain amount). —**наки́дываться,** *refl.* (*with* на + *acc.*) to attack; pounce (on).

накипа́ть *v. impfv.* [*pfv.* накипе́ть] **1,** (*of scum*) to form. **2,** *fig.* (*of passions*) to smolder.

на́кипь *n.f.* scum.

накла́д *n., in* в накла́де, *see* внакла́де.

накла́дка [*gen. pl.* -док] *n.* **1,** hairpiece; wig. **2,** protective plate, pad, or strap. —**тормозна́я накла́дка,** brake lining.

накладна́я *n., decl. as an adj.* invoice; bill of lading.

накладно́й *adj.* **1,** superimposed. **2,** (*of hair, a beard, etc.*) false. —**накладно́й карма́н,** patch pocket. —**накладны́е расхо́ды,** overhead (costs).

накла́дывать *v. impfv.* [*pfv.* наложи́ть] **1,** to lay on; lay over; superimpose. **2,** to apply (a bandage, makeup, etc.). **3,** to load (with); pack (with). **4,** to load; pack; pile (a quantity of something). —**накла́дывать на себя́ ру́ки,** to kill oneself; commit suicide. —**накла́дывать свой отпеча́ток на** (+ *acc.*), to leave its mark upon. —**накла́дывать себе́ на таре́лку** (+ *gen.*), to help oneself to.

наклевета́ть *v., pfv. of* клевета́ть.

накле́ивать *v. impfv.* [*pfv.* накле́ить] **1,** to glue on; paste on; affix. **2,** to paste up; post (a notice).

накле́йка [*gen. pl.* -е́ек] *n.* **1,** pasting on; gluing on. **2,** sticker; label. **3,** hinge (*for a postage stamp*).

накли́кать *v. impfv.* [*pfv.* накли́кать] *colloq.* to invite; court; bring on (trouble, disaster, etc.).

накли́кать *v. impfv.* [*pfv.* накли́кать] to invite; court; bring on (trouble, disaster, etc.).

накло́н *n.* **1,** inclination. **2,** slope; incline.

наклоне́ние *n.* **1,** inclination. **2,** *gram.* mood.

наклони́ть [*infl.* -клоню́, -кло́нишь] *v., pfv. of* наклоня́ть. —**наклони́ться,** *refl., pfv. of* наклоня́ться.

накло́нность *n.f.* inclination; tendency; leaning; propensity.

накло́нный *adj.* inclined; sloping; slanting.

наклоня́ть *v. impfv.* [*pfv.* наклони́ть] to incline; lean; tilt; bow. —**наклоня́ться,** *refl.* to bend over; lean over.

накова́льня [*gen. pl.* -лен] *n.* anvil. —**ме́жду мо́лотом и накова́льней,** between the devil and the deep blue sea.

нако́жный *adj.* appearing on the skin: нако́жная сыпь, skin rash.

наколе́нник *n.* kneepad.

наколо́ть *v. pfv.* [*infl.* -колю́, -ко́лешь] **1,** *pfv. of* нака́лывать. **2,** to chop; split (a quantity of wood). **3,** to slaughter; kill (a quantity of animals, fish, etc.). —**наколо́ться,** *refl., pfv. of* нака́лываться.

наконе́ц *adv.* at last; finally.

наконе́чник *n.* tip.

накопа́ть *v. pfv.* **1,** to dig. **2,** to dig (a quantity of something).

накопи́ть [*infl.* -коплю́, -ко́пишь] *v., pfv. of* копи́ть, накопля́ть, *and* нака́пливать. —**накопи́ться,** *refl., pfv. of* копи́ться, накопля́ться, *and* нака́пливаться.

накопле́ние *n.* accumulation.

накопля́ть *v. impfv.* [*pfv.* **накопи́ть**] to accumulate; amass. —**накопля́ться**, *refl.* to accumulate; pile up; build up.

накопти́ть *v. pfv.* [*infl.* -пчу́, -пти́шь] **1**, *pfv. of* **копти́ть** (*in sense #2*). **2**, to smoke (a quantity of ham, fish, glass, etc.).

накорми́ть *v., pfv. of* **корми́ть**.

накоротке́ *adv., colloq.* **1**, from close up; at close range. **2**, for a short time; for a moment. **3**, (*with* **с** + *instr.*) on friendly terms (with).

накра́пывать *v. impfv.* (*of rain*) to fall lightly. *Also impers.*: ста́ло накра́пывать, it began to drizzle.

накра́сить *v. pfv.* [*infl.* -шу, -сишь] **1**, *pfv. of* **накра́шивать**. **2**, to paint (a quantity of something). —**накра́ситься**, *refl., pfv. of* **кра́ситься** *and* **накра́шиваться**.

накра́сть *v. pfv.* [*infl. like* **красть**] to steal (a quantity of something).

накрахма́лить *v., pfv. of* **крахма́лить**.

накра́шивать *v. impfv.* [*pfv.* **накра́сить**] to paint (one's lips, face, etc.). —**накра́шиваться**, *refl., colloq.* to put on make-up.

накрени́ть *v., pfv. of* **крени́ть** *and* **накреня́ть**. —**накрени́ться**, *refl., pfv. of* **крени́ться** *and* **накреня́ться**.

накреня́ть *v. impfv.* [*pfv.* **накрени́ть**] **1**, *v.t.* to tip; tilt. **2**, *v.i., impers.* to tilt to one side: дом/ло́дку накрени́ло, the house/boat tilted to one side. —**накреня́ться**, *refl.* to tip over; list; tilt to one side.

на́крепко *adv.* **1**, firmly; fast. **2**, *colloq.* strictly. —**кре́пко-на́крепко**, *intensive form of* **кре́пко**: кре́пко-на́крепко засну́ть, to fall fast asleep.

на́крест *adv.* crosswise. *Also,* **крест-на́крест**.

накрича́ть *v. pfv.* [*infl.* -чу́, -чи́шь] to shout; (*with* **на** + *acc.*) shout at.

накрои́ть *v. pfv.* to cut out (a quantity of something).

накроши́ть *v. pfv.* [*infl.* -крошу́, -кро́шишь] to crumble; chop up (a quantity of something).

накрути́ть [*infl.* -кручу́, -кру́тишь] *v., pfv. of* **накру́чивать**.

накру́чивать *v. impfv.* [*pfv.* **накрути́ть**] (*with* **на** + *acc.*) to wind (onto); wind (around).

накрыва́ть *v. impfv.* [*pfv.* **накры́ть**] **1**, to cover. **2**, *mil.* to hit; strike. **3**, *colloq.* to catch in the act. **4**, *in* накрыва́ть (на) стол, to set the table. **5**, *in* накрыва́ть за́втрак/обе́д/у́жин, tó set the table for breakfast/dinner/supper. —**накрыва́ться**, *refl.* (*with instr.*) to cover oneself (with).

накры́ть [*infl.* -кро́ю, -кро́ешь] *v., pfv. of* **накрыва́ть**. —**накры́ться**, *refl., pfv. of* **накрыва́ться**.

накупи́ть *v. pfv.* [*infl.* -куплю́, -ку́пишь] to buy (a quantity of something).

накури́ть *v. pfv.* [*infl.* -курю́, -ку́ришь] to fill (a room) with smoke. —**накури́ться**, *refl.* to smoke to one's heart's content.

налага́ть *v. impfv.* [*pfv.* **наложи́ть**] to impose (a fine, penalty, duty, etc.). —**налага́ть аре́ст на иму́щество**, to seize (someone's) property. —**налага́ть запре́т на** (+ *acc.*), to place a ban on.

нала́дить [*infl.* -жу, -дишь] *v., pfv. of* **нала́живать**. —**нала́диться**, *refl., pfv. of* **нала́живаться**.

нала́дчик *n.* adjuster.

нала́живание *n.* adjustment; setting right.

нала́живать *v. impfv.* [*pfv.* **нала́дить**] to adjust; repair; put right. —**нала́живаться**, *refl.* to settle down; take shape; work out.

налакирова́ть *v. pfv.* [*infl.* -ру́ю, -ру́ешь] to varnish; lacquer.

налга́ть *v. pfv.* [*infl. like* **лгать**] **1**, to lie; tell lies. **2**, (*with* **на** + *acc.*) to tell lies about; slander.

нале́во *adv.* to the left; on the left.

налега́ть *v. impfv.* [*pfv.* **нале́чь**] (*with* **на** + *acc.*) **1**, to lean (on); put one's weight on. **2**, to wield (*vigorously*); ply (*with energy*). **3**, *colloq.* to apply oneself (to).

налегке́ *adv.* **1**, with little or no baggage or cargo: путеше́ствовать налегке́, to travel light. **2**, lightly dressed.

налеза́ть *v. impfv.* [*pfv.* **нале́зть**] *colloq.* **1**, to come swarming in. **2**, (*of clothes*) to fit.

нале́зть [*infl. like* **лезть**] *v., pfv. of* **налеза́ть**.

налепи́ть *v. pfv.* [*infl.* -леплю́, -ле́пишь] **1**, *pfv. of* **налепля́ть**. **2**, to make (a quantity of something by modeling).

налепля́ть *v. impfv.* [*pfv.* **налепи́ть**] *colloq.* to stick on; paste on.

налёт *n.* **1**, raid. **2**, holdup. **3**, thin layer; thin coating. **4**, *fig.* touch; tinge. —**с налёта**, **1**, on the run; at full speed. **2**, in a flash; with only a moment's thought.

налета́ть¹ *v. impfv.* [*pfv.* **налете́ть**] **1**, (*with* **на** + *acc.*) to fly into; fly onto; swoop down on; pounce on. **2**, (*with* **на** + *acc.*) to run into; smash into. **3**, (*of a storm*) to blow up.

налета́ть² *v. pfv.* to fly (a certain distance *or* amount of time).

налете́ть *v. pfv.* [*infl.* -чу́, -ти́шь] **1**, *pfv. of* **налета́ть¹**. **2**, to fly in (*in large numbers*).

налётчик *n.* robber; assailant.

нале́чь [*infl. like* **лечь**] *v., pfv. of* **налега́ть**.

налива́ть *v. impfv.* [*pfv.* **нали́ть**] **1**, to pour. **2**, (*with instr.*) to fill (with a liquid). **3**, (*with gen. or acc.*) to spill. —**налива́ться**, *refl.* **1**, (*with* **в** + *acc.*) (*of liquids*) to flow into; get into. **2**, (*with instr.*) to become filled with. **3**, (*of fruits*) to ripen. **4**, *in* нали́ться кро́вью, to become bloodshot.

нали́вка *n.* fruit liqueur.

наливно́й *adj.* **1**, liquid: наливно́й груз, liquid cargo. **2**, designed to carry liquids: наливно́е су́дно, tanker. **3**, fully ripe.

нали́м *n.* burbot (*fish*).

налинова́ть *v., pfv. of* **линова́ть**.

налипа́ть *v. impfv.* [*pfv.* **нали́пнуть**] (*with* **на** + *acc.*) (*of dirt, leaves, etc.*) to stick (to); collect (on).

нали́пнуть [*past* -ли́п, -ла] *v., pfv. of* **налипа́ть**.

нали́ть [*infl.* налью́, нальёшь; *past* на́лил *or* нали́л, налила́, на́лило *or* налило́] *v., pfv. of* **налива́ть**. —**нали́ться**, *refl., pfv. of* **налива́ться**.

налицо́ *adv.* present; on hand.

нали́чие *n.* presence; existence. —**быть в нали́чии**, to be available; be on hand.

нали́чность *n.f.* **1**, cash on hand. **2**, = **нали́чие**.

нали́чный *adj.* (*of money*) available; on hand. —**нали́чные**, *n. pl.* [*also,* **нали́чные де́ньги**] cash.

налови́ть *v. pfv.* [*infl.* -ловлю́, -ло́вишь] to catch (a quantity of something).

наловчи́ться *v.r. pfv.* (*with inf. or* **в** + *prepl.*) *colloq.* to become proficient (at); get the hang (of).

нало́г *n.* tax. —**нало́говый**, *adj.* tax (*attrib.*).

налогообложе́ние *n.* taxation.

налогоплате́льщик *n.* taxpayer.

наложе́ние *n.* **1,** application (*of a bandage, make-up, etc.*). **2,** imposition (*of a fine, tax, etc.*).

нало́женный *adj., in* **нало́женным платежо́м,** C.O.D.

наложи́ть [*infl.* -ложу́, -ло́жишь] *v., pfv. of* накла́дывать *and* налага́ть.

нало́жница *n., obs.* concubine.

наломáть *v. pfv.* to break (a quantity of something).

налощи́ть *v., pfv. of* лощи́ть.

налущи́ть *v. pfv.* to shell; husk (a quantity of something).

налюбова́ться *v.r. pfv.* [*infl.* -бу́юсь, -бу́ешься] (*with* на + *acc.*) to gaze at to one's heart's content: не могу́ налюбова́ться на э́ту карти́ну, I never get tired of looking at that picture.

нам *pron., dat. of* мы.

намагни́чивать *v. impfv.* [*pfv.* намагни́тить] to magnetize.

намáзать *v., pfv. of* мáзать. —**намáзаться,** *refl., pfv. of* мáзаться (*in sense #1*).

намалевáть *v., pfv. of* малевáть.

намарáть *v., pfv. of* марáть (*in sense #2*).

намáслить *v., pfv. of* мáслить.

намáтывать *v. impfv.* [*pfv.* намотáть] to wind onto; wind around. —**намотáть себе́ на ус,** *colloq.* to make a mental note of.

намáчивать *v. impfv.* [*pfv.* намочи́ть] **1,** to wet; moisten. **2,** to soak. **3,** (*with* на + *prepl.*) *colloq.* to make a puddle (on).

намёк *n.* hint.

намекáть *v. impfv.* [*pfv.* намекну́ть] **1,** (*with* на + *acc.*) to hint (at); allude (to). **2,** to suggest; infer; intimate (that).

наменя́ть *v. pfv.* **1,** to obtain (a quantity of something) by exchanging. **2,** to change (a quantity of money).

намеревáться *v.r. impfv.* to intend.

намéрен *adj., used predicatively* intending: что вы намéрены сдéлать?, what do you intend to do?

намéрение *n.* intention.

намéренный *adj.* intentional; deliberate. —**намéренно,** *adv.* intentionally; deliberately.

намерзáть *v. impfv.* [*pfv.* намёрзнуть] (*with* на + *prepl.*) (*of a layer of ice*) to form (on).

намёрзнуть [*past* -мёрз, -ла] *v., pfv. of* намерзáть.

намéртво *adv., colloq.* firmly; fast.

намести́ [*infl. like* мести́] *v., pfv. of* наметáть[1].

намéстник *n., obs.* **1,** deputy. **2,** provincial governor.

наметáть[1] *v. impfv.* [*pfv.* намести́] **1,** to sweep together (a quantity of something). **2,** (*of a storm, the wind, etc.*) to form (snowdrifts); drift (the snow). **3,** *impers.* to drift; pile up: намелó мнóго снéгу, large snowdrifts had formed.

наметáть[2] *v., pfv. of* намётывать.

намéтить [*infl.* -чу, -тишь] *v., pfv. of* мéтить (*in sense #1*) *and* намечáть. —**намéтиться,** *refl., pfv. of* намечáться.

намéтка [*gen. pl.* -ток] *n.* **1,** basting. **2,** basting thread. **3,** rough draft; outline.

намётывать *v. impfv.* [*pfv.* наметáть] **1,** to pile up (a quantity of something). **2,** *colloq.* (*with* глаз *or* рýку) to train: намётанный глаз, trained eye. Намётáть рýку на (+ *prepl.*), to become proficient at. **3,** to baste.

намечáть *v. impfv.* [*pfv.* намéтить] **1,** to mark. **2,** to plan; map out; outline. **3,** to set; schedule. **4,** to

nominate. —**намечáться,** *refl.* **1,** to appear; be visible. **2,** *fig.* to emerge; take shape. **3,** [*impfv. only*] to be planned; be scheduled.

нáми *pron., instr. of* мы.

намнóго *adv.* **1,** (*with comp. adjectives*) much; far. **2,** (*with verbs*) greatly; considerably.

намокáть *v. impfv.* [*pfv.* намóкнуть] to get wet; get soaked.

намóкнуть [*past* -мóк, -ла] *v., pfv. of* намокáть.

намолóть *v. pfv.* [*infl.* -мелю́, -мéлешь] to grind (a quantity of something).

намóрдник *n.* muzzle.

намóрщить *v., pfv. of* мóрщить. —**намóрщиться,** *refl., pfv. of* мóрщиться (*in sense #1*).

намотáть *v. pfv.* **1,** *pfv. of* мотáть *and* намáтывать. **2,** to wind (a quantity of something).

намочи́ть [*infl.* -мочу́, -мóчишь] *v., pfv. of* мочи́ть *and* намáчивать.

намýчиться *v.r. pfv., colloq.* **1,** to suffer; go through hell. **2,** (*with* с + *instr.*) to have a hell of a time with.

намы́ливать *v. impfv.* [*pfv.* намы́лить] **1,** to soap; lather. **2,** *in* намы́лить гóлову (+ *dat.*), *colloq.* to chew someone out. —**намы́ливаться,** *refl.* to soap oneself.

намы́лить *v., pfv. of* мы́лить *and* намы́ливать. —**намы́литься,** *refl., pfv. of* мы́литься *and* намы́ливаться.

намя́ть *v. pfv.* [*infl.* -мну, -мнёшь] *colloq.* **1,** to trample down; flatten. **2,** to irritate; chafe. —**намя́ть бокá** *or* шéю (+ *dat.*), *colloq.* to administer a beating to; beat up.

нанесéние *n.* **1,** inflicting; causing. **2,** tracing; plotting. **3,** applying; laying.

нанести́ [*infl. like* нести́] *v., pfv. of* наноси́ть.

нанизáть [*infl.* -нижу́, -ни́жешь] *v., pfv. of* низáть *and* нани́зывать.

нани́зывать *v. impfv.* [*pfv.* нанизáть] to string; thread.

наниматель *n.m.* **1,** tenant. **2,** employer.

нанимáть *v. impfv.* [*pfv.* наня́ть] **1,** to hire; employ. **2,** to hire; rent. —**нанимáться,** *refl.* to get a job.

нáново *adv., colloq.* anew; over again.

нанóс *n.* alluvium.

наноси́ть *v. impfv.* [*pfv.* нанести́; *pres.* -ношу́, -нóсишь] **1,** to inflict: нанести́ комý-нибудь удáр/пораже́ние, to inflict a blow/defeat on someone. **2,** to drift; pile up (snow, sand, etc.); (*of water*) wash up. **3,** to trace; plot (*on a map*). **4,** to apply a layer of. **5,** *impers.* to strike; run into: лóдку нанеслó на кáмень, the boat struck a rock. **6,** *in* наноси́ть визи́т (+ *dat.*), to pay a visit on.

нанóсный *adj.* **1,** alluvial. **2,** *fig.* alien; external.

наня́ть [*infl. like* поня́ть] *v., pfv. of* нанимáть. —**наня́ться,** *refl.* [*past* наня́лся, -лáсь] *pfv. of* нанимáться.

наоборóт *adv.* **1,** backwards. **2,** the other way round. **3,** (*with* и *or* и́ли) vice versa. **4,** on the contrary.

наобýм *adv., colloq.* **1,** without thinking. **2,** at random.

нáотмашь *adv.* **1,** (*with verbs of striking, throwing, etc.*) with a full sweep of one's arm. **2,** (*of one's arms*) stretched out; fully extended.

наотрéз *adv.* flatly; pointblank.

напáдать *v. pfv.* to fall (*in large quantities*).

напáдать *v. impfv.* [*pfv.* напáсть] (*with* на + *acc.*) **1,** to attack. **2,** to run across; come across; come upon. **3,** to come up with; hit upon (an idea). **4,** *colloq.*

to attack; assail; jump on. **5,** (*of a feeling*) to come over.

нападаю́щий *n., decl. as an adj., sports* forward (*offensive player*).

нападе́ние *n.* attack.

напа́дки [*gen.* **-док**] *n. pl.* (verbal) attacks.

напа́ивать *v. impfv.* [*pfv.* **напои́ть**] **1,** to give to drink. **2,** to make drunk. **3,** [*pfv.* **напая́ть**] to solder on.

напа́лм *n.* napalm. —**напа́лмовый,** *adj.* napalm.

напа́рник *n., colloq.* partner; buddy; mate.

напа́рывать *v. impfv.* [*pfv.* **напоро́ть**] *colloq.* to cut: напоро́ть но́гу на гвоздь, to cut one's foot on a nail. —**напа́рываться,** *refl.* (*with* **на** + *acc.*) *colloq.* **1,** to cut oneself (on). **2,** to run into; encounter.

напа́сть[1] *v. pfv.* [*infl. like* **пасть**] **1,** *pfv. of* **напада́ть**. **2,** to fall (*in large quantities*).

напа́сть[2] *n.f., colloq.* misfortune.

напая́ть *v., pfv. of* **напа́ивать** (*in sense #3*).

напе́в *n.* tune; melody; air.

напева́ть *v. impfv.* [*pfv.* **напе́ть**] **1,** to sing. **2,** to record; make (a record). **3,** [*impfv. only*] to hum.

напе́вный *adj.* melodious.

наперебо́й *adv., colloq.* **1,** interrupting one another. **2,** vying with one another; trying to outdo one another.

наперове́с *adv.* (*of a weapon*) pointed forward.

наперегонки́ *also,* **наперего́нки** *adv., colloq.* racing one another: бежа́ть наперегонки́, to race each other.

наперёд *adv., colloq.* **1,** forward. **2,** in advance. —**за́дом наперёд,** backwards: наде́ть шля́пу за́дом наперёд, to put one's hat on backwards.

наперекор *prep., with dat.* contrary to; in defiance of.

наперере́з *prep., with dat.* so as to cut across the path of; so as to intercept; so as to head off.

напереры́в *adv., colloq.* = **наперебо́й.**

наперечёт *adv., colloq.* **1,** (*with verbs of knowing*) inside out; like a book; (*with* **все**) every single one. **2,** few and far between.

наперсник *n., obs.* confidant.

наперсный *adj., in* **наперсный крест,** pectoral cross.

наперсток [*gen.* **-тка**] *n.* thimble.

наперстя́нка *n.* foxglove; digitalis.

напе́ть [*infl.* **-пою́, -поёшь**] *v., pfv. of* **напева́ть.**

напеча́тать *v., pfv. of* **печа́тать.** —**напеча́таться,** *refl., pfv. of* **печа́таться.**

напе́чь *v. pfv.* [*infl. like* **печь**] to bake (a quantity of something).

напива́ться *v.r. impfv.* [*pfv.* **напи́ться**] **1,** to drink one's fill. **2,** (*with gen.*) to have a drink of. **3,** to get drunk.

напили́ть *v. pfv.* [*infl.* **-пилю́, -пи́лишь**] to saw (a quantity of something).

напи́лок [*gen.* **-лка**] *n., colloq.* = **напи́льник.**

напи́льник *n.* file (*tool*).

напира́ть *v. impfv.* (*with* **на** + *acc.*) *colloq.* **1,** to press; put pressure on. **2,** to stress; emphasize.

написа́ние *n.* **1,** writing. **2,** spelling.

написа́ть *v., pfv. of* **писа́ть.**

напита́ть *v. pfv.* **1,** *pfv. of* **напи́тывать. 2,** *colloq.* to feed.

напи́ток [*gen.* **-тка**] *n.* drink; beverage.

напи́тывать *v. impfv.* [*pfv.* **напита́ть**] to saturate.

напи́ться [*infl. like* **пить**] *v.r., pfv. of* **напива́ться.**

напи́хивать *v. impfv.* [*pfv.* **напиха́ть**] *colloq.* to stuff; cram.

напи́чкать *v., pfv. of* **пи́чкать.**

наплавно́й *adj., in* **наплавно́й мост,** floating bridge.

напла́кать *v. pfv.* [*infl.* **-пла́чу, -пла́чешь**], *in* напла́кать себе́ глаза́, to have red eyes from crying. —**напла́каться,** *refl.* **1,** to have a good cry. **2,** (*with* **с** + *instr.*) *colloq.* to have trouble (with).

напластова́ние *n., geol.* bedding; stratification.

наплева́тельский *adj., colloq.* couldn't-care-less: наплева́тельское отноше́ние, couldn't-care-less attitude.

наплева́ть *v. pfv.* [*infl.* **-плю́ю, -плюёшь**] (*with* **на** + *acc.*) **1,** to spit on. **2,** *colloq.* not to give a damn: ему́ наплева́ть на э́то, he doesn't give a damn about it.

наплести́ *v. pfv.* [*infl. like* **плести́**] **1,** to weave (a quantity of something). **2,** *colloq.* to talk a lot of (nonsense).

наплы́в *n.* **1,** influx. **2,** excrescence (*on trees*).

напова́л *adv., in* уби́ть напова́л, to kill outright; kill on the spot.

наподо́бие *prep., with gen.* like; resembling.

напои́ть [*infl.* **-пою́, -по́ишь** *or* **-пои́шь**] *v., pfv. of* **пои́ть** *and* **напа́ивать.**

напока́з *adv.* **1,** on display. **2,** for show. —**выставля́ть напока́з, 1,** to put on display. **2,** to show off; flaunt.

наполза́ть *v. impfv.* [*pfv.* **наползти́**] *colloq.* (*with* **на** + *acc.*) to crawl onto.

наползти́ [*infl. like* **ползти́**] *v., pfv. of* **наполза́ть.**

наполне́ние *n.* (act of) filling.

наполни́тель *n.m.* filler.

наполня́ть *v. impfv.* [*pfv.* **напо́лнить**] to fill. —**наполня́ться,** *refl.* to be filled; become filled.

наполови́ну *adv.* **1,** half: наполови́ну пусто́й, half-empty. **2,** in half; by half: уменьши́ть наполови́ну, to reduce in/by half.

напома́дить *v., pfv. of* **пома́дить.** —**напома́диться,** *refl., pfv. of* **пома́диться.**

напомина́ние *n.* **1,** reminder. **2,** mention: при напомина́нии о..., at the mention of...

напомина́ть *v. impfv.* [*pfv.* **напо́мнить**] **1,** (*with dat.*) to remind: напомина́ть кому́-нибудь о встре́че, to remind someone about an appointment. Вы напомина́ете мне моего́ му́жа, you remind me of my husband. **2,** [*impfv. only*] to resemble: фо́рма ку́пола напомина́ет лу́ковицу, the shape of the dome resembles an onion.

напо́р *n.* pressure.

напо́ристый *adj.* assertive; aggressive.

напо́рный *adj.* pressure (*attrib.*).

напоро́ть *v. pfv.* [*infl.* **-порю́, -по́решь**] **1,** *pfv. of* **напа́рывать. 2,** (*with gen. or acc.*) to talk a lot of (nonsense). —**напоро́ться,** *refl., pfv. of* **напа́рываться.**

напо́ртить *v. pfv.* [*infl.* **-чу, -тишь**] *colloq.* **1,** to damage (a quantity of something). **2,** (*with dat.*) to harm.

напосле́док *adv., colloq.* **1,** finally; at last; in the end. **2,** in conclusion.

напра́вить [*infl.* **-влю, -вишь**] *v., pfv. of* **направля́ть.** —**напра́виться,** *refl., pfv. of* **направля́ться.**

направле́ние *n.* **1,** direction. **2,** trend. **3,** assignment. **4,** order; permit. **5,** *mil.* axis.

напра́вленность *n.f.* direction; orientation.

напра́вленный *adj.* **1,** purposeful. **2,** *radio* directional.

направля́ть *v. impfv.* [*pfv.* **напра́вить**] **1,** to direct. **2,** to aim (a blow); point (a weapon). **3,** to send. **4,** to sharpen. —**направля́ться,** *refl.* (*with* **в, на,** *or* **к**) to head for; make for.

напра́во *adv.* to the right; on the right.

напрактикова́ться *v.r. pfv.* [*infl.* -ку́юсь, -ку́ешься] (*with* в + *prepl.*) *colloq.* to become proficient (at); get the knack (of).

напра́слина *n., colloq.* false charge; false allegation.

напра́сно *adv.* in vain; for nothing. Вы напра́сно ждёте её, you're wasting your time waiting for her. Вы напра́сно обвиня́ете его́, you have no reason to accuse him.

напра́сный *adj.* **1,** vain; futile. **2,** (*of fears, anxiety, etc.*) needless; groundless.

напра́шиваться *v.r. impfv.* [*pfv.* напроси́ться] *colloq.* **1,** (*with* на + *acc.*) to invite oneself (to); (try to) get invited (to). Напра́шиваться в го́сти, to (try to) wangle an invitation. **2,** (*with* на + *acc.*) to ask for; look for; invite (trouble); fish for (a compliment). **3,** [*impfv. only*] to come to mind; suggest itself.

наприме́р *adv.* for example; for instance.

напрока́зить *v., pfv. of* прока́зить.

напрока́зничать *v., pfv. of* прока́зничать.

напрока́т *adv.* on a rental basis. —брать напрока́т, to rent; hire. —дава́ть *or* отдава́ть напрока́т, to rent; rent out. —сдава́ться напрока́т, to be for hire.

напролёт *adv., colloq.* through; long; straight: всю ночь напролёт, the whole night through/long; весь день напролёт, all day long; два дня напролёт, two days straight.

напроло́м *adv., colloq.* straight ahead (*regardless of obstacles*).

напропалу́ю *adv., colloq.* headlong; for all one is worth.

напроро́чить *v., pfv. of* проро́чить.

напроси́ться [*infl.* -прошу́сь, -про́сишься] *v.r., pfv. of* напра́шиваться.

напро́тив *adv.* **1,** opposite. **2,** across the street. **3,** on the contrary. —*prep., with gen.* opposite; facing.

на́прочь *adv., colloq.* completely.

напру́живать *v. impfv.* [*pfv.* напру́жить] *colloq.* to strain; make taut.

напряга́ть *v. impfv.* [*pfv.* напря́чь] to strain; exert. —напряга́ться, *refl.* **1,** to become taut. **2,** to strain oneself; exert oneself.

напряже́ние *n.* **1,** straining; exertion. **2,** tension; strain; stress. **3,** *electricity* tension; voltage.

напряжённость *n.f.* tension: междунаро́дная напряжённость, international tension.

напряжённый *adj.* **1,** tense; strained. **2,** intense; strenuous. **3,** (*of attention*) rapt.

напрями́к *adv., colloq.* **1,** straight; in a straight line. **2,** *fig.* to the point; pointblank.

напря́чь [*infl.* -прягу́, -пряжёшь, ...-прягу́т; *past* -пря́г, -прягла́, -прягло́] *v., pfv. of* напряга́ть. —напря́чься, *refl., pfv. of* напряга́ться.

напуга́ть *v. pfv.* to frighten; scare. —напуга́ться, *refl.* to become frightened; become scared.

напу́дрить *v., pfv. of* пу́дрить. —напу́дриться, *refl., pfv. of* пу́дриться.

напу́льсник *n.* wristband.

напуска́ть *v. impfv.* [*pfv.* напусти́ть] **1,** to let in. **2,** (*with* на + *acc.*) *colloq.* to sic (an animal) on. **3,** (*with* на + *acc.*) *colloq.* to strike (fear, terror, etc.) into. **4,** (*with* на себя́) *colloq.* to affect; assume an air of. **5,** *in* напуска́ть тума́ну, to confuse the issue. —напуска́ться, *refl.* (*with* на + *acc.*) *colloq.* to attack; pounce on.

напускно́й *adj.* affected; assumed.

напусти́ть [*infl.* -пущу́, -пу́стишь] *v., pfv. of* напуска́ть. —напусти́ться, *refl., pfv. of* напуска́ться.

напу́тать *v. pfv., colloq.* **1,** to make a mess of; botch. **2,** (*with* в + *prepl.*) to get (something) wrong; get (something) mixed up.

напу́тственный *adj.* parting; farewell.

напу́тствие *n.* parting words.

напу́тствовать *v. impfv. & pfv.* [*pres.* -ствую, -ству́ешь] (*with instr.*) to say (*when parting*).

напуха́ть *v. impfv.* [*pfv.* напу́хнуть] *colloq.* to swell up.

напу́хнуть [*past* -пу́х, -ла] *v., pfv. of* напуха́ть.

напы́житься *v.r., pfv. of* пы́житься.

напыли́ть *v., pfv. of* пыли́ть (*in sense #1*).

напы́щенность *n.f.* **1,** pomposity. **2,** bombast.

напы́щенный *adj.* **1,** pompous. **2,** bombastic; high-flown.

напя́ливать *v. impfv.* [*pfv.* напя́лить] **1,** to stretch (material) on a frame. **2,** *colloq.* to pull on (an item of clothing that is too small).

нарабо́тать *v. pfv., colloq.* **1,** to produce (a quantity of something). **2,** to earn (a sum of money). —нарабо́таться, *refl., colloq.* to do a lot of work; do enough work.

наравне́ *adv.* (*with* с + *instr.*) **1,** even (with); on a level (with). **2,** equally (with); on a par (with); on an equal footing (with).

нараспа́шку *adv., colloq.* unbuttoned; unfastened. —душа́ нараспа́шку, open-hearted; not one to hold back.

нараспе́в *adv.* in a singsong voice.

нараста́ние *n.* growth; expansion.

нараста́ть *v. impfv.* [*pfv.* нарасти́] **1,** (*with* на + *prepl.*) to grow (on); form (on). **2,** to grow; expand. **3,** to increase; build up; mount. **4,** (*of debts*) to pile up; (*of interest*) to accrue.

нарасти́ [*infl. like* расти́] *v., pfv. of* нараста́ть.

нарасти́ть [*infl.* -щу́, -сти́шь] *v., pfv. of* нара́щивать.

нарасхва́т *adv., colloq.* **1,** in great demand. **2,** *in* продава́ться нарасхва́т, to sell like hot cakes.

нара́щивание *n.* increase; build-up.

нара́щивать *v. impfv.* [*pfv.* нарасти́ть] **1,** [*impfv. only*] to increase; augment; step up; build up. **2,** to grow; develop (muscles, corns, etc.). **3,** to lengthen; extend.

нарва́л *n.* narwhal.

нарва́ть *v. pfv.* [*infl. like* рвать] **1,** *pfv. of* нарыва́ть. **2,** to pick (a quantity of something). **3,** to tear (a quantity of something). —нарва́ться, *refl., pfv. of* нарыва́ться.

нард *n.* nard; spikenard.

наре́зать [*infl.* -ре́жу, -ре́жешь] *v., pfv. of* нареза́ть.

нареза́ть *v. impfv.* [*pfv.* наре́зать] **1,** to cut; slice. **2,** to thread (a screw); rifle (a gun barrel).

наре́зка *n.* **1,** cutting; slicing. **2,** thread (*of a screw*).

нарека́ние *n.* censure; reprimand.

нарека́ть *v. impfv.* [*pfv.* наре́чь] *obs.* to name.

наре́чие *n.* **1,** adverb. **2,** dialect. —наре́чный, *adj.* adverbial.

наре́чь [*infl.* -реку́, -речёшь, ...-реку́т; *past* -рёк, -рекла́, -рекло́] *v., pfv. of* нарека́ть.

нарза́н *n.* a kind of mineral water; narzan.

нарисова́ть *v., pfv. of* рисова́ть.

нарица́тельный *adj., in* и́мя нарица́тельное, common noun.

наркóз *n.* **1,** anesthesia. **2,** anesthetic.

наркомáн *n.* drug addict. —**наркомáния,** *n.* drug addiction.

наркотизúровать *v. impfv. & pfv.* [*pres.* -рую, -руешь] to anesthetize.

наркóтик *n.* **1,** narcotic; drug. **2,** *colloq.* drug addict.

наркотúческий *adj.* narcotic. —**наркотúческие срéдства,** narcotics; drugs.

нарóд *n.* **1,** a people: совéтский нарóд, the Soviet people. **2,** the (common) people: человéк из нарóда, a man of the people. **3,** people: мнóго нарóду, a lot of people; a big crowd.

народúть *v. pfv.* [*infl.* -жý, -дúшь] *colloq.* to give birth to (a number of children). —**народúться,** *refl.,* *pfv. of* нарождáться.

нарóдник *n., hist.* Populist. —**нарóднический,** *adj.* Populist. —**нарóдничество,** *n.* Populism.

нарóдность *n.f.* **1,** nationality; people. **2,** national character; national roots.

нарóдный *adj.* **1,** people's. **2,** national. **3,** folk-: нарóдная пéсня, folk song.

нарождáться *v.r. impfv.* [*pfv.* народúться] **1,** *colloq.* to be born. **2,** *fig.* to arise; come into being.

нарóст *n.* growth; tumor.

нарочúтый *adj.* deliberate; intentional. —**нарочúто,** *adv.* deliberately; intentionally.

нарóчно *adv.* **1,** deliberately; on purpose. **2,** (*with* для) specifically (for); expressly (for). **3,** for spite; just to be contrary. **4,** *colloq.* for fun. —**как нарóчно,** as luck would have it.

нáрочный *n., decl. as an adj.* special messenger; courier.

нáрты [*gen.* нарт] *n. pl.* dog sled; reindeer sled.

нарубúть *v. pfv.* [*infl.* -рублю́, -рýбишь] to chop (a quantity of something).

нарýжно *adv., colloq.* outwardly.

нарýжное *n., decl. as an adj.* medicine to be taken externally.

нарýжность *n.f.* **1,** appearance; looks. **2,** exterior.

нарýжный *adj.* **1,** external; outward. **2,** (*of a wall*) outside. **3,** outward: нарýжное спокóйствие, outward calm.

нарýжу *adv.* ouside; outward(s); out. —**весь нарýжу,** (*of a person*) completely open about everything. —**вы́вести нарýжу,** to bring out into the open; bring to light. —**вы́йти нарýжу,** to come to the surface; come to light.

нарукáвник *n.* sleeve cover; sleeve protector.

нарукáвный *adj.* worn on the sleeve: нарукáвная повя́зка, armband.

нарумя́нить *v., pfv. of* румя́нить. —**нарумя́ниться,** *refl., pfv. of* румя́ниться (*in sense #1*).

нарýчники *n. pl.* [*sing.* нарýчник] handcuffs; manacles.

нарýчный *adj.* worn on the arm. —**нарýчные часы́,** wrist watch.

нарушáть *v. impfv.* [*pfv.* нарýшить] **1,** to violate; break. **2,** to disturb; disrupt.

наруше́ние *n.* **1,** violation; breach; infringement. **2,** disturbance; disruption.

нарушúтель *n.m.* violator.

нарýшить *v., pfv. of* нарушáть.

нарцúсс *n.* narcissus; daffodil.

нáры [*gen.* нар] *n. pl.* plank bed.

нары́в *n.* abscess; boil.

нарывáть *v. impfv.* [*pfv.* нарвáть] to become infected and swollen. —**нарывáться,** *refl.* (*with* на + *acc.*) *colloq.* to run into; bump into.

нары́ть *v. pfv.* [*infl.* -рóю, -рóешь] to dig (a quantity of something).

наря́д *n.* **1,** dress; attire; apparel. **2,** order; warrant. **3,** *mil.* detail. **4,** *mil.* duty.

нарядúть [*infl.* -ряжý, -рядúшь *or* -ря́дишь] *v., pfv. of* наряжáть. —**нарядúться,** *refl., pfv. of* наряжáться.

наря́дный *adj.* **1,** well-dressed. **2,** (*of an item of clothing*) good-looking; smart.

наря́ду *adv.* (*with* с + *instr.*) **1,** along (with); side by side (with). **2,** on a level (with); on a par (with). —**наря́ду с э́тим,** at the same time.

наряжáть *v. impfv.* [*pfv.* нарядúть] **1,** to dress; dress up. **2,** to order; assign; detail. —**наряжáться,** *refl.* to dress up.

нас *pron., gen. & prepl. of* мы.

насадúть *v. pfv.* [*infl.* -сажý, -сáдишь] **1,** *pfv. of* насáживать *and* насаждáть. **2,** to plant (a quantity of something). **3,** (*with* в + *acc.*) *colloq.* to stuff (people or animals) into.

насáдка [*gen. pl.* -док] *n.* **1,** putting on. **2,** attachment (*for a camera or other device*). **3,** bait.

насажáть *v. pfv.* = **насадúть** (*in senses #2 & #3*).

насаждáть *v. impfv.* [*pfv.* насадúть] to implant; instill.

насажде́ние *n.* **1,** planting. **2,** *fig.* implanting. **3,** *usu. pl.* plantings (*trees, plants, etc.*).

насáживать *v. impfv.* [*pfv.* насадúть] **1,** to plant. **2,** (*with* на + *acc.*) to put; fix; stick; fasten (onto a hook, spit, etc.).

насáливать *v. impfv.* [*pfv.* насолúть] **1,** to salt; pickle. **2,** (*with dat.*) *colloq.* to hurt; injure; spite.

насáхаривать *v. impfv.* [*pfv.* насáхарить] *colloq.* to sugar; put sugar into.

насвúстывать *v. impfv.* to whistle.

наседáть *v. impfv.* [*pfv.* насéсть] **1,** (*of dust*) to settle; collect. **2,** (*with* на + *acc.*) *colloq.* to pounce on; *fig.* press; put pressure on (someone).

насéдка [*gen. pl.* -док] *n.* brood hen.

насекáть *v. impfv.* [*pfv.* насéчь] **1,** to carve (*on a surface*). **2,** to carve up; slice.

насекóмое *n., decl. as an adj.* insect.

населéние *n.* population.

населённость *n.f.* population density.

населённый *adj.* populated.

населя́ть *v. impfv.* [*pfv.* населúть] **1,** to populate; settle. **2,** [*impfv. only*] to inhabit.

насéст *n.* roost; perch.

насéсть *v. pfv.* [*infl. like* сесть] **1,** *pfv. of* наседáть. **2,** (*of many people*) to sit down.

насéчка [*gen. pl.* -чек] *n.* **1,** notch; groove. **2,** inlay.

насéчь [*infl. like* сечь; *past* -сéк, -секлá, -секлó] *v., pfv. of* насекáть.

насéять *v. pfv.* to sow (a quantity of something).

насидéть [*infl.* -жý, -дúшь] *v., pfv. of* насúживать. —**насидéться,** *refl., colloq.* to sit a long time; sit long enough.

насúженный *adj., in* насúженное мéсто, place where one has always lived; one's home of many years.

насúживать *v. impfv.* [*pfv.* насидéть] to hatch (an egg).

наси́лие *n.* violence.

наси́ловать *v. impfv.* [*pfv.* изнаси́ловать; *pres.* -лую, -луешь] **1,** to force; coerce. **2,** to rape.

наси́лу *adv., colloq.* barely; with great difficulty.

наси́льник *n.* **1,** tyrant; oppressor. **2,** rapist.

наси́льно *adv.* by force; forcibly.

наси́льственный *adj.* forcible; violent.

наска́кивать *v. impfv.* [*pfv.* наскочи́ть] (*with* на + *acc.*) **1,** to run into; collide (with). **2,** to pounce on. **3,** *fig., colloq.* to jump on; assail.

насканда́лить *v., pfv. of* сканда́лить.

насквозь *adv.* **1,** through; right through. **2,** *fig.* through and through; to the core. —ви́деть наскво́зь, to see through (someone).

наско́к *n., colloq.* **1,** lunge. **2,** attack. —с наско́ку, **1,** with a swoop; by swooping down. **2,** on impulse; on the spur of the moment.

наско́лько *adv.* **1,** (*with adjectives and adverbs*) how: наско́лько э́то ве́рно?, how true is this? **2,** as far as: наско́лько я зна́ю, as far as I know.

на́скоро *adv., colloq.* hastily; hurriedly.

наскочи́ть [*infl.* -скочу́, -ско́чишь] *v., pfv. of* наска́кивать.

наскрести́ *v. pfv.* [*infl. like* скрести́] to scrape up; scrape together (*lit. & fig.*).

наску́чить *v. pfv.* (*with dat.*) *colloq.* to bore.

наслажда́ться *v.r. impfv.* [*pfv.* наслади́ться] (*with instr.*) to enjoy; take pleasure in.

наслажде́ние *n.* delight; pleasure; enjoyment.

насла́иваться *v.r. impfv.* [*pfv.* наслои́ться] to accumulate; pile up.

насла́ть *v. pfv.* [*infl.* -шлю́, -шлёшь] **1,** *pfv. of* насыла́ть. **2,** to send (a quantity of something).

насле́дие *n.* legacy; heritage.

наследи́ть *v., pfv. of* следи́ть (*in sense #6*).

насле́дник *n.* heir. —насле́дница, *n.* heiress.

насле́дный *adj., in* насле́дный принц/князь, crown prince.

насле́дование *n.* inheritance. —пра́во насле́дова- ния, succession.

насле́довать *v. impfv. & pfv.* [*pfv. also* унасле́до- вать; *pres.* -дую, -дуешь] **1,** to inherit. **2,** (*with dat.*) to succeed (someone) to the throne.

насле́дственность *n.f.* heredity.

насле́дственный *adj.* hereditary; inherited.

насле́дство *n.* inheritance. —получи́ть (что́-ни- будь) в насле́дство, to inherit.

наслое́ние *n.* **1,** stratification. **2,** layer.

наслои́ться *v.r., pfv. of* насла́иваться.

наслу́шаться *v.r. pfv.* (*with gen.*) **1,** to hear a lot of. **2,** to hear enough of.

наслы́шаться *v.r. pfv.* [*infl.* -шусь, -шишься] (*with* о) *colloq.* to hear enough (about).

насма́рку *adv., colloq., in* идти́/пойти́ насма́рку, to go awry; go down the drain.

на́смерть *adv.* **1,** to death; mortally. Разби́ться на́смерть, to be killed (*in a crash, fall, etc.*). **2,** to the death: сража́ться на́смерть, to fight to the death. **3,** *fig., colloq.* to an extreme degree: испуга́ть на́- смерть, to frighten to death; ненави́деть на́смерть, to hate with a passion.

насмеха́ться *v.r. impfv.* (*with* над) to mock; ridicule; deride.

насмеши́ть *v., pfv. of* смеши́ть.

насме́шка [*gen. pl.* -шек] *n.* **1,** taunt; gibe. **2,** *usu. pl.* ridicule; derision.

насме́шливый *adj.* **1,** (*of a person*) sarcastic. **2,** mocking; derisive.

насме́шник *n., colloq.* mocker.

насме́шничать *v. impfv., colloq.* to scoff; sneer; (*with* над) scoff at; deride.

насмея́ться *v.r. pfv.* [*infl.* -смею́сь, -смеёшься] **1,** *colloq.* to have a lot of laughs. **2,** (*with* над) to laugh at; make fun of; deride.

на́сморк *n.* (head) cold.

насмотре́ться *v.r. pfv.* [*infl.* -смотрю́сь, -смо́т- ришься] **1,** (*with gen.*) to see a lot of. **2,** (*with* на + *acc.*) to see enough of: не могу́ насмотре́ться на..., I can't see enough of...

насоли́ть [*infl. like* соли́ть] *v., pfv. of* наса́ливать.

насори́ть *v., pfv. of* сори́ть.

насо́с *n.* pump.

насо́сный *adj.* pump (*attrib.*); pumping.

на́спех *adv.* hastily; hurriedly; in a hurry.

наспле́тничать *v., pfv. of* спле́тничать.

наст *n.* frozen crust on snow.

настава́ть *v. impfv.* [*pfv.* наста́ть; *pres.* -стаёт] (*of time, a season, etc.*) to come.

настави́тельный *adj.* didactic.

наста́вить *v. pfv.* [*infl.* -влю, -вишь] **1,** *pfv. of* на- ставля́ть. **2,** to place (a quantity of something).

наставле́ние *n.* **1,** instructions. **2,** admonition. **3,** *mil.* manual.

наставля́ть *v. impfv.* [*pfv.* наста́вить] **1,** to lengthen. **2,** to aim; point. **3,** to teach; enlighten. —наставля́ть нос (+ *dat.*), to fool; dupe.

наста́вник *n.* teacher; tutor; mentor.

наста́ивать *v. impfv.* [*pfv.* настоя́ть] (*with* на + *prepl.*) to insist (on). —наста́ивать на своём, to insist on having one's own way. —настоя́ть на своём, to have one's way.

наста́ть [*infl.* -ста́нет] *v., pfv. of* настава́ть.

на́стежь *adv.* **1,** (*with verbs of opening*) wide. **2,** wide open.

насте́нный *adj.* wall (*attrib.*).

настига́ть *v. impfv.* [*pfv.* насти́гнуть *or* насти́чь] to overtake; catch up to.

насти́гнуть [*past* -сти́г, -ла] *v., pfv. of* настига́ть.

насти́л *n.* flooring.

настила́ть *v. impfv.* [*pfv.* настла́ть] to lay (a floor, carpet, etc.).

насти́лка *n., colloq.* flooring.

насти́чь [*infl. like* насти́гнуть] *v., pfv. of* настига́ть.

настла́ть [*infl.* -стелю́, -сте́лешь] *v., pfv. of* насти- ла́ть.

насто́й *n.* extract.

насто́йка *n.* **1,** (fruit) brandy: вишнёвая насто́йка, cherry brandy. **2,** tincture: насто́йка йо́да, tincture of iodine.

насто́йчивый *adj.* persistent; insistent. —насто́йчи- вость, *n.f.* persistence; perseverance.

насто́лько *adv.* **1,** (*with adjectives*) so: э́то бы́ло на- сто́лько невероя́тно, что..., it was so unbelievable that... **2,** (*with verbs*) so much: он насто́лько вы́рос, что..., he has grown so much that... —насто́лько..., наско́лько, as..., as: она́ насто́лько умна́, наско́ль- ко краси́ва, she is as intelligent as she is beautiful.

насто́льный *adj.* **1,** table (*attrib.*); desk (*attrib.*). **2,** *fig.* continually referred to: насто́льная кни́га, book

of ready reference; one's "bible". —**настóльный тéн-
нис,** table tennis.

насторáживать v. impfv. [pfv. **насторожи́ть**] **1,** to
put on one's guard. **2,** in насторожи́ть у́ши, to prick
up one's ears. —**насторáживаться,** refl. to prick up
one's ears; become alert.

насторожé adv. on the alert; on the lookout; on one's
guard.

насторóженный also, **насторожённый** adj. **1,**
watchful. **2,** guarded.

насторожи́ть v., pfv. of насторáживать. —**на-
сторожи́ться,** refl., pfv. of насторáживаться.

настоя́ние n. insistence.

настоя́тель n.m. **1,** abbot. **2,** dean (of a cathedral).
—**настоя́тельница,** n. mother superior.

настоя́тельный adj. **1,** insistent; persistent. **2,** vital;
urgent. —**настоя́тельно,** adv. urgently. —**настоя́-
тельность,** n.f. persistence.

настоя́ть [infl. -**стою́,** -**стои́шь**] v., pfv. of **настáивать.**

настоя́щее n., decl. as an adj. the present.

настоя́щий adj. **1,** present: в настоя́щее врéмя, at
the present time. **2,** the present; this. **3,** real; true;
genuine. —**настоя́щее врéмя,** gram. present tense.

настрадáться v.r.pfv. to suffer much.

настрáивать v. impfv. [pfv. **настрóить**] **1,** to tune
(a musical instrument); tune in (a radio). **2,** to adjust
(a device). **3,** to put (someone) in a certain mood: настрóить когó-нибудь на весёлый лад, to put someone in a happy frame of mind. ♦Often passive. Он
плóхо настрóен, he is in a bad mood. Я настрóен(а)
пойти́ в кинó, I am in the mood to go to the movies.
4, to influence; dispose: настрóить когó-нибудь в
пóльзу (or прóтив) чегó-нибудь, to influence someone in favor of (or against) something. Настрóить
(когó-нибудь) в свою́ пóльзу, to win over. Настрóить сы́на прóтив отцá, to turn a son against his father.
Он настрóен прóтив меня́, he has something against
me. —**настрáиваться,** refl. **1,** (with на + acc.) to tune
in (a program, station, etc.). **2,** (with к or прóтив)
to feel disposed (in a certain way toward or against).
3, (with inf.) to make up one's mind to; (with на + acc.)
decide upon.

настреля́ть v. pfv. to shoot (a quantity of something).
настрóго adv., colloq. strictly.

настроéние n. mood; frame of mind. —**у меня́ нет
настроéния** (+ inf.), I am not in the mood for...

настрóенность n.f. mood; attitude.

настрóить v. pfv. **1,** pfv. of **настрáивать. 2,** to build
(a quantity of something). —**настрóиться,** refl., pfv.
of настрáиваться.

настрóйка n. tuning.

настрóйщик n. tuner.

настрочи́ть v., pfv. of **строчи́ть** (in sense #2).

настря́пать v. pfv. to cook; whip up (a quantity of
something).

наступáтельный adj., mil. offensive.

наступáть v. impfv. [pfv. **наступи́ть**] **1,** (with на
+ acc.) to step on; tread on. **2,** [impfv. only] to attack;
assume the offensive; (with на + acc.) attack; advance
on or against. **3,** [impfv. only] (with на + acc.) to
harass; nag. **4,** [impfv. only] (of natural phenomena)
to advance. **5,** (of time, a season, etc.) to come.

наступи́ть [infl. -**ступлю́,** -**сту́пишь**] v., pfv. of наступáть.

наступлéние n. **1,** mil. offensive. **2,** coming (of a
season, time, etc.). До наступлéния темноты́, before nightfall.

насту́рция n. nasturtium.

насу́пить v. pfv. [infl. -**су́плю,** -**су́пишь**], in насу́-
пить брóви, to frown. —**насу́питься,** refl. to scowl;
frown.

нáсухо adv. dry: вы́тереть нáсухо, to wipe dry.

насуши́ть v. pfv. [infl. -**сушу́,** -**су́шишь**] to dry (a
quantity of something).

насу́щный adj. vital. —**насу́щный хлеб,** daily bread.

насчёт prep., with gen. about; regarding; concerning.
—**как насчёт** (+ gen.), how about...?; what about...?

насчи́тывать v. impfv. [pfv. **насчитáть**] **1,** to count.
2, [impfv. only] to number; consist of: áрмия насчи́-
тывала дéсять ты́сяч солдáт, the army numbered/
consisted of/10,000 soldiers. —**насчи́тываться,** refl.
[impfv. only] impers. to number: в гóроде насчи́ты-
вается сто ты́сяч жи́телей, the city's inhabitants
number 100,000; the city has a population of 100,000.

насылáть v. impfv. [pfv. **наслáть**] (of divine powers)
to send down; inflict (destruction, a calamity, etc.).

насыпáть [infl. -**сы́плю,** -**сы́плешь**] v., pfv. of **насыпáть.**

насыпáть v. impfv. [pfv. **насы́пать**] **1,** to sprinkle;
spread. **2,** to pour: насыпáть муки́ в мешóк, to pour
flour into a sack. **3,** to fill: насыпáть мешóк мукóй,
to fill a sack with flour. **4,** to build (out of dirt, sand,
etc.).

нáсыпь n.f. embankment.

насы́тить [infl. -**сы́щу,** -**сы́тишь**] v., pfv. of **насыщáть. —насы́титься,** refl., pfv. of насыщáться.

насыщáть v. impfv. [pfv. **насы́тить**] **1,** to satiate; sate.
2, to saturate. —**насыщáться,** refl. **1,** to be full; be
sated. **2,** to be saturated.

насыщéние n. **1,** satiation. **2,** saturation.

натáлкивать v. impfv. [pfv. **натолкну́ть**] **1,** colloq. to
push into/against/onto: натолкну́ть когó-нибудь на
стол, to push someone into/against the table. **2,** fig. to
lead (to): натáлкивать когó-нибудь на мысль, to lead
someone to think; give someone an idea. —**натáлки-
ваться,** refl. (with на + acc.) **1,** to run into; bump into;
strike. **2,** fig. to run into; encounter. **3,** fig. to run across;
come across.

натáптывать v. impfv. [pfv. **натоптáть**] (with на +
prepl.) colloq. to track up.

натаскáть v. pfv. **1,** pfv. of натáскивать. **2,** to bring,
drag, store, or steal (a quantity of something). **3,** colloq.
to cull; drag up (from various sources).

натáскивать v. impfv. [pfv. **натаскáть**] **1,** to train (a
dog). **2,** colloq. to coach; teach (quickly or superficially).
3, [pfv. натащи́ть] colloq. to pull on (an item of clothing); pull over.

натащи́ть v. pfv. [infl. -**тащу́,** -**тá́щишь**] **1,** pfv. of
натáскивать (in sense #3). **2,** = натаскáть (in sense
#2).

натвори́ть v. pfv., colloq. to do (something harmful):
что ты натвори́л?, what have you done?

нáте particle, colloq. here is; here you are.

натекáть v. impfv. [pfv. **натéчь**] (of water) to accumulate.

натéльный adj. worn next to the skin: натéльное
бельё, underwear.

натерéть v. pfv. [infl. like терéть] **1,** pfv. of натирáть.
2, to grate (a quantity of something). —**натерéться,**
refl., pfv. of натирáться.

натерпе́ться v.r. pfv. [infl. -терплю́сь, -те́рпишься] colloq. **1**, to suffer greatly. **2**, (with gen.) to suffer (a great deal of). —**натерпе́ться стра́ху**, to have a terrible fright.

нате́чь [infl. like течь] v., pfv. of **натека́ть**.

нате́шиться v.r. pfv., colloq. **1**, to enjoy oneself to the full. **2**, (with над) to have a good laugh (over).

натира́ть v. impfv. [pfv. **натере́ть**] **1**, to rub. **2**, to rub; irritate. Натере́ть себе́ мозо́ль, to get a corn. **3**, to polish. —**натира́ться**, refl. (with instr.) to rub oneself (with).

на́тиск n. onslaught; charge.

наткáть v. pfv. [infl. like ткать] to weave (a quantity of something).

наткну́ться v.r., pfv. of **натыка́ться**.

натолкну́ть v., pfv. of **ната́лкивать**. —**натолкну́ться**, refl., pfv. of **ната́лкиваться**.

натоло́чь v. pfv. [infl. like толо́чь] to pound; crush (a quantity of something).

натопи́ть v. pfv. [infl. -топлю́, -то́пишь] **1**, to heat well. **2**, to melt (a quantity of something).

натопта́ть [infl. -топчу́, -то́пчешь] v., pfv. of **натáп-тывать**.

наточи́ть v., pfv. of точи́ть (in sense #1).

натоща́к adv. on an empty stomach.

натр n., in е́дкий натр, caustic soda; sodium hydroxide.

натрави́ть [infl. -травлю́, -трáвишь] v., pfv. of **на-трáвливать**.

натрáвливать v. impfv. [pfv. **натрави́ть**] (with на + acc.) **1**, to sic (an animal on). **2**, colloq. to set (people against each other).

натренирова́ть v., pfv. of **тренирова́ть**. —**натре-нирова́ться**, refl., pfv. of **тренирова́ться**.

на́триевый adj. sodium (attrib.). —**на́триевая лáмпа**, sodium-vapor lamp. —**на́триевая сели́тра**, sodium nitrate.

на́трий n. sodium.

на́трое adv. in three; into three parts.

натруди́ть v. pfv. [infl. -тружу́, -тру́дишь or -тру-ди́шь] colloq. to overexert; wear out (a part of one's body).

нату́га n., colloq. strain; exertion.

на́туго adv., colloq. very tightly.

нату́живать v. impfv. [pfv. **нату́жить**] colloq. to strain; stretch; exert. —**нату́живаться**, refl., colloq. to make a supreme effort; bear down.

нату́жный adj., colloq. **1**, strenuous. **2**, strained. —**на-ту́жно**, adv., colloq. with great effort.

нату́ра n. **1**, nature; temperament; disposition. **2**, art real life: писа́ть с нату́ры, to paint from real life. **3**, model (one who poses). **4**, motion pictures location: на нату́ре, on location. —**нату́рой**, in kind: получа́ть жа́лованье нату́рой, to receive one's wages in kind.

натурализа́ция n. naturalization.

натурали́зм n. naturalism.

натурализова́ть v. impfv. & pfv. [pres. -зу́ю, -зу́-ешь] to naturalize (confer citizenship upon). —**нату-рализова́ться**, refl. to become naturalized.

натурали́ст n. naturalist. —**натуралисти́ческий**, adj. naturalist (attrib.); naturalistic.

натурáльный adj. **1**, natural (in various meanings). **2**, (of a product, material, etc.) natural; real. **3**, (of a person, gesture, etc.) natural; genuine. —**в натурáльную величину́**, life-size.

нату́рщик n.m. [fem. -щица] model (one who poses).

натыкать v. pfv., colloq. to stick in (a quantity of something).

натыка́ться v.r. impfv. [pfv. наткну́ться] (with на + acc.) **1**, to run into; run against (a sharp object). **2**, fig. to run into; encounter. **3**, colloq. to run across; come across; stumble upon.

натюрмо́рт n. still life.

натя́гивать v. impfv. [pfv. **натяну́ть**] **1**, to draw (a bow, reins, etc.). **2**, to draw tight; tighten. **3**, to pull on; slip on. **4**, to pull over: натяну́ть ша́пку нá уши, to pull one's cap over one's ears. —**натя́гиваться**, refl. to become taut.

натяже́ние n. pull; tension.

натя́жка n. **1**, stretching. **2**, fig. stretching of a point: с натя́жкой, by stretching a point.

натя́нутость n.f. tension; strain.

натя́нутый adj. **1**, strained. **2**, unnatural; forced.

натяну́ть [infl. -тяну́, -тя́нешь] v., pfv. of **натя́гивать**. —**натяну́ться**, refl., pfv. of **натя́гиваться**.

наугáд adv. **1**, at random. **2**, by guesswork.

наугóльник n. bevel; bevel square.

наудáчу adv. at random.

науди́ть v. pfv. [infl. -ужу́, -у́дишь] to catch (a quantity of fish).

нау́ка n. **1**, science. **2**, colloq. lesson: э́то тебе́ нау́ка!, let that be a lesson to you!

нау́ськивать v. impfv. [pfv. нау́ськать] colloq. **1**, to sic (a dog). **2**, to egg on; incite.

наутёк adv., colloq., in пусти́ться or бро́ситься нау-тёк, to take to one's heels.

наутофо́н n. foghorn.

нау́тро adv. the next morning.

научи́ть v., pfv. of учи́ть (in sense #1). —**научи́ться**, refl., pfv. of учи́ться (in sense #2).

нау́чный adj. scientific. —**нау́чно**, adv. scientifically.

нау́шник n. **1**, earlap; earmuff. **2**, earphone; headphone. **3**, colloq. informer; tattletale.

нау́шничать v. impfv., colloq. to spread malicious gossip.

нау́шничество n., colloq. malicious gossip.

наущ́ение n., obs. urging; instigation.

нафтали́н n. naphthalene.

нафто́л n. naphthol.

нахáл n.m. [fem. -ка] insolent person.

нахáльничать v. impfv., colloq. to be insolent; behave insolently.

нахáльный adj. impudent; insolent; impertinent.

нахáльство n. **1**, insolence; impudence; impertinence. **2**, effrontery; gall.

нахвáливать v. impfv. [pfv. нахвали́ть] colloq. to extol.

нахвали́ть [infl. -хвалю́, -хвáлишь] v., pfv. of **нах-вáливать**. —**нахвали́ться**, refl. (with instr.) to praise sufficiently: не могу́ им нахвали́ться, I cannot praise him too highly.

нахватáть v. pfv., colloq. to acquire; pick up (a quantity of something). —**нахватáться**, refl. (with gen.) colloq. to pick up (bits of knowledge, a few words of a language, etc.).

нахлéбник n. **1**, obs. boarder. **2**, parasite; hanger-on.

нахлестáть [infl. -хлещу́, -хлéщешь] v., pfv. of **нах-лёстывать**.

нахлёстывать v. impfv. [pfv. нахлестáть] colloq. to whip.

нахлобу́чивать *v. impfv.* [*pfv.* **нахлобу́чить**] *colloq.* to pull down (a hat) over one's eyes, ears, etc.

нахлобу́чка [*gen. pl.* **-чек**] *n., colloq.* scolding; bawling out; dressing-down.

нахлы́нуть *v. pfv.* **1,** (*of liquids*) to stream; flow; gush. **2,** (*of people*) to rush; throng; surge. **3,** *fig.* (*of thoughts*) to spring to mind.

нахму́ренный *adj.* **1,** frowning. **2,** gloomy.

нахму́рить *v., pfv. of* **хму́рить.** —**нахму́риться,** *refl., pfv. of* **хму́риться.**

находи́ть *v. impfv.* [*pfv.* **найти́**; *pres.* **-хожу́, -хо́дишь**] **1,** to find: найти́ свой портфе́ль, to find one's briefcase. Находи́ть до́вод убеди́тельным, to find an argument convincing. **2,** (*with* **на** + *acc.*) to strike; run into. **3,** (*with* **на** + *acc.*) to come upon. **4,** (*with* **на** + *acc.*) (*of emotions*) to come over. **5,** (*of clouds, twilight, etc.*) to gather. **6,** (*with* **на** + *acc.*) (*of clouds*) to cover; obscure. **7,** *impers.* (*of a crowd*) to gather: нашло́ мно́го наро́ду, a large crowd gathered. **8,** *in* найти́ свою́ смерть, to meet one's death/end. —**находи́ться,** *refl.* **1,** [*impfv. only*] to be; be found; be located. **2,** to be found; turn up. **3,** to come up with a quick answer; shoot back. Я не нашёлся, что отве́тить, I was at a loss as to how to answer.

нахо́дка [*gen. pl.* **-док**] *n.* a find.

нахо́дчивый *adj.* resourceful. —**нахо́дчивость,** *n.f.* resourcefulness.

нахожде́ние *n.* **1,** finding. **2,** being (somewhere).

нахо́хлиться *v.r., pfv. of* **хо́хлиться.**

нахохота́ться *v.r. pfv.* [*infl.* **-хочу́сь, -хо́чешься**] *colloq.* to have a good laugh.

нацара́пать *v., pfv. of* **цара́пать** (*in sense #2*).

нацеди́ть *v. pfv.* [*infl.* **-цежу́, -це́дишь**] to strain (a quantity of something).

наце́ливать *v. impfv.* [*pfv.* **наце́лить**] to aim (a weapon). —**наце́ливаться,** *refl.* **1,** to take aim. **2,** (*with inf.*) to get ready (to).

наце́нивать *v. impfv.* [*pfv.* **нацени́ть**] to mark up; raise the price of.

нацени́ть [*infl.* **-ценю́, -це́нишь**] *v., pfv. of* **наце́нивать.**

наце́нка *n.* markup; increase in price.

нацепи́ть [*infl.* **-цеплю́, -це́пишь**] *v., pfv. of* **нацепля́ть.**

нацепля́ть *v. impfv.* [*pfv.* **нацепи́ть**] (*with* **на** + *acc.*) to fasten to; hook onto; pin to.

наци́зм *n.* Nazism.

национализа́ция *n.* nationalization.

национализи́ровать *v. impfv. & pfv.* [*pres.* **-рую, -руешь**] to nationalize.

национали́зм *n.* nationalism. —**национали́ст,** *n.* nationalist. —**националисти́ческий,** *adj.* nationalist (*attrib.*); nationalistic.

национа́льность *n.f.* nationality.

национа́льный *adj.* national.

наци́ст *n.* Nazi. —**наци́стский,** *adj.* Nazi.

на́ция *n.* nation.

начади́ть *v., pfv. of* **чади́ть.**

нача́ло *n.* **1,** beginning: с са́мого нача́ла, from the very beginning; from the outset. **2,** origin; source. **3,** *pl.* basis: на доброво́льных нача́лах, on a voluntary basis. **4,** *pl.* principles: нача́ла хи́мии, principles of chemistry. —брать нача́ло, to originate; (*of a river*) rise. —вести́ своё нача́ло от, to have its origin in. —дать нача́ло (+ *dat.*), to give rise to. —для нача́ла, to

start with; for a start. —под нача́лом (+ *gen. or* у), under the direction of. —положи́ть нача́ло (+ *dat.*), **1,** to begin; initiate. **2,** to mark the beginning of. —по нача́лу, at first.

нача́льник *n.* chief; head; boss; superior. —**нача́льник ста́нции,** stationmaster —**нача́льник шта́ба,** chief of staff.

нача́льный *adj.* **1,** first; initial. **2,** (*of education, a school, etc.*) elementary; primary.

нача́льственный *adj.* overbearing; domineering.

нача́льство *n.* **1,** the authorities. **2,** command; direction. **3,** *colloq.* boss; chief.

нача́льствование *n.* command.

нача́льствовать *v. impfv.* [*pres.* **-ствую, -ствуешь**] (*with* **над**) *obs.* to command.

нача́тки *n. pl.* [*sing.* **нача́ток**] rudiments.

нача́ть [*infl.* **начну́, начнёшь;** *past* **на́чал, начала́, на́чало**] *v., pfv. of* **начина́ть.** —**нача́ться,** *refl.* [*past* **начался́, начала́сь, начало́сь**] *pfv. of* **начина́ться.**

начеку́ *adv.* on one's guard; on the alert.

начерни́ть *v., pfv. of* **черни́ть** (*in sense #1*).

на́черно *adv.* in the rough: писа́ть (что-нибудь) на́черно, to make a rough draft of.

начерта́ние *n.* **1,** tracing. **2,** outline.

начерта́тельный *adj., in* **начерта́тельная геоме́трия,** descriptive geometry.

начерта́ть *v. pfv.* **1,** *obs.* to trace; inscribe. **2,** *fig.* to set forth; outline.

начерти́ть *v., pfv. of* **черти́ть.**

начёс *n.* nap (*of cloth*).

начётчик *n.* pedant.

начина́ние *n.* project; undertaking.

начина́тельный *adj., gram.* inceptive: начина́тельный глаго́л, inceptive verb (*e.g.* забе́гать, to begin to run).

начина́ть *v. impfv.* [*pfv.* **нача́ть**] **1,** to begin; start (something). **2,** (*with inf.*) to begin (to); start (to). —**начина́ться,** *refl.* (*of something*) to begin; start.

начина́ющий *adj.* beginning. —*n.* beginner.

начина́я *prep.* (*with* **с** + *gen.*) beginning (with).

начини́ть *v. pfv.* **1,** [*infl.* **-чиню́, -чи́нишь**] *pfv. of* **начиня́ть. 2,** [*infl.* **-чиню́, -чи́нишь**] to mend (a quantity of something); sharpen (a quantity of pencils).

начи́нка *n.* stuffing; filling.

начиня́ть *v. impfv.* [*pfv.* **начини́ть**] to stuff.

начи́стить *v. pfv.* [*infl.* **-щу, -стишь**] **1,** *pfv. of* **начища́ть. 2,** to peel (a quantity of something).

на́чисто *adv.* **1,** clean: на́чисто вы́бритый, cleanshaven. Переписа́ть (что-нибудь) на́чисто, to make a clean copy of. **2,** *colloq.* completely; utterly. **3,** *colloq.* openly; candidly.

начистоту́ *adv.* frankly; without equivocation; straight from the shoulder.

начи́танный *adj.* well-read. —**начи́танность,** *n.f.* erudition.

начита́ть *v. pfv., colloq.* to read (a quantity of something). —**начита́ться,** *refl.* (*with gen.*) to read a great deal of.

начища́ть *v. impfv.* [*pfv.* **начи́стить**] *colloq.* to polish; shine.

наш [*fem.* **на́ша;** *neut.* **на́ше;** *pl.* **на́ши**] *poss. adj. & pron.* our; ours.

нашали́ть *v. pfv.* to be naughty; act up.

нашаты́рный *adj., in* **нашаты́рный спирт,** liquid ammonia.

нашаты́рь [*gen.* -тыря́] *n.m.* ammonium chloride.

нашепта́ть *v. pfv.* [*infl.* -шепчу́, -ше́пчешь] **1**, to whisper. **2**, (*with dat.*) to whisper in someone's ear.

наше́ствие *n.* invasion.

нашива́ть *v. impfv.* [*pfv.* наши́ть] to sew on.

наши́вка [*gen. pl.* -вок] *n., mil.* stripe; chevron.

нашивно́й *adj.* sewn-on.

наши́ть *v. pfv.* [*infl.* -шью́, -шьёшь] **1**, *pfv. of* нашива́ть. **2**, to sew (a quantity of something).

нашпигова́ть *v., pfv. of* шпигова́ть.

нашпи́ливать *v. impfv.* [*pfv.* нашпи́лить] **1**, to place (or stick) on a pin. **2**, to pin on.

нашуме́вший *adj.* sensational; much talked about; having caused quite a stir.

нашуме́ть *v. pfv.* [*infl.* -млю́, -ми́шь] **1**, to make a lot of noise. **2**, *fig.* to cause a sensation.

нащипа́ть *v. pfv.* [*infl.* -щиплю́, -щи́плешь] **1**, to pluck; pick (a quantity of something). **2**, *colloq.* to pinch.

нащу́пывать *v. impfv.* [*pfv.* нащу́пать] **1**, [*impfv. only*] to grope for; fumble for; feel about for. **2**, to feel (someone's pulse). **3**, to find; come upon (*after groping*). **4**, *fig.* to find; discover; detect. —**нащу́пывать по́чву**, to get the lay of the land; sound out the possibilities.

наэлектризова́ть *v., pfv. of* электризова́ть.

нае́бедничать *v., pfv. of* я́бедничать.

наяву́ *adv.* while awake; not in one's dreams.

на́яда *n.* naiad.

не *neg. particle* **1**, not: э́то не ве́рно, that is not true; лифт не рабо́тает, the elevator is not working. **2**, *inserted between such words as* ничего́, никто́, никогда́, *etc. and a verb following:* никто́ не зна́ет, no one knows. Мы почти́ никогда́ не ви́дим ее, we almost never see her. **3**, (*with imperatives*) don't: не забу́дьте!, don't forget! **4**, *occurring as a separate word when* не́чего, не́кого, *and their oblique case forms are separated to permit the insertion of a preposition in between:* ему́ не́ с кем игра́ть, he has no one to play with. **5**, (*with past tense verbal adverbs*) without: гла́зом не моргну́в, without batting an eye. **6**, (*with inf.*) will never; would never: его́ не узна́ть, you would never recognize him. —**не́ за что!**, not at all!; don't mention it! —**не то что** *or* **чтобы...**, it is not that...

неаккура́тность *n.f.* **1**, lack of punctuality. **2**, carelessness. **3**, sloppiness.

неаккура́тный *adj.* **1**, not punctual. **2**, careless; sloppy; inefficient. **3**, untidy.

неандерта́лец [*gen.* -льца] *n.* Neanderthal man. —**неандерта́льский**, *adj.* Neanderthal.

неаппети́тный *adj.* unappetizing.

небезопа́сный *adj.* somewhat dangerous; unsafe.

небезоснова́тельный *adj.* not without foundation.

небезразли́чный *adj.* **1**, not indifferent; interested. **2**, (*with dat. or* для) of interest (to).

небезызве́стный *adj.* not unknown; rather well-known.

небезынтере́сный *adj.* rather interesting.

небелёный *adj.* unbleached.

небе́сный *adj.* heavenly; celestial. —**небе́сный свод**, firmament.

неблагови́дный *adj.* unseemly; improper.

неблагода́рный *adj.* **1**, ungrateful. **2**, thankless. —**неблагода́рность**, *n.f.* ingratitude.

неблагожела́тельный *adj.* unfriendly; hostile. —**неблагожела́тельность**, *n.f.* ill will.

неблагозву́чие *n.* dissonance; disharmony. —**неблагозву́чный**, *adj.* dissonant; discordant.

неблагонадёжный *adj.* (politically) unreliable.

неблагополу́чие *n.* trouble; troubles.

неблагополу́чный *adj.* unhappy; unfortunate. —**неблагополу́чно**, *adv.* badly; in an unhappy way.

неблагопристо́йный *adj.* improper; indecent.

неблагоприя́тный *adj.* unfavorable.

неблагоразу́мие *n.* imprudence. —**неблагоразу́мный**, *adj.* imprudent; unwise; ill-advised.

неблагоро́дный *adj.* ignoble. —**неблагоро́дные мета́ллы**, base metals.

неблагоскло́нный *adj.* ill-disposed; unfavorably disposed. —**неблагоскло́нность**, *n.f.* unfavorable attitude.

неблагоустро́енный *adj.* (*of premises*) lacking amenities or conveniences.

неблестя́щий *adj.* not outstanding; mediocre.

нёбный *adj.* palatal. —**нёбная занаве́ска**, *anat.* uvula.

не́бо [*pl.* небеса́, небе́с, небеса́м] *n.* sky; heaven. —**ме́жду не́бом и землёй**, without a roof over one's head. —**на седьмо́м не́бе**, in seventh heaven. —**под откры́тым не́бом**, in the open air. —**попа́сть па́льцем в не́бо**, to be wide of the mark. —**превозноси́ть до небе́с**, to praise to the skies.

нёбо *n.* palate; roof of the mouth.

небога́тый *adj.* **1**, not rich; of modest means. **2**, modest; unpretentious. **3**, meager; scanty.

небоеспосо́бный *adj.* unfit for (military) action; disabled.

небольшо́й *adj.* **1**, small; not large; not great. **2**, (*of time, distance, etc.*) short. —**с небольши́м**, a little over; a little past: в три с небольши́м, a little after three.

небосво́д *n.* firmament.

небоскло́н *n.* lower part of the sky near the horizon.

небоскрёб *n.* skyscraper.

небо́сь *particle, colloq.* in all probability; most likely.

небре́жный *adj.* **1**, careless; negligent. **2**, sloppy; slipshod. **3**, casual. —**небре́жно**, *adv.* carelessly. —**небре́жность**, *n.f.* carelessness; negligence.

небри́тый *adj.* unshaven.

небыва́лый *adj.* **1**, unprecedented; unheard-of. **2**, fantastic; unreal.

небыли́ца *n.* tall story; cock-and-bull story.

небытие́ *n.* nonexistence.

небью́щийся *adj.* unbreakable; nonbreakable; shatterproof.

нева́жно *adv.* **1**, not well; poorly. **2**, *as an exclamation* never mind!; it doesn't matter!

нева́жный *adj.* **1**, unimportant. **2**, *colloq.* poor; not so good.

невдалеке́ *adv.* not far away; not far off.

невдомёк *adv., with dat., colloq.* having no idea: мне невдомёк, I had no idea; it never occurred to me.

неве́дение *n.* ignorance. —**держа́ть в неве́дении**, to keep in the dark.

неве́домо *adv., colloq.* there is no telling; there is no way of knowing.

неве́домый *adj.* **1**, unknown. **2**, mysterious.

неве́жа *n.m. & f.* boor; lout.

неве́жда *n.m. & f.* ignoramus.

неве́жество *n.* ignorance. —**неве́жественный**, *adj.* ignorant.

невежливый *adj.* impolite; rude. —**неве́жливость,** *n.f.* impoliteness; rudeness.

невезе́ние *n., colloq.* bad luck.

невезу́чий *adj., colloq.* unlucky.

невели́кий *adj., usu. used in short form* [*fem.* лика́; *neut.* -ли́ко *or* -лико́] **1,** small; not large. Невели́к ро́стом, short (*in height*). **2,** not great; slight; insignificant.

неве́рие *n.* **1,** disbelief. **2,** lack of faith.

неве́рно *adv.* **1,** incorrectly. **2,** with an uncertain gait.

неве́рность *n.f.* **1,** error; fallacy. **2,** infidelity.

неве́рный *adj.* **1,** incorrect; wrong; erroneous. **2,** unfaithful; untrue. **3,** unsteady; faltering. **4,** *in* неве́рная но́та, false note. —*n.* infidel.

невероя́тно *adv.* incredibly; unbelievably.

невероя́тность *n.f.* **1,** improbability. **2,** unbelievability. **3,** *pl.* unbelievable stories. —**до невероя́тности,** unbelievably; incredibly; to an incredible degree.

невероя́тный *adj.* incredible; unbelievable.

неве́рующий *adj.* nonbelieving; irreligious. —*n.* nonbeliever.

невесёлый *adj.* melancholy; sad; blue.

невесо́мый *adj.* weightless. —**невесо́мость,** *n.f.* weightlessness.

неве́ста *n.* **1,** fiancée. **2,** bride.

неве́стка [*gen. pl.* -ток]*n.* **1,** daughter-in-law. **2,** sister-in-law (*brother's wife or spouse's brother's wife*).

неве́сть *adv., colloq.* heaven knows; God knows.

невеще́ственный *adj.* immaterial.

невзви́деть *v. pfv., in* све́та невзви́деть, *colloq.* **1,** (*from shock or surprise*) to be stupefied. **2,** (*from pain*) to see stars.

невзго́да *n.* adversity; misfortune.

невзира́я на (*with acc.*) in spite of; regardless of.

невзлюби́ть *v. pfv.* [*infl.* -люблю́, -лю́бишь] to dislike; take a disliking to.

невзнача́й *adv., colloq.* by chance; accidentally.

невзно́с *n.* nonpayment of dues.

невзра́чный *adj.* ugly; homely; unattractive.

невзыска́тельный *adj.* undemanding.

не́видаль *n.f., colloq.* wonder; something to marvel at. —**вот** (*or* э́ка) **не́видаль!,** what's all the fuss?

неви́данный *adj.* extraordinary; unprecedented.

невиди́мка [*gen. pl.* -мок] *n.m. & f.* invisible man or creature. —*n.f.* invisible hairpin.

неви́димый *adj.* invisible.

неви́дный *adj.* **1,** invisible. **2,** *colloq.* insignificant. **3,** *colloq.* unattractive.

неви́дящий *adj.* **1,** unseeing; sightless; blind. **2,** (*of a look*) blank; absent; vacant.

неви́нность *n.f.* **1,** innocence. **2,** virginity.

неви́нный *adj.* **1,** innocent; guiltless. **2,** innocent; naïve; ingenuous. **3,** innocent; innocuous; harmless. **4,** innocent; virginal.

невино́вный *adj.* [*short form* -вен, -вна] innocent; not guilty. —**невино́вность,** *n.f.* innocence.

невку́сный *adj.* tasteless; unpalatable.

невменя́емый *adj., law* not responsible for one's actions.

невмеша́тельство *n.* noninterference; nonintervention.

невмоготу́ *adv., colloq.* too much; more than one can bear.

невнима́ние *n.* **1,** inattention. **2,** lack of consideration.

невнима́тельность *n.f.* **1,** carelessness. **2,** lack of consideration.

невнима́тельный *adj.* **1,** inattentive. **2,** inconsiderate.

невнуши́тельный *adj.* unimpressive.

невня́тный *adj.* indistinct; scarcely audible.

не́вод [*pl.* невода́] *n.* large fishing net.

невозвра́тный *adj.* **1,** irretrievable. **2,** (*of a loss*) irreparable.

невозвраще́нец [*gen.* -нца] *n.* defector.

невозде́ланный *adj.* untilled; uncultivated.

невоздержа́ние *n.* intemperance; immoderation.

невоздержанный *also,* **невоздёржный** *adj.* intemperate; immoderate. —**невоздёржанность; невоздёржность,** *n.f.* intemperance; immoderation.

невозмо́жно *adj., used predicatively* impossible: э́то практи́чески невозмо́жно, it is practically impossible.

невозмо́жное *n., decl. as an adj.* the impossible.

невозмо́жность *n.f.* impossibility. —**до невозмо́жности,** to the extreme.

невозмо́жный *adj.* impossible.

невозмути́мый *adj.* **1,** imperturbable; unflappable. **2,** (*of calm, quiet, etc.*) perfect; undisturbed. —**невозмути́мость,** *n.f.* imperturbability; coolness.

невознагради́мый *adj.* **1,** irreparable. **2,** that can never be repaid.

нево́лить *v. impfv., colloq.* to force; compel.

нево́льник *n.* slave. —**нево́льничество,** *n.* slavery. —**нево́льничий,** *adj.* [*fem.* -чья] slave (*attrib.*).

нево́льно *adv.* **1,** unintentionally. **2,** instinctively. **3,** against one's will.

нево́льный *adj.* **1,** unintentional; involuntary. **2,** involuntary; forced.

нево́ля *n.* **1,** slavery. **2,** captivity: размножа́ться в нево́ле, to breed in captivity. **3,** *colloq.* necessity.

невообрази́мый *adj.* inconceivable; unimaginable.

невооружённый *adj.* unarmed. —**невооружённым гла́зом,** with the naked (*or* unaided) eye.

невоспе́тый *adj.* unsung.

невоспи́танный *adj.* ill-bred; ill-mannered. —**невоспи́танность,** *n.f.* lack of upbringing.

невоспламеня́емый *adj.* incombustible; nonflammable.

невосполни́мый *adj.* irreparable.

невосприи́мчивый *adj.* **1,** slow to absorb or learn. **2,** (*with* к) immune (to). —**невосприи́мчивость,** *n.f.* immunity.

невостре́бованный *adj.* unclaimed.

невою́ющий *adj.* nonbelligerent.

невпопа́д *adv., colloq.* not to the point; он отвеча́л невпопа́д, his answers were not to the point.

невразуми́тельный *adj.* unintelligible.

невралги́я *n.* neuralgia. —**невралги́ческий,** *adj.* neuralgic.

неврастени́я *n.* nervous breakdown; nervous exhaustion; neurasthenia.

невреди́мый *adj.* unharmed; safe. —**цел и невреди́м,** safe and sound.

невре́дный *adj.* harmless.

неври́т *n.* neuritis.

невро́з *n.* neurosis.

невроло́гия *n.* neurology. —**невро́лог,** *n.* neurologist. —**неврологи́ческий,** *adj.* neurological.

невропато́лог *n.* neurologist.

невроти́ческий *adj.* neurotic.

невы́года *n.* **1,** disadvantage. **2,** loss.

невы́годно *adv.* **1,** not to one's advantage. **2,** at a loss. —*adj.*, *used predicatively* disadvantageous; not a good idea.

невы́годный *adj.* **1,** unprofitable. **2,** unfavorable; disadvantageous. **3,** unattractive.

невы́держанный *adj.* **1,** lacking self-control. **2,** uneven. **3,** (*of wine, cheese, etc.*) not aged; new. —**невы́держанность**, *n.f.* lack of self-control.

невыла́зный *adj.*, *colloq.* **1,** impassable. **2,** offering no way out.

невыноси́мый *adj.* unbearable; unendurable; insufferable. —**невыноси́мо**, *adv.* unbearably.

невыполне́ние *n.* nonfulfillment; failure to carry out.

невы́полненный *adj.* unfulfilled.

невыполни́мый *adj.* impracticable; unfeasible. —**невыполни́мость**, *n.f.* impracticability.

невырази́мый *adj.* inexpressible. —**невырази́мые**, *n. pl.*, *jocular* unmentionables.

невырази́тельный *adj.* inexpressive; unexpressive. —**невырази́тельность**, *n.f.* lack of expression.

невы́сказанный *adj.* unexpressed; unspoken.

невысо́кий *adj.* low. —**невысо́кого ка́чества**, low-grade; of poor quality.

невы́ход *n.* failure to appear.

не́га *n.* **1,** comfort; contentment; ease. **2,** bliss.

негати́в *n.*, *photog.* negative.

негати́вный *adj.* negative.

негашёный *adj.* **1,** (*of stamps*) uncanceled; unused. **2,** *in* негашёная и́звесть, quicklime.

не́где *adv.*, *used with inf.* nowhere; no place: мне не́где сесть, I have no place to sit.

неги́бкий *adj.* stiff; rigid; inflexible. —**неги́бкость**, *n.f.* stiffness.

негла́сный *adj.* secret.

неглиже́ *n. neut. indecl.* negligee.

неглубо́кий *adj.* **1,** shallow. **2,** *fig.* shallow; superficial.

неглу́пый *adj.* **1,** quite intelligent. **2,** (*of advice*) sound; sensible.

негну́щийся *adj.* stiff.

него́ (vo) *pron.*, *var.* of его́, *used after prepositions.*

него́дник *n.*, *colloq.* **1,** good-for-nothing. **2,** brat.

него́дность *n.f.* **1,** lack of fitness. **2,** uselessness. —**приходи́ть в него́дность**, **1,** to fall into disrepair. **2,** to become unusable.

него́дный *adj.* **1,** unfit. **2,** *colloq.* worthless; good-for-nothing.

негодова́ние *n.* indignation.

негодова́ть *v. impfv.* [*pres.* **-ду́ю, -ду́ешь**] to be indignant.

негоду́ющий *adj.* indignant.

негодя́й *n.* scoundrel.

негостеприи́мный *adj.* inhospitable.

негото́вый *adj.* unready.

негр *n.* Negro; black.

негра́мотный *adj.* **1,** illiterate. **2,** full of errors (*in grammar, spelling, etc.*). —**негра́мотность**, *n.f.* illiteracy.

негритёнок [*gen.* **-нка**; *pl.* **-тя́та, -тя́т**] *n.* Negro child; black child.

негритя́нка [*gen. pl.* **-нок**] *n.* Negro woman; black woman.

негритя́нский *adj.* Negro; black.

негро́идный *adj.* Negroid.

негро́мкий *adj.* low; not loud. —**негро́мко**, *adv.* in a low voice.

неда́вний *adj.* recent. —**до неда́внего вре́мени**, until recently.

неда́вно *adv.* recently; not long ago.

недалёкий *adj.* **1,** nearby; not far off. **2,** near (*in time*). В недалёком про́шлом, in the recent past. **3,** not very bright.

недалеко́ *also*, **недалёко** *adv.* not far. —*adj.* used predicatively not far: по́чта недалеко́ от вокза́ла, the post office is not far from the station.

недальнови́дный *adj.* shortsighted. —**недальнови́дность**, *n.f.* shortsightedness.

неда́ром *adv.* for a reason; not for nothing; (it is) no wonder.

недви́жимость *n.f.* real estate.

недви́жимый *also*, **недвижи́мый** *adj.* immovable. —**недви́жимое иму́щество**, real estate.

недвусмы́сленный *adj.* unequivocal; unambiguous. —**недвусмы́сленно**, *adv.* unequivocally.

недееспосо́бный *adj.* **1,** unable to function. **2,** *law* incompetent. —**недееспосо́бность**, *n.f.*, *law* incompetence.

недействи́тельный *adj.* **1,** *obs.* ineffective; ineffectual. **2,** invalid; null and void.

неделика́тный *adj.* indelicate; tactless. —**неделика́тность**, *n.f.* indelicacy; tactlessness.

недели́мый *adj.* **1,** indivisible. **2,** (*of numbers*) prime. —**недели́мость**, *n.f.* indivisibility.

неде́льный *adj.* a week's.

неде́ля *n.* week.

недержа́ние *n.*, *med.* incontinence.

недёшево *adv.*, *colloq.* not cheap: сто́ить недёшево, to cost a pretty penny.

недисциплини́рованный *adj.* undisciplined.

недобо́р *n.* shortage; shortfall.

недоброжела́тельный *adj.* unfriendly; hostile. —**недоброжела́тельность**, *n.f.*; **недоброжела́тельство**, *n.neut.* ill will.

недоброка́чественный *adj.* poor-quality; low-grade; inferior; shoddy. —**недоброка́чественность**, *n.f.* poor quality.

недобросо́вестность *n.f.* **1,** lack of conscientiousness; negligence. **2,** lack of integrity; bad faith.

недобросо́вестный *adj.* **1,** unconscientious. **2,** unscrupulous.

недо́брый *adj.* **1,** unkind; mean; malicious. **2,** evil; bad. —**недо́брое**, *n.* trouble: чу́ять недо́брое, to sense trouble; smell a rat.

недова́ривать *v. impfv.* [*pfv.* **недовари́ть**] to undercook.

недовари́ть [*infl.* **-варю́, -ва́ришь**] *v.*, *pfv. of* **недова́ривать**.

недове́рие *n.* **1,** distrust; mistrust. **2,** incredulity.

недове́рчивый *adj.* **1,** distrustful; mistrustful. **2,** incredulous. —**недове́рчивость**, *n.f.* distrust; mistrust.

недово́льный *adj.* [*short form* **-лен, -льна**] dissatisfied; discontented; displeased. —*n.* malcontent.

недово́льство *n.* dissatisfaction; discontent; displeasure.

недовыполне́ние *n.* failure to fulfill completely; underfulfillment.

недовыполня́ть *v. impfv.* [*pfv.* **недовы́полнить**] to fail to fulfill completely.

недога́дливый *adj.* slow to grasp things; dull; dense.

недогляде́ть *v. pfv.* [*infl.* **-жу́, -ди́шь**] *colloq.* **1,** to overlook. **2,** (*with* за + *instr.*) to fail to look after.

недоговáривать *v. impfv.* [*pfv.* **недоговори́ть**] to hold back; leave unsaid: вы чтó-то недоговáриваете, you're holding something back.

недоговорённость *n.f.* **1,** lack of agreement; lack of coordination. **2,** failure to tell all.

недоговори́ть *v., pfv. of* **недоговáривать.**

недодавáть *v. impfv.* [*pfv.* **недодáть;** *pres.* **-даю́, -даёшь**] to give less than the required amount: он мне недóдал три рубля́, he gave me three rubles less than he was supposed to.

недодáть [*infl. like* **дать;** *past* **недóдал, -далá, недóдало**] *v., pfv. of* **недодавáть.**

недодéланный *adj.* unfinished.

недодéлать *v. pfv.* to fail to do; fail to finish.

недодéлка [*gen. pl.* **-лок**] *n., colloq.* defect; imperfection.

недодержáть [*infl.* **-держу́, -дéржишь**] *v., pfv. of* **недодéрживать.**

недодéрживать *v. impfv.* [*pfv.* **недодержáть**] *photog.* to underexpose.

недодéржка *n., photog.* underexposure.

недоедáние *n.* malnutrition.

недоедáть *v. impfv.* to be underfed; be undernourished.

недожáривать *v. impfv.* [*pfv.* **недожáрить**] to undercook.

недозвóленный *adj.* unauthorized; unlawful; illicit.

недозрéлый *adj.* **1,** not fully ripe. **2,** *fig.* immature.

недои́мка [*gen. pl.* **-мок**] *n.* arrears; back rent; back taxes. —**недои́мщик,** *n.* person in arrears.

недокáзанный *adj.* unproved; unproven.

недоказу́емый *adj.* that cannot be proved.

недолгá *adv., in* (вот) и вся **недолгá,** *colloq.* and that's (all there is to) it!

недóлгий *adj.* short; brief.

недóлго *adv.* not long. —**недóлго ду́мая,** without pausing to think. —**недóлго и** (+ *inf.*), *colloq.* easily: недóлго и утону́ть, one could easily drown.

недолговéчный *adj.* short-lived; ephemeral.

недолюбливать *v. impfv.* to have little liking for; not particularly like.

недомогáние *n.* indisposition.

недомогáть *v. impfv.* to be unwell; be ailing; be indisposed.

недомóлвка [*gen. pl.* **-вок**] *n.* allusion; innuendo.

недомы́слие *n.* thoughtlessness; foolishness.

недонесéние *n.* failure to report a crime.

недонóсок [*gen.* **-ска**] *n.* prematurely born baby.

недонóшенный *adj.* born prematurely.

недооцéнивать *v. impfv.* [*pfv.* **недооцени́ть**] to underestimate.

недооцени́ть [*infl.* **-ценю́, -цéнишь**] *v., pfv. of* **недооцéнивать.**

недооцéнка *n.* underestimation.

недопечённый *adj.* half-baked.

недоплати́ть [*infl.* **-плачу́, -плáтишь**] *v., pfv. of* **недоплáчивать.**

недоплáчивать *v. impfv.* [*pfv.* **недоплати́ть**] to underpay: недоплати́ть пять рублéй, to underpay by five rubles.

недополучáть *v. impfv.* [*pfv.* **недополучи́ть**] to receive less than one should: недополучи́ть дéсять рублéй, to receive ten rubles less than one was supposed to.

недополучи́ть [*infl.* **-лучу́, -лу́чишь**] *v., pfv. of* **недополучáть.**

недопроизвóдство *n.* underproduction.

недопусти́мый *adj.* impermissible; intolerable.

недорабáтывать *v. impfv.* [*pfv.* **недорабóтать**] **1,** *v.i.* to work less than the required time. **2,** *v.t.* to fail to complete.

недорáзвитый *adj.* underdeveloped.

недоразумéние *n.* misunderstanding.

недóрого *adv.* inexpensively; for a reasonable price.

недорогóй *adj.* inexpensive.

недорóд *n.* poor harvest; crop failure.

недóросль *n.m.* ignorant young man.

недорóсток [*gen.* **-стка**] *n., colloq.* shrimp; runt.

недослы́шать *v. impfv. & pfv.* [*infl.* **-шу, -шишь**] **1,** [*v. pfv.*] to fail to hear entirely. **2,** [*v. impfv.*] *colloq.* to be somewhat hard of hearing.

недосмóтр *n.* oversight.

недосмотрéть *v. pfv.* [*infl.* **-смотрю́ -смóтришь**] *colloq.* **1,** to overlook. **2,** (*with* за + *instr.*) to fail to look after.

недоспáть [*infl. like* **спать**] *v., pfv. of* **недосыпáть.**

недоспéлый *adj.* not fully ripe.

недоставáть *v. impfv.* [*pfv.* **недостáть;** *pres.* **-стаёт**] *impers.* (*with gen.*) **1,** to be insufficient; be lacking: чегó вам недостаёт?, what are you lacking? Нам недостаёт дéнег, we are short of money. **2,** [*impfv. only*] to be missing: недостаёт двух страни́ц, two pages are missing. **3,** [*impfv. only*] to be missed: нам вас недоставáло, we missed you.

недостáток [*gen.* **-тка**] *n.* **1,** shortage; scarcity; lack. **2,** defect; shortcoming; deficiency.

недостáточно *adv.* not...enough; insufficiently. —*adj., used predicatively* not enough; insufficient: пять рублéй недостáточно, five rubles is not enough.

недостáточный *adj.* insufficient; inadequate. —**недостáточность,** *n.f.* insufficiency; inadequacy.

недостáть [*infl.* **-стáнет**] *v., pfv. of* **недоставáть.**

недостáча *n., colloq.* shortage.

недостаю́щий *adj.* missing: недостаю́щее звенó, missing link.

недостижи́мый *adj.* unattainable.

недостовéрный *adj.* of doubtful authenticity; unreliable.

недостóйно *adv.* badly; improperly. —*adj., used predicatively* (*with gen.*) unworthy of; beneath: это егó недостóйно, it is unworthy of him; it is beneath him.

недостóйный *adj.* [*short form* **-стóин, -стóйна**] **1,** unworthy: он её недостóин, he is unworthy of her. **2,** undignified. **3,** dishonorable.

недострóенный *adj.* (*of something being built*) unfinished.

недосту́пный *adj.* **1,** inaccessible. **2,** unattainable. **3,** distant; unapproachable. **4,** beyond one's comprehension. **5,** beyond one's means; more than one can afford. —**недосту́пность,** *n.f.* inaccessibility.

недосу́г *n., colloq., used impersonally with dat.* lack of (leisure) time: мне недосу́г, I am too busy.

недосчи́тываться *v.r. impfv.* [*pfv.* **недосчитáться**] (*with subject in gen.*) to be short; be missing.

недосыпáние *n.* lack of sleep.

недосыпáть *v. impfv.* [*pfv.* **недоспáть**] not to get enough sleep.

недосягáемый *adj.* **1,** unattainable. **2,** inaccessible.

недотёпа *n.m. & f., colloq.* maladroit person; clod.

недотрóга *n.* touch-me-not (*flower*). —*n.m. & f., colloq.* touchy person.

недоу́здок [*gen.* -дка] *n.* halter (*for a horse*).

недоумева́ть *v. impfv.* to be puzzled; be perplexed; be bewildered.

недоумева́ющий *adj.* puzzled; perplexed; bewildered.

недоуме́ние *n.* bewilderment; perplexity.

недоуме́нный *adj.* **1,** puzzling; perplexing; baffling. **2,** puzzled; perplexed.

недоу́чка [*gen. pl.* -чек] *n.m. & f., colloq.* person with little education.

недочёт *n.* **1,** shortage; deficit. **2,** defect; shortcoming.

не́дра [*gen.* недр] *n.pl.* **1,** bowels of the earth. **2,** *fig.* innermost depths.

недре́млющий *adj.* vigilant; watchful.

не́друг *n.* enemy; foe.

недружелю́бие *n.* unfriendliness. —**недружелю́бный,** *adj.* unfriendly.

неду́г *n.* ailment.

недурно́й *adj.* **1,** not bad. **2,** (*with* собо́й) not bad-looking. —**неду́рно,** *adv.* rather well.

недю́жинный *adj.* unusual; uncommon; outstanding; exceptional.

неё *pron.,* var. of **её,** *used after prepositions.*

неесте́ственный *adj.* unnatural.

нежда́нный *adj., colloq.* unexpected.

нежела́ние *n.* unwillingness; reluctance; disinclination.

нежела́тельный *adj.* undesirable.

не́жели *conj.,* archaic than.

нежена́тый *adj.* (*of a man*) unmarried; single.

не́женка [*gen. pl.* -нок] *n.m. & f., colloq.* sissy.

неживо́й *adj.* **1,** lifeless; dead. **2,** inorganic. **3,** listless; apathetic. **4,** (*of light*) faint.

нежи́зненный *adj.* **1,** unrealistic; impractical. **2,** unreal; weird.

нежило́й *adj.* **1,** unoccupied; vacant; unlived-in. **2,** unfit for occupation.

не́жить *v. impfv.* to pamper; coddle. —**не́житься,** *refl.* **1,** to lounge around; loll. **2,** to luxuriate; bask (in the sun).

не́жничать *v. impfv., colloq.* to be overly gentle.

не́жно *adv.* **1,** tenderly. **2,** gently.

не́жность *n.f.* **1,** tenderness; gentleness. **2,** *pl., colloq.* tender words.

не́жный *adj.* tender; gentle; delicate.

незабве́нный *adj.* unforgettable.

незаброни́рованный *adj.* unreserved: заброни́рованное ме́сто, unreserved seat.

незабу́дка [*gen. pl.* -док] *n.* forget-me-not.

незабыва́емый *adj.* unforgettable.

незавершённый *adj.* uncompleted; unfinished.

незави́дный *adj.* unenviable.

незави́симо *adv.* independently. —**незави́симо от,** regardless of; irrespective of.

незави́симость *n.f.* independence.

незави́симый *adj.* independent.

незави́сящий *adj., in* по незави́сящим от (+ *gen.*) обстоя́тельствам, due to circumstances beyond (one's) control.

незада́ча *n., colloq.* bad luck.

незада́чливый *adj., colloq.* unlucky; luckless.

незадо́лго *adv.* (*with* до) shortly (before); not long (before).

незаинтересо́ванный *adj.* disinterested.

незако́нно *adv.* unlawfully; illegally.

незаконнорождённый *adj.* (*of a child*) illegitimate.

незако́нный *adj.* unlawful; illegal; illegitimate. —**незако́нность,** *n.f.* illegality.

незако́нченный *adj.* unfinished.

незамедли́тельный *adj.* immediate.

незамени́мый *adj.* **1,** irreplaceable; indispensable. **2,** irreparable.

незаме́тно *adv.* **1,** without being seen. **2,** *fig.* imperceptibly; unnoticed: пройти́ незаме́тно, to pass unnoticed. —*adj., used predicatively* **1,** not noticeable: заме́тно, что́бы..., it is not noticeable that...; you could not tell that... **2,** (*with* для) unnoticed (by); without (someone) noticing it. Незаме́тно для себя́, without realizing it.

незаме́тный *adj.* **1,** imperceptible. **2,** inconspicuous. **3,** insignificant.

незаме́ченный *adj.* unnoticed.

незаму́жняя *adj.* (*of a woman*) unmarried.

незамыслова́тый *adj., colloq.* simple; unimaginative.

неза́нятый *adj.* unoccupied.

незапа́мятный *adj.* immemorial. —**с незапа́мятных времён,** since time immemorial.

неза́пертый *adj.* unlocked.

незапя́тнанный *adj.* unblemished; unsullied.

незара́зный *adj.* noncontagious.

незаря́женный *also,* **незаряжённый** *adj.* **1,** (*of a rifle, pistol, etc.*) unloaded. **2,** (*of a battery*) not charged.

незаселённый *adj.* unsettled.

незаслу́женный *adj.* undeserved.

незате́йливый *adj.* simple; unpretentious.

незауря́дный *adj.* outstanding.

неза́чем *adv.* (*with inf.*) *colloq.* there is no need (to); there is no point (in).

незащищённый *adj.* unprotected; undefended.

незва́ный *adj.* uninvited.

незде́шний *adj.* **1,** *colloq.* not of this place: я неде́шний, I am not from around here. **2,** *obs.* unearthly; supernatural.

нездоро́виться *v.r. impfv., impers.* (*with dat.*) to feel ill: мне нездоро́вится, I feel ill; I am not feeling well.

нездоро́вый *adj.* **1,** unwell. **2,** unhealthy; unwholesome.

нездоро́вье *n.* **1,** ill health. **2,** ailment.

неземно́й *adj.* unearthly.

незло́й *adj.* kind; good-natured.

незлопа́мятный *adj.* forgiving; not one to bear a grudge.

незнако́мец [*gen.* -мца] *n.m.* [*fem.* -мка] stranger.

незнако́мство *n.* lack of familiarity; unfamiliarity.

незнако́мый *adj.* **1,** unfamiliar; unknown. **2,** (*with* с + *instr.*) unacquainted (with). —*n., colloq.* stranger.

незна́ние *n.* ignorance.

незна́чащий *adj.* insignificant.

незначи́тельный *adj.* **1,** insignificant; very slight; negligible. **2,** insignificant; minor; trivial. —**незначи́тельность,** *n.f.* insignificance.

незре́лый *adj.* **1,** unripe; green. **2,** *fig.* immature. —**незре́лость,** *n.f.* immaturity.

незри́мый *adj.* invisible.

незря́чий *adj.* unseeing; sightless; blind.

незы́блемый *adj.* **1,** firm; solid. **2,** *fig.* steadfast; unwavering; unshakable.

неизбе́жный *adj.* inevitable; unavoidable. —**неизбе́жно,** *adv.* inevitably. —**неизбе́жность,** *n.f.* inevitability.

неизве́данный *adj.* **1,** unexplored. **2,** never before experienced.

неизве́стно *adj., used predicatively* unknown; not known: кто он тако́й – неизве́стно, who he is is not known.

неизве́стное *n., decl. as an adj., math.* unknown.

неизве́стность *n.f.* **1,** lack of information; uncertainty. Быть в неизве́стности (о), to be unaware (of); have no knowledge (of). **2,** obscurity: жить в неизве́стности, to live in obscurity.

неизве́стный *adj.* unknown. —*n.* unknown person; stranger.

неизглади́мый *adj.* indelible.

неи́зданный *adj.* unpublished.

неизлечи́мый *adj.* incurable.

неизме́нный *adj.* **1,** invariable; unchanging. **2,** unfailing; devoted. —**неизме́нно,** *adv.* invariably.

неизменя́емый *adj.* unalterable; unchanging; fixed.

неизмери́мый *adj.* immeasurable; unfathomable. —**неизмери́мо,** *adv.* immeasurably; infinitely.

неизъясни́мый *adj.* **1,** unexplainable. **2,** inexpressible.

неиме́ние *n., in* за неиме́нием (+ *gen.*), owing to the lack of; for want of. За неиме́нием лу́чшего, for want of anything better.

неимове́рный *adj.* incredible; fantastic.

неиму́щий *adj.* poor; indigent; needy.

неинтеллиге́нтный *adj.* not cultured; unsophisticated.

неинтере́сный *adj.* uninteresting.

неискорени́мый *adj.* ineradicable; ingrained.

неи́скренний *adj.* insincere. —**неи́скренность,** *n.f.* insincerity.

неискушённый *adj.* unsophisticated; inexperienced.

неисповеди́мый *adj.* inscrutable.

неисполне́ние *n.* nonperformance; failure to carry out; failure to obey.

неисполни́мый *adj.* **1,** impossible to carry out; impracticable. **2,** impossible to perform. **3,** unrealizable. Неисполни́мая мечта́, impossible dream. —**неисполни́мость,** *n.f.* impracticability.

неиспо́льзованный *adj.* unused.

неиспо́рченный *adj.* **1,** unspoiled. **2,** innocent; pure.

неисправи́мый *adj.* **1,** incorrigible. **2,** irreparable.

неиспра́вность *n.f.* **1,** disrepair. **2,** failure; malfunction(ing). **3,** carelessness.

неиспра́вный *adj.* **1,** defective; faulty; out of order. **2,** careless.

неиспы́танный *adj.* **1,** untried; untested. **2,** never before experienced.

неиссле́дованный *adj.* unexplored.

неиссяка́емый *adj.* inexhaustible.

ней́ство *n.* **1,** fury; rage. **2,** atrocity.

ней́ствовать *v. impfv.* [*pres.* -ствую, -ствуешь] **1,** to rage; rave. **2,** to run wild; go on a rampage. **3,** (*of a storm, the sea, etc.*) to rage.

ней́стовый *adj.* furious; violent.

неистощи́мый *adj.* inexhaustible.

неисцели́мый *adj.* incurable.

неисчерпа́емый *adj.* inexhaustible.

неисчисли́мый *adj.* countless; incalculable; innumerable.

ней *pers. pron., variant of* ей, *used after prepositions.*

нейло́н *n.* nylon. —**нейло́новый,** *adj.* nylon.

нейро́н *n.* neuron.

нейрохирурги́я *n.* neurosurgery. —**нейрохиру́рг,** *n.* neurosurgeon.

нейтрализа́ция *n.* neutralization.

нейтрализова́ть *v. impfv. & pfv.* [*pres.* -зу́ю, -зу́ешь] to neutralize.

нейтралите́т *n.* neutrality.

нейтра́льный *adj.* neutral.

нейтро́н *n.* neutron. —**нейтро́нный,** *adj.* neutron (*attrib.*): нейтро́нная бо́мба, neutron bomb.

неказ́истый *adj., colloq.* ugly; homely; unattractive.

неквалифици́рованный *adj.* unskilled.

не́кий *indef. pron.* a certain; someone named: вас спра́шивал не́кий Ивано́в, someone named Ivanov was asking for you.

не́когда *adv.* **1,** no time: мне не́когда, I have no time. **2,** once; formerly; at one time.

не́кого *indef. pron., gen. & acc.* [*dat.* не́кому; *instr.* не́кем; *prepl.* не́ (+ *prep.*) ком] *used with inf.* there is no one; there is nobody: не́кого посла́ть, there is no to send; мне не́кого спроси́ть, there is no one I can ask. *See also* не́кому.

неколеби́мый *adj.* = непоколеби́мый.

некомпете́нтный *adj.* incompetent; unqualified.

не́кому *indef. pron.* **1,** *dat. of* не́кого. **2,** there is no one: не́кому его́ замени́ть, there is no one to replace him.

неконституцио́нный *adj.* unconstitutional.

некороно́ванный *adj.* uncrowned.

некорре́ктный *adj.* improper; indecorous.

не́которые *indef. pron.* some; some people; certain people. —**не́которые из,** some of.

не́который *adj.* **1,** *pl.* some; certain: не́которые лю́ди, some/certain people. **2,** some; a certain amount of: не́которое сомне́ние, some doubt. —**не́которое вре́мя,** for some time; (for) a while. —**с не́которых пор,** for some time (now).

некраси́вый *adj.* **1,** ugly; unattractive. **2,** *colloq.* improper; not nice: э́то некраси́во, that's not nice.

некра́шеный *adj.* unpainted.

некре́пкий *adj.* **1,** not strong; not firm; flimsy. **2,** not robust. **3,** weak; diluted.

некрити́ческий *adj.* uncritical.

некро́з *n.* necrosis.

некроло́г *n.* obituary.

некста́ти *adv.* **1,** at the wrong time; at an inopportune moment. **2,** out of place; inappropriate.

некта́р *n.* nectar.

не́кто *indef. pron.* **1,** someone; somebody. **2,** a certain; someone named: вас спра́шивал не́кто Ивано́в, someone named Ivanov was asking for you.

не́куда *adv., used with inf.* nowhere; no place: мне е́хать не́куда, I have nowhere to go.

некульту́рный *adj.* **1,** uncivilized; uncultured. **2,** (*of plants*) uncultivated. —**некульту́рность,** *n.f.* lack of culture; lack of refinement.

некуря́щий *adj.* nonsmoking. —*n.* nonsmoker.

нела́дно *adv.* badly. —*adj., used predicatively* wrong: что́-то с ним нела́дно, something is wrong with him.

нела́дный *adj., colloq.* **1,** wrong: что́-то нела́дное происхо́дит, something wrong is going on. **2,** ungainly. —**нела́дное,** *n.* something wrong: чу́вствовать нела́дное, to sense that something is wrong.

нелады́ [*gen.* -до́в] *n. pl., colloq.* disagreements; friction; failure to get along: у них нелады́, they are not getting along.

нелакиро́ванный *adj.* not lacquered; unvarnished.

нела́сковый *adj.* cold; unfriendly.

нелега́льный *adj.* illegal. —**нелега́льно,** *adv.* illegally. —**нелега́льность,** *n.f.* illegality.

нелёгкий *adj.* **1,** not easy; hard; difficult. **2,** heavy; not light.

нелегко́ *adv.* not easily: языки́ даю́тся ему́ нелегко́, languages do not come easy to him.

неле́пость *n.f.* **1,** absurdity (*of something*). **2,** nonsense.

неле́пый *adj.* ridiculous; absurd.

неле́стный *adj.* unflattering; uncomplimentary.

нелётный *adj.* non-flying; unsuitable for flying.

нели́шний *adj.* useful; necessary. —**нели́шне,** *adj., used predicatively* useful; worthwhile: нели́шне отме́тить, что..., it is worth noting that...

нело́вкий *adj.* **1,** awkward; clumsy. **2,** awkward; uncomfortable; embarrassing: нело́вкое молча́ние, awkward silence.

нело́вко *adv.* awkwardly. —*adj., used predicatively* awkward; ill at ease: чу́вствовать себя́ нело́вко, to feel awkward/ill at ease/.

нело́вкость *n.f.* **1,** awkwardness. **2,** (an) indiscretion. **3,** (sense of) awkwardness; embarrassment.

нелоги́чный *adj.* illogical.

нелоя́льный *adj.* disloyal. —**нелоя́льность,** *n.f.* disloyalty.

нельзя́ *adv.* **1,** it is impossible; one cannot: нельзя́ сказа́ть, it is impossible to say; one cannot say. **2,** it is forbidden; one may not: нельзя́ кури́ть, smoking is forbidden. —**как нельзя́ лу́чше,** as well as possible. —**нельзя́ ли...,** can't you...?; couldn't you...?: нельзя́ ли поти́ше?, can't/couldn't you be a little more quiet?

нелюбе́зный *adj.* ungracious.

нелюби́мый *adj.* unloved.

нелюбо́вь [*infl. like* любо́вь] *n.f.* dislike.

нелюди́м *n.m.* [*fem.* -ка] unsociable person.

нелюди́мый *adj.* unsociable. —**нелюди́мость,** *n.f.* unsociability.

нём *pron., prepl. of* он *and* оно́.

нема́ло *adv.* **1,** (*with gen.*) quite a bit of; considerable. **2,** (*with verbs*) quite; quite a bit; quite a lot.

немалова́жный *adj.* of no small importance; not unimportant.

нема́лый *adj.* rather large; considerable.

немеблиро́ванный *adj.* unfurnished.

неме́дленный *adj.* immediate. —**неме́дленно,** *adv.* immediately; at once.

неме́для *adv.* immediately; at once.

Немези́да *n.* **1,** Nemesis (*Greek goddess*). **2,** (one's) nemesis.

неме́ркнущий *adj.* **1,** never fading. **2,** *fig.* undying.

неме́ть *v. impfv.* [*pfv.* онеме́ть] **1,** to be speechless; be dumbfounded. **2,** to become numb.

не́мец [*gen.* -мца] *n.m.* [*fem.* -мка] German. —**не́мецкий,** *adj.* German.

неми́лостивый *adj., obs.* **1,** ungracious. **2,** unmerciful.

неми́лость *n.f.* disfavor; disgrace.

немину́емый *adj.* inevitable; unavoidable. —**немину́емо,** *adv.* inevitably; unavoidably.

не́мка [*gen. pl.* -мок] *n.* German woman.

немно́гие *adj.* a few: в немно́гих слова́х, in a few words. —*indef. pron.* **1,** few people; not many people. **2,** the few: немно́гие, кто..., the few who... —**немно́гим,** *adv., used with comp. adjectives* a little.

немно́го *adv.* **1,** a little; a bit of. **2,** little; not much. **3,** a little; rather; somewhat.

немно́гое *n., in* то немно́гое, что..., the little that...; what little...

немногосло́вный *adj.* of few words; laconic.

немногочи́сленный *adj.* **1,** small (*in number of people, members, etc.*). **2,** *pl.* the few: немногочи́сленные доброво́льцы, the few volunteers.

немно́жко *adv., colloq.* = **немно́го.**

немну́щийся *adj.* (*of fabric*) crease-resistant.

немо́й *adj.* **1,** dumb; mute. **2,** (*of a film*) silent. —*n.* mute.

немолодо́й *adj.* not young.

немота́ *n.* inability to speak.

не́мочь *n.f., colloq.* sickness; illness.

немощёный *adj.* unpaved.

не́мощный *adj.* feeble.

не́мощь *n.f.* debility.

нему́ *pron., variant of* ему́, *used after prepositions.*

немудрено́ *adv.* no wonder: немудрено́, что он не отве́тил, no wonder he didn't answer.

немудрёный *adj., colloq.* simple; plain.

нему́дрый *adj.* **1,** not very bright. **2,** *colloq.* = **немудрёный.**

немы́слимый *adj.* unthinkable.

ненаблюда́тельный *adj.* unobservant.

ненави́деть *v. impfv.* [*pres.* -ви́жу, -ви́дишь] to hate; detest.

ненави́стник *n.* person who hates. —**ненави́стничество,** *n.* hostile attitude.

ненави́стный *adj.* hated; hateful; abhorrent.

не́нависть *n.f.* hatred; hate.

ненагля́дный *adj.* beloved.

ненадёжный *adj.* unreliable. —**ненадёжность,** *n.f.* unreliability.

ненадобность *n.f.* lack of need (for). —**за нена́добностью,** for lack of use. —**за нена́добностью** (+ *gen.*), there being no need (for).

ненадо́лго *adv.* for a short time; for a short while (*subsequent to the action expressed by the verb*): я уезжа́ю ненадо́лго, I am going away for a short time/while.

нена́званный *adj.* unnamed.

ненаказу́емый *adj.* not punishable by law.

ненаме́ренный *adj.* unintentional. —**ненаме́ренно,** *adv.* unintentionally.

ненападе́ние *n.* nonaggression.

ненаро́ком *adv., colloq.* by chance: он ненаро́ком зашёл, he just happened to drop in.

нена́стный *adj.* inclement.

нена́стье *n.* inclement weather.

ненасы́тный *adj.* insatiable.

ненасы́щенный *adj.* unsaturated.

ненатура́льный *adj.* **1,** artificial. **2,** unnatural.

ненау́чный *adj.* unscientific.

не́нец [*gen.* -нца] *n.m.* [*fem.* -нка] Nenets (*one of a people inhabiting northernmost Russia*). —**не́нецкий,** *adj.* Nenets.

ненорма́льный *adj.* abnormal. —**ненорма́льно,** *adv.* abnormally. —**ненорма́льность,** *n.f.* abnormality.

нену́жность *n.f.* **1,** uselessness. **2,** *usu. pl.* useless things.

нену́жный *adj.* unneeded; needless; unnecessary.

необду́манный *adj.* not thought out; rash.

необескура́женный *adj.* not discouraged; undismayed.

необеспе́ченный *adj.* without means; unprovided for.

необеспоко́енный *adj.* unworried; undisturbed.

необита́емый *adj.* uninhabited.

необозри́мый *adj.* boundless; vast. —**необозри́мость**, *n.f.* vastness.

необосно́ванный *adj.* **1,** groundless; unfounded. **2,** unsound.

необрабо́танный *adj.* **1,** uncultivated; untilled. **2,** crude; rough; unfinished.

необразо́ванный *adj.* uneducated. —**необразо́ванность**, *n.f.* lack of education.

необрати́мый *adj.* irreversible.

необу́зданный *adj.* unrestrained; unbridled.

необу́ченный *adj.* untrained.

необходи́мо *adj., used predicatively* necessary; essential: необходи́мо де́йствовать без промедле́ния, it is essential to act without delay. Необходи́мо приня́ть сро́чные ме́ры, urgent measures must be taken.

необходи́мое *n., decl. as an adj.* necessities; essentials: всё необходи́мое, all the necessities; everything one needs.

необходи́мость *n.f.* necessity; need. —**по необходи́мости**, out of necessity. —**при необходи́мости**, when necessary. —**предме́ты пе́рвой необходи́мости**, the barest necessities.

необходи́мый *adj.* necessary; essential.

необщи́тельный *adj.* unsociable; antisocial. —**необщи́тельность**, *n.f.* unsociability.

необъекти́вный *adj.* not objective; biased. —**необъекти́вность**, *n.f.* lack of objectivity.

необъя́вленный *adj.* (of a war) undeclared.

необъясни́мый *adj.* inexplicable; unexplainable; unaccountable.

необъя́тный *adj.* boundless; vast.

необыкнове́нный *adj.* unusual; uncommon; extraordinary. —**необыкнове́нно**, *adv.* unusually; uncommonly.

необыча́йность *n.f.* **1,** (with gen.) extraordinary nature (of). **2,** extraordinary event.

необыча́йный *adj.* extraordinary; exceptional.

необы́чный *adj.* unusual.

необяза́тельный *adj.* **1,** optional; not obligatory. **2,** (of a person) not obliging.

неограни́ченный *adj.* unlimited.

неодина́ковый *adj.* different; dissimilar.

неоднокра́тно *adv.* repeatedly; more than once. —**неоднокра́тный**, *adj.* repeated.

неоднородный *adj.* **1,** heterogeneous. **2,** dissimilar. —**неоднородность**, *n.f.* heterogeneity.

неодобре́ние *n.* disapproval.

неодобри́тельный *adj.* disapproving. —**неодобри́тельно**, *adv.* in disapproval.

неодоли́мый *adj.* **1,** (of a force, urge, etc.) irresistible. **2,** invincible.

неодушевлённый *adj.* inanimate.

неожи́данно *adv.* unexpectedly.

неожи́данность *n.f.* **1,** suddenness. **2,** unexpected development; surprise: кака́я прия́тная неожи́данность!, what a pleasant surprise!

неожи́данный *adj.* unexpected.

неоклассици́зм *n.* neoclassicism. —**неокласси́ческий**, *adj.* neoclassical.

неоконча́тельный *adj.* not final.

неоко́нченный *adj.* unfinished.

неолити́ческий *adj.* neolithic.

неологи́зм *n.* neologism.

нео́н *n.* neon. —**нео́новый**, *adj.* neon.

неопа́сный *adj.* not dangerous.

неопера́бельный *adj., med.* inoperable.

неопери́вшийся *adj.* **1,** unfledged. **2,** fig., colloq. callow.

неопису́емый *adj.* indescribable.

неопла́тный *adj.* **1,** that cannot be repaid. **2,** unable to pay one's debts.

неопла́ченный *adj.* unpaid.

неопо́знанный *adj.* unidentified.

неопра́вданный *adj.* **1,** unjustified; unwarranted. **2,** unfounded.

неопределённо *adv.* vaguely.

неопределённость *n.f.* **1,** vagueness. **2,** uncertainty.

неопределённый *adj.* **1,** indefinite; uncertain; indeterminate. **2,** vague; unclear. —**неопределённая фо́рма глаго́ла**, infinitive.

неопредели́мый *adj.* indefinable.

неопровержи́мый *adj.* irrefutable; incontrovertible; conclusive. —**неопровержи́мо**, *adv.* conclusively.

неопря́тный *adj.* untidy. —**неопря́тность**, *n.f.* untidiness.

неопублико́ванный *adj.* unpublished.

нео́пытный *adj.* inexperienced. —**нео́пытность**, *n.f.* inexperience; lack of experience.

неорганизо́ванный *adj.* unorganized; disorganized. —**неорганизо́ванность**, *n.f.* lack of organization; disorganization.

неоргани́ческий *adj.* inorganic.

неосведомлённый *adj.* uninformed. —**неосведомлённость**, *n.f.* lack of information; ignorance.

неосвещённый *adj.* unlighted; unlit.

неосла́бный *adj.* unflagging; unremitting. С неосла́бным внима́нием, with rapt attention. *Also,* **неослабева́ющий.**

неосмотри́тельный *adj.* imprudent; indiscreet. —**неосмотри́тельность**, *n.f.* imprudence; indiscretion.

неоснова́тельный *adj.* **1,** groundless; unfounded. **2,** colloq. frivolous; superficial; shallow.

неоспори́мый *adj.* indisputable; incontestable; undeniable.

неосторо́жно *adv.* carelessly.

неосторо́жность *n.f.* carelessness: по неосторо́жности, through carelessness.

неосторо́жный *adj.* careless; incautious.

неосуществи́мый *adj.* impracticable; infeasible. —**неосуществи́мость**, *n.f.* impracticability.

неося́заемый *adj.* intangible.

неотврати́мый *adj.* inevitable. —**неотврати́мость**, *n.f.* inevitability.

неотвя́зный *adj., colloq.* **1,** (of a thought, question, etc.) nagging. **2,** (of a person) bothersome; annoying. *Also,* **неотвя́зчивый.**

неотдели́мый *adj.* inseparable. —**неотдели́мость**, *n.f.* inseparability.

неотёсанный *adj., colloq.* crude; uncouth.

неотзы́вчивый *adj.* unresponsive.

не́откуда *adv., used with inf.* there is no place (from): мне не́откуда э́то доста́ть, there is no place I can get it from.

неотло́жка *n., colloq.* ambulance (service): вы́звать неотло́жку, to call an ambulance.

неотло́жный *adj.* urgent. —**неотло́жность**, *n.f.* urgency.

неотлу́чный *adj.* always present; ever-present. —**неотлу́чно**, *adv.* constantly.

неотполиро́ванный *adj.* unpolished.

неотрази́мый *adj.* irresistible. —**неотрази́мость**, *n.f.* irresistibility.

неотсту́пный *adj.* persistent; relentless. —**неотсту́пность**, *n.f.* persistence; relentlessness.

неотчётливый *adj.* indistinct. —**неотчётливость**, *n.f.* indistinctness.

неотшлифо́ванный *adj.* unpolished.

неотъе́млемый *adj.* inalienable. —**неотъе́млемая часть**, integral part.

неофи́т *n.* neophyte.

неофициа́льный *adj.* unofficial.

неохо́та *n.* reluctance; unwillingness. —**мне неохо́та** (+ *inf.*), I don't feel like...; I don't care to...

неохо́тно *adv.* reluctantly. —**неохо́тный**, *adj.* reluctant.

неоцени́мый *adj.* inestimable; invaluable.

неочи́щенный *adj.* unrefined; crude.

неощути́мый *adj.* imperceptible. *Also,* **неощути́тельный.**

непа́рный *adj.* odd (*one of an incomplete pair*).

непарти́йный *adj.* **1,** non-party; not belonging to the party. **2,** non-partylike; not befitting a member of the party.

непереводи́мый *adj.* untranslatable.

непередава́емый *adj.* indescribable; inexpressible.

непереноси́мый *adj.* unbearable.

непереходный *adj.* (*of a verb*) intransitive.

неперспекти́вный *adj.* having poor prospects; unpromising.

непеча́тный *adj., colloq.* unprintable (*i.e. obscene*).

непи́саный *adj.* unwritten.

неплатёж [*gen.* -тежа́] *n.* nonpayment.

неплатёжеспосо́бный *adj.* insolvent. —**неплатёжеспосо́бность**, *n.f.* insolvency.

неплате́льщик *n.* person who has not paid; defaulter.

неплодоро́дный *adj.* barren; infertile. —**неплодоро́дность**, *n.f.* barrenness; infertility.

непло́тно *adv.* not tightly: непло́тно закры́тый, not closed tightly. —**непло́тный**, *adj.* not dense; thin.

непло́хо *adv.* quite well; rather well. —*adj., used predicatively* not bad: э́то непло́хо, that's not bad.

неплохо́й *adj.* not (a) bad.

непобеди́мый *adj.* invincible; unconquerable. —**непобеди́мость**, *n.f.* invincibility.

непови́нный *adj.* innocent.

неповинове́ние *n.* disobedience; insubordination.

неповоро́тливый *adj.* clumsy. —**неповоро́тливость**, *n.f.* clumsiness.

неповтори́мый *adj.* inimitable; unique.

непого́да *n.* bad weather.

непого́жий *adj., colloq.* overcast; dreary.

непогреши́мый *adj.* infallible. —**непогреши́мость**, *n.f.* infallibility.

неподалёку *adv.* **1,** not far away; not far off. **2,** (*with* от) not far (from).

непода́тливый *adj.* unyielding; intractable.

неподви́жный *adj.* **1,** motionless; stationary; immobile. **2,** (*of a look, stare, etc.*) fixed. —**неподви́жно**, *adv.* motionless. —**неподви́жность**, *n.f.* immobility.

неподгото́вленный *adj.* **1,** unprepared. **2,** untrained.

неподде́льный *adj.* **1,** genuine; authentic. **2,** genuine; unfeigned; sincere.

неподку́пный *adj.* incorruptible. —**неподку́пность**, *n.f.* incorruptibility.

неподоба́ющий *adj.* improper; unseemly.

неподража́емый *adj.* inimitable.

неподтверждённый *adj.* unconfirmed.

неподходя́щий *adj.* unsuitable; inappropriate.

неподчине́ние *n.* insubordination. —**неподчине́ние суде́бному постановле́нию**, contempt of court.

непозволи́тельный *adj.* impermissible.

непоколеби́мый *adj.* unshakable; unwavering; steadfast. —**непоколеби́мость**, *n.f.* steadfastness.

непоко́рный *adj.* rebellious; recalcitrant; unruly. —**непоко́рность**, *n.f.* rebelliousness; recalcitrance.

непокры́тый *adj.* uncovered.

непола́дки *n. pl.* [*sing.* -дка] *colloq.* **1,** defects; bugs. **2,** arguments; squabbles.

неполнопра́вный *adj.* not enjoying full rights.

неполнота́ *n.* incompleteness.

неполноце́нный *adj.* inferior. —**неполноце́нность**, *n.f.* inferiority.

непо́лный *adj.* **1,** (*of a container*) partially filled; not completely full. **2,** incomplete. —**рабо́тать непо́лный день**, to work part-time.

непоме́рный *adj.* excessive; inordinate; exorbitant.

непонима́ние *n.* lack of understanding; failure to understand; incomprehension.

непоня́тно *adv.* incomprehensibly. —*adj., used predicatively* incomprehensible; impossible to understand: мне непоня́тно, как э́то случи́лось, I cannot understand how it happened.

непоня́тный *adj.* incomprehensible; unintelligible. —**непоня́тность**, *n.f.* incomprehensibility; unintelligibility.

непопада́ние *n.* miss (*in shooting*).

непоправи́мый *adj.* irreparable; irretrievable.

непопуля́рный *adj.* unpopular. —**непопуля́рность**, *n.f.* unpopularity.

непоро́чность *n.f.* innocence; purity; chastity.

непоро́чный *adj.* innocent; pure; chaste. —**непоро́чное зача́тие**, the Immaculate Conception.

непо́ртящийся *adj.* nonperishable.

непоря́док [*gen.* -дка] *n.* disorder.

непоря́дочный *adj.* dishonorable.

непосвящённый *adj.* uninitiated.

непосе́да *n.m. & f., colloq.* fidgety person; fidget.

непосе́дливый *adj.* restless; fidgety. —**непосе́дливость**, *n.f.* restlessness.

непосеще́ние *n.* (*with gen.*) failure to attend.

непоси́льный *adj.* exhausting; backbreaking.

непосле́довательный *adj.* inconsistent. —**непосле́довательность**, *n.f.* inconsistency.

непослуша́ние *n.* disobedience.

непослу́шный *adj.* disobedient.

непосре́дственный *adj.* **1,** immediate; direct. **2,** natural; spontaneous. —**непосре́дственно**, *adv.* immediately; directly. —**непосре́дственность,** *n.f.* spontaneity.

непостижи́мый *adj.* incomprehensible. —**непостижи́мость,** *n.f.* incomprehensibility.

непостоя́нный *adj.* inconstant; changeable; fickle. —**непостоя́нство,** *n.* inconstancy.

непоти́зм *n.* nepotism.

непотопля́емый *adj.* unsinkable.

непотре́бный *adj., obs.* indecent; obscene.

непохо́жий *adj.* (*with* на + *acc.*) unlike; different (from).

непоча́тый *adj.* untouched; unopened; unused. —**непоча́тый край** (+ *gen.*), no end (of); tons (of).

непочте́ние *n.* disrespect.

непочти́тельный *adj.* disrespectful. —**непочти́тельность,** *n.f.* disrespect.

непра́вда *n.* **1,** untruth; falsehood; lie. **2,** deception; trickery. —*interj.* not so! —**все́ми пра́вдами и непра́вдами,** by hook or by crook.

неправдоподо́бие *n.* improbability; unlikelihood.

неправдоподо́бный *adj.* **1,** improbable; unlikely. **2,** implausible.

непра́ведный *adj., obs.* unjust; unfair.

непра́вильно *adv.* incorrectly. —*adj., used predicatively* incorrect: бы́ло бы непра́вильно (+ *inf.*), it would be incorrect to...

непра́вильность *n.f.* **1,** error; fallacy. **2,** irregularity.

непра́вильный *adj.* **1,** wrong; incorrect. **2,** irregular. **3,** (*of a fraction*) improper.

неправомо́чный *adj.* not legally qualified; incompetent. —**неправомо́чность,** *n.f., law* incompetence.

неправота́ *n.* error.

непра́вый *adj., usu. used predicatively* wrong: она́ была́ непра́ва, she was wrong.

непракти́чный *adj.* impractical. —**непракти́чность,** *n.f.* impracticality.

непревзойдённый *adj.* unsurpassed; unexcelled.

непредви́денный *adj.* unforeseen.

непреднаме́ренный *adj.* unintentional; unpremeditated.

непредприи́мчивый *adj.* unenterprising.

непредсказу́емый *adj.* unpredictable.

непредубеждённый *adj.* unbiased; unprejudiced.

непредумы́шленный *adj.* unpremeditated. —**непредумы́шленное уби́йство,** manslaughter.

непредусмотри́тельный *adj.* lacking foresight; improvident. —**непредусмотри́тельность,** *n.f.* lack of foresight; improvidence.

непрекло́нный *adj.* inflexible; intransigent; adamant. —**непрекло́нность,** *n.f.* inflexibility; intransigence.

непрело́жный *adj.* immutable.

непреме́нно *adv.* **1,** absolutely; definitely; without fail. **2,** sure; bound: он непреме́нно опозда́ет, he is sure/bound to be late. —**непреме́нный,** *adj.* necessary; essential.

непребори́мый *adj.* irresistible.

непреодоли́мый *adj.* **1,** insurmountable; insuperable. **2,** irresistible.

непререка́емый *adj.* unquestionable; indisputable.

непреры́вный *adj.* continuous; uninterrupted. —**непреры́вно,** *adv.* continuously. —**непреры́вность,** *n.f.* continuity.

непреста́нный *adj.* incessant; continual. —**непреста́нно,** *adv.* incessantly; continually.

неприве́тливый *adj.* **1,** unfriendly; ungracious. **2,**

uninviting; forbidding. —**неприве́тливость,** *n.f.* unfriendliness; ungraciousness.

непривлека́тельный *adj.* unattractive.

непривы́чка *n.* not being used to something: с непривы́чки (+ к *or inf.*), not being used to...

непривы́чно *adv.* unusually. —*adj., used predicatively* (*with dat.*) unaccustomed; not used to: (мне) непривы́чно по́здно ложи́ться, I am not used to going to bed late.

непривы́чный *adj.* **1,** strange; unfamiliar. **2,** (*with* к) unaccustomed (to). **3,** inexperienced; untrained.

непригля́дный *adj.* unattractive; unsightly.

неприго́дный *adj.* unfit; unusable; useless. —**неприго́дность,** *n.f.* uselessness.

неприе́млемый *adj.* unacceptable. —**неприе́млемость,** *n.f.* unacceptability.

непризна́ние *n.* nonrecognition.

непри́знанный *adj.* unrecognized.

неприкаса́емые *n. pl., decl. as an adj.* untouchables (*in India*).

неприка́яннный *adj., colloq.* aimless; not knowing what to do with oneself.

неприкоснове́нность *n.f.* inviolability. —**дипломати́ческая неприкоснове́нность,** diplomatic immunity.

неприкоснове́нный *adj.* **1,** saved for an emergency: неприкоснове́нный запа́с, emergency reserve. **2,** *fig.* inviolable.

неприкра́шенный *adj.* plain; unadorned; unvarnished: неприкра́шенная пра́вда, the unvarnished truth.

неприкреплённый *adj.* unattached.

неприкры́тый *adj.* **1,** slightly open; ajar. **2,** uncovered; unprotected; undefended. **3,** *fig.* naked; barefaced; undisguised.

неприли́чие *n.* impropriety; indecency.

неприли́чный *adj.* improper; indecent. —**неприли́чно,** *adv.* improperly; indecently.

непримени́мый *adj.* inapplicable.

приме́тный *adj.* **1,** imperceptible. **2,** not noteworthy; ordinary.

непримеча́тельный *adj.* ordinary; undistinguished.

непримири́мый *adj.* irreconcilable. —**непримири́мость,** *n.f.* irreconcilability.

непринуждённый *adj.* natural; casual; relaxed; nonchalant. —**непринуждённость,** *n.f.* ease; abandon; nonchalance.

неприсоедине́ние *n.* nonalignment. —**неприсоедини́вшийся,** *adj.* nonaligned.

неприспосо́бленный *adj.* unable to adjust easily; maladjusted. —**неприспосо́бленность,** *n.f.* inability to adjust; maladjustment.

непристо́йность *n.f.* **1,** obscenity. **2,** *often pl.* an obscenity. —**непристо́йный,** *adj.* obscene.

непристу́пный *adj.* **1,** impregnable; unassailable. **2,** *fig.* (*of a person*) unapproachable.

непритво́рный *adj.* unfeigned; genuine.

непритяза́тельный *adj.* unpretentious; unassuming.

неприхотли́вый *adj.* unpretentious; simple; plain.

неприча́стность *n.f.* noninvolvement.

неприча́стный *adj.* [*short form* -стен, -стна] (*with* к) not implicated (in); not involved (in).

неприя́зненный *adj.* hostile; unfriendly.

неприя́знь *n.f.* hostility; enmity.

неприя́тель *n.m.* enemy. —**неприя́тельский,** *adj.* enemy (*attrib.*).

неприя́тно *adj., used predicatively* unpleasant: мне неприя́тно слы́шать э́то, it is unpleasant to hear it; I am distressed to hear it.

неприя́тность *n.f.* **1,** unpleasantness. **2,** *pl.* trouble.

неприя́тный *adj.* unpleasant; disagreeable.

непробива́емый *adj.* impenetrable.

непробу́дный *adj.* **1,** (*of sleep*) deep. **2,** *colloq.* (*of drinking*) unrestrained; (*of a drinker*) chronic.

непрове́ренный *adj.* unverified.

непроводни́к [*gen.* -ника́] *n., physics* nonconductor.

непрогля́дный *adj.* **1,** pitch-dark. **2,** (*of darkness, fog, etc.*) impenetrable.

непродолжи́тельный *adj.* short; of short duration. —**непродолжи́тельность,** *n.f.* shortness; short duration.

непродукти́вный *adj.* unproductive. —**непродукти́вность,** *n.f.* unproductiveness.

непроду́манный *adj.* not thought through; hasty; rash.

непрое́зжий *adj.* impassable.

непрозра́чный *adj.* opaque. —**непрозра́чность,** *n.f.* opacity; opaqueness.

непроизводи́тельный *adj.* **1,** unproductive. **2,** nonproductive. —**непроизводи́тельность,** *n.f.* unproductiveness.

непроизво́льный *adj.* involuntary.

непроизноси́мый *adj.* unpronounceable.

непрола́зный *adj., colloq.* impassable.

непромока́емый *adj.* waterproof. —**непромока́емый плащ,** raincoat.

непроница́емый *adj.* impenetrable. —**непроница́емость,** *n.f.* impenetrability.

непропорциона́льный *adj.* disproportionate. —**непропорциона́льно,** *adv.* disproportionately. —**непропорциона́льность,** *n.f.* disproportion.

непросвещённый *adj.* unenlightened.

непрости́тельный *adj.* unforgivable; inexcusable; unpardonable.

непроходи́мость *n.f.* **1,** impassability; impenetrability. **2,** *med.* obstruction; blockage.

непроходи́мый *adj.* **1,** impassable; impenetrable. **2,** *colloq.* utter.

непро́чный *adj.* **1,** not durable; flimsy. **2,** *fig.* tenuous. —**непро́чность,** *n.f.* flimsiness.

непро́шеный *adj.* **1,** uninvited. **2,** unsought; unsolicited.

непрямо́й *adj.* **1,** indirect. **2,** devious; evasive.

Непту́н *n.* Neptune.

непту́ний *n.* neptunium.

непу́тёвый *adj., colloq.* shiftless; good-for-nothing.

непью́щий *adj.* not drinking; who does not drink. —*n.* nondrinker.

неработоспосо́бный *adj.* disabled; incapacitated.

нерабо́чий *adj.* **1,** nonworking. **2,** off: нерабо́чий день, day off; нерабо́чее вре́мя, time off. **3,** *colloq.* not conducive to work.

нера́венство *n.* inequality.

неравноду́шный *adj.* [*short form* -шен, -шна] (*with* к) not indifferent (to).

неравноме́рный *adj.* uneven. —**неравноме́рно,** *adv.* unevenly. —**неравноме́рность,** *n.f.* unevenness.

неравнопра́вие *n.* lack of equal rights; inequality. —**неравнопра́вный,** *adj.* not enjoying equal rights; unequal.

нера́вный *adj.* unequal.

нераде́ние *n., obs.* = нераде́ивость.

неради́вый *adj.* lackadaisical. —**неради́вость,** *n.f.* lackadaisical attitude.

неразбери́ха *n., colloq.* confusion; chaos; disorder.

неразбо́рчивость *n.f.* **1,** illegibility. **2,** lack of discrimination.

неразбо́рчивый *adj.* **1,** illegible. **2,** not particular; undiscriminating. —**неразбо́рчивый в сре́дствах,** unscrupulous.

неразве́данный *adj.* unexplored; untapped.

нера́звитый *also,* **неразвито́й** *adj.* **1,** undeveloped. **2,** backward; retarded. —**нера́звитость,** *n.f.* backwardness; retardation.

неразга́данный *adj.* unsolved.

неразгово́рчивый *adj.* taciturn; uncommunicative. —**неразгово́рчивость,** *n.f.* taciturnity.

нераздели́мый *adj.* indivisible.

неразде́льный *adj.* **1,** (*of property*) commonly held. **2,** indivisible; inseparable.

неразличи́мый *adj.* **1,** indistinguishable. **2,** indiscernible.

неразлу́чный *adj.* inseparable. —**неразлу́чность,** *n.f.* inseparability.

неразре́занный *adj.* uncut.

неразрешённый *adj.* **1,** unsolved; unresolved. **2,** forbidden; prohibited.

неразреши́мый *adj.* insoluble.

неразруши́мый *adj.* indestructible.

неразры́вный *adj.* indissoluble.

неразу́мный *adj.* **1,** unreasonable; irrational. **2,** unwise; injudicious. —**неразу́мность,** *n.f.* unreasonableness; irrationality.

нераска́янный *adj., obs.* impenitent; unrepentant.

нерасположе́ние *n.* (*with* к) dislike (of/for).

нераспоряди́тельный *adj.* lacking administrative ability.

нераспростране́ние *n.* nonproliferation.

нерасска́занный *adj.* untold.

нерассуди́тельный *adj.* irrational; lacking common sense. —**нерассуди́тельность,** *n.f.* irrationality; lack of common sense.

нераствори́мый *adj.* insoluble; indissoluble.

нерасторжи́мый *adj.* indissoluble.

нерасторо́пный *adj.* sluggish; inert.

нерастро́ганный *adj.* unmoved.

нерасчётливость *n.f.* **1,** extravagance. **2,** lack of foresight; improvidence.

нерасчётливый *adj.* **1,** extravagant; wasteful. **2,** shortsighted; improvident.

нерациона́льный *adj.* inefficient.

нерв *n.* nerve.

нерви́ровать *v. impfv.* [*pres.* -рую, -руешь] to make nervous; unnerve.

нерви́ческий *adj., obs.* nervous.

не́рвничать *v. impfv.* to be nervous; become fidgety.

нервнобольно́й *adj.* suffering from a nervous disorder. —*n.* person suffering from a nervous disorder.

не́рвность *n.f.* nervousness.

не́рвный *adj.* **1,** nerve (*attrib.*): не́рвные кле́тки, nerve cells. **2,** nervous. **3,** irritable; high-strung. **4,** trying (on one's nerves). —**не́рвная систе́ма,** nervous system.

нерво́зный *adj.* nervous; high-strung. —**нерво́зность,** *n.f.* nervousness.

нереа́льный *adj.* **1,** unreal. **2,** unrealistic; impractical.

нерегуля́рный *adj.* irregular. —**нерегуля́рность,** *n.f.* irregularity.

неpе́дкий *adj.* not infrequent; not uncommon.

неpе́дко *adv.* quite often.

нерента́бельный *adj.* unprofitable.

не́рест *n.* spawning. —**нерести́лище,** *n.* spawning ground.

нерешённый *adj.* unresolved; unsolved.

нереши́мость *n.f.* indecision. —**быть в нереши́мости,** to be undecided.

нереши́тельность *n.f.* **1,** indecisiveness. **2,** indecision: быть в нереши́тельности, to be undecided. —**нереши́тельный,** *adj.* irresolute; indecisive.

нержаве́ющий *adj.* rust-resistant. —**нержаве́ющая сталь,** stainless steel.

неритми́чный *adj.* irregular; uneven.

неpо́бкий *adj.* not timid; brave.

неpо́вный *adj.* [*short form* **-вен, -вна́, -вно**] **1,** uneven. **2,** crooked. **3,** (*of one's pulse, breathing, etc.*) irregular. **4,** *fig.* erratic. —**неpо́вно,** *adv.* unevenly. —**неpо́вность,** *n.f.* unevenness.

неpо́вня *also,* **неровня́** *n.m. & f., colloq.* person not the equal of another.

не́рпа *n.* ringed seal.

нерукотво́рный *adj.* not created by human hands.

неpу́сский *adj.* non-Russian.

неруши́мый *adj.* inviolable; indissoluble. —**неруши́-мость,** *n.f.* inviolability.

неpя́ха *n.m. & f.* slovenly person; slob.

неpя́шливый *adj.* **1,** sloppy; slovenly. **2,** slipshod. —**неpя́шливость,** *n.f.;* **неpя́шество,** *n. neut.* sloppiness; slovenliness.

несбы́точный *adj.* unrealizable; vain.

несваре́ние *n., in* **несваре́ние желу́дка,** indigestion.

несве́дущий *adj.* **1,** ignorant; uninformed. **2,** (*with* **в** + *prepl.*) unfamiliar (with); unconversant (with); unversed (in); ungrounded (in).

несве́жий *adj.* **1,** not fresh; stale; spoiled. **2,** worn; dirty; soiled. **3,** worn; tired; drawn.

несвоевре́менно *adv.* **1,** at an inopportune time. **2,** too late.

несвоевре́менный *adj.* **1,** ill-timed; untimely. **2,** tardy; belated.

несвя́зный *adj.* rambling; disconnected; incoherent; disjointed. —**несвя́зность,** *n.f.* incoherence.

несгиба́емый *adj.* unbending; inflexible.

несгово́рчивый *adj.* uncooperative; intractable.

несгора́емый *adj.* fireproof; incombustible; noninflammable. —**несгора́емый шкаф,** safe. —**несгора́емый я́щик,** strongbox.

несде́ржанный *adj.* **1,** broken; unkept. **2,** unrestrained; violent.

несдоброва́ть *v. pfv., used in inf. only with dat. case:* ему́ несдоброва́ть; he is in for trouble.

несекре́тный *adj.* **1,** not secret. **2,** unclassified.

несе́ние *n.* performance; execution; carrying out.

несерьёзный *adj.* **1,** not serious. **2,** casual; lackadaisical. **3,** trivial; unimportant.

несессе́р (нэ-сэ-сэр) *n.* traveling case; toilet case.

несимметри́чный *adj.* asymmetrical. —**несимметри́чность,** *n.f.* asymmetry.

несказа́нный *adj.* indescribable; unspeakable.

нескла́дица *n., colloq.* incoherent talk; nonsense; prattle.

нескла́дный *adj.* **1,** awkward; ungainly. **2,** incoherent. **3,** discordant. **4,** absurd.

несклоня́емый *adj., gram.* indeclinable.

не́сколько *adj.* a few; some; several: не́сколько люде́й, a few people; в не́скольких слова́х, in a few words. —*adv.* somewhat: не́сколько удивлён, somewhat surprised.

несконча́емый *adj.* endless; unending; interminable.

нескро́мность *n.f.* **1,** immodesty. **2,** indiscretion.

нескро́мный *adj.* **1,** immodest. **2,** indiscreet. **3,** indecent.

нескрыва́емый *adj.* unconcealed; undisguised.

несла́женный *adj.* uncoordinated; disorganized.

несло́жный *adj.* uncomplicated; simple.

неслы́ханный *adj.* unheard-of.

неслы́шный *adj.* inaudible.

несме́лый *adj.* timid; diffident.

несменя́емый *adj.* **1,** ever-present; never removed. **2,** (*of a position*) permanent; (*of a person*) having tenure. —**несменя́емость,** *n.f.* irremovability from office; tenure.

несме́тный *adj.* countless; incalculable.

несмолка́емый *adj.* (*of a noise or sound*) incessant.

несмотря́ на (*with acc.*) despite; in spite of. —**несмотря́ ни на что,** despite all; in spite of everything.

несмыва́емый *adj.* indelible.

несмышлёный *adj., colloq.* slow to grasp things; dull; dense.

несно́сный *adj.* unbearable; unendurable.

несоблюде́ние *n.* failure to observe.

несовершенноле́тие *n.* minority (*being under legal age*).

несовершенноле́тний *adj.* under legal age. —*n.* minor.

несоверше́нный *adj.* **1,** imperfect. **2,** *gram.* imperfective: несоверше́нный вид, imperfective aspect.

несоверше́нство *n.* **1,** lack of perfection. **2,** *usu. pl.* imperfection.

несовмести́мый *adj.* incompatible. —**несовмести́мость,** *n.f.* incompatibility.

несогла́сие *n.* **1,** disagreement; difference of opinion. **2,** disagreement; discord. **3,** refusal; rejection.

несогла́сный *adj.* **1,** in disagreement. **2,** (*with* **с** + *instr.*) inconsistent (with). **3,** uncoordinated. **4,** discordant.

несогласо́ванный *adj.* uncoordinated. —**несогласо́ванность,** *n.f.* lack of coordination.

несозна́тельный *adj.* **1,** thoughtless; irresponsible. **2,** lacking political consciousness.

несоизмери́мый *adj.* incommensurable. —**несоизмери́мость,** *n.f.* incommensurability.

несокращённый *adj.* unabridged.

несокруши́мый *adj.* indestructible; unshakable.

несо́лоно *adv., in* **несо́лоно хлеба́вши,** having accomplished nothing.

несомне́нно *adv.* undoubtedly; doubtlessly; indubitably; unquestionably. —*adj., used predicatively* certain: одно́ несомне́нно, one thing is certain.

несомне́нный *adj.* undoubted; indubitable; unquestioned.

несообрази́тельный *adj.* slow to grasp things; dull; dense.

несообра́зный *adj.* **1,** incongruous. **2,** absurd. —**несообра́зность,** *n.f.* incongruity; absurdity.

несоотве́тствие *n.* discrepancy; disparity.

несоразме́рно *adv.* disproportionately. —**несоразме́рно с** (+ *instr.*), out of proportion to.

несоразме́рный *adj.* disproportionate; incommensurate. —**несоразме́рность,** *n.f.* disproportion.

несостоя́тельность *n.f.* **1,** insolvency; bankruptcy. **2,** fallacy.

несостоя́тельный *adj.* **1,** of modest means. **2,** insolvent; bankrupt. **3,** powerless; helpless. **4,** unsound; untenable.

несочу́вствующий *adj.* unsympathetic.

неспе́лый *adj.* unripe.

неспе́шный *adj.* unhurried.

неспоко́йно *adv.* anxiously. —*adj., used predicatively* uneasy: на душе́ у него́ неспоко́йно, he feels uneasy.

неспоко́йный *adj.* **1,** restless. **2,** anxious; uneasy.

неспорти́вный *adj.* unsportsmanlike.

неспосо́бность *n.f.* inability.

неспосо́бный *adj.* [*short form* -бен, -бна] **1,** not bright. **2,** (*with* к) having no aptitude (for). **3,** (with к *or* на) incapable (of).

несправедли́во *adv.* **1,** unjustly; unfairly. **2,** incorrectly; erroneously.

несправедли́вость *n.f.* injustice; unfairness.

несправедли́вый *adj.* **1,** unjust; unfair. **2,** incorrect.

неспровоци́рованный *adj.* unprovoked.

неспроста́ *adv., colloq.* for a definite reason; not by chance.

несравне́нно *adv.* **1,** incomparably. **2,** (*with comparisons*) far; infinitely. —**несравне́нный,** *adj.* incomparable; matchless; peerless.

несравни́мый *adj.* incomparable.

нестерпи́мый *adj.* unbearable; unendurable.

нестеснённый *adj.* uninhibited.

нести́ *v. impfv.* [*pfv.* понести́; *pres.* несу́, несёшь; *past* нёс, несла́, несло́] **1,** to carry. **2,** to carry swiftly; whisk. **3,** to suffer; sustain; incur. **4,** [*impfv. only*] to bear (responsibility). **5,** [*impfv. only*] to perform (duties). Нести́ слу́жбу, *mil.* to serve; see service. **6,** [*impfv. only*] to bring (death, freedom, ruin, etc.). **7,** *impers.* (*with instr.*) *colloq.* to blow: от окна́ несёт хо́лодом, there is a draft from the window. **8,** *impers.* (*with instr.*) to reek (of): от него́ несёт во́дкой, he reeks of vodka. **9,** *colloq.* to talk (nonsense). **10,** [*pfv.* снести́] to lay (eggs). —**нести́сь,** *refl.* **1,** to race; tear along. **2,** *colloq.* to rush; dash. **3,** to float; drift (*on water or through the air*). **4,** to be heard. **5,** [*pfv.* снести́сь] to lay eggs. *See also* носи́ть *and* носи́ться.

несто́йкий *adj.* **1,** unstable. **2,** (*of an odor*) slight; (*of perfume*) weak.

нестоя́щий *adj., colloq.* worthless; good-for-nothing.

нестроево́й *adj.* **1,** unfit for building purposes. **2,** *mil.* noncombatant. —*n., mil.* noncombatant.

нестро́йный *adj.* **1,** ungraceful; ungainly. **2,** irregular; disorderly. **3,** discordant.

несть *predicate, obs.* there is no... —**несть конца́** *or* числа́ (+ *dat.*), there is no end of...

несудохо́дный *adj.* unnavigable.

несура́зный *adj.* **1,** ridiculous; absurd. **2,** awkward; ungainly.

несусве́тный *adj., colloq.* **1,** utter; absolute; unmitigated. **2,** not of this world; not to be believed.

несу́шка [*gen. pl.* -шек] *n.* hen that lays eggs; layer.

несуще́ственный *adj.* minor; unimportant; inconsequential.

несуществу́ющий *adj.* nonexistent.

несхо́дный *adj.* different; dissimilar; disparate. —**несхо́дство,** *n.* difference; dissimilarity; disparity.

несчастли́вец [*gen.* -вца] *n.m.* [*fem.* -вица] *colloq.* unlucky person.

несчастли́вый *adj.* **1,** unhappy. **2,** unlucky; unfortunate.

несча́стный *adj.* **1,** unhappy. **2,** unfortunate. —**несча́стный слу́чай,** accident.

несча́стье *n.* misfortune. —**к несча́стью,** unfortunately.

несчётный *adj.* countless; innumerable.

несъедо́бный *adj.* inedible; uneatable.

нет *neg. particle.* **1,** no. **2,** not: нет ещё, not yet; почему́ нет?, why not? Вы идёте и́ли нет?, are you going or not? Я иду́, а он нет, I am going but he isn't. **3,** (*with gen.*) *indicating the absence of something:* нет вре́мени, there is no time. Его́ нет, he is not here. Там никого́ нет, there is no one there. У меня́ нет спи́чек, I don't have any matches. —**нет и нет** (*with gen.*), not a sign of (someone). —**нет-нет да и,** once in a while. —**своди́ть на нет,** to negate; nullify. —**своди́ться** *or* **сходи́ть на нет,** to come to naught.

нетакти́чный *adj.* tactless. —**нетакти́чность,** *n.f.* tactlessness.

нетала́нтливый *adj.* untalented; lacking talent.

нетвёрдо *adv.* not firmly: нетвёрдо держа́ться на нога́х, to be unsteady on one's feet.

нетвёрдый *adj.* **1,** not hard; soft. **2,** unsteady; shaky. **3,** irresolute; uncertain.

нетерпели́вый *adj.* impatient. —**нетерпели́во,** *adv.* impatiently. —**нетерпели́вость,** *n.f.* impatience.

нетерпе́ние *n.* impatience. —**ждать с нетерпе́нием, 1,** to await impatiently; await anxiously. **2,** to look forward to.

нетерпи́мость *n.f.* intolerance.

нетерпи́мый *adj.* **1,** intolerable. **2,** intolerant.

нетипи́чный *adj.* not typical.

нетле́нный *adj.* **1,** *obs.* imperishable. **2,** *fig.* eternal; immortal.

нетопы́рь [*gen.* -пыря́] *n.m.* pipistrelle (*bat*).

неторопли́вый *adj.* leisurely; unhurried. —**неторопли́во,** *adv.* leisurely.

нето́чность *n.f.* **1,** inaccuracy. **2,** *usu. pl.* inaccuracies.

нето́чный *adj.* inaccurate; inexact; imprecise.

нетре́бовательный *adj.* not demanding; undemanding.

нетре́звый *adj.* not sober; drunk: в нетре́звом ви́де, in a drunken state.

нетро́нутый *adj.* **1,** untouched; untapped. **2,** *fig.* pure; unsullied; virginal. **3,** unmoved.

нетру́дный *adj.* not difficult.

нетрудово́й *adj.* **1,** nonworking. **2,** unearned.

нетрудоспосо́бный *adj.* disabled; incapacitated. —**нетрудоспосо́бность,** *n.f.* disability; incapacity.

не́тто (нэ) *adj. & adv., indecl.* net: вес не́тто, net weight; цена́ не́тто, net price.

не́ту *particle, colloq.* = **нет.**

неубеди́тельный *adj.* unconvincing.

неу́бранный *adj.* **1,** (*of a room*) not straightened up; (*of a bed*) not made; (*of dishes*) not taken away. **2,** (*of crops*) not gathered; not harvested.

неуваже́ние *n.* disrespect; lack of respect.

неуважи́тельный *adj.* **1,** (*of a reason or excuse*) invalid. **2,** *colloq.* disrespectful.

неуве́ренность *n.f.* uncertainty; lack of confidence. —**неуве́ренный**, *adj.* uncertain.

неувяда́емый *adj.* **1**, *obs.* never fading. **2**, *fig.* undying. *Also,* **неувяда́ющий.**

неувя́зка [*gen. pl.* **-зок**] *n., colloq.* mix-up; slip-up; hitch.

неугаси́мый *adj.* **1**, unquenchable. **2**, *fig.* undying.

неуго́дный *adj.* disagreeable; objectionable.

неугомо́нный *adj., colloq.* **1**, indefatigable; always on the go. **2**, (*of a sound or noise*) incessant.

неуда́ча *n.* failure; reverse.

неуда́чливый *adj.* unlucky.

неуда́чник *n.* unlucky person; failure.

неуда́чно *adv.* **1**, unsuccessfully. **2**, poorly; badly.

неуда́чный *adj.* **1**, unsuccessful. **2**, unfortunate; having turned out badly.

неудержи́мый *adj.* irrepressible; uncontrollable.

неудиви́тельный *adj.* not surprising. —**неудиви́тельно**, *adj., used predicatively* not surprising: неудиви́тельно, что..., it is not surprising that...

неудо́бно *adv.* uncomfortably. —*adj., used predicatively* **1**, uncomfortable: мне неудо́бно так лежа́ть, I am uncomfortable lying that way. **2**, inconvenient. **3**, awkward.

неудо́бный *adj.* **1**, uncomfortable. **2**, inconvenient. **3**, awkward.

неудобовари́мый *adj.* indigestible.

неудобопроизноси́мый *adj.* difficult to pronounce; unpronounceable.

неудобочита́емый *adj.* difficult to read.

неудо́бство *n.* **1**, inconvenience; discomfort. **2**, awkwardness; embarrassment.

неудовлетворе́ние *n.* dissatisfaction.

неудовлетворённый *adj.* dissatisfied. —**неудовлетворённость**, *n.f.* dissatisfaction.

неудовлетвори́тельно *adv.* **1**, unsatisfactorily. **2**, (*as a school grade*) "unsatisfactory". —**неудовлетвори́тельный**, *adj.* unsatisfactory.

неудово́льствие *n.* displeasure.

неуёмный *adj., colloq.* **1**, irrepressible; indefatigable. **2**, (*of an emotion*) uncontrollable.

неуже́ли *interr. particle* really?; is it possible?

неужи́вчивый *adj.* hard to get along with.

неузнава́емость *n.f., in* до неузнава́емости, beyond recognition.

неузнава́емый *adj.* unrecognizable.

неука́занный *adj.* **1**, not indicated; unspecified. **2**, *obs.* not permitted.

неукло́нный *adj.* **1**, steady: неукло́нный рост, steady growth. **2**, steadfast; unwavering.

неуклю́жий *adj.* awkward; clumsy. —**неуклю́же**, *adv.* awkwardly; clumsily. —**неуклю́жесть**, *n.f.* awkwardness; clumsiness.

неукосни́тельный *adj.* absolute; total. —**неукосни́тельно**, *adv.* unfailingly.

неукроти́мый *adj.* **1**, untamable. **2**, uncontrollable. **3**, indomitable.

неулови́мый *adj.* **1**, elusive. **2**, barely audible or visible. —**неулови́мость**, *n.f.* elusiveness.

неуме́лый *adj.* clumsy; inept.

неуме́ние *n.* inability; lack of ability.

неуме́ренный *adj.* **1**, immoderate. **2**, intemperate. —**неуме́ренность**, *n.f.* immoderation.

неуме́стность *n.f.* **1**, impropriety. **2**, irrelevance.

неуме́стный *adj.* **1**, inappropriate; out of place; uncalled-for. **2**, irrelevant.

неу́мный *adj.* **1**, unintelligent. **2**, unwise.

неумоли́мый *adj.* **1**, implacable. **2**, inexorable.

неумолка́емый *adj.* (*of a sound or noise*) incessant.

неумо́лчный *adj.* = **неумолка́емый.**

неумы́шленный *adj.* unintentional.

неупла́та *n.* failure to pay; nonpayment.

неупла́ченный *adj.* unpaid; outstanding.

неупотреби́тельный *adj.* not in use.

неуравнове́шенный *adj.* unbalanced; unstable. —**неуравнове́шенность**, *n.f.* (mental) instability.

неурегули́рованный *adj.* (*of questions, issues, etc.*) unsettled; outstanding.

неурожа́й *n.* crop failure; poor harvest. —**неурожа́йный**, *adj., in* неурожа́йный год, year of poor harvest.

неуро́чный *adj.* untimely; inopportune.

неуря́дица *n., colloq.* **1**, confusion; disorder. **2**, squabbling; squabbles.

неуси́дчивый *adj.* **1**, restless. **2**, not diligent; not persevering.

неуспева́емость *n.f.* poor progress (*among pupils*); pupils' failure.

неуспева́ющий *adj.* (*of a student*) poor; not making satisfactory progress.

неуспе́х *n.* failure.

неуспе́шный *adj.* unsuccessful.

неуста́нный *adj.* **1**, untiring; tireless. **2**, unceasing; ceaseless.

неусто́йка *n.* **1**, *law* forfeit. **2**, *colloq.* failure.

неусто́йчивость *n.f.* instability.

неусто́йчивый *adj.* **1**, shaky; unstable; unsteady. **2**, fluctuating; variable; changeable.

неустрани́мый *adj.* **1**, irremovable. **2**, insurmountable. **3**, inevitable.

неустраши́мый *adj.* fearless; intrepid. —**неустраши́мость**, *n.f.* fearlessness; intrepidity.

неустро́енный *adj.* **1**, unsettled. **2**, poorly organized. **3**, not provided for. —**неустро́енность**, *n.f.* unsettled state.

неустро́йство *n.* disorder.

неусту́пчивый *adj.* unyielding; uncompromising. —**неусту́пчивость**, *n.f.* obstinacy; unwillingness to compromise.

неусы́пный *adj.* **1**, untiring; tireless. **2**, unflagging; constant.

неутеши́тельный *adj.* unencouraging; inauspicious.

неуте́шный *adj.* inconsolable; disconsolate.

неутоли́мый *adj.* unquenchable.

неутоми́мый *adj.* indefatigable; tireless. —**неутоми́мость**, *n.f.* indefatigability.

не́уч *n., colloq.* ignoramus.

неучти́вый *adj.* impolite; discourteous. —**неучти́вость**, *n.f.* impoliteness; discourtesy.

неую́тный *adj.* lacking in comforts. —**неую́тно**, *adj., used predicatively* uncomfortable: чу́вствовать себя́ неую́тно, to feel uncomfortable.

неуязви́мый *adj.* invulnerable. —**неуязви́мость**, *n.f.* invulnerability.

нефри́т *n.* **1**, nephritis. **2**, nephrite; jade.

нефтеналивно́й *adj.* carrying oil: нефтеналивно́е су́дно, oil tanker.

нефтено́сный *adj.* containing oil; yielding oil: нефтено́сный сла́нец, oil shale.

нефтеперегóнный *adj.*, *in* **нефтеперегóнный завóд**, oil refinery.

нефтепровóд *n.* oil pipeline.

нефтехими́ческий *adj.* petrochemical.

нефтехрани́лище *n.* oil storage tank.

нефть *n.f.* oil; petroleum.

нефтянóй *adj.* oil (*attrib.*); petroleum (*attrib.*).

нехарактéрный *adj.* not typical.

нехвáтка [*gen. pl.* **-ток**] *n.*, *colloq.* shortage.

нехи́трый *adj.* **1,** without guile; ingenuous. **2,** *colloq.* simple; unpretentious.

неходовóй *adj.* **1,** not in working order; out of commission. **2,** (*of merchandise*) not selling well; not in great demand.

нехорóший *adj.* bad. —**нехорóш собóй**, ugly; unattractive.

нехорошó *adv.* badly. —*adj.*, *used predicatively* **1,** not good; bad: нехорошó, что…, it's not good that… **2,** ill: емý стáло нехорошó, he began to feel ill.

нéхотя *adv.* **1,** unwillingly; reluctantly. **2,** accidentally; inadvertently.

нецелесообрáзный *adj.* **1,** inadvisable. **2,** pointless.

нецензýрный *adj.* unprintable; obscene.

нецеремóнный *adj.* unceremonious.

нецивилизóванный *adj.* uncivilized.

нечáянный *adj.* **1,** unexpected; chance. **2,** accidental; inadvertent. —**нечáянно,** *adv.* accidentally; inadvertently; by chance.

нéчего *indef. pron.*, *gen. & acc.* [*dat.* **нéчему;** *instr.* **нéчем;** *prepl.* **нé** (+ *prep.*) **чем**] *used with inf.* there is nothing: нéчего читáть, there is nothing to read. Мне нéчего дéлать, I have nothing to do. —*adv.*, *colloq. used with inf.* **1,** there is no need: нéчего беспокóиться, there is no need to worry. **2,** there is no point; it is no use: нéчего жáловаться, there is no point (*or* it's no use) complaining. —**нéчего и говори́ть; и говори́ть нéчего**, *see* **говори́ть.** —**нéчего сказáть, 1,** of course; to be sure. **2,** I must say! —**от нéчего дéлать,** having nothing better to do.

нечеловéческий *adj.* **1,** inhuman. **2,** superhuman.

нечёсаный *adj.* unkempt.

нечести́вый *adj.*, *obs.* wicked; unholy.

нечéстный *adj.* dishonest. —**нечéстно,** *adv.* dishonestly. —**нечéстность,** *n.f.* dishonesty.

нéчет *n.*, *colloq.* odd number.

нечёткий *adj.* **1,** unclear; illegible. **2,** careless; slipshod.

нечётный *adj.* (*of a number*) odd.

нечистокрóвный *adj.* half-blooded.

нечистоплóтный *adj.* **1,** dirty; sloppy. **2,** *fig.* unscrupulous; shady.

нечистотá [*pl.* **-тóты**] *n.* **1,** uncleanliness; impurity. **2,** *pl.* sewage. **3,** *pl.* impurities.

нечи́стый *adj.* **1,** unclean; dirty. **2,** impure; adulterated. **3,** (*of sounds or speech*) unclear. **4,** *fig.* dishonest; shady. —**нá руку нечи́ст,** light-fingered.

нéчисть *n.f.*, *colloq.* **1,** evil spirits. **2,** *fig.* scum.

нечленораздéльный *adj.* inarticulate; unintelligible.

нéчто *indef. pron.* something.

нечувстви́тельный *adj.* insensitive. —**нечувстви́тельность,** *n.f.* insensitivity.

нечýткий *adj.* **1,** insensitive; not keen; dull. **2,** insensitive; not caring; indifferent.

нешýточный *adj.*, *colloq.* not to be taken lightly: нешýточное дéло, no laughing matter.

нещáдный *adj.* merciless. —**нещáдно,** *adv.* mercilessly.

неэконóмный *adj.* uneconomical.

неэкспони́рованный *adj.* (*of film*) unexposed.

неэтили́рованный *adj.* (*of gasoline*) unleaded.

неэти́чный *adj.* unethical.

неэффекти́вность *n.f.* **1,** inefficacy. **2,** inefficiency.

неэффекти́вный *adj.* **1,** ineffective. **2,** inefficient.

нея́вка *n.* failure to appear.

нея́ркий *adj.* **1,** dim; faint. **2,** pale; subdued.

нея́сно *adv.* dimly; faintly. —*adj.*, *used predicatively* unclear: ещё нея́сно, что бýдет, it is still unclear as to what will happen.

нея́сность *n.f.* **1,** lack of clarity; vagueness. **2,** unclear point; ambiguity.

нея́сный *adj.* [*short form* **-сен, -снá, -сно**] **1,** unclear; indistinct. **2,** (*of sounds*) faint; indistinct. **3,** vague.

нея́сыть *n.f.* tawny owl.

ни *neg. particle* **1,** not a: на нéбе ни óблачка, there is not a cloud in the sky. ♦*Often used with* оди́н: он не сказáл ни одногó слóва, he did not say a single word. **2,** *occurring as a separate word when* никтó, ничтó, никакóй, *and their oblique case forms are separated to permit the insertion of a preposition in between:* ни за что на свéте, not for anything in the world. Он не отвечáл ни на какúе вопрóсы, he did not answer any questions. Я ни с кем не встрéтился, I did not meet anyone. —*indef. particle*, *equivalent to English* -ever: что ни *or* что бы ни, whatever; где ни *or* где бы ни, wherever. Кто бы он нú был, whoever he is. Кудá ни посмóтришь, wherever you look. —**ни…ни,** neither …nor: ни за ни прóтив, neither for nor against; ни тот ни другóй, neither one.

ни́ва *n.* **1,** field of grain. **2,** *fig.* field (of endeavor): на нúве просвещéния, in the field of education.

нивели́р *n.* level (*instrument*).

нивели́ровать *v. impfv. & pfv.* [*pres.* **-рую, -руешь**] to level.

нивелирóвка *n.* leveling.

нивя́ник *n.* (oxeye) daisy.

нигдé *adv.* nowhere; no place.

нигили́зм *n.* nihilism. —**нигили́ст,** *n.* nihilist. —**нигили́стический,** *adj.* nihilistic.

нидерлáндец [*gen.* **-дца**] *n.m.* [*fem.* **-дка**] Dutchman. —**нидерлáндский,** *adj.* Dutch; Netherlands (*attrib.*).

ни́же *adj.*, *comp. of* **ни́зкий.** —*adv.* below. —*prep.*, *with gen.* **1,** below: нúже нуля́, below zero. **2,** beneath: нúже егó достóинства, beneath his dignity.

нижеподписáвшийся *n.*, *decl. as an adj.* the undersigned.

нижеслéдующий *adj.* the following.

нижестоя́щий *adj.* (*of an organization, governmental body, etc.*) lower-level.

ни́жний *adj.* **1,** lower. **2,** bottom. —**ни́жнее бельё,** underwear. —**ни́жняя рубáшка,** undershirt. —**ни́жний этáж,** ground floor.

низ [*2nd loc.* **низý;** *pl.* **низы́**] *n.* **1,** bottom. **2,** *pl.*, *music* low notes. **3,** *pl.*, *colloq.* lower classes; lower strata.

низáть *v. impfv.* [*pfv.* **нанизáть;** *pres.* **нижý, ни́жешь**] to string; thread.

низвергáть *v. impfv.* [*pfv.* **низвéргнуть**] **1,** to throw (down); plunge. **2,** *fig.* to overthrow; bring down. —**низвергáться,** *refl.* (*of water*) to come rushing down; cascade down.

низвéргнуть [*past* -вéрг, -ла] *v.*, *pfv. of* низвергáть. —**низвéргнуться**, *refl.*, *pfv. of* низвергáться.
низвержéние *n.* overthrow.
низвестú [*infl. like* вестú] *v.*, *pfv. of* низводúть.
низводúть *v. impfv.* [*pfv.* низвестú; *pres.* -вожý, -вóдишь] **1,** to bring down. **2,** *fig.* (*with* до) to reduce (to).
низúна *n.* low-lying area. —**низúнный**, *adj.* low-lying.
нúзкий *adj.* [*short form* нúзок, низкá, нúзко; *comp.* нúже] **1,** low. **2,** (*of quality*) poor. **3,** base; despicable. **4,** (*of a sound, voice, etc.*) deep. —**нúзкого рóста**, short (*in height*).
нúзко *adv.* **1,** low: поклонúться нúзко, to bow low. **2,** despicably.
низкооплáчиваемый *adj.* low-paid.
низкопоклóнник *n.* sycophant.
низкопоклóнничать *v. impfv.* (*with* пéред) to grovel (before); bow and scrape (before).
низкопоклóнство *n.* servility.
низкопрóбный *adj.* **1,** (*of gold or silver*) base-alloy; low-grade. **2,** *fig.* low-grade; second-rate.
низкорóслый *adj.* undersized.
низкосóртный *adj.* low-quality; low-grade.
низлагáть *v. impfv.* [*pfv.* низложúть] to overthrow; depose; bring down.
низложéние *n.* overthrow.
низложúть [*infl.* -ложý, -лóжишь] *v.*, *pfv. of* низлагáть.
нúзменность *n.f.* **1,** lowland. **2,** baseness; meanness.
нúзменный *adj.* **1,** *geog.* low-lying. **2,** base; mean.
низовóй *adj.* **1,** low; close to the ground. **2,** located downstream. **3,** local; at the local level.
низóвье *n.* lower reaches (*of a river*).
нúзом *adv.* along the bottom; along the lower route.
нúзость *n.f.* baseness; meanness.
нúзший *adj.*, *superl. of* нúзкий, lowest. —**нúзшее образовáние**, elementary education.
никáк *adv.* (in) no way: я никáк не мог открыть дверь, there was no way I could open the door; I simply could not open the door. Никáк не могу вспомнить, I simply (*or* just) can't remember. Это никáк не помóжет, that won't help at all. —**никáк нельзя́**, absolutely impossible.
никакóй *adj.* not any; no: не мóжет быть никакóго сомнéния, there can be no doubt. Никаких извинéний!, no apologies!
нúкелевый *adj.* nickel.
никелировáть *v. impfv. & pfv.* [*pres.* -рýю, -рýешь] to plate with nickel; nickel-plate.
никелирóвка *n.* **1,** nickel-plating. **2,** nickle plate.
нúкель *n.m.* nickel.
никéм *pron.*, *instr. of* никтó.
нúкнуть *v. impfv.* [*pfv.* понúкнуть; *past* ник *or* нúкнул, нúкла] to droop.
никогдá *adv.* never. —**бóльше никогдá**, never again. —**как никогдá**, more than ever; as never before. —**никогдá ещё**, never before.
никогó *pron.*, *gen. & acc. of* никтó.
никóй *adj.*, *in* никóим óбразом *and* ни в кóем слýчае, under no circumstances.
никомý *pron.*, *dat. of* никтó.
никотúн *n.* nicotine. —**никотúнный**; **никотúновый**, *adj.* nicotine (*attrib.*).
никтó *indef. pron.* [*gen. & acc.* никогó; *dat.* никомý; *instr.* никéм; *prepl.* ни (+ *prep.*) ком] no one; nobody.

никудá *adv.* nowhere; no place. —**никудá не годúться**, to be of no use; be no good at all.
никудышный *adj.*, *colloq.* useless; worthless; good-for-nothing.
никчёмный *adj.*, *colloq.* useless; worthless; good-for-nothing. —**никчёмность**, *n.f.*, *colloq.* uselessness; worthlessness.
ним *pron.*, variant of им, used after prepositions.
нимáло *adv.* not at all; not in the least; not a bit.
нимб *n.* nimbus.
нúми *pron.*, variant of úми, used after prepositions.
нúмфа *n.* nymph.
нимфомáния *n.* nymphomania. —**нимфомáнка**, *n.* nymphomaniac.
ниóбий *n.* niobium.
ниодúмий *n.* neodymium.
ниоткýда *adv.* from nowhere; not from anywhere.
нипочём *adv.*, *colloq.* **1,** (*with dat.*) it is nothing (for someone): емý нипочём пройти двáдцать килóметров, it is nothing for him to walk twenty kilometers. **2,** dirt-cheap.
нúппель [*pl.* ниппеля́] *n.m.* nipple (*threaded pipe*).
нирвáна *n.* nirvana.
нисколько *adv.* not at all; not a bit; not in the least.
ниспадáть *v. impfv.* to hand down.
ниспровергáть *v. impfv.* [*pfv.* ниспровéргнуть] to overthrow.
ниспровéргнуть [*past* -вéрг, -ла] *v.*, *pfv. of* ниспровергáть.
ниспровержéние *n.* overthrow.
нисходя́щий *adj.* descending.
нúтка [*gen. pl.* -ток] *n.* **1,** thread. **2,** string (*of pearls, beads, etc.*). —**до нúтки**, **1,** (*with* всё) down to the last penny. **2,** (*with the verb* промóкнуть) to the skin. —**на живýю нúтку**, hastily; crudely. —**шит бéлыми нúтками**, transparent; poorly disguised.
нúточка [*gen. pl.* -чек] *n.*, *dim. of* нúтка.
нúточный *adj.* of or for thread.
нитрáт *n.* nitrate. —**нитрáтный**, *adj.* containing nitrate; nitrate (*attrib.*).
нитрúт *n.* nitrite.
нитроглицерúн *n.* nitroglycerin(e).
нить *n.f.* **1,** thread. **2,** filament. **3,** suture. —**потеря́ть нить разговóра**, to lose the thread of the conversation. —**проходúть крáсной нúтью** (*with* в + *prepl. or* чéрез) to be the dominant theme of; run through.
нúтяный *adj.* made of thread.
них *pers. pron.*, *var. of* их, used after prepositions.
ниц *adv.* with one's face touching the ground. —**пасть ниц**, to prostrate oneself.
ничегó *pron.*, *gen. of* ничтó, nothing: ничегó осóбенного, nothing special. —*adv. & adj.*, *colloq.* [*also*, **ничегó себé**] not bad; pretty good; pretty well. —**ничегó!**, no matter!; it doesn't matter!; never mind!
ничегонедéлание *n.*, *colloq.* idleness.
ничéй *indef. pron.* [*infl. like* чей] nobody's; no one's. —**ничья́ земля́**, no man's land.
ничéйный *adj.* **1,** *sports*; *games* drawn; tied. **2,** *colloq.* no man's: ничéйная земля́, no man's land.
ничéм *pron.*, *instr. of* ничтó.
ничемý *pron.*, *dat. of* ничтó.
ничкóм *adv.* prone; face down.
ничтó *indef. pron.* [*gen. & acc.* ничегó; *dat.* ничемý; *instr.* ничéм; *prepl.* ни (+ *prep.*) чём] nothing. *See also* ничегó.

ничтóжество *n.* nonentity; nobody.

ничтóжность *n.f.* **1,** insignificance. **2,** nonentity; nobody.

ничтóжный *adj.* **1,** (*of an amount*) insignificant; infinitesimal; paltry. **2,** insignificant; meaningless. **3,** (*of a person*) worthless; good-for-nothing.

ничýть *adv., colloq.* not at all; not the least; not a bit. —**ничýть не бывáло,** *colloq.* **1,** not at all; not in the least. **2,** but it was not that way; but that was not the case.

ничья́ [*gen., dat., & instr.* **ничьéй;** *acc.* **ничью́**] *n.*, *sports; games* tie; draw.

нúша *n.* niche; recess; alcove.

нища́ть *v. impfv.* [*pfv.* **обнища́ть**] to become impoverished.

нúщенка [*gen. pl.* **-нок**] *n.* beggar (woman).

нúщенский *adj.* **1,** beggarly. **2,** *fig.* paltry.

нúщенство *n.* **1,** begging. **2,** poverty; destitution.

нúщенствовать *v. impfv.* [*pres.* **-ствую, -ствуешь**] **1,** to beg; go begging. **2,** to live in poverty.

нищетá *n.* poverty.

нúщий *adj.* destitute; poverty-stricken. —*n.* beggar.

но *conj.* but.

Нóбелевский *adj.,* in **Нóбелевская прéмия,** Nobel Prize.

нобéлий *n.* nobelium.

новáтор *n.* innovator. —**новáторский,** *adj.* innovative. —**новáторство,** *n.* innovation.

новéйший *adj., superl. of* **нóвый,** newest; latest.

новéлла *n.* short story; novella.

новеллúст *n.* short story writer.

нóвенький *adj.* new. —*n.,* *colloq.* **1,** newcomer. **2,** freshman. —**что нóвенького?,** *colloq.* what's new?

новизнá *n.* novelty; newness.

новúнка [*gen. pl.* **-нок**] *n.* something new: кнúжные новúнки, new books. —**э́то мне в новúнку,** it is new to me; it is something I've never done before.

новичóк [*gen.* **-чка́**] *n.* **1,** novice. **2,** new boy *or* girl (*in school*).

новобрáнец [*gen.* **-нца**] *n.* recruit.

новобрáчный *n., decl. as an adj.* newlywed.

нововведéние *n.* innovation.

новогóдний *adj.* New Year's.

новогрéческий *adj.* modern Greek.

новозавéтный *adj.* New Testament (*attrib.*).

новозелáндец [*gen.* **-дца**] *n.m.* [*fem.* **-дка**] New Zealander. —**новозелáндский,** *adj.* New Zealand (*attrib.*).

новоиспечённый *adj., colloq.* **1,** newly made. **2,** newly appointed.

новокаúн *n.* novocaine. —**новокаúновый,** *adj.* novocaine.

новолýние *n.* new moon.

новомóдный *adj.* **1,** in the latest style. **2,** (*of words*) currently fashionable.

новообразовáние *n.* **1,** new formation; neoplasm; new growth. **3,** newly coined word.

новообращённый *adj.* newly converted (*to another religion*). —*n.* neophyte; convert; proselyte.

новоприбы́вший *adj.* newly arrived; recently arrived. —*n.* newcomer.

новорождённый *adj.* newborn. —*n.* newborn baby.

новосёл *n.* **1,** new settler. **2,** new tenant.

новосéлье *n.* **1,** new home. **2,** housewarming.

новострóйка [*gen. pl.* **-óек**] *n.* **1,** new building. **2,** construction project.

нóвость [*pl.* **нóвости, -стéй, -стя́м**] *n.f.* **1,** news. **2,** a novelty; something new. **3,** newness.

нóвшество *n.* innovation; novelty.

нóвый *adj.* [*short form* нов, нова́, нóво] **1,** new. **2,** (*of history, languages, etc.*) modern. —**Нóвый год,** the New Year. —**Нóвый свет,** the New World. —**нóвый стиль,** New Style (*of dates*). —**что нóвого?,** what's new?

новь *n.f.* virgin soil.

ногá [*acc.* **нóгу;** *pl.* **нóги, ног, нога́м**] *n.* **1,** leg. **2,** foot. —**быть без ног,** to be falling off one's feet. —**вверх нога́ми,** upside down; topsy-turvy. —**идтú в нóгу,** to keep in step. —**идтú в нóгу с,** to keep up with; keep pace with. —**идтú ногá зá ногу,** to amble along. —**к ногé!,** *mil.* order arms! —**на дрýжеской** (*or* на корóткой) **ногé с,** on good terms with. —**на нога́х, 1,** on one's feet. **2,** awake; up. **3,** on the go. **4,** up and about. —**на ра́вной ногé с,** on an equal footing with. —**ни ногóй,** never going to: мы тудá ни ногóй, we never set foot in there. —**однá нога́ здесь, другáя там,** be quick about it! —**со всех ног,** as fast as one's legs would carry one. —**с головы́ до ног,** from head to toe.

ногáец [*gen.* **-áйца**] *n.m.* [*fem.* **-áйка**] Nogai (*one of a people inhabiting the Caucasus*). —**ногáйский,** *adj.* Nogai.

ноготкú [*pl.* **-кóв**] *n. pl.* marigold.

нóготь [*gen.* **-гтя;** *pl.* **нóгти, -тéй, -тя́м**] *n.m.* nail; fingernail; toenail. —**до концá ногтéй,** to the tips of one's toes.

нож [*gen.* **ножá**] *n.* knife. —**быть на ножа́х,** to be at swords' points.

ножевóй *also,* **ножóвый** *adj.* knife (*attrib.*). —**ножевóй товáр; ножевы́е издéлия,** cutlery.

нóжик *n.* small knife.

нóжка [*gen. pl.* **-жек**] *n.* **1,** *dim. of* ногá. **2,** leg (*of a chair, table, etc.*). **3,** stem (*of a goblet*). **4,** stem (*of a mushroom*).

нóжницы [*gen.* **-ниц**] *n. pl.* **1,** scissors. **2,** shears.

ножнóй *adj.* foot (*attrib.*).

нóжны [*gen.* **нóжен**] *n. pl.* scabbard; sheath. *Also,* ножны́ [*gen.* ножóн].

ножóвка [*gen. pl.* **-вок**] *n.* handsaw; hacksaw.

ноздрева́тый *adj.* porous.

ноздря́ [*pl.* **нóздри, -рéй, -ря́м**] *n.* nostril.

нокáут *n., boxing* knockout.

нокаутúровать *v. impfv. & pfv.* [*pres.* **-рую, -руешь**] *boxing* to knock out.

нокдáун *n., boxing* knockdown.

ноктю́рн *n.* nocturne.

нолевóй *adj.* = **нулевóй.**

ноль [*gen.* **ноля́**] *n.m.* = **нуль.**

номенклатýра *n.* **1,** nomenclature. **2,** *USSR, colloq.* top-level governmental positions. —**номенклатýрный,** *adj.* (*of a post or the person holding it*) top-level.

нóмер [*pl.* **номерá**] *n.* **1,** number. **2,** issue (*of a newspaper*). **3,** size (*of an article of clothing*). **4,** hotel room. **5,** number; item (*on a program*). **6,** *colloq.* trick; ploy: нóмер не прошёл, the ploy didn't work.

номернóй *adj.* containing a number: номернóй знак, license plate.—*n.* room attendant (*in a hotel*).

номерóк [*gen.* **-рка́**] *n.* **1,** small room (*in a hotel*). **2,** check; ticket.

номина́л *n.*, *finance* par; face value.

номина́льный *adj.* nominal.

нора́ [*pl.* но́ры] *n.* hole; burrow (*of an animal*).

норве́жец [*gen.* -жца] *n.m.* [*fem.* -жка] Norwegian. —**норве́жский**, *adj.* Norwegian.

норд *n.*, *naut.* **1,** north. **2,** north wind.

норд-ве́ст *n.*, *naut.* **1,** northwest. **2,** northwester (*wind*).

но́рдовый *adj.*, *naut.* north.

норд-о́ст *n.*, *naut.* **1,** northeast. **2,** northeaster (*wind*).

но́рка [*gen. pl.* -рок] *n.* **1,** *dim. of* **нора́**. **2,** mink. —**но́рковый**, *adj.* mink (*attrib.*).

но́рма *n.* **1,** norm; standard. **2,** quota. **3,** rate. —**войти́ в но́рму**, to return to normal.

нормализа́ция *n.* normalization.

нормализова́ть *v. impfv. & pfv.* [*pres.* -зу́ю, -зу́ешь] **1,** to standardize. **2,** to normalize.

норма́ль *n.f.*, *math.* normal.

норма́льно *adv.* normally. —*adj.*, *used predicatively*, *colloq.* all right; O.K.: всё норма́льно, everything is all right/O.K. —**норма́льность**, *n.f.* normality. —**норма́льный**, *adj.* normal.

норма́ндский *adj.* Norman: Норма́ндское завое-ва́ние А́нглии, the Norman Conquest.—**Норма́ндские острова́**, Channel Islands.

норма́нн *n.* Norseman. —**норма́нский**; **норма́ннский**, *adj.* Norse.

нормати́в *n.* norm. —**нормати́вный**, *adj.* normative.

нормирова́ние *n.* **1,** standardization; setting of norms. **2,** rationing.

нормирова́ть *v. impfv. & pfv.* [*pres.* -ру́ю, -ру́ешь] **1,** to standardize; set. **2,** to ration.

но́ров *n.*, *colloq.* character; temperament; disposition. —**с но́ровом**, (*of a person*) stubborn; strong-willed; (*of a horse*) restive; balky.

норови́стый *adj.*, *colloq.* (*of a horse*) restive; balky.

норови́ть *v. impfv.* [*pres.* -влю́, -ви́шь] *colloq.* to try (to).

нос [*2nd loc.* носу́; *pl.* носы́] *n.* **1,** nose. **2,** *naut.* prow; bow. **3,** *geog.* point. —**води́ть за́ нос**, to lead (someone) on; string (someone) along; take in. —**из-под са́мого но́са**, from under one's very nose. —**на носу́**, near at hand; just around the corner: весна́ на носу́, spring is just around the corner. —**под са́мым но́сом**; **под носом**, under one's very nose. —**оста́вить с но́сом**, *colloq.* to leave (someone) holding the bag. —**оста́ться с но́сом**, *colloq.* to be left holding the bag. —**с но́са**; **с но́су**, *colloq.* apiece; a head.

носа́тый *adj.*, *colloq.* big-nosed.

но́сик *n.* **1,** *dim. of* **нос. 2,** spout (*on a teapot, watering can, etc.*).

носи́лки [*gen.* -лок] *n. pl.* stretcher; litter.

носи́льщик *n.* porter.

носи́тель *n.m.* **1,** transmitter (*e.g. of new ideas*). **2,** speaker (*of a certain language*). **3,** carrier (*of a disease*).

носи́ть *v. impfv.* [*pres.* ношу́, но́сишь] **1,** *indeterm. of* нести́. Носи́ть ору́жие, to bear arms. **2,** to wear. **3,** to bear (characteristics, traces, etc.). **4,** *in* носи́ть на рука́х, to dote on. —**носи́ться**, *refl.* **1,** *indeterm. of* нести́сь. **2,** to rush about; dash about. **3,** (*of clothing*) to wear: э́то пла́тье хорошо́ но́сится, this dress wears well. **4,** (*with* с + *instr.*) *colloq.* to fuss (over); make too much (of).

но́ска *n.* **1,** carrying. **2,** wearing; wear: от до́лгой но́ски, from long wear. **3,** laying (*of eggs*).

но́ский *adj.* **1,** *colloq.* giving long wear; durable. **2,** producing eggs in large quantity: но́ская ку́рица, a good layer.

носово́й *adj.* nose (*attrib.*); nasal. —**носово́й ко́нус**, nose cone. —**носово́й плато́к**, handkerchief.

носо́к [*gen.* -ска́] *n.* **1,** sock. **2,** toe (*of a shoe*).

носоро́г *n.* rhinoceros.

ностальги́я *n.* nostalgia. —**ностальги́ческий**, *adj.* nostalgic.

носу́ха *n.* coati.

но́та *n.* **1,** *music* note. **2,** *pl. music*: игра́ть по но́там, to play from music. **3,** *dipl.* note. —**разы́грывать (что́-нибудь) как по но́там**, to carry out like clockwork.

нота́риус *n.* notary public. —**нотариа́льный**, *adj.* notary (*attrib.*).

нота́ция *n.* **1,** notation. **2,** admonition; talking-to: чита́ть нота́цию (+ *dat.*), to give someone a talking-to.

но́тка [*gen. pl.* -ток] *n.* faint note; trace; hint; suggestion.

но́тный *adj. music* (*attrib.*): но́тный пюпи́тр, music stand. —**но́тный стан**, *music* staff.

нотоно́сец [*gen.* -сца] *n.*, *music* staff.

ночева́ть *v. impfv. & pfv.* [*pres.* -чу́ю, -чу́ешь] to spend the night.

ночёвка *n.*, *colloq.* spending the night.

ночле́г *n.* **1,** place to spend the night. **2,** spending the night: останови́ться на ночле́г, to stop for the night; spend the night.

ночле́жка [*gen. pl.* -жек] *n.*, *colloq.* = **ночле́жный дом**.

ночле́жный *adj.*, *in* **ночле́жный дом**, flophouse.

ночни́к [*gen.* -ника́] *n.* night light.

ночно́й *adj.* night (*attrib.*). —**ночно́й горшо́к**, chamber pot. —**ночно́й сто́лик**, night table.

ночь [*pl.* но́чи, ноче́й,ноча́м] *n.f.* night. —**на́ ночь, 1,** for the night; overnight. **2,** before going to bed. —**по ноча́м**, at night. —**споко́йной но́чи!**, good night! **но́чью** *adv.* at night.

но́ша *n.* **1,** load. **2,** *fig.* burden.

ноше́ние *n.* **1,** carrying; bearing. **2,** wearing.

но́щно *adv.*, *in* **де́нно и но́щно**, *colloq.* day and night.

но́ющий *adj.* (*of a pain*) gnawing; nagging.

ноя́брь [*gen.* -бря́] *n.m.* November. —**ноя́брьский**, *adj.* November (*attrib.*).

нрав *n.* disposition; temperament. —**быть** (*or* приходи́ться) **по нра́ву** (+ *dat.*), to please: всё ему́ не по нра́ву, nothing pleases him. *See also* **нра́вы**.

нра́виться *v.r. impfv.* [*pfv.* понра́виться; *pres.* -влюсь, -вишься] (*with dat.*) to please; be to the liking of: она́ мне нра́вится, I like her; пье́са мне не понра́вилась, I did not like (*or* enjoy) the play.

нравоуче́ние *n.* moral admonition.

нравоучи́тельный *adj.* moralizing; moralistic.

нра́вственно *adv.* morally.

нра́вственность *n.f.* **1,** morality. **2,** morals.

нра́вственный *adj.* moral.

нра́вы [*gen.* нрав] *n. pl.* customs; ways; way of life.

ну *interj.* **1,** well; well then; why; now: ну, я пошёл, well, I'm off; ну, коне́чно!, why of course! —а ну (+ *gen.*), to hell with...—**да ну?**, you don't say so! —**ну и...**, what...!: ну и пого́да!, what weather! —**ну и что?**, well, what of it?

нуга́ *n.* nougat.

ну́дный *adj.*, *colloq.* **1,** boring; tiresome. **2,** inane.

нужда́ [*pl.* ну́жды] *n.* **1,** (dire) need; dire straits: жить в нужде́, to live in dire straits. **2,** need; necessity: в слу́чае нужды́, in case of need; if need be. **3,** *pl.* needs: ну́жды населе́ния, the needs of the populace.

нужда́ться *v.r. impfv.* **1,** to be in need; be poor. **2,** (*with* в + *prepl.*) to need; be in need of.

ну́жно *adv.* **1,** (one) must; (one) has to; (one) needs to: э́то ну́жно сде́лать сейча́с, this must be done at once; мне ну́жно идти́, I have to go. **2,** needed: для чего́ э́то вам ну́жно?, what do you need that for?

ну́жный *adj.* [*short form* ну́жен, нужна́, ну́жно, ну́жны] **1,** necessary: ну́жные да́нные, the necessary data. Находи́ть ну́жным (+ *inf.*), to find it necessary to. **2,** needed: я здесь ну́жен (нужна́), I am needed here. **3,** (*with dat.*) one needs: ему́ ну́жен о́тдых, he needs rest; мне нужны́ де́ньги, I need money.

ну́-ка *interj., colloq.* well?; well then?; how about it?

нулево́й *adj.* zero (*attrib.*).

нуль [*gen.* нуля́] *n.m.* **1,** zero; naught. **2,** *fig.* (*of a person*) a nothing; a nobody. —своди́ть к нулю́, to negate; nullify. —своди́ться к нулю́, to come to naught.

нумера́тор *n.* numbering machine.

нумера́ция *n.* numeration; numbering.

нумеро́ванный *adj.* numbered. —**нумеро́ванное ме́сто**, reserved seat.

нумерова́ть *v. impfv.* [*pfv.* занумерова́ть *or* пронумерова́ть; *pres.* -ру́ю, -ру́ешь] to number.

нумизма́тика *n.* numismatics. —**нумизма́т**, *n.* numismatist. —**нумизмати́ческий**, *adj.* numismatic.

ну́нций *n.* nuncio.

нут *n.* chickpea.

ну́трия *n.* coypu; nutria.

нутро́ *n., colloq.* **1,** insides; innards. **2,** interior. **3,** essence. **4,** instinct. —**не по нутру́** (+ *dat.*), not to one's liking.

ны́не *adv.* now.

ны́нешний *adj., colloq.* present.

ны́нче *adv., colloq.* now; nowadays. —**не ны́нче — за́втра**, any day now.

нырну́ть *v., pfv. of* ныря́ть.

ныро́к [*gen.* -рка́] *n.* **1,** *colloq.* dive. **2,** pochard (*duck*).

ныря́льщик *n., colloq.* diver.

ныря́ть *v. impfv.* [*pfv.* нырну́ть] to dive.

ны́тик *n., colloq.* whiner.

ныть *v. impfv.* [*pres.* но́ю, но́ешь] **1,** to ache. **2,** *colloq.* to whine.

нытьё *n.* **1,** whining; complaining. **2,** dull pain.

нэп *n., abbrev. of* но́вая экономи́ческая поли́тика, N.E.P.; New Economic Policy (1921-27).

нюа́нс *n.* nuance.

ню́ни *n. pl., in* распуска́ть ню́ни, *colloq.* **1,** to start crying. **2,** to whine; start whining.

ню́ня *n.m. & f., colloq.* crybaby; whiner.

нюх *n., colloq.* **1,** sense of smell (*of an animal*). **2,** *fig.* (keen) sense: име́ть нюх на, to have a nose for.

ню́хательный *adj.* for smelling; to be smelled: ню́хательная соль, smelling salts. —**ню́хательный таба́к**, snuff.

ню́хать *v. impfv.* [*pfv.* поню́хать] to smell; sniff; take a whiff of.

ня́нчить *v. impfv.* to nurse; take care of. —**ня́нчиться**, *refl.* (*with* с + *instr.*) **1,** to nurse; take care of. **2,** *colloq.* to fuss with.

ня́нька [*gen. pl.* -нек] *n., colloq.* = ня́ня.

ня́ня *n.* **1,** nurse; nursemaid. **2,** *colloq.* nurse's aide.

О

О, о *n. neut.* fifteenth letter of the Russian alphabet.

о[1] *also,* об *and* обо *prep.* A, *with prepl.* about; of: говори́ть о поли́тике, to talk about politics; кни́га о Че́хове, a book about Chekhov. Он ду́мает то́лько о себе́, he thinks only of himself. В, *with acc.* **1,** against (*involving contact or collision*): опира́ться о сте́ну, to lean against the wall; во́лны бью́тся о бе́рег, the waves are beating against the shore. **2,** *in* бок о́ бок, side by side; рука́ о́б руку, hand in hand.

о[2] *interj.* oh!

о- *also,* об-, обо-, объ- *prefix* **1,** *indicating motion around:* обходи́ть, to walk around; оплыва́ть, to swim around. **2,** *indicating action affecting everyone present:* обноси́ть, to serve (everyone present). **3,** *indicating the gaining of an advantage:* обы́грывать, to beat; defeat; обсчи́тывать, to shortchange. **4,** (*with* -ся) *indicating a mistake or misstep:* ослы́шаться, to hear incorrectly; оступи́ться, to stumble. **5,** (*with* -ся) *indicating excess:* объеда́ться, to overeat.

оа́зис *n.* oasis.

об *prep.* = о (*used when the word following begins with a vowel*).

о́ба [*fem.* о́бе; *gen. & prepl.* обо́их, обе́их; *dat.* обо́им, обе́им; *instr.* обо́ими, обе́ими] *numeral, m. & neut.* (*nominative forms govern gen. sing.*) both: о́ба ма́льчика, both boys; обе́ими рука́ми, with both hands. —смотре́ть *or* гляде́ть в о́ба, **1,** to be on one's guard. **2,** (*with* в/на + *acc. or* за + *instr.*) to keep a watchful eye on.

обагря́ть *v. impfv.* [*pfv.* обагри́ть] to give a reddish or purplish hue to. —**обагря́ть кро́вью**, to stain with blood.

обалде́лый *adj., colloq.* dazed; groggy.

обалде́ть *v. pfv., colloq.* to lose one's wits.

обанкро́титься *v.r. pfv.* [*infl.* -чусь, -тишься] to go bankrupt.

обая́ние *n.* charm; attraction.

обая́тельный *adj.* charming; enchanting.

обва́л *n.* **1,** collapse; cave-in. **2,** slide; landslide.

обва́ливать *v. impfv.* **1,** [*pfv.* **обвали́ть**] to cause to collapse; bring down. **2,** [*pfv.* **обваля́ть**] to roll (in flour, bread crumbs, etc.). —**обва́ливаться,** *refl.* [*pfv.* **обвали́ться**] to collapse; cave in; come tumbling down.

обвали́ть [*infl.* -валю́, -ва́лишь] *v., pfv. of* **обва́ливать** (*in sense #1*). —**обвали́ться,** *refl., pfv. of* **обва́ливаться.**

обваля́ть *v., pfv. of* **обва́ливать** (*in sense #2*).

обва́ривать *v. impfv.* [*pfv.* **обвари́ть**] **1,** to pour boiling water over. **2,** to scald. —**обва́риваться,** *refl.* to scald oneself.

обвари́ть [*infl.* -варю́, -ва́ришь] *v., pfv. of* **обва́ривать.** —**обвари́ться,** *refl., pfv. of* **обва́риваться.**

обвева́ть *v. impfv.* [*pfv.* **обве́ять**] (*of the wind*) to blow upon; fan.

обвенча́ть *v., pfv. of* **венча́ть** (*in sense #2*). —**обвенча́ться,** *refl., pfv. of* **венча́ться** (*in sense #2*).

обвёртывать *v. impfv.* [*pfv.* **обверну́ть**] to wrap; bundle.

обве́сить [*infl.* -шу, -сишь] *v., pfv. of* **обве́шивать** (*in sense #1*).

обвести́ [*infl. like* вести́] *v., pfv. of* **обводи́ть.**

обве́тренный *adj.* **1,** weather-beaten; weather-worn. **2,** (*of one's hands, lips, etc.*) chapped.

обве́трить *v. pfv., usu. in the past passive part.,* to chap. —**обве́триться,** *refl.* **1,** to become weather-beaten. **2,** to become chapped.

обветша́лый *adj.* ramshackle; dilapidated.

обветша́ть *v., pfv. of* **ветша́ть.**

обве́шивать *v. impfv.* **1,** [*pfv.* **обве́сить**] to cheat in weighing. **2,** [*pfv.* **обве́шать**] *colloq.* to hang (with); cover (with).

обве́ять [*infl.* -ве́ю, -ве́ешь] *v., pfv. of* **обвева́ть.**

обвива́ть *v. impfv.* [*pfv.* **обви́ть**] to wind around. —**обвива́ться,** *refl.* (*with* вокру́г) to wind (around); twine (around); coil (around).

обвине́ние *n.* **1,** accusation; charge. **2,** *law* the prosecution.

обвини́тель *n.m.* **1,** accuser. **2,** prosecutor.

обвини́тельный *adj.* of accusation; accusatory. —**обвини́тельный акт; обвини́тельное заключе́ние,** (bill of) indictment. —**обвини́тельный пригово́р,** verdict of "guilty".

обвини́ть *v., pfv. of* **обвиня́ть.**

обвиня́емый *n., decl. as an adj.* the accused; defendant.

обвиня́ть *v. impfv.* [*pfv.* **обвини́ть**] (*with* в + *prepl.*) to accuse (of); charge (with).

обвиса́ть *v. impfv.* [*pfv.* **обви́снуть**] to hang down; droop.

обви́слый *adj., colloq.* drooping.

обви́снуть [*past* -ви́с, -ла] *v., pfv. of* **обвиса́ть.**

обви́ть [*infl.* обовью́, обовьёшь; *past fem.* обвила́] *v., pfv. of* **обвива́ть.** —**обви́ться,** *refl., pfv. of* **обвива́ться.**

обводи́ть *v. impfv.* [*pfv.* **обвести́;** *pres.* -вожу́, -во́дишь] **1,** to lead around; walk around; take around. **2,** *sports* to sidestep; dodge. **3,** to enclose; surround; ring. **4,** to circle; outline; draw a line around. **5,** *in* обводи́ть (что́-нибудь) взгля́дом *or* глаза́ми, to look around at. —**обвести́ (кого́-нибудь) вокру́г па́льца,** to twist around one's little finger.

обвола́кивать *v. impfv.* [*pfv.* **обволо́чь**] (*of smoke, clouds, etc.*) to envelop.

обволо́чь [*infl. like* волочь] *v., pfv. of* **обвола́кивать.**

обвора́живать *v. impfv.* [*pfv.* **обворожи́ть**] to charm; captivate; enchant.

обворова́ть [*infl.* -ру́ю, -ру́ешь] *v., pfv. of* **обворо́вывать.**

обворо́вывать *v. impfv.* [*pfv.* **обворова́ть**] *colloq.* to rob.

обворожи́тельный *adj.* charming; enchanting; bewitching.

обворожи́ть *v., pfv. of* **обвора́живать.**

обвяза́ть [*infl.* -вяжу́, -вя́жешь] *v., pfv. of* **обвя́зывать.** —**обвяза́ться,** *refl., pfv. of* **обвя́зываться.**

обвя́зывать *v. impfv.* [*pfv.* **обвяза́ть**] to tie around: обвяза́ть го́лову платко́м, to tie a kerchief around one's head. —**обвя́зываться,** *refl.* (*with instr.*) to tie (something) around oneself.

обго́н *n.* passing: обго́н запрещён!, no passing!

обгоня́ть *v. impfv.* [*pfv.* **обогна́ть**] **1,** to pass (*on the road, in a race, etc.*). **2,** *fig.* to outstrip; surpass; excel.

обгора́ть *v. impfv.* [*pfv.* **обгоре́ть**] **1,** to be partially burned. **2,** *colloq.* to get a bad sunburn.

обгоре́лый *adj.* charred; burnt; scorched.

обгоре́ть *v., pfv. of* **обгора́ть.**

обгрыза́ть *v. impfv.* [*pfv.* **обгры́зть**] to nibble (at).

обгры́зть [*infl. like* грызть] *v., pfv. of* **обгрыза́ть.**

обдава́ть *v. impfv.* [*pfv.* **обда́ть;** *past* -даю́, -даёшь] **1,** to douse (with water); splash (with mud). **2,** *impers.* to be seized with; be filled with: меня́ о́бдало хо́лодом, I suddenly felt very cold.

обда́ть [*infl. like* дать; *past* о́бдал, обдала́, о́бдало] *v., pfv. of* **обдава́ть.**

обде́лать *v., pfv. of* **обде́лывать.**

обдели́ть [*infl.* -делю́, -де́лишь] *v., pfv. of* **обделя́ть.**

обде́лывать *v. impfv.* [*pfv.* **обде́лать**] **1,** to finish; dress. **2,** to set (a precious stone). **3,** *colloq.* to arrange; manage; handle.

обделя́ть *v. impfv.* [*pfv.* **обдели́ть**] to cheat (someone) out of his rightful share; give (someone) less than his due.

обдира́ть *v. impfv.* [*pfv.* **ободра́ть**] **1,** to skin; flay. **2,** *colloq.* to lacerate. **3,** *colloq.* to wear out. **4,** *colloq.* to rob; fleece.

обдува́ть *v. impfv.* [*pfv.* **обду́ть**] **1,** (*of the wind*) to blow on. **2,** to blow off (dust, ashes, etc.). **3,** *colloq.* to swindle; dupe.

обду́манный *adj.* **1,** considered; carefully thought out. **2,** deliberate.

обду́мывать *v. impfv.* [*pfv.* **обду́мать**] to think over; consider carefully.

обду́ть [*infl.* -ду́ю, -ду́ешь] *v., pfv. of* **обдува́ть.**

о́бе *numeral, fem. of* о́ба.

обега́ть *v., pfv. of* **обега́ть** (*in sense #2*).

обега́ть *v. impfv.* [*pfv.* **обежа́ть**] **1,** to run around. **2,** [*pfv. also* **обе́гать**] to run all over; make the rounds of.

обе́д *n.* midday meal; dinner; lunch.

обе́дать *v. impfv.* [*pfv.* **пообе́дать**] to have dinner; have lunch.

обе́денный *adj.* dinner (*attrib.*); lunch (*attrib.*).

обедне́вший *adj.* impoverished.

обедне́ние *n.* impoverishment.

обедне́ть *v., pfv. of* **бедне́ть.**

обедни́ть *v., pfv. of* **обедня́ть.**

обе́дня [*gen. pl.* -ден] *n., relig.* Mass.

обедня́ть *v. impfv.* [*pfv.* **обедни́ть**] to impoverish.

обежа́ть [*infl. like* **бежа́ть**] *v., pfv. of* **обега́ть** (*in sense #1*).

обезбо́ливание *n.* anesthetization.

обезбо́ливать *v. impfv.* [*pfv.* **обезбо́лить**] to anesthetize.

обезбо́ливающий *adj.* anesthetic. —**обезбо́ливающее сре́дство**, anesthetic.

обезбо́лить *v., pfv. of* **обезбо́ливать**.

обезво́дить [*infl.* -жу, -дишь] *v., pfv. of* **обезво́живать**.

обезво́живание *n.* dehydration.

обезво́живать *v. impfv.* [*pfv.* **обезво́дить**] to dehydrate.

обезвре́живать *v. impfv.* [*pfv.* **обезвре́дить**] to render harmless.

обезгла́вить [*infl.* -влю, -вишь] *v., pfv. of* **обезгла́вливать**.

обезгла́вливание *n.* beheading; decapitation.

обезгла́вливать *v. impfv.* [*pfv.* **обезгла́вить**] to behead; decapitate.

обезде́нежеть *v. pfv., colloq.* to run out of money.

обездо́ленный *adj.* indigent; destitute.

обездо́ливать *v. impfv.* [*pfv.* **обездо́лить**] **1,** *obs.* to deprive of one's share. **2,** to leave destitute.

обезжи́ривать *v. impfv.* [*pfv.* **обезжи́рить**] to remove the fat from.

обеззара́живание *n.* disinfection; decontamination.

обеззара́живать *v. impfv.* [*pfv.* **обеззара́зить**] to disinfect; decontaminate.

обезземе́ливать [*pfv.* **обезземе́лить**] to dispossess of one's land.

обезле́сение *n.* deforestation.

обезле́сить *v. pfv.* to deforest.

обезли́чивать *v. impfv.* [*pfv.* **обезли́чить**] to rob of one's individuality; depersonalize.

обезлю́деть *v. pfv.* to become depopulated.

обезлю́дить *v. pfv.* to depopulate.

обезобра́живание *n.* disfigurement.

обезобра́живать *v. impfv.* [*pfv.* **обезобра́зить**] to disfigure.

обезопа́сить *v. pfv.* [*infl.* -шу, -сишь] to secure.

обезору́живать *v. impfv.* [*pfv.* **обезору́жить**] to disarm.

обезу́меть *v. pfv.* to lose one's senses; lose one's head.

обезья́на *n.* monkey; ape.

обезья́ний [*fem.* -нья] *adj.* **1,** monkey (*attrib.*). **2,** apelike.

обезья́нничать *v. impfv., colloq.* to ape; imitate.

обезьянообра́зный *adj.* ape-like.

обезьяночелове́к [*pl.* **обезьянолю́ди**] *n.* ape-man.

обели́ск *n.* obelisk.

обеля́ть *v. impfv.* [*pfv.* **обели́ть**] to vindicate; clear of a charge; prove the innocence of.

оберега́ть *v. impfv.* [*pfv.* **обере́чь**] to guard; protect.

обере́чь [*infl. like* **бере́чь**] *v., pfv. of* **оберега́ть**.

обёртывать *v., pfv. of* **обёртывать** *and* **обора́чивать**. —**оберну́ться**, *refl., pfv. of* **обёртываться** *and* **обора́чиваться**.

обёртка [*gen. pl.* -ток] *n.* **1,** wrapping; wrapper. **2,** cover (*for a book*).

оберто́н *n., music* overtone.

обёрточный *adj.* wrapping: **обёрточная бума́га**, wrapping paper.

обёртывание *n., med.* pack.

обёртывать *v. impfv.* [*pfv.* **оберну́ть**] **1,** (*with* вок-

рут) to wrap (around). **2,** (*with instr. or* в + *acc.*) to wrap (in). **3,** *in* **оберну́ть (кого́-нибудь) вокру́г па́льца**, to twist around one's little finger. —**обёртываться**, *refl.* = **обора́чиваться**.

обескро́вливать *v. impfv.* [*pfv.* **обескро́вить**] **1,** to drain of blood; bleed white. **2,** *fig.* to rob of vitality.

обескура́женность *n.f., colloq.* discouragement.

обескура́живать *v. impfv.* [*pfv.* **обескура́жить**] to discourage; dishearten.

обеспа́мятеть *v. pfv., colloq.* **1,** to lose one's memory. **2,** to lose consciousness. **3,** to lose one's senses.

обеспе́чение *n.* **1,** (*with instr.*) providing (with); supplying (with). **2,** ensuring; securing. **3,** (financial) security. **4,** security; guarantee.

обеспе́ченность *n.f.* **1,** (*with instr.*) supply: **обеспе́ченность учебниками**, supply of textbooks. **2,** (financial) security; material well-being.

обеспе́ченный *adj.* well-to-do.

обеспе́чивать *v. impfv.* [*pfv.* **обеспе́чить**] **1,** to ensure; secure. **2,** (*with instr.*) to provide (with); supply (with). **3,** to provide for; support. **4,** (*with* от) *obs.* to protect (from).

обеспоко́ить *v. pfv.* to worry; trouble; disturb. —**обеспоко́иться**, *refl.* to be worried; be disturbed.

обесси́леть *v. pfv.* to lose one's strength; become weak.

обесси́ливать *v. impfv.* [*pfv.* **обесси́лить**] to weaken; debilitate; rob of one's strength.

обессла́вить *v. pfv.* [*infl.* -влю, -вишь] to disgrace.

обессме́ртить *v. pfv.* [*infl.* -рчу, -ртишь] to immortalize.

обесцве́тить [*infl.* -чу, -тишь] *v., pfv. of* **обесцве́чивать**.

обесцве́чивание *n.* discoloration.

обесцве́чивать *v. impfv.* [*pfv.* **обесцве́тить**] to discolor.

обесце́нение *n.* depreciation.

обесце́нивать *v. impfv.* [*pfv.* **обесце́нить**] to cheapen; lessen the value of. —**обесце́ниваться**, *refl.* to depreciate; decrease in value.

обесче́стить *v., pfv. of* **бесче́стить**.

обе́т *n.* vow; pledge.

обетова́нный *adj., in* **обетова́нная земля́**, the Promised Land.

обеща́ние *n.* promise.

обеща́ть *v. impfv. & pfv.* **1,** (*with dat.*) to promise. **2,** *impers.* to promise: **день обеща́ет быть хоро́шим**, the day promises to be nice; it promises to be a nice day.

обжа́лование *n., law* appeal.

обжа́ловать *v. pfv.* [*infl.* -лую, -луешь] to appeal (a verdict, decision, etc.).

обже́чь [*infl.* **обожгу́, обожжёшь, ...обожгу́т**; *past* **обжёг, обожгла́**] *v., pfv. of* **обжига́ть**. —**обже́чься**, *refl., pfv. of* **обжига́ться**.

обжива́ть *v. impfv.* [*pfv.* **обжи́ть**] *colloq.* to make habitable. —**обжива́ться**, *refl., colloq.* to make oneself at home; feel at home.

обжига́тельный *adj.* used for burning or baking. —**обжига́тельная печь**, kiln.

обжига́ть *v. impfv.* [*pfv.* **обже́чь**] **1,** to burn. **2,** to bake (pottery, bricks, etc.). —**обжига́ться**, *refl.* **1,** to burn oneself. **2,** *fig.* to get burned; burn one's fingers.

обжи́ть [*infl.* **-живу́, -живёшь**; *past* **о́бжил, обжила́, о́бжило**] *v., pfv. of* **обжива́ть**. —**обжи́ться**, *refl.* [*past* **-жи́лся, -ла́сь, -ло́сь**] *pfv. of* **обжива́ться**.

обжо́ра *n.m. & f.*, *colloq.* glutton. —**обжо́рливый**, *adj.*, *colloq.* gluttonous. —**обжо́рство**, *n.*, *colloq.* gluttony.

обжу́ливать *v. impfv.* [*pfv.* **обжу́лить**] *colloq.* to swindle; cheat; gyp.

обзавести́сь [*infl. like* **вести́**] *v.r.*, *pfv. of* **обзаводи́ться**.

обзаводи́ться *v.r. impfv.* [*pfv.* **обзавести́сь**; *pres.* -**вожу́сь, -во́дишься**] (*with instr.*) *colloq.* **1,** to acquire; provide oneself with. **2,** to make (friends); start (a family). —**обзаводи́ться хозя́йством**, to set up house.

обзо́р *n.* **1,** observation. **2,** survey; roundup. **3,** field of vision.

обзыва́ть *v. impfv.* [*pfv.* **обозва́ть**] *colloq.* to call (someone something insulting): обозва́ть кого́-нибудь глупцо́м, to call someone a dunce.

обива́ть *v. impfv.* [*pfv.* **оби́ть**] **1,** to upholster; cover. **2,** to knock off; shake off. **3,** *colloq.* to wear out; wear thin. —**обива́ть (все) поро́ги**, to knock on every door.

оби́вка *n.* **1,** upholstering. **2,** upholstery.

оби́да *n.* **1,** offense; insult. **2,** offense; resentment. —**быть в оби́де на** (+ *acc.*), to be offended (*or* angry) with. —**не в оби́ду будь ска́зано**, no offense meant. —**не дать (кого́-нибудь) в оби́ду**, to allow no harm to come to. —**не дава́ться в оби́ду**, not to allow oneself to be pushed around.

оби́деть [*infl.* **оби́жу, оби́дишь**] *v.*, *pfv. of* **обижа́ть**. —**оби́деться**, *refl.*, *pfv. of* **обижа́ться**.

оби́дно *adj.*, *used predicatively* unfortunate; distressing: оби́дно э́то слы́шать, I am sorry to hear it. Оби́дно, что вы опозда́ли, it's a pity that you were late.

оби́дный *adj.* **1,** insulting; offensive. **2,** *colloq.* annoying.

оби́дчивый *adj.* touchy; sensitive. —**оби́дчивость**, *n.f.* touchiness.

оби́дчик *n.*, *colloq.* person who has offended someone.

обижа́ть *v. impfv.* [*pfv.* **оби́деть**] **1,** to offend; hurt the feelings of. **2,** *colloq.* to harm; wrong. —**обижа́ться**, *refl.* (*with* **на** + *acc.*) to take offense (at); be offended (by); resent.

оби́женный *adj.* **1,** offended. Вы оби́жены на меня́?, are you offended/angry/annoyed with me? **2,** resentful.

оби́лие *n.* abundance; plenty.

оби́льный *adj.* abundant; plentiful; bountiful. —**оби́льно**, *adv.* abundantly.

обиня́к [*gen.* -**няка́**] *n.*, *in* говори́ть обиняка́ми, to beat around the bush; **говори́ть без обиняко́в**, to speak straight to the point.

обира́ть *v. impfv.* [*pfv.* **обобра́ть**] *colloq.* **1,** to gather; pick. **2,** to rob; fleece.

обита́емый *adj.* inhabited.

обита́тель *n.m.* inhabitant.

обита́ть *v. impfv.* (*with* **в** + *prepl.*) to dwell (in); inhabit.

оби́тель *n.f.*, *obs.* monastery.

оби́тый *adj.* upholstered.

оби́ть [*infl.* **обобью́, обобьёшь**] *v.*, *pfv. of* **обива́ть**.

обихо́д *n.* **1,** everyday life; day-to-day existence. **2,** use: входи́ть в обихо́д, to come into use. —**предме́ты дома́шнего обихо́да**, (everyday) household items.

обихо́дный *adj.* everyday.

обка́пывать *v. impfv.*, *colloq.* **1,** [*pfv.* **обка́пать**] to stain (*by spilling drops of something on*). **2,** [*pfv.* **обкопа́ть**] to dig around.

обка́рмливать *v. impfv.* [*pfv.* **обкорми́ть**] to give (someone) too much to eat; stuff.

обка́тывать *v. impfv.* [*pfv.* **обката́ть**] **1,** to make round or smooth by rolling. **2,** to wear smooth. **3,** to break in (a car, motor, etc.).

обкла́дывать *v. impfv.* [*pfv.* **обложи́ть**] **1,** to surround (*by laying objects around*). **2,** to face (*with stone, marble, etc.*). **3,** (*of clouds*) to cover. *Also impers.:* не́бо обложи́ло ту́чами, the sky is overcast. **4,** to surround; lay siege to. **5,** *impers.* to become coated: у меня́ обложи́ло язы́к, my tongue is coated. —**обкла́дываться**, *refl.* (*with instr.*) to surround oneself (with).

обко́м *n.* regional committee (*contr. of* **областно́й комите́т**).

обкопа́ть *v.*, *pfv. of* **обка́пывать** (*in sense #2*).

обкорми́ть [*infl.* -**кормлю́, -ко́рмишь**] *v.*, *pfv. of* **обка́рмливать**.

обкра́дывать *v. impfv.* [*pfv.* **обокра́сть**] to rob.

обку́ривать *v. impfv.* [*pfv.* **обкури́ть**] **1,** to break in (a pipe). **2,** *colloq.* to stain by exposure to smoke.

обкури́ть [*infl.* -**курю́, -ку́ришь**] *v.*, *pfv. of* **обку́ривать**.

обку́сывать *v. impfv.* [*pfv.* **обкуса́ть**] to bite around the edges of; nibble.

обла́ва *n.* **1,** hunt (*involving surrounding, driving out, and shooting animals*). **2,** (police) raid; roundup; dragnet.

облага́ть *v. impfv.* [*pfv.* **обложи́ть**] to assess; tax. Облага́ть кого́-нибудь нало́гом, to impose a tax on.

облагора́живать *v. impfv.* [*pfv.* **облагоро́дить**] to ennoble.

облада́ние *n.* possession. —**облада́тель**, *n.m.* possessor.

облада́ть *v. impfv.* (*with instr.*) to possess; have.

о́блако [*pl.* **облака́, облако́в**] *n.* cloud.

обла́мывать *v. impfv.* [*pfv.* **обломо́ть** *or* **обломи́ть**] to break off.

обла́пить *v. pfv.* [*infl.* -**плю, -пишь**] *colloq.* (*of an animal*) to grab in its paws.

обласка́ть *v. pfv.* to show kindness toward.

областно́й *adj.* of an oblast; regional; provincial.

о́бласть [*pl.* **о́бласти, -сте́й, -стя́м**] *n.f.* **1,** oblast: моско́вская о́бласть, Moscow oblast. **2,** area; region. **3,** *fig.* field; sphere; domain.

обла́тка [*gen. pl.* -**ток**] *n.* **1,** capsule; tablet. **2,** *relig.* wafer.

облача́ть *v. impfv.* [*pfv.* **облачи́ть**] **1,** to robe; clothe (a clergyman). **2,** *colloq.* to dress up; deck out.

облаче́ние *n.* **1,** *relig.* vestment(s). **2,** *obs.* clothes.

облачи́ть *v.*, *pfv. of* **облача́ть**.

о́блачко [*pl.* **облачка́, -ко́в**] *n.*, *dim. of* **о́блако**.

о́блачность *n.f.* cloudiness.

о́блачный *adj.* **1,** cloud (*attrib.*): о́блачный покро́в, cloud cover. **2,** cloudy.

обла́ять *v. pfv.* [*infl.* -**ла́ю, -ла́ешь**] *colloq.* to bark furiously at.

облега́ть *v. impfv.* [*pfv.* **обле́чь**] **1,** to envelop; shroud. **2,** [*impfv. only*] (*of clothes*) to fit snugly; cling to.

облегча́ть *v. impfv.* [*pfv.* **облегчи́ть**] **1,** to lighten. **2,** to ease; facilitate. **3,** to ease; relieve; alleviate. —**облегча́ться**, *refl.* **1,** to lighten; become lighter. **2,** to become easier. **3,** to be relieved.

облегче́ние *n.* **1,** lightening; facilitating. **2,** (feeling of) relief.

облегчённый *adj.* **1,** made lighter. **2,** of relief: облегчённый вздох, sigh of relief. —**облегчённо**, *adv.* with (a sense of) relief.

облегчи́ть *v., pfv. of* **облегча́ть**. —**облегчи́ться**, *refl., pfv. of* **облегча́ться**.

обледене́лый *adj.* ice-covered; ice-coated.

обледене́ние *n.* icing up; icing over.

обледене́ть *v. pfv.* to ice up; be coated with ice.

облеза́ть *v. impfv.* [*pfv.* **обле́зть**] *colloq.* **1**, to lose one's fur; become mangy. **2**, (*of something painted*) to peel. **3**, (*of paint, varnish, etc.*) to peel off.

обле́злый *adj., colloq.* **1**, (*of an animal*) mangy. **2**, with the paint having worn off; shabby.

обле́зть [*infl. like* **лезть**] *v., pfv. of* **облеза́ть**.

облека́ть *v. impfv.* [*pfv.* **обле́чь**] **1**, *obs.* to clothe. **2**, to envelop; shroud. **3**, to vest (with power, authority, etc.). **4**, (*with* **в** + *acc.*) to express; couch (in certain language).

облени́ваться *v.r. impfv.* [*pfv.* **облени́ться**] to become lazy.

облени́ться [*infl.* -леню́сь, -ле́нишься] *v., pfv. of* **облени́ваться**.

облепи́ть [*infl.* -леплю́, -ле́пишь] *v., pfv. of* **облепля́ть**.

облепля́ть *v. impfv.* [*pfv.* **облепи́ть**] **1**, to stick to; cling to. **2**, to cover; plaster. **3**, *fig., colloq.* to swarm around.

облета́ть[1] *v. impfv.* [*pfv.* **облете́ть**] **1**, to fly around. **2**, to fly all over. **3**, *fig.* to spread all over: весть облете́ла весь го́род, the news spread all over town. **4**, (*of leaves*) to fall.

облета́ть[2] *v. pfv.* **1**, to fly all over. **2**, to test-fly.

облете́ть [*infl.* -чу́, -ти́шь] *v., pfv. of* **облета́ть**[1].

обле́чь *v. pfv.* **1**, [*infl. like* **ле́чь**] *pfv. of* **облега́ть**. **2**, [*infl. like* **те́чь**] *pfv. of* **облека́ть**.

обли́вание *n.* **1**, dousing (*with water*). **2**, douche.

облива́ть *v. impfv.* [*pfv.* **обли́ть**] **1**, to pour water over; douse. **2**, to cover (*with tears, sweat, etc.*). **3**, to soil; stain (*by spilling something on*): облива́ть ска́терть су́пом, to spill soup all over the tablecloth. —**облива́ть (кого́-нибудь) гря́зью** *or* **помо́ями**, to vilify; drag through the mud.

облига́ция *n., finance* bond.

облиза́ть [*infl.* -лижу́, -ли́жешь] *v., pfv. of* **обли́зывать**. —**облиза́ться**, *refl., pfv. of* **обли́зываться**.

обли́зывать *v. impfv.* [*pfv.* **облиза́ть**] **1**, to lick. **2**, *in* па́льчики обли́жешь, you'll love it! —**обли́зываться**, *refl.* **1**, to lick oneself. **2**, [*impfv. only*] to lick one's lips; *fig.* lick one's chops.

о́блик *n.* **1**, look; appearance. **2**, *fig.* character; make-up.

облиня́ть *v. pfv., colloq.* to fade.

обли́ть [*infl.* оболью́, обольёшь; *past* о́блил *or* обли́л, облила́, о́блило *or* обли́ло] *v., pfv. of* **облива́ть**.

облицева́ть [*infl.* -цую, -цуешь] *v., pfv. of* **облицо́вывать**.

облицо́вка *n.* facing; revetment.

облицо́вывать *v. impfv.* [*pfv.* **облицева́ть**] to face (*with stone, marble, etc.*).

облича́ть *v. impfv.* [*pfv.* **обличи́ть**] **1**, to expose (wrongs, misdeeds, etc.). **2**, [*impfv. only*] to reveal; indicate. Всё облича́ет в нём вое́нного, everything points to his being a military man.

обличе́ние *n.* exposure.

обличи́тель *n.m.* exposer. —**обличи́тельный**, *adj.* serving to expose something.

обличи́ть *v., pfv. of* **облича́ть**.

обли́чье *n., colloq.* look; appearance.

облобыза́ть *v. pfv., obs.* to kiss.

обложе́ние *n.* **1**, levying: обложе́ние нало́гами, levying of taxes. **2**, *obs.* siege.

обложи́ть [*infl.* -ложу́, -ло́жишь] *v., pfv. of* **обкла́дывать** *and* **облага́ть**. —**обложи́ться**, *refl., pfv. of* **обкла́дываться**.

обло́жка [*gen. pl.* -жек] *n.* **1**, cover (*of a book or magazine*). **2**, folder (*for papers*); case (*for documents*).

обложно́й *adj., in* обложно́й до́ждь, *colloq.* steady downpour.

облока́чиваться *v.r. impfv.* [*pfv.* **облокоти́ться**] (*with* на *or* о + *acc.*) to lean one's elbows (on *or* against).

облокоти́ться [*infl.* -кочу́сь, -ко́тишься *or* -коти́шься] *v.r., pfv. of* **облока́чиваться**.

облома́ть *v., pfv. of* **обла́мывать**.

обломи́ть [*infl.* -ломлю́, -ло́мишь] *v., pfv. of* **обла́мывать**.

обло́мовщина *n.* lethargy; apathy; sluggishness (*after* Обло́мов, *hero of the novel of the same name by Goncharov*).

обло́мок [*gen.* -мка] *n.* **1**, fragment. **2**, *pl.* wreckage; debris.

облупи́ть [*infl.* -луплю́, -лу́пишь] *v., pfv. of* **лупи́ть** (*in sense #1*) *and* **облу́пливать**. —**облупи́ться**, *refl., pfv. of* **лупи́ться** *and* **облу́пливаться**.

облу́пливать *v. impfv.* [*pfv.* **облупи́ть**] *colloq.* **1**, to peel; shell. **2**, *fig.* to swindle; fleece. —**облу́пливаться**, *refl.* (*of paint, plaster, etc.*) to come off; peel off.

облуча́ть *v. impfv.* [*pfv.* **облучи́ть**] to treat with rays; expose to rays.

облуче́ние *n.* irradiation; exposure to radiation; radiation treatment.

облучи́ть *v., pfv. of* **облуча́ть**.

облучо́к [*gen.* -чка́] *n.* coachman's seat.

облущи́ть *v., pfv. of* **лущи́ть**.

облысе́лый *adj.* bald.

облысе́ть *v., pfv. of* **лысе́ть**.

облюбова́ть *v. pfv.* [*infl.* -бую, -буешь] to choose; select; settle on.

обма́зать [*infl.* -ма́жу, -ма́жешь] *v., pfv. of* **обма́зывать**.

обма́зывать *v. impfv.* [*pfv.* **обма́зать**] **1**, to coat (with). **2**, to smear (with).

обма́кивать *v. impfv.* [*pfv.* **обмакну́ть**] to dip.

обма́н *n.* **1**, deception; deceit; fraud. **2**, illusion; delusion. —**обма́н зре́ния**; **опти́ческий обма́н**, optical illusion.

обма́нка *n., in* рогова́я обма́нка, hornblende; смоляна́я обма́нка, pitchblende.

обма́нный *adj.* fraudulent; deceitful.

обману́ть [*infl.* -ману́, -ма́нешь] *v., pfv. of* **обма́нывать**. —**обману́ться**, *refl., pfv. of* **обма́нываться**.

обма́нчивый *adj.* **1**, deceptive. **2**, illusory.

обма́нщик *n.* one who deceives; faker; cheat.

обма́нывать *v. impfv.* [*pfv.* **обману́ть**] **1**, to deceive. **2**, to trick; cheat. **3**, to disappoint; let down. **4**, to betray (someone's trust); fail to live up to (hopes, expectations, etc.). **5**, to be unfaithful to (one's spouse). **6**, to seduce. **7**, *in* обма́нывать себя́, to delude oneself. —**обма́нываться**, *refl.* **1**, to be deceived. **2**, to be mistaken.

обма́тывать *v. impfv.* [*pfv.* **обмота́ть**] to wind around; wrap around. —**обма́тываться**, *refl.* **1**, (*with* instr.) to wrap oneself in. **2,** (with вокру́г) to wrap around; be wrapped around.

обма́хивать v. impfv. [pfv. обмахну́ть] **1,** to fan. **2,** to brush off. **3,** to brush away. —**обма́хиваться,** refl. to fan oneself.

обма́чивать v. impfv. [pfv. обмочи́ть] to wet; moisten.

обмеле́ть v., pfv. of меле́ть.

обме́н n. exchange. —**обме́н веще́ств,** metabolism.

обме́нивать v. impfv. [pfv. обменя́ть] to exchange; trade; swap (one thing for another). —**обме́ниваться,** refl. **1,** (of two people) to trade; swap; make a trade. **2,** (with instr.) to exchange (similar things): обме́ниваться места́ми, to exchange places. Обме́ниваться впечатле́ниями, to compare notes.

обмени́ть v. pfv. [infl. -меню́, -ме́нишь] colloq. to exchange.

обме́нный adj. exchange (attrib.).

обменя́ть v., pfv. of обме́нивать. —**обменя́ться,** refl., pfv. of обме́ниваться.

обме́р n. **1,** measurement. **2,** colloq. dishonesty in measuring.

обмере́ть [infl. обомру́, обомрёшь; past о́бмер, обмерла́, о́бмерло] v., pfv. of обмира́ть.

обме́ривать v. impfv. [pfv. обме́рить] **1,** to measure. **2,** to cheat in measuring.

обмести́ [infl. like мести́] v., pfv. of обмета́ть¹.

обмета́ть¹ v. impfv. [pfv. обмести́] to sweep off; dust off; brush off.

обмета́ть² [infl. -мечу́, -ме́чешь] v., pfv. of обмё́тывать.

обмё́тывать v. impfv. [pfv. обмета́ть] sewing to overcast.

обмина́ть v. impfv. [pfv. обмя́ть] to press down; trample down.

обмира́ть v. impfv. [pfv. обмере́ть] colloq. **1,** to faint. **2,** to go numb (from fear, shock, etc.). **3,** (of one's heart) to skip a beat.

обмозгова́ть [infl. -гу́ю, -гу́ешь] v., pfv. of обмозго́вывать.

обмозго́вывать v. impfv. [pfv. обмозгова́ть] colloq. to think over; mull over.

обмола́чивать v. impfv. [pfv. обмолоти́ть] to thresh.

обмо́лвиться v.r. impfv. [infl. -влюсь, -вишься] **1,** to make a slip of the tongue. **2,** (with instr.) to utter.

обмо́лвка [gen. pl. -вок] n. slip of the tongue.

обмолоти́ть [infl. -лочу́, -ло́тишь] v., pfv. of обмола́чивать.

обмора́живать v. impfv. [pfv. обморо́зить] to get (a part of one's body) frostbitten: я обморо́зил себе́ ру́ки, my hands are frostbitten. —**обмора́живаться,** refl. to suffer frostbite.

обморо́жение also, обмороже́ние n. frostbite.

обморо́женный adj. frostbitten.

обморо́зить [infl. -жу, -зишь] v., pfv. of обмора́живать. —**обморо́зиться,** refl., pfv. of обмора́живаться.

о́бморок n. fainting spell. —**упа́сть в о́бморок,** to faint.

обморо́чить v., pfv. of моро́чить.

обмота́ть v., pfv. of обма́тывать. —**обмота́ться,** refl., pfv. of обма́тываться.

обмо́тки [gen. -ток] n. pl. puttees.

обмочи́ть [infl. -мочу́, -мо́чишь] v., pfv. of обма́чивать.

обмундирова́ние n. **1,** fitting out (with uniforms). **2,** uniform.

обмундирова́ть v. pfv. [infl. -ру́ю, -ру́ешь] to fit out (with uniforms).

обмундиро́вка n., colloq. = обмундирова́ние.

обмыва́ть v. impfv. [pfv. обмы́ть] to wash; bathe. —**обмыва́ться,** refl. to bathe (oneself).

обмы́лок [gen. -лка] n., colloq. remaining piece of a bar of soap.

обмы́ть [infl. -мо́ю, -мо́ешь] v., pfv. of обмыва́ть. —**обмы́ться,** refl., pfv. of обмыва́ться.

обмяка́ть v. impfv. [pfv. обмя́кнуть] colloq. **1,** to become soft. **2,** fig. to become flabby.

обмя́кнуть [past -мя́к, -ла] v., pfv. of обмяка́ть.

обмя́ть [infl. обомну́, обомнёшь] v., pfv. of обмина́ть.

обнагле́ть v., pfv. of нагле́ть.

обнадё́живать v. impfv. [pfv. обнадё́жить] to reassure; give hope to; raise the hopes of.

обнажа́ть v. impfv. [pfv. обнажи́ть] **1,** to bare; expose; uncover. **2,** to denude. **3,** to draw; unsheathe (a sword). **4,** fig. to reveal; lay bare. **5,** mil. to expose. —**обнажа́ться,** refl. **1,** to take off all one's clothes. **2,** to be exposed. **3,** to be denuded.

обнажё́нный adj. bare; naked; nude.

обнажи́ть v., pfv. of обнажа́ть. —**обнажи́ться,** refl., pfv. of обнажа́ться.

обнаро́дование n. promulgation.

обнаро́довать v. pfv. [infl. -дую, -дуешь] to promulgate.

обнару́жение also, обнаруже́ние n. **1,** discovery; detection. **2,** revelation; disclosure.

обнару́живать v. impfv. [pfv. обнару́жить] **1,** to reveal; display; show. **2,** to discover.

обна́шивать v. impfv. [pfv. обноси́ть] colloq. **1,** to wear in; break in (new clothes). **2,** to wear out (clothes). —**обна́шиваться,** refl., colloq. **1,** (of new clothes) to become broken in. **2,** (of clothes) to wear out.

обнести́ [infl. like нести́] v., pfv. of обноси́ть¹.

обнима́ть v. impfv. [pfv. обня́ть] **1,** to embrace; hug. **2,** fig. to engulf; envelop. **3,** fig. to take in; embrace. —**обнима́ться,** refl. (of two people) to embrace; hug.

обни́мка n., colloq., in в обни́мку, in each other's embrace.

обнища́лый adj. impoverished; destitute.

обнища́ние n. impoverishment; destitution.

обнища́ть v., pfv. of нища́ть.

обно́ва n., colloq. = обно́вка.

обнови́ть [infl. -влю́, -ви́шь] v., pfv. of обновля́ть.

обно́вка [gen. pl. -вок] n., colloq. article of clothing just bought; new acquisition; new outfit.

обновле́ние n. **1,** renovation. **2,** renewal. **3,** replenishment.

обновля́ть v. impfv. [pfv. обнови́ть] **1,** to renovate; refurbish; revamp. **2,** to renew; revitalize. **3,** to replenish. **4,** colloq. to wear for the first time.

обноси́ть¹ v. impfv. [pfv. обнести́; pres. -ношу́, -но́сишь] **1,** to carry around. **2,** to enclose; fence in. **3,** to serve (everyone): обноси́ть госте́й шампа́нским, to serve champagne to all the guests. **4,** to pass by (while serving); not serve.

обноси́ть² [infl. -ношу́, -но́сишь] v., pfv. of обна́-

шивать. —обноси́ться, refl. 1, pfv. of обна́шивать-ся. 2, to wear out all one's clothes.

обно́ски [gen. -сков] n. pl., colloq. old clothes.

обня́ть [infl. -ниму́, -ни́мешь; past о́бнял, обняла́, о́бняло] v., pfv. of обнима́ть. —обня́ться, refl. [past обня́лся or обнялся́, -ла́сь, -ло́сь, -ли́сь] pfv. of обнима́ться.

обо prep. = о (used before мне, всем, всей, and всех).

обобра́ть [infl. оберу́, оберёшь; past fem. обобрала́] v., pfv. of обира́ть.

обобща́ть v. impfv. [pfv. обобщи́ть] to summarize; synthesize.

обобще́ние n. 1, summarizing; synthesizing. 2, generalization.

обобществи́ть [infl. -влю́, -ви́шь] v., pfv. of обобществля́ть.

обобществле́ние n. socialization; collectivization.

обобществля́ть v. impfv. [pfv. обобществи́ть] to socialize; collectivize.

обобщи́ть v., pfv. of обобща́ть.

обогаща́ть v. impfv. [pfv. обогати́ть] to enrich. —обогаща́ться, refl. 1, to get rich; enrich oneself. 2, fig. to be enriched.

обогаще́ние n. enrichment.

обогна́ть [infl. обгоню́, обго́нишь; past fem. обогнала́] v., pfv. of обгоня́ть.

обогну́ть v., pfv. of огиба́ть.

обоготворе́ние n. deification.

обоготворя́ть v. impfv. [pfv. обоготвори́ть] to deify.

обогрева́ние n. heating.

обогрева́тель n.m. 1, heater. 2, defroster.

обогрева́ть v. impfv. [pfv. обогре́ть] to warm; heat. —обогрева́ться, refl. to warm up; get warm.

о́бод [pl. обо́дья, обо́дьев] n. rim (of a wheel).

ободо́к [gen. -дка́] n. 1, thin rim; ring. 2, band.

ободо́чный adj., in ободо́чная кишка́, anat. colon.

ободра́нец [gen. -нца] n., colloq. ragamuffin.

обо́дранный adj., colloq. ragged; torn; tattered.

ободра́ть [infl. обдеру́, обдерёшь; past fem. обдрала́] v., pfv. of обдира́ть.

ободре́ние n. encouragement; reassurance. —ободри́тельный, adj. encouraging; reassuring.

ободря́ть v. impfv. [pfv. ободри́ть] to cheer up; hearten; encourage; reassure. —ободря́ться, refl. to cheer up; take heart.

обо́его numeral, obs. of both. —ли́ца обо́его по́ла, people of both sexes.

обожа́ние n. adoration.

обожа́тель n.m., colloq. worshiper; admirer.

обожа́ть v. impfv. to adore; worship.

обожда́ть v. pfv. [infl. like ждать] colloq. to wait; wait a while.

обожестви́ть [infl. -влю́, -ви́шь] v., pfv. of обожествля́ть.

обожествле́ние n. deification.

обожествля́ть v. impfv. [pfv. обожестви́ть] to deify.

обо́з n. line; string; column (of vehicles).

обозва́ть [infl. обзову́, обзовёшь; past fem. обозвала́] v., pfv. of обзыва́ть.

обозли́ть v., pfv. of зли́ть. —обозли́ться, refl., pfv. of зли́ться.

обозна́ться v.r. pfv., colloq. to mistake someone for someone else.

обознача́ть v. impfv. [pfv. обозна́чить] 1, to mark;

indicate; designate. 2, [impfv. only] to mean; signify; denote. 3, to highlight; accentuate (visually). —обознача́ться, refl. 1, to appear; become visible. 2, to be felt; be sensed. 3, to become clear.

обозначе́ние n. 1, indication. 2, symbol; designation.

обозна́чить v., pfv. of обознача́ть. —обозна́читься, refl., pfv. of обознача́ться.

обозрева́тель n.m. commentator; columnist.

обозрева́ть v. impfv. [pfv. обозре́ть] 1, to look around; survey; view. 2, fig. to review; survey.

обозре́ние n. 1, viewing. 2, review; survey. 3, review (publication). 4, theat. revue.

обозре́ть [infl. -зрю́, -зри́шь] v., pfv. of обозрева́ть.

обозри́мый adj. visible. —в обозри́мом бу́дущем, in the foreseeable future.

обо́и [gen. обо́ев] n. pl. wallpaper.

обо́йма n. cartridge clip.

обо́йный adj. wallpaper (attrib.).

обойти́ [infl. обойду́, обойдёшь; past обошёл, обошла́, обошло́] v., pfv. of обходи́ть. —обойти́сь, refl., pfv. of обходи́ться.

обо́йщик n. 1, upholsterer. 2, paperhanger.

о́бок adv., colloq. alongside. —prep., with gen., colloq. alongside.

обокра́сть [infl. обкраду́, обкрадёшь] v., pfv. of обкра́дывать.

оболва́нить v. pfv., colloq. to dupe; make a fool of.

оболга́ть v. pfv. [infl. like лгать] to slander; calumniate.

оболо́чка [gen. pl. -чек] n. 1, shell (of a fruit or seed). 2, anat. membrane: сли́зистая оболо́чка, mucous membrane. 3, fig. shell: вне́шняя оболо́чка, one's outer shell. —ра́дужная оболо́чка, iris. —рогова́я оболо́чка, cornea. —се́тчатая оболо́чка, retina.

обо́лтус n., colloq. blockhead; oaf.

обольсти́тель n.m. seducer. —обольсти́тельный, adj. seductive.

обольсти́ть [infl. -льщу́, -льсти́шь] v., pfv. of обольща́ть. —обольсти́ться, refl., pfv. of обольща́ться.

обольща́ть v. impfv. [pfv. обольсти́ть] 1, to beguile. 2, to seduce. —обольща́ться, refl. 1, [impfv. only] to flatter oneself; delude oneself. 2, (with instr.) to be carried away (by): обольща́ться успе́хами, to be carried away by one's own success; let success go to one's head.

обольще́ние n. 1, seduction. 2, lure; temptation. 3, delusion.

обомле́ть v. pfv., colloq. to be stunned; freeze (in shock, surprise, etc.).

обомше́лый adj. moss-grown.

обоня́ние n. sense of smell. —обоня́тельный, adj. olfactory.

обоня́ть v. impfv. to smell (something).

обора́чивать v. impfv. [pfv. оберну́ть] to turn. —обора́чиваться, refl. 1, to turn around; look around. 2, fig. to turn out; work out. 3, colloq. to go and return. 4, colloq. to manage; get by.

оборва́нец [gen. -нца] n., colloq. vagabond; hobo.

обо́рванный adj. ragged; torn; tattered.

оборва́ть [infl. like рвать] v., pfv. of обрыва́ть. —оборва́ться, refl., pfv. of обрыва́ться.

обо́рвыш n., colloq. ragamuffin.

обо́рка [gen. pl. -рок] n. frill; flounce; ruffle.

оборо́на n. 1, defense. 2, defensive: быть в оборо́не, to be on the defensive. 3, defenses.

оборони́тельный *adj.* defensive.

оборони́ть *v., pfv. of* оборона́ть. —**оборони́ться,** *refl., pfv. of* оборона́ться.

оборо́нный *adj.* defense (*attrib.*).

оборона́ть *v. impfv.* [*pfv.* оборони́ть] to defend. —**оборона́ться,** *refl.* to defend oneself.

оборо́т *n.* **1,** revolution: сто оборо́тов в мину́ту, 100 r.p.m. **2,** *fig.* turn: оборо́т ре́чи, turn of speech. Приня́ть дурно́й оборо́т, to take a bad turn; take a turn for the worse. **3,** use; circulation: пуска́ть в оборо́т, to put into circulation. **4,** back; reverse side: смотри́ на оборо́те, please turn over. **5,** *finance* turnover. —**брать в оборо́т, 1,** to take in hand. **2,** to take to task.

о́боротень [*gen.* -тня] *n.m.* werewolf.

оборо́тливый *adj., colloq.* clever; resourceful. *Also,* **оборо́тистый.**

оборо́тный *adj.* **1,** *finance* circulating; negotiable. Оборо́тный капита́л, working capital. **2,** (*of a side*) back; reverse.

обору́дование *n.* **1,** equipping. **2,** equipment.

обору́довать *v. impfv. & pfv.* [*pres.* -дую, -дуешь] to equip.

обоснова́ние *n.* **1,** substantiation. **2,** basis; grounds.

обосно́ванный *adj.* sound; well-founded. —**обосно́ванность,** *n.f.* validity.

обоснова́ть [*infl.* -ную́, -нуёшь] *v., pfv. of* обосно́вывать. —**обоснова́ться,** *refl., pfv. of* обосно́вываться.

обосно́вывать *v. impfv.* [*pfv.* обоснова́ть] to substantiate. —**обосно́вываться,** *refl.* **1,** to be substantiated. **2,** to settle (*in a certain place*).

обосо́бить [*infl.* -блю, -бишь] *v., pfv. of* обособла́ть. —**обосо́биться,** *refl., pfv. of* обособла́ться.

обособле́ние *n.* isolation.

обосо́бленный *adj.* **1,** isolated; separate. **2,** solitary.

обособла́ть *v. impfv.* [*pfv.* обосо́бить] to isolate. —**обособла́ться,** *refl.* to stand apart; remain aloof.

обостре́ние *n.* **1,** intensification. **2,** aggravation; exacerbation.

обостре́нный *adj.* **1,** (*of facial features*) prominent. **2,** (*of the senses*) unusually keen. **3,** (*of relations*) strained.

обостра́ть *v. impfv.* [*pfv.* обостри́ть] **1,** to intensify; increase; heighten. **2,** to aggravate; exacerbate; strain. —**обостра́ться,** *refl.* **1,** to become more acute. **2,** (*of the senses*) to become keener. **3,** (*of pain*) to become more intense. **4,** (*of relations*) to be strained; worsen.

обо́чина *n.* **1,** side of a road; shoulder. **2,** curb.

обою́дный *adj.* mutual; reciprocal. —**обою́дно,** *adv.* mutually. —**обою́дность,** *n.f.* mutuality; reciprocity.

обоюдоо́стрый *adj.* double-edged.

обраба́тывать *v. impfv.* [*pfv.* обрабо́тать] **1,** to work; treat; process. **2,** to till; cultivate. **3,** to cleanse (a wound). **4,** to work up; put in final form. **5,** to refine; perfect. **6,** *colloq.* to work on; work over (someone); indoctrinate.

обрабо́тка *n.* **1,** working; treatment; processing. **2,** tillage; cultivation. **3,** refinement. **4,** *colloq.* indoctrination. —**брать в обрабо́тку,** to work on (someone); twist someone's arm.

обра́довать *v., pfv. of* ра́довать. —**обра́доваться,** *refl., pfv. of* ра́доваться.

о́браз *n.* **1,** image. **2,** way; mode; manner: о́браз жи́зни, way of life; о́браз мы́слей, way of thinking. О́браз правле́ния, form of government. **3,** [*pl.* образа́] icon. **4,** *used in forming adverbial expressions:* до́лжным

о́бразом, properly; коренны́м о́бразом, radically; суще́ственным о́бразом, substantially. —**гла́вным о́бразом,** chiefly; mainly; for the most part. —**каки́м о́бразом?,** how?; in what way? —**не́которым о́бразом,** of sorts; after a fashion. —**ника́ким о́бразом,** under no circumstances. —**ра́вным о́бразом,** by the same token. —**таки́м о́бразом, 1,** this way; like this. **2,** thus.

образе́ц [*gen.* -зца́] *n.* **1,** sample: образе́ц обо́ев, a wallpaper sample. **2,** model: образе́ц самоотве́рженности, a model of selflessness. **3,** pattern.

о́бразно *adv.* **1,** vividly. **2,** using imagery. —**о́бразно говоря́,** figuratively speaking.

о́бразность *n.f.* **1,** vividness. **2,** imagery.

о́бразный *adj.* **1,** vivid; colorful; graphic. **2,** using imagery.

образова́ние *n.* **1,** formation. **2,** education.

образо́ванный *adj.* educated; cultured; cultivated.

образова́тельный *adj.* educational.

образова́ть [*infl.* -зу́ю, -зу́ешь] *v., pfv. of* образо́вывать. —**образова́ться,** *refl., pfv. of* образо́вываться.

образо́вывать *v. impfv.* [*pfv.* образова́ть] to form. —**образо́вываться,** *refl.* **1,** to form; appear; come into being. **2,** *colloq.* to be all right: всё образу́ется, everything will be all right.

образу́мить *v. pfv.* [*infl.* -млю, -мишь] *colloq.* to bring to reason. —**образу́миться,** *refl., colloq.* to come to one's senses.

образцо́вый *adj.* model; exemplary.

обра́зчик *n.* **1,** sample. **2,** (*with gen.*) *fig., colloq.* sample (of); example (of).

обрамла́ть *v. impfv.* [*pfv.* обра́мить] to frame.

обраста́ть *v. impfv.* [*pfv.* обрасти́] (*with instr.*) **1,** to become overgrown (with). **2,** *colloq.* to be covered (with a layer of). **3,** *colloq.* to surround oneself (with).

обрасти́ [*infl. like* расти́] *v., pfv. of* обраста́ть.

обрати́мость *n.f.* **1,** reversibility. **2,** convertibility.

обрати́мый *adj.* **1,** reversible. **2,** convertible.

обрати́ть [*infl.* -щу́, -ти́шь] *v., pfv. of* обраща́ть. —**обрати́ться,** *refl., pfv. of* обраща́ться.

обра́тно *adv.* **1,** back. **2,** *colloq.* the other way round. **3,** *in* обра́тно пропорциона́льный (+ *dat.*), inversely proportional (to). —**биле́т туда́ и обра́тно,** round-trip ticket. —**пое́здка туда́ и обра́тно,** round trip.

обра́тное *n., decl. as an adj.* the opposite; the reverse.

обра́тный *adj.* **1,** reverse. **2,** opposite. **3,** return (*attrib.*): обра́тный а́дрес/биле́т/путь, return address/ticket/trip. С обра́тной по́чтой, by return mail. **4,** *math.* inverse.

обраща́ть *v. impfv.* [*pfv.* обрати́ть] **1,** to turn; direct. **2,** (*with* в + *acc.*) to turn (into); convert (into). —**обраща́ть внима́ние на** (+ *acc.*), to pay attention to. —**обраща́ть чье-нибудь внима́ние на** (+ *acc.*), to draw *or* call someone's attention to. —**обрати́ть в бе́гство,** to put to flight. —**обрати́ть в прах,** to reduce to dust (*or* ashes).

обраща́ться *v.r. impfv.* [*pfv.* обрати́ться] **1,** (*with* к) to apply (to); appeal (to); address. **2,** (*with* к) to turn to (*for advice or information*); consult; go to; see. **3,** (*with* в + *acc.*) to turn into; become. **4,** [*impfv. only*] to circulate; be in circulation. **5,** [*impfv. only*] (*with* с + *instr.*) to treat; handle (someone) in a certain way. **6,** [*impfv. only*] (*with* с + *instr.*) to handle; operate. **7,**

(*with* в + *acc.*) to convert (to another faith). —**обращаться в бегство**, to take flight.

обращение *n.* **1,** (*with* к) turning (toward). **2,** conversion. **3,** appeal. **4,** form of address: обращение на "ты", familiar form of address. **5,** (*with* с + *instr.*) treatment (of); handling (of). **6,** circulation.

обрез *n.* **1,** edge. **2,** sawed-off rifle. —**в обрез**, *colloq.* barely enough: у меня времени в обрез, I barely have enough time; I am pressed for time.

обрезание *n.* circumcision.

обрезание *n.* cutting; trimming.

обрезать [*infl.* -режу, -режешь] *v., pfv. of* обрезать *and* обрезывать. —**обрезаться**, *refl., pfv. of* обрезаться.

обрезать *v. impfv.* [*pfv.* обрезать] **1,** to trim; clip; prune. **2,** to cut (*accidentally*). **3,** *fig., colloq.* to cut short; interrupt. **4,** to circumcise. —**обрезаться**, *refl., colloq.* to cut oneself.

обрезок [*gen.* -зка] *n., usu. pl.* scrap (*of meat, paper, etc.*).

обрезывать *v. impfv.* = обрезать.

обрекать *v. impfv.* [*pfv.* обречь] (*with* на + *acc.*) to doom (to).

обременительный *adj.* burdensome; onerous.

обременять *v. impfv.* [*pfv.* обременить] to burden.

обрести [*infl.* обрету, обретёшь; *past* обрёл, обрела, обрело] *v., pfv. of* обретать.

обретать *v. impfv.* [*pfv.* обрести] to find.

обречённый *adj.* doomed. —**обречённость**, *n.f.* (impending) doom.

обречь [*infl.* -реку, -речёшь, ...-рекут; *past* -рёк, -рекла, -рекло] *v., pfv. of* обрекать.

обрисовать [*infl.* -сую, -суешь] *v., pfv. of* обрисовывать. —**обрисоваться**, *refl., pfv. of* обрисовываться.

обрисовывать *v. impfv.* [*pfv.* обрисовать] **1,** to draw a line around. **2,** to highlight. **3,** *fig.* to describe; portray. —**обрисовываться**, *refl.* **1,** to appear (in outline). **2,** *fig.* to become clear.

обрить *v. pfv.* [*infl.* обрею, обреешь] to shave; shave off. —**обриться**, *refl.* to shave one's head; shave off one's beard, mustache, etc.

оброк *n., hist.* tax paid by a peasant to the state for the use of land allotted to him; obrok.

обронить *v. pfv.* [*infl.* -роню, -ронишь] *colloq.* **1,** to drop. **2,** to let (a remark) drop.

обрубать *v. impfv.* [*pfv.* обрубить] **1,** to chop off; lop off. **2,** to chop the end off of.

обрубить [*infl.* -рублю, -рубишь] *v., pfv. of* обрубать.

обрубок [*gen.* -бка] *n.* stump.

обругать *v. pfv.* **1,** to curse out; call names. **2,** *colloq.* to criticize; attack; pan.

обрусеть *v. pfv.* to become Russified.

обруч [*pl.* обручи, обручей, -чам] *n.* hoop.

обручальный *adj.* engagement (*attrib.*). —**обручальное кольцо**, engagement ring; wedding ring.

обручать *v. impfv.* [*pfv.* обручить] to betroth; affiance. —**обручаться**, *refl.* (*with* с + *instr.*) to become engaged (to).

обручение *n.* engagement; betrothal.

обручить *v., pfv. of* обручать. —**обручиться**, *refl., pfv. of* обручаться.

обрушивать *v. impfv.* [*pfv.* обрушить] **1,** to bring down; send crashing to the ground. **2,** (*with* на + *acc.*) to bring down (on); rain (blows, bombs, etc.) on; hurl (epithets) at. —**обрушиваться**, *refl.* **1,** to collapse; cave in; come tumbling down. **2,** (*of the elements*) to pound; batter. **3,** (*with* на + *acc.*) to befall. **4,** (*with* на + *acc.*) to attack; pounce upon. **5,** (*with* на + *acc.*) to assail (*verbally*).

обрушить *v., pfv. of* обрушивать. —**обрушиться**, *refl., pfv. of* обрушиваться.

обрыв *n.* precipice.

обрывать *v. impfv.* [*pfv.* оборвать] **1,** to tear off; pluck. **2,** to break; snap. **3,** *fig.* to cut short; interrupt. —**обрываться**, *refl.* **1,** to break; snap. **2,** to slip; fall. **3,** *fig.* to stop suddenly; be suddenly cut short.

обрывистый *adj.* steep; precipitous.

обрывок [*gen.* -вка] *n.* **1,** scrap. **2,** *fig.* snatch (*of a song, conversation, etc.*). —**обрывочный**, *adj.* (*of thoughts, phrases, etc.*) disjointed.

обрызгивать *v. impfv.* [*pfv.* обрызгать] **1,** to spatter; splash. **2,** to sprinkle.

обрыскать *v. pfv., colloq.* to roam: обрыскать свет, to roam the world.

обрюзглый *adj.* flabby.

обрюзгнуть *v. pfv.* [*past* обрюзг, -ла] to become flabby.

обрюзгший *adj.* flabby.

обряд *n.* rite; ceremony. —**обрядовый**, *adj.* ritual; ceremonial.

обсадить [*infl.* -сажу, -садишь] *v., pfv. of* обсаживать.

обсаживать *v. impfv.* [*pfv.* обсадить] to plant around; plant along: обсаживать дорогу деревьями, to plant trees along a road.

обсерватория *n.* observatory.

обсесть *v. pfv.* [*infl. like* сесть] *colloq.* to sit around.

обскакать [*infl.* -скачу, -скачешь] *v., pfv. of* обскакивать.

обскакивать *v. impfv.* [*pfv.* обскакать] **1,** to gallop around. **2,** (*of a horse*) to outrun.

обскурант *n.* obscurant. —**обскурантизм**, *n.* obscurantism.

обследование *n.* **1,** inspection. **2,** *med.* checkup. —**обследователь**, *n.m.* inspector.

обследовать *v. impfv. & pfv.* [*pres.* -дую, -дуешь] to inspect.

обслуживание *n.* **1,** service. **2,** servicing; maintenance.

обслуживать *v. impfv.* [*pfv.* обслужить] **1,** to serve. **2,** to wait on. **3,** to service. **4,** [*impfv. only*] to operate (a machine).

обслужить [*infl.* -служу, -служишь] *v., pfv. of* обслуживать.

обсохнуть [*past* -сох, -ла] *v., pfv. of* обсыхать.

обставить [*infl.* -влю, -вишь] *v., pfv. of* обставлять.

обставлять *v. impfv.* [*pfv.* обставить] **1,** to surround (with). **2,** to furnish (a home, room, etc.). **3,** *fig.* to arrange; organize.

обстановка *n.* **1,** situation: международная обстановка, the international situation. **2,** *fig.* atmosphere; setting: в дружественной обстановке, in a friendly atmosphere. **3,** furniture. **4,** *theat.* set. —**перемена обстановки**, change of scenery (*fig.*).

обстирывать *v. impfv.* [*pfv.* обстирать] *colloq.* to do all the washing for.

обстоятельный *adj.* **1,** thorough; detailed. **2,** *colloq.* steady; reliable.

обстоя́тельство *n.* circumstance.

обстоя́ть *v. impfv.* to be; stand: как обстои́т де́ло с (+ *instr.*), how do matters stand with...? Вот как обстои́т де́ло, this is the way things stand; this is the way it is.

обстра́ивать *v. impfv.* [*pfv.* обстро́ить] 1, to surround (with buildings); line (with buildings). 2, to build; build up. —**обстра́иваться**, *refl., colloq.* 1, to build a house for oneself. 2, to be built up.

обстре́л *n.* fire; firing; shelling: попа́сть под обстре́л, to come under fire. —**взять под обстре́л**, to rake over the coals.

обстре́ливать *v. impfv.* [*pfv.* обстреля́ть] to fire upon; shell.

обстре́лянный *adj.* battle-hardened.

обстреля́ть *v., pfv. of* обстре́ливать.

обстро́ить *v., pfv. of* обстра́ивать. —**обстро́иться**, *refl., pfv. of* обстра́иваться.

обструкциони́зм *n.* obstructionism. —**обструкциони́ст**, *n.* obstructionist. —**обструкцио́нный**, *adj.* obstructionist.

обстру́кция *n.* obstruction; delaying tactics.

обступа́ть *v. impfv.* [*pfv.* обступи́ть] to surround; crowd around; cluster around.

обступи́ть [*infl.* -ступлю́, -сту́пишь] *v., pfv. of* обступа́ть.

обсуди́ть [*infl.* -сужу́, -су́дишь] *v., pfv. of* обсужда́ть.

обсужда́ть *v. impfv.* [*pfv.* обсуди́ть] to discuss.

обсужде́ние *n.* discussion.

обсу́шивать *v. impfv.* [*pfv.* обсуши́ть] to dry; dry out. —**обсу́шиваться**, *refl.* to dry oneself off; get dry.

обсуши́ть [*infl.* -сушу́, -су́шишь] *v., pfv. of* обсу́шивать. —**обсуши́ться**, *refl., pfv. of* обсу́шиваться.

обсчи́тывать *v. impfv.* [*pfv.* обсчита́ть] to short-change. —**обсчи́тываться**, *refl.* to make an error in counting; miscount.

обсы́пать [*infl.* -сы́плю, -сы́плешь] *v., pfv. of* обсы́па́ть.

обсыпа́ть *v. impfv.* [*pfv.* обсы́пать] to sprinkle (with).

обсыха́ть *v. impfv.* [*pfv.* обсо́хнуть] to dry; dry off. —**у него́ молоко́ на губа́х не обсо́хло**, he is still wet behind the ears.

обта́чивать *v. impfv.* [*pfv.* обточи́ть] to grind smooth.

обтека́емый *adj.* streamlined.

обтека́ть *v. impfv.* [*pfv.* обте́чь] 1, to flow around. 2, to bypass; skirt.

обтере́ть [*infl.* оботру́, оботрёшь; *past* обтёр, -ла] *v., pfv. of* обтира́ть. —**обтере́ться**, *refl., pfv. of* обтира́ться.

обтеса́ть [*infl.* -тешу́, -те́шешь] *v., pfv. of* обтёсывать.

обтёсывать *v. impfv.* [*pfv.* обтеса́ть] 1, to trim; rough-hew. 2, *fig., colloq.* to teach (someone) good manners.

обте́чь [*infl. like* те́чь] *v., pfv. of* обтека́ть.

обтира́ние *n.* rubdown.

обтира́ть *v. impfv.* [*pfv.* обтере́ть] 1, to wipe. 2, to wipe away. 3, to rub (with). —**обтира́ться**, *refl.* 1, to dry oneself. 2, to sponge oneself down. 3, *colloq.* to wear thin.

обточи́ть [*infl.* -точу́, -то́чишь] *v., pfv. of* обта́чивать.

обтрёпанный *adj.* 1, frayed; tattered. 2, shabbily dressed.

обтрепа́ть *v. pfv.* [*infl.* -треплю́, -тре́плешь] to fray. —**обтрепа́ться**, *refl.* to fray; become frayed.

обтя́гивать *v. impfv.* [*pfv.* обтяну́ть] 1, to cover; upholster. 2, (*of clothes*) to fit tightly; hug. —**обтя́гиваться**, *refl.* 1, to become covered. 2, (*of one's face*) to become drawn.

обтя́жка *n.* 1, covering. 2, cover. —**в обтя́жку**, close-fitting; tight-fitting.

обтяну́ть [*infl.* -тяну́, -тя́нешь] *v., pfv. of* обтя́гивать. —**обтяну́ться**, *refl., pfv. of* обтя́гиваться.

обува́ть *v. impfv.* [*pfv.* обу́ть] 1, to put on (someone's) shoes. 2, to put on (one's shoes). 3, to provide with shoes. —**обува́ться**, *refl.* to put on one's shoes.

обувно́й *adj.* shoe (*attrib.*).

о́бувь *n.f.* shoes; footwear.

обу́гливать *v. impfv.* [*pfv.* обу́глить] to char.

обу́за *n.* 1, burdensome chore. 2, burden.

обузда́ние *n.* restraint.

обу́здывать *v. impfv.* [*pfv.* обузда́ть] 1, to bridle (a horse). 2, *fig.* to restrain; curb.

обурева́ть *v. impfv.* (*of fears, doubts, etc.*) to seize; grip.

обусло́вливать *v. impfv.* [*pfv.* облусло́вить] 1, to condition; make conditional. 2, to cause; occasion. —**обусло́вливаться**, *refl.* (*with instr.*) 1, to be conditional (upon); be determined (by). 2, to be the result (of); be due (to).

обу́ть [*infl.* обу́ю, обу́ешь] *v., pfv. of* обува́ть. —**обу́ться**, *refl., pfv. of* обува́ться.

о́бух *also,* обу́х *n.* butt; butt end. —**бить/ударя́ть кого́-нибудь как о́бухом (обухо́м) по голове́**, to hit someone like a thunderbolt.

обуча́ть *v. impfv.* [*pfv.* обучи́ть] to teach; instruct; train: обуча́ть кого́-нибудь ремеслу́, to teach someone a trade. —**обуча́ться**, *refl.* 1, (*with dat.*) to learn: обуча́ться ремеслу́, to learn a trade. 2, [*impfv. only*] to study (in a certain institution).

обуче́ние *n.* 1, (*with gen.*) teaching; training (*of people*). Обуче́ние взро́слых, adult education. 2, (*with dat.*) teaching (*of a subject*); instruction (in): обуче́ние ремеслу́, teaching of a trade. Беспла́тное обуче́ние, free tuition.

обучи́ть [*infl.* -учу́, -у́чишь] *v., pfv. of* обуча́ть. —**обучи́ться**, *refl., pfv. of* обуча́ться.

обуя́ть *v. pfv.* (*of a feeling or physical state*) to seize; come over.

обха́живать *v. impfv., colloq.* 1, to walk all over. 2, to care for. 3, to play up to; cultivate.

обхва́т *n.* 1, circumference; girth: метр в обхва́те, a meter in circumference. 2, circumference equal to a span of the arm: дуб в три обхва́та, an oak tree three spans in circumference.

обхвати́ть [*infl.* -хвачу́, -хва́тишь] *v., pfv. of* обхва́тывать.

обхва́тывать *v. impfv.* [*pfv.* обхвати́ть] 1, to put one's arms around. 2, *fig.* to take in; embrace; encompass.

обхо́д *n.* 1, going around. 2, detour; bypass. 3, rounds; beat: идти́ в обхо́д, to make one's rounds. 4, *mil.* flanking movement. —**в обхо́д** (+ *gen.*), skirting; bypassing.

обходи́тельный *adj.* polite; courteous. —**обходи́тельность** *n.f.* politeness.

обходи́ть *v. imp v.* [*pfv.* обойти́; *pres.* -хожу́, -хо́дишь] 1, to go around; walk around. 2, *mil.* to outflank.

3, to walk around; bypass; avoid. **4,** to pass over; ignore. **5,** to circumvent; get around (a law, rule, etc.). **6,** to pass over; fail to promote. **7,** colloq. to pass; outpace. **8,** (with весь) to walk all over. **9,** (with все) to make the rounds of; go to every one of. **10,** to spread all over: но́вость обошла́ весь го́род, the news spread all over town. —обходи́ться, refl. **1,** (with с + instr.) to treat. **2,** colloq. to cost. **3,** colloq. to get along; manage. **4,** colloq. to turn out; work out.

обхо́дный adj. **1,** roundabout; circuitous: обхо́дным путём, by a roundabout way. **2,** mil. outflanking: обхо́дное движе́ние, outflanking movement.

обхо́дчик n. inspector. —путево́й обхо́дчик, R.R. trackwalker.

обхожде́ние n. **1,** behavior; manners; attitude. **2,** treatment.

обче́сться v.r. pfv. [infl. обочту́сь, обочтёшься; past обчёлся, обочла́сь] colloq. = обсчита́ться. —раз, два и обчёлся, you can count them on the fingers of one hand.

обчи́стить [infl. -чи́щу, -чи́стишь] v., pfv. of обчища́ть.

обчища́ть v. impfv. [pfv. обчи́стить] colloq. **1,** to clean. **2,** (in gambling) to clean out; take to the cleaners.

обша́ривать v. impfv. [pfv. обша́рить] colloq. to rummage; ransack.

обша́рпанный adj., colloq. dilapidated; run-down.

обшива́ть v. impfv. [pfv. обши́ть] **1,** (with instr.) to edge (with); border (with); trim (with). **2,** (with instr.) to plank (with boards). **3,** colloq. to sew all the clothes for.

обши́вка n. **1,** edging; bordering; trimming. **2,** plating; sheeting; planking.

обши́рный adj. vast; extensive. —обши́рность, n.f. extent; magnitude.

обши́ть [infl. обошью́, обошьёшь] v., pfv. of обшива́ть.

обшла́г [gen. sing. & nom. pl. обшлага́] n. cuff.

обща́ться v.r. impfv. (with с + instr.) to associate (with); consort (with); socialize (with).

общедосту́пный adj. **1,** available to all. **2,** understandable to all; popular. **3,** (of prices) moderate; reasonable.

общежи́тие n. **1,** dormitory. **2,** society; everyday life.

общеизве́стный adj. generally known; known to all. Общеизве́стно, что..., it is common knowledge that...

общенаро́дный adj. national; of all the people.

обще́ние n. association; contact; intercourse.

общеобразова́тельный adj. (of a school, subject, etc.) general; not specialized.

общепри́нятый adj. generally accepted; conventional.

обще́ственник n. person active in public life.

обще́ственность n.f. **1,** the public. **2,** public opinion. **3,** public-mindedness. **4,** socially active members.

обще́ственный adj. public; social.

о́бщество n. **1,** society; company: в о́бществе друзе́й, in the company of friends. **2,** society: лите-рату́рное о́бщество, literary society.

о́бщий adj. **1,** general; common. **2,** total; overall. —в о́бщем, in general; on the whole. —в о́бщем и це́лом, on the whole; all in all. —о́бщее ме́сто, platitude. —о́бщая су́мма; о́бщий ито́г, sum total; grand total. —не име́ть ничего́ о́бщего с, to have nothing in common with.

о́бщина also, общи́на n. **1,** community. **2,** commune.

общи́нный adj. communal.

общипа́ть [infl. -щиплю́, -щи́плешь] v., pfv. of щипа́ть (in sense #3) and общи́пывать.

общи́пывать v. impfv. [pfv. общипа́ть] to pluck.

общи́тельный adj. sociable; gregarious. —общи́тельность, n.f. sociability.

о́бщность n.f. commonality: о́бщность интере́сов, commonality of interests.

объего́ривать v. impfv. [pfv. объего́рить] colloq. to swindle; cheat; gyp.

объеда́ть v. impfv. [pfv. объе́сть] **1,** to eat around; nibble at. **2,** colloq. to eat out of house and home. —объеда́ться, refl. **1,** to overeat. **2,** (with instr. or gen.) to eat too much of.

объеде́ние n. **1,** overeating. **2,** colloq. something delicious; something out of this world.

объедине́ние n. **1,** unification. **2,** amalgamation; merger. **3,** union; association. **4,** mil. large formation (front, army, etc.).

объединённый adj. **1,** united: Объединённые На́ции, United Nations. **2,** joint: объединённый комите́т, joint committee.

объединя́ть v. impfv. [pfv. объедини́ть] **1,** to unite; unify. **2,** to combine (into one); amalgamate. **3,** to join; combine (forces, efforts, etc.). —объединя́ться, refl. to unite; combine; amalgamate.

объе́дки [gen. -ков] n.pl., colloq. leftovers; scraps.

объе́зд n. **1,** traveling around. **2,** detour.

объе́здить [infl. -е́зжу, -е́здишь] v., pfv. of объезжа́ть.

объе́здка n. breaking in (of a horse).

объе́здчик n. warden; ranger.

объезжа́ть v. impfv. **1,** [pfv. объе́хать] to go around; drive around; detour around. **2,** [pfv. объе́хать or объе́здить] to drive all over; travel throughout (a city, region, etc.). **3,** [pfv. объе́здить] to break in (a horse).

объе́кт n. **1,** object. **2,** establishment; installation. **3,** mil. objective.

объекти́в n. lens.

объекти́вный adj. objective. —объекти́вно, adv. objectively. —объекти́вность, n.f. objectivity.

объе́ктный adj., in объе́ктный паде́ж, objective case.

объём n. **1,** volume (of a geometric figure, trade, etc.). **2,** fig. scope; range.

объёмистый adj., colloq. large; bulky; voluminous.

объёмный adj. **1,** by volume. **2,** volumetric. **3,** (of an image, film, etc.) three-dimensional.

объе́сть [infl. like есть] v., pfv. of объеда́ть. —объе́сться, refl., pfv. of объеда́ться.

объе́хать [infl. -е́ду, -е́дешь] v., pfv. of объезжа́ть.

объяви́ть [infl. -явлю́, -я́вишь] v., pfv. of объявля́ть. —объяви́ться, refl., pfv. of объявля́ться.

объявле́ние n. **1,** declaration: объявле́ние войны́, declaration of war. **2,** announcement: объявле́ние о собра́нии, announcement of a meeting. **3,** advertisement. —доска́ объявле́ний, bulletin board.

объявля́ть v. impfv. [pfv. объяви́ть] **1,** to declare. **2,** (with acc. or о + prepl.) to announce. —объявля́ться, refl. **1,** colloq. to turn up; show up. **2,** (with instr.) to declare oneself to be.

объясне́ние n. **1,** explanation. **2,** face-to-face meeting (to settle something). **3,** in объясне́ние в любви́, declaration of love.

объясни́мый adj. explainable; explicable.

объясни́тельный adj. explanatory.

объясня́ть v. impfv. [pfv. **объясни́ть**] to explain. —**объясня́ться**, refl. **1**, (with с + instr.) to have a talk (with); have it out with. **2**, obs. to explain oneself; explain one's behavior. **3**, to become clear. **4**, [impfv. only] to express oneself; make oneself understood. **5**, [impfv. only] (with instr.) to be explained (by); be accounted for (by): чем э́то объясня́ется?, how do you account for this? Э́тим объясня́ется его́ поведе́ние, this accounts for his behavior. **6**, in **объясни́ться в любви́** (+ dat.), to make a declaration of love (to).

объя́тие n., usu. pl. embrace. —**с распростёртыми объя́тиями**, with open arms.

объя́ть v. pfv. [infl. **обойму́, обоймёшь**; past **объя́л, объя́ла**] **1**, to embrace. **2**, to engulf; envelop. **3**, (of an emotion) to fill; seize; come over.

обыва́тель n.m. **1**, obs. inhabitant; resident. **2**, person of narrow or petty interests. —**обыва́тельский**, adj. narrow; narrow-minded.

обы́грывать v. impfv. [pfv. **обыгра́ть**] to beat; defeat (in a game).

обы́денный adj. ordinary; everyday.

обыкнове́ние n. habit. —**по обыкнове́нию**, as usual; as is his/her custom or wont.

обыкнове́нно adv. usually.

обыкнове́нный adj. **1**, usual; customary. **2**, ordinary.

о́быск n. search (of a person, premises, etc.).

обыска́ть [infl. **обыщу́, обы́щешь**] v., pfv. of **обы́скивать**.

обы́скивать v. impfv. [pfv. **обыска́ть**] to search; conduct a search of.

обы́чай n. custom.

обы́чно adv. usually; generally; ordinarily. —**как обы́чно**, as usual.

обы́чный adj. **1**, usual; customary. Ра́ньше обы́чного, earlier than usual. **2**, ordinary. **3**, (of weapons) conventional. —**обы́чное пра́во**, common law.

обя́занность n.f. duty; responsibility.

обя́занный adj. **1**, (with inf.) obliged (to); required (to). **2**, (with dat.) obliged (to); indebted (to); obligated (to).

обяза́тельно adv. **1**, without fail. **2**, necessarily. **3**, as an interj. of course!; absolutely!

обяза́тельный adj. **1**, compulsory; obligatory; mandatory. **2**, obliging; accommodating.

обяза́тельство n. obligation; commitment. —**долгово́е обяза́тельство**, promissory note.

обяза́ть [infl. **обяжу́, обя́жешь**] v., pfv. of **обя́зывать**. —**обяза́ться**, refl., pfv. of **обя́зываться**.

обя́зывать v. impfv. [pfv. **обяза́ть**; pres. **-ваю, -ваешь** or **-зу́ю, -зу́ешь**] **1**, to oblige; obligate; bind; commit. **2**, to oblige; do (someone) a favor. —**обя́зываться**, refl. (with inf.) to pledge (to); undertake (to).

ова́л n. oval. —**ова́льный**, adj. oval.

ова́ция n. ovation: устро́ить ова́цию (+ dat.), to give an ovation (to).

овдове́ть v. pfv. (of a woman) to become widowed; (of a man) to become a widower.

овева́ть v. impfv. [pfv. **ове́ять**] **1**, (of the wind) to blow upon; fan. **2**, fig. to pervade; infuse.

ове́н [gen. овна́; pl. о́вны] n. **1**, obs. ram. **2**, cap. Aries.

овёс [gen. овса́] n. oats.

ове́чий [fem. **-чья**] adj. sheep (attrib.); sheep's. —**волк в ове́чьей шку́ре**, wolf in sheep's clothing.

ове́чка [gen. pl. **-чек**] n., dim. of **овца́**.

ове́ять [infl. **ове́ю, ове́ешь**] v., pfv. of **овева́ть**.

ОВИ́Р abbr. of **отде́л виз и регистра́ции**, visa and registration department; OVIR.

овладева́ть v. impfv. [pfv. **овладе́ть**] (with instr.) **1**, to seize; capture. **2**, to control; dominate. **3**, (of emotions) to seize; grip; come over. **4**, to master (a subject, theory, technique, etc.). —**овладе́ть собо́й**, to compose oneself; regain one's composure.

овладе́ние n. **1**, capture. **2**, mastery.

овладе́ть v., pfv. of **овладева́ть**.

о́вод [pl. о́воды or овода́] n. gadfly.

о́вощи [gen. овоще́й] n.pl. [sing. о́вощ] vegetables.

овощно́й adj. vegetable (attrib.).

овра́г n. ravine.

овся́нка [gen. pl. **-нок**] n. **1**, oatmeal. **2**, bunting (bird). Обыкнове́нная овся́нка, yellowhammer. Садо́вая овся́нка, ortolan.

овся́ный also, **овсяно́й** adj. oat (attrib.). —**овся́ная ка́ша; овся́ная крупа́**, oatmeal.

овуля́ция n. ovulation.

овца́ [pl. о́вцы, ове́ц, о́вцам] n. **1**, sheep. **2**, ewe.

овцебы́к n. musk ox.

овцево́д n. sheep farmer. —**овцево́дство**, n. sheep raising. —**овцево́дческий**, adj. pert. to the raising of sheep: овцево́дческая фе́рма, sheep farm.

овча́рка [gen. pl. **-рок**] n. sheep dog. —**неме́цкая овча́рка**, German shepherd.

овча́рня [gen. pl. **-рен**] n. sheepfold.

овчи́на also, **овчи́нка** n. sheepskin. —**овчи́нный**, adj. sheepskin.

ога́рок [gen. **-рка**] n. candle end.

огиба́ть v. impfv. [pfv. **обогну́ть**] **1**, to bend around; wind around. **2**, to round; go around; skirt.

оглавле́ние n. table of contents.

огласи́ть [infl. **-шу́, -си́шь**] v., pfv. of **оглаша́ть**.

огла́ска n. publicity.

оглаша́ть v. impfv. [pfv. **огласи́ть**] **1**, to announce; read out. **2**, obs. to divulge; make public. **3**, to fill (the air, a room, etc.) with a certain sound.

огло́бля [gen. pl. **-бель**] n. shaft (for harnessing a horse to a carriage).

огло́хнуть [past огло́х, **-ла**] v., pfv. of **гло́хнуть** (in sense #1).

оглуша́ть v. impfv. [pfv. **оглуши́ть**] **1**, to deafen. **2**, to stun.

оглуши́тельный adj. deafening.

оглуши́ть v., pfv. of **глуши́ть** (in sense #7) and **оглуша́ть**.

огляде́ть [infl. **-жу́, -ди́шь**] v., pfv. of **огля́дывать**. —**огляде́ться**, refl. **1**, pfv. of **огля́дываться** (in sense #1). **2**, fig. to get used to one's surroundings.

огля́дка n., obs. looking back. —**без огля́дки**, **1**, (with verbs of running) without looking back; like a jack rabbit. **2**, without second thoughts; without looking back. —**с огля́дкой**, with caution; cautiously.

огля́дывать v. impfv. [pfv. **огляде́ть** or **огляну́ть**] to look over; examine. —**огля́дываться**, refl. **1**, [pfv. огляде́ться] to look around. **2**, [pfv. огляну́ться] to look back; turn around and look.

огляну́ть [infl. **огляну́, огля́нешь**] v., pfv. of **огля́дывать**. —**огляну́ться**, refl., pfv. of **огля́дываться** (in sense #2).

огнево́й adj. **1**, fire (attrib.): огнева́я мощь, firepower. **2**, fiery. **3**, fiery red. —**огнево́й вал**, covering fire; barrage. —**огнева́я то́чка**, gun emplacement.

огнемёт *n.* flame thrower.

óгненный *adj.* **1,** fiery; ablaze. **2,** fiery red. **3,** *fig.* fiery; impassioned.

огнеопáсный *adj.* flammable; inflammable.

огнестрéльный *adj., in* огнестрéльное орýжие, firearm; firearms; огнестрéльная рáна, gunshot wound.

огнетушúтель *n.m.* fire extinguisher.

огнеупóрный *adj.* heat-resistant; refractory.

огó *interj.* oho!

оговáривать *v. impfv.* [*pfv.* оговорúть] **1,** to stipulate. **2,** to slander. —**оговáриваться,** *refl.* **1,** to point out in advance. **2,** to qualify one's statement. **3,** to make a slip of the tongue.

оговóр *n.* slander.

оговорúть *v., pfv. of* оговáривать. —**оговорúться,** *refl., pfv. of* оговáриваться.

оговóрка [*gen. pl.* -рок] *n.* **1,** reservation; stipulation; proviso; qualification. **2,** slip of the tongue.

оголённый *adj.* bare; nude.

оголúть *v., pfv. of* оголя́ть. —**оголúться,** *refl., pfv. of* оголя́ться.

оголтéлый *adj., colloq.* mad; rabid; fanatical.

оголя́ть *v. impfv.* [*pfv.* оголúть] **1,** to bare; expose. **2,** to denude. **3,** to draw; unsheathe (a sword). **4,** *mil.* to expose. —**оголя́ться,** *refl.* to be exposed.

огонёк [*gen.* -нькá] *n.* **1,** light; dot of light: огонькú гóрода, the lights of a city. **2,** *fig.* zest; verve. —**зайтú на огонёк** (*with* к), to drop in (on).

огóнь [*gen.* огня́] *n.m.* **1,** fire. **2,** light: огнú гóрода, the lights of a city. **3,** fire (*from a gun*): пулемётный огóнь, machine-gun fire. Откры́ть огóнь, to open fire. —**в огнé,** on fire; aflame; ablaze. —**днём с огнём** (**не найтú, не сыскáть,** *etc.*), seldom seen anywhere; not to be found anywhere. —**игрáть с огнём,** to play with fire. —**идтú/пойтú в огóнь и в вóду за** (+ *acc. or instr.*), to be willing to do anything for. —**мéжду двух огнéй,** between the devil and the deep blue sea. —**пройтú огóнь и вóду,** to have been through the mill.

огорáживать *v. impfv.* [*pfv.* огородúть] to fence in; enclose.

огорóд *n.* vegetable garden.

огородúть [*infl.* -рожý, -рóдишь *or* -родúшь] *v., pfv. of* огорáживать.

огорóдник *n.* truck farmer. —**огорóдничество,** *n.* truck farming.

огорóдный *adj.* garden (*attrib.*).

огорóшить *v. pfv., colloq.* to take aback.

огорчáть *v. impfv.* [*pfv.* огорчúть] to distress; grieve. —**огорчáться,** *refl.* to be distressed.

огорчéние *n.* distress; chagrin. —**огорчúтельный,** *adj.* distressing.

огорчúть *v., pfv. of* огорчáть. —**огорчúться,** *refl., pfv. of* огорчáться.

огрáбить *v., pfv. of* грáбить.

ограблéние *n.* robbery.

огрáда *n.* fence.

оградúть [*infl.* -жý, -дúшь] *v., pfv. of* ограждáть.

ограждáть *v. impfv.* [*pfv.* оградúть] **1,** *obs.* to fence in. **2,** to protect; shield.

ограждéние *n.* **1,** fencing in. **2,** protection. **3,** fence; barrier.

ограничéние *n.* limitation; restriction.

ограни́ченный *adj.* **1,** limited. **2,** (*of a person*) of limited intellect.

ограни́чивать *v. impfv.* [*pfv.* ограни́чить] to limit; restrict; confine. —**ограни́чиваться,** *refl.* (*with instr.*) **1,** to limit/restrict/confine oneself (to). **2,** to be limited (to).

ограничи́тельный *adj.* **1,** restrictive. **2,** *fig.* narrow: ограничи́тельное толковáние, narrow interpretation.

ограни́чить *v., pfv. of* ограни́чивать. —**ограни́читься,** *refl., pfv. of* ограни́чиваться.

огрéть *v.pfv., colloq.* to smack; whack.

огрéх *n., colloq.* fault; shortcoming; imperfection.

огрóмный *adj.* enormous; huge; tremendous; immense. —**огрóмность,** *n.f.* immensity.

огрубéлый *adj.* rough; coarse; callous(ed).

огрубéть *v., pfv. of* грубéть.

огрызáть *v. impfv.* [*pfv.* огры́зть] *colloq.* to nibble at. —**огрызáться,** *refl.* [*pfv.* огрызну́ться] **1,** (*with* на + *acc.*) (*of a dog*) to snap (at). **2,** *colloq.* to snap; retort sharply.

огры́зок [*gen.* -зка] *n.* **1,** leftover bit (*of an apple, piece of meat, etc.*). **2,** stub (*of a pencil*).

огры́зть [*infl. like* гры́зть] *v., pfv. of* огрызáть.

огýлом *adv., colloq.* **1,** indiscriminately; wholesale. **2,** in one lot; in a lump. **3,** all together; en masse.

огýльно *adv.* **1,** without grounds; unfairly. **2,** indiscriminately; wholesale.

огýльный *adj.* **1,** unfounded; groundless. **2,** *colloq.* indiscriminate; wholesale; sweeping.

огурéц [*gen.* -рцá] *n.* cucumber. —**огурéчный,** *adj.* cucumber (*attrib.*).

óда *n.* ode.

одáлживать *v. impfv.* [*pfv.* одолжи́ть] to lend.

одарённость *n.f.* gifts; talents; endowments.

одарённый *adj.* gifted.

одаря́ть *v. impfv.* [*pfv.* одари́ть] (*with instr.*) **1,** *obs.* to give (as a gift). **2,** to endow (with).

одевáть *v. impfv.* [*pfv.* одéть] to dress; clothe. —**одевáться,** *refl.* to dress; get dressed.

одéжда *n.* clothes; clothing.

одеколóн *n.* eau de Cologne.

оделя́ть *v. impfv.* [*pfv.* одели́ть] (*with instr.*) to present (with): оделя́ть детéй сластя́ми, to present sweets to the children.

одёр [*gen.* одрá] *n., colloq.* old horse; jade.

одёргивать *v. impfv.* [*pfv.* одёрнуть] **1,** to pull down; straighten (an article of clothing). **2,** *colloq.* to restrain; silence.

одеревенéлый *adj.* **1,** stiff; numb. **2,** *fig.* lifeless.

одеревенéть *v. pfv.* **1,** *pfv.of* деревенéть. **2,** *fig.* to become indifferent; become apathetic.

одержáть *v. pfv.* [*infl.* одержý, одéржишь] *in* одержáть побéду, to score a victory. —**одержáть верх,** *see* верх.

одержи́мость *n.f.* obsession; preoccupation.

одержи́мый *adj.* (*with instr.*) obsessed (by); possessed (by).

одёрнуть *v., pfv. of* одёргивать.

одéть [*infl.* одéну, одéнешь] *v., pfv. of* одевáть. —**одéться,** *refl., pfv. of* одевáться.

одея́ло *n.* blanket; cover.

одея́ние *n., obs.* clothing; raiment.

оди́н [*fem.* однá; *neut.* однó; *pl.* одни́; *gen.* одногó, однóй, одни́х; *acc. fem.* однý; *dat.* одномý, однóй,

одни́м; *instr.* одни́м, одно́й, одни́ми; *prepl.* одно́м, одно́й, одни́х] *numeral* one: оди́н биле́т, one ticket; одна́ ко́мната, one room; одни́ часы́, one watch. —*pron.* **1,** one: оди́н из са́мых лу́чших, one of the best. Оди́н друго́го удиви́тельнее, one more surprising than the next. **2,** *pl.* some; certain: одни́ бо́льше, чем други́е, some are larger than others. —*adj.* **1,** a; a certain. **2,** alone; by oneself: он живёт оди́н, he lives alone. **3,** only: в це́ркви бы́ли одни́ стару́шки, there were only old women in the church. **4,** the same: жить в одно́м до́ме, to live in the same house; они́ одни́х лет, they are the same age. —**все до одного́,** (everyone) to a man. —**все как оди́н,** one and all alike. —**ни оди́н,** not a single: он не сказа́л ни одного́ сло́ва, he did not say a single word. —**оди́н за други́м,** one by one; one after the other. —**оди́н и тот же,** the same. —**оди́н на оди́н,** face to face. —**оди́н то́лько,** alone: в одно́й то́лько Фра́нции, in France alone. —**по одному́,** one by one; one at a time. *See also* **одно́.**

одина́ково *adv.* **1,** identically. **2,** equally.

одина́ковый *adj.* identical. Они́ одина́кового ро́ста; они́ одина́ковы по ро́сту, they are of identical height; they are identical in height. —**в одина́ковой ме́ре,** in equal measure.

одина́рный *adj.* single.

оди́ннадцатый *ordinal numeral* eleventh.

оди́ннадцать [*gen., dat., & prepl.* -цати; *instr.* -цатью] *numeral* eleven.

одино́кий *adj.* **1,** lone; solitary. **2,** lonely; lonesome. **3,** single; unmarried. —*n.* single person; unmarried person.

одино́ко *adv.* **1,** alone. **2,** lonely: чу́вствовать себя́ одино́ко, to feel lonely.

одино́чество *n.* solitude; loneliness.

одино́чка [*gen. pl.* -чек] *n.m. & f.* lone person; person on his/her own. ♦*Often in compounds:* мать-одино́чка, unwed mother; single mother. —*n.f., colloq.* solitary (confinement) cell. —**в одино́чку,** alone; by oneself; on one's own. —**одино́чкой,** alone. —**по одино́чке,** one by one.

одино́чный *adj.* **1,** lone; solitary. **2,** for one person; single. —**одино́чный бой,** single combat. —**одино́чное заключе́ние,** solitary confinement.

одио́зный *adj.* odious; offensive.

одиссе́я *n.* odyssey.

одича́лый *adj.* (*of an animal, plant, etc.*) wild.

одича́ть *v., pfv. of* **дича́ть.**

одна́жды *adv.* **1,** once. **2,** once; one day; once upon a time.

одна́ко *conj.* however; but.

одно́ *numeral, neut. of* **оди́н.** —*pron.* one thing: одно́ несомне́нно, one thing is certain. —**одно́ и то же,** the same thing.

однобо́кий *adj.* **1,** lopsided. **2,** *fig.* one-sided.

однобо́ртный *adj.* single-breasted.

одновре́менно *also,* **одновреме́нно** *adv.* simultaneously; at the same time.

одновре́менность *also,* **одновреме́нность** *n.f.* simultaneity.

одновре́менный *also,* **одновреме́нный** *adj.* simultaneous.

одногла́зый *adj.* one-eyed.

одногоди́чный *adj.* one-year (*attrib.*).

одного́док [*gen.* -дка] *n.m.* [*fem.* -дка] *colloq.* = **одноле́ток.**

однодне́вный *adj.* one-day (*attrib.*).

однозна́чный *adj.* **1,** synonymous. **2,** having only one meaning. **3,** (*of a number*) one-digit.

одноимённый *adj.* of the same name.

однока́шник *n., colloq.* fellow student.

однокла́ссник *n.* classmate.

однокле́точный *adj.* one-celled.

одноколе́йный *adj.* single-track (*attrib.*).

одноко́лка *n.* gig.

однокомнатный *adj.* one-room (*attrib.*).

однокра́тный *adj., gram.* semelfactive: однокра́тный глаго́л, semelfactive verb (*e.g.* кри́кнуть).

одноку́рсник *n.* person enrolled in the same course; classmate.

одноле́тний *adj.* **1,** one-year (*attrib.*); one-year-old. **2,** *bot.* annual.

одноле́ток [*gen.* -тка] *n.m.* [*fem.* -тка] *colloq.* contemporary; person the same age.

одноме́стный *adj.* having one seat; having room for one; single-seat (*attrib.*).

однonóгий *adj.* one-legged.

однообра́зие *n.* monotony. —**однообра́зный,** *adj.* monotonous.

однопала́тный *adj.* unicameral.

однопо́лый *adj.* unisexual.

однорельсовый *adj.* single-rail (*attrib.*). —**одноре́льсовая желе́зная доро́га,** monorail.

однoро́дный *adj.* **1,** homogeneous. **2,** similar; uniform. —**одноро́дность,** *n.f.* homogeneity.

однору́кий *adj.* one-armed.

односельча́нин [*pl.* -ча́не, -ча́н] *n.m.* [*fem.* -ча́нка] person from the same village.

односло́жный *adj.* **1,** one-syllable; monosyllabic. **2,** *fig.* one-syllable; terse.

односпа́льный *adj., in* **односпа́льная крова́ть,** single bed.

односторо́нний *adj.* **1,** one-sided. **2,** unilateral. **3,** (*of movement, traffic, etc.*) one-way.

одноти́пный *adj.* of the same type.

однотомный *adj.* one-volume (*attrib.*).

одното́нный *adj.* **1,** monotone. **2,** single-colored. **3,** (*of a color*) solid.

однофами́лец [*gen.* -льца] *n.m.* [*fem.* -лица] person with the same (last) name.

одноцве́тный *adj.* one-color (*attrib.*); plain.

одноэта́жный *adj.* one-story.

одобре́ние *n.* approval.

одобри́тельный *adj.* approving. —**одобри́тельно,** *adv.* approvingly.

одобря́ть *v. impfv.* [*pfv.* **одо́брить**] to approve (of).

одолева́ть *v. impfv.* [*pfv.* **одоле́ть**] **1,** to overcome. **2,** *colloq.* to master.

одолжа́ть *v. impfv.* [*pfv.* **одолжи́ть**] **1,** to lend; loan. **2,** *obs.* to oblige; do (someone) a favor.

одолже́ние *n.* favor: сде́лать одолже́ние (+ *dat.*), to do someone a favor.

одолжи́ть *v., pfv. of* **одолжа́ть** *and* **ода́лживать.**

одома́шнивание *n.* domestication. *Also,* **одома́шнение.**

одома́шнивать *v. impfv.* [*pfv.* **одома́шнить**] to domesticate.

одо́метр *n.* odometer.

одонтоло́гия *n.* odontology.

одр [*gen.* одра́] *n.*, *obs.* bed. —**на сме́ртном одре́,** on one's deathbed.

одряхле́вший *adj.* decrepit; enfeebled.

одряхле́ть *v.*, *pfv. of* дряхле́ть.

одува́нчик *n.* dandelion.

оду́мываться *v.r. impfv.* [*pfv.* оду́маться] **1,** to change one's mind; think better of it. **2,** to collect oneself; come to one's senses.

одура́чить *v.*, *pfv. of* дура́чить.

одуре́лый *adj.*, *colloq.* dazed; groggy.

одуре́ние *n.*, *colloq.* stupor: пить до одуре́ния, to drink oneself into a stupor.

одуре́ть *v.*, *pfv. of* дуре́ть.

одурма́нить *v.*, *pfv. of* дурма́нить.

о́дурь *n.f.*, *colloq.* daze; trance; stupor.

одуря́ть *v. impfv.*, *colloq.* to cloud; befuddle (the mind).

одутлова́тый *adj.* puffy.

одухотворя́ть *v. impfv.* [*pfv.* одухотвори́ть] **1,** to ascribe intelligent powers to. **2,** to animate; inspire.

одушеви́ть [*infl.* -влю́, -ви́шь] *v.*, *pfv. of* одушевля́ть.

одушевле́ние *n.* enthusiasm; animation.

одушевлённый *adj.* **1,** animate. **2,** animated.

одушевля́ть *v. impfv.* [*pfv.* одушеви́ть] to animate.

оды́шка *n.* shortness of breath.

ожереби́ться *v.r.*, *pfv. of* жереби́ться.

ожере́лье *n.* necklace.

ожесточа́ть *v. impfv.* [*pfv.* ожесточи́ть] **1,** to harden. **2,** to embitter.

ожесточе́ние *n.* **1,** bitterness. **2,** *fig.* great zeal; great force.

ожесточённый *adj.* bitter; fierce.

ожесточи́ть *v.*, *pfv. of* ожесточа́ть.

ожива́ть *v. impfv.* [*pfv.* ожи́ть] **1,** to come back to life. **2,** *fig.* to perk up; come alive.

оживи́ть [*infl.* -влю́, -ви́шь] *v.*, *pfv. of* оживля́ть. —**ожи́виться,** *refl.*, *pfv. of* оживля́ться.

оживле́ние *n.* **1,** revival; resuscitation. **2,** animation.

оживлённый *adj.* **1,** animated; lively. **2,** (*of a street*) busy; (*of trade*) brisk. —**оживлённо,** *adv.* with great animation.

оживля́ть *v. impfv.* [*pfv.* оживи́ть] **1,** to bring back to life. **2,** to revive; resuscitate. **3,** *fig.* to liven up; enliven; brighten. —**оживля́ться,** *refl.* to perk up; come alive.

ожида́ние *n.* **1,** waiting; wait. **2,** expectation: сверх вся́кого ожида́ния, beyond all expectations. —**в ожида́нии** (+ *gen.*), while waiting; pending.

ожида́ть *v. impfv.* (with *gen.*) **1,** to expect. **2,** to wait for; await.

ожире́ние *n.* obesity.

ожире́ть *v.*, *pfv. of* жире́ть.

ожи́ть [*infl.* оживу́, оживёшь; *past* о́жил, ожила́, о́жило] *v.*, *pfv. of* ожива́ть.

ожо́г *n.* burn.

озабо́тить [*infl.* -чу, -тишь] *v.*, *pfv. of* озабо́чивать. —**озабо́титься,** *refl.*, *pfv. of* озабо́чиваться.

озабо́ченный *adj.* anxious; concerned; worried; apprehensive. —**озабо́ченность,** *n.f.* anxiety; concern.

озабо́чивать *v. impfv.* [*pfv.* озабо́тить] to cause (someone) anxiety. —**озабо́чиваться,** *refl.* (with *instr.*) to see to; attend to.

озагла́вливать *v. impfv.* [*pfv.* озагла́вить] to entitle.

озада́ченный *adj.* puzzled; perplexed; baffled. —**озада́ченность,** *n.f.* puzzlement; perplexity; bafflement.

озада́чивать *v. impfv.* [*pfv.* озада́чить] to perplex; baffle; confound; bewilder; take aback.

озаря́ть *v. impfv.* [*pfv.* озари́ть] **1,** to light up. **2,** *fig.* (*of a thought or idea*) to strike; dawn upon. —**озаря́ться,** *refl.* to light up.

озвере́лый *adj.* crazed.

озвере́ние *n.* brutality; ferocity.

озвере́ть *v.*, *pfv. of* звере́ть.

оздорови́тельный *adj.* health (*attrib.*); sanitary (*attrib.*).

оздорови́ть [*infl.* -влю́, -ви́шь] *v.*, *pfv. of* оздоровля́ть.

оздоровле́ние *n.* **1,** making healthier. **2,** *fig.* improvement.

оздоровля́ть *v. impfv.* [*pfv.* оздорови́ть] **1,** to make healthy; make healthier. **2,** *fig.* to improve.

озелене́ние *n.* planting of trees and shrubs.

озеленя́ть *v. impfv.* [*pfv.* озелени́ть] to plant trees and shrubs (in).

о́земь *adv.*, *colloq.* to the ground.

озёрный *adj.* of a lake; lake (*attrib.*).

о́зеро [*pl.* озёра, озёр] *n.* lake.

ози́мый *adj.* (*of crops*) winter. —**ози́мые,** *n. pl.* winter crops.

о́зимь *n.f.* winter crop(s).

озира́ть *v. impfv.* to look over. —**озира́ться,** *refl.* to look around.

озло́бить [*infl.* -блю, -бишь] *v.*, *pfv. of* озлобля́ть. —**озло́биться,** *refl.*, *pfv. of* озлобля́ться.

озлобле́ние *n.* bitterness; animosity.

озлобля́ть *v. impfv.* [*pfv.* озло́бить] to embitter. —**озлобля́ться,** *refl.* to become embittered.

ознако́мить [*infl.* -млю, -мишь] *v.*, *pfv. of* ознакомля́ть. —**ознако́миться,** *refl.*, *pfv. of* ознакомля́ться.

ознакомле́ние *n.* **1,** acquainting; familiarizing. **2,** acquaintance; familiarization.

ознакомля́ть *v. impfv.* [*pfv.* ознако́мить] (*with* с + *instr.*) to acquaint (with); familiarize (with). —**ознакомля́ться,** *refl.* (*with* с + *instr.*) to familiarize oneself (with); become familiar (with).

ознамена́вание *n.*, *in* **в ознаменова́ние** (+ *gen.*), in honor of; to mark; in commemoration of.

ознаменова́ть *v. pfv.* [*infl.* -ну́ю, -ну́ешь] **1,** *pfv. of* знаменова́ть. **2,** to mark. **3,** to celebrate; observe; commemorate.

означа́ть *v. impfv.* to mean; signify; denote.

озно́б *n.* shivering; chill.

озокери́т *n.* ozocerite.

озолоти́ть *v. pfv.* [*infl.* -чу́, -ти́шь] **1,** to give a golden color to. **2,** *colloq.* to shower with money, gifts, etc.

озо́н *n.* ozone. —**озо́новый,** *adj.* ozone (*attrib.*).

озорни́к [*gen.* -ника́] *n.*, *colloq.* mischief-maker.

озорнича́ть *v. impfv.*, *colloq.* to be naughty; make mischief.

озорно́й *adj.* mischievous.

озорство́ *n.* mischief.

озя́бнуть *v. pfv.* [*past* озя́б, -ла] *colloq.* to be cold; freeze.

ой *interj.* **1,** oh!; o! **2,** ouch!

ока́зывание *n.* rendering; providing; giving.

оказа́ть [*infl.* окажу́, ока́жешь] *v.*, *pfv. of* ока́зывать. —**оказа́ться,** *refl.*, *pfv. of* ока́зываться.

ока́зия *n.* **1,** *obs.* opportunity. **2,** *colloq.* unexpected event.

оказывать v. impfv. [pfv. **оказа́ть**] **1,** to render; provide (assistance, support, etc.). **2,** to give (preference, a welcome, reception, etc.). **3,** to exert; put; apply; bring to bear (pressure). **4,** to exert; have (influence). **5,** to accord (respect); put (confidence); extend (hospitality). **6,** to offer (resistance). —**оказываться,** refl. **1,** to find oneself (in a certain place). **2,** (with instr.) to turn out to be: он оказа́лся ста́рым знако́мым, he turned out to be an old acquaintance. **3,** impers. to turn out: оказа́лось, что..., it turned out that... **4,** to be: оказа́ться в большинстве́, to be in the majority. **5,** (with не) indicating the absence of something: в холоди́льнике проду́ктов не оказа́лось, there was no food in the refrigerator.

окаймля́ть v. impfv. [pfv. **окайми́ть**] to border; edge.

ока́лина n. dross.

окаменелость n.f. fossil.

окамене́лый adj. **1,** petrified. **2,** fig. stony; impassive.

окамене́ть v., pfv. of **камене́ть.**

окантова́ть v., pfv. of **кантова́ть.**

ока́нчивать v. impfv. [pfv. **око́нчить**] **1,** to finish; end; complete. **2,** to graduate (from). —**ока́нчиваться,** refl. **1,** to finish; end; be over. **2,** [impfv. only] (with instr.) to end (in); terminate (in).

о́канье n. pronunciation of unstressed Russian o as o rather than a.

ока́пи n.m. indecl. okapi.

ока́пывать v. impfv. [pfv. **окопа́ть**] **1,** to dig around. **2,** to dig a ditch around. —**ока́пываться,** refl. to dig in; entrench oneself.

окари́на n. ocarina.

окати́ть [infl. окачу́, ока́тишь] v., pfv. of **ока́чивать.**

о́кать v. impfv. to pronounce unstressed Russian o as o rather than a.

ока́чивать v. impfv. [pfv. **окати́ть**] (with instr.) to douse (with). —**окати́ть кого́-нибудь холо́дной водо́й,** to dampen one's enthusiasm.

океа́н n. ocean.

океаногра́фия n. oceanography. —**океано́граф,** n. oceanographer. —**океанографи́ческий,** adj. oceanographic.

океа́нский adj. ocean (attrib.); oceanic.

оки́дывать v. impfv. [pfv. **оки́нуть**] in оки́дывать взгля́дом (+acc.), to cast a glance (at).

о́кисел [gen. -сла] n. oxide.

окисле́ние n. oxidation.

окисля́ть v. impfv. [pfv. **окисли́ть**] to oxidize. —**окисля́ться,** refl. to oxidize; become oxidized.

о́кись n.f. oxide: о́кись железа́, ferric oxide.

оккульти́зм n. occultism. —**окку́льтный,** adj. occult.

оккупа́нт n. invader.

оккупа́ция n. (military) occupation. —**оккупацио́нный,** adj. occupying; of occupation: оккупацио́нная а́рмия, army of occupation.

оккупи́ровать v. impfv. & pfv. [pres. -рую, -руешь] mil. to occupy.

окла́д n. salary; wages; rate of pay.

оклевета́ть v. pfv. [infl. -вещу́, -ве́щешь] to slander; smear.

окле́ивать v. impfv. [pfv. **окле́ить**] to cover by pasting something on: окле́ивать ко́мнату обо́ями, to paper a room.

о́клик n. **1,** call. **2,** challenge (of a sentry).

оклика́ть v. impfv. [pfv. **окли́кнуть**] **1,** to call to; hail. **2,** (of a sentry) to challenge.

окно́ [pl. о́кна, о́кон, о́кнам] n. window.

о́ко [pl. о́чи, оче́й, оча́м] n., archaic eye. —о́ко за о́ко, зуб за зуб, an eye for an eye, a tooth for a tooth.

окова́ть [infl. окую́, окуёшь] v., pfv. of **око́вывать.**

око́вы [gen. око́в] n. pl. shackles; fetters.

око́вывать v. impfv. [pfv. **окова́ть**] **1,** to bind (with metal). **2,** fig. to shackle.

окола́чиваться v.r. impfv., colloq. to knock about; hang around.

околдова́ть [infl. -ду́ю, -ду́ешь] v., pfv. of **околдо́вывать.**

околдо́вывать v. impfv. [pfv. **околдова́ть**] to bewitch; cast a spell over.

околева́ть v. impfv. [pfv. **околе́ть**] (of animals) to die.

околёсица n., colloq. nonsense.

околе́ть v., pfv. of **околева́ть.**

око́лица n. **1,** fence surrounding a village. **2,** outskirts of a village.

околи́чности n. pl. [sing. околи́чность] obs. circumlocution. —без околи́чностей, plainly; to the point.

о́коло prep., with gen. **1,** near; close to. **2,** about; approximately. —adv. around; about: никого́ нет о́коло, there is no one around/about. —ходи́ть вокру́г да о́коло, to beat around the bush.

околопло́дник n. pericarp.

околосерде́чный adj., in околосерде́чная су́мка, pericardium.

околото́к [gen. -тка] n., obs. neighborhood; district.

околощитови́дный adj., in околощитови́дная железа́, parathyroid gland.

околпа́чивать v. impfv. [pfv. **околпа́чить**] colloq. to fool; dupe; make a fool of.

око́лыш n. hatband.

око́льный adj. roundabout; circuitous: око́льным путём, by a roundabout route.

оконе́чность n.f. extremity (of an island or continent).

око́нный adj. window (attrib.).

оконча́ние n. **1,** completion; termination. **2,** end. **3,** graduation. **4,** gram. ending. **5,** concluding installment: оконча́ние в сле́дующем но́мере, to be concluded in the next issue.

оконча́тельно adv. **1,** finally; definitively. **2,** utterly; completely. **3,** for good.

оконча́тельность n.f. finality.

оконча́тельный adj. final; definitive.

око́нчить v., pfv. of **ока́нчивать.** —**око́нчиться,** refl., pfv. of **ока́нчиваться.**

око́п n., mil. trench.

окопа́ть v., pfv. of **ока́пывать.** —**окопа́ться,** refl., pfv. of **ока́пываться.**

око́пный adj. trench (attrib.). —**око́пная война́,** trench warfare.

о́корок [pl. окорока́] n. ham; leg of veal; leg of mutton.

окостене́лый adj. **1,** ossified. **2,** numb; stiff.

окостене́ние n. ossification.

окостене́ть v., pfv. of **костене́ть.**

окоти́ться v.r., pfv. of **коти́ться.**

окочене́лый adj. **1,** numb (from the cold). **2,** (of a corpse) stiff.

окочене́ние n. rigidity. —тру́пное окочене́ние, rigor mortis.

окочене́ть v., pfv. of **кочене́ть.**

око́шко [pl. -шки, -шек] n., dim. of окно́.

о́кра *n.* okra; gumbo.

окра́ина *n.* **1,** outskirts (*of a city*). **2,** outlying areas.

окра́инный *adj.* outlying.

окра́сить [*infl.* -шу, -сишь] *v., pfv. of* окра́шивать.

окра́ска *n.* **1,** painting. **2,** color; coloring; coloration. **3,** *fig.* coloration; complexion. —**защи́тная** *or* **покрови́тельственная окра́ска,** protective coloration.

окра́шивать *v. impfv.* [*pfv.* окра́сить] to paint.

окре́пнуть [*past* окре́п, -ла] *v., pfv. of* кре́пнуть.

окрести́ть *v. pfv.* [*infl.* окрещу́, окре́стишь] **1,** *pfv. of* крести́ть (*in sense #1*). **2,** *colloq.* to nickname. —**окрести́ться,** *refl., pfv. of* крести́ться (*in sense #1*).

окре́стность *n.f., usu. pl.* environs; suburbs.

окре́стный *adj.* **1,** neighboring; adjacent. **2,** local; living nearby.

о́крик *n.* shout; cry.

окри́кнуть *v. pfv.* to shout to; call to.

окрова́вить *v. pfv.* [*infl.* -влю, -вишь] to stain with blood.

окрова́вленный *adj.* bloodstained.

окропля́ть *v. impfv.* [*pfv.* окропи́ть] to sprinkle; besprinkle.

окро́шка *n.* **1,** cold soup made from kvass with meat and vegetables. **2,** *colloq.* hodgepodge.

о́круг [*pl.* округа́] *n.* district.

окру́га *n., colloq.* neighborhood.

округли́ть *v., pfv. of* округля́ть. —**округли́ться,** *refl., pfv. of* округля́ться.

окру́глый *adj.* round; rounded.

округля́ть *v. impfv.* [*pfv.* округли́ть] **1,** to round; make round. **2,** to round off. **3,** *in* округля́ть глаза́, to stare wide-eyed. **4,** *colloq.* to enlarge (one's holdings). —**округля́ться,** *refl.* **1,** to become round. **2,** to fill out.

окружа́ть *v. impfv.* [*pfv.* окружи́ть] **1,** to surround; encircle. **2,** to gather round. **3,** to lavish: окружа́ть кого́-нибудь забо́той, to lavish care upon someone.

окружа́ющий *adj.* surrounding. —**окружа́ющее,** *n. neut.* one's surroundings: всё окружа́ющее, everything around one. —**окружа́ющие,** *n. pl.* those around one.

окруже́ние *n.* **1,** encirclement. **2,** surroundings; environment. **3,** entourage. —**в окруже́нии** (+ *gen.*), accompanied by; surrounded by; in the midst of.

окружи́ть *v., pfv. of* окружа́ть.

окружно́й *adj.* district (*attrib.*). —**окружна́я желе́зная доро́га,** suburban railway (*circling a city*). —**окружно́й суд,** circuit court.

окру́жность *n.f.* circumference.

окрути́ть [*inf.* окручу́, окру́тишь] *v., pfv. of* окру́чивать.

окру́чивать *v. impfv.* [*pfv.* окрути́ть] *colloq.* to wind around: окрути́ть про́волоку ле́нтой, to wind tape around a wire.

окрыля́ть *v. impfv.* [*pfv.* окрыли́ть] to inspire.

окры́ситься *v.r. pfv.* (*with* на + *acc.*) *colloq.* to snap (at).

окта́ва *n.* octave.

окта́н *n.* octane.

окте́т *n.* octet.

октя́брь [*gen.* -бря́] *n.m.* **1,** October. **2,** *cap.* the October Revolution (*of 1917*).

октя́брьский *adj.* **1,** October (*attrib.*). **2,** *cap.* of or pert. to the October Revolution.

окули́ст *n.* oculist.

окуля́р *n.* eyepiece.

окуна́ть *v. impfv.* [*pfv.* окуну́ть] (*with* в + *acc.*) to dip (something into a liquid). —**окуна́ться,** *refl.* (*with* в + *acc.*) **1,** to dip (into). **2,** *fig.* to be plunged into (darkness). **3,** *fig.* to be absorbed in; be engrossed in.

о́кунь [*pl.* о́куни, окуне́й, окуня́м] *n.m.* perch (*fish*).

окупа́ть *v. impfv.* [*pfv.* окупи́ть] to cover (a cost); cover the cost of. —**окупа́ться,** *refl.* **1,** to pay for itself. **2,** *fig.* to be justified; be worth it.

окупи́ть [*infl.* окуплю́, оку́пишь] *v., pfv. of* окупа́ть. —**окупи́ться,** *refl., pfv. of* окупа́ться.

оку́ривание *n.* fumigation.

оку́ривать *v. impfv.* [*pfv.* окури́ть] to fumigate.

окури́ть [*infl.* окурю́, оку́ришь] *v., pfv. of* оку́ривать.

оку́рок [*gen.* -рка] *n.* cigarette butt; cigar stub.

оку́тывать *v. impfv.* [*pfv.* оку́тать] **1,** to wrap. **2,** *fig.* to envelop; shroud.

ола́дья [*gen. pl.* -дий] *n.* pancake; fritter.

олеа́ндр *n.* oleander. —**олеа́ндровый,** *adj.* oleander (*attrib.*).

оледене́лый *adj.* frozen.

оледене́ть *v., pfv. of* ледене́ть.

оледени́ть *v., pfv. of* ледени́ть.

оленебы́к [*gen.* -быка́] *n.* eland (*antelope*).

оленево́д *n.* reindeer breeder. —**оленево́дство,** *n.* reindeer breeding. —**оленево́дческий,** *adj.* reindeer-breeding (*attrib.*).

оле́ний [*fem.* -нья] *adj.* **1,** deer (*attrib.*); deer's; reindeer (*attrib.*). **2,** deerskin. —**оле́ньи рога́,** antlers.

оле́нина *n.* venison.

олену́ха *n.* doe (*female deer*).

оле́нь *n.m.* deer. —**благоро́дный оле́нь,** red deer. —**се́верный оле́нь,** reindeer.

оли́ва *n.* **1,** olive. **2,** olive tree. *Also,* оли́вка.

оли́вковый *adj.* **1,** olive (*attrib.*). **2,** olive-green.

олига́рх *n.* oligarch. —**олигархи́ческий,** *adj.* oligarchic. —**олига́рхия,** *n.* oligarchy.

олимпиа́да *n.* **1,** Olympiad. **2,** Olympics.

олимпи́йский *adj.* Olympian; Olympic. —**Олимпи́йские и́гры,** Olympic Games.

оли́фа *n.* drying oil.

олицетворе́ние *n.* personification; embodiment.

олицетворя́ть *v. impfv.* [*pfv.* олицетвори́ть] to personify; embody.

о́лово *n.* tin. —**оловя́нный,** *adj.* tin.

о́лух *n., colloq.* oaf; dolt; blockhead.

о́луша *n.* gannet (*bird*).

ольха́ [*pl.* о́льхи] *n.* alder. —**ольхо́вый,** *adj.* alder (*attrib.*).

оля́пка [*gen. pl.* -пок] *n.* water ouzel; dipper.

ом *n.* ohm.

ома́р *n.* lobster.

оме́га *n.* omega.

оме́ла *n.* mistletoe.

омерзе́ние *n.* loathing.

омерзи́тельный *adj.* loathsome; disgusting; revolting.

омертве́лый *adj.* **1,** (*of tissues, cells, etc.*) dead. **2,** *fig.* stiff; numb. **3,** *fig.* deserted; lifeless.

омертве́ть *v., pfv. of* мертве́ть.

омёт *n.* stack of straw.

омле́т *n.* omelet.

о́мнибус *n., obs.* horse-drawn coach (*carrying paying passengers*).

омове́ние *n.* ablution.

омола́живать *v. impfv.* [*pfv.* **омолоди́ть**] to rejuvenate.

омоложе́ние *n.* rejuvenation.

омо́ним *n.* homonym.

омрача́ть *v. impfv.* [*pfv.* **омрачи́ть**] **1,** *obs.* to darken. **2,** to dull (the senses). **3,** to dampen; cast a pall over.

о́мут *n.* **1,** deep place in a river or lake. **2,** whirlpool. **3,** *fig.* maelstrom.

омыва́ть *v. impfv.* [*pfv.* **омы́ть**] **1,** to wash. **2,** [*impfv. only*] (of waves, the sea, etc.) to wash (the shore).

омы́ть [*infl.* **омо́ю, омо́ешь**] *v., pfv. of* **омыва́ть**.

он [*gen. & acc.* **его́**; *dat.* **ему́**; *instr.* **им**; *prepl.* **нём**] *pers. pron., 3rd person sing. masc.* he; (of inanimate objects) it.

она́ [*gen. & acc.* **её**; *dat.* **ей**; *instr.* **е́ю** *or* **ей**; *prepl.* **ней**] *pers. pron., 3rd person sing. fem.* she; (of inanimate objects) it.

она́гр *n.* onager.

онани́зм *n.* masturbation.

онани́ровать *v. impfv.* [*pres.* **-рую, -руешь**] to masturbate.

ондатра *n.* muskrat.

онеме́лый *adj.* **1,** numb; stiff. **2,** *obs.* dumb; mute.

онеме́ние *n.* **1,** numbness. **2,** inability to speak.

онеме́ть *v., pfv. of* **неме́ть**.

онёры *n. pl.* [*sing.* **онёра**] cards honors.

они́ [*gen. & acc.* **их**; *dat.* **им**; *instr.* **и́ми**; *prepl.* **них**] *pers. pron., 3rd person pl.* they.

о́никс *n.* onyx. —**о́никсовй,** *adj.* onyx.

о́но *see* **о́ный**.

оно́ [*infl. like* **он**] *pers. pron., 3rd person sing. neut.* it.

онтоло́гия *n.* ontology. —**онтологи́ческий,** *adj.* ontological.

ону́ча [*gen. pl.* **ону́ч**] *n.* piece of cloth wrapped around the foot and worn instead of a stocking.

о́ный *adj., obs.* that. —**во вре́мя о́но,** long ago; way back when.

опада́ть *v. impfv.* [*pfv.* **опа́сть**] **1,** (of leaves) to fall; (of fruit or petals) to fall off. **2,** (of wind) to subside. **3,** (of a swelling) to go down. **4,** *colloq.* (of one's face or cheeks) to become sunken.

опа́здывать *v. impfv.* [*pfv.* **опозда́ть**] to be late: опозда́ть в шко́лу/на рабо́ту/к обе́ду/, to be late for school/work/dinner. Опозда́ть с отве́том, to be late in answering. Опозда́ть на полчаса́, to be half an hour late.

опа́ивать *v. impfv.* [*pfv.* **опои́ть**] **1,** to give (an animal) too much to drink. **2,** to make (someone) drunk. **3,** *obs.* to poison.

опа́л *n.* opal.

опа́ла *n.* disgrace: быть в опа́ле, to be in disgrace.

опа́ливать *v. impfv.* [*pfv.* **опали́ть**] **1,** to scorch; sear. **2,** to singe (feathers, a chicken, etc.).

опали́ть *v., pfv. of* **пали́ть** (in sense # 1), **опаля́ть,** and **опа́ливать**.

опа́ловый *adj.* opal; opaline.

опа́льный *adj.* disgraced; in disgrace; in disfavor.

опаля́ть *v. impfv.* = **опа́ливать**.

опа́ра *n.* leavened dough.

опарши́веть *v., pfv. of* **парши́веть**.

опаса́ться *v.r. impfv.* **1,** (with gen.) to fear. **2,** (with gen. or inf.) to avoid; refrain from.

опасе́ние *n.* fear; apprehension.

опа́ска *n., colloq., in* с опа́ской, cautiously; без опа́ски, without fear.

опа́сливый *adj., colloq.* cautious; fearful.

опа́сно *adv.* dangerously. —*adj., used predicatively* dangerous: по э́той доро́ге опа́сно е́хать, it is dangerous to drive on this road.

опа́сность *n.f.* danger.

опа́сный *adj.* dangerous. —**опа́сная бри́тва,** straight razor.

опа́сть [*infl. like* **пасть**] *v., pfv. of* **опада́ть**.

опаха́ло *n.* large fan.

опе́ка *n.* guardianship; tutelage. —**Междунаро́дная опе́ка,** International Trusteeship. —**Сове́т по Опе́ке,** Trusteeship Council (of the United Nations).

опека́емый *n., decl. as an adj.* ward.

опека́ть *v. impfv.* **1,** to be the guardian of. **2,** *fig.* to watch over.

опеку́н [*gen.* **-куна́**] *n.* guardian. —**опеку́нский,** *adj.* of a guardian; guardian's; tutelary. —**опеку́нство,** *n.* guardianship.

о́пера *n.* opera.

операти́вный *adj.* **1,** operative; surgical: операти́вное вмеша́тельство, surgical intervention. **2,** *mil.* operations (attrib.); operational. **3,** effective; efficient.

опера́тор *n.* **1,** operator. **2,** cameraman. **3,** *obs.* surgeon.

операцио́нный *adj.* **1,** *med.* operating. **2,** *mil.* operations (attrib.). —**операцио́нная,** *n.* operating room.

опера́ция *n., med., mil., finance, etc.* operation.

опережа́ть *v. impfv.* [*pfv.* **опереди́ть**] **1,** to pass; outdistance; leave behind. **2,** to do something ahead of (someone); beat (someone) to it. **3,** to surpass; excel.

опере́ние *n.* plumage.

оперённый *adj.* feathered.

опере́тта *n.* operetta; musical comedy. —**опере́точный,** *adj.* of operetta; musical-comedy (attrib.).

опере́ть [*infl.* **обопру́, обопрёшь**; *past* **опёр, оперла́, оперло́**] *v., pfv. of* **опира́ть**. —**опере́ться,** *refl.* [*past* **опёрся, оперла́сь, оперло́сь**] *pfv. of* **опира́ться**.

опери́ровать *v. impfv.* [*pres.* **-рую, -руешь**] **1,** operate on. **2,** *mil.* to operate. **3,** (with instr.) to use.

опери́ться *v.r., pfv. of* **оперя́ться**.

о́перный *adj.* opera (attrib.); operatic.

оперя́ться *v.r. impfv.* [*pfv.* **опери́ться**] **1,** (of a bird) to become fully fledged. **2,** *fig.* to become independent; stand on one's own feet.

опеча́ленный *adj.* sad; sorrowful.

опеча́лить *v., pfv. of* **печа́лить**. —**опеча́литься,** *refl., pfv. of* **печа́литься**.

опеча́тать *v., pfv. of* **опеча́тывать**.

опеча́тка [*gen. pl.* **-ток**] *n.* misprint.

опеча́тывать *v. impfv.* [*pfv.* **опеча́тать**] to seal up.

опе́шить *v. pfv., colloq.* to be taken aback.

опива́ться *v.r. impfv.* [*pfv.* **опи́ться**] *colloq.* to drink to excess; have too much to drink; (with instr.) drink too much (of); have too much (of something) to drink.

о́пий *n.* opium. —**о́пийный,** *adj.* opium (attrib.).

опи́ливать *v. impfv.* [*pfv.* **опили́ть**] to saw.

опили́ть [*infl.* **опилю́, опи́лишь**] *v., pfv. of* **опи́ливать**.

опи́лки [*gen.* **-лок**] *n. pl.* **1,** filings. **2,** sawdust.

опира́ть *v. impfv.* [*pfv.* **опере́ть**] (with на *or* о + acc.) to lean (something) on *or* against. —**опира́ться,** *refl.* (with на *or* о + acc.) **1,** to lean on; lean against. **2,** *fig.* to rely on; depend on.

описа́ние *n.* description. —**описа́тельный,** *adj.* descriptive.

описа́ть [*infl.* опишу́, опи́шешь] *v., pfv. of* опи́сывать. —**описа́ться,** *refl.* to make a slip of the pen.

опи́ска [*gen. pl.* -сок] *n.* slip of the pen.

опи́сывать *v. impfv.* [*pfv.* описа́ть] **1,** to describe. **2,** to take inventory of. **3,** *math.* to circumscribe. **4,** to make; move in; describe (a circle, arc, etc.).

о́пись *n.f.* inventory.

опи́ться [*infl.* обопью́сь, обопьёшься; *past* опи́лся, опила́сь, опило́сь] *v.r., pfv. of* опива́ться.

о́пиум *n.* opium. —**о́пиумный,** *adj.* opium (*attrib.*).

опла́кать [*infl.* опла́чу, опла́чешь] *v., pfv. of* опла́кивать.

опла́кивать *v. impfv.* [*pfv.* опла́кать] to mourn; mourn the loss of.

опла́та *n.* pay; payment.

оплати́ть [*infl.* оплачу́, опла́тишь] *v., pfv. of* опла́чивать.

опла́чиваемый *adj.* paid: опла́чиваемый о́тпуск, paid vacation.

опла́чивать *v. impfv.* [*pfv.* оплати́ть] to pay.

оплева́ть [*infl.* оплюю́, оплюёшь] *v., pfv. of* оплёвывать.

оплёвывать *v. impfv.* [*pfv.* оплева́ть] *colloq.* to spit on (*lit. & fig.*).

оплести́ [*infl. like* плести́] *v., pfv. of* оплета́ть.

оплета́ть *v. impfv.* [*pfv.* оплести́] to entwine; string: оплести́ и́згородь колю́чей про́волокой, to entwine/string a fence with barbed wire.

оплеу́ха *n., colloq.* slap in the face.

оплеши́веть *v., pfv. of* плеши́веть.

оплодотворе́ние *n.* fertilization; impregnation; insemination.

оплодотворя́ть *v. impfv.* [*pfv.* оплодотвори́ть] to fertilize; impregnate.

опло́т *n.* bulwark; bastion.

оплоша́ть *v. pfv., colloq.* to make a mistake; slip up.

опло́шность *n.f.* mistake; blunder.

оплыва́ть *v. impfv.* [*pfv.* оплы́ть] **1,** to swim around; sail around. **2,** to swell up; become swollen. **3,** (*of a candle*) to drip.

оплы́ть [*infl. like* плыть] *v., pfv. of* оплыва́ть.

оповеща́ть *v. impfv.* [*pfv.* оповести́ть] to notify; inform.

оповеще́ние *n.* notification.

опо́ек [*gen.* опо́йка] *n.* calfskin.

опозда́ние *n.* **1,** lateness; tardiness. Нача́ть собра́ние с опозда́нием, to start the meeting late. **2,** delay.

опозда́ть *v., pfv. of* опа́здывать.

опознава́тельный *adj.* identification (*attrib.*); identifying. —**опознава́тельный знак, 1,** identification mark. **2,** landmark.

опознава́ть *v. impfv.* [*pfv.* опозна́ть; *pres.* -знаю́, знаёшь] to identify.

опозна́ние *n.* identification.

опозна́ть *v., pfv. of* опознава́ть.

опозо́рить *v., pfv. of* позо́рить. —**опозо́риться,** *refl., pfv. of* позо́риться.

опо́ить [*infl.* опою́, опо́ишь *or* опои́шь] *v., pfv. of* опа́ивать.

опо́йковый *adj.* calfskin (*attrib.*).

опола́скивать *v. impfv.* [*pfv.* ополосну́ть] to rinse.

ополза́ть *v. impfv.* [*pfv.* оползти́] **1,** to crawl around. **2,** (*of the ground or a building*) to slip; sink.

о́ползень [*gen.* -зня] *n.m.* landslide; mudslide.

оползти́ [*infl. like* ползти́] *v., pfv. of* ополза́ть.

ополосну́ть *v., pfv. of* опола́скивать.

ополча́ться *v.r. impfv.* [*pfv.* ополчи́ться] (*with* на + *acc. or* про́тив) **1,** to take up arms (against). **2,** *fig.* to assail; sail into.

ополче́нец [*gen.* -нца] *n.* militiaman.

ополче́ние *n.* militia.

ополчи́ться *v.r., pfv. of* ополча́ться.

опо́мниться *v.r. pfv.* **1,** to regain consciousness. **2,** to come to one's senses.

опо́р *n., in* во весь опо́р, at top speed; full tilt.

опо́ра *n.* **1,** support. **2,** basis. —**то́чка опо́ры, 1,** fulcrum. **2,** foothold: найти́ то́чку опо́ры, to gain a foothold.

опора́жнивать *v. impfv.* [*pfv.* опоро́жнить *or* опоро́жнить] to empty. —**опора́жниваться,** *refl.* to empty; become empty.

опо́рки *n. pl.* [*sing.* опо́рок] worn-out shoes.

опо́рный *adj.* supporting: опо́рная коло́нна, supporting column. —**опо́рный пункт,** *mil.* strong point.

опоро́жнить *also,* опорожни́ть *v., pfv. of* опора́жнивать *and* опорожня́ть. —**опоро́жниться,** *refl., pfv. of* опора́жниваться *and* опорожня́ться.

опорожня́ть *v. impfv.* = опора́жнивать. —**опорожня́ться,** *refl.* = опора́жниваться.

опоро́с *n.* farrow.

опоро́чить *v., pfv. of* поро́чить.

опо́ссум *n.* opossum.

опосты́леть *v. pfv.* (*with dat.*) *colloq.* to become hateful (to).

опохмеля́ться *v.r. impfv.* [*pfv.* опохмели́ться] *colloq.* to take a drink in order to cure a hangover.

опочи́ть *v. pfv.* [*infl.* -чи́ю, -чи́ешь] *obs.* **1,** to go to sleep. **2,** to die.

опошля́ть *v. impfv.* [*pfv.* опо́шлить] **1,** to vulgarize; debase. **2,** to make trite by overuse.

опоя́сать [*infl.* опоя́шу, опоя́шешь] *v., pfv. of* опоя́сывать. —**опоя́саться,** *refl., pfv. of* опоя́сываться.

опоя́сывать *v. impfv.* [*pfv.* опоя́сать] **1,** to gird. **2,** to circle; girdle. —**опоя́сываться, 1,** [*also,* опоя́сываться ремнём] to put on one's belt. **2,** *fig.* (*with instr.*) to be circled (by); be surrounded (by).

оппози́ция *n., polit.* opposition. —**оппозицио́нный,** *adj.* opposition (*attrib.*).

оппоне́нт *n.* opponent (*in a debate or argument*).

оппони́ровать *v. impfv.* (*with dat.*) to oppose (*in a discussion, debate, etc.*).

оппортуни́зм *n.* opportunism. —**оппортуни́ст,** *n.* opportunist. —**оппортунисти́ческий,** *adj.* opportunistic.

опра́ва *n.* **1,** mount; setting. **2,** frame; rim (*for eyeglasses*).

оправда́ние *n.* **1,** justification. **2,** excuse. **3,** *law* acquittal.

оправда́тельный *adj., in* оправда́тельный пригово́р, verdict of "not guilty".

оправда́ть *v., pfv. of* опра́вдывать. —**оправда́ться,** *refl., pfv. of* опра́вдываться.

опра́вдывать *v. impfv.* [*pfv.* оправда́ть] **1,** to justify. **2,** to excuse. **3,** to acquit. **4,** to live up to. **5,** *in* оправда́ть себя́, to prove its worth; prove worthwhile. —**опра́вдываться,** *refl.* **1,** to justify oneself; justify one's actions. **2,** to justify itself; be justified. **3,** to (try to) prove one's innocence. **4,** to prove to be correct. **5,** to be realized; materialize; come true.

оправить [*infl.* **-влю, -вишь**] *v., pfv. of* **оправлять.** —**оправиться,** *refl., pfv. of* **оправляться.**

оправка [*gen. pl.* **-вок**] *n.* mandrel.

оправлять *v. impfv.* [*pfv.* **оправить**] **1,** to straighten; adjust. **2,** to mount; set in a mount. —**оправляться,** *refl.* **1,** to straighten one's clothes; tidy oneself up. **2,** to recover; get well.

опрашивать *v. impfv.* [*pfv.* **опросить**] **1,** to poll; canvass. **2,** to question; examine.

определение *n.* **1,** determination. **2,** definition. **3,** *law* decision; ruling. **4,** *gram.* attribute; modifier.

определённо *adv.* definitely.

определённый *adj.* **1,** definite. **2,** certain: при определённых условиях, under certain conditions.

определитель *n.m.* **1,** determining factor. **2,** *math.* determinant.

определять *v. impfv.* [*pfv.* **определить**] **1,** to determine. **2,** to define. **3,** to fix; set. **4,** to diagnose (an illness). —**определяться,** *refl.* **1,** to be determined. **2,** to be formed; take shape. **3,** to determine one's position.

опреснение *n.* desalinization; desalination.

опреснять *v. impfv.* [*pfv.* **опреснить**] to desalinate.

опричнина *n., hist.* oprichnina (*period of terror during the reign of Tsar Ivan IV; also those charged with carrying it out*).

опробовать *v. pfv.* [*infl.* **-бую, -буешь**] to test.

опровергать *v. impfv.* [*pfv.* **опровергнуть**] **1,** to refute; rebut; disprove. **2,** to deny.

опровергнуть [*past* **-верг, -ла**] *v., pfv. of* **опровергать.**

опровержение *n.* **1,** refutation. **2,** denial. **3,** disclaimer; retraction.

опрокидывать *v. impfv.* [*pfv.* **опрокинуть**] to overturn; upset; tip over; knock over; topple. —**опрокидываться,** *refl.* **1,** to overturn; fall over; tip over; topple over. **2,** (*of a boat*) to capsize.

опрометчивый *adj.* rash; impetuous. —**опрометчиво,** *adv.* rashly; impetuously. —**опрометчивость,** *n.f.* rashness; impetuosity.

опрометью *adv.* headlong.

опрос *n.* **1,** questioning. **2,** poll; survey. **3,** quiz (*in school*).

опросить [*infl.* **опрошу, опросишь**] *v., pfv. of* **опрашивать.**

опросный *adj., in* опросный лист, questionnaire.

опростать *v. pfv., colloq.* to empty; empty the contents of.

опростоволоситься *v.r. pfv.* [*infl.* **-шусь, -сишься**] *colloq.* to make a fool of oneself.

опротестовать *v. pfv.* [*infl.* **-стую, -стуешь**] *law* to appeal; protest; contest.

опротиветь *v. pfv.* (with *dat.*) to become loathsome (to).

опрыскивать *v. impfv.* [*pfv.* **опрыскать**] **1,** to sprinkle. **2,** to spray.

опрятный *adj.* neat; tidy. —**опрятно,** *adv.* neatly. —**опрятность,** *n.f.* neatness; tidiness.

оптик *n.* optician; optometrist. —**оптика,** *n.* optics.

оптимальный *adj.* optimum.

оптимизм *n.* optimism. —**оптимист,** *n.* optimist. —**оптимистический,** *adj.* optimistic.

оптимум *n.* optimum.

оптический *adj.* optical.

оптовик [*gen.* **-вика**] *n.* wholesaler. —**оптовый,** *adj.* wholesale. —**оптом,** *adv.* wholesale.

опубликование *n.* **1,** publication. **2,** promulgation.

опубликовать *v. pfv.* [*infl.* **-кую, -куешь**] **1,** *pfv. of* **публиковать. 2,** to promulgate.

опунция *n.* prickly pear.

опус *n.* opus.

опускать *v. impfv.* [*pfv.* **опустить**] **1,** to lower; let down. **2,** (*with* в + *acc.*) to put (into); drop; deposit: опускать письмо в почтовый ящик, to mail a letter. **3,** to omit; leave out. —**как в воду опущенный,** dejected; crestfallen. —**опускать руки,** to become disheartened; lose heart.

опускаться *v.r. impfv.* [*pfv.* **опуститься**] **1,** to go down; descend; sink. **2,** *fig.* to go downhill; go to seed.

опустелый *adj.* deserted.

опустеть *v., pfv. of* **пустеть.**

опустить [*infl.* **опущу, опустишь**] *v., pfv. of* **опускать.** —**опуститься,** *refl., pfv. of* **опускаться.**

опустошать *v. impfv.* [*pfv.* **опустошить**] to devastate; ravage; lay waste.

опустошение *n.* devastation.

опустошительный *adj.* devastating.

опустошить *v., pfv. of* **опустошать.**

опутывать *v. impfv.* [*pfv.* **опутать**] **1,** to wind around; tie around: опутать что-нибудь веревкой, to tie/wind a string around something. **2,** *fig.* to entangle.

опухать *v. impfv.* [*pfv.* **опухнуть**] to swell (up); become swollen.

опухлый *adj., colloq.* swollen.

опухнуть [*past* **опух, -ла**] *v., pfv. of* **опухать.**

опухоль *n.f.* **1,** swelling. **2,** tumor.

опушать *v. impfv.* [*pfv.* **опушить**] **1,** to trim with fur. **2,** (*with instr.*) to cover with (fur, snow, frost, etc.).

опушка [*gen. pl.* **-шек**] *n.* **1,** edge of a forest. **2,** fur trimming.

опущение *n.* **1,** lowering; coming down. **2,** omission. **3,** *med.* prolapse.

опыление *n.* pollination.

опыливать *v. impfv.* [*pfv.* **опылить**] to dust (crops).

опылить *v., pfv. of* **опылять** *and* **опыливать.**

опылять *v. impfv.* [*pfv.* **опылить**] to pollinate.

опыт *n.* **1,** experience. **2,** experiment.

опытный *adj.* **1,** experienced. **2,** experimental.

опьянелый *adj., colloq.* intoxicated.

опьянение *n.* intoxication.

опьянеть *v., pfv. of* **пьянеть.**

опьянить *v., pfv. of* **пьянить** *and* **опьянять.**

опьянять *v. impfv.* [*pfv.* **опьянить**] to intoxicate; make drunk.

опять *adv.* again. —**опять-таки, 1,** again. **2,** and what is more.

орава *n., colloq.* **1,** crowd; mob. **2,** throng; horde.

оракул *n.* oracle.

орало *n., obs.* plow. —**перековать мечи на орала,** to beat swords into plowshares.

орангутанг *n.* orangutan.

оранжевый *adj.* orange.

оранжерея *n.* hothouse; greenhouse. —**оранжерейный,** *adj.* hothouse (*attrib.*).

оратор *n.* speaker; orator

оратория *n.* oratorio.

ораторский *adj.* oratorical. —**ораторское искусство,** oratory; public speaking.

орáторствовать v. impfv. [pres. -ствую, -ствуешь] colloq. to orate; perorate.

орáть v. impfv. [pres. орý, орёшь] colloq. to yell; scream.

орбúта n. 1, orbit. 2, eye socket. —**орбитáльный**, adj. orbital.

оргáзм n. orgasm.

óрган n. 1, physiol. organ: óрганы рéчи, organs of speech. 2, (governmental) organ; body: óрганы влáсти, organs of power; законодáтельный óрган, legislative body. 3, organ; publication.

оргáн n. organ (musical instrument).

организáтор n. organizer. —**организáторский**, adj. organizational.

организациóнный adj. of organization; organizational.

организáция n. 1, organization. 2, an organization.

органúзм n. 1, organism. 2, (one's) body; (one's) system.

организóванный adj. organized; well-organized. —**организóванно**, adv. in an organized manner. —**организóванность**, n.f. (good) organization.

организовáть v. impfv. & pfv. [pres. -зýю, -зýешь] to organize. —**организовáться**, refl. 1, to be organized. 2, to organize; get organized.

органúст n. organist.

органúческий adj. organic.

оргáнный adj., music organ (attrib.).

óргия n. orgy.

ордá [pl. óрды] n. horde. —**Золотáя ордá**, the Golden Horde.

óрден n. 1, [pl. орденá] order (medal): óрден Крáсного Знáмени, Order of the Red Banner. 2, [pl. óрдены] order (society): масóнский óрден, the Masonic Order.

орденонóсец [gen. -сца] n. holder of an order.

óрдер [pl. ордерá] n. 1, order; warrant; writ. 2, voucher.

ординáрец [gen. -рца] n., mil. orderly.

ординáрный adj. ordinary.

ординáта n., geom. ordinate.

орёл [gen. орлá] n. eagle. —**орёл úли рéшка?**, heads or tails?

ореóл n. 1, halo. 2, fig. aura.

орéх n. 1, nut. 2, walnut (tree & wood). —**достáться на орéхи** (+ dat.), colloq. to get it hot; get it good. —**разрáзделывать под орéх**, 1, to rake over the coals. 2, to rout.

орéховый adj. 1, nut (attrib.). 2, walnut (attrib.).

орéшек [gen. -шка] n., dim. of орéх. —**бýковый орéшек**, beechnut. —**чернúльный орéшек**, gallnut.

орéшник n. hazel (tree).

оригинáл n. 1, original: читáть в оригинáле, to read in the original. 2, colloq. queer bird; queer duck; unique character.

оригинáльничать v. impfv., colloq. to try to be clever.

оригинáльный adj. original. —**оригинáльность**, n.f. originality.

ориентáльный adj. oriental.

ориентáция n. orientation; getting one's bearings.

ориентúр n. landmark; reference point.

ориентúровать v. impfv. & pfv. [pres. -рую, -руешь] to orient. —**ориентúроваться**, refl. 1, [pfv. also сориентúроваться] to orient oneself; get one's bearings. 2, (with на + acc.) to be oriented (toward); direct one's efforts (toward).

ориентирóвка n. orientation; getting one's bearings. —**чýвство ориентирóвки**, sense of direction.

ориентирóвочно adv. 1, approximately. 2, tentatively.

ориентирóвочный adj. 1, reference (attrib.): ориентирóвочный пункт, reference point. 2, preliminary; tentative. 3, approximate.

оркéстр n. 1, orchestra. 2, orchestra pit.

оркестровáть v. impfv. & pfv. [pres. -стрýю, -стрýешь] to orchestrate.

оркестрóвка n. orchestration.

оркестрóвый adj. orchestral.

орлáн n. sea eagle; bald eagle.

орлёнок [gen. -нка; pl. орлáта, -лáт] n. eaglet.

орлúный adj. eagle (attrib.). —**орлúный нос**, aquiline nose.

орнáмент n. ornamental design; decorative pattern.

орнитолóгия n. ornithology. —**орнитóлог**, n. ornithologist. —**орнитологúческий**, adj. ornithological.

оробéлый adj. frightened; timid.

оробéть v. pfv. to become shy; lose one's nerve.

оросúтельный adj. irrigation (attrib.).

оросúть [infl. -шý, -сúшь] v., pfv. of орошáть.

орошáть v. impfv. [pfv. оросúть] to irrigate.

орошéние n. irrigation.

ортодоксáльный adj. orthodox. —**ортодóксия**, n. orthodoxy.

ортодонтúя n. orthodontia.

ортопéдия n. orthopedics. —**ортопéд**, n. orthopedics. —**ортопедúческий**, adj. orthopedic.

орýдие n. 1, instrument; implement. Орýдие пытки, instrument of torture. 2, fig. instrument; tool: орýдия производствá, instruments/tools of production. 3, fig. tool: орýдие в рукáх (+ gen.), a tool in the hands of. 4, mil. gun.

орудúйный adj., mil. gun (attrib.).

орýдовать v. impfv. [pres. -дую, -дуешь] colloq. 1, (with instr.) to handle; wield (an instrument). 2, (with instr.) to be in charge of; boss. 3, to be active; operate.

оружéйник n. gunsmith.

оружéйный adj. gun (attrib.); arms (attrib.); weapons (attrib.). —**оружéйный мáстер**, gunsmith. —**Оружéйная палáта**, the Armory (in the Kremlin).

орýжие n. 1, weapon. 2, weapons; arms. 3, in сúлой орýжия, by force of arms. 4, in товáрищ по орýжию, comrade in arms. —**бить (когó-нибудь) егó же орýжием**, to turn the tables on; beat (someone) at his own game.

орфогрáфия n. orthography; spelling. —**орфографúческий**, adj. orthographic; spelling (attrib.).

орхидéя (дэ) n. orchid.

осá [pl. óсы] n. wasp.

осáда n. siege. —**в осáде**, under siege.

осадúть [infl. осажý, осáдишь] v., pfv. of осаждáть and осáживать.

осáдка n. 1, sinking; settling. 2, draft (of a sailing vessel).

осáдный adj. siege (attrib.). —**осáдное положéние**, state of siege.

осáдок [gen. -дка] n. 1, sediment. 2, fig. aftertaste. 3, pl. precipitation. —**радиоактúвные осáдки**, (radioactive) fallout.

осáдочный adj. sedimentary.

осаждáть v. impfv. [pfv. осадúть] 1, to lay siege to;

besiege. **2,** *fig.* (*with instr.*) to besiege (with questions, requests, etc.).

оса́живать *v. impfv.* [*pfv.* **осади́ть**] **1,** to rein in (a horse). **2,** *v.i.* (*of an animal*) to stop short and retreat. **3,** to force back. **4,** *fig.* to silence; put in one's place.

оса́нистый *adj.* imposing; stately.

оса́нка *n.* carriage; bearing.

оса́нна *n.* hosanna.

осва́ивать *v. impfv.* [*pfv.* **осво́ить**] **1,** to master. **2,** to settle; open up; develop (new territory). **—осва́иваться,** *refl.* **1,** to (come to) feel at home. **2,** (*with* с + *instr.*) to get used to; adjust to. **3,** (*with* с + *instr.*) to familiarize oneself with.

осведоми́тель *n.m.* informer; informant. **—осведоми́тельный,** *adj.* pert. to information; information (*attrib.*).

осве́домить [*infl.* **-млю, -мишь**] *v., pfv. of* **осведомля́ть.**

осведомле́ние *n.* notification.

осведомлённый *adj.* well-informed; knowledgeable. **—осведомлённость,** *n.f.* knowledgeability.

осведомля́ть *v. impfv.* [*pfv.* **осве́домить**] to inform; notify. **—осведомля́ться,** *refl.* (*with* о) to inquire about.

освежа́ть *v. impfv.* [*pfv.* **освежи́ть**] to refresh; freshen (up); invigorate. **—освежа́ться,** *refl.* **1,** to be refreshed. **2,** to freshen up. **3,** to revive one's energies.

освежа́ющий *adj.* refreshing.

освежева́ть *v., pfv. of* **свежева́ть.**

освеже́ние *n.* refreshment.

освежи́тельный *adj.* refreshing.

освежи́ть *v., pfv. of* **освежа́ть. —освежи́ться,** *refl., pfv. of* **освежа́ться.**

освети́тельный *adj.* lighting (*attrib.*); illuminating.

освети́ть [*infl.* **-щу́, -ти́шь**] *v., pfv. of* **освеща́ть. —освети́ться,** *refl., pfv. of* **освеща́ться.**

освеща́ть *v. impfv.* [*pfv.* **освети́ть**] **1,** to light up; illuminate. **2,** *fig.* to elucidate; shed light on. **3,** to cover (a newspaper story).**—освеща́ться,** *refl.* to light up.

освеще́ние *n.* **1,** lighting; illumination. **2,** *fig.* interpretation. **3,** *fig.* coverage (*in the press*).

освещённость *n.f.* luminosity.

освиде́тельствовать *v. pfv.* [*infl.* **-ствую, -ству-ешь**] to examine.

освиста́ть [*infl.* **освищу́, освищешь**] *v., pfv. of* **освистывать.**

освистывать *v. impfv.* [*pfv.* **освиста́ть**] to hiss (a performer).

освободи́тель *n.m.* liberator; emancipator. **—освободи́тельный,** *adj.* liberation (*attrib.*); освободи́тельное движе́ние, liberation movement.

освободи́ть [*infl.* **-жу́, -ди́шь**] *v., pfv. of* **освобожда́ть. —освободи́ться,** *refl., pfv. of* **освобожда́ться.**

освобожда́ть *v. impfv.* [*pfv.* **освободи́ть**] **1,** to free; liberate. **2,** (*with* из) to release (from). **3,** (*with* от) to excuse (from); exempt (from). **4,** (*with* от) to relieve (of a position); remove (from office). **5,** to vacate. **6,** to clear; empty. **—освобожда́ться,** *refl.* **1,** to be freed; be released. **2,** to free oneself; get free. **3,** to be cleared; be vacated.

освобожде́ние *n.* **1,** liberation. **2,** release. **3,** evacuation. **4,** exemption.

освое́ние *n.* **1,** mastering; mastery. **2,** settling; developing (*of new territory*).

осво́ить *v., pfv. of* **осва́ивать. —осво́иться,** *refl., pfv. of* **осва́иваться.**

освяща́ть *v. impfv.* [*pfv.* **освяти́ть**] to sanctify; hallow; consecrate. **—освящённый века́ми,** time-honored.

освяще́ние *n.* sanctification; consecration.

осево́й *adj.* axial. **—осева́я ли́ния,** center line (*in a road*).

оседа́ть *v. impfv.* [*pfv.* **осе́сть**] **1,** to settle; sink. **2,** to settle; establish residence.

оседла́ть *v. pfv.* **1,** *pfv. of* **седла́ть. 2,** *colloq.* to sit astride; straddle. **3,** *fig.* to get control of; dominate.

осе́длость *n.f.* settled way of life. **—черта́ осе́длости,** the Pale of Settlement; the Jewish Pale.

осе́длый *adj.* settled: осе́длый о́браз жи́зни, settled way of life.

осека́ться *v.r. impfv.* [*pfv.* **осе́чься**] **1,** *obs.* (*of a gun*) to misfire. **2,** to stop short (*in speaking*); (*of one's voice*) to break off. **3,** *colloq.* to suffer a setback.

осёл [*gen.* **осла́**] *n.* donkey; ass.

осело́к [*gen.* **-лка́**] *n.* **1,** whetstone. **2,** *fig.* touchstone.

осемене́ние *n.* insemination.

осени́ть *v., pfv. of* **осеня́ть.**

осе́нний *adj.* autumn (*attrib.*); fall (*attrib.*).

о́сень *n.f.* autumn; fall.

о́сенью *adv.* in autumn; in (the) fall.

осеня́ть *v. impfv.* [*pfv.* **осени́ть**] **1,** to shade. **2,** (*of a thought*) to strike: меня́ осени́ла мысль, the thought struck me. **—осени́ть** (+ *acc.*) кре́стным зна́мением, to make the sign of the cross over.

осе́сть [*infl. like* **сесть**] *v., pfv. of* **оседа́ть.**

осети́н [*gen. pl.* **-ти́н**] *n.m.* [*fem.* **-ти́нка**] Ossetian (one of a people inhabiting the Caucasus). **—осети́нский,** *adj.* Ossetian.

осётр [*gen.* **осетра́**] *n.* sturgeon. **—осетри́на,** *n.* sturgeon (*used as food*). **—осетро́вый,** *adj.* sturgeon (*attrib.*).

осе́чка [*gen. pl.* **-чек**] *n.* misfire. **—дать осе́чку,** to misfire.

осе́чься [*infl. like* **сечь;** *past* **осёкся, -лась**] *v.r., pfv. of* **осека́ться.**

оси́ливать *v. impfv.* [*pfv.* **оси́лить**] *colloq.* **1,** to overpower. **2,** *fig.* to overcome. **3,** to manage; handle. **4,** to master (a subject); get through (a book).

оси́на *n.* aspen. **—оси́нник,** *n.* aspen grove.

оси́новый *adj.* aspen (*attrib.*). **—дрожа́ть как оси́новый лист,** to shake like a leaf.

оси́ный *adj.* wasp's. **—оси́ное гнездо́,** hornets' nest.

оси́плый *adj.* hoarse; husky.

оси́пнуть *v. pfv.* [*past* **оси́п, -ла**] to become hoarse.

осироте́лый *adj.* orphan (*attrib.*); orphaned.

осироте́ть *v., pfv. of* **сироте́ть.**

оска́л *n., in* **оска́л зубо́в,** bared teeth.

оска́лить *v. pfv., in* **оска́лить зу́бы,** to bare one's teeth; show one's teeth. **—оска́литься,** *refl.* = **оска́лить зу́бы.**

оскверне́ние *n.* desecration.

оскверня́ть *v. impfv.* [*pfv.* **оскверни́ть**] to desecrate; profane; defile.

оскла́биться *v.r. pfv.* [*infl.* **-блюсь, -бишься**] *colloq.* to grin.

оско́лок [*gen.* **-лка**] *n.* splinter; fragment.

оско́лочный *adj., mil.* **1,** fragmentation (*attrib.*): оско́лочная бо́мба, fragmentation bomb. **2,** shrapnel (*attrib.*): оско́лочная ра́на, shrapnel wound.

оско́мина *n.* soreness of the mouth. **—набива́ть**

оско́мину (+ *dat.*), **1,** to make one's mouth sore. **2,** *fig.* to bore to death.

оскопля́ть *v. impfv.* [*pfv.* оскопи́ть] to castrate.

оскорби́тельный *adj.* insulting; abusive.

оскорби́ть [*infl.* -блю́, -би́шь] *v., pfv. of* оскорбля́ть. —оскорби́ться, *refl., pfv. of* оскорбля́ться.

оскорбле́ние *n.* insult; affront. —оскорбле́ние де́йствием, assault and battery.

оскорбля́ть *v. impfv.* [*pfv.* оскорби́ть] to insult; offend. —оскорбля́ться, *refl.* to be insulted.

оскуде́ть *v., pfv. of* скуде́ть.

ослабе́ть *v., pfv. of* слабе́ть *and* ослабева́ть. **1,** to weaken; grow weak. **2,** to slacken. **3,** to loosen; come loose.

ослабе́лый *adj., colloq.* weakened; enfeebled.

ослабе́ть *v., pfv. of* слабе́ть *and* ослабева́ть.

осла́бить [*infl.* -блю, -бишь] *v., pfv. of* ослабля́ть.

ослабле́ние *n.* **1,** weakening. **2,** relaxation; slackening.

ослабля́ть *v. impfv.* [*pfv.* осла́бить] **1,** to weaken. **2,** to relax; slacken. **3,** to loosen.

осла́бнуть *v. pfv.* [*past* осла́б, -ла] *colloq.* = ослабе́ть.

осла́вить *v. pfv.* [*infl.* -влю, -вишь] *colloq.* to malign; defame. —осла́виться, *refl., colloq.* to get a bad reputation.

ослепи́тельный *adj.* blinding; dazzling.

ослепи́ть [*infl.* -плю́, -пи́шь] *v., pfv. of* ослепля́ть.

ослепле́ние *n.* **1,** (act of) blinding. **2,** *fig.* blindness.

ослепля́ть *v. impfv.* [*pfv.* ослепи́ть] **1,** to blind. **2,** to dazzle.

осле́пнуть *v. pfv.* [*past* осле́п, -ла] *v., pfv. of* сле́пнуть.

о́слик *n.* small donkey; burro.

осли́ный *adj.* donkey's.

осли́ца *n.* female donkey.

осложне́ние *n.* complication.

осложня́ть *v. impfv.* [*pfv.* осложни́ть] to complicate. —осложня́ться, *refl.* **1,** to become complicated. **2,** (*with instr.*) to be complicated (by).

ослуша́ние *n., obs.* disobedience.

ослу́шаться *v.r. pfv.* (*with gen.*) *colloq.* to disobey.

ослы́шаться *v.r. pfv.* [*infl.* -шусь, -шишься] to hear incorrectly.

ослы́шка *n., colloq.* something heard incorrectly.

осма́тривать *v. impfv.* [*pfv.* осмотре́ть] **1,** to examine; inspect. **2,** to see; visit (a museum, the sights, etc.). —осма́триваться, *refl.* to look around.

осме́ивать *v. impfv.* [*pfv.* осмея́ть] to ridicule; deride.

осмеле́ть *v., pfv. of* смеле́ть.

осме́ливаться *v.r. impfv.* [*pfv.* осме́литься] (*with inf.*) to dare; venture: осме́люсь сказа́ть, I dare say; I venture to say.

осмея́ние *n.* ridicule; derision; mockery.

осмея́ть [*infl.* осмею́, осмеёшь] *v., pfv. of* осме́ивать.

о́смий *n.* osmium.

о́смос *n.* osmosis.

осмо́тр *n.* examination; inspection; checkup.

осмотре́ть [*infl.* осмотрю́, осмо́тришь] *v., pfv. of* осма́тривать. —осмотре́ться, *refl., pfv. of* осма́триваться.

осмотри́тельный *adj.* wary; circumspect. —осмотри́тельность, *n.f.* circumspection.

осмо́трщик *n.* inspector.

осмысле́ние *n.* comprehension.

осмы́сленный *adj.* **1,** intelligent (*able to reason*). **2,** conscious.

осмы́сливать *v. impfv.* [*pfv.* осмы́слить] **1,** to comprehend; grasp. **2,** to interpret. *Also,* осмысля́ть.

оснасти́ть [*infl.* -щу́, -сти́шь] *v., pfv. of* оснаща́ть.

осна́стка *n.* **1,** fitting out. **2,** *naut.* rig; rigging.

оснаща́ть *v. impfv.* [*pfv.* оснасти́ть] to equip; fit out.

оснаще́ние *n.* **1,** equipping; fitting out. **2,** equipment.

осне́женный *also,* оснежённый *adj.* snow-covered.

осно́ва *n.* **1,** base. **2,** *fig.* basis. **3,** *pl.* fundamentals. **4,** *textiles* warp. **5,** *ling.* stem. —класть (что́-нибудь) в осно́ву; брать *or* принима́ть (что́-нибудь) за осно́ву, to take as a starting point. —лежа́ть в осно́ве; лечь в осно́ву (+ *gen.*), **1,** to form the basis of. **2,** to underlie. —осно́ва осно́в (+ *gen.*), the cornerstone (of).

основа́ние *n.* **1,** founding. **2,** foundation. **3,** *fig.* basis. **4,** reason; grounds: име́ть основа́ния ду́мать, что..., to have reasons to think that... На како́м основа́нии?, on what grounds? **5,** *chem.; math.* base. —до основа́ния, to the ground; to its foundations: разру́шить до основа́ния, to raze to the ground. —на основа́нии (+ *gen.*), on the basis of; on the strength of.

основа́тель *n.m.* founder.

основа́тельно *adv.* thoroughly; soundly.

основа́тельность *n.f.* **1,** soundness. **2,** thoroughness.

основа́тельный *adj.* **1,** sound; well-founded. **2,** sound; firm; stable. **3,** (*of a person*) solid; dependable. **4,** thorough. **5,** *colloq.* sizable.

основа́ть [*infl.* -ную́, -нуёшь] *v., pfv. of* осно́вывать. —основа́ться, *refl., pfv. of* осно́вываться.

основно́й *adj.* **1,** basic; fundamental; primary. **2,** main; principal; primary. —в основно́м, mainly; for the most part; in the main. —основна́я ма́сса, (+ *gen.*), the bulk (of).

основополага́ющий *adj.* fundamental.

основополо́жник *n.* founder (*of a school of thought*).

осно́вывать *v. impfv.* [*pfv.* основа́ть] **1,** to found. **2,** (*with* на + *prepl.*) to base (on). Это обвине́ние ни на чём не осно́вано, the charge is completely baseless. —осно́вываться, *refl.* **1,** [*impfv. only*] (*with* на + *prepl.*) to be based (on). **2,** to be formed. **3,** to settle (down).

осо́ба *n.f.* person.

осо́бенно *adv.* especially; particularly.

осо́бенность *n.f.* particular feature; distinctive feature. —в осо́бенности, in particular.

осо́бенный *adj.* special; particular; peculiar. —ничего́ осо́бенного, nothing special; nothing in particular.

особня́к [*gen.* -няка́] *n.* private house; mansion.

особняко́м *adv.* apart; by oneself. —держа́ться особняко́м, to remain aloof.

осо́бо *adv.* **1,** separately; apart. **2,** especially; particularly.

осо́бый *adj.* **1,** special; particular: осо́бый тип/ме́тод, special type/method. **2,** special; separate: осо́бая ко́мната, special/separate room.

о́собь *n.f.* **1,** individual. **2,** specimen.

осознава́ть *v. impfv.* [*pfv.* осозна́ть; *pres.* -знаю́, -знаёшь] to realize; become aware of.

осозна́ние *n.* realization; awareness.

осозна́ть [*infl.* -зна́ю, -зна́ешь] *v., pfv. of* осознава́ть.

осóка *n.* sedge.

осокóрь *n.m.* black poplar.

осоловéлый *adj., colloq.* bleary-eyed.

óспа *n.* **1,** pox. **2,** smallpox. **3,** *colloq.* pockmarks: изры́тый óспой, pockmarked. —вéтряная óспа, chicken pox. —корóвья óспа, cowpox. —чёрная óспа, (black) smallpox.

оспáривать *v. impfv.* [*pfv.* оспóрить] **1,** to challenge; dispute; contest. **2,** [*impfv. only*] to contend for; contest (a championship, prize, etc.).

óспенный *adj.* smallpox (*attrib.*).

óспина *n.* pockmark.

оспопрививáние *n.* vaccination.

оспори́мый *adj.* questionable; debatable.

оспóрить *v., pfv. of* оспáривать.

осрами́ть *v., pfv. of* срами́ть.

ост *n., naut.* **1,** east. **2,** east wind.

оставáться *v.r. impfv.* [*pfv.* остáться; *pres.* остаю́сь, остаёшься] **1,** to remain; stay. **2,** to be left; remain: скóлько врéмени остáлось?, how much time is left?; how much time remains? Остáться сиротóй, to be left an orphan. Дверь остáлась незáпертой, the door was left unlocked. Остаётся тóлько добáвить, что..., it remains only to add that... **3,** *impers.* (*with dat.*) to have: ему́ остáлось недóлго жить, he hasn't long to live. Нам не остаётся ничегó другóго, как..., we have no choice but to... —оставáться на вторóй год, to be left back (*in school*).

остáвить [*infl.* -влю, -вишь] *v., pfv. of* оставля́ть.

оставля́ть *v. impfv.* [*pfv.* остáвить] **1,** to leave. **2,** to give up; abandon. **3,** to keep; retain. —остáвьте!, stop it! —оставля́ть без внимáния, to disregard; take no notice of. —оставля́ть жела́ть мнóго лу́чшего, to leave much to be desired. —оставля́ть за собóй, to reserve: оставля́ть за собóй прáво, to reserve the right. —оставля́ть на вторóй год, to leave back (*in school*). —оставля́ть пóсле урóков, to keep in after school.

остальнóе *n., decl. as an adj.* the rest.

остальнóй *adj.* the other; the remaining; the rest of. —в остальнóм, in all other respects.

остальны́е *n. pl., decl. as an adj.* the others; the rest.

останáвливать *v. impfv.* [*pfv.* останови́ть] **1,** to stop; bring to a stop. **2,** *in* останáвливать взгляд на (+ *prepl.*), to rest one's gaze on. **3,** *in* останáвливать свой вы́бор на (+ *prepl.*), to choose; opt for. —останáвливаться, *refl.* **1,** to stop; come to a stop. **2,** to stay (at a hotel, with friends, etc.). **3,** (*with* на + *prepl.*) to dwell on (a subject, details, etc.). **4,** (*with* на + *prepl.*) to settle on; decide on. **5,** *in* ни пéред чем не останови́ться, to stop at nothing.

остáнки [*gen.* -ков] *n. pl.* remains (*of a human being*). —брéнные остáнки, mortal remains.

останови́ть [*infl.* -новлю́, -нóвишь] *v., pfv. of* останáвливать. —останови́ться, *refl., pfv. of* останáвливаться.

останóвка [*gen. pl.* -вок] *n.* **1,** stop; stopping. **2,** stop; stay. **3,** stop (*of or for a vehicle*): слéдующая останóвка, the next stop; автóбусная останóвка, bus stop.

остáток [*gen.* -тка] *n.* **1,** remainder; rest. **2,** *pl.* remains; vestiges. **3,** residue. **4,** *math.* remainder.

остáточный *adj.* **1,** remaining. **2,** vestigial. **3,** residual.

остáться [*infl.* остáнусь, остáнешься] *v.r., pfv. of* оставáться.

остеклянéть *v., pfv. of* стеклянéть.

остеолóгия (тэ) *n.* osteology. —остеóлог, *n.* osteologist.

остепени́ть *v. pfv.* to steady (someone) down. —остепени́ться, *refl.* to steady down; have sown one's wild oats.

остервенéлый *adj.* frenzied. —остервенéние, *n.* frenzy.

остервенéть *v. pfv.* to become enraged.

остервени́ть *v. pfv.* to enrage. —остервени́ться, *refl.* = остервенéть.

остерегáть *v. impfv.* [*pfv.* остерéчь] (*with* от) to warn (against); caution (against). —остерегáться, *refl.* **1,** to be careful. **2,** (*with gen.*) to beware (of); be wary (of). **3,** (*with gen. or inf.*) to avoid.

остерéчь [*infl. like* стерéчь] *v., pfv. of* остерегáть. —остерéчься, *refl., pfv. of* остерегáться.

óстов *n.* **1,** frame; framework. **2,** *anat.* skeleton.

остолбенéлый *adj., colloq.* stupefied; dumfounded. —остолбенéние, *n.* stupefaction; stupor.

остолбенéть *v., pfv. of* столбенéть.

остолóп *n., colloq.* blockhead; bonehead.

острóжно *adv.* carefully; cautiously. —*interj.* careful!; be careful!; look out!; watch out!; watch it!

осторóжность *n.f.* care; caution.

осторóжный *adj.* [*short form* -жен, -жна] careful; cautious.

осточертéть *v. pfv.* (*with dat.*) *colloq.* to make sick and tired: э́то мне осточертéло, I am sick and tired of it; I am fed up with it.

остраки́зм *n.* ostracism.

острáстка *n., colloq.* warning: для острáстки, as a warning.

острига́ть *v. impfv.* = стричь. —острига́ться, *refl.* = стри́чься.

остриё *n.* **1,** (sharp) point. **2,** cutting edge. **3,** *fig.* (*with gen.*) cutting edge (*of a joke, criticism, etc.*).

остри́ть *v.impfv.* **1,** to sharpen. **2,** to make jokes; crack jokes.

остри́чь [*infl. like* стричь] *v., pfv. of* стричь *and* острига́ть. —остри́чься, *refl., pfv. of* стри́чься *and* острига́ться.

óстро *adv.* **1,** (*with verbs of sharpening*) to a fine point. **2,** *fig.* sharply: óстро критиковáть, to sharply criticize. Óстро пáхнуть, to have a sharp/strong smell. Óстро нуждáться в, to be in dire need of.

óстров [*pl.* островá] *n.* island.

островитя́нин [*pl.* -тя́не] *n.m.* [*fem.* -тя́нка] islander.

островнóй *adj.* island (*attrib.*); insular.

островóк [*gen.* -вка́] *n.* small island.

острóг *n., obs.* jail.

острогá *n.* spear; harpoon: бить ры́бу острогóй, to spear a fish.

острогля́зый *adj., colloq.* sharp-eyed.

острогу́бцы [*gen. pl.* -цев] *n.pl.* cutting pliers.

остроконéчный *adj.* pointed; coming to a point.

остроли́ст *n.* holly.

острóта *n.* witticism; quip; wisecrack.

остротá *n.* sharpness; keenness; pungency.

остроу́мие *n.* wit.

остроу́мно *adv.* **1,** with great wit. **2,** cleverly.

остроу́мный *adj.* **1,** witty. **2,** clever; ingenious.

óстрый *adj.* **1,** sharp. **2,** acute. **3,** keen. **4,** pungent. **5,** (*of a situation, moment, etc.*) critical.

остря́к [*gen.* -ряка́] *n.* witty person; wit.

остудить [*infl.* остужу́, осту́дишь] *v.*, *pfv. of* студи́ть *and* остужа́ть.

остужа́ть *v. impfv.* [*pfv.* остуди́ть] to cool; chill.

оступа́ться *v.r. impfv.* [*pfv.* оступи́ться] to stumble.

оступи́ться [*infl.* оступлю́сь, осту́пишься] *v.r.*, *pfv. of* оступа́ться.

остыва́ть *v. impfv.* [*pfv.* осты́ть] **1,** to get cold. **2,** *fig.* to cool off; calm down. **3,** (*with* к) to grow cool towards. **4,** (*of strong emotions*) to cool.

осты́ть [*infl.* осты́ну, осты́нешь] *v.*, *pfv. of* остыва́ть.

осуди́ть [*infl.* осужу́, осу́дишь] *v.*, *pfv. of* осужда́ть.

осужда́ть *v. impfv.* [*pfv.* осуди́ть] **1,** to condemn; denounce. **2,** to convict. **3,** to condemn (*e.g.* to death); sentence.

осужде́ние *n.* **1,** condemnation; denunciation; censure. **2,** conviction.

осуждённый *n.*, *decl. as an adj.* convict.

осу́нуться *v.r. pfv.* to become drawn in the face.

осуша́ть *v. impfv.* [*pfv.* осуши́ть] **1,** to dry. **2,** to drain (a swamp, glass of wine, etc.). — осуша́ть (свои́) слё́зы, to stop crying. — осуша́ть слё́зы (+ *dat.*), to console.

осуше́ние *n.* drainage. — осуши́тельный, *adj.* drainage (*attrib.*).

осуши́ть [*infl.* осушу́, осу́шишь] *v.*, *pfv. of* осуша́ть.

осуществи́мый *adj.* feasible; practicable. — осуществи́мость, *n.f.* feasibility; practicability.

осуществи́ть [*infl.* -влю́, -ви́шь] *v.*, *pfv. of* осуществля́ть. — осуществи́ться, *refl.*, *pfv. of* осуществля́ться.

осуществле́ние *n.* realization; fulfillment; implementation.

осуществля́ть *v. impfv.* [*pfv.* осуществи́ть] **1,** to carry out; implement. **2,** to accomplish; realize. **3,** to exercise (a right, control, etc.). — осуществля́ться, *refl.* to be realized; come true.

осцилло́граф *n.* oscillograph.

осциллоско́п *n.* oscilloscope.

осцилля́тор *n.* oscillator.

осчастли́вить *v. pfv.* [*infl.* -влю, -вишь] to make happy.

осы́пать [*infl.* осы́плю, осы́плешь] *v.*, *pfv. of* осыпа́ть. — осы́паться, *refl.*, *pfv. of* осыпа́ться.

осыпа́ть *v. impfv.* [*pfv.* осы́пать] (*with instr.*) **1,** to sprinkle (with); strew (with). **2,** *fig.* to shower (with gifts); rain (blows); hurl (insults); heap (ridicule) upon. — осыпа́ться, *refl.* **1,** (*of plaster*) to peel off. **2,** to crumble. **3,** (*of leaves*) to fall. **4,** (*with instr.*) to be strewn with.

ось [*pl.* о́си, осе́й, ося́м] *n.f.* **1,** axis. **2,** axle.

осьмино́г *n.* octopus.

осяза́емый *adj.* tangible; palpable.

осяза́ние *n.* touch: чу́вство осяза́ния, sense of touch.

осяза́тельный *adj.* **1,** tactile. **2,** tangible.

осяза́ть *v. impfv.* to feel; perceive.

от *also,* ото *prep., with gen.* **1,** from: письмо́ от А́ни, a letter from Anya; от Москвы́ до Ленингра́да, from Moscow to Leningrad; счита́ть от одного́ до десяти́, to count from one to ten. Отходи́ть от стола́, to walk away from the table. **2,** *indicating cause:* дрожа́ть от стра́ха, to tremble from/with fear; умере́ть от ра́ка, to die of cancer. **3,** to; belonging to: ключ от ко́мнаты, the key to a room; пу́говица от пальто́, a button to a coat. **4,** for (*an illness*): что́-нибудь от

ка́шля, something for a cough; лечи́ть больно́го от я́звы, to treat a patient for an ulcer. **5,** of (*a certain date*): ва́ше письмо́ от седьмо́го ма́рта, your letter of March 7.

от- *also,* ото-, отъ-, *prefix* **1,** *indicating motion away, aside or back:* отходи́ть, to walk away; step back; отта́лкивать, to push away; push aside. **2,** *indicating separation, detachment, etc.:* отделя́ть, to separate; отреза́ть, to cut off. **3,** *indicating unfastening, unhooking, etc.:* отстёгивать, to unfasten; отпряга́ть, to unharness; отку́поривать, to uncork. **4,** *indicating response, return, etc.:* отвеча́ть, to answer; откликаться, to respond; отдава́ть, to give back; отпла́чивать, to pay back. **5,** *indicating rejection, refusal, etc.:* отка́зываться, to refuse; отверга́ть, to reject; отрека́ться, to renounce. **6,** *indicating completion of an action:* отобе́дать, to be finished with dinner; отде́лывать, to put into final form.

ота́пливать *v. impfv.* [*pfv.* отопи́ть] to heat (a building).

ота́ра *n.* flock (*of sheep*).

отбавля́ть *v. impfv.* [*pfv.* отба́вить] (*with gen.*) to pour off (a certain amount of). — хоть отбавля́й, more than enough; enough and then some.

отбараба́нить *v. pfv., colloq.* **1,** to stop drumming. **2,** to bang out (*on a musical instrument*). **3,** to rattle off (a speech, answers, etc.).

отбега́ть *v. impfv.* [*pfv.* отбежа́ть] to run away; run back.

отбежа́ть [*infl. like* бежа́ть] *v.*, *pfv. of* отбега́ть.

отбе́ливать *v. impfv.* [*pfv.* отбели́ть] to bleach.

отбели́ть [*infl.* отбелю́, отбе́лишь *or* отбели́шь] *v.*, *pfv. of* отбе́ливать.

отбива́ть *v. impfv.* [*pfv.* отби́ть] **1,** to break off. **2,** to beat off; repel; repulse (an attack); beat back (an attacker); parry; deflect (a blow). **3,** to recapture; retake. **4,** *colloq.* to take away; remove (a taste, odor, desire, etc.). **5,** to hurt; injure. **6,** to sharpen; whet. **7,** to beat (time); sound (a call). **8,** *sports* to return (a ball). — отбива́ться, *refl.* **1,** to be broken off. **2,** (*with* от) to fight off. **3,** to fall behind; (*with* от) stray (from). **4,** (*with* от) *colloq.* to drift away from; get away from. **5,** *in* отби́ться от рук, to get out of hand.

отбивно́й *adj.*, *in* отбивна́я котле́та, chop; cutlet. Бара́нья/свина́я отбивна́я, lamb/pork chop. Теля́чья отбивна́я, veal chop; veal cutlet.

отбира́ть *v. impfv.* [*pfv.* отобра́ть] **1,** to take away; take (from): отбира́ть конфе́ты у ребёнка, to take candy (away) from a child. **2,** to select.

отби́ть [*infl.* отобью́, отобьёшь] *v.*, *pfv. of* отбива́ть. — отби́ться, *refl.*, *pfv. of* отбива́ться.

отблагодари́ть *v. pfv.* **1,** to thank. **2,** to show one's appreciation to.

о́тблеск *n.* **1,** reflection. **2,** *fig.* (*with gen.*) spark (of); trace (of).

отбо́й *n.* **1,** *mil.* retreat: дава́ть *or* бить отбо́й, to sound retreat. **2,** the all-clear signal. — бить отбо́й, **1,** to beat a retreat. **2,** *fig.* to back down. — дать отбо́й, to ring off; hang up (the receiver). — отбо́ю нет от, no end of: у меня́ нет отбо́ю от предложе́ний, I've had no end of offers.

отбо́йный *adj.*, *in* отбо́йный молото́к, mechanical pick; пневмати́ческий отбо́йный молото́к, jackhammer.

отбо́р *n.* selection.

отбо́рный *adj.* **1,** select; choice. Отбо́рные войска́, crack troops. **2,** *colloq.* (*of swearwords*) choice; unprintable.

отбо́рочный *adj.* selection (*attrib.*). —отбо́рочные соревнова́ния, *sports* trials.

отбоя́риваться *v.r. impfv.* [*pfv.* отбоя́риться] (*with* от) *colloq.* to get out of; avoid.

отбра́сывать *v. impfv.* [*pfv.* отбро́сить] **1,** to throw aside; cast aside. **2,** *mil.* to throw back; hurl back. **3,** to cast (light, a shadow, etc.). **4,** *fig.* to cast aside (thoughts, doubts, etc.).

отбро́сить [*infl.* -шу, -сишь] *v., pfv. of* отбра́сывать.

отбро́сы [*gen.* -сов] *n.pl.* refuse; garbage.

отбыва́ть *v. impfv.* [*pfv.* отбы́ть] **1,** *v.i.* to leave; depart. **2,** *v.t.* to serve; serve out (time, a sentence, etc.).

отбы́тие *n.* **1,** departure. **2,** serving; completion (*of a sentence, term, etc.*).

отбы́ть [*infl.* -бу́ду, -бу́дешь; *past* о́тбыл, отбыла́, о́тбыло] *v., pfv. of* отбыва́ть.

отва́га *n.* courage; bravery.

отва́живать *v. impfv.* [*pfv.* отва́дить] (*with* от) *colloq.* **1,** to break (someone) of the habit (of). **2,** to drive off; scare off. —отва́живаться, *refl.* **1,** [*pfv.* отва́диться] (*with* от) *colloq.* to break the habit of; get out of the habit of. **2,** [*pfv.* отва́житься] to dare; venture.

отва́жный *adj.* courageous; brave. —отва́жно, *adv.* courageously; bravely.

отва́л *n.* **1,** casting off (*of a boat*). **2,** heap; dump: отва́л шла́ка, slag heap. —до отва́ла, to the bursting point.

отва́ливать *v. impfv.* [*pfv.* отвали́ть] **1,** to push aside. **2,** *v.i.* (*of a boat*) to cast off. **3,** *colloq.* to hand out (money). —отва́ливаться, *refl.* **1,** to fall off. **2,** *colloq.* to lean back.

отвали́ть [*infl.* -валю́, -ва́лишь] *v., pfv. of* отва́ливать. —отвали́ться, *refl., pfv. of* отва́ливаться.

отва́р *n.* decoction. —мясно́й отва́р, stock. —ри́совый отва́р, rice water.

отва́ривать *v. impfv.* [*pfv.* отвари́ть] to boil.

отвари́ть [*infl.* -варю́, -ва́ришь] *v., pfv. of* отва́ривать.

отварно́й *adj.* boiled.

отве́дывать *v. impfv.* [*pfv.* отве́дать] *colloq.* **1,** to try; taste. **2,** to taste; experience.

отвезти́ [*infl. like* везти́] *v., pfv. of* отвози́ть.

отверга́ть *v. impfv.* [*pfv.* отве́ргнуть] to reject; turn down.

отве́ргнуть [*past* -ве́рг, -ла] *v., pfv. of* отверга́ть.

отвердева́ть *v. impfv.* [*pfv.* отверде́ть] to harden; solidify.

отверде́лый *adj.* hard; hardened.

отверде́ть *v., pfv. of* отвердева́ть.

отве́рженный *adj. & n.* outcast.

отверну́ть *v., pfv. of* отвёртывать *and* отвора́чивать. —отверну́ться, *refl., pfv. of* отвёртываться *and* отвора́чиваться.

отве́рстие *n.* opening; hole.

отверте́ться [*infl.* -верчу́сь, -ве́ртишься] *v.r., pfv. of* отвёртываться (*in sense #3*).

отвёртка [*gen. pl.* -ток] *n.* screwdriver.

отвёртывать *v. impfv.* [*pfv.* отверну́ть] **1,** = отвора́чивать. **2,** to turn on (a faucet). **3,** to unscrew; screw off. —отвёртываться, *refl.* **1,** = отвора́чиваться. **2,** to come unscrewed. **3,** [*pfv.* отверте́ться] *colloq.* to get out of it; get off.

отве́с *n.* **1,** plumb. **2,** sheer cliff.

отве́сить [*infl.* -шу, -сишь] *v., pfv. of* отве́шивать.

отве́сный *adj.* sheer; vertical; perpendicular. —отве́сная скала́, cliff.

отвести́ [*infl. like* вести́] *v., pfv. of* отводи́ть.

отве́т *n.* answer; reply: в отве́т на (+ *acc.*), in answer/reply to. —без отве́та, unanswered: оста́вить/оста́ться без отве́та, to leave/remain unanswered. —(быть) в отве́те за (+ *acc.*), to be responsible for.

ответви́ться *v.r., pfv. of* ответвля́ться.

ответвле́ние *n.* branch; offshoot.

ответвля́ться *v.r. impfv.* [*pfv.* ответви́ться] to branch off.

отве́тить [*infl.* -чу, -тишь] *v., pfv. of* отвеча́ть.

отве́тный *adj.* **1,** return (*attrib.*): отве́тный визи́т, return visit. **2,** in reply: отве́тная речь, speech in reply. **3,** retaliatory.

отве́тственность *n.f.* responsibility: нести́ отве́тственность за (+ *acc.*), to bear the responsibility for.

отве́тственный *adj.* **1,** responsible: отве́тственный за рабо́ту, responsible for the work. **2,** crucial; (very) important. —отве́тственный рабо́тник, senior official. —отве́тственный реда́ктор, managing editor.

отве́тчик *n., law* defendant.

отвеча́ть *v. impfv.* [*pfv.* отве́тить] **1,** (*with dat.*) to answer; reply (to) (a person); (*with* на + *acc.*) (a question, letter, etc.). **2,** (*with* на + *acc.*) to respond to (a request, appeal, etc.). **3,** [*impfv. only*] (*with* за + *acc.*) to answer (for); be responsible (for). **4,** [*pfv. only*] (*with* за + *acc.*) to pay for: вы за э́то отве́тите!, you'll pay for this! **5,** [*impfv. only*] (*with dat.*) to meet; answer (needs, requirements, etc.). **6,** *in* отвеча́ть уро́к, to recite one's lesson.

отве́шивать *v. impfv.* [*pfv.* отве́сить] **1,** to weigh out. **2,** *colloq.* to deal; dish out (a blow). **3,** *in* отве́шивать покло́н, to make a bow.

отви́ливать *v. impfv.* [*pfv.* отвильну́ть] (*with* от) *colloq.* to avoid; dodge.

отви́нчивать *v. impfv.* [*pfv.* отвинти́ть] to unscrew; screw off.

отвиса́ть *v. impfv.* [*pfv.* отви́снуть] to hang down; sag; droop.

отви́слый *adj.* loose-hanging; drooping; flaccid.

отви́снуть [*past* -ви́с, -ла] *v., pfv. of* отвиса́ть.

отвлека́ть *v. impfv.* [*pfv.* отвле́чь] to distract; divert. —отвлека́ться, *refl.* **1,** to be distracted. **2,** (*with* от) to digress (from).

отвлече́ние *n.* **1,** distraction; diversion. **2,** *obs.* abstraction.

отвлечённый *adj.* abstract. —отвлечённо, *adv.* in an abstract manner; in the abstract.

отвле́чь [*infl. like* влечь] *v., pfv. of* отвлека́ть. —отвле́чься, *refl., pfv. of* отвлека́ться.

отво́д *n.* **1,** taking; delivering. **2,** draining off (*of water*). **3,** allocation (*of land*). **4,** diversion: для отво́да глаз, to divert attention. **5,** rejection (*of a candidate*); challenge (*to a witness*).

отводи́ть *v. impfv.* [*pfv.* отвести́; *pres.* -вожу́, -во́дишь] **1,** to take (someone on foot to a certain place). **2,** to lead away; take away. **3,** to deflect; ward off. **4,** to draw aside. **5,** to drain; drain off (water). **6,** to allot; set aside. **7,** to reject (someone's candidacy); challenge (a witness). —отводи́ть глаза́, to turn one's eyes away. —отводи́ть глаза́ (+ *dat.*), to mislead; delude; lead astray. —отводи́ть ду́шу, to unburden oneself.

отво́дный *adj.* drainage (*attrib.*); drain (*attrib.*).

отвоева́ть *v. pfv.* [*infl.* -воюю, -воюешь] **1**, *pfv. of* **отвоёвывать**. **2**, *colloq.* to fight (*for a certain length of time*). **3**, *colloq.* to finish fighting.

отвоёвывать *v. impfv.* [*pfv.* **отвоева́ть**] to win back (*in war*); retake.

отвози́ть *v. impfv.* [*pfv.* **отвезти́**; *pres.* -вожу́, -во́зишь] **1**, to take; drive (*someone to a certain place*). **2**, to take away; cart away.

отвора́чивать *v. impfv.* [*pfv.* **отверну́ть**] **1**, to turn away; turn aside. **2**, to turn down; fold down. **3**, *v.i.*, *colloq.* to turn; make a turn. —**отвора́чиваться**, *refl.* (*with* от) to turn away (from); turn one's back (on).

отвори́ть [*infl.* -творю́, -тво́ришь] *v., pfv. of* **отворя́ть**. —**отвори́ться**, *refl., pfv. of* **отворя́ться**.

отворо́т *n.* **1**, lapel. **2**, cuff.

отворя́ть *v. impfv.* [*pfv.* **отвори́ть**] to open. —**отворя́ться**, *refl.* to open; come open.

отврати́тельный *adj.* **1**, disgusting. **2**, *colloq.* miserable; rotten.

отвраща́ть *v. impfv.* [*pfv.* **отврати́ть**] **1**, *obs.* to turn away. **2**, to avert; ward off.

отвраще́ние *n.* disgust; repugnance; loathing; aversion.

отвыка́ть *v. impfv.* [*pfv.* **отвы́кнуть**] (*with* от) **1**, to become unaccustomed to. **2**, to get out of the habit of. **3**, to become estranged from.

отвы́кнуть [*past* -вы́к, -ла] *v., pfv. of* **отвыка́ть**.

отвяза́ть [*infl.* -вяжу́, -вя́жешь] *v., pfv. of* **отвя́зывать**. —**отвяза́ться**, *refl., pfv. of* **отвя́зываться**.

отвя́зывать *v. impfv.* [*pfv.* **отвяза́ть**] to untie; unfasten. —**отвя́зываться**, *refl.* **1**, to come untied; come loose. **2**, to break loose. **3**, (*with* от) *colloq.* to get rid of; rid oneself of; shake off. **4**, (*with* от) *colloq.* to leave alone; leave in peace.

отгада́ть *v., pfv. of* **отга́дывать**.

отга́дка [*gen. pl.* -док] *n.* answer; solution (*to a riddle*).

отга́дчик *n., colloq.* guesser.

отга́дывать *v. impfv.* [*pfv.* **отгада́ть**] **1**, to guess (*correctly*). **2**, to solve (a riddle).

отгиба́ть *v. impfv.* [*pfv.* **отогну́ть**] **1**, to unbend; straighten. **2**, to turn down; turn back.

отглаго́льный *adj., gram.* verbal: отглаго́льное существи́тельное, verbal noun.

отгла́живать *v. impfv.* [*pfv.* **отгла́дить**] to iron; press.

отгова́ривать *v. impfv.* [*pfv.* **отговори́ть**] (*with inf. or* от) **1**, to dissuade; talk out of. **2**, [*impfv. only*] to try to dissuade; try to talk out of. —**отгова́риваться**, *refl.* **1**, to beg off (*by giving excuses*). **2**, (*with instr.*) to plead (illness, ignorance, etc.).

отгово́рка [*gen. pl.* -рок] *n.* excuse.

отголо́сок [*gen.* -ска] *n.* **1**, echo. **2**, faint sound. **3**, sympathetic response. **4**, *pl.* repercussions; aftereffects; aftermath.

отгоня́ть *v. impfv.* [*pfv.* **отогна́ть**] to drive away; drive off.

отгора́живать *v. impfv.* [*pfv.* **отгороди́ть**] **1**, to fence off; partition off. **2**, *fig.* to shut off; isolate.

отгороди́ть [*infl.* -рожу́, -ро́дишь *or* -роди́шь] *v., pfv. of* **отгора́живать**.

отгреба́ть *v. impfv.* [*pfv.* **отгрести́**] **1**, *v.t.* to rake away. **2**, *v.i.* to row away.

отгреме́ть *v. pfv.* to die down; fall silent.

отгрести́ [*infl. like* грести́] *v., pfv. of* **отгреба́ть**.

отгружа́ть *v. impfv.* [*pfv.* **отгрузи́ть**] to ship.

отгрузи́ть [*infl.* -гружу́, -грузишь *or* -грузи́шь] *v., pfv. of* **отгружа́ть**.

отгру́зка *n.* shipment.

отгрыза́ть *v. impfv.* [*pfv.* **огры́зть**] to bite off; gnaw off.

отгры́зть [*infl. like* грызть] *v., pfv. of* **отгрыза́ть**.

отгу́л *n.* compensatory leave.

отгу́ливать *v. impfv.* [*pfv.* **отгуля́ть**] *colloq.* to take (time) off; take compensatory leave: отгу́ливать два дня, to take two days off; take two days compensatory leave.

отгуля́ть *v. pfv., colloq.* **1**, *pfv. of* **отгу́ливать**. **2**, to reach the end of (one's vacation). **3**, to celebrate (a holiday, wedding, etc.). **4**, to finish celebrating.

отдава́ть *v. impfv.* [*pfv.* **отда́ть**; *pres.* -даю́, -даёшь] **1**, to give back; return. **2**, to hand over; turn over. **3**, to devote: отдава́ть жизнь теа́тру, to devote one's life to the theater. **4**, (*with* в + *acc.*) to have (cleaned, repaired, etc.): отда́ть (что́-нибудь) в чи́стку/ремо́нт, to have (something) cleaned/repaired. **5**, *v.i.* (*of a gun*) to recoil. **6**, *v.i.* [*impfv. only*] (*with instr.*) to taste of; smell of; smack of. —**отдава́ть (кого́-нибудь) в шко́лу**, to put *or* place (someone) in school. —**отдава́ть долг**, to repay a debt. —**отдава́ть до́лжное**, *see* **до́лжное**. —**отдава́ть жизнь за** (+ *acc.*), to give one's life for. —**отдава́ть (кого́-нибудь) под суд**, to prosecute; bring to trial. —**отдава́ть после́дний долг** (+ *dat.*), to pay one's last respects to. —**отдава́ть предпочте́ние** (+ *dat.*), to give preference (to). —**отдава́ть прика́з**, to give an order. —**отдава́ть свой го́лос** (+ *dat.*), to cast one's vote (for). —**отдава́ть себе́ отчёт**, *see* **отчёт**. —**отдава́ть честь** (+ *dat.*), *mil.* to salute.

отдава́ться *v.r. impfv.* [*pfv.* **отда́ться**; *pres.* -даю́сь, -даёшься] **1**, (*with dat.*) to give oneself up (to). **2**, (*with dat.*) (*of a woman*) to give in (to). **3**, (*with dat.*) to devote oneself (to). **4**, (*of a sound*) to resound. **5**, (*of a pain*) to be felt. В мое́м се́рдце отдава́лось бо́лью, I felt sick at heart.

отдале́ние *n.* **1**, removal. **2**, estrangement. **3**, distance. —**в отдале́нии**, in the distance. —**на отдале́нии**, at a distance.

отдалённый *adj.* remote; distant. —**отдалённость**, *n.f.* remoteness.

отдаля́ть *v. impfv.* [*pfv.* **отдали́ть**] **1**, to remove; move away. **2**, to postpone; put off. **3**, to estrange; alienate. —**отдаля́ться**, *refl.* (*with* от) **1**, to drift away (from). **2**, to digress (from).

отда́ривать *v. impfv.* [*pfv.* **отдари́ть**] *colloq.* to give (a gift) in return.

отда́ть [*infl. like* дать; *past* о́тдал, отдала́, о́тдало] *v., pfv. of* **отдава́ть**. —**отда́ться**, *refl.* [*past* отда́лся, -ла́сь, -ло́сь] *pfv. of* **отдава́ться**.

отда́ча *n.* **1**, return. **2**, recoil; kick (*of a gun*).

отде́л *n.* **1**, section. **2**, department: отде́л зака́зов, order department.

отде́лать *v., pfv. of* **отде́лывать**. —**отде́латься**, *refl., pfv. of* **отде́лываться**.

отделе́ние *n.* **1**, separation. **2**, department; section; division; branch. Почто́вое отделе́ние, local post office. **3**, compartment; section. **4**, part (*of a concert, performance, etc.*). **5**, *mil.* squad. —**коте́льное отделе́ние**, boiler room. —**маши́нное отделе́ние**, engine room.

отдели́ть [*infl.* -делю́, -де́лишь] *v., pfv. of* **отделя́ть**. —**отдели́ться**, *refl., pfv. of* **отделя́ться**.

отде́лка *n.* **1,** finishing; decorating. **2,** trimming; trim.

отде́лывать *v. impfv.* [*pfv.* **отде́лать**] **1,** to put into final form. **2,** to decorate; trim. **3,** to finish (a surface). **4,** *colloq.* to rebuke; bawl out. —**отде́лываться**, *refl., colloq.* **1,** (*with* **от**) to finish; be done with; get out of the way. **2,** (*with* **от**) to get rid of. **3,** (*with instr.*) to get off (with). **4,** (*with an adverb*) to get off (cheap, easily, etc.).

отде́льно *adv.* **1,** separately; apart. **2,** individually.

отде́льность *n.f., in* **в отде́льности,** individually; separately.

отде́льный *adj.* **1,** separate. **2,** individual.

отделя́ть *v. impfv.* [*pfv.* **отдели́ть**] **1,** to separate. **2,** [*impfv. only*] to divide; serve as the boundary between. —**отделя́ться**, *refl.* (*with* **от**) **1,** to become separated from. **2,** to come off. **3,** to move away from.

отдёргивать *v. impfv.* [*pfv.* **отдёрнуть**] **1,** to pull back; draw back. **2,** to pull aside; draw aside.

отдира́ть *v. impfv.* [*pfv.* **отодра́ть**] to tear off; rip off.

отдохну́ть *v., pfv. of* **отдыха́ть**.

отдува́ть *v. impfv.* [*pfv.* **отду́ть**] **1,** to blow away. **2,** to puff up (one's cheeks). —**отдува́ться**, *refl.* **1,** to become puffed up. **2,** [*impfv. only*] to pant; puff. **3,** [*impfv. only*] (*with* **за** + *acc.*) *colloq.* to take the rap for.

отду́мывать *v. impfv.* [*pfv.* **отду́мать**] (*with inf.*) *colloq.* to change one's mind (about).

отду́ть [*infl.* -ду́ю, -ду́ешь] *v., pfv. of* **отдува́ть**. —**отду́ться**, *refl., pfv. of* **отдува́ться**.

отду́шина *n.* **1,** vent; air-vent. **2,** *fig.* outlet (*for one's emotions*).

о́тдых *n.* rest. —**дом о́тдыха,** rest home.

отдыха́ть *v. impfv.* [*pfv.* **отдохну́ть**] **1,** to rest. **2,** to be on vacation; take a vacation.

отдыша́ться *v.r. pfv.* [*infl.* -дышу́сь, -ды́шишься] to catch one's breath.

отёк *n., med.* edema.

отека́ть *v. impfv.* [*pfv.* **оте́чь**] **1,** to swell up; become swollen. **2,** to become numb. **3,** (*of a candle*) to drip.

оте́лится *v.r., pfv. of* **тели́ться**.

оте́ль (тэ) *n.m.* hotel.

отепля́ть *v. impfv.* [*pfv.* **отепли́ть**] to winterize.

оте́ц [*gen.* отца́] *n.* father. —**оте́ческий,** *adj.* fatherly; paternal.

оте́чественный *adj.* **1,** native. **2,** domestically produced. —**Вели́кая Оте́чественная война́,** the Great Patriotic War (*World War II*).

оте́чество *n.* native land; homeland; fatherland.

оте́чь [*infl. like* течь] *v., pfv. of* **отека́ть**.

отжа́ть [*infl.* отожму́, отожмёшь] *v., pfv. of* **отжима́ть**.

отже́чь [*infl.* отожгу́, отожжёшь, ...отожгу́т; *past* отжёг, отожгла́] *v., pfv. of* **отжига́ть**.

отжива́ть *v. impfv.* [*pfv.* **отжи́ть**] to die out; become a thing of the past. *See also* **отжи́ть**.

отжи́вший *adj.* **1,** having lived out one's life. **2,** out-of-date; obsolete.

отжига́ть *v. impfv.* [*pfv.* **отже́чь**] to anneal.

отжима́ть *v. impfv.* [*pfv.* **отжа́ть**] **1,** to wring out. **2,** to squeeze out (liquid). **3,** *colloq.* to push back; force back.

отжи́ть *v. pfv.* [*infl.* -живу́, -живёшь; *past* о́тжил, отжила́, о́тжило] **1,** *pfv. of* **отжива́ть. 2,** to have lived one's life. —**отжи́ть свой век,** to become a thing of the past; have had one's day.

отзвони́ть *v. pfv.* **1,** (*of a clock*) to strike (a certain hour). **2,** to stop ringing.

о́тзвук *n.* **1,** echo. **2,** faint sound. **3,** *fig.* sympathetic response. **4,** *fig.* reverberations.

о́тзыв *n.* **1,** review; comment: получи́ть благоприя́тные о́тзывы, to receive favorable reviews/comment. **2,** (character) reference. **3,** *fig.* responsive chord. **4,** reply (*to a password*).

отзы́в *n.* recall (*of an ambassador, representative, etc.*).

отзыва́ть *v. impfv.* [*pfv.* **отозва́ть**] **1,** to take aside. **2,** to recall (an ambassador.). **3,** *v.i.* [*impfv. only*] (*with instr.*) *colloq.* to have the taste of; smell faintly of. —**отзыва́ться**, *refl.* **1,** to answer. **2,** (*with* **на** + *acc.*) to respond to (an appeal, request, etc.). **3,** (*with* **на** + *prepl.*) to affect; have an effect on. **4,** (*with* **о**) to speak (well, badly, etc.) of.

отзы́вчивый *adj.* responsive; kindhearted; sympathetic. —**отзы́вчивость,** *n.f.* sympathy; kindheartedness; empathy.

отка́з *n.* **1,** refusal. **2,** repudiation; renunciation; disavowal. **3,** failure; breakdown: де́йствовать *or* рабо́тать без отка́за, to work perfectly. —**наби́тый до отка́за,** chock-full; filled to the brim.

отказа́ть [*infl.* -кажу́, -ка́жешь] *v., pfv. of* **отка́зывать.** —**отказа́ться,** *refl., pfv. of* **отка́зываться**.

отка́зывать *v. impfv.* [*pfv.* **отказа́ть**] **1,** to say no: он не уме́ет отка́зывать, he doesn't kow how to say no. **2,** (*with dat.*) to turn (someone) down: ему́ отказа́ли, they turned him down; he was turned down. **3,** (*with dat. and* **в** + *prepl.*) to refuse; deny: отка́зывать кому́-нибудь в по́мощи, to refuse help to someone; отка́зывать себе́ в са́мом необходи́мом, to deny oneself (even) the barest necessities. Ему́ нельзя́ отказа́ть в остроу́мии, you can't say he is not clever. **4,** *colloq.* (*of a machine*) to break down; fail to operate. **5,** *obs.* to leave; bequeath. —**отка́зываться,** *refl.* **1,** (*with inf.*) to refuse. **2,** (*with* **от**) to turn down; decline. **3,** (*with* **от**) to abandon; give up; relinquish. **4,** (*with* **от**) to renounce; repudiate; disavow; disown.

отка́лывать *v. impfv.* [*pfv.* **отколо́ть**] **1,** to chop off; break off. **2,** to unpin. —**отка́лываться,** *refl.* **1,** to break off; break away. **2,** *fig.* to break away; cut oneself off. **3,** to come unpinned.

отка́пывать *v. impfv.* [*pfv.* **откопа́ть**] **1,** to dig up; disinter; exhume. **2,** *fig., colloq.* to dig up; unearth.

отка́рмливать *v. impfv.* [*pfv.* **откорми́ть**] to fatten up.

отка́т *n.* recoil (*of a field gun*).

откати́ть [*infl.* -качу́, -ка́тишь] *v., pfv. of* **отка́тывать.** —**откати́ться,** *refl., pfv. of* **отка́тываться**.

отка́тывать *v. impfv.* [*pfv.* **откати́ть**] to roll (away, aside, *or* back). —**отка́тываться,** *refl.* **1,** to roll away; roll back. **2,** (*of troops*) to retreat; fall back. **3,** (*of a field gun*) to recoil.

отка́чивать *v. impfv.* [*pfv.* **откача́ть**] **1,** to pump out. **2,** to give artificial respiration to.

откачну́ться *v.r. pfv.* **1,** to swing to one side. **2,** to reel back; slump back.

отка́шливать *v. impfv.* [*pfv.* **отка́шляться**] to clear one's throat.

откидно́й *adj.* folding; collapsible.

отки́дывать *v. impfv.* [*pfv.* **отки́нуть**] **1,** to cast aside; throw aside; toss aside. **2,** (*with* **наза́д**) to throw back. **3,** to fold back; fold aside; raise; open. —**отки́дываться,** *refl.* to lean back; settle back.

откла́дывать *v. impfv.* [*pfv.* отложи́ть] **1,** to lay aside; put aside; set aside. **2,** to postpone; put off; defer. **3,** *chess* to adjourn (a game). **4,** to unhitch; unharness.

откла́ниваться *v.r. impfv.* [*pfv.* откла́няться] *obs.* to depart; take one's leave.

откле́ивать *v. impfv.* [*pfv.* откле́ить] to peel off (something stuck). —**откле́иваться,** *refl.* to come unstuck; come off.

о́тклик *n.* **1,** response. **2,** echo. **3,** *pl.* reaction; comments. **4,** *fig.* responsive chord.

отклика́ться *v.r. impfv.* [*pfv.* откли́кнуться] **1,** to answer; reply. **2,** (*with* на + *acc.*) to respond (to).

отклоне́ние *n.* **1,** rejection; denial. **2,** deviation; departure; digression. **3,** deflection.

отклони́ть [*infl.* -клоню́, -кло́нишь] *v., pfv. of* отклоня́ть. —**отклони́ться,** *refl., pfv. of* отклоня́ться.

отклоня́ть *v. impfv.* [*pfv.* отклони́ть] **1,** to deflect. **2,** to reject; turn down; decline. **3,** to deter; talk out of. —**отклоня́ться,** *refl.* (*with* от) to deviate (from); digress (from); stray (from).

отключа́ть *v. impfv.* [*pfv.* отключи́ть] to cut off; shut off; disconnect. —**отключа́ться,** *refl.* to become disconnected.

отокозыря́ть *v.pfv.* (*with dat.*) *colloq.* to salute.

отколоти́ть *v. pfv.* [*infl.* -лочу́, -ло́тишь] *colloq.* **1,** to knock off; hammer off. **2,** to beat up.

отколо́ть [*infl.* -колю́, -ко́лешь] *v., pfv. of* отка́лывать. —**отколо́ться,** *refl., pfv. of* отка́лываться.

откомандирова́ть [*infl.* -ру́ю, -ру́ешь] *v., pfv. of* откомандиро́вывать.

откомандиро́вывать *v. impfv.* [*pfv.* откомандиро́вать] **1,** to send (*on an assignment*). **2,** to assign; transfer.

откопа́ть *v., pfv. of* отка́пывать.

откорми́ть [*infl.* -кормлю́, -ко́рмишь] *v., pfv. of* отка́рмливать.

отко́с *n.* slope; side (*of a hill, embankment, etc.*): свали́ться под отко́с, to go/tumble over the embankment. Пусти́ть по́езд под отко́с, to derail a train. —**пойти́ под отко́с,** to fall apart; go to pieces.

открепля́ть *v. impfv.* [*pfv.* открепи́ть] **1,** to unfasten. **2,** to strike off the list.

открещиваться *v.r. impfv.* (*with* от) *colloq.* **1,** to try to avoid; shun. **2,** to disavow; disown.

открове́ние *n.* revelation.

открове́нничать *v. impfv.* (*with* с + *instr.*) *colloq.* to be frank (with); open up (to).

открове́нно *adv.* frankly. —**открове́нно говоря́,** frankly speaking; to be perfectly frank.

открове́нность *n.f.* frankness; candor.

открове́нный *adj.* **1,** frank; candid; outspoken. **2,** undisguised; unconcealed.

открути́ть [*infl.* -кручу́, -кру́тишь] *v., pfv. of* откру́чивать.

откру́чивать *v. impfv.* [*pfv.* открути́ть] to untwist; unscrew.

открыва́тель *n.m.* discoverer.

открыва́ть *v. impfv.* [*pfv.* откры́ть] **1,** to open. **2,** to uncover; reveal. **3,** to unveil (a monument). **4,** to discover. **5,** to reveal (a secret). **6,** to begin; launch. **7,** *colloq.* to turn on (water, gas, etc.). **8,** *in* откры́ть счёт, to score first; be the first to score. —**открыва́ться,** *refl.* **1,** to open; be opened. **2,** (*with* пе́ред) to open up

before one's eyes. **3,** *fig.* to be revealed; come to light. **4,** (*with dat.*) to open up to; confide in.

откры́тие *n.* **1,** opening. **2,** discovery.

откры́тка [*gen. pl.* -ток] *n.* postcard.

откры́то *adv.* openly.

откры́тый *adj.* **1,** open. **2,** (*of a dress*) low-cut. —**в откры́тую,** openly.

откры́ть [*infl.* -кро́ю, -кро́ешь] *v., pfv. of* открыва́ть. —**откры́ться,** *refl., pfv. of* открыва́ться.

отку́да *adv.* **1,** from where: отку́да вы?, where are you from? Он верну́лся туда́, отку́да он пришёл, he returned to the place from which he came. **2,** from what source?; how?: отку́да вы э́то зна́ете?, how do you (happen to) know that? Отку́да же я зна́ю?, how should I know? —**отку́да ни возьми́сь,** from out of nowhere; from out of the blue.

отку́да-либо *adv.* = отку́да-нибудь.

отку́да-нибудь *adv.* from somewhere or other.

отку́да-то *adv.* from somewhere.

о́ткуп *n.* tax farming. —**брать на о́ткуп,** to acquire exclusive rights to. —**отдава́ть на о́ткуп,** to farm out.

отку́поривать *v. impfv.* [*pfv.* отку́порить] to uncork; open.

откуси́ть [*infl.* -кушу́, -ку́сишь] *v., pfv. of* отку́сывать.

отку́сывать *v. impfv.* [*pfv.* откуси́ть] to bite off.

отлага́тельство *n.* delay. —**не терпе́ть отлага́тельства,** to brook no delay.

отлакирова́ть *v., pfv. of* лакирова́ть.

отла́мывать *v. impfv.* [*pfv.* отлома́ть *or* отломи́ть] to break off. —**отла́мываться,** *refl.* to break off; fall off; come off.

отлега́ть *v. impfv.* [*pfv.* отле́чь] (*of a pain, feeling, etc.*) to pass. —**у меня́ отлегло́ от се́рдца,** I felt relieved.

отлежа́ть [*infl.* -лежу́, -лежи́шь] *v., pfv. of* отлёживать. —**отлежа́ться,** *refl., pfv. of* отлёживаться.

отлёживать *v. impfv.* [*pfv.* отлежа́ть] to cause to become numb: я отлежа́л(а) но́гу, my foot has gone to sleep. —**отлёживаться,** *refl., colloq.* **1,** to recover (*after spending time in bed*). **2,** [*impfv. only*] to lie low.

отлёт *n.* departure (*by flying*). —**на отлёте, 1,** off at a distance. **2,** away from everything. **3,** about to leave. —**держа́ть (что́-нибудь) на отлёте,** to hold at arm's length.

отлета́ть *v. impfv.* [*pfv.* отлете́ть] **1,** to fly away; fly off. **2,** to be thrown (*from a blow or jolt*). **3,** to rebound; ricochet. **4,** *colloq.* to come off; come loose.

отлете́ть [*infl.* -чу́, -ти́шь] *v., pfv. of* отлета́ть.

отле́чь [*infl. like* лечь] *v., pfv. of* отлега́ть.

отли́в *n.* **1,** ebb; ebb tide. **2,** *fig.* ebb; decline; falling off. **3,** tint; fleck (*of color*). —**прили́в и отли́в,** ebb and flow of the tides. —**прили́вы и отли́вы,** tide; tides.

отлива́ть *v. impfv.* [*pfv.* отли́ть] **1,** to pour off. **2,** to pump out. **3,** to cast; found. **4,** *v.i.* (*of a liquid*) to flow; rush: кровь отлила́ от его́ лица́, the blood rushed from his face (*i.e.* he turned pale). **5,** *colloq.* to revive (*by throwing water on*). **6,** *v.i.* [*impfv. only*] (*with instr.*) to be streaked with (a certain color).

отли́вка *n.* founding; casting.

отлипа́ть *v. impfv.* [*pfv.* отли́пнуть] *colloq.* to come unstuck; come off.

отли́пнуть [*past* -ли́п, -ла] *v., pfv. of* отлипа́ть.

отли́ть [*infl.* отолью́, отольёшь; *past* о́тлил *or* отли́л, отлила́, о́тлило *or* отли́ло] *v., pfv. of* отлива́ть.

ОТЛИЧА́ТЬ *v. impfv.* [*pfv.* **ОТЛИЧИ́ТЬ**] **1,** to distinguish. **2,** to reward; honor. **3,** [*impfv. only*] to distinguish; set apart. **4,** [*impfv. only*] to single out. —**ОТЛИЧА́ТЬСЯ,** *refl.* **1,** to stand out. **2,** to distinguish oneself. **3,** [*impfv. only*] (*with* **от**) to differ (from). **4,** [*impfv. only*] (*with instr.*) to be remarkable (for); be notable (for). Он не отлича́ется умо́м, he is not particularly bright.

ОТЛИ́ЧИЕ *n.* **1,** difference; distinction. **2,** distinguished service. **3,** honors; distinction: око́нчить шко́лу с отли́чием, to graduate with honors. **4,** *in* знак отли́чия, *mil.* medal; decoration. —**в отли́чие от,** unlike; as opposed to; in contrast to; as distinct from.

ОТЛИЧИ́ТЕЛЬНЫЙ *adj.* distinguishing; distinctive.

ОТЛИЧИ́ТЬ *v., pfv. of* **ОТЛИЧА́ТЬ.** —**ОТЛИЧИ́ТЬСЯ,** *refl., pfv. of* **ОТЛИЧА́ТЬСЯ.**

ОТЛИ́ЧНИК *n.* **1,** A-student. **2,** outstanding worker.

ОТЛИ́ЧНО *adv.* excellently; very well. —*adj., used predicatively* excellent. —*n.indecl.* a grade of A (*in school*): сдать экза́мен на отли́чно, to get an A on an examination.

ОТЛИ́ЧНЫЙ *adj.* **1,** excellent. **2,** (*with* **от**) different (from).

ОТЛО́ГИЙ *adj.* not steep; gently sloping.

ОТЛОЖЕ́НИЕ *n.* **1,** *geol.* sediment. **2,** deposit: жировы́е отложе́ния, fatty deposits.

ОТЛОЖИ́ТЬ [*infl.* -ложу́, -ло́жишь] *v., pfv. of* **ОТКЛА́ДЫВАТЬ.**

ОТЛОЖНО́Й *adj.* (*of a collar*) turndown.

ОТЛОМА́ТЬ *v., pfv. of* **ОТЛА́МЫВАТЬ.** —**ОТЛОМА́ТЬСЯ,** *refl., pfv. of* **ОТЛА́МЫВАТЬСЯ.**

ОТЛОМИ́ТЬ [*infl.* -ломлю́, -ло́мишь] *v., pfv. of* **ОТЛА́МЫВАТЬ.** —**ОТЛОМИ́ТЬСЯ,** *refl., pfv. of* **ОТЛА́МЫВАТЬСЯ.**

ОТЛУПИ́ТЬ *v., pfv. of* **ЛУПИ́ТЬ** (*in sense #3*).

ОТЛУЧА́ТЬ *v. impfv.* [*pfv.* **ОТЛУЧИ́ТЬ**] **1,** *obs.* to remove; separate. **2,** *in* отлуча́ть от це́ркви, to excommunicate. —**ОТЛУЧА́ТЬСЯ,** *refl.* to go away; leave; absent oneself.

ОТЛУЧЕ́НИЕ *n.* **1,** *obs.* separation. **2,** *in* отлуче́ние от це́ркви, excommunication.

ОТЛУЧИ́ТЬ *v., pfv. of* **ОТЛУЧА́ТЬ.** —**ОТЛУЧИ́ТЬСЯ,** *refl., pfv. of* **ОТЛУЧА́ТЬСЯ.**

ОТЛУ́ЧКА *n.* absence: быть в отлу́чке, to be absent; be away. —**самово́льная отлу́чка,** absence without leave.

ОТЛЫ́НИВАТЬ *v. impfv.* (*with* **от**) *colloq.* to shirk.

ОТМА́ЛЧИВАТЬСЯ *v.r. impfv.* [*pfv.* **ОТМОЛЧА́ТЬСЯ**] *colloq.* to keep silent; say nothing.

ОТМА́ТЫВАТЬ *v. impfv.* [*pfv.* **ОТМОТА́ТЬ**] to wind off.

ОТМАХА́ТЬ [*infl.* -маха́ю, -маха́ешь] *v., pfv. of* **ОТМА́ХИВАТЬ** (*in sense #2*).

ОТМА́ХИВАТЬ *v. impfv.* **1,** [*pfv.* **ОТМАХНУ́ТЬ**] to brush away; chase away. **2,** [*pfv.* **ОТМАХА́ТЬ**] *colloq.* to cover (a certain distance). —**ОТМА́ХИВАТЬСЯ,** *refl.* [*pfv.* **ОТМАХНУ́ТЬСЯ**] **1,** to wave one's hand (*in disagreement or to object*). **2,** (*with* **от**) to brush away; chase away. **3,** (*with* **от**) *fig.* to brush aside; dismiss.

ОТМА́ЧИВАТЬ *v. impfv.* [*pfv.* **ОТМОЧИ́ТЬ**] to soak off.

ОТМЕЖЕВА́ТЬ [*infl.* -жую́, -жуёшь] *v., pfv. of* **ОТМЕЖЁВЫВАТЬ.** —**ОТМЕЖЕВА́ТЬСЯ,** *refl., pfv. of* **ОТМЕЖЁВЫВАТЬСЯ.**

ОТМЕЖЁВЫВАТЬ *v. impfv.* [*pfv.* **ОТМЕЖЕВА́ТЬ**] to mark off; delimit. —**ОТМЕЖЁВЫВАТЬСЯ,** *refl.* (*with* **от**) to dissociate oneself (from).

О́ТМЕЛЬ *n.f.* bank; shoal. —**песча́ная о́тмель,** sandbank; sand bar.

ОТМЕ́НА *n.* **1,** abolition. **2,** cancellation. **3,** repeal.

ОТМЕНИ́ТЬ [*infl.* -меню́, -ме́нишь] *v., pfv. of* **ОТМЕНЯ́ТЬ.**

ОТМЕ́ННЫЙ *adj.* excellent; splendid.

ОТМЕНЯ́ТЬ *v. impfv.* [*pfv.* **ОТМЕНИ́ТЬ**] **1,** to abolish. **2,** to cancel. **3,** to repeal; rescind.

ОТМЕРЕ́ТЬ [*infl.* отомрёт; *past* о́тмер, отмерла́, о́тмерло] *v., pfv. of* **ОТМИРА́ТЬ.**

ОТМЕРЗА́ТЬ *v. impfv.* [*pfv.* **ОТМЁРЗНУТЬ**] **1,** to perish from the frost. **2,** *colloq.* (*of one's hands, ears, etc.*) to be frozen.

ОТМЁРЗНУТЬ [*past* -мёрз, -ла] *v., pfv. of* **ОТМЕРЗА́ТЬ.**

ОТМЕ́РИВАТЬ *v. impfv.* [*pfv.* **ОТМЕ́РИТЬ**] to measure off. *Also,* **ОТМЕРЯ́ТЬ.**

ОТМЕСТИ́ [*infl. like* мести́] *v., pfv. of* **ОТМЕТА́ТЬ.**

ОТМЕ́СТКА *n., colloq.* revenge. —**в отме́стку,** in revenge; in retaliation.

ОТМЕТА́ТЬ *v. impfv.* [*pfv.* **ОТМЕСТИ́**] **1,** to sweep away; sweep off. **2,** *fig.* to reject; sweep aside.

ОТМЕ́ТИНА *n.* **1,** mark. **2,** spot of color (*on an animal or bird*).

ОТМЕ́ТИТЬ [*infl.* -чу, -тишь] *v., pfv. of* **ОТМЕЧА́ТЬ.** —**ОТМЕ́ТИТЬСЯ,** *refl., pfv. of* **ОТМЕЧА́ТЬСЯ.**

ОТМЕ́ТКА [*gen. pl.* -ток] *n.* **1,** mark; note. **2,** grade; mark (*in school*).

ОТМЕЧА́ТЬ *v. impfv.* [*pfv.* **ОТМЕ́ТИТЬ**] **1,** to mark. **2,** to note; take note of. **3,** to mark; celebrate; commemorate. —**ОТМЕЧА́ТЬСЯ,** *refl.* **1,** to register. **2,** to be noticed. **3,** to be noted.

ОТМИРА́ТЬ *v. impfv.* [*pfv.* **ОТМЕРЕ́ТЬ**] **1,** to die; die off. **2,** *fig.* to die out; disappear.

ОТМОКА́ТЬ *v. impfv.* [*pfv.* **ОТМО́КНУТЬ**] **1,** to get wet. **2,** to come off (*as a result of being wet*).

ОТМО́КНУТЬ [*past* -мок, -ла] *v., pfv. of* **ОТМОКА́ТЬ.**

ОТМОЛЧА́ТЬСЯ [*infl.* -чу́сь, -чи́шься] *v., pfv. of* **ОТМА́ЛЧИВАТЬСЯ.**

ОТМОРА́ЖИВАТЬ *v. impfv.* [*pfv.* **ОТМОРО́ЗИТЬ**] (*with* **себе́**) to get (a part of one's body) frostbitten: он отморо́зил себе́ нос, his nose was frostbitten.

ОТМОРО́ЖЕНИЕ *n.* frostbite.

ОТМОРО́ЗИТЬ [*infl.* -жу, -зишь] *v., pfv. of* **ОТМОРА́ЖИВАТЬ.**

ОТМОТА́ТЬ *v., pfv. of* **ОТМА́ТЫВАТЬ.**

ОТМОЧИ́ТЬ [*infl.* -мочу́, -мо́чишь] *v., pfv. of* **ОТМА́ЧИВАТЬ.**

ОТМЫВА́ТЬ *v. impfv.* [*pfv.* **ОТМЫ́ТЬ**] **1,** to wash off. **2,** to wash; wash clean. —**ОТМЫВА́ТЬСЯ,** *refl.* **1,** to wash oneself off. **2,** to come clean. **3,** to come off; come out (*when something is washed*).

ОТМЫКА́ТЬ *v. impfv.* [*pfv.* **ОТОМКНУ́ТЬ**] to unlock.

ОТМЫ́ТЬ [*infl.* -мо́ю, -мо́ешь] *v., pfv. of* **ОТМЫВА́ТЬ.** —**ОТМЫ́ТЬСЯ,** *refl., pfv. of* **ОТМЫВА́ТЬСЯ.**

ОТМЫ́ЧКА [*gen. pl.* -чек] *n.* **1,** master key; skeleton key. **2,** jimmy.

ОТНЕ́КИВАТЬСЯ *v.r. impfv., colloq.* to decline (by making excuses).

ОТНЕСТИ́ [*infl. like* нести́] *v., pfv. of* **ОТНОСИ́ТЬ.** —**ОТНЕСТИ́СЬ,** *refl., pfv. of* **ОТНОСИ́ТЬСЯ.**

ОТНИМА́ТЬ *v. impfv.* [*pfv.* **ОТНЯ́ТЬ**] **1,** to take away. **2,** to withdraw; remove (one's hand). **3,** to rob of (hope, faith, etc.). **4,** to take (a certain amount of time, effort, etc.). **5,** *colloq.* to amputate. **6,** *colloq.* to subtract; take away. —**ОТНИМА́ТЬСЯ,** *refl.* (*of a part of the body*) to become paralyzed.

относительно *adv.* relatively. —*prep., with gen.* regarding; concerning.

относительность *n.f.* relativity. —**теория относительности,** theory of relativity.

относительный *adj.* relative. —**относительное местоимение,** relative pronoun.

относить *v. impfv.* [*pfv.* **отнести;** *pres.* -ношу, -носишь] **1,** to take; carry; deliver (to a certain place). **2,** (*of the wind, current, etc.*) to carry away; sweep away. **3,** (*with* к) to attribute (to); ascribe (to); consider (among); place (among). Относить на счёт (+ *gen.*), to attribute to; put down to. —**относиться,** *refl.* (*with* к) **1,** to behave (toward); act (toward); treat. **2,** to react (toward); have a certain attitude (toward). **3,** [*impfv. only*] to belong to; be among. **4,** [*impfv. only*] to apply to; pertain to. Это не относится к делу, that is beside the point; that is irrelevant. **5,** [*impfv. only*] to date (from).

отношение *n.* **1,** (*with* к) attitude (toward). **2,** (*with* к) relation; relationship; connection: не иметь никакого отношения к, bear no relation(ship) to; have no connection with; have nothing to do with. **3,** *pl.* relations: международные отношения, international relations. Быть в хороших отношениях с, to be on good terms with. **4,** respect; regard; connection: в этом отношении, in this connection; во многих отношениях, in many respects. **5,** ratio. **6,** memorandum. —**в отношении** (+ *gen.*); **по отношению к,** with respect to; with regard to.

отныне *adv.* hereafter; henceforth; from now on.

отнюдь *adv.* [*usu.* отнюдь не] by no means; in no way.

отнятие *n.* **1,** taking away; seizure. **2,** amputation.

отнять [*infl.* отниму, отнимешь; *past* отнял, отняла, отняло] *v., pfv. of* **отнимать.** —**отняться,** *refl.* [*past* отнялся, -лась, -лось] *pfv. of* **отниматься.**

ото *prep.* = **от** (*used before words beginning with a double consonant*).

отобедать *v. pfv.* to have finished dinner.

отображать *v. impfv.* [*pfv.* **отобразить**] to reflect; depict; represent.

отображение *n.* reflection; representation.

отобразить [*infl.* -жу, -зишь] *v., pfv. of* **отображать.**

отобрать [*infl.* отберу, отберёшь; *past fem.* отобрала] *v., pfv. of* **отбирать.**

отовсюду *adv.* from everywhere.

отогнать [*infl.* отгоню, отгонишь; *past fem.* отогнала] *v., pfv. of* **отгонять.**

отогнуть *v., pfv. of* **отгибать.**

отогревать *v. impfv.* [*pfv.* **отогреть**] to warm. —**отогреваться,** *refl.* to warm oneself; warm up; get warm.

отодвигать *v. impfv.* [*pfv.* **отодвинуть**] **1,** to move aside; move away. **2,** *colloq.* to put off; postpone. **3,** *in* отодвигать на задний план, to relegate to the background. —**отодвигаться,** *refl.* **1,** to move aside; step aside. **2,** to move back; draw back. **3,** *colloq.* to be put off; be postponed.

отодрать [*infl.* отдеру, отдерёшь; *past fem.* отодрала] *v., pfv. of* **отдирать.**

отождествлять *also,* **отожествлять** *v. impfv.* [*pfv.* **отождествить** *or* **отожествить**] to equate.

отозвать [*infl.* отзову, отзовёшь; *past fem.* отозвала] *v., pfv. of* **отзывать.** —**отозваться,** *refl., pfv. of* **отзываться.**

отойти [*infl.* отойду, отойдёшь; *past* отошёл, отошла, отошло] *v., pfv. of* **отходить.**

отомкнуть *v., pfv. of* **отмыкать.**

отомстить *v., pfv. of* **мстить.**

отопительный *adj.* heating (*attrib.*). Отопительный сезон, season when heat is required.

отопить [*infl.* отоплю, отопишь] *v., pfv. of* **отапливать.**

отопление *n.* heating.

оторванность *n.f.* isolation; being cut off.

оторвать [*infl. like* рвать] *v., pfv. of* **отрывать.** —**оторваться,** *refl., pfv. of* **отрываться.**

оторопелый *adj., colloq.* dazed; dumfounded.

оторопеть *v. pfv., colloq.* to be struck dumb; be dumfounded.

оторопь *n.f., colloq.* confusion; panic; fright.

оторочка *n.* edging; trimming.

отослать [*infl.* отошлю, отошлёшь] *v., pfv. of* **отсылать.**

отоспаться [*infl.* -сплюсь, -спишься] *v.r., pfv. of* **отсыпаться.**

отощалый *adj., colloq.* emaciated.

отощать *v., pfv. of* **тощать.**

отпадать *v. impfv.* [*pfv.* **отпасть**] **1,** to fall off; come off; peel off. **2,** (*with* от) to drop out of (an organization). **3,** to cease to have significance; be no longer relevant. **4,** (*of a feeling*) to pass.

отпарировать *v. pfv.* [*infl.* -рую, -руешь] **1,** to parry (a blow). **2,** *fig.* to rebut (attacks, an argument, etc.). **3,** to retort.

отпарывать *v. impfv.* [*pfv.* **отпороть**] to snip off; slit off. —**отпарываться,** *refl.* to come off; tear off.

отпасть [*infl. like* пасть] *v., pfv. of* **отпадать.**

отпевание *n.* (religious) funeral service.

отпевать *v. impfv.* [*pfv.* **отпеть**] to hold a funeral service in honor of. *See also* **отпеть.**

отпереть [*infl.* отопру, отопрёшь; *past* отпер, отперла, отперло] *v., pfv. of* **отпирать.** —**отпереться,** *refl.* [*past* отпёрся *or* отперся, отперлась, отперлось] *pfv. of* **отпираться.**

отпетый *adj., colloq.* incorrigible.

отпеть *v. pfv.* [*infl.* -пою, -поёшь] **1,** *pfv. of* **отпевать. 2,** to sing; chant (a song, prayer, etc.). **3,** to stop singing; finish singing.

отпечатать *v., pfv. of* **отпечатывать.** —**отпечататься,** *refl., pfv. of* **отпечатываться.**

отпечаток [*gen.* -тка] *n.* **1,** print; imprint: отпечаток пальца, fingerprint. **2,** *fig.* imprint; mark: накладывать свой отпечаток на (+ *acc.*), to leave its mark upon.

отпечатывать *v. impfv.* [*pfv.* **отпечатать**] **1,** to print; run off. **2,** to type (something) on a typewriter. **3,** to make (fingerprints or footprints): отпечатать следы на песке, to make footprints in the sand.

отпивать *v. impfv.* [*pfv.* **отпить**] to take a sip of.

отпиливать *v. impfv.* [*pfv.* **отпилить**] to saw off.

отпилить [*infl.* -пилю, -пилишь] *v., pfv. of* **отпиливать.**

отпирательство *n.* persistent denial; refusal to confess.

отпирать *v. impfv.* [*pfv.* **отпереть**] to unlock. —**отпираться,** *refl.* **1,** to unlock; come unlocked. **2,** *colloq.* to deny; (*with* от) disavow.

отписать [*infl.* -пишу, -пишешь] *v., pfv. of* **отписывать.** —**отписаться,** *refl., pfv. of* **отписываться.**

отпи́ска [*gen. pl.* **-сок**] *n.* noncommittal answer; answer that is not really an answer.

отпи́сывать *v. impfv.* [*pfv.* **отписа́ть**] *obs.* 1, to confiscate. 2, to bequeath. —**отпи́сываться**, *refl., colloq.* to write a purely formal reply.

отпи́ть *v. pfv.* [*infl.* **отопью́, отопьёшь**; *past* **о́тпил, отпила́, о́тпило**] 1, *pfv. of* **отпива́ть**. 2, *colloq.* to finish drinking.

отпи́хивать *v. impfv.* [*pfv.* **отпихну́ть**] *colloq.* to push away; push aside; shove aside.

отпла́та *n.* repayment. —**в отпла́ту за**, in repayment for; in return for.

отплати́ть [*infl.* **-плачу́, -пла́тишь**] *v., pfv. of* **отпла́чивать**.

отпла́чивать *v. impfv.* [*pfv.* **отплати́ть**] (*with dat.*) to pay back; repay (someone).

отплёвывать *v. impfv.* [*pfv.* **отплю́нуть**] *colloq.* 1, *v.t.* to spit out. 2, *v.i.* to spit (a certain distance). —**отплёвываться**, *refl.* [*impfv. only*] to spit (*in disgust*).

отплыва́ть *v. impfv.* [*pfv.* **отплы́ть**] 1, to swim away. 2, (*of a ship*) to sail; depart.

отплы́тие *n.* sailing; departure.

отплы́ть [*infl. like* **плыть**] *v., pfv. of* **отплыва́ть**.

отплю́нуть *v., pfv. of* **отплёвывать**.

о́тповедь *n.f.* rebuke; reproof.

отполза́ть *v. impfv.* [*pfv.* **отползти́**] to crawl away.

отползти́ [*infl. like* **ползти́**] *v., pfv. of* **отполза́ть**.

отполирова́ть *v., pfv. of* **полирова́ть**.

отпо́р *n.* rebuff.

отпоро́ть [*infl.* **-порю́, -по́решь**] *v., pfv. of* **отпа́рывать**. —**отпоро́ться**, *refl., pfv. of* **отпа́рываться**.

отправи́тель *n.m.* sender.

отпра́вить [*infl.* **-влю, -вишь**] *v., pfv. of* **отправля́ть**. —**отпра́виться**, *refl., pfv. of* **отправля́ться**.

отпра́вка *n., colloq.* dispatch; shipment.

отправле́ние *n.* 1, sending; dispatch. 2, departure. 3, item of mail. 4, exercise; performance; discharge. 5, *pl.* functions (*of an organism*). —**то́чка отправле́ния**, point of departure.

отправля́ть *v. impfv.* [*pfv.* **отпра́вить**] 1, to send; dispatch. 2, [*impfv. only*] to discharge; perform. Отправля́ть правосу́дие, to administer justice. —**отправля́ться**, *refl.* 1, to leave; start out; set out. 2, [*impfv. only*] (*with* **от**) to proceed from (*in one's thinking*).

отправно́й *adj.* 1, dispatch (*attrib.*); shipping (*attrib.*). 2, initial. —**отправно́й пункт**; **отправна́я то́чка**, starting point.

отпра́здновать *v., pfv. of* **пра́здновать**.

отпра́шиваться *v.r. impfv.* [*pfv.* **отпроси́ться**] 1, [*usu. impfv.*] to request permission to be absent. 2, [*usu. pfv.*] to obtain permission to be absent: отпроси́ться на одну́ неде́лю, to get a week off.

отпроси́ться [*infl.* **-прошу́сь, -про́сишься**] *v.r., pfv. of* **отпра́шиваться**.

отпры́гивать *v. impfv.* [*pfv.* **отпры́гнуть**] to jump back; jump aside.

о́тпрыск *n.* 1, *bot.* shoot. 2, *fig., obs.* offspring.

отпряга́ть *v. impfv.* [*pfv.* **отпря́чь**] to unharness.

отпря́нуть *v. pfv.* to jump back; recoil.

отпря́чь [*infl.* **-прягу́, -пряжёшь, ...-прягу́т**; *past* **-пря́г, -прягла́, -прягло́**] *v., pfv. of* **отпряга́ть**.

отпу́гивать *v. impfv.* [*pfv.* **отпугну́ть**] to frighten away; frighten off.

о́тпуск [*pl.* **отпуска́**] *n.* 1, vacation: в о́тпуске (*or colloquially* в отпуску́), on vacation. 2, leave: о́тпуск по боле́зни, sick leave.

отпуска́ть *v. impfv.* [*pfv.* **отпусти́ть**] 1, to let go of. 2, to let go; release. 3, to loosen; slacken. 4, *v.i., colloq.* (*of pain*) to lessen; ease. 5, to grow (a beard, mustache, etc.). 6, to allot; allow. 7, to sell. 8, to remit (a sin). 9, *colloq.* to utter (a remark); crack (a joke).

отпускни́к [*gen.* **-ника́**] *n.* person on vacation; person on leave.

отпускно́й *adj.* vacation (*attrib.*).

отпусти́ть [*infl.* **-пущу́, -пу́стишь**] *v., pfv. of* **отпуска́ть**.

отпуще́ние *n.* 1, remission (*of sins*). 2, *in* отпуще́ние на во́лю, emancipation. —**козёл отпуще́ния**, scapegoat.

отраба́тывать *v. impfv.* [*pfv.* **отрабо́тать**] 1, to work off (a debt). 2, to perfect; polish.

отрабо́тать *v. pfv.* 1, *pfv. of* **отраба́тывать**. 2, to work (*for a certain length of time*). 3, *colloq.* to finish working; stop working.

отра́ва *n.* poison.

отрави́ть [*infl.* **отравлю́, отра́вишь**] *v., pfv. of* **отравля́ть**. —**отрави́ться**, *refl., pfv. of* **отравля́ться**.

отравле́ние *n.* poisoning. —**отравле́ние свинцо́м**, lead poisoning.

отравля́ть *v. impfv.* [*pfv.* **отрави́ть**] 1, to poison. 2, *fig.* to spoil; mar. —**отравля́ться**, *refl.* 1, to poison oneself; take poison. 2, to be poisoned; suffer poisoning.

отра́да *n.* joy; delight.

отра́дный *adj.* pleasing; gratifying. Отра́дно, что..., it is gratifying that...,

отража́тель *n.m.* reflector.

отража́ть *v. impfv.* [*pfv.* **отрази́ть**] 1, to reflect. 2, to repulse; repel; parry; ward off. —**отража́ться**, *refl.* 1, to be reflected. 2, (*with* **на** + *prepl.*) to affect; have an effect upon.

отраже́ние *n.* 1, reflection. 2, repulsing; repelling.

отрази́ть [*infl.* **-жу́, -зи́шь**] *v., pfv. of* **отража́ть**. —**отрази́ться**, *refl., pfv. of* **отража́ться**.

отрапортова́ть *v.pfv.* [*infl.* **-ту́ю, -ту́ешь**] to report.

отраслево́й *adj.* of a particular branch or field. —**отраслева́я библиогра́фия**, bibliography by subject.

о́трасль *n.f.* branch; field.

отраста́ть *v. impfv.* [*pfv.* **отрасти́**] (*of hair, nails, etc.*) to grow.

отрасти́ [*infl. like* **расти́**] *v., pfv. of* **отраста́ть**.

отрасти́ть [*infl.* **-щу́, -сти́шь**] *v., pfv. of* **отра́щивать**.

отра́щивать *v. impfv.* [*pfv.* **отрасти́ть**] 1, to let (one's hair, nails, etc.) grow. 2, to grow (a beard, paunch, etc.).

отреаги́ровать *v. pfv.* [*infl.* **-рую, -руешь**] to react.

отре́бье *n.* rabble. —**отре́бье о́бщества**, the dregs of society.

отрегули́ровать *v., pfv. of* **регули́ровать** (*in sense #2*).

отредакти́ровать *v., pfv. of* **редакти́ровать**.

отре́з *n.* 1, cut. 2, length (*of material*). 3, perforated line (*for tearing off something*).

отре́зать [*infl.* **-ре́жу, -ре́жешь**] *v., pfv. of* **отреза́ть** *and* **отре́зывать**.

отреза́ть *v. impfv.* [*pfv.* **отре́зать**] 1, to cut off. 2, *colloq.* to snap back (*when answering*). *Also,* **отре́зывать**.

отреве́ть *v., pfv. of* **треветь**.

отрезви́ть [*infl.* **-влю́, -ви́шь**] *v., pfv. of* **отрезвля́ть**. —**отрезви́ться**, *refl., pfv. of* **отрезвля́ться**.

отрезвля́ть *v. impfv.* [*pfv.* **отрезви́ть**] to sober; sober up. —**отрезвля́ться**, *refl.* to sober up; become sober.

отрезно́й *adj.* **1**, to be torn off. **2**, detachable.

отрéзок [*gen.* -зка] *n.* **1**, piece; length (*of material*). **2**, segment; section; part. Отрéзок вре́мени, segment/stretch/span of time.

отрéзывать *v.impfv.* = **отрезáть**.

отрекáться *v.r. impfv.* [*pfv.* **отре́чься**] (*with* от) **1**, to renounce; disavow; repudiate. **2**, *in* отрекáться от престóла, to abdicate.

отрекомендовáть *v.pfv.* [*infl.* -ду́ю, -ду́ешь] **1**, to recommend. **2**, *obs.* to introduce. —**отрекомендовáться**, *refl.* to introduce oneself.

отремонти́ровать *v.*, *pfv. of* **ремонти́ровать**.

отрéпье *n.*, *often pl.*, *colloq.* rags; tatters.

отречéние *n.* (*with* от) **1**, renunciation; disavowal; repudiation. **2**, *in* отречéние от престóла, abdication.

отрéчься [*infl.* -реку́сь, -речёшься, …-реку́тся; *past* -рёкся, -реклáсь, -реклóсь] *v.r.*, *pfv. of* **отрекáться**.

отрешáть *v. impfv.* [*pfv.* **отреши́ть**] *obs.* to remove; dismiss; suspend. —**отрешáться**, *refl.* (*with* от) **1**, to rid oneself of; get away from. **2**, to renounce.

отрешённый *adj.* **1**, aloof; isolated. **2**, (*of a look*) blank; distracted. —**отрешённость**, *n.f.* aloofness; isolation.

отреши́ть *v.*, *pfv. of* **отрешáть**. —**отреши́ться**, *refl.*, *pfv. of* **отрешáться**.

отрицáние *n.* **1**, denial. **2**, negation. **3**, *gram.* negative.

отрицáтельно *adv.* **1**, negatively. **2**, in the negative. **3**, adversely.

отрицáтельный *adj.* negative.

отрицáть *v. impfv.* to deny.

отрóг *n.* spur (*of a mountain range*).

óтроду *adv.* (*with* не) *colloq.* never in one's life; never in all one's born days.

отрóсток [*gen.* -стка] *n.* **1**, shoot; sprout. **2**, *anat.* outgrowth.

óтроческий *adj.* adolescent. —**óтрочество**, *n.* adolescence.

отрубáть *v. impfv.* [*pfv.* **отруби́ть**] to chop off.

óтруби [*gen.* -бéй] *n.pl.* bran.

отруби́ть *v. pfv.* [*infl.* -рублю́, -ру́бишь] **1**, *pfv. of* **отрубáть**. **2**, *colloq.* to snap back (*in answering*).

отру́гиваться *v.r. impfv.*, *colloq.* to answer back; answer curses with curses.

отры́в *n.* **1**, tearing off. **2**, break; hiatus. **3**, alienation; isolation. —в отры́ве от, isolated from; cut off from. —отры́в от земли́, **1**, takeoff. **2**, liftoff.

отрывáть *v. impfv.* [*pfv.* **оторвáть**] **1**, to tear off. **2**, (*with* от) to tear away (from): я не мог оторвáть мы́слей от э́того, I couldn't stop thinking about it. Я не моглá оторвáть глаз от э́того, I couldn't take my eyes off it. **3**, [*pfv.* **отры́ть**] to dig up; unearth.

отрывáться *v.r. impfv.* [*pfv.* **оторвáться**] **1**, to come off; be torn off. **2**, (*with* от) to break away (from); give (someone) the slip. **3**, *in* оторвáться от земли́, (*of a plane*) to take off. **4**, (*with* от) to lose touch (with); lose contact (with). **5**, (*with* от) to tear oneself away (from work, a book, etc.). —не отрывáясь, without a break; nonstop.

отры́вистый *adj.* **1**, (*of sounds*) staccato. **2**, (*of speech*) uneven; disjointed.

отрывнóй *adj.* **1**, that can be torn off. **2**, with sheets that can be torn off.

отры́вок [*gen.* -вка] *n.* **1**, passage; excerpt. **2**, frag-

ment; snatch: отры́вки разговóра, snatches of a conversation.

отры́вочный *adj.* **1**, fragmentary. **2**, disjointed.

отры́гивать *v. impfv.* [*pfv.* **отрыгну́ть**] to belch up.

отры́жка *n.* **1**, belch. **2**, *fig.*, *colloq.* vestige.

отры́ть [*infl.* -рóю, -рóешь] *v.*, *pfv. of* **отрывáть** (*in sense #3*).

отря́д *n.* **1**, *mil.* detachment. **2**, group: пионéрский отря́д, (young) pioneer group. **3**, *zool.* order.

отряжáть *v. impfv.* [*pfv.* **отряди́ть**] **1**, to dispatch; send (*on a certain assignment*). **2**, *mil.* to assign; detail.

отрясáть *v. impfv.* [*pfv.* **отрясти́**] to shake off. —**отрясти́ прах от свои́х ног**, to shake the dust from one's feet.

отрясти́ [*infl. like* трясти́] *v.*, *pfv. of* **отрясáть**.

отря́хивать *v. impfv.* [*pfv.* **отряхну́ть**] to shake off.

отсади́ть [*infl.* -сажу́, -сáдишь] *v.*, *pfv. of* **отсáживать**.

отсáживать *v. impfv.* [*pfv.* **отсади́ть**] **1**, to seat apart. **2**, to separate (animals, birds, etc.). **3**, to transplant.

отсáсывать *v. impfv.* [*pfv.* **отсосáть**] to draw off; draw out; suck out.

отсвéт *also*, **óтсвет** *n.* reflection.

отсвéчивать *v. impfv.* to shine; gleam (*by reflecting light*).

отсебя́тина *n.*, *colloq.* words of one's own.

отсéв *n.* **1**, sifting out (*lit. & fig.*). **2**, *fig.* dropping out: процéнт отсéва, dropout rate.

отсéивать *v. impfv.* [*pfv.* **отсéять**] **1**, to sift out. **2**, *fig.* to weed out; winnow out. —**отсéиваться**, *refl.* to drop out.

отсéк *n.* **1**, compartment. **2**, (space) module. —**бóмбовый отсéк**, bomb bay.

отсекáть *v. impfv.* [*pfv.* **отсéчь**] to chop off.

отсечéние *n.* chopping off. —**дать гóлову** (*or* рýку) **на отсечéние**, to stake one's life on it.

отсéчь [*infl. like* сечь; *past* -сéк, -секлá, -секлó] *v.*, *pfv. of* **отсекáть**.

отсéять [*infl.* -сéю, -сéешь] *v.*, *pfv. of* **отсéивать**.

отсидéть [*infl.* -жу́, -ди́шь] *v.*, *pfv. of* **отси́живать**. —**отсидéться**, *refl.*, *pfv. of* **отси́живаться**.

отси́живать *v. impfv.* [*pfv.* **отсидéть**] **1**, to make numb (*by sitting*): я отсидéл себé нóгу, my foot is asleep. **2**, *colloq.* to sit through: отсидéть весь спектáкль, to sit through the entire performance. **3**, to serve out; finish serving (a prison term). —**отси́живаться**, *refl.*, *colloq.* to take cover.

отскáбливать *v. impfv.* [*pfv.* **отскобли́ть**] to scrape off.

отскáкивать *v. impfv.* [*pfv.* **отскочи́ть**] **1**, to jump back; jump aside. **2**, to rebound; (*with* от) bounce off. **3**, *colloq.* to come off; fly off.

отскобли́ть [*infl.* -скоблю́, -скóблишь *or* -скобли́шь] *v.*, *pfv. of* **отскáбливать**.

отскочи́ть [*infl.* -скочу́, -скóчишь] *v.*, *pfv. of* **отскáкивать**.

отслáивать *v. impfv.* [*pfv.* **отслои́ть**] to remove layer by layer. —**отслáиваться**, *refl.* to come off in layers.

отслóйка *n.*, *in* отслóйка сетчáтки; отслóйка сéтчатой оболóчки, detached retina.

отслужи́ть *v. pfv.* [*infl.* -служу́, -слу́жишь] **1**, to serve out; finish serving. **2**, to be worn out (*from use*).

отсовéтовать *v. pfv.* [*infl.* -тую, -туешь] (*with dat. & inf.*) to dissuade (from); talk out of.

отсосáть [*infl.* -сосý, -сосёшь] *v., pfv. of* отсáсывать.

отсóхнуть [*past* -сóх, -ла] *v., pfv. of* отсыхáть.

отсрóчивать *v. impfv.* [*pfv.* отсрóчить] **1,** to postpone; defer. **2,** to extend (a passport, license, etc.).

отсрóчка [*gen. pl.* -чек] *n.* postponement; deferment; delay.

отставáние *n.* lag; lagging behind.

отставáть *v. impfv.* [*pfv.* отстáть; *pres.* -стаю́, -стаёшь] **1,** (*with* от) to lag behind; be behind; fall behind. **2,** (*of a clock or watch*) to be slow. **3,** to come off; peel off. **4,** (*with* от) *colloq.* to lose touch (with). **5,** (*with* от) *colloq.* to leave alone; leave in peace. —**отставáть от жи́зни/врéмени,** to be behind the times. —**отставáть от пóезда,** to fail to get back on a train in time.

отстáвить [*infl.* -влю, -вишь] *v., pfv. of* отставля́ть.

отстáвка *n.* **1,** resignation. **2,** retirement. —**в отстáвке,** retired. —**вы́йти** *or* **уйти́ в отстáвку. 1,** to resign. **2,** to retire.

отставля́ть *v. impfv.* [*pfv.* отстáвить] **1,** to move aside. **2,** *obs.* to discharge; dismiss. —**отстáвить!,** *mil.* as you were!

отставнóй *adj.* retired.

отстáивать *v. impfv.* [*pfv.* отстоя́ть] **1,** to defend. **2,** *fig.* to uphold (a principle); assert (one's rights). —**отстáиваться,** *refl.* (*of a liquid*) to settle. *See also* **отстоя́ть.**

отстáлый *adj.* **1,** backward. **2,** retarded. —**отстáлость,** *n.f.* backwardness.

отстáть [*infl.* -стáну, -стáнешь] *v., pfv. of* отставáть.

отстегáть *v., pfv. of* стегáть (*in sense* #2).

отстёгивать *v. impfv.* [*pfv.* отстегнýть] to unfasten; undo. —**отстёгиваться,** *refl.* to come unfastened; come undone.

отсти́рывать *v. impfv.* [*pfv.* отстирáть] to wash off; wash out. —**отсти́рываться,** *refl.* to come out in the wash.

отстоя́ть[1] *v. pfv.* [*infl.* -стою́, -стои́шь] **1,** *pfv. of* отстáивать. **2,** to stand through: отстоя́ть весь концéрт, to stand through the entire concert. —**отстоя́ться,** *refl., pfv. of* отстáиваться.

отстоя́ть[2] *v. impfv.* [*pres.* -стою́, -стои́шь] (*with* от) to be; be located (a certain distance from).

отстрáивать *v. impfv.* [*pfv.* отстрóить] **1,** to build; finish building. **2,** to rebuild (*after a disaster*).

отстранéние *n.* removal; dismissal.

отстраня́ть *v. impfv.* [*pfv.* отстрани́ть] **1,** to push aside. **2,** to remove; dismiss; suspend. —**отстраня́ться,** *refl.* **1,** to step aside. **2,** (*with* от) to avoid; dodge. **3,** (*with* от) to keep away (from); remain aloof (from).

отстрéливать *v. impfv.* [*pfv.* отстрели́ть] to shoot off. —**отстрéливаться,** *refl.* **1,** —**отстреля́ться,** to shoot back; fire back; (*with* от) fire back upon.

отстрели́ть [*infl.* -стрелю́, -стрéлишь] *v., pfv. of* отстрéливать.

отстреля́ться *v.r., pfv. of* отстрéливаться.

отстригáть *v. impfv.* [*pfv.* отстри́чь] to cut off (someone's hair).

отстри́чь [*infl. like* стри́чь] *v., pfv. of* отстригáть.

отстрóить *v., pfv. of* отстрáивать.

óтступ *n.* indentation; indentation (*in writing or printing*).

отступáть *v. impfv.* [*pfv.* отступи́ть] **1,** to step back. **2,** to recede. **3,** to retreat. **4,** to back down. **5,** (*with* от) to give up; abandon. **6,** (*with* от) to deviate (from); depart (from); digress (from). **7,** to indent. —**отсту-**

пáться, *refl.* (*with* от) to give up on; abandon; retreat from; turn one's back on.

отступи́ть [*infl.* -ступлю́, -стýпишь] *v., pfv. of* отступáть. —**отступи́ться,** *refl., pfv. of* отступáться.

отступлéние *n.* **1,** retreat. **2,** deviation; departure. **3,** digression.

отстýпник *n.* apostate. —**отстýпнический,** *adj.* apostate. —**отстýпничество,** *n.* apostasy.

отступнóе *n., decl. as an adj.* indemnity; compensation.

отступя́ *adv.* away; off: немнóго отступя́, a short distance away.

отсýтствие *n.* **1,** absence: в моё отсýтствие, in my absence. **2,** lack.

отсýтствовать *v. impfv.* [*pres.* -ствую, -ствуешь] **1,** to be absent: отсýтствовать на собрáнии, to be absent from a meeting. **2,** to be lacking: ули́ки отсýтствуют, evidence is lacking.

отсýтствующий *adj.* **1,** absent. **2,** (*of a look*) absent; blank; vacant. —*n.* absentee.

отсчёт *n.* **1,** counting out; marking off. **2,** reading (*on an instrument*). —**обрáтный отсчёт врéмени,** countdown. —**тóчка отсчёта,** reference point.

отсчи́тывать *v. impfv.* [*pfv.* отсчитáть] **1,** to count out: отсчитáть сто рублéй, to count out 100 rubles. **2,** to mark off; count off: отсчитáть дéсять шагóв, to mark off ten paces.

отсылáть *v. impfv.* [*pfv.* отослáть] **1,** to send off. **2,** to send away; dismiss. **3,** (*with* к) to refer (someone) to.

отсы́лка *n.* **1,** sending; dispatch. **2,** reference.

отсы́пать [*infl.* -сы́плю, -сы́плешь] *v., pfv. of* отсыпáть.

отсыпáть *v. impfv.* [*pfv.* отсы́пать] (*usu. with gen.*) to pour out (a quantity or portion of something).

отсыпáться *v.r. impfv.* [*pfv.* отоспáться] to catch up on one's sleep.

отсырéлый *adj.* damp; soggy.

отсырéть *v., pfv. of* сырéть.

отсыхáть *v. impfv.* [*pfv.* отсóхнуть] to wither.

отсю́да *adv.* **1,** from here. **2,** hence. Отсю́да слéдует, что..., from this it follows that...

оттáивать *v. impfv.* [*pfv.* оттáять] *v.t. & i.* to thaw; thaw out. —**оттáивать чьё-нибудь сéрдце,** to melt someone's heart.

оттáлкивать *v. impfv.* [*pfv.* оттолкнýть] **1,** to push back; push away; push aside. **2,** to repel; antagonize; alienate. —**оттáлкиваться,** *refl.* (*with* от) to push off (from shore, land, etc.).

оттáлкивающий *adj.* repulsive; repellent.

оттáскивать *v. impfv.* [*pfv.* оттащи́ть] **1,** to pull aside; drag aside. **2,** to pull away.

оттáчивать *v. impfv.* [*pfv.* отточи́ть] **1,** to sharpen; hone. **2,** *fig.* to polish; perfect.

оттащи́ть [*infl.* -тащý, -тáщишь] *v., pfv. of* оттáскивать.

оттáять [*infl.* -тáю, -тáешь] *v., pfv. of* оттáивать.

оттени́ть *v., pfv. of* оттеня́ть.

оттéнок [*gen.* -нка] *n.* **1,** tint; hue. **2,** shade; nuance. **3,** (*with gen.*) trace (of); tinge (of).

оттеня́ть *v. impfv.* [*pfv.* оттени́ть] **1,** to shade; shade in. **2,** *fig.* to set off.

óттепель *n.f.* thaw.

оттерéть [*infl.* оттрý, оттрёшь; *past* оттёр, -ла] *v., pfv. of* оттирáть.

оттесня́ть *v. impfv.* [*pfv.* **оттесни́ть**] **1,** to drive back; force back. **2,** *fig.* to force out; crowd out.

оттира́ть *v. impfv.* [*pfv.* **оттере́ть**] **1,** to rub off; rub out. **2,** to rub (one's hands, ears, etc.) until the feeling returns. **3,** *colloq.* to push aside; force aside.

о́ттиск *n.* **1,** imprint; print; impression. **2,** print; proof. **3,** reprint.

отти́скивать *v. impfv.* [*pfv.* **отти́снуть**] **1,** *colloq.* to push back. **2,** to imprint.

оттого́ *adv.* (*often* **оттого́ и**) that is why; which is why. —**оттого́ что,** because.

оттолкну́ть *v., pfv. of* **отта́лкивать.** —**оттолкну́ться,** *refl., pfv. of* **отта́лкиваться.**

оттома́нка [*gen. pl.* **-нок**] *n.* ottoman.

оттопы́ренный *adj.* protruding; prominent.

оттопы́ривать *v. impfv.* [*pfv.* **оттопы́рить**] *colloq.* to stick out. —**оттопы́риваться,** *refl., colloq.* to stick out; bulge; protrude.

отторга́ть *v. impfv.* [*pfv.* **отто́ргнуть**] to tear away; forcibly detach or separate.

отто́ргнуть [*past* **-то́рг** *or* **-то́ргнул, -то́ргла**] *v., pfv. of* **отторга́ть.**

отточи́ть [*infl.* **-точу́, -то́чишь**] *v., pfv. of* **отта́чивать.**

отту́да *adv.* from there.

оттузи́ть *v., pfv. of* **тузи́ть.**

оття́гивать *v. impfv.* [*pfv.* **оттяну́ть**] **1,** to draw aside; pull aside. **2,** *mil.* to draw off. **3,** to weigh down. **4,** to delay; put off. —**оття́гивать вре́мя,** to play for time; stall for time.

отта́жка [*gen. pl.* **-жек**] *n., colloq.* (deliberate) delay.

оттяну́ть [*infl.* **-тяну́, -тя́нешь**] *v., pfv. of* **оття́гивать.**

отума́нивать *v. impfv.* [*pfv.* **отума́нить**] **1,** to blur; dim; obscure. **2,** to dull; cloud (the senses).

отупе́лый *adj., colloq.* dazed.

отупе́ние *n.* daze; stupor; torpor.

отупе́ть *v. pfv.* to become dazed.

отутю́живать *v. impfv.* [*pfv.* **отутю́жить**] to iron; press.

отуча́ть *v. impfv.* [*pfv.* **отучи́ть**] (*with* **от** *or inf.*) to break (someone) of the habit of; train not to; wean away from. —**отуча́ться,** *refl.* (*with* **от** *or inf.*) to break oneself (of a habit); break the habit of.

отучи́ть [*infl.* **-учу́, -у́чишь**] *v., pfv. of* **отуча́ть.** —**отучи́ться,** *refl., pfv. of* **отуча́ться.**

отха́живать *v. impfv.* [*pfv.* **отходи́ть**] *colloq.* to nurse back to health.

отха́ркивать *v. impfv.* [*pfv.* **отха́ркнуть**] to cough up. —**отха́ркиваться,** *refl.* to clear one's throat.

отхвати́ть [*infl.* **-хвачу́, -хва́тишь**] *v., pfv. of* **отхва́тывать.**

отхва́тывать *v. impfv.* [*pfv.* **отхвати́ть**] *colloq.* to cut off; slice off; snip off.

отхлёбывать *v. impfv.* [*pfv.* **отхлебну́ть**] *colloq.* **1,** to take a sip of. **2,** (*with* **из**) to sip (from).

отхлеста́ть *v. pfv.* [*infl.* **-хлещу́, -хле́щешь**] *colloq.* to give (someone) a lashing; horsewhip.

отхлы́нуть *v. pfv.* to surge back.

отхо́д *n.* **1,** departure. **2,** *mil.* withdrawal. **3,** *fig.* departure; deviation; retreat. **4,** *pl.* waste; waste matter.

отходи́ть[1] *v. impfv.* [*pfv.* **отойти́**; *pres.* **-хожу́, -хо́дишь**] **1,** (*with* **от**) to walk away (from); step back (from). **2,** (*of a train*) to leave; depart. **3,** *mil.* to withdraw; fall back. **4,** (*with* **от**) to deviate (from); depart (from); digress (from). **5,** (*with* **от**) to drift away (from). **6,** to come off; peel off; (*of a stain*) come out. **7,** to

recover; come round. **8,** to calm down. **9,** (*with* **к**) (*of property*) to pass (to). **10,** *obs.* to pass; come to an end. —**отойти́ в про́шлое** *or* **в исто́рию,** to pass into history; become a thing of the past.

отходи́ть[2] [*infl.* **-хожу́, -хо́дишь**] *v., pfv. of* **отха́живать.**

отхо́дная *n., decl. as an adj.* prayer said for a dying person.

отхо́дчивый *adj.* disposed quickly to forgive; not such as to harbor a grudge.

отхо́жий *adj., in* **отхо́жее ме́сто,** outhouse; latrine.

отцвести́ [*infl. like* **цвести́**] *v., pfv. of* **отцвета́ть.**

отцвета́ть *v. impfv.* [*pfv.* **отцвести́**] **1,** to cease to bloom. **2,** *fig.* to lose its bloom; fade.

отцепи́ть [*infl.* **-цеплю́, -це́пишь**] *v., pfv. of* **отцепля́ть.** —**отцепи́ться,** *refl., pfv. of* **отцепля́ться.**

отцепля́ть *v. impfv.* [*pfv.* **отцепи́ть**] to unhook; uncouple. —**отцепля́ться,** *refl.* to come unhooked; come uncoupled.

отцеуби́йство *n.* patricide.

отцо́вский *adj.* **1,** one's father's. **2,** paternal. —**отцо́вство,** *n.* paternity; fatherhood.

отча́иваться *v.r. impfv.* [*pfv.* **отча́яться**] (*with inf. or* **в** + *prepl.*) to despair (of).

отча́ливать *v. impfv.* [*pfv.* **отча́лить**] (*of a boat*) to cast off.

отча́сти *adv.* partly; in part.

отча́яние *n.* despair.

отча́янно *adv.* **1,** desperately. **2,** *colloq.* frightfully.

отча́янный *adj.* **1,** desperate. **2,** *colloq.* reckless. **3,** *colloq.* frightful; awful.

отча́яться *v.r., pfv. of* **отча́иваться.**

отчего́ *adv.* why. —*conj.* and as a result; and because of that.

отчего́-нибудь *adv.* for some reason or other. *Also,* **отчего́-либо.**

отчего́-то *adv.* for some unknown reason.

отчека́нить *v., pfv. of* **чека́нить.**

отчёркивать *v. impfv.* [*pfv.* **отчеркну́ть**] to mark; mark off.

о́тчество *n.* patronymic (name).

отчёт *n.* account; report. —**отдава́ть себе́ отчёт в** (+ *prepl.*), to realize; be aware of.

отчётливый *adj.* distinct; clear. —**отчётливо,** *adv.* distinctly; clearly.

отчётность *n.f.* **1,** accounting; bookkeeping. **2,** accounts; records. —**прове́рка отчётности,** audit; auditing.

отчётный *adj.* **1,** of or pert. to a report. Отчётный докла́д, report. **2,** covered in a report: отчётный пери́од, the period covered.

отчи́зна *n., archaic* native land; fatherland.

о́тчий *adj., obs.* one's father's.

о́тчим *n.* stepfather.

отчисле́ние *n.* **1,** deduction. **2,** *pl.* money deducted; deductions. **3,** dismissal.

отчисля́ть *v. impfv.* [*pfv.* **отчи́слить**] **1,** to deduct. **2,** to dismiss.

отчи́стить [*infl.* **-щу, -стишь**] *v., pfv. of* **отчища́ть.**

отчи́тывать *v. impfv.* [*pfv.* **отчита́ть**] *colloq.* to tell off; give (someone) a talking-to. —**отчи́тываться,** *refl.* **1,** to report; give a report. **2,** (*with* **в** + *prepl.*) to account for.

отчища́ть *v. impfv.* [*pfv.* **отчи́стить**] **1,** to clean; scour. **2,** to remove (a stain, rust, etc.).

отчужда́ть v. impfv. [pfv. отчуди́ть] to alienate; estrange.

отчужде́ние n. alienation; estrangement.

отчужде́нность n.f. estrangement; aloofness; distance.

отшага́ть v. pfv., colloq. to walk (a certain distance).

отшагну́ть v. pfv., colloq. to step aside; step back.

отша́тываться v.r. impfv. [pfv. отшатну́ться] 1, to jump back; recoil. 2, (with от) fig. to turn one's back on.

отшвы́ривать v. impfv. [pfv. отшвырну́ть] colloq. to throw away; fling away.

отше́льник n. hermit; recluse. —отше́льнический, adj. (like that) of a hermit; solitary. —отше́льничество, n. solitary life.

отши́б n., in на отши́бе, 1, at a distance. 2, alone; by oneself. 3, (with от) apart (from); aloof (from).

отшиба́ть v. impfv. [pfv. отшиби́ть] colloq. 1, to hurt: отшиби́ть себе́ но́гу, to hurt one's leg. 2, impers. to lose (one's memory, appetite, etc.): у него́ отши́бло аппети́т, he lost his appetite.

отшиби́ть [infl. -бу́, -бёшь; past отши́б, -ла] v., pfv. of отшиба́ть.

отшлёпать v. pfv., colloq. to spank.

отшлифова́ть v., pfv. of шлифова́ть.

отшути́ться [infl. -шучу́сь, -шу́тишься] v.r., pfv. of отшу́чиваться.

отшу́чиваться v.r. impfv. [pfv. отшути́ться] colloq. to reply with a joke; come back with a joke.

отщепе́нец [gen. -нца] n. renegade.

отщепля́ть v. impfv. [pfv. отщепи́ть] to chip off. —отщепля́ться, refl. to chip off; be chipped off.

отщи́пывать v. impfv. [pfv. отщипну́ть] to pinch off (usu. a piece of bread).

отъеда́ть v. impfv. [pfv. отъе́сть] to bite off. —отъеда́ться, refl. to put on weight from good food.

отъе́зд n. departure. —быть в отъе́зде, to be away; be out of town.

отъезжа́ть v. impfv. [pfv. отъе́хать] to drive away; drive off; ride away; ride off.

отъе́сть [infl. like есть] v., pfv. of отъеда́ть. —отъе́сться, refl., pfv. of отъеда́ться.

отъе́хать [infl. -е́ду, -е́дешь] v., pfv. of отъезжа́ть.

отъя́вленный adj. arrant; unmitigated; out-and-out.

оты́грывать v. impfv. [pfv. отыгра́ть] to win back. —оты́грываться, refl. 1, to recoup one's losses. 2, colloq. to wiggle out of a situation.

отыска́ть [infl. отыщу́, оты́щешь] v., pfv. of оты́скивать. —отыска́ться, refl., pfv. of оты́скиваться.

оты́скивать v. impfv. [pfv. отыска́ть] 1, to find. 2, [impfv. only] to look for; search for; try to find. —оты́скиваться, refl. to be found; turn up.

отягоща́ть v. impfv. [pfv. отяготи́ть] to weigh down; burden.

отягча́ть v. impfv. [pfv. отягчи́ть] 1, to weigh down; burden. 2, to aggravate: отягча́ющие вину́ обстоя́тельства, aggravating circumstances.

отяжеле́ть v. pfv. to grow heavy; become heavy.

отяжеля́ть v. impfv. [pfv. отяжели́ть] 1, to make heavy. 2, to weigh down.

офице́р n. officer. —офице́рский, adj. officer (attrib.); officer's; officers'.

офице́рство n. 1, the officers. 2, officer's rank; commission.

официа́льный adj. 1, official. 2, fig. formal. —официа́льно, adv. officially.

официа́нт n. waiter.

официа́нтка [gen. pl. -ток] n. waitress.

официо́з n. semi-official publication.

официо́зный adj. semi-official.

оформи́тель n.m. 1, designer. 2, stage designer.

офо́рмить [infl. -млю, -мишь] v., pfv. of оформля́ть.

оформле́ние n. 1, design. 2, legalization. 3, processing (of documents). 4, taking on; hiring.

оформля́ть v. impfv. [pfv. офо́рмить] 1, to design; arrange; lay out. 2, to legalize; formalize; make official. 3, to process; validate (documents). 4, to take on; hire. —оформля́ться, refl. 1, to take shape. 2, to go through the formalities; complete the paperwork.

офо́рт n. etching.

офсе́т n. offset. —офсе́тный, adj. offset (attrib.): офсе́тная печа́ть, offset printing.

офтальмоло́гия n. ophthalmology. —офтальмо́лог, n. ophthalmologist.

ох interj. oh!; ah!

оха́ивать v. impfv. [pfv. оха́ять] colloq. to find fault with; run down.

о́ханье n. moaning; groaning.

оха́пка [gen. pl. -пок] n. armful. —в оха́пку; в оха́пке, in one's arms.

охарактеризова́ть v. pfv. [infl. -зу́ю, -зу́ешь] to characterize; describe.

о́хать v. impfv. [pfv. о́хнуть] to moan; groan.

оха́ять [infl. оха́ю, оха́ешь] v., pfv. of оха́ивать.

охва́т n. 1, encompassing. 2, scope; range. 3, mil. envelopment.

охвати́ть [infl. охвачу́, охва́тишь] v., pfv. of охва́тывать.

охва́тывать v. impfv. [pfv. охвати́ть] 1, (usu. with рука́ми) to put one's arms around; embrace. 2, to engulf; envelop: пла́мя охвати́ло зда́ние, flames engulfed the building. 3, (of emotions, feelings, etc.) to seize; grip. 4, fig. to take in; include; embrace; encompass. —охвати́ть (что́-нибудь) взгля́дом, to take in; survey. —охвати́ть (что́-нибудь) умо́м, to grasp; encompass in one's mind.

охладева́ть v. impfv. [pfv. охладе́ть] 1, (with к) to grow cold (toward). 2, (of feelings) to die down.

охлажда́ть v. impfv. [pfv. охлади́ть] 1, to cool; chill. 2, fig. to calm down. 3, fig. to dampen (one's ardor, enthusiasm, etc.). —охлажда́ться, refl. to cool; cool off; cool down.

охлажде́ние n. 1, cooling. 2, fig. coolness (toward someone).

охмеле́ть v.pfv., colloq. to become intoxicated.

о́хнуть v., pfv. of о́хать.

охо́та n. 1, hunt; hunting: идти́ на охо́ту, to go hunting. 2, wish; desire. Мне (не) охо́та (+ inf.), I (don't) feel like (reading, walking, etc.). —что за охо́та; охо́та вам (+ inf.), colloq. why do you want to...?; why bother...?; what's the use of...?

охо́титься v.r. impfv. [pres. -чусь, -тишься] (with на + acc. or за + instr.) to hunt; go hunting (for).

охо́тник n. 1, hunter. 2, volunteer. 3, (with до) enthusiast: быть охо́тником до ша́хмат, to be a chess enthusiast.

охо́тничий [fem. -чья] adj. hunting (attrib.). —охо́тничий до́мик, hunting lodge. —охо́тничий расска́з, fish story. —охо́тничья соба́ка, hunting dog; hound.

охо́тно adv. gladly; willingly.

óхра *n.* ocher.

охрáна *n.* **1,** guarding; protection. Быть под охрáной, to be under guard. **2,** guard; guards.

охранéние *n.* safeguarding; protection.

охранить *v., pfv. of* охранять.

охрáнка *n., colloq.* secret police in tsarist Russia; Okhranka.

охрáнный *adj.* safe-conduct: охрáнная грáмота; охрáнный лист, safe-conduct pass.

охранять *v. impfv.* [*pfv.* охранить] **1,** to guard. **2,** *fig.* to safeguard.

охрúплый *adj., colloq.* hoarse. *Also,* охрúпший.

охрúпнуть *v. pfv.* [*past* охрúп, -ла] to become hoarse.

оцарáпать *v. pfv.* to scratch.

оцелóт *n.* ocelot.

оцéнивать *v. impfv.* [*pfv.* оценить] **1,** to appraise; assess; evaluate. **2,** to estimate. **—оценить по достóинству, 1,** to assess properly. **2,** to appreciate; recognize the value of.

оценить [*infl.* оценю, оцéнишь] *v., pfv. of* оцéнивать.

оцéнка [*gen. pl.* -нок] *n.* **1,** (monetary) appraisal. **2,** assessment; appraisal; evaluation. **3,** grade; mark.

оцéнщик *n.* appraiser.

оцепенéлый *adj.* dazed; stunned.

оцепенéние *n.* stupor; torpor.

оцепенéть *v., pfv. of* цепенéть.

оцеплять *v. impfv.* [*pfv.* оцепить] to surround; seal off; cordon off.

очáг [*gen.* очагá] *n.* **1,** hearth; fireside. **2,** *fig.* center; hotbed; breeding ground.

очаровáние *n.* charm; fascination; enchantment.

очарóванный *adj.* **1,** charmed. **2,** spellbound.

очаровáтельный *adj.* charming.

очаровáть [*infl.* -рýю, -рýешь] *v., pfv. of* очарóвывать.

очарóвывать *v. impfv.* [*pfv.* очаровáть] to charm; captivate.

очевúдец [*gen.* -дца] *n.* eyewitness.

очевúдно *adv.* **1,** obviously. **2,** evidently. —*adj., used predicatively* obvious: бы́ло очевúдно, что..., it was obvious that...

очевúдный *adj.* [*short form* -ден, -дна] obvious.

очеловéчивать *v. impfv.* [*pfv.* очеловéчить] to humanize.

óчень *adv.* **1,** very. **2,** (*before verbs*) very much.

очервúветь *v., pfv. of* червúветь.

очереднóй *adj.* **1,** next; immediate; at hand. **2,** regular; regularly scheduled. **3,** ordinary; routine; just another.

очерёдность *n.f.* (prescribed) order; sequence.

óчередь [*pl.* óчереди, -дéй, -дям] *n.f.* **1,** turn: ждать своéй óчереди, to wait one's turn. **2,** line: стоять в óчереди, to stand in line. **3,** order; sequence. **4,** burst of fire: пулемётная óчередь, burst of machine-gun fire. **—в пéрвую óчередь,** first of all. **—в свою óчередь,** for one's part: я, в свою óчередь, for my part. **—на óчереди,** on the waiting list. **—не в послéднюю óчередь,** in no small measure.

óчерк *n.* essay. **—очеркúст,** *n.* essayist.

очернить *v., pfv. of* чернить (*in sense #2*).

очерствéлый *adj.* callous.

очерствéть *v., pfv. of* черствéть (*in sense #2*).

очерствлять *v. impfv.* [*pfv.* очерствúть] to harden (someone's heart).

очертáние *n.,* usu. *pl.* outline; contour.

очертить [*infl.* очерчý, очéртишь] *v., pfv. of* очéрчивать.

очéрчивать *v. impfv.* [*pfv.* очертить] **1,** to draw a line around. **2,** *fig.* to describe; outline; sketch. **—очертя гóлову,** headlong; rashly.

очёски [*gen.* -ков] *n. pl.* combings.

очинить [*infl.* очиню, очúнишь] *v., pfv. of* чинить (*in sense #2*).

очистúтельный *adj.* cleansing. **—очистúтельный завóд,** refinery.

очúстить [*infl.* -щу, -стишь] *v., pfv. of* чúстить (*in sense #4*) *and* очищáть. **—очúститься,** *refl., pfv. of* очищáться.

очúстка *n.* **1,** cleaning. **2,** clearing. **3,** purification. **—для очúстки сóвести,** to clear one's conscience.

очúстки [*gen.* -ков] *n. pl.* peelings: картóфельные очúстки, potato peelings.

очищáть *v. impfv.* [*pfv.* очúстить] **1,** to clean. **2,** to purify; refine. **3,** to cleanse; purge. **4,** to clear; clear up; clear out. **5,** *colloq.* to rob; clean out. **—очищáться,** *refl.* **1,** to clear; clear up. **2,** (*with* от) to become clear (of).

очищéние *n.* **1,** clearing. **2,** cleansing. **3,** purification.

очкú [*gen.* очкóв] *n. pl.* glasses; eyeglasses.

очкó [*pl.* очки, очкóв] *n.* **1,** point (*scored in a game*). **2,** pip (*on a playing card, die, domino, etc.*). **3,** small opening; mesh.

очковтирáтельство *n., colloq.* fakery.

очкóвый *adj., sports* based on points scored. **—очкóвая змея,** cobra.

очнýться *v.r. pfv.* **1,** to awaken. **2,** to regain consciousness.

óчный *adj.* **1,** in óчное обучéние, classroom instruction (*as opposed to correspondence courses*). **2,** in óчная стáвка, simultaneous questioning of witnesses or defendants (*in order to resolve contradictions*). **3,** in óчный цвет, pimpernel.

очумéть *v.pfv., colloq.* to lose one's head.

очутúться *v.r.pfv.* [*infl.* очýтишься; *1st person sing. not used*] to find oneself; wind up; end up (in a certain place).

очýхаться *v.r. pfv., colloq.* to come to; regain one's senses.

ошалéть *v., pfv. of* шалéть.

ошарáшивать *v. impfv.* [*pfv.* ошарáшить] *colloq.* to dumfound; flabbergast.

ошéйник *n.* collar (*for a dog*).

ошеломúтельный *adj.* stunning; staggering.

ошеломлять *v. impfv.* [*pfv.* ошеломúть] to stun; stagger.

ошельмовáть *v., pfv. of* шельмовáть.

ошибáться *v.r. impfv.* [*pfv.* ошибúться] **1,** to make a mistake. **2,** to be mistaken; be wrong.

ошибúться [*infl.* -бýсь, -бёшься; *past* ошúбся, ошúблась] *v.r., pfv. of* ошибáться.

ошúбка [*gen. pl.* -бок] *n.* mistake; error.

ошúбочно *adv.* **1,** erroneously; mistakenly. **2,** by mistake.

ошúбочный *adj.* erroneous; mistaken; fallacious. **—ошúбочность,** *n.f.* fallaciousness.

ошúкать *v. pfv., colloq.* to hiss; boo (a performer, play, etc.).

ошпáривать *v. impfv.* [*pfv.* ошпáрить] *colloq.* to scald. **—ошпáриваться,** *refl., colloq.* to scald oneself.

оштрафова́ть *v., pfv. of* **штрафова́ть**.

оштукату́рить *v., pfv. of* **штукату́рить**.

още́ниться *v.r., pfv. of* **щени́ться**.

още́иниться *v.r., pfv. of* **щети́ниться**.

ощипа́ть [*infl.* **ощиплю́, ощи́плешь**] *v., pfv. of* **щипа́ть** (*in sense #3*) *and* **ощи́пывать**.

ощи́пывать *v. impfv.* [*pfv.* **ощипа́ть**] **1,** to pluck. **2,** to pick (clean).

ощу́пывать *v. impfv.* [*pfv.* **ощу́пать**] to feel (*with one's fingers*).

о́щупь *n.f., in* **на о́щупь, 1,** to the touch. **2,** by touch.

о́щупью *adv.* by groping one's way: **идти́ о́щупью,** to grope one's way: **иска́ть о́щупью,** to grope for.

ощути́мый *adj.* **1,** perceptible; tangible; palpable. **2,** noticeable; marked; appreciable. *Also,* **ощути́тельный**.

ощуща́ть *v. impfv.* [*pfv.* **ощути́ть**] to feel; sense. —**ощуща́ться,** *refl.* [*impfv. only*] to be felt; be sensed.

ощуще́ние *n.* sensation; feeling.

оягни́ться *v.r., pfv. of* **ягни́ться**.

П

П, п *n. neut.* sixteenth letter of the Russian alphabet.

па *n. neut. indecl.* step (*in dancing*).

па́ва *n.* peahen.

павиа́н *n.* baboon.

павильо́н *n.* **1,** pavilion. **2,** film studio.

павли́н *n.* peacock. —**павли́ний,** *adj.* [*fem.* **-нья**] peacock (*attrib.*).

па́водок [*gen.* **-дка**] *n.* high water; flood.

па́вший *adj.* fallen.

пагина́ция *n.* pagination.

па́года *n.* pagoda.

па́губа *n., obs.* ruin; downfall.

па́губный *adj.* ruinous; pernicious; disastrous.

па́даль *n.f.* carrion.

па́дать *v. impfv.* [*pfv.* **упа́сть** *or* **пасть**] **1,** to fall: упа́сть на зе́млю, to fall to the ground. Пасть в бою́, to fall in battle. **2,** to decline; go down; fall: це́ны па́дают, prices are going down. —**па́дать ду́хом,** to lose heart. —**па́дать в о́бморок,** to faint.

па́дающий *adj.* falling. —**па́дающая звезда́,** shooting star. —**па́дающий мо́лот,** triphammer.

паде́ж [*gen.* **-дежа́**] *n., gram.* case.

падёж [*gen.* **-дежа́**] *n.* murrain.

паде́жный *adj., gram.* case (*attrib.*).

паде́ние *n.* **1,** fall. **2,** drop; decline. **3,** downfall. **4,** *physics* incidence.

па́дкий *adj.* [*short form* **па́док, па́дка**] (*with* **на** + *acc. or* **до**) having a weakness (for); susceptible (to): па́дкий на лесть, susceptible to flattery.

па́дуб *n.* holly.

паду́чий *adj., obs.* falling. —**паду́чая боле́знь,** *obs.* epilepsy.

па́дчерица *n.* stepdaughter.

па́дший *adj.* fallen. —**па́дшая же́нщина,** fallen woman.

паёк [*gen.* **пайка́**] *n.* ration.

паж [*gen.* **пажа́**] *n.* page; attendant.

паз [*2nd loc.* **пазу́**; *pl.* **пазы́**] *n.* **1,** crack; crevice. **2,** slot; groove; mortise.

па́зуха *n.* **1,** bosom. **2,** *anat.* sinus. **3,** *bot.* axil. —**держа́ть ка́мень за па́зухой,** to bear a grudge.

па́инька [*gen. pl.* **-нек**] *n.m. & f., colloq.* good child.

пай [*pl.* **пай**] *n.* share.

па́йка *n.* soldering.

па́йщик *n.* shareholder.

пакга́уз *n.* warehouse.

паке́т *n.* **1,** package. **2,** packet. **3,** paper bag.

пакетбо́т *n.* packet (*steamship*).

пакиста́нец [*gen.* **-нца**] *n.m.* [*fem.* **-нка**] Pakistani. —**пакиста́нский,** *adj.* Pakistani.

па́кля *n.* oakum; tow.

пакова́ть *v. impfv.* [*pfv.* **упакова́ть**; *pres.* **-ку́ю, -ку́ешь**] to pack (things).

па́костить *v. impfv.* [*pres.* **-щу, -стишь**] *colloq.* **1,** to soil; dirty. **2,** to spoil. **3,** (*with dat.*) to play dirty tricks on; do nasty things to.

па́костный *adj., colloq.* nasty; foul; vile.

па́кость *n.f., colloq.* **1,** dirty trick; mean trick. **2,** dirty word; obscenity.

пакт *n.* pact: пакт о ненападе́нии, nonaggression pact.

паланти́н *n.* (fur) stole.

пала́та *n.* **1,** house (*of a legislature*): пала́та представи́телей/о́бщин/ло́рдов, House of Representatives/Commons/Lords. **2,** bureau; chamber: торго́вая пала́та, chamber of commerce; пала́та мер и весо́в, Bureau of Weights and Measures. —**у него́ ума́ пала́та,** he is as smart as they come.

палатализа́ция *n.* palatalization.

палатализова́ть *v. impfv. & pfv.* [*pres.* **-зу́ю, -зу́ешь**] *phonet.* to palatalize.

пала́тальный *adj., phonet.* palatal.

пала́тка [*gen. pl.* **-ток**] *n.* **1,** tent. **2,** stall; booth.

пала́точный *adj.* tent (*attrib.*).

пала́ч [*gen.* **-лача́**] *n.* executioner; hangman; *fig.* butcher.

пала́ш [*gen.* **-лаша́**] *n.* broadsword.

па́левый *adj.* pale yellow; straw-colored.

палёный *adj.* singed; scorched.

палеоазиа́тский *adj.* Paleo-Asiatic.

палеогра́фия *n.* paleography. —**палео́граф,** *n.* paleographer. —**палеографи́ческий,** *adj.* paleograph[ic]

палеозо́йский *adj.* Paleozoic.

палеолити́ческий *adj.* paleolithic.

палеонтоло́гия *n.* paleontology. —**палеонто́лог**, *n.* paleontologist. —**палеонтологи́ческий**, *adj.* paleontological.

палести́нец [*gen.* -нца] *n.m.* [*fem.* -нка] Palestinian. —**палести́нский**, *adj.* Palestinian.

па́лец [*gen.* -льца] *n.* **1**, finger. Большо́й па́лец, thumb. **2**, *in* па́лец ноги́; па́лец на ноге́, toe. —знать (что́-нибудь) как свои́ пять па́льцев, to know like the back of one's hand. —па́льца в рот не клади́ (+ *dat.*), *colloq.* watch out for...!; be on your guard against...! —па́лец о па́лец не уда́рить, not to lift a finger. —пока́зывать *or* ука́зывать па́льцем на (+ *acc.*), to point one's finger at. —попа́сть па́льцем в не́бо, to be wide of the mark. —смотре́ть сквозь па́льцы на (+ *acc.*), to wink at; deliberately overlook; turn a blind eye to.

палиса́д *n.* palisade.

палиса́дник *n.* small garden.

палиса́ндр *n.* rosewood. —**палиса́ндровый**, *adj.* rosewood (*attrib.*).

пали́тра *n.* palette.

пали́ть *v. impfv.* **1**, [*pfv.* опали́ть] to singe (an animal). **2**, [*pfv.* спали́ть] to singe; scorch (*accidentally*). **3**, [*impfv. only*] (*of the sun*) to beat down. **4**, [*pfv.* вы́палить] *colloq.* to fire; shoot.

па́лка [*gen. pl.* -лок] *n.* **1**, stick. **2**, cane; walking stick. —из-под па́лки, under compulsion. —па́лка о двух конца́х, double-edged sword.

палла́дий *n.* palladium.

паллиати́в *n.* palliative. —**паллиати́вный**, *adj.* palliative.

пало́мник *n.* pilgrim.

пало́мничать *v. impfv.* to go on a pilgrimage.

пало́мничество *n.* pilgrimage. —**пало́мнический**, *adj.* pilgrim (*attrib.*); pilgrims'.

па́лочка [*gen. pl.* -чек] *n.* **1**, small stick: бараба́нная па́лочка, drumstick. **2**, baton; wand. **3**, bacillus.

па́лочный *adj.* with or using a stick. —па́лочная дисципли́на, discipline enforced with the rod.

па́лтус *n.* halibut.

па́луба *n.* deck (*of a ship*). —**па́лубный**, *adj.* deck (*attrib.*).

пальба́ *n., colloq.* firing: откры́ть пальбу́, to open fire.

па́льма *n.* palm (tree). —па́льма пе́рвенства, the crown; the chief laurels.

па́льмовый *adj.* palm (*attrib.*).

пальто́ *n. indecl.* overcoat.

па́льчик *n., dim. of* па́лец. —ма́льчик с па́льчик, Tom Thumb.

паля́щий *adj.* burning; scorching; searing.

пампа́сы [*gen.* -сов] *n. pl.* pampas.

памфле́т *n.* (political) pamphlet. —**памфлети́ст**, *n.* pamphleteer.

па́мятка [*gen. pl.* -ток] *n.* **1**, reminder. **2**, book of instructions.

па́мятливый *adj., colloq.* having a retentive memory. —**па́мятливость**, *n.f., colloq.* retentive memory.

па́мятник *n.* monument; memorial. —**надгро́бный па́мятник**, monument; (large) tombstone.

па́мятный *adj.* **1**, memorable. **2**, serving as a reminder: па́мятная кни́жка, memorandum book; notebook. **3**, memorial; commemorative: па́мятная доска́, memorial plaque; па́мятная ма́рка, commem-

orative stamp. —па́мятная запи́ска, memorandum; aide-mémoire. —па́мятный пода́рок, memento.

па́мятовать *v. impfv., in* па́мятуя о, remembering; recalling.

па́мять *n.f.* memory. —без па́мяти, **1**, unconscious. **2**, (*with verbs of running or racing*) madly; for all one is worth. **3**, (*with* от) madly in love with. **4**, (*with* люби́ть) to distraction. —в па́мять (+ *gen.*), in memory of. —на чье́й-нибудь па́мяти, in (*or* within) someone's memory. —на па́мять, **1**, by heart. **2**, from memory. **3**, as a keepsake. —по па́мяти, from memory. —по ста́рой па́мяти, **1**, by force of habit. **2**, (in) the old (*or* traditional) way. —приходи́ть на па́мять (+ *dat.*), to come to mind.

пана́ма *n.* Panama hat.

панаце́я *n.* panacea.

па́нда *n.* panda.

пандеми́я (дэ) *n.* pandemic.

панеги́рик *n.* panegyric; eulogy. —**панегири́ст**, *n.* panegyrist.

пане́ль *n.f.* **1**, pavement; sidewalk. **2**, paneling; wainscot.

панибра́тский *adj., colloq.* overly familiar. —**панибра́тство**, *n., colloq.* undue familiarity.

па́ника *n.* panic.

паникёр *n.* alarmist.

панихи́да *n.* funeral service; requiem.

пани́ческий *adj.* panicky; panic-stricken.

пано́птикум *n.* wax museum.

панора́ма *n.* panorama; panoramic view. —**панора́мный**, *adj.* panoramic.

пансио́н *n.* **1**, boarding house. **2**, room and board: жить на пансио́не, to receive room and board. **3**, *pre-rev.* boarding school.

пансиона́т *n.* (resort) hotel.

пансионе́р *n.* **1**, *pre-rev.* boarding-school student. **2**, boarder; roomer.

пантало́ны [*gen.* -ло́н] *n. pl.* **1**, *obs.* pants. **2**, (women's) drawers.

панталы́к *n., colloq., in* сбить с панталы́ку, to confuse; сби́ться с панталы́ку, to become confused.

пантеи́зм (тэ) *n.* pantheism. —**пантеи́ст**, *n.* pantheist. —**пантеисти́ческий**, *adj.* pantheistic.

пантео́н (тэ) *n.* pantheon.

панте́ра *n.* panther; leopard.

пантоми́ма *n.* pantomime. —**пантоми́мный; пантомими́ческий**, *adj.* pantomime.

панхромати́ческий *adj.* panchromatic.

па́нцирь *n.m.* **1**, armor; coat of mail. **2**, shell (*of a turtle*); armor (*of an armadillo*).

па́па *n.m.* **1**, papa; daddy. **2**, Pope.

папа́ха *n.* tall fur hat.

папа́ша *n.m., colloq.* daddy.

па́перть *n.f.* portico of a church.

папильо́тка [*gen. pl.* -ток] *n.* (hair) curler.

папиро́са *n.* cigarette.

папиро́сница *n.* cigarette case.

папиро́сный *adj.* cigarette (*attrib.*). —**папиро́сная бума́га**, tissue paper.

папи́рус *n.* papyrus.

па́пка [*gen. pl.* -пок] *n.* (cardboard) folder.

па́поротник *n.* fern.

па́прика *n.* paprika.

па́пский *adj.* papal. —**па́пство**, *n.* papacy.

па́пула *n.* papule.

папьé-машé *n. neut. indecl.* papier-mâché.

пар [*2nd loc.* парý; *pl.* парьí] *n.* **1,** steam. **2,** vapor. **3,** fallow land: лежáть под пáром, to lie fallow. —**на всех парáх, 1,** under a full head of steam. **2,** *fig.* at top speed.

пáра *n.* **1,** pair: пáра чулóк, pair of stockings. **2,** (married) couple: счастливая пáра, happy couple. **3,** (*with gen. or* к) mate (*other of a pair*): эта перчáтка — пáра (к) утéрянной, this glove is the mate to the one that was lost. **4,** (*with dat.*) *colloq.* suitable mate (for); good match (for): он ей не пáра, he is not a good match for her. **5,** (*with gen. pl.*) *colloq.* a few: мóжно попросить вас на пáру слов?, may I have a few words (*or* a word) with you? **6,** man's suit. —**стать** *or* **встать в пáры,** to line up in pairs. —**ходить** *or* **гулять пáрами,** to walk in pairs.

парáбола *n.* parabola. —**параболи́ческий,** *adj.* parabolic.

парáграф *n.* paragraph.

парáд *n.* parade.

парадигма *n.* paradigm.

парáдный *adj.* **1,** parade (*attrib.*). **2,** (*of clothes*) formal; dress. **3,** gala; festive. **4,** (*of an entrance, staircase, etc.*) main; front. —**парáдное,** *n.* front door.

парадóкс *n.* paradox. —**парадоксáльный,** *adj.* paradoxical.

паразит *n.* **1,** *biol.* parasite. **2,** *fig.* parasite; sponger. —**паразитизм,** *n.* parasitism. —**паразитический; паразитный,** *adj.* parasitic.

парализовáть *v. impfv. & pfv.* [*pres.* -зýю, -зýешь] to paralyze.

паралитик *n.* paralytic. —**паралитический,** *adj.* paralytic.

паралич [*gen.* -личá] *n.* paralysis. —**параличный,** *adj.* paralytic.

параллáкс *n.* parallax.

параллелепипед *n.* parallelepiped.

параллелизм *n.* parallelism.

параллелогрáмм *n.* parallelogram.

параллéль *n.f.* parallel.

параллéльно *adv.* **1,** (*with dat.*) parallel to: паралле́льно доро́ге, parallel to the road. **2,** (*with* с + *instr.*) *fig.* parallel to: паралле́льно с э́тим, parallel to this.

параллéльный *adj.* parallel.

парáметр *n.* parameter.

парамéция *n.* paramecium.

паранóик *n., colloq.* paranoiac. —**паранойческий,** *adj.* paranoid.

паранóйя *n.* paranoia.

парапéт *n.* parapet.

параплегия *n.* paraplegia.

паратиф *n.* paratyphoid (fever).

парафин *n.* paraffin. —**парафиновый,** *adj.* paraffin.

парафировать *v. impfv. & pfv.* [*pres.* -рую, -руешь] to initial (a treaty, document, etc.).

парашют (шу) *n.* parachute. Вы́броситься с парашю́том, to bail out. —**парашютизм,** *n.* parachute jumping (*as a sport*). —**парашютист,** *n.* parachutist; parachute jumper; paratrooper. —**парашютный,** *adj.* parachute (*attrib.*).

паращитовидный *adj., in* паращитови́дная железá, parathyroid gland.

парéз (рэ) *n.* paresis.

пáреный *adj.* steamed. —**деше́вле па́реной ре́пы,** *colloq.* dirt-cheap.

пáрень [*gen.* -рня; *pl.* пáрни, -нéй, -ня́м] *n.m., colloq.* fellow; lad; chap; guy.

пари *n. neut. indecl.* bet; wager.

парижáнин [*pl.* -жáне, -жáн] *n.m.* [*fem.* -жáнка] Parisian.

парижский *adj.* of Paris; Parisian.

парик [*gen.* -рикá] *n.* wig.

парикмáхер *n.* barber; hairdresser. —**парикмáхерская,** *n., decl. as an adj.* barbershop.

парильня [*gen. pl.* -лен] *n.* steam room.

парировать *v. impfv. & pfv.* [*pres.* -рую, -руешь] **1,** to parry; ward off. **2,** *fig.* to parry; counter.

паритéт *n.* parity. —**паритéтный,** *adj.* equal.

пáрить *v. impfv.* **1,** to steam. **2,** to stew. **3,** *impers.* to be sultry: сегóдня пáрит, it is sultry today. —**пáриться,** *refl.* **1,** to steam; sweat (*in a bath*). **2,** (*of food*) to stew.

парить *v. impfv.* to soar; glide.

пáрия *n.* pariah; outcast.

парк *n.* **1,** park. **2,** depot; yard. **3,** fleet; stock: автомоби́льный парк США, the total number of cars in the USA.

пáрка [*gen. pl.* -рок] *n.* parka.

паркéт *n.* parquetry; parquet. —**паркéтный,** *adj.* parquet.

парлáмент *n.* parliament. —**парламентари́зм,** *n.* parliamentarianism. —**парламентáрий,** *n.* member of parliament. —**парламентáрный,** *adj.* parliamentary.

парламентёр *n.* bearer of a flag of truce.

парлáментский *adj.* parliamentary.

парник [*gen.* -никá] *n.* hotbed.

парникóвый *adj.* hotbed (*attrib.*); hothouse (*attrib.*): парникóвые растéния, hothouse plants.

парнишка [*gen. pl.* -шек] *n.m., colloq.* lad; boy.

парнóй *adj.* **1,** (*of milk*) fresh from the cow; (*of meat*) freshly killed. **2,** *colloq.* stuffy; sultry.

пáрный *adj.* **1,** being one (*or* the other) of a pair. **2,** arranged or done in pairs. —**пáрная игрá,** doubles (*in tennis*).

паровóз *n.* locomotive.

паровóзный *adj.* locomotive (*attrib.*). —**паровóзное депó,** roundhouse.

паровóй *adj.* **1,** steam (*attrib.*); steam-driven: паровáя маши́на, steam engine. **2,** (*of food*) steamed. **3,** (*of land*) fallow.

пародировать *v. impfv. & pfv.* [*pres.* -рую, -руешь] to parody.

парóдия *n.* parody; travesty. —**пароди́ст,** *n.* parodist.

пароксизм *n.* paroxysm.

парóль *n.m.* password.

парóм *n.* ferry. —**парóмный,** *adj.* ferry (*attrib.*). —**парóмщик,** *n.* ferryman.

парообрáзный *adj.* vaporous.

парообразовáние *n.* vaporization; generation of steam.

парохóд *n.* ship; steamship. —**парохóдный,** *adj.* steamship (*attrib.*). —**парохóдство,** *n.* steamship line.

пáрочка [*gen. pl.* -чек] *n., colloq.* **1,** pair. **2,** couple.

пáрта *n.* school desk.

партбилéт *n.* Party (membership) card (*contr. of* партийный билéт).

партеногенéз (тэ, нэ) *n.* parthenogenesis.

партéр (тэ) *n., theat.* orchestra.

партиец [*gen.* -ийца] *n., colloq.* member of the (communist) party.

партиза́н [*gen. pl.* **-за́н**] *n.* partisan; guerrilla. —**партиза́нский**, *adj.* guerrilla (*attrib.*). —**партиза́нство**, *n.* guerrilla activity.

парти́йность *n.f.* **1,** party membership. **2,** party spirit. **3,** reflection of party principles (*in literature, art, etc.*).

парти́йный *adj.* party (*attrib.*); Party (*attrib.*).

партиту́ра *n.*, *music* score.

па́ртия *n.* **1,** (political) party. **2,** party; team; group. **3,** batch; lot; consignment. **4,** game. **5,** *music* part. **6,** *obs.* match; suitable mate.

партнёр *n.m.* [*fem.* **-нёрша**] **1,** partner. **2,** player. **3,** (one's) opponent (*in a game*).

парто́рг *n.* party organizer (*contr. of* **парти́йный организа́тор**).

па́рус [*pl.* **паруса́**] *n.* sail. —**на всех паруса́х**, (at) full speed.

паруси́на *n.* canvas. —**паруси́новый**, *adj.* canvas.

па́русник *n.* **1,** sailing vessel. **2,** sailfish. **3,** swallowtail (*butterfly*).

па́русный *adj.* sail (*attrib.*): па́русная ло́дка, sailboat.

Парфено́н *n.* Parthenon.

парфюме́рия *n.* perfumes. —**парфюме́р**, *n.* perfumer. —**парфюме́рный**, *adj.* perfume (*attrib.*).

парча́ *n.* brocade. —**парчо́вый**, *adj.* brocade; brocaded.

парша́ *n.* mange.

парши́веть *v. impfv.* [*pfv.* **запарши́веть** *or* **опарши́веть**] *colloq.* to become mangy.

парши́вый *adj.* **1,** mangy. **2,** *colloq.* rotten; lousy.

пас *n.*, *cards; sports* pass. —*predicate, colloq.* over one's head: в э́том де́ле я пас, this is way over my head; this is beyond me.

па́сека *n.* apiary; bee garden. —**па́сечник**, *n.* bee-keeper.

па́сквиль *n.m.* scurrilous piece of writing; libel; slander; hatchet job.

паску́дный *adj.*, *colloq.* foul; vile.

паслён *n.* nightshade.

па́смурный *adj.* **1,** overcast; dreary; dismal. **2,** gloomy; sullen; morose.

пасова́ть *v. impfv.* [*pfv.* **спасова́ть**; *pres.* **-су́ю, -су́ешь**] **1,** *cards* to pass. **2,** *fig.* (*with* **пе́ред**) to shrink (from); retreat in the face of. **3,** [*impfv. only*] *sports* to pass (a ball, puck, etc.).

па́спорт [*pl.* **паспорта́**] *n.* passport. —**па́спортный**, *adj.* passport (*attrib.*).

пасса́ж *n.* **1,** arcade. **2,** *music* passage.

пассажи́р *n.* passenger. —**пассажи́рский**, *adj.* passenger (*attrib.*).

пасса́т *n.* trade wind.

пасси́в *n.* **1,** *comm.* liabilities. **2,** *gram.* passive voice.

пасси́вный *adj.* **1,** passive. **2,** *econ.* unfavorable. —**пасси́вность**, *n.f.* passivity.

па́ссия *n.*, *obs.* passion; flame.

па́ста *n.* paste. —зубна́я па́ста, toothpaste.

па́стбище *n.* pasture. —**па́стбищный**, *adj.* pasture (*attrib.*); grazing (*attrib.*).

па́ства *n.* flock; congregation; parishioners.

пасте́ль (тэ) *n.f.* pastel. —**пасте́льный**, *adj.* pastel.

пастериза́ция (тэ) *n.* pasteurization.

пастеризова́ть (тэ) *v. impfv. & pfv.* [*pres.* **-зу́ю, -зу́ешь**] to pasteurize.

пастерна́к *n.* parsnip.

пасти́ *v. impfv.* [*pres.* **пасу́, пасёшь**; *past* **пас, пасла́, пасло́**] to tend; graze; herd. —**пасти́сь**, *refl.* to graze.

пастила́ [*pl.* **-ти́лы**] *n.* a confection made of fruit, sugar, and egg whites.

па́стор *n.* pastor; minister.

пастора́ль *n.f.* **1,** pastoral. **2,** pastorale. —**пастора́льный**, *adj.* pastoral.

пасту́х [*gen.* **-стуха́**] *n.* shepherd.

пасту́шеский *adj.* **1,** shepherd's. **2,** *obs.* pastoral.

пасту́ший [*fem.* **-шья**] *adj.* shepherd's.

пастушо́к [*gen.* **-шка́**] *n.* **1,** young shepherd. **2,** swain. **3,** rail (*bird*).

па́стырь *n.m.* **1,** *poetic* shepherd. **2,** pastor.

пасть[1] [*infl.* **паду́, падёшь**; *past* **пал, па́ла**] *v.*, *pfv. of* **па́дать.**

пасть[2] *n.f.* mouth (*of an animal*). —во́лчья пасть, cleft palate.

пастьба́ *n.* pasturage.

па́сха *n.* **1,** Easter. **2,** Passover. **3,** traditional Easter dish make of cottage cheese and other ingredients. —**пасха́льный**, *adj.* Easter (*attrib.*); Passover (*attrib.*); paschal.

па́сынок [*gen.* **-нка**] *n.* stepchild; stepson.

пасья́нс *n.*, *cards* solitaire.

пат *n.*, *chess* stalemate.

пате́нт *n.* patent. —**пате́нтный**, *adj.* patent (*attrib.*).

патенто́ванный *adj.* patent; patented.

патентова́ть *v. impfv. & pfv.* [*pres.* **-ту́ю, -ту́ешь**] to patent; take out a patent on.

патети́ческий (тэ) *adj.* passionate; impassioned.

патефо́н *n.* small portable phonograph. —**патефо́нный**, *adj.* phonograph (*attrib.*).

па́тио *n. indecl.* patio.

па́тлы [*gen.* **патл**] *n. pl.*, *colloq.* long disheveled locks of hair.

па́тока *n.* molasses; treacle.

патоло́гия *n.* pathology. —**пато́лог**, *n.* pathologist. —**патологи́ческий**, *adj.* pathological.

па́точный *adj.* **1,** made of molasses. **2,** *fig.* sugary; saccharine.

патриа́рх *n.* patriarch. —**патриарха́льный**, *adj.* patriarchal. —**патриарха́т**, *n.* patriarchy. —**патриа́рхия**, *n.* patriarchate.

патрио́т *n.* **1,** patriot. **2,** *fig.* supporter; booster. —**патриоти́зм**, *n.* patriotism. —**патриоти́ческий**, *adj.* patriotic.

патри́ций *n.* patrician.

патро́н *n.* **1,** *obs.* patron. **2,** cartridge. **3,** *mech.* chuck. **4,** socket (*for a bulb*).

патро́нник *n.* chamber (*of a gun*).

патро́нный *adj.* cartridge (*attrib.*).

патронта́ш *n.* ammunition belt.

патрули́ровать *v. impfv.* [*pres.* **-рую, -руешь**] to patrol.

патру́ль [*gen.* **-труля́**] *n.m.* patrol.

патру́льный *adj.* patrol (*attrib.*). —*n.* man on patrol.

па́уза *n.* **1,** pause. **2,** *music* rest.

пау́к [*gen.* **паука́**] *n.* spider.

паути́на *n.* spider web; cobweb.

па́фос *n.* fervor; zeal.

пах [*2nd loc.* **паху́**] *n.* groin.

па́харь *n.m.* plowman.

паха́ть *v. impfv.* [*pfv.* **вспаха́ть**; *pres.* **пашу́, па́шешь**] to plow.

па́хнуть *v. impfv.* [*past* **пах** *or* **па́хнул, па́хла**] **1,** (*with an adv.*) to smell (good, bad, nice, etc.). **2,** (*with instr.*) to smell (of).

пахну́ть v. pfv., usu. impers. (of air, a fragrance, etc.) to blow in: со двора́ пахну́ло хо́лодом, a gust of cold air blew in from the yard.

па́хота n. **1,** plowing. **2,** plowed land.

па́хотный adj. arable.

па́хта n. buttermilk.

па́хтать v. impfv. to churn.

паху́чий adj. strong-smelling. —**паху́честь,** n.f. strong smell; strong odor.

пацие́нт n.m. [fem. **-ка**] patient.

пацифи́зм n. pacifism. —**пацифи́ст,** n. pacifist. —**пацифи́стский,** adj. pacifist.

па́че n., obs. more. —**па́че того́; тем па́че,** the more so; all the more. —**па́че ча́яния,** contrary to (or beyond one's) expectations.

па́чка [gen. pl. **-чек**] n. **1,** pack; bundle; batch. **2,** tutu.

па́чкать v. impfv. [pfv. **запа́чкать** or **испа́чкать**] **1,** to soil; dirty; stain. **2,** [impfv. only] colloq. to daub. —**па́чкаться,** refl. to become dirty; become soiled.

пачкотня́ n., colloq. poorly painted picture; daub.

пачку́н [gen. **-куна́**] n., colloq. **1,** slovenly person. **2,** poor painter.

паша́ [gen. pl. **-ше́й**] n.m. pasha.

па́шня [gen. pl. **-шен**] n. plowed land; land under cultivation.

паште́т n. pâté.

па́юсный adj., in **па́юсная икра́,** pressed caviar.

пая́льник n. soldering iron.

пая́льный adj. soldering (attrib.). —**пая́льная ла́мпа,** blowtorch. —**пая́льная тру́бка,** blowpipe.

пая́льщик n. solderer.

пая́ние n. soldering.

пая́сничать v. impfv., colloq. to clown around.

пая́ть v. impfv. to solder.

пая́ц n. clown; buffoon.

певе́ц [gen. **-вца́**] n. singer.

певи́ца n. (female) singer.

певу́н [gen. **-вуна́**] n.m. [fem. **-ву́нья**] colloq. person who likes to sing.

певу́чий adj. melodious. —**певу́честь,** n.f. melodiousness.

пе́вчий adj., in **пе́вчая пти́ца,** songbird. —n. chorister; choirboy.

пега́нка [gen. pl. **-нок**] n. sheldrake.

пе́гий adj. piebald.

педаго́г n. teacher; pedagogue. —**педаго́гика,** n. pedagogy. —**педагоги́ческий,** adj. pedagogical.

педа́ль n.f. pedal.

педа́нт n. pedant. —**педанти́зм,** n. pedantry. —**педанти́чный,** adj. pedantic.

педера́стия n. sodomy.

педиатри́я n. pediatrics. —**педиа́тр,** n. pediatrician. —**педиатри́ческий,** adj. pediatric.

педикю́р n. pedicure; chiropody. —**педикю́рша,** n. (woman) chiropodist.

педо́метр n. pedometer.

пезе́та n. = **песе́та.**

пе́зо n. = **пе́со.**

пейза́ж n. **1,** landscape. **2,** landscape painting. —**пейзажи́ст,** n. landscape painter. —**пейза́жный,** adj. landscape (attrib.).

пека́н n. pecan.

пе́кари n.m. indecl. peccary.

пека́рный adj. baking (attrib.).

пека́рня [gen. pl. **-рен**] n. bakery.

пе́карь [pl. **пекаря́** or **пе́кари**] n.m. baker. —**пе́карский,** adj. baker's.

пеклёванный adj. (of flour) fine; finely ground. —**пеклёванный хлеб,** fine rye bread.

пе́кло n., colloq. **1,** intense heat. **2,** hell. **3,** fig. (with gen.) the heat (of); the thick (of).

пелена́ [gen. pl. **-лён**] n. cover; veil; shroud (of clouds, fog, snow, smoke, etc.).

пелена́ть v. impfv. [pfv. **спелена́ть** or **запелена́ть**] to diaper; swaddle.

пе́ленг n., navigation bearing.

пеленга́тор n. direction finder.

пеленгова́ть v. impfv. & pfv. [pres. **-гу́ю, -гу́ешь**] to take a bearing on.

пелёнка [gen. pl. **-нок**] n. diaper. —**с пелёнок,** from the cradle.

пелери́на n. cape.

пелика́н n. pelican.

пелла́гра n. pellagra.

пельме́ни n. pl. [sing. **пельме́нь,** m.] meat dumplings.

пе́мза n. pumice; pumice stone.

пе́на n. **1,** foam. **2,** lather; suds: **мы́льная пе́на,** soapsuds. **3,** scum.

пена́л n. pencil case.

пенёк [gen. **-нька́**] n. stump (of a tree).

пе́ние n. singing.

пе́нистый adj. foamy.

пе́нить v. impfv. [pfv. **вспе́нить**] to froth; cause to foam. —**пе́ниться,** refl. to froth; foam.

пеницилли́н n. penicillin.

пе́нка n. **1,** skin (forming on milk). **2,** [also, **морска́я пе́нка**] meerschaum. —**пе́нковый,** adj. meerschaum.

пе́нни n. neut. indecl. penny (in Great Britain).

пе́нный adj. foamy. —**пе́нный огнетуши́тель,** foam fire extinguisher.

пенопла́ст n. foam plastic; expanded plastic.

пенс n. penny (in Great Britain); pl. pence.

пе́нсия n. pension. Вы́йти or уйти́ на пе́нсию, to retire (or on a pension). —**пенсионе́р,** n. pensioner. —**пенсио́нный,** adj. pension (attrib.).

пенсне́ (нэ) n. neut. indecl. pince-nez.

Пентаго́н n. the Pentagon.

пента́метр n. pentameter.

пень [gen. **пня**] n.m. stump (of a tree). —**стоя́ть как пень,** to stand (there) like a dummy.

пенька́ n. hemp. —**пенько́вый,** adj. hemp (attrib.).

пеньюа́р n. peignoir.

пе́ня n. fine; penalty.

пеня́ть v. impfv. [pfv. **попеня́ть**] colloq. **1,** [impfv. only] (with на + acc.) to blame. **2,** (with dat.) to scold; chide.

пео́н n. peon. —**пеона́ж,** n. peonage.

пе́пел [gen. **пе́пла**] n. **1,** ashes. **2,** (volcanic) ash.

пепели́ще n. site of a fire.

пе́пельница n. ashtray.

пе́пельный adj. ash-colored.

пепси́н n. pepsin.

пепто́н n. peptone.

перве́йший adj., colloq. **1,** primary. **2,** the very best.

пе́рвенец [gen. **-нца**] n. first-born.

пе́рвенство n. **1,** championship. **2,** primacy.

пе́рвенствовать v. impfv. [pres. **-ствую, -ствуешь**] **1,** to come in first; finish first. **2,** (with над) to take precedence (over). **3,** (with ме́жду or среди́) to stand out (among); dominate.

перви́чный adj. primary; initial.

первобы́тный *adj.* **1,** primitive. **2,** primeval; pristine.

пе́рвое *n., decl. as an adj.* **1,** the first thing: пе́рвое, что на́до сде́лать, the first thing to be done. **2,** (*with dates*) first: сего́дня – пе́рвое ма́рта, today is March 1st. **3,** first course.

первозда́нный *adj.* primordial; primeval.

первоисто́чник *n.* original source; primary source.

первокла́ссный *adj.* first-class; first-rate.

первоку́рсник *n.* freshman.

первома́йский *adj.* May-Day (*attrib.*).

первонача́льный *adj.* **1,** original. **2,** initial; primary. **3,** elementary. —**первонача́льно,** *adv.* originally.

первообра́з *n.* prototype.

первоочередно́й *adj.* primary; immediate.

перворазря́дный *adj.* first-rate; first-class.

перворо́дный *adj.* **1,** *obs.* first-born. **2,** *fig.* pristine. —**перворо́дный грех,** original sin.

перворо́дство *n.* primogeniture.

первосвяще́нник *n.* high priest.

первосо́ртный *adj.* **1,** of the highest quality. **2,** *colloq.* first-rate; first-class.

первостепе́нный *adj.* paramount.

первоцве́т *n.* primrose.

пе́рвый *ordinal numeral & adj.* first: пе́рвая страни́ца, the first page. —*n.* **1,** the first. **2,** the former. —**в пе́рвую о́чередь,** first of all. —**из пе́рвых рук,** first-hand. —**пе́рвое вре́мя; на пе́рвых пора́х,** at first; in the beginning. —**пе́рвым де́лом; пе́рвым до́лгом,** *colloq.* first thing; first of all. *See also* **пе́рвое.**

перга́мент *n.* parchment. —**перга́ментный,** *adj.* parchment.

пере- *prefix* **1,** *indicating motion over or across:* перейти́ че́рез у́лицу, to cross the street; перелете́ть че́рез забо́р, to fly over the fence. **2,** *indicating motion to another place:* переле́чь на друго́й дива́н, to lie on another couch; переве́сить карти́ну на другу́ю сте́ну, to hang the picture on another wall. **3,** *indicating repetition of an action:* перечита́ть, to reread; перепрода́ть, to resell. **4,** *indicating excess:* перее́сть, to overeat; переплати́ть, to overpay. **5,** (*with pfv. verbs only*) *colloq., indicating thoroughness or completeness of an action:* переиска́ть, to search everywhere; перемо́кнуть, to get completely drenched. **6,** (*with pfv. verbs only*) *colloq., indicating outdoing someone:* перепи́ть, to outdrink; перехитри́ть, to outwit. **7,** (*with pfv. verbs only*) *colloq., used when the subject is all or many:* все цветы́ перемёрзли, all the flowers perished from the frost. **8,** (*with pfv. verbs only*) *colloq., used when the object is all or many:* перекупа́ть всех дете́й, to bathe all the children; переме́рить мно́го шляп, to try on many hats. **9,** (*with* -ся) *indicating reciprocity or exchange:* перепи́сываться, to correspond; перемиѓиваться, to wink at each other.

переадресова́ть [*infl.* -су́ю, -су́ешь] *v., pfv. of* **переадресо́вывать.**

переадресо́вывать *v. impfv.* [*pfv.* **переадресова́ть**] to readdress; forward.

перебази́ровать *v. pfv.* [*infl.* -рую, -руешь] to shift; transfer; relocate.

перебарщивать *v. impfv.* [*pfv.* **переборщи́ть**] *colloq.* to overdo it; go too far.

перебега́ть *v. impfv.* [*pfv.* **перебежа́ть**] **1,** to run across. **2,** to run from one place to another. **3,** to defect. —**перебега́ть доро́гу** (+ *dat.*), to stand in someone's way.

перебежа́ть [*infl. like* бежа́ть] *v., pfv. of* **перебега́ть.**

перебе́жка [*gen. pl.* -жек] *n.* **1,** run; rush; dash. **2,** defection. **3,** *sports* rerunning (*of a race*).

перебе́жчик *n.* defector; turncoat.

перебе́ливать *v. impfv.* [*pfv.* **перебели́ть**] **1,** to repaint; give a fresh coat of white paint. **2,** to make a clean copy of; put in final form.

перебели́ть [*infl.* -белю́, -бе́лишь *or* -бели́шь] *v., pfv. of* **перебе́ливать.**

перебеси́ться *v.r. pfv.* [*infl.* -бешу́сь, -бе́сишься] **1,** (*of dogs*) to become rabid. **2,** *colloq.* to settle down (*after leading a wild life*).

перебива́ть *v. impfv.* [*pfv.* **переби́ть**] **1,** to interrupt. **2,** to drown out. **3,** to reupholster. **4,** *colloq.* to snatch up (*ahead of someone else*). —**перебива́ться,** *refl.* **1,** to be smashed; be shattered. **2,** *colloq.* to manage; get along; make ends meet.

перебинтова́ть *v. pfv.* [*infl.* -ту́ю, -ту́ешь] **1,** to rebandage; change the bandage on. **2,** to bandage all of; bandage entirely.

перебира́ть *v. impfv.* [*pfv.* **перебра́ть**] **1,** to sort out. **2,** to go through; run through. **3,** to run one's fingers over. **4,** [*often,* **перебира́ть в па́мяти**] to turn (*or* run) over in one's mind. **5,** *printing* to reset. —**перебира́ться,** *refl., colloq.* **1,** to cross; get across. **2,** to move (*change residence*).

переби́ть *v. pfv.* [*infl.* -бью, -бьёшь] **1,** *pfv. of* **перебива́ть. 2,** to slaughter; massacre. **3,** to break; fracture. **4,** to break (all of something). —**переби́ться,** *refl., pfv. of* **перебива́ться.**

перебо́й *n.* interruption; irregularity: пульс с перебо́ями, irregular pulse.

переболе́ть[1] *v. pfv.* [*infl.* -ле́ю, -ле́ешь] (*with instr.*) **1,** to have had (a certain illness). **2,** (*of many people*) to come down with (a certain illness).

переболе́ть[2] *v. pfv.* [*infl.* -ли́т] *fig.* (*of one's heart*) to ache: се́рдце переболе́ло (*or* душа́ переболе́ла) за тебя́, my heart ached for you.

перебо́рка [*gen. pl.* -рок] *n.* **1,** sorting out. **2,** partition. **3,** *naut.* bulkhead.

перебороть *v. pfv.* [*infl.* -борю́, -бо́решь] to overcome. —**переборо́ть себя́,** to keep control of oneself.

переборщи́ть *v., pfv. of* **переба́рщивать.**

перебра́ниваться *v.r. impfv., colloq.* to exchange angry words.

перебра́нка *n., colloq.* squabble; hassle.

перебра́сывать *v. impfv.* [*pfv.* **перебро́сить**] **1,** to throw over. **2,** to throw across. **3,** to transport; transfer. —**перебра́сываться,** *refl.* **1,** to jump over. **2,** to spread. **3,** (*with instr.*) to exchange.

перебра́ть [*infl. like* брать] *v., pfv. of* **перебира́ть.** —**перебра́ться,** *refl., pfv. of* **перебира́ться.**

переброди́ть *v. pfv.* [*infl.* -брожу́, -бро́дишь] **1,** to ferment. **2,** *fig., colloq.* to mellow.

перебро́сить [*infl.* -шу, -сишь] *v., pfv. of* **перебра́сывать.** —**перебро́ситься,** *refl., pfv. of* **перебра́сываться.**

перебро́ска *n.* transfer.

перебыва́ть *v. pfv., used mainly in the past tense* **1,** to have been (in all or many places). **2,** (*with* у) to visit; go see (all or many people). **3,** (*of all or many people*) to have been (somewhere).

перева́л *n.* **1,** crossing. **2,** mountain pass.

перева́ливать *v. impfv.* [*pfv.* **перевали́ть**] **1,** to turn over on one's/its other side. **2,** to cross; traverse. **3,**

(*with* за + *acc.*) *colloq.* to exceed; (*of a person*) be past a certain age: ему́ перевали́ло за со́рок, he is past forty. —**перева́ливаться**, *refl.* **1,** to roll over. **2,** [*impfv. only*] to waddle.

перевали́ть [*infl.* -валю́, -ва́лишь] *v., pfv. of* перева́ливать. —**перевали́ться**, *refl., pfv. of* перева́ливаться.

перева́лка *n.* **1,** transfer of cargo; transshipment. **2,** transshipment point. **3,** *colloq.* waddle. —**перева́лочный**, *adj.* transfer (*attrib.*); transshipment (*attrib.*).

перева́ривать *v. impfv.* [*pfv.* перевари́ть] **1,** to recook. **2,** to overcook. **3,** to digest. **4,** *colloq.* to put up with; stomach.

перевари́ть [*infl.* -варю́, -ва́ришь] *v., pfv. of* перева́ривать.

перевезти́ [*infl. like* везти́] *v., pfv. of* перевози́ть.

переверну́ть *v., pfv. of* переверты́вать *and* перевора́чивать. —**переверну́ться**, *refl., pfv. of* переверты́ваться *and* перевора́чиваться.

переверте́ть [*infl.* -верчу́, -ве́ртишь] *v., pfv. of* переверты́вать (*in sense #5*).

переве́ртывание *n.* inversion.

переверты́вать *v. impfv.* [*pfv.* переверну́ть] **1,** to turn over; invert. **2,** *colloq.* to overturn; upset. **3,** to turn (a page). **4,** *colloq.* to change completely; transform. **5,** [*pfv.* переверте́ть] to turn too far; overwind (a watch). —**переверты́ваться**, *refl.* **1,** to turn over. **2,** to capsize.

переве́с *n.* **1,** superiority; preponderance. **2,** advantage; edge. **3,** *colloq.* excess weight.

переве́сить [*infl.* -шу, -сишь] *v., pfv. of* переве́шивать. —**переве́ситься**, *refl., pfv. of* переве́шиваться.

перевести́ [*infl. like* вести́] *v., pfv. of* переводи́ть. —**перевести́сь**, *refl., pfv. of* переводи́ться.

переве́шивать *v. impfv.* [*pfv.* переве́сить] **1,** to move by hanging elsewhere. **2,** to weigh again. **3,** *fig.* to outweigh. **4,** *v.i.* to prevail. —**переве́шиваться**, *refl.* (*with* в, на, *or* че́рез) to hang over; lean over.

перевива́ть *v. impfv.* [*pfv.* переви́ть] to interweave; intertwine.

перевира́ть *v. impfv.* [*pfv.* переврáть] *colloq.* to garble; misquote.

переви́ть [*infl. like* вить] *v., pfv. of* перевива́ть.

перево́д *n.* **1,** transfer. **2,** translation. **3,** remittance: де́нежный перево́д, money order. **4,** conversion (*to a different unit of measurement*). **5,** (*with gen.*) *colloq.* waste (of).

переводи́ть *v. impfv.* [*pfv.* перевести́; *pres.* -вожу́, -во́дишь] **1,** to lead across; take across. **2,** to transfer. **3,** to shift. **4,** to translate. **5,** to convert (to a different unit of measurement). **6,** to remit (money). **7,** *colloq.* to exterminate. **8,** *colloq.* to waste. **9,** *in* перевести́ дух *or* дыха́ние, to catch one's breath. —**переводи́ться**, *refl.* **1,** to switch; shift. **2,** *colloq.* to disappear; cease to exist. **3,** *colloq.* to be in short supply; be spent: у него́ де́ньги никогда́ не перево́дятся, he is never lacking for money.

переводно́й *adj.* **1,** of or for a money order. **2,** *in* переводна́я бума́га, carbon paper; переводна́я карти́нка, decal.

перево́дческий *adj.* of translating; of a translator.

перево́дчик *n.* translator; interpreter.

перево́з *n.* **1,** transporation. **2,** ferrying station.

перевози́ть *v. impfv.* [*pfv.* перевезти́; *pres.* -вожу́,

-во́зишь] **1,** to transport; move; convey. **2,** to take across; transport across; ferry across.

перево́зка *n.* transportation.

перево́зочный *adj., in* перево́зочные сре́дства, means of conveyance.

перево́зчик *n.* **1,** ferryman. **2,** *colloq.* mover. **3,** sandpiper.

перевооружа́ть *v. impfv.* [*pfv.* перевооружи́ть] to rearm (*supply with new arms*). —**перевооружа́ться**, *refl.* to rearm (*acquire new arms*).

перевооруже́ние *n.* rearmament.

перевооружи́ть *v., pfv. of* перевооружа́ть. —**перевооружи́ться**, *refl., pfv. of* перевооружа́ться.

перевоплоща́ть *v. impfv.* [*pfv.* перевоплоти́ть] to reincarnate.

перевоплоще́ние *n.* reincarnation.

перевора́чивать *v. impfv.* = переверты́вать. —**перевора́чиваться**, *refl.* = переверты́ваться.

переворо́т *n.* revolution; upheaval; coup. —госуда́рственный переворо́т, coup d'état.

переворо́шить *v. pfv., colloq.* **1,** to toss (hay). **2,** to mess up; disarrange. **3,** to turn over in one's mind. **4,** *fig.* to turn upside down.

перевоспита́ние *n.* re-education.

перевоспи́тывать *v. impfv.* [*pfv.* перевоспита́ть] to re-educate.

переврáть [*infl. like* врать] *v., pfv. of* перевира́ть.

перевы́боры [*gen.* -ров] *n. pl.* **1,** election. **2,** new election.

перевыполне́ние *n.* overfulfillment.

перевыполня́ть *v. impfv.* [*pfv.* перевы́полнить] to exceed; overfulfill.

перевяза́ть [*infl.* -вяжу́, -вя́жешь] *v., pfv. of* перевя́зывать. —**перевяза́ться**, *refl., pfv. of* перевя́зываться.

перевя́зка *n.* **1,** tying up. **2,** bandaging; dressing. **3,** *colloq.* bandage.

перевя́зочный *adj.* for the dressing of wounds: перевя́зочный пункт, place where wounds are dressed.

перевя́зывать *v. impfv.* [*pfv.* перевяза́ть] **1,** to tie; tie up. **2,** to bandage. **3,** to retie. **4,** to rebandage. **5,** to knit again. —**перевя́зываться**, *refl.* to bandage oneself.

пе́ревязь *n.f.* **1,** *mil.* shoulder belt. **2,** *med.* sling.

переги́б *n.* **1,** bend. **2,** *fig.* excess; extreme.

перегиба́ть *v. impfv.* [*pfv.* перегну́ть] **1,** to bend. **2,** *in* перегну́ть па́лку, to go too far; go overboard. —**перегиба́ться**, *refl.* to bend over; lean over.

перегласо́вка *n., phonet.* mutation.

перегля́дываться *v.r. impfv.* [*pfv.* перегляну́ться] to exchange glances.

перегляну́ться [*infl.* -гляну́сь, -гля́нешься] *v.r., pfv. of* перегля́дываться.

перегна́ть [*infl. like* гнать] *v., pfv. of* перегоня́ть.

перегнива́ть *v. impfv.* [*pfv.* перегни́ть] to rot through.

перегни́ть [*infl. like* гнить] *v., pfv. of* перегнива́ть.

перегно́й *n.* humus.

перегну́ть *v., pfv. of* перегиба́ть. —**перегну́ться**, *refl., pfv. of* перегиба́ться.

перегова́риваться *v.r. impfv.* **1,** to be engaged in conversation. **2,** (*with* с + *instr.*) to converse (with).

переговори́ть *v. pfv.* **1,** to talk; have a talk. **2,** *colloq.* to outtalk; talk down.

переговóры [*gen.* -ров] *n. pl.* **1,** negotiations. **2,** talks.

перего́н *n.* **1,** driving (*of cattle*). **2,** space between two stations. **3,** stage; leg (*of a journey*).

перего́нка *n.* distillation.

перего́нный *adj.* of or for distilling. —**перего́нный заво́д**, distillery. —**перего́нный куб**, still.

перегоня́ть *v. impfv.* [*pfv.* **перегна́ть**] **1,** to outdistance; outrun. **2,** *fig.* to outstrip; surpass; leave behind. **3,** to drive (to another place). **4,** *colloq.* to move; ship; transport. **5,** to distill.

перегора́живать *v. impfv.* [*pfv.* **перегороди́ть**] to partition (off).

перегора́ть *v. impfv.* [*pfv.* **перегоре́ть**] **1,** (*of a bulb, fuse, etc.*) to burn out. **2,** to be burned down to nothing. **3,** (*of a fire*) to burn itself out. **4,** *fig.* (*of emotions*) to die down.

перегороди́ть [*infl.* -рожу́, -ро́дишь *or* -роди́шь] *v., pfv. of* **перегора́живать**.

перегоро́дка [*gen. pl.* -док] *n.* **1,** partition. **2,** *fig.* barrier.

перегре́в *n.* overheating. *Also,* **перегрева́ние**.

перегрева́ть *v. impfv.* [*pfv.* **перегре́ть**] to overheat. —**перегрева́ться**, *refl.* **1,** to overheat; become overheated. **2,** to get too much sun.

перегружа́ть *v. impfv.* [*pfv.* **перегрузи́ть**] **1,** to load from one place to another. **2,** to overload; overburden. —**перегружа́ться**, *refl.* to be overloaded.

перегрузи́ть [*infl.* -гружу́, -гру́зишь *or* -грузи́шь] *v., pfv. of* **перегружа́ть**. —**перегрузи́ться**, *refl., pfv. of* **перегружа́ться**.

перегру́зка *n.* **1,** transfer of cargo; transshipment. **2,** overloading. —**перегру́зочный**, *adj.* transfer (*attrib.*); transshipment (*attrib.*).

перегруппирова́ть [*infl.* -ру́ю, -ру́ешь] *v., pfv. of* **перегруппиро́вывать**. —**перегруппирова́ться**, *refl., pfv. of* **перегруппиро́вываться**.

перегруппиро́вка *n.* regrouping.

перегруппиро́вывать *v. impfv.* [*pfv.* **перегруппирова́ть**] to regroup. —**перегруппиро́вываться**, *refl.* to regroup.

перегрыза́ть *v. impfv.* [*pfv.* **перегры́зть**] to gnaw through. —**перегрыза́ться**, *refl., colloq.* **1,** (*of animals*) to fight; scrap. **2,** *fig.* (*of people*) to squabble.

перегры́зть [*infl. like* **грызть**] *v., pfv. of* **перегрыза́ть**. —**перегры́зться**, *refl., pfv. of* **перегрыза́ться**.

пе́ред *prep., with instr.* **1,** in front of; before: сиде́ть пе́ред зе́ркалом, to sit in front of the mirror; предста́ть пе́ред судо́м, to appear before the court. **2,** before (*in time*): пе́ред обе́дом, before dinner. **3,** compared to: э́то ничто́ пе́ред..., that's nothing compared to... —**пе́ред тем, как**, before: пе́ред тем, как вы́йти и́з дому, before leaving the house; пе́ред тем, как он вы́шел и́з дому, before he left the house.

перёд [*gen.* пе́реда; *pl.* переда́] *n.* front.

передава́ть *v. impfv.* [*pfv.* **переда́ть**; *pres.* -даю́, -даёшь] **1,** to hand over; (*at the table*) to pass. **2,** to transmit; convey. Переда́йте ему́ (от меня́) приве́т, give him my regards. Переда́йте ей, что..., tell her that... **3,** to refer; turn over (a matter). **4,** to turn over; transfer (property). **5,** to transmit: передава́ть по ра́дио, to broadcast; передава́ть по телеви́дению, to televise. **6,** *colloq.* to overpay.

переда́точный *adj.* transmission (*attrib.*); gear (*attrib.*): переда́точный реме́нь, transmission belt; переда́точное число́, gear ratio.

переда́тчик *n.* **1,** transmitter. **2,** messenger.

переда́ть [*infl. like* **дать**; *past* пе́редал, -дала́, пе́редало] *v., pfv. of* **передава́ть**.

переда́ча *n.* **1,** transmission. **2,** transfer. **3,** broadcast. **4,** *mech.* transmission; gear; drive. **5,** parcel (*for a hospital patient, prisoner, etc.*). **6,** *sports* pass.

передвига́ть *v. impfv.* [*pfv.* **передви́нуть**] to move; shift (*from one place to another*). —**передвига́ться**, *refl.* **1,** to move. **2,** [*impfv. only*] to move about; walk.

передвиже́ние *n.* **1,** movement; transportation. **2,** movement; locomotion. —**сре́дства передвиже́ния**, means of conveyance.

передви́жка *n., colloq.* movement. —**библиоте́ка-передви́жка**, mobile library; bookmobile.

передвижно́й *adj.* **1,** movable. **2,** traveling; mobile.

передви́нуть *v., pfv. of* **передвига́ть**. —**передви́нуться**, *refl., pfv. of* **передвига́ться**.

переде́л *n.* redistribution.

переде́лать *v. pfv.* **1,** *pfv. of* **переде́лывать**. **2,** *colloq.* to do (all or everything).

переде́ли́ть [*infl.* -делю́, -де́лишь] *v., pfv. of* **переде́ля́ть**.

переде́лка *n.* **1,** alteration; doing over. **2,** adaptation (*of a book, play, etc.*). **3,** fix; mess; jam: попа́сть в переде́лку, to get into a mess.

переде́лывать *v. impfv.* [*pfv.* **переде́лать**] **1,** to alter (a garment). **2,** to redo; do over. **3,** to remake; make into something else.

переделя́ть *v. impfv.* [*pfv.* **передели́ть**] to redistribute.

передёргивать *v. impfv.* [*pfv.* **передёрнуть**] **1,** to pull; tug on; jerk. **2,** *impers.* to wince: его́ передёрнуло от э́тих слов, he winced on hearing those words. **3,** *colloq.* to cheat (at cards); juggle (facts).

передержа́ть [*infl.* -держу́, -де́ржишь] *v., pfv. of* **передёрживать**.

передёрживать *v. impfv.* [*pfv.* **передержа́ть**] **1,** to keep in too long. **2,** *photog.* to overexpose. **3,** to retake (an examination).

переде́ржка *n.* **1,** *photog.* overexposure. **2,** *colloq.* misstatement; distortion of the facts.

передёрнуть *v., pfv. of* **передёргивать**.

пере́дний *adj.* front. —**пере́дний план**, foreground.

пере́дник *n.* apron.

пере́дняя *n., decl. as an adj.* vestibule; hall.

передо *prep.* = **пе́ред** (*used mainly in the combination* **передо мной**).

передова́я *n., decl. as an adj.* **1,** lead article. **2,** *mil.* front line.

передоверя́ть *v. impfv.* [*pfv.* **передове́рить**] to transfer (legal title, power of attorney, etc.).

передови́к [*gen.* -вика́] *n.* outstanding worker.

передови́ца *n., colloq.* = **передова́я статья́**.

передово́й *adj.* **1,** forward. Передово́й отря́д, advance guard. **2,** advanced; progressive. —**передова́я статья́**, lead article.

передо́к [*gen.* -дка́] *n.* **1,** front (*of a vehicle*). **2,** vamp (*of a shoe*).

передо́хнуть *v. pfv.* [*past* -до́х, -ла] *colloq.* (*of many animals*) to die.

передохну́ть *v. pfv.* **1,** to take a breath. **2,** *colloq.* to pause for breath; take a short rest.

передра́знивать *v. impfv.* [*pfv.* **передразни́ть**] to mimic; imitate.

передразни́ть [*infl.* -дразню́, -дра́знишь] *v., pfv. of* **передра́знивать**.

передра́ться *v.r. pfv.* [*infl. like* **драть**] (*of many people*) to fight; scrap.

передря́га *n., colloq.* scrape; row: попа́сть в передря́гу, to get into a scrape.

переду́мывать *v. impfv.* [*pfv.* **переду́мать**] **1**, to change one's mind. **2**, (*with acc. or* **о**) *colloq.* to think over carefully.

переды́шка [*gen. pl.* **-шек**] *n.* breathing space; respite.

перееда́ть *v. impfv.* [*pfv.* **перее́сть**] **1**, to overeat. **2**, to corrode; eat away.

перее́зд *n.* **1**, (act of) crossing. **2**, crossing (*place to cross*). **3**, move; moving (*to another residence*).

переезжа́ть *v. impfv.* [*pfv.* **перее́хать**] **1**, to cross. **2**, to move (to another residence). **3**, *colloq.* to run over.

перее́сть [*infl. like* **есть**] *v., pfv. of* **перееда́ть**.

перее́хать [*infl. like* **е́хать**] *v., pfv. of* **переезжа́ть**.

пережа́ривать *v. impfv.* [*pfv.* **пережа́рить**] to overcook; overdo.

пережда́ть [*infl. like* **ждать**] *v., pfv. of* **пережида́ть**.

пережева́ть [*infl.* **-жую́, -жуёшь**] *v., pfv. of* **пережёвывать**.

пережёвывать *v. impfv.* [*pfv.* **пережева́ть**] **1**, to chew. **2**, [*impfv. only*] *fig.* to keep repeating.

пережени́ть *v. pfv.* [*infl.* **-женю́, -же́нишь**] *colloq.* to marry off (many or all one's sons). —**пережени́ться**, *refl.* (*of many men*) to get married.

переже́чь *v. pfv.* [*infl. like* **жечь**] **1**, *pfv. of* **пережига́ть**. **2**, to burn (all or much of something).

пережива́ние *n., usu. pl.* **1**, (emotional) experiences. **2**, sufferings; tribulations.

пережива́ть *v. impfv.* [*pfv.* **пережи́ть**] **1**, to go through; experience. **2**, to survive. **3**, to outlive. **4**, *v.i.* [*impfv. only*] *colloq.* to be upset.

пережига́ть *v. impfv.* [*pfv.* **переже́чь**] **1**, to heat to excess. **2**, to burn out (a bulb, fuse, etc.). **3**, *colloq.* to burn too much (fuel, electricity, etc.).

пережида́ть *v. impfv.* [*pfv.* **пережда́ть**] to wait out; wait until (something) is over.

пережито́е *n., decl. as an adj.* past experiences; what one has experienced or gone through.

пережи́ток [*gen.* **-тка**] *n.* vestige; remnant; survival.

пережи́ть [*infl. like* **жить**; *past* **пе́режил** *or* **пережи́л, -жила́, пе́режило** *or* **пережи́ло**] *v., pfv. of* **пережива́ть**.

перезабы́ть *v. pfv.* [*infl.* **-бу́ду, -бу́дешь**] *colloq.* to forget (much or everything).

перезаключа́ть *v. impfv.* [*pfv.* **перезаключи́ть**] renew (a contract).

перезаряди́ть [*infl.* **-ряжу́, -ря́дишь** *or* **-ряди́шь**] *v., pfv. of* **перезаряжа́ть**.

перезаряжа́ть *v. impfv.* [*pfv.* **перезаряди́ть**] **1**, to recharge. **2**, to overcharge. **3**, to reload.

перезво́н *n.* ringing of bells.

перезимова́ть *v. pfv.* [*infl.* **-му́ю, -му́ешь**] to winter; spend the winter.

перезрева́ть *v. impfv.* [*pfv.* **перезре́ть**] to become overripe.

перезре́лый *adj.* overripe.

перезре́ть *v. pfv., pfv. of* **перезрева́ть**.

переигра́ть *v. pfv.* **1**, *pfv. of* **переи́грывать**. **2**, to play; perform (all or many of something).

переи́грывать *v. impfv.* [*pfv.* **переигра́ть**] **1**, to replay. **2**, *colloq.* to outplay. **3**, *theat., colloq.* to overplay (a part); overact.

переизбира́ть *v. impfv.* [*pfv.* **переизбра́ть**] to re-elect.

переизбра́ние *n.* re-election.

переизбра́ть [*infl. like* **брать**] *v., pfv. of* **переизбира́ть**.

переиздава́ть *v. impfv.* [*pfv.* **переизда́ть**; *pres.* **-даю́, -даёшь**] to republish; reissue.

переизда́ние *n.* **1**, republication. **2**, new edition.

переизда́ть [*infl. like* **дать**] *v., pfv. of* **переиздава́ть**.

переименова́ть *v. pfv.* [*infl.* **-ну́ю, -ну́ешь**] to rename.

перейм́чивый *adj., colloq.* imitative.

переина́чивать *v. impfv.* [*pfv.* **переина́чить**] *colloq.* to modify; alter.

перейти́ [*infl.* **перейду́, перейдёшь**; *past* **перешёл, перешла́**] *v., pfv. of* **переходи́ть**.

перека́лывать *v. impfv.* [*pfv.* **переколо́ть**] to pin (somewhere else). *See also* **переколо́ть**.

перека́пывать *v. impfv.* [*pfv.* **перекопа́ть**] **1**, to dig (all of something). **2**, to dig again. **3**, to dig across.

перека́рмливать *v. impfv.* [*pfv.* **перекорми́ть**] to overfeed.

перека́т *n.* **1**, *usu. pl.* sharp sound; crack (*of shots being fired*); clap (*of thunder*). **2**, sandbank; shoal.

перекати́-по́ле *n.* tumbleweed.

перекати́ть [*infl.* **-качу́, -ка́тишь**] *v., pfv. of* **перека́тывать**. —**перекати́ться**, *refl., pfv. of* **перека́тываться**.

перека́тывать *v. impfv.* [*pfv.* **перекати́ть**] to roll (from one place to another). —**перека́тываться**, *refl.* to roll (over, across, etc.).

перека́шивать *v. impfv.* [*pfv.* **перекоси́ть**] *usu. impers.* to distort; warp; twist: (лицо́) его́ перекоси́ло, his face became distorted. —**перека́шиваться**, *refl.* to become distorted; become warped.

переквалифика́ция *n.* retraining.

переквалифици́ровать *v. impfv. & pfv.* [*pres.* **-рую, -руешь**] to retrain. —**переквалифици́роваться**, *refl.* to be retrained; learn a new trade.

переки́дывать *v. impfv.* [*pfv.* **переки́нуть**] = **переки́нуть** = **перебра́сывать**. —**переки́дываться**, *refl.* = **перебра́сываться**.

перекипа́ть *v. impfv.* [*pfv.* **перекипе́ть**] **1**, to boil too long. **2**, *fig., colloq.* to calm down.

пе́рекись *n.f.* peroxide: пе́рекись водоро́да, hydrogen peroxide.

перекла́дина *n.* **1**, crossbeam; crossbar; transom. **2**, *sports* horizontal bar.

перекла́дывать *v. impfv.* [*pfv.* **переложи́ть**] **1**, to move (from one place to another). **2**, *fig.* to shift (a job, responsibility, etc.). **3**, (*with instr.*) to pack (with); interlay (with). **4**, to pile up again. **5**, *music; lit.* to rearrange; (*with* **в** *or* **на** + *acc.*) set (to music); put (into verse). **6**, *colloq.* to put too much (salt, sugar, etc.).

перекле́ивать *v. impfv.* [*pfv.* **перекле́ить**] **1**, to glue again; paste again. **2**, to glue; paste (somewhere else).

переклика́ть *v. impfv., colloq.* to call the roll. —**перекликаться**, *refl.* **1**, to call; shout (to one another). **2**, (*with* **с** + *instr.*) *fig.* to have certain things in common (with).

перекли́чка *n.* roll call: де́лать перекли́чку, to call the roll.

переключа́тель *n.m.* switch: переключа́тель све́та, light switch.

переключа́ть v. impfv. [pfv. **переключи́ть**] to switch; shift. —**переключа́ться**, refl. (with на + acc.) to switch (to); shift (to).

переключе́ние n. switch; switching over; change-over.

переключи́ть v., pfv. of **переключа́ть**. —**переключи́ться**, refl., pfv. of **переключа́ться**.

перекова́ть [infl. -кую́, -куёшь] v., pfv. of **перекó́вывать**.

перекó́вывать v. impfv. [pfv. **перекова́ть**] 1, to re-forge. 2, fig. to remold. 3, to make a new shoe for (a horse).

переколо́ть v. pfv. [infl. -колю́, -ко́лешь] 1, pfv. of **перека́лывать**. 2, to prick in many places. 3, to slaughter; massacre. 4, to chop (all or much of something).

переконструи́ровать v. impfv. & pfv. [pres. -рую, руешь] to redesign.

перекопа́ть v., pfv. of **перека́пывать**.

перекорми́ть [infl. -кормлю́, -ко́рмишь] v., pfv. of **перека́рмливать**.

перекó́ры [gen. -ров] n.pl., colloq. squabble.

перекоси́ть [infl. -кошу́, -коси́шь] v., pfv. of **перека́шивать**. —**перекоси́ться**, refl., pfv. of **перека́шиваться**.

перекочева́ть [infl. -чую, -чуешь] v., pfv. of **перекочёвывать**.

перекочёвывать v. impfv. [pfv. **перекочева́ть**] to wander; migrate (from one place to another).

перекó́шенный adj. 1, twisted out of shape. 2, (of one's face) twisted; contorted.

перекра́ивать v. impfv. [pfv. **перекрои́ть**] 1, to cut again. 2, to refashion; revamp. 3, in **перекра́ивать ка́рту ми́ра**, to recarve the map of the world.

перекра́сить v. pfv. [infl. -шу, -сишь] 1, pfv. of **перекра́шивать**. 2, to paint (all or many things). —**перекра́ситься**, refl., pfv. of **перекра́шиваться**.

перекра́шивать v. impfv. [pfv. **перекра́сить**] to paint (something) a different color; repaint. —**перекра́шиваться**, refl. 1, to change color. 2, fig., colloq. to hide one's true colors.

перекрести́ть [infl. -крещу́, -кре́стишь] v., pfv. of **крести́ть** (in sense #3) and **перекре́щивать**. —**перекрести́ться**, refl., pfv. of **крести́ться** (in sense #2) and **перекре́щиваться**.

перекрё́стный adj. cross. —**перекрё́стный допро́с**, cross-examination. —**перекрё́стный ого́нь**, crossfire. —**перекрё́стная ссы́лка**, cross-reference.

перекрё́сток [gen. -стка] n. intersection; crossing. —**крича́ть на всех перекрё́стках**, to shout from the rooftops.

перекре́щивать v. impfv. [pfv. **перекрести́ть**] 1, to make the sign of the cross over. 2, colloq. to rename; rechristen. 3, colloq. to lie across; crisscross. —**перекре́щиваться**, refl. to intersect; crisscross.

перекрича́ть v. pfv. [infl. -чу́, -чи́шь] to shout down.

перекрои́ть v., pfv. of **перекра́ивать**.

перекрути́ть [infl. -кручу́, -кру́тишь] v., pfv. of **перекру́чивать**.

перекру́чивать v. impfv. [pfv. **перекрути́ть**] colloq. 1, to twist. 2, to twist too far; turn too far.

перекрыва́ть v. impfv. [pfv. **перекры́ть**] 1, to cover again; re-cover. 2, colloq. to exceed. 3, to block; bar. 4, to dam (a river).

перекры́ть [infl. -кро́ю, -кро́ешь] v., pfv. of **перекрыва́ть**.

перекувырну́ть v. pfv., colloq. to upset; overturn. —**перекувырну́ться**, refl., colloq. 1, to tip over; topple over. 2, to turn a somersault (in the air).

перекупа́ть[1] v. impfv. [pfv. **перекупи́ть**] colloq. 1, to buy by outbidding someone else. 2, to buy back.

перекупа́ть[2] v. pfv., colloq. 1, to bathe too long. 2, to bathe (all or many people). —**перекупа́ться**, refl., colloq. to bathe too long; stay in the water too long.

перекупи́ть [infl. -куплю́, -ку́пишь] v., pfv. of **перекупа́ть**[1].

переку́пщик n. one who buys for resale; dealer.

переку́р n., colloq. smoke break.

перекуси́ть v. pfv. [infl. -кушу́, -ку́сишь] 1, to bite in half. 2, to bite through. 3, colloq. to have a bite to eat.

перела́мывать v. impfv. [pfv. **переломи́ть**] 1, to break in two; fracture. 2, to alter; transform. 3, colloq. to overcome; conquer (a feeling). —**перела́мываться**, refl. to be broken in two; be fractured.

перелеза́ть v. impfv. [pfv. **переле́зть**] to climb over.

переле́зть [infl. like **лезть**] v., pfv. of **перелеза́ть**.

переле́ска n. hepatica.

переле́сок [gen. -ска] n. coppice; copse.

перелё́т n. 1, (long) flight. 2, migration (of birds). 3, overshooting (of a target).

перелета́ть v. impfv. [pfv. **перелете́ть**] 1, to fly over; fly across. 2, to fly (from one place to another).

перелете́ть [infl. -чу́, -ти́шь] v., pfv. of **перелета́ть**.

перелё́тный adj. (of a bird) migratory.

переле́чь v. pfv. [infl. like **лечь**] to lie down (somewhere else).

перели́в n. 1, flowing. 2, usu. pl. play (of colors). 3, usu. pl. modulation.

перелива́ние n. 1, pouring (from one container to another). 2, transfusion: **перелива́ние крóви**, blood transfusion.

перелива́ть v. impfv. [pfv. **перели́ть**] 1, to pour (from one vessel to another). 2, in **перелива́ть кровь** (+ dat.), to give a blood transfusion (to). 3, to recast. 4, [impfv. only] to gleam; glisten. —**перелива́ться**, refl. 1, to flow (from one place to another). 2, to overflow. 3, [impfv. only] to gleam; glisten. 4, [impfv. only] (of sounds) to modulate.

перели́вчатый adj. 1, (of colors) iridescent. 2, (of a voice) lilting.

перели́стывать v. impfv. [pfv. **перелиста́ть**] to leaf through.

перели́ть [infl. like **лить**] v., pfv. of **перелива́ть**. —**перели́ться**, refl., pfv. of **перелива́ться**.

перелицева́ть [infl. -цу́ю, -цу́ешь] v., pfv. of **перелицо́вывать**.

перелицо́вывать v. impfv. [pfv. **перелицева́ть**] 1, to alter by turning inside out. 2, fig., colloq. to give a new face to.

перелови́ть v. pfv. [infl. -ловлю́, -ло́вишь] to catch (all or many of something).

переложе́ние n. 1, (with в or на + acc.) setting (to); turning into (verse, music, etc.). 2, music arrangement; transposition.

переложи́ть [infl. -ложу́, -ло́жишь] v., pfv. of **перекла́дывать**.

перелó́м n. 1, break; fracture. 2, fig. critical period; turning point. 3, fig. sudden change.

переломá́ть v. pfv. to break (all or many things). —**переломá́ться**, refl. (of many things) to be broken.

переломи́ть [*infl.* -ломлю́, -ло́мишь] *v., pfv. of* перела́мывать. —переломи́ться, *refl., pfv. of* перела́мываться.

переломо́мный *adj.* critical; crucial.

перема́зать *v. pfv.* [*infl.* -ма́жу, -ма́жешь] *colloq.* to smear; make dirty. —перема́заться, *refl., colloq.* to get all dirty.

перема́нивать *v. impfv.* [*pfv.* перемани́ть] to entice; win over.

перемани́ть [*infl.* -маню́, -ма́нишь] *v., pfv. of* перема́нивать.

перема́тывать *v. impfv.* [*pfv.* перемота́ть] 1, to wind (onto something else). 2, to rewind.

перема́хивать *v. impfv.* [*pfv.* перемахну́ть] *colloq.* to jump over.

перемежа́ть *v. impfv.* 1, to alternate: перемежа́ть рабо́ту (с) о́тдыхом, to alternate work and rest. 2, to intersperse: перемежа́ть расска́з анекдо́тами, to intersperse a story with anecdotes. —перемежа́ться, *refl.* to alternate.

перемежа́ющийся *adj.* intermittent.

переме́на *n.* 1, change. 2, recess; break (*between classes*).

перемени́ть *v. pfv.* [*infl.* -меню́, -ме́нишь] to change. —перемени́ться, *refl.*, to change. 2, (with к) to change one's attitude (toward); act differently (toward). 3, (*with instr.*) to change; exchange; trade.

переме́нный *adj.* variable. —переме́нная величина́, *math.* variable. —переме́нный ток, alternating current. —с переме́нным успе́хом, with varying (degrees of) success.

переме́нчивый *adj., colloq.* changeable.

перемерза́ть *v. impfv.* [*pfv.* перемёрзнуть] 1, to freeze up; freeze solid. 2, *colloq.* to freeze; be frozen.

перемёрзнуть *v. pfv.* [*past* -мёрз, -ла] 1, *pfv. of* перемерза́ть. 2, (*of all of something, usu. plants*) to perish from the frost.

переме́ривать *v. impfv.* [*pfv.* переме́рить] 1, to remeasure. 2, to try on again.

переме́рить *v. pfv.* 1, *pfv. of* переме́ривать. 2, to measure (all or many things). 3, to try on (all or many things).

перемести́ть [*infl.* -щу́, -сти́шь] *v., pfv. of* переме-ща́ть. —перемести́ться, *refl., pfv. of* переме-ща́ться.

переме́тить *v. pfv.* [*infl.* -чу, -тишь] 1, *pfv. of* переме-ча́ть. 2, to mark (all or many of something).

переметну́ться *v.r. pfv., colloq.* 1, to jump across; dart across. 2, to defect (to the enemy).

переме́тный *adj., in* переме́тная сума́, saddlebag.

перемеча́ть *v. impfv.* [*pfv.* переме́тить] to mark again.

переме́шивать *v. impfv.* [*pfv.* перемеша́ть] 1, to mix. 2, to stir. 3, to mix up; disarrange. 4, *colloq.* to mix up; confuse. —переме́шиваться, *refl.* 1, (with с + *instr.*) to mix (with); blend (with). 2, to get mixed up.

перемеща́ть *v. impfv.* [*pfv.* перемести́ть] to move; shift; transfer. —перемеща́ться, *refl.* to move.

перемеще́ние *n.* 1, shift; movement. 2, displacement. 3, transfer.

перемещённый *adj., in* перемещённые ли́ца, displaced persons.

переми́гиваться *v.r. impfv.* [*pfv.* перемигну́ться] to wink to each other.

перемина́ться *v.r. impfv., colloq.* (*often with* с ноги́ на́ ногу) to shift from foot to foot (*in anxiety*).

переми́рие *n.* truce; armistice.

перемога́ть *v. impfv., colloq.* to fight off (drowsiness, an illness, etc.). —перемога́ться, *refl., colloq.* to try to fight off an illness.

перемо́лвить *v. pfv.* [*infl.* -влю, -вишь] *colloq., in* перемо́лвить сло́во с (+ *instr.*), to have a word with.

перемота́ть *v., pfv. of* перема́тывать.

перемыва́ть *v. impfv.* [*pfv.* перемы́ть] to wash again. —перемыва́ть ко́сточки (+ *dat.*), to say malicious things about.

перемы́ть *v. pfv.* [*infl.* -мо́ю, -мо́ешь] 1, *pfv. of* перемыва́ть. 2, to wash (all or many of something).

перемы́чка [*gen. pl.* -чек] *n.* 1, crosspiece. 2, lintel. 3, bulkhead.

перенапряга́ть *v. impfv.* [*pfv.* перенапря́чь] to overexert.

перенапряже́ние *n.* overexertion.

перенапря́чь [*infl. like* напря́чь] *v., pfv. of* перенапряга́ть.

перенаселе́ние *n.* overpopulation.

перенаселённый *adj.* overpopulated. —перенаселённость, *n.f.* overpopulation.

перенаселя́ть *v. impfv.* [*pfv.* перенасели́ть] to overpopulate.

перенесе́ние *n.* 1, moving; shifting; transferring. 2, postponement; putting off. 3, enduring.

перенести́ [*infl. like* нести́] *v., pfv. of* переноси́ть. —перенести́сь, *refl., pfv. of* переноси́ться.

перенима́ть *v. impfv.* [*pfv.* переня́ть] *colloq.* to adopt; copy; imitate.

перено́с *n.* 1, moving; shifting; transferring. 2, *in* перено́с сло́ва, dividing a word at the end of a line; word division. 3, hyphen (*at the end of a line*).

переноси́ть *v. impfv.* [*pfv.* перенести́; *pres.* -ношу́, -но́сишь] 1, to carry across; carry somewhere else. 2, to move; shift; transfer. 3, to postpone; put off. 4, to endure; bear; stand: переноси́ть жару́, to endure the heat. Я не переношу́ его́, I can't stand him. 5, to come through (an illness, operation, etc.). 6, *in* переноси́ть сло́во, to carry over part of a word to the next line. —переноси́ться, *refl.* 1, *colloq.* to dash from one place to another; (*with* через) dash across. 2, (*of thoughts, attention, etc.*) to shift. 3, to shift one's thoughts; turn one's thoughts.

перено́сица *n.* bridge of the nose.

перено́сный *adj.* 1, portable. 2, figurative: в перено́сном смы́сле, in the figurative sense.

перено́счик *n.* 1, carrier. 2, carrier (*of a disease*). 3, *obs.* spreader of gossip.

переночева́ть *v. pfv.* [*infl.* -чу́ю, -чу́ешь] to spend the night.

перенумерова́ть *v.pfv.* [*infl.* -ру́ю, -ру́ешь] 1, to renumber. 2, to number (all or many of something).

переня́ть [*infl.* перейму́, переймёшь; *past* пе́ренял, -няла́, пе́реняло] *v., pfv. of* перенима́ть.

переобору́дование *n.* re-equipping.

переобору́довать *v. impfv. & pfv.* [*pres.* -дую, -дуешь] to re-equip.

переобременя́ть *v. impfv.* [*pfv.* переобремени́ть] to overburden.

переобува́ть *v. impfv.* [*pfv.* переобу́ть] to change someone's shoes: переобу́ть ребёнка, to change a child's shoes. Переобу́ть боти́нки, to change (one's) shoes. —**переобува́ться**, *refl.* **1**, to change (one's) shoes. **2**, (with в + *acc.*) to change into (different shoes). **3**, to put one's shoes back on.

переобу́ть [*infl.* -бу́ю, -бу́ешь] *v., pfv. of* **переобува́ть**. —**переобу́ться**, *refl., pfv. of* **переобува́ться**.

переодева́ть *v. impfv.* [*pfv.* **переоде́ть**] **1**, to change (someone's) clothes. **2**, *colloq.* to change (an article of clothing). **3**, (*with instr. or* в + *acc.*) to dress (as); disguise (as). —**переодева́ться**, *refl.* **1**, to change clothes. **2**, (*with* в + *acc.*) to change (into). **3**, (*with instr. or* в + *acc.*) to dress up (as); disguise oneself (as).

переоде́ть [*infl.* -де́ну, -де́нешь] *v., pfv. of* **переодева́ть**. —**переоде́ться**, *refl., pfv. of* **переодева́ться**.

переоце́нивать *v. impfv.* [*pfv.* **переоцени́ть**] **1**, to reappraise; reassess. **2**, to overestimate; overrate.

переоцени́ть [*infl.* -ценю́, -це́нишь] *v., pfv. of* **переоце́нивать**.

переоце́нка *n.* **1**, reappraisal; reassessment. **2**, overestimation.

перепада́ть *v. impfv.* [*pfv.* **перепа́сть**] **1**, (*of rain, snow, etc.*) to fall intermittently. **2**, (*with dat.*) *colloq.* to come one's way.

перепа́ивать *v. impfv.* [*pfv.* **перепои́ть**] **1**, to give (an animal) too much to drink. **2**, *colloq.* to make (a person) drunk.

перепа́лка [*gen. pl.* -лок] *n., colloq.* **1**, exchange of gunfire. **2**, squabble; wrangle.

перепа́сть [*infl. like* пасть] *v., pfv. of* **перепада́ть**.

перепа́чкать *v. impfv.* to get (something) all dirty. —**перепа́чкаться**, *refl.* to get all dirty.

перепе́в *n.* **1**, hum. **2**, *fig.* repetition; rehash.

пе́репел [*pl.* перепела́] *n.* quail.

перепелена́ть *v. pfv.* to change (a baby).

перепёлка [*gen. pl.* -лок] *n.* female quail.

перепеля́тник *n.* sparrow hawk.

перепе́рчивать *v. impfv.* [*pfv.* **перепе́рчить**] to put too much pepper in.

перепеча́тать *v., pfv. of* **перепеча́тывать**.

перепеча́тка [*gen. pl.* -ток] *n.* **1**, (act of) reprinting. **2**, reprint.

перепеча́тывать *v. impfv.* [*pfv.* **перепеча́тать**] **1**, to reprint. **2**, to retype.

перепива́ть *v. impfv.* [*pfv.* **перепи́ть**] *colloq.* **1**, to have too much to drink. **2**, to outdrink. —**перепива́ться**, *refl., colloq.* to get completely drunk.

перепи́ливать *v. impfv.* [*pfv.* **перепили́ть**] to saw in two.

перепили́ть *v. pfv.* [*infl.* -пилю́, -пи́лишь] **1**, *pfv. of* **перепи́ливать**. **2**, to saw (all of something).

переписа́ть [*infl.* -пишу́, -пи́шешь] *v., pfv. of* **перепи́сывать**.

перепи́ска *n.* **1**, copying. **2**, correspondence. Быть в перепи́ске с, to correspond with.

перепи́счик *n.* copier; copyist.

перепи́сывать *v. impfv.* [*pfv.* **переписа́ть**] **1**, to rewrite. **2**, to copy over. **3**, to make a list of. —**перепи́сываться**, *refl.* [*impfv. only*] to correspond (*by mail*).

пе́репись *n.f.* census.

перепи́ть [*infl. like* пить] *v., pfv. of* **перепива́ть**. —**перепи́ться**, *refl., pfv. of* **перепива́ться**.

переплавля́ть *v. impfv.* [*pfv.* **перепла́вить**] **1**, (*with* в *or* на + *acc.*) to melt down (into something else). **2**, to float; transport by floating downstream.

перепла́та *n., colloq.* overpayment.

переплати́ть [*infl.* -плачу́, -пла́тишь] *v., pfv. of* **перепла́чивать**.

перепла́чивать *v. impfv.* [*pfv.* **переплати́ть**] to overpay.

переплести́ [*infl. like* плести́] *v., pfv. of* **переплета́ть**. —**переплести́сь**, *refl., pfv. of* **переплета́ться**.

переплёт *n.* **1**, cover; binding (*of a book*). **2**, sash: око́нный переплёт, window sash. **3**, *colloq.* fix; mess; jam: попа́сть в переплёт, to get into a mess.

переплета́ть *v. impfv.* [*pfv.* **переплести́**] **1**, to bind (a book). **2**, to interlace; interweave; intertwine. **3**, to lock together; interlock (one's fingers, arms, etc.). **4**, to braid again. —**переплета́ться**, *refl.* **1**, to become intertwined. **2**, *fig.* to be intertwined; be interwoven.

переплете́ние *n.* **1**, interlacing; interweaving. **2**, *textiles* weave; texture.

переплётная *n., decl. as an adj.* bindery.

переплётный *adj.* bookbinding (*attrib.*). —**переплётное де́ло**, bookbinding.

переплётчик *n.* bookbinder.

переплыва́ть *v. impfv.* [*pfv.* **переплы́ть**] **1**, to swim across. **2**, to sail across.

переплы́ть [*infl. like* плыть] *v., pfv. of* **переплыва́ть**.

переподгота́вливать *v. impfv.* [*pfv.* **переподгото́вить**] to provide with additional training; give (someone) a refresher course.

переподгото́вка *n.* additional training; refresher course.

перепои́ть *v. pfv.* [*infl.* -пою́, -по́ишь *or* -пои́шь] **1**, *pfv. of* **перепа́ивать**. **2**, to give (everyone or many people) something to drink.

переполза́ть *v. impfv.* [*pfv.* **переползти́**] to crawl across; creep across.

переползти́ [*infl. like* ползти́] *v., pfv. of* **переполза́ть**.

переполне́ние *n.* **1**, overfilling. **2**, overcrowding.

перепо́лненный *adj.* crowded; jammed; packed.

переполня́ть *v. impfv.* [*pfv.* **переполни́ть**] **1**, to overfill. **2**, to overcrowd. **3**, *fig.* to overwhelm (with emotion). —**переполня́ться**, *refl.* to be filled to overflowing; be crowded/packed/jammed.

переполо́х *n.* **1**, alarm; panic. **2**, turmoil; commotion.

переполоши́ть *v. pfv., colloq.* to throw into a panic. —**переполоши́ться**, *refl., colloq.* to be thrown into a panic.

перепо́нка [*gen. pl.* -нок] *n.* **1**, membrane. **2**, *zool.* web. —**бараба́нная перепо́нка**, eardrum.

перепо́нчатый *adj., zool.* webbed: перепо́нчатые ла́пы, webbed feet.

перепоруча́ть *v. impfv.* [*pfv.* **перепоручи́ть**] to turn over; hand over; entrust.

перепоручи́ть [*infl.* -ручу́, -ру́чишь] *v., pfv. of* **перепоруча́ть**.

перепра́ва *n.* **1**, crossing (*of a river*). **2**, place to cross (a river).

переправля́ть *v. impfv.* [*pfv.* **перепра́вить**] **1**, to carry across; ferry across. **2**, to forward. **3**, *colloq.* to correct. —**переправля́ться**, *refl.* to cross; make one's way across.

перепрева́ть *v. impfv.* [*pfv.* **перепре́ть**] **1**, to rot. **2**, (*of food*) to be overcooked.

перепре́лый *adj.* rotten.

перепре́ть *v., pfv. of* **перепрева́ть**.

перепро́бовать *v. pfv.* [*infl.* -бую, -буешь] to try; taste (all or many of something).

перепродава́ть v. impfv. [pfv. **перепрода́ть**; pres. -да́ю, -даёшь] to resell.

перепрода́жа n. resale.

перепрода́ть [infl. like **прода́ть**] v., pfv. of **перепродава́ть**.

перепроизво́дство n. overproduction.

перепры́гивать v. impfv. [pfv. **перепры́гнуть**] 1, to jump over; jump across. 2, to jump from place to place; jump from one thing to another.

перепу́г n., colloq. fright.

перепуга́ть v. pfv. to frighten; scare. —**перепуга́ться**, refl. to be frightened; be terrified.

перепу́тать v., pfv. of **пу́тать** and **перепу́тывать**. —**перепу́таться**, refl., pfv. of **пу́таться** and **перепу́тываться**.

перепу́тывать v. impfv. [pfv. **перепу́тать**] 1, to tangle. 2, to mix up; disarrange. 3, to confuse; get (two or more things) mixed up. —**перепу́тываться**, refl. 1, to become (en)tangled. 2, to get mixed up. 3, to get confused.

перепу́тье n. crossroads. —**на перепу́тье**, at the crossroads.

перераба́тывать v. impfv. [pfv. **перерабо́тать**] 1, to process; refine. 2, (with в or на + acc.) to make (into); convert (into). 3, to rework; revise. 4, to work overtime. 5, colloq. to overwork; tire oneself out.

перерабо́тка n. 1, processing; refining. 2, reworking; revision. 3, colloq. overtime work.

перераспределе́ние n. redistribution.

перераспределя́ть v. impfv. [pfv. **перераспредели́ть**] to redistribute.

перераста́ние n. 1, outgrowing. 2, (with в + acc.) development (into); mil. escalation (into).

перераста́ть v. impfv. [pfv. **перерасти́**] 1, to outgrow. 2, (with в + acc.) to develop (into); evolve (into).

перерасти́ [infl. like **расти́**] v., pfv. of **перераста́ть**.

перерасхо́д n. overexpenditure.

перерасхо́довать v. impfv. & pfv. [pres. -дую, -дуешь] to use too much (of).

перерва́ть [infl. like **рвать**] v., pfv. of **перерыва́ть** (in sense #1).

перере́зать v. pfv. [infl. -ре́жу, -ре́жешь] 1, pfv. of **перереза́ть**. 2, colloq. to kill (all or many of something).

перереза́ть v. impfv. [pfv. **перере́зать**] 1, to cut (usu. in two). 2, to cut off (a road, army, etc.).

перереша́ть v. impfv. [pfv. **перереши́ть**] colloq. 1, to change one's mind. 2, to solve in a different manner.

перерисова́ть [infl. -су́ю, -су́ешь] v., pfv. of **перерисо́вывать**.

перерисо́вывать v. impfv. [pfv. **перерисова́ть**] to draw again; make a copy of.

перерожда́ть v. impfv. [pfv. **перероди́ть**] to regenerate; make a new man of. —**перерожда́ться**, refl. 1, colloq. to be reborn. 2, to be (completely) regenerated; become a new person. 3, to degenerate.

перерожде́ние n. 1, regeneration. 2, degeneration.

переро́сток [gen. -стка] n. youngster who is slow to develop (and therefore older than his classmates).

переруба́ть v. impfv. [pfv. **переруби́ть**] to cut in two; chop in two.

переруби́ть v. pfv. [infl. -рублю́, -ру́бишь] 1, pfv. of **переруба́ть**. 2, to cut down (all or many of something).

переруга́ть v. pfv., colloq. to swear at (everyone).

—**переруга́ться**, refl., colloq. to swear at each other; cuss each other out.

переру́гиваться v.r. impfv., colloq. to swear at each other; swear back and forth.

переры́в n. recess; break. —**с переры́вами**, intermittently; off and on.

перерыва́ть v. impfv. 1, [pfv. **перерва́ть**] to break; snap. 2, [pfv. **переры́ть**] to dig up; fig. rummage through.

переры́ть [infl. -ро́ю, -ро́ешь] v., pfv. of **перерыва́ть** (in sense #2).

переряди́ть [infl. -ряжу́, -ря́дишь] v., pfv. of **переряжа́ть**. —**переряди́ться**, refl., pfv. of **переряжа́ться**.

переряжа́ть v. impfv. [pfv. **переряди́ть**] (with instr. or в + acc.) colloq. to dress up (as); disguise (as). —**переряжа́ться**, refl., colloq. 1, to disguise oneself. 2, (with instr. or в + acc.) to dress up (as); disguise oneself (as).

пересади́ть [infl. -сажу́, -са́дишь] v., pfv. of **переса́живать**.

переса́дка [gen. pl. -док] n. 1, change (of trains, planes, etc.). 2, transplant; transplantation.

переса́живать v. impfv. [pfv. **пересади́ть**] 1, to seat somewhere else; move; transfer. 2, to transplant; graft. —**переса́живаться**, refl. [pfv. **пересе́сть**] 1, to change one's seat. 2, to change trains; change planes.

переса́ливать v. impfv. [pfv. **пересоли́ть**] 1, to put too much salt in. 2, fig., colloq. to go too far; overdo it.

пересдава́ть v. impfv. [pfv. **пересда́ть**; pres. -сдаю́, -сдаёшь] 1, to rent again; sublet. 2, cards to deal again. 3, colloq. to retake (an examination).

пересда́ть [infl. like **дать**] v., pfv. of **пересдава́ть**.

пересека́ть v. impfv. [pfv. **пересе́чь**] 1, to cross; traverse. 2, to cross; intersect. 3, in пересека́ть путь or доро́гу (+ dat.), to bar the way (to). —**пересека́ться**, refl. to cross (each other); intersect (each other).

переселе́нец [gen. -нца] n. 1, migrant. 2, settler.

переселе́ние n. 1, migration; transmigration. 2, moving; resettlement. —**переселе́ние душ**, relig. transmigration.

переселя́ть v. impfv. [pfv. **пересели́ть**] to move; resettle. —**переселя́ться**, refl. 1, to migrate. 2, to move; relocate.

пересе́сть [infl. like **сесть**] v., pfv. of **переса́живаться**.

пересече́ние n. 1, crossing. 2, intersection.

пересечённый adj. (of terrain) rough; broken; rugged.

пересе́чь [infl. like **сечь**; past -се́к, -секла́, -секло́] v., pfv. of **пересека́ть**. —**пересе́чься**, refl., pfv. of **пересека́ться**.

переси́живать v. impfv. [pfv. **пересиде́ть**] colloq. 1, to sit longer than; stay longer than. 2, to sit too long; stay too long. 3, to sit out; wait out.

переси́ливать v. impfv. [pfv. **переси́лить**] 1, to overpower. 2, fig. to overcome; master.

переска́з n. 1, retelling. 2, exposition.

пересказа́ть v. pfv. [infl. -скажу́, -ска́жешь] 1, pfv. of **переска́зывать**. 2, to tell (all or many of something).

переска́зывать v. impfv. [pfv. **пересказа́ть**] to retell.

переска́кивать v. impfv. [pfv. **перескочи́ть**] 1, to jump over; jump across. 2, to jump from place to place;

jump from one thing to another. **3,** *fig., colloq.* to skip over (*when reading or telling something*).

перескочи́ть [*infl.* -скочу́, -ско́чишь] *v., pfv. of* **переска́кивать.**

пересла́ть [*infl.* -шлю́, -шлёшь] *v., pfv. of* **пересыла́ть.**

пересма́тривать *v. impfv.* [*pfv.* **пересмотре́ть**] **1,** to look over; go over again. **2,** to re-examine; reconsider; review. **3,** to revise.

пересме́иваться *v.r. impfv., colloq.* to look at each other and giggle.

пересме́шник *n.* **1,** mockingbird. **2,** *colloq.* one who likes to tease.

пересмо́тр *n.* **1,** reconsideration; review. **2,** revision.

пересмотре́ть [*infl.* -смотрю́, -смо́тришь] *v., pfv. of* **пересма́тривать.**

переснима́ть *v. impfv.* [*pfv.* **пересня́ть**] **1,** to make a copy of (a photograph). **2,** to reshoot (a film, scene, etc.).

пересня́ть [*infl. like* **снять**] *v., pfv. of* **переснима́ть.**

пересоздава́ть *v. impfv.* [*pfv.* **пересозда́ть**; *pres.* -даю́, -даёшь] to re-create.

пересозда́ть [*infl. like* **дать**] *v., pfv. of* **пересоздава́ть.**

пересо́л *n.* excess of salt.

пересоли́ть [*infl.* -солю́, -со́лишь *or* -соли́шь] *v., pfv. of* **переса́ливать.**

пересо́хнуть [*past* -со́х, -ла] *v., pfv. of* **пересыха́ть.**

переспа́ть *v. pfv.* [*infl. like* **спать**] *colloq.* **1,** to oversleep. **2,** to spend the night (somewhere).

переспева́ть *v. impfv.* [*pfv.* **переспе́ть**] to become overripe.

переспе́лый *adj.* overripe.

переспе́ть *v., pfv. of* **переспева́ть.**

переспо́рить *v. pfv.* to win an argument from; get the best of in an argument.

переспра́шивать *v. impfv.* [*pfv.* **переспроси́ть**] to ask again.

переспроси́ть *v. pfv.* [*infl.* -спрошу́, -спро́сишь] **1,** *pfv. of* **переспра́шивать. 2,** *colloq.* to ask (many people or everyone).

пересо́рить *v. pfv., colloq.* to cause a quarrel between. —**пересо́риться**, *refl. (of many people)* to quarrel.

перестава́ть *v. impfv.* [*pfv.* **переста́ть**; *pres.* -стаю́, -стаёшь] to stop; cease.

переставля́ть *v. impfv.* [*pfv.* **переста́вить**] **1,** to move (from one place to another). **2,** to rearrange; transpose. —**переставля́ть но́ги**, to plod along. —**е́ле переставля́ть но́ги**, to be scarcely able to walk.

переста́ивать *v. impfv.* [*pfv.* **перестоя́ть**] **1,** to be left standing too long (and turn sour). **2,** *colloq.* to wait out; wait till something passes.

перестано́вка [*gen. pl.* -вок] *n.* **1,** rearrangement; transposition. **2,** *math.* permutation.

перестара́ться *v.r. pfv., colloq.* to try too hard; overdo it.

переста́ть [*infl.* -ста́ну, -ста́нешь] *v., pfv. of* **перестава́ть.**

перестила́ть *v. impfv.* [*pfv.* **перестла́ть**] **1,** to remake (a bed). **2,** to re-lay (a floor).

перестира́ть *v. pfv.* **1,** *pfv. of* **перести́рывать. 2,** to wash; launder (all of something).

перести́рывать *v. impfv.* [*pfv.* **перестира́ть**] to wash again; launder again.

перестла́ть [*infl.* -стелю́, -сте́лешь] *v., pfv. of* **перестила́ть.**

перестоя́ть [*infl.* -стою́, -стои́шь] *v., pfv. of* **переста́ивать.**

перестрада́ть *v. pfv.* **1,** to suffer a great deal. **2,** to suffer through; go through.

перестра́ивать *v. impfv.* [*pfv.* **перестро́ить**] **1,** to rebuild; reconstruct. **2,** to reorganize. **3,** *mil.* to re-form. **4,** to tune. —**перестра́иваться**, *refl.* **1,** to change one's methods of work. **2,** *mil.* to re-form.

перестрахова́ть [*infl.* -ху́ю, -ху́ешь] *v., pfv. of* **перестрахо́вывать.** —**перестрахова́ться**, *refl., pfv. of* **перестрахо́вываться.**

перестрахо́вка *n.* **1,** reinsurance. **2,** *colloq.* excessive caution. —**для перестрахо́вки**, to be on the safe side.

перестрахо́вщик *n., colloq.* person who never takes any chances.

перестрахо́вывать *v. impfv.* [*pfv.* **перестрахова́ть**] to reinsure. —**перестрахо́вываться**, *refl.* **1,** to reinsure oneself. **2,** *fig., colloq.* to play safe; make extra sure.

перестре́ливаться *v.r. impfv.* to exchange shots; exchange gunfire.

перестре́лка [*gen. pl.* -лок] *n.* exchange of gunfire.

перестреля́ть *v. pfv.* **1,** to shoot (all or many of something). **2,** *colloq.* to use up (*in shooting*).

перестро́ить *v., pfv. of* **перестра́ивать.** —**перестро́иться**, *refl., pfv. of* **перестра́иваться.**

перестро́йка *n.* **1,** rebuilding; reconstruction. **2,** reorganization. **3,** retuning.

пересту́киваться *v.r. impfv.* (*of prisoners*) to communicate with each other by tapping.

переступа́ть *v. impfv.* [*pfv.* **переступи́ть**] **1,** to step across; step over. **2,** [*impfv. only*] to walk; step; move. **3,** *fig.* to overstep; transgress. —**переступа́ть с ноги́ на́ ногу**, to shift from foot to foot.

переступи́ть [*infl.* -ступлю́, -сту́пишь] *v., pfv. of* **переступа́ть.**

пересу́ды [*gen.* -дов] *n. pl., colloq.* gossip.

пересу́шивать *v. impfv.* [*pfv.* **пересуши́ть**] **1,** to dry again. **2,** to dry too much.

пересуши́ть *v. pfv.* [*infl.* -сушу́, -су́шишь] **1,** *pfv. of* **пересу́шивать. 2,** to dry (all of something).

пересчёт *n.* recount; recounting.

пересчи́тывать *v. impfv.* [*pfv.* **пересчита́ть**] **1,** to count. **2,** to recount.

пересыла́ть *v. impfv.* [*pfv.* **пересла́ть**] to send; remit; forward by mail.

пересы́лка *n.* **1,** sending; forwarding. **2,** remittance (*of money*). **3,** postage: плати́ть за пересы́лку, to pay the postage.

пересыпа́ть [*infl.* -сы́плю, -сы́плешь] *v., pfv. of* **пересыпа́ть.**

пересыпа́ть *v. impfv.* [*pfv.* **пересы́пать**] **1,** to pour (into another container). **2,** (*with instr.*) to sprinkle (with); *fig.* intersperse (with). **3,** *colloq.* to pour too much.

пересыха́ть *v. impfv.* [*pfv.* **пересо́хнуть**] **1,** to dry up; become dry. **2,** *impers.* to become parched: у меня́ в го́рле пересо́хло, my throat is parched.

перета́пливать *v. impfv.* [*pfv.* **перетопи́ть**] **1,** to light (a stove) again. **2,** to melt; melt down.

перетаска́ть *v. pfv., colloq.* **1,** to carry; haul (from one place to another). **2,** to carry off; steal.

перета́скивать *v. impfv.* [*pfv.* **перетащи́ть**] **1,** to drag over; drag across. **2**, to drag (from one place to another); move (something heavy).

перетасова́ть [*infl.* -су́ю, -су́ешь] *v., pfv. of* **перетасо́вывать.**

перетасо́вка *n.* shuffling; reshuffle.

перетасо́вывать *v. impfv.* [*pfv.* **перетасова́ть**] **1**, to shuffle (cards). **2**, *fig., colloq.* to shuffle; reshuffle; move around.

перетащи́ть [*infl.* -тащу́, -та́щишь] *v., pfv. of* **перета́скивать.**

перетере́ть *v. pfv.* [*infl. like* **тере́ть**] **1**, *pfv. of* **перетира́ть**. **2**, to wipe (all of something). —**перетере́ться**, *refl., pfv. of* **перетира́ться.**

перетерпе́ть *v. pfv.* [*infl.* -терплю́, -те́рпишь] *colloq.* to endure; suffer.

перетира́ть *v. impfv.* [*pfv.* **перетере́ть**] **1**, to break; wear through (a rope). **2**, to grind; grate. —**перетира́ться**, *refl.* (*of a rope*) to wear through.

перето́лки [*gen.* -ков] *n.pl., colloq.* gossip.

перетолкова́ть *v. pfv.* [*infl.* -ку́ю, -ку́ешь] **1**, *pfv. of* **перетолко́вывать**. **2**, *colloq.* to talk (with many people); talk over (many things).

перетолко́вывать *v. impfv.* [*pfv.* **перетолкова́ть**] to misinterpret; misconstrue.

перетопи́ть [*infl.* -топлю́, -то́пишь] *v., pfv. of* **перета́пливать.**

перетряса́ть *v. impfv.* [*pfv.* **перетрясти́**] **1**, to shake out. **2**, to rummage through.

перетрясти́ [*infl. like* **трясти́**] *v., pfv. of* **перетряса́ть.**

перетря́хивать *v. impfv.* [*pfv.* **перетряхну́ть**] to shake out.

пере́ть *v. impfv.* [*pres.* пру, прёшь; *past* пёр, -ла] *colloq.* **1**, to go; make one's way. **2**, to force one's way. **3**, to haul. **4**, to come out; stream out.

перетя́гивать *v. impfv.* [*pfv.* **перетяну́ть**] **1**, to pull (from one place to another). **2**, *v.i., colloq.* to make it (to a certain place). **3**, *fig., colloq.* to win over (to one's side). **4**, (*with instr.*) to tie tightly (with). **5**, to retighten. **6**, *v.i.* to weigh more. —**перетя́гиваться**, *refl.* (*with instr.*) to tie (something) tightly around one's waist.

перетяну́ть [*infl.* -тяну́, -тя́нешь] *v., pfv. of* **перетя́гивать**. —**перетяну́ться**, *refl., pfv. of* **перетя́гиваться.**

переубежда́ть *v. impfv.* [*pfv.* **переубеди́ть**] to change (someone's mind); make (someone) change his mind. —**переубежда́ться**, *refl.* to change one's mind.

переу́лок [*gen.* -лка] *n.* side street.

переустра́ивать *v. impfv.* [*pfv.* **переустро́ить**] **1**, to reconstruct. **2**, to reorganize.

переустро́йство *n.* **1**, reconstruction. **2**, reorganization.

переутоми́ть [*infl.* -млю́, -ми́шь] *v., pfv. of* **переутомля́ть**. —**переутоми́ться**, *refl., pfv. of* **переутомля́ться.**

переутомле́ние *n.* exhaustion; fatigue; overwork.

переутомля́ть *v. impfv.* [*pfv.* **переутоми́ть**] to tire out; wear out. —**переутомля́ться**, *refl.* to tire oneself out; wear oneself out.

переуче́сть [*infl. like* **уче́сть**] *v., pfv. of* **переучи́тывать.**

переучёт *n.* stock-taking; inventory.

переу́чивать *v. impfv.* [*pfv.* **переучи́ть**] **1**, to teach again; retrain. **2**, to study again; study a second time.

—**переу́чиваться**, *refl.* **1**, to be retrained; undergo retraining. **2**, (*with dat.*) to relearn.

переучи́тывать *v. impfv.* [*pfv.* **переуче́сть**] to take stock of; take inventory of.

переучи́ть [*infl.* -учу́, -у́чишь] *v., pfv. of* **переу́чивать**. —**переучи́ться**, *refl., pfv. of* **переу́чиваться.**

перефрази́ровать *v. impfv. & pfv.* [*pres.* -рую, -руешь] to reword; rephrase; paraphrase.

перефразиро́вка *n.* paraphrase.

перехва́ливать *v. impfv.* [*pfv.* **перехвали́ть**] to praise excessively; give undue praise to.

перехвали́ть [*infl.* -хвалю́, -хва́лишь] *v., pfv. of* **перехва́ливать.**

перехва́т *n., colloq.* interception. —**перехва́т телефо́нных сообще́ний**, wiretapping.

перехвати́ть [*infl.* -хвачу́, -хва́тишь] *v., pfv. of* **перехва́тывать.**

перехва́тчик *n.* one who intercepts something. —**истреби́тель-перехва́тчик**, *aero.* interceptor.

перехва́тывать *v. impfv.* [*pfv.* **перехвати́ть**] **1**, to intercept. **2**, to grab. **3**, to tie around: перехвати́ть но́гу жгуто́м, to tie a tourniquet around one's leg. **4**, *fig.* to traverse. **5**, to stop; cut off (one's breathing, voice, etc.). **6**, *colloq.* to borrow for a short time. **7**, *v.i., colloq.* to have a quick bite to eat. **8**, *v.i., colloq.* to go too far; overdo it.

перехитри́ть *v. pfv.* to outwit; outsmart; outfox.

перехо́д *n.* **1**, (act of) crossing. **2**, crossing (*place to cross*). **3**, passage; passageway. **4**, *mil.* day's march. **5**, shift; switch. **6**, transition. **7**, conversion (*to another religion*).

переходи́ть *v. impfv.* [*pfv.* **перейти́**; *pres.* -хожу́, -хо́дишь] **1**, to cross. **2**, to go; walk; pass (from one place to another). **3**, to shift; switch. **4**, to pass (into the hands of). **5**, (*with* в + *acc.*) to turn into. **6**, (*with* в + *acc.*) to adopt; be converted to (another religion).

перехо́дный *adj.* **1**, connecting. **2**, transitional. **3**, (*of a grade*) passing. **4**, (*of a verb*) transitive.

переходя́щий *adj.* **1**, transitory. **2**, *finance* carried over to the following year. —**переходя́щие дожди́**, intermittent showers. —**переходя́щий ку́бок**, challenge cup.

пе́рец [*gen.* -рца] *n.* pepper.

перецара́пать *v. pfv.* to scratch severely. —**перецара́паться**, *refl.* **1**, to scratch each other. **2**, *colloq.* to scratch oneself.

пе́речень [*gen.* -чня] *n.m.* list; enumeration; inventory.

перечёркивать *v. impfv.* [*pfv.* **перечеркну́ть**] to cross out.

перечерти́ть [*infl.* -черчу́, -че́ртишь] *v., pfv. of* **перече́рчивать.**

перече́рчивать *v. impfv.* [*pfv.* **перечерти́ть**] **1**, to draw again. **2**, to copy.

перече́сть *v. pfv.* [*infl.* -чту́, -чтёшь; *past* -чёл, -чла́] *colloq.* = **перечита́ть** *and* **пересчита́ть.**

перечини́ть *v. pfv.* [*infl.* -чиню́, -чи́нишь] **1**, to repair; mend (all or many of something). **2**, to repair again; mend.

перечисле́ние *n.* **1**, enumeration. **2**, transfer.

перечисля́ть *v. impfv.* [*pfv.* **перечи́слить**] **1**, to enumerate. **2**, to transfer.

перечита́ть *v. pfv.* **1**, *pfv. of* **перечи́тывать**. **2**, to read (all or many of something).

перечи́тывать v. impfv. [pfv. перечита́ть or пере-че́сть] to reread.

пере́чить v. impfv. (with dat.) colloq. to contradict.

пе́речница n. pepper shaker.

пе́речный adj. pepper (attrib.).

перечу́вствовать v. pfv. [infl. -ствую, -ствуешь] to experience; live through; go through (a great deal).

переша́гивать v. impfv. [pfv. перешагну́ть] 1, to step over. 2, fig. to overcome. 3, (with за + acc.) to be past (a certain age).

переше́ек [gen. -ше́йка] n. isthmus; neck of land.

перешёптываться v.r. impfv. to whisper to each other.

перешиба́ть v. impfv. [pfv. перешиби́ть] colloq. to break; fracture.

перешиби́ть [infl. -бу́, -бёшь; past -ши́б, -ла́] v., pfv. of перешиба́ть.

перешива́ть v. impfv. [pfv. переши́ть] to alter (by sewing).

переши́ть [infl. -шью, -шьёшь] v., pfv. of переши-ва́ть.

перещеголя́ть v. pfv., colloq. to outdo; surpass.

переэкзаменова́ть v. pfv. [infl. -ную, -нуешь] to give (someone) a second examination. —переэкза-менова́ться, refl. to take an examination for a second time.

переэкзамено́вка n. repeat examination (for one who has failed the first time).

перигей n. perigee.

пеоигелий n. perihelion.

пери́ла [gen. -ри́л] n.pl. banister; railing.

пери́метр n. perimeter.

пери́на n. feather bed.

пери́од n. 1, period (of time). 2, (historical) period.

перио́дика n. periodicals.

периоди́ческий adj. 1, [also, периоди́чный] peri-odic. 2, (of a publication) periodical. 3, (of a decimal) repeating. —периоди́чески, adv. periodically.

перипети́я n., usu. pl. vicissitudes; ups and downs.

периско́п n. periscope.

периста́льтика n. peristalsis. —перистальти́чес-кий, adj. peristaltic.

перисти́ль n.m. peristyle.

пе́ристый adj. 1, feathered. 2, bot. pinnate. 3, (of clouds) fleecy.

перитони́т n. peritonitis.

перифери́я n. 1, periphery. 2, outlying districts; the provinces. —перифери́йный, adj. provincial. —пери-фери́ческий, adj. peripheral.

перифра́за also, перифра́з n. periphrasis.

пёрка [gen. pl. -рок] n. drill bit.

перка́ль n.m. or f. percale. —перка́левый, adj. per-cale.

перл n., obs. pearl.

перламу́тр n. mother-of-pearl. —перламу́тровый, adj. mother-of-pearl (attrib.).

пе́рлинь also, перли́нь n.m. hawser.

пе́рловый adj., obs. made of pearls; pearl (attrib.).

перло́вый adj. 1, in перло́вая крупа́, pearl barley. 2, made of pearl barley.

перлюстра́ция n. secret opening of mail.

пермане́нт n. permanent wave.

пермане́нтный adj. permanent.

перна́тый adj. feathered. —перна́тые, n.pl. birds.

перо́ [pl. пе́рья, пе́рьев] n. 1, feather. 2, pen. —взять-

ся за перо́, to take pen in hand. —вы́йти из-под пера́ (+ gen.), to emerge from the pen of.

перочи́нный adj., in перочи́нный нож (но́жик), penknife.

перпендикуля́р n. perpendicular. —перпендику-ля́рный, adj. perpendicular.

перро́н n. platform (in a railroad station).

перс n.m. [fem. персия́нка] Persian. —перси́дский, adj. Persian.

пе́рсик n. 1, peach. 2, peach tree. —пе́рсиковый, adj. peach (attrib.).

персо́на n. person. —со́бственной персо́ной, in person.

персона́ж n. character; personage.

персона́л n. personnel. —персона́льный, adj. per-sonal.

перспекти́ва n. 1, perspective. 2, vista; view. 3, pros-pect: в перспекти́ве, in prospect. 4, pl. prospects; outlook.

перспекти́вный adj. 1, perspective. 2, long-term; long-range. 3, having good prospects; promising.

перст [gen. перста́] n., obs. finger. —оди́н как перст, all alone in the world.

пе́рстень [gen. -стня] n.m. ring set with a stone.

пертурба́ция n., astron. & fig. perturbation.

перуа́нский adj. Peruvian.

перфе́кт (пэ, фэ) n., gram. perfect; the perfect tense.

перфока́рта n. punch card.

перфора́тор n. 1, perforator; punch. 2, drill. —пер-фора́ция, n. perforation.

перфори́ровать v. impfv. & pfv. [pres. -рую, -ру-ешь] to perforate.

перхо́та n., colloq. tickling sensation in one's throat.

пе́рхоть n.f. dandruff.

перцо́вка n. pepper brandy.

перцо́вый adj. pepper (attrib.).

перча́тка [gen. pl. -ток] n. glove. —бро́сить перча́т-ку, to throw down the gauntlet.

пе́рчить v. impfv. to put pepper in or on.

перши́ть v impfv., impers., colloq. to have a tickling sensation in one's throat: у меня́ перши́т в го́рле, I have a tickling sensation in my throat; my throat tickles.

пёрышко [gen. pl. -шек] n. small feather.

пёс [gen. пса] n. dog.

пе́сенка [gen. -нок] n., dim. of пе́сня. —его́ пе́-сенка спе́та, he is done for; he has had it.

пе́сенник n. 1, member of a chorus. 2, songwriter. 3, songbook.

песе́та n. peseta (monetary unit of Spain).

песе́ц [gen. -сца́] n. polar fox.

песка́рь [gen. -каря́] n.m. gudgeon (fish).

песнопе́ние n. 1, religious song; hymn; chant. 2, obs. poem; poetry.

песнь n.f. 1, obs. song. 2, canto. —Песнь Пе́сней, Song of Songs.

пе́сня [gen. pl. -сен] n. song. —до́лгая пе́сня, a long story. —ста́рая пе́сня, the same old story. —тяну́ть всё ту же пе́сню, to harp on the same string.

пе́со n. indecl. peso (monetary unit of a number of Latin American countries).

песо́к [gen. -ска́] n. sand. —золото́й песо́к, gold dust. —са́харный песо́к, granulated sugar.

песо́чник n. sandpiper.

песо́чница n. sandbox.

песо́чный *adj.* **1,** sand (*attrib.*). **2,** *colloq.* sand-colored; sandy. **3,** (*of pastry*) short: песо́чный торт, shortcake. —**песо́чные часы́,** hourglass.

пессими́зм *n.* pessimism. —**пессими́ст,** *n.* pessimist. —**пессимисти́ческий,** *adj.* pessimistic.

пест [*gen.* песта́] *n.* pestle.

пе́стик *n.* **1,** *dim. of* пест. **2,** *bot.* pistil.

пе́стовать *v. impfv.* [*pfv.* вы́пестовать; *pres.* -тую, -туешь] **1,** *obs.* to nurse. **2,** *fig.* to nurture.

пестре́ть[1] *v. impfv.* [*pres.* -ре́ет] **1,** (*of something brightly colored or multicolored*) to appear; strike the eye. **2,** (*with instr.*) to be bright (with); be gay (with).

пестре́ть[2] *v. impfv.* [*pres.* -ри́т] **1,** to be everywhere; be all over. **2,** to turn up continually.

пестри́ть *v. impfv.* **1,** to make colorful. **2,** (*with instr.*) to sprinkle (with); intersperse (with). **3,** (*with instr.*) to abound (in); be filled (with); be replete (with). **4,** *impers.* to be dazzled: у меня́ пестри́ло в глаза́х, I was dazzled.

пестрота́ *n.* **1,** diversity of colors. **2,** *fig.* diversity; diverse nature.

пёстрый *adj.* **1,** multicolored; motley. **2,** *fig.* mixed; diverse; motley; heterogeneous.

песча́ник *n.* sandstone.

песча́нка [*gen. pl.* -нок] *n.* **1,** gerbil. **2,** sanderling.

песча́ный *adj.* **1,** sand (*attrib.*): песча́ная о́тмель, sandbank. **2,** sandy.

песчи́нка [*gen. pl.* -нок] *n.* grain of sand.

пета́рда *n.* **1,** petard. **2,** firecracker.

пе́телька [*gen. pl.* -лек] *n.* **1,** *dim. of* пе́тля. **2,** eyelet.

пети́ция *n.* petition.

петли́ца *n.* **1,** buttonhole (*in a lapel*). **2,** colored patch or stripe (*on a uniform*).

пе́тля [*gen.pl.* -тель] *n.* **1,** loop. **2,** noose. **3,** buttonhole. **4,** stitch: спусти́ть пе́тлю, to drop a stitch. **5,** hinge (*of a door*). **6,** *aero.* [*often* мёртвая пе́тля] loop: де́лать (мёртвую) пе́тлю, to loop the loop. —**лезть в пе́тлю,** to risk one's neck.

петля́ть *v. impfv., colloq.* **1,** to weave; zigzag. **2,** *fig.* to equivocate; prevaricate.

петру́шка *n.f.* parsley. —*n.m.* **1,** puppet show. **2,** chief character in this show.

пету́ния *also,* пету́нья *n.* petunia.

пету́х [*gen.* -туха́] *n.* rooster; cock. —**встава́ть с петуха́ми,** to get up at the crack of dawn. —**пусти́ть кра́сного петуха́,** to start a fire.

пету́ший [*fem.* -шья] *adj.* rooster's; cock's. —**пету́ший гребешо́к,** cockscomb (*plant*).

петуши́ный *adj.* rooster (*attrib.*); cock (*attrib.*). —**петуши́ный бой,** cockfight; cockfighting. —**петуши́ный гре́бень,** cockscomb.

петуши́ться *v.r. impfv., colloq.* to get on one's high horse.

петушо́к [*gen.* -шка́] *n.* cockerel.

петь *v. impfv.* [*pfv.* спеть *or* пропе́ть; *pres.* пою́, поёшь] to sing.

пехо́та *n.* infantry. —**морска́я пехо́та,** the marines.

пехоти́нец [*gen.* -нца] *n.* infantryman; foot soldier. —**морско́й пехоти́нец,** marine.

пехо́тный *adj.* infantry (*attrib.*).

печа́лить *v. impfv.* [*pfv.* опеча́лить] to sadden. —**печа́литься,** *refl.* to be sad; be saddened; grieve.

печа́ль *n.f.* sorrow; sadness.

печа́льный *adj.* [*short form* -лен, -льна] sad. —**печа́льно,** *adv.* sadly.

печа́тание *n.* printing.

печа́тать *v. impfv.* [*pfv.* напеча́тать] **1,** to print. **2,** *in* печа́тать на маши́нке, to type. **3,** to publish. **4,** to have (something) published. —**печа́таться,** *refl.* to have something published.

печа́тка [*gen. pl.* -ток] *n.* signet.

печа́тник *n.* printer.

печа́тный *adj.* **1,** printing (*attrib.*): печа́тный стано́к, printing press. **2,** printed. **3,** published. —**печа́тные бу́квы,** block letters. —**печа́тный лист,** signature (*of 16 pages*). —**печа́тное сло́во,** the printed word.

печа́ть *n.f.* **1,** seal; stamp. **2,** printing: кни́га сейча́с в печа́ти, the book is being printed right now. **3,** type; print. **4,** the press: освеща́ться в печа́ти, to be covered in the press. —**выходи́ть из печа́ти,** to come off the press; come out.

пече́ние *n.* baking.

печёнка *n.* liver (*meat*).

печёночник *n.* liverwort.

печёночница *n.* hepatica.

печёночный *adj.* liver (*attrib.*); hepatic.

печёный *adj.* baked.

пе́чень *n.f., anat.* liver.

пече́нье *n.* pastry; cookies.

пе́чка [*gen. pl.* -чек] *n.* stove.

печно́й *adj.* stove (*attrib.*).

печу́рка [*gen. pl.* -рок] *n.* small portable stove.

печь[1] *v. impfv.* [*pfv.* испе́чь; *pres.* пеку́, печёшь, ...пеку́т; *past* пёк, пекла́, пекло́] **1,** to bake. **2,** [*impfv. only*] (*of the sun*) to beat down on; (*intrans.*) to be burning hot. —**пе́чься,** *refl.* **1,** to bake; be baked. **2,** [*impfv. only*] (*with* о) to care (about).

печь[2] [*2nd loc.* печи́; *pl.* пе́чи, пече́й, печа́м] *n.f.* **1,** stove; oven. **2,** furnace: до́менная печь, blast furnace. —**обжига́тельная печь,** kiln.

пешехо́д *n.* pedestrian. —**пешехо́дный,** *adj.* pedestrian (*attrib.*).

пе́ший *adj.* traveling on foot.

пе́шка [*gen. pl.* -шек] *n., chess & fig.* pawn.

пешко́м *adv.* on foot.

пеще́ра *n.* cave; cavern.

пеще́рный *adj.* cave (*attrib.*): пеще́рный челове́к, cave man.

пиани́но *n. indecl.* upright piano.

пиани́ссимо *adv. & n. indecl.* pianissimo.

пиани́ст *n.m.* [*fem.* -ни́стка] pianist.

пиа́но *adv., music* piano; soft.

пиано́ла *n.* player piano.

пиа́стр *n.* piaster (*monetary unit of several Middle Eastern countries*).

пивна́я *n., decl. as an adj.* tavern; saloon; pub.

пивно́й *adj.* beer (*attrib.*).

пи́во *n.* beer.

пивова́р *n.* brewer. —**пивоваре́ние,** *n.* brewing. —**пивова́ренный,** *adj.* brewing (*attrib.*): пивова́ренный заво́д, brewery.

пи́галица *n.* lapwing; pewit.

пигме́й *n.* pygmy.

пигме́нт *n.* pigment. —**пигмента́ция,** *n.* pigmentation.

пиджа́к [*gen.* -жака́] *n.* (man's) suit jacket; coat.

пижа́ма *n.* pajamas.

пижо́н *n., colloq.* fop; dandy.

пик *n.* **1,** mountain peak. **2,** peak (*of work, traffic, etc.*). —**часы́ пик,** rush hours.

пи́ка *n.* lance; pike. —**в пи́ку** (+ *dat.*), in order to spite someone.

пика́нтный *adj.* **1,** piquant; pungent. **2,** *fig.* spicy. —**пика́нтность,** *n.f.* piquancy.

пика́п *n.* pickup truck.

пике́ *n. neut. indecl.* **1,** piqué. **2,** *aero.* dive. —**пике́йный,** *adj.* piqué.

пике́т *n.* **1,** picket line. **2,** *mil.* picket. **3,** bench mark. **4,** piquet (*card game*).

пикети́ровать *v. impfv.* [*pres.* -рую, -руешь] to picket.

пике́тчик *n.* picket (*one who pickets*).

пи́ки [*gen.* пик] *n. pl.*, *cards* spades.

пики́рование *n.*, *aero.* dive; diving.

пики́ровать *v. impfv. & pfv.* [*pres.* -рую, -руешь] *aero.* to dive; go into a dive.

пики́роваться *v.r. impfv.* [*pres.* -руюсь, -руешься] to squabble; bicker; trade insults.

пики́ровка *n.* squabbling; bickering.

пики́ровщик *n.* dive bomber.

пики́рующий *adj.*, *in* **пики́рующий бомбардиро́вщик,** dive bomber.

пи́кколо *n. indecl.* piccolo.

пикни́к [*gen.* -ника́] *n.* picnic.

пи́кнуть *v. pfv.*, *colloq.*, *usu. used negatively*, to object: он и пи́кнул не успе́л, before he had a chance to say "no".

пи́ковый *adj.* **1,** *cards* of spades: пи́ковая да́ма, queen of spades. **2,** *colloq.* awkward; sticky: пи́ковое положе́ние, awkward situation. —**остава́ться при пи́ковом интере́се,** to be left holding the bag.

пиктогра́мма *n.* pictograph. —**пиктогра́фия,** *n.* pictography. —**пиктографи́ческий,** *adj.* pictographic.

пи́кули [*gen.* -лей] *n.pl.* pickles.

пи́кша *n.* haddock.

пила́ [*pl.* пи́лы] *n.* saw.

пила́в *n.* pilaf.

пила́-ры́ба *n.* sawfish.

пилёный *adj.* sawed. —**пилёный са́хар,** lump sugar.

пилигри́м *n.*, *obs.* pilgrim.

пили́кать *v. impfv.*, *colloq.* to scrape (on a musical instrument).

пили́ть *v. impfv.* [*pres.* пилю́, пи́лишь] **1,** to saw. **2,** *fig.* to nag.

пи́лка [*gen. pl.* -лок] *n.* **1,** sawing. **2,** small handsaw. **3,** nail file.

пи́ллерс *n.*, *naut.* stanchion.

пило́н *n.* pylon.

пило́т *n.* pilot. —**пилота́ж,** *n.* piloting; flying.

пилоти́ровать *v. impfv.* [*pres.* -рую, -руешь] to pilot.

пило́тка [*gen. pl.* -ток] *n.*, *mil.* overseas cap.

пи́льщик *n.* sawyer; woodcutter.

пилю́ля *n.* pill.

пиля́стра *also,* **пиля́стр** *n.* pilaster.

пина́ть *v. impfv.* [*pfv.* пнуть] *colloq.* to kick.

пингви́н *n.* penguin.

пинг-по́нг *n.* ping-pong.

пи́ния *n.* stone pine.

пино́к [*gen.* -нка́] *n.*, *colloq.* kick.

пи́нта *n.* pint.

пинце́т *n.* tweezers.

пио́н *n.* peony.

пионе́р *n.* pioneer. —**пионе́рский,** *adj.* pioneer (*attrib.*).

пиоре́я *n.* pyorrhea.

пипе́тка [*gen. pl.* -ток] *n.* eye dropper; medicine dropper.

пир [*2nd loc.* пиру́; *pl.* пиры́] *n.* feast; banquet. —**пир горо́й; пир на весь мир,** lavish banquet; sumptuous feast.

пирами́да *n.* pyramid. —**пирамида́льный,** *adj.* pyramidal.

пира́т *n.* pirate. —**пира́тский,** *adj.* pirate (*attrib.*); piratical. —**пира́тство,** *n.* piracy.

пири́т *n.* pyrite.

пирова́ть *v. impfv.* [*pres.* -ру́ю, -ру́ешь] to feast; have a feast.

пиро́г [*gen.* -рога́] *n.* pie.

пиро́жное *n.*, *decl. as an adj.* pastry.

пирожо́к [*gen.* -жка́] *n.* small pie; patty.

пирома́ния *n.* pyromania.

пироте́хника *n.* pyrotechnics.

пи́рров *adj.*, *in* **пи́ррова побе́да,** Pyrrhic victory.

пирс *n.* pier.

пиру́шка [*gen. pl.* -шек] *n.*, *colloq.* lively party.

пируэ́т *n.* pirouette.

пи́ршество *n.*, *obs.* sumptuous feast.

писа́ка *n.m. & f.*, *colloq.* poor writer; hack writer; scribbler.

писа́ние *n.* writing. —**свяще́нное писа́ние,** Holy Scripture; Holy Writ.

пи́саный *adj.* handwritten. —**пи́саная краса́вица,** picture of beauty.

писа́рь [*pl.* писаря́] *n.m.*, *usu. mil.* clerk.

писа́тель *n.m.* [*fem.* -ница] writer. —**писа́тельский,** *adj.* writer; writer's. —**писа́тельство,** *n.*, *colloq.* writing; being a writer.

писа́ть *v. impfv.* [*pfv.* **написа́ть;** *pres.* **пишу́, пи́шешь**] **1,** to write. **2,** to paint. **3,** *in* писа́ть на маши́нке, to type. —**писа́ться,** *refl.* [*impfv. only*] **1,** to be spelled: как пи́шется э́то сло́во?, how is this word spelled? **2,** *impers.* (*with dat.*) to feel like writing: мне сего́дня не пи́шется, I don't feel like writing today; I can't get myself to do any writing today.

писе́ц [*gen.* -сца́] *n.* scribe.

писк *n.* peep; cheep.

пискли́вый *adj.* squeaky.

пи́скнуть *v.*, *pfv. of* пища́ть.

писсуа́р *n.* urinal.

пистоле́т *n.* pistol; gun. —**пистоле́т-пулемёт,** submachine gun.

пистоле́тный *adj.* pistol (*attrib.*).

писто́н *n.* **1,** percussion cap. **2,** *music* piston.

пису́лька [*gen. pl.* -лек] *n.*, *colloq.* short letter; note.

писчебума́жный *adj.* stationery (*attrib.*).

пи́счий *adj.* writing (*attrib.*): пи́счая бума́га, writing paper.

письмена́ [*gen.* -мён] *n. pl.* characters; letters.

пи́сьменно *adv.* in writing.

пи́сьменность *n.f.* **1,** written language; system of writing. **2,** literature; literary texts (*of an ancient people*).

пи́сьменный *adj.* **1,** writing (*attrib.*): пи́сьменный стол, desk. **2,** written: пи́сьменная про́сьба, written request.

письмо́ [*pl.* пи́сьма, пи́сем] *n.* **1,** letter: писа́ть письмо́, to write a letter. **2,** writing: чте́ние и письмо́, reading and writing. **3,** script: ара́бское письмо́, the Arabic script.

письмоно́сец [*gen.* -сца] *n.* mailman.

питáние *n.* **1,** feeding. **2,** food; diet; nourishment; nutrition. **3,** power supply.

питáтельный *adj.* **1,** nourishing; nutritious. **2,** feeding (*attrib.*). —**питáтельная средá,** culture medium.

питáть *v. impfv.* **1,** to feed; nourish. **2,** to supply (with energy). **3,** *fig.* to harbor (a feeling); have a feeling of. —**питáться,** *refl.* **1,** to eat; take one's meals. **2,** (*with instr.*) to feed (on).

питóмец [*gen.* -мца] *n.m.* [*fem.* -мица] **1,** charge; ward. **2,** pupil. **3,** graduate; alumnus.

питóмник *n.* **1,** nursery (*for plants*). **2,** farm (*for breeding and raising animals*).

питóн *n.* python.

пить *v. impfv.* [*pfv.* **вы́пить;** *pres.* **пью, пьёшь;** *past fem.* **пилá**] to drink. Я хочý пить, I am thirsty. —**как пить дать,** *colloq.* for sure.

питьё *n.* **1,** drinking: гóдный для питья́, fit to drink. **2,** drink; beverage.

питьевóй *adj.* drinking (*attrib.*): питьевáя водá, drinking water. —**питьевáя сóда,** baking soda; bicarbonate of soda.

пифагóров *adj.,* in **пифагóрова теорéма,** Pythagorean theorem.

пихáть *v. impfv.* [*pfv.* **пихнýть**] *colloq.* **1,** to push; shove. **2,** (*with* **в** + *acc.*) to stuff (into); cram (into).

пи́хта *n.* fir. —**пи́хтовый,** *adj.* fir (*attrib.*).

пиццикáто *adv. & n. indecl.* pizzicato.

пи́чкать *v. impfv.* [*pfv.* **напи́чкать**] (*with instr.*) *colloq.* to stuff (with food, drink, medicine, etc.).

пичýга *n., colloq.* small bird. *Also,* **пичýжка.**

пиччикáто *adv. & n. indecl.* pizzicato.

пи́шущий *adj.,* in **пи́шущая маши́нка,** typewriter.

пи́ща *n.* food. —**пи́ща для умá/размышлéния,** food for thought.

пищáль *n.f.* arquebus; harquebus.

пищáть *v. impfv.* [*pfv.* **пи́скнуть;** *pres.* **пищý, пищи́шь**] to peep; cheep.

пищевáрéние *n.* digestion. —**расстрóйство пищевáрéния,** indigestion.

пищевари́тельный *adj.* digestive. —**пищевари́тельный канáл,** alimentary canal.

пищевóд *n.* gullet; esophagus.

пищевóй *adj.* food (*attrib.*).

пищýха *n.* **1,** pika (*animal*). **2,** creeper (*bird*).

пия́вка [*gen. pl.* -вок] *n.* leech.

плав *n.,* in **на плавý,** afloat.

плáвание *n.* **1,** swimming. **2,** voyage.

плáвательный *adj.* swimming (*attrib.*).

плáвать *v. impfv.* **1,** *indeterm. of* **плыть. 2,** to float (*not sink*). **3,** *colloq.* to flounder; be at sea.

плáвающий *adj.* **1,** swimming. **2,** floating. **3,** (*of a vehicle*) amphibious.

плáвень [*gen.* -вня] *n.m., metall.* flux.

плавикóвый *adj.,* in **плавикóвая кислотá,** hydrofluoric acid; **плавикóвый шпат,** fluorspar; fluorite.

плави́льный *adj.* melting (*attrib.*); smelting (*attrib.*). —**плави́льный котёл,** melting pot.

плави́льня [*gen. pl.* -лен] *n.* smelting plant. —**плави́льщик,** *n.* smelter.

плáвить *v. impfv.* [*pres.* -влю, -вишь] to melt; smelt. —**плáвиться,** *refl.* to melt.

плáвка *n.* melting; smelting.

плáвки [*gen.* -вок] *n. pl.* swimming trunks.

плáвкий *adj.* capable of being melted.

плавлéние *n.* melting. —**тóчка плавлéния,** melting point.

плавни́к [*gen.* -никá] *n.* **1,** fin (*of a fish*). **2,** driftwood.

плáвный *adj.* **1,** (*of movements*) smooth; graceful. **2,** (*of sounds or speech*) smooth; fluent. —**плáвность,** *n.f.* smoothness.

плавýнчик *n.* phalarope.

плавýчесть *n.f.* buoyancy.

плавýчий *adj.* **1,** floating. **2,** buoyant. —**плавýчая бáза,** *naut.* tender. —**плавýчая льди́на,** ice field.

плагиáт *n.* plagiarism. —**плагиáтор,** *n.* plagiarist.

плáзма *n.* plasma.

плакáт *n.* poster; placard.

плáкать *v. impfv.* [*pres.* **плáчу, плáчешь**] to cry; weep. —**плáкаться,** *refl.* (*with* **на** + *acc.*) *colloq.* to cry (about); bemoan.

плáкса *n.m. & f., colloq.* crybaby.

плакси́вый *adj., colloq.* whining.

плакýчий *adj.* **1,** *obs.* whining. **2,** (*of trees*) weeping: плакýчая и́ва, weeping willow.

пламенéть *v. impfv.* to blaze; flame.

плáменный *adj.* **1,** flaming; fiery. **2,** *fig.* fiery; ardent.

плáмя [*gen., dat., & prepl.* **плáмени;** *instr.* **плáменем**] *n. neut.* flame; blaze.

план *n.* **1,** plan. **2,** diagram: план кварти́ры, floor plan of an apartment; план гóрода, city map. **3,** *fig.* aspect; context. —**зáдний план,** background. —**крýпный план,** close-up. —**перéдний план,** foreground. —**учéбный план,** curriculum.

планёр *n., aero.* glider. —**планери́зм,** *n.* gliding. —**планери́ст,** *n.* glider pilot. —**планёрный,** *adj.* gliding (*attrib.*).

планéта *n.* planet.

планетáрий *n.* planetarium.

планéтный *adj.* planetary.

планимéтрия *n.* plane geometry.

плани́рование *n.* **1,** planning. **2,** *aero.* gliding; glide.

плани́ровать *v. impfv.* [*pfv.* **сплани́ровать;** *pres.* -рую, -руешь] **1,** [*pfv.* **запланировать**] to plan. **2,** *aero.* to glide; glide down.

планировáть *v. impfv.* [*pfv.* **распланировáть;** *pres.* -рую, -руешь] to lay out.

планирóвка *n.* **1,** planning. **2,** laying out. **3,** layout; design.

планирóвщик *n.* planner; one who lays out a city, town, etc.

плáнка [*gen. pl.* -нок] *n.* **1,** plank; strip. **2,** bar; crossbar (*used in high jumping*).

планктóн *n.* plankton.

планови́к [*gen.* -викá] *n.* (economic) planner.

плáновый *adj.* **1,** planned: плáновое хозя́йство, planned economy. **2,** planning (*attrib.*): плáновый отдéл, planning department.

планомéрный *adj.* planned; systematic.

плантáтор *n.* plantation owner; planter. —**плантáция,** *n.* plantation.

планшéт *n.* map case.

планши́р *n.* gunwale.

пласт [*gen.* -стá] *n.* **1,** layer. **2,** *geol.* stratum. —**лежáть пластóм,** (*of a sick person*) to be flat on one's back.

плáстик *n.* plastic.

плáстика *n.* **1,** plastic arts. **2,** grace of movement.

плáстиковый *adj.* plastic. —**плáстиковая бóмба,** plastic bomb.

пласти́нка [*gen. pl.* -нок] *n.* **1,** metal plate. **2,** phonograph record. **3,** photographic plate. **4,** blade (*of a leaf*). —**кровяны́е пласти́нки,** platelets.

пласти́ческий *adj.* **1,** plastic. **2,** (*of movements of the body*) rhythmical; graceful.

пласти́чный *adj.* **1,** plastic. **2,** supple; pliant; plastic. **3,** rhythmical; graceful.

пластма́сса *n.* plastic. —**пластма́ссовый,** *adj.* plastic.

пла́стырь *n.m.* plaster (*applied to a sore or wound*).

пла́та *n.* **1,** pay; payment. **2,** fee; charge: **входна́я пла́та,** admission charge. —**зарабо́тная пла́та,** pay; wages; salary. —**кварти́рная пла́та,** rent.

плата́н *n.* plane tree.

платёж [*gen.* -тежа́] *n.* payment. —**нало́женным платежо́м,** C.O.D.

платёжеспосо́бный *adj.* solvent. —**платёжеспосо́бность,** *n.f.* solvency.

платёжный *adj.* pay (*attrib.*); payment (*attrib.*). —**платёжный бала́нс,** balance of payments. —**платёжная ве́домость,** payroll.

плате́льщик *n.* payer.

пла́тина *n.* platinum. —**пла́тиновый,** *adj.* platinum.

плати́ть *v. impfv.* [*pfv.* **заплати́ть;** *pres.* **плачу́, пла́тишь**] to pay: **плати́ть кому́-нибудь за** (+ *acc.*), to pay someone for (something). —**плати́ться,** *refl.* [*pfv.* **поплати́ться**] to pay; pay the penalty: **поплати́ться жи́знью за** (+ *acc.*), to pay for (something) with one's life.

пла́тный *adj.* **1,** requiring payment. **2,** paying. **3,** paid.

плато́ *n. indecl.* plateau.

плато́к [*gen.* -тка́] *n.* kerchief. —**носово́й плато́к,** handkerchief. —**ше́йный плато́к,** neckerchief.

платони́ческий *adj.* platonic.

платфо́рма *n.* **1,** platform. **2,** flatcar. **3,** (political) platform.

пла́тье *n.* **1,** [*gen. pl.* -тьев] dress; gown. **2,** clothes; clothing.

платяно́й *adj.* clothes (*attrib.*). —**платяно́й шкаф,** wardrobe.

плафо́н *n.* **1,** decorated ceiling. **2,** shade (*for a lamp suspended from a ceiling*).

пла́ха *n.* **1,** block; log. **2,** execution block.

плац [*2nd loc.* плацу́] *n.* parade ground.

плацда́рм *n.* **1,** bridgehead; beachhead. **2,** springboard; jumping-off place; staging area.

плаце́нта *n.* placenta.

плацка́рта *n.* reserved seat coupon (*for a train*). —**плацка́ртный,** *adj.* reserved.

плач *n.* weeping; crying.

плаче́вный *adj.* **1,** mournful; sad. **2,** lamentable; deplorable; sorry.

плашмя́ *adv.* flat: **лежа́ть плашмя́,** to lie flat.

плащ [*gen.* плаща́] *n.* **1,** cloak. **2,** raincoat.

плебе́й *n.* plebeian. —**плебе́йский,** *adj.* plebeian.

плебисци́т *n.* plebiscite.

плебс *n.* the common people; hoi polloi.

плева́ *n.* membrane. —**де́вственная плева́,** hymen.

плева́тельница *n.* spittoon; cuspidor.

плева́ть *v. impfv.* [*pfv.* **плю́нуть;** *pres.* **плюю́, плюёшь**] **1,** to spit. **2,** (*with* на + *acc.*) *colloq.* to ignore; shrug off; brush off. **3,** (*with inf.*) *colloq.* not to give a damn: **ему́ плева́ть на э́то,** he doesn't give a damn about it. —**плева́ться,** *refl.* [*impfv. only*] *colloq.* = **плева́ть.**

пле́вел *n.* **1,** darnel. **2,** *fig.* weed.

плево́к [*gen.* -вка́] *n.* spit; spittle; sputum.

пле́вра *n.* pleura. —**плевра́льный,** *adj.* pleural.

плеври́т *n.* pleurisy.

плёвый *adj., colloq.* **1,** miserable; rotten. **2,** trifling; insignificant.

плед *n.* lap robe; steamer rug.

плексигла́с *n.* plexiglass.

плектр *n.* plectrum.

племенно́й *adj.* **1,** tribal. **2,** pedigreed. **3,** breeding (*attrib.*); stud (*attrib.*).

пле́мя [*gen., dat., & prepl.* пле́мени; *instr.* пле́менем; *pl.* племена́, -мён, -мена́м] *n. neut.* tribe.

племя́нник *n.* nephew.

племя́нница *n.* niece.

плен [*2nd loc.* плену́] *n.* captivity. —**брать/взять в плен,** to take (someone) prisoner. —**попа́сть в плен,** to be taken prisoner.

плена́рный *adj.* plenary.

плене́ние *n., obs.* **1,** taking prisoner; capture. **2,** captivity.

плени́тельный *adj.* captivating; enchanting.

плени́ть *v. pfv.* **1,** *pfv. of* **пленя́ть. 2,** *obs.* to take prisoner. —**плени́ться,** *refl., pfv. of* **пленя́ться.**

плёнка [*gen. pl.* -нок] *n.* **1,** thin layer (*of ice, dust, fat, etc.*). **2,** *photog.* film. **3,** tape: **записа́ть на плёнку,** to tape; tape-record. **4,** pellicle.

пле́нник *n.* prisoner; captive.

пле́нный *adj.* captive. —*n.* prisoner; captive.

плёночный *adj.* film (*attrib.*). —**плёночный фотоаппара́т,** roll-film camera.

пле́нум *n.* plenum; plenary session.

пленя́ть *v. impfv.* [*pfv.* **плени́ть**] to captivate; enchant. —**пленя́ться,** *refl.* (*with instr.*) to be captivated (by); be fascinated (with).

плёс *n.* stretch; section (*of a river*).

пле́сень *n.f.* mold.

плеск *n.* **1,** splash; splashing. **2,** lapping (*of waves*).

плеска́ть *v. impfv.* [*pfv.* **плесну́ть;** *pres.* **плещу́, пле́щешь**] **1,** *v.i.* (*of water or other liquids*) to splash. **2,** *v.t.* to splash: **плеска́ть во́ду** (*or* водо́й) **на́ пол,** to splash water on the floor. **3,** *v.i.* (*of waves*) to lap (against something). —**плеска́ться,** *refl.* [*impfv. only*] **1,** to splash. **2,** to spill.

пле́сневеть *v. impfv.* [*pfv.* **запле́сневеть**] to grow moldy.

плесну́ть *v., pfv. of* **плеска́ть.**

плести́ *v. impfv.* [*pfv.* **сплести́;** *pres.* **плету́, плетёшь;** *past* **плёл, плела́, плело́**] **1,** to weave; braid; plait. **2,** *colloq.* to weave (intrigues); spin (a tale); utter (nonsense). —**плести́ть,** *refl.* [*impfv. only*] *colloq.* to plod along; trudge along.

плете́ние *n.* **1,** weaving. **2,** wickerwork.

плетёнка [*gen. pl.* -нок] *n., colloq.* **1,** wicker basket. **2,** wicker enclosure. **3,** twist (*of bread*).

плетёный *adj.* wicker (*attrib.*); wattled.

плете́нь [*gen.* -тня́] *n.m.* wattle fence. —**навести́ тень на плете́нь,** to confuse the issue.

плётка [*gen. pl.* -ток] *n.* lash.

плеть [*pl.* плети, -те́й, -тя́м] *n.f.* lash.

плечево́й *adj.* shoulder (*attrib.*).

пле́чико [*pl.* -ки, -ков] *n.* **1,** *dim. of* плечо́. **2,** shoulder strap. **3,** *pl.* clothes hanger; coat hanger.

плечи́стый *adj.* broad-shouldered.

плечо́ [*pl.* пле́чи, плеч, плеча́м] *n.* shoulder. —**вы-**

носи́ть на свои́х плеча́х, to carry on one's shoulders; bear the full burden of. —за плеча́ми, **1**, behind one. **2**, close at hand. —име́ть го́лову на плеча́х, to have a good head on one's shoulders. —не по плечу́ (+ *dat.*), *colloq.* too much for; beyond one. —плечо́м к плечу́, shoulder to shoulder —с плеч доло́й, off one's back; over and done with.

плеши́веть v. impfv. [pfv. **оплеши́веть**] to grow bald.

плеши́вый adj. bald. —**плеши́вость,** n.f. baldness.

плешь n.f. bald spot.

плея́да n. brilliant assemblage; galaxy. —**Плея́ды,** n. pl., astron. Pleiades.

пли́нтус n. plinth.

плиссе́ (сэ) n. neut. indecl. accordion pleats. —adj., indecl. with accordion pleats.

плиссирова́ть v. impfv. [pres. -ру́ю, -ру́ешь] to pleat; make pleats in.

плита́ [pl. пли́ты] n. **1**, slab. **2**, flagstone. **3**, (electric) stove; range. —**моги́льная плита́,** gravestone.

пли́тка [gen. pl. -ток] n. **1**, thin slab; tile. **2**, bar (of chocolate). **3**, small stove.

плитня́к [gen. -няка́] n. flagstone. —**плитняко́вый,** adj. flagstone.

пли́точный adj. tiled: пли́точный пол, tiled floor.

плове́ц [gen. -вца́] n.m. [fem. пловчи́ха] swimmer.

плод [gen. плода́] n. **1**, fruit. **2**, fetus. **3**, fig. fruit: плоды́ на́ших трудо́в, the fruits of our labor. —**плод воображе́ния,** product (or figment) of the imagination.

плоди́ть v. impfv. [pres. пложу́, плоди́шь] **1**, to produce. **2**, fig. to generate; engender. —**плоди́ться,** refl. to propagate; multiply; breed.

пло́дный adj. **1**, of a fruit. **2**, producing fruit. **3**, fertilized. **4**, fetal.

плодови́тый adj. **1**, (of animals) prolific; fertile; fecund. **2**, (of a writer, composer, etc.) prolific. —**плодови́тость,** n.f. fertility.

плодово́дство n. fruit growing.

плодо́вый adj. **1**, fruit (attrib.). **2**, fruit-bearing.

плодоноси́ть v. impfv. [pres. -но́сит] to bear fruit.

плодоно́сный adj. fruit-bearing.

плодоро́дие n. fertility.

плодоро́дный adj. fertile.

плодотво́рный adj. fruitful; productive.

пло́мба n. **1**, seal (for a door or package). **2**, filling (for a tooth).

пломби́р n. ice cream topped with fruit.

пломбирова́ть v. impfv. [pfv. **запломбирова́ть;** pres. -ру́ю, -ру́ешь] **1**, to seal. **2**, to fill (a tooth).

пло́ский adj. [short form -сок, -ска́, -ско; comp. пло́ще] **1**, flat. **2**, fig. flat; vapid; banal. —**пло́ская стопа́,** flatfoot. —**пло́ский червь,** flatworm.

плоского́рье n. plateau; tableland.

плоскогру́дый adj. flat-chested.

плоскогу́бцы [gen. -цев] n. pl. pliers.

плоскодо́нка [gen. pl. -нок] n., colloq. flat-bottomed boat.

плоскодо́нный adj. flat-bottomed.

плоскосто́пие n. flatfoot; fallen arches.

пло́скость [pl. пло́скости, -стей, -стя́м] n.f. **1**, flatness. **2**, plane. **3**, fig. plane; level; sphere. **4**, fig. platitude; banality.

плот [gen. плота́; 2nd loc. плоту́] n. raft.

плотва́ n. roach (fish).

плоти́на n. dam.

пло́тник n. carpenter.

пло́тничать v. impfv. to work as a carpenter.

пло́тничество n. carpentry.

пло́тничий [fem. -чья] adj. carpenter's (attrib.). Also, **пло́тничный.**

пло́тно adv. **1**, tightly. **2**, densely. **3**, in пое́сть пло́тно, to eat heartily.

пло́тность n.f. **1**, density. **2**, solidity.

пло́тный adj. [short form -тен, -тна́, -тно] **1**, dense; compact. **2**, (of material) closely woven. **3**, colloq. stocky; solidly built. **4**, colloq. (of a meal) hearty.

плотоя́дный adj. carnivorous. —**плотоя́дное живо́тное,** carnivore.

пло́тский adj., obs. carnal.

плоть n.f. flesh. —**во плоти́,** in the flesh. —**плоть и кровь моя́,** my own flesh and blood. —**плоть от пло́ти мое́й,** flesh of my flesh. —**кра́йняя плоть,** anat. foreskin.

пло́хо adv. badly; poorly. Пло́хо па́хнуть, to smell bad. —adj., used predicatively **1**, bad: э́то пло́хо, that's bad. **2**, (with dat.) ill; not well: ему́ пло́хо, he is not well. **3**, (with dat.) in a bad way: ей пло́хо, she is in a bad way.

плохо́й adj. [short form плох, плоха́, пло́хо, пло́хи or плохи́; comp. ху́же] bad; poor.

плоша́ть v. impfv. (usu. used negatively) colloq. to make a mistake.

площа́дка [gen. pl. -док] n. **1**, ground; site; area: площа́дка для игр, playground; строи́тельная площа́дка, building site. **2**, sports court: те́ннисная/баскетбо́льная площа́дка, tennis/basketball court. **3**, landing (of a staircase). **4**, platform (of a railway car or streetcar): пускова́я or ста́ртовая площа́дка, launching pad.

площадно́й adj. coarse; crude; vulgar; of the gutter.

пло́щадь [pl. пло́щади, -де́й, -дя́м] n.f. **1**, area. **2**, space: жила́я пло́щадь, living space. **3**, square: Кра́сная пло́щадь, Red Square.

плуг [pl. плуги́] n. plow.

плу́нжер n. plunger.

плут [gen. плута́] n. cheat; swindler.

плута́ть v. impfv., colloq. to stray; wander.

плути́шка [gen. pl. -шек] n.m. imp; rascal.

плу́тни [gen. -ней] n. pl., colloq. tricks.

плутова́тый adj. crafty; cunning.

плутова́ть v. impfv. [pfv. сплутова́ть; pres. -ту́ю, -ту́ешь] colloq. to cheat.

плутовско́й adj. **1**, crooked; underhanded. **2**, (of one's face, eyes, etc.) roguish. **3**, lit. picaresque.

плутовство́ n. **1**, cheating. **2**, trickery.

плутокра́т n. plutocrat. —**плутократи́ческий,** adj. plutocratic. —**плутокра́тия,** n. plutocracy.

Плуто́н n. Pluto (the planet).

плуто́ний n. plutonium.

плыть v. impfv. [pfv. поплы́ть; pres. плыву́, плывёшь; past fem. плыла́] **1**, to swim. **2**, to sail. **3**, to float. —**плыть сто́я,** to tread water. See also **пла́вать.**

плюга́вый adj., colloq. **1**, ugly; miserable-looking. **2**, fig. trivial; piddling.

плюма́ж n. plume (on a hat.).

плю́нуть v., pfv. of **плева́ть.**

плюс n. **1**, plus sign. **2**, fig., colloq. plus; advantage. —adv. plus: два плюс три равно́ пяти́, two plus three equals five. Плюс пять гра́дусов, five degrees above freezing.

ПЛЮСНА́ [*pl.* плю́сны, -сен] *n.* metatarsus. —**плюс-невой**, *adj.* metatarsal.

ПЛЮ́ХАТЬСЯ *v.r. impfv.* [*pfv.* плю́хнуться] (*with* в *or* на + *acc.*) *colloq.* to flop into/onto.

ПЛЮШ *n.* plush (*fabric*). —**плю́шевый**, *adj.* plush.

ПЛЮ́ШКА [*gen. pl.* -шек] *n.* sweet roll; bun.

ПЛЮЩ [*gen.* плюща́] *n.* ivy. —**плюще́вой**, *adj.* ivy (*attrib.*).

ПЛЯЖ *n.* beach. —**пля́жный**, *adj.* beach (*attrib.*).

ПЛЯС *n., colloq.* dance.

ПЛЯСА́ТЬ *v. impfv.* [*pfv.* спляса́ть; *pres.* пляшу́, пля́-шешь] to dance.

ПЛЯ́СКА [*gen. pl.* -сок] *n.* dance. —**пля́ска свято́го Ви́тта; ви́ттова пля́ска**, Saint Vitus' dance.

ПЛЯСОВО́Й *adj.* dance (*attrib.*); dancing. —**плясова́я**, *n.* dance tune.

ПЛЯСУ́Н [*gen.* -суна́] *n.m.* [*fem.* -су́нья] *colloq.* dancer.

ПНЕВМАТИ́ЧЕСКИЙ *adj.* pneumatic.

ПНУТЬ *v., pfv. of* **пина́ть**.

ПО *prep.* A, *with dat.* **1,** along: идти́ по у́лице, to walk along the street. **2,** about; around; through: ходи́ть по ко́мнате, to pace about the room; е́здить по стране́, to travel around/through a country. **3,** in *or* to various places: ходи́ть по магази́нам, to go shopping; раз-мести́ть това́ры по по́лкам, to arrange the merchan-dise on the shelves. **4,** in the direction of: по ве́тру, with the wind; по тече́нию, downstream. **5,** by: по оши́бке, by mistake; по желе́зной доро́ге, by rail; по профе́ссии, by profession. **6,** through; due to; on account of: не по мое́й вине́, through no fault of mine; отсу́тствовать по боле́зни, to be absent on account of illness. **7,** according to: по пра́вилам, according to the rules; по мои́м часа́м, according to my watch. **8,** in the field of: кни́га по иску́сству, art book; чемпио́н по бо́ксу, boxing champion. **9,** to; for the purpose of: кампа́ния по привлече́нию тури́стов, campaign to attract tourists; опера́ция по удале́нию пу́ли, ope-ration to remove a bullet. **10,** *with verbs of striking:* уда́рить кулако́м по́ столу, to bang one's fist on the table. **11,** *with expressions of time* each; every; on: по вечера́м, each evening; по среда́м, on Wednesdays. B, *with acc.* **1,** *with expressions of time* through: с ию́ля по сентя́брь, from July through September. По сей день, to this day. **2,** up to; down to (*on one's body*): ко́сы по по́яс, braids down to one's waist; грязь была́ по коле́но, the mud was knee-deep. **3,** on (*a side or direction*): по ту сто́рону, on the other side; по ле́вую ру́ку, on the left. **4,** *obs.* for; to fetch: идти́ по́ воду, to go for water. C, *with prepl.* on; upon; after: по сме́рти отца́, on the death of his father; по оконча́нии университе́та, upon graduation from the university. D, *with dat. or acc.* **1,** each; apiece: де́ти получи́ли по я́блоку, each child received an apple. Чле́ны получи́ли по два биле́та, each member received two tickets. Я купи́л четы́ре кни́ги по рублю́, I bought four books at one ruble each. **2,** by; in: по одному́, one by one; по́ двое, two by two; по́ два, in twos. —**по мне**, as far as I am concerned.

ПО- *prefix* **1,** *used to form the perfective aspect:* по-бледне́ть, *pfv. of* бледне́ть. **2,** *indicating the beginning of an action:* побежа́ть, to begin to run. **3,** *indicating action of short duration:* почита́ть, to read for a while. **4,** (*with* -ива *or* -ыва *verbs*) *indicating action performed intermittently:* попи́сывать, to write from time to time. **5,** (*with comp. adjectives*) a little: погро́мче, a little

louder. **6,** *in various combinations:* по-мо́ему, in my opinion; по-ра́зному, in different ways; говори́ть по-ру́сски, to speak Russian.

ПОБАГРОВЕ́ТЬ *v., pfv. of* багрове́ть.

ПОБА́ИВАТЬСЯ *v.r. impfv.* (*with gen. or inf.*) *colloq.* to be somewhat afraid.

ПОБА́ЛИВАТЬ *v. impfv., colloq.* to ache a little; ache on and off; ache now and then.

ПОБЕ́Г *n.* **1,** escape. **2,** *bot.* sprout; shoot.

ПОБЕ́ГАТЬ *v. pfv.* to do a little running.

ПОБЕГУ́ШКИ *n. pl., in* быть на побегу́шках, *colloq.* **1,** to run errands. **2,** (*with* у) to be at someone's beck and call.

ПОБЕ́ДА *n.* victory.

ПОБЕДИ́ТЕЛЬ *n.m.* victor; winner.

ПОБЕДИ́ТЬ [*infl.* -ди́шь, -ди́т; *1st person sing. not used*] *v., pfv. of* побежда́ть.

ПОБЕ́ДНЫЙ *adj.* **1,** victory (*attrib.*); of victory. **2,** vic-torious; triumphant.

ПОБЕДОНО́СНЫЙ *adj.* victorious; triumphant.

ПОБЕЖА́ТЬ *v. pfv.* [*infl. like* бежа́ть] **1,** *pfv. of* бежа́ть. **2,** to begin to run.

ПОБЕЖДА́ТЬ *v. impfv.* [*pfv.* победи́ть] **1,** to defeat; vanquish; conquer. **2,** *v.i.* to triumph; win. **3,** *fig.* to conquer; overcome.

ПОБЕЛЕ́ТЬ *v., pfv. of* беле́ть.

ПОБЕЛИ́ТЬ *v., pfv. of* бели́ть (*in sense #1*).

ПОБЕ́ЛКА *n.* whitewashing.

ПОБЕРЕ́ЧЬ *v. pfv.* [*infl. like* бере́чь] **1,** to save; preserve. **2,** to take care of. **3,** to watch; look after. —**побе-ре́чься**, *refl.* to take care of oneself.

ПОБЕСЕ́ДОВАТЬ *v. pfv.* [*infl.* -дую, -дуешь] to have a chat.

ПОБЕСПОКО́ИТЬ *v. pfv.* to trouble; disturb. —**побес-поко́иться**, *refl.* **1,** to trouble oneself. **2,** to be con-cerned.

ПОБИРА́ТЬСЯ *v.r. impfv., colloq.* to beg; live by begging.

ПОБИ́ТЬ *v. pfv.* [*infl.* -бью, -бьёшь] **1,** *pfv. of* бить (*in senses #2 & #3*). **2,** to beat up. **3,** to kill; slaughter; destroy. **4,** (*of rain, hail, etc.*) to beat down; flatten; (*of frost*) to nip. **5,** *sports* to break (a record). —**поби́ться**, *refl.* **1,** to break; be broken. **2,** (*of fruit*) to be bruised; be damaged.

ПОБЛАГОДАРИ́ТЬ *v., pfv. of* благодари́ть.

ПОБЛА́ЖКА *n., colloq.* indulgence. —**дава́ть побла́ж-ку** (+ *dat.*), to be lenient with.

ПОБЛЕДНЕ́ТЬ *v., pfv. of* бледне́ть.

ПОБЛЁКЛЫЙ *adj.* faded.

ПОБЛЁКНУТЬ *v., pfv. of* блёкнуть.

ПОБЛИ́ЗОСТИ *adv.* nearby. —**побли́зости от**, near.

ПОБОЖИ́ТЬСЯ *v.r., pfv. of* божи́ться.

ПОБО́Й [*gen.* -бо́ев] *n. pl.* beating.

ПОБО́ИЩЕ *n.* **1,** *obs.* bloody battle. **2,** brawl. —**ледо́вое побо́ище**, Battle on the Ice (*famous battle fought on the ice of Lake Peipus in 1242*).

ПОБОЛТА́ТЬ *v. pfv.* **1,** *colloq.* to have a chat. **2,** *colloq.* to shake; agitate. **3,** (*with instr.*) to dangle.

ПОБО́ЛЬШЕ *adj.* a little larger. —*adv.* a little more.

ПОБО́РНИК *n.* champion; defender.

ПОБОРО́ТЬ *v. pfv.* [*infl.* -борю́, -бо́решь] **1,** to defeat; conquer. **2,** *fig.* to overcome (a feeling). —**поборо́ть себя́**, to control oneself.

ПОБО́РЫ [*gen.* -ров] *n. pl.* **1,** bribery. **2,** extortion.

ПОБО́ЧНЫЙ *adj.* **1,** occurring or done on the side; secondary; incidental: побо́чный проду́кт, by-product; побо́чные эффе́кты, side effects; побо́чная рабо́та, sideline. **2**, obs. illegitimate.

побоя́ться v.r. pfv. (with gen. or inf.) to be afraid.

побрани́ть v. pfv. to scold slightly; chide. —**побрани́ться**, refl. to have a quarrel.

побрата́ться v.r., pfv. of брата́ться.

побра́ть v. pfv. [infl. like брать] colloq. to take (all or many of something). —**чёрт побери́!**, what the hell!

побре́згать v., pfv. of бре́згать.

побрести́ v. pfv. [infl. like брести́] to trudge.

побри́ть v., pfv. of брить. —**побри́ться**, refl., pfv. of бри́ться.

поброди́ть v. pfv. [infl. -брожу́, -бро́дишь] colloq. to wander (for a while).

поброса́ть v. pfv. **1**, to throw; toss. **2**, to forsake; desert.

побряку́шка [gen. pl. -шек] n., colloq. **1**, trinket. **2**, (child's) rattle.

побуди́тельный adj. serving to cause or induce. —**побуди́тельная причи́на**, motive; incentive.

побуди́ть [infl. -жу́, -ди́шь] v., pfv. of побужда́ть.

побу́дка n. reveille.

побужда́ть v. impfv. [pfv. побуди́ть] to impel; induce; prompt; motivate.

побужде́ние n. **1**, urge: внеза́пное побужде́ние, a sudden urge. **2**, motive; reason: из коры́стных побужде́ний, for selfish motives/reasons. **3**, initiative: по со́бственному побужде́нию, on one's own initiative; on one's own.

побуре́ть v., pfv. of буре́ть.

побыва́ть v. pfv. **1**, (with в or на + prepl.) to visit; have been (to a place or to many places). **2**, (with у) to visit; go see (a person).

побы́вка n., colloq. **1**, short visit; stay. **2**, mil. furlough; leave.

побы́ть v. pfv. [infl. -бу́ду, -бу́дешь; past по́был, побыла́, по́было] to stay (somewhere).

пова́дить v. pfv. [infl. -ва́жу, -ва́дишь] colloq. to train. —**пова́диться**, refl., colloq. **1**, (with inf.) to get into the habit of. **2**, (with a prep.) to go all the time; drop in on constantly.

пова́дка [gen. pl. -док] n., colloq. **1**, habit; mannerism. **2**, pl. manner; ways.

пова́дно adv., colloq., in **чтобы не́ было** (+ dat.) **пова́дно** (+ inf.), so as to be certain that one will not do it again.

повали́ть[1] [infl. -валю́, -ва́лишь] v., pfv. of вали́ть[1] (in sense #1). —**повали́ться**, refl., pfv. of вали́ться.

повали́ть[2] v. pfv. [infl. -ва́лит] colloq. **1**, to flock; throng. **2**, (of snow) to begin to fall heavily; (of smoke) begin to pour out.

пова́льный adj. general; mass.

поваля́ть v., pfv. of валя́ть (in sense #1). —**поваля́ться**, refl., pfv. of валя́ться.

по́вар [pl. повара́] n. cook.

пова́ренный adj. culinary. —**пова́ренная кни́га**, cookbook. —**пова́ренная соль**, common salt; table salt.

по-ва́шему adv. **1**, in your opinion. **2**, as you wish: пусть бу́дет по-ва́шему, have it your way.

пове́дать v. pfv. to announce; reveal; disclose.

поведе́ние n. behavior; conduct.

повезти́ v., pfv. of везти́.

повелева́ть v. impfv. [pfv. повеле́ть] **1**, (with dat.) to order; command. **2**, [impfv. only] (with instr.) to rule; rule over.

повеле́ние n. command.

повеле́ть [infl. -велю́, -вели́шь] v., pfv. of повелева́ть.

повели́тель n.m. **1**, sovereign; ruler. **2**, colloq. lord and master.

повели́тельный adj. imperious; peremptory. —**повели́тельное наклоне́ние**, gram. imperative mood.

повенча́ть v., pfv. of венча́ть (in sense #2). —**повенча́ться**, refl., pfv. of венча́ться (in sense #2).

поверга́ть v. impfv. [pfv. пове́ргнуть] **1**, obs. to knock down; topple. **2**, obs. to defeat. **3**, (with в + acc.) to plunge into (a state, mood, etc.).

пове́ргнуть [past -ве́рг, -ла] v., pfv. of поверга́ть.

пове́ренный n., decl. as an adj. **1**, attorney. **2**, confidant. —**пове́ренный в дела́х**, chargé d'affaires.

пове́рить v., pfv. of ве́рить and поверя́ть.

пове́рка n. **1**, check. **2**, roll call. —**на пове́рку**, in actual fact; in reality.

поверну́ть v., pfv. of повёртывать and повора́чивать. —**поверну́ться**, refl., pfv. of повёртываться and повора́чиваться.

поверте́ть v. pfv. [infl. -верчу́, -ве́ртишь] **1**, to turn slightly. **2**, to turn this way and that. —**поверте́ться**, refl. to turn; turn this way and that.

повёртывать v. impfv. = повора́чивать. —**повёртываться**, refl. = повора́чиваться.

пове́рх prep., with gen. over. —adv. above; overhead.

пове́рхностный adj. **1**, surface (attrib.). **2**, superficial. —**пове́рхностно**, adv. superficially. —**пове́рхностность**, n.f. superficiality.

пове́рхность n.f. surface.

по́верху adv., colloq. on top; on the surface.

пове́рье n. popular belief; superstition.

поверя́ть v. impfv. [pfv. пове́рить] **1**, to confide; entrust. **2**, obs. to check; verify.

пове́са n.m. playboy.

повеселе́ть v., pfv. of веселе́ть.

повесели́ть v. pfv. to amuse; entertain. —**повесели́ться**, refl. to have fun.

пове́сить [infl. -шу, -сишь] v., pfv. of ве́шать. —**пове́ситься**, refl., pfv. of ве́шаться.

повествова́ние n. narration; narrative.

повествова́тельный adj. **1**, narrative. **2**, gram. declarative.

повествова́ть v. impfv. [pres. -ству́ю, -ству́ешь] to tell; relate; narrate.

повести́ v. pfv. [infl. like вести́] **1**, pfv. of вести́ and поводи́ть[1]. **2**, to begin; start; launch. **3**, to manage; handle.

повести́сь v.r. pfv. [infl. like вести́] **1**, impers. to be the custom: и́сстари повело́сь (+ inf.), since ancient times it has been the custom to... **2**, (with с + instr.) colloq. to take up with (someone).

пове́стка [gen. pl. -ток] n. notice; notification. —**пове́стка в суд**, summons; subpoena. —**пове́стка дня**, agenda.

по́весть [pl. по́вести, -сте́й, -стя́м] n.f. story; tale.

пове́трие n. **1**, obs. epidemic. **2**, colloq. rage; craze; fad.

пове́шение n. hanging (method of execution).

пове́ять v. pfv. **1**, to begin to blow. **2**, impers. (with instr.) to be in the air: пове́яло весно́й, spring was in the air; пове́яло прохла́дой, there was a coolness in the air.

повздо́рить v., pfv. of вздо́рить.

повзросле́ть v. pfv. to grow up; become an adult.

повива́льный adj., in **повива́льная ба́бка**, obs. midwife.

повида́ть v., pfv. of вида́ть. —**повида́ться**, refl., pfv. of вида́ться.

по-ви́димому adv. apparently; evidently.

пови́дло n. jam.

пови́нная n., decl. as an adj. admission; confession (of guilt). —**принести́ пови́нную**, to confess one's guilt. —**яви́ться** or **прийти́ с пови́нной**, to give oneself up.

пови́нность n.f. obligation; duty. —**во́инская пови́нность**, military conscription; the draft.

пови́нный adj. [short form пови́нен, -нна] (with в + prepl.) guilty (of). See also **пови́нная**.

повинова́ться v.r. impfv. & pfv. [pres. -ну́юсь, -ну́ешься] (with dat.) to obey.

повинове́ние n. obedience.

повиса́ть v. impfv. [pfv. пови́снуть] **1,** to hang; remain suspended. **2,** (with на + prepl.) to hang onto; cling to. **3,** to hang down; droop. —**повиса́ть в во́здухе, 1,** to remain poised in midair. **2,** fig. to be up in the air.

пови́снуть [past -ви́с, -ла] v., pfv. of повиса́ть.

повиту́ха n., obs., colloq. midwife.

повле́чь v., pfv. of влечь.

повлия́ть v., pfv. of влия́ть.

по́вод[1] n. grounds; cause; reason. —**по по́воду** (+ gen.), regarding; with regard to. —**по э́тому по́воду**, in this connection.

по́вод[2] [2nd loc. поводу́; pl. пово́дья, пово́дьев] n. rein. —**быть на поводу́ у**, to be under the thumb of. —**вести́ на поводу́**, to lead by the nose. —**идти́/пойти́ на поводу́ у**, to knuckle under to.

поводи́ть[1] v. impfv. [pfv. повести́; pres. -вожу́, -во́дишь] (with instr.) **1,** to move; wiggle. Он и бро́вью не повёл, he didn't bat an eye. **2,** to run along the surface of something: поводи́ть па́льцами по мате́рии, to run one's fingers over the material.

поводи́ть[2] v. pfv. [infl. -вожу́, -во́дишь] to lead (a person); walk (a horse).

поводо́к [gen. -дка́] n. leash.

поводы́рь [gen. -дыря́] n.m. **1,** one who leads a blind person. **2,** colloq. guide.

пово́зка [gen. pl. -зок] n. wagon.

повойник n. kerchief worn around the head by married peasant women in old Russia.

поволо́ка n., in глаза́ с поволо́кой, languishing eyes.

повора́чивать v. impfv. [pfv. поверну́ть] **1,** v.t. to turn: поверну́ть кран, to turn the faucet. **2,** v.i. to turn: поверну́ть напра́во, to turn right. —**куда́** (or **как**) **ни поверни́**, any way you look at it.

повора́чиваться v.r. impfv. [pfv. поверну́ться] **1,** to turn: ключ не повора́чивается, the key won't turn. **2,** [often with кругом] to turn around. **3,** fig. to turn out. —**поверну́ться спино́й к**, to turn one's back on (figuratively). —**у меня́ язы́к не поверну́лся**, I couldn't bring myself (to tell him, say it, etc.).

поворожи́ть v., pfv. of ворожи́ть.

поворо́т n. **1,** turn: круто́й поворо́т, sharp turn. **2,** fig. turn; change; turning point.

поворо́тливость n.f. **1,** agility. **2,** maneuverability.

поворо́тливый adj. **1,** nimble, agile. **2,** (of a vehicle) maneuverable.

поворо́тный adj. **1,** rotary; turning; swivel (attrib.):

поворо́тный круг, turntable; поворо́тное сиде́нье, swivel seat. **2,** fig. turning; decisive: поворо́тный пункт, turning point.

повреди́ть [infl. -жу́, -ди́шь] v., pfv. of вреди́ть and поврежда́ть.

поврежда́ть v. impfv. [pfv. повреди́ть] to hurt; injure; damage.

поврежде́ние n. **1,** damage. **2,** injury.

повремени́ть v. pfv., colloq. **1,** (with с + instr.) to delay; hold off (doing something). **2,** to wait.

повреме́нный adj. **1,** periodic. **2,** (of work, pay, etc.) by the hour, day, week, etc.

повседне́вный adj. daily; day-to-day; everyday.

повсеме́стный adj. general; to be found everywhere. —**повсеме́стно**, adv. everywhere.

повста́нец [gen. -нца] n. rebel; insurgent. —**повста́нческий**, adj. rebel (attrib.); insurgent.

повстреча́ть v. pfv., colloq. to run into; meet. —**повстреча́ться**, refl. (with с + instr.) colloq. to run into; meet.

повсю́ду adv. everywhere.

повторе́ние n. **1,** repetition. **2,** recurrence. **3,** review.

повтори́тельный adj. repeat (attrib.). —**повтори́тельный курс**, refresher course.

повтори́ть v., pfv. of повторя́ть. —**повтори́ться**, refl., pfv. of повторя́ться.

повто́рный adj. a second; repeat (attrib.). —**повто́рно**, adv. for the second time; once again.

повторя́ть v. impfv. [pfv. повтори́ть] **1,** to repeat. **2,** to review; go over. **3,** to equal; tie (a record). —**повторя́ться**, refl. **1,** to happen again. **2,** to sound again; be heard again. **3,** to repeat itself. **4,** [impfv. only] to repeat oneself.

повыша́ть v. impfv. [pfv. повы́сить] **1,** to raise. **2,** to increase; heighten. **3,** to improve; enhance. **4,** to promote; give a promotion to. —**повыша́ться**, refl. **1,** to rise. **2,** to increase. **3,** to be promoted.

повыше́ние n. **1,** rise; increase. Повыше́ние зарпла́ты, pay raise. **2,** in повыше́ние по слу́жбе, promotion.

повы́шенный adj. increased; heightened. Повы́шенная температу́ра, a (slight) temperature.

повяза́ть [infl. -вяжу́, -вя́жешь] v., pfv. of повя́зывать. —**повяза́ться**, refl., pfv. of повя́зываться.

повя́зка [gen. pl. -зок] n. **1,** band. **2,** bandage.

повя́зывать v. impfv. [pfv. повяза́ть] to tie. —**повя́зываться**, refl. (with instr.) to tie (something) around oneself.

пога́нить v. impfv., colloq. **1,** to soil; get dirty. **2,** fig. to defile.

пога́нка [gen. pl. -нок] n. **1,** toadstool. **2,** grebe (bird).

пога́ный adj. **1,** (of food) inedible; impure. **2,** colloq. foul; vile. —**пога́ное ведро́**, garbage pail.

погаса́ть v. impfv. [pfv. пога́снуть] **1,** (of lights, a fire, etc.) to go out. **2,** fig. to dim; fade.

погаси́ть [infl. -гашу́, -га́сишь] v., pfv. of гаси́ть and погаша́ть.

пога́снуть [past пога́с, -ла] v., pfv. of га́снуть and погаса́ть.

погаша́ть v. impfv. [pfv. погаси́ть] **1,** to cancel (a stamp). **2,** to pay off (a debt, loan, etc.).

погаше́ние n. **1,** cancellation (of a stamp). **2,** paying off.

погиба́ть v. impfv. [pfv. поги́бнуть] **1,** to be killed; perish. **2,** (of a ship or plane) to go down.

погибнуть [*past* -гиб, -ла] *v.*, *pfv.* of **гибнуть** and **погибать**.

погладить *v.*, *pfv.* of **гладить** (*in sense #2*).

поглаживать *v. impfv.* to stroke from time to time.

поглощать *v. impfv.* [*pfv.* **поглотить**] **1**, to absorb; take in; soak up. **2**, to consume; use up. **3**, to engulf. **4**, *fig.* to absorb; engross. **5**, *fig.* to devour (books, stories, etc.).

поглощение *n.* absorption.

поглупеть *v.*, *pfv.* of **глупеть**.

поглядеть *v.*, *pfv.* of **глядеть**. —**поглядеться**, *refl.*, *pfv.* of **глядеться**.

поглядывать *v. impfv.* **1**, to glance from time to time. **2**, (*with* за + *instr.*) *colloq.* to keep an eye on.

погнать *v. pfv.* [*infl. like* **гнать**] to drive. —**погнаться**, *refl.* (*with* за + *instr.*) to chase after; take off after.

погнуть *v. pfv.* to bend. —**погнуться**, *refl.* to bend; become bent.

погнушаться *v.r.*, *pfv.* of **гнушаться**.

поговаривать *v. impfv.*, *colloq.* to talk: поговаривают, что..., there is talk that...; it is rumored that...

поговорить *v. pfv.* to have a talk.

поговорка [*gen. pl.* -рок] *n.* saying.

погода *n.* weather. —**делать погоду**, to make the difference. —**ждать у моря погоды**, to wait for a miracle to happen.

погодить *v. pfv.* [*infl.* -гожу, -годишь] *colloq.* to wait a while. —**немного погодя**, a little while later.

погодный *adj.* **1**, yearly. **2**, weather (*attrib.*).

погодок [*gen.* -дка] *n.* one of a pair of siblings a year apart in age: Иван и Ольга погодки, Ivan and Olga are a year apart in age.

погожий *adj.* (*of the weather*) fine: погожий день, a fine day.

поголовный *adj.* general; total; all-inclusive. —**поголовно**, *adv.* to a man: все поголовно, everyone to the last man.

поголовье *n.* total amount of livestock.

поголубеть *v.*, *pfv.* of **голубеть**.

погон *n.*, *mil.* shoulder strap.

погонщик *n.* driver; drover.

погоня *n.* **1**, pursuit; chase. **2**, pursuers. **3**, *fig.* pursuit: погоня за счастьем, pursuit of happiness.

погонять *v. impfv.* **1**, to drive; urge on (animals). **2**, *colloq.* to hurry; rush (someone).

погорелец [*gen.* -льца] *n.* person made homeless by a fire.

погореть *v. pfv.* **1**, *colloq.* to lose everything in a fire. **2**, *colloq.* to burn down. **3**, *colloq.* (*of many things*) to be burned. **4**, to burn for a while.

погост *n.* village cemetery.

погостить *v. pfv.* [*infl.* -щу, -стишь] (*with* у) to stay for a while (at the home of).

пограничник *n.* border guard.

пограничный *adj.* border (*attrib.*); boundary (*attrib.*); frontier (*attrib.*).

погреб [*pl.* погреба] *n.* cellar. —**пороховой погреб**, **1**, powder magazine. **2**, *fig.* powder keg.

погребальный *adj.* funeral (*attrib.*).

погребать *v. impfv.* [*pfv.* **погрести**] to bury; inter.

погребение *n.* burial.

погремушка [*gen. pl.* -шек] *n.* (child's) rattle.

погрести *v. pfv.* [*infl. like* **грести**] **1**, *pfv.* of **погребать**. **2**, to row (*for a while*).

погреть *v. pfv.* to warm (*for a while*). —**погреться**, *refl.* to warm oneself (*for a while*); warm up a little.

погрешить *v.*, *pfv.* of **грешить** (*in sense #2*).

погрешность *n.f.* error.

погрозить *v. pfv.* [*infl.* -жу, -зишь] to make a threatening gesture: погрозить пальцем (+ *dat.*), to shake one's finger at.

погром *n.* **1**, massacre. **2**, pogrom. —**погромный**, *adj.* (*of a speech*) rabble-rousing. —**погромщик**, *n.* one taking part in a pogrom; thug.

погружать *v. impfv.* [*pfv.* **погрузить**] **1**, to dip; immerse. **2**, *fig.* to plunge: город был погружён в темноту, to city was plunged into darkness. **3**, *fig.* to absorb; engross: весь погружён в работу, completely absorbed in one's work; погружён в размышления, lost in thought. —**погружаться**, *refl.* (*with* в + *acc.*) **1**, to sink (into); be submerged (in). **2**, *fig.* to be plunged into (darkness); become absorbed in (one's work); be lost in (thought).

погружение *n.* immersion; submersion.

погрузить [*infl.* -гружу, -грузишь *or* -грузишь] *v.*, *pfv.* of **грузить** (*in sense #2*) and **погружать**. —**погрузиться**, *refl.*, *pfv.* of **грузиться** and **погружаться**.

погрузка *n.* loading. —**погрузочный**, *adj.* loading (*attrib.*).

погрязать *v. impfv.* [*pfv.* **погрязнуть**] (*with* в + *prepl.*) to become mired in; get bogged down in.

погрязнуть *v. pfv.* [*past* -гряз, -ла] **1**, *pfv.* of **погрязать**. **2**, *fig.* (*with* в + *prepl.*) to wallow (in).

погубить *v.*, *pfv.* of **губить**.

погудка [*gen. pl.* -док] *n.*, *colloq.* **1**, tune; melody. **2**, story; tale. —**старая погудка на новый лад**, the same old story with a new twist.

погуливать *v. impfv.*, *colloq.* **1**, to stroll; walk up and down. **2**, to carouse (*from time to time*).

погулять *v. pfv.* to go for a walk; take a walk.

погустеть *v.*, *pfv.* of **густеть**.

под *also*, **подо** *prep.* A, *with instr.* **1**, under (*with verbs of location*): быть под водой, to be under water; сидеть под деревом, to be sitting under a tree. **2**, (*in various figurative senses*) under: под присягой, under oath; под чужим именем, under an assumed name. **3**, in the environs of (a city): жить под Москвой, to live in the environs of Moscow. B, *with acc.* **1**, under (*with verbs of motion*): мяч закатился под диван, the ball rolled under the couch; поставьте чемодан под кровать, put the suitcase under the bed. **2**, (*with numbers denoting age*) under; not yet: ему под сорок, he is under/not yet/forty. **3**, (*with certain nouns*) toward: под вечер, toward evening. **4**, to the sound of: танцевать под музыку, to dance to the music. **5**, in imitation: мебель под красное дерево, furniture in imitation mahogany. C, *with acc. or instr.* (*of a container*) used to hold: банка под варенье (*or* под вареньем), jelly jar.

под- *also*, **подо-**, **подъ-** *prefix* **1**, *indicating motion upward or from under*: подбрасывать, to toss up; подпирать, to prop up. **2**, *indicating motion under*: подлезть под диван, to crawl under the couch. **3**, *indicating motion toward*: подходить, to approach. **4**, *indicating action to a slight degree*: поджарить, to fry lightly; подмёрзнуть, to be slightly frozen. **5**, *indicating the adding of something*: подливать сливок в кофе, to add some cream to the coffee. **6**, *indicating stealth*: подслушивать, to eavesdrop. **7**, joining in; going along: подпева́ть, to join in singing. **8,** (*with nouns*) under; sub-: подпо́лье, underground; подразделе́-ние, subdivision. **9,** (*with adjectives*) on the outskirts of: подмоско́вный, on the outskirts of Moscow.

подава́льщик *n.* waiter; server. —**подава́льщица,** *n.* waitress.

подава́ть *v. impfv.* [*pfv.* **пода́ть;** *pres.* -даю́, -даёшь] **1,** (*with certain nouns*) to give: пода́ть сове́т/сигна́л/кома́нду, to give advice/a signal/a command/. **2,** to serve (food, a meal, etc.). **3,** *v.i.* to give alms. **4,** to bring; deliver (a vehicle). **5,** to hand in; submit; file; lodge; register. **6,** to help on with: подава́ть кому́-ни-будь пальто́, to help someone on with his (her) coat. **7,** *tennis* to serve. —**подава́ть в отста́вку,** to submit (*or* tender) one's resignation. —**подава́ть в суд, 1,** to sue; go to court. **2,** (*with* на + *acc.*) to bring (*or* file) suit against. —**подава́ть го́лос, 1,** to announce one's pres-ence. **2,** to cast one's vote. —**подава́ть наде́жду, 1,** to offer hope. **2,** to give (*or show*) promise. —**подава́ть приме́р,** to set an example. —**подава́ть при́знаки жи́зни,** to show signs of life. —**подава́ть ру́ку,** to offer (*or* extend) one's hand. —**не подава́ть ви́ду,** not to show; not let on. —**руко́й пода́ть,** a stone's throw (from).

подава́ться *v.r. impfv.* [*pfv.* **пода́ться;** *pres.* -даю́сь, -даёшься] **1,** to be served. **2,** to move. **3,** *colloq.* to yield; give way. **4,** (*with* в *or* на + *acc.*) to leave (for); set out (for).

подави́ть [*infl.* -давлю́, -да́вишь] *v., pfv. of* **подавля́ть.** —**подави́ться,** *refl., pfv. of* **дави́ться.**

подавле́ние *n.* suppression.

пода́вленный *adj.* **1,** (*of a sound*) muffled. **2,** (*of a feeling*) suppressed. **3,** depressed; despondent. —**по-да́вленность.** *n.f.* depression; despondency.

подавля́ть *v. impfv.* [*pfv.* **подави́ть**] **1,** to press down; weigh down. **2,** to suppress; put down; crush. **3,** to suppress; repress (a feeling, laugh, etc.). **4,** to depress; dispirit. **5,** to overwhelm.

подавля́ющий *adj.* **1,** overwhelming: подавля́ющее большинство́, overwhelming majority. **2,** depressing.

пода́вно *adv.* (*usu.* и **пода́вно**) *colloq.* even more (so): весно́й там жа́рко, а ле́том и пода́вно, it's hot there in spring and even more so in summer.

пода́гра *n.* gout.

пода́льше *adv., colloq.* a little farther.

подари́ть *v., pfv. of* **дари́ть.**

пода́рок [*gen.* -рка] *n.* gift; present. Получи́ть что́-нибудь в пода́рок, to receive something as a gift.

пода́тель *n.m.* bearer.

пода́тливый *adj.* **1,** pliable; malleable. **2,** *fig.* pliable; amenable.

по́дать *n.f.,* pre-rev. tax. —**податно́й,** *adj.* tax (*attrib.*).

пода́ть [*infl. like* **дать;** *past* по́дал, подала́, по́дало] *v., pfv. of* **подава́ть.** —**пода́ться,** *refl.* [*past* пода́лся, -ла́сь, -ло́сь] *pfv. of* **подава́ться.**

пода́ча *n.* **1,** giving; presenting; handing in. **2,** supply; delivery. **3,** *tennis* serve; service.

пода́чка [*gen. pl.* -чек] *n., colloq.* handout.

пода́яние *n., obs.* alms.

подбавля́ть *v. impfv.* [*pfv.* **подба́вить**] (*with gen.*) to add a little (of something).

подбега́ть *v. impfv.* [*pfv.* **подбежа́ть**] (*with* к) to come running (up to).

подбежа́ть [*infl. like* **бежа́ть**] *v., pfv. of* **подбега́ть.**

подбива́ть *v. impfv.* [*pfv.* **подби́ть**] **1,** to nail on. **2,**

to line (a garment). **3,** *mil.* to cripple; knock out. **4,** *col-loq.* to incite; put up to. —**подби́ть глаз** (+ *dat.*), to give (someone) a black eye.

подбира́ть *v. impfv.* [*pfv.* **подобра́ть**] **1,** to pick up. **2,** to tuck up. **3,** to draw up (the edge of a garment); put up (one's hair). **4,** to draw in (reins, one's stomach, etc.). **5,** to purse (one's lips). **6,** to select; choose. —**подбира́ться,** *refl.* **1,** to be selected; be chosen. **2,** (*with* к) to sneak up to *or* on. **3,** (*with* под + *acc.*) *colloq.* to crawl under. **4,** *colloq.* to draw oneself up; straighten up. **5,** *colloq.* to draw oneself in; huddle up.

подби́ть [*infl.* **подобью́, подобьёшь**] *v., pfv. of* **подби-ва́ть.**

подбодря́ть *v. impfv.* [*pfv.* **подбодри́ть**] to cheer up; hearten. —**подбодря́ться,** *refl.* to cheer up; take heart.

подбо́р *n.* **1,** selection; selecting. **2,** selection; assort-ment. —**как на подбо́р,** choice: я́блоки как на под-бо́р, choice apples.

подбо́рка *n.* **1,** selection. **2,** group of related articles under a single heading in a newspaper.

подборо́док [*gen.* -дка] *n.* chin.

подбоче́ниться *v.r. pfv., colloq.* to place one's hands on one's hips.

подбра́сывать *v. impfv.* [*pfv.* **подбро́сить**] **1,** to throw up; toss up. **2,** (*with* под + *acc.*) to throw under; toss under. **3,** to throw in; throw on (more of some-thing). **4,** to slip; place surreptitiously. **5,** to abandon (a child). **6,** to shake; toss up and down. *Also impers.:* маши́ну/пассажи́ров си́льно подбра́сывало, the car/passengers was/were tossed all around (*or* kept bouncing up and down).

подбро́сить [*infl.* -шу, -сишь] *v., pfv. of* **подбра́сы-вать.**

подва́л *n.* **1,** basement. **2,** special article (*in a newspa-per*).

подва́льный *adj.* basement (*attrib.*).

подвезти́ [*infl. like* **везти́**] *v., pfv. of* **подвози́ть.**

подвене́чный *adj.* wedding (*attrib.*); bridal.

подверга́ть *v. impfv.* [*pfv.* **подве́ргнуть**] (*with dat.*) to subject (to); expose (to). —**подверга́ться,** *refl.* (*with dat.*) to be subjected (to); be exposed (to); undergo.

подве́ргнуть [*past* -ве́рг, -ла] *v., pfv. of* **подверга́ть.** —**подве́ргнуться,** *refl., pfv. of* **подверга́ться.**

подве́рженный *adj.* (*with dat.*) subject (to); liable (to); prone (to); susceptible (to). —**подве́рженность,** *n.f.* susceptibility.

подвёртывать *v. impfv.* [*pfv.* **подверну́ть**] **1,** to turn up; fold up. **2,** to tuck under; fold under. **3,** to sprain; twist: подверну́ть себе́ но́гу, to sprain/twist/turn one's ankle. **4,** to tighten; screw tight. —**подвёрты-ваться,** *refl.* **1,** to be turned inward. **2,** *colloq.* to turn up; show up; appear.

подве́сить [*infl.* -шу, -сишь] *v., pfv. of* **подве́ши-вать.**

подве́ска [*gen. pl.* -сок] *n.* **1,** hanging up. **2,** *mech.* suspension. **3,** pendant.

подвесно́й *adj.* hanging; suspended. —**подвесна́я доро́га,** aerial railway. —**подвесно́й мост,** suspen-sion bridge. —**подвесно́й мото́р,** outboard motor.

подвести́ [*infl. like* **вести́**] *v., pfv. of* **подводи́ть.**

подве́тренный *adj.* leeward.

подве́шивать *v. impfv.* [*pfv.* **подве́сить**] to hang; suspend.

подвива́ть *v. impfv.* [*pfv.* **подви́ть**] to curl slightly.

по́двиг *n.* feat; exploit.

подви́гать *v. pfv.* (*with instr.*) to move (a part of one's body) slightly; wiggle. —**подви́гаться**, *refl.* to move a little.

подвига́ть *v. impfv.* [*pfv.* **подви́нуть**] **1**, to move. **2**, *fig., colloq.* to give a push to; get (something) moving. —**подвига́ться**, *refl.* **1**, to move. **2**, to move over. **3**, to edge (toward, forward, etc.). **4**, *fig.* to make progress.

подви́д *n.* subspecies.

подви́жник *n.* **1**, religious ascetic. **2**, (*with gen.*) champion (of).

подвижно́й *adj.* mobile. —**подвижно́й соста́в**, rolling stock.

подви́жность *n.f.* **1**, mobility. **2**, liveliness.

подви́жный *adj.* lively; active; quick.

подвиза́ться *v.r. impfv.* to work (in a certain field): подвиза́ться на своём по́прище, to ply one's trade.

подвинти́ть [*infl.* -чу́, -ти́шь] *v., pfv. of* **подви́нчивать**.

подви́нуть *v., pfv. of* **подвига́ть**. —**подви́нуться**, *refl., pfv. of* **подвига́ться**.

подви́нчивать *v. impfv.* [*pfv.* **подвинти́ть**] to tighten; screw tight.

подви́ть [*infl.* **подовью́**, **подовьёшь**; *past fem.* **подвила́**] *v., pfv. of* **подвива́ть**.

подвла́стный *adj.* (*with dat.*) subject (to); under the control (of).

подво́да *n.* cart; wagon.

подводи́ть *v. impfv.* [*pfv.* **подвести́**; *pres.* -вожу́, -во́дишь] **1**, (*with к*) to lead up to; bring to. **2**, *mil.* to bring up (reserves). **3**, to extend: подводи́ть доро́гу к реке́, to extend a road as far as the river. **4**, (*with под + acc.*) to place under; place beneath (for support); lay (a foundation, mine, etc.). **5**, (*with под + acc.*) to place; subsume (in a certain category). **6**, to adjust (a clock). **7**, to touch up (*with make-up*): подвести́ бро́ви, to pencil one's eyebrows. **8**, *colloq.* to let down; disappoint. —**подводи́ть бала́нс**, to strike a balance. —**подводи́ть ито́г** *or* **ито́ги** (+ *dat.*), to add up; total; *fig.* sum up. —**подводи́ть к концу́**, to complete; finish. —у меня́ живо́т подвело́, I have an empty feeling in my stomach.

подво́дный *adj.* **1**, underwater. **2**, submarine (*attrib.*). —**подво́дный ка́мень**, **1**, reef. **2**, *fig.* pitfall. —**подво́дное крыло́**, hydrofoil. —**подво́дная ло́дка**, submarine. —**подво́дная скала́**, reef. —**подво́дное тече́ние**, undercurrent; undertow.

подво́з *n.* supply; delivery; transport.

подвози́ть *v. impfv.* [*pfv.* **подвезти́**; *pres.* -вожу́, -во́зишь] **1**, to transport; bring; deliver. **2**, to pick up along the way; give (someone) a lift.

подворо́тня [*gen. pl.* -тен] *n.* **1**, space beneath a gate. **2**, board covering this space.

подво́х *n., colloq.* (dirty or sneaky) trick.

подвы́пивший *adj., colloq.* tipsy; high; tight.

подвяза́ть [*infl.* -вяжу́, -вя́жешь] *v., pfv. of* **подвя́зывать**. —**подвяза́ться**, *refl., pfv. of* **подвя́зываться**.

подвя́зка [*gen. pl.* -зок] *n.* garter.

подвя́зывать *v. impfv.* [*pfv.* **подвяза́ть**] **1**, to tie up (*so as not to fall*). **2**, to tie around oneself. —**подвя́зываться**, *refl.* (*with instr.*) to tie (something) around oneself.

подгиба́ть *v. impfv.* [*pfv.* **подогну́ть**] **1**, to fold over; tuck in. **2**, to bend (one's knees). **3**, *in* подгиба́ть но́ги

под себя́, to tuck one's legs under one. —**подгиба́ться**, *refl.* **1**, to be turned up; be folded up. **2**, (*of one's legs or knees*) to bend; sag.

подгляде́ть *v. pfv.* [*infl.* -гляжу́, -гляди́шь] **1**, *pfv. of* **подгля́дывать**. **2**, to catch sight of; spot; detect.

подгля́дывать *v. impfv.* [*pfv.* **подгляде́ть**] **1**, to watch secretly. **2**, (*with в + acc.*) to peep through. **3**, (*with за + instr.*) to peep at.

подгнива́ть *v. impfv.* [*pfv.* **подгни́ть**] **1**, to rot from under; rot on the bottom. **2**, to rot slightly.

подгни́ть [*infl. like* гни́ть] *v., pfv. of* **подгнива́ть**.

подгова́ривать *v. impfv.* [*pfv.* **подговори́ть**] (*with inf. or на + acc.*) to incite (to); put up to.

подголо́сок [*gen.* -ска] *n.* **1**, *music* second part; supporting voice. **2**, *fig., colloq.* yes man.

подгоня́ть *v. impfv.* [*pfv.* **подогна́ть**] **1**, to drive; steer (to a certain place). **2**, to drive on; urge on. **3**, to adjust; fit. **4**, *colloq.* to time; schedule.

подгора́ть *v. impfv.* [*pfv.* **подгоре́ть**] (*of food*) to be slightly burnt.

подгоре́лый *adj.* slightly burnt.

подгоре́ть *v., pfv. of* **подгора́ть**.

подгота́вливать *v. impfv.* [*pfv.* **подгото́вить**] **1**, to prepare. **2**, to train. —**подгота́вливаться**, *refl.* (*with к*) to prepare (for); get ready (for).

подготови́тельный *adj.* preparatory.

подгото́вить [*infl.* -влю, -вишь] *v., pfv. of* **подгота́вливать** *and* **подготовля́ть**. —**подгото́виться**, *refl., pfv. of* **подгота́вливаться** *and* **подготовля́ться**.

подгото́вка *n.* **1**, preparation. **2**, training. **3**, grounding; background.

подгото́вленность *n.f.* preparedness.

подготовля́ть *v. impfv.* = **подгота́вливать**. —**подготовля́ться**, *refl.* = **подгота́вливаться**.

подгру́док [*gen.* -дка] *n.* dewlap; jowl.

подгру́ппа *n.* subgroup.

подгу́зник *n.* diaper.

поддава́ть *v. impfv.* [*pfv.* **подда́ть**; *pres.* поддаю́, поддаёшь] **1**, to strike; kick. **2**, (*with gen.*) *colloq.* to increase; step up. **3**, *colloq.* (*in certain games*) to give away (a card, piece, etc.). —**поддава́ться**, *refl.* (*with dat.*) **1**, to give in (to); yield (to); succumb (to). **2**, [*impfv. only*] to respond (to treatment); lend itself (to translation); (*with не*) defy (description).

поддавки́ [*gen.* -ко́в] *n. pl.* giveaway checkers.

подда́кивать *v. impfv.* [*pfv.* **подда́кнуть**] (*with dat.*) *colloq.* to say yes (to); agree (with); nod assent (to).

по́дданный *n., decl. as an adj.* subject; citizen: англи́йский по́дданный, British subject; америка́нский по́дданный, American citizen.

по́дданство *n.* citizenship.

подда́ть [*infl. like* да́ть; *past* по́ддал, -дала́, по́ддало] *v., pfv. of* **поддава́ть**. —**подда́ться**, *refl.* [*past* подда́лся, -ла́сь, -ло́сь] *pfv. of* **поддава́ться**.

поддева́ть *v. impfv.* [*pfv.* **подде́ть**] **1**, to raise slightly (*from underneath*). **2**, to hook; snag. **3**, (*with под + acc.*) *colloq.* to put on; wear (underneath). **4**, *fig., colloq.* to needle (someone).

поддёвка [*gen. pl.* -вок] *n.* man's long coat with a fitted waist.

подде́лать *v., pfv. of* **подде́лывать**. —**подде́латься**, *refl., pfv. of* **подде́лываться**.

подде́лка [*gen. pl.* -лок] *n.* forgery.

подде́лыватель *n.m.* forger; counterfeiter.

подде́лывать *v. impfv.* [*pfv.* **подде́лать**] to forge;

counterfeit. —**подде́лываться**, *refl.* **1,** (*with* **под** + *acc.*) to imitate; pose (as). **2,** (*with* **к**) *colloq.* to ingratiate oneself (with); play up to.

подде́льный *adj.* **1,** forged; counterfeit. **2,** artificial; imitation (*attrib.*).

поддержа́ние *n.* maintenance.

поддержа́ть [*infl.* **поддержу́, подде́ржишь**] *v., pfv. of* **подде́рживать**.

подде́рживать *v. impfv.* [*pfv.* **поддержа́ть**] **1,** to support; hold up. **2,** to support: подде́рживать кандида́та, to support a candidate. Подде́рживать предложе́ние, to support a proposal; second a motion. **3,** to maintain; keep up (order, a correspondence, etc.).

подде́ржка *n.* support.

подде́ть [*infl.* **подде́ну, подде́нешь**] *v., pfv. of* **поддева́ть**.

поддра́знивать *v. impfv.* [*pfv.* **поддразни́ть**] to tease.

поддразни́ть [*infl.* **-дразню́, -дра́знишь**] *v., pfv. of* **поддра́знивать**.

поддува́ло *n.* ash pit (*of a furnace*).

поддува́ть *v. impfv., impers.* to blow slightly: от окна́ поддува́ет, there is a slight draft from the window.

поде́йствовать *v., pfv. of* **де́йствовать** (*in sense #4*).

поде́лать *v. pfv., colloq.* to do. —ничего́ не поде́лаешь, there is nothing you can do about it.

подели́ть *v., pfv. of* **дели́ть**. —**подели́ться**, *refl., pfv. of* **дели́ться** (*in senses #2 & #3*).

поде́лка [*gen. pl.* **-лок**] *n.* **1,** *usu. pl.* odd jobs. **2,** homemade article.

подело́м *adv., colloq.* deservedly; properly. —ему́/ей подело́м, it serves him/her right.

поде́лывать *v. impfv., colloq., in* что (вы) поде́лываете?, how are you doing?; how are you getting along?

подёнка [*gen. pl.* **-нок**] *n.* mayfly.

подённый *adj.* by the day. —*n.* dayworker; day laborer. —**подённая**, *n., colloq.* daywork.

подёнщик *n.m.* [*fem.* **-щица**] dayworker; day laborer. —**подёнщина**, *n.* daywork.

подёргать *v. pfv.* (*with acc. or* **за** + *acc.*) to pull at (*a number of times*).

подёргивание *n.* (nervous) twitch.

подёргивать *v. impfv.* **1,** (*with acc. or* **за** + *acc.*) to pull (at). **2,** (*with instr.*) to twitch. *Also impers.:* его́ подёргивало, he was twitching. —**подёргиваться**, *refl.* to twitch.

поде́ржанный *adj.* secondhand; used.

подержа́ть *v. pfv.* [*infl.* **-держу́, -де́ржишь**] **1,** to hold (*for a while*). **2,** to keep (*for a while*). —**подержа́ться**, *refl.* **1,** (*with* **за** + *acc.*) to hold onto (*for a while*). **2,** to hold out (*for a while*).

подёрнуть *v. pfv.* **1,** to cover (with a thin layer of something). **2,** to shroud; envelop.

подешеве́ть *v., pfv. of* **дешеве́ть**.

поджа́ривать *v. impfv.* [*pfv.* **поджа́рить**] **1,** to roast; broil; fry (*lightly*). **2,** to toast (bread).

поджа́ристый *adj.* brown; nice and brown.

поджа́рить *v., pfv. of* **поджа́ривать**.

поджа́рый *adj., colloq.* lean; wiry.

поджа́ть [*infl.* **подожму́, подожмёшь**] *v., pfv. of* **поджима́ть**.

поджелу́дочный *adj.* pancreatic. —**поджелу́дочная железа́**, pancreas.

подже́чь [*infl.* **подожгу́, подожжёшь, ...подожгу́т**; *past* **поджёг, подожгла́**] *v., pfv. of* **поджига́ть**.

поджига́тель *n.m.* **1,** arsonist. **2,** *fig.* instigator. —**поджига́тель войны́**, warmonger.

поджига́ть *v. impfv.* [*pfv.* **подже́чь**] **1,** to set fire to; set on fire. **2,** *colloq.* to burn (food) slightly.

поджида́ть *v. impfv.* (*with gen.*) to wait for; await.

поджи́лки [*gen.* **-лок**] *n. pl., colloq.* tendons of the knee. —у меня́ поджи́лки затрясли́сь, my knees were shaking; I was quaking in my boots.

поджима́ть *v. impfv.* [*pfv.* **поджа́ть**] to draw up (one's legs); purse (one's lips); put (one's tail) between one's legs.

поджо́г *n.* arson.

подзаголо́вок [*gen.* **-вка**] *n.* subtitle; subheading.

подзадо́ривать *v. impfv.* [*pfv.* **подзадо́рить**] *colloq.* to goad; egg on.

подзаты́льник *n., colloq.* blow on the back of the head.

подзащи́тный *n., decl. as an adj., law* client.

подземе́лье *n.* underground cave, cell, or vault.

подзе́мный *adj.* underground; subterranean. —**подзе́мный толчо́к**, earth tremor.

подзерка́льник *n.* pier table.

подзо́л *n.* podzol.

подзо́рный *adj., in* **подзо́рная труба́**, spyglass.

подзыва́ть *v. impfv.* [*pfv.* **подозва́ть**] to call to; beckon.

поди́ *v., imperative of* **пойти́**, *colloq.:* поди́ прочь!, go away! Поди́ поспо́рь с ним!, go argue with him!; just try arguing with him! —*particle, colloq.* probably; I dare say.

подиви́ться *v.r., pfv. of* **диви́ться**.

подира́ть *v. impfv., usu. in* подира́ть по ко́же, to go up and down one's spine. —моро́з по ко́же подира́ет (*with* **у**), to get the creeps (*or* shivers); get chills up and down one's spine.

подка́лывать *v. impfv.* [*pfv.* **подколо́ть**] **1,** to pin up. **2,** (*with* **к**) to append (to). **3,** *colloq.* to needle; twit. **4,** (*with gen.*) to chop up some more of.

подка́пывать *v. impfv.* [*pfv.* **подкопа́ть**] **1,** to undermine. —**подка́пываться**, *refl.* **1,** (*with* **под** + *acc.*) to dig under. **2,** to tunnel under. **3,** *fig., colloq.* to undercut (someone).

подкара́уливать *v. impfv.* [*pfv.* **подкарау́лить**] *colloq.* to watch for; be on the lookout for.

подка́рмливать *v. impfv.* [*pfv.* **подкорми́ть**] *colloq.* **1,** to feed. **2,** to fatten up.

подкати́ть [*infl.* **-качу́, -ка́тишь**] *v., pfv. of* **подка́тывать**. —**подкати́ться**, *refl., pfv. of* **подка́тываться**.

подка́тывать *v. impfv.* [*pfv.* **подкати́ть**] (*with* **к**) **1,** *v.t.* to roll (a ball, barrel, etc.) up to; drive (a vehicle) up to. **2,** *v.i., colloq.* to roll up to; pull up to. **3,** *v.i., colloq.* to press against: у меня́ ком подкати́л к го́рлу (*or impers.* у меня́ подкати́ло к го́рлу), I felt a lump in my throat. —**подка́тываться**, *refl.* **1,** (*with* **к**) to roll over to. **2,** (*with* **под** + *acc.*) to roll under. **3,** (*with* **к**) *colloq.* to roll up to; pull up to.

подка́шивать *v. impfv.* [*pfv.* **подкоси́ть**] **1,** to cut; trim (grass). **2,** to knock off one's feet; (*of a bullet*) cut down. **3,** *fig.* to demoralize. —**подка́шиваться**, *refl.* (*of one's legs*) to give way.

подки́дывать *v. impfv.* [*pfv.* **подки́нуть**] **1,** to throw up; toss up. **2,** to slip; place surreptitiously. **3,** to abandon (a child).

подки́дыш *n.* abandoned child; foundling.

подки́нуть *v., pfv. of* **подки́дывать**.

подкла́дка [*gen. pl.* -док] *n.* lining.

подкладно́й *adj.* placed underneath. —подкладно́е су́дно, bedpan.

подкла́дывать *v. impfv.* [*pfv.* подложи́ть] **1,** (*with* под + *acc.*) to place under; lay under. **2,** (*with* к) to apply (to); append (to). **3,** (*with gen.*) to add; put some more. **4,** to put furtively; slip; stick; plant. **5,** (*with* под + *acc.*) *colloq.* to line: подкла́дывать шёлк под пальто́, to line a coat with silk.

подкла́сс *n.* subclass.

подкле́ивать *v. impfv.* [*pfv.* подкле́ить] **1,** to glue under; paste under. **2,** to glue up; paste up.

подключа́ть *v. impfv.* [*pfv.* подключи́ть] to connect; hook up. —подключа́ться, *refl.* **1,** to be connected. **2,** (*with* к) *colloq.* to join.

подко́ва *n.* horseshoe.

подкова́ть [*infl.* -кую́, -куёшь] *v., pfv. of* подко́вывать.

подко́вывать *v. impfv.* [*pfv.* подкова́ть] **1,** to shoe (a horse). **2,** *fig., colloq.* to train; ground: хорошо́ подко́ван в фи́зике, well-grounded in physics.

подко́жный *adj.* hypodermic.

подколо́дный *adj., in* змея́ подколо́дная, *colloq.* snake in the grass.

подколо́ть [*infl.* -колю́, -ко́лешь] *v., pfv. of* подка́лывать.

подкоми́ссия *n.* subcommittee.

подкомите́т *n.* subcommittee.

подко́п *n.* **1,** undermining. **2,** underground passage; tunnel. **3,** *pl., colloq.* schemes; machinations.

подкопа́ть *v., pfv. of* подка́пывать. —подкопа́ться, *refl., pfv. of* подка́пываться.

подкорми́ть [*infl.* -кормлю́, -ко́рмишь] *v., pfv. of* подка́рмливать.

подко́с *n.* strut; cross brace.

подкоси́ть [*infl.* -кошу́, -ко́сишь] *v., pfv. of* подка́шивать. —подкоси́ться, *refl., pfv. of* подка́шиваться.

подкра́дываться *v.r. impfv.* [*pfv.* подкра́сться] (*with* к) to sneak up to *or* on; steal up to.

подкра́сить [*infl.* -шу, -сишь] *v., pfv. of* подкра́шивать. —подкра́ситься, *refl., pfv. of* подкра́шиваться.

подкра́сться [*infl. like* красть] *v.r., pfv. of* подкра́дываться.

подкра́шивать *v. impfv.* [*pfv.* подкра́сить] to touch up. —подкра́шиваться, *refl., colloq.* to put on some make-up.

подкрепи́ть [*infl.* -плю́, -пи́шь] *v., pfv. of* подкрепля́ть.

подкрепле́ние *n.* **1,** reinforcement. **2,** *pl., mil.* reinforcements. **3,** *colloq.* sustenance. —в подкрепле́ние (+ *gen.*), to support (an argument, assertion, etc.).

подкрепля́ть *v. impfv.* [*pfv.* подкрепи́ть] **1,** to reinforce. **2,** to fortify (with food, drink, etc.). **3,** *fig.* to support; bolster. —подкрепля́ться, *refl.* to fortify oneself (*with food or drink*).

по́дкуп *n.* **1,** bribery. **2,** graft.

подкупи́ть *v. impfv.* [*pfv.* подкупи́ть] **1,** to bribe. **2,** *fig.* to win over. **3,** (*with gen.*) *colloq.* to buy an additional quantity of.

подкупа́ющий *adj.* winning; appealing; engaging.

подкупи́ть [*infl.* -куплю́, -ку́пишь] *v., pfv. of* подкупа́ть.

подла́живаться *v.r. impfv.* [*pfv.* подла́диться] *col-loq.* **1,** (*with* под + *acc. or* к) to adapt (to); adjust (to). **2,** (*with* к) to try to please; play up to.

подла́мывать *v. impfv.* [*pfv.* подломи́ть] to break. —подла́мываться, *refl.* **1,** to give way; cave in; collapse. **2,** (*of one's legs, knees, etc.*) to buckle.

по́дле *prep., with gen.* beside; alongside of; near. —*adv.* alongside; nearby.

подлежа́ть *v. impfv.* [*pres.* -жу́, -жи́шь] (*with dat.*) to be subject to; be liable to.

подлежа́щее *n., decl. as an adj., gram.* subject.

подлежа́щий *adj.* (*with dat.*) subject (to); liable (to).

подлеза́ть *v. impfv.* [*pfv.* подле́зть] (*with* под + *acc.*) to crawl under.

подле́зть [*infl. like* лезть] *v., pfv. of* подлеза́ть.

подле́сок [*gen.* -ска] *n.* underbrush; undergrowth.

подлета́ть *v. impfv.* [*pfv.* подлете́ть] (*with* к) **1,** to fly up to. **2,** *colloq.* to rush up to.

подлете́ть [*infl.* -чу́, -ти́шь] *v., pfv. of* подлета́ть.

подле́ц [*gen.* -леца́] *n.* scoundrel.

подлива́ть *v. impfv.* [*pfv.* подли́ть] (*with gen.*) to add a little more (*by pouring*). —подлива́ть ма́сла в ого́нь, to add fuel to the fire; pour oil on the flames.

подли́вка *n.* sauce; gravy.

подли́за *n.m. & f., colloq.* bootlicker.

подли́зываться *v.r. impfv.* [*pfv.* подлиза́ться] (*with* к) *colloq.* to lick (someone's) boots.

по́длинник *n.* original: чита́ть в по́длиннике, to read in the original.

по́длинный *adj.* **1,** original. **2,** genuine; authentic. **3,** true; real. —по́длинно, *adv.* truly; really. —по́длинность, *n.f.* authenticity.

подли́ть [*infl.* подолью́, подольёшь; *past fem.* подлила́] *v., pfv. of* подлива́ть.

по́дличать *v. impfv.* **1,** to be mean; do mean things. **2,** to be servile; (*with* пе́ред) cater to; play up to.

по́дло *adv.* despicably.

подло́г *n.* forgery.

подло́дка [*gen. pl.* -док] *n., colloq.* submarine (*contr. of* подво́дная ло́дка).

подложи́ть [*infl.* -ложу́, -ло́жишь] *v., pfv. of* подкла́дывать.

подло́жный *adj.* forged; counterfeit.

подлоко́тник *n.* armrest.

подломи́ть [*infl.* -ломлю́, -ло́мишь] *v., pfv. of* подла́мывать. —подломи́ться, *refl., pfv. of* подла́мываться.

по́длость *n.f.* **1,** meanness; baseness. **2,** mean trick; dirty trick.

по́длый *adj.* mean; base; miserable; despicable.

подма́зать [*infl.* -ма́жу, -ма́жешь] *v., pfv. of* подма́зывать. —подма́заться, *refl., pfv. of* подма́зываться.

подма́зывать *v. impfv.* [*pfv.* подма́зать] **1,** to grease. **2,** *colloq.* to grease the palm of. —подма́зываться, *refl., colloq.* **1,** to put on some make-up. **2,** (*with* к) to play up to; curry favor with.

подманда́тный *adj., in* подманда́тная террито́рия, mandated territory.

подмасте́рье [*gen. pl.* -рьев] *n.m.* apprentice.

подма́хивать *v. impfv.* [*pfv.* подмахну́ть] *colloq.* to sign hurriedly; sign without reading.

подма́чивать *v. impfv.* [*pfv.* подмочи́ть] **1,** to wet slightly. **2,** *colloq.* to damage (one's reputation).

подме́на *also,* подме́н *n.* (improper or illegal) substitution.

подмени́ть [*infl.* -меню́, -ме́нишь] *v., pfv. of* подменя́ть.

подменя́ть *v. impfv.* [*pfv.* подмени́ть] **1,** to remove (stealthily) and replace with something else: подменя́ть чей-нибудь экзаменацио́нный биле́т свои́м, to replace someone's exam paper with one's own; substitute one's own exam paper for someone else's. Кто-то подмени́л мне шля́пу, someone took my hat (and left his own instead). **2,** to replace; take the place of (*for a short time*).

подмерза́ть *v. impfv.* [*pfv.* подмёрзнуть] to freeze slightly; become slightly frozen.

подмёрзнуть [*past* -мёрз, -ла] *v., pfv. of* подмерза́ть.

подмести́ [*infl. like* мести́] *v., pfv. of* подмета́ть.

подмета́льщик *n.m.* [*fem.* -щица] sweeper.

подмета́ть *v. impfv.* [*pfv.* подмести́] to sweep.

подме́тить [*infl.* -чу, -тишь] *v., pfv. of* подмеча́ть.

подмётка [*gen. pl.* -ток] *n.* sole (*of a shoe*). —в подмётки не годи́ться (+ *dat.*), to be unable to hold a candle to.

подмеча́ть *v. impfv.* [*pfv.* подме́тить] to notice; spot; detect.

подме́шивать *v. impfv.* [*pfv.* подмеша́ть] (*with gen.*) to add a little (*by mixing*).

подми́гивать *v. impfv.* [*pfv.* подмигну́ть] (*with dat.*) to wink (at).

подмина́ть *v. impfv.* [*pfv.* подмя́ть] (*often with под себя́*) **1,** to pin down. **2,** *fig.* to crush.

подмо́га *n., colloq.* help.

подмока́ть *v. impfv.* [*pfv.* подмо́кнуть] to get slightly wet.

подмо́кнуть [*past* -мо́к, -ла] *v., pfv. of* подмока́ть.

подмора́живать *v. impfv.* [*pfv.* подморо́зить] **1,** to freeze slightly; put in the refrigerator for a while. **2,** *impers.* to freeze up: но́чью подморо́зило, there was some frost during the night.

подмоско́вный *adj.* located near (*or* on the outskirts of) Moscow.

подмо́стки [*gen.* -ков] *n. pl.* **1,** scaffold. **2,** the stage: на подмо́стках, on the stage; before the footlights.

подмо́ченный *adj.* **1,** slightly wet. **2,** *colloq.* (*of one's reputation*) damaged.

подмочи́ть [*infl.* -мочу́, -мо́чишь] *v., pfv. of* подма́чивать.

подмыва́ть *v. impfv.* [*pfv.* подмы́ть] **1,** to wash (*from underneath*). **2,** to wash away. **3,** [*impfv. only*] *impers. colloq.* to be dying to: меня́ так и подмыва́ет сказа́ть ей, I am dying to tell her.

подмы́ть [*infl.* -мо́ю, -мо́ешь] *v., pfv. of* подмыва́ть.

подмы́шка [*gen. pl.* -шек] *n.* armpit.

подмы́шник *n.* (perspiration) shield (*sewn to the armhole of a dress*).

подмя́ть [*infl.* подомну́, подомнёшь] *v., pfv. of* подмина́ть.

поднадзо́рный *adj.* under surveillance. —*n.* person under surveillance.

поднебе́сье *n.* the heavens; the skies.

поднево́льный *adj.* **1,** dependent. **2,** (*of labor*) forced.

поднесе́ние *n.* **1,** giving (*of a gift*). **2,** *obs.* gift.

поднести́ [*infl. like* нести́] *v., pfv. of* подноси́ть.

поднима́ть *v. impfv.* [*pfv.* подня́ть] **1,** to raise; lift. **2,** to pick up. **3,** to take up; carry up. **4,** *fig.* to rouse: поднима́ть на борьбу́, to rouse to action. **5,** *fig.* to raise (a fuss); start a revolt). **6,** to plow up: поднима́ть

целину́, to plow up (*or* turn up) virgin soil. —поднима́ть на во́здух, to blow up; blow sky-high. —поднима́ть на́ смех, to hold up to ridicule. —поднима́ть ру́ку на (+ *acc.*), to lift a hand against.

поднима́ться *v.r. impfv.* [*pfv.* подня́ться] **1,** to go up; rise. **2,** (*with на* + *acc.*) to mount; ascend. **3,** *fig.* to arise; break out; develop. —рука́ не поднима́ется (*with у and inf.*), one cannot bring oneself (to).

подновля́ть *v. impfv.* [*pfv.* поднови́ть] to freshen up; touch up.

подного́тная *n., decl. as an adj., colloq., in* вся подного́тная, inside information; all there is to know.

подно́жие *n.* **1,** foot (*of a mountain*). **2,** pedestal.

подно́жка [*gen. pl.* -жек] *n.* **1,** running board. **2,** дава́ть подно́жку (+ *dat.*), *colloq.* to trip (someone) up.

подно́жный *adj.* situated or placed under one's feet. —подно́жный корм, pasturage.

подно́с *n.* tray.

подноси́ть *v. impfv.* [*pfv.* поднести́; *pres.* -ношу́, -но́сишь] **1,** (*with к*) to bring (to); carry (to). **2,** (*with к*) to hold up (to); lift up (to). **3,** to give; present (a gift).

подно́счик *n.* **1,** *mil.* carrier; handler. **2,** server of drinks (*in a tavern*).

подноше́ние *n.* **1,** giving; presenting. **2,** gift; present.

подны́ривать *v. impfv.* [*pfv.* поднырну́ть] (*with под* + *acc.*) to dive under.

подня́тие *n.* raising; lifting.

подня́ть [*infl.* -ниму́, -ни́мешь; *past* по́днял, подня́ла, по́дняло] *v., pfv. of* поднима́ть. —подня́ться, *refl.* [*past* подня́лся *or* подня́лся, -ла́сь, -ло́сь] *pfv. of* поднима́ться.

подо *prep.* = под.

подоба́ть *v. impfv.* (*with dat.*) to befit; become.

подоба́ющий *adj.* proper; befitting; becoming.

подо́бие *n.* (*with gen.*) something resembling; semblance (of); likeness (of).

подо́бно *prep., with dat.* like: подо́бно отцу́, он..., like his father, he... —подо́бно тому́ как, just as.

подо́бный *adj.* [*short form* подо́бен, -бна] **1,** (*with dat.*) similar (to); like. **2,** such. **3,** *geom.* (*of figures*) similar. —и тому́ подо́бное, and so on; and so forth; and the like; et cetera. —ничего́ подо́бного, nothing of the sort; nothing of the kind.

подобостра́стие *n.* obsequiousness; servility. —подобостра́стный *adj.* obsequious; servile.

подобра́ть [*infl.* подберу́, подберёшь; *past fem.* подобрала́] *v., pfv. of* подбира́ть. —подобра́ться, *refl., pfv. of* подбира́ться.

подобре́ть *v., pfv. of* добре́ть (*in sense #1*).

подобру́-поздоро́ву *adv., colloq.* (*with verbs of leaving*) while the going (*or* getting) is good.

подогна́ть [*infl.* подгоню́, подго́нишь; *past fem.* подогнала́] *v., pfv. of* подгоня́ть.

подогну́ть *v., pfv. of* подгиба́ть. —подогну́ться, *refl., pfv. of* подгиба́ться.

подогрева́ть *v. impfv.* [*pfv.* подогре́ть] **1,** to warm up. **2,** to reheat; warm over.

пододвига́ть *v. impfv.* [*pfv.* пододви́нуть] (*with к*) to move up (to); move closer (to). —пододвига́ться, *refl.* (*with к*) to move over (to); move closer (to).

пододея́льник *n.* blanket cover.

подожда́ть *v., pfv. of* ждать.

подозва́ть [*infl.* подзову́, подзовёшь; *past fem.* подозвала́] *v., pfv. of* подзыва́ть.

подозрева́емый *adj.* suspect(ed); under suspicion. —*n.* suspect.

подозрева́ть *v. impfv.* (*with* в + *prepl.*) to suspect (of).

подозре́ние *n.* suspicion.

подозри́тельный *adj.* suspicious. —**подозри́тельно,** *adv.* suspiciously.

подои́ть *v., pfv. of* **дои́ть.**

подо́йник *n.* milk pail.

подойти́ [*infl.* **подойду́, подойдёшь;** *past* **подошёл, подошла́, подошло́**] *v., pfv. of* **подходи́ть.**

подоко́нник *n.* window sill.

подо́л *n.* lap (*of a skirt*).

подо́лгу *adv.* for a long time; for hours on end.

подольща́ться *v.r. impfv.* [*pfv.* **подольсти́ться**] (*with* к) to ingratiate oneself (with).

подо́нки [*gen.* -ков] *n. pl.* dregs; residue. —**подо́нки о́бщества,** dregs of society.

подопе́чный *adj.* under the care of a guardian. —*n.* ward; charge. —**подопе́чная террито́рия,** trust territory.

подоплёка *n.* underlying cause; underlying basis.

подо́пытный *adj.* experimental; used for experimental purposes. —**подо́пытный кро́лик,** guinea pig.

подорва́ть [*infl. like* **рвать**] *v., pfv. of* **подрыва́ть.**

подорожа́ть *v., pfv. of* **дорожа́ть.**

подоро́жник *n.* plantain.

подоро́жный *adj.* situated along a road.

подосла́ть [*infl.* -шлю́, -шлёшь] *v., pfv. of* **подсыла́ть.**

подосно́ва *n.* true cause; underlying cause.

подоспе́ть *v. pfv., colloq.* **1,** (*of time*) to come. **2,** to arrive in time; come at the right time.

подостла́ть [*infl.* **подстелю́, -сте́лешь**] *v., pfv. of* **подстила́ть.**

подоткну́ть *v., pfv. of* **подтыка́ть.**

подотчётный *adj.* **1,** (*of money*) on account. **2,** (*with dat.*) accountable (to). —**подотчётность,** *n.f.* accountability.

подо́хнуть [*past* -до́х, -ла] *v., pfv. of* **до́хнуть.**

подохо́дный *adj., in* **подохо́дный нало́г,** income tax.

подо́шва *n.* **1,** sole (*of a shoe*). **2,** *colloq.* sole (*of the foot*). **3,** foot (*of a mountain*).

подпада́ть *v. impfv.* [*pfv.* **подпа́сть**] (*with* под + *acc.*) to fall under; come under (the power, influence, etc. of someone).

подпа́ивать *v. impfv.* [*pfv.* **подпои́ть**] *colloq.* to give (someone) too much to drink; intentionally make (someone) drunk.

подпа́ливать *v. impfv.* [*pfv.* **подпали́ть**] *colloq.* **1,** to singe; scorch. **2,** to set fire to; set on fire.

подпа́лина *n.* **1,** *colloq.* burn mark. **2,** spot; dapple.

подпали́ть *v., pfv. of* **подпа́ливать.**

подпа́сок [*gen.* -ска] *n.* shepherd boy.

подпа́сть [*infl. like* **пасть**] *v., pfv. of* **подпада́ть.**

подпева́ла *n.m. & f., colloq.* lackey; yes man.

подпева́ть *v. impfv.* **1,** to sing along; join in singing. **2,** (*with dat.*) to sing along with. **3,** (*with dat.*) *fig., colloq.* to echo; parrot.

подпере́ть [*infl.* **подопру́, -прёшь;** *past* **подпёр, -ла**] *v., pfv. of* **подпира́ть.** —**подпере́ться,** *refl., pfv. of* **подпира́ться.**

подпи́ливать *v. impfv.* [*pfv.* **подпили́ть**] **1,** to saw at the base of. **2,** to shorten (*by sawing*).

подпили́ть [*infl.* -пилю́, -пи́лишь] *v., pfv. of* **подпи́ливать.**

подпира́ть *v. impfv.* [*pfv.* **подопре́ть**] to prop up. —**подпира́ться,** *refl., colloq.* to prop oneself up.

подписа́ние *n.* signing.

подписа́ть [*infl.* -пишу́, -пи́шешь] *v., pfv. of* **подпи́сывать.** —**подписа́ться,** *refl., pfv. of* **подпи́сываться.**

подпи́ска [*gen. pl.* -сок] *n.* **1,** subscription. **2,** signed statement; written pledge.

подписно́й *adj.* subscription (*attrib.*).

подпи́счик *n.* subscriber.

подпи́сывать *v. impfv.* [*pfv.* **подписа́ть**] **1,** to sign. **2,** to write at the bottom; add at the end. **3,** (*with* на + *acc.*) to take out a subscription for (someone) to (a publication). —**подпи́сываться,** *refl.* **1,** to sign one's name. **2,** (*with* на + *acc.*) to subscribe (to).

по́дпись *n.f.* **1,** signature. **2,** caption.

подплыва́ть *v. impfv.* [*pfv.* **подплы́ть**] (*with* к) **1,** to swim up to. **2,** to sail up to.

подплы́ть [*infl. like* **плыть**] *v., pfv. of* **подплыва́ть.**

подпои́ть [*infl.* -пою́, -по́ишь *or* -пои́шь] *v., pfv. of* **подпа́ивать.**

подполза́ть *v. impfv.* [*pfv.* **подползти́**] **1,** (*with* к) to crawl up to; creep up to. **2,** (*with* под + *acc.*) to crawl under; creep under.

подползти́ [*infl. like* **ползти́**] *v., pfv. of* **подполза́ть.**

подполко́вник *n.* lieutenant colonel.

подпо́лье *n.* **1,** cellar. **2,** *fig.* underground: уйти́ в подпо́лье, to go underground. —**подпо́льный,** *adj.* underground (*attrib.*). —**подпо́льщик,** *n.* member of the underground.

подпо́ра *n.* prop; support. *Also* **подпо́рка.**

подпо́рный *adj.* supporting. —**подпо́рная сте́нка,** retaining wall.

подпору́чик *n., pre-rev.* second lieutenant.

подпо́чва *n.* subsoil.

подпоя́сать [*infl.* -поя́шу, -поя́шешь] *v., pfv. of* **подпоя́сывать.** —**подпоя́саться,** *refl., pfv. of* **подпоя́сываться.**

подпоя́сывать *v. impfv.* [*pfv.* **подпоя́сать**] to put a belt on; tie a belt around. —**подпоя́сываться,** *refl.* to put one's belt on.

подпра́вить [*infl.* -влю, -вишь] *v., pfv. of* **подправля́ть.**

подправля́ть *v. impfv.* [*pfv.* **подпра́вить**] to fix up; straighten; put right.

подпру́га *n.* bellyband; surcingle.

подпры́гивать *v. impfv.* [*pfv.* **подпры́гнуть**] **1,** to jump up and down. **2,** to bounce up and down; bob up and down.

подпуска́ть *v. impfv.* [*pfv.* **подпусти́ть**] **1,** to allow to approach; allow to come near. **2,** *colloq.* to add. **3,** *colloq.* to utter; get in.

подпусти́ть [*infl.* -пущу́, -пу́стишь] *v., pfv. of* **подпуска́ть.**

подраба́тывать *v. impfv.* [*pfv.* **подрабо́тать**] *colloq.* **1,** to work up; work out. **2,** to earn on the side.

подра́внивать *v. impfv.* [*pfv.* **подровня́ть**] **1,** to level; make even. **2,** to trim (one's hair, beard, etc.).

подра́гивать *v. impfv., colloq.* **1,** to quiver. **2,** (*with instr.*) to shake (a part of one's body).

подража́ние *n.* imitation. —**подража́тель,** *n.m.* imitator. —**подража́тельный,** *adj.* imitative.

подража́ть *v. impfv.* (*with dat.*) to imitate.

подразделе́ние *n.* **1,** subdivision. **2,** *mil.* subunit.

подразделя́ть *v. impfv.* [*pfv.* **подразделить**] to subdivide. —**подразделя́ться,** *refl.* to subdivide; be subdivided.

подразумева́ть *v. impfv.* to mean; have in mind. —**подразумева́ться,** *refl.* to be meant; be understood.

подраста́ть *v. impfv.* [*pfv.* **подрасти́**] to grow; grow up.

подрасти́ [*infl. like* **расти́**] *v., pfv. of* **подраста́ть.**

подра́ться *v.r. pfv.* [*infl. like* **драть**] to fight; get into a fight.

подре́зать [*infl.* -**ре́жу,** -**ре́жешь**] *v., pfv. of* **подреза́ть.**

подреза́ть *v. impfv.* [*pfv.* **подре́зать**] to cut; trim; clip; prune.

подрисова́ть [*infl.* -**су́ю,** -**су́ешь**] *v., pfv. of* **подрисо́вывать.**

подрисо́вывать *v. impfv.* [*pfv.* **подрисова́ть**] **1,** to touch up. **2,** to paint in.

подро́бно *adv.* in detail.

подро́бность *n.f.* detail.

подро́бный *adj.* detailed.

подровня́ть *v., pfv. of* **подра́внивать.**

подро́сток [*gen.* -**стка**] *n.* adolescent; teenager.

подруба́ть *v. impfv.* [*pfv.* **подрубить**] **1,** to chop (*at the base*). **2,** to hem.

подруби́ть [*infl.* -**рублю́,** -**ру́бишь**] *v., pfv. of* **подруба́ть.**

подру́га *n.* (female) friend.

подружи́ться *v.r., pfv. of* **дружи́ться.**

подру́ливать *v. impfv.* [*pfv.* **подрули́ть**] *aero.* (*with* **к**) to taxi up to.

подрумя́нивать *v. impfv.* [*pfv.* **подрумя́нить**] **1,** to redden; flush. **2,** to put some rouge on. **3,** to brown; toast. —**подрумя́ниваться,** *refl.* **1,** to flush; become flushed. **2,** to put on some rouge. **3,** (*of food*) to become nice and brown.

подру́чный *adj.* **1,** on hand; handy. **2,** improvised; makeshift. **3,** assistant. —*n.* assistant.

подры́в *n.* **1,** blowing up. **2,** *fig.* undermining.

подрыва́ть *v. impfv.* [*pfv.* **подорва́ть**] **1,** to blow up. **2,** *fig.* to undermine. **3,** [*pfv.* **подры́ть**] to dig under; dig the ground from under.

подрывни́к [*gen.* -**ника́**] *n.* demolition expert.

подрывно́й *adj.* **1,** demolition (*attrib.*); blasting (*attrib.*). **2,** *fig.* subversive.

подры́ть [*infl.* -**ро́ю,** -**ро́ешь**] *v., pfv. of* **подрыва́ть** (*in sense #3*).

подря́д *n.* contract. —*adv.* in a row; in succession.

подряди́ть [*infl.* -**жу́,** -**ди́шь**] *v., pfv. of* **подряжа́ть.**

подря́дный *adj.* contract (*attrib.*); done on contract.

подря́дчик *n.* contractor.

подряжа́ть *v. impfv.* [*pfv.* **подряди́ть**] to hire.

подсади́ть [*infl.* -**сажу́,** -**са́дишь**] *v., pfv. of* **подса́живать.**

подса́живать *v. impfv.* [*pfv.* **подсади́ть**] (*with* **в** *or* **на** + *acc.*) **1,** to help (someone) into *or* onto. **2,** (*with* **к**) to seat next to. **3,** (*with gen.*) to plant (an additional quantity of something). —**подса́живаться,** *refl.* [*pfv.* **подсе́сть**] (*with* **к**) to sit down near; take a seat near.

подса́ливать *v. impfv.* [*pfv.* **подсоли́ть**] to salt lightly; add a little salt to.

подсве́чник *n.* candlestick.

подсева́ть *v. impfv.* [*pfv.* **подсе́ять**] (*with gen.*) to sow (an additional quantity of something).

подсека́ть *v. impfv.* [*pfv.* **подсе́чь**] to chop off; chop down (*at the base*).

подсе́сть [*infl. like* **сесть**] *v., pfv. of* **подса́живаться.**

подсе́чь [*infl. like* **сечь;** *past* -**се́к,** -**ла́,** -**ло́**] *v., pfv. of* **подсека́ть.**

подсе́ять [*infl.* -**се́ю,** -**се́ешь**] *v., pfv. of* **подсева́ть.**

подси́живать *v. impfv.* [*pfv.* **подсиде́ть**] *colloq.* **1,** to lie in wait for. **2,** to plot against; scheme against.

подси́нивать *v. impfv.* [*pfv.* **подсини́ть**] **1,** to color blue. **2,** to rinse in bluing; blue.

подсини́ть *v., pfv. of* **сини́ть** *and* **подси́нивать.**

подска́бливать *v. impfv.* [*pfv.* **подскобли́ть**] to scrape off.

подсказа́ть [*infl.* -**скажу́,** -**ска́жешь**] *v., pfv. of* **подска́зывать.**

подска́зывать *v. impfv.* [*pfv.* **подсказа́ть**] **1,** (*with dat.*) to prompt: не подска́зывать!, no prompting! **2,** to suggest (an idea, solution, etc.).

подскака́ть [*infl.* -**скачу́,** -**ска́чешь**] *v., pfv. of* **подска́кивать** (*in sense #4*).

подска́кивать *v. impfv.* [*pfv.* **подскочи́ть**] **1,** to jump up. **2,** *colloq.* (*of prices, temperature, etc.*) to shoot up; soar; skyrocket. **3,** (*with* **к**) to run up to; come running up to. **4,** [*pfv.* **подскака́ть**] (*with* **к**) to come galloping up to.

подскобли́ть [*infl.* -**скоблю́,** -**ско́блишь** *or* -**скобли́шь**] *v., pfv. of* **подска́бливать.**

подскочи́ть [*infl.* -**скочу́,** -**ско́чишь**] *v., pfv. of* **подска́кивать.**

подсла́щивать *v. impfv.* [*pfv.* **подсласти́ть**] to sweeten.

подсле́дственный *adj.* under investigation.

подслепова́тый *adj.* having poor vision.

подслу́живаться *v.r. impfv.* [*pfv.* **подслужи́ться**] (*with* **к**) *colloq.* to curry favor (with); play up to.

подслужи́ться [*infl.* -**служу́сь,** -**слу́жишься**] *v.r., pfv. of* **подслу́живаться.**

подслу́шать *v., pfv. of* **подслу́шивать.**

подслу́шивание *n.* eavesdropping. —**пункт/пост подслу́шивания,** listening post.

подслу́шивать *v. impfv.* [*pfv.* **подслу́шать**] **1,** to overhear. **2,** [*impfv. only*] to eavesdrop.

подсма́тривать *v. impfv.* [*pfv.* **подсмотре́ть**] **1,** to watch secretly. **2,** (*with* **в** + *acc.*) to peep through. **3,** (*with* **за** + *instr.*) to spy on.

подсме́иваться *v.r. impfv.* (*with* **над**) to make fun of.

подсмотре́ть *v. pfv.* [*infl.* -**смотрю́,** -**смо́тришь**] **1,** *pfv. of* **подсма́тривать.** **2,** to catch sight of; spot; detect.

подсне́жник *n.* snowdrop.

подсо́бный *adj.* auxiliary; subsidiary; accessory; additional.

подсо́вывать *v. impfv.* [*pfv.* **подсу́нуть**] **1,** (*with* **под** + *acc.*) to put under; shove under. **2,** *colloq.* to slip; put furtively. **3,** *colloq.* to palm off.

подсозна́ние *n.* the subconscious. —**подсозна́тельный,** *adj.* subconscious.

подсоли́ть [*infl.* -**солю́,** -**со́лишь** *or* -**соли́шь**] *v., pfv. of* **подса́ливать.**

подсо́лнечник *n.* sunflower. —**подсо́лнечный,** *adj.* sunflower (*attrib.*).

подсо́лнух *n., colloq.* **1,** sunflower. **2,** *usu. pl.* sunflower seeds.

подсо́хнуть [*past* -**со́х,** -**ла**] *v., pfv. of* **подсыха́ть.**

подспо́рье *n., colloq.* help; support.

подспу́дный *adj.* hidden; secret; latent. —подспу́дно, *adv.* secretly.

подста́вить [*infl.* -влю, -вишь] *v., pfv. of* подставля́ть.

подста́вка [*gen. pl.* -вок] *n.* stand; support.

подставля́ть *v. impfv.* [*pfv.* подста́вить] 1, (*with* под + *acc.*) to place under. 2, (*with* к) to place near (to). Подста́вить стул (+ *dat.*), to bring up a chair for. 3, (*with dat.*) to turn toward: подставля́ть лицо́ со́лнцу, to turn one's face toward the sun. 4, to expose; leave vulnerable. 5, to substitute. —подставля́ть другу́ю щёку, to turn the other cheek. —подставля́ть но́жку (+ *dat.*), to trip (someone) up.

подставно́й *adj.* 1, placed near or under. 2, false. —подставно́е лицо́, dummy; front.

подстака́нник *n.* glass holder (*for use when drinking*).

подстано́вка *n., math.* substitution.

подста́нция *n.* substation.

подстёгивать *v. impfv.* [*pfv.* подстегну́ть] 1, *colloq.* to fasten (on). 2, to urge on; whip (a horse). 3, *fig., colloq.* to stir up; spur on.

подстерега́ть *v. impfv.* [*pfv.* подстере́чь] to lie in wait for.

подстере́чь [*infl. like* стере́чь] *v., pfv. of* подстерега́ть.

подстила́ть *v. impfv.* [*pfv.* подостла́ть] (*with* под + *acc.*) to lay under; spread under.

подсти́лка [*gen. pl.* -лок] *n.* bedding.

подстра́ивать *v. impfv.* [*pfv.* подстро́ить] 1, (*with* к) to build on to. 2, *colloq.* to cook up. 3, *in* подстро́ить шу́тку/по́длость/па́кость (+ *dat.*), to play a dirty trick on.

подстрека́тель *n.m.* instigator. —подстрека́тельство, *n.* instigation.

подстрека́ть *v. impfv.* [*pfv.* подстрекну́ть] 1, to incite; goad; egg on; put up to. 2, to arouse (a feeling).

подстре́ливать *v. impfv.* [*pfv.* подстрели́ть] to wound (an animal); wing (a bird).

подстрели́ть [*infl.* -стрелю́, -стре́лишь] *v., pfv. of* подстре́ливать.

подстрига́ть *v. impfv.* [*pfv.* подстри́чь] to clip; trim; crop. —подстрига́ться, *refl.* to get a haircut; get a trim.

подстри́чь [*infl. like* стричь] *v., pfv. of* подстрига́ть.

подстро́ить *v., pfv. of* подстра́ивать.

подстро́чник *n.* word-for-word translation.

подстро́чный *adj.* 1, (*of a translation*) word-for-word. 2, placed under a line or at the bottom of a page: подстро́чное примеча́ние, footnote.

по́дступ *n.* approach.

подступа́ть *v. impfv.* [*pfv.* подступи́ть] 1, (*with* к) to approach. 2, [*often with* к го́рлу *or* к се́рдцу] (*of emotions, tears, etc.*) to come; come over; (*of a lump*) to form. —подступа́ться, *refl.* (*with* к) to approach.

подступи́ть [*infl.* -ступлю́, -сту́пишь] *v., pfv. of* подступа́ть. —подступи́ться, *refl., pfv. of* подступа́ться.

подсуди́мый *n., decl. as an adj.* defendant.

подсу́дный *adj.* (*with dat.*) within the jurisdiction (of). —подсу́дность, *n.f.* jurisdiction.

подсу́мок [*gen.* -мка] *n.* cartridge pouch.

подсу́нуть *v., pfv. of* подсо́вывать.

подсу́шивать *v. impfv.* [*pfv.* подсуши́ть] to dry (something) a little.

подсуши́ть [*infl.* -сушу́, -су́шишь] *v., pfv. of* подсу́шивать.

подсчёт *n.* 1, count(ing). 2, *pl.* calculations.

подсчи́тывать *v. impfv.* [*pfv.* подсчита́ть] to count up; calculate; compute.

подсыла́ть *v. impfv.* [*pfv.* подосла́ть] to send on a secret mission.

подсы́пать [*infl.* -сы́плю, -сы́плешь] *v., pfv. of* подсыпа́ть.

подсыпа́ть *v. impfv.* [*pfv.* подсы́пать] (*with gen. or acc.*) to add a little (of something) by sprinkling.

подсыха́ть *v. impfv.* [*pfv.* подсо́хнуть] to dry out a little.

подта́ивать *v. impfv.* [*pfv.* подта́ять] to melt a little; melt slightly.

подта́лкивать *v. impfv.* [*pfv.* подтолкну́ть] 1, to push slightly; shove slightly; nudge. 2, *fig.* to prompt; encourage; spur on.

подта́пливать *v. impfv.* [*pfv.* подтопи́ть] to heat slightly; warm slightly.

подта́скивать *v. impfv.* [*pfv.* подтащи́ть] (*with* к) to pull up to; drag up to.

подтасова́ть [*infl.* -су́ю, -су́ешь] *v., pfv. of* подтасо́вывать.

подтасо́вка *n.* 1, dishonest shuffling (*of cards*). 2, *fig.* juggling (*of facts*)

подтасо́вывать *v. impfv.* [*pfv.* подтасова́ть] 1, to shuffle (cards) dishonestly. 2, *fig.* to juggle (facts)

подта́чивать *v. impfv.* [*pfv.* подточи́ть] 1, to sharpen. 2, to eat away; corrode. 3, *fig.* to undermine; sap.

подтащи́ть [*infl.* -тащу́, -та́щишь] *v., pfv. of* подта́скивать.

подта́ять [*infl.* -та́ет] *v., pfv. of* подта́ивать.

подтверди́ть [*infl.* -жу́, -ди́шь] *v., pfv. of* подтвержда́ть.

подтвержда́ть *v. impfv.* [*pfv.* подтверди́ть] to confirm; corroborate. Подверждáть получе́ние (+ *gen.*), to acknowledge receipt of.

подтвержде́ние *n.* confirmation; corroboration.

подтёк *n.* 1, streak. 2, bruise.

подтека́ть *v. impfv.* [*pfv.* подте́чь] 1, (*with* под + *acc.*) to flow under; run under. 2, *colloq.* (*of a container*) to leak.

подте́кст *n.* underlying theme.

подтере́ть [*infl.* подотру́, -трёшь; *past* подтёр, -ла] *v., pfv. of* подтира́ть.

подте́чь [*infl. like* течь] *v., pfv. of* подтека́ть.

подтира́ть *v. impfv.* [*pfv.* подтере́ть] to wipe up.

подтолкну́ть *v., pfv. of* подта́лкивать.

подтопи́ть [*infl.* -топлю́, -то́пишь] *v., pfv. of* подта́пливать.

подточи́ть [*infl.* -точу́, -то́чишь] *v., pfv. of* подта́чивать.

подтру́нивать *v. impfv.* [*pfv.* подтруни́ть] (*with* над) to poke fun at.

подтыка́ть *v. impfv.* [*pfv.* подоткну́ть] to tuck in; tuck under.

подтя́гивать *v. impfv.* [*pfv.* подтяну́ть] 1, to tighten; pull tight. 2, (*with* к) to pull up to; drag up to. 3, (*with* под + *acc.*) to pull under; drag under. 4, *mil.* to bring up (troops). 5, to get after; clamp down on. 6, *v.i.* to join in singing. —подтя́гиваться, *refl.* 1, to tighten one's belt. 2, to pull oneself up. 3, (*of troops*) to move up. 4, *fig., colloq.* to catch up with the rest.

подтя́жка [*gen. pl.* -жек] *n.* suspender.

ПОДТЯ́НУТЫЙ *adj.* smart; neat; fresh.

ПОДТЯНУ́ТЬ [*infl.* -тяну́, -тя́нешь] *v.*, *pfv. of* подтя́гивать. —**подтяну́ться**, *refl.*, *pfv. of* подтя́гиваться.

ПОДУ́МАТЬ *v. pfv.* **1**, *pfv. of* ду́мать. **2**, to think for a moment. —**и не поду́маю!**, I wouldn't dream of it! —**поду́мать то́лько!**, just think!; just imagine!

ПОДУ́МЫВАТЬ *v. impfv.* (*with inf. or* о) *colloq.* to be thinking of; be considering (a possibility).

ПОДУРНЕ́ТЬ *v.*, *pfv. of* дурне́ть.

ПОДУ́ТЬ *v. pfv.* **1**, *pfv. of* ду́ть. **2**, to begin to blow.

ПОДУ́ЧИВАТЬ *v. impfv.* [*pfv.* подучи́ть] *colloq.* **1**, to teach. **2**, to learn. **3**, to egg on; put up to. —**поду́чиваться**, *refl.* (with dat. or inf.) colloq. to learn.

ПОДУЧИ́ТЬ [*infl.* -учу́, -у́чишь] *v.*, *pfv. of* поду́чивать. —**подучи́ться**, *refl.*, *pfv. of* поду́чиваться.

ПОДУ́ШЕЧКА [*gen. pl.* -чек] *n.*, *dim. of* поду́шка. —**поду́шечка для була́вок**, pincushion.

ПОДУШИ́ТЬ *v. pfv.* [*infl.* -душу́, -ду́шишь] to perfume; put some perfume on. —**подуши́ться**, *refl.* to put on some perfume.

ПОДУ́ШКА [*gen. pl.* -шек] *n.* pillow; cushion. —**поду́шка для штемпеле́й**, stamp pad; ink pad.

ПОДУ́ШНЫЙ *adj.*, *in* поду́шный нало́г; поду́шная по́дать, poll tax; tax per head.

ПОДФА́РНИК *n.* parking light.

ПОДХАЛИ́М *m.* toady; sycophant.

ПОДХАЛИ́МНИЧАТЬ *v. impfv.*, *colloq.* **1**, to be servile; bow and scrape. **2**, (with пе́ред) to curry favor with; play up to.

ПОДХАЛИ́МСТВО *n.* toadyism.

ПОДХВАТИ́ТЬ [*infl.* -хвачу́, -хва́тишь] *v.*, *pfv. of* подхва́тывать.

ПОДХВА́ТЫВАТЬ *v. impfv.* [*pfv.* подхвати́ть] **1**, to catch; grasp; snatch. **2**, *colloq.* to catch; pick up (an illness). **3**, to pick up (information, an expression, etc.). **4**, to join in (singing, a conversation, etc.).

ПОДХЛЁСТЫВАТЬ *v. impfv.* [*pfv.* подхлестну́ть] **1**, to whip; urge on (a horse). **2**, *fig.*, *colloq.* to spur on.

ПОДХО́Д *n.* approach.

ПОДХОДИ́ТЬ *v. impfv.* [*pfv.* подойти́; *pres.* -хожу́, -хо́дишь] **1**, (with к) to approach; come up; walk up to. **2**, to approach; come near. **3**, to do; be suitable. **4**, (*with dat.*) to suit; fit; be right for.

ПОДХОДЯ́ЩИЙ *adj.* suitable; proper; appropriate; right.

ПОДЦЕПИ́ТЬ [*infl.* -цеплю́, -це́пишь] *v.*, *pfv. of* подцепля́ть.

ПОДЦЕПЛЯ́ТЬ *v. impfv.* [*pfv.* подцепи́ть] **1**, to hook on; couple. **2**, *fig.*, *colloq.* to get; acquire; catch.

ПОДЧА́С *adv.* sometimes; at times.

ПОДЧЁРКИВАТЬ *v. impfv.* [*pfv.* подчеркну́ть] **1**, to underline. **2**, to emphasize; stress.

ПОДЧИНЕ́НИЕ *n.* **1**, subordination. Быть в подчине́нии у, to be subordinate to. **2**, submission. **3**, subjugation.

ПОДЧИНЁННЫЙ *adj. & n.* subordinate. —**подчинённость**, *n.f.* subordination.

ПОДЧИНИ́ТЬ *v. pfv.* [*pfv.* подчини́ть] **1**, to subjugate; subdue. **2**, (*with dat.*) to subordinate (to); subject (to). **3**, (*with dat.*) to place under the command or jurisdiction of. —**подчиня́ться**, *refl.* (with dat.) to submit (to); yield (to); obey.

ПОДЧИ́СТИТЬ [*infl.* -щу, -стишь] *v.*, *pfv. of* подчища́ть.

ПОДЧИ́СТКА *n.* **1**, cleaning up. **2**, *colloq.* erasure.

ПОДЧИ́ТЧИК *n.* [*usu.* корре́ктор-подчи́тчик] copyholder.

ПОДЧИЩА́ТЬ *v. impfv.* [*pfv.* подчи́стить] **1**, to clean up. **2**, to erase; rub out.

ПОДШИВА́ТЬ *v. impfv.* [*pfv.* подши́ть] **1**, to sew in; sew on. **2**, to sew a hem in. **3**, to sole (a shoe). **4**, to file (newspapers, documents, etc.).

ПОДШИ́ВКА [*gen. pl.* -вок] *n.* **1**, hemming. **2**, soling (of shoes). **3**, filing. **4**, *colloq.* file: газе́тная подши́вка, newspaper file.

ПОДШИ́ПНИК *n.*, *mech.* bearing: ша́риковый подши́пник, ball bearing.

ПОДШИ́ТЬ [*infl.* подошью́, -шьёшь] *v.*, *pfv. of* подшива́ть.

ПОДШТА́ННИКИ [*gen.* -ков] *n. pl.*, *colloq.* men's drawers.

ПОДШУТИ́ТЬ [*infl.* -шучу́, -шу́тишь] *v.*, *pfv. of* подшу́чивать.

ПОДШУ́ЧИВАТЬ *v. impfv.* [*pfv.* подшути́ть] (*with* над) **1**, to make fun of. **2**, to play a trick on.

ПОДЪЕ́ЗД *n.* **1**, approach. **2**, entrance; doorway.

ПОДЪЕЗДНО́Й *adj.* of approach. —**подъездна́я доро́га**, access road.

ПОДЪЕЗЖА́ТЬ *v. impfv.* [*pfv.* подъе́хать] (*with* к) to drive up to; ride up to; draw up to; pull up to.

ПОДЪЁМ *n.* **1**, raising; lifting. **2**, ascent; upgrade. **3**, *fig.* rise; upsurge. **4**, enthusiasm. **5**, instep. **6**, reveille. —**лёгок на подъём**, always ready to get up and go. —**тяжёл на подъём**, hard to get moving.

ПОДЪЁМНИК *n.* lift; hoist.

ПОДЪЁМНЫЙ *adj.* lifting (*attrib.*). —**подъёмный кран**, crane. —**подъёмный мост**, drawbridge. —**подъёмная си́ла**, **1**, lifting capacity. **2**, *aero.* lift.

ПОДЪЕ́ХАТЬ [*infl. like* е́хать] *v.*, *pfv. of* подъезжа́ть.

ПОДЫ́ГРЫВАТЬ *v. impfv.* [*pfv.* подыгра́ть] (*with dat.*) *colloq.* to accompany (on a musical instrument). —**поды́грываться**, *refl.* (with к) colloq. to play up to.

ПОДЫМА́ТЬ *v. impfv.* = поднима́ть.

ПОДЫСКА́ТЬ [*infl.* подыщу́, поды́щешь] *v.*, *pfv. of* поды́скивать.

ПОДЫ́СКИВАТЬ *v. impfv.* [*pfv.* подыска́ть] **1**, to find. **2**, [*impfv. only*] to look for; seek; try to find.

ПОДЫТО́ЖИВАТЬ *v. impfv.* [*pfv.* подыто́жить] **1**, to add up; total. **2**, to sum up.

ПОДЫША́ТЬ *v. pfv.* [*infl.* -дышу́, -ды́шишь] (*with instr.*) to breathe; take a breath of.

ПОЕДА́ТЬ *v. impfv.* [*pfv.* пое́сть] **1**, to eat up. **2**, (of insects, rodents, etc.) to eat; devour.

ПОЕДИ́НОК [*gen.* -нка] *n.* duel.

ПОЕ́ДОМ *also*, пое́дом *adv.*, *colloq. in* есть (кого́-нибудь) пое́дом, to make someone's life miserable (by nagging).

ПО́ЕЗД [*pl.* поезда́] *n.* train.

ПОЕ́ЗДИТЬ *v. pfv.* [*infl.* -е́зжу, -е́здишь] to travel about; travel widely.

ПОЕ́ЗДКА [*gen. pl.* -док] *n.* trip.

ПОЕЗДНО́Й *adj.* train (*attrib.*).

ПОЕ́СТЬ [*infl. like* есть] *v.*, *pfv. of* есть (*in sense #2*) *and* поеда́ть.

ПОЕ́ХАТЬ *v. pfv.* [*infl.* пое́ду, пое́дешь] **1**, *pfv. of* е́хать. **2**, (of a vehicle) to start moving. —**пое́хали!**, let's go!; let's get started!; let's be off!

ПОЖАЛЕ́ТЬ *v.*, *pfv. of* жале́ть.

ПОЖА́ЛОВАТЬ *v.*, *pfv. of* жа́ловать. —**пожа́ловаться**, *refl.*, *pfv. of* жа́ловаться.

ПОЖА́ЛУЙ *particle* **1**, possibly; probably: пожа́луй, вы пра́вы, you may be right; you are probably right. **2**, well, all right! (*indicating reluctant consent*).

пожа́луйста *particle* **1,** please! **2,** you're welcome!; don't mention it! **3,** certainly!; by all means!

пожа́р *n.* a fire: лесно́й пожа́р, forest fire.

пожа́рище *n.* scene of a fire; burned-out area.

пожа́рник *n.* fireman.

пожа́рный *adj.* fire (*attrib.*). —*n.* fireman. —**пожа́рная ле́стница**, fire escape. —**пожа́рная маши́на**, fire engine.

пожа́тие *n.* handshake.

пожа́ть *v. pfv.* **1,** [*infl.* -жму́, -жмёшь] *pfv. of* жать¹ (*in sense #2*) *and* пожима́ть. **2,** [*infl.* -жну́, -жнёшь] *pfv. of* пожина́ть.

пожева́ть *v. pfv.* [*infl.* -жую́, -жуёшь] to chew.

пожела́ние *n.* wish: наилу́чшие пожела́ния, best wishes.

пожела́ть *v., pfv. of* жела́ть.

пожелте́лый *adj.* yellowed.

пожелте́ть *v., pfv. of* желте́ть.

пожени́ться *v.r. pfv.* [*infl.* -же́нится] (*of two people*) to get married.

поже́ртвование *n.* contribution; donation.

поже́ртвовать *v., pfv. of* же́ртвовать.

пожи́ва *n., colloq.* easy money.

пожива́ть *v. impfv., in* как вы пожива́ете?, how are you?; how are you getting along?

поживи́ться *v.r. pfv.* [*infl.* -влю́сь, -ви́шься] *colloq.* **1,** (*with instr.*) to make money (off of *or* out of). **2,** (*with* за счёт) to profit (at the expense of).

пожи́зненный *adj.* life (*attrib.*); for life; lifetime (*attrib.*): пожи́зненное заключе́ние, life imprisonment. —**пожи́зненно**, *adv.* for life: назнача́ться пожи́зненно, to be appointed for life.

пожило́й *adj.* getting on in years.

пожима́ние *n.* shaking (of hands); shrug (of the shoulder).

пожима́ть *v. impfv.* [*pfv.* пожа́ть] **1,** to shake: пожима́ть ру́ку (+ *dat.*), to shake someone's hand. **2,** *in* пожима́ть плеча́ми, to shrug one's shoulders.

пожина́ть *v. impfv.* [*pfv.* пожа́ть] **1,** *obs.* to reap. **2,** *fig.* to reap; gain: пожина́ть ла́вры, to reap the laurels.

пожира́ть *v. impfv.* [*pfv.* пожра́ть] **1,** to devour; consume. **2,** *colloq.* to eat; gobble.

пожи́тки [*pl.* -ков] *n. pl., colloq.* belongings.

пожи́ть *v. pfv.* [*infl.* -живу́, -живёшь; *past* по́жил, пожила́, по́жило] **1,** to live for a while. **2,** *colloq.* to live it up. —**поживём — уви́дим**, we'll see what happens.

пожра́ть [*infl. like* жрать] *v., pfv. of* пожира́ть.

пожури́ть *v., pfv. of* жури́ть.

по́за *n.* **1,** pose; position. **2,** *fig.* affectation; pretense.

позаба́вить *v. pfv.* [*infl.* -влю, -вишь] to amuse; entertain. —**позаба́виться**, *refl., colloq.* to have a little fun.

позабо́титься *v.r., pfv. of* забо́титься.

позабыва́ть *v. impfv.* [*pfv.* позабы́ть] *colloq.* to forget all about; completely forget.

позабы́ть [*infl.* -бу́ду, -бу́дешь] *v., pfv. of* позабыва́ть.

позави́довать *v., pfv. of* зави́довать.

поза́втракать *v., pfv. of* за́втракать.

позавчера́ *adv.* the day before yesterday.

позади́ *adv.* behind. —*prep., with gen.* behind.

позаи́мствовать *v., pfv. of* займствовать.

позапро́шлый *adj.* before last: позапро́шлый год, the year before last.

позари́ться *v.r., pfv. of* за́риться.

позва́ть *v., pfv. of* звать.

позволе́ние *n.* permission. —**с позволе́ния сказа́ть, 1,** if I may say so. **2,** if you could call it that.

позволи́тельный *adj.* permissible.

позволя́ть *v. impfv.* [*pfv.* позво́лить] (*with dat.*) **1,** to allow; permit. **2,** to enable; make it possible for. —**позво́льте, 1,** (*with inf.*) allow me to... **2,** excuse me!; I beg your pardon! —**позво́лить себе́, 1,** (*with inf.*) to venture (to); take the liberty of. **2,** to allow oneself; be able to afford: не могу́ себе́ э́того позво́лить, I can't afford it.

позвони́ть *v., pfv. of* звони́ть.

позвоно́к [*gen.* -нка́] *n.* vertebra.

позвоно́чник *n.* spine; backbone.

позвоно́чный *adj.* vertebrate; vertebral. Позвоно́чный столб, spinal column. —**позвоно́чные**, *n. pl.* vertebrates.

по́здний *adj.* late. —**до по́здней но́чи**, till late at night.

по́здно *adv.* late. —*adj., used predicatively* late: уже́ по́здно, it is already late.

поздоро́ваться *v.r., pfv. of* здоро́ваться.

поздорове́ть *v., pfv. of* здорове́ть.

поздоро́виться *v.r. pfv., colloq., impers., used negatively with dat.* to be bad for: ему́ не поздоро́вится от э́того, it will be bad for him; he will come out the worse for it.

поздрави́тельный *adj.* congratulatory.

поздра́вить [*infl.* -влю, -вишь] *v., pfv. of* поздравля́ть.

поздравле́ние *n.* congratulation. Прими́те мои́ поздравле́ния, (please) accept my congratulations.

поздравля́ть *v. impfv.* [*pfv.* поздра́вить] **1,** to congratulate. **2,** (*on holidays, birthdays, etc.*) to wish a happy...: поздра́вить кого́-нибудь с Но́вым го́дом, to wish someone a happy New Year.

позелене́ть *v., pfv. of* зелене́ть.

позёр *n.* play-actor. —**позёрство**, *n.* play-acting.

по́зже *adv., comp. of* по́здно, later.

пози́ровать *v. impfv.* [*pres.* -рую, -руешь] to pose.

позити́в *n., photog.* positive.

позитиви́зм *n.* positivism.

позити́вный *adj.* positive.

позитро́н *n.* positron.

позицио́нный *adj.* positional.

пози́ция *n.* **1,** position. **2,** *fig.* position; viewpoint: изложи́ть свою́ пози́цию, to state one's position.

познава́тельный *adj.* cognitive.

познава́ть *v. impfv.* [*pfv.* позна́ть; *pres.* -зна́ю, -зна́ешь] **1,** to get to know. **2,** to experience. —**познава́ться**, *refl.* [*impfv. only*] to become known; become recognized (*for what one is*).

познако́мить *v., pfv. of* знако́мить. —**познако́миться**, *refl., pfv. of* знако́миться.

позна́ние *n.* **1,** cognition. **2,** *pl.* knowledge. —**тео́рия позна́ния**, epistemology.

позна́ть [*infl.* -зна́ю, -зна́ешь] *v., pfv. of* познава́ть.

позоло́та *n.* gilding; gilt.

позолоти́ть *v., pfv. of* золоти́ть.

позоло́ченный *adj.* gilded; gilt.

позо́р *n.* shame; disgrace.

позо́рить *v. impfv.* [*pfv.* опозо́рить] to disgrace. —**позо́риться**, *refl.* to disgrace oneself.

позо́рище *n., colloq.* shameful event; disgrace; scandal.

позóрный *adj.* disgraceful; shameful. —позóрный столб, pillory.

позумéнт *n.* galloon; braid.

позы́в *n.* urge; desire.

позывнóй *adj., in* позывнóй сигнáл, call sign. —позывны́е, *n. pl.* call sign.

поигрáть *v. pfv.* to play (*for a while*).

поимённо *adv.* by name.

поимённый *adj.* of names: поимённый спи́сок, list of names. —поимённое голосовáние, roll-call vote.

поименовáть *v. pfv.* [*infl.* -ну́ю, -ну́ешь] 1, to call; name. 2, to mention; list.

пои́мка *n.* catching; capture.

поинтересовáться *v.r. pfv.* [*infl.* -су́юсь, -су́ешься] 1, (*with instr.*) to show an interest (in). 2, to inquire; ask.

пóиск *n., often pl.* 1, search; quest. 2, retrieval (*of information*). 3, *mil.* reconnaissance raid. —в пóисках (+ *gen.*), in search of. —пойти́ *or* отпрáвиться на пóиски (+ *gen.*), to set out in search of.

поискáть *v. pfv.* [*infl.* -ищу́, -и́щешь] to look for.

поискóвый *also,* пóисковый *adj.* 1, search (*attrib.*): поискóвая грýппа, search party. 2, exploring; prospecting.

пои́стине *adv.* truly; indeed.

пои́ть *v. impfv.* [*pfv.* напои́ть; *pres.* пою́, пóишь *or* пои́шь] 1, to give (someone) something to drink. 2, to water (cattle).

пóйло *n.* mash; swill.

пóйма *n.* flood plain.

поймáть *v., pfv. of* лови́ть.

пóйнтер [*pl.* пойнтерá] *n.* pointer (*dog*).

пойти́ *v. pfv.* [*infl.* пойду́, пойдёшь; *past* пошёл, пошлá, пошлó] 1, *pfv. of* идти́. 2, to begin to walk; set out. 3, (*of a vehicle*) to start moving. 4, (*of rain, snow, etc.*) to begin to fall: пошёл дождь, it began to rain. 5, (*of a liquid*) to begin to flow. 6, (*with* на + *acc.*) to do; take the step of: он не пойдёт на э́то, he won't do (something like) that. 7, (*with inf.*) *colloq.* to begin (to). 8, *past tense only, giving imperative meaning,* go!; leave!; go away! Пошёл вон!, away with you!; be off. —я пошёл, *colloq.* I'm leaving; I'm off. —éсли (уж) на то пошлó, for that matter; if it comes to that.

покá *adv.* for the time being; for the present; for the moment; for now. —*conj.* 1, while: покá я ждал, while I was waiting. 2, as long as: покá я бýду жив, as long as I live. 3, (*with* не) until: покá онá не придёт, until she comes. 4, (*with* не) before: покá не пóздно, before it is too late. —*interj.* [*also,* ну, покá] *colloq.* so long! —покá ещё; покá что, 1, for the time being; for the present. 2, so far; thus far; as yet.

покáз *n.* showing; demonstration.

показáние *n.* 1, *usu.pl.* evidence; testimony. 2, affidavit; deposition. 3, *usu. pl.* reading (*on an instrument*).

показáтель *n.m.* 1, index; indicator. 2, *pl.* figures. 3, *math.* exponent.

показáтельный *adj.* 1, indicative; significant; revealing. 2, model (*attrib.*); demonstration (*attrib.*). —показáтельный суд, show trial.

показáть [*infl.* -кажý, -кáжешь] *v., pfv. of* покáзывать. —показáться, *refl.* 1, *pfv. of* казáться. 2, *pfv. of* покáзываться.

показнóй *adj.* 1, for show; done for effect. 2, ostentatious.

показýха *n., colloq.* show; window dressing.

покáзывать *v. impfv.* [*pfv.* показáть] 1, to show. 2, (*with* на + *acc.*) to point at; point to. 3, to register; read. 4, to show; display (a quality, emotion, etc.). 5, *sports* to achieve (a certain result). 6, to stick out (one's tongue); turn (one's back); thumb (one's nose). 7, to perform (a trick, play, etc.). 8, to testify; (*with* на + *acc.*) testify against. 9, (*with dat.*) *colloq.* to show; teach (someone) a lesson. —не покáзывать ви́ду, not to show; not let on. —показáть (комý-нибудь) на дверь, to show (someone) the door (*i.e.* order out). —показáть пример (+ *dat.*), to serve as an example to. —показáть себя́, 1, to prove oneself; show one's worth. 2, (*with instr.*) to prove to be; show oneself to be.

покáзываться *v.r. impfv.* [*pfv.* показáться] 1, to appear; come into view. 2, to show up; turn up. Показáться врачý, to see a doctor. —покáзываться на глазáх у, (*of tears*) to come to one's eyes. —покáзываться на глазá (+ *dat.*), to show one's face to; allow oneself to be seen by.

покáлывать *v. impfv., colloq.* 1, to prick. 2, *impers.* to have an intermittent pain: у меня́ покáлывает в бокý, I have an intermittent pain in my side.

покáмест *adv. & conj., colloq.* = покá.

покарáть *v., pfv. of* карáть.

покатáть *v., pfv. of* катáть (*in sense #2*). —покатáться, *refl., pfv. of* катáться (*in sense #2*).

покати́ть *v., pfv. of* кати́ть. —покати́ться, *refl.* 1, *pfv. of* кати́ться. 2, *in* покати́ться сó смеху, *colloq.* to roar with laughter.

покáтость *n.f.* slope; incline.

покáтываться *v.r. impfv., colloq., in* покáтываться сó смеху, *colloq.* to roar with laughter.

покáтый *adj.* 1, slanting; sloping. 2, *in* покáтый лоб, receding forehead.

покачáть *v. pfv.* 1, to rock; swing. 2, *in* покачáть головóй, to shake one's head. —покачáться, *refl.* 1, to rock. 2, to swing back and forth. 3, *in* покачáться на качéлях, to ride a swing.

покáчивать *v. impfv.* to rock slightly. —покáчиваться, *refl.* to rock, toss, or waver slightly.

покачнýть *v. pfv.* 1, to shake. 2, to tip; tilt. —покачнýться, *refl.* 1, to sway. 2, to lurch. 3, to tilt. 4, *fig., colloq.* to take a turn for the worse.

покáшливать *v. impfv.* to have a slight cough; cough intermittently.

покáшлять *v. pfv.* to cough (*momentarily*).

покая́ние *n.* 1, (religious) confession. 2, repentance; penitence.

покая́нный *adj.* of repentance; repentant; penitent.

покáяться *v.r., pfv. of* кáяться.

поквартáльный *adj.* quarterly. —поквартáльно, *adv.* quarterly.

поквитáться *v.r. pfv.* (*with* с + *instr.*) *colloq.* to get even (with); settle scores (with).

пóкер *n.* poker (*card game*).

покидáть *v. impfv.* [*pfv.* поки́нуть] to leave; desert; abandon; forsake.

покладáя *verbal adv., in* рабóтать не покладáя рук, to work untiringly.

поклáдистый *adj.* amenable; agreeable.

поклáжа *n.* 1, load. 2, baggage; luggage.

поклёп *n., colloq.* slander; calumny.

поклóн *n.* 1, bow. 2, regards; greetings; best wishes. —идти́ на поклóн к, to go begging to.

поклонéние *n.* (*with dat.*) worship (of): поклонéние и́долам, worship of idols.

поклони́ться [*infl.* -клоню́сь, -кло́нишься] *v.r., pfv. of* кла́няться.

покло́нник *n.* **1,** admirer. **2,** devotee. **3,** suitor. **4,** *relig.* worshiper.

поклоня́ться *v.r. impfv.* (*with dat.*) to worship.

покля́сться *v.r., pfv. of* кля́сться.

поко́иться *v.r. impfv.* **1,** (*with* на + *prepl.*) to rest (on). **2,** to repose; lie: здесь поко́ится..., here lies...

поко́й *n.* **1,** peace (of mind): оставля́ть в поко́е, to leave in peace. **2,** quiet. **3,** rest: в состоя́нии поко́я, in a state of rest. **4,** *obs.* room; apartment. —**ве́чный поко́й,** eternal rest. —**приёмный поко́й,** reception office (*in a hospital*). —**уходи́ть на поко́й,** to retire.

поко́йник *n.m.* [*fem.* -ница] the deceased.

поко́йницкая *n., decl. as an adj.* morgue; mortuary.

поко́йный *adj.* **1,** calm; tranquil; serene. **2,** (*of a deceased person*) the late. —*n.* the deceased.

поколеба́ть *v., pfv. of* колеба́ть. —**поколеба́ться,** *refl., pfv. of* колеба́ться.

поколе́ние *n.* generation.

поколоти́ть *v. pfv.* [*infl.* -лочу́, -ло́тишь] *colloq.* **1,** to beat; whip; thrash. **2,** (*with* в + *acc. or* по) to bang (on).

поколо́ть *v. pfv.* [*infl.* -колю́, -ко́лешь] **1,** to prick. **2,** to slaughter. **3,** to chop (all or a quantity of something).

поко́нчить *v. pfv.* (*with* с + *instr.*) **1,** to finish. **2,** to put an end to. —**поко́нчить жизнь самоуби́йством; поко́нчить с собо́й,** to commit suicide. —**поко́нчить счёты с** (+ *instr.*), to break off with.

покоре́ние *n.* conquest.

покори́тель *n.m.* conqueror. —**покори́тель серде́ц,** lady-killer.

покори́ть *v., pfv. of* покоря́ть. —**покори́ться,** *refl., pfv. of* покоря́ться.

покорми́ть *v., pfv. of* корми́ть.

поко́рный *adj.* **1,** submissive; obedient. **2,** humble: поко́рная про́сьба, humble request. —**поко́рно,** *adv.* humbly. —**поко́рность,** *n.f.* submissiveness.

покоро́бить *v., pfv. of* коро́бить. —**покоро́биться,** *refl., pfv. of* коро́биться.

покоря́ть *v. impfv.* [*pfv.* покори́ть] **1,** to conquer; subdue. **2,** *fig.* to win the heart of. —**покоря́ться,** *refl.* (*with dat.*) **1,** to submit (to). **2,** to resign oneself (to).

поко́с *n.* **1,** mowing. **2,** meadow.

покоси́ть[1] *v. pfv.* [*infl.* -кошу́, -ко́сишь] *colloq.* to mow; cut.

покоси́ть[2] *v. pfv.* [*infl.* -кошу́, -коси́шь] **1,** to tilt. **2,** (*with acc. or instr.*) to cock (one's eye). —**покоси́ться,** *refl., pfv. of* коси́ться.

покра́сить *v., pfv. of* кра́сить.

покрасне́ть *v., pfv. of* красне́ть.

покриви́ть *v., pfv. of* криви́ть. —**покриви́ться,** *refl., pfv. of* криви́ться.

покри́кивать *v. impfv., colloq.* to shout.

покро́в *n.* **1,** cover; covering. **2,** *fig.* cover; cloak; mantle: под покро́вом но́чи, under cover of night. **3,** *obs.* coverlet. —**ко́жный покро́в,** skin. —**леднико́вый покро́в,** icecap. —**о́блачный покро́в,** cloud cover. —**по́чвенный покро́в,** topsoil. —**сне́жный покро́в,** blanket of snow.

покрови́тель *n.m.* patron; protector; sponsor.

покрови́тельственный *adj.* **1,** protective. **2,** patronizing. —**покрови́тельственная окра́ска,** protective coloration. —**покрови́тельственный тари́ф,** protective tariff.

покрови́тельство *n.* patronage; sponsorship. Под покрови́тельством (+ *gen.*), under the auspices of.

покрови́тельствовать *v. impfv.* [*pres.* -ствую, -ствуешь] (*with dat.*) to patronize; sponsor.

покро́й *n.* cut (*of a garment*). —**все на оди́н покро́й,** all alike.

покроши́ть *v. pfv.* [*infl.* -крошу́, -кро́шишь] **1,** to chop up. **2,** to crumble.

покружи́ть *v. pfv.* [*infl.* -кружу́, -кру́жишь] **1,** *v.t.* to spin around. **2,** *v.i.* to wander (*for a while*). **3,** *v.i.* (*of an aircraft*) to circle several times. —**покружи́ться,** *refl.* **1,** to spin around. **2,** to wander (*for a while*). **3,** (*of a bird*) to circle.

покрути́ть *v. pfv.* [*infl.* -кручу́, -кру́тишь] (*with acc. or instr.*) to twist.

покрыва́ло *n.* **1,** cloth cover. **2,** bedspread; counterpane. **3,** covering; layer: нефтяно́е покрыва́ло, oil slick.

покрыва́ть *v. impfv.* [*pfv.* покры́ть] **1,** to cover. **2,** to coat (with paint, lacquer, etc.). **3,** to hide; cover up; shield. **4,** to cover; defray (expenses, losses, etc.). **5,** to drown out.

покры́тие *n.* **1,** (act of) covering. **2,** covering; coating; surface. **3,** defrayal (*of expenses*); discharge (*of debts*). **4,** roofing.

покры́ть [*infl.* -кро́ю, -кро́ешь] *v., pfv. of* крыть *and* покрыва́ть.

покры́шка [*gen. pl.* -шек] *n.* **1,** tire. **2,** *colloq.* cover; lid.

поку́да *adv. & conj., colloq.* = пока́.

покупа́тель *n.m.* buyer; customer.

покупа́тельный *adj.* buying (*attrib.*); purchasing (*attrib.*): покупа́тельная спосо́бность, purchasing power.

покупа́ть *v. impfv.* [*pfv.* купи́ть] to buy; purchase.

поку́пка [*gen. pl.* -пок] *n.* **1,** purchase; (act of) purchasing. **2,** a purchase: де́лать поку́пки, to go shopping.

покупно́й *adj.* **1,** purchased; bought. **2,** *in* покупна́я цена́, purchase price.

покури́ть *v. pfv.* [*infl.* -курю́, -ку́ришь] to have a smoke.

покуса́ть *v. pfv.* to bite; sting.

покуси́ться [*infl.* -шу́сь, -си́шься] *v.r., pfv. of* покуша́ться.

поку́шать *v., pfv. of* ку́шать.

покуша́ться *v.r. impfv.* [*pfv.* покуси́ться] (*with* на + *acc.*) **1,** to make an attempt upon: покуси́ться на чью́-нибудь жизнь, to make an attempt on someone's life. **2,** to encroach (upon).

покуше́ние *n.* (*with* на + *acc.*) attempted assassination of; attempt on the life of.

пол *n.* **1,** [*2nd loc.* полу́; *pl.* полы́, поло́в] floor. **2,** [*pl.* по́лы, поло́в] sex.

пол- *prefix* **1,** half: полчаса́, half an hour. **2,** *colloq.* (*in telling time*) half (*before the next hour*): полшесто́го, half-past five.

пола́ [*pl.* по́лы] *n.* **1,** flap (*of a garment*). **2,** flap; fold (*of a tent*). —**из-под полы́,** (*of a purchase, sale, etc.*) under the table (*or* counter).

полага́ть *v. impfv.* to think; believe; suppose. На́до полага́ть, one may assume; it may be assumed. —**полага́ться,** *refl.* **1,** *impers.* to be proper; be in order; be expected. Как полага́ется, as it should be; as expected. Не полага́ется, not supposed to; not the thing to do. **2,** (*with dat.*) to be due to; be payable to. **3,** [*pfv.* положи́ться] (*with* на + *acc.*) to rely on.

пола́дить *v. pfv.* [*infl.* -ла́жу, -ла́дишь] *colloq.* **1,** to reach an agreement. **2,** to get along.

пола́комиться *v.r., pfv. of* ла́комиться.

полбеды́ *n.f., colloq.,* in **э́то ещё полбеды́**, it's not so terrible; it's no calamity.

полве́ка [*gen.* полуве́ка] *n.m.* half a century. В тече́ние полуве́ка, for half a century.

полго́да [*gen.* полуго́да] *n.m.* half a year. Бо́льше полуго́да, more than half a year.

по́лдень [*gen.* полу́дня] *n.m.* noon. —**полдне́вный,** *adj.* noon (*attrib.*); midday (*attrib.*).

по́лдник *n.* mid-afternoon snack.

полдоро́ги *n.f.* halfway point: на полдоро́ге, halfway; at the halfway point.

полдю́жины *n.f.* half a dozen.

по́ле [*pl.* поля́, поле́й] *n.* **1,** field. **2,** *fig.* field (*of activity*). **3,** background (*of a painting*). **4,** *pl.* brim (*of a hat*). **5,** *pl.* margin. —**по́ле би́твы; по́ле бо́я; по́ле сраже́ния,** battlefield. —**по́ле зре́ния,** field of vision.

полеве́ть *v., pfv. of* леве́ть.

полёвка [*gen. pl.* -вок] *n.* vole.

полево́дство *n.* field crop farming.

полево́й *adj.* field (*attrib.*). —**полева́я мышь,** field mouse. —**полевы́е цветы́,** wildflowers.

полего́ньку *adv., colloq.* slowly; little by little.

полегча́ть *v., pfv. of* легча́ть.

полежа́ть *v. pfv.* [*infl.* -лежу́, -лежи́шь] to lie for a while; lie down for a while.

поле́зно *adj., used predicatively* **1,** useful. **2,** healthy; good: по́сле обе́да поле́зно отдохну́ть, it is good to rest after dinner.

поле́зность *n.f.* usefulness.

поле́зный *adj.* [*short form* -зен, -зна] **1,** useful; helpful. **2,** wholesome. **3,** good (for): поле́зный для здоро́вья, good for one's health. —**чем могу́ быть поле́зен (поле́зна)?,** what can I do for you?

поле́зть *v. pfv.* [*infl. like* лезть] **1,** *pfv. of* лезть. **2,** to begin to climb.

полемизи́ровать *v. impfv.* [*pres.* -рую, -руешь] to engage in polemics.

поле́мика *n.* polemics. —**полеми́ст,** *n.* polemicist. —**полеми́ческий,** *adj.* polemic(al).

полени́ться *v.r. pfv.* [*infl.* -леню́сь, -ле́нишься] (*with inf.*) to be too lazy (to).

поле́нница *n.* stack of logs; stack of firewood.

поле́но [*pl.* поле́нья, -ньев] *n.* log (*for burning*).

поле́сье *n.* marshy woodlands.

полёт *n.* flight; flying. —**полёт фанта́зии,** flight of fantasy.

полета́ть *v. pfv.* to fly (*for a while*).

полете́ть *v. pfv.* [*infl.* -чу́, -ти́шь] **1,** *pfv. of* лете́ть. **2,** to begin to fly; take off. **3,** *colloq.* to fall.

полётный *adj.* flight (*attrib.*); flying.

полечи́ть *v. pfv.* [*infl.* -лечу́, -ле́чишь] to treat (*for a while*). —**полечи́ться,** *refl.* to be treated; get some treatment.

поле́чь *v. pfv.* [*infl. like* лечь] (*of all or many people*) **1,** *colloq.* to lie down. **2,** to be killed (*in battle*).

по́лзать *v. impfv., indeterm. of* ползти́.

ползко́м *adv.* by crawling; on all fours.

ползти́ *v. impfv.* [*pfv.* поползти́; *pres.* ползу́, ползёшь; *past* полз, ползла́, ползло́] **1,** to crawl. **2,** to creep (along). **3,** to trickle. **4,** *colloq.* (*of fabric*) to come apart.

ползу́н [*gen.* -зуна́] *n., colloq.* baby still in the crawling stage.

ползуно́к [*gen.* -нка́] *n., colloq.* **1,** = ползу́н. **2,** *pl.* crawlers (*baby's garment*).

ползу́чий *adj.* (*of a plant*) creeping: ползу́чее расте́ние, creeper.

полиа́ндрия *n.* polyandry.

полива́ть *v. impfv.* [*pfv.* поли́ть] to water (plants). —**полива́ться,** *refl.* (*with instr.*) to pour (water) on oneself.

поли́вка *n.* watering (*of plants*).

полига́мия *n.* polygamy. —**полигами́ческий; полига́мный,** *adj.* polygamous.

полигло́т *n.* polyglot.

полиго́н *n.* **1,** firing range. **2,** training ground. —**испыта́тельный полиго́н,** proving ground.

полиграфия *n.* printing. —**полиграфи́ческий,** *adj.* printing (*attrib.*).

поликли́ника *n.* polyclinic.

полиме́р *n.* polymer. —**полиме́рный,** *adj.* polymeric.

полинези́ец [*gen.* -и́йца] *n.m.* [*fem.* -и́йка] Polynesian. —**полинези́йский,** *adj.* Polynesian.

полиня́лый *adj.* faded.

полиня́ть *v., pfv. of* линя́ть (*in sense #1*).

полиомиели́т *n.* poliomyelitis.

поли́п *n.* polyp.

полирова́льный *adj.* polishing (*attrib.*). —**полирова́льная маши́на,** buffing machine.

полиро́ванный *adj.* polished.

полирова́ть *v. impfv.* [*pfv.* отполирова́ть; *pres.* -ру́ю, -ру́ешь] to polish.

полиро́вка *n.* **1,** polishing. **2,** polish; gloss; finish. —**полиро́вочный,** *adj.* polishing (*attrib.*). —**полиро́вщик,** *n.* polisher.

по́лис *n., in* страхово́й по́лис, insurance policy.

полисме́н *n.* policeman (*in the U.S. or Great Britain*).

полиста́ть *v. pfv.* to flip through.

полистиро́л *n.* polystyrene.

политбюро́ *n. indecl.* Politburo.

политеи́зм (тэ) *n.* polytheism. —**политеи́ст,** *n.* polytheist. —**политеисти́ческий,** *adj.* polytheistic.

полите́хникум *n.* polytechnic school.

политехни́ческий *adj.* polytechnic.

политзаключённый *n., decl. as an adj.* political prisoner.

поли́тик *n.* politician.

поли́тика *n.* **1,** policy. **2,** politics.

политика́н *n.* (unscrupulous) politician.

полити́ческий *adj.* political. —**полити́ческий де́ятель,** political figure; politician.

полити́чный *adj., colloq.* politic; diplomatic.

политру́к *n.* political instructor in the Soviet armed forces (*contr. of* полити́ческий руководи́тель).

политу́ра *n.* polish; varnish.

поли́ть *v. pfv.* [*infl.* -лью́, -льёшь; *past* по́лил *or* поли́л, полила́, по́лило *or* поли́ло] **1,** *pfv. of* полива́ть. **2,** (*of rain*) to begin to come down. —**поли́ться,** *refl.* [*past* поли́лся, полила́сь, полило́сь *or* поли́лось] **1,** *pfv. of* полива́ться. **2,** to begin to flow.

полице́йский *adj.* police (*attrib.*). —*n.* policeman.

поли́ция *n.* police.

поли́чное *n., decl. as an adj., in* с поли́чным, red-handed: пойма́ть/попа́сться с поли́чным, to catch/be caught/red-handed.

полиэтиле́н *n.* polyethylene. —**полиэтиле́новый,** *adj.* polyethylene.

полиэфи́р *n.* polyester. —**полиэфи́рный,** *adj.* polyester.

полк [*gen.* **полка́**; *2nd loc.* **полку́**] *n.* regiment. —**на́-шего полку́ при́было**, our numbers have grown.

по́лка [*gen. pl.* **-лок**] *n.* **1**, shelf. **2**, berth.

полко́вник *n.* colonel.

полково́дец [*gen.* **-дца**] *n.* military leader.

полково́й *adj.* regimental.

полне́ть *v. impfv.* [*pfv.* **пополне́ть**] to put on weight; get fat.

полни́ть *v. impfv., colloq.* to make (someone) look fat.

по́лно *predicate, colloq.* **1**, enough!; stop! **2**, don't be silly!

полно́ *adv., colloq.* filled; packed: в за́ле бы́ло полно́ наро́да, the hall was packed with people.

полнове́сный *adj.* **1**, full-weight. **2**, heavy; weighty.

полновла́стие *n.* full power; absolute power. —**полновла́стный**, *adj.* having full or absolute power.

полново́дный *adj.* (*of a river or lake*) at a high level.

полново́дье *n.* high water.

полногру́дый *adj.* buxom.

полнокро́вие *n., med.* plethora.

полнокро́вный *adj.* full-blooded; red-blooded.

полнолу́ние *n.* full moon.

полнометра́жный *adj.* (*of a film*) feature-length.

полномо́чие *n.* authority; power. —**полномо́чный**, *adj.* plenipotentiary.

полнопра́вие *n.* full rights; equality. —**полнопра́в-ный**, *adj.* enjoying full rights: полнопра́вный член, full member.

по́лностью *adv.* **1**, in full. **2**, fully; completely.

полнота́ *n.* **1**, fullness; completeness. **2**, obesity; corpulence. —**для полноты́ карти́ны**, to complete the picture. —**от полноты́ се́рдца**, out of the fullness of one's heart. —**со всей полното́й; во всей полноте́**, in its entirety.

полноце́нный *adj.* **1**, worth its full value. **2**, *fig.* full-fledged.

по́лночь [*gen.* **полу́ночи** *or* **по́лночи**] *n.f.* midnight. —**полно́чный**, *adj.* midnight (*attrib.*).

по́лный *adj.* [*short form* **по́лон, полна́, по́лно** *or* **полно́**] **1**, full. **2**, complete; total. **3**, fat; stout. —**в по́лной ме́ре**, fully; in full measure.

по́ло *n. indecl.* polo. —**во́дное по́ло**, water polo.

полови́к [*gen.* **-вика́**] *n.* floor mat; doormat.

полови́на *n.* **1**, half. **2**, (*with ordinal numbers*) half-past: полови́на тре́тьего, half-past two. **3**, middle: в полови́не ме́сяца, in the middle of the month.

полови́нный *adj.* half; half a; a half: полови́нная до́ля, a half share. —**полови́нная но́та**, half note. —**в полови́нном соста́ве**, at half strength.

полови́нчатый *adj.* halfway; indecisive.

полови́ца *n.* floorboard.

поло́вник *n., colloq.* ladle.

полово́дье *n.* high water (*resulting from the melting of snow*).

полово́й *adj.* **1**, sexual; sex (*attrib.*). **2**, floor (*attrib.*).

по́лог *n.* **1**, canopy. **2**, *fig.* cover.

поло́гий *adj.* not steep; gently sloping.

положе́ние *n.* **1**, position: сидя́чее положе́ние, sitting position. **2**, situation: отча́янное положе́ние, desperate situation. **3**, status. **4**, tenet; thesis; proposition. **5**, regulations. **6**, provision. —**в (интере́сном) положе́нии**, pregnant. —**положе́ние веще́й/дел**, state of affairs. —**входи́ть в (чьё-нибудь) положе́ние**, to put oneself in someone's place; empathize with.

поло́женный *adj.* agreed-upon; prescribed.

поло́жено *short form neut. of past passive part. of* **положи́ть** (*with dat.*) *colloq.* (one) should; (one) is supposed to. —**как поло́жено**, as one should; as it should be.

положи́тельно *adv.* **1**, positively: положи́тельно заряжённое ядро́, a positively charged nucleus. **2**, positively; favorably. **3**, positively; absolutely: положи́тельно некраси́в, positively ugly; положи́тельно ничего́, absolutely nothing.

положи́тельный *adj.* **1**, positive. **2**, affirmative. **3**, *colloq.* absolute; utter.

положи́ть [*infl.* **-ложу́, -ло́жишь**] *v., pfv. of* **класть**. —**поло́жим**, let us say; let us assume. —**положи́ть коне́ц** (+ *dat.*), to put an end to. —**положи́ть слова́ на му́зыку**, to set words to music.

положи́ться [*infl.* **-ложу́сь, -ло́жишься**] *v. r., pfv. of* **полага́ться** (*in sense #3*).

по́лоз [*pl.* **поло́зья, -зьев**] *n.* runner (*of a sleigh*).

полома́ть *v. pfv.* **1**, to break. **2**, *colloq.* to disrupt. **3**, *colloq., pfv. of* **лома́ть** (*in sense #5*). —**полома́ться**, *refl.* **1**, to break; break down. **2**, *pfv. of* **лома́ться** (*in sense #5*).

поло́мка [*gen. pl.* **-мок**] *n.* **1**, breakage. **2**, breakdown (*of a machine*). **3**, broken part.

поломо́йка [*gen. pl.* **-мо́ек**] *n., colloq.* woman who washes floors.

полоне́з *n.* polonaise.

поло́ний *n.* polonium.

полони́ть *v. pfv., archaic* to take prisoner.

полоса́ [*acc.* **полосу́** *or* **по́лосу**; *pl.* **по́лосы, поло́с, -са́м**] *n.* **1**, strip (*of metal, paper, etc.*). **2**, stripe (*in a design*). **3**, strip (*of land*); lane (*of a highway*). **4**, belt; region; zone. **5**, band (*of frequencies, the spectrum, etc.*). **6**, welt (*from a blow*). **7**, (*with gen.*) period (*of*); spell (*of*): полоса́ хоро́шей пого́ды, spell of good weather. **8**, page (*of a newspaper, book, etc.*).

полоса́тик *n.* rorqual (*whale*).

полоса́тый *adj.* striped.

поло́ска [*gen. pl.* **-сок**] *n., dim. of* **полоса́**. —**в поло́ску**, striped.

полоска́ние *n.* **1**, rinsing; gargling. **2**, mouthwash.

полоска́тельница *n.* slop basin.

полоска́ть *v. impfv.* [*pfv.* **вы́полоскать** *or* **прополо-ска́ть**; *pres.* **-лощу́, -ло́щешь**] **1**, to rinse. **2**, *in* полоска́ть го́рло, to gargle. —**полоска́ться**, *refl.* [*impfv. only*] **1**, to splash about (*in water*). **2**, (*of a flag, sail, etc.*) to flutter.

по́лость [*pl.* **по́лости, -сте́й, -стя́м**] *n.f.* **1**, cavity. **2**, lap robe.

полоте́нце [*gen. pl.* **-нец**] *n.* towel.

полотёр *n.* floor-polisher.

поло́тнище *n.* **1**, width (*of cloth*): простыня́ в два поло́тнища, a sheet of two widths. **2**, leaf (*of a door, gate, etc.*).

полотно́ [*pl.* **поло́тна, поло́тен**] *n.* **1**, linen. **2**, canvas; painting. **3**, roadbed. **4**, blade (*of a saw, axe, etc.*).

полотня́ный *adj.* linen.

поло́ть *v. impfv.* [*pfv.* **вы́полоть**; *pres.* **полю́, по́-лешь**] **1**, to weed (a garden). **2**, to pull up (weeds).

полоу́мие *n., colloq.* madness. —**полоу́мный**, *adj., colloq.* mad; crazy.

полпути́ *n.m.* halfway point: на полпути́, halfway; at the halfway point; midway.

полсло́ва [*gen.* **полсло́ва** *or* **полусло́ва**] *n. neut.* **1**, a (brief) word: мо́жно вас на полсло́ва?, may I have a word with you? **2**, a word half uttered: останови́ться на полусло́ве, to stop short (*when speaking*); прерва́ть на полусло́ве, to cut (someone) short. —**ни полсло́ва**, not a single word.

полста́вки *n.f.*, *in* **на полста́вки**, part-time.

полти́нник *n.*, *colloq.* fifty kopecks; fifty-kopeck coin.

полтора́ [*fem.* **полторы́**; *gen.*, *dat.*, *instr.*, & *prepl.* **полу́тора**] *numeral* one and a half.

полтора́ста [*gen.*, *dat.*, *instr.*, & *prepl.* **полу́тораста**] *numeral* one hundred and fifty.

полуавтомати́ческий *adj.* semiautomatic.

полубессозна́тельный *adj.* semiconscious.

полубо́г *n.* demigod.

полуботи́нок [*gen.* -нка; *gen. pl.* -нок] *n.* shoe.

полувое́нный *adj.* paramilitary.

полуго́дие *n.* half a year; half of a calendar year. —**полугоди́чный**; **полугодово́й**, *adj.* half-year (*attrib.*); six-month (*attrib.*). —**полугодова́лый**, *adj.* six-month-old.

полуголо́дный *adj.* half-starved.

полугра́мотный *adj.* semiliterate.

полуде́нный *adj.* noon (*attrib.*); midday (*attrib.*).

полуди́ть *v.*, *pfv. of* **луди́ть**.

полуживо́й *adj.* more dead than alive.

полузабытьё [*2nd loc.* -тьи́] *n.* (state of) semi-consciousness.

полузащи́тник *n.*, *sports* halfback.

полукро́вка [*gen. pl.* -вок] *n.* half-breed.

полукро́вный *adj.* half-blooded.

полукру́г *n.* semicircle. —**полукру́глый**, *adj.* semicircular.

полулежа́ть *v. impfv.* [*pres.* -жу́, -жи́шь] to recline.

полумёртвый *adj.* half-dead; more dead than alive.

полуме́сяц *n.* half-moon.

полуме́сячный *adj.* half a month's.

полумра́к *n.* semidarkness.

полуно́чник *n.*, *colloq.* night owl.

полуно́чничать *v. impfv.*, *colloq.* to stay up most of the night; burn the midnight oil.

полуно́чный *also*, **полуно́чный** *adj.* midnight (*attrib.*).

полуоборо́т *n.* half-turn.

полуо́стров [*pl.* **полуострова́**] *n.* peninsula. —**полуостровно́й**, *adj.* peninsular.

полуотво́ренный *adj.* half-open; ajar. *Also*, **полуоткры́тый**.

полуприце́п *n.* semitrailer.

полупроводни́к [*gen.* -ника́] *n.* semiconductor.

полупрозра́чный *adj.* translucent.

полуразру́шенный *adj.* tumble-down; ramshackle.

полураспа́д *n.*, *in* **пери́од полураспа́да**, half-life.

полусве́т *n.* dim light.

полусме́рть *n.f.*, *in* **до полусме́рти**, (half) to death: испуга́ть до полусме́рти, to frighten (half) to death. —**изби́ть до полусме́рти**, to beat within an inch of one's life.

полусозна́тельный *adj.* semiconscious.

полусо́н [*gen.* -сна́] *n.* state of being half asleep: в полусне́, half asleep. —**полусо́нный**, *adj.* half asleep.

полуста́нок [*gen.* -нка] *n.* small station; way station.

полуте́нь [*2nd loc.* -тени́] *n.f.* penumbra.

полуто́н *n.* **1**, *music* half tone. **2**, *art* halftone.

полутьма́ *n.* semidarkness.

полуфабрика́т *n.* **1**, semi-finished product. **2**, *pl.* partially prepared food.

полуфина́л *n.* semifinal; semifinals. —**полуфинали́ст**, *n.* semifinalist. —**полуфина́льный**, *adj.* semifinal.

получасово́й *adj.* half-hour (*attrib.*).

получа́тель *n.m.* recipient.

получа́ть *v. impfv.* [*pfv.* **получи́ть**] **1**, to receive; get. **2**, to obtain; get. **3**, to gain. **4**, *colloq.* to catch; get (a cold, illness, etc.). —**получа́ться**, *refl.* **1**, to be received; be obtained. **2**, to come about; result. **3**, to come out; turn out.

получе́ние *n.* **1**, receiving; receipt. **2**, obtaining.

получи́ть [*infl.* -лучу́, -лу́чишь] *v.*, *pfv. of* **получа́ть**. —**получи́ться**, *refl.*, *pfv. of* **получа́ться**.

полу́чка *n.*, *colloq.* **1**, (act of) receiving; receipt. **2**, sum (*of money*). **3**, pay; paycheck.

полуша́рие *n.* hemisphere.

полу́шка [*gen. pl.* -шек] *n.*, *pre-rev.* old coin worth 1/4 of a kopeck. —**ни полу́шки**, not a penny; not a plug nickel.

полушу́бок [*gen.* -бка] *n.* short sheepskin coat.

полушутя́ *adv.* half in jest.

полцены́ *n.f.* half-price: купи́ть за полцены́, to buy at half-price.

полчаса́ [*gen.* **получа́са**] *n.m.* half an hour. Ка́ждые полчаса́, every half-hour.

по́лчище *n.* **1**, horde. **2**, *fig.* swarm.

по́лый *adj.* hollow. —**по́лая вода́**, floodwaters.

по́лымя *n. neut.*, *in* **из огня́ да в по́лымя**, out of the frying pan into the fire.

полы́нный *adj.* wormwood (*attrib.*). —**полы́нная во́дка**, absinthe.

полы́нь *n.f.* wormwood; sagebrush.

полынья́ [*gen. pl.* -не́й] *n.* unfrozen patch of water in the ice; polynya.

полысе́ть *v.*, *pfv. of* **лысе́ть**.

полыха́ть *v. impfv.* to blaze.

по́льза *n.* use; benefit; good. Кака́я от э́того по́льза?, what good will it do? —**в по́льзу** (+ *gen.*), **1**, in favor of. **2**, for; for the sake of; on behalf of. —**быть** *or* **идти́ на по́льзу** (+ *dat.*), to do (someone) good; be good for.

по́льзование *n.* **1**, use. **2**, (with *instr.*) enjoyment (of).

по́льзоваться *v.r. impfv.* [*pfv.* **воспо́льзоваться**; *pres.* -зуюсь, -зуешься] (with *instr.*) **1**, to use; make use of; take advantage of. **2**, [*impfv. only*] to enjoy (an advantage, good health, etc.).

по́лька [*gen. pl.* -лек] *n.* **1**, Polish woman. **2**, polka (*dance*).

по́льский *adj.* Polish.

польсти́ть *v.*, *pfv. of* **льстить**.

полюби́ть *v. pfv.* [*infl.* -люблю́, -лю́бишь] **1**, to come to love; fall in love with. **2**, to come to like; grow fond of. —**полюби́ться**, *refl.* (with *dat.*) *colloq.* to catch the fancy of.

полюбова́ться *v.r.*, *pfv. of* **любова́ться**.

полюбо́вный *adj.* (of an agreement, settlement, etc.) amicable. —**полюбо́вно**, *adv.* amicably.

полюбопы́тствовать *v.*, *pfv. of* **любопы́тствовать**.

по́люс *n.* pole: Се́верный по́люс, North Pole; Ю́жный по́люс, South Pole. Они́ — два по́люса, they are poles apart.

поля́к *n.* Pole.

поля́на *n.* clearing (*in the woods*); glade.

поляризáция *n.* polarization.

поляризовáть *v. impfv. & pfv.* [*pres.* -зýю, -зýешь] to polarize.

полярность *n.f.* polarity.

полярный *adj.* polar. —**Полярная звездá**, the North Star. —**Полярный круг**, the Arctic *or* Antarctic Circle.

помáда *n.* pomade. —**губнáя помáда**, lipstick.

помáдить *v. impfv.* [*pfv.* напомáдить; *pres.* -мáжу, -мáдишь] **1**, to pomade (one's hair). **2**, to paint (one's lips). —**помáдиться**, *refl.* **1**, to pomade one's hair. **2**, to put on lipstick.

помáдка *n.* fruit candy.

помáзание *n.*, *relig.* anointment.

помáзать [*infl.* -мáжу, -мáжешь] *v.*, *pfv. of* мáзать (*in sense #1*) *and* помáзывать.

помазóк [*gen.* -зкá] *n.* small brush; shaving brush.

помáзывать *v. impfv.* [*pfv.* помáзать] to anoint.

помалéньку *adv.*, *colloq.* **1**, at a leisurely pace; without hurrying. **2**, modestly; жить помалéньку, to live modestly. **3**, tolerable; all right.

помáлкивать *v. impfv.*, *colloq.* to keep quiet; hold one's tongue.

поманить *v.*, *pfv. of* манить.

помáрка [*gen. pl.* -рок] *n.* pencil mark; correction.

помахáть *v. pfv.* [*infl.* -машý, -мáшешь] **1**, (*with dat.*) to wave (to). **2**, (*with instr.*) to wave (something).

помáхивать *v. impfv.* (*with instr.*) **1**, to wave (*back and forth*). **2**, to wag; swish (one's tail).

помéдлить *v. pfv.* (*with inf. or* с + *instr.*) to delay; be slow.

помелó *n.* broom (*for cleaning out stoves and chimneys*).

помéньше *adj.* a little smaller. —*adv.* a little less.

поменять *v.*, *pfv. of* менять. —**поменяться**, *refl.*, *pfv. of* меняться.

померáнец [*gen.* -нца] *n.* wild bitter orange. —**померáнцевый**, *adj.* orange (*attrib.*).

померéть [*infl.* помрý, помрёшь; *past* пóмер, померлá, пóмерло] *v.*, *pfv. of* помирáть.

померéщиться *v.r.*, *pfv. of* мерéщиться.

помёрзнуть *v. pfv.* [*past* -мёрз, -ла] *colloq.* to perish from the frost.

помéрить *v. pfv.* to try on. —**помéриться**, *refl.*, *pfv. of* мéриться.

помéркнуть *v.*, *pfv. of* мéркнуть.

помертвéлый *adj.* **1**, deathly pale. **2**, lifeless.

помертвéть *v.*, *pfv. of* мертвéть.

поместительный *adj.* spacious; roomy. —**поместительность**, *n.f.* spaciousness; roominess.

поместить [*infl.* -щý, -стишь] *v.*, *pfv. of* помещáть. —**поместиться**, *refl.*, *pfv. of* помещáться.

помéстный *adj.* **1**, estate (*attrib.*). **2**, landed: помéстное дворянство, landed gentry.

помéстье *n.* estate; manor.

пóмесь *n.f.* **1**, hybrid; cross. **2**, *colloq.* mixture (*of two different elements*).

помéсячный *adj.* monthly. —**помéсячно**, *adv.* monthly; each month; by the month.

помёт *n.* **1**, dung; droppings. **2**, litter; brood.

помéта *n.* mark; note.

помéтить [*infl.* -чу, -тишь] *v.*, *pfv. of* мéтить (*in sense #1*) *and* помечáть.

помéтка [*gen. pl.* -ток] *n.* mark; note.

помéха *n.* **1**, hindrance; obstacle. **2**, interruption. **3**, *pl.* static; interference.

помечáть *v. impfv.* [*pfv.* помéтить] **1**, to mark. **2**, to date; write the date on.

помéшанный *adj.* **1**, mad; crazy; insane. **2**, (*with* на + *prepl.*) *colloq.* addicted (to); hooked (on). —*n.* madman; lunatic.

помешáтельство *n.* madness; insanity.

помешáть *v.*, *pfv. of* мешáть. —**помешáться**, *refl.* **1**, to go mad; go crazy. **2**, (*with* на + *prepl.*) *colloq.* to develop a passion (for); become a nut (about).

помещáть *v. impfv.* [*pfv.* поместить] **1**, to place; put. **2**, to house; lodge; accommodate. **3**, to invest. **4**, to publish (*in a newspaper, magazine, etc.*). —**помещáться**, *refl.* **1**, [*impfv. only*] to be; be placed; be situated. **2**, to be housed; be lodged. **3**, to fit: помещáться за столóм, to fit around the table.

помещéние *n.* **1**, placing; placement. **2**, quarters; accommodations; housing. **3**, premises.

помéщик *n.* landowner.

помéщичий [*fem.* -чья] *adj.* **1**, of or pert. to a landowner. **2**, manorial. —**помéщичий дом**, manor house.

помидóр *n.* tomato. —**помидóрный**, *adj.* tomato (*attrib.*).

помилование *n.* **1**, pardon; forgiveness. **2**, clemency; a pardon.

помиловать *v. pfv.* [*infl.* -лую, -луешь] to pardon. —**Гóсподи, помилуй!**, Lord have mercy!

помимо *prep.*, *with gen.* **1**, besides; apart from; aside from. **2**, without the knowledge of. —**помимо всегó прóчего**, in addition to/apart from/everything else; all else aside.

помин *n.*, *obs.* mention. —**и в помине нет** (*preceded by gen.*), there is not a trace of; (something is) not to be found anywhere. —**и помину нет** (*preceded by* о + *prepl.*), there is no trace/mention/question of; (something is) out of the question. —**лёгок на помине**, talk of the devil.

поминáть *v. impfv.* [*pfv.* помянуть] **1**, to remember; recall. **2**, (*with* о) to mention. **3**, to pray for. **4**, to give (*or* attend) a funeral repast in memory of. —**поминáть добрóм** (+ *acc.*), to speak well of. —**не поминáй (меня) лихом**, don't think ill of me. —**поминáй как звáли**, he (she, it) disappeared without a trace.

поминки [*gen.* -нок] *n. pl.* funeral repast.

поминутный *adj.* **1**, by the minute. **2**, continual; constant. —**поминутно**, *adv.* continually; constantly.

помирáть *v. impfv.* [*pfv.* померéть] *colloq.* to die. —**помирáть сó смеху**, *colloq.* to die laughing.

помирить *v.*, *pfv. of* мирить. —**помириться**, *refl.*, *pfv. of* мириться.

пóмнить *v. impfv.* **1**, to remember. **2**, *in* не пóмнить себя, to get carried away; lose control of oneself; (*with* от) be beside oneself (with). —**пóмниться**, *refl.* **1**, (*with dat.*) to remember: мне пóмнится, I remember; I seem to remember. **2**, *impers.*, *colloq.* to remember (*said of oneself*): как пóмнится, as I recall.

помнóгу *adv.*, *colloq.* **1**, a lot. **2**, (*with gen.*) many.

помножáть *v. impfv.* [*pfv.* помнóжить] **1**, *math.* to multiply. **2**, *fig.* to increase; augment.

помнóжить *v.*, *pfv. of* мнóжить *and* помножáть.

помогáть *v. impfv.* [*pfv.* помóчь] (*with dat.*) to help.

по-мóему *adv.* in my opinion.

помóи [*gen.* -мóев] *n. pl.* kitchen waste; dirty dishwater. —**обливáть помóями**, to vilify; drag through the mud.

помóйка [*gen. pl.* -móек] *n.*, *colloq.* garbage pit.

помойный *adj.* garbage (*attrib.*): помойное ведро, garbage pail. —**помойная яма**, cesspool.

помол *n.* **1,** grinding. **2,** grind: мелкого помола, finely ground; fine-ground.

помолвить *v. pfv.* [*infl.* -влю, -вишь] (*with* с + *instr.*) *obs.* to betroth (to).

помолвка *n.* engagement; betrothal.

помолиться *v.r.,* *pfv. of* молиться (*in sense #1*).

помолодеть *v.,* *pfv. of* молодеть.

помолчать *v. pfv.* [*infl.* -чу, -чишь] to be silent (*for a while*).

поморщиться *v.r.,* *pfv. of* морщиться (*in sense #2*).

поморье *n.* coastal region.

помост *n.* dais; podium.

помочи [*gen.* -чей] *n. pl.* suspenders. —**быть** *or* **ходить на помочах у** (+ *gen.*), to be tied to someone's apron strings. —**водить на помочах**, to keep on a leash (*fig.*).

помочить *v.pfv.* [*infl.* -мочу, -мочишь] to moisten slightly. —**помочиться**, *refl., pfv. of* мочиться.

помочь [*infl. like* мочь] *v., pfv. of* помогать.

помощник *n.m.* [*fem.* -ница] assistant; helper. Помощник директора, assistant director.

помощь *n.f.* help; aid; assistance. —**на помощь!**, help! —**при помощи; с помощью** (+ *gen.*), with the help of; by means of.

помпа *n.* **1,** pump. **2,** pomp.

помпезный *adj.* lavish; extravagant.

помпон *n.* pompon.

помрачнеть *v., pfv. of* мрачнеть.

помутить *v., pfv. of* мутить (*in sense #2*). —**помутиться**, *refl., pfv. of* мутиться.

помутнение *n.* clouding; dimming.

помутнеть *v., pfv. of* мутнеть.

помучить *v. pfv.* to tease; torment; make suffer. —**помучиться**, *refl.* to suffer.

помчать *v., pfv. of* мчать. —**помчаться**, *refl., pfv. of* мчаться.

помыкать *v. impfv.* (*with instr.*) *colloq.* to order about.

помысел [*gen.* -сла] *n.* thought; idea; intention.

помыслить *v., pfv. of* помышлять.

помыть *v., pfv. of* мыть. —**помыться**, *refl., pfv. of* мыться.

помышлять *v. impfv.* [*pfv.* помыслить] (*with* о) to think (about); contemplate.

помянуть [*infl.* -мяну, -мянешь] *v., pfv. of* поминать. —**помяните моё слово**, mark my words!

помятый *adj.* **1,** crumpled; creased. **2,** (*of one's face*) lined; wrinkled.

помять *v., pfv. of* мять (*in senses #2 & #4*). —**помяться**, *refl., pfv. of* мяться.

понадеяться *v. r. pfv.* (*with* на + *acc.*) to count on.

понадобиться *v.r. pfv.* [*infl.* -блюсь, -бишься] (*with dat.*) **1,** to be needed: если вам это когда-нибудь понадобится, if you ever have need of it. **2,** to be necessary.

понапрасну *adv., colloq.* **1,** in vain. **2,** for no reason; for nothing.

понаслышке *adv., colloq.* through hearsay.

поначалу *adv., colloq.* at first.

по-нашему *adv.* in our opinion.

поневоле *adv., colloq.* against one's will; willy-nilly.

понедельник *n.* Monday.

понедельный *adj.* weekly. —**понедельно**, *adv.* weekly; each week; by the week.

понемногу *adv.* **1,** a little at a time. **2,** little by little.

понести *v. pfv.* [*infl. like* нести] **1,** *pfv. of* нести. **2,** (*of a horse*) to bolt. —**понестись**, *refl.* **1,** *pfv. of* нестись. **2,** to dash off.

пони *n.m. indecl.* pony.

понижать *v. impfv.* [*pfv.* понизить] **1,** to lower; reduce. **2,** to demote. —**понижаться**, *refl.* to go down; drop; decline.

понижение *n.* **1,** lowering; reduction. **2,** drop; fall; decline. **3,** *in* понижение в должности (*or* по службе), demotion.

понизить [*infl.* -жу, -зишь] *v., pfv. of* понижать. —**понизиться**, *refl., pfv. of* понижаться.

понизу *adv.* low; close to the ground.

поникать *v. impfv.* [*pfv.* поникнуть] **1,** to droop. **2,** *in* поникать головой, to hang one's head.

поникнуть [*past* -ник, -ла] *v., pfv. of* никнуть *and* поникать.

понимание *n.* **1,** understanding; comprehension. **2,** interpretation.

понимать *v. impfv.* [*pfv.* понять] **1,** to understand: понимать по-русски, to understand Russian. Понять намёк, to take a hint. **2,** to realize: он сразу понял, что..., he immediately realized that... **3,** [*impfv. only*] (*with acc. or* в + *prepl.*) to have an understanding of; know something about: я ничего не понимаю в спорте, I know nothing about sports.

поножовщина *n., colloq.* fight involving the use of knives.

пономарь [*gen.* -маря] *n.m.* sexton.

понос *n.* diarrhea.

поносить[1] *v. impfv.* [*pres.* -ношу, -носишь] to vilify; revile; defame.

поносить[2] *v. pfv.* [*infl.* -ношу, -носишь] to carry (*for a while*).

поношение *n.* **1,** vilification; defamation. **2,** *usu. pl.* verbal abuse. **3,** disgrace.

поношенный *adj.* **1,** worn; shabby; threadbare. **2,** *colloq.* somewhat the worse for wear.

понравиться *v.r., pfv. of* нравиться.

понтификат *n.* pontificate.

понтон *n.* pontoon. —**понтонный**, *adj.* pontoon (*attrib.*): понтонный мост, pontoon bridge.

понуждать *v. impfv.* [*pfv.* понудить] to force; compel.

понуждение *n.* compulsion.

понукать *v. impfv.* **1,** to urge on (an animal). **2,** *colloq.* to hurry; rush.

понурить *v. pfv.* to hang (one's head). —**понуриться**, *refl.* to hang one's head; look despondent.

понурый *adj.* **1,** downcast; despondent. **2,** bowed; bent.

пончик *n.* doughnut.

пончо *n. indecl.* poncho.

поныне *adv., archaic* until now.

понюхать *v., pfv. of* нюхать.

понюшка [*gen. pl.* -шек] *n., colloq.* pinch of snuff.

понятие *n.* concept; notion; idea.

понятливый *adj.* bright; clever; sharp.

понятно *adv.* **1,** clearly; intelligibly. **2,** *colloq.* naturally; understandably. —*adj., used predicatively* **1,** understandable: это понятно, that is understandable. **2,** I understand. **3,** *interrogatively* do you understand?; is that understood? **4,** obvious: совершенно понятно, что..., it is quite obvious that...

ПОНЯ́ТНОСТЬ *n.f.* intelligibility.

ПОНЯ́ТНЫЙ *adj.* **1**, understandable; comprehensible; intelligible. **2**, understandable; justified; justifiable. —**поня́тное де́ло**, *colloq.* naturally; understandably.

ПОНЯТО́Й *n.*, *decl. as an adj.* witness (*present during a search or when something is being counted.*).

ПОНЯ́ТЬ [*infl.* пойму́, поймёшь; *past* по́нял, поняла́, по́няло] *v.*, *pfv. of* понима́ть.

ПООБЕ́ДАТЬ *v.*, *pfv. of* обе́дать.

ПООБЕЩА́ТЬ *v. pfv.* to promise.

ПООДА́ЛЬ *adv.* at a distance: держа́ться поода́ль, to keep one's distance.

ПООДИНО́ЧКЕ *adv.* one at a time; one by one.

ПООЧЕРЁДНЫЙ *adj.* alternating; done in turn. —**поочерёдно**, *adv.* in turn.

ПООЩРЕ́НИЕ *n.* encouragement.

ПООЩРИ́ТЕЛЬНЫЙ *adj.* serving to encourage: поощри́тельная улы́бка, a smile of encouragement. Поощри́тельная пре́мия, incentive bonus.

ПООЩРЯ́ТЬ *v. impfv.* [*pfv.* поощри́ть] to encourage; stimulate.

ПОП [*gen.* попа́] *n.*, *colloq.* priest.

ПОПАДА́НИЕ *n.* hit: прямо́е попада́ние, direct hit.

ПОПАДА́ТЬ *v. impfv.* [*pfv.* попа́сть] **1**, (*with* в *or* на + *acc.*) to get (to a place). **2**, (*with* в + *acc.*) to get into (a building, college, situation, trouble, etc.). **3**, (*with* в + *acc.*) to fall into (a trap, someone's hands, etc.). **4**, (*with* в + *acc.*) to end up (in); wind up (in). **5**, (*with* на + *acc.*) to catch; make; be on time for (a train, bus, etc.). **6**, (*with* в *or* под + *acc.*) to get caught in: попа́сть в мете́ль, to get caught in a snowstorm; попа́сть под дождь, to get caught in the rain. **7**, (*with* под + *acc.*) to be run over (by). **8**, (*with* на + *acc.*) to find; come upon: попа́сть на рабо́ту, to land a job. **9**, (*with* в + *acc.*) (*of a missile*) to hit; strike: попа́сть в цель, to hit the target. Пу́ля попа́ла ему́ в грудь, the bullet struck him in the chest. **10**, (*with instr. and* в + *acc.*) to get (something into a small opening): попа́сть ключо́м в замо́к, to get the key into the lock. **11**, (*with* под + *acc.*) to come under (suspicion, someone's influence, etc.). **12**, *impers.* (*with dat.*) *colloq.* to get a scolding; catch it: мне попадёт от отца́, I'll catch it from my father. —попа́сть в плен, to be taken prisoner. —попа́сть в ру́ки (+ *gen.*), to come/fall into the hands of. Мне попа́л(а) в ру́ки (+ *nom.*), I came across... —попа́сться (*or* попа́сться) по́д руку (+ *dat.*), to turn up (*by chance*): всё, что ему́ попада́ло по́д руку, anything (*or* whatever) he could get his hands on. —попа́сть под суд, to be brought to trial. —где попа́ло; куда́ попа́ло, anywhere; wherever one happens to be. —как попа́ло, helter-skelter; in a hit or miss fashion. —кто попа́ло, anyone; the first one who comes along. —что попа́ло, anything; anything that comes along.

ПОПАДА́ТЬСЯ *v.r. impfv.* [*pfv.* попа́сться] **1**, to be caught: попа́сться на кра́же, to be caught stealing. **2**, (*with dat.*) *colloq.* to come across: мне попа́лась интере́сная кни́га, I came across an interesting book. —попада́ться на глаза́ (+ *dat.*), to catch someone's eye. —попа́сться на у́дочку, to swallow the bait. —пе́рвый попа́вшийся, the first one to come along.

ПОПАДЬЯ́ *n.*, *colloq.* priest's wife.

ПОПА́РНО *adv.* in pairs; two by two.

ПОПА́СТЬ [*infl. like* пасть] *v.*, *pfv. of* попада́ть. —попа́сться, *refl.*, *pfv. of* попада́ться.

ПОПА́ХИВАТЬ *v. impfv.* (*with instr.*) *colloq.* to smell slightly (of).

ПОПЕНЯ́ТЬ *v.*, *pfv. of* пеня́ть.

ПОПЕРЁК *adv.* across. —*prep.*, *with gen.* across; athwart. —знать вдоль и попере́к, to know inside out. —стать попере́к го́рла (+ *dat.*), to stick in someone's throat. —стоя́ть попере́к доро́ги (+ *dat.*), to stand in someone's way.

ПОПЕРЕМЕ́ННО *adv.* alternately; in turn.

ПОПЕРЕ́ЧИНА *n.* crossbeam; crossbar; crosspiece.

ПОПЕРЕ́ЧНИК *n.* diameter.

ПОПЕРЕ́ЧНЫЙ *adj.* transverse; cross-: попере́чный разре́з; попере́чное сече́ние, cross section. Попере́чная пила́, cross-cut saw. —ка́ждый встре́чный и попере́чный, any (*or* every) Tom, Dick, or Harry.

ПОПЕРХНУ́ТЬСЯ *v.r. pfv.* (*with instr.*) to choke (on).

ПОПЕЧЕ́НИЕ *n.* care; charge: быть на попече́нии (+ *gen.*), to be in the care/charge of; име́ть (+ *acc.*) на попече́нии, to have charge of.

ПОПЕЧИ́ТЕЛЬ *n.m.* guardian; trustee. —попечи́тельство, *n.* guardianship; trusteeship.

ПОПИВА́ТЬ *v. impfv.*, *colloq.* **1**, *v.t.* to drink (something) slowly. **2**, *v.i.* to drink from time to time.

ПОПИРА́ТЬ *v. impfv.* [*pfv.* попра́ть] to trample upon; violate; flout.

ПОПИСА́ТЬ *v. pfv.* [*infl.* -пишу́, -пи́шешь] to write (*for a while*).

ПОПИ́СЫВАТЬ *v. impfv.*, *colloq.* to write occasionally; write from time to time.

ПОПИ́ТЬ *v. pfv.* [*infl.* -пью́, -пьёшь; *past* по́пил *or* попи́л, попила́, по́пило *or* попи́ло] *colloq.* **1**, (*with gen.*) to have a drink of. **2**, to have something to drink.

ПОПЛА́ВАТЬ *v. pfv.* to go for a swim; have a swim.

ПОПЛАВО́К [*gen.* -вка́] *n.* **1**, float (*marker*). **2**, fishing float; bob. **3**, *colloq.* floating restaurant.

ПОПЛА́КАТЬ *v. pfv.* [*infl.* -пла́чу, -пла́чешь] to have a brief cry; shed a few tears.

ПОПЛАТИ́ТЬСЯ *v.r.*, *pfv. of* плати́ться.

ПОПЛЕСТИ́СЬ *v.r. pfv.* [*infl. like* плести́] to trudge along.

ПОПЛИ́Н *n.* poplin. —попли́новый, *adj.* poplin.

ПОПЛЫ́ТЬ *v. pfv.* [*infl. like* плыть] **1**, *pfv. of* плыть. **2**, to begin to swim. **3**, to begin to drift.

ПОПЛЯСА́ТЬ *v. pfv.* [*infl.* -пляшу́, -пля́шешь] *colloq.* to dance (*for a while*).

ПОПО́ВИЧ *n.*, *colloq.* priest's son.

ПОПО́ВНА [*gen. pl.* -вен] *n.*, *colloq.* priest's daughter.

ПОПО́ВНИК *n.* (oxeye) daisy.

ПОПО́ЗЖЕ *adv.* a little later.

ПОПО́ЙКА [*gen. pl.* -о́ек] *n.*, *colloq.* drinking bout.

ПОПОЛА́М *adv.* **1**, in half; in two. **2**, half and half: снег попола́м с дождём, half snow, half rain.

ПО́ПОЛЗЕНЬ [*gen.* -зня] *n.m.* nuthatch (*bird*).

ПОПОЛЗНОВЕ́НИЕ *n.* impulse; inclination.

ПОПОЛЗТИ́ *v. pfv.* [*infl. like* ползти́] **1**, *pfv. of* ползти́. **2**, to begin to crawl.

ПОПОЛНЕ́НИЕ *n.* **1**, replenishment. **2**, *mil.*, *often pl.* reinforcements; additional personnel.

ПОПО́ЛНИТЬ *v.*, *pfv. of* попо́лнеть.

ПОПОЛНЯ́ТЬ *v. impfv.* [*pfv.* попо́лнить] **1**, to replenish (a supply of something). **2**, to supply with more of something. **3**, *fig.* to expand; broaden; enlarge. **4**, *mil.* to reinforce; beef up.

ПОПОЛУ́ДНИ *adv.* in the afternoon; p.m.

ПОПО́МНИТЬ *v. pfv.*, *colloq.* to remember. —попо́мните моё сло́во!, mark my words!

попóна *n.* horsecloth.

попóртить *v. pfv.* [*infl.* -чу, -тишь] *colloq.* to damage slightly.

попóтчевать *v., pfv. of* пóтчевать.

поправéть *v., pfv. of* правéть.

поправи́мый *adj.* 1, (*of an error*) rectifiable. 2, (*of a situation*) not beyond repair; not hopeless.

попрáвить [*infl.* -влю, -вишь] *v., pfv. of* поправля́ть. —попрáвиться, *refl., pfv. of* поправля́ться.

попрáвка [*gen. pl.* -вок] *n.* 1, correction. 2, amendment. 3, repair. 4, adjustment. 5, recovery: у негó дéло идёт на попрáвку, he is on the road to recovery; he is on the mend.

поправлéние *n.* 1, correcting; correction. 2, adjustment. 3, straightening out; putting right.

поправля́ть *v. impfv.* [*pfv.* попрáвить] 1, to correct. 2, to repair; fix; mend. 3, to straighten; adjust; set right; put right. 4, to restore (one's health). —поправля́ться, *refl.* 1, to correct oneself. 2, to improve; get better. 3, to get well; recover. 4, to put on weight.

попрáть *v., used in the past tense only, pfv. of* попирáть.

по-прéжнему *adv.* as before.

попрёк *n., colloq.* critical remark. Вéчные попрёки, endless nagging.

попрекáть *v. impfv.* [*pfv.* попрекну́ть] *colloq.* to reproach.

пóприще *n.* field (of endeavor): научное пóприще, the scientific field.

попрóбовать *v., pfv. of* прóбовать.

попроси́ть *v., pfv. of* проси́ть. —попроси́ться, *refl., pfv. of* проси́ться.

пóпросту *adv.* simply. —пóпросту говоря́, to put it bluntly; in plain words.

попрошáйка [*gen. pl.* -шáек] *n.m. & f., colloq.* beggar.

попрошáйничать *v. impfv., colloq.* to beg.

попрошáйничество *n., colloq.* begging.

попрощáться *v.r., pfv. of* прощáться.

попры́гать *v. pfv.* 1, to jump. 2, to hop.

попры́гивать *v. impfv., colloq.* to hop about; hop around.

попрыгу́н *n.m.* [*fem.* -гу́нья] *colloq.* fidgety person; fidget.

попря́тать *v. pfv.* [*infl.* -пря́чу, -пря́чешь] *colloq.* to hide (all or many of something). —попря́таться, *refl., colloq.* (*of all or many of something*) to hide.

попугáй *n.* parrot.

попугáть *v. pfv., colloq.* to frighten a little; scare.

попу́дрить *v. pfv.* to powder. —попу́дриться, *refl.* to powder one's nose.

популяризáция *n.* popularization.

популяризи́ровать *v. impfv. & pfv.* [*pres.* -рую, -руешь] to popularize. *Also,* популяризовáть [*pres.* -зу́ю, -зу́ешь].

популя́рно *adv.* in understandable terms; in a way that is easy to understand.

популя́рность *n.f.* popularity.

популя́рный *adj.* [*short form* -я́рен, -я́рна] 1, popular. 2, written or set forth in understandable terms.

попурри́ *n. neut. indecl.* music medley.

попусти́тельство *n.* 1, tolerance (of); permissive attitude (toward). 2, connivance.

попусти́тельствовать *v. impfv.* [*pres.* -ствую, -ствуешь] (*with dat.*) to permit; tolerate; put up with; do nothing about.

пóпусту *adv., colloq.* to no purpose; for nothing. *Also,* по-пустóму.

попу́тно *adv.* 1, at the same time; while one is (*or* was) at it. 2, in passing: попу́тно отмéтить, to mention in passing.

попу́тный *adj.* 1, going the same way. 2, situated along the way: попу́тная стáнция, way station. 3, *fig.* passing: попу́тное замечáние, a passing remark. —попу́тный вéтер, favorable wind; tail wind.

попу́тчик *n.* 1, traveling companion. 2, *polit.* fellow traveler.

попытáть *v. pfv., colloq.* to try: попытáть счáстья, to try one's luck. —попытáться, *refl., pfv. of* пытáться.

попы́тка [*gen. pl.* -ток] *n.* attempt; try.

попы́хивать *v. impfv., colloq.* 1, to give off occasional puffs of smoke. 2, (*with instr.*) to puff on (a cigar, pipe, etc.).

попя́титься *v.r., pfv. of* пя́титься.

попя́тный *adj., obs.* backward; reverse. —идти́ на попя́тный *or* попя́тную, *colloq.* to go back on one's word.

пóра *n.* pore.

порá [*acc.* пóру] *n.* 1, time. 2, *impers.* it is time: нам порá домóй, it is time for us to be going home. —в (сáмую) пóру, at (just) the right time. —в ту пóру, then; at that time. —в э́ту пóру, now; at this time. —до каки́х пор?, until when? —до поры́ до врéмени, for the time being. —до сих пор, until now; up to now. —до тех пор, until then. —до тех пор покá, as long as. —до тех пор покá не, until the time when. —на пéрвых порáх, at first. —с дáвних пор, for a long time. —с каки́х пор?, since when? —с нéкоторых пор, for some time now. —с тех пор, since then. —с тех пор, как, since.

порабóтать *v. pfv.* to do some work.

поработи́тель *n.m.* enslaver; oppressor.

порабощáть *v. impfv.* [*pfv.* поработи́ть] to enslave.

порабощéние *n.* enslavement.

поравня́ть *v. pfv., colloq.* to make equal; place on an equal footing. —поравня́ться, *refl.* (*with* с + *instr.*) to pull alongside (of); draw even (with).

порáдовать *v. pfv.* [*infl.* -дую, -дуешь] to gladden; make happy. —порáдоваться, *refl.* to be glad; be happy.

поражáть *v. impfv.* [*pfv.* порази́ть] 1, to strike; smite. 2, to hit (a target). 3, to strike; astonish. 4, (*of an illness*) to strike; affect. 5, to defeat; rout.

поражéнец [*gen.* -нца] *n.* defeatist.

поражéние *n.* 1, defeat. 2, damage; destruction.

поражéнчество *n.* defeatism. —поражéнческий, *adj.* defeatist.

порази́тельный *adj.* striking; astonishing. —порази́тельно, *adv.* strikingly.

порази́ть [*infl.* -жу́, -зи́шь] *v., pfv. of* поражáть.

по-рáзному *adv.* differently; in different ways.

порáнить *v. pfv.* to wound; injure. —порáниться, *refl.* to injure oneself; hurt oneself.

порáньше *adv.* a little earlier.

пораски́нуть *v. pfv., colloq., in* пораски́нуть умóм, to think it over.

порастáть *v. impfv.* [*pfv.* порасти́] (*with instr.*). to become overgrown (with).

порасти́ [*infl. like* расти́] *v., pfv. of* порастáть.

порвáть *v. pfv.* [*infl. like* рвать] 1, *pfv. of* рвать *and* порывáть. 2, to break; disrupt (communications). —порвáться, *refl.* 1, *pfv.* of рвáться *and* порывáться. 2, to break; snap.

поредéть *v., pfv. of* редéть.

поре́з *n.* cut.

поре́зать *v. pfv.* [*infl.* -ре́жу, -ре́жешь] **1,** to cut (*accidentally*). **2,** to slice. —поре́заться, *refl.* to cut oneself.

поре́й *n.* leek.

порекомендова́ть *v., pfv. of* рекомендова́ть.

по́ристый *adj.* porous. —по́ристость, *n.f.* porosity.

порица́ние *n.* condemnation; censure.

порица́ть *v. impfv.* to condemn; censure.

по́рка *n.* **1,** unstitching. **2,** *colloq.* whipping; thrashing; flogging.

порногра́фия *n.* pornography. —порнографи́чес-кий, *adj.* pornographic.

по́ровну *adv.* equally; in equal parts.

поро́г *n.* **1,** threshold; doorstep. **2,** *usu. pl.* rapids (*of a river*). —на поро́ге, at hand; just around the corner. **2,** (*with gen.*) on the brink of. —обива́ть (все) поро́ги, to knock on every door.

поро́да *n.* **1,** breed; strain. **2,** *fig.* breed; type (*of person*). —го́рная поро́да, *geol.* rock.

поро́дистый *adj.* thoroughbred; pedigreed.

породи́ть [*infl.* -жу́, -ди́шь] *v., pfv. of* порожда́ть.

породни́ть *v., pfv. of* родни́ть. —породни́ться, *refl., pfv. of* родни́ться.

порожда́ть *v. impfv.* [*pfv.* породи́ть] **1,** *obs.* to give birth to; beget. **2,** to give rise to; generate; engender.

порожде́ние *n.* product; result.

поро́жистый *adj.* (*of a river*) full of rapids.

поро́жний *adj., colloq.* empty. —перелива́ть из пусто́го в поро́жнее, to engage in idle chatter.

порожня́к *[gen.* -няка́] *n.* empty trains; empty cars. —порожняко́м, *adv., colloq.* empty; without cargo; without passengers.

по́рознь *adv.* separately; apart.

порозове́ть *v., pfv. of* розове́ть.

поро́й *adv.* at times; occasionally; now and then.

поро́к *n.* **1,** vice. **2,** defect.

поросёнок *[gen.* -нка; *pl.* -ся́та, -ся́т] *n.* piglet; suckling pig.

по́росль *n.f.* **1,** sprouts; shoots. **2,** thicket. **3,** *colloq.* growth of hair.

порося́тина *n.* suckling pig (*served as food*).

поро́ть *v. impfv.* [*pres.* порю́, по́решь] **1,** [*pfv.* вы́пороть] *colloq.* to whip; flog. **2,** [*pfv.* распоро́ть] to unstitch. **3,** [*impfv. only*] *colloq.* to talk (nonsense).

по́рох *n.* powder; gunpowder. —не ню́хать по́роху, never to have been in combat. —па́хнет по́рохом, war is in the air. —тра́тить по́рох да́ром, to waste one's energies. —у него́ по́роху не хвата́ет, he hasn't got it in him; he is not up to it.

порохово́й *adj.* powder (*attrib.*); gunpowder (*attrib.*): порохова́я бо́чка, powder keg.

поро́чить *v. impfv.* [*pfv.* опоро́чить] **1,** to sully; besmirch (*someone's reputation*). **2,** to disparage; run down. **3,** to discredit.

поро́чность *n.f.* depravity.

поро́чный *adj.* **1,** perverted; depraved. **2,** faulty; unsound. —поро́чный круг, vicious circle.

поро́ша *n.* fresh snow; newly-fallen snow.

пороши́ть *v. impfv.* **1,** (*of snow*) to fall lightly. **2,** *impers.* to be snowing lightly.

порошкообра́зный *adj.* powdery.

порошо́к *[gen.* -шка́] *n.* **1,** powder. **2,** *in* моло́чный порошо́к, powdered milk; яи́чный порошо́к, powdered eggs. —стере́ть в порошо́к, to make mincemeat of.

порт *[2nd loc.* порту́; *pl.* по́рты, -то́в, -та́м] *n.* port.

порта́л *n.* portal.

портати́вный *adj.* portable.

портве́йн *n.* port (wine).

по́ртик *n.* portico.

по́ртить *v. impfv.* [*pfv.* испо́ртить; *pres.* по́рчу, по́ртишь] **1,** to spoil; damage; mar; impair. **2,** to corrupt. —по́ртиться, *refl.* **1,** to spoil; decay. **2,** to deteriorate. **3,** to stop working; break down. **4,** (*of the weather*) to turn bad.

портмоне́ (нэ) *n. neut. indecl., obs.* purse.

портни́ха *n.* dressmaker.

портно́вский *adj.* tailor's.

портно́й *n., decl. as an adj.* tailor.

портня́жничать *v. impfv., colloq.* to be a tailor; work as a tailor.

портня́жный *adj.* tailor's. —портня́жное де́ло, tailoring.

портови́к *[gen.* -вика́] *n.* dock worker.

порто́вый *adj.* port (*attrib.*). —порто́вый го́род, seaport. —порто́вый рабо́чий, dock worker.

портре́т *n.* portrait. —портрети́ст, *n.* portrait painter. —портре́тный, *adj.* portrait (*attrib.*).

портсига́р *n.* cigarette case.

португа́лец *[gen.* -льца] *n.m.* [*fem.* -лка] Portuguese. —португа́льский, *adj.* Portuguese.

портула́к *n.* portulaca; purslane.

портупе́я *n.* sword belt.

портфе́ль *n.m.* **1,** briefcase; portfolio. **2,** portfolio; office: мини́стр без портфе́ля, minister without portfolio.

портше́з *n.* sedan chair.

портье́ *n.m. indecl.* desk clerk (*in a hotel*).

портье́ра *n.* heavy curtain (*for a door or window*).

портя́нка *[gen. pl.* -нок] *n.* foot wrapping (*worn in place of socks*).

поруби́ть *v. pfv.* [*infl.* -рублю́, -ру́бишь] **1,** to chop down. **2,** to chop.

пору́бка *n.* chopping down (*of trees*).

поруга́ние *n.* humiliation.

поруга́ть *v. pfv.* to tell off; curse out. —поруга́ться, *refl.* **1,** (*with* с + *instr.*) to quarrel (with); have words (with). **2,** to swear; curse.

пору́ка *n.* bail; surety; guarantee. Брать на пору́ки, to bail (someone) out. —отпуска́ть на пору́ки, to release on bail. —кругова́я пору́ка, **1,** collective responsibility. **2,** covering up for each other.

поруча́ть *v. impfv.* [*pfv.* поручи́ть] (*with dat.*) **1,** to instruct; charge; commission. **2,** to entrust.

поруче́ние *n.* assignment; mission; errand.

пору́чик *n., pre-rev.* lieutenant.

поручи́тель *n.m.* person who vouches for another; sponsor.

поручи́тельство *n.* **1,** statement vouching for another person; reference. **2,** bail.

поручи́ть [*infl.* -ручу́, -ру́чишь] *v., pfv. of* поруча́ть. —поручи́ться, *refl., pfv. of* руча́ться.

пору́чни *[gen.* -ней] *n. pl.* handrail.

порфи́р *n.* porphyry.

порха́ть *v. impfv.* [*pfv.* порхну́ть] to flit.

порцио́нный *adj.* à la carte.

по́рция *n.* portion; helping.

по́рча *n.* **1,** damage; spoilage. **2,** *fig.* deterioration.

по́ршень *[gen.* -шня] *n.m.* piston.

поршнево́й *adj.* piston (*attrib.*).

поры́в *n.* **1,** gust (*of wind*). **2,** fit; burst (*of emotion*). **3,** impulse.

порыва́ть *v. impfv.* [*pfv.* **порва́ть**] **1,** *v.i.* (*with* с + *instr.*) to break (with). **2,** *v.t.* to break off; sever (ties, relations, etc.). —**порыва́ться,** *refl.* **1,** (*of ties, relations, etc.*) to be broken off. **2,** [*impfv. only*] to try to move; try to get up. **3,** [*impfv. only*] (*with inf.*) to try (to); strive (to).

поры́вистый *adj.* **1,** (*of the wind*) gusty. **2,** (*of movements*) jerky. **3,** (*of a person*) impetuous; impulsive.

порыже́ть *v., pfv. of* **рыже́ть.**

поры́ться *v.r., pfv. of* **ры́ться.**

поря́дковый *adj., in* **поря́дковое числи́тельное,** ordinal number; **поря́дковый но́мер,** serial number.

поря́дком *adv., colloq.* **1,** rather; pretty. **2,** properly.

поря́док [*gen.* -**дка**] *n.* **1,** order; sequence: по поря́дку, in order; in sequence; in succession. **2,** (*proper*) order: всё в поря́дке, everything is in order; everything is all right (*or* o.k.). **3,** procedure. **4,** order; regime: ста́рый поря́док, the old order. **5,** *mil.* order; formation. **6,** *in* в спе́шном поря́дке, in short order; в обяза́тельном поря́дке, without fail; в служе́бном поря́дке, in line of duty. —**в поря́дке** (+ *gen.*), as; by way of. —**в поря́дке веще́й,** in the nature of things. —**идти́ свои́м поря́дком,** to take its normal course. —**поря́дка** (+ *gen.*), on the order of; approximately.

поря́дочно *adv.* **1,** honestly. **2,** *colloq.* quite a bit; quite a while; quite a ways. **3,** *colloq.* fairly well.

поря́дочность *n.f.* honesty; decency.

поря́дочный *adj.* **1,** honest; decent. **2,** fairly good; decent. **3,** considerable; sizable. **4,** utter; out-and-out.

посади́ть [*infl.* -**сажу́,** -**са́дишь**] *v., pfv. of* **сажа́ть.**

поса́дка *n.* **1,** (*act of*) planting. **2,** *pl.* plantings. **3,** boarding; embarkation. **4,** landing (*of an aircraft*). **5,** manner of sitting (*when riding*).

поса́дочный *adj.* **1,** planting (*attrib.*). **2,** boarding (*attrib.*). **3,** landing (*attrib.*).

поса́пывать *v. impfv., colloq.* to breathe heavily; sniff; snort.

поса́сывать *v. impfv., colloq.* to suck (on *or* at).

посва́тать *v., pfv. of* **сва́тать.** —**посва́таться,** *refl., pfv. of* **сва́таться.**

посвеже́ть *v., pfv. of* **свеже́ть.**

посвети́ть *v. pfv.* [*infl.* -**свечу́,** -**све́тишь**] **1,** *pfv. of* **свети́ть** (*in sense #2*). **2,** to shine (*for a while*).

посветле́ть *v., pfv. of* **светле́ть.**

по́свист *n.* whistle; whistling.

посвиста́ть *v. pfv.* [*infl.* -**свищу́,** -**сви́щешь**] to whistle; give a whistle. *Also,* **посвисте́ть** [*infl.* -**свищу́,** -**свисти́шь**].

посви́стывание *n.* whistling.

посви́стывать *v. impfv.* to whistle (*softly or from time to time*).

по-сво́ему *adv.* in one's own way.

по-сво́йски *adv., colloq.* **1,** in one's own way. **2,** as a friend.

посвяти́ть [*infl.* -**щу́,** -**ти́шь**] *v., pfv. of* **посвяща́ть.**

посвяща́ть *v. impfv.* [*pfv.* **посвяти́ть**] **1,** (*with dat.*) to devote (to); dedicate (to). **2,** (*with* в + *acc.*) to let in on: посвяти́ть кого́-нибудь в та́йну, to let someone in on a secret. **3,** (*with* в + *nom. pl.*) to ordain: посвяти́ть кого́-нибудь в свяще́нники, to ordain someone as priest.

посвяще́ние *n.* **1,** dedication. **2,** letting (someone) in on (a secret). **3,** consecration; ordination; initiation.

посе́в *n.* **1,** sowing. **2,** *usu. pl.* crops.

посевна́я *n., decl. as an adj., colloq.* sowing campaign.

посевно́й *adj.* sowing (*attrib.*). —**посевна́я пло́щадь,** area under cultivation.

поседе́лый *adj.* turned gray.

поседе́ть *v., pfv. of* **седе́ть.**

посейча́с *adv., colloq.* until now; up to now.

поселе́нец [*gen.* -**нца**] *n.* **1,** settler. **2,** *pre-rev.* exile (*person sent into exile*).

поселе́ние *n.* **1,** settling. **2,** settlement. **3,** *pre-rev.* exile.

посели́ть *v., pfv. of* **поселя́ть.** —**посели́ться,** *refl., pfv. of* **поселя́ться.**

поселко́вый *adj.* village (*attrib.*).

посёлок [*gen.* -**лка**] *n.* village; community; settlement.

поселя́ть *v. impfv.* [*pfv.* **посели́ть**] **1,** to settle. **2,** *fig.* to arouse; engender. —**поселя́ться,** *refl.* to settle; take up residence.

посему́ *adv., obs.* therefore.

посеребри́ть *v., pfv. of* **серебри́ть.** —**посеребри́ться,** *refl., pfv. of* **серебри́ться.**

посереди́не *adv.* in the middle. —*prep., with gen.* in the middle of.

посере́ть *v., pfv. of* **сере́ть.**

посети́тель *n.m.* visitor.

посети́ть [*infl.* -**щу́,** -**ти́шь**] *v., pfv. of* **посеща́ть.**

посе́товать *v., pfv. of* **се́товать.**

посеща́емость *n.f.* (regularity) of attendance.

посеща́ть *v. impfv.* [*pfv.* **посети́ть**] **1,** to visit. **2,** to attend.

посеще́ние *n.* **1,** visit. **2,** attendance.

посе́ять *v., pfv. of* **се́ять.**

посиде́ть *v. pfv.* [*infl.* -**жу́,** -**ди́шь**] to sit (*for a while*).

поси́льный *adj.* **1,** within one's power to do. **2,** (*of help, payment, etc.*) whatever one can give.

посине́ть *v., pfv. of* **сине́ть.**

поскака́ть *v. pfv.* [*infl.* -**скачу́,** -**ска́чешь**] **1,** to hop off (*to another place*). **2,** to gallop off.

поскользну́ться *v.r., pfv.* to slip (*and fall*).

поско́льку *conj.* **1,** since; inasmuch as; as long as. **2,** as far as; to the extent that.

по́сконь *n.f.* male hemp. —**поско́нный,** *adj.* hemp (*attrib.*).

поскупи́ться *v.r., pfv. of* **скупи́ться.**

послабле́ние *n., often pl.* relaxation of discipline; leniency.

посла́нец [*gen.* -**нца**] *n.* messenger; envoy.

посла́ние *n.* message.

посла́нник *n.* envoy; minister.

по́сланный *n., decl. as an adj.* messenger; envoy.

посла́ть [*infl.* **пошлю́, пошлёшь**] *v., pfv. of* **слать** *and* **посыла́ть.**

по́сле *prep., with gen.* **1,** after: по́сле обе́да, after dinner. **2,** since: по́сле его́ возвраще́ния, since his return. —*adv.* afterward. —**по́сле того́, как,** after: по́сле того́, как он ушёл, after he left. —**по́сле того́, что,** after; in view of. —**по́сле чего́,** whereupon.

послевое́нный *adj.* postwar.

после́д *n.* afterbirth.

после́дить *v. pfv.* [*infl.* -**жу́,** -**ди́шь**] (*with* за + *instr.*) to watch; look after.

после́дний *adj.* **1,** last. **2,** past: за после́днюю неде́лю, during the past week. **3,** recent: в *or* за после́дние го́ды, in recent years. **4,** the latest: после́дние изве́стия, the latest news. **5,** the latter. **6,** the lowest; the worst. —**в** or **за после́днее вре́мя**, recently; lately; of late. —**до после́днего**, to the last; to the utmost; to the bitter end. —**после́дними слова́ми**, in the crudest possible language.

после́дователь *n.m.* follower.

после́довательно *adv.* **1,** consecutively; in succession. **2,** consistently.

после́довательность *n.f.* **1,** succession; sequence. **2,** consistency.

после́довательный *adj.* **1,** consecutive; successive. **2,** consistent.

после́довать *v., pfv. of* **сле́довать** (*in senses #1 & #2*).

после́дствие *n.* consequence. —**оставля́ть без после́дствий**, to fail to act on; take no action on.

после́дующий *adj.* subsequent.

после́дыш *n., colloq.* **1,** youngest child in a family. **2,** *fig.* last to propound a certain (reactionary) doctrine.

послеза́втра *adv.* the day after tomorrow.

послеобе́денный *adj.* after-dinner.

послеопераци́онный *adj.* postoperative. —**послеопераци́онная пала́та**, recovery room.

послереволюци́онный *adj.* post-revolutionary.

послеродово́й *adj.* postnatal.

послесло́вие *n.* epilogue; postscript.

посло́вица *n.* proverb. —**войти́ в посло́вицу**, to become proverbial.

послужи́ть *v. pfv.* [*infl.* -**служу́, -слу́жишь**] **1,** *pfv. of* **служи́ть**. **2,** to serve (*for a while*).

послужно́й *adj., in* **послужно́й спи́сок**, service record.

послуша́ние *n.* obedience.

послу́шать *v., pfv. of* **слу́шать** (*in sense #2*). —**послу́шаться**, *refl., pfv. of* **слу́шаться**.

по́слушник *n., eccles.* novice.

послу́шный *adj.* obedient.

послы́шаться *v.r., pfv. of* **слы́шаться**.

послюни́ть *v., pfv. of* **слюни́ть**.

посма́тривать *v. impfv.* to look from time to time.

посме́иваться *v.r. impfv.* **1,** to chuckle. **2,** (*with* **над**) to poke fun at.

посме́нный *adj.* shift (*attrib.*): **посме́нная рабо́та**, shift work. —**посме́нно**, *adv.* in shifts.

посме́ртно *adv.* posthumously.

посме́ртный *adj.* posthumous. —**посме́ртная ма́ска**, death mask.

посме́ть *v., pfv. of* **сметь**.

посме́шище *n.* laughingstock. —**выставля́ть (кого́-нибудь) на посме́шище**, to make a laughingstock of.

посмея́ться *v.r. pfv.* [*infl.* -**смею́сь, -смеёшься**] **1,** to laugh a little. **2,** (*with* **над**) to poke fun at.

посмотре́ть *v., pfv. of* **смотре́ть**. —**посмотре́ться**, *refl., pfv. of* **смотре́ться**.

посо́бие *n.* **1,** allowance; benefits: **посо́бие по безрабо́тице**, unemployment benefits. **2,** textbook. **3,** *pl.* study aids: **нагля́дные посо́бия**, visual aids.

посо́бник *n.* accomplice. —**посо́бничество**, *n.* complicity.

посо́веститься *v.r., pfv. of* **со́веститься**.

посове́товать *v., pfv. of* **сове́товать**. —**посове́товаться**, *refl., pfv. of* **сове́товаться**.

посо́л [*gen.* -**сла́**] *n.* ambassador.

посоли́ть *v., pfv. of* **соли́ть**.

посолове́лый *adj., colloq.* bleary-eyed.

посолове́ть *v. pfv., colloq.* to become bleary-eyed.

посо́льский *adj.* **1,** ambassadorial. **2,** embassy (*attrib.*).

посо́льство *n.* embassy.

по́сох *n.* **1,** staff; crook. **2,** crosier.

посо́хнуть *v. pfv.* [*past* -**со́х, -ла**] (*of all or many things*) to wither.

поспа́ть *v. pfv.* [*infl. like* **спать**] to sleep a bit; take a nap.

поспева́ть *v. impfv.* [*pfv.* **поспе́ть**] **1,** to ripen. **2,** *colloq.* to be on time. **3,** (*with* **за** + *instr.*) to keep up with; keep pace with.

поспе́ть *v., pfv. of* **спеть**[1] *and* **поспева́ть**.

поспеши́ть *v., pfv. of* **спеши́ть**. —**поспеши́шь — люде́й насмеши́шь**, haste makes waste.

поспе́шный *adj.* hasty; hurried. —**поспе́шно**, *adv.* hastily; hurriedly; in a hurry. —**поспе́шность**, *n.f.* haste.

поспо́рить *v., pfv. of* **спо́рить**.

посрами́ть [*infl.* -**млю́, -ми́шь**] *v., pfv. of* **посрамля́ть**.

посрамле́ние *n.* disgrace.

посрамля́ть *v. impfv.* [*pfv.* **посрами́ть**] to disgrace.

посреди́ *prep., with gen.* in the middle of. —*adv.* in the middle.

посреди́не *adv. & prep.* = **посереди́не**.

посре́дник *n.* **1,** middleman; intermediary. **2,** mediator; go-between.

посре́дничать *v. impfv.* to mediate; serve as a go-between.

посре́дничество *n.* mediation. —**посре́днический**, *adj.* mediation (*attrib.*); middleman (*attrib.*); intermediary.

посре́дственно *adv.* so-so; not particularly well. —*n. indecl.* "fair"; "mediocre" (*school grade*).

посре́дственность *n.f.* **1,** mediocrity. **2,** mediocre person; a mediocrity.

посре́дственный *adj.* mediocre.

посре́дство *n., in* **при посре́дстве** *and* **че́рез посре́дство** (+ *gen.*), **1,** through; by means of. **2,** through the intercession of; thanks to.

посре́дством *prep., with gen.* through; by means of.

поссо́рить *v., pfv. of* **ссо́рить**. —**поссо́риться**, *refl., pfv. of* **ссо́риться**.

пост [*gen.* **поста́**; *2nd loc.* **посту́**] *n.* **1,** post: **наблюда́тельный пост**, observation post. **2,** post; position: **пост дире́ктора**, the post/position of director. **3,** *relig.* fast. —**вели́кий пост**, Lent.

поста́вить [*infl.* -**влю, -вишь**] *v., pfv. of* **ста́вить** *and* **поставля́ть**.

поста́вка [*gen. pl.* -**вок**] *n.* delivery.

поставля́ть *v. impfv.* [*pfv.* **поста́вить**] to supply.

поставщи́к [*gen.* -**щика́**] *n.* supplier.

постаме́нт *n.* pedestal; base.

постанови́ть [*infl.* -**новлю́, -но́вишь**] *v., pfv. of* **постановля́ть**.

постано́вка *n.* **1,** *theat.* production. **2,** position; carriage (*of a part of the body*). **3,** organization. **4,** stating; posing: **постано́вка вопро́са**, the way a question is put. **5,** *in* **постано́вка го́лоса**, voice training.

постановле́ние *n.* **1,** decision; resolution. **2,** decree.

постановля́ть *v. impfv.* [*pfv.* **постанови́ть**] to decide; resolve; decree.

постано́вочный *adj., theat.* production (*attrib.*).

постано́вщик *n., theat.* director.

постара́ться *v.r., pfv. of* **стара́ться**.

постаре́ть *v.*, *pfv. of* **старе́ть**.

посте́ль *n.f.* bed. —**посте́льный**, *adj.* bed (*attrib.*).

постепе́нный *adj.* gradual. —**постепе́нно**, *adv.* gradually.

постесня́ться *v.r.*, *pfv. of* **стесня́ться** (*in sense #2*).

постига́ть *v. impfv.* [*pfv.* **пости́гнуть** *or* **пости́чь**] **1**, to comprehend; grasp. **2**, (*of misfortune*) to befall; overtake.

пости́гнуть [*past* -сти́г, -ла] *v.*, *pfv. of* **постига́ть**.

постиже́ние *n.* comprehension; grasp.

постижи́мый *adj.* comprehensible.

постила́ть *v. impfv.* [*pfv.* **постла́ть**] to lay (a rug, tablecloth, etc.); make (a bed).

постира́ть *v. pfv.*, *colloq.* to wash; launder.

пости́ться *v.r. impfv.* [*pres.* **пощу́сь**, **пости́шься**] to fast.

пости́чь [*infl. like* **пости́гнуть**] *v.*, *pfv. of* **постига́ть**.

постла́ть [*infl. like* **стлать**] *v.*, *pfv. of* **стлать** *and* **постила́ть**.

по́стник *n.* person who fasts.

по́стничать *v. impfv.*, *colloq.* to fast.

по́стный *adj.* **1**, fast (*attrib.*): по́стный день, fast day. **2**, containing no milk or meat. **3**, *colloq.* (*of meat*) lean. **4**, *fig.* dreary. **5**, *fig.* pious; sanctimonious.

постово́й *adj.* **1**, duty (*attrib.*); sentry (*attrib.*): постовая бу́дка, sentry box. **2**, on duty: постово́й милиционе́р, policeman on duty. —*n.* man on duty.

посто́й *n.* quartering; billeting (*of troops*). —**ста́вить на посто́й**, to billet.

посто́льку *conj.*, in посто́льку, поско́льку, insofar as; to the extent that.

посторони́ться *v.r.*, *pfv. of* **сторони́ться**.

посторо́нний *adj.* outside; foreign; extraneous. —*n.* stranger; outsider.

постоя́лец [*gen.* -льца] *n.*, *obs.* lodger; guest (*at a hotel or inn*).

постоя́лый *adj.*, in постоя́лый двор, *obs.* inn; hostelry.

постоя́нно *adv.* constantly; continually.

постоя́нный *adj.* **1**, constant. **2**, permanent. **3**, regular; steady. —**постоя́нная а́рмия**, standing army. —**постоя́нный ток**, direct current.

постоя́нство *n.* constancy.

постоя́ть *v. pfv.* [*infl.* -стою́, -стои́шь] **1**, to stand (*for a while*). **2**, (*with* за + *acc.*) to stand up for. —**посто́й!**; **посто́йте!**, wait a minute!; stop!

пострада́вший *n.*, *decl. as an adj.* victim (*of a disaster*).

пострада́ть *v. pfv.* **1**, *pfv. of* **страда́ть**. **2**, to be injured; be damaged; suffer damage.

постре́л *n.*, *colloq.* imp; rascal; brat.

постре́ливать *v. impfv.* to fire an occasional shot.

постреля́ть *v. pfv.* **1**, *v.i.* to fire a gun (*for a while*); do some shooting. **2**, *v.t.*, *colloq.* to shoot (many of something); bag.

пострига́ть *v. impfv.* [*pfv.* **постри́чь**] **1**, to cut (one's hair, beard, etc.). **2**, to give (someone) a haircut. —**пострига́ться**, *refl.* **1**, to cut one's hair. **2**, to get a haircut.

постри́чь [*infl. like* **стричь**] *v.*, *pfv. of* **пострига́ть**. —**постри́чься**, *refl.*, *pfv. of* **пострига́ться**.

постро́ение *n.* **1**, building; construction. **2**, *mil.* formation.

постро́ить *v.*, *pfv. of* **стро́ить**. —**постро́иться**, *refl.*, *pfv. of* **стро́иться**.

постро́йка [*gen. pl.* -о́ек] *n.* **1**, building; edifice. **2**, building; construction.

постро́мка [*gen. pl.* -мок] *n.* trace (*of a harness*).

постскри́птум *n.* postscript; P.S.

посту́кивать *v. impfv.* to tap; rap; knock.

постула́т *n.* postulate.

постули́ровать *v. impfv. & pfv.* [*pres.* -рую, -руешь] to postulate.

поступа́тельный *adj.* forward; progressive.

поступа́ть *v. impfv.* [*pfv.* **поступи́ть**] **1**, to act. **2**, (*with* с + *instr.*) to treat. **3**, (*with* в *or* на + *acc.*) to join; enter; enlist (in). Поступа́ть на рабо́ту, to take a job; go to work. Поступа́ть на ку́рсы, to enroll in courses. **4**, to arrive; be received; come in. **5**, *in* поступи́ть в прода́жу, to go on sale; поступи́ть в произво́дство, to go into production. —**поступа́ться**, *refl.* (*with instr.*) to waive; forgo.

поступи́ть [*infl.* -ступлю́, -сту́пишь] *v.*, *pfv. of* **поступа́ть**. —**поступи́ться**, *refl.*, *pfv. of* **поступа́ться**.

поступле́ние *n.* **1**, joining; entering. **2**, receipt. **3**, coming in; arrival. **4**, *pl.* receipts.

посту́пок [*gen.* -пка] *n.* act; deed.

по́ступь *n.f.* walk; gait.

постуча́ть *v.*, *pfv. of* **стуча́ть**. —**постуча́ться**, *refl.*, *pfv. of* **стуча́ться**.

постыди́ться *v.r.*, *pfv. of* **стыди́ться**.

посты́дный *adj.* shameful; disgraceful.

посты́лый *adj.*, *colloq.* repellent; odious.

посу́да *n.* **1**, dishes: мыть посу́ду, to wash the dishes. **2**, ware: эмали́рованная посу́да, enamelware. **3**, utensils. **4**, *colloq.* vessel; utensil.

посу́дина *n.*, *colloq.* **1**, vessel; container. **2**, boat; tub.

посуди́ть *v. pfv.* [*infl.* -сужу́, -су́дишь] to judge: посуди́те са́ми, judge for yourself.

посу́дный *adj.* **1**, for dishes; dish (*attrib.*). **2**, china (*attrib.*): посу́дный шкаф, china closet.

посудомо́ечный *adj.*, in посудомо́ечная маши́на, dishwasher.

посудомо́йка [*gen. pl.* -мо́ек] *n.*, *colloq.* dishwasher.

посу́л *n.*, *colloq.* promise.

посули́ть *v.*, *pfv. of* **сули́ть**.

по́суху *adv.*, *colloq.* over dry land.

посчастли́виться *v.r. pfv.*, *impers.* (*with dat.*) to be lucky.

посчита́ть *v. pfv.* **1**, to count. **2**, *colloq.* to consider. —**посчита́ться**, *refl.* **1**, *pfv. of* **счита́ться** (*in sense #1*). **2**, (*with* с + *instr.*) to get even (with); settle scores (with).

посыла́ть *v. impfv.* [*pfv.* **посла́ть**] to send.

посы́лка [*gen. pl.* -лок] *n.* **1**, package; parcel. **2**, sending; mailing. **3**, premise. —**быть на посы́лках**, to run errands.

посы́лочный *adj.* **1**, for a package or packages. **2**, mail-order: посы́лочная торго́вля, mail-order business.

посы́льный *n.*, *decl. as an adj.* messenger.

посы́пать [*infl.* -сы́плю, -сы́плешь] *v.*, *pfv. of* **посыпа́ть**. —**посы́паться**, *refl.* **1**, to begin to fall. **2**, (*of questions, blows, etc.*) to rain down.

посыпа́ть *v. impfv.* [*pfv.* **посы́пать**] to sprinkle.

посяга́тельство *n.* encroachment; infringement.

посяга́ть *v. impfv.* [*pfv.* **посягну́ть**] (*with* на + *acc.*) to infringe (upon); encroach (upon).

пот [*2nd loc.* поту́] *n.* perspiration; sweat: весь в поту́, all perspired. —**в по́те лица́**, by the sweat of one's brow. —**пóтом и крóвью,** by one's own sweat and blood.

потайнóй *adj.* secret; hidden.

потакáние *n.* (*with dat.*) *colloq.* indulgence (of); catering (to).

потакáть *v. impfv.* (*with dat.*) *colloq.* to indulge; cater to.

потанцевáть *v. pfv.* [*infl.* -цýю, -цýешь] to dance (*for a while*); have a dance: потанцýем?, shall we dance?

потаскýха *n., colloq.* strumpet; tart.

потасóвка [*gen. pl.* -вок] *n., colloq.* **1,** brawl; fight. **2,** whipping; beating.

потáчка [*gen. pl.* -чек] *n., colloq.* favor; indulgence.

потáш [*gen.* -ташá] *n.* potash. —**потáшный,** *adj.* potash (*attrib.*).

потащи́ть *v., pfv. of* тащи́ть. —**потащи́ться,** *refl., pfv. of* тащи́ться.

потвóрство *n.* (*with dat.*) leniency (toward); indulgence (of).

потвóрствовать *v. impfv.* [*pres.* -ствую, -ствуешь] (*with dat.*) to indulge; be lenient (toward); look the other way (at).

потёк *n.* streak.

потёмки [*gen.* -мок] *n. pl.* darkness.

потёмкинский *adj., in* **потёмкинская дерéвня,** Potemkin village.

потемнéние *n.* darkening.

потемнéть *v., pfv. of* темнéть (*in sense #1*).

потенциáл (тэ) *n.* potential. —**потенциáльный,** *adj.* potential.

потеплéние *n.* warming.

потеплéть *v., pfv. of* теплéть.

потерéть *v. pfv.* [*infl. like* терéть] to rub. —**потерéться,** *refl., pfv. of* терéться.

потерпéвший *adj., law* aggrieved: потерпéвшая сторонá, the aggrieved party. —*n., law* victim: потерпéвший от пожáра, victim of a fire.

потерпéть *v. pfv.* [*infl.* -терплю́, -тéрпишь] **1,** *pfv. of* терпéть (*in sense #3*). **2,** to be patient. **3,** (*usu. neg.*) to tolerate; put up with.

потёртость *n.f.* sore spot (*caused by rubbing or chafing*).

потёртый *adj.* shabby; threadbare.

потéря *n.* **1,** loss. **2,** waste (*of time, money, etc.*). **3,** *pl.* losses; casualties.

потéрянный *adj.* **1,** lost. **2,** confused; bewildered. **3,** *colloq.* gone to the dogs. —**как потéрянный,** like a lost soul.

потерять *v., pfv. of* терять. —**потеряться,** *refl., pfv. of* теряться.

потесни́ть *v., pfv. of* тесни́ть (*in sense #1*). —**потесни́ться,** *refl.* to crowd together; squeeze together (*so as to make room for someone else*).

потéть *v. impfv.* **1,** [*pfv.* вспотéть] to perspire; sweat. **2,** [*pfv.* запотéть] *colloq.* to become misty; steam up.

потéха *n.* **1,** fun; amusement. **2,** funny incident; funny thing.

потéчь *v. pfv.* [*infl. like* течь] **1,** to begin to flow. **2,** to begin to leak.

потешáть *v. impfv., colloq.* to entertain; amuse. —**потешáться,** *refl.* **1,** *colloq.* to amuse oneself. **2,** (*with* над) to make fun of.

потéшить *v., pfv. of* тéшить. —**потéшиться,** *refl., pfv. of* тéшиться.

потéшный *adj., colloq.* funny; amusing.

потирáть *v. impfv.* to rub. —**потирáть рýки,** to rub one's hands (*with glee, worry, etc.*).

потихóньку *adv., colloq.* **1,** quietly; silently. **2,** secretly; on the sly. **3,** slowly; gradually.

потни́к [*gen.* -никá] *n.* saddlecloth.

потни́ца *n.* prickly heat; heat rash.

пóтный *adj.* **1,** sweaty; covered with perspiration. **2,** steamed up; misted up.

потовóй *adj.* sweat (*attrib.*): потовы́е желéзы, sweat glands.

потогóнный *adj.* **1,** inducing perspiration. **2,** involving sweatshop conditions: потогóнная фáбрика, sweatshop. —**потогóнное,** *n.* something taken to induce perspiration.

потóк *n.* stream; torrent; flood.

потолковáть *v. pfv.* [*infl.* -кýю, -кýешь] *colloq.* to talk (*for a while*); have a talk.

потолóк [*gen.* -лкá] *n.* ceiling. —**взять с потолкá,** to take (*e.g.* facts) out of the air. —**плевáть в потолóк,** to sit around doing nothing.

потолстéть *v., pfv. of* толстéть.

потóм *adv.* **1,** then; next. **2,** afterward(s); later (on).

потóмок [*gen.* -мка] *n.* descendant; offspring.

потóмственный *adj.* **1,** *obs.* hereditary; ancestral. **2,** by birth: потóмственный дворяни́н, a nobleman by birth. Он потóмственный актёр, he comes from a long line of actors.

потóмство *n.* **1,** progeny. **2,** posterity.

потомý *adv.* which is why. —**потомý...и,** that is why: потомý я и спрáшиваю, that's why I ask. —**потомý что,** because.

потонýть *v., pfv. of* тонýть (*in sense #1*).

потóп *n.* **1,** *Bib.* flood. **2,** *colloq.* flood; deluge.

потопи́ть *v., pfv. of* топи́ть (*in sense #4*).

потоплéние *n.* sinking.

потоптáть *v. pfv.* [*infl.* -топчý, -тóпчешь] to trample down.

поторáпливать *v. impfv., colloq.* to hurry; urge on. —**поторáпливаться,** *refl., colloq.* to hurry: поторáпливайтесь!, hurry up!; get a move on!

поторопи́ть *v., pfv. of* торопи́ть. —**поторопи́ться,** *refl., pfv. of* торопи́ться.

потóчный *adj.* done on an assembly line: потóчное произвóдство, assembly-line production.

потрáва *n.* damage done to crops by cattle.

потрави́ть *v., pfv. of* трави́ть (*in sense #2*).

потрáтить *v., pfv. of* трáтить. —**потрáтиться,** *refl., pfv. of* трáтиться.

потрафлять *v. impfv.* [*pfv.* потрáфить] (*with dat.*) *colloq.* to please; satisfy.

потреби́тель *n.m.* consumer. —**потреби́тельский,** *adj.* consumer (*attrib.*); consumers'.

потреби́ть [*infl.* -блю́, -би́шь] *v., pfv. of* потребля́ть.

потреблéние *n.* consumption. —**товáры ширóкого потреблéния,** consumer goods.

потребля́ть *v. impfv.* [*pfv.* потреби́ть] to consume.

потрéбность *n.f.* need; requirement.

потрéбный *adj.* necessary; required; requisite.

потрéбовать *v., pfv. of* трéбовать. —**потрéбоваться,** *refl., pfv. of* трéбоваться.

потревóжить *v., pfv. of* тревóжить (*in sense #2*).

потрёпанный *adj.* tattered; shabby; threadbare.

потрепáть *v. pfv.* [*infl.* -треплю́, -трéплешь] **1,** *pfv.*

of трепа́ть. **2**, *mil.* to inflict heavy losses on. **3**, *fig.* to scar.

потре́скаться *v.r., pfv. of* тре́скаться.

потре́скивать *v. impfv.* to crackle.

потро́гать *v. pfv.* to touch; feel; finger.

потроха́ [*gen.* -хо́в] *n. pl.* giblets.

потроши́ть *v. impfv.* [*pfv.* вы́потрошить] to eviscerate; disembowel.

потруди́ться *v.r. pfv.* [*infl.* -тружу́сь, -тру́дишься] **1**, to work (*for a while*). **2**, (*with inf.*) to bother (to); take the trouble (to).

потряса́ть *v. impfv.* [*pfv.* потрясти́] **1**, to shake. **2**, (*with instr.*) to shake; brandish. **3**, *fig.* to shake; shock; stagger; stun.

потряса́ющий *adj.* **1**, staggering; stunning. **2**, tremendous; stupendous. **3**, *colloq.* marvelous; fabulous.

потрясе́ние *n.* **1**, shock. **2**, upheaval.

потрясти́ [*infl. like* трясти́] *v., pfv. of* потряса́ть.

потря́хивать *v. impfv.* (*with acc. or instr.*) *colloq.* to shake.

поту́ги [*gen.* -ту́г] *n. pl.* **1**, spasms. Родовы́е поту́ги, birth pains; labor pains. **2**, *fig.* vain attempts.

потупля́ть *v. impfv.* [*pfv.* поту́пить] to lower (one's eyes, head, etc.). —потупля́ться, *refl.* to lower one's eyes; lower one's head.

потускне́лый *adj.* dull; tarnished.

потускне́ть *v., pfv. of* тускне́ть.

потусторо́нний *adj., in* потусторо́нний мир, the next world.

потуха́ть *v. impfv.* [*pfv.* поту́хнуть] **1**, (*of something burning*) to go out. **2**, to die out; fade away.

поту́хнуть [*past* -ту́х, -ла] *v., pfv. of* ту́хнуть (*in sense #1*) *and* потуха́ть.

поту́хший *adj.* **1**, dull; lifeless. **2**, (*of a volcano*) extinct.

потучне́ть *v., pfv. of* тучне́ть.

потуши́ть *v., pfv. of* туши́ть (*in sense #1*).

по́тчевать *v. impfv.* [*pfv.* попо́тчевать; *pres.* -чую, -чуешь] (*with instr.*) *colloq.* to treat to (food, drink, etc.).

потяга́ться *v.r., pfv. of* тяга́ться.

потя́гивать *v. impfv.* **1**, to pull at; tug at. **2**, to draw on (a cigarette, pipe, etc.). **3**, to sip. —потя́гиваться, *refl.* [*pfv.* потяну́ться] to stretch; take a stretch.

потяну́ть *v., pfv. of* тяну́ть. —потяну́ться, *refl., pfv. of* тяну́ться (*in sense #3*) *and* потя́гиваться.

поу́жинать *v., pfv. of* у́жинать.

поумне́ть *v., pfv. of* умне́ть.

поуро́чный *adj.* **1**, of *or* for a lesson. **2**, (*of payment*) by the lesson.

поутру́ *adv., colloq.* in the morning.

поуча́ть *v. impfv.* **1**, to teach; instruct. **2**, to preach to; lecture.

поуче́ние *n.* **1**, edification: в поуче́ние (+ *dat.*), for the edification of. **2**, sermon; homily.

поучи́тельный *adj.* instructive.

поучи́ть *v. pfv.* [*infl.* -учу́, -у́чишь] to teach (*for a while*).

поха́бный *adj., colloq.* dirty; lewd; obscene.

поха́живать *v. impfv., colloq.* **1**, to walk back and forth; pace. **2**, (*with* к) to drop in on (*from time to time*).

похвала́ *n.* praise.

похвали́ть *v., pfv. of* хвали́ть. —похвали́ться, *refl., pfv. of* хвали́ться.

похвальба́ *n., colloq.* bragging; boasting.

похва́льный *adj.* laudable; commendable; admirable; praiseworthy. —похва́льная гра́мота, certificate of good work and conduct (*in school*).

похваля́ться *v.r. impfv.* (*with instr.*) *colloq.* to boast (about); brag (about).

похва́статься *v.r., pfv. of* хва́statься.

похити́тель *n.m.* **1**, thief. **2**, kidnaper; abductor. **3**, hijacker.

похища́ть *v. impfv.* [*pfv.* похи́тить] **1**, to steal. **2**, to kidnap; abduct. **3**, to hijack.

похище́ние *n.* **1**, theft. **2**, kidnaping; abduction. **3**, hijacking.

похлёбка *n.* pottage.

похло́пать *v., pfv. of* хло́пать.

похлопота́ть *v., pfv. of* хлопота́ть.

похло́пывать *v. impfv., colloq.* to clap; tap; pat.

похме́лье *n.* hangover.

похо́д *n.* **1**, excursion; outing; hike. Туристи́ческий похо́д, hiking expedition; walking tour. Лы́жный/ло́дочный похо́д, skiing/boat trip. **2**, march. **3**, *mil.* campaign. **4**, campaign; drive. —кресто́вый похо́д, *hist.* crusade.

похода́тайствовать *v., pfv. of* хода́тайствовать.

походи́ть[1] *v. impfv.* [*pres.* -хожу́, -хо́дишь] (*with* на + *acc.*) to resemble; look like; be like.

походи́ть[2] *v. pfv.* [*infl.* -хожу́, -хо́дишь] to walk (*for a while*); take a walk.

похо́дка *n.* walk; gait.

похо́дный *adj., mil.* **1**, field (*attrib.*): похо́дная ку́хня, (mobile) field kitchen. **2**, march (*attrib.*); marching.

похо́дя *adv., colloq.* **1**, hastily; on the run. **2**, at the same time; while one is (was) at it. **3**, casually; without thinking twice about it.

похожде́ние *n.* adventure.

похо́жий *adj.* (*with* на + *acc.*) similar (to); like; alike. Э́то на него́ не похо́же, that's not like him. Похо́же, что бу́дет дождь, it looks like rain.

похолода́ние *n.* drop in temperature; cold snap.

похолода́ть *v. pfv., impers.* to get cold; turn cold.

похолоде́ть *v., pfv. of* холоде́ть.

похорони́ть *v., pfv. of* хорони́ть.

похоро́нный *adj.* funeral (*attrib.*).

по́хороны [*gen.* -ро́н; *dat.* -рона́м] *n. pl.* funeral.

похороше́ть *v., pfv. of* хороше́ть.

похотли́вый *adj.* lustful; lewd; lascivious. —похотли́вость, *n.f.* lewdness; lasciviousness.

похотни́к [*gen.* -ника́] *n.* clitoris.

по́хоть *n.f.* lust.

похуде́ть *v., pfv. of* худе́ть.

поцелова́ть *v., pfv. of* целова́ть. —поцелова́ться, *refl., pfv. of* целова́ться.

поцелу́й *n.* kiss.

почасово́й *adj.* by the hour; hourly.

поча́ток [*gen.* -тка] *n.* ear (*of corn*).

по́чва *n.* **1**, soil; ground. **2**, *fig.* basis; foundation: не име́ть (под собо́й) по́чвы, to be without foundation. —на по́чве (+ *gen.*), due to; owing to; on account of. —выбива́ть по́чву из-под чьи́х-нибудь ног, to cut the ground from under someone's feet. —подгота́вливать по́чву для, to prepare the ground for; pave the way for; set the stage for. —теря́ть по́чву под нога́ми, to feel the ground slipping from beneath one's feet.

по́чвенный *adj.* soil (*attrib.*).

почвове́д *n.* soil scientist. —почвове́дение, *n.* soil science.

почём *adv., colloq.* how much is?; how much are?; what is the price of? —почём знать?, who knows?; how is one to know? —почём я зна́ю?, how should I know?

почему́ *adv.* 1, *interr.* why? 2, *rel.* why: я не зна́ю, почему́ он э́то сказа́л, I don't know why he said that. —*conj.* which is why. —вот почему́, that is why. —почему́ бы не (+ *inf.*), why not...?: почему́ бы не спроси́ть её?, why not ask her? —почему́ нет?, why not?

почему́-либо *adv.* for some reason; for any reason. *Also,* почему́-нибудь.

почему́-то *adv.* for some reason or other.

по́черк *n.* handwriting.

почерне́лый *adj.* darkened; blackened.

почерне́ть *v., pfv. of* черне́ть.

почерпа́ть *v. impfv.* [*pfv.* почерпну́ть] 1, *colloq.* to draw (water). 2, *fig.* to glean; cull.

почерстве́ть *v., pfv. of* черстве́ть (*in sense #1*).

почеса́ть *v., pfv. of* чеса́ть. —почеса́ться, *refl., pfv. of* чеса́ться (*in sense #2*).

по́чести [*gen.* -стей] *n.pl.* honor; homage: ока́зывать *or* воздава́ть по́чести (+ *dat.*), to pay homage to.

почёсывать *v. impfv., colloq.* to scratch occasionally. —почёсываться, *refl., colloq.* to scratch oneself occasionally.

почёт *n.* honor; respect; esteem.

почётный *adj.* 1, honored; of honor: почётное ме́сто, place of honor. 2, honorary. 3, honorable. —почётный карау́л, guard of honor; honor guard.

по́чечный *adj.* kidney (*attrib.*); renal.

почива́ть *v. impfv.* [*pfv.* почи́ть] *obs.* 1, to sleep. 2, [*impfv. only*] to lie; repose (in one's grave). —почива́ть (почи́ть) на ла́врах, to rest on one's laurels.

почи́вший *n., decl. as an adj.* the deceased.

почи́н *n.* 1, initiative. 2, *colloq.* start; beginning.

почини́ть *v., pfv. of* чини́ть (*in sense #1*).

почи́нка *n.* mending; repair.

почи́стить *v., pfv. of* чи́стить.

почита́й *adv., colloq.* 1, almost. 2, probably.

почита́тель *n.m.* admirer.

почита́ть¹ *v. impfv.* 1, to respect; honor; revere. 2, *obs.* to consider.

почита́ть² *v. pfv.* 1, to read (*for a while*). 2, *colloq.* to read (a book, article, etc.).

почи́тывать *v. impfv., colloq.* to read from time to time.

почи́ть [*infl.* -чи́ю, -чи́ешь] *v., pfv. of* почива́ть.

по́чка [*gen. pl.* -чек] *n.* 1, bud. 2, kidney.

по́чта *n.* 1, mail. 2, post office. —дипломати́ческая по́чта, diplomatic pouch.

почтальо́н *n.* mailman; postman.

почта́мт *n.* main post office.

почте́ние *n.* 1, respect; deference. 2, reverence. —с почте́нием, (*at the close of a letter*) respectfully yours.

почте́нный *adj.* 1, worthy. 2, venerable. 3, *colloq.* considerable.

почти́ *adv.* almost; nearly. —почти́ что = почти́.

почти́тельность *n.f.* respect; deference.

почти́тельный *adj.* respectful; reverent; deferential. —держа́ться на почти́тельном расстоя́нии, to keep at a distance; keep one's distance.

почти́ть *v. pfv.* [*infl. like* чтить] to honor.

почтме́йстер *n., obs.* postmaster.

почто́вый *adj.* postal; mail (*attrib.*). —почто́вая бума́га, stationery. —почто́вый го́лубь, carrier pigeon; homing pigeon. —почто́вая ка́рточка, postcard. —почто́вая ма́рка, postage stamp. —почто́вые расхо́ды, postage. —почто́вый ште́мпель, postmark. —почто́вый я́щик, mailbox.

почу́вствовать *v., pfv. of* чу́вствовать. —почу́вствоваться, *refl., pfv. of* чу́вствоваться.

почу́диться *v.r., pfv. of* чу́диться.

почу́ять *v., pfv. of* чу́ять.

пошаба́шить *v., pfv. of* шаба́шить.

поша́ливать *v. impfv., colloq.* to act up.

пошатну́ть *v. pfv.* to shake. —пошатну́ться, *refl.* 1, to stagger. 2, to be shaken. 3, *fig.* (*of one's health*) to be impaired.

поша́тывать *v. impfv.* 1, to shake. 2, *impers.* to totter: его́ поша́тывает, he is unsteady on his feet. —поша́тываться, *refl.* 1, to sway; totter; wobble. 2, (*of a tooth*) to be loose.

пошевели́ть *v., pfv. of* шевели́ть. —пошевели́ться, *refl., pfv. of* шевели́ться.

поши́б *n., colloq.* manner; style. —одного́ поши́ба, two of a kind; from the same mold.

поши́вка *n.* sewing.

поши́вочный *adj., in* поши́вочная мастерска́я, tailor's shop; dressmaker's shop.

по́шлина *n.* duty; customs.

по́шлость *n.f.* 1, pettiness. 2, trite remark; banality.

по́шлый *adj.* 1, common; petty; shallow. 2, coarse; vulgar. 3, banal; trite.

пошля́к [*gen.* -ляка́] *n., colloq.* common *or* shallow person.

пошту́чный *adj.* by the piece. —пошту́чно, *adv.* by the piece.

пошуме́ть *v. pfv.* [*infl.* -млю́, -ми́шь] to make (some) noise.

пошути́ть *v., pfv. of* шути́ть.

поща́да *n.* mercy.

пощади́ть *v., pfv. of* щади́ть.

пощекота́ть *v., pfv. of* щекота́ть.

пощёчина *n.* slap in the face.

пощи́пывать *v. impfv.* 1, to pinch from time to time. 2, *impers.* to prick; tingle: у меня́ щёки пощи́пывает, my cheeks are tingling.

пощу́пать *v., pfv. of* щу́пать.

поэ́зия *n.* poetry. —поэ́ма *n.* (long) poem.

поэ́т *n.* poet.

поэта́пный *adj.* phased. —поэта́пно, *adv.* in stages.

поэте́сса (тэ) *n.* poetess.

поэти́ческий *adj.* poetic.

поэ́тому *adv.* therefore.

появи́ться [*infl.* -явлю́сь, -я́вишься] *v.r., pfv. of* появля́ться.

появле́ние *n.* appearance.

появля́ться *v.r. impfv.* [*pfv.* появи́ться] to appear.

по́яс [*pl.* пояса́] *n.* 1, belt. 2, waist: кла́няться в по́яс, to bow from the waist. 3, [*pl.* по́ясы] zone: часово́й по́яс, time zone. —спаса́тельный по́яс, life belt; life preserver.

поясне́ние *n.* explanation.

поясни́тельный *adj.* explanatory.

поясни́ть *v., pfv. of* поясня́ть.

поясни́ца *n.* small of the back. —поясни́чный, *adj.* lumbar.

поясно́й *adj.* **1,** belt (*attrib.*). **2,** to the waist; from the waist. **3,** zonal. —**поясно́й портре́т,** half-length portrait.

поясня́ть *v. impfv.* [*pfv.* **поясни́ть**] to explain; elucidate.

прабабка [*gen. pl.* **-бок**] *n.* great-grandmother. *Also,* **праба́бушка.**

пра́вда *n.* truth. Это пра́вда, that is true; that's the truth. Пра́вда ли, что...?, is it true that...? —*adv.* **1,** really; indeed. **2,** true; admittedly; to be sure. **3,** *in questions,* isn't that so?; don't you think so? —**все́ми пра́вдами и непра́вдами,** by hook or by crook. —**по пра́вде говоря́; по пра́вде сказа́ть,** to tell the truth...

правди́вый *adj.* **1,** (*of a person*) truthful. **2,** (*of a story, answer, etc.*) true; truthful. —**правди́вость,** *n.f.* truthfulness; veracity.

правдоподо́бие *n.* plausibility; credibility; verisimilitude. —**правдоподо́бный,** *adj.* plausible; believable; credible.

пра́ведник *n.* righteous man.

пра́ведный *adj.* **1,** righteous. **2,** just. —**пра́ведность,** *n.f.* righteousness.

праве́ть *v. impfv.* [*pfv.* **поправе́ть**] to shift to the right; become more conservative.

пра́вило *n.* **1,** rule: пра́вило орфогра́фии, spelling rule. **2,** *pl.* rules; regulations: пра́вила безопа́сности, rules of safety; safety regulations. —**как пра́вило,** as a rule. —**взять себе́ за пра́вило** (+ *inf.*), to make it a rule (to).

пра́вильно *adv.* **1,** correctly. **2,** properly. **3,** regularly; evenly. —*adj., used predicatively* right; correct: соверше́нно пра́вильно, absolutely right.

пра́вильность *n.f.* **1,** rightness; correctness. **2,** regularity.

пра́вильный *adj.* **1,** right; correct. **2,** proper. **3,** regular: пра́вильный глаго́л, regular verb; пра́вильные черты́ лица́, regular features. —**пра́вильная дробь,** proper fraction.

прави́тель *n.m.* ruler.

прави́тельство *n.* government. —**прави́тельственный,** *adj.* governmental; government (*attrib.*).

пра́вить *v. impfv.* [*pres.* **-влю, -вишь**] **1,** (*with instr.*) to rule; govern. **2,** (*with instr.*) to drive; steer. **3,** (*with acc.*) to read; correct (something written). **4,** (*with acc.*) to sharpen; hone.

пра́вка *n.* reading; correcting: пра́вка корректу́ры, proofreading.

правле́ние *n.* **1,** government; rule. **2,** management; board of directors.

пра́внук *n.* great-grandson.

пра́внучка [*gen. pl.* **-чек**] *n.* great-granddaughter.

пра́во [*pl.* **права́**] *n.* **1,** right: пра́во на труд, the right to work; пра́во го́лоса, the right to vote. **2,** law: уголо́вное пра́во, criminal law. Изуча́ть пра́во, to study law. **3,** *pl., colloq.* (driver's) license. —*particle, colloq.* **1,** really. **2,** believe me! —**на права́х** (+ *gen.*), as; in the capacity of. —**по пра́ву,** rightfully; deservedly.

правове́рный *adj.* orthodox; faithful.

правово́й *adj.* legal; of (the) law.

правоме́рный *adj.* legitimate.

правомо́чный *adj., law* competent.

правонаруше́ние *n.* offense; violation of the law. —**правонаруши́тель,** *n.m.* offender; lawbreaker; wrongdoer.

правописа́ние *n.* orthography; spelling.

правосла́вие *n.* the Orthodox faith.

правосла́вный *adj.* orthodox. —*n.* member of the Orthodox Church.

правосу́дие *n.* justice.

правота́ *n.* rightness; correctness.

пра́вый *adj.* **1,** right; right-hand. **2,** *polit.* right; right-wing. **3,** *naut.* starboard. **4,** [*short form* **прав, права́, пра́во, пра́вы**] right; correct. **5,** (*of a cause*) just. —*n.* right-winger; rightist.

пра́вящий *adj.* ruling: пра́вящие круги́, ruling circles.

прагмати́зм *n.* pragmatism. —**прагмати́ст,** *n.* pragmatist. —**прагмати́ческий,** *adj.* pragmatic.

пра́дед *n.* **1,** great-grandfather. **2,** *pl.* ancestors; forefathers.

пра́зднество *n.* **1,** festival; celebration. **2,** *pl.* festivities.

пра́здник *n.* **1,** holiday: с пра́здником!, happy holiday! **2,** celebration. —**бу́дет и на на́шей у́лице пра́здник,** our day will come.

пра́здничный *adj.* **1,** holiday (*attrib.*). **2,** festive.

пра́здно *adv.* idly.

пра́зднование *n.* celebration.

пра́здновать *v. impfv.* [*pfv.* **отпра́здновать;** *pres.* **-ную, -нуешь**] to celebrate.

пра́здный *adj.* idle. —**пра́здность,** *n.f.* idleness.

празеоди́м *n.* praseodymium.

пра́ктик *n.* **1,** practical worker. **2,** practical person.

пра́ктика *n.* **1,** practice: на пра́ктике, in practice. **2,** practical experience. **3,** practical work. **4,** *obs.* practice (*of a physician or lawyer*).

практика́нт *n.* person undergoing practical training; trainee.

практикова́ть *v. impfv.* [*pres.* **-ку́ю, -ку́ешь**] **1,** *v.t.* to practice; try out. **2,** *v.i., obs.* (*of a physician, lawyer, etc.*) to practice. —**практикова́ться,** *refl.* **1,** (*with в* + *prepl.*) to practice. **2,** to be practiced; be done.

пра́ктикум *n.* practical work; practical training.

практи́чески *adv.* **1,** in a practical manner; practically. **2,** practically; virtually; for all practical purposes.

практи́ческий *adj.* practical: практи́ческий челове́к/курс/о́пыт, practical person/course/experience.

практи́чный *adj.* practical: практи́чный челове́к/костю́м/автомоби́ль, practical person/suit/car. —**практи́чность,** *n.f.* practicality.

пра́отец [*gen.* **-тца**] *n., obs.* forefather; ancestor.

пра́порщик *n., mil.* **1,** warrant officer. **2,** *pre-rev.* ensign; lieutenant.

прапраба́бка [*gen. pl.* **-бок**] *n.* great-great-grandmother. *Also,* **прапраба́бушка.**

прапра́внук *n.* great-great-grandson.

прапра́внучка [*gen. pl.* **-чек**] *n.* great-great-granddaughter.

прапра́дед *n.* great-great-grandfather.

прах *n.* **1,** *poetic* dust. **2,** (earthly) remains. —**мир пра́ху его́,** may he rest in peace. —**обрати́ть** *or* **преврати́ть в прах,** to reduce to dust (*or* ashes). —**пойти́ пра́хом,** to go to the dogs.

пра́чечная *n., decl. as an adj.* laundry.

пра́чка [*gen. pl.* **-чек**] *n.* laundress.

праща́ *n.* sling (*for hurling stones*).

пра́щур *n.* ancestor; forefather.

пре- *prefix* **1,** *indicating a high degree:* превозноси́ть, to extol; пресыща́ть, to satiate. **2,** *indicating excess:* преувели́чивать, to exaggerate. **3,** *indicating transfor-*

mation: превраща́ть, to turn into. **4,** *indicating the overcoming of something:* преодолева́ть/превозмога́ть, to overcome. **5,** (*with adjectives*) *indicating a high degree:* престаре́лый, very old.

преа́мбула *n.* preamble.

пребыва́ние *n.* **1,** (one's) stay: во вре́мя на́шего пребыва́ния в Пари́же, during our stay in Paris. **2,** tenure: пребыва́ние в до́лжности, tenure in office. —**ме́сто постоя́нного пребыва́ния,** permanent residence.

пребыва́ть *v. impfv.* to be.

превали́ровать *v. impfv.* [*pres.* -рую, -руешь] **1,** to predominate. **2,** (*with* над) to dominate; take precedence over.

превенти́вный *adj.* preventive.

превзойти́ [*infl.* -взойду́, -взойдёшь; *past* -взошёл, -взошла́, -взошло́] *v., pfv. of* превосходи́ть.

превозмога́ть *v. impfv.* [*pfv.* превозмо́чь] to overcome.

превозмо́чь [*infl. like* мочь] *v., pfv. of* превозмога́ть.

превознести́ [*infl. like* нести́] *v., pfv. of* превозноси́ть.

превозноси́ть *v. impfv.* [*pfv.* превознести́; *pres.* -ношу́, -но́сишь] to extol. —**превозноси́ть до небе́с,** to praise to the skies.

превосходи́тельство *n.* Excellency: ва́ше превос-ходи́тельство, Your Excellency.

превосходи́ть *v. impfv.* [*pfv.* превзойти́; *pres.* -хожу́, -хо́дишь] **1,** to excel. **2,** to exceed; surpass. —**превосходи́ть (самого́) себя́,** to outdo oneself.

превосхо́дный *adj.* **1,** excellent; superb. **2,** *gram.* superlative: превосхо́дная сте́пень, superlative degree.

превосхо́дство *n.* superiority.

преврати́ть [*infl.* -щу́, -ти́шь] *v., pfv. of* превраща́ть. —**преврати́ться,** *refl., pfv. of* превраща́ться.

превра́тно *adv.* incorrectly: превра́тно истолкова́ть, to misinterpret.

превра́тность *n.f.* **1,** error; fallacy. **2,** *pl.* vicissitudes: превра́тности судьбы́, the vicissitudes of life.

превра́тный *adj.* **1,** wrong; incorrect; erroneous. **2,** *obs.* (*of luck, fate, etc.*) fickle; capricious.

превраща́ть *v. impfv.* [*pfv.* преврати́ть] (*with* в + *acc.*) **1,** to turn into; convert into. **2,** to reduce to (rubble, ashes, etc.). —**превраща́ться,** *refl.* (*with* в + *acc.*) to turn to; turn into; become.

превраще́ние *n.* **1,** conversion. **2,** transformation.

превы́сить [*infl.* -шу, -сишь] *v., pfv. of* превыша́ть.

превыша́ть *v. impfv.* [*pfv.* превы́сить] to exceed.

превыше́ние *n.* **1,** exceeding. **2,** excess.

прегра́да *n.* obstacle; barrier.

прегради́ть [*infl.* -жу́, -ди́шь] *v., pfv. of* прегражда́ть.

прегражда́ть *v. impfv.* [*pfv.* прегради́ть] to block; bar; obstruct.

прегражде́ние *n.* blocking; barring; obstructing.

прегреше́ние *n., obs.* sin; transgression; iniquity.

пред *prep.* = **пе́ред.**

пред- *prefix, indicating prior action:* предви́деть, to foresee; предвосхища́ть, to anticipate.

предава́ть *v. impfv.* [*pfv.* преда́ть; *pres.* -даю́, -даёшь] **1,** to betray. **2,** (*with dat.*) to commit (to): предава́ть (что́-нибудь) огню́, to commit to the flames. **3,** *in* предава́ть гла́сности, to make public; предава́ть сме́рти, to put to death; предава́ть суду́, to prosecute; put on trial. —**предава́ться,** *refl.* (*with dat.*) to give way to; indulge in.

преда́ние *n.* **1,** legend. **2,** (*with dat.*) committing (to); putting (to).

пре́данность *n.f.* devotion; dedication.

пре́данный *adj.* devoted; dedicated. —**пре́данный вам,** yours truly.

преда́тель *n.m.* traitor.

преда́тельский *adj.* **1,** traitorous; treasonable. **2,** treacherous.

преда́тельство *n.* **1,** betrayal. **2,** treachery. **3,** treason.

преда́ть [*infl. like* дать; *past* пре́дал, предала́, пре́дало] *v., pfv. of* предава́ть. —**преда́ться,** *refl.* [*past* преда́лся, -ла́сь, -ло́сь] *pfv. of* предава́ться.

предвари́тельно *adv.* beforehand; in advance; ahead of time.

предвари́тельный *adj.* **1,** preliminary. **2,** advance; prior.

предваря́ть *v. impfv.* [*pfv.* предвари́ть] **1,** to anticipate. **2,** *obs.* to forewarn.

предве́стие *n.* omen; augury; portent.

предве́стник *n.* harbinger; precursor; forerunner.

предвеща́ть *v. impfv.* to portend; presage; augur. Предвеща́ть хоро́шее, to augur well; bode well.

предвзя́тость *n.f.* prejudice; bias. —**предвзя́тый,** *adj.* preconceived.

предви́дение *n.* **1,** foresight. **2,** anticipation: в предви́дении (+ *gen.*), in anticipation of. **3,** prediction.

предви́деть *v. impfv.* [*pres.* -ви́жу, -ви́дишь] to foresee.

предвкуси́ть [*infl.* -вкушу́, -вку́сишь] *v., pfv. of* предвкуша́ть.

предвкуша́ть *v. impfv.* [*pfv.* предвкуси́ть] to anticipate with pleasure; look forward to.

предвкуше́ние *n.* **1,** foretaste. **2,** anticipation.

предводи́тель *n.m.* leader. —**предводи́тельство,** *n.* leadership.

предводи́тельствовать *v. impfv.* [*pres.* -ствую, -ствуешь] **1,** to be the leader; be in charge. **2,** (*with instr.*) to lead; command; be the leader of.

предвое́нный *adj.* prewar.

предвосхища́ть *v. impfv.* [*pfv.* предвосхи́тить] to anticipate.

предвосхище́ние *n.* anticipation.

предвы́борный *adj.* election (*attrib.*).

предго́рье *n.* foothill.

преддве́рие *n.* **1,** entrance. **2,** *fig.* (*with gen.*) period immediately preceding.

преде́л *n.* **1,** limit. **2,** *pl.* bounds: вы́йти за преде́лы (+ *gen.*), to go beyond the bounds of. **3,** (*with gen.*) height (of); acme (of); pinnacle (of): преде́л жела́ний, the pinnacle of one's desires. —**в преде́лах** (+ *gen.*), within. —**за преде́лами** (+ *gen.*), outside; beyond.

преде́льно *adv.* utterly; to the extreme.

преде́льный *adj.* **1,** boundary (*attrib.*): преде́льная ли́ния, boundary line. **2,** maximum: преде́льный во́зраст, maximum age. Преде́льный срок, time limit. **3,** *fig.* utmost: с преде́льной быстрото́й, with the utmost speed.

предержа́щий *adj., in* вла́сти предержа́щие, *obs.* the powers that be; the authorities.

предзнаменова́ние *n.* omen; augury; portent.

предика́т *n.*, *gram.* predicate. —**предикати́вный**, *adj.*, *gram.* predicative.

предисло́вие *n.* preface; foreword.

предлага́ть *v. impfv.* [*pfv.* **предложи́ть**] **1**, to offer. **2**, to propose. **3**, to suggest. **4**, to pose (a question, riddle, etc.). **5**, to order (someone to do something).

предло́г *n.* **1**, pretext; excuse. **2**, preposition.

предложе́ние *n.* **1**, offer. **2**, proposal; proposition. **3**, suggestion. **4**, motion (*made at a meeting*). **5**, *gram.* sentence; clause. **6**, *econ.* supply: спрос и предло-же́ние, supply and demand.

предложи́ть [*infl.* -ложу́, -ло́жишь] *v.*, *pfv. of* **предла-га́ть.**

предло́жный *adj., in* **предло́жный паде́ж,** preposi-tional case.

предме́стье *n.* suburb.

предме́т *n.* **1**, object: неодушевлённый предме́т, inanimate object. **2**, article; item: предме́т ро́скоши, luxury item. **3**, object; target: предме́т насме́шек, object of ridicule. **4**, subject; topic. **5**, subject (*in school*). —**на предме́т** (+ *gen.*), for; for the purpose of.

предме́тный *adj.* **1**, subject (*attrib.*): предме́тный катало́г, subject catalogue. **2**, material; physical. —**предме́тное стекло́,** slide (*for a microscope*). —**предме́тный указа́тель,** index. —**предме́тный уро́к,** object lesson.

предмо́стный *adj.* located at the foot of a bridge. —**предмо́стное укрепле́ние,** bridgehead.

предназнача́ть *v. impfv.* [*pfv.* **предназна́чить**] (*with* на + *acc. or* для) **1**, to mean; intend; design (for). **2**, to set aside; earmark (for).

предназначе́ние *n.* **1**, mission; calling. **2**, *obs.* fate; destiny.

предназна́чить *v.*, *pfv. of* **предназнача́ть.**

преднаме́ренный *adj.* premeditated; intentional; deliberate. —**преднаме́ренно,** *adv.* intentionally; deliberately. —**преднаме́ренность,** *n.f.* premedita-tion.

предначерта́ние *n.* prescription; requirement.

предначерта́ть *v. pfv.* to destine; predetermine; foreordain.

предо *prep.* = **пред** *and* **пе́ред.**

пре́док [*gen.* -дка] *n.* ancestor; forefather.

предопределе́ние *n.* **1**, predetermination. **2**, *obs.* predestination.

предопределя́ть *v. impfv.* [*pfv.* **предопредели́ть**] to predetermine; predestine; foreordain.

предоста́вить [*infl.* -влю, -вишь] *v.*, *pfv. of* **предо-ставля́ть.**

предоставле́ние *n.* granting; giving.

предоставля́ть *v. impfv.* [*pfv.* **предоста́вить**] **1**, to grant; give. **2**, to leave (*to do something*): нам предо-ста́вили э́то сде́лать, it was left for us to do. —**предо-ставля́ть самому́ себе́,** to leave on one's own; leave to one's own devices.

предостерега́ть *v. impfv.* [*pfv.* **предостере́чь**] (*with* от) to warn (against); caution (against).

предостереже́ние *n.* warning; caution.

предостере́чь [*infl. like* **стере́чь**] *v.*, *pfv. of* **предо-стерега́ть.**

предосторо́жность *n.f.* **1**, caution; precaution. **2**, *usu. pl.* precautions. —**ме́ры предосторо́жности,** precautionary measures.

предосуди́тельный *adj.* reprehensible; blamewor-thy.

предотвраща́ть *v. impfv.* [*pfv.* **предотврати́ть**] to avert; prevent.

предотвраще́ние *n.* prevention; preventing; avert-ing.

предохране́ние *n.* protection.

предохрани́тель *n.m.* safety device; safety catch; safety lock.

предохрани́тельный *adj.* **1**, precautionary; preven-tive. **2**, safety (*attrib.*): предохрани́тельный кла́пан, safety valve.

предохраня́ть *v. impfv.* [*pfv.* **предохрани́ть**] to protect.

предписа́ние *n.* order: предписа́ния врача́, doc-tor's orders.

предписа́ть [*infl.* -пишу́, -пи́шешь] *v.*, *pfv. of* **пред-пи́сывать.**

предпи́сывать *v. impfv.* [*pfv.* **предписа́ть**] **1**, to order; direct. **2**, to prescribe.

предпле́чье *n.* forearm.

предплюсна́ [*pl.* -плю́сны, -плю́сен] *n., anat.* tar-sus. —**предплюсневой,** *adj.* tarsal.

предполага́емый *adj.* **1**, planned. **2**, supposed; pre-sumed.

предполага́ть *v. impfv.* [*pfv.* **предположи́ть**] **1**, to suppose; assume; presume. **2**, [*impfv. only*] to intend; plan. **3**, [*impfv. only*] to presuppose. —**предполага́ть-ся,** *refl.* [*impfv. only*] **1**, to be planned. **2**, *impers.* to be assumed: предполага́лось, что..., it was assumed that...

предположе́ние *n.* **1**, supposition; assumption. **2**, plan; project.

предположи́тельно *adv.* **1**, by making an assump-tion; hypothetically. **2**, supposedly; presumably; prob-ably.

предположи́тельный *adj.* hypothetical; conjectu-ral.

предположи́ть [*infl.* -ложу́, -ло́жишь] *v.*, *pfv. of* **предполага́ть.**

предпосла́ть [*infl.* -шлю́, -шлёшь] *v.*, *pfv. of* **пред-посыла́ть.**

предпосле́дний *adj.* next to last.

предпосыла́ть *v. impfv.* [*pfv.* **предпосла́ть**] (*with* dat.) to preface: предпосыла́ть расска́зу анекдо́т, to preface one's story with an anecdote. Предпосы-ла́ть не́сколько слов к расска́зу, to preface one's story with a few words.

предпосы́лка [*gen. pl.* -лок] *n.* **1**, prerequisite; pre-condition. **2**, premise.

предпоче́сть [*infl.* -чту́, -чтёшь; *past* -чёл, -чла́, -чло́] *v.*, *pfv. of* **предпочита́ть.**

предпочита́ть *v. impfv.* [*pfv.* **предпоче́сть**] to pre-fer.

предпочте́ние *n.* preference.

предпочти́тельный *adj.* **1**, preferable; preferred. Си́ний цвет предпочти́тельнее зелёного, blue is preferable to green. **2**, (*of a tariff*) preferential.

предприи́мчивый *adj.* enterprising. —**предприи́м-чивость,** *n.f.* enterprise; initiative.

предпринима́тель *n.m.* entrepreneur; business-man.

предпринима́тельство *n.* enterprise: свобо́дное предпринима́тельство, free enterprise.

предпринима́ть *v. impfv.* [*pfv.* **предприня́ть**] **1**, to undertake. **2**, to make (an attempt, efforts, etc.). **3**, to take (steps, measures, action, etc.). **4,** to mount (an attack, offensive, etc.).

предприня́ть [*infl. like* **приня́ть**] *v., pfv. of* **предпринима́ть**.

предприя́тие *n.* **1,** undertaking; venture. **2,** enterprise: промы́шленное предприя́тие, an industrial enterprise.

предрасполага́ть *v. impfv.* [*pfv.* **предрасположи́ть**] (*with* к *or* в по́льзу) to predispose (toward *or* in favor of).

предрасположе́ние *n.* (*with* к) predisposition (to *or* toward).

предрасполо́женный *adj.* (*with* к) predisposed (to).

предрасположи́ть [*infl.* -ложу́, -ло́жишь] *v., pfv. of* **предрасполага́ть**.

предрассу́док [*gen.* -дка] *n.* prejudice.

предрека́ть *v. impfv.* [*pfv.* **предре́чь**] **1,** to predict. **2,** to portend.

предре́чь [*infl. like* **пе́чь**] *v., pfv. of* **предрека́ть**.

предреша́ть *v. impfv.* [*pfv.* **предреши́ть**] **1,** to decide beforehand. **2,** to prejudge. **3,** to predetermine.

предродово́й *adj.* prenatal.

председа́тель *n.m.* chairman. —**председа́тельский**, *adj.* chairman's. —**председа́тельство**, *n.* chairmanship.

председа́тельствовать *v. impfv.* [*pres.* -ствую, -ствуешь] to preside.

предсе́рдие *n.* auricle (*of the heart*).

предсказа́ние *n.* prediction.

предсказа́тель *n.m.* forecaster; prognosticator.

предсказа́ть [*infl.* -скажу́, -ска́жешь] *v., pfv. of* **предска́зывать**.

предска́зуемый *adj.* predictable.

предска́зывать *v. impfv.* [*pfv.* **предсказа́ть**] to predict.

предсме́ртный *adj.* **1,** occurring just before death; death (*attrib.*). **2,** (*of words, a wish, etc.*) dying.

представи́тель *n.m.* **1,** representative. **2,** spokesman.

представи́тельный *adj.* **1,** representative. **2,** impressive; imposing.

представи́тельство *n.* **1,** representation. **2,** representative office: вое́нное представи́тельство, military representative's office.

предста́вить [*infl.* -влю, -вишь] *v., pfv. of* **представля́ть**. —**предста́виться**, *refl., pfv. of* **представля́ться**.

представле́ние *n.* **1,** presentation; submission. **2,** idea; notion. **3,** picture (*in one's mind*). **4,** performance; show. **5,** representation (*formal statement*).

представля́ть *v. impfv.* [*pfv.* **предста́вить**] **1,** to present; submit. **2,** to introduce; present (a person). **3,** (*with* себе́) to imagine. **4,** [*impfv. only*] to represent. **5,** [*impfv. only*] (*often with* собо́й) to be; represent; constitute: представля́ть (собо́й) опа́сность (для), to represent a danger (to). Представля́ть угро́зу, to pose a threat. Представля́ть интере́с (для), to be of interest (to). Представля́ть тру́дности *or* затрудне́ния, to present difficulties. Что он собо́й представля́ет?, what sort of person is he?; what is he like? —**представля́ться**, *refl.* **1,** to introduce oneself. **2,** (*of an opportunity*) to arise; present itself. **3,** (*with dat.*) to appear (before). **4,** (*with dat.*) to seem (to). **5,** (*with instr.*) *colloq.* to pretend (to be).

предста́тельный *adj., in* предста́тельная железа́, prostate gland.

предста́ть *v. pfv.* [*infl.* -ста́ну, -ста́нешь] (*with* пе́ред) to appear (before).

предстоя́ть *v. impfv.* [*pres.* -стои́т] **1,** to lie ahead; be in the offing. **2,** (*with dat.*) to be in store (for). Нам предстои́т холо́дная зима́, we are in for a cold winter. **3,** (*with dat. and inf.*) to have to: мне предстои́т пое́хать туда́, I shall have to go there.

предстоя́щий *adj.* forthcoming; impending.

предте́ча *n.m. & f., archaic* forerunner; precursor. —Иоа́нн Предте́ча, John the Baptist.

предубежда́ть *v. impfv.* [*pfv.* **предубеди́ть**] *obs.* to prejudice.

предубежде́ние *n.* prejudice; bias. —**предубеждённый**, *adj.* prejudiced; biased.

предуга́дывать *v. impfv.* [*pfv.* **предугада́ть**] **1,** to guess; divine. **2,** to foresee; anticipate.

предупреди́тельный *adj.* **1,** precautionary; preventive. **2,** warning (*attrib.*): предупреди́тельный вы́стрел, warning shot. **3,** considerate; thoughtful; attentive.

предупреди́ть [*infl.* -жу́, -ди́шь] *v., pfv. of* **предупрежда́ть**.

предупрежда́ть *v. impfv.* [*pfv.* **предупреди́ть**] **1,** to warn. **2,** to notify. **3,** to prevent. **4,** to anticipate. **5,** to beat (someone) to it.

предупрежде́ние *n.* **1,** warning. **2,** notification; notice. **3,** prevention.

предусма́тривать *v. impfv.* [*pfv.* **предусмотре́ть**] **1,** to foresee; envisage; anticipate. **2,** [*impfv. only*] to provide for; stipulate.

предусмотре́ть [*infl.* -смотрю́, -смо́тришь] *v., pfv. of* **предусма́тривать**.

предусмотри́тельный *adj.* having foresight; farsighted. —**предусмотри́тельность**, *n.f.* foresight.

предчу́вствие *n.* presentiment; premonition; foreboding.

предчу́вствовать *v. impfv.* [*pres.* -ствую, -ствуешь] **1,** to have a premonition about. **2,** (*with* что) to have a feeling that...

предше́ственник *n.* **1,** predecessor. **2,** forerunner; precursor.

предше́ствовать *v. impfv.* [*pres.* -ствую, -ствуешь] (*with dat.*) to precede.

предше́ствующий *adj.* preceding; previous.

предъяви́тель *n.m.* bearer (*of a document*). —**предъяви́тель и́ска**, plaintiff.

предъяви́ть [*infl.* -явлю́, -я́вишь] *v., pfv. of* **предъявля́ть**.

предъявле́ние *n.* **1,** presentation (*of a document*). **2,** bringing (*of a suit, charges, etc.*).

предъявля́ть *v. impfv.* [*pfv.* **предъяви́ть**] **1,** to present; produce; show (a document). **2,** to bring (a lawsuit); press; prefer (charges). **3,** to make (demands); assert (one's rights).

предыду́щий *adj.* previous. —**предыду́щее**, *n.* the foregoing.

прее́мник *n.* successor.

прее́мственность *n.f.* **1,** succession. **2,** continuity.

прее́мственный *adj.* successive.

прее́мство *n.* succession.

пре́жде *adv.* **1,** before; formerly. **2,** first. —*prep., with gen.* before; ahead of. —**пре́жде всего́**, first of all; first and foremost. —**пре́жде чем**, before.

преждевре́менный *adj.* **1,** premature. **2,** untimely. —**преждевре́менно,** *adv.* prematurely.

пре́жний *adj.* **1,** former. **2,** previous. —**в пре́жнее вре́мя; в пре́жние времена́,** in former times.

презента́бельный *adj.* presentable; proper.

презервати́в *n.* contraceptive device; contraceptive.

президе́нт *n.* president. —**президе́нтский,** *adj.* presidential. —**президе́нтство,** *n.* presidency.

прези́диум *n.* presidium.

презира́ть *v. impfv.* [*pfv.* **презре́ть**] **1,** [*impfv. only*] to despise; scorn; hold in contempt. **2,** to disregard; scorn.

презре́ние *n.* (with к) **1,** contempt; scorn (for someone). **2,** disdain; disregard (of danger, death, etc.).

презре́нный *adj.* contemptible; despicable. —**презре́нный мета́лл,** filthy lucre.

презре́ть [*infl.* -зрю́, -зри́шь] *v., pfv. of* **презира́ть** (*in sense #2*).

презри́тельный *adj.* scornful; contemptuous; disdainful.

презу́мпция *n.* presumption.

преиму́щественно *adv.* mainly; chiefly; primarily.

преиму́щественный *adj.* **1,** primary; paramount. **2,** preferred.

преиму́щество *n.* advantage: преиму́щество пе́ред сопе́рником, advantage over one's rival. —**по преиму́ществу,** mainly; chiefly; primarily.

преиспо́дняя *n., decl. as an adj., obs.* hell; the nether world.

преиспо́лненный *adj.* (*with gen.*) filled (with); full (of).

преисполня́ть *v. impfv.* [*pfv.* **преиспо́лнить**] **1,** to fill. **2,** *fig.* to imbue.

прейскура́нт *n.* price list; catalogue. —**прейскура́нтный,** *adj.* of a price list: прейскура́нтная цена́, list price.

преклоне́ние *n.* (with пе́ред) worship (of); admiration (of); reverence (for).

преклони́ть [*infl.* -клоню́, -кло́нишь] *v., pfv. of* **преклоня́ть.** —**преклони́ться,** *refl., pfv. of* **преклоня́ться.**

прекло́нный *adj.* (*of age*) old; advanced.

преклоня́ть *v. impfv.* [*pfv.* **преклони́ть**] **1,** to bend (one's knees); bow (one's head). **2,** *in* преклоня́ть коле́на (*or* коле́ни) пе́ред, to kneel before; bow down to. —**преклоня́ться,** *refl.* (*with* пе́ред) **1,** to kneel (before); bow down (to). **2,** to worship; revere. **3,** to admire; take off one's hat to.

прекосло́вить *v. impfv.* [*pres.* -влю, -вишь] (*with dat.*) to contradict.

прекра́сно *adv.* **1,** marvelously. Она́ прекра́сно вы́глядит, she looks marvelous/wonderful. **2,** perfectly well: я прекра́сно зна́ю, что..., I know perfectly well that... **3,** *as an interj.* wonderful!; fine!; perfect!

прекра́сное *n., decl. as an adj.* the beautiful; that which is beautiful.

прекра́сный *adj.* **1,** beautiful. **2,** excellent; wonderful. **3,** *in* прекра́сный пол, the fair sex. —**в оди́н прекра́сный день,** one fine day. —**ра́ди чьих-нибудь прекра́сных глаз,** for love.

прекрати́ть [*infl.* -щу́, -ти́шь] *v., pfv. of* **прекраща́ть.** —**прекрати́ться,** *refl., pfv. of* **прекраща́ться.**

прекраща́ть *v. impfv.* [*pfv.* **прекрати́ть**] to halt; cease; break off; terminate; suspend; discontinue. —**прекраща́ться,** *refl.* to end; stop; cease.

прекраще́ние *n.* halt; cessation; suspension. —**прекраще́ние огня́,** cease-fire. —**прекраще́ние пре́ний,** cloture.

прела́т *n.* prelate.

преле́стный *adj.* charming; delightful; lovely.

пре́лесть *n.f.* **1,** charm. **2,** a delight: пря́мо пре́лесть!, it's an absolute delight; it's simply delightful.

преломи́ть [*infl.* -ломлю́, -ло́мишь] *v., pfv. of* **преломля́ть.**

преломле́ние *n.* refraction.

преломля́ть *v. impfv.* [*pfv.* **преломи́ть**] to refract.

пре́лый *adj.* rotten.

прель *n.f.* rot; mold.

прельсти́ть [*infl.* -льщу́, -льсти́шь] *v., pfv. of* **прельща́ть.** —**прельсти́ться,** *refl., pfv. of* **прельща́ться.**

прельща́ть *v. impfv.* [*pfv.* **прельсти́ть**] **1,** to charm; captivate. **2,** to tempt; entice; lure. —**прельща́ться,** *refl.* (*with instr.*) to be enticed (by); fall for.

прелюбоде́й *n.* adulterer. —**прелюбоде́йка,** *n.* adulteress. —**прелюбоде́йный,** *adj.* adulterous.

прелюбоде́йствовать *v. impfv.* [*pres.* -ствую, -ствуешь] to commit adultery.

прелюбодея́ние *n.* adultery.

прелю́дия *n.* **1,** *music* prelude. **2,** *fig.* (*with* к) prelude (to).

премиа́льный *adj.* bonus (*attrib.*). —**премиа́льные,** *n. pl.* bonus.

преми́нуть *v. pfv., used negatively with inf.* not to fail (to).

премирова́ть *v. impfv. & pfv.* [*pres.* -ру́ю, -ру́ешь] to give a bonus to; award a prize to.

пре́мия *n.* **1,** prize. **2,** bonus. **3,** premium.

прему́дрость *n.f.* **1,** *obs.* wisdom. **2,** *usu. pl.* mysteries; intricacies. —**невелика́ прему́дрость,** it's not that difficult.

прему́дрый *adj.* **1,** *obs.* possessing great wisdom. **2,** abstruse; arcane.

премье́р *n.* **1,** premier. **2,** leading actor; star performer.

премье́ра *n.* première.

премье́р-мини́стр *n.* prime minister.

премье́рша *n., colloq., theat.* leading lady.

пренебрега́ть *v. impfv.* [*pfv.* **пренебре́чь**] (*with instr.*) **1,** to scorn; disdain; look down on. **2,** to disregard; ignore (rules, advice, etc.). **3,** to neglect (one's duties, health, etc.).

пренебреже́ние *n.* **1,** scorn; disdain. **2,** disregard. **3,** neglect.

пренебрежи́тельный *adj.* scornful; disdainful.

пренебре́чь [*infl.* -брегу́, -бреже́шь, ...-брегу́т; *past* -брёг, -брегла́, -брегло́] *v., pfv. of* **пренебрега́ть.**

пре́ния [*gen.* -ний] *n.pl.* debate.

преоблада́ние *n.* **1,** predominance. **2,** preponderance.

преоблада́ть *v. impfv.* **1,** to predominate. **2,** (*with* над) to prevail over.

преоблада́ющий *adj.* predominant; prevailing.

преобража́ть *v. impfv.* [*pfv.* **преобрази́ть**] **1,** to transform. **2,** to transfigure.

преображе́ние *n.* **1,** transformation. **2,** *relig.* the Transfiguration.

преобрази́ть [*infl.* -жу́, -зи́шь] *v., pfv. of* **преобража́ть.**

преобразова́ние *n.* **1,** transformation. **2,** *pl.* reforms.

преобразова́тель *n.m.* **1,** reformer. **2,** *electricity* transformer.

преобразова́ть [*infl.* -зу́ю, -зу́ешь] *v., pfv. of* **преобразо́вывать**.

преобразо́вывать *v. impfv.* [*pfv.* **преобразова́ть**] **1,** to transform; reorganize; reform. **2,** *electricity; physics* to transform.

преодолева́ть *v. impfv.* [*pfv.* **преодоле́ть**] to overcome; surmount.

преодоле́ние *n.* overcoming; surmounting.

преодоле́ть *v., pfv. of* **преодолева́ть**.

преодоли́мый *adj.* surmountable.

препара́т *n.* **1,** laboratory specimen. **2,** preparation; compound.

препина́ние *n., in* **зна́ки препина́ния,** punctuation marks.

препира́тельство *n.* squabble; hassle.

препира́ться *v.r. impfv.* to squabble; wrangle.

преподава́ние *n.* teaching.

преподава́тель *n.m.* [*fem.* -ница] teacher. —**преподава́тельский,** *adj.* teaching (*attrib.*).

преподава́ть *v. impfv.* [*pres.* -даю́, -даёшь] to teach.

преподнести́ [*infl. like* нести́] *v., pfv. of* **преподноси́ть**.

преподноси́ть *v. impfv.* [*pfv.* **преподнести́;** *pres.* -ношу́, -но́сишь] **1,** to present (a gift, award, etc.). **2,** *colloq.* to give (a surprise, bad news, etc.). **3,** to present (facts, material, etc.).

преподо́бие *n.* Reverence (*title*). —**преподо́бный,** *adj.* Reverend.

препо́на *n., obs.* obstacle; impediment.

препроводи́ть [*infl.* -вожу́, -води́шь *or* -во́дишь] *v., pfv. of* **препровожда́ть**.

препровожда́ть *v. impfv.* [*pfv.* **препроводи́ть**] **1,** to send. **2,** to forward.

препровожде́ние *n.* **1,** sending; forwarding. **2,** passing (*of time*).

препя́тствие *n.* **1,** obstacle. **2,** *sports* obstacle; hurdle: бег/ска́чка с препя́тствиями, hurdle/steeplechase race.

препя́тствовать *v. impfv.* [*pfv.* **воспрепя́тствовать;** *pres.* -ствую, -ствуешь] (*with dat.*) to hinder; impede.

прерва́ть [*infl. like* рвать] *v., pfv. of* **прерыва́ть**. —**прерва́ться,** *refl., pfv. of* **прерыва́ться**.

пререка́ние *n., usu. pl.* squabble; argument.

пререка́ться *v.r. impfv.* to argue; squabble; bicker.

пре́рия *n.* prairie.

прерогати́ва *n.* prerogative.

прерыва́ние *n.* interruption.

прерыва́тель *n.m.* circuit breaker.

прерыва́ть *v. impfv.* [*pfv.* **прерва́ть**] **1,** to interrupt. **2,** to break; break off; sever. —**прерыва́ться,** *refl.* **1,** to be interrupted. **2,** (*of one's voice*) to break.

преры́вистый *adj.* irregular; intermittent.

пресви́тер *n.* presbyter.

пресвитериа́нин [*pl.* -иа́не, -иа́н] *n.* Presbyterian. *Also,* **пресвитериа́нец** [*gen.* -нца; *fem.* -нка].

пресвитериа́нский *adj.* Presbyterian.

пресека́ть *v. impfv.* [*pfv.* **пресе́чь**] **1,** to put a stop to. **2,** to head off; nip: пресека́ть в ко́рне, to nip in the bud. **3,** to cut short. —**пресека́ться,** *refl.* **1,** to stop. **2,** to end. **3,** (*of one's voice*) to break.

пресе́чь [*infl. like* се́чь; *past* -сёк, -секла́ *or* -се́кла, -секло́ *or* -сёкло] *v., pfv. of* **пресека́ть**. —**пресе́чься,** *refl., pfv. of* **пресека́ться**.

пресле́дование *n.* **1,** pursuit. **2,** persecution. **3,** prosecution.

пресле́дователь *n.m.* **1,** persecutor. **2,** pursuer.

пресле́довать *v. impfv.* [*pres.* -дую, -дуешь] **1,** to pursue. **2,** to persecute. **3,** *fig.* (*of a thought, melody, etc.*) to haunt. **4,** to prosecute.

пресловут́ый *adj.* notorious; famous.

пресмыка́ться *v.r. impfv.* (*with* **пе́ред**) to grovel (before).

пресмыка́ющееся *n., decl. as an adj.* reptile.

пресново́дный *adj.* fresh-water.

пре́сный *adj.* **1,** (*of water*) fresh. **2,** (*of bread or dough*) unleavened. **3,** (*of food*) tasteless. **4,** *fig.* insipid; vapid.

пресс *n.* press (*machine*).

пре́сса *n.* the press.

пресс-конфере́нция *n.* press conference; news conference.

прессова́ние *n.* pressing.

прессова́ть *v. impfv.* [*pfv.* **спрессова́ть;** *pres.* -су́ю, -су́ешь] to press.

прессо́вка *n.* pressing.

прессовщи́к [*gen.* -щика́] *n.* presser; pressman.

пресс-папье́ *n. neut. indecl.* **1,** paperweight. **2,** blotter.

преста́виться *v.r. pfv., obs.* to die; pass away.

престаре́лый *adj.* very old; aged. —**дом для престаре́лых,** old age home.

прести́ж *n.* prestige.

прести́жный *adj.* **1,** prestigious. **2,** of prestige: прести́жный вопро́с, matter of prestige.

пре́сто *n. indecl. & adj., music* presto.

престо́л *n.* throne. —**па́пский престо́л,** Holy/Apostolic See.

престолонасле́дие *n.* succession (to the throne).

престо́льный *adj.* throne (*attrib.*). —**престо́льный пра́здник,** patron saint's day.

преступа́ть *v. impfv.* [*pfv.* **преступи́ть**] *obs.* to break; overstep (the law).

преступи́ть [*infl.* -ступлю́, -сту́пишь] *v., pfv. of* **преступа́ть**.

преступле́ние *n.* crime.

престу́пник *n.* criminal.

престу́пность *n.f.* **1,** crime: рост престу́пности, the rise in crime. **2,** criminal nature; criminality. —**де́тская престу́пность,** juvenile delinquency.

престу́пный *adj.* criminal.

пресыща́ть *v. impfv.* [*pfv.* **пресы́тить**] to satiate; surfeit.

пресыще́ние *n.* satiation; satiety; surfeit.

претворя́ть *v. impfv.* [*pfv.* **претвори́ть**] *obs.* to change; transform. —**претворя́ть в жизнь,** to make a reality of; put into practice.

претенде́нт *n.* (*with* на + *acc.*) **1,** contender; aspirant. **2,** applicant; claimant. **3,** challenger. **4,** pretender (to the throne).

претендова́ть *v. impfv.* [*pres.* -ду́ю, -ду́ешь] (*with* на + *acc.*) **1,** to lay claim to. **2,** to seek; aspire to. **3,** to have pretensions of.

прете́нзия *n.* **1,** claim. **2,** complaint; grievance. **3,** pretension. —**быть в прете́нзии на** (+ *acc.*), to have something against; have it in for. —**с прете́нзиями,** pretentious.

претенцио́зный (тэ) *adj.* pretentious. —**претенци-о́зность,** *n.f.* pretentiousness.

претерпева́ть *v. impfv.* [*pfv.* **претерпе́ть**] **1,** to suffer; endure. **2,** to undergo (changes).

претерпе́ть [*infl.* -**терплю́, -те́рпишь**] *v., pfv. of* **претерпева́ть.**

прети́ть *v. impfv.* (*with dat.*) to sicken; disgust. *Also impers.*: мне прети́т от э́того, I'm sick of it; it makes me sick.

преткнове́ние *n., in* ка́мень преткнове́ния, stumbling block.

пре́тор *n.* praetor.

преть *v. impfv.* [*pfv.* **сопре́ть**] to rot.

преувеличе́ние *n.* exaggeration.

преувели́чивать *v. impfv.* [*pfv.* **преувели́чить**] to exaggerate.

преуменьша́ть *v. impfv.* [*pfv.* **преуме́ньши́ть** *or* **преуме́ньшить**] **1,** to underestimate; underrate. **2,** to understate; minimize; play down.

преуменьше́ние *n.* underestimation.

преуме́ньши́ть *also,* **преуме́ньшить** *v., pfv. of* **преуменьша́ть.**

преуспева́ть *v. impfv.* [*pfv.* **преуспе́ть**] **1,** to succeed; be successful. **2,** [*impfv. only*] to thrive; prosper.

префе́кт *n.* prefect. —**префекту́ра,** *n.* prefecture.

префера́нс *n.* preference (*card game*).

пре́фикс *n.* prefix. —**префикса́ция,** *n.* prefixion.

преходя́щий *adj.* transient; transitory; ephemeral; momentary.

прецеде́нт *n.* precedent.

при *prep., with prepl.* **1,** near; by; at: при впаде́нии реки́ Оки́ в Во́лгу, where the Oka River flows into the Volga. Быть при́ смерти, to be near death. **2,** attached to: я́сли при заво́де, nursery attached to a factory; указа́тель при кни́ге, index to a book. **3,** in the presence of: при мне, in my presence; при свиде́телях, in the presence of witnesses. **4,** during: при жи́зни (+ *gen.*), during the life of; при Ива́не Гро́зном, during the reign of Ivan the Terrible. **5,** under (*a ruler or regime*): при Ста́лине, under Stalin; жить при коммуни́зме, to live under communism. **6,** at; on; upon; when: при упомина́нии о, at the mention of; при перехо́де че́рез у́лицу, when crossing the street. **7,** on the person of: докуме́нты при себе́, documents on one's person. **8,** having; possessing: быть при деньга́х, to have plenty of money. **9,** under; in view of; given: при таки́х усло́виях, under such conditions. **10,** (*with* всём *or* всей) for all; despite: при всём том, for all that. При всём моём жела́нии, much as I would like to. —**ни при чём** (*often preceded by* тут), **1,** innocent. **2,** having nothing to do with it; irrelevant. **3,** *in* оста́ться ни при чём, to be left with nothing. —**при чём тут** (+ *nom.*), what has this to do with...? —**при э́том,** here; in the process; in so doing.

при- *prefix* **1,** *indicating arrival:* приходи́ть, to come; прилета́ть, to arrive (*by plane*). **2,** *indicating attachment:* привя́зывать, to tie to; пришива́ть, to sew on. **3,** *indicating addition:* прибавля́ть, to add; прикупа́ть, to buy some more. **4,** *indicating partial or slight action:* приотворя́ть, to open slightly; приспуска́ть, to lower slightly.

приба́вить [*infl.* -**влю, -вишь**] *v., pfv. of* **прибавля́ть.** —**приба́виться,** *refl., pfv. of* **прибавля́ться.**

приба́вка [*gen. pl.* -**вок**] *n.* **1,** adding; addition. **2,** something added; addition. **3,** increase; raise (*in pay*).

прибавле́ние *n.* **1,** adding; addition. **2,** something added; addition. **3,** increase (*in weight*); rise (*of water*).

прибавля́ть *v. impfv.* [*pfv.* **приба́вить**] **1,** to add: прибавля́ть соль (*or* со́ли) к су́пу, to add salt to the soup; прибавля́ть не́сколько слов, to add a few words. **2,** (*with acc. or gen.*) to increase. **3,** *in* прибавля́ть в ве́се, *colloq.* to put on weight. —**прибавля́ться,** *refl.* **1,** to be added. **2,** to increase; rise. **3,** (*of the day*) to grow longer. **4,** (*of the moon*) to wax.

приба́вочный *adj.* **1,** additional. **2,** *econ.* surplus: приба́вочная сто́имость, surplus value.

прибалти́йский *adj.* Baltic.

прибау́тка [*gen. pl.* -**ток**] *n.* humorous saying.

прибега́ть *v. impfv.* **1,** [*pfv.* **прибежа́ть**] to come running. **2,** [*pfv.* **прибе́гнуть**] (*with* к) to resort to.

прибе́гнуть [*past* -**бе́г** *or* -**бе́гнул, -бе́гла**] *v., pfv. of* **прибега́ть** (*in sense #2*).

прибедня́ться *v. impfv.* [*pfv.* **прибедни́ться**] *colloq.* **1,** to pretend to be poorer than one is. **2,** to play down one's achievements; be excessively modest.

прибежа́ть [*infl. like* **бежа́ть**] *v., pfv. of* **прибега́ть** (*in sense #1*).

прибе́жище *n.* refuge.

приберега́ть *v. impfv.* [*pfv.* **прибере́чь**] to put aside; hold aside.

прибере́чь [*infl. like* **бере́чь**] *v., pfv. of* **приберега́ть.**

прибива́ть *v. impfv.* [*pfv.* **приби́ть**] **1,** to nail; nail down. **2,** (*of wind, rain, etc.*) to beat down; flatten. —**приби́ть к бе́регу,** *usu. impers.* to wash ashore: ло́дку приби́ло к бе́регу, the boat was washed ashore.

прибира́ть *v. impfv.* [*pfv.* **прибра́ть**] *colloq.* **1,** to put in order; tidy up. **2,** to put away. —**прибра́ть к рука́м, 1,** to take (someone) in hand. **2,** to seize; expropriate.

приби́ть [*infl.* -**бью, -бьёшь**] *v., pfv. of* **прибива́ть.**

приближа́ть *v. impfv.* [*pfv.* **прибли́зить**] to bring near; bring nearer. —**приближа́ться,** *refl.* **1,** to draw near. **2,** (*with* к) to approach; near. **3,** (*with* к) to approximate.

приближе́ние *n.* **1,** bringing near. **2,** approach.

приближённый *adj.* **1,** (*of people*) close; trusted. **2,** *math.* approximate; rough. —*n.* close associate (*of a ruler or high-ranking person*).

приблизи́тельно *adv.* approximately; roughly. —**приблизи́тельный,** *adj.* approximate.

прибли́зить [*infl.* -**жу, -зишь**] *v., pfv. of* **приближа́ть.** —**прибли́зиться,** *refl., pfv. of* **приближа́ться.**

прибо́й *n.* surf; breakers.

прибо́р *n.* **1,** instrument; device; apparatus; appliance. **2,** set: бри́твенный прибо́р, shaving set. Черни́льный прибо́р, inkstand. **3,** (*place*) setting. Накры́ть стол на шесть прибо́ров, to set the table for six.

прибо́рный *adj., in* прибо́рная доска́, instrument panel; dashboard.

прибра́ть [*infl. like* **брать**] *v., pfv. of* **прибира́ть.**

прибре́жный *adj.* **1,** offshore. **2,** coastal.

прибыва́ть *v. impfv.* [*pfv.* **прибы́ть**] **1,** to arrive. **2,** to increase in size or number; grow larger: толпа́ всё прибыва́ла, the crowd kept getting larger and larger. **3,** (*of water*) to rise; (*of the moon*) to wax.

при́быль *n.f.* **1,** profit. **2,** *colloq.* benefit; gain. **3,** increase; rise. —**при́быльный,** *adj.* profitable; lucrative.

прибы́тие *n.* arrival.

прибы́ть [*infl.* -бу́ду, -бу́дешь; *past* при́был, прибыла́, при́было] *v., pfv. of* прибыва́ть.

привал *n.* **1,** halt; rest. **2,** resting place.

прива́ливать *v. impfv.* [*pfv.* привали́ть] **1,** (*with* к) to lean (a heavy object) against. **2,** *colloq.* to arrive in great numbers. **3,** (*with dat.*) *colloq.* (of luck) to strike; descend on. —**прива́ливаться,** *refl.* (*with* к) *colloq.* to lean against.

привали́ть [*infl.* -валю́, -ва́лишь] *v., pfv. of* прива́ливать. —**привали́ться,** *refl., pfv. of* прива́ливаться.

прива́тный *adj., obs.* private.

приведе́ние *n.* **1,** bringing. **2,** citing; adducing. **3,** putting (in order, motion, etc.).

привезти́ [*infl. like* везти́] *v., pfv. of* привози́ть.

привере́дливый *adj., colloq.* choosy; finicky; fussy.

приве́рженец [*gen.* -нца] *n.* adherent; supporter.

приве́рженность *n.f.* **1,** adherence. **2,** devotion. —**приве́рженный,** *adj.* (*with dat.*) devoted (to); loyal (to).

привёртывать *v. impfv.* [*pfv.* приверну́ть] **1,** to tighten (a screw). **2,** (*with* к) to screw (onto). **3,** to turn down (a flame, lamp, etc.).

приве́сить [*infl.* -шу, -сишь] *v., pfv. of* приве́шивать.

привести́ [*infl. like* вести́] *v., pfv. of* приводи́ть. —**привести́сь,** *refl., pfv. of* приводи́ться.

приве́т *n.* regards; greetings. —*interj., colloq.* hello there!; hi!

приве́тливый *adj.* friendly; amiable; affable. —**приве́тливость,** *n.f.* friendliness; amiability; affability.

приве́тственный *adj.* of welcome; welcoming.

приве́тствие *n.* greeting.

приве́тствовать *v. impfv.* [*pres.* -ствую, -ствуешь] **1,** to greet; welcome. **2,** to welcome (a proposal, decision, etc.).

приве́шивать *v. impfv.* [*pfv.* приве́сить] to hang up.

привива́ть *v. impfv.* [*pfv.* приви́ть] **1,** to graft. **2,** (*with dat.*) to inoculate: привива́ть кому́-нибудь холе́ру, to inoculate someone for cholera. **3,** *fig.* to instill (in): привива́ть кому́-нибудь хоро́шие мане́ры, to instill good manners in someone. —**привива́ться,** *refl.* **1,** (of a vaccine) to take. **2,** *fig.* to take root; take hold; (of a name, word, style, etc.) catch on.

приви́вка *n.* inoculation: сде́лать приви́вку (+ *dat.*), to inoculate. —**приви́вка о́спы,** (smallpox) vaccination.

привиде́ние *n.* ghost; apparition.

приви́деться *v.r. pfv.* (*with dat.*) *colloq.* to appear in one's dreams: мне приви́делось, I dreamt.

привилегиро́ванный *adj.* privileged.

привиле́гия *n.* privilege.

приви́нчивать *v. impfv.* [*pfv.* привинти́ть] **1,** to screw on. **2,** (*with* к) to screw onto.

привира́ть *v. impfv.* [*pfv.* привра́ть] *colloq.* **1,** *v.i.* to lie. **2,** *v.t.* to make up; add (fictional details).

приви́ть [*infl. like* вить] *v., pfv. of* привива́ть. —**приви́ться,** *refl.* [*past* -ви́лся, -ла́сь, -ло́сь] *pfv. of* привива́ться.

при́вкус *n.* **1,** aftertaste. **2,** taste; flavor. **3,** *fig.* touch; trace; tinge.

привлека́тельный *adj.* attractive. —**привлека́тельность,** *n.f.* attractiveness.

привлека́ть *v. impfv.* [*pfv.* привле́чь] **1,** to attract. **2,** to bring in; call in. **3,** to win over: привлека́ть на свою́ сто́рону, to win over to one's side. —**привлека́ть к**

суду́, to arraign; bring to trial. —**привлека́ть к отве́ту** *or* **к отве́тственности,** to bring to account *or* justice.

привлече́ние *n.* **1,** attracting. **2,** bringing in; calling in. —**привлече́ние к отве́тственности,** bringing to account. —**привлече́ние к суду́,** arraignment.

привле́чь [*infl. like* влечь] *v., pfv. of* привлека́ть.

приво́д *n.* **1,** (forcible) arrest. **2,** *mech.* drive.

приводи́ть *v. impfv.* [*pfv.* привести́; *pres.* -вожу́, -во́дишь] **1,** to bring (on foot). **2,** (of a road, tracks, etc.) to lead (somewhere). **3,** (*with* к) to lead (to a certain result). **4,** (*with* в + *acc.*) to bring to a certain state or condition: приводи́ть в поря́док, to put in order; приводи́ть в движе́ние, to set in motion; приводи́ть в смяте́ние, to throw into confusion. **5,** to cite; adduce. —**приводи́ть в де́йствие,** to start (*e.g.* a machine) going. —**приводи́ть в исполне́ние,** to carry out. —**приводи́ть в себя́** (*or* в чу́вство), **1,** to revive; resuscitate; bring around. **2,** to bring back to reality (a person lost in thought). —**приводи́ть к о́бщему знамена́телю,** to reduce to a common denominator.

приводи́ться *v.r. impfv.* [*pfv.* привести́сь; *pres.* -во́дится] *impers.* (*with dat. & inf.*) *colloq.* to happen to; have occasion to: мне не привело́сь быть там, I have not had occasion to be there.

приводне́ние *n.* landing on water; splashdown.

приводни́ться *v.r., pfv. of* приводня́ться.

приводно́й *adj., mech.* drive (*attrib.*); transmission (*attrib.*): приводно́й вал, drive shaft; приводно́й реме́нь, transmission belt.

приводня́ться *v.r. impfv.* [*pfv.* приводни́ться] to land on water.

приво́з *n.* **1,** bringing in; delivery. **2,** *colloq.* a shipment.

привози́ть *v. impfv.* [*pfv.* привезти́; *pres.* -вожу́, -во́зишь] to bring (by vehicle).

привозно́й *adj.* imported. *Also,* приво́зный.

приво́лье *n.* **1,** wide open spaces. **2,** freedom to move about.

приво́льный *adj.* **1,** open; spacious. **2,** free.

привора́живать *v. impfv.* [*pfv.* приворожи́ть] to bewitch; charm.

привра́тник *n.* gatekeeper; doorkeeper.

привра́ть [*infl. like* врать] *v., pfv. of* привира́ть.

привска́кивать *v. impfv.* [*pfv.* привскочи́ть] to jump up.

привскочи́ть [*infl.* -вскочу́, -вско́чишь] *v., pfv. of* привска́кивать.

привстава́ть *v. impfv.* [*pfv.* привста́ть; *pres.* -стаю́, -стаёшь] to rise (halfway).

привста́ть [*infl.* -вста́ну, -вста́нешь] *v., pfv. of* привстава́ть.

привыка́ть *v. impfv.* [*pfv.* привы́кнуть] (*with* к *or inf.*) **1,** to be *or* get used to; grow accustomed to. **2,** to be *or* get into the habit of.

привы́кнуть [*past* -вы́к, -ла] *v., pfv. of* привыка́ть.

привы́чка [*gen. pl.* -чек] *n.* habit. Это вошло́ у меня́ в привы́чку, it has become a habit with me. Не в мои́х привы́чках по́здно ложи́ться, I don't usually go to bed late.

привы́чный *adj.* **1,** habitual; usual; customary. **2,** (*with* к) *colloq.* used to; accustomed (to). **3,** *colloq.* (of a person) of set habits; (of an eye, hands, etc.) practiced.

привя́занность *n.f.* (*with* к) (emotional) attachment (to). —**привя́занный,** *adj.* attached.

привяза́ть [*infl.* -вяжу́, -вя́жешь] *v., pfv. of* привя́зывать. —**привяза́ться,** *refl., pfv. of* привя́зываться.

привязно́й *adj.* fastened; secured. —**привязно́й ре-ме́нь,** seat belt.

привя́зчивый *adj., colloq.* **1,** easily forming attachments. **2,** annoying; bothersome.

привя́зывать *v. impfv.* [*pfv.* **привяза́ть**] **1,** (*with* к) to tie (to); bind (to); attach (to). **2,** (*with* к себе́) to win over. —**привя́зываться,** *refl.* (*with* к) **1,** to become attached (to). **2,** to attach oneself (to). **3,** *colloq.* to pester.

при́вязь *n.f.* **1,** leash. **2,** tether.

пригвожда́ть *v. impfv.* [*pfv.* **пригвозди́ть**] (*with* к) **1,** to nail (to). **2,** *fig.* to nail (to); rivet (to); chain (to): пригвождённый к ме́сту, nailed/riveted to the spot.

пригиба́ть *v. impfv.* [*pfv.* **пригну́ть**] to bend; bend down (a tree, branch, etc.). —**пригиба́ться,** *refl.* to bend down.

пригла́живать *v. impfv.* [*pfv.* **пригла́дить**] **1,** to smooth. **2,** to slick down (one's hair).

пригласи́тельный *adj.* conveying an invitation. —**пригласи́тельный биле́т,** ticket of admission (*to invited guests only*).

пригласи́ть [*infl.* -шу́, -си́шь] *v., pfv. of* **приглаша́ть.**

приглаша́ть *v. impfv.* [*pfv.* **пригласи́ть**] to invite.

приглаше́ние *n.* invitation.

приглашённый *adj.* invited. —*n.* person invited; invited guest. —**приглашённый дирижёр,** guest conductor.

приглуша́ть *v. impfv.* [*pfv.* **приглуши́ть**] to muffle; deaden; absorb (sound).

пригляде́ть [*infl.* -жу́, -ди́шь] *v., pfv. of* **пригля́дывать.** —**пригляде́ться,** *refl., pfv. of* **пригля́дываться.**

пригля́дывать *v. impfv.* [*pfv.* **пригляде́ть**] *colloq.* **1,** (*with* за + *instr.*) to look after; keep an eye on. **2,** to pick out. —**пригля́дываться,** *refl., colloq.* **1,** (*with* к) to stare (at); scrutinize. **2,** (*with* к) to get used to. **3,** (*with dat.*) to pall (on); become boring (to).

пригляну́ться *v.r. pfv.* [*infl.* -гляну́сь, -гля́нешься] (*with dat.*) *colloq.* to catch the fancy of.

пригна́ть [*infl. like* гнать] *v., pfv. of* **пригоня́ть.**

пригну́ть *v., pfv. of* **пригиба́ть.** —**пригну́ться,** *refl., pfv. of* **пригиба́ться.**

пригова́ривать *v. impfv.* [*pfv.* **приговори́ть**] **1,** (*with* к) to sentence (to); condemn (to). **2,** [*impfv. only*] *colloq.* to repeat; keep saying.

пригово́р *n.* **1,** verdict. **2,** sentence.

приговори́ть *v., pfv. of* **пригова́ривать.**

пригоди́ться *v.r. pfv.* [*infl.* -жу́сь, -ди́шься] (*with dat.*) to come in handy; be useful (to); stand in good stead.

приго́дный *adj.* (*with* к *or* для) fit (for); suitable (for). —**приго́дность,** *n.f.* fitness; suitability.

пригоня́ть *v. impfv.* [*pfv.* **пригна́ть**] **1,** to drive home; bring in (cattle). **2,** to fit; adjust.

пригора́ть *v. impfv.* [*pfv.* **пригоре́ть**] to be slightly burnt.

пригоре́лый *adj.* burnt.

пригоре́ть *v., pfv. of* **пригора́ть.**

при́город *n.* suburb. —**при́городный,** *adj.* suburban.

приго́рок [*gen.* -рка] *n.* hillock; knoll.

при́горшня *also,* **приго́ршня** [*gen. pl.* -шней] *n.* handful.

приготови́тельный *adj.* preparatory.

приготови́ть [*infl.* -влю, -вишь] *v., pfv. of* **гото́вить** *and* **приготовля́ть.** —**приготови́ться,** *refl., pfv. of* **гото́виться** *and* **приготовля́ться.**

приготовле́ние *n.* **1,** preparation. **2,** *pl.* preparations.

приготовля́ть *v. impfv.* [*pfv.* **пригото́вить**] **1,** to prepare. **2,** to cook. —**приготовля́ться,** *refl.* (*with* к) to prepare (for); get ready (for).

пригрева́ть *v. impfv.* [*pfv.* **пригре́ть**] **1,** to warm. **2,** *fig., colloq.* to give shelter to.

пригре́зиться *v.r., pfv. of* **гре́зиться.**

пригре́ть *v., pfv. of* **пригрева́ть.**

пригрози́ть *v. pfv.* [*infl.* -жу́, -зи́шь] (*with dat.*) to threaten.

пригу́бить *v. pfv.* [*infl.* -блю, -бишь] to take a sip of; taste.

придава́ть *v. impfv.* [*pfv.* **прида́ть**; *pres.* -даю́, -даёшь] **1,** to give; impart. **2,** to attach (significance, importance, etc.). **3,** *mil.* to assign; attach (to a certain unit).

придави́ть [*infl.* -давлю́, -да́вишь] *v., pfv. of* **прида́вливать.**

прида́вливать *v. impfv.* [*pfv.* **придави́ть**] **1,** to press down upon; weigh down. **2,** (*with* к) to press (something) against (something).

прида́ние *n.* **1,** giving; imparting. **2,** *mil.* assigning; attaching.

прида́ное *n., decl. as an adj.* **1,** dowry. **2,** trousseau. **3,** layette.

прида́ток [*gen.* -тка] *n.* appendage; adjunct.

прида́точный *adj.,* in **прида́точное предложе́ние,** dependent clause; subordinate clause.

прида́ть [*infl. like* дать; *past* при́дал, придала́, при́дало] *v., pfv. of* **придава́ть.**

прида́ча *n.* **1,** giving; imparting. **2,** *mil.* assigning; attaching. **3,** addition. —**в прида́чу,** besides; in addition; to boot; into the bargain.

придвига́ть *v. impfv.* [*pfv.* **придви́нуть**] (*with* к) to move (something) toward; move (something) closer to. —**придвига́ться,** *refl.* (*with* к) to move closer (to).

придво́рный *adj.* court (*attrib.*). —*n.* courtier.

приде́лывать *v. impfv.* [*pfv.* **приде́лать**] (*with* к) to attach (to); fasten (to).

придержа́ть [*infl.* -держу́, -де́ржишь] *v., pfv. of* **приде́рживать.**

приде́рживать *v. impfv.* [*pfv.* **придержа́ть**] **1,** to hold; hold still; hold in place. **2,** *colloq.* to hold back; withhold. **3,** *in* придержа́ть язы́к, to hold one's tongue. —**приде́рживаться,** *refl.* [*impfv. only*] **1,** (*with* за + *acc.*) to hold onto. **2,** (*with gen.*) to keep to; stick to: приде́рживаться пра́вой стороны́, to keep/stick to the right. **3,** *fig.* (*with gen.*) to stick to; adhere to (a subject, opinion, agreement, etc.).

приди́ра *n.m. & f., colloq.* faultfinder; quibbler.

придира́ться *v.r., impfv.* [*pfv.* **придра́ться**] (*with* к) to find fault (with); carp (at); pick on.

приди́рка [*gen. pl.* -рок] *n.* cavil; quibble.

приди́рчивый *adj.* captious; carping; hypercritical.

придоро́жный *adj.* roadside; wayside.

придра́ться [*infl. like* драть] *v.r., pfv. of* **придира́ться.**

приду́мывать *v. impfv.* [*pfv.* **приду́мать**] to think of; think up; devise.

придуркова́тый *adj., colloq.* dumb; stupid.

при́дурь *n.f., colloq.,* in с при́дурью, slightly touched in the head.

придуши́ть *v. pfv.* [*infl.* -душу́, -ду́шишь] *colloq.* to strangle; choke.

придыха́ние *n., phonet.* aspiration. —**придыха́-
тельный,** *adj.* aspirate.

приеда́ться *v.r. impfv.* [*pfv.* **прие́сться**] (*with dat.*)
colloq. to pall (on); become boring (to).

прие́зд *n.* arrival. —**с прие́здом!**, welcome!

приезжа́ть *v. impfv.* [*pfv.* **прие́хать**] to come (*by
vehicle*); arrive.

прие́зжий *adj.* **1**, newly arrived. **2**, visiting; touring.
—*n.* newcomer.

прие́м *n.* **1**, receiving. **2**, admission. **3**, reception; welcome. **4**, reception (*social gathering*). **5**, dose. **6**, method; technique. **7**, trick; ploy. **8**, *radio; television* reception. —**в оди́н прие́м, 1**, in one gulp. **2**, in one
sitting.

прие́млемый *adj.* acceptable.

прие́мная *n., decl. as an adj.* waiting room.

прие́мник *n.* (radio) receiver.

прие́мный *adj.* **1**, receiving (*attrib.*); reception (*attrib.*).
Прие́мные часы́, office hours. **2**, admission (*attrib.*).
Прие́мная коми́ссия, selection committee. **3**, (*of a
parent*) foster; adoptive; (*of a child*) adopted.

прие́мыш *n., colloq.* adopted child.

прие́сться [*infl. like* **есть**] *v.r., pfv. of* **приеда́ться.**

прие́хать [*infl.* **-е́ду, -е́дешь**] *v., pfv. of* **приезжа́ть.**

прижа́ть [*infl.* **-жму́, -жмёшь**] *v., pfv. of* **прижима́ть.**
—**прижа́ться,** *refl., pfv. of* **прижима́ться.**

прижече́ь [*infl. like* **жечь**] *v., pfv. of* **прижига́ть.**

прижива́льщик *n.m.* [*fem.* **-ва́лка**] sponger; hanger-
on.

прижива́ться *v.r. impfv.* [*pfv.* **прижи́ться**] to become acclimated.

прижига́ние *n.* cauterization.

прижига́ть *v. impfv.* [*pfv.* **прижече́ь**] to cauterize.

прижи́зненный *adj.* occurring in one's lifetime; occurring before one's death.

прижима́ть *v. impfv.* [*pfv.* **прижа́ть**] **1**, (*with* **к**) to
press (to *or* against). **2**, (*with* **к**) to pin (to): прижима́ть
к земле́, to pin to the ground; pin down. Прижима́ть
к стене́, to pin/drive against the wall; *fig.* drive into a
corner. **3**, *fig., colloq.* to put pressure on. —**прижи-
ма́ться,** *refl.* (*with* **к**) to snuggle up to; cuddle up to;
nestle close to.

прижи́мистый *adj., colloq.* tight-fisted.

прижи́ть [*infl. like* **жить**; *past* **-жи́лся, -ла́сь,
-ло́сь**] *v.r., pfv. of* **прижива́ться.**

приз [*pl.* **призы́**] *n.* prize.

призаду́мываться *v.r. impfv.* [*pfv.* **призаду́мать-
ся**] to become thoughtful; become pensive.

призанима́ть *v. impfv.* [*pfv.* **призаня́ть**] *colloq.* to
borrow.

призаня́ть [*infl. like* **заня́ть**] *v., pfv. of* **призанима́ть.**

призва́ние *n.* vocation; calling.

призва́ть [*infl. like* **звать**] *v., pfv. of* **призыва́ть.**

призе́мистый *adj.* stocky; thickset; heavyset; squat.

приземле́ние *n.* landing.

приземля́ть *v. impfv.* [*pfv.* **приземли́ть**] to land (a
plane). —**приземля́ться,** *refl.* to land; touch down.

призёр *n.* prizewinner.

при́зма *n.* prism. —**призмати́ческий,** *adj.* prismatic.

признава́ть *v. impfv.* [*pfv.* **призна́ть**; *pres.* **-зна́ю,
-зна́ешь**] **1**, to recognize. **2**, to admit; acknowledge.
3, to declare; pronounce; find: его́ призна́ли душе́в-
нобольны́м, he was declared insane. —**признава́ть-
ся,** *refl.* **1**, to confess (that). **2**, (*with* **в** + *prepl.*) to
confess (to): признава́ться в преступле́нии, to

confess to a crime. **3**, *in* призна́ться в любви́, to make
a declaration of love.

при́знак *n.* sign; indication; symptom.

призна́ние *n.* **1**, confession; admission; acknowledgment. **2**, recognition: получи́ть призна́ние, to receive
recognition. **3**, *in* призна́ние в любви́, declaration of
love.

при́знанный *adj.* recognized; acknowledged.

призна́тельный *adj.* grateful; appreciative. —**при-
зна́тельность,** *n.f.* gratitude; appreciation.

призна́ть [*infl.* **-зна́ю, -зна́ешь**] *v., pfv. of* **призна-
ва́ть.** —**призна́ться,** *refl., pfv. of* **признава́ться.**

призово́й *adj.* prize (*attrib.*).

при́зрак *n.* specter; ghost; apparition.

при́зрачный *adj.* **1**, ghostly; eerie. **2**, unreal; illusory.

призы́в *n.* **1**, appeal; call. **2**, slogan. **3**, *mil.* call-up.

призыва́ть *v. impfv.* [*pfv.* **призва́ть**] **1**, (*with inf.*) to
call upon (to); urge (to). **2**, (*with* **на** + *acc. or* **к**) to
call (for); appeal (for). **3**, *mil.* to call up; draft. **4**, *past
passive part. only*, A, to destine: он при́зван быть вра-
чо́м, he is destined to be a doctor. B, to intend: рабо́та
при́звана воспи́тывать люде́й, the work is intended
to teach people. —**призыва́ть к отве́ту,** to call to
account.

призывни́к [*gen.* **-ника́**] *n.* draftee; inductee; conscript.

призывно́й *adj.* of or pert. to the military draft: при-
зывно́й во́зраст, draft age; призывна́я коми́ссия,
selective service commission; призывно́й пункт, draft
board; induction center.

при́иск *n., often pl.* mine: алма́зные при́иски, diamond mines.

прийти́ [*infl.* **приду́, придёшь**; *past* **пришёл, при-
шла́, пришло́**] *v., pfv. of* **приходи́ть.** —**прийти́сь,**
refl., pfv. of **приходи́ться.**

прика́з *n.* order; command. —**по прика́зу** (+ *gen.*),
by order of.

приказа́ние *n.* order; command.

приказа́ть [*infl.* **-кажу́, -ка́жешь**] *v., pfv. of* **прика́-
зывать.**

прика́зчик *n., obs.* **1**, salesman; clerk. **2**, steward (*on
a large estate*).

прика́зывать *v. impfv.* [*pfv.* **приказа́ть**] (*with dat.*) to
order; command. —**приказа́ть до́лго жить,** *colloq.*
to die; depart this world.

прика́лывать *v. impfv.* [*pfv.* **приколо́ть**] **1**, (*with* **к**)
to pin (to). **2**, *colloq.* to stab to death.

прика́нчивать *v. impfv.* [*pfv.* **прико́нчить**] *colloq.* **1**,
to terminate; wind up. **2**, to finish off (a quantity of food
or drink). **3**, to kill; finish off.

прикарма́нивать *v. impfv.* [*pfv.* **прикарма́нить**] *colloq.* to pocket.

прикаса́ться *v.r. impfv.* [*pfv.* **прикосну́ться**] (*with* **к**)
to touch.

прикати́ть [*infl.* **-качу́, -ка́тишь**] *v., pfv. of* **прика́-
тывать.** —**прикати́ться,** *refl., pfv. of* **прика́тываться.**

прика́тывать *v. impfv.* [*pfv.* **прикати́ть**] **1**, *v.t.* to roll
(something somewhere). **2**, *v.i., colloq.* to come rolling
up; arrive. —**прика́тываться,** *refl.* (*with* **к**) to roll up to.

прики́дывать *v. impfv.* [*pfv.* **прики́нуть**] *colloq.* **1**, to
add; throw in; toss in. **2**, to estimate; reckon. **3**, to try
on. —**прики́дываться,** *refl.* (*with instr.*) *colloq.* to pretend (to be).

прикла́д *n.* **1**, rifle butt. **2**, *sewing* findings.

прикладно́й *adj.* applied: прикладны́е нау́ки, applied sciences.

прикла́дывать *v. impfv.* [*pfv.* приложи́ть] (*with* к) **1,** to put (against); place (against). **2,** to apply (to); affix (to). **3,** *in* приложи́ть ру́ку к, to have a hand in; put one's hand to. **4,** *in* ума́ не приложу́, I have no idea; I can't imagine; I am at a loss. —**прикла́дываться,** *refl.* **1,** (*with instr. and* к) to put (one's eye, ear, etc.) to. **2,** (*with* к) to kiss reverently. **3,** to take aim.

прикле́ивать *v. impfv.* [*pfv.* прикле́ить] (*with* к) to glue (to); paste (to). —**прикле́иваться,** *refl.* (*with* к) to stick (to).

приклёпывать *v. impfv.* [*pfv.* приклепа́ть] to rivet.

приклони́ть *v. pfv.* [*infl.* -клоню́, -кло́нишь] to lay (one's head): ему́ не́где го́лову приклони́ть, he has nowhere to lay his head.

приключа́ться *v.r. impfv.* [*pfv.* приключи́ться] *colloq.* to happen; occur.

приключе́ние *n.* **1,** adventure. **2,** incident. —**приключе́нческий,** *adj.* adventure (*attrib.*).

приключи́ться *v.r., pfv. of* приключа́ться.

прикова́ть [*infl.* -кую́, -куёшь] *v., pfv. of* прико́вывать.

прико́вывать *v. impfv.* [*pfv.* прикова́ть] **1,** (*with* к) to chain (to). **2,** (*with* к) *fig.* to tie down; nail; rivet (to a place): прикова́ть к ме́сту, to rivet to the spot. **3,** *fig.* to fix (one's gaze); rivet (one's attention). —**прико́ванный к посте́ли,** bedridden.

прико́л *n., naut., in* на прико́ле, **1,** tied up; moored. **2,** idle; laid up.

прикола́чивать *v. impfv.* [*pfv.* приколоти́ть] to nail down; fasten with nails.

приколоти́ть [*infl.* -лочу́, -ло́тишь] *v., pfv. of* прикола́чивать.

приколо́ть [*infl.* -колю́, -ко́лешь] *v., pfv. of* прика́лывать.

прикомандирова́ть *v. pfv.* [*infl.* -ру́ю, -ру́ешь] (*with* к) to assign (to).

прико́нчить *v., pfv. of* прика́нчивать.

прикорну́ть *v. pfv., colloq.* to curl up; settle down (*for a nap*).

прикоснове́ние *n.* **1,** touch. **2,** *fig.* involvement.

прикосну́ться *v.r., pfv. of* прикаса́ться.

прикра́сить [*infl.* -шу, -сишь] *v., pfv. of* прикра́шивать.

прикра́сы *n. pl.* [*sing.* прикра́са] *colloq.* embellishments (*in telling or describing something*): без прикра́с, without embellishment.

прикра́шивать *v. impfv.* [*pfv.* прикра́сить] to embellish; embroider; exaggerate.

прикрепи́ть [*infl.* -плю́, -пи́шь] *v., pfv. of* прикрепля́ть. —**прикрепи́ться,** *refl., pfv. of* прикрепля́ться.

прикрепле́ние *n.* **1,** fastening; attaching. **2,** assigning. **3,** registration.

прикрепля́ть *v. impfv.* [*pfv.* прикрепи́ть] (*with* к) **1,** to fasten (to); attach (to). **2,** to assign (to); attach (to). —**прикрепля́ться,** *refl.* (*with* к) **1,** to fasten (onto). **2,** to register (at).

прикри́кивать *v. impfv.* [*pfv.* прикри́кнуть] (*with* на + *acc.*) to shout (at).

прикрыва́ть *v. impfv.* [*pfv.* прикры́ть] **1,** to close (*but not tightly*). **2,** to cover (*but not completely*). **3,** to cover up; conceal. **4,** to shield; protect. **5,** *colloq.* to close down; liquidate. —**прикрыва́ться,** *refl.* **1,** (*with instr.*) to cover *or* shield oneself (with). **2,** (*of a door,*

window, *etc.*) to close. **3,** *fig.* (*with instr.*) to cover up one's actions (by); take refuge (in).

прикры́тие *n.* **1,** concealment. **2,** protection. **3,** cover; shelter. **4,** *mil.* cover.

прикры́ть [*infl.* -кро́ю, -кро́ешь] *v., pfv. of* прикрыва́ть. —**прикры́ться,** *refl., pfv. of* прикрыва́ться.

прикупа́ть *v. impfv.* [*pfv.* прикупи́ть] to buy some more of.

прикупи́ть [*infl.* -куплю́, -ку́пишь] *v., pfv. of* прикупа́ть.

прику́ривать *v. impfv.* [*pfv.* прикури́ть] **1,** to light up; light a cigarette. **2,** to get a light from another cigarette.

прикури́ть [*infl.* -курю́, -ку́ришь] *v., pfv. of* прику́ривать.

прику́с *n., dent.* bite.

прикуси́ть [*infl.* -кушу́, -ку́сишь] *v., pfv. of* прику́сывать.

прику́сывать *v. impfv.* [*pfv.* прикуси́ть] to bite (one's tongue, lip, etc.).

прила́вок [*gen.* -вка] *n.* counter.

прилага́тельный *adj., in* и́мя прилага́тельное, adjective. —**прилага́тельное,** *n., decl. as an adj.* adjective.

прилага́ть *v. impfv.* [*pfv.* приложи́ть] **1,** (*with* к) to attach (to); append (to); enclose (in). **2,** to apply; exert: прилага́ть все уси́лия, to make every effort.

прила́живать *v. impfv.* [*pfv.* прила́дить] to fit; adjust.

приласка́ть *v. pfv.* **1,** to caress; pet. **2,** to be nice to. —**приласка́ться,** *refl.* (*with* к) **1,** to snuggle up to. **2,** to make up to.

прилега́ть *v. impfv.* (*with* к) **1,** to adjoin; lie adjacent (to). **2,** (*of clothes*) to fit; fit snugly.

прилега́ющий *adj.* adjoining; adjacent; contiguous.

прилежа́ние *n.* diligence.

приле́жный *adj.* diligent. —**приле́жно,** *adv.* diligently. —**приле́жность,** *n.f.* diligence.

прилепи́ть [*infl.* -леплю́, -ле́пишь] *v., pfv. of* прилепля́ть. —**прилепи́ться,** *refl., pfv. of* прилепля́ться.

прилепля́ть *v. impfv.* [*pfv.* прилепи́ть] (*with* к) to stick (to); affix (to). —**прилепля́ться,** *refl.* (*with* к) to stick (to).

прилёт *n.* arrival (*of air passengers or birds*).

прилета́ть *v. impfv.* [*pfv.* прилете́ть] **1,** to come flying in; arrive by plane. **2,** (*of a plane*) to arrive.

прилете́ть [*infl.* -чу́, -ти́шь] *v., pfv. of* прилета́ть.

приле́чь *v. pfv.* [*infl. like* лечь] to lie down for a while.

прили́в *n.* **1,** rising tide. **2,** rush (*of blood*). **3,** *fig.* influx. **4,** *fig.* wave; surge; burst. —**прили́в и отли́в,** ebb and flow of the tides. —**прили́вы и отли́вы,** tide; tides.

прилива́ть *v. impfv.* [*pfv.* прили́ть] **1,** to flow. **2,** (*of blood*) to rush.

прили́вный *adj.* tidal.

прили́занный *adj., colloq.* sleek.

прилипа́ние *n.* adhesion.

прилипа́ть *v. impfv.* [*pfv.* прили́пнуть] (*with* к) to stick (to); adhere (to).

прили́пнуть [*past* -ли́п, -ла] *v., pfv. of* прилипа́ть.

прили́пчивый *adj.* **1,** sticky. **2,** *fig., colloq.* catching; contagious. **3,** *fig., colloq.* bothersome; pesky.

прили́ть [*infl. like* лить] *v., pfv. of* прилива́ть.

прили́чие *n.* **1,** propriety; decency; decorum. **2,** *pl.* the proprieties; rules of propriety.

прили́чно *adv.* **1,** decently; properly. **2,** *colloq.* quite well.

прили́чный *adj.* **1,** decent; proper. **2,** *colloq.* decent; passable.

приложе́ние *n.* **1,** application. **2,** enclosure. **3,** supplement; appendix. **4,** *gram.* apposition.

приложи́ть [*infl.* -ложу́, -ло́жишь] *v., pfv. of* прилага́ть *and* прикла́дывать. —**приложи́ться,** *refl., pfv. of* прикла́дываться.

прилуне́ние *n.* moon landing.

прилуни́ться *v.r. pfv. of* луни́ться.

прильну́ть *v., pfv. of* льну́ть.

примадо́нна *n.* prima donna.

прима́нивать *v. impfv.* [*pfv.* примани́ть] to entice; lure; decoy.

примани́ть [*infl.* -маню́, -ма́нишь] *v., pfv. of* прима́нивать.

прима́нка *n.* **1,** bait; lure. **2,** *fig.* lure; attraction.

прима́с *n., eccles.* primate.

прима́т *n.* **1,** primacy. **2,** *pl., zool.* primates.

примелька́ться *v.r. pfv.* (*with dat.*) to become (overly) familiar to: го́род мне примелька́лся, I have seen (more than) enough of the city.

примене́ние *n.* application; use; employment. —**в примене́нии к,** as applied to.

примени́мый *adj.* applicable. —**примени́мость,** *n.f.* applicability.

примени́тельно *adv.* (*with* к) as it applies to; with reference to.

примени́ть [*infl.* -меню́, -ме́нишь] *v., pfv. of* применя́ть. —**примени́ться,** *refl., pfv. of* применя́ться.

применя́ть *v. impfv.* [*pfv.* примени́ть] to apply; employ; use. —**применя́ться,** *refl.* **1,** to be used. **2,** (*with* к) to adjust (to).

приме́р *n.* example. —**для приме́ра,** as an example. —**к приме́ру,** for example. —**не в приме́р,** **1,** (*with dat.*) unlike; as distinct from. **2,** (*with comp. adjectives*) much more; far more. —**по приме́ру** (+ *gen.*), after/following the example of.

примерза́ть *v. impfv.* [*pfv.* примёрзнуть] (*with* к) to freeze (to).

примёрзнуть [*past* -мёрз, -ла] *v., pfv. of* примерза́ть.

приме́рить *v., pfv. of* примеря́ть.

приме́рка *n.* **1,** trying on. **2,** fitting: сде́лать приме́рку, to have a fitting.

приме́рно *adv.* **1,** in an exemplary manner. **2,** approximately. **3,** *colloq.* for example.

приме́рный *adj.* **1,** exemplary; model. **2,** approximate.

приме́рочная *n., decl. as an adj.* dressing room (*for trying on clothes*).

примеря́ть *v. impfv.* [*pfv.* приме́рить] to try on.

при́месь *n.f.* **1,** admixture. **2,** *fig., colloq.* touch; dash; trace.

приме́та *n.* **1,** mark; sign. **2,** omen. —**брать на приме́ту,** to take note of. —**име́ть на приме́те,** to have an eye on.

примета́ть *v., pfv. of* приметывать.

приме́тить [*infl.* -чу, -тишь] *v., pfv. of* примеча́ть.

приме́тливый *adj., colloq.* observant.

приме́тный *adj.* **1,** noticeable; perceptible. **2,** conspicuous.

примётывать *v. impfv.* [*pfv.* примета́ть] to stitch; baste.

примеча́ние *n.* note; footnote; explanatory note.

примеча́тельный *adj.* noteworthy; notable.

примеча́ть *v. impfv.* [*pfv.* приме́тить] *colloq.* **1,** to notice. **2,** to note; take note of; make a mental note of.

приме́шивать *v. impfv.* [*pfv.* примеша́ть] to add (something to something) by mixing.

примина́ть *v. impfv.* [*pfv.* примя́ть] to crush; flatten; trample down.

примире́ние *n.* reconciliation.

примири́тель *n.m.* conciliator. —**примири́тельный,** *adj.* conciliatory.

примири́ть *v., pfv. of* мири́ть *and* примиря́ть. —**примири́ться,** *refl., pfv. of* мири́ться *and* примиря́ться.

примиря́ть *v. impfv.* [*pfv.* примири́ть] to reconcile. —**примиря́ться,** *refl.* **1,** to become reconciled (*after a quarrel*). **2,** (*with* с + *instr.*) to become reconciled (to); reconcile oneself (to).

примити́вный *adj.* primitive.

примкну́ть *v., pfv. of* примыка́ть. —**при́мкнутые штыки́,** fixed bayonets.

примо́лкнуть *v. pfv.* [*past* -мо́лк, -ла] *colloq.* to fall silent.

примо́рский *adj.* **1,** seaside (*attrib.*). **2,** maritime.

примо́рье *n.* area near the seashore.

примости́ться *v.r. pfv.* [*infl.* -щу́сь, -сти́шься] *colloq.* to settle down; perch (*in an uncomfortable place*).

примо́чка [*gen. pl.* -чек] *n.* wash: примо́чка для глаз, eyewash.

при́мула *n.* primrose.

при́мус *n.* small kerosene stove.

примча́ться *v.r. pfv.* [*infl.* -мчу́сь, -мчи́шься] to arrive on the run; come tearing along.

примыка́ть *v. impfv.* [*pfv.* примкну́ть] (*with* к) **1,** to join; side with. **2,** [*impfv. only*] to adjoin; abut. —**примыка́ть/примкну́ть штыки́,** to fix bayonets.

примя́ть [*infl.* -мну́, -мнёшь] *v., pfv. of* примина́ть.

принадлежа́ть *v. impfv.* [*pres.* -лежу́, -лежи́шь] **1,** (*with dat.*) to belong to. **2,** (*with* к) to belong to; be a member of. —**принадлежа́ть к числу́** (+ *gen.*), to be among; number among.

принадле́жность *n.f.* **1,** *pl.* accessories; articles; gear. **2,** (*with* к) belonging (to); affiliation (with). **3,** characteristic; attribute.

принале́чь *v. pfv.* [*infl. like* лечь] (*with* на + *acc.*) *colloq.* **1,** to lean (on). **2,** *fig.* to apply oneself (to).

принаряжа́ть *v. impfv.* [*pfv.* принаряди́ть] *colloq.* to dress up; deck out. —**принаряжа́ться,** *refl., colloq.* to get dressed up.

принево́ливать *v. impfv.* [*pfv.* принево́лить] *colloq.* to force; make; compel.

принесе́ние *n.* **1,** bringing. **2,** *in* принесе́ние прися́ги, taking of the oath. **3,** *in* принесе́ние поздравле́ний, offering of congratulations.

принести́ [*infl. like* нести́] *v., pfv. of* приноси́ть.

принижа́ть *v. impfv.* [*pfv.* прини́зить] **1,** to humiliate; humble. **2,** to disparage; belittle.

приниже́ние *n.* **1,** humiliation. **2,** disparagement.

прини́женный *adj.* **1,** humble. **2,** humiliating.

прини́зить [*infl.* -жу, -зишь] *v., pfv. of* принижа́ть.

приника́ть *v. impfv.* [*pfv.* прини́кнуть] (*with* к) to press against; nestle close to. Прини́кнуть губа́ми к (чему́-нибудь), to press one's lips against.

прини́кнуть [*past* -ник, -ла] *v., pfv. of* приника́ть.

принима́ть *v. impfv.* [*pfv.* приня́ть] **1,** to accept. **2,** to receive (a person *or* persons). **3,** to admit; allow to enter. **4,** to take (food, medicine, measures, a bath, etc.). **5,** to assume; take on. **6,** to take over. **7,** to adopt (a resolution, amendment, etc.); pass (a law). **8,** to adopt (a religion, citizenship, etc.). **9,** [*impfv. only*] to receive; pick up (a signal). **10,** (*with* за + *acc.*) to take for; mistake for. **11,** [*impfv. only*] to deliver (a baby). —**принима́ть во внима́ние** *or* **в расчёт** *or* **к све́дению,** to take account of; take into account; take into consideration. —**принима́ть (бли́зко) к се́рдцу,** to take to heart. —**принима́ть на ве́ру,** to take on faith. —**принима́ть на свой счёт,** to take personally. —**принима́ть реше́ние,** to make a decision. —**принима́ть сто́рону** (+ *gen.*), to take someone's side. —**принима́ть уча́стие** (*with* в + *prepl.*), to take part (in); participate (in).

принима́ться *v.r. impfv.* [*pfv.* **приня́ться**] **1,** (*with inf. or* за + *acc.*) to begin; set about. **2,** (*of a plant*) to take root; (*of a vaccine*) to take.

принора́вливать *v. impfv.* [*pfv.* **приноро́вить**] (*with* к) *colloq.* **1,** to adapt (to). **2,** to time to coincide with. —**принора́вливаться,** *refl.* (*with* к) *colloq.* **1,** to adjust (to). **2,** to get the knack of.

приноси́ть *v. impfv.* [*pfv.* **принести́;** *pres.* -ношу́, -но́сишь] **1,** to bring. **2,** to yield; bear. **3,** to offer (an apology, one's thanks, etc.). —**приноси́ть (что́-нибудь) в же́ртву,** to sacrifice. —**приноси́ть же́ртву,** to make a sacrifice. —**приноси́ть по́льзу,** to be of use; be of benefit. —**приноси́ть прися́гу,** to take the oath.

приноше́ние *n.* offering; gift.

принуди́тельный *adj.* **1,** (*of labor*) forced. **2,** (*of measures*) coercive.

прину́дить [*infl.* -жу, -дишь] *v.*, *pfv. of* **принужда́ть.**

принужда́ть *v. impfv.* [*pfv.* **прину́дить**] to force; compel.

принужде́ние *n.* compulsion; coercion; duress: по принужде́нию, under duress.

принуждённый *adj.* forced; constrained; unnatural. —**принуждённость,** *n.f.* constraint.; stiffness; lack of spontaneity.

принц *n.* prince. —**принце́сса,** *n.* princess.

при́нцип *n.* principle. —**в при́нципе,** in principle. —**из при́нципа,** on principle.

принципиа́льно *adv.* **1,** in principle. **2,** fundamentally.

принципиа́льность *n.f.* adherence to principle.

принципиа́льный *adj.* **1,** of principle: принципиа́льный челове́к, man of principle. **2,** fundamental: име́ть принципиа́льное значе́ние, to-be of fundamental importance.

приню́хиваться *v.r. impfv.* [*pfv.* **приню́хаться**] (*with* к) *colloq.* **1,** to sniff. **2,** to get used to the smell of.

приня́тие *n.* **1,** acceptance. **2,** receiving. **3,** admission; admittance. **4,** taking (*of food, medicine, measures, an oath, etc.*). **5,** assumption; taking on. **6,** making (*a decision*).

при́нятый *past passive part. of* **приня́ть,** accepted. Это не при́нято, that is (just) not done. У нас не при́нято (+ *inf.*), it is not our custom (or practice) to...

приня́ть [*infl.* приму́, при́мешь; *past* при́нял, приняла́, при́няло] *v.*, *pfv. of* **принима́ть.** —**приня́ться,** *refl.* [*past* принялся́, -ла́сь, -ло́сь] *pfv. of* **принима́ться.**

приободря́ть *v. impfv.* [*pfv.* **приободри́ть**] to cheer

up; hearten. —**приободря́ться,** *refl.* to cheer up; feel better.

приобрести́ [*infl.* -брету́, -брете́шь; *past* -брёл, -брела́, -брело́] *v.*, *pfv. of* **приобрета́ть.**

приобрета́ть *v. impfv.* [*pfv.* **приобрести́**] to acquire; gain.

приобрете́ние *n.* acquisition.

приобща́ть *v. impfv.* [*pfv.* **приобщи́ть**] **1,** (*with* к) to introduce (to); acquaint (with); initiate (into). **2,** (*with* к) to attach (to); append (to). **3,** to administer the sacrament to. —**приобща́ться,** *refl.* (*with* к) to join; enter into; become a part of.

приоде́ть *v. pfv.* [*infl.* -де́ну, -де́нешь] *colloq.* to dress (someone) up. —**приоде́ться,** *refl.*, *colloq.* to get dressed up.

прио́р *n.*, *eccles.* prior.

приорите́т *n.* **1,** being first. Ему́ принадлежи́т приорите́т откры́тия (+ *gen.*), to him belongs the distinction of having invented... **2,** priority.

приоса́ниваться *v.r. impfv.* [*pfv.* **приоса́ниться**] *colloq.* to assume a dignified air.

приостана́вливать *v. impfv.* [*pfv.* **приостанови́ть**] to halt; interrupt; suspend. —**приостана́вливаться,** *refl.* to stop for a moment; pause.

приостанови́ть [*infl.* -новлю́, -но́вишь] *v.*, *pfv. of* **приостана́вливать.** —**приостанови́ться,** *refl.*, *pfv. of* **приостана́вливаться.**

приостано́вка *n.* halt; suspension.

приостановле́ние *n.* halt; suspension. —**приостановле́ние исполне́ния пригово́ра,** stay of execution.

приотвори́ть [*infl.* -ворю́, -во́ришь] *v.*, *pfv. of* **приотворя́ть.** —**приотвори́ться,** *refl.*, *pfv. of* **приотворя́ться.**

приотворя́ть *v. impfv.* [*pfv.* **приотвори́ть**] *v.t.* to open slightly. —**приотворя́ться,** *refl.* (*of a door*) to open slightly.

приоткрыва́ть *v. impfv.* [*pfv.* **приоткры́ть**] *v.t.* to open slightly. —**приоткрыва́ться,** *refl.* (*of a door*) to open slightly.

приоткры́ть [*infl.* -кро́ю, -кро́ешь] *v.*, *pfv. of* **приоткрыва́ть.**

приохо́тить *v. pfv.* [*infl.* -хо́чу, -хо́тишь] to instill (in someone) an appreciation for: приохо́тить кого́-нибудь к чте́нию, to instill in someone a taste for reading. —**приохо́титься,** *refl.* (*with* к) *colloq.* to take to.

припада́ть *v. impfv.* [*pfv.* **припа́сть**] **1,** (*with* к) to press (oneself) close to. Припада́ть у́хом к земле́, to press one's ear to the ground. **2,** (*with* на + *acc.*) to drop (to): припа́сть на одно́ коле́но, to drop to one knee. **3,** [*impfv. only*] *colloq.* to be slightly lame; (*with* на + *acc.*) limp slightly (on).

припа́док [*gen.* -дка] *n.* fit; attack.

припа́дочный *adj.* **1,** of an attack or fit. **2,** *colloq.* subject to attacks. —*n.* person subject to attacks.

припа́ивать *v. impfv.* [*pfv.* **припая́ть**] (*with* к) to solder (to).

припа́йка *n.* soldering.

припа́рка [*gen. pl.* -рок] *n.*, *usu. pl.* poultice.

припаса́ть *v. impfv.* [*pfv.* **припасти́**] *colloq.* to store (up); lay in a supply of.

припасти́ [*infl. like* пасти́] *v.*, *pfv. of* **припаса́ть.**

припа́сть [*infl. like* пасть] *v.*, *pfv. of* **припада́ть.**

припа́сы [*gen.* -сов] *n. pl.* supplies. —**боевы́е** *or* огнестре́льные припа́сы, ammunition. —съестны́е припа́сы, provisions; rations.

припая́ть v., pfv. of припа́ивать.

припе́в n. refrain.

припева́ть v. impfv., colloq. to sing (while doing something).

припева́ючи adv., colloq., in жить припева́ючи, to live in clover.

припёк n. intense heat from the sun: на припёке, in the hot sun; right in the sun.

припека́ть v. impfv. (of the sun) to be very hot; beat down.

припере́ть [infl. like пере́ть] v., pfv. of припира́ть.

припира́ть v. impfv. [pfv. припере́ть] 1, (with к) to place (something) firmly against (something). 2, to secure: припира́ть дверь сту́лом, to secure a door by placing a chair against it. 3, colloq. to set (a door or window) ajar. —припере́ть к стене́, to drive against the wall; drive into a corner.

приписа́ть [infl. -пишу́, -пи́шешь] v., pfv. of припи́сывать. —приписа́ться, refl., pfv. of припи́сываться.

припи́ска [gen. pl. -сок] n. 1, postscript. 2, codicil. 3, registration. 4, pl. falsification of figures.

припи́сывать v. impfv. [pfv. приписа́ть] 1, to add (to something written). 2, (with к) to register (at). 3, (with dat.) to ascribe (to); attribute (to). —припи́сываться, refl. 1, (with dat.) to be attributed (to). 2, to register.

припла́та n. extra charge; surcharge.

приплати́ть [infl. -плачу́, -пла́тишь] v., pfv. of припла́чивать.

припла́чивать v. impfv. [pfv. приплати́ть] to pay (a certain amount) extra.

приплод n. litter; offspring.

приплыва́ть v. impfv. [pfv. приплы́ть] (with к) to swim up to; reach by swimming.

приплы́ть [infl. like плыть] v., pfv. of приплыва́ть.

приплю́снутый adj. flat; flattened.

приплю́щивать v. impfv. [pfv. приплю́снуть] to flatten.

припля́сывать v. impfv. to dance up and down.

приподнима́ть v. impfv. [pfv. приподня́ть] to raise slightly. —приподнима́ться, refl. 1, to raise oneself slightly. 2, to sit up.

припо́днятый adj. 1, (of one's mood) elated; exultant. 2, (of style, language, etc.) elevated.

приподня́ть [infl. like подня́ть] v., pfv. of приподнима́ть. —приподня́ться, refl., pfv. of приподнима́ться.

припо́й n. solder.

приполза́ть v. impfv. [pfv. приползти́] (with к) to crawl to; reach by crawling.

приползти́ [infl. like ползти́] v., pfv. of приполза́ть.

припомина́ть v. impfv. [pfv. припо́мнить] to remember; recall; recollect.

припра́ва n. seasoning; flavoring; relish; dressing; condiment.

припра́вить [infl. -влю, -вишь] v., pfv. of приправля́ть.

приправля́ть v. impfv. [pfv. припра́вить] to season; flavor.

припря́тать [infl. -пря́чу, -пря́чешь] v., pfv. of припря́тывать.

припря́тывать v. impfv. [pfv. припря́тать] colloq. 1, to put away; store. 2, fig. to hide; conceal.

припу́гивать v. impfv. [pfv. припугну́ть] colloq. to frighten; scare; intimidate.

припу́дривать v. impfv. [pfv. припу́дрить] to powder. —припу́дриваться, refl. to powder oneself.

припуска́ть v. impfv. [pfv. припусти́ть] colloq. 1, (with к) to allow to come near; let at. 2, to urge on (a horse). 3, to let out (a garment). 4, v.i. to quicken one's pace. 5, v.i. (of rain) to come down harder. —припуска́ться, refl., colloq. to quicken one's pace.

припусти́ть [infl. -пущу́, -пу́стишь] v., pfv. of припуска́ть. —припусти́ться, refl., pfv. of припуска́ться.

припуха́ть v. impfv. [pfv. припу́хнуть] to be slightly swollen.

припу́хлый adj. slightly swollen. —припу́хлость, n.f. slight swelling.

припу́хнуть [past -пу́х, -ла] v., pfv. of припуха́ть.

прираба́тывать v. impfv. [pfv. прирабо́тать] to earn (extra money).

при́работок [gen. -тка] n. extra money earned.

прира́внивать v. impfv. [pfv. приравня́ть] (with к) to equate (with).

прираста́ть v. impfv. [pfv. прирасти́] 1, (with к) to grow on to. 2, (with к) fig. to become rooted to; become frozen to. 3, to increase; grow.

прирасти́ [infl. like расти́] v., pfv. of прираста́ть.

прираще́ние n. 1, increase. 2, increment.

приревнова́ть v. pfv. [infl. -ну́ю, -ну́ешь] to be jealous of.

прире́зать [infl. -ре́жу, -ре́жешь] v., pfv. of прире́зать and прире́зывать.

прире́зать v. impfv. [pfv. прире́зать] 1, to cut (someone's) throat. 2, to slaughter (animals). 3, to add on (a piece of land). Also, прире́зывать.

приро́да n. 1, nature: дары́ приро́ды, the gifts of nature; изуча́ть приро́ду, to study nature. 2, climate; environment (of a region): суро́вая приро́да Сиби́ри, the harsh climate (or rugged environment) of Siberia. 3, colloq. (a person's) nature. Челове́ческая приро́да, human nature. —в приро́де веще́й, in the nature of things. —от приро́ды, from birth. —по приро́де, by nature.

приро́дный adj. 1, natural. 2, innate; inborn; inherent.

прирождённый adj. 1, innate; inborn. 2, (of a person) born: прирождённый поэ́т, a born poet.

приро́ст n. increase; growth.

прируча́ть v. impfv. [pfv. приручи́ть] to tame; domesticate.

прируче́ние n. taming; domestication.

приручённый adj. tame.

приручи́ть v., pfv. of прируча́ть.

приса́дка n. additive.

приса́живаться v.r. impfv. [pfv. присе́сть] to sit down; have a seat; take a seat.

приса́ливать v. impfv. [pfv. присоли́ть] colloq. to add a touch of salt to.

приса́сываться v.r. impfv. [pfv. присоса́ться] (with к) 1, to adhere to (by suction). 2, fig., colloq. to worm one's way into.

присва́ивать v. impfv. [pfv. присво́ить] 1, to appropriate; take for one's own. 2, to pass off as one's own. 3, (with dat.) to award (a degree to); confer (a title on); give (a name to).

при́свист n. whistle; whistling.

присви́стывать v. impfv. [pfv. присви́стнуть] to whistle.

присвоéние *n.* **1,** appropriation. **2,** conferring.

присвóить *v., pfv. of* присвáивать.

приседáние *n.* **1,** squat. **2,** *obs.* curtsy.

приседáть *v. impfv.* [*pfv.* присéсть] **1,** to squat; crouch. **2,** *obs.* to curtsy.

присéст *n., obs.* sitting. —в (*or* за) одúн присéст, at one sitting; at a stretch.

присéсть [*infl. like* сесть] *v., pfv. of* присáживаться *and* приседáть.

прúсказка [*gen. pl.* -зок] *n.* **1,** introduction; prelude. **2,** saying.

прискакáть *v. pfv.* [*infl.* -скачý, -скáчешь] to arrive at a gallop.

прискóрбие *n., obs.* sorrow; regret. —к моемý прискóрбию, to my regret.

прискóрбный *adj.* **1,** sad; sorrowful. **2,** regrettable; deplorable.

прискýчить *v. pfv., colloq.* **1,** to become boring. **2,** (*with dat.*) to bore.

прислáть [*infl.* -шлю, -шлёшь] *v., pfv. of* присылáть.

прислонять *v. impfv.* [*pfv.* прислонúть] (*with* к) **1,** to lean; rest (something) against. **2,** to place; stand (something) against. —прислонáться, *refl.* (*with* к) to lean against; rest against.

прислýга *n.* **1,** *obs.* servant; maid. **2,** *obs.* servants. **3,** *mil.* crew; team.

прислýживать *v. impfv.* **1,** to be a servant. **2,** (*with dat.*) *colloq.* to wait on. —прислýживаться, *refl.* (*with dat. or* к) to play up to.

прислýжник *n.* **1,** *obs.* servant. **2,** *colloq.* lackey.

прислýшиваться *v.r. impfv.* [*pfv.* прислýшаться] (*with* к) **1,** to listen (to). **2,** to heed. **3,** *colloq.* to get used to the sound of.

присмáтривать *v. impfv.* [*pfv.* присмотрéть] **1,** (*with* за + *instr.*) to look after; keep an eye on. **2,** [*impfv. only*] to look for. —присмáтриваться, *refl.* (*with* к) **1,** to look closely (at). **2,** to grow accustomed to.

присмирéть *v. pfv.* to calm down; grow quiet.

присмóтр *n.* supervision.

присмотрéть *v. pfv.* [*infl.* -смотрю, -смóтришь] **1,** *pfv. of* присмáтривать. **2,** to find. —присмотрéться, *refl., pfv. of* присмáтриваться.

приснúться *v.r., pfv. of* снúться.

присоединéние *n.* **1,** addition. **2,** joining. **3,** annexation.

присоединять *v. impfv.* [*pfv.* присоединúть] (*with* к) **1,** to add (something) to. **2,** to join (something) to. **3,** to annex (to). —присоединяться, *refl.* (*with* к) **1,** to be added to. **2,** to join. **3,** to endorse; subscribe to.

присолúть [*infl.* -солю, -сóлишь *or* -солúшь] *v., pfv. of* присáливать.

присосáться *v.r., pfv. of* присáсываться.

присосéдиться *v.r. pfv.* [*infl.* -жусь, -дишься] (*with* к) *colloq.* to sit down next to.

присóсок [*gen.* -ска] *n., bot., zool.* sucker. *Also,* присóска.

присóхнуть [*past* -сóх, -ла] *v., pfv. of* присыхáть.

приспéть *v. pfv., colloq.* (*of time*) to be ripe.

приспéшник *n.* henchman.

приспосáбливать *v. impfv.* = приспособлять. —приспосáбливаться, *refl.* = приспособляться.

приспособить [*infl.* -блю, -бишь] *v., pfv. of* приспособлять *and* приспосáбливать. —приспособиться, *refl., pfv. of* приспособляться *and* приспосáбливаться.

приспособлéние *n.* **1,** device. **2,** adaptation; adjustment.

приспособляемость *n.f.* adaptability.

приспособлять *v. impfv.* [*pfv.* приспособить] **1,** to adapt. **2,** (*with* под + *acc.*) to convert (into). —приспособляться, *refl.* (*with* к) to adjust (to); become adjusted (to); adapt (to).

приспускáть *v. impfv.* [*pfv.* приспустúть] **1,** to lower slightly. **2,** to lower (a flag) to half-mast.

приспустúть [*infl.* -спущý, -спýстишь] *v., pfv. of* приспускáть.

прúстав [*pl.* приставá] *n., pre-rev.* police officer. —судéбный прúстав, *pre-rev.* bailiff.

приставáние *n., usu. pl.* nagging; pestering.

приставáть *v. impfv.* [*pfv.* пристáть; *pres.* -стаю, -стаёшь] (*with* к) **1,** to stick (to); adhere (to). **2,** *colloq.* to nag; pester. **3,** *colloq.* to join. **4,** (*of a boat*) to put in (to); pull up (to). **5,** *colloq.* (*of a disease*) to be transmitted (to). *See also* пристáть.

пристáвить [*infl.* -влю, -вишь] *v., pfv. of* приставлять.

пристáвка [*gen. pl.* -вок] *n.* **1,** prefix. **2,** attachment; accessory.

приставлять *v. impfv.* [*pfv.* пристáвить] **1,** (*with* к) to place (against); lean (against). **2,** to add on. **3,** *colloq.* to appoint to look after.

приставнóй *adj.* attached.

пристáвочный *adj.* **1,** prefixed. **2,** (*of a collar, cuffs, etc.*) detachable.

прúстальный *adj.* (*of a look*) intent; (*of attention*) rapt. —прúстально, *adv.* intently.

пристáнище *n.* refuge; shelter; haven.

прúстань [*pl.* прúстани, -нéй, -нáм] *n.f.* dock; pier; wharf.

пристáть *v. pfv.* [*infl.* -стáну, -стáнешь] **1,** *pfv. of* приставáть. **2,** *impers.* (*with dat.*) *colloq.* to befit; become.

пристёгивать *v. impfv.* [*pfv.* пристегнýть] to fasten; button; hook; buckle; pin. —пристёгиваться, *refl.* to hook on.

пристóйный *adj.* proper; decorous.

пристрáивать *v. impfv.* [*pfv.* пристрóить] **1,** (*with* к) to build on (to); add on (to). **2,** *colloq.* to place; find a job for. —пристрáиваться, *refl., colloq.* **1,** to ensconce oneself; perch. **2,** to get a job. **3,** (*with* к) to get into formation (with).

пристрáстие *n.* (*with* к) **1,** predilection; bent. **2,** partiality; bias.

пристрастúть *v. pfv.* [*infl.* -щý, -стúшь] *colloq.* to develop (in someone) a love of: пристрастúть когó-нибудь к кнúгам, to develop in someone a love of books. —пристрастúться, *refl.* (*with* к) to develop a passion (for).

пристрáстный *adj.* **1,** partial; biased. **2,** (*with* к) partial (to); drawn (to). —пристрáстно, *adv.* in a biased manner. —пристрáстность, *n.f.* partiality; bias.

пристрáчивать *v. impfv.* [*pfv.* пристрочúть] (*with* к) to sew on (to).

пристрéливать *v. impfv.* **1,** [*pfv.* пристрелúть] to shoot; kill. **2,** [*pfv.* пристрелять] to zero in (a weapon); zero in on (a target). —пристрéливаться, *refl.* [*pfv.* пристреляться] to zero in.

пристрелúть [*infl.* -стрелю, -стрéлишь] *v., pfv. of* пристрéливать (*in sense #1*).

пристре́лка *n.* zeroing in (*of a weapon*); zeroing in on (*a target*).

пристреля́ть *v., pfv. of* **пристре́ливать** (*in sense #2*). —**пристреля́ться**, *refl., pfv. of* **пристре́ливаться**.

пристро́ить *v., pfv. of* **пристра́ивать**. —**пристро́иться**, *refl., pfv. of* **пристра́иваться**.

пристро́йка [*gen. pl.* -**стро́ек**] *n.* annex; extension.

пристрочи́ть [*infl.* -**строчу́**, -**строчи́шь** *or* -**стро́чишь**] *v., pfv. of* **пристра́чивать**.

пристру́нивать *v. impfv.* [*pfv.* **пристру́нить**] *colloq.* to clamp down on; crack down on.

присту́кивать *v. impfv.* [*pfv.* **присту́кнуть**] (*with instr.*) **1**, to rap. **2**, to click (one's heels).

при́ступ *n.* **1**, fit; attack. **2**, *mil.* attack; assault.

приступа́ть *v. impfv.* [*pfv.* **приступи́ть**] (*with* к) to proceed (to); begin; set about. —**приступа́ться**, *refl.* (*with* к) *colloq.* to approach; come near (to).

приступи́ть [*infl.* -**ступлю́**, -**сту́пишь**] *v., pfv. of* **приступа́ть**. —**приступи́ться**, *refl., pfv. of* **приступа́ться**.

пристыди́ть *v., pfv. of* **стыди́ть**.

присуди́ть [*infl.* -**сужу́**, -**су́дишь**] *v., pfv. of* **присужда́ть**.

присужда́ть *v. impfv.* [*pfv.* **присуди́ть**] **1**, (*with* к) to sentence (to). **2**, to award; confer.

присужде́ние *n.* awarding; conferring.

прису́тствие *n.* presence: в моём прису́тствии, in my presence. —**прису́тствие ду́ха**, presence of mind.

прису́тствовать *v. impfv.* [*pres.* -**ствую**, -**ствуешь**] to be present: присутствовать на собра́нии/в за́ле/при разгово́ре/, to be present at a meeting/in the hall/during a conversation/.

прису́тствующий *n., decl. as an adj.* person present.

прису́щий *adj.* (*with dat.*) inherent (in): с прису́щим ему́ добродушием, with his inherent good nature.

присчи́тывать *v. impfv.* [*pfv.* **присчита́ть**] to add on.

присыла́ть *v. impfv.* [*pfv.* **присла́ть**] to send.

присыпа́ть [*infl.* -**сы́плю**, -**сы́плешь**] *v., pfv. of* **присыпа́ть**.

присыпа́ть *v. impfv.* [*pfv.* **присы́пать**] **1**, (*with gen.*) to pour some more (of). **2**, to sprinkle (a surface): присыпа́ть что-нибудь песко́м, to sprinkle something with sand.

присы́пка *n.* **1**, sprinkling. **2**, powder: де́тская присы́пка, baby powder.

присыха́ть *v. impfv.* [*pfv.* **присо́хнуть**] (*with* к) to stick (to); adhere (*in drying*).

прися́га *n.* oath. —**дава́ть прися́гу**, to swear. —**приводи́ть** (кого́-нибудь) к прися́ге, to swear in; administer the oath to. —**приноси́ть** *or* **принима́ть прися́гу**, to take the oath.

присяга́ть *v. impfv.* [*pfv.* **присягну́ть**] to swear.

прися́жный *n., decl. as an adj.* **1**, juror. **2**, *pl.* jury.

притаи́ть *v. pfv., colloq.* **1**, to conceal. **2**, to harbor. —**притаи́ться**, *refl.* to hide.

прита́птывать *v. impfv.* [*pfv.* **притопта́ть**] to trample; trample down.

прита́скивать *v. impfv.* [*pfv.* **притащи́ть**] to bring in; drag in. —**прита́скиваться**, *refl., colloq.* to drag oneself along.

притащи́ть [*infl.* -**тащу́**, -**та́щишь**] *v., pfv. of* **прита́скивать**. —**притащи́ться**, *refl., pfv. of* **прита́скиваться**.

притвори́ть [*infl.* -**творю́**, -**тво́ришь**] *v., pfv. of* **притворя́ть**. —**притвори́ться**, *refl.* **1**, [*infl.* -**творится**]

pfv. of **притворя́ться** (*in sense #1*). **2**, [*infl.* -**творю́сь**, -**тво́ришься**] *pfv. of* **притворя́ться** (*in sense #2*).

притво́рный *adj.* feigned; pretended. —**притво́рно**, *adv.* pretending to: притво́рно рассерди́ться, to pretend to be angry.

притво́рство *n.* sham; pretense. —**притво́рщик**, *n.* faker.

притворя́ть *v. impfv.* [*pfv.* **притвори́ть**] to close; shut. —**притворя́ться**, *refl.* **1**, to be closed; be shut. **2**, (*with instr.*) to pretend (to be).

притека́ть *v. impfv.* [*pfv.* **прите́чь**] **1**, to leak in. **2**, *fig.* to filter in.

притерпе́ться *v.r. pfv.* [*infl.* -**терплю́сь**, -**те́рпишься**] (*with* к) *colloq.* to get used to; learn to live with.

притёртый *adj.* ground in; ground smooth. —**притёртое стекло́**, ground glass.

притесне́ние *n.* oppression.

притесни́тель *n.m.* oppressor.

притесня́ть *v. impfv.* [*pfv.* **притесни́ть**] to oppress; keep down.

прите́чь [*infl. like* **течь**] *v., pfv. of* **притека́ть**.

прити́скивать *v. impfv.* [*pfv.* **прити́снуть**] (*with* к) to press (something) against (something).

притиха́ть *v. impfv.* [*pfv.* **прити́хнуть**] **1**, to quiet down; (*of noise*) die down. **2**, to subside; abate.

прити́хнуть [*past* -**ти́х**, -**ла**] *v., pfv. of* **притиха́ть**.

приткну́ть *v. pfv., colloq.* to stick; put; lay. —**приткну́ться**, *refl., colloq.* to find room for oneself; find a place to stay.

прито́к *n.* **1**, inflow (*of water, air, etc.*). **2**, *fig.* influx. **3**, *fig.* surge (*of energy, an emotion, etc.*). **4**, tributary.

прито́лока *n.* lintel.

прито́м *conj.* besides; moreover; furthermore.

прито́н *n.* den: иго́рный прито́н, gambling den.

притопну́ть *v., pfv. of* **прито́пывать**.

притопта́ть [*infl.* -**топчу́**, -**то́пчешь**] *v., pfv. of* **прита́птывать**.

прито́пывать *v. impfv.* [*pfv.* **прито́пнуть**] (*with instr.*) **1**, to stamp (one's foot). **2**, to tap (one's foot in time to music).

притормози́ть *v. pfv.* [*infl.* -**жу́**, -**зи́шь**] to slow down (*trans. & intrans.*).

прито́рный *adj.* sugary; saccharine.

притра́гиваться *v.r. impfv.* [*pfv.* **притро́нуться**] (*with* к) to touch.

притупи́ть [*infl.* -**туплю́**, -**ту́пишь**] *v., pfv. of* **притупля́ть**. —**притупи́ться**, *refl., pfv. of* **притупля́ться**.

притупля́ть *v. impfv.* [*pfv.* **притупи́ть**] **1**, to blunt. **2**, *fig.* to dull (the mind, senses, etc.). —**притупля́ться**, *refl.* **1**, to become dull. **2**, *fig.* to fade; wane.

притуши́ть *v. pfv.* [*infl.* -**тушу́**, -**ту́шишь**] *colloq.* **1**, to put out; extinguish. **2**, to dim (lights).

при́тча *n.* **1**, parable. **2**, *in exclamations, colloq.* strange thing: что за при́тча!, what a strange thing! —**при́тча во язы́цех**, the talk of the town.

притяга́тельный *adj.* attractive; magnetic.

притя́гивать *v. impfv.* [*pfv.* **притяну́ть**] **1**, to pull in (a boat). **2**, to attract; draw. **3**, *colloq.* to summon: притяну́ть к отве́ту, to call to account. —**притя́нутый за́ волосы**, farfetched.

притяжа́тельный *adj., gram.* possessive.

притяже́ние *n.* attraction; gravitation; gravity.

притяза́ние *n.* (*with* на + *acc.*) claim (to).

притяза́тельный *adj.* demanding; exacting.

притяну́ть [*infl.* -тяну́, -тя́нешь] *v.*, *pfv. of* **притя́-гивать**.

приукра́шивать *v. impfv.* [*pfv.* **приукра́сить**] *colloq.* **1**, to decorate; spruce up; brighten up. **2**, to embellish (a story, an account, etc.). —**приукра́шиваться**, *refl.*, *colloq.* to spruce up.

приуро́чивать *v. impfv.* [*pfv.* **приуро́чить**] (*with* к) to time (for); time to coincide (with).

приуча́ть *v. impfv.* [*pfv.* **приучи́ть**] (*with* к *or inf.*) **1**, to teach (to); train (to). **2**, to inure (to). —**приуча́ться**, *refl.* (*with* к *or inf.*) **1**, to train oneself (to). **2**, to get used to.

приучи́ть [*infl.* -учу́, -у́чишь] *v.*, *pfv. of* **приуча́ть**. —**приучи́ться**, *refl.*, *pfv. of* **приуча́ться**.

прифронтово́й *adj.*, *mil.* forward; front-line. —**прифронтова́я полоса́**, forward area.

прихва́рывать *v. impfv.* [*pfv.* **прихворну́ть**] *colloq.* to be ailing; be unwell.

прихвастну́ть *v. pfv.*, *colloq.* to brag a little; boast a little.

прихвати́ть [*infl.* -хвачу́, -хва́тишь] *v.*, *pfv. of* **прихва́тывать**.

прихва́тывать *v. impfv.* [*pfv.* **прихвати́ть**] *colloq.* **1**, to grab; grip. **2**, to take along. **3**, to tie up; fasten. **4**, (*of frost*) to nip; damage.

прихворну́ть *v.*, *pfv. of* **прихва́рывать**.

при́хвостень [*gen.* -тня] *n.m.*, *colloq.* toady; sycophant.

прихлеба́тель *n.m.*, *colloq.* parasite; sponger.

прихлёбывать *v. impfv.* [*pfv.* **прихлебну́ть**] *colloq.* to sip.

прихло́пывать *v. impfv.* [*pfv.* **прихло́пнуть**] **1**, to slap; bang. **2**, to slam (shut). **3**, *colloq.* to catch: прихло́пнуть па́лец две́рью, to catch one's finger in a door. **4**, [*impfv. only*] to clap (*in rhythm*).

прихлы́нуть *v. pfv.* to rush; surge.

прихо́д *n.* **1**, coming; arrival. **2**, income; receipts. **3**, parish; congregation.

приходи́ть *v. impfv.* [*pfv.* **прийти́**; *pres.* -хожу́, -хо́дишь] **1**, to come; arrive. **2**, (*with* к) to come to; arrive at; reach (a decision, conclusion, agreement, etc.). **3**, (*with* в + *acc.*) to reach a certain state or condition: приходи́ть в у́жас, to be horrified; приходи́ть в ве́тхость, to fall into disrepair. —**приходи́ть в го́лову** (+ *dat.*), to come to mind; occur to. —**приходи́ть в себя́**, to regain consciousness; come to.

приходи́ться *v.r. impfv.* [*pfv.* **прийти́сь**; *pres.* -хожу́сь, -хо́дишься] **1**, (*with* по) to fit: сапоги́ пришли́сь по ноге́, the shoes fitted well. **2**, (*with* по) (*of a blow or flying object*) to land (on); fall (on). **3**, (*with* на + *acc.*) to fall (*on a certain date*). **4**, *impers.* (*with dat. and inf.*) to have to: ему́ придётся подожда́ть, he will have to wait. **5**, *impers.* (*with dat. and inf.*) to happen to; have occasion to: мне ча́сто приходи́лось (+ *inf.*) I frequently had occasion to... Удивля́ться не приходится, one should not (*or* there is no reason to) be surprised. **6**, *impers.* (*with dat. and adverb*) to have a certain time of it: ему́ пришло́сь тяжело́ *or* нелегко́, he has had a hard time of it. **7**, *impers.* (*with* на + *acc.*) to number; account for: на ка́ждую же́нщину приходи́лось по тро́е мужчи́н, there were three men for every woman. Четвёртого всего́ экспорта приходится на нефть, oil accounts for one-fourth of all exports. **8**, *impers.* to be due: на ка́ждого пришло́сь по рублю́, each person had to pay a ruble. С

вас прихо́дится пять рубле́й, you owe five rubles. **9**, [*impfv. only*] to be related in a certain way: кем он вам прихо́дится?, how is he related to you? **10**, *in* приходи́ться по вку́су (+ *dat.*), to be to someone's taste; приходи́ться по душе́ (+ *dat.*), to suit; please; be to one's liking. —**где придётся**, wherever one can. —**как придётся**, in whatever way one can. —**чем придётся**, with whatever happens to be on hand.

прихо́дный *adj.* receipts (*attrib.*): прихо́дная кни́га, receipts book.

прихо́довать *v. impfv.* [*pfv.* **заприхо́довать**; *pres.* -дую, -дуешь] *bookkeeping* to credit (*enter on the credit side of the ledger*).

прихо́до-расхо́дный *adj.*, *in* прихо́до-расхо́дная кни́га, receipts and disbursements book.

прихо́дский *adj.* parish (*attrib.*). —**прихо́дская шко́ла**, parochial school.

прихожа́нин [*pl.* -жа́не, -жа́н] *n.m.* [*fem.* -жа́нка] parishioner.

прихо́жая *n.*, *decl. as an adj.* vestibule; hall.

прихора́шивать *v. impfv.*, *colloq.* to spruce up; doll up. —**прихора́шиваться**, *refl.*, *colloq.* to spruce up.

прихотли́вый *adj.* **1**, (*of a person*) whimsical; capricious. **2**, (*of a design*) quaint; intricate. **3**, (*of a dream*) fanciful.

при́хоть *n.f.* whim; whimsy; caprice.

прихра́мывать *v. impfv.* to limp slightly.

прице́л *n.* sight (*on a gun*). —**взять на прице́л**, to take aim at; draw a bead on.

прице́ливание *n.* aiming (*of a weapon*).

прице́ливаться *v.r. impfv.* [*pfv.* **прице́литься**] **1**, to take aim. **2**, (*with* в + *acc.*) to aim (at).

прице́льный *adj.* **1**, aiming; sighting: прице́льное приспособле́ние, sighting device. **2**, aimed: прице́льный ого́нь, aimed fire.

прице́ниваться *v.r. impfv.* [*pfv.* **прицени́ться**] (*with* к) *colloq.* to ask the price of.

прицени́ться [*infl.* -еню́сь, -е́нишься] *v.r.*, *pfv. of* **прице́ниваться**.

прице́п *n.* trailer.

прицепи́ть [*infl.* -цеплю́, -це́пишь] *v.*, *pfv. of* **прицепля́ть**. —**прицепи́ться**, *refl.*, *pfv. of* **прицепля́ться**.

прице́пка [*gen. pl.* -пок] *n.* **1**, hitching; hooking. **2**, *colloq.* cavil; quibble.

прицепля́ть *v. impfv.* [*pfv.* **прицепи́ть**] (*with* к) **1**, to hitch (to); hook (to). **2**, *colloq.* to pin (to). —**прицепля́ться**, *refl.* (*with* к) **1**, to be hitched (to); hook (onto). **2**, to stick (to); cling (to). **3**, *fig.*, *colloq.* to join. **4**, *fig.*, *colloq.* to attach oneself to. **5**, *fig.*, *colloq.* to pick on.

прицепно́й *adj.* towed; that needs to be towed.

прича́л *n.* **1**, mooring; moorage. **2**, mooring line. **3**, berth (*at a pier*).

прича́ливать *v. impfv.* [*pfv.* **прича́лить**] **1**, *v.t.* to moor. **2**, *v.i.* (*with* к) to tie up (at).

прича́льный *adj.* mooring (*attrib.*): прича́льный кана́т, mooring line.

прича́стие *n.* **1**, *gram.* participle. **2**, *relig.* communion; Eucharist.

прича́стить [*infl.* -щу́, -сти́шь] *v.*, *pfv. of* **причаща́ть**. —**прича́ститься**, *refl.*, *pfv. of* **причаща́ться**.

прича́стный *adj.* **1**, (*with* к) involved (in); being a party to; connected (with); concerned (with). **2**, *gram.* participial. —**прича́стность**, *n.f.* involvement.

причаща́ть v. impfv. [pfv. **причасти́ть**] to give communion to. —**причаща́ться**, refl. to receive communion.

причём conj. **1,** in which connection. **2,** at that. ♦Often not translated: супру́ги развели́сь, причём сын оста́лся у отца́, the couple was divorced, the son remaining with the father.

причеса́ть [infl. -чешу́, -че́шешь] v., pfv. of **причёсывать**. —**причеса́ться**, refl., pfv. of **причёсываться**.

причёска [gen. pl. -сок] n. hairdo.

причёсывать v. impfv. [pfv. **причеса́ть**] to comb. —**причёсываться**, refl. **1,** to comb one's hair. **2,** to have one's hair done.

причи́на n. **1,** cause. **2,** reason: по э́той причи́не, for this reason. —**безо вся́кой причи́ны**, for no reason whatever.

причини́ть v., pfv. of **причиня́ть**.

причи́нный adj. causal; causative. —**причи́нность**, n.f. causality.

причиня́ть v. impfv. [pfv. **причини́ть**] to cause: причиня́ть вред (+ dat.), to cause damage to.

причисля́ть v. impfv. [pfv. **причи́слить**] (with к) **1,** to add (to). **2,** to number (among). —**причисля́ться**, refl. (with к) to belong to.

причита́ние n. lamentation.

причита́ть v. impfv. to wail; moan (in grief). —**причита́ться**, refl. **1,** (with dat.) to be owed (to); be due (to). **2,** (with с + gen.) to owe; be obliged to pay: с вас причита́ется три рубля́, you owe three rubles.

причмо́кивать v. impfv. [pfv. **причмо́кнуть**] to smack one's lips. Also, **причмо́кивать губа́ми**.

причу́да n. whim; whimsy; caprice.

причу́дливый adj. **1,** quaint; intricate. **2,** colloq. whimsical; capricious.

пришвартова́ть v., pfv. of **швартова́ть**. —**пришвартова́ться**, refl., pfv. of **швартова́ться**.

пришёлец [gen. -льца] n. newcomer.

пришёптывать v. impfv. to whisper.

прише́ствие n. coming; appearance; advent. —**до второ́го прише́ствия**, till doomsday.

пришибленный adj., colloq. crushed; crestfallen.

пришива́ть v. impfv. [pfv. **приши́ть**] to sew on.

приши́ть [infl. -шью́, -шьёшь] v., pfv. of **пришива́ть**.

при́шлый adj. having come from somewhere else; newly arrived.

пришпи́ливать v. impfv. [pfv. **пришпи́лить**] **1,** to pin on. **2,** (with к) to pin to.

пришпо́ривать v. impfv. [pfv. **пришпо́рить**] **1,** to spur (a horse). **2,** fig., colloq. to spur on; urge on.

прищёлкивать v. impfv. [pfv. **прищёлкнуть**] (with instr.) to snap; crack.

прищемля́ть v. impfv. [pfv. **прищеми́ть**] to catch: прищеми́ть па́лец две́рью, to catch one's finger in a door.

прище́пка [gen. pl. -пок] n. clothespin.

прищу́ривать v. impfv. [pfv. **прищу́рить**], in прищу́ривать глаза́, to squint. —**прищу́риваться**, refl. to squint.

прию́т n. **1,** shelter; refuge. **2,** pre-rev. orphanage; foundling home.

приюти́ть v. pfv. [infl. -ючу́, -юти́шь] to shelter; give refuge to. —**приюти́ться**, refl. to take shelter.

прия́тель n.m. [fem. -ница] friend. —**прия́тельский**, adj. friendly.

прия́тно adv. pleasantly. —adj., used predicatively pleasant; nice: прия́тно э́то слы́шать, it is nice to hear it. Мне бу́дет прия́тно (+ inf.), I will be happy to...; it will be a pleasure to...

прия́тный adj. [short form -я́тен, -я́тна] pleasant; pleasing; nice.

про prep., with acc. about: говори́ть про дру́га, to talk about a friend. —**про запа́с**, see **запа́с**. —**про себя́**, to oneself: чита́ть про себя́, to read to oneself.

про- prefix **1,** indicating motion through: пробира́ться сквозь толпу́, to make one's way through a crowd. **2,** indicating motion past: прое́хать ми́мо ста́нции, to ride past the station. **3,** indicating thoroughness of an action: просу́шивать, to dry thoroughly. **4,** indicating failure, error, etc.: проигра́ть, to lose; промахну́ться, to miss; провали́ться, to fail; просчита́ться, to miscalculate. **5,** (with pfv. verbs only) indicating action performed over or throughout a certain period of time: прожи́ть три го́да за грани́цей, to live abroad for three years; проспа́ть всё у́тро, to sleep through the entire morning. **6,** (with adjectives) pro-: проамерика́нский, pro-American.

проанализи́ровать v., pfv. of **анализи́ровать**.

про́ба n. **1,** test; trial. **2,** sample. **3,** a unit of fineness of precious metals based on 96 parts for pure metals: зо́лото пятьдеся́т шесто́й про́бы, 14-karat gold. **4,** hallmark (of precious metals). —**высо́кой/вы́сшей про́бы**, of a high/the highest/ order. —**ни́зкой** or **ни́зшей про́бы**, of the worst type.

пробавля́ться v.r. impfv. (with instr.) colloq. to get along (on); subsist (on).

проба́лтывать v. impfv. [pfv. **проболта́ть**] colloq. to blab; blurt out; let out. —**проба́лтываться**, refl., colloq. to shoot off one's mouth; let the cat out of the bag; spill the beans.

пробе́г n. **1,** run. **2,** race. —**про́бный пробе́г**, test run; road test.

пробе́гать v. pfv. to run (for a certain length of time).

пробега́ть v. impfv. [pfv. **пробежа́ть**] **1,** to run; (with по) run along; run down; (with че́рез) run through; (with ми́мо) run past. **2,** (with по) to pass over; sweep over. **3,** (with instr. and по) to run (something over something): пробежа́ть па́льцами по клавиату́ре, to run one's fingers over the keyboard. **4,** to glance over; run through; scan.

пробежа́ть [infl. like **бежа́ть**] v., pfv. of **пробега́ть**. —**пробежа́ться**, refl. (with по) to run about; race about.

пробе́жка [gen. pl. -жек] n. run.

пробе́л n. **1,** blank space; blank. **2,** fig. gap: пробе́лы в зна́ниях, gaps in one's knowledge.

пробива́ть v. impfv. [pfv. **проби́ть**] **1,** to make a hole in; pierce. **2,** to break through; breach. **3,** to make (a hole). **4,** colloq. to lay (a road); clear (a path). —**пробива́ть себе́ доро́гу**, **1,** to force one's way through. **2,** fig. to make one's way in the world.

пробива́ться v.r. impfv. [pfv. **проби́ться**] **1,** (with к, сквозь or че́рез) to force one's way (to or through); break through (to). **2,** (with в + acc. or сквозь) to seep through; filter through. **3,** (of plants, hair, etc.) to push through; come out; appear.

пробивно́й adj., colloq. aggressive; pushy.

пробира́ть v. impfv. [pfv. **пробра́ть**] colloq. **1,** (of cold) to penetrate; (of fear) to seize. **2,** to bawl out.

—**пробираться**, *refl.* **1,** to make one's way. **2,** to sneak; steal (*into or* through).

пробирка [*gen. pl.* -рок] *n.* test tube.

пробирный *adj.* pert. to the analyzing of precious metals. —**пробирный камень**, touchstone.

пробить [*infl.* -бью, -бьёшь] *v., pfv. of* **бить** *and* **пробивать**. —**пробиться**, *refl., pfv. of* **пробиваться**.

пробка [*gen. pl.* -бок] *n.* **1,** cork. **2,** plug; stopper. **3,** *fig.* jam; congestion. **4,** fuse. —**глуп как пробка**, dumb as they come.

пробковый *adj.* cork (*attrib.*). —**пробковый пояс**, life belt.

проблема *n.* problem.

проблематика *n.* problems. —**проблематический**; **проблематичный**, *adj.* problematic(al).

проблеск *n.* **1,** flash; gleam. **2,** *fig.* glimmer (*of hope*).

проблуждать *v. pfv.* to wander (*for a certain length of time*).

пробный *adj.* **1,** test (*attrib.*); trial (*attrib.*). **2,** sample (*attrib.*). —**пробный камень**, touchstone. —**пробный шар**, trial balloon.

пробовать *v. impfv.* [*pfv.* **попробовать**; *pres.* -бую, -буешь] **1,** to try. **2,** to test. **3,** to taste.

прободение *n., med.* perforation. —**прободной**, *adj., med.* perforated: прободная язва, perforated ulcer.

пробоина *n.* hole; breach.

пробой *n.* hasp.

проболеть *v. pfv.* **1,** [*infl.* -ею, -еешь] to be ill (*for a certain length of time*). **2,** [*infl.* -лит] to hurt (*for a certain length of time*).

проболтать *v. pfv.* **1,** *pfv. of* **пробалтывать**. **2,** (*of two people*) to talk (*for a certain length of time*). —**проболтаться**, *refl., pfv. of* **пробалтываться**.

пробор *n.* part (*in one's hair*).

пробормотать *v., pfv. of* **бормотать**.

пробочник *n., colloq.* corkscrew.

пробрать [*infl. like* **брать**] *v., pfv. of* **пробирать**. —**пробраться**, *refl., pfv. of* **пробираться**.

пробродить *v. pfv.* [*infl.* -брожу, -бродишь] to wander (*for a certain length of time*).

пробубнить *v., pfv. of* **бубнить**.

пробудить *v. pfv.* **1,** [*infl.* -бужу, -будишь] *pfv. of* **пробуждать** (*in sense* #1). **2,** [*infl.* -бужу, -будишь] *pfv. of* **будить** (*in sense* #2) *and* **пробуждать** (*in sense* #2). —**пробудиться**, *refl., pfv. of* **пробуждаться**.

пробуждать *v. impfv.* [*pfv.* **пробудить**] **1,** to wake up; awaken. **2,** *fig.* to rouse; arouse. —**пробуждаться**, *refl.* **1,** to wake up. **2,** *fig.* to be aroused; be awakened.

пробуждение *n.* awakening.

пробуравить *v., pfv. of* **буравить**.

пробурить *v., pfv. of* **бурить**.

пробурчать *v., pfv. of* **бурчать**.

пробыть *v. pfv.* [*infl.* -буду, -будешь; *past* пробыл, пробыла, пробыло] to stay (*for a certain length of time*); spend (*a certain amount of time*).

провал *n.* **1,** collapse; cave-in. **2,** depression; hole. **3,** failure. **4,** exposure (*of illegal activity*). **5,** lapse: провал памяти, lapse of memory.

проваливать *v. impfv.* [*pfv.* **провалить**] **1,** to cause to collapse; cause to cave in. **2,** *fig., colloq.* to ruin; make a mess of. **3,** *fig., colloq.* to fail (a student). **4,** *fig., colloq.* to reject.—**проваливаться**, *refl.* **1,** (*with* в + *acc.*) to fall (into). **2,** to collapse; cave in; come tumbling down. **3,** to fail. **4,** *colloq.* to disappear.

5, *in* как сквозь землю провалиться, to vanish into thin air.

провалить [*infl.* -валю, -валишь] *v., pfv. of* **проваливать**. —**провалиться**, *refl., pfv. of* **проваливаться**.

провансаль *n.m.* mayonnaise. —**капуста провансаль**, pickled cabbage with a dressing added.

прованский *adj., in* прованское масло, olive oil.

проваривать *v. impfv.* [*pfv.* **проварить**] to boil thoroughly; cook thoroughly.

проварить [*infl.* -варю, -варишь] *v., pfv. of* **проваривать**.

проведать *v., pfv. of* **проведывать**.

проведение *n.* **1,** guiding; conducting. **2,** building; construction. **3,** installation. **4,** conducting; carrying out; holding.

проведывать *v. impfv.* [*pfv.* **проведать**] *colloq.* **1,** to call on; pay a visit on. **2,** to find out; learn.

провезти [*infl. like* **везти**] *v., pfv. of* **провозить**.

провентилировать *v., pfv. of* **вентилировать**.

проверенный *adj.* tested; of proven ability.

проверить *v., pfv. of* **проверять**.

проверка [*gen. pl.* -рок] *n.* **1,** check; checking. **2,** verification. **3,** testing.

провернуть *v., pfv. of* **провёртывать**.

проверочный *adj.* **1,** control (*attrib.*). **2,** test (*attrib.*): проверочная работа, test paper (*in school*).

провёртывать *v. impfv.* [*pfv.* **провернуть**] *colloq.* **1,** to drill; bore (a hole). **2,** to drill a hole in.

проверять *v. impfv.* [*pfv.* **проверить**] **1,** to check. **2,** to test.

провести *v. pfv.* [*infl. like* **вести**] **1,** *pfv. of* **проводить²**. **2,** *colloq.* to trick; take in.

проветривание *n.* ventilation.

проветривать *v. impfv.* [*pfv.* **проветрить**] to air out; ventilate. —**проветриваться**, *refl.* **1,** to be aired out. **2,** *colloq.* to get some fresh air.

провеять *v., pfv. of* **веять** (*in sense* #4).

провидение *n.* foresight; vision.

провидение *n., relig.* Providence. —**провиденциальный**, *adj.* providential.

провидеть *v. impfv.* [*pres.* -вижу, -видишь] to foresee.

провидец [*gen.* -дца] *n.* prophet; seer.

провизия *n.* food; provisions.

провизор *n.* pharmacist.

провиниться *v.r. pfv.* (*with* в + *prepl.*) to be guilty (of); do (something) wrong.

провинность *n.f., colloq.* **1,** fault. **2,** misdeed.

провинциал *n.* a provincial; hick. —**провинциализм**, *n.* provincialism. —**провинциальный**, *adj.* provincial.

провинция *n.* **1,** province. **2,** the provinces.

провисать *v. impfv.* [*pfv.* **провиснуть**] to be weighed down; sag.

провиснуть [*past* -вис, -ла] *v., pfv. of* **провисать**.

провод [*pl.* провода] *n.* **1,** wire. **2,** (telephone) line: прямой провод, direct line. —**быть на проводе**, to be calling; be on the line.

проводимость *n.f.* conductivity.

проводить¹ [*infl.* -вожу, -водишь] *v., pfv. of* **провожать**.

проводить² *v. impfv.* [*pfv.* **провести**; *pres.* -вожу, -водишь] **1,** to lead; guide; conduct; take; steer. **2,** (*with instr. and* по) to run (one's hand, fingers, etc.) over the surface of. **3,** to build; construct (a railroad, canal, etc.). **4,** to install (a telephone, electricity, etc.). **5,** to conduct (a meeting, investigation, etc.); carry out (reforms); hold (elections). **6,** to spend (time). Хорошо́ провести́ вре́мя, to have a good time. **7,** to draw (a line, boundary, etc.). **8,** to draw; make (a distinction, comparison, etc.). **9,** to get (a proposal, bill, etc.) through. **10,** [*impfv. only*] to conduct (electricity, heat, etc.). —провести́ в жизнь, to put into practice; make a reality of. *See also* провести́.

прово́дка *n.* **1,** guiding; conducting. **2,** building; construction. **3,** installation. **4,** wiring.

проводни́к [*gen.* -ника́] *n.* **1,** guide. **2,** conductor (*on a train*). **3,** physics conductor.

про́воды [*gen.* -дов] *n. pl.* send-off.

провожа́тый *n.,* decl. as an adj. guide; escort.

провожа́ть *v. impfv.* [*pfv.* проводи́ть] **1,** to accompany. **2,** (*with* в *or* на + *acc.*) to see (someone) off (at). **3,** (*with* до) to walk to; see to: проводи́ть (кого́-нибудь) до гости́ницы/две́ри, to walk (someone) to the hotel; see to the door. **4,** to send off (to the army, war, etc.). **5,** to follow (*with one's eyes*).

прово́з *n.* **1,** transport; delivery. **2,** smuggling in. —пла́та за прово́з, freight charges; carrying charges.

провозгласи́ть [*infl.* -шу́, -си́шь] *v., pfv. of* провозглаша́ть.

провозглаша́ть *v. impfv.* [*pfv.* провозгласи́ть] **1,** to proclaim. **2,** to propose (a toast).

провозглаше́ние *n.* proclamation.

провози́ть[1] *v. impfv.* [*pfv.* провезти́; *pres.* -вожу́, -во́зишь] **1,** to transport; convey. **2,** to smuggle (in).

провози́ть[2] *v. pfv.* [*infl.* -вожу́, -во́зишь] to convey; carry; deliver (*for a certain length of time*). —провози́ться, *refl.* (*with* с + *instr.*) to be busy with; concern oneself with (*for a certain length of time*).

провока́тор *n.* **1,** agent provocateur. **2,** instigator.

провока́ция *n.* provocation. —провокацио́нный, *adj.* provocative.

про́волка *n.* wire. —колю́чая про́волка, barbed wire.

про́волочка [*gen. pl.* -чек] *n.* **1,** short piece of wire. **2,** fine wire.

проволо́чка [*gen. pl.* -чек] *n., colloq.* delay.

про́волочный *adj.* wire (*attrib.*).

провоня́ть *v. pfv., colloq.* **1,** *v.i.* to smell; stink. **2,** *v.t.* to smell up; stink up.

прово́рный *adj.* **1,** agile; nimble; adroit; dexterous. **2,** quick; swift; brisk.

проворова́ться *v.r. pfv.* [*infl.* -ру́юсь, -ру́ешься] *colloq.* to be caught stealing.

прово́рство *n.* **1,** agility; dexterity. **2,** promptness.

проворча́ть *v. pfv.* [*infl.* -чу́, -чи́шь] to mumble; grumble.

провоци́ровать *v. impfv. & pfv.* [*pfv. also* спровоци́ровать; *pres.* -ру́ю, -ру́ешь] to provoke.

провы́ть *v. pfv.* [*infl.* -во́ю, -во́ешь] to howl; wail.

провя́лить *v., pfv. of* вя́лить.

прога́дывать *v. impfv.* [*pfv.* прогада́ть] *colloq.* to miscalculate.

прога́лина *n., colloq.* **1,** clearing; glade. **2,** space; gap.

проги́б *n.* sagging; sag.

прогиба́ть *v. impfv.* [*pfv.* прогну́ть] to bend; weigh down; cause to sag. —прогиба́ться, *refl.* to bend; sag.

прогла́дить *v. pfv.* [*infl.* -жу, -дишь] **1,** *pfv. of* прогла́живать. **2,** to iron (*for a certain length of time*).

прогла́живать *v. impfv.* [*pfv.* прогла́дить] to iron.

прогла́тывать *v. impfv.* [*pfv.* проглоти́ть] to swallow. —проглоти́ть язы́к, to keep quiet; hold one's tongue. —язы́к проглоти́шь, it will make your mouth water.

проглоти́ть [*infl.* -глочу́, -гло́тишь] *v., pfv. of* прогла́тывать.

прогляде́ть *v. pfv.* [*infl.* -жу́, -ди́шь] **1,** *pfv. of* прогля́дывать (*in sense #1*). **2,** to overlook. **3,** to gaze at; stare at (*for a certain length of time*).

прогля́дывать *v. impfv.* **1,** [*pfv.* прогляде́ть] *colloq.* to look over; skim; scan. **2,** [*pfv.* проглянуть] to appear; come partly into view; peep.

проглянуть [*infl.* -гляну́, -гля́нешь] *v., pfv. of* прогля́дывать (*in sense #2*).

прогна́ть [*infl. like* гнать] *v., pfv. of* прогоня́ть.

прогнива́ть *v. impfv.* [*pfv.* прогни́ть] to rot through.

прогни́ть [*infl. like* гнить] *v., pfv. of* прогнива́ть.

прогно́з *n.* prognosis; forecast.

прогну́ть *v., pfv. of* прогиба́ть. —прогну́ться, *refl., pfv. of* прогиба́ться.

прогова́ривать *v. impfv.* [*pfv.* проговори́ть] to say; utter. —прогова́риваться, *refl.* to let the cat out of the bag; spill the beans.

проговори́ть *v. pfv.* **1,** *pfv. of* прогова́ривать. **2,** to talk; converse (*for a certain length of time*). —проговори́ться, *refl., pfv. of* прогова́риваться.

проголода́ться *v.r. pfv.* to be hungry; get hungry.

проголосова́ть *v., pfv. of* голосова́ть.

прого́н *n.* **1,** driving (*of animals*). **2,** girder. **3,** stairwell.

прогоня́ть *v. impfv.* [*pfv.* прогна́ть] **1,** to drive (animals). **2,** to drive away; chase away. **3,** *fig., colloq.* to dispel. **4,** *colloq.* to fire; dismiss.

прогора́ть *v. impfv.* [*pfv.* прогоре́ть] **1,** (*of wood*) to be burned completely. **2,** to be damaged (*by fire*). **3,** *fig., colloq.* to go bankrupt; go broke.

прого́рклый *adj.* rancid.

прого́ркнуть [*past* -го́рк, -ла] *v., pfv. of* го́ркнуть.

програ́мма *n.* **1,** program. **2,** syllabus.

программи́рование *n.* (computer) programming.

программи́ровать *v. impfv.* [*pfv.* запрограмми́ровать; *pres.* -рую, -руешь] to program.

программи́ст *n.* (computer) programmer.

програ́ммный *adj.* **1,** program (*attrib.*): програ́ммная му́зыка, program music. **2,** programmed.

прогрева́ть *v. impfv.* [*pfv.* прогре́ть] to warm up; make warm. —прогрева́ться, *refl.* to warm up; become warm.

прогреме́ть *v. pfv.* [*infl.* -млю́, -ми́шь] to thunder; ring out.

прогре́сс *n.* progress.

прогресси́вный *adj.* progressive.

прогресси́ровать *v. impfv.* [*pres.* -рую, -руешь] **1,** to progress; make progress. **2,** (*of an illness*) to grow progressively worse.

прогре́ссия *n., math.* progression.

прогре́ть *v., pfv. of* прогрева́ть. —прогре́ться, *refl., pfv. of* прогрева́ться.

прогрыза́ть *v. impfv.* [*pfv.* прогры́зть] to gnaw through.

прогры́зть [*infl. like* грызть] *v., pfv. of* прогрыза́ть.

прогуде́ть *v. pfv.* [*infl.* -жу́, -ди́шь] **1,** to buzz; hum; drone. **2,** (*of a horn or factory whistle*) to sound; blow.

прогу́л *n.* unexcused absence from work or school; truancy.

прогу́ливать *v. impfv.* [*pfv.* прогуля́ть] **1,** to miss;

fail to show up for: прогу́ливать уро́ки, to play hooky; play truant. **2,** [*impfv. only*] to walk; take for a walk. —**прогу́ливаться,** *refl.* to take a walk; go for a stroll.

прогу́лка [*gen. pl.* **-лок**] *n.* **1,** walk; stroll. **2,** outing; ride; drive.

прогу́лочный *adj.* excursion (*attrib.*); pleasure (*attrib.*). —**прогу́лочная па́луба,** promenade deck. —**прогу́лочный шаг,** leisurely pace.

прогу́льщик *n.* **1,** shirker. **2,** truant.

прогуля́ть *v. pfv.* **1,** *pfv. of* **прогу́ливать. 2,** to walk; stroll (*for a certain length of time*). —**прогуля́ться,** *refl., pfv. of* **прогу́ливаться.**

продава́ть *v. impfv.* [*pfv.* **прода́ть;** *pres.* **-да́ю, -даёшь**] **1,** to sell. **2,** to sell out; betray. —**продава́ться,** *refl.* **1,** [*impfv. only*] to sell; be selling (*well, poorly, etc.*). **2,** [*impfv. only*] to be for sale. **3,** to sell oneself. **4,** to be a traitor; (*with dat.*) sell out to.

продаве́ц [*gen.* **-вца́**] *n.* seller; salesman; salesperson.

продави́ть [*infl.* **-давлю́, -да́вишь**] *v., pfv. of* **прода́вливать.**

прода́вливать *v. impfv.* [*pfv.* **продави́ть**] to bend in; cause to sag in the middle.

продавщи́ца *n.* saleslady; salesgirl.

прода́жа *n.* sale. —**в прода́же,** in stock; available. —**нет в прода́же,** out of stock; not on sale.

прода́жность *n.f.* corruption; venality.

прода́жный *adj.* **1,** sale (*attrib.*); selling (*attrib.*): прода́жная цена́, selling price. **2,** for sale. **3,** corrupt; venal. —**прода́жная же́нщина,** prostitute.

прода́ть [*infl. like* **дать;** *past* **про́дал, продала́, про́дало**] *v., pfv. of* **продава́ть.** —**прода́ться,** *refl.* [*past* **прода́лся, -ла́сь, -ло́сь**] *pfv. of* **продава́ться.**

продвига́ть *v. impfv.* [*pfv.* **продви́нуть**] **1,** to move (something) forward. **2,** (*with* к) to move toward; (*with* че́рез) move through. **3,** to promote; advance. **4,** *colloq.* to move along; expedite. —**продвига́ться,** *refl.* **1,** to move forward; move ahead; advance. **2,** *fig.* to advance; move up. **3,** *colloq.* to move along; make progress.

продвиже́ние *n.* **1,** movement. **2,** advancement; promotion.

продви́нутый *adj.* advanced.

продви́нуть *v., pfv. of* **продвига́ть.** —**продви́нуться,** *refl., pfv. of* **продвига́ться.**

продева́ть *v. impfv.* [*pfv.* **проде́ть**] to pass through: продева́ть ни́тку в иго́лку, to thread a needle.

продекламировать *v., pfv. of* **деклами́ровать.**

проде́лать *v., pfv. of* **проде́лывать.**

проде́лка [*gen. pl.* **-лок**] *n.* prank; trick.

проде́лывать *v. impfv.* [*pfv.* **проде́лать**] **1,** to make (a hole). **2,** to do; perform. **3,** to play (a trick).

продемонстри́ровать *v. pfv.* [*infl.* **-рую, -руешь**] to demonstrate; display; show.

продёргивать *v. impfv.* [*pfv.* **продёрнуть**] *colloq.* to pass through: продёргивать ни́тку в иго́лку, to thread a needle.

продержа́ть *v. pfv.* [*infl.* **-держу́, -де́ржишь**] to hold; keep (*for a certain length of time*). —**продержа́ться,** *refl.* **1,** to remain (*in a certain position*). **2,** to last. **3,** to hold out.

продёрнуть *v., pfv. of* **продёргивать.**

проде́ть [*infl.* **-де́ну, -де́нешь**] *v., pfv. of* **продева́ть.**

продешеви́ть *v. pfv.* [*infl.* **-влю́, -ви́шь**] to sell (something) cheap.

продиктова́ть *v., pfv. of* **диктова́ть.**

продира́ть *v. impfv.* [*pfv.* **продра́ть**] *colloq.* to tear; wear through. —**продира́ться,** *refl., colloq.* **1,** to be torn; be worn through. **2,** to make one's way; force one's way.

продлева́ть *v. impfv.* [*pfv.* **продли́ть**] to prolong; extend.

продле́ние *n.* extension; prolongation.

продли́ть *v., pfv. of* **продлева́ть.** —**продли́ться,** *refl., pfv. of* **дли́ться.**

продово́льственный *adj.* food (*attrib.*). —**продово́льственный магази́н,** grocery store. —**продово́льственные това́ры,** foodstuffs.

продово́льствие *n.* food; provisions.

продолби́ть *v., pfv. of* **долби́ть** (*in sense #1*).

продолгова́тый *adj.* oblong.

продолжа́тель *n.m.* continuer.

продолжа́ть *v. impfv.* [*pfv.* **продо́лжить**] **1,** [*usu. impfv.*] to continue. **2,** [*usu. pfv.*] to extend; prolong. —**продолжа́ться,** *refl.* to last; continue; go on.

продолже́ние *n.* **1,** continuation. **2,** sequel. —**в продолже́ние** (+ *gen.*), during; in the course of. —**продолже́ние сле́дует,** to be continued.

продолжи́тельность *n.f.* length; duration. —**продолжи́тельность жи́зни,** life expectancy.

продолжи́тельный *adj.* prolonged; long.

продо́лжить *v., pfv. of* **продолжа́ть.** —**продо́лжиться,** *refl., pfv. of* **продолжа́ться.**

продо́льный *adj.* **1,** longitudinal. **2,** *naut.* fore-and-aft. —**продо́льная пила́,** ripsaw.

продохну́ть *v. pfv., colloq.* to take a deep breath. —**не** (*or* **нельзя́**) **продохну́ть,** it's impossible to breathe.

продра́ть [*infl. like* **драть**] *v., pfv. of* **продира́ть.** —**продра́ться,** *refl., pfv. of* **продира́ться.**

продро́гнуть *v. pfv.* [*past* **-дро́г, -ла**] to be chilled to the bone.

продува́ть *v. impfv.* [*pfv.* **проду́ть**] **1,** to blow out; clean out by blowing. **2,** [*impfv. only*] (*of a wind, draft, etc.*) *colloq.* to blow through. **3,** *impers.* to be chilled through (*by the wind*): меня́ продуло, I am chilled (from the wind).

продувно́й *adj., colloq.* sly; crafty.

проду́кт *n.* **1,** product. **2,** *pl.* food products; groceries: моло́чные проду́кты, dairy products; заморо́женные проду́кты, frozen food(s).

продукти́вный *adj.* productive. —**продукти́вность,** *n.f.* productivity.

продукто́вый *adj.* food (*attrib.*). —**продукто́вый магази́н,** grocery store.

проду́кция *n.* production; output.

проду́манный *adj.* considered; carefully thought out.

проду́мывать *v. impfv.* [*pfv.* **проду́мать**] to think out; think through.

проду́ть [*infl.* **-ду́ю, -ду́ешь**] *v., pfv. of* **продува́ть.**

продыря́вливать *v. impfv.* [*pfv.* **продыря́вить**] *colloq.* **1,** to make a hole in. **2,** to wear holes in. —**продыря́вливаться,** *refl., colloq.* to develop holes; become full of holes.

продю́сер (сэ) *n.* producer (*of a motion picture*).

проеда́ть *v. impfv.* [*pfv.* **проéсть**] **1,** to eat away; corrode. **2,** *colloq.* to spend (one's money) on food.

проéзд *n.* **1,** passage; getting across: туда́ нет проéзда, you cannot get there; there is no way to get there. **2,** trip: де́ньги на проéзд, money for the trip.

Плáта за проéзд, fare. Скóлько стóит проéзд в...?, what is the fare to...? **3,** passage; passageway. **4,** street; thoroughfare. —**проéздом,** *colloq.* passing through.

проéздить *v. pfv.* [*infl.* **-éзжу, -éздишь**] **1,** to travel (*for a certain length of time*). **2,** *colloq.* to spend (a certain amount of money) on a trip.

проезднóй *adj.,* in **проезднáя плáта,** fare; **проезднóй билéт,** ticket.

проезжáть *v. impfv.* [*pfv.* **проéхать**] **1,** to ride; drive (along, through, past, etc.). **2,** (*with* **мимо**) to pass (by). **3,** to go (right) past (*inadvertently*). **4,** to cover (a certain distance).

проéзжий *adj.* **1,** passing by; passing through. **2,** (*of a road*) fit for traffic; used for traffic. —*n.* person passing through.

проéкт *n.* **1,** project; plan; design. **2,** draft: проéкт резолюции, draft resolution.

проектировать *v. impfv.* [*pfv.* **спроектировать;** *pres.* **-рую, -руешь**] **1,** to design. **2,** [*impfv. only*] to plan. **3,** *math.* to project. **4,** to project (*onto a screen*).

проектирóвщик *n.* designer.

проéктный *adj.* **1,** planning (*attrib.*). **2,** planned; projected. —**проéктная мóщность, 1,** planned production capacity (*of a factory*). **2,** rated capacity (*of a machine*).

проéктор *n.* projector.

проекциóнный *adj.,* in **проекциóнный аппарáт** *or* **фонáрь,** projector.

проéкция *n.* projection.

проём *n.* opening (*for a door, window, etc.*).

проéсть [*infl. like* **есть**] *v., pfv. of* **проедáть.**

проéхать [*infl. like* **éхать**] *v., pfv. of* **проезжáть.** —**проéхаться,** *refl., colloq.* to go for a ride; go for a drive.

прожáренный *adj.* (*of meat*) well-done.

прожáривать *v. impfv.* [*pfv.* **прожáрить**] to roast thoroughly; fry thoroughly.

прождáть *v. pfv.* [*infl. like* **ждать**] to wait (*for a certain length of time*).

прожевáть [*infl.* **-жую, -жуёшь**] *v., pfv. of* **прожёвывать.**

прожёвывать *v. impfv.* [*pfv.* **прожевáть**] to chew well; chew thoroughly.

прожектёр *n.* promoter of impractical schemes.

прожéктор *n.* searchlight; floodlight.

прожéчь [*infl. like* **жечь**] *v., pfv. of* **прожигáть.**

прожжённый *adj., colloq.* arch; arrant; out-and-out.

проживáние *n.* **1,** residing; residence. **2,** squandering.

проживáть *v. impfv.* [*pfv.* **прожить**] **1,** [*impfv. only*] to live; reside. **2,** to spend; run through (a sum of money).

прожигáть *v. impfv.* [*pfv.* **прожéчь**] **1,** to burn: прожигáть дыру в (+ *prepl.*), to burn a hole in. **2,** to burn through. —**прожигáть жизнь,** to lead a dissolute life.

прожилка [*gen. pl.* **-лок**] *n.* vein; streak.

прожитие *n.,* in **на прожитие,** to live on: дéньги на прожитие, money to live on.

прожиточный *adj.,* in **прожиточный минимум,** living wage; subsistence wage.

прожить *v. pfv.* [*infl.* **-живу, -живёшь;** *past* **прóжил, прожилá, прóжило**] **1,** *pfv. of* **проживáть** (*in sense* #2). **2,** to live (*for a certain length of time*).

прожóрливый *adj.* voracious; gluttonous.

прожужжáть *v. pfv.* [*infl.* **-жжу, -жжишь**] to buzz.

—**прожужжáть уши** (+ *dat.*), to tell (someone) over and over.

прóза *n.* prose.

прозáик *n.* writer of prose.

прозаический *adj.* **1,** prose (*attrib.*). **2,** [*also,* **прозаичный**] prosaic. **3,** practical; businesslike.

прозвáние *n.* nickname.

прозвáть [*infl. like* **звать**] *v., pfv. of* **прозывáть.**

прозвенéть *v. pfv.* [*infl.* **-нит, -нят**] to ring out; resound.

прóзвище *n.* nickname.

прозвонить *v. pfv.* **1,** (*of a bell*) to ring. **2,** to announce by ringing a bell.

прозвучáть *v., pfv. of* **звучáть.**

прозевáть *v., pfv. of* **зевáть** (*in sense* #3).

прозелит *n.* proselyte.

прозимовáть *v., pfv. of* **зимовáть.**

прозорливый *adj.* sagacious; perspicacious. —**прозорливость,** *n.f.* sagacity; perspicacity.

прозрáчный *adj.* **1,** transparent. **2,** (*of water, air, etc.*) clear. **3,** (*of material*) very thin; gauzy. —**прозрáчность,** *n.f.* transparency.

прозревáть *v. impfv.* [*pfv.* **прозрéть**] **1,** to regain one's sight. **2,** *fig.* to see things clearly; see the light.

прозрéние *n.* **1,** recovery of one's sight. **2,** *fig.* insight; discernment.

прозрéть [*infl.* **-зрю, -зришь**] *v., pfv. of* **прозревáть.**

прозывáть *v. impfv.* [*pfv.* **прозвáть**] to nickname.

прозябáть *v. impfv.* to vegetate (*lit. & fig.*).

прозябнуть *v. pfv.* [*past* **-зяб, -ла**] *colloq.* to be frozen; be chilled to the bone.

проигрáть *v., pfv. of* **проигрывать. 2,** to play (*for a certain length of time*). —**проигрáться,** *refl., pfv. of* **проигрываться.**

проигрыватель *n.m.* record player.

проигрывать *v. impfv.* [*pfv.* **проигрáть**] **1,** to lose. **2,** to gamble away. **3,** *colloq.* to play; perform. —**проигрываться,** *refl.* to gamble away all one's money.

проигрыш *n.* **1,** loss; defeat. **2,** losses (*in gambling*). —**быть в прóигрыше,** to be the loser; end up losing.

прóигрышный *adj.* losing.

произведéние *n.* **1,** making (*of something*). **2,** work (*of art or literature*). **3,** *math.* product.

произвести [*infl. like* **вести**] *v., pfv. of* **производить.**

производитель *n.m.* **1,** producer. **2,** sire. —**производитель рабóт,** construction superintendent.

производительный *adj.* productive. —**производительность,** *n.f.* productivity.

производить *v. impfv.* [*pfv.* **произвести;** *pres.* **-вожу, -вóдишь**] **1,** [*usu. impfv.*] to produce; manufacture. **2,** to conduct; carry out. **3,** to produce; cause; create. **4,** to make (an impression, calculation, repairs, etc.). **5,** to produce; give birth to. Производить на свет, to bring into the world. **6,** (*with* **в** + *nom. pl.*) to promote (to): егó произвели в капитáны, he was promoted to captain.

производный *adj.* derivative. —**производная,** *n.,* *math.* derivative. —**производное,** *n., chem.* derivative.

производственный *adj.* production (*attrib.*); industrial.

произвóдство *n.* **1,** production. **2,** manufacture. **3,** conducting; carrying out. **4,** promotion.

произвóл *n.* **1,** arbitrary rule; tyranny; despotism. **2,** arbitrariness. —**оставлять** *or* **бросáть на произвóл судьбы,** to leave to the mercy of fate.

произво́льный *adj.* **1,** arbitrary. **2,** *physiol.* voluntary. —**произво́льно,** *adv.* arbitrarily.

произнесе́ние *n.* **1,** pronouncing (*of a sentence*). **2,** giving (*of a speech*).

произнести́ [*infl. like* нести́] *v., pfv. of* произноси́ть.

произноси́ть *v. impfv.* [*pfv.* произнести́; *pres.* -но́шу, -но́сишь] **1,** to pronounce. **2,** to utter (a word); deliver (a speech, sermon, toast, etc.).

произноше́ние *n.* pronunciation.

произойти́ [*infl.* -изойдёт; *past* -изошёл, -изошла́] *v., pfv. of* происходи́ть.

произраста́ть *v. impfv.* [*pfv.* произрасти́] to sprout; spring up.

произрасти́ [*infl. like* расти́] *v., pfv. of* произраста́ть.

проиллюстри́ровать *v., pfv. of* иллюстри́ровать.

проинформи́ровать *v., pfv. of* информи́ровать.

про́иски [*gen.* -сков] *n. pl.* intrigues; schemes; machinations.

проистека́ть *v. impfv.* [*pfv.* происте́чь] (*with* из *or* от) to arise (out of); stem (from); spring (from); result (from).

происте́чь [*infl. like* течь] *v., pfv. of* проистека́ть.

происходи́ть *v. impfv.* [*pfv.* произойти́; *pres.* -хожу́, -хо́дишь] **1,** to happen; occur; take place. **2,** (*with* от) to result (from); be the result (of). **3,** (*with* от *or* из) to be descended (from).

происхожде́ние *n.* **1,** origin. **2,** parentage; descent; extraction; ancestry. Англича́нин по происхожде́нию, of English origin; English by birth.

происше́ствие *n.* incident.

пройдо́ха *n.m. & f., colloq.* sly person; rascal.

про́йма *n.* armhole.

пройти́ [*infl.* пройду́, пройдёшь; *past* прошёл, прошла́, прошло́] *v., pfv. of* проходи́ть. —**пройти́сь,** *refl., pfv. of* проха́живаться.

прок [*2nd gen.* про́ку] *n., colloq.* use; good: како́й прок в э́том?; что про́ку от э́того?, what's the good of it?

прокажённый *adj.* leprous. —*n.* leper.

прока́за *n.* **1,** leprosy. **2,** prank; trick.

прока́зить *v. impfv.* [*pfv.* напрока́зить; *pres.* -жу, -зишь] *colloq.* = прока́зничать.

прока́зливый *adj., colloq.* mischievous.

прока́зник *n.* mischief-maker; prankster.

прока́зничать *v. impfv.* [*pfv.* напрока́зничать] to play pranks; horse around.

прока́лывать *v. impfv.* [*pfv.* проколо́ть] to prick; pierce; puncture.

проканите́литься *v.r., pfv. of* каните́литься.

прока́пывать *v. impfv.* [*pfv.* прокопа́ть] **1,** to dig (a canal, ditch, etc.). **2,** to dig through.

прока́т *n.* **1,** rental. **2,** rolling (*of metal*). **3,** rolled metal.

проката́ть *v., pfv. of* прока́тывать.

прокати́ть *v. pfv.* [*infl.* -качу́, -ка́тишь] **1,** to roll. **2,** to take for a ride. **3,** *v.i.* to roll by; roll past. **4,** *colloq.* to fail to elect; reject at the polls. **5,** *colloq.* to berate; roundly condemn. —**прокати́ться,** *refl.* **1,** to roll; roll along. **2,** to go for a ride. **3,** (*with* по) to sweep across; sweep over.

прока́тка *n.* rolling (*of metal*).

прока́тный *adj.* **1,** for rent; rented; rental (*attrib.*). **2,** of or pert. to the rolling of metal: прока́тный стан, rolling mill. **3,** (*of metal*) rolled.

прока́тывать *v. impfv.* [*pfv.* проката́ть] **1,** to roll flat; press. **2,** to roll (metal).

прока́шливаться *v.r. impfv.* [*pfv.* прока́шляться] to clear one's throat.

прокипяти́ть *v. pfv.* [*infl.* -чу́, -ти́шь] to boil (thoroughly).

проки́снуть [*past* -ки́с, -ла] *v., pfv. of* ки́снуть.

прокла́дка *n.* **1,** laying (*of a road, pipe, etc.*). **2,** padding. **3,** washer; gasket.

прокла́дывать *v. impfv.* [*pfv.* проложи́ть] **1,** to lay; build (a road, pipeline, etc.). **2,** to make; form (a path, trail, etc.). **3,** (*with instr.*) to interlay (with); pack (with). —**прокла́дывать путь, 1,** to blaze a trail. **2,** (*with dat.*) to pave the way (for). —**прокла́дывать себе́ доро́гу,** to make one's way in the world.

проклама́ция *n.* leaflet.

проклами́ровать *v. impfv. & pfv.* [*pres.* -рую, -руешь] to proclaim.

прокле́ивать *v. impfv.* [*pfv.* прокле́ить] to smear; cover (*with paste or glue*).

проклина́ть *v. impfv.* [*pfv.* прокля́сть] to damn; curse.

прокля́сть [*infl.* -кляну́, -клянёшь; *past* про́клял, -кляла́, про́кляло] *v., pfv. of* проклина́ть.

прокля́тие *n.* **1,** curse: налага́ть прокля́тие на, to place a curse on. **2,** damnation; perdition. **3,** curse word; swearword. —*interj.* damn it!; damn it all!

про́клятый *past passive part. of* прокля́сть: будь я про́клят (про́клята), е́сли..., I'll be damned if...

прокля́тый *adj.* cursed; damned; accursed.

проко́л *n.* puncture.

проколо́ть [*infl.* -колю́, -ко́лешь] *v., pfv. of* прока́лывать.

прокомменти́ровать *v. pfv.* [*infl.* -рую, -руешь] to comment on; provide commentary on.

прокомпости́ровать *v., pfv. of* компости́ровать.

проконспекти́ровать *v., pfv. of* конспекти́ровать.

проко́нсул *n.* proconsul.

проконсульти́ровать *v., pfv. of* консульти́ровать. —**проконсульти́роваться,** *refl., pfv. of* консульти́роваться.

проконтроли́ровать *v., pfv. of* контроли́ровать.

прокопа́ть *v., pfv. of* прока́пывать.

прокопте́лый *adj., colloq.* sooty; covered with soot.

проко́рм *n.* nourishment; sustenance.

прокорми́ть *v. pfv.* [*infl.* -кормлю́, -ко́рмишь] to feed; provide sustenance for. —**прокорми́ться,** *refl., colloq.* **1,** to feed oneself; sustain oneself. **2,** (*with instr.*) to subsist (on).

прокорректи́ровать *v., pfv. of* корректи́ровать.

проко́с *n.* swath.

прокра́дываться *v.r. impfv.* [*pfv.* прокра́сться] to sneak; steal; creep (into, through, etc.).

прокра́сться [*infl. like* красть] *v.r., pfv. of* прокра́дываться.

прокрича́ть *v. pfv.* [*infl.* -чу́, -чи́шь] **1,** to shout. **2,** *fig.* to trumpet; crow.

прокурату́ра *n.* office of the public prosecutor.

прокуро́р *n.* public prosecutor. —**прокуро́рский,** *adj.* public prosecutor's.

прокуси́ть [*infl.* -кушу́, -ку́сишь] *v., pfv. of* проку́сывать.

проку́сывать *v. impfv.* [*pfv.* прокуси́ть] to bite through.

прокути́ть *v. pfv.* [*infl.* -кучу́, -ку́тишь] **1**, *v.t.* to squander; dissipate. **2**, *v.i.* to go on a binge.

прола́мывать *v. impfv.* [*pfv.* проломи́ть] **1**, to break through; make a hole in. **2**, to fracture (one's skull). —прола́мываться, *refl.* to break; give way.

пролега́ть *v. impfv.* (*of a road*) to lie; run; pass.

пролежа́ть *v. pfv.* [*infl.* -лежу́, -лежи́шь] to lie (*for a certain length of time*).

про́лежень [*gen.* -жня] *n.m.* bedsore.

пролеза́ть *v. impfv.* [*pfv.* проле́зть] **1**, (*with* сквозь *or* че́рез) to climb through. **2**, (*with* в + *acc.*) to fit through; get through; go through. **3**, (*with* в + *acc.*) *colloq.* to worm one's way into.

проле́зть [*infl. like* ле́зть] *v., pfv. of* пролеза́ть.

пролёт *n.* **1**, flight. **2**, open space. **3**, span (*of a bridge*). **4**, *archit.* bay. **5**, stairwell. **6**, *colloq.* distance between two railway stations.

пролетариа́т *n.* proletariat. —пролета́рий, *n.* proletarian; worker. —пролета́рский, *adj.* proletarian.

пролета́ть *v. impfv.* [*pfv.* пролете́ть] **1**, to fly; (*with* над) fly over; (*with* че́рез) fly across; (*with* ми́мо) fly past. **2**, to fly (a certain distance). **3**, *fig.* (*of time*) to fly by.

пролете́ть [*infl.* -чу́, -ти́шь] *v., pfv. of* пролета́ть.

проле́тка [*gen. pl.* -ток] *n.* open carriage.

проли́в *n.* strait; channel.

пролива́ть *v. impfv.* [*pfv.* проли́ть] **1**, to spill. **2**, to shed (light, tears, blood, etc.). —пролива́ться, *refl.* (*of a liquid*) to spill.

проливно́й *adj.* (*of rain*) driving; torrential.

проли́ть [*infl.* -лью́, -льёшь; *past* про́лил *or* проли́л, пролила́, про́лило *or* проли́ло] *v., pfv. of* пролива́ть. —проли́ться, *refl., pfv. of* пролива́ться.

проло́г *n.* prologue.

проложи́ть [*infl.* -ложу́, -ло́жишь] *v., pfv. of* прокла́дывать.

проло́м *n.* break; breach.

проломи́ть [*infl.* -ломлю́, -ло́мишь] *v., pfv. of* прола́мывать. —проломи́ться, *refl., pfv. of* прола́мываться.

прома́зать [*infl.* -ма́жу, -ма́жешь] *v., pfv. of* ма́зать (*in sense #6*) *and* прома́зывать.

прома́зывать *v. impfv.* [*pfv.* прома́зать] **1**, to oil; grease. **2**, *colloq.* to miss (*in shooting or games*).

прома́сливать *v. impfv.* [*pfv.* прома́слить] to treat with oil.

прома́тывать *v. impfv.* [*pfv.* промота́ть] *colloq.* to squander; dissipate.

про́мах *n.* **1**, miss (*in shooting*). **2**, *fig.* blunder. —ма́лый не про́мах, nobody's fool.

промахну́ться *v.r. pfv.* **1**, to miss (*in striking, shooting, etc.*). **2**, *colloq.* to make a blunder.

прома́чивать *v. impfv.* [*pfv.* промочи́ть] to drench; soak.

промедле́ние *n.* delay.

проме́длить *v. pfv.* to delay; procrastinate.

проме́жность *n.f.* crotch.

промежу́ток [*gen.* -тка] *n.* **1**, space (*between two objects*). **2**, interval (*of time*).

промежу́точный *adj.* **1**, intermediate. **2**, intervening; interim. —промежу́точные вы́боры, off-year elections.

промелькну́ть *v. pfv.* **1**, to flash by; flash past. **2**, (*of a thought*) to flash across one's mind. **3**, *fig.* to appear momentarily; be faintly perceptible.

проме́нивать *v. impfv.* [*pfv.* променя́ть] to exchange; trade; barter.

промерза́ть *v. impfv.* [*pfv.* промёрзнуть] **1**, to be frozen solid. **2**, *colloq.* to be chilled through.

промёрзлый *adj.* frozen.

промёрзнуть [*past* -мёрз, -ла] *v., pfv. of* промерза́ть.

проме́ривать *v. impfv.* [*pfv.* проме́рить] to measure; survey.

промеря́ть *v. impfv.* = проме́ривать.

Промете́й *n.* Prometheus.

проме́тий *n.* promethium.

проме́шкать *v. pfv., colloq.* to linger; dawdle.

промо́зглый *adj.* dank; damp.

промока́тельный *adj., in* промока́тельная бума́га, blotting paper.

промока́ть *v. impfv.* [*pfv.* промо́кнуть] **1**, to get wet; get soaked; get drenched. **2**, [*impfv. only*] to be not waterproof: плащ промока́ет, the raincoat is not waterproof. **3**, *v.t.* [*pfv.* промокну́ть] to blot; dry (ink).

промока́шка [*gen. pl.* -шек] *n., colloq.* blotter.

промо́кнуть [*past* -мо́к, -ла] *v., pfv. of* промока́ть.

промокну́ть [*past* -мокну́л] *v., pfv. of* промока́ть (*in sense #3*).

промо́лвить *v. pfv.* [*infl.* -влю, -вишь] to utter; say.

промолча́ть *v. pfv.* [*infl.* -чу́, -чи́шь] to keep silent; say nothing.

проморга́ть *v. pfv., colloq.* **1**, to fail to notice. **2**, to miss; let slip by.

промота́ть *v., pfv. of* прома́тывать.

промочи́ть [*infl.* -мочу́, -мо́чишь] *v., pfv. of* прома́чивать.

промтова́рный *adj., in* промтова́рный магази́н, general store (*selling clothes, manufactured items, etc.*).

промтова́ры [*gen.* -ров] *n. pl.* manufactured goods (*contr. of* промы́шленные това́ры).

промча́ться *v.r. pfv.* [*infl.* -чу́сь, -чи́шься] to flash by; race by; speed by.

промыва́ть *v. impfv.* [*pfv.* промы́ть] **1**, to wash; cleanse; bathe. **2**, to pan (gold).

про́мысел [*gen.* -сла] *n.* **1**, trade: пушно́й про́мысел, fur trade. Куста́рный про́мысел, cottage industry. **2**, hunting; catching. Рыбный про́мысел, fishing. **3**, *pl.* fields; mines: нефтяны́е про́мыслы, oil fields; соляны́е про́мыслы, salt mines.

про́мысл *n., relig.* Providence.

промысло́вый *adj.* **1**, commercial. **2**, sold commercially: промысло́вая пти́ца, game bird; промысло́вая ры́ба, food fish. **3**, producers': промысло́вая коопера́ция, producers' cooperative.

промы́ть [*infl.* -мо́ю, -мо́ешь] *v., pfv. of* промыва́ть.

промы́шленник *n.* manufacturer; industrialist.

промы́шленность *n.f.* industry. —промы́шленный, *adj.* industrial.

промышля́ть *v. impfv.* (*with instr.*) to earn one's living (by); make a living (from).

промя́млить *v., pfv. of* мя́млить.

прона́шивать *v. impfv.* [*pfv.* пpoноси́ть] to wear out (clothes). —прона́шиваться, *refl.* (*of clothes*) to wear out.

пронести́ [*infl. like* нести́] *v., pfv. of* пpoноси́ть[1]. —пронести́сь, *refl., pfv. of* проноси́ться.

пронза́ть *v. impfv.* [*pfv.* пронзи́ть] to pierce; impale

пронзи́тельный *adj.* piercing.

пронзи́ть [*infl.* -нжу́, -нзи́шь] *v., pfv. of* пронза́ть.

пронза́ть [*infl.* -нижу́, -ни́жешь] *v., pfv. of* прони́зывать.

прони́зывать *v. impfv.* [*pfv.* пронизи́ть] **1,** to pierce. **2,** *fig.* to penetrate; permeate.

проника́ть *v. impfv.* [*pfv.* прони́кнуть] (*with* в + *acc.*) **1,** to penetrate. **2,** to get to; reach. **3,** *fig.* to delve into; (try to) fathom. —**проника́ться,** *refl.* (*with instr.*) to be imbued (with); be filled (with).

проникнове́ние *n.* **1,** penetration. **2,** feeling; sincerity.

проникнове́нный *adj.* heartfelt; earnest. —**проникнове́нность,** *n.f.* feeling; sincerity.

прони́кнуть [*past* -ни́к, -ла] *v., pfv. of* проника́ть. —**прони́кнуться,** *refl., pfv. of* проника́ться.

пронима́ть *v. impfv.* [*pfv.* проня́ть] *colloq.* **1,** (*of* cold, wind, *etc.*) to penetrate. **2,** *fig.* to move; touch; affect.

проница́емый *adj.* permeable. —**проница́емость,** *n.f.* permeability.

проница́тельный *adj.* **1,** astute; shrewd; penetrating; perspicacious. **2,** (*of a look*) penetrating. —**проница́тельность,** *n.f.* astuteness; perspicacity; acumen; insight.

проноси́ть[1] *v. impfv.* [*pfv.* пронести́; *pres.* -ношу́, -но́сишь] **1,** to carry. **2,** (*with* че́рез) to carry through; (*with* ми́мо) carry past. **3,** to carry quickly; whisk. **4,** to smuggle (something) into, past, *or* out of. **5,** *impers.* to pass: грозу́ пронесло́, the storm passed. —**проноси́ться,** *refl.* **1,** to rush past; flash by; sweep over. **2,** (*of a rumor*) to spread; (*of time*) to fly by.

проноси́ть[2] *v. pfv.* [*infl.* -ношу́, -но́сишь] **1,** *pfv. of* прона́шивать. **2,** to carry (*for a certain length of time*). **3,** to wear (*for a certain length of time*). —**проноси́ться,** *refl.* **1,** *pfv. of* прона́шиваться. **2,** (*of clothes*) to last (*a certain length of time*).

пронумерова́ть *v., pfv. of* нумерова́ть.

проны́ра *n.m. & f., colloq.* one always able to gain access; wire-puller. —**проны́рливый,** *adj., colloq.* sneaky; slippery; able to worm one's way in.

проню́хивать *v. impfv.* [*pfv.* проню́хать] *colloq.* to hear about; get wind of.

проня́ть [*infl. like* поня́ть] *v., pfv. of* пронима́ть.

прообраз *n.* prototype.

пропага́нда *n.* **1,** propaganda. **2,** (*with gen.*) propagandizing (of).

пропаганди́ровать *v. impfv.* [*pres.* -рую, -руешь] to propagandize.

пропаганди́ст *n.* propagandist. —**пропаганди́стский,** *adj.* propagandistic; propaganda (*attrib.*).

пропада́ть *v. impfv.* [*pfv.* пропа́сть] **1,** to disappear; be missing: где вы пропада́ли?, куда́ вы пропа́ли?, where did you disappear to?; where have you been? У меня́ пропа́л зо́нтик, my umbrella has disappeared; I've lost my umbrella. **2,** to die; perish. **3,** to be lost; be done for. **4,** to be wasted. —**пиши́ пропа́ло,** it's hopeless. —**пропади́ про́падом!,** *colloq.* damn it all!

пропа́жа *n.* **1,** disappearance; loss. **2,** *colloq.* lost object; missing thing.

пропа́лывать *v. impfv.* [*pfv.* прополо́ть] to weed.

пропа́н *n.* propane.

про́пасть [*pl.* про́пасти, -сте́й, -стя́м] *n.f.* **1,** abyss; chasm. **2,** *fig.* gulf; chasm. **3,** (*with gen.*) *colloq.* lots of; tons of. —**на краю́ про́пасти,** on the brink of disaster.

пропа́сть [*infl. like* пасть] *v., pfv. of* пропада́ть.

пропа́хнуть *v. pfv.* [*past* -па́х, -ла] (*with instr.*) to become permeated with the smell of; reek (of).

пропа́щий *adj., colloq.* **1,** lost; gone for good. **2,** hopeless.

пропека́ть *v. impfv.* [*pfv.* пропе́чь] to bake (*thoroughly*). —**пропека́ться,** *refl.* to be baked thoroughly.

пропе́ллер *n.* propeller.

пропе́ть *v. pfv.* [*infl.* -пою́, -поёшь] **1,** *pfv. of* петь. **2,** to sing (*for a certain length of time*).

пропе́чь [*infl. like* печь] *v., pfv. of* пропека́ть. —**пропе́чься,** *refl., pfv. of* пропека́ться.

пропива́ть *v. impfv.* [*pfv.* пропи́ть] to drink away; squander by drinking.

пропи́ливать *v. impfv.* [*pfv.* пропили́ть] to saw through.

пропили́ть [*infl.* -пилю́, -пи́лишь] *v., pfv. of* пропи́ливать.

прописа́ть [*infl.* -пишу́, -пи́шешь] *v., pfv. of* пропи́сывать. —**прописа́ться,** *refl., pfv. of* пропи́сываться.

пропи́ска [*gen. pl.* -сок] *n.* **1,** registration. **2,** residence permit.

прописно́й *adj.* **1,** *in* прописна́я бу́ква, capital letter. **2,** conventional: прописна́я мора́ль, conventional morality. —**прописна́я и́стина,** truism.

пропи́сывать *v. impfv.* [*pfv.* прописа́ть] **1,** to prescribe (medicine). **2,** to register. —**пропи́сываться,** *refl.* to register (*e.g.* in a hotel).

про́пись *n.f.* sample of writing. —**про́писью,** *adv.* written out: написа́ть число́ про́писью, to write out a number (*using letters*).

пропита́ние *n.* **1,** subsistence: сре́дства пропита́ния, means of subsistence. **2,** food; sustenance.

пропи́тывать *v. impfv.* [*pfv.* пропита́ть] to saturate; impregnate.

пропи́ть *v. pfv.* [*infl.* -пью́, -пьёшь; *past* про́пил *or* пропи́л, пропила́, про́пило *or* пропи́ло] **1,** *pfv. of* пропива́ть. **2,** to drink (*for a certain length of time*).

пропла́вать *v. pfv.* to swim (*for a certain length of time*).

пропла́кать *v. pfv.* [*infl.* -пла́чу, -пла́чешь] to cry (*for a certain length of time*). —**пропла́кать глаза́,** *colloq.* to cry one's eyes out.

проплыва́ть *v. impfv.* [*pfv.* проплы́ть] **1,** to swim; sail; float; drift. **2,** (*with acc. or* ми́мо) to swim past; sail past. **3,** to swim; sail (a certain distance).

проплы́ть [*infl. like* плыть] *v., pfv. of* проплыва́ть.

пропове́дник *n.* **1,** preacher. **2,** *fig.* advocate; exponent; proponent.

пропове́довать *v. impfv.* [*pres.* -дую, -дуешь] **1,** to preach; propagate (a religion, idea, etc.). **2,** *v.i.* to preach (*deliver a sermon*).

про́поведь *n.f.* **1,** sermon. **2,** spreading; propagation.

пропо́йца *n.m. & f., colloq.* drunkard; drunk.

пропо́лзать *v. impfv.* [*pfv.* прополэти́] to crawl; creep.

прополэти́ [*infl. like* ползти́] *v., pfv. of* пропо́лзать.

пропо́лка *n.* weeding.

прополоска́ть *v., pfv. of* полоска́ть.

прополо́ть [*infl.* -полю́, -по́лешь] *v., pfv. of* пропа́лывать.

пропорциона́льно *adv.* **1,** proportionally; proportionately. **2,** (*with dat.*) proportionately with; in proportion to. —**пропорциона́льность,** *n.f.* proportion.

пропорциона́льный *adj.* **1,** proportional; proportionate. **2,** well-proportioned.

пропо́рция *n.* proportion.

пропоте́ть *v. pfv.* **1,** to perspire heavily. **2,** *colloq.* (*of an item of clothing*) to become drenched with perspiration.

про́пуск *n.* **1,** admission; admittance. **2,** passing through; letting through. **3,** omission. **4,** failure to attend; absence. **5,** blank; gap. **6,** [*pl.* -ска́] pass; permit. **7,** [*pl.* -ска́] password.

пропуска́ть *v. impfv.* [*pfv.* пропусти́ть] **1,** to admit; let in; let pass; let through. **2,** to serve; accommodate (a certain number of people). **3,** *sports* to allow (a goal, point to be scored, etc.). **4,** to let in (light, water, etc.). **5,** to pass through; run through; put through. **6,** to omit; leave out. **7,** to skip; pass over. **8,** to miss; fail to attend. **9,** to miss; let slip by.

пропускно́й *adj.* admission (*attrib.*). —пропускна́я бума́га, blotting paper. —пропускна́я спосо́бность, (carrying) capacity.

пропусти́ть [*infl.* -пущу́, -пу́стишь] *v., pfv. of* пропуска́ть.

прора́б *n.* construction superintendent (*contr. of* производи́тель рабо́т).

прораба́тывать *v. impfv.* [*pfv.* прорабо́тать] *colloq.* **1,** to work over; study carefully. **2,** to give (someone) a going over.

прорабо́тать *v. pfv.* **1,** *pfv. of* прораба́тывать. **2,** to work (*for a certain length of time*).

прораста́ние *n.* germination; sprouting.

прораста́ть *v. impfv.* [*pfv.* прорасти́] to germinate; sprout.

прорасти́ [*infl. like* расти́] *v., pfv. of* прораста́ть.

прорва́ть [*infl. like* рвать] *v., pfv. of* прорыва́ть[1]. —прорва́ться, *refl., pfv. of* прорыва́ться.

проре́з *n.* cut; slit; opening.

проре́зать [*infl.* -ре́жу, -ре́жешь] *v., pfv. of* проре́зать. —проре́заться, *refl., pfv. of* проре́заться.

прореза́ть *v. impfv.* [*pfv.* проре́зать] to cut; cut through. —прореза́ться, *refl.* (*of teeth*) to cut through: у ребёнка прореза́ются зу́бы, the child is teething.

прорези́нивать *v. impfv.* [*pfv.* прорези́нить] to rubberize.

про́резь *n.f.* cut; slit; opening.

прорепети́ровать *v., pfv. of* репети́ровать.

проре́ха *n.* **1,** tear. **2,** *colloq.* shortcoming; deficiency.

прорецензи́ровать *v., pfv. of* рецензи́ровать.

проржа́веть *v. pfv.* to rust through.

прорица́ние *n.* prophecy; prediction. —прорица́тель, *n.m.* prophet.

прорица́ть *v. impfv.* to prophesy.

проро́к *n.* prophet.

пророни́ть *v. pfv.* [*infl.* -роню́, -ро́нишь] **1,** to utter: не пророни́ть ни сло́ва, not to utter a word. **2,** to miss: он бои́тся пророни́ть сло́во, he is afraid to miss a word. —не пророни́ть (ни) слезы́ *or* слези́нки, not to shed a tear.

проро́ческий *adj.* prophetic. —проро́чество, *n.* prophecy.

проро́чить *v. impfv.* [*pfv.* напроро́чить] to prophesy.

проруба́ть *v. impfv.* [*pfv.* проруби́ть] to cut through; hack through.

проруби́ть [*infl.* -рублю́, -ру́бишь] *v., pfv. of* проруба́ть.

про́рубь *n.f.* hole in the ice.

проры́в *n.* **1,** bursting. **2,** breach. **3,** *mil.* breakthrough. **4,** *fig.* hitch; lag (*in production*).

прорыва́ть[1] *v. impfv.* [*pfv.* прорва́ть] **1,** to tear. **2,** to break through. **3,** *impers.* to burst: плоти́ну прорва́ло, the dam burst. —прорыва́ться, *refl.* **1,** to tear; break; burst. **2,** to break through; (*with* из) break out of.

прорыва́ть[2] *v. impfv.* [*pfv.* проры́ть] to dig (a hole, tunnel, canal, etc.).

проры́ть [*infl.* -ро́ю, -ро́ешь] *v., pfv. of* прорыва́ть[2].

проса́ливать *v. impfv.* **1,** [*pfv.* проса́лить] to grease. **2,** [*pfv.* просоли́ть] to salt.

проса́чивание *n.* **1,** seepage. **2,** penetration; infiltration.

проса́чиваться *v.r. impfv.* [*pfv.* просочи́ться] **1,** to seep. **2,** (*with* в + *acc.*) to penetrate; infiltrate. **3,** *fig.* (*of news, a rumor, etc.*) to leak out; (*with* в + *acc.*) filter (into).

просве́рливать *v. impfv.* [*pfv.* просверли́ть] **1,** to drill; bore (a hole). **2,** to drill through; drill a hole in.

просверли́ть *v., pfv. of* сверли́ть (*in sense #1*) *and* просве́рливать.

просве́т *n.* **1,** narrow shaft of light (*shining through an opening onto a surface*). **2,** *fig.* bright spot (*in a situation, one's life, etc.*). **3,** open space; empty space. **4,** opening; crack (*in a door or window*). **5,** *mil.* stripe (*on shoulder insignia*).

просвети́тельный *adj.* educational.

просвети́ть *v. pfv.* **1,** [*infl.* -свечу́, -све́тишь] *pfv. of* просве́чивать. **2,** [*infl.* -свещу́, -свети́шь] *pfv. of* просвеща́ть.

просветле́ние *n.* **1,** brightening (*of the sky*). **2,** *fig.* lucid moment.

просветле́ть *v., pfv. of* светле́ть.

просве́чивание *n.* X-raying; X-ray examination.

просве́чивать *v. impfv.* [*pfv.* просвети́ть] **1,** (*of the sun*) to light up. **2,** to X-ray. **3,** [*impfv. only*] to be translucent. **4,** [*impfv. only*] (*with* сквозь) to appear through; shine through.

просвеща́ть *v. impfv.* [*pfv.* просвети́ть] to enlighten.

просвеще́ние *n.* **1,** enlightenment. **2,** education.

просвира́ *n., Orth. Ch.* communion bread.

просви́рник *n.* marsh mallow. *Also,* просвирня́к [*gen.* -няка́].

просвиста́ть [*infl.* -свищу́, -сви́щешь] *v., pfv. of* просви́стывать. *Also,* просвисте́ть [*infl.* -свищу́, -свисти́шь].

просви́стывать *v. impfv.* [*pfv.* просвиста́ть *or* просвисте́ть] to whistle.

про́седь *n.f.* streaks of gray.

просе́ивать *v. impfv.* [*pfv.* просе́ять] to sift.

про́сека *n.* cleared path in a forest.

просёлок [*gen.* -лка] *n.* country road; byroad.

просёлочный *adj., in* просёлочная доро́га, = просёлок.

просе́ять [*infl.* -се́ю, -се́ешь] *v., pfv. of* просе́ивать.

просиде́ть [*infl.* -жу́, -ди́шь] *v., pfv. of* проси́живать.

проси́живать *v. impfv.* [*pfv.* просиде́ть] **1,** to sit (*for a certain length of time*). **2,** to stay (*for a certain length of time*). **3,** to wear out the seat of; wear out by sitting on.

про́синь *n.f.* bluish tint.

проси́тель *n.m., obs.* applicant; suppliant.

проси́тельный *adj.* pleading; suppliant.

проси́ть *v. impfv.* [*pfv.* **попроси́ть**; *pres.* **прошу́, про́сишь**] **1,** to ask: попроси́те его́ войти́, ask him to come in. **2,** to ask for; request: проси́ть кни́гу, to ask for a book; проси́ть разреше́ния, to ask (for) permission; проси́ть (о) по́мощи, to ask for help. **3,** to beg: проси́ть проще́ния, to beg someone's pardon. Я вас о́чень прошу́!, please!; I beg of you! **4,** to invite; call; ask. **5,** [*impfv. only*] to ask; charge (a price). **6,** (*with* за + *acc.*) to plead for (someone). —**прошу́ вас!**, please go ahead!; (*when serving food*) please help yourself!; (*when offering a chair*) please have a seat!; (*when entering a doorway*) after you!

проси́ться *v.r. impfv.* [*pfv.* **попроси́ться**; *pres.* **прошу́сь, про́сишься**] **1,** (*with inf. or* в/на + *acc.*) to ask (for); apply (for); ask permission (to). **2,** [*impfv. only*] (*with* на + *acc.*): проси́ться на язы́к, to be on the tip of one's tongue; проси́ться на карти́ну, to cry out to be painted.

проси́ть *v. pfv.* **1,** (*of the sun*) to begin to shine. **2,** *fig.* (*with instr.*) to beam (with joy); light up (with a smile).

проскака́ть *v. pfv.* [*infl.* -скачу́, -ска́чешь] **1,** to gallop. **2,** (*with* ми́мо) to gallop past.

проска́кивать *v. impfv.* [*pfv.* **проскочи́ть**] **1,** *v.t.* to race through; race past. Проскочи́ть светофо́р, to go through a traffic light. **2,** (*with* сквозь) to get through; slip through. **3,** to slip (into a small opening). **4,** *colloq.* (*of time*) to slip by. **5,** *colloq.* (*of mistakes*) to creep in.

проска́льзывание *n.* slippage.

проска́льзывать *v. impfv.* [*pfv.* **проскользну́ть**] **1,** to slip (through a small opening). **2,** to slip; sneak (into, past, through, etc.).

просклоня́ть *v., pfv. of* **склоня́ть** (*in sense* #5).

проскользну́ть *v., pfv. of* **проска́льзывать.**

проскочи́ть [*infl.* -скочу́, -ско́чишь] *v., pfv. of* **проска́кивать.**

проскрипе́ть *v., pfv. of* **скрипе́ть.**

проскурня́к [*gen.* -няка́] *n.* marsh mallow.

проскуча́ть *v. pfv.* to be bored (*for a certain length of time*).

просла́вить [*infl.* -влю, -вишь] *v., pfv. of* **прославля́ть.** —**просла́виться**, *refl., pfv. of* **прославля́ться.**

прославле́ние *n.* glorification.

просла́вленный *adj.* celebrated; renowned.

прославля́ть *v. impfv.* [*pfv.* **просла́вить**] **1,** to make famous. **2,** to glorify; celebrate (*in song, poetry, etc.*). —**прославля́ться**, *refl.* (*with instr.*) to become famous (for).

проследи́ть [*infl.* -жу́, -ди́шь] *v., pfv. of* **просле́живать.**

просле́живать *v. impfv.* [*pfv.* **проследи́ть**] **1,** to follow; trail; shadow. **2,** *fig.* to trace; trace the development of. **3,** (*with* за + *instr.*) *colloq.* to monitor; keep tabs on.

прослези́ться *v.r. pfv.* [*infl.* -жу́сь, -зи́шься] to shed a few tears.

просло́йка [*gen. pl.* -о́ек] *n.* **1,** layer. **2,** *fig.* social stratum.

прослужи́ть *v. pfv.* [*infl.* -служу́, -слу́жишь] **1,** to serve (*for a certain length of time*). **2,** (*of a product*) to last (*for a certain length of time*).

прослу́шать *v. pfv.* **1,** *pfv. of* **слу́шать** (*in sense* #4). and **прослу́шивать. 2,** *colloq.* to fail to hear; fail to catch; miss.

прослу́шивать *v. impfv.* [*pfv.* **прослу́шать**] **1,** to listen to (*from beginning to end*). **2,** *med.* to examine (*by listening to*). **3,** to "bug" (a room); tap (a telephone).

прослы́ть *v., pfv. of* **слыть.**

прослы́шать *v. pfv.* [*infl.* -шу, -шишь] (*with* о) *colloq.* to hear (about).

просма́тривать *v. impfv.* [*pfv.* **просмотре́ть**] **1,** to look over; glance over; scan. **2,** to examine; view. **3,** to overlook; miss. —**просма́триваться**, *refl.* [*impfv. only*] to be visible.

просмо́тр *n.* **1,** examination. **2,** viewing: предвари́тельный просмо́тр, preview. **3,** oversight; error.

просмотре́ть [*infl.* -смотрю́, -смо́тришь] *v., pfv. of* **просма́тривать.**

просну́ться *v.r., pfv. of* **просыпа́ться.**

про́со *n.* millet.

просо́вывать *v. impfv.* [*pfv.* **просу́нуть**] to stick; thrust (into, through, etc.).

просо́дия *n.* prosody. —**просоди́ческий**, *adj.* prosodic.

просоли́ть [*infl.* -солю́, -со́лишь *or* -соли́шь] *v., pfv. of* **проса́ливать** (*in sense* #2).

просо́хнуть [*past* -со́х, -ла] *v., pfv. of* **просыха́ть.**

просочи́ться *v.r., pfv. of* **проса́чиваться.**

проспа́ть *v. pfv.* [*infl. like* **спать**] **1,** *pfv. of* **просыпа́ть**[2]. **2,** to sleep (*for a certain length of time*). —**проспа́ться**, *refl., colloq.* to sleep it off.

проспе́кт *n.* **1,** broad street; avenue: Не́вский проспе́кт, the Nevsky Prospekt (*main street of Leningrad*). **2,** outline; prospectus. **3,** advertisement: рекла́мные проспе́кты, advertisements; promotional material.

проспо́рить *v. pfv.* **1,** to lose (*in a bet*). **2,** to argue (*for a certain length of time*).

проспряга́ть *v., pfv. of* **спряга́ть.**

просро́ченный *adj.* **1,** overdue. **2,** expired.

просро́чивать *v. impfv.* [*pfv.* **просро́чить**] **1,** to be behind in. **2,** to exceed (a time limit). **3,** to allow to expire: мой па́спорт просро́чен, my passport has expired.

просро́чка *n.* **1,** delinquency (*in paying*). **2,** expiration.

проста́вить [*infl.* -влю, -вишь] *v., pfv. of* **простав-ля́ть.**

проставля́ть *v. impfv.* [*pfv.* **проста́вить**] to write in; fill in; enter.

проста́ивать *v. impfv.* [*pfv.* **простоя́ть**] **1,** to stand; stay (*for a certain length of time*). **2,** to stand idle; sit idle; lie idle. **3,** to stand; remain.

проста́к [*gen.* -стака́] *n.* simpleton.

проста́та *n.* prostate (gland).

просте́йшие *n. pl., decl. as an adj.* protozoa.

просте́нок [*gen.* -нка] *n.* space between windows; pier.

простере́ть [*past* -стёр, -ла; *future rarely used*] *v., pfv. of* **простира́ть**[1]. —**простере́ться**, *refl., pfv. of* **простира́ться.**

простёртый *adj.* **1,** (*of one's hand or arm*) outstretched. **2,** stretched out on the floor or ground.

просте́цкий *adj., colloq.* simple; humble; unpretentious.

простира́ть[1] *v. impfv.* [*pfv.* **простере́ть**] to stretch out; hold out; extend. —**простира́ться**, *refl.* to extend; stretch.

простира́ть[2] *v., pfv. of* **прости́рывать.**

прости́рывать *v. impfv.* [*pfv.* **простира́ть**] *colloq.* to wash; launder.

прости́тельный *adj.* pardonable; forgivable; excusable.

проститу́тка [*gen. pl.* -ток] *n.* prostitute. —**проститу́ция**, *n.* prostitution.

прости́ть [*infl.* прощу́, прости́шь] *v., pfv. of* проща́ть. —**прости́ться**, *refl., pfv. of* проща́ться.

про́сто *adv.* simply. —*adj., used predicatively* simple: Это не так про́сто, it's not so simple. Вам про́сто критикова́ть, it is easy for you to criticize. —**про́сто-на́просто**, simply (*used for emphasis*). —**про́сто так**, **1**, as usual; in the usual manner. **2**, for no particular reason.

простова́тый *adj., colloq.* **1**, simple-minded. **2**, naïve; ingenuous.

простоволо́сый *adj., colloq.* bareheaded.

простоду́шие *n.* simple-heartedness.

простоду́шный *adj.* **1**, simple-hearted. **2**, artless; ingenuous.

просто́й[1] *adj.* [*short form* прост, проста́, про́сто; *comp.* про́ще] **1**, simple. **2**, plain: просто́й материа́л, plain material; проста́я пи́ща, plain food. **3**, mere: просто́й сме́ртный, mere mortal. —**просты́м гла́зом**, with the naked eye. —**просто́е число́**, prime number.

просто́й[2] *n.* idle time; downtime.

простоква́ша *n.* thick sour milk; clabber.

простонаро́дье *n., obs.* the common people. —**простонаро́дный**, *adj., obs.* of the common people.

простона́ть *v. pfv.* [*infl.* -стону́, -сто́нешь] to groan; moan.

просто́р *n.* **1**, space; expanse. **2**, range; scope; freedom.

простор́ечие *n.* vernacular; common speech. —**простор́ечный**, *adj.* vernacular.

просто́рный *adj.* spacious; roomy.

простосерде́чие *n.* simple-heartedness. —**простосерде́чный**, *adj.* simple-hearted.

простота́ *n.* simplicity.

простофи́ля *n.m. & f., colloq.* nincompoop.

простоя́ть [*infl.* -сто́ю, -сто́ишь] *v., pfv. of* проста́ивать.

простра́нный *adj.* **1**, vast; extensive. **2**, (*of a speech, letter, etc.*) lengthy; wordy; long-winded.

простра́нство *n.* space. —**простра́нственный**, *adj.* spatial.

простра́ция *n.* prostration.

простра́чивать *v. impfv.* [*pfv.* прострочи́ть] to stitch.

простре́л *n.* lumbago.

простре́ливать *v. impfv.* [*pfv.* прострели́ть] **1**, to shoot through. **2**, [*impfv. only*] to rake with (machine-gun) fire.

прострели́ть [*infl.* -стрелю́, -стре́лишь] *v., pfv. of* простре́ливать.

прострочи́ть *v., pfv. of* строчи́ть (*in sense #1*) *and* простра́чивать.

просту́да *n.* a cold.

простуди́ть [*infl.* -стужу́, -сту́дишь] *v., pfv. of* простужа́ть. —**простуди́ться**, *refl., pfv. of* простужа́ться.

просту́дливый *adj., colloq.* susceptible to colds; easily catching cold.

просту́дный *adj.* of or from a cold.

простужа́ть *v. impfv.* [*pfv.* простуди́ть] to allow to catch cold. —**простужа́ться**, *refl.* to catch cold.

просту́женный *adj.* **1**, having a cold: я просту́жен(а), I have a cold. **2**, showing the effects of a cold.

просту́кивать *v. impfv.* [*pfv.* просту́кать] to tap.

проступа́ть *v. impfv.* [*pfv.* проступи́ть] **1**, to ooze. **2**, to appear; become faintly visible.

проступи́ть [*infl.* -сту́пит] *v., pfv. of* проступа́ть.

просту́пок [*gen.* -пка] *n.* **1**, misdeed; offense. **2**, *law* misdemeanor.

простуча́ть *v. pfv.* [*infl.* -чу́, -чи́шь] **1**, to tap out (a message). **2**, to come rolling by; come rattling by.

простыва́ть *v. impfv.* [*pfv.* просты́ть] *colloq.* to get cold. —**его́ и след просты́л**, he vanished without a trace.

просты́нный *adj.* of or for sheets: просты́нное полотно́, sheeting.

простыня́ [*pl.* про́стыни, -сты́нь, -стыня́м] *n.* sheet; bed sheet.

просты́ть [*infl.* -сты́ну, -сты́нешь] *v., pfv. of* простыва́ть.

просу́нуть *v., pfv. of* просо́вывать.

просу́шивать *v. impfv.* [*pfv.* просуши́ть] to dry (thoroughly). —**просу́шиваться**, *refl.* to dry out thoroughly.

просуши́ть [*infl.* -сушу́, -су́шишь] *v., pfv. of* просу́шивать.

просуществова́ть *v. pfv.* [*infl.* -ству́ю, -ству́ешь] **1**, to exist; subsist. **2**, to last; endure.

просце́ниум *n.* proscenium.

просчёт *n.* **1**, error (*in counting or calculation*). **2**, *fig.* miscalculation.

просчита́ть *v., pfv. of* просчи́тывать. —**просчита́ться**, *refl., pfv. of* просчи́тываться.

просчи́тывать *v. impfv.* [*pfv.* просчита́ть] **1**, to count. **2**, to miscount. —**просчи́тываться**, *refl.* **1**, to miscount. **2**, *fig.* to miscalculate.

про́сып *also*, **просы́п** *n., colloq.*, *in* спать без про́сыпу/про́сыпа, to sleep on and on; sleep like a log.

просы́пать [*infl.* -сы́плю, -сы́плешь] *v., pfv. of* просыпа́ть[1].

просыпа́ть[1] *v. impfv.* [*pfv.* просы́пать] to spill.

просыпа́ть[2] *v. impfv.* [*pfv.* проспа́ть] **1**, to oversleep. **2**, *colloq.* to sleep through. —**просыпа́ться**, *refl.* [*pfv.* просну́ться] to wake up.

просыха́ть *v. impfv.* [*pfv.* просо́хнуть] to dry out.

про́сьба *n.* request. У меня́ к вам про́сьба, I have a favor to ask of you. Про́сьба не кури́ть!, you are requested not to smoke.

прося́ной *adj.* millet (*attrib.*).

прося́щий *adj.* pleading; supplicating.

протагони́ст *n.* protagonist.

протакти́ний *n.* protactinium.

прота́лина *n.* thawed patch; place where the snow has melted.

прота́лкивать *v. impfv.* [*pfv.* протолкну́ть] **1**, to push; press; force (into, through, forward, etc.). **2**, *colloq.* to expedite (a matter); give (something) a little push. —**прота́лкиваться**, *refl.* [*pfv.* протолка́ться *or* протолкну́ться] *colloq.* to force one's way; elbow one's way.

протанцева́ть *v. pfv.* [*infl.* -цу́ю, -цу́ешь] **1**, to dance. **2**, to dance (*for a certain length of time*).

прота́пливать *v. impfv.* [*pfv.* протопи́ть] **1**, to heat properly; heat sufficiently. **2**, [*impfv. only*] to heat slightly; warm slightly.

прота́птывать *v. impfv.* [*pfv.* протопта́ть] **1**, to beat (a path). **2,** *colloq.* to wear holes in (a carpet, pair of socks, etc.).

протара́нить *v., pfv. of* **тара́нить.**

прота́скивать *v. impfv.* [*pfv.* **протащи́ть**] **1,** to drag. **2,** to drag through; pull through. **3,** *colloq.* to push through (a law, resolution, etc.). **4,** *colloq.* to give (someone) a going over (*in the press*).

прота́чивать *v. impfv.* [*pfv.* **проточи́ть**] to eat through; gnaw through.

протащи́ть [*infl.* -тащу́, -та́щишь] *v., pfv. of* **прота́скивать.**

прота́ять *v. pfv.* [*infl.* -та́ет] to melt.

протеже́ (тэ) *n.m. & f., indecl.* protégé.

проте́з (тэ) *n.* prosthetic device; artificial limb. —**зубно́й проте́з,** denture.

проте́зный (тэ) *adj.* prosthetic.

протеи́н (тэ) *n.* protein. —**протеи́новый,** *adj.* protein (*attrib.*).

протека́ть *v. impfv.* [*pfv.* **проте́чь**] **1,** to flow. **2,** to leak; seep. **3,** to leak; have a leak. **4,** (*of time, life, etc.*) to pass; go by. **5,** (*of an event, illness, etc.*) to proceed. Боле́знь протека́ет без осложне́ний, the illness is taking its normal course.

проте́ктор *n.* **1,** *obs.* protector; patron. **2,** tread (*on tires*).

протектора́т *n.* protectorate.

протекциони́зм *n.* protectionism.

проте́кция *n.* patronage; influence.

протере́ть [*infl. like* тере́ть] *v., pfv. of* **протира́ть.** —**протере́ться,** *refl., pfv. of* **протира́ться.**

проте́ст *n.* protest.

протеста́нт *n.* **1,** Protestant. **2,** protester. —**протестанти́зм; протеста́нство,** *n.* Protestantism. —**протеста́нтский,** *adj.* Protestant.

протестова́ть *v. impfv.* [*pres.* -ту́ю, -ту́ешь] (*with* про́тив) to protest.

проте́чь [*infl. like* течь] *v., pfv. of* **протека́ть.**

про́тив *prep., with gen.* **1,** against. **2,** opposite; facing. **3,** against; contrary to. **4,** against; compared to. —*predicate,* against: я не про́тив, I am not against it. —*n., colloq.* con: все за и про́тив, all the pros and cons. —**ничего́ не име́ть про́тив,** to have no objection (to).

про́тивень [*gen.* -вня] *n.m.* baking sheet; roasting pan.

проти́виться *v.r. impfv.* [*pfv.* **воспроти́виться;** *pres.* -влюсь, -вишься] (*with dat.*) to oppose; resist.

проти́вник *n.* **1,** enemy. **2,** opponent; adversary.

проти́вно *adv.* in a disgusting way. Проти́вно па́хнуть, have a disgusting odor. —*adj., used predicatively* disgusting; revolting: мне проти́вно (+ *inf.*), I find it disgusting/revolting to have to... —*prep., with dat., obs.* against; contrary to.

проти́вный *adj.* **1,** *obs.* opposite; facing. **2,** contrary. **3,** opposing. **4,** disgusting; repugnant. —**в проти́вном слу́чае,** otherwise; failing which.

противоа́томный *adj., in* противоа́томная защи́та, defense/protection against nuclear attack.

противове́с *n.* counterbalance; counterweight. —**в противове́с** (+ *dat.*), in contrast to; as distinct from. —**для противове́са,** for balance.

противовозду́шный *adj., in* противовозду́шная оборо́на, air defense.

противога́з *n.* gas mask.

противоде́йствие *n.* opposition; counteraction.

противоде́йствовать *v. impfv.* [*pres.* -ствую, -ствуешь] (*with dat.*) to oppose; counteract.

противоесте́ственный *adj.* unnatural; perverted.

противозако́нный *adj.* illegal; unlawful. —**противозако́нность,** *n.f.* illegality.

противозача́точный *adj.* contraceptive. —**противозача́точные сре́дства,** contraceptives.

противолежа́щий *adj.* **1,** opposite; facing. **2,** (*of an angle*) alternate.

противопехо́тный *adj., mil.* anti-personnel.

противопожа́рный *adj.* fire-prevention (*attrib.*).

противополо́жное *n., decl. as an adj.* the opposite.

противополо́жность *n.f.* **1,** opposition; contrast. **2,** opposite: пряма́я противополо́жность, exact opposite. —**в противополо́жность** (+ *dat.*), **1,** unlike; in contrast to. **2,** as opposed to; in contradistinction to.

противополо́жный *adj.* **1,** opposite: в противополо́жном направле́нии, in the opposite direction. **2,** opposite; contrary: противополо́жные взгля́ды, opposite views.

противопоста́вить [*infl.* -влю, -вишь] *v., pfv. of* **противопоставля́ть.**

противопоставле́ние *n.* **1,** contrasting. **2,** opposition.

противопоставля́ть *v. impfv.* [*pfv.* **противопоста́вить**] (*with dat.*) **1,** to compare (to); contrast (with). **2,** to oppose: противопоставля́ть си́ле си́лу, to oppose force with force.

противоречи́вый *adj.* contradictory; conflicting.

противоре́чие *n.* contradiction.

противоре́чить *v. impfv.* (*with dat.*) **1,** to contradict (someone). **2,** to contradict; be contrary to; be at variance with.

противостоя́ние *n., astron.* opposition.

противостоя́ть *v. impfv.* [*pres.* -стою́, -стои́шь] (*with dat.*) **1,** to resist; withstand. **2,** to oppose; be opposed to.

противота́нковый *adj.* antitank.

противоя́дие *n.* antidote.

протира́ть *v. impfv.* [*pfv.* **протере́ть**] **1,** to wear a hole in. **2,** to wipe; wipe clean. **3,** to strain; grate. —**протира́ться,** *refl.* to be worn through.

проти́скивать *v. impfv.* [*pfv.* **проти́снуть**] to force; press; squeeze (something) into *or* through. —**проти́скиваться,** *refl.* to squeeze into; squeeze through; squeeze between.

проткну́ть *v., pfv. of* **протыка́ть.**

протодья́кон *n., Orth. Ch.* archdeacon.

прото́к *n.* **1,** channel. **2,** *anat.* duct.

протоко́л *n.* **1,** minutes (*of a meeting*). **2,** report (*of an incident, interrogation, etc.*). **3,** protocol (*between states*).

протолка́ться *v.r., pfv. of* **прота́лкиваться.**

протолкну́ть *v., pfv. of* **прота́лкивать.** —**протолкну́ться,** *refl., pfv. of* **прота́лкиваться.**

прото́н *n.* proton.

протопи́ть [*infl.* -топлю́, -то́пишь] *v., pfv. of* **прота́пливать.**

протопла́зма *n.* protoplasm.

протопта́ть [*infl.* -топчу́, -то́пчешь] *v., pfv. of* **прота́птывать.**

проторённый *adj.* (*of a road or path*) beaten; well-trodden.

проторя́ть *v. impfv.* [*pfv.* **протори́ть**] *usu. in* протори́ть путь *or* доро́гу, **1,** to beat a path. **2,** *fig.* to open the way.

прототи́п *n.* prototype.

проточить [*infl.* -точу́, -то́чишь] *v., pfv. of* прота́чивать.

прото́чный *adj.* (*of water*) running; flowing; (*of a pond*) not stagnant; fed by springs.

протра́ва *n.* mordant.

протрезви́ть [*infl.* -влю́, -ви́шь] *v., pfv. of* протрезвля́ть. —**протрезви́ться**, *refl., pfv. of* протрезвля́ться.

протрезвля́ть *v. impfv.* [*pfv.* протрезви́ть] to sober up; make sober. —**протрезвля́ться**, *refl.* to sober up; become sober.

протруби́ть *v., pfv. of* труби́ть.

протуха́ть *v. impfv.* [*pfv.* проту́хнуть] to spoil; rot.

проту́хнуть [*past* -ту́х, -ла] *v., pfv. of* ту́хнуть (*in sense #2*) *and* протуха́ть.

проту́хший *adj.* rotten.

протыка́ть *v. impfv.* [*pfv.* проткну́ть] to pierce.

протя́гивать *v. impfv.* [*pfv.* протяну́ть] **1,** to extend; stretch (a rope, wire, etc.). **2,** to stretch out; hold out; offer; extend. **3,** to sustain (a note, sound, etc.). —**протя́гиваться**, *refl.* **1,** to reach out. **2,** to stretch; extend. **3,** *colloq.* to stretch out. **4,** *colloq.* to last; go on. *See also* протяну́ть.

протяже́ние *n.* length; extent. —**на протяже́нии** (+ *gen.*), for; over a period of.

протяжённость *n.f.* length; extent.

протя́жный *adj.* (*of speech, a sound, etc.*) slow; prolonged.

протяну́ть *v. pfv.* [*infl.* -тяну́, -тя́нешь] **1,** *pfv. of* протя́гивать. **2,** *colloq.* to delay; drag out. **3,** *v.i., colloq.* to hold out; live a while longer. **4,** *in* протяну́ть но́ги, *colloq.* to kick the bucket. —**протяну́ться**, *refl., pfv. of* протя́гиваться.

проучи́ть *v. pfv.* [*infl.* -учу́, -у́чишь] **1,** *colloq.* to teach (someone) a (good) lesson. **2,** to teach (*for a certain length of time*). —**проучи́ться**, *refl.* to study (*for a certain length of time*).

профа́н *n.* ignoramus.

профана́ция *n.* profanation.

профани́ровать *v. impfv. & pfv.* [*pres.* -рую, -руешь] to profane.

профессиона́л *n.* professional.

профессиона́льный *adj.* professional. —**профессиона́льная боле́знь**, occupational disease. —**профессиона́льное образова́ние**, vocational training.

профе́ссия *n.* profession. —**челове́к свобо́дной профе́ссии**, professional man (*in private practice*).

профе́ссор [*pl.* профессора́] *n.* professor. Профе́ссор исто́рии, professor of history; history professor. —**профе́ссорский**, *adj.* professorial. —**профе́ссорство**, *n.* professorship.

профессу́ра *n.* **1,** professorship. **2,** professors.

профила́ктика *n.* **1,** *med.* prophylaxis. **2,** preventive measures: пожа́рная профила́ктика, fire prevention. —**профилакти́ческий**, *adj.* prophylactic.

про́филь *n.m.* **1,** profile. **2,** *fig.* type: худо́жники разли́чного про́филя, painters of various types/styles/schools. Специали́ст широ́кого про́филя, broad specialist.

профо́рма *n., colloq.* formality. —**для профо́рмы**, as a matter of form.

профсою́з *n.* trade union (*contr. of* профессиона́льный сою́з). —**профсою́зный**, *adj.* trade-union (*attrib.*).

проха́живаться *v.r. impfv.* [*pfv.* пройти́сь] **1,** to walk; stroll. **2,** (*with* насчёт *or* по а́дресу) *colloq.* to make slighting remarks about; take a swipe at.

прохвати́ть [*infl.* -хвачу́, -хва́тишь] *v., pfv. of* прохва́тывать.

прохва́тывать *v.impfv.* [*pfv.* прохвати́ть] *colloq.* **1,** (*of cold, wind, etc.*) to penetrate. **2,** *impers.* to get a chill: меня́ прохвати́ло в откры́той маши́не, I got a chill in the open car.

прохво́ст *n., colloq.* scoundrel.

прохла́да *n.* cool; coolness: вече́рняя прохла́да, the cool of the evening.

прохла́дец *also,* прохла́дца *n., in* с прохла́дцем; с прохла́дцей, *colloq.* leisurely; without making much effort.

прохлади́тельный *adj.* cooling; refreshing.

прохлади́ться [*infl.* -жу́сь, -ди́шься] *v.r., pfv. of* прохлажда́ться.

прохла́дно *adv.* coolly. —*adj., used predicatively* **1,** cool: сего́дня прохла́дно, it is cool today. **2,** chilly: мне прохла́дно, I am chilly.

прохла́дный *adj.* cool.

прохла́дца *n. see* прохла́дец.

прохлажда́ться *v.r. impfv.* [*pfv.* прохлади́ться] *colloq.* **1,** to cool off. **2,** [*impfv. only*] to idle; loaf.

прохо́д *n.* **1,** passing. **2,** passage; passageway. **3,** aisle. **4,** *in* за́дний прохо́д, anus. **5,** *in* пра́во прохо́да, right of way. —**не дава́ть прохо́да** (+ *dat.*), to give someone no peace. —**прохо́да нет от**, there is no getting away from...

проходи́мец [*gen.* -мца] *n., colloq.* scoundrel; crook; rogue.

проходи́мость *n.f.* **1,** ability (of a surface) to carry traffic. **2,** ability (of a vehicle) to travel cross-country.

проходи́мый *adj.* passable.

проходи́ть[1] *v. impfv.* [*pfv.* пройти́; *pres.* -хожу́, -хо́дишь] **1,** to walk (along, through, past, into, etc.). **2,** (*with* ми́мо) to pass (by). **3,** to go (right) past (*inadvertently*). **4,** (*with* че́рез) to pass through. **5,** (*with* в + *acc.*) to fit into; fit through. **6,** to cover (a certain distance); traverse (a route or path); walk the length of (*e.g.* a street). **7,** (*of roads, a border, etc.*) to run; extend. **8,** to pass; elapse; go by. **9,** (*of pain, rain, etc.*) to pass; stop. **10,** to go: заседа́ние прошло́ уда́чно, the meeting went well. **11,** to undergo (treatment, training, etc.); complete (a course). **12,** *colloq.* to study.

проходи́ть[2] *v. pfv.* [*infl.* -хожу́, -хо́дишь] to walk (*for a certain length of time*).

проходна́я *n., decl. as an adj.* checkpoint (*at the entrance to a factory or other building*).

проходно́й *adj.* (*of a room, courtyard, etc.*) connecting; communicating. —**проходно́й балл**, lowest passing score (*on an entrance examination*). —**проходна́я бу́дка**, entrance gate; checkpoint. —**проходна́я пе́шка**, *chess* passed pawn.

прохожде́ние *n.* passing; passage.

прохо́жий *n.* **1,** passing. **2,** passing through; in transit. —*n.* passer-by.

прохрипе́ть *v. pfv.* [*infl.* -плю́, -пи́шь] to utter in a hoarse voice.

прохуди́ться *v.r. pfv., colloq.* to wear out.

процвета́ние *n.* prosperity.

процвета́ть *v. impfv.* to prosper; flourish; thrive.

процеди́ть [*infl.* -цежу́, -це́дишь] *v., pfv. of* **проце́живать.**

процеду́ра *n.* **1,** procedure. **2,** *usu. pl., med.* treatment (*baths, massages, etc.*). —**процеду́рный,** *adj.* procedural.

проце́живать *v. impfv.* [*pfv.* **процеди́ть**] **1,** to strain; filter. **2,** to mutter.

проце́нт *n.* **1,** percent: два́дцать проце́нтов, twenty percent. **2,** percentage. **3,** *pl.* interest.

проце́нтный *adj.* **1,** percentage (*attrib.*). **2,** interest-bearing.

проце́сс *n.* **1,** process. **2,** [*often* суде́бный проце́сс] A, trial. B, lawsuit. **3,** *med.* condition. Проце́сс в лёгких, tuberculosis of the lungs.

проце́ссия *n.* procession.

процити́ровать *v., pfv. of* **цити́ровать.**

прочерти́ть [*infl.* -черчу́, -че́ртишь] *v., pfv. of* **проче́рчивать.** —**прочерти́ться,** *refl., pfv. of* **проче́рчиваться.**

проче́рчивать *v. impfv.* [*pfv.* **прочерти́ть**] to draw (a line). —**проче́рчиваться,** *refl.* to stand out.

прочеса́ть [*infl.* -чешу́, -че́шешь] *v., pfv. of* **прочё́сывать.**

проче́сть [*infl.* -чту́, -чтёшь; *past* -чёл, -чла́, -чло́] *v., pfv. of* **чита́ть.**

прочё́сывать *v. impfv.* [*pfv.* **прочеса́ть**] **1,** to comb (flax, fiber, etc.). **2,** *fig., colloq.* to comb; search.

про́чий *adj.* other. —**про́чие,** *n. pl.* the others. —**и про́чее,** and so on; and so forth. —**ме́жду про́чим,** by the way. —**поми́мо всего́ про́чего,** *see* **поми́мо.** —**при про́чих ра́вных усло́виях,** other things being equal.

прочи́стить [*infl.* -щу, -стишь] *v., pfv. of* **прочища́ть.**

прочита́ть *v. pfv.* **1,** *pfv. of* **чита́ть. 2,** to read (*for a certain length of time*).

про́чить *v. impfv.* **1,** to intend; have in mind: про́чить кого́-нибудь в зятья́, to have someone in mind to one's son-in-law. **2,** to predict: ему́ про́чат блестя́щее бу́дущее, a brilliant future is being predicted for him.

прочища́ть *v. impfv.* [*pfv.* **прочи́стить**] **1,** to clean out. **2,** to clear (a road, forest, etc.).

про́чно *adv.* firmly; solidly; securely.

про́чность *n.f.* **1,** strength; durability. **2,** soundness; solidity.

про́чный *adj.* **1,** firm; durable. **2,** *fig.* (*of peace, a friendship, etc.*) lasting.

прочте́ние *n.* **1,** reading. **2,** reciting. **3,** giving (*of lectures*).

прочу́вствовать *v. pfv.* [*infl.* -ствую, -ствуешь] **1,** to feel deeply. **2,** to experience; live through.

прочь *adv.* away; off: ру́ки прочь!, hands off! —*interj.* begone! Прочь отсю́да!, get away from here! Прочь с доро́ги!, get out of the way! —**быть не прочь** (+ *inf.*), not to mind; not be averse to.

проше́дшее *n., decl. as an adj.* the past.

проше́дший *adj.* last; past. —**проше́дшее вре́мя,** *gram.* the past tense.

проше́ние *n., obs.* application; petition; formal request.

прошепта́ть *v., pfv. of* **шепта́ть.**

проше́ствие *n., in* по проше́ствии (+ *gen.*), with the passage (of); upon the expiration (of).

прошива́ть *v. impfv.* [*pfv.* **проши́ть**] **1,** to sew; stitch. **2,** *colloq.* to riddle (with bullets); rack (with a bomb).

проши́вка *n.* lace trim.

проши́ть [*infl.* -шью, -шьёшь] *v., pfv. of* **прошива́ть.**

прошлого́дний *adj.* last year's.

про́шлое *n., decl. as an adj.* the past. —**отойти́ в про́шлое,** to become a thing of the past.

про́шлый *adj.* **1,** last: в про́шлом году́, last year. **2,** past: про́шлые во́йны/оши́бки, past wars/mistakes.

прошмы́гивать *v. impfv.* [*pfv.* **прошмыгну́ть**] *colloq.* to sneak; slip (into, past, etc.).

проштуди́ровать *v., pfv. of* **штуди́ровать.**

проща́й *interj.* farewell!; adieu! *Also,* **проща́йте.**

проща́льный *adj.* parting; farewell (*attrib.*).

проща́ние *n.* parting; farewell. —**на проща́ние,** at parting.

проща́ть *v. impfv.* [*pfv.* **прости́ть**] to forgive; excuse; pardon. —**проща́ться,** *refl.* [*pfv.* **прости́ться** *or* **попроща́ться**] (*with* с + *instr.*) to say goodbye (to); bid farewell.

про́ще *adj., comp. of* **просто́й.**

проще́ние *n.* forgiveness; pardon: прошу́ проще́ния!, I beg your pardon!

прощу́пывать *v. impfv.* [*pfv.* **прощу́пать**] **1,** to feel. **2,** *fig.* to reconnoiter. **3,** *fig.* to size up. —**прощу́пывать по́чву,** to get the lay of the land; sound out the possibilities.

проэкзаменова́ть *v., pfv. of* **экзаменова́ть.** —**проэкзаменова́ться,** *refl., pfv. of* **экзаменова́ться.**

прояви́тель *n.m., photog.* developer.

прояви́ть [*infl.* -явлю́, -я́вишь] *v., pfv. of* **проявля́ть.** —**прояви́ться,** *refl., pfv. of* **проявля́ться.**

проявле́ние *n.* **1,** display; manifestation. **2,** *photog.* developing.

проявля́ть *v. impfv.* [*pfv.* **прояви́ть**] **1,** to show; display (a quality or emotion). **2,** *photog.* to develop. —**прояви́ть себя́, 1,** to show one's worth. **2,** (*with instr.*) to prove to be.

проявля́ться *v.r. impfv.* [*pfv.* **прояви́ться**] to reveal itself; manifest itself.

проя́снеть *v. pfv., colloq.* (*of the sky*) to clear up.

проясне́ть *v. pfv.* **1,** to become clear. **2,** to brighten up.

проясня́ть *v. impfv.* [*pfv.* **проясни́ть**] to make clear. —**проясня́ться,** *refl.* **1,** to clear up. **2,** *fig.* to become clear. **3,** to brighten up.

пруд [*gen.* пруда́; *2nd loc.* пруду́] *n.* pond.

пруди́ть *v. impfv.* [*pfv.* **запруди́ть;** *pres.* пружу́, пру́дишь *or* пруди́шь] to dam up. —**хоть пруд пруди́,** plenty; galore.

пружи́на *n.* **1,** spring. **2,** *in* гла́вная пружи́на, mainspring. —**нажа́ть на все пружи́ны,** to pull out all the stops.

пружи́нистый *adj.* springy; resilient.

пружи́нить *v. impfv.* to be springy; be resilient. —**пружи́ниться,** *refl., colloq.* = **пружи́нить.**

пружи́нный *adj.* spring (*attrib.*): пружи́нный матра́с, spring mattress.

пруса́к [*gen.* -сака́] *n.* Croton bug; German cockroach.

прусса́к [*gen.* -ссака́] *n.* Prussian. —**пру́сский,** *adj.* Prussian.

прут [*gen.* пру́та *or* прута́; *pl.* пру́тья, пру́тьев] *n.* **1,** twig. **2,** rod.

пры́гание *also,* пры́ганье *n.* jumping.

пры́гать *v. impfv.* [*pfv.* **пры́гнуть**] **1,** to jump; leap. **2,** to bounce. —**пры́гать на одно́й ноге́,** to hop.

прыгу́н [*gen.* -гуна́] *n.* jumper.

прыжо́к [*gen.* -жка́] *n.* jump; leap. —**прыжки́ в во́ду,** diving. —**прыжо́к в во́ду,** dive. —**прыжо́к в высоту́,** high jump. —**прыжо́к в длину́,** broad jump. —**прыжо́к с ме́ста,** standing broad jump. —**прыжо́к с разбе́га,** running broad jump. —**прыжо́к с шесто́м,** pole vault. —**тройно́й прыжо́к,** hop, step, and jump.

пры́скать *v. impfv.* [*pfv.* пры́снуть] (*with instr.*) *colloq.* to sprinkle.

пры́снуть *v. pfv., colloq.* **1,** *pfv. of* пры́скать. **2,** (*of blood*) to gush. **3,** to dart; dash. **4,** to burst out laughing.

пры́ткий *adj.* [*comp.* пры́тче] *colloq.* quick; nimble; agile.

прыть *n.f., colloq.* **1,** speed. **2,** energy; vim; pep. —**во всю прыть,** at full speed.

прыщ [*gen.* -ща́] *n.* pimple.

прыща́вый *adj., colloq.* pimply.

пряде́ние *n.* spinning.

пря́деный *adj.* spun.

пряди́льный *adj.* spinning (*attrib.*).

пряди́льщик *n.m.* [*fem.* -щица] *n.* spinner.

прядь *n.f.* strand (*of hair*).

пря́жа *n.* yarn.

пря́жка [*gen. pl.* -жек] *n.* buckle.

пря́лка [*gen. pl.* -лок] *n.* **1,** distaff. **2,** spinning wheel.

пряма́я *n., decl. as an adj.* straight line. —**по прямо́й,** as the crow flies.

прямизна́ *n.* straightness.

прямико́м *adv., colloq.* **1,** straight; in a straight line. **2,** straight to the point.

пря́мо *adv.* **1,** straight. **2,** straight ahead. **3,** right; directly. **4,** openly; frankly. **5,** *colloq.* really; truly. **6,** *colloq.* simply; just: я пря́мо не зна́ю, I just don't know.

прямоду́шие *n.* directness; straightforwardness. —**прямоду́шный,** *adj.* direct; straightforward.

прямо́й *adj.* **1,** straight. **2,** erect; upright. **3,** direct. **4,** straightforward. **5,** *in* прямо́й у́гол, right angle. —**прямо́й расчёт** *or* **смысл** (+ *inf.*), *colloq.* there is every reason to...; it makes a lot of sense to... *See also* пряма́я.

прямолине́йный *adj.* **1,** rectilinear. **2,** *fig.* straightforward.

прямота́ *n.* directness; straightforwardness.

прямоуго́льник *n.* rectangle. —**прямоуго́льный,** *adj.* rectangular.

пря́ник *n.* cake: медо́вый пря́ник, honey cake. Имби́рный пря́ник, gingerbread. —**поли́тика кнута́ и пря́ника,** the carrot and the stick.

пря́ность *n.f.* spice. —**пря́ный,** *adj.* spicy.

прясть *v. impfv.* [*pfv.* спрясть; *pres.* пряду́, прядёшь; *past* прял, пряла́ *or* пря́ла, пря́ло] to spin (cloth, yarn, etc.).

пря́тание *also,* **пря́танье** *n.* hiding.

пря́тать *v. impfv.* [*pfv.* спря́тать; *pres.* пря́чу, пря́чешь] to hide; conceal. —**пря́таться,** *refl.* to hide; be hiding.

пря́тки [*gen.* -ток] *n. pl.* hide-and-seek.

пря́ха *n.* (woman) spinner.

псало́м [*gen.* -лма́] *n.* psalm.

псалты́рь *n.m. or f.* [*gen.* -ты́ри *or* -тыря́] Psalter.

пса́рня [*gen. pl.* -рен] *n.* kennel.

псевдони́м *n.* pseudonym; pen name.

пси́на *n., colloq.* **1,** dogmeat. **2,** smell of a dog.

псих *n., colloq.* madman; lunatic; nut.

психиатри́я *n.* psychiatry. —**психиа́тр,** *n.* psychiatrist. —**психиатри́ческий,** *adj.* psychiatric.

пси́хика *n.* psyche. —**психи́ческий,** *adj.* psychic.

психоана́лиз *n.* psychoanalysis. —**психоаналити́ческий,** *adj.* psychoanalytic(al).

психо́з *n.* psychosis.

психоло́гия *n.* psychology. —**психо́лог,** *n.* psychologist. —**психологи́ческий,** *adj.* psychological.

психопа́т *n.* psychopath. —**психопати́ческий,** *adj.* psychopathic. —**психопати́я,** *n.* psychopathy.

психосомати́ческий *adj.* psychosomatic.

психотерапи́я *n.* psychotherapy. —**психотерапе́вт,** *n.* psychotherapist.

психоти́ческий *adj.* psychotic.

псориа́з *n.* psoriasis.

пта́шка [*gen. pl.* -шек] *n., colloq.* little bird; birdie. —**ра́нняя пта́шка,** early bird.

птене́ц [*gen.* -нца́] *n.* baby bird; nestling; fledgling.

птерода́ктиль *n.m.* pterodactyl.

пти́ца *n.* bird. —**дома́шняя пти́ца,** poultry.

птицево́д *n.* poultry farmer; poultry breeder. —**птицево́дство,** *n.* poultry farming; poultry breeding.

птицело́в *n.* fowler. —**птицело́вство,** *n.* fowling.

пти́чий [*fem.* -чья] *adj.* **1,** bird (*attrib.*); bird's. **2,** birdlike. **3,** *in* пти́чий двор, barnyard. —**вид с пти́чьего полёта,** bird's-eye view. —**жить на пти́чьих права́х,** to live from hand to mouth.

пти́чка [*gen. pl.* -чек] *n.* **1,** *dim. of* пти́ца. **2,** check; check mark; tick [✔].

пти́чник *n.* poultry yard; hen house.

пу́блика *n.* **1,** (the) public. **2,** audience. **3,** *colloq.* people.

публика́ция *n.* **1,** publication. **2,** (published) announcement; notice.

публикова́ть *v. impfv.* [*pfv.* опубликова́ть; *pres.* -ку́ю, -ку́ешь] to publish.

публици́ст *n.* commentator; columnist; publicist.

публи́чно *adv.* publicly; in public.

публи́чный *adj.* public. —**публи́чный дом,** brothel.

пу́гало *n.* **1,** scarecrow. **2,** *fig.* bugaboo; bugbear.

пу́ганый *adj.* frightened.

пуга́ть *v. impfv.* [*pfv.* испуга́ть] to frighten; scare. —**пуга́ться,** *refl.* (*with gen.*) to be frightened (of); be scared (of).

пуга́ч [*gen.* -гача́] *n.* toy pistol.

пугли́вый *adj.* easily frightened; fearful; timorous.

пу́говица *n.* button.

пуд [*pl.* пуды́] *n.* old Russian unit of weight equal to approx. 36 pounds; pood.

пу́дель *n.m.* poodle.

пу́динг *n.* pudding.

пу́дра *n.* powder. —**са́харная пу́дра,** powdered sugar.

пу́дреница *n.* (lady's) compact.

пу́дрить *v. impfv.* [*pfv.* напу́дрить] to powder. —**пу́дриться,** *refl.* to powder one's face; powder one's nose.

пуза́тый *adj., colloq.* potbellied.

пу́зо *n., colloq.* belly; paunch.

пузырёк [*gen.* -рька́] *n.* **1,** small bottle; vial. **2,** bubble.

пузы́риться *v.r. impfv., colloq.* **1,** to bubble. **2,** (*of clothes*) to billow.

пузы́рь [*gen.* -зыря́] *n.m.* **1,** bubble. **2,** *colloq.* blister. **3,** bladder: жёлчный пузы́рь, gall bladder; мочево́й пузы́рь, urinary bladder. **4,** bag: пузы́рь со льдом, ice bag.

пук [*pl.* пуки́] *n.* bunch; bundle; tuft; wisp.

пулево́й *adj.* bullet (*attrib.*).

пулемёт *n.* machine gun. —**пулемётный,** *adj.* machine-gun (*attrib.*). —**пулемётчик,** *n.* machine gunner.

пулестойкий *adj.* bulletproof. *Also,* **пуленепробиваемый; пуленепроницаемый.**

пуловер *n.* pullover.

пульверизатор *n.* atomizer; sprayer.

пульпа *n.* pulp (*of a tooth*).

пульс *n.* pulse.

пульсар *n.* pulsar.

пульсация *n.* pulsation.

пульсировать *v. impfv.* [*pres.* -рует] to pulsate.

пульт *n.* **1,** music stand: дирижёрский пульт, conductor's stand. **2,** console; control panel.

пуля *n.* bullet.

пулярка [*gen. pl.* -рок] *n.* fattened chicken.

пума *n.* puma.

пункт *n.* **1,** point: поворотный пункт, turning point. Самый северный пункт страны, the northernmost point in the country. **2,** station; post; center: медицинский пункт, first-aid station; наблюдательный пункт, observation post; призывной пункт, induction center. **3,** point; paragraph; item (*in a document*). **4,** *in* пункты обвинения, counts (*of an indictment*). —по пунктам; пункт за пунктом, point by point.

пунктир *n.* dotted line. —**пунктирный,** *adj., in* пунктирная линия, = пунктир.

пунктуальный *adj.* punctual. —**пунктуальность,** *n.f.* punctuality.

пунктуация *n.* punctuation.

пункция *n., med.* puncture; tapping.

пуночка [*gen. pl.* -чек] *n.* snow bunting.

пунцовый *adj.* crimson.

пунш *n.* punch.

пуп [*gen.* пупа] *n., colloq.* navel; bellybutton.

пупавка [*gen. pl.* -вок] *n.* camomile.

пуповина *n.* umbilical cord.

пупок [*gen.* -пка] *n.* navel.

пупочный *adj.* umbilical.

пупырышек [*gen.* -шка] *n., colloq.* pimple. —**пупырчатый,** *adj., colloq.* pimply.

пурга *n.* blizzard; snowstorm.

пуризм *n.* purism. —**пурист,** *n.* purist.

пуританин [*pl.* -тане, -тан] *n.m.* [*fem.* -танка] **1,** *hist.* Puritan. **2,** puritan.

пуританский *adj.* **1,** Puritan. **2,** puritanical.

пурпурный *adj.* purple; crimson. *Also,* **пурпуровый.**

пуск *n.* **1,** starting; setting in motion. **2,** launching.

пускай *particle* = **пусть.**

пускать *v. impfv.* [*pfv.* пустить] **1,** to let go (of). **2,** to let (someone) go (somewhere). **3,** to let in; admit. **4,** to take in (lodgers). **5,** to start up; switch on; set in motion. **6,** to throw; toss. **7,** to fire; shoot. **8,** to blow (smoke, bubbles, etc.). **9,** (*with* в + *acc.*) to put into production, into circulation, on sale, etc.). **10,** to sprout (buds, shoots, etc.). **11,** *colloq.* to start; set afloat (a rumor, gossip, etc.). —**пускать в дело,** to put to use. —**пускать в ход,** *see* **ход.** —**пускать корни,** *see* **корень.** —**пускать кровь** (+ *dat.*), to bleed (someone). —**пускать себе пулю в лоб,** to blow one's brains out.

пускаться *v.r. impfv.* [*pfv.* пуститься] **1,** to set out; set off. **2,** to dash; race. **3,** (*with inf.*) to begin (to); start (to). **4,** (*with* в *or* на + *acc.*) to enter into; embark upon.

пусковой *adj.* starting (*attrib.*); launching (*attrib.*). —**пусковая установка,** launcher.

пустельга *n.* kestrel.

пустеть *v. impfv.* [*pfv.* опустеть] to become empty; become deserted.

пустить [*infl.* пущу, пустишь] *v., pfv. of* пускать. —**пуститься,** *refl., pfv. of* пускаться.

пусто *adj., used predicatively* empty; deserted: на улицах было пусто, the streets were empty/deserted.

пустовать *v. impfv.* [*pres.* -стует] to be empty; stand empty.

пустоголовый *adj., colloq.* empty-headed.

пустозвон *n., colloq.* windbag.

пустой *adj.* [*short form* пуст, пуста, пусто] **1,** empty. **2,** *fig.* empty; vain; hollow. **3,** *fig.* lacking depth; shallow. —**пустое место, 1,** blank space. **2,** a nothing; nonentity; nobody. —**пустая трата** (+ *gen.*), a waste (of). —**с пустыми руками,** empty-handed.

пустомеля *n.m. & f., colloq.* windbag.

пустопорожний *adj., colloq.* empty.

пустослов *n., colloq.* windbag. —**пустословие,** *n., colloq.* idle talk; twaddle; hot air.

пустословить *v. impfv.* [*pres.* -влю, -вишь] *colloq.* to babble; chatter.

пустота [*pl.* пустоты] *n.* **1,** emptiness. **2,** vacuum. **3,** *fig.* void.

пустотелый *adj.* hollow.

пустоцвет *n.* **1,** sterile flower. **2,** *fig.* person who has amounted to nothing.

пустошь *n.f.* uncultivated plot of land.

пустынник *n.* hermit.

пустынный *adj.* **1,** desert (*attrib.*). **2,** uninhabited; deserted. **3,** bleak; desolate.

пустыня *n.* **1,** desert. **2,** wilderness; wasteland.

пустырь [*gen.* -стыря] *n.m.* abandoned lot; neglected plot of land.

пусть *particle* let: пусть он говорит, let him speak. Пусть икс равен игреку, let x equal y. —*conj.* **1,** though: задача, пусть трудная, но выполнима, the task, though difficult, can be accomplished. **2,** granted; so what if...?: пусть он мне помог, разве это дает право (+ *inf.*), so what if he helped me? Does that give him the right to...? —**пусть будет по-вашему,** have it your way. —**пусть будет так,** so be it.

пустяк [*gen.* -тяка] *n.* **1,** trifle. **2,** *pl.* nonsense. —**пара пустяков,** child's play. —**пустяки!,** never mind!; it's nothing!

пустяковый *adj., colloq.* trifling; trivial.

путаник *n., colloq.* muddle-headed person.

путаница *n.* mess; muddle; jumble.

путаный *adj.* **1,** tangled. **2,** confused; rambling; incoherent. **3,** *colloq.* (*of a person*) confused; mixed up.

путать *v. impfv.* **1,** [*pfv.* запутать, спутать, *or* перепутать] to tangle. **2,** [*pfv.* перепутать] to mix up (*objects previously in order*). **3,** [*pfv.* спутать *or* запутать] to confuse; mix (someone) up. **4,** [*pfv.* спутать *or* перепутать] to confuse; get (two or more things) mixed up. **5,** [*impfv. only*] to ramble (*in speech*). **6,** [*pfv.* запутать *or* впутать] (*with* в + *acc.*) *colloq.* to involve (in); embroil (in). **7,** [*pfv.* спутать] to hobble; fetter (a horse). —**путаться,** *refl.* **1,** [*pfv.* с-, за-, пере-] to become (en)tangled. **2,** [*pfv.* с-, пере-] *colloq.* to become confused. **3,** [*pfv.* в-] (*with* в + *acc.*) *colloq.* to interfere (in); meddle (in). **4,** [*pfv.* с-] (*with* с + *instr.*) *colloq.* to consort (with); keep company (with).

путёвка [*gen. pl.* -вок] *n.* **1,** pass; permit; authorization. **2,** ticket for a group tour; place in a tourist group. —**путёвка в жизнь,** a start in life.

путеводи́тель *n.m.* guidebook.

путево́дный *adj.* guiding. —**путево́дная звезда́,** guiding star; lodestar. —**путево́дная нить,** clue.

путево́й *adj.* **1,** travel (*attrib.*): путевы́е заме́тки, travel notes. **2,** *R.R.* track (*attrib.*): путево́й обхо́дчик, trackman; lineman. —**путева́я ка́рта,** road map. —**путева́я ско́рость,** ground speed.

путе́ец [*gen.* -те́йца] *n.* railway engineer.

путём *prep., with gen.* by means of; by.

путепрово́д *n.* overpass.

путеше́ственник *n.* traveler.

путеше́ствие *n.* trip; journey; voyage.

путеше́ствовать *v. impfv.* [*pres.* -ствую, -ствуешь] to travel.

пу́тник *n.* traveler.

пу́тный *adj., colloq.* **1,** sensible. **2,** worthwhile. —из него́ ничего́ пу́тного не вы́йдет, he'll never amount to anything.

путч *n.* putsch.

пу́ты [*gen.* пут] *n. pl.* fetters; shackles (*lit. & fig.*).

путь [*gen., dat., & prepl.* пути́; *instr.* путём; *pl.* пути́, путе́й, путя́м] *n.m.* **1,** way; route: на обра́тном пути́, on the way back. Око́льным путём, by a roundabout way/route. **2,** journey; traveling: два дня пути́, a two-day journey; two days of traveling. Отпра́виться в путь, to start/set out on a journey. Счастли́вого пути́!, bon voyage! **3,** *fig.* path: и́збранный путь, one's chosen path. **4,** *fig.* track: на ло́жном пути́, on the wrong track. **5,** way; means; method: каки́м путём?, in what way?; by what means? **6,** *R.R.* track: запа́сный путь, sidetrack; siding. **7,** *pl., anat.* passage; tract: дыха́тельные пути́, respiratory tract. —по пути́, **1,** [*also,* в пути́] on the way; along the way; en route. **2,** (*with dat.*) going one's way: мне с ва́ми по пути́, I am going your way. *See also* путём.

пуф *n.* padded stool; hassock.

пух *n.* down; fluff; fuzz. —в пух и прах, **1,** thoroughly; utterly. **2,** (*with verbs of dressing*) in one's finest. —ни пу́ха ни пера́!, good luck!

пу́хлый *adj.* chubby; pudgy; plump.

пу́хнуть *v. impfv.* [*past* пух, -ла] to swell.

пухови́к [*gen.* -вика́] *n.* feather bed.

пухо́вка [*gen. pl.* -вок] *n.* powder puff.

пухо́вый *adj.* made of down; downy.

пучегла́зый *adj., colloq.* goggle-eyed.

пучи́на *n.* ocean depths.

пучо́к [*gen.* -чка́] *n.* **1,** bunch (*of flowers*); tuft (*of grass*). **2,** wisp (*of hay, straw, etc.*). **3,** beam: пучо́к све́та, beam of light. **4,** bun: носи́ть во́лосы пучко́м, to wear one's hair in a bun.

пу́шечный *adj.* gun (*attrib.*); cannon (*attrib.*). —пу́шечное мя́со, cannon fodder. —пу́шечное ядро́, cannon ball.

пуши́нка [*gen. pl.* -нок] *n.* **1,** bit of fluff. **2,** tiny flake (*of snow*).

пуши́стый *adj.* downy; fluffy; fuzzy.

пуши́ть *v. impfv.* [*pfv.* распуши́ть] to fluff (up).

пу́шка [*gen. pl.* -шек] *n.* **1,** gun. **2,** cannon. —как из пу́шки, punctually; right on time.

пушка́рь [*gen.* -каря́] *n.m., obs.* gunner; artilleryman.

пушни́на *n.* fur; furs.

пушно́й *adj.* **1,** fur (*attrib.*). **2,** fur-bearing.

пушо́к [*gen.* -шка́] *n.* fluff; fuzz.

пу́ща *n.* dense forest.

пу́ще *adv., colloq.* more.

пу́щий *adj., obs.* **1,** greatest. **2,** *preceded by* для, greater: для пу́щей ва́жности, for greater effect.

пуэрторика́нец [*gen.* -нца] *n.m.* [*fem.* -нка] Puerto Rican. —пуэрторика́нский, *adj.* Puerto Rican.

пчела́ [*pl.* пчёлы] *n.* bee.

пчели́ный *adj.* bee (*attrib.*). —пчели́ный воск, beeswax.

пчелово́д *n.* beekeeper. —пчелово́дство, *n.* beekeeping.

пче́льник *n.* apiary.

пшени́ца *n.* wheat. —твёрдая пшени́ца, durum wheat.

пшени́чный *adj.* wheat (*attrib.*).

пшено́ *n.* millet.

пыж [*gen.* пыжа́] *n.* wad (*used in loading a firearm*).

пыжи́к *n.* baby reindeer.

пы́житься *v.r. impfv.* [*pfv.* напы́житься] *colloq.* **1,** to make every effort; strain every nerve. **2,** to act high and mighty.

пыл [*2nd loc.* пылу́] *n.* ardor. —в пылу́ (+ *gen.*), in the heat of (battle, an argument, etc.); in a moment of (anger, passion, etc.). —с пы́лу, с жа́ру, piping hot.

пыла́ть *v. impfv.* **1,** to flame; blaze. **2,** (*of one's face*) to glow. **3,** (*with instr.*) to burn (with love, rage, etc.).

пылесо́с *n.* vacuum cleaner.

пыли́нка [*gen. pl.* -нок] *n.* speck of dust.

пыли́ть *v. impfv.* **1,** *v.i.* [*pfv.* напыли́ть] to raise (a cloud of) dust. **2,** *v.t.* [*pfv.* запыли́ть] to get dust on. —пыли́ться, *refl.* [*pfv.* запыли́ться] to get dusty; gather dust.

пы́лкий *adj.* ardent; fervent; fiery. —пы́лкость, *n.f.* ardor; fervor.

пыль [*2nd loc.* пыли́] *n.f.* dust. —пуска́ть пыль в глаза́, **1,** to put on a false front. **2,** (*with dat.*) to throw dust in someone's eyes.

пы́льник *n.* **1,** *bot.* anther. **2,** smock to protect against dust; duster. **3,** light summer overcoat.

пы́льный *adj.* **1,** dust (*attrib.*). **2,** dusty.

пыльца́ *n.* pollen.

пыта́ть *v. impfv.* **1,** to torture. **2,** *fig.* to torment.

пыта́ться *v.r. impfv.* [*pfv.* попыта́ться] to attempt; try; endeavor.

пы́тка [*gen. pl.* -ток] *n.* **1,** torture. **2,** *fig.* torture; agony; sheer hell.

пытли́вый *adj.* inquisitive. —пытли́вость, *n.f.* inquisitiveness.

пы́хать *v. impfv.* [*pres.* пы́шу, пы́шешь] *colloq.* **1,** to blaze. **2,** (*with instr.*) to radiate: пы́хать сча́стьем, to radiate happiness. Он пы́шет здоро́вьем, he is the picture of health.

пыхте́ние *n.* panting; puffing.

пыхте́ть *v. impfv.* [*pres.* пыхчу́, пыхти́шь] to puff; pant.

пы́шка [*gen. pl.* -шек] *n.* **1,** bun. **2,** *colloq.* plump child.

пы́шный *adj.* **1,** sumptuous; magnificent. **2,** fluffy. **3,** (*of vegetation*) luxuriant; lush. **4,** pompous; high-flown. —пы́шность, *n.f.* sumptuousness; splendor; pomp.

пьедеста́л *n.* pedestal.

пье́са *n.* (stage) play.

пью́щий *adj.* (*of a person*) who drinks. —*n.* drinker.

пьяне́ть *v. impfv.* [*pfv.* опьяне́ть] to get drunk.

пьяни́ть *v. impfv.* [*pfv.* опьяни́ть] to intoxicate; make drunk.

пья́ница *n.m. & f.* drunkard.

пья́нство *n.* drunkenness.

пья́нствовать *v. impfv.* [*pres.* -ствую, -ствуешь] to drink too much; be frequently drunk.

пья́ный *adj. & n.* drunk.

пэр *n.* peer. —**пэ́рство**, *n.* title of peer.

пюпи́тр *n.* stand: но́тный пюпи́тр, music stand.

пюре́ (рэ) *n. neut. indecl.* purée. —**я́блочное пюре́**, applesauce. —**карто́фельное пюре́**, mashed potatoes.

пядь [*pl.* пя́ди, -де́й, -дя́м] *n.f.* span (*distance from thumb to forefinger*). —**пядь земли́**, dot of land. —**не отда́ть** *or* **не уступи́ть ни пя́ди земли́**, not to yield an inch. —**будь он семи́ пяде́й во лбу**, even if he were a genius/the smartest man in the world/.

па́лить *v. impfv.*, *colloq.*, *in* па́лить глаза́ на (+ *acc.*), to stare at.

па́льцы [*gen.* -лец] *n. pl.* tambour (*embroidery frame*).

пясть *n.f.* metacarpus.

пята́ [*pl.* пя́ты, пят, пята́м] *n.* **1**, *obs.* heel. **2**, abutment. —**до пят**, (*of a garment*) extending down to one's ankles. —**по пята́м**, on someone's heels. —**под пято́й** (+ *gen.*), under the heel of.

пята́к [*gen.* -така́] *n.*, *colloq.* five-kopeck piece.

пятачо́к [*gen.* -чка́] *n.*, *colloq.* **1**, = пята́к. **2**, pig's snout.

пя́тая *n.*, *decl. as an adj.* fifth: одна́ пя́тая, one-fifth.

пятёрка *n.* **1**, the numeral 5. **2**, *colloq.* anything numbered 5. **3**, a grade of "five", signifying "excellent". **4**, *cards* five. **5**, *colloq.* five-ruble note.

пятерня́ *n.*, *colloq.* one's hand.

пя́теро *collective numeral* five.

пятибо́рье *n.* pentathlon.

пятигра́нник *n.* pentahedron.

пятидесятиле́тие *n.* **1**, fiftieth anniversary; fiftieth birthday. **2**, fifty-year period.

пятидесятиле́тний *adj.* **1**, fifty-year (*attrib.*). **2**, fifty-year-old.

пятидеся́тница *n.* Pentecost.

пятидеся́тый *ordinal number* fiftieth.

пятидне́вный *adj.* five-day (*attrib.*).

пятикни́жие *n.* the Pentateuch.

пятиконе́чный *adj.* (*of a star*) five-pointed.

пятикра́тный *adj.* fivefold.

пятиле́тие *n.* **1**, fifth anniversary; fifth birthday. **2**, five-year period.

пятиле́тка [*gen. pl.* -ток] *n.* five-year plan.

пятиле́тний *adj.* **1**, five-year (*attrib.*). **2**, five-year-old.

пятирублёвка [*gen. pl.* -вок] *n.*, *colloq.* five-ruble note.

пятисо́тый *ordinal numeral* five-hundredth.

пятисто́пный *adj.* pentameter. —**пятисто́пный стих**, pentameter. —**пятисто́пный ямб**, iambic pentameter.

пя́титься *v.r. impfv.* [*pfv.* попя́титься; *pres.* -чусь, -тишься] **1**, to back up; move backwards. **2**, *colloq.* to back out; (*with* от) go back on.

пятиуго́льник *n.* pentagon. —**пятиуго́льный**, *adj.* pentagonal.

пя́тка [*gen. pl.* -ток] *n.* heel. —**лиза́ть пя́тки** (+ *dat.*), to lick someone's boots. —**наступа́ть на пя́тки** (+ *dat.*), to be close on the heels of. —**показа́ть пя́тки**, to take to one's heels. —**у меня́ душа́ ушла́ в пя́тки**, my heart sank.

пятна́дцатый *ordinal numeral* fifteenth.

пятна́дцать [*gen., dat., & prepl.* -цати; *instr.* -цатью] *numeral* fifteen.

пятна́ть *v. impfv.* [*pfv.* запятна́ть] **1**, to spot; stain. **2**, *fig.* to sully; tarnish.

пятна́шки [*gen.* -шек] *n. pl.* tag (*game*).

пятни́стый *adj.* spotted.

пя́тница *n.* Friday.

пятно́ [*pl.* пя́тна, пя́тен] *n.* spot; stain; blemish.

пя́тнышко [*pl.* -шки, -шек] *n.*, *dim. of* пятно́.

пято́к [*gen.* -тка́] *n.* (*with gen. pl.*) *colloq.* five (*similar objects*).

пя́тый *ordinal numeral* fifth.

пять [*gen., dat., & prepl.* пяти́; *instr.* пятью́] *numeral* five.

пятьдеся́т [*gen., dat., & prepl.* пяти́десяти; *instr.* пятью́десятью] *numeral* fifty.

пятьсо́т [*gen.* пятисо́т; *dat.* пятиста́м; *instr.* пятью́ста́ми; *prepl.* пятиста́х] *numeral* five hundred.

пя́тью *adv.* five times: пя́тью пять — два́дцать пять, five times five is 25.

Р

Р, р *n. neut.* seventeenth letter of the Russian alphabet.

раб [*gen.* раба́] *n.m.* [*fem.* раба́] slave.

рабовладе́лец [*gen.* -льца] *n.* slaveowner. —**рабовладе́льческий**, *adj.* slave-owning.

раболе́пный *adj.* servile. —**раболе́пие**; **раболе́пство**, *n.* servility.

раболе́пствовать *v. impfv.* [*pres.* -ствую, -ству-ешь] (*with* пе́ред) to be servile (to); kowtow (to); grovel (before).

рабо́та *n.* **1**, work. **2**, job: меня́ть рабо́ту, to change jobs. **3**, *in* курсова́я рабо́та, term paper. **4**, *pl.* work; operations: строи́тельные рабо́ты, construction work; спаса́тельные рабо́ты, rescue operations. **5**, *pl.* works (*of an artist, writer, etc.*). **6**, workmanship: превосхо́дной рабо́ты, of superb workmanship.

—**брать в работу, 1,** to take in hand. **2,** to take to task.

работать *v. impfv.* **1,** to work. **2,** (*with instr.*) to use; handle; wield (a tool). **3,** (*of a device*) to work; function; operate. **4,** to be open (*to the public*). **5,** *in* **работать над собой,** to work to improve oneself. —**работаться,** *refl., impers.* **1,** *indicating the progress of work:* сегодня хорошо работается, the work is going well today. **2,** (*with dat.*) to feel like working: мне сегодня не работается, I don't feel like working today; I can't get down to work today.

работник *n.* **1,** worker: отличный работник, excellent worker. Работник искусства, person who works in the arts. Научный работник, person engaged in scientific research. **2,** employee; official: работник посольства, embassy employee/official. Руководящий работник, person in a supervisory position.

работница *n.* woman worker.

работный *adj., obs.* working (*attrib.*). —**работный дом,** workhouse.

работодатель *n.m.* employer.

работорговец [*gen.* -вца] *n.* slave trader. —**работорговля,** *n.* slave trade.

работоспособный *adj.* **1,** able-bodied. **2,** hard-working; industrious. —**работоспособность,** *n.f.* ability to work; capacity for work.

работяга *n.m. & f., colloq.* hard worker.

работящий *adj., colloq.* hard-working; industrious.

рабочий *adj.* work (*attrib.*); working; worker's. —*n.* worker; workman. —**рабочий день,** workday. —**рабочий класс,** the working class. —**рабочие руки,** workmen; hands. —**рабочая сила,** manpower. —**рабочий скот,** draft animals. —**рабочий сцены,** stage-hand. —**в рабочем порядке,** in the course of work; (while) on the job.

рабский *adj.* **1,** slave (*attrib.*). **2,** servile; slavish.

рабство *n.* slavery; servitude; bondage.

рабыня *n.* slave; bondwoman.

раввин *n.* rabbi. —**раввинский,** *adj.* rabbinical.

равенство *n.* equality.

равнение *n., mil.* alignment.

равнина *n.* plain.

равнинный *adj.* **1,** of the plains. **2,** (*of terrain*) flat.

равно *adv.* equally. —*adj., used predicatively* (*with dat.*) equal (to): два плюс три равно пяти, two plus three equals five. —**всё равно, 1,** it is all the same; it makes no difference. **2,** still; all the same; nevertheless. —**всё равно, что,** just the same as. —**равно и; равно как,** as well as.

равнобедренный *adj., math.* isosceles.

равновесие *n.* balance; equilibrium. —**вывести из равновесия,** to disconcert; rattle.

равноденствие *n.* equinox.

равнодушие *n.* indifference.

равнодушный *adj.* [*short form* -шен, -шна] (*with* к) indifferent (to). —**равнодушно,** *adv.* with indifference.

равнозначный *adj.* equivalent.

равномерный *adj.* even; uniform.

равноправие *n.* equal rights; equality.

равноправный *adj.* **1,** equal; enjoying equal rights. **2,** equitable.

равносильный *adj.* **1,** of equal strength. **2,** (*with dat.*) equivalent (to); tantamount (to).

равносторонний *adj.* equilateral.

равноугольный *adj.* equiangular.

равноценный *adj.* **1,** equal in price. **2,** of equal value.

равный *adj.* [*short form* равен, равна, равно, равны] equal. —*n.* equal: первый среди равных, first among equals. —**на равной ноге с,** on an equal footing with. —**при прочих равных условиях,** other things being equal. —**равным образом,** by the same token.

равнять *v. impfv.* [*pfv.* сравнять] **1,** to make equal; equalize. **2,** [*impfv. only*] (*with* с + *instr.*) to equate (with). —**равняться,** *refl.* [*impfv. only*] **1,** (*with dat.*) to equal. **2,** (*with dat.*) to amount to; be tantamount to. **3,** (*with* с + *instr.*) *colloq.* to compete (with); compare (with). **4,** (*with* по) to emulate. **5,** *mil.* to dress.

рагу *n. neut. indecl.* ragout; stew.

рад *adj., used predicatively* (*with inf., dat., or* что) glad; pleased: очень рад (рада) познакомиться с вами!, pleased to meet you! Я рад случаю (+ *inf.*), I am glad/pleased to have the opportunity to...

радар *n.* radar. —**радарный,** *adj.* radar (*attrib.*).

раджа *n.m.* rajah.

ради *prep., with gen.* for; for the sake of. —**ради бога!,** *see* бог.

радиальный *adj.* radial.

радиатор *n.* radiator.

радиация *n.* radiation.

радий *n.* radium. —**радиевый,** *adj.* radium.

радикал *n.* **1,** *polit.* radical. **2,** *math.* radical sign. **3,** *chem.* radical. —**радикализм,** *n.* radicalism.

радикальный *adj.* **1,** *polit.* radical. **2,** radical; drastic. —**радикально,** *adv.* radically.

радио *n. indecl.* **1,** radio: по радио, on/over the radio. **2,** = радиоприёмник.

радиоактивный *adj.* radioactive. —**радиоактивность,** *n.f.* radioactivity.

радиовещание *n.* broadcasting. —**радиовещательный,** *adj.* broadcasting.

радиограмма *n.* radio message; radiogram.

радиола *n.* radio-phonograph.

радиология *n.* radiology. —**радиолог,** *n.* radiologist.

радиолокатор *n.* radar (set). —**радиолокация,** *n.* radar; detection by radar. —**радиолокационный,** *adj.* radar (*attrib.*).

радиолюбитель *n.m.* amateur radio operator; ham.

радиомаяк [*gen.* -маяка] *n.* (radio) beacon.

радиопеленгатор *n.* (radio) direction finder.

радиопередатчик *n.* radio transmitter.

радиопередача *n.* radio broadcast; radio transmission.

радиоприёмник *n.* radio: включить радиоприёмник, to turn on the radio.

радиосвязь *n.f.* radio communication.

радиослушатель *n.m.* (radio) listener.

радиостанция *n.* radio station.

радиотелеграфия *n.* radiotelegraphy.

радиотелефон *n.* radiotelephone. —**радиотелефония,** *n.* radiotelephony.

радиотерапия *n.* radiotherapy.

радиотехник *n.* radio mechanic. —**радиотехника,** *n.* radio engineering.

радировать *v. impfv. & pfv.* [*pres.* -рую, -руешь] to radio.

радист *n.* radio operator.

радиус *n.* radius. —**радиус действия,** range (*of an aircraft, missile, etc.*).

радовать *v. impfv.* [*pfv.* обрадовать; *pres.* -дую,

-дуешь] to gladden; make happy. —**ра́доваться**, *refl.* to be glad; be happy; rejoice. Ра́доваться изве́стию, to be happy about the news; rejoice over the news.

радо́н *n.* radon.

ра́достно *adv.* with joy. —*adj., used predicatively* (*with dat.*) delighted: мне бы́ло ра́достно, что..., I was delighted that...

ра́достный *adj.* joyful; joyous. Ра́достное изве́стие, joyful news; glad tidings.

ра́дость *n.f.* joy; gladness.

ра́дуга *n.* rainbow.

ра́дужность *n.f.* iridescence.

ра́дужный *adj.* 1, iridescent; opalescent. 2, *fig.* bright; rosy. 3, (*of hopes, spirits, etc.*) high. —**ра́дужная оболо́чка**, *anat.* iris.

раду́шие *n.* cordiality; hospitality.

раду́шный *adj.* cordial. —**раду́шно**, *adv.* cordially.

раж *n., colloq.* passion; frenzy. —**войти́ в раж**, to become very emotional; get all worked up.

раз [*pl.* разы́, раз] *n.* 1, time: два ра́за, two times. 2, *in counting,* one: раз, два, три, one, two, three. —*adv.* once: раз по́здно ве́чером, once late at night. —*conj., colloq.* since; if: раз не зна́ешь, не говори́, if you don't know, don't talk. —**в са́мый раз**, 1, the right time. 2, the right size. —**вся́кий раз, когда́,** every time; whenever. —**ещё раз,** again; once again. —**как раз,** just; exactly; precisely: как раз то, что мне ну́жно, just what I need. —**не раз,** more than once. —**ни ра́зу,** not a single time. —**раз за ра́зом,** time after time; time and again.

раз- *also,* **рас-, разо-, разъ-,** *prefix* 1, *indicating breaking asunder:* разбива́ть, to smash. 2, (*with* -ся) *indicating dispersal:* разъезжа́ться, to depart (*in various directions*). 3, *indicating distribution:* раздава́ть, to hand out. 4, *indicating undoing or unfastening:* развя́зывать, to untie. 5, *indicating reversal of action:* разлюби́ть, to cease to love. 6, (*with* -ся) [*with pfv. verbs only*] *indicating warming up to one's activity:* разговори́ться, to warm to one's subject.

разба́вить [*infl.* -влю, -вишь] *v., pfv. of* разбавля́ть.

разбавля́ть *v. impfv.* [*pfv.* разба́вить] to dilute.

разбаза́ривать *v. impfv.* [*pfv.* разбаза́рить] *colloq.* to squander.

разба́лтывать *v. impfv.* [*pfv.* разболта́ть] *colloq.* 1, to shake up; stir. 2, to work loose; knock loose. 3, to give away (a secret). —**разба́лтываться**, *refl., colloq.* 1, to come loose. 2, to get carried away (*while speaking*). 3, *fig.* to get out of hand.

разбе́г *n.* running approach (*before jumping, diving, taking off, etc.*). —**с разбе́га; с разбе́гу,** while running at full speed. —**прыжо́к с разбе́га/разбе́гу,** running broad jump.

разбега́ться *v.r. impfv.* [*pfv.* разбежа́ться] 1, to scatter; disperse. 2, to run at top speed. 3, to make a running approach. —**у меня́ глаза́ разбежа́лись,** I didn't know where to look first.

разбежа́ться [*infl. like* бежа́ть] *v.r., pfv. of* разбега́ться.

разбереди́ть *v., pfv. of* береди́ть.

разбива́ть *v. impfv.* [*pfv.* разби́ть] 1, to break; smash; shatter. 2, to hurt badly; fracture. 3, to defeat; crush. 4, to demolish (an argument, theory, etc.). 5, to divide; break up. 6, to lay out (a garden, park, etc.). 7, to pitch (a tent); set up (camp). —**разбива́ться**, *refl.* 1, to break; be smashed. 2, to break up; split up. 3,

(*of a plane*) to crash. 4, to be badly hurt. 5, *in* разби́ться на́смерть, to be killed (*in a crash, fall, etc.*).

разби́вка *n.* 1, dividing up. 2, laying out.

разбинтова́ть [*infl.* -ту́ю, -ту́ешь] *v., pfv. of* разбинто́вывать.

разбинто́вывать *v. impfv.* [*pfv.* разбинтова́ть] to unbandage.

разбира́тельство *n.* investigation. —**суде́бное разбира́тельство,** trial.

разбира́ть *v. impfv.* [*pfv.* разобра́ть] 1, to take apart; dismantle. 2, to analyze; examine; look into. 3, to sort out. 4, to buy up. 5, to make out; discern. 6, to make out; decipher (something written). 7, *gram.* to parse. 8, *colloq.* (*of an emotion*) to seize; come over. 9, [*impfv. only*] *colloq.* to stop to choose; take time to choose. —**разбира́ться**, *refl.* (*with* в + *prepl.*) to understand; have an understanding of.

разбитно́й *adj., colloq.* 1, capable; adept. 2, sprightly; outgoing.

разби́тый *adj.* 1, broken. 2, defeated. 3, ruined; shattered. 4, worn out; jaded. —**разби́т паралично́м,** paralyzed.

разби́ть [*infl.* разобью́, разобьёшь] *v., pfv. of* бить (*in sense #4*) *and* разбива́ть. —**разби́ться**, *refl., pfv. of* разбива́ться.

разбогате́ть *v., pfv. of* богате́ть.

разбо́й *n.* robbery. —**разбо́йник**, *n.* robber.

разбо́йничать *v. impfv.* to commit robberies.

разбо́йничий [*fem.* -чья] *adj.* robbers'. *Also,* **разбо́йнический.**

разболе́ться *v.r. pfv., colloq.* 1, [*infl.* -е́юсь, -е́ешься] to become seriously ill. 2, [*infl.* -и́тся] to begin to hurt.

разболта́ть *v., pfv. of* разба́лтывать. —**разболта́ться**, *refl., pfv. of* разба́лтываться.

разбомби́ть *v. pfv.* [*infl.* -блю́, -би́шь] to destroy; wipe out (*by bombing*); bomb out.

разбо́р *n.* 1, taking apart. 2, analysis. 3, investigation. 4, sorting out. 5, selectivity: без разбо́ра, indiscriminately. 6, *gram.* parsing. 7, *colloq.* quality; caliber.

разбо́рка *n.* 1, taking apart; dismantling. 2, sorting out.

разбо́рный *adj.* 1, collapsible. 2, (*of furniture*) sectional.

разбо́рчиво *adv.* legibly.

разбо́рчивость *n.f.* 1, discrimination. 2, legibility.

разбо́рчивый *adj.* 1, discriminating. 2, legible.

разбрани́ть *v. pfv., colloq.* to scold; bawl out; berate. —**разбрани́ться**, *refl.* (*with* с + *instr.*) *colloq.* to quarrel (with).

разбра́сывать *v. impfv.* [*pfv.* разброса́ть] to scatter. —**разбра́сываться**, *refl.* 1, to stretch out. 2, *fig.* to do too many things at once; spread oneself thin.

разбреда́ться *v.r. impfv.* [*pfv.* разбрести́сь] (*of many people*) to wander off (*in different directions*).

разбрести́сь [*infl. like* брести́] *v.r., pfv. of* разбреда́ться.

разбро́д *n.* 1, confusion; disorder. 2, discord; dissension.

разбро́санный *adj.* 1, scattered; dispersed. 2, *colloq.* disconnected; incoherent.

разброса́ть *v., pfv. of* разбра́сывать. —**разброса́ться**, *refl., pfv. of* разбра́сываться.

разбры́згивать *v. impfv.* [*pfv.* разбры́згать] to

splash; sprinkle; spray. —**разбры́згиваться**, *refl.* to splash; spatter.

разбуди́ть *v., pfv. of* **буди́ть** (*in sense #1*).

разбуха́ть *v. impfv.* [*pfv.* **разбу́хнуть**] to swell.

разбу́хнуть [*past* -бу́х, -ла] *v., pfv. of* **бу́хнуть**[1] *and* **разбуха́ть**.

разбушева́ться *v.r. impfv.* [*infl.* -шу́юсь, -шу́ешься] **1**, (*of a storm, the sea, etc.*) to rage. **2**, *colloq.* to become enraged; fly into a rage.

разва́л *n.* collapse; breakdown.

разва́ливать *v. impfv.* [*pfv.* **развали́ть**] **1**, to tear down. **2**, *fig.* to ruin; make a mess of. —**разва́ливаться**, *refl.* **1**, to collapse; come tumbling down. **2**, to fall apart; go to pieces. **3**, *colloq.* to sprawl out.

разва́лина *n.* **1**, *pl.* ruins. **2**, *colloq.* (physical) wreck.

развали́ть [*infl.* -валю́, -ва́лишь] *v., pfv. of* **разва́ливать**. —**развали́ться**, *refl., pfv. of* **разва́ливаться**.

разва́ривать *v. impfv.* [*pfv.* **развари́ть**] to boil until soft.

развари́ть [*infl.* -варю́, -ва́ришь] *v., pfv. of* **разва́ривать**.

ра́зве *particle* **1**, really? **2**, (*with inf.*) perhaps one should...; shouldn't one...? **3**, (*with* не) isn't it...?: ра́зве не я́сно, что..., isn't it clear that...? —*conj., obs.* unless. —**ра́зве то́лько**; **ра́зве что**, except: ра́зве то́лько на кра́йнем се́вере, except in the extreme north. Он почти́ не постаре́л, ра́зве что стал чу́точку седе́е, he has hardly aged at all except for becoming a bit grayer.

развева́ть *v. impfv.* to blow about; cause to wave. —**развева́ться**, *refl.* to flutter.

разве́дать *v., pfv. of* **разве́дывать**.

разведе́ние *n.* raising; breeding.

разведённый *adj.* divorced. —*n.* divorced man. —**разведённая**, *n.* divorcée.

разве́дка *n.* **1**, (gathering of) intelligence. **2**, intelligence service. **3**, reconnaissance. **4**, prospecting; exploration.

разве́дочный *adj.* **1**, exploratory. **2**, reconnaissance (*attrib.*); intelligence (*attrib.*).

разве́дчик *n.* **1**, *mil.* scout. **2**, intelligence agent. **3**, prospector. **4**, reconnaissance plane.

разве́дывательный *adj.* intelligence (*attrib.*); reconnaissance (*attrib.*).

разве́дывать *v. impfv.* [*pfv.* **разве́дать**] **1**, (*with* о) *colloq.* to find out (about). **2**, *mil.* to reconnoiter. **3**, to prospect; explore.

развезти́ [*infl. like* везти́] *v., pfv. of* **развози́ть**.

разве́ивать *v. impfv.* [*pfv.* **разве́ять**] **1**, (*of the wind*) to scatter; disperse. **2**, *fig.* to dispel.

развенчивать *v. impfv.* [*pfv.* **развенча́ть**] to discredit.

развёрнутый *adj.* **1**, *mil.* deployed; extended. **2**, all-out; full-scale. **3**, detailed; comprehensive.

развернуть *v., pfv. of* **развёртывать** *and* **развора́чивать** (*in sense #1*). —**разверну́ться**, *refl., pfv. of* **развёртываться** *and* **развора́чиваться**.

развёрстка *n.* **1**, apportionment; allotment. **2**, assessment (*of a tax*).

развёртка [*gen. pl.* -ток] *n.* reamer.

развёртывание *n.* **1**, unfolding; unwrapping; unrolling. **2**, *mil.* deployment. **3**, *fig.* development.

развёртывать *v. impfv.* [*pfv.* **разверну́ть**] **1**, to unfold; unwrap. **2**, to unroll; unfurl. **3**, *mil.* to deploy. **4**, to launch (a campaign, movement, etc.). **5**, to de-

velop; expand. —**развёртываться**, *refl.* **1**, to come unfolded; come unrolled; come undone. **2**, *mil.* to deploy. **3**, *fig.* to develop.

развесели́ть *v. pfv.* to cheer up; gladden. —**развесели́ться**, *refl.* to cheer up; become cheerful.

развесёлый *adj., colloq.* gay; merry; jolly.

разве́систый *adj.* (*of a tree*) spreading.

разве́сить [*infl.* -шу, -сишь] *v., pfv. of* **разве́шивать**.

разве́ска *n.* weighing.

развесно́й *adj.* sold by weight.

развести́ [*infl. like* вести́] *v., pfv. of* **разводи́ть**. —**развести́сь**, *refl., pfv. of* **разводи́ться**.

разветви́ть [*infl.* -влю́, -ви́шь] *v., pfv. of* **разветвля́ть**. —**разветви́ться**, *refl., pfv. of* **разветвля́ться**.

разветвле́ние *n.* fork (*in a road*).

разветвля́ться *v.r. impfv.* [*pfv.* **разветви́ться**] **1**, (*of a tree or bush*) to form branches. **2**, (*of a road*) to fork; divide.

разве́шивать *v. impfv.* [*pfv.* **разве́сить**] **1**, to weigh out. **2**, [*pfv. also* **разве́шать**] to hang out (a number of objects). **3**, (*of a tree*) to spread (its branches).

разве́ять *v., pfv. of* **разве́ивать**.

развива́ть *v. impfv.* [*pfv.* **разви́ть**] **1**, to develop. **2**, to unwind; unravel. —**развива́ться**, *refl.* **1**, to develop. **2**, to come unwound.

разви́лина *n.* fork (*in a road or branches of a tree*).

разви́листый *adj.* forked.

разви́лка [*gen. pl.* -лок] *n.* fork (*in a road*).

развинти́ть [*infl.* -чу́, -ти́шь] *v., pfv. of* **разви́нчивать**. —**развинти́ться**, *refl., pfv. of* **разви́нчиваться**.

разви́нченный *adj.* **1**, unscrewed. **2**, (*of one's gait*) unsteady. **3**, *colloq.* unnerved.

разви́нчивать *v. impfv.* [*pfv.* **развинти́ть**] to unscrew. —**разви́нчиваться**, *refl.* **1**, to come unscrewed; come loose. **2**, *colloq.* to go to pieces. **3**, *colloq.* (*of one's nerves*) to be shot.

разви́тие *n.* development. —**разви́тие собы́тий**, course of events.

развито́й *adj.* [*short form* ра́звит, развита́, ра́звито] **1**, highly developed. **2**, mature.

разви́ть [*infl.* разовью́, разовьёшь; *past fem.* развила́] *v., pfv. of* **развива́ть**. —**разви́ться**, *refl., pfv. of* **развива́ться**.

развлека́тельный *adj.* done purely for pleasure or entertainment; entertainment (*attrib.*).

развлека́ть *v. impfv.* [*pfv.* **развле́чь**] to entertain; amuse. —**развлека́ться**, *refl.* to amuse oneself; seek diversion.

развлече́ние *n.* amusement; entertainment; diversion; recreation.

развле́чь [*infl. like* влечь] *v., pfv. of* **развлека́ть**. —**развле́чься**, *refl., pfv. of* **развлека́ться**.

разво́д *n.* **1**, divorce. В разво́де, divorced. **2**, posting (*of sentries*). **3**, breeding. *See also* **разво́ды**.

разводи́ть *v. impfv.* [*pfv.* **развести́**; *pres.* -вожу́, -во́дишь] **1**, to take; conduct (*each to his place*). **2**, *mil.* to post (sentries). **3**, to separate; pull apart. **4**, to dilute; dissolve. **5**, to raise; breed. **6**, to grow; cultivate (plants). **7**, to build; make (a fire). **8**, *in* разводи́ть рука́ми, to throw up one's hands. —**разводи́ться**, *refl.* **1**, (*with* с + *instr.*) to divorce; get a divorce from. **2**, to breed; multiply.

разво́дка *n., colloq.* separating. Разво́дка моста́, opening up of a drawbridge.

разводно́й *adj., in* **разводно́й мост**, drawbridge.

разво́ды [*gen.* -до́в] *n. pl.* **1,** design; pattern. **2,** *colloq.* streaks; stains.

разво́з *n.* delivery; conveyance; transport.

развози́ть *v. impfv.* [*pfv.* развезти́; *pres.* -вожу́, -во́зишь] **1,** to deliver; convey; transport (*each to his or its destination*). **2,** *impers., colloq.* to become impassable: доро́гу развезло́, the road became impassable.

разво́зка *n., colloq.* delivery; conveyance; transport.

разволнова́ть *v. pfv.* [*infl.* -ну́ю, -ну́ешь] to upset; throw into a state. —**разволнова́ться,** *refl.* to become highly upset.

развора́чивать *v. impfv.* **1,** [*pfv.* разверну́ть] to turn (a vehicle) around. **2,** [*pfv.* развороти́ть] *colloq.* to upset; throw into disorder. —**развора́чиваться,** *refl.* [*pfv.* разверну́ться] to turn around (*in a vehicle*).

разворова́ть [*infl.* -ру́ю, -ру́ешь] *v., pfv. of* разворо́вывать.

разворо́вывать *v. impfv.* [*pfv.* разворова́ть] *colloq.* to steal; make off with.

разворо́т *n.* **1,** U-turn. **2,** turn (*in a road*). **3,** (*with gen.*) *colloq.* development (of). **4,** inside (*of something that folds over*). **5,** double page; centerfold.

развороти́ть [*infl.* -рочу́, -ро́тишь] *v., pfv. of* развора́чивать (*in sense #2*).

развра́т *n.* debauchery; depravity.

развраща́ть [*infl.* -щу́, -ти́шь] *v., pfv. of* развраща́ть. —**разврати́ться,** *refl., pfv. of* развраща́ться.

развра́тник *n.* profligate; lecher; libertine; rake; roué.

развра́тничать *v. impfv.* to lead a dissolute life.

развра́тный *adj.* dissolute; profligate.

развраща́ть *v. impfv.* [*pfv.* разврати́ть] to corrupt; deprave; debauch. —**развраща́ться,** *refl.* **1,** to become corrupted. **2,** to give way to debauchery.

развраще́ние *n.* (*with gen.*) corruption (of).

развращённый *adj.* corrupt; depraved; dissolute. —**развращённость,** *n.f.* depravity.

развью́чивать *v. impfv.* [*pfv.* развью́чить] to unload (a pack animal).

развяза́ть [*infl.* -вяжу́, -вя́жешь] *v., pfv. of* развя́зывать. —**развяза́ться,** *refl., pfv. of* развя́зываться.

развя́зка [*gen. pl.* -зок] *n.* **1,** outcome; upshot. **2,** climax; dénouement.

развя́зный *adj.* overly familiar; forward.

развя́зывать *v. impfv.* [*pfv.* развяза́ть] **1,** to untie. **2,** *fig., colloq.* to free; release. —**развяза́ть войну́,** to unleash a war. —**развяза́ть язы́к, 1,** (*with dat.*) to loosen someone's tongue. **2,** to start talking.

развя́зываться *v.r. impfv.* [*pfv.* развяза́ться] **1,** to come untied; come loose; come undone. **2,** *fig.* (*with* с + *instr.*) *colloq.* to get rid of; finish with.

разгада́ть *v., pfv. of* разга́дывать.

разга́дка [*gen. pl.* -док] *n.* **1,** solving; unraveling. **2,** solution.

разга́дывать *v. impfv.* [*pfv.* разгада́ть] **1,** to solve; unravel. **2,** to figure out; divine.

разга́р *n.* high point; height: в разга́р сезо́на, at the height of the season. —в (по́лном *or* са́мом) разга́ре, at its height; in full swing.

разгиба́ть *v. impfv.* [*pfv.* разогну́ть] to unbend; straighten. —рабо́тать, не разгиба́я спины́, to work without letup.

разгиба́ться *v.r. impfv.* [*pfv.* разогну́ться] to straighten up.

разгильдя́й *n., colloq.* slob.

разглаго́льствовать *v. impfv.* [*pres.* -ствую, -ству-ешь] *colloq.* to speak at length; hold forth.

разгла́живать *v. impfv.* [*pfv.* разгла́дить] **1,** to smooth out. **2,** to press; iron.

разглаша́ть *v. impfv.* [*pfv.* разгласи́ть] to divulge; make known.

разглаше́ние *n.* divulging; divulgence.

разгляде́ть *v. pfv.* [*infl.* -жу́, -ди́шь] to discern; make out.

разгля́дывать *v. impfv.* to examine closely; look over.

разгне́ванный *adj.* furious; enraged; incensed.

разгне́вать *v. pfv.* to infuriate; enrage. —**разгне́-ваться,** *refl.* to fly into a rage.

разгова́ривать *v. impfv.* to talk; speak; converse. Разгова́ривать по-ру́сски, to speak Russian. Они́ не разгова́ривают друг с дру́гом, they don't talk to each other; they are not on speaking terms.

разгове́ться *v.r. pfv.* to break the Lenten fast.

разгово́р *n.* **1,** conversation. **2,** talk: то́лько и разгово́ру, что об э́том, it's all people are talking about. **3,** subject: перемени́ть разгово́р, to change the subject. Э́то друго́й разгово́р, that's another matter; that's something else again. —**без разгово́ров!; и ника́ких разгово́ров!,** and no argument!; I want to hear nothing more about it!

разговори́ться *v.r. pfv., colloq.* **1,** to get into a conversation; get to talking. **2,** to warm to one's subject.

разгово́рник *n.* phrase book.

разгово́рный *adj.* **1,** conversational. **2,** colloquial. —**разгово́рная бу́дка,** telephone booth.

разгово́рчивый *adj.* talkative; loquacious. —**разго-во́рчивость,** *n.f.* loquaciousness.

разго́н *n.* **1,** dispersal. **2,** momentum. —в разго́не, (*of a number of people*) away on an errand or assignment. —с разго́на, full speed; full tilt.

разгоня́ть *v. impfv.* [*pfv.* разогна́ть] **1,** to disperse; break up. **2,** *fig.* to dispel (a feeling). **3,** to drive at high speed; race. —**разгоня́ться,** *refl.* to gather momentum.

разгора́живать *v. impfv.* [*pfv.* разгороди́ть] to partition off; fence off.

разгора́ться *v.r. impfv.* [*pfv.* разгоре́ться] **1,** to begin to burn properly. **2,** (*of one's cheeks*) to become flushed. **3,** *fig.* (*of passions, an argument, etc.*) to flare.

разгороди́ть [*infl.* -рожу́, -ро́дишь *or* -роди́шь] *v., pfv. of* разгора́живать.

разгорячи́ть *v., pfv. of* горячи́ть. —**разгорячи́ться,** *refl., pfv. of* горячи́ться.

разгра́бить *v. pfv.* [*infl.* -блю, -бишь] to rob; loot; ransack.

разграбле́ние *n.* plundering; looting.

разграниче́ние *n.* **1,** delimitation. **2,** differentiation.

разграни́чивать *v. impfv.* [*pfv.* разграни́чить] **1,** to delimit; demarcate. **2,** to distinguish; differentiate.

разграфи́ть *v., pfv. of* графи́ть.

разгреба́ть *v. impfv.* [*pfv.* разгрести́] to rake aside; shovel aside.

разгрести́ [*infl. like* грести́] *v., pfv. of* разгреба́ть.

разгро́м *n.* **1,** crushing defeat; rout. **2,** destruction; devastation. **3,** *colloq.* havoc; chaos.

разгроми́ть *v., pfv. of* громи́ть.

разгружа́ть *v. impfv.* [*pfv.* разгрузи́ть] **1,** to unload (a vehicle, vessel, etc.). **2,** *fig., colloq.* to relieve (of part of one's work). —**разгружа́ться,** *refl.* to unload; discharge cargo.

разгрузи́ть [*infl.* -гружу́, -гру́зишь *or* -грузи́шь] *v., pfv. of* **разгружа́ть.** —**разгрузи́ться,** *refl., pfv. of* **разгружа́ться.**

разгру́зка *n.* unloading.

разгрыза́ть *v. impfv.* [*pfv.* **разгры́зть**] to bite in two; crack between one's teeth.

разгры́зть [*infl. like* грызть] *v., pfv. of* **разгрыза́ть.**

разгу́л *n.* **1,** carousing. **2,** *fig.* (*with gen.*) wave: разгу́л наси́лия, wave of violence.

разгу́ливать *v. impfv.* [*pfv.* **разгуля́ть**] *colloq.* **1,** [*impfv. only*] to take a stroll. **2,** to dispel (a feeling). **3,** to amuse so as to keep awake. —**разгу́ливаться,** *refl., colloq.* **1,** to live it up; let oneself go. **2,** to become wide-awake. **3,** (*of the weather*) to clear up.

разгу́лье *n., colloq.* revelry.

разгу́льный *adj., colloq.* wild; fast; loose.

разгуля́ть *v., pfv. of* **разгу́ливать.** —**разгуля́ться,** *refl., pfv. of* **разгу́ливаться.**

раздава́ть *v. impfv.* [*pfv.* **разда́ть;** *pres.* -да́ю, -да-ёшь] to distribute; give out; hand out. —**раздава́ться,** *refl.* **1,** to be heard; resound; ring out. **2,** to move aside; make way. **3,** *colloq.* to become fatter; fill out.

раздави́ть *v. pfv.* [*infl.* -давлю́, -да́вишь] **1,** *pfv. of* **дави́ть** (*in senses* #4 & #5). **2,** to overwhelm; crush.

раздари́вать *v. impfv.* [*pfv.* **раздари́ть**] to give away (*as gifts*).

раздари́ть [*infl.* -дарю́, -да́ришь] *v., pfv. of* **разда́-ривать.**

разда́точный *adj.* distributing; distribution (*attrib.*).

разда́ть [*infl. like* дать; *past* ро́здал *or* разда́л, раздала́, ро́здало *or* разда́ло] *v., pfv. of* **раздава́ть.** —**разда́ться,** *refl.* [*past* разда́лся, -дала́сь, -дало́сь *or* -да́лось] *pfv. of* **раздава́ться.**

разда́ча *n.* distribution.

раздва́ивать *v. impfv.* [*pfv.* **раздвои́ть**] to divide in half. —**раздва́иваться,** *refl.* to divide; be divided.

раздвига́ть *v. impfv.* [*pfv.* **раздви́нуть**] **1,** to draw apart; spread apart; pull apart. **2,** to draw aside; move aside. **3,** to push one's way through (a crowd). **4,** to extend (a table). —**раздвига́ться,** *refl.* **1,** (*of a curtain*) to part; (*of a crowd*) to step aside; make way. **2,** [*impfv. only*] (*of a table*) to expand; open up.

раздвижно́й *adj.* **1,** expandable; extensible: раздвижно́й стол, expandable table. **2,** sliding: раздвижна́я дверь, sliding door; раздвижно́й за́навес, draw curtain.

раздви́нуть *v., pfv. of* **раздвига́ть.** —**раздви́нуть-ся,** *refl., pfv. of* **раздвига́ться.**

раздвое́ние *n.* split; division. —**раздвое́ние ли́ч-ности,** split personality.

раздво́енный *adj.* divided; double. —**раздво́енное копы́то,** cloven hoof.

раздвои́ть *v., pfv. of* **раздва́ивать.** —**раздвои́ться,** *refl., pfv. of* **раздва́иваться.**

раздева́лка [*gen. pl.* -лок] *n., colloq.* cloakroom; checkroom.

раздева́льня [*gen. pl.* -лен] *n.* **1,** cloakroom; check-room. **2,** dressing room; locker room.

раздева́ние *n.* undressing.

раздева́ть *v. impfv.* [*pfv.* **разде́ть**] to undress. —**раз-дева́ться,** *refl.* **1,** to get undressed. **2,** to take off one's coat.

разде́л *n.* **1,** division; dividing up. **2,** section; part (*of a book, article, etc.*).

разде́лать *v., pfv. of* **разде́лывать.** —**разде́латься,** *refl., pfv. of* **разде́лываться.**

разделе́ние *n.* division.

раздели́тельный *adj.* **1,** dividing. **2,** *gram.* partitive; disjunctive.

раздели́ть [*infl.* -делю́, -де́лишь] *v., pfv. of* **дели́ть** *and* **разделя́ть.** —**раздели́ться,** *refl., pfv. of* **де-ли́ться** *and* **разделя́ться.**

разде́лывать *v. impfv.* [*pfv.* **разде́лать**] **1,** to dress; prepare (*for cooking*). **2,** (*with* под + *acc.*) to finish (in imitation wood grain, marble, etc.). —**разде́лы-ваться,** *refl.* (*with* с + *instr.*) *colloq.* **1,** to settle (debts); settle up with (someone). **2,** to get even with; settle scores with.

разде́льный *adj.* **1,** separate. **2,** (*of speech*) clear; distinct.

разделя́ть *v. impfv.* [*pfv.* **раздели́ть**] **1,** to divide. **2,** to share. **3,** to separate. —**разделя́ться,** *refl.* **1,** to divide; be divided. **2,** to break up; split up. **3,** [*impfv. only*] (*with* на + *acc.*) to fall into (different categories).

разде́ть [*infl.* -де́ну, -де́нешь] *v., pfv. of* **раздева́ть.** —**разде́ться,** *refl., pfv. of* **раздева́ться.**

раздира́ть *v. impfv.* [*pfv.* **раздодра́ть**] **1,** to tear to pieces. **2,** [*impfv. only*] *fig.* to tear apart. —**разди-ра́ться,** *refl., colloq.* to tear; rip.

раздира́ющий *adj.* heart-rending; heartbreaking.

раздобре́ть *v., pfv. of* **добре́ть** (*in sense* #2).

раздобыва́ть *v. impfv.* [*pfv.* **раздобы́ть**] *colloq.* to obtain; wangle; get hold of.

раздобы́ть [*infl. like* быть; *past fem.* -была́] *v., pfv. of* **раздобыва́ть.**

раздо́лье *n.* **1,** open space; expanse. **2,** *fig.* freedom.

раздо́льный *adj., colloq.* **1,** vast; spacious; far-flung. **2,** *fig.* free; carefree.

раздо́р *n., often pl.* discord; dissension.

раздоса́довать *v. pfv.* [*infl.* -дую, -дуешь] *colloq.* to vex.

раздража́ть *v. impfv.* [*pfv.* **раздражи́ть**] **1,** to irri-tate; annoy. **2,** to irritate (the skin, eyes, etc.). —**раз-дража́ться,** *refl.* to become irritated.

раздраже́ние *n.* irritation.

раздражи́тель *n.m.* irritant.

раздражи́тельный *adj.* irritable. —**раздражи́тель-ность,** *n.f.* irritability.

раздражи́ть *v., pfv. of* **раздража́ть.** —**раздра-жи́ться,** *refl., pfv. of* **раздража́ться.**

раздразни́ть *v. pfv.* [*infl.* -дразню́, -дра́знишь] **1,** to tease; provoke. **2,** to whet (a desire, one's appe-tite, etc.).

раздроби́ть [*infl.* -блю́, -би́шь] *v., pfv. of* **дроби́ть** *and* **раздробля́ть.** —**раздроби́ться,** *refl., pfv. of* **дроби́ться** *and* **раздробля́ться.**

раздро́бленность *n.f.* disunity; division; fragmenta-tion.

раздробля́ть *v. impfv.* [*pfv.* **раздроби́ть**] **1,** to smash; splinter. **2,** *fig.* to fragment; splinter. **3,** to re-duce; convert (into smaller units). —**раздробля́ться,** *refl.* to splinter.

раздува́ть *v. impfv.* [*pfv.* **разду́ть**] **1,** to fan (a fire). **2,** to inflate. **3,** to stir up; whip up; foment. **4,** *colloq.* to exaggerate; blow up. **5,** *impers., colloq.* to be puffed up: у него́ разду́ло щёку, his cheek is puffed up. —**раздува́ться,** *refl.* **1,** to swell up; become swollen. **2,** to bulge.

раздумать v. pfv. to change one's mind. —**раздумываться**, refl. (with о) colloq. to begin to reflect (on).

раздумывать v. impfv. to ponder; think; deliberate. —**не раздумывая**, without a moment's hesitation.

раздумье n. 1, thought; meditation. 2, usu. pl. thoughts. 3, second thoughts; doubts.

раздутый adj., colloq. 1, swollen; puffed up. 2, inflated; excessive. 3, exaggerated; overblown.

раздуть [infl. -дую, -дуешь] v., pfv. of раздувать. —**раздуться**, refl., pfv. of раздуваться.

разевать v. impfv. [pfv. разинуть] colloq. to open (one's mouth) wide. —**разинув рот**, open-mouthed.

разжалобить v. pfv. [infl. -блю, -бишь] to move to pity; stir.

разжалование n., obs. demotion.

разжаловать v. pfv. [infl. -лую, -луешь] obs. to demote.

разжать [infl. разожму, разожмёшь] v., pfv. of разжимать. —**разжаться**, refl., pfv. of разжиматься.

разжевать [infl. -жую, -жуёшь] v., pfv. of разжёвывать.

разжёвывать v. impfv. [pfv. разжевать] to chew; masticate.

разжечь [infl. разожгу, разожжёшь, ...разожгут; past разжёг, разожгла] v., pfv. of разжигать. —**разжечься**, refl., pfv. of разжигаться.

разжигание n. 1, kindling. 2, fig. igniting (of conflicts); unleashing (of war).

разжигать v. impfv. [pfv. разжечь] 1, to kindle; light. 2, fig. to kindle; inflame. 3, fig. to unleash (a war). —**разжигаться**, refl. to catch (fire); start burning.

разжижать v. impfv. [pfv. разжидить] colloq. to dilute.

разжижение n. dilution.

разжимать v. impfv. [pfv. разжать] to unclench; relax; release. —**разжиматься**, refl. to open; part; relax.

разжиреть v., pfv. of жиреть.

разжиться v.r. pfv. [infl. like жить; past -жился, -жилась, -жилось] colloq. to get rich.

разинуть v., pfv. of разевать.

разиня n.m. & f., colloq. scatterbrain.

разительный adj. striking.

разить v. impfv. [pres. ражу, разишь] 1, to strike. 2, to defeat; crush. 3, impers. (with instr.) colloq. to reek (of): от него разит водкой, he reeks of vodka.

разлагать v. impfv. [pfv. разложить] 1, to separate (or break down) into (its) constituent parts. 2, math. to expand. 3, fig. to corrupt. —**разлагаться**, refl. 1, to decompose; decay. 2, to degenerate. 3, to disintegrate; collapse; go to pieces.

разлад n. 1, lack of coordination; disorder. 2, discord; dissension.

разлаживать v. impfv. [pfv. разладить] colloq. 1, to put out of commission. 2, to disrupt. —**разлаживаться**, refl., colloq. 1, to go out of commission. 2, fig. to go bad.

разламывать v. impfv. 1, [pfv. разломать] to tear down. 2, [pfv. разломать or разломить] to break (into parts or pieces). —**разламываться**, refl. to break apart.

разлениться v.r. pfv. [infl. -ленюсь, -ленишься] colloq. to become utterly lazy.

разлетаться v.r. impfv. [pfv. разлететься] 1, to fly in all directions; scatter into the air. 2, fig. (of news) to spread. 3, to shatter. 4, fig. (of hopes, dreams, etc.)

to vanish; be shattered; be dashed. 5, (with в + acc. or к) colloq. to rush; dash (into or up to).

разлечься v.r. pfv. [infl. like лечь] colloq. to stretch out.

разлив n. 1, bottling. 2, overflowing. 3, high water; spring flood. —**в разлив**, for consumption on the premises.

разливание n. pouring.

разливательный adj., in разливательная ложка, ladle.

разливать v. impfv. [pfv. разлить] 1, to spill. 2, to pour (into many containers). 3, fig. to spread; diffuse. 4, in (их) водой не разольёшь, the two of them are inseparable. —**разливаться**, refl. 1, to spill. 2, (of a river) to overflow its banks. 3, to spread. 4, [impfv. only] colloq. to sing (melodiously); say (with feeling); sob (bitterly).

разливной adj. (of beer) on draft; on tap.

разлиновать v. pfv. [infl. -ную, -нуешь] to rule; line.

разлить [infl. разолью, разольёшь; past fem. разлила] v., pfv. of разливать. —**разлиться**, refl., pfv. of разливаться.

различать v. impfv. [pfv. различить] 1, to distinguish; tell apart. 2, to discern; make out. —**различаться**, refl. [impfv. only] to differ.

различие n. 1, difference: различие во взглядах, difference of opinion. 2, distinction: делать/проводить различие, to make/draw a distinction. —**знаки различия**, insignia.

различимый adj. 1, distinguishable. 2, discernible.

различительный adj. distinctive; distinguishing.

различить v., pfv. of различать.

различный adj. 1, different; differing. 2, various; diverse.

разложение n. 1, decomposition. 2, fig. decay; degeneration; disintegration.

разложить [infl. -ложу, -ложишь] v., pfv. of раскладывать and разлагать.

разлом n. 1, breaking up. 2, break.

разломать v., pfv. of разламывать. —**разломаться**, refl., pfv. of разламываться.

разломить [infl. -ломлю, -ломишь] v., pfv. of разламывать (in sense #2). —**разломиться**, refl., pfv. of разламываться.

разлука n. 1, separation. Жить в разлуке, to be separated. 2, parting.

разлучать v. impfv. [pfv. разлучить] to separate; part. —**разлучаться**, refl. to part company; separate.

разлюбить v. pfv. [infl. -люблю, -любишь] to cease to love; no longer love.

размагничивать v. impfv. [pfv. размагнитить] to demagnetize.

размазать [infl. -мажу, -мажешь] v., pfv. of размазывать. —**размазаться**, refl., pfv. of размазываться.

размазня n., colloq. 1, gruel. 2, wishy-washy person.

размазывать v. impfv. [pfv. размазать] 1, to spread; smear. 2, colloq. to pad (a story, report, etc.). —**размазываться**, refl. to smear.

размалывать v. impfv. [pfv. размолоть] to grind.

разматывать v. impfv. [pfv. размотать] to unwind; unreel. —**разматываться**, refl. to unwind; become unwound.

размах n. 1, swing; sweep (of one's arm). 2, span:

размах крыльев, wingspan. **3,** *fig.* range; scope. —**со всего размаху,** with all one's might.

разма́хивать *v. impfv.* [*pfv.* **размахну́ть**] (*with instr.*) **1,** [*impfv. only*] to wave; swing; brandish. **2,** to draw back (*in order to strike with*). —**разма́хиваться,** *refl.* to draw back one's arm (*in order to strike someone or something*); haul off.

размахну́ть *v., pfv. of* **разма́хивать.** —**размахну́ться,** *refl., pfv. of* **разма́хиваться.**

разма́чивать *v. impfv.* [*pfv.* **размочи́ть**] to soak; steep.

разма́шистый *adj., colloq.* **1,** (*of a motion*) sweeping. **2,** (*of handwriting*) sprawling. **3,** (*of an expanse of land*) broad.

размежева́ть [*infl.* -жу́ю, -жу́ешь] *v., pfv. of* **размежёвывать.**

размежёвывать *v. impfv.* [*pfv.* **размежева́ть**] to delimit.

размельча́ть *v. impfv.* [*pfv.* **размельчи́ть**] to crush; grind; reduce to small particles.

разме́н *n.* exchange. —**разме́н де́нег,** changing of money.

разме́нивать *v. impfv.* [*pfv.* **разменя́ть**] to change (money). —**разме́ниваться,** *refl., colloq.* **1,** (*with instr.*) to exchange. **2,** to waste one's energies.

разме́нный *adj.* change (*attrib.*): **разме́нная ка́сса,** change booth. —**разме́нная моне́та,** small change.

разменя́ть *v., pfv. of* **разме́нивать.** —**разменя́ться,** *refl., pfv. of* **разме́ниваться.**

разме́р *n.* **1,** size: **разме́р ко́мнаты,** the size of a room. Я ношу́ боти́нки деся́того разме́ра, I wear a size ten shoe. **2,** amount. В двойно́м разме́ре, twice as much. Ссу́да в разме́ре ты́сячи до́лларов, a $1000 loan. **3,** *often pl.* scale; extent; proportions. **4,** *pros.* meter. **5,** *music* measure.

разме́ренный *adj.* measured.

размеря́ть *v. impfv.* [*pfv.* **разме́рить**] to measure.

размеси́ть [*infl.* -мешу́, -ме́сишь] *v., pfv. of* **разме́шивать** (*in sense #1*).

размести́ [*infl. like* **мести́**] *v., pfv. of* **размета́ть**[1].

размести́ть [*infl.* -щу́, -сти́шь] *v., pfv. of* **размеща́ть.** —**размести́ться,** *refl., pfv. of* **размеща́ться.**

размета́ть[1] *v. impfv.* [*pfv.* **размести́**] **1,** to sweep; sweep clean. **2,** to sweep away; sweep up.

размета́ть[2] [*infl.* -мечу́, -ме́чешь] *v., pfv. of* **размё-тывать.** —**размета́ться,** *refl.* **1,** to lie with one's arms and legs outstretched. **2,** (*of one's hair*) to hang loosely.

разме́тить [*infl.* -чу, -тишь] *v., pfv. of* **размеча́ть.**

разме́тка [*gen. pl.* -ток] *n.* **1,** marking. **2,** mark.

размётывать *v. impfv.* [*pfv.* **размета́ть**] **1,** to scatter; disperse. **2,** to destroy; demolish. **3,** to stretch out; spread apart.

размеча́ть *v. impfv.* [*pfv.* **разме́тить**] to mark; mark up; mark out.

разме́шивать *v. impfv.* **1,** [*pfv.* **размеси́ть**] to knead. **2,** [*pfv.* **размеша́ть**] to stir.

размеща́ть *v. impfv.* [*pfv.* **размести́ть**] **1,** to place; arrange; station (*many people or items*). **2,** to find lodging for; quarter (*troops*). **3,** to distribute; assign. **4,** to place (*orders*); float (*a loan*). —**размеща́ться,** *refl.* **1,** (*of many people*) to take their places; take seats. **2,** to be quartered.

размеще́ние *n.* **1,** placement; arrangement; station-ing. **2,** distribution. **3,** quartering; billeting (*of troops*). **4,** placing (*of orders*); floating (*of a loan*).

размина́ть *v. impfv.* [*pfv.* **размя́ть**] **1,** to mash; knead. **2,** *colloq.* to stretch (one's legs). —**размина́ться,** *refl., colloq.* **1,** to stretch one's legs. **2,** to limber up.

размини́ровать *v. impfv. & pfv.* [*pres.* -рую, -руешь] to clear of mines.

разми́нка *n., colloq.* limbering up; warm-up.

размину́ться *v.r. pfv., colloq.* **1,** to miss one another; fail to meet. **2,** (*of letters*) to cross in the mail. **3,** to pass by each other (*in a narrow place*).

размножа́ть *v. impfv.* [*pfv.* **размно́жить**] **1,** to make copies of. **2,** to raise; breed. —**размножа́ться,** *refl.* to multiply; reproduce; breed; propagate.

размноже́ние *n.* **1,** copying; reproducion. **2,** reproduction; propagation.

размно́жить *v., pfv. of* **размножа́ть.** —**размно́житься,** *refl., pfv. of* **размножа́ться.**

размозжи́ть *v. pfv.* to smash; shatter.

размока́ть *v. impfv.* [*pfv.* **размо́кнуть**] to become soggy.

размо́кнуть [*past* -мо́к, -ла] *v., pfv. of* **размока́ть.**

размо́л *n.* **1,** grinding; milling. **2,** *in* кру́пного размо́ла, coarse; ме́лкого размо́ла, finely ground.

размо́лвка [*gen. pl.* -вок] *n.* spat; tiff.

размоло́ть [*infl.* -мелю́, -ме́лешь] *v., pfv. of* **размалывать.**

размора́живать *v. impfv.* [*pfv.* **разморо́зить**] to defrost; unfreeze. —**размора́живаться,** *refl.* to defrost; melt.

размота́ть *v., pfv. of* **разма́тывать.** —**размота́ться,** *refl., pfv. of* **разма́тываться.**

размочи́ть [*infl.* -мочу́, -мо́чишь] *v., pfv. of* **разма́чивать.**

размы́в *n.* washing away; erosion.

размыва́ть *v. impfv.* [*pfv.* **размы́ть**] **1,** to wash away; wash out: вода́ размы́ла доро́гу, the water/flood-waters washed out the road. **2,** to erode.

размыка́ть *v. impfv.* [*pfv.* **разомкну́ть**] **1,** to open. **2,** to break (a circuit).

размы́ть [*infl.* -мо́ю, -мо́ешь] *v., pfv. of* **размыва́ть.**

размышле́ние *n.* reflection; meditation; thought. —**по зре́лом размышле́нии,** on second thought.

размышля́ть *v. impfv.* to reflect; meditate; ponder.

размягча́ть *v. impfv.* [*pfv.* **размягчи́ть**] to soften.

размягче́ние *n.* softening.

размягчи́ть *v., pfv. of* **размягча́ть.**

размякнуть [*past* -мя́к, -ла] *v., pfv. of* **мя́кнуть.**

размя́ть [*infl.* размну́, размнёшь] *v., pfv. of* **мять** (*in sense #1*) *and* **размина́ть.** —**размя́ться,** *refl., pfv. of* **размина́ться.**

разнаря́дка [*gen. pl.* -док] *n.* order; voucher.

разна́шивать *v. impfv.* [*pfv.* **разноси́ть**] to break in (shoes).

разнести́ [*infl. like* **нести́**] *v., pfv. of* **разноси́ть**[1] —**разнести́сь,** *refl., pfv. of* **разноси́ться.**

разнима́ть *v. impfv.* [*pfv.* **разня́ть**] *colloq.* to separate; pull apart.

ра́зниться *v.r. impfv.* to differ.

ра́зница *n.* difference. —**больша́я ра́зница,** it makes a big difference. —**кака́я ра́зница?,** what difference does it make?

разнобо́й *n.* lack of coordination; inconsistency.

разнови́дность *n.f.* a variety.

разновре́менный *adj.* occurring at different times.

разногла́сие *n.* **1,** disagreement. **2,** discrepancy.

разноголо́сица *n., colloq.* **1,** dissonance. **2,** disagreement. **3,** discrepancy.

разноголо́сый *adj.* discordant.

ра́зное *n., decl. as an adj.* **1,** various things. **2,** (*as a heading*) miscellaneous.

разнообра́зие *n.* variety; diversity.

разнообра́зить *v. impfv.* [*pres.* -жу, -зишь] to vary; diversify.

разнообра́зный *adj.* diverse; varied.

разноречи́вый *adj.* conflicting; contradictory.

разноро́дный *adj.* heterogeneous. —**разноро́дность,** *n.f.* heterogeneity.

разно́с *n.* **1,** carrying; delivery. **2,** *colloq.* sharp rebuke; dressing-down.

разноси́ть[1] *v. impfv.* [*pfv.* разнести́; *pres.* -ношу́, -но́сишь] **1,** to carry; deliver (*each to its place*). **2,** to distribute; hand around. **3,** to enter; record. **4,** *colloq.* to scatter; disperse. **5,** *colloq.* to spread. **6,** *colloq.* to shatter; destroy. **7,** *colloq.* to berate; upbraid. **8,** *colloq.* to criticize; excoriate; pan. **9,** *impers., colloq.* to swell: у меня́ щёку разнесло́, my cheek is swollen. —**разноси́ться,** *refl.* **1,** to spread rapidly. **2,** to sound; resound.

разноси́ть[2] [*infl.* -ношу́, -но́сишь] *v., pfv. of* разна́шивать.

разно́ска *n., colloq.* distribution; handing out.

разно́сный *adj., colloq.* scathing; blistering.

разносторо́нний *adj.* **1,** *math.* scalene. **2,** multifaceted; versatile. **3,** (*of education*) all-round. —**разносторо́нность,** *n.f.* versatility.

ра́зность *n.f.* **1,** *obs.* difference. **2,** *math.* difference. —**ра́зные ра́зности,** various things; this and that.

разно́счик *n.* **1,** delivery man. **2,** peddler.

разноцве́тный *adj.* of different colors.

разношёрстный *adj.* **1,** (*of animals*) of different colors. **2,** *fig., colloq.* motley.

разну́зданный *adj.* **1,** (*of a horse*) unbridled. **2,** *fig.* rowdy; unruly.

разну́здывать *v. impfv.* [*pfv.* разнузда́ть] to unbridle.

ра́зный *adj.* **1,** different; differing: ра́зные вку́сы, different/differing tastes. **2,** different; not the same: говори́ть на ра́зных языка́х, to speak different languages; not speak the same language. **3,** various: ра́зные тео́рии, various theories. **4,** *colloq.* all sorts of: ра́зная ру́хлядь, all sorts of junk. *See also* ра́зное.

разню́хивать *v. impfv.* [*pfv.* разню́хать] *colloq.* **1,** to smell out. **2,** *fig.* to smell about; nose about.

разня́ть [*infl.* -ниму́, -ни́мешь; *past* разня́л *or* ро́знял, разняла́, разня́ло *or* ро́зняло] *v., pfv. of* разнима́ть.

разоблача́ть *v. impfv.* [*pfv.* разоблачи́ть] to expose; unmask.

разоблаче́ние *n.* exposure.

разоблачи́ть *v., pfv. of* разоблача́ть.

разобра́ть [*infl.* разберу́, разберёшь; *past fem.* разобрала́] *v., pfv. of* разбира́ть. —**разобра́ться,** *refl., pfv. of* разбира́ться.

разобща́ть *v. impfv.* [*pfv.* разобщи́ть] **1,** to cut off. **2,** to alienate; estrange.

ра́зовый *adj.* one-time; for one-time use only.

разогна́ть [*infl.* разгоню́, разго́нишь; *past fem.* разогнала́] *v., pfv. of* разгоня́ть. —**разогна́ться,** *refl., pfv. of* разгоня́ться.

разогну́ть *v., pfv. of* разгиба́ть. —**разогну́ться,** *refl., pfv. of* разгиба́ться.

разогрева́ть *v. impfv.* [*pfv.* разогре́ть] **1,** to heat up; warm up. **2,** to reheat; warm over: разогре́тый обе́д, warmed-over dinner. —**разогрева́ться,** *refl.* to get hot; get warm.

разоде́ть *v. pfv.* [*infl.* -оде́ну, -оде́нешь] *colloq.* to dress up. —**разоде́ться,** *refl., colloq.* to dress up; get dressed up.

разодра́ть [*infl.* раздеру́, раздерёшь; *past fem.* разодрала́] *v., pfv. of* раздира́ть. —**разодра́ться,** *refl.* **1,** *pfv. of* раздира́ться. **2,** *colloq.* to have a fight.

разозли́ть *v., pfv. of* злить. —**разозли́ться,** *refl., pfv. of* зли́ться.

разойти́сь [*infl.* разойду́сь, разойдёшься; *past* разошёлся, разошла́сь] *v.r., pfv. of* расходи́ться.

ра́зом *adv., colloq.* **1,** at once; at the same time. **2,** at once; instantly. **3,** at once; in one gulp; with one stroke.

разомкну́ть *v., pfv. of* размыка́ть.

разорва́ть [*infl. like* рвать] *v., pfv. of* разрыва́ть. —**разорва́ться,** *refl., pfv. of* разрыва́ться.

разоре́ние *n.* **1,** destruction; devastation. **2,** bankruptcy; ruin.

разори́тельный *adj.* devastating; ruinous.

разори́ть *v., pfv. of* разоря́ть. —**разори́ться,** *refl., pfv. of* разоря́ться.

разоружа́ть *v. impfv.* [*pfv.* разоружи́ть] *v.t.* to disarm. —**разоружа́ться,** *refl.* to disarm.

разоруже́ние *n.* disarmament.

разоружи́ть *v., pfv. of* разоружа́ть. —**разоружи́ться,** *refl., pfv. of* разоружа́ться.

разоря́ть *v. impfv.* [*pfv.* разори́ть] **1,** to ravage; devastate. **2,** to ruin. —**разоря́ться,** *refl.* **1,** to be ruined. **2,** to lose everything; go broke.

разосла́ть [*infl.* -шлю́, -шлёшь] *v., pfv. of* рассыла́ть.

разоспа́ться *v.r. pfv.* [*infl. like* спать] *colloq.* to fall fast asleep.

разостла́ть [*infl.* расстелю́, рассте́лешь] *v., pfv. of* расстила́ть.

разочарова́ние *n.* disappointment; disillusionment; disenchantment.

разочаро́ванный *adj.* disappointed; disillusioned; disenchanted.

разочарова́ть [*infl.* -ру́ю, -ру́ешь] *v., pfv. of* разоча́ровывать. —**разочарова́ться,** *refl., pfv. of* разоча́ровываться.

разочаро́вывать *v. impfv.* [*pfv.* разочарова́ть] to disappoint; disillusion. —**разочаро́вываться,** *refl.* (*with* в + *prepl.*) to be disappointed (with); become disillusioned (with).

разраба́тывать *v. impfv.* [*pfv.* разрабо́тать] **1,** to work out; develop (a plan, theory, device, etc.). **2,** to cultivate (land). **3,** to work (a mine); mine (a certain mineral).

разрабо́тка *n.* **1,** development. **2,** cultivation (*of land*). **3,** mining; extraction.

разра́внивать *v. impfv.* [*pfv.* разровня́ть] to level.

разража́ться *v.r. impfv.* [*pfv.* разрази́ться] **1,** to break out. **2,** (*with instr.*) to burst into (tears, laughter, etc.).

разраста́ться *v.r. impfv.* [*pfv.* разрасти́сь] to grow; expand; increase in size.

разрасти́сь [*infl. like* расти́] *v.r.*, *pfv. of* разраста́ться.

разрежа́ть *v. impfv.* [*pfv.* разреди́ть] **1,** to thin out. **2,** to rarefy (the air).

разре́з *n.* **1,** cut; split. **2,** *med.* incision. **3,** section: попере́чный разре́з, cross section. **4,** *fig.* sense: aspect: в друго́м разре́зе, in a different sense/way/ light. —в разре́зе (+ *gen.*), in the light of.

разре́зать [*infl.* -ре́жу, -ре́жешь] *v.*, *pfv. of* разреза́ть.

разреза́ть *v. impfv.* [*pfv.* разре́зать] **1,** to cut; slit. **2,** to lance. **3,** to bisect; divide in half.

разреша́ть *v. impfv.* [*pfv.* разреши́ть] **1,** (with *dat.*) to permit; allow. **2,** to solve (a problem). **3,** to settle; resolve (a dispute, conflict, etc.). —разреша́ться, *refl.* **1,** [*impfv. only*] (with *dat.*) to be permitted; be allowed: ему́ не разреша́ется (+ *inf.*), he is not permitted/ allowed to... **2,** to be solved; be settled. **3,** *in* разреши́ться от бре́мени (+ *instr.*), to give birth to; be delivered of.

разреше́ние *n.* **1,** permission: с ва́шего разреше́ния, with your permission. **2,** solution; resolution; settlement. **3,** *colloq.* permit.

разреши́мый *adj.* solvable.

разреши́ть *v.*, *pfv. of* разреша́ть. —разреши́ться, *refl.*, *pfv. of* разреша́ться.

разрисова́ть *v. pfv.* [*infl.* -су́ю, -су́ешь] to draw all over: сте́ны бы́ли разрисо́ваны цвета́ми, the walls had flowers drawn all over them.

разровня́ть *v.*, *pfv. of* разра́внивать.

разро́зненный *adj.* **1,** (of a set) incomplete; (of one of such a set) odd. **2,** uncoordinated.

разро́знивать *v. impfv.* [*pfv.* разро́знить] to break; break up (a set of something).

разруба́ть *v. impfv.* [*pfv.* разруби́ть] **1,** to chop up. **2,** to cut up.

разруби́ть [*infl.* -рублю́, -ру́бишь] *v.*, *pfv. of* разруба́ть.

разруга́ть *v. pfv.*, *colloq.* **1,** to berate; chastise. **2,** to tear apart; pan (a book, play, etc.). —разруга́ться, *refl.*, *colloq.* to quarrel.

разру́ха *n.* (economic) ruin.

разруша́ть *v. impfv.* [*pfv.* разру́шить] **1,** to destroy; demolish. **2,** *fig.* to wreck (one's plans, hopes, etc.); ruin (one's health). —разруша́ться, *refl.* **1,** to be destroyed; collapse. **2,** *fig.* to be ruined.

разруше́ние *n.* **1,** destruction (*act of destroying*). **2,** *pl.* destruction (*heavy damage*).

разруши́тель *n.m.* destroyer; wrecker.

разруши́тельный *adj.* destructive.

разру́шить *v.*, *pfv. of* разруша́ть. —разру́шиться, *refl.*, *pfv. of* разруша́ться.

разры́в *n.* **1,** break; rupture. **2,** breaking (of relations); breakup. **3,** burst (of a shell). **4,** gap.

разрыва́ть *v. impfv.* [*pfv.* разорва́ть] **1,** to tear; tear open; tear up. **2,** to blow up. **3,** *impers.* to burst: котёл разорва́ло, the boiler burst. **4,** *fig.* to break off; sever (relations, ties, etc.). **5,** *v.i.* (with с + *instr.*) *colloq.* to break (with someone). **6,** [*pfv.* разры́ть] to dig; dig up. —разрыва́ться, *refl.* [*pfv.* разорва́ться] **1,** to tear; be torn. **2,** to break; snap. **3,** to burst; explode; go off. **4,** (of relations) to be broken off.

разрывно́й *adj.* explosive.

разрыда́ться *v.r. pfv.* to burst into tears; begin to sob.

разры́ть [*infl.* -ро́ю, -ро́ешь] *v.*, *pfv. of* разрыва́ть (*in sense* #6).

разрыхля́ть *v. impfv.* [*pfv.* разрыхли́ть] to loosen (soil, dirt, etc.).

разря́д *n.* **1,** category. **2,** class; rank: спортсме́н пе́рвого разря́да, top-class athlete; сле́сарь тре́тьего разря́да, metalworker of the third rank. **3,** discharge (*of electricity, a weapon, etc.*).

разряди́ть [*infl.* -ряжу́, -ря́дишь *or* -ряди́шь] *v.*, *pfv. of* разряжа́ть. —разряди́ться, *refl.*, *pfv. of* разряжа́ться.

разря́дка *n.* **1,** unloading (*of a weapon*); using up (*of a battery*). **2,** *fig.* relaxation; lessening (*of tension*); détente.

разряжа́ть *v. impfv.* [*pfv.* разряди́ть] **1,** to unload (a weapon). **2,** to use up; run down (a battery). **3,** *fig.* to relax (tension); defuse (a situation). Разряди́ть атмосфе́ру, to clear the air. **4,** *colloq.* to dress up; deck out. —разряжа́ться, *refl.* **1,** (of a battery) to run down. **2,** *fig.* to become less tense. **3,** *colloq.* to get dressed up.

разубежда́ть *v. impfv.* [*pfv.* разубеди́ть] (*with* в + *prepl.*) to change someone's mind (about); convince to the contrary. —разубежда́ться, *refl.* (*with* в + *prepl.*) to change one's mind (about).

разува́ть *v. impfv.* [*pfv.* разу́ть] to take off (someone's) shoes. —разува́ться, *refl.* to take off one's shoes.

разуверя́ть *v. impfv.* [*pfv.* разуве́рить] (*with* в + *prepl.*) to disillusion (about); disabuse (of); change someone's mind (about). —разуверя́ться, *refl.* (*with* в + *prepl.*) to lose faith (in); lose hope (of).

разузнава́ть *v. impfv.* [*pfv.* разузна́ть; *pres.* -зна́ю, -знаёшь] *colloq.* **1,** [*impfv. only*] to make inquiries; try to find out. **2,** to find out.

разукра́шивать *v. impfv.* [*pfv.* разукра́сить] *colloq.* to adorn; embellish.

разукрупня́ть *v. impfv.* [*pfv.* разукрупни́ть] to break up into smaller units.

ра́зум *n.* reason; intellect. —у меня́ ум за ра́зум захо́дит, I am at my wits' end.

разуме́ние *n.*, *obs.* understanding.

разуме́ть *v. impfv.* **1,** to mean. **2,** *obs.* to understand.

разуме́ться *v.r. impfv.* to be understood; be taken to mean. —разуме́ется, naturally; of course. —само́ собо́й разуме́ется, it goes without saying.

разу́мно *adv.* sensibly; rationally. —*adj.*, used predicatively reasonable: э́то вполне́ разу́мно, that is entirely reasonable.

разу́мный *adj.* **1,** intelligent; rational. **2,** clever. **3,** reasonable; sensible; logical.

разу́ть [*infl.* -зу́ю, -зу́ешь] *v.*, *pfv. of* разува́ть. —разу́ться, *refl.*, *pfv. of* разува́ться.

разу́чивать *v. impfv.* [*pfv.* разучи́ть] to learn. —разу́чиваться, *refl.* to forget; forget how (to); lose one's ability (to).

разучи́ть [*infl.* -учу́, -у́чишь] *v.*, *pfv. of* разу́чивать. —разучи́ться, *refl.*, *pfv. of* разу́чиваться.

разъеда́ть *v. impfv.* [*pfv.* разъе́сть] to eat away; corrode.

разъедине́ние *n.* **1,** separation. **2,** disconnecting. **3,** disengagement.

разъединя́ть *v. impfv.* [*pfv.* разъедини́ть] **1,** to separate. **2,** to disconnect. —разъединя́ться, *refl.* **1,** to come apart. **2,** to disengage.

разъе́зд *n.* **1,** departure (*of people in different directions*). **2,** *pl.* travels: в разъе́здах, traveling; on the move. **3,** *mil.* mounted patrol. **4,** *R.R.* short stretch of double track.

разъездно́й *adj.* **1,** traveling. **2,** for traveling.

разъезжа́ть *v. impfv.* to travel. —**разъезжа́ться,** *refl.* [*pfv.* разъе́хаться] **1,** to depart (*in various directions*). **2,** to pass by each other; miss each other; fail to meet. **3,** to be able to pass by each other (*on a narrow street, road, etc.*). **4,** (*of a married couple*) to separate; break up. **5,** *colloq.* to fall apart; come apart.

разъе́сть [*infl. like* есть] *v., pfv. of* разъеда́ть.

разъе́хаться [*infl.* разъе́дусь, разъе́дешься] *v.r., pfv. of* разъезжа́ться.

разъяря́ть *v. impfv.* [*pfv.* разъяри́ть] to enrage; infuriate.

разъясне́ние *n.* explanation; clarification.

разъясни́тельный *adj.* explanatory.

разъясня́ть *v. impfv.* [*pfv.* разъясни́ть] to explain; elucidate; clarify. —**разъясня́ться,** *refl.* to become clear; be cleared up.

разы́грывать *v. impfv.* [*pfv.* разыгра́ть] **1,** to perform; put on. **2,** to play (*a certain card, chess opening, etc.*). **3,** to raffle (off). **4,** to pose as; play the role of. **5,** *colloq.* to fool; make a fool of. —**разы́грываться,** *refl.* **1,** to play; frolic. **2,** *colloq.* (*of a performer*) to warm to one's part. **3,** *fig.* to increase in intensity; build up.

разыска́ть *v. pfv.* [*infl.* разыщу́, разы́щешь] **1,** *pfv. of* разы́скивать. **2,** to find.

разы́скивать *v. impfv.* [*pfv.* разыска́ть] to search for; hunt for; seek.

рай [*2nd loc.* раю́] *n.* paradise.

райко́м *n.* district committee (*contr. of* райо́нный комите́т).

райо́н *n.* **1,** area; region. **2,** district (*of a city*). **3,** subdivision of an oblast; rayon. —**райо́нный,** *adj.* district (*attrib.*).

ра́йский *adj.* heavenly. —**ра́йская пти́ца,** bird of paradise.

рак *n.* **1,** crawfish. **2,** cancer (*disease*). **3,** *cap., astron.* Cancer: тро́пик Ра́ка, Tropic of Cancer.

ра́ка *n.* shrine (*of a saint*).

раке́та *n.* **1,** rocket. **2,** missile.

раке́тка [*gen. pl.* -ток] *n.* (tennis) racket.

раке́тный *adj.* rocket (*attrib.*); missile (*attrib.*).

ра́ковина *n.* **1,** shell. **2,** sink. **3,** bandstand. —**ушна́я ра́ковина,** auricle (*of the ear*).

ра́ковый *adj.* **1,** of (a) crawfish. **2,** cancer (*attrib.*); cancerous.

ракообра́зное *n., decl. as an adj.* crustacean.

раку́рс *also,* ра́курс *n.* **1,** *art* foreshortening. В раку́рсе, foreshortened. **2,** *fig.* perspective.

раку́шка [*gen. pl.* -шек] *n.* shell; sea shell.

ра́ма *n.* frame.

ра́мка [*gen. pl.* -мок] *n.* **1,** small frame. **2,** *pl.* limits; bounds. —**в ра́мках** (+ *gen.*), within the framework of.

ра́мочный *adj.* frame (*attrib.*).

ра́мпа *n., theat.* footlights.

ра́на *n.* wound.

ранг *n.* rank.

рангоу́т *n., naut.* masts and spars. —**рангоу́тный,** *adj., in* рангоу́тное де́рево, *naut.* spar.

ра́нее *adv.* earlier; sooner.

ране́ние *n.* **1,** wounding; injuring. **2,** wound; injury: получи́ть ране́ние, to be wounded; be injured.

ра́неный *adj.* wounded; injured. —*n.* wounded man; casualty. Ухо́д за ра́неными, care of the wounded.

ра́нец [*gen.* -нца] *n.* knapsack. **2,** satchel.

ранжи́р *n., in* по ранжи́ру, in size order.

ра́нить *v. impfv. & pfv.* to wound; injure. Он был ра́нен в но́гу, he was wounded in the leg.

ра́нний *adj.* early.

ра́но *adv.* early. —*adj., used predicatively* early: ещё ра́но, it is still early. —**ра́но и́ли по́здно,** sooner or later.

рант [*2nd loc.* ранту́] *n.* welt (*of a shoe*).

ра́нчо *n. indecl.* ranch.

рань *n.f., colloq.* early morning hours: в таку́ю рань, at such an ungodly hour.

ра́ньше *adv.* **1,** earlier; sooner. **2,** before. **3,** (*with gen.*) before; ahead of. **4,** before; formerly. —**ра́ньше вре́мени; ра́ньше сро́ка,** ahead of time; ahead of schedule.

рапи́ра *n.* rapier; foil.

рапо́рт *n.* report.

рапортова́ть *v. impfv. & pfv.* [*pres.* -ту́ю, -ту́ешь] to report.

рапс *n.* rape (*plant*). —**ра́псовый,** *adj.* rape (*attrib.*): ра́псовое ма́сло, rape oil.

рапсо́дия *n.* rhapsody.

рас- *prefix, var. of* раз- (*used before voiceless consonants*).

ра́са *n.* race: жёлтая ра́са, the yellow race.

раси́зм *n.* racism. —**раси́ст,** *n.* racist. —**раси́стский,** *adj.* racist.

раска́иваться *v.r. impfv.* [*pfv.* раска́яться] to repent; be sorry.

раскалённый *adj.* scorching; burning; red-hot.

раскали́ть *v., pfv. of* раскаля́ть. —**раскали́ться,** *refl., pfv. of* раскаля́ться.

раска́лывать *v. impfv.* [*pfv.* расколо́ть] **1,** to split; cleave. **2,** *fig.* to split; divide. —**раска́лываться,** *refl.* to split; split up.

раскаля́ть *v. impfv.* [*pfv.* раскали́ть] to make red-hot. —**раскаля́ться,** *refl.* to become red-hot.

раска́пывать *v. impfv.* [*pfv.* раскопа́ть] **1,** to dig; dig up. **2,** to excavate. **3,** *fig., colloq.* to dig up; unearth.

раска́рмливать *v. impfv.* [*pfv.* раскорми́ть] to fatten (up).

раска́т *n.* peal; clap; burst (*of thunder, laughter, etc.*).

раската́ть *v., pfv. of* раска́тывать[1].

раска́тистый *adj.* rolling; resounding.

раскати́ть [*infl.* -качу́, -ка́тишь] *v., pfv. of* раска́тывать[2]. —**раскати́ться,** *refl., pfv. of* раска́тываться.

раска́тывать[1] *v. impfv.* [*pfv.* раската́ть] **1,** to unroll. **2,** to smooth out; level. **3,** to roll (dough).

раска́тывать[2] *v. impfv.* [*pfv.* раскати́ть] to set in motion by rolling. —**раска́тываться,** *refl.* **1,** to gather speed. **2,** to roll about. **3,** to resound.

раска́чивать *v. impfv.* [*pfv.* раскача́ть] **1,** to rock. **2,** [*impfv. only*] (*with instr.*) to swing. **3,** *fig., colloq.* to rouse to action. —**раска́чиваться,** *refl.* **1,** to swing back and forth. **2,** [*impfv. only*] *colloq.* to sway (*while walking*). **3,** *fig., colloq.* to bestir oneself; get (oneself) moving.

раска́шляться *v.r. pfv.* to have a fit of coughing.

раска́яние *n.* repentance; remorse.

раска́яться [*infl.* -ка́юсь, -ка́ешься] *v.r., pfv. of* раска́иваться.

расквартирова́ние *n.* quartering; billeting.

расквартирова́ть *v. pfv.* [*infl.* -ру́ю, -ру́ешь] to quarter; billet.

расква́шивать *v. impfv.* [*pfv.* расква́сить] *colloq.* to smash in; bloody: расква́сить нос (+ *dat.*), to bloody someone's nose.

расквита́ться *v.r. pfv.* (*with* с + *instr.*) *colloq.* **1,** to settle one's debts (with); square one's accounts (with). **2,** to get even (with).

раскида́ть *v., pfv. of* раски́дывать (*in sense* #4).

раски́дистый *adj.* (*of a tree*) spreading.

раски́дывать *v. impfv.* [*pfv.* раски́нуть] **1,** to spread; spread out. **2,** to pitch (a tent); set up (camp). **3,** *in* раски́дывать умо́м, *colloq.* to ponder. **4,** [*pfv.* раскида́ть] to scatter. —**раски́дываться,** *refl.* [*pfv.* раски́нуться] **1,** to stretch; extend (*over a wide area*). **2,** *colloq.* to stretch out; sprawl.

раски́нуть *v., pfv. of* раски́дывать. —**раски́нуться,** *refl., pfv. of* раски́дываться.

раскиса́ть *v. impfv.* [*pfv.* раски́снуть] *colloq.* **1,** to become soggy; become limp. **2,** *fig.* to become listless; become apathetic. **3,** *fig.* to become very emotional.

раски́снуть [*past* -ки́с, -ла] *v., pfv. of* раскиса́ть.

раскла́дка *n.* **1,** laying out; spreading. **2,** making (of a fire, bed, etc.). **3,** apportionment.

раскладно́й *adj.* folding.

раскладу́шка [*gen. pl.* -шек] *n., colloq.* cot.

раскла́дывать *v. impfv.* [*pfv.* разложи́ть] **1,** to put (each in its place); put away. **2,** to lay out; spread out. **3,** to distribute; apportion. **4,** to make; build (a fire). —**раскла́дываться,** *refl., colloq.* to lay one's things out.

раскла́ниваться *v.r. impfv.* [*pfv.* раскла́няться] **1,** to bow. **2,** (*of a performer*) to take a bow. **3,** (*with* с + *instr.*) *colloq.* to take leave of.

расклеивать *v. impfv.* [*pfv.* раскле́ить] **1,** to unglue; unseal. **2,** to post (a notice, placard, etc.) in many places. —**раскле́иваться,** *refl.* **1,** to come unstuck; come apart. **2,** *fig., colloq.* to fall through. **3,** *fig. colloq.* to feel run-down.

расклейка *n.* posting; hanging up.

раско́ванный *adj.* uninhibited; unconstrained. Чу́вствовать себя́ раско́ванно, to feel uninhibited; feel free to do what one pleases.

расковать [*infl.* -ку́ю, -ку́ешь] *v., pfv. of* раско́вывать.

раско́вывать *v. impfv.* [*pfv.* расковать] **1,** to unshoe (a horse). **2,** to unchain; unshackle.

раско́л *n.* split; schism; cleavage.

расколо́ть [*infl.* -колю́, -ко́лешь] *v., pfv. of* коло́ть (*in sense* #4) *and* раска́лывать. —**расколо́ться,** *refl., pfv. of* раска́лываться.

раско́льник *n.* **1,** religious dissenter. **2,** *fig.* person exerting a divisive influence; splitter.

раско́льнический *adj.* schismatic; divisive.

раскопа́ть *v., pfv. of* раска́пывать.

раско́пки [*gen.* -пок] *n.pl.* excavations.

раскорми́ть [*infl.* -кормлю́, -ко́рмишь] *v., pfv. of* раска́рмливать.

раскоря́ка *n.m. & f., colloq.* bowlegged person.

раско́сый *adj.* (*of one's eyes*) slanting.

раскоше́ливаться *v.r. impfv.* [*pfv.* раскоше́литься] *colloq.* to pay up; loosen one's purse strings.

раскра́дывать *v. impfv.* [*pfv.* раскра́сть] to rob; steal.

раскра́ивать *v. impfv.* [*pfv.* раскро́ить] to cut out.

раскра́сить [*infl.* -шу, -сишь] *v., pfv. of* раскра́шивать.

раскра́ска *n.* **1,** coloring. **2,** coloration.

раскрасне́ться *v.r. pfv.* to blush; become flushed; turn red.

раскра́сть [*infl. like* красть] *v., pfv. of* раскра́дывать.

раскра́шивать *v. impfv.* [*pfv.* раскра́сить] to paint; color.

раскрепоща́ть *v. impfv.* [*pfv.* раскрепости́ть] to emancipate.

раскрепоще́ние *n.* emancipation.

раскритикова́ть *v. pfv.* [*infl.* -ку́ю, -ку́ешь] to criticize severely.

раскрича́ться *v.r. pfv.* [*infl.* -чу́сь, -чи́шься] *colloq.* **1,** to start shouting. **2,** (*with* на + *acc.*) to start swearing (at); call (someone) a lot of names.

раскро́ить *v., pfv. of* раскра́ивать.

раскроши́ть *v. pfv.* [*infl.* -крошу́, -кро́шишь] to crumble.

раскрути́ть [*infl.* -кручу́, -кру́тишь] *v., pfv. of* раскру́чивать. —**раскрути́ться,** *refl., pfv. of* раскру́чиваться.

раскру́чивать *v. impfv.* [*pfv.* раскрути́ть] to untwist. —**раскру́чиваться,** *refl.* to come untwisted.

раскрыва́ть *v. impfv.* [*pfv.* раскры́ть] **1,** to open. **2,** to uncover; expose; bare. **3,** to reveal. **4,** to discover. **5,** *in* раскры́ть свои́ ка́рты, to reveal (*or* tip) one's hand. —**раскрыва́ться,** *refl.* **1,** to open. **2,** to uncover oneself; expose onself. **3,** to be uncovered; be exposed. **4,** to come out; come to light. **5,** to reveal one's secrets; tell one's story.

раскры́тие *n.* **1,** opening. **2,** exposure. **3,** revelation; disclosure.

раскры́ть [*infl.* -кро́ю, -кро́ешь] *v., pfv. of* раскрыва́ть. —**раскры́ться,** *refl., pfv. of* раскрыва́ться.

раскупа́ть *v. impfv.* [*pfv.* раскупи́ть] to buy up.

раскупи́ть [*infl.* -куплю́, -ку́пишь] *v., pfv. of* раскупа́ть.

раску́поривать *v. impfv.* [*pfv.* раску́порить] to uncork.

раску́ривать *v. impfv.* [*pfv.* раскури́ть] **1,** to get (a pipe, cigarette, etc.) lighted. **2,** [*impfv. only*] *colloq.* to pass the time smoking.

раскури́ть [*infl.* -курю́, -ку́ришь] *v., pfv. of* раску́ривать.

раскуси́ть *v. pfv.* [*infl.* -кушу́, -ку́сишь] **1,** *pfv. of* раску́сывать. **2,** *fig., colloq.* to see through (someone).

раску́сывать *v. impfv.* [*pfv.* раскуси́ть] to bite; bite into pieces.

раску́тывать *v. impfv.* [*pfv.* раску́тать] to unwrap.

ра́совый *adj.* racial; race (*attrib.*).

распа́д *n.* **1,** disintegration; breakup. **2,** *chem.; physics* decay.

распада́ться *v.r. impfv.* [*pfv.* распа́сться] **1,** to disintegrate; fall apart. **2,** *fig.* to break up.

распа́ивать *v. impfv.* [*pfv.* распая́ть] to unsolder.

распакова́ть [*infl.* -ку́ю, -ку́ешь] *v., pfv. of* распако́вывать. —**распакова́ться,** *refl., pfv. of* распако́вываться.

распако́вка *n.* unpacking.

распако́вывать *v. impfv.* [*pfv.* распакова́ть] to unpack. —**распако́вываться**, *refl.*, *colloq.* to unpack; get unpacked.

распаля́ть *v. impfv.* [*pfv.* распали́ть] **1**, *colloq.* to make burning hot. **2**, *fig.* to fire up.

распа́ривать *v. impfv.* [*pfv.* распа́рить] **1**, to steam; stew. **2**, *colloq.* to cause to sweat.

распа́рывать *v. impfv.* [*pfv.* распоро́ть] **1**, to unstitch. **2**, to rip open. —**распа́рываться**, *refl.* to rip; split.

распа́сться [*infl. like* пасть] *v.r., pfv. of* распада́ться.

распаха́ть [*infl.* -пашу́, -па́шешь] *v., pfv. of* распа́хивать (*in sense #1*).

распа́хивать *v. impfv.* **1**, [*pfv.* распаха́ть] to plow; plow up. **2**, [*pfv.* распахну́ть] to throw open; fling open. —**распа́хиваться**, *refl.* [*pfv.* распахну́ться] to swing open; fly open.

распахну́ть *v., pfv. of* распа́хивать (*in sense #2*). —**распахну́ться**, *refl., pfv. of* распа́хиваться.

распашо́нка [*gen. pl.* -нок] *n.* baby's short-sleeved undershirt that opens down the back.

распая́ть *v., pfv. of* распа́ивать.

распева́ть *v. impfv., colloq.* to sing (*loudly or gaily*).

распека́ть *v. impfv.* [*pfv.* распе́чь] *colloq.* to tell off; upbraid.

распе́ться *v.r. pfv.* [*infl.* -пою́сь, -поёшься] *colloq.* **1**, (*of a singer*) to warm up. **2**, to sing away.

распеча́тывать *v. impfv.* [*pfv.* распеча́тать] to unseal; break the seal of.

распе́чь [*infl. like* печь] *v., pfv. of* распека́ть.

распива́ть *v. impfv.* [*pfv.* распи́ть] *colloq.* **1**, to drink up (together with someone else). **2**, [*impfv. only*] to drink slowly; linger over.

распи́ливать *v. impfv.* [*pfv.* распили́ть] to saw up.

распили́ть [*infl.* -пилю́, -пи́лишь] *v., pfv. of* распи́ливать.

распина́ть *v. impfv.* [*pfv.* распя́ть] to crucify. —**распина́ться**, *refl.* [*impfv. only*] *colloq.* **1**, (*with* за + *acc.*) to go to bat for. **2**, (*with* о) to crow (about).

расписа́ние *n.* schedule; timetable.

расписа́ть [*infl.* -пишу́, -пи́шешь] *v., pfv. of* расписывать. —**расписа́ться**, *refl., pfv. of* расписываться.

распи́ска [*gen. pl.* -сок] *n.* (written) receipt.

расписно́й *adj., colloq.* painted (*with designs*).

распи́сывать *v. impfv.* [*pfv.* расписа́ть] **1**, to write down; note down; copy down; enter (a number of items). **2**, to schedule; assign. **3**, to paint; decorate. **4**, *fig., colloq.* to describe in glowing terms. —**распи́сываться**, *refl.* **1**, to sign one's name. **2**, *colloq.* to register one's marriage. **3**, (*with* в + *prepl.*) *colloq.* to openly admit; openly advertise.

распи́ть [*infl.* разопью́, разопьёшь; *past* распи́л *or* ро́спил, распила́, распи́ло *or* ро́спило] *v., pfv. of* распива́ть.

распи́хивать *v. impfv.* [*pfv.* распиха́ть] *colloq.* **1**, to push aside; force one's way through. **2**, to shove; stuff.

распла́вить [*infl.* -влю, -вишь] *v., pfv. of* расплавля́ть.

распла́вленный *adj.* molten.

расплавля́ть *v. impfv.* [*pfv.* распла́вить] to melt; melt down.

распла́каться *v.r. pfv.* [*infl.* -пла́чусь, -пла́чешься] to burst into tears.

распланиро́вать *v. pfv.* [*infl.* -рую, -руешь] to plan out (one's day, work, etc.).

распланирова́ть [*infl.* -ру́ю, -ру́ешь] *v., pfv. of* плани́ровать.

распла́стывать *v. impfv.* [*pfv.* распласта́ть] **1**, to slice into layers. **2**, to spread; spread out; spread flat. —**распла́стываться**, *refl.* to lie flat.

распла́та *n.* **1**, payment. **2**, *fig.* retribution. —**день** (*or* час) распла́ты, day of reckoning.

расплати́ться [*infl.* -плачу́сь, -пла́тишься] *v.r., pfv. of* распла́чиваться.

распла́чиваться *v.r. impfv.* [*pfv.* расплати́ться] **1**, (*with* с + *instr.*) to pay off; settle accounts (with). **2**, (*with* с + *instr.*) to get even (with). **3**, (*with* за + *acc.*) to pay (for); take the punishment (for).

расплеска́ть [*infl.* -плещу́, -пле́щешь] *v., pfv. of* расплёскивать. —**расплеска́ться**, *refl., pfv. of* расплёскиваться.

расплёскивать *v. impfv.* [*pfv.* расплеска́ть] to spill. —**расплёскиваться**, *refl.* (*of a liquid*) to spill.

расплести́ [*infl. like* плести́] *v., pfv. of* расплета́ть.

расплета́ть *v. impfv.* [*pfv.* расплести́] to untwist; unbraid.

расплоди́ть *v. pfv.* [*infl.* -жу́, -ди́шь] to breed. —**расплоди́ться**, *refl.* to breed; multiply.

расплыва́ться *v.r. impfv.* [*pfv.* расплы́ться] **1**, (*of a liquid*) to run; (*of something in the air*) to spread. **2**, *fig.* to become blurred. **3**, *fig., colloq.* to grow fat. **4**, *fig.* (*of a smile, look of satisfaction, etc.*) to spread across one's face. —**расплыва́ться в улы́бке**, (*of one's face*) to break into a smile.

расплы́вчатый *adj.* **1**, indistinct. **2**, *fig.* vague.

расплы́ться [*infl. like* плыть] *v.r., pfv. of* расплыва́ться.

расплю́щивать *v. impfv.* [*pfv.* расплю́щить] to flatten; crush; squash.

распознава́ть *v. impfv.* [*pfv.* распозна́ть; *pres.* -знаю́, -знаёшь] **1**, to recognize; identify. **2**, to diagnose (an illness). **3**, to discern; make out.

распозна́ть [*infl.* -зна́ю, -зна́ешь] *v., pfv. of* распознава́ть.

располага́ть *v. impfv.* **1**, (*with instr.*) to have; have at one's disposal. **2**, (*with instr.*) to make use of; do with. **3**, (*with* к) to be conducive to. **4**, *obs.* to intend; plan. **5**, [*pfv.* расположи́ть] to arrange; station; post. **6**, [*pfv.* расположи́ть] (*often with* к себе́) to win over. —**располага́ться**, *refl.* [*pfv.* расположи́ться] **1**, to settle down; sit down. **2**, *in* располага́ться ла́герем, to camp; encamp; set up camp. **3**, [*impfv. only*] *obs.* to intend; plan.

располага́ющий *adj.* pleasing; attractive.

расползаться *v.r. impfv.* [*pfv.* расползти́сь] **1**, to crawl; crawl away (*in different directions*). **2**, *colloq.* to come apart at the seams.

расползти́сь [*infl. like* ползти́] *v.r., pfv. of* располза́ться.

расположе́ние *n.* **1**, arrangement; layout; disposition. **2**, location; position. **3**, favor; sympathies; liking. **4**, (*with* к) inclination (toward); tendency (toward). **5**, *colloq.* mood; desire: у меня́ нет расположе́ния (+ *inf.*), I am not in the mood to... —**расположе́ние ду́ха**, mood; frame of mind.

располо́женный *adj.* **1**, located; situated. **2**, (*with* к) fond (of). **3**, (*with* к) inclined (to); disposed (toward). **4**, (*with inf.*) of a mood (to); in the mood (for).

располо́жить [*infl.* -ложу́, -ло́жишь] *v.*, *pfv. of* располага́ть (*in senses #5 & #6*). —**расположи́ться**, *refl.* 1, *pfv. of* располага́ться. 2, (*with inf.*) *obs.* to decide (to); make up one's mind (to).

распоро́ть [*infl.* -порю́, -по́решь] *v.*, *pfv. of* поро́ть (*in sense #2*) *and* распа́рывать.—**распоро́ться**, *refl.*, *pfv. of* распа́рываться.

распоряди́тель *n.m.* manager; superintendent; person in charge.

распоряди́тельный *adj.* efficient; businesslike.

распоряди́ться [*infl.* -жу́сь, -ди́шься] *v.r.*, *pfv. of* распоряжа́ться.

распоря́док [*gen.* -дка] *n.* order; routine.

распоряжа́ться *v.r. impfv.* [*pfv.* распоряди́ться] 1, (*with inf. or* о) to order (*that something be done*). 2, [*impfv. only*] to be in charge; give orders; (*with instr.*) be in charge of; direct; manage. 3, (*with instr.*) to handle; do with (money, property, etc.).

распоряже́ние *n.* 1, (*with instr.*) disposition (of). 2, order; command. 3, disposal: име́ть в своём распоряже́нии, to have at one's disposal; предоста́вить в распоряже́ние (+ *gen.*), to place at the disposal of.

распоя́сать [*infl.* -поя́шу, -поя́шешь] *v.*, *pfv. of* распоя́сывать. —**распоя́саться**, *refl.*, *pfv. of* распоя́сываться.

распоя́сывать *v. impfv.* [*pfv.* распоя́сать] to ungird. —**распоя́сываться**, *refl.* 1, to take off one's belt. 2, *fig.*, *colloq.* to cast off all restraint; let oneself go.

распра́ва *n.* (*with* с + *instr.*) harsh treatment (of); savage punishment (of); reprisals (against).

распра́вить [*infl.* -влю, -вишь] *v.*, *pfv. of* расправля́ть. —**распра́виться**, *refl.*, *pfv. of* расправля́ться.

расправля́ть *v. impfv.* [*pfv.* распра́вить] 1, to smooth out. 2, to straighten. 3, *in* расправля́ть кры́лья, to spread one's wings (*lit. & fig.*). —**расправля́ться**, *refl.* 1, to get smoothed out. 2, (*with* с + *instr.*) to deal with (*severely or cruelly*). 3, (*with* с + *instr.*) *colloq.* to dispose of; finish off. 4, *in* расправля́ться без суда́, to take the law into one's own hands.

распределе́ние *n.* distribution; allocation.

распредели́тель *n.m.* 1, distributor (*person*). 2, distribution center. 3, *mech.* distributor.

распредели́тельный *adj.* distribution (*attrib.*); distributing; distributive. —**распредели́тельный вал**, camshaft. —**распредели́тельный щит**, switchboard.

распределя́ть *v. impfv.* [*pfv.* распредели́ть] to distribute; allocate.

распродава́ть *v. impfv.* [*pfv.* распрода́ть; *pres.* -даю́, -даёшь] to sell out; sell completely.

распрода́жа *n.* sale; clearance sale.

распрода́ть [*infl. like* прода́ть] *v.*, *pfv. of* распродава́ть.

распростере́ть [*past* -стёр, -ла, *not used in future*] *v.*, *pfv. of* распростира́ть. —**распростере́ться**, *refl.*, *pfv. of* распростира́ться.

распростёртый *adj.* 1, outstretched. 2, prostrate. —**с распростёртыми объя́тиями**, with open arms.

распростира́ть *v. impfv.* [*pfv.* распростере́ть] to stretch out; spread; extend. —**распростира́ться**, *refl.* 1, to lie with arms outstretched. 2, *fig.* to stretch; extend.

распрости́ться *v.r. pfv.* [*infl.* -щу́сь, -сти́шься] (*with* с + *instr.*) *colloq.* to say goodbye (to); bid farewell (to); take leave (of).

распростране́ние *n.* 1, spreading. 2, dissemination. 3, expansion; extension. 4, prevalence; distribution: име́ть большо́е распростране́ние, to be widespread. О́бласть распростране́ния живо́тного, area over which an animal is to be found.

распространённый *adj.* widespread; prevalent.

распространя́ть *v. impfv.* [*pfv.* распространи́ть] 1, to spread. 2, to disseminate. 3, to expand. 4, to extend. 5, to give off. —**распространя́ться**, *refl.* 1, to spread. 2, to extend. 3, (*with* о) *colloq.* to dwell at great length (upon). 4, *in* распространя́ться на те́му, to dwell/enlarge/expand on a subject.

ра́спря *n.*, *usu. pl.* discord; contention; strife.

распряга́ть *v. impfv.* [*pfv.* распря́чь] to unharness.

распрямля́ть *v. impfv.* [*pfv.* распрями́ть] to straighten; unbend. —**распрямля́ться**, *refl.* to straighten up.

распря́чь [*infl.* -прягу́, -пряжёшь, ...-прягу́т; *past* -пря́г, -прягла́, -прягло́] *v.*, *pfv. of* распряга́ть.

распу́гивать *v. impfv.* [*pfv.* распуга́ть] *colloq.* to frighten away; scare away.

распуска́ть *v. impfv.* [*pfv.* распусти́ть] 1, to dismiss; disband; dissolve. 2, to loosen; let out (reins); let down (one's hair). 3, to open; spread; unfurl. 4, *colloq.* to be too lenient with; let get out of hand. 5, *colloq.* to spread (rumors, gossip, etc.). 6, *colloq.* to dissolve; melt. 7, *in* распуска́ть язы́к, *colloq.* to speak too freely. 8, *in* распуска́ть со́пли, слю́ни, ню́ни, *see* со́пли, слю́ни, ню́ни. —**распуска́ться**, *refl.* 1, (*of buds*) to open. 2, *colloq.* to come undone. 3, *colloq.* to become flabby. 4, *colloq.* to let oneself go. 5, *colloq.* to get out of hand.

распусти́ть [*infl.* -пущу́, -пу́стишь] *v.*, *pfv. of* распуска́ть. —**распусти́ться**, *refl.*, *pfv. of* распуска́ться.

распу́тать *v.*, *pfv. of* распу́тывать. —**распу́таться**, *refl.*, *pfv. of* распу́тываться.

распу́тица *n.* time of year when roads are impassable.

распу́тник *n.* profligate; lecher; libertine.

распу́тничать *v. impfv.* to lead a dissolute life.

распу́тный *adj.* dissolute; profligate; licentious.

распу́тство *n.* profligacy; licentiousness; dissoluteness.

распу́тывать *v. impfv.* [*pfv.* распу́тать] 1, to untangle; disentangle; unravel. 2, *fig.* to unravel. —**распу́тываться**, *refl.* 1, to come untangled. 2, *fig.*, *colloq.* to be cleared up; be settled. 3, *fig.*, *colloq.* to disentangle oneself (*from a situation*). 4, *in* распу́таться с долга́ми, to free oneself of debt.

распу́тье *n.* crossroads. —**на распу́тье**, at the crossroads.

распуха́ть *v. impfv.* [*pfv.* распу́хнуть] 1, to swell; swell up. 2, to bulge.

распу́хнуть [*past* -пу́х, -ла] *v.*, *pfv. of* распуха́ть.

распуши́ть *v.*, *pfv. of* пуши́ть.

распу́щенность *n.f.* 1, lack of discipline; laxity. 2, dissoluteness; dissipation.

распу́щенный *adj.* 1, (*of one's hair*) loose; hanging down. 2, *colloq.* undisciplined. 3, dissolute.

распыли́тель *n.m.* sprayer; atomizer.

распыля́ть *v. impfv.* [*pfv.* распыли́ть] 1, to pulverize. 2, to spray. 3, to disperse; scatter.

распя́тие *n.* 1, crucifixion. 2, crucifix.

распя́ть [*infl.* -пну́, -пнёшь] *v.*, *pfv. of* распина́ть.

расса́да *n.* seedlings.

рассади́ть [*infl.* -сажу́, -са́дишь] *v.*, *pfv. of* расса́-
живать.

расса́дник *n.* **1,** nursery (*for plants*). **2,** *fig.* center
(*of learning*); breeding ground (*of crime, infection, etc.*).

расса́живать *v. impfv.* [*pfv.* рассади́ть] **1,** to seat
(*each in his place*). **2,** to separate; seat apart. **3,** to plant
farther apart. —расса́живаться, *refl.* [*pfv.* рассе́сть-
ся] (*of many people*) to take their (respective) seats.

расса́сываться *v.r. impfv.* [*pfv.* рассоса́ться] **1,** (*of
a tumor*) to dissolve. **2,** *colloq.* (*of a crowd*) to melt
away.

рассвести́ [*infl.* -светёт; *past* -свело́] *v.*, *pfv. of* рас-
света́ть.

рассве́т *n.* dawn; daybreak.

рассвета́ть *v. impfv.* [*pfv.* рассвести́] *impers.* to
dawn: рассвета́ет, day is dawning; day is breaking.

рассвирепе́ть *v.*, *pfv. of* свирепе́ть.

рассода́ться *v.r. impfv.* [*pfv.* рассе́сться] to crack.

рассёдлывать *v. impfv.* [*pfv.* расседла́ть] to unsaddle.

рассе́ивание *n.* scattering; dispersion; dispersal.

рассе́ивать *v. impfv.* [*pfv.* рассе́ять] **1,** to disperse.
2, to diffuse (light). **3,** *fig.* to dispel (doubts, fears,
etc.). **4,** *fig.* to take someone's mind off things. —рас-
се́иваться, *refl.* **1,** to scatter; disperse. **2,** (*of fog*)
to lift; (*of clouds*) to disappear. **3,** to get one's mind
off things.

рассека́ть *v. impfv.* [*pfv.* рассе́чь] **1,** to cleave; split.
2, to slash; gash. **3,** to cut in two.

рассекре́чивать *v. impfv.* [*pfv.* рассекре́тить] to
declassify.

рассе́лина *n.* cleft; fissure.

расселя́ть *v. impfv.* [*pfv.* рассели́ть] **1,** to settle
(many people). **2,** to separate; settle separately. —рас-
селя́ться, *refl.* to settle in different places.

рассерди́ть *v.*, *pfv. of* серди́ть. —рассерди́ться,
refl., *pfv. of* серди́ться.

рассе́сться [*infl. like* сесть] *v.r.*, *pfv. of* расса́жи-
ваться *and* рассода́ться.

рассе́чь [*infl. like* сечь; *past* -сёк, -секла́, -секло́] *v.*,
pfv. of рассека́ть.

рассе́яние *n.* **1,** dispersion. **2,** diffusion (*of light*).
3, dispelling (*of doubts, rumors, etc.*).

рассе́янный *adj.* **1,** scattered; dispersed. **2,** (*of light*)
diffused. **3,** absent-minded. —рассе́янно, *adv.* absent-
mindedly; absently. —рассе́янность, *n.f.* absent-
mindedness.

рассе́ять [*infl.* -се́ю, -се́ешь] *v.*, *pfv. of* рассе́ивать.
—рассе́яться, *refl.*, *pfv. of* рассе́иваться.

расска́з *n.* **1,** story; tale. **2,** account.

рассказа́ть [*infl.* -скажу́, -ска́жешь] *v.*, *pfv. of* рас-
ка́зывать.

расска́зчик *n.* narrator; storyteller.

расска́зывание *n.* telling; narration.

расска́зывать *v. impfv.* [*pfv.* рассказа́ть] to tell;
relate; recount.

рассла́бить [*infl.* -блю, -бишь] *v.*, *pfv. of* расслаб-
ля́ть.

расслабле́ние *n.* weakness; debility. *Also,* рас-
сла́бленность, *n.f.*

рассла́бленный *adj.* **1,** weak; debilitated. **2,** (*of a
gait*) unsure; unsteady.

расслабля́ть *v. impfv.* [*pfv.* рассла́бить] **1,** to
weaken; debilitate. **2,** to relax (muscles).

рассла́ивать *v. impfv.* [*pfv.* расслои́ть] to stratify.

рассле́дование *n.* investigation; inquiry.

рассле́довать *v. impfv. & pfv.* [*pres.* -дую, -дуешь]
to investigate; inquire into.

расслое́ние *n.* stratification: расслое́ние о́бщества,
stratification of society.

расслои́ть *v.*, *pfv. of* рассла́ивать.

расслы́шать *v. pfv.* [*infl.* -шу, -шишь] to hear; catch.

рассма́тривать *v. impfv.* [*pfv.* рассмотре́ть] **1,** to
examine; scrutinize. **2,** to consider; take up; examine.
3, [*impfv. only*] (*with* как) to regard (as); consider (to
be). *See also* рассмотре́ть.

рассмеши́ть *v.*, *pfv. of* смеши́ть.

рассмея́ться *v.r. pfv.* [*infl.* -смею́сь, -смеёшься]
to burst out laughing.

рассмотре́ние *n.* examination; consideration.

рассмотре́ть *v. pfv.* [*infl.* -смотрю́, -смо́тришь]
1, *pfv. of* рассма́тривать. **2,** to discern; make out;
spot.

рассо́л *n.* brine.

рассо́льник *n.* soup with pickled cucumbers.

рассо́рить *v. pfv.* to set to quarreling; cause a quarrel
between. —рассо́риться, *refl.* (*with* с + *instr.*) to
have a falling-out (with).

рассортирова́ть *v.*, *pfv. of* сортирова́ть.

рассортиро́вка *n.* sorting out.

рассоса́ться [*infl. like* соса́ть] *v.r.*, *pfv. of* расса́сы-
ваться.

рассо́хнуться [*past* -со́хся, -со́хлась] *v.r.*, *pfv. of*
рассыха́ться.

расспра́шивать *v. impfv.* [*pfv.* расспроси́ть] to
question.

расспроси́ть [*infl.* -спрошу́, -спро́сишь] *v.*, *pfv. of*
расспра́шивать.

расспро́сы [*gen.* -сов] *n. pl.* questions; questioning.

рассро́чивать *v. impfv.* [*pfv.* рассро́чить] to spread
(payments) over a period of time.

рассро́чка *n.*, *usu. in* в рассро́чку, on the installment
plan; on time.

расстава́ние *n.* parting; taking leave.

расстава́ться *v.r. impfv.* [*pfv.* расста́ться; *pres.* -ста-
ю́сь, -стаёшься] (*with* с + *instr.*) **1,** to part (with). **2,**
to leave (a place). **3,** *fig.* to give up (an idea, dream, etc.).

расста́вить [*infl.* -влю, -вишь] *v.*, *pfv. of* расстав-
ля́ть.

расставля́ть *v. impfv.* [*pfv.* расста́вить] **1,** to place;
arrange. **2,** to assign (personnel); post (sentries). **3,** to
spread; move apart.

расстано́вка *n.* **1,** placement; arrangement. **2,** intermittent pauses. —говори́ть с расстано́вкой, to speak
in measured tones.

расста́ться [*infl.* -ста́нусь, -ста́нешься] *v.r.*, *pfv. of*
расстава́ться.

расстёгивать *v. impfv.* [*pfv.* расстегну́ть] to unfasten; unbutton; unhook; undo. —расстёгиваться,
refl. **1,** to come undone. **2,** to unbutton one's coat.

расстила́ть *v. impfv.* [*pfv.* разостла́ть] to spread out.
—расстила́ться, *refl.* **1,** to be spread out. **2,** to stretch;
extend.

расстоя́ние *n.* distance.

расстра́ивать *v. impfv.* [*pfv.* расстро́ить] **1,** to throw
into disorder; break up. **2,** to impair; damage; ruin;
shatter. **3,** to disrupt; upset. **4,** to frustrate; thwart; foil.
5, to upset (*emotionally*); disturb. **6,** to throw out of
tune. **7,** *in* расстра́ивать желу́док, to upset one's
stomach; cause indigestion. **8,** *in* расстро́ить сва́дьбу,

to break off one's engagement. —расстра́иваться, refl. 1, to be thrown into disorder. 2, to collapse; break down. 3, to fall through. 4, to become upset. 5, to get out of tune.

расстре́л n. execution by a firing squad.

расстре́ливать v. impfv. [pfv. **расстреля́ть**] 1, to execute by a firing squad. 2, to shoot up; rake with fire. 3, to use up; exhaust (one's ammunition).

расстри́га n.m. unfrocked monk; unfrocked priest.

расстрига́ть v. impfv. [pfv. **расстри́чь**] to unfrock; defrock.

расстри́чь [infl. like стричь] v., pfv. of расстрига́ть.

расстро́енный adj. 1, disorganized; thrown into disorder. 2, upset (emotionally). 3, (of one's health) impaired. 4, out of tune.

расстро́ить v., pfv. of расстра́ивать. —расстро́иться, refl., pfv. of расстра́иваться.

расстро́йство n. 1, upsetting; disruption. 2, disorder; disarray. 3, med. disorder. 4, colloq. discomfiture; distress. —расстро́йство желу́дка, upset stomach. —расстро́йство пищеваре́ния, indigestion.

расступа́ться v.r. impfv. [pfv. **расступи́ться**] 1, to step aside; make way. 2, to part; open.

расступи́ться [infl. -ступлю́сь, -сту́пишься] v.r., pfv. of расступа́ться.

рассуди́тельный adj. reasonable; sensible; judicious; prudent. —рассуди́тельность, n.f. prudence; discretion; good sense.

рассуди́ть v. pfv. [infl. -сужу́, -су́дишь] 1, to settle a dispute between. 2, (with что) to decide (that); come to the conclusion (that). 3, to think; reflect.

рассу́док [gen. -дка] n. 1, reason. 2, sanity. 3, common sense. —в по́лном рассу́дке, in full possession of one's faculties.

рассу́дочный adj. rational.

рассужда́ть v. impfv. 1, to reason. 2, (with о) to discuss. 3, (with о) to discourse (on); expound (on).

рассужде́ние n. 1, reasoning. 2, pl. discussion; comments; remarks. 3, pl. objections; arguments; без (вся́ких) рассужде́ний, without any arguments.

рассу́чивать v. impfv. [pfv. **рассучи́ть**] 1, to untwist. 2, to roll down (one's sleeves).

рассучи́ть [infl. -сучу́, -су́чишь] v., pfv. of рассу́чивать.

рассчи́танный adj. 1, calculated; intentional. 2, (with на + acc.) intended (for); designed (for); meant (for).

рассчи́тывать v. impfv. [pfv. **рассчита́ть**] 1, to calculate. 2, to figure; plan. 3, to dismiss; discharge; fire. 4, [impfv. only] to intend; expect. 5, [impfv. only] (with на + acc.) to count on. —рассчи́тываться, refl. 1, (with с + instr.) to settle up with (someone); pay off (one's debts). 2, (with с + instr.) to settle scores (with); get even (with). 3, colloq. to lose one's job. 4, [impfv. only] (with за + acc.) to answer for; pay for.

рассыла́ть v. impfv. [pfv. **разосла́ть**] to send out; mail out; circulate.

рассы́лка n. sending out; mailing out.

рассы́льный n., decl. as an adj. errand boy.

рассы́пать [infl. -сы́плю, -сы́плешь] v., pfv. of рассыпа́ть. —рассы́паться, refl., pfv. of рассыпа́ться.

рассыпа́ть v. impfv. [pfv. **рассы́пать**] to spill; scatter; strew. —рассыпа́ться, refl. 1, to spill; be strewn. 2, to crumble; fall to pieces. 3, to scatter; disperse. 4, (of one's hair) to hang loosely. 5, (with в + prepl.) colloq. to shower (with praises, compliments, etc.): рассы-

па́ться кому́-нибудь в комплиме́нтах, to shower someone with compliments. Рассыпа́ться в извине́ниях, to apologize profusely.

рассы́пчатый adj. friable; crumbly.

рассыха́ться v.r. impfv. [pfv. **рассо́хнуться**] to crack (as a result of drying up).

раста́лкивать v. impfv. [pfv. **растолка́ть**] colloq. 1, to push (everyone) aside. 2, to awaken; arouse (by shaking).

раста́пливать v. impfv. [pfv. **растопи́ть**] 1, to light (a stove). 2, to melt. —раста́пливаться, refl. 1, (of a stove) to light. 2, to melt.

раста́птывать v. impfv. [pfv. **растопта́ть**] to trample; crush.

растаска́ть v., pfv. of раста́скивать (in senses #1 & #2).

раста́скивать v. impfv. [pfv. **растащи́ть**] 1, [pfv. also растаска́ть] to carry away; remove (one at a time, bit by bit). 2, [pfv. also растаска́ть] to steal; make off with. 3, colloq. to pull apart; separate.

раста́чивать v. impfv. [pfv. **расточи́ть**] to chisel out.

растащи́ть [infl. -тащу́, -та́щишь] v., pfv. of раста́скивать.

раста́ять v., pfv. of та́ять.

раство́р n. solution: щелочно́й раство́р, alkaline solution. —строи́тельный раство́р, mortar.

растворе́ние n. dissolution; solution.

раствори́мый adj. soluble. —раствори́мость, n.f. solubility.

раствори́тель n.m. solvent.

раствори́ть v. pfv. 1, [infl. -творю́, -тво́ришь] pfv. of растворя́ть (in sense #1). 2, [infl. -творю́, -твори́шь] pfv. of растворя́ть (in sense #2). —раствори́ться, refl. [same distinction in stress] pfv. of растворя́ться.

растворя́ть v. impfv. [pfv. **раствори́ть**] 1, to open. 2, to dissolve. —растворя́ться, refl. 1, (of a door, window, etc.) to open; swing open. 2, (of a substance) to dissolve.

растворя́ющий adj. solvent.

растека́ться v.r. impfv. [pfv. **расте́чься**] 1, (of liquids) to run; spread. 2, (of a crowd) to set out (in various directions). 3, (with по) (of a smile, feeling, etc.) to come over (one's face, body, etc.). 4, [impfv. only] colloq. to go into unnecessary detail.

расте́ние n. plant.

растениево́дство n. plant growing; plant cultivation.

растере́ть [infl. разотру́, разотрёшь; past растёр, -ла] v., pfv. of растира́ть.

расте́рзанный adj. 1, torn to shreds. 2, disheveled.

растерза́ть v. pfv. 1, to tear to pieces. 2, to torment. Растерза́ть чье-нибудь се́рдце, to tear at one's heart; tear one's heart out.

расте́рянный adj. confused; bewildered. —расте́рянно, adv. in bewilderment. —расте́рянность, n.f. confusion; bewilderment.

растеря́ть v. pfv. to lose (many things). —растеря́ться, refl. 1, (of many things) to be lost. 2, to become confused; be bewildered; become flustered.

расте́чься [infl. like течь] v.r., pfv. of растека́ться.

расти́ v. impfv. [pfv. **вы́расти**; pres. расту́, растёшь; past рос, росла́, росло́] 1, to grow. 2, to grow up. 3, to grow; increase; rise; go up.

растира́ние n. 1, grinding. 2, rubbing; massaging.

растира́ть v. impfv. [pfv. **растере́ть**] 1, to grind (into small particles). **2,** to rub (onto the surface of something). **3,** to rub; massage.

расти́тельность *n.f.* **1,** vegetation. **2,** *colloq.* hair (*on one's face or body*).

расти́тельный *adj.* plant (*attrib.*); vegetable (*attrib.*). —**расти́тельное ма́сло,** vegetable oil.

расти́ть *v. impfv.* [*pfv.* **вы́растить;** *pres.* **ращу́, расти́шь**] **1,** to raise; bring up (children). **2,** to train (personnel). **3,** to raise; grow; cultivate (plants).

растлева́ть *v. impfv.* [*pfv.* **растли́ть**] **1,** to violate; ravish (a minor). **2,** *fig.* to corrupt.

растле́ние *n.* **1,** violation; rape (*of a minor*). **2,** decay; decadence.

растле́нный *adj.* corrupt; decadent.

растли́ть *v., pfv. of* **растлева́ть.**

растолка́ть *v., pfv. of* **раста́лкивать.**

растолкова́ть [*infl.* **-ку́ю, -ку́ешь**] *v., pfv. of* **растолко́вывать.**

растолко́вывать *v. impfv.* [*pfv.* **растолкова́ть**] to explain.

растоло́чь *v., pfv. of* **толо́чь.**

растолсте́ть *v. pfv.* to grow fat; put on a lot of weight.

растопи́ть [*infl.* **-топлю́, -то́пишь**] *v., pfv. of* **топи́ть** (*in sense #3*) *and* **раста́пливать.** —**растопи́ться,** *refl., pfv. of* **раста́пливаться.**

расто́пка *n.* **1,** lighting (*of a stove*). **2,** *colloq.* kindling wood.

растопта́ть [*infl.* **-топчу́, -то́пчешь**] *v., pfv. of* **раста́птывать.**

растопы́ривать *v. impfv.* [*pfv.* **растопы́рить**] *colloq.* to spread apart.

расторга́ть *v. impfv.* [*pfv.* **расто́ргнуть**] to annul; abrogate.

расто́ргнуть [*past* **-то́рг** *or* **-то́ргнул, -то́ргла**] *v., pfv. of* **расторга́ть.**

расторже́ние *n.* annulment; abrogation.

расторо́пный *adj.* capable; competent; efficient. —**расторо́пность,** *n.f.* capability; competence; efficiency.

расточа́ть *v. impfv.* [*pfv.* **расточи́ть**] **1,** to squander; dissipate. **2,** to lavish; shower: расточа́ть похвалы́ (+ *dat.*), to lavish praise upon.

расточе́ние *n.* squandering; dissipation.

расточи́тель *n.m.* squanderer; spendthrift.

расточи́тельный *adj.* extravagant; wasteful. —**расточи́тельность,** *n.f.* extravagance; wastefulness.

расточи́ть *v. pfv.* **1,** [*infl.* **-точу́, -то́чишь**] *pfv. of* **расточа́ть. 2,** [*infl.* **-точу́, -то́чишь**] *pfv. of* **раста́чивать.**

растрави́ть [*infl.* **-травлю́, -тра́вишь**] *v., pfv. of* **растравля́ть.**

растравля́ть *v. impfv.* [*pfv.* **растрави́ть**] **1,** to irritate; *fig.* rub salt on (a wound). **2,** *colloq.* to revive; reopen (something unpleasant).

растранжи́рить *v., pfv. of* **транжи́рить.**

растра́та *n.* **1,** squandering; waste. **2,** embezzlement.

растра́тить [*infl.* **-чу, -тишь**] *v., pfv. of* **растра́чивать.**

растра́тчик *n.* embezzler.

растра́чивать *v. impfv.* [*pfv.* **растра́тить**] **1,** to squander; dissipate. **2,** to embezzle.

растрево́жить *v. pfv.* **1,** to alarm; upset. **2,** to stir up; disturb.

растрёпа *n.m. & f., colloq.* slovenly person; slob.

растрёпанный *adj.* **1,** disheveled. **2,** tattered.

растрепа́ть *v. pfv.* [*infl.* **-треплю́, -тре́плешь**] **1,** to mess up; muss. **2,** to wear out; tatter.

растре́скаться *v.r. pfv.* to crack all over.

растро́ганный *adj.* deeply touched; deeply moved.

растро́гать *v. pfv.* to move; touch; affect deeply. —**растро́гаться,** *refl.* to be (deeply) touched; be (deeply) moved.

растру́б *n.* **1,** flare (*of a garment, bell, etc.*). **2,** bell (*of a musical instrument*).

растряса́ть *v. impfv.* [*pfv.* **растрясти́**] **1,** to strew; scatter. **2,** *fig., colloq.* to waste; spend needlessly. **3,** *impers.* to be shaken up (*while riding*): его́ растрясло́, he was shaken up.

растрясти́ [*infl. like* **трясти́**] *v., pfv. of* **растряса́ть.**

растя́гивать *v. impfv.* [*pfv.* **растяну́ть**] **1,** to stretch. **2,** to strain; sprain. **3,** to spread out. **4,** to prolong; drag out. **5,** *in* растя́гивать слова́, to drawl. —**растя́гиваться,** *refl.* **1,** to stretch; become stretched. **2,** to extend; be stretched out. **3,** *colloq.* to stretch out. **4,** *colloq.* to tumble headlong. **5,** to be stretched out; be dragged out (*over a period of time*).

растяже́ние *n.* strain; sprain.

растяжи́мость *n.f.* **1,** stretchability. **2,** tensile strength.

растяжи́мый *adj.* **1,** stretchable. **2,** *fig.* loose; imprecise.

растя́жка *n.* stretching: отда́ть ту́фли на растя́жку, to have one's shoes stretched.

растя́нутый *adj.* **1,** stretched out; extended. **2,** *fig.* long-winded; verbose.

растяну́ть [*infl.* **-тяну́, -тя́нешь**] *v., pfv. of* **растя́гивать.** —**растяну́ться,** *refl., pfv. of* **растя́гиваться.**

растя́па *n.m. & f., colloq.* dolt; dope; dullard.

расфасова́ть *v., pfv. of* **фасова́ть.**

расфасо́вка *n.* packaging.

расформирова́ть [*infl.* **-ру́ю, -ру́ешь**] *v., pfv. of* **расформиро́вывать.**

расформиро́вывать *v. impfv.* [*pfv.* **расформирова́ть**] to disband.

расха́живать *v. impfv.* to pace back and forth.

расхва́ливать *v. impfv.* [*pfv.* **расхвали́ть**] to extol; rave about; praise to the skies.

расхвали́ть [*infl.* **-хвалю́, -хва́лишь**] *v., pfv. of* **расхва́ливать.**

расхва́рываться *v.r. impfv.* [*pfv.* **расхвора́ться**] *colloq.* to become ill.

расхва́статься *v.r. pfv., colloq.* to brag endlessly.

расхва́тывать *v. impfv.* [*pfv.* **расхвата́ть**] *colloq.* to buy up; snap up; snatch up.

расхвора́ться *v.r., pfv. of* **расхва́рываться.**

расхити́тель *n.m.* embezzler (*of public property*).

расхища́ть *v. impfv.* [*pfv.* **расхи́тить**] to steal; embezzle; misappropriate.

расхище́ние *n.* theft; embezzlement; misappropriation.

расхля́банный *adj., colloq.* **1,** rickety; wobbly. **2,** *fig.* lax; slack. —**расхля́банность,** *n.f., colloq.* laxity.

расхо́д *n.* **1,** *usu. pl.* expenses. **2,** (*with gen.*) expenditure (of); consumption (of); outlay (of). —**в расхо́де,** *colloq.* in use (*and therefore unavailable*). —**вы́вести** *or* пусти́ть в расхо́д, *colloq.* to shoot; execute.

расходи́ться *v.r. impfv.* [*pfv.* **разойти́сь;** *pres.* **-хожу́сь, -хо́дишься**] **1,** to depart (*in different directions*); disperse. **2,** to pass by each other; miss each other; fail to meet. **3,** to be able to pass by each other (*in a narrow place*). **4,** to part company; (*of a married couple*) separate; break up. **5,** to come apart. **6,** to divide; diverge. **7,** to differ; be at variance. Расходи́ться во мне́ниях, to be of different opinions. **8,** (*of an item*) to sell; be sold out; (*of money*) to be spent. **9,** to gather speed. **10,** *fig.* to get worked up.

расхо́дный *adj.* expense (*attrib.*).

расхо́дование *n.* **1,** spending. **2,** expenditure.

расхо́довать *v. impfv.* [*pfv.* израсхо́довать; *pres.* -дую, -дуешь] **1,** to spend; expend. **2,** *colloq.* to use (up); consume (fuel).

расхожде́ние *n.* **1,** divergence. **2,** discrepancy. **3,** difference: расхожде́ние во мне́ниях, difference of opinion.

расхо́жий *adj., colloq.* **1,** everyday; for everyday use or wear. **2,** in great demand; in great vogue.

расхола́живать *v. impfv.* [*pfv.* расхолоди́ть] to dim the enthusiasm of; dampen the ardor of.

расхоте́ть *v. pfv.* [*infl.* like хоте́ть] *colloq.* to want no longer; lose all desire (to *or* for). —**расхоте́ться**, *refl., impers.* (*with dat.*) *colloq.* = расхоте́ть.

расхохота́ться *v.r. pfv.* [*infl.* -хохочу́сь, -хохо́чешься] to burst out laughing; roar with laughter.

расцара́пывать *v. impfv.* [*pfv.* расцара́пать] to scratch (severely).

расцвести́ [*infl.* like цвести́] *v., pfv. of* расцвета́ть.

расцве́т *n.* **1,** flowering; blooming; blossoming. **2,** *fig.* flowering; golden age. **3,** *fig.* peak; prime: в расцве́те сил *or* своего́ тала́нта, at the peak of one's powers; в расцве́те лет, in the prime of life.

расцвета́ть *v. impfv.* [*pfv.* расцвести́] **1,** to flower; blossom; bloom. **2,** *fig.* (*of a person*) to blossom. **3,** *fig.* (*of one's face*) to light up. **4,** *fig.* to flourish.

расцвети́ть [*infl.* -цвечу́, -цвети́шь] *v., pfv. of* расцве́чивать.

расцве́тка *n.* color scheme; color combination.

расцве́чивать *v. impfv.* [*pfv.* расцвети́ть] *colloq.* to deck; adorn (*with something colorful*).

расцелова́ть *v. pfv.* [*infl.* -лу́ю, -лу́ешь] to kiss fervently; shower with kisses.

расце́нивать *v. impfv.* [*pfv.* расцени́ть] **1,** to price; set a price on. **2,** to assess; estimate; rate. **3,** (*with* как) to regard (as); consider (to be).

расцени́ть [*infl.* -ценю́, -це́нишь] *v., pfv. of* расце́нивать.

расце́нка *n.* **1,** appraisal; valuation. **2,** price; rate. **3,** *usu. pl.* wage rate.

расцепи́ть [*infl.* -цеплю́, -це́пишь] *v., pfv. of* расцепля́ть. —**расцепи́ться**, *refl., pfv. of* расцепля́ться.

расцепля́ть *v. impfv.* [*pfv.* расцепи́ть] to unhook; unhitch; uncouple. —**расцепля́ться**, *refl.* to come unhitched.

расчеса́ть [*infl.* -чешу́, -че́шешь] *v., pfv. of* расчёсывать. —**расчеса́ться**, *refl., pfv. of* расчёсываться.

расчёска [*gen. pl.* -сок] *n., colloq.* comb.

расче́сть *v. pfv.* [*infl.* разочту́, разочтёшь; *past* расчёл, разочла́, разочло́] *colloq.* = рассчита́ть. —**расче́сться**, *refl., colloq.* = рассчита́ться.

расчёсывать *v. impfv.* [*pfv.* расчеса́ть] **1,** to comb. **2,** to scratch (and thus further irritate). —**расчёсываться**, *refl., colloq.* to comb one's hair.

расчёт *n.* **1,** calculation; reckoning: по моему́ расчёту, by my calculations. Это не входи́ло в мой расчёты, that did not enter into my calculations; I had not allowed for that. **2,** payment; settlement. Быть в рас-

чёте с, to be all even with. **3,** discharge; dismissal: дать расчёт (+ *dat.*), to dismiss; fire. **4,** *fig.* retribution: с ним бу́дет коро́ткий расчёт, retribution will be swift. **5,** assumption; expectation: в расчёте на (+ *acc.*), on the expectation of. С таки́м расчётом, что..., on the assumption that...; with the idea that... **6,** selfish consideration: брак по расчёту, marriage for money; marriage of convenience. **7,** *colloq.* benefit; advantage: нет расчёта (+ *inf.*), there is no point in... **8,** *mil.* crew. —**принима́ть в расчёт**, *see* принима́ть.

расчётливость *n.f.* **1,** thrift. **2,** prudence.

расчётливый *adj.* **1,** thrifty. **2,** prudent.

расчётный *adj.* **1,** calculation (*attrib.*). **2,** of payments; pay (*attrib.*). —**расчётная пала́та**, clearing house.

расчи́стить [*infl.* -щу, -стишь] *v., pfv. of* расчища́ть.

расчи́стка *n.* clearing (*of land, roads, etc.*).

расчиха́ться *v.r. pfv., colloq.* to have a fit of sneezing.

расчища́ть *v. impfv.* [*pfv.* расчи́стить] to clear; rid of obstacles.

расчлене́ние *n.* **1,** division. **2,** dismemberment.

расчленя́ть *v. impfv.* [*pfv.* расчлени́ть] **1,** to divide. **2,** to dismember. **3,** to break down (*into component parts*).

расчу́вствоваться *v.r. pfv.* [*infl.* -ствуюсь, -ствуешься] *colloq.* to be deeply touched.

расша́ркиваться *v.r. impfv.* [*pfv.* расша́ркаться] **1,** to bow, scraping one's feet. **2,** (*with* пе́ред) *colloq.* to bow and scrape (before).

расша́танный *adj.* **1,** wobbly; rickety. **2,** (*of one's health*) seriously impaired; (*of one's nerves*) shattered.

расша́тывать *v. impfv.* [*pfv.* расшата́ть] **1,** to shake loose; knock loose. **2,** to make unsteady; make wobbly. **3,** *fig.* to undermine; impair. —**расша́тываться**, *refl.* **1,** to come loose. **2,** to be (*or* become) rickety. **3,** *fig.* to break down; collapse; go to pieces. **4,** *fig.* (*of one's nerves*) to be shattered; (*of one's health*) to give way.

расшвы́ривать *v. impfv.* [*pfv.* расшвыря́ть] *colloq.* to toss in all directions.

расшевели́ть *v. pfv., colloq.* to stir; rouse.

расшиба́ть *v. impfv.* [*pfv.* расшиби́ть] *colloq.* to hurt; bruise; stub. —**расшиба́ться**, *refl., colloq.* to hurt oneself.

расшиби́ть [*infl.* -бу́, -бёшь; *past* -ши́б, -ла] *v., pfv. of* расшиба́ть. —**расшиби́ться**, *refl., pfv. of* расшиба́ться.

расшива́ть *v. impfv.* [*pfv.* расши́ть] **1,** to rip open. **2,** to embroider.

расшире́ние *n.* **1,** widening; broadening. **2,** expansion. **3,** *med.* dilation. —**расшире́ние вен**, varicose veins.

расширя́ть *v. impfv.* [*pfv.* расши́рить] **1,** to widen; broaden. **2,** to enlarge. **3,** *fig.* to broaden; expand. —**расширя́ться**, *refl.* to widen; broaden; expand.

расши́ть [*infl.* разошью́, разошьёшь] *v., pfv. of* расшива́ть.

расшифрова́ть [*infl.* -ру́ю, -ру́ешь] *v., pfv. of* расшифро́вывать.

расшифро́вка *n.* decipherment.

расшифро́вывать *v. impfv.* [*pfv.* расшифрова́ть] to decipher; decode.

расшнурова́ть [*infl.* -ру́ю, -ру́ешь] *v., pfv. of* расшнуро́вывать.

расшнуро́вывать *v. impfv.* [*pfv.* расшнурова́ть] to unlace; untie.

расшуме́ться *v.r. pfv.* [*infl.* -млю́сь, -ми́шься] *colloq.* to become noisy; raise a rumpus.

расще́лина *n.* cleft; crevice; fissure.

расщепи́ть [*infl.* -плю́, -пи́шь] *v.*, *pfv. of* расщепля́ть. —**расщепи́ться**, *refl., pfv. of* расщепля́ться.

расщепле́ние *n.* **1,** splitting: расщепле́ние а́тома, splitting of the atom. **2,** fission: расщепле́ние ядра́, nuclear fission.

расщепля́ть *v. impfv.* [*pfv.* **расщепи́ть**] to split. —**расщепля́ться**, *refl.* to split; be split.

ратификацио́нный *adj.* ratification (*attrib.*): ратификацио́нные гра́моты, instruments of ratification.

ратифика́ция *n.* ratification.

ратифици́ровать *v. impfv. & pfv.* [*pres.* -рую, -руешь] to ratify.

ра́тник *n., obs.* warrior; soldier.

ра́тный *adj., obs.* military.

ра́товать *v. impfv.* [*pres.* -тую, -туешь] **1,** *obs.* to fight in battle. **2,** (*with* за + *acc.*) to fight for; advocate; (*with* про́тив) inveigh (against).

ра́туша *n.* town hall; city hall.

рать *n.f., archaic* **1,** army. **2,** battle.

ра́унд *n., boxing* round.

рафина́д *n.* lump sugar.

рафини́ровать *v. impfv. & pfv.* [*pres.* -рую, -руешь] to refine.

раха́т-луку́м *n.* Turkish delight.

рахи́т *n.* rickets.

рацио́н *n.* ration.

рационализа́ция *n.* application of modern means of efficiency; streamlining.

рационализи́ровать *v. impfv. & pfv.* [*pres.* -рую, -руешь] to apply modern methods of efficiency to; streamline.

рационали́зм *n.* rationalism.

рационали́ст *n.* **1,** rationalist. **2,** rational person. —**рационалисти́ческий**, *adj.* rationalistic.

рациона́льный *adj.* **1,** rational. **2,** efficient. **3,** *math.* rational. —**рациона́льность**, *n.f.* rationality.

ра́ция *n.* portable two-way radio; walkie-talkie.

ра́чий (*fem.* **-чья**) *adj.* of (a) crawfish. —**ра́чьи глаза́**, bulging eyes.

рачи́тельный *adj., obs.* zealous; diligent.

ра́шпер *n.* gridiron; grill.

ра́шпиль *n.m.* rasp.

рвану́ть *v. pfv.* **1,** to tug; jerk. **2,** *colloq.* to dart; dash. **3,** *colloq.* to start with a jerk; lurch forward. —**рвану́ться**, *refl.* = **рвану́ть** (*in senses #2 & #3*).

рва́ный *adj.* **1,** torn; full of holes. **2,** uneven; jagged. **3,** *in* рва́ная ра́на, laceration.

рвань *n.f., colloq.* **1,** tatters; rags. **2,** riffraff.

рвать *v. impfv.* [*pres.* рву, рвёшь; *past fem.* рвала́] **1,** [*pfv.* порва́ть] to tear; tear up. **2,** [*pfv.* порва́ть] to break; snap. **3,** to pull out; tear out; snatch. **4,** to pull off; yank off. **5,** to pick; pluck (flowers). **6,** [*pfv.* порва́ть] to break off; sever (ties, relations, etc.). **7,** to blow up. **8,** [*pfv.* вы́рвать] *impers., colloq.* to vomit; throw up: его́ рвёт, he is throwing up. —**рвать и мета́ть**, to be in a rage; rant and rave. —**рвать на себе́ во́лосы**, to tear one's hair. —**рвать на ча́сти**, to harass; harry; beset.

рва́ться *v.r. impfv.* [*pfv.* порва́ться; *pres.* рвусь; рвёшься; *past* рва́лся, рвала́сь, рвало́сь *or* рва́лось, рвали́сь *or* рва́лись] **1,** to tear; become torn. **2,** (*of a rope, thread, etc.*) to break; snap. **3,** [*impfv.*

only] to burst; explode. **4,** (*of ties, relations, etc.*) to be broken off. **5,** [*impfv. only*] (*with various prepositions*) to thirst for; be dying for.

рвач [*gen.* рвача́] *n., colloq.* crook; chiseler.

рве́ние *n.* zeal; ardor.

рво́та *n.* vomiting.

рво́тный *adj.* **1,** pert. to vomiting: рво́тная ма́сса, vomit. **2,** inducing vomiting; emetic: рво́тное сре́дство, an emetic. —**рво́тное**, *n.* emetic.

рдест *n.* pondweed.

рдеть *v. impfv.* (*of anything red*) to glow.

ре *n. neut., music* re; D.

реабилита́ция *n.* rehabilitation.

реабилити́ровать *v. impfv. & pfv.* [*pres.* -рую, -руешь] to rehabilitate.

реаге́нт *n.* reagent.

реаги́ровать *v. impfv.* [*pres.* -рую, -руешь] (*with* на + *acc.*) to react (to).

реакти́в *n.* reagent.

реакти́вный *adj.* **1,** reactive. **2,** jet; jet-propelled. **3,** rocket (*attrib.*): реакти́вная устано́вка, rocket launcher. Реакти́вный снаря́д, missile.

реа́ктор *n.* reactor.

реакционе́р *n.* reactionary.

реакцио́нный *adj.* reactionary.

реа́кция *n.* **1,** reaction (*in various senses*). **2,** *polit.* reaction; extreme conservatism.

реализа́ция *n.* **1,** realization; achievement. **2,** selling; converting to cash.

реали́зм *n.* realism.

реализова́ть *v. impfv. & pfv.* [*pres.* -зу́ю, -зу́ешь] **1,** to realize; bring about; see fulfilled. **2,** to sell; convert into cash. —**реализова́ться**, *refl.* to be realized; materialize.

реали́ст *n.* realist. —**реалисти́ческий**, *adj.* realistic.

реа́льность *n.f.* reality.

реа́льный *adj.* [*short form* реа́лен, реа́льна] **1,** real. **2,** realistic; practical. —**реа́льное учи́лище**, pre-rev. secondary school stressing scientific subjects (*as opposed to the classics*).

реанима́ция *n.* reanimation; resuscitation.

ребёнок [*gen.* -нка; *pl.* ребя́та, ребя́т] *n.* child; baby.

рёберный *adj.* rib (*attrib.*).

ребо́рда *n.* flange (*of a wheel*).

ребри́стый *adj.* **1,** having prominent ribs. **2,** ribbed.

ребро́ [*pl.* рёбра, рёбер] *n.* **1,** rib. **2,** edge. —**поста́вить вопро́с ребро́м**, to put a question pointblank.

ре́бус *n.* **1,** rebus. **2,** *fig.* enigma.

ребя́та [*gen.* ребя́т] *n. pl.* **1,** *pl. of* ребёнок. **2,** *colloq.* lads; boys.

ребяти́шки [*gen.* -шек] *n. pl., colloq.* children; kids.

ребя́ческий *adj.* **1,** child's; of a child. **2,** childish.

ребя́чество *n.* **1,** *obs.* childhood. **2,** childishness.

ребя́чий [*fem.* -чья] *adj., colloq.* **1,** child's; children's. **2,** childish.

ребя́читься *v.r. impfv., colloq.* to behave childishly.

рёв *n.* **1,** roar. **2,** *colloq.* howl (*of a child*).

рева́нш *n.* **1,** revenge (*after a defeat*): взять рева́нш, to gain revenge. **2,** *in* матч-рева́нш, return match. —**реванши́зм**, *n.* revanchism. —**реванши́ст**, *n.* revanchist.

ревéнь [*gen.* ревеня́] *n.m.* rhubarb. —**ревённый**, *adj.* rhubarb.

реверáнс *n.* curtsy.

реверберáция *n.* reverberation.

реве́ть *v. impfv.* [*pres.* реву́, ревёшь] **1,** to roar. **2,**

fig. (*of a storm, the sea, etc.*) to rage. **3,** *colloq.* to howl; bawl.

ревизиони́зм *n.* revisionism. —**ревизиони́ст,** *n.* revisionist. —**ревизиони́стский,** *adj.* revisionist (*attrib.*).

реви́зия *n.* **1,** inspection. **2,** audit; auditing. **3,** revision. —**ревизио́нный,** *adj.* inspection (*attrib.*); auditing.

ревизова́ть *v. impfv. & pfv.* [*pres.* -зу́ю, -зу́ешь] **1,** to inspect. **2,** to audit. **3,** to revise.

ревизо́р *n.* inspector.

ревмати́зм *n.* rheumatism. —**ревма́тик,** *n.,* *colloq.* rheumatic. —**ревмати́ческий,** *adj.* rheumatic.

ревмя́ *adv.* в ревмя́ реве́ть, *colloq.* to howl.

ревни́вец [*gen.* -вца] *n., colloq.* jealous person.

ревни́вый *adj.* jealous. —**ревни́во,** *adv.* jealously.

ревни́тель *n.m., obs.* ardent supporter.

ревнова́ть *v. impfv.* [*pres.* -ну́ю, -ну́ешь] to be jealous of: он ревну́ет жену́ к Са́ше, he is jealous of Sasha because his wife likes him; he is jealous over the fact that his wife likes Sasha.

ре́вностный *adj.* ardent; zealous.

ре́вность *n.f.* **1,** jealousy. **2,** *obs.* zeal; ardor.

револьве́р *n.* revolver.

револьве́рный *adj.* revolver (*attrib.*). —**револьве́рный стано́к,** turret lathe.

революционе́р *n.* revolutionary; revolutionist.

революционизи́ровать *v. impfv. & pfv.* [*pres.* -рую, -руешь] to revolutionize.

револю́ция *n.* revolution. —**революцио́нный,** *adj.* revolutionary.

реву́н [*gen.* -вуна́] *n.* **1,** *colloq.* child who is always crying or yelling. **2,** howling monkey.

ревю́ *n. neut. indecl.* revue.

рега́лии *n. pl.* [*sing.* рега́лия] regalia.

рега́та *n.* regatta.

ре́гби (рэ) *n. neut. indecl.* rugby.

регенера́ция *n.* regeneration. —**регенерати́вный,** *adj.* regenerative.

ре́гент *n.* **1,** regent. **2,** director of a church choir. —**ре́гентство,** *n.* regency.

регио́н *n.* region. —**региона́льный,** *adj.* regional.

реги́стр *n.* **1,** register; list. **2,** *music* register. **3,** *music* stop (*of an organ, reed instrument, etc.*).

регистра́тор *n.* registering clerk; registrar. —**регистрату́ра,** *n.* registration office; registry.

регистра́ция *n.* registration. —**регистрацио́нный,** *adj.* registration (*attrib.*).

регистри́ровать *v. impfv.* [*pfv.* зарегистри́ровать; *pres.* -рую, -руешь] to register; record. —**регистри́роваться,** *refl.* **1,** to register. **2,** to register one's marriage.

регла́мент *n.* **1,** *obs.* regulations; rules. **2,** order of business; agenda. **3,** *colloq.* speaker's allotted time.

регламента́ция *n.* regulation.

регламенти́ровать *v. impfv. & pfv.* [*pres.* -рую, -руешь] to regulate.

регла́н *n.* raglan.

регре́сс *n.* regression; retrogression. —**регресси́вный,** *adj.* regressive; retrogressive.

регресси́ровать *v. impfv.* [*pres.* -рую, -руешь] to regress; retrogress.

регули́рование *n.* regulation; adjustment.

регули́ровать *v. impfv.* [*pres.* -рую, -руешь] **1,** to regulate. **2,** [*pfv.* отрегули́ровать] to adjust.

регулиро́вка *n.* **1,** regulation. **2,** adjustment.

регуля́рный *adj.* regular. —**регуля́рно,** *adv.* regularly. —**регуля́рность,** *n.f.* regularity.

регуля́тор *n., mech.* regulator; governor.

редакти́рование *n.* editing.

редакти́ровать *v. impfv.* [*pfv.* отредакти́ровать; *pres.* -рую, -руешь] to edit.

реда́ктор *n.* editor. —**реда́кторский,** *adj.* editorial; editor's.

редакцио́нный *adj.* editorial; editing (*attrib.*). —**редакцио́нная колле́гия,** editorial board. —**редакцио́нная статья́,** editorial.

реда́кция *n.* **1,** editing. Под реда́кцией (+ *gen.*), edited by... **2,** wording. **3,** version; edition: первонача́льная реда́кция, original version/edition. **4,** editorial staff. **5,** editorial office: письмо́ в реда́кцию, letter to the editor.

реде́ть *v. impfv.* [*pfv.* **пореде́ть**] to thin out.

реди́с *n.* **1,** radish (*plant*). **2,** radishes.

реди́ска [*gen. pl.* -сок] *n.* radish.

ре́дкий *adj.* [*comp.* ре́же] **1,** rare. **2,** (*of trains, visits, etc.*) infrequent. **3,** (*of a forest, vegetation, etc.*) sparse. **4,** (*of hair*) thin; (*of teeth*) widely spaced.

ре́дко *adv.* rarely; seldom. —**ре́дко когда́,** very rarely; very seldom.

редколле́гия *n.* = редакцио́нная колле́гия.

ре́дкостный *adj.* rare.

ре́дкость *n.f.* **1,** rarity. **2,** a rarity. **3,** thinness; sparseness. —**на ре́дкость,** exceptionally: зима́ была́ на ре́дкость холо́дной, the winter was exceptionally cold.

реду́кция *n.* reduction (*in various technical senses*).

реду́т *n.* redoubt.

ре́дька *n.* radish.

редю́йт *n.* redoubt.

рее́стр *n.* register; list; log.

ре́же *adj., comp. of* ре́дкий. —*adv., comp. of* ре́дко.

режи́м *n.* **1,** regime. **2,** regimen: больни́чный режи́м, hospital regimen. **3,** procedures: режи́м безопа́сности, safety procedures. **4,** conditions: температу́рный режи́м, temperature conditions.

режиссёр *n., theat.* director.

режисси́ровать *v. impfv.* [*pres.* -рую, -руешь] *theat.* to direct.

режиссу́ра *n.* **1,** direction (*of a play or film*). **2,** directors.

ре́жущий *adj.* **1,** cutting. **2,** (*of a pain*) sharp.

реза́к [*gen.* -зака́] *n.* large knife; cutter.

ре́зальщик *n.* cutter (*person*).

ре́зание *n.* cutting.

ре́заный *adj.* **1,** cut. **2,** sliced.

ре́зать *v. impfv.* [*pres.* ре́жу, ре́жешь] **1,** to cut. **2,** to slice. **3,** *colloq.* to cut open (*surgically*). **4,** to carve; engrave. **5,** [*pfv.* заре́зать] to kill; slaughter. **6,** [*pfv.* сре́зать] *sports* to slice (a ball). —**ре́зать глаз** *or* глаза́, to offend the eye. —**ре́зать у́хо** *or* слух, to grate on one's ears.

ре́заться *v.r. impfv.* [*pres.* ре́жусь, ре́жешься] **1,** to cut; be cut; be able to be cut. **2,** *colloq.* to fight (*with swords*). **3,** *colloq.* (*of teeth*) to cut through: у ребёнка ре́жутся зу́бы, the child is teething.

резви́ться *v.r. impfv.* [*pres.* -влю́сь, -ви́шься] to romp; frolic; rollick.

ре́звость *n.f.* **1,** playfulness. **2,** speed (*of a horse*).

ре́звый *adj.* **1,** playful; frisky. **2,** (*of a horse*) fast; fast-running.

резеда́ *n.* mignonette.

резе́кция *n., med.* resection.

резе́рв *n.* **1,** reserve: резе́рвы зерна́, reserves of grain. Име́ть в резе́рве, to have in reserve. **2,** *mil.* reserve; reserves.

резерва́ция *n.* (Indian) reservation.

резерви́ровать *v. impfv. & pfv.* [*pres.* -рую, -руешь] to keep in reserve.

резерви́ст *n.* reservist.

резе́рвный *adj.* reserve (*attrib.*).

резервуа́р *n.* reservoir.

резе́ц [*gen.* -зца́] *n.* **1,** cutting tool; cutter. **2,** incisor (*tooth*).

резиде́нт *n.* **1,** resident governor. **2,** resident alien. **3,** chief of a country's intelligence operations in another country.

резиде́нция *n.* residence.

рези́на *n.* rubber.

рези́нка [*gen. pl.* -нок] *n.* **1,** eraser. **2,** elastic band. **3,** rubber band. **4,** garter. —жева́тельная рези́нка, chewing gum.

рези́новый *adj.* rubber.

ре́зка *n.* cutting.

ре́зкий *adj.* [*short form* ре́зок, резка́, ре́зко; *comp.* ре́зче] **1,** (*of a voice*) shrill. **2,** (*of an odor*) pungent. **3,** (*of light*) glaring. **4,** (*of cold, wind, etc.*) biting. **5,** (*of features*) sharp. **6,** (*of movements*) jerky. **7,** (*of words, criticism, etc.*) harsh. **8,** (*of a change*) abrupt; drastic. **9,** (*of a person, manners, etc.*) abrupt; brusque.

ре́зко *adv.* **1,** sharply. **2,** harshly. **3,** abruptly.

ре́зкость *n.f.* **1,** harshness; sharpness; abruptness. **2,** sharpness; clarity; definition. **3,** *pl.* harsh words.

резно́й *adj.* carved.

резня́ *n.* slaughter; massacre; butchery; carnage.

резолю́ция *n.* resolution.

резо́н *n.*, *colloq.* reason.

резона́нс *n.* **1,** resonance. **2,** *fig.* reaction; response.

резона́тор *n.* resonator.

резонёр *n.* sermonizer; preacher.

резони́ровать *v. impfv.* [*pres.* -рую, -руешь] to resound.

резо́нный *adj.*, *colloq.* reasonable.

результа́т *n.* **1,** result. **2,** *sports* (one's) score; showing: показа́ть лу́чший результа́т, to achieve the best score. —в результа́те, **1,** as a result. **2,** (*with gen.*) as a result of.

результати́вный *adj.* effective; successful.

ре́зче *adj.*, *comp. of* ре́зкий.

ре́зчик *n.* carver; engraver.

резь *n.f.* sharp pain.

резьба́ *n.* **1,** carving. **2,** thread (*of a screw*).

резюме́ (мэ) *n. neut. indecl.* résumé.

резюми́ровать *v. impfv. & pfv.* [*pres.* -рую, -руешь] to summarize; sum up.

рейд *n.* **1,** *naut.* roadstead. **2,** *mil.* raid. **3,** unannounced investigation.

ре́йка [*gen. pl.* ре́ек] *n.* **1,** strip of wood. **2,** measuring rod. —зубча́тая ре́йка, rack (*for a pinion*).

рейс *n.* **1,** trip; voyage: пе́рвый рейс, maiden voyage. **2,** flight: рейс сто во́семь, flight 108.

рейсши́на *n.* T square.

рейту́зы [*gen.* -ту́з] *n. pl.* **1,** riding breeches. **2,** long knit pants.

река́ [*acc.* реку́ *or* ре́ку; *pl.* ре́ки, рек, река́м *or* ре́кам] *n.* river.

ре́квием *n.* requiem.

реквизи́ровать *v. impfv. & pfv.* [*pres.* -рую, -руешь] to requisition; commandeer.

реквизи́т *n.*, *theat.* properties; stage props.

реквизи́ция *n.* requisitioning.

рекла́ма *n.* **1,** advertising; publicity. **2,** advertisement; commercial. **3,** sign: нео́новая рекла́ма, neon sign.

реклами́ровать *v. impfv. & pfv.* [*pres.* -рую, -руешь] to advertise; publicize.

рекла́мный *adj.* advertising (*attrib.*); publicity (*attrib.*); promotional. —рекла́мный щит, billboard.

рекогносци́ровать *v. impfv. & pfv.* [*pres.* -рую, -руешь] to reconnoiter.

рекогносциро́вка *n.* reconnaissance. —рекогносциро́вочный, *adj.* reconnaissance (*attrib.*).

рекоменда́тельный *adj.* of recommendation: рекоменда́тельное письмо́, letter of recommendation.

рекоменда́ция *n.* recommendation: дать рекоменда́цию, to make a recommendation.

рекомендова́ть *v. impfv. & pfv.* [*pfv. also* порекомендова́ть; *pres.* -ду́ю, -ду́ешь] to recommend. —рекомендова́ться, *refl.* **1,** [*impfv. only*] to be recommended. **2,** [*pfv. also* отрекомендова́ться] to introduce oneself.

реконструи́ровать *v. impfv. & pfv.* [*pres.* -рую, -руешь] to reconstruct.

реконстру́кция *n.* reconstruction. —реконструкти́вный, *adj.* reconstruction (*attrib.*).

реко́рд *n.* record: поста́вить реко́рд, to set a record.

рекорди́ст *n.* **1,** record holder. **2,** (*of an animal*) prize-winner.

реко́рдный *adj.* record (*attrib.*); record-breaking.

рекордсме́н *n.* record holder.

ре́крут *n.*, *pre-rev.* recruit.

ре́ктор *n.* rector (*of a university*).

реле́ (рэ) *n. neut. indecl.*, *electricity* relay.

религио́зный *adj.* religious.

рели́гия *n.* religion.

рели́квия *n.* relic.

рели́кт *n.* relic; ancient artifact.

релье́ф *n.*, *art; topog.* relief.

релье́фно *adv.* in relief.

релье́фный *adj.* **1,** carved in relief. **2,** (*of a surface, design, etc.*) raised. **3,** *fig.* vivid; graphic. —релье́фная ка́рта, relief map.

рельс *n.*, *R.R.* rail; track. —ре́льсовый, *adj.* rail (*attrib.*).

рема́рка [*gen. pl.* -рок] *n.* **1,** note. **2,** *theat.* stage direction.

ремённый *adj.* **1,** of, from, or for a belt. **2,** *mech.* belt (*attrib.*): ремённый приво́д; ремённая переда́ча, belt drive.

реме́нь [*gen.* ремня́] *n.m.* **1,** strap. **2,** belt. —привязно́й реме́нь, seat belt. —реме́нь вентиля́тора, fan belt.

реме́сленник *n.* craftsman; artisan.

реме́сленный *adj.* **1,** craft (*attrib.*). **2,** *fig.* pedestrian; unimaginative. —реме́сленное учи́лище, vocational school.

ремесло́ [*pl.* ремёсла, -сел] *n.* trade; craft.

ремешо́к [*gen.* -шка́] *n.* small strap.

реми́ссия *n.*, *med.* remission.

ремо́нт *n.* repair; repairs. Быть в ремо́нте, to be under (*or* undergoing) repair.

ремонти́ровать *v. impfv. & pfv.* [*pfv. also* отремонти́ровать; *pres.* -ру́ю, -ру́ешь] to repair; renovate; refurbish; overhaul; recondition.

ремо́нтный *adj.* repair (*attrib.*).

ренега́т *n.* renegade; turncoat. —ренега́тство, *n.* desertion; apostasy.

ре́ний *n.* rhenium.

рено́нс *n., cards* revoke.

ре́нта *n., econ.* rent. —ежего́дная ре́нта, annuity.

рента́бельный *adj.* profitable; paying. Рента́бельное предприя́тие, going concern.

рентге́н *n., colloq.* 1, X-rays. 2, X-ray machine.

рентге́нов *adj., in* рентге́новы лучи́, X-rays.

рентге́новский *adj.* X-ray (*attrib.*).

рентгеногра́мма *n.* X-ray; X-ray photograph.

рентгеноло́гия *n.* radiology. —рентгено́лог, *n.* radiologist.

рентгеноскопи́я *n.* X-raying; X-ray examination.

рентгенотерапи́я *n.* X-ray therapy.

реорганиза́ция *n.* reorganization.

реорганизова́ть *v. impfv. & pfv.* [*pres.* -зу́ю, -зу́ешь] to reorganize.

реоста́т *n.* rheostat.

ре́па *n.* turnip.

репара́ции *n. pl.* [*sing.* -ция] reparations. —репарацио́нный, *adj.* reparations (*attrib.*).

репатриа́нт *n.* repatriate. —репатриа́ция, *n.* repatriation.

репатрии́ровать *v. impfv. & pfv.* [*pres.* -ру́ю, -ру́ешь] to repatriate.

репе́йник *n.* 1, burdock. 2, bur.

репе́р *n.* bench mark.

репертуа́р *n.* repertoire. —репертуа́рный, *adj.* repertory (*attrib.*).

репети́ровать *v. impfv.* [*pfv.* прорепети́ровать; *pres.* -ру́ю, -ру́ешь] 1, to rehearse. 2, [*impfv. only*] to coach; tutor.

репети́тор *n.* tutor; coach. —репети́торский, *adj.* tutoring (*attrib.*); tutorial. —репети́торство, *n.* tutoring.

репети́ция *n.* rehearsal. —репетицио́нный, *adj.* rehearsal (*attrib.*).

ре́плика *n.* 1, retort; rejoinder. 2, *theat.* cue.

реполо́в *n.* linnet.

репорта́ж *n.* 1, report (*in the news media*). 2, reporting.

репортёр *n.* reporter.

репресси́вный *adj.* repressive.

репресси́ровать *v. impfv. & pfv.* [*pres.* -ру́ю, -ру́ешь] to subject to repression.

репре́ссия *n.* repression.

репри́за *n.* reprise.

репроду́ктор *n.* loudspeaker.

репроду́кция *n.* reproduction; copy.

репута́ция *n.* reputation.

ре́пчатый *adj., in* ре́пчатый лук, onion.

ресни́ца *n.* eyelash.

респекта́бельный *adj.* respectable. —респекта́-бельность, *n.f.* respectability.

респира́тор *n.* respirator.

респу́блика *n.* republic.

республика́нец [*gen.* -нца] *n.* republican.

республика́нский *adj.* 1, republican. 2, of a republic of the USSR.

рессо́ра *n.* spring (*on a vehicle*). —рессо́рный, *adj.* on springs; having springs.

реставра́тор *n.* restorer (*of works of art*).

реставра́ция *n.* restoration.

реставри́ровать *v. impfv. & pfv.* [*pres.* -ру́ю, -ру́ешь] to restore.

рестора́н *n.* restaurant. —рестора́нный, *adj.* restaurant (*attrib.*).

ресу́рс *n.* 1, *pl.* resources: приро́дные ресу́рсы, natural resources. 2, resort; recourse: после́дний ресу́рс, last resort.

рети́вый *adj.* zealous. —рети́во, *adv.* zealously. —рети́вость, *n.f.* zeal.

рети́на *n.* retina.

ретирова́ться *v.r impfv. & pfv.* [*pres.* -ру́юсь, -ру́ешься] *colloq.* to retire; withdraw.

рето́рта *n.* retort (*vessel*).

ретроспекти́вный *adj.* retrospective. —ретроспе́к-ция, *n.* retrospection.

ретушёр *n.* retoucher.

ретуши́ровать *v. impfv. & pfv.* [*pres.* -ру́ю, -ру́ешь] *photog.* to retouch.

ре́тушь *n.f.* retouching.

рефера́т *n.* 1, synopsis; abstract. 2, paper; essay.

рефере́ндум *n.* referendum.

рефере́нт *n.* 1, reader; reviewer. 2, adviser; consultant.

рефери́ровать *v. impfv. & pfv.* [*pres.* -ру́ю, -ру́ешь] to abstract; make a synopsis of.

рефле́кс *n.* reflex.

рефлекти́вный *adj.* = рефлекто́рный.

рефле́ктор *n.* 1, reflector. 2, reflecting telescope.

рефлекто́рный *adj.* reflex: рефлекто́рная реа́к-ция, reflex reaction.

рефо́рма *n.* reform. —реформа́тор, *n.* reformer.

реформа́тский *adj., in* реформа́тская це́рковь, Reformed Church.

реформа́ция *n., hist.* the Reformation.

реформи́ровать *v. impfv. & pfv.* [*pres.* -ру́ю, -ру́ешь] to reform.

рефра́ктор *n.* refracting telescope; refractor.

рефра́кция *n.* refraction.

рефре́н *n.* refrain.

рефрижера́тор *n.* refrigerator.

рехну́ться *v.r. pfv., colloq.* to go mad; go crazy.

рецензе́нт *n.* reviewer; critic.

рецензи́ровать *v. impfv.* [*pfv.* прорецензи́ровать; *pres.* -ру́ю, -ру́ешь] to review.

реце́нзия *n.* review: реце́нзия на кни́гу (*or* о кни́ге), book review.

реце́пт *n.* 1, prescription. 2, recipe.

рецесси́вный *adj., biol.* recessive.

рециди́в *n.* 1, recurrence. 2, *med.* relapse. 3, *law* second offense.

рецидиви́зм *n.* recidivism. —рецидиви́ст, *n.* recidivist.

речево́й *adj.* speech (*attrib.*).

рече́ние *n.* expression; locution.

речи́стый *adj., colloq.* 1, eloquent. 2, talkative.

речитати́в *n., music* recitative. —говори́ть *or* чита́ть речитати́вом, to intone.

ре́чка [*gen. pl.* -чек] *n.* small river.

речно́й *adj.* river (*attrib.*).

речь [*pl.* ре́чи, рече́й, реча́м] *n.f.* 1, speech: о́рганы ре́чи, organs of speech. 2, a speech: произноси́ть речь, to make a speech. —речь идёт о, the question is one of; it is a question of. —**об э́том не мо́жет быть и ре́чи**, that is out of the question.

реша́ть v. impfv. [pfv. **реши́ть**] **1**, (with inf.) to decide (to). **2**, to decide (an issue, the outcome of something, etc.). **3**, to solve. —**реша́ться**, refl. **1**, (with inf.) to make up one's mind (to); (with **на** + acc.) decide on. **2**, (with inf.) to dare (to); bring oneself (to). **3**, to be decided.

реша́ющий adj. deciding; decisive. —**с реша́ющим го́лосом**, voting: член с реша́ющим го́лосом, voting member.

реше́ние n. **1**, decision. **2**, solution.

решётка [gen. pl. -**ток**] n. grating; grate; lattice; grille. Ками́нная решётка, fire screen. —**посади́ть за решётку**, to put behind bars; imprison. —**сиде́ть за решёткой**, to be behind bars.

решето́ [pl. **решёта**] n. strainer; sieve.

решётчатый adj. lattice (attrib.); latticed.

реши́мость n.f. determination; resoluteness; resolve.

реши́тельно adv. **1**, decisively. **2**, strongly; emphatically; categorically. **3**, absolutely.

реши́тельность n.f. **1**, decisiveness. **2**, determination.

реши́тельный adj. **1**, (of a person, action, result, moment, etc.) decisive. **2**, (of an answer) definite. **3**, (of a refusal, protest, gesture, etc.) emphatic.

реши́ть v., pfv. of **реша́ть**. —**реши́ться**, refl., pfv. of **реша́ться**.

ре́шка n., in **орёл и́ли ре́шка?**, heads or tails?

ре́ять v. impfv. [pres. **ре́ю, ре́ешь**] **1**, to soar; glide. **2**, to hover. **3**, to flutter.

ржа́веть v. impfv. [pfv. **заржа́веть**] to rust.

ржа́вчина n. rust.

ржа́вый adj. **1**, rusty. **2**, rust-colored.

ржа́ние n. neighing.

ржа́нка [gen. pl. -**нок**] n. plover.

ржано́й adj. rye (attrib.): ржано́й хлеб, rye bread.

ржать v. impfv. [pres. **ржёт**] to neigh.

ри́га n. threshing barn.

ри́за n. **1**, chasuble. **2**, metal plating on an icon.

ри́зница n. sacristy; vestry.

рикоше́т n. ricochet; rebound. —**рикоше́том**, on the rebound.

рикошети́ровать v. impfv. & pfv. [pres. -**рует**] to ricochet.

ри́кша [gen. pl. **рикш**] n. **1**, n.f. rickshaw. **2**, n.m. rickshaw driver.

ри́млянин [pl. **ри́мляне, ри́млян**] n.m. [fem. **ри́млянка**] Roman.

ри́мский adj. Roman.

ринг n. boxing ring.

ри́нуться v.r. pfv. **1**, to dash; rush: ри́нуться к вы́ходу, to dash/rush for the exit. Ри́нуться помо́чь (+ dat.), to rush to help (someone). **2**, fig. (with **в** + acc.) to plunge into (a task, battle, etc.).

рис n. rice.

риск n. risk. Идти́ на риск, to take a risk; take a chance. —**на свой страх и риск**, at one's own risk.

рискну́ть v. pfv. **1**, pfv. of **рискова́ть**. **2**, (with inf.) to dare (to); venture (to).

риско́ванный adj. **1**, risky. **2**, risqué.

рискова́ть v. impfv. [pfv. **рискну́ть**; pres. -**ку́ю, -ку́ешь**] **1**, to take a chance; take chances. **2**, (with instr.) to risk. **3**, (with inf.) to risk; run the risk of.

рисова́льный adj. drawing (attrib.).

рисова́льщик n. (graphic) artist.

рисова́ние n. drawing.

рисова́ть v. impfv. [pfv. **нарисова́ть**; pres. -**су́ю, -су́ешь**] **1**, to draw. **2**, fig. to paint; portray. —**рисова́ться**, refl. [impfv. only] **1**, to appear; loom; be silhouetted. **2**, fig. (with dat.) to appear (to); seem (to). **3**, to show off.

рисо́вка n. **1**, obs. drawing. **2**, showing off; pretentiousness.

ри́совый adj. rice (attrib.).

рису́нок [gen. -**нка**] n. **1**, a drawing. **2**, design; pattern. **3**, (when accompanying a scientific article) figure.

ритм n. rhythm.

ри́тмика n. **1**, rhythm. **2**, rhythmics.

ритми́ческий adj. rhythmic; rhythmical.

ритми́чный adj. rhythmic; rhythmical. —**ритми́чность**, n.f. rhythm.

рито́рика n. rhetoric. —**ритори́ческий**, adj. rhetorical.

ритуа́л n. ritual. —**ритуа́льный**, adj. ritual.

риф n. reef.

рифлёный adj. corrugated; fluted.

ри́фма n. rhyme.

рифма́ч [gen. -**мача́**] n., colloq. rhymer; rhymester.

рифмова́ть v. impfv. [pres. -**му́ю, -му́ешь**] to rhyme; make (something) rhyme. —**рифмова́ться**, refl. (of words, sounds, etc.) to rhyme.

рифмоплёт n., colloq. rhymer; rhymester.

ро́ба n. overalls.

ро́ббер n., cards rubber.

робе́ть v. impfv. to be timid; be shy.

ро́бкий adj. [short form ро́бок, робка́, ро́бко; comp. ро́бче] timid; shy. —**не из ро́бкого деся́тка**, not the timid type.

ро́бко adv. timidly.

ро́бость n.f. timidity; shyness.

ро́бот n. robot.

ров [gen. **рва**; 2nd loc. **рву**] n. ditch. —**крепостно́й ров**, moat.

рове́сник n. person one's own age; contemporary.

ро́вно adv. **1**, evenly. **2**, exactly; precisely: ро́вно в де́сять часо́в, at ten o'clock sharp. **3**, colloq. absolutely: ро́вно ничего́, absolutely nothing.

ро́вность n.f. **1**, evenness. **2**, fig. equanimity.

ро́вный adj. [short form ро́вен, ровна́, ро́вно] **1**, even; level. **2**, straight. **3**, even; steady; equable. **4**, fig. even-tempered. —**для ро́вного счёта**, to make it come out even. —**ро́вным счётом**, **1**, exactly. **2**, only. —**ро́вным счётом ничего́**, absolutely nothing.

ро́вня also, **ровня́** n.m. & f., colloq. (one's) equal.

ровня́ть v. impfv. [pfv. **сровня́ть**] to even; level.

рог [pl. **рога́**] n. **1**, horn; antler. **2**, horn: труби́ть в рог, to blow a horn. —**брать быка́ за рога́**, to take the bull by the horns. —**наставля́ть рога́** (+ dat.), colloq. to cuckold.

рога́стый adj., colloq. having large horns or antlers.

рога́тка [gen. pl. -**ток**] n. **1**, bar; barrier. **2**, fig. obstacle. **3**, slingshot.

рога́тый adj. horned. —**кру́пный/ме́лкий рога́тый скот**, see скот.

рога́ч [gen. -**гача́**] n. **1**, stag; hart. **2**, stag beetle.

рогови́ца n. cornea.

роговой adj. **1**, made of horn. **2**, (of glasses) horn-rimmed. **3**, horny. **4**, music for (the) horn. —**рогова́я обма́нка**, hornblende. —**рогова́я оболо́чка**, cornea.

рого́жа *n.* matting.

рого́з *n.* cattail.

рогоно́сец [*gen.* -сца] *n., colloq.* cuckold.

род *n.* **1,** family. **2,** birth; origin; stock. **3,** sort; kind. **4,** gender. **5,** genus. **6,** *in* челове́ческий род, the human race. **7,** *in* род заня́тий *or* де́ятельности, line of work; occupation; profession. **8,** *in* род войск, *mil.* arm of service. —вести́ свой род от..., to trace one's ancestry back to... —в не́котором ро́де, to a certain extent; in a certain sense; in a way. —в своём ро́де, in his way; in its way. —вся́кого ро́да (+ *nom.*), all sorts of. —из ро́да в род, from generation to generation. —от роду, of age: ему́ два́дцать лет от роду, he is twenty years of age. —своего́ ро́да, a kind of. —тако́го ро́да (+ *nom.*), such. —что́-то в э́том ро́де, something like that. *See also* ро́дом *and* ро́ды.

ро́дий *n.* rhodium.

роди́льница *n.* woman who has just given birth.

роди́льный *adj.* **1,** maternity (*attrib.*): роди́льное отделе́ние, maternity ward; delivery room. **2,** puerperal: роди́льная горя́чка, puerperal fever.

роди́мый *adj., colloq.* **1,** native. **2,** one's own. —роди́мое пятно́, birthmark.

ро́дина *n.* native land; homeland; motherland.

роди́нка [*gen. pl.* -нок] *n.* mole; birthmark.

роди́тели [*gen.* -лей] *n. pl.* parents.

роди́тельный *adj., in* роди́тельный паде́ж, genitive case.

роди́тельский *adj.* parental; parents'.

роди́ть *v. pfv.* [*infl.* рожу́, роди́шь; *past fem.* родила́] **1,** *pfv. of* рожа́ть *and* рожда́ть; to sire; father; beget. —роди́ться, *refl., pfv. of* рожда́ться.

родни́к [*gen.* -ника́] *n.* spring (*of water*). —роднико́вый, *adj.* spring (*attrib.*).

родни́ть *v. impfv.* [*pfv.* сродни́ть *or* породни́ть] to unite; bring together. —родни́ться, *refl.* [*pfv.* породни́ться] (*with* с + *instr.*) to become related to.

родно́й *adj.* **1,** related by blood. Родно́й брат, brother (*as opposed to* двою́родный брат — cousin). **2,** native: родна́я дере́вня, one's native village. Родно́й го́род, home town. **3,** *in direct address,* my dear. —родны́е, *n. pl.* relatives.

родня́ *n.* **1,** relatives. **2,** *colloq.* relative.

родови́тый *adj.* of noble birth. —родови́тость, *n.f.* noble birth.

родово́й *adj.* **1,** family (*attrib.*). **2,** ancestral. **3,** tribal. **4,** *biol.* generic. **5,** *gram.* gender (*attrib.*). **6,** birth (*attrib.*): родовы́е поту́ги, birth pains; labor pains.

рододе́ндрон (дэ) *n.* rhododendron.

ро́дом *adv.* by birth: он ро́дом из Фра́нции, he is a native of France; he is a Frenchman by birth.

родонача́льник *n.* **1,** progenitor. **2,** *fig.* father; founder.

родосло́вие *n.* genealogy; pedigree; lineage. *Also,* родосло́вная.

родосло́вный *adj.* genealogical. —родосло́вное де́рево, family tree.

ро́дственник *n.* relative; relation.

ро́дственный *adj.* **1,** family (*attrib.*): ро́дственные свя́зи, family ties; ties of kinship. **2,** (*of languages, peoples, sciences, etc.*) related. **3,** *fig.* warm; cordial.

родство́ *n.* **1,** relationship; kinship: быть в родстве́ с, to be related to. **2,** *colloq.* relatives. **3,** affinity.

ро́ды [*gen.* ро́дов] *n. pl.* birth; childbirth.

ро́жа *n.* **1,** erysipelas (*skin disease*). **2,** *colloq.* ugly face; ugly mug; ugly puss.

рожа́ть *v. impfv.* [*pfv.* роди́ть] **1,** *v.i.* to give birth; have a baby. **2,** *v.t.* to give birth to; bear.

рожда́емость *n.f.* birth rate.

рожда́ть *v. impfv.* [*pfv.* роди́ть] **1,** = рожа́ть. **2,** *fig.* to give rise to; engender. —рожда́ться, *refl.* to be born.

рожде́ние *n.* birth. —день рожде́ния, birthday.

рождённый *past passive part. of* роди́ть, born: рождённый для сце́ны, born for the stage.

рожде́ственский *adj.* Christmas (*attrib.*).

рождество́ *n.* Christmas.

роже́ница *also,* рожени́ца *n.* woman giving birth.

рожо́к [*gen.* -жка́; *pl.* ро́жки, ро́жек *in sense #1;* рожки́, рожко́в *in other senses*] *n.* **1,** small horn. **2,** *music* horn. **3,** shoehorn. **4,** nursing bottle. —англи́йский рожо́к, English horn. —га́зовый рожо́к, gas burner. —слухово́й рожо́к, ear trumpet.

рожь [*gen., dat., & prepl.* ржи; *instr.* ро́жью] *n.f.* rye.

ро́за *n.* **1,** rose. **2,** rosebush.

ро́зан *n., colloq.* rose.

ро́звальни [*gen.* -ней] *n. pl.* low wide sled.

ро́зга [*gen. pl.* ро́зог] *n.* rod (*for whipping*).

ро́зговенье *n.* first day following a period of fasting.

розе́тка [*gen. pl.* -ток] *n.* **1,** rosette. **2,** small jam dish. **3,** electric outlet.

розмари́н *n.* rosemary.

ро́зница *n., in* в ро́зницу, retail. —ро́зничный, *adj.* retail.

ро́зно *adv., obs.* apart; separately.

рознь *n.f.* **1,** dissension; discord. **2,** (*with dat.*) *indicating diversity of similar things:* челове́к челове́ку — рознь, there are all kinds of people; there are people, and then there are people.

розове́ть *v. impfv.* [*pfv.* порозове́ть] **1,** to turn pink. **2,** [*impfv. only*] (*of anything rose or pink*) to appear; be seen.

розовощёкий *adj.* rosy-cheeked.

ро́зовый *adj.* **1,** rose (*attrib.*). **2,** rose-colored; pink. **3,** *fig.* rosy. —сквозь ро́зовые очки́, through rose-colored glasses.

ро́зыгрыш *n.* **1,** drawing (*in a lottery*). **2,** *sports* play; competition. **3,** draw; tie; drawn game.

ро́зыск *n.* **1,** search. **2,** investigation. —уголо́вный ро́зыск, department of criminal investigation.

рои́ться *v.r. impfv.* to swarm.

рой [*pl.* рои́] *n.* swarm.

рок *n.* fate.

рокирова́ть *v. impfv. & pfv.* [*pres.* -ру́ю, -ру́ешь] *chess* to castle. *Also,* рокирова́ться.

рокиро́вка *n., chess* castling: де́лать рокиро́вку, to castle.

роково́й *adj.* fatal.

рококо́ *n. indecl.* rococo.

ро́кот *n.* **1,** roar; rumble. **2,** murmur.

рокота́ть *v. impfv.* [*pres.* -кочу́, -ко́чешь] to rumble; resound.

ро́лик *n.* **1,** roller; caster. **2,** *pl.* roller skates. **3,** reel (*for movie film*).

ро́ликовый *adj.* roller (*attrib.*). —ро́ликовые коньки́, roller skates. —ро́ликовый подши́пник, roller bearing.

роль [*pl.* ро́ли, роле́й, роля́м] *n.f.* role; part. —игра́ть роль, to play a role/part.

ром *n.* rum.

рома́н *n.* **1**, novel. **2**, *colloq.* romance; love affair.

романи́ст *n.* **1**, novelist. **2**, specialist in Romance philology.

рома́нс *n., music* romance.

рома́нский *adj.* **1**, Romance: рома́нские языки́, Romance languages. **2**, Romanesque.

романизи́ровать *v. impfv. & pfv.* [*pres.* -рую, -руешь] to romanticize.

романти́зм *n.* romanticism.

рома́нтик *n.* romanticist.

рома́нтика *n.* **1**, romanticism. **2**, romance; romantic appeal.

романти́ческий *adj.* romantic. *Also*, **романти́чный**.

рома́шка [*gen. pl.* -шек] *n.* camomile.

ромб *n.* rhombus. —**ромби́ческий**, *adj.* rhombic.

ромбо́ид *n.* rhomboid.

ро́мовый *adj.* rum (*attrib.*).

ромште́кс (тэ) *n.* rump steak.

ро́ндо *n. indecl.* rondo.

роня́ть *v. impfv.* [*pfv.* урони́ть] **1**, to drop. **2**, [*impfv. only*] to shed (leaves, tears, etc.). **3**, *fig.* to demean: роня́ть/урони́ть себя́, to demean oneself.

ро́пот *n.* **1**, murmur (*of disapproval*); grumbling. **2**, murmuring; rustling; rippling.

ропта́ть *v. impfv.* [*pres.* ропщу́, ро́пщешь] to grumble; murmur.

роса́ *n.* dew.

роси́нка [*gen. pl.* -нок] *n.* dewdrop.

роси́стый *adj.* dewy.

роско́шествовать *v. impfv.* [*pres.* -ствую, -ствуешь] to live in luxury; live sumptuously. *Also*, **роско́шничать**.

роско́шный *adj.* luxurious; sumptuous.

ро́скошь *n.f.* luxury.

ро́слый *adj.* strapping; husky; burly.

ро́сный *adj., in* ро́сный ла́дан, benzoin.

росома́ха *n.* wolverine.

ро́спись *n.f.* painting; mural.

ро́спуск *n.* dismissal; dissolution.

росси́йский *adj.* Russian.

ро́ссказни [*gen.* -ней] *n. pl., colloq.* tale; yarn; cock-and-bull story.

ро́ссыпь *n.f.* (mineral) deposit.

рост *n.* **1**, growth. **2**, height. Высо́кого ро́ста, tall. Ни́зкого ро́ста, short. Он ро́стом шесть фу́тов, he is six feet tall. Существо́ в рост челове́ка, a creature the height of a man. **3**, rise; increase. **4**, length (*of a garment*): брю́ки сороково́го разме́ра пе́рвого ро́ста, trousers size forty short. —во весь рост, **1**, to one's full height. **2**, (*of a portrait*) full-length. **3**, *fig.* in all its magnitude. —не по ро́сту, (*of a garment*) not the right size. —по ро́сту, according to size; in size order.

ро́стбиф *n.* roast beef.

ростовщи́к [*gen.* -щика́] *n.* **1**, moneylender. **2**, usurer. —**ростовщи́ческий**, *adj.* usurious. —**ростовщи́чество**, *n.* usury.

росто́к [*gen.* -тка́] *n.* sprout; shoot.

ро́счерк *n.* flourish. —одни́м ро́счерком пера́, with a stroke of the pen.

рося́нка *n.* sundew.

росяно́й *adj.* dew (*attrib.*).

рот [*gen.* рта; *2nd loc.* рту] *n.* mouth. Во рту, in one's mouth. Изо рта, from one's mouth. —во весь рот, **1**, at the top of one's lungs. **2**, from ear to ear. —набра́ть воды́ в рот, to keep silent; keep mum. —не брать в рот (+ *gen.*), not to touch (a certain food or drink). —смотре́ть в рот (+ *dat.*), to listen spellbound (to someone).

ро́та *n., mil.* company.

рота́нг *n.* rattan. —**рота́нговый**, *adj.* rattan.

рота́тор *n.* mimeograph.

ротацио́нный *adj.* rotary. —**ротацио́нная (печа́тная) маши́на**, rotary press.

ро́тный *adj., mil.* company (*attrib.*). —*n.* company commander.

ротово́й *adj.* of the mouth; oral.

ротозе́й *n., colloq.* **1**, onlooker; bystander. **2**, dimwit; dullard.

ротозе́йство *n., colloq.* extreme absent-mindedness.

рото́нда *n.* rotunda.

ро́тор *n.* rotor.

ро́ща *n.* grove.

роялли́зм *n.* royalism. —**роялли́ст**, *n.* royalist. —**роялли́стский**, *adj.* royalist.

роя́ль *n.m.* piano.

ртуть *n.f.* mercury. —**ртутный**, *adj.* mercury (*attrib.*).

руба́нок [*gen.* -нка] *n.* plane (*tool*).

руба́ха *n.* shirt.

руба́шка [*gen. pl.* -шек] *n.* **1**, shirt. **2**, casing. **3**, back (*of a playing card*). —ночна́я руба́шка, **1**, nightshirt. **2**, nightgown. —роди́ться в руба́шке, to be born with a silver spoon in one's mouth.

рубе́ж [*gen.* -бежа́] *n.* **1**, border; boundary. **2**, *mil.* line: огнево́й рубе́ж, firing line. —за рубежо́м, abroad.

рубе́ц [*gen.* -бца́] *n.* **1**, scar; welt. **2**, hem. **3**, rumen; paunch (*of an animal*). **4**, tripe.

руби́дий *n.* rubidium.

Рубико́н *n., in* перейти́ Рубико́н, to cross the Rubicon.

руби́н *n.* ruby. —**руби́новый**, *adj.* ruby (*attrib.*).

руби́ть *v. impfv.* [*pres.* рублю́, ру́бишь] **1**, to chop. **2**, to chop down; cut down; fell. **3**, to slash. **4**, to build (*out of logs*). —**руби́ться**, *refl.* to fight with swords.

руби́ще *n.* rags; tatters.

ру́бка [*gen. pl.* -бок] *n.* **1**, chopping; felling. **2**, *naut.* deckhouse. —боева́я ру́бка, conning tower. —рулева́я ру́бка, pilothouse.

рублёвка [*gen. pl.* -вок] *n., colloq.* one-ruble note. —**рублёвый**, *adj.* ruble (*attrib.*); one-ruble (*attrib.*).

ру́бленый *adj.* **1**, chopped. **2**, made of logs.

рубль [*gen.* рубля́] *n.m.* ruble.

ру́брика *n.* heading.

рубцева́ться *v.r. impfv.* [*pfv.* зарубцева́ться; *pres.* -цу́ется] (*of a wound*) to form a scar.

ру́бчатый *adj.* (*of material*) ribbed.

ру́бчик *n.* **1**, *dim. of* рубе́ц. **2**, rib; ridge (*on material*).

ру́гань *n.f.* swearing; profanity.

руга́тельный *adj.* abusive. —**руга́тельство**, *n.* swearword; expletive.

руга́ть *v. impfv.* [*pfv.* вы́ругать] to curse out; swear at. —**руга́ться**, *refl.* [*impfv. only*] **1**, to swear; curse. **2**, to swear at one another.

руда́ [*pl.* ру́ды] *n.* ore.

рудиме́нт *n.* rudimentary organ. —**рудимента́рный**, *adj.* rudimentary.

рудни́к [*gen.* -ника́] *n.* mine. —**руднико́вый; руд-
ни́чный**, *adj.* mine (*attrib.*).

ру́дный *adj.* ore (*attrib.*); of ore.

рудоко́п *n., obs.* miner.

руже́йник *n.* gunsmith.

руже́йный *adj.* gun (*attrib.*); rifle (*attrib.*).

ружьё [*pl.* ру́жья, ру́жей, ру́жьям] *n.* **1**, gun. **2**,
in various set expressions, arms: быть под ружьём,
to be under arms; призыва́ть под ружьё, to call to
arms.

руи́ны *n. pl.* [*sing.* руи́на] ruins.

рука́ [*acc.* ру́ку; *pl.* ру́ки, рук, рука́м] *n.* **1**, hand.
2, arm. —**в рука́х**, in one's hands. —**из пе́рвых рук**,
(*of information*) firsthand. —**из рук вон (пло́хо)**, atro-
ciously; miserably. —**из рук в ру́ки**, from hand to hand.
—**на рука́х**, **1**, in one's arms. **2**, *fig.* on one's hands.
—**на́ руку** (+ *dat.*), to one's liking. —**не с руки́**
(+ *dat.*), inconvenient (for); inappropriate (for). —**от
рук** (+ *gen.*), at the hands of. —**от руки́**, in longhand.
—**по рука́м!**, it's a deal! —**по руке́**, the right size.
—**под руко́й**, on hand; at hand. —**по́д руку**, **1**, arm
in arm. **2**, *in* говори́ть кому́-нибудь по́д руку, to speak
to someone when he (she) is busy. —**рука́ в ру́ку;
рука́ о́б руку**, hand in hand. —**ру́ки вверх!**, hands
up! —**ру́ки прочь!**, hands off! —**руко́й пода́ть**, a
stone's throw.

рука́в [*gen. sing. & nom. pl.* рукава́] *n.* **1**, sleeve. **2**,
branch (*of a river*). **3**, hose. —**спустя́ рукава́**, carelessly; in a slipshod manner.

рукави́ца *n.* mitten.

руководи́тель *n.m.* **1**, leader. **2**, supervisor; head.

руководи́ть *v. impfv.* [*pres.* -вожу́, -води́шь] (*with
instr.*) **1**, to direct; manage; run. **2**, to lead; head. **3**, to
guide; supervise. —**руководи́ться**, *refl.* (*with instr.*)
to be guided (by).

руково́дство *n.* **1**, leadership. **2**, guidance; supervision. **3**, guide: руково́дство к де́йствию, guide to
action. **4**, manual; handbook. **5**, leaders.

руково́дствоваться *v.r. impfv.* [*pres.* -ствуюсь,
-ствуешься] (*with instr.*) to be guided (by).

руководя́щий *adj.* **1**, leading; guiding. **2**, senior;
supervisory. —**руководя́щий комите́т**, steering committee.

рукоде́лие *n.* needlework. —**рукоде́льница**, *n.*
needleworker.

рукомо́йник *n.* washstand.

рукопа́шный *adj., in* рукопа́шный бой, hand-to-
hand fighting/combat.

рукопи́сный *adj.* **1**, manuscript (*attrib.*). **2**, handwritten. **3**, cursive.

ру́копись *n.f.* manuscript.

рукоплеска́ние *n., usu. pl.* applause.

рукоплеска́ть *v. impfv.* [*pres.* -плещу́, -пле́щешь]
to applaud.

рукопожа́тие *n.* handshake.

рукоположе́ние *n., Orth. Ch.* ordination.

рукоя́тка [*gen. pl.* -ток] *n.* handle. *Also*, **рукоя́ть**,
n.f.

рула́да *n., music* roulade.

рулево́й *adj.* rudder (*attrib.*); steering (*attrib.*). —*n.*
helmsman.

руле́т *n.* meat (*or* potato) loaf.

руле́тка [*gen. pl.* -ток] *n.* **1**, tape measure. **2**, roulette;
roulette wheel.

рули́ть *v. impfv., aero.* to taxi.

руло́н *n.* roll; bolt (*of cloth*).

руль [*gen.* руля́] *n.m.* **1**, rudder; helm. **2**, steering
wheel. **3**, handlebar(s). —**за рулём**, at (*or* behind) the
wheel. —**стать за руль**, to take the helm. —**стоя́ть у
руля́**, to be at the helm.

ру́мба *n.* rumba.

румы́н [*gen. pl.* румы́н] *n.m.* [*fem.* -мы́нка] Romanian. —**румы́нский**, *adj.* Romanian.

румя́на [*gen.* -мя́н] *n.pl.* rouge.

румя́нец [*gen.* -нца] *n.* color in one's face; redness
in one's cheeks.

румя́нить *v. impfv.* [*pfv.* наруმя́нить] **1**, to rouge;
apply rouge to. **2**, [*pfv. also* заруმя́нить] to redden;
put color in; give a reddish glow to. —**румя́ниться**,
refl. **1**, [*pfv.* наруმя́ниться] to put on rouge. **2**, [*pfv.*
заруმя́ниться] to turn red; flush.

румя́ный *adj.* ruddy; rosy.

руно́ [*pl.* ру́на] *n.* fleece. —**золото́е руно́**, the Golden
Fleece.

ру́ны *n. pl.* [*sing.* ру́на] runes. —**руни́ческий**, *adj.*
runic.

ру́пия *n.* rupee.

ру́пор *n.* **1**, megaphone. **2**, *fig.* mouthpiece.

руса́к [*gen.* -сака́] *n.* **1**, European hare. **2**, *colloq.*
Russian.

руса́лка [*gen. pl.* -лок] *n.* mermaid.

руси́ст *n.* specialist in the Russian language.

русифика́ция *n.* Russification.

русифици́ровать *v. impfv. & pfv.* [*pres.* -рую, -ру-
ешь] to Russify.

ру́сло *n.* **1**, river bed; channel. **2**, *fig.* course; direction.

русофи́л *n.* Russophile.

русофо́б *n.* Russophobe. —**русофо́бство**, *n.* Russophobia.

ру́сский *adj.* Russian: ру́сский язы́к, the Russian
language. —*n.* Russian (*person*).

русскоязы́чный *adj.* Russian-language (*attrib.*).

ру́сый *adj.* **1**, (*of hair*) light brown. **2**, (*of a person*) with
light brown hair.

руте́ний *n.* ruthenium.

рути́на *n.* resistance to change; conservatism. —**ру-
тинёр**, *n.* conservative; traditionalist. —**рути́нный**,
adj. staid; conservative; traditional.

ру́хлядь *n.f., colloq.* junk.

ру́хнуть *v. pfv.* **1**, to collapse; come tumbling down.
2, *fig.* (*of hopes, plans, etc.*) to collapse; fall through;
come to naught.

руча́тельство *n.* guarantee.

руча́ться *v.r. impfv.* [*pfv.* поручи́ться] (*with* за +
acc.) to vouch for; guarantee.

ручеёк [*gen.* -чейка́] *n., dim. of* ручей.

руче́й [*gen.* -чья́] *n.* brook; stream.

ру́чка [*gen. pl.* -чек] *n.* **1**, *dim. of* рука́. **2**, handle;
knob. **3**, arm (*of a chair, sofa, etc.*). **4**, penholder. **5**,
pen. —**автомати́ческая ру́чка**, fountain pen.

ручно́й *adj.* **1**, hand (*attrib.*). **2**, manual. **3**, tame; domesticated. —**ручны́е часы́**, wrist watch.

ру́шить *v. impfv.* to tear down. —**ру́шиться**, *refl.* **1**,
to collapse; come tumbling down. **2**, *fig.* to collapse;
fall through.

ры́ба *n.* **1**, fish. **2**, *pl., cap.* Pisces. —**ни ры́ба ни мя́со**,
neither fish nor fowl.

рыба́к [*gen.* -бака́] *n.* (commercial) fisherman.

рыба́лка *n., colloq.* fishing: идти́ на рыба́лку, to
go fishing.

рыба́цкий *adj.* fishing (*attrib.*); fisherman's. *Also,* рыба́чий [*fem.* -чья].

рыба́чить *v. impfv.* to fish.

рыбе́шка [*gen. pl.* -шек] *n., colloq.* small fish.

ры́бий [*fem.* -бья] *adj.* fish (*attrib.*). —ры́бий жир, cod-liver oil. —ры́бий клей, isinglass.

ры́бка [*gen. pl.* -бок] *n., dim. of* ры́ба. —золота́я ры́бка, goldfish.

ры́бный *adj.* fish (*attrib.*). —ры́бная ло́вля, fishing.

рыболо́в *n.* fisherman; angler. —рыболо́вный, *adj.* fishing (*attrib.*). —рыболо́вство, *n.* fishing (*as an economic activity*).

рыво́к [*gen.* -вка́] *n.* **1,** jerk. **2,** spurt. **3,** *weightlifting* snatch.

рыга́ть *v. impfv.* [*pfv.* рыгну́ть] to belch.

рыда́ние *n.* sobbing.

рыда́ть *v. impfv.* to sob.

рыжеволо́сый *adj.* redheaded.

рыже́ть *v. impfv.* [*pfv.* порыже́ть] to become red; turn red.

ры́жий *adj.* **1,** red. **2,** redheaded. **3,** (*of a horse*) chestnut. —*n., colloq.* circus clown.

ры́жик *n.* a variety of edible mushroom.

рык *n.* roar.

рыка́ть *v. impfv.* to roar.

ры́ло *n.* **1,** snout. **2,** *colloq.* mug; puss; kisser.

ры́льце [*gen. pl.* -лец] *n.* **1,** *dim. of* ры́ло. **2,** *bot.* stigma.

ры́нда *n.* ship's bell.

ры́нок [*gen.* -нка] *n.* market. —ры́ночный, *adj.* market (*attrib.*).

рыса́к [*gen.* -сака́] *n.* trotter (*horse*).

ры́сий [*fem.* -сья] *adj.* **1,** lynx (*attrib.*). **2,** (*of one's eyes*) piercing.

рыси́стый *adj., in* рыси́стые бега́, trotting races; рыси́стая ло́шадь, trotter.

рыси́ть *v. impfv.* (*of a horse*) to trot.

ры́скать *v. impfv.* [*pres.* ры́щу, ры́щешь] **1,** to prowl; be on the prowl. **2,** *colloq.* to wander about; roam.

рысца́ *n.* slow trot; jog trot.

рысь *n.f.* **1,** lynx; bobcat. **2,** trot: ры́сью (*or* на рыся́х), at a trot.

ры́твина *n.* rut; pothole.

рыть *v. impfv.* [*pfv.* вы́рыть; *pres.* ро́ю, ро́ешь] **1,** to dig. **2,** to dig up.

рытьё *n.* digging.

ры́ться *v.r. impfv.* [*pfv.* поры́ться; *pres.* ро́юсь, ро́ешься] (*with* в + *prepl.*) **1,** [*impfv. only*] to dig (in the dirt, sand, etc.). **2,** to search; rummage; ransack. —ры́ться/поры́ться в па́мяти, to rack one's brains; try hard to remember.

рыхле́ть *v. impfv.* to become soft; lose its firmness.

рыхли́ть *v. impfv.* [*pfv.* взрыхли́ть] to loosen; turn up (soil, dirt, etc.).

ры́хлый *adj.* loose; crumbly; friable.

ры́царский *adj.* **1,** knight's; knights'. **2,** chivalrous.

ры́царство *n.* **1,** knights. **2,** knighthood. **3,** chivalry.

ры́царь *n.m.* knight.

рыча́г [*gen.* -чага́] *n.* lever.

рыча́ние *n.* growling; snarling.

рыча́ть *v. impfv.* [*pres.* -чи́т] to growl; snarl.

рья́ный *adj.* zealous. —рья́но, *adv.* zealously. —рья́ность, *n.f.* zeal.

рэ́кет *n.* racket. —рэкети́р, *n.* racketeer.

рюкза́к [*gen.* -зака́] *n.* knapsack.

рю́мка [*gen. pl.* -мок] *n.* small liquor glass.

рю́мочка [*gen. pl.* -чек] *n., dim. of* рю́мка.

ряби́на *n.* **1,** mountain ash; rowan tree. **2,** rowanberries. **3,** pockmark.

ряби́ть *v. impfv.* **1,** to ripple (*trans. & intrans.*). **2,** (*usu. with* в глаза́х) to dance before one's eyes. *Also impers.:* у меня́ в глаза́х ряби́т, things are dancing (*or* flashing) before my eyes.

рябо́й *adj.* **1,** pockmarked. **2,** spotted.

ря́бчик *n.* hazel grouse; hazel hen.

рябь *n.f.* ripples.

ря́вкать *v. impfv.* [*pfv.* ря́вкнуть] *colloq.* to roar; bellow.

ряд [*gen.* ря́да, *but after* 2, 3, & 4 ряда́; *2nd loc.* ряду́; *pl.* ряды́] *n.* **1,** row. **2,** *mil.* file. **3,** *pl., mil.* ranks. **4,** row of stalls (*in a market*). **5,** [*prepl.* в ря́де] series; number: це́лый ряд (+ *gen.*), a whole series of; в ря́де слу́чаев, in a number of cases. —в ряд/ряду́, abreast. —в ряду́ (+ *gen.*), among. —из ря́да вон выходя́щий, exceptional; out of the ordinary. —стоя́ть в одно́м ряду́ с, to be/rank on a par with.

рядово́й *adj.* **1,** common; ordinary; average. **2,** *mil.* of the rank and file: рядово́й соста́в, the rank and file; enlisted personnel. —*n., mil.* private.

ря́дом *adv.* **1,** alongside. **2,** next to each other; side by side. **3,** nearby. **4,** next door. —ря́дом с (+ *instr.*), **1,** next to; beside; alongside. **2,** next door to.

ря́са *n.* monk's habit; cassock; frock.

ря́ска *n.* duckweed.

С

С, с *n. neut.* eighteenth letter of the Russian alphabet.

с *also*, **со** *prep.* A, *with instr.* **1**, with: я пойду с вами, I'll go with you; читать с трудом, to read with difficulty. **2**, and: мы с тобой, you and I; три с половиной, three and a half; хлеб с маслом, bread and butter. **3**, on (*a specified train, plane etc.*): уехать с ранним поездом, to leave on the early-morning train. **4**, *used in greetings:* с праздником!, happy holiday!; с Новым годом!, Happy New Year! B, *with gen.* **1**, off; down from; down: сойти с рельсов, to go off the tracks; упасть с лестницы, to fall down the stairs; достать книгу с полки, to take a book from the shelf. **2**, from: с вокзала, from the station; с работы, from work. С самого начала, from the very beginning. С головы до ног, from head to toe. С русского на английский, from Russian to English. **3**, *indicating cause:* кататься со смеху, to roar with laughter; умирать с голоду, to die of hunger. **4**, with: с вашего разрешения, with your permission. **5**, since: с детства, since childhood; с тех пор, since then. С, *with acc.* about; approximately: с месяц, about a month; величиной с дом, about the size of a house.
—с тем, чтобы, *see* чтобы.

с- *also*, **со-**, **съ-**, *prefix* **1**, *indicating motion off or down:* сойти с лестницы, to go down the stairs; соскользнуть со стола, to slip off the table. **2**, *indicating removal from a surface:* соскабливать, to scrape off. **3**, *indicating bringing or gathering together:* собирать, to gather; соединять, to unite. **4**, (*with* -ся) *indicating coming together from various places:* съезжаться, to gather; assemble (*from various places*). **5**, *indicating joining or fastening together:* связывать, to tie together. **6**, (*with pfv. verbs only*) *indicating motion to a place and back:* сбегать, to run (*to a place and return*). **7**, (*with* -ся) *indicating harmony in doing something:* спеваться, to sing in harmony; срабатываться, to achieve harmony in work.

саам *n.m.* [*fem.* **саамка**] Lapp; Laplander. —**саамский**, *adj.* Lapp; Lappish.

сабля [*gen. pl.* -бель] *n.* saber. —**сабельный**, *adj.* saber (*attrib.*).

саботаж *n.* sabotage. —**саботажник**, *n.* saboteur.

саботажничать *v. impfv.*, *colloq.* = **саботировать**.

саботировать *v. impfv. & pfv.* [*pres.* -рую, -руешь] to sabotage.

саван *n.* **1**, shroud. **2**, *fig.* cover; blanket; mantle (*of snow, ice, fog, etc.*).

саванна *n.* savanna; savannah.

саврасый *adj.* (*of a horse*) light brown with a black mane and tail.

сага *n.* saga.

сагитировать *v.*, *pfv. of* агитировать (*in sense #2*).

сад [*2nd loc.* саду; *pl.* сады] *n.* garden. —ботанический сад, botanical gardens. —детский сад, kindergarten. —фруктовый сад, orchard. —яблоневый сад, apple orchard.

садизм *n.* sadism.

садик *n.*, *dim. of* сад.

садист *n.* sadist. —**садистский**, *adj.* sadistic.

садить *v. impfv.* [*pres.* сажу, садишь] *colloq.* = сажать.

садиться *v.r. impfv.* [*pfv.* сесть; *pres.* сажусь, садишься] **1**, to sit; sit down; take a seat. Садитесь!, sit down!; have a seat! Сесть за стол/работу, to sit down at a table; sit (*or* get) down to work. Сесть в постели, to sit up in bed. **2**, (*with* в *or* на + *acc.*) to take; board; get on (a train, bus, etc.); get into (a car); get on(to); mount (a horse). **3**, (*of a bird, insect, etc.*) to alight; perch. **4**, (*of dust, fog, etc.*) to settle. **5**, (*of an airplane*) to land. **6**, (*of the sun, stars, etc.*) to set. **7**, (*of a building, foundation, etc.*) to sink. **8**, (*of material*) to shrink.

саднить *v. impfv.* **1**, to scratch; abrade. **2**, to smart; sting; burn. В горле саднит, my throat feels scratchy.

садовник *n.* gardener.

садовод *n.* horticulturist; gardener. —**садоводство**, *n.* horticulture; gardening. —**садоводческий**, *adj.* horticultural.

садовый *adj.* **1**, garden (*attrib.*). **2**, cultivated. —садово-парковое искусство, landscape architecture.

садок [*gen.* -дка] *n.* **1**, fish tank. **2**, pen; coop; warren.

сажа *n.* soot. —в саже, sooty.

сажалка [*gen. pl.* -лок] *n.* planter (*machine*).

сажать *v. impfv.* [*pfv.* посадить] **1**, to plant. **2**, to seat; sit (someone) down. **3**, to place; put. **4**, to set down; land (an aircraft). **5**, to put in prison. **6**, *colloq.* to make (a stain, blot, etc.). —сажать/посадить в клетку, to cage. —сажать/посадить на кол, to impale on a stake. —сажать/посадить на цепь, to chain; chain up. —сажать/посадить под арест, to place under arrest.

саженец [*gen.* -нца] *n.* seedling.

сажень *also*, **сажень** *n.f.* old Russian unit of length equal to approx. 7 feet. —морская сажень, fathom.

сазан *n.* carp (*fish*).

сайга́ *also*, **сайга́к** *n.* a variety of antelope; saiga.

са́йка [*gen. pl.* **са́ек**] *n.* roll (*of bread*).

саквоя́ж *n.* traveling bag.

сакрамента́льный *adj.* **1,** ritual (*attrib.*). **2,** sacred. **3,** traditional.

сакс *n., hist.* Saxon.

саксау́л *n.* tree native to Central Asia; saxaul.

саксо́нский *adj.* Saxon.

саксофо́н *n.* saxophone.

сала́зки [*gen.* **-зок**] *n. pl.* small sled; toboggan.

салама́ндра *n.* salamander.

сала́т *n.* **1,** lettuce. **2,** salad. —**сала́тник,** *n.* salad bowl.

сала́тный *adj.* **1,** lettuce (*attrib.*); salad (*attrib.*). **2,** light green.

са́лить *v. impfv.* to grease.

са́лки [*gen.* **-лок**] *n. pl.* tag (*game*).

са́ло *n.* **1,** fat; lard. **2,** grease. **3,** tallow. **4,** thin ice.

сало́н *n.* **1,** salon. **2,** lounge (*in a hotel, on a train, ship, etc.*). **3,** passenger section (*on an airplane*). **4,** showroom. —**сало́н-ваго́н,** parlor car.

сало́нный *adj.* light; trivial: сало́нный разгово́р, small talk.

салфе́тка [*gen. pl.* **-ток**] *n.* napkin.

са́льдо *n. indecl., bookkeeping* balance. —**акти́вное/ отрица́тельное са́льдо торго́вого бала́нса,** trade surplus/deficit.

са́льность *n.f.* profanity; obscenity.

са́льный *adj.* **1,** tallow (*attrib.*). **2,** greasy. **3,** salacious. —**са́льные же́лезы,** sebaceous glands.

са́льто *n. indecl.* somersault. *Also,* **са́льто-морта́ле.**

салю́т *n.* salute.

салютова́ть *v. impfv. & pfv.* [*pres.* **-ту́ю, -ту́ешь**] (*with dat.*) to salute.

сала́ми *n.f. indecl.* salami.

сам *emphatic pron.* [*fem.* **сама́**; *neut.* **само́**; *pl.* **са́ми**; *gen.* **самого́, само́й, сами́х**; *dat.* **самому́, само́й, сами́м**; *acc. fem.* **саму́** *or* **самоё**; *instr.* **сами́м, само́й, сами́ми**; *prepl.* **само́м, само́й, сами́х**] oneself; myself; yourself; himself; herself; ourselves, etc.: я сам э́то сде́лаю, I'll do it myself. Письмо́ от самого́ президе́нта, a letter from the President himself. —**быть сами́м собо́й,** to be oneself. Будь сам (сама́) собо́й!, be yourself! —**сам не свой (сама́ не своя́),** not oneself; out of sorts. —**сам по себе́, 1,** oneself; in and of itself; per se. **2,** independently; on one's own. —**сам собо́й,** by itself; of itself.

сама́н *n.* adobe. —**сама́нный,** *adj.* adobe.

сама́рий *n.* samarium.

саме́ц [*gen.* **-мца́**] *n.* male (*of animals*): саме́ц оле́ня, male deer; buck.

самизда́т *n.* underground publication of manuscripts (*in the USSR*).

са́мка [*gen. pl.* **-мок**] *n.* female (*of animals*): са́мка оле́ня, female deer; doe.

само- *prefix* self-.

самоана́лиз *n.* self-analysis; introspection.

самобы́тный *adj.* original; distinctive.

самова́р *n.* samovar.

самовла́стие *n.* **1,** *obs.* one-man rule. **2,** *fig.* despotism. —**самовла́стный,** *adj.* despotic.

самовлюблённый *adj.* conceited.

самовнуше́ние *n.* autosuggestion.

самовозгора́ние *n.* spontaneous combustion.

самово́лие *n.* arbitrariness; high-handedness.

самово́льный *adj.* **1,** self-willed. **2,** arbitrary; high-

handed. **3,** unauthorized: самово́льная отлу́чка, absence without leave. —**самово́льно,** *adv.* without permission.

самовоспламене́ние *n.* spontaneous combustion.

самого́н *n.* homemade whiskey.

самодви́жущийся *adj.* self-propelled.

самоде́льный *adj.* homemade.

самодержа́вие *n.* autocracy. —**самодержа́вный,** *adj.* autocratic.

самоде́ржец [*gen.* **-жца**] *n.* autocrat.

самоде́ятельность *n.f.* **1,** individual initiative. **2,** amateur activities; amateur production.

самоде́ятельный *adj.* **1,** independent. **2,** amateur.

самоди́йский *adj.* Samoyed.

самодисципли́на *n.* self-discipline.

самодовле́ющий *adj.* self-contained; independent.

самодово́льный *adj.* self-satisfied; self-complacent; smug. —**самодово́льство,** *n.* self-satisfaction; self-complacency; smugness.

самоду́р *n.* high-handed person. —**самоду́рство,** *n.* high-handedness.

самозарожде́ние *n.* spontaneous generation.

самозащи́та *n.* self-defense.

самозва́нец [*gen.* **-нца**] *n.m.* [*fem.* **-нка**] impostor; pretender.

самозва́нный *also,* **самозва́ный** *adj.* pseudo-; false; self-styled.

самока́т *n.* scooter.

самокри́тика *n.* self-criticism. —**самокрити́ческий,** *adj.* self-critical.

самолёт *n.* plane; airplane; aircraft.

самоли́чно *adv., colloq.* oneself; personally.

самолюби́вый *adj.* proud. —**самолю́бие,** *n.* pride; self-respect.

самомне́ние *n.* conceit.

самонаблюде́ние *n.* introspection.

самонадея́нный *adj.* self-assured; presumptuous. —**самонадея́нность,** *n.f.* self-assurance; presumption.

самоназва́ние *n.* self-designation.

самооблада́ние *n.* self-control; equanimity; composure.

самообма́н *n.* self-deception.

самооборо́на *n.* self-defense.

самообслу́живание *n.* self-service.

самоопределе́ние *n.* self-determination.

самоотверже́ние *n.* = самоотве́рженность.

самоотве́рженный *adj.* selfless. —**самоотве́рженность,** *n.f.* selflessness.

самоотрече́ние *n.* self-denial.

самоочеви́дный *adj.* self-evident.

самопи́сец [*gen.* **-сца**] *n.* recorder: бортово́й самопи́сец, flight recorder.

самопи́ска [*gen. pl.* **-сок**] *n., colloq.* fountain pen.

самопоже́ртвование *n.* self-sacrifice.

самопроизво́льный *adj.* spontaneous. —**самопроизво́льность,** *n.f.* spontaneity.

самопу́ск *n.* self-starter.

саморо́док [*gen.* **-дка**] *n.* **1,** nugget. **2,** *fig.* person with exceptional natural talent.

самоса́д *n., colloq.* home-grown tobacco.

самосва́л *n.* dump truck.

самосожже́ние *n.* self-immolation.

самосозна́ние *n.* consciousness.

самосохране́ние *n.* self-preservation.

самостоя́тельный *adj.* independent. —**самостоя́-тельно,** *adv.* independently. —**самостоя́тельность,** *n.f.* independence.

самостре́л *n.* **1,** crossbow. **2,** self-inflicted wound (*made to evade military service*). **3,** *colloq.* soldier with a self-inflicted wound.

самосу́д *n.* mob law; lynching.

самотёк *n.* aimless unplanned progression; drift: пусти́ть де́ло на самотёк, to let matters take their course.

самотёком *adv.* **1,** (*of the movement of liquids*) by gravity. **2,** *fig.* spontaneously; on its own momentum.

самоуби́йство *n.* suicide: поко́нчить жизнь самоуби́йством, to commit suicide. —**самоуби́йствен-ный,** *adj.* suicidal.

самоуби́йца *n.m. & f.* person who has committed suicide.

самоуваже́ние *n.* self-respect; self-esteem.

самоуве́ренный *adj.* self-confident; self-assured. —**самоуве́ренность,** *n.f.* self-confidence; self-assurance.

самоуничтоже́ние *n.* self-destruction.

самоуправле́ние *n.* self-government. —**самоуправля́ющийся,** *adj.* self-governing.

самоупра́вный *adj.* arbitrary. —**самоупра́вство,** *n.* arbitrariness.

самоучи́тель *n.m.* manual of self-instruction.

самоу́чка [*gen. pl.* **-чек**] *n.m. & f., colloq.* self-taught person; self-educated person.

самохва́льство *n., colloq.* boasting; self-congratulation.

самохо́дка [*gen. pl.* **-док**] *n., colloq.* self-propelled gun.

самохо́дный *adj.* self-propelled.

самоцве́т *n.* semiprecious stone. —**самоцве́тный,** *adj.* semiprecious.

самоце́ль *n.f.* end in itself.

самочи́нный *adj.* **1,** arbitrary. **2,** done on one's own initiative.

самочу́вствие *n.* general physical and mental state. Как ва́ше самочу́вствие?, how do you feel (in general)?

самура́й *n.* samurai.

самши́т *n.* box tree.

са́мый *adj.* **1,** the very: до са́мого конца́, to the very end. **2,** *in* тот са́мый *or* тот же са́мый, the same: тот са́мый челове́к, the same person. **3,** *used in forming superlatives:* са́мый ва́жный вопро́с, the most important question. **4,** *in* са́мое бо́льшее, the most; at (the) most; са́мое по́зднее, at the latest.

сан *n.* rank; title. —**посвяща́ть в духо́вный сан,** to ordain (*as a clergyman*).

санато́рий *n.* sanitarium; sanatorium.

сангвини́ческий *adj.* excitable; mercurial.

санда́л *n.* sandalwood.

санда́лия *n.* sandal.

санда́ловый *adj.* sandalwood.

са́ни [*gen.* сане́й; *dat.* саня́м] *n. pl.* sleigh; sled.

санита́р *n.* **1,** (medical) orderly. **2,** [*also,* **санита́р-носи́льщик**] stretcher-bearer.

санита́рия *n.* sanitation.

санита́рный *adj.* **1,** sanitary: санита́рное состоя́ние, sanitary conditions. **2,** *mil.* medical: санита́рный батальо́н, medical battalion. —**санита́рное су́дно,** hospital ship. —**санита́рная су́мка,** first-aid kit.

са́нки [*gen.* **-нок**] *n. pl., colloq.* sled; sleigh.

санкциони́ровать *v. impfv. & pfv.* [*pres.* -ру́ю, -ру́ешь] to sanction.

са́нкция *n.* **1,** sanction; approval. **2,** *pl.* sanctions.

са́нный *adj.* sled (*attrib.*); sleigh (*attrib.*).

санови́тый *adj.* = сано́вный.

сано́вник *n.* dignitary; high official.

сано́вный *adj.* **1,** high-ranking; distinguished. **2,** stately; dignified.

санскри́т *n.* Sanskrit. —**санскри́тский,** *adj.* Sanskrit.

сантигра́мм *n.* centigram.

санти́м *n.* centime.

сантиме́тр *n.* **1,** centimeter. **2,** tape measure.

сап *n.* glanders.

са́па *n., mil.* trench; sap. —**ти́хой са́пой,** on the sly.

сапёр *n., mil.* sapper.

сапо́г [*gen.* -пога́; *gen. pl.* -по́г] *n.* boot.

сапо́жник *n.* shoemaker.

сапо́жный *adj.* shoe (*attrib.*).

сапса́н *n.* peregrine falcon.

сапфи́р *n.* sapphire. —**сапфи́рный; сапфи́ровый,** *adj.* sapphire.

сара́й *n.* shed. —**дровяно́й сара́й,** woodshed. —**каре́тный сара́й,** coach house. —**ло́дочный сара́й,** boathouse.

саранча́ *n.* **1,** locusts. **2,** a (single) locust.

сарафа́н *n., pre-rev.* peasant woman's dress.

сарде́лька [*gen. pl.* **-лек**] *n.* small sausage.

сарди́на *n.* sardine. *Also,* **сарди́нка.**

сардони́ческий *adj.* sardonic.

са́ржа *n.* serge. —**са́ржевый,** *adj.* serge.

сарка́зм *n.* sarcasm.

саркасти́ческий *adj.* sarcastic. —**саркасти́чески,** *adv.* sarcastically.

саркофа́г *n.* sarcophagus.

са́рыч [*gen.* -рыча́] *n.* buzzard.

сатана́ *n.* Satan. —**сатани́нский,** *adj.* satanic.

сателли́т *n.* satellite.

сати́н *n.* sateen. —**сати́новый,** *adj.* sateen.

сати́р *n.* satyr.

сати́ра *n.* satire. —**сати́рик,** *n.* satirist. —**сатири́ческий,** *adj.* satirical.

сатра́п *n.* satrap. —**сатра́пия,** *n.* satrapy.

Сату́рн *n.* Saturn.

сафло́р *n.* safflower.

сафья́н *n.* morocco; morocco leather. —**сафья́н-ный; сафья́новый,** *adj.* morocco.

са́хар *n.* sugar.

сахари́н *n.* saccharin.

са́харистый *adj.* containing sugar; rich in sugar.

са́харница *n.* sugar bowl.

са́харный *adj.* **1,** sugar (*attrib.*). **2,** *fig.* sugary; honeyed. —**са́харная боле́знь,** diabetes. —**са́харная голова́,** sugar loaf. —**са́харный заво́д,** sugar refinery. —**са́харный песо́к,** granulated sugar. —**са́харная пу́дра,** powdered sugar. —**са́харная свёкла,** sugar beet. —**са́харный тростни́к,** sugar cane.

сахаро́за *n.* sucrose.

сачо́к [*gen.* -чка́] *n.* net with a hoop on a long handle.

сба́вить [*infl.* -влю, -вишь] *v., pfv. of* сбавля́ть.

сба́вка *n., colloq.* reduction.

сбавля́ть *v. impfv.* [*pfv.* сба́вить] **1,** to take off (from a price). **2,** to reduce (a price, speed, etc.). —**сбавля́ть вес** *or* в ве́се, to lose weight.

сбаланси́рованный *adj.* balanced.

сбаланси́ровать v. pfv. [infl. -ру́ю, -ру́ешь] **1,** pfv. of баланси́ровать. **2,** to regain one's balance.

сбе́гать v. pfv., colloq. **1,** to run (somewhere and return). **2,** (with за + instr.) to run and fetch.

сбега́ть v. impfv. [pfv. сбежа́ть] **1,** to run down. **2,** to run away; escape. **3,** to disappear; fade (from one's face). —сбега́ться, refl. (of many people) to come running.

сбежа́ть [infl. like бежа́ть] v., pfv. of сбега́ть. —сбежа́ться, refl., pfv. of сбега́ться.

сберега́тельный adj. savings (attrib.). —сберега́тельная ка́сса, savings bank. —сберега́тельная кни́жка, bankbook; passbook.

сберега́ть v. impfv. [pfv. сбере́чь] **1,** to guard; protect. **2,** to save; conserve. **3,** to put aside (for future use).

сбереже́ние n. **1,** (with gen.) conservation (of). **2,** pl. savings.

сбере́чь [infl. like бере́чь] v., pfv. of сберега́ть.

сберка́сса n. savings bank (contr. of сберега́тельная ка́сса).

сберкни́жка [gen. pl. -жек] n. bankbook; passbook (contr. of сберега́тельная кни́жка).

сбива́ть v. impfv. [pfv. сбить] **1,** to knock off: сбить (кого́-нибудь) с ног, to knock off one's feet. **2,** to shoot down. **3,** to throw off; disconcert. **4,** to knock together. **5,** to wear down (shoes, heels, etc.). **6,** to reduce; bring down. **7,** to churn (butter); whip (cream, eggs, etc.). —сбива́ть с пути́, to lead astray. —сбива́ть с то́лку, to confuse.

сбива́ться v.r. impfv. [pfv. сби́ться] **1,** to slip off; slip out of position. **2,** to become confused; be disconcerted. **3,** to be off; be wrong. **4,** (of footwear) to become worn down. **5,** to crowd together; huddle together. —сбива́ться с ног, to be exhausted; be falling off one's feet. —сбива́ться с ноги́, to break step. —сбива́ться с пути́, to go astray; lose one's way. —сбива́ться с то́лку, to become confused.

сби́вчивый adj. **1,** confusing; muddled. **2,** inconsistent; contradictory.

сбить [infl. собью́, собьёшь] v., pfv. of сбива́ть. —сби́ться, refl., pfv. of сбива́ться.

сближа́ть v. impfv. [pfv. сбли́зить] to draw together; bring closer together. —сближа́ться, refl. **1,** to draw nearer; come closer together. **2,** (with с + instr.) to become close friends (with).

сближе́ние n. **1,** coming together; drawing together. **2,** rapprochement. **3,** mil. approach; closing in. **4,** obs. resemblance.

сбли́зить [infl. -жу, -зишь] v., pfv. of сближа́ть. —сбли́зиться, refl., pfv. of сближа́ться.

сбо́ку adv. **1,** from the side; from one side. **2,** on the side; on one side. —prep., with gen. beside; alongside.

сболтну́ть v. pfv., colloq. to blurt out.

сбор n. **1,** collection. **2,** gathering. **3,** theat. receipts. Де́лать по́лные сбо́ры, to play to packed houses. **4,** duty; toll; levy. **5,** meeting; gathering; assembly. **6,** mil. muster. **7,** short course of instruction. **8,** pl. preparations (for a trip). —в сбо́ре, present; on hand.

сбо́рище n., colloq. gathering; crowd.

сбо́рка [gen. pl. -рок] n. **1,** assembly; putting together. **2,** gather (in clothing).

сбо́рная n., decl. as an adj. = сбо́рная кома́нда.

сбо́рник n. collection; anthology.

сбо́рный adj. **1,** gathering (attrib.); meeting (attrib.);

assembly (attrib.). **2,** mixed; combined; of various kinds. **3,** prefabricated. —сбо́рная кома́нда, combined team; all-star team.

сбо́рочный adj. assembly (attrib.).

сбо́рщик n. **1,** collector (of taxes, signatures, etc.). **2,** picker (of cotton). **3,** assembler.

сбра́сывать v. impfv. [pfv. сбро́сить] **1,** to throw off; throw down. **2,** to drop (bombs). **3,** fig. to overthrow. **4,** to shed. **5,** fig. to shake off (apathy, an illness, etc.). **6,** (with в + acc.) colloq. to toss (into). **7,** cards to discard. **8,** finance to dump. —сбра́сывать со счето́в, to rule out; count out.

сбрива́ть v. impfv. [pfv. сбрить] to shave off.

сбрить [infl. сбре́ю, сбре́ешь] v., pfv. of сбрива́ть.

сброд n., colloq. rabble; riffraff.

сбро́сить [infl. -шу, -сишь] v., pfv. of сбра́сывать.

сбру́я n. harness.

сбыва́ть v. impfv. [pfv. сбыть] **1,** to sell; market. **2,** to get rid of. Сбыва́ть с рук, to get off one's hands. **3,** v.i. (of rising waters) to recede. —сбыва́ться, refl. to come true; be realized.

сбыт n. sale.

сбыть [infl. like быть] v., pfv. of сбыва́ть. —сбы́ться, refl. [past сбы́лся, сбыла́сь, сбыло́сь] pfv. of сбыва́ться.

сва́дебный adj. wedding (attrib.).

сва́дьба [gen. pl. -деб] n. wedding.

сва́йный adj. built on piles.

сва́ливать v. impfv. [pfv. свали́ть] **1,** to knock down. **2,** to throw down. **3,** to toss together; toss into a pile. **4,** colloq. to overthrow. **5,** fig. to throw off; cast off. **6,** (with на + acc.) colloq. to shift; dump (work, blame, etc.) on(to) someone else. **7,** colloq. (of sleep) to overcome; (of an illness) to strike. **8,** v.i., colloq. (of a large crowd) to depart. **9,** v.i., colloq. to abate. —сва́ливаться, refl. **1,** to fall. **2,** to collapse; come tumbling down. **3,** colloq. to lean; tilt. **4,** colloq. to appear from nowhere. **5,** colloq. to fall ill. **6,** colloq. (of cattle) to die.

свали́ть [infl. свалю́, сва́лишь] v., pfv. of вали́ть[1] and сва́ливать. —свали́ться, refl., pfv. of вали́ться and сва́ливаться.

сва́лка [gen. pl. -лок] n. **1,** dump; dumping ground. **2,** colloq. brawl; scuffle.

сваля́ть v., pfv. of валя́ть (in sense #3).

сва́ривать v. impfv. [pfv. свари́ть] to weld together.

свари́ть [infl. сварю́, сва́ришь] v., pfv. of вари́ть and сва́ривать.

сва́рка n. welding.

сварли́вый adj. quarrelsome; cantankerous.

сварно́й adj. welded.

сва́рочный adj. welding (attrib.). —сва́рочное желе́зо, wrought iron.

сва́рщик n. welder.

сва́стика n. swastika.

сват n. **1,** matchmaker. **2,** father of one's son-in-law or daughter-in-law.

сва́тать v. impfv. [pfv. посва́тать or сосва́тать] **1,** to match up; arrange a match for; (with dat. or за + acc.) match (someone) up with. **2,** to propose to; ask for one's hand; request permission to marry. —сва́таться, refl. [pfv. посва́таться] (with за + acc. or к) to propose to.

сватовство́ n. matchmaking.

сва́тья n. mother of one's son-in-law or daughter-in-law.

сваха *n.* matchmaker.

свая *n.* pile: мост на сваях, bridge on piles.

сведение *n.* 1, *usu. pl.* information. 2, *pl.* knowledge. —доводить до (чьего-нибудь) сведения, to inform; bring to the attention of: довожу до вашего сведения, I beg to inform you. —доходить до (чьего-нибудь) сведения, to come to the attention of. —к вашему сведению, for your information. —принимать к сведению, *see* принимать.

сведение *n.* 1, leading down; leading away. 2, joining together; bringing together. 3, removal (*of stains*). 4, reduction; squaring; reconciling. 5, cramp.

сведущий *adj.* knowledgeable; well-versed.

свежевать *v. impfv.* [*pfv.* освежевать; *pres.* -жую, жуешь] to skin; dress (an animal).

свежесть *n.f.* 1, freshness. 2, cool air. —не первой свежести, 1, not very fresh. 2, (*of clothes*) not very clean.

свежеть *v. impfv.* [*pfv.* посвежеть] 1, to become cool; become chilly; cool off. 2, *naut.* (*of the wind*) to blow up. 3, (*of a person*) to take on a healthy color.

свежий *adj.* [*short form* свеж, свежа, свежо, свежи *or* свежи] 1, fresh. 2, cool; chilly. 3, the latest: свежий номер, the latest issue. —на свежую голову, with a fresh mind. —на свежую память, while (something is) still fresh in one's memory. —со свежими силами, with renewed strength *or* vigor.

свезти *v. pfv.* [*infl. like* везти] 1, *pfv. of* свозить. 2, to take; drive (to a certain place). 3, to take; drive (to and back).

свёкла *n.* 1, beets. 2, a (single) beet.

свекловица *n.* sugar beet. —свекловичный, *adj.* beet (*attrib.*); sugar-beet (*attrib.*); beet-sugar (*attrib.*).

свеклосахарный *adj.* beet-sugar (*attrib.*).

свекольник *n.* 1, beet soup. 2, beet tops.

свекольный *adj.* 1, beet (*attrib.*). 2, beet-colored.

свёкор [*gen.* -кра] *n.* father-in-law (*husband's father*).

свекровь *n.f.* mother-in-law (*husband's mother*).

свергать *v. impfv.* [*pfv.* свергнуть] 1, *obs.* to throw down. 2, to overthrow.

свергнуть [*past* сверг, -ла] *v.*, *pfv. of* свергать.

свержение *n.* overthrow.

сверить *v.*, *pfv. of* сверять.

сверкание *n.* 1, sparkle. 2, glare.

сверкать *v. impfv.* [*pfv.* сверкнуть] 1, to sparkle; glitter; shine. 2, (*of lightning*) to flash.

сверлильный *adj.* boring (*attrib.*); drilling (*attrib.*).

сверлить *v. impfv.* 1, [*pfv.* просверлить] to drill; drill a hole in; bore through. 2, *impers.* to cause a gnawing pain: у меня сверлит в ухе, I have a gnawing pain in my ear. 3, (*of a thought*) to haunt; weigh on one's mind. 4, *in* сверлить (кого-нибудь) глазами, to stare right through (someone).

сверло [*pl.* свёрла] *n.* drill (*tool*).

сверлящий *adj.* 1, (*of a pain*) gnawing. 2, (*of a sound*) shrill; piercing.

свернуть *v.*, *pfv. of* свёртывать *and* сворачивать. —свернуться, *refl.*, *pfv. of* свёртываться.

сверстать *v.*, *pfv. of* верстать.

сверстник *n.* person one's own age; contemporary; peer.

свёрток [*gen.* -тка] *n.* 1, roll (*of paper, material, etc.*). 2, package.

свёртывание *n.* 1, rolling up. 2, curtailment. 3, coagulation.

свёртывать *v. impfv.* [*pfv.* свернуть] 1, to roll up. 2, to curtail; cut back. 3, *in* свернуть шею (+ *dat.*), to wring someone's neck; свернуть себе шею, to break one's neck; get killed. —свёртываться, *refl.*, 1, to roll up; curl up. 2, to congeal; curdle; coagulate.

сверх *prep.*, *with gen.* 1, over. 2, in addition to; over and above; in excess of. 3, *fig.* beyond: сверх сил, beyond one's strength; сверх всякого ожидания, beyond all expectations. —сверх всего, on top of everything (else). —сверх того, moreover; furthermore.

сверх- *prefix* super-.

сверхдержава *n.* superpower.

сверхзвуковой *adj.* supersonic.

сверхплановый *adj.* in excess of the plan; over and above the plan.

сверхприбыль *n.f.* excess profits.

сверхсрочный *adj.* 1, additional; extra: сверхсрочная служба, additional time in service. 2, *colloq.* extremely urgent.

сверху *adv.* 1, from above; from the top. 2, on top. —сверху донизу, from top to bottom.

сверхурочный *adj.* overtime (*attrib.*). —сверхурочно, *adv.* overtime: работать сверхурочно, to work overtime. —сверхурочные, *n. pl.* overtime (pay).

сверхчеловек *n.* superman. —сверхчеловеческий, *adj.* superhuman.

сверхчувствительный *adj.* supersensitive.

сверхштатный *adj.* supernumerary.

сверхъестественный *adj.* supernatural.

сверчок [*gen.* -чка] *n.* cricket (*insect*).

свершать *v. impfv.* [*pfv.* свершить] = совершать.

сверять *v. impfv.* [*pfv.* сверить] to check; compare; collate.

свесить *v. pfv.* [*infl.* -шу, -сишь] 1, *pfv. of* свешивать. 2, *colloq.* to weigh. —свеситься, *refl.*, *pfv. of* свешиваться.

свести [*infl. like* вести] *v.*, *pfv. of* сводить. —свестись, *refl.*, *pfv. of* сводиться.

свет¹ [*2nd loc.* на свету] *n.* light. —в свете (+ *gen.*), in the light of. —при свете (+ *gen.*), by the light of. —чуть свет, at the crack of dawn.

свет² *n.* 1, world. 2, society: высший свет, high society. —ни за что на свете, not for (anything in) the world. —тот свет, the next (*or* other) world. —выйти в свет, to come out; be published. —появиться на свет, to come into the world; be born. —производить на свет, to bring into the world. —увидеть свет, 1, to see the light of day; be published. 2, = появиться на свет.

светать *v. impfv.*, *impers.* to dawn: светает, day is dawning; day is breaking; it is getting light.

светило *n.* 1, heavenly body. 2, *fig.* luminary.

светильник *n.* (oil) lamp.

светить *v. impfv.* [*pres.* свечу, светишь] 1, (*of the sun, moon, etc.*) to shine. 2, [*pfv.* посветить] (*with instr.*) to shine (a light); (*with dat.*) shine a light on; hold up a light for. —светиться, *refl.* (*of lights, stars, one's eyes, etc.*) to shine.

светлеть *v. impfv.* [*pfv.* посветлеть *or* просветлеть] to brighten (up); become bright.

светло *adj.* *used predicatively* light: уже светло, it is light already.

светло- *prefix, used with colors,* light: светло-зелёный, light green.

светловолóсый *adj.* light-haired; fair-haired.

свéтлость *n.f.* **1,** lightness; brightness. **2,** (*with* вáша, егó, её, *etc.*) lordship; grace: вáша свéтлость, your lordship; your grace.

свéтлый *adj.* **1,** light. **2,** bright. **3,** (*of liquids, glass, etc.*) clear. **4,** *fig.* lucid: свéтлый ум, lucid mind. **5,** *fig.* happy; radiant. —**свéтлая лúчность,** fine person. —**свéтлая пáмять,** blessed memory.

светля́к [*gen.* **-ляка́**] *n.* firefly; lightning bug.

светлячóк [*gen.* **-чка́**] *n.* = светля́к.

световóй *adj.* **1,** light (*attrib.*). **2,** luminous. **3,** illuminated. —**световóй год,** light year.

светомаскирóвка *n.* blackout.

светонепроница́емый *adj.* lightproof.

светопреставлéние *n.* the end of the world.

светофóр *n.* traffic light.

свéточ *n.* **1,** *obs.* torch. **2,** *fig.* (*with gen.*) torch: свéточ úстины, the torch of truth. **3,** *fig.* luminary; leading light.

светочувствúтельный *adj., photog.* sensitive to light.

свéтский *adj.* **1,** fashionable. **2,** refined; polite. **3,** secular; lay.

светя́щийся *adj.* luminous; luminescent.

свечá [*pl.* **свéчи, свечéй, свечáм**] *n.* **1,** candle. При свéте свечи́; при свечáх, by candlelight. **2,** (unit of) candlepower. **3,** *in* запальна́я свечá, spark plug. **4,** suppository. —**игрá не стóит свеч,** the game is not worth the candle.

свечéние *n.* **1,** luminescence. **2,** fluorescence. **3,** phosphorescence.

свéчка [*gen. pl.* **-чек**] *n.* **1,** candle. **2,** suppository.

свечнóй *adj.* candle (*attrib.*).

свéшать *v., pfv. of* вéшать (*in sense #3*).

свéшивать *v. impfv.* [*pfv.* **свéсить**] **1,** (*with* с + *gen.*) to hang (something from something). **2,** to let down; lower (a rope); dangle (one's legs). —**свéшиваться,** *refl.* **1,** to hang down; dangle. **2,** *colloq.* (*with* из) to lean out of; (*with* чéрез) lean over.

свива́льник *n.* swaddling clothes.

свива́ть *v. impfv.* [*pfv.* **свить**] **1,** to twist. **2,** to weave. **3,** to roll; roll up. **4,** [*impfv. only*] to swaddle. —**свива́ться,** *refl.* to roll up.

свида́ние *n.* **1,** appointment; date; meeting; rendezvous. **2,** visit (*with a prisoner, patient, etc.*). —**до свида́ния!,** goodbye! —**до скóрого свида́ния!,** see you soon!

свидéтель *n.m.* witness.

свидéтельство *n.* **1,** evidence. **2,** testimony. **3,** certificate; license: свидéтельство о рождéнии, birth certificate; бра́чное свидéтельство, marriage license.

свидéтельствовать *v. impfv.* [*pres.* **-ствую, -ствуешь**] **1,** to testify; give evidence. **2,** (*with* о) to attest to; bear witness to. —**свидéтельствовать почтéние** (+ *dat.*), *obs.* to pay one's respects to.

свина́рник *n.* pigpen; pigsty.

свинéц [*gen.* **-нца́**] *n.* lead.

свини́на *n.* pork.

свúнка [*gen. pl.* **-нок**] *n.* **1,** little pig. **2,** mumps. —**морска́я свúнка,** guinea pig.

свинóй *adj.* **1,** pig (*attrib.*); hog (*attrib.*). **2,** pork (*attrib.*).

свинома́тка [*gen. pl.* **-ток**] *n.* sow (*pig*).

свинопа́с *n.* swineherd.

свúнский *adj., colloq.* swinish.

свúнство *n., colloq.* **1,** squalor; filth. **2,** despicable act. **3,** scandal; outrage.

свинти́ть [*infl.* **-чу́, -ти́шь**] *v., pfv. of* свúнчивать.

свинцóвый *adj.* **1,** lead (*attrib.*). **2,** leaden; dull gray. —**свинцóвые бели́ла,** white lead; ceruse. —**свинцóвый блеск,** galena.

свúнчивать *v. impfv.* [*pfv.* **свинти́ть**] **1,** to screw together. **2,** *colloq.* to unscrew.

свинья́ [*pl.* **свúньи, свинéй, свúньям**] *n.* **1,** pig; hog; swine. **2,** *in* морска́я свинья́, porpoise. —**подложи́ть свинью́** (+ *dat.*), to play a dirty trick on.

свирéль *n.f.* reed (*primitive musical instrument*).

свирепéть *v. impfv.* [*pfv.* **рассвирепéть**] to become violent; become enraged.

свирéпость *n.f.* ferocity.

свирéпствовать *v. impfv.* [*pres.* **-ствую, -ствуешь**] **1,** to go on a rampage; wreak havoc. **2,** (*of a storm, fire, etc.*) to rage.

свирéпый *adj.* fierce; ferocious.

свиристéль *n.m.* waxwing (*bird*).

свиса́ть *v. impfv.* [*pfv.* **свúснуть**] to hang down; droop.

свúснуть [*past* **свис, -ла**] *v., pfv. of* свиса́ть.

свист *n.* **1,** whistle; whistling. **2,** hiss; hissing.

свиста́ть *v. impfv.* [*pres.* **свищу́, свúщешь**] = свистéть.

свистéть *v. impfv.* [*pfv.* **свúстнуть;** *pres.* **свищу́, свисти́шь**] **1,** to whistle. **2,** to hiss.

свистóк [*gen.* **-стка́**] *n.* whistle (*instrument or sound*).

свистопля́ска *n., colloq.* bedlam; chaos.

свисту́лька [*gen. pl.* **-лек**] *n., colloq.* whistle; tin whistle.

свисту́н [*gen.* **-туна́**] *n., colloq.* whistler (*one who whistles*).

свистя́щий *adj. & n.* sibilant.

свúта *n.* suite; retinue.

свúтер (тэ) *n.* sweater.

свúток [*gen.* **-тка**] *n.* **1,** roll. **2,** scroll.

свить [*infl.* **совью́, совьёшь;** *past fem.* **свила́**] *v., pfv. of* вить *and* свива́ть. —**свúться,** *refl., pfv. of* свива́ться.

свихну́ть *v. pfv., colloq.* to dislocate. —**свихну́ться,** *refl., colloq.* **1,** to go mad; go nuts. **2,** to go astray.

свищ [*gen.* **свища́**] *n.* **1,** knothole. **2,** *med.* fistula.

свия́зь *n.f.* widgeon (*duck*).

свобóда *n.* freedom; liberty. —**на свобóде, 1,** at liberty; at large. **2,** at one's leisure. —**выпуска́ть** *or* **отпуска́ть на свобóду,** to set free.

свобóдно *adv.* **1,** freely. **2,** easily. **3,** loosely. **4,** fluently. **5,** in a relaxed manner. —*adj., used predicatively* unoccupied: здесь свобóдно?, is this seat taken?

свобóдный *adj.* [*short form* **-ден, -дна**] **1,** free. **2,** vacant; unoccupied. **3,** loose. **4,** (*of time*) spare; free. **5,** free and easy; relaxed.

свободолюби́вый *adj.* freedom-loving. —**свободолюби́е,** *n.* love of freedom.

свободомы́слие *n.* free thought.

свободомы́слящий *adj.* freethinking. —*n.* freethinker.

свод *n.* **1,** code: свод зако́нов, code of laws. **2,** *archit.* arch. —**небéсный свод,** the firmament.

своди́ть¹ *v. impfv.* [*pfv.* **свести́;** *pres.* **свожу́, свóдишь**] **1,** to lead down; take down; help (someone) down. **2,** to take (a person somewhere on foot). **3,** to lead away. **4,** to join; tie together. **5,** *fig.* to bring together. **6,** to remove (a stain, wart, etc.). **7,** (*with* **на** + *acc. or* **к** *or* **до**) to reduce: своди́ть к ми́нимуму, to reduce to a minimum. **8,** (*with* **в** + *acc.*) to incorporate (into): своди́ть в табли́цу, to tabulate. **9,** to square; settle: своди́ть счёты с, to settle scores with. **10,** *fig.* to turn; switch (a conversation, one's thoughts, etc.). **11,** to cramp. *Also impers.:* у меня́ свело́ но́гу, I have a cramp in my leg. —**не своди́ть глаз с** (+ *gen.*), not take one's eyes off... —**своди́ть в моги́лу,** to be the death of. —**своди́ть дру́жбу с,** to make friends with. —**своди́ть концы́ с конца́ми,** to make ends meet. —**своди́ть на нет,** to negate; nullify. —**своди́ть с ума́,** to drive mad; drive out of one's mind.

СВОДИ́ТЬ² *v. pfv.* [*infl.* **свожу́, сво́дишь**] to take to and back; lead to and back.

СВОДИ́ТЬСЯ *v.r. impfv.* [*pfv.* **свести́сь;** *pres.* **сво́дится**] to come (down) to: своди́ться на нет *or* к нулю́, to come to naught. Всё де́ло сво́дится к э́тому, the whole thing comes (*or* boils) down to this.

СВО́ДКА [*gen. pl.* **-док**] *n.* summary. Сво́дка пого́ды, weather report; weather forecast.

СВО́ДНИК *n.* procurer; pimp.

СВО́ДНИЧАТЬ *v. impfv.* to pander.

СВО́ДНИЧЕСТВО *n.* procuring.

СВО́ДНЫЙ *adj.* combined; consolidated; composite. —**сво́дный брат, 1,** stepbrother. **2,** half brother. —**сво́дная сестра́, 1,** stepsister. **2,** half sister.

СВО́ДЧАТЫЙ *adj.* arched; vaulted.

СВОЕВО́ЛИЕ *n.* arbitrariness; high-handedness; capriciousness.

СВОЕВО́ЛЬНЫЙ *adj.* strong-willed; headstrong.

СВОЕВРЕ́МЕННЫЙ *adj.* timely; opportune. —**своевре́менно,** *adv.* in time. —**своевре́менность,** *n.f.* timeliness.

СВОЕКОРЫ́СТИЕ *n.* self-interest. —**своекоры́стный,** *adj.* self-seeking.

СВОЕНРА́ВИЕ *n.* arbitrariness; capriciousness. —**своенра́вный,** *adj.* arbitrary; capricious.

СВОЕОБРА́ЗИЕ *n.* distinctive quality.

СВОЕОБРА́ЗНЫЙ *adj.* distinctive; singular; peculiar.

СВОЗИ́ТЬ¹ *v. impfv.* [*pfv.* **свезти́;** *pres.* **свожу́, сво́зишь**] **1,** to gather together (*in one place*). **2,** to drive down. **3,** to take away; cart away. *See also* **свезти́.**

СВОЗИ́ТЬ² *v. pfv.* [*infl.* **свожу́, сво́зишь**] to drive; take (someone) to and back.

СВОЙ [*infl. like* **мой**] *poss. adj. & pron., used when the possessor is the subject of the sentence.* **1,** one's; my; his; her; their: снять свою́ шля́пу, to take off one's hat. **2,** one's own: у них своя́ маши́на, they have their own car; they have a car of their own. —**свой,** *n. pl.* one's own people. —**брать своё, 1,** to succeed; prevail. **2,** to take its toll. —**доби́ться своего́,** to gain one's objective; get one's way. —**наста́ивать на своём,** to insist on having one's own way. —**настоя́ть на своём,** to have one's own way. —**оста́ться при свои́х,** to break even (*in gambling*). —**получи́ть своё,** to get one's just reward. —**стоя́ть на своём,** to stand one's ground.

СВО́ЙСТВЕННИК *n.* relative by marriage; in-law.

СВО́ЙСТВЕННЫЙ *adj.* (*with dat.*) characteristic: со сво́йственным ему́ ю́мором, with his characteristic humor. Челове́ку сво́йственно ошиба́ться, to err is human.

СВО́ЙСТВО *n.* property; attribute; characteristic.

СВОЙСТВО́ *n.* relationship by marriage.

СВОЛА́КИВАТЬ *v. impfv.* [*pfv.* **своло́чь**] *colloq.* to drag; drag off; drag down.

СВО́ЛОЧЬ *n.f., vulg.* **1,** riffraff; rabble. **2,** swine; scoundrel.

СВОЛО́ЧЬ [*infl.* **-локу́, -лочёшь, ...-локу́т;** *past* **-лок, -локла́, -локло́**] *v., pfv. of* **свола́кивать.**

СВО́РА *n.* **1,** leash. **2,** pack (*of dogs, wolves, etc.*). **3,** gang.

СВОРА́ЧИВАТЬ *v. impfv.* [*pfv.* **сверну́ть**] **1,** *v.i.* to turn: свора́чивать с доро́ги/в переу́лок/, to turn off the road/down a side street/. **2,** *v.t., colloq.* to turn: свора́чивать маши́ну нале́во, to turn a car to the left.

СВОЯ́К [*gen.* **свояка́**] *n.* brother-in-law (*wife's sister's husband*).

СВОЯ́ЧЕНИЦА *n.* sister-in-law (*wife's sister*).

СВЫКА́ТЬСЯ *v.r. impfv.* [*pfv.* **свы́кнуться**] (*with* **с** + *instr.*) to get used to.

СВЫ́КНУТЬСЯ [*past* **свы́кся, свы́клась**] *v.r., pfv. of* **свыка́ться.**

СВЫСОКА́ *adv.* **1,** *obs.* from on high. **2,** with disdain: смотре́ть на (+ *acc.*) свысока́, to look down on.

СВЫ́ШЕ *adv.* from above; from on high. —*prep., with gen.* **1,** over; more than. **2,** beyond: свы́ше мои́х сил, beyond me; more than I can handle.

СВЯ́ЗАННЫЙ *adj.* **1,** related; connected. **2,** (*of movements*) awkward; (*of speech*) halting. *See also* **свя́зывать** (*sense #5*).

СВЯЗА́ТЬ [*infl.* **свяжу́, свя́жешь**] *v., pfv. of* **вяза́ть** *and* **свя́зывать.** —**связа́ться,** *refl., pfv. of* **свя́зываться.**

СВЯЗИ́СТ *n.* **1,** *mil.* signalman. **2,** telephone or telegraph worker.

СВЯ́ЗКА [*gen. pl.* **-зок**] *n.* **1,** bunch; bundle. **2,** ligament. —**глаго́л-свя́зка,** linking verb. —**голосовы́е свя́зки,** vocal cords.

СВЯЗНО́Й *adj.* liaison (*attrib.*); communications (*attrib.*). —*n.* messenger.

СВЯ́ЗНЫЙ *adj.* coherent; connected. —**свя́зность,** *n.f.* coherence.

СВЯЗУ́ЮЩИЙ *adj.* connecting.

СВЯ́ЗЫВАТЬ *v. impfv.* [*pfv.* **связа́ть**] **1,** to tie; bind; tie together. **2,** to connect; link; join. **3,** to put in touch with. **4,** *fig.* to bind: свя́зан обеща́нием, bound by a promise. Судьба́ их связа́ла, fate bound them together. **5,** *past passive part. only,* A, to connect; associate: всё, что свя́зано с э́тим, everything connected/associated/having to do/with it. B, to involve; entail: э́то свя́зано с ри́ском, it involves/entails risk. —**связа́ть свою́ судьбу́ с,** to cast one's lot with. —**связа́ть по рука́м и нога́м, 1,** to bind hand and foot. **2,** *fig.* to tie someone's hands.

СВЯ́ЗЫВАТЬСЯ *v.r. impfv.* [*pfv.* **связа́ться**] (*with* **с** + *instr.*) **1,** to contact; get in touch (with). **2,** *colloq.* to get involved (with).

СВЯЗЬ *n.f.* **1,** connection. **2,** tie; link: торго́вые свя́зи, trade ties. **3,** contact; touch: потеря́ть связь с, to lose contact/touch with. **4,** (illicit) affair; liaison. **5,** communication(s). **6,** *pl.* (personal) contacts; connections. **7,** coupling; tie. **8,** *mil.* liaison. —**в связи́ с** (+ *instr.*), **1,** in connection with. **2,** because of; owing to. —**в связи́ с э́тим, 1,** in this connection. **2,** as a result. —**в э́той связи́,** in this connection.

СВЯТЕ́ЙШЕСТВО *n.* Holiness: его́ святе́йшество, His Holiness.

святи́лище *n.* **1,** *obs.* temple; sanctuary. **2,** *fig.* revered place.

свя́тки [*gen.* -ток] *n. pl.* yuletide; the period from Christmas through January 6th.

свя́то *adv.* **1,** as if sacred: свя́то чтить что́-нибудь, to hold something sacred. **2,** scrupulously: свя́то соблюда́ть что́-нибудь, to observe something scrupulously.

свято́й *adj.* holy; sacred. —*n.* saint. —**свята́я и́стина**, gospel truth. —**свята́я святы́х**, holy of holies.

свя́тость *n.f.* holiness; sanctity.

святота́тство *n.* sacrilege. —**святота́тственный**, *adj.* sacrilegious.

святота́тствовать *v. impfv.* [*pres.* -ствую, -ствуешь] to commit sacrilege.

свя́точный *adj.* Christmas (*attrib.*).

свято́ша *n.m. & f.* pious hypocrite.

свя́тцы [*gen.* -цев] *n. pl.* church calendar.

святы́ня *n.* sacred object; holy place.

свяще́нник *n.* **1,** priest. **2,** clergyman.

свяще́ннический *adj.* **1,** priestly; sacerdotal. **2,** clergyman's; clergy's.

свяще́нный *adj.* sacred; holy.

свяще́нство *n.* priesthood.

сгиб *n.* **1,** bend. **2,** crook; joint.

сгиба́ть *v. impfv.* [*pfv.* согну́ть] to bend. —**сгиба́ться**, *refl.* **1,** (of an object) to bend. **2,** (of a person) to bend over.

сги́нуть *v. pfv., colloq.* to disappear; vanish.

сгла́дить [*infl.* -жу, -дишь] *v., pfv. of* сгла́живать.

сгла́живать *v. impfv.* [*pfv.* сгла́дить] **1,** to smooth; smooth out. **2,** *fig.* to smooth over.

сгла́зить *v.* [*infl.* -жу, -зишь] to jinx; put a hex on; give (someone) the evil eye.

сглупи́ть *v. pfv.* [*infl.* -плю́, -пи́шь] *colloq.* to do or say something foolish.

сгнить *v., pfv. of* гнить.

сгнои́ть *v., pfv. of* гнои́ть.

сгова́риваться *v.r. impfv.* [*pfv.* сговори́ться] **1,** to arrange (to do something). Та́йно сговори́ться (+ *inf.*), to secretly conspire to... **2,** to reach an agreement: с ним тру́дно сговори́ться, it is hard to reach an agreement with him; he is hard to deal with.

сго́вор *n.* **1,** conspiracy. **2,** collusion. **3,** *obs.* agreement; understanding. **4,** *obs.* betrothal.

сговори́ться *v.r., pfv. of* сгова́риваться.

сгово́рчивый *adj.* amenable.

сгоня́ть *v. impfv.* [*pfv.* согна́ть] **1,** to drive away; drive off; chase away; chase off. **2,** to drive together; round up. **3,** *colloq.* to take off (weight).

сгора́ние *n.* combustion. —**дви́гатель вну́треннего сгора́ния**, internal-combustion engine.

сгора́ть *v. impfv.* [*pfv.* сгоре́ть] **1,** to burn (up); be burned (up); burn down. **2,** (of fuel, firewood, etc.) to be consumed. **3,** (of vegetation) to wither; shrivel. **4,** *fig.* to burn oneself out. **5,** *fig.* (with от or с + *gen.*) to be dying (of shame, curiosity, etc.).

сго́рбить *v., pfv. of* го́рбить. —**сго́рбиться**, *refl., pfv. of* го́рбиться.

сго́рбленный *adj.* hunched; stooped.

сгоре́ть [*infl.* -рю́, -ри́шь] *v., pfv. of* сгора́ть.

сгоряча́ *adv.* in the heat of the moment; in a fit of temper.

сгреба́ть *v. impfv.* [*pfv.* сгрести́] **1,** to rake; sweep. **2,** *colloq.* to sweep off; brush off; shovel off.

сгрести́ [*infl. like* грести́] *v., pfv. of* сгреба́ть.

сгруди́ться *v.r. pfv., colloq.* to congregate; cluster.

сгружа́ть *v. impfv.* [*pfv.* сгрузи́ть] to unload.

сгрузи́ть [*infl.* сгружу́, сгру́зишь *or* сгрузи́шь] *v., pfv. of* сгружа́ть.

сгруппирова́ть *v., pfv. of* группирова́ть. —**сгруппирова́ться**, *refl., pfv. of* группирова́ться.

сгрыза́ть *v. impfv.* [*pfv.* сгрызть] to chew up.

сгрызть [*infl. like* грызть] *v., pfv. of* сгрыза́ть.

сгуби́ть *v. pfv.* [*infl.* сгублю́, сгу́бишь] *colloq.* to ruin.

сгусти́ть [*infl.* -щу́, -сти́шь] *v., pfv. of* сгуща́ть. —**сгусти́ться**, *refl., pfv. of* сгуща́ться.

сгу́сток [*gen.* -тка] *n.* **1,** clot: сгу́сток кро́ви, blood clot. **2,** *fig.* bundle: сгу́сток эне́ргии, bundle of energy.

сгуща́ть *v. impfv.* [*pfv.* сгусти́ть] **1,** to thicken; make thick. **2,** to condense. **3,** to clot; coagulate (blood). —**сгуща́ть кра́ски**, **1,** to (grossly) exaggerate. **2,** to make things out to be worse than they are.

сгуща́ться *v.r. impfv.* [*pfv.* сгусти́ться] to thicken; condense; clot; coagulate.

сгуще́ние *n.* thickening; coagulation; clotting.

сгущённый *adj.*, *in* сгущённое молоко́, condensed milk; evaporated milk.

сда́бривать *v. impfv.* [*pfv.* сдо́брить] to season; flavor; spice.

сдава́ть *v. impfv.* [*pfv.* сдать; *pres.* сдаю́, сдаёшь] **1,** to hand in; turn in. **2,** to hand over; turn over. **3,** to rent; lease; let. **4,** to surrender; give up. **5,** *cards* to deal. **6,** *v.i., colloq.* to decline (in health). **7,** *v.i., colloq.* to break down; give out. **8,** *in* сдава́ть экза́мен, to take an examination; сдать экза́мен, to pass an examination. —**сдава́ться**, *refl.* **1,** to surrender; give up. **2,** (in a game, esp. chess) to resign. **3,** [*impfv. only*] to be for rent. **4,** [*impfv. only*] (with dat.) *colloq.* to seem; appear.

сдави́ть [*infl.* сдавлю́, сда́вишь] *v., pfv. of* сда́вливать.

сда́вливать *v. impfv.* [*pfv.* сдави́ть] **1,** to squeeze. **2,** to constrict.

сда́точный *adj.* delivery (*attrib.*).

сдать [*infl. like* дать] *v., pfv. of* сдава́ть. —**сда́ться**, *refl.* [*past* сда́лся, сдала́сь, сдало́сь] *pfv. of* сдава́ться.

сда́ча *n.* **1,** handing over; handing in; turning in. **2,** returning; giving back. **3,** renting; leasing. **4,** surrender; giving up. **5,** taking (of an examination). **6,** *cards* deal; dealing. **7,** change (money given back). **8,** *fig., colloq.* riposte. —**дава́ть сда́чи** (with dat.), **1,** to hit back; strike back. **2,** to give (someone) tit for tat.

сдва́ивать *v. impfv.* [*pfv.* сдво́ить] to double.

сдвиг *n.* **1,** shift; change. **2,** *fig.* progress; step forward; change for the better. **3,** *geol.* fault.

сдвига́ть *v. impfv.* [*pfv.* сдви́нуть] **1,** to move (from a certain place). **2,** to move together; draw together. **3,** *in* сдви́нуть бро́ви, to knit one's brows.

сдвига́ться *v.r. impfv.* [*pfv.* сдви́нуться] **1,** to move; budge. **2,** to move closer together. —**сдвига́ться с ме́ста**, **1,** to move; budge. **2,** *fig.* to make headway.

сдво́ить *v., pfv. of* сдва́ивать.

сде́лать *v., pfv. of* де́лать. —**сде́латься**, *refl., pfv. of* де́латься (in senses #3 & #4).

сде́лка [*gen. pl.* -лок] *n.* transaction; bargain; deal.

сде́льный *adj.* by the piece. —**сде́льная рабо́та**, piecework.

сде́льщик *n.* pieceworker.

сде́льщина *n.* piecework.

сдёргивать *v. impfv.* [*pfv.* **сдёрнуть**] to pull off.

сде́ржанный *adj.* restrained; reserved. —**сде́ржанность**, *n.f.* restraint; reserve.

сдержа́ть *v. pfv.* [*infl.* **сдержу́, сде́ржишь**] 1, *pfv. of* **сде́рживать**. 2, to keep (one's word, a promise, etc.). —**сдержа́ться**, *refl., pfv. of* **сде́рживаться**.

сде́рживать *v. impfv.* [*pfv.* **сдержа́ть**] 1, to restrain; hold back; hold in check. 2, to hold back; suppress; repress (tears, laughter, a feeling, etc.). 3, to withstand. —**сде́рживаться** *n.f. refl.* to restrain oneself.

сдёрнуть *v., pfv. of* **сдёргивать**.

сдира́ть *v. impfv.* [*pfv.* **содра́ть**] 1, to strip; tear off; remove. 2, *colloq.* to cheat; "rip off".

сдо́ба *n.* 1, shortening. 2, sweet rolls; buns.

сдо́бный *adj.* (*of pastry*) rich. —**сдо́бная бу́лка**, bun.

сдо́брить *v., pfv. of* **сда́бривать**.

сдоброва́ть *v. pfv., in* ему́ (ей) не сдоброва́ть, it will not turn out well for him (her).

сдо́хнуть *v. pfv.* [*past* **сдох, -ла**] (*of animals*) to die.

сдружи́ть *v. pfv.* [*infl.* **сдружу́, сдру́жишь** *or* **сдру́жишь**] to bring together; make friends of. —**сдружи́ться**, *refl.* to become friends.

сдува́ть *v. impfv.* [*pfv.* **сдуть**] *v.t.* to blow away; blow off. *Also impers. and intrans.:* у него́ шля́пу сду́ло, his hat blew off. —**как ве́тром сду́ло**, disappeared completely.

сду́ру *adv., colloq.* foolishly; stupidly.

сдуть [*infl.* **сду́ю, сду́ешь**] *v., pfv. of* **сдува́ть**.

сё *dem. pron.* [*gen.* **сего́**] *used only in certain idiomatic expressions.* —**то-сё; то и сё; то да сё**, this and that: поговори́ть о том, о сём, to talk about this and that. —**ни то ни сё**, ordinary; nondescript. —**ни с того́ ни с сего́**, for no apparent reason; without rhyme or reason.

сеа́нс *n.* 1, performance; show. 2, sitting (*for a portrait*). 3, session. —**сеа́нс одновреме́нной игры́**, simultaneous chess exhibition.

себе́ *pron., dat. & prepl. of* себя́. *See* себя́.

себесто́имость *n.f.* (prime) cost.

себя́ *refl. pron.* [*dat. & prepl.* **себе́**; *instr.* **собо́й**] oneself (myself, yourself, himself, etc.): недооцени́ть себя́, to underestimate oneself; владе́ть собо́й, control oneself; отвеча́ть за себя́, answer for oneself; ду́мать то́лько о себе́, think only of oneself. —**быть сами́м собо́й**, *see* сам. —**вне себя́**, beside oneself: вне себя́ от ра́дости, beside oneself with joy. —**к себе́**, 1, to one's home. 2, (*sign on doors*) "pull". —**ме́жду собо́й**, among oneselves. —**не по себе́** (+ *dat.*), not to be feeling well. —**от себя́**, 1, for oneself; personally. 2, (*sign on doors*) "push". —**про себя́**, to oneself: чита́ть про себя́, to read to oneself. —**сам по себе́**, *see* сам. —**сам собо́й**, by itself; of itself. —**так себе́**, so-so. —**у себя́**, at home.

себялю́бец [*gen.* **-бца**] *n.* self-centered person.

себялюби́вый *adj.* selfish; self-centered. —**себялю́бие**, *n.* selfishness; egoism.

сев *n.* sowing.

се́вер *n.* north.

се́верный *adj.* northern; North; northerly.

се́веро-восто́к *n.* northeast. —**се́веро-восто́чный**, *adj.* northeast; northeastern; northeasterly.

се́веро-за́пад *n.* northwest. —**се́веро-за́падный**, *adj.* northwest; northwestern; northwesterly.

северя́нин [*pl.* **-я́не, -я́н**] *n.m.* [*fem.* **-я́нка**] northerner.

севооборо́т *n.* crop rotation.

севрю́га *n.* a variety of sturgeon.

сегме́нт *n., math.* segment.

сего́дня (vo) *adv.* today. Сего́дня у́тром, this morning. Сего́дня ве́чером, this evening; tonight. —**не сего́дня-за́втра**, any day now.

сего́дняшний (vo) *adj.* today's. —**сего́дняшний день**, today.

сегрега́ция *n.* segregation.

седа́лище *n., obs.* seat; place to sit.

седа́лищный *adj.* sciatic: седа́лищный нерв, sciatic nerve.

седе́льник *n.* saddler.

седе́льный *adj.* saddle (*attrib.*).

седе́ть *v. impfv.* [*pfv.* **поседе́ть**] to turn gray.

седи́ли *n.m.* cedilla.

седина́ [*pl.* **седи́ны**] *n., often pl.* gray hair. —**дожи́ть до седи́н**, to live to be old and gray.

седла́ть *v. impfv.* [*pfv.* **оседла́ть**] to saddle.

седло́ [*pl.* **сёдла, сёдел**] *n.* saddle.

седлови́на *n.* depression; dip.

седоволо́сый *adj.* gray-haired; white-haired. *Also,* **седовла́сый**.

седо́й *adj.* 1, (*of hair*) gray; white. 2, gray-haired; white-haired. —**дожи́ть до седы́х воло́с**, to live to be old and gray.

седо́к [*gen.* **-дока́**] *n.* 1, rider; horseman. 2, rider; passenger (*in a carriage*).

седьма́я *n., decl. as an adj.* seventh: одна́ седьма́я, one-seventh.

седьмо́й *ordinal numeral* seventh.

сеза́м *n.* sesame. —**сеза́мовый**, *adj.* sesame.

сезо́н *n.* season. —**сезо́нный**, *adj.* season (*attrib.*); seasonal.

сей *dem. pron.* [*fem.* **сия́**; *neut.* **сие́**; *pl.* **сии́**; *gen.* **сего́, сей, сих**; *acc. fem.* **сию́**; *dat.* **сему́, сей, сим**; *instr.* **сим, сей, си́ми**; *prepl.* **сём, сей, сих**] *obs.* this. —**до сих пор**, until now. —**на сей раз**, this time. —**по сей день**, to this day. —**при сём**, hereto; herewith. —**сего́ го́да**, (*with dates* — *usu. abbr. to* c.г.) of this year. —**сим**, hereby. —**сию́ мину́ту**, this minute; this instant.

сейсми́ческий *adj.* seismic.

сейсмо́граф *n.* seismograph.

сейсмоло́гия *n.* seismology. —**сейсмо́лог**, *n.* seismologist. —**сейсмологи́ческий**, *adj.* seismological.

сейф *n.* safe.

сейча́с *adv.* 1, now; right now; at present: он сейча́с за́нят, he is busy right now. 2, right now; right away; at once; immediately: я сейча́с верну́сь, I'll be right back. 3, just; just now: она́ сейча́с звони́ла, she just called. —**сейча́с же**, 1, right now; immediately; at once. 2, right away; immediately (*in the past*).

се́канс *n., trig.* secant.

сека́ч [*gen.* **-кача́**] *n.* chopper (*tool*).

секве́стр *n.* sequestration.

секвестрова́ть *v. impfv. & pfv.* [*pres.* **-ру́ю, -ру́ешь**] to sequester.

секво́йя *n.* sequoia; redwood.

секи́ра *n.* poleax.

секре́т *n.* secret: большо́й секре́т, a big secret. Держа́ть (что́-нибудь) в секре́те, to keep (something) secret. —**по секре́ту**, confidentially; in confidence.

—под больши́м (*or* по́лным) секре́том, in strict confidence.

секретариа́т *n.* secretariat.

секрета́рский *adj.* secretarial.

секрета́рствовать *v. impfv.* [*pres.* -ствую, -ству-ешь] to serve as secretary.

секрета́рь [*gen.* -таря́] *n.m.* [*fem.* -та́рша] secretary. —генера́льный секрета́рь, *see* генера́льный. —госуда́рственный секрета́рь, secretary of state.

секрете́р (тэ) *n.* desk; writing table.

секре́тничать *v. impfv., colloq.* **1,** to keep things secret. **2,** to talk confidentially.

секре́тно *adv.* secretly; in secret. —соверше́нно секре́тно, top secret.

секре́тность *n.f.* secrecy.

секре́тный *adj.* secret.

секре́ция *n.* secretion. —железа́ вну́тренней секре́ции, ductless gland; endocrine gland.

секс *n.* sex.

се́кста *n., music* sixth.

секста́нт *n.* sextant.

сексте́т *n.* sextet.

сексуа́льный *adj.* sexual. —сексуа́льность, *n.f.* sexuality.

се́кта *n.* sect.

секта́нт *n.* sectarian. —секта́нтский, *adj.* sectarian. —секта́нтство, *n.* sectarianism.

се́ктор *n.* sector.

секуляриза́ция *n.* secularization.

секуляризи́ровать *v. impfv. & pfv.* [*pres.* -рую, -руешь] to secularize.

секу́нда *n.* **1,** second (*of time or angular measurement*). **2,** *music* second.

секунда́нт *n.* second (*in a duel, chess match, etc.*).

секу́ндный *adj.* **1,** second (*attrib.*): секу́ндная стре́лка, second hand (*on a watch*). **2,** lasting only a second; momentary.

секундоме́р *n.* stopwatch.

секу́щая *n., decl. as an adj., geom.* secant.

секцио́нный *adj.* sectional.

се́кция *n.* section.

селёдка [*gen. pl.* -док] *n., colloq.* herring. —селё-дочный, *adj.* herring (*attrib.*).

селезёнка *n.* spleen. —селезёночный, *adj.* splenetic.

се́лезень [*gen.* -зня] *n.m.* drake; male duck.

селе́кция *n.* breeding (*of plants and animals*).

селе́н *n.* selenium.

селе́ние *n.* village; settlement.

селени́т *n.* selenite.

сели́тра *n.* saltpeter; niter. —аммиа́чная *or* аммо́ниевая сели́тра, ammonium nitrate. —ка́лиевая *or* кали́йная сели́тра, potassium nitrate. —на́триевая сели́тра, sodium nitrate.

сели́тряный *adj.* saltpeter (*attrib.*); nitric.

сели́ть *v. impfv.* to settle. —сели́ться, *refl.* to settle; take up residence.

село́ [*pl.* сёла] *n.* village. —ни к селу́ ни к го́роду, apropos of nothing; for no apparent reason.

сельдере́й *n.* celery. —сельдере́йный, *adj.* celery (*attrib.*).

сельдь [*pl.* се́льди, -де́й, -дя́м] *n.f.* herring. —как се́льди в бо́чке, like sardines.

се́льский *adj.* **1,** rural. **2,** village (*attrib.*). —се́льское хозя́йство, agriculture.

сельскохозя́йственный *adj.* agricultural; farm (*attrib.*).

сельсове́т *n.* village soviet (*contr. of* се́льский сове́т).

се́льтерский *adj., in* се́льтерская вода́, seltzer water.

сема́нтика *n.* semantics. —семанти́ческий, *adj.* semantic.

семафо́р *n.* semaphore.

сёмга *n.* smoked salmon; lox.

семе́йный *adj.* family (*attrib.*).

семе́йственность *n.f.* **1,** attachment to family; family spirit. **2,** nepotism.

семе́йственный *adj.* attached to one's family; home-loving.

семе́йство *n.* **1,** = семья́. **2,** *biol.* family.

семени́ть *v. impfv., colloq., in* семени́ть нога́ми, to trip (along); walk with mincing steps.

семенни́к [*gen.* -ника́] *n.* **1,** seed plant. **2,** testicle.

семенно́й *adj.* **1,** seed (*attrib.*). **2,** seminal.

семёрка *n.* **1,** the numeral 7. **2,** *colloq.* anything numbered 7. **3,** *cards* seven.

се́меро *collective numeral* seven.

семе́стр *n.* semester.

се́мечко [*gen. pl.* -чек] *n.* **1,** *dim. of* се́мя. **2,** *pl.* sunflower seeds.

семидесятиле́тие *n.* **1,** seventieth anniversary; seventieth birthday. **2,** seventy-year period.

семидесятиле́тний *adj.* **1,** seventy-year (*attrib.*). **2,** seventy-year-old.

семидеся́тый *ordinal numeral* seventieth.

семидне́вный *adj.* seven-day (*attrib.*).

семикра́тный *adj.* sevenfold.

семиле́тие *n.* **1,** seventh anniversary; seventh birthday. **2,** seven-year period.

семиле́тка [*gen. pl.* -ток] *n.* **1,** seven-year school. **2,** Seven-Year Plan.

семиле́тний *adj.* **1,** seven-year (*attrib.*). **2,** seven-year-old.

семина́р *n.* seminar.

семина́рия *n.* seminary. —семинари́ст, *n.* seminary student; seminary graduate.

семисо́тый *ordinal numeral* seven-hundredth.

семи́тский *adj.* Semitic. *Also,* семити́ческий.

семиуго́льник *n.* heptagon. —семиуго́льный, *adj.* heptagonal.

семичасово́й *adj.* seven-hour: семичасово́й рабо́чий день, seven-hour working day.

семна́дцать *numeral* seventeen. —семна́дцатый, *ordinal numeral* seventeenth.

семь [*gen., dat., & prepl.* семи́; *instr.* семью́] *numeral* seven.

се́мьдесят [*gen., dat., & prepl.* семи́десяти; *instr.* семью́десятью] *numeral* seventy.

семьсо́т [*gen.* семисо́т; *dat.* семиста́м; *instr.* семьюста́ми; *prepl.* семиста́х] *numeral* seven hundred.

се́мью *adv.* seven times: се́мью пять — три́дцать пять, seven times five is 35.

семья́ [*pl.* се́мьи, се́мей, се́мьям] *n.* family.

семьяни́н *n.* family man.

се́мя [*gen., dat., & prepl.* се́мени; *instr.* се́менем; *pl.* семена́, семя́н, семена́м] *n. neut.* **1,** seed. **2,** semen. —пойти́ в семена́, (*of a plant*) to go to seed.

семядо́ля *n.* cotyledon.

семяизлия́ние *n.* ejaculation.

семяпо́чка [*gen. pl.* -чек] *n., bot.* ovule.

сена́т *n.* senate. —**сена́тор,** *n.* senator. —**сена́тор-ский,** *adj.* senator's; senatorial. —**сена́тский,** *adj.* senate (*attrib.*).

сенберна́р (сэ) *n.* Saint Bernard (*dog*).

се́ни [*gen.* сене́й] *n. pl.* entrance hall; vestibule.

сенни́к [*gen.* -ника́] *n.* straw mattress.

сенно́й *adj.* hay (*attrib.*). —**сенна́я лихора́дка,** hay fever.

се́но *n.* hay. —**соба́ка на се́не,** dog in the manger.

сенова́л *n.* hayloft.

сеноко́с *n.* **1,** haymaking. **2,** hayfield.

сеноко́силка [*gen. pl.* -лок] *n.* machine for mowing hay.

сенса́ция *n.* sensation. —**сенсацио́нный,** *adj.* sensational.

сенсо́рный (сэ) *adj.* sensory.

сентенцио́зный (сэ,тэ) *adj.* sententious.

сенте́нция (сэ, тэ) *n.* maxim; adage.

сентимента́льничать (сэ) *v. impfv.* **1,** to be sentimental. **2,** to be soft; be lenient.

сентимента́льный (сэ) *adj.* sentimental. —**сентимента́льность,** *n.f.* sentimentality.

сентя́брь [*gen.* -бря́] *n.m.* September. —**сентя́брь-ский,** *adj.* September (*attrib.*).

сень [*2nd loc.* сени́] *n.f., archaic* canopy. —**под се́нью** (+ *gen.*), under the protection of.

сепарати́зм *n.* separatism. —**сепарати́ст,** *n.* separatist. —**сепарати́стский,** *adj.* separatist.

сепара́тный *adj., polit.* separate: сепара́тный мир, separate peace.

сепара́тор *n.* separator.

се́пия (сэ) *n.* **1,** sepia. **2,** cuttlefish.

се́псис (сэ) *n.* sepsis.

се́птима (сэ) *n., music* seventh.

септи́ческий (сэ) *adj.* septic.

се́ра *n.* sulfur. —**ушна́я се́ра,** earwax.

сера́ль *n.m.* seraglio.

серафи́м *n.* seraph.

серб *n.m.* [*fem.* се́рбка] Serb.

сербохорва́тский *adj.* Serbo-Croatian.

се́рбский *adj.* Serbian.

сербскохорва́тский *adj.* Serbo-Croatian.

серва́нт *n.* sideboard.

серви́з *n.* set (*of dishes or silverware*): фарфо́ровый серви́з, set of china.

сервирова́ть *v. impfv. & pfv.* [*pres.* -ру́ю, -ру́ешь] **1,** to set (a table). **2,** to serve (a meal).

сервиро́вка [*often with* стола́] *n.* **1,** (act of) setting (a table). **2,** table arrangement.

серде́чник *n., colloq.* **1,** person with a heart ailment. **2,** heart specialist.

серде́чно *adv.* **1,** cordially; warmly. **2,** sincerely.

серде́чно-сосу́дистый *adj.* cardiovascular.

серде́чность *n.f.* warmth; cordiality.

серде́чный *adj.* **1,** heart (*attrib.*); cardiac. **2,** hearty; cordial. **3,** warmhearted; kind. **4,** heartfelt; sincere. **5,** of the heart; love (*attrib.*); romantic.

серди́тый *adj.* (*with* на + *acc.*) angry (at). —**серди́-то,** *adv.* angrily.

серди́ть *v. impfv.* [*pfv.* рассерди́ть; *pres.* сержу́, се́рдишь] to anger; make angry. —**серди́ться,** *refl.* (*with* на + *acc.*) to be angry (at); become angry (with).

сердобо́лие *n., obs.* compassion. —**сердобо́льный,** *adj., colloq.* tenderhearted.

се́рдце [*pl.* сердца́, серде́ц, сердца́м] *n.* heart. —**всем се́рдцем,** with all one's heart. —**в сердца́х,** *colloq.* in a fit of anger. —**от всего́ се́рдца,** from the bottom of one's heart. —**от полноты́ се́рдца,** in the fullness of one's heart. —**от чи́стого се́рдца,** in all sincerity. —**по́ сердцу** (+ *dat.*), to one's liking. —**брать за́ сердце,** to move deeply. —**положа́ ру́ку на́ сердце,** in all honesty. —**принима́ть (бли́зко) к се́рдцу,** to take to heart.

сердцебие́ние *n.* **1,** heartbeat. **2,** palpitation of the heart.

сердцеви́дка [*gen. pl.* -док] *n.* cockle (*mollusk*).

сердцеви́дный *adj.* heart-shaped.

сердцеви́на *n.* **1,** core. **2,** *fig.* core; heart.

сердцее́д *n., colloq.* lady-killer.

серебри́стый *adj.* silvery.

серебри́ть *v. impfv.* [*pfv.* посеребри́ть] to silver; silver-plate. —**серебри́ться,** *refl.* to become silvery.

серебро́ *n.* silver.

сере́бряник *n.* silversmith.

сере́бряный *adj.* silver. —**сере́бряных дел ма́стер,** silversmith.

середи́на *n.* middle. —**золота́я середи́на,** the golden mean; happy medium.

середи́нный *adj.* **1,** middle. **2,** *fig.* halfway; compromise (*attrib.*).

серёдка [*gen. pl.* -док] *n., colloq.* middle; center.

середня́к [*gen.* -няка́] *n.* middle-class peasant.

серёжка [*gen. pl.* -жек] *n.* **1,** earring. **2,** catkin. **3,** *colloq.* wattle (*on fowl*).

серена́да *n.* serenade.

сере́ть *v. impfv.* [*pfv.* посере́ть] to turn gray.

сержа́нт *n.* sergeant. —**сержа́нтский,** *adj.* sergeant's.

сери́йный *adj.* **1,** (*of production*) mass. **2,** mass-produced.

се́рия *n.* **1,** series. **2,** set (*of postage stamps*). **3,** part (*of a film*): кинофи́льм в трех се́риях, three-part film.

сермя́га *n.* **1,** a coarse undyed cloth. **2,** robe made of this cloth.

се́рна *n.* chamois.

серни́стый *adj.* **1,** containing sulfur: серни́стые краси́тели, sulfur dyes. **2,** sulfurous; sulfide (of): серни́стая кислота́, sulfurous acid; серни́стый водоро́д, hydrogen sulfide.

сернобы́к [*gen.* -быка́] *n.* oryx.

сернокислый *adj.* sulfate (of): сернокислый аммо́ний/ба́рий/на́трий, ammonium/barium/sodium sulfate. —**сернокислая соль,** sulfate.

се́рный *adj.* **1,** sulfur (*attrib.*). **2,** sulfuric.

сероводоро́д *n.* hydrogen sulfide.

сероло́гия *n.* serology.

серп [*gen.* серпа́] *n.* sickle. —**серп луны́,** crescent moon.

серпанти́н *n.* (paper) streamer.

сертифика́т *n.* certificate.

се́рый *adj.* **1,** gray. **2,** *fig.* dull; drab.

серьга́ [*pl.* се́рьги, серёг, серьга́м] *n.* earring.

серьёзно *adv.* **1,** seriously. Я говорю́ серьезно, I'm serious. **2,** (*in direct address*) seriously?; really?

серьёзность *n.f.* seriousness.

серьёзный *adj.* [*short form* -зен, -зна] serious.

се́ссия *n.* session.

сестра́ [*pl.* сёстры, сестёр, сёстрам] *n.* sister. —ме-дици́нская сестра́, (hospital) nurse.

сестрёнка [*gen. pl.* -нок] *n.* little sister.

сёстрин *adj.* one's sister's.

сестри́ца *also*, сестри́чка *n.*, *dim.* of сестра́.

сесть [*infl.* ся́ду, ся́дешь; *past* сел, се́ла] *v.*, *pfv.* of сади́ться.

сет (сэ) *n.*, *tennis* set.

се́тка [*gen. pl.* -ток] *n.* 1, net. 2, netting. 3, window screen. 4, *colloq.* string bag. 5, grid.

се́тование *n.* 1, complaining. 2, *usu. pl.* complaint.

се́товать *v. impfv.* [*pfv.* посе́товать; *pres.* -тую, туешь] 1, (*with* на + *acc. or a dependent clause*) to complain. 2, (*with* о *or a dependent clause*) to lament; bewail; bemoan.

се́ттер (сэ, тэ) *n.* setter.

сетча́тка *n.* retina.

се́тчатый *adj.* made of netting or gauze. —се́тчатая оболо́чка, retina.

сеть [*2nd loc.* сети́; *pl.* се́ти, сете́й, сетя́м] *n.f.* 1, net. 2, network.

сече́ние *n.* section: кони́ческое сече́ние, conic section; попере́чное сече́ние, cross section.

се́чка [*gen. pl.* -чек] *n.* 1, chopping knife. 2, fine-cut straw; chaff.

сечь *v. impfv.* [*pres.* секу́, сече́шь, ...секу́т] 1, [*impfv. only; past* сек, секла́, секло́] to cut to pieces; slash. 2, [*pfv.* вы́сечь, *past* сек, се́кла, се́кло] to whip; flog. —се́чься, *refl.* [*impfv. only*] [*past* се́кся, секла́сь, секло́сь] 1, (*of hair*) to be brittle; break. 2, (*of fabric*) to tear; fray.

се́ялка [*gen. pl.* -лок] *n.* seeding machine; seeder.

се́янец [*gen.* -нца] *n.* seedling.

се́ятель *n.m.* sower.

се́ять *v. impfv.* [*pfv.* посе́ять; *pres.* се́ю, се́ешь] to sow.

сжа́литься *v.r. pfv.* (*with* над) to take pity on.

сжа́тие *n.* 1, compression. 2, constriction. 3, grip; grasp.

сжа́тость *n.f.* conciseness.

сжа́тый *adj.* 1, (*of air*) compressed. 2, (*of fists*) clenched. 3, concise. —в сжа́тые сро́ки, in a short space of time.

сжать[1] [*infl.* сожму́, сожмёшь] *v.*, *pfv.* of сжима́ть. —сжа́ться, *refl.*, *pfv.* of сжима́ться.

сжать[2] [*infl.* сожну́, сожнёшь] *v.*, *pfv.* of жать[2].

сжечь [*infl.* сожгу́, сожжёшь,...сожгу́т; *past* жёг, сожгла́, сожгло́] *v.*, *pfv.* of жечь *and* сжига́ть.

сжива́ть *v. impfv.* [*pfv.* сжить] 1, *colloq.* to make (someone) move out (*by making life unbearable*). 2, *in* сжива́ть со све́та *or* со све́ту, to be the death of. —сжива́ться, *refl.* (*with* с + *instr.*) *colloq.* 1, to make friends with; become friendly with. 2, to get used to.

сжига́ть *v. impfv.* [*pfv.* сжечь] to burn.

сжижа́ть *v. impfv.* [*pfv.* сжиди́ть] to liquefy.

сжиже́ние *n.* liquefaction.

сжи́женный *adj.* liquefied.

сжима́ть *v. impfv.* [*pfv.* сжать] 1, to squeeze. 2, to clench (one's fist, teeth, etc.). 3, to compress. 4, to constrict (one's throat). 5, *fig.* to reduce; condense. —сжима́ться, *refl.* 1, to be compressed; be clenched. 2, to shrink; contract. 3, to tighten; close. 4, to shrink; huddle up (from cold, fear, etc.).

сжить [*infl. like* жить] *v.*, *pfv.* of сжива́ть. —сжи́ться, *refl.* [*past* сжи́лся, -ла́сь, -ло́сь] *pfv.* of сжива́ться.

сза́ди *adv.* 1, behind. 2, from behind; from the rear. —*prep.*, *with gen.* behind.

сзыва́ть *v. impfv.* = созыва́ть.

си *n. neut.*, *music* si; ti; B.

сиа́мский *adj.* Siamese.

сибари́т *n.* sybarite. —сибари́тский, *adj.* sybaritic.

сиби́рский *adj.* Siberian. —сиби́рская ко́шка, Persian cat. —сиби́рская я́зва, anthrax.

сибиря́к [*gen.* -яка́] *n.m.* [*fem.* -я́чка] Siberian.

си́вка [*gen. pl.* -вок] *n.m. & f.*, *colloq.* gray horse. —*n.f.* golden plover. —си́вка глупая, dotterel.

сиву́ха *n.* raw vodka.

си́вый *adj.* 1, (*of a horse*) gray. 2, *colloq.* (*of hair*) gray.

сиг [*gen.* сига́] *n.* whitefish.

сига́ра *n.* cigar.

сигаре́та *n.* cigarette. —сигаре́тный, *adj.* cigarette (*attrib.*).

сига́рный *adj.* cigar (*attrib.*).

сигна́л *n.* signal.

сигнализа́тор *n.* signaling device.

сигнализа́ция *n.* 1, signaling. 2, alarm system. 3, signaling system.

сигнализи́ровать *v. impfv. & pfv.* [*pres.* -рую, -руешь] 1, to signal. 2, *fig.* (*with acc. or* о) to warn (of).

сигна́льный *adj.* signal (*attrib.*). —сигна́льный ого́нь, signal light; beacon.

сигна́льщик *n.* signalman; flagman.

сигнату́ра *n.* label (*on a medicine bottle*).

сиде́лка [*gen. pl.* -лок] *n.* nurse.

сиде́ние *n.* sitting.

си́день [*gen.* -дня] *n.m.*, *obs.* stay-at-home. —си́днем сиде́ть, to stay home all the time.

сиде́нье *n.* seat.

сиде́ть *v. impfv.* [*pres.* сижу́, сиди́шь] 1, to sit; be sitting: сиде́ть на полу́, be sitting on the floor. Сиде́ть за уро́ками, to sit doing one's lessons. Сиде́ть без де́ла, to sit around doing nothing. 2, (*with certain nouns*) to be: сиде́ть на дие́те, to be on a diet. 3, (*of clothes*) to fit. 4, to be in prison. —сиде́ться, *refl.*, *used negatively with dat.* to be restless; be unable to sit for long (in a certain place): ему́ не сиди́тся на ме́сте, he can't sit still.

сидр *n.* cider. —си́дровый, *adj.* cider (*attrib.*).

сидя́чий *adj.* 1, sitting. 2, sedentary. —сидя́чая забасто́вка, sit-down strike.

сие́на *n.* sienna.

сиза́ль *n.m.* sisal.

си́зый *adj.* blue-gray.

сикомо́р *n.* sycamore.

си́ла *n.* 1, strength. 2, force: си́ла уда́ра, the force of a blow. Си́лой ору́жия, by force of arms. 3, power: лошади́ная си́ла, horsepower. Си́ла печа́тного сло́ва, the power of the printed word. 4, effect; force: вступа́ть в си́лу, to go into effect/force. 5, *pl.*, *mil.* forces: вооружённые си́лы, armed forces. 6, *pl.* forces; elements: реакцио́нные си́лы, reactionary forces/elements. —быть (не) в си́лах, (not) to be able; (not) have the strength (*fig.*). —в ме́ру сил; по ме́ре сил, as far as one is able. —всё, что в (чьи́х-нибудь) си́лах, everything in one's power. —все́ми си́лами, in every way. —в си́лу (+ *gen.*), on the strength of; by virtue of. —изо всех сил, with all one's might.

—не под сúлу (+ *dat.*), too much for; beyond one. **—от сúлы**, at the most. **—чéрез сúлу**, with the utmost difficulty; by forcing oneself. **—что есть сил**, for all one is worth.

силáч [*gen.* -лачá] *n.* strong man.

силикагéль *n.m.* silica gel.

силикáт *n.* silicate.

силикóн *n.* silicone.

сúлиться *v.r. impfv., colloq.* to try; make an effort.

силлогúзм *n.* syllogism. **—силлогистúческий; силлогúчный**, *adj.* syllogistic.

силовóй *adj.* power (*attrib.*): силовáя стáнция, power station; power plant.

силóк [*gen.* -лкá] *n.* snare.

силомéр *n.* dynamometer.

сúлос *n.* **1,** silage. **2,** silo. **—сúлосный**, *adj.* silage (*attrib.*).

силуэ́т *n.* silhouette.

сúльно *adv.* **1,** strongly; powerfully. **2,** very much; greatly.

сúльный *adj.* [*short form* сúлен *or* силён, сильнá, сúльно, сúльны *or* сильнь́] **1,** strong; powerful. **2,** severe; intense; violent. **3,** (*of a student*) good.

сильф *n.* sylph. **—сильфúда**, *n.* sylphid.

СИМ *see* сей.

симбиóз *n.* symbiosis.

сúмвол *n.* symbol.

символизúровать *v. impfv. & pfv.* [*pres.* -рую, -руешь] to symbolize; be symbolic of.

символúзм *n.* symbolism.

симвóлика *n.* **1,** symbolism. **2,** symbols.

символúческий *adj.* symbolic. *Also*, **символúчный**.

симметрúя *n.* symmetry. **—симметрúческий; симметрúчный**, *adj.* symmetrical.

симпатизúровать *v. impfv.* [*pres.* -рую, -руешь] (*with dat.*) **1,** to like; be fond of. **2,** to be in sympathy with.

симпатúческий *adj., anat.; physiol.* sympathetic: симпатúческая нéрвная систéма, sympathetic nervous system. **—симпатúческие чернúла**, invisible ink.

симпатúчный *adj.* likable; nice.

симпáтия *n.* **1,** (*with* к) liking (for). **2,** *pl.* sympathies: симпáтии слýшателей, the sympathies of the audience.

симпóзиум *n.* symposium.

симптóм *n.* symptom. **—симптоматúческий**, *adj., med.* symptomatic.

симптоматúчный *adj.* **1,** symptomatic; significant; indicative of something. **2,** = **симптоматúческий**.

симулúровать *v. impfv. & pfv.* [*pres.* -рую, -руешь] to simulate; feign.

симулянт *n.* **1,** simulator. **2,** malingerer.

симуляция *n.* **1,** simulation. **2,** malingering.

симфонúческий *adj.* **1,** symphony (*attrib.*). **2,** symphonic.

симфóния *n.* symphony.

синагóга *n.* synagogue.

синдикáт *n.* syndicate.

синдрóм *n.* syndrome.

синевá *n.* **1,** blue color. **2,** blue expanse. **—синевá под глазáми**, blue circles under one's eyes.

синевáтый *adj.* bluish.

синеглáзый *adj.* blue-eyed.

синекýра *n.* sinecure.

синéль *n.f.* chenille.

синéть *v. impfv.* [*pfv.* посинéть] **1,** to turn blue; become blue. **2,** [*impfv. only*] (*of anything blue*) to appear.

сúний *adj.* (dark) blue.

синúльный *adj., in* синúльная кислотá, prussic acid.

синúть *v. impfv.* [*pfv.* подсинúть] **1,** to dye blue. **2,** to rinse in bluing; blue.

синúца *n.* titmouse; tomtit.

синкóпа *n.* **1,** *music* syncopation. **2,** *gram.* syncope.

синкопúровать *v. impfv. & pfv.* [*pres.* -рую, -руешь] *music* to syncopate.

синóд *n.* synod. **—синодáльный**, *adj.* synodal.

синóним *n.* synonym. **—синонимúческий; синонимúчный**, *adj.* synonymous.

синóптика *n.* weather forecasting. **—синóптик**, *n.* weather forecaster.

синоптúческий *adj.* pert. to weather forecasting: синоптúческая кáрта, weather map.

сúнтаксис *n.* syntax. **—синтаксúческий**, *adj.* syntactical.

сúнтез (тэ) *n.* **1,** synthesis. **2,** *physics* fusion.

синтезúровать (тэ) *v. impfv. & pfv.* [*pres.* -рую, руешь] to synthesize.

синтетúческий (тэ) *adj.* synthetic.

синтоúзм *n.* Shinto; Shintoism.

сúнус *n.* **1,** *math.* sine. **2,** *anat.* sinus. **—синуúт; синусúт**, *n.* sinusitis.

синхронизáция *n.* synchronization.

синхронизúровать *v. impfv. & pfv.* [*pres.* -рую, руешь] to synchronize.

синхронúческий *adj.* synchronic.

синхрóнный *adj.* synchronous. **—синхрóнный перевóд**, simultaneous translation.

синь *n.f.* blue color.

сúнька *n.* **1,** blueing. **2,** blueprint.

синю́ха *n.* cyanosis.

синю́шность *n.f.* = синю́ха.

синяк [*gen.* -якá] *n.* **1,** bruise; black-and-blue mark. **2,** *in* синякú под глазáми, dark patches under one's eyes. **—избивáть до синякóв**, to beat black-and-blue.

сионúзм *n.* Zionism. **—сионúст**, *n.* Zionist. **—сионúстский**, *adj.* Zionist.

сип *n.* griffon vulture.

сипéть *v. impfv.* [*pres.* сиплю́, сипúшь] **1,** (*of something hot*) to hiss. **2,** to speak in a hoarse voice. **3,** *impers.* to be hoarse: у меня́ в гóрле сипúт, my throat is hoarse.

сúплый *adj.* hoarse; husky.

сúпнуть *v. impfv.* [*past* сип *or* сúпнул, сúпла] to become hoarse.

сипу́ха *n.* barn owl.

сирéна *n.* siren.

сирéнь *n.f.* lilac. **—сирéневый**, *adj.* lilac.

сúречь *conj., archaic* that is to say.

сирúец [*gen.* -úйца] *n.m.* [*fem.* -úйка] Syrian. **—сирúйский**, *adj.* Syrian.

сирóкко *n.m. indecl.* sirocco.

сирóп *n.* syrup.

сиротá [*pl.* сирóты] *n.m. & f.* orphan. **—крýглый** *or* **крýглая сиротá**, child who has lost both parents.

сиротéть *v. impfv.* [*pfv.* осиротéть] to be orphaned.

сиротлúвый *adj.* lonely.

сирóтский *adj.* orphan (*attrib.*); orphan's. **—сирóтский дом** *or* **прию́т**, orphanage; orphan asylum.

сирóтство *n.* orphanhood.

система *n.* system.

систематизи́ровать *v. impfv. & pfv.* [*pres.* -ру́ю, ру́ешь] to systematize.

системати́ческий *adj.* systematic. —**системати́чески,** *adv.* systematically.

си́стола *n.* systole. —**систоли́ческий,** *adj.* systolic.

си́тец [*gen.* си́тца] *n.* printed cotton fabric; chintz.

си́течко [*gen. pl.* -чек] *n.* filter; strainer.

си́тник *n.* **1,** rush (*plant*). **2,** *colloq.* bread made of sifted flour.

си́то *n.* sieve; strainer.

ситуа́ция *n.* situation.

си́тцевый *adj.* made of printed cotton; chintz (*attrib.*).

си́филис *n.* syphilis. —**сифили́тик,** *n., colloq.* syphilitic. —**сифилити́ческий,** *adj.* syphilitic.

сифо́н *n.* siphon.

сия́ние *n.* **1,** glow. **2,** halo. **3,** *fig.* radiance. —**се́верное сия́ние,** northern lights; aurora borealis.

сия́ть *v. impfv.* to shine; beam; glow.

скабрёзный *adj.* indecent; off-color; bawdy; dirty. —**скабрёзность,** *n.f.* dirty word; *pl.* indecent language.

сказ *n.* epic tale.

сказа́ние *n.* folk legend.

ска́занное *n., decl. as an adj.* what has been said.

сказа́ть [*infl.* скажу́, ска́жешь] *v., pfv. of* говори́ть. —**е́сли не сказа́ть** (+ *adj.*), if not... —**мо́жно сказа́ть,** you might say. —**не́чего сказа́ть,** *see* не́чего. —**сказа́ть своё сло́во,** to have one's say; make one's presence felt. —**так сказа́ть,** so to speak; as it were. —**хоте́ть сказа́ть,** to mean. —**что́бы** (*or* е́сли) **не сказа́ть бо́льше,** to say the least.

сказа́ться [*infl.* скажу́сь, ска́жешься] *v.r., pfv. of* ска́зываться.

скази́тель *n.m.* teller of folk tales.

ска́зка [*gen. pl.* -зок] *n.* tale.

ска́зочник *n.* storyteller.

ска́зочный *adj.* **1,** fairy-tale (*attrib.*). **2,** fabulous; fantastic.

сказу́емое *n., decl. as an adj., gram.* predicate.

ска́зываться *v.r. impfv.* [*pfv.* сказа́ться] **1,** *colloq.* to be told. **2,** (*with* в + *prepl.*) to be manifest (in); be seen (in). **3,** (*with* на + *prepl.*) to have an effect (upon); tell (on *or* upon). **4,** (*with instr.*) *colloq.* to pose as; pretend to be. **5,** *obs.* to give warning; give notice.

скака́лка [*gen. pl.* -лок] *n.* jump rope.

скака́ть *v. impfv.* [*pres.* скачу́, ска́чешь] **1,** to jump; skip. **2,** to gallop (*on horseback*). **3,** (*of a horse*) to race. —**скака́ть на одно́й ноге́,** to hop.

скаково́й *adj.* racing (*attrib.*). —**скакова́я ло́шадь,** racehorse.

скаку́н [*gen.* -куна́] *n.* fast horse; racer.

скала́ [*pl.* ска́лы] *n.* **1,** rock. **2,** [*often* отве́сная скала́] cliff. —**подво́дная скала́,** reef.

скали́стый *adj.* rocky.

ска́лить *v. impfv., in* ска́лить зу́бы, **1,** to bare one's teeth. **2,** *colloq.* to laugh; smile; grin.

ска́лка [*gen. pl.* -лок] *n.* rolling pin.

ска́лывать *v. impfv.* [*pfv.* сколо́ть] **1,** to chop away; chip away. **2,** to pin together.

скальки́ровать *v., pfv. of* кальки́ровать.

скалькули́ровать *v., pfv. of* калькули́ровать.

скальп *n.* scalp (*taken from the head of an enemy*).

ска́льпель *n.m.* scalpel.

скальпи́ровать *v. impfv. & pfv.* [*pres.* -ру́ю, -ру́ешь] to scalp.

скаме́ечка [*gen. pl.* -чек] *n.* small bench.

скаме́йка [*gen. pl.* -ме́ек] *n.* bench. —**скаме́йка для ног,** footstool.

скамья́ [*pl.* скамьи́ *or* ска́мьи, скаме́й, скамья́м] *n.* **1,** bench. **2,** *in* скамья́ подсуди́мых, the dock. —**со шко́льной скамьи́,** right out of school.

сканда́л *n.* **1,** scandal. **2,** row; brawl.

скандализи́ровать *v. impfv. & pfv.* [*pres.* -ру́ю, -ру́ешь] to scandalize.

скандали́ст *n.* trouble-maker; rowdy.

сканда́лить *v. impfv.* [*pfv.* наскanда́лить] to make a fuss; kick up a row.

сканда́льный *adj.* **1,** scandalous. **2,** rowdy; boisterous. **3,** *colloq.* (*of a person*) always making a fuss.

ска́ндий *n.* scandium.

скандина́в *n.m.* [*fem.* -на́вка] Scandinavian. —**скандина́вский,** *adj.* Scandinavian.

сканди́ровать *v. impfv. & pfv.* [*pres.* -ру́ю, -ру́ешь] **1,** to scan (verse). **2,** to enunciate. **3,** (*of a crowd*) to chant.

ска́пливать *v. impfv.* [*pfv.* скопи́ть] to save up; amass. —**ска́пливаться,** *refl.* **1,** to pile up; accumulate. **2,** to gather; congregate.

скарабе́й *n.* scarab.

скарб *n., colloq.* household belongings.

ска́редный *adj., colloq.* miserly; stingy.

скарлати́на *n.* scarlet fever. —**скарлати́нный,** *adj., colloq.* of scarlet fever.

ска́рмливать *v. impfv.* [*pfv.* скорми́ть] to feed: ска́рмливать се́но лошадя́м, to feed hay to the horses.

скат *n.* **1,** slope; incline. **2,** ramp; slide. **3,** *zool.* ray; skate.

ската́ть *v., pfv. of* ска́тывать (*in sense #1*).

ска́терть [*pl.* ска́терти, -те́й, -тя́м] *n.f.* tablecloth. —**ска́тертью доро́га!,** good riddance!

скати́ть [*infl.* скачу́, ска́тишь] *v., pfv. of* ска́тывать (*in sense #2*). —**скати́ться,** *refl., pfv. of* ска́тываться.

ска́тывать *v. impfv.* **1,** [*pfv.* ската́ть] to roll up (*into a ball or bundle*). **2,** [*pfv.* скати́ть] to roll down (a slope). —**ска́тываться,** *refl.* [*pfv.* скати́ться] **1,** to roll down; slide down. **2,** *fig.* (*with* в, на, *or* к) to slide into; slip into.

ска́ут *n.* boy scout.

скафа́ндр *n.* **1,** diving suit. **2,** space suit.

ска́чка [*gen. pl.* -чек] *n.* **1,** horse race. **2,** *pl.* the races.

скачкообра́зный *adj.* uneven; spasmodic.

скачо́к [*gen.* -чка́] *n.* **1,** jump; leap. **2,** *fig.* sudden change. —**скачка́ми,** by leaps and bounds.

ска́шивать *v. impfv.* [*pfv.* скоси́ть] **1,** to mow; cut. **2,** *fig.* to strike down; cut down. **3,** to twist; tilt. **4,** to cock (one's eye). **5,** to bevel; miter.

сква́жина *n.* chink; slit. —**замо́чная сква́жина,** keyhole. —**нефтяна́я сква́жина,** oil well.

сквайр *n.* squire.

сквалы́га *n.m. & f., colloq.* cheapskate; skinflint. *Also,* **сквалы́жник,** *n.m.*

сква́ттер (тэ) *n.* squatter.

сквер *n.* public garden.

скве́рно *adv.* badly; bad.

скверносло́в *n.* foul-mouthed person. —**скверносло́вие,** *n.* foul language.

сквернословить v. impfv. [pres. -влю, -вишь] to swear; use foul language.

скверный adj. **1,** foul; nasty. **2,** vulgar; indecent. **3,** colloq. bad; awful; lousy.

сквитать v. pfv., obs. to repay. —**сквитаться**, refl. (with с + instr.) colloq. **1,** to settle up (with). **2,** to settle scores (with).

сквозить v. impfv. **1,** impers. to be drafty: здесь сквозит, there is a draft in here. **2,** (with через) (of wind) to blow through; get through; (of light) pass through; filter through. **3,** to be transparent; admit light. **4,** (with сквозь) to be seen (through). **5,** fig. to creep in: в его ответе сквозило раздражение, a trace of irritation crept into his answer.

сквозной adj. **1,** (of a hole or wound) going all the way through. **2,** thin; sheer. —**сквозной ветер**, draft.

сквозняк [gen. -няка́] n. draft: сидеть на сквозняке, to be (or sit) in a draft.

сквозь prep., with acc. through: пробираться сквозь толпу, to make one's way through a crowd.

скворец [gen. -рца] n. starling.

скворечник n. bird house (for starlings). Also, **скворечня** [gen. pl. -чен].

скелет n. skeleton. —**скелетный**, adj. skeletal.

скептик n. skeptic. —**скептицизм**, n. skepticism. —**скептический**, adj. skeptical.

скерцо n. indecl. scherzo.

скетч n. sketch; skit.

скидка [gen. pl. -док] n. **1,** discount; reduction. **2,** fig. (with на + acc.) allowance (for).

скидывать v. impfv. [pfv. скинуть] **1,** to throw off; throw down. **2,** fig., colloq. to overthrow. **3,** colloq. to take off. **4,** fig. to shake off (laziness, a feeling, etc.). **5,** to take off; knock off (from a price). —**скидывать со счетов**, to rule out; count out.

скиния n., Bib. tabernacle.

скинуть v., pfv. of скидывать.

скипетр n. scepter.

скипидар n. turpentine. —**скипидарный**, adj. turpentine (attrib.).

скирд [gen. скирда́; pl. скирды́, -до́в, -да́м] n. haystack. Also, **скирда́** [pl. ски́рды, скирд, -да́м].

скисать v. impfv. [pfv. скиснуть] **1,** to turn sour. **2,** fig., colloq. to lose heart; lose interest.

скиснуть [past скис, -ла] v., pfv. of скисать.

скиталец [gen. -льца] n. wanderer. —**скитание**, n. wandering.

скитаться v.r. impfv. to wander; roam.

скиф n. **1,** Scythian. **2,** skiff. —**скифский**, adj. Scythian.

склад n. **1,** supply; stock; store. **2,** warehouse; storehouse; depot. **3,** way; mode; tenor: склад жизни, way of life. **4,** style (of writing or speaking). **5,** build; physique. **6,** in склад ума́, mentality; turn of mind. —**ни скла́ду ни ла́ду**, no sense whatever. See also **склады**.

складка [gen. pl. -док] n. **1,** fold; crease; pleat. **2,** wrinkle. —**в складку**, pleated.

складно adv. smoothly.

складной adj. folding; collapsible.

складный adj., colloq. **1,** well-built; well-proportioned. **2,** (of speech) smooth; (of something written) well put together.

складчатый adj. pleated.

складчина n. pooling of resources. —**в складчину**, jointly.

склады [gen. -до́в] n. pl., obs. syllables. —**читать по складам**, to read a syllable at a time.

складывать v. impfv. [pfv. сложить] **1,** to lay together; pile (up). **2,** to pack. **3,** to fold. **4,** math. to add. **5,** to compose. **6,** to set down; lay down. —**сидеть сложа руки**, to sit with one's hands folded (i.e. doing nothing). —**сложить голову за** (+ acc.), to lay down one's life (for). —**сложить оружие**, to lay down one's arms.

складываться v.r. impfv. [pfv. сложиться] **1,** to form; take shape. **2,** to develop. **3,** to fold. **4,** colloq. to pool one's resources.

склеивать v. impfv. [pfv. склеить] to glue together; paste together. —**склеиваться**, refl. to stick together.

склеить v., pfv. of клеить and склеивать. —**склеиться**, refl., pfv. of клеиться and склеиваться.

склеп n. burial vault; crypt.

склёпывать v. impfv. [pfv. склепать] to rivet.

склероз n. sclerosis. —**склеротический**, adj. sclerotic.

скликать [infl. скличу, скличешь] v., pfv. of скликать.

скликать v. impfv. [pfv. скликать] colloq. to call together; summon.

склока n. squabble; row.

склон n. slope; incline. —**на склоне лет**, in the twilight of one's life.

склонение n. **1,** inclining; disposing. **2,** gram. declension. **3,** astron. declination.

склонить [infl. склоню́, скло́нишь] v., pfv. of склонять. —**склониться**, refl., pfv. of склоняться.

склонность n.f. (with к) **1,** inclination (toward); tendency (toward); disposition (toward). **2,** aptitude (for); talent (for); bent (for).

склонный adj. [short form -нен, -нна́, -нно] (with к or inf.) inclined (to); given (to); prone (to).

склоняемый adj., gram. declinable.

склонять v. impfv. [pfv. склонить] **1,** to incline; bend; bow. **2,** in склонять голову перед, to bow to; yield to. **3,** in склонять в свою пользу, to win over; склонять на свою сторону, to win over to one's side. **4,** fig. to persuade. **5,** [pfv. просклонять] gram. to decline. —**склоняться**, refl. **1,** to bend; bend over. **2,** (with перед) to submit (to); yield (to). **3,** (with на + acc. or к) to lean (toward); be inclined (toward). **4,** (with на + acc. or к) colloq. to agree (to). **5,** [impfv. only] gram. to be declined.

склочный adj., colloq. argumentative; contentious.

склянка [gen. pl. -нок] n. **1,** small bottle; vial. **2,** naut. bell: восемь склянок, eight bells.

скоба́ [pl. ско́бы, скоб, скоба́м] n. bracket; staple.

скобка [gen. pl. -бок] n. **1,** = скоба́. **2,** pl. parentheses. **3,** [also, квадра́тные скобки] brackets. —**в скобках**, parenthetically.

скоблить v. impfv. [pres. скоблю, скоблишь or скоблишь] to scrape.

скобяной adj. hardware (attrib.): скобяной товар; скобяные изделия, hardware.

скованность n.f. awkwardness; constraint.

скованный adj. awkward; constrained. —**скованный льдами**, (of a river) frozen over; icebound.

сковать [infl. скую, скуёшь] v., pfv. of сковывать.

сковорода́ [*pl.* ско́вороды, сковоро́д, -рода́м] *n.* frying pan.

сковоро́дка [*gen. pl.* -док] *n., colloq.* frying pan.

ско́вывать *v. impfv.* [*pfv.* скова́ть] **1,** to make; forge. **2,** to forge together; *fig.* unite. **3,** to chain; shackle. **4,** to constrain. **5,** *mil.* to tie down. **6,** to freeze: лёд скова́л ре́ку, the river was frozen over.

скола́чивать *v. impfv.* [*pfv.* сколоти́ть] **1,** to nail together. **2,** to knock together (*i.e.* build). **3,** *fig., colloq.* to put together; form. **4,** *colloq.* to scrape together (money).

сколоти́ть [*infl.* -лочу́, -ло́тишь] *v., pfv. of* скола́чивать.

сколо́ть [*infl.* сколю́, ско́лешь] *v., pfv. of* ска́лывать.

сколь *adv., obs.* how.

скольже́ние *n.* sliding; slippage; skid(ding).

скользи́ть *v. impfv.* [*pfv.* скользну́ть; *pres.* -льжу́, -льзи́шь] **1,** to slide. **2,** to glide (*along a surface*). **3,** to slip. —скользи́ть по верха́м *or* по пове́рхности, to skim the surface.

ско́льзкий *adj.* [*short form* -зок, -зка́, -зко] **1,** slippery. **2,** *fig.* tricky; treacherous. **3,** *fig.* ticklish; delicate. —ско́льзко, *adj., used predicatively* slippery: на у́лицах ско́льзко, the streets are slippery.

скользну́ть *v. pfv.* **1,** *pfv. of* скользи́ть. **2,** (*with* по) (*of a bullet*) to graze; glance off. **3,** to slip (into, by, past, under, etc.).

скользя́щий *adj.* sliding: скользя́щая шкала́, sliding scale. —скользя́щий уда́р, glancing blow. —скользя́щий у́зел, slipknot.

ско́лько *adv.* how much?; how many?: ско́лько миль?, how many miles? Ско́лько э́то сто́ит?, how much does it cost? —во ско́лько?, *colloq.* (at) what time? —ско́лько вре́мени, *see* вре́мя. —ско́лько ни, however much; as much as. —ско́лько хоти́те; ско́лько уго́дно, as much as you like.

ско́лько-нибудь *adv.* **1,** (*with gen.*) any...at all. **2,** (*with verbs and adjectives*) the least bit.

скома́ндовать *v. pfv.* [*infl.* -дую, -дуешь] to order; command.

скомбини́ровать *v., pfv. of* комбини́ровать.

ско́мкать *v., pfv. of* ко́мкать.

скоморо́х *n., colloq.* buffoon; clown. —скоморо́шество, *n., colloq.* buffoonery.

скомпили́ровать *v., pfv. of* компили́ровать.

скомпонова́ть *v., pfv. of* компонова́ть.

скомпромети́ровать *v., pfv. of* компромети́ровать.

сконструи́ровать *v., pf v. of* констру́ировать.

сконфу́женный *adj.* confused; flustered; embarrassed; bewildered.

сконфу́зить *v., pfv. of* конфу́зить. —сконфу́зиться, *refl., pfv. of* конфу́зиться.

сконцентри́ровать *v., pfv. of* концентри́ровать. —сконцентри́роваться, *refl., pfv. of* концентри́рироваться.

сконча́ться *v.r. pfv.* to die; pass away.

скопа́ *n.* osprey.

скопе́ц [*gen.* -пца́] *n.* **1,** castrated man or boy. **2,** *hist.* member of the *skoptsy*, a religious sect practicing castration.

скопидо́м *n., colloq.* cheapskate; skinflint. —скопидо́мство, *n., colloq.* miserliness.

скопи́ровать *v., pfv. of* копи́ровать.

скопи́ть [*infl.* скоплю́, ско́пишь] *v., pfv. of* ска́пливать. —скопи́ться, *refl., pfv. of* ска́пливаться.

ско́пище *n.* crowd; throng.

скопле́ние *n.* **1,** accumulating; accumulation. **2,** crowd; accumulation; concentration.

ско́пом *adv., colloq.* in a group; in a crowd; en masse.

скорбе́ть *v. impfv.* [*pres.* -блю́, -би́шь] to grieve; mourn.

ско́рбный *adj.* sorrowful; mournful. —ско́рбно, *adv.* sorrowfully; sadly.

скорбь *n.f.* grief; sorrow.

скоре́е *also,* скоре́й *adj., comp. of* ско́рый. —*adv.* **1,** *comp. of* ско́ро. **2,** hurry up! Иди́ скоре́й!, come quickly! **3,** rather; sooner. **4,** more likely. **5,** more: скоре́е похо́ж на, more like. —скоре́е всего́, most probably; most likely.

скорлупа́ [*pl.* -лу́пы] *n.* shell (*of an egg, nut, etc.*). —уйти́ в свою́ скорлупу́, to withdraw into one's shell.

скорми́ть [*infl.* скормлю́, ско́рмишь] *v., pfv. of* ска́рмливать.

скорня́жный *adj.* fur (*attrib.*).

скорня́к [*gen.* -няка́] *n.* furrier.

ско́ро *adv.* **1,** fast; quickly. **2,** soon. —не ско́ро, not for some time; not for a long time.

скорогово́рка [*gen. pl.* -рок] *n.* **1,** rapid speech; patter. **2,** tongue twister.

скоро́мный *adj.* not to be eaten on fast days. —скоро́мный день, non-fast day.

скоропали́тельный *adj., colloq.* hasty; rash.

ско́ропись *n.f.* cursive writing.

скороподъёмность *n.f., aero.* rate of climb.

скоропо́ртящийся *adj.* perishable.

скоропости́жный *adj.* (*of death*) sudden.

скороспе́лый *adj.* **1,** early-ripening; fast-maturing. **2,** *fig., colloq.* hasty; premature.

скоростни́к [*gen.* -ника́] *n.* high-speed worker.

скоростно́й *adj.* **1,** of speed; speed (*attrib.*). **2,** high-speed. —скоростно́й бег на конька́х, speed skating.

скоростре́льный *adj.* (*of a gun*) rapid-firing.

ско́рость [*pl.* ско́рости, -сте́й, -стя́м] *n.f.* **1,** speed; velocity. **2,** gear: переключа́ться на пе́рвую ско́рость, to shift into first gear.

скоросшива́тель *n.m.* binder (*for papers*).

скорота́ть *v., pfv. of* корота́ть.

скороте́чный *adj.* transitory; short-lived.

скорохо́д *n.* **1,** *obs.* footman. **2,** *colloq.* fast runner.

скорпио́н *n.* **1,** scorpion. **2,** *cap.* Scorpio.

ско́рчить *v., pfv. of* ко́рчить. —ско́рчиться, *refl., pfv. of* ко́рчиться.

ско́рый *adj.* **1,** fast; quick; swift; speedy. **2,** impending; forthcoming. —в ско́ром бу́дущем, in the near future. —в ско́ром вре́мени, before long; shortly. —на ско́рую ру́ку, **1,** in a slapdash manner. **2,** in a hurry; on the run. —ско́рая по́мощь, **1,** first aid. **2,** *colloq.* ambulance.

скос *n.* **1,** slope; slant. **2,** bevel; miter.

скоси́ть *v. pfv.* **1,** [*infl.* скошу́, ско́сишь] *pfv. of* коси́ть[1] *and* ска́шивать (*in senses #1 & #2*). **2,** [*infl.* скошу́, ско́сишь] *pfv. of* коси́ть[2] *and* ска́шивать (*in senses #3, 4, 5*).

скот [*gen.* скота́; *acc.* скот] *n.* cattle; livestock. —ме́лкий рога́тый скот, sheep and goats. —кру́пный рога́тый скот, cattle (*cows, oxen, etc.*). —рабо́чий скот, draft animals.

скоти́на *n., colloq.* **1,** = скот. **2,** animal.

скóтник *n.* **1,** person who tends cattle. **2,** *colloq.* cattle yard.

скóтный *adj.* cattle (*attrib.*). —**скóтный двор, 1,** stockyard. **2,** farmyard.

скотобóйня [*gen. pl.* -бóен] *n.* slaughterhouse.

скотовóд *n.* cattle breeder. —**скотовóдство,** *n.* cattle raising; cattle breeding. —**скотовóдческий,** *adj.* cattle-breeding (*attrib.*).

скотолóжство *n.* sodomy.

скотопригóнный *adj., in* **скотопригóнный двор,** stockyard.

скóтский *adj.* **1,** cattle (*attrib.*). **2,** *fig.* like that of an animal.

скóтство *n.* **1,** animal-like existence. **2,** *colloq.* crudity; barbarity.

скрáдывать *v. impfv.* to conceal.

скрáшивать *v. impfv.* [*pfv.* **скрáсить**] **1,** to make more attractive. **2,** *fig.* to soften the effect of; tone down; relieve. **3,** *fig.* to brighten up (one's life, existence, etc.).

скребни́ца *n.* currycomb.

скребóк [*gen.* -бкá] *n.* scraper.

скрéжет *n.* **1,** grinding; grating; clanking. **2,** grinding; gnashing (*of teeth*).

скрежетáть *v. impfv.* [*pres.* **скрежещу́, скрежé-щешь**] **1,** *v.i.* to grind; grate; clank. **2,** (*with instr.*) to grind; gnash (one's teeth).

скрéпа *n.* **1,** clamp; brace. **2,** *fig.* tie; bond. **3,** countersignature.

скрепи́ть [*infl.* -плю́, -пи́шь] *v., pfv. of* **скрепля́ть.**

скрéпка [*gen. pl.* -пок] *n.* paper clip.

скрепля́ть *v. impfv.* [*pfv.* **скрепи́ть**] **1,** to fasten together; clamp together. **2,** *fig.* to cement (a friendship, ties, etc.). **3,** to countersign. —**скрепя́ сéрдце,** reluctantly; grudgingly.

скрести́ *v. impfv.* [*pres.* **скребу́, скребёшь;** *past* **скрёб, скреблá, скреблó**] to scrape. —**скрести́сь,** *refl.* (*of a cat, mouse, etc.*) to scratch; make a scratching noise.

скрести́ть [*infl.* -щу́, -сти́шь] *v., pfv. of* **скрéщивать.**

скрещéние *n.* **1,** crossing: скрещéние шпаг, crossing of swords. **2,** crossing; intersection.

скрéщивание *n.* **1,** crossing. **2,** crossbreeding.

скрéщивать *v. impfv.* [*pfv.* **скрести́ть**] **1,** to cross; place crosswise. **2,** to cross; crossbreed. —**скрéщивать шпáги** *or* **мечи́,** to cross swords.

скриви́ть *v., pfv. of* **криви́ть.** —**скриви́ться,** *refl., pfv. of* **криви́ться.**

скрижáль *n.f.* **1,** tablet (*bearing a sacred text*). **2,** *pl.* (*with gen.*) annals (of).

скрип *n.* squeak; creak.

скрипáч [*gen.* -пачá] *n.m.* [*fem.* -пáчка] violinist.

скрипéть *v. impfv.* [*pfv.* **проскрипéть;** *pres.* -плю́, -пи́шь] to squeak; creak.

скрипи́чный *adj.* violin (*attrib.*). —**скрипи́чный ключ,** treble clef.

скри́пка [*gen. pl.* -пок] *n.* violin. —**игрáть пéрвую скри́пку,** to play the leading role; be top dog. —**игрáть втóрую скри́пку,** to play second fiddle.

скрипу́чий *adj., colloq.* squeaky; creaky.

скрои́ть *v., pfv. of* **крои́ть.**

скрóмник *n.* modest person.

скрóмничать *v. impfv.* to be excessively modest.

скрóмный *adj.* modest. —**скрóмно,** *adv.* modestly. —**скрóмность,** *n.f.* modesty.

скрупулёзный *adj.* scrupulous; meticulous.

скрути́ть *v. pfv.* [*infl.* **скручу́, скру́тишь**] **1,** *pfv. of* **крути́ть** (*in sense #2*) *and* **скру́чивать. 2,** *colloq.* to subdue; bend to one's will. **3,** *colloq.* (*of an illness*) to lay (someone) low.

скру́чивать *v. impfv.* [*pfv.* **скрути́ть**] **1,** to twist (cloth, rope, etc.). **2,** to roll (a cigarette). **3,** to tie up; bind securely. **4,** *in* скрути́ть ру́ки кому́-нибудь за спиной, to tie/twist someone's arms behind his back.

скрывáть *v. impfv.* [*pfv.* **скрыть**] to hide; conceal. —**скрывáться,** *refl.* **1,** to hide; be hiding. **2,** to disappear: скрывáться из виду, to disappear from view; pass out of sight. **3,** [*impfv. only*] to be concealed. **4,** *colloq.* to steal away; make off.

скры́тие *n.* hiding; concealment.

скры́тничать *v. impfv., colloq.* to be secretive.

скры́тность *n.f.* **1,** secretiveness. **2,** *colloq.* secrecy.

скры́тный *adj.* secretive.

скры́тый *adj.* **1,** hidden; concealed. **2,** latent.

скрыть [*infl.* **скрóю, скрóешь**] *v., pfv. of* **скрывáть.** —**скры́ться,** *refl., pfv. of* **скрывáться.**

скрю́чивать *v. impfv.* [*pfv.* **скрю́чить**] *colloq.* **1,** to bend. **2,** *impers.* to be bent: егó скрю́чило от бóли, he was doubled up in pain. —**скрю́чиваться,** *refl., colloq.* to be bent; be doubled up.

скря́га *n.m. & f.* miser; skinflint.

скря́жничать *v. impfv., colloq.* to be a miser.

скудéть *v. impfv.* [*pfv.* **оскудéть**] to become depleted.

скýдный *adj.* scanty; meager. —**скýдность; скýдость,** *n.f.* scarcity; paucity.

скýка *n.* boredom.

скулá [*pl.* **скýлы**] *n.* cheekbone.

скулáстый *adj.* having high cheekbones.

скули́ть *v. impfv.* to whine; whimper.

скýльптор *n.* sculptor.

скульптýра *n.* sculpture.

скульптýрный *adj.* **1,** sculptural; sculptor's. **2,** *fig.* statuesque.

скýмбрия *n.* mackerel.

скунс *n.* skunk. —**скýнсовый,** *adj.* skunk (*attrib.*).

скупáть *v. impfv.* [*pfv.* **скупи́ть**] to buy up.

скупердя́й *n., colloq.* cheapskate; skinflint; tightwad.

скупéц [*gen.* -пцá] *n.* miser.

скупи́ть [*infl.* **скуплю́, скýпишь**] *v., pfv. of* **скупáть.**

скупи́ться *v.r. impfv.* [*pfv.* **поскупи́ться;** *pres.* **скуплю́сь, скýпишься**] **1,** to be stingy. **2,** to scrimp; skimp. **3,** (*with на* + *acc. pl.*) to stint; be sparing with.

скупóй *adj.* **1,** stingy. **2,** (*of light, soil, sun, etc.*) poor; weak; (*of rainfall, supplies, rations, etc.*) meager. **3,** (*with на* + *acc. pl.*) sparing (with). —**скýпо,** *adv.* stingily. —**скýпость,** *n.f.* stinginess.

скýпщик *n.* buyer (*of items for resale*).

скуфья́ [*gen. pl.* -фéй] *n.* skullcap. *Also,* **скуфéйка** [*gen. pl.* -фéек].

скучáть *v. impfv.* **1,** to be bored. **2,** (*with по* + *dat., but prepl. with pers. pronouns*) to miss; long for; yearn for.

скучáющий *adj.* bored.

скýченный *adj.* congested; overcrowded. —**скýченность,** *n.f.* congestion; overcrowding.

скýчиваться *v.r. impfv.* [*pfv.* **скýчиться**] *colloq.* to crowd together; cluster.

скýчно *adv.* in a boring manner. —*adj., used predicatively* **1,** bored: мне скýчно, I am bored. **2,** boring: скýчно сидéть одномý, it is boring to be alone.

скучный *adj.* **1,** boring; tiresome; tedious. **2,** bored.

скушать *v. pfv.* to eat; eat up.

слабеть *v. impfv.* [*pfv.* ослабеть] **1,** to weaken; become weak; grow weak. **2,** (*of one's health, eyesight, etc.*) to fail; get worse. **3,** to slacken; subside.

слабина *n.* **1,** slack (*in a rope*). **2,** weak spot.

слабительный *adj.* cathartic; purgative. —**слабительное,** *n.* laxative.

слабить *v. impfv., impers.* to have diarrhea: его слабит, he has diarrhea.

слабо *adv.* **1,** weakly; faintly. **2,** poorly.

слабоволие *n.* weakness of will. —**слабовольный,** *adj.* weak-willed.

слаборазвитый *adj.* (*of countries*) underdeveloped.

слабосилие *n.* weakness; lack of strength.

слабосильный *adj.* **1,** weak; feeble. **2,** low-powered.

слабость *n.f.* weakness. Иметь слабость к, to have a weakness for.

слабоумие *n.* feeble-mindedness.

слабоумный *adj.* feeble-minded. —*n.* feeble-minded person; imbecile; moron.

слабый *adj.* **1,** weak. **2,** faint; slight. **3,** poor; weak; bad. **4,** loose; lax; slack.

слава *n.* **1,** glory. **2,** fame. **3,** reputation. **4,** *colloq.* rumors; talk. —**во славу** (+ *gen.*), to the glory of. —**на славу,** marvelously; wonderfully well: удаться на славу, to be a great success. —**слава богу!,** see бог.

славист *n.* Slavicist. —**славистика,** *n.* Slavic studies.

славить *v. impfv.* [*pres.* -влю, -вишь] **1,** to glorify. **2,** to sing the praises of. —**славиться,** *refl.* (*with instr. or* как) to be famous (for *or* as); be renowned (for).

славка [*gen. pl.* -вок] *n.* warbler.

славно *adv., colloq.* wonderfully. —*adj., used predicatively, colloq.* nice; wonderful: как славно!, how nice!; how wonderful!

славный *adj.* **1,** glorious. **2,** famous; renowned. **3,** *colloq.* nice.

славословие *n.* **1,** glorification. **2,** *pl.* paeans of praise.

славянин [*pl.* -яне, -ян] *n.m.* [*fem.* -янка] Slav.

славянофил *n.* Slavophile.

славянский *adj.* Slavic; Slavonic.

слагаемое *n., decl. as an adj.* element; component.

слагать *v. impfv.* [*pfv.* сложить] **1,** to compose. **2,** (*with* с себя) to give up; relinquish; decline. —**слагаться,** *refl.* [*impfv. only*] (*with* из) to be composed of; consist of.

слад *n., colloq., in* сладу нет с (+ *instr.),* he (she) is impossible; there is no dealing with him (her).

сладить [*infl.* -жу, -дишь] *v., pfv. of* слаживать.

сладкий *adj.* [*short form* -док, -дка, -дко; *comp.* слаще] sweet. —**сладкое мясо,** sweetbread.

сладко *adv.* sweetly; sweet.

сладкое *n., decl. as an adj.* **1,** sweets. **2,** dessert.

сладкоежка [*gen. pl.* -жек] *n.m. & f., colloq.* person with a sweet tooth.

сладкозвучный *adj.* sweet-sounding.

сладкоречивый *adj.* smooth-spoken.

сладостный *adj.* sweet.

сладострастие *n.* sensuality. —**сладострастный,** *adj.* sensual.

сладость *n.f.* **1,** sweetness. **2,** *pl.* sweets. **3,** *fig., colloq.* delight.

слаженный *adj.* harmonious; well-coordinated. —**слаженность,** *n.f.* harmony.

слаживать *v. impfv.* [*pfv.* сладить] *colloq.* **1,** to arrange. **2,** (*with* с + *instr.*) to handle; cope (with).

слазить *v. pfv.* [*infl.* слажу, слазишь] **1,** to climb up (to an attic, onto a roof, etc.). **2,** to go down (to a cellar, basement, etc.).

слалом *n.* slalom.

сланец [*gen.* -нца] *n.* slate; shale. —**сланцевый,** *adj.* slate (*attrib.*); shale (*attrib.*).

сластёна *n.m. & f., colloq.* person with a sweet tooth.

сласти [*gen.* -стей; *dat.* -стям] *n. pl.* sweets.

сластолюбивый *adj.* sensual.

слать *v. impfv.* [*pfv.* послать; *pres.* шлю, шлёшь] to send.

слащавый *adj.* sugary; honeyed.

слаще *adj., comp. of* сладкий.

слева *adv.* **1,** from the left. **2,** to (*or* on) the left.

слегка *adv.* **1,** slightly; a little. **2,** lightly; gently.

след [*gen.* следа *or* следа; *dat.* следу; *2nd loc.* следу; *pl.* следы] *n.* **1,** track: свежие следы, fresh tracks. **2,** trail: напасть на след (+ *gen.*), to come upon the trail of... **3,** trace: от этого не осталось ни следа, not a trace of it remains. **4,** footprint; footstep. **5,** mark; scar: следы шин, tire marks; следы оспы, smallpox scars. *See also* следом.

следить *v. impfv.* [*pres.* слежу, следишь] (*with* за + *instr.*) **1,** to follow (*with one's eye*). **2,** to watch; look after; keep an eye on. **3,** to see that (order, discipline, etc.) is maintained. **4,** *fig.* to follow; keep abreast of. **5,** to keep under surveillance. **6,** [*pfv.* наследить] *colloq.* to leave footmarks: следить сапогами на полу, to track up the floor.

следование *n.* **1,** following. **2,** movement; travel. —**поезд дальнего следования,** long-distance train.

следователь *n.m.* investigator.

следовательно *adv.* consequently.

следовать *v. impfv.* [*pres.* -дую, -дуешь] **1,** [*pfv.* последовать] (*with* за + *instr.*) to follow; come *or* go after: следовать за проводником, to follow the guide. Лето следует за весной, summer follows spring. **2,** [*pfv.* последовать] (*with dat.*) to follow (rules, advice, an example, etc.). **3,** *impers.* (*with* из) to follow (from): из этого следует, что..., from this it follows that... **4,** (*with* в *or* до) (*of a train or ship*) to be bound for. **5,** *impers.* one should: следует отметить, что..., it should be noted that... Как и следовало ожидать, as was to be expected. **6,** *impers.* (*with* с + *gen.*) to be owed; be due: сколько с меня следует?, how much do I owe? —**как следует,** properly. —**кому следует,** to the proper person. —**куда следует,** to the proper quarter.

следом *adv.* **1,** right behind; in someone's footsteps. **2,** immediately afterward. —**следом за** (+ *instr.*), **1,** right behind; close behind. **2,** right after; immediately after.

следопыт *n.* **1,** hunter (who tracks down animals). **2,** *fig.* pioneer; trailblazer.

следственный *adj.* of inquiry; investigatory.

следствие *n.* **1,** consequence; result. **2,** investigation; inquiry. —**причина и следствие,** cause and effect.

следуемый *adj.* due: следуемая мне сумма, the amount due me.

следующий *adj.* **1,** next: на следующий день, the next day. **2,** following: следующим образом, in the following manner. —**следующее,** *n.* the following.

слежа́ться [*infl.* -жи́ться] *v.r.*, *pfv. of* слёживаться.

слеже́ние *n.*, *aerospace* tracking; monitoring. —ста́нция слеже́ния, tracking station.

слёживаться *v.r. impfv.* [*pfv.* слежа́ться] **1**, to become firmly packed. **2**, to become rumpled (*from lying around a long time*).

слёжка *n.* surveillance: установи́ть слёжку за (+ *instr.*), to place under surveillance.

слеза́ [*pl.* слёзы, слёз, слеза́м] *n.* tear: быть в слеза́х, to be in tears.

слеза́ть *v. impfv.* [*pfv.* слезть] (*with* с + *gen.*) **1**, to climb down (from). **2**, to dismount (from). **3**, *colloq.* to get off (a train, bus, etc.). **4**, *colloq.* (*of paint, skin, etc.*) to come off.

слези́нка [*gen. pl.* -нок] *n.* tear; teardrop.

слези́ться *v.r. impfv.* (*of one's eyes*) to water; tear.

слезли́вый *adj.* **1**, easily moved to tears. **2**, tearful. **3**, *fig.* overly sentimental; maudlin.

слёзный *adj.* **1**, tear (*attrib.*); lachrymal: слёзный прото́к, tear duct. **2**, *colloq.* plaintive.

слезоточи́вый *adj.* (*of one's eyes*) teary. —слезоточи́вый газ, tear gas.

слезть [*infl. like* лезть] *v.*, *pfv. of* слеза́ть.

слепе́нь [*gen.* -пня́] *n.m.* horsefly.

слепе́ц [*gen.* -пца́] *n.* blind man.

слепи́ть[1] *v. impfv.* [*pres.* слеплю́, слепи́шь] **1**, *obs.* to blind. **2**, to dazzle.

слепи́ть[2] [*infl.* слеплю́, сле́пишь] *v.*, *pfv. of* лепи́ть (*in sense #2*) *and* слепля́ть. —слепи́ться, *refl.*, *pfv. of* слепля́ться.

слепля́ть *v. impfv.* [*pfv.* слепи́ть] to glue together; paste together. —слепля́ться, *refl.* to stick together; become stuck.

сле́пнуть *v. impfv.* [*pfv.* осле́пнуть; *past* слеп *or* сле́пнул, сле́пла] to go blind; lose one's eyesight.

сле́по *adv.* blindly.

слепо́й *adj.* blind. —*n.* blind man.

слепо́к [*gen.* -пка] *n.* cast; mold.

слепорождённый *adj.* blind from birth.

слепота́ *n.* blindness.

слепы́ш [*gen.* -пыша́] *n.* mole rat.

сле́сарный *adj.* metalworking (*attrib.*); locksmith (*attrib.*). *Also*, сле́сарский.

сле́сарь [*pl.* слесаря́ *or* сле́сари] *n.m.* **1**, metalworker. **2**, locksmith.

слёт *n.* **1**, flight (*of birds*). **2**, *fig.* gathering; meeting; rally.

слета́ть[1] *v. impfv.* [*pfv.* слете́ть] **1**, (*with* с + *gen.*) to fly down (from). **2**, to fly away. **3**, (*with* с + *gen.*) to slip off; fall off. **4**, *colloq.* to jump down. **5**, *fig.* (*of a feeling*) to pass; disappear. **6**, *in* слета́ть с губ/уст/языка́, to escape one's lips. —слета́ться, *refl.* to fly in (*from many places*); come flying in.

слета́ть[2] *v. pfv.* to fly (*to a certain place and return*).

слете́ть [*infl.* -чу́, -ти́шь] *v.*, *pfv. of* слета́ть[1]. —слете́ться, *refl.*, *pfv. of* слета́ться.

слечь *v. pfv.* [*infl. like* лечь] to take ill; take to one's bed.

сли́ва *n.* **1**, plum. **2**, plum tree.

слива́ть *v. impfv.* [*pfv.* слить] **1**, to pour off; pour out. **2**, to pour together. **3**, *fig.* to combine; merge. —слива́ться, *refl.* **1**, (*of rivers*) to meet; converge. **2**, (*of organizations*) to merge. **3**, (*of sounds, colors, etc.*) to blend. Слива́ться с фо́ном, to melt into the background.

сли́вки [*gen.* -вок] *n. pl.* cream. —сли́вки о́бщества, the cream of society.

сли́вовый *adj.* plum (*attrib.*).

сли́вочник *n.* creamer; cream pot.

сли́вочный *adj.* **1**, cream (*attrib.*). **2**, creamy. —сли́вочное моро́женое, ice cream. —сли́вочный сыр, cream cheese.

сливя́нка *n.* plum brandy.

слиза́ть [*infl.* слижу́, сли́жешь] *v.*, *pfv. of* сли́зывать.

сли́зень [*gen.* -зня] *n.m.*, *zool.* slug.

сли́зистый *adj.* **1**, slimy. **2**, *anat.* mucous: сли́зистая оболо́чка, mucous membrane.

слизня́к [*gen.* -няка́] *n.*, *zool.* slug.

сли́зывать *v. impfv.* [*pfv.* слиза́ть] to lick off.

слизь *n.f.* **1**, mucus. **2**, [*also*, расти́тельная слизь] mucilage. **3**, slime.

слиня́лый *adj.*, *colloq.* faded.

слиня́ть *v. pfv.*, *colloq.* to fade.

слипа́ться *v.r. impfv.* [*pfv.* сли́пнуться] **1**, to stick together. **2**, [*impfv. only*] (*of one's eyes*) to be heavy with sleep: у меня́ глаза́ слипа́ются, I can hardly keep my eyes open.

сли́пнуться [*past* сли́пся, сли́плась] *v.r.*, *pfv. of* слипа́ться.

сли́тно *adv.* **1**, together. **2**, (*of a way of spelling*) as one word.

сли́тный *adj.* **1**, continuous; unbroken. **2**, (*of spelling*) as one word.

сли́ток [*gen.* -тка] *n.* **1**, ingot; bar. **2**, *pl.* bullion: зо́лото в сли́тках, gold bullion.

слить [*infl.* солью́, сольёшь; *past fem.* слила́] *v.*, *pfv. of* слива́ть. —сли́ться, *refl.* [*past* сли́лся, -ла́сь, -ло́сь] *pfv. of* слива́ться.

слича́ть *v. impfv.* [*pfv.* сличи́ть] to compare (against each other).

сли́шком *adv.* **1**, too. **2**, (*with certain verbs*) too much; excessively. —сли́шком мно́го, too much; too many.

слия́ние *n.* **1**, blending (*of styles, colors, etc.*). **2**, confluence (*of rivers*). **3**, merger; amalgamation; union.

слобода́ [*pl.* сло́боды, слобо́д, слобода́м] *n.*, *hist.* settlement inhabited by tradesmen or free peasants.

слова́к *n.m.* [*fem.* -ва́чка] Slovak.

слова́рный *adj.* **1**, dictionary (*attrib.*). **2**, lexical.

слова́рь [*gen.* -варя́] *n.m.* **1**, dictionary. **2**, vocabulary.

слова́цкий *adj.* Slovak.

слове́нец [*gen.* -нца] *n.m.* [*fem.* -нка] Slovene. —слове́нский [*adj.*] Slovenian.

слове́сник *n.* **1**, teacher of Russian language and literature. **2**, *obs.* philologist.

слове́сность *n.f.*, *obs.* **1**, literature. **2**, philology.

слове́сный *adj.* **1**, verbal; oral. **2**, *obs.* philological.

слове́чко [*gen. pl.* -чек] *n.*, *dim. of* сло́во. —замо́лвить *or* заки́нуть слове́чко за (+ *acc.*), to put in a word for.

сло́вник *n.* word list (*for a dictionary*); subject list (*for an encyclopedia*).

сло́вно *conj.* **1**, as if; as though. **2**, like.

сло́во [*pl.* слова́, слов, слова́м] *n.* **1**, word. **2**, one's word: сдержа́ть (своё) сло́во, to keep one's word. **3**, the floor: проси́ть сло́ва, to ask for the floor. —в двух слова́х, in a few words; briefly. —други́ми слова́ми, in other words. —игра́ слов, play on words. —к сло́ву (сказа́ть), by the way. —на слова́х, **1**, orally. **2**, in words. —одни́м сло́вом, in a word. —от сло́ва до сло́ва, from beginning to end. —по слова́м (+ *gen.*), according to. —слов нет, *colloq.* there is no denying; it must be said that... —сло́во в сло́во, word for word. —сло́во за́ сло́во, gradually; as the conversation progressed. —сло́вом, in a word. —с пе́рвого сло́ва, right at the outset (of the conversation). —челове́к сло́ва, a man of his word.

словоохо́тливый *adj.* talkative; loquacious.

словосочета́ние *n.* combination of words. —усто́йчивое словосочета́ние, set expression.

слог [*pl.* сло́ги, слого́в, слога́м] *n.* **1**, syllable. **2**, *obs.* style.

слогово́й *adj.* syllabic.

слоёный *adj.* puff (*attrib.*); flaky. —слоёный пиро́г, puff pastry. —слоёное те́сто, puff paste.

сложе́ние *n.* **1**, *math.* addition. **2**, build; physique.

сложённый *adj.* built: хорошо́ сложенный ю́ноша, well-built young man.

сложи́ть [*infl.* сложу́, сло́жишь] *v.*, *pfv.* of скла́дывать *and* слага́ть. —сложи́ться, *refl.*, *pfv.* of скла́дываться.

сло́жно *adv.* in a complicated way.

сложноподчинённый *adj.*, *in* сложноподчинённое предложе́ние, complex sentence.

сложносочинённый *adj.*, *in* сложносочинённое предложе́ние, compound sentence.

сло́жность *n.f.* **1**, complexity. **2**, *pl.* difficulties. —в о́бщей сло́жности, in all; a total of; all told.

сло́жный *adj.* **1**, complex; complicated. **2**, difficult. **3**, intricate. **4**, (*of words, interest, etc.*) compound.

сло́йстый *adj.* stratified; laminated. —сло́йстые облака́, strati.

слой [*pl.* сло́и, слоёв] *n.* **1**, layer. **2**, coat (*of paint*). **3**, *geol.* stratum. **4**, (social) stratum: все сло́и населе́ния, all strata (*or* segments) of the population.

сло́йка [*gen. pl.* сло́ек] *n.* puff (*piece of pastry*).

слом *n.* tearing down; dismantling; demolition.

слома́ть *v.*, *pfv.* of лома́ть. —слома́ться, *refl.*, *pfv.* of лома́ться (*in sense* #1).

сломи́ть *v. pfv.* [*infl.* сломлю́, сло́мишь] **1**, to break; smash; shatter. **2**, to defeat; crush. **3**, *fig.* to break (a person, one's spirit, will, resistance, etc.). **4**, *in* сломя́ го́лову, at breakneck speed; like mad. —сломи́ться, *refl.*, *colloq.* to break.

слон [*gen.* слона́] *n.* **1**, elephant. **2**, *chess* bishop. **3**, *in* морско́й слон, sea elephant; elephant seal. —де́лать из му́хи слона́, to make a mountain out of a molehill.

слонёнок [*gen.* -нка; *pl.* -ня́та, -ня́т] *n.* baby elephant; young elephant.

слони́ха *n.* she-elephant.

слоно́вость *n.f.* elephantiasis.

слоно́вый *adj.* elephant (*attrib.*). —слоно́вая боле́знь, elephantiasis. —слоно́вая кость, ivory.

слоня́ться *v.r. impfv.*, *colloq.* to loiter; drift (*from place to place*).

сло́пать *v.*, *pfv.* of ло́пать.

слуга́ [*pl.* слу́ги] *n.m.* servant; manservant.

служа́нка [*gen. pl.* -нок] *n.* servant; maid.

слу́жащий *n.*, *decl. as an adj.* employee; office worker.

слу́жба *n.* **1**, service. **2**, work; job. **3**, church service. —сослужи́ть слу́жбу, *see* сослужи́ть.

служе́бный *adj.* **1**, office (*attrib.*); official. **2**, auxiliary; secondary.

служе́ние *n.* serving; service.

служи́тель *n.m.* **1**, *obs.* servant. **2**, attendant. —служи́тель ку́льта, clergyman.

служи́ть *v. impfv.* [*pfv.* послужи́ть; *pres.* служу́, слу́жишь] **1**, to serve. **2**, (*with dat.*) to serve; be in the service of. **3**, (*with instr.*) to serve (as); function (as). **4**, *v.t.* [*impfv. only*] *eccl.* to officiate at; conduct (a service, mass, etc.). **5**, [*impfv. only*] (*of a dog*) to beg.

слупи́ть *v.*, *pfv.* of лупи́ть.

слух *n.* **1**, (sense of) hearing. **2**, ear for music: игра́ть по слу́ху, to play by ear. Абсолю́тный слух, absolute/perfect pitch. **3**, rumor. —ни слу́ху ни ду́ху (*with* о *or* от), there hasn't been a word from... —превраща́ться в слух, to be all ears; listen with rapt attention.

слухово́й *adj.* hearing (*attrib.*); auditory. —слухово́й аппара́т, hearing aid. —слухово́е окно́, dormer window. —слухово́й рожо́к; слухова́я тру́бка, ear trumpet.

слу́чай *n.* **1**, case: в тако́м слу́чае, in that case. **2**, opportunity; chance. **3**, incident; occurrence: несча́стный слу́чай, an accident. **4**, chance; luck: де́ло слу́чая, a matter of chance. —во вся́ком слу́чае, in any case; at any rate. —в кра́йнем слу́чае, if worst comes to worst; as a last resort. —в лу́чшем слу́чае, at best. —в проти́вном слу́чае, otherwise; failing which. —в слу́чае (+ *gen.*), in case of; in the event of. —в слу́чае чего́, **1**, in which case. **2**, in the event of trouble. —в том слу́чае, е́сли..., in case... —в ху́дшем слу́чае, at worst. —на вся́кий слу́чай, just in case. —на слу́чай (+ *gen.*), in case of; so as to be prepared for. —на слу́чай, е́сли..., in case...; so as to be prepared when... —ни в ко́ем слу́чае, under no circumstances. —от слу́чая к слу́чаю, from time to time. —по слу́чаю, **1**, (*with gen.*) on the occasion of. **2**, (*with gen.*) on account of; owing to. **3**, by chance; by luck. —при слу́чае, when the opportunity presents itself.

случа́йно *adv.* **1**, by chance; by accident; accidentally. **2**, *in questions*, by any chance.

случа́йность *n.f.* **1**, (*with gen.*) accidental nature (*of something*). **2**, chance occurrence; accident: чи́стая случа́йность, pure accident.

случа́йный *adj.* [*short form* -ча́ен, -ча́йна] **1**, chance; accidental; random. **2**, (*of earnings, expenses, etc.*) incidental.

случа́ть *v. impfv.* [*pfv.* случи́ть] to mate (animals).

случа́ться *v.r. impfv.* [*pfv.* случи́ться] **1**, to happen; occur. **2**, (*with* с + *instr.*) to happen to: что случи́лось с ним?, what happened to him? **3**, *impers.* (*with dat. and inf.*) to happen to; have occasion to. **4**, *colloq.* to happen to be; turn up.

случи́ть *v.*, *pfv.* of случа́ть.

случи́ться *v.r.*, *pfv.* of случа́ться.

слу́шание *n.* **1**, listening. **2**, attending (*a lecture*); taking (*a course*). **3**, *law* hearing.

слу́шатель *n.m.* **1**, listener. **2**, student. **3**, *pl.* audience.

слу́шать *v. impfv.* **1**, to listen (to). **2**, [*pfv.* послу́шать] *fig.* to listen to; heed. **3**, to hear (a case). **4**, [*pfv.* прослу́шать] to attend (a lecture); take (a course). —слу́шаю!, **1**, (*when answering the phone*) hello! **2**, (*on receiving an order*) very well!; I understand!

слу́шаться *v.r. pfv.* [*pfv.* послу́шаться] **1**, (*with gen.*) to obey. **2**, (*with gen.*) to heed (advice). **3**, [*impfv. only*] *law* (*of a case*) to be heard.

слыть *v. impfv.* [*pfv.* прослы́ть; *pres.* слыву́, слывёшь; *past fem.* слыла́] (*with instr.*) to be reputed to be; have a reputation for.

слыхáть *v. impfv., colloq., used in the past tense,* to hear.

слы́шать *v. impfv.* [*pfv.* услы́шать; *pres.* слы́шу, слы́шишь] to hear. —**слы́шаться,** *refl.* [*pfv.* послы́шаться] **1,** to be heard. **2,** [*impfv. only*] *fig.* to be felt; be sensed.

слы́шимость *n.f.* **1,** audibility. **2,** (*on radio or TV*) reception. **3,** (*on the telephone*) connection.

слы́шно *adv.* audibly. —*adj., used predicatively* **1,** audible: егó не слы́шно, he can't be heard. Мне ничегó не слы́шно, I can't hear a thing. Слы́шно, как мýха пролетúт, you could hear a pin drop. **2,** heard; rumored: что слы́шно?, what's new?

слы́шный *adj.* [*short form* слы́шен, -шнá, -шно] audible.

слюдá *n.* mica. —**слюдянóй,** *adj.* mica (*attrib.*).

слюнá *n.* saliva.

слюни [*gen.* слюнéй] *n. pl., colloq.* saliva. —**пускáть слюни,** to drool; drivel; slobber. —**распускáть слюни,** *colloq.* **1,** to start crying. **2,** to complain; whine. **3,** to be moved.

слюни́ть *v. impfv.* [*pfv.* послюни́ть] to moisten with saliva.

слюнки [*gen. pl.* -нок] *n. pl., colloq.* = слюни. —у меня слюнки текýт, my mouth is watering.

слю́нный *adj.* salivary.

слюня́вый *adj., colloq.* driveling.

сля́коть *n.f.* slush. —**сля́котный,** *adj.* slushy.

смáзать [*infl.* смáжу, смáжешь] *v., pfv. of* смáзывать.

смáзка *n.* **1,** grease. **2,** greasing; lubrication.

смазли́вый *adj., colloq.* pretty; good-looking.

смáзочный *adj.* lubrication (*attrib.*); lubricating: смáзочный материáл, lubricant.

смáзчик *n.* grease monkey.

смáзывание *n.* **1,** oiling; greasing; lubrication. **2,** painting; swabbing. **3,** blurring; slurring over.

смáзывать *v. impfv.* [*pfv.* смáзать] **1,** to oil; grease; lubricate. **2,** to paint; swab. **3,** to wipe off. **4,** *colloq.* to blur (a picture). **5,** *fig., colloq.* to slur over; gloss over.

смак *n., colloq.* relish; gusto: есть со смáком, to eat with relish/gusto.

смаковáть *v. impfv.* [*pres.* -кýю, -кýешь] *colloq.* to savor; relish.

смáнивать *v. impfv.* [*pfv.* сманúть] *colloq.* **1,** to entice. **2,** to lure away.

сманúть [*infl.* сманю́, смáнишь] *v., pfv. of* смáнивать.

смастерúть *v., pfv. of* мастерúть.

смáтывать *v. impfv.* [*pfv.* смотáть] **1,** to wind; wind in. **2,** (*with* с + *gen.*) to wind off; unwind (from). **3,** *in* смáтывать ýдочки, *colloq.* to take off; vamoose. —**смáтываться,** *refl., colloq.* **1,** to take off; vamoose. **2,** (*with* в + *acc.*) to run down to; dash down to (*and return*).

смáхивать *v. impfv.* **1,** [*pfv.* смахнýть] to brush off; brush away. **2,** [*impfv. only*] (*with* на + *acc.*) *colloq.* to look like; resemble.

смáчивать *v. impfv.* [*pfv.* смочúть] to moisten.

смáчный *adj., colloq.* tasty. —**смáчно,** *adv., colloq.* with relish; with gusto.

смежáть *v. impfv.* [*pfv.* смежúть] to close (one's eyes).

смéжный *adj.* **1,** adjacent; contiguous; adjoining. **2,** allied; related. —**смéжность,** *n.f.* contiguity.

смекáлистый *adj., colloq.* clever; sharp; quick-witted.

смекáлка *n., colloq.* shrewdness; native intelligence.

смекáть *v. impfv.* [*pfv.* смекнýть] *còlloq.* to catch on; get the point.

смелéть *v. impfv.* [*pfv.* осмелéть] to become bolder; grow bolder.

смéло *adv.* **1,** boldly. **2,** *colloq.* with full confidence; safely.

смéлость *n.f.* boldness; daring; audacity; temerity.

смéлый *adj.* bold; daring; audacious.

смельчáк [*gen.* -чакá] *n.* daredevil.

смéна *n.* **1,** changing; replacement. Смéна карáула, changing of the guard. **2,** alternation (*of the seasons, day and night, etc.*). **3,** shift (*of work or duty*); session (*of school*). **4,** change; set: две смéны белья́, two changes/sets of underwear. **5,** a replacement: найтú смéну, to find a replacement. **6,** the rising generation. —**идтú** *or* **приходúть на смéну** (+ *dat.*), to replace; take the place of.

сменúть [*infl.* сменю́, смéнишь] *v., pfv. of* сменя́ть[1]. —**сменúться,** *refl., pfv. of* сменя́ться.

смéнный *adj.* **1,** shift (*attrib.*). **2,** removable; replaceable.

сменя́емый *adj.* removable; replaceable.

сменя́ть[1] *v. impfv.* [*pfv.* сменúть] **1,** to change. **2,** to replace; relieve; remove. **3,** to replace; take the place of. —**сменя́ться,** *refl.* **1,** to be replaced. **2,** (*with* с + *gen.*) to be relieved of. **3,** (*with instr.*) to give way to: лéто сменúлось óсенью, summer gave way to autumn.

сменя́ть[2] *v. pfv., colloq.* to exchange; trade.

смердéть *v. impfv.* [*pres.* -ржý, -рдúшь] to stink.

смерзáться *v.r. impfv.* [*pfv.* смёрзнуться] to freeze together.

смёрзнуться [*past* смёрзся, смёрзлась] *v.r., pfv. of* смерзáться.

смéрить *v. pfv., colloq.* to measure. —**смéрить (когó-нибудь) взгля́дом** *or* **глазáми,** to look over (from head to toe).

смеркáться *v.r. impfv.* [*pfv.* смéркнуться] *impers.* to get dark: смеркáется, it is getting dark; dusk is falling.

смертéльно *adv.* **1,** mortally; fatally; to death. **2,** terribly: смертéльно устáл, terribly tired. Смертéльно скýчно, deadly dull.

смертéльный *adj.* **1,** deadly; mortal; fatal; lethal. **2,** (*of an insult*) grievous. **3,** (*of boredom, exhaustion, etc.*) utter.

смéртник *n.* prisoner condemned to death.

смéртность *n.f.* death rate; mortality (rate). —**дéтская смéртность,** infant mortality.

смéртный *adj.* **1,** death (*attrib.*). **2,** mortal. —*n.* mortal: простые смéртные, mere mortals. —**смéртная казнь,** the death penalty; capital punishment.

смертонóсный *adj.* lethal; fatal; mortal.

смерть [*pl.* смéрти, -тéй, -тя́м] *n.f.* death. —**дó смерти,** to death: мне скýчно дó смерти, I am bored to death. —**при смерти,** near death.

смерч *n.* **1,** whirlwind. **2,** tornado. **3,** waterspout.

смесúтель *n.m.* mixer; blender.

смести́ [*infl. like* мести́] *v., pfv. of* сметáть[1].

сместúть [*infl.* -щý, -стúшь] *v., pfv. of* смещáть.

смесь *n.f.* mixture; blend.

смéта *n.* estimate.

сметáна *n.* sour cream.

сметáть¹ *v. impfv.* [*pfv.* **смести́**] **1**, to sweep away; sweep off. **2**, *fig.* (*of a fire, wind, etc.*) to sweep away.

сметáть² *v. pfv.* **1**, [*infl.* **-тáю,-тáешь**] *pfv. of* **метáть²** *and* **смётывать** (*in sense #1*). **2**, [*infl.* **смечу́, смéчешь**] *pfv. of* **смётывать** (*in sense #2*).

смётка *n., colloq.* quick-wittedness; savvy.

смётливый *adj.* bright; clever; quick-witted.

смéтный *adj.* estimated.

смётывать *v. impfv.* [*pfv.* **сметáть**] **1**, to baste together. **2**, to stack (hay, straw, etc.).

сметь *v. impfv.* [*pfv.* **посмéть**] to dare: никто́ не смел возрази́ть, no one dared raise an objection. —**как вы смéете!**, how dare you! —**не смéйте** (+ *inf.*)!, don't you dare...!

смех *n.* laughter; laugh. —**для** *or* **рáди смéха**, (just) for fun. —**как** (*or* **слóвно**) **нá смех**, as if to mock someone; as if to rub it in. —**не до смéху** (+ *dat.*), (one is) in no mood for laughter. —**поднимáть нá смех**, to hold up to ridicule. —**умирáть сó смеху**, to die laughing.

смехотвóрный *adj.* laughable; ludicrous; ridiculous.

смéшанный *adj.* **1**, mixed. **2**, hybrid.

смешáть *v., pfv. of* **мешáть** (*in sense #3*) *and* **смéшивать.** —**смешáться,** *refl., pfv. of* **мешáться** *and* **смéшиваться.**

смешéние *n.* **1**, mixing. **2**, mixture; blend. **3**, confusion. —**смешéние языкóв,** babel of tongues.

смéшивание *n.* mixing.

смéшивать *v. impfv.* [*pfv.* **смешáть**] **1**, to mix; blend. **2**, to mix up (*objects previously in order*). **3**, to get (two persons or things) mixed up; confuse with each other. —**смéшиваться,** *refl.* **1**, to mix; blend; merge. **2**, (*with* **с** + *instr.*) to blend in (with); melt (into); disappear (into). **3**, (*of objects*) to get mixed up. **4**, *colloq.* (*of a person*) to become confused; get mixed up.

смеши́ть *v. impfv.* [*pfv.* **насмеши́ть** *or* **рассмеши́ть**] to make (someone) laugh.

смешли́вый *adj.* easily moved to laughter.

смешнó *adv.* in a funny way. —*adj., used predicatively* funny: э́то не смешнó, that is not funny. Мне не смешнó, I do not find it funny; I am not amused.

смешнóй *adj.* **1**, funny; amusing. **2**, ridiculous; ludicrous. —**до смешнóго**, ridiculously; to the extreme.

смешóк [*gen.* **-шкá**] *n., colloq.* **1**, chuckle. **2**, *pl.* taunts; digs.

смещáть *v. impfv.* [*pfv.* **смести́ть**] **1**, to displace. **2**, to remove (*from office*).

смещéние *n.* **1**, removal; dismissal; displacement. **2**, *in* смещéние поня́тий, confusion of (two) concepts.

смея́ться *v.r. impfv.* [*pres.* **смею́сь, смеёшься**] **1**, to laugh. **2**, (*with dat.*) to laugh at: смея́ться шýтке, to laugh at a joke. **3**, (*with* **над**) to make fun of. **4**, (*with* **над**) to laugh off; scoff at. **5**, *colloq.* to joke.

сми́ловаться *v.r. pfv.* [*infl.* **-луюсь, -луешься**] *obs.* (*with* **над**) to have pity (on); take pity (on); have mercy (on).

смирéние *n.* **1**, humility. **2**, meekness. **3**, (sense of) resignation.

смирéнный *adj.* humble; meek. —**смирéнно,** *adv.* humbly. —**смирéнность,** *n.f.* humility.

смири́тельный *adj., in* **смири́тельная рубáшка,** strait jacket.

смири́ть *v., pfv. of* **смиря́ть.** —**смири́ться,** *refl., pfv. of* **смиря́ться.**

сми́рно *adv.* quietly; still: сидéть сми́рно, to sit still.

—*interj., mil.* attention! —**стóйка сми́рно,** position of attention.

сми́рный *adj.* quiet; mild-mannered.

смиря́ть *v. impfv.* [*pfv.* **смири́ть**] to suppress; repress; curb. —**смиря́ться,** *refl.* **1**, to submit; give in. **2**, (*with* **с** + *instr.*) to reconcile oneself (to).

смóква *n.* fig.

смóкинг *n.* tuxedo; dinner jacket.

смокóвница *n.* fig tree.

смолá [*pl.* **смóлы**] *n.* **1**, resin. **2**, pitch; tar.

смолёный *adj.* tarred.

смоли́стый *adj.* resinous.

смоли́ть *v. impfv.* [*pfv.* **вы́смолить**] to pitch; tar.

смолкáть *v. impfv.* [*pfv.* **смóлкнуть**] **1**, to fall silent. **2**, (*of noise, sounds, etc.*) to die away; stop; cease.

смóлкнуть [*past* **смолк, -ла**] *v., pfv. of* **смолкáть.**

смóлоду *adv.* **1**, since one's youth. **2**, in one's youth.

смолчáть *v. pfv.* [*infl.* **-чý, -чи́шь**] *colloq.* to be silent; hold one's tongue.

смоль *n.f., in* **чёрный как смоль,** jet-black.

смоляно́й *adj.* resin (*attrib.*); pitch (*attrib.*); tar (*attrib.*).

смонти́ровать *v., pfv. of* **монти́ровать.**

сморкáть *v. impfv.* [*pfv.* **вы́сморкать**], *in* сморкáть нос, to blow one's nose. —**сморкáться,** *refl.* to blow one's nose.

сморóдина *n.* currants. —**сморóдинный,** *adj.* currant (*attrib.*); made of currants.

сморчóк [*gen.* **-чкá**] *n.* morel (*mushroom*).

смóрщенный *adj.* wrinkled.

смóрщивать *v. impfv.* [*pfv.* **смóрщить**] to wrinkle. —**смóрщиваться,** *refl.* **1**, to become wrinkled. **2**, to shrivel.

смóрщить *v., pfv. of* **мóрщить** *and* **смóрщивать.** —**смóрщиться,** *refl., pfv. of* **мóрщиться** (*in senses #2 & #3*) *and* **смóрщиваться.**

смотáть *v., pfv. of* **смáтывать.** —**смотáться,** *refl., pfv. of* **смáтываться.**

смотр *n.* **1**, [*2nd loc.* **смотрý;** *pl.* **смотры́**] review; parade. **2**, [*no 2nd loc.; pl.* **смóтры**] public showing.

смотрéть *v. impfv.* [*pfv.* **посмотрéть;** *pres.* **смотрю́, смóтришь**] **1**, to look. **2**, (*with* **на** + *acc.*) to look at. **3**, to look over; have a look at; examine. **4**, to watch; see (television, a movie, game, etc.). **5**, (*with* **на** + *acc.*) *fig.* to regard; look upon. **6**, [*impfv. only*] (*with* **в** *or* **на** + *acc.*) to look out on; face. **7**, [*impfv. only*] to appear; peep out. **8**, (*with* **за** + *instr.*) to look after; keep an eye on. **9**, [*impfv. only*] (*with instr.*) *colloq.* to look like. —**смотри́(те), 1**, watch out!; take care! **2**, see how!; look how! —**смотря́ где,** it depends (on) where. —**смотря́ как,** it depends. —**смотря́ когда́,** it depends (on) when. —**смотря́ по** (+ *dat.*), depending on.

смотрéться *v.r. impfv.* [*pfv.* **посмотрéться;** *pres.* **смотрю́сь, смóтришься**] to look at oneself: смотрéться в зéркало, to look at oneself in the mirror.

смотри́тель *n.m.* guard; watchman; keeper.

смотровóй *adj.* **1**, observation (*attrib.*): смотровáя вы́шка, observation tower. **2**, *mil.* inspection (*attrib.*); review (*attrib.*).

смочи́ть [*infl.* **смочý, смóчишь**] *v., pfv. of* **смáчивать.**

смочь *v., pfv. of* **мочь.**

смошéнничать *v., pfv. of* **мошéнничать.**

смрад *n.* stench. —**смра́дный,** *adj.* stinking.

сму́глый *adj.* dark; swarthy; dark-complexioned.

сму́та *n.* **1,** *obs.* (civil) strife. **2,** *colloq.* dissension. **3,** distress.

смути́ть [*infl.* -щу́, -ти́шь] *v., pfv. of* смуща́ть. —**смути́ться,** *refl., pfv. of* смуща́ться.

сму́тно *adv.* vaguely; dimly.

сму́тный *adj.* **1,** dim; hazy; vague. **2,** troubled. **3,** marked by civil strife. —**сму́тное вре́мя,** *hist.* The Time of Troubles (1605-13).

смутья́н *n., colloq.* fomenter of civil strife; agitator.

смуща́ть *v. impfv.* [*pfv.* смути́ть] **1,** to embarrass; disconcert. **2,** to trouble; bother; disturb; perturb. —**смуща́ться,** *refl.* to be embarrassed.

смуще́ние *n.* embarrassment.

смыва́ть *v. impfv.* [*pfv.* смыть] to wash away; wash off. —**смыва́ться,** *refl.* **1,** to wash off; come off. **2,** *colloq.* to disappear; take off.

смыка́ть *v. impfv.* [*pfv.* сомкну́ть] to close (ranks, one's eyes, etc.). —**смыка́ться,** *refl.* **1,** to close. **2,** to close in. **3,** (*with* с + *instr.*) to join; make contact with. **4,** *fig.* to close ranks; unite.

смысл *n.* **1,** sense. **2,** meaning. —**в смы́сле** (+ *gen.*), **1,** in the sense of. **2,** as regards. —**нет смы́сла** (+ *inf.*), there is no sense (*or* no point) in...

смы́слить *v. impfv., colloq.* to understand.

смыслово́й *adj.* semantic.

смыть [*infl.* смо́ю, смо́ешь] *v., pfv. of* смыва́ть. —**смы́ться,** *refl., pfv. of* смыва́ться.

смы́чка *n.* **1,** joining; linking; coupling. **2,** *fig.* joining together; unifying.

смычко́вый *adj.* (*of musical instruments*) played with a bow.

смычо́к [*gen.* -чка́] *n., music* bow.

смышлёный *adj., colloq.* bright; clever; smart.

смягча́ть *v. impfv.* [*pfv.* смягчи́ть] **1,** to soften. **2,** to alleviate; mitigate; assuage. **3,** to tone down. —**смягча́ться,** *refl.* **1,** to soften; become soft. **2,** to abate; relent; ease. **3,** (*of the weather*) to become mild.

смягче́ние *n.* **1,** softening. **2,** mitigation.

смягчи́ть *v., pfv. of* смягча́ть. —**смягчи́ться,** *refl., pfv. of* смягча́ться.

смяте́ние *n.* **1,** confusion. **2,** panic.

смятённый *adj., obs.* troubled.

смять *v. pfv.* [*infl.* сомну́, сомнёшь] **1,** *pfv. of* мять (*in senses* #2 & #3). **2,** to trample upon; trample down. **3,** *mil.* to crush; overrun. **4,** *fig.* to crush; overwhelm. —**смя́ться,** *refl., pfv. of* мя́ться (*in sense* #1).

снабди́ть [*infl.* -бжу́, -бди́шь] *v., pfv. of* снабжа́ть.

снабжа́ть *v. impfv.* [*pfv.* снабди́ть] (*with instr.*) to supply (with); furnish (with); provide (with).

снабже́ние *n.* supply; supplying; provision.

сна́добье *n., colloq.* medicinal herb.

сна́йпер *n.* **1,** sharpshooter. **2,** sniper.

снару́жи *adv.* **1,** from the outside; on the outside. **2,** outwardly.

снаря́д *n.* **1,** shell; projectile; missile. **2,** apparatus; device; machine. —**гимнасти́ческие снаря́ды,** gymnastic apparatus.

снаряди́ть [*infl.* -жу́, -ди́шь] *v., pfv. of* снаряжа́ть.

снаря́дный *adj.* shell (*attrib.*); ammunition (*attrib.*).

снаряжа́ть *v. impfv.* [*pfv.* снаряди́ть] **1,** to equip; outfit. **2,** *colloq.* to send; dispatch.

снаряже́ние *n.* **1,** equipping; outfitting. **2,** equipment; outfit.

снасть [*pl.* сна́сти, -сте́й, -стя́м] *n.f.* tackle: рыбо-ло́вная снасть, fishing tackle.

снача́ла *adv.* **1,** at first; in the beginning. **2,** first (*before doing something else*). **3,** over again; from the beginning.

сна́шивать *v. impfv.* [*pfv.* сноси́ть] to wear out (clothes). —**сна́шиваться,** *refl.* (*of clothes*) to wear out.

снег [*2nd loc.* снегу́; *pl.* снега́] *n.* snow. —**как снег на́ голову,** out of a clear blue sky.

снеги́рь [*gen.* -гиря́] *n.m.* bullfinch.

снегово́й *adj.* **1,** snow (*attrib.*). **2,** (*of mountains*) snowcapped.

снегоочисти́тель *n.m.* snowplow.

снегопа́д *n.* snowfall.

снегосту́п *n.* snowshoe.

снегохо́д *n.* snowmobile.

снегу́рочка *n.* snow maiden. *Also,* **снегу́рка.**

снеда́ть *v. impfv.* **1,** *obs., colloq.* to eat. **2,** *fig.* to gnaw; consume; torment.

снедь *n.f., obs.* food.

снежи́нка [*gen. pl.* -нок] *n.* snowflake.

снежи́ть *v. impfv., colloq.* to snow.

сне́жный *adj.* **1,** snow (*attrib.*). **2,** snowy. —**сне́жная ба́ба,** snowman.

снежо́к [*gen.* -жка́] *n.* **1,** light snow. **2,** snowball. —**игра́ть в снежки́,** to throw snowballs.

снести́ [*infl. like* нести́] *v., pfv. of* нести́ (*in sense* #10) *and* сноси́ть[1]. —**снести́сь,** *refl., pfv. of* нести́сь (*in sense* #5) *and* сноси́ться[1].

снижа́ть *v. impfv.* [*pfv.* сни́зить] **1,** to lower; reduce. **2,** to bring down; land (an airplane). —**снижа́ться,** *refl.* **1,** (*of prices, temperature, etc.*) to go down; come down; drop; fall. **2,** (*of an airplane*) to land.

сниже́ние *n.* **1,** lowering; reduction. **2,** descent (*of an airplane*).

сни́зить [*infl.* -жу, -зишь] *v., pfv. of* снижа́ть. —**сни́зиться,** *refl., pfv. of* снижа́ться.

снизойти́ [*infl.* снизойду́, снизойдёшь; *past* снизошёл, снизошла́] *v., pfv. of* снисходи́ть.

сни́зу *adv.* **1,** from below. **2,** from the bottom. —**сни́зу до́верху,** from top to bottom. —**смотре́ть на** (+ *acc.*) **сни́зу вверх,** to look up to someone.

сни́кнуть *v. pfv.* [*past* сник, -ла] **1,** (*of plants*) to droop. **2,** *fig.* to die down. **3,** *fig., colloq.* to feel depressed.

снима́ть *v. impfv.* [*pfv.* снять] **1,** to take down; remove. **2,** to take off; remove (clothing, jewelry, make-up, etc.). **3,** to withdraw (a motion, one's candidacy, etc.). **4,** to remove; drop (from an agenda, from production, etc.). **5,** to lift (a ban or siege); dismiss (a charge); remit (a punishment). **6,** to dismiss (from a job); remove (from office). **7,** to gather in (a harvest). **8,** to photograph; take a picture of. **9,** to rent. —**снима́ть коло́ду,** to cut the cards. —**снима́ть ко́пию с** (+ *gen.*), to make a copy of. —**снима́ть ме́рку с** (+ *gen.*), to take someone's measurements. —**снима́ть показа́ния** (+ *gen.*), to take evidence from. —**снима́ть тру́бку,** to pick up the receiver (*of a telephone*).

снима́ться *v.r. impfv.* [*pfv.* сня́ться] **1,** (*with* с + *gen.*) to come off (of); come loose (from). **2,** (*with* +*gen.*) to leave; depart (from). **3,** to be photographed; have one's picture taken. —**снима́ться с ла́геря,** to break camp. —**снима́ться с я́коря,** to weigh anchor.

сни́мок [*gen.* -мка] *n.* picture; photograph; snapshot.

снискáть *v. pfv.* [*infl.* снищу́, сни́щешь] to gain; win.

снисходи́тельность *n.f.* **1,** condescension. **2,** leniency.

снисходи́тельный *adj.* **1,** condescending. **2,** lenient.

снисходи́ть *v. impfv.* [*pfv.* снизойти́; *pres.* -хожу́, -хо́дишь] **1,** (*with* к, до, *or inf.*) to condescend (to); deign (to). **2,** (*with* к) to show sympathy (toward); be tolerant (of).

снисхожде́ние *n.* **1,** condescension. **2,** leniency.

сни́ться *v.r. impfv.* [*pfv.* присни́ться] (*with dat.*) to appear in one's dreams: вы мне сни́лись, I dreamt (*or* had a dream) about you. Мне сни́лось, что..., I dreamt that...

сноб *n.* snob. —**сноби́зм,** *n.* snobbery; snobbishness.

сно́ва *adv.* again; once again; over again; anew.

сновáть *v. impfv.* [*pres.* сную́, снуёшь] **1,** (*of ships*) to ply back and forth. **2,** to scamper about.

сновиде́ние *n.* dream.

сногсшибáтельный *adj.*, *colloq.* stunning; staggering.

сноп [*gen.* снопá] *n.* **1,** sheaf. **2,** shaft (*of light*).

снорови́стый *adj.*, *colloq.* clever; smart.

сноро́вка *n.* skill; knack; ability.

снос *n.* **1,** *aero.; naut.* drift. **2,** tearing down; demolition. **3,** *colloq.* wear: э́тому сно́су нет, you can't wear it out. —**быть на сно́сях**, *colloq.* to be about to give birth.

сноси́ть[1] *v. impfv.* [*pfv.* снести́; *pres.* сношу́, сно́сишь] **1,** to carry down. **2,** to take; deliver. **3,** to cut off; chop off. **4,** (*of the wind*) to blow off; blow away; (*of water*) to wash away. **5,** to tear down (a building). **6,** to endure. **7,** *cards* to discard. —**сноси́ться,** *refl.* (*with* с + *instr.*), to communicate (with); get in touch (with).

сноси́ть[2] *v. pfv.* [*infl.* сношу́, сно́сишь] **1,** *pfv. of* снáшивать. **2,** *colloq.* to carry (*to a certain place and back*). —**сноси́ться,** *refl.*, *pfv. of* снáшиваться.

сно́ска [*gen. pl.* -сок] *n.* footnote.

сно́сно *adv.* **1,** fairly well; tolerably well. **2,** so-so.

сно́сный *adj.* **1,** tolerable; bearable. **2,** *colloq.* tolerable; passable; fairly good.

снотво́рный *adj.* **1,** taken to induce sleep: снотво́рная таблéтка, sleeping pill. **2,** *fig.* soporific.

снохá [*pl.* сно́хи] *n.* daughter-in-law.

сноше́ние *n.*, *usu. pl.* relations; dealings; intercourse.

сня́тие *n.* **1,** removal. **2,** dismissal. **3,** gathering in (*of a harvest*). **4,** lifting (*of a ban, siege, etc.*). **5,** making (*of copies*).

снято́й *adj.*, *in* сня́тое молоко́, skim milk.

снять [*infl.* сниму́, сни́мешь; *past fem.* сняла́] *v.*, *pfv. of* снимáть. —**сня́ться,** *refl.* [*past* сня́лся, -лáсь, -ло́сь] *pfv. of* снимáться.

со *prep.* = с.

со- *prefix* **1,** = с-. **2,** *corresponds to English prefix* co-: соáвтор, coauthor; сосуществовáние, coexistence.

соáвтор *n.* coauthor. —**соáвторство,** *n.* coauthorship.

собáка *n.* **1,** dog. **2,** *in* морскáя собáка, dogfish. —**вот где собáка зары́та!**, so that's what it's all about! —**он на э́том собáку съел,** he knows this subject inside out.

собáчий [*fem.* -чья] *adj.* **1,** dog (*attrib.*). **2,** *fig.*, *colloq.* a dog's: собáчья жизнь, a dog's life. —**собáчий хо́лод,** brutal cold.

собáчка [*gen. pl.* -чек] *n.* **1,** little dog; doggy. **2,** trigger. **3,** pawl; pallet.

собáчник *n.*, *colloq.* dog lover.

собесéдник *n.* **1,** person to whom one was speaking. **2,** (*after an adj.*) person to talk to.

собесéдование *n.* conversation; discussion.

собирáние *n.* gathering; collecting.

собирáтель *n.m.* collector.

собирáтельный *adj.*, *gram.* collective.

собирáтельство *n.* **1,** collecting (*as a hobby*). **2,** *anthropology* gathering.

собирáть *v. impfv.* [*pfv.* собрáть] **1,** to gather (people, firewood, information, etc.). **2,** to collect (books, taxes, etc.). **3,** to pick (fruit); gather in (a harvest). **4,** to assemble; put together (a machine, collection, etc.). **5,** to put together; pack: собирáть вéщи в я́щик, to pack things into a box. **6,** to receive; poll (votes). **7,** to gather; take in (a garment). **8,** *colloq.* to get (someone) ready to go somewhere: собирáть детéй в шко́лу, to get the children ready for school. **9,** *in* собирáть на стол, *colloq.* to set the table. **10,** to collect (one's thoughts); summon up (one's strength, courage, etc.).

собирáться *v.r. impfv.* [*pfv.* собрáться] **1,** to gather; assemble. **2,** to prepare; get ready: собирáться в доро́гу/о́тпуск, to get ready for a trip; get ready to go on vacation. **3,** (*of a storm*) to be gathering; be in the offing. **4,** [*impfv. only*] (*with inf.*) to intend (to). **5,** [*impfv. only*] (*with inf.*) to be about to. **6,** [*pfv. only*] (*with inf.*) to make up one's mind (to). **7,** (*with* с + *instr.*) to collect (one's thoughts); summon up (one's strength, courage, etc.).

соблаговоли́ть *v. pfv.* (*with inf.*) *obs.* to deign (to).

соблáзн *n.* temptation.

соблазни́тель *n.m.* **1,** tempter. **2,** seducer.

соблазни́тельный *adj.* **1,** tempting. **2,** seductive.

соблазня́ть *v. impfv.* [*pfv.* соблазни́ть] **1,** to tempt. **2,** to seduce. —**соблазня́ться,** *refl.* to be tempted.

соблюдáть *v. impfv.* [*pfv.* соблюсти́] to observe; abide by.

соблюдéние *n.* observance.

соблюсти́ [*infl.* -блюду́, -блюдёшь] *v.*, *pfv. of* блюсти́ *and* соблюдáть.

собо́й *also*, **собо́ю** *pron.*, *instr. of* себя́.

соболéзнование *n.* condolence; condolences.

соболéзновать *v. impfv.* [*pres.* -ную, -нуешь] (*with dat.*) to commiserate (with).

собо́лий [*fem.* -лья] *adj.* sable (*attrib.*).

соболи́ный *adj.* sable (*attrib.*).

со́боль *n.m.* sable.

собо́р *n.* **1,** cathedral. **2,** *hist.* assembly: зéмский собо́р, zemski sobor (*legislative assembly in old Russia*). **3,** *relig.* council: вселéнский собо́р, ecumenical council.

собо́рный *adj.* cathedral (*attrib.*).

собо́рование *n.* extreme unction.

собо́ю *pron.* = собо́й.

собрáние *n.* **1,** meeting. **2,** assembly. **3,** collection. —**собрáние сочинéний**, collected works.

со́бранный *adj.* **1,** tensed up; intense; concentrated. **2,** straight; erect. **3,** precise; efficient.

собрáт [*pl.* собрáтья, собрáтьев *or* собрáтий] *n.* **1,** colleague. **2,** *colloq.* counterpart.

собрáть [*infl. like* брать] *v.*, *pfv. of* собирáть. —**собрáться,** *refl.* [*past* собрáлся, -лáсь, -ло́сь *or* -лось, -ли́сь *or* -лись] *pfv. of* собирáться.

со́бственник *n.* owner; proprietor.

со́бственнический *adj.* **1**, proprietary. **2**, acquisitive; possessive.

со́бственно *particle* **1**, actually; in fact. **2**, proper: со́бственно го́род, the city proper. —**со́бственно говоря́**, strictly speaking.

собственнору́чный *adj.* handwritten. Собственнору́чная по́дпись, autograph. —**собственнору́чно**, *adv.* with one's own hands.

со́бственность *n.f.* **1**, property. **2**, ownership.

со́бственный *adj.* one's own. —**в со́бственном смы́сле**, in the true (*or* literal) sense. —**и́мя со́бственное**, proper noun. —**со́бственной персо́ной**, in person.

собуты́льник *n.,* *colloq.* drinking companion.

собы́тие *n.* event.

сова́ [*pl.* со́вы] *n.* owl.

сова́ть *v. impfv.* [*pfv.* су́нуть; *pres.* сую́, суёшь] to stick; slip; thrust. —**сова́ться**, *refl.* (*with* в + *acc.*) *colloq.* **1**, to plunge (into). **2**, to force one's way (into). **3**, to butt (into); poke one's nose (into).

совере́н *n.* sovereign (*British coin*).

соверша́ть *v. impfv.* [*pfv.* соверши́ть] **1**, to make (a trip, deal, mistake, etc.). **2**, to commit (a crime, sin, aggression, etc.). **3**, to carry out (a mission, raid, etc.). **4**, to accomplish (a feat, miracle, etc.).

соверше́ние *n.* **1**, accomplishment; completion. **2**, commission; perpetration (*of a crime*).

соверше́нно *adv.* completely; entirely; absolutely; perfectly; utterly.

совершенноле́тие *n.* majority; coming of age. —**совершенноле́тний**, *adj.* of age.

соверше́нный *adj.* **1**, perfect. **2**, absolute; utter. —**соверше́нный вид**, *gram.* perfective aspect.

соверше́нство *n.* perfection. —**в соверше́нстве**, perfectly; to perfection.

соверше́нствование *n.* improvement; perfecting.

соверше́нствовать *v. impfv.* [*pfv.* усоверше́нствовать; *pres.* -ствую, -ствуешь] to improve; perfect; refine.

соверши́ть *v.,* *pfv. of* соверша́ть.

со́вестить *v. impfv.* [*pres.* -щу, -стишь] *colloq.* to shame; chide. —**со́веститься**, *refl.* [*pfv.* посо́веститься] *colloq.* to be ashamed.

со́вестливый *adj.* conscientious; scrupulous.

со́вестно *adj.,* *used predicatively* (*with dat.*) ashamed: мне бы́ло со́вестно, I was ashamed.

со́весть *n.f.* conscience. —**на со́весть**, conscientiously. —**по со́вести (говоря́)**, to tell the truth; to be honest; in all honesty.

сове́т *n.* **1**, advice; counsel. **2**, council. **3**, soviet: Верхо́вный Сове́т, the Supreme Soviet.

сове́тник *n.* adviser.

сове́товать *v. impfv.* [*pfv.* посове́товать; *pres.* -тую, -туешь] (*with dat.*) to advise. —**сове́товаться**, *refl.* (*with* с + *instr.*) to consult; seek the advice of.

совето́лог *n.* specialist on the Soviet Union; Kremlinologist.

сове́тский *adj.* Soviet. —**Сове́тский Сою́з**, the Soviet Union.

сове́тчик *n.* adviser.

совеща́ние *n.* conference.

совеща́тельный *adj.* consultative; deliberative. —**пра́во совеща́тельного го́лоса**, voice but no vote. —**член с совеща́тельным го́лосом**, nonvoting member.

совеща́ться *v.r. impfv.* **1**, to deliberate. **2**, (*with* с + *instr.*) to confer (with).

сови́ный *adj.* **1**, owl's. **2**, owlish.

совлада́ть *v. pfv.* (*with* с + *instr.*) *colloq.* to cope with; handle; control. —**совлада́ть с собо́й**, to control oneself; get control of oneself.

совладе́лец [*gen.* -льца] *n.* co-owner; joint owner.

совладе́ние *n.* joint ownership.

совмести́мый *adj.* compatible. —**совмести́мость**, *n.f.* compatibility.

совмести́тельство *n.* holding of more than one job. Рабо́тать по совмести́тельству, to hold down two jobs.

совмести́ть [*infl.* -щу́, -сти́шь] *v.,* *pfv. of* совмеща́ть.

совме́стно *adv.* jointly; together.

совме́стный *adj.* joint; combined. —**совме́стное обуче́ние**, coeducation.

совмеща́ть *v. impfv.* [*pfv.* совмести́ть] to combine.

Совнарко́м *n.,* *contr. of* Сове́т Наро́дных Комисса́ров, Council of People's Commissars; Sovnarkom; (*replaced in 1946 by the Council of Ministers*).

совнархо́з *n.,* *contr. of* сове́т наро́дного хозя́йства, council of the national economy; sovnarkhoz (*regional economic councils established in 1957*).

сово́к [*gen.* -вка́] *n.* scoop. —**садо́вый сово́к**, trowel. —**сово́к для му́сора**, dustpan.

совокупле́ние *n.* copulation; coition.

совокупля́ться *v.r. impfv.* to copulate.

совоку́пно *adv.,* *obs.* together.

совоку́пность *n.f.* aggregate; sum total.

совоку́пный *adj.,* *obs.* joint; combined.

совпада́ть *v. impfv.* [*pfv.* совпа́сть] **1**, to coincide. **2**, to agree; tally.

совпаде́ние *n.* **1**, coincidence. **2**, identity; concurrence; harmony (*of interests, opinions, etc.*). **3**, combination (*of circumstances*).

совпа́сть [*infl. like* пасть] *v.,* *pfv. of* совпада́ть.

соврати́тель *n.m.* seducer.

соврати́ть [*infl.* -щу́, -ти́шь] *v.,* *pfv. of* совраща́ть.

совра́ть *v.,* *pfv. of* врать.

совраща́ть *v. impfv.* [*pfv.* соврати́ть] **1**, to pervert; **2**, to seduce.

совраще́ние *n.* perversion; seduction.

совреме́нник *n.* contemporary.

совреме́нность *n.f.* **1**, modernity. **2**, the present.

совреме́нный *adj.* **1**, contemporary. **2**, modern.

совсе́м *adv.* **1**, quite. **2**, completely; entirely. —**не совсе́м**, not entirely. —**совсе́м не**, not at all; not in the least.

совхо́з *n.* state farm (*contr. of* сове́тское хозя́йство).

согла́сие *n.* **1**, consent; assent. **2**, agreement. **3**, harmony.

согласи́тельный *adj.* conciliation (*attrib.*): согласи́тельная коми́ссия, conciliation committee.

согласи́ться [*infl.* -шу́сь, -си́шься] *v.r.,* *pfv. of* соглаша́ться.

согла́сно *adv.* in harmony. —*prep.,* *with dat. or* с + *instr.* according to; in accordance with.

согла́сный *adj.* [*short form* -сен, -сна] **1**, (*with* с + *instr.*) in agreement: я с ва́ми согла́сен (согла́сна), I agree with you. **2**, (*with* на + *acc.*) agreeable: он согла́сен на все усло́вия, he agrees (*or* is agreeable) to all the conditions. **3,** harmonious. **4,** *phonet.* consonantal: согла́сная бу́ква, consonant. —*n.* consonant.

согласова́ние *n.* **1,** coordination. **2,** *gram.* agreement. Согласова́ние времён, sequence of tenses.

согласо́ванный *adj.* coordinated; concerted. —**согла́сованность,** *n.f.* coordination.

согласова́ть [*infl* -су́ю, -су́ешь] *v., pfv. of* согла́-со́вывать.

согласова́ться *v.r. impfv. & pfv.* [*pres.* -су́ется] (*with* с + *instr.*) **1,** to be in conformance (with); be in keeping (with). **2,** *gram.* to agree (with).

согласо́вывать *v. impfv.* [*pfv.* согласова́ть] **1,** to coordinate. **2,** *gram.* to make agree.

соглаша́тель *n.m.* compromiser; appeaser. —**согла-ша́тельский,** *adj.* of compromise; of appeasement. —**соглаша́тельство,** *n.* policy of compromise; appeasement.

соглаша́ться *v.r. impfv.* [*pfv.* согласи́ться] **1,** (*with* с + *instr.*) to agree (with). **2,** (*with inf. or* на + *acc.*) to agree (to); consent (to).

соглаше́ние *n.* agreement.

согна́ть [*infl.* сгоню́, сго́нишь; *past fem.* согнала́] *v., pfv. of* сгоня́ть.

со́гнутый *adj.* **1,** bent. **2,** bent over; stooped.

согну́ть *v., pfv. of* гнуть *and* сгиба́ть. —**согну́ться,** *refl., pfv. of* гну́ться *and* сгиба́ться.

согрева́ние *n.* warming; heating.

согрева́ть *v. impfv.* [*pfv.* согре́ть] to warm; heat. —**согрева́ться,** *refl.* to get warm; warm up.

согреши́ть *v., pfv. of* греши́ть.

со́да *n.* soda: каусти́ческая со́да, caustic soda.

соде́йствие *n.* assistance; help.

соде́йствовать *v. impfv. & pfv.* [*pres.* -ствую, -ству-ешь] (*with dat.*) **1,** to assist. **2,** to further; promote; contribute to.

содержа́ние *n.* **1,** support; maintenance; upkeep. **2,** content: фо́рма и содержа́ние, form and content. Бога́тое содержа́ние белка́, high protein content. **3,** *colloq.* contents (*of a container*). **4,** contents (*of a book, letter, etc.*); subject matter. **5,** table of contents. **6,** pay; wages; salary.

содержа́нка [*gen. pl.* -нок] *n.* kept woman.

содержа́тель *n.m., obs.* owner; operator.

содержа́тельный *adj.* rich in content; informative; meaty.

содержа́ть *v. impfv.* [*pres.* -держу́, -де́ржишь] **1,** to contain. **2,** to support (a family, children, etc.). **3,** to keep (*in a certain state*): содержа́ть в испра́вности, to keep in working order. **4,** to keep; (forcibly) confine: содержа́ть под аре́стом, to keep under arrest. **5,** *obs.* to own; operate (a business). —**содер-жа́ться,** *refl.* **1,** to be kept; be maintained. **2,** to be contained: в мя́се соде́ржатся белки́, meat contains proteins.

содержи́мое *n., decl. as an adj.* contents.

со́довый *adj.* soda (*attrib.*).

содо́м *n., colloq.* uproar; commotion.

содра́ть [*infl.* сдеру́, сдерёшь; *past fem.* содрала́] *v., pfv. of* драть (*in sense #4*) *and* сдира́ть.

содрога́ние *n.* shudder.

содрога́ться *v.r. impfv.* [*pfv.* содрогну́ться] to shudder.

содру́жество *n.* **1,** cooperation; harmony. **2,** association; union. —Брита́нское содру́жество на́ций, British Commonwealth of Nations.

со́евый *adj.* soybean (*attrib.*). —со́евые бобы́, soybeans.

соедине́ние *n.* **1,** joining; uniting. **2,** linking; connecting. **3,** joint. **4,** *chem.* compound. **5,** *mil.* large unit (*division-size or larger*).

соединённый *adj.* united. —Соединённые Шта́ты, the United States.

соедини́тельный *adj.* connecting. —**соедини́тель-ная ткань,** connective tissue.

соединя́ть *v. impfv.* [*pfv.* соедини́ть] **1,** to connect; hook up. **2,** to unite. Соединя́ть си́лы, to join forces. **3,** to link; connect; join. **4,** to combine. —**соединя́ться,** *refl.* **1,** to unite; be united. **2,** to be linked; be connected. **3,** to be combined.

сожале́ние *n.* **1,** regret. **2,** pity. —к сожале́нию, unfortunately.

сожале́ть *v. impfv.* **1,** (*with* о *or a dependent clause*) to regret. **2,** (*with* о) *obs.* to pity; feel sorry for.

сожже́ние *n.* burning.

сожи́тель *n.m.* [*fem.* -ница] **1,** roommate. **2,** *colloq.* lover. —**сожи́тельство,** *n.* cohabitation.

сожи́тельствовать *v. impfv.* [*pres.* -ствую, -ству-ешь] to live together.

сожра́ть *v., pfv. of* жрать.

созва́ниваться *v.r. impfv.* [*pfv.* созвони́ться] (*with* с + *instr.*) *colloq.* to call (someone) on the telephone; be in touch by phone.

созва́ть [*infl. like* звать] *v., pfv. of* созыва́ть *and* сзыва́ть.

созве́здие *n.* constellation.

созвони́ться *v.r., pfv. of* созва́ниваться.

созву́чие *n.* **1,** *music* consonance. **2,** harmony; concord. **3,** assonance.

созву́чный *adj.* **1,** (*of sounds*) harmonious; assonant. **2,** (*with dat.*) in keeping with; in tune with.

создава́ть *v. impfv.* [*pfv.* созда́ть; *pres.* -даю́, -даёшь] **1,** to create. **2,** *short form past passive part. only* (*with* для), made (for); cut out (for): со́зданы друг для дру́га, made for each other; не со́здан для э́того, not cut out for this. —**создава́ться,** *refl.* to be created; arise; develop. У меня́ создало́сь впечатле́ние, что..., I got the impression that...

созда́ние *n.* **1,** creation (*act of creating*). **2,** creation; work. **3,** creature.

созда́тель *n.m.* creator; originator.

созда́ть [*infl. like* дать; *past* со́здал, создала́, со́здало] *v., pfv. of* создава́ть. —**созда́ться,** *refl.* [*past* -да́лся, -дала́сь, -дало́сь *or* -да́лось] *pfv. of* создава́ться.

созерца́ние *n.* contemplation. —**созерца́тельный,** *adj.* contemplative.

созерца́ть *v. impfv.* to contemplate.

созида́ние *n.* creation. —**созида́тель,** *n.m.* creator. —**созида́тельный,** *adj.* creative.

созида́ть *v. impfv.* to create.

сознава́ть *v. impfv.* [*pfv.* созна́ть; *pres.* -знаю́, -зна-ёшь] to realize; recognize; be conscious of; be aware of. —**сознава́ться,** *refl.* (*with* в + *prepl.*) to confess (to).

созна́ние *n.* **1,** consciousness: приходи́ть в созна́-ние, to regain consciousness. Без созна́ния, unconscious. **2,** awareness; realization; recognition; consciousness. **3,** *obs.* confession.

сознательно *adv.* consciously; deliberately.

сознательность *n.f.* consciousness; awareness: кла́ссовая созна́тельность, class consciousness; полити́ческая созна́тельность, political awareness.

сознательный *adj.* **1,** conscious. **2,** deliberate.

сознать [*infl.* -зна́ю, -зна́ешь] *v., pfv. of* сознава́ть. —**созна́ться,** *refl., pfv. of* сознава́ться.

созрева́ние *n.* ripening; maturation.

созрева́ть *v. impfv.* [*pfv.* созре́ть] to ripen; mature.

созре́ть *v., pfv. of* зреть¹ *and* созрева́ть.

созыв *n.* calling; convening.

созыва́ть *v. impfv.* [*pfv.* созва́ть] **1,** to call together; invite; summon. **2,** to call; convene.

соизволя́ть *v. impfv.* [*pfv.* соизво́лить] (*with inf.*) *obs.* to deign (to).

соизмери́мый *adj.* commensurable.

соиска́ние *n.* (*with gen.*) competition (*for an award or degree*).

соиска́тель *n.m.* competitor; rival.

со́йка [*gen. pl.* со́ек] *n.* jay (*bird*).

сойти́ [*infl.* сойду́, сойдёшь; *past* сошёл, сошла́, сошло́] *v., pfv. of* сходи́ть. —**сойти́сь,** *refl., pfv. of* сходи́ться.

сок *n.* **1,** juice. **2,** sap. —**в по́лном соку́,** in the prime of life.

сока́мерник *n.* cellmate.

соковыжима́лка [*gen. pl.* -лок] *n.* squeezer; juicer.

со́кол *n.* falcon. —**гол как соко́л** (*with different stress*), poor as a church mouse.

соколи́ный *adj.* falcon's. —**соколи́ная охо́та,** falconry.

сократи́ть [*infl.* -щу́, -ти́шь] *v., pfv. of* сокраща́ть. —**сократи́ться,** *refl., pfv. of* сокраща́ться.

сокраща́ть *v. impfv.* [*pfv.* сократи́ть] **1,** to reduce; curtail. **2,** to shorten. **3,** to abridge; condense. **4,** to abbreviate. **5,** *colloq.* to dismiss; fire. **6,** *math.* to cancel. —**сокраща́ться,** *refl.* **1,** to become *or* grow shorter. **2,** to be shortened. **3,** to be reduced. **4,** *physiol.* to contract.

сокраще́ние *n.* **1,** reduction; curtailment. **2,** shortening. **3,** abridgment; condensation. **4,** abbreviation. **5,** contraction (*of muscles*). **6,** *math.* cancellation. **7,** *colloq.* discharge; dismissal.

сокращённо *adv.* for short.

сокрове́нный *adj.* **1,** secret; hidden. **2,** *fig.* (*of one's thoughts, feelings, etc.*) innermost.

сокро́вище *n.* treasure. —**ни за каки́е сокро́вища,** not for (anything in) the world.

сокро́вищница *n.* treasure house.

сокруша́ть *v. impfv.* [*pfv.* сокруши́ть] **1,** to shatter; smash; destroy. **2,** to distress; upset. —**сокруша́ться,** *refl.* [*impfv. only*] (*with* о) to grieve; lament; be distressed (over).

сокруше́ние *n.* **1,** smashing; destruction. **2,** distress.

сокрушённый *adj.* grieving; grief-stricken. —**сокру-шённо,** *adv.* sorrowfully.

сокруши́тельный *adj.* **1,** (*of a blow*) crushing; crippling; shattering. **2,** (*of a feeling*) overwhelming.

сокруши́ть *v., pfv. of* сокруша́ть.

сокры́тие *n.* concealment.

солга́ть *v., pfv. of* лгать.

солда́т [*gen. pl.* -да́т] *n.* soldier. —**солда́тик,** *n.* toy (*or* tin) soldier. —**солда́тка,** *n.* soldier's wife. —**солда́тский,** *adj.* soldier's.

солева́ренный *adj., in* солева́ренный заво́д, saltworks. *Also,* **солева́рный.**

солева́рня [*gen. pl.* -рен] *n.* saltworks.

солево́й *adj.* saline.

соле́ние *n.* salting; pickling.

соленóид *n.* solenoid.

солёность *n.f.* salinity; saltiness.

солёный *adj.* **1,** salt (*attrib.*): солёная вода́, salt water. **2,** salty. **3,** salted; pickled. **4,** *fig., colloq.* spicy; racy; risqué. *See also* со́лон.

соле́нье *n., usu. pl.* salted foods.

солеци́зм *n.* solecism.

солидаризи́роваться *v.r. impfv. & pfv.* [*pres.* -ру́-юсь, -руешься] (*with* с + *instr.*) to express one's solidarity with; make common cause with.

солида́рность *n.f.* solidarity.

солида́рный *adj.* **1,** united; as one; of one mind. **2,** (*with* с + *instr.*) in full agreement (with); at one (with).

соли́дно *adv.* **1,** solidly. **2,** in a serious tone or manner. **3,** in a sizable amount: соли́дно зараба́тывать, to earn good money.

соли́дный *adj.* [*short form* -ден, -дна] **1,** solid; firm. **2,** sound; thorough. **3,** reputable; well-established. **4,** imposing; impressive. **5,** mature; middle-aged. **6,** *colloq.* large; stout. **7,** *colloq.* sizable; considerable.

соли́ст *n.m.* [*fem.* соли́стка] soloist.

солите́р (тэ) *n.* large diamond; solitaire.

солитёр *n.* tapeworm.

соли́ть *v. impfv.* [*pfv.* посоли́ть; *pres.* солю́, со́лишь *or* соли́шь] **1,** to salt. **2,** to pickle.

со́лка *n.* salting; pickling.

со́лнечно *adv.* like the sun. —*adj.,* used predicatively sunny: бы́ло со́лнечно и тепло́, it was sunny and warm.

со́лнечный *adj.* **1,** sun (*attrib.*); solar. **2,** sunny. —**со́л-нечное пятно́,** sunspot. —**со́лнечный свет,** sunlight; sunshine. —**со́лнечное сплете́ние,** solar plexus. —**со́лнечный уда́р,** sunstroke. —**со́лнечные часы́,** sundial.

со́лнце (сонц) *n.* sun.

солнцезащи́тный *adj.* serving as protection against the sun: солнцезащи́тные очки́, sunglasses.

солнцепёк *n.* blazing sun; heat of the sun.

солнцестоя́ние *n.* solstice.

со́ло *n. indecl.* solo.

солове́й [*gen.* -вья́] *n.* nightingale.

соловьи́ный *adj.* nightingale (*attrib.*); nightingale's.

со́лод *n.* malt.

соло́дка *n.* licorice.

солодо́вый *adj.* malt (*attrib.*). —**солодо́вый са́хар,** maltose.

соло́ма *n.* straw.

соло́менный *adj.* **1,** straw (*attrib.*). **2,** (*of a roof*) thatched. **3,** straw-colored. —**соло́менная вдова́,** grass widow.

соло́минка [*gen. pl.* -нок] *n.* a straw. —**хвата́ться за соло́минку,** to grasp at a straw.

со́лон *adj., short form of* солёный, **1,** salty: у меня́ во рту со́лоно, I have a salty taste in my mouth. **2,** *fig.* involving misfortune or adversity: ему́ со́лоно (*or* со́лон) пришло́сь, he came to grief. —**не со́лоно хлеба́вши,** having accomplished nothing.

солоне́ц [*gen.* -нца́] *n.* dark alkaline soil.

солони́на *n.* corned beef.

соло́нка [*gen. pl.* -нок] *n.* salt shaker; saltcellar.

СО́ЛОНО adj. see **со́лон**.

СОЛОНОВА́ТЫЙ adj. brackish.

СОЛОНЧА́К [gen. **-чака́**] n. saline soil; salt marsh.

СОЛЬ[1] n.f. **1**, salt. **2**, (with gen.) colloq. the point: вся соль расска́за, the whole point of the story.

СОЛЬ[2] n. neut. indecl., music sol; G.

СО́ЛЬНЫЙ adj. solo.

СОЛЬФЕ́ДЖИО n. indecl. solfeggio.

СОЛЯ́НКА n. **1**, saltwort. **2**, a thick soup with meat or fish.

СОЛЯНО́Й adj. salt (attrib.); saline.

СОЛЯ́НЫЙ adj., in соля́ная кислота́, hydrochloric acid.

СОЛЯ́РИЙ n. solarium.

СОМ [gen. сома́] n. sheatfish.

СОМАТИ́ЧЕСКИЙ adj. somatic.

СО́МКНУТЫЙ adj. (of a formation, order, etc.) close.

СОМКНУ́ТЬ v., pfv. of смыка́ть. —**сомкну́ться**, refl., pfv. of смыка́ться.

СОМНЕВА́ТЬСЯ v.r. impfv. (with в + prepl. or a dependent clause) to doubt; have doubts; be in doubt. Вы мо́жете не сомнева́ться в э́том, you can be sure of that.

СОМНЕ́НИЕ n. doubt. —**без (вся́кого) сомне́ния**, without a doubt. —**вне (вся́кого) сомне́ния**, beyond (any) doubt.

СОМНИ́ТЕЛЬНО adj., used predicatively doubtful: о́чень сомни́тельно, что́бы..., it is very doubtful whether...

СОМНИ́ТЕЛЬНЫЙ adj. **1**, doubtful; dubious; questionable. **2**, shady; suspicious.

СОМНО́ЖИТЕЛЬ n.m., math. factor.

СОН [gen. сна] n. **1**, sleep. **2**, dream. —**ви́деть сон**, to have a dream. —**ви́деть (что́- or кого́-нибудь) во сне**, to have a dream about. —**сквозь сон**, in one's sleep; while half asleep. —**сон в ру́ку**, the dream came true. —**со сна**, being half asleep (or awake): он со сна ничего́ не по́нял, he was too sleepy to understand anything. —**у меня́ сна ни в одно́м глазу́**, I am not the least bit sleepy.

СОНА́ТА n. sonata.

СОНЕ́Т n. sonnet.

СОНЛИ́ВЫЙ adj. sleepy; drowsy. —**сонли́вость**, n.f. sleepiness; drowsiness.

СОНМ n. **1**, huge throng. **2**, (with gen.) multitude (of).

СО́ННЫЙ adj. **1**, sleepy; drowsy. **2**, sleeping. —**со́нная боле́знь**, sleeping sickness.

СО́НЯ n. dormouse. —n.m. & f., colloq. sleepyhead.

СООБРАЖА́ТЬ v. impfv. [pfv. **сообрази́ть**] **1**, to think; reflect. **2**, to figure out. Хорошо́ сообража́ть, to be quick to figure things out; be quick-witted. **3**, [impfv. only] (with в + prepl.) colloq. to know something about (a subject).

СООБРАЖЕ́НИЕ n. **1**, ability to reason. **2**, usu. pl. thoughts; views (on a subject). **3**, usu. pl. considerations; reasons: по фина́нсовым соображе́ниям, for financial reasons. **4**, obs. thinking; thought: поступа́ть без соображе́ния, to act without thinking/thought. —**принима́ть в соображе́ние**, to take into consideration.

СООБРАЗИ́ТЕЛЬНЫЙ adj. clever; quick-witted. —**сообрази́тельность**, n.f. cleverness; quickness of wit.

СООБРАЗИ́ТЬ [infl. **-жу́, -зи́шь**] v., pfv. of сообража́ть.

СООБРА́ЗНО prep., with dat. or с + instr. in accordance with; in conformity with.

СООБРА́ЗНОСТЬ n.f. conformity.

СООБРА́ЗНЫЙ adj. (with с + instr.) conforming to; in keeping with. —**ни с чем не сообра́зный**, absurd; ridiculous.

СООБРАЗОВА́ТЬ v. impfv. & pfv. [pres. **-зу́ю, -зу́ешь**] (with с + instr.) to make (something) conform (to). —**сообразова́ться**, refl. (with с + instr.) **1**, to conform to. **2**, to take account of.

СООБЩА́ adv. jointly; together; in concert.

СООБЩА́ТЬ v. impfv. [pfv. **сообщи́ть**] **1**, to report; announce; convey: сообща́ть изве́стие, to report the news; сообща́ть реше́ние or о реше́нии, announce a decision. Газе́ты сообща́ют, что..., the newspapers report that... **2**, (with dat.) to inform; tell. **3**, to impart; transmit. —**сообща́ться**, refl. [impfv. only] **1**, to be reported. **2**, (with с + instr.) to communicate (with). **3**, (with с + instr.) to be linked (with). **4**, (of rooms) to connect.

СООБЩЕ́НИЕ n. **1**, report; message; communication. **2**, communication(s). Пути́ сообще́ния, communications (railway, road, etc.).

СООБЩЕСТВО n. association (of people). —**в соо́бществе с**, in the company of.

СООБЩИ́ТЬ v., pfv. of сообща́ть.

СОО́БЩНИК n. accomplice.

СООРУДИ́ТЬ [infl. **-жу́, -ди́шь**] v., pfv. of сооружа́ть.

СООРУЖА́ТЬ v. impfv. [pfv. **сооруди́ть**] to erect; build.

СООРУЖЕ́НИЕ n. **1**, erection; construction. **2**, building; structure. **3**, mil. installation; pl. works.

СООТВЕ́ТСТВЕННО adv. **1**, accordingly. **2**, respectively. —prep., with dat. or с + instr. according to; in accordance with.

СООТВЕ́ТСТВЕННЫЙ adj. **1**, (with dat.) corresponding (to). **2**, appropriate; proper.

СООТВЕ́ТСТВИЕ n. accordance; conformity. —**в соотве́тствии с** (+ instr.), in accordance with. —**приводи́ть в соотве́тствие с**, to bring into conformity (or into line) with.

СООТВЕ́ТСТВОВАТЬ v. impfv. [pres. **-ствую, -ствуешь**] (with dat.) to correspond (to); conform (to).

СООТВЕ́ТСТВУЮЩИЙ adj. **1**, corresponding. **2**, appropriate; proper; suitable. —**соотве́тствующим о́бразом**, accordingly.

СООТЕ́ЧЕСТВЕННИК n. compatriot; fellow countryman.

СООТНЕСТИ́ [infl. like нести́] v., pfv. of соотноси́ть.

СООТНОСИ́ТЕЛЬНЫЙ adj. correlative.

СООТНОСИ́ТЬ v. impfv. [pfv. **соотнести́**; pres. **-ношу́, -но́сишь**] to correlate. —**соотноси́ться**, refl. [impfv. only] to correspond.

СООТНОШЕ́НИЕ n. **1**, correlation. **2**, ratio. —**соотноше́ние сил**, correlation of forces; balance of forces.

СОПЕ́РНИК n. rival.

СОПЕ́РНИЧАТЬ v. impfv. (with с + instr.) **1**, to compete (with). **2**, to vie (with). **3**, to compare (with); rival; equal.

СОПЕ́РНИЧЕСТВО n. rivalry.

СОПЕ́ТЬ v. impfv. [pres. **-плю́, -пи́шь**] to sniffle; wheeze.

СО́ПКА [gen. pl. **-пок**] n. **1**, hill or mountain with a rounded summit (in the Asian USSR). **2**, volcano (on Kamchatka Peninsula).

СО́ПЛИ [gen. **сопле́й**] n. pl., vulg. snot.

СОПЛИ́ВЫЙ adj., colloq. snotty.

СОПЛО́ [pl. **со́пла, со́пел** or **сопл**] n. nozzle.

СОПОСТА́ВИТЬ [infl. **-влю, -вишь**] v., pfv. of сопоставля́ть.

СОПОСТАВЛЕ́НИЕ n. comparison.

сопоставля́ть *v. impfv.* [*pfv.* сопоста́вить] to compare; contrast.

сопра́но *n. neut. indecl.* soprano (*voice*). —*n. fem. indecl.* soprano (*singer*). —сопра́нный; сопра́новый, *adj.* soprano.

сопреде́льный *adj.* neighboring; adjacent; contiguous.

сопредседа́тель *n.m.* co-chairman.

сопре́ть *v.,* *pfv. of* преть.

соприкаса́ться *v.r. impfv.* [*pfv.* соприкосну́ться] **1**, to touch; border (each other); be contiguous. **2**, (*with* с + *instr.*) to border; adjoin. **3**, (*with instr.*) to touch; bump: соприкосну́ться лба́ми, to touch/bump foreheads.

соприкоснове́ние *n.* **1**, contiguity. **2**, contact. —то́чки соприкоснове́ния, things in common; areas of common interest.

соприкосну́ться *v.r.,* *pfv. of* соприкаса́ться.

сопроводи́тельный *adj.* accompanying. —сопроводи́тельное письмо́, covering letter.

сопроводи́ть [*infl.* -жу́, -ди́шь] *v.,* *pfv. of* сопровожда́ть.

сопровожда́ть *v. impfv.* [*pfv.* сопроводи́ть] to accompany. —сопровожда́ться, *refl.* [*impfv. only*] (*with instr.*) to be accompanied (by).

сопровожде́ние *n.* **1**, (act of) accompanying: в сопровожде́нии (+ *gen.*), accompanied by; без сопровожде́ния, unaccompanied. **2**, *music* accompaniment. **3**, *mil.* escort.

сопротивле́ние *n.* resistance.

сопротивля́емость *n.f.* resistance (*ability to resist*).

сопротивля́ться *v.r. impfv.* (*with dat.*) to resist.

сопряжённый *adj.* (*with* с + *instr.*) involving; entailing: э́то сопряжено́ с больши́ми расхо́дами, it involves/entails great expense.

сопу́тствовать *v. impfv.* [*pres.* -ствую, -ствуешь] (*with dat.*) to accompany. Ему́ во всём сопу́тствует уда́ча, he is successful at everything he tries.

сопу́тствующий *adj.* attendant; concomitant.

сор *n.* rubbish; refuse; litter. —выноси́ть сор из избы́, to wash one's dirty linen in public; tell tales out of school.

соразме́рить *v.,* *pfv. of* соразмеря́ть.

соразме́рно *prep.,* with dat. or с + instr. commensurate with.

соразме́рный *adj.* **1**, commensurate; proportionate. **2**, well-proportioned. —соразме́рность, *n.f.* proportion; balance.

соразмеря́ть *v. impfv.* [*pfv.* соразме́рить] to make commensurate (with); balance.

сора́тник *n.* comrade in arms.

сорване́ц [*gen.* -нца́] *n.,* *colloq.* hoodlum; brat; (*of a girl*) tomboy.

сорва́ть [*infl. like* рвать] *v.,* *pfv. of* срыва́ть. —сорва́ться, *refl.,* *pfv. of* срыва́ться.

сорвиголова́ [*infl. like* голова́] *n.m. & f., colloq.* daredevil.

сорганизова́ть *v. pfv.* [*infl.* -зу́ю, -зу́ешь] *colloq.* to organize.

со́рго *n. indecl.* sorghum.

соревнова́ние *n.* **1**, competition. **2**, *pl., sports* competition; contest.

соревнова́ться *v.r. impfv.* [*pres.* -ну́юсь, -ну́ешься] to compete.

сориенти́роваться *v.r.,* *pfv. of* ориенти́роваться (*in sense #1*).

сори́нка [*gen. pl.* -нок] *n.* speck of dust.

сори́ть *v. impfv.* [*pfv.* насори́ть] **1**, to litter. **2**, [*impfv. only*] (*with instr.*) to squander: сори́ть деньга́ми, to toss money around.

со́рный *adj.* rubbish (*attrib.*); refuse (*attrib.*). —со́рная трава́, weed; weeds.

сорня́к [*gen.* -няка́] *n.* weed.

соро́дич *n.* **1**, relative. **2**, fellow countryman.

со́рок [*gen., dat., instr., & prepl.* сорока́] *numeral* forty.

соро́ка *n.* magpie.

сорокале́тие *n.* **1**, fortieth anniversary; fortieth birthday. **2**, forty-year period.

сорокале́тний *adj.* **1**, forty-year (*attrib.*). **2**, forty-year-old.

сороково́й *ordinal numeral* fortieth.

сороконо́жка [*gen. pl.* -жек] *n., colloq.* centipede.

сорокопу́т *n.* shrike.

соро́чка [*gen. pl.* -чек] *n.* **1**, shirt. Ночна́я соро́чка, nightgown; nightshirt. **2**, chemise. **3**, back (*of a playing card*). —роди́ться в соро́чке, to be born with a silver spoon in one's mouth.

сорт [*pl.* сорта́] *n.* **1**, sort; kind. **2**, quality; grade: пе́рвого со́рта, top-quality; high-grade.

сортирова́ть *v. impfv.* [*pfv.* рассортирова́ть; *pres.* -ру́ю, -ру́ешь] to sort; assort.

сортиро́вка *n.* sorting.

сортиро́вочный *adj.* sorting (*attrib.*). —сортиро́вочная ста́нция, *R.R.* switchyard.

сортиро́вщик *n.* sorter.

сортово́й *adj.* high-quality.

соса́ние *n.* sucking.

соса́тельный *adj.* sucking (*attrib.*).

соса́ть *v. impfv.* [*pres.* сосу́, сосёшь] to suck.

сосва́тать *v.,* *pfv. of* сва́тать.

сосе́д [*pl.* сосе́ди, -дей, -дям] *n.m.* [*fem.* -се́дка] neighbor. —сосе́дний, *adj.* neighboring; adjacent; next. —сосе́дский, *adj.* the neighbors'.

сосе́дство *n.* **1**, proximity. **2**, *obs.* neighbors. —по сосе́дству с, adjacent to; adjoining.

соси́ска [*gen. pl.* -сок] *n.* frankfurter.

со́ска [*gen. pl.* -сок] *n.* **1**, nipple (*of a nursing bottle*). **2**, pacifier.

соска́бливать *v. impfv.* [*pfv.* соскобли́ть] to scrape off.

соска́кивать *v. impfv.* [*pfv.* соскочи́ть] (*with* с + *gen.*) **1**, to jump off; jump down (from). **2**, to come off.

соска́льзывать *v. impfv.* [*pfv.* соскользну́ть] **1**, to slide down. **2**, to slip off.

соскобли́ть [*infl.* -скоблю́, -скоблишь *or* -скобли́шь] *v.,* *pfv. of* соска́бливать.

соскользну́ть *v.,* *pfv. of* соска́льзывать.

соскочи́ть [*infl.* -скочу́, -ско́чишь] *v.,* *pfv. of* соска́кивать.

соску́читься *v.r. pfv.* **1**, to become bored. **2**, = скуча́ть (*in sense #2*).

сослага́тельный *adj., in* сослага́тельное наклоне́ние, subjunctive mood.

сосла́ть [*infl.* сошлю́, сошлёшь] *v.,* *pfv. of* ссыла́ть. —сосла́ться, *refl.,* *pfv. of* ссыла́ться.

со́слепа *also,* **со́слепу** *adv., colloq.* because one is unable to see; because of one's poor eyesight.

сосло́вие *n.* estate; class. —дворя́нское сосло́вие, the nobility. —духо́вное сосло́вие, the clergy.

—**крестья́нское сосло́вие,** the peasantry. —**купе́ческое сосло́вие,** the merchants.

сосло́вный *adj.* class (*attrib.*).

сослужи́вец [*gen.* -вца] *n.* colleague; fellow worker.

сослужи́ть *v. pfv.* [*infl.* -служу́, -слу́жишь], *in* сослужи́ть слу́жбу (+ *dat.*), **1,** to do (someone) a favor. **2,** (*with* хоро́шую) to stand in good stead; (*with* плоху́ю) to do (someone) a disservice; not serve (someone) well.

сосна́ [*pl.* со́сны, со́сен] *n.* pine; pine tree. —**сосно́вый,** *adj.* pine (*attrib.*).

сосну́ть *v. pfv.*, *colloq.* to take a nap.

сосня́к [*gen.* -няка́] *n.* pine forest.

сосо́к [*gen.* -ска́] *n.* nipple; teat.

сосредото́чение *n.* (act of) concentration. —**сосредото́ченность,** *n.f.* (degree of) concentration.

сосредото́ченный *adj.* **1,** concentrated. **2,** lost in concentration. **3,** (*of a look*) intent; (*of attention*) rapt.

сосредото́чивать *v. impfv.* [*pfv.* сосредото́чить] to concentrate. —**сосредото́чиваться,** *refl.* **1,** to be concentrated. **2,** (*with* на + *prepl.*) to concentrate (on).

соста́в *n.* **1,** composition; make-up. **2,** staff; personnel. Ли́чный соста́в, personnel. **3,** *in certain expressions,* strength: чи́сленный соста́в, numerical strength. В по́лном соста́ве, at full strength. **4,** trains; cars: това́рный соста́в, freight cars; подвижно́й соста́в, rolling stock. **5,** (chemical) compound. **6,** *in* соста́в исполни́телей, *theat.* cast. **7,** *in* соста́в преступле́ния, corpus delicti. —**в соста́ве** (+ *gen.*), consisting of: коми́ссия в соста́ве трёх челове́к, a committee of three. —**входи́ть в соста́в** (+ *gen.*), to form a part of; be a member of.

состави́тель *n.m.* compiler.

соста́вить [*infl.* -влю, -вишь] *v., pfv. of* составля́ть. —**соста́виться,** *refl., pfv. of* составля́ться.

составле́ние *n.* **1,** compilation. **2,** drawing up; drafting. **3,** formation.

составля́ть *v. impfv.* [*pfv.* соста́вить] **1,** to put together (*in one place*). **2,** to form (a group, collection, opinion, etc.). **3,** to compile (a list, dictionary, etc.). **4,** to compose; draft; draw up. **5,** to be; represent; constitute. **6,** to total; amount; come to. **7,** *in* составля́ть компа́нию (+ *dat.*), to keep (someone) company. —**составля́ться,** *refl.* **1,** to be formed. **2,** to be built up; accumulate.

составно́й *adj.* **1,** compound; composite. **2,** component; constituent: составна́я часть, component/constituent part. **3,** sectional. —**составна́я карти́нка,** jigsaw puzzle.

соста́рить *v., pfv. of* ста́рить. —**соста́риться,** *refl., pfv. of* ста́риться.

состоя́ние *n.* **1,** state; condition: состоя́ние здоро́вья, state of health; в плохо́м состоя́нии, in poor condition. **2,** fortune: нажива́ть состоя́ние, to make a fortune. —**быть в состоя́нии** (+ *inf.*), to be in a position to.

состоя́тельность *n.f.* **1,** wealth. **2,** soundness (*of an argument*).

состоя́тельный *adj.* **1,** well-to-do. **2,** well-founded.

состоя́ть *v. impfv.* [*pres.* -сто́ю, -стои́шь] **1,** (*with* из) to consist of. **2,** (*with instr. or various prepositions*) to be (*with reference to one's status*): состоя́ть чле́ном (+ *gen.*), to be a member of; состоя́ть в бра́ке, to be married. **3,** (*with* в + *prepl.*) to belong to. **4,** (*with*

в + *prepl.*) to be; consist of; lie in: ра́зница состои́т в том, что..., the difference is that...

состоя́ться *v.r. pfv.* [*infl.* -стои́тся] to take place; be held.

сострада́ние *n.* compassion. —**сострада́тельный,** *adj.* compassionate.

состряга́ть *v. impfv.* [*pfv.* состри́чь] to cut off; clip off.

состри́ть *v. pfv.* to crack; make a wisecrack.

состри́чь [*infl. like* стричь] *v., pfv. of* состряга́ть.

состро́ить *v. pfv., colloq.* to make (a face).

состря́пать *v., pfv. of* стря́пать.

состяза́ние *n.* competition; contest; match.

состяза́ться *v.r. impfv.* to compete.

сосу́д *n.* **1,** vessel; container. **2,** *anat.* vessel. —**сосу́дистый,** *adj.* vascular.

сосу́лька [*gen. pl.* -лек] *n.* icicle.

сосу́н [*gen.* -суна́] *n,* suckling. *Also,* сосуно́к [*gen.* -нка́]

сосуществова́ние *n.* coexistence.

сосуществова́ть *v. impfv.* [*pres.* -ству́ю, -ству́ешь] to coexist.

сосчита́ть *v., pfv. of* счита́ть (*in sense #1*).

сот *n., gen. pl. of* сто: не́сколько сот, several hundred.

со́тая *n., decl. as an adj.* hundredth: одна́ со́тая, one-hundredth.

сотворе́ние *n.* creation (*of the world*). —**от сотворе́ния ми́ра,** since the world began; since the beginning of time.

сотвори́ть *v., pfv. of* твори́ть.

со́тенный *adj., colloq.* hundred-ruble (*attrib.*).

сотёрн (тэ) *n.* sauterne.

сотка́ть *v., pfv. of* ткать.

со́тня [*gen. pl.* -тен] *n.* **1,** one hundred. **2,** *pl.* (*with gen.*) hundreds (of): со́тни ты́сяч люде́й, hundreds of thousands of people.

сотова́рищ *n.* associate; colleague.

со́товый *adj.* of or from a honeycomb.

сотру́дник *n.* **1,** collaborator; colleague; associate. **2,** official. **3,** (*with gen.*) contributor (*to a newspaper, magazine, etc.*). —**нау́чный сотру́дник,** research assistant.

сотру́дничать *v. impfv.* **1,** (*with* с + *instr.*) to cooperate (with); collaborate (with). **2,** (*with* в + *prepl.*) to contribute to; write for (a publication).

сотру́дничество *n.* **1,** cooperation; collaboration. **2,** (*with* в + *prepl.*) contributing (to a publication).

сотряса́ть *v. impfv.* [*pfv.* сотрясти́] to shake; rock. —**сотряса́ться,** *refl.* to shake; tremble.

сотрясе́ние *n.* **1,** shaking; vibration. **2,** shock; impact. —**сотрясе́ние мо́зга,** brain concussion.

сотрясти́ [*infl. like* трясти́] *v., pfv. of* сотряса́ть. —**сотрясти́сь,** *refl., pfv. of* сотряса́ться.

со́ты *n. pl.* [*sing.* сот] honeycomb.

со́тый *ordinal numeral* hundredth.

со́ус *n.* sauce; gravy; dressing. —**со́усник,** *n.* gravy boat.

соуча́стие *n.* complicity. —**соуча́стник,** *n.* accomplice.

соучени́к [*gen.* -ника́] *n.m.* [*fem.* -ни́ца] fellow classmate.

софа́ [*pl.* со́фы] *n.* sofa.

софи́зм *n.* sophism. —**софи́ст,** *n.* sophist. —**софи́стика,** *n.* sophistry. —**софисти́ческий,** *adj.* sophistic.

соха́ [*pl.* со́хи] *n.* old wooden plow.

сóхнуть *v. impfv.* [*pfv.* **вы́сохнуть**; *past* **сох** *or* **сóх-**
нул, сóхла] **1,** to dry; become dry. **2,** to dry up. **3,**
to wither. **4,** *colloq.* to grow thin.

сохранéние *n.* **1,** preservation; conservation. **2,** keeping; retention. **3,** safekeeping: отдавáть на сохранéние, to turn over for safekeeping.

сохрани́ть *v., pfv. of* **сохраня́ть.** —**сохрани́ться,**
refl., pfv. of **сохраня́ться.**

сохрáнность *n.f.* **1,** safety. **2,** state of preservation.
—в сохрáнности, safe; intact.

сохрáнный *adj.* **1,** safe: в сохрáнном мéсте, in a
safe place. **2,** safe; unharmed.

сохраня́ть *v. impfv.* [*pfv.* **сохрани́ть**] **1,** to preserve;
maintain. **2,** to keep; retain. **3,** to conserve. **4,** to protect. **5,** *in* сохраня́ть за собóй, to reserve. —**сохра-**
ня́ться, *refl.* **1,** to be preserved; remain; survive. **2,**
(*of food*) to keep; not spoil. **3,** *colloq.* (*of a person*)
to be well-preserved.

соцвéтие *n.* raceme.

социализáция *n.* socialization.

социализи́ровать *v. impfv. & pfv.* [*pres.* **-рую, -ру-**
ешь] to socialize.

социали́зм *n.* socialism. —**социали́ст,** *n.* socialist.
—**социалисти́ческий,** *adj.* socialist; socialistic.

социáльный *adj.* social.

социолóгия *n.* sociology. —**социóлог,** *n.* sociologist.
—**социологи́ческий,** *adj.* sociological.

сочéльник *n.* **1,** Christmas Eve. **2,** Twelfth Night.

сочетáние *n.* combination. —в сочетáнии с, in conjunction with.

сочетáть *v. impfv. & pfv.* to combine. —**сочетáться,**
refl. **1,** to be combined. **2,** to match; go well together;
(*with* с + *instr.*) go well with.

сочинéние *n.* **1,** (act of) composing. **2,** (literary) work.
3, composition (*written for school*).

сочини́тель *n.m.* **1,** *archaic* writer; composer. **2,** *col-*
loq. liar; storyteller.

сочини́тельный *adj., gram.* coordinate: сочини́-
тельный сою́з, coordinate conjunction.

сочиня́ть *v. impfv.* [*pfv.* **сочини́ть**] **1,** to compose. **2,**
to make up; concoct; invent.

сочи́ть *v. impfv.* to exude. —**сочи́ться,** *refl.* to ooze;
trickle.

сóчный *adj.* **1,** juicy; succulent. **2,** *fig.* rich; lush. —**сóч-**
ность, *n.f.* juiciness; succulence.

сочу́вственный *adj.* sympathetic. —**сочу́вственно,**
adv. sympathetically.

сочу́вствие *n.* sympathy.

сочу́вствовать *v. impfv.* [*pres.* **-ствую, -ствуешь**]
(*with dat.*) **1,** to sympathize (with); feel sorry for; feel
for. **2,** to sympathize (with); be in sympathy (with).

сóшка [*gen. pl.* **-шек**] *n.* prop; support (*for a gun*).
—мéлкая сóшка, small fry; pipsqueak.

сошни́к [*gen.* **-никá**] *n.* plowshare.

сощу́рить *v., pfv. of* **щу́рить.** —**сощу́риться,** *refl.,*
pfv. of **щу́риться.**

сою́з *n.* **1,** union. **2,** alliance. **3,** *gram.* conjunction.
—в сою́зе с, in league with.

сою́зник *n.m.* [*fem.* **-ница**] ally. Фрáнция – наш со-
ю́зник (*or* нáша сою́зница), France is our ally.

сою́зный *adj.* **1,** union (*attrib.*). **2,** federal. **3,** allied.

сóя *n.* **1,** soybean (*plant*). **2,** *colloq.* soy sauce.

спагéтти *n. neut. indecl.* spaghetti.

спад *n.* **1,** falling off; decline. **2,** *econ.* recession; slump.
3, receding (*of water*).

спадáть *v. impfv.* [*pfv.* **спасть**] **1,** (*with* с + *gen.*)
to fall off; fall down from. **2,** (*of water, swelling, etc.*)
to go down. **3,** [*impfv. only*] to hang down. **4,** to subside; abate.

спазм *also,* **спáзма** *n.* spasm. —**спазмати́ческий,**
adj. spasmodic.

спáивать *v. impfv.* **1,** [*pfv.* **спая́ть**] to solder (together); *fig.* unite. **2,** [*pfv.* **спо́ить**] *colloq.* to make drunk;
make a drunkard of.

спáйка *n.* **1,** soldering. **2,** soldered joint. **3,** *fig.* unity;
cohesion.

спали́ть *v., pfv. of* **пали́ть** (*in sense #2*).

спáльный *adj.* sleeping (*attrib.*). —**спáльное мéсто,**
berth.

спáльня [*gen. pl.* **-лен**] *n.* bedroom.

спаниéль *n.m.* spaniel.

спаньё *n., colloq.* sleeping.

спáренный *adj.* dual; twin.

спáржа *n.* asparagus. —**спáржевый,** *adj.* asparagus
(*attrib.*).

спáривание *n.* mating.

спáривать *v. impfv.* [*pfv.* **спáрить**] **1,** to pair; couple.
2, to mate. —**спáриваться,** *refl.* **1,** *colloq.* to pair off.
2, to mate.

спартакиáда *n.* Spartacist Games.

спартáнец [*gen.* **-нца**] *n.m.* [*fem.* **-нка**] Spartan.
—**спартáнский,** *adj.* Spartan.

спáрывать *v. impfv.* [*pfv.* **споро́ть**] to remove; take
off (*by cutting the stitches*).

спасáние *n.* saving; rescuing.

спасáтель *n.m.* **1,** rescue worker. **2,** lifeguard.

спасáтельный *adj.* rescue (*attrib.*). —**спасáтельный**
жилéт, life jacket. —**спасáтельный круг,** life buoy.
—**спасáтельная лóдка** *or* **шлю́пка,** lifeboat. —**спа-**
сáтельный пóяс, life belt; life preserver.

спасáть *v. impfv.* [*pfv.* **спасти́**] to save; rescue. —**спа-**
сáться, *refl.* **1,** to be saved. **2,** to escape.

спасéние *n.* **1,** saving; rescue. **2,** escape. **3,** salvation.

спаси́бо *particle* thank you; thanks. Большóе (вам)
спаси́бо!, thank you very much! —за (однó) спа-
си́бо, without asking anything in return. —и на том
спаси́бо, we should be grateful at least for that.

спаси́тель *n.m.* **1,** savior; rescuer. **2,** *relig.* Savior.

спаси́тельный *adj.* that which saves; bringing salvation.

спасовáть *v., pfv. of* **пасовáть.**

спасти́ [*infl.* **спасу́, спасёшь;** *past* **спас, спаслá,**
спаслó] *v., pfv. of* **спасáть.** —**спасти́сь,** *refl., pfv. of*
спасáться.

спасти́ческий *adj.* spastic.

спасть [*infl. like* **пасть**] *v., pfv. of* **спадáть.**

спать *v. impfv.* [*pres.* **сплю, спишь, спит, спим,**
спи́те, спят; *past fem.* **спалá**] to sleep. —**спáться,**
refl. [*past* **спалóсь**] *impers.* (*with dat.*) *colloq.* to be
able to sleep: мне не спи́тся, I can't fall asleep; мне
плóхо спалóсь, I didn't sleep well.

спáянный *adj.* united; close-knit. —**спáянность,** *n.f.*
unity; cohesion.

спая́ть *v., pfv. of* **спáивать** (*in sense #1*).

спевáться *v.r. impfv.* [*pfv.* **спéться**] **1,** to achieve harmony in singing. **2,** *colloq.* to get along.

спéвка *n.* choir practice.

спектáкль *n.m.* show; performance.

спектр *n.* spectrum. —**спектрáльный,** *adj.* spectral.

спектроско́п *n.* spectroscope. —**спектроскопи́ческий**, *adj.* spectroscopic.

спекули́ровать *v. impfv.* [*pres.* -ру́ю, -руешь] (*with instr. or* на + *prepl.*) **1,** to speculate (in). **2,** to exploit; capitalize (on); take advantage of.

спекуля́нт *n.* **1,** speculator. **2,** *fig.* exploiter; opportunist.

спекуляти́вный *adj.* **1,** speculative. **2,** (*of prices*) artificially high.

спекуля́ция *n.* **1,** speculation. **2,** (*with* на + *prepl.*) taking advantage of.

спелена́ть *v., pfv. of* пелена́ть.

спе́лый *adj.* ripe. —**спе́лость**, *n.f.* ripeness.

сперва́ *adv., colloq.* first; at first.

спе́реди *adv.* **1,** in front. **2,** from the front. —*prep., with gen.* in (*or* from) the front of.

спере́ть *v. pfv.* [*infl.* сопру́, сопрёшь; *past* спёр, -ла] *colloq.* to steal; swipe.

спе́рма *n.* sperm.

спёртый *adj., colloq.* (*of air*) close; stuffy.

спеси́вый *adj.* haughty; arrogant; high and mighty.

спесь *n.f.* haughtiness; arrogance. —**сбива́ть спесь с** (+ *gen.*), to take (someone) down a peg.

спеть[1] *v. impfv.* [*pfv.* поспе́ть; *pres.* спе́ет] to ripen; become ripe.

спеть[2] [*infl.* спою́, споёшь] *v., pfv. of* петь. —**спе́ться**, *refl., pfv. of* спева́ться.

спех *n., colloq.* hurry. —**мне не к спе́ху**, I'm in no hurry.

специализа́ция *n.* specialization.

специализи́ровать *v. impfv. & pfv.* [*pres.* -ру́ю, -руешь] to make specialized; assign a specialty to. —**специализи́роваться**, *refl.* (*with* в + *prepl. or* по) to specialize (in).

специали́ст *n.* specialist; expert.

специа́льно *adv.* **1,** specially: специа́льно подгото́влен, specially trained. **2,** especially: специа́льно для вас, especially for you.

специа́льность *n.f.* **1,** specialty; field of specialization: рабо́тать по специа́льности, to work in one's field. **2,** profession: инжене́р по специа́льности, an engineer by profession.

специа́льный *adj.* **1,** special. **2,** specialized.

специ́фика *n.* (specific) nature.

спецификация *n.* specification.

специфи́ческий *adj.* specific.

спе́ция *n.* spice.

спецоде́жда *n.* overalls.

спе́шивать *v. impfv.* [*pfv.* спе́шить] to order to dismount; force to dismount. —**спе́шиваться**, *refl.* to dismount.

спе́шить *v., pfv. of* спе́шивать. —**спе́шиться**, *refl., pfv. of* спе́шиваться.

спеши́ть *v. impfv.* [*pfv.* поспеши́ть] **1,** to hurry; rush. **2,** [*impfv. only*] to be in a hurry. **3,** (*with inf.*) to hasten (to). **4,** [*impfv. only*] (*of a timepiece*) to be fast. —**не спеша́**, at a leisurely pace; deliberately.

спе́шка *n., colloq.* hurry; rush; haste. —**в спе́шке**, in one's (*or* everyone's) haste.

спе́шно *adv.* in a hurry; hastily.

спе́шность *n.f.* **1,** urgency. **2,** haste.

спе́шный *adj.* **1,** urgent; pressing. **2,** hurried; hasty. —**спе́шная по́чта**, special delivery.

спива́ться *v.r. impfv.* [*pfv.* спи́ться] to take to drink; become an alcoholic.

спидо́метр *n.* speedometer.

спи́кер *n.* speaker (*of the House of Commons or House of Representatives*).

спи́ливать *v. impfv.* [*pfv.* спили́ть] **1,** to saw down. **2,** to saw off.

спили́ть [*infl.* спилю́, спи́лишь] *v., pfv. of* спи́ливать.

спина́ [*acc.* спи́ну; *pl.* спи́ны] *n.* back. —**за спино́й** (+ *gen.*), behind someone's back. —**спино́й к**, with one's back to.

спи́нка [*gen. pl.* -нок] *n.* **1,** *dim. of* спина́. **2,** back (*of a garment, piece of furniture, etc.*).

спинно́й *adj.* spinal; dorsal. —**спинно́й мозг**, spinal cord. —**спинно́й хребе́т**, spine; backbone; spinal column.

спинномозгово́й *adj.* spinal.

спира́ль *n.f.* spiral. —**спира́льный**, *adj.* spiral.

спири́т *n.* spiritualist (*one who believes in communication with the dead*). —**спирити́зм**, *n.* spiritualism. —**спирити́ческий**, *adj.* spiritualistic.

спиритуали́зм *n., philos.* spiritualism. —**спиритуали́ст**, *n.* spiritualist.

спирт *n.* **1,** alcohol: древе́сный спирт, wood alcohol. **2,** spirits: камфа́рный спирт, spirits of camphor. —**нашаты́рный спирт**, liquid ammonia.

спиртно́е *n., decl. as an adj., colloq.* alcohol.

спиртно́й *adj.* alcoholic.

спирто́вка [*gen. pl.* -вок] *n.* spirit lamp.

спиртово́й *adj.* spirit (*attrib.*); alcohol (*attrib.*).

списа́ть [*infl.* спишу́, спи́шешь] *v., pfv. of* спи́сывать. —**списа́ться**, *refl., pfv. of* спи́сываться.

спи́сок [*gen.* -ска] *n.* list.

спи́сывать *v. impfv.* [*pfv.* списа́ть] **1,** to copy. **2,** (*with* с + *gen.*) to base on (*when writing or painting*): спи́сан с живо́го лица́, based on a real-life person. **3,** (*with* у) to copy (from); crib (from). **4,** *finance* to write off. —**спи́сываться**, *refl.* (*with* с + *instr.*) to write to; get in touch with (*by mail*).

спито́й *adj., colloq.* (*of tea or coffee*) weak.

спи́ться [*infl.* сопью́сь, сопьёшься; *past* спи́лся, спила́сь, спило́сь] *v.r., pfv. of* спива́ться.

спи́хивать *v. impfv.* [*pfv.* спихну́ть] *colloq.* **1,** to push off. **2,** *fig.* to shove aside; kick out.

спи́ца *n.* **1,** spoke. **2,** knitting needle.

спич *n.* (short) speech.

спи́чечница *n.* **1,** *obs.* matchbox. **2,** matchbox holder.

спи́чечный *adj.* match (*attrib.*): спи́чечная коро́бка, matchbox.

спи́чка [*gen. pl.* -чек] *n.* match.

сплав *n.* **1,** alloy. **2,** floating (*of timber*).

спла́вить [*infl.* -влю, -вишь] *v., pfv. of* сплавля́ть.

сплавля́ть *v. impfv.* [*pfv.* спла́вить] **1,** to fuse; alloy. **2,** *fig.* to bind together; forge together. **3,** to float (something) downstream. **4,** *colloq.* to get rid of; unload.

сплавно́й *adj.* (*of timber*) floating.

сплани́ровать *v., pfv. of* плани́ровать.

спла́чивать *v. impfv.* [*pfv.* сплоти́ть] **1,** to fasten together; join. **2,** *fig.* to rally; unite. **3,** *in* сплачивать ряды́, to close ranks. —**спла́чиваться**, *refl.* **1,** to cluster (together). **2,** *fig.* to rally; unite; be united.

сплёвывать *v. impfv.* [*pfv.* сплюну́ть] to spit; spit out.

сплести́ [*infl. like* плести́] *v., pfv. of* плести́ *and* сплета́ть. —**сплести́сь**, *refl., pfv. of* сплета́ться.

сплета́ть *v. impfv.* [*pfv.* сплести́] **1,** to weave. **2,** to entwine; intertwine. —**сплетáться,** *refl.* **1,** to become entwined; become tangled. **2,** *fig.* to become intertwined.

сплетéние *n.* **1,** junction. **2,** tangle. **3,** *anat.* plexus: сóлнечное сплетéние, solar plexus. **4,** *fig.* combination: сплетéние обстоя́тельств, combination of circumstances. —**сплетéние лжи,** web of lies.

сплéтник *n.m.* [*fem.* **-ница**] gossip (*person*).

сплéтничать *v. impfv.* [*pfv.* **насплéтничать**] to gossip.

сплéтня [*gen. pl.* **-тен**] *n.* gossip; item of gossip.

сплеча́ *adv.* **1,** with a full sweep of the arm. **2,** in haste; without thought. —**руби́ть сплеча́,** to shoot from the hip.

сплоти́ть [*infl.* **-чу́, -ти́шь**] *v., pfv. of* **спла́чивать.** —**сплоти́ться,** *refl., pfv. of* **спла́чиваться.**

сплохова́ть *v. pfv.* [*infl.* **-ху́ю, -ху́ешь**] *colloq.* to make a blunder.

сплочéние *n.* rallying; uniting.

сплочённость *n.f.* unity; solidarity; cohesion.

сплочённый *adj.* **1,** solid. **2,** united.

сплошнóй *adj.* **1,** solid; continuous; unbroken. **2,** complete; total. **3,** *colloq.* pure; utter; sheer.

сплошь *adv.* all over; completely. —**сплошь и (**or **да) ря́дом,** *colloq.* very often.

сплутова́ть *v., pfv. of* **плутова́ть.**

сплыва́ть *v. impfv.* [*pfv.* **сплыть**] *colloq.* **1,** to swim downstream; float downstream. **2,** to overflow; run over. —**бы́ло да сплы́ло,** it came and it went; it's gone for good.

сплыть [*infl. like* **плыть**] *v., pfv. of* **сплыва́ть.**

сплю́нуть *v., pfv. of* **сплёвывать.**

сплю́снутый *adj.* flat; flattened. *Also,* **сплю́щенный.**

сплю́щивать *v. impfv.* [*pfv.* **сплю́щить**] to flatten. —**сплю́щиваться,** *refl.* to become flat; flatten out.

спляса́ть *v., pfv. of* **пляса́ть.**

сподви́жник *n.* associate; comrade-in-arms.

сподру́чный *adj., colloq.* convenient; handy.

спозара́нку *adv., colloq.* early in the morning.

спои́ть [*infl.* **спою́, спои́шь** or **спои́шь**] *v., pfv. of* **спа́ивать** (*in sense #2*).

споко́йно *adv.* calmly; peacefully. —*adj., used predicatively* quiet; peaceful: здесь споко́йно, it is quiet/peaceful here. —**спи́те споко́йно!,** sleep well! —**у меня́ на душе́ споко́йно,** my mind is at ease.

споко́йный *adj.* [*short form* **-ко́ен, -ко́йна**] **1,** calm; tranquil; quiet; peaceful. **2,** (*of light, color, etc.*) restful. **3,** *colloq.* comfortable. —**споко́йной но́чи!,** good night!

споко́йствие *n.* **1,** quiet; calm; tranquillity. **2,** public order. **3,** composure; equanimity.

спола́скивать *v. impfv.* [*pfv.* **сполосну́ть**] *colloq.* to rinse; rinse out.

сполза́ть *v. impfv.* [*pfv.* **сползти́**] **1,** to climb down; crawl down. **2,** to slip off; slip down. **3,** to trickle down. **4,** to slope down. **5,** (*of an expression, smile, etc.*) to fade (from one's face).

сползти́ [*infl. like* **ползти́**] *v., pfv. of* **сполза́ть.**

сполна́ *adv.* in full.

сполосну́ть *v., pfv. of* **спола́скивать.**

сполóх *n.* **1,** flash of lightning. **2,** *pl.* northern lights.

спонта́нный *adj.* spontaneous.

спор *n.* **1,** argument. **2,** dispute; controversy. —**спóру нет,** there is no question; there's no denying.

спóра *n.* spore.

споради́ческий *adj.* sporadic.

спóрить *v. impfv.* [*pfv.* **поспóрить**] **1,** to argue. **2,** to deny: не спóрю, что..., I don't deny that... **3,** *colloq.* to bet. **4,** (*with* с *or* прóтив) *fig.* to fight. **5,** to compete.

спóриться *v.r. impfv., colloq.* to go well; work out well; turn out well.

спóрный *adj.* **1,** controversial. **2,** debatable; moot. **3,** unsettled; outstanding. **4,** disputed.

спорóть [*infl.* **спорю́, спóрешь**] *v., pfv. of* **спа́рывать.**

спорт *n.* sports.

спорти́вный *adj.* sports (*attrib.*); sporting; athletic. —**из спорти́вного интере́са,** for the fun of it.

спортсме́н *n.m.* [*fem.* **-ме́нка**] athlete; sportsman. —**спортсме́нский,** *adj.* sportsmanlike.

спорхну́ть *v. pfv.* **1,** to fly away; flit away. **2,** to land suddenly.

спóрщик *n.* person who likes to argue.

спóрый *adj., colloq.* **1,** (*of work, movements, etc.*) smooth. **2,** profitable.

спорынья́ *n.* ergot.

спóсоб *n.* way; method.

спосóбность *n.f.* **1,** ability. **2,** *usu. pl.* (*with* к) aptitude (for); faculty (for). У́мственные спосóбности, mental faculties. **3,** capacity; power: пропускна́я спосóбность, carrying capacity; покупа́тельная спосóбность, purchasing power.

спосóбный *adj.* [*short form* **-бен, -бна**] **1,** able; bright; talented. **2,** (*with* к) good (at); having a gift (for). **3,** (*with* к, на, *or inf.*) capable (of).

спосóбствовать *v. impfv.* [*pres.* **-ствую, -ствуешь**] (*with dat.*) to further; promote; contribute to.

спотыка́ться *v.r. impfv.* [*pfv.* **споткну́ться**] to stumble; trip.

спохвати́ться [*infl.* **-хвачу́сь, -хва́тишься**] *v.r., pfv. of* **спохва́тываться.**

спохва́тываться *v.r. impfv.* [*pfv.* **спохвати́ться**] *colloq.* to remember suddenly.

спра́ва *adv.* **1,** from the right. **2,** to (*or* on) the right.

справедли́во *adv.* fairly; justly.

справедли́вость *n.f.* justice; fairness. —**справедли́вости ра́ди,** in all fairness. —**отда́ть справедли́вость** (+ *dat.*), to give credit to; give (someone) his due.

справедли́вый *adj.* **1,** just; fair. **2,** just; justifiable; justified. **3,** correct; valid.

спра́вить [*infl.* **-влю, -вишь**] *v., pfv. of* **справля́ть.** —**спра́виться,** *refl., pfv. of* **справля́ться.**

спра́вка [*gen. pl.* **-вок**] *n.* **1,** *usu. pl.* reference: для спра́вок, for reference purposes. **2,** information. **3,** certificate. —**наводи́ть спра́вки о,** to make inquiries about.

справля́ть *v. impfv.* [*pfv.* **спра́вить**] *colloq.* to celebrate (an occasion). Справля́ть сва́дьбу, to hold a wedding. —**справля́ться,** *refl.* **1,** (*with* о) to inquire (about). **2,** (*with* в + *prepl.*) to consult (a book, dictionary, etc.). **3,** (*with* с + *instr.*) to cope with; handle.

спра́вочник *n.* reference book; directory.

спра́вочный *adj.* reference (*attrib.*); information (*attrib.*); inquiry (*attrib.*).

спра́шивать *v. impfv.* [*pfv.* **спроси́ть**] **1,** (*with acc. or* у) to ask (someone). **2,** (*with acc. or* о) to ask (about). **3,** to ask for. **4,** to ask for (someone); ask to see. **5,** to call on (a pupil). **6,** *colloq.* to ask; charge (a price). **7,** (*with* с + *gen.*) *colloq.* to hold accountable. —**спра́-**

шиваться, *refl.* **1**, (*with* у) *colloq.* to ask permission (of). **2**, [*impfv. only*] *impers.*: спрашивается, one may ask; the question arises.

спрессовать *v., pfv. of* прессовать.

спринт *n.* sprint. —**спринтер**, *n.* sprinter.

спринцевать *v. impfv.* [*pres.* -цую, -цуешь] to syringe.

спринцовка *n.* **1**, syringing. **2**, syringe.

спроваживать *v. impfv.* [*pfv.* спровадить] *colloq.* to escort out; send on one's way; send packing.

спровоцировать *v., pfv. of* провоцировать.

спроектировать *v., pfv. of* проектировать.

спрос *n., econ.* demand: спрос и предложение, supply and demand. —**без спроса; без спросу**, without permission.

спросить [*infl.* спрошу, спросишь] *v., pfv. of* спрашивать. —**спроситься**, *refl., pfv. of* спрашиваться.

спросонок *adv., colloq.* half-awake; being only half-awake.

спроста *adv., colloq.* **1**, out of naïveté. **2**, on the spur of the moment; just like that.

спрут *n.* octopus.

спрыгивать *v. impfv.* [*pfv.* спрыгнуть] (*with* с + *gen.*) to jump off; jump down (from).

спрыскивать *v. impfv.* [*pfv.* спрыснуть] *colloq.* to sprinkle.

спрягать *v. impfv.* [*pfv.* проспрягать] to conjugate (a verb).

спряжение *n., gram.* conjugation.

спрясть *v., pfv. of* прясть.

спрятать *v., pfv. of* прятать. —**спрятаться**, *refl., pfv. of* прятаться.

спугивать *v. impfv.* [*pfv.* спугнуть] to frighten off; frighten away.

спуд *n., in* под спудом, hidden; under wraps; из-под спуда, from hiding; from under wraps.

спуск *n.* **1**, lowering. **2**, descent; going down. **3**, descent; slope. —**не давать спуска** (+ *dat.*), *colloq.* to give someone no quarter.

спускать *v. impfv.* [*pfv.* спустить] **1**, to lower; let down. **2**, to launch (a ship). **3**, to release; let loose. **4**, to let the air out of; let the water out of. **5**, *v.i.* (*of a tire*) to go flat. **6**, *colloq.* to pardon; forgive. **7**, *colloq.* to sell; unload. **8**, *colloq.* to squander; throw away. **9**, *in* спускать курок, to pull the trigger. **10**, *in* спускать петлю, to drop a stitch. —**спускаться**, *refl.* **1**, to go down; descend. **2**, (*of a plane, bird, etc.*) to land. **3**, to sail downstream. **4**, (*of fog, dusk, etc.*) to descend; fall. **5**, [*impfv. only*] to hang down. **6**, [*impfv. only*] to slope down.

спускной *adj.* drain (*attrib.*): спускной кран, drain cock.

спусковой *adj.* = спускной. —**спусковой крючок**, trigger.

спустить [*infl.* спущу, спустишь] *v., pfv. of* спускать. —**спуститься**, *refl., pfv. of* спускаться.

спустя *prep.*, with acc. after.

спутанный *adj.* **1**, tangled. **2**, confused; muddled; incoherent.

спутать *v., pfv. of* путать. —**спутаться**, *refl., pfv. of* путаться.

спутник *n.* **1**, traveling companion. **2**, satellite.

спьяна *also*, спьяну *adv., colloq.* while drunk.

спятить *v. pfv.* [*infl.* спячу, спятишь] *colloq.* to go crazy; go nuts.

спячка *n.* **1**, [*usu.* зимняя спячка] hibernation. **2**, *colloq.* drowsiness; lethargy.

срабатывать *v. impfv.* [*pfv.* сработать] *colloq.* **1**, to make; turn out. **2**, (*of a device, machine, etc.*) to work; operate. —**срабатываться**, *refl.* **1**, (*of a machine*) to wear out. **2**, to work well together.

сработанность *n.f.* **1**, harmony in work. **2**, wear (and tear).

сработать *v., pfv. of* срабатывать. —**сработаться**, *refl., pfv. of* срабатываться.

сравнение *n.* **1**, comparison. **2**, simile. —**по сравнению с; в сравнении с**, compared to; in comparison with. —**не идёт (ни) в (какое) сравнение с**, cannot compare to.

сравнивать *v. impfv.* **1**, [*pfv.* сравнить] to compare. **2**, [*pfv.* сравнять] to make equal. Сравнять счёт, to tie the score. **3**, [*pfv.* сровнять] to even; level. Сровнять с землёй, to raze to the ground.

сравнимый *adj.* comparable. —**ни с чем не сравнимый**, incomparable; in a class by itself.

сравнительно *adv.* **1**, comparatively. **2**, (*with* с + *instr.*) compared to.

сравнительный *adj.* comparative.

сравнить *v., pfv. of* сравнивать (*in sense #1*). —**сравниться**, *refl.* (*with* с + *instr.*) to compare: никто не может сравниться с ней, no one can compare to her.

сравнять *v., pfv. of* равнять *and* сравнивать (*in sense #2*). —**сравняться**, *refl.* (*with* с + *instr.*) to become the equal of; achieve equality with.

сражать *v. impfv.* [*pfv.* сразить] **1**, to strike down. **2**, *fig.* (*of news*) to stagger. —**сражаться**, *refl.* to fight (*in batttle*).

сражение *n.* battle.

сразить [*infl.* -жу, -зишь] *v., pfv. of* сражать. —**сразиться**, *refl., pfv. of* сражаться.

сразу *adv.* **1**, at once; immediately; right away. **2**, all at once. **3**, just: сразу за (+ *instr.*), just beyond *or* behind. —**сразу после** (+ *gen.*), **1**, right after. **2**, just past.

срам *n., colloq.* shame.

срамить *v. impfv.* [*pfv.* осрамить; *pres.* -млю, -мишь] *colloq.* to shame; disgrace.

срамник [*gen.* -ника] *n., colloq.* shameless person.

срамной *adj., obs.* indecent.

срастание *n.* knitting (*of bones*).

срастаться *v.r. impfv.* [*pfv.* срастись] to grow together; (*of bones*) knit.

срастись [*infl. like* расти] *v.r., pfv. of* срастаться.

срастить [*infl.* -щу, -стишь] *v., pfv. of* сращивать.

сращение *n.* **1**, joining together. **2**, growing together.

сращивание *n.* **1**, setting (*of a bone*). **2**, joining; splicing. **3**, *fig.* merging.

сращивать *v. impfv.* [*pfv.* срастить] **1**, to set (a broken bone). **2**, to join together; splice. **3**, *fig.* to merge; intertwine.

сребреник *n.* ancient silver coin; piece of silver.

среда *n.* **1**, [*acc.* среду] Wednesday. **2**, [*acc.* среду] surroundings; environment; *physics* medium. —**окружающая среда**, the environment.

среди *prep.*, with gen. **1**, in the middle of. **2**, among. —**среди** (*or* средь) **бела дня**, in broad daylight.

средина *n.* = середина. —**срединный**, *adj.* = серединный.

средне *adv., colloq.* fair; so-so.

средне- *prefix* **1**, central: среднеазиатский, Central

Asian. **2,** middle: среднеангли́йский язы́к, Middle English.

средневеко́вье *n.* the Middle Ages. —**средневеко́вый,** *adj.* medieval.

сре́днее *n., decl. as an adj.* average: вы́ше/ни́же сре́днего, above/below average. —**в сре́днем,** on the average.

сре́дний *adj.* **1,** middle. **2,** medium. **3,** average; mean. **4,** average; mediocre. **5,** *gram.* neuter. **6,** (*of school or education*) secondary. —**сре́дние века́,** the Middle Ages. —**сре́дних лет,** middle-aged. —**сре́дней руки́,** ordinary; of no particular distinction.

средото́чие *n.* focus; focal point; center; hub.

сре́дство *n.* **1,** means; way. **2,** *pl.* means: сре́дства произво́дства, means of production; челове́к со сре́дствами, man of means. **3,** *pl.* funds. **4,** medication; preparation; remedy: возбужда́ющее сре́дство, stimulant; сре́дство от ка́шля, cough remedy; сре́дство от насеко́мых, insecticide.

средь *prep.* = среди́.

срез *n.* **1,** cut; slice; section. **2,** microscopic section.

сре́зать [*infl.* сре́жу, сре́жешь] *v., pfv. of* ре́зать (*in sense #6*) *and* среза́ть. —**сре́заться,** *refl., pfv. of* среза́ться.

среза́ть *v. impfv.* [*pfv.* сре́зать] **1,** to cut off; cut away. **2,** to strike down; cut down. **3,** *fig.* to reduce; cut down. **4,** to cut off (*while speaking*). **5,** to slice (a ball). **6,** *colloq.* to flunk (a student). **7,** *in* среза́ть у́гол, to take a shortcut. —**среза́ться,** *refl.* (*with* на + *prepl.*) to flunk (an examination).

сре́зывать *v. impfv.* = среза́ть.

срисова́ть [*infl.* -су́ю, -су́ешь] *v., pfv. of* срисо́вывать.

срисо́вывать *v. impfv.* [*pfv.* срисова́ть] to copy.

сровня́ть *v., pfv. of* ровня́ть *and* сра́внивать (*in sense #3*).

сродни́ *adv.* (*with dat.*) *colloq.* **1,** related (to). **2,** *fig.* akin (to).

сродни́ть *v., pfv. of* родни́ть. —**сродни́ться,** *refl.* (*with* с + *instr.*) **1,** to become close to. **2,** to get used to.

сро́дный *adj.* related.

сродство́ *n.* relationship; affinity.

сро́ду *adv., colloq.* **1,** since one was born; always. **2,** (*fol. by* не) never (in one's whole life).

срок *n.* **1,** (period of) time: в коро́ткий срок, in a short time. Срок ожида́ния, waiting period. **2,** term: избира́ться сро́ком на четы́ре го́да, to be elected for a four-year term. **3,** date: намеча́ть срок, to set the date. **4,** deadline. —**в срок; к сро́ку,** in time; on time; on schedule. —**до сро́ка; ра́ньше сро́ка,** ahead of time; ahead of schedule. —**кра́йний/после́дний/преде́льный срок,** deadline.

сро́чно *adv.* **1,** urgently. **2,** immediately; without delay.

сро́чность *n.f.* **1,** urgency. **2,** *colloq.* hurry.

сро́чный *adj.* **1,** urgent; pressing: сро́чное де́ло, urgent matter. Сро́чный зака́з, rush order. **2,** prompt. **3,** for a fixed period: сро́чная слу́жба, service for a fixed period; regular tour of duty.

сруб *n.* **1,** felling (of timber): продава́ть на сруб, to sell for timber. **2,** frame; framework. **3,** log cabin.

сруба́ть *v. impfv.* [*pfv.* сруби́ть] to chop down; fell.

сруби́ть *v. pfv.* [*infl.* срублю́, сру́бишь] **1,** *pfv. of* сруба́ть. **2,** to build (*of logs*).

срыв *n.* failure; breakdown; collapse.

срыва́ть *v. impfv.* [*pfv.* сорва́ть] **1,** to tear off; tear

away. **2,** to pick; pluck. **3,** to frustrate; disrupt; thwart; foil. **4,** *fig., colloq.* to win (applause); steal (a kiss); wangle (money). **5,** (*with* на + *prepl.*) to vent (one's feelings) on. **6,** *in* сорва́ть банк, to break the bank. **7,** *in* сорва́ть го́лос, to strain one's voice. **8,** [*pfv.* срыть] to level with the ground; raze to the ground. —**срыва́ться,** *refl.* **1,** to come off; come loose. **2,** (*with* с + *gen.*) to fall (from); slip (from). **3,** to break loose. **4,** (*with* с + *gen.*) to spring up (from); depart suddenly (from). **5,** (*of sounds*) to ring out; resound. **6,** *fig., colloq.* to fail; fall through. **7,** (*of one's voice*) to break. **8,** *in* срыва́ться с губ *or* с языка́, to escape one's lips.

срыть [*infl.* сро́ю, сро́ешь] *v., pfv. of* срыва́ть (*in sense #8*).

сря́ду *adv., colloq.* in a row; consecutively.

сса́дина *n.* scratch; abrasion.

ссади́ть [*infl.* ссажу́, сса́дишь] *v., pfv. of* сса́живать.

сса́живать *v. impfv.* [*pfv.* ссади́ть] **1,** to scratch. **2,** to help down; help (someone) get down. **3,** to put off; make (someone) get off.

ссо́ра *n.* quarrel. —**быть в ссо́ре (с),** to have had a falling-out (with).

ссо́рить *v. impfv.* [*pfv.* поссо́рить] to cause a quarrel between. —**ссо́риться,** *refl.* to quarrel.

ссо́хнуться [*past* ссо́хся, -лась] *v.r., pfv. of* ссыха́ться.

СССР *abbr. of* Сою́з Сове́тских Социалисти́ческих Респу́блик, Union of Soviet Socialist Republics; USSR.

ссу́да *n.* loan. —**безвозвра́тная ссу́да,** outright grant.

ссуди́ть [*infl.* ссужу́, ссу́дишь] *v., pfv. of* ссужа́ть.

ссужа́ть *v. impfv.* [*pfv.* ссуди́ть] to loan; lend.

ссуту́лить *v., pfv. of* суту́лить. —**ссуту́литься,** *refl., pfv. of* суту́литься.

ссыла́ть *v. impfv.* [*pfv.* сосла́ть] to banish; exile. —**ссыла́ться,** *refl.* (*with* на + *acc.*) **1,** to cite; quote; refer (to); allude (to). **2,** to cite (*as an excuse*); plead; allege.

ссы́лка [*gen. pl.* -лок] *n.* **1,** reference: перекрёстная ссы́лка, cross reference. **2,** exile; banishment.

ссы́лочный *adj.* reference (*attrib.*).

ссы́льный *adj.* in exile. —*n.* exile.

ссыпа́ть [*infl.* ссы́плю, ссы́плешь] *v., pfv. of* ссыпа́ть.

ссыпа́ть *v. impfv.* [*pfv.* ссы́пать] to pour.

ссыха́ться *v.r. impfv.* [*pfv.* ссо́хнуться] **1,** to shrink. **2,** to warp; become warped. **3,** to cake; become caked.

стабилиза́тор *n.* stabilizer.

стабилиза́ция *n.* stabilization.

стабилизи́ровать *v. impfv. & pfv.* [*pres.* -рую, -руешь] to stabilize. —**стабилизи́роваться,** *refl.* to stabilize; become stabilized.

стаби́льность *n.f.* stability.

стаби́льный *adj.* stable. —**стаби́льный уче́бник,** standard textbook.

ста́вень [*gen.* -вня] *n.m.* shutter.

ста́вить *v. impfv.* [*pfv.* поста́вить; *pres.* -влю, -вишь] **1,** to stand; place; set; put. **2,** to install. **3,** to apply (*to a part of one's body*). **4,** to affix (a seal, signature, etc.). **5,** to stage; produce; put on. **6,** to bet; stake. **7,** *with various nouns,* to set: ста́вить реко́рд, to set a record; ста́вить часы́/буди́льник, to set a watch/ alarm clock/; ста́вить себе́ зада́чу, to set a task for oneself; ста́вить себе́ це́лью, to set as one's goal.

—**ставить вопрос**, to pose a question. —**ставить в пример**, to hold up as an example. —**ставить диагноз**, to make a diagnosis. —**ставить отметки**, to give grades. —**ставить условия**, to lay down conditions.

ставка *n.* **1,** stake; stakes. **2,** rate: ставка процента, rate of interest. **3,** wage. **4,** *fig.* reliance: делать ставку на (+ *acc.*), to count on. **5,** *mil.* headquarters.

ставленник *n.* protégé.

ставня [*gen. pl.* -вен] *n.* shutter.

стадиальный *adj.* occurring in stages. *Also,* **стадийный**.

стадион *n.* stadium.

стадия *n.* stage. —**по стадиям**, in stages.

стадный *adj.* (*of animals*) living in herds; gregarious. —**стадный инстинкт**, herd instinct.

стадо [*pl.* стада] *n.* herd; flock.

стаж *n.* length of service. Служащий с большим стажем, employee with a long record of service. Надбавка к зарплате за стаж, pay increase for length of service.

стажёр *n.* person undergoing on-the-job training.

стажировка *n.* practical training; on-the-job training.

стаивать *v. impfv.* [*pfv.* стаять] to melt.

стайка [*gen. pl.* стаек] *n., dim. of* стая, small flock; small group.

стакан *n.* glass: стакан воды, glass of water.

стаккато *adv.* staccato.

стаксель *n.m.* staysail.

сталагмит *n.* stalagmite.

сталактит *n.* stalactite.

сталевар *n.* steelworker.

сталелитейный *adj.* pert. to the making of steel: сталелитейный завод, steel mill.

сталелитейщик *n.* steelworker.

сталеплавильный *adj.* pert. to the melting of steel: сталеплавильная печь, steel-melting furnace.

сталкивать *v. impfv.* [*pfv.* столкнуть] **1,** to push off; push away; push down; push into. **2,** to cause to collide. **3,** *colloq.* to bring together. —**сталкиваться**, *refl.* (*with* с + *instr.*) **1,** to collide. **2,** *fig.* to clash. **3,** to run into; encounter.

сталь *n.f.* steel. —**стальной**, *adj.* steel; of steel.

стамеска [*gen. pl.* -сок] *n.* chisel.

стан *n.* **1,** figure; build. **2,** mill: прокатный стан, rolling mill. **3,** camp. —**нотный стан**, *music* staff.

стандарт *n.* **1,** standard. **2,** *fig.* stereotype.

стандартизация *n.* standardization.

стандартизировать *v. impfv. & pfv.* [*pres.* -рую, -руешь] to standardize. *Also,* **стандартизовать** [*pres.* -зую, -зуешь].

стандартный *adj.* **1,** standard; standardized. **2,** *fig.* standard; conventional.

станина *n.* mount; base.

станиоль *n.m.* tin foil.

станица *n.* **1,** large Cossack village. **2,** flock (*of birds*).

станковый *adj.* machine (*attrib.*). —**станковый пулемёт**, heavy *or* medium machine gun.

становиться *v.r. impfv.* [*pfv.* стать; *pres.* становлюсь, становишься] **1,** to stand: станьте передо мной, stand in front of me. **2,** (*with instr.*) to become; get: стать друзьями, to become friends. Стать холодно, to get cold. Стать лучше, to get better. —**стать в очередь**, to get on line. —**стать в позу**, to strike a pose. —**стать на колени**, to kneel (down). —**стать на ноги**, to get on one's feet. —**стать на путь** (+ *gen.*),

to embark on a path of... —**стать на сторону** (+ *gen.*), to side with; take the side of. *See also* **стать**.

становление *n.* (*with gen.*) formation (of): становление характера, formation of character.

становой *adj., pre-rev.* district (*attrib.*). —**становой хребет**; **становая жила**, backbone; mainstay.

станок [*gen.* -нка] *n.* **1,** machine; machine tool: печатный станок, printing press; ткацкий станок, loom; токарный станок, lathe. **2,** gun mount.

станочник *n.* machine operator; machine tool operator.

станс *n.* stanza.

станционный *adj.* station (*attrib.*).

станция *n.* **1,** station: железнодорожная/заправочная станция, railroad/filling station. **2,** *R.R.* yard: товарная станция, freight yard; сортировочная станция, switchyard. —**телефонная станция**, telephone exchange.

стаптывать *v. impfv.* [*pfv.* стоптать] **1,** to wear down (shoes, heels, etc.). **2,** *colloq.* to trample. —**стаптываться**, *refl.* (*of shoes, heels, etc.*) to wear down; become worn down.

старание *n.* effort: прилагать все старания, to exert every effort.

старатель *n.m.* prospector for gold; gold digger.

старательный *adj.* diligent; assiduous; painstaking. —**старательно**, *adv.* diligently; painstakingly. —**старательность**, *n.f.* diligence; application.

стараться *v.r. impfv.* [*pfv.* постараться] to try; endeavor.

старение *n.* aging.

стареть *v. impfv.* [*pfv.* постареть] **1,** to grow old; get old; age. **2,** [*impfv. only*] to become obsolete; become antiquated.

старец [*gen.* -рца] *n.* (venerable) old man.

старик [*gen.* -рика] *n.* old man.

старина *n.f.* **1,** ancient times; olden times: в старину, in ancient/olden times. **2,** old ways; old customs: по старине, the old way; the traditional way. **3,** relic of the past. —*n.m., colloq.* old man! old boy! —**тряхнуть стариной**, to relive one's youth.

старинка *n., in* по старинке, the old way.

старинный *adj.* **1,** old; ancient. **2,** antique.

старить *v. impfv.* [*pfv.* состарить] to age; make old. —**стариться**, *refl.* to age; grow old.

старичок [*gen.* -чка] *n.* little old man.

старовер *n., hist.* Old Believer.

стародавний *adj.* **1,** (*of times*) olden. **2,** (*of an object, custom, etc.*) very old.

старожил *n.* long-time resident.

старозаветный *adj.* **1,** old-fashioned. **2,** antiquated.

старомодный *adj.* old-fashioned.

старообразный *adj.* old-looking.

старообрядец [*gen.* -дца] *n., hist.* Old Believer.

староста *n.m.* **1,** village elder. **2,** monitor (*in school*). —**церковный староста**, churchwarden.

старость *n.f.* old age. —**на старости лет**, in one's old age.

старт *n.* **1,** *sports* start. **2,** starting line. **3,** *aero.* take-off. **4,** blast-off.

стартер *n., mech. & sports* starter.

стартовать *v. impfv. & pfv.* [*pres.* -тую, -туешь] **1,** *sports* to start. **2,** *aero.* to take off. **3,** (*of a space vehicle*) to blast off.

ста́ртовый *adj.* **1,** *sports* starting. **2,** launching: ста́р-товая площа́дка, launching pad.

стару́ха *n.* old woman.

стару́шка [*gen. pl.* -шек] *n.* old woman.

ста́рческий *adj.* **1,** of old age. **2,** senile.

ста́рше *adj., comp. of* ста́рый *and* ста́рший.

старшекла́ссник *n.* pupil in his senior year.

старшеку́рсник *n.* senior (*in college*).

ста́рший *adj., used only as a modifier* **1,** older; elder. **2,** oldest; eldest. **3,** senior; head. —*n.* **1,** chief; man in charge. **2,** *pl.* adults. **3,** *pl.* one's elders. —**ста́рший лейтена́нт,** first lieutenant.

старшина́ [*pl.* старши́ны] *n.m.* **1,** *mil.* master sergeant. **2,** *naval* petty officer. **3,** *pre-rev.* foreman (*of a shop, jury, etc.*). —**старшина́ дипломати́ческого ко́рпуса,** dean of the diplomatic corps.

старшинство́ *n.* seniority.

ста́рый *adj.* old. —**ста́рое,** *n.* the old; the past.

старьё *n., colloq.* old things; junk.

старьёвщик *n.* old-clothes dealer; junkman.

ста́скивать *v. impfv.* [*pfv.* стащи́ть] **1,** to pull off; drag off. **2,** to pull into; drag into.

стасова́ть *v., pfv. of* тасова́ть.

ста́тика *n.* statics.

стати́ст *n., theat.* extra; supernumerary.

стати́стик *n.* statistician. —**стати́стика,** *n.* statistics. —**статисти́ческий,** *adj.* statistical.

стати́ческий *adj., physics; electricity* static.

стати́чный *adj.* static (*not in motion*).

ста́тный *adj.* graceful; shapely.

ста́тус *n.* status.

ста́тус-кво́ *n.m. indecl.* status quo.

стату́т *n.* statute.

стату́этка [*gen. pl.* -ток] *n.* statuette; figurine.

ста́туя *n.* statue.

стать[1] *v. pfv.* [*infl.* ста́ну, ста́нешь] **1,** *pfv. of* станови́ться. **2,** (*of a watch, machine, etc.*) to stop; stop running. **3,** (*of a river*) to freeze over. **4,** [*past tense only*] (*with inf.*) to begin (to); start. **5,** [*future tense only*] (*with inf.*) *indicates the future:* он не ста́нет есть, he won't eat. **6,** (*with* с + *instr.*) to happen (to); become (of). **7,** *impers.* (*with* не) to die: его́ не ста́ло, he died; he was no more. **8,** *colloq.* to cost. —**во что бы то ни ста́ло,** at all costs. —**ста́ло быть,** consequently.

стать[2] [*pl.* ста́ти, -те́й, -тя́м] *n.f.* figure; build. —**под стать** (+ *dat.*), **1,** right (for). **2,** like. **3,** befitting; becoming. —**с како́й ста́ти?,** why?; what for?

ста́ться *v.r. pfv.* [*infl.* ста́нется] (*with* с + *instr.*) *colloq.* to happen (to); become (of).

статья́ [*gen. pl.* -те́й] *n.* **1,** article. **2,** article; clause; paragraph (*of a constitution, treaty, etc.*). **3,** entry (*in a dictionary*). **4,** item: статья́ расхо́да, expense item. —**по всем статья́м,** in all respects.

стаха́новец [*gen.* -вца] *n.* Stakhanovite. —**стаха́новский,** *adj.* Stakhanovite (*attrib.*).

стациона́р *n.* permanent establishment: больни́ца-стациона́р, permanent hospital.

стациона́рный *adj.* **1,** stationary. **2,** permanent. —**стациона́рный больно́й,** hospital patient (*as opposed to an outpatient*).

стача́ть *v., pfv. of* тача́ть.

ста́чечник *n.* striker. —**ста́чечный,** *adj.* strike (*attrib.*).

ста́чивать *v. impfv.* [*pfv.* сточи́ть] to dull (a cutting instrument) through long use: сто́ченная бри́тва, dull razor.

ста́чка [*gen. pl.* -чек] *n.* strike.

стащи́ть [*infl.* стащу́, ста́щишь] *v., pfv. of* тащи́ть (*in sense #5*) *and* ста́скивать.

ста́я *n.* flock (*of birds*); school (*of fish*); pack (*of dogs*).

ста́ять [*infl.* ста́ет] *v., pfv. of* ста́ивать.

ствол [*gen.* ствола́] *n.* **1,** trunk (*of a tree*). **2,** barrel (*of a gun*).

створ *n.* = ство́рка.

створа́живать *v. impfv.* [*pfv.* створо́жить] to curdle. —**створа́живаться,** *refl.* (*of a substance*) to curdle.

ство́рка [*gen. pl.* -рок] *n.* **1,** leaf; fold (*of a door, gate, mirror, etc.*). **2,** valve (*of a mollusk*).

створо́жить *v., pfv. of* створа́живать. —**створо́житься,** *refl., pfv. of* створа́живаться.

ство́рчатый *adj.* folding. —**ство́рчатое окно́,** casement window.

стеари́н *n.* stearin.

стеати́т *n.* steatite.

сте́бель [*gen.* -бля; *pl.* сте́бли, -бле́й, -бля́м] *n.m.* stem; stalk.

стёганка [*gen. pl.* -нок] *n., colloq.* quilted jacket.

стёганый *adj.* quilted. —**стёганое одея́ло,** quilt.

стега́ть *v. impfv.* **1,** [*pfv.* вы́стегать] to quilt. **2,** [*pfv.* отстега́ть *and* стегну́ть] to whip; lash.

стежо́к [*gen.* -жка́] *n.* stitch.

стезя́ *n., obs.* path; way; road.

стека́ть *v. impfv.* [*pfv.* стечь] to flow down. —**стека́ться,** *refl.* **1,** to flow together. **2,** *fig.* to flock together; congregate; throng.

стекленеть *v. impfv.* [*pfv.* остеклене́ть] **1,** to become like glass. **2,** (*of one's eyes*) to become glassy.

стекло́ [*pl.* стёкла, стёкол] *n.* glass. —**око́нное стекло́,** windowpane. —**пере́днее стекло́,** windshield. —**увеличи́тельное стекло́,** magnifying glass.

стекловолокно́ *n.* fiberglass.

стеклоду́в *n.* glass blower.

стеклоочисти́тель *n.m.* windshield wiper.

стекля́нный *adj.* **1,** glass. **2,** (*of a stare*) glassy.

стекля́рус *n.* bugles; bugle beads.

стеко́льный *adj.* glass (*attrib.*): стеко́льный заво́д, glassworks.

стеко́льщик *n.* glazier.

стели́ть *v. impfv.* [*pres.* стелю́, сте́лешь] = стлать. —**стели́ться,** *refl.* = стла́ться.

стелла́ж [*gen.* -лажа́] *n.* **1,** shelves. **2,** rack.

сте́лька [*gen. pl.* -лек] *n.* **1,** insole; inner sole. —**пья́н как сте́лька; пьян в сте́льку,** *colloq.* dead drunk.

стемне́ть *v., pfv. of* темне́ть (*in sense #2*).

стена́ [*acc.* сте́ну; *pl.* сте́ны, стен, стена́м] *n.* wall. —**стена́ в сте́ну,** right next door. —**жить** *or* **сиде́ть в четырёх стена́х,** to sit home all the time. —**лезть на́ стену,** *see* лезть.

стена́ть *v. impfv., obs.* to moan; groan.

стенгазе́та *n.* wall newspaper.

стенд (тэ) *n.* stand.

сте́ндовый (тэ) *adj., in* сте́ндовая стрельба́, trap-shooting.

сте́нка [*gen. pl.* -нок] *n.* **1,** *dim. of* стена́. **2,** side (*of a container*). **3,** *anat.* wall. —**поста́вить к сте́нке,** *colloq.* to execute; shoot.

стенно́й *adj.* wall (*attrib.*). —**стенно́й шкаф,** built-in closet.

стенобитный *adj., hist.* used to batter down walls: стенобитный таран, battering-ram.

стенограмма *n.* transcript (of a lecture, report, etc.) taken down in shorthand.

стенограф *n.* stenographer.

стенографировать *v. impfv.* [*pres.* -рую, -руешь] to take down in shorthand.

стенографист *n.m.* [*fem.* -фистка] stenographer.

стенография *n.* shorthand; stenography. —**стенографический**, *adj.* shorthand (*attrib.*); stenographic.

стенокардия *n.* angina pectoris.

стенопись *n.f.* mural; mural painting.

стеньга *n.* topmast.

степенный *adj.* sedate; staid.

степень [*pl.* степени, -ней, -ням] *n.f.* **1**, extent; degree: в значительной степени, to a considerable extent. **2**, academic degree. **3**, *gram.* degree. **4**, *math.* power: десять в пятой степени, ten to the fifth power. —**в высшей степени** (+ *adj.*), extraordinarily; most. —**ни в малейшей степени**, not in the least.

степной *adj.* steppe (*attrib.*).

степь [*2nd loc.* степи; *pl.* степи, -пей, -пям] *n.f.* steppe.

стервятник *n.* Egyptian vulture.

стереометрия *n.* solid geometry.

стереоскоп *n.* stereoscope. —**стереоскопический**, *adj.* stereoscopic. —**стереоскопия**, *n.* stereoscopy.

стереотип *n.* stereotype.

стереотипировать *v. impfv. & pfv.* [*pres.* -рую, -руешь] *printing* to stereotype.

стереотипный *adj.* stereotyped.

стереофонический *adj.* stereophonic.

стереть [*infl.* сотру, сотрёшь; *past* стёр, -ла] *v., pfv.* of стирать. —**стереться**, *refl., pfv.* of стираться.

стеречь *v. impfv.* [*pres.* стерегу, стережёшь, ...стерегут; *past* стерёг, стерегла, стерегло] to guard; watch.

стержень [*gen.* -жня] *n.m.* **1**, rod; bar. **2**, pivot. **3**, *fig.* core; heart.

стержневой *adj.* (*of a question or issue*) key; pivotal.

стерилизатор *n.* sterilizer. —**стерилизация**, *n.* sterilization.

стерилизовать *v. impfv. & pfv.* [*pres.* -зую, -зуешь] to sterilize.

стерильный *adj.* sterile; sterilized. —**стерильность**, *n.f.* sterility.

стерлинг *n.* sterling. Фунт стерлингов, the pound sterling. —**стерлинговый**, *adj.* sterling (*attrib.*).

стерлядь [*pl.* стерляди, -дей, -дям] *n.f.* sterlet (*fish*).

стерня *n.* **1**, harvested field (*with only the stubble remaining*). **2**, stubble. *Also,* **стернь**, *n.f.*

стероид *n.* steroid.

стерпеть *v. pfv.* [*infl.* стерплю, стерпишь] to bear; endure. —**стерпеться**, *refl.* (*with* с + *instr.*) *colloq.* to get used to; come to accept.

стёртый *adj.* **1**, effaced. **2**, worn smooth. **3**, *fig.* trite.

стеснение *n.* **1**, uneasiness; inhibition; constraint. **2**, constriction; feeling of tightness. **3**, *usu. pl.* restrictions; constraints.

стеснённый *adj.* **1**, crowded together. **2**, (*of breathing*) labored. **3**, uneasy; inhibited. **4**, straitened: в стеснённых обстоятельствах, in straitened circumstances. **5**, (*fol. by* в + *prepl.*) short of; squeezed (for): стеснён(ный) в средствах, squeezed for money.

стеснительность *n.f.* shyness; diffidence.

стеснительный *adj.* **1**, tight-fitting; constricting. **2**, confining; restrictive. **3**, shy; inhibited.

стеснить *v., pfv.* of теснить (*in sense #2*) *and* стеснять. —**стесниться**, *refl., pfv.* of тесниться (*in sense #1*) *and* стесняться (*in senses #3 & #4*).

стеснять *v. impfv.* [*pfv.* стеснить] **1**, to crowd; cramp. **2**, to hinder; hamper. **3**, to confine; restrict. **4**, to constrain; inhibit. **5**, to constrict. **6**, (*with себя*) to stint: не стеснять себя в средствах, not stint oneself. —**стесняться**, *refl.* **1**, [*impfv. only*] to feel uneasy; feel awkward; feel self-conscious. **2**, [*pfv.* постесняться] (*with inf.*) to be afraid (to); be ashamed (to); (*with gen.*) by shy (in the presence of); be afraid (of). **3**, [*pfv.* стесниться] to crowd; crowd together; be crowded together. **4**, [*pfv.* стесниться] (*with* в + *prepl.*) to spare; use sparingly: не стесняться в средствах, not stint oneself; не стесняться в выражениях, not mince words.

стетоскоп *n.* stethoscope.

стечение *n.* **1**, flowing together. **2**, coming together; gathering (*of people*). **3**, combination (*of circumstances*).

стечь [*infl. like* течь] *v., pfv.* of стекать. —**стечься**, *refl., pfv.* of стекаться.

стибрить *v. pfv., colloq.* to swipe; pilfer; filch.

стилет *n.* stiletto.

стилизация *n.* stylization.

стилизовать *v. impfv. & pfv.* [*pres.* -зую, -зуешь] to stylize.

стилист *n.* stylist. —**стилистика**, *n.* stylistics. —**стилистический**, *adj.* stylistic.

стиль *n.m.* **1**, style. **2**, *swimming* stroke.

стильный *adj.* **1**, period (*attrib.*): стильная мебель, period furniture. **2**, *colloq.* stylish; chic.

стиляга *n.m. & f.* stilyaga (*young man or woman adopting modish clothes and often evading social responsibility*).

стимул *n.* stimulus; incentive.

стимулирование *n.* stimulation.

стимулировать *v. impfv. & pfv.* [*pres.* -рую, -руешь] to stimulate.

стипендия *n.* grant; scholarship.

стиральный *adj.* washing (*attrib.*): стиральная машина, washing machine. —**стиральный порошок**, soap powder; detergent.

стирать *v. impfv.* [*pfv.* стереть] **1**, to wipe off. **2**, to erase. **3**, to rub; chafe; irritate. **4**, [*pfv.* выстирать] to wash; launder. —**стираться**, *refl.* [*pfv.* стереться] **1**, to be effaced; be obliterated; wear away. **2**, to become worn down; wear thin. **3**, [*impfv. only*] to wash: рубашка не стирается, the shirt is not washable.

стирка *n.* wash; washing; laundering. —**отдавать (что-нибудь) в стирку**, to have (something) washed; send out to be laundered.

стирол *n.* styrene.

стискивать *v. impfv.* [*pfv.* стиснуть] **1**, to squeeze. **2**, to hem in. **3**, to constrict. **4**, to grit (one's teeth).

стих [*gen.* стиха] *n.* **1**, verse. **2**, *pl.* poetry; poems.

стихарь [*gen.* -харя] *n.m.* surplice.

стихать *v. impfv.* [*pfv.* стихнуть] **1**, to grow still; become silent. **2**, to die down; subside; abate.

стихийность *n.f.* spontaneity.

стихийный *adj.* **1**, elemental. **2**, spontaneous. —**стихийное бедствие**, natural disaster.

стихи́я *n.* element. —**быть в свое́й стихи́и,** to be in one's element.

сти́хнуть [*past* стих, -ла] *v., pfv. of* **стиха́ть.**

стихоплёт *n., colloq.* rhymer; rhymester.

стихосложе́ние *n.* versification.

стихотворе́ние *n.* short poem.

стихотво́рный *adj.* **1,** poetical. **2,** in verse.

стишо́к [*gen.* -шка́] *n., dim. of* стих.

стлать *v. impfv.* [*pfv.* **постла́ть**; *pres.* стелю́, сте́лешь] to lay (a tablecloth, carpet, etc.); make (a bed). —**стла́ться,** *refl.* [*impfv. only*] **1,** to stretch; extend. **2,** (*of a plant*) to creep.

сто [*gen., dat., instr., & prepl.* ста; *gen. pl.* сот] *numeral* hundred.

стог [*2nd loc.* сто́гу; *pl.* стога́] *n.* stack: стог се́на, haystack.

сто́ик *n.* stoic.

сто́имость *n.f.* **1,** cost. **2,** *econ.* value: приба́вочная сто́имость, surplus value.

сто́ить *v. impfv.* **1,** to cost. **2,** (*with gen.*) to be worth: сто́ить больши́х де́нег, to be worth a lot of money. Не сто́ит труда́, it's not worth the trouble. **3,** (*with gen.*) to be worthy of. **4,** (*with inf.*) to be worth (while): кни́гу сто́ит проче́сть, the book is worth (while) reading. Не сто́ит с ним спо́рить, it is not worth arguing with him. **5,** (*with gen.*) to take (a certain amount of effort): ему́ сто́ило больши́х уси́лий (+ *inf.*), it took great effort on his part to... —**сто́ит то́лько** (+ *inf.*), one has only to...

стоици́зм *n.* stoicism.

стои́ческий *adj.* stoical. —**стои́чески,** *adv.* stoically.

сто́йка [*gen. pl.* сто́ек] *n.* **1,** [*also,* сто́йка сми́рно] position of attention. **2,** handstand. **3,** post; upright; stanchion. **4,** strut; prop. **5,** counter; bar.

сто́йкий *adj.* **1,** durable; hardy; long-lasting. **2,** *chem.* stable. **3,** *fig.* steadfast; staunch.

сто́йко *adv.* **1,** stoically. **2,** firmly. Сто́йко держа́ться, to stand firm; stand fast.

сто́йкость *n.f.* **1,** durability; hardinesss. **2,** *fig.* fortitude; steadfastness.

сто́йло *n.* stall.

стоймя́ *adv.* upright.

сток *n.* **1,** flow; drainage. **2,** drain; gutter.

сто́кер *n.* stoker (*machine*).

стокра́т *adv., archaic* a hundred times. —**стокра́тный,** *adj.* hundredfold: в стокра́тном разме́ре, a hundredfold.

стол [*gen.* стола́] *n.* **1,** table. **2,** board; meals: кварти́ра и стол, room and board. **3,** food; cooking. **4,** diet. **5,** department; office; bureau: стол зака́зов, order department. —**пи́сьменный стол,** desk.

столб [*gen.* столба́] *n.* **1,** pole; post; pillar. **2,** column (*of air, smoke, etc.*). —**позвоно́чный столб,** spinal column.

столбене́ть *v. impfv.* [*pfv.* **остолбене́ть**] *colloq.* to freeze (*from terror, shock, etc.*).

столбе́ц [*gen.* -бца́] *n.* column (*of print, figures, etc.*).

сто́лбик *n.* **1,** small column. **2,** column (*of print, figures, etc.*). **3,** *in* сто́лбик ртути, column of mercury. **4,** *bot.* style.

столбня́к [*gen.* -няка́] *n.* **1,** tetanus. **2,** *colloq.* stupor; trance.

столе́тие *n.* **1,** century. **2,** centenary; centennial.

столе́тний *adj.* **1,** hundred-year (*attrib.*). **2,** hundred-year-old. —**столе́тняя война́,** the Hundred Years' War. —**столе́тний юбиле́й,** hundredth anniversary.

столе́тник *n.* century plant.

сто́лик *n.* small table.

столи́ца *n.* capital (*city*). —**столи́чный,** *adj.* of a capital; capital (*attrib.*).

столкнове́ние *n.* **1,** collision. **2,** clash; conflict.

столкну́ть *v., pfv. of* **ста́лкивать.** —**столкну́ться,** *refl., pfv. of* **ста́лкиваться.**

столкова́ться *v.r. pfv.* [*infl.* -ку́юсь, -ку́ешься] *colloq.* to agree; reach agreement.

столова́ться *v.r. impfv.* [*pres.* -лу́юсь, -лу́ешься] to board; take meals.

столо́вая *n., decl. as an adj.* **1,** dining room. **2,** dining hall.

столо́вый *adj.* **1,** table (*attrib.*). **2,** dining-room (*attrib.*). —**столо́вая гора́,** mesa. —**столо́вая ло́жка,** tablespoon; soupspoon. —**столо́вые прибо́ры,** tableware; flatware.

столо́чь *v. pfv.* [*infl. like* толо́чь] *colloq.* to pound; crush; pulverize.

столп [*gen.* столпа́] *n.* **1,** *obs.* = столб. **2,** *fig.* pillar: столпы́ о́бщества, the pillars of society.

столпи́ться *v.r. pfv.* to crowd; congregate.

столпотворе́ние *n., in* вавило́нское столпотворе́ние, **1,** chaos. **2,** babel.

столь *adv.* so: это не столь ва́жно, it's not so important.

сто́лько *adv.* so much; so many. —**сто́лько (же)...,** ско́лько (и), as much as; as many as.

столя́р [*gen.* -яра́] *n.* joiner; cabinetmaker.

столя́рничать *v. impfv.* to be a cabinetmaker.

столя́рный *adj.* joiner's.

стоматоло́гия *n.* stomatology; dentistry. —**стомато́лог,** *n.* stomatologist; dentist.

стон *n.* groan; moan.

стона́ть *v. impfv.* [*pres.* стону́, сто́нешь] to groan; moan.

стоп *interj.* stop!

стопа́ [*pl.* сто́пы *in sense* #1; стопы́ *in other senses*] *n.* **1,** foot. **2,** *pros.* foot: метри́ческая стопа́, metric foot. **3,** pile (*of objects*). **4,** ream (*of paper*). —**идти́ по стопа́м** (+ *gen.*), to follow in the footsteps of. —**направля́ть свои́ стопы́,** to wend one's way.

сто́пка [*gen. pl.* -пок] *n.* **1,** pile. **2,** small glass (*for wine or vodka*).

сто́пор *n., mech.* stop; catch.

сто́порить *v. impfv.* [*pfv.* **застопорить**] to stop (an engine, machine, etc.). —**сто́пориться,** *refl.* **1,** to stop; jam; become inoperative. **2,** *fig., colloq.* to come to a standstill.

сто́порный *adj., mech.* stop (*attrib.*); arresting; locking.

стопроце́нтный *adj.* one-hundred-percent (*attrib.*).

стоп-сигна́л *n.* stoplight; brake light.

стопта́ть [*infl.* стопчу́, сто́пчешь] *v., pfv. of* **ста́птывать.** —**стопта́ться,** *refl., pfv. of* **ста́птываться.**

сторгова́ться *v.r. pfv.* [*infl.* -гу́юсь, -гу́ешься] to agree on a price (*after bargaining*).

стори́цей *also,* стори́цею *adv.* many times over: окупа́ться стори́цей, to pay for itself many times over.

сто́рож [*pl.* сторожа́] *n.* watchman; guard.

сторожево́й *adj.* watch (*attrib.*); sentry (*attrib.*). —**сторожева́я ба́шня** (*or* вы́шка), watchtower. —**сторожево́й ка́тер,** patrol boat. —**сторожево́й пёс,** watchdog.

сторожи́ть v. impfv. to guard; watch.

сторо́жка [gen. pl. -жек] n. hut; cabin; lodge (of a watchman, warden, etc.).

сторона́ [acc. сто́рону; pl. сто́роны, сторо́н, сторона́м] n. **1,** side. **2,** direction: в ту сто́рону, in that direction; that way. **3,** fig. aspect: положи́тельная сторона́, positive aspect. **4,** law party. **5,** land; country. —в стороне́ (от), apart (from); aloof (from). —в сто́рону, aside. —в сто́рону (+ gen.), in the direction of. —на все четы́ре сто́роны, wherever one wishes to go. —на стороне́, elsewhere; in another place. —на́ сторону, (with verbs of selling) on the side. —по ту сто́рону (+ gen.), on the other side (of). —со всех сторо́н, **1,** on all sides; from all sides. **2,** from all aspects. —с одно́й стороны́..., с друго́й стороны́..., on the one hand..., on the other hand... —со стороны́, **1,** from a distance; without being directly involved. **2,** from elsewhere; from another place. —со стороны́ (+ gen.), **1,** from the direction of. **2,** on the part of. Со свое́й стороны́ я..., for my part, I... Óчень ми́ло с ва́шей стороны́, very kind on your part; very kind of you. **3,** (of relatives) on the side of. —стороно́й, **1,** by: проходи́ть стороно́й, to pass by; bypass. **2,** on one side: обходи́ть (что́-нибудь) стороно́й, to side-step. **3,** fig. indirectly; secondhand. —встать or стать на сто́рону (+ gen.), to side with; take the side of. —держа́ться or остава́ться в стороне́, to remain aloof; remain on the sidelines.

сторони́ться v.r. impfv. [pfv. посторони́ться; pres. сторонюсь, сторо́нишься] **1,** to stand aside; step aside; make way. **2,** [impfv. only] (with gen.) to avoid; shun.

сторо́нний adj., obs. = посторо́нний. —сторо́нний наблюда́тель, outside/detached observer.

сторо́нник n. supporter; advocate.

сторублёвка [gen. pl. -вок] n., colloq. hundred-ruble note.

сторублёвый adj. **1,** hundred-ruble (attrib.). **2,** costing or worth one hundred rubles.

стоскова́ться v.r. pfv. [infl. -ку́юсь, -ку́ешься] (with по + dat., but prepl. with pers. pronouns) colloq. to miss; long for.

сточи́ть [infl. сточу́, сто́чишь] v., pfv. of ста́чивать.

сто́чный adj. drainage (attrib.). —сто́чные во́ды, sewage. —сто́чная кана́ва, gutter. —сто́чная труба́, sewer.

стошни́ть v. pfv., impers. to vomit; throw up: меня́ стошни́ло, I threw up.

сто́я adv. (used after verbs) standing up; on one's feet.

стояк [gen. -яка́] n. upright post.

стоя́ние n. standing: до́лгое стоя́ние в о́череди, a long stand in line.

стоя́нка [gen. pl. -нок] n. **1,** stop. **2,** stopping place. **3,** stand (for taxis, carriages, etc.). **4,** parking (of cars). **5,** parking lot.

стоя́ть v. impfv. [pres. стою́, стои́шь] **1,** to stand; be standing. **2,** to stand; be situated: дом стои́т на холму́, the house stands (or sits) on a hill. **3,** to be: маши́на стои́т в гараже́, the car is in the garage. Стоя́ть у вла́сти, to be in power. ♦Also in many other constructions: стои́т си́льный моро́з, there is a heavy frost. Пого́да стоя́ла тёплая, the weather was warm. Зима́ стоя́ла холо́дная, it was a cold winter. Стоя́л коне́ц ию́ня, it was late June. Стоя́ла тишина́, it was quiet. **4,** to stop; cease to function: мои́ часы́ стоя́т,

my watch has stopped. Рабо́та стои́т, work has stopped; work is at a standstill. **5,** (with за + acc.) to stand for; favor; be in favor of. —стой!; сто́йте!, **1,** stop! **2,** wait a minute! —стоя́ть на своём, to stand one's ground.

стоя́чий adj. **1,** standing; upright; erect. **2,** (of water) stagnant.

сто́ящий adj., colloq. worthwhile.

страви́ть [infl. стравлю́, стра́вишь] v., pfv. of стра́вливать.

стра́вливать v. impfv. [pfv. страви́ть] **1,** to set (two animals) against each other. **2,** colloq. to provoke a fight or argument between (two people).

страда́ n. **1,** extra hard work performed at harvest time. **2,** fig. hard work. **3,** season of hard work.

страда́лец [gen. -льца] n. sufferer.

страда́льческий adj. of suffering.

страда́ние n. suffering.

страда́тельный adj., gram. passive: страда́тельный зало́г, passive voice.

страда́ть v. impfv. [pfv. пострада́ть] **1,** to suffer: страда́ть от жары́, to suffer from the heat; страда́ть бессо́нницей, to suffer from insomnia. Страда́ть за свои́ убежде́ния, to suffer for one's beliefs. **2,** [impfv. only] (with за + acc.) to feel for. **3,** [impfv. only] colliq. to be poor; be deficient: у него́ страда́ет орфогра́фия, he is poor at spelling. See also пострада́ть.

стра́дный adj. (of time) busy; hectic.

страж n., obs. guard; guardian.

стра́жа n. **1,** obs. guard; watch. **2,** (with под) custody: быть под стра́жей, to be in custody; брать под стра́жу, take into custody; содержа́ть под стра́жей, hold in custody. —быть на стра́же, **1,** to be on guard. **2,** (with gen.) to guard; be guarding.

страна́ [pl. стра́ны] n. country. —страна́ све́та, cardinal point; point of the compass.

страни́ца n. page.

стра́нник n. wanderer.

стра́нно adv. strangely. —adj., used predicatively strange: как ни стра́нно, strange as it seems.

стра́нность n.f. **1,** strangeness. **2,** usu. pl. peculiarity; quirk; eccentricity.

стра́нный adj. strange; odd. —стра́нное де́ло, it is strange; it's a strange thing.

странове́дение n. area studies.

стра́нствие n. traveling; wandering. Also, стра́нствование.

стра́нствовать v. impfv. [pres. -ствую, -ствуешь] to wander; roam.

стра́стно adv. **1,** passionately. **2,** ardently.

страстно́й adj. pert. to the week before Easter. —страстна́я неде́ля, holy week. —страстно́й четве́рг, Holy Thursday. —страстна́я пя́тница, Good Friday.

стра́стность n.f. passion; ardor.

стра́стный adj. **1,** passionate; impassioned. **2,** ardent; fervent. **3,** avid; enthusiastic.

страсть [pl. стра́сти, -сте́й, -стя́м] n.f. **1,** passion. **2,** usu. pl., colloq. horrors. —adv. [usu. fol. by как or како́й] colloq. awfully (much); terribly (much).

стратаге́ма n. stratagem.

страте́гия n. strategy. —страте́г, n. strategist. —страти́ческий, adj. strategic.

стратифика́ция n. stratification.

стратосфе́ра n. stratosphere.

стра́ус *n.* ostrich. —**стра́усовый**, *adj.* ostrich (*attrib.*).

страх *n.* fear. —**на свой страх**, at one's risk. —**под стра́хом сме́рти**, on pain of death.

страхова́ние *n.* insurance.

страхова́ть *v. impfv.* [*pfv.* **застрахова́ть**] **1**, to insure. **2**, *fig.* to safeguard. —**страхова́ться**, *refl.* to insure oneself; (*with* **от**) take out insurance (against).

страхо́вка *n.* insurance.

страхово́й *adj.* insurance (*attrib.*).

страхо́вщик *n.* insurer.

страши́лище *n., colloq.* fright; horrible sight.

страши́ть *v. impfv.* to frighten. —**страши́ться**, *refl.* (*with gen.*) to be afraid (of); fear.

стра́шно *adv.* terribly; awfully. —*adj., used predicatively* **1**, terrible; horrible; awful. **2**, (*with dat.*) afraid: мне стра́шно, I am afraid.

стра́шный *adj.* terrible; horrible; dreadful; frightful; awful.

стре́жень [*gen.* **-жня**] *n.m.* part of a river where the current is strongest.

стрекоза́ [*pl.* **-ко́зы**] *n.* dragonfly; darning needle.

стре́кот *n.* chirping. *Also,* **стрекота́ние**.

стрекота́ть *v. impfv.* [*pres.* **-кочу́, -ко́чешь**] to chirp.

стрела́ [*pl.* **стре́лы**] *n.* **1**, arrow. **2**, boom (*of a derrick*). —**стрело́й**, straight (*or* swift) as an arrow.

стреле́ц [*gen.* **-льца́**] *n., hist.* member of a special military corps in the 16th and 17th centuries; strelets. **2**, *cap.* Sagittarius.

стре́лка [*gen. pl.* **-лок**] *n.* **1**, *dim. of* **стрела́**. **2**, arrow (*pointing to something*). **3**, hand (*of a clock or watch*): мину́тная стре́лка, minute hand. **4**, needle (*of a compass, dial, etc.*). **5**, *R.R.* switch. **6**, spit (*of land*).

стрелко́вый *adj.* rifle (*attrib.*); shooting (*attrib.*). **2**, *mil.* rifle (*attrib.*). —**стрелко́вое де́ло**, musketry. —**стрелко́вое ору́жие**, small arms.

стрелови́дный *adj.* **1**, arrow-shaped. **2**, *aero.* swept-back.

стрело́к [*gen.* **-лка́**] *n.* **1**, shot; marksman: хоро́ший стрело́к, a good shot. **2**, *mil.* gunner.

стре́лочник *n., R.R.* switchman.

стрельба́ [*pl.* **стре́льбы**] *n.* **1**, shooting; firing. **2**, *pl.* firing practice. —**откры́ть стрельбу́**, to open fire; start shooting.

стре́льбище *n.* firing range.

стрельну́ть *v. pfv.* **1**, to fire a shot. **2**, *colloq.* to dash; dart (*away or out of sight*).

стре́льчатый *adj.* arched. —**стре́льчатое окно́**, lancet window.

стре́ляный *adj.* **1**, shot; killed. **2**, (*of a weapon*) having been fired; (*of a shell or cartridge*) spent. **3**, having been under fire. —**стре́ляный воробе́й**, *colloq.* old hand.

стреля́ть *v. impfv.* [*pfv.* **вы́стрелить**] **1**, to shoot; fire: не стреля́йте!, don't shoot! **2**, (*with* **в** + *acc. or* **по**) to shoot at; fire at. **3**, (*with* **из**) to fire (a weapon). **4**, [*impfv. only*] to shoot (and kill): стреля́ть у́ток, to shoot ducks. **5**, [*impfv. only*] to crackle. **6**, [*impfv. only*] (*with instr.*) *colloq.* to crack (a whip). **7**, [*impfv. only*] *impers., colloq.* to have a shooting pain: у меня́ стреля́ет в у́хе, I have a shooting pain in my ear. —**стреля́ть глаза́ми**, **1**, to glance around. **2**, to make eyes.

стремгла́в *adv.* headlong.

стреми́тельный *adj.* **1**, very fast; rapid. **2**, dynamic; energetic. —**стреми́тельно**, *adv.* rapidly; headlong.

стреми́ться *v.r. impfv.* [*pres.* **стремлю́сь, стре-мишься**] **1**, (*with* **к**) to seek; aim for; strive for; aspire to. **2**, (*with inf.*) to try (to). **3**, (*with* **в** *or* **на** + *acc.*) to try to get to (a place); try to get into (a school or college). **4**, *obs.* to rush.

стремле́ние *n.* **1**, (*with* **к**) striving (for). **2**, aspiration. **3**, longing; yearning; urge.

стремни́на *n.* rapids (*on a river*).

стре́мя [*gen., dat., & prepl.* **стре́мени**; *instr.* **стре́менем**; *pl.* **стремена́, стремя́н, стремена́м**] *n. neut.* stirrup.

стремя́нка [*gen. pl.* **-нок**] *n.* stepladder.

стрено́жить *v., pfv. of* **трено́жить**.

стре́пет *n.* little bustard.

стрептоко́кк *n.* streptococcus.

стрептомици́н *n.* streptomycin.

стресс *n.* (emotional) stress.

стреха́ [*pl.* **стре́хи**] *n.* eaves.

стригу́щий *adj., in* стригу́щий лиша́й, ringworm.

стриж [*gen.* **стрижа́**] *n.* swift (*bird*).

стри́женый *adj.* **1**, (*of hair*) short; closely cropped; (*of a person*) with closely cropped hair. **2**, (*of sheep*) shorn. **3**, (*of a lawn, trees, etc.*) trimmed.

стри́жка [*gen. pl.* **-жек**] *n.* **1**, clipping. **2**, shearing. **3**, haircut. —**маши́нка для стри́жки**, clippers.

стрипти́з *n.* striptease.

стрихни́н *n.* strychnine.

стричь *v. impfv.* [*pfv.* **остри́чь**; *pres.* **стригу́, стри-жёшь, ...стригу́т**; *past* **стриг, -ла**] **1**, to cut (one's hair, beard, etc.). **2**, to give (someone) a haircut. **3**, to shear; trim; clip. —**стри́чься**, *refl.* **1**, to cut one's hair. **2**, to get a haircut. **3**, to wear one's hair a certain way: стри́чься ко́ротко, to wear one's hair short.

стробоско́п *n.* stroboscope.

строга́льный *adj.* (*of a machine or tool*) planing. —**строга́льщик**, *n.* planer.

строга́ть *v. impfv.* [*pfv.* **вы́строгать**] to plane (wood).

стро́гий *adj.* [*comp.* **стро́же**] **1**, (*of a person, rule, etc.*) strict. **2**, (*of rules, measures, etc.*) stringent. **3**, (*of a look, voice, etc.*) stern. **4**, (*of criticism, a sentence, etc.*) severe.

стро́го *adv.* **1**, strictly: стро́го говоря́, strictly speaking; стро́го воспреща́ется, strictly forbidden. **2**, severely.

стро́гость *n.f.* **1**, strictness. **2**, severity.

строево́й *adj.* **1**, *mil.* drill (*attrib.*): строево́й расчёт, drill team. **2**, *mil.* front-line: строево́й офице́р, front-line officer. **3**, (*of material*) building: строево́й лес, lumber; timber. —**строева́я подгото́вка**, drill. —**строева́я сто́йка**, position of attention.

строе́ние *n.* **1**, a building. **2**, (*with gen.*) structure (of).

строи́тель *n.m.* builder. —**строи́тельный**, *adj.* building (*attrib.*); construction (*attrib.*).

строи́тельство *n.* **1**, (act of) building; construction. **2**, construction project. **3**, construction site.

стро́ить *v. impfv.* [*pfv.* **постро́ить**] **1**, to build; construct. **2**, (*with* **на** + *prepl.*) to base (on). **3**, to make (plans, assumptions, etc.). **4**, to organize; plan. **5**, [*impfv. only*] to make (an expression on one's face): стро́ить гла́зки, to make eyes; стро́ить грима́сы, to make faces. **6**, *mil.* to form. **7**, *in* стро́ить себе́ иллю́зии, to create illusions for oneself; delude oneself. **8**, *in* стро́ить из себя́ (+ *acc.*), to make oneself out to be. —**стро́иться**, *refl.* **1**, to be built. **2**, to build a house for oneself. **3**, (*with* **на** + *prepl.*) to be based (on). **4**, *mil.* to form; line up.

строй *n.* **1,** [*2nd loc.* строю́; *pl.* строи́, строёв] *mil.* formation. **2,** system: обще́ственный строй, social system. **3,** tone; pitch; key (*of a musical instrument*). **4,** *gram.* structure. **5,** pattern: строй мышле́ния, pattern of thinking. —**вводи́ть в строй,** to put into service; put into operation. —**вступа́ть в строй,** to go into operation. —**выбыва́ть из стро́я,** *see* **выбыва́ть.** —**выводи́ть из стро́я,** to put out of operation; put out of commission. —**выходи́ть из стро́я,** to break down; be disabled. —**прогоня́ть кого́-нибудь сквозь строй,** to make someone run the gauntlet.

стро́йка [*gen. pl.* стро́ек] *n.* **1,** (act of) building; construction. **2,** construction project; construction site.

стро́йный *adj.* **1,** graceful; slender; trim; svelte. **2,** (*of rows or columns*) regular; even. **3,** logical; coherent; consistent. **4,** harmonious.

строка́ [*acc.* строку́ *or* стро́ку; *pl.* стро́ки, строк, строка́м] *n.* line (*of writing*). —**чита́ть ме́жду строк,** to read between the lines.

стро́нций *n.* strontium.

стропи́ло *n.* rafter.

стропти́вый *adj.* obstinate; contrary.

строфа́ [*pl.* стро́фы] *n.* stanza.

строчи́ть *v. impfv.* [*pres.* строчу́, стро́чишь *or* строчи́шь] **1,** [*pfv.* простро́чить] to stitch. **2,** [*pfv.* настрочи́ть] *colloq.* to scribble; dash off. **3,** [*impfv. only*] *colloq.* to fire in rapid succession; blaze away.

стро́чка [*gen. pl.* -чек] *n.* **1,** = **строка́. 2,** stitch: ажу́рная стро́чка, hemstitch.

строчно́й *adj.* (*of a letter*) small; lower-case. *Also,* **стро́чный.**

струг *n.* plane (*tool*).

стру́жка [*gen. pl.* -жек] *n.* **1,** *usu. pl.* shavings. **2,** excelsior. —**мы́льная стру́жка,** soap flakes.

стру́иться *v.r. impfv.* to stream; pour.

стру́йка [*gen. pl.* стру́ек] *n.* **1,** stream; trickle. **2,** wisp (*of smoke*).

стру́йный *adj.* jet (*attrib.*). —**стру́йное тече́ние,** jet stream.

структу́ра *n.* structure. —**структу́рный,** *adj.* structural.

струна́ [*pl.* стру́ны] *n.* **1,** string (*of a musical instrument, tennis racket, etc.*). **2,** *fig.* chord: заде́ть чувстви́тельную струну́, to strike a sensitive chord. —**игра́ть на сла́бых стру́нах (кого́-нибудь),** to play on someone's weaknesses.

стру́нка [*gen. pl.* -нок] *n.* = **струна́. —вы́тянуться** *or* **стать в стру́нку,** to stand at attention. —**ходи́ть по стру́нке (у),** to toe the line (for).

стру́нный *adj.* **1,** string (*attrib.*): стру́нный кварте́т, string quartet. **2,** (*of a musical instrument*) stringed.

струп [*pl.* стру́пья, стру́пьев] *n.* scab.

стру́сить *v., pfv. of* **тру́сить.**

стручко́вый *adj.* leguminous. —**стручко́вый горо́х,** peas in the pod. —**стручко́вый пе́рец,** red pepper. —**стручко́вая фасо́ль,** string beans.

стручо́к [*gen.* -чка́] *n.* pod.

струя́ [*pl.* стру́и] *n.* spurt; jet; stream; current. —**бить струёй,** to spurt; jet,

стря́пать *v. impfv.* [*pfv.* состря́пать] *colloq.* **1,** to cook. **2,** *fig.* to cook up.

стряпня́ *n., colloq.* **1,** cooking. **2,** concoction.

стряса́ть *v. impfv.* [*pfv.* стрясти́] to shake off.

стрясти́ [*infl. like* трясти́] *v., pfv. of* **стряса́ть.**

—**стрясти́сь,** *refl.* (*with* с + *instr.*) *colloq.* (*of a misfortune*) to happen to; befall.

стря́хивать *v. impfv.* [*pfv.* стряхну́ть] **1,** to shake off. **2,** to shake down (a thermometer).

студе́нт *n.m.* [*fem.* -де́нтка] student. —**студе́нческий,** *adj.* student (*attrib.*); students'.

студе́нчество *n.* **1,** students. **2,** student days; student life.

студёный *adj., colloq.* very cold; freezing; icy.

сту́день [*gen.* -дня] *n.m.* aspic (*of meat or fish*).

студи́ть *v. impfv.* [*pfv.* остуди́ть; *pres.* стужу́, сту́дишь] *colloq.* to cool; chill.

сту́дия *n.* studio.

сту́жа *n., colloq.* severe cold.

стук *n.* **1,** knock: стук в дверь, knock at the door. **2,** clatter.

сту́кать *v. impfv.* [*pfv.* сту́кнуть] **1,** to knock; rap. **2,** to hit; strike. Сту́кнуть кулако́м по́ столу, to bang one's fist on the table. —**сту́каться,** *refl.* (*with instr.*) to bang; bump; knock: сту́кнуться голова́ми, to bump heads. Сту́кнуться голово́й о дверь, to bang one's head on the door. *See also* **сту́кнуть.**

стука́ч [*gen.* -кача́] *n., colloq.* informer; stool pigeon.

сту́кнуть *v. pfv.* **1,** *pfv. of* **сту́кать. 2,** *colloq.* (*of time*) to come. **3,** *impers.* (*with dat.*) *colloq.*, *indicating attainment of a certain age:* ему́ уже́ сту́кнуло се́мьдесят лет, he is already seventy. —**сту́кнуться,** *refl., pfv. of* **сту́каться.**

стул *n.* **1,** [*pl.* сту́лья, сту́льев] chair. **2,** *med.* stool. —**сиде́ть ме́жду двух сту́льев,** to fall between two stools.

стульча́к [*gen.* -чака́] *n.* toilet seat.

сту́льчик *n., dim. of* **стул.** —**высо́кий де́тский сту́льчик,** highchair.

сту́па *n.* mortar (*bowl*).

ступа́ть *v. impfv.* [*pfv.* ступи́ть] **1,** to step. **2,** [*impfv. only*] to walk. —**нога́ не ступа́ет (куда́-нибудь),** not set foot in (a certain place). *See also* **ступи́ть.**

ступе́нчатый *adj.* stepped; graded.

ступе́нь *n.f.* **1,** step (*on a staircase*). **2,** *fig.* step; stage. **3,** *fig.* level.

ступе́нька [*gen. pl.* -нек] *n.* **1,** step (*on a staircase*). **2,** rung (*of a ladder*).

ступи́ть *v. pfv.* [*infl.* ступлю́, сту́пишь] **1,** *pfv. of* **ступа́ть. 2,** (*with* на + *acc.*) to set foot on.

сту́пица *n.* hub (*of a wheel*).

сту́пка [*gen. pl.* -пок] *n.* = **сту́па.**

ступня́ *n.* **1,** foot. **2,** sole (*of the foot*).

сту́пор *n.* stupor.

стуча́ть *v. impfv.* [*pfv.* постуча́ть; *pres.* -чу́, -чи́шь] **1,** to knock; rap. **2,** (*of one's teeth*) to chatter; (*of one's heart*) to throb. —**стуча́ться,** *refl.* to knock; rap.

стушева́ться *v.r., pfv. of* **тушева́ться** *and* **стушёвываться.**

стушёвываться *v.r. impfv.* [*pfv.* стушева́ться] *colloq.* **1,** to become indistinct; fade away. **2,** to withdraw into the background. **3,** (*with* пе́ред) to be overshadowed (by). **4,** to become flustered.

стуши́ть *v., pfv. of* **туши́ть** (*in sense #2*).

стыд [*gen.* стыда́] *n.* shame.

стыди́ть *v. impfv.* [*pfv.* пристыди́ть; *pres.* стыжу́, стыди́шь] to shame; put to shame. —**стыди́ться,** *refl.* [*pfv.* постыди́ться] (*with gen.*) to be ashamed (of).

стыдли́вый *adj.* bashful; modest; self-conscious. —**стыдли́вость,** *n.f.* bashfulness; modesty.

сты́дно *adj., used predicatively* it is a shame. —**сты́дно!**, shame on you! —**мне сты́дно**, I am ashamed. —**как вам не сты́дно!**, aren't you ashamed!

сты́дный *adj.* shameful.

стык *n.* **1,** joint. **2,** junction.

стыкова́ться *v.r. pfv.* [*infl.* -**ку́ется**] (*of space vehicles*) to dock.

стыко́вка *n.* docking (*of space vehicles*).

сты́нуть *v. impfv.* [*past* стыл, сты́ла] = **стыть.**

стыть *v. impfv.* [*pfv.* **осты́ть**; *pres.* **сты́ну, сты́нешь**] **1,** to cool off; get cold. **2,** to freeze; become frozen. **3,** *fig.* (*of an emotion*) to cool.

сты́чка [*gen. pl.* -**чек**] *n.* **1,** skirmish; clash. **2,** *colloq.* squabble; altercation.

стю́ард *n.* steward (*aboard ship or aloft*). —**стюарде́сса**, (дэ) *n.* stewardess.

стяг *n.* banner; standard.

стя́гивать *v. impfv.* [*pfv.* **стяну́ть**] **1,** to tighten; draw tight. **2,** to gather; concentrate. **3,** to pull off; remove. —**стя́гиваться**, *refl.* **1,** to tighten; become tight. **2,** to assemble; congregate.

стяжа́тель *n.m.* money-grubber. —**стяжа́тельство**, *n.* making money.

стяжа́ть *v. impfv. & pfv.* **1,** to amass (*wealth*). **2,** to win; gain (*fame, respect, etc.*).

стяну́ть *v. pfv.* [*infl.* **стяну́, стя́нешь**] **1,** *pfv. of* **стя́гивать. 2,** *colloq.* to swipe; pilfer. —**стяну́ться**, *refl.*, *pfv. of* **стя́гиваться.**

суахи́ли *n.m. indecl.* Swahili.

субаре́нда *n.* sublease.

суббо́та *n.* **1,** Saturday. **2,** Sabbath.

суббо́тний *adj.* **1,** Saturday (*attrib.*). **2,** Sabbath (*attrib.*).

суббо́тник *n.* voluntary unpaid work performed on days off (*originally on Saturday*).

субконтине́нт *n.* subcontinent.

сублима́т *n.* sublimate. —**сублима́ция**, *n., chem.* sublimation.

сублими́ровать *v. impfv. & pfv.* [*pres.* -**рую, -руешь**] *chem.* to sublimate.

субордина́ция *n.* deference to rank: соблюда́ть субордина́цию, to defer to rank.

субподря́д *n.* subcontract. —**субподря́дчик**, *n.* subcontractor.

субсиди́ровать *v. impfv. & pfv.* [*pres.* -**рую, -руешь**] to subsidize.

субси́дия *n.* subsidy.

субста́нция *n.* substance.

субстра́т *n.* substratum.

субти́льный *adj., colloq.* frail; delicate.

субти́тр *n., motion pictures* subtitle.

субтро́пики [*gen.* -**ков**] *n. pl.* subtropics. —**субтропи́ческий**, *adj.* subtropical.

субъе́кт *n.* **1,** subject. **2,** *colloq.* fellow; person; character.

субъективи́зм *n.* **1,** subjectivism. **2,** subjectivity.

субъекти́вный *adj.* subjective. —**субъекти́вность**, *n.f.* subjectivity.

сува́льда *n.* tumbler (*of a lock*).

сувени́р *n.* souvenir.

суверен *n.* sovereign. —**суверените́т**, *n.* sovereignty. —**суверенный**, *adj.* sovereign.

сугли́нок [*gen.* -**нка**] *n.* loam. —**сугли́нистый**, *adj.* loamy.

сугро́б *n.* snowdrift.

сугу́бо *adv.* especially; particularly.

сугу́бый *adj.* **1,** *obs.* double. **2,** special; particular.

суд [*gen.* **суда́**] *n.* **1,** court (*of law*). **2,** trial: суд над кём-нибудь, the trial of... **3,** judgment; verdict. **4,** *in* вое́нный суд, court-martial. **5,** *in* стра́шный суд, Judgment Day. —**пока́ суд да де́ло**, in the meantime; while we're waiting.

суда́к [*gen.* -**дака́**] *n.* pike perch.

суда́рыня *n., obs.* madam.

су́дарь *n.m., obs.* sir.

суда́чить *v. impfv., colloq.* to gossip.

суде́бный *adj.* **1,** court (*attrib.*). **2,** legal; judicial. **3,** forensic. —**суде́бная оши́бка**, miscarriage of justice. —**суде́бный проце́сс**, trial.

суде́йский *adj.* **1,** judge's. **2,** referee's; umpire's.

суди́лище *n.* (unfair) trial.

суди́мость *n.f., law* previous conviction.

суди́ть *v. impfv.* [*pres.* **сужу́, су́дишь**] **1,** (*often with* о) to judge. **2,** to try (*in court*). **3,** *sports* to referee; umpire. **4,** *in* су́дя по (+ *dat., but prepl. with pers. pronouns*) judging by. —**суди́ться**, *refl.* **1,** to go to court. **2,** (*with* с + *instr.*) to sue. **3,** to be tried (*in court*). *See also* **суждено́.**

су́дно *n.* **1,** [*pl.* **суда́, судо́в**] vessel; ship. **2,** [*pl.* **су́дна, су́ден**], *in* подкладно́е су́дно, bedpan.

су́дный *adj., obs.* of a court; judicial. —**Су́дный день**, Judgment Day.

судове́рфь *n.f.* shipyard.

судовладе́лец [*gen.* -**льца**] *n.* shipowner.

судово́й *adj.* ship (*attrib.*); ship's.

судо́к [*gen.* -**дка́**] *n.* **1,** gravy boat. **2,** cruet stand. **3,** *pl.* set of interlocking pots for carrying food.

судомо́йка [*gen. pl.* -**мо́ек**] *n.* (woman) dishwasher. —**судомо́йня**, *n.* [*gen. pl.* -**мо́ен**] scullery.

судопроизво́дство *n.* legal proceedings.

су́дорога *n.* **1,** cramp. **2,** convulsion.

су́дорожный *adj.* **1,** convulsive. **2,** *fig.* feverish; frantic; hectic.

судостро́ение *n.* shipbuilding. —**судостро́итель**, *n.m.* shipbuilder. —**судостро́ительный**, *adj.* shipbuilding (*attrib.*).

судоустро́йство *n.* judicial system.

судохо́дный *adj.* **1,** shipping (*attrib.*). **2,** navigable. —**судохо́дность**, *n.f.* navigability.

судохо́дство *n.* shipping; navigation.

судьба́ [*pl.* **су́дьбы, су́деб, су́дьбам**] *n.* **1,** fate; fortune; destiny. **2,** (one's) fate; (one's) lot. —**во́лею судеб**, by the will of fate. —**каки́ми судьба́ми?**, what brings you here? —**не судьба́, 1,** it was not to be; it was not in the cards. **2,** (*with dat. and inf.*) (one was) not fated (*or* destined) to: ему́ не судьба́ возврати́ться, he was not destined to return.

судья́ [*pl.* **су́дьи, суде́й, су́дьям**] *n.m.* **1,** judge. **2,** *sports* referee; umpire.

суеве́рие *n.* superstition. —**суеве́рный**, *adj.* superstitious.

суета́ *n.* **1,** fuss; bustle. **2,** trifle; triviality. —**суета́ суе́т**, vanity of vanities.

суети́ться *v.r. impfv.* [*pres.* **суечу́сь, суети́шься**] to bustle about.

суетли́вый *adj.* **1,** restless; fidgety. **2,** bustling.

сужде́ние *n.* judgment; opinion.

суждено́ *short form neut. of past passive part. of* **суди́ть**, fated; destined: нам не суждено́ бы́ло вы́играть, we were not fated to win.

сужéние n. narrowing; contraction; constriction.

сýживать v. impfv. [pfv. сýзить] **1,** to narrow. **2,** to take in (a garment). —**сýживаться,** refl. to narrow; become narrow; contract.

сýзить [infl. сýжу, сýзишь] v., pfv. of **сýживать.** —**сýзиться,** refl., pfv. of **сýживаться.**

сук [gen. сукá; 2nd loc. сукý; pl. сýчья, сýчьев or сукú, сукóв] n. **1,** bough. **2,** knot (in wood).

сýка n. bitch. —**сýкин,** adj., in **сýкин сын,** vulg. son of a bitch.

сукнó [pl. сýкна, сýкон] n. smooth woolen cloth. —**класть под сукнó,** to shelve; pigeonhole.

сукóнка [gen. pl. -нок] n. cloth; rag.

сукóнный adj. **1,** cloth (attrib.). **2,** (of language, speech, etc.) dull; vapid; uninspired.

сулемá n. mercuric chloride; corrosive sublimate.

сулúть v. impfv. [pfv. посулúть] **1,** obs. to promise. **2,** [impfv. only] to portend; augur.

султáн n. **1,** sultan. **2,** plume. **3,** column (of steam, smoke, etc.).

султанáт n. sultanate.

султáнка [gen. pl. -нок] n. red mullet.

сульфаниламúдный adj., in **сульфаниламúдные препарáты,** sulfa drugs.

сульфáт n. sulfate.

сульфúд n. sulfide.

сумá n., obs. bag. —**ходúть с сумóй,** to beg for a living.

сумасбрóд n. nut; screwball.

сумасбрóдный adj. **1,** crazy; touched; unbalanced. **2,** mad; wild; reckless. —**сумасбрóдство,** n. erratic behavior.

сумасшéдший adj. mad; crazy; insane. —n. madman; insane person. —**сумасшéдший дом,** insane asylum.

сумасшéствие n. madness; insanity.

суматóха n. bustle; tumult; commotion.

суматóшный adj., colloq. **1,** bustling. **2,** tumultuous; hectic. Also, **суматóшливый.**

сумáх n. sumac.

сумбýр n. confusion. —**сумбýрный,** adj. confused.

сýмеречный adj. **1,** twilight (attrib.). **2,** (of light) dim; dull.

сýмерки [gen. -рек] n. pl. twilight; dusk.

сумéть v. pfv. (with inf.) to be able; manage; succeed.

сýмка [gen. pl. -мок] n. **1,** bag: сýмка для покýпок, shopping bag. **2,** handbag; purse; pocketbook. **3,** zool. pouch. —**санитáрная сýмка,** first-aid kit.

сýмма n. **1,** sum; total. **2,** sum; amount (of money).

суммáрный adj. **1,** total. **2,** general; generalized.

суммúровать v. impfv. & pfv. [pres. -рую, -руешь] **1,** to add up; total. **2,** to sum up; summarize.

сýмочка [gen. pl. -чек] n. handbag; purse; pocketbook.

сýмрак n. semidarkness. —**сýмрачный,** adj. gloomy.

сýмчатый adj. & n. marsupial.

сумя́тица n., colloq. **1,** bustle; commotion. **2,** confusion; turmoil.

сундýк [gen. -дукá] n. trunk; chest.

сýнуть v., pfv. of совáть. —**сýнуться,** refl., pfv. of совáться.

суп [pl. супы́] n. soup.

супермáркет n. supermarket.

супероблóжка [gen. pl. -жек] n. dust jacket.

супертáнкер n. supertanker.

сýпесь n.f. loam. Also, **сýпесок** [gen. -ска].

супинáтор n. arch support.

сýпить v. impfv. [pres. сýплю, сýпишь] colloq. to knit (one's brows).

сýпник n. soup tureen. Also, **сýпница.**

суповóй adj. soup (attrib.). —**суповáя лóжка,** soup ladle.

супрýг n. husband; spouse. —**супрýга,** n. wife; spouse. —**супрýги,** n. pl. husband and wife; married couple.

супрýжеский adj. marital; matrimonial; married; conjugal. —**супрýжество,** n. married life; matrimony.

сургýч [gen. -гучá] n. sealing wax. —**сургýчный,** adj. of sealing wax.

сурдúнка n., music mute. —**под сурдúнку,** quietly; secretly; on the sly.

сурéпица n. rape (plant). —**сурéпный,** adj. rape (attrib.): сурéпное мáсло, rape oil.

сýрик n. red lead.

сурóво adv. **1,** severely. **2,** sternly.

сурóвость n.f. severity; harshness.

сурóвый adj. **1,** (of climate, winter, etc.) harsh; severe; rigorous. **2,** (of life, truth, measures, etc.) harsh. **3,** (of punishment, a sentence, etc.) harsh; severe. **4,** (of a person, look, voice, etc.) stern. **5,** (of cloth) unbleached.

сурóк [gen. -ркá] n. marmot; woodchuck; ground hog.

суррогáт n. substitute: суррогáт сáхара, sugar substitute. —**суррогáтный,** adj. substitute; ersatz.

сурьмá n. antimony.

сусáльный adj., in сусáльное зóлото, gold leaf; сусáльное серебрó, silver leaf.

сýслик n. a kind of ground squirrel; suslik.

сýсло n. mash. —**виногрáдное сýсло,** new wine.

сустáв n., anat. joint.

суставнóй adj. of the joints. —**суставнóй ревматúзм,** rheumatic fever.

сутенёр n. gigolo.

сýтки [gen. -ток] n. pl. twenty-four-hour period; day: трóе сýток, three days (and nights). —**крýглые сýтки,** round the clock.

сýтолока n. bustle; commotion.

сýточный adj. a day's. —**сýточные,** n. pl. per diem.

сутýлить v. impfv. [pfv. ссутýлить] to hunch: сутýлить спúну, to hunch one's back. —**сутýлиться,** refl. to stoop; slouch.

сутýлый adj. round-shouldered; stooped. —**сутýлость,** n.f. stoop; slouch.

суть[1] n.f. essence. —**по сýти дéла,** in essence; as a matter of fact. —**суть дéла,** the heart (or crux) of the matter.

суть[2] v., archaic, 3rd person of быть: такúе дéйствия суть нéчто инóе, чем..., such actions are something different from...

суфлé n. neut. indecl. soufflé.

суфлёр n., theat. prompter.

суфлúровать v. impfv. [pres. -рую, -руешь] theat. (with dat.) to prompt.

суфражúстка [gen. pl. -ток] n. suffragette.

сýффикс n. suffix.

сухáрь [gen. -харя́] n.m. zwieback; rusk.

сухáя n., decl. as an adj., sports, colloq. shutout.

сýхо adv. **1,** dryly: сказáть сýхо, to say dryly. **2,** coldly: прин́ять гостéй сýхо, to receive the guests coldly. —adj., used predicatively dry: бы́ло сýхо, it was dry.

сухове́й *n.* hot dry wind.

сухожи́лие *n.* tendon.

сухо́й *adj.* [*comp.* су́ше] **1**, dry. **2**, dried. **3**, dried-up. **4**, arid. **5**, thin; skinny. **6**, cold; aloof. **7**, (*of a reception, tone, etc.*) cold; chilly. **8**, dry; dull. —вы́йти сухи́м из воды́, to emerge unscathed. —держа́ть по́рох сухи́м, to keep one's powder dry. *See also* суха́я.

сухопа́рый *adj., colloq.* lean; skinny.

сухопу́тный *adj.* land (*attrib.*); ground (*attrib.*); overland.

су́хость *n.f.* **1**, dryness. **2**, coldness; aloofness.

сухоща́вый *adj., colloq.* lean; skinny.

сучёный *adj.* twisted.

сучи́ть *v. impfv.* [*pres.* сучу́, су́чишь] **1**, to twist. **2**, (*with instr.*) *colloq.* to flap.

сучкова́тый *adj.* **1**, knotty. **2**, gnarled.

сучо́к [*gen.* -чка́] *n.* **1**, twig. **2**, knot (*in wood*). —без сучка́, без задо́ринки, without a hitch.

су́ша *n.* land; dry land.

су́ше *adj., comp. of* сухо́й.

суше́ние *n.* drying.

сушёный *adj.* dried.

суше́нье *n.* dried fruit.

суши́лка [*gen. pl.* -лок] *n.* **1**, dryer. **2**, drying room.

суши́льный *adj.* drying (*attrib.*).

суши́льня [*gen. pl.* -лен] *n.* drying room.

суши́ть *v. impfv.* [*pfv.* вы́сушить; *pres.* сушу́, су́шишь] to dry; make dry. —суши́ться, *refl.* to dry; become dry.

су́шка [*gen. pl.* -шек] *n.* **1**, drying. **2**, bagel.

сушь *n.f., colloq.* **1**, dry spell. **2**, dry place; dry land. **3**, dry reading matter.

суще́ственно *adv.* substantially.

суще́ственный *adj.* **1**, substantial; fundamental. **2**, vital; essential. —суще́ственным о́бразом, substantially.

существи́тельный *adj., in* и́мя существи́тельное, noun. —существи́тельное, *n.* noun.

существо́ *n.* **1**, essence; gist. **2**, being; creature. —по существу́, **1**, in essence; in effect; essentially. **2**, to the point: говори́ть по существу́, to speak to the point.

существова́ние *n.* existence.

существова́ть *v. impfv.* [*pres.* -ству́ю, -ству́ешь] to exist.

су́щий *adj.* **1**, *obs.* existing. **2**, *colloq.* pure; utter; downright; absolute.

су́щность *n.f.* essence. —в су́щности, **1**, essentially; in essence. **2**, *in* в су́щности говоря́, as a matter of fact; as a practical matter. —по са́мой свое́й су́щности, by its (their) very nature.

сфабрикова́ть *v. pfv.* [*infl.* -ку́ю, -ку́ешь] *colloq.* **1**, to forge. **2**, *pfv. of* фабрикова́ть (*in sense #3*).

сфальши́вить *v., pfv. of* фальши́вить.

сфантази́ровать *v., pfv. of* фантази́ровать (*in sense #2*).

сфе́ра *n.* **1**, sphere. **2**, *fig.* sphere; realm; domain. **3**, *pl.* circles: деловы́е сфе́ры, business circles. —сфе́ра влия́ния, sphere of influence.

сфери́ческий *adj.* spherical.

сферо́ид *n.* spheroid. —сфероида́льный, *adj.* spheroidal.

сфинкс *n.* sphinx.

сформирова́ть *v., pfv. of* формирова́ть. —сформирова́ться, *refl., pfv. of* формирова́ться.

сформова́ть *v., pfv. of* формова́ть.

сформули́ровать *v., pfv. of* формули́ровать.

сфотографи́ровать *v., pfv. of* фотографи́ровать. —сфотографи́роваться, *refl., pfv. of* фотографи́роваться.

схвати́ть [*infl.* схвачу́, схва́тишь] *v., pfv. of* хвата́ть (*in sense #1*) *and* схва́тывать. —схвати́ться, *refl., pfv. of* хвата́ться (*in sense #1*) *and* схва́тываться.

схва́тка [*gen. pl.* -ток] *n.* **1**, fight; skirmish. **2**, *pl.* cramps; pains.

схва́тывать *v. impfv.* [*pfv.* схвати́ть] **1**, to seize; grab. **2**, *colloq.* to catch (a cold, illness, etc.). **3**, (*of an illness*) to strike: его́ схвати́ла подагра, he was stricken with gout. **4**, *fig., colloq.* to grasp; comprehend. **5**, *fig.* (*of an artist, portrait, etc.*) to capture. —схва́тываться, *refl.* **1**, (*with* за + *acc.*) to seize; grab; grasp; snatch. **2**, to fight; battle; (*with* с + *instr.*) grapple (with); come to grips (with).

схе́ма *n.* **1**, diagram; chart. **2**, outline. **3**, *electronics* circuit.

схемати́ческий *adj.* **1**, schematic; diagrammatic. **2**, sketchy.

схи́зма *n.* schism.

схитри́ть *v., pfv. of* хитри́ть.

схлы́нуть *v. pfv.* **1**, (*of water*) to rush back; sweep back. **2**, *fig.* (*of emotions*) to subside.

сход *n.* **1**, going down; descent. **2**, coming off. **3**, *colloq.* descent; slope. **4**, *pre-rev.* meeting; assembly.

сходи́ть[1] *v. impfv.* [*pfv.* сойти́; *pres.* схожу́, схо́дишь] **1**, to go down; descend. **2**, to get off; disembark. **3**, (*with* с + *gen.*) to go off (a road, tracks, etc.). **4**, (*of paint, dirt, skin, etc.*) to come off; peel off. **5**, (*with* за + *acc.*) to pass for; be taken for. **6**, *colloq.* to go; come off: всё сошло́ хорошо́, everything went well. —сходи́ть на бе́рег, to go ashore. —сходи́ть на нет, to come to naught. —сходи́ть с рук, to go unnoticed; go unpunished; (*with dat.*) get away with: э́то сходи́ло ему́ с рук, he got away with it. —сходи́ть с ума́, to go out of one's mind; lose one's mind; go mad.

сходи́ть[2] *v. pfv.* [*infl.* схожу́, схо́дишь] to go (*to a certain place and return*).

сходи́ться *v.r. impfv.* [*pfv.* сойти́сь; *pres.* схожу́сь, схо́дишься] **1**, to meet. **2**, to gather. **3**, (*with* с + *instr.*) to become friends (with); become intimate (with). **4**, to coincide. **5**, to tally. **6**, *colloq.* to agree. —сходи́ться (*or* не сходи́ться) во вку́сах, to have similar (*or* different) tastes. —сходи́ться (*or* не сходи́ться) хара́ктерами, to be compatible (*or* incompatible).

схо́дка [*gen. pl.* -док] *n., pre-rev.* meeting; assembly.

схо́дни [*gen.* -ней] *n. pl.* gangplank.

схо́дный *adj.* **1**, similar. **2**, *colloq.* (*of a price*) fair; reasonable.

схо́дство *n.* similarity; likeness; resemblance.

схо́жесть *n.f., colloq.* similarity; resemblance.

схо́жий *adj., colloq.* similar.

сца́пать *v. pfv., colloq.* to grab; grab hold of.

сцара́пывать *v. impfv.* [*pfv.* сцара́пать] to scrape off.

сцеди́ть [*infl.* сцежу́, сце́дишь] *v., pfv. of* сце́живать.

сце́живать *v. impfv.* [*pfv.* сцеди́ть] to strain off.

сце́на *n.* **1**, stage: выступа́ть на сце́не, to appear on (the) stage. **2**, scene: фина́льная сце́на, the final scene. **3**, *colloq.* scene: устро́ить сце́ну, to make a scene. —сойти́ со сце́ны, 1, to retire from the stage. 2, (of a play) no longer be performed. 3, fig. to pass from the scene. —уйти́ со сце́ны, to retire from the stage. —яви́ться/появи́ться/вы́ступить на сце́ну, to appear on the scene.

сцена́рий n. scenario. —сцена́рист, n. scenario writer.

сцени́ческий adj. stage (attrib.); scenic.

сцени́чный adj. suitable for the stage.

сцепи́ть [infl. сцеплю́, сце́пишь] v., pfv. of сцепля́ть. —сцепи́ться, refl., pfv. of сцепля́ться.

сцепле́ние n. 1, coupling. 2, clutch. 3, fig. combination (of circumstances).

сцепля́ть v. impfv. [pfv. сцепи́ть] to couple. —сцепля́ться, refl. 1, to engage; mesh. 2, colloq. to grapple; be locked in combat.

сцепно́й adj. coupling (attrib.).

счастли́вец [gen. -вца] n.m. [fem. -вица] lucky person.

счастли́во also, сча́стливо adv. 1, happily. 2, luckily: счастли́во отде́латься, to get off lucky. —interj. good luck!; all the best!

счастли́вчик n., colloq. = счастли́вец.

счастли́вый adj. [short form сча́стлив or счастли́в] 1, happy. 2, lucky; fortunate. —счастли́вого пути́!, bon voyage!

сча́стье n. 1, happiness. 2, (good) luck; (good) fortune. Ва́ше сча́стье, что..., you are lucky/fortunate that... —к сча́стью; по сча́стью, fortunately. —на сча́стье, 1, for (good) luck. 2, (with gen.) luckily for. На моё сча́стье, luckily for me.

счесть [infl. сочту́, сочтёшь; past счёл, сочла́, сочло́] v., pfv. of счита́ть (in sense #3). —сче́сться, refl., pfv. of счита́ться (in sense #4).

счёт [2nd loc. на счету́; pl. счета́, except in sense #6] n. 1, counting: вести́ счёт (+ dat.), to keep count of. 2, calculation; reckoning. 3, account. 4, bill; (in a restaurant) check. 5, sports score. 6, pl. accounts; scores: своди́ть счёты с, to settle scores with. —без счёту, countless. —в два счёта, colloq. in a jiffy. —в коне́чном счёте, in the final analysis. —в счёт (+ gen.), against; to be applied against. —за счёт (+ gen.), 1, by using; by taking from. 2, at the expense of. —на счёт, 1, (with gen.) at the expense of. 2, (with a possessive pronoun) about; concerning. —на счету́, in ка́ждый ... на счету́, every ... counts. —на хоро́шем счету́ у, in good standing with; in the good graces of. —на э́тот счёт, on this point; on that score. —счёту нет (+ dat.), more than one knows what to do with.

счётный adj. 1, calculating (attrib.): счётная маши́на, adding machine. 2, accounts (attrib.): счётная кни́га, accounts book.

счетово́д n. bookkeeper; accountant. —счетово́дный, adj. bookkeeping (attrib.); accounting (attrib.). —счетово́дство, n. bookkeeping; accounting.

счётчик n. 1, meter: га́зовый счётчик, gas meter. 2, counter (person). —счётчик Ге́йгера, Geiger counter.

счёты [gen. -тов] n. pl. abacus.

счисле́ние n. 1, obs. calculation; computation. 2, math. numbering: десяти́чная систе́ма счисле́ния, decimal system. 3, naut. reckoning: счисле́ние пути́, dead reckoning.

счи́стить [infl. -щу, -стишь] v., pfv. of счища́ть.

счи́танные adj. only a few.

счита́ть v. impfv. 1, [pfv. сосчита́ть] to count: счи́тать до десяти́, to count to ten. Не счита́я..., not counting... 2, to do arithmetic: счита́ть в уме́, to do figures in one's head. 3, [pfv. счесть] (with instr. or за + acc.) to consider; regard; look upon: счита́ть что-нибудь ну́жным, to consider something necessary; счита́ть за честь, to consider it an honor. 4, to believe; think; feel: я счита́ю, что..., I believe that... —счита́ться, refl. 1, [pfv. посчита́ться] (with с + instr.) to consider; take into consideration; take into account. Не счита́ться с, to ignore. 2, (with instr.) to be considered; be regarded. 3, passive of счита́ть: э́то не счита́ется, that doesn't count. Счита́ется, что..., it is believed (or thought) that... 4, [pfv. сче́сться] (with с + instr.) colloq. to settle (up) with.

счи́тывание n., computer science reading; readout.

счища́ть v. impfv. [pfv. счи́стить] to clear away.

США abbr. of Соединённые Шта́ты Аме́рики, United States of America; USA.

сшиба́ть v. impfv. [pfv. сшиби́ть] colloq. 1, to knock off. 2, to knock down. —сшиба́ться, refl., colloq. 1, to collide. 2, to get into a fight.

сшиби́ть [infl. -бу́, -бёшь; past сшиб, -ла] v., pfv. of сшиба́ть. —сшиби́ться, refl., pfv. of сшиба́ться.

сшива́ть v. impfv. [pfv. сшить] 1, to sew together. 2, med. to suture. 3, to join together; fasten together. 4, to make (by fastening together planks).

сшить [infl. сошью́, сошьёшь] v., pfv. of шить and сшива́ть.

съеда́ть v. impfv. [pfv. съесть] to eat; eat up.

съеде́ние n. being eaten alive. —отдава́ть or оставля́ть на съеде́ние (+ dat.), 1, to leave to be eaten alive by. 2, fig. to leave at the mercy of.

съедо́бный adj. edible.

съёживаться v.r. impfv. [pfv. съёжиться] 1, to shrivel; shrink. 2, to huddle up; cringe. 3, to become haggard.

съёжиться v.r., pfv. of ёжиться and съёживаться.

съезд n. convention; congress.

съе́здить v. pfv. [infl. съе́зжу, съе́здишь] to go (to a place and return); make a trip (to).

съезжа́ть v. impfv. [pfv. съе́хать] (with с + gen.) 1, to go down; ride down; drive down. 2, to go off; drive off. 3, obs. to leave; drive off. 4, colloq. to move out. 5, colloq. to come off; slip off. —съезжа́ться, refl. 1, to meet; run into each other. 2, to gather; assemble.

съёмка [gen. pl. -мок] n. 1, taking down; removal. 2, survey; surveying: возду́шная съёмка, aerial survey. 3, shooting (of a picture).

съёмный adj. removable; detachable.

съёмочный adj., motion pictures shooting (attrib.). —съёмочная площа́дка, (movie) set.

съёмщик n. tenant; renter.

съестно́й adj. food (attrib.). —съестно́е, n. food; victuals.

съесть [infl. like есть] v., pfv. of есть (in sense #1) and съеда́ть.

съе́хать [infl. съе́ду, съе́дешь] v., pfv. of съезжа́ть. —съе́хаться, refl., pfv. of съезжа́ться.

съязви́ть v., pfv. of язви́ть (in sense #3).

сы́воротка n. 1, whey. 2, med. serum.

сы́гранность n.f. coordination; teamwork.

сыгра́ть v. pfv. 1, pfv. of игра́ть. 2, in сыгра́ть шу́тку с, to play a joke/trick on. —сыгра́ться, refl. to play well together; develop teamwork.

сы́змала *also,* **сы́змалу** *adv., colloq.* since childhood.

сы́знова *adv., colloq.* all over again; anew; afresh.

сын [*pl.* **сыновья́, -ве́й, -вья́м**] *n.* son.

сыни́шка *n.m., dim. of* сын.

сыно́вний *adj.* filial.

сыно́к [*gen.* -нка́] *n., colloq.* **1,** son. **2,** sonny.

сы́пать *v. impfv.* [*pres.* **сы́плю, сы́плешь**] **1,** to pour (a dry substance). **2,** (*with acc. or instr.*) to shower; rain (blows, insults, etc.); spout (words, information, etc.). **3,** *v.i.* (*of rain, snow, etc.*) to fall; come down. **4,** *in* сы́пать деньга́ми, to toss money around. —**сы́паться,** *refl.* **1,** (*of a dry substance*) to pour; spill. **2,** to flake off; peel off. **3,** to fly about. **4,** (*of rain, snow, etc.*) to fall; come down. **5,** *fig.* to rain down; stream in; pour in.

сыпно́й *adj., in* сыпно́й тиф, typhus.

сыпня́к [*gen.* -няка́] *n., colloq.* typhus.

сыпу́чий *adj.* friable; crumbly; loose. — **ме́ры сыпу́-чих тел,** dry measures. —**сыпу́чий песо́к,** quicksand.

сыпь *n.f.* rash.

сыр [*pl.* **сыры́**] *n.* cheese.

сыре́ть *v. impfv.* [*pfv.* **отсыре́ть**] to become damp.

сыре́ц [*gen.* -рца́] *n., usu. used in compounds,* product in its raw state: шёлк-сыре́ц, raw silk. Нефть-сыре́ц, crude oil.

сы́рник *n.* cheese pancake.

сы́рный *adj.* cheese (*attrib.*).

сыроёжка [*gen. pl.* -жек] *n.* a variety of mushroom; russula.

сыро́й *adj.* **1,** damp. **2,** (*of food*) raw; uncooked; (*of water*) unboiled. **3,** not completely cooked or baked; half-done. **4,** in rough form; unfinished.

сыромя́ть *n.f.* rawhide. —**сыромя́тный,** *adj.* rawhide.

сы́рость *n.f.* dampness.

сырьё *n.* raw material(s).

сыск *n., pre-rev.* criminal investigation.

сыска́ть *v. pfv.* [*infl.* **сыщу́, сы́щешь**] *colloq.* to find.

сыскно́й *adj., pre-rev.* of criminal investigation.

сы́тно *adv.* heartily. Сы́тно пое́сть, have a hearty meal.

сы́тный *adj.* (*of food or a meal*) filling.

сы́тость *n.f.* satiety.

сы́тый *adj.* full (*from eating*). —**сыт по го́рло, 1,** stuffed to the gills. **2,** (*with instr.*) sick and tired of.

сыч [*gen.* сыча́] *n.* little owl.

сычу́г [*gen.* -чуга́] *n.* **1,** fourth stomach of a ruminant animal. **2,** rennet.

сычу́жина *n.* rennin.

сычу́жный *adj.* rennet (*attrib.*). —**сычу́жный фер-ме́нт,** rennin.

сы́щик *n.* detective.

сэконо́мить *v., pfv. of* эконо́мить.

сэр *n.* sir.

сэт *n., tennis* set.

сюда́ *adv., expressing direction* here; this way.

сюже́т *n.* **1,** subject; subject matter. **2,** *lit.* plot. **3,** *colloq.* topic.

сюже́тный *adj.* **1,** of a plot: сюже́тное разви́тие, development of a plot. **2,** having a strong plot.

сюзере́н *n.* suzerain. —**сюзеренитёт,** *n.* suzerainty. —**сюзере́нный,** *adj.* suzerain.

сюи́та *n., music* suite.

сюрпри́з *n.* a surprise. —**сюрпри́зный,** *adj.* surprise (*attrib.*).

сюрреали́зм *n.* surrealism. —**сюрреали́ст,** *n.* surrealist. —**сюрреалисти́ческий,** *adj.* surrealistic.

сюрту́к [*gen.* -тука́] *n.* frock coat.

сюсю́канье *n., colloq.* lisp; lisping.

сюсю́кать *v. impfv., colloq.* to lisp.

сяк *adv., in* так и сяк; то так то сяк, **1,** this way or that; one way or the other. **2,** fair; so-so.

сям *adv., in* там и сям; то там то сям, here and there.

Т

Т, т *n. neut.* nineteenth letter of the Russian alphabet.

та *adj., fem. of* тот.

таба́к [*gen.* -бака́] *n.* tobacco. —**де́ло таба́к,** *colloq.* things are in a bad way; things are in a sorry state.

табаке́рка [*gen. pl.* -рок] *n.* snuffbox.

табаково́д *n.* tobacco grower. —**табаково́дство,** *n.* tobacco growing. —**табаково́дческий,** *adj.* tobacco-growing.

таба́чный *adj.* tobacco (*attrib.*).

та́бель *n.m.* **1,** table; chart. **2,** [*also,* та́бель успева́емости] report card. **3,** sign-out board. —*n.f., in* та́бель о ра́нгах, *hist.* Table of Ranks.

та́бельный *adj.* shown on a table. —**та́бельная дос-ка́,** time board. —**та́бельные часы́,** time clock.

та́бельщик *n.* one who records the hours worked by employees; timekeeper.

табле́тка [*gen. pl.* -ток] *n.* tablet; pill.

табли́ца *n.* table: табли́ца умноже́ния, multiplication table.

табли́чка [*gen. pl.* -чек] *n.* tablet; plaque.

табли́чный *adj.* tabular.

табло́ *n. indecl.* (electronic) indicator panel; scoreboard.

табльдо́т *n.* table d'hôte.

та́бор *n.* gypsy band.

табу́ *n. neut. indecl.* taboo.

табуля́тор *n.* tabulating machine; tabulator.

табу́н [*gen.* -буна́] *n.* herd; flock. —**табу́нщик,** *n.* herdsman.

табуре́т *n.* stool.

табуре́тка [*gen. pl.* -ток] *n.* stool.

та́волга *n.* meadowsweet.

таврёный *adj.* branded.

таври́ть *v. impfv.* to brand (cattle).

тавро́ [*pl.* та́вра, тавр, тавра́м] *n.* brand (*on cattle*).

тавтоло́гия *n.* tautology. —**тавтологи́ческий**, *adj.* tautological; redundant.

тага́н *n.* trivet.

таджи́к *n.m.* [*fem.* -жи́чка] Tadzhik. —**таджи́кский**, *adj.* Tadzhik.

таёжный *adj.* of the taiga; in the taiga.

таз [*2nd loc.* тазу́; *pl.* тазы́] *n.* **1,** basin. Умыва́льный таз, washbasin. **2,** pelvis.

та́зовый *adj.* pelvic. —**та́зовая кость**, hipbone.

таи́нственность *n.f.* mystery.

таи́нственный *adj.* **1,** mysterious. **2,** secret.

таи́нство *n.* **1,** *obs.* secret; mystery. **2,** sacrament.

таи́ть *v. impfv.* **1,** to conceal; hide. **2,** to harbor (a thought, feeling, grudge, etc.). **3,** *in* таи́ть в себе́, *fig.* to hold; be fraught with. —**таи́ться**, *refl.* **1,** to hide; be hiding. **2,** to lurk. **3,** to withhold information; not tell the whole story.

тайга́ *n.* taiga.

тайко́м *adv.* secretly; surreptitiously; on the sly. —**тайко́м от**, without the knowledge of; without telling.

тайм *n.* period (*of a game*).

та́йна *n.* **1,** secret: глубо́кая та́йна, a deep secret. Держа́ть (что́-нибудь) в та́йне, to keep (something) secret. **2,** mystery.

тайни́к [*gen.* -ника́] *n.* **1,** hiding place; cache. **2,** hideout; hideaway. —**в тайника́х се́рдца**, in the innermost recesses of one's heart.

та́йно *adv.* secretly; in secret.

та́йнопись *n.f.* secret writing.

та́йный *adj.* secret.

та́йский *adj.* Thai.

тайфу́н *n.* typhoon.

так *adv.* **1,** this way; that way; like this; like that: не говори́те так, don't talk like that. **2,** (*before short-form adjectives*) so: э́то не так стра́шно, it's not so terrible. **3,** so; true; correct: э́то не совсе́м так, that is not entirely correct. **4,** then; in that case. —*particle* so; then; thus; therefore. —**не так**, wrong; amiss: что́-то не так, something is wrong. —**не так ли?**, isn't that so?; don't you think so? —**так же**, (in) the same way. —**так же... как и**, as... as. —**так и быть**, so be it. —**так и не** (+ *verb*), never. —**так и так**, either way. —**так как**, since; inasmuch as. —**так себе́**, so-so. —**так что**, so; and so.

такела́ж *n., naut.* rigging.

та́кже *adv.* also; too; as well.

-таки *particle*, used for emphasis. —**всё-таки**, still; all the same. —**опя́ть-таки**, *see* опя́ть.

тако́в *indef. pron.* [*fem.* такова́; *neut.* таково́; *pl.* таковы́] **1,** such/that is; such/those are: таковы́ фа́кты, such are the facts; those are the facts. **2,** like that; the same; alike: все моряки́ таковы́, all sailors are like that. —**и был тако́в**, *colloq.* and off he went; and away he went.

таково́й *indef. pron.* such; the same: за отсу́тствием таково́го, in the absence of the same. —**как таково́й**, as such.

тако́й *indef. adj.* such; such a: тако́й челове́к, such a person; таки́е ве́щи, such things. —*indef. pron.* the sort of person: он тако́й, что..., he is the sort of person who... —*adv.* (*used before long-form adjectives only*) so; such: она́ така́я краси́вая, she is so beautiful;

така́я краси́вая де́вушка, such a beautiful girl. —**и всё тако́е**, *colloq.* and all that. —**кто тако́й?**, who is it? Кто вы тако́й?, who are you? —**таки́м о́бразом**, *see* о́браз. —**тако́е**, such a thing. —**тако́й же**, the same. —**тако́й же** (+ *adj.*) **как**, as... as. —**что ж (тут) тако́е** (*or* тако́го)?, what of it? —**что тако́е?**, what's the matter?; what's going on? —**что тако́е** (+ *nom.*), what is a...? —**что э́то тако́е?**, what is this?

тако́й-то *adj.* **1,** so-and-so. **2,** such and such.

та́кса *n.* **1,** (set) rate. **2,** dachshund.

такси́ *n. neut. indecl.* taxi; cab.

таксо́метр *n.* taximeter.

таксомото́р *n.* taxi.

таксоно́мия *n.* taxonomy. —**таксономи́ческий**, *adj.* taxonomic.

такт *n.* **1,** *music* bar; measure. **2,** rhythm; beat; time: в такт, in time. В такт му́зыке, in time to the music. Отбива́ть такт, to beat time. Сби́ться с та́кта, to lose the beat. **3,** tact.

та́к-таки *particle, colloq.* **1,** still; anyway. **2,** really. —**та́к-таки всё**, absolutely everything.

та́ктик *n.* tactician.

та́ктика *n.* tactics. —**такти́ческий**, *adj.* tactical.

такти́чный *adj.* tactful. —**такти́чно**, *adv.* tactfully. —**такти́чность**, *n.f.* tactfulness; tact.

тала́нт *n.* talent. —**тала́нтливый**, *adj.* talented.

талисма́н *n.* talisman.

та́лия *n.* waist.

та́ллий *n.* thallium.

талму́д *n.* Talmud. —**талмуди́зм**, *n.* dogmatism; fundamentalism; talmudism.

талмуди́ст *n.* **1,** Talmudic scholar. **2,** dogmatist; fundamentalist. —**талмуди́стский**, *adj.* dogmatic; doctrinaire. —**талмуди́ческий**, *adj.* Talmudic.

тало́н *n.* coupon. —**поса́дочный тало́н**, boarding pass.

та́лый *adj.* melting; melted.

тальк *n.* **1,** talc; talcum. **2,** talcum powder. —**та́льковый**, *adj.* talc (*attrib.*); talcum (*attrib.*).

там *adv.* there; in that place. —**там, где**, where; the place where. —**там же**, in that place; (*in footnotes*) ibid.

тамада́ *n.m.* toastmaster.

тамари́нд *n.* tamarind.

тамари́ск *n.* tamarisk.

та́мбур *n.* **1,** vestibule. **2,** platform (*of a railway car*). **3,** chain stitch.

тамбури́н *n.* tambourine.

та́мбурный *adj., in* та́мбурный шов; та́мбурная стро́чка, chain stitch.

тамо́женник *n.* customs official. —**тамо́женный**, *adj.* customs (*attrib.*).

тамо́жня *n.* customs; custom house.

та́мошний *adj., colloq.* of that place; local.

тампо́н *n.* tampon.

тамта́м *n.* tom-tom.

тана́гра *n.* tanager.

та́нгенс *n., trig.* tangent. —**тангенциа́льный**, *adj.* tangential.

та́нго *n. indecl.* tango.

та́ндем (дэ) *n.* tandem.

та́нец [*gen.* -нца] *n.* **1,** dance. **2,** *pl.* dance (*affair with dancing*): пойти́ на та́нцы, to go to a dance.

тани́н *n.* tannin. —**тани́нный**, *adj.* tannic.

танк *n.* **1,** *mil.* tank. **2,** tank; cistern.

та́нкер *n.* tanker.

танке́тка [*gen. pl.* -ток] *n.* **1**, *mil.* light tank. **2**, wedge heel. **3**, *pl.* wedge-heeled shoes.

танки́ст *n.* member of a tank crew.

та́нковый *adj., mil.* tank (*attrib.*).

танта́л *n.* tantalum.

танцева́льный *adj.* dance (*attrib.*); dancing (*attrib.*): танцева́льный ве́чер, dance.

танцева́ть *v. impfv.* [*pres.* -цу́ю, -цу́ешь] to dance.

танцо́вщик *n.m.* [*fem.* -щица] (ballet) dancer.

танцо́р *n.* dancer.

тапёр *n.* pianist engaged for a dance.

тапио́ка *n.* tapioca.

тапи́р *n.* tapir.

та́почки [*gen.* -чек] *n. pl.* [*sing.* та́почка] **1**, slippers. **2**, sneakers.

та́ра *n.* **1**, container (*for safeguarding or transporting*). **2**, wrapping material; packing material. **3**, *comm.* tare.

тараба́нить *v. impfv., colloq.* to clatter.

тараба́рщина *n., colloq.* gibberish.

тарака́н *n.* cockroach.

тара́н *n.* **1**, battering-ram. **2**, *mech.* ram.

тара́нить *v. impfv.* [*pfv.* протара́нить] to ram.

таранта́с *n.* large four-wheeled carriage; tarantass.

тара́нтул *n.* tarantula.

тара́нь *n.f.* roach (*fish*).

тарара́м *n., colloq.* uproar; hubbub; hullabaloo.

тарата́йка [*gen. pl.* -та́ек] *n.* two-wheeled carriage.

тарато́рить *v. impfv., colloq.* to jabber; chatter.

тарахте́ть *v. impfv.* [*pres.* -хчу́, -хти́шь] *colloq.* **1**, to clatter. **2**, *fig.* to chatter.

тара́щить *v. impfv.* [*pfv.* вы́таращить] *colloq., in* тара́щить глаза́, to stare; gape.

таре́лка [*gen. pl.* -лок] *n.* **1**, plate; dish. **2**, *pl.* cymbals. —быть в свое́й таре́лке, to be in one's element. —быть не в свое́й таре́лке, **1**, to be out of sorts; be not quite oneself. **2**, to feel ill at ease; feel uneasy.

таре́лочка [*gen. pl.* -чек] *n., dim. of* таре́лка. —стрельба́ по таре́лочкам, trapshooting.

тари́ф *n.* **1**, tariff. **2**, rate. —**тари́фный**, *adj.* tariff (*attrib.*).

та́ры-ба́ры *n. pl. indecl., colloq.* chatter; tittle-tattle.

таска́ть *v. impfv.* **1**, *indeterm. of* тащи́ть. **2**, to carry. **3**, *colloq.* to wear (for a long time). **4**, (*with* за + *acc.*) *colloq.* to pull (by): таска́ть (кого́-нибудь) за́ уши, to pull (someone) by the ears. —**таска́ться**, *refl., colloq.* **1**, to wander; amble. **2**, (*with* по) to make the rounds of. **3**, to hang around. **4**, (*with* с + *instr.*) to carry around (*on one's person*). **5**, (*with* за + *instr.*) to chase after (women). **6**, (*with* с + *instr.*) to have an affair (with).

тасова́ть *v. impfv.* [*pfv.* стасова́ть; *pres.* -су́ю, -су́ешь] to shuffle (cards).

тасо́вка *n.* shuffling; shuffle (*of cards*).

ТАСС *n.m.* Tass (*abbr. of* Телегра́фное Аге́нство Сове́тского Сою́за).

тата́рин [*pl.* тата́ры, тата́р] *n.m.* [*fem.* тата́рка] Tatar. —**тата́рский**, *adj.* Tatar.

тату́ировать *v. impfv. & pfv.* [*pres.* -рую, -руешь] to tattoo.

татуиро́вка *n.* **1**, tatooing. **2**, tattoo.

тафта́ *n.* taffeta. —**тафтяно́й**, *adj.* taffeta.

тахо́метр *n.* tachometer.

тахта́ *n.f.* ottoman; divan.

тача́нка [*gen. pl.* -нок] *n.* **1**, light open carriage. **2**, machine-gun cart.

тача́ть *v. impfv.* [*pfv.* вы́тачать *or* стача́ть] to stitch.

та́чка [*gen. pl.* -чек] *n.* wheelbarrow.

тащи́ть *v. impfv.* [*pfv.* потащи́ть; *pres.* тащу́, та́щишь] **1**, to pull; draw; tow. **2**, to drag; haul; lug. **3**, [*pfv.* вы́тащить] to pull out. **4**, [*pfv.* вы́тащить] to drag (someone) somewhere against his will. **5**, [*pfv.* вы́тащить *or* стащи́ть] *colloq.* to swipe; pilfer. —**тащи́ться**, *refl.* **1**, to drag along; trail along (the ground). **2**, *colloq.* to drag oneself along. **3**, *colloq.* to go (somewhere) reluctantly; drag oneself. *See also* таска́ть.

та́яние *n.* melting.

та́ять *v. impfv.* [*pfv.* раста́ять; *pres.* та́ю, та́ешь] **1**, to melt; thaw. **2**, (*of clouds, smoke, etc.*) to dissipate. **3**, *fig.* to fade; wane; dwindle; ebb. **4**, *fig.* to fade from view. **5**, [*impfv. only*] (*of a person*) to waste away.

тварь *n.f., obs.* **1**, creature. **2**, wretch; bum.

тверде́ть *v. impfv.* [*pfv.* затверде́ть] to harden; become hard.

тверди́ть *v. impfv.* [*pres.* твержу́, тверди́шь] **1**, to repeat (*or* keep saying) over and over again; (*with* о) talk endlessly about. **2**, [*pfv.* затверди́ть *or* вы́твердить] to memorize (*through repetition*).

твёрдо *adv.* firmly; firm. Твёрдо вы́учить, to learn thoroughly. Твёрдо запо́мнить, to remember well.

твёрдока́менный *adj.* callous; insensitive; hard-boiled.

твердоло́бый *adj., colloq.* **1**, thickheaded. **2**, dyed-in-the-wool.

твёрдость *n.f.* **1**, hardness; firmness. **2**, *fig.* resoluteness; steadfastness.

твёрдый *adj.* [*comp.* тве́рже] **1**, hard. **2**, solid. **3**, firm. **4**, fixed; set. **5**, *fig.* steadfast; resolute. —**твёрдый знак**, hard sign (ъ).

тверды́ня *n.* **1**, stronghold. **2**, *fig.* bulwark.

тве́рже *adj., comp. of* твёрдый.

твид *n.* tweed.

твой [*infl. like* мой] *poss. adj. & pron.* your; yours (*familiar*).

творе́ние *n.* **1**, *obs.* creation; creating. **2**, creation; product; work. **3**, *obs.* creature; being.

творе́ц [*gen.* -рца́] *n.* creator; maker.

твори́тельный *adj., in* твори́тельный паде́ж, instrumental case.

твори́ть *v. impfv.* [*pfv.* сотвори́ть] **1**, to create. **2**, to perform; do. **3**, *in* твори́ть чудеса́, to work miracles. —**твори́ться**, *refl.* [*impfv. only*] *colloq.* to be going on.

творо́г [*gen.* -рога́] *n.* **1**, curds. **2**, cottage cheese. *Also*, тво́рог [*gen.* тво́рога].

творо́жник *n.* curd pancake; cottage-cheese pancake.

тво́рческий *adj.* creative.

тво́рчество *n.* **1**, creative activity. **2**, works (*of an author*).

те *adj., pl. of* тот.

т.е. *abbr. of* то есть, that is; i.e.

теа́тр *n.* **1**, theater: идти́ в теа́тр, to go to the theater. **2**, *mil.* theater: теа́тр вое́нных де́йствий, theater of (military) operations.

театра́л *n.m.* [*fem.* -тра́лка] theatergoer; playgoer.

театра́льный *adj.* **1**, theater (*attrib.*); theatrical. **2**, overly dramatic; histrionic. —**театра́льность**, *n.f.* theatrics; histrionics.

тебе́ *pron., dat. & prepl. of* ты.

тебя́ *pron., gen. & acc. of* ты.

тевто́н *n.* Teuton. —**тевто́нский,** *adj.* Teutonic.

теза́урус *n.* thesaurus.

те́зис (тэ) *n.* thesis.

тёзка [*gen. pl.* -зок] *n.m.* & *f.* namesake.

тейзм (тэ) *n.* theism. —**тейст,** *n.* theist. —**теисти́ческий,** *adj.* theistic.

текст *n.* **1,** text. **2,** *music* words; lyrics; libretto.

тексти́ль *n.m.* textiles. —**тексти́льный,** *adj.* textile (*attrib.*). —**тексти́льщик,** *n.* textile worker.

текстово́й *adj.* textual.

текстуа́льный *adj.* **1,** textual. **2,** literal; word-for-word.

теку́честь *n.f.* **1,** fluidity. **2,** fluctuation. **3,** turnover (*of personnel*).

теку́чий *adj.* **1,** fluid; flowing; running. **2,** fluctuating; constantly changing.

теку́щий *adj.* **1,** current; present. **2,** routine; everyday. —**теку́щий ремо́нт,** routine repairs; preventive maintenance. —**теку́щий счёт,** (liquid) bank account; checking account.

телеви́дение *n.* television. —**телевизио́нный,** *adj.* television (*attrib.*).

телеви́зор *n.* television set.

теле́га *n.* cart; wagon.

телегра́мма *n.* telegram.

телегра́ф *n.* **1,** telegraph. **2,** telegraph office.

телеграфи́ровать *v. impfv.* & *pfv.* [*pres.* -рую, -руешь] to telegraph; wire; cable.

телеграфи́ст *n.* telegraph operator; telegrapher. —**телегра́фия,** *n.* telegraphy.

телегра́фный *adj.* telegraph (*attrib.*); telegraphic.

теле́жка [*gen. pl.* -жек] *n.* light cart; handcart.

телезри́тель *n.m.* (television) viewer.

телека́мера *n.* television camera.

телеме́тр *n.* telemeter. —**телеметри́я,** *n.* telemetry.

телёнок [*gen.* -нка; *pl.* теля́та, теля́т] *n.* calf.

телеобъекти́в *n.* telephoto lens.

телеоло́гия *n.* teleology. —**телеологи́ческий,** *adj.* teleological.

телепа́тия *n.* telepathy. —**телепати́ческий,** *adj.* telepathic.

телепереда́ча *n.* **1,** television transmission. **2,** telecast.

телеско́п *n.* telescope. —**телескопи́ческий,** *adj.* telescopic. —**телеско́пный,** *adj.* telescope (*attrib.*).

теле́сный *adj.* **1,** bodily; corporal. **2,** flesh-colored. **3,** corporeal.

телесту́дия *n.* television studio.

телета́йп *n.* teletype.

телефо́н *n.* telephone. —**телефо́н-автома́т,** *n.* public telephone; pay phone.

телефони́ровать *v. impfv.* & *pfv.* [*pres.* -рую, -руешь] (*with dat.*) to telephone; phone; call.

телефони́ст *n.m.* [*fem.* -и́стка] telephone operator.

телефони́я *n.* telephony.

телефо́нный *adj.* **1,** telephone (*attrib.*). **2,** telephonic.

теле́ц [*gen.* -льца́] *n.* **1,** *obs.* calf. **2,** *cap.* Taurus.

тели́ться *v.r. impfv.* [*pfv.* отели́ться; *pres.* те́лится] to calve.

тёлка [*gen. pl.* -лок] *n.* heifer.

теллу́р *n.* tellurium.

те́ло [*pl.* тела́, тел, тела́м] *n.* body. —**держа́ть в чёрном те́ле,** to work (someone) to the bone. —**душо́й и те́лом,** utterly; totally; body and soul. —**ни душо́й ни те́лом не винова́т,** completely innocent.

телогре́йка [*gen. pl.* -гре́ек] *n.* padded jacket.

телодвиже́ние *n.* body movement; gesture.

телосложе́ние *n.* build; physique.

телохрани́тель *n.m.* bodyguard.

те́льный *adj., colloq.* worn next to the skin.

те́льце *n.* **1,** [*pl.* те́льца, те́лец] little body. **2,** [*pl.* тельца́, теле́ц] corpuscle.

теля́тина *n.* veal.

теля́чий [*fem.* -чья] *adj.* **1,** calf (*attrib.*); calf's. **2,** veal (*attrib.*). —**теля́чий восто́рг,** childish glee.

тем *adj., instr. sing.* & *dat. pl.* of **тот.** —*adv., used with comp. degree of adjectives:* so much the: **тем лу́чше,** so much the better. **2,** (*with* **чем**) the... the: **тем ра́ньше, тем лу́чше,** the sooner the better. —**тем бо́лее,** *see* **бо́лее.** —**тем не ме́нее,** nevertheless. —**тем са́мым,** thus; thereby.

те́ма *n.* **1,** subject; topic; theme. **2,** *music* theme: **те́ма с вариа́циями,** theme with variations.

тема́тика *n.* subject matter. —**темати́ческий,** *adj.* thematic; topical.

тембр (тэ) *n.* timbre.

те́мень *n.f., colloq.* darkness.

темне́ть *v. impfv.* **1,** [*pfv.* потемне́ть] to become dark; darken. **2,** [*pfv.* стемне́ть] *impers.* to get dark: темне́ет, it is getting dark. **3,** [*impfv. only*] (*of anything dark*) to appear; loom.

темни́ть *v. impfv.* to darken; make darker.

темни́ца *n., obs.* prison; dungeon.

темно́ *adj., used predicatively* dark: в ко́мнате бы́ло темно́, it was dark in the room.

тёмно- *prefix, used with colors,* dark: тёмно-зелёный, dark green.

темноволо́сый *adj.* dark-haired.

темноко́жий *adj.* dark-skinned.

темнота́ *n.* dark; darkness.

тёмный *adj.* **1,** dark. **2,** gloomy; dismal. **3,** obscure; vague. **4,** shady; unsavory; suspicious. **5,** ignorant.

темп *n.* **1,** *music* tempo. **2,** pace; rate; tempo.

те́мпера (тэ) *n.* tempera; distemper.

темпера́мент *n.* **1,** temperament. **2,** zest; verve; vibrancy. Челове́к с темпера́ментом, spirited/vibrant person.

темпера́ментный *adj.* **1,** temperamental. **2,** spirited; vibrant.

температу́ра *n.* temperature.

температу́рить *v. impfv., colloq.* to have a temperature.

температу́рный *adj.* temperature (*attrib.*).

темь *n.f., colloq.* darkness.

те́мя [*gen., dat.,* & *prepl.* те́мени; *instr.* те́менем] *n. neut.* top of the head.

тенденцио́зность (тэ, дэ) *n.f.* **1,** tendentiousness. **2,** biased attitude; biased approach.

тенденцио́зный (тэ, дэ) *adj.* **1,** tendentious. **2,** biased; slanted.

тенде́нция (тэ, дэ) *n.* **1,** tendency. **2,** bias.

те́ндер (тэ, дэ) *n.* **1,** *R.R.* tender. **2,** *naut.* cutter.

теневой *adj.* shady. —**теневая сторона́** (+ *gen.*), the dark side (of).

тенёта [*gen.* -нёт] *n. pl.* net; snare.

тени́стый *adj.* shady.

те́ннис (тэ) *n.* tennis. —**тенниси́ст,** *n.* tennis player.

те́нниска (тэ) [*gen. pl.* -сок] *n., colloq.* sport shirt; polo shirt.

те́ннисный (тэ) *adj.* tennis (*attrib.*).

те́нор [*pl.* тенора́] *n.* tenor. —теноро́вый, *adj.* tenor (*attrib.*).

тент (тэ) *n.* awning.

тень (*2nd loc.* тени́; *pl.* те́ни, тене́й, теня́м] *n.f.* 1, shade. 2, shadow. 3, *fig.* trace (of sadness, doubt, etc.) on one's face. 4, *fig.* grain; particle (*of truth*); shadow; particle (*of doubt*). 5, ghost. —броса́ть тень на (+ *acc.*), to cast aspersions on. —держа́ться в тени́, to remain in the background. —от него́ оста́лась одна́ тень, he is only a shadow of his former self.

теокра́тия (тэ) *n.* theocracy. —теократи́ческий, *adj.* theocratic.

теоло́гия (тэ) *n.* theology. —телеологи́ческий, *adj.* theological.

теоре́ма *n.* theorem.

теоретизи́ровать *v. impfv.* [*pres.* -рую, -руешь] to theorize.

теоре́тик *n.* theoretician; theorist.

теорети́ческий *adj.* theoretical. —теорети́чески, *adv.* theoretically.

тео́рия *n.* theory. —в тео́рии, in theory; theoretically.

теосо́фия (тэ) *n.* theosophy. —теосо́ф, *n.* theosophist. —теосо́фский; теософи́ческий, *adj.* theosophical.

тепе́решний *adj., colloq.* present; today's; present-day. Тепе́решняя жизнь, life today.

тепе́рь *adv.* now.

тепле́ть *v. impfv.* [*pfv.* потепле́ть] to become warm; get warm; warm up.

те́плиться *v.r. impfv.* to flicker; glimmer.

тепли́ца *n.* hothouse; greenhouse. —тепли́чный, *adj.* hothouse (*attrib.*).

тепло́ *n.* 1, warmth. 2, *physics* heat. —*adv.* warmly. —*adj.,* used predicatively warm: сего́дня тепло́, it is warm today; мне тепло́, I am warm.

теплова́тый *adj.* tepid; lukewarm.

теплово́з *n.* diesel locomotive.

теплово́й *adj.* heat (*attrib.*); thermal; caloric. —теплово́й уда́р, heatstroke.

теплокро́вный *adj.* warm-blooded.

тепломе́р *n.* calorimeter.

теплопрово́дный *adj.* heat-conducting.

теплосто́йкий *adj.* heat-resistant.

теплота́ *n.* 1, heat. 2, warmth.

теплохо́д *n.* motor ship.

теплу́шка [*gen. pl.* -шек] *n., colloq.* heated freight car used to carry people.

тёплый *adj.* 1, warm. 2, *fig.* warm; cordial. —тёплое месте́чко, soft job.

теплы́нь *n.f., colloq.* warm weather; mild weather.

терапе́вт *n.* internist. —терапевти́ческий, *adj.* therapeutic.

терапи́я *n.* 1, internal medicine. 2, therapy.

те́рбий *n.* terbium.

тереби́ть *v. impfv.* [*pres.* -блю́, -би́шь] 1, to pull at; tug at. 2, *fig., colloq.* to pester; nag.

те́рем [*pl.* терема́] *n.* tower in old Russian mansions where women were kept in seclusion.

тере́ть *v. impfv.* [*pres.* тру, трёшь; *past* тёр, -ла] 1, to rub. 2, to grate; grind. 3, to chafe (*trans. & intrans.*). —тере́ться, *refl.* [*pfv.* потере́ться] 1, *colloq.* to rub oneself. 2, (*with* о + *acc.*) to rub against. 3, *fig., colloq.* to hang around.

терза́ние *n.* torment; anguish; agony.

терза́ть *v. impfv.* 1, to tear apart; tear to pieces. 2, to torment. —терза́ться, *refl.* to suffer; be tormented.

тёрка [*gen. pl.* -рок] *n.* grater.

те́рмин *n.* term: техни́ческий те́рмин, technical term.

термина́л *n.* computer terminal.

терминоло́гия *n.* terminology.

терми́т *n.* 1, termite. 2, Thermit.

терми́ческий *adj.* thermal.

термодина́мика *n.* thermodynamics. —термодинами́ческий, *adj.* thermodynamic.

термо́метр *n.* thermometer.

термопа́ра *n.* thermocouple.

те́рмос (тэ) *n.* thermos (bottle).

термоста́т (тэ) *n.* thermostat.

термоя́дерный *adj.* thermonuclear.

тёрн *n.* 1, blackthorn. 2, sloe; sloes.

терни́стый *adj.* 1, *obs.* thorny. 2, *fig.* thorny; full of pitfalls: терни́стый путь, thorny path.

терно́вник *n.* blackthorn.

терпели́вый *adj.* patient. —терпели́во, *adv.* patiently. —терпели́вость, *n.f.* patience; forbearance.

терпе́ние *n.* patience.

терпе́ть *v. impfv.* [*pres.* терплю́, те́рпишь] 1, to endure; bear; stand. 2, to tolerate; stand; put up with. 3, [*pfv.* потерпе́ть] to suffer; sustain (a defeat, losses, etc.). 4, *in* вре́мя те́рпит, there is plenty of time; вре́мя не те́рпит, there is no time to be lost. —терпе́ться, *refl.* [*impfv. only*] used negatively with the dative case and inf. to be impatient (to); be unable to wait (to): ему́ не терпе́лось нача́ть, he couldn't wait to begin.

терпи́мо *adv.* with tolerance: относи́ться терпи́мо к, to be tolerant of. —*adj.,* used predicatively, *colloq.* tolerable; bearable.

терпи́мость *n.f.* tolerance. —дом терпи́мости, brothel.

терпи́мый *adj.* 1, tolerant. 2, tolerable.

те́рпкий *adj.* [*comp.* те́рпче] tart; acrid; astringent. —те́рпкость, *n.f.* astringency; acerbity.

террако́та (тэ) *n.* terra cotta.

террако́товый (тэ) *adj.* 1, terra-cotta. 2, reddish brown.

терра́са *n.* terrace. —терра́сный, *adj.* terraced.

территориа́льный *adj.* territorial.

террито́рия *n.* 1, territory. 2, premises; grounds (*of a building, factory, etc.*).

терро́р *n.* terror.

терроризи́ровать *v. impfv. & pfv.* [*pres.* -рую, -руешь] to terrorize.

террори́зм *n.* terrorism. —террори́ст, *n.* terrorist. —террористи́ческий, *adj.* terrorist (*attrib.*).

тёртый *adj.* 1, grated. 2, *fig., colloq.* experienced; worldly-wise. —тёртый кала́ч, experienced person; old hand.

те́рция (тэ) *n., music* third.

терье́р (тэ) *n.* terrier.

теря́ть *v. impfv.* [*pfv.* потеря́ть] 1, to lose. 2, to waste (time, words, etc.). 3, to shed (leaves). 4, *v.i.* (*with* в + *prepl.*) to lose; suffer; be the worse for: теря́ть в ве́се, to lose weight; теря́ть в перево́де, to suffer in translation; теря́ть в чьём-нибудь мне́нии, to go down in someone's estimation. —теря́ть го́лову, to lose one's head. Не теря́ть головы́, to keep one's head. —теря́ть из виду (*or* из ви́да), to lose sight of; lose track of. —теря́ть си́лу, 1, to lose one's vigor.

2, to expire; become invalid. —**теря́ть управле́ние, 1,** (*with instr.*) to lose control (of). **2,** to go out of control.

теря́ться *v.r. impfv.* [*pfv.* **потеря́ться**] **1,** to be lost; get lost. **2,** [*impfv. only*] (*of one's eyesight, memory, etc.*) to fail; fade. **3,** to become flustered; panic.

тёс *n.* boards; planks.

теса́к [*gen.* -**сака́**] *n.* cutlass.

теса́ние *n.* cutting; hewing.

тёсаный *adj.* cut; hewn.

теса́ть *v. impfv.* [*pres.* **тешу́, те́шешь**] to cut; hew.

тесёмка [*gen. pl.* -**мок**] *n.* braid.

теси́на *n.* board; plank.

тёска *n.* cutting; hewing.

тесло́ [*pl.* **тёсла, тёсел**] *n.* adz.

тесни́на *n.* **1,** gorge; ravine. **2,** defile.

тесни́ть *v. impfv.* **1,** [*pfv.* **потесни́ть**] to crowd; cramp. **2,** [*pfv.* **стесни́ть**] to constrict (the throat, chest, etc.). *Also impers.:* мне тесни́т грудь, I feel a tightness in my chest. **3,** [*impfv. only*] (*of clothes*) to be too tight. —**тесни́ться,** *refl.* **1,** [*pfv.* **стесни́ться**] to crowd; cluster. **2,** to crowd together; move closer to each other. **3,** to be crowded (together). **4,** to jostle each other.

те́сно *adv.* **1,** close together. **2,** closely: те́сно свя́занный, closely connected. —*adj., used predicatively* **1,** crowded: здесь те́сно, it is crowded here. **2,** tight: мне те́сно в плеча́х, it feels tight in the shoulders.

теснота́ *n.* crowded conditions; close quarters.

те́сный *adj.* [*short form* **те́сен, тесна́, те́сно**] **1,** crowded; cramped. **2,** tight; compact; close. **3,** *fig.* close; intimate. **4,** (*of clothes*) tight.

тесо́вый *adj.* board (*attrib.*); plank (*attrib.*).

те́сто *n.* dough. —**из друго́го те́ста,** of a different breed; made of different stuff.

тесть *n.m.* father-in-law (*wife's father*).

тесьма́ *n.* braid.

тётенька *n., colloq.* aunt; aunty.

те́терев [*pl.* **тетерева́**] *n.* black grouse.

тетеревя́тник *n.* [*often* **я́стреб-тетеревя́тник**] goshawk.

тете́рка [*gen. pl.* -**рок**] *n.* female black grouse; gray hen.

тете́ря *n.* **1,** *regional* black grouse. **2,** *colloq., in* со́нная тете́ря, sleepyhead; лени́вая тете́ря, lazybones.

тетива́ *n.* bowstring.

тётка [*gen. pl.* -**ток**] *n.* aunt.

тетра́дка [*gen. pl.* -**док**] *n.* notebook.

тетра́дный *adj.* notebook (*attrib.*).

тетра́дь *n.f.* notebook.

тётушка *n., dim. of* тётка *and* тётя.

тётя [*gen. pl.* -**тей**] *n.* aunt.

тёфтели [*gen.* -**лей**] *n. pl.* meatballs.

техне́ций *n.* technetium.

те́хник *n.* technician.

те́хника *n.* **1,** technology. **2,** technique. **3,** (technical) equipment.

те́хникум *n.* technical school.

техни́ческий *adj.* technical. —**техни́чески,** *adv.* technically.

техно́лог *n.* **1,** technologist. **2,** production engineer.

технологи́ческий *adj.* **1,** technological. **2,** production (*attrib.*): технологи́ческий пото́к, production line. —**технологи́ческая ка́рта,** production chart; flow sheet.

техноло́гия *n.* technology; engineering.

тече́ние *n.* **1,** flow; flowing. **2,** current: по тече́нию; про́тив тече́ния, with/against the current (*or* tide). **3,** *fig.* course (*of events, an illness, etc.*). **4,** *fig.* trend; tendency. —**в тече́ние** (+ *gen.*), **1,** in the course of; during. **2,** for; over a period of. **3,** within (a certain amount of time). —**с тече́нием вре́мени,** with the passage of time; in the course of time.

те́чка *n.* heat (*in animals*).

течь[1] *v. impfv.* [*pres.* **теку́, течёшь, ...теку́т;** *past* **тёк, текла́, текло́**] **1,** to flow. **2,** to stream. **3,** to leak. **4,** *fig.* (*of time, life, etc.*) to pass; flow by. —**у меня́ из носу течёт,** my nose is running. —**у меня́ кровь течёт из носу,** my nose is bleeding.

течь[2] *n.f.* leak: дать течь, to spring a leak.

те́шить *v. impfv.* [*pfv.* **поте́шить**] *colloq.* **1,** to amuse; entertain. **2,** to gratify; please. **3,** to console. —**те́шиться,** *refl.* **1,** to amuse oneself. **2,** (*with* над) *colloq.* to make fun of; poke fun at. **3,** (*with instr.*) to console oneself (in *or* by); take consolation (in).

тёща *n.* mother-in-law (*wife's mother*).

тиа́ра *n.* tiara.

тибе́тский *adj.* Tibetan.

ти́гель [*gen.* -**гля**] *n.m.* crucible.

тигр *n.* tiger.

тигрёнок [*gen.* -**нка;** *pl.* **тигря́та, тигря́т**] *n.* tiger cub.

тигри́ца *n.* tigress.

тигро́вый *adj.* tiger (*attrib.*); tiger's.

тик *n.* **1,** (nervous) tic. **2,** teak (*wood*). **3,** ticking (*cloth*).

ти́канье *n.* ticking (*of a clock*).

ти́кать *v. impfv.* (*of a clock*) to tick.

ти́ккер *n.* ticker.

ти́ковый *adj.* **1,** teak (*attrib.*). **2,** made with ticking.

ти́льда *n.* tilde.

тимиа́н *n.* = тимья́н.

тимофе́евка *n.* timothy; timothy grass.

тимпа́н *n., music* timpani.

тимья́н *also,* **тимиа́н** *n.* thyme.

ти́на *n.* pond scum. —**ти́нистый,** *adj.* filled with pond scum.

тинкту́ра *n.* tincture.

тип *n.* **1,** type. **2,** phylum. **3,** [*acc.* ти́па] *colloq.* character; odd person.

типа́ж [*gen.* **типажа́**] *n.* model; prototype.

типи́ческий *adj.* typical.

типи́чно *adv.* typically. —*adj., used predicatively* typical: э́то типи́чно для него́, that's typical of him.

типи́чный *adj.* typical.

типово́й *adj.* **1,** model. **2,** standard; standardized.

типо́граф *n.* printer; typographer. —**типогра́фия,** *n.* printing house. —**типогра́фский,** *adj.* typographic(al); printer's.

типу́н [*gen.* -**пуна́**] *n.* pip (*bird disease*).

тир *n.* shooting gallery.

тира́да *n.* tirade.

тира́ж [*gen.* **тиража́**] *n.* **1,** drawing (*in a lottery*). **2,** circulation (*of a periodical*). **3,** printing (*of a book*); number of copies printed. —**вы́йти в тира́ж,** to be no longer able to work; be ready for retirement.

тира́н *n.* tyrant.

тира́нить *v. impfv.* **1,** to tyrannize; oppress. **2,** to torment.

тирани́я *n.* tyranny. —**тирани́ческий,** *adj.* tyrannical.

тира́нство *n.* tyranny.

тира́нствовать *v. impfv.* [*pres.* -ствую, -ствуешь] to be a tyrant.

тире́ (рэ) *n. neut. indecl.* dash.

тис *n.* yew.

ти́скать *v. impfv.* [*pfv.* ти́снуть] *colloq.* to squeeze; press.

тиски́ [*gen.* -ско́в] *n. pl.* vise: зажа́ть в тиски́, to grip in a vise. —в тиска́х (+ *gen.*), in the grips of.

тисне́ние *n.* 1, stamping; embossing. 2, imprint; design.

тиснёный *adj.* stamped; embossed.

ти́снуть *v., pfv. of* ти́скать.

тита́н *n.* 1, titan. 2, titanium. 3, large boiler. —**тита-ни́ческий**, *adj.* titanic.

титр *n., motion pictures* title; subtitle.

ти́тул *n.* title.

титуло́ванный *adj.* titled.

титулова́ть *v. impfv. & pfv.* [*pres.* -лую, -луешь] to call; address (someone) by his title.

ти́тульный *adj., printing* title (*attrib.*): ти́тульный лист, title page.

тиф *n.* typhus. —**брюшно́й тиф,** typhoid. —**возвра́т-ный тиф,** relapsing fever. —**сыпно́й тиф,** typhus.

тифо́зный *adj.* typhoid; typhus (*attrib.*).

ти́хий *adj.* [*comp.* ти́ше] 1, soft; low. 2, quiet; still. 3, calm; tranquil. 4, quiet; retiring. 5, slow.

ти́хо *adv.* 1, quietly. 2, softly. 3, slowly. —*adj., used predicatively* quiet: здесь ти́хо, it is quiet here.

тихомо́лком *adv., colloq.* quietly; without making a sound.

тихо́нько *adv., colloq.* quietly; softly.

тихо́ня *n.m. & f., colloq.* timid person; meek person.

ти́ше *adj., comp. of* ти́хий. —*adv., comp. of* ти́хо. —*interj.* quiet!; please be quiet!

тишина́ *n.* quiet; silence; stillness.

тишь [*2nd loc.* тиши́] *n.f.* quiet; stillness. —**тишь да гладь,** peace and quiet.

тка́ный *adj.* woven.

ткань *n.f.* 1, cloth; fabric. 2, *anat.* tissue.

тканьё *n.* 1, weaving. 2, cloth. 3, woven design.

ткать *v. impfv.* [*pfv.* сотка́ть; *pres.* тку, ткёшь; *past fem.* ткала́ or тка́ла] 1, to weave. 2, *in* ткать паути́ну, to spin a web.

тка́цкий *adj.* weaving (*attrib.*); weaver's. —**тка́цкий стано́к,** loom.

ткач [*gen.* ткача́] *n.m.* [*fem.* -чи́ха] weaver.

ткну́ть *v., pfv. of* ты́кать. —**ткну́ться,** *refl., pfv. of* ты́каться.

тле́ние *n.* 1, rotting; decay. 2, smoldering.

тле́нный *adj.* mortal.

тлетво́рный *adj.* 1, noxious. 2, *fig.* pernicious; delete-rious.

тлеть *v. impfv.* 1, to rot; decay. 2, to smolder. —**тле́ть-ся,** *refl., colloq.* to smolder.

тля *n.* plant louse.

тмин *n.* caraway. —**тми́нный,** *adj.* caraway (*attrib.*).

то *dem. adj. & pron., neut. of* тот, that: в то вре́мя, at that time. То бы́ли незабыва́емые мину́ты, those were unforgettable moments. —*conj.* then: е́сли он не хо́чет, то не угова́ривайте его́, if he does not want to, then don't try to persuade him. —**а то; не то,** or; or else; otherwise. —**а то и,** or maybe: челове́к две́сти, а то и бо́льше, some 200 people, or maybe more. —**и то,** and even; at that. —**не то..., не то,** half... half; a combination of... —**не то что; не то**

чтобы, it is not (so much) that... —**то есть,** that is; that is to say. —**то ли..., то ли,** either..., or; a combi-nation of... —**то..., то,** now: он живёт то в го́роде, то в дере́вне, he divides his time between the city and the country. —**то, что...,** 1, what... 2, the fact that...

тобо́й *also,* **тобо́ю** *pron., instr. of* ты.

това́р *n.* 1, goods; merchandise. 2, commodity.

това́рищ *n.* 1, comrade. 2, friend. 3, (*with* по) fellow: това́рищ по рабо́те, fellow worker. —**това́рищ по несча́стью,** comrade in distress; fellow sufferer. —**това́рищ по ору́жию,** comrade in arms.

това́рищеский *adj.* comradely; friendly.

това́рищество *n.* 1, comradeship; fellowship. 2, company; society; association.

това́рный *adj.* 1, goods (*attrib.*); commodity (*attrib.*). 2, *R.R.* freight (*attrib.*): това́рный по́езд, freight train.

товарообме́н *n.* barter.

товарооборо́т *n.* commodity turnover.

то́га *n.* toga.

тогда́ *adv.* 1, then; at that time. 2, then; in that case. —**тогда́ как,** while; whereas. —**тогда́, когда́...,** when...

тогда́шний *adj., colloq.* of that time; at that time.

того́ (во) *adj., gen. of* тот.

тожде́ственный *adj.* identical. —**тожде́ствен-ность,** *n.f.* identity; sameness.

то́ждество *n.* identity: то́ждество взгля́дов, identity of views.

то́же *adv.* 1, also; too. 2, (*with neg. verbs*) either: я то́же не зна́ю, I don't know either.

той *adj., fem. gen., dat., prepl., & instr. of* тот.

ток *n.* 1, current (*of air, water, etc.*). 2, *electricity* cur-rent. 3, [*2nd loc.* току́; *pl.* тока́] threshing floor. 4, mating (*of birds*). 5, [*2nd loc.* току́; *pl.* тока́] mating ground. 6, toque. —**ток кро́ви,** bloodstream.

тока́рный *adj.* lathe (*attrib.*). —**тока́рный стано́к,** lathe.

то́карь [*pl.* то́кари or токаря́] *n.m.* lathe operator; turner.

токова́ние *n.* mating call.

токова́ть *v. impfv.* [*pres.* -ку́ет] (*of a bird*) to utter its mating call.

токоприёмник *n.* trolley (*device for conducting cur-rent*).

токсеми́я *n.* toxemia.

токсиколо́гия *n.* toxicology. —**токсико́лог,** *n.* toxi-cologist. —**токсикологи́ческий,** *adj.* toxicological.

токси́н *n.* toxin.

токси́ческий *adj.* toxic.

тол *n.* TNT; trinitrotoluene.

толи́ка *n.* (*with gen.*) *colloq.* small amount (of). —**ма́-лую толи́ку,** a little; tiny bit.

толк *n.* 1, sense. 2, good; use. 3, *pl.* talk; rumors. 4, sect; group. —**бе́з толку,** 1, without making any sense. 2, for nothing; to no purpose. —**взять в толк,** to understand; figure out. —**знать толк в** (+ *prepl.*), to know well; be a connoisseur of. —**сбива́ть с то́лку,** to confuse. —**сбива́ться с то́лку,** to become confused. —**с то́лком,** showing good sense; intelligently. *See also* **то́лком.**

толка́ние *n.* pushing. —**толка́ние ядра́,** *sports* shot-put.

толка́ть *v. impfv.* [*pfv.* толкну́ть] 1, to push; shove. 2, to poke; prod. 3, (*with* на + *acc.*) to incite (to);

put up to. **4,** *in* **толка́ть ядро́,** *sports* to put the shot. —**толка́ться,** *refl.* **1,** [*impfv. only*] to push one another; jostle; shove. **2,** (*with* о + *acc.*) *colloq.* to strike (against). **3,** (*with* в + *acc.*) *colloq.* to knock on the door of; try to get into. **4,** [*impfv. only*] *colloq.* to knock about; idle; loaf.

толка́ч [*gen.* -кача́] *n.,* *colloq.* person who cuts through red tape; fixer; expediter.

толкну́ть *v.,* *pfv.* of **толка́ть.** —**толкну́ться,** *refl.,* *pfv.* of **толка́ться.**

толкова́ние *n.* **1,** interpretation. **2,** commentary.

толкова́тель *n.m.* interpreter; commentator.

толкова́ть *v. impfv.* [*pres.* -ку́ю, -ку́ешь] **1,** to interpret. **2,** *colloq.* to explain. **3,** *colloq.* to talk; converse.

толко́вый *adj.* **1,** intelligent; clever. **2,** clear; intelligible. —**толко́вый слова́рь,** defining dictionary.

то́лком *adv., colloq.* **1,** plainly; clearly. **2,** in earnest: засе́сть то́лком за уро́ки, to sit down to one's lessons in earnest. **3,** properly. То́лком всё разгляде́ть, to have a good look around. Никто́ то́лком не знал, nobody really knew.

толкотня́ *n., colloq.* crush (*of people*).

толку́чий *adj., in* **толку́чий ры́нок,** *colloq.* flea market. —**толку́чка,** *n., colloq.* flea market.

толокно́ *n.* oatmeal.

толо́чь *v. impfv.* [*pfv.* **растоло́чь** *or* **истоло́чь;** *pres.* толку́, толчёшь, ...толку́т; *past* толо́к, толкла́, толкло́] **1,** to pound; crush; pulverize. **2,** *in* толо́чь во́ду в сту́пе, to waste one's time; beat the air. —**толо́чься,** *refl.* [*impfv. only*] *colloq.* **1,** to move about (*in a small area*). **2,** to crowd; mill about. **3,** to hang around.

толпа́ [*pl.* то́лпы] *n.* crowd.

толпи́ться *v.r. impfv.* to crowd; throng.

толсте́ть *v. impfv.* [*pfv.* **потолсте́ть**] to get fat; put on weight.

толсти́ть *v. impfv., colloq.* to make (someone) look fat.

толсто́вка [*gen. pl.* -вок] *n.* long belted blouse (*as worn by Tolstoy*).

толстогу́бый *adj.* thick-lipped.

толстоко́жий *adj.* thick-skinned. —**тостоко́жее живо́тное,** pachyderm.

толстосу́м *n., colloq.* rich man; moneybags.

толсту́ха *n., colloq.* fat woman.

то́лстый [*comp.* то́лще] **1,** thick. **2,** fat; stout. **3,** (*of cloth*) heavy. —**то́лстая кишка́,** large intestine.

толстя́к [*gen.* -стяка́] *n., colloq.* fat man.

толуо́л *n.* toluene.

толчёный *adj.* ground: толчёный минда́ль, ground almonds.

толчея́ *n., colloq.* crush (*of people*).

толчо́к [*gen.* -чка́] *n.* **1,** push; shove. **2,** jolt; bump. **3,** shock; tremor. **4,** *fig.* spur; impetus. **5,** *weightlifting* clean and jerk.

то́лща *n.* **1,** thick mass; layer. **2,** *fig.* the masses.

то́лще *adj., comp.* of **то́лстый.**

толщина́ *n.* **1,** thickness. **2,** corpulence.

толь *n.m.* tarred roofing paper.

то́лько *adv.* **1,** only: то́лько три дня, only three days. **2,** not until; not till: то́лько в после́днюю мину́ту, not until/till the last minute. **3,** alone: то́лько в э́том году́, this year alone. **4,** just: он то́лько пришёл, he just arrived. **5,** (*with* не) *used in exclamations for emphasis:* где то́лько он не быва́л!, where *hasn't* he been?; is there anywhere he hasn't been? Чего́ то́лько

не приду́мывают лю́ди!, what people won't think of! —*conj.* only: с удово́льствием, то́лько не сего́дня, with pleasure, only not today. —*particle* just: поду́мать то́лько!, just think! Вы то́лько попро́буйте э́тот ко́фе!, just taste this coffee! —**да и то́лько,** *see* **да.** —**едва́ то́лько,** = **как то́лько.** —**как то́лько,** as soon as. —**лишь то́лько,** = **как то́лько.** —**оди́н то́лько,** *see* **оди́н.** —**сто́ит то́лько** (+ *inf.*), one has only to... —**то́лько бы, 1,** if only. **2,** (*with* не + *inf.*) one must simply not; the one thing we must not do is... —**то́лько и,** the only thing: об э́том то́лько и говори́ли, it was all they talked about. —**то́лько что,** just: я то́лько что пришёл, I just arrived.

том[1] *adj., prepl.* of **тот.**

том[2] [*pl.* тома́] *n.* volume.

томага́вк *n.* tomahawk.

тома́т *n.* tomato. —**тома́тный,** *adj.* tomato (*attrib.*).

то́мик *n., dim.* of **том.**

томи́тельный *adj.* **1,** oppressive; agonizing. **2,** tedious; tiring.

томи́ть *v. impfv.* [*pfv.* **истоми́ть;** *pres.* томлю́, то́мишь] **1,** to tire; exhaust. **2,** (*of heat, thirst, etc.*) to oppress. —**томи́ться,** *refl.* [*impfv. only*] **1,** to suffer. **2,** to languish (*in prison, captivity, etc.*). **3,** (*with* по) to pine (for).

томле́ние *n.* **1,** anguish; suffering. **2,** languor.

то́мность *n.f.* languor.

то́мный *adj.* languid; languorous.

тому́ *adj., dat.* of **тот.** —**тому́ наза́д,** ago.

тон [*pl.* тона́ *or* то́ны] *n.* **1,** (musical) tone. **2,** tone of voice. **3,** tone; shade. **4,** *fig.* tone: тон письма́, the tone of the letter. **5,** form: э́то счита́ется дурны́м то́ном, it is considered poor form. —**в тон, 1,** (*with dat.*) in harmony with; in tune with; in keeping with. **2,** in the same tone of voice; in kind. —**не в тон,** off key. —**повы́сить тон,** to raise one's voice. —**попа́сть в тон,** to strike the right note. —**сба́вить тон,** to quiet down.

тона́льность *n.f., music* key: тона́льность до дие́з, key of C sharp.

тона́льный *adj.* tonal.

то́ненький *adj., colloq.* thin.

тонзу́ра *n.* tonsure.

тонизи́ровать *v. impfv.* [*pres.* -рую, -руешь] *physiol.* to tone up.

тони́ческий *adj.* tonic.

то́нкий *adj.* [*comp.* то́ньше; *superl.* тонча́йший] **1,** thin. **2,** (*of thread, linen, etc.*) fine. **3,** (*of the senses*) keen. **4,** (*of food, wines, etc.*) fine. **5,** fine; subtle; nice. **6,** astute; keen; perceptive.

то́нко *adv.* **1,** thinly; thin. **2,** finely. **3,** subtly.

тонкоко́жий *adj.* thin-skinned.

то́нкость *n.f.* **1,** thinness. **2,** fineness. **3,** subtlety. **4,** keenness (*of the senses*). **5,** fine point; subtlety; nicety. —**до то́нкостей,** minutely; down to the fine points.

то́нна *n.* ton.

тонна́ж *n.* tonnage.

тонне́ль (нэ) *n.m.* tunnel.

то́нус *n., physiol.* tone: мы́шечный то́нус, muscle tone.

тону́ть *v. impfv.* [*pres.* тону́, то́нешь] **1,** [*pfv.* **потону́ть**] to sink. **2,** [*pfv.* **утону́ть**] to drown.

то́ньше *adj., comp.* of **то́нкий.**

топа́з *n.* topaz. —**топа́зовый,** *adj.* topaz.

то́пать *v. impfv.* [*pfv.* **то́пнуть**] (*with instr.*) to stamp (one's feet).

топи́ть *v. impfv.* [*pres.* **топлю́, то́пишь**] **1,** to heat (a building). **2,** to stoke (a furnace). **3,** [*pfv.* **растопи́ть**] to melt. **4,** [*pfv.* **потопи́ть**] to sink. **5,** [*pfv.* **утопи́ть**] to drown. —**топи́ться,** *refl.* **1,** (*of a stove*) to burn; be lit. **2,** to melt. **3,** [*pfv.* **утопи́ться**] to drown oneself.

то́пка *n.* **1,** heating. **2,** melting. **3,** furnace.

то́пкий *adj.* [*comp.* **то́пче**] swampy; marshy.

топлёный *adj.* **1,** melted. **2,** baked.

то́пливо *n.* fuel. —**то́пливный,** *adj.* fuel (*attrib.*).

то́пнуть *v.*, *pfv.* of **то́пать.**

топогра́фия *n.* topography. —**топо́граф,** *n.* topographer. —**топографи́ческий,** *adj.* topographical.

то́полевый *adj.* poplar (*attrib.*).

топо́логия *n.* topology.

то́поль [*pl.* **тополя́**] *n.m.* poplar.

топо́р [*gen.* **топора́**] *n.* ax.

топо́рик *n.* hatchet.

топори́ще *n.* ax handle.

топо́рный *adj.* **1,** of an ax; ax (*attrib.*). **2,** (*of a piece of furniture*) crudely made. **3,** (*of workmanship*) crude. **4,** (*of a person*) unpolished; unrefined; uncouth.

топо́рщить *v. impfv.* to make (hair, fur, etc.) stand on end. —**топо́рщиться,** *refl.* (*of one's hair*) to bristle; (*of material*) to pucker.

то́пот *n.* tramp; tramping; stamping; clatter.

топота́ть *v. impfv.* [*pres.* **-почу́, -по́чешь**] *colloq.* **1,** [*also,* **топота́ть нога́ми**] to stamp one's feet. **2,** to tramp along.

то́псель *n.m.* topsail.

топта́ние *n.* trampling. —**топта́ние на ме́сте,** marking time.

топта́ть *v. impfv.* [*pres.* **топчу́, то́пчешь**] **1,** to trample; trample down. **2,** to stamp out (a fire). **3,** *colloq.* to soil; track dirt on. **4,** *in* **топта́ть в грязь,** to drag through the mud. —**топта́ться,** *refl.* **1,** to shift from foot to foot. **2,** *colloq.* to walk about; hang about. **3,** *in* **топта́ться на ме́сте,** mark time.

топча́к [*gen.* **-чака́**] *n.* treadmill.

топь *n.f.* swamp; marsh; bog.

то́ра *n.* Torah.

то́рба *n.* feedbag.

торг [*2nd loc.* **торгу́**; *pl.* **торги́**] *n.* **1,** trade. **2,** bargaining. **3,** deal. **4,** *obs.* market. **5,** *pl.* auction.

торга́ш [*gen.* **-гаша́**] *n.*, *colloq.* petty tradesman; huckster.

торгова́ть *v. impfv.* [*pres.* **-гу́ю, -гу́ешь**] **1,** to do business. **2,** (*of a store*) to be open (for business). **3,** (*with instr.*) to deal in; sell. **4,** (*with* **с** + *instr.*) to trade (with another country). —**торгова́ться,** *refl.* to bargain; haggle; dicker.

торго́вец [*gen.* **-вца**] *n.* merchant; tradesman. У́личный торго́вец, street vendor.

торго́вля *n.* trade; business; commerce.

торго́вый *adj.* **1,** trade (*attrib.*); commercial. **2,** (*of a ship, fleet, etc.*) merchant. —**торго́вая пала́та,** chamber of commerce. —**торго́вый центр,** shopping center.

тореадо́р *n.* toreador.

торе́ц [*gen.* **-рца́**] *n.* **1,** butt end. **2,** (wooden) paving block.

торже́ственно *adv.* **1,** with great solemnity. **2,** solemnly. —**торже́ственность,** *n.f.* solemnity.

торже́ственный *adj.* **1,** solemn. **2,** festive; gala. **3,** ceremonial. **4,** triumphal.

торжество́ *n.* **1,** celebration; *pl.* festivities. **2,** triumph; victory. **3,** (feeling of) triumph; exultation.

торжествова́ть *v. impfv.* [*pfv.* **восторжествова́ть**; *pres.* **-ству́ю, -ству́ешь**] **1,** (*with* **над**) to triumph (over). **2,** [*impfv. only*] to rejoice; exult. **3,** [*impfv. only*] *obs.* to celebrate (a holiday, victory, etc.).

торжеству́ющий *adj.* triumphant; exultant.

то́ри *n.m. indecl.* Tory.

то́рий *n.m.* thorium.

торма́шки *n.pl.*, *in* **вверх торма́шки** *and* **вверх торма́шками, 1,** head over heels. **2,** upside-down; topsy-turvy.

торможе́ние *n.* braking.

то́рмоз *n.* **1,** [*pl.* **тормоза́**] brake. **2,** [*pl.* **то́рмозы**] *fig.* brake; obstacle; hindrance.

тормози́ть *v. impfv.* [*pfv.* **затормози́ть**; *pres.* **-можу́, -мози́шь**] **1,** to brake; apply the brakes (to). **2,** *fig.* to hinder; hamper; impede; retard.

тормозно́й *adj.* brake (*attrib.*): тормозно́й башма́к, brake shoe. —**тормозно́й конду́ктор,** brakeman. —**тормозна́я раке́та,** retro-rocket.

тормоши́ть *v. impfv.*, *colloq.* **1,** to pull at; tug at. **2,** *fig.* to bother; pester.

то́рный *adj.* (*of a road*) even; smooth; worn down; well-trodden.

торова́тый *adj.*, *obs.* generous.

торопи́ть *v. impfv.* [*pfv.* **поторопи́ть**; *pres.* **торопли́ю, торо́пишь**] **1,** to hurry (up); rush. **2,** to hasten; speed up. —**торопи́ться,** *refl.* **1,** to hurry; rush. **2,** to be in a hurry.

торопли́вый *adj.* **1,** hasty; hurried. **2,** always in a hurry; bustling. —**торопли́во,** *adv.* hastily; hurriedly. —**торопли́вость,** *n.f.* haste; hurry.

торо́с *n.* hummock (*in an ice field*).

торпе́да *n.* torpedo.

торпеди́ровать *v. impfv. & pfv.* [*pres.* **-рую, -руешь**] to torpedo.

торпе́дный *adj.* torpedo (*attrib.*). —**торпе́дный ка́тер,** PT boat.

торс *n.* torso.

торт *n.* cake.

торф *n.* peat. —**торфяно́й,** *adj.* peat (*attrib.*).

торча́ть *v. impfv.* [*pres.* **-чу́, -чи́шь**] **1,** to stick out; jut out; protrude. **2,** *colloq.* to hang around. —**торча́ть пе́ред глаза́ми,** to be ever present; never go away.

торчко́м *adv.*, *colloq.* on end; erect; upright.

торше́р *n.* floor lamp.

тоска́ *n.* **1,** melancholy. **2,** boredom; ennui. **3,** (*with* **по**) longing (for); yearning (for); nostalgia (for).

тоскли́вый *adj.* **1,** melancholy; depressed. **2,** dreary; dismal; depressing.

тоскова́ть *v. impfv.* [*pres.* **-ку́ю, -ку́ешь**] **1,** to be melancholy; be depressed. **2,** (*with* **по** + *dat.*, *but prepl. for pers. pronouns*) to miss; long for. —**тоскова́ть по до́му,** to be homesick.

тост *n.* toast: предлага́ть тост, to propose a toast.

то́стер (тэ) *n.* toaster.

тот [*fem.* **та**; *neut.* **то**; *pl.* **те**; *gen.* **того́, той, тех**; *dat.* **тому́, той, тем**; *acc. fem.* **ту**; *instr.* **тем, той, те́ми**; *prepl.* **том, той, тех**] *dem. adj.* **1,** that: в тот день, on that day. **2,** (*with* **кото́рый**) the... that: э́та та кни́га, кото́рую вы иска́ли?, is this the book you were looking for? **3,** the right: э́то тот дом?, is this the right house? Я набра́л не тот но́мер, I dialed the wrong number. **4,** the other; the far: по ту сто́рону (+ *gen.*), on the other side of. —*dem. pron.* **1,** that one; that. **2,** the latter. **3,** (*fol. by* кто) he (who); the one (who). **4,** (*fol. by* кото́рый) the one (that). —**и тот и друго́й,** both. —**не тот, так друго́й,** if not one, then the other. —**ни тот ни друго́й,** neither; neither one. —**тот и́ли ино́й,** some... or other; one... or another. —**тот же; тот са́мый; тот же са́мый,** the same. *See also* **то** *and* **тем.**

тотализа́тор *n.* **1,** totalizator; pari-mutuel machine. **2,** pari-mutuel betting.

тоталитари́зм *n.* totalitarianism. —**тоталита́рный,** *adj.* totalitarian.

тота́льный *adj.* total. —**тота́льная война́,** total war.

тоте́м (тэ) *n.* totem. —**тотеми́зм,** *n.* totemism.

то́-то *particle, colloq.* **1,** that's just the point. **2,** aha!; what did I tell you! **3,** that is why; that is how. **4,** how!: то́-то бы́ло краси́во, how beautiful it was!

то́тчас *adv.* immediately; at once.

точе́ние *n.* sharpening.

точёный *adj.* **1,** sharpened. **2,** shaped in a lathe. **3,** *fig.* (*of features*) chiseled.

точи́лка [*gen. pl.* -лок] *n.* **1,** sharpener. **2,** *colloq.* pencil sharpener.

точи́ло *n.* grindstone; whetstone.

точи́льный *adj.* sharpening (*attrib.*). —**точи́льный ка́мень,** grindstone; whetstone. —**точи́льный реме́нь,** strop.

точи́льщик *n.* grinder; knife grinder.

точи́ть *v. impfv.* [*pres.* точу́, то́чишь] **1,** [*pfv.* наточи́ть] to sharpen; hone. **2,** [*pfv.* вы́точить] to turn (*in a lathe*). **3,** to eat away. **4,** (*of water*) to wear away. **5,** *fig.* to oppress; wear down. —**точи́ть зу́бы на** (+ *acc.*), to have it in for; bear a grudge against.

то́чка [*gen. pl.* -чек] *n.* **1,** dot. **2,** point (*in space*): са́мая высо́кая то́чка, the highest point. Отправна́я то́чка, starting point. **3,** period. **4,** *in* две то́чки, colon; то́чка с запято́й, semicolon. **5,** *in* то́чка кипе́ния/замерза́ния, boiling/freezing point. **6,** *in* то́чка зре́ния, point of view; viewpoint. **7,** sharpening. —*interj.* enough!; that will do! —**бить в одну́ то́чку,** to concentrate on one thing. —**до то́чки,** thoroughly; down to the last detail. —**доходи́ть до то́чки,** to reach the breaking point; reach the end of one's rope; be at the end of one's tether. —**мёртвая то́чка,** *see* **мёртвый.** —**попа́сть в (са́мую) то́чку,** to hit the nail on the head. —**ста́вить то́чку на** (+ *prepl.*), to finish; close the books on. —**ста́вить то́чки над "и",** to dot the "i's" and cross the "t's". —**то́чка в то́чку,** perfectly; to the letter.

то́чно *adv.* exactly; precisely; accurately. —*conj.* **1,** like; as. **2,** as if; as though. —**так то́чно!,** *mil.* yes, sir!

то́чность *n.f.* **1,** exactness; precision. **2,** accuracy. **3,** punctuality. —**в то́чности,** exactly; precisely; to the letter. —**с то́чностью до,** within.

то́чный *adj.* **1,** exact; precise. **2,** accurate. **3,** punctual. —**то́чные прибо́ры,** precision instruments.

точь-в-точь *adv.* exactly.

тошни́ть *v. impfv., impers.* to be nauseous; feel nauseous: меня́ тошни́т, I feel nauseous.

то́шно *adj., used predicatively* nauseating; sickening: мне то́шно смотре́ть на э́то, it sickens me to look at it.

тошнота́ *n.* nausea. —**тошнотво́рный,** *adj.* nauseating; sickening.

то́шный *adj., colloq.* **1,** nauseating. **2,** bothersome; tiresome.

тоща́ть *v. impfv.* [*pfv.* отоща́ть] *colloq.* to become very thin; become gaunt; waste away.

то́щий *adj.* **1,** emaciated; gaunt. **2,** empty. **3,** poor; meager.

тпру *interj.* whoa!

трава́ [*pl.* тра́вы] *n.* **1,** grass. **2,** herb. —**со́рная трава́,** weed; weeds.

трави́нка [*gen. pl.* -нок] *n.* blade of grass.

трави́ть *v. impfv.* [*pres.* травлю́, тра́вишь] **1,** [*pfv.* вы́травить] to exterminate; poison. **2,** [*pfv.* потрави́ть] to trample (down). **3,** [*pfv.* затрави́ть] to hunt (down); *fig.* hound; persecute. **4,** [*pfv.* вы́травить] to etch. **5,** [*pfv.* вы́травить] *naut.* to let out; pay out (a rope, cable, etc.). —**трави́ться,** *refl.* [*impfv. only*] *colloq.* to take poison.

травле́ние *n.* etching.

тра́вля *n.* **1,** hunt; hunting. **2,** *fig.* hounding; persecution.

тра́вма *n.* injury; trauma. —**травмати́ческий,** *adj.* traumatic. —**травматоло́гия,** *n.* traumatology.

травми́ровать *v. impfv. & pfv.* [*pres.* -рую, -руешь] **1,** to injure; damage. **2,** to traumatize.

травоя́дный *adj.* herbivorous.

травяни́стый *adj.* **1,** herbaceous. **2,** grassy. **3,** *fig., colloq.* tasteless.

травяно́й *adj.* **1,** grass (*attrib.*). **2,** grassy.

траге́дия *n.* tragedy.

траги́зм *n.* tragedy; tragic element.

тра́гик *n.* tragedian.

трагикоме́дия *n.* tragicomedy. —**трагикоми́ческий,** *adj.* tragicomic.

траги́ческий *adj.* tragic. —**траги́чески,** *adv.* tragically.

траги́чный *adj.* tragic. —**траги́чно,** *adv.* tragically. —**траги́чность,** *n.f.* tragedy; tragic nature.

тради́ция *n.* tradition. —**традицио́нный,** *adj.* traditional.

траекто́рия *n.* trajectory. —**траекто́рия полёта,** flight path.

тракт *n., obs.* highway. —**желу́дочно-кише́чный тракт,** alimentary canal. —**пищевари́тельный тракт,** digestive tract.

тракта́т *n.* **1,** treatise; tract. **2,** treaty.

тракти́р *n., obs.* tavern; inn. —**тракти́рщик,** *n., obs.* innkeeper.

трактова́ть *v. impfv.* [*pres.* -ту́ю, -ту́ешь] **1,** to interpret. **2,** (*with* о) to treat; discuss (a certain subject).

тракто́вка *n.* treatment; interpretation.

тра́ктор [*pl.* тра́кторы *or* трактора́] *n.* tractor. —**тракто́рист,** *n.* tractor driver. —**тра́кторный,** *adj.* tractor (*attrib.*).

трал *n.* trawl.

тра́лить *v. impfv.* to trawl.

тра́льщик *n.* **1,** trawler. **2,** minesweeper.

трамбова́ть *v. impfv.* [*pfv.* утрамбова́ть; *pres.* -бу́ю, -бу́ешь] to beat down; smooth down.

трамва́й *n.* streetcar; trolley; tram. —**трамва́йный,** *adj.* streetcar (*attrib.*); trolley (*attrib.*); tram (*attrib.*).

трампли́н *n.* **1,** diving board; springboard. **2,** *fig.* springboard; starting point. —**лы́жный трампли́н,** ski jump.

транжи́р *n.*, *colloq.* spendthrift.

транжи́рить *v. impfv.* [*pfv.* **растранжи́рить**] *colloq.* to squander.

транзи́стор *n.* transistor.

транзи́т *n.* transit. —**транзи́тный**, *adj.* transit (*attrib.*).

транс *n.* trance.

трансатланти́ческий *adj.* transatlantic.

трансконтинента́льный *adj.* transcontinental.

транскри́пция *n.*, *ling.*; *music* transcription.

трансли́ровать *v. impfv. & pfv.* [*pres.* -рую, -руешь] to transmit; broadcast.

транслитера́ция *n.* transliteration.

транслитери́ровать *v. impfv. & pfv.* [*pres.* -рую, -руешь] to transliterate.

трансля́ция *n.* transmission; broadcast. —**трансляцио́нный**, *adj.* transmission (*attrib.*); broadcasting.

трансокеа́нский *adj.* transoceanic.

транспара́нт *n.* **1,** lined paper (*placed under unlined paper*). **2,** banner; streamer.

транспони́ровать *v. impfv. & pfv.* [*pres.* -рую, -руешь] *music* to transpose.

транспониро́вка *n.*, *music* transposition.

тра́нспорт *n.* **1,** transport. **2,** transportation. **3,** shipment; consignment. **4,** supply ship; troopship; troop transport.

транспо́рт *n.*, *bookkeeping* carrying forward.

транспорта́бельный *adj.* transportable.

транспортёр *n.* **1,** conveyor. **2,** *mil.* transporter; carrier.

транспорти́р *n.* protractor.

транспорти́ровать *v. impfv. & pfv.* [*pres.* -рую, -руешь] **1,** to transport. **2,** *bookkeeping* to carry forward.

транспортиро́вка *n.* transporting; transportation.

тра́нспортник *n.* transport worker.

тра́нспортный *adj.* transport (*attrib.*).

транссиби́рский *adj.* trans-Siberian.

трансформа́тор *n.* **1,** *electricity* transformer. **2,** *theat.* quick-change artist.

трансформа́ция *n.* transformation.

трансформи́ровать *v. impfv. & pfv.* [*pres.* -рую, -руешь] to transform; convert.

трансцендента́льный *adj.* transcendental.

трансценде́нтный *adj.* **1,** *philos.* transcendent. **2,** *math.* transcendental.

транше́йный *adj.* trench (*attrib.*). —**транше́йная стопа́**, trench foot.

транше́я *n.* trench.

трап *n.* **1,** ship's ladder. **2,** boarding ramp.

тра́пеза *also,* **трапе́за** *n.* food; meal (*originally referring to that served in a monastery*).

тра́пезная *also,* **трапе́зная** *n.*, *decl. as an adj.* refectory (*in a monastery*).

тра́пезный *also,* **трапе́зный** *adj.* meal (*attrib.*); dining (*attrib.*).

трапе́ция *n.* **1,** *geom.* trapezoid. **2,** trapeze.

тра́сса *n.* **1,** route. **2,** path (*of a bullet, missile, etc.*). **3,** road; highway.

трасса́нт *n.*, *comm.* drawer.

трасси́ровать *v. impfv. & pfv.* [*pres.* -рую, -руешь] to trace (*on a map or chart*).

трасси́рующий *adj.* tracer (*attrib.*): трасси́рущая пу́ля, tracer bullet.

тра́та *n.* **1,** spending. **2,** expenditure; expense. **3,** (preceded by an adj.) waste: пуста́я тра́та вре́мени, waste of time.

тра́тить *v. impfv.* [*pfv.* **истра́тить** *or* **потра́тить**; *pres.* тра́чу, тра́тишь] **1,** to spend (money). **2,** to expend (time, energy, etc.). **3,** to use up. **4,** to waste. —**тра́титься**, *refl.* **1,** to spend money. **2,** to be spent.

тра́улер *n.* trawler.

тра́ур *n.* **1,** mourning. **2,** mourning clothes. —**наде́ть тра́ур**, to go into mourning. —**носи́ть тра́ур по** (+ *dat.*), to be in mourning for.

тра́урница *n.* mourning cloak (*butterfly*).

тра́урный *adj.* **1,** mourning (*attrib.*); funeral (*attrib.*). **2,** *fig.* mournful; sorrowful.

трафаре́т *n.* **1,** stencil. **2,** *fig.* stereotype.

трафаре́тный *adj.* **1,** stenciled. **2,** *fig.* conventional; stereotyped.

трах *interj.* bang!

трахе́я *n.* trachea. —**трахе́йный**, *adj.* tracheal.

тра́хнуть *v. pfv.*, *colloq.* **1,** to fire; shoot. **2,** (*of a sound, shot, etc.*) to ring out. **3,** to bang; smash; whack. —**тра́хнуться**, *refl.*, *colloq.* (*with* о + *acc.*) to bang (into *or* against).

трахо́ма *n.* trachoma.

тре́ба *n.* **1,** sacrifice; offering. **2,** religious ceremony (*wedding, christening, etc.*) performed by a clergyman.

тре́бование *n.* **1,** demand. **2,** *pl.* requirements: отвеча́ть тре́бованиям, to meet the requirements. **3,** requisition; order.

тре́бовательный *adj.* demanding; exacting.

тре́бовать *v. impfv.* [*pfv.* **потре́бовать**; *pres.* тре́бую, тре́буешь] **1,** (with gen., acc., *or* чтобы) to demand. **2,** (with acc.) to demand to see (a permit, passport, etc.). **3,** (with gen.) to require; need; call for. **4,** (with acc.) to summon; send for; call in. —**тре́боваться**, *refl.* to be needed; be required.

требуха́ *n.* entrails.

трево́га *n.* **1,** alarm: быть в трево́ге, to be alarmed. **2,** alarm signal: бить трево́гу, to sound the alarm. **3,** alert: поднима́ть по трево́ге, to place on alert.

трево́жить *v. impfv.* **1,** [*pfv.* **встрево́жить**] to alarm; worry; trouble. **2,** [*pfv.* **потрево́жить**] to disturb; interrupt. —**трево́житься**, *refl.* [*pfv.* **встрево́житься**] to become alarmed; become worried.

трево́жный *adj.* **1,** anxious; uneasy; troubled. **2,** of alarm: трево́жный взгляд, a look of alarm. **3,** alarming. **4,** alarm (*attrib.*): трево́жный сигна́л, alarm signal.

треволне́ние *n.*, *colloq.* **1,** worry; agitation. **2,** *pl.* vicissitudes.

тре́звенник *n.*, *colloq.* teetotaler.

трезве́ть *v. impfv.* [*pfv.* **отрезве́ть**] to sober up; become sober.

трезво́н *n.* **1,** sound of church bells. **2,** long ringing of a bell. **3,** *fig.*, *colloq.* talk; gossip. **4,** *fig.*, *colloq.* row; ruckus.

трезво́нить *v. impfv.* **1,** to ring; sound; peal. **2,** *fig.*, *colloq.* to trumpet; proclaim. **3,** (with о) *colloq.* to spread rumors (about).

тре́звость *n.f.* **1,** sobriety. **2,** temperance; abstinence. —**тре́звость ума́**, cool-headedness.

трезву́чие *n.*, *music* triad.

тре́звый *adj.* **1,** sober; not drunk. **2,** *colloq.* who does not drink; teetotaling. **3,** *fig.* sober; realistic.

трезу́бец [*gen.* -бца] *n.* trident.

трек *n.*, *sports* track. —**тре́ковый**, *adj.* track (*attrib.*).

трель *n.f.* trill; warble.

тре́моло *n. indecl.* tremolo.

тренажёр *n.* trainer; simulator.

тре́нер *n.* trainer; coach.

тре́нзель *n.m.* snaffle.

тре́ние *n.* **1,** rubbing; rubbing together. **2,** friction. **3,** *pl., fig.* friction; conflict.

трениро́ванный *adj.* trained.

тренирова́ть *v. impfv.* [*pfv.* **натренирова́ть**; *pres.* -ру́ю, -ру́ешь] to train; coach. —**тренирова́ться**, *refl.* to train; undergo training.

трениро́вка *n.* **1,** training. **2,** practice; workout. —**трениро́вочный**, *adj.* training (*attrib.*).

трено́га *n.* **1,** tripod. **2,** three-legged shackle (*for a horse*).

трено́гий *adj.* three-legged.

трено́жить *v. impfv.* [*pfv.* **стрено́жить**] to hobble (a horse).

трено́жник *n.* tripod.

тре́нькать *v. impfv., colloq.* to strum.

трепа́к [*gen.* -пака́] *n.* trepak.

трепа́ло *n.* scutch; swingle. *Also,* **трепа́лка.**

тре́паный *adj., colloq.* **1,** torn; tattered; ragged; frayed. **2,** disheveled; unkempt.

трепа́ть *v. impfv.* [*pres.* **треплю́, тре́плешь**] **1,** [*pfv.* **потрепа́ть**] to dishevel (*by pulling or tugging at*). **2,** [*pfv.* **потрепа́ть**] (*of the wind*) to blow about. **3,** [*pfv.* **потрепа́ть**] (*with* по + *dat.*) to pat; stroke. **4,** [*pfv.* **истрепа́ть**] *colloq.* to fray; wear out. **5,** [*impfv. only*] (*with* за + *acc.*) to pull (someone's hair, ears, etc.). **6,** [*impfv. only*] *colloq.* to whip; whack. **7,** [*impfv. only*] (*of illness, fever, etc.*) to rack. **8,** [*impfv. only*] to scutch. **9,** *in* трепа́ть не́рвы (+ *dat.*), to jangle someone's nerves. **10,** *in* трепа́ть языко́м, *colloq.* to babble; chatter. —**трепа́ться,** *refl.* **1,** [*impfv. only*] to flutter. **2,** [*pfv.* **истрепа́ться**] *colloq.* to become frayed; wear out.

тре́пет *n.* **1,** quivering; trembling. **2,** tremor; palpitation. **3,** *fig.* trepidation.

трепета́ние *n.* **1,** quivering; trembling. **2,** palpitation.

трепета́ть *v. impfv.* [*pres.* **трепещу́, трепе́щешь**] **1,** to quiver. **2,** (*of one's heart*) to palpitate. **3,** to flicker. **4,** to tremble (*with an emotion*).

тре́петно *adv.* **1,** with a quiver. **2,** with trepidation.

тре́петный *adj.* **1,** quivering; fluttering; flickering. **2,** of trepidation; trembling. **3,** timid; fearful.

тре́пка [*gen. pl.* -пок] *n., colloq.* **1,** beating; thrashing. **2,** scolding; bawling out; dressing-down. —**тре́пка не́рвов,** strain on one's nerves.

треск *n.* **1,** crack; cracking sound. **2,** crackle; crackling sound. **3,** *colloq.* fuss; hullabaloo. —**провали́ться с тре́ском,** to fail ignominiously; be a complete flop.

треска́ *n.* cod; codfish.

тре́скаться *v.r. impfv.* [*pfv.* **потре́скаться**] **1,** to crack. **2,** to chap; become chapped.

треско́вый *adj.* cod (*attrib.*); codfish (*attrib.*).

трескотня́ *n., colloq.* **1,** crackle; rattle. **2,** chirping (*of insects*). **3,** *fig.* chatter.

треску́чий *adj., colloq.* **1,** crackling. **2,** (*of a sound*) grating; harsh. **3,** (*of frost*) sharp; harsh. **4,** *fig.* high-flown; high-sounding; pretentious.

тре́снуть *v. pfv.* **1,** *v.i.* to crack; burst. **2,** *colloq.* to bang (on *or* against). **3,** *colloq.* to hit; smack. —**тре́снуться,** *refl., colloq.* to bang: тре́снуться голово́й о перекла́дину, **to** bang one's head on a crossbar.

трест *n., econ.* trust.

трете́йский *adj.* of arbitration: трете́йский суд, court of arbitration.

тре́тий [*fem.* -тья] *ordinal numeral* third. —**тре́тьего дня,** the day before yesterday. *See also* **тре́тье.**

трети́ровать *v. impfv.* [*pres.* -рую, -руешь] to slight; snub.

трети́чный *adj.* tertiary.

треть [*pl.* тре́ти, -те́й, -та́м] *n.f.* a third: две тре́ти, two thirds (2/3).

тре́тье *n., decl. as an adj.* third course; dessert.

третьесо́ртный *adj.* third-rate.

третьестепе́нный *adj.* **1,** insignificant. **2,** third-rate.

треуго́лка [*gen. pl.* -лок] *n.* cocked hat.

треуго́льник *n.* triangle. —**треуго́льный,** *adj.* triangular.

трефно́й *adj.* (*of food*) non-kosher. —**трефно́е,** *n.* non-kosher food.

тре́фовый *also,* **трефо́вый** *adj., cards* of clubs: тре́фовый туз, ace of clubs.

тре́фы [*gen.* треф] *n. pl., cards* clubs.

трёхвале́нтный *adj.* trivalent.

трёхгла́вый *adj.* three-headed. —**трёхгла́вая мы́шца,** triceps.

трёхгоди́чный *adj.* three-year (*attrib.*).

трёхгодова́лый *adj.* three-year-old.

трёхгра́нник *n.* trihedron. —**трёхгра́нный,** *adj.* trihedral.

трёхдне́вный *adj.* three-day (*attrib.*).

трёхколёсный *adj.* three-wheel(ed). —**трёхколёсный велосипе́д,** tricycle.

трёхко́мнатный *adj.* three-room.

трёхле́тие *n.* **1,** third anniversary; third birthday. **2,** three-year period.

трёхле́тний *adj.* **1,** three-year (*attrib.*). **2,** three-year-old.

трёхме́рный *adj.* three-dimensional.

трёхме́сячный *adj.* **1,** three-month (*attrib.*). **2,** three-month-old.

трёхнеде́льный *adj.* **1,** three-week (*attrib.*). **2,** three-week-old.

трёхсло́жный *adj.* three-syllable.

трёхсотле́тие *n.* three-hundredth anniversary; tercentenary. —**трёхсотле́тний,** *adj.* three-hundred-year (*attrib.*); tercentenary.

трёхсо́тый *ordinal numeral* three-hundredth.

трёхсторо́нний *adj.* **1,** three-sided. **2,** trilateral; tripartite; three-way.

трёхцве́тный *adj.* three-colored; tricolored.

трёхчасово́й *adj.* **1,** three-hour (*attrib.*). **2,** *colloq.* three-o'clock (*attrib.*).

трёхчле́н *n.* trinomial. —**трёхчле́нный,** *adj.* trinomial.

трёхэта́жный *adj.* three-story.

треща́ние *n.* **1,** cracking; crackling. **2,** chirping. **3,** chattering.

треща́ть *v. impfv.* [*pres.* трещу́, трещи́шь] **1,** to crack. **2,** to crackle. **3,** to chirp. **4,** to ring loudly; make a racket. **5,** *colloq.* to chatter. **6,** *colloq.* (*of one's head*) to be splitting. **7,** *fig.* to be on the verge of collapse.

тре́щина *n.* **1,** crack; split. **2,** fissure. **3,** *fig.* rift; split; breach. —**дать тре́щину,** to crack.

трещо́тка [*gen. pl.* -ток] *n.* **1,** rattle (*for making a noise*). **2,** ratchet. **3,** *colloq.* chatterbox.

три [*gen. & prepl.* трёх; *dat.* трём; *instr.* тремя́] *numeral* three.

триа́да *n.* triad.

триангуля́ция *n.* triangulation.

триа́совый *adj.* Triassic.

трибу́н *n.* tribune.

трибу́на *n.* **1,** speaker's rostrum. **2,** grandstand; stands.

трибуна́л *n.* tribunal.

тривиа́льный *adj.* trite; banal. —**тривиа́льность,** *n.f.* banality.

тригономе́трия *n.* trigonometry. —**тригонометри́ческий,** *adj.* trigonometric.

три́девять *numeral, colloq., in* **за три́девять земе́ль,** at the other end of the world.

тридцатиле́тний *adj.* **1,** thirty-year (*attrib.*). **2,** thirty-year-old.

тридца́тый *ordinal numeral* thirtieth.

три́дцать [*gen., dat., & prepl.* -цати́; *instr.* -цатью] *numeral* thirty.

три́жды *adv.* three times; thrice.

тризм *n.* lockjaw.

трико́ *n. indecl.* **1,** tricot. **2,** tights.

трикота́ж *n.* **1,** knitted fabric. **2,** knitted wear.

трикота́жный *adj.* **1,** knitting (*attrib.*). **2,** knitted.

триктра́к *n.* backgammon.

трили́стник *n.* trefoil; shamrock.

триллио́н *n.* trillion (*U.S.*); billion (*Brit.*).

трило́гия *n.* trilogy.

триме́стр *n.* trimester.

трина́дцатый *ordinal numeral* thirteenth.

трина́дцать *numeral* thirteen.

тринитротолуо́л *n.* trinitrotoluene.

три́о *n. indecl.* trio.

трио́д *n.* triode.

трио́ль *n.f., music* triplet.

три́ппер *n.* gonorrhea.

три́птих *n.* triptych.

три́ста [*gen.* трёхсо́т; *dat.* трёмста́м; *instr.* тремяста́ми; *prepl.* трёхста́х] *numeral* three hundred.

три́тий *n.* tritium.

трито́н *n., zool.* triton; newt.

триумви́р *n.* triumvir. —**триумвира́т,** *n.* triumvirate.

триу́мф *n.* triumph. —**триумфа́льный,** *adj.* triumphal.

трихи́на *n.* trichina.

трихинеллёз *n.* trichinosis.

тро́гательный *adj.* touching; moving; poignant. —**тро́гательность,** *n.f.* poignancy.

тро́гать *v. impfv.* [*pfv.* тро́нуть] **1,** to touch. **2,** bother; disturb. **3,** to touch; move; affect (*emotionally*). **4,** *v.i.* to start moving. —**тро́гаться,** *refl.* **1,** to start moving. **2,** [*often* тро́нуться в путь] to set out; start out. **3,** (*of ice*) to begin to break up. **4,** to be touched; be moved (*emotionally*). *See also* тро́нуть.

тро́е [*infl. like* дво́е] *collective numeral* three.

троекра́тный *adj.* done or happening three times; three-time.

тро́ица *n.* **1,** Trinity. **2,** *colloq.* Whitsunday.

тро́ицын *adj., in* тро́ицын день, Whitsunday.

тро́йка *n.* **1,** the numeral 3. **2,** *colloq.* anything numbered 3. **3,** troika. **4,** a grade of "three", signifying "satisfactory". **5,** *cards* three. **6,** *colloq.* [*also,* костю́м-тро́йка] three-piece suit.

тройно́й *adj.* triple; threefold; three-way.

тро́йня *n.* triplets.

тро́йственный *adj.* **1,** triple. **2,** tripartite.

троллейбус *n.* trolley bus. —**тролле́йбусный,** *adj.* trolley-bus (*attrib.*).

тролль *n.m., folklore* troll.

тромб *n.* blood clot. —**тромбо́з,** *n.* thrombosis.

тромбо́н *n.* trombone. —**тромбони́ст,** *n.* trombonist.

трон *n.* throne. —**тро́нный,** *adj.* throne (*attrib.*).

тро́нутый *adj.* **1,** [*short form only*] touched; moved (*emotionally*). **2,** *colloq.* touched in the head; wacky.

тро́нуть *v. pfv.* **1,** *pfv. of* тро́гать. **2,** to touch; affect: тро́нутый моро́зом, touched (*or* nipped) by the frost. —**тро́нуться,** *refl.* **1,** *pfv. of* тро́гаться. **2,** *colloq.* to be slightly touched (*or* wacky).

троп *n.* trope.

тропа́ [*pl.* тро́пы, троп, тропа́м *or* тро́пам] *n.* path.

тро́пик *n.* **1,** tropic: тро́пик Ра́ка, Tropic of Cancer; тро́пик Козеро́га, Tropic of Capricorn. **2,** *pl.* tropics.

тропи́нка [*gen. pl.* -нок] *n.* path.

тропи́ческий *adj.* tropical. —**тропи́ческий по́яс,** Torrid Zone.

тропосфе́ра *n.* troposphere.

трос *n.* rope; cable.

трости́нка [*gen. pl.* -нок] *n.* thin reed.

тростни́к [*gen.* -ника́] *n.* reed; rush; cane. —**са́харный тростни́к,** sugar cane.

тростнико́вый *adj.* **1,** reed (*attrib.*); rush (*attrib.*); cane (*attrib.*). **2,** overgrown with reeds; reedy.

тро́сточка [*gen. pl.* -чек] *n.* cane; walking stick.

трость [*pl.* тро́сти, -сте́й, -стя́м] *n.f.* cane; walking stick.

троти́л *n.* trinitrotoluene.

тротуа́р *n.* sidewalk; pavement.

трофе́й *n.* **1,** trophy; memento. **2,** *pl.* spoils; booty. —**трофе́йный,** *adj.* captured (*in war*).

трохе́й *n.* trochee. —**трохеи́ческий,** *adj.* trochaic.

троюро́дный *adj., denoting relationships of cousins:* троюро́дный брат; троюро́дная сестра́, second cousin.

троя́кий *adj.* triple; threefold.

троя́нский *adj.* Trojan.

труба́ [*pl.* тру́бы] *n.* **1,** pipe. Дымова́я труба́, chimney; smokestack. **2,** trumpet. **3,** *anat.* tube. —**вы́лететь в трубу́,** *colloq.* to go broke. —**пусти́ть в трубу́,** *colloq.* **1,** to bankrupt; ruin. **2,** to squander; dissipate.

трубаду́р *n.* troubadour.

труба́ч [*gen.* -бача́] *n.* trumpeter; trumpet player.

труби́ть *v. impfv.* [*pfv.* протруби́ть; *pres.* трублю́, труби́шь] **1,** (*with* в + *acc.*) to blow (a trumpet). **2,** to sound; signal; announce. **3,** to sound; blare. **4,** (*with* о) *colloq.* to trumpet; crow about.

тру́бка [*gen. pl.* -бок] *n.* **1,** tube; pipe. **2,** receiver (*of a telephone*). Возьми́те тру́бку!, pick up the phone! Я переда́м тру́бку (+ *dat.*), I'll put... on. **3,** pipe (*for smoking*). **4,** fuse. **5,** roll (*of material*).

трубкозу́б *n.* aardvark.

тру́бный *adj.* **1,** pipe (*attrib.*). **2,** trumpet (*attrib.*).

трубопрово́д *n.* conduit; pipeline.

трубочи́ст *n.* chimney sweep.

тру́бочный *adj.* pipe (*attrib.*): тру́бочный таба́к, pipe tobacco.

тру́бчатый *adj.* tubular.

труд [*gen.* труда́] *n.* **1,** labor. **2,** effort; trouble; difficulty: не сто́ит труда́, it's not worth the trouble. **3,** (written) work (*usually of a scientific nature*). —**дать себе́** (*or* **взять на себя́**) **труд,** to take the trouble. —**с трудо́м, 1,** with difficulty. **2,** hardly; scarcely; barely.

труди́ться *v.r. impfv.* [*pres.* **тружу́сь, тру́дишься**] **1,** to work; labor; toil. **2,** *colloq.* to bother; take the trouble.

тру́дно *adv.* with difficulty. Тру́дно произноси́мое сло́во, a difficult (*or* hard) word to pronounce. —*adj., used predicatively* difficult; hard: тру́дно сказа́ть, it is difficult/hard to say. Мне тру́дно пове́рить э́тому, I find that hard to believe.

тру́дность *n.f.* difficulty.

тру́дный *adj.* [*short form* **-ден, -дна́, -дно**] difficult; hard.

трудово́й *adj.* **1,** labor (*attrib.*). **2,** working. **3,** earned: трудовы́е дохо́ды, earned income. —**трудова́я кни́жка,** work-record book.

трудоде́нь [*gen.* **-дня́**] *n.m.* workday (*unit of payment on collective farms*).

трудоёмкий *adj.* **1,** labor-intensive. **2,** time-consuming.

трудолюби́вый *adj.* hard-working; industrious. —**трудолю́бие,** *n.* industry; industriousness.

трудоспосо́бный *adj.* able to work; able-bodied. —**трудоспосо́бность,** *n.f.* ability to work.

трудоустро́йство *n.* job placement.

трудя́щийся *adj.* working; laboring. —*n.* worker; laborer.

тру́женик *n.* worker; toiler.

труни́ть *v. impfv.* (*with* **над**) *colloq.* to make fun of; kid.

труп *n.* dead body; corpse; cadaver.

трупиа́л *n.* oriole.

тру́пный *adj.* **1,** of or like a corpse. **2,** (*of an odor*) putrid. —**тру́пное окочене́ние,** rigor mortis. —**тру́пный яд,** ptomaine.

тру́ппа *n.* company; troupe.

трус *n.m.* [*fem.* **-си́ха**] coward.

тру́сики [*gen.* **-ков**] *n. pl.* **1,** shorts. **2,** undershorts; underpants; panties.

тру́сить *v. impfv.* [*pfv.* **стру́сить**; *pres.* **тру́шу, тру́сишь**] to be a coward; be afraid; get cold feet.

труси́ть *v. impfv.* [*pres.* **трушу́, труси́шь**] *colloq.* to trot; jog.

труси́ха *n., fem. of* **трус.**

трусли́вый *adj.* cowardly.

тру́сость *n.f.* cowardice.

трусца́ *n., colloq.* trot.

трусы́ [*gen.* **-со́в**] *n. pl.* **1,** shorts. **2,** undershorts; underpants.

трут *n.* tinder.

тру́тень [*gen.* **-тня**] *n.m.* drone.

труха́ *n.* **1,** dust; flakes; bits (*of hay, straw, rotted wood, etc.*). **2,** *fig.* trash; rubbish.

трухля́вый *adj.* moldering; rotten.

трущо́ба *n.* **1,** thicket. **2,** out-of-the-way place. **3,** slum.

трын-трава́ *predicate* (*with dat.*) *colloq.* all the same: ему́ всё трын-трава́, it's all the same to him.

трюи́зм *n.* truism.

трюк *n.* trick; stunt. —**трю́ковый,** *adj.* trick (*attrib.*).

трюм *n.* hold (*of a ship*).

трюмо́ *n. indecl.* pier glass.

трю́фель [*pl.* **трю́фели, -ле́й, -ля́м**] *n.m.* **1,** truffle. **2,** *pl.* chocolate truffles.

тряпи́чник *n.* ragman.

тряпи́чный *adj.* rag (*attrib.*).

тря́пка [*gen. pl.* **-пок**] *n.* **1,** rag. **2,** *pl., colloq.* clothes; finery. **3,** *colloq.* milksop; weakling.

тряпьё *n.* rags.

тряси́на *n.* quagmire.

тря́ска *n.* bumpiness; shaking.

тря́ский *adj.* **1,** (*of a vehicle*) that shakes a lot; shaky. **2,** (*of a road*) bumpy.

трясогу́зка [*gen. pl.* **-зок**] *n.* wagtail (*bird*).

трясти́ *v. impfv.* [*pfv.* **тряхну́ть**; *pres.* **трясу́, трясёшь**; *past* **тряс, трясла́, трясло́**] **1,** to shake: трясти́ де́рево, to shake a tree; трясти́ голово́й, to shake one's head. **2,** to shake out. **3,** *impers.* (*of a person*) to be shaking: его́ всего́ трясёт, he is shaking all over. **4,** (*of a vehicle*) to shake. —**трясти́сь,** *refl.* **1,** to shake. **2,** to tremble. **3,** *colloq.* to bounce along. **4,** (*with* **над**) *colloq.* to guard with one's life; watch like a hawk.

тсс *interj.* hush!

тсу́га *n.* hemlock (*tree*).

ту *adj., fem. acc. of* **тот.**

туале́т *n.* **1,** dress; clothes. **2,** toilet; grooming. **3,** dressing table; vanity. **4,** rest room; washroom.

туале́тный *adj.* toilet (*attrib.*). —**туале́тный сто́лик,** dressing table; vanity.

ту́ба *n.* tuba.

туберкулёз *n.* tuberculosis. —**туберкулёзный,** *adj.* tubercular; tuberculous.

туберо́за *n.* tuberose.

туви́нец [*gen.* **-нца**] *n.m.* [*fem.* **-нка**] Tuvinian (*one of a people inhabiting southern Siberia*). —**туви́нский,** *adj.* Tuvinian.

ту́го *adv.* **1,** tight; tightly. **2,** *colloq.* with difficulty; slowly. —*adj., used predicatively, colloq.* short of: с деньга́ми мне ту́го, I am short of money.

тугоду́м *n., colloq.* dimwit.

туго́й *adj.* [*comp.* **ту́же**] **1,** tight; taut. **2,** tightly filled; stuffed. **3,** slow to grasp things; dense; dull. —**туго́й на де́ньги,** tight with one's money. —**туго́й на язы́к,** slow of speech; inarticulate. —**туго́й на́ ухо,** hard of hearing.

тугоу́хий *adj.* hard of hearing; partially deaf.

туда́ *adv., expressing direction,* there: посмотри́те туда́!, look over there! Положи́те э́то туда́!, put it (over) there! —**не туда́,** to the wrong place; in the wrong direction. Вы не туда́ попа́ли, you've got the wrong number (*on the telephone*). —**ни туда́ ни сюда́,** neither backward nor forward; unable to move. —**туда́ и обра́тно,** there and back. Биле́т туда́ и обра́тно, round-trip ticket. Пое́здка туда́ и обра́тно, round trip. —**туда́ и сюда́,** back and forth.

туда́-сюда́ *adv., colloq.* **1,** here and there; around and about. **2,** all right; so-so; passable.

ту́же *adj., comp. of* **туго́й.**

тужи́ть *v. impfv.* [*pres.* **тужу́, ту́жишь**] *colloq.* to grieve.

ту́житься *v.r. impfv., colloq.* to exert oneself; make a great effort.

тужу́рка [*gen. pl.* **-рок**] *n.* man's double-breasted jacket.

туз [*gen. & acc.* **туза́**] *n.* **1,** *cards* ace. **2,** *colloq.* bigwig.

тузе́мец [*gen.* **-мца**] *n.m.* [*fem.* **-мка**] native. —**тузе́мный,** *adj.* native; indigenous.

тузи́ть *v. impfv.* [*pfv.* **оттузи́ть**; *pres.* **тужу́, тузи́шь**] *colloq.* to thrash; pommel.

тука́н *n.* toucan.

ту́кать *v. impfv.* [*pfv.* **ту́кнуть**] *colloq.* **1,** to slam. **2,** to tap; clack. —**ту́каться,** *refl.* (*with* **о** + *acc.*) *colloq.* to bang into.

ту́лий *n.* thulium.

ту́ловище *n.* trunk; torso.

тулу́п *n.* sheepskin coat.

тулья́ [*gen. pl.* -ле́й] *n.* crown (*of a hat*).

тума́к [*gen.* -мака́; *acc.* тума́к *or* -мака́] *n., colloq.* punch; wallop; clout.

тума́н *n.* fog.

тума́нить *v. impfv.* [*pfv.* затума́нить] to cloud; obscure. —**тума́ниться,** *refl.* **1,** to be obscured by fog. **2,** (*of one's eyes*) to become dim; (*of the senses*) to become muddled.

тума́нность *n.f.* **1,** fog; fogginess. **2,** *fig.* vagueness; obscurity. **3,** *astron.* nebula.

тума́нный *adj.* **1,** foggy; misty. **2,** *fig.* hazy; vague.

ту́мба *n.* **1,** curbside stone or post. **2,** stand; pedestal.

ту́мбочка [*gen. pl.* -чек] *n.* night table.

тунг *n.* tung tree. —**ту́нговый,** *adj.* tung (*attrib.*): ту́нговое ма́сло, tung oil.

ту́ндра *n.* tundra. —**ту́ндровый,** *adj.* tundra (*attrib.*).

туне́ц [*gen.* -нца́] *n.* tuna.

туне́ядец [*gen.* -дца] *n.* parasite; sponger. —**туне-я́дство,** *n.* parasitism.

туни́ка *n.* tunic (*worn in ancient times*).

тунне́ль (нэ) *n.m.* tunnel.

тупе́ть *v. impfv.* **1,** to become dull. **2,** (*of the senses*) to become clouded.

ту́пик *n.* puffin (*bird*).

тупи́к [*gen.* тупика́] *n.* **1,** blind alley; dead-end street. **2,** *fig.* impasse; deadlock. —**зайти́ в тупи́к,** to reach an impasse; be deadlocked. —**ста́вить в тупи́к,** to put on the spot; throw for a loss. —**стать в тупи́к,** to be on the spot; be at a loss.

тупи́ть *v. impfv.* [*pfv.* иступи́ть *or* затупи́ть; *pres.* туплю́, ту́пишь] to blunt; dull; take the edge off. —**тупи́ться,** *refl.* to dull; become dull.

тупи́ца *n.m. & f., colloq.* dimwit; dullard; dolt.

тупоголо́вый *adj., colloq.* dimwitted; thickheaded.

тупо́й *adj.* **1,** dull; blunt. **2,** (*of pain, sounds, etc.*) dull. **3,** (*of a person*) dull; obtuse. **4,** (*of a look, expression, etc.*) vacant; blank. —**тупо́й у́гол,** obtuse angle. —**ту-по́е ударе́ние,** grave accent.

ту́пость *n.f.* **1,** dullness; bluntness. **2,** dullness; obtuseness.

тупоу́мие *n.* dullness; obtuseness. —**тупоу́мный,** *adj.* thickheaded; dimwitted.

тур *n.* **1,** turn (*in dancing*). **2,** round (*of a tournament, negotiations, etc.*). **3,** stage; phase. **4,** aurochs.

тура́ *n., chess* rook; castle.

турба́за *n.* tourist center. —**молодёжная турба́за,** youth hostel.

турби́на *n.* turbine. —**турби́нный,** *adj.* turbine (*attrib.*).

турбовинтово́й *adj.* turboprop (*attrib.*).

турбореакти́вный *adj.* turbojet (*attrib.*).

туре́цкий *adj.* Turkish. —**туре́цкий бараба́н,** bass drum. —**туре́цкий горо́х,** chickpea.

тури́зм *n.* tourism. —**тури́ст,** *n.* tourist.

туристи́ческий *adj.* **1,** tourist (*attrib.*). **2,** walking (*attrib.*); hiking (*attrib.*): туристи́ческий похо́д, walking tour; hiking expedition.

тури́стский *adj.* tourist (*attrib.*).

туркме́н [*gen. pl.* -ме́н] *n.m.* [*fem.* -ме́нка] Turkmen (*one of a people inhabiting the Turkmen S.S.R.*). —**туркме́нский,** *adj.* Turkmen.

турмали́н *n.* tourmaline.

ту́рман *n.* tumbler pigeon.

турне́ (нэ) *n. neut. indecl.* tour.

турни́к [*gen.* -ника́] *n., sports* horizontal bar.

турнике́т *n.* turnstile.

турни́р *n.* tournament.

ту́рок [*gen.* ту́рка; *gen. pl.* ту́рок] *n.m.* [*fem.* турча́н-ка] Turk.

турухта́н *n.* ruff (*bird*).

ту́скло *adv.* dimly.

ту́склость *n.f.* dullness; dimness.

ту́склый *adj.* **1,** (*of light*) dim. **2,** (*of metals*) dull; lackluster. **3,** dreary; overcast. **4,** *fig.* colorless; insipid.

тускне́ть *v. impfv.* [*pfv.* потускне́ть] **1,** to grow dim; lose its luster. **2,** *fig.* to fade; wane. **3,** [*impfv. only*] (*with* пе́ред) to pale (before).

тут *adv., expressing location,* here. —**(быть) тут как тут,** *colloq.* to appear like clockwork; be Johnny on the spot. —**не тут-то бы́ло,** it was not to be. —**там и тут,** here and there. —**тут же,** then and there; there and then.

туто́вник *n.* mulberry tree.

ту́товый *adj.* mulberry (*attrib.*). —**ту́товый шелко-пря́д,** silkworm. —**ту́товая я́года,** mulberry.

ту́фелька [*gen. pl.* -лек] *n.* **1,** small shoe; fancy shoe. **2,** paramecium.

ту́фля [*gen. pl.* -фель] *n.* shoe: ту́фли на высо́ких каблука́х, high-heeled shoes. —**дома́шние ту́фли,** (bedroom) slippers.

ту́хлый *adj.* rotten; spoiled; tainted.

тухля́тина *n., colloq.* **1,** food which has spoiled or become rotten. **2,** foul odor from such food.

ту́хнуть *v. impfv.* [*past* тух *or* ту́хнул, ту́хла] **1,** [*pfv.* поту́хнуть] (*of something burning*) to go out. **2,** [*pfv.* проту́хнуть] to spoil; rot.

ту́ча *n.* cloud; storm cloud.

тучне́ть *v. impfv.* [*pfv.* потучне́ть] to grow fat; put on weight.

ту́чность *n.f.* **1,** obesity; corpulence. **2,** richness; fertility.

ту́чный *adj.* **1,** fat; stout; obese. **2,** (*of soil*) rich; fertile. **3,** (*of grass, grain, a meadow, etc.*) lush.

туш *n.* flourish (*of trumpets*).

ту́ша *n.* carcass.

туше́ *n. neut. indecl.* touch (*when playing a musical instrument*).

тушева́ть *v. impfv.* [*pfv.* затушева́ть; *pres.* -шу́ю, -шу́ешь] **1,** to shade; add shading to. **2,** *fig.* to soften; tone down. —**тушева́ться,** *refl.* [*pfv.* стушева́ться] *colloq.* to become flustered.

тушёвка *n.* shading.

туше́ние *n.* **1,** extinguishing. **2,** stewing.

тушёный *adj.* stewed; braised.

туши́ть *v. impfv.* [*pres.* тушу́, ту́шишь] **1,** [*pfv.* поту-ши́ть] to put out; extinguish (a fire, candle, etc.); turn out; turn off (a light). **2,** [*pfv.* стуши́ть] to stew; braise.

тушка́нчик *n.* jerboa.

тушь *n.f.* **1,** India ink. **2,** mascara.

тща́тельный *adj.* careful; painstaking. —**тща́тельно,** *adv.* carefully; painstakingly. —**тща́тельность,** *n.f.* care.

тщеду́шие *n.* frailty. —**тщеду́шный,** *adj.* frail.

тщесла́вие *n.* vanity. —**тщесла́вный,** *adj.* vain.

тще́тный *adj.* vain; futile. —**тще́тно,** *adv.* vainly; in vain. —**тще́тность,** *n.f.* futility.

ТЩИ́ТЬСЯ *v.r. impfv.* (*with inf.*) to try (to); endeavor (to); take pains (to).

ТЫ [*gen. & acc.* **тебя́**; *dat. & prepl.* **тебе́**; *instr.* **тобо́й** *or* **тобо́ю**] *pers. pron., 2nd person sing.* you (*familiar*). —**быть с** с (+ *instr.*) **на ты**, to address each other as "ты" (*as opposed to* "вы").

ТЫ́КАТЬ[1] *v. impfv.* [*pfv.* **ткнуть**; *pres.* **ты́чу, ты́чешь**] *colloq.* **1,** to stick; thrust. **2,** to poke; jab. —**ты́каться**, *refl., colloq.* **1,** (*with* **в** + *acc.*) to bang into. **2,** (*with instr.*) to stick; poke (one's nose, head, etc.) into. **3,** to rush about; bustle about.

ТЫ́КАТЬ[2] *v. impfv.* [*pres.* **ты́каю, ты́каешь**] *colloq.* to address someone using the familiar pronoun **ты**.

ТЫ́КВА *n.* pumpkin. —**ты́квенный**, *adj.* pumpkin (*attrib.*).

ТЫЛ [*2nd loc.* **тылу́**; *pl.* **тылы́**] *n., mil.* **1,** rear. **2,** rear services. —**тылово́й**, *adj.* rear.

ТЫ́ЛЬНЫЙ *adj.* rear; back. —**ты́льная сторона́ руки́**, back of the hand.

ТЫН *n.* paling; fence.

ТЫ́СЯЧА *numeral* thousand.

ТЫ́СЯЧЕКРА́ТНЫЙ *adj.* thousandfold.

ТЫСЯЧЕЛЕ́ТИЕ *n.* **1,** millennium. **2,** thousandth anniversary.

ТЫСЯЧЕЛЕ́ТНИЙ *adj.* **1,** thousand-year (*attrib.*). **2,** thousand-year-old.

ТЫ́СЯЧНАЯ *n., decl. as an adj.* thousandth: одна́ ты́сячная, one-thousandth.

ТЫ́СЯЧНЫЙ *ordinal numeral* thousandth. —*adj.* consisting of many thousands: ты́сячная толпа́, a crowd of many thousands.

ТЫЧИ́НКА *n.* stamen.

ТЫЧО́К [*gen.* **-чка́**] *n., colloq.* **1,** poke; jab. **2,** something sticking up in the air.

ТЬМА *n.* **1,** darkness. **2,** (*with gen.*) *colloq.* a host (of); a multitude (of).

ТЬФУ *interj.* bah!; phooey!

ТЮБЕТЕ́ЙКА [*gen. pl.* **-те́ек**] *n.* skullcap (*worn in Central Asia*).

ТЮ́БИК *n.* tube (*for glue, toothpaste, etc.*).

ТЮ́БИНГ *n.* tubing; piping.

ТЮК [*gen.* **тюка́**] *n.* **1,** bale. **2,** bundle.

ТЮ́КАТЬ *v. impfv.* [*pfv.* **тю́кнуть**] *colloq.* to bang.

ТЮ́ЛЕВЫЙ *adj.* tulle.

ТЮЛЕ́НЕВЫЙ *adj.* **1,** seal (*attrib.*). **2,** sealskin.

ТЮЛЕ́НИЙ [*fem.* **-нья**] *adj.* seal (*attrib.*).

ТЮЛЕ́НЬ *n.m.* seal (*sea animal*).

ТЮЛЬ *n.m.* tulle.

ТЮЛЬПА́Н *n.* tulip. —**тюльпа́нный**, *adj.* tulip (*attrib.*).

ТЮРБА́Н *n.* turban.

ТЮРБО́ *n. indecl.* turbot.

ТЮРЕ́МНЫЙ *adj.* prison (*attrib.*); jail (*attrib.*). —**тюре́мное заключе́ние**, imprisonment.

ТЮРЕ́МЩИК *n.* jailer.

ТЮ́РКСКИЙ *adj.* Turkic.

ТЮРЬМА́ [*pl.* **тю́рьмы, тю́рем**] *n.* jail; prison.

ТЮФЯ́К [*gen.* **тюфяка́**] *n.* straw mattress.

ТЯ́ВКАТЬ *v. impfv.* [*pfv.* **тя́вкнуть**] to yelp.

ТЯГ *n., in* дать тя́гу, *colloq.* to take to one's heels; make tracks.

ТЯ́ГА *n.* **1,** pulling; towing. **2,** pulling power; traction. **3,** thrust (*of an engine*). **4,** rod: соедини́тельная тя́га, connecting rod. **5,** draft (*of a chimney*). **6,** (*with* **к**) bent (for); craving (for).

ТЯГА́ТЬСЯ *v.r. impfv.* [*pfv.* **потяга́ться**] (*with* **с** + *instr.*) to compete (with); contend (with); vie (with).

ТЯГА́Ч [*gen.* **тягача́**] *n.* tractor (*for hauling trailers*). —**артиллери́йский тяга́ч**, artillery mover. —**тяга́ч с прице́пом**, tractor-trailer.

ТЯ́ГЛО *n.* **1,** *hist.* tax; impost; assessment. **2,** [*also*, **живо́е тя́гло**] draft animals.

ТЯ́ГЛОВЫЙ *adj.* **1,** *hist.* taxed. **2,** (*of animals*) draft.

ТЯ́ГЛЫЙ *adj.* (*of animals*) draft.

ТЯ́ГОВЫЙ *adj.* **1,** tractive. **2,** used to haul: тя́говый кана́т, hauling rope.

ТЯ́ГОСТНЫЙ *adj.* **1,** burdensome; onerous. **2,** painful; distressing.

ТЯ́ГОСТЬ *n.f.* burden: быть в тя́гость (+ *dat.*), to be a burden (to).

ТЯГОТА́ [*pl.* **тя́готы**] *n.* **1,** burden. **2,** *pl.* (*with gen.*) the rigors (of): тя́готы пути́, the rigors of traveling.

ТЯГОТЕ́НИЕ *n.* **1,** *physics* gravity. **2,** (*with* **к**) gravitation (toward). **3,** (*with* **к**) *fig.* bent (for); liking (for).

ТЯГОТЕ́ТЬ *v. impfv.* **1,** (*with* **к**) to gravitate (toward); be drawn (to). **2,** (*with* **над**) to hang over; tower over. **3,** *fig.* (*with* **над**) to hang over; weigh upon.

ТЯГОТИ́ТЬ *v. impfv.* [*pres.* **-гощу́, -готи́шь**] **1,** to burden; weigh down. **2,** (*of an article of clothing*) to bother; make uncomfortable. —**тяготи́ться**, *refl.* (*with instr.*) to be burdened (by); feel (something) as a burden.

ТЯГУ́ЧЕСТЬ *n.f.* **1,** stretchability. **2,** malleability. **3,** viscosity.

ТЯГУ́ЧИЙ *adj.* **1,** stretchable. **2,** malleable; ductile. **3,** viscous. **4,** *fig.* slow; drawn-out. **5,** *fig.* dull; boring; monotonous.

ТЯ́ЖБА *n., obs.* lawsuit; litigation.

ТЯЖЕЛЕ́ТЬ *v. impfv.* to become heavy; grow heavy.

ТЯЖЕЛО́ *adv.* **1,** heavily. **2,** gravely; seriously; severely. —*adj., used predicatively* (*often with dat.*) **1,** hard; difficult. **2,** miserable; wretched. **3,** grievous; painful.

ТЯЖЕЛОАТЛЕ́Т *n.* **1,** wrestler. **2,** weightlifter.

ТЯЖЕЛОВЕ́С *n., sports* heavyweight.

ТЯЖЕЛОВЕ́СНЫЙ *adj.* heavy; ponderous.

ТЯЖЁЛЫЙ *adj.* **1,** heavy. **2,** hard; difficult. **3,** grave; serious; severe. **4,** painful; grievous; distressing. **5,** (*of thoughts, a feeling, odor, etc.*) oppressive. **6,** (*of a style of writing*) ponderous.

ТЯ́ЖЕСТЬ *n.f.* **1,** weight. **2,** load. **3,** *physics* gravity. **4,** heaviness. **5,** gravity; severity.

ТЯ́ЖКИЙ *adj.* **1,** *obs.* heavy. **2,** grave; severe. **3,** distressing. —**пусти́ться во все тя́жкие**, **1,** to let oneself go. **2,** to go all out.

ТЯНУ́ТЬ *v. impfv.* [*pfv.* **потяну́ть**; *pres.* **тяну́, тя́нешь**] **1,** to pull; tug. **2,** to haul; tow. **3,** to stretch; extend. **4,** to draw; attract. **5,** *colloq.* to drag (someone) somewhere against his will. **6,** (*with* **с** + *instr.*) to delay: тяну́ть с отве́том, to delay in answering. **7,** [*impfv. only*] to drag out; prolong. **8,** [*impfv. only*] to sustain; prolong (a note, song, etc.). **9,** (*of a chimney*) to draw. **10,** to sustain oneself; subsist. **11,** *usu. impers.* to blow gently; waft. **12,** to weigh (so much). **13,** *impers.* to long to: его́ тя́нет домо́й, he is longing to go home. —**тяну́ться**, *refl.* [*impfv. only*] **1,** to stretch. **2,** to stretch; extend (*over a distance*). **3,** [*pfv.* **потяну́ться**] (*with* **за** *or* **к**) to reach for; reach out for. **4,** to follow along; follow in succession. **5,** to move slowly along. **6,** to last; drag on. **7,** (*with* **к**) to be drawn toward. **8,** (*of clouds, smoke, etc.*) to drift. **9,** (*with* **за** + *instr.*) *colloq.* to try to keep up with.

ТЯНУ́ЧКА *n.* taffy.

ТЯ́ПКА [*gen. pl.* **-пок**] *n.* chopping knife; cleaver.

ТЯ́ТЯ *n.m., colloq.* dad; pop.

У

У, у *n. neut.* twentieth letter of the Russian alphabet.

у *prep., with gen.* **1,** by; at; near: стоя́ть у окна́, to stand at/by/near the window. **2,** at the home of: жить у родны́х, to live with one's relatives. **3,** *indicating possession:* у меня́ три бра́та, I have three brothers. **4,** from: узна́ть что́-нибудь у сосе́да, to find out something from one's neighbor.

у- *prefix* **1,** *indicating movement away:* убега́ть, to run away. **2,** *indicating the imparting of a quality or attribute:* удлиня́ть, to lengthen; углубля́ть, to deepen. **3,** *indicating reduction:* убавля́ть, to reduce; ушива́ть, to take in. **4,** *indicating covering of a surface:* усыпа́ть, to strew; bestrew; устила́ть, to cover; overlay.

уба́вить [*infl.* -влю, -вишь] *v., pfv. of* убавля́ть. —**уба́виться,** *refl., pfv. of* убавля́ться.

убавля́ть *v. impfv.* [*pfv.* уба́вить] **1,** to reduce; lower. **2,** *in* убавля́ть в ве́се, *colloq.* to lose weight. —**убавля́ться,** *refl.* **1,** to be reduced in size; become smaller. **2,** to decrease; diminish.

убаю́кать *v., pfv. of* баю́кать *and* убаю́кивать.

убаю́кивать *v. impfv.* [*pfv.* убаю́кать] **1,** to lull to sleep. **2,** *fig.* to lull.

убега́ть *v. impfv.* [*pfv.* убежа́ть] **1,** to run away; flee. **2,** to escape. **3,** [*impfv. only*] (*of inanimate objects*) to extend; retreat; disappear (into the distance).

убеди́тельно *adv.* **1,** convincingly; persuasively. **2,** earnestly: убеди́тельно прошу́ вас, I urge you; I beg you.

убеди́тельность *n.f.* persuasiveness.

убеди́тельный *adj.* **1,** convincing; persuasive. **2,** (*of a request*) urgent; earnest.

убеди́ть [*infl.* -ди́шь, -ди́т; *1st person sing. not used*] *v., pfv. of* убежда́ть. —**убеди́ться,** *refl., pfv. of* убежда́ться.

убежа́ть [*infl. like* бежа́ть] *v., pfv. of* убега́ть.

убежда́ть *v. impfv.* [*pfv.* убеди́ть] **1,** (*with* в + *prepl.*) to convince (of). **2,** (*with inf.*) to persuade (to). **3,** [*impfv. only*] to try to persuade; urge. —**убежда́ться,** *refl.* (*with* в + *prepl. or a dependent clause*) **1,** to become convinced (of *or* that). **2,** to make sure (of *or* that). **3,** *in* сам убеди́ться, to see for oneself.

убежде́ние *n.* **1,** persuasion. **2,** belief; conviction.

убеждённо *adv.* with conviction. —**убеждённость,** *n.f.* conviction; certainty.

убеждённый *adj.* **1,** convinced. **2,** staunch; confirmed.

убе́жище *n.* **1,** refuge. **2,** asylum: пра́во убе́жища, right of asylum. **3,** *mil.* shelter; dugout.

убере́чь *v. pfv.* [*infl. like* бере́чь] to protect.

убива́ть *v. impfv.* [*pfv.* уби́ть] to kill. —**убива́ться,** *refl., colloq.* **1,** to be killed. **2,** to hurt oneself. **3,** [*impfv. only*] to work oneself to the bone; "kill oneself". **4,** [*impfv. only*] to grieve; mourn.

уби́йственный *adj.* **1,** deadly. **2,** murderous; unbearable. **3,** (*of a result or consequences*) disastrous. **4,** (*of news, criticism, a look, etc.*) devastating.

уби́йство *n.* murder; assassination.

уби́йца *n.m. & f.* killer; murderer; assassin.

убира́ть *v. impfv.* [*pfv.* убра́ть] **1,** to take away; remove. **2,** to put away. **3,** to delete; take out. **4,** to clean up; tidy up; straighten up. **5,** *in* убра́ть со стола́, to clear the table. **6,** to make (a bed). **7,** *colloq.* to take in (a garment). **8,** to gather in; harvest. **9,** to decorate; adorn. —**убира́ться,** *refl., colloq.* **1,** to clear out; beat it; vamoose. **2,** to clean up; tidy up.

уби́тый *adj.* **1,** killed; murdered. **2,** *fig.* crushed (*in spirit*): уби́тый го́рем, heartbroken; broken-hearted. —*n.* dead man; person who has been killed. —**спать как уби́тый,** to sleep like a log.

уби́ть [*infl.* убью́, убьёшь] *v., pfv. of* убива́ть. —**уби́ться,** *refl., pfv. of* убива́ться.

ублажа́ть *v. impfv.* [*pfv.* ублажи́ть] *colloq.* to indulge; cater to.

ублю́док [*gen.* -дка] *n., colloq.* **1,** cur; mongrel. **2,** cur (*contemptible person*).

убо́гий *adj.* **1,** wretched; squalid. **2,** crippled; disfigured. **3,** *fig.* empty; sterile.

убо́гость *n.f.* **1,** utter poverty; squalor. **2,** *fig.* emptiness; sterility; poverty.

убо́жество *n.* **1,** utter poverty; squalor. **2,** *fig.* emptiness; sterility; poverty. **3,** *obs.* physical disability; deformity.

убо́й *n.* slaughtering; slaughter (*of animals*). —**корми́ть (как) на убо́й,** to stuff to the gills. —**посыла́ть (кого́-нибудь) на убо́й,** to send off to be slaughtered.

убо́йный *adj.* **1,** (*of animals*) to be slaughtered; intended for slaughter; (*of a place*) slaughtering (*attrib.*). **2,** *mil.* (*of power, energy, etc.*) destructive; lethal.

убо́р *n., archaic* attire. —**головно́й убо́р,** headdress.

убо́ристый *adj.* (*of writing, type, etc.*) close.

убо́рка *n.* **1,** cleaning up; tidying up. **2,** gathering in; harvesting.

убо́рная *n., decl. as an adj.* **1,** lavatory; washroom. **2,** *theat.* dressing room.

убо́рочный *adj.* harvesting (*attrib.*). —**убо́рочная маши́на,** harvester.

убо́рщик *n.* janitor; porter. —**убо́рщица,** *n.* cleaning woman; maid.

убра́нство *n.* **1,** furnishings. **2,** *obs.* dress; attire.

убра́ть [*infl. like* брать] *v., pfv. of* убира́ть. —убра́ться, *refl., pfv. of* убира́ться.

убыва́ть *v. impfv.* [*pfv.* убы́ть] **1,** to decrease; wane; recede; subside. **2,** to leave; take leave.

у́быль *n.f.* **1,** decrease. **2,** loss. —идти́ на у́быль, to wane; ebb; subside.

убы́ток [*gen.* -тка] *n.* **1,** loss: продава́ть в убы́ток (*or* с убы́тком), to sell at a loss. **2,** *pl.* losses; damages.

убы́точный *adj.* unprofitable.

убы́ть [*infl.* убу́ду, убу́дешь; *past* у́был, убыла́, у́было] *v., pfv. of* убыва́ть.

уважа́емый *adj.* **1,** respected; honored. **2,** (*in direct address or salutations*) dear.

уважа́ть *v. impfv.* to respect.

уваже́ние *n.* respect. —с уваже́нием, sincerely yours (*in letters*).

уважи́тельный *adj.* **1,** valid; legitimate. **2,** respectful; deferential.

ува́жить *v. pfv., colloq.* **1,** to comply with; honor (a request). **2,** to humor; be nice to.

у́валень [*gen.* -льня] *n.m., colloq.* lout; lummox.

ува́риваться *v.r. impfv.* [*pfv.* увари́ться] *colloq.* to be thoroughly cooked.

увари́ться [*infl.* ува́рится] *v.r., pfv. of* ува́риваться.

уве́домить [*infl.* -млю, -мишь] *v., pfv. of* уведомля́ть.

уведомле́ние *n.* notification; notice.

уведомля́ть *v. impfv.* [*pfv.* уве́домить] to notify; inform.

увезти́ [*infl. like* везти́] *v., pfv. of* увози́ть.

увекове́чение *n.* immortalization; perpetuation.

увекове́чивать *v. impfv.* [*pfv.* увекове́чить] **1,** to immortalize. **2,** to perpetuate.

увеличе́ние *n.* **1,** increase. **2,** magnification; *photog.* enlargement.

увели́чивать *v. impfv.* [*pfv.* увели́чить] **1,** to increase. **2,** to magnify; *photog.* enlarge. —увели́чиваться, *refl.* to increase; grow.

увеличи́тель *n.m., photog.* enlarger.

увеличи́тельный *adj.* magnifying. —увеличи́тельный аппара́т, enlarger. —увеличи́тельное стекло́, magnifying glass.

увели́чить *v., pfv. of* увели́чивать. —увели́читься, *refl., pfv. of* увели́чиваться.

увенча́ть *v., pfv. of* венча́ть (*in sense* #1) *and* увенчивать. —увенча́ться, *refl., pfv. of* венча́ться (*in sense* #1) *and* уве́нчиваться.

уве́нчивать *v. impfv.* [*pfv.* увенча́ть] to crown. —уве́нчиваться, *refl.* **1,** *obs.* to be crowned. **2,** (*with instr.*) to culminate (in): увенча́ться успе́хом, to succeed; be crowned with success.

уве́рение *n.* assurance.

уве́ренность *n.f.* **1,** confidence. **2,** assurance; certainty.

уве́ренный *adj.* [*short form* уве́рен, -ена] **1,** sure; certain; confident. **2,** [*usu. short form*] (*with* в + *prepl.*) sure (of); certain (of).

уве́рить *v., pfv. of* уверя́ть. —уве́риться, *refl., pfv. of* уверя́ться.

уверну́ться *v.r., pfv. of* увёртываться.

уве́ровать *v. pfv.* [*infl.* -рую, -руешь] (*with* в + *acc.*) to come to believe (in).

увёртка [*gen. pl.* -ток] *n., colloq.* subterfuge; dodge; ruse; trick.

увёртливый *adj.* shifty; evasive.

увёртываться *v.r. impfv.* [*pfv.* увернуться] (*with* от) to evade; dodge.

увертю́ра *n., music* overture.

уверя́ть *v. impfv.* [*pfv.* уве́рить] to assure. —уверя́ться, *refl.* **1,** to make sure. **2,** to become convinced.

увеселе́ние *n.* entertainment; amusement.

увесели́тельный *adj.* amusement (*attrib.*); entertainment (*attrib.*); pleasure (*attrib.*).

увеселя́ть *v. impfv.* to entertain; amuse.

уве́систый *adj.* weighty; heavy.

увести́ [*infl. like* вести́] *v., pfv. of* уводи́ть.

уве́чить *v. impfv.* to mutilate; maim.

уве́чье *n.* (serious) injury.

уве́шивать *v. impfv.* [*pfv.* уве́шать] to hang; cover with hangings: уве́шать сте́ну карти́нами, to hang a wall with pictures.

увеща́ние *n.* admonition; exhortation; remonstrance.

увещева́ть *v. impfv.* to admonish; exhort; remonstrate. *Also,* увеща́ть.

увива́ть *v. impfv.* [*pfv.* уви́ть] to wind around; twine around. —увива́ться, *refl.* [*impfv. only*] *colloq.* to hang around.

увида́ть *v. pfv., used only in the past tense, colloq.* to see; catch sight of. —увида́ться, *refl., colloq.* to see each other.

уви́деть *v. pfv.* [*infl.* уви́жу, уви́дишь] **1,** *pfv. of* ви́деть. **2,** to catch sight of. —уви́деться, *refl., pfv. of* ви́деться.

уви́ливать *v. impfv.* [*pfv.* увильну́ть] (*with* от) *colloq.* **1,** to avoid; dodge. **2,** to evade; get out of (*doing something*). **3,** [*impfv. only*] to try to get out of.

уви́ть [*infl. like* вить] *v., pfv. of* увива́ть.

увлажне́ние *n.* **1,** moistening. **2,** moisture.

увлажня́ть *v. impfv.* [*pfv.* увлажни́ть] to moisten; dampen; humidify.

увлека́тельный *adj.* fascinating; absorbing.

увлека́ть *v. impfv.* [*pfv.* увле́чь] **1,** to carry away; carry off. **2,** *fig.* to carry away; engross. **3,** *fig.* to fascinate; enthrall. **4,** *fig.* to enchant; captivate. —увлека́ться, *refl.* **1,** (*with instr.*) to develop an enthusiasm for. **2,** (*with instr.*) to become engrossed in; be wrapped up in. **3,** (*with instr.*) to fall for; become infatuated with. **4,** to get carried away.

увлека́ющийся *adj.* easily carried away; easily falling in love.

увлече́ние *n.* **1,** enthusiasm. **2,** (*with instr.*) passion (for); fascination (with). **3,** (*with instr.*) infatuation (with); crush (on).

увлечённый *adj.* enthusiastic. —увлечённо, *adv.* with enthusiasm.

увле́чь [*infl. like* влечь] *v., pfv. of* увлека́ть. —увле́чься, *refl., pfv. of* увлека́ться.

уво́д *n.* **1,** evacuation; withdrawal. **2,** theft.

уводи́ть *v. impfv.* [*pfv.* увести́; *pres.* увожу́, уво́дишь] **1,** to lead away; take away. **2,** to carry off; steal.

уво́з *n.* **1,** carting away. **2,** abduction.

увози́ть *v. impfv.* [*pfv.* увезти́; *pres.* увожу́, уво́зишь] **1,** to take away (*by conveyance*). **2,** to abduct.

уволо́кивать *v. impfv.* [*pfv.* уволо́чь] *colloq.* **1,** to drag away. **2,** to carry off; abduct. **3,** to make off with; steal.

уво́лить *v., pfv. of* увольня́ть. —уво́литься, *refl., pfv. of* увольня́ться.

уволо́чь [*infl. like* воло́чь] *v., pfv. of* увола́кивать.

увольнёние *n.* discharge; dismissal.

увольнительный *adj., in* **увольнительная записка; увольнительное свидетельство,** pass; written leave of absence.

увольнять *v. impfv.* [*pfv.* **уволить**] **1,** to dismiss; discharge; lay off; fire. **2,** (*with* **от**) to spare (from); relieve (of). —**увольняться,** *refl.* **1,** to be discharged; get one's discharge. **2,** to be released; be excused.

увы *interj.* alas!

увядать *v. impfv.* [*pfv.* **увянуть**] to fade; wither.

увядший *adj.* faded; withered.

увязать[1] [*infl.* **увяжу, увяжешь**] *v., pfv. of* **увязывать.** —**увязаться,** *refl., pfv. of* **увязываться.**

увязать[2] *v. impfv.* [*pfv.* **увязнуть;** *pres.* **-заю, -заешь**] **1,** to get stuck. **2,** *fig.* to become mired; get bogged down.

увязка *n.* **1,** tying up. **2,** *fig.* coordination; tying together.

увязнуть [*past* **увяз, -ла**] *v., pfv. of* **вязнуть** *and* **увязать**[2].

увязывать *v. impfv.* [*pfv.* **увязать**] **1,** to tie up; pack up. **2,** *fig.* to coordinate; reconcile; square. —**увязываться,** *refl.* **1,** (*with* **с** + *instr.*) to tie in with. **2,** (*with* **за** + *instr.*) *colloq.* to follow; haunt; dog.

увянуть [*past* **увял, увяла**] *v., pfv. of* **вянуть** *and* **увядать.**

угадать *v., pfv. of* **угадывать.**

угадчик *n., colloq.* guesser.

угадывать *v. impfv.* [*pfv.* **угадать**] to guess.

угадываться *v.r. impfv.* to be sensed; be felt; be seen.

угар *n.* **1,** carbon-monoxide fumes. **2,** carbon-monoxide poisoning. **3,** *fig.* ecstasy; fever; intoxication.

угарный *adj.* **1,** carbon-monoxide (*attrib.*); containing carbon monoxide. **2,** *fig.* feverish; frenzied. —**угарный газ,** carbon monoxide.

угасание *n.* fading; waning; dying out.

угасать *v. impfv.* [*pfv.* **угаснуть**] **1,** to go out; die out. **2,** *fig.* to fade; wane; ebb.

угаснуть [*past* **угас, -ла**] *v., pfv. of* **гаснуть** *and* **угасать.**

углевод *n.* carbohydrate.

углеводород *n.* hydrocarbon.

углекислота *n.* carbonic acid.

углекислый *adj.* carbonate (of): **углекислый кальций,** calcium carbonate; **углекислый натрий,** sodium carbonate. —**углекислый газ,** carbon dioxide. —**углекислая соль,** carbonate.

углекоп *n., obs.* coal miner.

углерод *n.* carbon.

углеродистый *adj.* **1,** carbon: **углеродистая сталь,** carbon steel. **2,** carbide (of): **углеродистый кальций,** calcium carbide.

угловатый *adj.* **1,** angular. **2,** *fig.* awkward.

угловой *adj.* **1,** corner (*attrib.*). **2,** angular: **угловая скорость,** angular velocity.

углубить [*infl.* **-блю, -бишь**] *v., pfv. of* **углублять.** —**углубиться,** *refl., pfv. of* **углубляться.**

углублёние *n.* **1,** deepening. **2,** hollow; depression; dip.

углублённый *adj.* **1,** sunken. **2,** *fig.* in-depth. **3,** *fig.* (*with* **в** + *acc.*) engrossed (in).

углублять *v. impfv.* [*pfv.* **углубить**] to deepen. —**углубляться,** *refl.* **1,** to deepen; become deeper. **2,** (*with* **в** + *acc.*) to go deep (into); sink (into). **3,** *fig.* (*with* **в** + *acc.*) to go deep into; delve (into). **4,** *fig.* (*with*

в + *acc.*) to become absorbed (in). **5,** *in* **углубиться в себя,** to withdraw into oneself.

углядёть *v. pfv.* [*infl.* **-жу, -дишь**] *colloq.* **1,** to see; spot. **2,** (*with* **за** + *instr.*) to look after; keep an eye on.

угнать [*infl. like* **гнать**] *v., pfv. of* **угонять.** —**угнаться,** *refl.* (*with* **за** + *instr.*) [*usu. in neg. sentences*] to keep up (with); keep pace (with).

угнездиться *v.r. pfv., colloq.* to nestle.

угнетатель *n.m.* oppressor.

угнетать *v. impfv.* **1,** to oppress. **2,** to depress.

угнетёние *n.* **1,** oppression. **2,** depression; dejection.

угнетённый *adj.* **1,** oppressed. **2,** depressed.

угова́ривать *v. impfv.* [*pfv.* **уговорить**] **1,** to persuade. **2,** [*impfv. only*] to try to persuade; coax. —**уговариваться,** *refl., colloq.* to agree; arrange.

уговор *n.* **1,** *often pl.* persuasion; attempt at persuasion: **уговоры на него не действуют,** attempts to persuade him are useless. **2,** *colloq.* agreement; arrangement; understanding.

уговорить *v., pfv. of* **уговаривать.** —**уговориться,** *refl., pfv. of* **уговариваться.**

угода *n., in* **в угоду** (+ *dat.*), (in order) to please.

угодить *v. pfv.* [*infl.* **угожу, угодишь**] **1,** *pfv. of* **угождать. 2,** (*with various prepositions*) *colloq.* to fall (into); step (into); land (in); end up (in). **3,** (*with* **в** + *acc.*) *colloq.* to hit; strike: **пуля угодила ему в плечо,** the bullet struck him in the shoulder. **4,** (*with instr.*) *colloq.* to cause to strike; bang: **угодить головой в стекло,** to bang into the glass with one's head.

угодливый *adj.* obsequious. —**угодливость,** *n.f.* obsequiousness.

угодник *n.* **1,** *colloq.* sycophant. **2,** saint.

угодничать *v. impfv.* (*with* **перед**) *colloq.* to curry favor (with); play up to.

угодничество *n.* obsequiousness; servility.

угодно *predicate (with dat.)* wished; desired: **что вам угодно?,** what would you like? **Как вам угодно,** as you wish; just as you like. **Сколько душе угодно,** as much as one's heart desires. —*particle* any-; -ever one likes: **что угодно,** anything/whatever you like; **где** (*or* **куда**) **угодно,** anywhere/wherever you like. **Какой угодно** (+ *noun*), any ...you like. —**если угодно,** perhaps.

угодный *adj.* (*with dat.*) pleasing (to).

угодье *n., often pl.* land (*with reference to its use*): **травяное угодье,** grassland; **лесные угодья,** forests.

угождать *v. impfv.* [*pfv.* **угодить**] (*with dat. or* **на** + *acc.*) to please. *See also* **угодить.**

угол [*gen.* **угла;** *2nd loc.* **углу**] *n.* **1,** corner: **в углу,** in the corner; **на углу,** on the (street) corner. **2,** angle. **3,** place to live: **иметь свой угол,** to have a home of one's own. **4,** (*with an adj.*) remote place: **глухой угол,** out-of-the-way place; **медвёжий угол,** godforsaken place. —**за углом,** around the corner. —**из-за угла, 1,** from around the corner. **2,** from behind; without warning. —**из угла в угол,** (*with verbs of walking or pacing*) up and down; back and forth. —**под углом в** (+ *acc.*), at an angle of. —**по углам,** (*with verbs of talking or whispering*) in secret; in the corridors.

уголёк [*gen.* **-лька**] *n.* small piece of coal.

уголовник *n.* criminal.

уголовный *adj.* criminal: **уголовное право,** criminal law.

уголовщина *n., colloq.* **1,** criminal act. **2,** criminals; the underworld.

уголок [*gen.* **-лка**] *n.* **1,** *dim. of* **угол. 2,** cozy corner;

nook. —кра́сный уголо́к, recreation and reading room.

у́голь [*gen.* у́гля *or* угля́; *pl.* у́гли, у́глей *or* угле́й, у́глям *or* угля́м] *n.m.* **1,** coal. **2,** (piece of) coal: горя́чие у́гли, live coals; live embers. —быть *or* сиде́ть как на у́гольях, to be on tenterhooks.

уго́льник *n.* **1,** try square. **2,** triangle (*drawing instrument*).

у́гольный *adj.* coal (*attrib.*). —у́гольная кислота́, carbonic acid.

у́гольщик *n.* coal miner.

угомони́ть *v. pfv., colloq.* to calm; calm down. —угомони́ться, *refl., colloq.* to calm down; become calm.

уго́н *n.* **1,** driving away; sending away. **2,** hijacking (*of an aircraft*).

угоня́ть *v. impfv.* [*pfv.* угна́ть] **1,** to drive away. **2,** *colloq.* to steal (cattle). **3,** to hijack (an aircraft).

угора́здить *v. pfv., colloq., impers.* **1,** to make; prompt; possess: как э́то вас угора́здило сде́лать э́то?, what on earth made you do it? **2,** (*used sarcastically*) to manage to: его́ угора́здило заболе́ть, he managed to get sick.

угора́ть *v. impfv.* [*pfv.* угоре́ть] **1,** to be overcome by fumes; get carbon-monoxide poisoning. **2,** *colloq.* to go mad.

угоре́лый *adj., colloq.* mad; crazy. —бежа́ть как угоре́лый, to run like mad.

угоре́ть [*infl.* -рю́, -ри́шь] *v., pfv. of* угора́ть.

у́горь [*gen.* угря́] *n.m.* **1,** eel. **2,** blackhead; *pl.* acne.

угости́ть [*infl.* -щу́, -сти́шь] *v., pfv. of* угоща́ть. —угости́ться, *refl., pfv. of* угоща́ться.

угото́вить *v. pfv.* [*infl.* -влю, -вишь] *obs.* to prepare.

угоща́ть *v. impfv.* [*pfv.* угости́ть] to treat: угоща́ть друзе́й обе́дом, to treat one's friends to dinner. —угоща́ться, *refl., colloq.* **1,** to partake oneself. Угоща́йтесь, пожа́луйста!, help yourself! **2,** (*with instr.*) to help oneself to.

угоще́ние *n.* **1,** entertaining; treating. **2,** food; refreshments.

угрева́тый *adj.* covered with blackheads; pimply.

угрожа́ть *v. impfv.* (*with dat.*) to threaten: угрожа́ть кому́-нибудь ору́жием, to threaten someone with a weapon. Стране́ угрожа́ет го́лод, the country is threatened with (*or* faces) famine.

угрожа́ющий *adj.* threatening; menacing.

угро́за *n.* threat; menace. —ста́вить под угро́зу, to endanger; jeopardize.

угрызе́ние *n., in* угрызе́ния со́вести, pangs of conscience.

угрю́мый *adj.* **1,** sullen; gloomy; morose. **2,** bleak; forbidding. —угрю́мость, *n.f.* sullenness; gloominess; moroseness.

уда́в *n.* boa (*snake*).

удава́ться *v.r. impfv.* [*pfv.* уда́ться; *pres.* удаётся] **1,** to be successful; be a success; turn out well. **2,** *impers.* (*with dat. and inf.*) to succeed: ему́ удало́сь доста́ть биле́ты, he succeeded in getting the tickets.

удави́ть *v. pfv.* [*infl.* удавлю́, уда́вишь] to strangle. —удави́ться, *refl., colloq.* to hang oneself.

удавле́ние *n.* strangling; strangulation.

удале́ние *n.* **1,** withdrawal. **2,** removal. **3,** extraction. **4,** distance.

удалённый *adj.* remote. —удалённость, *n.f.* remoteness; distance.

удале́ц [*gen.* -льца́] *n.* daring person.

удали́ть *v., pfv. of* удаля́ть. —удали́ться, *refl., pfv. of* удаля́ться.

удало́й *also*, уда́лый *adj.* **1,** bold; daring. **2,** dashing.

у́даль *n.f.* boldness; daring; bravado.

уда́льство́ *n., colloq.* = у́даль.

удаля́ть *v. impfv.* [*pfv.* удали́ть] **1,** to move away; move farther away. **2,** to remove; take away. **3,** to remove; force to leave: удаля́ть ученика́ из кла́сса, to send a pupil out of the room. **4,** to remove; extract (a tooth, splinter, etc.). —удаля́ться, *refl.* **1,** to move away. Удаля́ться от те́мы, to wander from the subject. **2,** (*with* от) to get away (from); isolate oneself (from). **3,** to withdraw; retire.

уда́р *n.* **1,** blow. **2,** stroke (*of a clock, bell, etc.*). **3,** *mil.* attack; thrust; strike; blow. **4,** *sports* shot; stroke. **5,** bolt (*of thunder or lightning*). **6,** *med.* stroke. **7,** *in* уда́р судьбы́, stroke of bad luck. —быть в уда́ре, *colloq.* to be in good form. —быть под уда́ром, to be vulnerable; be under the gun. —ста́вить под уда́р, to endanger; jeopardize.

ударе́ние *n.* **1,** accent; stress. **2,** accent mark. **3,** *fig.* emphasis: де́лать ударе́ние на (+ *prepl.*), to stress; emphasize.

уда́рить *v., pfv. of* ударя́ть. —уда́риться, *refl., pfv. of* ударя́ться.

уда́рник *n.* **1,** firing pin. **2,** drummer. **3,** shock worker; pace-setting worker.

уда́рный *adj.* **1,** striking (*attrib.*); percussion (*attrib.*). **2,** shock (*attrib.*): уда́рная волна́/брига́да, shock wave/brigade. **3,** urgent. **4,** (*of a syllable*) stressed.

ударя́ть *v. impfv.* [*pfv.* уда́рить] **1,** to strike; hit: уда́рить ло́шадь кнуто́м, to strike the horse with a whip. Уда́рить кого́-нибудь по лицу́, to slap someone in the face. **2,** (*with instr.*) to bang; pound: уда́рить кулако́м по́ столу, to bang/pound one's fist on the table. **3,** (*of an illness, emotion, etc.*) to strike. **4,** (*with* на + *acc. or* по) to attack. *Also intrans.*: уда́рить со всех сторо́н, to attack from all sides. **5,** *fig.* (*with* по) to strike a blow against; combat. **6,** (*with* в + *acc.*) to beat (a drum); ring (a bell); sound (an alarm). **7,** to ring out; resound. Уда́рил гром, there was a clap of thunder. **8,** (*of a clock*) to strike (a certain hour). —не уда́рить лицо́м в грязь, not disgrace oneself. —ударя́ть в го́лову (+ *dat.*), (*of alcoholic beverages*) to go to one's head. —уда́рить по рука́м, to strike a bargain.

ударя́ться *v.r. impfv.* [*pfv.* уда́риться] **1,** (*with* о *or* в + *acc.*) to strike; bang (into *or* against); bump (into). Ло́дка уда́рилась о скалу́, the boat struck a rock. Уда́риться голово́й о дверь, to bang one's head on the door. **2,** (*with* в + *acc.*) *colloq.* to break into; burst into; give way to (tears, panic, etc.). —уда́риться в кра́йность, to go to an extreme.

уда́ться [*infl. like* дать; *past* уда́лся, -ла́сь, -ло́сь] *v.r., pfv. of* удава́ться.

уда́ча *n.* **1,** success. **2,** good luck.

уда́чливый *adj.* **1,** lucky. **2,** successful.

уда́чник *n., colloq.* lucky man.

уда́чно *adv.* **1,** successfully. **2,** well. **3,** aptly. —*adj., used predicatively* fortunate: уда́чно, что..., it is fortunate that...

уда́чный *adj.* **1,** successful. **2,** apt; appropriate; felicitous.

удва́ивать *v. impfv.* [*pfv.* удво́ить] **1,** to double. **2,** *fig.* to redouble. —удва́иваться, *refl.* to double.

удвое́ние *n.* doubling; redoubling.

удвоить v., pfv. of **удваивать**. —**удвоиться**, refl., pfv. of **удваиваться**.

удел n. **1**, hist. princely domain. **2**, fate; lot; destiny.

уделить [infl. **уделю, уделишь**] v., pfv. of **уделять**.

удельный adj., physics specific: удельная теплота, specific heat. —**удельный вес**, **1**, specific gravity. **2**, relative amount (as against a total); proportion; percentage.

уделять v. impfv. [pfv. **уделить**] **1**, to spare (a small amount of something). **2**, to give; devote (time, attention, etc.).

удерж n., colloq., in **без удержу**, **1**, without restraint; with abandon. **2**, (with verbs of crying) uncontrollably. —**ему** (or **на него**) **нет удержу**, there is nothing to stop him; there is no holding him back. —**не знать удержу**, to know no restraint.

удержание n. **1**, keeping; retention. **2**, holding back; withholding. **3**, deduction; withholding (of money).

удержать [infl. **удержу, удержишь**] v., pfv. of **удерживать**. —**удержаться**, refl., pfv. of **удерживаться**.

удерживать v. impfv. [pfv. **удержать**] **1**, to hold up; keep from falling. **2**, to restrain; hold back. **3**, to keep; retain. **4**, to deduct; withhold. —**удерживаться**, refl. **1**, to keep one's feet. **2**, to hold out. **3**, to restrain oneself. **4**, (with **от**) to keep (from); help: я не мог удержаться от смеха, I couldn't help laughing.

удесятерять v. impfv. [pfv. **удесятерить**] to increase tenfold.

удешевить [infl. **-влю, -вишь**] v., pfv. of **удешевлять**.

удешевлять v. impfv. [pfv. **удешевить**] to reduce the price of.

удивительно adv. **1**, surprisingly; remarkably. **2**, marvelously. **3**, extremely. —adj., used predicatively surprising: удивительно, что... it is surprising that...

удивительный adj. **1**, surprising. **2**, wonderful; marvelous. **3**, remarkable.

удивить [infl. **-влю, -вишь**] v., pfv. of **удивлять**. —**удивиться**, refl., pfv. of **удивляться**.

удивление n. surprise: к моему удивлению, to my surprise. —**на удивление**, **1**, first-rate. **2**, splendidly. **3**, fol. by an adj. or adv. surprisingly. **4**, in всем на удивление, to the surprise of everyone.

удивлённый adj. surprised. —**удивлённо**, adv. in surprise.

удивлять v. impfv. [pfv. **удивить**] to surprise. —**удивляться**, refl. (with dat.) to be surprised (at).

удила [gen. **удил**] n. pl. bit. —**закусить удила**, to take the bit in one's teeth.

удилище n. fishing rod.

удильщик n. angler.

удирать v. impfv. [pfv. **удрать**] colloq. to take off; run away.

удить v. impfv. [pres. **ужу, удишь**] to fish for: удить рыбу, to fish. —**удиться**, refl. (of fish) to bite.

удлинение n. **1**, lengthening. **2**, extension.

удлинённый adj. **1**, lengthened. **2**, oblong; elongated.

удлинитель n.m. extension cord. —**удлинительный**, adj. extension (attrib.): удлинительный шнур, extension cord.

удлинять v. impfv. [pfv. **удлинить**] **1**, to lengthen; make longer. **2**, to extend; prolong. —**удлиняться**, refl. to lengthen; become (or get) longer.

удмурт n.m. [fem. **удмуртка**] Udmurt (one of a people inhabiting central European Russia). —**удмуртский**, adj. Udmurt.

удобно adv. comfortably. —adj., used predicatively **1**, (with dat.) comfortable: вам удобно?, are you comfortable? **2**, (with dat.) convenient: когда вам будет удобно?, when will it be convenient for you? **3**, all right: удобно ли спросить его об этом?, is it all right to ask him about it?

удобный adj. [short form **-бен, -бна**] **1**, comfortable. **2**, convenient.

удобо- prefix easy to: удобочитаемый, easy to read; удобоисполнимый, easy to carry out.

удобоваримый adj. digestible. —**удобоваримость**, n.f. digestiblity.

удобрение n. **1**, fertilization. **2**, fertilizer.

удобрять v. impfv. [pfv. **удобрить**] to fertilize (soil).

удобство n. **1**, comfort. **2**, convenience: со всеми удобствами, with all the conveniences.

удовлетворение n. satisfaction; gratification.

удовлетворённый adj. satisfied; contented. —**удовлетворённость**, n.f. satisfaction; contentment.

удовлетворительно adv. **1**, satisfactorily. **2**, (as a school grade) "satisfactory".

удовлетворительный adj. satisfactory.

удовлетворять v. impfv. [pfv. **удовлетворить**] **1**, to satisfy; make (someone) content. **2**, to satisfy; assuage (one's hunger, curiosity, etc.). **3**, to grant; comply with (a wish, request, etc.). **4**, to meet; satisfy: удовлетворять требование, to meet a demand. Удовлетворять требованиям, to meet/satisfy/answer the requirements. **5**, (with instr.) to supply (with); furnish (with). —**удовлетворяться**, refl. (with instr.) to be satisfied (with).

удовольствие n. pleasure. С удовольствием!, with pleasure!; I'll be glad to! К общему удовольствию, to everyone's delight. —**жить в своё удовольствие**, to live a life of ease.

удовольствоваться v.r., pfv. of **довольствоваться**.

удод n. hoopoe.

удой n. **1**, yield of milk. **2**, milking.

удойный adj. (of a cow) giving much milk.

удорожать v. impfv. [pfv. **удорожить**] to raise the price of.

удостаивать v. impfv. [pfv. **удостоить**] **1**, (with gen.) to award; confer (a title, degree, etc.). **2**, (with instr.) to favor (with): он не удостоил нас ответом, he did not favor us with an answer. —**удостаиваться**, refl. **1**, (with gen.) to be awarded; be given; be granted (something). **2**, (with inf.) to have the honor of; have the good fortune to.

удостоверение n. **1**, certification; attestation. **2**, certificate. —**удостоверение личности**, identity card.

удостоверять v. impfv. [pfv. **удостоверить**] **1**, to certify; attest. **2**, to witness (a signature). —**удостоверяться**, refl. (with **в** + prepl. or a dependent clause) to make sure (of or that).

удостоить v., pfv. of **удостаивать**. —**удостоиться**, refl., pfv. of **удостаиваться**.

удосуживаться v.r. impfv. [pfv. **удосужиться**] colloq. to find time (to); get around to.

удочерять v. impfv. [pfv. **удочерить**] to adopt (a girl).

удочка [gen. pl. **-чек**] n. fishing rod (with the line attached). —**закинуть удочку**, to drop a hint; put out a feeler. —**пойма́ть на у́дочку**, to trick; hoodwink. —**попа́сться на у́дочку**, to swallow (or take) the bait.

удра́ть [infl. like **драть**] v., pfv. of **удира́ть**.

удружи́ть v. pfv. (with dat.) colloq. to do (someone) a favor.

удруча́ть v. impfv. [pfv. **удручи́ть**] to depress; dispirit.

удручённый adj. depressed; dejected; despondent.

удручи́ть v., pfv. of **удруча́ть**.

удуша́ть v. impfv. [pfv. **удуши́ть**] 1, to suffocate; smother. 2, fig. to stifle.

удуше́ние n. suffocation; asphyxiation.

удуши́ть [infl. удушу́, уду́шишь] v., pfv. of **удуша́ть**.

уду́шливый adj. stifling. —**удушливый газ**, choking gas.

уду́шье n. difficulty in breathing.

уедине́ние n. solitude; seclusion.

уединённый adj. solitary; secluded.

уединя́ть v. impfv. [pfv. **уедини́ть**] to seclude; isolate. —**уединя́ться**, refl. to withdraw; seclude oneself; closet oneself.

уе́зд n., hist. district. —**уе́здный**, adj. district (attrib.).

уезжа́ть v. impfv. [pfv. **уе́хать**] to leave; go away; depart (by conveyance).

уе́хать [infl. уе́ду, уе́дешь] v., pfv. of **уезжа́ть**.

уж[1] adv. = **уже́**. —particle, used for emphasis: это уж просто безобра́зие, it's simply disgraceful; не так уж хо́лодно сего́дня, it's not all that cold today.

уж[2] [gen. ужа́] n. any of several kinds of nonpoisonous snakes. —**обыкнове́нный уж**, grass snake. —**водяно́й уж**, water snake.

ужа́лить v., pfv. of **жа́лить**.

у́жас n. 1, horror; terror. 2, pl. horrors: у́жасы войны́, the horrors of war. 3, colloq. horrible thing; horrible situation: про́сто у́жас!, it's simply horrible!

ужаса́ть v. impfv. [pfv. **ужасну́ть**] to terrify; horrify. —**ужаса́ться**, refl. to be terrified; be horrified.

ужа́сно adv. terribly; awfully. —adj., used predicatively terrible; awful: э́то ужа́сно, that's terrible; that's awful.

ужасну́ть v., pfv. of **ужаса́ть**. —**ужасну́ться**, refl. pfv. of **ужаса́ться**.

ужа́сный adj. terrible; horrible; frightful; awful; dreadful.

у́же adj., comp. of **у́зкий**.

уже́ adv. 1, already. 2, (in interr. sentences) yet. —**уже́ не**, no longer; any longer; anymore.

уже́ние n. fishing; angling.

ужива́ться v.r. impfv. [pfv. **ужи́ться**] (with с + instr.) to get along (with).

уживчивый adj. easygoing; easy to get along with.

ужи́мка [gen. pl. -мок] n., usu. pl. grimace.

у́жин n. supper.

у́жинать v. impfv. [pfv. **поу́жинать**] to have supper.

ужи́ться [infl. like жить; past ужи́лся, -ла́сь, -ло́сь] v.r., pfv. of **ужива́ться**.

узаконе́ние n. 1, legalization. 2, obs. law; statute.

узако́нивать v. impfv. [pfv. **узако́нить**] to legalize; legitimize. Also, **узаконя́ть**.

узбе́к n.m. [fem. -бе́чка] n. Uzbek. —**узбе́кский**, adj. Uzbek.

узда́ [pl. у́зды] n. 1, bridle. 2, fig. restraint; check: держа́ть в узде́, to keep in check.

узде́чка [gen. pl. -чек] n. bridle.

у́зел [gen. узла́] n. 1, knot. 2, junction 3, fig. hub. 4,

---

bundle; pack. 5, node. 6, naut. knot (measure of speed). 7, mech. unit.

узело́к [gen. -лка́] n. 1, small knot. 2, nodule.

у́зенький adj., colloq. narrow.

у́зкий adj. [short form у́зок, узка́, у́зко, у́зки or узки́; comp. у́же] 1, narrow. 2, (of clothes, shoes, etc.) tight: ю́бка мне узка́, the skirt is tight on me. 3, fig. narrow-minded. —**у́зкое ме́сто**, bottleneck.

у́зко adv. 1, tightly. 2, fig. from a narrow perspective. —adj., used predicatively narrow; tight: здесь у́зко, it is narrow/tight in here.

узкоколе́йный adj., R.R. narrow-gauge.

узколо́бый adj. narrow-minded.

узлова́тый adj. (of a rope, thread, etc.) full of knots; knotted.

узлово́й adj. 1, junction (attrib.): узлова́я ста́нция, (railway) junction. 2, fig. key; pivotal: узлово́й вопро́с, key/ pivotal question.

узнава́ние n. recognition.

узнава́ть v. impfv. [pfv. **узна́ть**; pres. узнаю́, узна́ешь] 1, to recognize. 2, to find out; learn. 3, to try to find out; inquire. 4, to experience; know. 5, to get to know.

узна́ть [infl. узна́ю, узна́ешь] v., pfv. of **узнава́ть**.

у́зник n. prisoner.

узо́р n. pattern; design. —**узо́рчатый**, adj. having a design; figured.

у́зость n.f. narrowness.

узре́ть v. pfv. [infl. узрю́, у́зришь or узри́шь] 1, pfv. of зреть[2]. 2, to see; realize; perceive.

узурпа́тор n. usurper. —**узурпа́ция**, n. usurpation.

узурпи́ровать v. impfv. & pfv. [pres. -рую, -руешь] to usurp.

у́зы [gen. уз] n. pl. bonds; ties: у́зы дру́жбы, bonds/ties of friendship.

уйгу́р n.m. [fem. -гу́рка] Uigur (one of a people inhabiting Central Asia and China). —**уйгу́рский**, adj. Uigur.

у́йма n., colloq. (with gen.) a lot (of); heaps (of); tons (of).

уйти́ [infl. уйду́, уйдёшь; past ушёл, ушла́, ушло́] v., pfv. of **уходи́ть**.

указ n. decree; edict; ukase. —**не указ** (+ dat.), not such that it (or one) must be obeyed: никто́ ему́ не указ, he doesn't take orders from anyone.

указа́ние n. 1, indication; indicating. 2, usu. pl. instructions; directions.

ука́занный adj. indicated: на ука́занном ме́сте, at the place indicated.

указа́тель n.m. 1, indicator; pointer. 2, index. 3, directory.

указа́тельный adj. serving to indicate. —**указа́тельное местоиме́ние**, demonstrative pronoun. —**указа́тельный па́лец**, index finger. —**указа́тельный столб**, signpost.

указа́ть [infl. укажу́, ука́жешь] v., pfv. of **ука́зывать**.

ука́зка [gen. pl. -зок] n. 1, pointer. 2, colloq. orders: по ука́зке (+ gen.), on orders from.

указчик n., colloq. one who gives orders.

ука́зывать v. impfv. [pfv. **указа́ть**] 1, to point (in a certain direction); (with на + acc.) point to; point at. 2, to point out; indicate (a road, place, etc.). 3, (with на + acc.) to point out (mistakes, shortcomings, etc.). 4, to indicate (one's name, certain information, etc.).

укати́ть v., pfv. of **ука́тывать**[1].

укати́ть [*infl.* укачу́, ука́тишь] *v., pfv. of* ука́тывать[2]. —укати́ться, *refl., pfv. of* ука́тываться.

ука́тывать[1] *v. impfv.* [*pfv.* ука́ть] **1**, to roll (a surface). **2**, to wear (a road) smooth.

ука́тывать[2] *v. impfv.* [*pfv.* укати́ть] **1**, *v.t.* to roll away; remove by rolling. **2**, *v.i., colloq.* to leave; take off. —ука́тываться, *refl.* **1**, to roll away. **2**, *colloq.* (*of a vehicle*) to drive off.

ука́чивать *v. impfv.* [*pfv.* укача́ть] **1**, to rock to sleep. **2**, *impers.* to experience motion sickness: меня́ укача́ло, I became seasick, carsick, etc.

укла́д *n.* **1**, mode; tenor: укла́д жи́зни, way/mode/tenor of life. **2**, system: феода́льный укла́д, feudal system.

укла́дка *n.* **1**, laying. **2**, piling; stacking. **3**, arranging; setting (*of one's hair*).

укла́дчик *n.* **1**, packer. **2**, layer (*of floors, tracks, etc.*).

укла́дывать *v. impfv.* [*pfv.* уложи́ть] **1**, to lay; lay down (gently). **2**, [*also,* укла́дывать спать] to put to bed. **3**, to order to bed: (*of an illness*) lay up. **4**, to pile up; stack. **5**, to arrange; set (one's hair). **6**, to pack. **7**, to lay; cover (a surface with a certain material). **8**, *colloq.* to kill. —укла́дываться, *refl.* **1**, [*pfv.* уложи́ться] *colloq.* to pack; pack up. **2**, [*pfv.* уложи́ться] (*with* в + *acc. or prepl.*) to fit (into); go (into). **3**, [*pfv.* уле́чься] to go to sleep. **4**, уле́чься] (*of objects*) to lie correctly; lie as desired. *See also* уле́чься.

укло́н *n.* **1**, slope; incline. **2**, *fig.* bias; slant. **3**, *fig.* (political) deviation. —под укло́н, downhill; downward.

уклоне́ние *n.* **1**, deviation; digression. **2**, evasion; avoidance.

уклони́ться [*infl.* уклоню́сь, уклони́шься] *v.r., pfv. of* уклоня́ться.

укло́нчивый *adj.* evasive. —укло́нчивость, *n.f.* evasiveness.

уклоня́ться *v.r. impfv.* [*pfv.* уклони́ться] (*with* от) **1**, to dodge; duck. **2**, to evade; avoid. **3**, to deviate (from); digress (from).

уклю́чина *n.* oarlock.

уко́л *n.* **1**, prick. **2**, *med.* injection. **3**, *fig.* gibe; dig.

уколо́ть *v. pfv.* [*infl.* уколю́, уко́лешь] **1**, to prick. **2**, *fig.* to wound; pique.

укомплектова́ние *n.* **1**, manning; staffing. **2**, bringing up to full strength.

укомплектова́ть *v., pfv. of* комплектова́ть.

уко́р *n.* reproach. —уко́ры со́вести, pangs of conscience. —не в уко́р будь ска́зано, no criticism implied.

укора́чивать *v. impfv.* [*pfv.* укороти́ть] to shorten.

укорени́вшийся *adj.* deep-seated; ingrained.

укореня́ть *v. impfv.* [*pfv.* укорени́ть] **1**, to root; implant. **2**, *fig.* to root; ingrain. —укореня́ться, *refl.* **1**, to take root. **2**, *fig.* to become ingrained.

укори́зна *n.* reproach. —укори́зненный, *adj.* of reproach; reproachful.

укори́ть *v., pfv. of* укоря́ть.

укороти́ть [*infl.* -чу́, -ти́шь] *v., pfv. of* укора́чивать.

укоря́ть *v. impfv.* [*pfv.* укори́ть] (*with* в + *prepl.*) to reproach (for).

укра́дкой *adv.* stealthily; furtively.

украи́нец [*gen.* -нца] *n.m.* [*fem.* -нка] Ukrainian. —украи́нский, *adj.* Ukrainian.

укра́сить [*infl.* -шу, -сишь] *v., pfv. of* украша́ть.

укра́сть *v., pfv. of* красть.

украша́ть *v. impfv.* [*pfv.* укра́сить] to decorate; adorn; embellish.

украше́ние *n.* **1**, (act of) decorating; decoration. **2**, decoration; adornment; embellishment. **3**, adornment; embellishment; ornament.

укрепи́ть [*infl.* -плю́, -пи́шь] *v., pfv. of* укрепля́ть. —укрепи́ться, *refl., pfv. of* укрепля́ться.

укрепле́ние *n.* **1**, strengthening; consolidation; reinforcement. **2**, *mil.* fortification.

укрепля́ть *v. impfv.* [*pfv.* укрепи́ть] **1**, to strengthen; reinforce. **2**, to fortify. **3**, to consolidate. **4**, to invigorate. **5**, to build up (one's strength, confidence, etc.). **6**, to tighten (discipline). —укрепля́ться, *refl.* **1**, to become stronger. **2**, to take up a fortified position. **3**, *fig.* to become firmly established. **4**, *fig.* (*with* в + *prepl.*) to become firm (in): укрепи́ться в свои́х убежде́ниях, to become firm in one's beliefs. Укрепи́ться в наме́рении (+ *inf.*), to become ever more determined to...

укро́мный *adj.* secluded.

укро́п *n.* dill.

укроти́тель *n.m.* tamer: укроти́тель львов, lion tamer.

укроти́ть [*infl.* -щу́, -ти́шь] *v., pfv. of* укроща́ть.

укроща́ть *v. impfv.* [*pfv.* укроти́ть] **1**, to tame. **2**, to curb; restrain; subdue.

укроще́ние *n.* **1**, taming. **2**, curbing; restraining; subduing.

укрупне́ние *n.* **1**, enlargement. **2**, amalgamation.

укрупня́ть *v. impfv.* [*pfv.* укрупни́ть] to combine into larger units.

укрыва́тельство *n.* concealment (*of a crime*); harboring; hiding (*of a criminal*).

укрыва́ть *v. impfv.* [*pfv.* укры́ть] **1**, to cover. **2**, to conceal; harbor; shelter. —укрыва́ться, *refl.* **1**, to cover oneself up. **2**, to take cover; take shelter; take refuge. **3**, to escape one's notice: от него́ ничто́ не укро́ется, nothing escapes him.

укры́тие *n.* **1**, concealment. **2**, shelter. —под укры́тием (+ *gen.*), under cover of.

укры́ть [*infl.* укро́ю, укро́ешь] *v., pfv. of* укрыва́ть. —укры́ться, *refl., pfv. of* укрыва́ться.

у́ксус *n.* vinegar. —у́ксусница, *n.* vinegar cruet.

уксусноки́слый *adj., in* уксусноки́слая соль, acetate.

у́ксусный *adj.* vinegar (*attrib.*); acetic. —у́ксусная кислота́, acetic acid.

уку́поривать *v. impfv.* [*pfv.* уку́порить] **1**, to cork up. **2**, *colloq.* to pack.

уку́с *n.* bite; sting.

укуси́ть [*infl.* укушу́, уку́сишь] *v., pfv. of* куса́ть.

уку́тывать *v. impfv.* [*pfv.* уку́тать] (*with* в + *acc.*) to wrap (in).

ула́вливать *v. impfv.* [*pfv.* улови́ть] **1**, to catch; perceive; detect. **2**, to grasp (the meaning of something). **3**, *colloq.* to entice. **4**, *colloq.* to seize: улови́ть моме́нт, to seize the moment. **5**, to pick up (a radio signal).

ула́дить [*infl.* -жу, -дишь] *v., pfv. of* ула́живать. —ула́диться, *refl., pfv. of* ула́живаться.

ула́живание *n.* settlement; reconciliation; adjustment.

ула́живать *v. impfv.* [*pfv.* ула́дить] **1**, to settle (a matter). **2**, to settle; reconcile; compose; adjust (differences). —ула́живаться, *refl.* to be settled.

ула́мывать *v. impfv.* [*pfv.* уломать] *colloq.* **1**, to persuade; induce; prevail upon. **2**, [*impfv. only*] to try to persuade.

у́лей [*gen.* у́лья] *n.* beehive.

улепётывать *v. impfv.* [*pfv.* улепетну́ть] *colloq.* to take to one's heels; skedaddle.

улета́ть *v. impfv.* [*pfv.* улете́ть] to fly away; fly off.

улете́ть [*infl.* -чу́, -ти́шь] *v., pfv. of* улета́ть.

улету́чиваться *v.r. impfv.* [*pfv.* улету́читься] **1,** to evaporate. **2,** *colloq.* to vanish.

уле́чься *v.r. pfv.* [*infl. like* лечь] **1,** *pfv. of* укла́дываться (*in senses #3 & #4*). **2,** (*of dust*) to settle. **3,** *fig.* to subside; die down.

улизну́ть *v. pfv., colloq.* to slip away; sneak away; steal away.

ули́ка *n.* piece of evidence; *pl.* evidence.

ули́тка [*gen. pl.* -ток] *n.* snail.

у́лица *n.* street. —**на у́лице; на у́лицу,** outside; outdoors. —**с у́лицы,** from outside; from outdoors.

улича́ть *v. impfv.* [*pfv.* уличи́ть] **1,** to convict; prove guilty. **2,** (*with* в + *prepl.*) to catch (*in the act of doing something*).

у́личка [*gen. pl.* -чек] *n., colloq.* small street; narrow street.

у́личный *adj.* street (*attrib.*).

уло́в *n.* catch (*quantity caught*).

улови́мый *adj.* perceptible; audible.

улови́ть [*infl.* уловлю́, уло́вишь] *v., pfv. of* ула́вливать.

уло́вка [*gen. pl.* -вок] *n.* trick; ruse.

уложе́ние *n., hist.* code of law.

уложи́ть [*infl.* уложу́, уло́жишь] *v., pfv. of* укла́дывать. —**уложи́ться,** *refl., pfv. of* укла́дываться (*in senses #1 & #2*).

уломать *v., pfv. of* ула́мывать.

у́лочка [*gen. pl.* -чек] *n., colloq.* small street; narrow street.

улуча́ть *v. impfv.* [*pfv.* улучи́ть] to find (time); seize (a moment).

улучша́ть *v. impfv.* [*pfv.* улу́чшить] to improve; better. —**улучша́ться,** *refl.* to improve; get better.

улучше́ние *n.* **1,** improvement; improving. **2,** *pl.* improvements.

улу́чшить *v., pfv. of* улучша́ть. —**улу́чшиться,** *refl., pfv. of* улучша́ться.

улыба́ться *v.r. impfv.* [*pfv.* улыбну́ться] **1,** to smile. **2,** (*with dat.*) *fig.* to smile on: судьба́ ему́ улыбну́лась, fortune smiled on him. **3,** [*impfv. only*] (*with dat.*) *colloq.* to appeal to: мысль мне не улыба́ется, the idea doesn't appeal to me.

улы́бка [*gen. pl.* -бок] *n.* smile.

улыбну́ться *v.r., pfv. of* улыба́ться.

улы́бчивый *adj., colloq.* smiling.

ультима́тум *n.* ultimatum.

ультра- *prefix* ultra-.

ультразвуково́й *adj.* ultrasonic.

ультрамари́н *n.* ultramarine. —**ультрамари́новый,** *adj.* ultramarine.

ультрасовреме́нный *adj.* ultramodern.

ультрафиоле́товый *adj., in* ультрафиоле́товые лучи́, ultraviolet rays.

улюлю́ *interj.* halloo!

улюлю́кать *v. impfv.* to halloo.

ум [*gen.* ума́] *n.* **1,** mind. **2,** intellect. —**без ума́,** (*with verbs of loving*) madly. —**без ума́ от,** crazy about. —**в своём уме́,** in one's right mind. —**в уме́, 1,** in one's mind. **2,** in one's head: счита́ть в уме́, to do figures in one's head. —**из ума́ вон,** completely slipped one's

mind. —**на уме́,** on one's mind. —**себе́ на уме́,** shrewd; crafty. —**с умо́м,** *colloq.* intelligently. —**сходи́ть с ума́,** to go out of one's mind; go mad.

умале́ние *n.* belittling; derogation.

умали́ть *v., pfv. of* умаля́ть.

умалишённый *adj.* mad; insane. —*n.* madman; lunatic. —**дом умалишённых,** insane asylum.

ума́лчивать *v. impfv.* [*pfv.* умолча́ть] (*with* о) to keep silent (about); say nothing (about); fail to mention.

умаля́ть *v. impfv.* [*pfv.* умали́ть] **1,** to belittle; minimize. **2,** to detract from; diminish.

ума́сливать *v. impfv.* [*pfv.* ума́слить] *colloq.* to butter up.

ума́ять *v. pfv., colloq.* to exhaust; wear out. —**ума́яться,** *refl., colloq.* to become exhausted; become worn out.

у́мбра *n.* umber.

уме́лец [*gen.* -льца] *n.* skilled craftsman.

уме́лый *adj.* able; skillful. —**уме́ло,** *adv.* ably; skillfully.

уме́ние *n.* ability; skill.

уменьша́емое *n., decl. as an adj., math.* minuend.

уменьша́ть *v. impfv.* [*pfv.* уме́ньшить *or* уменьши́ть] to reduce; decrease; lessen. —**уменьша́ться,** *refl.* to decrease; diminish; decline.

уменьше́ние *n.* reduction; decrease; decline; diminution.

уменьши́тельный *adj., gram.* diminutive. —**уменьши́тельное и́мя,** familiar first name (*e.g.* То́ля *for* Анато́лий).

уме́ньшить *also,* уменьши́ть *v., pfv. of* уменьша́ть. —**уме́ньшиться; уменьши́ться,** *refl., pfv. of* уменьша́ться.

уме́ренный *adj.* **1,** moderate. **2,** temperate. —**уме́ренность,** *n.f.* moderation.

умере́ть [*infl.* умру́, умрёшь; *past* у́мер, умерла́, у́мерло] *v., pfv. of* умира́ть.

уме́рить *v., pfv. of* умеря́ть.

умертви́ть [*infl.* умерщвлю́, умертви́шь] *v., pfv. of* умерщвля́ть.

уме́рший *n., decl. as an adj.* the deceased.

умерщвле́ние *n.* killing. —**умерщвле́ние пло́ти,** mortification of the flesh.

умерщвля́ть *v. impfv.* [*pfv.* умертви́ть] **1,** to kill. **2,** to deaden. —**умерщвля́ть плоть,** to mortify the flesh.

умеря́ть *v. impfv.* [*pfv.* уме́рить] to moderate; temper.

умести́ть [*infl.* -щу́, сти́шь] *v., pfv. of* умеща́ть. —**умести́ться,** *refl., pfv. of* умеща́ться.

уме́стно *adv.* appropriately; aptly.—*adj., used predicatively* appropriate: бы́ло бы уме́стно (+ *inf.*), it would be appropriate to...; it would be a good idea to...

уме́стность *n.f.* timeliness; relevance; pertinence.

уме́стный *adj.* appropriate; timely; relevant; pertinent.

уме́ть *v. impfv.* (*with inf.*) to know how (to); be able (to).

умеща́ть *v. impfv.* [*pfv.* умести́ть] to fit; get: умести́ть всё в чемода́н(е), to fit/get everything into the suitcase. —**умеща́ться,** *refl.* to fit; go (into *or* onto).

умиле́ние *n.* deep feeling; deep emotion. Слёзы умиле́ния, tears of emotion. —**приходи́ть в умиле́ние,** to be deeply moved.

умили́тельный *adj.* moving; touching; affecting.

умили́ть *v., pfv. of* умиля́ть. —**умили́ться,** *refl., pfv. of* умиля́ться.

уми́лостивить *v. pfv.* [*infl.* -влю, -вишь] to placate; mollify; propitiate.

уми́льный *adj.* **1,** touching; affecting. **2,** ingratiating; obsequious.

умиля́ть *v. impfv.* [*pfv.* умили́ть] to move; touch; affect. —**умиля́ться,** *refl.* to be moved; be touched.

умира́ние *n.* dying..

умира́ть *v. impfv.* [*pfv.* умере́ть] to die.

умира́ющий *adj.* dying. —*n.* dying man.

умиротворе́ние *n.* pacification; appeasement.

умиротворя́ть *v. impfv.* [*pfv.* умиротвори́ть] to pacify; appease.

умля́ут *n.* umlaut.

умне́ть *v. impfv.* [*pfv.* поумне́ть] to become wiser; grow wiser.

у́мник *n., colloq.* **1,** clever man; clever child. **2,** smart aleck; wise guy.

у́мница *n.m. & f., colloq.* clever person.

у́мничать *v. impfv., colloq.* to show off one's intelligence.

умножа́ть *v. impfv.* [*pfv.* умно́жить] **1,** *math.* to multiply. **2,** to increase; augment. —**умножа́ться,** *refl.* to multiply; increase in number.

умноже́ние *n.* **1,** *math.* multiplication. **2,** increase.

умно́жить *v., pfv. of* мно́жить *and* умножа́ть. —**умно́житься,** *refl., pfv. of* мно́житься *and* умножа́ться.

у́мный *adj.* [*short form* умён, умна́, у́мно *or* умно́, у́мны *or* умны́] intelligent; clever; smart.

умозаключа́ть *v. impfv.* [*pfv.* умозаключи́ть] to conclude; deduce.

умозаключе́ние *n.* conclusion; deduction.

умозаключи́ть *v., pfv. of* умозаключа́ть.

умозре́ние *n.* speculation; conjecture.

умозри́тельный *adj.* speculative.

умоисступле́ние *n.* frenzy: припа́док умоисступле́ния, fit of frenzy.

умоли́ть *v. pfv.* [*infl.* умолю́, умо́лишь] to persuade; prevail upon.

у́молк *n., in* без у́молку, endlessly; incessantly.

умолка́ть *v. impfv.* [*pfv.* умо́лкнуть] **1,** to fall silent. **2,** (*of noise, sounds, etc.*) to die away; stop; cease.

умо́лкнуть [*past* умо́лк, -ла] *v., pfv. of* умолка́ть.

умолча́ние *n.* **1,** silence; keeping silent. **2,** *pl.* (deliberate) omissions; things left unsaid.

умолча́ть [*infl.* -чу́, -чи́шь] *v., pfv. of* ума́лчивать.

умоля́ть *v. impfv.* to beg; plead with; implore; beseech; entreat.

умонастрое́ние *n.* frame of mind.

умопомеша́тельство *n.* mental derangement; insanity.

умопомраче́ние *n.* daze; trance; stupor.

умопомрачи́тельный *adj., colloq.* stunning; stupendous; fantastic.

умо́ра *n., colloq.* a scream; a riot: э́то умо́ра, it's a scream/riot.

умори́тельный *adj., colloq.* screamingly funny; hilarious.

умори́ть *v. pfv., colloq.* **1,** to kill. **2,** to exhaust; wear out. —**умори́ть го́лодом,** to starve (someone) to death. —**умори́ть со́ смеху,** to have (someone) in stitches.

у́мственный *adj.* mental; intellectual. —**у́мственно,** *adv.* mentally: у́мственно отста́лый, mentally retarded.

умудря́ть *v. impfv.* [*pfv.* умудри́ть] to make wiser.

—**умудря́ться,** *refl.* **1,** to become wiser. **2,** (*with inf.*) *colloq.* to manage (to); contrive (to).

умча́ть *v. pfv.* [*infl.* умчу́, умчи́шь] to whisk away. —**умча́ться,** *refl.* to dash away; speed away.

умыва́льник *n.* washstand; washbasin; washbowl.

умыва́льный *adj.* wash (*attrib.*); washing (*attrib.*).

умыва́ние *n.* washing.

умыва́ть *v. impfv.* [*pfv.* умы́ть] to wash. —**умыва́ться,** *refl.* to wash (one's hands and face).

умыка́ть *v. impfv.* [*pfv.* умыкну́ть] *colloq.* to steal.

у́мысел [*gen.* -сла] *n.* design; intention; purpose. Злой у́мысел, malicious intent. —**с у́мыслом,** on purpose; deliberately.

умы́ть [*infl.* умо́ю, умо́ешь] *v., pfv. of* умыва́ть. —**умы́ться,** *refl., pfv. of* умыва́ться.

умы́шленный *adj.* intentional; deliberate; premeditated. —**умы́шленно,** *adv.* deliberately; intentionally; purposely.

умягча́ть *v. impfv.* [*pfv.* умягчи́ть] **1,** to soften. **2,** *fig.* to mollify.

унаво́зить *v., pfv. of* наво́зить.

унасле́довать *v. pfv.* [*infl.* -дую, -дуешь] to inherit.

унести́ [*infl. like* нести́] *v., pfv. of* уноси́ть. —**унести́сь,** *refl., pfv. of* уноси́ться.

униа́т *n.* Uniat. —**униа́тский,** *adj.* Uniat.

универма́г *n.* department store (*contr. of* универса́льный магази́н).

универса́льность *n.f.* universality.

универса́льный *adj.* **1,** universal. **2,** all-round. **3,** multi-purpose; all-purpose. —**универса́льный магази́н,** department store. —**универса́льное сре́дство,** panacea.

университе́т *n.* university. —**университе́тский,** *adj.* university (*attrib.*).

унижа́ть *v. impfv.* [*pfv.* уни́зить] **1,** to humiliate. **2,** to degrade; humble; abase. —**унижа́ться,** *refl.* **1,** to humble oneself. **2,** (*with* до) to stoop to.

униже́ние *n.* **1,** humiliation. **2,** degradation; abasement. **3,** indignity.

уни́женный *adj.* **1,** humiliated. **2,** humble; abject.

униза́ть [*infl.* унижу́, уни́жешь] *v., pfv. of* уни́зывать.

унизи́тельный *adj.* humiliating; degrading.

уни́зить [*infl.* -жу, -зишь] *v., pfv. of* унижа́ть. —**уни́зиться,** *refl., pfv. of* унижа́ться.

уни́зывать *v. impfv.* [*pfv.* униза́ть] to stud (*with* jewels).

уника́льный *adj.* unique.

у́никум *n.* unique person; unique object.

унима́ть *v. impfv.* [*pfv.* уня́ть] **1,** to quiet; calm; pacify. **2,** to stop; suppress. —**унима́ться,** *refl.* **1,** to quiet down; calm down. **2,** to stop; subside; abate; die down.

унисо́н *n.* unison. —**в унисо́н,** in unison.

унита́з *n.* toilet.

унифика́ция *n.* standardization.

унифици́ровать *v. impfv. & pfv.* [*pres.* -рую, -руешь] to standardize.

уничижи́тельный *adj.* pejorative.

уничтожа́ть *v. impfv.* [*pfv.* уничто́жить] **1,** to destroy; annihilate; obliterate; wipe out. **2,** to eliminate; abolish; do away with.

уничтожа́ющий *adj.* **1,** destructive; devastating. **2,** *fig.* scathing; devastating; withering.

уничтоже́ние *n.* **1,** destruction; annihilation. **2,** elimination; abolition.

уничто́жить *v., pfv. of* уничтожа́ть.

у́ния *n.* union (*of countries or churches*).

уноси́ть *v. impfv.* [*pfv.* унести́; *pres.* уношу́, уно́сишь] **1,** to carry away; carry off. **2,** *fig.* to take (lives). **3,** *colloq.* to make off with. **4,** *in* уноси́ть но́ги, to escape; get away. —**уноси́ться,** *refl.* **1,** to speed away; dash off. **2,** *fig.* (*of thoughts*) to go back. **3,** *fig.* (*of time*) to fly by.

у́нтер-офице́р *n.* noncommissioned officer.

у́нция *n.* ounce.

уныва́ть *v. impfv.* to lose heart; be dejected; be discouraged.

уны́лый *adj.* **1,** downcast; despondent; dejected. **2,** cheerless; dreary; dismal.

уны́ние *n.* despondency; dejection.

уня́ть [*infl.* уйму́, уймёшь; *past* уня́л, уняла́, уня́ло] *v., pfv. of* унима́ть. —**уня́ться,** *refl., pfv. of* уня́ться.

упа́д *n., in* до упа́ду, till one is about to drop.

упа́док [*gen.* -дка] *n.* decline; decay. —**упа́док ду́ха,** despondency; depression. —**упа́док сил,** weakness; loss of strength.

упа́дочничество *n.* decadence. —**упа́дочнический,** *adj.* decadent.

упа́дочный *adj.* **1,** decadent. **2,** depressed: упа́дочное настрое́ние, depression.

упакова́ть [*infl.* -ку́ю, -ку́ешь] *v., pfv. of* пакова́ть *and* упако́вывать. —**упакова́ться,** *refl., pfv. of* упако́вываться.

упако́вка *n.* **1,** packing. **2,** packing material. —**упако́вочный,** *adj.* packing (*attrib.*).

упако́вщик *n.* packer.

упако́вывать *v. impfv.* [*pfv.* упакова́ть] to pack. —**упако́вываться,** *refl.* to pack; get packed; pack one's things.

упасти́ *v. pfv.* [*infl. like* спасти́] *archaic* to save. —**упаси́ бог!; бо́же упаси́!, 1,** God forbid!; heaven forbid! **2,** perish the thought!

упа́сть [*infl. like* пасть] *v., pfv. of* па́дать.

упека́ть *v. impfv.* [*pfv.* упе́чь] *colloq.* **1,** to bake thoroughly. **2,** to send away; banish. **3,** *in* упека́ть в тюрьму́, to toss into jail.

упере́ть [*infl. like* пере́ть] *v., pfv. of* упира́ть. —**упере́ться,** *refl., pfv. of* упира́ться.

упе́чь [*infl. like* пе́чь] *v., pfv. of* упека́ть.

упива́ться *v.r. impfv.* [*pfv.* упи́ться] **1,** *colloq.* to get drunk. **2,** (*with instr.*) to delight in; revel in.

упира́ть *v. impfv.* [*pfv.* упере́ть] **1,** to place firmly (on *or* against): упира́ть ле́стницу в сте́ну, to place a ladder against the wall. **2,** to fix (one's eyes on something): упира́ть взгляд в дверь, to fix one's eyes on the door. **3,** *v.i.* (*with* на + *acc.*) *colloq.* to lay stress on. —**упира́ться,** *refl.* **1,** (*with instr.*) to give a push with. **2,** (*with instr.*) to plant firmly (on *or* against): упира́ться нога́ми в зе́млю, to plant one's feet firmly on the ground. **3,** (*with instr.*) *colloq.* to fix (one's eyes on something): упере́ться взгля́дом в дверь, to fix one's eyes on the door. **4,** (*with* в + *acc.*) *colloq.* to run into; come up against. **5,** *fig.,* *colloq.* to balk; resist.

уписа́ть [*infl.* упишу́, упи́шешь] *v., pfv. of* упи́сывать.

упи́сывать *v. impfv.* [*pfv.* уписа́ть] *colloq.* to eat; gobble up.

упи́танный *adj.* well-fed; fat; plump.

упи́ться [*infl. like* пить; *past* упи́лся, -ла́сь, -ло́сь] *v.r., pfv. of* упива́ться.

упла́та *n.* payment.

уплати́ть [*infl.* уплачу́, упла́тишь] *v., pfv. of* упла́чивать.

упла́чивать *v. impfv.* [*pfv.* уплати́ть] to pay.

уплотне́ние *n.* **1,** packing down; compression. **2,** hard spot. **3,** *in* уплотне́ние рабо́чего дня, tightening up the schedule of the working day.

уплотни́тель *n.m.* seal.

уплотня́ть *v. impfv.* [*pfv.* уплотни́ть] **1,** to pack down (dirt, sand, etc.). **2,** to make more compact; make more crowded. **3,** *fig.* to crowd more into: уплотня́ть рабо́чий день, to crowd more into the working day. —**уплотня́ться,** *refl.* **1,** to be packed down. **2,** to become more crowded. **3,** to give up part of one's living space.

уплыва́ть *v. impfv.* [*pfv.* уплы́ть] **1,** to swim away. **2,** to sail away; sail off. **3,** to float away. **4,** (*of time*) to slip by.

уплы́ть [*infl. like* плыть] *v., pfv. of* уплыва́ть.

упова́ние *n., obs.* hope.

упова́ть *v. impfv., obs.* **1,** to hope. **2,** (*with* на + *acc.*) to hope for. **3,** (*with* на + *acc.*) to count on.

уподо́бить [*infl.* -блю, -бишь] *v., pfv. of* уподобля́ть. —**уподо́биться,** *refl., pfv. of* уподобля́ться.

уподобля́ть *v. impfv.* [*pfv.* уподо́бить] to liken: уподобля́ть поли́тику ша́хматам, to liken politics to chess. —**уподобля́ться,** *refl.* (*with dat.*) to become like; come to resemble.

упое́ние *n.* rapture; ecstasy.

упои́тельный *adj.* ravishing; intoxicating.

упоко́й *n., in* за упоко́й (+ *gen.*), for the repose of.

уполза́ть *v. impfv.* [*pfv.* уползти́] **1,** to crawl away. **2,** to move away (*slowly*); drift away.

уползти́ [*infl. like* ползти́] *v., pfv. of* уполза́ть.

уполномо́ченный *adj.* authorized. —*n.* authorized agent; representative; plenipotentiary.

уполномо́чивать *v. impfv.* [*pfv.* уполномо́чить] to authorize; empower.

уполномо́чие *n., in* по уполномо́чию (+ *gen.*), by authority of.

уполномо́чить *v., pfv. of* уполномо́чивать.

упомина́ние *n.* mentioning; mention: при (одно́м) упомина́нии (+ *gen. or with* о), at the (very) mention of.

упомина́ть *v. impfv.* [*pfv.* упомяну́ть] to mention.

упо́мнить *v. pfv., colloq.* to remember.

упомяну́ть [*infl.* -мяну́, -мя́нешь] *v., pfv. of* упомина́ть.

упо́р *n.* **1,** support: для упо́ра, for support. **2,** prop; support. —**в упо́р,** pointblank. —**де́лать упо́р на** (+ *acc. or prepl.*), to emphasize; lay stress on.

упо́рный *adj.* stubborn; persistent.

упо́рство *n.* stubbornness; persistence; perseverance.

упо́рствовать *v. impfv.* [*pres.* -ствую, -ствуешь] **1,** to be stubborn. **2,** to persist; persevere.

упорхну́ть *v. pfv.* to fly away; flit away.

упоря́доченный *adj.* orderly; efficient; well organized.

упоря́дочить *v. pfv.* to put in order; put right; normalize.

употреби́тельный *adj.* widely-used; in common use.

употреби́ть [*infl.* -блю́, -би́шь] *v., pfv. of* употребля́ть. —**употреби́ться,** *refl., pfv. of* употребля́ться.

употребле́ние *n.* use.

употребля́ть v. impfv. [pfv. **употреби́ть**] to use. —**употребля́ться**, refl. to be used.

упра́ва n. **1**, pre-rev. council; board. **2**, colloq. justice: иска́ть упра́вы, to seek justice. Найти́ упра́ву на (+ acc.), to see justice done in the case of.

управи́тель n.m., obs. manager; steward.

упра́виться [infl. -влюсь, -вишься] v.r., pfv. of **управля́ться**.

управле́ние n. **1**, (with instr.) management (of); administration (of). **2**, (with instr.) driving (a car); conducting (a ship); steering (a ship). **3**, mech. control: дистанцио́нное управле́ние, remote control. Рыча́г управле́ния, control lever. **4**, government: ме́стное управле́ние, local government. **5**, (governmental) board; bureau; administration; agency; directorate.

управле́нческий adj. administrative.

управля́емый adj. guided; управля́емый снаря́д, guided missile.

управля́ть v. impfv. (with instr.) **1**, to operate (a machine); drive (a car). **2**, to manage; administer; run. **3**, to rule; govern. **4**, to control. **5**, to conduct (an orchestra). **6**, gram. to govern. —**управля́ться**, refl. [pfv. **упра́виться**] colloq. **1**, (with с + instr.) to finish (with). **2**, (with с + instr.) to cope with; deal with; handle. **3**, [impfv. only] (of a vehicle) to ride; handle (a certain way).

управля́ющий n., decl. as an adj. manager.

упражне́ние n. exercise.

упражня́ть v. impfv. to exercise; train. —**упражня́ться**, refl. (with в or на + prepl.) to practice.

упраздне́ние n. abolition.

упраздня́ть v. impfv. [pfv. **упраздни́ть**] to abolish.

упра́шивать v. impfv. to beg; entreat.

упрева́ть v. impfv. [pfv. **упре́ть**] colloq. to be well-cooked.

упрежда́ть v. impfv. [pfv. **упреди́ть**] obs. **1**, to warn. **2**, to anticipate. —**упрежда́ющий уда́р**, preemptive strike.

упрёк n. reproach; rebuke; reproof. —**ста́вить (что́-нибудь) в упрёк** (+ dat.), to hold something against someone.

упрека́ть v. impfv. [pfv. **упрекну́ть**] (with в + prepl.) to reproach; rebuke: упрека́ть кого́-нибудь в неблагода́рности, to reproach someone for his (her) ingratitude.

упре́ть v., pfv. of **упрева́ть**.

упроси́ть v. pfv. [infl. упрошу́, упро́сишь] to persuade; talk into; prevail upon.

упрости́ть [infl. -щу́, -сти́шь] v., pfv. of **упроща́ть**.

упро́чение n. strengthening; consolidation.

упро́чивать v. impfv. [pfv. **упро́чить**] to strengthen; consolidate. —**упро́чиваться**, refl. to become firmly established.

упроща́ть v. impfv. [pfv. **упрости́ть**] **1**, to simplify. **2**, to oversimplify.

упроще́ние n. simplification. —**упрощённый**, adj. simplified. —**упроще́нство; упроще́нчество**, n. oversimplification. —**упрощённческий**, adj. oversimplified; simplistic.

упру́гий adj. elastic; resilient; springy. —**упру́гость**, n.f. elasticity; resilience.

упря́жка [gen. pl. -жек] n. **1**, team (of horses, dogs, etc.). **2**, harness.

упряжно́й adj. harness (attrib.). —**упряжна́я ло́шадь**, draft horse.

у́пряжь n.f. harness.

упря́мец [gen. -мца] n., colloq. stubborn person.

упря́миться v.r. impfv. [pfv. **заупря́миться**; pres. -млюсь, -мишься] to be stubborn; balk.

упря́мство n. stubbornness; obstinacy.

упря́мый adj. **1**, stubborn; obstinate. **2**, persistent.

упря́тать [infl. упря́чу, упря́чешь] v., pfv. of **упря́тывать**.

упря́тывать v. impfv. [pfv. **упря́тать**] colloq. **1**, to hide; put away. **2**, in упря́тывать в тюрьму́, to toss into prison.

упуска́ть v. impfv. [pfv. **упусти́ть**] **1**, to lose hold of; let slip out of one's hands. **2**, to let slip by; miss; lose (a chance, opportunity, etc.). —**упуска́ть и́з виду**, to lose sight of; overlook; fail to realize.

упусти́ть [infl. упущу́, упу́стишь] v., pfv. of **упуска́ть**.

упуще́ние n. omission; oversight.

упы́рь [gen. упыря́] n.m., colloq. vampire.

ура́ interj. hurrah!; hurray!

уравне́ние n. **1**, equalization. **2**, math. equation.

ура́внивать v. impfv. **1**, [pfv. **уравня́ть**] to equalize; make equal. **2**, [pfv. **уровня́ть**] to level; even.

уравни́тельный adj. **1**, equalizing. **2**, applied equally to all.

уравнове́сить [infl. -шу, -сишь] v., pfv. of **уравнове́шивать**.

уравнове́шенный adj. **1**, balanced. **2**, fig. even-tempered. —**уравнове́шенность**, n.f. even temper.

уравнове́шивать v. impfv. [pfv. **уравнове́сить**] **1**, to balance. **2**, fig. to counterbalance; offset.

уравня́ть v., pfv. of **ура́внивать** (in sense #1).

урага́н n. hurricane.

уразумева́ть v. impfv. [pfv. **уразуме́ть**] to understand.

ура́н n. **1**, uranium. **2**, cap. Uranus.

ура́новый adj. uranium (attrib.).

урва́ть [infl. like рвать] v., pfv. of **урыва́ть**.

урду́ n.m. indecl. Urdu.

урегули́рование n. settlement.

урегули́ровать v. pfv. [infl. -рую, -руешь] to settle (an issue, dispute, etc.).

уре́зать [infl. уре́жу, уре́жешь] v., pfv. of **уре́зывать** and **уреза́ть**.

урезо́нивать v. impfv. [pfv. **урезо́нить**] colloq. **1**, to bring to reason. **2**, [impfv. only] to reason with; try to persuade.

уре́зывать v. impfv. [pfv. **уре́зать**] **1**, colloq. to shorten (by cutting off a part). **2**, to reduce; cut; curtail. **3**, to abridge (someone's rights). **4**, in уре́зывать себя́ в (+ prepl.), to stint oneself (in). Also, **уреза́ть**.

уреми́я n. uremia. —**уреми́ческий**, adj. uremic.

уре́тра n. urethra.

у́рна n. **1**, urn. **2**, refuse container. —**избира́тельная у́рна**, ballot box.

у́ровень [gen. -вня] n.m. **1**, level: у́ровень мо́ря, sea level. **2**, fig. standard: жи́зненный у́ровень, standard of living. **3**, level (instrument). —**быть на у́ровне**, colloq. to be up to the mark; be up to par. —**идти́ в у́ровень с ве́ком**, to keep up with the times.

уровня́ть v., pfv. of **ура́внивать** (in sense #2).

уро́д n. **1**, freak; monster. **2**, ugly person. **3**, monstrosity.

уроди́ть v. pfv. [infl. -жу́, -ди́шь] to bear; yield. —**уроди́ться**, refl. **1**, to come up; grow; ripen. **2**, colloq. to be born. 3, (with в + acc.) colloq. to take after; resemble.

уро́дливость n.f. 1, ugliness. 2, deformity.

уро́дливый adj. 1, deformed; misshapen. 2, extremely ugly; hideous. 3, fig. wrong; improper; distorted.

уро́довать v. impfv. [pfv. изуро́довать; pres. -дую, -дуешь] 1, to disfigure. 2, fig. to corrupt.

уро́дский adj., colloq. ugly; hideous.

уро́дство n. 1, deformity. 2, ugliness. 3, abnormality.

урожа́й n. harvest; crop.

урожа́йность n.f. productivity; yield.

урожа́йный adj. 1, (of ground, soil, etc.) productive; fertile. 2, (of crops) high-yield. 3, (of a year, season, etc.) good (for crops); productive.

урождённая adj. née.

уроже́нец [gen. -нца] n.m. [fem. -нка] native.

уро́к n. lesson.

уроло́гия n. urology. —уро́лог, n. urologist. —уроло́гический, adj. urological.

уро́н n. 1, damage; harm. 2, losses; casualties.

урони́ть [infl. уроню́, уро́нишь] v., pfv. of роня́ть.

уро́чище n. natural boundary.

уро́чный adj. 1, obs. fixed; set; agreed-upon. 2, usual; customary.

урча́ние n. rumbling.

урча́ть v. impfv. [pres. -чу́, -чи́шь] to rumble.

урыва́ть v. impfv. [pfv. урва́ть] colloq. 1, to snatch; grab. 2, fig. to find (time).

уры́вками adv., colloq. in snatches; by fits and starts.

урю́к n. dried apricots.

ус [pl. усы́] n. 1, whisker (of an animal). 2, bot. runner. —кито́вый ус, whalebone. See also усы́.

усади́ть [infl. усажу́, уса́дишь] v., pfv. of уса́живать.

уса́дка n. shrinkage.

уса́дьба [gen. pl. -деб] n. 1, country estate. 2, farmstead.

уса́живать v. impfv. [pfv. усади́ть] 1, to seat; sit; offer a seat to. 2, (with за + acc.) to sit (someone) down to. 3, to plant (with). —уса́живаться, refl. [pfv. усе́сться] 1, to sit down; take a seat. 2, (with за + acc. or inf.) to sit down to; settle down to.

уса́тый adj. 1, with a mustache. 2, (of an animal) having whiskers.

уса́ч [gen. усача́] n., colloq. man with a (big) mustache.

усва́ивать v. impfv. [pfv. усво́ить] 1, to master. 2, to acquire (a habit, instinct, etc.). 3, to adopt (a custom, manner, etc.). 4, to digest; assimilate.

усво́ение n. 1, mastering. 2, acquiring. 3, assimilation.

усво́ить v., pfv. of усва́ивать.

усе́ивать v. impfv. [pfv. усе́ять] to dot; stud: не́бо усе́яно звёздами, the sky is studded with stars.

усека́ть v. impfv. [pfv. усе́чь] to truncate.

усе́рдие n. zeal.

усе́рдный adj. 1, zealous. 2, diligent.

усе́рдствовать v. impfv. [pres. -ствую, -ствуешь] 1, to show great zeal; work hard. 2, (with inf.) to take pains (to).

усе́сться [infl. like сесть] v.r., pfv. of уса́живаться.

усе́чь [infl. like сечь; past усёк, -ла́, -ло́] v., pfv. of усека́ть.

усе́ять [infl. усе́ю, усе́ешь] v., pfv. of усе́ивать.

усиде́ть v. pfv. [infl. -жу́, -ди́шь] 1, to keep one's seat. 2, to sit; stay (in one place). 3, colloq. to keep a job.

уси́дчивый adj. assiduous. —уси́дчивость, n.f. assiduousness.

у́сик n. 1, small mustache. 2, zool. feeler. 3, bot. tendril.

усиле́ние n. 1, strengthening; reinforcement. 2, intensification. 3, amplification (of sound).

уси́ленно adv. 1, with great force. 2, hard; diligently; in earnest: уси́ленно гото́виться к экза́менам, to study hard for one's examinations. 3, colloq. with great effort; with great difficulty.

уси́ленный adj. 1, increased; extra. 2, intense; strenuous. 3, (of requests, questions, etc.) repeated; persistent.

уси́ливать v. impfv. [pfv. уси́лить] 1, to strengthen; reinforce. 2, to increase; intensify. 3, to amplify (sound). —уси́ливаться, refl. 1, to become stronger. 2, to increase; become more intense. 3, (of rain) to come down harder. 4, [impfv. only] (with inf.) obs. to strive (to); endeavor (to).

уси́лие n. effort: прилага́ть все уси́лия, to make every effort. —де́лать над собо́й уси́лие, to force oneself.

усили́тель n.m. amplifier; booster.

уси́лить v., pfv. of уси́ливать. —уси́литься, refl., pfv. of уси́ливаться.

ускака́ть v. pfv. [infl. ускачу́, уска́чешь] 1, to skip away; hop away. 2, to gallop off.

ускольза́ть v. impfv. [pfv. ускользну́ть] 1, to slip out: ускользну́ть из рук, to slip out of one's hands. 2, to slip away; sneak away; steal away. 3, (with от) to elude; evade; give (someone) the slip. 4, in ускользну́ть от чьего́-нибудь внима́ния, to escape one's notice. 5, (with от) colloq. to avoid giving (an answer, explanation, etc.).

ускоре́ние n. acceleration.

ускори́тель n.m. 1, accelerator. 2, rocketry booster.

ускоря́ть v. impfv. [pfv. уско́рить] 1, to accelerate; speed up; quicken. 2, to hasten; bring on sooner. —ускоря́ться, refl. 1, to pick up speed; accelerate. 2, to be speeded up.

усла́вливаться v. = усло́вливаться.

усла́да n., obs. pleasure; delight.

услади́ть [infl. -жу́, -ди́шь] v., pfv. of услажда́ть.

услажда́ть v. impfv. [pfv. услади́ть] obs. 1, to delight; bring pleasure to. 2, to brighten up. 3, to relieve; mitigate.

усла́ть [infl. ушлю́, ушлёшь] v., pfv. of усыла́ть.

уследи́ть v. pfv. [infl. -жу́, -ди́шь] (with за + instr.) 1, to keep an eye on. 2, to follow; keep track of.

усло́вие n. 1, condition: непреме́нное усло́вие, essential condition. Ста́вить усло́вия, to lay down conditions. 2, pl. conditions: усло́вия труда́, working conditions. 3, pl. terms; provisions (of a treaty, contract, etc.): на льго́тных усло́виях, on favorable terms. 4, obs. agreement: заключи́ть усло́вие, to conclude an agreement. —в усло́виях (+ gen.), under conditions of... —ни при каки́х усло́виях, under no circumstances. —при про́чих ра́вных усло́виях, other things being equal. —при таки́х усло́виях, under such conditions. —при усло́вии, что..., on condition that; provided.

усло́виться [infl. -влюсь, -вишься] v.r., pfv. of усло́вливаться.

усло́вленный adj. 1, agreed-upon. 2, [short form only] agreed: как усло́влено, as agreed.

усло́вливаться v.r. impfv. [pfv. усло́виться] to agree; arrange: усло́виться встре́титься, to agree/ arrange to meet. Усло́виться о цене́, to agree on the price.

усло́вно *adv.* conditionally; tentatively. Он получи́л год усло́вно, he was given a year on probation; he was given a one-year suspended sentence.

усло́вность *n.f.* convention; conventionality.

усло́вный *adj.* **1,** agreed-upon; prearranged. **2,** conventional. **3,** conditional; provisional. **4,** relative. **5,** (*of a line*) imaginary. **6,** *art* symbolic. **7,** *gram.* conditional. —усло́вный пригово́р, suspended sentence. —усло́вный рефле́кс, conditioned reflex.

усложне́ние *n.* complication.

усложня́ть *v.* *impfv.* [*pfv.* усложни́ть] to complicate. —усложня́ться, *refl.* to become complicated.

услу́га *n.* **1,** favor; good turn: оказа́ть услу́гу (+ *dat.*), to do (someone) a favor. Плоха́я услу́га, disservice; ill turn. **2,** *pl.* services: предлага́ть свои́ услу́ги, to offer one's services. **3,** *pl.* facilities. —к ва́шим услу́гам, at your disposal.

услу́живать *v.* *impfv.* [*pfv.* услужи́ть] (*with dat.*) **1,** to help; oblige; accommodate; do something for. **2,** [*impfv. only*] *obs.* to serve; be a servant to.

услужи́ть [*infl.* услужу́, услу́жишь] *v.*, *pfv. of* услу́живать.

услу́жливый *adj.* obliging; helpful; accommodating.

услыха́ть *v.* *pfv.* [*infl. like* слы́шать] = услы́шать.

услы́шать *v.*, *pfv. of* слы́шать.

усма́тривать *v.* *impfv.* [*pfv.* усмотре́ть] **1,** (*with* за + *instr.*) to look after; keep an eye on. **2,** (*with* в + *prepl.*) to see (in); see (as): усма́тривать в ко́м-нибудь сопе́рника, to see someone as a rival. **3,** *colloq.* to see; spot.

усмеха́ться *v.r.* *impfv.* [*pfv.* усмехну́ться] to smile; grin.

усме́шка *n.* **1,** smile; grin. **2,** sneer; smirk.

усмире́ние *n.* **1,** suppression. **2,** pacification.

усмиря́ть *v.* *impfv.* [*pfv.* усмири́ть] **1,** to pacify; quiet. **2,** to suppress; put down.

усмотре́ние *n.* discretion; judgment.

усмотре́ть [*infl.* усмотрю́, усмо́тришь] *v.*, *pfv. of* усма́тривать.

усну́ть *v.* *pfv.* to fall asleep.

усоверше́нствование *n.* **1,** improvement; refinement. **2,** advanced training: ку́рсы усоверше́нствования, advanced training program.

усоверше́нствовать *v.*, *pfv. of* соверше́нствовать.

усомни́ться *v.r.* *pfv.* (*with* в + *prepl.*) to doubt; have doubts about.

усоно́гий *adj.*, *in* усоно́гий рак, barnacle.

усо́пший *adj.*, *obs.* deceased. —*n.*, *obs.* the deceased.

усо́хнуть [*past* усо́х, -ла] *v.*, *pfv. of* усыха́ть.

успева́емость *n.f.* progress (*in one's studies*). —та́бель успева́емости, report card.

успева́ть *v.* *impfv.* [*pfv.* успе́ть] **1,** (*with inf.*) to have time (to). **2,** (*with* на + *acc. or* к) *colloq.* to be on time (for). **3,** (*with* в + *prepl.*) *obs.* to be successful (in). **4,** [*impfv. only*] to make progress (*in one's studies*).

успе́ние *n.*, *relig.* **1,** death; passing. **2,** Assumption. —успе́нский, *adj.* Assumption (*attrib.*): Успе́нский собо́р, Cathedral of the Assumption.

успе́ть *v.*, *pfv. of* успева́ть. —успе́ется, *impers.*, *colloq.* there's plenty of time!

успе́х *n.* **1,** success. **2,** *pl.* progress: де́лать успе́хи, to make progress. —как ва́ши успе́хи?, how are you getting along? —с тем же успе́хом, might (just) as well.

успе́шный *adj.* successful. —успе́шно, *adv.* successfully. —успе́шность, *n.f.* success.

успока́ивать *v.* *impfv.* [*pfv.* успоко́ить] **1,** to calm; calm down. **2,** to quiet; quiet down (a child, group, etc.). **3,** to relieve; soothe (pain); calm (one's nerves); settle (one's stomach). **4,** to allay (suspicion, doubts, etc.). —успока́иваться, *refl.* **1,** to calm down. **2,** (*of pain, a storm, etc.*) to subside; abate. **3,** *colloq.* to be satisfied.

успокое́ние *n.* **1,** calming; quieting; soothing. **2,** peace of mind; tranquillity.

успокои́тельный *adj.* **1,** calming; soothing. **2,** reassuring. —успокои́тельное сре́дство, sedative; tranquilizer.

успоко́ить *v.*, *pfv. of* успока́ивать. —успоко́иться, *refl.*, *pfv. of* успока́иваться.

уста́ [*gen.* уст] *n.pl.*, *obs.* mouth. —из пе́рвых уст, firsthand. —из уст (+ *gen.*), from the mouth of; from. —из уст в уста́, by word of mouth. —у всех на уста́х, on everyone's lips.

уста́в *n.* **1,** regulations; statutes. **2,** charter: уста́в ООН, United Nations Charter. **3,** *mil.* manual: боево́й уста́в, field manual.

устава́ть *v.* *impfv.* [*pfv.* уста́ть; *pres.* устаю́, устаёшь] to tire; get tired. —не устава́я, tirelessly.

уста́вить [*infl.* -влю, -вишь] *v.*, *pfv. of* уставля́ть. —уста́виться, *refl.*, *pfv. of* уставля́ться.

уставля́ть *v.* *impfv.* [*pfv.* уста́вить] *colloq.* **1,** to place; arrange. **2,** (*with instr.*) to cover (with); fill (with); cram (with). **3,** to point; direct; aim. —уставля́ться, *refl.*, *colloq.* **1,** (*with* в + *acc.*) to fit (into); go (into). **2,** (*with instr.*) to be crowded (with); be crammed (with). **3,** (*with* на + *acc.*) to stare (at).

уста́вный *adj.* regulation; prescribed.

уста́лость *n.f.* fatigue.

уста́лый *adj.* tired.

у́сталь *n.f.*, *obs.* = уста́лость. —без у́стали, tirelessly. —не знать у́стали, to be tireless; be indefatigable.

устана́вливать *v.* *impfv.* [*pfv.* установи́ть] **1,** to install. **2,** to establish. **3,** to set; fix. —устана́вливаться, *refl.* **1,** to be established. **2,** to be formed. **3,** to set in.

установи́ть [*infl.* -новлю́, -но́вишь] *v.*, *pfv. of* устана́вливать. —установи́ться, *refl.*, *pfv. of* устана́вливаться.

устано́вка [*gen. pl.* -вок] *n.* **1,** placing; mounting; installation. **2,** plant; unit: силова́я устано́вка, power plant; холоди́льная устано́вка, refrigeration unit; бурова́я устано́вка, drilling rig; дождева́льная устано́вка, sprinkler system. **3,** mount: оруди́йная устано́вка, gun mount. **4,** launcher: раке́тная устано́вка, rocket launcher. **5,** adjustment: то́нкая устано́вка, fine adjustment. **6,** setting: устано́вка высотоме́ра, altimeter setting. **7,** directive; instructions. **8,** precept; tenet: идеологи́ческие устано́вки, ideological precepts/tenets.

установле́ние *n.* establishment.

устарева́ть *v.* *impfv.* [*pfv.* устаре́ть] to become obsolete; become antiquated.

устаре́вший *adj.* obsolete; outmoded; outdated; out-of-date; antiquated. *Also,* устаре́лый.

устаре́ть *v.*, *pfv. of* устарева́ть.

уста́ть [*infl.* уста́ну, уста́нешь] *v.*, *pfv. of* устава́ть.

устерега́ть *v.* *impfv.* [*pfv.* устере́чь] *colloq.* to guard.

устере́чь [*infl. like* стере́чь] *v.*, *pfv. of* устерега́ть.

устила́ть *v. impfv.* [*pfv.* устла́ть] to cover; overlay.

устла́ть [*infl.* устелю́, усте́лешь] *v.*, *pfv. of* устила́ть.

у́стный *adj.* oral; verbal. —**у́стно**, *adv.* orally; verbally.

усто́й *n.* **1**, abutment (*of a bridge*). **2**, foundation. **3**, *pl.*, *fig.* foundation; basis. **4**, *colloq.* cream forming on the surface of milk.

усто́йчивый *adj.* stable; steady. —**усто́йчивость**, *n.f.* stability.

устоя́ть *v. pfv.* [*infl.* устою́, устои́шь] **1**, to remain on one's feet; keep one's balance. **2**, to hold out; stand firm; stand one's ground. **3**, (*with* пе́ред *or* про́тив) to withstand; resist. —**устоя́ться**, *refl.* **1**, (*of liquids*) to settle. **2**, *fig.* to become fixed; become firmly established: устоя́вшиеся взгля́ды, set views.

устра́ивать *v. impfv.* [*pfv.* устро́ить] **1**, to arrange; organize. **2**, to arrange; settle; put in order. **3**, to place (in a job, school, etc.). **4**, to put up (in lodgings). **5**, to build; make; construct. **6**, *colloq.* to make; create (a scene, scandal, etc.). **7**, *colloq.* to suit: э́то меня́ вполне́ устра́ивает, that suits me fine. —**устра́иваться**, *refl.* **1**, to work out: всё устро́илось, everything worked out. **2**, to settle down (in a comfortable place): устро́иться на дива́не, to settle down on the couch. **3**, to get settled (in a house or apartment). **4**, to get a job. **5**, to manage; make out; get along; get by.

устране́ние *n.* removal; elimination.

устраня́ть *v. impfv.* [*pfv.* устрани́ть] to remove; eliminate. —**устраня́ться**, *refl.* **1**, (*with* от) to withdraw (from); retire (from). **2**, to disappear.

устраша́ть *v. impfv.* [*pfv.* устраши́ть] to frighten; scare. —**устраша́ться**, *refl.* to be frightened.

устреми́ть [*infl.* -млю́, -ми́шь] *v.*, *pfv. of* устремля́ть. —**устреми́ться**, *refl.*, *pfv. of* устремля́ться.

устремле́ние *n.* **1**, surge; onrush. **2**, aspiration.

устремля́ть *v. impfv.* [*pfv.* устреми́ть] to direct; fix (one's gaze, attention, etc.). —**устремля́ться**, *refl.* **1**, to rush; dash; (*with* вниз) swoop down. **2**, (*with* на + *acc. or* к) to be directed (toward); (*of one's eyes*) be fixed (on); (*of a person*) concentrate (on).

у́стрица *n.* oyster. —**у́стричный**, *adj.* oyster (*attrib.*).

устро́итель *n.m.* organizer.

устро́ить *v.*, *pfv. of* устра́ивать. —**устро́иться**, *refl.*, *pfv. of* устра́иваться.

устро́йство *n.* **1**, arranging; organizing. **2**, arrangement; layout. **3**, (political or social) system. **4**, mechanism; device.

усту́п *n.* ledge.

уступа́ть *v. impfv.* [*pfv.* уступи́ть] **1**, *v.t.* to yield; give up; let have; cede. **2**, *v.i.* (*with dat.*) to yield (to); succumb (to); give in (to); give way (to). **3**, *v.i.* (*with dat.*) to be inferior (to); be second (to). **4**, *v.t.*, *colloq.* to sell (*at a reduced price*); let go; let have: уступи́ть что́-нибудь за шесть до́лларов, to let something go for six dollars. **5**, *v.t.*, *colloq.* to deduct; take off (*from a price*): уступи́ть два рубля́, to deduct/take off/two rubles.

уступи́тельный *adj.*, *gram.* concessive.

уступи́ть [*infl.* уступлю́, усту́пишь] *v.*, *pfv. of* уступа́ть.

усту́пка [*gen. pl.* -пок] *n.* **1**, yielding; giving up. **2**, concession: идти́ на (*or* де́лать) усту́пки, to make concessions. **3**, discount; reduction.

усту́пчивый *adj.* amenable; compliant.

устыди́ть *v. pfv.* [*infl.* -жу́, -ди́шь] to shame; put

to shame. —**устыди́ться**, *refl.* (*with gen.*) to be ashamed (of).

у́стье [*gen. pl.* у́стьев] *n.* **1**, mouth (*of a river*). **2**, opening; mouth.

усугуби́ть [*infl.* -блю́, -би́шь] *v.*, *pfv. of* усугубля́ть. *Also,* усугу́бить [*infl.* -блю, -бишь].

усугубля́ть *v. impfv.* [*pfv.* усугуби́ть *or* усугу́бить] **1**, to increase; heighten; intensify; redouble. **2**, to (further) aggravate; make (even) worse.

усы́ [*gen.* усо́в] *n. pl.* [*sing.* ус] **1**, mustache. **2**, whiskers (*of an animal*).

усыла́ть *v. impfv.* [*pfv.* усла́ть] to send away.

усынови́ть [*infl.* -влю́, -ви́шь] *v.*, *pfv. of* усыновля́ть.

усыновле́ние *n.* adoption (*of a child*).

усыновля́ть *v. impfv.* [*pfv.* усынови́ть] to adopt (a child).

усыпа́льница *n.* burial vault.

усы́пать [*infl.* усы́плю, усы́плешь] *v.*, *pfv. of* усыпа́ть.

усыпа́ть *v. impfv.* [*pfv.* усы́пать] **1**, to strew; bestrew. **2**, *fig.* to stud: не́бо усы́пано звёздами, the sky is studded with stars.

усыпи́тельный *adj.* soporific.

усыпи́ть [*infl.* -плю́, -пи́шь] *v.*, *pfv. of* усыпля́ть.

усыпля́ть *v. impfv.* [*pfv.* усыпи́ть] **1**, to put to sleep; lull to sleep. **2**, *fig.* to lull (someone's attention); allay (suspicions).

усыпля́ющий *adj.* = усыпи́тельный.

усыха́ть *v. impfv.* [*pfv.* усо́хнуть] **1**, to wither. **2**, *colloq.* to become wizened.

ута́ивать *v. impfv.* [*pfv.* утаи́ть] **1**, to conceal; hold back; withhold. **2**, to hide. **3**, to steal; appropriate.

ута́йка *n.*, *colloq.* concealment. —**без ута́йки**, without concealing anything; without holding anything back.

ута́птывать *v. impfv.* [*pfv.* утопта́ть] to trample down.

ута́скивать *v. impfv.* [*pfv.* утащи́ть] **1**, to carry away; drag away. **2**, *colloq.* to drag (someone) somewhere against his will. **3**, *colloq.* to make off with; steal.

утащи́ть [*infl.* утащу́, ута́щишь] *v.*, *pfv. of* ута́скивать.

у́тварь *n.f.* utensils.

утверди́тельный *adj.* affirmative. —**утверди́тельно**, *adv.* affirmatively; in the affirmative.

утверди́ть [*infl.* -жу́, -ди́шь] *v.*, *pfv. of* утвержда́ть. —**утверди́ться**, *refl.*, *pfv. of* утвержда́ться.

утвержда́ть *v. impfv.* [*pfv.* утверди́ть] **1**, [*impfv. only*] to maintain; assert; claim; contend. **2**, to approve; confirm; ratify. **3**, to establish firmly. **4**, (*with* в + *prepl.*) to convince (of). Утверди́ть кого́-нибудь во мне́нии, что…, to reinforce someone's opinion that… —**утвержда́ться**, *refl.* **1**, to become firmly established. **2**, (*with* в + *prepl.*) to become firm in (one's views, intention, etc.).

утвержде́ние *n.* **1**, assertion; claim; contention. **2**, approval; confirmation.

утека́ть *v. impfv.* [*pfv.* уте́чь] **1**, (*of a liquid or gas*) to leak; escape. **2**, (*of time*) to pass; fly by. —**мно́го воды́ утекло́ с тех пор**, a lot of water has flown under the bridge since then.

утёнок [*gen.* -нка; *pl.* утя́та, утя́т] *n.* duckling. —**га́дкий утёнок**, ugly duckling.

утепля́ть *v. impfv.* [*pfv.* утепли́ть] **1**, to warm; heat. **2**, to winterize.

утере́ть [*infl. like* тере́ть] *v.*, *pfv. of* утира́ть.

утерпе́ть *v. pfv.* [*infl.* утерплю́, уте́рпишь] to restrain oneself.

уте́ря *n.* loss (*of papers, documents, etc.*).

утеря́ть *v. pfv.* to lose; mislay.

утёс *n.* cliff.

утёсистый *adj.* **1,** rocky; craggy. **2,** steep; precipitous.

уте́ха *n., colloq.* **1,** pleasure; delight; fun. **2,** comfort; consolation.

уте́чка *n.* **1,** loss; leakage. **2,** *fig.* outflow; drain.

уте́чь [*infl. like* течь] *v., pfv. of* утека́ть.

утеша́ть *v. impfv.* [*pfv.* уте́шить] to console; comfort. —**утеша́ться**, *refl.* **1,** to console oneself. **2,** (*with instr.*) to take consolation (in). **3,** to calm down; pull oneself together.

утеше́ние *n.* consolation; comfort; solace.

утеши́тель *n.m.* comforter.

утеши́тельный *adj.* comforting; consoling. —**утеши́тельный приз,** consolation prize.

уте́шить *v., pfv. of* утеша́ть. —**уте́шиться,** *refl., pfv. of* утеша́ться.

утилиза́ция *n.* utilization.

утилизи́ровать *v. impfv. & pfv.* [*pres.* -рую, -ру-ешь] to utilize.

утилитари́зм *n.* utilitarianism. —**утилита́рный,** *adj.* utilitarian.

ути́ль *n.m.* scrap. —**ути́льный,** *adj.* scrap (*attrib.*).

утильсырьё *n.* = ути́ль.

ути́ный *adj.* duck (*attrib.*); duck's.

утира́ть *v. impfv.* [*pfv.* утере́ть] **1,** to wipe away (tears, sweat, etc.). **2,** to wipe (one's face, brow, etc.). —**утере́ть нос** (+ *dat.*), *colloq.* to show up; get the better of.

утиха́ть *v. impfv.* [*pfv.* ути́хнуть] to subside; abate; die down; calm down.

ути́хнуть [*past* ути́х, -ла] *v., pfv. of* утиха́ть.

утихоми́ривать *v. impfv.* [*pfv.* утихоми́рить] *colloq.* to calm; pacify; placate. —**утихоми́риваться,** *refl., colloq.* **1,** to calm down. **2,** to abate.

у́тка [*gen. pl.* у́ток] *n.* **1,** duck. **2,** *fig.* canard. **3,** *colloq.* bedpan.

уткну́ть *v. pfv., colloq.* **1,** to plant firmly. **2,** to hide; bury. —**уткну́ться,** *refl., colloq.* **1,** (*with* в + *acc.*) to bury oneself in (a pillow, book, etc.). **2,** (*with instr. and* в + *acc.*) to bury (a part of oneself) in. **3,** (*with* в + *acc.*) to bang into; strike.

утконо́с *n.* (duck-billed) platypus.

утле́гарь *n.m.* jib boom; outrigger.

у́тлый *adj.* **1,** (*of a boat*) rickety. **2,** wretched. **3,** *obs.* decrepit.

уто́к [*gen.* утка́] *n., textiles* woof; weft; filling.

утоле́ние *n.* (*with gen.*) **1,** appeasing (*of hunger*); quenching (*of thirst*). **2,** *fig.* relief (of).

утоли́ть *v., pfv. of* утоля́ть.

утолща́ть *v. impfv.* [*pfv.* утолсти́ть] to thicken.

утолще́ние *n.* bulge.

утоля́ть *v. impfv.* [*pfv.* утоли́ть] **1,** to appease; assuage (one's hunger); quench (one's thirst). **2,** *fig.* to relieve; alleviate.

утоми́тельный *adj.* **1,** tiring; fatiguing. **2,** tiresome; dull.

утоми́ть [*infl.* -млю́, -ми́шь] *v., pfv. of* утомля́ть. —**утоми́ться,** *refl., pfv. of* утомля́ться.

утомле́ние *n.* fatigue.

утомлённый *adj.* tired.

утомля́ть *v. impfv.* [*pfv.* утоми́ть] to tire. —**утомля́ться,** *refl.* to tire; become tired; get tired.

утону́ть [*infl.* утону́, уто́нешь] *v., pfv. of* тону́ть (*in sense #2*) *and* утопа́ть.

утонча́ть *v. impfv.* [*pfv.* утончи́ть] **1,** to thin; make thinner. **2,** *fig.* to refine; cultivate.

утончённый *adj.* refined; cultivated. —**утончён-ность,** *n.f.* refinement.

утончи́ть *v., pfv. of* утонча́ть.

утопа́ть *v. impfv.* [*pfv.* утону́ть] **1,** to drown. **2,** [*impfv. only*] (*with* в + *prepl.*) to be rolling in (money, wealth, etc.); be bathed in (light, verdure, etc.).

утопа́ющий *n., decl. as an adj.* drowning man.

утопи́зм *n.* utopianism.

утопи́ть *v., pfv. of* топи́ть (*in sense #5*). —**утопи́ться,** *refl., pfv. of* топи́ться (*in sense #3*).

уто́пия *n.* utopia. —**утопи́ческий,** *adj.* utopian.

утопле́ние *n.* drowning.

уто́пленник *n.* drowned man.

утопта́ть [*infl.* утопчу́, уто́пчешь] *v., pfv. of* ута́пты-вать.

у́точка [*gen. pl.* -чек] *n., dim. of* у́тка. —**ходи́ть у́точ-кой,** to waddle.

уточне́ние *n.* **1,** making (something) more precise. **2,** a clarification: внести́ уточне́ния в прое́кт, to make some clarifications in the draft; make some things in the draft more precise.

уточня́ть *v. impfv.* [*pfv.* уточни́ть] **1,** to make more precise. **2,** to state more precisely. **3,** to find out more about.

утра́ивать *v. impfv.* [*pfv.* утро́ить] to triple; treble. —**утра́иваться,** *refl.* to triple; increase threefold.

утрамбова́ть *v., pfv. of* трамбова́ть.

утра́та *n.* loss.

утра́тить [*infl.* -чу, -тишь] *v., pfv. of* утра́чивать.

утра́чивать *v. impfv.* [*pfv.* утра́тить] to lose.

у́тренний *adj.* morning (*attrib.*).

у́тренник *n.* **1,** morning performance. **2,** early-morning frost.

у́треня *n.* matin; morning prayer.

утри́ровать *v. impfv. & pfv.* [*pres.* -рую, -руешь] to exaggerate.

утриро́вка *n.* exaggeration.

у́тро [*gen.* у́тра *but* утра́ *after* с, до, *and the time of day; dat.* у́тру *but* утру́ *after* к] *n.* morning. Шесть часо́в утра́, six o'clock in the morning. —**к утру́; под у́тро,** toward morning. —**по утра́м,** each morning. —**с утра́ до ве́чера,** from morning till night. *See also* у́тром.

утро́ба *n.* belly; womb.

утро́бный *adj.* **1,** uterine. **2,** (*of sounds*) deep; from the belly.

утро́ить *v., pfv. of* утра́ивать. —**утро́иться,** *refl., pfv. of* утра́иваться.

у́тром *adv.* in the morning. —**вчера́/за́втра/сего́дня у́тром,** yesterday/tomorrow/this morning.

утружда́ть *v. impfv.* **1,** to bother; trouble. **2,** to over-burden; tire. **3,** *in* утружда́ть себя́, to extend oneself; go to a lot of trouble. —**утружда́ться,** *refl.* = утруж-да́ть себя́. Не утружда́йтесь!, don't trouble yourself!; don't go to a lot of trouble!

утучня́ть *v. impfv.* [*pfv.* утучни́ть] to fatten; fatten up.

утю́г [*gen.* утюга́] *n.* an iron (*for ironing*).

утю́жить *v. impfv.* [*pfv.* вы́утюжить] to iron; press.

утю́жка *n.* ironing; pressing.

утяжелять *v. impfv.* [*pfv.* **утяжелить**] to make heavier; increase the weight of.

утянуть *v. pfv.* [*infl.* **утяну́, утя́нешь**] *colloq.* **1,** to drag away; drag off. **2,** to drag (someone) somewhere against his will.

уха́ *n.* fish soup.

уха́б *n.* pothole. —**уха́бистый**, *adj.* full of potholes; bumpy.

ухажёр *n., colloq.* **1,** ladies' man; philanderer. **2,** suitor; admirer.

уха́живание *n.* **1,** looking after; caring for; tending. **2,** courting; paying court to. **3,** *pl.* advances.

уха́живать *v. impfv.* (*with* за + *instr.*) **1,** to look after; take care of; care for; tend. **2,** to court; pay court to; woo. **3,** to play up to.

у́харь *n.m., colloq.* dashing fellow; gay blade. —**у́харский**, *adj., colloq.* dashing. —**у́харство**, *n., colloq.* bravado; bluster.

у́хать *v. impfv.* [*pfv.* **у́хнуть**] *colloq.* **1,** to cry out; gasp. **2,** (*of an owl*) to hoot. **3,** to make a loud noise; ring out; resound.

ухва́т *n.* oven prongs.

ухвати́ть [*infl.* **ухвачу́, ухва́тишь**] *v., pfv. of* **ухва́тывать.** —**ухвати́ться**, *refl., pfv. of* **ухва́тываться.**

ухва́тка [*gen. pl.* **-ток**] *n., colloq.* **1,** movement of the body. **2,** knack. **3,** manner; way.

ухва́тывать *v. impfv.* [*pfv.* **ухвати́ть**] to grasp. —**ухва́тываться**, *refl.* (*with* за + *acc.*) **1,** to grasp; grab hold of. **2,** *fig., colloq.* to tackle (a job, task, etc.). **3,** *fig., colloq.* to jump at (an idea, suggestion, opportunity, etc.).

ухитря́ться *v.r. impfv.* [*pfv.* **ухитри́ться**] (*with inf.*) *colloq.* to manage (to); contrive (to).

ухищре́ние *n.* device; trick.

ухищря́ться *v.r. impfv.* to contrive; scheme.

ухло́пать *v. pfv., colloq.* **1,** to kill. **2,** to squander.

ухмы́лка [*gen. pl.* **-лок**] *n., colloq.* grin; smirk.

ухмыля́ться *v.r. impfv.* [*pfv.* **ухмыльну́ться**] *colloq.* to grin; smirk.

у́хнуть *v., pfv. of* **у́хать.**

у́хо [*pl.* **у́ши, уше́й, уша́м**] *n.* ear. —**во все у́ши слу́шать**, to be all ears. —**в одно́ у́хо вошло́, в друго́е вы́шло**, in one ear and out the other. —**и у́хом не вести́**, not to pay the least attention. —**по́ уши в** (+ *prepl.*), up to one's ears; head over heels (*in work, love, debt, etc.*). —**пропуска́ть ми́мо уше́й**, to ignore; pay no attention to.

ухо́д *n.* **1,** leaving; departure. **2,** quitting: уход с рабо́ты, quitting one's job. **3,** care: уход за ра́неными/маши́ной, care of the wounded; care of a car.

уходи́ть *v. impfv.* [*pfv.* **уйти́**; *pres.* **ухожу́, ухо́дишь**] **1,** to leave; go away: уйти́ из до́ма, to leave the house; уйти́ от жены́, to leave one's wife; уйти́ в шко́лу, to leave for school. **2,** to quit; retire: уйти́ с рабо́ты, to quit one's job; уйти́ со сце́ны, to retire from the stage; уйти́ на пе́нсию, to retire. **3,** (*with* от) to escape (from); elude. **4,** (*of time*) to pass. **5,** (*with* на + *acc.*) to go into: мно́го рабо́ты ушло́ в э́то, a lot of work went into that. **6,** (*with* в + *acc.*) to sink (into). **7,** (*with* в + *acc.*) *fig.* to become absorbed (in). **8,** *colloq.* to boil over. —**уходи́ть в себя́**, to withdraw into oneself.

ухудша́ть *v. impfv.* [*pfv.* **уху́дшить**] to worsen; make worse. —**ухудша́ться**, *refl.* to worsen; become worse; deteriorate.

ухудше́ние *n.* worsening; deterioration.

уху́дшить *v., pfv. of* **ухудша́ть.** —**уху́дшиться**, *refl., pfv. of* **ухудша́ться.**

уцеле́ть *v. pfv.* **1,** to escape injury; escape damage. **2,** to survive.

уце́нивать *v. impfv.* [*pfv.* **уцени́ть**] to mark down (merchandise).

уцени́ть [*infl.* **уценю́, уце́нишь**] *v., pfv. of* **уце́нивать.**

уцепи́ть *v. pfv.* [*infl.* **уцеплю́, уце́пишь**] *colloq.* to grab. —**уцепи́ться**, *refl.* (*with* за + *acc.*) **1,** to grab hold of. **2,** *fig., colloq.* to jump at (an idea, offer, etc.).

уча́ствовать *v. impfv.* [*pres.* **-ствую, -ствуешь**] (*with* в + *prepl.*) **1,** to participate (in); take part (in). **2,** to share (in).

уча́стие *n.* **1,** (*with* в + *prepl.*) participation (in). **2,** (*with* в + *prepl.*) sharing (in). **3,** (*with* к) sympathy (for); concern (for). —**принима́ть уча́стие в** (+ *prepl.*), **1,** to take part in. **2,** to take an interest in (someone); show concern for.

участи́ть [*infl.* **-щу́, -сти́шь**] *v., pfv. of* **учаща́ть.** —**участи́ться**, *refl., pfv. of* **учаща́ться.**

участко́вый *adj.* district (*attrib.*). —*n., colloq.* district militia officer.

уча́стливый *adj.* sympathetic.

уча́стник *n.* participant. Уча́стник конфере́нции, conferee. Уча́стник состяза́ния, contestant.

уча́сток [*gen.* **-стка**] *n.* **1,** plot (*of land*). **2,** section (*of a road, pipeline, etc.*). **3,** area; portion (*of a surface*). **4,** *mil.* sector. **5,** *fig.* area; field; sphere. **6,** district. **7,** *pre-rev.* police district.

у́часть *n.f.* fate; lot.

учаща́ть *v. impfv.* [*pfv.* **участи́ть**] to increase the frequency of; make more frequent. —**учаща́ться**, *refl.* **1,** to become more frequent. **2,** (*of one's pulse*) to quicken.

уча́щийся *n., decl. as an adj.* student; pupil.

учёба *n.* **1,** studies. **2,** training.

уче́бник *n.* textbook.

уче́бный *adj.* **1,** educational: уче́бное заведе́ние, educational institution. **2,** teaching: уче́бные посо́бия, teaching aids. **3,** *mil.* training: уче́бное по́ле, training ground. —**уче́бный год**, school year; academic year. —**уче́бный план**, curriculum. —**уче́бная стрельба́**, firing practice.

уче́ние *n.* **1,** studies; studying; learning. **2,** apprenticeship. **3,** teaching. **4,** *mil.* exercise. **5,** doctrine. **6,** (*with gen.*) the teachings (of).

учени́к [*gen.* **-ника́**] *n.m.* [*fem.* **-ни́ца**] **1,** pupil. **2,** apprentice. **3,** disciple.

учени́ческий *adj.* **1,** pupil's; pupils'. **2,** crude; amateurish.

учени́чество *n.* **1,** time spent as a student. **2,** apprenticeship.

учёность *n.f.* learning; erudition.

учёный *adj.* **1,** learned; erudite; scholarly. **2,** scientific. **3,** academic. **4,** (*of animals*) trained. —*n.* **1,** scientist. **2,** scholar. —**учёный секрета́рь**, academic secretary. —**учёная сте́пень**, (college) degree.

уче́сть [*infl.* **учту́, учтёшь**; *past* **учёл, учла́, учло́**] *v., pfv. of* **учи́тывать.**

учёт *n.* **1,** stock-taking; inventory. **2,** record: учет осмо́тра, record of inspection. **3,** registration: брать на учёт, to register. Быть *or* состоя́ть на учёте, to be registered; be on the books. **4,** consideration; taking into account: с учётом (+ *gen.*), in consideration of; taking into account.

учетверя́ть *v. impfv.* [*pfv.* **учетвери́ть**] to quadruple. —**учетверя́ться,** *refl.* to quadruple; be quadrupled.

учётный *adj.* **1,** record (*attrib.*); registration (*attrib.*). **2,** *finance* discount (*attrib.*).

учи́лище *n.* (specialized) school: ремёсленное учи́лище, vocational school.

учини́ть [*infl.* **учиню́, учини́шь**] *v., pfv. of* **чини́ть** (*in sense #3*) *and* **учиня́ть.**

учиня́ть *v. impfv.* [*pfv.* **учини́ть**] **1,** to carry out (reprisals); conduct (an interrogation). **2,** *colloq.* to make (a scene); create (a scandal).

учи́тель [*pl.* **учителя́**] *n.m.* [*fem.* **учи́тельница**] teacher.

учи́тельский *adj.* teachers'. —**учи́тельская,** *n.* teachers' room.

учи́тельство *n.* **1,** teaching. **2,** teachers.

учи́тельствовать *v. impfv.* [*pres.* **-ствую, -ствуешь**] to teach; be a teacher.

учи́тывать *v. impfv.* [*pfv.* **уче́сть**] **1,** to consider; take into consideration; take into account; take account of. **2,** to take stock of. **3,** *in* учи́тывать ве́ксель, to discount a note.

учи́ть *v. impfv.* [*pfv.* **вы́учить**; *pres.* **учу́, у́чишь**] **1,** [*pfv. also* **научи́ть**] (*with dat. or inf.*) to teach: учи́ть (кого́-нибудь) англи́йскому языку́, to teach (someone) English; учи́ть кого́-нибудь пла́вать, to teach someone how to swim. **2,** (*with acc.*) to study; learn; memorize (a lesson, role, etc.). —**учи́ться,** *refl.* **1,** [*impfv. only*] (*with dat.*) to study: учи́ться ру́сскому языку́, to study Russian. **2,** [*pfv.* **вы́учиться** *or* **научи́ться**] (*with dat. or inf.*) to learn: вы́учиться/научи́ться ру́сскому языку́, to learn Russian; учи́ться пла́вать, to learn (how) to swim. **3,** [*impfv. only*] to study; be a student.

учреди́тель *n.m.* founder.

учреди́тельный *adj.* constituent: учреди́тельное собра́ние, constituent assembly.

учрежда́ть *v. impfv.* [*pfv.* **учреди́ть**] to found; establish.

учрежде́ние *n.* **1,** founding; establishment. **2,** insti-tution; establishment: культу́рное учрежде́ние, cultural institution. **3,** (social) institution: отжи́вшее уч-режде́ние, outmoded institution.

учти́вый *adj.* polite; courteous. —**учти́вость,** *n.f.* politeness; courtesy.

учу́ять *v. pfv.* [*infl.* **учу́ю, учу́ешь**] *colloq.* to smell; sense.

уша́нка [*gen. pl.* **-нок**] *n.* cap with earflaps.

уша́стый *adj., colloq.* with big ears.

уша́т *n.* tub (*carried on a pole inserted through handles*).

у́ши *n., pl. of* у́хо.

уши́б *n.* injury; bruise.

ушиба́ть *v. impfv.* [*pfv.* **ушиби́ть**] to hurt; injure; bruise: ушиби́ть себе́ па́лец, to hurt one's finger. —**ушиба́ться,** *refl.* to hurt oneself.

ушиби́ть [*infl.* **-бу́, -бёшь;** *past* **уши́б, -ла**] *v., pfv. of* ушиба́ть. —**ушиби́ться,** *refl., pfv. of* ушиба́ться.

уши́бленный *adj.* injured.

ушива́ть *v. impfv.* [*pfv.* **уши́ть**] to take in (a garment).

уши́ть [*infl.* **ушью́, ушьёшь**] *v., pfv. of* ушива́ть.

у́шко [*pl.* **у́шки, у́шек**] *n., dim. of* у́хо.

ушко́ [*pl.* **ушки́, ушко́в**] *n.* **1,** = у́шко. **2,** eye (*of a needle*). **3,** tab; hook.

ушни́к [*gen.* **-ника́**] *n., colloq.* ear specialist.

ушно́й *adj.* ear (*attrib.*).

уще́лье *n.* gorge; ravine; canyon.

ущеми́ть [*infl.* **-млю́, -ми́шь**] *v., pfv. of* ущемля́ть.

ущемле́ние *n.* **1,** jamming; catching. **2,** *fig.* restriction; abridgment. **3,** *med.* strangulation.

ущемля́ть *v. impfv.* [*pfv.* **ущеми́ть**] **1,** to jam; catch: ущеми́ть па́лец две́рью, to catch one's finger in the door. **2,** to abridge (someone's rights); restrict (someone's freedom). **3,** to oppress. **4,** to hurt; aggrieve. **5,** to hurt; wound (someone's pride).

уще́рб *n.* harm; damage. —**в уще́рб** (+ *dat.*), to the detriment of. —**на уще́рбе,** on the wane.

уще́рбный *adj.* waning.

ущипну́ть *v. pfv.* to pinch.

уэ́льский *adj.* Welsh.

ую́т *n.* comfort.

ую́тный *adj.* cozy; comfortable.

уязви́мый *adj.* vulnerable. —**уязви́мость,** *n.f.* vulnerability.

уязвля́ть *v. impfv.* [*pfv.* **уязви́ть**] **1,** *obs.* to sting; wound. **2,** *fig.* to hurt; pique.

уясня́ть *v. impfv.* [*pfv.* **уясни́ть**] **1,** (*often with* себе́) to get a clear idea of. **2,** *obs.* to explain.

Ф, ф *n. neut.* 21st letter of the Russian alphabet.

фа *n. neut., music* fa; F

фа́брика *n.* factory.

фабрика́нт *n.* factory owner; manufacturer.

фабрика́т *n.* manufactured item; finished product.

фабрика́ция *n.* manufacture; fabrication.

фабрикова́ть *v. impfv.* [*pres.* -ку́ю, -ку́ешь] **1,** *obs.* to manufacture. **2,** *colloq.* to turn out; crank out (*in large numbers*). **3,** [*pfv.* **сфабрикова́ть**] *colloq.* to fabricate; make up: сфабрико́ванные обвине́ния, trumped-up charges.

фабри́чный *adj.* **1,** factory (*attrib.*). **2,** factory-made. —*n., obs.* factory worker. —**фабри́чная ма́рка,** trademark.

фа́була *n.* plot (*of a story*).

фавн *n.* faun.

фаво́р *n.* favor: быть в фаво́ре у, to be in someone's favor; be in someone's good graces.

фавори́т *n.* favorite.

фавори́зм *n.* favoritism.

фаго́т *n.* bassoon. —**фаготи́ст,** *n.* bassoonist.

фагоци́т *n.* phagocyte.

фа́за *n.* phase.

фаза́н *n.* pheasant. —**фаза́ний,** *adj.* [*fem.* -нья] pheasant (*attrib.*); pheasant's.

фа́зис *n.* phase.

фа́кел *n.* torch.

фа́кельный *adj.* of a torch. —**фа́кельное ше́ствие,** torchlight procession.

фа́кельщик *n.* **1,** torchbearer. **2,** one who puts something to the torch.

факси́миле *n. neut. indecl.* facsimile.

факт *n.* fact. Факт, что..., it is a fact that... Факт тот, что..., the fact of the matter is... —**поста́вить пе́ред фа́ктом,** to present with a fait accompli.

факти́чески *adv.* in fact; to all intents and purposes.

факти́ческий *adj.* **1,** actual. **2,** factual. **3,** de facto: факти́ческое призна́ние, de facto recognition. —**факти́ческий брак,** common-law marriage.

фа́ктор *n.* factor.

факто́рия *n.* trading post.

факту́ра *n.* **1,** texture; finish. **2,** *art* manner of execution. **3,** *comm.* invoice; bill.

факультати́вный *adj.* optional; elective.

факульте́т *n.* university department; faculty.

фал *n.* halyard.

фала́нга *n.* phalanx.

фа́лда *n.* tail (*of a coat*); coattail.

фалли́ческий *adj.* phallic.

фалло́пиев *adj., in* **фалло́пиевы тру́бы,** Fallopian tubes.

фа́ллос *n.* phallus.

фальсифика́ция *n.* **1,** falsificaton. **2,** forgery. **3,** adulteration. —**фальсифика́тор,** *n.* falsifier.

фальсифици́ровать *v. impfv. & pfv.* [*pres.* -рую, -руешь] **1,** to falsify. **2,** to distort. **3,** to adulterate.

фальце́т *n.* falsetto. —**фальце́тный,** *adj.* falsetto.

фальши́вить *v. impfv.* [*pfv.* **сфальши́вить;** *pres.* -влю, -вишь] **1,** to be insincere; play the hypocrite. **2,** to play or sing off key.

фальши́вка [*gen. pl.* -вок] *n., colloq.* forged document; forgery.

фальши́во *adv.* **1,** falsely. **2,** off key.

фальшивомоне́тчик *n.* counterfeiter.

фальши́вый *adj.* **1,** false. **2,** forged; counterfeit. **3,** false; insincere.

фальшь *n.f.* **1,** cheating; dishonesty. **2,** falseness; hypocrisy; insincerity. **3,** *music* false note(s); being off key.

фами́лия *n.* last name; family name; surname.

фами́льный *adj.* family (*attrib.*).

фамилья́рничать *v. impfv.* (with **с** + *instr.*) *colloq.* to be overly familiar (with); take liberties (with).

фамилья́рный *adj.* familiar; unceremonious. —**фамилья́рно,** *adv.* unceremoniously. —**фамилья́рность,** *n.f.* familiarity.

фанабе́рия *n., colloq.* arrogance; snobbery.

фанати́зм *n.* fanaticism. —**фана́тик,** *n.* fanatic. —**фанати́ческий; фанати́чный,** *adj.* fanatic; fanatical.

фане́ра *n.* **1,** veneer (*thin layer of wood*). **2,** plywood. —**фане́рный,** *adj.* plywood (*attrib.*).

фант *n., usu. pl.* forfeits (*game*).

фантазёр *n.* dreamer; visionary.

фантази́ровать *v. impfv.* [*pres.* -рую, -руешь] **1,** to indulge in fantasy. **2,** [*pfv.* **сфантази́ровать**] to make up; dream up. **3,** to make things up. **4,** to improvise.

фанта́зия *n.* **1,** fantasy; fancy. **2,** imagination. **3,** *colloq.* whim; fancy. **4,** *music* fantasy.

фантасмаго́рия *n.* phantasmagoria. —**фантасмагори́ческий,** *adj.* phantasmagoric.

фанта́ст *n.* **1,** visionary. **2,** writer or artist treating the fantastic.

фанта́стика *n.* fantasy. —**нау́чная фанта́стика,** science fiction.

фантасти́ческий *adj.* fantastic. *Also,* **фантасти́чный.**

фанто́м *n.* phantom.

фанфа́ра *n.* **1,** trumpet; bugle. **2,** fanfare; flourish.

фанфаро́н *n., colloq.* braggart.

фа́ра *n.* headlight.

фарао́н *n.* **1,** Pharoah. **2,** *cards* faro.

фарва́тер (тэ) *n.* waterway; channel.

Фаренге́йт *n.* Fahrenheit: со́рок гра́дусов по Фаренге́йту, forty degrees Fahrenheit.

фарисе́й *n.* pharisee. —**фарисе́йский,** *adj.* pharisaic.

фармаколо́гия *n.* pharmacology. —**фармако́лог,** *n.* pharmacologist. —**фармакологи́ческий,** *adj.* pharmacological.

фармакопе́я *n.* pharmacopeia.

фармаце́вт *n.* pharmacist. —**фармаце́втика,** *n.* pharmaceutics. —**фармацевти́ческий,** *adj.* pharmaceutical.

фарма́ция *n.* pharmacy (*preparation of drugs*).

фарс *n.* farce.

фа́ртинг *n.* farthing.

фа́ртук *n.* apron.

фарфо́р *n.* china; porcelain. —**фарфо́ровый,** *adj.* china; porcelain.

фарцо́вщик *n., colloq.* black marketeer (*reselling merchandise and currency acquired from foreigners*).

фарш *n.* stuffing; mince.

фарширо́ванный *adj.* stuffed.

фарширова́ть *v. impfv.* [*pres.* -ру́ю, -ру́ешь] to stuff.

фас *n.* **1,** front (*of one's face*). **2,** *obs.* front (*of an object, building, etc.*). —в фас; фа́сом, full face.

фаса́д *n.* **1,** front (*of a building*). **2,** façade.

фасе́тка [*gen. pl.* -ток] *n.* facet (*of a gem*). *Also,* фасе́т.

фасова́ть *v. impfv.* [*pfv.* расфасова́ть; *pres.* -су́ю, -су́ешь] to package (food).

фасо́вка *n.* packaging. —**фасо́вочный,** *adj.* packaging (*attrib.*).

фасо́левый *adj.* of (kidney) beans; bean (*attrib.*): фасо́левый суп, bean soup.

фасо́ль *n.f.* **1,** kidney beans. **2,** a (single) kidney bean.

фасо́н *n.* **1,** cut (*of a garment*). **2,** fashion; style. **3,** *colloq.* style; manner.

фасо́нистый *adj., colloq.* fashionable; stylish.

фасо́нный *adj.* shaped.

фат *n.* fop.

фата́ *n.* bridal veil.

фатали́зм *n.* fatalism. —**фатали́ст,** *n.* fatalist.

фаталисти́ческий *adj.* **1,** fatalistic. **2,** fatal; inevitable.

фата́льный *adj.* **1,** fatal. **2,** of resignation: фата́льный вид, air of resignation.

фатова́тый *adj.* foppish.

фатовство́ *n.* foppery.

фа́уна *n.* fauna.

фаши́зм *n.* fascism. —**фаши́ст,** *n.* fascist. —**фаши́стский,** *adj.* fascist.

фаэто́н *n.* phaeton.

фая́нс *n.* glazed pottery; delftware. —**фая́нсовый,** *adj.* made of delftware.

февра́ль [*gen.* -раля́] *n.m.* February. —**февра́льский,** *adj.* February (*attrib.*).

федерали́зм *n.* federalism. —**федерали́ст,** *n.* federalist.

федера́льный *adj.* federal.

федерати́вный *adj.* federated; federal.

федера́ция *n.* federation.

фееpи́ческий *adj.* **1,** *theat.* based on a fairy tale. **2,** *fig.* magical; fabulous. **3,** *colloq.* enchanting.

фее́рия *n.* **1,** *theat.* play or ballet based on a fairy tale. **2,** *fig.* enchanting spectacle.

фейерве́рк *n.* fireworks.

фельдма́ршал *n.* field marshal.

фе́льдшер [*pl.* фельдшера́] *n.* medical assistant.

фельето́н *n.* humorous or satirical article. —**фельетони́ст,** *n.* writer of such articles. —**фельето́нный,** *adj.* humorous; satirical.

фемини́зм *n.* feminism. —**фемини́ст; фемини́стка,** *n.* feminist. —**фемини́стский; феминисти́ческий,** *adj.* feminist (*attrib.*).

фен *n.* hair dryer.

фе́никс *n.* phoenix.

фенобарбита́л *n.* phenobarbital.

фено́л *n.* phenol.

фено́мен *n.* phenomenon; marvel; whiz.

феномена́льный *adj.* phenomenal.

фе́нхель *n.m.* fennel.

фео́д *n.* fief.

феода́л *n.* feudal lord. —**феодали́зм,** *n.* feudalism. —**феода́льный,** *adj.* feudal.

ферзь [*gen. & acc.* ферзя́] *n.m., chess* queen. —**фе́рзевый,** *adj.* queen's.

фе́рма *n.* **1,** farm. **2,** girder; truss.

ферме́нт *n.* ferment; enzyme.

фе́рмер *n.* farmer. —**фе́рмерский,** *adj.* farmer's; farmers'.

фе́рмерство *n.* **1,** farming. **2,** farmers.

фе́рмий *n.* fermium.

ферму́ар *n., obs.* **1,** clasp. **2,** necklace.

ферроти́пия *n.* ferrotype; tintype.

феру́ла *n.* ferule.

фе́ска [*gen. pl.* -сок] *n.* fez.

фестива́ль *n.m.* festival. —**фестива́льный,** *adj.* festival (*attrib.*).

фесто́н *n.* **1,** *pl.* scallops (*on material*). **2,** festoon (*ornamental carving*). —**фесто́нный; фесто́нчатый,** *adj.* scalloped.

фети́ш *n.* fetish.

фетишизи́ровать *v. impfv.* [*pres.* -рую, -руешь] to make a fetish of.

фетр *n.* felt. —**фе́тровый,** *adj.* felt.

фехтова́ние *n., sports* fencing. —**фехтова́льный,** *adj.* fencing (*attrib.*). —**фехтова́льщик,** *n.* fencer.

фехтова́ть *v. impfv.* [*pres.* -ту́ю, -ту́ешь] *sports* to fence.

фешене́бельный (нэ) *adj.* fashionable; high-class.

фе́я *n.* fairy.

фи *interj.* fie!; tut!; pshaw!

фиа́кр *n.* (hired) carriage.

фиа́лка [*gen. pl.* -лок] *n.* violet (*flower*).

фиа́ско *n. indecl.* fiasco.

фи́бра *n.* **1,** *obs.* fiber. **2,** *usu. pl., fig.* fiber: все́ми фи́брами души́, with every fiber of one's soul.

фибро́зный *adj.* fiber (*attrib.*); fibrous.

фи́га *n.* **1,** fig. **2,** fig tree. **3,** *colloq.* fig (*insulting gesture*).

фигля́р *n.* **1,** *obs.* (circus) acrobat; performer of tricks. **2,** *colloq.* buffoon.

фи́говый *adj.* fig (*attrib.*). —фи́говый листо́к, fig leaf.

фигу́ра *n.* **1,** figure. **2,** *chess* piece. **3,** *cards* face card.

фигура́льный *adj.* figurative; metaphorical.

фигури́ровать *v. impfv.* [*pres.* -рую, -руешь] to figure; appear.

фигури́ст *n.m.* [*fem.* -и́стка] figure skater.

фигу́рка [*gen. pl.* -рок] *n.* **1,** *dim. of* **фигу́ра. 2,** figurine.

фигу́рный *adj.* **1,** figure (*attrib.*): фигу́рное ката́ние на конька́х, figure skating. **2,** (*of a pattern*) figured.

фи́дер (дэ) *n., electricity* feeder.

фи́зик *n.* physicist.

фи́зика *n.* physics.

физиоло́гия *n.* physiology. —**физио́лог,** *n.* physiologist. —**физиологи́ческий,** *adj.* physiological.

физионо́мия *n.* **1,** face. **2,** facial expression; look. **3,** physiognomy.

физиотерапи́я *n.* physiotherapy; physical therapy. —**физиотерапе́вт,** *n.* (physio)therapist.

физи́чески *adv.* physically.

физи́ческий *adj.* **1,** physical. **2,** physics (*attrib.*); of physics.

физкульту́ра *n.* physical training; physical education (*contr. of* физи́ческая культу́ра).

физкульту́рный *adj.* athletic. —**физкульту́рный зал,** gymnasium. —**физкульту́рный костю́м,** gym suit.

фикса́ж *n., photog.* fixing agent; hypo.

фикси́ровать *v. impfv. & pfv.* [*pfv. also* зафикси́ровать] *pres.* -рую, -руешь] **1,** to fix; set. **2,** to record (*on paper, film, etc.*). **3,** to fix (one's gaze, attention, etc.). **4,** *photog.* to fix.

фикти́вный *adj.* **1,** fictitious. **2,** forged. —**фикти́вный брак,** pro forma marriage (*carried out to meet a certain legal requirement*).

фи́кус *n.* **1,** fig tree. **2,** rubber plant (*ornamental house plant*).

фи́кция *n.* fiction; invention; fabrication.

филакте́рия *n.* phylactery.

филантро́пия *n.* philanthropy. —**филантро́п,** *n.* philanthropist. —**филантропи́ческий,** *adj.* philanthropic.

филармо́ния *n.* philharmonic society. —**филармони́ческий,** *adj.* philharmonic.

филатели́я (тэ) *n.* philately. —**филатели́ст,** *n.* philatelist. —**филателисти́ческий,** *adj.* philatelic.

филе́ *n. neut. indecl.* filet; sirloin.

филе́нка [*gen. pl.* -нок] *n.* panel. —**филе́ночный; филе́нчатый,** *adj.* paneled.

филёр *n.* detective; agent.

филиа́л *n.* branch (*of a store, institution, etc.*). —**филиа́льный,** *adj.* branch (*attrib.*).

филигра́нный *adj.* **1,** filigree. **2,** *fig.* meticulous.

филигра́нь *n.f.* filigree.

фи́лин *n.* eagle owl.

фили́ппика *n.* philippic.

филиппи́нский *adj.* Philippine.

филоде́ндрон (дэ) *n.* philodendron.

филоло́гия *n.* philology. —**фило́лог,** *n.* philologist. —**филологи́ческий,** *adj.* philological.

филосо́фия *n.* philosophy. —**фило́соф,** *n.* philosopher. —**филосо́фский,** *adj.* philosophic(al).

филосо́фствовать *v. impfv.* [*pres.* -ствую, -ствуешь] to philosophize.

фильм *n.* film; movie; motion picture.

фильмоте́ка *n.* film library.

фильтр *n.* filter.

фильтра́ция *n.* filtration; filtering.

фильтрова́льный *adj.* filter (*attrib.*); filtering.

фильтрова́ть *v. impfv.* [*pres.* -рую, -руешь] **1,** to filter. **2,** *fig., colloq.* to screen; select.

фимиа́м *n.* incense. —**кури́ть фимиа́м** (+ *dat.*), to sing the praises of.

фина́л *n.* **1,** finale. **2,** *sports* finals; final round. —**фина́лист,** *n.* finalist. —**фина́льный,** *adj.* final.

финанси́ровать *v. impfv. & pfv.* [*pres.* -рую, -руешь] to finance.

финанси́ст *n.* financier.

фина́нсовый *adj.* financial; fiscal.

фина́нсы [*gen.* -сов] *n. pl.* finance; finances.

фи́ник *n.* date (*fruit*).

финики́йский *adj.* Phoenician.

фи́никовый *adj.* date (*attrib.*). —**фи́никовая па́льма,** date palm.

фини́фть *n.f., obs.* enamel.

фи́ниш *n.* **1,** finish (*of a race*). **2,** finish line.

финиши́ровать *v. impfv. & pfv.* [*pres.* -рую, -руешь] *sports* to finish.

фи́нишный *adj.* finish (*attrib.*): фи́нишная ле́нта (*or* ле́нточка), the tape.

фи́нка [*gen. pl.* -нок] *n.* **1,** *fem. of* финн. **2,** *colloq.* knife; dagger.

финн *n.m.* [*fem.* фи́нка] Finn.

фи́нно-уго́рский *adj.* Finno-Ugric.

фи́нский *adj.* Finnish.

финт *n., sports* feint.

финти́ть *v. impfv.* [*pres.* -чу́, -ти́шь] *colloq.* to be tricky; resort to deception.

финтифлю́шка [*gen. pl.* -шек] *n., colloq.* knick-knack.

фиоле́товый *adj.* violet; purple.

фио́рд *n.* fiord.

фи́рма *n.* business firm.

фи́рменный *adj.* company (*attrib.*); house (*attrib.*). —**фи́рменное блю́до,** specialty of the house.

фисгармо́ния *n.* harmonium.

фиска́л *n., colloq.* tattler; talebearer.

фиска́лить *v. impfv., colloq.* to tattle; tell tales.

фиста́шка *n.* pistachio. —**фиста́шковый,** *adj.* pistachio.

фи́стула *also,* фистула́ *n.* **1,** *med.* fistula. **2,** falsetto.

фити́ль [*gen.* -тиля́] *n.m.* wick.

фи́шка [*gen. pl.* -шек] *n.* chip (*used in games*).

флаг *n.* flag. —**под фла́гом** (+ *gen.*), **1,** (*of a ship*) flying the flag of. **2,** *fig.* under the banner of. **3,** *fig.* in the guise of.

фла́гман *n.* **1,** flag officer. **2,** flagship.

фла́гманский *adj.,* in фла́гманский кора́бль, flagship; фла́гманский самолёт, lead aircraft.

флагшто́к *n.* flagpole.

фла́жный *adj.* flag (*attrib.*).

флажо́к [*gen.* -жка́] *n.* small flag.

флако́н *n.* small bottle.

флама́ндец [*gen.* -дца] *n.m.* [*fem.* -дка] Fleming. —**флама́ндский,** *adj.* Flemish.

флами́нго *n.m. indecl.* flamingo.

фланг *n., mil.* flank. —**фланго́вый,** *adj.* flanking.

флане́ль *n.f.* flannel. —**флане́левый,** *adj.* flannel.

фла́нец [*gen.* -нца] *n.* flange.

флани́ровать *v. impfv.* [*pres.* -рую, -руешь] *colloq.* to stroll; saunter.

фланки́ровать *v. impfv. & pfv.* [*pres.* -рую, -руешь] *mil.* to flank.

флеби́т *n.* phlebitis.

флéгма *n.* **1,** phlegm; sluggishness; apathy. **2,** *colloq.* phlegmatic person.

флегмáтик *n.* phlegmatic person. —**флегматический; флегматичный,** *adj.* phlegmatic.

флéйта *n.* flute. —**флейтист,** *n.* flutist.

флéксия *n. gram.* inflection. —**флективный,** *adj.* inflected.

флёр *n.* crepe.

флигель [*pl.* **флигеля**] *n.m.* **1,** wing (*of a building*). **2,** annex.

флирт *n.* flirting; flirtation.

флиртовáть *v. impfv.* [*pres.* -**тýю, -тýешь**] to flirt.

флокс *n.* phlox.

фломáстер *n.* soft-tip pen.

флóра *n.* flora.

флорин *n.* florin.

флот *n.* **1,** fleet. **2,** navy. —**воéнно-морскóй флот,** navy. —**воздýшный флот,** air force. —**торгóвый флот,** merchant fleet; merchant marine.

флотилия *n.* **1,** flotilla. **2,** fleet: китобóйная флотилия, whaling fleet.

флóтский *adj.* naval.

флоэ́ма *n.* phloem.

флуоресцéнция *n.* fluorescence.

флуоресцировать *v. impfv.* [*pres.* -**рует**] to fluoresce.

флюгáрка [*gen. pl.* -**рок**] *n.* **1,** ship's emblem. **2,** *colloq.* weather vane.

флюгер [*pl.* **флюгерá**] *n.* weather vane.

флюоресцéнция *n.* = флуоресцéнция. —**флюоресцировать,** *v.* = флуоресцировать.

флюс *n.* **1,** gumboil. **2,** *metall.* flux.

фляга *n.* flask; canteen. *Also,* **фляжка.**

фóбия *also,* **фобия** *n.* phobia.

фойé *n. neut. indecl.* lobby (*of a theater*).

фок *n.* foresail.

фок-мáчта *n.* foremast.

фокстерьéр (тэ) *n.* fox terrier.

фокстрóт *n.* fox trot.

фóкус *n.* **1,** *physics; photog.* focus. **2,** *fig.* focal point; center. **3,** trick.

фокусировать *v. impfv. & pfv.* [*pres.* -**рую, -руешь**] to focus.

фóкусник *n.* magician; conjurer; prestidigitator.

фóкусничать *v. impfv., colloq.* to play tricks.

фóкусный *adj.* focal.

фóкус-пóкус *n., colloq.* hocus-pocus.

фол *n., sports* foul.

фолиáнт *n.* large book; volume; folio.

фóлио *n. indecl.* folio.

фолликул *n.* follicle.

фóльга *n.* foil: алюминиевая фóльга, aluminum foil.

фольклóр *n.* folklore. —**фольклорист,** *n.* specialist in folklore.

фон *n.* background.

фонáрик *n., dim. of* **фонáрь.**

фонáрный *adj.* lamp (*attrib.*); lantern (*attrib.*). —**фонáрный столб,** lamppost.

фонáрщик *n., obs.* lamplighter.

фонáрь [*gen.* -**наря**] *n.m.* **1,** lantern. **2,** (*in combinations*) -light: зáдний/кармáнный/ýличный фонáрь, taillight/flashlight/street light/. **3,** *in* проекциóнный фонáрь, projector. **4,** bay window; skylight. **5,** *colloq.* black eye.

фонд *n.* **1,** fund: фонд зарабóтной плáты, wage fund. **2,** *pl.* stocks; securities. **3,** fund; foundation: фонд пóмощи, relief fund.

фóндовый *adj.* stock (*attrib.*). —**фóндовая биржа,** stock exchange; stock market.

фонéма (нэ) *n.* phoneme. —**фонематический,** *adj.* phonemic.

фонéтика (нэ) *n.* phonetics. —**фонетический,** *adj.* phonetic.

фонолóгия *n.* phonology.

фонотéка *n.* record library.

фонтáн *n.* fountain.

фонтанировать *v. impfv.* [*pres.* -**рует**] to gush; gush forth.

фонтáнчик *n.* **1,** *dim. of* **фонтáн. 2,** water fountain; drinking fountain.

фóра *n., sports* advantage; head start (*given a weaker player*). —**таблица фор,** table of handicaps.

форéйтор *n.* postilion.

форéль *n.f.* trout.

фóрзац *n.* flyleaf.

фóрма *n.* **1,** form. **2,** shape. **3,** mold. **4,** uniform. —**быть в фóрме,** to be in good form. —**для фóрмы,** for form's sake. —**по всей фóрме, 1,** properly. **2,** really and truly.

формализм *n.* formalism. —**формалист,** *n.* formalist. —**формалистический,** *adj.* formalistic.

формальдегид *n.* formaldehyde.

формáльно *adv.* formally; officially; legally.

формáльность *n.f.* formality; technicality.

формáльный *adj.* formal.

формáт *n.* format; size.

формáция *n.* **1,** structure. **2,** *geol.* formation.

фóрменный *adj.* **1,** uniform (*attrib.*). **2,** *obs.* formal; official. **3,** *colloq.* real; regular; downright.

формировáние *n.* **1,** forming; formation. **2,** *mil.* unit.

формировáть *v. impfv.* [*pfv.* **сформировáть;** *pres.* -**рую, -руешь**] **1,** to form; mold. **2,** to form; organize. —**формировáться,** *refl.* **1,** to form; be formed. **2,** to mature; develop.

формовáть *v. impfv.* [*pfv.* **сформовáть;** *pres.* -**мýю, -мýешь**] to shape; mold; model.

фóрмула *n.* formula.

формулировать *v. impfv. & pfv.* [*pfv. also* **сформулировать;** *pres.* -**рую, -руешь**] to word; phrase; formulate.

формулирóвка *n.* **1,** formulation. **2,** formula. **3,** wording.

формуляр *n.* **1,** *pre-rev.* record of service. **2,** maintenance log. **3,** charge card (*inserted in a library book*).

форпóст *n.* outpost.

форс *n., colloq.* show; swank; ostentation. —**для фóрса,** to show off.

форсированный *adj.* accelerated. —**форсированный марш,** *mil.* forced march.

форсировать *v. impfv. & pfv.* [*pres.* -**рую, -руешь**] **1,** to speed up. **2,** *mil.* to make a forced crossing of (*e.g. a river*).

форсýнка [*gen. pl.* -**нок**] *n.* sprayer; injector.

форт [*2nd loc.* **фортý;** *pl.* **фóрты**] *n.* fort.

фóрте (тэ) *adv., music* forte.

фóртель *n.m., colloq.* trick.

фортепьяно *n. indecl.* piano. —**фортепьянный,** *adj.* piano (*attrib.*).

фортиссимо *adv.* fortissimo.

фортифика́ция *n.* fortification. —**фортификаци-о́нный**, *adj.* fortification (*attrib.*).

фо́рточка [*gen. pl.* **-чек**] *n.* small hinged window pane.

форту́на *n.* fortune.

фо́рум *n.* forum.

форшла́г *n., music* grace note.

форште́вень (штэ) [*gen.* **-вня**] *n.m., naut.* stem.

фосге́н *n.* phosgene.

фосфа́т *n.* phosphate. —**фосфа́тный; фосфа́то-вый**, *adj.* phosphate (*attrib.*).

фо́сфор *n.* phosphorus.

фосфоресце́нция *n.* phosphorescence. —**фосфо-ресци́рующий**, *adj.* phosphorescent.

фо́сфорный *adj.* phosphoric; phosphorous.

фо́то *n. indecl., colloq.* photo; photograph.

фотоаппара́т *n.* camera.

фотогени́чный *adj.* photogenic.

фотогравю́ра *n.* photogravure; photoengraving.

фото́граф *n.* photographer.

фотографи́ровать *v. impfv.* [*pfv.* **сфотографи́ро-вать**; *pres.* **-рую, -руешь**] **1,** to photograph; take a picture of. **2,** [*impfv. only*] to take a picture; take pictures. —**фотографи́роваться**, *refl.* to be photo-graphed; have one's picture taken.

фотографи́ческий *adj.* photographic.

фотогра́фия *n.* **1,** photography. **2,** photograph. **3,** photographer's studio.

фотока́рточка [*gen. pl.* **-чек**] *n., colloq.* photograph; snapshot.

фотоко́пия *n.* photocopy.

фотолюби́тель *n.m.* amateur photographer.

фото́метр *n.* photometer.

фото́н *n.* photon.

фотоси́нтез (тэ) *n.* photosynthesis.

фотосни́мок [*gen.* **-мка**] *n.* photograph; snapshot.

фотоста́т *n.* photostat machine.

фотосфе́ра *n.* photosphere.

фотоэлектри́ческий *adj.* photoelectric.

фотоэлеме́нт *n.* photoelectric cell; electric eye.

фо́фан *n., colloq.* dope; jerk.

фрагме́нт *n.* fragment. —**фрагмента́рный**, *adj.* fragmentary.

фра́за *n.* **1,** sentence. **2,** phrase.

фразеоло́гия *n.* phraseology. —**фразеологи́чес-кий**, *adj.* phraseological.

фразёр *n.* phrasemonger. —**фразёрство**, *n.* phrase-mongering.

фрак *n.* tail coat; tails.

фраки́йский *adj.* Thracian.

фракцио́нный *adj.* **1,** factional. **2,** factious.

фра́кция *n.* (political) faction.

фрамбе́зия *n.* yaws.

фраму́га *n.* transom.

франк *n.* **1,** franc (*monetary unit*). **2,** *hist.* Frank.

франки́ровать *v. impfv. & pfv.* [*pres.* **-рую, -руешь**] to prepay the postage (on).

франкмасо́н *n.* freemason. —**франкмасо́нство**, *n.* freemasonry.

франт *n.* dandy; fop.

франти́ть *v. impfv.* [*pres.* **-чу́, -ти́шь**] *colloq.* to dress like a dandy.

франтова́тый *adj., colloq.* foppish.

фра́нций *n.* francium.

францу́з *n.m.* [*fem.* **-цу́женка**] Frenchman. —**фран-цу́зский**, *adj.* French.

фрахт *n.* **1,** freight. **2,** freight charges.

фрахтова́ть *v. impfv.* [*pfv.* **зафрахтова́ть**; *pres.* **-ту́ю, -ту́ешь**] to charter.

фра́чный *adj.* of or for a tail coat; worn with a tail coat.

фрега́т *n.* frigate.

фре́за *also*, **фреза́** *n.* milling cutter.

фре́зерный *adj.* milling (*attrib.*): фре́зерный стано́к, milling machine.

фрезерова́ние *n.* milling.

фрезерова́ть *v. impfv. & pfv.* [*pres.* **-ру́ю, -ру́ешь**] to cut; mill (metal).

фре́йлина *n.* lady in waiting.

френоло́гия *n.* phrenology.

френч *n.* service jacket.

фре́ска [*gen. pl.* **-сок**] *n.* fresco. —**фре́сковый**, *adj.* fresco (*attrib.*).

фриво́льный *adj.* ribald.

фриз *n.* frieze.

фрикаде́лька (дэ) [*gen. pl.* **-лек**] *n.* ball of minced meat or fish cooked in soup.

фрикасе́ (сэ) *n. neut. indecl.* fricassee.

фрикати́вный *adj.* fricative.

фронт [*pl.* **фро́нты, фронто́в, фронта́м**] *n.* **1,** *mil.* front. **2,** *meteorology* front: тёплый фронт, warm front. **3,** *fig.* front: еди́ный фронт, united front. —**стать во фронт**, to stand at attention.

фронта́льный *adj.* frontal.

фронтиспи́с *n.* frontispiece.

фронтови́к [*gen.* **-вика́**] *n.* front-line soldier.

фронтово́й *adj., mil.* front (*attrib.*); front-line.

фронто́н *n.* pediment.

фрукт *n.* **1,** piece of fruit. **2,** *pl.* fruit.

фрукто́вый *adj.* fruit (*attrib.*). —**фрукто́вый сад**, or-chard.

фрустра́ция *n.* frustration.

фтор *n.* fluorine.

фтори́д *n.* fluoride.

фто́ристый *adj.* fluoride (of): фто́ристый на́трий, sodium fluoride.

фу *interj.* **1,** (*of disgust, contempt, etc.*) ugh! **2,** (*of fatigue, relief, etc.*) whew!

фу́га *n., music* fugue.

фуга́с *n.* land mine.

фуга́ска [*gen. pl.* **-сок**] *n., colloq.* **1,** land mine. **2,** demolition bomb.

фуга́сный *adj.* high-explosive. —**фуга́сная бо́мба**, demolition bomb.

фуже́р *n.* tall wine glass.

фу́кать *v. impfv.* [*pfv.* **фу́кнуть**] *colloq.* **1,** to snort. **2,** to blow. **3,** (*of an engine, locomotive, etc.*) to puff.

фукси́н *n.* fuchsin; magenta.

фу́ксия *n.* fuchsia.

фунда́мент *n.* foundation.

фундамента́льный *adj.* **1,** solid; sturdy. **2,** (*of knowledge*) thorough; profound. **3,** (*of research, a work, study, etc.*) basic. —**фундамента́льная биб-лиоте́ка**, main library.

фунду́к [*gen.* **-дука́**] *n.* filbert.

фуникулёр *n.* **1,** funicular railway. **2,** cable car.

функциона́льный *adj.* functional.

функциони́ровать *v. impfv.* [*pres.* **-рую, -руешь**] to function.

фу́нкция *n.* function.

фунт *n.* pound (*unit of weight; monetary unit*).

фу́нтик *n.*, *colloq.* cone-shaped paper bag.

фу́ра *n.* **1**, wagon. **2**, van.

фура́ж [*gen.* -ража́] *n.* fodder; forage.

фура́жка [*gen. pl.* -жек] *n.* service cap.

фура́жный *adj.* forage (*attrib.*); fodder (*attrib.*).

фурго́н *n.* van.

фу́рия *n.* **1**, *myth.* Fury. **2**, *colloq.* shrew; virago.

фуро́р *n.* furor; sensation.

фуру́нкул *n.*, *med.* boil.

фут *n.* foot (*12 inches*).

футбо́л *n.* soccer. —**футболи́ст**, *n.* soccer player.

футбо́лка [*gen. pl.* -лок] *n.* sport shirt.

футбо́льный *adj.* soccer (*attrib.*).

футля́р *n.* case: футля́р для очко́в, eyeglass case.

фу́товый *adj.* one foot in length; one-foot (*attrib.*).

футури́зм *n.* futurism. —**футуристи́ческий**, *adj.* futuristic.

фуфа́йка [*gen. pl.* -фа́ек] *n.* jersey.

фы́рканье *n.* snorting; snort.

фы́ркать *v. impfv.* [*pfv.* **фы́ркнуть**] **1**, to snort. **2**, (*of an engine, locomotive, etc.*) to puff. **3**, *colloq.* to chuckle. **4**, *colloq.* to grumble. **5**, (*with* на + *acc.*) *colloq.* to sneer (at).

фюзеля́ж *n.* fuselage.

X

X, x *n. neut.* 22nd letter of the Russian alphabet.

ха́живать *v. impfv.*, *colloq.* to go (*regularly*).

хака́с *n.m.* [*fem.* -ка́ска] Khakass (*one of a people inhabiting southern Siberia*). —**хака́сский**, *adj.* Khakass.

ха́ки *n. neut. indecl. & adj.* khaki.

хала́т *n.* **1**, oriental robe. **2**, bathrobe. **3**, (surgeon's) gown; (artist's) smock. —**рабо́чий хала́т**, overalls.

хала́тность *n.f.* **1**, indifference. **2**, negligence.

хала́тный *adj.* indifferent; lackadaisical; negligent.

халва́ *n.* a paste made of nuts, sugar, and oil; halva.

хали́ф *n.* caliph. —**халифа́т**, *n.* caliphate.

халту́ра *n.*, *colloq.* **1**, work performed (*or* money earned) on the side. **2**, hackwork. —**халту́рный**, *adj.*, *colloq.* hack. —**халту́рщик**, *n.*, *colloq.* hack worker; hack.

халцедо́н *n.* chalcedony.

хам *n.*, *colloq.* cad; boor.

хамелео́н *n.* chameleon.

хами́тский *adj.* Hamitic.

ха́мский *adj.*, *colloq.* boorish. —**ха́мство**, *n.*, *colloq.* boorishness.

хан *n.* khan.

хандра́ *n.* melancholy; depression.

хандри́ть *v. impfv.* to be depressed; have the blues; be down in the dumps.

ханжа́ *n.m. & f.* self-righteous person; hypocrite. —**ха́нжеский**; **ханжеско́й**, *adj.* sanctimonious; self-righteous. —**ха́нжество**; **ханжество́**, *n.* sanctimony; self-righteousness.

ханжи́ть *v. impfv.*, *colloq.* to play the hypocrite; put on an act.

ха́нство *n.* khanate.

хао́с *n.* chaos. —**хаоти́ческий**, *adj.* chaotic.

хаоти́чный *adj.* chaotic. —**хаоти́чность**, *n.f.* chaotic nature.

ха́пать *v. impfv.* [*pfv.* **ха́пнуть**] *colloq.* **1**, to grab; snatch. **2**, to steal; swipe.

хараки́ри *n. neut. indecl.* hara-kiri.

хара́ктер *n.* **1**, character; personality; disposition. **2**, nature (*of something*): хара́ктер рабо́ты, the nature of the work. **3**, (strength of) character: проявля́ть хара́ктер, to show *or* demonstrate character. Челове́к с хара́ктером, strong-willed person. **4**, character (*in a story, play, etc.*). —**вы́держать хара́ктер**, to stand firm. —**носи́ть (како́й-нибудь) хара́ктер**, to be... (in nature): носи́ть вре́менный хара́ктер, to be temporary (in nature).

характеризова́ть *v. impfv. & pfv.* [*pres.* -зу́ю, -зу́ешь] **1**, to describe; characterize. **2**, to be characteristic of; be typical of. —**характеризова́ться**, *refl.* [*impfv. only*] (*with instr.*) to be characterized (by); be marked (by).

характери́стика *n.* **1**, description; characterization. **2**, character reference.

характе́рно *adv.* in one's own distinctive way. —*adj.*, *used predicatively* **1**, (*with* для) characteristic (of). **2**, significant: характе́рно, что..., it is significant that...

характе́рный *adj.* **1**, typical; characteristic. **2**, distinctive. **3**, *theat.* character (*attrib.*).

харза́ *n.* yellow-throated marten.

ха́ркать *v. impfv.* [*pfv.* **ха́ркнуть**] *colloq.* to expectorate; spit. Ха́ркать кро́вью, to spit blood.

ха́ртия *n.* charter. —**Вели́кая ха́ртия во́льностей**, Magna Carta.

харче́вня [*gen. pl.* -вен] *n.*, *obs.* (cheap) eating place.

харчи́ [*gen.* -че́й] *n. pl.*, *colloq.* food; grub.

харчо́ *n. indecl.* mutton soup.

ха́ря *n.*, *colloq.* face; mug; puss.

ха́та *n.* peasant's hut. —**моя́ ха́та с кра́ю**, it has nothing to do with me.

ха́ять *v. impfv.* [*pres.* ха́ю, ха́ешь] *colloq.* to find fault with; run down.

хвала́ *n.* praise.

хвале́бный *adj.* **1**, laudatory. **2**, (*of a song, hymn, etc.*) of praise.

хвали́ть *v. impfv.* [*pfv.* **похвали́ть**; *pres.* **хвалю́**, хва́лишь] to praise. —**хвали́ться**, *refl.* (*with instr.*) to boast (about *or* of); brag (about).

хва́статься *v.r. impfv.* [*pfv.* **похва́статься**] (*with instr.*) to boast (about *or* of); brag (about).

хвастли́вый *adj.* boastful. —**хвастли́вость**, *n.f.* boastfulness.

хвастовство́ *n.* boasting; bragging.

хвасту́н [*gen.* -**стуна́**] *n.m.* [*fem.* -**сту́нья**] *colloq.* braggart.

хват *n., colloq.* dashing fellow; gay blade.

хвата́ть *v. impfv.* **1**, [*pfv.* **схвати́ть**] to seize; grab; grasp; snatch. **2**, [*pfv.* **хвати́ть**] *impers.* (*with gen.*) to suffice; be enough; last: вре́мени не хвата́ет, there is not enough time. Этого нам хва́тит на ме́сяц, that will last us a month. Хва́тит!, enough! На сего́дня хва́тит, that will be enough for today. С меня́ хва́тит!, I've had enough! Хва́тит тебе́ пла́кать!, enough of your crying! **3**, [*impfv. only*] *impers.* A, to be missing: не хвата́ет двух страни́ц, two pages are missing. B, to miss (someone): мне вас не хвата́ет, I miss you. —**насколько хвата́ет глаз**, as far as the eye can see. *See also* **хвати́ть**.

хвата́ться *v.r. impfv.* (*with за* + *acc.*) **1**, [*pfv.* **схвати́ться**] to grab; grasp. **2**, [*impfv. only*] to take up; seize upon; embrace. —**хвата́ться за́ голову** (*in horror or despair*). —**хвата́ться за соло́минку**, to grasp at a straw. —**хвата́ться за ум**, to come to one's senses.

хвати́ть *v. pfv.* [*infl.* **хвачу́**, **хва́тишь**] **1**, *pfv. of* **хвата́ть** (*in sense #2*). **2**, *colloq.* to strike; hit. **3**, *colloq.* to experience; suffer. **4**, *colloq.* to drink; guzzle. **5**, *in* **хвати́ть че́рез край**, to go too far; overstate one's case. —**хвати́ться**, *refl.* (*with gen.*) *colloq.* to miss; notice the absence of.

хва́тка *n.* **1**, grip; grasp. **2**, skill. —**мёртвая хва́тка**, mortal grip; iron grip.

хво́йный *adj.* **1**, coniferous. **2**, pine (*attrib.*).

хвора́ть *v. impfv., colloq.* to be ill; be ailing.

хво́рост *n.* **1**, brushwood. **2**, pastry sticks.

хворости́на *n.* switch; stick; rod.

хво́рый *adj., colloq.* sickly; ailing.

хворь *n.f., colloq.* illness; ailment.

хвост [*gen.* **хвоста́**] *n.* **1**, tail. **2**, tail end; tag end. **3**, *colloq.* line; queue: стоя́ть в хвосте́, to stand in line.

хвоста́тый *adj.* having a tail.

хво́стик *n., dim. of* **хвост**. —**с хво́стиком**, plus a little more: пятьдеся́т лет с хво́стиком, fifty plus (years).

хвостово́й *adj.* tail (*attrib.*).

хвощ [*gen.* **хвоща́**] *n.* horsetail (*plant*).

хвоя́ *n.* **1**, pine needles. **2**, branches of a pine tree.

хе́рес *n.* sherry.

херуви́м *n.* cherub. —**херуви́мский**, *adj.* cherubic.

хе́тты [*gen.* -**тов**] *n. pl.* Hittites. —**хе́ттский**, *adj.* Hittite.

хиба́рка [*gen. pl.* -**рок**] *n.* shanty; hovel. *Also*, **хиба́ра**.

хи́жина *n.* hut; shack.

хиле́ть *v. impfv., colloq.* to fade; decline; become sickly.

хи́лый *adj.* sickly; feeble.

химе́ра *n.* chimera. —**химери́ческий**, *adj.* chimerical.

хи́мик *n.* chemist.

химика́лии [*gen.* -**лий**] *n. pl.* chemicals.

химиотерапи́я *n.* chemotherapy.

хими́ческий *adj.* chemical. —**хими́ческий каранда́ш**, indelible pencil. —**хими́ческая чи́стка**, dry cleaning.

хи́мия *n.* chemistry.

химчи́стка *n., colloq.* **1**, dry cleaning. **2**, dry cleaning establishment; dry cleaner's (*contr. of* **хими́ческая чи́стка**).

хи́на *n.* quinine.

хи́нди *n.m. indecl.* Hindi.

хини́н *n.* quinine.

хи́нный *adj.* quinine (*attrib.*). —**хи́нное де́рево**, cinchona (*tree*).

хире́ть *v. impfv.* [*pfv.* **захире́ть**] *colloq.* **1**, to decline in health. **2**, (*of plants*) to wither.

хирома́нт *n.* palmist; palm reader. —**хирома́нтия**, *n.* palmistry.

хиру́рг *n.* surgeon. —**хирурги́ческий**, *adj.* surgical. —**хирурги́я**, *n.* surgery.

хитре́ц [*gen.* -**треца́**] *n.* cunning person.

хитреца́ *n., colloq.* shrewdness; cunning. *Also*, **хитри́нка**.

хитри́ть *v. impfv.* [*pfv.* **схитри́ть**] **1**, to use cunning; resort to guile. **2**, (*with с* + *instr.*) to try to outwit. **3**, *colloq.* to maneuver; contrive.

хи́тро *adv.* **1**, slyly. **2**, *colloq.* cleverly.

хитросплете́ние *n., usu. pl.* **1**, intricacies; complexities. **2**, schemes; stratagems.

хи́трость *n.f.* **1**, cunning; guile. **2**, ingenuity. **3**, ruse; trick. —**не велика́ хи́трость**, it takes no great skill.

хитроу́мие *n.* cleverness.

хитроу́мный *adj.* **1**, clever. **2**, ingenious. **3**, intricate.

хи́трый *adj.* [*short form* **хитёр**, **хитра́**, **хи́тро**] **1**, sly; crafty; cunning; wily. **2**, *colloq.* clever; ingenious.

хихи́канье *n.* giggling.

хихи́кать *v. impfv.* to giggle.

хище́ние *n.* theft; embezzlement; misappropriation.

хи́щник *n.* **1**, beast of prey; bird of prey. **2**, *fig.* predator.

хи́щнический *adj.* **1**, (*of instincts, habits, etc.*) predatory. **2**, rapacious. **3**, destructive (*to the environment*).

хи́щничество *n.* **1**, preying on others. **2**, plundering.

хи́щный *adj.* predatory; rapacious. —**хи́щная пти́ца**, bird of prey.

хладнокро́вие *n.* equanimity; composure.

хладнокро́вно *adv.* **1**, calmly. **2**, in cold blood.

хладнокро́вный *adj.* **1**, cool; calm; collected. **2**, (*of an act*) cold-blooded.

хлам *n.* rubbish; refuse; trash.

хлеб *n.* **1**, bread. **2**, loaf of bread. **3**, [*pl.* **хлеба́**] grain.

хлеба́ть *v. impfv.* [*pfv.* **хлебну́ть**] to gulp (down). *See also* **хлебну́ть**.

хле́бец [*gen.* -**бца**] *n.* small loaf of bread.

хле́бница *n.* breadbasket.

хлебну́ть *v. pfv.* **1**, *pfv. of* **хлеба́ть**. **2**, *colloq.* to drink; have a drop to drink: хлебну́ть ли́шнего, to have a drop too much to drink. **3**, *fig.* (*with gen.*) *colloq.* to experience; know: хлебну́ть го́ря, to have known much sorrow.

хле́бный *adj.* **1**, bread (*attrib.*). **2**, of grain; grain (*attrib.*). **3**, rich in grain. **4**, *colloq.* profitable; lucrative.

хлебопёк *n.* baker.

хлеборо́б *n.* farmer.

хлебосо́л *n.* hospitable person; good host. —**хлебосо́льный**, *adj.* hospitable. —**хлебосо́льство**, *n.* hospitality.

хлеб-со́ль [*gen.* **хлеба-со́ли**] *n.m. or f.* **1**, bread and salt (*symbol of hospitality*). **2,** hospitality. **—***interj.* hearty appetite!

хлев [*2nd loc.* хлеву́; *pl.* хлева́] *n.* **1,** barn (*for livestock*). **2,** *colloq.* pigsty.

хлеста́ть *v. impfv.* [*pfv.* хлестну́ть; *pres.* хлещу́, хле́щешь] **1,** to whip; lash; flog. **2,** (*of rain*) to come down in torrents. **3,** (*with* в *or* о + *acc.*) to beat against. **4,** *fig.* to flay; castigate; excoriate.

хлёсткий *adj.* [*comp.* хлёстче] **1,** (*of a wind*) biting; (*of a sound, blow, etc.*) sharp. **2,** *fig.* biting; scathing; trenchant.

хлестну́ть *v.,* *pfv. of* хлеста́ть.

хли́пкий *adj., colloq.* **1,** rickety. **2,** frail. **3,** watery.

хлоп *interj.* bang!

хло́панье *n.* banging; slamming; clapping.

хло́пать *v. impfv.* [*pfv.* похло́пать *or* хло́пнуть] **1,** to slap; bang: хло́пать кого́-нибудь по спине́, to slap someone on the back; хло́пать кулако́м по столу́, to bang one's fist on the table. **2,** (*with instr.*) to slam (a door); crack (a whip); flap (one's wings). **3,** (*of a cork*) to pop; (*of a shot*) to ring out. **4,** to clap; applaud; (*with dat.*) applaud (someone). **—хло́пать в ладо́ши,** to clap one's hands. **—хло́пать глаза́ми** *or* уша́ми, to look blank.

хло́паться *v.r. impfv.* [*pfv.* хло́пнуться] *colloq.* to fall down; flop.

хло́пец [*gen.* -пца] *n., colloq.* boy; lad; youth.

хлопково́д *n.* cotton grower. **—хлопково́дство,** *n.* cotton growing. **—хлопково́дческий,** *adj.* cotton-growing.

хло́пковый *adj.* cotton. **—хло́пковое ма́сло,** cottonseed oil.

хлопкоочисти́тельный *adj., in* хлопкоочисти́-тельная маши́на, cotton gin.

хло́пнуть *v., pfv. of* хло́пать. **—хло́пнуться** *refl., pfv. of* хло́паться.

хло́пок [*gen.* -пка] *n.* cotton.

хлопо́к [*gen.* -пка́] *n.* **1,** loud noise; bang; sound (*of a shot*); pop (*of a cork*). **2,** slap; pat (*on the back*). **3,** *pl.* clapping; applause.

хлопота́ть *v. impfv.* [*pfv.* похлопота́ть; *pres.* -почу́, -по́чешь] **1,** [*impfv. only*] to fuss; bustle about. **2,** (*with* о) to seek; try to get. **3,** (*with* чтобы) to make efforts (to); try to see to it that. **4,** (*with* за + *acc.*) to make efforts; intercede (on behalf of).

хлопотли́вый *adj.* **1,** busy; bustling. **2,** difficult; demanding; onerous.

хло́потный *adj., colloq.* = хлопотли́вый (*in sense #2*).

хлопотня́ *n., colloq.* bustling about; feverish activity.

хлопоту́н [*gen.* -туна́] *n.m.* [*fem.* -ту́нья] *colloq.* hustler; busybody.

хло́поты [*gen.* хлопо́т; *dat.* хлопота́м] *n. pl.* **1,** chores. **2,** efforts. **3,** worries; cares.

хлопу́шка [*gen. pl.* -шек] *n.* **1,** fly swatter. **2,** cracker (*party favor*).

хлопча́тник *n.* cotton plant.

хлопчатобума́жный *adj.* cotton.

хло́пья [*gen.* -пьев] *n. pl.* flakes: хло́пья сне́га, snowflakes; кукуру́зные хло́пья, corn flakes.

хлор *n.* chlorine.

хлори́д *n.* chloride.

хлори́рование *n.* chlorination.

хлори́ровать *v. impfv. & pfv.* [*pres.* -рую, -руешь] to chlorinate.

хлори́стый *adj.* **1,** chlorous. **2,** *in compounds, …* chloride: хлори́стый аммо́ний/ка́лий/на́трий, ammonium/potassium/sodium chloride.

хло́рный *adj.* chloric. **—хло́рная и́звесть,** chloride of lime. **—хло́рная кислота́,** perchloric acid.

хлорофи́лл *n.* chlorophyll.

хлорофо́рм *n.* chloroform.

хлороформи́ровать *v. impfv. & pfv.* [*pres.* -рую, -руешь] to chloroform.

хлы́нуть *v. pfv.* **1,** to stream; gush; pour; rush. **2,** (*of rain*) to come down in torrents. **3,** (*of a crowd*) to stream; surge.

хлыст [*gen.* хлыста́] *n.* **1,** whip. **2,** *hist.* member of a religious sect that practiced flagellation; khlyst.

хлыщ [*gen.* хлыща́] *n., colloq.* fop; dandy.

хлю́пать *v. impfv., colloq.* to splash; make a splashing sound. **—хлю́пать но́сом,** to sniff.

хлю́пкий *adj., colloq.* **1,** soggy. **2,** rickety. **3,** frail.

хлябь *n.f.* **1,** *archaic* abyss. **2,** *colloq.* mud.

хля́стик *n.* half-belt (*at the back of a coat*).

хмелёк [*gen.* -лька́] *n., dim. of* хмель. **—под хмелько́м,** tipsy; high.

хмеле́ть *v. impfv., colloq.* to become tipsy; get high.

хмель *n.m.* **1,** hop (*plant*). **2,** hops. **3,** *colloq.* intoxication: во хмелю́, intoxicated.

хмельно́й *adj.* **1,** intoxicated. **2,** intoxicating. **—хмельно́е,** *n.* alcohol; liquor.

хму́рить *v. impfv.* [*pfv.* нахму́рить] **1,** to knit (one's brows). **2,** *in* хму́рить лицо́, to frown. **—хму́риться,** *refl.* **1,** to frown. **2,** to be overcast.

хму́рый *adj.* **1,** (*of a person*) gloomy; somber; sullen. **2,** (*of the weather, sky, etc.*) gloomy; overcast; dismal.

хна *n.* henna.

хны́канье *n., colloq.* whining; whimpering.

хны́кать *v. impfv.* [*pres.* хны́чу, хны́чешь *or* хны́каю, хны́каешь] *colloq.* to whine; whimper.

хо́бби *n. neut. indecl., colloq.* hobby.

хо́бот *n.* trunk (*of an elephant*).

ход *n.* **1,** motion: за́дний ход, reverse motion. **2,** speed: замедля́ть ход, to reduce one's speed; slow down. **3,** operation (*of a machine*). **4,** [*pl.* хо́ды *or* ходы́] stroke (*of an engine, piston, etc.*). **5,** *fig.* course; progress: ход собы́тий, course of events. Ход мы́слей, train of thought. **6,** [*pl.* хо́ды *or* ходы́] move (*in chess*); lead (*in cards*). На сороково́м ходу́, on the fortieth move. **7,** [*pl.* хо́ды] move; maneuver. **8,** [*pl.* ходы́] entrance; door: пара́дный/че́рный ход, front/back door. **9,** [*pl.* ходы́] passage; passageway. **10,** *fig.* chance of success: ему́ хо́ду нет, he has no chance. **11,** *obs.* procession. **—в большо́м ходу́,** in great demand. **—в по́лном ходу́,** in full swing. **—в хо́де** (+ *gen.*), in the course of; during. **—в ход** (+ *dat.*), to start up; set in motion. **—дать хо́ду,** *colloq.* to take to one's heels. **—знать все ходы́ и вы́ходы,** to know all the ins and outs. **—идти́ по́лным хо́дом,** to proceed apace. **—идти́ свои́м хо́дом, 1,** to proceed under one's own power *or* steam. **2,** to proceed at one's own pace. **—на по́лном ходу́,** (at) full speed. **—на ходу́, 1,** in operation. **2,** quickly; on the run. While something is in motion. **—не дава́ть хо́ду** (+ *dat.*), to give someone no chance. **—пойти́ в ход, 1,** to come into use; come into play. **2,** to become much in demand. **—по́лный ход!,** full speed ahead! **—пусти́ть в ход, 1,** to start; set in motion. **2,** *in* пусти́ть в ход все. сре́дства, to move heaven and earth; leave no stone unturned. —с хóду, without stopping; while in motion.

ходáтай n. intercessor.

ходáтайство n. **1**, application; solicitation; petition. **2**, intercession.

ходáтайствовать v. impfv. [pfv. **походáтайствовать**; pres. -ствую, -ствуешь] **1**, (with о) to apply (for); petition (for); solicit. **2**, (with за + acc.) to intercede (on behalf of).

хóдики [gen. -ков] n.pl., colloq. wall clock (driven by weights).

ходи́ть v. impfv. [pres. хожý, хóдишь] **1**, indeterm. of идти́. **2**, to walk; be able to walk. **3**, (of trains, buses, etc.) to run; operate. **4**, (of news, rumors, etc.) to be going around. **5**, (with в + prepl.) to wear: ходи́ть в очкáх, to wear glasses. **6**, (with за + instr.) to look after; care for.

хóдкий adj., colloq. **1**, agile. **2**, (of a vehicle, ship, etc.) fast-moving. **3**, (of merchandise) fast-selling. **4**, (of an expression) currently popular.

ходовóй adj. **1**, mech. working; operational. **2**, performance (attrib.): ходовы́е испытáния, performance tests. Ходовы́е кáчества маши́ны, performance of a car. **3**, colloq. popular; fast-selling. **4**, colloq. (of an expression, anecdote, etc.) currently popular. —**ходовáя пружи́на**, mainspring (of a watch).

ходóк [gen. -докá] n. **1**, walker. **2**, colloq. regular visitor (to). **3**, (with на + acc. or по) colloq. person who is adroit (with or at). **4**, obs. envoy; delegate.

ходýли [gen. -лей] n. pl. [sing. ходýля] stilts.

ходýлочник n. stilt (bird).

ходýльный adj. stilted.

ходýн [gen. -дунá] n., colloq. walker. —**ходи́ть ходунóм**, **1**, to shake violently. **2**, fig. to be in a whirl.

ходунки́ [gen. -кóв] n. pl. walker (device).

ходьбá n. walking; walk: полчасá ходьбы́, half an hour's walk.

ходя́чий adj. **1**, walking. **2**, (of a sick person) able to walk; ambulatory. **3**, fig. current; currently popular.

хожде́ние n. **1**, walking; going: хожде́ние в кинó, going to the movies. **2**, circulation (of money). **3**, fig. use; currency: име́ть широ́кое хожде́ние, to be in wide use; enjoy wide currency.

хозрасчёт n. self-supporting basis; operation without government support (contr. of **хозя́йственный расчёт**).

хозя́ин [pl. хозя́ева, хозя́ев] n. **1**, owner. **2**, master. **3**, (preceded by an adj.) (good, bad, etc.) administrator; manager. **4**, employer; boss. **5**, landlord. **6**, host. —**хозя́ева по́ля**, sports the home team. —**хозя́ин своегó сло́ва**, man of his word.

хозя́йка [gen. pl. -яек] n., fem. of **хозя́ин**. —**дома́шняя хозя́йка**, housewife.

хозя́йничать v. impfv. **1**, to be in charge; run things. **2**, to keep house. **3**, colloq. to throw one's weight around.

хозя́йский adj. **1**, master's. **2**, proprietary: хозя́йское отноше́ние к, a proprietary attitude toward. **3**, fig. careful: хозя́йским глáзом, with a careful eye. **4**, fig. imperious. —**де́ло хозя́йское**, colloq. it's up to you (to decide).

хозя́йственник n. administrator; manager.

хозя́йственность n.f. efficiency (in running a household).

хозя́йственный adj. **1**, economic. **2**, household (at-

trib.). **3**, thrifty; economical. —**хозя́йственное мы́ло**, kitchen soap. —**хозя́йственная сýмка**, shopping bag.

хозя́йство n. **1**, economy. **2**, [usu. **дома́шнее хозя́йство**] housekeeping. **3**, equipment; property. **4**, household equipment. **5**, farm. —**се́льское хозя́йство**, agriculture.

хозя́йствование n. management.

хозя́йствовать v. impfv. [pres. -ствую, -ствуешь] **1**, to manage; be a manager. **2**, to keep house.

хозя́йчик n., colloq. small proprietor.

хоккеи́ст n. hockey player.

хокке́й n. hockey. —**хокке́йный**, adj. hockey (attrib.).

хóленый adj. well-groomed.

холе́ра n. cholera.

холе́рик n. temperamental, high-strung person. —**холери́ческий**, adj. choleric; temperamental; high-strung.

холе́рный adj. cholera (attrib.).

холестери́н n. cholesterol.

хóлить v. impfv. to take care of.

хóлка n. withers.

холл n. **1**, (meeting) hall. **2**, lobby.

холм [gen. холмá] n. hill.

хóлмик n. small hill; knoll.

холми́стый adj. hilly.

хóлод [pl. холодá] n. **1**, cold. **2**, pl. cold weather: пе́рвые холодá, first cold weather.

холодáть v. impfv., impers. to get cold; turn cold.

холоде́ть v. impfv. [pfv. **похолоде́ть**] **1**, to grow cold. **2**, fig. to turn cold (from fear, horror, etc.).

холоде́ц [gen. -дцá] n., colloq. aspic (of meat or fish).

холоди́льник n. refrigerator; icebox.

холоди́льный adj. refrigeration (attrib.); refrigerating.

холоди́ть v. impfv. [pres. -жý, -ди́шь] to cool; chill.

холо́дненький adj., colloq. chilly; nippy.

холодне́ть v. impfv., impers. to get cold; turn cold.

хóлодно adv. coldly. —adj., used predicatively cold: здесь хóлодно, it is cold here; мне хóлодно, I am cold.

холоднова́тый adj., colloq. rather cool.

холоднокрóвный adj., zool. cold-blooded.

хóлодность n.f. coldness.

холóдный adj. [short form хóлоден, холоднá, хóлодно] **1**, cold. **2**, unheated. **3**, (of a garment, blanket, etc.) light; thin; not providing sufficient warmth. —**холóдное орýжие**, plain weapon (sword, bayonet, etc.).

холодóк [gen. -дкá] n., colloq. **1**, coolness; chill. **2**, cool breeze. **3**, cool place. **4**, cool (of the day, evening, etc.). **5**, fig. chill; coolness (in relations).

холóп n. **1**, hist. serf; bondsman. **2**, fig. lackey; stooge.

холóпский adj. **1**, hist. serf's. **2**, fig. servile.

холóпство n. **1**, hist. serfdom. **2**, fig. servility.

холóпствовать v. impfv. [pres. -ствую, -ствуешь] **1**, to be servile. **2**, (with пе́ред) to kowtow to.

холости́ть v. impfv. [pfv. **вы́холостить**; pres. -лощý, -лости́шь] to castrate; geld (an animal).

холостóй adj. **1**, (of a man) single; unmarried. **2**, bachelor (attrib.). **3**, mech. idle: холостóй ход, idling. **4**, blank: холостóй патрóн, blank cartridge.

холостя́к [gen. -стякá] n. bachelor. —**холостя́цкий**, adj., colloq. bachelor (attrib.); bachelor's.

холоще́ние n. castration.

холощёный adj. castrated; gelded.

холст [gen. холстá] n. **1**, linen. **2**, sackcloth; burlap. **3**, painting canvas.

холсти́на *n.* = холст.

холсти́нка *n.* **1,** piece of cloth. **2,** linen or cotton fabric.

холу́й *n., colloq.* lackey; flunky; stooge.

холщо́вый *adj.* **1,** linen. **2,** burlap.

хо́ля *n., colloq.* loving care. —**жить в хо́ле,** to be lovingly cared for.

хому́т [*gen.* -мута́] *n.* collar (*for a horse*).

хомя́к [*gen.* -мяка́] *n.* hamster.

хор [*pl.* хоры́ *or* хо́ры] *n.* **1,** chorus. **2,** choir. —**хо́ром,** in a chorus; in unison; all together. *See also* **хо́ры.**

хора́л *n.* chorale.

хорва́т *n.m.* [*fem.* -ва́тка] Croat. —**хорва́тский,** *adj.* Croatian.

хо́рда *n., math.* chord.

хоре́й *n.* trochee. —**хоре́йческий,** *adj.* trochaic.

хорёк [*gen.* -рька́] *n.* polecat; fitch; ferret.

хореогра́фия *n.* choreography. —**хорео́граф,** *n.* choreographer. —**хореографи́ческий,** *adj.* choreographic.

хоре́я *n.* chorea.

хори́ст *n.* member of a choir; chorister.

хормейстер *n.* choirmaster.

хорово́д *n.* round dance with singing.

хорово́й *adj.* choral.

хорони́ть *v. impfv.* [*pfv.* **похорони́ть;** *pres.* -роню́, -ро́нишь] to bury; inter.

хорохо́риться *v.r. impfv., colloq.* to swagger; bluster.

хоро́шенький *adj.* **1,** pretty; attractive; cute. **2,** *colloq.* good. **3,** *colloq., ironic* fine; nice; pretty: хоро́шенькая исто́рия, a pretty mess.

хороше́нько *adv., colloq.* properly; thoroughly. Хороше́нько отдохну́ть, to have a good rest. Сту́кните хороше́нько!, give a good knock!

хороше́ть *v. impfv.* [*pfv.* **похороше́ть**] to get prettier; become more attractive.

хоро́ший *adj.* [*short form* хоро́ш, хороша́, хорошо́, хоро́ши] **1,** good. **2,** nice. **3,** (*short form only, usu. with* собо́й) pretty; attractive; good-looking.

хорошо́ *adv.* well: хорошо́ себя́ чу́вствовать, to feel well. Хорошо́ ска́зано!, well said! Хорошо́ па́хнуть, to smell good. —*adj., used predicatively* **1,** good; fine; nice: э́то хорошо́, that's good/nice. Хорошо́, что..., it's a good thing that... **2,** (*with dat.*) satisfied; happy: вам бу́дет хорошо́ там, you'll be happy there; you'll like it there. —*particle* all right; O.K.; very well. —*n. indecl.* "good" (*school grade*).

хо́ры [*gen.* хо́ров] *n. pl.* gallery; balcony.

хорь [*gen.* хоря́] *n.m.* = хорёк.

хорько́вый *adj.* fitch (*attrib.*).

хоте́ть *v. impfv.* [*pres.* хочу́, хо́чешь, хо́чет, хоти́м, хоти́те, хотя́т] **1,** to want: что вы хоти́те?, what do you want? **2,** to like; wish: хоти́те ещё ча́шку ко́фе?, would you like another cup of coffee? Де́лайте, как хоти́те, do as you like/wish/please. —**хо́чешь не хо́чешь,** like it or not.

хоте́ться *v.r. impfv.* [*pres.* хо́чется] *impers.* (*with dat.*) **1,** to want: мне хо́чется поговори́ть с ним, I want to have a talk with him. **2,** to feel like: ему́ не хо́чется идти́, he doesn't feel like going.

хоть *conj.* **1,** although; though. **2,** if you like. **3,** at least. **4,** even if. **5,** for example. **6,** any-: хоть что, anything; хоть где, anywhere. **7,** *used with an imperative verb in a number of idiomatic expressions:* хоть убе́й, for the life of me; хоть отбавля́й, plenty; ample; more than

enough. —**хоть бы, 1,** even if. **2,** if only. —**хоть бы и так,** *colloq.* **1,** what of it?; what if it is? **2,** even so. —**хоть бы что** (+ *dat.*), *colloq.* couldn't care less. —**хоть куда́,** *colloq.* first-rate.

хотя́ *conj.* **1,** although. **2,** though. —**хотя́ бы, 1,** if only. **2,** even if. **3,** at least.

хохла́тый *adj.* crested.

хохла́ч [*gen.* -лача́] *n.* hooded seal.

хо́хлиться *v.r. impfv.* [*pfv.* **нахо́хлиться**] **1,** (*of a bird*) to ruffle its feathers. **2,** *fig., colloq.* to sulk.

хохо́л [*gen.* хохла́] *n.* **1,** crest (*of a bird*). **2,** topknot. **3,** *obs., colloq.* Ukrainian.

хохоло́к [*gen.* -лка́] *n., dim. of* хохо́л (*in senses #1 & #2*).

хо́хот *n.* loud laughter.

хохота́ть *v. impfv.* [*pres.* хохочу́, хохо́чешь] to laugh loudly.

хохоту́н [*gen.* -туна́] *n.m.* [*fem.* -ту́нья] *colloq.* merry fellow; one easily moved to laughter.

храбре́ц [*gen.* -бреца́] *n.* brave man.

храбри́ться *v.r. impfv., colloq.* to pretend not to be afraid; keep a stiff upper lip.

хра́брый *adj.* brave. —**хра́бро,** *adv.* bravely. —**хра́брость,** *n.f.* bravery.

храм *n.* temple. —Храм Васи́лия Блаже́нного, St. Basil's Cathedral (*on Red Square*).

хране́ние *n.* storage; safekeeping. —**ка́мера хране́ния (багажа́),** baggage room.

храни́лище *n.* storehouse; depository; respository.

храни́тель *n.m.* **1,** keeper; custodian. **2,** curator (*of a museum*).

храни́ть *v. impfv.* **1,** to keep: храни́ть письмо́/та́йну, to keep a letter/secret. Храни́ть что́-нибудь в се́йфе, to keep something in a safe. **2,** to maintain (silence, a custom, etc.).

храп *n.* **1,** snore; snoring. **2,** snorting (*of a horse*).

храпе́ть *v. impfv.* [*pres.* -плю́, -пи́шь] **1,** to snore. **2,** (*of a horse*) to snort.

храпови́к [*gen.* -вика́] *n.* ratchet. —**храпово́й,** *adj.* ratchet (*attrib.*).

храпу́н [*gen.* -пуна́] *n., colloq.* snorer.

хребе́т [*gen.* -бта́] *n.* **1,** spine; backbone. **2,** mountain range.

хрен *n.* horseradish.

хрестома́тия *n.* reader (*book*).

хризанте́ма (тэ) *n.* chrysanthemum.

хрип *n.* wheeze. —**предсме́ртный хрип,** death rattle.

хрипе́ть *v. impfv.* [*pres.* -плю́, -пи́шь] **1,** to wheeze. **2,** to be hoarse.

хри́плый *adj.* hoarse. —**хри́пло,** *adv.* hoarsely; in a hoarse voice.

хри́пнуть *v. impfv.* [*past* хрип *or* хри́пнул, хри́пла] to become hoarse.

хрипота́ *n.* hoarseness.

христиани́н [*pl.* -тиа́не, -тиа́н] *n.m.* [*fem.* -тиа́нка] Christian. —**христиа́нский,** *adj.* Christian. —**христиа́нство,** *n.* Christianity.

Христо́с [*gen.* Христа́] *n.* Christ.

хром *n.* **1,** chromium. **2,** chrome. **3,** chrome leather.

хромати́чесикй *adj.* chromatic.

хрома́ть *v. impfv.* **1,** to limp. **2,** *colloq.* to be deficient. **3,** *colloq.* to be weak; be poor (*in a certain school subject*): он хрома́ет по орфогра́фии *or* у него́ хрома́ет орфогра́фия, he is poor in spelling. —**хрома́ть на о́бе но́ги,** to flounder.

хроми́рование *n.* chrome plating.

хроми́ровать *v. impfv. & pfv.* [*pres.* -ру́ю, -ру́ешь] to plate with chrome; chrome-plate.

хро́мистый *adj.* chrome (*attrib.*): хро́мистая сталь, chrome steel.

хроми́т *n.* chromite.

хро́мовый *adj.* chrome (*attrib.*). —хро́мовая кислота́, chromic acid.

хромо́й *adj.* lame. —*n.* lame person.

хромоно́гий *adj.* lame.

хромосо́ма *n.* chromosome.

хромота́ *n.* lameness.

хро́ник *n.*, *colloq.* chronically ill person.

хро́ника *n.* 1, chronicle. 2, news items. 3, newsreel.

хроника́льный *adj.* chronicle (*attrib.*); in chronicle form. —хроника́льный фильм, newsreel.

хрони́ческий *adj.* 1, chronic. 2, chronically ill.

хроноло́гия *n.* chronology. —хронологи́ческий, *adj.* chronological.

хроно́метр *n.* 1, *obs.* timepiece. 2, chronometer.

хронометра́ж *n.* time (and motion) study. —хронометражи́ст, *n.* time-study man.

хронометри́ровать *v. impfv. & pfv.* [*pres.* -ру́ю, -ру́ешь] to time; clock.

хронометри́ст *n.* timer; timekeeper.

хру́пкий *adj.* [*short form* -пок, -пка́, -пко] 1, fragile; brittle. 2, frail; delicate.

хру́пкость *n.f.* 1, fragility. 2, frailty.

хруст *n.* crunch; crunching sound.

хруста́лик *n.* 1, *colloq.* something made of crystal. 2, lens of the eye.

хруста́ль [*gen.* -сталя́] *n.m.* 1, crystal. 2, item made of crystal.

хруста́льный *adj.* 1, crystal. 2, like crystal.

хруста́н *n.* dotterel.

хрусте́ть *v. impfv.* [*pfv.* хру́стнуть; *pres.* хрущу́, хрусти́шь] to crunch.

хрущ [*gen.* хруща́] *n.* cockchafer.

хрю́канье *n.* grunting.

хрю́кать *v. impfv.* [*pfv.* хрю́кнуть] to grunt.

хряк [*gen.* хряка́] *n.* male hog.

хрящ [*gen.* хряща́] *n.* cartilage. —хрящева́тый, *adj.* cartilaginous. —хрящево́й, *adj.* cartilage (*attrib.*).

худе́ть *v. impfv.* [*pfv.* похуде́ть] to get thin; lose weight.

ху́до *n.*, *obs.*, *colloq.* harm. —*adv.* badly; poorly: ху́до оде́тый, poorly dressed. —*adj., used predicatively* (*with dat.*) 1, bad; in a bad way. 2, unwell: ему́ ху́до, he is not feeling well.

худоба́ *n.* thinness; leanness.

худо́жественность *n.f.* artistic value; artistry.

худо́жественный *adj.* 1, art (*attrib.*); of art. 2, artistic. —худо́жественная литерату́ра, fiction. —худо́жественный фильм, feature film.

худо́жество *n.* 1, *obs.* art. 2, *colloq.* trick; prank.

худо́жник *n.m.* [*fem.* -ница] 1, artist. 2, painter.

худо́й *adj.* 1, [*comp.* ху́же] bad. 2, [*comp.* худе́е] thin; skinny. 3, [*comp.* худе́е] *colloq.* worn; tattered; full of holes. —на худо́й коне́ц, *colloq.* if worst comes to worst. *See also* ху́же.

худоща́вый *adj.* thin; lean; skinny.

худше́е *n.*, *decl. as an adj.* 1, the worse: переме́на к ху́дшему, change for the worse. 2, the worst: пригото́виться к ху́дшему, to be prepared for the worst.

ху́дший *adj.*, *used only as a modifer, comp. and superl.* of плохо́й and худо́й, worse; worst. —в ху́дшем слу́чае, at worst.

ху́же *adj.*, *comp. of* плохо́й and худо́й, worse. —*adv.*, *comp. of* пло́хо and ху́до, worse. —тем ху́же, so much the worse. —ху́же всего́, worst of all. —ху́же всего́ то, что..., the worst of it is that...

хула́ *n.* (verbal) abuse.

хулига́н *n.* hooligan; hoodlum.

хулига́нить *v. impfv.* to behave like a hooligan or hoodlum.

хулига́нский *adj.* like that of a hooligan or hoodlum.

хулига́нство *n.* hooliganism; disorderly conduct.

хули́тель *n.m.* detractor.

хули́ть *v. impfv.* to disparage.

ху́нта *n.* junta.

хурма́ *n.* persimmon.

ху́тор [*pl.* хутора́] *n.* farm. —хуторско́й, *adj.* farm (*attrib.*).

Ц

Ц, ц *n. neut.* 23rd letter of the Russian alphabet.

ца́пать *v. impfv.* [*pfv.* ца́пнуть] *colloq.* to grab; snatch.

ца́пля [*gen. pl.* -пель] *n.* heron. —бе́лая ца́пля, egret.

ца́пнуть *v.*, *pfv. of* ца́пать.

цара́пать *v. impfv.* 1, [*pfv.* цара́пнуть] to scratch. 2, [*pfv.* нацара́пать] *colloq.* to scribble; scrawl. —цара́паться, *refl.* [*impfv. only*] 1, to scratch; make scratching sounds; have a tendency to scratch. 2, to scratch each other.

цара́пина *n.* scratch.

цара́пнуть *v.*, *pfv. of* цара́пать.

царе́вич *n.* tsarevitch.

царе́вна [*gen. pl.* -вен] *n.* tsarevna.

цареуби́йство *n.* regicide.

цари́зм *n.* tsarism.

цари́ть *v. impfv.* 1, *obs.* (*of a monarch*) to reign. 2, *fig.* (*of silence*) to reign; (*of conditions*) to prevail.

цари́ца *n.* 1, tsarina. 2, *fig.* (*with gen.*) queen (of):

цари́ца мод, queen of fashion. —цари́ца ба́ла, belle of the ball.

ца́рский *adj.* **1,** of the tsar; tsar's. **2,** tsarist. **3,** *fig.* regal.

ца́рственный *adj.* regal; majestic.

ца́рство *n.* **1,** kingdom; realm. **2,** reign. **3,** *fig.* kingdom: живо́тное ца́рство, animal kingdom. —венча́ние на ца́рство, coronation.

ца́рствование *n.* reign. —в ца́рствование (+ *gen.*), during the reign of.

ца́рствовать *v. impfv.* [*pres.* -ствую, -ствуешь] to reign.

царь [*gen.* царя́] *n.m.* **1,** tsar. **2,** *fig.* king: царь звере́й, king of beasts.

цвести́ *v. impfv.* [*pres.* цвету́, цветёшь; *past* цвёл, цвела́, цвело́] **1,** to bloom; blossom; flower. **2,** (*with instr.*) *fig.* to be the picture of (beauty, health, etc.). **3,** *fig.* to flourish.

цвет *n.* **1,** [*pl.* цвета́] color. **2,** [*pl.* цветы́] (*sing. rare*) flower. —во цве́те лет, in one's prime; in the prime of life. —в по́лном цвету́, in full bloom.

цвете́ние *n.* blooming; blossoming; flowering.

цвети́стый *adj.* **1,** colorful. **2,** *fig.* flowery; florid.

цветко́вый *adj.* (*of plants*) flowering.

цветни́к [*gen.* -ника́] *n.* flower bed; flower garden.

цветно́й *adj.* colored; color (*attrib.*). —цветна́я капу́ста, cauliflower. —цветно́й каранда́ш, crayon. —цветны́е мета́ллы, non-ferrous metals. —цветно́е стекло́, stained glass.

цветово́дство *n.* floriculture.

цветово́й *adj.* color (*attrib.*).

цвето́к [*gen.* -тка́; *pl.* цветы́, цвето́в, цвета́м] *n.* flower.

цветоло́же *n., bot.* receptacle.

цветоно́жка [*gen. pl.* -жек] *n., bot.* pedicel.

цвето́чек [*gen.* -чка] *n., dim. of* цвето́к.

цвето́чница *n.* flower girl.

цвето́чный *adj.* flower (*attrib.*); floral.

цвету́щий *adj.* **1,** flowering; blossoming; blooming. **2,** *fig.* healthy; robust. **3,** *fig.* flourishing; prospering.

цеди́лка [*gen. pl.* -лок] *n., colloq.* strainer.

цеди́ть *v. impfv.* [*pres.* цежу́, це́дишь] **1,** to strain; filter. **2,** to pour slowly (*through a narrow opening*). **3,** to sip. **4,** *colloq.* to utter (*often slowly and with suppressed anger*).

це́дра *n.* dried lemon or orange peel.

це́зий *n.* cesium.

цейтно́т *n., chess* time trouble.

целе́бный *adj.* **1,** medicinal; curative. **2,** healthful; salubrious.

целево́й *adj.* having a particular purpose. —целева́я устано́вка, aim; objective.

целенапра́вленный *adj.* purposeful.

целесообра́зный *adj.* advisable; expedient. —целесообра́зность, *n.f.* advisability; expediency.

целеустремлённый *adj.* purposeful.

целико́м *adv.* **1,** whole: проглоти́ть целико́м, to swallow whole. **2,** wholly; entirely. —целико́м и по́лностью, completely; fully.

целина́ *n.* virgin land; virgin soil.

цели́нный *adj.* virgin: цели́нные зе́мли, virgin lands.

цели́тельный *adj.* healing; curative.

це́лить *v. impfv.* (*with* в + *acc.*) to aim (at). *Also,* це́литься, *refl.*

целлофа́н *n.* cellophane. —целлофа́новый, *adj.* cellophane.

целлуло́ид *n.* celluloid. —целлуло́идный, *adj.* celluloid.

целлюло́за *n.* cellulose. —целлюло́зный, *adj.* cellulose.

целова́ть *v. impfv.* [*pfv.* поцелова́ть; *pres.* -лу́ю, -лу́ешь] to kiss. —целова́ться, *refl.* (*of two people*) to kiss.

це́лое *n., decl. as an adj.* **1,** whole; the whole. **2,** *math.* whole number; integer.

целому́дренный *adj.* chaste. —целому́дрие, *n.* chastity.

це́лостность *n.f.* unity. —территориа́льная це́лостность, territorial integrity.

це́лостный *adj.* unified; integrated.

це́лость *n.f.* **1,** (*with gen.*) the safety (of). **2,** wholeness; unity. —в це́лости, intact. —в це́лости и сохра́нности, safe and sound.

це́лый *adj.* **1,** whole; entire. **2,** intact; undamaged. **3,** safe; unharmed: цел и невреди́м, safe and sound. —в це́лом, **1,** on the whole. **2,** as a whole. —в о́бщем и це́лом, on the whole; all in all. —по це́лым дням; це́лыми дня́ми, for days on end. *See also* це́лое.

цель *n.f.* **1,** target; mark. **2,** aim; goal; object; purpose. —с це́лью; в це́лях (+ *gen. or with inf.*), with the aim of; for the purpose of. —с э́той це́лью, toward this end.

це́льность *n.f.* unity; wholeness.

це́льный *adj.* **1,** whole; of one piece. **2,** single; unified; integrated. **3,** (*of a person, his nature, etc.*) sound; steady; solid. **4,** complete; finished. **5,** (*of milk, blood, etc.*) whole.

Це́льсий *n.* Celsius; Centigrade: де́сять гра́дусов по Це́льсию, ten degrees Celsius/Centigrade.

цеме́нт *n.* cement.

цементи́ровать *v. impfv. & pfv.* [*pres.* -рую, -руешь] **1,** to cement. **2,** to caseharden.

цеме́нтный *adj.* cement.

цена́ [*acc.* це́ну; *pl.* це́ны] *n.* **1,** price. **2,** *fig.* worth. Знать це́ну (+ *dat.*), to know the worth (*or* value) of. —цено́й (+ *gen.*), at the cost of. —цены́ нет (+ *dat.*), priceless.

ценз *n.* requirement: возрастно́й ценз, age requirement.

це́нзор *n.* censor.

цензу́ра *n.* **1,** censorship. **2,** censorship office.

цензу́рный *adj.* **1,** censorship (*attrib.*). **2,** able to pass censorship; printable.

цени́тель *n.m.* judge; connoisseur.

цени́ть *v. impfv.* [*pres.* ценю́, це́нишь] **1,** *obs.* to appraise; evaluate. **2,** to judge. **3,** to appreciate. **4,** to value; prize.

це́нник *n.* price list.

це́нность *n.f.* **1,** value. **2,** *pl.* valuables. **3,** *pl.* values.

це́нный *adj.* **1,** valuable. **2,** (*of a parcel*) having a stated value. —це́нные бума́ги, securities.

цент *n.* cent.

це́нтнер *n.* centner (*100 kilograms*).

центр *n.* center.

централиза́ция *n.* centralization.

централи́зм *n.* centralism. —демократи́ческий централи́зм, democratic centralism.

централизо́ванный *adj.* centralized.

централизова́ть *v. impfv. & pfv.* [*pres.* -зу́ю, -зу́-ешь] to centralize.

центра́льный *adj.* central.

центробе́жный *adj.* centrifugal: центробе́жная си́ла, centrifugal force.

центрово́й *adj.* center (*attrib.*); central. —*n.* center (*on a basketball team*).

центростреми́тельный *adj.* centripetal.

цеп [*gen.* цепа́] *n.* flail.

цепене́ть *v. impfv.* [*pfv.* оцепене́ть] to become numb; become rigid.

це́пкий *adj.* [*short form* це́пок, цепка́, це́пко] **1,** prehensile; tenacious. **2,** *fig.* keen; perceptive. **3,** (*of one's memory*) retentive. **4,** *fig., colloq.* persistent; dogged.

це́пкость *n.f.* tenacity.

цепля́ться *v.r impfv.* (*with* за + *acc.*) to cling (to).

цепно́й *adj.* chain (*attrib.*). —**цепно́е колесо́,** sprocket wheel. —**цепна́я реа́кция,** chain reaction.

цепо́чка [*gen. pl.* -чек] *n.* **1,** small chain: цепо́чка для часо́в, watch chain. **2,** row; line; file: цепо́чкой, in a line.

цеппели́н *n.* zeppelin.

цепь [*2nd loc.* цепи́; *pl.* це́пи, цепе́й, цепя́м] *n.f.* **1,** chain. **2,** *fig.* (*with gen.*) chain (*of mountains, islands, events, etc.*). **3,** *electricity* circuit.

церебра́льный *adj.* cerebral. —**церебра́льный парали́ч,** cerebral palsy.

церемониа́л *n.* ceremonial; ritual. —**церемониа́льный,** *adj.* ceremonial.

церемо́ниться *v.r. impfv.* to stand on ceremony.

церемо́ния *n.* **1,** ceremony. **2,** *pl., colloq.* ceremony; formalities. Без дальне́йших церемо́ний, without further ado. —**церемо́нный,** *adj.* ceremonious.

це́рий *n.* cerium.

церковнославя́нский *adj.* Church Slavonic.

церко́вный *adj.* of the church; church (*attrib.*).

це́рковь [*gen., dat., & prepl.* це́ркви; *instr.* це́рковью; *pl.* це́ркви, церкве́й, церква́м] *n.f.* church.

цесаре́вич *n.* crown prince (*in tsarist Russia*).

цеса́рка [*gen. pl.* -рок] *n.* guinea fowl; guinea hen.

цех *n.* **1,** shop (*in a factory*). **2,** *hist.* guild.

цехово́й *adj.* shop (*attrib.*). —**цехово́й профсою́з,** craft union.

цеце́ *n.f. indecl.* [*often* му́ха цеце́] tsetse fly.

циа́н *n.* cyanogen.

циани́д *n.* cyanide.

циани́стый *adj.* cyanic. —**циани́стый ка́лий,** potassium cyanide.

циа́новый *adj.* cyanic.

циано́з *n.* cyanosis.

цивилиза́ция *n.* civilization.

цивилизо́ванный *adj.* civilized.

цивилизова́ть *v. impfv. & pfv.* [*pres.* -зу́ю, -зу́ешь] to civilize.

циви́льный *adj., obs.* civilian.

цига́рка [*gen. pl.* -рок] *n., colloq.* hand-rolled cigarette.

циге́йка *n.* fur of the tsigai sheep (*a common variety in the USSR*).

цика́да *n.* cicada.

цикл *n.* cycle.

цикламе́н *n.* cyclamen.

цикли́ческий *adj.* cyclical. *Also,* **цикли́чный.**

цикло́н *n.* cyclone. —**циклони́ческий,** *adj.* cyclonic.

циклотро́н *n.* cyclotron.

цико́рий *n.* chicory. —**цико́рный,** *adj.* chicory (*attrib.*).

цику́та *n.* water hemlock.

цили́ндр *n.* **1,** cylinder. **2,** top hat. —**цилиндри́ческий,** *adj.* cylindrical.

цимба́лы [*gen.* -ба́л] *n. pl.* dulcimer.

цинга́ *n.* scurvy.

цини́зм *n.* cynicism. —**ци́ник,** *n.* cynic.

цини́ческий *adj.* = **цини́чный.**

цини́чный *adj.* **1,** cynical. **2,** indecent; off-color. —**цини́чность,** *n.f.* cynicism.

цинк *n.* zinc. —**ци́нковый,** *adj.* zinc (*attrib.*).

ци́нния *n.* zinnia.

цино́вка [*gen. pl.* -вок] *n.* mat.

цирк *n.* circus.

цирка́ч [*gen.* -кача́] *n., colloq.* circus performer.

цирково́й *adj.* circus (*attrib.*).

цирко́н *n.* zircon.

цирко́ний *n.* zirconium.

циркули́ровать *v. impfv.* [*pres.* -рую, -руешь] to circulate.

ци́ркуль *n.m.* pair of compasses (*for drawing*).

циркуля́р *n.* circular; directive.

циркуля́ция *n.* circulation.

цирро́з *n.* cirrhosis.

цирю́льник *n., obs.* barber.

цирю́льня [*gen. pl.* -лен] *n., obs.* barbershop.

цисте́рна *n.* **1,** cistern; tank. **2,** tank car.

цитаде́ль (дэ) *n.f.* citadel.

цита́та *n.* quotation.

ци́тирование *n.* quoting; citing.

цити́ровать *v. impfv.* [*pfv.* процити́ровать; *pres.* -рую, -руешь] to quote; cite.

цитоло́гия *n.* cytology. —**цитологи́ческий,** *adj.* cytological.

ци́тра *n.* zither.

цитра́т *n.* citrate.

ци́трус *n.* citrus.

ци́трусовый *adj.* citrus. —**ци́трусовые,** *n. pl.* citrus plants.

цифербла́т *n.* dial (*of an instrument*); face (*of a clock*).

ци́фра *n.* number; numeral; figure.

цифрово́й *adj.* numerical. —**цифрова́я вычисли́тельная маши́на,** digital computer.

ци́церо *n. neut. or m. indecl., typog.* pica.

цо́кать *v. impfv.* [*pfv.* цо́кнуть] to clatter; clank.

цо́коль *n.m.* socle.

цо́кот *n.* clatter; clank.

цуг *n.* team of horses harnessed in tandem or in pairs. —**цу́гом,** in tandem.

цука́т *n.* candied fruit; candied peel.

цыга́н [*pl.* цыга́не, цыга́н, цыга́нам] *n.m.* [*fem.* цыга́нка] Gypsy. —**цыга́нский,** *adj.* Gypsy.

цы́пки [*gen.* -пок] *n. pl., colloq.* red spots (*on the skin*).

цыпле́нок [*gen.* -нка; *pl.* цыпля́та, цыпля́т] *n.* chicken; chick.

цы́почки *n. pl.* tiptoes. —**стать на цы́почки,** to stand on one's tiptoes. —**ходи́ть на цы́почках,** to tiptoe.

Ч

Ч, ч *n. neut.* 24th letter of the Russian alphabet.

чаба́н [*gen.* -бана́] *n.* shepherd.

чабёр [*gen.* -бра́] *n.* savory (*plant*). *Also,* **ча́бер** [*gen.* -бра].

чабре́ц *also,* **чебре́ц** [*gen.* -реца́] *n.* thyme.

ча́вкать *v. impfv.* **1,** to munch; eat noisily. **2,** to tramp; tread noisily.

чад [*2nd loc.* чаду́] *n.* **1,** fumes. **2,** daze: быть (как) в чаду, to be in a daze.

чади́ть *v. impfv.* [*pfv.* **начади́ть**; *pres.* **чажу́, чади́шь**] **1,** to smoke; emit fumes. **2,** (*with instr.*) to give off (*while smoking, cooking, etc.*).

ча́дный *adj.* **1,** smoky. **2,** smoking. **3,** *fig.* dazed. **4,** *fig.* deadening.

ча́до *n., archaic* offspring; child.

чадра́ *n.* veil worn by Moslem women.

чаёвничать *v. impfv., colloq.* to (leisurely) drink tea.

чаевы́е *n. pl., decl. as an adj.* tip; gratuity.

чаепи́тие *n.* drinking of tea.

чаи́нка [*gen. pl.* -нок] *n.* tea leaf.

чай [*2nd gen.* ча́ю] *n.* tea. —**дать на чай** (+ *dat.*), to tip (someone).

ча́йка [*gen. pl.* ча́ек] *n.* gull; sea gull.

ча́йная *n., decl. as an adj.* tearoom.

ча́йник *n.* teakettle; teapot.

ча́йница *n.* tea caddy.

ча́йный *adj.* tea (*attrib.*). —**ча́йная ло́жка,** teaspoon. —**ча́йная ча́шка,** teacup.

чал *n.* mooring line.

ча́лить *v. impfv.* to moor (a ship).

ча́лка [*gen. pl.* -лок] *n.* mooring line.

чалма́ *n.* turban.

ча́лый *adj.* roan.

чан [*pl.* чаны́] *n.* vat.

ча́ра *n., archaic* goblet.

ча́рка [*gen. pl.* -рок] *n., archaic* cup.

чарова́ть *v. impfv.* [*pres.* -ру́ю, -ру́ешь] to charm; captivate.

чаровни́ца *n.* charming woman; enchantress.

чароде́й *n.* **1,** sorcerer; magician. **2,** *fig.* charmer. —**чароде́йка,** *n.* sorceress; *fig.* enchantress. —**чаро-де́йство,** *n.* sorcery; witchcraft.

чару́ющий *adj.* charming; captivating; enchanting.

ча́ры [*gen.* чар] *n. pl.* **1,** *obs.* magic charm. **2,** charm; charms.

час [*gen.* ча́са, *but after* 2, 3, & 4 часа́; *pl.* часы́, часо́в] *n.* **1,** hour. **2,** (*in telling time*) o'clock: пять часо́в, five o'clock; в семь часо́в, at seven o'clock. Час дня, 1 P.M.; час но́чи, 1 A.M. —**в до́брый час!**, good luck! —**в кото́ром часу́?**, (at) what time? —**кото́рый (тепе́рь) час?**, what time is it? —**расти́ не по дням, а по часа́м,** to grow by the hour; shoot up like a beanstalk. —**с ча́су на час,** at any hour; at any moment. —**час от часу,** by the hour; by the minute: ему́ стано́вится лу́чше час от часу, he is getting better by the minute; he is improving steadily. —**час от часу не ле́гче!**, things are getting worse by the minute. *See also* **часы́.**

часо́вня [*gen. pl.* -вен] *n.* chapel.

часово́й *adj.* **1,** lasting an hour; hour-long. **2,** hourly; per hour. **3,** *colloq.* one-o'clock (*attrib.*). **4,** clock (*attrib.*); watch (*attrib.*). —*n.* sentry. —**часово́й по́яс,** time zone. —**часова́я стре́лка,** hour hand. —**часовы́е стре́лки,** hands of a clock. —**по часово́й стре́лке,** clockwise. —**про́тив часово́й стре́лки,** counterclockwise.

часовщи́к [*gen.* -щика́] *n.* watchmaker.

часте́нько *adv., colloq.* fairly often.

части́ца *n.* **1,** small part. **2,** particle: части́ца пы́ли, particle of dust. **3,** *gram.* particle.

части́чный *adj.* partial. —**части́чно,** *adv.* partly; partially.

ча́стник *n., colloq.* private trader.

ча́стное *n., decl. as an adj.* **1,** *math.* quotient. **2,** the particular.

ча́стность *n.f.* detail. —**в ча́стности,** in particular; specifically.

ча́стный *adj.* **1,** private. **2,** particular; individual. —**ча́стный ито́г,** subtotal. —**ча́стным о́бразом,** privately. *See also* **ча́стное.**

ча́сто *adv.* **1,** often; frequently. **2,** densely; close together.

частоко́л *n.* fence; paling.

частота́ *n.* **1,** frequency: частота́ слу́чаев, frequency of cases. **2,** [*pl.* часто́ты] *physics; radio* frequency: ультравысо́кая частота́, ultrahigh frequency.

часто́тный *adj.* frequency (*attrib.*).

часту́шка [*gen. pl.* -шек] *n.* ditty; jingle.

ча́стый *adj.* [*comp.* ча́ще] **1,** frequent. **2,** quick; rapid; rapid-fire. **3,** dense; thick. **4,** set close together; close. **5,** (*of a comb, sieve, etc.*) fine. **6,** (*of rain*) steady.

часть [*pl.* ча́сти, часте́й, частя́м] *n.f.* **1,** part: ра́вные ча́сти, equal parts; запасны́е ча́сти, spare parts. Ча́сти те́ла, parts of the body. **2,** *mil.* unit. **3,** department: уче́бная часть, teaching department. **4,** *colloq.* field; sphere: не по мое́й ча́сти, out of my line/pro-vince. —**бо́льшая часть** (+ *gen.*), most (of). —**боль-**

шей ча́стью; по бо́льшей ча́сти, for the most part. —по частя́м, in parts; piecemeal.

ча́стью adv. partly; in part.

часы́ [gen. часо́в] n. pl. 1, clock; watch. 2, mil. sentry duty: стоя́ть на часа́х, to stand guard. 3, in песо́чные часы́, hourglass; со́лнечные часы́, sundial. —рабо́тать как часы́, to work like clockwork; perform flawlessly.

ча́хлый adj. 1, (of a person) sickly. 2, (of plants) withered.

ча́хнуть v. impfv. [pfv. зача́хнуть; past чах or ча́хнул, ча́хла, ча́хло] 1, (of plants) to wither; wilt. 2, (of persons) to become weak; fade; waste away.

чахо́тка n., colloq. consumption; tuberculosis. —чахо́точный, adj., colloq. consumptive.

ча́ша n. 1, drinking bowl (used in olden times). Кругова́я ча́ша, loving cup. 2, large bowl. —ча́ша весо́в, scale: склони́ть ча́шу весо́в в по́льзу (+ gen.), to tip the scales in favor of. —ча́ша терпе́ния, one's patience.

чашели́стик n. sepal.

ча́шечка [gen. pl. -чек] n. 1, small cup. 2, bot. calyx. —коле́нная ча́шечка, kneecap.

ча́шка [gen. pl. -шек] n. cup. —коле́нная ча́шка, kneecap.

ча́ща n. dense forest.

ча́ще adj., comp. of ча́стый. —adv., comp. of ча́сто. —ча́ще всего́, most often; usually.

чащо́ба n., colloq. = ча́ща.

ча́яние n. hope; expectation. —па́че ча́яния, see па́че.

ча́ять v. impfv. [pres. ча́ю, ча́ешь] obs. to expect; hope. —души́ не ча́ять в (+ prep.), to idolize; adore; dote upon.

чва́ниться v.r. impfv. to swagger; boast.

чванли́вый adj. conceited; pretentious.

чва́нный adj. arrogant; conceited.

чва́нство n. arrogance; conceit.

чебре́ц n. = чабре́ц.

чебуре́к n. mutton pie (Caucasian dish).

чего́ (vo) pron., gen. of что. —adv., colloq. why?; what for?: чего́ я туда́ пойду́?, why should I go there? —до чего́, how!: до чего́ она́ краси́ва!, how lovely she is! —по́сле чего́, after which. —чего́ бы не, what: чего́ бы он не дал за э́то!, what he wouldn't give for that! —чего́ до́брого, for all one knows.

чей [fem. чья; neut. чьё; pl. чьи; gen. чьего́, чьей, чьих; acc. fem. чью; dat. чьему́, чьей, чьим; instr. чьим, чьей, чьи́ми; prepl. чьём, чьей, чьих] poss. pron. 1, interr. whose?: чья э́та шля́па?, whose hat is this? 2, rel. whose: челове́к, чьё и́мя изве́стно всем, a man whose name is known to all.

чей-либо [infl. like чей] indef. pron. = чей-нибудь.

чей-нибудь [infl. like чей] indef. pron. someone's; somebody's; anyone's; anybody's.

чей-то [infl. like чей] indef. pron. someone's; somebody's.

чек n. 1, check. 2, bill; receipt.

чека́ n. pin; linchpin.

Чека́ n. fem. indecl., contr. of Чрезвыча́йная коми́ссия, Cheka (Soviet security agency, 1917-22).

чека́н n. stamp; punch; die.

чека́нить v. impfv. [pfv. отчека́нить] 1, to mint; coin. 2, to engrave; emboss. 3, fig. to articulate.

чека́нка n. 1, minting (of coins); mintage. 2, embossed design.

чека́нный adj. 1, engraving. 2, engraved; embossed. 3, fig. precise; crisp.

чеки́ст n. member of the Cheka.

че́ковый adj. check (attrib.); checking. —че́ковая кни́жка, checkbook.

челе́ста n. celesta.

чёлка n. bangs (of hair): носи́ть чёлку, to wear bangs.

чёлн [gen. челна́; pl. челны́ or чёлны] n. canoe.

челно́к [gen. -нока́] n. 1, = чёлн. 2, shuttle. —челно́чный, adj. shuttle (attrib.).

чело́ [pl. чёла] n., archaic forehead; brow. —бить чело́м (+ dat.), 1, to bow humbly before. 2, to beseech. 3, to thank earnestly.

челове́к [gen. pl. челове́к; other pl. forms rarely used] n. 1, person; man. 2, man; mankind: челове́к — разу́мное существо́, man is a rational being.

человеконенави́стник n. misanthrope. —человеконенави́стнический, adj. misanthropic. —человеконенави́стничество, n. misanthropy.

человекообра́зный adj. anthropomorphous; anthropoid.

человекоподо́бный adj. anthropoid; manlike.

челове́ко-ча́с [pl. -часы́, -часо́в] n. man-hour.

челове́ческий adj. 1, human. 2, humane. —челове́ческий род, the human race.

челове́чество n. mankind; humanity.

челове́чный adj. humane. —челове́чность, n.f. humaneness; humanity.

че́люсть n.f. 1, jaw; jawbone. 2, denture; set of false teeth. —челюстно́й, adj. jaw (attrib.); jawbone (attrib.).

че́лядь n.f. servants.

чем pron., instr. of что. —conj. 1, than: лу́чше по́здно, чем никогда́, better late than never. Бо́льше чем когда́-либо ра́ньше, more than ever before. 2, (with тем) the..., the...: чем ра́ньше, тем лу́чше, the sooner the better. 3, (with inf.) instead of; rather than.

чём pron., prepl. of что.

чемери́ца n. hellebore.

чемода́н n. suitcase. —чемода́нчик, n. small suitcase.

чемпио́н n. champion. —чемпиона́т, n. championship (tournament). —чемпио́нский, adj. championship (attrib.). —чемпио́нство, n. championship.

чему́ pron., dat. of что.

чепе́ц [gen. -пца́] n. cap worn indoors by elderly women, usually tied under the chin.

чепуха́ n., colloq. 1, nonsense. 2, trifling matter. 3, trifling amount.

че́пчик n. 1, dim. of чепе́ц. 2, (baby's) bonnet.

червеобра́зный adj. vermiform. —червеобра́зный отро́сток, vermiform appendix.

че́рви [gen. -ве́й] n. pl., cards hearts.

черви́веть v. impfv. [pfv. очерви́веть] to become wormy.

черви́вый adj. worm-eaten; wormy.

черво́нец [gen. -нца] n. 1, pre-rev. three-ruble gold coin. 2, ten-ruble note in use from 1922 through 1947.

черво́нный adj. 1, archaic red; scarlet. 2, cards of hearts: черво́нный туз, ace of hearts. —черво́нное зо́лото, pure gold.

червото́чина n. 1, wormhole. 2, fig. flaw.

че́рвы [gen. черв] n. pl. = че́рви.

червь [gen. червя́; pl. че́рви, черве́й, червя́м] n.m. worm.

червя́к [*gen.* -вяка́] *n.* = **червь.** —**замори́ть червя-**
ка́, *colloq.* to have a bite to eat.

червя́чный *adj., mech.* worm (*attrib.*): червя́чная
шестерня́, worm gear.

червячо́к [*gen.* -чка́] *n.* small worm. —**замори́ть**
червячка́, *colloq.* to have a bite to eat.

черда́к [*gen.* -дака́] *n.* attic. —**черда́чный,** *adj.* attic
(*attrib.*).

черёд [*gen.* череда́] *n.*, *colloq.* **1,** (one's) turn. **2,** time:
наста́л черёд (+ *inf.*), the time has come to... —**идти́**
свои́м чередо́м, to take its normal course.

череда́ *n.* **1,** *obs.* = **черёд. 2,** column; file. **3,** *fig.*
sequence; chain. **4,** bur marigold (*flower*).

чередова́ние *n.* alternation.

чередова́ть *v. impfv.* [*pres.* -ду́ю, -ду́ешь] to alternate. —**чередова́ться,** *refl.* to alternate; take turns.

че́рез *prep., with acc.* **1,** across: перейти́ че́рез у́ли-
цу, to walk across the street; cross the street. **2,** over:
перепры́гнуть че́рез забо́р, to jump over the fence.
3, through: идти́ че́рез лес, to walk through the forest.
4, via; by way of: е́хать че́рез Минск, to go by way of
Minsk. **5,** in (*expressing time from the present*): я при-
ду́ че́рез де́сять мину́т, I'll come in ten minutes. **6,**
after (*an interval of*): верну́ться че́рез год, to return
after a year; че́рез де́сять лет по́сле войны́, ten years
after the war. **7,** through; with the aid of: говори́ть
че́рез перево́дчика, to speak through an interpreter.
8, *indicating intervals of two:* че́рез день, every other
day. Они́ живу́т че́рез дом от нас, they live two
houses away from us. **9,** *indicating a specified interval:*
печа́тать че́рез два интерва́ла, to double-space. Они́
живу́т че́рез три до́ма отсю́да, they live three houses
away.

черёмуха *n.* a kind of cherry tree.

черено́к [*gen.* -нка́] *n.* **1,** handle; haft. **2,** cutting;
graft.

че́реп [*pl.* черепа́] *n.* skull; cranium.

черепа́ха *n.* **1,** turtle; tortoise. **2,** tortoise shell.

черепа́ховый *adj.* **1,** turtle (*attrib.*). **2,** tortoise-shell
(*attrib.*).

черепа́ший [*fem.* -шья] *adj.* **1,** turtle (*attrib.*); turtle's.
2, *fig.* snail-like: черепа́шьим ша́гом, at a snail's pace.

черепи́ца *n.* (unglazed) tile. —**черепи́чный,** *adj.* tile
(*attrib.*); tiled.

черепно́й *adj.* cranial. —**черепна́я коро́бка,** cranium.

черепо́к [*gen.* -пка́] *n.* fragment of pottery. —**раз-**
би́ться в черепки́, to be smashed to smithereens.

черессе́дельник *n.* saddle girth.

чересчу́р *adv.* **1,** too. **2,** (*with verbs*) too much. —**че-**
ресчу́р мно́го, too much; too many.

чере́шневый *adj.* cherry (*attrib.*).

чере́шня [*gen. pl.* -шен] *n.* **1,** sweet cherries. **2,** a
(single) sweet cherry. **3,** cherry tree.

черешо́к [*gen.* -шка́] *n.* **1,** petiole. **2,** = **черено́к.**

черка́ть *also,* **чёркать** *v. impfv.* [*pfv.* черкну́ть] *col-*
loq. **1,** (*with* по) to scratch; leave a mark on. **2,** [*impfv.*
only] to cross out (a word or words); mark up (a page).

черке́с *n.m.* [*fem.* **черке́шенка**] Circassian. —**черке́с-**
ский, *adj.* Circassian.

черкну́ть *v. pfv., colloq.* **1,** *pfv. of* **черка́ть. 2,** to write;
dash off: черкни́те мне не́сколько слов, drop me
a line.

черне́ть *v. impfv.* [*pfv.* почерне́ть] **1,** to turn black.
2, [*impfv. only*] (*of anything black*) to appear; loom.

черни́ка *n.* **1,** blueberries; huckleberries; whortleber-

ries. **2,** a single such berry. **3,** a bush yielding any of
these berries.

черни́ла [*gen.* -ни́л] *n. pl.* ink.

черни́льница *n.* inkwell.

черни́льный *adj.* ink (*attrib.*). —**черни́льный каран-**
да́ш, indelible pencil. —**черни́льный оре́шек,** gallnut.

черни́ть *v. impfv.* **1,** [*pfv.* начерни́ть] to blacken;
make black. **2,** [*pfv.* очерни́ть] to blacken; slander;
defame.

черни́чный *adj.* blueberry (*attrib.*); huckleberry (*at-*
trib.); whortleberry (*attrib.*).

чёрно-бе́лый *adj.* black-and-white.

чёрно-бу́рый *adj.* dark brown. —**чёрно-бу́рая ли-**
си́ца, silver fox.

чернови́к [*gen.* -вика́] *n.* rough draft; rough copy.

черново́й *adj.* (*of something written*) rough; preliminary.

черного́рец [*gen.* -рца] *n.m.* [*fem.* -рка] Montenegrin. —**черного́рский,** *adj.* Montenegrin.

чернозём *n.* rich black topsoil of central European Russia; chernozem.

черноко́жий *adj.* dark-skinned; black. —*n.* black man;
black.

черном́азый *adj., colloq.* swarthy; dark-complexioned.

чернорабо́чий *adj.* unskilled. —*n.* unskilled laborer.

черносли́в *n.* prunes.

чернота́ *n.* blackness; darkness.

чёрный *adj.* **1,** black. **2,** (*of a door, yard, staircase,*
etc.) back. **3,** *fig.* dark; somber. —*n.* **1,** black; negro. **2,**
neut. black (clothes): она́ была́ вся в чёрном, she was
all in black. **3,** *pl., chess* black: игра́ть чёрными, to
be black; play the black pieces. —**бере́чь на чёр-**
ный день, to put aside for a rainy day. —**чёрное**
де́рево, ebony. —**чёрная доска́,** blackboard. —**чёр-**
ный дрозд, blackbird. —**чёрные мета́ллы,** ferrous
metals. —**чёрная рабо́та,** menial work; dirty work.
—**чёрный ры́нок,** black market. —**чёрный спи́сок,**
blacklist. —**чёрным по бе́лому,** in black and white;
in the clearest possible terms.

чернь *n.f., obs.* rabble; riffraff.

черпа́к [*gen.* -пака́] *n.* scoop.

черпа́лка [*gen. pl.* -лок] *n., colloq.* scoop.

че́рпать *v. impfv.* [*pfv.* черпну́ть] **1,** to draw (water);
scoop up (dirt, sand, etc.). **2,** [*impfv. only*] *fig.* to draw;
derive; cull.

черстве́ть *v. impfv.* **1,** [*pfv.* зачерстве́ть *or* по-
черстве́ть] (*of bread*) to become stale. **2,** [*pfv.* очерст-
ве́ть] to become callous; become hardhearted.

чёрствый *adj.* **1,** stale. **2,** callous; hardhearted.
—**чёрствость,** *n.f.* callousness.

чёрт [*pl.* че́рти, черте́й, черт́ям] *n.* devil. —**до чёрта,**
colloq. **1,** awfully. **2,** (*with gen.*) plenty (of); galore.
—**иди́ к чёрту!,** go to hell! —**к чёрту!,** to hell with
it! —**како́го чёрта** (+ *subject & verb*), what the hell
is/does...? —**на кой чёрт?,** *colloq.* what the hell for?
—**ни черта́,** *colloq.* not a thing. —**чёрт возьми́!; чёрт**
побери́!, what the hell? —**чёрт (его́) зна́ет!,** God
knows! —**чёрт с** (+ *instr.*), to hell with...!

черта́ *n.* **1,** line. **2,** boundary. В черте́ го́рода, within
the city limits. **3,** *pl.* features: черты́ лица́, facial features. **4,** trait; feature; characteristic. —**в о́бщих чер-**
та́х, in general terms; in broad outline.

чертёж [*gen.* -тежа́] *n.* drawing; draft; design.

чертёжник *n.* draftsman.

чертёжный *adj.* drawing (*attrib.*).

чертёнок [*gen.* -нка; *pl.* -тенята, -тенят] *n.*, *colloq.* little devil; imp.

чертить *v. impfv.* [*pfv.* начертить; *pres.* черчу, чёртишь] to draw (a line, figure, map, diagram, etc.).

чёртов *adj.* of the devil; devil's. —**чёртова дюжина,** baker's dozen. —**чёртово колесо,** Ferris wheel.

чертовски *adv.*, *colloq.* awfully: чертовски рад, awfully glad. Чертовски сердит, mad as hell. Чертовски голоден, famished. Чертовски далеко, a hell of a long way.

чертовский *adj.* **1,** of the devil; devilish. **2,** *colloq.* hellish; damnable.

чертовщина *n.* **1,** devils. **2,** *fig.*, *colloq.* something awful or ridiculous.

чертог *n.*, *obs.* **1,** chamber. **2,** palace.

чертополох *n.* thistle.

чёрточка [*gen. pl.* -чек] *n.* **1,** line. **2,** hyphen.

чертыхаться *v.r. impfv.* [*pfv.* чертыхнуться] *colloq.* to swear; curse.

черчение *n.* drawing. —**техническое черчение,** mechanical drawing.

чесалка [*gen. pl.* -лок] *n.* combing (*or* carding) machine.

чесальный *adj.* combing (*attrib.*); carding (*attrib.*).

чесание *n.* combing; carding.

чесать *v. impfv.* [*pfv.* почесать; *pres.* чешу, чёшешь] **1,** to scratch (*to relieve an itch*). **2,** [*impfv. only*] *colloq.* to comb (hair). **3,** [*impfv. only*] to comb; card (flax, cotton, etc.). —**чесать затылок** (*or* в затылке), *colloq.* to scratch one's head (*in puzzlement*). —**чесать язык** (*or* языком), *colloq.* to babble; prattle.

чесаться *v.r. impfv.* [*pres.* чешусь, чёшешься] **1,** to itch: у меня чёшется спина, my back itches. *Also fig.* у него чёшутся руки (+ *inf.*), he is itching to... **2,** [*pfv.* почесаться] to scratch oneself (*to relieve itching*). **3,** *colloq.* to comb one's hair.

чеснок [*gen.* -нока] *n.* garlic. —**чесночный,** *adj.* garlic (*attrib.*).

чесотка *n.* scabies; mange.

чествование *n.* **1,** honoring. **2,** celebration (*in honor of someone*).

чествовать *v. impfv.* [*pres.* -ствую, -ствуешь] to honor; pay tribute to.

честить *v. impfv.* [*pres.* чещу, честишь] **1,** *obs.* to honor. **2,** *obs.* to call (by a name or title). **3,** *ironic*, *colloq.* to curse out; vilify.

честно *adv.* honestly. —**честно говоря,** to be honest...; in all honesty.

честной *adj.*, *obs.* honored.

честность *n.f.* honesty.

честный *adj.* honest. —**честное слово!,** word of honor!; honest to goodness!

честолюбец [*gen.* -бца] *n.* ambitious person.

честолюбивый *adj.* ambitious. —**честолюбие,** *n.* ambition.

честь *n.f.* **1,** honor: в честь (+ *gen.*), in honor of. **2,** credit: делать честь (+ *dat.*), to be a credit to. —**отдавать честь** (+ *dat.*), to salute. —**пора и честь знать, 1,** it's time to stop. **2,** it's time we were going. —**с честью,** with distinction; with flying colors. —**честь честью,** properly.

чёт *n.*, *colloq.* even number.

чета *n.* **1,** pair; couple. **2,** married couple. —**не чета**

(+ *dat.*), **1,** not the equal of; no match for. **2,** too good for; head and shoulders above.

четверг [*gen.* -верга] *n.* Thursday. —**после дождичка в четверг,** *colloq.* who knows when?

четвереньки *n. pl.*, *in* на четвереньках, on one's hands and knees; on all fours.

четвёрка *n.* **1,** the numeral 4. **2,** *colloq.* anything numbered 4. **3,** team of four horses. **4,** a grade of "four", signifying "good". **5,** *cards* four.

четверной *adj.* quadruple; fourfold.

четверня *n.* **1,** team of four horses. **2,** *colloq.* quadruplets.

четверо [*gen. & prepl.* -рых; *dat.* -рым; *instr.* -рыми] *collective numeral* four.

четвероногий *adj.* four-legged. —**четвероногое,** *n.* quadruped.

четверостишие *n.* quatrain.

четвертак [*gen.* -така] *n.*, *obs.* twenty-five kopecks.

четвёртка [*gen. pl.* -ток] *n.*, *obs.* quarter.

четвертной *adj.* **1,** *in* четвертная нота, *music* quarter note. **2,** (*of a grade*) for a (school) quarter. **3,** *obs.* twenty-five-ruble. —**четвертная,** *n.*, *obs.* twenty-five-ruble note.

четвертование *n.* (execution by) quartering.

четвертовать *v. impfv. & pfv.* [*pres.* -тую, -туешь] to quarter (*as a method of execution*).

четвёртый *ordinal numeral* fourth.

четверть *n.f.* quarter; fourth: три четверти, three quarters; three fourths (¾). Четверть шестого, a quarter past five; без четверти семь, a quarter to seven.

четвертьфинал *n.* quarterfinal. —**четвертьфинальный,** *adj.* quarterfinal.

чётки [*gen.* -ток] *n. pl.* rosary (*beads*).

чёткий *adj.* [*short form* чёток, четка, чётко; *comp.* чётче] **1,** clear; distinct. **2,** clear-cut. **3,** precise. **4,** efficient.

чётко *adv.* **1,** clearly; distinctly. **2,** smartly: чётко шагать, to step smartly.

чёткость *n.f.* **1,** clarity. **2,** precision. **3,** efficiency.

чётный *adj.* (*of a number*) even.

четыре [*gen. & prepl.* четырёх; *dat.* четырём; *instr.* четырьмя] *numeral* four.

четырежды *adv.* four times.

четыреста [*gen.* четырёхсот; *dat.* четырёмстам; *instr.* четырьмястами; *prepl.* четырёхстах] *numeral* four hundred.

четырёхгодичный *adj.* four-year (*attrib.*).

четырёхголосный *adj.*, *music* four-part.

четырёхгранник *n.* tetrahedron. —**четырёхгранный,** *adj.* tetrahedral.

четырёхдневный *adj.* four-day (*attrib.*).

четырёхклассный *adj.* (*of schools or courses*) four-year.

четырёхколёсный *adj.* four-wheel(ed).

четырёхкратный *adj.* fourfold; quadruple.

четырёхлетие *n.* **1,** fourth anniversary; fourth birthday. **2,** four-year period.

четырёхлетний *adj.* **1,** four-year (*attrib.*). **2,** four-year-old.

четырёхмесячный *adj.* **1,** four-month (*attrib.*). **2,** four-month-old.

четырёхнедельный *adj.* **1,** four-week (*attrib.*). **2,** four-week-old.

четырёхсотлетие *n.* four-hundredth anniversary.

—**четырёхсотле́тний**, *adj.* four-hundred-year (*attrib.*).

четырёхсо́тый *ordinal numeral* four-hundredth.

четырёхсто́пный *adj.* tetrameter. —**четырёхсто́пный стих**, tetrameter. —**четырёхсто́пный ямб**, iambic tetrameter.

четырёхсторо́нний *adj.* four-sided; quadrilateral.

четырёхуго́льник *n.* quadrangle. —**четырёхуго́льный**, *adj.* quadrangular.

четырёхэта́жный *adj.* four-story.

четы́рнадцатый *ordinal numeral* fourteenth.

четы́рнадцать *numeral* fourteen.

чех *n.m.* [*fem.* **че́шка**] Czech.

чехарда́ *n.* leapfrog.

чехо́л [*gen.* **чехла́**] *n.* **1,** cover; slip cover. **2,** case.

чехослова́цкий *adj.* Czechoslovak.

чечеви́ца *n.* **1,** lentil. **2,** *obs.* lens. —**чечеви́чный**, *adj.* lentil (*attrib.*).

чече́нец [*gen.* **-нца**] *n.m.* [*fem.* **-нка**] Chechen (*one of a people inhabiting the Caucasus*). —**чече́нский**, *adj.* Chechen.

чече́тка [*gen. pl.* **-ток**] *n.* **1,** tap dance. **2,** redpoll (*bird*).

че́шский *adj.* Czech.

чешу́йчатый *adj.* scaly.

чешуя́ *n.* scales (*of a fish, snake, etc.*).

чи́бис *n.* lapwing; pewit.

чиж [*gen.* **чижа́**] *n.* siskin (*bird*).

чили́ец [*gen.* **-и́йца**] *n.m.* [*fem.* **-и́йка**] Chilean. —**чили́йский**, *adj.* Chilean.

чин [*pl.* **чины́**] *n.* rank; grade. —**чин чи́ном**, properly.

чина́р *also,* **чина́ра** *n.* Oriental plane tree.

чини́ть *v. impfv.* **1,** [*pfv.* **почини́ть**; *pres.* **чиню́, чи́нишь**] to fix; mend; repair. **2,** [*pfv.* **очини́ть**; *pres.* **чиню́, чи́нишь**] to sharpen (a pencil). **3,** [*pfv.* **учини́ть**; *pres.* **чиню́, чи́нишь**] to carry out. Чини́ть препя́тствия (+ *dat.*), to put obstacles in someone's way.

чини́ться *v.r. impfv., obs.* to stand on ceremony.

чи́нный *adj.* decorous; sedate. —**чи́нность**, *n.f.* decorum; propriety.

чино́вник *n.* **1,** official; functionary. **2,** bureaucrat.

чино́внический *adj.* **1,** official's; officials'. **2,** bureaucratic.

чино́вничество *n.* **1,** officials; officialdom. **2,** bureaucracy.

чино́вничий [*fem.* **-чья**] *adj.* = **чино́внический**.

чино́вный *adj., obs.* high-ranking.

чи́псы [*gen.* **-сов**] *n. pl.* potato chips.

чи́рей [*gen.* **чи́рья**] *n., colloq.* boil; abscess.

чири́канье *n.* chirping; twittering.

чири́кать *v. impfv.* to chirp; twitter.

чи́ркать *v. impfv.* [*pfv.* **чи́ркнуть**] **1,** (*with* **о** + *acc. or* **по**) to rub (something) against. **2,** (*with instr.*) to strike (a match).

чиро́к [*gen.* **-рка́**] *n.* teal.

чи́сленно *adv.* numerically.

чи́сленность *n.f.* number; size; numerical strength. —**чи́сленностью в** (+ *acc.*), numbering.

чи́сленный *adj.* numerical.

числи́тель *n.m.* numerator.

числи́тельное *n., decl. as an adj., gram.* numeral. *Also,* **и́мя числи́тельное**.

чи́слить *v. impfv.* **1,** *obs.* to count; calculate. **2,** to list; put down; record. **3,** (*with instr.*) to consider; regard (as). —**чи́слиться**, *refl.* **1,** to be listed; be put down; be recorded. **2,** (*with* **за** + *instr.*) to be put down under the name of; *fig.* be attributed to. **3,** to number: в го́роде чи́слится сто ты́сяч челове́к, the city has a population of 100,000. **4,** (*with instr.*) to be considered; be regarded (as).

число́ [*pl.* **чи́сла, чи́сел**] *n.* **1,** number: чётное число́, even number. **2,** number; quantity. **3,** date; day (*of the month*): како́е сего́дня число́?, what is today's date? В после́дних чи́слах декабря́, in the last days of December. **4,** *gram.* number: еди́нственное число́, singular; мно́жественное число́, plural. **5,** *pl., cap., Bib.* (book of) Numbers. —**в том числе́**, including. —**в числе́** (+ *gen.*), among.

числово́й *adj.* numerical.

чи́стик *n.* guillemot (*bird*).

чи́стилище *n.* purgatory.

чи́стильщик *n.* cleaner. —**чи́стильщик сапо́г**, shoeshine boy; bootblack.

чи́стить *v. impfv.* [*pfv.* **почи́стить** *or* **вы́чистить**; *pres.* **чи́щу, чи́стишь**] **1,** to clean. **2,** to clean out; clear out. **3,** to clear (a road); dredge (a river). **4,** [*pfv.* **очи́стить**] to peel; pare. **5,** to shine (shoes); brush (one's teeth). **6,** *fig., colloq.* to purge.

чи́стка *n.* **1,** cleaning. **2,** purge.

чи́сто *adv.* **1,** cleanly; neatly. **2,** purely. **3,** just like: она́ рассужда́ет чи́сто по-же́нски, she reasons just like a woman. —*adj., used predicatively* clean: здесь чи́сто, it is clean here. —**чи́сто-на́чисто**, spotlessly clean.

чистови́к [*gen.* **-вика́**] *n., colloq.* final draft.

чистово́й *adj.* (*of a copy, manuscript, etc.*) final; clean.

чистога́н *n., colloq.* cash.

чистокро́вный *adj.* thoroughbred.

чистописа́ние *n.* penmanship.

чистопло́тный *adj.* clean; neat; tidy; cleanly.

чистопоро́дный *adj.* thoroughbred.

чистосерде́чие *n.* open-heartedness; sincerity. —**чистосерде́чный**, *adj.* open-hearted; sincere.

чистота́ *n.* **1,** cleanliness. **2,** purity.

чи́стый *adj.* [*comp.* **чи́ще**] **1,** clean. **2,** pure. **3,** clear. **4,** (*of income, weight, etc.*) net. **5,** *colloq.* pure; sheer; utter. —**чи́стой** *or* **чисте́йшей воды́**, of the first water; of the first order. —**чи́стое по́ле**, open country.

чита́льный *adj., in* **чита́льный зал**, reading room.

чита́льня [*gen. pl.* **-лен**] *n.* reading room.

чита́тель *n.m.* reader. —**чита́тельский**, *adj.* reader's; readers'.

чита́ть *v. impfv.* [*pfv.* **прочита́ть** *or* **проче́сть**] **1,** to read. **2,** to recite (a poem, prayer, etc.). **3,** to give; deliver (a lecture, sermon, etc.); give; teach (a course). —**чита́ться**, *refl.* [*impfv. only*] **1,** to be read. **2,** to be legible. **3,** (*of a book*) to read (easily, quickly, etc.). **4,** (*used negatively with dat.*) not to feel like reading.

чи́тка *n.* reading.

чих *n., colloq.* sneeze.

чиха́нье *n.* sneezing.

чиха́ть *v. impfv.* [*pfv.* **чихну́ть**] to sneeze.

чи́ще *adj., comp. of* **чи́стый**.

член *n.* **1,** member. **2,** limb (*of the body*). **3,** part (*of a sentence*). **4,** *gram.* article. **5,** *math.* term. —**член-корреспонде́нт**, corresponding/associate member (*of an academy*).

члени́ть *v. impfv.* to divide into parts.

членовреди́тельство *n.* **1,** (deliberate) mutilation (of someone). **2,** self-mutilation.

членоразде́льный *adj.* articulate.

чле́нский *adj.* membership (*attrib.*); чле́нские взно́сы, membership dues.

чле́нство *n.* membership.

чмо́кать *v. impfv.* [*pfv.* **чмо́кнуть**] **1,** [*also,* **чмо́кать губа́ми**] to smack one's lips. **2,** *colloq.* to give (someone) a loud kiss. **3,** to make a squirting sound.

чо́каться *v.r. impfv.* [*pfv.* **чо́кнуться**] to clink glasses (*when making a toast*).

чо́порный *adj.* strait-laced; prim and proper.

чрева́тый *adj.* (*with instr.*) fraught (with): чрева́тый опа́сными после́дствиями, fraught with dangerous consequences.

чре́во *n., archaic* **1,** stomach. **2,** womb.

чревовеща́ние *n.* ventriloquism. **—чревовеща́тель,** *n.m.* ventriloquist.

чреда́ *n., obs.* turn.

чрез *prep.* = **че́рез.**

чрезвыча́йный *adj.* **1,** extraordinary. **2,** emergency: чрезвыча́йное положе́ние, state of emergency. **—чрезвыча́йно,** *adv.* extremely; extraordinarily.

чрезме́рный *adj.* excessive. **—чрезме́рно,** *adv.* excessively.

чте́ние *n.* reading. Чте́ние ле́кций, lecturing.

чтец [*gen.* **чтеца́**] *n.* reader; reciter.

чти́во *n., colloq.* (piece of) literary trash.

чтить *v. impfv.* [*pres.* **чту, чтишь, ...чтят** *or* **чтут**] **1,** to honor. **2,** to revere.

что [*gen.* **чего́;** *dat.* **чему́;** *instr.* **чем;** *prepl.* **чём**] *pron.* **1,** *interr.* what?: что э́то зна́чит?, what does this mean? О чём он говори́т?, what is he talking about? **2,** *rel.* which; that: пе́рвое, что пришло́ мне в го́лову, the first thing that came into my head. Никто́ не подошёл к телефо́ну, что о́чень необы́чно, no one answered the telephone, which is very unusual. **3,** *indef.* (*with* **есть**) quite a lot; quite a bit: а́втору есть что рассказа́ть, the author has quite a lot to tell. Сожале́ть ему́ есть о чём, he has quite a lot to be sorry about. Выбира́ть бы́ло из чего́, there was quite a lot to choose from. **—***conj.* that: я уве́рен, что он говори́т пра́вду, I am sure that he is telling the truth. Э́то так про́сто, что ка́ждый поймёт, it is so simple that anyone can understand it. **—***adv.* why?; how come?: что ты тако́й весёлый?, why are you so merry? Что же ты молчи́шь?, why are you (or how come you're) so quiet? **—не́ за что!,** don't mention it! **—ни за что, 1,** not for anything. **2,** for nothing; in vain. **—ни к чему́, 1,** of no use. **2,** (*with inf.*) there is no need to. **3,** for no reason. **—ни с чем, 1,** empty-handed. **2,** *in* оста́ться ни с чем, to be left with nothing; be left destitute. **—ну и что?,** *colloq.* well, so what?; what of it? **—что (бы) ни,** whatever: что ни де́лаешь; что бы ты ни де́лал, whatever you do. **—что вы!, 1,** how can you say that! **2,** *in* ну, что вы!, oh go on! **3,** *in* нет, что вы!, not at all! **—что до,** as for. **—что за** (+ *nom.*), **1,** what is?: что за кни́ги, what are those books over there? **2,** what kind of?; what sort of: что он за челове́к?, what sort of person is he?; what is he like? **—что к чему́,** (*with verbs of knowing, understanding, etc.*) what's what; what's going on. **—что ли,** perhaps. **—что с ва́ми?,** what's the matter with you? *See also* **чего́** *and* **чем.**

чтобы *also,* **чтоб** *conj.* **1,** *with inf.* in order to; so as to: чтобы приходи́ть во́время, in order to be on time; чтобы не меша́ть гостя́м, so as not to disturb the guests. **2,** *used to introduce a dependent clause:* скажи́те ему́, чтобы он ушёл, tell him to go away. Я не ви́дел, чтобы кто-нибудь входи́л, I didn't see anyone enter. Она́ лю́бит, чтобы ей льсти́ли, she likes to be flattered. **—***particle, used to express a peremptory command:* чтобы э́того бо́льше не́ было!, this must not happen again! **—для того́, чтобы; с тем, чтобы, 1,** (*with inf.*) in order to; so as to. **2,** (*with a dependent clause*) so that; in order that.

что́-либо *indef. pron.* = **что́-нибудь.**

что́-нибудь *indef. pron.* something; anything.

что́-то *indef. pron.* something. **—***adv., colloq.* somehow: мне что́-то не спало́сь, I somehow couldn't sleep.

чуб [*pl.* **чубы́**] *n.* forelock.

чуба́рый *adj.* (*of a horse*) dappled.

чува́ш *n.m.* [*fem.* **чува́шка**] Chuvash (*one of a people inhabiting central European Russia*). **—чува́шский,** *adj.* Chuvash.

чу́вственный *adj.* **1,** sense (*attrib.*): чу́вственное восприя́тие, sense perception. **2,** sensual. **—чу́вственность,** *n.f.* sensuality.

чувстви́тельность *n.f.* sensitivity.

чувстви́тельный *adj.* **1,** sensitive. **2,** sentimental. **3,** noticeable; perceptible. **4,** severe; keenly felt. **—чувстви́тельный нерв,** sensory nerve.

чу́вство *n.* **1,** sense: пять чувств, the five senses. Чу́вство ю́мора, sense of humor. **2,** feeling: прия́тное чу́вство, a pleasant feeling. **3,** consciousness. **—лиши́ться чувств,** to lose consciousness. **—привести́ в чу́вство,** to revive; bring around. **—прийти́ в чу́вство,** to regain consciousness; come to. **—упа́сть без чувств,** to faint away.

чу́вствовать *v. impfv.* [*pfv.* **почу́вствовать;** *pres.* **-ствую, -ствуешь**] **1,** to feel. **2,** to sense. **3,** (*with* себя́) to feel (*a certain way*): как вы себя́ чу́вствуете?, how do you feel? Чу́вствовать себя́ больны́м, to feel ill. **4,** *in* чу́вствовать за́пах (+ *gen.*), to smell (something). **—чу́вствоваться,** *refl.* **1,** to be felt. **2,** to be sensed.

чугу́н [*gen.* **-гуна́**] *n.* **1,** cast iron. **2,** iron pot. **—чугу́нный,** *adj.* cast-iron.

чугунолите́йный *adj.* iron (*attrib.*). **—чугунолите́йный заво́д,** ironworks.

чуда́к [*gen.* **-дака́**] *n.m.* [*fem.* **-да́чка**] strange person; queer bird.

чудакова́тый *adj.* odd; queer; peculiar; eccentric.

чуда́ческий *adj.* odd; queer; eccentric.

чуда́чество *n.* **1,** peculiarity; quirk. **2,** *pl.* shenanigans; monkey business.

чудеса́ *n., pl. of* **чу́до.**

чуде́сно *adv.* **1,** miraculously. **2,** marvelously; wonderfully. **3,** *as an interj.* wonderful!

чуде́сный *adj.* **1,** miraculous. **2,** wonderful; marvelous.

чуди́ть *v. impfv., colloq.* to behave oddly; act up.

чу́диться *v.r. impfv.* [*pfv.* **почу́диться**] *impers.* to seem: мне чу́дится, it seems to me.

чу́дище *n., obs.* monster.

чу́дно *adv.* **1,** wonderfully; marvelously. **2,** *as an interj.* wonderful!

чудно́ *adv., colloq.* **1,** strangely; oddly. **2,** *as an interj.* (it is) strange!

чудно́й *adj., colloq.* odd; strange; queer.

чу́дный *adj.* wonderful; marvelous.

чу́до [*pl.* чудеса́, чуде́с, чудеса́м] *n.* miracle; wonder. —**чу́дом,** by a miracle. —**чу́до приро́ды,** freak of nature.

чудо́вище *n.* monster.

чудо́вищность *n.f.* (*with gen.*) monstrosity (of); enormity (of).

чудо́вищный *adj.* monstrous.

чудоде́й *n., obs.* miracle worker; magician.

чудоде́йственный *adj.* wonder-working; miraculous.

чудотво́рец [*gen.* -рца] *n.* miracle worker. —**чудотво́рный,** *adj.* wonder-working; miraculous.

чужа́к [*gen.* -жака́] *n., colloq.* stranger; newcomer.

чужби́на *n.* foreign land; foreign soil.

чужда́ться *v.r. impfv.* (*with gen.*) to avoid; shun; keep away from.

чу́ждый *adj.* **1,** (*often with dat.*) alien (to); foreign (to). **2,** (*with gen.*) devoid (of); free (from).

чужезе́мец [*gen.* -мца] *n., obs.* foreigner. —**чужезе́мный,** *adj., obs.* foreign.

чужестра́нец [*gen.* -нца] *n., obs.* foreigner. —**чужестра́нный,** *adj., obs.* foreign.

чужо́й *adj.* **1,** someone else's. **2,** foreign; alien. **3,** strange; unfamiliar. —*n.* **1,** stranger. **2,** *neut.* something belonging to someone else.

чу́кча [*gen. pl.* -чей] *n.m. & f.* [*fem. also* чукча́нка] Chukchi (*one of a people inhabiting northeasternmost Siberia*). —**чуко́тский,** *adj.* Chukchi.

чула́н *n.* storeroom; pantry.

чуло́к [*gen.* -лка́; *gen. pl.* чуло́к] *n.* stocking. —**чуло́чный,** *adj.* stocking (*attrib.*); hose (*attrib.*).

чума́ *n.* plague.

чума́зый *adj., colloq.* dirty.

чумно́й *adj.* **1,** of the plague; plague (*attrib.*). **2,** afflicted with the plague. —*n.* person afflicted with the plague.

чура́ться *v.r. impfv., colloq.* to avoid.

чурба́н *n.* block (*of wood*).

чу́рка [*gen. pl.* -рок] *n.* block (*of wood*); strip (*of metal*).

чу́ткий *adj.* [*short form* чу́ток, чутка́, чу́тко; *comp.* чу́тче] **1,** keen; sensitive. **2,** (*of sleep*) light. **3,** sympathetic; kind.

чу́тко *adv.* **1,** closely: чу́тко прислу́шиваться, to listen closely. **2,** sympathetically. **3,** *in* чу́тко спать, to be a light sleeper.

чу́ткость *n.f.* **1,** keenness; sensitivity. **2,** sympathy; consideration.

чу́точка *n., colloq., in* чу́точку, a little; a bit. —**ни чу́точки,** not a bit; not in the least.

чуть *adv.* **1,** hardly; scarcely; barely. **2,** (just) a little; (very) slightly. —*conj.* as soon as. —**чуть ли не,** almost; nearly; just about: чуть ли не ка́ждый день, almost every day. —**чуть ли не; чуть бы́ло не,** almost; nearly: он чуть не упа́л, he almost fell. —**чуть свет,** at the crack of dawn. —**чуть то́лько,** as soon as. —**чуть что,** at the drop of a hat.

чутьё *n.* **1,** scent; sense of smell (*of an animal*). **2,** *fig.* flair; instinct; feel.

чуть-чу́ть *adv.* a tiny bit. —**чуть-чу́ть не,** = **чуть не.**

чу́чело *n.* **1,** stuffed animal; stuffed bird. **2,** scarecrow.

чу́шка [*gen. pl.* -шек] *n., colloq.* baby pig. —**чугу́н в чу́шках,** pig iron.

чушь *n.f., colloq.* nonsense.

чу́ять *v. impfv.* [*pfv.* почу́ять; *pres.* чу́ю, чу́ешь] **1,** to smell; scent. **2,** *fig.* to sense. —**ног под собо́й не чу́ять, 1,** to be utterly exhausted. **2,** to be walking on air.

чьё *pron., neut. of* чей. —**чья,** *pron., fem. of* чей.

Ш, ш *n. neut.* 25th letter of the Russian alphabet.

ша́баш *n.* sabbath. —**ша́баш ведьм,** witches' sabbath.

шаба́шить *v. impfv.* [*pfv.* пошаба́шить] *colloq.* to quit work; knock off work.

ша́бер *n.* scraper.

шабло́н *n.* **1,** mold. **2,** stencil. **3,** *fig.* stereotype.

шабло́нный *adj.* **1,** standard. **2,** *fig.* stereotyped; trite.

ша́вка [*gen. pl.* -вок] *n., colloq.* small dog.

шаг [*gen.* ша́га, *but after* 2, 3, & 4 шага́; *pl.* шаги́, шаго́в] *n.* **1,** step: сде́лать шаг, to take a step. **2,** pace: отсчита́ть де́сять шаго́в, to mark off ten paces. **3,** *pl.* (sound of) footsteps. **4,** pace (*rate of speed when walking*): уско́рить шаг *or* приба́вить ша́гу, to quicken one's pace. **5,** step; action: риско́ванный шаг, risky step. —**два шага́; в двух шага́х (от),** a few steps away (from); a stone's throw (from). —**на ка́ждом шагу́,** at every step; at every turn. —**ни на шаг, 1,** not a step; not one step. **2,** not at all; not a bit. —**ни ша́гу,** not a step; not one step. —**у́зки в шагу́,** tight in the seat. —**шаг за ша́гом,** step by step.

шага́ть *v. impfv.* [*pfv.* шагну́ть] **1,** to step. **2,** to stride; pace. **3,** *fig.* to progress; make progress.

ша́гом *adv.* at a walk. —**ша́гом марш!,** forward march!

шагоме́р *n.* pedometer.

ша́йба *n.* **1,** *mech.* washer. **2,** *sports* puck.

ша́йка [*gen. pl.* ша́ек] *n.* **1,** gang; band. **2,** small wash-basin.

шака́л *n.* jackal.

шала́нда *n.*, *naut.* lighter; scow.

шала́ш [*gen.* -лаша́] *n.* hut; cabin.

шале́ (лэ) *n. neut. indecl.* chalet.

шале́ть *v. impfv.* [*pfv.* ошале́ть] *colloq.* to go crazy.

шали́ть *v. impfv.* to act up; misbehave; be naughty.

шаловли́вый *adj.* **1,** playful. **2,** mischievous. —**ша-ловли́вость,** *n.f.* playfulness.

шалопа́й *n.*, *colloq.* playboy; good-for-nothing.

ша́лость *n.f.* prank; trick.

шало́т *n.* shallot.

шалу́н [*gen.* -луна́] *n.* rascal; imp.

шалфе́й *n.* sage (*plant*).

ша́лый *adj.*, *colloq.* crazy; nuts.

шаль *n.f.* shawl.

шально́й *adj.*, *colloq.* **1,** crazy; mad. **2,** (*of a bullet, bomb, etc.*) stray; random.

шама́н *n.* shaman. —**шама́нство,** *n.* shamanism.

ша́мкать *v. impfv.*, *colloq.* to mumble.

шампа́нское *n.*, *decl. as an adj.* champagne.

шампу́нь *n.m.* shampoo.

шанкр *n.* chancre. —**мя́гкий шанкр,** soft chancre; chancroid. —**твёрдый шанкр,** hard chancre; chancre.

шанс *n.* chance: ша́нсы на успе́х, chances of success.

шансоне́тка [*gen. pl.* -ток] *n.* **1,** light comic song. **2,** cabaret singer.

шанта́ж [*gen.* -тажа́] *n.* blackmail.

шантажи́ровать *v. impfv.* [*pres.* -ру́ю, -руешь] to blackmail.

шантажи́ст *n.* blackmailer.

ша́пка [*gen. pl.* -пок] *n.* **1,** cap; hat. **2,** (*with gen.*) shock (*of hair*); clump (*of grass*). **3,** *journalism* headline; masthead.

ша́почка [*gen. pl.* -чек] *n.*, *dim. of* ша́пка. —Кра́с-ная ша́почка, Little Red Riding Hood.

ша́почник *n.* hatter.

ша́почный *adj.* **1,** hat (*attrib.*). **2,** *in* ша́почное зна-ко́мство, nodding acquaintance. —прийти́ к ша́поч-ному разбо́ру, to arrive just when everyone is leaving.

шар [*gen.* ша́ра, *but after* 2, 3, & 4 шара́; *pl.* шары́, шаро́в] *n.* **1,** sphere. **2,** ball. —возду́шный шар, bal-loon. —земно́й шар, the earth; the globe. —про́бный шар, trial balloon.

шараба́н *n.* gig (*carriage*).

шара́да *n.* charade.

шара́хать *v. impfv.* [*pfv.* шара́хнуть] *colloq.* **1,** to smack. **2,** to shoot. —**шара́хаться,** *refl.*, *colloq.* **1,** to jump aside (*from fear or surprise*). **2,** [*impfv. only*] (*with* от) to shun; keep away from.

шарж *n.* caricature; lampoon.

шаржи́ровать *v. impfv.* [*pres.* -ру́ю, -руешь] to car-icature; lampoon.

ша́рик *n.* **1,** *dim. of* шар. **2,** marble: игра́ть в ша́рики, to play marbles. —кровяны́е ша́рики, blood cor-puscles.

ша́риковый *adj.* ball-shaped. —ша́риковый под-ши́пник, ball bearing. —ша́риковая ру́чка, ball-point pen.

шарикоподши́пник *n.* ball bearing.

ша́рить *v. impfv.* to feel; fumble; grope; rummage.

ша́рканье *n.* shuffling (*of feet*).

ша́ркать *v. impfv.* [*pfv.* ша́ркнуть] **1,** [*impfv. only*] (*with* по) to shuffle (along). **2,** (*with instr.*) to shuffle (one's feet).

шарлата́н *n.* charlatan; quack. —**шарлата́нский,** *adj.*

quack; fraudulent. —**шарлата́нство,** *n.* quackery; charlatanism.

шарма́нка [*gen. pl.* -нок] *n.* barrel organ. —**шарма́н-щик,** *n.* organ grinder.

шарни́р *n.* hinge; joint.

шарова́ры [*gen.* -ва́р] *n. pl.* **1,** loose trousers gathered at the ankles (*part of the national costume of certain peoples*). **2,** (sports) pants: лы́жные шарова́ры, ski pants.

шарови́дный *adj.* spherical.

шарово́й *adj.* spherical. —**шарово́й шарни́р,** ball-and-socket joint.

шарообра́зный *adj.* spherical.

шарф *n.* scarf.

шасси́ *n. neut. indecl.* **1,** chassis. **2,** *aero.* undercar-riage; landing gear.

шата́ние *n.* **1,** swaying; wobbling. **2,** *fig.* wavering; vacillation. **3,** *colloq.* roaming; wandering.

шата́ть *v. impfv.* **1,** to shake; rock. **2,** *impers.* to reel; stagger: его́ шата́ло, he was reeling. —**шата́ться,** *refl.* **1,** to be loose; be unsteady. **2,** to reel; stagger. **3,** to sway. **4,** *colloq.* to roam about; knock about.

шате́н (тэ) *n.m.* [*fem.* -те́нка] person with brown hair.

шатёр [*gen.* -тра́] *n.* large tent.

ша́ткий *adj.* **1,** shaky; unsteady; rickety; wobbly. **2,** *fig.* shaky; precarious. **3,** *fig.* wavering; vacillating. —ни ша́тко ни ва́лко, fair to middling.

шату́н [*gen.* -туна́] *n.* connecting rod.

ша́фер [*pl.* шафера́] *n.* best man (*at a wedding*).

шафра́н *n.* saffron. —**шафра́нный,** *adj.* saffron (*at-trib.*).

шах *n.* **1,** shah. **2,** *chess* check.

шахмати́ст *n.* chess player.

ша́хматный *adj.* **1,** chess (*attrib.*). **2,** like a checker-board; in checkerboard fashion. **3,** *colloq.* checked; checkered.

ша́хматы [*gen.* -мат] *n. pl.* **1,** chess. **2,** chess set.

ша́хта *n.* **1,** mine; pit. **2,** shaft. **3,** silo (*for a missile*).

шахтёр *n.* miner. —**шахтёрский,** *adj.* miner's; miners'.

ша́хтный *adj.* mine (*attrib.*).

ша́шечница *n.*, *colloq.* checkerboard.

ша́шечный *adj.* for or pert. to checkers; checkers (*attrib.*).

ша́шка [*gen. pl.* -шек] *n.* **1,** saber; sword. **2,** checker piece. **3,** *pl.* checkers (*game*). **4,** paving block. **5,** block; slab; cartridge (*containing an explosive charge*). —ды-мова́я ша́шка, smudge pot.

шашлы́к [*gen.* -лыка́] *n.* shashlik; shish kebab.

ша́шни [*gen.* -ней] *n. pl.*, *colloq.* **1,** tricks; pranks. **2,** (love) affairs.

шва́бра *n.* mop.

шваль *n.f.*, *colloq.* **1,** trash; junk. **2,** good-for-nothing. **3,** riffraff; rabble.

шварто́в *n.* mooring line; *pl.* moorings.

швартова́ть *v. impfv.* [*pfv.* пришвартова́ть; *pres.* -ту́ю, -ту́ешь] to moor (a ship). —**швартова́ться,** *refl.* to moor; tie up.

швед *n.m.* [*fem.* шве́дка] Swede. —**шве́дский,** *adj.* Swedish.

швейник *n.* worker in a garment factory.

швейный *adj.* sewing (*attrib.*). —швейная маши́на, sewing machine. —швейная фа́брика, clothing (*or* garment) factory.

швейца́р *n.* doorman.

швейца́рец [*gen.* -рца] *n.m.* [*fem.* -рка] Swiss. —**швейца́рский**, *adj.* Swiss.

швец [*gen.* швеца́] *n., obs., regional* **1**, tailor. **2**, shoemaker. —**и швец, и жнец, и в дуду́ игре́ц**, jack-of all-trades.

швея́ *n.* seamstress.

шво́рень [*gen.* -рня] *n.m.* pivot; kingpin.

швырну́ть *v., pfv. of* швыря́ть.

швыро́к [*gen.* -рка́] *n.* **1**, toss. **2**, logs; firewood. **3**, object tossed in the air for firing practice.

швыря́ние *n.* tossing; flinging; hurling.

швыря́ть *v. impfv.* [*pfv.* швырну́ть] **1**, (*with acc. or instr.*) to toss; fling; hurl. **2**, *impers.* to toss: ло́дку швыря́ло на волна́х, the boat was tossing on the waves. **3**, *in* швыря́ть де́ньги *or* деньга́ми, to toss (*or* throw) money around. —**швыря́ться**, *refl.* [*impfv. only*] (*with instr.*) *colloq.* **1**, to toss; hurl (at one another). **2**, *fig.* to trifle with.

шевели́ть *v. impfv.* [*pfv.* пошевели́ть *or* шевельну́ть; *pres.* шевелю́, шеве́лишь *or* шевели́шь] **1**, (*with instr.*) to move; wiggle. **2**, (*with acc.*) to stir. **3**, *in* шевели́ть мозга́ми, to use one's brains. —**шевели́ться**, *refl.* **1**, to move; stir. **2**, *fig.* to show signs of life.

шевельну́ть *v., pfv. of* шевели́ть. —**шевельну́ться**, *refl., pfv. of* шевели́ться.

шевелю́ра *n.* head of hair.

шевио́т *n.* cheviot. —**шевио́товый**, *adj.* cheviot.

шевро́ *n. indecl.* kidskin. —**шевро́вый**, *adj.* kidskin; kid.

шевро́н *n., mil.* chevron; stripe.

шеде́вр (дэ) *n.* masterpiece.

шезло́нг *n.* chaise longue.

ше́йка [*gen. pl.* ше́ек] *n.* **1**, *dim. of* ше́я. **2**, neck; narrow part. —**ше́йка ма́тки**, cervix.

ше́йный *adj.* **1**, neck (*attrib.*). **2**, *anat.* cervical. —**ше́йный плато́к**, neckerchief.

шейх *n.* sheik.

ше́лест *n.* rustle; rustling.

шелесте́ть *v. impfv.* [*pres.* -ти́т] to rustle.

шёлк [*pl.* шелка́] *n.* silk. —**в долгу́ как в шелку́**, up to one's ears in debt.

шелкови́нка [*gen. pl.* -нок] *n.* (piece of) silk thread.

шелкови́стый *adj.* silky; silken.

шелкови́ца *n.* mulberry.

шелкови́чный *adj.* mulberry (*attrib.*). —**шелкови́чный червь**, silkworm.

шелково́дство *n.* sericulture.

шёлковый *adj.* **1**, silk. **2**, (*of hair*) silken. **3**, *fig., colloq.* meek; docile.

шелкопря́д *n.* **1**, silkworm. **2**, moth: непа́рный шелкопря́д, gypsy moth.

шелла́к *n.* shellac.

шелохну́ть *v. pfv.* (*with acc. or instr.*) to move (slightly). —**шелохну́ться**, *refl.* to move; stir.

шелуди́вый *adj., colloq.* mangy.

шелуха́ *n.* husk; peel; hull.

шелуши́ть *v. impfv.* to shell; peel; husk. —**шелуши́ться**, *refl.* (*of paint, one's skin, etc.*) to peel.

ше́льма *n.m. & f., colloq.* scoundrel; rascal.

шельме́ц [*gen.* -меца́] *n., colloq.* = ше́льма.

шельмова́ть *v. impfv.* [*pfv.* ошельмова́ть; *pres.* -му́ю, -му́ешь] *colloq.* to disparage; run down.

шемя́кин *adj., in* шемя́кин суд, unfair trial.

шепеля́вить *v. impfv.* [*pres.* -влю, -вишь] to lisp; pronounce *s* as *sh* and *z* as *zh*.

шепеля́вый *adj.* lisping. —**шепеля́вость**, *n.f.* lisp.

шепну́ть *v., pfv. of* шепта́ть.

шёпот *n.* whisper. —**шёпотом**, *adv.* in a whisper.

шептала́ *n.* dried peaches; dried apricots.

шепта́ние *n.* whispering.

шепта́ть *v. impfv.* [*pfv.* прошепта́ть *or* шепну́ть; *pres.* шепчу́, ше́пчешь] to whisper. —**шепта́ться**, *refl.* [*impfv. only*] to whisper (to each other).

шепту́н [*gen.* -туна́] *n., colloq.* **1**, whisperer. **2**, spreader of gossip.

шербе́т *n.* sherbet.

шере́нга *n.* **1**, rank; column; file. **2**, (*with gen.*) row (of); line (of).

шери́ф *n.* sheriff.

шерохова́тость *n.f.* **1**, roughness. **2**, rough edge. **3**, *pl., fig.* rough edges; disagreements.

шерохова́тый *adj.* **1**, rough. **2**, *fig.* crude.

шерсти́нка [*gen. pl.* -нок] *n.* strand of wool.

шерсти́стый *adj.* woolly.

шерсти́ть *v. impfv.* (*of rough material*) to irritate the skin; itch.

шерсть *n.f.* **1**, wool. **2**, hair; fur (*of an animal*). —**про́тив ше́рсти**, against the grain. —**гла́дить про́тив ше́рсти**, to rub the wrong way.

шерстяно́й *adj.* wool; woolen.

шерша́вить *v. impfv.* to become rough.

шерша́вый *adj.* rough.

ше́ршень [*gen.* -шня] *n.m.* hornet.

шест [*gen.* шеста́] *n.* pole.

шеста́я *n., decl. as an adj.* sixth: одна́ шеста́я, one-sixth.

ше́ствие *n.* procession. —**замыка́ть ше́ствие**, to bring up the rear.

ше́ствовать *v. impfv.* [*pres.* -ствую, -ствуешь] to march; parade.

шестёрка *n.* **1**, the numeral 6. **2**, *colloq.* anything numbered 6. **3**, group of six. **4**, team of six horses. **5**, *cards* six.

шестерня́ *n.* **1**, [*gen. pl.* -рён] gear; cogwheel; pinion. **2**, [*gen. pl.* -не́й] *colloq.* team of six horses.

ше́стеро *collective numeral* six.

шестидеся́тый *ordinal numeral* sixtieth.

шестидне́вный *adj.* six-day (*attrib.*).

шестикра́тный *adj.* sixfold.

шестиме́сячный *adj.* **1**, six-month (*attrib.*). **2**, six-month-old.

шестисо́тый *ordinal numeral* six-hundredth.

шестиуго́льник *n.* hexagon. —**шестиуго́льный**, *adj.* hexagonal.

шестна́дцатый *ordinal numeral* sixteenth.

шестна́дцать *numeral* sixteen.

шесто́й *ordinal numeral* sixth.

шесто́к [*gen.* -тка́] *n.* **1**, hearth (*of a Russian stove*). **2**, perch; roost.

шесть [*gen., dat., & prepl.* шести́; *instr.* шестью́] *numeral* six.

шестьдеся́т [*gen., dat., & prepl.* шести́десяти; *instr.* шестью́десятью] *numeral* sixty.

шестьсо́т [*gen.* шестисо́т; *dat.* шестиста́м; *instr.* шестьюста́ми; *prepl.* шестиста́х] *numeral* six hundred.

ше́стью *adv.* six times: ше́стью шесть – три́дцать шесть, six times six is 36.

шеф *n.* **1,** *colloq.* boss; chief. **2,** patron; sponsor. —**шеф-по́вар,** chef.

ше́фство *n.* patronage; sponsorship.

ше́фствовать *v. impfv.* [*pres.* **-ствую, -ствуешь**] (*with* **над**) to be a patron of; sponsor.

ше́я *n.* neck. —**бро́ситься на ше́ю** (+ *dat.*), to throw one's arms around someone's neck. —**ве́шаться на ше́ю** (+ *dat.*), to throw oneself at. —**гнуть ше́ю пе́ред,** to kowtow to. —**по (са́мую) ше́ю,** up to one's neck (*in work, debt, etc.*). —**получи́ть по ше́е,** to get it in the neck. —**сади́ться на ше́ю** (+ *dat.*); **сиде́ть на ше́е у,** to live off; sponge off; be a burden to. —**слома́ть (себе́) ше́ю, 1,** to break one's neck. **2,** *fig.* to fall on one's face.

ши́бкий *adj., colloq.* fast; swift; quick.

ши́бко *adv., colloq.* **1,** fast. **2,** very; very much.

ши́ворот *n., in* **за ши́ворот,** by the scruff of the neck. —**ши́ворот-навы́ворот,** topsy-turvy.

шизофрени́я *n.* schizophrenia. —**шизофре́ник,** *n.* schizophrenic. —**шизофрени́ческий,** *adj.* schizophrenic.

шик *n.* stylishness: **оде́т с ши́ком,** stylishly dressed. Счита́ться ши́ком, to be considered chic.

шика́рно *adv.* **1,** smartly. **2,** *as an interj., colloq.* splendid!

шика́рный *adj.* **1,** smart; chic. **2,** *colloq.* fine; grand.

ши́кать *v. impfv.* [*pfv.* **ши́кнуть**] *colloq.* **1,** (*with* **на** + *acc.*) to shoo away by saying шш. **2,** (*with* **на** + *acc.*) to hush; say шш to. **3,** (*with dat.*) to hiss (a performer).

ши́ллинг *n.* shilling.

ши́ло [*pl.* **ши́лья, ши́льев**] *n.* awl.

шилоклю́вка [*gen. pl.* **-вок**] *n.* avocet (*bird*).

шилохво́сть *n.f.* pintail (*duck*).

шимпанзе́ (зэ) *n.m. indecl.* chimpanzee.

ши́на *n.* **1,** tire. **2,** *med.* splint.

шине́ль *n.f.* overcoat.

шинка́рь [*gen.* **-каря́**] *n.m., obs.* tavern keeper.

шинкова́ть *v. impfv.* [*pres.* **-ку́ю, -ку́ешь**] to chop; shred (cabbage).

ши́нный *adj.* tire (*attrib.*).

шино́к [*gen.* **-нка́**] *n., obs.* tavern.

шинши́лла *n.* chinchilla.

шиньо́н *n.* chignon.

шип [*gen.* **шипа́**] *n.* **1,** thorn. **2,** tenon. **3,** spike; cleat.

шипе́ние *n.* hissing; sizzling; fizzing.

шипе́ть *v. impfv.* [*pres.* **шиплю́, шипи́шь**] to hiss; sizzle; fizz.

шипо́вник *n.* wild rose.

шипу́честь *n.f.* effervescence.

шипу́чий *adj.* sparkling; effervescent. —**шипу́чее,** *n.* sparkling beverage.

шипу́чка *n., colloq.* sparkling beverage.

шипя́щий *adj.* **1,** hissing. **2,** *phonet.* sibilant. —*n., phonet.* sibilant.

ши́ре *adj., comp. of* **широ́кий.**

ширина́ *n.* width; breadth. В три ме́тра ширино́й, three meters wide. Име́ть три ме́тра в ширину́, to be three meters wide.

шири́нка *n., colloq.* fly (*on trousers*).

ши́рить *v. impfv.* **1,** *colloq.* to widen; make wider; open wider. **2,** *fig.* to expand. —**ши́риться,** *refl.* to expand.

ши́рма *n.* **1,** screen. **2,** *fig.* screen; cover.

широ́кий *adj.* [*short form* **широ́к, широка́, широко́** *or* **широ́ко, широки́** *or* **широ́ки;** *comp.* **ши́ре**] **1,** wide; broad. **2,** loose; loose-fitting. **3,** extensive. **4,** generous. **5,** lavish; grand. **6,** *in* **широ́кая пу́блика,** the general public; **широ́кий чита́тель,** the general/average reader. **7,** *in* **това́ры широ́кого потребле́ния,** consumer goods. —**жить на широ́кую но́гу,** to live in grand style.

широко́ *adv.* **1,** widely; wide. **2,** broadly. —**жить широко́,** to live in grand style.

широковеща́ние *n.* broadcasting.

широковеща́тельный *adj.* **1,** broadcasting (*attrib.*). **2,** *fig.* high-sounding.

ширококоле́йный *adj., R.R.* broad-gauge.

широкопле́чий *adj.* broad-shouldered.

широкоуго́льный *adj.* wide-angle.

широта́ [*pl.* **широ́ты**] *n.* **1,** *colloq.* width. **2,** breadth; broad scope; wide range. **3,** latitude.

ширпотре́б *n., colloq.* **1,** mass consumption. **2,** consumer goods.

ширь *n.f.* expanse; open space. —**во всю ширь, 1,** to its full extent. **2,** *fig.* to the fullest.

шить *v. impfv.* [*pfv.* **сшить;** *pres.* **шью, шьёшь**] **1,** to sew. **2,** [*impfv. only*] to embroider. **3,** [*impfv. only*] *colloq.* to have one's clothes made (somewhere). —**он ни шьёт ни по́рет,** he keeps hemming and hawing.

шитьё *n.* **1,** sewing. **2,** needlework. **3,** embroidery.

ши́фер *n.* slate. —**ши́ферный,** *adj.* slate (*attrib.*).

шифо́н *n.* chiffon. —**шифо́новый,** *adj.* chiffon.

шифонье́рка [*gen. pl.* **-рок**] *n.* chiffonier.

шифр *n.* **1,** cipher; code. **2,** call number.

шифрова́льщик *n.* cipher clerk; cryptographer.

шифро́ванный *adj.* in code; coded.

шифрова́ть *v. impfv.* [*pfv.* **зашифрова́ть;** *pres.* **-ру́ю, -ру́ешь**] to encipher; code; encode.

шифро́вка *n.* **1,** enciphering; encoding. **2,** *colloq.* coded message.

шиш [*gen.* **шиша́**] *n., colloq.* **1,** fig (*insulting gesture*). **2,** nothing; nil.

ши́шка [*gen. pl.* **-шек**] *n.* **1,** *bot.* cone. **2,** bump; lump. **3,** *colloq.* big shot.

шишкова́тый *adj.* knobby.

шишкови́дный *adj.* cone-shaped; pineal.

шкала́ [*pl.* **шка́лы**] *n.* **1,** scale; dial. **2,** *fig.* scale: **шкала́ за́работной пла́ты,** wage scale.

шка́лик *n.* **1,** old Russian unit of liquid measure equal to about $\frac{1}{8}$ of a pint. **2,** small vodka glass or bottle of this capacity.

шка́нцы [*gen.* **-нцев**] *n. pl.* quarterdeck.

шкату́лка [*gen. pl.* **-лок**] *n.* small box.

шкаф [*2nd loc.* **шкафу́;** *pl.* **шкафы́**] *n.* closet; cabinet; cupboard. —**кни́жный шкаф,** bookcase. —**несгора́емый шкаф,** safe. —**платяно́й шкаф,** wardrobe.

шка́фик *also,* **шка́фчик** *n.* small closet; small cabinet.

шквал *n.* squall. —**шква́листый,** *adj.* gusty.

шква́рки [*gen.* **-рок**] *n. pl.* cracklings.

шкво́рень [*gen.* **-рня**] *n.m.* pivot; kingbolt; kingpin.

шкив [*pl.* **шкивы́**] *n.* pulley.

шки́пер *n.* skipper; captain.

шко́ла *n.* **1,** school. Шко́ла-интерна́т, boarding school. **2,** schooling; training: пройти́ хоро́шую шко́лу, to receive thorough training. —**суро́вая шко́ла жи́зни,** the bitter experience of life; the school of hard knocks.

шко́лить v. impfv. [pfv. **вы́школить**] colloq. to school; train; discipline.

шко́льник n. schoolboy. —**шко́льница**, n. schoolgirl.

шко́льнический adj. schoolboy (attrib.); typical of a schoolboy.

шко́льничество n. schoolboyish behavior; schoolboy pranks; shenanigans.

шко́льный adj. school (attrib.).

шку́ра n. skin; hide; pelt. —**быть в чье́й-нибудь шку́ре**, to be in someone's shoes. —**дели́ть шку́ру неуби́того медве́дя**, to count one's chickens before they are hatched. —**драть шку́ру с** (+ gen.), 1, to tan someone's hide. 2, to exploit mercilessly; bleed white. —**дрожа́ть за свою́ шку́ру**, to worry about one's own skin. —**испы́тывать (что́-нибудь) на сво-е́й шку́ре**, to experience (something) personally. —**спасти́ свою́ шку́ру**, to save one's skin. —**спусти́ть шку́ру с** (+ gen.), to tan someone's hide.

шку́рка n. 1, dim. of шку́ра. 2, sandpaper.

шку́рник n., colloq. self-seeker; one who looks out only for himself.

шку́рный adj., colloq. selfish; self-seeking.

шлагба́ум n. barrier; gate.

шлак n. slag.

шланг n. hose.

шлейф n. train (of a dress).

шлем n. 1, helmet. 2, cards slam.

шлёпанцы n. pl. [sing. **шлёпанец**] colloq. bedroom slippers.

шлёпать v. impfv. [pfv. **шлёпнуть**] 1, to smack; slap; spank. 2, (with instr.) to make a noise with. 3, [impfv. only] colloq. to shuffle; tramp. 4, [impfv. only] (with по) colloq. to tramp; slosh (through water, mud, etc.). —**шлёпаться**, refl., colloq. to tumble; flop; plop.

шлёпка n., colloq. spanking.

шлёпнуть v., pfv. of шлёпать. —**шлёпнуться**, refl., pfv. of шлёпаться.

шлепо́к [gen. -пка́] n. slap; smack.

шлифова́льный adj. polishing (attrib.).

шлифова́льщик n. polisher.

шлифова́ть v. impfv. [pfv. **отшлифова́ть**; pres. -фу́ю -фу́ешь] 1, to polish. 2, to grind.

шлифо́вка n. polishing. —**шлифо́вщик**, n. polisher.

шлюз n. 1, sluice. 2, lock (in a canal). —**шлю́зный**, adj. sluice (attrib.).

шлюп n. sloop.

шлю́пка [gen. pl. -пок] n. boat. —**спаса́тельная шлю́пка**, lifeboat.

шлю́ха n., colloq. slut.

шля́па n. hat. —**де́ло в шля́пе**, it's in the bag.

шля́пка [gen. pl. -пок] n. 1, dim. of шля́па. 2, head (of a nail). 3, cap (of a mushroom).

шля́пник n. hatter.

шля́пный adj. hat (attrib.). —**шля́пный ма́стер**, hatter.

шля́ться v.r. impfv., colloq. to wander about; gad about; gallivant.

шмель [gen. шмеля́] n.m. bumblebee.

шмы́гать v. impfv. [pfv. **шмыгну́ть**] 1, colloq. to bustle; scurry. 2, [impfv. only] (with instr.) to scrape: шмы́гать нога́ми по́ полу, to scrape one's feet on the floor. —**шмы́гать но́сом**, to sniff the air.

шмыгну́ть v. pfv. 1, pfv. of шмы́гать. 2, to dart; slip.

шнитт-лу́к n. chive.

шни́цель n.m. schnitzel.

шно́ркель n.m. snorkel.

шнур [gen. шнура́] n. 1, cord; lace. 2, electric cord. 3, fuse.

шнурова́ть v. impfv. [pfv. **зашнурова́ть**; pres. -ру́ю, -ру́ешь] to lace; tie.

шнуро́вка n. lacing.

шнуро́к [gen. -рка́] n. lace: шнуро́к для боти́нок, shoelace.

шныря́ть v. impfv., colloq. 1, to scurry; scamper. 2, to poke about; prowl around; snoop about. 3, in шныря́ть глаза́ми, to cast one's eyes about.

шов [gen. шва] n. 1, seam. 2, stitch; suture. 3, mech. joint. —**треща́ть по (всем) швам**, to come apart at the seams.

шовини́зм n. chauvinism. —**шовини́ст**, n. chauvinist. —**шовинисти́ческий**, adj. chauvinistic.

шок n., med. shock.

шоки́ровать v. impfv. [pres. -рую, -руешь] to shock.

шокола́д n. chocolate. —**шокола́дный**, adj. chocolate.

шо́мпол [pl. шомпола́] n. ramrod.

шо́рник n. saddler; harness-maker.

шо́рный adj. saddle (attrib.); harness (attrib.); saddler's.

шо́рох n. rustle; rustling.

шо́рты [gen. шорт] n. pl. shorts.

шо́ры [gen. шор] n. pl. blinkers; blinders.

шоссе́ (сэ) n. neut. indecl. highway.

шоссе́йный (сэ) adj. road (attrib.); highway (attrib.). —**шоссе́йная доро́га**, highway.

шосси́ровать v. impfv. & pfv. [pres. -рую, -руешь] to make into a highway.

шотла́ндец [gen. -дца] n.m. [fem. -дка] Scotchman; Scotsman.

шотла́ндка [gen. pl. -док] n. 1, fem. of шотла́ндец. 2, tartan; plaid.

шотла́ндский adj. Scottish; Scotch.

шофёр n. driver; chauffeur. —**шофёрский**, adj. driver's; chauffeur's.

шпа́га n. sword.

шпага́т n. 1, string; cord; twine. 2, gymnastics split.

шпа́жный adj. of a sword.

шпаклева́ть v. impfv. [pfv. **зашпаклева́ть**; pres. -люю, -люешь] to putty; seal up.

шпаклёвка n. 1, puttying; sealing up. 2, putty.

шпа́ла n. railroad tie.

шпале́ра n., usu. pl. 1, trellis. 2, row of trees along a road. 3, mil. rows; columns. 4, obs. wallpaper.

шпанго́ут n. frame (of a ship, airplane, etc.).

шпа́нка n. Spanish fly.

шпа́нский adj., obs. Spanish. —**шпа́нская му́шка**, Spanish fly.

шпарга́лка [gen. pl. -лок] n., colloq. pony; crib (concealed student's notes).

шпа́рить v. impfv., colloq. 1, to pour boiling water on. 2, to scald.

шпат n. spar. —**алма́зный шпат**, corundum. —**плави́ковый шпат**, fluorspar; fluorite. —**полево́й шпат**, feldspar.

шпа́тель (тэ) n.m. 1, spatula. 2, palette knife; putty knife.

шпене́к [gen. -нька́] n. peg; prong.

шпигова́ть v. impfv. [pfv. **нашпигова́ть**; pres. -гу́ю, -гу́ешь] to lard.

шпик *n.* **1,** small cubes of lard. **2,** *colloq.* sleuth; secret agent.

шпиль *n.m.* **1,** spire; steeple. **2,** capstan.

шпи́лька [*gen. pl.* -лек] *n.* **1,** hairpin. **2,** *mech.* pin; stud. **3,** tack; brad. **4,** *fig.* sarcastic comment; dig.

шпина́т *n.* spinach. —**шпина́тный,** *adj.* spinach (*attrib.*).

шпингале́т *n.* latch; catch; bolt.

шпи́ндель (дэ) *n.m.* spindle; shaft.

шпио́н *n.* spy.

шпиона́ж *n.* espionage.

шпио́нить *v. impfv.* to spy.

шпио́нский *adj.* espionage (*attrib.*); spy (*attrib.*).

шпио́нство *n.* spying.

шпиц *n.* **1,** *obs.* spire; steeple. **2,** spitz (*dog*).

шпон *n., printing* lead; slug.

шпо́нка [*gen. pl.* -нок] *n., mech.* key; dowel.

шпо́ра *n.* spur.

шпо́рник *n.* delphinium; larkspur.

шприц *n.* (hypodermic) syringe.

шпро́ты [*gen.* шпрот] *n. pl.* sprats.

шпу́лька [*gen. pl.* -лек] *n.* spool; bobbin.

шпунт [*gen.* шпунта́] *n.* groove.

шпыня́ть *v. impfv., colloq.* **1,** to poke; jab. **2,** *fig.* to nag; needle.

шрам *n.* scar.

шрапне́ль *n.f.* shrapnel. —**шрапне́льный,** *adj.* shrapnel (*attrib.*).

шрифт [*pl.* шрифты́] *n.* print; type.

штаб [*pl.* штабы́] *n., mil.* staff; headquarters.

шта́бель [*pl.* штабеля́] *n.m.* pile; stack.

штаб-кварти́ра *n.* headquarters (building).

штабно́й *adj.* staff (*attrib.*). —*n.* staff officer.

штаке́тник *n.* **1,** fence. **2,** pickets (*forming a fence*).

штамп *n.* **1,** *mech.* die. **2,** (rubber) stamp. **3,** imprint. **4,** *fig.* stereotype. **5,** *fig.* cliché.

штампова́льный *adj., mech.* punching; stamping. —**штампова́льный пресс,** punch press.

штампо́ванный *adj.* **1,** pressed; shaped. **2,** *fig.* stock; trite.

штампова́ть *v. impfv.* [*pres.* -пу́ю, -пу́ешь] **1,** to stamp. **2,** *mech.* to punch; press; shape. **3,** *fig., colloq.* to grind out.

штампо́вка *n.* **1,** stamping. **2,** punching; pressing.

штампо́вочный *adj., mech.* punching; stamping. —**штампо́вочный пресс,** punch press.

шта́нга *n.* **1,** rod; bar. **2,** *sports* barbell. **3,** *sports* crossbar (*between goal posts*).

штанги́ст *n.* weightlifter.

штанда́рт *n., obs.* standard; banner.

штани́на *n., colloq.* pants leg; trouser leg.

штани́шки [*gen. pl.* -шек] *n. pl., colloq.* short pants.

штаны́ [*gen.* -но́в] *n. pl., colloq.* trousers; pants.

штат *n.* **1,** state: Соединённые Шта́ты Аме́рики, the United States of America. **2,** (permanent) staff: сокраще́ние шта́тов, staff reduction.

штати́в *n.* **1,** stand; base. **2,** *photog.* tripod.

шта́тный *adj.* staff (*attrib.*); permanent.

шта́тский *adj. & n.* civilian.

штевень [*gen.* -вня] *n.m.* stem *or* sternpost (*of a ship*).

штемпелева́ть (тэ) *v. impfv.* [*pfv.* заштемпелева́ть; *pres.* -лю́ю, -лю́ешь] to stamp; postmark.

штемпель [*pl.* штемпеля́] *n.m.* **1,** rubber stamp. **2,**

imprint made with a rubber stamp. —**почто́вый штемпель,** postmark.

штемпельный (тэ) *adj.* stamp (*attrib.*); stamping (*attrib.*). —**штемпельная поду́шка,** stamp pad; ink pad.

штепсель (тэ) [*pl.* штепселя́] *n.m.* **1,** electric plug. **2,** *colloq.* electric outlet.

штепсельный (тэ) *adj.* of an electric plug or outlet. —**штепсельная ви́лка,** electric plug. —**штепсельная розе́тка,** electric outlet.

штибле́ты *n. pl.* [*sing.* штибле́та] (men's) shoes; boots.

штилево́й *adj., naut.* calm. —**штилевы́е по́лосы,** *naut.* the doldrums.

штиль *n.m., naut.* calm.

штифт [*gen.* штифта́] *n.* pin; peg; dowel.

шток *n., mech.* rod: шток по́ршня, piston rod.

штокро́за *n.* hollyhock.

што́пальный *adj.* darning (*attrib.*): што́пальная игла́, darning needle.

што́пать *v. impfv.* [*pfv.* зашто́пать] to darn.

што́пка *n.* **1,** darning. **2,** *colloq.* darning thread.

што́пор *n.* **1,** corkscrew. **2,** *aero.* spin. —**што́пор на хвост,** tailspin.

што́ра *n.* window shade; blind.

шторм *n.* storm; gale (*at sea*).

штормова́ть *v. impfv.* [*pres.* -му́ю, -му́ешь] to weather a storm.

штормово́й *adj.* **1,** storm (*attrib.*). **2,** stormy. —**ве́тер штормово́й си́лы,** wind of gale force.

штоф *n.* **1,** damask. **2,** old Russian unit of liquid measure equal to about 2½ pints. **3,** *obs.* wine bottle of this capacity.

што́фный *adj.* damask.

штраф *n.* **1,** fine. **2,** penalty.

штрафно́й *adj.* **1,** penalty (*attrib.*). **2,** penal. —**штрафно́й бросо́к,** *basketball* free throw. —**штрафно́й уда́р,** *soccer* penalty kick.

штрафова́ть *v. impfv.* [*pfv.* оштрафова́ть; *pres.* -фу́ю, -фу́ешь] **1,** to fine. **2,** to penalize.

штрейкбре́хер *n.* strikebreaker.

штри́пка [*gen. pl.* -пок] *n.* strap for fastening trousers to footwear.

штрих [*gen.* штриха́] *n.* **1,** stroke (*in drawing*). **2,** *fig.* detail; feature.

штрихова́ть *v. impfv.* [*pfv.* заштрихова́ть; *pres.* -ху́ю, -ху́ешь] *drawing* to shade; hatch.

штрихо́вка *n.* drawing shading; hatching.

штуди́ровать *v. impfv.* [*pfv.* проштуди́ровать; *pres.* -рую, -руешь] to study.

шту́ка *n.* **1,** piece; item; unit: пять штук яи́ц, five eggs. **2,** *colloq.* thing. **3,** *colloq.* trick. —**за шту́ку,** apiece; each.

штука́рь [*gen.* -каря́] *n.m., colloq.* jokester; prankster.

штукату́р *n.* plasterer.

штукату́рить *v. impfv.* [*pfv.* оштукату́рить] to plaster.

штукату́рка *n.* **1,** plaster. **2,** plastering. —**штукату́рный,** *adj.* plaster (*attrib.*); plastering (*attrib.*).

штурва́л *n.* steering wheel (*of a ship or aircraft*). —**за штурва́лом,** at the helm; at the controls.

штурва́льный *adj.* steering (*attrib.*). —*n.* man at the wheel; helmsman.

штурм *n., mil.* storm; assault.

шту́рман *n.* navigator.

штурмова́ть *v. impfv.* [*pres.* -му́ю, -му́ешь] *mil.* to storm.

штурмови́к [*gen.* -вика́] *n.* **1,** low-flying attack aircraft. **2,** storm trooper (*in Nazi Germany*).

штурмо́вка *n.* strafing.

штурмово́й *adj.* assault (*attrib.*). —**штурмова́я авиа́ция, 1,** ground-attack aircraft. **2,** ground-attack forces.

шту́цер [*pl.* штуцера́] *n.* carbine.

шту́чка [*gen. pl.* -чек] *n.*, *dim. of* шту́ка.

шту́чный *adj.* by the piece; sold by the piece.

штык [*gen.* штыка́] *n.* bayonet. —**встре́тить** *or* **приня́ть в штыки́,** to meet with extreme hostility; be up in arms over.

штыково́й *adj.* bayonet (*attrib.*).

штырь [*gen.* штыря́] *n.m.* pin; dowel.

шу́ба *n.* fur coat.

шубе́йка [*gen. pl.* -бе́ек] *n.*, *colloq.* short fur coat.

шуга́ *n.* drift ice.

шу́лер [*pl.* шулера́] *n.* cardsharp; cheat. —**шу́лерский,** *adj.* cheating; dishonest. —**шу́лерство,** *n.* cheating; foul play.

шум *n.* **1,** noise. **2,** *fig.* fuss: подня́ть шум, to make/raise a fuss. **3,** *fig.* stir; sensation: вы́звать шум; наде́лать шу́ма, to cause a sensation; cause quite a stir. **4,** *in* шум в се́рдце, heart murmur; шум в уша́х, buzzing in one's ears. —**мно́го шу́ма из ничего́,** much ado about nothing.

шуме́ть *v. impfv.* [*pres.* -млю́, -ми́шь] **1,** to make (a) noise; be noisy. **2,** *fig., colloq.* to make a fuss. —**у меня́ шуми́т в уша́х,** I have a buzzing in my ears.

шуми́ха *n.*, *colloq.* fuss; uproar; clamor; hullabaloo.

шумли́вый *adj.* **1,** noisy; boisterous. **2,** *colloq.* high-sounding.

шу́мно *adv.* noisily. —*adj.*, *used predicatively* noisy: здесь сли́шком шу́мно, it is too noisy in here.

шу́мный *adj.* **1,** noisy. **2,** lively; bustling. **3,** *fig.* causing a sensation: шу́мный успе́х, huge/sensational success.

шумови́к [*gen.* -вика́] *n.*, *theat.* sound-effects man.

шумо́вка [*gen. pl.* -во́к] *n.* straining spoon; skimmer.

шумово́й *adj.* sound (*attrib.*). —**шумовы́е эффе́кты,** sound effects.

шумо́к [*gen.* -мка́] *n.*, *colloq.* slight noise. —**под шумо́к,** secretly; on the sly.

шу́рин *n.* brother-in-law (*wife's brother*).

шуру́п *n.* screw.

шурша́ние *n.* rustling.

шурша́ть *v. impfv.* [*pres.* -шу́, -ши́шь] to rustle.

шу́стрый *adj.*, *colloq.* smart; bright.

шут [*gen.* шута́] *n.* jester; buffoon.

шути́ть *v. impfv.* [*pfv.* пошути́ть; *pres.* шучу́, шу́тишь] **1,** to joke; jest: вы шу́тите!, you're joking! **2,** (*with* с + *instr.*) to play (with). **3,** (*with* над) to make fun of. **4,** [*impfv. only*] (*with instr.*) to trifle with. —**шути́ть с огнём,** to play with fire. —**шу́тки шути́ть,** to joke.

шути́ха *n.* **1,** *fem. of* шут. **2,** rocket (*firework*).

шу́тка [*gen. pl.* -ток] *n.* joke. —**в шу́тку,** in jest; as a joke. —**не до шу́ток,** it's no joke; it's no laughing matter. Ему́ не до шу́ток, he is in no mood for jokes. —**не на шу́тку,** really; genuinely; seriously. —**с ним шу́тки пло́хи,** he is not to be trifled with; you don't fool around with him. —**сыгра́ть шу́тку с,** to play a joke/trick on. —**шу́тки в сто́рону; кро́ме шу́ток,** joking aside.

шутли́вый *adj.* **1,** *colloq.* jocular; full of fun. **2,** (*of a remark, song, etc.*) humorous; facetious.

шутни́к [*gen.* -ника́] *n.* joker; jokester.

шутовско́й *adj.* **1,** of a jester. Шутовско́й колпа́к, fool's cap. **2,** mischievous; prankish.

шутовство́ *n.* buffoonery.

шу́точный *adj.* **1,** humorous; facetious. **2,** (*usu. neg.*) trifling: э́то не шу́точное де́ло, it's no trifling (*or* laughing) matter.

шутя́ *adv.* **1,** in jest; for fun. **2,** easily; without any difficulty. —**не шутя́,** seriously; in earnest.

шушу́каться *v.r. impfv.*, *colloq.* to whisper (to each other).

шхе́ры [*gen.* шхер] *n. pl.* rocky islets along a rugged coast.

шху́на *n.* schooner.

шш *interj.* shh!

Щ, щ *n. neut.* 26th letter of the Russian alphabet.

щаве́левый *adj.* sorrel (*attrib.*). —**щаве́левая кислота́,** oxalic acid.

щаве́ль [*gen.* -веля́] *n.m.* sorrel.

щади́ть *v. impfv.* [*pfv.* пощади́ть; *pres.* щажу́, щади́шь] **1,** to spare; spare the life of; have mercy on. **2,** to spare: не щади́ть уси́лий, to spare no effort; щади́ть чьё-нибудь самолю́бие, to spare someone's pride.

щебёнка *n.*, *colloq.* = ще́бень.

ще́бень [*gen.* -бня] *n.m.* macadam. —**щебёночный,** *adj.* macadam(ized).

щебет *n.* twitter; chirping. *Also,* щебета́ние.

щебета́ть *v. impfv.* [*pres.* -бечу́, -бе́чешь] **1,** to twitter; chirp. **2,** *colloq.* to chatter.

щего́л [*gen.* -гла́] *n.* goldfinch.

щеголева́тый *adj.* stylish; dapper.

щёголь *n.m.* dandy; fop.

щегольну́ть *v., pfv. of* **щеголя́ть.**

щегольско́й *adj.* **1,** smart; handsome; elegant. **2,** dashing; jaunty.

щегольство́ *n.* **1,** foppery; dandyism. **2,** showing off.

щеголя́ть *v. impfv.* [*pfv.* **щегольну́ть**] **1,** [*impfv. only*] to wear fancy clothes. **2,** (*with* в + *prepl.*) *colloq.* to sport. **3,** (*with instr.*) *colloq.* to show off; flaunt.

ще́дрый *adj.* generous. —**ще́дро,** *adv.* generously. —**ще́дрость,** *n.f.* generosity.

щека́ [*acc.* **щёку;** *pl.* **щёки, щёк, щека́м**] *n.* cheek. —**уплета́ть** *or* **упи́сывать за о́бе щеки́,** to eat ravenously; devour; gobble up.

щеко́лда *n.* door latch.

щекота́ние *n.* tickling sensation.

щекота́ть *v. impfv.* [*pfv.* **пощекота́ть;** *pres.* **-кочу́, -ко́чешь**] to tickle.

щеко́тка *n.* **1,** tickling. **2,** tickling sensation. —**боя́ться щеко́тки,** to be ticklish.

щекотли́вый *adj.* ticklish; delicate. —**щекотли́вость,** *n.f.* ticklishness; delicacy.

щеко́тно *adj., used predicatively* tickling: мне щеко́тно, it tickles.

щеко́тный *adj.* causing a tickling sensation.

щели́стый *adj., colloq.* full of cracks.

щёлк *n., colloq.* snap; crack; click.

щёлка [*gen. pl.* **-лок**] *n.* crack; slit.

щёлканье *n.* **1,** snapping; cracking; clicking. **2,** warbling (*of birds*).

щёлкать *v. impfv.* [*pfv.* **щёлкнуть**] **1,** to flick: щёлкнуть кого-нибудь по́ носу, to give someone a flick on the nose. **2,** (*of a lock, shutter, etc.*) to click. **3,** (*with instr.*) to crack (a whip); snap (one's fingers, a shutter, etc.); click (one's tongue); turn (a key) with a click. **4,** to crack (nuts). **5,** [*impfv. only*] (*of a bird*) to warble.

щелкопёр *n., obs.* hack writer.

щёлок *n.* lye.

щелочно́й *adj.* alkaline. —**щёлочность,** *n.f.* alkalinity.

щёлочь *n.f.* alkali.

щелчо́к [*gen.* **-чка́**] *n.* **1,** flick; fillip. **2,** click; crack. **3,** *colloq.* slight; snub.

щель [*2nd loc.* **щели́;** *pl.* **щели, щелей, щелям**] *n.f.* **1,** crack; slit. **2,** slot (*for a coin*). **3,** *mil.* slit trench. —**голосова́я щель,** glottis.

щеми́ть *v. impfv.* **1,** to constrict. **2,** to ache; hurt. **3,** *fig.* to oppress; weigh on.

щемя́щий *adj.* oppressive; nagging.

щени́ться *v.r. impfv.* [*pfv.* **ощени́ться**] to have pups.

щено́к [*gen.* **-нка́;** *pl.* **-нки́, -нко́в** *or* **щеня́та, щеня́т**] *n.* pup; puppy.

щепа́ [*pl.* **ще́пы, щеп, щепа́м**] *n.* **1,** chip of wood. **2,** chips; kindling. **3,** shingles (*for a roof*).

щепа́ть *v. impfv.* [*pres.* **щеплю́, ще́плешь**] to chop; cleave.

щепети́льный *adj.* punctilious.

ще́пка [*gen. pl.* **-пок**] *n.* chip; sliver. —**худо́й как ще́пка,** thin as a rail.

щепо́тка [*gen. pl.* **-ток**] *n.* = **щепо́ть.**

щепо́ть *also,* **ще́поть** *n.f.* **1,** three fingers (the thumb, index, and middle finger) held together. **2,** pinch: щепо́ть со́ли, pinch of salt.

щерба́тый *adj.* **1,** chipped. **2,** with teeth missing. **3,** *colloq.* pockmarked.

щерби́на *n.* **1,** chip; nick. **2,** place where a tooth is missing. **3,** pockmark.

щети́на *n.* **1,** bristles. **2,** stubble (*of beard*). —**щети́нистый,** *adj.* bristly.

щети́ниться *v.r. impfv.* [*pfv.* **ощети́ниться**] to bristle.

щётка [*gen. pl.* **-ток**] *n.* **1,** brush. **2,** fetlock.

щёточный *adj.* brush (*attrib.*).

щёчный *adj.* cheek (*attrib.*).

щи [*gen.* **щей**] *n. pl.* cabbage soup. —**попа́сть как кур во́ щи,** to get into a jam; get into hot water.

щи́колотка [*gen. pl.* **-ток**] *n.* ankle.

щипа́ть *v. impfv.* [*pres.* **щиплю́, щи́плешь**] **1,** [*pfv.* **щипну́ть**] to pinch. **2,** [*impfv. only*] to burn; sting. **3,** [*pfv.* **общипа́ть** *or* **ощипа́ть**] to pluck. **4,** [*impfv. only*] to nibble. —**щипа́ться,** *refl. impfv.] colloq.* **1,** to pinch. **2,** to pinch each other.

щипко́вый *adj., in* **щипко́вые инструме́нты,** instruments played by plucking.

щипко́м *adv.* pizzicato.

щипну́ть *v., pfv. of* **щипа́ть** (*of sense #1*).

щипо́к [*gen.* **-пка́**] *n.* pinch; nip; tweak.

щипцы́ [*gen.* **-цо́в**] *n. pl.* tongs. —**хирурги́ческие щипцы́,** forceps. —**щипцы́ для зави́вки,** curling irons. —**щипцы́ для оре́хов,** nutcracker.

щи́пчики [*gen.* **-ков**] *n. pl.* tweezers.

щит [*gen.* **щита́**] *n.* **1,** shield. **2,** screen; guard: щит от гря́зи, mudguard. **3,** board; panel: распредели́тельный щит, switchboard; щит управле́ния, control panel. **4,** shell (*of a turtle*). **5,** *basketball* backboard. —**верну́ться на щите́,** to return home defeated. —**верну́ться со щито́м,** to return home victorious. —**поднима́ть на щит,** to extol; praise to the skies.

щитови́дный *adj.* thyroid: щитови́дная железа́, thyroid gland.

щито́к [*gen.* **-тка́**] *n.* **1,** *dim. of* **щит. 2,** panel. **3,** *sports* shinguard.

щитомо́рдник *n.* copperhead (*snake*).

щу́ка *n.* pike (*fish*).

щуп *n.* **1,** probe. **2,** dipstick.

щу́пальце [*gen. pl.* **-лец**] *n.* tentacle.

щу́пать *v. impfv.* [*pfv.* **пощу́пать**] to feel; touch. —**щу́пать** (+ *acc.*) **глаза́ми,** to look over; scan.

щу́плый *adj., colloq.* puny; thin; frail.

щу́рить *v. impfv.* [*pfv.* **сощу́рить**], *in* **щу́рить глаза́,** to squint. —**щу́риться,** *refl.* to squint.

щу́чий [*fem.* **-чья**] *adj.* pike's. —**как по щу́чьему веле́нию,** as if by magic.

Ъ

Ъ, ъ *n. neut., called* **твёрдый знак**, 27th letter of the Russian alphabet.

Ы

Ы, ы *n. neut.* 28th letter of the Russian alphabet.

Ь

Ь, ь *n. neut., called* **мягкий знак**, 29th letter of the Russian alphabet.

Э

Э, э *n. neut., also called* **э оборо́тное**, thirtieth letter of the Russian alphabet.

эбе́новый *adj.* ebony. —**эбе́новое де́рево**, ebony.

эбони́т *n.* ebonite; vulcanite.

эвакуа́ция *n.* evacuation. —**эвакуацио́нный**, *adj.* evacuation (*attrib.*).

эвакуи́ровать *v. impfv. & pfv.* [*pres.* -ру́ю, -руешь] to evacuate.

эве́н *n.m.* [*fem.* **эве́нка**] Even (*one of a people inhabiting eastern Siberia*).

эве́нк *n.m.* [*fem.* **эвенки́йка**] Evenk (*one of a people inhabiting eastern Siberia*). —**эвенки́йский**, *adj.* Evenki.

эве́нский *adj.* Even: **эве́нский язы́к**, the Even language (*see* **эве́н**).

эвкали́пт *n.* eucalyptus. —**эвкали́птовый**, *adj.* eucalyptus (*attrib.*).

ЭВМ *abbr. of* **электро́нная вычисли́тельная маши́на**, (electronic) computer.

эволюциони́ровать *v. impfv. & pfv.* [*pres.* -ру́ю, -руешь] to evolve.

эволю́ция *n.* evolution. —**эволюцио́нный**, *adj.* evolutionary.

э́врика *interj.* eureka!

эвфеми́зм *n.* euphemism. —**эвфемисти́ческий**, *adj.* euphemistic.

эгалита́рный *adj.* egalitarian.

эги́да *n.* aegis: **под эги́дой** (+ *gen.*), under the aegis (of).

эго́изм *n.* egoism; selfishness. —**эго́ист**; **эго́истка**, *n.* egoist; egotist. —**эгоисти́ческий**; **эгоисти́чный**, *adj.* egoistic; egotistical; selfish.

эготи́зм *n.* egotism.

эдельве́йс (дэ) *n.* edelweiss.

Эде́м (дэ) *n.* Eden.

эй *interj.* hey!

эйнште́йний (тэ) *n.* einsteinium.

эйфори́я *n.* euphoria.

эква́тор *n.* equator. —**экваториа́льный**, *adj.* equatorial.

эквивале́нт *n.* equivalent. —**эквивале́нтность**, *n.f.* equivalence. —**эквивале́нтный**, *adj.* equivalent.

эквилибри́ст *n.* tightrope walker; high-wire artist. —**эквилибри́стика**, *n.* balancing act; tightrope walking.

экзальта́ция *n.* exaltation; ecstasy. —**экзальти́рованный**, *adj.* in a state of exaltation; ecstatic.

экза́мен *n.* examination. —**экзамена́тор**, *n.* examiner. —**экзаменацио́нный**, *adj.* examination (*attrib.*).

экзаменова́ть *v. impfv.* [*pfv.* **проэкзаменова́ть**; *pres.* -ну́ю, -нуешь] to examine. —**экзаменова́ться**, *refl.* to take an examination.

экзеку́ция *n., obs.* **1,** whipping; flogging; corporal punishment. **2,** execution.

экзе́ма (зэ) *n.* eczema.

экземпля́р (зэ) *n.* **1,** copy (*one of many*): **в трёх экземпля́рах**, in three copies; in triplicate. **2,** specimen: **ре́дкий экземпля́р**, rare specimen.

экзистенциали́зм *n.* existentialism. —**экзистенциали́ст**, *n.* existentialist. —**экзистенциа́льный**, *adj.* existential(ist).

экзо́тика *n.* exotic things; exotic objects. —**экзоти́ческий**, *adj.* exotic.

экиво́к *n., usu. pl.* ambiguity: **говори́ть с экиво́ками**, to talk in ambiguities; **говори́ть без экиво́ков**, to talk straight to the point.

э́кий *adj., colloq.* what a...!

экипа́ж *n.* **1,** carriage. **2,** crew.

экипирова́ть *v. impfv. & pfv.* [*pres.* -ру́ю, -руешь] to equip.

экипиро́вка *n.* **1,** equipping. **2,** equipment.

эклекти́зм *n.* eclecticism. —**экле́ктик**, *n.* eclectic. —**эклекти́ческий**; **эклекти́чный**, *adj.* eclectic.

экле́р *n.* éclair.

экли́птика *n., astron.* ecliptic.

эколо́гия *n.* ecology. —**экологи́ческий**, *adj.* ecological.

эконо́м *n., obs.* **1,** thrifty person. **2,** manager of a household; steward. **3,** economist.

эконо́мика *n.* **1,** economics. **2,** economy (*of a country*). —**экономи́ст**, *n.* economist.

эконо́мить *v. impfv.* [*pfv.* **сэконо́мить**; *pres.* -млю, -мишь] **1,** to save: **эконо́мить вре́мя**, to save time; **эконо́мить на материа́лах**, to save on materials. **2,** [*impfv. only*] to economize.

экономи́ческий *adj.* economic.

экономи́чный *adj.* (*of a device, method, etc.*) economical.

эконо́мия *n.* **1,** economy; thrift: **соблюда́ть эконо́мию**, to be economical; economize. **2,** (*with gen.*) saving (of): **эконо́мия то́плива**, saving of fuel; fuel economy. **3,** savings; amount saved (*by economizing*): **эконо́мия соста́вила...**, the savings amounted to...

эконо́мка [*gen. pl.* -мок] *n., obs.* housekeeper.

эконо́мничать *v. impfv., colloq.* to economize; scrimp; watch one's pennies.

эконо́мный *adj.* economical; thrifty.

экра́н *n.* **1**, screen. **2**, the screen (*motion pictures*). **3**, shield: тепловой экра́н, heat shield.

экраниза́ция *n.* filming.

экранизи́ровать *v. impfv. & pfv.* [*pres.* -рую, -руешь] to make into a movie.

экскава́тор *n.* steam shovel.

э́кскурс *n.* digression.

экскурса́нт *n.* person on an excursion; sightseer.

экску́рсия *n.* **1**, excursion; sightseeing tour. **2**, tourist group; sightseeing party. —экскурсио́нный, *adj.* excursion (*attrib.*).

экскурсово́д *n.* tour guide.

экспли́брис *n.* bookplate.

экспанси́вый *adj.* expansive; effusive.

экспансиони́зм *n.* expansionism. —экспансиони́стский, *adj.* expansionist.

экспа́нсия *n.* (territorial) expansion.

экспатриа́ция *n.* expatriation. —экспатриа́нт, *n.* expatriate.

экспатрии́ровать *v. impfv. & pfv.* [*pres.* -рую, -руешь] to expatriate.

экспеди́ция *n.* expedition. —экспедицио́нный, *adj.* expeditionary.

экспериме́нт *n.* experiment. —эксперимента́льный, *adj.* experimental. —эксперименти́рование, *n.* experimentation.

эксперименти́ровать *v. impfv.* [*pres.* -рую, -руешь] to experiment.

экспе́рт *n.* expert.

эксперти́за *n.* **1**, examination by experts. **2**, committee of experts.

экспе́ртный *adj.* **1**, expert. **2**, of experts.

эксплуата́тор *n.* exploiter. —эксплуата́торский, *adj.* exploiter (*attrib.*); exploiting.

эксплуата́ция *n.* **1**, exploitation. **2**, operation. —эксплуатацио́нный, *adj.* operating; operational.

эксплуати́ровать *v. impfv.* [*pres.* -рую, -руешь] **1**, to exploit; take advantage of. **2**, to operate; run.

экспози́метр *n., photog.* exposure meter; light meter.

экспози́ция *n.* **1**, layout; display. **2**, *photog.* exposure.

экспона́т *n.* exhibit.

экспоне́нт *n.* **1**, exhibitor. **2**, *math.* exponent.

экспони́ровать *v. impfv. & pfv.* [*pres.* -рую, -руешь] **1**, to exhibit. **2**, *photog.* to expose.

экспоно́метр *n., photog.* exposure meter; light meter.

э́кспорт *n.* **1**, export. **2**, exports. —экспортёр, *n.* exporter.

экспорти́ровать *v. impfv. & pfv.* [*pres.* -рую, -руешь] to export.

э́кспортный *adj.* export (*attrib.*).

экспре́сс *n.* express (*train, ship, bus, etc.*).

экспресси́вный *adj.* expressive.

экспре́ссия *n.* expression; expressiveness.

экспро́мт *n.* something composed on the spur of the moment; something one just dashed off. —экспро́мтом, *adv.* impromptu; extemporaneously.

экспроприа́ция *n.* expropriation.

экспроприи́ровать *v. impfv. & pfv.* [*pres.* -рую, -руешь] to expropriate.

экста́з *n.* ecstasy. —экстати́ческий, *adj.* ecstatic.

экстерн (тэ) *n.* student allowed to take examinations without attending classes.

экстерриториа́льный *adj.* extraterritorial.

экстравага́нтный *adj.* eccentric; bizarre; outlandish.

экстраги́ровать *v. impfv. & pfv.* [*pres.* -рую, -руешь] to extract.

экстра́кт *n.* extract.

экстра́кция *n.* extraction.

экстраордина́рный *adj.* extraordinary.

экстраполи́ровать *v. impfv. & pfv.* [*pres.* -рую, -руешь] to extrapolate.

экстраполя́ция *n.* extrapolation.

экстреми́зм *n.* extremism. —экстреми́ст, *n.* extremist. —экстреми́стский, *adj.* extremist.

э́кстренный *adj.* **1**, urgent. **2**, special. —э́кстренно, *adv.* urgently.

эксце́нтрик *n.* **1**, clown. **2**, *obs.* eccentric (person). **3**, *mech.* cam.

эксцентри́ческий *adj.* **1**, = эксцентри́чный. **2**, *theat.* comical; improbable. **3**, *math.* eccentric.

эксцентри́чный *adj.* eccentric; odd. —эксцентри́чность, *n.f.* eccentricity.

эксце́сс *n., usu. pl.* excesses.

эктопла́зма *n.* ectoplasm.

эласти́чный *adj.* **1**, elastic. **2**, supple. —эласти́чность, *n.f.* elasticity.

элева́тор *n.* **1**, grain elevator. **2**, lift; hoist.

элега́нтный *adj.* elegant. —элега́нтно, *adv.* elegantly. —элега́нтность, *n.f.* elegance.

элеги́ческий *adj.* **1**, elegiac. **2**, [*also,* элеги́чный] *fig.* melancholy.

эле́гия *n.* **1**, elegy. **2**, *fig.* melancholy.

электризова́ть *v. impfv. & pfv.* [*pfv. also* наэлектризова́ть; *pres.* -зую, -зу́ешь] **1**, to electrify; charge with electricity. **2**, *fig.* to electrify; thrill.

эле́ктрик *n.* electrician. —инжене́р-эле́ктрик, electrical engineer.

элетри́к *adj. indecl.* grayish blue.

электрифика́ция *n.* electrification.

электрифици́ровать *v. impfv. & pfv.* [*pres.* -рую, -руешь] to electrify; provide with electric power.

электри́ческий *adj.* electric. —электри́ческий стул, electric chair.

электри́чество *n.* electricity.

электри́чка [*gen. pl.* -чек] *n., colloq.* **1**, electric railway. **2**, electric train.

электро- *prefix* electric(al): электропо́езд, electric train; электроте́хник, electrical engineer.

электрово́з *n.* electric locomotive.

электро́д *n.* electrode.

электродви́гатель *n.m.* electric motor.

электрока́р *n.* electric (*i.e.* battery-operated) vehicle for carrying loads or baggage.

электрокардиогра́мма *n.* electrocardiogram. —электрокардио́граф, *n.* electrocardiograph.

электро́лиз *n.* electrolysis.

электроли́ния *n.* electric power line.

электроли́т *n.* electrolyte.

электромагнети́зм *n.* electromagnetism. —электромагни́т, *n.* electromagnet. —электромагни́тный, *adj.* electromagnetic.

электромонтёр *n.* electrician.

электро́н *n.* electron.

электро́ника *n.* electronics.

электро́нный *adj.* **1**, electron (*attrib.*). **2**, electronic. —электро́нная ла́мпа, electron tube; vacuum tube.

электропита́ние *n.* power supply.

электроста́нция *n.* power station.

электроста́тика *n.* electrostatics. —электростати́ческий, *adj.* electrostatic.

электроте́хник *n.* electrical engineer. —электроте́хника, *n.* electrical engineering.

электроэнéргия n. electrical energy; electric power.

элемéнт n. **1**, element. **2**, *electricity* cell: сухóй элемéнт, dry cell. **3**, *colloq.* character: подозрúтельный элемéнт, suspicious character.

элементáрный adj. elementary.

элерóн n. aileron.

эликсúр n. elixir.

элúта n. elite.

эллúнский adj. Hellenic.

эллúпс n. **1**, ellipse. **2**, = э́ллипсис.

эллúпсис n., *ling.* ellipsis.

эллипсóид n. ellipsoid.

эллиптúческий adj. elliptical.

эль n.m. ale.

эльф n. elf.

эмáлевый adj. enamel (*attrib.*); enameled.

эмалирóванный adj. enameled.

эмалировáть v. *impfv.* [*pres.* -рýю, -рýешь] to enamel.

эмáль n.f. enamel.

эманáция n. emanation.

эмансипáтор n. emancipator. —**эмансипáция**, n. emancipation.

эмансипúровать v. *impfv.* & *pfv.* [*pres.* -рую, -руешь] to emancipate.

эмбáрго n. *indecl.* embargo.

эмблéма n. emblem. —**эмблематúческий**, adj. emblematic.

эмболúя n. embolism.

эмбриолóгия n. embryology. —**эмбриóлог**, n. embryologist.

эмбриóн n. embryo. —**эмбрионáльный**, adj. embryonic.

эмигрáнт n. émigré; emigrant. —**эмигрáнтский**, adj. émigré (*attrib.*).

эмигрáция n. **1**, emigration. **2**, émigrés. —**в эмигрáции**, abroad; in a foreign land (*to which one has emigrated*).

эмигрúровать v. *impfv.* & *pfv.* [*pres.* -рую, -руешь] to emigrate.

эмúр n. emir. —**эмирáт**, n. emirate.

эмиссáр n. emissary.

эмúссия n. **1**, *finance* issuance; emission. **2**, *electronics* emission.

эмóция n. emotion. —**эмоционáльный**, adj. emotional.

эмпирúзм n. empiricism. —**эмпúрик**, n. empiricist. —**эмпирúческий**, adj. empirical.

э́му n.m. *indecl.* emu.

эмýльсия n. emulsion.

эмфизéма (зэ) n. emphysema.

эндемúческий adj. endemic.

эндокрúнный adj. endocrine.

эндокринолóгия n. endocrinology.

э́ндшпиль n.m., *chess* end game.

энергéтика n. energy. —**энергетúческий**, adv. energy (*attrib.*).

энергúчный adj. **1**, (*of a person*) energetic. **2**, (*of measures, protests, etc.*) forceful; vigorous; energetic. —**энергúчно**, adv. energetically; vigorously.

энéргия n. **1**, energy. **2**, (electric) power.

э́нный adj. **1**, any; an unspecified; a certain. **2**, *colloq.* unlimited; endless: э́нное колúчество, an endless amount. —**в э́нной стéпени**, to the nth degree.

э́нский adj. X (*used to designate something that cannot be identified*).

энтерúт n. enteritis.

энтомолóгия n. entomology. —**энтомóлог**, n. entomologist. —**энтомологúческий**, adj. entomological.

энтузиáзм n. enthusiasm. —**энтузиáст**, n. enthusiast.

энцефалúт n. encephalitis.

энцúклика n. encyclical.

энциклопéдия n. encyclopedia. —**энциклопедúст**, n. encyclopedist. —**энциклопедúческий**, adj. encyclopedic.

эпигóн n. imitator; copier.

эпигрáмма n. epigram. —**эпиграмматúческий**, adj. epigrammatic.

эпúграф n. epigraph.

эпидéмия n. epidemic. —**эпидемúческий**, adj. epidemic.

эпидéрмис (дэ) n. epidermis.

эпизóд n. episode.

эпизодúческий adj. **1**, episodic. **2**, occasional; sporadic.

э́пик n. epic poet.

эпикурéец [*gen.* -éйца] n. epicurean. —**эпикурéйский**, adj. epicurean.

эпилéпсия n. epilepsy. —**эпилéптик**, n. epileptic. —**эпилептúческий**, adj. epileptic.

эпилóг n. epilogue.

эпúстола n. epistle. —**эпистолáрный**, adj. epistolary.

эпитáфия n. epitaph.

эпитéлий (тэ) n. epithelium. —**эпителиáльный**, adj. epithelial.

эпúтет n. epithet.

эпицéнтр n. epicenter.

эпúческий adj. epic.

эполéта n. epaulet. *Also*, **эполéт**.

эпопéя n. epic; epic work.

эпóха n. epoch; age; era. —**эпохáльный**, adj. epochal.

э́ра n. era. —**до нáшей э́ры**, B.C.: в двухсóтом годý до нáшей э́ры, in 200 B.C.—**нáшей э́ры**, A.D.: в двухсóтом годý нáшей э́ры, in 200 A.D.

э́рбий n. erbium.

эрг n. erg.

эрéкция n., *physiol.* erection.

э́рика n. brier; heath.

Эрмитáж n. the Hermitage Museum (*in Leningrad*).

эрóзия n. erosion.

эротúзм n. eroticism.

эрóтика n. **1**, sensuality. **2**, erotic literature. —**эротúческий**, adj. erotic.

эрудúрованный adj. erudite.

эрудúция n. erudition. —**эрудúт**, n. erudite person.

эрцгéрцог n. archduke. —**эрцгерцогúня**, n. archduchess. —**эрцгéрцогство**, n. archduchy.

эскáдра n., *naval* squadron.

эскáдренный adj. squadron (*attrib.*). —**эскáдренный миноносец**, destroyer.

эскадрúлья [*gen. pl.* -лий] n. (air) squadron.

эскадрóн n. (cavalry) squadron. —**эскадрóнный**, adj. squadron (*attrib.*).

эскалáтор n. escalator.

эскалáция n. escalation.

эскáрп n., *mil.* escarpment.

эсквáйр n. esquire.

эскúз n. **1**, sketch. **2**, draft; outline. —**эскúзный**, adj. rough; preliminary; in outline form.

эскимо́ *n. indecl.* ice cream on a stick.

эскимо́с *n.m.* [*fem.* -мо́ска] Eskimo. —эскимо́с-
ский, *adj.* Eskimo.

эско́рт *n., mil.* escort.

эскорти́ровать *v. impfv.* [*pres.* -рую, -руешь] *mil.* to
escort.

эсми́нец [*gen.* -нца] *n., naval* destroyer (*contr. of*
эска́дренный миноно́сец).

эспера́нто *n. indecl.* Esperanto.

эсплана́да *n.* esplanade.

эссе́нция *n.* **1,** essence: ро́мовая эссе́нция, essence
of rum. **2,** *fig.* essence.

эстака́да *n.* **1,** trestle; overpass. **2,** pier.

эстафе́та *n.* **1,** relay race. **2,** baton (*used in a relay
race*). —эстафе́тный, *adj.* relay (*attrib.*); used in a
relay race.

эсте́тика (тэ) *n.* esthetics. —эсте́т, *n.* esthete. —эсте-
ти́ческий, *adj.* esthetic.

эсто́нец [*gen.* -нца] *n.m.* [*fem.* -нка] Estonian.
—эсто́нский, *adj.* Estonian.

эстраго́н *n.* tarragon.

эстра́да *n.* **1,** stage; platform. **2,** vaudeville. —эстра́д-
ный, *adj.* vaudeville (*attrib.*).

эта́ж [*gen.* этажа́] *n.* floor; story.

этаже́рка [*gen. pl.* -рок] *n.* bookcase.

э́так *adv., colloq.* **1,** so; like this; like that. **2,** about;
approximately; some. —и так и э́так, this way and that.

э́такий *adj., colloq.* **1,** such; such a... **2,** what a...!

этало́н *n.* **1,** standard (*of measurement*). **2,** *fig.* model.

эта́п *n.* **1,** stage; leg (*of a journey*). **2,** *fig.* stage; phase.
3, halting place (*for troops, or prisoners going into
exile*). **4,** group of prisoners traveling under guard.
—по эта́пу, under guard; under escort.

э́тика *n.* ethics.

этике́т *n.* etiquette.

этике́тка [*gen. pl.* -ток] *n.* label.

эти́л *n.* ethyl.

этиле́н *n.* ethylene.

этили́рованный *adj.* (*of gasoline*) leaded.

эти́ловый *adj.* ethyl (*attrib.*).

этимоло́гия *n.* etymology. —этимо́лог, *n.* etymologist. —этимологи́ческий, *adj.* etymological.

эти́ческий *adj.* ethical. *Also,* эти́чный.

этни́ческий *adj.* ethnic.

этногра́фия *n.* ethnography. —этно́граф, *n.* ethnographer. —этнографи́ческий, *adj.* ethnographic.

этноло́гия *n.* ethnology. —этно́лог, *n.* ethnologist.
—этнологи́ческий, *adj.* ethnological.

э́то *dem. adj., neut. of* э́тот, this: э́то сло́во, this word.
—*dem. pron.* **1,** this; that; it: что э́то?, what is this?
Я уже́ знал об э́том, I already knew about it. Что
вы хоти́те э́тим сказа́ть?, what do you mean by that?
2, this is; that is; it is: э́то дуб, this is an oak tree;
э́то — желу́ди, these are acorns. Это о́чень про́сто,
this (that, it) is very simple. **3,** (*of neuter nouns only*)
this one. —*particle* **1,** (the one) who: кто э́то звони́л?,
who was that who called? Это он вы́болтал секре́т?,
was it *he* who spilled the beans? **2,** *used as an intensifier:* что э́то с ва́ми?, what's the matter with you?
Куда́ э́то он пошёл?, where on earth has he gone?

э́тот [*fem.* э́та; *neut.* э́то; *pl.* э́ти; *gen.* э́того, э́той,
э́тих; *dat.* э́тому, э́той, э́тим; *acc. fem.* э́ту; *instr.*
э́тим, э́той, э́тими; *prepl.* э́том, э́той, э́тих] *dem.
adj.* this: э́тот дом, this house; э́та кни́га, this book;
э́то сло́во, this word; э́ти лю́ди, these people. —*dem.
pron.* this one.

этру́сский *adj.* Etruscan.

этю́д *n.* **1,** *art* sketch. **2,** essay. **3,** *music* étude. **4,**
chess problem.

эфеме́рный *adj.* ephemeral.

эфе́с *n.* hilt (*handle of a sword*).

эфио́п *n.m.* [*fem.* эфио́пка] Ethiopian. —эфио́п-
ский, *adj.* Ethiopian.

эфи́р *n.* **1,** ether (*upper regions of the atmosphere*).
2, *chem.* ether: эти́ловый эфи́р, ether; ethyl ether.
3, *radio* air: выходи́ть в эфи́р, to go on the air. Пе-
реда́ть в эфи́р, to broadcast. —прямо́й эфи́р,
live broadcasting.

эфи́рный *adj.* **1,** ether (*attrib.*). **2,** ethereal. —эфи́р-
ное ма́сло, essential oil.

эффе́кт *n.* **1,** effect. **2,** *pl.* effects: шумовы́е эф-
фе́кты, sound effects. —с эффе́ктом, with emphasis;
with a flourish.

эффекти́вный *adj.* **1,** effective. **2,** efficient. —эф-
фекти́вно, *adv.* effectively; efficiently. —эффекти́в-
ность, *n.f.* effectiveness; efficiency.

эффе́ктный *adj.* striking; showy; flashy.

э́хо *n.* echo.

эхоло́т *n.* sonic depth finder.

эшафо́т *n.* scaffold.

эшело́н *n.* **1,** *mil.* echelon. **2,** special train.

Ю

Ю, ю *n. neut.* 31st letter of the Russian alphabet.

юбиле́й *n.* anniversary; jubilee. —**юбиле́йный**, *adj.* anniversary (*attrib.*).

юбиля́р *n.* person or institution whose anniversary is being celebrated.

ю́бка [*gen. pl.* -бо́к] *n.* skirt. —**ни́жняя ю́бка**, half slip; petticoat. —**ю́бка клёш**, flared skirt.

ю́бочка [*gen. pl.* -чек] *n.* short skirt. —**шотла́ндская ю́бочка**, kilt.

ювели́р *n.* jeweler.

ювели́рный *adj.* **1,** jewelry (*attrib.*); jeweler's (*attrib.*). **2,** *fig.* finely wrought; exquisite.

юг *n.* south.

ю́го-восто́к *n.* southeast. —**ю́го-восто́чный**, *adj.* southeast; southeastern; southeasterly.

ю́го-за́пад *n.* southwest. —**ю́го-за́падный**, *adj.* southwest; southwestern; southwesterly.

югосла́в *n.m.* [*fem.* -сла́вка] Yugoslav. —**югосла́вский**, *adj.* Yugoslav; Yugoslavian.

южа́нин [*pl.* южа́не, южа́н] *n.m.* [*fem.* южа́нка] southerner.

ю́жный *adj.* southern; South; southerly.

ю́зом *adv.* into a skid: **пойти́ ю́зом**, to skid.

ю́кка *n.* yucca.

юла́ *n.* **1,** top (*toy*). **2,** *colloq.* fidgety person; fidgety child.

юлиа́нский *adj., in* **юлиа́нский календа́рь**, Julian calendar.

юли́ть *v. impfv., colloq.* **1,** to keep moving about. **2,** (*of an insect*) to flit. **3,** (*with* **пе́ред**) to play up to; ingratiate oneself (with). **4,** to equivocate.

ю́мор *n.* humor.

юморе́ска *n.* humoresque.

юмори́ст *n.* humorist. —**юмористи́ческий**, *adj.* humorous.

ю́нга *n.* cabin boy.

юне́ц [*gen.* юнца́] *n., colloq.* youth; lad.

ю́нкер *n.* **1,** [*pl.* ю́нкеры] junker. **2,** [*pl.* юнкера́] *prerev.* military cadet.

ю́ность *n.f.* youth.

ю́ноша [*gen. pl.* -шей] *n.m.* youth (*young man*).

ю́ношеский *adj.* **1,** youth (*attrib.*). **2,** youthful.

ю́ношество *n.* **1,** youth; young people. **2,** youth (*time when one is young*).

ю́ный *adj.* young; youthful.

юпи́тер *n.* **1,** Jupiter. **2,** *l.c.* floodlight.

юр *n., in* **на (са́мом) юру́**, **1,** in an open (*or* exposed) place. **2,** *colloq.* in the midst (*or* center) of everything.

юриди́ческий *adj.* juridical; legal; judicial. —**юриди́ческий факульте́т**, department/faculty of law; law school.

юрисди́кция *n.* jurisdiction.

юриско́нсульт *n.* legal adviser (*to a company, institution, etc.*).

юриспруде́нция *n.* jurisprudence.

юри́ст *n.* lawyer.

ю́ркий *adj.* **1,** nimble; agile. **2,** *fig., colloq.* clever; sharp.

юркну́ть *also,* **ю́ркнуть** *v. pfv.* to dart; scamper.

юро́дивый *adj.* touched; cracked; crazy.

юро́дство *n.* **1,** madness; derangement. **2,** irrational act.

юро́дствовать *v. impfv.* [*pres.* -ствую, -ствуешь] to act like a madman.

юро́к [*gen.* юрка́] *n.* brambling.

ю́рский *adj.* Jurassic.

ю́рта *n.* nomad's tent.

юсти́ция *n.* justice. —**мини́стр юсти́ции**, Minister of Justice; (*U.S.*) Attorney General.

ют *n.* quarterdeck.

юти́ться *v.r. impfv.* [*pres.* ючу́сь, юти́шься] **1,** to nestle. **2,** to huddle. **3,** to be cooped up.

юфть *n.f.* Russia leather.

Я

Я, я *n. neut.* 32nd letter of the Russian alphabet. —**от А до Я**, from A to Z.

я [*gen. & acc.* **меня**; *dat. & prepl.* **мне**; *instr.* **мной** *or* **мною**] *pers. pron.*, 1st person *sing.* I.

я́беда *n.m. & f., colloq.* **1,** tattler. **2,** spreader of malicious gossip. —*n.f., obs.* malicious gossip.

я́бедник *n., colloq.* spreader of malicious gossip.

я́бедничать *v. impfv.* [*pfv.* **ная́бедничать**] (*with* **на** + *acc.*) *colloq.* **1,** to tell (on); tattle (on). **2,** to spread malicious gossip (about).

я́бедничество *n., colloq.* spreading of malicious gossip.

я́блоко [*pl.* **я́блоки, я́блок**] *n.* apple. —**в я́блоках**, dappled: **се́рый в я́блоках**, dapple-gray. —**глазно́е я́блоко**, eyeball. —**я́блоко мише́ни**, bull's-eye. —**я́блоко раздо́ра**, apple of discord; bone of contention.

я́блоневый *adj.* of apple trees. **Я́блоневый цвет**, apple blossom. **Я́блоневый сад**, apple orchard. *Also,* **я́блонный**.

я́блоня *n.* apple tree.

я́блочко [*gen. pl.* **-чек**] *n., dim. of* **я́блоко.**

я́блочный *adj.* apple (*attrib.*); of apples.

яви́ть [*infl.* **явлю́, я́вишь**] *v., pfv. of* **явля́ть.** —**яви́ться**, *refl., pfv. of* **явля́ться.**

я́вка [*gen. pl.* **-вок**] *n.* **1,** appearance; attendance. **2,** secret meeting. **3,** secret meeting place.

явле́ние *n.* **1,** phenomenon. **2,** occurrence. **3,** *theat.* scene.

явля́ть *v. impfv.* [*pfv.* **яви́ть**] **1,** to show; reveal. **2,** *in* **явля́ть собо́й,** *colloq.* to be. —**явля́ться,** *refl.* **1,** to appear; report: **яви́ться на рабо́ту,** to appear at work; report for work. **2,** (*with instr.*) to be: **явля́ться по́лной неожи́данностью,** to be a complete surprise.

я́вный *adj.* **1,** overt; open: **я́вная вражда́,** overt/open hostility. **2,** obvious: **э́то я́вное недоразуме́ние,** this is an obvious (*or* is obviously a) misunderstanding. —**я́вно,** *adv.* obviously.

я́вор *n.* sycamore; Eurasian maple.

я́вочный *adj.* **1,** secret; clandestine. **2,** *in* **я́вочный пункт; я́вочная ба́за,** *mil.* reporting office (*for recruits*). —**я́вочным поря́дком,** without prior permission.

я́вственный *adj.* clear; distinct.

я́вствовать *v. impfv.* [*pres.* **-ствует**] to be clear; be apparent; be obvious.

явь *n.f.* reality.

ягдта́ш *n.* game bag.

я́гель *n.m.* reindeer moss.

ягнёнок [*gen.* **-нка;** *pl.* **ягня́та, ягня́т**] *n.* lamb.

ягни́ться *v.r. impfv.* [*pfv.* **оягни́ться**] (*of a ewe*) to give birth.

ягня́тник *n.* bearded vulture.

я́года *n.* **1,** berry. **2,** *in* **ви́нная я́года,** fig. —**одного́ по́ля я́года,** birds of a feather.

я́годицы *n. pl.* [*sing.* **я́годица**] buttocks.

я́годник *n.* **1,** berry patch. **2,** berry bush. **3,** *colloq.* one who likes to pick berries.

я́годный *adj.* berry (*attrib.*).

ягуа́р *n.* jaguar.

яд *n.* **1,** poison. **2,** *fig.* venom.

я́дерный *adj.* nuclear.

ядови́тый *adj.* **1,** poison; poisonous; venomous; toxic. **2,** *fig.* venomous; vicious; malicious.

ядохимика́т *n.* pesticide.

ядрёный *adj., colloq.* **1,** (*of a plant*) hearty; (*of a fruit*) juicy. **2,** (*of a person*) robust; vigorous; hale and hearty. **3,** bracing; invigorating.

я́дрица *n.* unground buckwheat.

ядро́ [*pl.* **я́дра, я́дер, я́драм**] *n.* **1,** kernel. **2,** core. **3,** nucleus. **4,** *fig.* heart; core. **5,** *mil.* ball: **пу́шечное ядро́,** cannon ball. **6,** *sports* shot: **толка́ть ядро́,** to put the shot.

я́зва *n.* **1,** ulcer; sore. **2,** *fig.* curse; plague. —**сиби́рская я́зва,** anthrax.

я́звенный *adj.* ulcerous. —**я́звенная боле́знь,** peptic ulcer.

язви́тельный *adj.* caustic; biting; cutting; sarcastic.

язви́ть *v. impfv.* [*pres.* **язвлю́, язви́шь**] **1,** *obs.* to sting. **2,** *fig., obs.* to taunt. **3,** [*pfv.* **съязви́ть**] to say sarcastically.

язы́к [*gen.* **языка́**] *n.* **1,** tongue. **2,** language. **3,** clapper (*of a bell*). **4,** *mil.* prisoner (*to be interrogated*). —**найти́ о́бщий язы́к,** to find common ground. —**говори́ть на ра́зных языка́х,** to be speaking different languages; be on different wavelengths.

языка́стый *adj., colloq.* sharp-tongued.

языкове́д *n.* linguist. —**языкове́дение,** *n.* linguistics.

языково́й *adj.* linguistic; language (*attrib.*).

языко́вый *adj.* tongue (*attrib.*).

языкозна́ние *n.* linguistics.

язы́ческий *adj.* heathen; pagan. —**язы́чество,** *n.* paganism.

язычко́вый *adj., phonet.* uvular. —**язычко́вый инструме́нт,** reed instrument.

язы́чник *n.* heathen; pagan.

язычо́к [*gen.* **-чка́**] *n.* **1,** *dim. of* **язы́к. 2,** tongue (of a shoe). **3,** uvula. **4,** *music* reed. **5,** catch; fastener.

язь [*gen.* **язя́**] *n.m.* a fish of the carp family.

яи́чко [*gen. pl.* -чек] *n.* **1,** *dim. of* яйцо́. **2,** testicle.

яи́чник *n., anat.* ovary.

яи́чница *n.* [*also,* яи́чница-глазу́нья] fried eggs. —**яи́чница-болту́нья,** scrambled eggs.

яи́чный *adj.* egg (*attrib.*).

яйцеви́дный *adj.* egg-shaped.

яйцево́д *n.* oviduct.

яйцекладу́щий *adj.* oviparous.

яйцекле́тка *n., biol.* ovule.

яйцеро́дный *adj.* oviparous.

яйцо́ [*pl.* я́йца, яи́ц, я́йцам] *n.* egg. —**яйцо́-пашо́т,** poached egg.

як *n.* yak.

я́кобы *conj.* that (*implying skepticism about a statement*): говоря́т, я́кобы он ско́ро уезжа́ет, they say (that) he is leaving soon. —*particle* supposedly; allegedly: письмо́, я́кобы напи́санное им, a letter allegedly written by him.

я́корный *adj.* of an anchor. —**я́корное ме́сто; я́корная стоя́нка,** (place of) anchorage.

я́корь [*pl.* якоря́] *n.m.* **1,** anchor. **2,** *electricity* armature. —**стать на я́корь,** to anchor. —**стоя́ть на я́коре,** to stand/lie at anchor. —**я́корь спасе́ния,** last hope; last means of salvation.

яку́т *n.m.* [*fem.* яку́тка] Yakut (*one of a people inhabiting northeastern Siberia*). —**яку́тский,** *adj.* Yakut.

якша́ться *v.r. impfv.* (*with* с + *instr.*) *colloq.* to hobnob (with); rub elbows (with).

ял *n.* yawl.

я́лик *n.* skiff; dinghy; wherry.

я́ловый *adj.* (*of cows, sheep, etc.*) dry; giving no milk.

я́ма *n.* hole; pit. —**возду́шная я́ма,** air pocket. —**выгребна́я я́ма,** cesspool. —**долгова́я я́ма,** debtors' prison.

ямб *n.* iamb. —**четырёхсто́пный ямб,** iambic tetrameter. —**пятисто́пный ямб,** iambic pentameter.

ямби́ческий *adj.* iambic.

я́мка [*gen. pl.* -мок] *n.* **1,** *dim. of* я́ма. **2,** dimple.

я́мочка [*gen. pl.* -чек] *n.* dimple.

ямс *n.* yam.

ямщи́к [*gen.* -щика́] *n.* stagecoach driver.

янва́рь [*gen.* января́] *n.m.* January. —**янва́рский,** *adj.* January (*attrib.*).

я́нки *n.m. indecl.* Yankee.

янта́рь [*gen.* -таря́] *n.m.* amber. —**янта́рный,** *adj.* amber.

япо́нец [*gen.* -нца] *n.m.* [*fem.* -нка] Japanese (man): он япо́нец, he is Japanese. —**япо́нский,** *adj.* Japanese.

яр [*2nd loc.* яру́] *n.* **1,** cliff. **2,** ravine.

яра́нга *n.* tent made of reindeer hides.

ярд *n.* yard (*36 inches*).

яре́мный *adj., in* **яре́мная ве́на,** jugular vein.

я́ркий *adj.* [*short form* я́рок, ярка́, я́рко; *comp.* я́рче] **1,** bright; brilliant. **2,** *fig.* striking; vivid; graphic. **3,** *fig.* brilliant; outstanding.

я́рко *adv.* **1,** brightly; brilliantly. **2,** clearly; distinctly.

я́рко- *prefix, used with colors,* bright: я́рко-кра́сный, bright red.

я́ркость *n.f.* brightness; brilliance.

ярлы́к [*gen.* -лыка́] *n.* label; tag.

ярлычо́к [*gen.* -чка́] *n., dim. of* ярлы́к.

я́рмарка [*gen. pl.* -рок] *n.* (trade) fair. —**я́рмарочный,** *adj.* fair (*attrib.*).

ярмо́ [*pl.* я́рма] *n.* **1,** yoke (*for oxen*). **2,** *fig.* yoke (*of oppression*).

яровиза́ция *n.* vernalization.

яровизи́ровать *v. impfv. & pfv.* [*pres.* -рую, -руешь] to vernalize.

ярово́й *adj.* (*of crops*) spring (*attrib.*): ярова́я пшени́ца, spring wheat.

я́ростный *adj.* **1,** furious. **2,** violent.

я́рость *n.f.* fury; rage.

я́рус *n.* tier. —**я́русный,** *adj.* tiered.

я́рый *adj.* **1,** furious; violent. **2,** fervent; zealous.

ярь-медя́нка [*gen.* я́ри-медя́нки] *n.* verdigris.

я́сельный *adj.* nursery (*attrib.*).

я́сеневый *adj.* ash (*attrib.*).

я́сень *n.m.* ash (*tree*).

я́сли [*gen.* я́слей] *n. pl.* **1,** manger. **2,** nursery; day nursery.

яснеть *v. impfv.* to become clear; clear up.

я́сно *adv.* clearly. —*adj., used predicatively* clear: всё я́сно?, is everything clear? Сего́дня я́сно, it is a clear day today. —*particle* **1,** I see; I understand. **2,** *colloq.* of course.

яснови́дение *n.* clairvoyance. —**яснови́дец,** *n.* [*gen.* -дца] clairvoyant (person). —**яснови́дящий,** *adj.* clairvoyant.

я́сность *n.f.* clarity.

я́сный *adj.* [*short form* я́сен, ясна́, я́сно, я́сны *or* ясны́] clear. —**я́сное де́ло,** of course; it goes without saying. —**ясне́е я́сного,** as clear as day; crystal-clear.

я́ства *n. pl.* [*sing.* я́ство] food; victuals.

я́стреб [*pl.* ястреба́ *or* я́стребы] *n.* hawk.

ястреби́ный *adj.* **1,** hawk's. **2,** hawklike.

ястребо́к [*gen.* -бка́] *n.* **1,** *dim. of* я́стреб. **2,** *colloq.* fighter plane.

ятага́н *n.* scimitar.

ять *n.m.* name of the old letter Ѣ of the Russian alphabet, replaced in 1918 by the letter е. —**на ять,** *colloq.* **1,** first-rate. **2,** perfectly; to a T.

я́хонт *n., obs.* **1,** ruby. **2,** sapphire.

я́хта *n.* yacht.

яхтсме́н *n.* yachtsman.

яче́йка [*gen. pl.* ячее́к] *n.* **1,** tiny opening (*one of many*). **2,** socket (*of a tooth*). **3,** cell (*of a communist party*). **4,** foxhole.

ячме́нный *adj.* barley (*attrib.*).

ячме́нь [*gen.* -меня́] *n.m.* **1,** barley. **2,** sty (*on one's eye*).

я́чневый *adj.* made of fine-ground barley.

я́шма *n.* jasper. —**я́шмовый,** *adj.* jasper (*attrib.*).

я́щер *n.* pangolin.

я́щерица *n.* lizard.

я́щик *n.* **1,** box. **2,** drawer. **3,** *in* му́сорный я́щик, garbage can; почто́вый я́щик, mailbox. —**откла́дывать в до́лгий я́щик,** to put off indefinitely. —**сыгра́ть в я́щик,** *colloq.* to die; kick the bucket.

я́щур *n.* foot-and-mouth disease.

A Glossary
of Proper Nouns

CONTINENTS

Africa	Áфрика
America	Амéрика
Antarctica	Антарктѝда (continent)
	Антáрктика (South Polar Region)
Asia	Áзия
Eurasia	Еврáзия
Europe	Еврóпа

COUNTRIES

Afghanistan	Афганистáн
Albania	Албáния
Algeria	Алжѝр
Angola	Ангóла
Argentina	Аргентѝна
Australia	Австрáлия
Austria	Áвстрия
Bahrain	Бахрéйн
Bangladesh	Бангладéш
Barbados	Барбáдос
Belgium	Бéльгия
Belize	Белѝз
Benin	Бенѝн
Bhutan	Бутáн
Bolivia	Болѝвия
Botswana	Ботсвáна
Brazil	Бразѝлия
Bulgaria	Болгáрия
Burma	Бѝрма
Burundi	Бурýнди
Cambodia	Камбóджа
Cameroon	Камерýн
Canada	Канáда
Chad	Чад
Chile	Чѝли
China	Китáй
Colombia	Колýмбия
Congo	Кóнго
Costa Rica	Кóста-Рѝка
Cuba	Кýба
Cyprus	Кипр
Czechoslovakia	Чехословáкия

Denmark	Дáния
Dominican Republic	Доминикáнская респýблика
Ecuador	Эквадóр
Egypt	Егѝпет (*gen.* -пта)
El Salvador	Сальвадóр
Ethiopia	Эфиóпия
Fiji	Фѝджи
Finland	Финлáндия
France	Фрáнция
Gabon	Габóн
Gambia	Гáмбия
Germany	Гермáния
Ghana	Гáна
Great Britain	Великобритáния
Greece	Грéция
Guatemala	Гватемáла
Guinea	Гвинéя
Guyana	Гайáна
Haiti	Гайти
Honduras	Гондурáс
Hungary	Вéнгрия
Iceland	Ислáндия
India	Ѝндия
Indonesia	Индонéзия
Iran	Ирáн
Iraq	Ирáк
Ireland	Ирлáндия
Israel	Изрáиль (*m.*).
Italy	Итáлия
Ivory Coast	Бéрег Слонóвой Кóсти
Jamaica	Ямáйка
Japan	Япóния
Jordan	Иордáния
Kenya	Кéния
Korea	Корéя
Kuwait	Кувéйт
Laos	Лаóс
Lebanon	Ливáн
Lesotho	Лесóто
Liberia	Либéрия
Libya	Лѝвия
Luxembourg	Люксембýрг

Malagasy Republic	Малагасийская Республика	Upper Volta	Ве́рхняя Во́льта
Malawi	Мала́ви	Uruguay	Уругва́й
Malaysia	Мала́йзия		
Mali	Мали́	Venezuela	Венесуэ́ла
Malta	Ма́льта	Vietnam	Вьетна́м
Mauritania	Маврита́ния		
Mauritius	Маври́кий	Yemen	Йе́мен
Mexico	Ме́ксика	Yugoslavia	Югосла́вия
Mongolia	Монго́лия		
Morocco	Маро́кко	Zaire	Заи́р
Mozambique	Мозамби́к	Zambia	За́мбия
		Zimbabwe	Зимба́бве

Namibia	Нами́бия
Nepal	Непа́л
Netherlands	Нидерла́нды
New Zealand	Но́вая Зела́ндия
Nicaragua	Никара́гуа
Niger	Ни́гер
Nigeria	Ниге́рия
Norway	Норве́гия

TERRITORIES, REGIONS, PRINCIPALITIES

Andorra	Андо́рра
Armenia	Арме́ния
Oman	Ома́н
		Bavaria	Бава́рия
Pakistan	Пакиста́н	Bessarabia	Бессара́бия
Panama	Пана́ма	Bosnia	Бо́сния
Paraguay	Парагва́й	Britanny	Брета́нь (f.)
Peru	Перу́	Burgundy	Бургу́ндия
Philippines	Филиппи́ны		
Poland	По́льша	Cape Cod	Кейп-Ко́д
Portugal	Португа́лия	Cape of Good Hope	мыс До́брой Наде́жды
		Cornwall	Ко́рнуолл
Qatar	Ка́тар	Crimea	Крым
		Croatia	Хорва́тия
Romania	Румы́ния		
Rwanda	Руа́нда	Dalmatia	Далма́ция
Saudi Arabia	Сауди́вская Ара́вия	England	А́нглия
Senegal	Сенега́л	Eritrea	Эритре́я
Sierra Leone	Сье́рра-Лео́не	Estonia	Эсто́ния
Singapore	Сингапу́р		
Somalia	Сомали́	Flanders	Фла́ндрия
South Africa	Ю́жно-Африка́нская Респу́блика		
		Galicia	Гали́ция
Soviet Union	Сове́тский Сою́з	Georgia	Гру́зия
Spain	Испа́ния	Gibraltar	Гибралта́р
Sri Lanka	Шри Ла́нка	Greenland	Гренла́ндия
Sudan	Суда́н		
Surinam	Surinám	Holland	Голла́ндия
Swaziland	Сва́зиленд	Hong Kong	Гонко́нг
Sweden	Шве́ция		
Switzerland	Швейца́рия	Indochina	Индокита́й
Syria	Си́рия		
		Kashmir	Кашми́р
Taiwan	Тайва́нь (m.)		
Tanzania	Танза́ния	Labrador	Лабрадо́р
Thailand	Таила́нд	Latvia	Ла́твия
Togo	То́го	Liechtenstein	Ли́хтенштейн
Trinidad and Tobago	Тринида́д и Тоба́го	Lithuania	Литва́
Tunisia	Туни́с		
Turkey	Ту́рция	Macao	Мака́о
		Macedonia	Македо́ния
Uganda	Уга́нда	Manchuria	Маньчжу́рия
United States	Соединённые Шта́ты	Melanesia	Мелане́зия
		Mesopotamia	Месопота́мия
		Micronesia	Микроне́зия
		Monaco	Мона́ко

| New England | Нóвая Áнглия |
| Normandy | Нормáндия |

| Oceania | Океáния |

Palestine	Палестúна
Patagonia	Патагóния
Persia	Пéрсия
Phoenicia	Финикúя
Polynesia	Полинéзия
Prussia	Прýссия
Punjab	Пенджáб

| Russia | Россúя |

Saar	Саáр
San Marino	Сан-Марúно
Saxony	Саксóния
Scandinavia	Скандинáвия
Scotland	Шотлáндия
Serbia	Сéрбия
Siam	Сиáм
Siberia	Сибúрь (f.)
Silesia	Силéзия
Sinai	Синáйский полуóстров
Slovakia	Словáкия
Slovenia	Словéния

Tibet	Тибéт
Tuscany	Тоскáна
Tyrol	Тирóль (m.)

| Ukraine | Украúна |
| Ulster | Óльстер |

| Wales | Уэльс |

| Yucatan | Юкатáн |

ISLAND GROUPS

Aleutian Islands	Алеýтские островá
Antilles	Антúльские островá
Azores	Азóрские островá
Bahamas	Багáмские островá
Balearic Islands	Балеáрские островá
Canary Islands	Канáрские островá
Cape Verde Islands	островá Зелёного Мыса
Channel Islands	Нормáндские островá
Falkland Islands	Фолклéндские островá
Faroe Islands	Фарéрские островá
Galapagos Islands	островá Галáпагос
Leeward Islands	Подвéтренные островá

Maldive Islands	Мальдúвские островá
Mariana Islands	Мариáнские островá
Marshall Islands	Мáршалловы островá
Orkney Islands	Оркнéйские островá
Ryukyu Islands	островá Рюкю
Samoa	Самóа
Seychelles	Сейшéльские островá
Shetland Islands	Шетлáндские островá
Solomon Islands	Соломóновы островá
Virgin Islands	Виргúнские островá
Windward Islands	Навéтренные островá

ISLANDS

Antigua	Антúгуа
Aruba	Арýба
Bali	Бáли
Bermuda	Бермýдские островá
Borneo	Борнéо
Corfu	Кóрфу
Corsica	Кóрсика
Crete	Крит
Curacao	Кюрасáо
Easter Island	óстров Пáсхи
Guadalcanal	Гуадалканáл
Guadeloupe	Гваделýпа
Guam	Гуам
Hokkaido	Хоккáйдо
Honshu	Хóнсю
Iwo Jima	Иводзúма
Java	Ява
Leyte	Лéйте
Long Island	Лонг-Áйленд
Luzon	Лусóн
Madagascar	Мадагаскáр
Madeira	Мадéйра
Majorca	Мальóрка, Майóрка
Man, Isle of	óстров Мэн
Martinique	Мартинúка
Mindanao	Минданáо
New Guinea	Нóвая Гвинéя
Okinawa	Окинáва
Puerto Rico	Пуэрто-Рúко
Réunion	Реюньóн
Rhodes	Рóдос

Sakhalin	Сахалин	Rhode Island	Род-Айленд
Sardinia	Сардиния		
Sicily	Сицилия	South Carolina	Южная Каролина
Sumatra	Суматра	South Dakota	Южная Дакота
Tahiti	Тайти	Tennessee	Теннесси
Tasmania	Тасмания	Texas	Техас
Timor	Тимор		
		Utah	Юта
Vancouver	Ванкувер		
		Vermont	Вермонт
Zanzibar	Занзибар	Virginia	Виргиния

STATES of the UNION

		Washington	Вашингтон
		West Virginia	Западная Виргиния
Alabama	Алабама	Wisconsin	Висконсин
Alaska	Аляска	Wyoming	Вайоминг
Arizona	Аризона		
Arkansas	Арканзас		

CANADIAN PROVINCES

California	Калифорния		
Colorado	Колорадо	Alberta	Альберта
Connecticut	Коннектикут		
		British Columbia	Британская Колумбия
Delaware	Делавэр		
		Manitoba	Манитоба
Florida	Флорида		
		New Brunswick	Нью-Брансуик
Georgia	Джорджия	Newfoundland	Ньюфаундленд
		Nova Scotia	Новая Шотландия
Hawaii	Гавайи		
		Ontario	Онтарио
Idaho	Айдахо		
Illinois	Иллинойс	Prince Edward Island	остров Принца
Indiana	Индиана		Эдуарда
Iowa	Айова		
		Quebec	Квебек
Kansas	Канзас		
Kentucky	Кентукки	Saskatchewan	Саскачеван

CITIES

Louisiana	Луизиана		
		Acapulco	Акапулько
Maine	Мэн	Accra	Аккра
Maryland	Мэриленд	Addis Ababa	Аддис-Абеба
Massachusetts	Массачусетс	Albany	Олбани
Michigan	Мичиган	Alexandria	Александрия
Minnesota	Миннесота	Algiers	Алжир
Mississippi	Миссисипи	Amman	Амман
Missouri	Миссури	Amsterdam	Амстердам
Montana	Монтана	Ankara	Анкара
		Antwerp	Антверпен
Nebraska	Небраска	Archangel	Архангельск
Nevada	Невада	Asunción	Асунсьон
New Hampshire	Нью-Хэмпшир	Athens	Афины
New Jersey	Нью-Джерси	Atlanta	Атланта
New Mexico	Нью-Мексико	Auckland	Окленд
New York	Нью-Йорк		
North Carolina	Северная Каролина	Baghdad	Багдад
North Dakota	Северная Дакота	Baku	Баку
		Baltimore	Балтимор
Ohio	Огайо	Bangkok	Бангкок
Oklahoma	Оклахома	Barcelona	Барселона
Oregon	Орегон	Beirut	Бейрут
		Belfast	Белфаст
Pennsylvania	Пенсильвания	Belgrade	Белград

Berlin	Берл435н	Hague, The	Гаа́га
Berne	Берн	Haifa	Ха́йфа
Bethlehem	Вифлее́м	Halifax	Га́лифакс
Birmingham	Би́рмингем	Hamburg	Га́мбург
Bogotá	Богота́	Hanoi	Хано́й
Bombay	Бомбе́й	Hanover	Ганно́вер
Bonn	Бонн	Harbin	Харби́н
Bordeaux	Бордо́	Havana	Гава́на
Boston	Бо́стон	Helsinki	Хе́льсинки
Brasília	Брази́лия	Hiroshima	Хироси́ма
Brazzaville	Браззави́ль (*m.*)	Honolulu	Гонолу́лу
Brisbane	Бри́сбен	Houston	Хью́стон
Brussels	Брюссе́ль (*m.*)		
Bucharest	Бухаре́ст	Indianapolis	Индиана́полис
Budapest	Будапе́шт	Irkutsk	Ирку́тск
Buenos Aires	Буэ́нос-А́йрес	Istanbul	Стамбу́л
Buffalo	Бу́ффало		
		Jericho	Иерихо́н
Cairo	Каи́р	Jerusalem	Иерусали́м
Calcutta	Кальку́тта	Johannesburg	Йоха́ннесбург
Calgary	Ка́лгари		
Cambridge	Ке́мбридж	Kabul	Кабу́л
Canberra	Ка́нберра	Kansas City	Ка́нзас-Си́ти
Cannes	Канн	Karachi	Кара́чи
Canterbury	Ке́нтербери	Katmandu	Катманду́
Canton	Канто́н	Kazan	Каза́нь (*f.*)
Capetown	Ке́йптаун	Kharkov	Ха́рьков
Caracas	Кара́кас	Khartoum	Харту́м
Cardiff	Ка́рдифф	Kiev	Ки́ев
Casablanca	Касабла́нка	Kingston	Ки́нгстон
Chicago	Чика́го	Kinshasa	Кинша́са
Cincinnati	Цинцинна́ти	Kishinev	Кишинёв
Cleveland	Кли́вленд	Kuala Lumpur	Куа́ла-Лу́мпур
Cologne	Кёльн	Kuibyshev	Ку́йбышев
Colombo	Коло́мбо	Kyoto	Кио́то
Conakry	Ко́накри		
Copenhagen	Копенга́ген	Lagos	Ла́гос
Cracow	Кра́ков	Lahore	Лахо́р
		Lancaster	Ла́нкастер
Dacca	Да́кка	Las Vegas	Лас-Ве́гас
Dakar	Дака́р	Leeds	Лидс
Dallas	Да́ллас	Le Havre	Гавр
Damascus	Дама́ск	Leicester	Ле́стер
Dar es Salaam	Дар-эс-Сала́м	Leipzig	Ле́йпциг
Denver	Де́нвер	Leningrad	Ленингра́д
Des Moines	Де-Мо́йн	Lhasa	Лха́са
Detroit	Детро́йт	Lima	Ли́ма
Djakarta	Джака́рта	Lisbon	Лиссабо́н
Dover	Дувр	Little Rock	Литл-Ро́к
Dresden	Дре́зден	Liverpool	Ливерпу́ль (*m.*)
Dublin	Ду́блин	London	Ло́ндон
Dubrovnik	Дубро́вник	Los Angeles	Лос-А́нджелес
		Louisville	Лу́исвилл
Edinburgh	Э́динбург	Luanda	Луа́нда
Edmonton	Э́дмонтон	Lucerne	Люце́рн
		Lusaka	Луса́ка
Florence	Флоре́нция	Lvov	Львов
Fort Worth	Форт-Уэ́рт		
Frankfurt	Фра́нкфурт	Madrid	Мадри́д
		Managua	Мана́гуа
Geneva	Жене́ва	Manchester	Ма́нчестер
Genoa	Ге́нуя	Manila	Мани́ла
Glasgow	Гла́зго	Marseilles	Марсе́ль (*m.*)
Gorky	Го́рький		
Guadalajara	Гвадалаха́ра		

Mecca	Мекка	Raleigh	Роли
Melbourne	Мельбурн	Rangoon	Рангун
Memphis	Мемфис	Rawalpindi	Равалпинди
Mexico City	Мехико	Regina	Риджайна
Miami	Майами	Reno	Рино
Milan	Милан	Reykjavik	Рейкьявик
Milwaukee	Милуоки	Richmond	Ричмонд
Minneapolis	Миннеаполис	Riga	Рига
Minsk	Минск	Rio de Janeiro	Рио-де-Жанейро
Mobile	Мобил	Riyadh	Эр-Рияд
Montevideo	Монтевидео	Rochester	Рочестер
Montreal	Монреаль (m.)	Rome	Рим
Moscow	Москва	Rotterdam	Роттердам
Munich	Мюнхен		
Murmansk	Мурманск	Saigon	Сайгон
		St. Louis	Сент-Луис
Nairobi	Найроби	St. Paul	Сент-Пол
Naples	Неаполь (m.)	Salisbury	Солсбери
Nashville	Нашвилл	Salt Lake City	Солт-Лейк-Сити
Nassau	Нассау	Samarkand	Самарканд
Nazareth	Назарет	San Diego	Сан-Диего
Newark	Ньюарк	San Francisco	Сан-Франциско
New Delhi	Дели	San Juan	Сан-Хуан
New Orleans	Новый Орлеан	Santiago	Сантьяго
New York	Нью-Йорк	São Paulo	Сан-Паулу
Nice	Ницца	Seattle	Сиэтл
Nicosia	Никосия	Seoul	Сеул
Nottingham	Ноттингем	Seville	Севилья
Novosibirsk	Новосибирск	Shanghai	Шанхай
Nuremberg	Нюрнберг	Sofia	София
		Stockholm	Стокгольм
Oakland	Окленд	Sydney	Сидней
Odessa	Одесса		
Omaha	Омаха	Taipei	Тайбэй
Osaka	Осака	Tallin	Таллин
Oslo	Осло	Tashkent	Ташкент
Ottawa	Оттава	Tbilisi	Тбилиси
Oxford	Оксфорд	Teheran	Тегеран
		Tel Aviv	Тель-Авив
Paris	Париж	Tirana	Тирана
Peking	Пекин	Tokyo	Токио
Perth	Перт	Toronto	Торонто
Philadelphia	Филадельфия	Trieste	Триест
Phnom Penh	Пномпень (m.)	Tripoli	Триполи
Phoenix	Финикс	Tulsa	Талса
Pisa	Пиза	Tunis	Тунис
Pittsburgh	Питсбург	Turin	Турин
Plymouth	Плимут		
Port-au-Prince	Порт-о-Пренс	Ulan Bator	Улан-Батор
Portland	Портленд		
Portsmouth	Портсмут	Vancouver	Ванкувер
Prague	Прага	Venice	Венеция
Pretoria	Претория	Versailles	Версаль (m.)
Providence	Провиденс	Victoria	Виктория
Pyongyang	Пхеньян	Vienna	Вена
		Vientiane	Вьентьян
		Vilnius	Вильнюс
Quebec	Квебек	Vladivostok	Владивосток
Quito	Кито	Volgograd	Волгоград

Warsaw	Варша́ва	Japan, of	Япо́нское мо́ре
Washington	Вашингто́н		
Wellington	Ве́ллингтон	Mediterranean	Средизе́мное мо́ре
Wilmington	Уи́лмингтон		
Winnipeg	Ви́ннипег	North	Се́верное мо́ре
Yerevan	Ерева́н	Okhotsk, of	Охо́тское мо́ре
Yokohama	Йокоха́ма		
York	Йорк	Red	Кра́сное мо́ре
Zurich	Цю́рих	South China	Ю́жно-Кита́йское мо́ре

SECTIONS OF CITIES

		White	Бе́лое мо́ре
Bronx	Бронкс		
Brooklyn	Бру́клин	Yellow	Жёлтое мо́ре

LAKES

Coney Island	Ко́ни-А́йленд		
		Albert	Альбе́рт
Harlem	Га́рлем		
Hollywood	Голливу́д	Baikal	Байка́л
Manhattan	Манха́ттан	Chad	Чад
Montmartre	Монма́ртр		
		Erie	Э́ри
Queens	Квинс		
		Great Bear	Большо́е Медве́жье о́зеро
Soho	Со́хо		
		Great Salt	Большо́е Солёное о́зеро
Westminster	Ве́стминстер		

OCEANS

		Great Slave	Большо́е Нево́льничье о́зеро
Arctic	Се́верный Ледови́тый океа́н		
		Huron	Гуро́н
Atlantic	Атланти́ческий океа́н		
		Ladoga	Ла́дожское о́зеро
Indian	Инди́йский океа́н		
		Michigan	Мичига́н
Pacific	Ти́хий океа́н		
		Onega	Оне́жское о́зеро

SEAS

		Ontario	Онта́рио
Adriatic	Адриати́ческое мо́ре		
Aegean	Эге́йское мо́ре	Superior	Ве́рхнее о́зеро
Aral	Ара́льское мо́ре		
Azov, of	Азо́вское мо́ре	Tanganyika	Тангани́йка
		Titicaca	Титика́ка
Baltic	Балти́йское мо́ре		
Bering	Бе́рингово мо́ре	Victoria	Викто́рия
Black	Чёрное мо́ре		

RIVERS

Caribbean	Кари́бское мо́ре		
Caspian	Каспи́йское мо́ре	Amazon	Амазо́нка
		Amur	Аму́р
Dead	Мёртвое мо́ре		
		Columbia	Колу́мбия
Irish	Ирла́ндское мо́ре	Congo	Ко́нго

Danube	Дунáй
Delaware	Дéлавэр
Dnieper	Днепр
Dniester	Днестр
Don	Дон
Elbe	Эльба
Euphrates	Евфрáт
Ganges	Ганг
Hudson	Гудзóн
Indus	Инд
Irrawaddy	Ирáвади
Irtysh	Иртыш
Jordan	Иордáн
Lena	Лéна
Loire	Луáра
Mackenzie	Маккéнзи
Mekong	Мекóнг
Mississippi	Миссисúпи
Missouri	Миссýри
Niger	Нúгер
Nile	Нил
Ob	Обь
Oder	Óдер
Ohio	Огáйо
Orinoco	Оринóко
Paraná	Паранá
Po	По
Potomac	Потóмак
Rhine	Рейн
Rhone	Рóна
Rio Grande	Рúо-Грáнде
St. Lawrence	Святóго Лаврéнтия
Seine	Сéна
Susquehanna	Саскуэхáнна
Thames	Тéмза
Tigris	Тигр
Vistula	Вúсла
Volga	Вóлга
Volta	Вóльта
Yangtze	Янцзы
Yellow	Жёлтая
Yenisei	Енисéй
Yukon	Юкон
Zambezi	Замбéзи

GULFS, BAYS, STRAITS, CHANNELS, CANALS

Bengal, Bay of	Бенгáльский залúв
Bering Strait	Бéрингов пролúв
Biscay, Bay of	Бискáйский залúв
Bosp(h)orus	Босфóр
English Channel	Ла-Мáнш
Gibraltar, Strait of	Гибралтáрский пролúв
Hudson Bay	Гудзóнов залúв
Magellan, Strait of	Магеллáнов пролúв
Mexico, Gulf of	Мексикáнский залúв
Panama Canal	Панáмский канáл
Persian Gulf	Персúдский залúв
Suez Canal	Суэцкий канáл

MOUNTAIN RANGES

Adirondack Mountains	Адирóндак
Allegheny Mountains	Аллегáны
Alps	Áльпы
Andes	Áнды
Appalachian Mountains	Аппалáчи
Carpathian Mountains	Карпáты
Catskill Mountains	гóры Кáтскилл
Caucasus	Кавкáз
Himalayas	Гималáи
Pyrenees	Пиренéи
Rocky Mountains	Скалúстые гóры
Ural Mountains	Урáл

MOUNTAIN PEAKS

Elbrus	Эльбрýс
Etna	Этна
Everest	Эверéст
Fuji, Fujiyama	Фудзияма
Kilimanjaro	Килиманджáро
Matterhorn	Мáттерхорн
Mauna Loa	Мáуна-Лóа

McKinley	Мак-Кинли	Descartes	Декарт
Mont Blanc	Монблан	Dickens	Диккенс
		Diderot	Дидро
Pike's Peak	Пайкс-Пик	Diogenes	Диоген
Popocatepetl	Попокатепетль	Disraeli	Дизраэли
		Dostoyevsky	Достоевский
Rainier	Рейнир	Dvorak	Дворжак
Sinai	Синай	Edison	Эдисон
		Einstein	Эйнштейн
Vesuvius	Везувий	Eisenhower	Эйзенхауэр
		Erasmus	Эразм
Whitney	Уитни		
		Faulkner	Фолкнер

FAMOUS NAMES

		Flaubert	Флобер
		Franco	Франко
Aesop	Эзоп	Franklin	Франклин
Andropov	Андропов	Freud	Фрейд
Aristotle	Аристотель		
Atatürk	Ататюрк	Galileo	Галилей
Attila	Аттила	Gandhi	Ганди
		Garibaldi	Гарибальди
Bach	Бах	Genghis Khan	Чингисхан
Balzac	Бальзак	Goethe	Гёте
Beethoven	Бетховен	Gogol	Гоголь
Bismarck	Бисмарк	Grieg	Григ
Bolivar	Боливар	Gutenberg	Гутенберг
Brahms	Брамс		
Brezhnev	Брежнев	Hammarskjöld	Хаммаршельд
Buddha	Будда	Hannibal	Ганнибал
		Hawthorne	Хоторн
Caesar	Цезарь	Haydn	Гайдн
Calvin	Кальвин	Hegel	Гегель
Carter	Картер	Hemingway	Хемингуэй
Caruso	Карузо	Hippocrates	Гиппократ
Cervantes	Сервантес	Hitler	Гитлер
Chaplin	Чаплин	Homer	Гомер
Charlemagne	Карл Великий	Hugo	Гюго
Chaucer	Чосер		
Chekhov	Чехов	Jefferson	Джефферсон
Chopin	Шопен	Joan of Arc	Жанна д'Арк
Christ	Христос	Joyce	Джойс
Churchill	Черчилль		
Cicero	Цицерон	Kafka	Кафка
Clausewitz	Клаузевиц	Keats	Китс
Clemenceau	Клемансо	Kennedy	Кеннеди
Columbus	Колумб	Khrushchev	Хрущёв
Confucius	Конфуций	Kipling	Киплинг
Copernicus	Коперник		
Cortés	Кортес	Lenin	Ленин
Curie	Кюри	Lincoln	Линкольн
		Longfellow	Лонгфелло
Dante	Данте	Luther	Лютер
Darwin	Дарвин		
da Vinci	да Винчи	MacArthur	Макартур
Debussy	Дебюсси	Machiavelli	Макиавелли
de Gaulle	де Голль	Magellan	Магеллан
Demosthenes	Демосфен	Manet	Мане

Mao Tse-tung	Máo Цзэ-дýн	Schweitzer	Швéйцер
Marshall	Мáршалл	Shakespeare	Шекспúр
Marx	Маркс	Shaw	Шóу
Metternich	Méттерних	Shostakovich	Шостакóвич
Michelangelo	Микелáнджело	Socrates	Сокрáт
Milton	Мúльтон	Solzhenitsyn	Солженúцын
Mohammed	Мухáммед	Sophocles	Софóкл
Molière	Мольéр	Stalin	Стáлин
Monet	Монé	Strauss	Штрáус
Mozart	Мóцарт		
Mussolini	Муссолúни	Talleyrand	Талейрáн
		Tamerlane	Тимýр
Napoleon	Наполеóн	Tchaikovsky	Чайкóвский
Newton	Ньютон	Tennyson	Тéннисон
Nixon	Нúксон	Thackeray	Тéккерей
		Tito	Тúто
Pasternak	Пастернáк	Tolstoy	Толстóй
Pasteur	Пастéр	Trotsky	Трóцкий
Picasso	Пикáссо	Truman	Трýмэн
Plato	Платóн	Turgenev	Тургéнев
Proust	Пруст		
Pushkin	Пýшкин	van Gogh	ван Гог
		Virgil	Вергúлий
Raphael	Рафаэ́ль	Voltaire	Вольтéр
Reagan	Рéйган		
Rembrandt	Рéмбрандт	Wagner	Вáгнер
Renoir	Ренуáр	Washington	Вáшингтон
Robespierre	Робеспьéр	Webster	Уэ́бстер
Rockefeller	Рокфéллер	Whitman	Уúтмен
Rodin	Родéн	Wilson	Вúльсон
Roosevelt	Рýзвельт	Wright	Райт
Rousseau	Руссó		
Rubens	Рýбенс	Zola	Золя́